ANNUAL STATEMENT STUDIES

FINANCIAL RATIO BENCHMARKS

Volume II

2019 2020

RMA
Annual Statement Studies®
Copyright, Ordering, Licensing, and Use of Data Information

To **obtain permission** to copy, quote, reproduce, replicate, disseminate, or distribute the Statement Studies® data/material please fax or email a brief letter stating who you are and how you intend to use the Statement Studies® data to: Statement Studies Information Products at fax number 215-446-4101 or via email to studies@rmahq.org. Depending on the requested use, RMA may require a license agreement and royalty fee.

A **License Agreement is required** if you wish to use or incorporate any portion of the data, in whole or in part in other products that will in turn be sold to others, such as in software oriented or derived products, scholarly publications, or training materials.

To **purchase** a copy, or additional copies, of the Statement Studies® data in book or online format, contact RMA's Customer Relations at 1-800-677-7621. Regional data presented in the same fashion as you see in this book is only available in eStatement Studies.

If you have a **question regarding the data** please reference the detailed explanatory notes provided in the Introduction section of the enclosed product. If you are unable to find the answer to your question please contact us by e-mail at: studies@rmahq.org. Be sure to include your detailed question along with your telephone number, fax number, and email address.

The Risk Management Association
1801 Market Street, Suite 300
Philadelphia, PA 19103
© 2019 by RMA
ISBN# 978-1-57070-352-2

TABLE OF CONTENTS

Information on Copyright, Ordering, Licensing, and use of Data iii
List of Participating Institutions vi
Introduction to Statement Studies and Organization of Content viii
Definition of Ratios x
Explanation of Noncontractor Balance Sheet and Income Data xix
Explanation of Contractor—Percentage-of-Completion Basis of Accounting xx
IDP Sample Report xxiii
NAICS Codes Appearing in the Statement Studies 27
Full Descriptions of Industries Appearing in the Statement Studies 33

	Description Index	Data Set Begins On
Agriculture, Forestry, Fishing and Hunting	33	97
Mining	35	167
Utilities	35	183
Construction—General Industries Format*	36	201
Manufacturing	39	263
Wholesale Trade	57	763
Retail Trade	62	903
Transportation and Warehousing	66	1019
Information	68	1095
Finance and Insurance	70	1131
Real Estate and Rental and Leasing	72	1189
Professional, Scientific and Technical Services	74	1233
Management of Companies and Enterprises	78	1317
Administrative and Support and Waste Management and Remediation Services	78	1323
Educational Services	81	1391
Health Care and Social Assistance	82	1413
Arts, Entertainment and Recreation	86	1491
Accommodation and Food Services	87	1531
Other Services (Except Public Administration)	89	1559
Public Administration	91	1627
Construction—Percentage of Completion Basis of Accounting*	93	1655

Supplemental Information:

Text—Key Word Index of Industries Appearing in the Statement Studies I
Construction Financial Management Association Data IX
RMA's Credit & Lending Dictionary XIX

*General Industries Format means that a valid construction NAICS was assigned to the subject companies contained in the sample; however, the financial statements were prepared using a general or traditional manufacturing or service industries presentation of results versus using a percentage-of-completion method of accounting. Industries found in the percentage-of-completion presentation follow the presentation used by RMA in the past.

About RMA

Founded in 1914, The Risk Management Association is a not-for-profit, member-driven professional association whose sole purpose is to advance the use of sound risk principles in the financial services industry. RMA promotes an enterprise approach to risk management that focuses on credit risk, market risk, and operational risk.

Headquartered in Philadelphia, Pennsylvania, RMA has 2,500 institutional members that include banks of all sizes as well as nonbank financial institutions. They are represented in the association by 18,000 risk management professionals who are chapter members in financial centers throughout North America, Europe, and Asia/Pacific. Visit RMA on the Web at www.rmahq.org.

vi

RMA ACKNOWLEDGES AND THANKS THE FOLLOWING INSTITUTIONS, CONTRIBUTORS TO THE 2019 STATEMENT STUDIES DATA SUBMISSION PROGRAM.

Alabama
BBVA Compass
Regions Bank

Arizona
Arizona Bank & Trust
First Fidelity Bank

California
Bank of the West
Central Valley Community Bank
Farmers and Merchants Bank of
    Central Valley California
Merchants Bank & Trust
Montecito Bank & Trust
Pinnacle Bank
Premier Valley Bank
Presidio Bank

Colorado
Citywide Banks
First National Bank of Omaha
Independent Bank

Connecticut
Dime Bank
Jewett City Savings Bank
Peoples United Bank
The Milford Bank

Florida
CenterState Bank
The Bank of Tampa

Georgia
SunTrust Banks, Inc.

Hawaii
Central Pacific Bank
First Hawaiian Bank

Idaho
First Interstate Bank
Idaho First Bank
Washington Trust Bank

Illinois
Devon Bank
First Midwest Bank
First National Bank of Omaha
Glenview State Bank
Illinois Bank & Trust

Indiana
First Federal Savings Bank
First Financial Bank
Old National Bank

Iowa
Dubuque Bank & Trust
Farmers State Bank

Kansas
Bank of Blue Valley
Conway Bank NA
Emprise Bank
First National Bank of Omaha
INTRUST Bank, N.A.

Kentucky
Central Bank & Trust Co.
Community Trust Bank, Inc.

Louisiana
Business First Bank
Whitney Bank

Maine
Bangor Savings Bank
First National Bank
Kennebunk Savings

Maryland
Harford Bank
The Bank of Glen Burnie

Massachusetts
Brookline Bancorp
Eastern Bank
Fall River Five dba BankFive
Pittsfield Cooperative Bank
Santander Bank, N.A.

Michigan
Chemical Bank a division of
    TCF National Bank
Comerica Bank
Commercial Bank
First National Bank of Michigan
First State Bank
Huron Community Bank

Minnesota
BankCherokee
BlackRidgeBANK
Bremer Bank, National Association
Citizens Independent Bank
Community Resource Bank
Fidelity Bank
First Minnetonka City Bank
Minnesota Bank & Trust
Minnwest Bank
North Star Bank
Stearns Bank N.A.

Mississippi
BancorpSouth
Hancock Bank
The Peoples Bank
Trustmark National Bank

Missouri
Academy Bank, N.A.
Cass Commercial Bank
Central Bancompany
Commerce Bank NA
Royal Banks of Missouri

Montana
First Interstate Bank
Rocky Mountain Bank

Nebraska
First National Bank of Omaha
Mutual of Omaha Bank
Union Bank and Trust Company

New Jersey
Peapack-Gladstone Bank
TD Bank, N.A.

New Mexico
New Mexico Bank & Trust

New York
Canandaigua National Bank & Trust
CIT Group
Community Bank, NA
Lake Shore Savings Bank
M&T Bank
NBT Bank, N.A.
Steuben Trust Company
Tompkins Trust Company

North Carolina
BB&T
TowneBank

North Dakota
Bell Bank
BlackRidgeBANK

Ohio
First Financial Bank
Huntington National Bank

Oklahoma
First Fidelity Bank
First United Bank & Trust Co

Oregon
First Interstate Bank
People's Bank of Commerce
Washington Trust Bank

Pennsylvania
1st Summit Bank
Community Bank
First Columbia Bank & Trust Co.
First Commonwealth Bank
Firstrust Bank
Fulton Bank
Gemino Healthcare Finance, LLC
Kish Bank
Orrstown Bank
PeoplesBank, a Codorus
    Valley Company
QNB Bank
Republic Bank
S&T Bank
Somerset Trust Company
Washington Financial Bank

Puerto Rico
Oriental Bank

Rhode Island
Citizens Financial Group

South Dakota
First Interstate Bank
First PREMIER Bank
The First National Bank in
    Sioux Falls

Tennessee
First Tennessee Bank, N.A.
Pinnacle Bank

Texas
American Bank, N.A.
American National Bank of Texas
Comerica Bank
Extraco Banks, N.A.
First Bank & Trust
First United Bank & Trust Co
Frost Bank
Independent Bank
Texas Capital Bank
Woodforest National Bank

Utah
Cache Valley Bank
Zions Bancorporation

Vermont
Community National Bank
Mascoma Bank
National Bank of Middlebury
The Bank of Bennington
The Brattleboro Savings and
    Loan Association
Union Bank

Virginia
First Community Bank
Sonabank
TowneBank
United Bankshares, Inc.

Washington
Columbia Bank
First Interstate Bank
HomeStreet Bank
Mountain Pacific Bank
Northwest Farm Credit Services
Washington Trust Bank

West Virginia
United Bankshares, Inc.
WesBanco Bank, Inc.

Wisconsin
Associated Bank N.A.
Bank of Sun Prairie
First Bank Financial Centre
First National Bank and
    Trust Company
Horicon Bank
Johnson Bank
State Bank Financial
Wisconsin Bank & Trust

Wyoming
First Interstate Bank

Introduction to Annual Statement Studies: Financial Ratio Benchmarks, 2019-2020 and General Organization of Content

The notes below will explain the presentation of *Annual Statement Studies: Financial Ratio Benchmarks*, describe how the book is organized, and answer most of your questions.

The Quality You Expect from RMA: RMA is the most respected source of objective, unbiased information on issues of importance to credit risk professionals. In its 100th year, RMA's *Annual Statement Studies®* has been the industry standard for comparison financial data. Material contained in today's Annual Statement Studies was first published in the March 1919 issue of the Federal Reserve Bulletin. In the days before computers, the *Annual Statement Studies* data was recorded in pencil on yellow ledger paper! Today, it features data for over 781 industries derived <u>directly</u> from more than 260,000 statements of financial institutions' borrowers and prospects.

- **Data That Comes Straight from Original Sources:** The more than 260,000 statements used to produce the composites presented here come directly from RMA member institutions and represent the financials from their commercial customers and prospects. RMA does not know the names of the individual entities. In fact, to ensure confidentiality, company names are removed before the data is even delivered to RMA. The raw data making up each composite is not available to any third party.

- **Data Presented in Common Size:** *Annual Statement Studies: Financial Ratio Benchmarks* contains composite financial data. Balance sheet and income statement information is shown in common size format, with each item a percentage of total assets and sales. RMA computes common size statements for each individual statement in an industry group, then aggregates and averages all the figures. In some cases, because of computer rounding, the figures to the right of the decimal point do not balance exactly with the totals shown. A minus sign beside the value indicates credits and losses.

- **Includes the Most Widely Used Ratios:** Nineteen of the most widely used ratios in the financial services industry accompany the balance sheet information, including various types of liquidity, coverage, leverage, and operating ratios.

- **Organized by the NAICS for Ease of Use:** This edition is organized according to the 2017 North American Industry Classification System (NAICS), a product of the U.S. Office of Management and Budget. At the top of each page of data, you will find the NAICS. Please note, in the revised 2017 catalog some industries were merged to create its new 2017 NAICS. In these instances, RMA recalculated aggregate historical reporting. For detailed 2017 and 2012 NAICS mapping, please visit the RMA site or: http://www.census.gov/eos/www/naics/

- **Twenty Sections Outline Major Types of Businesses:** To provide further delineation, the book is divided into 20 sections outlining major lines of businesses. If you know the NAICS number you are looking for, use the NAICS-page guide provided in the front of this book. In general, the book is arranged in ascending NAICS numerical order. For your convenience, full descriptions of each NAICS are presented in this book. In addition, you will find a text-based index near the end of the book.

- **If You Do Not Know the NAICS Code You Are Looking for...** If you do not know the precise industry NAICS you are looking for, contact the Census Bureau at 1-888-75NAICS or naics@census.gov. Describe the activity of the establishment for which you need an industry code and you will receive a reply. Another source to help you assign the correct NAICS industry name and number can be found at www.census.gov/epcd/www/naics.html.

- **Can't Find the Industry You Want?** There are a number of reasons you may not find the industry you are looking for (i.e., you know you need industry xxxxxx but it is not in the product). Many times we have information on an industry, but it is not published because the sample size was too small or there were significant questions concerning the data. (For an industry to be displayed in the *Annual Statement Studies: Financial Ratio Benchmarks*, there must be at least 30 valid statements submitted to RMA.) In other instances, we simply do not have the data. Generally, most of what we receive is published.

- **Composite Data Not Shown?** When there are fewer than 10 financial statements in a particular asset or sales size category, the composite data is not shown because a sample this small is not considered representative and could be misleading. However, all the data for that industry is shown in the All Sizes column. The total number of statements for each size category is shown in bold print at the top of each column. In addition, the number of statements used in a ratio array will differ from the number of statements in a sample because certain elements of data may not be present in all financial statements. In these cases, the number of statements used is shown in parentheses to the left of the array.

- **Presentation of the Data on Each Page-Spread:** For all non-contracting spread statements, the data for a particular industry appears on both the left and right pages. The heading Current Data Sorted by Assets is in the five columns on the left side. The center section of the double-page presentation contains the Comparative Historical Data, with the All Sizes column for the current year shown under the heading 4/1/18-3/31/19. Comparable data from past editions of the *Annual Statement Studies: Financial Ratio Benchmarks* also appears in this section. Current Data Sorted by Sales is displayed in the five columns to the far right.

- **Companies with Less than $250 Million in Total Assets:** In our presentation, we used companies having less than $250 million in total assets—except in the case of contractors who use the percentage-of-completion method of accounting. *The section for contractors using the percentage-of-completion method of accounting contains data only sorted by revenue.* There is no upper limit placed on revenue size for any industry. Its information is found on only one page.

- **Page Headers:** The information shown at the top of each page includes the following: 1) the identity of the industry group; 2) its North American Industry Classification System (NAICS); 3) a breakdown by size categories of the types of financial statements reported; 4) the number of statements in each category; 5) the dates of the statements used; and 6) the size categories. For instance, 16 (4/1-9/30/18) means that 16 statements with fiscal dates between April 1 and September 30, 2018, make up part of the sample.

- **Page Footers:** At the bottom of each page, we have included the sum of the sales (or revenues) and total assets for all the financial statements in each size category. This data allows recasting of the common size statements into dollar amounts. To do this, divide the number at the bottom of the page by the number of statements in that size category. Then multiply the result by the percentages in the common size statement. Please note: The dollar amounts will be an approximation because RMA computes the balance sheet and income statement percentages for each individual statement in an industry group, then aggregates and averages all the figures.

- **Our Thanks to CFMA:** RMA appreciates the cooperation of the Construction Financial Management Association in permitting us to reproduce excerpts from its *Construction Industry Annual Financial Survey*. This data complements the RMA contractor industry data. For more details on this data, please visit www.cfma.org.

- **Recommended for Use as General Guidelines:** RMA recommends you use *Annual Statement Studies: Financial Ratio Benchmarks* data only as general guidelines and not as absolute industry norms. There are several reasons why the data may not be fully representative of a given industry:

1. **Data Not Random** — The financial statements used in the *Annual Statement Studies: Financial Ratio Benchmarks* are not selected by any random or statistically reliable method. RMA member banks voluntarily submit the raw data they have available each year with no limitation on company size.

2. **Categorized by Primary Product Only** — Many companies have varied product lines; however, the *Annual Statement Studies: Financial Ratio Benchmarks* categorizes them by their primary product NAICS number only.

3. **Small Samples** — Some of the industry samples are small in relation to the total number of firms for a given industry. A relatively small sample can increase the chances that some composites do not fully represent an industry.

4. **Extreme Statements** — An extreme or outlier statement can occasionally be present in a sample, causing a disproportionate influence on the industry composite. This is particularly true in a relatively small sample.

5. **Operational Differences** — Companies within the same industry may differ in their method of operations, which in turn can directly influence their financial statements. Since they are included in the sample, these statements can significantly affect the composite calculations.

6. **Additional Considerations** — There are other considerations that can result in variations among different companies engaged in the same general line of business. These include different labor markets, geographical location, different accounting methods, quality of products handled, sources and methods of financing, and terms of sale.

For these reasons, RMA does not recommend using the *Annual Statement Studies: Financial Ratio Benchmarks* figures as absolute norms for a given industry. Rather, you should use the figures only as general guidelines and as a supplement to the other methods of financial analysis. RMA makes no claim regarding how representative the figures printed in this book are.

DEFINITION OF RATIOS

Introduction

On each data page, below the common size balance sheet and income statement information, you will find a series of ratios computed from the financial statement data.

Here is how these figures are calculated for any given ratio:

1. The ratio is computed for each financial statement in the sample.

2. These values are arrayed (listed) in an order from the strongest to the weakest. In interpreting ratios, the "strongest" or "best" value is not always the largest numerical value, nor is the "weakest" always the lowest numerical value. (For certain ratios, there may be differing opinions as to what constitutes a strong or a weak value. RMA follows general banking guidelines consistent with sound credit practice to resolve this problem.)

3. The array of values is divided into four groups of equal size. The description of each ratio appearing in the *Statement Studies* provides details regarding the arraying of the values.

What Are Quartiles?

Each ratio has three points, or "cutoff values," that divide an array of values into four equal-sized groups called quartiles, as shown below. The quartiles include the upper quartile, upper-middle quartile, lower-middle quartile, and the lower quartile. The upper quartile is the cutoff value where one-quarter of the array of ratios falls between it and the strongest ratio. The median is the midpoint—that is, the middle cutoff value where half of the array falls above it and half below it. The lower quartile is the point where one-quarter of the array falls between it and the weakest ratio. In many cases, the average of two values is used to arrive at the quartile value. You will find the median and quartile values on all *Statement Studies* data pages in the order indicated in the chart below.

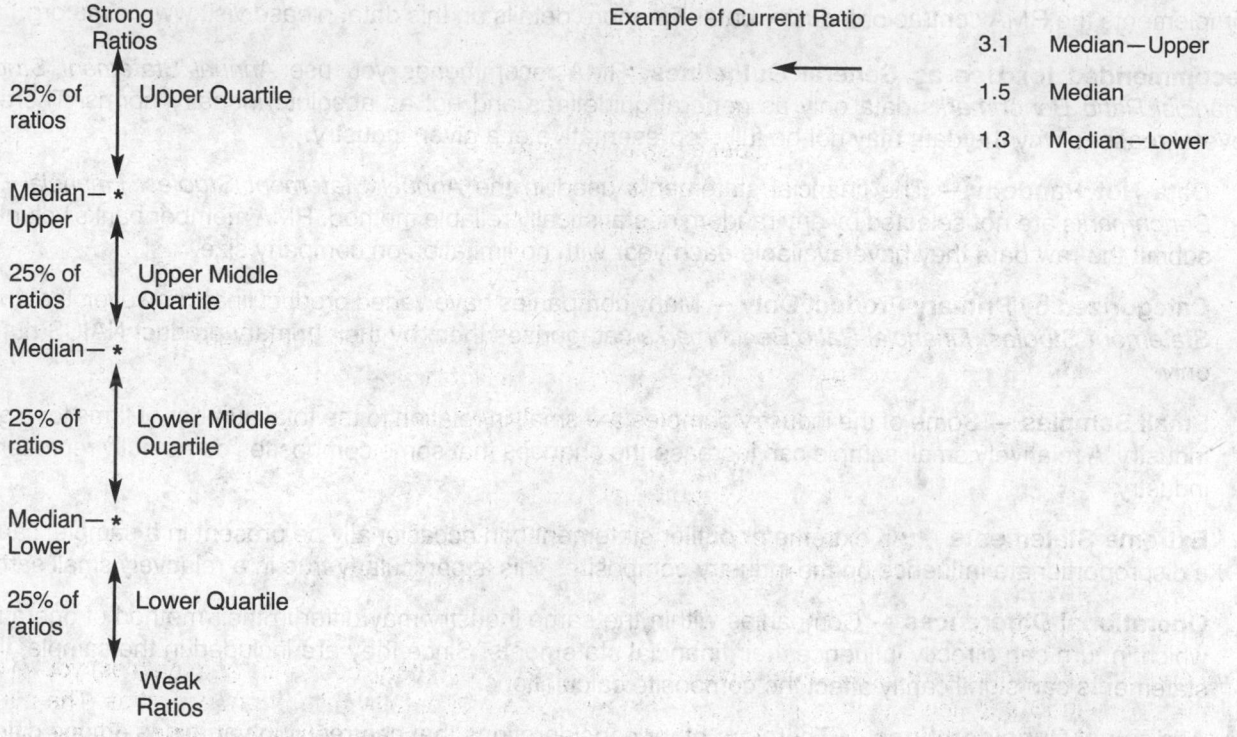

Why Use Medians/Quartiles Instead of the Average?

There are several reasons why medians and quartiles are used instead of an average. Medians and quartiles eliminate the influence of an "outlier" (an extremely high or low value compared to the rest of the values). They also more accurately reflect the ranges of ratio values than a straight averaging method would.

It is important to understand that the spread (range) between the upper and lower quartiles represents the middle 50% of all the companies in a sample. Therefore, ratio values greater than the upper quartile or less than the lower quartile may begin to approach "unusual" values.

Nonconventional Values:

For some ratio values, you will occasionally see an entry that is other than a conventional number. These entries are defined as follows:

(1) UND — This stands for "undefined," the result of the denominator in a ratio calculation approaching zero.

(2) NM — This may occasionally appear as a quartile or median for the ratios sales/working capital, debt/worth, and fixed/worth. It stands for "no meaning" in cases where the dispersion is so small that any interpretation is meaningless.

(3) 999.8 — When a ratio value equals 1,000 or more, it also becomes an "unusual" value and is given the "999.8" designation. This is considered to be a close enough approximation to the actual unusually large value.

Linear versus Nonlinear Ratios:

An array that is ordered in ascending sequence or in descending sequence is linear. An array that deviates from true ascending or true descending when its values change from positive to negative (low to high positive, followed by high to low negative) is non-linear.

A specific example of a nonlinear ratio would be the Sales/Working Capital ratio. In other words, when the Sales/Working Capital ratio is positive, then the top quartile would be represented by the lowest positive ratio. However, if the ratio is negative, the top quartile will be represented by the highest negative ratio! In a nonlinear array such as this, the median could be either positive or negative because it is whatever the middle value is in the particular array of numbers.

Nonlinear Ratios
Sales/Working Capital

Fixed/Worth

Debt/Worth

Linear Ratios
Current Ratio

Quick Ratio

Sales Receivables

Days' Receivables

Cost of Sales/Inventory

Days' Inventory

Cost of Sales/Payables

Days' Payables

EBIT/Interest

Net Profit + Deprec, Depletion, Amort/Current Maturities Long-Term Debt

% Profits Before Taxes/Tangible Net Worth

% Profits Before Taxes/Total Assets

Sales/Net Fixed Assets

Sales/Total Assets

% Depreciation, Depletion, Amortization/Sales

% Officers', Directors', Owners' Compensation/Sales

Important Notes on Ratios:

Turnover Ratios — For certain ratios (sales/receivables, cost of sales/inventory, cost of sales/payables) you will see two numbers, one in **BOLD** and one in regular type. These ratios are generally called turnover ratios. The number in **BOLD** represents **the number of days** and the number in regular type is **the number of times**. Please see the definition of sales/receivables on the following pages for a more complete description of the two types of calculations and what each means.

Inventory Presentations — **Inventory presentations** are based on fiscal year-end point-in-time balances, not averages. In addition, our data capture does not permit us to know what method of inventory accounting (LIFO or FIFO, for instance) was used.

The following ratios contained in the *Statement Studies* are grouped into five principal categories: liquidity, coverage, leverage, operating, and specific expense items.

LIQUIDITY RATIOS

Liquidity is a measure of the quality and adequacy of current assets to meet current obligations as they come due. In other words, can a firm quickly convert its assets to cash — without a loss in value — in order to meet its immediate and short-term obligations? For firms such as utilities that can readily and accurately predict their cash inflows, liquidity is not nearly as critical as it is for firms like airlines or manufacturing businesses that can have wide fluctuations in demand and revenue streams. These ratios provide a level of comfort to lenders in case of liquidation.

1. Current Ratio

How to Calculate: Divide total current assets by total current liabilities.

$$\frac{\text{Total Current Assets}}{\text{Total Current Liabilities}}$$

How to Interpret: This ratio is a rough indication of a firm's ability to service its current obligations. Generally, the higher the current ratio, the greater the "cushion" between current obligations and a firm's ability to pay them. While a stronger ratio shows that the numbers for current assets exceed those for current liabilities, the composition and quality of current assets are critical factors in the analysis of an individual firm's liquidity.

The ratio values are arrayed from the highest positive to the lowest positive.

2. Quick Ratio

How to Calculate: Add cash and equivalents to trade receivables. Then, divide by total current liabilities.

$$\frac{\text{Cash \& Equivalents + Trade Receivables (net)}}{\text{Total Current Liabilities}}$$

How to Interpret: Also known as the "acid test" ratio, this is a stricter, more conservative measure of liquidity than the current ratio. This ratio reflects the degree to which a company's current liabilities are covered by its most liquid current assets, the kind of assets that can be converted quickly to cash and at amounts close to book value. Inventory and other less liquid current assets are removed from the calculation. Generally, if the ratio produces a value that's less than 1 to 1, it implies a "dependency" on inventory or other "less" current assets to liquidate short-term debt.

The ratio values are arrayed from the highest positive to the lowest positive.

3. Sales/Receivables

How to Calculate: Divide net sales by trade receivables.

$$\frac{\text{Net Sales}}{\text{Trade Receivables (net)}}$$

Please note — In the contractor section, both accounts receivable-progress billings and accounts receivable-current retention are included in the receivables figure used in calculating the revenues/receivables and receivables/payables ratios.

How to Interpret: This ratio measures the number of times trade receivables turn over during the year. The higher the turnover of receivables, the shorter the time between sale and cash collection.

> For example, a company with sales of $720,000 and receivables of $120,000 would have a sales/receivables ratio of 6.0. This means receivables turn over six times a year. If a company's receivables appear to be turning more slowly than the rest of the industry, further research is needed and the quality of the receivables should be examined closely.

Cautions — A problem with this ratio is that it compares one day's receivables, shown at statement date, to total annual sales and does not take into consideration seasonal fluctuations. An additional problem in interpretation may arise when there is a large proportion of cash sales to total sales.

When the receivables figure is zero, the quotient will be undefined (UND) and represents the best possible ratio. The ratio values are therefore arrayed starting with undefined (UND) and then from the numerically highest value to the numerically lowest value. The only time a zero will appear in the array is when the sales figure is low and the quotient rounds off to zero. By definition, this ratio cannot be negative.

4. Days' Receivables

The sales/receivables ratio will have a figure printed in bold type directly to the left of the array. This figure is the days' receivables.

How to Calculate the Days' Receivables: Divide the sales/receivables ratio into 365 (the number of days in one year).

$$\frac{365}{\text{Sales/Receivable ratio}}$$

How to Interpret the Days' Receivables: This figure expresses the average number of days that receivables are outstanding. Generally, the greater the number of days outstanding, the greater the probability of delinquencies in accounts receivable. A comparison of a company's daily receivables may indicate the extent of a company's control over credit and collections.

Please note — You should take into consideration the terms offered by a company to its customers because these may differ from terms within the industry.

> *For example*, using the sales/receivable ratio calculated above, 365 ÷ 6 = 61 (i.e., the average receivable is collected in 61 days).

5. Cost of Sales/Inventory

How to Calculate: Divide cost of sales by inventory.

$$\frac{\text{Cost of Sales}}{\text{Inventory}}$$

How to Interpret: This ratio measures the number of times inventory is turned over during the year.

High Inventory Turnover — On the positive side, high inventory turnover can indicate greater liquidity or superior merchandising. Conversely, it can indicate a shortage of needed inventory for sales.

Low Inventory Turnover — Low inventory turnover can indicate poor liquidity, possible overstocking, or obsolescence. On the positive side, it could indicate a planned inventory buildup in the case of material shortages.

Cautions — A problem with this ratio is that it compares one day's inventory to cost of goods sold and does not take seasonal fluctuations into account. When the inventory figure is zero, the quotient will be undefined (UND) and represents the best possible ratio. The ratio values are arrayed starting with undefined (UND) and then from the numerically highest value to the numerically lowest value. The only time a zero will appear in the array is when the figure for cost of sales is very low and the quotient rounds off to zero.

Please note — For service industries, the cost of sales is included in operating expenses. In addition, please note that the data collection process does not differentiate the method of inventory valuation.

6. Days' Inventory

The days' inventory is the figure printed in bold directly to the left of the cost of sales/inventory ratio.

How to Calculate the Days' Inventory: Divide the cost of sales/inventory ratio into 365 (the number of days in one year).

$$\frac{365}{\text{Cost of Sales/Inventory ratio}}$$

How to Interpret: Dividing the inventory turnover ratio into 365 days yields the average length of time units are in inventory.

7. Cost of Sales/Payables

How to Calculate: Divide cost of sales by trade payables.

$$\frac{\text{Cost of Sales}}{\text{Trade Payables}}$$

Please note — In the contractor section, both accounts payable-trade and accounts payable-retention are included in the payables figure used in calculating the cost of revenues/payables and receivables/payables ratios.

How to Interpret: This ratio measures the number of times trade payables turn over during the year. The higher the turnover of payables, the shorter the time between purchase and payment. If a company's payables appear to be turning more slowly than the industry, then the company may be experiencing cash shortages, disputing invoices with suppliers, enjoying extended terms, or deliberately expanding its trade credit. The ratio comparison of company to industry suggests the existence of these or other possible causes. If a firm buys on 30-day terms, it is reasonable to expect this ratio to turn over in approximately 30 days.

Cautions — A problem with this ratio is that it compares one day's payables to cost of goods sold and does not take seasonal fluctuations into account. When the payables figure is zero, the quotient will be undefined (UND) and represents the best possible ratio. The ratio values are arrayed starting with undefined (UND) and then from the numerically highest to the numerically lowest value. The only time a zero will appear in the array is when the figure for cost of sales is very low and the quotient rounds off to zero.

8. Days' Payables

The days' payables is the figure printed in bold type directly to the left of the cost of sales/payables ratio.

How to Calculate the Days' Payables: Divide the cost of sales/payables ratio into 365 (the number of days in one year).

$$\frac{365}{\text{Cost of Sales/Payables ratio}}$$

How to Interpret: Division of the payables turnover ratio into 365 days yields the average length of time trade debt is outstanding.

9. Sales/Working Capital

How to Calculate: Divide net sales by net working capital (current assets less current liabilities equals net working capital).

$$\frac{\text{Net Sales}}{\text{Net Working Capital}}$$

How to Interpret: Because it reflects the ability to finance current operations, working capital is a measure of the margin of protection for current creditors. When you relate the level of sales resulting from operations to the underlying working capital, you can measure how efficiently working capital is being used.

Low ratio (close to zero) — A low ratio may indicate an inefficient use of working capital.

High ratio (high positive or high negative) — A very high ratio often signifies overtrading, which is a vulnerable position for creditors.

Please note — The sales/working capital ratio is a nonlinear array. In other words, it is an array that is NOT ordered from highest positive to highest negative as is the case for linear arrays. The ratio values are arrayed from the lowest positive to the highest positive, to undefined (UND), and then from the highest negative to the lowest negative. If working capital is zero, the quotient is undefined (UND).

If the sales/working capital ratio is positive, then the top quartile would be represented by the lowest positive ratio. However, if the ratio is negative, the top quartile will be represented by the *highest* negative ratio! In a nonlinear array such as the sales/working capital ratio, the median could be either positive or negative because it is whatever the middle value is in the particular array of numbers.

Cautions — When analyzing this ratio, you need to focus on working capital, not on the sales figure. Although sales cannot be negative, working capital can be. If you have a large, positive working capital number, the ratio will be small and positive — which is good. Because negative working capital is bad, if you have a large, negative working capital number, the sales/working capital ratio will be small *and* negative — which is NOT good. Therefore, the lowest positive ratio is the best and the lowest negative ratio is the worst. If working capital is a small negative number, the ratio will be large, which is the best of the negatives.

COVERAGE RATIOS

Coverage ratios measure a firm's ability to service its debt. In other words, how well does the flow of a company's funds cover its short-term financial obligations? In contrast to liquidity ratios that focus on the possibility of liquidation, coverage ratios seek to provide lenders a comfort level based on the belief the firm will remain a viable enterprise.

1. Earnings Before Interest and Taxes (EBIT)/Interest

How to Calculate: Divide earnings (profit) before annual interest expense and taxes by annual interest expense.

$$\frac{\text{Earnings Before Interest \& Taxes}}{\text{Annual Interest Expense}}$$

How to Interpret: This ratio measures a firm's ability to meet interest payments. A high ratio may indicate that a borrower can easily meet the interest obligations of a loan. This ratio also indicates a firm's capacity to take on additional debt.

Please note — Only statements reporting annual interest expense were used in the calculation of this ratio. The ratio values are arrayed from the highest positive to the lowest positive and then from the lowest negative to the highest negative.

2. Net Profit + Depreciation, Depletion, Amortization/Current Maturities Long-Term Debt

How to Calculate: Add net profit to depreciation, depletion, and amortization expenses. Then, divide by the current portion of long-term debt.

$$\frac{\text{Net Profit + Depreciation, Depletion, Amortization Expenses}}{\text{Current Portion of Long-Term Debt}}$$

How to Interpret: This ratio reflects how well cash flow from operations covers current maturities. Because cash flow is the primary source of debt retirement, the ratio measures a firm's ability to service principal repayment and take on additional debt. Even though it is a mistake to believe all cash flow is available for debt service, this ratio is still a valid measure of the ability to service long-term debt.

Please note — Only data for corporations with the following items was used:

(1) Profit or loss after taxes (positive, negative, or zero).

(2) A positive figure for depreciation/depletion/amortization expenses.

(3) A positive figure for current maturities of long-term debt.

Ratio values are arrayed from the highest to the lowest positive and then from the lowest to the highest negative.

LEVERAGE RATIOS

How much protection do a company's assets provide for the debt held by its creditors? Highly leveraged firms are companies with heavy debt in relation to their net worth. These firms are more vulnerable to business downturns than those with lower debt-to-worth positions. While leverage ratios help measure this vulnerability, keep in mind that these ratios vary greatly depending on the requirements of particular industry groups.

1. Fixed/Worth

How to Calculate: Divide fixed assets (net of accumulated depreciation) by tangible net worth (net worth minus intangibles).

$$\frac{\text{Net Fixed Assets}}{\text{Tangible Net Worth}}$$

How to Interpret: This ratio measures the extent to which owner's equity (capital) has been invested in plant and equipment (fixed assets). A lower ratio indicates a proportionately smaller investment in fixed assets in relation to net worth and a better "cushion" for creditors in case of liquidation. Similarly, a higher ratio would indicate the opposite situation. The presence of a substantial number of fixed assets that are leased — and not appearing on the balance sheet — may result in a deceptively lower ratio.

Fixed assets may be zero, in which case the quotient is zero. If tangible net worth is zero, the quotient is undefined (UND). If tangible net worth is negative, the quotient is negative.

Please note — Like the sales/working capital ratio discussed above, this fixed/worth ratio is a nonlinear array. In other words, it is an array that is NOT ordered from highest positive to highest negative as a linear array would be. The ratio values are arrayed from the lowest positive to the highest positive, to undefined (UND), and then from the highest negative to the lowest negative.

If the Fixed/Worth ratio is positive, then the top quartile would be represented by the lowest positive ratio. However, if the ratio is negative, the top quartile will be represented by the *highest negative* ratio! In a nonlinear array such as this, the median could be either positive or negative because it is whatever the middle value is in the particular array of numbers.

2. Debt/Worth

How to Calculate: Divide total liabilities by tangible net worth.

$$\frac{\text{Total Liabilities}}{\text{Tangible Net Worth}}$$

How to Interpret: This ratio expresses the relationship between capital contributed by creditors and that contributed by owners. Basically, it shows how much protection the owners are providing creditors. The higher the ratio, the greater the risk being assumed by creditors. A lower ratio generally indicates greater long-term financial safety. Unlike a highly leveraged firm, a firm with a low debt/worth ratio usually has greater flexibility to borrow in the future.

Tangible net worth may be zero, in which case the ratio is undefined (UND). Tangible net worth may also be negative, which results in the quotient being negative. The ratio values are arrayed from the lowest to highest positive, to undefined, and then from the highest to lowest negative.

Please note — Like the sales/working capital ratio discussed above, this debt/worth ratio is a nonlinear array. In other words, it is an array that is NOT ordered from highest positive to highest negative as a linear array would be. The ratio values are arrayed from the lowest positive to the highest positive, to undefined (UND), and then from the highest negative to the lowest negative.

If the debt/worth ratio is positive, then the top quartile would be represented by the lowest positive ratio. However, if the ratio is negative, the top quartile will be represented by the *highest negative* ratio! In a nonlinear array such as this, the median could be either positive or negative because it is whatever the middle value is in the particular array of numbers.

OPERATING RATIOS

Operating ratios are designed to assist in the evaluation of management performance.

1. % Profits Before Taxes/Tangible Net Worth

How to Calculate: Divide profit before taxes by tangible net worth. Then, multiply by 100.

$$\frac{\text{Profit Before Taxes}}{\text{Tangible Net Worth}} \times 100$$

How to Interpret: This ratio expresses the rate of return on tangible capital employed. While it can serve as an indicator of management performance, you should always use it in conjunction with other ratios. Normally associated with effective management, a high return could actually point to an undercapitalized firm. Conversely, a low return that's usually viewed as an indicator of inefficient management performance could actually reflect a highly capitalized, conservatively operated business.

This ratio has been multiplied by 100 because it is shown as a percentage.

Profit before taxes may be zero, in which case the ratio is zero. Profits before taxes may be negative, resulting in negative quotients. Firms with negative tangible net worth have been omitted from the ratio arrays. Negative ratios will therefore only result in the case of negative profit before taxes. If the tangible net worth is zero, the quotient is undefined (UND). If there are fewer than 10 ratios for a particular size class, the result is not shown. The ratio values are arrayed starting with undefined (UND), then from the highest to the lowest positive values, and finally from the lowest to the highest negative values.

2. % Profits Before Taxes/Total Assets

How to Calculate: Divide profit before taxes by total assets and multiply by 100.

$$\frac{\text{Profit Before Taxes}}{\text{Total Assets}} \times 100$$

How to Interpret: This ratio expresses the pre-tax return on total assets and measures the effectiveness of management in employing the resources available to it. If a specific ratio varies considerably from the ranges found in this book, the analyst will need to examine the makeup of the assets and take a closer look at the earnings figure. A heavily depreciated plant and a large amount of intangible assets or unusual income or expense items will cause distortions of this ratio.

This ratio has been multiplied by 100 since it is shown as a percentage. If profit before taxes is zero, the quotient is zero. If profit before taxes is negative, the quotient is negative. These ratio values are arrayed from the highest to the lowest positive and then from the lowest to the highest negative.

3. Sales/Net Fixed Assets

How to Calculate: Divide net sales by net fixed assets (net of accumulated depreciation).

$$\frac{\text{Net Sales}}{\text{Net Fixed Assets}}$$

How to Interpret: This ratio is a measure of the productive use of a firm's fixed assets. Largely depreciated fixed assets or a labor-intensive operation may cause a distortion of this ratio.

If the net fixed figure is zero, the quotient is undefined (UND). The only time a zero will appear in the array will be when the net sales figure is low and the quotient rounds off to zero. These ratio values cannot be negative.

They are arrayed from undefined (UND) and then from the highest to the lowest positive values.

4. Sales/Total Assets

How to Calculate: Divide net sales by total assets.

$$\frac{\text{Net Sales}}{\text{Total Assets}}$$

How to Interpret: This ratio is a general measure of a firm's ability to generate sales in relation to total assets. It should be used only to compare firms within specific industry groups and in conjunction with other operating ratios to determine the effective employment of assets.

The only time a zero will appear in the array will be when the net sales figure is low and the quotient rounds off to zero. The ratio values cannot be negative. They are arrayed from the highest to the lowest positive values.

EXPENSE TO SALES RATIOS

The following two ratios relate specific expense items to net sales and express this relationship as a percentage. Comparisons are convenient because the item, net sales, is used as a constant. Variations in these ratios are most pronounced between capital- and labor-intensive industries.

1. % Depreciation, Depletion, Amortization/Sales

How to Calculate: Divide annual depreciation, amortization, and depletion expenses by net sales and multiply by 100.

$$\frac{\text{Depreciation, Amortization, Depletion Expenses}}{\text{Net Sales}} \times 100$$

2. % Officers', Directors', Owners' Compensation/Sales

How to Calculate: Divide annual officers', directors', owners' compensation by net sales and multiply by 100. Include total salaries, bonuses, commissions, and other monetary remuneration to all officers, directors, and/or owners of the firm during the year covered by the statement. This includes drawings of partners and proprietors.

$$\frac{\text{Officers', Directors', Owners' Compensation}}{\text{Net Sales}} \times 100$$

Only statements showing a positive figure for each of the expense categories shown above were used. The ratios are arrayed from the lowest to highest positive values.

Explanation of Noncontractor Balance Sheet and Income Data

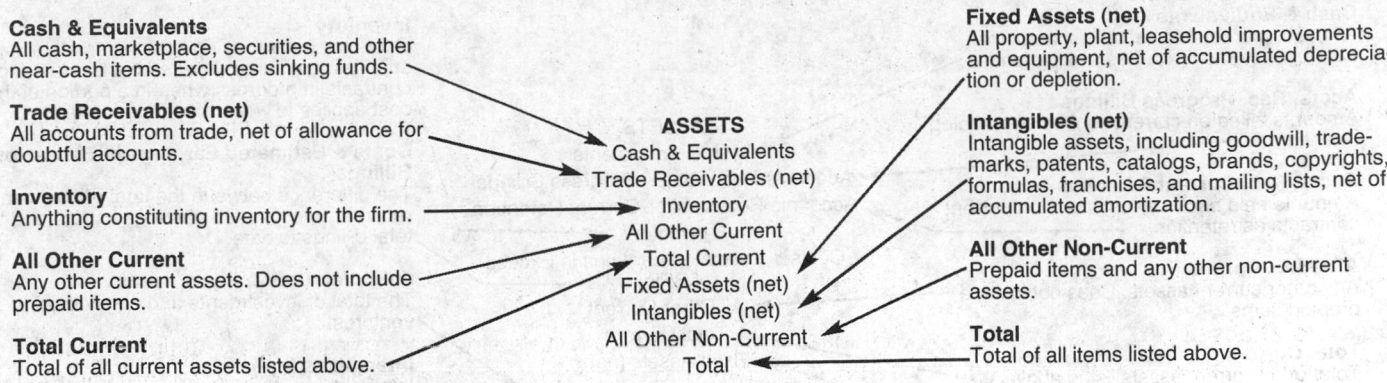

Cash & Equivalents
All cash, marketplace, securities, and other near-cash items. Excludes sinking funds.

Trade Receivables (net)
All accounts from trade, net of allowance for doubtful accounts.

Inventory
Anything constituting inventory for the firm.

All Other Current
Any other current assets. Does not include prepaid items.

Total Current
Total of all current assets listed above.

ASSETS
Cash & Equivalents
Trade Receivables (net)
Inventory
All Other Current
Total Current
Fixed Assets (net)
Intangibles (net)
All Other Non-Current
Total

Fixed Assets (net)
All property, plant, leasehold improvements and equipment, net of accumulated depreciation or depletion.

Intangibles (net)
Intangible assets, including goodwill, trademarks, patents, catalogs, brands, copyrights, formulas, franchises, and mailing lists, net of accumulated amortization.

All Other Non-Current
Prepaid items and any other non-current assets.

Total
Total of all items listed above.

Notes Payable—Short Term
All short-term note obligations, including bank and commercial paper. Does not include trade notes payable.

Current Maturities—L/T/D
That portion of long-term obligations that is due within the next fiscal year.

Trade Payables
Open accounts due to the trade.

Income Taxes Payable
Income taxes including current portion of deferred taxes.

All Other Current
Any other current liabilities, including bank overdrafts and accrued expenses.

LIABILITIES
Notes Payable-Short Term
Cur. Mat.-L/T/D
Trade Payables
Income Taxes Payable
All Other Current
Total Current
Long-Term Debt
Deferred Taxes
All Other Non-Current
Net Worth
Total Liabilities & Net Worth

Total Current
Total of all current liabilities listed above.

Long-Term Debt
All senior debt, including bonds, debentures, bank debt, mortgages, deferred portions of long-term debt, and capital lease obligations.

Deferred Taxes
All deferred taxes.

All Other Non-Current
Any other non-current liabilities, including subordinated debt, and liability reserves.

Net Worth
Difference between Total Liabilities and Total Assets. Minority interest is included here.

Total Liabilities & Net Worth
Total of all items listed above.

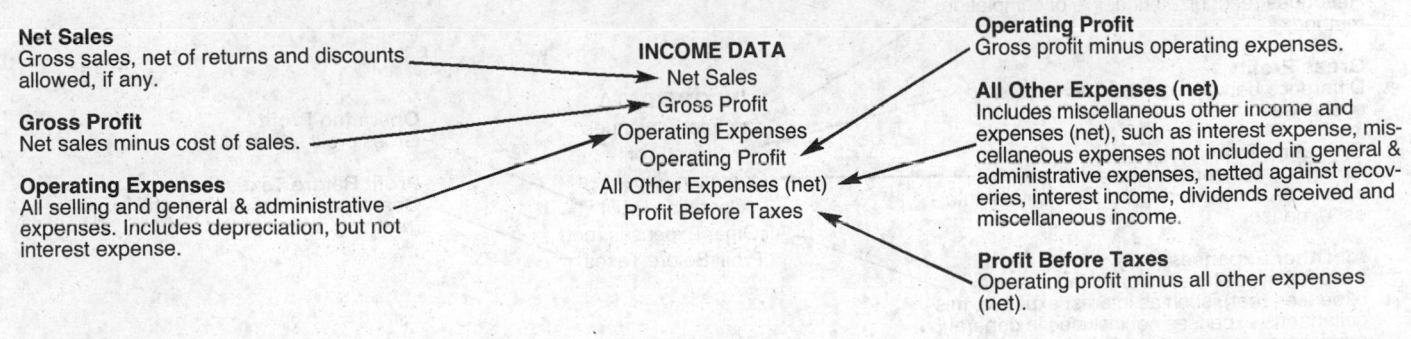

Net Sales
Gross sales, net of returns and discounts allowed, if any.

Gross Profit
Net sales minus cost of sales.

Operating Expenses
All selling and general & administrative expenses. Includes depreciation, but not interest expense.

INCOME DATA
Net Sales
Gross Profit
Operating Expenses
Operating Profit
All Other Expenses (net)
Profit Before Taxes

Operating Profit
Gross profit minus operating expenses.

All Other Expenses (net)
Includes miscellaneous other income and expenses (net), such as interest expense, miscellaneous expenses not included in general & administrative expenses, netted against recoveries, interest income, dividends received and miscellaneous income.

Profit Before Taxes
Operating profit minus all other expenses (net).

Explanation of Contractor Percentage-of-Completion Basis of Accounting Balance Sheet and Income Data

Cash & Equivalents
All cash, marketable securities, and other near-cash items. Excludes sinking funds.

Accts. Rec.-Progress Billings
Amounts billed on current contracts excluding retention.

Accts. Rec.-Current Retention
Amounts held back by customers on current contracts as retention.

All Other Current
Any other current assets. Does not include prepaid items.

Total Current
Total of all current assets listed above.

Fixed Assets (net)
All property, plant, leasehold improvements and equipment, net of accumulated depreciation or depletion.

All Other Non-Current
Prepaid items and other non-current assets.

Inventory
Costs attributable to equipment, small tools, supplies, and other deferred costs related to contracts in progress wherein a portion of the cost applies to work not yet performed.

Costs & Estimated Earnings in Excess of Billings
The difference between the total of costs and recognized estimated earnings to date and the total billings to date.

Joint Ventures & Investments
The total of investments and equity in joint ventures.

Intangibles (net)
Intangible assets, including goodwill, trade-marks, patents, catalogs, brands, copyrights, formulas, franchises, and mailing lists, net of accumulated amortization.

Total
Total of all items listed above.

ASSETS
Cash & Equivalents
Accounts Receivable—Progress Billings
Accounts Receivable—Current Retention
Inventory
Costs & Estimated Earnings in Excess of Billings
All Other Current
Total Current
Fixed Assets (net)
Joint Ventures & Investments
Intangibles (net)
All Other Non-Current
Total

Notes Payable—Short Term
All short-term note obligations, including bank and commercial paper. Does not include trade notes payable.

Accounts Payable—Trade
Open accounts and note obligations due to the trade.

Accounts Payable—Retention
Amounts held back as retention in payments to subcontractors on current contracts.

Long-Term Debt
All senior debt, including bonds, debentures, bank debt, mortgages, deferred portions of long-term debt, and capital lease obligations.

Deferred Taxes
Total of all deferred taxes.

All Other Non-Current
Any other non-current liabilities, including subordinated debt, and liability reserves.

Billings in Excess of Costs & Est. Earn.
The difference between the total billings to date and the total of costs and recognized estimated earnings to date.

Income Taxes Payable
Income taxes including current portion of deferred taxes.

Current Maturities—LTD
That portion of long-term obligations that is due within the next fiscal year.

All Other Current
Any other current liabilities, including bank overdrafts and accrued expenses.

Total Current
Total of all current liabilities listed above.

Net Worth
Difference between total assets and total liabilities. Minority interest is included here.

Total Liabilities & Net Worth
Total of all items listed above.

LIABILITIES
Notes Payable—Short Term
Accounts Payable—Trade
Accounts Payable—Retention
Billings in Excess of Costs & Estimated Earnings
Income Taxes Payable
Current Maturities—LTD
All Other Current
Total Current
Long-Term Debt
Deferred Taxes
All Other Non-Current
Net Worth
Total Liabilities & Net Worth

Contract Revenues
Revenues recognized under % of completion method.

Gross Profit
Difference between contract revenues and cost of sales.

Operating Expenses
All selling and general and administrative expenses. Includes depreciation, but not interest expense.

All Other Expenses (net)
Includes miscellaneous other income and expenses (net), such as interest expense, miscellaneous expenses not included in general & administrative expenses, netted against recoveries, interest income, dividends received and miscellaneous income.

Operating Profit
Gross profit minus operating expenses.

Profit Before Taxes
Operating profit minus all other expenses (net).

INCOME DATA
Contract Revenues
Gross Profit
Operating Expenses
Operating Profit
All Other Expenses (net)
Profit Before Taxes

For further analysis, please refer to *Industry Default Probabilities and Cash Flow Measures*

If you think *Financial Ratio Benchmarks* is a valuable resource, wait until you see its companion study. Now in its thirteenth year and bigger than ever, *Industry Default Probabilities and Cash Flow Measures* is a major expansion of our *Annual Statement Studies*. These benchmarks add substantial value to the critical analysis of cash flow for private companies.

The latest edition of *Industry Default Probabilities and Cash Flow Measures* includes many new industries, stronger statements, five years of historical data sorted by assets and sales. In short, it is more like our traditional *Statement Studies*.

Industry Default Probabilities and Cash Flow Measures includes:
- Cash flow measures on a common-size percentage scale. Ratios include:
  - Cash from Trading
  - Cash after Operations
  - Net Cash after Operations
  - Cash after Debt Amortization
  - Debt Service P&I Coverage
  - Interest Coverage (Operating Cash)
- Change in position, normalized, year over year, for eight financial statement line items. Ratios include:
  - Change in Inventory
  - Total Current Assets (TCA)
  - Total Assets (TA)
  - Retained Earnings (RE)
  - Net Sales (NS)
  - Cost of Goods Sold (CGS)
  - Profit before Interest & Taxes (PBIT)
  - Depreciation/Depletion/Amortization (DDA)
- Trend data available for the past five years.
- Other ratios:
  - Sustainable Growth Rate
  - Funded Debt/EBITDA
  - Data arrayed by asset and sales size.

Access to the Industry Default Probabilities and Cash Flow Measures is only available in the eStatement Studies online database. A copy of a sample report can be found on the next page. For more information on how to upgrade to eStatement Studies, please see the inside back cover, or contact us at 1-800-677-7621.

INDUSTRY DEFAULT PROBABILITIES AND CASH FLOW MEASURES SAMPLE REPORT

AGRICULTURE—Soybean Farming NAICS 111110

Current Data Sorted by Assets						Type of Statement	Comparative Historical Data	
		1	4	1	1	Unqualified	10	20
	2	3	3			Reviewed	5	19
	2	1				Compiled	5	12
6	8	6	1			Tax Returns	25	30
2	5	9	3	2		Other	33	52
	7 (4/1-9/30/17)		53 (10/1/17-3/31/18)				4/1/13-3/31/14	4/1/14-3/31/15
0-500M	500M-2MM	2-10MM	10-50MM	50-100MM	100-250MM	Assets Size	ALL	ALL
8	17	20	11	3	1	Number of Statements	78	133
%	%	%	%	%	%		%	%

0-500M	500M-2MM	2-10MM	10-50MM	50-100MM	100-250MM	CASH FLOW MEASURES	4/1/13-3/31/14 ALL	4/1/14-3/31/15 ALL
%	%	%	%	%	%		%	%
						Cash from Trading/Sales		
	17.2	38.9	25.1			Cash after Operations/Sales	25.3	26.4
	6.5	19.3	9.7				(76) 10.5	10.0
	-16.9	3.9	-1.7				4.8	3.2
	16.7	28.1	23.8			Net Cash after Operations/Sales	25.8	26.3
	5.3	15.0	9.0				(76) 10.7	11.7
	-.3	2.6	2.1				5.3	3.9
	12.6	5.6	4.9			Net Cash after Debt Amortization/Sales	12.5	8.7
	(16) 5.7	.9	-2.2				(76) 4.1	2.2
	-3.0	-11.2	-6.7				-2.3	-2.6
	14.7	2.4	29.3			Debt Service P&I Coverage	7.1	6.0
	(14) 9.6	(16) 1.3	(10) 2.2				(68) 2.8	(120) 2.4
	-.2	.1	.0				.8	1.1
	51.9	22.1	59.6			Interest Coverage (Operating Cash)	18.4	24.1
	(13) 8.3	(16) 5.7	(10) 16.3				(66) 5.1	(118) 7.0
	-3.3	.5	2.2				1.3	2.5
		48.0				Δ Inventory	31.5	22.9
		(10) -.5					(43) 6.0	(66) 4.1
		-17.4					-6.6	-5.9
	28.6	31.7	4.9			Δ Total Current Assets	47.0	49.4
	2.8	10.5	-6.2				14.1	9.1
	-35.1	-20.4	-26.1				-13.4	-12.6
	36.3	20.8	8.3			Δ Total Assets	26.9	24.1
	3.1	3.1	-1.9				6.1	4.9
	-5.8	-7.7	-5.7				-3.5	-3.7
	111.1	32.9	6.6			Δ Retained Earnings	82.3	36.6
	(15) 10.8	(19) 4.2	-15.0				(76) 17.1	(131) 10.1
	-72.0	-38.7	-91.3				-.8	-4.3
	34.7	13.8	16.5			Δ Net Sales	27.9	23.3
	-2.5	6.9	5.4				10.0	3.2
	-11.7	.3	-7.8				-2.3	-6.3
						Δ Cost of Goods Sold		
	96.1	88.0	73.5			Δ Profit before Int. & Taxes	120.8	82.7
	(16) -.7	13.6	-7.4				35.5	(131) 14.9
	-44.8	-34.1	-47.6				-18.0	-35.3
	67.7	12.6	100.7			Δ Depr./Depl./Amort.	11.3	21.1
	(12) -21.3	(18) 2.3	7.7				(69) -4.7	(110) .0
	-81.6	-15.8	-31.1				-33.6	-16.3
	64.9	50.4	12.5			**RATIOS** Sustainable Growth Rate	16.1	26.3
	.0	17.7	-.1				(77) .1	(131) 5.6
	-39.7	-.2	-11.5				-17.7	-7.9
	.0	.6	.5			Funded Debt/EBITDA	.5	.6
	1.0	1.4	8.2				2.1	2.2
	3.4	8.3	15.4				5.9	7.6
9580M	42882M	289548M	468863M	141379M	56029M	Net Sales ($)	1170146M	3006125M
2078M	21645M	95307M	207335M	218849M	105246M	Total Assets ($)	874532M	1601154M

M = $ thousand   MM = $ million

AGRICULTURE—Soybean Farming NAICS 111110

Comparative Historical Data			Type of Statement	Current Data Sorted by Sales					
14	6	7	Unqualified		1	1			5
13	5	8	Reviewed		1		2	3	2
9	8	3	Compiled		1	1	1		
31	23	21	Tax Returns	5	12	2	2		
50	40	21	Other	5	4		3	4	5
4/1/15-3/31/16 ALL	4/1/16-3/31/17 ALL	4/1/17-3/31/18 ALL		7 (4/1-9/30/17)			53 (10/1/17-3/31/18)		
			Sales Size	0-1MM	1-3MM	3-5MM	5-10MM	10-25MM	25MM & OVER
117	82	60	Number of Statements	10	19	4	8	7	12
%	%	%		%	%	%	%	%	%

Hist 1	Hist 2	Hist 3	CASH FLOW MEASURES	0-1MM	1-3MM	3-5MM	5-10MM	10-25MM	25MM & OVER
%	%	%		%	%				%
			Cash from Trading/Sales						
25.2	18.7	22.0	Cash after Operations/Sales	98.9	22.7				9.8
10.0	5.0	6.7		19.0	18.9				6.3
3.6	-2.1	-1.9		-15.4	3.6				1.9
24.1	18.4	20.4	Net Cash after Operations/Sales	90.5	27.2				9.6
(116) 10.0	5.8	7.5		1.0	17.1				7.1
4.5	.0	1.1		-19.1	4.9				1.9
14.5	5.7	8.8	Net Cash after Debt Amortization/Sales	3.0	11.8				3.7
(116) 2.7	(81) .7	(59) .0		-15.4	8.8				-1.0
-3.5	-6.0	-6.7		-65.5	-2.6				-5.4
8.9	8.9	11.9	Debt Service P&I Coverage		13.4				13.1
(95) 2.6	(70) 1.9	(50) 1.7			(16) 7.4				(11) 2.4
.7	.0	.0			.5				.6
21.5	22.4	23.9	Interest Coverage (Operating Cash)		42.8				30.4
(90) 6.0	(64) 5.8	(49) 5.1			(15) 10.9				(11) 13.1
2.2	.0	.0			1.8				1.2
13.8	25.6	38.4	Δ Inventory						
(49) .0	(42) -1.0	(27) 1.6							
-17.5	-19.5	-15.4							
47.1	38.8	23.3	Δ Total Current Assets	-15.8	39.4				11.7
4.4	3.7	2.1		-49.2	13.7				.5
-15.0	-17.3	-25.0		-80.4	-26.1				-10.4
27.3	16.8	21.0	Δ Total Assets	34.7	33.9				9.3
3.3	-.4	2.4		7.1	8.3				-2.8
-4.0	-9.0	-7.7		-61.7	-5.6				-5.5
45.7	44.3	35.5	Δ Retained Earnings	28.5	135.5				5.6
(112) 8.3	(80) 4.1	(57) 4.5		11.8	(16) 10.6				-12.3
-9.3	-24.5	-39.5		-52.3	-.3				-51.2
17.7	19.2	14.5	Δ Net Sales	7.8	49.8				30.1
.2	4.5	6.0		-.6	11.8				9.7
-14.7	-9.5	-4.9		-30.2	-3.1				-.8
			Δ Cost of Goods Sold						
90.4	85.5	101.7	Δ Profit before Int. & Taxes	101.4	188.1				55.8
(116) 11.9	12.0	(59) 6.5		15.5	(18) 30.3				-25.6
-44.7	-46.3	-44.8		-72.9	-10.1				-68.9
29.4	28.5	36.4	Δ Depr./Depl./Amort.		30.6				43.8
(89) .0	(70) -5.6	(49) .0			(16) -15.8				(10) 21.4
-34.0	-55.5	-26.8			-37.5				-17.1

Hist 1	Hist 2	Hist 3	RATIOS	0-1MM	1-3MM	3-5MM	5-10MM	10-25MM	25MM & OVER
24.5	19.8	27.4	Sustainable Growth Rate	4.5	42.7				22.3
6.5	(81) 1.4	.3		-.9	2.2				.6
-7.0	-7.0	-13.8		-32.4	-24.5				-17.0
.3	.3	.3	Funded Debt/EBITDA	2.7	.2				.5
2.4	2.1	2.3		9.0	1.0				1.9
6.7	10.5	9.1		NM	2.8				10.2
2343689M	1692251M	1008281M	Net Sales ($)	5415M	34506M	17030M	56384M	130791M	764155M
1662679M	922447M	650460M	Total Assets ($)	24514M	51377M	12629M	44808M	123974M	393158M

© RMA 2018   M = $ thousand   MM = $ million

RETAIL TRADE

Current Data Sorted by Assets   Comparative Historical Data

Type of Statement	0-500M	500M-2MM	2-10MM	10-50MM	50-100MM	100-250MM	ALL	ALL
Unqualified	1			8	15	12	6	102	91
Reviewed	1	1	25	102	12	6	218	158
Compiled		2	13	17	2	2	68	48
Tax Returns		10	59	50	1		245	215
Other	10	16	490	1029	98	50	1279	1488
		145 (4/1-9/30/18)		1,893 (10/1/18-3/31/19)			4/1/14-3/31/15	4/1/15-3/31/16
	0-500M	500M-2MM	2-10MM	10-50MM	50-100MM	100-250MM	ALL	ALL
NUMBER OF STATEMENTS	12	29	595	1213	125	64	1912	2000
	%	%	%	%	%	%	%	%
ASSETS								
Cash & Equivalents	7.5	13.9	11.6	13.1	13.0	13.7	12.4	12.5
Trade Receivables (net)	13.2	5.0	5.8	6.2	7.7	6.3	7.1	6.6
Inventory	52.5	53.3	67.8	60.8	53.1	48.1	59.8	61.8
All Other Current	3.9	.2	1.8	2.0	2.4	3.0	2.3	2.0
Total Current	77.1	72.4	87.0	82.0	76.2	71.1	81.6	83.0
Fixed Assets (net)	17.3	14.1	6.3	8.0	12.7	16.3	9.8	8.9
Intangibles (net)	1.0	5.4	2.6	3.4	4.2	6.5	3.5	3.1
All Other Non-Current	3.6	8.1	4.2	6.5	6.9	6.1	5.1	5.0
Total	100.0	100.0	100.0	100.0	100.0	100.0	100.0	100.0
LIABILITIES								
Notes Payable-Short Term	47.7	27.3	55.9	53.8	48.9	29.5	51.3	51.7
Cur. Mat.-L.T.D.	3.4	3.0	1.8	1.2	1.0	1.0	1.8	2.0
Trade Payables	29.3	15.3	5.7	6.1	5.4	18.4	5.0	5.7
Income Taxes Payable	.0	.0	.0	.1	.0	.0	.1	.1
All Other Current	4.2	7.1	11.1	9.7	11.7	10.3	9.8	9.9
Total Current	84.6	52.7	74.5	70.8	67.0	59.3	67.9	69.3
Long-Term Debt	17.7	11.5	6.2	5.6	7.9	11.2	6.0	5.8
Deferred Taxes	.0	.0	.1	.1	.4	.3	.1	.1
All Other Non-Current	3.8	11.0	2.2	2.3	1.3	4.3	3.9	3.0
Net Worth	-7.1	24.7	17.0	21.0	23.4	24.9	22.1	21.8
Total Liabilities & Net Worth	100.0	100.0	100.0	100.0	100.0	100.0	100.0	100.0
INCOME DATA								
Net Sales	100.0	100.0	100.0	100.0	100.0	100.0	100.0	100.0
Gross Profit	20.0	26.8	10.8	9.7	11.0	12.6	11.8	11.1
Operating Expenses	18.0	24.6	11.7	9.9	10.1	11.5	11.3	10.7
Operating Profit	2.0	2.3	-.9	-.2	.9	1.1	.5	.4
All Other Expenses (net)	-.5	-.4	-1.2	-1.6	-1.1	-.9	-1.1	-1.2
Profit Before Taxes	2.5	2.6	.3	1.3	2.0	2.0	1.6	1.6
RATIOS								
Current	1.3	2.0	1.3	1.3	1.3	1.3	1.3	1.3
	1.2	1.4	1.1	1.1	1.1	1.2	1.2	1.2
	1.0	1.1	1.0	1.0	1.0	1.1	1.1	1.1
Quick	.4	1.0	.3	.4	.4	.5	.4	.4
	.3	.2	.2	.2	.3	.3	(1910) .3	(1996) .3
	.1	.1	.1	.2	.2	.2	.2	.2
Sales/Receivables	4 99.0	1 478.6	2 147.6	3 117.8	5 79.6	2 190.9	3 117.6	3 131.2
	13 29.0	3 129.8	5 78.0	6 63.4	8 45.3	6 63.5	6 62.2	5 68.0
	23 16.1	8 45.7	9 42.7	10 36.0	15 24.1	13 28.9	10 37.0	9 40.1
Cost of Sales/Inventory	68 5.4	35 10.4	69 5.3	63 5.8	63 5.8	64 5.7	55 6.6	58 6.3
	83 4.4	91 4.0	89 4.1	81 4.5	79 4.6	79 4.6	72 5.1	74 4.9
	130 2.8	126 2.9	114 3.2	104 3.5	94 3.9	94 3.9	94 3.9	96 3.8
Cost of Sales/Payables	0 UND	1 335.3	2 228.4	2 232.7	2 155.3	3 110.6	2 194.7	2 211.4
	0 UND	6 59.0	3 125.6	3 116.6	4 86.2	9 42.0	3 109.2	3 117.1
	12 30.1	29 12.4	7 55.4	6 63.2	8 48.6	62 5.9	6 61.4	5 66.8
Sales/Working Capital	10.8	6.6	14.2	17.3	16.4	14.2	15.6	15.9
	26.3	17.8	25.7	30.7	30.9	24.1	27.2	27.2
	NM	NM	83.6	83.8	118.8	61.5	62.9	61.3
EBIT/Interest		8.7	4.4	15.8	13.3	12.0	16.1	22.1
	(20) 1.7	(419) 1.7	(871) 3.8	(98) 4.5	(52) 5.9		(1273) 4.6	(1363) 5.9
		1.0	.3	1.5	2.7	2.4	1.9	2.2
Net Profit + Depr., Dep., Amort./Cur. Mat. L/T/D			22.4	6.6	6.9		9.7	11.2
		(11) 1.3	(38) 3.9	(13) 3.0			(87) 4.1	(88) 3.8
			.7	2.0	1.9		1.4	1.6
Fixed/Worth	.3	.1	.1	.1	.2	.3	.1	.1
	1.1	.2	.3	.4	.5	.7	.4	.3
	NM	2.1	1.0	1.0	1.3	1.6	1.0	1.0
Debt/Worth	3.0	1.0	2.7	2.9	2.6	2.7	2.4	2.5
	6.6	2.4	5.5	5.1	4.0	3.9	4.6	4.7
	NM	20.4	17.3	11.1	7.3	9.1	10.3	10.0
% Profit Before Taxes/Tangible Net Worth		56.0	31.6	40.7	48.6	40.7	52.5	50.0
	(23) 6.5	(498) 12.3	(1093) 21.9	(119) 23.8	(60) 24.0		(1740) 26.4	(1833) 27.4
		.4	-.8	9.1	13.4	11.4	11.5	11.0
% Profit Before Taxes/Total Assets	13.6	18.4	5.2	6.9	7.5	8.4	8.9	9.0
	2.9	2.0	1.5	3.8	4.8	4.7	4.8	4.9
	.0	.1	-1.2	1.1	2.7	1.9	1.7	1.7
Sales/Net Fixed Assets	67.5	180.4	211.6	149.6	94.8	58.3	155.3	157.1
	21.3	54.5	89.0	64.8	42.4	31.8	65.9	68.4
	12.4	20.5	40.5	29.5	13.6	8.4	27.4	29.7
Sales/Total Assets	3.3	3.6	3.9	3.6	3.3	3.3	4.1	4.1
	2.6	2.9	3.1	3.0	2.7	2.6	3.4	3.3
	2.1	2.4	2.5	2.4	2.1	2.0	2.6	2.7
% Depr., Dep., Amort./Sales		.1	.1	.1	.2	.2	.1	.1
	(21) .2	(459) .2	(1039) .2	(119) .3	(54) .3		(1626) .2	(1683) .2
		.5	.4	.4	.5	.5	.4	.4
% Officers', Directors' Owners' Comp/Sales		1.2	.3	.2	.2		.3	.2
	(14) 1.7	(357) .5	(743) .4	(64) .4	(19) .2		(1047) .5	(1186) .4
		2.9	.9	.6	.5	.3	1.0	.8
Net Sales ($)	6014M	125022M	12962141M	79099499M	23978024M	24553790M	134741512M	140187718M
Total Assets ($)	1677M	39972M	4004358M	26401072M	8348391M	9540048M	42118935M	43794224M

© RMA 2019

M = $ thousand MM = $ million
See Pages viii through xx for Explanation of Ratios and Data

Comparative Historical Data | Current Data Sorted by Sales

3/31/17 ALL	3/31/18 ALL	3/31/19 ALL	Type of Statement	0-1MM	1-3MM	3-5MM	5-10MM	10-25MM	25MM & OVER
40	55	42	Unqualified		1		2	4	37
136	206	147	Reviewed	1		1		15	128
53	58	36	Compiled		2		1	8	25
151	195	120	Tax Returns		4	3	9	37	67
981	2009	1693	Other	11	5	16	53	327	1281
4/1/16-3/31/17 ALL	4/1/17-3/31/18 ALL	4/1/18-3/31/19 ALL		145 (4/1-9/30/18)			1,893 (10/1/18-3/31/19)		
1361	2523	2038	**NUMBER OF STATEMENTS**	12	12	20	65	391	1538
%	%	%	**ASSETS**	%	%	%	%	%	%
12.6	13.8	12.7	Cash & Equivalents	5.5	17.6	12.6	11.1	11.0	13.2
6.6	6.7	6.2	Trade Receivables (net)	15.5	8.5	3.9	4.8	5.3	6.5
62.1	58.1	61.8	Inventory	50.7	42.4	49.8	66.6	67.4	60.6
2.3	1.7	2.0	All Other Current	2.3	1.6	.4	4.0	1.6	2.0
83.6	80.3	82.6	Total Current	74.0	70.1	66.7	86.5	85.2	82.2
9.1	9.4	8.2	Fixed Assets (net)	15.6	21.4	19.5	4.1	7.1	8.4
3.3	3.4	3.3	Intangibles (net)	5.9	3.5	6.2	4.5	3.3	3.2
3.9	6.9	5.8	All Other Non-Current	3.5	5.1	7.6	5.0	4.3	6.2
100.0	100.0	100.0	Total	100.0	100.0	100.0	100.0	100.0	100.0
			LIABILITIES						
53.4	51.0	52.9	Notes Payable-Short Term	47.9	9.7	34.7	56.9	55.1	52.8
2.0	1.3	1.4	Cur. Mat.-L.T.D.	4.0	.6	3.2	1.1	1.5	1.4
5.9	5.5	6.6	Trade Payables	10.1	27.3	12.7	5.4	5.9	6.5
.1	.1	.0	Income Taxes Payable	.0	.1	.0	.0	.0	.0
8.7	10.6	10.2	All Other Current	5.3	8.8	3.7	10.7	11.8	9.8
70.1	68.5	71.1	Total Current	67.3	46.5	54.4	74.1	74.3	70.7
6.4	6.5	6.3	Long-Term Debt	7.1	22.3	10.7	10.9	6.4	5.9
.1	.1	.1	Deferred Taxes	.0	.0	.9	.0	.1	.1
3.6	3.1	2.4	All Other Non-Current	13.9	1.6	8.1	2.9	2.7	2.2
19.9	21.8	20.0	Net Worth	10.7	29.6	25.8	12.1	16.5	21.1
100.0	100.0	100.0	Total Liabilities & Net Worth	100.0	100.0	100.0	100.0	100.0	100.0
			INCOME DATA						
100.0	100.0	100.0	Net Sales	100.0	100.0	100.0	100.0	100.0	100.0
11.5	10.4	10.5	Gross Profit	24.4	33.7	23.6	13.7	10.5	9.9
11.3	10.9	10.8	Operating Expenses	19.1	29.6	21.9	14.8	11.7	10.0
.2	-.6	-.3	Operating Profit	5.3	4.1	1.6	-1.1	-1.2	-.1
-1.0	-1.9	-1.4	All Other Expenses (net)	.0	.5	-.4	-.3	-1.2	-1.5
1.3	1.3	1.1	Profit Before Taxes	5.3	3.6	2.0	-.8	.1	1.4
			RATIOS						
1.3	1.3	1.3	Current	1.3	10.8	1.8	1.4	1.3	1.3
1.2	1.2	1.1		1.2	3.1	1.3	1.2	1.1	1.1
1.1	1.0	1.0		1.0	1.2	1.1	1.0	1.0	1.0
.4	.4	.4	Quick	.4	4.3	.7	.3	.3	.4
(1360) .3	(2517) .3	.2		.2	1.0	.2	.2	.2	.3
.2	.2	.2		.1	.1	.1	.1	.1	.2
3 133.1	3 105.6	3 125.6	Sales/Receivables	1 532.2	0 UND	1 475.4	3 138.7	2 155.8	3 119.0
6 59.2	6 59.4	6 65.6		12 30.8	7 55.9	4 99.8	5 62.0	5 74.9	6 63.5
10 35.4	10 35.3	10 36.2		22 16.3	16 23.3	13 27.7	13 27.9	9 40.1	10 36.1
63 5.8	60 6.1	65 5.6	Cost of Sales/Inventory	68 5.4	15 24.1	37 9.9	96 3.8	79 4.6	62 5.9
81 4.5	78 4.7	83 4.4		83 4.4	114 3.2	118 3.1	130 2.8	104 3.5	79 4.6
104 3.5	96 3.8	107 3.4		130 2.8	261 1.4	228 1.6	182 2.0	130 2.8	99 3.7
2 203.0	2 208.5	2 219.9	Cost of Sales/Payables	0 UND	3 132.1	1 498.0	2 212.4	2 210.1	2 219.0
3 107.5	3 110.3	3 114.9		0 UND	15 25.0	5 80.7	4 90.8	3 111.4	3 115.8
6 56.5	6 61.5	6 56.6		3 105.7	83 4.4	30 12.3	14 26.9	8 45.9	6 61.7
15.0	15.9	15.9	Sales/Working Capital	10.8	1.9	5.1	8.5	13.4	17.4
25.3	27.6	28.4		26.3	4.0	16.6	16.4	25.2	30.5
55.9	79.9	84.2		NM	21.7	28.0	NM	78.6	86.7
10.6	16.9	10.7	EBIT/Interest			20.8	1.8	3.8	15.0
(964) 3.4	(1651) 4.7	(1466) 3.2				(16) 1.5	(47) 1.1	(277) 1.6	(1110) 4.0
1.5	1.5	1.2				-.1	-1.6	.2	1.6
7.3	7.4	7.1	Net Profit + Depr., Dep., Amort./Cur. Mat. L/T/D						7.0
(66) 3.7	(85) 4.0	(71) 3.3						(61)	3.4
1.8	1.2	1.7							1.9
.2	.1	.1	Fixed/Worth	.1	.1	.1	.1	.1	.1
.4	.4	.4		.7	.4	.2	.4	.4	.4
1.0	1.1	1.1		2.7	1.6	2.4	4.7	1.3	1.0
2.9	2.5	2.8	Debt/Worth	2.7	.4	2.0	2.9	3.0	2.8
5.1	4.6	5.0		5.1	1.0	3.3	9.7	6.0	4.9
11.3	10.3	11.8		15.7	4.9	9.5	-44.6	17.3	10.4
42.5	41.7	38.8	% Profit Before Taxes/Tangible Net Worth	51.6	10.6	54.0	13.3	25.5	42.1
(1224) 20.2	(2293) 20.2	(1802) 19.5		(10) 17.6	(10) 5.9	(17) 4.0	(46) 2.8	(326) 9.4	(1393) 22.6
5.9	5.9	5.7		.0	.0	.2	-15.9	-2.7	9.9
7.1	7.6	6.6	% Profit Before Taxes/Total Assets	11.3	9.9	15.1	1.1	4.1	7.3
3.6	3.5	3.4		3.4	2.5	2.1	-.3	.9	4.0
.8	.8	.5		.0	.9	.0	-4.1	-1.6	1.4
143.7	148.7	158.0	Sales/Net Fixed Assets	UND	52.3	85.1	216.8	181.4	151.2
58.5	59.4	67.1		22.7	22.4	32.5	85.7	69.9	67.6
28.2	24.4	30.1		7.9	4.9	8.1	39.5	30.0	30.4
3.8	3.7	3.7	Sales/Total Assets	2.7	3.3	2.8	2.9	3.4	3.8
3.1	3.1	3.0		2.3	1.7	2.3	2.2	2.7	3.1
2.5	2.4	2.4		1.6	1.0	1.0	1.6	2.2	2.5
.1	.1	.1	% Depr., Dep., Amort./Sales		.1	.1	.1	.1	.1
(1137) .2	(2163) .2	(1697) .2			(10) .4	(12) .3	(43) .3	(301) .2	(1326) .2
.4	.4	.4			1.3	.7	.7	.4	.4
.3	.2	.2	% Officers', Directors' Owners' Comp/Sales				.5	.3	.2
(760) .5	(1472) .4	(1199) .4					(30) 1.1	(235) .6	(922) .3
.9	.7	.7					1.5	.9	.6
94822742M	186202058M	140724490M	Net Sales ($)	3154M	26005M	79187M	491301M	7174040M	132950803M
31721304M	63802639M	48335518M	Total Assets ($)	7540M	27786M	79188M	270312M	2964134M	44986558M

M = $ thousand   MM = $ million
See Pages viii through xx for Explanation of Ratios and Data

Current Data Sorted by Assets

Comparative Historical Data

							Type of Statement			
		1	5	8	6	2	Unqualified		14	20
	2	4	12	11	2		Reviewed		25	23
	42	15	23	5			Compiled		67	55
	23	77	45	10		1	Tax Returns		185	210
		55	82	38	4		Other		193	139
		39 (4/1-9/30/18)		434 (10/1/18-3/31/19)					4/1/14-3/31/15	4/1/15-3/31/16
	0-500M	500M-2MM	2-10MM	10-50MM	50-100MM	100-250MM			ALL	ALL
	67	152	167	72	12	3	NUMBER OF STATEMENTS		484	447
	%	%	%	%	%	%	ASSETS		%	%
	15.4	10.2	8.2	6.0	3.4		Cash & Equivalents		8.8	8.2
	4.2	8.6	16.2	23.7	62.9		Trade Receivables (net)		15.1	15.6
	61.5	63.5	58.5	53.5	10.3		Inventory		58.1	59.1
	.5	2.5	1.3	4.9	11.4		All Other Current		2.9	1.9
	81.6	84.9	84.3	87.9	88.1		Total Current		84.9	84.7
	10.0	9.0	9.2	7.5	7.5		Fixed Assets (net)		9.0	9.5
	3.8	.4	1.5	.8	.7		Intangibles (net)		.9	1.0
	4.6	5.7	5.1	3.8	3.7		All Other Non-Current		5.3	4.7
	100.0	100.0	100.0	100.0	100.0		Total		100.0	100.0
							LIABILITIES			
	31.1	33.3	36.3	40.0	54.0		Notes Payable-Short Term		36.2	38.0
	2.4	3.2	1.1	2.3	1.8		Cur. Mat.-L.T.D.		2.2	2.4
	8.5	5.3	6.3	3.3	1.8		Trade Payables		5.8	6.1
	.0	.1	.0	.1	.3		Income Taxes Payable		.1	.3
	14.4	11.8	12.4	11.9	3.1		All Other Current		12.7	11.5
	56.4	53.6	56.1	57.5	60.9		Total Current		57.1	58.2
	14.3	11.2	10.6	7.2	6.2		Long-Term Debt		10.7	9.6
	.0	.0	.0	.1	.5		Deferred Taxes		.0	.0
	27.5	8.9	4.9	8.4	9.6		All Other Non-Current		8.7	6.5
	1.8	26.2	28.4	26.8	22.9		Net Worth		23.6	25.6
	100.0	100.0	100.0	100.0	100.0		Total Liabilties & Net Worth		100.0	100.0
							INCOME DATA			
	100.0	100.0	100.0	100.0	100.0		Net Sales		100.0	100.0
	22.7	18.4	19.3	19.3	43.6		Gross Profit		20.9	20.2
	19.9	17.6	16.3	15.6	35.4		Operating Expenses		18.4	17.4
	2.8	.9	3.0	3.7	8.3		Operating Profit		2.6	2.8
	.8	.1	.7	.9	3.0		All Other Expenses (net)		.4	.5
	2.0	.7	2.3	2.8	5.3		Profit Before Taxes		2.1	2.2
							RATIOS			
	3.4	2.9	2.3	1.8	1.5				2.7	2.8
	1.6	1.6	1.4	1.4	1.4		Current		1.5	1.4
	1.0	1.2	1.1	1.2	1.3				1.1	1.1
	.8	.9	.9	1.1	1.4				.8	1.0
	.3	(151) .3	.3	.3	1.3		Quick	(480)	.3	(446) .3
	.1	.1	.1	.2	1.1				.1	.1
0	UND	0 UND	1 703.1	2 184.7	203 1.8			0	UND	0 UND
0	UND	1 255.2	5 74.8	8 45.3	332 1.1		Sales/Receivables	3	118.9	4 97.3
5	76.3	7 52.7	15 24.3	30 12.1	406 .9			13	28.3	13 27.7
24	15.0	53 6.9	46 7.9	54 6.7	50 7.3			41	9.0	46 8.0
61	6.0	74 4.9	74 4.9	70 5.2	64 5.7		Cost of Sales/Inventory	64	5.7	66 5.5
114	3.2	104 3.5	107 3.4	101 3.6	91 4.0			94	3.9	99 3.7
0	UND	0 UND	1 640.5	1 419.2	8 47.6			0	UND	0 UND
0	UND	1 292.0	4 101.4	4 101.7	11 33.6		Cost of Sales/Payables	2	188.1	2 189.5
5	68.1	6 60.8	10 35.5	10 35.1	19 19.7			8	48.1	8 47.8
	8.3	6.8	6.2	4.7	2.3				5.9	5.9
	16.6	15.9	15.5	10.0	3.5		Sales/Working Capital		15.2	14.7
	264.3	38.8	44.8	22.7	4.5				55.1	50.9
	8.3	4.9	6.9	6.0	3.5				7.0	8.3
(45)	2.6	(120) 1.8	(132) 2.7	(64) 2.6	2.2		EBIT/Interest	(402)	2.6	(366) 3.1
	.5	1.0	1.2	1.6	.9				1.2	1.4
							Net Profit + Depr., Dep.,		13.0	5.2
							Amort./Cur. Mat. L/T/D	(18)	1.4	(14) 1.4
									.0	.2
	.0	.0	.0	.0	.0				.0	.0
	.1	.1	.1	.1	.0		Fixed/Worth		.1	.1
	4.4	1.0	.7	.5	.8				.9	.7
	1.1	1.1	1.1	1.9	2.7				1.2	1.3
	5.2	2.8	3.3	3.3	3.3		Debt/Worth		3.0	3.1
	-3.9	13.6	9.7	7.4	5.8				10.5	9.0
	89.9	51.9	56.1	37.1	53.2				54.7	49.5
(44)	30.8	(126) 18.4	(151) 20.4	(68) 23.1	(11) 28.8		% Profit Before Taxes/Tangible Net Worth	(418)	21.0	(390) 21.1
	17.9	2.7	4.7	7.0	14.0				5.4	5.7
	26.4	12.0	10.9	8.6	6.9				11.8	12.9
	10.4	4.4	5.0	5.1	5.6		% Profit Before Taxes/Total Assets		4.5	5.1
	.0	.3	1.2	1.7	.2				.6	1.2
	UND	UND	619.0	563.8	216.4				745.9	637.2
	458.2	206.1	120.7	104.0	91.9		Sales/Net Fixed Assets		126.9	127.2
	52.0	30.4	30.5	22.3	18.5				34.1	32.6
	8.7	5.4	5.0	4.3	1.1				5.8	5.8
	5.0	3.9	3.4	2.8	.9		Sales/Total Assets		4.0	4.0
	3.1	2.5	1.8	1.1	.6				2.3	2.0
	.2	.1	.1	.1	.2				.1	.1
(22)	.4	(74) .3	(94) .2	(42) .2	(11) .3		% Depr., Dep., Amort./Sales	(299)	.2	(285) .2
	.8	.6	.4	.6	1.3				.6	.5
	1.2	.9	.4	.3					.8	.8
(30)	2.9	(91) 1.5	(75) .8	(25) .4			% Officers', Directors' Owners' Comp/Sales	(242)	1.4	(236) 1.4
	4.9	2.7	1.3	.8					2.7	2.6
	111867M	754375M	2856704M	4442841M	886394M	284329M	Net Sales ($)		8665104M	8286951M
	17978M	173505M	793415M	1560887M	907496M	345513M	Total Assets ($)		2805123M	2983668M

M = $ thousand   MM = $ million
See Pages viii through xx for Explanation of Ratios and Data

Comparative Historical Data | Current Data Sorted by Sales

Type of Statement

	4/1/16-3/31/17 ALL	4/1/17-3/31/18 ALL	4/1/18-3/31/19 ALL	0-1MM	1-3MM	3-5MM	5-10MM	10-25MM	25MM & OVER
					39 (4/1-9/30/18)		434 (10/1/18-3/31/19)		
Unqualified	19	13	22		1		4	3	14
Reviewed	28	36	29		2	1	6	7	13
Compiled	52	40	45		4	7	14	13	7
Tax Returns	179	166	174	20	46	29	37	24	18
Other	179	206	203	16	24	24	43	46	50
NUMBER OF STATEMENTS	457	461	473	36	77	61	104	93	102
	%	%	%	%	%	%	%	%	%
ASSETS									
Cash & Equivalents	10.7	9.8	9.4	7.6	13.1	9.6	9.0	10.1	6.7
Trade Receivables (net)	14.9	12.8	14.7	12.5	10.0	12.4	14.2	13.6	22.0
Inventory	56.1	58.2	58.3	56.8	51.7	61.2	58.1	63.2	57.6
All Other Current	3.0	2.4	2.4	.0	.9	2.9	3.0	3.0	2.9
Total Current	84.7	83.3	84.7	76.8	75.6	86.1	84.3	89.9	89.2
Fixed Assets (net)	10.0	10.3	8.9	12.1	15.2	7.3	9.7	5.8	6.1
Intangibles (net)	1.2	1.4	1.3	3.3	2.8	1.3	.4	.8	1.0
All Other Non-Current	4.1	5.0	5.0	7.7	6.4	5.3	5.6	3.5	3.8
Total	100.0	100.0	100.0	100.0	100.0	100.0	100.0	100.0	100.0
LIABILITIES									
Notes Payable-Short Term	33.5	36.2	35.6	22.0	32.2	30.5	36.2	38.1	43.2
Cur. Mat.-L.T.D.	2.7	2.3	2.2	3.1	2.6	2.8	2.4	2.1	1.0
Trade Payables	6.1	6.2	5.7	10.1	5.6	4.0	5.7	5.4	5.3
Income Taxes Payable	.2	.1	.1	.0	.0	.0	.1	.1	.1
All Other Current	13.7	13.4	12.2	19.4	10.9	9.4	13.1	12.0	11.7
Total Current	56.3	58.2	55.8	54.6	51.4	46.7	57.6	57.7	61.3
Long-Term Debt	10.6	10.3	10.7	10.5	19.0	13.9	9.2	8.7	5.8
Deferred Taxes	.0	.1	.0	.0	.0	.0	.0	.1	.1
All Other Non-Current	7.0	10.8	10.0	19.7	11.9	14.2	10.4	4.1	7.8
Net Worth	26.0	20.5	23.5	15.1	17.8	25.2	22.8	29.4	25.1
Total Liabilities & Net Worth	100.0	100.0	100.0	100.0	100.0	100.0	100.0	100.0	100.0
INCOME DATA									
Net Sales	100.0	100.0	100.0	100.0	100.0	100.0	100.0	100.0	100.0
Gross Profit	20.4	19.2	20.2	29.2	22.6	21.0	20.7	16.7	17.4
Operating Expenses	17.5	17.1	17.6	27.4	20.7	17.6	18.4	14.5	13.8
Operating Profit	2.8	2.1	2.6	1.8	1.9	3.4	2.3	2.2	3.6
All Other Expenses (net)	.3	.8	.7	.7	.5	.3	.8	.4	1.1
Profit Before Taxes	2.5	1.3	1.9	1.1	1.4	3.1	1.5	1.8	2.5
RATIOS									
Current	2.6	2.3	2.5	5.2	2.9	4.1	2.1	2.2	1.6
	1.4	1.4	1.4	1.7	1.5	2.2	1.4	1.4	1.4
	1.1	1.1	1.2	1.0	1.1	1.2	1.2	1.1	1.2
Quick	1.0	.9	1.0	1.4	1.1	1.2	.8	.9	1.1
	(455) .3	(458) .3	(472) .3	.2	.4	.4	(103) .2	.3	.3
	.1	.1	.1	.0	.2	.1	.1	.1	.2
	0 UND	0 UND	0 UND	0 UND	0 UND	0 UND	0 UND	0 UND	2 197.1
Sales/Receivables	4 88.7	3 114.9	3 109.0	0 UND	3 115.8	1 684.0	3 108.9	3 133.7	7 52.1
	13 27.2	13 29.1	13 27.5	30 12.2	12 31.7	7 51.8	12 29.8	12 31.2	16 22.2
	42 8.6	45 8.1	49 7.5	68 5.4	49 7.4	49 7.4	52 7.0	43 8.4	49 7.4
Cost of Sales/Inventory	64 5.7	69 5.3	72 5.1	140 2.6	72 5.1	76 4.8	76 4.8	69 5.3	64 5.7
	94 3.9	99 3.7	104 3.5	304 1.2	111 3.3	104 3.5	104 3.5	101 3.6	87 4.2
	0 UND	0 UND	0 UND	0 UND	0 UND	0 UND	0 999.8	0 UND	1 303.1
Cost of Sales/Payables	2 166.6	3 128.4	2 174.4	0 UND	1 654.5	1 701.0	4 92.3	4 202.9	4 88.4
	8 43.6	10 35.5	9 42.2	30 12.2	6 60.8	4 83.1	11 31.8	8 48.4	9 38.8
	5.6	6.7	6.1	2.2	6.8	4.2	6.8	6.6	6.4
Sales/Working Capital	14.8	15.8	13.8	7.2	17.1	12.5	15.5	13.6	16.6
	59.1	48.8	36.7	136.3	67.1	22.2	46.4	32.7	32.0
	9.1	5.5	5.4	8.3	3.4	9.5	5.0	7.9	6.3
EBIT/Interest	(363) 3.0	(389) 2.3	(376) 2.4	(25) 2.5	(61) 1.3	(47) 2.6	(86) 2.1	(70) 2.6	(87) 3.2
	1.3	1.1	1.1	-2.1	.3	1.0	1.1	1.3	1.7
Net Profit + Depr., Dep.,	11.7	28.7	25.4						24.5
Amort./Cur. Mat. L/T/D	(13) 3.4	(15) 5.2	(15) 1.5						(11) 1.4
	1.4	1.3	.1						-.7
	.0	.0	.0	.0	.0	.0	.0	.0	.0
Fixed/Worth	.2	.2	.1	.0	.3	.1	.1	.1	.1
	.8	1.2	.7	.7	4.0	.7	1.0	.4	.5
	1.1	1.5	1.3	.5	1.2	1.0	1.3	1.1	2.0
Debt/Worth	3.1	3.8	3.3	1.8	3.6	1.8	3.7	3.3	3.8
	9.0	13.0	11.3	-19.4	-56.0	15.5	10.7	8.5	7.9
% Profit Before Taxes/Tangible	51.9	43.4	51.7	51.1	49.0	59.0	51.2	61.1	51.1
Net Worth	(395) 22.6	(384) 19.5	(403) 22.8	(26) 20.7	(57) 14.6	(49) 20.4	(92) 18.5	(84) 23.8	(95) 28.8
	5.5	4.7	5.2	-2.7	1.8	4.4	4.7	6.1	12.8
% Profit Before Taxes/Total	14.3	10.5	11.8	17.8	10.8	15.6	11.9	11.8	10.5
Assets	5.9	4.0	5.3	7.0	2.5	4.4	5.1	5.6	5.6
	1.2	.0	.8	-8.6	-.8	1.0	.8	1.4	2.2
	762.6	646.7	982.4	UND	999.8	UND	984.3	822.5	651.8
Sales/Net Fixed Assets	120.2	116.1	144.3	384.0	70.5	268.7	180.9	132.4	188.7
	30.1	26.4	30.7	16.0	12.3	26.4	27.4	45.7	45.9
	5.6	5.3	5.2	3.0	5.3	5.4	5.2	5.7	5.6
Sales/Total Assets	3.9	3.8	3.6	1.5	3.1	3.7	3.5	3.8	4.1
	2.3	1.9	2.0	1.1	2.0	2.2	1.9	2.7	2.2
	.1	.1	.1	.4	.2	.1	.1	.0	.1
% Depr., Dep., Amort./Sales	(277) .2	(271) .2	(245) .2	(11) .7	(41) .5	(25) .3	(55) .2	(50) .1	(63) .2
	.5	.5	.6	3.0	.9	.5	.6	.4	.4
	.7	.7	.6		1.2	1.0	.8	.3	.3
% Officers', Directors' Owners' Comp/Sales	(248) 1.4	(246) 1.3	(223) 1.1		(40) 2.5	(39) 1.7	(53) 1.2	(42) .8	(41) .5
	2.9	2.6	2.5		3.8	2.8	2.4	1.3	.8
Net Sales ($)	9605481M	10288727M	9336510M	20010M	148624M	225972M	752880M	1450665M	6738359M
Total Assets ($)	3695336M	3671962M	3798794M	18601M	63634M	94559M	337543M	529524M	2754933M

© RMA 2019

M = $ thousand   MM = $ million
See Pages viii through xx for Explanation of Ratios and Data

Current Data Sorted by Assets   Comparative Historical Data

Type of Statement	0-500M	500M-2MM	2-10MM	10-50MM	50-100MM	100-250MM		4/1/14-3/31/15 ALL	4/1/15-3/31/16 ALL
Unqualified		2	1	2	2	4		8	5
Reviewed	1	11	11	26	5	1		37	31
Compiled	4	9	20	9				53	40
Tax Returns	4	13	15	3	1			51	55
Other			85	90	13	10		158	161
		39 (4/1-9/30/18)		303 (10/1/18-3/31/19)					
NUMBER OF STATEMENTS	9	35	132	130	21	15		307	292
	%	%	%	%	%	%		%	%
ASSETS									
Cash & Equivalents		13.9	10.4	9.9	10.4	8.7		11.1	11.7
Trade Receivables (net)		4.1	2.4	3.2	2.6	7.8		2.9	2.9
Inventory		62.0	74.9	74.6	72.1	65.5		72.5	72.6
All Other Current		3.1	1.0	1.4	1.3	1.4		1.7	1.7
Total Current		83.2	88.7	89.2	86.3	83.4		88.3	88.8
Fixed Assets (net)		12.1	7.6	7.3	8.5	12.6		8.0	7.7
Intangibles (net)		2.8	2.6	1.7	3.4	2.6		2.1	1.9
All Other Non-Current		1.9	1.1	1.8	1.7	1.4		1.6	1.5
Total		100.0	100.0	100.0	100.0	100.0		100.0	100.0
LIABILITIES									
Notes Payable-Short Term		28.8	51.5	56.3	62.4	46.2		51.6	50.9
Cur. Mat.-L.T.D.		6.5	2.6	1.2	.4	2.1		1.3	1.2
Trade Payables		5.2	5.0	3.0	2.8	8.6		3.9	4.3
Income Taxes Payable		.3	.1	.1	.1	.0		.1	.1
All Other Current		6.3	8.3	4.7	4.3	10.3		7.6	6.7
Total Current		47.0	67.6	65.3	69.9	67.3		64.5	63.2
Long-Term Debt		22.9	6.0	3.8	5.8	5.6		6.1	5.9
Deferred Taxes		.0	.1	.0	.2	.6		.1	.0
All Other Non-Current		4.7	3.4	2.8	3.5	1.6		5.3	3.9
Net Worth		25.3	22.9	28.1	20.7	24.9		23.9	27.0
Total Liabilties & Net Worth		100.0	100.0	100.0	100.0	100.0		100.0	100.0
INCOME DATA									
Net Sales		100.0	100.0	100.0	100.0	100.0		100.0	100.0
Gross Profit		27.4	22.1	19.8	19.0	20.1		21.9	21.3
Operating Expenses		24.3	18.7	15.2	15.1	14.6		18.2	17.3
Operating Profit		3.1	3.4	4.6	3.9	5.5		3.7	4.0
All Other Expenses (net)		.9	1.1	.9	1.2	1.2		.6	.5
Profit Before Taxes		2.2	2.3	3.7	2.7	4.3		3.1	3.5
RATIOS									
Current		3.8	1.6	1.5	1.3	1.5		1.6	1.6
		1.7	1.3	1.3	1.2	1.1		1.3	1.3
		1.1	1.1	1.2	1.1	1.1		1.2	1.2
Quick		.9	.3	.3	.2	.3		.3	.4
		.4	.2	.2	.2	.2		.2	.2
		.1	.1	.1	.1	.1		.1	.1
Sales/Receivables		0 UND	0 999.8	1 451.2	2 209.7	3 133.9		0 843.5	0 750.5
		0 999.8	2 169.4	3 119.4	3 107.4	7 51.0		2 166.1	2 176.0
		2 179.6	5 69.4	6 50.4	6 57.0	15 24.9		6 64.9	5 71.3
Cost of Sales/Inventory		46 7.9	130 2.8	126 2.9	135 2.7	122 3.0		118 3.1	114 3.2
		114 3.2	159 2.3	152 2.4	159 2.3	152 2.4		146 2.5	140 2.6
		174 2.1	203 1.8	192 1.9	192 1.9	166 2.2		203 1.8	192 1.9
Cost of Sales/Payables		0 UND	1 551.4	2 233.5	1 251.7	3 118.5		1 276.5	1 255.8
		2 209.6	3 145.9	4 88.3	5 75.8	8 46.8		3 110.8	3 104.8
		6 61.4	8 44.0	9 41.1	9 41.5	19 19.1		8 45.9	9 42.8
Sales/Working Capital		4.0	7.4	6.9	8.7	7.6		6.6	6.6
		10.1	11.1	12.0	14.6	19.9		11.0	10.5
		43.8	20.7	16.8	27.6	40.0		19.7	19.9
EBIT/Interest		3.9	5.0	5.4	4.0	8.4		6.9	8.2
	(30)	2.2	(126) 2.6	(123) 3.1	(19) 2.2	3.4		(289) 3.7	(278) 4.1
		.8	1.3	2.0	1.2	1.9		2.0	2.2
Net Profit + Depr., Dep., Amort./Cur. Mat. L/T/D								15.4	44.7
								(22) 9.2	(16) 8.2
								2.0	3.2
Fixed/Worth		.0	.1	.0	.1	.2		.1	.1
		.3	.2	.1	.3	.3		.2	.2
		1.6	.5	.4	.8	.7		.6	.5
Debt/Worth		.8	1.9	2.1	3.1	1.9		2.1	1.9
		2.3	3.8	3.2	4.6	5.6		3.4	3.4
		32.4	8.6	5.1	9.7	11.0		6.9	5.9
% Profit Before Taxes/Tangible Net Worth		45.7	52.2	45.2	60.6	53.3		58.6	54.9
	(30)	18.3	(120) 30.1	(128) 26.6	(20) 27.9	32.6		(284) 29.8	(273) 34.9
		.3	9.6	12.3	10.7	22.6		13.2	15.5
% Profit Before Taxes/Total Assets		10.2	10.0	10.9	9.1	9.2		12.1	12.4
		4.3	5.0	6.1	3.6	6.8		5.8	7.1
		-.3	1.0	2.6	1.3	4.0		2.2	2.7
Sales/Net Fixed Assets		184.1	251.4	228.1	109.2	90.7		166.0	201.4
		47.6	67.3	55.6	53.3	69.2		62.2	62.0
		19.2	30.2	27.7	24.5	9.3		26.7	26.3
Sales/Total Assets		5.0	2.6	2.6	2.3	2.4		2.7	2.9
		2.6	2.2	2.2	2.0	2.3		2.1	2.3
		1.9	1.9	1.8	1.8	2.0		1.8	1.9
% Depr., Dep., Amort./Sales		.2	.1	.1	.2	.2		.2	.1
	(24)	.4	(78) .3	(95) .3	(20) .3	(14) .3		(225) .3	(207) .2
		1.1	.6	.5	.6	.6		.5	.5
% Officers', Directors' Owners' Comp/Sales		1.6	.7	.4				.8	.7
	(24)	2.3	(68) 1.1	(62) .7				(164) 1.6	(144) 1.3
		4.1	1.8	1.3				3.0	2.6
Net Sales ($)	18309M	141571M	1639902M	5966889M	3434987M	4989449M		10438631M	10283870M
Total Assets ($)	2157M	42910M	734008M	2726389M	1590020M	2243672M		4452973M	4213445M

M = $ thousand   MM = $ million
See Pages viii through xx for Explanation of Ratios and Data

Comparative Historical Data | Current Data Sorted by Sales

Historical columns: **4/1/16-3/31/17 ALL** · **4/1/17-3/31/18 ALL** · **4/1/18-3/31/19 ALL**
Current columns: **39 (4/1-9/30/18)** spanning 0-1MM / 1-3MM — **303 (10/1/18-3/31/19)** spanning 3-5MM / 5-10MM / 10-25MM / 25MM & OVER

4/1/16-3/31/17 ALL	4/1/17-3/31/18 ALL	4/1/18-3/31/19 ALL		0-1MM	1-3MM	3-5MM	5-10MM	10-25MM	25MM & OVER
			Type of Statement						
9	11	9	Unqualified				1		8
34	44	45	Reviewed		2		3	12	28
39	57	41	Compiled	1	7	7	5	13	8
53	47	32	Tax Returns	2	3	7	7	9	4
168	192	215	Other	2	8	10	37	51	107
303	351	342	**NUMBER OF STATEMENTS**	5	20	24	53	85	155
%	%	%	**ASSETS**	%	%	%	%	%	%
12.0	12.8	10.9	Cash & Equivalents		20.0	9.4	8.5	11.8	10.4
2.7	4.0	3.2	Trade Receivables (net)		.9	1.2	4.9	2.5	3.4
72.9	67.0	72.4	Inventory		56.4	74.2	73.3	73.3	74.3
.9	1.3	1.4	All Other Current		.7	1.6	1.1	.8	1.4
88.6	85.0	87.8	Total Current		78.0	86.4	87.9	88.4	89.6
8.0	10.5	8.4	Fixed Assets (net)		17.1	10.1	8.1	7.2	7.2
2.2	2.3	2.2	Intangibles (net)		3.2	2.7	2.5	2.4	2.0
1.2	2.2	1.5	All Other Non-Current		1.6	.9	1.6	2.0	1.3
100.0	100.0	100.0	Total		100.0	100.0	100.0	100.0	100.0
			LIABILITIES						
52.2	45.9	50.2	Notes Payable-Short Term		19.5	39.3	47.2	53.0	56.9
.8	1.9	2.3	Cur. Mat.-L.T.D.		7.0	5.7	2.2	2.5	1.1
3.7	6.4	4.3	Trade Payables		5.9	8.1	5.5	3.3	3.6
.1	.1	.2	Income Taxes Payable		.1	.1	.5	.2	.1
7.7	8.2	6.5	All Other Current		6.6	4.0	7.9	8.7	5.3
64.5	62.6	63.4	Total Current		39.0	57.2	63.3	67.6	66.9
4.6	6.6	7.0	Long-Term Debt		17.4	17.0	12.7	3.3	3.9
.0	.0	.1	Deferred Taxes		.0	.0	.1	.0	.1
3.1	4.5	3.8	All Other Non-Current		10.1	3.1	6.6	2.1	2.8
27.8	26.3	25.7	Net Worth		33.5	22.7	17.3	27.1	26.3
100.0	100.0	100.0	Total Liabilities & Net Worth		100.0	100.0	100.0	100.0	100.0
			INCOME DATA						
100.0	100.0	100.0	Net Sales		100.0	100.0	100.0	100.0	100.0
21.4	23.9	21.5	Gross Profit		29.9	25.7	21.1	21.8	19.0
17.1	18.8	17.6	Operating Expenses		25.5	21.5	17.8	17.4	15.0
4.3	5.1	3.9	Operating Profit		4.3	4.2	3.3	4.4	4.1
.5	.9	1.0	All Other Expenses (net)		1.0	1.0	1.2	.9	.9
3.8	4.2	2.9	Profit Before Taxes		3.3	3.2	2.1	3.5	3.1
			RATIOS						
1.6	1.6	1.6	Current		5.8	2.5	1.8	1.5	1.5
1.3	1.3	1.3			1.9	1.3	1.3	1.3	1.3
1.2	1.2	1.1			1.2	1.1	1.1	1.1	1.1
.4	.4	.3	Quick		2.8	.3	.4	.4	.3
.2	.2	.2			.6	.1	.2	.2	.2
.1	.1	.1			.1	.0	.1	.1	.1
0 999.8	0 906.7	0 999.8	Sales/Receivables		0 UND	0 UND	0 999.8	1 478.7	1 400.8
2 167.9	2 175.2	2 163.1			0 UND	0 910.5	2 162.1	2 174.4	3 118.4
5 68.1	6 58.2	6 57.1			4 94.1	3 144.4	9 42.0	5 77.0	7 51.2
111 3.3	101 3.6	122 3.0	Cost of Sales/Inventory		78 4.7	118 3.1	118 3.1	122 3.0	122 3.0
146 2.5	140 2.6	152 2.4			152 2.4	174 2.1	159 2.3	159 2.3	146 2.5
182 2.0	174 2.1	192 1.9			243 1.5	261 1.4	215 1.7	192 1.9	174 2.1
1 367.2	1 333.7	1 331.7	Cost of Sales/Payables		0 UND	1 392.2	0 UND	1 256.2	2 217.9
3 112.1	3 107.6	3 114.8			0 UND	3 116.5	1 276.2	3 109.0	5 80.3
8 47.0	11 32.9	8 43.4			8 44.4	7 51.9	5 71.3	8 44.3	9 40.2
7.4	7.1	7.1	Sales/Working Capital		3.4	4.3	6.5	7.5	7.5
12.4	11.9	11.6			7.7	8.7	11.0	11.5	12.3
19.8	21.1	20.3			23.0	33.8	21.6	21.5	19.2
8.1	8.3	5.2	EBIT/Interest		3.5	4.2	5.1	5.5	5.5
(286) 4.4	(330) 4.0	(319) 2.9			(17) 2.4	(21) 1.9	(49) 2.2	(80) 3.0	(148) 3.0
2.4	2.0	1.6			.5	.7	1.0	1.7	1.9
10.7	40.9	33.2	Net Profit + Depr., Dep., Amort./Cur. Mat. L/T/D						87.8
(19) 6.6	(26) 7.1	(26) 10.8							(15) 13.5
2.4	3.3	2.7							2.9
.1	.1	.1	Fixed/Worth		.0	.1	.1	.1	.1
.2	.2	.2			.3	.3	.3	.2	.2
.5	.7	.5			3.3	.8	.7	.4	.4
1.9	1.7	1.8	Debt/Worth		.7	1.4	1.5	1.7	2.3
3.4	3.4	3.5			2.3	4.8	4.7	2.9	3.6
6.1	6.4	7.2			11.7	14.0	25.0	6.9	5.9
61.4	59.4	50.3	% Profit Before Taxes/Tangible Net Worth		67.2	28.2	46.2	61.7	47.9
(291) 34.7	(324) 31.0	(321) 28.8			(18) 26.9	(20) 11.6	(44) 31.0	(82) 33.4	(152) 27.4
17.6	13.6	11.3			.4	-8.7	1.3	12.2	13.8
13.2	13.4	10.8	% Profit Before Taxes/Total Assets		14.6	7.6	8.7	12.5	10.9
7.5	6.9	5.8			6.1	1.5	4.8	6.8	6.2
4.0	2.9	1.8			-.1	-1.1	-.1	2.7	2.0
183.5	205.6	225.9	Sales/Net Fixed Assets		UND	167.5	219.4	259.0	225.3
65.9	60.8	59.3			48.7	33.0	64.7	58.9	66.0
29.3	21.9	27.4			6.9	16.1	29.7	33.2	28.5
2.9	2.9	2.6	Sales/Total Assets		3.4	2.6	2.7	2.8	2.6
2.4	2.3	2.2			1.9	2.2	2.2	2.3	2.3
2.0	1.9	1.9			1.1	1.3	1.9	1.9	1.9
.1	.1	.1	% Depr., Dep., Amort./Sales		.2	.1	.1	.1	.1
(217) .3	(240) .3	(236) .3			(14) .8	(15) .7	(31) .3	(52) .3	(121) .2
.6	.6	.6			5.4	1.2	.6	.5	.4
.7	.6	.6	% Officers', Directors' Owners' Comp/Sales		1.9	1.6	.9	.6	.4
(152) 1.3	(161) 1.2	(170) 1.0			(13) 3.3	(15) 2.3	(24) 1.3	(47) 1.0	(70) .7
2.4	2.3	1.9			4.1	4.2	2.0	1.6	1.3
12673164M	13642018M	16191107M	Net Sales ($)	2511M	38452M	97171M	400359M	1410116M	14242498M
5249936M	6026051M	7339156M	Total Assets ($)	2731M	33689M	77896M	190650M	687721M	6346469M

Current Data Sorted by Assets   Comparative Historical Data

0-500M	500M-2MM	2-10MM	10-50MM	50-100MM	100-250MM	Type of Statement	4/1/14-3/31/15 ALL	4/1/15-3/31/16 ALL
				1	3	Unqualified	2	5
	3	11	10			Reviewed	22	18
3	16	18	4			Compiled	30	30
8	20	19	4			Tax Returns	46	37
14	25	52	23	1	2	Other	74	69
	34 (4/1-9/30/18)		203 (10/1/18-3/31/19)					
25	64	100	41	2	5	NUMBER OF STATEMENTS	174	159
%	%	%	%	%	%	ASSETS	%	%
22.5	11.9	7.4	8.6			Cash & Equivalents	9.8	9.6
7.8	7.6	3.4	3.1			Trade Receivables (net)	4.8	4.5
42.2	58.5	69.3	61.8			Inventory	62.4	62.2
3.1	1.5	1.9	2.3			All Other Current	1.4	2.8
75.5	79.4	82.1	75.8			Total Current	78.4	79.1
19.5	16.8	14.0	14.9			Fixed Assets (net)	15.9	15.0
1.1	.4	1.7	4.7			Intangibles (net)	1.3	2.1
3.9	3.4	2.2	4.6			All Other Non-Current	4.4	3.8
100.0	100.0	100.0	100.0			Total	100.0	100.0
						LIABILITIES		
16.5	18.8	36.9	39.8			Notes Payable-Short Term	36.6	37.8
2.4	1.6	.8	2.1			Cur. Mat.-L.T.D.	1.9	2.9
3.5	13.5	8.4	11.2			Trade Payables	6.0	5.7
.0	.2	.0	.0			Income Taxes Payable	.0	.1
47.2	12.0	8.3	7.8			All Other Current	12.8	10.1
69.6	46.0	54.3	60.9			Total Current	57.2	56.5
9.7	23.2	12.1	10.5			Long-Term Debt	13.8	12.4
.0	.0	.0	.0			Deferred Taxes	.1	.0
6.4	9.7	3.7	2.5			All Other Non-Current	5.4	7.0
14.3	21.1	29.9	26.1			Net Worth	23.4	23.9
100.0	100.0	100.0	100.0			Total Liabilities & Net Worth	100.0	100.0
						INCOME DATA		
100.0	100.0	100.0	100.0			Net Sales	100.0	100.0
41.0	31.0	25.8	21.6			Gross Profit	27.8	27.4
33.6	25.7	21.1	17.3			Operating Expenses	23.7	23.1
7.4	5.2	4.7	4.3			Operating Profit	4.1	4.3
.6	1.2	.8	.0			All Other Expenses (net)	.8	.8
6.7	4.0	3.9	4.3			Profit Before Taxes	3.3	3.5
						RATIOS		
6.1	3.7	2.0	1.4				1.8	1.8
1.7	1.7	1.3	1.2			Current	1.3	1.3
.9	1.2	1.2	1.1				1.1	1.2
2.0	.8	.4	.3				.4	.4
.7	.3	.2	.2			Quick	.2	.2
.2	.1	.1	.1				.1	.1
0 UND	0 UND	0 997.7	1 411.4				1 292.6	1 356.8
1 350.6	3 127.1	2 151.8	4 82.1			Sales/Receivables	5 73.7	3 107.5
9 40.8	15 23.6	11 34.4	8 45.5				10 34.9	10 34.8
4 84.8	60 6.1	135 2.7	146 2.5				111 3.3	111 3.3
33 11.1	135 2.7	182 2.0	174 2.1			Cost of Sales/Inventory	166 2.2	159 2.3
126 2.9	243 1.5	228 1.6	215 1.7				215 1.7	215 1.7
0 UND	0 UND	1 391.1	3 105.1				2 221.1	1 492.4
0 UND	5 77.3	5 80.7	9 40.9			Cost of Sales/Payables	5 80.9	5 70.6
10 38.1	46 8.0	14 26.1	23 16.1				13 29.1	13 27.4
7.4	3.8	4.7	6.5				5.9	5.8
19.2	8.1	9.2	15.0			Sales/Working Capital	9.8	10.6
UND	24.6	13.0	30.8				21.2	19.6
6.8	10.6	6.6	6.9				8.5	8.9
(13) 2.8	(61) 3.3	(93) 3.5	(40) 4.6			EBIT/Interest	(160) 3.0	(146) 3.6
1.5	1.5	2.0	2.3				1.7	1.7
						Net Profit + Depr., Dep.,	4.7	7.1
						Amort./Cur. Mat. L/T/D	(15) 1.7	(13) 3.1
							1.1	1.3
.1	.1	.1	.1				.1	.1
.2	.6	.3	.5			Fixed/Worth	.4	.3
7.7	11.0	1.0	1.7				1.8	1.4
.2	1.4	1.4	1.8				1.7	1.5
2.3	3.3	3.1	3.7			Debt/Worth	3.4	3.0
UND	96.3	6.3	9.0				9.0	8.1
109.3	70.7	45.0	43.3			% Profit Before Taxes/Tangible	47.2	44.1
(19) 56.6	(54) 33.5	(94) 20.2	(34) 23.9			Net Worth	(152) 25.4	(140) 22.4
34.6	8.0	10.3	17.0				11.3	10.1
47.7	12.5	10.7	10.1				9.8	11.3
27.3	7.6	6.1	6.9			% Profit Before Taxes/Total Assets	5.0	5.6
5.5	1.6	2.6	3.2				2.0	2.0
494.1	244.3	126.9	119.0				85.4	88.2
50.8	28.9	32.0	40.4			Sales/Net Fixed Assets	34.1	36.9
14.9	8.8	9.2	5.5				9.2	11.2
10.7	3.7	2.4	2.0				2.9	2.9
5.8	2.2	1.9	1.7			Sales/Total Assets	1.9	2.1
2.7	1.5	1.4	1.3				1.3	1.4
	.4	.3	.2				.3	.3
	(37) .8	(59) .8	(26) .5			% Depr., Dep., Amort./Sales	(120) .6	(103) .8
	2.4	1.9	1.7				1.8	1.7
3.7	1.6	.8	.6				1.0	1.0
(11) 5.8	(30) 2.7	(44) 1.5	(21) .8			% Officers', Directors' Owners' Comp/Sales	(96) 1.9	(83) 2.0
6.7	7.1	2.7	1.7				4.1	4.0
35827M	211704M	970694M	1303344M	404358M	827849M	Net Sales ($)	2025658M	2184680M
6359M	76128M	504764M	796772M	116759M	828195M	Total Assets ($)	1235460M	1265619M

M = $ thousand   MM = $ million
See Pages viii through xx for Explanation of Ratios and Data

Comparative Historical Data | Current Data Sorted by Sales

Type of Statement									
	4	5	3	Unqualified		3	3	6	5	3
	17	23	25	Reviewed	4	10	6	6	12	8
	36	55	41	Compiled						3
	43	51	51	Tax Returns	3	16	6	13	11	2
	69	140	117	Other	14	20	12	25	30	16

	4/1/16-3/31/17 ALL	4/1/17-3/31/18 ALL	4/1/18-3/31/19 ALL		34 (4/1-9/30/18)			203 (10/1/18-3/31/19)		
					0-1MM	1-3MM	3-5MM	5-10MM	10-25MM	25MM & OVER
NUMBER OF STATEMENTS	169	274	237		21	49	27	50	58	32

ASSETS (%)

	ALL	ALL	ALL		0-1MM	1-3MM	3-5MM	5-10MM	10-25MM	25MM & OVER
Cash & Equivalents	10.6	13.6	10.7		12.5	13.4	11.2	9.8	8.8	9.5
Trade Receivables (net)	4.1	5.4	5.0		7.1	8.4	5.1	3.8	3.1	3.3
Inventory	64.2	53.8	61.3		38.5	53.0	61.0	68.6	72.3	57.9
All Other Current	2.0	2.5	2.0		3.4	2.1	3.1	.8	1.8	2.4
Total Current	80.9	75.3	79.0		61.5	76.9	80.3	83.1	86.1	73.1
Fixed Assets (net)	14.7	18.4	16.1		33.2	17.7	15.4	12.7	10.3	19.2
Intangibles (net)	1.9	1.8	1.8		1.8	1.6	3.1	.4	1.4	3.9
All Other Non-Current	2.5	4.5	3.1		3.6	3.9	1.2	3.7	2.3	3.8
Total	100.0	100.0	100.0		100.0	100.0	100.0	100.0	100.0	100.0

LIABILITIES

	ALL	ALL	ALL		0-1MM	1-3MM	3-5MM	5-10MM	10-25MM	25MM & OVER
Notes Payable-Short Term	38.2	24.0	30.0		18.6	18.4	22.0	31.8	42.8	35.7
Cur. Mat.-L.T.D.	3.3	1.4	1.5		3.5	1.1	1.7	.7	.8	3.2
Trade Payables	6.7	10.3	9.5		5.8	11.3	14.0	9.0	7.6	9.6
Income Taxes Payable	.0	.1	.1		.0	.1	.0	.2	.1	.0
All Other Current	10.3	12.1	13.7		27.1	16.9	14.3	10.9	10.0	10.6
Total Current	58.5	47.8	54.7		55.0	47.8	51.9	52.7	61.3	59.0
Long-Term Debt	11.0	14.8	14.9		21.5	19.4	21.4	12.5	8.6	13.3
Deferred Taxes	.0	.0	.0		.0	.0	.0	.0	.0	.0
All Other Non-Current	4.4	9.6	5.3		8.9	12.2	3.1	3.4	3.0	1.5
Net Worth	26.1	27.8	25.0		14.5	20.7	23.6	31.3	27.1	26.2
Total Liabilities & Net Worth	100.0	100.0	100.0		100.0	100.0	100.0	100.0	100.0	100.0

INCOME DATA

	ALL	ALL	ALL		0-1MM	1-3MM	3-5MM	5-10MM	10-25MM	25MM & OVER
Net Sales	100.0	100.0	100.0		100.0	100.0	100.0	100.0	100.0	100.0
Gross Profit	26.0	31.3	28.0		51.1	34.8	27.4	23.1	21.9	21.7
Operating Expenses	22.0	26.4	22.9		41.3	29.5	22.3	18.9	17.6	17.3
Operating Profit	3.9	4.9	5.1		9.8	5.3	5.2	4.2	4.3	4.4
All Other Expenses (net)	.7	.9	.8		1.8	1.1	1.2	.6	.4	.7
Profit Before Taxes	3.3	4.0	4.3		8.0	4.2	4.0	3.7	3.9	3.7

RATIOS

	ALL	ALL	ALL		0-1MM	1-3MM	3-5MM	5-10MM	10-25MM	25MM & OVER
Current	1.8	2.8	2.2		4.9	4.7	2.3	2.2	1.6	1.4
	1.4	1.5	1.3		1.7	1.7	1.4	1.5	1.3	1.2
	1.1	1.2	1.2		.8	1.2	1.2	1.2	1.2	1.0
Quick	.4	.8	.5		2.0	1.4	.6	.4	.4	.3
	.2 (273)	.3	.2		.7	.3	.3	.2	.2	.2
	.1	.1	.1		.2	.1	.1	.1	.1	.1
Sales/Receivables	1 443.8	1 697.2	0 999.8		0 UND	0 UND	0 UND	1 443.4	0 999.8	1 402.6
	3 118.9	3 107.6	3 125.2		1 256.0	5 80.3	4 90.0	3 131.0	2 151.8	4 84.0
	10 36.9	13 27.3	11 33.1		28 13.0	20 18.1	17 21.8	8 48.5	8 47.1	11 33.1
Cost of Sales/Inventory	104 3.5	54 6.7	96 3.8		33 11.1	63 5.8	60 6.1	107 3.4	130 2.8	107 3.4
	152 2.4	140 2.6	166 2.2		118 3.1	166 2.2	159 2.3	166 2.2	174 2.1	166 2.2
	203 1.8	215 1.7	228 1.6		228 1.6	304 1.2	182 2.0	228 1.6	215 1.7	203 1.8
Cost of Sales/Payables	1 369.0	2 217.9	1 519.1		0 UND	0 UND	1 281.9	0 UND	2 160.2	2 160.8
	5 77.4	8 47.9	5 77.2		1 310.0	6 61.3	5 77.4	3 124.2	5 70.5	6 59.2
	11 32.5	36 10.1	17 21.1		28 13.0	46 8.0	60 6.1	8 43.8	14 26.3	20 18.4
Sales/Working Capital	6.0	4.6	5.2		5.1	3.1	4.9	4.8	5.9	7.2
	11.0	9.7	10.1		12.0	7.7	7.7	10.4	10.3	15.9
	22.7	28.9	20.1		-46.4	45.3	17.7	15.6	17.8	45.7
EBIT/Interest	9.0	8.5	7.5		7.6	10.8	9.8	6.2	6.8	8.2
	(158) 3.4	(242) 3.8	(213) 3.8		(14) 2.8	(38) 2.6	(25) 3.3	(48) 3.7	(57) 3.7	(31) 6.4
	1.8	1.6	1.8		1.6	1.5	1.3	2.2	2.1	4.1
Net Profit + Depr., Dep., Amort./Cur. Mat. L/T/D	4.2	8.4	11.0							
	(15) 1.7	(17) 3.0	(15) 3.4							
	.6	1.0	1.2							
Fixed/Worth	.1	.1	.1		.2	.1	.1	.1	.1	.1
	.3	.4	.4		1.5	.6	.4	.3	.3	.8
	1.4	2.2	1.9		12.6	8.4	1.4	1.2	.9	1.8
Debt/Worth	1.7	1.1	1.4		.5	.7	1.7	.9	1.7	2.2
	3.2	2.7	3.2		4.0	2.6	4.8	2.9	3.5	3.6
	7.6	12.0	8.3		NM	UND	9.2	5.8	6.7	5.5
% Profit Before Taxes/Tangible Net Worth	52.6	54.8	49.4		154.1	42.3	66.4	50.8	48.7	42.3
	(157) 26.8	(234) 22.3	(208) 25.6		(16) 69.4	(39) 17.3	(26) 35.7	(46) 24.7	(53) 21.9	(28) 24.1
	9.8	9.4	12.2		14.2	7.9	9.6	12.3	11.7	17.9
% Profit Before Taxes/Total Assets	10.9	12.6	11.8		30.3	15.0	12.0	11.8	10.4	10.4
	5.6	6.1	7.2		17.2	4.3	7.5	7.5	6.1	7.4
	2.2	1.4	2.6		3.1	1.4	1.4	3.3	2.8	4.5
Sales/Net Fixed Assets	111.4	99.0	121.3		64.0	64.9	270.4	218.4	146.6	95.7
	34.0	25.9	29.8		8.2	23.4	29.8	53.9	45.2	19.6
	10.7	8.1	8.1		1.8	8.0	10.2	9.8	17.7	4.9
Sales/Total Assets	2.7	3.2	2.8		3.9	3.0	2.8	2.8	2.6	2.8
	2.1	2.1	2.0		2.4	1.6	2.2	2.2	2.0	1.7
	1.6	1.4	1.4		.9	1.2	1.5	1.5	1.7	1.3
% Depr., Dep., Amort./Sales	.4	.4	.3		.7	.4	.4	.3	.2	.4
	(118) .7	(181) .9	(135) .8		(10) 2.5	(23) 1.4	(19) .8	(29) .7	(32) .5	(22) 1.0
	1.3	1.9	2.1		5.0	2.6	1.4	1.9	1.1	1.7
% Officers', Directors' Owners' Comp/Sales	1.0	1.0	.8			2.3	1.8	.6	.7	.4
	(82) 2.2	(108) 2.1	(108) 1.8			(23) 3.5	(12) 2.9	(20) 1.0	(32) 1.2	(14) .9
	3.7	4.0	3.7			7.2	4.4	1.7	2.6	1.6
Net Sales ($)	2553275M	3674228M	3753776M		13911M	100616M	103521M	362755M	954086M	2218887M
Total Assets ($)	1406878M	1930466M	2328977M		8307M	63228M	57944M	184055M	504511M	1510932M

© RMA 2019

M = $ thousand　MM = $ million

See Pages viii through xx for Explanation of Ratios and Data

Current Data Sorted by Assets | Comparative Historical Data

0-500M	500M-2MM	2-10MM	10-50MM	50-100MM	100-250MM	Type of Statement	4/1/14-3/31/15 ALL	4/1/15-3/31/16 ALL
	1	1		9	6	3	Unqualified	32	34
1	2	20	27	4	1	Reviewed	70	75
3	12	32	9			Compiled	78	74
12	33	56	13			Tax Returns	122	97
13	37	137	57	11	9	Other	231	226
	59 (4/1-9/30/18)		449 (10/1/18-3/31/19)					
29	85	245	115	21	13	NUMBER OF STATEMENTS	533	506
%	%	%	%	%	%	**ASSETS**	%	%
15.3	13.6	10.3	9.3	7.5	4.4	Cash & Equivalents	10.0	9.6
4.7	5.8	6.0	10.1	8.5	10.5	Trade Receivables (net)	7.6	7.3
47.3	62.8	61.4	48.7	37.7	49.7	Inventory	55.2	55.7
.5	1.5	1.5	2.6	1.7	4.4	All Other Current	1.7	2.2
67.9	83.7	79.2	70.6	55.3	69.0	Total Current	74.4	74.8
20.4	10.8	10.8	17.1	24.2	18.6	Fixed Assets (net)	14.7	15.4
5.6	4.0	5.4	5.8	12.9	10.3	Intangibles (net)	5.6	5.4
6.1	1.5	4.5	6.5	7.6	2.1	All Other Non-Current	5.3	4.5
100.0	100.0	100.0	100.0	100.0	100.0	Total	100.0	100.0
						LIABILITIES		
28.9	18.0	31.8	27.0	26.3	25.8	Notes Payable-Short Term	29.3	30.2
1.1	3.3	2.5	2.8	2.6	7.3	Cur. Mat.-L.T.D.	3.5	3.5
5.2	24.4	12.0	11.3	7.5	5.2	Trade Payables	11.3	9.8
.0	.1	.1	.1	.2	.3	Income Taxes Payable	.1	.1
7.7	9.5	10.1	9.4	10.5	13.9	All Other Current	10.5	10.3
42.9	55.4	56.4	50.6	47.1	52.4	Total Current	54.6	53.9
25.1	16.4	9.7	12.9	12.7	13.7	Long-Term Debt	10.9	12.6
.0	.0	.0	.2	.0	.4	Deferred Taxes	.2	.2
10.7	6.1	4.7	1.7	3.3	1.7	All Other Non-Current	5.8	4.9
21.3	22.2	29.1	34.6	36.9	31.8	Net Worth	28.5	28.4
100.0	100.0	100.0	100.0	100.0	100.0	Total Liabilties & Net Worth	100.0	100.0
						INCOME DATA		
100.0	100.0	100.0	100.0	100.0	100.0	Net Sales	100.0	100.0
34.9	27.9	22.4	22.4	19.4	21.5	Gross Profit	23.1	23.2
31.0	24.9	20.1	19.3	15.6	17.3	Operating Expenses	20.3	20.2
3.9	3.1	2.3	3.1	3.8	4.3	Operating Profit	2.8	3.0
1.3	1.0	.4	.2	.5	.9	All Other Expenses (net)	.1	.3
2.6	2.1	1.9	2.9	3.3	3.4	Profit Before Taxes	2.7	2.7
						RATIOS		
6.5	3.2	1.9	1.9	1.4	1.4		1.9	1.8
2.4	1.4	1.3	1.4	1.2	1.3	Current	1.3	1.3
1.2	1.2	1.1	1.1	.8	1.1		1.1	1.1
2.2	.9	.6	.5	.7	.5		.6	.6
(28) .7	.2	(244) .2	.3	.3	.3	Quick	.3	(505) .3
.1	.1	.1	.2	.2	.2		.1	.1
0 UND	0 UND	1 271.7	6 59.5	8 48.1	10 37.5		2 216.9	2 192.8
0 UND	2 195.6	4 81.3	11 34.0	12 29.6	13 28.3	Sales/Receivables	6 65.1	6 66.2
7 49.8	10 36.7	12 30.1	23 16.0	20 18.2	30 12.0		14 25.5	14 26.0
8 47.3	74 4.9	94 3.9	65 5.6	41 8.8	85 4.3		65 5.6	69 5.3
41 9.0	126 2.9	135 2.7	99 3.7	68 5.4	122 3.0	Cost of Sales/Inventory	94 3.9	101 3.6
114 3.2	228 1.6	182 2.0	146 2.5	122 3.0	135 2.7		140 2.6	152 2.4
0 UND	3 128.6	4 97.2	7 51.9	9 39.9	5 76.4		5 69.9	5 78.3
3 124.3	16 22.4	9 40.7	13 27.6	14 26.1	10 35.6	Cost of Sales/Payables	10 35.0	10 37.4
10 36.0	85 4.3	27 13.6	29 12.7	19 19.7	18 19.9		22 16.6	20 18.4
6.6	4.7	6.2	7.1	10.2	7.8		7.5	7.3
20.9	9.4	11.4	12.3	20.1	14.6	Sales/Working Capital	15.2	14.3
107.7	22.5	30.6	27.6	-43.6	38.6		47.4	35.0
15.2	4.4	7.4	12.4	30.4	7.3		10.3	9.2
(20) 2.6	(71) 1.5	(222) 2.8	(105) 5.1	4.8	(12) 3.6	EBIT/Interest	(493) 4.4	(459) 3.6
-.4	-.1	1.0	1.8	2.7	1.7		1.6	1.6
		22.2	11.6				10.1	6.0
		(12) 9.0	(11) 1.1			Net Profit + Depr., Dep., Amort./Cur. Mat. L/T/D	(56) 2.3	(55) 1.9
		4.1	.9				1.2	1.2
.0	.1	.1	.1	.3	.3		.1	.1
.4	.3	.3	.4	.8	.7	Fixed/Worth	.4	.4
-2.4	-1.8	1.1	1.3	4.0	6.5		1.7	1.5
.2	1.0	1.4	1.1	.9	2.0		1.4	1.4
3.9	3.0	3.2	2.5	3.1	3.8	Debt/Worth	3.2	3.0
-4.5	-11.1	9.2	5.3	12.6	95.9		8.6	8.7
81.0	45.9	36.8	36.3	38.3	64.9		44.2	46.3
(18) 38.4	(59) 18.9	(214) 14.9	(103) 20.3	(18) 26.3	(11) 23.2	% Profit Before Taxes/Tangible Net Worth	(457) 23.7	(446) 22.5
-7.4	.3	4.0	9.4	19.3	14.1		9.6	8.1
31.6	11.3	8.1	11.5	13.3	10.1		11.8	9.7
14.6	2.6	3.5	7.0	8.8	4.4	% Profit Before Taxes/Total Assets	6.4	5.1
-2.0	-2.1	.0	1.9	3.2	1.6		1.6	1.2
999.8	110.9	147.6	96.6	22.5	40.5		99.1	92.6
170.0	42.7	43.2	28.0	10.4	14.6	Sales/Net Fixed Assets	41.5	33.4
10.9	16.8	21.5	7.0	4.6	6.6		11.8	11.2
7.8	4.0	2.7	3.0	2.5	2.7		3.5	3.4
4.5	2.5	2.2	2.1	2.3	2.0	Sales/Total Assets	2.6	2.4
2.5	1.6	1.7	1.6	1.9	1.3		1.9	1.8
.3	.2	.2	.3		.5		.3	.3
(13) 1.6	(48) .6	(176) .6	(89) .5	(20) 1.0	(11) .7	% Depr., Dep., Amort./Sales	(414) .6	(397) .6
10.1	1.2	1.2	1.5	1.8	4.3		1.3	1.2
1.2	1.0	.9	.4				.9	.9
(13) 2.8	(42) 2.3	(118) 1.5	(33) 1.2			% Officers', Directors' Owners' Comp/Sales	(222) 1.5	(212) 1.5
7.6	3.9	2.3	2.4				2.7	2.5
49127M	307883M	2913225M	5536362M	3339040M	4357189M	Net Sales ($)	20224280M	18506196M
7886M	102972M	1198717M	2284407M	1460578M	2121566M	Total Assets ($)	8387910M	7625794M

M = $ thousand   MM = $ million
See Pages viii through xx for Explanation of Ratios and Data

Comparative Historical Data | Current Data Sorted by Sales

4/1/16-3/31/17 ALL	4/1/17-3/31/18 ALL	4/1/18-3/31/19 ALL	Type of Statement	0-1MM	1-3MM	3-5MM	5-10MM	10-25MM	25MM & OVER
31	26	19	Unqualified		1				18
53	66	55	Reviewed	1		2	9	16	27
58	86	56	Compiled	2	7	9	14	13	11
94	134	114	Tax Returns	10	17	12	40	28	7
226	339	264	Other	6	23	37	50	84	64
				59 (4/1-9/30/18)			449 (10/1/18-3/31/19)		
NUMBER OF STATEMENTS									
462	651	508		19	48	60	113	141	127
%	%	%	**ASSETS**	%	%	%	%	%	%
10.4	11.2	10.6	Cash & Equivalents	7.0	11.6	11.7	11.6	9.4	10.8
7.4	7.5	7.0	Trade Receivables (net)	4.2	7.0	4.6	4.9	7.0	10.6
55.9	56.3	56.7	Inventory	52.1	60.7	61.7	61.2	57.8	48.1
1.9	2.1	1.8	All Other Current	.0	1.1	2.3	2.2	.7	2.9
75.6	77.1	76.1	Total Current	63.3	80.4	80.2	79.9	74.9	72.4
13.5	13.5	13.6	Fixed Assets (net)	29.8	13.1	10.7	8.9	14.4	15.8
5.8	5.2	5.7	Intangibles (net)	4.8	6.0	4.7	5.5	5.4	6.8
5.2	4.3	4.6	All Other Non-Current	2.1	.6	4.4	5.7	5.3	5.0
100.0	100.0	100.0	Total	100.0	100.0	100.0	100.0	100.0	100.0
			LIABILITIES						
28.9	25.5	27.8	Notes Payable-Short Term	37.0	19.3	18.6	28.9	33.5	26.8
3.3	2.4	2.7	Cur. Mat.-L.T.D.	1.5	3.1	2.5	2.7	2.5	3.2
10.4	15.0	13.2	Trade Payables	12.1	11.2	22.7	15.5	9.7	11.4
.1	.1	.1	Income Taxes Payable	.0	.0	.0	.1	.1	.1
9.7	9.7	9.8	All Other Current	14.9	7.1	7.4	11.9	8.8	10.4
52.5	52.7	53.6	Total Current	65.6	40.8	51.2	59.1	54.6	51.9
11.9	11.7	12.7	Long-Term Debt	26.2	21.0	16.0	6.8	12.5	11.3
.2	.2	.1	Deferred Taxes	.0	.0	.0	.0	.1	.1
5.6	6.7	4.5	All Other Non-Current	11.2	6.3	9.6	5.7	2.4	1.6
29.8	28.7	29.1	Net Worth	-3.0	31.9	23.2	28.4	30.4	35.0
100.0	100.0	100.0	Total Liabilities & Net Worth	100.0	100.0	100.0	100.0	100.0	100.0
			INCOME DATA						
100.0	100.0	100.0	Net Sales	100.0	100.0	100.0	100.0	100.0	100.0
22.9	23.2	23.9	Gross Profit	39.2	33.1	24.9	22.6	23.1	19.7
20.9	20.8	21.1	Operating Expenses	35.8	28.5	22.5	20.6	20.7	16.3
2.0	2.5	2.8	Operating Profit	3.5	4.6	2.4	2.0	2.3	3.5
.3	.5	.5	All Other Expenses (net)	3.3	.7	1.3	.5	.1	.2
1.7	2.0	2.3	Profit Before Taxes	.2	3.9	1.0	1.6	2.3	3.3
			RATIOS						
2.0	2.1	2.1		1.8	4.8	3.1	1.8	1.8	1.9
1.4	1.4	1.4	Current	1.3	1.8	1.5	1.3	1.3	1.3
1.1	1.1	1.1		.6	1.2	1.1	1.1	1.1	1.1
.6	.7	.6		.7	1.2	1.0	.5	.5	.6
.3	.3	(506) .2	Quick	.1	(47) .3	(59) .3	.2	.2	.3
.1	.1	.1		.0	.1	.1	.1	.1	.2
2 189.1	1 269.5	1 249.8		0 UND	0 UND	0 UND	1 588.0	3 110.8	6 57.5
6 60.4	6 63.0	6 60.4	Sales/Receivables	0 959.0	2 152.2	2 178.9	3 109.2	6 57.8	11 34.0
15 24.8	15 25.1	15 24.0		12 30.7	18 19.8	15 24.6	8 47.1	16 23.2	22 16.8
72 5.1	68 5.4	76 4.8		41 9.0	87 4.2	79 4.6	87 4.2	87 4.2	54 6.7
107 3.4	111 3.3	118 3.1	Cost of Sales/Inventory	118 3.1	182 2.0	146 2.5	130 2.8	122 3.0	85 4.3
159 2.3	166 2.2	174 2.1		365 1.0	228 1.6	215 1.7	166 2.2	166 2.2	122 3.0
5 76.9	5 77.5	4 83.8		0 UND	2 206.7	2 151.9	4 103.7	5 76.4	7 53.5
10 37.8	11 33.9	11 33.5	Cost of Sales/Payables	11 31.9	7 54.2	24 15.5	11 33.5	9 40.3	13 28.4
20 18.2	32 11.4	30 12.0		174 2.1	32 11.5	87 4.2	30 12.1	23 15.9	24 15.2
6.9	6.2	6.2		3.3	3.8	4.5	6.7	6.7	8.1
12.0	13.3	11.9	Sales/Working Capital	11.8	6.1	9.8	11.2	14.4	15.0
32.3	37.5	31.6		-5.2	10.2	31.1	31.3	34.2	31.6
7.5	7.0	8.2		2.8	6.2	4.3	5.1	7.5	13.8
(422) 2.7	(591) 2.8	(451) 3.3	EBIT/Interest	(15) .7	(41) 2.5	(47) 1.5	(103) 2.3	(129) 3.8	(116) 6.3
1.2	1.1	1.0		-.8	.6	-.1	.8	1.3	2.4
4.3	5.1	11.4	Net Profit + Depr., Dep.,					14.0	10.0
(46) 1.3	(55) 1.9	(33) 4.0	Amort./Cur. Mat. L/T/D					(12) 5.8	(18) 2.6
.5	.4	1.0						1.5	.3
.1	.1	.1		.0	.1	.1	.1	.1	.2
.3	.4	.3	Fixed/Worth	5.4	.4	.4	.2	.4	.4
1.5	1.8	1.5		-1.9	60.2	-6.2	.9	1.2	1.5
1.3	1.3	1.2		1.8	.5	.7	1.4	1.3	1.1
3.0	3.1	3.0	Debt/Worth	-10.6	2.3	4.3	3.5	2.9	2.7
8.3	12.0	12.1		-3.3	NM	-19.1	15.0	8.3	6.4
40.9	41.0	39.7	% Profit Before Taxes/Tangible		42.9	47.9	36.2	35.2	45.7
(399) 15.8	(538) 17.1	(423) 19.2	Net Worth		(36) 20.3	(43) 17.5	(97) 10.8	(124) 18.8	(114) 26.3
3.3	4.3	5.9			3.9	-1.8	-.6	7.6	13.8
9.7	10.0	10.8	% Profit Before Taxes/Total	8.4	14.7	12.1	6.1	9.5	13.9
3.5	4.1	4.5	Assets	-1.1	7.5	2.2	2.5	4.3	7.7
.3	.3	.2		-10.0	-.5	-1.0	-.4	1.2	3.1
103.0	114.7	118.6		UND	78.5	182.3	213.9	102.5	98.3
40.7	39.5	37.9	Sales/Net Fixed Assets	10.6	29.9	41.9	58.7	37.6	27.2
14.1	13.5	12.9		1.9	9.6	19.8	26.2	11.0	10.1
3.2	3.2	3.0		2.8	3.7	3.2	2.9	2.8	3.3
2.3	2.4	2.2	Sales/Total Assets	1.4	2.0	2.1	2.2	2.2	2.5
1.7	1.7	1.7		.9	1.4	1.5	1.7	1.7	1.9
.3	.2	.3		2.6	.2	.3	.2	.3	.3
(348) .6	(463) .5	(357) .6	% Depr., Dep., Amort./Sales	(10) 4.6	(26) .7	(36) .7	(82) .5	(96) .7	(107) .5
1.1	1.1	1.3		14.1	1.5	1.4	1.0	1.3	1.3
.9	.9	.9	% Officers', Directors'		1.9	1.0	.9	.8	.5
(176) 1.6	(255) 1.6	(209) 1.6	Owners' Comp/Sales		(22) 3.1	(22) 1.6	(62) 1.6	(69) 1.2	(27) 1.0
3.1	2.8	2.8			5.6	3.9	2.3	2.2	
17660802M	18587570M	16502826M	Net Sales ($)	10494M	90574M	237496M	830839M	2229213M	13104210M
7553261M	7976756M	7176126M	Total Assets ($)	8356M	50424M	136367M	399174M	1092704M	5489101M

© RMA 2019

M = $ thousand   MM = $ million

See Pages viii through xx for Explanation of Ratios and Data

Current Data Sorted by Assets

Comparative Historical Data

Type of Statement	0-500M	500M-2MM	2-10MM	10-50MM	50-100MM	100-250MM	4/1/14-3/31/15 ALL	4/1/15-3/31/16 ALL
Unqualified				4	2	4	21	19
Reviewed		2	8	4	2		28	27
Compiled	1	7	14	6			64	33
Tax Returns	40	56	19	8			175	172
Other	25	36	42	23	5	3	140	176
		32 (4/1-9/30/18)		279 (10/1/18-3/31/19)				
NUMBER OF STATEMENTS	66	101	83	45	9	7	428	427

	0-500M %	500M-2MM %	2-10MM %	10-50MM %	50-100MM %	100-250MM %	ALL %	ALL %
ASSETS								
Cash & Equivalents	20.9	11.0	10.4	5.0			11.0	11.5
Trade Receivables (net)	8.4	10.6	15.5	14.2			13.4	13.4
Inventory	39.3	46.8	48.2	48.4			44.7	43.0
All Other Current	2.7	1.3	2.3	1.3			2.0	2.3
Total Current	71.2	69.8	76.4	68.8			71.2	70.2
Fixed Assets (net)	16.1	18.2	13.2	19.6			17.7	18.5
Intangibles (net)	2.0	4.6	5.4	2.9			4.8	5.2
All Other Non-Current	10.6	7.4	5.1	8.7			6.3	6.0
Total	100.0	100.0	100.0	100.0			100.0	100.0
LIABILITIES								
Notes Payable-Short Term	13.3	10.5	12.2	13.4			12.5	13.0
Cur. Mat.-L.T.D.	2.4	2.1	1.9	1.9			2.7	2.1
Trade Payables	11.9	15.4	18.8	16.5			17.7	20.0
Income Taxes Payable	.1	.3	.1	.0			.1	.1
All Other Current	19.7	10.3	8.8	13.1			9.2	9.1
Total Current	47.4	38.6	41.9	45.0			42.2	44.4
Long-Term Debt	33.2	22.8	12.5	22.6			16.5	15.6
Deferred Taxes	.0	.0	.1	.1			.1	.1
All Other Non-Current	9.1	8.2	4.1	2.1			10.5	7.5
Net Worth	10.3	30.5	41.3	30.3			30.8	32.4
Total Liabilities & Net Worth	100.0	100.0	100.0	100.0			100.0	100.0
INCOME DATA								
Net Sales	100.0	100.0	100.0	100.0			100.0	100.0
Gross Profit	41.0	39.0	36.7	33.4			37.1	36.6
Operating Expenses	39.3	35.4	31.8	31.0			32.8	32.6
Operating Profit	1.7	3.6	4.8	2.4			4.2	4.0
All Other Expenses (net)	-.1	.4	.0	.8			.4	.3
Profit Before Taxes	1.8	3.2	4.8	1.6			3.9	3.7

RATIOS

	0-500M	500M-2MM	2-10MM	10-50MM			ALL	ALL
Current	6.2	3.6	2.7	3.3			3.1	3.1
	2.4	2.1	1.8	1.7			1.8	1.8
	1.2	1.1	1.3	1.1			1.2	1.1
Quick	2.1	1.1	1.1	.9			1.2	1.2
	.7	.6	.6	.5			.6	.5
	.2	.3	.3	.3			.3	.3
Sales/Receivables	0 UND	2 203.8	5 77.6	17 22.1			2 154.1	3 137.4
	1 257.9	12 30.9	18 20.1	25 14.6			16 23.5	15 25.1
	9 38.6	24 15.3	35 10.3	35 10.4			29 12.4	29 12.4
Cost of Sales/Inventory	6 65.3	38 9.7	49 7.4	74 4.9			40 9.1	38 9.7
	39 9.4	99 3.7	101 3.6	174 2.1			85 4.3	76 4.8
	118 3.1	174 2.1	140 2.6	281 1.3			166 2.2	159 2.3
Cost of Sales/Payables	0 UND	5 75.2	15 23.6	30 12.0			10 35.4	11 32.9
	2 234.6	25 14.4	36 10.1	49 7.5			29 12.7	29 12.4
	25 14.7	51 7.1	56 6.5	78 4.7			53 6.9	55 6.6
Sales/Working Capital	7.4	4.1	3.8	2.8			4.8	5.0
	16.6	8.1	7.9	7.7			9.9	10.1
	72.5	58.8	18.9	40.0			38.2	49.3
EBIT/Interest	19.0	19.0	42.5	8.2			16.7	16.0
	(37) 5.6	(76) 4.8	(71) 6.0	(43) 2.3			(352) 5.6	(346) 4.6
	.2	1.5	2.1	1.1			2.1	1.7
Net Profit + Depr., Dep., Amort./Cur. Mat. L/T/D			8.5	5.2			6.8	10.3
		(13) 4.3	(14) 2.0				(47) 2.9	(46) 2.6
		.9	.0				1.4	1.5
Fixed/Worth	.0	.1	.0	.2			.1	.1
	.3	.5	.2	.7			.3	.4
	-9.6	4.9	.7	1.4			1.8	2.1
Debt/Worth	.3	.7	.8	1.0			.8	.7
	1.4	1.5	1.4	2.8			2.0	1.9
	-16.7	82.9	3.7	6.2			7.8	9.7
% Profit Before Taxes/Tangible Net Worth	71.4	51.7	59.3	21.5			53.0	50.9
	(46) 31.6	(77) 22.5	(76) 22.1	(41) 11.4			(356) 22.3	(356) 23.4
	7.8	6.5	7.7	2.3			8.9	6.5
% Profit Before Taxes/Total Assets	33.3	16.8	17.2	6.9			17.7	17.8
	10.2	7.2	7.7	2.7			6.9	6.8
	-3.4	1.2	2.7	.2			2.3	1.4
Sales/Net Fixed Assets	595.9	154.5	106.7	30.2			125.6	75.4
	45.0	39.3	45.5	13.9			34.7	30.3
	17.8	10.9	18.8	5.5			12.0	12.2
Sales/Total Assets	9.1	4.2	3.7	2.1			4.2	4.4
	5.5	2.6	2.6	1.5			2.7	2.7
	3.1	1.9	2.1	1.0			1.9	1.8
% Depr., Dep., Amort./Sales	.4	.5	.4	.9			.5	.5
	(35) 1.2	(56) 1.0	(55) .9	(41) 1.3			(289) .9	(297) 1.0
	2.1	1.8	1.6	2.2			1.7	1.8
% Officers', Directors', Owners' Comp/Sales	2.8	1.6	1.0	.7			1.7	1.8
	(34) 5.0	(65) 3.1	(44) 1.4	(21) .8			(219) 3.1	(213) 2.9
	7.0	4.9	3.1	1.9			5.8	5.0
Net Sales ($)	100208M	329026M	1157096M	1862380M	1386733M	1559473M	9649176M	9710932M
Total Assets ($)	16669M	103478M	399112M	1084703M	679229M	965240M	4153303M	4520859M

M = $ thousand   MM = $ million
See Pages viii through xx for Explanation of Ratios and Data

RETAIL—Automotive Parts and Accessories Stores NAICS 441310

Comparative Historical Data / Current Data Sorted by Sales

4/1/16-3/31/17	4/1/17-3/31/18	4/1/18-3/31/19	Type of Statement	0-1MM	1-3MM	3-5MM	5-10MM	10-25MM	25MM & OVER
17	12	10	Unqualified						10
21	26	16	Reviewed		1	1	1	8	5
36	27	28	Compiled	1	5	3	3	12	4
140	133	123	Tax Returns	22	51	17	19	7	7
137	151	134	Other	13	30	12	24	26	29
4/1/16-3/31/17 ALL	4/1/17-3/31/18 ALL	4/1/18-3/31/19 ALL		32 (4/1-9/30/18)			279 (10/1/18-3/31/19)		
351	349	311	NUMBER OF STATEMENTS	36	87	33	47	53	55
%	%	%	**ASSETS**	%	%	%	%	%	%
10.5	10.6	11.6	Cash & Equivalents	17.9	14.4	10.4	12.6	8.5	6.0
13.8	13.4	12.1	Trade Receivables (net)	8.1	8.6	13.6	14.6	14.2	14.9
47.1	45.5	45.7	Inventory	48.1	41.2	51.8	43.4	49.6	46.0
2.0	1.7	2.0	All Other Current	.2	3.0	.9	1.7	1.7	2.5
73.4	71.2	71.4	Total Current	74.4	67.2	76.6	72.4	74.1	69.4
16.8	19.4	16.7	Fixed Assets (net)	12.4	23.3	13.2	10.3	15.5	17.8
4.6	3.8	4.0	Intangibles (net)	3.1	3.3	3.0	5.2	4.0	5.2
5.2	5.6	7.9	All Other Non-Current	10.2	6.2	7.1	12.0	6.4	7.5
100.0	100.0	100.0	Total	100.0	100.0	100.0	100.0	100.0	100.0
			LIABILITIES						
11.2	13.6	12.1	Notes Payable-Short Term	9.2	12.2	8.4	12.4	17.0	10.9
3.2	2.8	2.2	Cur. Mat.-L.T.D.	2.0	2.5	2.7	1.3	2.2	2.6
17.3	16.7	16.0	Trade Payables	5.5	15.4	14.7	17.2	19.4	20.0
.1	.2	.1	Income Taxes Payable	.0	.3	.1	.1	.1	.1
8.8	10.4	12.3	All Other Current	28.3	9.6	11.7	12.9	7.0	10.8
40.6	43.6	42.7	Total Current	45.0	40.0	37.6	44.0	45.7	44.4
17.8	19.4	21.8	Long-Term Debt	42.9	27.5	13.5	14.5	14.5	17.2
.2	.0	.1	Deferred Taxes	.0	.0	.0	.1	.1	.2
6.7	7.0	6.2	All Other Non-Current	8.3	11.4	3.5	4.6	3.2	2.5
34.7	29.9	29.3	Net Worth	3.8	21.2	45.5	36.7	36.5	35.8
100.0	100.0	100.0	Total Liabilities & Net Worth	100.0	100.0	100.0	100.0	100.0	100.0
			INCOME DATA						
100.0	100.0	100.0	Net Sales	100.0	100.0	100.0	100.0	100.0	100.0
38.9	35.7	37.5	Gross Profit	43.6	41.2	36.1	34.9	35.5	32.8
34.1	32.0	34.3	Operating Expenses	43.1	37.7	31.7	30.4	32.3	29.8
4.7	3.7	3.3	Operating Profit	.5	3.5	4.4	4.6	3.3	3.1
.3	.4	.3	All Other Expenses (net)	.7	.3	-.2	.0	.4	.5
4.4	3.3	3.0	Profit Before Taxes	-.2	3.2	4.6	4.5	2.9	2.6
			RATIOS						
3.7	3.7	3.5	Current	9.1	3.9	6.2	3.3	2.5	2.7
1.9	1.9	2.0		3.4	2.0	2.4	1.9	1.7	1.6
1.3	1.2	1.2		1.5	1.1	1.5	1.2	1.2	1.2
1.2	1.3	1.1	Quick	2.3	1.3	1.2	1.3	.8	.8
(350) .6	(348) .6	.6		.9	.6	.7	.8	.5	.4
.3	.3	.3		.1	.2	.3	.3	.2	.2
4 96.1	4 96.7	3 139.2	Sales/Receivables	0 UND	0 UND	1 434.4	4 98.8	5 67.7	9 42.6
15 23.6	17 21.3	13 27.2		4 101.4	7 53.1	12 30.9	15 24.7	21 17.0	24 15.4
28 13.0	31 11.7	28 13.1		18 19.8	24 15.3	23 15.6	37 9.9	31 11.9	33 11.1
45 8.2	38 9.7	39 9.3	Cost of Sales/Inventory	27 13.4	36 10.1	26 13.8	19 19.4	50 7.3	56 6.5
96 3.8	89 4.1	94 3.9		140 2.6	76 4.8	85 4.3	89 4.1	111 3.3	96 3.8
192 1.9	166 2.2	174 2.1		281 1.3	152 2.4	159 2.3	159 2.3	174 2.1	192 1.9
12 29.9	7 54.1	6 60.5	Cost of Sales/Payables	0 UND	0 UND	2 234.6	5 78.2	22 16.3	21 17.5
33 11.0	28 12.9	27 13.3		3 126.0	21 17.2	24 14.9	25 14.7	44 8.3	45 8.1
54 6.8	53 6.9	54 6.8		26 13.9	53 6.9	41 9.0	52 7.0	61 6.0	72 5.1
4.0	4.0	4.1	Sales/Working Capital	2.2	4.9	4.0	3.8	5.5	4.2
8.4	10.0	10.0		5.8	11.6	6.8	8.9	12.0	10.9
25.2	31.3	36.5		20.8	99.6	24.4	27.4	40.9	49.3
16.1	13.6	14.0	EBIT/Interest	9.5	14.7	14.7	52.3	18.3	9.1
(287) 5.1	(296) 4.3	(243) 4.4		(19) 2.8	(59) 4.4	(23) 6.0	(41) 7.3	(48) 4.1	(53) 3.0
2.3	1.3	1.1		-.2	.8	2.3	2.0	1.1	1.2
6.6	8.0	7.4	Net Profit + Depr., Dep., Amort./Cur. Mat. L/T/D					6.4	8.1
(40) 2.0	(45) 2.3	(37) 3.3						(10) 1.0	(20) 2.7
1.3	.8	.5						.4	.4
.1	.1	.1	Fixed/Worth	.0	.1	.0	.1	.1	.2
.3	.4	.4		.2	.9	.1	.2	.4	.4
1.3	2.0	1.8		NM	-2.6	.6	.6	1.0	1.4
.7	.7	.7	Debt/Worth	.3	.6	.5	.6	.9	1.0
1.8	1.9	1.7		1.8	2.0	.9	1.4	1.8	2.3
6.1	8.5	8.5		-8.8	-17.8	3.1	6.8	5.4	4.7
46.9	40.8	47.2	% Profit Before Taxes/Tangible Net Worth	44.0	54.7	42.5	76.5	41.5	33.4
(302) 19.2	(285) 16.6	(256) 18.5		(25) 24.6	(61) 28.1	(30) 16.7	(41) 28.0	(47) 16.1	(52) 12.8
5.6	5.4	5.6		3.0	11.1	10.7	6.2	2.0	4.2
17.9	15.5	16.2	% Profit Before Taxes/Total Assets	17.8	20.2	21.9	24.8	13.5	10.9
6.9	5.1	6.7		3.0	7.9	7.7	9.7	4.5	3.7
1.8	.9	.7		-13.7	.0	2.6	2.4	.6	.3
89.9	70.7	114.7	Sales/Net Fixed Assets	227.9	124.8	434.6	137.9	74.4	55.9
31.1	24.9	30.1		24.0	30.2	98.4	53.7	23.0	21.0
13.9	10.2	12.5		12.1	9.5	24.5	21.3	11.5	8.3
3.9	3.8	4.4	Sales/Total Assets	5.1	4.8	4.7	4.8	3.9	3.0
2.5	2.6	2.6		2.0	3.0	2.9	2.6	2.7	2.1
1.6	1.7	1.7		1.2	1.9	2.1	2.0	1.7	1.5
.5	.5	.5	% Depr., Dep., Amort./Sales	.6	.6	.2	.3	.8	.5
(246) 1.0	(240) 1.1	(203) 1.1		(21) 1.2	(49) 1.2	(16) .9	(29) .7	(38) 1.1	(50) 1.1
1.8	1.9	2.0		2.2	2.1	1.9	1.7	1.6	2.2
1.6	1.5	1.1	% Officers', Directors' Owners' Comp/Sales	4.2	2.1	1.6	1.0	.8	.7
(169) 2.8	(182) 3.0	(166) 2.6		(17) 6.6	(49) 3.9	(22) 2.3	(32) 2.0	(29) 1.4	(17) .9
4.8	6.0	5.0		8.4	6.6	3.8	5.6	2.6	1.6
7059268M	11238849M	6394916M	Net Sales ($)	19093M	166468M	130559M	344848M	836483M	4897465M
3461073M	4513630M	3248431M	Total Assets ($)	9764M	65074M	49567M	167847M	397644M	2558535M

M = $ thousand   MM = $ million
See Pages viii through xx for Explanation of Ratios and Data

Current Data Sorted by Assets   Comparative Historical Data

						Type of Statement		
1	8	15	4	3	2	Unqualified		
3	1	13	17	2	1	Reviewed	11	11
19	8	6	4	1		Compiled	40	25
					1	Tax Returns	30	27
14	11	28	15	2	6	Other	47	65
							80	66

0-500M	500M-2MM	2-10MM	10-50MM	50-100MM	100-250MM		4/1/14-3/31/15 ALL	4/1/15-3/31/16 ALL
	30 (4/1-9/30/18)		155 (10/1/18-3/31/19)					
37	28	62	40	8	10	**NUMBER OF STATEMENTS**	208	194
%	%	%	%	%	%	**ASSETS**	%	%
24.2	17.5	7.1	5.4		2.0	Cash & Equivalents	8.0	11.5
9.0	13.5	14.5	15.0		5.2	Trade Receivables (net)	15.6	15.4
24.3	34.3	44.5	42.0		21.8	Inventory	39.0	37.2
4.9	5.1	2.8	2.0		1.3	All Other Current	2.5	2.1
62.3	70.4	68.9	64.4		30.5	Total Current	65.0	66.1
25.9	19.7	21.4	25.0		58.1	Fixed Assets (net)	24.2	21.8
5.6	3.2	3.9	4.3		1.9	Intangibles (net)	4.0	5.4
6.2	6.6	5.8	6.4		9.6	All Other Non-Current	6.8	6.7
100.0	100.0	100.0	100.0		100.0	Total	100.0	100.0
						LIABILITIES		
18.7	9.3	12.3	9.0		6.6	Notes Payable-Short Term	10.3	10.0
3.5	1.1	2.4	2.3		3.7	Cur. Mat.-L.T.D.	2.6	2.9
18.6	21.0	24.3	23.3		13.5	Trade Payables	26.9	29.5
.3	.3	.1	.1		.0	Income Taxes Payable	.2	.1
15.0	12.9	8.6	8.4		8.5	All Other Current	9.9	9.9
56.2	44.6	47.7	43.1		32.3	Total Current	49.8	52.4
19.9	5.7	10.7	14.8		49.0	Long-Term Debt	17.0	17.3
.0	.0	.2	.5		.0	Deferred Taxes	.2	.2
4.8	2.6	3.6	1.6		7.3	All Other Non-Current	4.8	4.7
19.1	47.2	37.9	40.1		11.3	Net Worth	28.2	25.4
100.0	100.0	100.0	100.0		100.0	Total Liabilties & Net Worth	100.0	100.0
						INCOME DATA		
100.0	100.0	100.0	100.0		100.0	Net Sales	100.0	100.0
45.8	42.2	36.7	34.6		36.3	Gross Profit	36.3	36.0
40.7	38.3	33.1	32.0		31.1	Operating Expenses	33.0	33.8
5.1	3.9	3.6	2.6		5.2	Operating Profit	3.3	2.2
.2	.2	-.2	.1		2.4	All Other Expenses (net)	.1	-.1
4.9	3.7	3.8	2.5		2.8	Profit Before Taxes	3.2	2.4
						RATIOS		
2.3	2.9	2.2	2.0		1.3		2.0	2.3
1.5	1.4	1.5	1.5		1.2	Current	1.4	1.4
.8	1.0	1.1	1.2		.7		1.0	.9
1.2	1.3	.7	.7		.4		.7	.9
.7	.7	.5	.5		.2	Quick	(207) .5	.5
.3	.3	.3	.2		.1		.3	.3
1 610.3	4 81.4	7 51.1	11 34.4		3 143.0		6 60.3	6 60.4
3 117.2	9 39.0	18 20.5	21 17.4		5 74.4	Sales/Receivables	15 24.0	16 23.4
8 47.2	21 17.3	29 12.4	27 13.3		10 38.1		27 13.5	27 13.7
12 29.5	28 12.9	51 7.1	70 5.2		47 7.7		40 9.1	38 9.7
24 15.2	46 8.0	85 4.3	85 4.3		68 5.4	Cost of Sales/Inventory	70 5.2	63 5.8
43 8.5	96 3.8	118 3.1	104 3.5		114 3.2		99 3.7	87 4.2
0 UND	16 23.2	27 13.7	27 13.3		21 17.2		28 13.1	25 14.5
21 17.6	27 13.3	45 8.2	50 7.3		36 10.2	Cost of Sales/Payables	41 8.8	41 8.8
36 10.1	49 7.5	56 6.5	61 6.0		59 6.2		61 6.0	65 5.6
11.4	7.1	6.7	7.8		21.5		8.7	7.8
34.8	19.6	13.3	12.7		29.3	Sales/Working Capital	21.0	17.2
-54.7	NM	70.4	39.3		-20.0		278.5	-86.4
14.3	54.3	18.1	14.2		4.1		20.9	17.0
(23) 6.3	(21) 6.1	(57) 6.3	6.3		3.1	EBIT/Interest	(188) 7.7	(166) 6.7
1.3	1.6	2.9	2.2		1.1		2.4	1.5
			8.0			Net Profit + Depr., Dep.,	7.0	6.4
		(14)	5.0			Amort./Cur. Mat. L/T/D	(46) 4.2	(30) 3.8
			3.2				2.1	2.1
.3	.1	.2	.3		2.5		.2	.2
1.0	.3	.5	.6		6.2	Fixed/Worth	.7	.6
NM	1.3	1.3	1.5		-54.9		2.7	3.1
.9	.5	.8	1.0		2.5		.8	.8
2.3	1.1	1.6	1.7		9.3	Debt/Worth	2.3	2.5
NM	2.5	4.9	3.5		-76.4		6.9	8.3
120.9	44.5	41.0	25.5			% Profit Before Taxes/Tangible	40.1	44.1
(28) 66.8	(24) 27.0	(57) 15.9	(37) 14.4			Net Worth	(170) 21.7	(155) 20.8
16.7	10.6	8.1	6.2				10.1	5.5
45.5	27.3	13.1	9.8		7.4	% Profit Before Taxes/Total	13.2	12.6
22.2	11.7	6.7	5.0		5.7	Assets	7.2	6.4
4.2	2.9	3.6	2.1		.4		2.1	.9
142.8	51.1	54.8	23.8		12.2		41.0	47.4
38.9	30.4	21.3	15.2		2.3	Sales/Net Fixed Assets	21.3	22.2
11.6	19.3	9.4	9.5		1.5		9.6	10.6
8.6	5.1	3.8	3.2		3.1		4.4	4.4
5.3	3.7	3.1	2.9		1.6	Sales/Total Assets	3.0	3.2
3.0	2.8	2.2	2.1		1.2		2.2	2.3
.3	.4	.7	1.0				.6	.8
(20) .9	(23) 1.0	(49) 1.0	(38) 1.3			% Depr., Dep., Amort./Sales	(174) 1.0	(149) 1.3
1.5	1.6	1.9	1.9				1.8	1.8
2.1	2.7	1.1					1.2	1.3
(15) 3.7	(13) 4.0	(16) 1.6				% Officers', Directors' Owners' Comp/Sales	(81) 3.6	(74) 2.7
7.8	4.4	2.5					5.1	6.1
56988M	106434M	905084M	2692508M	1917550M	3840626M	Net Sales ($)	11153866M	8806633M
10044M	28225M	303752M	1007982M	585217M	1827512M	Total Assets ($)	4218194M	3186406M

M = $ thousand   MM = $ million
See Pages viii through xx for Explanation of Ratios and Data

Comparative Historical Data   Current Data Sorted by Sales

	4/1/16-3/31/17 ALL	4/1/17-3/31/18 ALL	4/1/18-3/31/19 ALL	Type of Statement	0-1MM	1-3MM	3-5MM	5-10MM	10-25MM	25MM & OVER
	11	7	9	Unqualified					1	8
	39	34	44	Reviewed		5	2	6	8	23
	25	28	22	Compiled		3		4	8	7
	53	50	34	Tax Returns	4	20	1	6	1	2
	86	82	76	Other	6	13	8	6	19	24
					30 (4/1-9/30/18)			155 (10/1/18-3/31/19)		
	214	201	185	**NUMBER OF STATEMENTS**	10	41	11	22	37	64
	%	%	%	**ASSETS**	%	%	%	%	%	%
	11.6	11.8	11.3	Cash & Equivalents	20.6	23.2	16.0	8.9	6.7	4.7
	14.0	15.0	13.0	Trade Receivables (net)	6.3	9.2	17.3	12.4	16.3	14.0
	38.1	34.0	37.4	Inventory	17.4	28.2	25.3	47.2	43.4	41.6
	1.7	2.8	3.3	All Other Current	.4	5.8	6.9	.7	4.2	1.8
	65.3	63.6	64.9	Total Current	44.8	66.4	65.6	69.3	70.6	62.1
	23.3	25.0	24.6	Fixed Assets (net)	49.2	19.1	31.2	20.0	21.4	26.5
	3.9	5.0	4.2	Intangibles (net)	5.9	5.5	.2	6.3	2.9	3.9
	7.5	6.3	6.3	All Other Non-Current	.4	9.0	3.0	4.4	5.1	7.5
	100.0	100.0	100.0	Total	100.0	100.0	100.0	100.0	100.0	100.0
				LIABILITIES						
	11.3	10.0	12.2	Notes Payable-Short Term	6.7	17.8	11.6	7.7	15.8	9.2
	2.4	3.1	2.4	Cur. Mat.-L.T.D.	1.6	3.4	.5	1.0	3.1	2.3
	27.2	23.5	22.2	Trade Payables	15.6	17.2	17.8	23.1	27.5	23.7
	.1	.1	.2	Income Taxes Payable	.0	.3	.7	.0	.2	.1
	8.8	13.0	10.5	All Other Current	8.7	16.9	12.3	7.3	6.5	9.9
	49.8	49.7	47.5	Total Current	32.6	55.6	42.9	39.1	53.1	45.2
	13.9	15.3	14.7	Long-Term Debt	19.5	14.9	13.5	9.7	11.9	17.3
	.2	.2	.2	Deferred Taxes	.0	.0	.0	.0	.1	.4
	4.8	5.0	3.4	All Other Non-Current	9.4	3.2	.7	5.8	2.7	2.7
	31.2	29.8	34.3	Net Worth	38.8	26.3	42.9	45.5	32.2	34.5
	100.0	100.0	100.0	Total Liabilities & Net Worth	100.0	100.0	100.0	100.0	100.0	100.0
				INCOME DATA						
	100.0	100.0	100.0	Net Sales	100.0	100.0	100.0	100.0	100.0	100.0
	36.2	37.3	38.4	Gross Profit	48.7	46.4	40.3	37.2	35.4	33.4
	33.7	33.7	34.7	Operating Expenses	41.8	41.5	33.7	33.6	32.7	30.9
	2.5	3.6	3.7	Operating Profit	6.9	4.9	6.7	3.5	2.7	2.5
	.0	.1	.2	All Other Expenses (net)	1.2	.1	.7	-.5	-.4	.5
	2.5	3.5	3.5	Profit Before Taxes	5.7	4.8	6.0	4.0	3.1	2.0
				RATIOS						
	2.0	2.3	2.1		8.4	2.4	2.9	3.5	1.9	1.8
	1.3	1.4	1.4	Current	1.5	1.4	1.9	1.8	1.4	1.4
	1.0	1.0	1.1		.7	.9	1.3	1.4	1.1	1.1
	.8	1.0	.9		6.0	1.3	1.7	.9	.7	.6
	.5	.5	.5	Quick	.5	.7	1.1	.6	.4	.4
	.3	.3	.3		.2	.3	.3	.4	.3	.2
	5 71.6	5 75.5	4 87.1		0 UND	1 416.4	5 72.5	1 288.2	8 48.3	6 61.2
	15 24.0	15 24.7	11 32.6	Sales/Receivables	4 87.3	5 74.5	16 22.7	12 29.8	17 21.4	18 19.8
	25 14.7	26 14.1	24 15.3		10 36.4	12 29.5	24 14.9	24 15.2	31 11.9	27 13.7
	40 9.2	33 10.9	38 9.6		8 43.6	18 20.7	18 20.3	39 9.4	51 7.2	57 6.4
	68 5.4	64 5.7	69 5.3	Cost of Sales/Inventory	32 11.5	27 13.5	31 11.7	101 3.6	78 4.7	81 4.5
	91 4.0	94 3.9	101 3.6		68 5.4	59 6.2	69 5.3	140 2.6	111 3.3	104 3.5
	26 14.3	18 20.4	21 17.2		0 UND	0 UND	10 37.5	5 69.4	33 11.0	29 12.7
	41 8.8	36 10.1	38 9.6	Cost of Sales/Payables	27 13.3	27 13.5	18 20.0	37 9.9	49 7.5	49 7.5
	62 5.9	61 6.0	55 6.6		62 5.9	36 10.1	31 11.9	64 5.7	56 6.5	58 6.3
	8.8	7.7	8.0		6.5	10.9	8.2	5.5	6.9	9.8
	20.2	21.6	17.4	Sales/Working Capital	27.9	34.8	22.0	7.6	15.8	18.7
	-265.5	UND	121.2		-14.7	-64.4	68.1	38.2	75.8	86.8
	11.9	14.2	15.3			20.4		40.2	19.0	11.1
	(179) 5.3	(169) 5.7	(159) 5.4	EBIT/Interest		(26) 4.7		(20) 11.3	(35) 5.4	4.4
	1.7	1.8	2.1			1.1		5.9	2.8	1.8
	7.8	7.2	8.6	Net Profit + Depr., Dep.,						11.5
	(35) 4.6	(34) 3.1	(30) 5.3	Amort./Cur. Mat. L/T/D					(22)	7.2
	2.1	1.5	3.5							4.2
	.2	.2	.2		.5	.1	.1	.1	.2	.3
	.7	.7	.6	Fixed/Worth	1.7	.5	.4	.5	.7	.7
	2.5	3.0	1.9		6.3	NM	2.4	1.9	1.3	2.4
	.9	.8	.8		.8	.6	.6	.5	1.1	1.1
	2.2	1.8	1.8	Debt/Worth	2.2	1.3	.8	1.5	1.9	2.2
	7.5	8.0	5.2		7.5	NM	3.1	4.0	5.2	4.3
	46.8	46.0	48.6	% Profit Before Taxes/Tangible		89.4	142.8	40.9	45.0	25.9
	(185) 20.1	(169) 17.9	(159) 19.4	Net Worth	(31) 30.5	(10) 37.8	(20) 26.0	(33) 17.2	(56) 15.4	
	7.7	5.9	10.0			11.3	9.0	14.9	8.1	4.4
	12.6	15.0	16.5	% Profit Before Taxes/Total	27.8	36.5	34.2	15.9	13.7	8.9
	5.9	6.8	7.4	Assets	20.8	18.4	8.5	11.4	6.5	5.1
	1.5	1.5	2.5		-7.5	3.1	3.8	4.8	3.0	.7
	39.5	38.3	43.2		16.9	135.5	108.2	49.3	67.9	25.6
	19.5	18.2	20.6	Sales/Net Fixed Assets	4.9	38.9	41.8	23.1	23.3	16.9
	10.2	9.0	9.4		2.9	15.8	4.9	9.6	8.9	9.7
	4.3	4.0	4.4		3.0	8.2	5.2	4.1	4.4	3.5
	3.2	3.0	3.2	Sales/Total Assets	2.7	4.5	3.6	2.9	3.3	3.0
	2.3	2.0	2.3		2.3	3.1	2.1	2.1	2.2	2.1
	.8	.9	.7			.4		.6	.8	.9
	(174) 1.3	(163) 1.4	(143) 1.1	% Depr., Dep., Amort./Sales	(28) .9		(17) 1.0	(30) 1.2	(56) 1.3	
	2.1	2.0	1.9		1.6		1.2	2.3	2.0	
	1.3	1.0	1.2	% Officers', Directors',		2.1		1.4		.4
	(78) 2.9	(58) 3.3	(56) 2.3	Owners' Comp/Sales	(22) 3.8		(11) 2.1		(13) .8	
		5.9	4.2			7.6		4.0		
	9111021M	8391870M	9519190M	Net Sales ($)	6560M	79163M	45232M	160409M	563015M	8664811M
	3461291M	3339542M	3762732M	Total Assets ($)	2743M	24373M	15943M	59122M	218154M	3442397M

Current Data Sorted by Assets   **Comparative Historical Data**

Type of Statement								
	1	2	4	14	5	8	Unqualified	37	44
		5	23	19		2	Reviewed	66	55
	1	16	30	7		1	Compiled	74	71
	17	46	32	3		1	Tax Returns	156	152
	14	33	44	40	10	7	Other	208	211

	0-500M	500M-2MM	2-10MM	10-50MM	50-100MM	100-250MM		4/1/14-3/31/15 ALL	4/1/15-3/31/16 ALL
		71 (4/1-9/30/18)			314 (10/1/18-3/31/19)				
NUMBER OF STATEMENTS	33	102	133	83	15	19		541	533
ASSETS	%	%	%	%	%	%		%	%
Cash & Equivalents	22.5	12.6	12.2	9.6	8.3	13.9		12.8	12.8
Trade Receivables (net)	4.3	8.4	10.8	12.3	21.1	7.2		11.9	10.3
Inventory	41.4	54.7	39.7	36.9	31.1	28.9		44.4	44.2
All Other Current	1.4	1.6	3.2	2.9	4.6	2.9		2.5	2.0
Total Current	69.5	77.3	65.8	61.7	65.1	52.8		71.6	69.3
Fixed Assets (net)	16.9	16.6	22.6	28.0	22.2	38.4		19.7	20.5
Intangibles (net)	3.4	2.5	3.9	3.8	2.8	3.8		2.9	2.5
All Other Non-Current	10.1	3.5	7.7	6.5	10.0	5.0		5.8	7.8
Total	100.0	100.0	100.0	100.0	100.0	100.0		100.0	100.0
LIABILITIES									
Notes Payable-Short Term	6.2	9.6	6.9	6.5	4.1	6.5		8.8	8.4
Cur. Mat.-L.T.D.	5.8	2.1	2.8	1.7	.8	1.2		2.5	2.1
Trade Payables	7.0	17.1	14.2	13.6	11.6	9.4		16.7	14.8
Income Taxes Payable	.0	.2	.1	.1	.2	.2		.1	.1
All Other Current	20.5	17.8	22.7	23.9	18.8	13.7		17.0	19.9
Total Current	39.5	46.9	46.7	45.7	35.6	30.9		45.1	45.2
Long-Term Debt	14.7	11.7	19.1	13.7	14.2	18.1		12.1	13.7
Deferred Taxes	.0	.0	.2	.1	.0	.1		.1	.1
All Other Non-Current	4.5	9.8	5.3	7.4	9.5	3.3		8.2	8.0
Net Worth	41.3	31.7	28.8	33.0	40.8	47.5		34.5	33.0
Total Liabilties & Net Worth	100.0	100.0	100.0	100.0	100.0	100.0		100.0	100.0
INCOME DATA									
Net Sales	100.0	100.0	100.0	100.0	100.0	100.0		100.0	100.0
Gross Profit	52.8	45.6	42.2	43.2	47.5	47.3		43.2	44.2
Operating Expenses	46.2	42.2	37.7	39.8	43.0	43.7		38.6	39.3
Operating Profit	6.6	3.4	4.5	3.3	4.5	3.6		4.6	4.8
All Other Expenses (net)	.4	.0	.5	.6	1.1	.0		.1	.4
Profit Before Taxes	6.2	3.3	4.0	2.7	3.4	3.6		4.4	4.5
RATIOS									
Current	10.3	3.2	2.6	2.2	2.9	2.5		2.9	2.8
	2.8	1.9	1.4	1.4	1.5	1.4		1.7	1.6
	1.3	1.1	1.0	1.0	1.2	1.1		1.2	1.1
Quick	4.4	1.1	1.0	.8	1.6	1.0		1.0	1.0
	.7	.4	.5	.5	.6	.5		(540) .5	(531) .4
	.3	.1	.1	.1	.2	.5		.2	.1
Sales/Receivables	0 UND	0 UND	0 UND	0 770.0	3 114.1	1 430.4		0 999.8	0 UND
	0 UND	2 180.3	3 115.5	3 139.8	12 31.3	7 49.7		3 136.6	2 147.1
	11 33.5	13 28.1	16 23.3	21 17.6	89 4.1	12 31.6		18 20.2	12 30.2
Cost of Sales/Inventory	14 25.5	73 5.0	59 6.2	58 6.3	73 5.0	96 3.8		59 6.2	61 6.0
	62 5.9	126 2.9	107 3.4	89 4.1	118 3.1	111 3.3		104 3.5	104 3.5
	166 2.2	192 1.9	159 2.3	122 3.0	159 2.3	146 2.5		159 2.3	159 2.3
Cost of Sales/Payables	0 UND	12 31.5	13 28.1	15 23.7	24 15.0	25 14.6		16 23.2	14 26.3
	1 379.0	23 15.6	27 13.6	29 12.4	36 10.1	51 7.2		29 12.5	29 12.7
	19 19.1	40 9.1	42 8.7	44 8.3	49 7.4	66 5.5		47 7.8	43 8.4
Sales/Working Capital	4.8	5.3	6.4	7.3	3.6	4.9		5.4	5.7
	9.8	9.9	16.3	22.7	11.2	9.0		11.1	12.6
	40.4	26.7	127.1	-141.0	33.8	29.5		41.4	59.9
EBIT/Interest	61.8	18.9	18.2	32.1	23.8	5.2		30.3	30.2
	(21) 10.1	(78) 5.8	(115) 4.4	(73) 6.7	6.7	(16) 2.5		(422) 7.7	(408) 6.8
	2.2	1.9	1.7	1.1	1.4	.7		2.2	2.5
Net Profit + Depr., Dep., Amort./Cur. Mat. L/T/D			15.3	20.6				10.3	7.6
			(19) 1.7	(17) 10.9				(65) 4.3	(58) 3.6
			.5	2.2				1.6	1.7
Fixed/Worth	.0	.1	.2	.3	.2	.4		.1	.1
	.2	.3	.7	.8	.5	.6		.5	.5
	1.1	1.7	2.4	2.2	1.9	1.8		1.7	1.8
Debt/Worth	.3	.7	1.0	.8	.6	.6		.7	.7
	.9	1.5	1.8	2.2	1.9	1.3		1.7	1.6
	12.4	8.3	9.5	6.6	4.8	2.6		5.4	6.0
% Profit Before Taxes/Tangible Net Worth	136.3	58.2	55.5	40.2	32.8	23.3		57.7	61.0
	(29) 44.6	(82) 25.8	(112) 25.9	(72) 18.6	(14) 19.6	(17) 8.2		(468) 25.6	(463) 27.7
	16.3	9.5	6.0	7.3	10.4	1.1		9.2	10.2
% Profit Before Taxes/Total Assets	39.5	20.6	14.6	14.2	10.8	13.6		21.1	19.9
	19.1	8.0	6.8	8.5	8.9	2.9		9.4	9.2
	7.0	2.0	1.5	.5	.4	.1		2.6	2.7
Sales/Net Fixed Assets	UND	116.7	59.7	42.2	19.3	6.3		66.3	70.2
	37.9	28.1	20.7	13.8	13.6	4.3		24.9	24.9
	13.1	14.9	5.9	5.3	7.2	2.6		9.5	8.6
Sales/Total Assets	6.3	3.9	3.6	3.7	3.1	2.1		4.1	4.1
	3.6	2.9	2.4	2.6	1.9	1.4		2.8	2.8
	2.3	2.0	1.5	1.8	1.3	1.0		1.9	1.8
% Depr., Dep., Amort./Sales	.4	.4	.6	.6	.8	1.3		.4	.4
	(15) .8	(61) .7	(104) .9	(73) 1.1	(14) 1.1	(15) 1.9		(408) .8	(387) .8
	2.1	1.4	1.6	1.4	1.7	3.7		1.4	1.4
% Officers', Directors' Owners' Comp/Sales	2.9	1.9	.9	.6				1.6	1.4
	(16) 4.2	(44) 3.4	(58) 2.2	(24) 1.1				(232) 2.7	(230) 2.7
	9.7	6.7	3.9					5.1	6.1
Net Sales ($)	48326M	323229M	1560258M	5491173M	2215431M	5032962M		18592800M	21909377M
Total Assets ($)	9710M	110158M	591766M	1956624M	1044162M	3013609M		8354190M	10108385M

M = $ thousand   MM = $ million
See Pages viii through xx for Explanation of Ratios and Data

Comparative Historical Data | Current Data Sorted by Sales

Type of Statement									
Unqualified	25	28	34	1	2			5	26
Reviewed	60	48	49		6	4	9	9	21
Compiled	59	61	55	1	11	9	10	14	10
Tax Returns	128	147	99	15	31	20	21	8	4
Other	167	192	148	5	28	14	21	26	54
	4/1/16-3/31/17 ALL	4/1/17-3/31/18 ALL	4/1/18-3/31/19 ALL	71 (4/1-9/30/18)		314 (10/1/18-3/31/19)			
				0-1MM	1-3MM	3-5MM	5-10MM	10-25MM	25MM & OVER
NUMBER OF STATEMENTS	439	476	385	22	78	47	61	62	115
	%	%	%	%	%	%	%	%	%
ASSETS									
Cash & Equivalents	12.2	12.5	12.6	12.9	12.3	14.1	14.8	12.2	11.1
Trade Receivables (net)	10.2	9.6	10.1	4.1	6.6	12.5	8.3	12.4	12.5
Inventory	45.5	44.5	42.3	42.0	50.4	43.5	44.4	39.3	36.9
All Other Current	3.0	3.0	2.6	.4	1.7	.8	3.4	3.6	3.5
Total Current	70.8	69.6	67.6	59.4	70.9	70.9	70.9	67.4	64.0
Fixed Assets (net)	20.4	20.9	22.5	25.0	21.7	22.2	17.5	17.9	27.7
Intangibles (net)	3.5	4.0	3.4	5.3	2.5	2.8	3.0	6.7	2.5
All Other Non-Current	5.3	5.5	6.5	10.3	4.9	4.1	8.7	7.9	5.8
Total	100.0	100.0	100.0	100.0	100.0	100.0	100.0	100.0	100.0
LIABILITIES									
Notes Payable-Short Term	8.5	8.6	7.4	6.5	9.2	6.2	8.9	7.0	6.1
Cur. Mat.-L.T.D.	2.2	1.9	2.5	8.9	2.8	2.5	1.2	2.1	1.8
Trade Payables	14.1	16.3	13.9	6.5	12.9	13.0	15.8	16.2	14.0
Income Taxes Payable	.3	.2	.1	.1	.0	.4	.0	.1	.1
All Other Current	19.3	20.1	20.9	14.7	16.6	19.7	21.9	25.7	22.4
Total Current	44.4	47.0	44.7	36.8	41.5	41.7	47.9	51.2	44.4
Long-Term Debt	13.4	15.2	15.3	26.8	15.2	13.9	10.8	14.9	16.5
Deferred Taxes	.1	.0	.1	.0	.0	.1	.1	.3	.0
All Other Non-Current	9.1	7.8	6.9	5.2	11.0	6.9	3.7	5.2	7.2
Net Worth	33.1	30.0	32.9	31.3	32.2	37.4	37.6	28.4	31.9
Total Liabilities & Net Worth	100.0	100.0	100.0	100.0	100.0	100.0	100.0	100.0	100.0
INCOME DATA									
Net Sales	100.0	100.0	100.0	100.0	100.0	100.0	100.0	100.0	100.0
Gross Profit	45.2	45.0	44.7	55.0	49.0	41.5	42.4	40.5	44.5
Operating Expenses	40.9	40.7	40.6	44.7	45.4	38.2	38.2	37.5	40.4
Operating Profit	4.3	4.3	4.1	10.4	3.6	3.3	4.1	3.0	4.1
All Other Expenses (net)	.0	.2	.4	1.9	.5	-.5	.2	.5	.5
Profit Before Taxes	4.3	4.1	3.7	8.5	3.1	3.8	4.0	2.5	3.6
RATIOS									
	2.7	2.9	2.8	3.8	3.9	4.4	2.2	2.1	2.3
Current	1.7	1.6	1.5	2.6	2.1	1.9	1.5	1.3	1.4
	1.1	1.1	1.1	1.1	1.1	1.1	1.1	1.0	1.0
	1.0	1.0	1.0	2.0	1.2	1.5	1.0	.9	.9
Quick	.4 (475)	.4	.5	.3	.4	.6	.4	.6	.5
	.1	.1	.1	.1	.1	.2	.1	.1	.2
	0 UND	0 UND	0 UND	0 UND	0 UND	0 UND	0 UND	0 UND	0 770.0
Sales/Receivables	3 137.2	2 162.2	3 136.9	0 UND	3 130.9	1 570.0	3 109.4	2 152.6	3 115.5
	14 26.2	14 26.1	14 25.9	12 29.8	11 33.6	23 15.7	15 23.6	26 13.8	13 27.9
	64 5.7	60 6.1	62 5.9	30 12.0	101 3.6	65 5.6	43 8.5	51 7.2	61 6.0
Cost of Sales/Inventory	104 3.5	104 3.5	107 3.4	130 2.8	135 2.7	101 3.6	122 3.0	99 3.7	96 3.8
	166 2.2	159 2.3	159 2.3	304 1.2	215 1.7	146 2.5	192 1.9	146 2.5	122 3.0
	14 26.4	13 29.0	12 30.0	0 UND	4 93.5	6 59.7	16 22.8	18 19.8	18 20.7
Cost of Sales/Payables	27 13.4	29 12.4	26 13.8	7 56.0	21 17.3	18 19.9	29 12.5	28 13.0	31 11.8
	45 8.2	47 7.8	43 8.4	35 10.4	33 10.9	36 10.1	44 8.3	54 6.7	47 7.8
	5.6	5.9	5.8	3.9	3.8	5.7	6.9	7.2	6.8
Sales/Working Capital	11.2	12.6	13.3	6.9	8.1	9.0	12.8	21.7	18.6
	48.7	54.1	77.2	NM	30.1	47.3	36.6	-97.7	122.1
	30.8	24.4	19.3	11.8	11.8	30.6	18.0	29.0	28.3
EBIT/Interest	(355) 7.6	(388) 6.5	(318) 5.2	(18) 4.8	(59) 4.7	(36) 4.5	(48) 5.1	(55) 6.6	(102) 6.9
	2.6	1.8	1.5	1.3	1.4	1.3	2.7	1.1	1.4
	10.2	6.4	15.4						21.6
Net Profit + Depr., Dep., Amort./Cur. Mat. L/T/D	(51) 3.3	(51) 3.4	(49) 3.4					(27)	4.6
	.9	1.4	1.3						3.0
	.2	.1	.1	.1	.1	.1	.1	.1	.3
Fixed/Worth	.6	.5	.6	.4	.3	.7	.4	.6	.7
	1.5	2.3	1.9	4.0	1.8	3.3	1.2	2.3	1.9
	.7	.7	.7	.5	.5	.5	.9	1.0	.7
Debt/Worth	1.6	1.9	1.6	1.2	1.4	1.9	1.5	2.5	1.9
	6.8	7.1	7.4	17.7	7.4	15.9	4.0	11.1	5.0
	63.1	64.7	53.8	144.2	47.9	64.0	57.9	54.7	42.5
% Profit Before Taxes/Tangible Net Worth	(377) 29.6	(396) 26.6	(326) 24.5	(19) 36.0	(63) 19.7	(38) 36.4	(55) 26.1	(50) 28.8	(101) 19.4
	10.1	7.1	8.1	8.8	6.2	7.0	10.1	8.0	4.2
	21.0	19.6	17.5	22.2	14.9	23.1	17.7	15.0	15.8
% Profit Before Taxes/Total Assets	9.0	8.9	7.9	12.9	6.9	9.8	7.7	7.5	9.0
	2.8	1.7	1.3	-.3	.9	1.1	1.9	.7	1.1
	54.6	60.2	60.9	149.9	82.8	60.4	91.8	68.5	36.7
Sales/Net Fixed Assets	20.7	22.3	19.3	15.6	22.5	23.8	22.6	23.9	13.5
	9.2	9.0	6.2	4.5	9.0	5.9	8.8	8.5	5.3
	4.0	4.2	3.7	3.3	3.6	4.5	3.6	3.8	4.0
Sales/Total Assets	2.8	2.8	2.6	1.8	2.4	2.7	2.9	2.5	2.8
	1.8	1.7	1.6	.9	1.6	1.6	1.6	1.8	1.7
	.5	.4	.5	1.4	.4	.5	.3	.6	.6
% Depr., Dep., Amort./Sales	(347) .9	(358) .9	(282) 1.0	(12) 2.6	(51) .8	(30) 1.1	(45) .7	(43) .8	(101) 1.2
	1.6	1.6	1.6	7.1	1.7	1.5	1.4	1.3	1.7
	1.3	1.2	1.2		2.1	1.7	1.0	.9	.5
% Officers', Directors', Owners' Comp/Sales	(175) 2.6	(200) 2.8	(146) 2.6	(37) 5.0	(16) 3.1	(26) 2.4	(28) 1.4	(30) .9	
	5.4	5.4	5.4		8.3	4.1	3.8	3.1	3.8
Net Sales ($)	16416140M	16195744M	14671379M	13549M	161446M	185386M	446387M	985832M	12878779M
Total Assets ($)	7339558M	6536437M	6726029M	9902M	90068M	85566M	199035M	471997M	5869461M

Current Data Sorted by Assets   Comparative Historical Data

Type of Statement

Type of Statement	0-500M	500M-2MM	2-10MM	10-50MM	50-100MM	100-250MM	4/1/14-3/31/15 ALL	4/1/15-3/31/16 ALL
Unqualified			3		1			
Reviewed		1	6	7			8	24
Compiled	1	5	5	3			25	29
Tax Returns	11	36	14				25	29
Other	12	18	24	8		1	97	107
							74	104
	30 (4/1-9/30/18)		126 (10/1/18-3/31/19)					
NUMBER OF STATEMENTS	24	60	52	18	1	1	229	273

	%	%	%	%	%	%	%	%
ASSETS								
Cash & Equivalents	21.3	16.8	10.2	6.7			10.3	13.2
Trade Receivables (net)	25.9	16.7	24.7	23.7			26.0	24.0
Inventory	19.2	38.2	38.5	37.1			35.8	33.7
All Other Current	4.9	2.1	2.8	2.0			2.7	2.3
Total Current	71.3	73.8	76.2	69.5			74.8	73.2
Fixed Assets (net)	11.2	13.5	15.3	20.6			15.4	14.8
Intangibles (net)	1.4	4.1	2.0	2.8			2.2	3.4
All Other Non-Current	16.1	8.6	6.6	7.1			7.6	8.7
Total	100.0	100.0	100.0	100.0			100.0	100.0
LIABILITIES								
Notes Payable-Short Term	9.5	8.7	8.6	14.0			11.2	12.8
Cur. Mat.-L.T.D.	1.9	1.5	1.2	1.8			1.9	1.9
Trade Payables	26.0	13.6	18.5	15.6			22.3	19.9
Income Taxes Payable	.1	.2	.0	.4			.1	.1
All Other Current	31.0	24.2	22.3	11.8			16.1	17.4
Total Current	68.5	48.1	50.6	43.6			51.5	52.2
Long-Term Debt	14.9	14.3	8.2	12.4			15.9	10.7
Deferred Taxes	.0	.0	.0	.1			.1	.1
All Other Non-Current	7.3	5.5	4.1	7.0			10.7	7.9
Net Worth	9.3	32.1	37.0	37.0			21.7	29.1
Total Liabilties & Net Worth	100.0	100.0	100.0	100.0			100.0	100.0
INCOME DATA								
Net Sales	100.0	100.0	100.0	100.0			100.0	100.0
Gross Profit	35.2	35.3	34.0	30.2			35.3	34.3
Operating Expenses	31.5	32.0	31.3	28.5			31.7	30.8
Operating Profit	3.8	3.2	2.6	1.8			3.5	3.5
All Other Expenses (net)	.7	-.1	-.1	.1			.1	.0
Profit Before Taxes	3.1	3.3	2.7	1.6			3.4	3.5

RATIOS

	0-500M	500M-2MM	2-10MM	10-50MM	50-100MM	100-250MM	4/1/14-3/31/15 ALL	4/1/15-3/31/16 ALL
Current	4.7	4.0	2.7	2.0			2.7	2.8
	1.4	1.6	1.6	1.6			1.7	1.6
	.7	1.0	1.1	1.2			1.1	1.1
Quick	2.7	1.4	1.3	1.4			1.3	1.3
	.8	.6	.7	.5			.7	.8
	.3	.3	.4	.3			.3	.4
Sales/Receivables	0 UND	2 173.1	8 45.9	17 21.3			6 58.3	6 60.8
	12 30.3	11 32.9	23 16.2	29 12.6			22 16.3	19 19.1
	26 14.1	27 13.3	38 9.6	36 10.0			36 10.2	35 10.5
Cost of Sales/Inventory	2 148.3	27 13.6	38 9.7	40 9.1			20 18.7	20 18.7
	13 29.1	52 7.0	54 6.7	73 5.0			45 8.1	40 9.1
	27 13.4	101 3.6	122 3.0	107 3.4			101 3.6	78 4.7
Cost of Sales/Payables	7 50.7	7 53.0	16 23.1	15 24.2			13 27.7	15 25.1
	19 19.5	20 18.3	23 15.9	21 17.0			24 15.1	23 16.1
	37 9.8	36 10.2	40 9.1	43 8.5			39 9.4	35 10.3
Sales/Working Capital	9.6	6.1	5.6	7.2			7.0	7.5
	18.3	14.3	12.6	13.1			12.8	15.7
	-28.2	409.5	63.6	30.4			53.0	86.2
EBIT/Interest	18.2	10.0	25.1	12.5			19.3	34.2
	(16) 11.0	(39) 3.0	(43) 6.7	3.8			(175) 7.3	(220) 9.8
	3.0	-.3	2.3	2.3			2.6	2.8
Net Profit + Depr., Dep., Amort./Cur. Mat. L/T/D							11.8	21.8
							(23) 3.0	(28) 4.7
							1.8	1.2
Fixed/Worth	.1	.1	.1	.1			.1	.1
	.2	.3	.3	.5			.3	.3
	NM	1.5	1.1	1.2			1.8	1.8
Debt/Worth	.8	.6	.7	.7			.8	.7
	2.1	1.9	1.9	1.8			1.8	2.2
	NM	16.6	3.4	2.9			12.7	8.1
% Profit Before Taxes/Tangible Net Worth	66.3	70.3	56.3	29.0			57.5	72.8
	(18) 36.5	(48) 32.0	(48) 24.8	(15) 21.6			(184) 27.5	(220) 34.2
	7.5	5.0	9.8	3.2			8.0	9.9
% Profit Before Taxes/Total Assets	28.7	23.0	21.1	10.1			21.3	22.6
	14.6	7.3	10.0	4.8			8.9	9.9
	.2	.5	2.1	1.4			2.8	3.1
Sales/Net Fixed Assets	214.0	121.4	90.5	62.7			138.8	121.4
	91.2	58.5	43.8	11.7			59.5	48.4
	32.3	17.2	15.0	8.3			18.7	21.4
Sales/Total Assets	8.9	4.3	4.8	3.3			5.4	5.1
	5.6	3.3	3.2	3.0			3.6	3.7
	4.1	2.6	2.3	2.0			2.5	2.6
% Depr., Dep., Amort./Sales	.2	.3	.2	.6			.3	.3
	(10) .5	(38) .4	(37) .6	(16) .9			(156) .6	(187) .6
	.9	1.5	1.7	1.2			1.1	1.1
% Officers', Directors' Owners' Comp/Sales	2.2	2.6	1.0				1.9	1.7
	(17) 4.6	(42) 3.5	(21) 1.8				(115) 3.4	(140) 3.0
	7.6	6.1	5.1				5.5	6.0
Net Sales ($)	45181M	237344M	826275M	868310M	292547M	125478M	5906385M	6625298M
Total Assets ($)	7327M	68206M	235946M	318464M	73800M	119259M	1426770M	1927309M

M = $ thousand   MM = $ million
See Pages viii through xx for Explanation of Ratios and Data

Comparative Historical Data / Current Data Sorted by Sales

Type of Statement

Type of Statement	4/1/16-3/31/17	4/1/17-3/31/18	4/1/18-3/31/19	0-1MM	1-3MM	3-5MM	5-10MM	10-25MM	25MM & OVER
Unqualified	4	7	4					3	1
Reviewed	21	22	14		1		2	1	10
Compiled	23	16	14		3	3	2	4	2
Tax Returns	74	70	61	4	20	13	14	10	
Other	74	89	63	3	17	9	10	9	15
	4/1/16-3/31/17 ALL	4/1/17-3/31/18 ALL	4/1/18-3/31/19 ALL	30 (4/1-9/30/18)			126 (10/1/18-3/31/19)		
NUMBER OF STATEMENTS	196	204	156	7	41	25	28	27	28

Main Data

	4/1/16-3/31/17 ALL %	4/1/17-3/31/18 ALL %	4/1/18-3/31/19 ALL %	0-1MM %	1-3MM %	3-5MM %	5-10MM %	10-25MM %	25MM & OVER %
ASSETS									
Cash & Equivalents	12.9	14.0	13.9		19.9	12.3	14.9	12.4	6.9
Trade Receivables (net)	23.3	23.9	21.7		18.6	23.1	15.6	24.6	30.0
Inventory	35.6	34.2	35.4		33.2	29.6	38.2	40.5	36.8
All Other Current	2.1	2.3	2.7		3.6	2.3	3.6	1.6	2.7
Total Current	73.9	74.4	73.8		75.3	67.3	72.3	79.1	76.4
Fixed Assets (net)	15.7	15.6	14.6		15.6	15.8	13.8	11.9	16.8
Intangibles (net)	2.7	4.0	2.8		1.1	9.6	2.2	.3	2.7
All Other Non-Current	7.7	5.9	8.8		7.9	7.3	11.8	8.7	4.2
Total	100.0	100.0	100.0		100.0	100.0	100.0	100.0	100.0
LIABILITIES									
Notes Payable-Short Term	10.3	7.8	9.5		8.8	12.3	3.3	10.6	13.5
Cur. Mat.-L.T.D.	1.9	1.8	1.5		1.3	2.7	.7	1.4	1.3
Trade Payables	19.6	17.7	17.5		15.9	19.4	16.2	17.6	20.6
Income Taxes Payable	.1	.2	.1		.1	.3	.0	.0	.3
All Other Current	21.0	20.7	23.0		26.8	24.1	25.0	25.9	14.2
Total Current	53.0	48.2	51.6		52.9	58.8	45.2	55.5	49.9
Long-Term Debt	8.8	9.7	12.1		11.8	18.3	13.5	5.6	10.3
Deferred Taxes	.1	.0	.0		.0	.0	.0	.0	.1
All Other Non-Current	5.6	5.4	5.4		4.4	6.4	4.5	1.9	5.2
Net Worth	32.5	36.7	30.9		30.9	16.5	36.7	36.9	34.5
Total Liabilties & Net Worth	100.0	100.0	100.0		100.0	100.0	100.0	100.0	100.0
INCOME DATA									
Net Sales	100.0	100.0	100.0		100.0	100.0	100.0	100.0	100.0
Gross Profit	34.1	33.9	34.3		35.7	35.1	34.0	32.1	30.8
Operating Expenses	30.1	30.3	31.3		32.2	35.2	29.1	29.0	27.6
Operating Profit	4.0	3.6	3.0		3.5	-.1	4.9	3.1	3.1
All Other Expenses (net)	.1	-.3	.1		.3	.0	-.2	-.5	.2
Profit Before Taxes	3.9	3.9	3.0		3.2	-.1	5.1	3.5	2.9
RATIOS									
Current	2.5	2.6	2.8	4.5	1.8	3.4	2.5	2.0	
	1.6	1.6	1.6	2.2	1.2	1.8	1.5	1.5	
	1.1	1.1	1.1	1.0	.8	1.3	1.1	1.1	
Quick	1.2	1.5	1.4	2.0	1.0	1.1	1.3	1.4	
	.7	.8	.6	.6	.5	.6	.6	.7	
	.3	.4	.3	.3	.3	.3	.3	.3	
Sales/Receivables	7 52.9	7 55.9	6 63.2	2 182.0	8 43.8	0 999.8	8 43.6	21 17.7	
	18 20.4	19 18.8	18 20.6	11 34.2	16 23.2	9 42.1	21 17.5	29 12.6	
	32 11.5	33 10.9	33 10.9	26 14.3	34 10.7	33 11.0	34 10.6	41 8.9	
Cost of Sales/Inventory	22 16.9	21 17.7	25 14.7	16 23.4	14 26.2	28 13.0	39 9.4	36 10.2	
	42 8.7	42 8.6	47 7.7	37 9.9	51 7.1	55 6.6	47 7.7	47 7.7	
	81 4.5	79 4.6	101 3.6	89 4.1	114 3.2	76 4.8	99 3.7	104 3.5	
Cost of Sales/Payables	14 26.0	14 26.9	12 31.3	3 142.3	14 26.2	3 109.8	14 25.4	20 18.4	
	25 14.4	22 16.5	21 17.1	19 19.7	28 12.9	20 18.2	19 19.5	25 14.5	
	37 9.8	33 11.0	39 9.3	38 9.7	46 7.9	42 8.7	37 9.9	40 9.1	
Sales/Working Capital	7.9	7.4	6.2	5.9	10.0	5.4	8.2	7.0	
	17.1	15.4	13.9	13.5	25.8	12.8	10.9	13.6	
	100.9	108.7	74.7	NM	-42.0	107.6	69.4	32.2	
EBIT/Interest	33.4	40.0	16.1		19.5	5.3	18.1	37.2	17.8
	(157) 10.0	(155) 11.8	(118) 5.3		(25) 7.1	(18) 2.0	(17) 3.0	(25) 13.7	(26) 5.0
	4.0	3.3	1.8		2.3	-1.3	.9	5.5	2.8
Net Profit + Depr., Dep., Amort./Cur. Mat. L/T/D	14.5	13.1	3.3						
	(20) 8.4	(20) 7.9	(11) 1.6						
	2.4	3.2	1.0						
Fixed/Worth	.1	.1	.1		.1	.2	.0	.1	.1
	.4	.3	.3		.3	1.1	.2	.2	.6
	1.3	1.1	1.3		1.4	-.8	1.1	.5	1.3
Debt/Worth	.9	.7	.7		.4	1.6	.4	.7	.9
	1.8	2.0	1.9		1.9	3.4	1.6	1.5	2.4
	5.9	6.3	6.1		5.8	-4.9	8.5	2.2	3.4
% Profit Before Taxes/Tangible Net Worth	77.6	74.3	59.3		60.7	41.3	75.2	52.9	46.5
	(168) 32.5	(178) 34.0	(131) 26.9		(38) 34.8	(15) 13.6	(23) 34.8	(25) 24.0	(24) 26.0
	10.3	8.1	6.7		9.9	1.8	5.5	11.7	11.8
% Profit Before Taxes/Total Assets	21.4	24.6	21.2		21.0	12.1	30.7	21.3	17.7
	9.7	10.9	8.4		8.4	1.5	10.9	9.6	8.6
	3.7	3.0	1.5		1.1	-1.5	1.0	2.4	2.4
Sales/Net Fixed Assets	109.2	96.6	101.3		125.9	72.1	144.5	150.2	89.3
	46.9	52.9	50.3		59.5	53.6	61.3	44.1	31.2
	18.0	19.8	16.1		19.8	10.7	18.6	17.3	9.4
Sales/Total Assets	5.3	5.0	5.0		5.0	4.3	4.9	4.8	5.4
	3.8	3.8	3.3		3.5	3.0	3.8	3.6	3.3
	2.8	2.7	2.6		2.9	2.5	2.6	2.6	2.4
% Depr., Dep., Amort./Sales	.3	.3	.3		.3	.3	.2	.2	.4
	(136) .6	(135) .6	(103) .6		(22) .6	(17) .8	(16) .4	(21) .4	(23) .8
	1.1	1.2	1.4		1.5	2.1	1.5	1.1	1.1
% Officers', Directors' Owners' Comp/Sales	1.7	1.4	1.8		2.5	2.2	1.5	.5	.7
	(95) 3.6	(97) 3.3	(87) 3.2		(28) 4.5	(16) 3.5	(16) 3.3	(11) 1.1	(11) 1.0
	6.3	5.5	6.6		6.8	5.9	4.2	2.3	2.6
Net Sales ($)	5929702M	4118838M	2395135M	5111M	88417M	99897M	210127M	422428M	1569155M
Total Assets ($)	1022563M	985611M	823002M	3685M	27426M	39035M	67404M	124907M	560545M

M = $ thousand   MM = $ million
See Pages viii through xx for Explanation of Ratios and Data

Current Data Sorted by Assets   Comparative Historical Data

Type of Statement	0-500M	500M-2MM	2-10MM	10-50MM	50-100MM	100-250MM		4/1/14-3/31/15 ALL	4/1/15-3/31/16 ALL
Unqualified			1	4	1			6	12
Reviewed			2	2				11	8
Compiled	1	3	6	1				19	16
Tax Returns	15	24	6	1				67	79
Other	10	16	17	10	3	2		85	76
		19 (4/1-9/30/18)		106 (10/1/18-3/31/19)					
NUMBER OF STATEMENTS	26	43	32	18	4	2		188	191
	%	%	%	%	%	%		%	%
ASSETS									
Cash & Equivalents	29.5	19.3	11.9	12.7				17.3	16.4
Trade Receivables (net)	2.2	10.5	16.5	13.2				11.1	10.9
Inventory	38.5	42.5	49.0	42.4				41.3	40.9
All Other Current	3.0	2.7	3.8	4.5				3.3	4.3
Total Current	73.3	75.0	81.2	72.8				73.0	72.4
Fixed Assets (net)	14.9	15.7	12.8	12.6				16.1	15.6
Intangibles (net)	6.6	5.4	4.6	7.3				5.7	5.0
All Other Non-Current	5.2	3.8	1.3	7.3				5.3	7.1
Total	100.0	100.0	100.0	100.0				100.0	100.0
LIABILITIES									
Notes Payable-Short Term	11.5	7.2	8.3	10.0				12.0	9.2
Cur. Mat.-L.T.D.	2.6	2.3	.7	2.5				2.0	1.7
Trade Payables	8.8	14.7	14.3	24.6				16.9	17.4
Income Taxes Payable	.0	.0	.0	.2				.2	.0
All Other Current	13.5	10.8	18.7	14.4				17.6	18.6
Total Current	36.5	35.0	42.0	51.7				48.6	46.8
Long-Term Debt	13.2	12.2	7.9	8.0				14.5	13.3
Deferred Taxes	.0	.0	.0	.0				.1	.1
All Other Non-Current	4.3	3.7	4.6	5.6				8.8	8.3
Net Worth	46.0	49.0	45.4	34.7				28.1	31.5
Total Liabilities & Net Worth	100.0	100.0	100.0	100.0				100.0	100.0
INCOME DATA									
Net Sales	100.0	100.0	100.0	100.0				100.0	100.0
Gross Profit	49.7	46.5	40.9	42.8				44.7	46.5
Operating Expenses	44.9	40.7	38.2	38.6				39.3	41.4
Operating Profit	4.8	5.8	2.7	4.2				5.4	5.1
All Other Expenses (net)	.3	.2	1.0	.2				.4	.2
Profit Before Taxes	4.5	5.7	1.7	4.0				5.0	4.9
RATIOS									
Current	8.3	4.2	3.3	2.5				2.6	3.3
	2.1	2.4	2.3	1.5				1.8	1.9
	1.1	1.3	1.4	1.0				1.2	1.2
Quick	6.1	1.7	1.4	1.0				1.2	1.4
	.9	.9	.7	.3				.5	.6
	.3	.3	.3	.1				.2	.2
Sales/Receivables	0 UND	0 UND	5 70.9	0 999.8				0 UND	0 UND
	0 UND	2 240.9	22 16.6	7 48.9				4 88.9	5 69.7
	1 325.0	21 17.2	36 10.0	37 9.9				24 15.4	19 18.9
Cost of Sales/Inventory	13 28.1	41 8.8	81 4.5	18 20.4				43 8.5	36 10.0
	39 9.4	96 3.8	135 2.7	94 3.9				94 3.9	99 3.7
	91 4.0	174 2.1	182 2.0	140 2.6				166 2.2	166 2.2
Cost of Sales/Payables	0 UND	14 26.1	20 17.9	23 16.0				8 43.6	11 32.0
	0 UND	24 15.2	35 10.3	47 7.7				28 13.1	28 13.0
	20 17.9	40 9.2	42 8.6	65 5.6				54 6.7	53 6.9
Sales/Working Capital	7.2	4.2	4.2	3.4				5.0	4.5
	15.6	7.4	6.5	11.0				9.8	9.7
	92.9	32.3	11.2	NM				29.4	53.6
EBIT/Interest	30.5	31.4	24.2	17.0				37.9	34.9
	(16) 7.1	(31) 19.5	(24) 6.1	(13) 4.1				(139) 7.2	(132) 7.0
	1.5	3.1	1.0	-2.1				1.8	1.9
Net Profit + Depr., Dep., Amort./Cur. Mat. L/T/D									
Fixed/Worth	.0	.1	.1	.1				.1	.1
	.5	.3	.2	.3				.4	.4
	8.7	1.3	.7	2.6				2.9	3.8
Debt/Worth	.2	.3	.5	.6				.8	.6
	1.2	1.0	1.2	2.8				1.8	1.8
	26.7	4.4	5.5	9.8				10.7	24.4
% Profit Before Taxes/Tangible Net Worth	254.9	47.1	39.1	63.5				68.4	62.3
	(21) 29.6	(39) 27.3	(30) 13.4	(16) 17.8				(154) 27.7	(150) 27.9
	9.3	12.1	.2	3.3				8.5	4.8
% Profit Before Taxes/Total Assets	54.9	26.4	16.4	17.6				25.7	26.7
	11.2	12.9	5.5	6.1				9.8	9.2
	3.1	4.6	.2	.2				2.2	1.3
Sales/Net Fixed Assets	UND	126.4	119.8	93.6				84.4	103.3
	101.7	33.0	35.9	47.8				26.5	32.3
	20.6	15.0	15.4	13.9				14.5	14.1
Sales/Total Assets	7.7	3.9	3.0	3.6				3.9	4.3
	5.7	2.9	2.4	2.3				2.7	2.8
	4.4	2.1	1.7	1.8				1.8	1.9
% Depr., Dep., Amort./Sales	.1	.2	.3	.5				.3	.3
	(11) .7	(30) .7	(24) .6	(14) .7				(121) .7	(113) .9
	2.0	1.3	.9	1.5				1.5	1.7
% Officers', Directors' Owners' Comp/Sales	1.8	2.0	1.2					2.6	2.5
	(13) 4.0	(27) 3.5	(17) 2.5					(76) 5.1	(85) 4.2
	6.5	7.4	6.7					8.9	6.6
Net Sales ($)	46532M	138468M	345610M	956029M	543980M	620556M		3990142M	3642968M
Total Assets ($)	8098M	43525M	153821M	341062M	288855M	473015M		1517956M	1533085M

Comparative Historical Data | Current Data Sorted by Sales

4/1/16-3/31/17 ALL	4/1/17-3/31/18 ALL	4/1/18-3/31/19 ALL	Type of Statement	0-1MM	1-3MM	3-5MM	5-10MM	10-25MM	25MM & OVER
					19 (4/1-9/30/18)			106 (10/1/18-3/31/19)	
7	9	6	Unqualified					1	5
9	8	4	Reviewed					2	2
14	12	11	Compiled		4	2	1	3	1
52	55	46	Tax Returns	5	20	11	5	4	1
45	63	58	Other	5	15	4	10	13	11
127	147	125	**NUMBER OF STATEMENTS**	10	39	17	16	23	20
%	%	%	**ASSETS**	%	%	%	%	%	%
15.3	13.2	17.8	Cash & Equivalents	26.8	23.4	21.0	14.5	11.9	9.1
11.8	12.6	10.3	Trade Receivables (net)	2.9	6.0	9.8	10.4	21.7	9.8
42.2	41.4	43.3	Inventory	31.7	43.6	43.2	49.7	43.7	43.1
3.8	3.0	3.2	All Other Current	.1	3.2	1.1	7.1	2.5	4.5
73.1	70.3	74.7	Total Current	61.5	76.2	75.2	81.7	79.7	66.6
17.1	19.5	14.4	Fixed Assets (net)	21.5	16.2	10.9	13.5	10.5	15.7
4.5	4.1	6.8	Intangibles (net)	11.0	4.6	6.7	3.8	6.7	11.8
5.4	6.1	4.0	All Other Non-Current	5.9	2.9	7.3	1.0	3.1	6.0
100.0	100.0	100.0	Total	100.0	100.0	100.0	100.0	100.0	100.0
			LIABILITIES						
9.9	10.4	8.9	Notes Payable-Short Term	7.9	9.2	11.0	5.1	7.4	11.8
1.6	2.3	1.9	Cur. Mat.-L.T.D.	1.1	2.4	1.0	3.5	.9	1.9
14.9	15.2	15.0	Trade Payables	2.2	8.3	18.8	13.2	24.9	21.3
.1	.0	.0	Income Taxes Payable	.0	.0	.0	.0	.1	.1
21.1	14.0	14.0	All Other Current	13.7	12.6	8.3	19.4	15.7	15.4
47.6	41.9	39.8	Total Current	25.0	32.6	39.1	41.1	48.9	50.4
13.9	13.4	10.8	Long-Term Debt	20.2	10.1	14.5	12.2	6.0	8.4
.0	.2	.1	Deferred Taxes	.0	.0	.0	.0	.0	.6
5.8	10.5	4.6	All Other Non-Current	7.9	3.2	1.6	9.8	2.9	6.0
32.6	34.0	44.7	Net Worth	46.9	54.1	44.7	36.9	42.2	34.6
100.0	100.0	100.0	Total Liabilities & Net Worth	100.0	100.0	100.0	100.0	100.0	100.0
			INCOME DATA						
100.0	100.0	100.0	Net Sales	100.0	100.0	100.0	100.0	100.0	100.0
45.3	45.7	45.2	Gross Profit	52.8	50.9	39.0	43.6	38.5	44.5
41.7	41.4	40.9	Operating Expenses	47.7	44.6	34.3	39.7	36.4	41.8
3.6	4.4	4.3	Operating Profit	5.1	6.3	4.7	3.9	2.1	2.8
.6	.7	.4	All Other Expenses (net)	.9	-.1	.1	.9	1.1	.1
3.0	3.7	4.0	Profit Before Taxes	4.2	6.4	4.6	3.1	1.0	2.6
			RATIOS						
3.3	3.1	3.5	Current	12.5	18.4	2.8	3.5	2.5	2.3
2.0	1.7	2.0		5.1	2.5	1.8	2.2	1.7	1.3
1.1	1.1	1.2		.9	1.3	1.2	1.5	1.1	.9
1.5	1.3	1.5	Quick	7.8	4.8	1.7	1.3	1.0	.8
.5	(145) .5	.7		1.9	.9	1.0	.6	.7	.2
.2	.2	.2		.2	.3	.2	.2	.3	.1
0 999.8	0 UND	0 UND	Sales/Receivables	0 UND	0 UND	0 UND	0 UND	15 24.9	1 327.6
6 65.1	5 68.7	3 112.1		0 UND	1 363.1	1 536.4	8 48.4	22 16.7	1 95.8
24 14.9	25 14.4	22 16.6		11 33.8	10 35.4	25 14.7	28 13.0	36 10.0	14 26.2
31 11.8	41 8.9	39 9.4	Cost of Sales/Inventory	19 19.7	27 13.7	30 12.3	85 4.3	47 7.7	32 11.3
101 3.6	114 3.2	94 3.9		89 4.1	87 4.2	60 6.1	107 3.4	99 3.7	107 3.4
182 2.0	203 1.8	174 2.1		215 1.7	228 1.6	126 2.9	159 2.3	182 2.0	174 2.1
10 38.2	14 25.6	13 28.8	Cost of Sales/Payables	0 UND	0 UND	18 19.9	14 25.6	25 14.4	42 8.7
23 15.7	28 13.2	27 13.4		0 UND	17 21.1	28 12.9	23 15.7	38 9.7	58 6.3
42 8.7	58 6.3	46 8.0		17 22.1	31 11.7	40 9.2	37 9.8	54 6.8	68 5.4
4.9	5.1	4.8	Sales/Working Capital	2.6	4.1	5.5	4.8	5.0	5.4
9.5	11.0	8.3		6.9	8.0	8.1	6.3	7.7	20.2
35.4	45.4	40.2		NM	39.9	93.3	14.6	26.0	NM
30.1	19.3	24.3	EBIT/Interest		32.7	51.2	24.2	35.7	11.2
(94) 4.9	(117) 5.7	(89) 6.9		(26) 16.0	(13) 16.9	(13) 1.9	(14) 12.2	(17) 4.1	
1.1	1.1	1.4			4.3	4.9	.0	-2.4	.0
		4.5	Net Profit + Depr., Dep., Amort./Cur. Mat. L/T/D						
	(15) 3.8								
		1.3							
.1	.1	.1	Fixed/Worth	.0	.0	.1	.1	.1	.2
.4	.4	.3		1.3	.2	.3	.3	.2	.5
2.0	1.5	1.3		-104.3	1.1	1.9	6.6	.7	2.7
.5	.7	.5	Debt/Worth	.1	.2	.5	.6	.6	1.0
1.4	2.1	1.3		1.9	.7	1.1	3.6	1.3	3.6
11.8	6.4	6.5		-213.2	2.7	5.0	23.9	4.2	11.8
48.3	68.2	55.9	% Profit Before Taxes/Tangible Net Worth		58.7	55.9	35.9	47.1	69.5
(101) 18.0	(128) 26.7	(110) 24.3		(35) 24.4	(15) 36.3	(15) 12.2	(21) 20.8	(17) 16.1	
2.8	7.4	5.4			8.9	14.0	-13.6	-2.3	3.4
18.0	22.2	19.8	% Profit Before Taxes/Total Assets	54.9	25.3	27.6	18.3	15.0	10.7
8.5	9.4	7.9		4.8	12.9	13.8	3.8	7.7	6.6
.6	.9	1.5		-3.3	5.5	5.9	-.9	-.3	-3.7
50.0	67.2	135.5	Sales/Net Fixed Assets	UND	357.6	499.0	195.5	212.0	85.0
25.3	27.8	33.1		26.5	29.8	48.8	44.2	44.9	14.7
13.6	12.0	14.6		6.6	14.5	24.7	17.3	22.7	9.7
4.2	4.1	4.5	Sales/Total Assets	5.3	5.5	6.2	3.5	3.2	3.4
2.6	2.7	2.7		2.5	3.6	3.7	2.7	2.4	2.2
1.7	1.9	1.9		.7	2.1	2.4	1.8	1.9	1.7
.5	.6	.3	% Depr., Dep., Amort./Sales		.4	.2		.3	.6
(86) 1.1	(88) 1.1	(83) .7		(24) .7	(13) .7		(16) .7	(16) 1.3	
1.9	2.1	1.4			1.3			1.3	1.8
1.7	2.1	1.6	% Officers', Directors' Owners' Comp/Sales		2.6	1.3	1.7		
(53) 3.7	(02) 4.3	(60) 3.3		(23) 5.0	(11) 2.4	(13) 2.5			
7.2	7.0	6.6		7.6	5.2	3.5			
2571295M	2552283M	2651175M	Net Sales ($)	6255M	76766M	65520M	120795M	335670M	2046169M
1000676M	1319489M	1308376M	Total Assets ($)	5429M	28279M	18677M	51459M	146050M	1058482M

M = $ thousand   MM = $ million
See Pages viii through xx for Explanation of Ratios and Data

Current Data Sorted by Assets　　　　　　　　　　Comparative Historical Data

							Type of Statement			
				4	1	1	Unqualified		2	4
	1	1	2	3		Reviewed		9	6
5	8	8	2			Compiled		10	9
8	10	4	1			Tax Returns		31	30
5	14	18	7	1		Other		36	34
	24 (4/1-9/30/18)		80 (10/1/18-3/31/19)					4/1/14-3/31/15	4/1/15-3/31/16
0-500M	500M-2MM	2-10MM	10-50MM	50-100MM	100-250MM			ALL	ALL
18	33	31	16	5	1	NUMBER OF STATEMENTS		88	83
%	%	%	%	%	%	ASSETS		%	%
16.8	15.0	16.6	19.1			Cash & Equivalents		13.9	13.3
4.9	12.0	13.7	8.5			Trade Receivables (net)		12.2	12.9
41.3	48.9	49.3	41.4			Inventory		49.8	48.2
5.6	2.8	3.2	2.5			All Other Current		2.0	1.4
68.6	78.7	82.9	71.5			Total Current		78.0	75.8
21.0	13.2	10.0	24.9			Fixed Assets (net)		13.5	13.6
5.5	4.4	1.4	.9			Intangibles (net)		4.3	4.5
5.0	3.7	5.6	2.7			All Other Non-Current		4.3	6.1
100.0	100.0	100.0	100.0			Total		100.0	100.0
						LIABILITIES			
10.1	11.3	11.5	6.3			Notes Payable-Short Term		11.6	10.4
2.1	1.2	.7	.6			Cur. Mat.-L.T.D.		2.8	2.1
12.2	16.7	20.7	12.0			Trade Payables		21.8	20.0
.1	.1	.3	.1			Income Taxes Payable		.1	.1
14.1	14.7	21.7	22.7			All Other Current		14.8	15.7
38.7	44.0	54.8	41.8			Total Current		51.2	48.3
36.7	14.1	6.1	6.7			Long-Term Debt		11.6	10.4
.0	.0	.4	.2			Deferred Taxes		.2	.2
17.8	7.8	3.2	3.1			All Other Non-Current		9.3	7.0
6.7	34.2	35.5	48.3			Net Worth		27.7	34.2
100.0	100.0	100.0	100.0			Total Liabilities & Net Worth		100.0	100.0
						INCOME DATA			
100.0	100.0	100.0	100.0			Net Sales		100.0	100.0
38.5	31.2	27.2	32.0			Gross Profit		33.3	34.5
37.0	27.6	24.3	29.3			Operating Expenses		30.0	31.6
1.6	3.6	2.9	2.7			Operating Profit		3.3	2.9
1.9	.3	.0	.2			All Other Expenses (net)		.1	.1
-.4	3.2	2.9	2.5			Profit Before Taxes		3.1	2.9
						RATIOS			
9.0	2.8	2.2	2.4					2.6	2.9
1.6	1.7	1.4	1.7			Current		1.5	1.7
1.2	1.4	1.2	1.3					1.2	1.1
1.6	1.3	1.0	.8					1.0	1.0
.4	.6	.4	.6			Quick		.5	.5
.2	.2	.3	.4					.2	.2

0	UND	1	607.3	5	68.5	4	98.8					Sales/Receivables	3	109.1	4	88.2
0	UND	7	52.6	13	27.7	7	49.4						8	43.1	11	33.6
8	44.7	17	21.8	22	16.7	13	28.3						21	17.7	24	15.5
19	19.1	49	7.5	62	5.9	51	7.2					Cost of Sales/Inventory	53	6.9	51	7.2
59	6.2	79	4.6	87	4.2	74	4.9						78	4.7	79	4.6
152	2.4	107	3.4	118	3.1	104	3.5						114	3.2	135	2.7
0	UND	8	47.1	12	30.0	10	37.0					Cost of Sales/Payables	11	31.9	14	25.6
16	22.7	20	18.7	30	12.1	20	18.4						27	13.3	30	12.2
56	6.5	48	7.6	50	7.3	33	11.2						51	7.2	58	6.3

8.3	5.9	4.8	5.8			Sales/Working Capital		6.2	5.1
12.7	8.9	9.9	12.5					11.8	12.3
36.4	20.8	29.3	22.6					33.3	34.5

			8.2		71.9			EBIT/Interest		18.7	30.0
	(27)		4.7	(28)	8.9				(75)	6.7	(70)	7.2
			2.2		3.0					2.5	1.7

						Net Profit + Depr., Dep., Amort./Cur. Mat. L/T/D			11.3
								(12)	3.6
									1.0

.1	.2	.1	.1			Fixed/Worth		.1	.1
.6	.3	.2	.6					.4	.2
-11.9	NM	.5	.9					1.6	.9
.9	.7	.7	.5			Debt/Worth		1.1	.8
8.5	2.3	2.4	1.2					2.2	1.8
-3.2	NM	5.3	2.4					12.5	8.0

	104.7		54.4		81.2		26.1			% Profit Before Taxes/Tangible Net Worth		52.7		39.8
(11)	12.3	(25)	21.9		19.2		21.9				(72)	22.2	(70)	16.9
	-19.4		7.0		7.9		12.2					9.3		12.2

13.1	20.7	10.7	14.3			% Profit Before Taxes/Total Assets		15.1	12.2
2.5	7.7	5.9	7.2					5.6	5.9
-21.6	2.3	3.0	4.9					1.8	1.6
183.7	100.1	120.3	59.0			Sales/Net Fixed Assets		93.8	127.9
31.9	36.4	49.8	13.5					34.6	47.5
8.1	18.8	17.4	6.7					18.5	16.7
6.6	4.0	3.7	3.9			Sales/Total Assets		4.3	4.0
3.0	3.2	3.0	3.0					3.2	3.1
2.0	2.4	2.0	2.3					2.5	2.2

	.5		.4		.4		.5			% Depr., Dep., Amort./Sales		.3		.3
(11)	1.7	(23)	.7	(20)	.6	(14)	1.0				(62)	.6	(51)	.6
	3.5		1.2		.9		1.3					1.1		1.1

			2.0		1.0			% Officers', Directors' Owners' Comp/Sales			1.1		1.4
		(23)	2.9	(10)	1.4				(48)	2.5	(39)	2.8
			4.5		2.5					3.7		4.4

22845M	128598M	539558M	1388699M	775829M	183278M	Net Sales ($)		2679221M	1881773M
5627M	37239M	179673M	442723M	342493M	136360M	Total Assets ($)		1191692M	804827M

M = $ thousand　　　MM = $ million
See Pages viii through xx for Explanation of Ratios and Data

Comparative Historical Data | Current Data Sorted by Sales

			Type of Statement						
1	6	6	Unqualified				6		
7	3	7	Reviewed			1	5		
15	24	23	Compiled	2	8	3	2	6	2
29	30	23	Tax Returns	4	9	4	1	3	2
28	60	45	Other	2	10	3	7	11	12
4/1/16-	4/1/17-	4/1/18-			24 (4/1-9/30/18)			80 (10/1/18-3/31/19)	
3/31/17	3/31/18	3/31/19							
ALL	ALL	ALL		0-1MM	1-3MM	3-5MM	5-10MM	10-25MM	25MM & OVER
80	123	104	**NUMBER OF STATEMENTS**	8	27	10	11	21	27
%	%	%	**ASSETS**	%	%	%	%	%	%
13.8	14.8	16.3	Cash & Equivalents		15.1	31.5	13.9	15.6	16.6
11.0	10.7	10.9	Trade Receivables (net)		10.0	8.0	11.5	13.6	12.0
48.9	46.2	46.1	Inventory		47.9	42.1	55.8	47.5	43.6
1.2	3.4	3.3	All Other Current		1.8	6.0	3.9	2.2	2.2
74.9	75.1	76.6	Total Current		74.9	87.5	85.0	78.9	74.5
15.3	15.8	15.6	Fixed Assets (net)		17.4	9.0	7.5	11.8	19.8
4.5	2.2	3.6	Intangibles (net)		5.4	.0	4.0	1.1	3.6
5.3	6.9	4.2	All Other Non-Current		2.3	3.6	3.6	8.3	2.1
100.0	100.0	100.0	Total		100.0	100.0	100.0	100.0	100.0
			LIABILITIES						
12.9	12.4	9.8	Notes Payable-Short Term		10.9	7.3	5.5	14.0	5.9
1.6	1.5	1.2	Cur. Mat.-L.T.D.		.7	.2	2.1	.7	1.4
17.5	21.3	16.4	Trade Payables		14.1	14.0	25.6	18.7	14.9
.1	.1	.2	Income Taxes Payable		.1	.1	.2	.2	.3
18.0	18.4	17.8	All Other Current		15.7	15.5	19.9	16.7	23.2
50.1	53.6	45.4	Total Current		41.5	37.1	53.3	50.4	45.7
9.6	13.4	14.2	Long-Term Debt		21.5	5.7	9.7	7.0	6.3
.3	.1	.1	Deferred Taxes		.0	.0	.0	.5	.1
4.7	7.8	7.7	All Other Non-Current		9.0	5.8	4.0	3.3	5.2
35.3	25.0	32.5	Net Worth		28.0	51.3	33.0	38.7	42.6
100.0	100.0	100.0	Total Liabilties & Net Worth		100.0	100.0	100.0	100.0	100.0
			INCOME DATA						
100.0	100.0	100.0	Net Sales		100.0	100.0	100.0	100.0	100.0
33.0	31.9	31.2	Gross Profit		33.3	31.7	26.9	27.0	30.1
30.4	28.9	28.2	Operating Expenses		30.3	26.1	23.6	24.2	26.5
2.6	3.0	3.0	Operating Profit		3.0	5.6	3.3	2.9	3.6
.0	.2	.5	All Other Expenses (net)		.3	.4	.2	.1	.2
2.7	2.8	2.6	Profit Before Taxes		2.7	5.2	3.2	2.8	3.5
			RATIOS						
2.6	2.2	2.5			5.8	4.9	2.3	2.2	2.4
1.5	1.4	1.6	Current		1.7	2.8	1.5	1.7	1.6
1.1	1.1	1.3			1.2	1.5	1.4	1.2	1.3
.9	.9	1.0			3.3	3.4	.9	1.0	1.1
(79) .4	.5	.5	Quick		.5	1.2	.4	.6	.6
.3	.2	.3			.3	.4	.1	.3	.4
4 91.0	3 112.7	2 178.6		0 UND	0 UND	4 87.7	6 59.7	5 71.6	
11 33.4	9 41.2	9 41.7	Sales/Receivables	8 48.4	1 394.7	13 28.3	13 27.6	12 31.3	
23 16.2	16 23.5	19 18.9		17 21.9	4 87.4	24 15.5	23 15.6	22 16.4	
62 5.9	40 9.1	51 7.2		56 6.5	32 11.3	42 8.7	46 8.0	60 6.1	
78 4.7	74 4.9	78 4.7	Cost of Sales/Inventory	79 4.6	76 4.8	87 4.2	85 4.3	76 4.8	
130 2.8	114 3.2	114 3.2		140 2.6	96 3.8	203 1.8	111 3.3	101 3.6	
9 40.3	12 31.3	9 40.0		0 UND	0 UND	15 24.9	12 30.1	13 28.5	
23 15.6	25 14.6	23 15.9	Cost of Sales/Payables	15 23.8	14 26.8	36 10.2	25 14.4	22 16.5	
47 7.8	47 7.7	44 8.3		49 7.4	29 12.8	74 4.9	41 8.8	40 9.2	
6.2	6.4	5.3			6.4	4.5	5.2	4.9	5.0
13.4	15.1	10.6	Sales/Working Capital		10.8	8.3	9.1	13.6	13.8
45.6	47.6	23.0			32.7	16.6	17.6	34.2	28.0
15.3	23.7	19.9			7.9			62.9	30.4
(61) 5.6	(90) 7.0	(76) 6.3	EBIT/Interest	(21) 2.7			(19) 8.2	(16) 8.1	
1.7	2.0	2.3			1.7			2.6	4.5
11.2		5.5							
(12) 3.8		(12) 3.3	Net Profit + Depr., Dep., Amort./Cur. Mat. L/T/D						
1.2		1.0							
.1	.1	.1			.2	.0	.1	.1	.2
.3	.3	.3	Fixed/Worth		.5	.2	.2	.2	.6
1.2	1.4	1.2			-1.8	.3	.6	.4	1.0
.8	.7	.7			.9	.4	.7	.6	.7
2.1	2.1	2.3	Debt/Worth		3.9	1.2	2.3	2.4	1.5
9.2	10.0	6.6			-12.6	2.5	9.0	5.0	3.1
33.7	49.8	53.2			53.7	60.1	79.4	68.7	53.2
(69) 17.4	(102) 20.4	(88) 22.0	% Profit Before Taxes/Tangible Net Worth	(19) 12.3	16.9	(10) 14.2	25.6	(26) 24.5	
6.5	7.5	8.4			6.6	7.7	2.9	10.2	17.1
13.1	15.0	14.4			18.3	21.6	10.2	10.8	15.9
7.1	6.5	6.6	% Profit Before Taxes/Total Assets		7.7	7.6	5.6	7.8	11.5
1.6	.9	2.3			1.8	2.4	2.2	3.5	5.9
83.6	102.0	93.6			75.9	162.0	153.2	76.3	73.0
36.8	38.3	36.5	Sales/Net Fixed Assets		28.1	95.0	83.6	36.7	24.3
16.7	13.9	13.4			13.2	24.8	35.3	15.8	7.9
4.1	4.5	4.0			3.8	5.9	4.0	4.1	4.0
3.2	3.3	3.0	Sales/Total Assets		3.2	3.8	3.0	3.0	3.0
2.0	2.2	2.2			2.4	2.4	2.0	2.1	2.3
.4	.3	.5			.6			.4	.5
(65) .6	(89) .6	(73) .8	% Depr., Dep., Amort./Sales	(18) .9			(15) .6	(22) .8	
1.0	1.0	1.2			2.1			.9	1.0
1.7	1.5	1.5			2.0			.7	
(40) 3.1	(61) 2.9	(44) 2.5	% Officers', Directors' Owners' Comp/Sales	(16) 2.5		(10) 1.4			
5.1	5.2	4.5			5.7			3.9	
2280632M	2939896M	3038807M	Net Sales ($)	4284M	55201M	37688M	77470M	321684M	2542480M
960178M	1103878M	1144115M	Total Assets ($)	2120M	19091M	11773M	33327M	116384M	961420M

© RMA 2019

M = $ thousand   MM = $ million
See Pages viii through xx for Explanation of Ratios and Data

Current Data Sorted by Assets   Comparative Historical Data

Type of Statement	0-500M	500M-2MM	2-10MM	10-50MM	50-100MM	100-250MM		4/1/14-3/31/15 ALL	4/1/15-3/31/16 ALL
Unqualified	1	2	7	4	3	2		21	14
Reviewed	3	4	15	11	1			25	24
Compiled	27	16	15	5				24	19
Tax Returns	10	31	38	11	4	6		83	78
Other								90	114
	43 (4/1-9/30/18)			173 (10/1/18-3/31/19)					
NUMBER OF STATEMENTS	41	53	75	31	8	8		243	249
	%	%	%	%	%	%		%	%
ASSETS									
Cash & Equivalents	18.6	13.9	14.4	11.8				16.5	15.4
Trade Receivables (net)	11.5	14.7	20.8	27.6				23.2	23.1
Inventory	37.7	39.4	35.2	30.6				32.1	32.5
All Other Current	1.4	1.7	5.6	4.7				2.5	3.6
Total Current	69.2	69.7	76.0	74.7				74.3	74.6
Fixed Assets (net)	20.5	14.5	14.4	11.4				12.8	12.8
Intangibles (net)	4.6	6.1	4.8	6.8				6.4	6.6
All Other Non-Current	5.6	9.7	4.8	7.1				6.6	6.0
Total	100.0	100.0	100.0	100.0				100.0	100.0
LIABILITIES									
Notes Payable-Short Term	17.5	7.8	10.0	11.7				10.2	11.4
Cur. Mat.-L.T.D.	4.2	2.6	1.1	1.4				2.0	1.4
Trade Payables	15.1	22.7	21.4	25.1				26.6	24.3
Income Taxes Payable	.8	.1	.0	.1				.1	.3
All Other Current	18.7	18.2	15.4	12.7				10.8	12.0
Total Current	56.3	51.4	48.0	50.9				49.7	49.2
Long-Term Debt	22.7	10.7	7.8	6.6				13.3	14.1
Deferred Taxes	.0	.2	.1	.0				.1	.2
All Other Non-Current	10.1	3.1	4.8	4.7				7.4	5.0
Net Worth	10.8	34.6	39.4	37.7				29.6	31.5
Total Liabilties & Net Worth	100.0	100.0	100.0	100.0				100.0	100.0
INCOME DATA									
Net Sales	100.0	100.0	100.0	100.0				100.0	100.0
Gross Profit	43.8	39.0	36.3	33.9				37.6	37.0
Operating Expenses	39.0	35.1	31.4	30.8				32.9	32.5
Operating Profit	4.7	3.9	4.9	3.2				4.6	4.5
All Other Expenses (net)	2.9	-.1	-.2	.1				.4	.4
Profit Before Taxes	1.9	4.0	5.1	3.1				4.2	4.1
RATIOS									
Current	2.5	3.7	2.5	2.8				2.5	2.6
	1.5	1.5	1.6	1.3				1.5	1.6
	.7	.8	1.2	1.0				1.1	1.1
Quick	1.1	1.2	1.2	1.5				1.3	1.4
	.5	.5	.6	.8				.8	.8
	.2	.2	.4	.3				.4	.3
Sales/Receivables	0 UND	1 254.1	5 79.7	17 21.0				4 102.2	4 103.5
	2 159.0	7 54.2	19 18.8	36 10.1				20 18.7	15 24.7
	16 23.0	23 16.1	34 10.7	45 8.1				40 9.1	40 9.1
Cost of Sales/Inventory	8 46.7	18 20.2	20 17.9	19 19.2				13 28.9	15 25.1
	27 13.7	64 5.7	56 6.5	42 8.7				40 9.1	38 9.5
	96 3.8	107 3.4	96 3.8	118 3.1				85 4.3	85 4.3
Cost of Sales/Payables	0 UND	10 36.1	11 33.7	17 21.3				13 28.8	13 29.1
	12 31.4	29 12.5	29 12.8	29 12.7				33 11.1	28 13.0
	37 9.9	57 6.4	56 6.5	65 5.6				62 5.9	51 7.1
Sales/Working Capital	10.4	6.8	6.4	5.8				8.0	6.9
	41.0	16.8	15.5	15.5				17.7	17.7
	-35.4	-34.8	44.4	-164.9				68.6	137.1
EBIT/Interest	16.3	31.7	20.7	29.1				31.9	41.1
	(23) 3.4	(36) 6.3	(57) 6.5	(24) 6.6				(193) 8.7	(186) 8.3
	-.1	1.5	3.1	3.0				1.8	2.2
Net Profit + Depr., Dep., Amort./Cur. Mat. L/T/D								7.1	18.8
								(22) 4.0	(18) 4.6
								1.7	2.1
Fixed/Worth	.1	.1	.1	.1				.1	.1
	.7	.5	.3	.4				.3	.3
	-3.6	NM	1.3	1.2				5.1	1.4
Debt/Worth	1.1	.5	.7	.4				.8	.7
	2.4	1.7	1.5	3.3				2.2	2.6
	-10.2	NM	10.0	7.9				89.5	15.3
% Profit Before Taxes/Tangible Net Worth	130.1	91.8	67.9	74.4				76.5	85.9
	(28) 52.8	(40) 25.6	(65) 35.8	(26) 22.2				(185) 29.6	(197) 30.6
	15.4	6.3	9.2	8.0				9.8	9.4
% Profit Before Taxes/Total Assets	34.5	20.6	21.5	16.3				22.6	22.1
	10.3	9.9	11.4	5.7				9.2	11.1
	-1.6	2.6	3.6	1.9				2.0	2.5
Sales/Net Fixed Assets	228.7	266.2	177.5	73.1				239.5	262.4
	48.0	51.8	62.7	23.6				55.2	57.0
	15.9	16.0	16.0	14.3				20.7	21.6
Sales/Total Assets	11.0	6.6	4.9	3.7				5.5	5.5
	5.9	3.9	3.3	2.7				3.7	3.9
	3.9	2.8	1.9	1.9				2.5	2.4
% Depr., Dep., Amort./Sales	.3	.2	.2	.3				.2	.2
	(27) .7	(33) .7	(52) .4	(26) .7				(159) .7	(150) .5
	1.4	2.8	1.0	1.6				1.6	1.3
% Officers', Directors' Owners' Comp/Sales	.9	1.7	.9					1.3	1.3
	(21) 3.2	(22) 3.2	(29) 1.7					(131) 3.1	(112) 3.1
	5.1	5.6	2.6					5.4	6.7
Net Sales ($)	57152M	272888M	1361318M	1713333M	1464819M	2577507M		10186076M	14331317M
Total Assets ($)	9253M	56094M	337347M	591230M	586353M	1202888M		3325612M	4130834M

M = $ thousand   MM = $ million
See Pages viii through xx for Explanation of Ratios and Data

Comparative Historical Data | Current Data Sorted by Sales

Type of Statement									
	4/1/16-3/31/17	4/1/17-3/31/18	4/1/18-3/31/19	43 (4/1-9/30/18)			173 (10/1/18-3/31/19)		
	ALL	ALL	ALL	0-1MM	1-3MM	3-5MM	5-10MM	10-25MM	25MM & OVER
Unqualified	15	12	9						9
Reviewed	16	38	22	1	2	3	1	4	11
Compiled	22	32	27	2	3	3	3	10	6
Tax Returns	64	61	58	8	26	5	10	6	3
Other	81	113	100	7	10	13	24	6	26
NUMBER OF STATEMENTS	198	256	216	18	41	24	38	40	55
ASSETS	%	%	%	%	%	%	%	%	%
Cash & Equivalents	17.3	14.8	14.8	14.7	14.7	11.0	16.6	17.2	13.6
Trade Receivables (net)	21.6	19.0	18.7	13.4	9.7	13.5	19.0	21.5	27.4
Inventory	30.3	35.9	35.2	32.1	38.8	45.9	32.0	36.6	30.1
All Other Current	2.7	3.7	3.4	.8	3.8	3.4	3.1	4.5	3.3
Total Current	72.0	73.5	72.2	61.0	67.0	73.9	70.7	79.7	74.5
Fixed Assets (net)	14.4	14.1	14.8	25.4	15.7	18.2	16.5	9.9	11.5
Intangibles (net)	7.0	6.6	6.5	2.6	9.6	2.8	5.3	5.5	8.7
All Other Non-Current	6.6	5.8	6.5	11.0	7.7	5.2	7.5	4.9	5.2
Total	100.0	100.0	100.0	100.0	100.0	100.0	100.0	100.0	100.0
LIABILITIES									
Notes Payable-Short Term	7.8	9.6	10.7	22.8	11.1	12.4	6.3	11.0	8.6
Cur. Mat.-L.T.D.	2.6	2.3	2.2	.5	4.3	3.0	1.6	1.9	1.4
Trade Payables	22.3	21.8	21.4	16.6	15.0	18.7	18.3	27.1	27.0
Income Taxes Payable	.2	.2	.2	1.0	.4	.1	.1	.0	.0
All Other Current	13.7	15.5	15.9	4.9	25.1	15.7	12.9	17.2	14.0
Total Current	46.7	49.4	50.4	45.9	55.8	49.8	39.2	57.2	51.1
Long-Term Debt	11.5	9.9	11.6	32.3	11.8	16.2	8.2	7.8	8.0
Deferred Taxes	.2	.2	.1	.0	.0	.2	.3	.0	.1
All Other Non-Current	6.7	7.6	5.2	.4	12.2	2.9	4.7	3.0	4.7
Net Worth	34.9	32.9	32.6	21.4	20.2	30.9	47.7	32.0	36.2
Total Liabilities & Net Worth	100.0	100.0	100.0	100.0	100.0	100.0	100.0	100.0	100.0
INCOME DATA									
Net Sales	100.0	100.0	100.0	100.0	100.0	100.0	100.0	100.0	100.0
Gross Profit	39.9	36.6	38.5	58.3	42.8	41.1	36.1	29.2	36.3
Operating Expenses	35.0	32.6	34.3	46.7	39.7	38.4	31.4	26.9	32.0
Operating Profit	4.9	4.0	4.2	11.6	3.1	2.7	4.8	2.3	4.3
All Other Expenses (net)	.3	.4	.5	6.3	.1	-.7	.0	-.1	.3
Profit Before Taxes	4.6	3.6	3.7	5.3	3.0	3.4	4.8	2.4	4.0
RATIOS									
Current	3.0	2.5	2.6	5.3	2.6	2.3	3.0	2.5	2.3
	1.6	1.5	1.5	1.5	1.6	1.6	1.8	1.6	1.4
	1.1	1.1	1.0	.8	.7	1.0	1.3	1.0	1.0
Quick	1.5	1.1	1.3	2.7	.8	1.0	1.8	1.4	1.2
	.8	.7	.6	.6	.4	.4	.8	.7	.8
	.3	.4	.3	.2	.2	.2	.4	.4	.5
Sales/Receivables	2 167.8	3 112.4	3 109.1	0 UND	0 UND	2 150.5	3 108.1	5 76.6	10 34.8
	18 20.8	14 25.8	13 27.5	5 78.4	2 193.8	9 41.0	14 26.3	19 19.5	29 12.4
	41 8.8	36 10.0	35 10.3	32 11.5	20 18.2	33 10.9	42 8.7	33 11.1	45 8.2
Cost of Sales/Inventory	10 37.1	15 24.1	15 23.7	31 11.7	12 30.9	54 6.7	9 39.7	17 22.1	17 21.7
	38 9.5	53 6.9	56 6.5	83 4.4	33 11.2	101 3.6	57 6.4	52 7.0	39 9.3
	81 4.5	107 3.4	104 3.5	118 3.1	118 3.1	126 2.9	85 4.3	81 4.5	114 3.2
Cost of Sales/Payables	13 28.5	13 27.8	10 36.0	4 83.5	0 UND	13 28.1	11 34.4	11 33.7	15 23.9
	29 12.6	32 11.3	27 13.4	20 18.3	10 35.5	42 8.6	25 14.7	28 13.0	33 11.0
	51 7.1	58 6.3	57 6.4	63 5.8	46 8.0	56 6.5	57 6.4	55 6.6	69 5.3
Sales/Working Capital	7.0	6.9	6.7	5.5	10.2	6.5	4.8	7.7	8.9
	16.4	14.3	16.7	16.1	42.6	8.6	9.2	18.7	19.7
	80.4	130.5	-440.3	-19.8	-22.3	NM	80.0	NM	183.1
EBIT/Interest	35.9	23.5	19.5	4.0	18.8	9.9	10.6	42.9	26.4
	(151) 7.7	(191) 5.7	(153) 5.7	(11) .3	(23) 5.6	(20) 4.7	(24) 5.7	(32) 7.6	(43) 6.4
	2.5	1.4	2.0	-1.3	1.6	1.4	1.0	2.2	3.2
Net Profit + Depr., Dep., Amort./Cur. Mat. L/T/D	8.9	5.1	11.8						
	(21) 3.7	(30) 2.4	(18) 4.1						
	1.7	1.0	2.2						
Fixed/Worth	.1	.1	.1	.1	.1	.0	.0	.1	.1
	.3	.3	.4	1.3	.7	.5	.2	.3	.5
	2.0	2.7	2.7	-60.5	-1.2	11.8	1.4	NM	1.4
Debt/Worth	.7	.8	.7	.7	.8	.9	.4	.6	.9
	1.9	2.5	2.0	3.6	1.9	1.6	1.1	1.9	3.1
	11.1	19.2	20.9	-121.8	-8.0	15.5	3.6	NM	10.2
% Profit Before Taxes/Tangible Net Worth	66.8	66.9	78.1	96.2	123.6	85.1	50.5	70.8	82.3
	(161) 34.5	(201) 29.2	(170) 31.6	(13) 48.5	(27) 39.0	(20) 15.7	(34) 24.5	(30) 36.1	(46) 36.9
	9.5	7.6	8.5	6.9	17.5	1.8	5.5	5.7	12.3
% Profit Before Taxes/Total Assets	21.8	22.4	19.6	23.8	25.3	12.3	24.8	18.8	19.6
	8.8	8.4	9.6	4.3	10.9	6.3	12.2	8.1	10.1
	2.1	.9	2.2	-7.0	2.4	-2.0	1.9	2.5	4.7
Sales/Net Fixed Assets	162.9	130.1	145.5	54.0	144.6	145.9	309.7	92.2	182.1
	42.3	44.4	48.0	16.3	51.8	28.9	70.0	60.7	42.8
	16.4	17.5	14.9	6.8	19.8	10.8	14.6	28.5	14.8
Sales/Total Assets	4.9	4.9	5.2	4.6	9.9	4.3	5.2	5.5	4.9
	3.5	3.3	3.5	3.0	4.4	2.9	3.0	4.1	3.2
	2.4	2.1	2.2	1.6	3.0	1.7	1.9	3.2	2.1
% Depr., Dep., Amort./Sales	.2	.2	.2	.8	.4	.2	.2	.2	.2
	(143) .6	(172) .6	(147) .7	(12) 1.8	(26) .7	(14) .7	(29) .4	(25) .6	(41) .7
	1.5	1.3	1.4	2.5	1.3	2.6	2.1	1.0	1.3
% Officers', Directors' Owners' Comp/Sales	1.2	1.2	1.0		.9	3.0	1.5	.9	.5
	(95) 2.5	(94) 2.5	(81) 2.0		(20) 3.4	(11) 3.6	(13) 2.1	(13) 1.5	(17) 1.1
	5.8	4.5	4.1		5.4	4.7	2.6	1.0	2.3
Net Sales ($)	7513692M	7926067M	7447017M	10699M	73966M	93246M	276393M	657164M	6335549M
Total Assets ($)	2727153M	2958786M	2783165M	6833M	23147M	44363M	114011M	231669M	2363142M

© RMA 2019

M = $ thousand   MM = $ million
See Pages viii through xx for Explanation of Ratios and Data

Current Data Sorted by Assets   Comparative Historical Data

Type of Statement

	0-500M	500M-2MM	2-10MM	10-50MM	50-100MM	100-250MM	Type of Statement	4/1/14-3/31/15 ALL	4/1/15-3/31/16 ALL
			2	5	2	6	Unqualified	25	18
		2	12	14		1	Reviewed	52	39
		3	11	2			Compiled	37	32
	5	11	10	1	4	1	Tax Returns	38	33
	3	3	16	18			Other	52	68
	8	19	51	40	6	8	**NUMBER OF STATEMENTS**	204	190

Current periods: 21 (4/1-9/30/18) · 111 (10/1/18-3/31/19)

Common Size (%)

0-500M	500M-2MM	2-10MM	10-50MM	50-100MM	100-250MM		4/1/14-3/31/15 ALL	4/1/15-3/31/16 ALL
%	%	%	%	%	%	**ASSETS**	%	%
	5.7	8.7	7.2			Cash & Equivalents	8.2	8.3
	13.8	22.9	21.7			Trade Receivables (net)	25.2	22.2
	47.6	41.2	35.5			Inventory	36.2	38.2
	1.1	2.6	1.7			All Other Current	1.9	2.3
	68.1	75.3	66.1			Total Current	71.6	71.1
	18.4	17.2	26.1			Fixed Assets (net)	19.4	18.8
	.5	1.5	3.3			Intangibles (net)	2.4	3.7
	13.0	6.0	4.6			All Other Non-Current	6.6	6.5
	100.0	100.0	100.0			Total	100.0	100.0
						LIABILITIES		
	11.1	8.0	14.1			Notes Payable-Short Term	10.5	10.4
	1.1	2.3	2.4			Cur. Mat.-L.T.D.	2.1	1.9
	14.1	14.8	11.1			Trade Payables	16.4	16.4
	.0	.1	.0			Income Taxes Payable	.1	.1
	10.2	11.6	7.8			All Other Current	7.0	12.4
	36.4	36.9	35.3			Total Current	36.0	41.0
	9.7	8.7	11.0			Long-Term Debt	12.7	12.5
	.0	.1	.3			Deferred Taxes	.3	.3
	13.6	2.5	1.7			All Other Non-Current	8.1	7.1
	40.3	51.8	51.7			Net Worth	42.9	39.2
	100.0	100.0	100.0			Total Liabilities & Net Worth	100.0	100.0
						INCOME DATA		
	100.0	100.0	100.0			Net Sales	100.0	100.0
	30.9	27.5	29.8			Gross Profit	28.2	29.5
	27.7	25.1	25.8			Operating Expenses	25.6	26.7
	3.2	2.4	4.0			Operating Profit	2.5	2.8
	-.2	-.2	-.1			All Other Expenses (net)	-.3	-.2
	3.4	2.6	4.1			Profit Before Taxes	2.8	3.0

RATIOS

0-500M	500M-2MM	2-10MM	10-50MM	50-100MM	100-250MM		4/1/14-3/31/15 ALL	4/1/15-3/31/16 ALL
	3.7	3.8	2.6			Current	3.4	3.1
	2.1	2.4	1.8				2.0	2.0
	1.1	1.4	1.4				1.5	1.4
	1.6	1.4	1.2			Quick	1.7	1.5
	.7	.8	.8				.9 (189)	.8
	.0	.5	.5				.5	.5
0 UND	16 22.8	13 28.0				Sales/Receivables	19 19.7	17 21.1
21 17.7	26 14.0	31 11.8					32 11.3	29 12.5
31 11.7	39 9.4	41 9.0					47 7.8	41 8.9
36 10.1	39 9.4	47 7.8				Cost of Sales/Inventory	46 8.0	49 7.5
104 3.5	81 4.5	68 5.4					66 5.5	72 5.1
126 2.9	107 3.4	91 4.0					104 3.5	104 3.5
10 34.9	14 27.0	14 25.5				Cost of Sales/Payables	15 24.6	15 23.7
20 18.3	24 15.3	18 20.2					25 14.5	23 15.6
29 12.4	36 10.0	30 12.1					37 9.9	38 9.7
	4.9	4.5	6.3			Sales/Working Capital	4.5	5.0
	8.2	6.4	9.7				8.1	7.8
	79.5	14.2	14.2				14.6	14.5
	24.3	31.3	17.1			EBIT/Interest	14.3	15.8
	(16) 6.5	(47) 6.0	(37) 5.8				(182) 5.5	(169) 6.0
	2.6	2.1	3.1				2.1	2.3
		11.6	7.0			Net Profit + Depr., Dep., Amort./Cur. Mat. L/T/D	5.8	13.2
		(16) 4.0	(12) 4.2				(44) 3.3	(38) 3.4
		1.6	2.3				1.8	1.3
	.2	.2	.3			Fixed/Worth	.2	.2
	.3	.2	.6				.4	.4
	1.2	.5	.9				.8	.9
	.5	.5	.5			Debt/Worth	.6	.6
	1.3	.9	1.0				1.2	1.3
	8.5	1.8	2.0				3.0	3.4
	44.2	27.6	29.8			% Profit Before Taxes/Tangible Net Worth	27.9	30.3
	(17) 12.0	10.2	(38) 17.5				(192) 13.5	(173) 14.4
	5.6	2.5	6.1				5.8	5.5
	13.0	14.1	16.4			% Profit Before Taxes/Total Assets	10.9	12.2
	6.5	4.8	6.6				5.3	5.5
	2.5	1.9	2.8				2.0	2.4
	78.9	40.8	17.7			Sales/Net Fixed Assets	39.0	37.8
	28.3	18.6	12.7				18.6	16.8
	12.9	10.4	6.9				9.4	9.1
	4.0	3.4	3.1			Sales/Total Assets	3.4	3.4
	2.7	2.5	2.8				2.7	2.7
	2.3	2.0	1.9				2.1	2.2
	.3	.6	1.0			% Depr., Dep., Amort./Sales	.5	.5
	(14) .8	(44) .9	(37) 1.2				(177) .9	(165) .9
	1.8	1.2	1.6				1.3	1.5
	1.2	.7				% Officers', Directors' Owners' Comp/Sales	1.2	1.2
	(14) 2.4	(33) 1.7					(104) 2.1	(84) 1.9
	3.6						3.9	3.2
16376M	86523M	808363M	2726364M	963089M	2451045M	Net Sales ($)	7940458M	6388835M
2774M	26454M	283148M	1037481M	384413M	1281479M	Total Assets ($)	3376348M	2787775M

M = $ thousand   MM = $ million
See Pages viii through xx for Explanation of Ratios and Data

Comparative Historical Data   Current Data Sorted by Sales

Type of Statement / Number of Statements

4/1/16-3/31/17 ALL	4/1/17-3/31/18 ALL	4/1/18-3/31/19 ALL	Type of Statement	0-1MM	1-3MM	3-5MM	5-10MM	10-25MM	25MM & OVER
20	22	15	Unqualified			1		1	14
38	34	28	Reviewed		1	4	5	6	16
19	18	17	Compiled			8	2	4	6
32	22	27	Tax Returns	1	5	2	8	5	1
54	58	45	Other		2	2	2	14	22
				1	21 (4/1-9/30/18)			111 (10/1/18-3/31/19)	
163	154	132	NUMBER OF STATEMENTS	1	8	17	17	30	59

Assets / Liabilities / Income Data

4/1/16-3/31/17 ALL %	4/1/17-3/31/18 ALL %	4/1/18-3/31/19 ALL %		0-1MM %	1-3MM %	3-5MM %	5-10MM %	10-25MM %	25MM & OVER %
			ASSETS						
9.2	7.3	8.4	Cash & Equivalents			5.3	8.5	10.4	6.7
22.2	22.6	19.6	Trade Receivables (net)			14.9	18.6	21.4	22.6
39.0	39.0	39.8	Inventory			49.3	40.3	39.2	37.7
1.5	2.2	1.9	All Other Current			1.0	.5	4.3	1.5
71.9	71.2	69.7	Total Current			70.4	67.8	75.4	68.6
18.7	19.3	21.4	Fixed Assets (net)			20.4	20.8	17.8	22.6
2.7	3.9	2.3	Intangibles (net)			.6	.7	1.6	3.9
6.7	5.6	6.6	All Other Non-Current			8.6	10.7	5.3	4.9
100.0	100.0	100.0	Total			100.0	100.0	100.0	100.0
			LIABILITIES						
9.6	11.2	10.6	Notes Payable-Short Term			17.2	7.9	7.5	11.6
2.1	2.1	2.1	Cur. Mat.-L.T.D.			.6	1.9	2.7	2.1
15.4	15.4	13.2	Trade Payables			11.0	11.6	15.5	13.0
.1	.1	.1	Income Taxes Payable			.0	.0	.1	.1
11.5	12.7	9.8	All Other Current			8.4	9.1	13.1	9.3
38.8	41.6	35.8	Total Current			37.3	30.5	38.9	36.0
11.2	11.3	11.7	Long-Term Debt			11.4	13.8	8.0	12.1
.2	.2	.2	Deferred Taxes			.0	.1	.1	.3
8.7	6.1	4.7	All Other Non-Current			11.8	2.2	4.0	1.9
41.1	40.9	47.7	Net Worth			39.4	53.3	49.0	49.7
100.0	100.0	100.0	Total Liabilities & Net Worth			100.0	100.0	100.0	100.0
			INCOME DATA						
100.0	100.0	100.0	Net Sales			100.0	100.0	100.0	100.0
28.8	28.9	29.0	Gross Profit			32.9	30.6	27.5	27.9
25.7	25.9	25.9	Operating Expenses			27.8	29.5	25.1	24.3
3.1	3.0	3.1	Operating Profit			5.1	1.1	2.4	3.6
-.2	.0	.0	All Other Expenses (net)			.7	-.9	-.3	.0
3.3	3.0	3.2	Profit Before Taxes			4.4	2.0	2.7	3.6

Ratios

4/1/16-3/31/17 ALL	4/1/17-3/31/18 ALL	4/1/18-3/31/19 ALL		0-1MM	1-3MM	3-5MM	5-10MM	10-25MM	25MM & OVER
3.6	3.2	3.3	Current			3.2	6.8	4.2	3.1
2.2	2.0	2.2				2.1	2.8	2.3	1.9
1.5	1.4	1.4				1.2	1.5	1.4	1.5
1.9	1.3	1.4	Quick			1.7	2.4	1.4	1.2
.8	.8	.8				.7	1.0	.9	.8
.5	.5	.5				.2	.4	.6	.4
17 / 21.8	16 / 22.5	11 / 33.5	Sales/Receivables	0 / UND		7 / 53.8	14 / 25.4	17 / 21.4	
28 / 13.0	30 / 12.2	26 / 14.0		21 / 17.3		27 / 13.7	27 / 13.7	31 / 11.9	
37 / 9.8	42 / 8.7	38 / 9.6		30 / 12.0		42 / 8.7	40 / 9.2	38 / 9.5	
47 / 7.8	45 / 8.2	45 / 8.2	Cost of Sales/Inventory	21 / 17.2		62 / 5.9	37 / 9.9	46 / 7.9	
68 / 5.4	72 / 5.1	73 / 5.0		104 / 3.5		89 / 4.1	81 / 4.5	65 / 5.6	
96 / 3.8	99 / 3.7	104 / 3.5		130 / 2.8		107 / 3.4	107 / 3.4	85 / 4.3	
14 / 26.9	15 / 24.7	14 / 26.9	Cost of Sales/Payables	6 / 56.5		10 / 35.6	15 / 23.9	15 / 24.7	
21 / 17.0	24 / 15.4	21 / 17.2		11 / 34.2		17 / 21.6	24 / 15.4	19 / 18.9	
34 / 10.8	35 / 10.3	32 / 11.4		29 / 12.5		37 / 9.8	38 / 9.7	31 / 11.9	
4.6	4.6	4.8	Sales/Working Capital			3.9	4.2	4.1	5.8
7.7	8.4	7.8				6.0	5.0	6.4	9.0
16.0	15.4	14.3				58.0	12.0	14.3	14.2
22.9	14.4	25.6	EBIT/Interest			13.9	28.0	36.8	19.8
(147) 7.4	(136) 5.5	(118) 6.4				(16) 3.9	(15) 3.7	(28) 7.6	(53) 7.1
2.8	2.2	2.6				2.4	-6.5	1.8	3.6
11.7	5.0	7.9	Net Profit + Depr., Dep., Amort./Cur. Mat. L/T/D						7.0
(28) 5.3	(30) 3.0	(34) 4.0						(16)	4.9
1.2	.5	2.3							2.5
.2	.2	.2	Fixed/Worth			.1	.2	.1	.3
.4	.5	.4				.2	.5	.3	.5
.8	.9	.8				.7	1.0	.7	.8
.5	.5	.5	Debt/Worth			.5	.2	.6	.6
1.2	1.3	1.0				.9	.9	1.0	1.2
3.1	3.3	2.2				6.0	2.2	1.9	2.4
30.4	29.9	30.9	% Profit Before Taxes/Tangible Net Worth			52.8	26.4	28.4	31.8
(150) 16.0	(141) 14.6	(126) 15.3				(15) 9.4	(16) 8.7	9.3	(57) 18.9
5.3	4.5	5.7				5.0	2.1	1.1	11.0
13.8	11.6	13.5	% Profit Before Taxes/Total Assets			9.7	10.5	11.2	15.5
7.1	5.9	6.3				5.0	3.2	4.0	6.9
2.4	1.7	2.2				.8	-.9	.5	4.3
34.9	37.6	31.6	Sales/Net Fixed Assets			125.8	19.6	55.2	19.7
19.8	15.1	14.9				35.8	12.8	17.3	12.8
9.7	8.6	7.9				15.8	9.0	10.0	7.6
3.5	3.3	3.4	Sales/Total Assets			4.1	3.1	3.3	3.3
2.7	2.6	2.6				2.5	2.5	2.6	2.8
2.2	2.1	2.1				2.1	2.0	1.7	2.1
.6	.6	.7	% Depr., Dep., Amort./Sales			.3	.7	.7	.9
(134) 1.0	(126) 1.1	(112) 1.1				(10) .6	(16) .9	(24) 1.0	(56) 1.1
1.4	1.5	1.5				1.9	1.3	1.4	1.5
.9	1.1	.8	% Officers', Directors' Owners' Comp/Sales			1.8	1.5	.6	.4
(71) 2.0	(58) 2.3	(59) 1.7				(11) 2.5	(13) 2.3	(19) 1.2	(14) .8
3.8	3.6	3.4				3.6	4.3		

| 6582034M | 8175611M | 7051760M | Net Sales ($) | 901M | 16067M | 63629M | 123422M | 470902M | 6376839M |
| 3051151M | 3481176M | 3015749M | Total Assets ($) | 425M | 6051M | 50744M | 50823M | 197876M | 2709830M |

M = $ thousand   MM = $ million
See Pages viii through xx for Explanation of Ratios and Data

Current Data Sorted by Assets | | | | | | | Comparative Historical Data

© RMA 2019

0-500M	500M-2MM	2-10MM	10-50MM	50-100MM	100-250MM		4/1/14-3/31/15 ALL	4/1/15-3/31/16 ALL
		1	1			Type of Statement		
		1	1			Unqualified		
1	6					Reviewed		1
3	4	1	3			Compiled	3	11
3	4					Tax Returns	18	16
	3 (4/1-9/30/18)		22 (10/1/18-3/31/19)			Other	7	10
7	10	3	5			NUMBER OF STATEMENTS	28	38
%	%	%	%	%	%	**ASSETS**	%	%
	8.4			D A T A	D A T A	Cash & Equivalents	11.6	10.6
	34.9					Trade Receivables (net)	17.4	22.3
	36.2					Inventory	40.1	35.9
	2.6			N	N	All Other Current	1.5	6.8
	82.1			O	O	Total Current	70.6	75.7
	16.5			T	T	Fixed Assets (net)	14.9	14.2
	1.0					Intangibles (net)	6.7	5.4
	.5			A	A	All Other Non-Current	7.9	4.8
	100.0			V	V	Total	100.0	100.0
				A I L A B L E	A I L A B L E	**LIABILITIES**		
	10.2					Notes Payable-Short Term	8.7	12.3
	.4					Cur. Mat.-L.T.D.	2.2	1.7
	21.8					Trade Payables	24.6	28.8
	.0					Income Taxes Payable	.1	.0
	6.3					All Other Current	9.0	9.5
	38.7					Total Current	44.6	52.3
	5.2					Long-Term Debt	20.4	8.9
	.0					Deferred Taxes	.1	.1
	7.9					All Other Non-Current	4.9	10.2
	48.1					Net Worth	30.1	28.5
	100.0					Total Liabilties & Net Worth	100.0	100.0
						INCOME DATA		
	100.0					Net Sales	100.0	100.0
	40.8					Gross Profit	37.5	36.9
	35.5					Operating Expenses	34.1	34.9
	5.3					Operating Profit	3.4	2.0
	-.3					All Other Expenses (net)	.0	.0
	5.6					Profit Before Taxes	3.5	2.0
						RATIOS		
	2.9						2.5	2.5
	2.6					Current	1.5	1.5
	1.8						1.2	1.3
	1.6						1.0	1.2
	1.2					Quick	.6	.6
	.6						.3	.4
23	15.7						3 111.3	13 27.1
31	11.6					Sales/Receivables	13 28.3	28 13.1
69	5.3						29 12.5	35 10.5
62	5.9						35 10.5	43 8.4
76	4.8					Cost of Sales/Inventory	62 5.9	69 5.3
111	3.3						83 4.4	99 3.7
19	19.2						23 16.1	28 13.0
42	8.6					Cost of Sales/Payables	32 11.3	45 8.2
51	7.2						51 7.1	70 5.2
	4.6						7.7	7.5
	6.9					Sales/Working Capital	13.3	10.8
	10.5						60.7	24.4
							22.7	14.2
						EBIT/Interest	(26) 7.5	(28) 7.9
							4.0	2.2
						Net Profit + Depr., Dep., Amort./Cur. Mat. L/T/D		
	.0						.1	.1
	.2					Fixed/Worth	.4	.5
	.6						2.0	-21.3
	.4						1.0	1.2
	.7					Debt/Worth	3.5	2.8
	4.2						5.9	-114.9
							68.3	55.9
						% Profit Before Taxes/Tangible Net Worth	(24) 26.8	(28) 25.3
							12.4	5.6
	35.6						18.4	17.8
	11.4					% Profit Before Taxes/Total Assets	11.0	6.4
	1.8						4.8	1.3
	192.5						129.7	94.5
	24.4					Sales/Net Fixed Assets	53.8	35.0
	12.7						15.1	12.7
	3.7						4.7	4.0
	3.2					Sales/Total Assets	4.0	3.1
	2.6						2.7	2.3
							.5	.4
						% Depr., Dep., Amort./Sales	(15) 1.6	(27) .7
							2.2	1.6
							1.6	1.8
						% Officers', Directors' Owners' Comp/Sales	(20) 2.8	(21) 2.8
							5.9	6.5
5790M	37026M	39866M	371204M			Net Sales ($)	164457M	442857M
2042M	12527M	11604M	144854M			Total Assets ($)	51505M	145938M

M = $ thousand   MM = $ million
See Pages viii through xx for Explanation of Ratios and Data

Comparative Historical Data | Current Data Sorted by Sales

			Type of Statement	0-1MM	1-3MM	3-5MM	5-10MM	10-25MM	25MM & OVER
1	1	2	Unqualified	1			1	1	1
1	1	3	Reviewed	2	4	1	1		1
12	8	9	Compiled	2	2	3	2	1	3
8	10	11	Tax Returns		3 (4/1-9/30/18)		22 (10/1/18-3/31/19)		
4/1/16-3/31/17	4/1/17-3/31/18	4/1/18-3/31/19	Other	0-1MM	1-3MM	3-5MM	5-10MM	10-25MM	25MM & OVER
ALL	ALL	ALL							
22	20	25	**NUMBER OF STATEMENTS**	5	6	4	4	1	5
%	%	%	**ASSETS**	%	%	%	%	%	%
7.6	11.3	7.8	Cash & Equivalents						
19.2	17.9	27.3	Trade Receivables (net)						
48.9	42.1	44.9	Inventory						
4.0	2.0	2.4	All Other Current						
79.8	73.3	82.3	Total Current						
15.6	19.3	13.5	Fixed Assets (net)						
1.9	2.4	2.6	Intangibles (net)						
2.7	5.0	1.7	All Other Non-Current						
100.0	100.0	100.0	Total						
			LIABILITIES						
18.4	21.1	9.9	Notes Payable-Short Term						
4.0	1.6	1.8	Cur. Mat.-L.T.D.						
18.9	25.4	21.1	Trade Payables						
.0	.1	.0	Income Taxes Payable						
7.7	7.9	9.0	All Other Current						
48.9	56.1	41.8	Total Current						
19.2	23.2	25.5	Long-Term Debt						
.0	.0	.0	Deferred Taxes						
8.5	3.7	5.3	All Other Non-Current						
23.3	17.0	27.3	Net Worth						
100.0	100.0	100.0	Total Liabilties & Net Worth						
			INCOME DATA						
100.0	100.0	100.0	Net Sales						
37.1	42.8	40.5	Gross Profit						
36.3	42.0	36.6	Operating Expenses						
.8	.9	3.9	Operating Profit						
.2	-.3	.3	All Other Expenses (net)						
.6	1.2	3.6	Profit Before Taxes						
			RATIOS						
2.7	2.3	3.0							
1.9	1.5	2.5	Current						
1.3	1.1	1.4							
1.0	1.1	1.5							
.5	.5	1.0	Quick						
.2	.2	.6							
6 63.5	11 33.2	18 20.1							
20 18.7	21 17.1	28 12.9	Sales/Receivables						
46 7.9	36 10.1	52 7.0							
68 5.4	44 8.3	72 5.1							
101 3.6	96 3.8	96 3.8	Cost of Sales/Inventory						
166 2.2	159 2.3	130 2.8							
22 16.4	29 12.8	20 18.1							
42 8.7	55 6.6	42 8.7	Cost of Sales/Payables						
51 7.1	68 5.4	55 6.6							
5.6	6.5	5.2							
8.4	12.2	7.1	Sales/Working Capital						
21.5	62.1	12.1							
15.6	8.8	31.6							
(19) 5.8	(19) 3.5	(24) 4.8	EBIT/Interest						
1.1	1.0	1.2							
			Net Profit + Depr., Dep., Amort./Cur. Mat. L/T/D						
.1	.2	.1							
.5	.4	.3	Fixed/Worth						
1.3	18.0	.7							
1.0	.7	.6							
3.2	2.4	1.3	Debt/Worth						
9.2	83.8	7.7							
53.2	71.6	77.3							
(19) 14.4	(16) 8.8	(20) 18.3	% Profit Before Taxes/Tangible Net Worth						
.4	1.8	2.8							
10.4	11.7	28.7							
5.0	3.8	6.5	% Profit Before Taxes/Total Assets						
-5.2	-3.9	.6							
76.1	106.0	111.7							
31.6	20.2	29.2	Sales/Net Fixed Assets						
10.9	12.3	16.6							
3.4	4.0	3.7							
2.8	2.8	3.2	Sales/Total Assets						
1.9	2.0	2.5							
.4	.4	.3							
(14) .8	(13) .9	(17) .7	% Depr., Dep., Amort./Sales						
1.7	1.8	1.8							
	1.8	2.1							
(10)	4.5	(14) 3.8	% Officers', Directors' Owners' Comp/Sales						
	7.7	9.6							
251288M	241799M	453886M	Net Sales ($)	2652M	12014M	15875M	30212M	21929M	371204M
111232M	123115M	171027M	Total Assets ($)	1240M	4698M	5608M	8415M	6212M	144854M

M = $ thousand   MM = $ million
See Pages viii through xx for Explanation of Ratios and Data

Current Data Sorted by Assets | Comparative Historical Data

Type of Statement	0-500M	500M-2MM	2-10MM	10-50MM	50-100MM	100-250MM		4/1/14-3/31/15 ALL	4/1/15-3/31/16 ALL
Unqualified			1	6	1	3		7	12
Reviewed		3	5	8				28	27
Compiled	1	8	14	2				55	51
Tax Returns	7	49	16	2				91	104
Other	8	49	39	14	5	2		95	116
		21 (4/1-9/30/18)		222 (10/1/18-3/31/19)					
NUMBER OF STATEMENTS	16	109	75	32	6	5		276	310
	%	%	%	%	%	%	ASSETS	%	%
	8.1	8.7	8.4	5.2			Cash & Equivalents	7.4	8.0
	6.9	8.9	10.7	12.9			Trade Receivables (net)	11.4	9.7
	67.6	54.8	44.7	40.0			Inventory	50.6	51.4
	.0	2.2	2.2	3.7			All Other Current	1.3	1.6
	82.6	74.7	66.1	61.7			Total Current	70.6	70.7
	8.3	12.0	20.4	25.8			Fixed Assets (net)	15.8	15.9
	3.1	4.1	4.4	4.3			Intangibles (net)	3.2	3.7
	6.0	9.2	9.1	8.2			All Other Non-Current	10.4	9.7
	100.0	100.0	100.0	100.0			Total	100.0	100.0
							LIABILITIES		
	18.4	6.3	6.4	12.1			Notes Payable-Short Term	9.1	8.1
	2.7	3.2	2.2	2.5			Cur. Mat.-L.T.D.	2.6	2.8
	9.3	11.3	10.1	10.6			Trade Payables	13.0	13.1
	.0	.1	.1	.2			Income Taxes Payable	.1	.1
	7.3	6.9	8.4	6.0			All Other Current	7.2	6.2
	37.7	27.8	27.1	31.4			Total Current	32.0	30.2
	14.5	20.7	19.7	15.4			Long-Term Debt	17.7	19.3
	.0	.0	.0	.5			Deferred Taxes	.1	.1
	19.2	12.1	3.4	5.1			All Other Non-Current	8.1	11.7
	28.6	39.3	49.8	47.6			Net Worth	42.2	38.6
	100.0	100.0	100.0	100.0			Total Liabilties & Net Worth	100.0	100.0
							INCOME DATA		
	100.0	100.0	100.0	100.0			Net Sales	100.0	100.0
	39.2	37.4	36.5	36.1			Gross Profit	37.7	37.5
	35.6	34.5	31.5	32.0			Operating Expenses	33.7	34.9
	3.5	2.9	5.0	4.1			Operating Profit	4.0	2.7
	.5	-.7	-.2	.0			All Other Expenses (net)	-.2	-.7
	3.0	3.6	5.3	4.1			Profit Before Taxes	4.2	3.4
							RATIOS		
	7.1	6.0	4.6	3.5				4.8	5.5
	2.8	3.8	2.9	2.1			Current	2.5	2.9
	2.0	2.3	1.9	1.2				1.5	1.6
	.8	1.3	1.3	1.2				1.3	1.4
	(15) .3	.6	.8	.7			Quick	.5	(309) .7
	.2	.3	.3	.2				.2	.2
	1 261.1	2 180.8	4 99.7	8 44.8				4 100.7	4 88.6
	9 38.8	6 58.0	12 29.9	14 25.4			Sales/Receivables	10 36.8	10 38.4
	18 19.9	19 19.0	25 14.8	29 12.7				25 14.4	21 17.2
	101 3.6	99 3.7	87 4.2	60 6.1				87 4.2	94 3.9
	182 2.0	146 2.5	140 2.6	118 3.1			Cost of Sales/Inventory	135 2.7	140 2.6
	281 1.3	182 2.0	182 2.0	152 2.4				182 2.0	192 1.9
	0 UND	7 51.7	13 27.2	15 23.6				13 28.5	14 25.8
	6 65.7	21 17.5	24 15.2	22 16.3			Cost of Sales/Payables	25 14.5	26 14.2
	28 12.9	34 10.6	37 9.8	41 8.9				42 8.7	40 9.1
	2.5	3.2	3.6	4.6				3.7	3.5
	4.4	4.6	5.1	6.7			Sales/Working Capital	5.8	5.0
	14.3	7.6	7.6	22.3				10.6	10.2
	10.6	14.8	22.0	11.3				11.5	14.0
	(13) 7.3	(92) 5.8	(66) 4.9	(31) 5.6			EBIT/Interest	(235) 4.8	(273) 4.7
	.0	2.1	1.8	2.0				1.8	1.9
		6.6	6.8				Net Profit + Depr., Dep.,	6.6	5.8
		(11) 2.9	(11) 3.1				Amort./Cur. Mat. L/T/D	(35) 2.1	(39) 3.0
		.9	1.1					.8	1.3
	.1	.0	.1	.3				.1	.1
	.3	.2	.3	.5			Fixed/Worth	.3	.3
	.4	1.1	.8	1.2				.9	1.1
	.4	.4	.6	.5				.5	.6
	1.9	1.2	1.0	1.2			Debt/Worth	1.3	1.6
	8.0	5.9	2.2	3.1				3.9	4.4
	60.3	40.1	39.7	32.7			% Profit Before Taxes/Tangible	35.1	34.0
	(13) 29.8	(95) 20.5	(72) 20.8	(30) 21.8			Net Worth	(252) 16.7	(268) 15.9
	3.0	7.4	6.5	10.6				5.4	6.0
	16.0	17.5	15.7	10.9			% Profit Before Taxes/Total	12.7	12.0
	8.8	9.1	8.2	8.1			Assets	6.0	5.8
	-.1	2.5	2.3	4.3				1.8	1.8
	80.5	172.6	61.2	37.5				86.1	81.2
	42.9	38.7	15.7	12.2			Sales/Net Fixed Assets	27.8	27.3
	22.5	12.6	5.1	4.6				8.2	7.8
	3.6	3.0	2.7	2.6				3.2	2.9
	2.3	2.2	2.0	2.1			Sales/Total Assets	2.2	2.2
	1.7	1.9	1.4	1.7				1.7	1.7
		.4	.6	.6				.4	.4
		(67) 1.0	(55) 1.4	(27) 1.4			% Depr., Dep., Amort./Sales	(207) .9	(230) 1.1
		2.3	2.2	2.1				1.8	2.1
		1.7	1.0					1.8	1.9
		(60) 3.0	(38) 2.6				% Officers', Directors'	(142) 3.6	(163) 3.3
		5.5	4.0				Owners' Comp/Sales	5.4	5.7
	18748M	281804M	670004M	1371327M	849729M	1528553M	Net Sales ($)	3570816M	4123182M
	6132M	117803M	305113M	639894M	353365M	848990M	Total Assets ($)	1694123M	1958522M

M = $ thousand   MM = $ million
See Pages viii through xx for Explanation of Ratios and Data

Comparative Historical Data

Current Data Sorted by Sales

Type of Statement

4/1/16-3/31/17	4/1/17-3/31/18	4/1/18-3/31/19	Type of Statement	0-1MM	1-3MM	3-5MM	5-10MM	10-25MM	25MM & OVER
13	9	11	Unqualified				1		10
21	23	16	Reviewed		1	2	4	3	6
41	32	25	Compiled		6	4	8	7	4
72	60	74	Tax Returns	6	36	13	13	2	
85	98	117	Other	7	48	13	17	13	19
ALL	ALL	ALL		21 (4/1-9/30/18)		222 (10/1/18-3/31/19)			

4/1/16-3/31/17 ALL	4/1/17-3/31/18 ALL	4/1/18-3/31/19 ALL		0-1MM	1-3MM	3-5MM	5-10MM	10-25MM	25MM & OVER
232	222	243	**NUMBER OF STATEMENTS**	13	91	32	43	25	39
%	%	%	**ASSETS**	%	%	%	%	%	%
7.1	8.7	7.8	Cash & Equivalents	4.6	8.5	9.3	8.8	7.7	5.3
8.8	10.1	9.9	Trade Receivables (net)	4.0	7.0	11.8	10.3	11.3	15.4
51.1	47.6	50.5	Inventory	66.5	52.0	55.0	47.5	43.2	45.9
1.5	1.6	2.3	All Other Current	.8	2.5	1.9	3.2	1.3	2.0
68.5	68.0	70.5	Total Current	76.0	70.0	78.1	69.8	63.5	68.6
16.2	17.5	16.7	Fixed Assets (net)	10.3	15.4	10.3	17.0	26.5	20.7
4.0	4.1	4.4	Intangibles (net)	5.7	5.7	1.8	3.0	2.8	5.5
11.3	10.5	8.5	All Other Non-Current	8.1	8.9	9.8	10.2	7.2	5.2
100.0	100.0	100.0	Total	100.0	100.0	100.0	100.0	100.0	100.0
			LIABILITIES						
8.3	5.9	8.2	Notes Payable-Short Term	19.2	7.0	4.8	5.2	8.0	13.3
2.5	2.6	2.7	Cur. Mat.-L.T.D.	4.6	3.2	1.4	2.4	3.6	1.6
11.0	12.2	11.0	Trade Payables	7.3	9.3	11.0	13.4	8.2	15.1
.1	.2	.1	Income Taxes Payable	.1	.1	.1	.2	.1	.3
7.1	7.8	7.3	All Other Current	5.5	8.0	5.5	6.6	9.3	7.6
29.0	28.6	29.3	Total Current	36.6	27.6	22.7	27.8	29.2	37.8
19.5	21.0	19.1	Long-Term Debt	23.3	24.7	9.3	17.2	20.5	14.0
.1	.2	.1	Deferred Taxes	.0	.0	.0	.1	.2	.5
9.6	6.9	8.7	All Other Non-Current	24.5	12.4	7.5	4.0	3.8	3.9
41.8	43.3	42.8	Net Worth	15.7	35.3	60.4	51.0	46.3	43.9
100.0	100.0	100.0	Total Liabilities & Net Worth	100.0	100.0	100.0	100.0	100.0	100.0
			INCOME DATA						
100.0	100.0	100.0	Net Sales	100.0	100.0	100.0	100.0	100.0	100.0
37.4	37.4	37.0	Gross Profit	41.4	37.9	35.3	36.9	40.0	33.2
34.1	34.3	33.2	Operating Expenses	39.6	34.2	31.3	33.4	34.2	29.7
3.3	3.0	3.8	Operating Profit	1.8	3.7	4.0	3.5	5.8	3.5
-.3	-.5	-.3	All Other Expenses (net)	.3	-.3	-1.2	-.5	.0	-.1
3.6	3.5	4.1	Profit Before Taxes	1.5	4.0	5.2	4.0	5.7	3.5
			RATIOS						
6.0	5.1	5.2	Current	4.8	6.6	6.0	5.1	3.6	3.0
3.1	3.0	3.0		2.6	3.8	4.5	3.0	2.9	1.8
1.7	1.8	1.8		2.2	2.0	2.6	1.9	1.7	1.2
1.3	1.4	1.3	Quick	.7	1.3	2.1	1.3	1.0	1.2
.6	.7 (242)	.6		(12) .3	.6	.9	.7	.7	.5
.2	.3	.2		.1	.2	.5	.2	.3	.2
3 106.4	4 96.5	3 121.0	Sales/Receivables	2 223.2	2 146.8	2 171.1	3 119.5	2 155.4	7 49.5
8 47.4	11 32.0	9 41.6		12 31.5	6 62.1	9 40.2	13 28.3	8 43.1	13 27.8
18 20.0	22 16.3	21 17.3		19 18.8	14 26.7	38 9.7	24 15.5	24 14.9	29 12.6
96 3.8	89 4.1	94 3.9	Cost of Sales/Inventory	215 1.7	111 3.3	99 3.7	99 3.7	65 5.6	63 5.8
140 2.6	130 2.8	140 2.6		261 1.4	152 2.4	140 2.6	118 3.1	122 3.0	114 3.2
192 1.9	182 2.0	182 2.0		304 1.2	182 2.0	174 2.1	174 2.1	182 2.0	152 2.4
11 33.0	12 29.2	10 38.4	Cost of Sales/Payables	1 254.8	6 58.7	8 46.6	14 27.0	11 33.4	18 19.9
24 15.0	22 16.6	23 16.0		16 23.5	18 20.7	16 15.9	26 13.8	23 16.0	30 12.1
38 9.6	40 9.2	38 9.7		46 8.0	32 11.4	32 11.3	46 7.9	33 11.2	47 7.8
3.6	3.6	3.5	Sales/Working Capital	2.2	3.2	3.0	3.7	4.6	6.2
5.3	5.3	5.0		2.9	4.6	4.0	5.9	5.5	10.6
9.6	8.6	8.9		4.2	7.1	6.8	7.8	13.5	19.8
15.9	14.8	14.9	EBIT/Interest	7.7	14.7	22.8	12.9	18.4	20.9
(206) 4.8	(191) 5.2	(213) 5.8		(12) 3.9	(81) 5.5	(23) 12.6	(35) 6.6	4.5	(37) 5.8
2.0	1.9	1.9		-.8	2.0	2.1	1.6	2.6	2.1
4.8	5.3	6.8	Net Profit + Depr., Dep.,						38.8
(28) 2.7	(34) 3.0	(36) 3.8	Amort./Cur. Mat. L/T/D						(13) 6.0
1.5	.9	2.2							4.1
.1	.1	.1	Fixed/Worth	.2	.0	.0	.0	.2	.3
.3	.3	.3		.4	.3	.1	.2	.5	.5
1.2	1.1	1.1		NM	1.4	.4	1.1	1.1	1.1
.5	.5	.5	Debt/Worth	1.2	.6	.3	.4	.8	.6
1.5	1.3	1.2		3.8	1.3	.5	.8	1.2	1.8
3.9	3.7	3.8		NM	5.9	1.4	3.0	2.8	4.0
33.9	32.1	39.7	% Profit Before Taxes/Tangible	88.0	45.4	34.3	37.4	48.0	33.2
(205) 17.9	(200) 16.7	(220) 20.8	Net Worth	(10) 11.7	(77) 22.7	(31) 18.3	(41) 14.3	18.8	(36) 22.9
7.3	3.7	7.4		-6.6	8.7	4.8	2.3	11.5	12.3
13.6	13.0	15.5	% Profit Before Taxes/Total Assets	9.2	17.1	17.4	15.2	14.8	13.1
6.6	5.8	8.3		5.9	10.1	9.0	8.2	7.1	8.3
2.2	1.6	2.3		6.0	2.5	2.1	.7	4.2	4.2
75.9	78.5	79.9	Sales/Net Fixed Assets	56.0	150.1	153.3	77.3	39.7	57.0
21.6	23.9	22.0		22.5	29.6	45.2	20.0	15.0	13.0
9.4	7.1	7.9		8.4	8.7	15.6	5.9	3.1	6.5
3.0	3.1	2.9	Sales/Total Assets	2.0	2.8	3.2	3.0	3.2	3.1
2.3	2.1	2.1		1.6	2.0	2.2	2.1	2.2	2.4
1.6	1.5	1.7		1.2	1.6	1.9	1.6	1.6	1.9
.5	.5	.5	% Depr., Dep., Amort./Sales		.5	.2	.6	.5	.8
(166) 1.1	(167) 1.2	(169) 1.3			(56) 1.5	(24) .6	(32) 1.4	(17) 1.0	(34) 1.5
2.0	2.1	2.2			2.7	1.2	2.2	1.8	2.1
1.7	1.5	1.4	% Officers', Directors'		1.8	1.2	1.3	.9	
(132) 3.1	(109) 2.6	(112) 2.8	Owners' Comp/Sales		(51) 3.1	(18) 2.5	(21) 2.5	(10) 3.4	
4.9	4.2	4.3			5.7	3.6	4.0	4.3	
3341950M	3551194M	4720165M	Net Sales ($)	8589M	182143M	121103M	300520M	371221M	3736589M
1647651M	1674160M	2271297M	Total Assets ($)	5936M	98920M	56467M	154803M	212523M	1742648M

M = $ thousand   MM = $ million
See Pages viii through xx for Explanation of Ratios and Data

Current Data Sorted by Assets   Comparative Historical Data

0-500M	500M-2MM	2-10MM	10-50MM	50-100MM	100-250MM	Type of Statement	4/1/14-3/31/15 ALL	4/1/15-3/31/16 ALL
		4	14	4	1	Unqualified	27	27
	5	36	22	2		Reviewed	74	80
4	8	35	7	1		Compiled	81	62
34	59	45	10			Tax Returns	150	193
14	49	79	50	6	11	Other	218	222
	58 (4/1-9/30/18)		442 (10/1/18-3/31/19)					
52	121	199	103	13	12	NUMBER OF STATEMENTS	550	584
%	%	%	%	%	%	ASSETS	%	%
24.0	14.5	8.2	7.0	8.4	9.8	Cash & Equivalents	10.3	11.9
17.7	23.6	27.2	26.9	23.1	26.7	Trade Receivables (net)	27.7	25.7
21.5	35.1	35.7	33.9	29.2	18.9	Inventory	33.6	31.6
4.3	3.4	1.5	1.9	2.5	2.4	All Other Current	2.0	1.6
67.5	76.6	72.6	69.6	63.1	57.8	Total Current	73.6	70.8
20.2	14.2	17.2	19.4	25.6	14.0	Fixed Assets (net)	16.5	17.4
2.5	3.3	2.0	5.1	2.1	22.2	Intangibles (net)	2.9	3.9
9.8	6.0	8.2	5.9	9.1	6.0	All Other Non-Current	7.1	7.8
100.0	100.0	100.0	100.0	100.0	100.0	Total	100.0	100.0
						LIABILITIES		
16.6	9.4	9.4	11.9	7.6	4.8	Notes Payable-Short Term	12.4	10.5
2.0	1.5	1.8	3.4	1.3	1.0	Cur. Mat.-L.T.D.	2.6	2.5
18.6	19.0	16.1	15.8	14.1	13.5	Trade Payables	18.6	17.4
.3	.1	.2	.1	.2	.1	Income Taxes Payable	.1	.3
17.9	9.9	10.6	8.3	9.2	8.2	All Other Current	11.0	11.0
55.4	39.9	38.1	39.5	32.4	27.6	Total Current	44.7	41.6
19.6	13.7	11.6	12.4	10.9	23.5	Long-Term Debt	12.9	14.4
.0	.0	.2	.3	.0	.4	Deferred Taxes	.2	.2
10.6	8.2	4.8	3.9	2.9	4.7	All Other Non-Current	7.4	6.9
14.3	38.1	45.2	44.0	53.8	43.8	Net Worth	34.7	37.0
100.0	100.0	100.0	100.0	100.0	100.0	Total Liabilities & Net Worth	100.0	100.0
						INCOME DATA		
100.0	100.0	100.0	100.0	100.0	100.0	Net Sales	100.0	100.0
40.4	37.2	28.5	27.4	22.5	30.4	Gross Profit	30.2	31.4
36.1	32.7	24.7	23.4	18.5	23.9	Operating Expenses	26.6	27.4
4.3	4.5	3.9	4.0	4.0	6.5	Operating Profit	3.6	3.9
.2	.4	-.1	-.2	.1	1.7	All Other Expenses (net)	.0	.0
4.1	4.2	4.0	4.2	3.9	4.8	Profit Before Taxes	3.5	4.0
						RATIOS		
3.4	4.4	4.1	3.1	3.3	3.2	Current	2.9	3.1
1.5	2.0	2.1	1.9	2.2	1.8		1.8	1.9
.8	1.2	1.4	1.3	1.2	1.2		1.2	1.3
2.1	2.0	1.9	1.5	2.0	2.0	Quick	1.5	1.9
.9	1.0	1.0	.9	1.1	1.2		.9	1.0
.4	.5	.5	.6	.5	.7		.5	.5
0 UND	6 65.3	20 18.6	24 15.2	23 15.9	25 14.4	Sales/Receivables	18 19.9	15 24.9
9 39.9	24 15.1	31 11.6	35 10.5	34 10.7	38 9.7		32 11.5	30 12.0
26 13.8	41 8.9	42 8.6	46 7.9	49 7.4	47 7.7		47 7.7	45 8.1
0 UND	18 20.4	36 10.1	40 9.1	45 8.1	18 20.7	Cost of Sales/Inventory	28 13.0	24 15.0
18 20.2	56 6.5	57 6.4	59 6.2	54 6.8	46 8.0		54 6.7	52 7.0
78 4.7	114 3.2	89 4.1	87 4.2	72 5.1	81 4.5		91 4.0	89 4.1
0 UND	10 37.1	13 28.6	16 23.5	13 28.0	14 26.3	Cost of Sales/Payables	14 25.3	15 24.7
6 66.2	25 14.4	20 18.3	25 14.7	25 14.8	20 18.1		25 14.8	24 15.2
36 10.1	51 7.2	35 10.4	40 9.2	31 11.8	47 7.7		40 9.1	41 8.9
8.8	4.5	5.1	5.1	5.5	4.8	Sales/Working Capital	5.7	5.5
20.0	9.1	8.5	7.7	7.3	10.5		9.7	9.6
-35.8	24.2	16.3	17.1	18.1	20.3		25.0	22.1
22.5	53.6	31.4	22.4	38.1	10.7	EBIT/Interest	18.9	26.8
(35) 7.1	(98) 9.2	(177) 7.4	(96) 7.6	(12) 9.0	(10) 6.1		(475) 6.5	(493) 8.6
-2.1	2.5	2.1	3.0	3.6	-.5		2.1	3.0
		5.3	9.3			Net Profit + Depr., Dep., Amort./Cur. Mat. L/T/D	7.4	10.2
		(30) 2.0	(23) 2.5				(75) 3.5	(75) 3.5
		.5	1.0				1.6	2.1
.1	.1	.1	.2	.2	.2	Fixed/Worth	.1	.1
.7	.2	.3	.4	.5	.8		.4	.3
-1.3	.9	.8	1.1	.9	NM		1.1	1.1
.7	.4	.5	.6	.3	.9	Debt/Worth	.7	.6
4.5	1.6	1.2	1.5	.8	3.6		1.8	1.6
-6.6	5.3	3.5	3.1	2.2	NM		5.1	5.4
216.1	58.1	42.3	33.5	27.9		% Profit Before Taxes/Tangible Net Worth	51.4	55.6
(35) 36.8	(103) 23.6	(186) 18.0	(94) 20.3	12.6			(475) 20.1	(509) 23.2
11.8	8.8	6.5	8.9	10.8			8.0	10.7
39.6	23.3	19.4	15.3	12.6	16.6	% Profit Before Taxes/Total Assets	17.1	19.4
14.9	8.8	7.8	7.7	7.8	12.9		7.9	9.5
-1.1	2.9	2.2	3.1	4.2	-1.9		2.2	3.5
201.3	147.7	55.4	40.3	24.4	36.1	Sales/Net Fixed Assets	97.0	86.6
50.8	37.4	24.8	20.2	7.6	25.5		28.2	28.6
18.2	17.5	11.9	8.9	4.9	10.4		12.0	11.5
9.2	4.3	3.9	3.4	3.4	3.1	Sales/Total Assets	4.1	4.1
5.1	3.1	2.9	2.8	2.0	2.1		2.9	2.9
3.1	2.3	2.0	1.8	1.5	1.2		2.1	2.1
.6	.3	.5	.6	.7		% Depr., Dep., Amort./Sales	.4	.4
(29) 1.0	(70) .7	(160) .9	(90) 1.1	1.5			(418) .8	(434) .9
2.1	1.7	1.5	1.7	1.8			1.6	1.7
3.6	2.4	1.1	.6			% Officers', Directors' Owners' Comp/Sales	1.4	1.4
(31) 6.8	(69) 4.1	(102) 2.2	(26) 1.3				(247) 2.6	(265) 3.1
9.2	6.9	3.5	2.7				5.1	5.6
96670M	446693M	3020026M	5832462M	2131780M	4238973M	Net Sales ($)	18041489M	15457102M
14844M	138224M	991594M	2253166M	952469M	1681230M	Total Assets ($)	5866231M	7023668M

M = $ thousand   MM = $ million
See Pages viii through xx for Explanation of Ratios and Data

Comparative Historical Data

Current Data Sorted by Sales

			Type of Statement	0-1MM	1-3MM	3-5MM	5-10MM	10-25MM	25MM & OVER
21	26	23	Unqualified	1		2	14	4	19
84	66	65	Reviewed					19	29
49	50	55	Compiled	3	2	9	13	17	11
169	147	148	Tax Returns	16	41	30	20	30	11
192	219	209	Other	10	26	21	32	51	69
4/1/16-3/31/17	4/1/17-3/31/18	4/1/18-3/31/19		58 (4/1-9/30/18)			442 (10/1/18-3/31/19)		
ALL	ALL	ALL							
515	508	500	**NUMBER OF STATEMENTS**	30	69	62	79	121	139
%	%	%	**ASSETS**	%	%	%	%	%	%
12.6	11.0	11.2	Cash & Equivalents	13.9	17.9	13.2	12.4	9.1	7.4
24.7	26.6	25.1	Trade Receivables (net)	11.9	21.1	22.4	25.2	27.1	29.5
32.1	32.4	33.2	Inventory	30.7	32.6	34.3	28.6	35.0	34.4
1.9	1.9	2.4	All Other Current	3.7	3.0	2.7	2.5	1.6	2.3
71.3	71.9	71.8	Total Current	60.2	74.7	72.6	68.7	72.8	73.6
17.6	17.6	17.4	Fixed Assets (net)	26.0	12.5	18.6	19.0	17.5	16.3
4.1	4.3	3.5	Intangibles (net)	5.6	2.9	2.8	2.4	3.6	4.0
6.9	6.2	7.3	All Other Non-Current	8.3	10.0	6.0	9.8	6.1	6.0
100.0	100.0	100.0	Total	100.0	100.0	100.0	100.0	100.0	100.0
			LIABILITIES						
10.4	10.1	10.5	Notes Payable-Short Term	20.0	12.4	6.5	6.3	11.3	11.0
2.9	2.3	2.1	Cur. Mat.-L.T.D.	2.6	1.5	1.7	1.8	2.2	2.5
17.5	17.4	16.9	Trade Payables	17.5	17.6	19.9	14.2	17.3	16.2
.2	.2	.1	Income Taxes Payable	.1	.2	.1	.3	.1	.1
9.8	9.1	10.6	All Other Current	6.2	12.3	14.1	9.1	10.1	10.5
40.8	39.2	40.2	Total Current	46.5	43.9	42.3	31.7	41.0	40.3
13.9	14.3	13.4	Long-Term Debt	21.4	14.9	19.5	10.6	13.2	9.9
.2	.2	.2	Deferred Taxes	.0	.0	.0	.4	.1	.2
6.4	7.2	6.0	All Other Non-Current	18.0	7.7	5.1	8.8	3.6	3.5
38.7	39.0	40.2	Net Worth	14.0	33.5	33.1	48.5	42.1	46.1
100.0	100.0	100.0	Total Liabilities & Net Worth	100.0	100.0	100.0	100.0	100.0	100.0
			INCOME DATA						
100.0	100.0	100.0	Net Sales	100.0	100.0	100.0	100.0	100.0	100.0
31.7	32.4	31.5	Gross Profit	49.1	36.4	35.0	32.1	28.1	26.5
27.4	27.8	27.3	Operating Expenses	43.3	32.2	30.5	27.8	24.7	22.1
4.3	4.6	4.2	Operating Profit	5.7	4.2	4.4	4.3	3.4	4.3
.1	.1	.1	All Other Expenses (net)	1.4	.3	.4	-.6	.0	.0
4.1	4.4	4.1	Profit Before Taxes	4.3	3.9	4.0	5.0	3.4	4.3
			RATIOS						
3.3	3.4	3.7		2.8	4.6	5.1	4.9	3.0	3.0
2.0	2.0	2.0	Current	1.5	2.1	1.9	2.2	1.8	1.9
1.3	1.3	1.3		.8	1.1	1.2	1.4	1.3	1.4
1.8	1.9	1.8		1.8	2.7	1.8	2.4	1.9	1.5
1.0	1.0	1.0	Quick	.6	.9	.9	1.2	1.0	.9
.5	.5	.5		.3	.3	.5	.6	.6	.6
16 23.5	18 19.8	16 23.5		0 UND	5 68.7	6 57.5	15 24.0	21 17.3	24 15.0
29 12.5	30 12.3	29 12.4	Sales/Receivables	7 54.8	24 15.2	20 18.0	29 12.4	34 10.8	32 11.5
44 8.3	45 8.2	42 8.6		31 11.9	41 9.0	33 10.9	45 8.2	48 7.6	43 8.4
27 13.6	29 12.4	29 12.4		0 UND	12 31.1	18 20.6	21 17.7	36 10.2	38 9.6
51 7.1	55 6.6	54 6.7	Cost of Sales/Inventory	62 5.9	61 6.0	64 5.7	47 7.7	57 6.4	51 7.1
89 4.1	96 3.8	91 4.0		118 3.1	111 3.3	111 3.3	85 4.3	89 4.1	76 4.8
14 26.2	14 25.7	12 29.8		0 UND	12 31.2	8 44.3	8 45.5	15 24.9	13 27.8
24 15.5	24 15.0	21 17.6	Cost of Sales/Payables	17 21.7	25 14.4	23 16.1	17 21.3	24 15.3	21 17.7
40 9.1	41 8.9	41 8.9		52 7.0	49 7.4	45 8.2	35 10.5	41 9.0	37 9.8
5.5	5.3	5.3		5.8	4.1	4.4	4.3	5.6	6.4
9.2	8.5	8.7	Sales/Working Capital	14.1	9.1	9.8	7.6	8.7	8.4
22.7	18.6	19.8		-34.5	64.2	70.7	18.1	16.6	17.7
28.6	27.9	29.9		11.0	32.9	61.2	27.0	22.5	35.0
(446) 8.8	(439) 8.0	(428) 7.8	EBIT/Interest	(19) 3.3	(56) 7.1	(51) 8.9	(65) 8.0	(111) 5.1	(126) 9.9
3.1	2.8	2.4		-4.6	2.4	2.0	2.2	2.2	3.6
8.7	9.2	5.3					3.9	8.5	9.6
(70) 3.1	(73) 2.9	(66) 2.3	Net Profit + Depr., Dep., Amort./Cur. Mat. L/T/D				(12) .8	(20) 2.3	(26) 2.9
1.4	1.2	.9					.1	1.0	1.3
.1	.1	.1		.0	.0	.1	.1	.1	.2
.4	.3	.3	Fixed/Worth	.7	.2	.3	.3	.4	.3
1.2	1.1	1.0		-1.0	2.2	7.5	.8	.9	.7
.6	.7	.5		1.2	.4	.5	.4	.6	.6
1.6	1.4	1.4	Debt/Worth	5.4	1.3	1.8	.9	1.6	1.2
4.8	4.3	4.4		-7.0	151.1	35.6	2.9	3.9	2.9
52.3	44.6	47.7		39.1	67.6	75.2	49.9	35.7	42.3
(444) 24.2	(446) 22.5	(440) 21.1	% Profit Before Taxes/Tangible Net Worth	(20) 15.6	(55) 32.7	(50) 20.6	(75) 16.8	(111) 18.3	(129) 23.5
11.3	9.1	8.1		-1.2	8.7	7.8	6.3	6.1	11.8
19.8	19.8	20.0		21.6	23.3	28.3	20.5	14.7	18.7
9.2	10.2	8.3	% Profit Before Taxes/Total Assets	4.3	10.0	7.1	8.8	5.9	9.9
3.5	3.0	2.4		-6.2	2.0	2.8	2.0	2.2	3.9
72.4	70.1	66.2		162.7	198.9	137.4	64.8	54.9	46.1
25.1	23.2	27.2	Sales/Net Fixed Assets	17.1	40.9	37.2	22.1	25.2	25.4
11.8	11.3	12.0		5.3	17.9	13.9	10.1	12.4	11.7
4.1	4.0	4.0		3.4	4.1	5.0	3.9	3.8	3.9
2.9	2.9	2.9	Sales/Total Assets	2.4	3.0	3.5	2.8	2.9	3.1
2.2	2.2	2.0		1.1	2.1	2.3	1.9	2.1	2.1
.5	.4	.5		1.1	.5	.3	.4	.6	.4
(390) .9	(382) 1.0	(371) 1.0	% Depr., Dep., Amort./Sales	(18) 2.8	(38) 1.0	(39) .6	(57) .9	(98) 1.1	(121) .8
1.7	1.8	1.7		7.0	2.0	1.5	1.5	1.9	1.5
1.4	1.4	1.4		6.9	3.5	1.9	2.3	1.0	.5
(247) 3.0	(242) 2.9	(230) 2.8	% Officers', Directors', Owners' Comp/Sales	(14) 9.3	(40) 5.0	(40) 2.8	(43) 2.8	(54) 1.9	(39) 1.3
5.0	5.8	4.9		15.4	8.1	5.8	4.2	3.2	1.8
16820749M	17341582M	15766604M	Net Sales ($)	18556M	141915M	247035M	565162M	1925259M	12868677M
7109080M	7146039M	6031527M	Total Assets ($)	13570M	57870M	87952M	250262M	788012M	4833861M

M = $ thousand   MM = $ million
See Pages viii through xx for Explanation of Ratios and Data

Current Data Sorted by Assets   Comparative Historical Data

Type of Statement	0-500M	500M-2MM	2-10MM	10-50MM	50-100MM	100-250MM	4/1/14-3/31/15 ALL	4/1/15-3/31/16 ALL
Unqualified					2		1	1
Reviewed	1	3	2		1		12	12
Compiled	10	14	7	8			13	9
Tax Returns		6	8	7		5	30	39
Other			11				23	35
	7 (4/1-9/30/18)			78 (10/1/18-3/31/19)				
NUMBER OF STATEMENTS	11	23	28	15	3	5	79	96
	%	%	%	%	%	%	%	%
ASSETS								
Cash & Equivalents	13.9	11.3	6.9	4.3			8.3	8.5
Trade Receivables (net)	6.7	4.0	7.1	9.4			7.5	8.1
Inventory	65.2	54.9	70.1	66.5			63.6	67.5
All Other Current	.0	1.3	2.4	1.3			.6	1.6
Total Current	85.8	71.6	86.4	81.4			80.0	85.7
Fixed Assets (net)	8.9	22.5	8.5	13.9			14.3	9.0
Intangibles (net)	3.3	1.7	.8	2.6			1.2	1.5
All Other Non-Current	1.9	4.3	4.2	2.1			4.5	3.7
Total	100.0	100.0	100.0	100.0			100.0	100.0
LIABILITIES								
Notes Payable-Short Term	20.8	12.7	37.7	33.5			20.0	25.2
Cur. Mat.-L.T.D.	2.7	1.4	.9	4.5			1.0	2.2
Trade Payables	7.9	17.0	12.0	12.8			22.9	19.5
Income Taxes Payable	.1	.3	.0	.1			.0	.1
All Other Current	5.8	9.0	14.9	8.8			8.7	7.9
Total Current	37.3	40.4	65.6	59.7			52.5	54.9
Long-Term Debt	20.5	21.9	8.9	6.5			13.1	9.7
Deferred Taxes	.0	.0	.0	.3			.1	.1
All Other Non-Current	4.7	4.1	1.8	4.8			4.1	3.8
Net Worth	37.3	33.6	23.7	28.7			30.2	31.5
Total Liabilities & Net Worth	100.0	100.0	100.0	100.0			100.0	100.0
INCOME DATA								
Net Sales	100.0	100.0	100.0	100.0			100.0	100.0
Gross Profit	36.1	30.6	22.4	22.4			26.3	24.5
Operating Expenses	35.1	26.1	20.0	19.5			24.0	21.4
Operating Profit	1.0	4.5	2.4	2.9			2.4	3.1
All Other Expenses (net)	.7	.4	.4	-.1			.2	-.2
Profit Before Taxes	.4	4.1	2.0	3.0			2.2	3.3
RATIOS								
Current	5.5	4.5	1.5	1.6			2.0	2.1
	2.1	1.7	1.3	1.5			1.5	1.5
	1.5	1.1	1.2	1.1			1.2	1.3
Quick	.7	1.0	.3	.4			.5	.6
	.5	.3	.1	.2			(78) .2	.2
	.2	.1	.1	.1			.1	.1
Sales/Receivables	0 UND	0 UND	1 286.2	11 33.6			3 142.8	2 175.5
	2 169.3	3 137.5	7 51.5	15 25.0			6 58.2	7 53.2
	12 31.2	11 33.1	21 17.6	24 15.5			17 21.3	14 25.4
Cost of Sales/Inventory	72 5.1	79 4.6	101 3.6	118 3.1			89 4.1	101 3.6
	89 4.1	146 2.5	159 2.3	152 2.4			140 2.6	140 2.6
	203 1.8	174 2.1	243 1.5	166 2.2			182 2.0	182 2.0
Cost of Sales/Payables	0 UND	0 UND	2 159.9	5 74.3			10 37.0	6 63.8
	0 UND	26 13.9	10 36.7	22 16.5			26 14.2	19 18.8
	12 30.7	57 6.4	27 13.3	39 9.4			85 4.3	48 7.6
Sales/Working Capital	4.2	6.1	7.4	5.9			6.3	5.8
	9.5	13.2	10.2	7.9			9.6	8.6
	15.3	33.5	25.1	20.1			20.6	16.2
EBIT/Interest		22.6	9.9	21.7			14.9	16.6
	(22) 5.6		(27) 4.3	(14) 6.6			(69) 5.7	(85) 6.7
		2.1	1.6	3.1			2.7	2.6
Net Profit + Depr., Dep., Amort./Cur. Mat. L/T/D							8.5	12.4
							(10) 4.3	(12) 4.6
							2.0	1.5
Fixed/Worth	.0	.1	.1	.2			.1	.1
	.2	.5	.2	.5			.3	.2
	.8	2.1	1.1	1.3			1.0	.7
Debt/Worth	1.5	1.1	1.9	1.0			1.1	1.0
	2.9	2.5	3.4	3.5			2.4	2.5
	4.6	7.3	15.2	8.6			5.5	5.3
% Profit Before Taxes/Tangible Net Worth	80.6	91.6	47.3	44.7			32.5	40.2
	30.4	(22) 20.9	20.3	18.8			(72) 17.4	(88) 19.5
	-27.0	9.2	3.5	7.1			9.5	8.1
% Profit Before Taxes/Total Assets	25.7	14.8	7.8	8.7			8.3	10.5
	7.2	4.4	4.0	4.1			5.2	4.9
	-4.8	1.4	.7	2.2			1.8	2.3
Sales/Net Fixed Assets	910.0	65.3	127.7	45.2			80.5	117.4
	64.5	21.1	42.8	38.1			29.0	57.5
	14.4	4.8	21.7	13.6			13.2	22.6
Sales/Total Assets	4.8	3.5	3.0	2.6			2.9	3.7
	3.7	2.4	2.2	2.2			2.4	2.6
	2.2	1.5	1.6	1.6			1.7	2.0
% Depr., Dep., Amort./Sales		.6	.3	.5			.4	.3
	(16)	1.1	(20) .6	.9			(62) .7	(66) .6
		2.8	1.0	1.5			1.4	.9
% Officers', Directors' Owners' Comp/Sales		2.5	1.0				1.8	1.2
	(15)	3.7	(17) 1.5				(42) 3.2	(46) 2.5
		5.1	2.4				5.2	5.6
Net Sales ($)	12801M	67137M	303741M	764541M	366888M	978331M	1929217M	3694910M
Total Assets ($)	3225M	26200M	133687M	359717M	227210M	725214M	877550M	1649719M

© RMA 2019

M = $ thousand   MM = $ million
See Pages viii through xx for Explanation of Ratios and Data

Comparative Historical Data / Current Data Sorted by Sales

4/1/16-3/31/17 ALL	4/1/17-3/31/18 ALL	4/1/18-3/31/19 ALL	Type of Statement	0-1MM	1-3MM	3-5MM	5-10MM	10-25MM	25MM & OVER
5	8	2	Unqualified						2
14	11	10	Reviewed					3	7
14	14	11	Compiled	1	2	1	1	5	1
30	29	32	Tax Returns	5	14	3	7	3	
26	28	30	Other		6		8	6	10
					7 (4/1-9/30/18)		78 (10/1/18-3/31/19)		
89	90	85	NUMBER OF STATEMENTS	6	22	4	16	17	20
%	%	%	ASSETS	%	%	%	%	%	%
7.1	8.0	8.1	Cash & Equivalents		10.3		10.9	4.1	4.9
7.1	7.2	6.5	Trade Receivables (net)		4.2		7.4	7.6	8.2
69.0	67.8	65.2	Inventory		60.3		64.8	74.0	68.9
.8	1.0	1.8	All Other Current		.7		3.4	.7	2.8
83.9	83.9	81.6	Total Current		75.6		86.6	86.4	84.8
11.0	10.6	13.2	Fixed Assets (net)		16.4		9.2	9.9	10.3
2.1	1.8	1.9	Intangibles (net)		2.7		.8	1.5	2.5
2.9	3.7	3.4	All Other Non-Current		5.4		3.4	2.2	2.4
100.0	100.0	100.0	Total		100.0		100.0	100.0	100.0
			LIABILITIES						
27.4	27.4	27.7	Notes Payable-Short Term		13.3		39.3	34.8	31.3
3.3	2.3	2.0	Cur. Mat.-L.T.D.		2.0		.6	2.1	2.9
21.0	19.9	14.2	Trade Payables		14.5		11.9	10.6	19.8
.0	.1	.1	Income Taxes Payable		.2		.0	.0	.0
5.1	9.2	10.0	All Other Current		9.8		6.8	21.2	5.9
56.8	58.9	54.0	Total Current		39.9		58.6	68.8	59.8
10.8	9.3	13.3	Long-Term Debt		23.2		10.3	7.0	6.3
.0	.1	.1	Deferred Taxes		.0		.0	.0	.3
7.3	3.6	3.4	All Other Non-Current		4.3		3.0	.4	4.5
25.0	28.2	29.1	Net Worth		32.6		28.1	23.7	29.1
100.0	100.0	100.0	Total Liabilities & Net Worth		100.0		100.0	100.0	100.0
			INCOME DATA						
100.0	100.0	100.0	Net Sales		100.0		100.0	100.0	100.0
25.6	24.1	26.2	Gross Profit		32.5		23.8	21.7	21.5
22.9	21.3	23.3	Operating Expenses		30.1		21.2	19.3	18.9
2.7	2.9	2.9	Operating Profit		2.4		2.6	2.4	2.6
.3	.2	.3	All Other Expenses (net)		.4		.3	.3	.0
2.4	2.7	2.6	Profit Before Taxes		2.0		2.2	2.1	2.6
			RATIOS						
1.7	1.8	2.0	Current		4.6		1.9	1.4	1.7
1.4	1.4	1.4			1.7		1.5	1.3	1.4
1.2	1.2	1.2			1.2		1.2	1.0	1.2
.4	.4	.5	Quick		.8		.5	.2	.4
.2	.2	.2			.4		.1	.1	.2
.1	.1	.1			.2		.1	.1	.1
3 120.9	2 152.0	2 231.9	Sales/Receivables		0 UND		1 346.4	3 121.3	7 49.3
8 47.1	8 45.0	9 41.4			2 178.5		5 73.6	13 28.8	13 28.9
17 21.9	16 22.5	18 20.7			13 28.5		20 18.0	20 17.9	23 15.6
107 3.4	94 3.9	87 4.2	Cost of Sales/Inventory		79 4.6		51 7.1	126 2.9	122 3.0
152 2.4	140 2.6	152 2.4			130 2.8		146 2.5	152 2.4	159 2.3
228 1.6	192 1.9	215 1.7			174 2.1		261 1.4	243 1.5	203 1.8
5 70.1	7 55.6	1 259.9	Cost of Sales/Payables		0 UND		0 791.9	3 129.3	10 36.6
19 19.0	22 16.8	12 30.7			8 47.5		6 56.5	10 37.2	30 12.2
69 5.3	60 6.1	40 9.2			57 6.4		27 13.3	35 10.5	68 5.4
5.5	6.3	6.2	Sales/Working Capital		5.5		6.2	7.8	5.6
8.6	9.6	9.2			13.3		11.1	9.2	7.6
18.8	30.4	20.1			32.6		18.9	189.5	18.6
10.2	11.4	18.3	EBIT/Interest		18.3		15.6	20.6	17.7
(85) 5.3	(85) 4.6	(79) 4.2			(19) 3.4		(15) 5.0	5.5	(19) 3.4
2.2	2.0	1.7			.8		1.7	1.4	3.1
		14.1	Net Profit + Depr., Dep.,						
	(11)	2.9	Amort./Cur. Mat. L/T/D						
		1.8							
.1	.1	.1	Fixed/Worth		.1		.1	.1	.2
.3	.3	.3			.3		.2	.3	.3
.8	1.3	1.2			1.9		1.3	1.3	.5
1.6	1.3	1.5	Debt/Worth		1.0		1.1	2.0	1.5
2.9	2.8	3.2			4.1		3.0	3.4	3.0
6.5	6.3	7.6			14.8		16.5	19.9	5.5
29.4	33.3	46.8	% Profit Before Taxes/Tangible		98.3		57.8	39.8	34.3
(79) 17.5	(79) 17.4	(84) 20.0	Net Worth		(21) 31.6		21.9	18.9	18.7
5.4	8.0	7.5			5.2		4.7	4.4	11.3
9.1	8.1	9.6	% Profit Before Taxes/Total		17.7		9.3	7.5	7.3
4.3	4.3	4.2	Assets		5.1		2.6	6.1	4.2
1.1	1.5	1.2			.1		.8	.9	2.6
72.5	98.2	82.5	Sales/Net Fixed Assets		329.8		251.7	66.1	64.8
34.8	35.8	33.1			36.3		117.4	38.4	27.2
19.3	15.4	13.1			11.9		17.0	27.5	12.1
3.0	3.2	3.0	Sales/Total Assets		3.7		3.5	2.6	2.6
2.2	2.3	2.2			2.7		2.4	1.7	2.1
1.7	1.7	1.6			1.9		1.7	1.5	1.6
.5	.5	.5	% Depr., Dep., Amort./Sales		.3			.4	.6
(68) .8	(66) .8	(66) .7			(13) .9			(15) .6	.7
1.2	1.3	1.4			2.8			1.0	1.2
1.3	1.2	1.1	% Officers', Directors'		2.1			.9	
(41) 2.6	(41) 2.4	(44) 2.1	Owners' Comp/Sales		(15) 3.7			(10) 1.9	
5.5	4.8	3.9			5.1				
4633611M	4198953M	2493439M	Net Sales ($)	4358M	42072M	18200M	116905M	235044M	2076860M
1971705M	1947272M	1475253M	Total Assets ($)	2759M	18707M	7723M	50816M	142582M	1252666M

© RMA 2019

M = $ thousand   MM = $ million
See Pages viii through xx for Explanation of Ratios and Data

Current Data Sorted by Assets   Comparative Historical Data

Type of Statement

Type of Statement	0-500M	500M-2MM	2-10MM	10-50MM	50-100MM	100-250MM		4/1/14-3/31/15 ALL	4/1/15-3/31/16 ALL
Unqualified			1	4	2	4		12	9
Reviewed		1	12	17	1			22	15
Compiled	3	15	9	1				46	36
Tax Returns	18	24	12	3				58	60
Other	28	38	36	15	2			66	82
		43 (4/1-9/30/18)		203 (10/1/18-3/31/19)					
NUMBER OF STATEMENTS	49	78	70	40	5	4		204	202

	0-500M %	500M-2MM %	2-10MM %	10-50MM %	50-100MM %	100-250MM %		ALL %	ALL %
ASSETS									
Cash & Equivalents	20.2	10.9	10.6	5.7				10.0	11.2
Trade Receivables (net)	6.0	10.4	13.2	12.1				10.6	10.8
Inventory	33.6	40.2	39.8	41.5				37.4	39.7
All Other Current	2.1	2.1	2.4	3.5				1.8	1.8
Total Current	62.0	63.7	66.0	62.8				59.7	63.5
Fixed Assets (net)	25.9	27.3	24.1	27.6				29.4	27.8
Intangibles (net)	4.4	3.5	2.1	3.7				2.1	2.9
All Other Non-Current	7.7	5.5	7.8	5.9				8.7	5.8
Total	100.0	100.0	100.0	100.0				100.0	100.0
LIABILITIES									
Notes Payable-Short Term	9.2	9.8	11.0	16.8				10.1	10.1
Cur. Mat.-L.T.D.	3.0	2.6	2.3	1.7				4.1	3.6
Trade Payables	15.2	20.3	16.6	13.7				14.1	15.6
Income Taxes Payable	.2	.2	.1	.3				.1	.1
All Other Current	20.9	8.6	8.0	7.3				12.6	9.2
Total Current	48.6	41.5	38.0	39.9				41.0	38.5
Long-Term Debt	44.8	24.8	13.3	16.2				18.4	21.6
Deferred Taxes	.0	.0	.1	.1				.1	.2
All Other Non-Current	15.5	6.7	3.8	5.7				8.2	10.5
Net Worth	-8.9	27.0	44.8	38.1				32.3	29.3
Total Liabilities & Net Worth	100.0	100.0	100.0	100.0				100.0	100.0
INCOME DATA									
Net Sales	100.0	100.0	100.0	100.0				100.0	100.0
Gross Profit	39.8	38.3	35.4	31.3				37.3	37.6
Operating Expenses	34.2	34.1	30.6	28.5				33.6	34.1
Operating Profit	5.6	4.3	4.8	2.8				3.7	3.5
All Other Expenses (net)	1.3	.9	.3	.7				.4	.4
Profit Before Taxes	4.3	3.4	4.5	2.2				3.3	3.1

RATIOS

	0-500M	500M-2MM	2-10MM	10-50MM	50-100MM	100-250MM		ALL	ALL
Current	3.3	3.3	3.6	2.9				2.9	3.0
	2.0	1.7	1.7	1.5				1.6	1.7
	.9	1.1	1.2	1.1				1.0	1.2
Quick	1.3	1.1	1.3	1.0				1.3	1.1
	.5	.5	.6	.5				.5	.5
	.2	.1	.3	.1				.1	.2
Sales/Receivables	0 UND	2 232.0	3 121.7	8 46.7				1 267.2	2 233.8
	0 UND	7 55.2	14 26.1	21 17.7				7 55.2	8 43.3
	6 57.7	19 18.8	27 13.4	33 10.9				23 15.8	21 17.0
Cost of Sales/Inventory	7 50.0	42 8.6	47 7.8	63 5.8				42 8.6	42 8.6
	34 10.8	78 4.7	89 4.1	89 4.1				73 5.0	76 4.8
	104 3.5	159 2.3	146 2.5	166 2.2				126 2.9	140 2.6
Cost of Sales/Payables	0 UND	10 38.4	13 27.5	13 27.3				6 59.9	11 34.5
	1 437.0	25 14.4	29 12.4	24 14.9				24 15.4	25 14.5
	47 7.8	59 6.2	44 8.3	49 7.4				44 8.3	46 8.0
Sales/Working Capital	8.4	6.1	4.5	5.9				5.8	5.3
	22.2	13.3	8.4	11.2				12.6	10.9
	-25.6	104.7	28.1	21.1				173.8	37.5
EBIT/Interest	12.8	10.4	29.0	7.6				14.6	12.2
	(37) 5.4	(68) 3.3	(60) 6.3	(36) 2.4				(173) 4.8	(173) 4.6
	1.2	1.2	2.3	1.4				1.6	1.8
Net Profit + Depr., Dep., Amort./Cur. Mat. L/T/D			4.5	6.0				4.5	7.0
		(10) 2.0	(13) 2.5					(25) 2.4	(37) 2.7
			.8	1.5				.8	2.1
Fixed/Worth	.2	.3	.2	.3				.2	.3
	.9	.9	.5	.8				.8	.8
	-1.7	6.5	1.2	1.8				2.9	3.6
Debt/Worth	1.0	1.0	.5	.8				.7	.6
	4.1	2.1	1.2	2.2				1.7	1.8
	-3.9	16.5	3.6	4.8				7.0	7.2
% Profit Before Taxes/Tangible Net Worth	89.4	60.8	38.0	24.7				44.1	39.6
	(29) 50.0	(62) 22.4	(65) 19.1	(38) 13.2				(168) 18.1	(166) 18.0
	7.0	6.9	6.4	3.1				6.0	7.4
% Profit Before Taxes/Total Assets	29.2	16.5	20.2	7.7				14.8	14.9
	14.8	5.5	7.0	4.2				7.1	7.0
	-.6	1.2	2.8	.8				1.7	1.7
Sales/Net Fixed Assets	124.1	44.2	36.1	23.7				44.5	38.7
	25.6	16.8	16.2	9.1				12.2	13.2
	8.2	5.6	6.4	4.7				5.1	4.8
Sales/Total Assets	6.5	4.0	3.5	2.7				3.9	3.8
	3.8	2.7	2.5	1.9				2.6	2.5
	2.6	1.6	1.7	1.5				1.7	1.7
% Depr., Dep., Amort./Sales	.5	.6	.3	1.1				.7	.8
	(24) 1.4	(51) 1.5	(55) 1.3	(37) 1.8				(162) 1.3	(159) 1.5
	2.5	2.7	2.5	3.4				2.9	3.1
% Officers', Directors' Owners' Comp/Sales	3.2	2.0	1.2	.6				2.0	1.3
	(22) 6.5	(32) 3.3	(28) 2.3	(10) .9				(85) 3.6	(83) 2.6
	9.3	4.8	4.7	2.5				7.0	5.5
Net Sales ($)	52409M	252864M	782323M	1630782M	812664M	1096770M		3648657M	5755581M
Total Assets ($)	11693M	83849M	307931M	786198M	343550M	660651M		1698319M	2382240M

M = $ thousand   MM = $ million

See Pages viii through xx for Explanation of Ratios and Data

Comparative Historical Data | | | | Current Data Sorted by Sales

			Type of Statement						
12	8	11	Unqualified			2	4	1	10
17	21	30	Reviewed					9	15
25	60	29	Compiled	2	9	5	8	4	1
58	74	57	Tax Returns	15	14	13	8	6	1
78	138	119	Other	21	25	18	21	19	15
4/1/16-3/31/17	4/1/17-3/31/18	4/1/18-3/31/19			43 (4/1-9/30/18)			203 (10/1/18-3/31/19)	
ALL	ALL	ALL		0-1MM	1-3MM	3-5MM	5-10MM	10-25MM	25MM & OVER
190	301	246	**NUMBER OF STATEMENTS**	38	48	38	41	39	42
%	%	%	**ASSETS**	%	%	%	%	%	%
10.2	12.6	11.6	Cash & Equivalents	21.2	10.2	9.7	15.3	7.4	6.7
9.6	10.4	10.4	Trade Receivables (net)	3.5	8.9	12.7	13.7	11.5	12.4
44.9	44.8	39.6	Inventory	29.4	40.3	38.1	41.1	43.3	44.3
2.5	1.6	2.5	All Other Current	3.0	1.9	2.8	1.8	1.8	3.6
67.2	69.5	64.1	Total Current	57.2	61.3	63.3	71.8	64.0	67.0
24.9	22.4	26.0	Fixed Assets (net)	34.3	25.2	26.7	18.2	26.0	26.4
2.4	2.8	3.3	Intangibles (net)	3.0	4.2	4.0	2.6	3.6	2.2
5.5	5.3	6.6	All Other Non-Current	5.6	9.3	6.0	7.4	6.3	4.4
100.0	100.0	100.0	Total	100.0	100.0	100.0	100.0	100.0	100.0
			LIABILITIES						
9.8	9.5	11.2	Notes Payable-Short Term	8.1	9.0	16.9	6.8	14.6	12.3
4.1	2.8	2.4	Cur. Mat.-L.T.D.	2.3	3.3	2.4	2.1	2.6	1.6
12.8	19.7	17.1	Trade Payables	15.5	16.4	18.9	19.7	17.6	14.9
.4	.1	.2	Income Taxes Payable	.2	.3	.1	.2	.2	.3
8.8	9.8	10.7	All Other Current	16.8	16.2	7.0	7.5	6.6	9.4
36.0	42.0	41.6	Total Current	43.0	45.0	45.3	36.3	41.6	38.5
18.4	18.3	23.7	Long-Term Debt	50.0	28.2	20.0	17.1	11.7	15.8
.3	.0	.1	Deferred Taxes	.0	.0	.1	.1	.1	.1
8.8	8.0	7.3	All Other Non-Current	18.5	6.2	6.3	3.2	7.5	3.4
36.5	31.6	27.2	Net Worth	-11.4	20.5	28.3	43.2	39.1	42.2
100.0	100.0	100.0	Total Liabilities & Net Worth	100.0	100.0	100.0	100.0	100.0	100.0
			INCOME DATA						
100.0	100.0	100.0	Net Sales	100.0	100.0	100.0	100.0	100.0	100.0
36.8	35.2	36.6	Gross Profit	44.3	38.1	35.4	36.0	30.7	35.1
32.9	31.0	32.1	Operating Expenses	35.2	33.7	33.4	30.9	27.4	32.0
3.9	4.2	4.5	Operating Profit	9.0	4.4	2.0	5.1	3.3	3.1
.3	.4	.7	All Other Expenses (net)	1.3	1.8	-.2	.4	.4	.5
3.6	3.8	3.7	Profit Before Taxes	7.7	2.5	2.2	4.7	2.9	2.6
			RATIOS						
4.0	3.4	3.3		3.7	3.2	1.9	4.5	2.9	2.9
2.0	1.8	1.7	Current	2.0	1.8	1.5	2.2	1.5	1.8
1.3	1.2	1.1		.8	1.1	1.0	1.4	1.1	1.2
1.2	1.4	1.2		2.7	1.1	1.1	1.9	1.4	1.0
.5	(300) .5	.5	Quick	.5	.4	.5	.9	.4	.5
.2	.2	.2		.1	.1	.1	.4	.1	.1
1 304.0	1 286.9	1 395.3		0 UND	0 921.0	2 159.0	1 255.9	3 119.1	5 75.5
6 62.0	7 49.0	7 48.9	Sales/Receivables	0 UND	8 48.3	5 66.7	13 27.6	13 28.2	16 22.2
23 16.1	23 15.6	23 15.7		6 60.7	21 17.2	22 16.8	30 12.1	27 13.4	33 11.1
56 6.5	44 8.3	39 9.4		0 UND	36 10.0	33 10.9	38 9.5	48 7.6	62 5.9
91 4.0	94 3.9	78 4.7	Cost of Sales/Inventory	64 5.7	99 3.7	64 5.7	73 5.0	96 3.8	94 3.9
146 2.5	166 2.2	146 2.5		166 2.2	182 2.0	114 3.2	146 2.5	140 2.6	159 2.3
8 47.0	8 46.7	8 47.7		0 UND	4 91.5	9 41.4	10 38.2	12 31.3	17 22.1
20 18.4	27 13.6	25 14.7	Cost of Sales/Payables	0 UND	23 15.8	24 15.3	31 11.9	30 12.3	29 12.5
41 9.0	54 6.7	54 6.8		89 4.1	59 6.2	45 8.2	56 6.5	42 8.6	54 6.8
4.8	5.3	6.0		5.6	5.3	8.8	5.3	6.1	5.1
8.6	9.8	12.4	Sales/Working Capital	17.7	12.2	19.1	8.5	13.3	11.2
19.8	27.9	54.2		-14.8	126.6	112.9	23.0	78.1	19.6
18.5	13.9	13.0		8.3	10.2	12.2	31.7	15.0	18.8
(173) 6.3	(256) 4.3	(209) 3.8	EBIT/Interest	(23) 2.9	(45) 3.4	(33) 3.5	(34) 8.7	(37) 3.6	(37) 4.2
1.9	1.7	1.6		.9	1.4	.3	2.7	2.1	1.6
6.0	6.1	5.4						4.3	8.2
(34) 3.8	(45) 2.6	(39) 2.5	Net Profit + Depr., Dep., Amort./Cur. Mat. L/T/D				(10)	1.6 (17)	2.7
1.6	1.3	1.5						-.5	1.9
.2	.2	.2		.4	.3	.2	.1	.3	.3
.6	.6	.8	Fixed/Worth	1.9	.9	.7	.4	.7	.0
1.8	1.6	2.3		-1.4	90.4	1.7	2.0	1.5	1.4
.5	.7	.8		1.1	.9	.8	.4	.7	.6
1.4	1.7	2.0	Debt/Worth	4.4	3.1	1.4	1.4	2.0	1.8
4.3	6.9	10.9		4.0	NM	15.0	3.7	5.3	3.7
36.4	40.8	50.0		76.0	77.4	49.3	58.5	25.5	31.3
(165) 16.0	(255) 17.5	(203) 19.2	% Profit Before Taxes/Tangible Net Worth	(23) 50.0	(36) 31.8	(33) 9.5	(35) 23.3	(35) 13.5	(41) 17.1
5.6	6.2	6.6		3.6	10.3	.5	9.4	5.8	6.0
13.8	14.4	18.8		33.5	19.5	15.7	21.4	11.7	12.1
7.1	6.1	5.7	% Profit Before Taxes/Total Assets	9.8	6.1	4.5	10.3	4.7	5.0
2.0	1.6	1.5		.0	1.1	-1.0	3.7	2.2	.9
45.6	67.4	42.3		89.8	52.7	49.9	76.6	38.7	23.3
13.5	17.5	15.4	Sales/Net Fixed Assets	8.3	13.7	19.3	26.8	13.7	10.4
6.6	6.9	6.2		3.7	5.5	9.2	12.6	4.9	6.7
3.7	3.8	3.8		3.8	3.5	5.3	4.5	3.6	3.0
2.5	2.6	2.6	Sales/Total Assets	2.2	2.4	3.3	3.3	2.5	2.4
1.8	1.7	1.7		1.3	1.5	2.2	1.8	1.6	1.8
.8	.5	.6		.7	.7	.3	.3	.7	1.1
(141) 1.4	(209) 1.1	(175) 1.6	% Depr., Dep., Amort./Sales	(21) 2.1	(29) 1.7	(28) .9	(25) .5	(33) 1.7	(39) 1.8
2.9	2.2	2.6		3.1	3.0	2.6	2.4	2.6	2.4
1.5	1.1	1.6		6.4	2.8	1.7	1.4	1.0	
(71) 3.0	(114) 2.7	(92) 3.1	% Officers', Directors' Owners' Comp/Sales	(11) 7.9	(23) 4.8	(21) 2.9	(19) 2.5	(12) 1.4	
5.8	5.5	5.4		11.9	6.7	4.1	4.2	3.2	
4514356M	5641032M	4627812M	Net Sales ($)	24090M	86914M	145392M	283855M	596813M	3490748M
2119782M	2483597M	2193872M	Total Assets ($)	12324M	45848M	53391M	116177M	277531M	1688601M

© RMA 2019   M = $ thousand   MM = $ million
See Pages viii through xx for Explanation of Ratios and Data

Current Data Sorted by Assets   Comparative Historical Data

Type of Statement	4/1/14-3/31/15	4/1/15-3/31/16
Unqualified	56	55
Reviewed	57	56
Compiled	131	114
Tax Returns	235	204
Other	282	311

1 6 28 28 **0-500M**	3 19 74 79 96 (4/1-9/30/18) **500M-2MM**	8 21 26 49 108 **2-10MM**	15 19 7 5 73 562 (10/1/18-3/31/19) **10-50MM**	13 23 **50-100MM**	18 2 33 **100-250MM**		4/1/14-3/31/15 **ALL**	4/1/15-3/31/16 **ALL**
63	175	212	119	36	53	**NUMBER OF STATEMENTS**	761	740
%	%	%	%	%	%	**ASSETS**	%	%
13.8	18.6	19.6	15.1	10.7	6.2	Cash & Equivalents	14.7	16.1
2.1	3.3	3.3	4.1	4.3	7.5	Trade Receivables (net)	3.7	4.1
51.2	39.5	26.1	20.2	20.5	23.3	Inventory	32.0	30.3
1.6	2.0	2.0	2.7	3.8	3.9	All Other Current	2.8	2.8
68.6	63.5	51.0	42.0	39.4	40.9	Total Current	53.1	53.3
20.2	24.1	30.6	37.6	40.7	44.4	Fixed Assets (net)	30.7	31.1
3.8	5.5	6.9	9.8	12.1	8.2	Intangibles (net)	5.9	7.1
7.4	7.0	11.6	10.6	7.9	6.5	All Other Non-Current	10.2	8.5
100.0	100.0	100.0	100.0	100.0	100.0	Total	100.0	100.0
						LIABILITIES		
7.0	8.0	1.6	2.3	2.6	4.3	Notes Payable-Short Term	3.3	5.2
1.9	3.3	3.9	3.8	3.7	3.6	Cur. Mat.-L.T.D.	3.3	3.1
17.5	20.3	17.7	15.7	14.5	16.7	Trade Payables	19.1	17.9
.1	.2	.1	.2	.2	.1	Income Taxes Payable	.2	.2
12.6	12.3	8.0	8.6	12.3	12.9	All Other Current	11.9	11.0
39.1	44.1	31.4	30.5	33.3	37.7	Total Current	37.8	37.4
16.4	18.8	22.9	20.7	20.5	26.5	Long-Term Debt	20.7	20.9
.1	.0	.1	.4	.7	.8	Deferred Taxes	.2	.2
21.0	7.4	8.4	7.5	7.3	7.2	All Other Non-Current	9.2	8.2
23.5	29.8	37.2	40.8	38.2	27.9	Net Worth	32.2	33.3
100.0	100.0	100.0	100.0	100.0	100.0	Total Liabilities & Net Worth	100.0	100.0
						INCOME DATA		
100.0	100.0	100.0	100.0	100.0	100.0	Net Sales	100.0	100.0
28.4	26.7	28.3	29.4	29.3	28.8	Gross Profit	26.7	27.3
26.6	25.0	26.2	27.8	27.6	27.9	Operating Expenses	25.4	25.4
1.8	1.7	2.0	1.6	1.8	1.0	Operating Profit	1.4	1.9
-.3	-.8	-.8	-.5	.3	.3	All Other Expenses (net)	-.4	-.4
2.1	2.5	2.8	2.1	1.5	.6	Profit Before Taxes	1.8	2.3
						RATIOS		
5.4	4.4	3.2	2.1	1.8	1.5		2.7	2.8
2.7	2.0	1.8	1.4	1.2	1.0	Current	1.5	1.6
1.2	1.0	1.1	.9	.9	.8		1.0	1.0
1.7	1.4	1.7	1.1	.7	.5		1.0	1.2
(61) .5	(174) .6	.6	.5	.4	.3	Quick	(756) .5	(735) .5
.1	.2	.3	.3	.2	.1		.2	.2
0 UND	0 UND	0 UND	1 496.4	1 427.9	2 192.0		0 UND	0 UND
0 UND	0 999.8	1 544.5	2 176.8	3 138.1	5 74.9	Sales/Receivables	1 462.5	1 440.2
0 999.8	2 209.8	3 134.3	5 67.1	4 83.8	8 45.5		3 120.3	4 102.8
17 21.1	18 20.3	18 20.5	18 20.2	18 20.1	22 16.4		18 20.6	18 20.6
31 11.6	27 13.6	23 15.6	25 14.5	24 15.4	30 12.3	Cost of Sales/Inventory	24 15.0	24 15.1
43 8.4	34 10.7	32 11.3	33 11.2	33 10.9	35 10.4		34 10.6	34 10.6
0 UND	3 129.5	9 40.6	12 30.3	13 27.6	16 22.6		7 48.9	7 53.1
4 85.3	10 37.6	16 22.8	20 18.6	17 21.2	20 18.5	Cost of Sales/Payables	14 25.2	14 25.7
13 29.1	18 20.5	21 17.0	25 14.6	22 16.9	25 14.5		23 15.6	22 16.9
11.9	13.1	14.2	14.8	18.9	26.3		16.4	14.8
20.9	27.4	23.3	36.8	67.1	999.8	Sales/Working Capital	35.8	32.0
87.4	-271.2	260.5	-214.2	-128.3	-46.6		-426.8	999.8
20.3	26.8	20.9	12.4	10.5	5.9		17.3	22.7
(34) 3.5	(120) 8.6	(158) 7.0	(106) 5.8	(32) 3.3	(51) 2.0	EBIT/Interest	(595) 5.5	(576) 6.3
-.2	1.3	2.3	1.3	2.0	.3		1.5	2.1
		7.1	6.7	9.5			5.3	8.2
	(24) 2.0	(35) 3.5	(18) 3.4			Net Profit + Depr., Dep., Amort./Cur. Mat. L/T/D	(98) 2.9	(95) 3.4
		.7	1.5	1.3			1.4	1.7
.1	.2	.3	.6	.8	1.2		.4	.3
.4	.6	.8	1.1	1.4	2.4	Fixed/Worth	1.1	1.0
1.9	5.1	3.4	5.4	3.3	8.0		7.6	4.7
.4	.4	.5	.9	.9	2.2		.6	.6
.9	1.4	1.4	1.7	2.9	4.4	Debt/Worth	1.8	1.8
-33.8	38.1	7.0	9.0	5.6	12.4		18.9	16.9
83.8	64.3	50.9	41.4	56.8	38.2		49.8	64.9
(47) 22.2	(136) 31.1	(174) 22.8	(101) 15.5	(31) 13.3	(44) 14.4	% Profit Before Taxes/Tangible Net Worth	(595) 22.7	(593) 30.2
7.9	10.1	8.0	5.0	4.9	-3.3		6.6	10.2
33.2	25.4	20.5	11.2	7.5	6.4		18.1	20.3
10.2	11.2	10.2	5.2	3.7	3.1	% Profit Before Taxes/Total Assets	7.0	9.2
.0	2.0	2.4	1.2	1.4	-1.4		1.1	2.6
371.7	135.2	43.8	23.1	17.6	13.1		64.3	55.0
51.3	41.2	19.8	11.4	11.3	9.4	Sales/Net Fixed Assets	21.6	21.2
23.0	18.1	9.4	5.6	6.7	6.6		9.4	9.1
11.6	9.4	7.1	5.2	5.1	4.8		8.0	8.0
8.5	7.1	4.9	4.0	4.3	4.1	Sales/Total Assets	5.5	5.4
5.0	5.1	3.4	2.6	3.1	3.7		3.6	3.4
.3	.3	.5	.8	1.2	.7		.4	.5
(38) .6	(119) .6	(170) .9	(114) 1.3	(33) 1.5	(14) 1.6	% Depr., Dep., Amort./Sales	(629) .9	(598) 1.0
1.7	1.2	1.5	1.9	1.8	2.3		1.5	1.6
1.2	.8	.6	.5				.6	.6
(28) 2.6	(80) 1.4	(71) .9	(27) .8			% Officers', Directors' Owners' Comp/Sales	(306) 1.2	(240) 1.3
4.5	2.5	1.8	1.2				2.5	2.8
164167M	1532954M	4917952M	10981087M	11429525M	39493659M	Net Sales ($)	64713293M	66517495M
17899M	209525M	969504M	2697080M	2696047M	9419776M	Total Assets ($)	14814154M	15961913M

M = $ thousand   MM = $ million
See Pages viii through xx for Explanation of Ratios and Data

© RMA 2019

Comparative Historical Data / Current Data Sorted by Sales

			Type of Statement						
53	61	55	Unqualified		1		1	4	49
45	45	45	Reviewed			2	3	10	30
69	64	58	Compiled		5	4	9	21	19
199	181	156	Tax Returns	6	22	19	37	55	17
259	318	344	Other	7	17	29	48	86	157
4/1/16-3/31/17	4/1/17-3/31/18	4/1/18-3/31/19			96 (4/1-9/30/18)			562 (10/1/18-3/31/19)	
ALL	ALL	ALL		0-1MM	1-3MM	3-5MM	5-10MM	10-25MM	25MM & OVER
625	669	658	**NUMBER OF STATEMENTS**	13	45	54	98	176	272
%	%	%	**ASSETS**	%	%	%	%	%	%
16.4	16.2	16.4	Cash & Equivalents	14.2	16.9	15.3	19.0	20.5	13.1
3.8	3.8	3.7	Trade Receivables (net)	.3	1.1	1.2	4.0	4.2	4.4
29.3	28.5	30.5	Inventory	47.7	39.2	37.4	34.9	31.3	24.7
2.1	2.6	2.3	All Other Current	6.3	.2	2.0	2.3	2.3	2.6
51.5	51.1	52.9	Total Current	68.4	57.4	56.0	60.2	58.2	44.8
31.6	30.9	30.8	Fixed Assets (net)	26.3	27.4	25.9	25.0	26.0	37.7
7.2	8.1	7.1	Intangibles (net)	2.9	6.0	6.7	6.3	6.4	8.4
9.6	9.9	9.2	All Other Non-Current	2.5	9.2	11.5	8.6	9.3	9.1
100.0	100.0	100.0	Total	100.0	100.0	100.0	100.0	100.0	100.0
			LIABILITIES						
3.8	4.1	4.2	Notes Payable-Short Term	2.8	8.6	2.5	10.2	3.1	2.5
3.7	3.3	3.5	Cur. Mat.-L.T.D.	.3	1.8	2.9	1.8	4.9	3.8
18.1	18.2	17.8	Trade Payables	1.3	9.1	12.0	10.2	22.5	17.9
.2	.1	.1	Income Taxes Payable	.0	.1	.2	.0	.2	.2
11.7	11.6	10.3	All Other Current	15.5	8.7	13.0	13.4	9.0	9.6
37.5	37.2	36.0	Total Current	19.9	28.3	30.6	43.6	39.6	33.9
22.4	20.9	20.9	Long-Term Debt	18.3	16.4	24.8	19.0	22.6	20.7
.3	.2	.2	Deferred Taxes	.3	.0	.0	.0	.1	.4
7.9	9.1	9.0	All Other Non-Current	49.0	13.5	5.2	6.3	7.5	9.1
31.9	32.6	33.9	Net Worth	12.5	41.9	39.5	31.0	30.2	35.9
100.0	100.0	100.0	Total Liabilties & Net Worth	100.0	100.0	100.0	100.0	100.0	100.0
			INCOME DATA						
100.0	100.0	100.0	Net Sales	100.0	100.0	100.0	100.0	100.0	100.0
28.7	28.8	28.2	Gross Profit	28.6	32.9	25.7	27.6	27.7	28.4
26.8	27.2	26.4	Operating Expenses	26.9	29.6	23.2	25.4	26.4	26.9
1.8	1.6	1.7	Operating Profit	1.7	3.3	2.4	2.2	1.4	1.5
-.3	-.4	-.5	All Other Expenses (net)	.4	-.5	-.3	-1.1	-.9	-.2
2.1	2.0	2.3	Profit Before Taxes	1.3	3.8	2.7	3.3	2.2	1.7
			RATIOS						
2.8	2.8	2.9		13.9	6.1	4.8	5.3	3.1	2.0
1.6	1.6	1.6	Current	5.7	2.9	2.2	2.1	1.8	1.3
1.0	.9	1.0		2.4	1.2	1.1	.9	1.1	.9
1.3	1.3	1.3		2.7	3.0	1.6	2.5	1.5	.8
(624) .5	(668) .5	(655) .5	Quick	.7	1.0	(52) .5	(97) .7	.6	.4
.2	.2	.2		.3	.2	.2	.2	.3	.2
0 UND	0 UND	0 UND		0 UND	0 UND	0 UND	0 UND	0 UND	1 646.1
1 475.6	1 391.5	1 431.9	Sales/Receivables	0 UND	0 UND	0 UND	0 999.3	1 639.4	2 180.7
4 101.5	4 99.3	3 109.0		0 UND	0 UND	1 557.6	4 102.6	3 142.4	5 72.4
18 20.1	18 20.2	18 19.9		22 16.7	16 22.2	22 16.3	22 16.7	17 21.0	18 20.1
26 14.3	25 14.7	25 14.5	Cost of Sales/Inventory	51 7.1	32 11.4	32 11.5	27 13.7	22 16.4	24 15.0
35 10.4	34 10.6	34 10.8		96 3.8	46 8.0	43 8.4	32 11.3	31 11.6	33 11.2
7 50.6	7 53.1	7 50.9		0 UND	0 UND	0 UND	4 92.1	9 39.3	11 31.9
15 24.3	16 22.9	15 24.6	Cost of Sales/Payables	0 UND	5 78.2	7 52.8	11 32.2	16 23.0	18 20.1
22 16.5	23 16.0	22 16.8		2 188.7	12 31.0	13 27.6	18 20.4	22 16.7	24 14.9
13.0	13.2	14.6		6.1	11.0	11.5	9.6	14.7	19.4
33.5	32.6	29.6	Sales/Working Capital	10.6	17.3	25.6	21.4	25.5	43.4
-351.5	-128.8	-338.5		17.7	71.4	212.6	-207.4	276.3	-113.7
18.5	17.6	18.1			25.5	14.7	23.6	27.3	11.7
(503) 5.3	(517) 5.3	(501) 5.6	EBIT/Interest	(33) 7.0	(31) 3.9	(66) 7.8	(132) 9.1	(233) 4.2	
1.3	1.1	1.3			1.9	.6	2.0	1.1	1.2
6.9	4.7	7.3						9.6	8.3
(85) 3.2	(93) 2.7	(91) 3.3	Net Profit + Depr., Dep., Amort./Cur. Mat. L/T/D				(20) 2.3	(60) 3.4	
1.6	1.6	1.4						.7	1.5
.4	.4	.3		.2	.1	.2	.2	.3	.7
1.1	1.1	.9	Fixed/Worth	.4	.5	.6	.6	.7	1.4
6.9	13.1	4.3		.0	3.0	3.7	NM	2.8	5.4
.6	.6	.6		.3	.3	.3	.3	.6	.9
1.9	1.8	1.8	Debt/Worth	.8	.7	1.2	1.3	1.4	2.4
20.8	39.7	10.1		5.3	5.1	9.8	-21.8	8.3	9.7
49.6	47.8	56.5	% Profit Before Taxes/Tangible Net Worth	75.1	64.7	77.3	49.8	55.7	54.5
(485) 22.6	(513) 19.8	(533) 21.8		(12) 10.0	(37) 23.1	(44) 31.5	(72) 29.4	(140) 23.0	(228) 16.7
7.4	6.1	6.5		5.9	10.9	9.5	11.0	8.2	5.0
18.1	17.8	18.9		11.3	26.1	26.6	24.3	22.8	11.9
7.4	6.9	7.6	% Profit Before Taxes/Total Assets	5.3	13.5	10.0	11.0	10.3	5.2
1.2	.9	1.6		1.2	3.1	1.8	2.0	1.7	1.3
57.4	51.3	48.8		124.3	136.3	69.1	143.9	84.9	23.7
18.6	19.3	19.8	Sales/Net Fixed Assets	27.9	30.9	29.5	32.0	28.8	13.2
8.4	8.7	9.5		10.0	9.7	10.7	14.3	13.7	7.8
7.4	7.4	7.6		8.2	8.5	8.0	8.3	9.0	6.1
4.9	4.9	5.1	Sales/Total Assets	3.6	5.4	5.5	5.9	6.0	4.5
3.2	3.4	3.6		2.4	3.2	3.1	3.6	4.2	3.3
.5	.5	.5			.4	.4	.2	.5	.7
(496) 1.0	(526) 1.0	(488) .9	% Depr., Dep., Amort./Sales	(29) .9	(41) .9	(67) .7	(133) .8	(211) 1.2	
1.7	1.7	1.6		2.4	1.5	1.4	1.4	1.7	
.8	.6	.7		1.6	1.2	.8	.6	.5	
(227) 1.5	(229) 1.1	(213) 1.2	% Officers', Directors' Owners' Comp/Sales	(22) 2.7	(18) 1.6	(37) 1.4	(73) 1.0	(57) .8	
3.2	2.5	2.3		5.1	2.1	2.1	2.1	1.2	
61011992M	62755080M	68519344M	Net Sales ($)	8189M	90902M	223944M	733965M	2825207M	64637137M
14459266M	15290979M	16009831M	Total Assets ($)	2468M	29529M	55055M	193553M	577224M	15152002M

© RMA 2019

M = $ thousand   MM = $ million
See Pages viii through xx for Explanation of Ratios and Data

Current Data Sorted by Assets · Comparative Historical Data

0-500M	500M-2MM	2-10MM	10-50MM	50-100MM	100-250MM	Type of Statement	4/1/14-3/31/15 ALL	4/1/15-3/31/16 ALL
		1	5	2	2	Unqualified	9	7
1	1	2	1			Reviewed	14	12
3	4	1	1			Compiled	16	24
47	21	12	1		2	Tax Returns	109	130
26	14	10	7		3	Other	53	50
	12 (4/1-9/30/18)			154 (10/1/18-3/31/19)				
77	**40**	**26**	**14**	**2**	**7**	**NUMBER OF STATEMENTS**	**201**	**223**
%	%	%	%	%	%	**ASSETS**	%	%
24.8	15.6	8.9	7.7			Cash & Equivalents	16.8	16.5
2.3	1.2	3.2	4.0			Trade Receivables (net)	2.3	3.2
41.4	23.8	15.8	16.3			Inventory	32.4	28.2
1.4	2.0	3.3	2.8			All Other Current	2.0	1.4
69.9	42.6	31.2	30.8			Total Current	53.5	49.2
15.7	35.8	56.8	60.2			Fixed Assets (net)	34.6	34.2
11.3	10.6	4.3	3.6			Intangibles (net)	6.2	8.1
3.1	10.9	7.7	5.4			All Other Non-Current	5.6	8.5
100.0	100.0	100.0	100.0			Total	100.0	100.0
						LIABILITIES		
10.3	4.9	2.3	2.3			Notes Payable-Short Term	8.2	10.1
.7	.7	1.2	3.7			Cur. Mat.-L.T.D.	2.5	2.5
9.9	8.8	8.4	11.7			Trade Payables	11.7	10.2
.7	.0	.0	.0			Income Taxes Payable	.1	.2
15.5	9.9	23.5	6.2			All Other Current	12.3	13.4
37.1	24.2	35.3	23.9			Total Current	34.8	36.4
9.6	18.1	38.4	27.8			Long-Term Debt	23.3	22.5
.0	.0	.3	.4			Deferred Taxes	.3	.3
8.2	10.9	10.2	8.8			All Other Non-Current	10.4	13.3
45.1	46.7	15.8	39.2			Net Worth	31.1	27.5
100.0	100.0	100.0	100.0			Total Liabilties & Net Worth	100.0	100.0
						INCOME DATA		
100.0	100.0	100.0	100.0			Net Sales	100.0	100.0
23.4	19.8	20.3	19.1			Gross Profit	17.9	21.8
21.5	16.9	17.5	16.7			Operating Expenses	16.8	21.1
1.8	2.9	2.8	2.4			Operating Profit	1.1	.7
-1.2	-1.6	-.1	.6			All Other Expenses (net)	-.6	-.7
3.0	4.6	2.9	1.8			Profit Before Taxes	1.7	1.5
						RATIOS		
9.5	7.1	3.6	3.0				4.7	6.1
2.5	2.5	2.2	1.3			Current	1.9	1.8
1.2	1.3	.7	.8				.9	.9
3.1	2.9	1.6	2.1				1.4	2.0
.9	.5	.6	.4			Quick	(200) .5	(222) .6
.2	.2	.2	.2				.2	.2
0 UND	0 UND	0 UND	1 429.8				0 UND	0 UND
0 UND	0 UND	0 999.8	3 110.5			Sales/Receivables	0 UND	0 UND
0 UND	0 863.6	2 181.1	5 68.7				1 305.9	2 238.9
9 41.8	9 42.3	10 36.9	10 37.5				7 53.3	8 44.9
16 22.5	16 22.8	16 22.5	12 29.3			Cost of Sales/Inventory	13 29.1	17 21.1
27 13.3	43 8.4	24 14.9	39 9.4				26 13.8	35 10.5
0 UND	0 816.0	0 UND	8 44.3				0 UND	0 UND
0 UND	6 57.7	6 62.2	11 32.6			Cost of Sales/Payables	4 86.1	5 75.9
5 74.1	13 28.4	10 34.9	19 19.6				9 40.0	12 31.3
14.6	11.1	17.7	10.5				17.4	13.4
37.6	26.9	34.5	90.7			Sales/Working Capital	63.7	38.0
153.4	90.7	-62.8	-92.6				-396.3	-133.8
31.5	27.2	9.1	7.2				10.8	10.0
(38) 11.5	(22) 4.5	(21) 4.1	(13) 3.2			EBIT/Interest	(133) 3.8	(131) 3.4
1.6	1.7	2.1	1.6				1.3	1.5
							5.2	7.9
						Net Profit + Depr., Dep., Amort./Cur. Mat. L/T/D	(12) 2.5	(15) 1.6
							1.0	1.1
.0	.2	1.4	1.1				.2	.2
.3	.9	4.5	1.9			Fixed/Worth	1.0	1.4
1.3	2.6	-12.5	3.1				8.5	-18.9
.2	.2	1.6	.9				.5	.6
1.4	1.1	4.4	1.8			Debt/Worth	2.3	2.6
7.0	3.9	-26.3	4.1				267.8	-24.1
212.2	60.1	57.1	27.2				62.2	70.6
(64) 63.0	(33) 23.3	(18) 37.5	(13) 11.4			% Profit Before Taxes/Tangible Net Worth	(153) 27.5	(159) 28.8
17.2	14.7	19.1	5.4				6.0	6.9
42.8	26.3	11.9	8.5				20.7	19.2
21.7	12.5	7.7	4.5			% Profit Before Taxes/Total Assets	7.1	7.1
3.8	5.2	2.8	1.8				1.7	1.3
UND	140.1	25.6	16.0				226.3	144.1
272.0	18.4	6.5	6.7			Sales/Net Fixed Assets	33.9	19.8
29.7	5.4	2.0	2.3				7.9	6.2
19.8	7.3	7.2	6.6				13.5	10.4
10.2	4.0	3.3	3.7			Sales/Total Assets	7.2	4.9
5.2	2.1	1.5	1.6				3.6	2.5
.2	.4	.7	.4				.3	.3
(34) .4	(28) .7	(17) 1.1	(11) 1.5			% Depr., Dep., Amort./Sales	(134) .8	(165) 1.0
1.1	1.6	2.3	2.0				1.7	2.3
1.1	.8						.9	.7
(36) 1.9	(20) 1.4					% Officers', Directors' Owners' Comp/Sales	(78) 2.0	(101) 1.8
2.8	2.4						3.3	3.2
174262M	221694M	489283M	1282850M	683686M	4154294M	Net Sales ($)	12097096M	8580223M
15306M	41262M	99252M	315486M	136938M	1095532M	Total Assets ($)	2031625M	1806429M

M = $ thousand   MM = $ million
See Pages viii through xx for Explanation of Ratios and Data

Comparative Historical Data | Current Data Sorted by Sales

	4/1/16-3/31/17 ALL	4/1/17-3/31/18 ALL	4/1/18-3/31/19 ALL	Type of Statement	0-1MM	1-3MM	3-5MM	5-10MM	10-25MM	25MM & OVER
	2	4	5	Unqualified			1	1	1	5
	12	6	9	Reviewed						6
	12	8	9	Compiled		3	3		2	1
	110	107	83	Tax Returns	16	32	14	10	6	5
	50	58	60	Other	8	18	10	8	3	13
					24 12 (4/1-9/30/18)	53	28 154 (10/1/18-3/31/19)	21	10	30
	186	183	166	NUMBER OF STATEMENTS	24	53	28	21	10	30
	%	%	%	**ASSETS**	%	%	%	%	%	%
	15.0	15.5	18.0	Cash & Equivalents	23.2	22.0	14.5	14.2	24.1	10.6
	3.3	2.1	2.3	Trade Receivables (net)	.0	2.7	.9	1.2	3.1	5.5
	31.0	34.6	29.5	Inventory	27.1	35.3	37.8	23.3	25.1	19.2
	2.1	1.4	2.0	All Other Current	.2	1.8	2.4	3.9	.5	2.7
	51.3	53.6	51.8	Total Current	50.5	61.8	55.5	42.5	52.8	38.0
	33.8	30.0	32.4	Fixed Assets (net)	28.2	21.8	30.4	38.9	44.8	47.4
	8.1	8.6	9.9	Intangibles (net)	18.3	12.3	2.5	10.4	1.4	8.3
	6.7	7.8	5.9	All Other Non-Current	2.9	4.0	11.5	8.1	.9	6.3
	100.0	100.0	100.0	Total	100.0	100.0	100.0	100.0	100.0	100.0
				LIABILITIES						
	7.0	10.1	6.5	Notes Payable-Short Term	9.1	9.8	4.2	6.3	5.0	1.5
	2.7	1.6	1.2	Cur. Mat.-L.T.D.	.6	.3	.8	1.5	1.6	3.2
	11.3	10.0	10.1	Trade Payables	3.1	7.0	13.8	10.5	11.2	17.1
	.1	.3	.4	Income Taxes Payable	.0	.7	.8	.0	.0	.0
	8.6	13.4	14.1	All Other Current	15.9	11.7	11.2	31.2	4.4	10.7
	29.7	35.3	32.3	Total Current	28.8	29.4	30.7	49.7	22.2	32.6
	26.9	20.8	18.6	Long-Term Debt	19.1	11.3	23.8	21.8	27.5	21.0
	.2	.1	.1	Deferred Taxes	.0	.0	.0	.0	.0	.8
	8.3	10.0	9.3	All Other Non-Current	5.8	11.4	9.4	8.2	2.3	11.6
	34.9	33.8	39.7	Net Worth	46.4	47.8	36.1	20.3	48.0	33.9
	100.0	100.0	100.0	Total Liabilities & Net Worth	100.0	100.0	100.0	100.0	100.0	100.0
				INCOME DATA						
	100.0	100.0	100.0	Net Sales	100.0	100.0	100.0	100.0	100.0	100.0
	19.5	20.9	21.4	Gross Profit	30.9	24.5	16.7	18.2	16.3	16.6
	17.5	19.6	19.0	Operating Expenses	28.0	22.0	13.4	17.0	14.7	14.8
	2.0	1.3	2.4	Operating Profit	2.9	2.5	3.3	1.2	1.6	1.8
	-.6	-.9	-.9	All Other Expenses (net)	-1.6	-1.8	-.7	.0	.3	.0
	2.7	2.2	3.2	Profit Before Taxes	4.5	4.3	4.0	1.1	1.3	1.8
				RATIOS						
	4.8	5.0	5.4	Current	11.6	10.8	3.3	4.8	5.1	2.2
	2.0	1.8	2.2		3.3	3.3	2.1	2.3	2.4	1.2
	1.2	1.1	1.1		1.0	1.4	1.2	.7	1.6	.8
	1.4	2.0	2.2	Quick	3.9	3.9	.9	2.7	2.6	1.1
	.5	(180) .6	.7		.8	1.2	.4	.4	1.2	.5
	.2	.2	.2		.2	.2	.2	.1	.5	.3
	0 UND	0 UND	0 UND	Sales/Receivables	0 UND	0 UND	0 UND	0 UND	0 UND	2 243.2
	0 UND	0 UND	0 UND		0 UND	0 UND	0 UND	0 UND	1 432.5	3 129.7
	1 254.6	1 504.7	1 332.2		0 UND	0 UND	0 UND	1 476.8	2 212.2	4 83.6
	9 42.4	10 36.9	9 39.3	Cost of Sales/Inventory	24 14.9	11 32.2	7 54.9	6 57.4	5 76.6	10 37.5
	15 24.6	17 21.0	16 23.5		33 11.0	17 21.1	12 30.9	10 36.9	14 26.0	12 31.7
	25 14.4	32 11.4	27 13.6		63 5.8	27 13.5	19 19.0	24 14.9	26 14.1	19 19.1
	0 UND	0 UND	0 UND	Cost of Sales/Payables	0 UND	0 UND	0 UND	0 UND	0 UND	2 148.0
	4 87.3	3 108.1	4 97.8		0 UND	0 821.0	5 80.0	4 98.4	9 42.3	7 54.7
	11 34.5	11 32.3	11 34.4		0 UND	6 63.6	10 36.6	11 34.6	11 33.9	16 22.8
	16.6	14.1	15.1	Sales/Working Capital	8.7	10.2	28.2	18.3	12.8	35.5
	39.9	40.6	38.1		18.5	24.1	51.5	40.7	22.5	94.8
	172.5	365.2	240.7		UND	86.1	130.7	-288.6	NM	-100.0
	9.0	10.6	16.3	EBIT/Interest	6.7	28.3	18.9	59.3		11.0
	(115) 3.5	(103) 4.0	(102) 5.3		(10) 2.2	(26) 9.0	(17) 6.4	(16) 10.6		(27) 4.1
	1.9	1.6	1.9		-3.7	2.2	2.7	3.6		2.0
	6.1			Net Profit + Depr., Dep., Amort./Cur. Mat. L/T/D						
	(10) 2.0									
	1.0									
	.2	.0	.1	Fixed/Worth	.0	.0	.0	.5	.1	1.1
	1.2	.8	.9		1.0	.5	.8	1.3	1.6	1.9
	7.1	3.5	3.9		UND	1.9	3.2	-10.6	4.2	NM
	.5	.6	.4	Debt/Worth	.1	.2	.9	.7	.2	1.1
	1.8	1.9	1.7		1.2	1.5	2.2	1.7	1.2	2.3
	33.1	9.0	7.3		UND	5.3	5.0	-5.9	4.7	NM
	78.6	77.4	90.4	% Profit Before Taxes/Tangible Net Worth	69.6	153.4	108.4	84.7		54.1
	(146) 30.7	(146) 28.0	(134) 35.9		(19) 34.1	(44) 35.2	(25) 61.1	(14) 51.4		(23) 22.8
	10.4	10.6	13.7		8.6	14.8	31.6	21.8		8.1
	25.7	28.4	28.9	% Profit Before Taxes/Total Assets	20.9	33.9	44.1	31.0	39.0	11.0
	9.2	9.2	10.8		8.0	13.8	15.8	17.9	5.1	6.4
	3.2	2.4	3.4		-.8	4.4	8.8	7.2	-.1	2.1
	196.9	999.8	558.0	Sales/Net Fixed Assets	730.8	UND	803.3	110.6	UND	20.7
	30.9	37.4	24.4		31.2	74.8	98.3	19.5	9.5	12.4
	6.5	7.3	6.1		5.9	16.9	5.0	4.6	5.1	5.6
	12.4	13.1	11.6	Sales/Total Assets	5.5	14.5	28.1	9.4	12.6	8.1
	6.0	6.3	5.7		3.4	7.6	7.7	6.7	7.1	5.0
	3.1	3.2	2.9		1.5	3.2	2.3	3.3	3.2	3.5
	.3	.3	.4	% Depr., Dep., Amort./Sales	.3	.3	.1	.3		.8
	(131) 1.0	(103) .8	(97) .8		(12) 1.3	(24) .7	(18) .6	(15) .5		(22) 1.1
	1.8	1.6	1.7		2.2	1.4	1.3	1.7		1.8
	.9	.9	.8	% Officers', Directors' Owners' Comp/Sales	1.8	1.3	.9			
	(82) 1.8	(78) 1.9	(70) 1.6		(11) 2.9	(23) 2.2	(18) 1.2			
	3.2	3.8	2.6		4.8	2.7	1.8			
	6262155M	5504233M	7006069M	Net Sales ($)	14925M	97983M	109336M	143925M	154905M	6484995M
	1425707M	1205945M	1703776M	Total Assets ($)	6848M	27445M	26125M	32777M	41788M	1568793M

M = $ thousand   MM = $ million
See Pages viii through xx for Explanation of Ratios and Data

Current Data Sorted by Assets   Comparative Historical Data

						Type of Statement	3	3
						Unqualified		
						Reviewed	1	2
		2				Compiled	9	11
9	4	1				Tax Returns	32	21
4	4	1				Other	18	21
	5 (4/1-9/30/18)		25 (10/1/18-3/31/19)	1	4		4/1/14-3/31/15	4/1/15-3/31/16
0-500M	500M-2MM	2-10MM	10-50MM	50-100MM	100-250MM		ALL	ALL
13	8	4		1	4	NUMBER OF STATEMENTS	63	58
%	%	%	%	%	%	**ASSETS**	%	%
21.3						Cash & Equivalents	16.3	18.2
2.8						Trade Receivables (net)	6.2	10.5
24.1						Inventory	20.1	22.7
11.8		D				All Other Current	1.9	.9
60.0		A				Total Current	44.5	52.4
35.7		T				Fixed Assets (net)	34.0	32.1
2.7		A				Intangibles (net)	14.1	9.7
1.6		N				All Other Non-Current	7.4	5.9
100.0		O				Total	100.0	100.0
		T				**LIABILITIES**		
12.3						Notes Payable-Short Term	14.4	14.3
4.4		A				Cur. Mat.-L.T.D.	2.5	3.6
8.3		V				Trade Payables	16.7	13.1
.0		A				Income Taxes Payable	.1	.1
36.7		I				All Other Current	12.5	9.3
61.6		L				Total Current	46.3	40.4
27.7		A				Long-Term Debt	18.0	19.4
.0		B				Deferred Taxes	.0	.0
12.5		L				All Other Non-Current	19.5	14.7
-1.9		E				Net Worth	16.3	25.6
100.0						Total Liabilities & Net Worth	100.0	100.0
						INCOME DATA		
100.0						Net Sales	100.0	100.0
42.1						Gross Profit	33.5	30.7
39.6						Operating Expenses	31.8	26.5
2.5						Operating Profit	1.7	4.2
.6						All Other Expenses (net)	.8	.7
1.9						Profit Before Taxes	.9	3.5
						RATIOS		
8.1							2.3	2.8
1.4						Current	1.1	1.6
.5							.4	.9
1.8							1.5	1.7
.8						Quick	(62) .5	.8
.2							.1	.2
0 UND							0 UND	0 UND
0 UND						Sales/Receivables	0 UND	1 551.6
1 253.6							4 89.3	11 33.5
5 71.4							7 49.1	6 63.0
12 29.5						Cost of Sales/Inventory	15 24.1	12 29.7
20 18.3							36 10.0	31 11.7
0 UND							0 UND	0 UND
0 UND						Cost of Sales/Payables	9 41.3	9 40.2
14 25.4							28 12.9	20 18.1
23.4							20.4	18.7
44.7						Sales/Working Capital	86.3	35.3
-24.2							-15.8	-82.9
							9.0	28.9
						EBIT/Interest	(47) 2.7	(45) 6.5
							-.2	2.5
						Net Profit + Depr., Dep., Amort./Cur. Mat. L/T/D		
.2							.3	.2
UND						Fixed/Worth	2.0	1.4
-1.4							-1.7	-31.2
.3							.7	.7
UND						Debt/Worth	3.9	2.4
-3.4							-3.4	-47.5
						% Profit Before Taxes/Tangible Net Worth	68.1	67.8
							(36) 15.4	(42) 35.8
							1.9	12.2
21.2							15.0	25.6
5.7						% Profit Before Taxes/Total Assets	6.9	12.0
-15.4							-1.4	4.4
80.7							84.2	131.8
36.6						Sales/Net Fixed Assets	18.3	19.1
6.4							7.3	8.3
12.8							8.4	7.8
7.4						Sales/Total Assets	4.9	5.2
4.1							2.7	3.5
							.6	.4
						% Depr., Dep., Amort./Sales	(46) 1.2	(42) 1.1
							2.0	2.0
							1.9	.8
						% Officers', Directors' Owners' Comp/Sales	(29) 3.9	(21) 1.5
							6.2	3.8
22674M	27170M	53229M		172290M	1392527M	Net Sales ($)	1357085M	1555603M
2823M	7130M	13614M		74437M	636084M	Total Assets ($)	553519M	656444M

M = $ thousand   MM = $ million

See Pages viii through xx for Explanation of Ratios and Data

Comparative Historical Data / Current Data Sorted by Sales

Type of Statement									
2	**1**		Unqualified					1	1
	1		Reviewed						
6	**4**	**2**	Compiled						
13	**15**	**14**	Tax Returns	3	7	2	2		
13	**18**	**14**	Other	3	2	4			5
4/1/16-3/31/17	4/1/17-3/31/18	4/1/18-3/31/19		5 (4/1-9/30/18)			25 (10/1/18-3/31/19)		
ALL	ALL	ALL		0-1MM	1-3MM	3-5MM	5-10MM	10-25MM	25MM & OVER
34	39	30	**NUMBER OF STATEMENTS**	6	9	6	2	1	6
%	%	%	**ASSETS**	%	%	%	%	%	%
23.1	20.6	20.2	Cash & Equivalents						
8.3	9.2	5.6	Trade Receivables (net)						
17.1	20.9	16.7	Inventory						
2.4	4.8	7.4	All Other Current						
51.0	55.5	50.0	Total Current						
29.8	28.3	35.1	Fixed Assets (net)						
11.2	7.5	10.8	Intangibles (net)						
8.0	8.7	4.2	All Other Non-Current						
100.0	100.0	100.0	Total						
			LIABILITIES						
6.6	8.3	7.4	Notes Payable-Short Term						
3.6	2.6	2.8	Cur. Mat.-L.T.D.						
12.5	8.8	9.4	Trade Payables						
.2	.1	.0	Income Taxes Payable						
9.4	12.2	25.3	All Other Current						
32.3	32.0	44.9	Total Current						
23.5	22.0	28.2	Long-Term Debt						
.1	.1	.4	Deferred Taxes						
9.6	8.3	6.7	All Other Non-Current						
34.5	37.7	19.9	Net Worth						
100.0	100.0	100.0	Total Liabilties & Net Worth						
			INCOME DATA						
100.0	100.0	100.0	Net Sales						
38.4	39.1	42.5	Gross Profit						
34.5	36.7	38.7	Operating Expenses						
3.9	2.4	3.9	Operating Profit						
.4	.4	1.5	All Other Expenses (net)						
3.5	2.1	2.4	Profit Before Taxes						
			RATIOS						
6.5	6.3	3.5							
2.0	2.6	1.4	Current						
.8	.8	.8							
2.9	3.2	1.7							
1.2	.8	1.0	Quick						
.2	.3	.2							
0 UND	0 UND	0 UND							
2 186.0	3 112.9	1 295.8	Sales/Receivables						
12 30.9	15 25.0	8 45.8							
9 39.0	8 44.9	7 49.0							
22 16.8	21 17.2	19 19.2	Cost of Sales/Inventory						
33 11.2	35 10.5	27 13.6							
0 UND	1 301.5	0 UND							
9 39.7	9 39.7	7 53.9	Cost of Sales/Payables						
22 16.9	24 15.1	25 14.4							
9.2	9.0	18.0							
23.3	20.2	40.2	Sales/Working Capital						
-59.2	-55.3	-42.0							
20.0	36.4	21.4							
(27) 7.4	(28) 11.3	(20) 4.0	EBIT/Interest						
1.3	.0	1.9							
			Net Profit + Depr., Dep., Amort./Cur. Mat. L/T/D						
.4	.1	.5							
1.0	.6	1.8	Fixed/Worth						
5.5	2.3	-1.8							
.6	.5	.7							
2.1	1.4	7.1	Debt/Worth						
15.3	4.7	-6.1							
96.4	58.3	119.4							
(27) 48.1	(34) 24.2	(20) 31.4	% Profit Before Taxes/Tangible Net Worth						
9.8	2.1	8.5							
23.4	24.0	13.1							
10.7	9.7	8.8	% Profit Before Taxes/Total Assets						
1.0	.4	3.0							
46.4	263.9	59.4							
15.8	19.6	12.5	Sales/Net Fixed Assets						
7.1	6.9	6.1							
7.0	7.7	7.6							
4.6	4.5	5.1	Sales/Total Assets						
2.2	1.9	2.1							
.8	.8	.7							
(19) 1.6	(20) 1.6	(17) 1.6	% Depr., Dep., Amort./Sales						
2.2	3.4	3.1							
2.6	1.0	2.0							
(16) 4.3	(16) 3.4	(16) 5.1	% Officers', Directors' Owners' Comp/Sales						
6.3	5.3	7.9							
2424152M	1826914M	1667890M	Net Sales ($)	3756M	18682M	22802M	13593M	16377M	1592680M
1072506M	922883M	734088M	Total Assets ($)	1847M	9214M	3570M	3160M	2363M	713934M

© RMA 2019

M = $ thousand   MM = $ million
See Pages viii through xx for Explanation of Ratios and Data

Current Data Sorted by Assets   Comparative Historical Data

0-500M	500M-2MM	2-10MM	10-50MM	50-100MM	100-250MM	Type of Statement	4/1/14-3/31/15 ALL	4/1/15-3/31/16 ALL
						Unqualified		
	1	2	2			Reviewed	1	1
		3	2			Compiled	4	4
1	6	2	1			Tax Returns	9	9
3	1	5	4			Other	14	17
							14	14
4	8	12	9			**NUMBER OF STATEMENTS**	42	45
%	%	%	%	%	%	**ASSETS**	%	%
		24.0		D	D	Cash & Equivalents	13.9	14.1
		27.1		A	A	Trade Receivables (net)	21.2	17.6
		11.9		T	T	Inventory	16.4	20.7
		1.4		A	A	All Other Current	4.9	2.9
		64.3				Total Current	56.5	55.4
		14.9		N	N	Fixed Assets (net)	30.4	30.9
		6.9		O	O	Intangibles (net)	6.6	5.1
		13.9		T	T	All Other Non-Current	6.7	8.7
		100.0				Total	100.0	100.0
				A	A	**LIABILITIES**		
		.8		V	V	Notes Payable-Short Term	3.2	7.1
		.7		A	A	Cur. Mat.-L.T.D.	1.4	2.1
		23.9		I	I	Trade Payables	22.8	22.7
		.0		L	L	Income Taxes Payable	.1	.0
		16.1		A	A	All Other Current	24.6	13.4
		41.6		B	B	Total Current	52.2	45.4
		17.2		L	L	Long-Term Debt	17.1	14.6
		.0		E	E	Deferred Taxes	.4	.2
		.0				All Other Non-Current	1.8	12.7
		41.1				Net Worth	28.4	27.0
		100.0				Total Liabilities & Net Worth	100.0	100.0
						INCOME DATA		
		100.0				Net Sales	100.0	100.0
		26.0				Gross Profit	28.9	29.6
		22.4				Operating Expenses	24.7	25.3
		3.7				Operating Profit	4.2	4.3
		.1				All Other Expenses (net)	-.2	.9
		3.5				Profit Before Taxes	4.4	3.4
						RATIOS		
		2.7					2.2	1.8
		1.8				Current	1.3	1.2
		1.1					1.0	.9
		2.1					1.3	1.1
		1.1				Quick	.8	.8
		.6					.3	.3
	0	884.2					0 UND	0 UND
	3	125.5				Sales/Receivables	3 126.3	1 607.1
	32	11.5					24 15.3	20 18.6
	3	116.1					4 82.3	5 74.1
	8	47.2				Cost of Sales/Inventory	8 43.2	11 32.8
	13	29.1					21 17.8	20 17.9
	6	56.2					7 51.5	3 123.1
	13	27.9				Cost of Sales/Payables	14 25.6	16 23.0
	26	14.0					30 12.3	24 15.5
		14.1					19.8	22.9
		25.8				Sales/Working Capital	43.3	80.2
		149.7					-281.1	-123.8
							39.5	45.4
						EBIT/Interest	(30) 8.2	(34) 13.3
							1.7	2.5
						Net Profit + Depr., Dep., Amort./Cur. Mat. L/T/D		
		.2					.3	.3
		.4				Fixed/Worth	.7	.8
		NM					3.0	UND
		.4					.7	.8
		1.0				Debt/Worth	1.6	2.2
		NM					7.0	UND
							66.4	80.6
						% Profit Before Taxes/Tangible Net Worth	(35) 33.3	(35) 48.0
							6.0	25.1
		30.8					27.3	28.7
		20.8				% Profit Before Taxes/Total Assets	13.2	14.6
		1.8					1.1	4.7
		282.9					93.5	108.4
		49.6				Sales/Net Fixed Assets	22.0	33.2
		19.2					10.7	14.5
		8.7					9.7	10.6
		7.0				Sales/Total Assets	6.2	7.1
		4.2					3.4	4.6
							.5	.2
						% Depr., Dep., Amort./Sales	(29) .8	(34) .6
							1.3	1.3
							1.5	1.9
						% Officers', Directors' Owners' Comp/Sales	(24) 2.6	(20) 2.7
							5.1	4.3
6299M	64476M	435221M	670303M			Net Sales ($)	1507366M	1795749M
738M	8131M	53642M	177957M			Total Assets ($)	477228M	480339M

Comparative Historical Data · Current Data Sorted by Sales

Type of Statement

4/1/16-3/31/17 ALL	4/1/17-3/31/18 ALL	4/1/18-3/31/19 ALL	Type of Statement	0-1MM	1-3MM	3-5MM	5-10MM	10-25MM	25MM & OVER
1	2		Unqualified						
3	2	5	Reviewed					1	4
9	8	5	Compiled					2	3
14	10	10	Tax Returns					3	1
13	18	13	Other	1	3	5	2	2	6
					6 (4/1-9/30/18)			27 (10/1/18-3/31/19)	
40	38	33	NUMBER OF STATEMENTS	1	3	5	2	8	14

Assets

%	%	%	ASSETS	%	%	%	%	%	%
21.9	13.3	16.9	Cash & Equivalents						20.3
16.9	20.6	20.8	Trade Receivables (net)						28.9
20.5	20.3	16.4	Inventory						13.6
.9	2.6	1.6	All Other Current						2.6
60.1	56.8	55.7	Total Current						65.4
28.2	33.7	30.6	Fixed Assets (net)						24.0
5.9	4.9	5.7	Intangibles (net)						5.2
5.8	4.7	8.0	All Other Non-Current						5.4
100.0	100.0	100.0	Total						100.0

Liabilities

			LIABILITIES						
9.9	9.3	2.8	Notes Payable-Short Term						3.2
2.8	1.7	3.2	Cur. Mat.-L.T.D.						4.9
22.2	26.3	23.2	Trade Payables						29.3
.0	.0	.5	Income Taxes Payable						.1
21.8	12.8	10.5	All Other Current						11.9
56.7	50.2	40.2	Total Current						49.3
20.5	20.9	17.6	Long-Term Debt						12.2
.1	.1	.0	Deferred Taxes						.1
7.3	3.5	2.7	All Other Non-Current						.4
15.4	25.3	39.5	Net Worth						38.0
100.0	100.0	100.0	Total Liabilities & Net Worth						100.0

Income Data

			INCOME DATA						
100.0	100.0	100.0	Net Sales						100.0
32.3	28.8	26.4	Gross Profit						19.4
28.8	26.4	23.2	Operating Expenses						16.5
3.5	2.4	3.3	Operating Profit						2.9
.1	.2	.3	All Other Expenses (net)						.4
3.4	2.2	3.0	Profit Before Taxes						2.5

Ratios

			RATIOS						
2.2	1.8	2.5							2.1
1.2	1.1	1.3	Current						1.2
.8	.8	.8							.9
1.4	1.1	1.7							1.9
.9	.6	1.0	Quick						1.0
.3	.3	.4							.4
0 UND	0 UND	0 UND							1 669.2
1 535.0	2 198.6	1 537.3	Sales/Receivables						15 25.1
22 16.7	24 15.4	26 13.9							33 11.1
1 545.4	4 84.1	4 92.8							3 127.1
14 26.5	12 30.4	10 36.1	Cost of Sales/Inventory						8 47.2
23 15.7	21 17.0	22 16.5							16 23.2
0 966.5	8 48.3	7 54.6							10 36.6
15 24.6	19 19.2	17 22.1	Cost of Sales/Payables						16 23.3
25 14.5	28 13.2	26 14.3							34 10.7
21.4	24.3	15.0							14.4
86.5	65.2	51.6	Sales/Working Capital						60.0
-60.7	-137.1	-65.1							-221.8
97.0	50.8	126.5							160.0
(31) 18.2	(30) 10.0	(23) 6.9	EBIT/Interest						(12) 7.3
7.1	3.0	3.7							2.5
			Net Profit + Depr., Dep., Amort./Cur. Mat. L/T/D						
.3	.2	.2							.1
1.3	.9	.6	Fixed/Worth						.3
-5.2	-11.1	2.0							1.4
1.0	.9	.6							.9
2.9	2.5	1.1	Debt/Worth						2.8
-11.2	-11.8	7.9							7.9
103.4	91.0	60.3							70.8
(26) 39.4	(27) 33.4	(28) 23.8	% Profit Before Taxes/Tangible Net Worth						21.8
26.2	8.5	12.4							8.9
33.9	27.8	24.5							25.5
20.0	11.5	10.8	% Profit Before Taxes/Total Assets						8.2
8.5	1.6	1.4							.9
121.6	67.6	278.7							393.1
34.9	27.4	24.8	Sales/Net Fixed Assets						63.7
13.4	12.3	7.8							10.3
11.2	9.4	8.1							7.5
6.5	6.7	6.1	Sales/Total Assets						5.8
5.1	5.2	2.4							3.1
.2	.1	.4							.1
(30) .7	(28) .8	(26) .8	% Depr., Dep., Amort./Sales						(11) .7
.9	1.4	2.0							1.8
1.5	1.4	1.5							
(16) 2.8	(16) 3.2	(13) 1.7	% Officers', Directors' Owners' Comp/Sales						
5.0	7.0	3.4							
1451460M	2091529M	1176299M	Net Sales ($)	28M	4895M	19738M	13722M	133586M	1004330M
379524M	483457M	240468M	Total Assets ($)	11M	1486M	6313M	4567M	23331M	204760M

M = $ thousand   MM = $ million
See Pages viii through xx for Explanation of Ratios and Data

Current Data Sorted by Assets   Comparative Historical Data

Type of Statement	0-500M	500M-2MM	2-10MM	10-50MM	50-100MM	100-250MM		9 4/1/14-3/31/15	2 4/1/15-3/31/16
Unqualified									
Reviewed		1	2						2
Compiled		8	1	1				9	2
Tax Returns	5	7	3	1				32	51
Other	10	3 (4/1-9/30/18)	4	41 (10/1/18-3/31/19)				26	18
								ALL	ALL
NUMBER OF STATEMENTS	15	16	10	3				67	73
	%	%	%	%	%	%	ASSETS	%	%
	28.9	18.9	16.7				Cash & Equivalents	12.0	20.3
	7.5	5.3	16.6				Trade Receivables (net)	4.9	4.3
	8.2	10.1	4.0	D	D		Inventory	6.0	5.7
	4.1	4.5	1.9	A	A		All Other Current	1.1	.9
	48.7	38.9	39.2	T	T		Total Current	24.0	31.1
	41.4	35.9	38.2	A	A		Fixed Assets (net)	50.6	42.4
	5.6	15.5	8.6				Intangibles (net)	12.1	9.5
	4.3	9.7	14.0	N	N		All Other Non-Current	13.4	16.9
	100.0	100.0	100.0	O	O		Total	100.0	100.0
				T	T		LIABILITIES		
	9.6	7.8	9.1				Notes Payable-Short Term	6.4	9.2
	2.5	5.9	4.0	A	A		Cur. Mat.-L.T.D.	2.7	3.0
	12.1	8.0	9.4	V	V		Trade Payables	8.0	15.6
	.0	.1	.0	A	A		Income Taxes Payable	.1	.2
	12.1	12.4	12.7	I	I		All Other Current	17.8	13.1
	36.3	34.2	35.2	L	L		Total Current	35.0	41.1
	23.5	20.5	38.3	A	A		Long-Term Debt	28.5	31.9
	.0	.0	.0	B	B		Deferred Taxes	.0	.0
	26.6	6.7	7.1	L	L		All Other Non-Current	14.7	15.4
	13.6	38.6	19.4	E	E		Net Worth	21.8	11.5
	100.0	100.0	100.0				Total Liabilities & Net Worth	100.0	100.0
							INCOME DATA		
	100.0	100.0	100.0				Net Sales	100.0	100.0
	59.6	53.3	55.0				Gross Profit	50.8	53.2
	49.7	46.0	48.1				Operating Expenses	45.3	48.8
	9.9	7.3	6.9				Operating Profit	5.4	4.4
	.4	.2	3.1				All Other Expenses (net)	.8	.3
	9.5	7.1	3.8				Profit Before Taxes	4.6	4.1
							RATIOS		
	4.4	3.1	1.9					2.2	3.6
	1.4	1.6	.7				Current	1.1	1.3
	.8	.9	.2					.4	.5
	4.4	2.7	1.6					1.2	3.0
	.7	1.1	.6				Quick	(66) .7	1.1
	.4	.4	.1					.3	.3
	0 UND	0 UND	1 612.6					0 UND	0 UND
	1 416.4	1 331.1	2 148.2				Sales/Receivables	0 UND	0 UND
	14 26.9	6 63.6	22 16.8					1 330.7	2 149.5
	3 129.3	1 371.7	1 346.2					1 314.9	1 265.8
	8 45.8	8 45.6	7 51.6				Cost of Sales/Inventory	7 55.3	5 70.1
	54 6.7	21 17.7	13 27.2					11 32.2	11 33.0
	0 UND	1 294.4	13 27.4					0 UND	0 UND
	15 25.1	12 29.6	25 14.8				Cost of Sales/Payables	5 69.3	6 59.7
	41 8.8	26 14.3	31 11.7					27 13.3	33 11.1
	15.3	11.5	12.4					36.1	14.8
	58.4	27.9	-68.5				Sales/Working Capital	496.0	80.9
	-33.0	-70.1	-7.5					-16.1	-30.7
		21.9						13.5	23.7
		(12) 7.9					EBIT/Interest	(51) 4.6	(53) 6.1
		2.9						1.0	1.1
							Net Profit + Depr., Dep., Amort./Cur. Mat. L/T/D		
	.5	.5	1.4					1.1	.7
	.9	.8	6.9				Fixed/Worth	2.7	1.7
	-.6	NM	-13.7					-3.5	-2.1
	.3	.5	3.7					1.2	.6
	1.0	2.8	9.3				Debt/Worth	4.1	3.3
	-1.9	-14.5	-46.6					-5.8	-3.6
	147.3	63.1					% Profit Before Taxes/Tangible	103.1	75.7
	(10) 77.6	(11) 47.0					Net Worth	(43) 43.0	(49) 35.1
	50.6	13.2						8.3	7.3
	68.9	32.1	34.6					25.0	30.7
	48.5	16.2	16.6				% Profit Before Taxes/Total Assets	10.3	12.7
	5.5	4.6	7.8					1.9	-1.0
	20.2	27.3	18.6					12.8	25.7
	10.3	11.9	9.4				Sales/Net Fixed Assets	7.4	10.7
	5.3	4.3	5.5					3.9	4.9
	6.2	5.0	5.4					5.1	6.2
	4.2	3.2	3.4				Sales/Total Assets	3.3	3.6
	2.8	1.5	1.2					1.6	2.5
								1.8	1.4
							% Depr., Dep., Amort./Sales	(50) 3.0	(59) 2.2
								4.8	4.5
								1.9	2.1
							% Officers', Directors' Owners' Comp/Sales	(29) 3.5	(37) 4.2
								5.4	6.2
	17135M	66808M	154430M	174312M			Net Sales ($)	429485M	208424M
	3900M	18113M	46229M	50858M			Total Assets ($)	249237M	68214M

Comparative Historical Data | Current Data Sorted by Sales

Type of Statement

4/1/16-3/31/17 ALL	4/1/17-3/31/18 ALL	4/1/18-3/31/19 ALL	Type of Statement	0-1MM	1-3MM	3-5MM	5-10MM	10-25MM	25MM & OVER
1		1	Unqualified						1
		2	Reviewed					2	
6	5	2	Compiled			2			
35	24	17	Tax Returns	5	4	2	2	3	1
29	21	22	Other	4	10	2	2	1	3
					3 (4/1-9/30/18)		41 (10/1/18-3/31/19)		
71	52	44	NUMBER OF STATEMENTS	9	14	6	4	6	5

Data

4/1/16-3/31/17 ALL %	4/1/17-3/31/18 ALL %	4/1/18-3/31/19 ALL %		0-1MM %	1-3MM %	3-5MM %	5-10MM %	10-25MM %	25MM & OVER %
			ASSETS						
20.9	22.9	21.2	Cash & Equivalents		27.0				
4.8	4.8	8.4	Trade Receivables (net)		3.8				
6.8	5.7	7.5	Inventory		4.0				
3.0	2.6	3.6	All Other Current		3.7				
35.6	36.0	40.7	Total Current		38.5				
38.5	44.2	38.2	Fixed Assets (net)		44.8				
13.8	7.6	12.7	Intangibles (net)		6.5				
12.1	12.3	8.4	All Other Non-Current		10.2				
100.0	100.0	100.0	Total		100.0				
			LIABILITIES						
11.6	4.3	8.2	Notes Payable-Short Term		5.1				
2.4	3.9	4.8	Cur. Mat.-L.T.D.		5.0				
6.4	7.5	9.0	Trade Payables		5.9				
.2	.3	.0	Income Taxes Payable		.1				
12.4	15.6	12.1	All Other Current		19.6				
33.1	31.7	34.7	Total Current		35.6				
27.2	20.1	30.4	Long-Term Debt		19.4				
.0	.0	.0	Deferred Taxes		.0				
11.1	7.3	13.6	All Other Non-Current		17.7				
28.6	40.9	21.4	Net Worth		27.3				
100.0	100.0	100.0	Total Liabilities & Net Worth		100.0				
			INCOME DATA						
100.0	100.0	100.0	Net Sales		100.0				
59.9	56.5	55.6	Gross Profit		56.4				
52.2	48.8	47.7	Operating Expenses		45.3				
7.7	7.7	8.0	Operating Profit		11.2				
1.0	.5	1.1	All Other Expenses (net)		.6				
6.7	7.2	6.9	Profit Before Taxes		10.6				
			RATIOS						
4.1	2.8	2.3			4.6				
1.5	1.2	1.2	Current		1.2				
.6	.6	.6			.7				
3.2	1.9	1.7			4.4				
1.2	.9	.7	Quick		.7				
.3	.3	.4			.5				
0 UND	0 UND	0 UND			0 UND				
0 UND	0 UND	2 210.6	Sales/Receivables		0 UND				
5 70.1	3 104.5	13 27.1			5 74.7				
4 97.0	1 473.8	2 194.8			0 UND				
8 44.3	6 57.5	7 52.3	Cost of Sales/Inventory		5 78.3				
19 19.0	12 30.4	26 14.1			10 35.9				
0 UND	0 UND	2 208.1			0 UND				
14 26.5	0 UND	17 21.3	Cost of Sales/Payables		2 165.3				
24 15.0	24 15.0	30 12.2			15 23.9				
10.5	16.8	13.8			13.9				
32.8	111.9	70.3	Sales/Working Capital		529.1				
-27.8	-45.1	-21.1			-29.0				
34.3	50.1	18.4							
(50) 11.3	(37) 12.0	(30) 6.8	EBIT/Interest						
2.4	3.8	1.6							
			Net Profit + Depr., Dep., Amort./Cur. Mat. L/T/D						
.6	.5	.7			.6				
1.4	1.2	1.8	Fixed/Worth		1.2				
-4.0	7.0	-1.8			NM				
.4	.4	.6			.6				
2.9	1.3	4.9	Debt/Worth		1.3				
-5.2	8.5	-3.9			NM				
138.0	110.1	128.9			135.5				
(51) 68.2	(40) 61.2	(27) 57.1	% Profit Before Taxes/Tangible Net Worth		(11) 63.1				
29.1	30.8	33.2			54.7				
40.5	43.4	43.8			59.0				
17.3	30.2	18.6	% Profit Before Taxes/Total Assets		43.2				
5.7	8.4	8.3			17.9				
19.3	18.0	19.0			12.2				
10.9	9.6	11.4	Sales/Net Fixed Assets		9.8				
5.5	5.3	5.9			4.5				
5.0	6.2	5.2			6.2				
3.4	3.6	3.9	Sales/Total Assets		4.0				
2.2	2.4	2.5			2.1				
1.5	1.4	1.6							
(48) 2.3	(41) 2.1	(27) 2.2	% Depr., Dep., Amort./Sales						
3.9	4.1	3.7							
1.7	1.9	1.5							
(32) 3.6	(24) 3.5	(18) 2.4	% Officers', Directors' Owners' Comp/Sales						
6.2	6.0	5.2							
535154M	324020M	412685M	Net Sales ($)	6403M	23085M	24248M	30816M	89917M	238216M
237919M	220139M	119100M	Total Assets ($)	6351M	8847M	8475M	11155M	22170M	62102M

M = $ thousand   MM = $ million
See Pages viii through xx for Explanation of Ratios and Data

Current Data Sorted by Assets   Comparative Historical Data

							Type of Statement		
			1				Unqualified		
	1	2					Reviewed	2	2
		2					Compiled	2	3
4		2					Tax Returns	5	5
2		4	4	1			Other	7	8
	3 (4/1-9/30/18)		20 (10/1/18-3/31/19)					10	14
								4/1/14-	4/1/15-
0-500M	500M-2MM	2-10MM	10-50MM	50-100MM	100-250MM			3/31/15	3/31/16
6	1	10	5	1			NUMBER OF STATEMENTS	26 ALL	32 ALL
%	%	%	%	%	%	%	ASSETS	%	%
		6.5					Cash & Equivalents	12.5	17.6
		7.9					Trade Receivables (net)	10.8	7.8
		27.9					Inventory	23.9	22.2
		.2					All Other Current	7.0	1.0
		42.5					Total Current	54.2	48.6
		36.8					Fixed Assets (net)	33.4	36.7
		15.8					Intangibles (net)	5.8	7.7
		4.9					All Other Non-Current	6.5	7.1
		100.0					Total	100.0	100.0
							LIABILITIES		
		6.9					Notes Payable-Short Term	7.5	12.6
		3.7					Cur. Mat.-L.T.D.	3.5	2.7
		10.5					Trade Payables	10.6	9.8
		.1					Income Taxes Payable	.2	.1
		9.2					All Other Current	6.1	7.1
		30.5					Total Current	27.9	32.3
		28.1					Long-Term Debt	22.8	20.8
		.0					Deferred Taxes	.0	.1
		4.7					All Other Non-Current	4.9	5.0
		36.7					Net Worth	44.4	41.8
		100.0					Total Liabilities & Net Worth	100.0	100.0
							INCOME DATA		
		100.0					Net Sales	100.0	100.0
		41.0					Gross Profit	45.4	47.2
		36.7					Operating Expenses	40.7	41.3
		4.2					Operating Profit	4.6	5.9
		2.5					All Other Expenses (net)	.5	1.0
		1.7					Profit Before Taxes	4.1	4.9
							RATIOS		
		3.5						4.6	4.8
		1.3					Current	2.2	2.1
		.5						1.0	1.1
		.7						1.8	2.1
		.3					Quick	.8	.9
		.2						.4	.5
	0	UND						0 UND	0 999.8
	3	132.4					Sales/Receivables	6 59.8	5 73.4
	23	15.7						30 12.3	20 18.1
	19	19.0						27 13.4	26 14.3
	39	9.3					Cost of Sales/Inventory	54 6.7	46 7.9
	146	2.5						101 3.6	89 4.1
	4	97.9						9 39.0	2 229.7
	12	31.0					Cost of Sales/Payables	21 17.7	15 23.6
	38	9.6						49 7.5	49 7.5
		9.2						4.9	5.9
		31.9					Sales/Working Capital	8.1	13.3
		-30.6						-152.8	249.4
		11.3						32.8	33.1
		5.5					EBIT/Interest	(23) 7.5	(30) 8.1
		.9						1.7	1.4
							Net Profit + Depr., Dep., Amort./Cur. Mat. L/T/D		
		.6						.5	.4
		1.1					Fixed/Worth	.9	1.2
		-9.6						1.7	18.8
		.6						.4	.3
		3.0					Debt/Worth	1.3	1.5
		-24.2						5.2	43.3
								42.2	54.9
							% Profit Before Taxes/Tangible Net Worth	(23) 30.5	(25) 31.1
								10.8	15.6
		42.5						22.7	27.5
		9.1					% Profit Before Taxes/Total Assets	13.6	11.5
		.4						3.5	1.9
		26.1						19.4	21.7
		7.3					Sales/Net Fixed Assets	7.2	7.4
		4.0						4.3	4.4
		3.6						3.1	3.4
		2.5					Sales/Total Assets	2.3	2.5
		1.8						1.7	1.9
								.8	.8
							% Depr., Dep., Amort./Sales	(19) 2.0	(27) 2.2
								3.6	3.3
									2.9
							% Officers', Directors' Owners' Comp/Sales		(13) 4.6
									6.8
7281M	5189M	135426M	181374M	402404M			Net Sales ($)	1274836M	1325179M
1608M	883M	43370M	90990M	94031M			Total Assets ($)	307385M	331244M

D A T A   N O T   A V A I L A B L E (shown in columns 50-100MM / 100-250MM area)

M = $ thousand   MM = $ million
See Pages viii through xx for Explanation of Ratios and Data

Comparative Historical Data | **Current Data Sorted by Sales**

Type of Statement									
	1	2	1					1	
Unqualified	1	2	3				1	2	
Reviewed	6	3	2			1	1	1	
Compiled	6	6	6	2	2	1	1	1	
Tax Returns	13	11	11	2	2		2	2	5
Other						3 (4/1-9/30/18)	20 (10/1/18-3/31/19)		
	4/1/16-3/31/17	4/1/17-3/31/18	4/1/18-3/31/19	0-1MM	1-3MM	3-5MM	5-10MM	10-25MM	25MM & OVER
	ALL	ALL	ALL						
NUMBER OF STATEMENTS	27	24	23	2	4	1	5	6	5
	%	%	%	%	%	%	%	%	%
ASSETS									
Cash & Equivalents	17.4	17.5	16.9						
Trade Receivables (net)	4.0	8.4	10.5						
Inventory	19.8	18.2	23.1						
All Other Current	2.0	3.5	.9						
Total Current	43.2	47.6	51.5						
Fixed Assets (net)	35.7	31.6	32.3						
Intangibles (net)	12.7	11.6	11.9						
All Other Non-Current	8.3	9.2	4.3						
Total	100.0	100.0	100.0						
LIABILITIES									
Notes Payable-Short Term	4.3	4.3	4.9						
Cur. Mat.-L.T.D.	3.0	2.9	1.9						
Trade Payables	7.9	6.5	10.3						
Income Taxes Payable	.2	.3	.1						
All Other Current	8.0	12.9	9.3						
Total Current	23.5	27.0	26.5						
Long-Term Debt	28.4	13.3	20.7						
Deferred Taxes	.1	.0	.0						
All Other Non-Current	6.6	7.5	2.7						
Net Worth	41.4	52.2	50.1						
Total Liabilities & Net Worth	100.0	100.0	100.0						
INCOME DATA									
Net Sales	100.0	100.0	100.0						
Gross Profit	53.2	42.8	45.6						
Operating Expenses	44.9	35.0	35.6						
Operating Profit	8.4	7.8	10.0						
All Other Expenses (net)	1.4	.5	1.5						
Profit Before Taxes	7.0	7.3	8.5						
RATIOS									
Current	3.5	7.7	5.4						
	1.9	1.7	2.8						
	1.0	.9	1.2						
Quick	1.5	3.9	3.6						
	.9	1.0	.9						
	.4	.2	.3						
Sales/Receivables	0 UND	0 UND	0 UND						
	1 641.0	6 62.2	4 100.0						
	10 37.5	21 17.0	16 23.4						
Cost of Sales/Inventory	34 10.6	10 35.0	9 39.0						
	53 6.9	40 9.1	42 8.7						
	63 5.8	72 5.1	72 5.1						
Cost of Sales/Payables	3 108.3	0 UND	1 362.9						
	17 21.0	2 156.6	8 45.0						
	31 11.6	23 15.7	18 19.9						
Sales/Working Capital	8.5	5.0	5.8						
	16.9	18.2	15.9						
	-434.0	-64.0	90.6						
EBIT/Interest	37.5	40.4	22.4						
	(24) 7.0	(20) 8.0	(19) 6.7						
	1.5	2.4	1.9						
Net Profit + Depr., Dep., Amort./Cur. Mat. L/T/D									
Fixed/Worth	.3	.1	.2						
	1.0	.8	.8						
	-16.6	20.8	1.2						
Debt/Worth	.4	.3	.5						
	1.6	1.2	.8						
	-8.1	45.1	4.3						
% Profit Before Taxes/Tangible Net Worth	120.9	65.1	97.3						
	(19) 33.3	(20) 36.5	(20) 46.5						
	4.4	15.0	16.5						
% Profit Before Taxes/Total Assets	31.3	33.9	45.0						
	11.3	13.0	24.0						
	2.4	3.7	4.6						
Sales/Net Fixed Assets	25.2	109.1	75.3						
	6.2	8.7	7.7						
	4.0	4.9	4.6						
Sales/Total Assets	4.2	4.4	5.5						
	2.3	2.7	2.9						
	1.7	1.7	1.8						
% Depr., Dep., Amort./Sales	1.1	1.0	.3						
	(17) 2.8	(18) 3.1	(18) 2.4						
	4.9	4.6	3.5						
% Officers', Directors' Owners' Comp/Sales	2.4	1.7	1.0						
	(11) 6.8	(12) 3.7	(10) 2.0						
	15.1	8.5	8.0						
Net Sales ($)	406580M	794650M	731674M	1238M	6043M	3962M	31226M	88657M	600548M
Total Assets ($)	274246M	424598M	230882M	425M	1183M	3314M	12245M	59583M	154132M

© RMA 2019   M = $ thousand   MM = $ million
See Pages viii through xx for Explanation of Ratios and Data

Current Data Sorted by Assets　　　　　　　　　　Comparative Historical Data

	0-500M	500M-2MM	2-10MM	10-50MM	50-100MM	100-250MM	Type of Statement	4/1/14-3/31/15 ALL	4/1/15-3/31/16 ALL
Unqualified					2	1		6	1
Reviewed						1		9	9
Compiled	2	2	2	4				21	16
Tax Returns	24	17	5	3		1		93	126
Other	16	26	14	6				97	88

Date ranges: 17 (4/1-9/30/18)　　113 (10/1/18-3/31/19)

0-500M	500M-2MM	2-10MM	10-50MM	50-100MM	100-250MM		4/1/14-3/31/15 ALL	4/1/15-3/31/16 ALL
42	45	25	13	3	2	**NUMBER OF STATEMENTS**	226	240
%	%	%	%	%	%	**ASSETS**	%	%
25.6	14.8	17.4	15.8			Cash & Equivalents	20.7	16.7
2.3	5.2	12.8	9.4			Trade Receivables (net)	6.8	5.8
7.0	11.0	24.2	24.0			Inventory	18.3	17.6
1.3	3.2	3.8	1.0			All Other Current	1.5	1.7
36.1	34.3	58.2	50.3			Total Current	47.3	41.8
36.6	40.6	29.6	34.8			Fixed Assets (net)	34.0	34.9
14.2	12.9	4.7	12.3			Intangibles (net)	8.1	10.5
13.1	12.2	7.6	2.6			All Other Non-Current	10.6	12.9
100.0	100.0	100.0	100.0			Total	100.0	100.0
						LIABILITIES		
9.2	7.6	6.5	4.9			Notes Payable-Short Term	7.4	11.0
6.1	2.2	4.8	4.5			Cur. Mat.-L.T.D.	3.0	2.7
5.1	7.9	19.2	10.4			Trade Payables	13.9	12.9
.4	.1	.0	.0			Income Taxes Payable	.1	.3
29.0	5.6	10.1	5.7			All Other Current	15.8	19.3
49.9	23.4	40.6	25.7			Total Current	40.1	46.2
34.0	33.8	16.5	21.0			Long-Term Debt	25.7	27.0
.0	.0	.8	.6			Deferred Taxes	.1	.2
10.5	2.1	5.9	6.1			All Other Non-Current	8.5	9.5
5.6	40.6	36.2	46.7			Net Worth	25.6	17.2
100.0	100.0	100.0	100.0			Total Liabilities & Net Worth	100.0	100.0
						INCOME DATA		
100.0	100.0	100.0	100.0			Net Sales	100.0	100.0
62.4	50.4	44.1	31.5			Gross Profit	48.1	50.2
55.4	43.4	41.4	31.4			Operating Expenses	43.8	46.3
7.0	7.0	2.7	.2			Operating Profit	4.3	3.9
1.6	.6	.0	.7			All Other Expenses (net)	.7	.4
5.4	6.4	2.6	-.5			Profit Before Taxes	3.6	3.4
						RATIOS		
3.4	4.8	2.2	3.3				2.9	2.6
1.5	1.9	1.7	1.5			Current	1.4	1.2
.4	.6	1.0	.7				.6	.5
2.6	4.3	1.3	1.8				1.9	1.4
.8	.7	.7	.6			Quick	(224) .8	.6
.2	.2	.4	.4				.2	.2
0 UND	0 UND	0 UND	0 UND				0 UND	0 UND
0 UND	0 999.8	7 50.2	4 90.9			Sales/Receivables	0 UND	0 UND
0 UND	8 45.8	25 14.4	32 11.5				6 64.6	6 66.3
0 UND	3 142.7	15 24.1	10 37.4				5 68.5	6 60.3
7 55.8	10 36.5	28 13.0	27 13.5			Cost of Sales/Inventory	15 24.2	17 21.5
17 21.6	33 11.2	85 4.3	51 7.2				39 9.4	38 9.6
0 UND	0 UND	19 19.4	5 66.7				2 152.3	0 UND
0 UND	6 58.4	31 11.9	16 22.8			Cost of Sales/Payables	17 21.5	14 26.2
13 27.6	22 16.6	54 6.8	33 11.2				38 9.7	31 11.7
23.3	11.0	9.8	8.0				10.9	13.8
143.1	31.0	17.5	16.7			Sales/Working Capital	35.9	79.4
-17.9	-29.9	NM	-40.5				-35.2	-19.6
10.3	24.6	26.2	18.1				11.6	15.8
(26) 4.2	(30) 6.5	(21) 3.3	(10) 2.4			EBIT/Interest	(163) 4.8	(171) 4.8
2.0	1.7	-.3	1.1				1.3	1.1
						Net Profit + Depr., Dep., Amort./Cur. Mat. L/T/D		
.2	.3	.3	.4				.2	.3
1.9	1.2	.7	1.0			Fixed/Worth	1.0	1.5
-1.1	7.8	4.2	NM				UND	-4.6
.5	.4	.6	.5				.7	.8
7.8	1.7	1.4	1.9			Debt/Worth	2.1	2.7
-2.7	50.8	9.2	NM				UND	-9.4
261.7	86.2	43.9	18.7				95.2	107.1
(25) 75.9	(38) 50.6	(20) 24.8	(10) 9.0			% Profit Before Taxes/Tangible Net Worth	(170) 37.6	(164) 47.5
36.5	24.8	-1.6	2.6				8.3	15.4
51.3	26.6	22.1	13.4				31.5	30.3
26.0	19.7	6.2	2.9			% Profit Before Taxes/Total Assets	10.4	14.2
2.9	5.0	-1.0	1.4				1.4	1.6
50.7	25.3	33.7	70.3				48.1	46.9
21.2	7.0	10.8	7.4			Sales/Net Fixed Assets	15.2	13.3
9.6	4.9	6.4	3.6				6.8	5.5
7.5	4.2	4.5	4.7				6.2	6.5
5.1	2.8	3.1	2.6			Sales/Total Assets	3.6	3.8
3.4	2.2	2.2	1.4				2.2	2.3
.7	1.3	.6	.9				.7	.7
(30) 1.5	(28) 2.5	(23) 1.8	(11) 2.4			% Depr., Dep., Amort./Sales	(171) 1.6	(176) 1.9
4.8	4.4	2.7	5.9				3.3	3.8
1.8	2.3	.4					1.7	1.5
(25) 4.6	(21) 4.7	(11) 2.5				% Officers', Directors' Owners' Comp/Sales	(109) 3.7	(121) 3.3
7.6	6.2	3.7					6.0	6.1
50211M	141130M	411802M	619408M	359055M	1272336M	Net Sales ($)	5097605M	3020489M
9534M	44328M	125284M	236508M	232235M	349914M	Total Assets ($)	1507099M	1246748M

M = $ thousand　　MM = $ million
See Pages viii through xx for Explanation of Ratios and Data

Comparative Historical Data | | | Type of Statement | ## Current Data Sorted by Sales

4/1/16-3/31/17 ALL	4/1/17-3/31/18 ALL	4/1/18-3/31/19 ALL	Type of Statement	0-1MM	1-3MM	3-5MM	5-10MM	10-25MM	25MM & OVER
					17 (4/1-9/30/18)			113 (10/1/18-3/31/19)	
2	5	3	Unqualified	1	3		1	2	3
9	8	7	Reviewed					2	5
12	10	11	Compiled						4
84	60	47	Tax Returns	10	25	3	6	2	2
62	66	62	Other	10	24	3	9	10	6
169	149	130	**NUMBER OF STATEMENTS**	21	52	5	16	16	20
%	%	%	**ASSETS**	%	%	%	%	%	%
21.4	17.2	18.9	Cash & Equivalents	21.2	21.1		13.9	22.4	14.4
4.1	6.5	6.6	Trade Receivables (net)	.9	4.5		8.5	10.0	14.6
15.8	17.0	13.7	Inventory	7.4	5.2		32.0	22.1	21.6
2.0	2.0	2.4	All Other Current	.0	3.2		2.6	3.8	2.0
43.2	42.7	41.6	Total Current	29.6	33.9		57.0	58.3	52.6
38.4	37.5	36.3	Fixed Assets (net)	46.4	35.1		27.4	30.5	34.8
10.1	12.2	11.9	Intangibles (net)	16.6	14.5		8.5	5.1	10.7
8.2	7.6	10.3	All Other Non-Current	7.6	16.4		7.1	6.1	1.9
100.0	100.0	100.0	Total	100.0	100.0		100.0	100.0	100.0
			LIABILITIES						
7.7	7.6	7.5	Notes Payable-Short Term	10.9	5.6		11.0	3.7	7.6
3.2	3.3	4.8	Cur. Mat.-L.T.D.	6.6	3.2		3.5	6.3	7.4
10.2	11.8	9.5	Trade Payables	4.1	4.2		18.9	17.5	14.7
.3	.6	.2	Income Taxes Payable	.5	.2		.0	.0	.1
16.6	11.9	13.9	All Other Current	23.9	15.8		11.8	8.4	6.8
38.0	35.2	35.9	Total Current	45.9	29.1		45.3	36.0	36.6
32.5	29.1	28.7	Long-Term Debt	40.9	32.4		23.4	16.2	18.2
.2	.1	.2	Deferred Taxes	.0	.0		.1	.8	.8
16.2	5.9	5.9	All Other Non-Current	10.1	5.9		.5	10.2	3.1
12.9	29.7	29.3	Net Worth	3.3	32.7		30.7	36.9	41.3
100.0	100.0	100.0	Total Liabilties & Net Worth	100.0	100.0		100.0	100.0	100.0
			INCOME DATA						
100.0	100.0	100.0	Net Sales	100.0	100.0		100.0	100.0	100.0
50.6	48.7	50.6	Gross Profit	62.4	59.8		41.4	46.4	30.0
44.9	43.0	45.2	Operating Expenses	56.2	51.6		37.3	42.7	29.0
5.7	5.7	5.4	Operating Profit	6.2	8.3		4.1	3.6	1.1
.8	.9	.8	All Other Expenses (net)	3.5	.4		.5	-.7	.4
4.9	4.8	4.6	Profit Before Taxes	2.7	7.8		3.5	4.3	.7
			RATIOS						
2.8	3.5	3.6	Current	3.6	5.6		2.5	3.2	2.1
1.4	1.5	1.6		.9	1.9		1.4	1.7	1.3
.8	.7	.7		.4	.5		.7	1.1	.8
1.8	2.2	2.3	Quick	3.0	4.7		1.1	2.1	1.2
.8	.8	.7		.6	1.2		.3	1.0	.7
.3	.3	.3		.2	.3		.1	.4	.4
0 UND	0 UND	0 UND	Sales/Receivables	0 UND	0 UND		0 UND	0 UND	0 999.8
0 UND	0 999.8	0 UND		0 UND	0 UND		1 547.7	1 257.1	10 37.1
5 68.9	11 33.9	9 40.7		0 UND	3 114.3		25 14.8	30 12.2	34 10.6
7 55.7	7 50.3	3 115.9	Cost of Sales/Inventory	0 UND	2 172.5		7 53.5	9 41.1	17 21.7
18 20.6	20 18.1	13 27.3		13 27.3	6 61.9		47 7.8	23 15.6	25 14.5
40 9.2	47 7.8	34 10.6		30 12.0	14 25.8		87 4.2	91 4.0	45 8.1
2 239.4	3 114.2	0 UND	Cost of Sales/Payables	0 UND	0 UND		5 81.0	16 22.2	12 31.6
12 31.4	14 27.0	13 28.9		0 UND	5 76.8		33 10.9	33 11.1	16 23.4
29 12.7	33 11.0	29 12.8		14 25.8	13 27.1		54 6.7	68 5.4	36 10.2
12.9	11.2	10.9	Sales/Working Capital	17.4	12.2		10.8	8.5	9.2
39.3	31.5	30.9		-56.9	33.1		48.7	14.5	34.2
-47.9	-52.4	-34.6		-10.7	-35.7		-34.1	89.2	-63.4
15.3	12.2	12.4	EBIT/Interest	11.2	10.0		53.2	99.7	6.9
(122) 4.5	(110) 3.8	(91) 3.7		(16) 2.9	(28) 5.9		(14) 9.2	(13) 2.1	(15) 2.7
.4	1.3	1.6		-2.0	2.3		4.9	.4	1.3
3.8		2.7	Net Profit + Depr., Dep., Amort./Cur. Mat. L/T/D						
(11) 1.7		(11) 1.8							
1.1		1.2							
.5	.4	.4	Fixed/Worth	1.1	.2		.3	.3	.4
1.7	1.4	1.3		5.0	1.0		1.0	.6	1.6
-4.8	-8.2	UND		-1.0	4.4		751.9	NM	NM
.8	.6	.5	Debt/Worth	1.6	.3		.7	.3	1.0
3.4	2.8	2.6		13.0	1.4		2.6	1.3	2.3
10.3	-15.0	-19.2		-2.7	86.1		758.1	NM	NM
101.9	88.4	73.9	% Profit Before Taxes/Tangible Net Worth	234.4	167.5		63.3	52.6	24.9
(118) 48.9	(106) 39.4	(97) 41.9		(11) 59.4	(41) 57.0		(13) 43.9	(12) 38.0	(15) 9.8
10.4	11.9	12.3		-.5	28.3		12.3	17.6	6.1
32.0	24.7	28.5	% Profit Before Taxes/Total Assets	38.5	42.4		25.5	32.4	13.3
12.1	9.5	13.3		7.9	24.2		18.1	9.8	5.7
.7	2.0	2.5		-0.9	9.3		3.8	.6	1.2
32.0	34.2	38.5	Sales/Net Fixed Assets	35.2	37.8		52.9	36.1	90.6
13.0	11.8	12.3		9.1	16.1		23.6	10.3	10.4
4.5	4.3	5.8		3.3	5.9		10.6	6.2	4.6
6.4	5.2	5.0	Sales/Total Assets	5.7	5.3		6.0	4.6	5.2
3.5	3.0	3.2		3.2	3.2		4.0	3.1	2.8
2.0	1.9	2.2		1.6	2.4		2.7	2.0	1.6
.8	.7	.9	% Depr., Dep., Amort./Sales	.9	1.2		.8	.3	1.0
(121) 2.3	(104) 1.9	(95) 1.9		(13) 5.3	(36) 2.1		(13) 1.3	(14) 1.4	(16) 1.7
4.1	3.5	3.6		8.5	3.4		1.9	3.8	3.2
1.6	1.6	1.8	% Officers', Directors' Owners' Comp/Sales		1.9				
(77) 3.7	(71) 3.6	(62) 3.8			(30) 4.1				
6.0	6.9	6.2			8.2				
2185240M	3322779M	2853942M	Net Sales ($)	10460M	97364M	19676M	106839M	242249M	2377354M
1089734M	1128283M	997803M	Total Assets ($)	5523M	32315M	12154M	28817M	89256M	829738M

M = $ thousand   MM = $ million
See Pages viii through xx for Explanation of Ratios and Data

Current Data Sorted by Assets | Comparative Historical Data

	0-500M	500M-2MM	2-10MM	10-50MM	50-100MM	100-250MM	Type of Statement	4/1/14-3/31/15 ALL	4/1/15-3/31/16 ALL
	3	1	5		2	1	Unqualified	6	6
			7	6			Reviewed	19	18
	1	1	5	1			Compiled	30	20
	62	48	12		1	2	Tax Returns	169	166
	18	31	12	15	2	1	Other	111	99
		28 (4/1-9/30/18)		209 (10/1/18-3/31/19)					
	84	81	41	22	5	4	NUMBER OF STATEMENTS	335	309
	%	%	%	%	%	%	**ASSETS**	%	%
	17.1	15.2	11.6	10.8			Cash & Equivalents	13.4	11.8
	.5	.6	1.9	10.0			Trade Receivables (net)	3.0	2.0
	51.7	49.5	47.9	38.3			Inventory	48.3	49.0
	1.5	2.5	1.8	2.4			All Other Current	1.9	1.8
	70.7	67.8	63.1	61.6			Total Current	66.6	64.6
	13.1	10.9	24.1	17.8			Fixed Assets (net)	15.0	16.1
	11.8	19.5	8.7	16.8			Intangibles (net)	14.7	14.1
	4.3	1.8	4.1	3.8			All Other Non-Current	3.8	5.2
	100.0	100.0	100.0	100.0			Total	100.0	100.0
							LIABILITIES		
	8.2	4.5	6.0	7.0			Notes Payable-Short Term	9.7	11.5
	1.5	2.4	1.8	3.3			Cur. Mat.-L.T.D.	2.7	2.1
	9.8	12.6	18.8	19.7			Trade Payables	15.5	15.6
	.1	.1	.0	.1			Income Taxes Payable	.2	.2
	15.9	6.6	7.3	7.2			All Other Current	11.1	12.8
	35.5	26.2	33.9	37.2			Total Current	39.1	42.2
	10.3	19.2	19.3	13.7			Long-Term Debt	17.3	18.6
	.0	.0	.0	.0			Deferred Taxes	.0	.0
	13.6	11.8	10.4	2.6			All Other Non-Current	9.6	10.3
	40.6	42.8	36.3	46.5			Net Worth	34.0	28.9
	100.0	100.0	100.0	100.0			Total Liabilities & Net Worth	100.0	100.0
							INCOME DATA		
	100.0	100.0	100.0	100.0			Net Sales	100.0	100.0
	25.0	25.2	23.7	27.7			Gross Profit	25.4	24.3
	23.0	21.0	20.8	23.3			Operating Expenses	22.2	21.3
	2.0	4.3	2.9	4.4			Operating Profit	3.3	3.0
	-.7	.0	.6	.6			All Other Expenses (net)	.1	.1
	2.7	4.2	2.3	3.8			Profit Before Taxes	3.2	2.9
							RATIOS		
	11.1	10.9	5.2	2.4			Current	5.5	5.2
	3.8	3.3	1.7	1.6				2.1	2.0
	1.5	1.5	1.2	1.2				1.2	1.2
	2.3	1.6	1.0	1.2			Quick	1.3	1.1
	(83) .6	.7	.3	.4				(333) .4	(305) .4
	.2	.2	.1	.2				.1	.1
	0 UND	0 UND	0 UND	0 999.8			Sales/Receivables	0 UND	0 UND
	0 UND	0 UND	0 UND	4 81.7				0 UND	0 UND
	0 UND	0 999.8	2 165.8	42 8.6				2 210.5	0 736.8
	26 14.0	47 7.8	59 6.2	45 8.2			Cost of Sales/Inventory	41 8.9	41 8.9
	48 7.6	74 4.9	76 4.8	87 4.2				62 5.9	63 5.8
	74 4.9	104 3.5	111 3.3	118 3.1				99 3.7	96 3.8
	0 UND	0 UND	9 42.8	18 20.5			Cost of Sales/Payables	0 UND	0 UND
	0 UND	6 60.1	26 13.9	29 12.5				10 37.7	15 24.4
	7 51.7	31 11.6	51 7.2	56 6.5				33 11.1	34 10.7
	7.6	4.5	5.1	6.0			Sales/Working Capital	6.1	6.3
	10.8	6.9	11.0	9.2				12.2	12.7
	35.1	18.1	45.7	36.1				35.1	52.0
	10.0	22.1	20.8	10.3			EBIT/Interest	12.8	11.8
	(39) 4.5	(50) 4.7	(36) 3.9	(19) 4.6				(224) 5.2	(192) 4.2
	1.3	1.6	2.0	1.3				1.7	1.4
							Net Profit + Depr., Dep., Amort./Cur. Mat. L/T/D	4.8	3.4
								(14) 1.2	(10) .7
								-.2	-.2
	.0	.0	.1	.1			Fixed/Worth	.0	.0
	.2	.3	.5	.9				.3	.5
	2.1	-1.6	1.6	1.6				35.0	-10.2
	.2	.4	.5	.7			Debt/Worth	.7	.6
	1.1	2.3	1.8	1.9				2.1	2.7
	-9.1	-4.3	22.9	22.6				-20.2	-10.6
	72.6	78.9	57.4	63.9			% Profit Before Taxes/Tangible Net Worth	59.7	69.7
	(61) 34.4	(53) 28.7	(33) 17.2	(18) 31.8				(242) 31.2	(216) 30.3
	3.8	10.7	3.9	5.3				8.3	8.2
	30.4	19.4	19.7	13.2			% Profit Before Taxes/Total Assets	19.2	19.0
	12.0	9.9	5.0	5.9				8.9	8.1
	.9	2.5	1.1	1.5				1.8	1.3
	999.8	312.4	83.6	84.3			Sales/Net Fixed Assets	277.9	302.9
	109.6	51.3	19.6	39.1				59.7	55.8
	28.6	22.1	4.8	5.5				16.0	14.8
	8.1	4.7	4.1	3.0			Sales/Total Assets	5.3	5.0
	4.8	2.8	2.5	2.2				3.3	3.5
	3.5	2.0	1.7	1.7				2.1	2.2
	.3	.2	.3	.4			% Depr., Dep., Amort./Sales	.3	.3
	(41) .8	(51) .6	(32) .5	(17) 1.0				(208) .7	(179) .7
	1.6	1.4	1.3	1.4				1.5	1.8
	2.3	1.5	.8				% Officers', Directors' Owners' Comp/Sales	1.3	1.2
	(43) 3.8	(34) 2.4	(22) 1.3					(157) 2.6	(140) 2.1
	5.6	3.9	2.6					4.6	4.2
	121085M	246117M	521784M	1133986M	1297454M	3625303M	Net Sales ($)	9277451M	5125744M
	21770M	75532M	166454M	482011M	392377M	677729M	Total Assets ($)	2497810M	1420752M

M = $ thousand   MM = $ million
See Pages viii through xx for Explanation of Ratios and Data

Comparative Historical Data · Current Data Sorted by Sales

			Type of Statement						
6	11	12	Unqualified	2	3		2	1	4
9	11	13	Reviewed					6	7
18	12	8	Compiled	1		1	1	3	2
152	137	125	Tax Returns	25	62	19	12	3	4
97	103	79	Other	8	31	9	9		15
4/1/16-3/31/17 ALL	4/1/17-3/31/18 ALL	4/1/18-3/31/19 ALL		28 (4/1-9/30/18)		209 (10/1/18-3/31/19)			
				0-1MM	1-3MM	3-5MM	5-10MM	10-25MM	25MM & OVER
282	274	237	NUMBER OF STATEMENTS	36	96	29	24	20	32
%	%	%	ASSETS	%	%	%	%	%	%
12.1	13.6	14.6	Cash & Equivalents	13.9	14.7	19.6	13.9	14.1	11.0
2.3	2.6	1.7	Trade Receivables (net)	.5	.7	.2	2.1	4.6	5.7
48.0	46.7	48.6	Inventory	46.8	50.6	48.1	52.7	47.1	42.6
1.7	2.1	2.0	All Other Current	2.5	1.7	2.2	.3	2.4	2.8
64.2	65.1	66.8	Total Current	63.7	67.8	70.1	69.0	68.2	62.2
16.2	18.3	15.1	Fixed Assets (net)	16.0	12.7	12.0	20.1	18.8	17.8
14.7	12.1	14.7	Intangibles (net)	16.4	16.5	16.3	7.5	6.6	16.1
4.9	4.6	3.4	All Other Non-Current	3.9	3.0	1.7	3.4	6.4	3.9
100.0	100.0	100.0	Total	100.0	100.0	100.0	100.0	100.0	100.0
			LIABILITIES						
7.5	8.7	6.3	Notes Payable-Short Term	11.9	5.8	3.6	3.8	7.7	4.6
2.4	2.3	2.1	Cur. Mat.-L.T.D.	2.6	1.9	1.8	.8	1.0	4.3
15.7	14.2	13.5	Trade Payables	3.0	11.3	14.6	19.4	26.0	18.6
.1	.1	.1	Income Taxes Payable	.1	.1	.4	.0	.0	.1
15.1	15.0	10.4	All Other Current	18.7	9.9	7.9	3.2	10.2	10.2
40.8	40.3	32.3	Total Current	36.3	29.0	28.3	27.2	44.9	37.8
21.7	17.5	17.0	Long-Term Debt	10.6	16.1	19.9	19.4	11.3	25.9
.0	.0	.0	Deferred Taxes	.0	.0	.0	.0	.0	.0
6.7	11.7	11.1	All Other Non-Current	12.8	13.4	10.1	8.6	8.7	6.5
30.8	30.5	39.6	Net Worth	40.3	41.5	41.7	44.8	35.2	29.8
100.0	100.0	100.0	Total Liabilities & Net Worth	100.0	100.0	100.0	100.0	100.0	100.0
			INCOME DATA						
100.0	100.0	100.0	Net Sales	100.0	100.0	100.0	100.0	100.0	100.0
25.0	26.3	25.1	Gross Profit	28.2	25.8	20.9	21.5	26.3	25.4
21.6	23.7	22.0	Operating Expenses	26.3	22.0	18.9	18.4	23.2	21.8
3.4	2.6	3.1	Operating Profit	1.9	3.8	2.0	3.0	3.1	3.6
.2	.1	-.1	All Other Expenses (net)	-.3	-.2	.0	-.2	.4	.4
3.2	2.5	3.2	Profit Before Taxes	2.2	3.9	2.0	3.3	2.8	3.2
			RATIOS						
5.1	4.8	6.8	Current	5.7	14.5	10.8	7.2	2.3	2.3
1.9	2.0	2.6		3.3	3.8	2.6	2.8	1.4	1.8
1.2	1.1	1.3		1.2	1.7	1.4	1.5	1.2	1.1
.9	1.2	1.5	Quick	1.7	2.3	2.2	1.2	.8	1.0
(281) .4	(273) .4	(236) .5		.6	(95) .6	.7	.5	.3	.4
.1	.1	.2		.2	.2	.1	.2	.1	.2
0 UND	0 UND	0 UND	Sales/Receivables	0 UND	0 UND	0 UND	0 UND	0 UND	0 999.8
0 UND	0 UND	0 UND		0 UND	0 UND	0 UND	0 UND	1 349.5	3 125.5
1 578.8	1 313.0	1 582.2		0 UND	0 UND	0 UND	0 780.1	4 98.9	6 57.7
34 10.6	38 9.7	42 8.7	Cost of Sales/Inventory	45 8.2	38 9.6	24 15.1	48 7.6	51 7.1	44 8.3
57 6.4	59 6.2	65 5.6		76 4.8	68 5.4	59 6.2	63 5.8	61 6.0	63 5.8
91 4.0	94 3.9	94 3.9		111 3.3	94 3.9	94 3.9	85 4.3	107 3.4	91 4.0
0 UND	0 UND	0 UND	Cost of Sales/Payables	0 UND	0 UND	0 UND	1 307.5	12 29.4	14 25.4
12 31.0	15 24.8	8 44.2		0 UND	0 787.0	5 70.8	20 18.3	32 11.4	27 13.4
32 11.5	36 10.2	30 12.0		5 75.1	26 14.2	38 9.5	42 8.7	58 6.3	38 9.6
6.7	6.1	5.4	Sales/Working Capital	5.2	4.8	6.4	5.4	6.1	6.6
15.0	12.1	9.6		9.1	8.4	12.6	10.1	14.2	12.3
79.4	70.4	27.0		18.8	18.4	26.2	27.6	47.1	77.1
12.6	13.8	12.7	EBIT/Interest	9.6	20.1	24.8	17.1	50.6	11.2
(192) 4.9	(194) 5.0	(153) 4.3		(14) 5.8	(54) 4.2	(21) 1.6	(18) 6.8	(17) 3.3	(29) 4.6
1.7	1.5	1.5		1.3	2.3	.3	1.3	2.0	1.1
3.8	8.0	13.3	Net Profit + Depr., Dep., Amort./Cur. Mat. L/T/D						
(10) 2.9	(14) 2.7	(10) 2.0							
1.7	1.7	.9							
.0	.1	.0	Fixed/Worth	.0	.0	.0	.1	.2	.1
.4	.6	.4		.3	.3	.2	.4	.8	1.0
-17.1	-7.0	4.2		UND	-2.3	1.7	2.3	3.6	2.5
.7	.5	.4	Debt/Worth	.3	.3	.3	.3	.8	.8
3.0	2.4	1.8		1.5	1.5	2.5	1.1	3.2	2.3
-12.3	-12.3	-9.3		-6.8	-4.8	-7.8	6.1	57.2	NM
60.2	51.4	66.0	% Profit Before Taxes/Tangible Net Worth	66.7	57.1	115.5	83.5	68.2	58.9
(198) 22.1	(190) 24.8	(170) 28.0		(24) 20.8	(64) 24.8	(21) 33.0	(21) 21.4	(16) 24.6	(24) 33.9
6.3	7.1	6.1		4.8	11.7	3.2	1.5	6.7	3.8
18.3	17.3	22.5	% Profit Before Taxes/Total Assets	22.3	23.5	28.9	20.7	17.4	20.5
8.4	7.3	9.4		7.9	11.3	6.5	4.9	4.1	6.7
1.9	.9	1.3		.8	3.0	2.4	.7	1.5	.4
231.5	152.9	312.4	Sales/Net Fixed Assets	UND	420.9	UND	215.2	100.6	76.8
54.6	32.8	51.3		76.1	77.3	51.0	48.2	35.4	37.4
16.0	14.6	14.5		9.9	21.2	24.4	5.6	12.0	7.7
5.2	5.1	5.3	Sales/Total Assets	5.0	5.4	6.5	5.8	4.3	4.4
3.4	3.3	3.3		3.1	3.6	4.5	3.1	3.4	2.8
2.2	2.1	2.2		1.7	2.3	2.6	2.1	2.0	2.1
.3	.4	.3	% Depr., Dep., Amort./Sales	.6	.3	.3	.2	.2	.4
(167) .7	(175) .7	(148) .7		(19) 1.2	(47) .8	(20) .7	(22) .4	(16) .3	(24) .7
1.8	1.9	1.4		3.7	1.4	1.4	.9	.9	1.4
1.7	1.5	1.3	% Officers', Directors' Owners' Comp/Sales	3.5	2.3	.8	1.2	.7	
(130) 2.7	(126) 2.6	(105) 2.6		(11) 4.3	(51) 3.3	(14) 1.4	(11) 1.6	(10) 1.3	
4.1	4.2	4.3		6.3	5.3	4.1	2.2	1.9	
5630713M	7217972M	6945729M	Net Sales ($)	24046M	167662M	114374M	167138M	322309M	6150200M
1596827M	1927277M	1815873M	Total Assets ($)	10974M	59829M	33000M	54380M	134401M	1523289M

M = $ thousand   MM = $ million
See Pages viii through xx for Explanation of Ratios and Data

Current Data Sorted by Assets   Comparative Historical Data

						Type of Statement		
		1	5	3	3	Unqualified	14	14
	1	5	6	2		Reviewed	23	17
7	14	9	4			Compiled	64	51
26	64	26	2			Tax Returns	190	188
21	45	35	15	5	4	Other	146	162
	35 (4/1-9/30/18)		268 (10/1/18-3/31/19)				4/1/14-3/31/15	4/1/15-3/31/16
0-500M	500M-2MM	2-10MM	10-50MM	50-100MM	100-250MM		ALL	ALL
54	124	76	32	10	7	**NUMBER OF STATEMENTS**	437	432
%	%	%	%	%	%	**ASSETS**	%	%
20.5	17.1	12.5	14.9	6.5		Cash & Equivalents	16.0	16.6
9.6	21.5	29.5	32.8	28.6		Trade Receivables (net)	23.5	23.3
41.5	28.2	23.3	19.5	18.0		Inventory	29.6	29.9
4.1	1.6	1.8	1.5	1.3		All Other Current	1.6	2.3
75.7	68.4	67.1	68.6	54.5		Total Current	70.7	72.1
13.8	10.0	10.8	10.8	6.7		Fixed Assets (net)	12.5	11.5
4.0	13.8	13.8	12.8	33.4		Intangibles (net)	9.2	8.9
6.5	7.8	8.2	7.8	5.3		All Other Non-Current	7.6	7.5
100.0	100.0	100.0	100.0	100.0		Total	100.0	100.0
						LIABILITIES		
16.3	10.7	10.7	10.1	2.2		Notes Payable-Short Term	7.4	11.1
3.6	4.4	2.0	2.5	1.4		Cur. Mat.-L.T.D.	2.5	2.5
32.3	25.5	30.3	28.5	38.0		Trade Payables	25.7	25.7
.0	.1	.2	.3	.0		Income Taxes Payable	.2	.1
18.4	7.4	8.1	9.0	7.0		All Other Current	9.3	11.5
70.5	48.1	51.4	50.5	48.6		Total Current	45.1	50.8
16.2	23.8	16.0	12.7	14.7		Long-Term Debt	15.0	15.4
.0	.0	.0	.0	.0		Deferred Taxes	.0	.0
2.8	2.4	3.5	5.7	1.4		All Other Non-Current	6.8	8.2
10.4	25.7	29.2	31.1	35.3		Net Worth	33.1	25.6
100.0	100.0	100.0	100.0	100.0		Total Liabilities & Net Worth	100.0	100.0
						INCOME DATA		
100.0	100.0	100.0	100.0	100.0		Net Sales	100.0	100.0
32.7	25.0	24.3	30.7	25.1		Gross Profit	28.0	28.9
29.9	20.6	21.9	25.5	16.2		Operating Expenses	22.7	24.9
2.7	4.5	2.5	5.2	8.9		Operating Profit	5.3	4.0
-.2	.0	.1	-.3	.2		All Other Expenses (net)	.3	-.1
3.0	4.5	2.4	5.5	8.7		Profit Before Taxes	5.0	4.1
						RATIOS		
3.5	3.0	2.0	2.3	1.6			3.3	3.0
1.6	1.7	1.4	1.5	1.2		Current	1.7	1.7
.7	1.0	1.0	1.0	.8			1.1	1.1
1.6	1.6	1.3	1.7	1.1			1.6	1.5
.4	(123) .9	(75) .9	.9	.8		Quick (436)	.9	.9
.1	.5	.5	.6	.3			.6	.5
0 UND	0 910.6	14 25.2	23 16.1	6 56.6			3 122.1	2 175.5
1 391.2	15 24.5	22 16.9	33 11.1	33 11.1		Sales/Receivables	16 23.4	16 22.6
6 63.3	23 15.9	34 10.8	50 7.3	44 8.3			26 13.9	26 13.8
15 24.5	16 23.2	13 28.6	13 28.8	9 38.8			16 23.5	16 23.4
28 12.9	26 14.0	25 14.5	21 17.0	18 20.4		Cost of Sales/Inventory	27 13.7	27 13.4
49 7.5	37 9.9	37 9.8	47 7.8	32 11.5			40 9.1	40 9.1
0 UND	3 133.2	14 25.3	22 16.8	27 13.7			7 55.0	9 42.5
13 29.1	16 23.1	29 12.7	36 10.1	34 10.6		Cost of Sales/Payables	20 18.1	21 17.5
30 12.2	34 10.8	43 8.4	57 6.4	57 6.4			35 10.3	33 10.9
12.9	12.1	14.5	9.1	16.1			9.7	10.7
59.0	20.5	26.3	16.9	20.4		Sales/Working Capital	21.7	20.8
-31.1	-246.2	NM	154.1	-136.6			111.7	175.2
19.4	24.4	15.0	25.4				32.7	37.9
(26) 5.7	(88) 3.8	(59) 3.5	(26) 7.5			EBIT/Interest (293) / (301)	7.5	10.3
-4.1	.9	.8	.3				2.1	1.9
							8.4	5.4
						Net Profit + Depr., Dep., Amort./Cur. Mat. L/T/D (29) / (25)	3.1	2.6
							1.8	.7
.0	.1	.1	.2	.2			.1	.1
.2	.4	.6	.4	2.3		Fixed/Worth	.3	.3
-1.9	-.5	77.8	5.7	-.2			4.5	3.2
.5	.9	1.2	1.2	3.0			.7	.7
3.5	3.8	4.7	4.8	7.9		Debt/Worth	2.6	2.5
-4.9	-4.1	999.8	24.2	-2.8			47.4	-26.4
129.5	86.3	94.9	98.2				120.6	104.8
(34) 66.3	(77) 41.7	(58) 38.6	(25) 54.8			% Profit Before Taxes/Tangible Net Worth (336) / (314)	40.9	42.4
31.7	8.4	8.9	12.7				12.1	13.6
73.0	36.4	17.7	23.6	26.4			34.7	32.7
22.1	12.4	5.7	13.5	15.0		% Profit Before Taxes/Total Assets	11.8	12.9
-6.4	1.2	.7	.0	1.4			2.1	1.8
UND	365.0	231.5	83.7	270.9			337.7	377.8
278.6	88.5	89.8	44.4	79.3		Sales/Net Fixed Assets	83.2	91.8
41.2	36.5	31.2	22.2	27.1			30.9	29.3
12.8	7.6	5.7	4.5	4.5			7.2	7.9
8.3	5.5	4.7	3.3	3.5		Sales/Total Assets	5.0	5.3
4.4	3.6	3.2	2.3	1.9			3.5	3.3
.1	.1	.2	.2				.2	.2
(25) .4	(67) .4	(44) .5	(24) .6			% Depr., Dep., Amort./Sales (279) / (269)	.4	.4
.8	.8	1.0	1.0				1.0	1.0
1.5	2.2	.7					1.6	1.7
(28) 3.7	(73) 3.3	(39) 1.5				% Officers', Directors' Owners' Comp/Sales (238) / (221)	2.8	3.0
6.9	5.1	2.8					5.4	5.2
130383M	767288M	1730636M	2174059M	2467617M	2931978M	Net Sales ($)	14334541M	15947896M
15117M	136182M	372282M	635988M	748981M	1073253M	Total Assets ($)	3980048M	4111052M

© RMA 2019

M = $ thousand   MM = $ million
See Pages viii through xx for Explanation of Ratios and Data

Comparative Historical Data | Current Data Sorted by Sales

Type of Statement

Hist 1	Hist 2	Hist 3	Type of Statement	0-1MM	1-3MM	3-5MM	5-10MM	10-25MM	25MM & OVER
10	10	12	Unqualified				2	3	12
22	17	14	Reviewed						9
34	35	34	Compiled	2	4	10	6	9	3
144	143	118	Tax Returns	5	15	31	36	21	10
167	147	125	Other	7	20	23	14	23	38
4/1/16-3/31/17 ALL	4/1/17-3/31/18 ALL	4/1/18-3/31/19 ALL		35 (4/1-9/30/18)			268 (10/1/18-3/31/19)		
377	352	303	NUMBER OF STATEMENTS	14	39	64	58	56	72

4/1/16-3/31/17 ALL %	4/1/17-3/31/18 ALL %	4/1/18-3/31/19 ALL %		0-1MM %	1-3MM %	3-5MM %	5-10MM %	10-25MM %	25MM & OVER %
			ASSETS						
16.5	17.0	15.6	Cash & Equivalents	19.8	18.4	17.6	14.7	15.7	12.3
25.1	23.6	22.9	Trade Receivables (net)	8.2	8.2	19.7	22.0	27.5	33.7
28.3	29.1	27.9	Inventory	33.9	28.7	32.7	34.2	22.0	21.5
1.7	2.1	2.2	All Other Current	2.5	4.6	2.2	1.5	.8	2.3
71.6	71.7	68.5	Total Current	64.4	59.9	72.1	72.3	66.0	69.8
10.8	11.4	10.8	Fixed Assets (net)	29.3	15.3	9.2	9.6	9.0	8.7
11.9	11.2	13.2	Intangibles (net)	4.9	11.2	12.0	10.6	18.7	14.8
5.7	5.7	7.4	All Other Non-Current	1.5	13.7	6.7	7.5	6.3	6.8
100.0	100.0	100.0	Total	100.0	100.0	100.0	100.0	100.0	100.0
			LIABILITIES						
8.4	10.4	11.3	Notes Payable-Short Term	14.2	22.7	7.8	11.6	8.9	9.3
2.7	2.6	3.3	Cur. Mat.-L.T.D.	1.0	1.0	5.5	3.8	4.3	1.8
26.1	23.0	28.6	Trade Payables	17.3	18.0	23.1	34.5	29.9	35.7
.1	.1	.1	Income Taxes Payable	.0	.0	.1	.1	.0	.3
9.4	9.4	9.7	All Other Current	35.7	10.0	8.3	8.2	7.2	8.7
46.7	45.5	53.0	Total Current	68.3	51.7	44.8	58.2	50.3	55.8
19.3	16.5	19.0	Long-Term Debt	13.5	33.2	24.7	15.3	17.1	11.8
.1	.0	.0	Deferred Taxes	.0	.0	.0	.0	.0	.1
3.9	5.6	3.0	All Other Non-Current	6.3	2.4	3.2	1.4	3.2	3.8
30.0	32.3	24.9	Net Worth	11.9	12.7	27.3	25.0	29.4	28.5
100.0	100.0	100.0	Total Liabilities & Net Worth	100.0	100.0	100.0	100.0	100.0	100.0
			INCOME DATA						
100.0	100.0	100.0	Net Sales	100.0	100.0	100.0	100.0	100.0	100.0
27.1	26.8	26.8	Gross Profit	44.6	33.7	26.0	24.8	23.6	24.5
23.3	23.1	23.0	Operating Expenses	43.3	30.4	20.7	20.8	20.4	20.7
3.8	3.7	3.9	Operating Profit	1.3	3.3	5.3	4.0	3.2	3.8
-.3	-.2	.0	All Other Expenses (net)	.3	.1	.1	-.4	-.2	.3
4.1	3.9	3.9	Profit Before Taxes	1.0	3.2	5.2	4.4	3.4	3.5
			RATIOS						
3.1	3.6	2.6	Current	2.9	4.4	4.1	2.2	2.0	1.8
1.7	1.7	1.5		1.9	1.6	2.1	1.3	1.4	1.3
1.1	1.1	1.0		.6	.7	1.3	.9	1.0	1.0
1.8	2.0	1.5	Quick	1.6	2.1	2.3	1.0	1.4	1.3
1.0	1.0	(301) .8		.4	.6	(63) 1.1	.6	(71) .9	.9
.5	.5	.4		.1	.2	.5	.3	.5	.5
7 53.2	3 135.0	2 219.9	Sales/Receivables	0 UND	0 UND	0 821.4	1 389.8	10 35.7	17 21.8
18 20.5	16 22.4	17 21.7		0 UND	2 171.9	13 28.8	14 26.5	19 19.7	28 12.9
28 13.2	25 14.7	30 12.3		27 13.6	14 26.1	26 14.1	22 16.7	29 12.5	42 8.7
16 22.9	15 24.7	14 25.7	Cost of Sales/Inventory	33 11.0	22 16.8	19 19.2	16 22.8	8 48.2	11 34.3
27 13.7	26 14.1	26 14.2		51 7.2	41 9.0	29 12.6	24 15.0	19 19.1	20 18.7
37 9.8	38 9.5	39 9.4		101 3.6	61 6.0	38 9.6	33 11.2	31 11.8	31 11.7
11 33.0	8 46.0	9 39.5	Cost of Sales/Payables	0 UND	0 UND	1 664.1	11 32.6	16 23.5	23 16.2
21 17.7	17 21.2	24 15.5		28 13.0	8 46.4	15 23.6	22 16.4	26 14.3	32 11.5
35 10.4	34 10.7	38 9.6		46 7.9	35 10.3	27 13.5	38 9.7	33 11.0	54 6.8
10.2	10.0	13.0	Sales/Working Capital	11.5	9.8	10.1	16.0	14.5	13.8
17.7	18.3	23.5		54.9	39.9	15.9	33.6	26.6	27.8
166.7	89.6	-213.7		-5.0	-23.8	42.2	-58.0	-530.7	157.5
31.0	37.7	20.2	EBIT/Interest		14.8	41.6	30.0	16.0	25.4
(276) 6.6	(264) 7.4	(214) 4.3		(20) 1.0	(43) 7.3	(46) 4.3	(41) 3.3	(57) 7.3	
1.7	2.6	.8			-4.5	2.2	1.5	-2.0	1.0
5.7	4.7	1.7	Net Profit + Depr., Dep., Amort./Cur. Mat. L/T/D						
(29) 2.6	(21) 2.4	(13) .9							
.8	1.2	-.6							
.1	.1	.1	Fixed/Worth	.0	.0	.0	.0	.1	.2
.4	.4	.4		1.0	1.0	.3	.6	.3	.5
-2.5	-5.2	-1.5		-1.3	-.7	-1.1	-.8	2.6	77.8
.7	.6	1.0	Debt/Worth	.7	.8	.4	1.0	1.1	1.6
2.5	2.6	4.4		4.3	19.6	3.0	3.6	4.1	5.6
-11.8	-17.8	-6.7		-5.3	-3.2	-4.6	-5.3	-13.0	999.8
100.4	96.4	107.8	% Profit Before Taxes/Tangible Net Worth		93.0	122.4	85.6	75.9	144.4
(261) 46.7	(251) 42.8	(204) 45.8		(21) 37.0	(42) 48.7	(37) 50.2	(41) 34.9	(55) 57.2	
12.4	11.8	12.9			11.7	16.8	8.4	2.7	21.6
31.5	31.9	31.7	% Profit Before Taxes/Total Assets	50.7	28.5	42.6	41.2	26.3	20.5
13.0	13.3	11.9		9.4	9.8	15.6	12.3	6.7	8.9
2.2	2.5	.8		40.9	5.3	5.0	1.7	.2	.8
315.6	382.5	357.5	Sales/Net Fixed Assets	UND	999.8	299.2	594.0	250.5	222.9
83.8	85.8	89.0		31.2	85.2	94.1	170.2	105.2	75.3
30.6	33.0	33.5		13.3	17.8	34.8	42.1	36.7	29.8
7.1	7.3	7.2	Sales/Total Assets	8.7	6.6	7.7	8.7	7.7	5.9
5.0	5.0	4.8		4.6	4.1	4.8	6.3	5.2	4.1
3.4	3.6	3.4		1.9	2.5	3.5	4.6	3.7	3.2
.1	.1	.1	% Depr., Dep., Amort./Sales		.3	.1	.2	.1	.1
(236) .5	(209) .4	(170) .4		(17) .6	(38) .4	(27) .3	(31) .5	(48) .5	
1.0	.9	.9			1.8	.7	.9	1.0	.9
1.7	1.5	1.4	% Officers', Directors' Owners' Comp/Sales		2.6	2.8	2.1	1.1	.3
(188) 2.6	(169) 2.6	(142) 2.8		(16) 3.8	(40) 3.8	(36) 2.9	(28) 1.7	(16) .6	
4.8	4.3	4.6			7.3	5.5	4.2	2.7	1.3
13294288M	13077445M	10201961M	Net Sales ($)	7842M	76756M	255078M	419298M	848240M	8594747M
3496667M	3119907M	2981803M	Total Assets ($)	3733M	24867M	59276M	93116M	300198M	2500613M

Current Data Sorted by Assets   Comparative Historical Data

						Type of Statement		
		2	2		3	Unqualified	12	7
	1	2	4			Reviewed	6	10
7	12	2	3		1	Compiled	10	11
5	7	7		3		Tax Returns	40	41
	7 (4/1-9/30/18)	14	74 (10/1/18-3/31/19)		4	Other	41	45
0-500M	500M-2MM	2-10MM	10-50MM	50-100MM	100-250MM		4/1/14-3/31/15 ALL	4/1/15-3/31/16 ALL
12	20	25	13	3	8	NUMBER OF STATEMENTS	109	114
%	%	%	%	%	%	ASSETS	%	%
30.7	22.9	17.1	19.1			Cash & Equivalents	18.8	16.8
2.8	8.9	18.4	19.7			Trade Receivables (net)	12.2	11.0
30.1	41.5	39.0	38.2			Inventory	46.0	43.6
3.4	1.0	3.1	10.3			All Other Current	3.1	3.9
67.0	74.4	77.6	87.2			Total Current	80.2	75.4
24.5	8.0	8.2	9.0			Fixed Assets (net)	9.0	12.1
3.9	6.8	10.2	3.2			Intangibles (net)	4.7	6.4
4.5	10.7	4.0	.6			All Other Non-Current	6.1	6.1
100.0	100.0	100.0	100.0			Total	100.0	100.0
						LIABILITIES		
22.8	9.0	10.9	6.9			Notes Payable-Short Term	7.8	6.3
3.5	.2	2.0	.9			Cur. Mat.-L.T.D.	1.0	1.9
8.7	9.9	26.8	14.7			Trade Payables	17.1	14.7
.0	.2	.3	.0			Income Taxes Payable	.3	.1
13.9	18.2	12.3	7.8			All Other Current	7.7	8.4
48.9	37.4	52.3	30.4			Total Current	33.8	31.5
7.1	4.1	11.0	4.9			Long-Term Debt	8.6	15.7
.0	.0	.0	.0			Deferred Taxes	.1	.3
8.3	12.7	5.4	6.4			All Other Non-Current	6.8	6.0
35.7	45.8	31.3	58.4			Net Worth	50.7	46.4
100.0	100.0	100.0	100.0			Total Liabilties & Net Worth	100.0	100.0
						INCOME DATA		
100.0	100.0	100.0	100.0			Net Sales	100.0	100.0
62.1	43.7	40.4	48.7			Gross Profit	41.8	48.0
51.2	35.9	35.6	38.3			Operating Expenses	32.6	40.1
10.8	7.8	4.9	10.4			Operating Profit	9.2	8.0
1.2	.7	.9	.1			All Other Expenses (net)	.4	.4
9.7	7.1	4.0	10.3			Profit Before Taxes	8.8	7.5
						RATIOS		
5.8	15.0	2.1	6.0				5.5	6.5
2.5	2.7	1.5	4.4			Current	2.5	2.5
.7	1.2	1.1	1.6				1.5	1.4
5.7	6.5	1.2	3.5				1.7	2.0
.6	1.4	.7	1.0			Quick	.8	.8
.2	.2	.3	.2				.4	.3
0 UND	0 UND	0 UND	0 UND				0 UND	0 UND
0 UND	0 UND	9 38.8	34 10.8			Sales/Receivables	4 101.2	3 110.8
0 UND	1 258.4	36 10.2	68 5.4				27 13.6	33 10.9
0 UND	16 22.2	36 10.0	91 4.0				47 7.8	62 5.9
15 23.8	78 4.7	56 6.5	215 1.7			Cost of Sales/Inventory	104 3.5	122 3.0
135 2.7	122 3.0	152 2.4	281 1.3				174 2.1	182 2.0
0 UND	0 UND	7 54.7	35 10.5				9 42.0	12 31.6
0 UND	0 UND	36 10.1	47 7.7			Cost of Sales/Payables	28 13.1	28 12.9
0 UND	24 15.0	60 6.1	61 6.0				54 6.8	55 6.6
5.7	3.7	5.9	2.1				3.9	3.7
14.8	13.2	18.6	3.9			Sales/Working Capital	6.5	7.0
NM	36.8	94.9	4.6				18.1	15.1
		8.4					46.5	58.6
	(20)	4.2				EBIT/Interest	(67) 11.5	(81) 15.6
		1.5					4.4	3.6
						Net Profit + Depr., Dep.,		10.2
						Amort./Cur. Mat. L/T/D	(10)	4.9
								1.4
.0	.0	.0	.0				.0	.0
.5	.2	.1	.1			Fixed/Worth	.1	.2
.8	.6	1.0	.3				.4	.9
.1	.1	1.0	.2				.3	.2
1.0	1.3	6.1	.6			Debt/Worth	1.0	1.0
7.5	20.4	21.2	2.2				2.7	4.9
160.4	66.4	140.7	69.2				87.4	70.2
(10) 103.9	(16) 8.4	(20) 61.3	(12) 36.4			% Profit Before Taxes/Tangible Net Worth	(97) 43.1	(96) 36.9
55.2	-2.0	4.5	25.3				12.8	8.1
87.3	35.0	24.0	33.4				42.3	40.8
26.3	4.1	10.5	15.9			% Profit Before Taxes/Total Assets	15.7	16.2
5.3	-1.7	1.9	11.4				5.4	3.8
325.0	377.3	999.8	182.4				565.7	272.9
24.7	91.9	107.3	45.6			Sales/Net Fixed Assets	95.4	39.3
8.6	23.6	35.2	11.8				22.2	14.9
5.9	8.0	5.8	2.5				4.2	3.8
4.6	3.5	3.6	1.6			Sales/Total Assets	2.8	2.6
3.4	2.2	2.3	1.4				2.1	2.0
	.4	.1					.2	.3
	(11) .6	(18) .5				% Depr., Dep., Amort./Sales	(60) .5	(69) .8
	2.0	1.0					1.7	1.8
	1.5	.4					1.3	1.4
	(10) 2.7	(12) 1.0				% Officers', Directors' Owners' Comp/Sales	(46) 3.7	(40) 2.3
	4.6	6.1					5.9	3.9
15070M	104427M	421681M	518730M	162749M	1395294M	Net Sales ($)	3170609M	4394157M
3264M	21577M	110613M	272597M	199069M	1099036M	Total Assets ($)	1498132M	2137429M

M = $ thousand   MM = $ million
See Pages viii through xx for Explanation of Ratios and Data

Comparative Historical Data | Current Data Sorted by Sales

						Type of Statement						
	7		5		5	Unqualified				4		5
	6		6		6	Reviewed				3		2
	5		9		7	Compiled			1	3		3
	26		39		26	Tax Returns			3	5		3
	36		42		37	Other	4	9	2	5	7	12
	4/1/16-3/31/17		4/1/17-3/31/18		4/1/18-3/31/19		3	9	1			
	ALL		ALL		ALL			7 (4/1-9/30/18)		74 (10/1/18-3/31/19)		
							0-1MM	1-3MM	3-5MM	5-10MM	10-25MM	25MM & OVER
	80		**101**		**81**	NUMBER OF STATEMENTS	**7**	**18**	**3**	**9**	**19**	**25**
	%		%		%		%	%	%	%	%	%
						ASSETS						
	16.2		17.8		19.1	Cash & Equivalents	24.0				19.7	13.4
	9.5		13.1		13.7	Trade Receivables (net)	.0				20.0	20.6
	41.5		43.0		36.5	Inventory	39.6				42.7	34.0
	3.4		3.4		3.7	All Other Current	2.9				5.9	3.2
	70.6		77.3		73.1	Total Current	66.5				88.2	71.2
	14.7		10.6		10.8	Fixed Assets (net)	14.3				6.6	7.8
	8.6		8.4		8.9	Intangibles (net)	6.1				4.1	12.2
	6.1		3.7		7.3	All Other Non-Current	13.2				1.2	8.8
	100.0		100.0		100.0	Total	100.0				100.0	100.0
						LIABILITIES						
	8.8		10.4		11.2	Notes Payable-Short Term	9.0				12.0	9.3
	1.9		2.1		1.4	Cur. Mat.-L.T.D.	.3				2.5	.7
	13.3		13.2		16.4	Trade Payables	5.5				24.3	20.1
	.1		.1		.2	Income Taxes Payable	.2				.0	.3
	8.5		8.5		13.1	All Other Current	11.9				8.8	15.2
	32.5		34.3		42.3	Total Current	26.9				47.6	45.6
	8.1		7.3		8.5	Long-Term Debt	9.4				6.9	9.3
	.4		.3		.0	Deferred Taxes	.0				.0	.1
	8.1		7.8		8.4	All Other Non-Current	7.5				3.0	7.7
	50.8		50.3		40.7	Net Worth	56.2				42.5	37.3
	100.0		100.0		100.0	Total Liabilities & Net Worth	100.0				100.0	100.0
						INCOME DATA						
	100.0		100.0		100.0	Net Sales	100.0				100.0	100.0
	46.0		45.5		46.0	Gross Profit	48.1				33.5	44.7
	38.9		38.7		38.1	Operating Expenses	38.8				26.8	38.1
	7.1		6.8		7.9	Operating Profit	9.3				6.8	6.6
	1.0		.7		1.1	All Other Expenses (net)	.9				.6	1.7
	6.1		6.2		6.8	Profit Before Taxes	8.5				6.2	4.9
						RATIOS						
	5.1		5.6		4.7		17.9				6.2	2.9
	2.3		2.5		2.0	Current	2.7				2.3	1.5
	1.4		1.5		1.2		1.3				1.4	1.1
	1.8		1.8		2.1		6.5				2.7	1.3
	.8		.9		.7	Quick	1.4				.9	.6
	.3		.4		.3		.3				.3	.2
0	UND	0	UND	0	UND		0	UND			0	UND	3	106.9
2	157.8	6	59.5	4	101.3	Sales/Receivables	0	UND			12	29.6	26	14.0
28	13.2	38	9.7	34	10.6		0	UND			43	8.4	66	5.5
58	6.3	52	7.0	36	10.0		0	UND			22	16.4	50	7.3
107	3.4	122	3.0	87	4.2	Cost of Sales/Inventory	101	3.6			56	6.5	107	3.4
182	2.0	192	1.9	159	2.3		159	2.3			203	1.8	215	1.7
4	98.2	3	133.3	0	UND		0	UND			14	26.6	25	14.6
22	16.9	29	12.4	28	12.9	Cost of Sales/Payables	0	UND			38	9.5	43	8.5
51	7.1	47	7.8	50	7.3		7	53.1			57	6.4	61	6.0
	4.1		3.5		4.2		3.5				3.2	4.1
	7.2		7.1		9.6	Sales/Working Capital	6.4				11.1	8.2
	18.9		14.2		48.8		63.1				26.0	67.2
	25.0		44.3		17.1						18.8	29.5
(52)	7.9	(63)	8.1	(51)	5.0	EBIT/Interest				(14)	5.9	(18)	4.9
	1.7		.9		.9						3.0	-.5
						Net Profit + Depr., Dep., Amort./Cur. Mat. L/T/D						
	.0		.0		.0		.1				.0	.0
	.2		.1		.2	Fixed/Worth	.2				.0	.2
	.7		.7		.8		.8				.2	NM
	.2		.2		.3		.2				.2	.8
	1.1		.9		1.6	Debt/Worth	.6				1.3	2.6
	2.9		4.3		12.9		5.0				6.1	NM
	69.2		75.0		106.1		100.0				101.2	81.5
(69)	29.9	(86)	35.1	(65)	45.0	% Profit Before Taxes/Tangible Net Worth	(15)	10.8			(18)	51.3	(19)	39.1
	5.8		14.3		6.8		.9				9.1	24.9
	26.0		40.0		32.3		34.6				33.0	19.0
	11.6		14.8		11.0	% Profit Before Taxes/Total Assets	8.2				15.9	7.9
	2.3		3.1		1.0		.4				2.9	1.1
	446.8		529.7		214.4		UND				999.8	116.8
	45.1		47.9		49.4	Sales/Net Fixed Assets	30.0				199.9	40.1
	11.6		15.8		17.9		9.8				45.6	16.4
	3.7		4.3		4.9		5.0				6.3	3.2
	2.7		2.7		2.8	Sales/Total Assets	2.9				3.8	1.6
	1.6		1.6		1.5		1.4				2.6	1.2
	.2		.2		.2		.4				.1	.1
(44)	1.1	(57)	.5	(54)	.6	% Depr., Dep., Amort./Sales	(11)	1.6			(12)	.2	(17)	.6
	2.3		1.3		1.2		2.2				1.0	1.5
	1.4		1.2		1.1							
(29)	2.9	(46)	2.4	(31)	2.9	% Officers', Directors' Owners' Comp/Sales						
	5.6		4.8		5.6							
2870813M		3473584M		2617951M		Net Sales ($)	5004M	36025M	11504M	66594M	339724M	2159100M
2111510M		1830301M		1706156M		Total Assets ($)	2407M	18339M	3318M	24418M	112896M	1544778M

M = $ thousand   MM = $ million
See Pages viii through xx for Explanation of Ratios and Data

Current Data Sorted by Assets   Comparative Historical Data

Current sample periods: 1 (4/1–9/30/18) · 25 (10/1/18–3/31/19)

0-500M	500M-2MM	2-10MM	10-50MM	50-100MM	100-250MM	Type of Statement / Item	4/1/14-3/31/15 ALL	4/1/15-3/31/16 ALL
						Type of Statement		
						Unqualified		
			1			Reviewed	2	3
1		2				Compiled	3	8
9	2	1		1		Tax Returns	21	21
1	6	2				Other	15	22
11	8	5	1	1		**NUMBER OF STATEMENTS**	41	57
%	%	%	%	%	%	**ASSETS**	%	%
28.8						Cash & Equivalents	19.2	16.5
3.9						Trade Receivables (net)	7.1	9.2
28.8						Inventory	35.4	29.1
5.0						All Other Current	1.6	2.0
66.5						Total Current	63.3	56.8
16.3						Fixed Assets (net)	21.7	19.7
8.8						Intangibles (net)	8.0	12.4
8.4						All Other Non-Current	7.0	11.1
100.0						Total	100.0	100.0
						LIABILITIES		
12.5						Notes Payable-Short Term	9.8	12.4
7.1						Cur. Mat.-L.T.D.	2.4	1.9
17.5						Trade Payables	17.7	16.6
.0						Income Taxes Payable	.1	.1
3.6						All Other Current	12.2	13.3
40.7						Total Current	42.2	44.2
23.8						Long-Term Debt	23.6	10.8
.0						Deferred Taxes	.0	.0
1.7						All Other Non-Current	5.2	9.3
33.8						Net Worth	29.0	35.6
100.0						Total Liabilities & Net Worth	100.0	100.0
						INCOME DATA		
100.0						Net Sales	100.0	100.0
61.4						Gross Profit	53.9	56.4
57.1						Operating Expenses	45.9	51.4
4.3						Operating Profit	8.1	4.9
.9						All Other Expenses (net)	-.1	.3
3.4						Profit Before Taxes	8.1	4.6
						RATIOS		
3.9						Current	2.7	2.8
2.0							1.6	1.5
1.0							1.0	.9
1.7						Quick	1.0	1.8
1.0							.6	.6
.3							.2	.2
0 UND						Sales/Receivables	0 UND	0 UND
0 UND							5 77.1	3 106.7
9 38.8							14 26.4	19 19.7
27 13.5						Cost of Sales/Inventory	35 10.5	28 13.2
40 9.2							79 4.6	69 5.3
74 4.9							152 2.4	111 3.3
0 UND						Cost of Sales/Payables	7 49.7	0 UND
14 26.1							30 12.0	26 13.8
57 6.4							74 4.9	63 5.8
4.6						Sales/Working Capital	7.9	8.0
20.0							18.3	22.7
UND							314.7	-50.5
						EBIT/Interest	62.8	40.1
							(31) 22.8	(40) 5.3
							3.4	1.3
						Net Profit + Depr., Dep., Amort./Cur. Mat. L/T/D		
.0						Fixed/Worth	.1	.1
.1							.6	.5
-1.9							2.2	3.1
.2						Debt/Worth	.5	.6
1.1							1.2	1.9
-4.7							19.7	-13.4
						% Profit Before Taxes/Tangible Net Worth	119.6	74.4
							(32) 53.9	(42) 29.8
							28.8	8.0
27.7						% Profit Before Taxes/Total Assets	44.7	21.0
14.9							23.2	11.5
-7.0							5.7	1.3
UND						Sales/Net Fixed Assets	69.1	116.3
167.0							23.1	34.5
8.4							10.3	12.7
9.5						Sales/Total Assets	5.3	4.8
4.1							3.2	3.4
3.2							2.5	2.2
						% Depr., Dep., Amort./Sales	.4	.5
							(27) 1.0	(38) 1.4
							1.8	2.1
						% Officers', Directors' Owners' Comp/Sales	2.2	3.2
							(23) 5.0	(18) 7.7
							10.9	19.9
10516M	27693M	65968M	46021M	40626M		Net Sales ($)	777005M	567588M
2357M	8362M	24126M	15735M	50022M		Total Assets ($)	285565M	230177M

M = $ thousand   MM = $ million

See Pages viii through xx for Explanation of Ratios and Data

Comparative Historical Data | Current Data Sorted by Sales

			Type of Statement						1
2	2	1	Unqualified						1
2		2	Reviewed						1
5	5	4	Compiled		2	2			
26	13	15	Tax Returns	8	4		3		
15	15	4	Other	1			2		1
4/1/16-	4/1/17-	4/1/18-			1 (4/1-9/30/18)		25 (10/1/18-3/31/19)		
3/31/17	3/31/18	3/31/19		0-1MM	1-3MM	3-5MM	5-10MM	10-25MM	25MM & OVER
ALL	ALL	ALL							
50	35	26	NUMBER OF STATEMENTS	9	6	2	5	1	3
%	%	%	ASSETS	%	%	%	%	%	%
19.0	18.5	18.5	Cash & Equivalents						
8.2	9.2	5.9	Trade Receivables (net)						
29.3	36.1	28.9	Inventory						
1.7	1.4	3.1	All Other Current						
58.2	65.2	56.4	Total Current						
19.0	23.8	21.5	Fixed Assets (net)						
5.5	3.7	12.2	Intangibles (net)						
17.2	7.4	9.9	All Other Non-Current						
100.0	100.0	100.0	Total						
			LIABILITIES						
9.5	13.3	11.5	Notes Payable-Short Term						
2.4	5.2	4.7	Cur. Mat.-L.T.D.						
15.3	13.0	14.9	Trade Payables						
.1	.1	.0	Income Taxes Payable						
23.9	22.6	5.0	All Other Current						
51.2	54.7	36.1	Total Current						
13.9	20.6	23.9	Long-Term Debt						
.1	.0	.0	Deferred Taxes						
4.1	10.8	10.2	All Other Non-Current						
30.5	13.8	29.8	Net Worth						
100.0	100.0	100.0	Total Liabilties & Net Worth						
			INCOME DATA						
100.0	100.0	100.0	Net Sales						
56.9	52.6	55.7	Gross Profit						
51.2	47.0	50.2	Operating Expenses						
5.7	5.6	5.5	Operating Profit						
-.3	.2	.7	All Other Expenses (net)						
6.0	5.5	4.7	Profit Before Taxes						
			RATIOS						
2.7	1.9	3.7							
1.6	1.4	1.6	Current						
.8	.9	1.0							
1.7	1.1	1.6							
.8	.5	.7	Quick						
.2	.2	.3							
0	UND	0	UND	0	UND		Sales/Receivables		
6	63.0	2	241.3	0	UND				
14	25.9	13	29.1	14	26.4				
35	10.3	31	11.6	28	13.2		Cost of Sales/Inventory		
69	5.3	89	4.1	48	7.6				
118	3.1	182	2.0	94	3.9				
5	70.4	2	174.0	0	UND		Cost of Sales/Payables		
31	11.6	29	12.5	17	21.1				
73	5.0	63	5.8	62	5.9				
9.9	9.4	6.1	Sales/Working Capital						
21.0	18.8	19.0							
-23.9	-80.2	UND							
	77.8		29.0		22.8		EBIT/Interest		
(33)	13.9	(22)	10.1	(20)	4.7				
	2.4		4.1		1.6				
			Net Profit + Depr., Dep., Amort./Cur. Mat. L/T/D						
.1	.0	.1	Fixed/Worth						
.4	.7	.9							
-12.9	UND	NM							
.3	1.0	.9	Debt/Worth						
1.6	2.5	3.4							
-36.0	-9.2	NM							
	64.4		96.7		190.1		% Profit Before Taxes/Tangible Net Worth		
(36)	27.8	(25)	29.6	(20)	30.7				
	12.5		6.0		8.8				
25.9	50.9	25.0	% Profit Before Taxes/Total Assets						
11.1	12.5	14.1							
3.5	2.9	.3							
80.5	179.0	187.4	Sales/Net Fixed Assets						
26.1	28.7	25.2							
9.8	7.0	7.9							
5.4	5.3	4.6	Sales/Total Assets						
2.9	3.2	3.5							
1.9	1.7	1.8							
	.5		.3		1.0		% Depr., Dep., Amort./Sales		
(36)	1.4	(24)	1.1	(14)	1.8				
	2.9		2.7		3.3				
	1.7		2.6		1.6		% Officers', Directors' Owners' Comp/Sales		
(25)	3.9	(15)	4.6	(13)	5.1				
	7.9		10.5		12.0				
724335M	307355M	190824M	Net Sales ($)	4675M	11436M	8182M	32215M	21225M	113091M
361295M	145656M	100602M	Total Assets ($)	1973M	4289M	3333M	12692M	8461M	69854M

© RMA 2019

M = $ thousand   MM = $ million
See Pages viii through xx for Explanation of Ratios and Data

Current Data Sorted by Assets							Comparative Historical Data	
						Type of Statement		
		1	2			Unqualified	4	3
		1	3			Reviewed	2	2
	1	2				Compiled	3	14
2	7	4				Tax Returns	20	13
14	8	14	3	5		Other	32	32
	9 (4/1-9/30/18)		58 (10/1/18-3/31/19)				4/1/14-3/31/15 ALL	4/1/15-3/31/16 ALL
0-500M	500M-2MM	2-10MM	10-50MM	50-100MM	100-250MM			
16	16	22	8	5		**NUMBER OF STATEMENTS**	61	64
%	%	%	%	%	%	**ASSETS**	%	%
34.3	13.0	12.9			DATA NOT AVAILABLE	Cash & Equivalents	17.7	15.9
.0	13.8	32.3				Trade Receivables (net)	12.2	11.5
40.1	38.9	35.3				Inventory	33.5	32.9
.3	2.4	1.8				All Other Current	3.3	4.1
74.8	68.1	82.3				Total Current	66.7	64.4
8.9	15.1	9.9				Fixed Assets (net)	18.3	16.9
1.7	7.5	1.2				Intangibles (net)	4.7	10.8
14.7	9.3	6.6				All Other Non-Current	10.3	7.9
100.0	100.0	100.0				Total	100.0	100.0
						LIABILITIES		
5.9	16.5	11.6				Notes Payable-Short Term	9.2	10.3
5.2	1.3	1.9				Cur. Mat.-L.T.D.	2.1	2.7
5.3	14.4	30.9				Trade Payables	16.3	16.0
.0	.0	.0				Income Taxes Payable	.3	.1
8.7	10.9	10.4				All Other Current	7.4	14.7
25.1	43.2	54.9				Total Current	35.5	43.7
41.1	17.0	10.7				Long-Term Debt	17.3	14.2
.0	.0	.0				Deferred Taxes	.0	.3
8.8	6.8	3.0				All Other Non-Current	9.8	8.3
25.1	32.9	31.4				Net Worth	37.4	33.4
100.0	100.0	100.0				Total Liabilties & Net Worth	100.0	100.0
						INCOME DATA		
100.0	100.0	100.0				Net Sales	100.0	100.0
49.9	45.7	40.7				Gross Profit	45.3	47.2
38.8	42.0	36.0				Operating Expenses	38.1	39.1
11.1	3.7	4.7				Operating Profit	7.2	8.1
.5	1.3	.9				All Other Expenses (net)	.9	.8
10.6	2.5	3.8				Profit Before Taxes	6.3	7.3
						RATIOS		
13.9	13.6	3.1					4.1	4.3
5.5	2.1	1.9				Current	1.9	1.7
1.8	1.2	1.0					1.3	1.1
5.2	6.9	1.4					1.6	1.7
3.2	1.2	.8				Quick	.8	(63) .7
.5	.1	.6					.5	.2
0 UND	0 UND	10 37.0					0 UND	0 UND
0 UND	0 999.8	40 9.2				Sales/Receivables	2 182.4	3 118.7
0 UND	25 14.4	63 5.8					25 14.5	21 17.2
28 13.0	56 6.5	49 7.4					30 12.1	21 17.1
74 4.9	81 4.5	73 5.0				Cost of Sales/Inventory	62 5.9	55 6.6
91 4.0	122 3.0	130 2.8					118 3.1	104 3.5
0 UND	0 UND	23 16.0					2 222.7	6 56.8
0 UND	10 37.2	55 6.6				Cost of Sales/Payables	23 15.7	23 15.8
0 UND	36 10.1	91 4.0					47 7.8	45 8.2
5.2	4.9	5.4					5.1	6.8
6.6	10.3	8.7				Sales/Working Capital	12.8	14.6
41.6	94.4	50.9					35.3	216.3
	52.6	30.5					13.8	29.8
	(12) 4.3	(17) 4.4				EBIT/Interest	(40) 6.4	(44) 6.0
	-1.0	1.1					2.6	1.7
						Net Profit + Depr., Dep., Amort./Cur. Mat. L/T/D		
.0	.0	.0					.1	.1
.1	.1	.1				Fixed/Worth	.4	.4
.6	-4.4	3.3					1.3	-50.3
.2	.2	.6					.6	.5
.6	3.1	2.7				Debt/Worth	1.4	1.9
2.5	-3.3	21.2					4.7	-72.0
102.0	59.8	74.1					72.7	97.4
(13) 71.0	(10) 26.2	(19) 22.8				% Profit Before Taxes/Tangible Net Worth	(52) 34.8	(47) 42.1
3.2	6.4	5.9					13.3	18.8
66.4	34.0	27.6					33.4	45.3
33.8	8.8	7.0				% Profit Before Taxes/Total Assets	12.1	13.6
.5	-1.7	.2					4.4	3.3
725.0	UND	393.5					285.7	262.6
179.4	71.4	120.3				Sales/Net Fixed Assets	25.4	41.5
44.3	26.2	20.6					13.9	12.7
5.2	5.9	3.6					5.1	5.7
4.3	3.5	3.2				Sales/Total Assets	3.0	3.8
3.5	2.1	1.7					2.2	2.1
		.2					.6	.2
		(10) .5				% Depr., Dep., Amort./Sales	(38) 1.2	(36) .8
		.6					1.9	2.2
							1.1	1.4
						% Officers', Directors' Owners' Comp/Sales	(15) 2.4	(24) 2.6
							5.8	4.9
16729M	87557M	345006M	725276M	767789M		Net Sales ($)	1774280M	1637772M
3050M	16678M	120067M	216185M	359164M		Total Assets ($)	699911M	669201M

M = $ thousand MM = $ million

See Pages viii through xx for Explanation of Ratios and Data

Comparative Historical Data | Current Data Sorted by Sales

4/1/16-3/31/17 ALL	4/1/17-3/31/18 ALL	4/1/18-3/31/19 ALL	Type of Statement	0-1MM	1-3MM	3-5MM	5-10MM	10-25MM	25MM & OVER
6	6	3	Unqualified						3
2	2	4	Reviewed				1		3
1	3	3	Compiled					3	
28	11	13	Tax Returns	1	3	3	2	4	
40	37	44	Other	12	5	6	3	8	10
				12	9 (4/1-9/30/18) 5	6	3	58 (10/1/18-3/31/19) 8	10
77	59	67	**NUMBER OF STATEMENTS**	13	8	9	6	15	16
%	%	%	**ASSETS**	%	%	%	%	%	%
15.9	16.0	17.6	Cash & Equivalents	25.5				10.7	13.1
10.2	13.2	17.2	Trade Receivables (net)	.0				31.9	19.6
35.1	34.8	37.1	Inventory	36.7				40.2	34.9
2.6	3.6	2.3	All Other Current	.0				2.0	4.8
63.7	67.6	74.2	Total Current	62.3				84.8	72.4
20.6	16.4	12.7	Fixed Assets (net)	12.0				9.2	15.8
10.9	11.9	4.9	Intangibles (net)	7.7				1.0	9.8
4.7	4.2	8.3	All Other Non-Current	18.0				4.9	2.1
100.0	100.0	100.0	Total	100.0				100.0	100.0
			LIABILITIES						
11.3	16.7	10.1	Notes Payable-Short Term	15.9				13.4	8.9
2.2	1.8	2.8	Cur. Mat.-L.T.D.	4.7				2.4	2.5
16.5	16.2	18.7	Trade Payables	2.4				39.1	19.9
.1	.1	.1	Income Taxes Payable	.0				.0	.2
14.1	14.6	11.0	All Other Current	8.5				10.5	13.8
44.3	49.5	42.6	Total Current	31.5				65.3	45.4
18.3	14.4	20.4	Long-Term Debt	54.1				11.1	12.4
.5	.3	.4	Deferred Taxes	.0				.0	1.9
9.7	3.0	6.2	All Other Non-Current	10.8				3.0	6.4
27.1	32.8	30.4	Net Worth	3.6				20.6	33.9
100.0	100.0	100.0	Total Liabilities & Net Worth	100.0				100.0	100.0
			INCOME DATA						
100.0	100.0	100.0	Net Sales	100.0				100.0	100.0
50.4	46.2	44.4	Gross Profit	52.5				32.6	43.5
45.5	40.6	38.7	Operating Expenses	43.6				28.0	40.3
4.9	5.6	5.7	Operating Profit	8.9				4.6	3.2
.6	.5	1.4	All Other Expenses (net)	1.7				1.1	2.8
4.3	5.1	4.4	Profit Before Taxes	7.2				3.5	.4
			RATIOS						
4.0	2.7	5.7		15.9				2.2	2.0
1.4	1.8	1.9	Current	4.6				1.6	1.6
1.0	1.2	1.1		1.4				1.0	1.0
1.3	1.2	2.4		5.1				1.2	1.3
.5	.7	1.0	Quick	1.2				.7	.7
.3	.3	.4		.3				.3	.4
0 UND	0 UND	0 UND		0 UND				8 43.3	6 61.7
3 133.3	2 155.1	8 43.3	Sales/Receivables	0 UND				22 16.9	29 12.5
27 13.4	31 11.6	41 8.9		0 UND				52 7.0	48 7.6
33 11.0	32 11.3	36 10.0		34 10.8				27 13.7	36 10.0
76 4.8	66 5.5	74 4.9	Cost of Sales/Inventory	83 4.4				68 5.4	70 5.2
126 2.9	99 3.7	111 3.3		107 3.4				111 3.3	122 3.3
4 89.8	11 34.0	0 UND		0 UND				22 16.3	24 15.4
29 12.5	23 16.1	23 16.0	Cost of Sales/Payables	0 UND				54 6.8	47 7.7
50 7.3	47 7.7	60 6.1		0 UND				87 4.2	63 5.8
5.7	6.4	5.5		5.0				6.2	5.8
17.7	12.9	9.5	Sales/Working Capital	6.7				12.6	13.3
413.4	43.3	52.0		99.2				132.0	NM
21.8	16.3	29.2						29.2	9.8
(62) 5.2	(42) 5.9	(47) 6.4	EBIT/Interest					(13) 4.4	(11) 4.0
.7	1.0	1.1						.6	1.3
8.0			Net Profit + Depr., Dep.,						
(11) 3.1			Amort./Cur. Mat. L/T/D						
1.7									
.0	.1	.0		.0				.0	.1
.7	.3	.1	Fixed/Worth	.0				.1	.5
-3.2	3.0	2.7		-.7				5.0	15.5
.9	.7	.5		.4				.9	1.0
3.7	2.3	1.6	Debt/Worth	.7				3.0	2.9
-12.2	16.1	36.2		-3.0				23.3	31.3
154.5	97.6	77.5	% Profit Before Taxes/Tangible					74.7	77.3
(49) 34.5	(47) 23.1	(52) 23.9	Net Worth					(13) 23.5	(13) 22.8
12.0	4.2	5.9						3.2	-50.4
27.8	24.7	37.7	% Profit Before Taxes/Total	50.7				24.4	17.1
8.9	9.5	9.5	Assets	30.1				6.3	8.4
.6	.5	.7		5.0				.2	-6.6
181.4	222.1	300.3		UND				717.0	113.1
27.8	48.6	83.6	Sales/Net Fixed Assets	262.0				130.0	56.3
7.0	15.8	23.5		40.8				31.4	9.2
5.5	4.6	4.3		4.4				4.8	3.6
3.0	3.2	3.3	Sales/Total Assets	3.7				3.6	2.8
1.9	2.2	2.2		1.6				2.6	2.3
.4	.4	.4							.3
(46) .9	(34) .7	(31) .9	% Depr., Dep., Amort./Sales						(12) 1.3
2.3	1.9	1.6							2.2
1.4	.8	1.2	% Officers', Directors'						
(23) 3.6	(18) 2.7	(23) 2.9	Owners' Comp/Sales						
7.1	7.6	5.4							
3593060M	4869525M	1942357M	Net Sales ($)	7903M	13530M	35381M	39300M	266387M	1579856M
1395211M	1343512M	715144M	Total Assets ($)	3535M	4742M	16325M	11380M	78269M	600893M

M = $ thousand   MM = $ million
See Pages viii through xx for Explanation of Ratios and Data

		Current Data Sorted by Assets						Comparative Historical Data	
Type of Statement									
Unqualified				1	1			3	4
Reviewed			2					4	2
Compiled			1					6	4
Tax Returns	12	4	1					26	26
Other	8	9	14	3	1	1		48	41
	0-500M	4 (4/1-9/30/18) 500M-2MM	2-10MM	55 (10/1/18-3/31/19) 10-50MM	50-100MM	100-250MM		4/1/14-3/31/15 ALL	4/1/15-3/31/16 ALL
NUMBER OF STATEMENTS	20	13	18	5	2	1		87	77
	%	%	%	%	%	%		%	%
ASSETS									
Cash & Equivalents	30.5	15.9	13.8					13.9	11.6
Trade Receivables (net)	4.8	19.3	24.0					20.8	23.0
Inventory	18.3	24.8	22.2					21.1	23.0
All Other Current	5.7	1.6	1.7					4.4	4.2
Total Current	59.4	61.7	61.7					60.1	61.9
Fixed Assets (net)	26.5	15.2	16.1					24.0	21.6
Intangibles (net)	9.3	5.0	14.1					5.4	6.8
All Other Non-Current	4.8	18.1	8.1					10.4	9.8
Total	100.0	100.0	100.0					100.0	100.0
LIABILITIES									
Notes Payable-Short Term	20.4	11.1	9.3					20.1	11.0
Cur. Mat.-L.T.D.	4.3	1.6	2.2					2.5	4.5
Trade Payables	8.9	21.2	21.6					15.9	20.1
Income Taxes Payable	.0	.1	.9					.0	.0
All Other Current	22.0	6.0	11.5					12.3	11.4
Total Current	55.6	40.0	45.7					50.8	47.1
Long-Term Debt	22.7	19.0	12.9					11.3	9.3
Deferred Taxes	.0	.0	.0					.0	.3
All Other Non-Current	15.5	.6	1.2					19.4	10.2
Net Worth	6.2	40.5	40.3					18.5	33.1
Total Liabilties & Net Worth	100.0	100.0	100.0					100.0	100.0
INCOME DATA									
Net Sales	100.0	100.0	100.0					100.0	100.0
Gross Profit	63.7	52.1	50.4					54.4	55.4
Operating Expenses	47.7	41.4	37.4					48.5	50.6
Operating Profit	15.9	10.7	13.0					5.9	4.8
All Other Expenses (net)	.8	.9	.4					.6	.2
Profit Before Taxes	15.1	9.8	12.6					5.3	4.6
RATIOS									
Current	7.3	4.3	1.8					3.4	2.7
	1.0	2.0	1.2					1.5	1.4
	.4	1.1	.9					.8	1.0
Quick	2.1	3.1	1.1					1.7	1.6
	.5	1.2	.7					(86) .9	1.0
	.1	.4	.5					.4	.4
Sales/Receivables	0 UND	0 UND	1 333.4					0 UND	6 64.3
	0 UND	21 17.2	32 11.5					13 27.1	29 12.6
	0 UND	43 8.4	69 5.3					53 6.9	51 7.2
Cost of Sales/Inventory	0 UND	0 UND	30 12.0					0 UND	23 15.6
	24 15.4	34 10.7	49 7.5					24 15.0	50 7.3
	91 4.0	107 3.4	104 3.5					81 4.5	126 2.9
Cost of Sales/Payables	0 UND	0 UND	12 30.1					0 UND	19 19.3
	5 73.6	0 UND	57 6.4					33 11.2	51 7.1
	41 8.9	42 8.7	94 3.9					76 4.8	111 3.3
Sales/Working Capital	10.2	4.4	9.5					5.4	5.4
	NM	6.0	25.2					19.6	18.2
	-9.5	NM	-259.3					-34.2	NM
EBIT/Interest	13.3		24.6					34.9	17.7
	(12) 6.9		(14) 7.0					(66) 7.5	(55) 6.3
	1.7		2.7					-.5	-.2
Net Profit + Depr., Dep., Amort./Cur. Mat. L/T/D									
Fixed/Worth	.1	.0	.2					.1	.2
	NM	.1	.6					.6	.6
	-.5	.6	NM					-28.6	33.1
Debt/Worth	.2	.5	.8					.5	.6
	NM	2.0	2.1					1.3	2.3
	-2.3	4.6	NM					-20.0	107.1
% Profit Before Taxes/Tangible Net Worth	175.2	108.4	118.2					71.1	82.2
	(10) 71.7	(12) 52.1	(14) 54.0					(64) 30.4	(60) 40.9
	33.2	11.8	18.4					3.9	3.6
% Profit Before Taxes/Total Assets	76.1	48.6	65.6					27.4	25.2
	27.9	11.9	14.9					13.6	7.4
	8.2	.0	2.8					.8	-1.1
Sales/Net Fixed Assets	777.3	489.6	64.9					106.0	58.5
	22.3	88.3	21.1					21.0	17.5
	7.0	7.6	11.0					6.5	7.6
Sales/Total Assets	5.3	5.0	3.6					4.2	3.8
	3.9	2.6	2.8					3.1	2.7
	2.0	.7	1.6					1.9	1.6
% Depr., Dep., Amort./Sales	.3		.2					.7	.6
	(11) .9		(14) 1.2					(51) 1.5	(50) 1.9
	2.9		3.7					3.7	3.6
% Officers', Directors' Owners' Comp/Sales								2.2	1.6
								(40) 4.7	(27) 5.0
								12.2	10.5
Net Sales ($)	19059M	35206M	235205M	264225M	323507M	869962M		899516M	1350862M
Total Assets ($)	4419M	11832M	90179M	94636M	151350M	204690M		379530M	570861M

Comparative Historical Data | Current Data Sorted by Sales

Type of Statement									
Unqualified	4	4	2					2	2
Reviewed	3	3	3					1	1
Compiled	6	4	1						1
Tax Returns	24	25	17	10	5	1	1		
Other	25	29	36	6	7	3	5	10	5
	4/1/16-3/31/17 ALL	4/1/17-3/31/18 ALL	4/1/18-3/31/19 ALL	0-1MM	1-3MM 4 (4/1-9/30/18)	3-5MM	5-10MM	10-25MM 55 (10/1/18-3/31/19)	25MM & OVER
NUMBER OF STATEMENTS	62	65	59	16	12	4	6	13	8

	%	%	%	%	%	%	%	%	%
ASSETS									
Cash & Equivalents	20.0	17.2	20.7	31.4	22.4			17.8	
Trade Receivables (net)	22.6	21.5	17.1	3.8	12.8			20.8	
Inventory	20.2	18.1	21.1	9.6	24.5			21.2	
All Other Current	2.3	1.4	2.9	6.3	2.8			2.1	
Total Current	65.1	58.2	61.8	51.1	62.5			61.9	
Fixed Assets (net)	16.9	23.7	20.6	29.4	20.4			19.1	
Intangibles (net)	10.0	9.6	8.7	11.4	2.1			9.8	
All Other Non-Current	8.1	8.5	8.9	8.1	15.1			9.2	
Total	100.0	100.0	100.0	100.0	100.0			100.0	
LIABILITIES									
Notes Payable-Short Term	18.4	9.6	12.7	20.3	11.9			9.8	
Cur. Mat.-L.T.D.	2.8	2.4	3.3	2.3	5.8			2.3	
Trade Payables	18.3	19.0	17.1	3.1	14.6			19.9	
Income Taxes Payable	.0	.1	.3	.0	.1			.1	
All Other Current	10.0	9.7	13.4	10.5	25.1			11.3	
Total Current	49.6	40.8	46.8	36.1	57.6			43.5	
Long-Term Debt	12.4	26.9	18.1	31.3	15.4			15.1	
Deferred Taxes	.1	.1	.0	.0	.0			.0	
All Other Non-Current	11.4	13.5	6.0	.8	25.4			1.5	
Net Worth	26.5	18.7	29.1	31.8	1.7			40.0	
Total Liabilties & Net Worth	100.0	100.0	100.0	100.0	100.0			100.0	
INCOME DATA									
Net Sales	100.0	100.0	100.0	100.0	100.0			100.0	
Gross Profit	55.0	54.7	55.5	73.2	54.8			48.1	
Operating Expenses	49.5	49.4	42.5	51.6	47.2			38.8	
Operating Profit	5.4	5.3	12.9	21.5	7.6			9.2	
All Other Expenses (net)	.7	.6	.9	1.3	.8			.4	
Profit Before Taxes	4.7	4.8	12.1	20.3	6.7			8.8	
RATIOS									
Current	2.6	2.2	3.8	6.2	5.6			2.6	
	1.6	1.6	1.3	1.3	2.0			1.2	
	.9	1.0	.8	.5	.6			.9	
Quick	1.9	1.6	2.0	2.9	3.1			1.1	
	1.0	1.0	.7	.6	1.2			.8	
	.5	.3	.4	.2	.2			.4	
Sales/Receivables	1 442.6	1 443.6	0 UND	0 UND	0 UND			1 421.7	
	27 13.7	27 13.5	6 63.2	0 UND	2 217.5			32 11.3	
	61 6.0	56 6.5	41 9.0	0 UND	35 10.5			55 6.6	
Cost of Sales/Inventory	19 19.1	16 23.1	18 20.5	0 UND	19 19.4			21 17.3	
	45 8.2	39 9.4	36 10.1	0 UND	33 11.1			35 10.5	
	99 3.7	83 4.4	89 4.1	126 2.9	78 4.7			79 4.6	
Cost of Sales/Payables	5 68.8	12 29.6	0 UND	0 UND	0 UND			10 36.4	
	51 7.2	51 7.1	31 11.8	0 UND	20 18.2			63 5.8	
	94 3.9	87 4.2	69 5.3	21 17.3	36 10.1			89 4.1	
Sales/Working Capital	6.4	7.9	5.7	5.0	4.8			8.5	
	13.1	18.7	22.1	34.9	10.0			27.3	
	-67.9	-539.8	-36.3	-23.4	-20.0			-183.5	
EBIT/Interest	28.8	21.2	15.9	13.3				13.9	
	(41) 5.9	(50) 6.9	(40) 6.5	(11) 7.5				(10) 7.0	
	.2	.9	2.4	2.7				3.2	
Net Profit + Depr., Dep., Amort./Cur. Mat. L/T/D									
Fixed/Worth	.1	.2	.1	.2	.0			.1	
	.4	.7	.4	2.0	.4			.7	
	3.7	11.2	16.1	-.8	NM			9.9	
Debt/Worth	.7	.9	.4	.3	.3			.8	
	2.7	1.8	2.4	2.0	2.3			1.7	
	NM	NM	-27.5	-3.6	NM			28.6	
% Profit Before Taxes/Tangible Net Worth	91.7	87.1	104.3					166.6	
	(47) 33.9	(49) 41.5	(44) 53.9					(11) 37.0	
	16.3	16.0	25.6					19.9	
% Profit Before Taxes/Total Assets	35.9	30.0	64.7	76.1	28.2			52.4	
	10.4	12.1	20.1	38.4	10.6			9.7	
	.2	1.5	5.5	12.0	-.1			4.1	
Sales/Net Fixed Assets	113.3	98.7	109.8	53.9	390.2			64.7	
	33.0	24.7	25.3	19.6	41.9			25.3	
	8.9	7.5	10.5	3.7	11.4			8.5	
Sales/Total Assets	4.4	4.2	4.3	4.3	4.7			3.7	
	2.9	2.9	3.3	2.1	3.9			3.3	
	1.4	1.8	1.7	1.3	2.6			1.8	
% Depr., Dep., Amort./Sales	.2	.7	.3					.2	
	(39) 1.1	(39) 2.0	(38) .9					(11) 1.3	
	3.8	4.0	2.7					4.8	
% Officers', Directors' Owners' Comp/Sales	2.1	3.7	2.1						
	(20) 7.0	(24) 6.2	(20) 3.2						
	13.4	9.4	11.6						
Net Sales ($)	1599690M	1523086M	1747164M	6744M	22407M	16732M	41049M	194587M	1465645M
Total Assets ($)	800139M	848542M	557106M	3818M	7657M	5876M	19175M	75185M	445395M

© RMA 2019

M = $ thousand   MM = $ million
See Pages viii through xx for Explanation of Ratios and Data

Current Data Sorted by Assets						Type of Statement	Comparative Historical Data	
2		4	29	9	37	Unqualified	67	66
1	8	26	36	10	1	Reviewed	83	82
13	36	29	19	1		Compiled	137	126
163	116	51	4		2	Tax Returns	413	377
64	111	116	69	32	32	Other	466	446
	128 (4/1-9/30/18)		893 (10/1/18-3/31/19)				4/1/14-3/31/15	4/1/15-3/31/16
0-500M	500M-2MM	2-10MM	10-50MM	50-100MM	100-250MM		ALL	ALL
243	271	226	157	52	72	NUMBER OF STATEMENTS	1166	1097
%	%	%	%	%	%	**ASSETS**	%	%
21.7	19.2	12.6	12.0	10.1	7.8	Cash & Equivalents	15.9	15.9
2.9	2.1	4.8	6.8	7.2	4.6	Trade Receivables (net)	5.0	3.7
41.1	16.1	10.6	13.0	8.5	6.3	Inventory	18.3	16.5
2.1	3.0	2.7	2.1	2.8	1.8	All Other Current	1.7	2.0
67.8	40.5	30.8	33.8	28.5	20.5	Total Current	40.8	38.1
19.4	44.2	52.3	52.3	57.7	65.6	Fixed Assets (net)	45.0	46.2
8.1	8.3	8.1	6.0	7.1	8.8	Intangibles (net)	7.9	7.8
4.7	7.0	8.8	7.8	6.7	5.0	All Other Non-Current	6.4	8.0
100.0	100.0	100.0	100.0	100.0	100.0	Total	100.0	100.0
						LIABILITIES		
5.1	2.8	2.2	3.4	1.9	2.5	Notes Payable-Short Term	3.6	3.7
2.1	2.8	2.7	3.1	2.8	2.9	Cur. Mat.-L.T.D.	3.2	3.0
14.8	9.0	8.7	14.9	12.0	7.9	Trade Payables	11.7	10.5
.2	.2	.1	.1	.1	.1	Income Taxes Payable	.2	.1
15.6	8.9	6.2	6.8	8.3	5.2	All Other Current	9.6	8.3
37.8	23.7	19.9	28.4	25.1	18.6	Total Current	28.2	25.6
15.9	37.5	39.2	33.0	35.0	39.2	Long-Term Debt	34.5	33.2
.0	.0	.2	.7	.7	.3	Deferred Taxes	.3	.3
14.7	7.8	6.1	2.5	2.8	4.0	All Other Non-Current	8.7	8.6
31.6	30.9	34.6	35.5	36.4	37.9	Net Worth	28.4	32.4
100.0	100.0	100.0	100.0	100.0	100.0	Total Liabilities & Net Worth	100.0	100.0
						INCOME DATA		
100.0	100.0	100.0	100.0	100.0	100.0	Net Sales	100.0	100.0
14.9	16.3	15.8	15.3	16.1	15.0	Gross Profit	13.2	15.3
14.0	13.9	12.7	13.6	13.6	11.5	Operating Expenses	11.3	13.0
.8	2.4	3.0	1.7	2.5	3.5	Operating Profit	1.9	2.4
-1.0	-.3	.2	.0	-.1	.4	All Other Expenses (net)	.0	-.1
1.8	2.7	2.8	1.7	2.6	3.1	Profit Before Taxes	1.9	2.5
						RATIOS		
6.1	4.8	3.6	1.8	1.7	1.6		3.6	3.5
2.6	2.4	2.0	1.2	1.1	1.0	Current	1.6	1.7
1.3	1.2	1.1	.8	.7	.7		.9	.9
2.2	2.5	2.1	1.1	1.0	1.0		1.9	1.9
(240) .8	(270) 1.1	1.0	.6	.6	.5	Quick	(1165) .8	(1094) .8
.2	.4	.5	.3	.4	.3		.3	.3
0 UND	0 UND	0 UND	1 303.5	2 225.1	2 242.2		0 UND	0 UND
0 UND	0 UND	1 367.6	3 125.4	3 113.3	3 144.9	Sales/Receivables	0 745.4	0 858.0
1 632.4	1 354.5	4 94.1	5 67.7	9 42.2	5 67.4		3 120.7	3 123.5
7 52.9	7 53.9	6 62.0	6 63.1	5 67.1	4 82.4		5 80.6	5 70.3
11 34.6	10 36.7	9 40.4	9 42.2	9 41.5	6 61.9	Cost of Sales/Inventory	7 51.6	9 41.8
16 22.2	16 22.9	13 28.4	14 26.2	11 34.1	9 42.0		11 32.2	13 27.9
0 UND	0 UND	2 168.0	6 56.5	8 46.6	6 58.2		1 585.4	1 367.3
2 183.6	4 103.6	6 64.0	10 37.7	11 33.6	8 44.7	Cost of Sales/Payables	4 83.2	5 72.2
7 53.2	7 51.9	10 37.8	15 24.4	17 21.2	11 34.3		9 41.5	10 34.8
23.4	17.1	20.2	29.5	28.4	40.2		28.5	23.9
43.8	31.2	36.7	112.1	294.8	NM	Sales/Working Capital	65.6	52.6
122.3	141.3	200.8	-103.8	-67.0	-55.2		-389.0	-414.9
26.3	10.6	8.7	9.3	11.3	9.4		10.0	13.0
(100) 9.2	(194) 4.1	(207) 4.4	(152) 4.8	(51) 4.2	(68) 4.0	EBIT/Interest	(899) 4.5	(841) 5.0
2.2	1.6	2.0	2.5	2.1	2.6		2.0	2.3
		8.8	5.4	10.8	7.2	Net Profit + Depr., Dep.,	5.9	7.7
		(24) 3.4	(42) 3.6	(16) 4.1	(20) 4.1	Amort./Cur. Mat. L/T/D	(132) 2.8	(128) 3.6
		1.9	2.1	2.8	1.9		1.7	1.9
.0	.4	.9	1.0	1.4	1.5		.5	.5
.3	2.0	2.0	1.7	2.1	2.3	Fixed/Worth	1.8	1.8
3.4	106.8	10.1	3.9	4.1	13.1		13.7	7.0
.4	.7	1.0	1.0	1.2	1.1		.8	.8
1.5	2.5	2.5	2.0	2.5	2.2	Debt/Worth	2.6	2.3
38.5	UND	16.3	6.1	5.1	14.8		43.0	13.1
85.9	99.9	41.4	39.4	35.1	35.6	% Profit Before Taxes/Tangible	60.3	60.2
(185) 46.7	(204) 30.1	(182) 20.5	(136) 18.1	(49) 21.9	(60) 22.4	Net Worth	(902) 26.5	(890) 29.1
16.4	12.7	8.6	8.4	12.9	13.5		11.4	13.5
38.0	22.1	12.7	10.8	10.6	13.2	% Profit Before Taxes/Total	17.1	19.6
16.1	9.3	7.3	5.7	7.0	8.2	Assets	8.2	8.9
5.0	2.8	3.1	3.0	3.3	4.4		2.9	3.4
UND	63.4	18.5	19.0	10.6	8.2		89.3	63.4
170.6	13.8	6.3	9.6	6.9	5.2	Sales/Net Fixed Assets	15.5	10.9
48.0	4.0	3.1	5.0	3.9	3.2		5.6	4.5
21.5	9.2	6.2	8.2	6.1	5.1		13.3	10.1
14.2	5.3	3.5	4.9	3.9	3.5	Sales/Total Assets	6.5	5.0
8.6	2.7	1.9	3.1	2.5	2.4		3.7	2.9
.1	.5	.7	.7	.8	.9		.4	.5
(127) .4	(192) .9	(168) 1.2	(150) 1.1	1.3	(49) 1.3	% Depr., Dep., Amort./Sales	(873) .8	(836) 1.0
.8	1.9	1.9	1.6	1.7	1.6		1.4	1.7
.6	.6	.5	.2				.3	.5
(115) 1.1	(117) 1.2	(80) .8	(26) .4			% Officers', Directors'	(431) .7	(426) .9
1.8	2.1	1.5	.9			Owners' Comp/Sales	1.4	1.6
849177M	1935383M	5130587M	20544869M	17093199M	48999554M	Net Sales ($)	124555986M	98669798M
62609M	304928M	1005401M	3674309M	3666546M	12251385M	Total Assets ($)	19950060M	20266393M

M = $ thousand   MM = $ million
See Pages viii through xx for Explanation of Ratios and Data

Comparative Historical Data | Current Data Sorted by Sales

4/1/16-3/31/17 ALL	4/1/17-3/31/18 ALL	4/1/18-3/31/19 ALL	Type of Statement	0-1MM	1-3MM	3-5MM	5-10MM	10-25MM	25MM & OVER
69	66	81	Unqualified		1	2	2	2	74
76	63	82	Reviewed	1	3	6	5	7	60
107	77	98	Compiled		6	17	22	24	29
374	386	336	Tax Returns	9	110	88	78	37	14
425	434	424	Other	10	39	66	84	60	165
				128 (4/1-9/30/18)	893 (10/1/18-3/31/19)				
1051	1026	1021	NUMBER OF STATEMENTS	20	159	179	191	130	342

ASSETS (%)

4/1/16-3/31/17	4/1/17-3/31/18	4/1/18-3/31/19		0-1MM	1-3MM	3-5MM	5-10MM	10-25MM	25MM & OVER
15.1	16.5	16.0	Cash & Equivalents	8.5	15.1	16.8	20.5	20.7	11.9
4.2	4.6	4.1	Trade Receivables (net)	.7	2.0	2.0	2.1	5.0	7.0
18.4	18.1	19.3	Inventory	30.9	31.4	24.7	17.3	14.9	12.8
1.9	1.9	2.5	All Other Current	.0	1.0	2.5	3.6	3.4	2.4
39.6	41.1	41.8	Total Current	40.1	49.5	46.1	43.6	44.0	34.2
46.2	43.9	43.6	Fixed Assets (net)	40.2	37.7	38.6	40.5	38.7	52.6
7.6	8.0	7.8	Intangibles (net)	10.8	8.2	9.0	8.4	6.8	6.9
6.6	7.0	6.8	All Other Non-Current	8.9	4.5	6.3	7.5	10.5	6.3
100.0	100.0	100.0	Total	100.0	100.0	100.0	100.0	100.0	100.0

LIABILITIES

4/1/16-3/31/17	4/1/17-3/31/18	4/1/18-3/31/19		0-1MM	1-3MM	3-5MM	5-10MM	10-25MM	25MM & OVER
3.4	2.8	3.2	Notes Payable-Short Term	5.8	5.0	3.2	2.0	2.7	3.2
2.8	2.7	2.7	Cur. Mat.-L.T.D.	.9	2.3	2.1	3.1	2.9	2.9
11.0	11.7	11.3	Trade Payables	10.0	10.1	8.9	9.4	11.2	14.3
.2	.2	.1	Income Taxes Payable	.0	.1	.1	.3	.3	.1
9.0	9.5	9.3	All Other Current	11.3	11.5	10.2	8.7	9.9	7.8
26.3	26.9	26.6	Total Current	28.0	29.0	24.4	23.5	26.8	28.3
31.8	32.2	32.1	Long-Term Debt	18.5	33.7	29.9	34.6	31.9	31.9
.3	.2	.2	Deferred Taxes	.0	.0	.0	.0	.0	.6
7.8	7.3	7.7	All Other Non-Current	8.0	8.4	14.4	8.0	9.1	3.3
33.8	33.4	33.4	Net Worth	45.5	28.8	31.3	34.0	32.1	35.9
100.0	100.0	100.0	Total Liabilities & Net Worth	100.0	100.0	100.0	100.0	100.0	100.0

INCOME DATA

4/1/16-3/31/17	4/1/17-3/31/18	4/1/18-3/31/19		0-1MM	1-3MM	3-5MM	5-10MM	10-25MM	25MM & OVER
100.0	100.0	100.0	Net Sales	100.0	100.0	100.0	100.0	100.0	100.0
16.8	15.9	15.6	Gross Profit	27.0	16.8	15.4	15.5	16.0	14.4
14.5	13.7	13.4	Operating Expenses	23.2	15.7	13.2	12.5	13.9	12.3
2.3	2.2	2.1	Operating Profit	3.8	1.1	2.1	3.0	2.1	2.0
-.2	-.2	-.3	All Other Expenses (net)	-1.8	-.9	-.5	.1	.0	.0
2.5	2.4	2.4	Profit Before Taxes	5.6	2.1	2.7	2.9	2.2	2.0

RATIOS

4/1/16-3/31/17	4/1/17-3/31/18	4/1/18-3/31/19		0-1MM	1-3MM	3-5MM	5-10MM	10-25MM	25MM & OVER
3.5	3.5	3.6	Current	4.5	6.8	6.4	4.8	3.9	1.8
1.6	1.7	1.7		2.4	2.3	2.8	2.5	1.9	1.2
1.0	1.0	1.0		1.0	1.1	1.4	1.2	1.1	.8
1.7	1.9	1.9	Quick	2.2	2.2	2.5	2.7	2.5	1.1
(1048) .7	(1022) .8	(1017) .8		.2	(157) .7	(177) 1.1	1.3	1.0	.6
.3	.4	.3		.1	.2	.4	.5	.5	.3
0 UND	0 UND	0 UND	Sales/Receivables	0 UND	0 UND	0 UND	0 UND	0 UND	1 307.4
1 647.5	1 643.3	1 707.8		0 UND	0 UND	0 UND	0 UND	1 688.9	3 132.0
4 97.2	4 92.3	3 123.9		0 UND	1 365.7	1 455.6	1 359.1	4 94.4	6 65.6
6 56.6	6 61.7	6 60.3	Cost of Sales/Inventory	14 25.8	10 37.7	7 51.6	6 61.3	6 76.5	5 68.4
10 36.2	9 38.9	9 39.2		54 6.7	16 23.3	10 35.9	9 42.6	7 50.9	8 45.9
15 23.8	15 24.2	14 25.9		99 3.7	24 15.4	15 24.7	12 31.1	12 30.9	11 32.2
1 305.6	1 436.1	1 336.3	Cost of Sales/Payables	0 UND	0 UND	0 UND	1 640.3	2 173.8	6 58.4
6 57.7	6 56.8	6 65.6		6 66.3	1 345.5	2 151.3	4 81.5	5 72.6	9 41.4
12 30.9	12 30.3	10 35.3		27 13.3	7 55.4	7 51.4	7 51.9	10 35.1	13 27.6
22.0	21.0	21.5	Sales/Working Capital	7.6	17.2	19.6	17.7	22.8	31.7
51.8	47.0	46.0		11.1	33.5	34.0	32.3	46.9	166.4
-603.6	-925.0	-999.8		NM	122.3	92.4	132.5	230.2	-88.0
11.4	10.5	11.1	EBIT/Interest		9.5	9.1	14.0	15.0	11.8
(786) 4.5	(748) 4.5	(772) 4.5			(98) 3.0	(102) 4.1	(139) 5.4	(102) 5.0	(324) 5.2
2.1	2.2	2.2			1.3	1.9	2.1	1.9	2.6
6.8	7.0	7.2	Net Profit + Depr., Dep., Amort./Cur. Mat. L/T/D						7.4
(118) 3.1	(107) 3.5	(111) 3.6						(92)	3.8
1.9	2.2	2.0							2.2
.5	.5	.5	Fixed/Worth	.0	.1	.2	.3	.4	1.0
1.6	1.7	1.6		.9	1.6	1.2	1.5	1.5	1.9
6.1	8.1	7.4		5.6	-40.5	106.8	7.3	24.7	4.1
.7	.8	.8	Debt/Worth	.6	.6	.4	.6	.8	1.0
2.1	2.1	2.1		1.8	2.9	1.5	2.5	2.0	2.0
11.6	15.6	15.6		89.8	-39.0	UND	16.8	46.8	5.9
51.1	61.3	59.0	% Profit Before Taxes/Tangible Net Worth	47.9	77.1	65.4	97.8	72.4	38.3
(861) 25.9	(815) 26.5	(816) 26.5		(17) 11.7	(115) 31.6	(135) 30.4	(152) 32.7	(100) 29.8	(297) 21.9
11.7	11.9	11.4		1.6	11.3	12.7	12.1	10.9	11.4
18.0	17.7	17.1	% Profit Before Taxes/Total Assets	12.0	25.3	23.3	24.7	20.7	11.6
8.2	8.4	8.5		2.9	10.6	10.4	12.3	9.6	7.0
3.1	3.2	3.2		.1	2.3	3.1	4.0	3.5	3.4
52.1	68.9	70.1	Sales/Net Fixed Assets	UND	415.7	314.4	90.3	68.2	20.5
9.8	11.5	13.1		9.0	26.7	24.7	21.3	17.7	9.2
4.1	4.5	4.7		1.2	4.2	3.8	4.5	6.0	4.9
9.3	9.5	10.2	Sales/Total Assets	2.4	13.4	15.4	12.5	11.2	8.2
4.6	5.1	5.5		1.7	6.0	6.7	5.6	6.4	5.0
2.6	2.9	2.9		.9	2.8	2.7	2.8	3.2	3.3
.5	.5	.5	% Depr., Dep., Amort./Sales		.5	.2	.4	.4	.7
(828) 1.1	(769) 1.1	(738) 1.0		(100) 1.0	(111) .8	(116) 1.0	(101) .9	(303) 1.1	
1.9	1.8	1.6			2.1	1.9	1.7	1.5	1.5
.5	.5	.5	% Officers', Directors' Owners' Comp/Sales		1.0	.6	.6	.5	
(403) 1.0	(398) 1.0	(351) 1.0		(70) 1.7	(80) .9	(85) 1.1	(47) .8	(67) .5	
1.7	1.9	1.8			2.6	1.7	1.5	1.3	1.2

4/1/16-3/31/17	4/1/17-3/31/18	4/1/18-3/31/19		0-1MM	1-3MM	3-5MM	5-10MM	10-25MM	25MM & OVER
76308631M	89762359M	94552769M	Net Sales ($)	12719M	330184M	697976M	1319899M	2056061M	90135930M
19794515M	19418281M	20965178M	Total Assets ($)	9549M	84637M	204670M	322746M	502893M	19840683M

M = $ thousand   MM = $ million
See Pages viii through xx for Explanation of Ratios and Data

Current Data Sorted by Assets   Comparative Historical Data

	0-500M	500M-2MM	2-10MM	10-50MM	50-100MM	100-250MM	Type of Statement	5 4/1/14- 3/31/15 ALL	7 4/1/15- 3/31/16 ALL
	1 7 7	3 2 6 6	4 3 4 11	4 1 3 5	1	1	Unqualified	5	7
							Reviewed	9	.10
							Compiled	10	12
		8 (4/1-9/30/18)		68 (10/1/18-3/31/19)			Tax Returns	47	35
					2	5	Other	39	37
NUMBER OF STATEMENTS	15	17	22	13	3	6		110	101
	%	%	%	%	%	%	**ASSETS**	%	%
Cash & Equivalents	35.1	31.0	11.8	10.6				17.0	18.4
Trade Receivables (net)	3.0	5.4	7.9	8.5				10.0	11.0
Inventory	28.8	13.0	4.9	6.9				14.6	16.3
All Other Current	8.9	10.2	.8	2.0				2.2	3.3
Total Current	75.8	59.7	25.4	28.1				43.8	48.9
Fixed Assets (net)	16.9	30.0	52.3	40.7				39.3	35.0
Intangibles (net)	5.0	5.3	2.0	8.9				7.4	7.0
All Other Non-Current	2.2	5.0	20.3	22.3				9.5	9.0
Total	100.0	100.0	100.0	100.0				100.0	100.0
							LIABILITIES		
Notes Payable-Short Term	3.3	2.7	1.1	5.3				5.5	3.7
Cur. Mat.-L.T.D.	.6	1.6	4.7	2.4				2.6	2.4
Trade Payables	6.3	8.7	7.6	12.5				12.4	14.0
Income Taxes Payable	1.1	.0	.0	.1				.1	.0
All Other Current	16.8	23.0	4.3	3.6				9.1	8.5
Total Current	28.2	35.9	17.7	23.9				29.7	28.7
Long-Term Debt	11.7	16.7	40.9	18.8				29.9	23.3
Deferred Taxes	.0	.0	.0	2.0				.3	.0
All Other Non-Current	21.8	6.5	3.3	9.3				6.2	4.6
Net Worth	38.2	40.9	38.0	46.1				34.0	43.4
Total Liabilties & Net Worth	100.0	100.0	100.0	100.0				100.0	100.0
							INCOME DATA		
Net Sales	100.0	100.0	100.0	100.0				100.0	100.0
Gross Profit	14.2	19.1	18.1	11.6				15.2	17.2
Operating Expenses	13.2	17.0	14.2	10.5				13.4	14.6
Operating Profit	1.1	2.1	3.8	1.1				1.8	2.6
All Other Expenses (net)	-1.5	-.6	-1.2	.0				-.1	-.2
Profit Before Taxes	2.5	2.7	5.1	1.1				1.9	2.8
							RATIOS		
Current	9.3	4.1	2.2	2.3				3.6	3.2
	3.9	2.1	1.5	1.3				1.6	1.7
	1.5	1.1	.7	.9				.9	1.0
Quick	3.1	2.4	1.7	1.8				2.4	2.2
	1.4	1.2	1.1	.7				1.0	1.0
	.6	.7	.5	.4				.4	.3
Sales/Receivables	0 UND	0 UND	0 UND	3 107.7				0 UND	0 UND
	0 UND	0 999.8	2 148.0	6 61.7				2 214.7	2 162.9
	0 UND	2 160.6	12 29.4	14 25.9				5 71.2	8 48.3
Cost of Sales/Inventory	5 74.5	5 78.6	2 165.9	2 233.8				3 112.1	4 100.5
	10 36.9	8 48.0	5 68.9	8 45.8				6 61.2	7 53.2
	13 27.7	12 29.2	10 37.8	13 29.1				9 41.2	14 26.7
Cost of Sales/Payables	0 UND	2 217.8	3 119.7	10 35.7				2 238.0	2 176.0
	1 554.1	4 82.5	7 52.8	12 30.5				5 67.6	8 44.9
	3 113.3	10 37.0	11 34.6	16 23.2				9 40.5	12 29.6
Sales/Working Capital	12.9	15.9	20.5	8.6				24.7	19.2
	31.5	26.6	49.7	85.5				55.3	43.8
	60.8	NM	-70.2	-153.2				-246.6	UND
EBIT/Interest		80.3	7.4	4.8				14.0	18.8
		(12) 6.4	(19) 3.6	(12) 3.1				(87) 4.8	(79) 6.4
		1.8	1.9	.1				2.0	3.1
Net Profit + Depr., Dep., Amort./Cur. Mat. L/T/D								12.6	13.0
								(12) 3.6	(11) 4.5
								1.5	1.3
Fixed/Worth	.0	.2	1.0	.2				.3	.1
	.2	.9	1.6	1.4				1.2	.8
	3.6	8.8	3.2	2.8				6.3	3.4
Debt/Worth	.3	.5	1.1	.6				.8	.6
	1.5	1.1	2.6	2.2				1.7	1.4
	3.3	12.3	4.1	4.5				28.9	5.3
% Profit Before Taxes/Tangible Net Worth	67.1	87.7	50.0	25.2				53.8	62.5
	(13) 37.0	(14) 43.4	23.0	18.0				(86) 31.0	(90) 32.2
	22.8	1.0	7.1	-2.0				9.8	16.3
% Profit Before Taxes/Total Assets	29.1	52.7	15.4	7.4				18.7	19.9
	24.1	20.5	8.1	3.5				8.1	10.5
	9.6	.0	2.7	-1.2				3.3	5.4
Sales/Net Fixed Assets	UND	177.4	11.4	25.9				124.1	234.0
	444.5	38.8	6.5	9.6				14.6	18.9
	46.9	7.8	4.1	6.5				7.6	6.0
Sales/Total Assets	19.8	11.4	4.4	4.7				12.9	11.0
	11.2	6.7	3.4	3.9				6.3	5.7
	5.8	3.8	1.9	1.4				3.9	3.1
% Depr., Dep., Amort./Sales		.2	.8	.7				.3	.3
		(12) .6	(18) 1.6	(12) .9				(84) .7	(76) .9
		1.7	2.4	1.1				1.3	1.7
% Officers', Directors' Owners' Comp/Sales			.5					.5	.6
			(10) 1.8					(48) 1.1	(45) 1.1
			3.0					2.8	2.5
Net Sales ($)	55357M	120230M	491118M	1643691M	908976M	2729667M		13026562M	12492821M
Total Assets ($)	4450M	18270M	124174M	364612M	216302M	902011M		1750078M	2500224M

M = $ thousand   MM = $ million
See Pages viii through xx for Explanation of Ratios and Data

Comparative Historical Data

Current Data Sorted by Sales

Type of Statement

	4/1/16-3/31/17 ALL	4/1/17-3/31/18 ALL	4/1/18-3/31/19 ALL	0-1MM	1-3MM	3-5MM	5-10MM	10-25MM	25MM & OVER
Unqualified	9	8	6					1	5
Reviewed	15	17	8		1		1	2	4
Compiled	10	6	9		2	1	2		4
Tax Returns	27	24	17	2	5	1	6	3	
Other	29	32	36		1	6	9	7	13
					8 (4/1-9/30/18)		68 (10/1/18-3/31/19)		
NUMBER OF STATEMENTS	90	87	76	2	9	8	18	13	26
	%	%	%	%	%	%	%	%	%
ASSETS									
Cash & Equivalents	14.9	15.5	20.3				30.2	14.3	12.9
Trade Receivables (net)	5.8	8.2	6.7				1.4	6.8	10.4
Inventory	16.7	13.6	12.1				17.2	5.9	7.8
All Other Current	4.4	3.6	5.1				8.2	1.3	2.1
Total Current	41.9	40.9	44.2				56.9	28.3	33.3
Fixed Assets (net)	39.5	41.6	39.3				30.5	38.0	50.7
Intangibles (net)	9.3	7.3	4.9				4.7	7.6	5.1
All Other Non-Current	9.3	10.2	11.6				7.8	26.0	10.9
Total	100.0	100.0	100.0				100.0	100.0	100.0
LIABILITIES									
Notes Payable-Short Term	2.9	4.5	3.5				.6	6.3	4.3
Cur. Mat.-L.T.D.	2.0	2.3	2.6				4.0	3.0	2.5
Trade Payables	12.7	13.2	8.6				6.9	6.3	13.4
Income Taxes Payable	.1	.1	.2				.0	.0	.0
All Other Current	10.8	8.8	10.8				20.7	8.7	4.1
Total Current	28.5	28.9	25.7				32.3	24.3	24.4
Long-Term Debt	28.9	25.8	25.2				18.3	28.4	29.5
Deferred Taxes	.2	.3	.4				.0	.0	1.1
All Other Non-Current	9.5	9.1	8.4				5.7	3.6	5.4
Net Worth	32.8	36.0	40.3				43.8	43.7	39.6
Total Liabilties & Net Worth	100.0	100.0	100.0				100.0	100.0	100.0
INCOME DATA									
Net Sales	100.0	100.0	100.0				100.0	100.0	100.0
Gross Profit	19.8	17.1	16.6				17.0	15.5	13.9
Operating Expenses	16.8	15.1	14.1				13.5	13.0	11.7
Operating Profit	3.0	2.0	2.4				3.5	2.6	2.2
All Other Expenses (net)	.0	-.3	-.7				.0	-.7	.3
Profit Before Taxes	3.0	2.3	3.1				3.5	3.3	1.9
RATIOS									
	2.7	2.7	3.4				4.1	2.0	2.1
Current	1.7	1.4	1.7				2.0	1.4	1.6
	.8	.8	.9				.8	.7	.9
	1.5	1.6	1.9				1.9	1.6	1.6
Quick	.7	.8	1.2				1.3	1.2	1.0
	.3	.4	.5				.6	.3	.5
	0 UND	0 UND	0 UND				0 UND	1 436.1	3 109.9
Sales/Receivables	1 634.8	2 173.2	2 163.2				0 UND	3 116.9	6 58.4
	5 76.5	11 34.2	10 36.5				0 845.1	16 23.4	12 30.6
	5 78.1	4 82.0	4 97.8				4 86.4	2 199.0	3 107.7
Cost of Sales/Inventory	9 41.4	7 49.7	8 45.8				7 50.8	5 72.0	7 49.5
	17 21.9	12 31.3	11 33.1				11 32.1	10 36.9	10 37.3
	3 113.1	3 124.3	2 187.8				1 410.4	2 146.8	8 46.3
Cost of Sales/Payables	8 45.3	9 40.9	7 52.8				3 120.7	8 45.5	11 34.4
	14 25.4	14 25.5	11 32.6				7 52.3	11 33.7	15 24.6
	22.2	21.4	16.1				23.7	15.7	20.6
Sales/Working Capital	54.2	61.6	35.1				39.6	94.1	49.7
	-116.6	-119.1	-147.8				-59.1	-60.1	-158.6
	18.6	7.5	7.4				27.2	25.1	4.7
EBIT/Interest	(66) 4.7	(66) 3.9	(56) 3.6				(11) 5.6	(11) 5.8	(22) 2.9
	2.4	1.9	1.8				3.2	.0	1.8
	12.5		4.6						
Net Profit + Depr., Dep., Amort./Cur. Mat. L/T/D	(10) 5.4		(11) 2.7						
	3.0		1.4						
	.3	.5	.3				.0	.2	1.0
Fixed/Worth	1.3	1.5	1.3				.8	1.3	1.7
	5.7	4.4	3.5				2.6	3.3	2.9
	.7	.6	.5				.4	.6	1.2
Debt/Worth	1.9	2.3	1.8				1.1	2.7	2.3
	32.1	9.2	3.9				4.0	4.1	3.8
	74.4	58.9	49.2				89.7	82.1	25.1
% Profit Before Taxes/Tangible Net Worth	(73) 28.6	(75) 27.6	(71) 24.7				(16) 57.9	(12) 31.8	19.0
	11.4	10.1	6.3				31.8	-1.1	7.8
	22.8	18.3	20.5				50.9	19.3	8.3
% Profit Before Taxes/Total Assets	8.3	6.6	8.1				18.2	13.4	4.8
	3.2	1.7	2.0				6.1	.3	2.7
	84.9	47.9	58.9				UND	36.2	16.2
Sales/Net Fixed Assets	15.3	12.0	10.8				68.0	12.1	9.0
	4.3	5.2	5.0				5.7	4.7	3.5
	8.6	7.9	9.6				14.1	6.3	5.5
Sales/Total Assets	4.9	5.1	4.4				7.2	3.1	4.2
	2.7	2.9	2.5				3.5	1.3	2.6
	.6	.4	.6					.4	.7
% Depr., Dep., Amort./Sales	(62) 1.1	(65) .9	(55) 1.0					(10) .7	(24) 1.0
	2.1	1.7	1.7					1.4	1.8
	.8	.4	.5						
% Officers', Directors', Owners' Comp/Sales	(35) 1.7	(30) .9	(27) 1.2						
	2.5	2.0	2.6						
Net Sales ($)	6559457M	9311934M	5949039M	1455M	18852M	33970M	133272M	192435M	5569055M
Total Assets ($)	2102087M	2271035M	1629819M	219M	13451M	8920M	27953M	82909M	1496367M

© RMA 2019

M = $ thousand   MM = $ million
See Pages viii through xx for Explanation of Ratios and Data

Current Data Sorted by Assets

Comparative Historical Data

						Type of Statement		
1				1				
1	1		1	1		1		
	1	1	1				Unqualified	3	4
3	2	2	2	1			Reviewed	3	3
2		5		1	3	4	Compiled	4	5
							Tax Returns	6	12
							Other	18	20

0-500M	500M-2MM	2-10MM	10-50MM	50-100MM	100-250MM			4/1/14-3/31/15 ALL	4/1/15-3/31/16 ALL
	6 (4/1-9/30/18)			29 (10/1/18-3/31/19)					
7	7	9	4	3	5	NUMBER OF STATEMENTS		34	44
%	%	%	%	%	%			%	%

						ASSETS			
						Cash & Equivalents		11.2	15.7
						Trade Receivables (net)		12.5	6.4
						Inventory		49.7	47.9
						All Other Current		2.3	2.0
						Total Current		75.6	71.9
						Fixed Assets (net)		9.2	14.5
						Intangibles (net)		4.3	7.2
						All Other Non-Current		10.9	6.4
						Total		100.0	100.0

						LIABILITIES			
						Notes Payable-Short Term		12.2	15.9
						Cur. Mat.-L.T.D.		1.3	2.2
						Trade Payables		20.4	13.4
						Income Taxes Payable		.3	.1
						All Other Current		8.6	8.0
						Total Current		42.8	39.6
						Long-Term Debt		15.4	11.2
						Deferred Taxes		.2	.1
						All Other Non-Current		25.8	9.6
						Net Worth		15.8	39.5
						Total Liabilities & Net Worth		100.0	100.0

						INCOME DATA			
						Net Sales		100.0	100.0
						Gross Profit		46.4	48.9
						Operating Expenses		42.8	46.3
						Operating Profit		3.6	2.7
						All Other Expenses (net)		.7	1.0
						Profit Before Taxes		2.9	1.6

						RATIOS			
								3.8	4.2
						Current		2.2	2.3
								1.2	1.2
								1.4	.9
						Quick		.7	.6
								.1	.2
							0		UND	0	UND
						Sales/Receivables	2	233.6	1	640.0
							27	13.3	9	40.9
							70	5.2	99	3.7
						Cost of Sales/Inventory	130	2.8	140	2.6
							203	1.8	228	1.6
							11	32.1	7	49.3
						Cost of Sales/Payables	36	10.1	31	11.7
							89	4.1	65	5.6
								4.4		2.9
						Sales/Working Capital		8.9		6.1
								21.6		12.9
								18.3		12.5
						EBIT/Interest	(26)	6.8	(29)	3.2
								2.4		1.4
						Net Profit + Depr., Dep., Amort./Cur. Mat. L/T/D				
								.0		.1
						Fixed/Worth		.3		.3
								1.2		1.7
								.8		.4
						Debt/Worth		2.3		1.5
								12.6		14.9
								63.8		36.2
						% Profit Before Taxes/Tangible Net Worth	(28)	34.6	(35)	15.5
								16.0		4.7
								22.1		12.0
						% Profit Before Taxes/Total Assets		8.2		5.8
								3.6		1.6
								184.7		85.1
						Sales/Net Fixed Assets		42.1		26.2
								11.8		12.2
								3.7		3.0
						Sales/Total Assets		2.8		2.0
								1.4		1.4
								.3		.3
						% Depr., Dep., Amort./Sales	(24)	.6	(32)	.9
								1.0		2.1
								2.2		2.8
						% Officers', Directors' Owners' Comp/Sales	(16)	3.6	(20)	5.8
								5.9		11.2

7611M	30685M	129886M	197299M	378611M	2097759M	Net Sales ($)		2606258M	3095026M
2515M	9295M	39378M	67503M	228387M	968348M	Total Assets ($)		744824M	1328225M

© RMA 2019

M = $ thousand   MM = $ million

See Pages viii through xx for Explanation of Ratios and Data

Comparative Historical Data | Current Data Sorted by Sales

			Type of Statement	0-1MM	1-3MM	3-5MM	5-10MM	10-25MM	25MM & OVER
3	2	3	Unqualified		1			1	1
2	2	4	Reviewed		1		1	1	
4	3	2	Compiled			2			
7	14	8	Tax Returns	3	2	1		1	1
19	20	18	Other	1	1	2	3	1	9
4/1/16-3/31/17	4/1/17-3/31/18	4/1/18-3/31/19		6 (4/1-9/30/18)			29 (10/1/18-3/31/19)		
ALL	ALL	ALL							
35	41	35	**NUMBER OF STATEMENTS**	4	5	6	4	5	11
%	%	%	**ASSETS**	%	%	%	%	%	%
15.6	13.6	15.4	Cash & Equivalents						5.5
9.4	7.2	11.5	Trade Receivables (net)						23.3
44.5	46.4	43.1	Inventory						28.2
2.2	3.2	2.1	All Other Current						3.5
71.6	70.4	72.2	Total Current						60.4
16.5	17.4	15.4	Fixed Assets (net)						24.1
3.5	3.0	5.0	Intangibles (net)						10.2
8.4	9.2	7.4	All Other Non-Current						5.3
100.0	100.0	100.0	Total						100.0
			LIABILITIES						
17.3	15.2	18.6	Notes Payable-Short Term						11.7
2.8	3.5	1.4	Cur. Mat.-L.T.D.						3.7
24.5	19.7	18.1	Trade Payables						17.7
.1	.1	.0	Income Taxes Payable						.1
16.1	21.4	14.8	All Other Current						16.0
60.8	59.9	52.9	Total Current						49.4
23.7	8.1	9.1	Long-Term Debt						21.1
.5	.0	.0	Deferred Taxes						.0
4.0	3.2	12.0	All Other Non-Current						32.9
11.0	28.8	26.0	Net Worth						-3.5
100.0	100.0	100.0	Total Liabilities & Net Worth						100.0
			INCOME DATA						
100.0	100.0	100.0	Net Sales						100.0
47.1	47.2	47.8	Gross Profit						51.4
45.4	45.5	46.6	Operating Expenses						50.7
1.7	1.6	1.3	Operating Profit						.7
2.7	.8	1.0	All Other Expenses (net)						2.7
-.9	.9	.3	Profit Before Taxes						-2.0
			RATIOS						
2.2	3.3	3.7	Current						1.5
1.4	1.3	1.6							1.1
.8	.8	.9							.9
.8	1.0	1.5	Quick						1.1
.3	.3	.4							.4
.1	.1	.2							.1
0 999.8	0 UND	0 UND	Sales/Receivables						11 33.0
5 68.0	1 410.0	2 237.2							15 24.0
26 13.8	6 65.5	17 20.9							38 9.7
76 4.8	96 3.8	72 5.1	Cost of Sales/Inventory						4 81.5
122 3.0	146 2.5	118 3.1							122 3.0
166 2.2	215 1.7	203 1.8							192 1.9
17 21.6	15 24.0	28 12.9	Cost of Sales/Payables						35 10.4
39 9.3	35 10.5	40 9.1							41 8.8
101 3.6	91 4.0	72 5.1							72 5.1
5.9	4.4	3.1	Sales/Working Capital						15.3
12.6	15.9	14.0							29.8
-26.7	-24.0	-32.5							-32.5
16.7	27.8	22.1	EBIT/Interest						11.5
(29) 3.2	(30) 2.6	(28) 4.7							-1.1
-1.4	-1.9	-2.9							-2.5
			Net Profit + Depr., Dep., Amort./Cur. Mat. L/T/D						
.1	.1	.1	Fixed/Worth						1.5
.6	.5	.3							11.2
2.3	2.2	11.2							-.3
1.1	.4	.6	Debt/Worth						2.7
2.5	1.8	1.7							42.1
6.9	NM	-6.8							-1.9
54.6	25.5	42.8	% Profit Before Taxes/Tangible Net Worth						
(28) 28.8	(31) 10.4	(25) 6.5							
5.0	-1.4	-11.8							
17.0	14.9	20.2	% Profit Before Taxes/Total Assets						26.4
6.3	3.2	2.5							-5.1
-24.5	-7.3	-6.0							-22.7
82.1	71.9	78.9	Sales/Net Fixed Assets						25.8
20.6	23.2	24.1							8.0
11.1	7.7	8.0							6.1
3.7	3.3	3.4	Sales/Total Assets						4.3
2.7	2.2	2.1							2.0
1.8	1.7	1.7							1.7
.4	.6	.5	% Depr., Dep., Amort./Sales						
(25) .9	(27) 1.4	(20) 1.3							
1.7	2.3	1.6							
4.8	2.6	1.3	% Officers', Directors' Owners' Comp/Sales						
(14) 6.6	(18) 5.5	(11) 2.9							
11.2	8.7	7.1							
1534015M	1196718M	2841851M	Net Sales ($)	2458M	9775M	25036M	28148M	91406M	2685028M
780169M	590332M	1315426M	Total Assets ($)	1452M	2687M	14205M	10826M	46241M	1240015M

Current Data Sorted by Assets   Comparative Historical Data

0-500M	500M-2MM	2-10MM	10-50MM	50-100MM	100-250MM	Type of Statement	4/1/14-3/31/15 ALL	4/1/15-3/31/16 ALL
		6	1	1	5	Unqualified	8	12
	1	2	3			Reviewed	8	7
	2					Compiled	8	6
6	2	2			1	Tax Returns	24	36
14	3	9	8	2	7	Other	45	62
	8 (4/1-9/30/18)		67 (10/1/18-3/31/19)					
20	8	19	12	3	13	**NUMBER OF STATEMENTS**	93	123
%	%	%	%	%	%	**ASSETS**	%	%
15.0		15.9	18.5		6.3	Cash & Equivalents	14.5	19.9
1.6		8.2	12.5		3.5	Trade Receivables (net)	4.4	7.0
49.0		41.3	39.1		31.3	Inventory	44.8	40.0
.4		11.8	2.7		3.7	All Other Current	2.8	2.9
66.0		77.3	72.8		44.8	Total Current	66.4	69.7
23.2		11.6	19.5		32.8	Fixed Assets (net)	21.3	18.8
7.9		8.5	.1		9.2	Intangibles (net)	5.4	3.2
3.0		2.7	7.7		13.2	All Other Non-Current	6.9	8.2
100.0		100.0	100.0		100.0	Total	100.0	100.0
						LIABILITIES		
38.5		11.4	5.0		5.3	Notes Payable-Short Term	9.7	8.2
1.4		1.9	1.8		.8	Cur. Mat.-L.T.D.	1.3	2.0
12.7		21.4	18.3		13.4	Trade Payables	20.1	15.4
.0		.4	.0		.4	Income Taxes Payable	.1	.1
16.6		18.0	13.2		13.1	All Other Current	12.6	11.6
69.2		53.1	38.3		33.0	Total Current	43.8	37.3
23.8		11.8	12.9		23.5	Long-Term Debt	15.1	11.6
.0		.2	.0		.0	Deferred Taxes	.1	.1
15.3		2.0	14.2		20.1	All Other Non-Current	10.0	11.3
-8.3		32.9	34.6		23.4	Net Worth	31.0	39.7
100.0		100.0	100.0		100.0	Total Liabilities & Net Worth	100.0	100.0
						INCOME DATA		
100.0		100.0	100.0		100.0	Net Sales	100.0	100.0
45.7		48.0	54.6		45.5	Gross Profit	47.0	46.0
43.1		44.9	46.4		48.6	Operating Expenses	44.1	41.0
2.6		3.1	8.2		-3.1	Operating Profit	3.0	5.0
1.6		.2	.5		2.0	All Other Expenses (net)	.8	.8
1.0		2.9	7.7		-5.1	Profit Before Taxes	2.1	4.1
						RATIOS		
5.7		2.5	2.8		1.9		3.1	4.3
1.7		1.5	2.3		1.2	Current	1.9	2.2
.5		1.1	1.2		.9		1.1	1.1
.8		1.0	1.4		.8		1.0	2.0
.5		.4	.7		.3	Quick	.4 (122)	.7
.1		.1	.3		.1		.1	.2
0 UND		0 UND	0 UND		0 UND		0 UND	0 UND
0 UND		5 71.3	10 38.0		3 106.7	Sales/Receivables	0 999.8	0 UND
0 UND		21 17.3	25 14.6		7 51.2		5 78.6	6 56.8
21 17.7		81 4.5	64 5.7		42 8.7		61 6.0	43 8.4
104 3.5		114 3.2	166 2.2		83 4.4	Cost of Sales/Inventory	107 3.4	68 5.4
118 3.1		182 2.0	243 1.5		130 2.8		140 2.6	126 2.9
0 UND		28 13.1	29 12.8		31 11.8		21 17.4	1 454.0
0 UND		46 7.9	46 7.9		39 9.3	Cost of Sales/Payables	39 9.3	23 16.1
19 19.6		78 4.7	76 4.8		56 6.5		68 5.4	53 6.9
7.9		5.3	3.8		12.9		6.1	5.2
16.6		12.7	6.8		13.7	Sales/Working Capital	10.1	9.9
-12.1		33.2	24.7		NM		41.5	49.1
42.7		27.0	121.4		2.0		19.8	33.9
(15) 8.1		(18) 3.5	(11) 34.4		(12) -3.0	EBIT/Interest	(69) 3.9	(84) 6.8
.2		.3	4.7		-32.0		-1.6	1.1
								52.7
						Net Profit + Depr., Dep., Amort./Cur. Mat. L/T/D	(11)	6.0
								1.2
.1		.1	.1		.9		.2	.1
1.5		.4	.6		2.0	Fixed/Worth	.5	.3
-.3		-3.0	NM		-1.6		3.4	1.5
.7		.7	.5		1.5		.6	.4
7.3		4.0	1.7		4.7	Debt/Worth	2.1	1.3
-2.0		-6.9	NM		-5.5		156.1	10.9
188.8		99.0					41.9	67.8
(12) 77.6		(14) 42.9				% Profit Before Taxes/Tangible Net Worth	(71) 21.3	(101) 27.0
47.6		22.7					.7	5.4
43.2		22.3	46.2		6.2		18.6	28.4
6.5		10.6	13.4		-8.2	% Profit Before Taxes/Total Assets	6.1	7.8
-13.0		.2	-.2		-17.3		-1.9	.3
103.8		108.6	49.1		9.8		46.5	93.0
38.5		34.8	16.4		6.8	Sales/Net Fixed Assets	18.1	36.0
9.9		18.7	8.2		5.8		9.0	11.0
9.9		3.6	3.2		2.7		4.1	5.0
4.2		2.9	2.6		2.5	Sales/Total Assets	2.8	3.4
2.2		1.8	1.4		1.4		2.1	2.2
.1		.4	.3				.5	.3
(10) .9		(13) .6	(11) 1.0			% Depr., Dep., Amort./Sales	(65) 1.1	(80) .7
5.1		1.7	1.8				2.3	1.7
							1.6	1.6
						% Officers', Directors' Owners' Comp/Sales	(39) 3.2	(50) 3.4
							6.1	6.3
34753M	23804M	287525M	554582M	698745M	5030366M	Net Sales ($)	6795821M	8485523M
5401M	9286M	107435M	245200M	202045M	2274173M	Total Assets ($)	2670825M	3299536M

M = $ thousand   MM = $ million
See Pages viii through xx for Explanation of Ratios and Data

Comparative Historical Data | Current Data Sorted by Sales

4/1/16-3/31/17 ALL	4/1/17-3/31/18 ALL	4/1/18-3/31/19 ALL		0-1MM	1-3MM	3-5MM	5-10MM	10-25MM	25MM & OVER
			Type of Statement	8 (4/1-9/30/18)		67 (10/1/18-3/31/19)			
10	6	13	Unqualified				2	4	7
7	6	6	Reviewed				1	3	2
5		2	Compiled		1				
23	22	11	Tax Returns	2	6	1	1	1	1
51	62	43	Other	8	7	2	2	6	18
96	96	75	**NUMBER OF STATEMENTS**	10	14	3	6	14	28
%	%	%	**ASSETS**	%	%	%	%	%	%
15.4	16.1	14.9	Cash & Equivalents	11.8	18.4			16.2	12.9
4.7	5.2	5.5	Trade Receivables (net)	3.2	.1			8.9	7.4
44.1	40.8	41.8	Inventory	45.7	49.3			40.4	36.4
2.5	2.9	4.3	All Other Current	.3	1.4			11.7	3.2
66.8	65.0	66.5	Total Current	61.0	69.2			77.2	60.0
20.3	22.1	21.8	Fixed Assets (net)	21.4	21.5			12.4	27.3
6.4	5.6	6.2	Intangibles (net)	15.3	6.7			3.6	4.6
6.6	7.3	5.5	All Other Non-Current	2.3	2.5			6.9	8.1
100.0	100.0	100.0	Total	100.0	100.0			100.0	100.0
			LIABILITIES						
17.9	11.4	16.7	Notes Payable-Short Term	24.9	16.3			13.5	4.6
1.6	1.1	1.4	Cur. Mat.-L.T.D.	2.7	1.2			.9	1.1
16.1	15.3	16.2	Trade Payables	5.0	8.8			25.8	15.0
.2	.1	.2	Income Taxes Payable	.0	.0			.2	.3
17.3	16.6	15.8	All Other Current	5.0	24.6			11.5	14.7
53.0	44.5	50.2	Total Current	37.6	51.0			51.8	35.7
13.4	16.3	17.3	Long-Term Debt	39.5	9.7			7.9	19.5
.0	.2	.1	Deferred Taxes	.0	.0			.2	.1
8.8	6.8	12.3	All Other Non-Current	17.7	11.7			5.3	17.1
24.8	32.2	20.1	Net Worth	5.3	27.5			34.8	27.6
100.0	100.0	100.0	Total Liabilities & Net Worth	100.0	100.0			100.0	100.0
			INCOME DATA						
100.0	100.0	100.0	Net Sales	100.0	100.0			100.0	100.0
46.7	46.5	48.3	Gross Profit	49.9	45.1			50.4	48.2
45.4	42.9	45.9	Operating Expenses	47.3	45.0			43.4	46.2
1.2	3.6	2.4	Operating Profit	2.6	.1			6.9	2.0
1.4	.6	1.0	All Other Expenses (net)	2.3	.5			.9	1.4
-.2	2.9	1.4	Profit Before Taxes	.4	-.4			6.1	.6
			RATIOS						
2.8	3.2	2.6		6.8	3.7			3.2	2.4
1.7	1.7	1.5	Current	2.7	1.7			1.4	1.8
1.2	1.1	1.1		.8	.7			1.1	1.2
.9	1.1	.8		.8	.9			1.1	.8
.3	.4	.5	Quick	.6	.3			.5	.5
.1	.1	.1		.1	.0			.1	.2
0 UND	0 UND	0 UND		0 UND	0 UND			0 UND	0 811.2
0 UND	0 UND	0 999.8	Sales/Receivables	0 UND	0 UND			5 67.2	4 84.7
6 60.2	4 88.2	7 51.9		1 359.8	0 UND			12 31.4	12 29.5
56 6.5	49 7.4	61 6.0		101 3.6	46 8.0			78 4.7	57 6.4
83 4.4	85 4.3	111 3.3	Cost of Sales/Inventory	114 3.2	107 3.4			126 2.9	99 3.7
159 2.3	166 2.2	166 2.2		174 2.1	126 2.9			182 2.0	146 2.5
4 83.4	0 UND	13 27.5		0 UND	0 UND			30 12.3	29 12.8
25 14.8	22 16.6	31 11.8	Cost of Sales/Payables	0 UND	11 32.3			47 7.7	38 9.6
48 7.6	60 6.1	62 5.9		21 17.7	21 17.4			104 3.5	61 6.0
6.1	5.4	6.5		3.5	11.5			5.2	6.9
12.3	15.1	13.5	Sales/Working Capital	8.0	17.5			14.1	13.2
80.8	84.5	46.1		-184.4	-14.4			274.9	32.4
14.6	16.5	24.1						57.3	35.5
(73) 1.5	(71) 4.0	(64) 3.2	EBIT/Interest					(13) 6.6	(25) .7
-2.4	.0	-1.8						3.1	-18.7
22.2									
(11) 4.5			Net Profit + Depr., Dep., Amort./Cur. Mat. L/T/D						
1.9									
.1	.1	.2		.1	.2			.1	.3
.6	.7	1.0	Fixed/Worth	.9	1.4			.3	1.3
7.3	2.4	-4.1		-.3	-13.8			NM	NM
.7	.7	.8		.7	.7			.5	.9
1.9	1.7	3.0	Debt/Worth	2.5	4.6			2.8	2.6
22.2	16.2	-7.4		-1.7	-68.1			NM	NM
59.1	48.7	81.3			174.6			126.8	36.1
(74) 16.6	(75) 25.0	(54) 27.4	% Profit Before Taxes/Tangible Net Worth	(10) 66.6				(11) 52.7	(21) -1.6
-9.8	3.8	-10.9			-7.6			26.6	-58.1
21.2	16.8	26.3		46.8	36.0			33.6	14.6
3.3	7.2	5.4	% Profit Before Taxes/Total Assets	-1.8	6.8			14.8	.9
-8.0	-.6	-9.6		-10.8	-10.2			5.6	-15.0
78.8	73.8	65.0		94.4	120.5			83.5	17.6
18.9	23.5	18.3	Sales/Net Fixed Assets	19.0	50.9			34.2	9.8
7.0	6.3	6.8		5.0	14.7			14.1	5.8
4.2	4.0	3.8		3.4	7.9			3.6	3.4
3.0	2.8	2.7	Sales/Total Assets	2.3	4.0			2.9	2.6
1.9	1.8	1.7		1.3	2.2			2.1	1.5
.5	.4	.4							.4
(64) .9	(51) .9	(45) 1.0	% Depr., Dep., Amort./Sales					(16)	1.4
2.0	1.7	2.5							2.3
1.6	1.8	2.2							
(39) 2.9	(12) 3.3	(26) 4.0	% Officers', Directors' Owners' Comp/Sales						
4.7	6.5	6.1							
6311827M	7183572M	6629775M	Net Sales ($)	5428M	27595M	12370M	41563M	240451M	6302368M
2802169M	2913470M	2843540M	Total Assets ($)	2449M	12170M	3775M	14731M	92919M	2717496M

M = $ thousand   MM = $ million
See Pages viii through xx for Explanation of Ratios and Data

Current Data Sorted by Assets | Comparative Historical Data

Current-data column periods: **7 (4/1-9/30/18)** and **60 (10/1/18-3/31/19)**
Historical column periods: **4/1/14-3/31/15 ALL** and **4/1/15-3/31/16 ALL**

	0-500M	500M-2MM	2-10MM	10-50MM	50-100MM	100-250MM		4/1/14-3/31/15 ALL	4/1/15-3/31/16 ALL
Type of Statement									
Unqualified			1	1		4		7	11
Reviewed			4	2				8	5
Compiled	1	1	2					5	8
Tax Returns	8	5	8					30	37
Other	5	3	4	8	3	6		30	37
NUMBER OF STATEMENTS	14	10	19	11	3	10		80	98
	%	%	%	%	%	%	**ASSETS**	%	%
Cash & Equivalents	19.1	16.8	12.2	16.0		11.3		15.4	14.0
Trade Receivables (net)	.0	2.5	3.8	2.3		5.5		4.4	4.9
Inventory	53.2	31.5	47.2	46.6		37.9		52.8	49.7
All Other Current	3.2	1.6	.6	3.9		3.6		2.1	2.5
Total Current	75.4	52.5	63.9	68.8		58.3		74.7	71.1
Fixed Assets (net)	20.5	23.5	24.9	22.8		26.6		15.3	18.9
Intangibles (net)	3.2	13.6	2.3	4.4		10.1		5.0	2.7
All Other Non-Current	1.0	10.5	8.9	4.0		5.0		5.0	7.3
Total	100.0	100.0	100.0	100.0		100.0		100.0	100.0
							LIABILITIES		
Notes Payable-Short Term	46.4	17.2	4.3	9.3		3.4		5.1	6.0
Cur. Mat.-L.T.D.	4.5	6.2	2.3	2.6		.9		2.2	2.1
Trade Payables	2.5	6.1	21.5	25.6		23.3		17.3	18.1
Income Taxes Payable	.0	.0	.0	.1		.0		.1	.4
All Other Current	15.2	3.0	11.4	12.7		18.8		9.5	7.7
Total Current	68.7	32.4	39.5	50.2		46.5		34.3	34.2
Long-Term Debt	27.3	27.1	14.2	9.0		20.8		9.8	10.8
Deferred Taxes	.0	.0	.0	.2		.3		.1	.2
All Other Non-Current	1.5	20.0	9.3	2.7		10.8		10.5	9.8
Net Worth	2.4	20.5	37.0	37.8		21.7		45.3	44.9
Total Liabilities & Net Worth	100.0	100.0	100.0	100.0		100.0		100.0	100.0
							INCOME DATA		
Net Sales	100.0	100.0	100.0	100.0		100.0		100.0	100.0
Gross Profit	42.0	55.0	43.3	49.0		49.1		47.2	45.1
Operating Expenses	37.8	48.3	41.2	46.3		46.0		42.3	39.5
Operating Profit	4.2	6.7	2.1	2.7		3.1		4.9	5.6
All Other Expenses (net)	.6	.0	-.2	.6		2.2		.8	1.1
Profit Before Taxes	3.7	6.6	2.3	2.1		.8		4.2	4.5
							RATIOS		
Current	3.1	5.7	3.5	2.6		1.8		4.5	3.5
	1.6	1.8	1.6	1.3		1.3		2.4	2.2
	.6	1.1	1.2	1.2		.8		1.3	1.5
Quick	1.5	2.7	.9	.8		.6		1.2	1.0
	.3	.5	.4	.2		.2		.5	.5
	.1	.2	.1	.1		.1		.1	.1
Sales/Receivables	0 UND	0 UND	0 UND	0 UND		0 UND		0 UND	0 UND
	0 UND	0 UND	2 160.3	4 101.9		8 47.8		1 729.9	0 742.0
	0 UND	0 UND	7 52.3	4 82.5		15 24.9		6 63.7	4 87.5
Cost of Sales/Inventory	45 8.2	32 11.5	96 3.8	54 6.7		87 4.2		81 4.5	87 4.2
	96 3.8	78 4.7	126 2.9	111 3.3		101 3.6		140 2.6	130 2.8
	126 2.9	166 2.2	166 2.2	166 2.2		159 2.3		215 1.7	182 2.0
Cost of Sales/Payables	0 UND	0 UND	24 15.4	14 26.5		51 7.2		11 33.3	14 25.8
	0 UND	0 UND	38 9.7	38 9.5		76 4.8		41 8.9	43 8.5
	4 94.1	17 21.0	70 5.2	66 5.5		91 4.0		66 5.5	65 5.6
Sales/Working Capital	7.4	4.7	4.9	7.2		8.6		3.1	4.1
	22.6	10.8	9.7	22.6		14.4		7.4	7.4
	-14.7	NM	23.8	37.5		-27.6		18.5	19.4
EBIT/Interest	58.0		6.6					17.7	19.2
	(11) 13.5	(16) 2.3						(59) 6.0	(64) 5.2
	6.0		1.0					1.7	1.5
Net Profit + Depr., Dep., Amort./Cur. Mat. L/T/D									11.0
									(11) 2.3
									.4
Fixed/Worth	.0	.1	.2	.3		.3		.1	.1
	.5	5.9	.9	.5		1.9		.3	.3
	-2.0	-.7	2.1	.8		-.4		1.2	1.1
Debt/Worth	.6	1.3	.5	.5		1.5		.3	.4
	1.5	NM	1.8	1.4		3.9		1.2	1.1
	-4.7	-3.3	10.7	1.8		-3.0		4.3	3.1
% Profit Before Taxes/Tangible Net Worth			16.8	64.5				46.5	44.3
			(15) 7.0	(10) 22.9				(69) 17.2	(91) 15.8
			.6	6.8				2.7	3.1
% Profit Before Taxes/Total Assets	37.6	26.5	7.4	18.7		17.0		21.7	18.9
	20.9	11.9	3.3	4.9		1.5		6.9	6.9
	12.0	-2.6	-.1	1.8		-11.7		1.3	1.5
Sales/Net Fixed Assets	227.3	92.2	50.6	22.7		21.9		88.9	71.9
	32.2	33.0	26.2	16.7		12.4		24.7	18.9
	9.6	9.6	11.9	9.5		5.7		11.5	7.5
Sales/Total Assets	5.1	3.3	3.2	4.7		2.7		3.8	3.7
	3.7	2.6	2.7	3.9		2.3		2.6	2.7
	2.7	1.7	1.6	2.3		1.9		1.6	1.7
% Depr., Dep., Amort./Sales			.6					.3	.3
			(16) .7					(54) .8	(71) 1.1
			1.5					2.6	1.8
% Officers', Directors' Owners' Comp/Sales			1.6					1.5	1.7
			(11) 3.5					(30) 3.9	(46) 2.7
			5.2					5.2	4.0
Net Sales ($)	15958M	27975M	233996M	861563M	392925M	4195028M		5570640M	6292157M
Total Assets ($)	3420M	9465M	79708M	268914M	229525M	1908412M		2343794M	2648996M

Comparative Historical Data | Current Data Sorted by Sales

	4/1/16-3/31/17 ALL	4/1/17-3/31/18 ALL	4/1/18-3/31/19 ALL	Type of Statement	0-1MM	1-3MM	3-5MM	5-10MM	10-25MM	25MM & OVER
	4	5	6	Unqualified				1	1	4
	9	5	6	Reviewed				1	3	2
	7	5	4	Compiled	1	1		1		1
	29	19	22	Tax Returns	5	11		3	2	1
	26	28	29	Other	2	5	1	2	1	18
						7 (4/1-9/30/18)	1	60 (10/1/18-3/31/19)		
NUMBER OF STATEMENTS	75	62	67		8	17	1	8	7	26
	%	%	%	**ASSETS**	%	%	%	%	%	%
Cash & Equivalents	14.5	15.4	15.3			15.3				15.0
Trade Receivables (net)	2.9	2.9	2.9			.0				4.7
Inventory	46.7	44.1	44.5			35.6				42.9
All Other Current	2.1	3.3	2.3			2.6				3.2
Total Current	66.2	65.8	65.0			53.5				65.9
Fixed Assets (net)	22.4	21.7	23.2			33.4				22.7
Intangibles (net)	4.8	6.3	5.8			10.5				6.4
All Other Non-Current	6.6	6.2	6.0			2.7				5.0
Total	100.0	100.0	100.0			100.0				100.0
				LIABILITIES						
Notes Payable-Short Term	6.3	9.9	15.8			20.1				7.4
Cur. Mat.-L.T.D.	2.5	1.7	3.1			4.9				1.8
Trade Payables	11.5	13.4	15.5			1.4				23.2
Income Taxes Payable	.1	.1	.0			.0				.0
All Other Current	9.8	13.8	12.0			12.2				13.7
Total Current	30.3	38.9	46.3			38.6				46.2
Long-Term Debt	21.2	12.2	19.5			30.6				15.4
Deferred Taxes	.2	.2	.1			.0				.2
All Other Non-Current	7.5	4.1	8.2			1.3				9.1
Net Worth	40.8	44.6	25.9			29.5				29.1
Total Liabilties & Net Worth	100.0	100.0	100.0			100.0				100.0
				INCOME DATA						
Net Sales	100.0	100.0	100.0			100.0				100.0
Gross Profit	47.9	48.4	47.0			49.0				47.8
Operating Expenses	41.5	44.1	43.4			43.6				45.1
Operating Profit	6.4	4.3	3.6			5.4				2.7
All Other Expenses (net)	1.2	.8	.6			.1				1.3
Profit Before Taxes	5.2	3.4	3.0			5.3				1.5
				RATIOS						
Current	5.4	4.1	3.2			4.2				2.7
	2.7	1.8	1.5			1.9				1.4
	1.5	1.3	1.1			1.0				1.0
Quick	1.7	.9	.9			1.7				.8
	.5	.4	.3			.5				.3
	.2	.2	.1			.2				.1
Sales/Receivables	0 UND	0 UND	0 UND			0 UND				0 UND
	0 999.8	0 999.8	0 UND			0 UND				4 85.2
	4 82.0	7 55.6	7 54.7			0 UND				14 26.5
Cost of Sales/Inventory	89 4.1	94 3.9	60 6.1			42 8.6				85 4.3
	126 2.9	118 3.1	114 3.2			74 4.9				111 3.3
	182 2.0	215 1.7	166 2.2			152 2.4				166 2.2
Cost of Sales/Payables	1 264.0	4 91.7	0 UND			0 UND				31 11.6
	23 15.8	34 10.8	28 13.2			0 UND				53 6.9
	59 6.2	73 5.0	68 5.4			2 150.9				79 4.6
Sales/Working Capital	3.8	4.5	5.2			7.4				5.8
	6.6	9.0	11.8			8.8				14.4
	14.3	27.9	260.7			NM				NM
EBIT/Interest	28.9	25.6	29.7			58.0				26.9
	(58) 5.2	(47) 5.1	(55) 4.9			(15) 7.5				(21) 4.3
	1.0	.7	.9			3.5				-1.6
Net Profit + Depr., Dep., Amort./Cur. Mat. L/T/D										
Fixed/Worth	.2	.1	.2			.1				.3
	.4	.3	.7			1.4				.7
	1.8	1.4	-2.4			NM				-.9
Debt/Worth	.3	.4	.7			.5				.7
	1.1	1.2	1.8			1.5				1.8
	3.9	3.7	-9.4			-3.6				-8.4
% Profit Before Taxes/Tangible Net Worth	47.3	50.5	52.5			79.7				58.3
	(61) 19.9	(55) 14.1	(48) 22.5			(12) 29.4				(19) 25.1
	5.9	2.0	5.6			11.1				7.3
% Profit Before Taxes/Total Assets	22.5	20.0	20.1			23.0				16.1
	6.6	5.2	7.4			13.8				6.2
	.5	.3	.2			5.2				-7.1
Sales/Net Fixed Assets	36.4	49.3	49.1			71.2				22.5
	19.4	18.1	19.5			22.2				14.1
	6.5	7.5	9.5			2.6				8.6
Sales/Total Assets	3.6	3.5	3.9			4.0				4.0
	2.3	2.5	2.7			2.8				2.4
	1.4	1.7	2.1			1.5				2.0
% Depr., Dep., Amort./Sales	.5	.5	.6			.4				1.0
	(56) 1.2	(42) 1.0	(42) 1.0			(10) 1.5				(16) 1.3
	2.8	2.2	1.8			3.5				1.8
% Officers', Directors' Owners' Comp/Sales	1.7	1.2	1.8			2.5				
	(33) 3.0	(22) 2.4	(25) 3.1			(10) 3.3				
	7.8	5.8	6.2			8.1				
Net Sales ($)	5191126M	4993511M	5727445M		4075M	28209M	3037M	63626M	113361M	5515137M
Total Assets ($)	2314804M	2088092M	2499444M		3754M	15078M	99M	23040M	34336M	2423137M

M = $ thousand   MM = $ million
See Pages viii through xx for Explanation of Ratios and Data

Current Data Sorted by Assets   Comparative Historical Data

0-500M	500M-2MM	2-10MM	10-50MM	50-100MM	100-250MM	Type of Statement	4/1/14-3/31/15 ALL	4/1/15-3/31/16 ALL
					1	Unqualified	1	4
1		1				Reviewed	1	3
7	8	3				Compiled	6	6
2	4	4	4		2	Tax Returns	21	26
		6				Other	14	24
	4 (4/1-9/30/18)		39 (10/1/18-3/31/19)					
10	12	14	4		3	NUMBER OF STATEMENTS	43	63
%	%	%	%	%	%	ASSETS	%	%
22.9	16.2	12.8				Cash & Equivalents	18.2	16.0
3.8	1.0	6.8				Trade Receivables (net)	4.9	8.0
52.0	27.0	38.3				Inventory	42.4	46.1
.2	2.7	7.3				All Other Current	3.2	1.9
78.9	47.0	65.1				Total Current	68.6	72.0
11.5	42.8	22.0				Fixed Assets (net)	21.9	18.8
1.2	2.1	10.1				Intangibles (net)	3.5	4.8
8.5	8.2	2.8				All Other Non-Current	5.9	4.4
100.0	100.0	100.0				Total	100.0	100.0
						LIABILITIES		
16.0	1.3	7.6				Notes Payable-Short Term	10.6	10.2
1.2	3.5	1.6				Cur. Mat.-L.T.D.	1.9	5.3
19.8	7.9	11.9				Trade Payables	23.4	12.8
.0	.0	.3				Income Taxes Payable	1.1	.3
22.9	3.5	7.4				All Other Current	11.6	9.0
59.9	16.3	28.9				Total Current	48.8	37.6
10.0	19.5	12.8				Long-Term Debt	17.4	14.3
.0	.0	.2				Deferred Taxes	.0	.0
2.1	14.1	9.5				All Other Non-Current	15.0	11.2
28.1	50.1	48.7				Net Worth	18.9	36.9
100.0	100.0	100.0				Total Liabilities & Net Worth	100.0	100.0
						INCOME DATA		
100.0	100.0	100.0				Net Sales	100.0	100.0
55.7	56.2	52.2				Gross Profit	48.8	48.6
49.8	38.7	46.0				Operating Expenses	41.8	42.2
5.9	17.5	6.2				Operating Profit	6.9	6.4
.6	1.4	-.7				All Other Expenses (net)	.7	.5
5.3	16.1	6.9				Profit Before Taxes	6.3	5.9
						RATIOS		
5.6	9.4	4.8				Current	4.2	4.6
1.7	2.6	2.3					2.2	2.3
.7	1.3	1.7					1.0	1.3
1.4	3.5	1.7				Quick	1.3	1.3
.4	.5	.7					.4	.5
.2	.3	.2					.2	.1
0 UND	0 UND	0 UND				Sales/Receivables	0 UND	0 UND
0 UND	0 UND	4 87.0					0 UND	3 137.9
5 79.8	2 164.6	11 33.8					5 72.4	11 31.8
44 8.3	94 3.9	91 4.0				Cost of Sales/Inventory	43 8.4	76 4.8
83 4.4	107 3.4	122 3.0					99 3.7	126 2.9
182 2.0	126 2.9	166 2.2					152 2.4	174 2.1
0 UND	0 UND	0 UND				Cost of Sales/Payables	0 UND	2 149.3
34 10.8	7 51.2	38 9.5					14 26.1	23 16.1
78 4.7	69 5.3	72 5.1					39 9.4	57 6.4
4.0	3.7	4.3				Sales/Working Capital	4.9	4.2
NM	8.2	6.4					11.5	7.2
-33.6	25.4	10.6					999.8	29.6
		18.1				EBIT/Interest	29.3	24.8
	(12) 8.0						(33) 5.6	(47) 5.1
		2.5					2.6	1.6
						Net Profit + Depr., Dep., Amort./Cur. Mat. L/T/D		
.0	.2	.1				Fixed/Worth	.1	.1
.3	.8	.3					.6	.6
-.7	2.8	.7					6.4	4.5
.4	.2	.3				Debt/Worth	.5	.5
10.8	.8	1.5					3.9	1.5
-8.1	2.8	3.4					54.8	19.5
	85.1	34.5				% Profit Before Taxes/Tangible Net Worth	94.9	76.1
	55.7	(13) 23.4					(35) 52.4	(52) 27.2
	35.5	6.4					31.6	10.8
67.9	42.4	17.5				% Profit Before Taxes/Total Assets	37.5	29.5
29.7	27.8	10.0					13.2	10.9
-5.7	14.5	1.9					3.0	2.3
UND	15.9	34.5				Sales/Net Fixed Assets	90.6	93.3
45.0	4.0	16.6					29.1	22.1
14.9	1.1	9.2					9.1	8.2
9.1	2.7	3.0				Sales/Total Assets	4.3	3.9
3.5	1.4	2.0					3.2	2.5
2.1	.8	1.3					1.8	1.5
		.9				% Depr., Dep., Amort./Sales	.6	.9
	(10) 2.0						(29) 1.3	(45) 1.3
		3.0					2.6	2.3
						% Officers', Directors' Owners' Comp/Sales	1.4	2.7
							(21) 3.5	(29) 4.3
							7.7	8.5
15411M	20044M	159971M	147593M		1022953M	Net Sales ($)	1034844M	1526616M
2903M	12348M	73563M	79459M		548802M	Total Assets ($)	379915M	775454M

M = $ thousand   MM = $ million
See Pages viii through xx for Explanation of Ratios and Data

Comparative Historical Data | Current Data Sorted by Sales

			Type of Statement						
	1	1	Unqualified					1	1
2	1	1	Reviewed					1	
5	5	4	Compiled	1		1	1	1	
19	23	19	Tax Returns	5	9		3	2	
27	23	18	Other	1	5		3	2	7
4/1/16-	4/1/17-	4/1/18-			4 (4/1-9/30/18)			39 (10/1/18-3/31/19)	
3/31/17	3/31/18	3/31/19		0-1MM	1-3MM	3-5MM	5-10MM	10-25MM	25MM & OVER
ALL	ALL	ALL							
53	53	43	NUMBER OF STATEMENTS	7	14	1	7	6	8
%	%	%	ASSETS	%	%	%	%	%	%
16.5	15.4	15.0	Cash & Equivalents		18.5				
7.6	5.2	4.7	Trade Receivables (net)		2.0				
41.8	40.0	38.3	Inventory		31.8				
3.0	3.5	4.0	All Other Current		2.4				
69.0	64.1	62.0	Total Current		54.7				
23.1	21.9	24.5	Fixed Assets (net)		32.1				
2.6	7.4	7.5	Intangibles (net)		2.6				
5.3	6.7	6.0	All Other Non-Current		10.6				
100.0	100.0	100.0	Total		100.0				
			LIABILITIES						
9.4	9.0	7.4	Notes Payable-Short Term		.8				
3.2	3.5	1.8	Cur. Mat.-L.T.D.		3.2				
12.4	12.0	12.1	Trade Payables		8.0				
.2	.1	.2	Income Taxes Payable		.0				
9.7	10.3	11.1	All Other Current		9.2				
34.9	35.0	32.7	Total Current		21.2				
16.4	14.7	14.1	Long-Term Debt		16.1				
.0	.0	.1	Deferred Taxes		.0				
9.5	10.7	8.3	All Other Non-Current		13.0				
39.2	39.6	44.9	Net Worth		49.7				
100.0	100.0	100.0	Total Liabilties & Net Worth		100.0				
			INCOME DATA						
100.0	100.0	100.0	Net Sales		100.0				
50.2	48.8	54.2	Gross Profit		56.7				
43.9	42.0	44.1	Operating Expenses		37.2				
6.2	6.9	10.1	Operating Profit		19.5				
.6	.3	.4	All Other Expenses (net)		.5				
5.7	6.6	9.7	Profit Before Taxes		19.0				
			RATIOS						
4.3	4.4	4.4			10.9				
2.4	2.4	2.3	Current		2.7				
1.4	1.0	1.3			1.1				
1.5	1.3	1.4			3.7				
.6	.7	(42) .5	Quick		.9				
.2	.2	.2			.3				
0 UND	0 UND	0 UND		0 UND					
3 128.7	0 999.8	2 177.1	Sales/Receivables	0 UND					
11 34.7	8 47.4	8 45.4		2 172.9					
76 4.8	66 5.5	79 4.6		69 5.3					
114 3.2	104 3.5	122 3.0	Cost of Sales/Inventory	101 3.6					
182 2.0	203 1.8	203 1.8		114 3.2					
4 100.3	0 UND	4 95.0		0 UND					
26 14.0	22 16.8	35 10.5	Cost of Sales/Payables	7 52.2					
66 5.5	50 7.3	64 5.7		56 6.5					
4.2	4.2	4.4			4.1				
6.4	7.7	7.0	Sales/Working Capital		8.8				
23.8	NM	23.1			NM				
28.3	15.9	19.2			126.3				
(44) 7.8	(36) 5.3	(32) 8.5	EBIT/Interest		(10) 18.9				
1.6	1.3	2.3			11.2				
			Net Profit + Depr., Dep., Amort./Cur. Mat. L/T/D						
.2	.1	.1			.2				
.5	.4	.3	Fixed/Worth		.8				
2.5	12.4	3.2			3.9				
.6	.3	.5			.2				
1.5	1.1	1.1	Debt/Worth		.8				
6.7	120.6	12.6			5.4				
63.9	71.1	79.0	% Profit Before Taxes/Tangible Net Worth		113.0				
(48) 23.8	(41) 22.7	(37) 36.1			(13) 64.9				
10.6	5.6	11.5			50.2				
19.2	25.9	31.4	% Profit Before Taxes/Total Assets		46.7				
9.5	10.3	17.1			31.1				
3.7	1.6	3.8			22.9				
60.7	53.9	37.3			36.0				
16.3	20.8	17.4	Sales/Net Fixed Assets		7.9				
6.7	7.2	5.7			1.9				
3.4	3.4	3.1			3.6				
2.4	2.4	2.1	Sales/Total Assets		2.3				
1.7	1.4	1.3			.9				
.8	.8	.7							
(37) 1.8	(39) 1.3	(26) 1.5	% Depr., Dep., Amort./Sales						
2.7	2.8	2.9							
1.8	2.4	2.7	% Officers', Directors' Owners' Comp/Sales		4.1				
(27) 3.8	(25) 3.9	(21) 4.2			(10) 4.3				
6.3	4.5	4.9			4.7				
1915807M	2421269M	1365972M	Net Sales ($)	4043M	22678M	4626M	50222M	86654M	1197749M
796030M	1108545M	717075M	Total Assets ($)	3102M	14314M	3966M	22659M	35604M	637430M

© RMA 2019

M = $ thousand   MM = $ million
See Pages viii through xx for Explanation of Ratios and Data

Current Data Sorted by Assets   Comparative Historical Data

						Type of Statement		
	1		6			Unqualified	9	7
		3	2			Reviewed	12	12
	3	4	1			Compiled	24	26
12	14	5	3		1	Tax Returns	68	65
8	12	12	9	3	2	Other	69	75
	20 (4/1-9/30/18)		81 (10/1/18-3/31/19)				4/1/14-3/31/15	4/1/15-3/31/16
0-500M	500M-2MM	2-10MM	10-50MM	50-100MM	100-250MM		ALL	ALL
20	30	24	21	3	3	**NUMBER OF STATEMENTS**	182	185
%	%	%	%	%	%	**ASSETS**	%	%
25.6	21.7	15.9	8.1			Cash & Equivalents	17.2	15.3
7.2	8.6	9.5	13.7			Trade Receivables (net)	9.3	8.6
46.4	40.4	39.7	36.8			Inventory	43.8	43.2
.5	3.9	4.1	4.8			All Other Current	2.7	2.1
79.6	74.7	69.2	63.3			Total Current	73.0	69.2
16.3	11.8	22.9	24.3			Fixed Assets (net)	17.2	18.9
.6	7.1	2.2	9.6			Intangibles (net)	3.6	4.7
3.5	6.4	5.7	2.8			All Other Non-Current	6.2	7.1
100.0	100.0	100.0	100.0			Total	100.0	100.0
						LIABILITIES		
20.7	13.8	11.9	7.9			Notes Payable-Short Term	12.3	12.2
4.7	1.4	1.8	1.2			Cur. Mat.-L.T.D.	1.4	1.7
25.6	20.6	18.9	21.9			Trade Payables	18.3	17.8
.0	.0	.0	.2			Income Taxes Payable	.1	.2
20.8	10.4	5.6	5.7			All Other Current	13.4	15.5
71.8	46.2	38.3	36.9			Total Current	45.5	47.4
11.5	8.5	12.4	12.4			Long-Term Debt	13.2	14.9
.0	.0	.0	.1			Deferred Taxes	.1	.1
4.9	4.3	.8	10.0			All Other Non-Current	5.2	9.7
11.8	41.0	48.5	40.6			Net Worth	36.0	27.9
100.0	100.0	100.0	100.0			Total Liabilties & Net Worth	100.0	100.0
						INCOME DATA		
100.0	100.0	100.0	100.0			Net Sales	100.0	100.0
48.2	53.5	48.0	51.2			Gross Profit	47.5	48.7
41.2	47.4	40.0	45.7			Operating Expenses	42.6	43.6
7.0	6.1	7.9	5.5			Operating Profit	5.0	5.1
2.4	.8	1.1	1.0			All Other Expenses (net)	.6	.8
4.7	5.3	6.9	4.5			Profit Before Taxes	4.4	4.2
						RATIOS		
1.7	3.7	3.3	2.6				3.8	3.3
1.2	2.0	1.7	1.7			Current	1.9	1.6
.8	1.3	1.3	1.2				1.2	1.1
.9	1.6	1.2	1.1				1.6	1.1
.5	.8	.4	.3			Quick	.7	.5
.1	.4	.3	.2				.2	.2
0 UND	0 UND	0 999.8	0 999.8				0 UND	0 UND
0 UND	1 327.8	4 91.1	2 165.3			Sales/Receivables	1 265.5	2 215.0
17 20.9	15 23.9	22 16.5	49 7.4				20 18.3	22 16.7
29 12.8	46 8.0	69 5.3	94 3.9				52 7.0	64 5.7
140 2.6	96 3.8	135 2.7	135 2.7			Cost of Sales/Inventory	104 3.5	114 3.2
203 1.8	159 2.3	228 1.6	243 1.5				192 1.9	215 1.7
0 UND	1 347.8	12 31.7	43 8.5				7 50.5	10 38.2
42 8.7	26 13.9	34 10.8	60 6.1			Cost of Sales/Payables	30 12.0	34 10.8
83 4.4	64 5.7	85 4.3	87 4.2				70 5.2	63 5.8
7.7	5.7	4.8	5.1				4.6	4.6
20.4	9.4	6.4	8.1			Sales/Working Capital	9.5	10.1
-19.2	27.1	27.5	25.9				40.8	46.3
12.9	35.8	40.6	15.9				25.6	19.0
(14) 6.3	(23) 6.7	(18) 5.6	(20) 8.8			EBIT/Interest	(132) 11.3	(135) 6.2
1.3	.4	1.5	1.2				1.8	1.0
						Net Profit + Depr., Dep., Amort./Cur. Mat. L/T/D	14.5	11.2
							(14) 6.5	(16) 7.7
							3.0	2.1
.0	.0	.1	.3				.1	.1
.6	.1	.4	.7			Fixed/Worth	.3	.4
2.3	.6	.9	1.3				1.2	1.9
.9	.4	.4	.9				.4	.7
3.8	1.0	1.2	1.5			Debt/Worth	1.6	2.1
UND	NM	2.4	3.3				4.4	11.7
126.3	107.1	39.3	49.1				72.3	49.7
(15) 26.0	(23) 35.8	(23) 16.0	(19) 23.9			% Profit Before Taxes/Tangible Net Worth	(155) 33.3	(152) 23.9
-8.2	12.0	7.7	2.6				9.3	7.5
29.5	35.5	19.6	21.5				26.5	19.0
9.6	16.7	5.9	10.1			% Profit Before Taxes/Total Assets	11.2	8.2
-1.3	5.8	1.9	.6				3.1	.9
UND	737.9	91.0	23.2				154.1	79.8
68.1	59.5	13.7	11.7			Sales/Net Fixed Assets	31.4	25.9
11.8	16.6	7.9	4.7				9.1	8.6
4.3	5.2	3.3	2.7				4.3	3.8
2.9	3.1	2.3	2.0			Sales/Total Assets	2.7	2.4
2.0	2.0	1.7	1.4				1.7	1.5
.3	.1	.7	1.1				.3	.5
(13) .9	(16) .4	(18) 1.0	(17) 1.7			% Depr., Dep., Amort./Sales	(120) 1.1	(126) 1.3
3.5	1.2	3.2	2.1				1.9	2.2
	1.8	.9					2.4	2.5
	(22) 5.2	(13) 2.7				% Officers', Directors' Owners' Comp/Sales	(78) 4.0	(78) 4.0
	8.4	5.5					6.8	7.8
17262M	114039M	280469M	1188742M	272358M	1204715M	Net Sales ($)	2535286M	2661795M
5731M	29604M	116809M	519444M	246004M	523307M	Total Assets ($)	1197784M	1328976M

M = $ thousand   MM = $ million
See Pages viii through xx for Explanation of Ratios and Data

Comparative Historical Data   Current Data Sorted by Sales

			Type of Statement						
					1				6
								2	3
					1		3	2	2
				8	12	5	6	1	3
				4	13	3	5	10	11
8	7	7	Unqualified						
7	11	5	Reviewed						
18	13	8	Compiled						
59	39	35	Tax Returns		20 (4/1-9/30/18)			81 (10/1/18-3/31/19)	
80	57	46	Other						
4/1/16-3/31/17 ALL	4/1/17-3/31/18 ALL	4/1/18-3/31/19 ALL		0-1MM	1-3MM	3-5MM	5-10MM	10-25MM	25MM & OVER
172	127	101	**NUMBER OF STATEMENTS**	12	27	8	14	15	25
%	%	%	**ASSETS**	%	%	%	%	%	%
14.0	15.5	17.3	Cash & Equivalents	31.9	14.6		23.5	14.2	8.3
9.7	7.4	9.3	Trade Receivables (net)	10.7	6.9		4.1	10.5	13.8
45.3	42.0	40.5	Inventory	44.4	37.3		45.0	47.0	37.0
3.2	1.8	3.4	All Other Current	.1	3.1		5.0	4.6	3.4
72.2	66.7	70.6	Total Current	87.1	61.8		77.7	76.3	62.5
16.6	19.3	18.9	Fixed Assets (net)	6.7	24.0		10.7	16.2	24.9
5.0	7.7	5.7	Intangibles (net)	.8	8.0		5.0	2.7	9.5
6.1	6.3	4.8	All Other Non-Current	5.5	6.1		6.7	4.9	3.0
100.0	100.0	100.0	Total	100.0	100.0		100.0	100.0	100.0
			LIABILITIES						
15.0	11.3	13.5	Notes Payable-Short Term	21.1	13.0		14.5	9.7	8.0
1.5	1.7	2.2	Cur. Mat.-L.T.D.	6.2	2.4		1.0	1.3	1.6
20.8	14.6	20.7	Trade Payables	23.3	16.4		15.8	20.4	22.8
.2	.1	.1	Income Taxes Payable	.0	.0		.0	.0	.2
10.0	9.5	10.4	All Other Current	26.3	9.3		7.7	5.0	8.8
47.3	37.2	46.8	Total Current	77.0	41.2		38.9	36.4	41.4
14.0	15.1	11.0	Long-Term Debt	11.1	13.8		6.4	12.4	8.0
.1	.1	.0	Deferred Taxes	.0	.0		.0	.0	.0
4.6	7.4	5.6	All Other Non-Current	5.4	5.8		1.0	1.2	12.5
34.0	40.2	36.6	Net Worth	6.6	39.3		53.6	49.9	38.1
100.0	100.0	100.0	Total Liabilties & Net Worth	100.0	100.0		100.0	100.0	100.0
			INCOME DATA						
100.0	100.0	100.0	Net Sales	100.0	100.0		100.0	100.0	100.0
48.2	48.4	50.0	Gross Profit	50.6	53.6		46.5	50.3	48.7
43.7	42.4	43.5	Operating Expenses	41.4	45.6		42.0	42.3	43.5
4.5	6.0	6.5	Operating Profit	9.1	8.0		4.5	7.9	5.2
.7	1.1	1.3	All Other Expenses (net)	4.2	.7		.5	1.1	1.1
3.8	4.9	5.2	Profit Before Taxes	5.0	7.3		4.0	6.9	4.1
			RATIOS						
2.7	4.0	3.1	Current	2.9	2.4		3.3	3.9	2.5
1.7	1.9	1.7		1.2	1.7		2.0	2.0	1.5
1.1	1.2	1.2		.8	1.1		1.4	1.3	1.2
1.0	1.2	1.0	Quick	1.0	1.0		1.5	1.2	1.0
.4	.5	.5		.7	.5		.5	.6	.3
.1	.2	.2		.2	.2		.2	.3	.2
0 UND	0 UND	0 UND	Sales/Receivables	0 UND	0 UND		0 UND	1 635.8	0 999.8
2 158.5	2 237.3	2 232.2		0 UND	0 UND		4 91.6	2 165.3	3 107.2
20 18.1	16 22.7	21 17.6		33 11.0	12 30.1		8 46.6	33 11.1	37 9.9
45 8.2	59 6.2	59 6.2	Cost of Sales/Inventory	34 10.6	31 11.8		31 11.9	70 5.2	94 3.9
122 3.0	122 3.0	135 2.7		152 2.4	114 3.2		146 2.5	126 2.9	135 2.7
203 1.8	203 1.8	203 1.8		281 1.3	182 2.0		228 1.6	281 1.3	159 2.3
14 26.6	8 44.5	10 37.4	Cost of Sales/Payables	0 UND	0 914.0		5 66.9	26 13.9	31 11.7
41 8.9	32 11.5	41 8.9		15 25.0	26 14.0		35 10.3	31 11.7	54 6.7
76 4.8	61 6.0	74 4.9		96 3.8	63 5.8		50 7.3	94 3.9	74 4.9
5.1	4.7	5.3	Sales/Working Capital	3.0	5.6		5.4	4.6	5.7
10.7	9.0	8.7		17.9	12.8		6.8	6.4	9.1
71.9	39.7	30.2		-19.2	63.6		11.6	28.9	28.3
23.2	21.7	24.7	EBIT/Interest		26.3		63.1	52.9	42.9
(134) 6.0	(105) 7.3	(79) 6.4			(25) 6.8		(10) 5.2	(10) 4.2	(21) 9.5
1.4	1.1	1.5			3.2		.5	1.3	1.2
13.8			Net Profit + Depr., Dep., Amort./Cur. Mat. L/T/D						
(10) 9.3									
4.4									
.1	.1	.1	Fixed/Worth	.0	.1		.0	.1	.2
.3	.4	.4		.1	.6		.1	.3	.7
1.9	1.6	1.3		UND	2.1		.7	.6	1.5
.7	.6	.7	Debt/Worth	.7	.8		.3	.5	.7
1.8	1.7	1.4		4.3	1.1		1.1	1.1	1.5
8.6	6.5	4.8		5.2	9.6		4.0	1.6	3.9
69.8	62.7	53.0	% Profit Before Taxes/Tangible Net Worth		82.9		51.1	54.9	45.6
(138) 29.2	(106) 29.4	(84) 25.7			(21) 28.2		18.4	(14) 18.1	(21) 29.5
7.2	6.4	6.6			.6		4.1	6.1	13.2
28.5	21.9	23.8	% Profit Before Taxes/Total Assets	23.1	30.0		21.6	35.6	21.5
10.8	11.2	10.6		9.6	14.3		7.6	8.5	10.6
1.1	1.8	1.4		-12.9	3.7		1.2	1.0	.6
93.1	102.8	210.5	Sales/Net Fixed Assets	UND	56.8		311.5	92.0	23.2
29.2	26.3	18.7		290.1	18.7		82.6	22.6	12.0
11.4	8.9	7.8		31.0	6.2		10.5	8.1	5.4
3.9	3.8	3.5	Sales/Total Assets	3.5	3.2		4.5	3.8	2.9
2.8	2.5	2.5		2.6	2.5		3.0	2.4	2.2
1.8	1.7	1.8		1.5	1.6		1.8	1.7	1.8
.4	.3	.3	% Depr., Dep., Amort./Sales		.3		.1	.3	1.2
(108) .9	(82) 1.1	(69) 1.2			(18) 1.1		(11) .7	(11) .8	(19) 1.7
2.2	2.4	2.1			2.8		2.2	1.3	3.6
2.1	1.6	1.7	% Officers', Directors' Owners' Comp/Sales		5.7				
(72) 3.8	(54) 4.3	(50) 4.6			(18) 6.7				
6.9	7.5	8.2			9.9				
3620125M	4014208M	3077585M	Net Sales ($)	5718M	45265M	32241M	99918M	219945M	2674498M
1581069M	1794671M	1440899M	Total Assets ($)	2400M	22526M	14769M	47746M	106557M	1246901M

   M = $ thousand   MM = $ million
See Pages viii through xx for Explanation of Ratios and Data

Current Data Sorted by Assets   Comparative Historical Data

	0-500M	500M-2MM	2-10MM	10-50MM	50-100MM	100-250MM		Type of Statement	4/1/14-3/31/15 ALL	4/1/15-3/31/16 ALL
Unqualified			1						5	6
Reviewed		1		1					13	8
Compiled		1	5	5					7	8
Tax Returns	8	14	6			1			27	36
Other	2	5	8	5	1	4			47	53
		9 (4/1-9/30/18)		59 (10/1/18-3/31/19)						
NUMBER OF STATEMENTS	10	21	20	11	1	5			99	111
	%	%	%	%	%	%		ASSETS	%	%
Cash & Equivalents	28.7	12.0	8.9	6.7					12.3	8.4
Trade Receivables (net)	7.7	6.1	7.0	8.8					6.0	7.0
Inventory	43.5	53.6	63.8	58.4					55.4	55.5
All Other Current	.6	2.1	1.3	2.3					1.9	1.6
Total Current	80.5	73.8	80.9	76.2					75.6	72.5
Fixed Assets (net)	8.6	14.2	14.9	16.5					14.7	15.6
Intangibles (net)	3.3	2.6	1.6	5.8					4.6	4.2
All Other Non-Current	7.5	9.4	2.6	1.5					5.2	7.7
Total	100.0	100.0	100.0	100.0					100.0	100.0
								LIABILITIES		
Notes Payable-Short Term	13.0	6.7	14.5	5.3					8.6	11.0
Cur. Mat.-L.T.D.	.2	2.3	2.4	.3					1.6	1.3
Trade Payables	28.5	24.6	22.9	19.5					24.7	23.7
Income Taxes Payable	.0	.0	.0	.0					.1	.1
All Other Current	10.8	26.6	10.1	15.2					13.2	14.5
Total Current	52.4	60.2	49.8	40.3					48.2	50.6
Long-Term Debt	4.6	11.6	6.5	9.4					9.4	10.3
Deferred Taxes	.0	.0	.0	.0					.3	.4
All Other Non-Current	.0	5.5	7.9	5.1					10.6	7.8
Net Worth	43.0	22.7	35.8	45.2					31.5	31.0
Total Liabilities & Net Worth	100.0	100.0	100.0	100.0					100.0	100.0
								INCOME DATA		
Net Sales	100.0	100.0	100.0	100.0					100.0	100.0
Gross Profit	43.0	42.6	45.8	44.9					41.3	41.1
Operating Expenses	34.9	38.4	44.1	41.5					39.1	38.8
Operating Profit	8.0	4.1	1.7	3.4					2.1	2.3
All Other Expenses (net)	.5	.4	.5	3.5					.7	.4
Profit Before Taxes	7.5	3.8	1.2	-.1					1.5	1.9
								RATIOS		
Current	7.4	3.8	3.4	3.5					2.9	2.8
	2.0	1.5	1.7	1.8					1.7	1.5
	1.0	.9	1.2	1.3					1.3	1.1
Quick	2.0	.9	.9	1.4					.8	.6
	1.1	.2	.1	.3					.3 (110)	.3
	.4	.1	.1	.1					.1	.1
Sales/Receivables	0 UND	0 UND	0 UND	3 145.0					0 UND	0 UND
	0 UND	2 242.5	1 682.9	6 60.4					1 256.2	2 211.9
	9 41.0	12 30.2	11 32.4	17 21.6					15 24.9	14 25.3
Cost of Sales/Inventory	0 UND	114 3.2	135 2.7	126 2.9					79 4.6	94 3.9
	68 5.4	166 2.2	159 2.3	166 2.2					135 2.7	140 2.6
	166 2.2	243 1.5	243 1.5	228 1.6					182 2.0	192 1.9
Cost of Sales/Payables	0 UND	23 15.8	35 10.4	31 11.7					31 11.8	31 11.6
	21 17.1	56 6.5	52 7.0	49 7.5					54 6.8	55 6.6
	41 8.8	83 4.4	83 4.4	81 4.5					79 4.6	81 4.5
Sales/Working Capital	3.6	3.6	3.4	3.1					5.3	5.2
	10.4	12.3	7.5	6.9					8.1	11.5
	NM	NM	29.4	18.2					18.1	53.6
EBIT/Interest		13.8	17.0						14.2	14.5
		(14) 5.4	(18) 2.7						(68) 5.0	(79) 4.7
		1.2	-.2						-.2	.2
Net Profit + Depr., Dep., Amort./Cur. Mat. L/T/D									8.5	10.0
									(13) 2.0	(17) 6.7
									1.0	1.8
Fixed/Worth	.0	.0	.1	.2					.1	.2
	.1	.2	.4	.4					.3	.4
	.8	NM	1.6	1.4					1.1	1.9
Debt/Worth	.2	.8	.7	.3					.9	.7
	.5	4.2	1.9	1.7					1.7	1.8
	NM	NM	8.4	8.1					4.7	19.2
% Profit Before Taxes/Tangible Net Worth		35.5	13.5						39.6	37.6
	(16) 25.3	(17) 7.0							(83) 15.1	(90) 18.5
		2.6	-6.4						3.0	6.5
% Profit Before Taxes/Total Assets	39.3	17.2	6.1	14.4					12.9	13.0
	16.2	3.9	2.0	6.8					5.1	6.9
	8.9	-.1	-2.2	-4.1					.7	-.3
Sales/Net Fixed Assets	UND	704.8	34.1	21.2					88.6	58.3
	68.9	53.6	21.7	19.1					22.6	19.1
	28.5	9.7	11.3	11.4					12.7	10.1
Sales/Total Assets	7.3	3.7	3.5	2.8					3.5	3.1
	3.2	1.9	2.7	2.3					2.7	2.5
	2.5	1.2	1.9	1.6					2.0	1.9
% Depr., Dep., Amort./Sales		.1	.4	.9					.5	.5
		(14) .5	(17) 1.2	(10) 1.5					(72) .9	(81) .9
		2.4	1.4	2.2					2.0	2.2
% Officers', Directors' Owners' Comp/Sales		1.1	3.3						1.4	1.6
	(13) 2.8	(10) 3.9							(40) 3.0	(47) 2.8
		5.7	6.4						5.6	4.4
Net Sales ($)	11071M	56471M	202827M	716734M	197270M	1837951M			3877042M	4583403M
Total Assets ($)	2027M	23847M	84301M	299987M	94347M	822350M			1676964M	2149965M

M = $ thousand   MM = $ million
See Pages viii through xx for Explanation of Ratios and Data

Comparative Historical Data | Current Data Sorted by Sales

Type of Statement	1	5	3		1			2
Unqualified	5	6	5				1	4
Reviewed	5	6	7		1		5	1
Compiled	23	22	28	7	9	3	9	
Tax Returns	37	35	25	3	5		2	10
Other	4/1/16-	4/1/17-	4/1/18-		9 (4/1-9/30/18)		59 (10/1/18-3/31/19)	
	3/31/17	3/31/18	3/31/19	0-1MM	1-3MM	3-5MM	5-10MM	10-25MM	25MM & OVER
	ALL	ALL	ALL						

	ALL	ALL	ALL	0-1MM	1-3MM	3-5MM	5-10MM	10-25MM	25MM & OVER
NUMBER OF STATEMENTS	71	74	68	10	16	3	11	11	17
ASSETS	%	%	%	%	%	%	%	%	%
Cash & Equivalents	8.6	11.4	12.6	15.3	14.7		17.8	6.7	8.1
Trade Receivables (net)	7.2	4.6	7.1	14.1	6.5		3.5	3.6	8.1
Inventory	56.7	55.3	55.5	45.8	45.9		63.9	69.2	55.3
All Other Current	1.8	1.4	2.1	.6	1.4		2.2	1.9	4.1
Total Current	74.3	72.8	77.3	75.8	68.5		87.5	81.4	75.6
Fixed Assets (net)	16.3	15.4	14.2	5.8	23.5		6.5	13.9	16.7
Intangibles (net)	5.1	6.4	3.3	2.7	2.8		2.5	.9	6.1
All Other Non-Current	4.3	5.5	5.2	15.7	5.2		3.5	3.8	1.6
Total	100.0	100.0	100.0	100.0	100.0		100.0	100.0	100.0
LIABILITIES									
Notes Payable-Short Term	13.8	13.0	9.6	5.6	6.4		7.2	17.8	5.2
Cur. Mat.-L.T.D.	2.0	2.0	1.6	.3	1.8		5.0	.8	.7
Trade Payables	25.8	21.1	23.5	22.7	24.3		23.0	28.6	20.0
Income Taxes Payable	.0	.0	.0	.0	.0		.0	.0	.1
All Other Current	9.5	14.7	16.1	8.4	36.9		8.4	7.0	13.5
Total Current	51.1	50.8	50.8	37.0	69.4		43.6	54.4	39.5
Long-Term Debt	14.7	12.5	8.7	3.6	14.5		6.1	7.6	10.2
Deferred Taxes	.4	.4	.0	.0	.0		.0	.0	.0
All Other Non-Current	10.3	5.6	5.7	2.6	4.9		1.0	11.9	6.9
Net Worth	23.4	30.7	34.7	56.8	11.2		49.3	26.2	43.4
Total Liabilties & Net Worth	100.0	100.0	100.0	100.0	100.0		100.0	100.0	100.0
INCOME DATA									
Net Sales	100.0	100.0	100.0	100.0	100.0		100.0	100.0	100.0
Gross Profit	44.9	44.3	43.7	38.5	45.3		39.4	50.0	43.0
Operating Expenses	42.0	42.5	40.0	33.9	40.4		34.8	47.6	40.1
Operating Profit	2.9	1.8	3.7	4.6	4.9		4.5	2.3	2.9
All Other Expenses (net)	.7	.7	.9	1.2	.1		.3	.8	2.2
Profit Before Taxes	2.2	1.1	2.8	3.5	4.8		4.2	1.5	.7
RATIOS									
	2.5	2.5	3.5	7.4	3.3		4.4	2.0	3.0
Current	1.4	1.5	1.8	2.5	1.2		3.0	1.5	1.8
	1.2	1.0	1.2	1.2	.6		1.1	1.3	1.4
	.6	.6	1.1	2.1	1.0		1.1	.5	1.2
Quick	(70) .3	.3	.3	1.5	.3		.3	.1	.3
	.1	.1	.1	.2	.0		.1	.0	.1

													Sales/Receivables												

Sales/Receivables	0 UND	0 UND	0 UND	0 UND	0 UND		0 UND	0 UND	2 156.1
	3 132.8	1 426.8	2 182.6	0 UND	1 362.9		1 315.8	0 785.4	5 68.6
	18 20.8	6 57.4	12 31.2	118 3.1	12 29.8		6 64.3	11 33.9	17 22.1
Cost of Sales/Inventory	107 3.4	99 3.7	111 3.3	0 UND	135 2.7		101 3.6	152 2.4	118 3.1
	152 2.4	152 2.4	152 2.4	159 2.3	166 2.2		130 2.8	159 2.3	146 2.5
	192 1.9	203 1.8	215 1.7	261 1.4	281 1.3		192 1.9	261 1.4	228 1.6
Cost of Sales/Payables	34 10.7	31 11.7	24 15.2	14 26.3	5 74.6		23 16.1	42 8.6	37 9.9
	60 6.1	53 6.9	49 7.5	38 9.7	33 11.2		46 7.9	61 6.0	49 7.5
	85 4.3	81 4.5	81 4.5	215 1.7	76 4.8		56 6.5	104 3.5	83 4.4
Sales/Working Capital	6.1	5.0	3.7	3.3	3.5		3.3	4.0	4.5
	11.3	11.4	7.1	3.9	25.1		5.6	7.8	6.5
	38.1	222.2	23.1	18.6	-7.1		82.3	19.8	11.6
EBIT/Interest	10.7	12.6	17.0					9.3	66.6
	(52) 3.6	(57) 4.4	(51) 4.3					2.0	(14) 4.3
	1.0	-1.9	1.1					-.1	.7
Net Profit + Depr., Dep., Amort./Cur. Mat. L/T/D	9.3								
	(14) 3.4								
	1.8								
Fixed/Worth	.2	.2	.1	.0	.3		.0	.3	.2
	.5	.6	.4	.0	1.0		.0	.5	.5
	7.4	4.4	1.4	.2	-.4		.2	1.2	1.1
Debt/Worth	1.0	1.0	.5	.2	.9		.3	1.4	.6
	2.8	2.7	1.8	.5	7.7		.5	2.1	1.7
	41.0	20.1	9.4	4.1	-3.7		5.7	9.1	6.0
% Profit Before Taxes/Tangible Net Worth	49.2	50.2	34.7	41.3	38.7			9.3	35.2
	(55) 18.4	(61) 20.7	(55) 16.3	28.0	(10) 17.2			(10) 2.8	(14) 21.3
	3.3	.3	3.8	14.7	-1.0			-13.7	9.6
% Profit Before Taxes/Total Assets	12.4	16.1	15.1	34.9	17.1		23.2	2.8	14.8
	4.7	5.4	5.2	8.7	6.4		5.5	1.1	5.9
	-.6	-3.9	.3	3.7	-1.1		4.3	-2.8	-2.1
Sales/Net Fixed Assets	61.9	56.2	93.4	UND	159.0		401.5	28.7	22.7
	19.5	20.5	22.1	68.9	17.5		167.7	21.7	19.1
	9.4	12.9	11.6	28.5	5.3		12.7	19.6	8.6
Sales/Total Assets	3.3	3.4	3.3	3.1	3.0		4.2	3.6	2.8
	2.5	2.2	2.4	2.4	1.8		2.7	3.0	2.3
	1.9	1.8	1.8	1.0	1.2		2.5	1.9	1.8
% Depr., Dep., Amort./Sales	.4	.5	.4		.1			.6	.6
	(56) 1.0	(61) .9	(52) 1.0		(12) 1.6			(10) 1.2	(15) 1.2
	2.3	2.8	1.7		2.6			1.4	2.0
% Officers', Directors' Owners' Comp/Sales	1.5	1.8	1.8						
	(36) 3.1	(36) 3.5	(33) 3.4						
	5.2	6.1	6.1						
Net Sales ($)	3414761M	3097131M	3022324M	6013M	28080M	11398M	74365M	150513M	2751955M
Total Assets ($)	1619276M	1618909M	1326859M	5569M	16459M	2775M	26033M	59339M	1216684M

© RMA 2019   M = $ thousand   MM = $ million
See Pages viii through xx for Explanation of Ratios and Data

Current Data Sorted by Assets   Comparative Historical Data

Type of Statement	0-500M	500M-2MM	2-10MM	10-50MM	50-100MM	100-250MM		4/1/14-3/31/15 ALL	4/1/15-3/31/16 ALL
Unqualified			2	5	3	1		14	11
Reviewed			7	7	1			25	16
Compiled	2	6	16	6				46	35
Tax Returns	12	25	16	2				80	92
Other	7	16	19	21	7	5		79	107
		38 (4/1-9/30/18)		148 (10/1/18-3/31/19)					
NUMBER OF STATEMENTS	21	47	60	41	11	6		244	261
ASSETS	%	%	%	%	%	%		%	%
Cash & Equivalents	27.4	9.2	10.1	7.8	1.9			8.8	9.3
Trade Receivables (net)	1.6	4.0	3.4	5.1	9.7			5.2	5.3
Inventory	59.8	73.2	71.0	68.7	60.8			64.8	66.0
All Other Current	.7	2.0	1.8	2.2	1.5			1.9	1.7
Total Current	89.4	88.4	86.3	83.9	73.9			80.7	82.4
Fixed Assets (net)	7.1	4.9	9.2	10.7	17.8			11.2	10.6
Intangibles (net)	.2	1.9	.5	.2	4.1			2.0	1.7
All Other Non-Current	3.2	4.8	4.0	5.1	4.2			6.2	5.3
Total	100.0	100.0	100.0	100.0	100.0			100.0	100.0
LIABILITIES									
Notes Payable-Short Term	16.8	10.4	11.8	11.8	13.1			11.5	8.9
Cur. Mat.-L.T.D.	1.7	.5	.8	2.2	1.5			2.4	1.3
Trade Payables	20.9	21.8	17.2	20.0	18.8			19.3	17.3
Income Taxes Payable	1.3	.0	.1	.0	.0			.2	.2
All Other Current	7.3	10.2	9.5	9.4	10.2			9.7	11.3
Total Current	48.0	42.9	39.3	43.5	43.7			43.0	38.9
Long-Term Debt	16.3	7.7	9.7	6.4	13.7			9.3	8.4
Deferred Taxes	.0	.0	.1	.1	.1			.1	.2
All Other Non-Current	6.2	5.1	2.2	4.4	4.3			7.8	7.8
Net Worth	29.1	44.3	48.7	45.6	38.2			39.8	44.7
Total Liabilities & Net Worth	100.0	100.0	100.0	100.0	100.0			100.0	100.0
INCOME DATA									
Net Sales	100.0	100.0	100.0	100.0	100.0			100.0	100.0
Gross Profit	50.1	40.2	41.9	37.2	43.7			42.8	42.3
Operating Expenses	43.8	36.5	37.8	31.3	43.5			37.9	37.7
Operating Profit	6.4	3.8	4.1	5.9	.2			4.9	4.6
All Other Expenses (net)	.0	.3	.4	.2	.0			.5	.4
Profit Before Taxes	6.3	3.5	3.7	5.7	.2			4.4	4.2
RATIOS									
Current	8.2	7.5	3.4	3.2	2.9			3.7	4.3
	2.8	2.6	2.3	2.0	1.7			2.0	2.3
	1.5	1.7	1.6	1.5	1.2			1.4	1.6
Quick	3.0	.9	.6	.6	.3			.8	.8
	.6	.3	.3	.3	.2			(242) .2	(259) .3
	.1	.1	.1	.1	.1			.1	.1
Sales/Receivables	0 UND	0 UND	0 UND	1 565.0	2 242.1			0 UND	0 UND
	0 UND	0 UND	3 134.2	6 63.0	10 38.0			1 254.4	3 131.6
	2 159.6	4 86.0	8 44.7	17 21.0	29 12.7			10 37.8	14 26.9
Cost of Sales/Inventory	45 8.1	122 3.0	192 1.9	192 1.9	243 1.5			146 2.5	140 2.6
	203 1.8	261 1.4	304 1.2	281 1.3	332 1.1			281 1.3	281 1.3
	332 1.1	406 .9	456 .8	365 1.0	456 .8			406 .9	406 .9
Cost of Sales/Payables	0 UND	0 UND	33 10.9	36 10.1	55 6.6			29 12.5	24 15.0
	0 UND	30 12.3	59 6.2	54 6.7	99 3.7			55 6.6	59 6.2
	89 4.1	107 3.4	99 3.7	104 3.5	118 3.1			96 3.8	94 3.9
Sales/Working Capital	2.5	2.3	2.0	2.4	2.7			2.5	2.4
	5.5	4.7	3.5	3.2	4.0			4.2	3.8
	12.0	10.0	5.4	8.8	10.5			9.2	7.3
EBIT/Interest	23.5	25.1	12.2	24.6	7.7			14.4	21.0
	(15) 7.8	(37) 5.7	(54) 4.2	(35) 7.0	3.6			(210) 4.7	(220) 5.6
	.7	1.4	1.3	2.4	-.3			1.4	1.0
Net Profit + Depr., Dep., Amort./Cur. Mat. L/T/D								5.9	4.1
							(34)	(34) 3.2	(32) 1.8
								.8	1.1
Fixed/Worth	.0	.0	.0	.1	.2			.1	.1
	.0	.0	.1	.2	.4			.2	.2
	.3	.2	.4	.4	1.5			.6	.4
Debt/Worth	.3	.4	.4	.6	.9			.6	.5
	1.3	.8	1.1	1.2	2.0			1.4	1.2
	2.4	6.6	2.2	2.4	3.6			4.9	3.0
% Profit Before Taxes/Tangible Net Worth	125.3	39.8	17.9	32.5	10.2			36.8	26.4
	(19) 30.8	(40) 19.4	(58) 8.2	(39) 14.8	(10) 5.0			(219) 13.9	(241) 10.1
	13.2	.5	2.1	6.9	-14.5			2.8	1.0
% Profit Before Taxes/Total Assets	29.4	18.1	10.6	15.6	5.9			11.8	11.1
	19.2	7.6	3.3	6.0	3.6			5.0	4.5
	4.4	.2	.7	2.9	-1.8			.8	.4
Sales/Net Fixed Assets	UND	UND	72.7	53.5	14.2			63.8	81.4
	UND	118.7	23.4	18.6	10.0			23.5	24.5
	36.8	41.9	10.2	10.4	7.7			9.9	10.4
Sales/Total Assets	5.3	3.9	1.9	2.0	1.7			2.3	2.3
	2.7	1.6	1.5	1.5	1.4			1.6	1.6
	1.6	1.2	1.0	1.2	1.1			1.1	1.1
% Depr., Dep., Amort./Sales		.1	.4	.5				.3	.4
		(23) .4	(43) .9	(38) 1.0				(182) .8	(183) 1.0
		1.2	1.3	1.8				1.7	1.6
% Officers', Directors' Owners' Comp/Sales	6.5	2.2	2.5	1.1				2.1	1.9
	(15) 7.7	(29) 4.4	(33) 4.5	(10) 1.7				(129) 4.8	(121) 4.3
	11.0	6.4	6.3	4.3				7.4	7.9
Net Sales ($)	15653M	137995M	463554M	1674069M	1189167M	1598772M		6052726M	5368684M
Total Assets ($)	4696M	52060M	291937M	892752M	853392M	977546M		3400738M	3140580M

© RMA 2019

M = $ thousand   MM = $ million
See Pages viii through xx for Explanation of Ratios and Data

Comparative Historical Data | Current Data Sorted by Sales

4/1/16-3/31/17 ALL	4/1/17-3/31/18 ALL	4/1/18-3/31/19 ALL	Type of Statement	0-1MM	1-3MM	3-5MM	5-10MM	10-25MM	25MM & OVER
12	7	11	Unqualified				1	1	9
22	21	15	Reviewed		1		4	5	5
42	35	30	Compiled	4	6	3	5	7	5
79	72	55	Tax Returns	11	21	10	9	2	2
91	79	75	Other	7	15	6	10	14	23
				38 (4/1-9/30/18)		148 (10/1/18-3/31/19)			
246	214	186	**NUMBER OF STATEMENTS**	22	43	19	29	29	44
%	%	%	**ASSETS**	%	%	%	%	%	%
9.4	10.2	10.9	Cash & Equivalents	18.4	13.4	9.0	9.8	9.5	7.1
4.1	4.6	4.1	Trade Receivables (net)	2.6	4.7	.7	3.3	4.6	6.1
67.7	64.3	68.7	Inventory	72.1	66.1	75.8	69.4	72.7	63.1
2.3	1.8	1.8	All Other Current	1.5	1.7	.2	2.3	2.2	2.3
83.4	80.8	85.5	Total Current	94.6	85.9	85.7	84.7	89.0	78.6
10.2	10.5	9.1	Fixed Assets (net)	2.1	8.2	7.8	9.0	7.4	15.4
2.0	3.1	1.0	Intangibles (net)	.2	1.6	.4	1.5	.2	1.2
4.4	5.6	4.4	All Other Non-Current	3.1	4.2	6.1	4.7	3.5	4.8
100.0	100.0	100.0	Total	100.0	100.0	100.0	100.0	100.0	100.0
			LIABILITIES						
10.4	9.8	11.9	Notes Payable-Short Term	13.0	10.6	11.5	9.0	16.1	12.1
1.8	1.9	1.2	Cur. Mat.-L.T.D.	1.7	.7	.9	.5	1.7	1.7
16.7	15.7	19.3	Trade Payables	12.3	20.7	24.3	21.3	17.0	19.6
.2	.1	.2	Income Taxes Payable	1.2	.1	.0	.1	.0	.0
12.6	11.8	9.6	All Other Current	7.3	9.0	13.1	5.2	11.6	11.6
41.6	39.2	42.3	Total Current	35.6	41.1	50.0	36.0	46.4	45.0
10.7	10.9	10.1	Long-Term Debt	9.9	13.2	10.7	7.7	4.9	12.1
.1	.1	.1	Deferred Taxes	.0	.0	.0	.1	.1	.1
6.1	7.6	4.3	All Other Non-Current	2.2	6.0	3.4	1.8	3.3	6.2
41.5	42.1	43.2	Net Worth	52.0	39.7	35.9	54.4	45.3	36.6
100.0	100.0	100.0	Total Liabilities & Net Worth	100.0	100.0	100.0	100.0	100.0	100.0
			INCOME DATA						
100.0	100.0	100.0	Net Sales	100.0	100.0	100.0	100.0	100.0	100.0
42.6	42.6	41.7	Gross Profit	47.5	45.4	40.3	38.7	35.3	42.2
38.1	38.5	37.4	Operating Expenses	41.6	41.0	33.8	36.4	30.1	38.5
4.5	4.0	4.4	Operating Profit	5.9	4.3	6.5	2.2	5.2	3.7
.7	1.0	.3	All Other Expenses (net)	.4	.2	.8	.1	-.1	.6
3.7	3.0	4.1	Profit Before Taxes	5.5	4.1	5.7	2.1	5.3	3.1
			RATIOS						
3.5	3.8	3.9	Current	9.1	7.5	4.4	3.1	3.2	2.9
2.1	2.1	2.3		3.2	2.8	2.2	2.2	2.2	1.8
1.5	1.4	1.6		1.7	1.7	1.6	1.6	1.5	1.2
.6	.8	.7	Quick	2.7	1.1	.6	.7	.6	.6
(244) .2	.3	.3		.3	.6	.1	.2	.3	.3
.1	.1	.1		.1	.2	.1	.1	.1	.1
0 UND	0 UND	0 UND	Sales/Receivables	0 UND	0 UND	0 UND	0 UND	1 565.0	1 484.1
2 163.5	2 182.2	2 152.7		0 UND	0 846.3	0 UND	1 384.3	6 60.4	6 57.8
12 29.3	9 40.4	9 41.7		4 92.4	8 45.8	4 97.1	9 41.6	15 24.2	17 21.7
166 2.2	159 2.3	166 2.2	Cost of Sales/Inventory	166 2.2	130 2.8	192 1.9	166 2.2	192 1.9	174 2.1
261 1.4	261 1.4	281 1.3		304 1.2	281 1.3	304 1.2	261 1.4	281 1.3	261 1.4
406 .9	406 .9	406 .9		521 .7	521 .7	456 .8	406 .9	365 1.0	365 1.0
28 13.1	24 15.5	22 16.3	Cost of Sales/Payables	0 UND	1 415.7	33 11.0	35 10.4	20 18.0	38 9.6
53 6.9	52 7.0	54 6.7		0 UND	45 8.1	62 5.9	61 6.0	43 8.5	68 5.4
94 3.9	85 4.3	101 3.6		96 3.8	118 3.1	91 4.0	114 3.2	72 5.1	111 3.3
2.3	2.3	2.4	Sales/Working Capital	2.0	1.6	2.7	2.5	2.4	2.9
3.9	4.0	4.1		2.9	3.2	4.9	4.6	3.2	5.4
7.5	8.8	8.2		7.9	8.3	7.3	5.9	6.6	12.3
13.1	11.7	15.3	EBIT/Interest	17.4	22.6	21.8	11.6	16.5	19.5
(227) 5.2	(192) 4.7	(157) 5.7		(13) 4.6	(36) 4.2	7.8	(24) 4.8	(26) 6.0	(39) 5.8
1.3	1.2	1.5		-.7	1.1	2.5	1.3	2.3	1.1
7.9	5.6	5.1	Net Profit + Depr., Dep., Amort./Cur. Mat. L/T/D						
(40) 2.5	(31) 2.6	(13) 2.7							
1.4	.4	1.0							
.1	.1	.0	Fixed/Worth	.0	.0	.0	.0	.0	.2
.2	.2	.1		.0	.0	.2	.1	.1	.3
.6	.5	.4		.1	.2	.6	.4	.2	1.0
.5	.5	.4	Debt/Worth	.2	.3	.4	.4	.5	.8
1.3	1.3	1.1		1.0	.9	1.2	.9	.8	2.0
3.7	3.4	2.6		1.9	2.6	4.3	1.4	2.6	3.7
25.4	26.0	29.5	% Profit Before Taxes/Tangible Net Worth	81.5	32.0	34.9	15.8	27.3	34.9
(224) 10.5	(194) 10.1	(170) 11.6		(20) 23.0	(39) 11.6	(17) 12.5	(28) 6.6	(27) 15.5	(39) 9.9
1.9	2.6	2.5		-.4	.6	3.7	1.2	7.0	3.1
11.1	10.8	14.3	% Profit Before Taxes/Total Assets	25.2	15.1	23.1	10.1	13.4	13.6
4.5	4.3	5.9		10.8	6.0	4.7	3.5	7.3	5.6
.5	.6	1.0		-.6	.3	2.1	.7	1.9	.9
74.6	76.8	168.5	Sales/Net Fixed Assets	UND	609.5	122.9	76.1	261.3	21.9
24.4	24.8	32.1		UND	55.9	47.4	34.4	30.8	11.7
10.4	10.7	11.7		150.3	18.9	20.3	9.2	14.4	8.2
2.2	2.3	2.4	Sales/Total Assets	2.8	3.2	2.4	2.7	2.3	2.3
1.6	1.6	1.6		1.6	1.6	1.6	1.7	1.7	1.7
1.1	1.1	1.1		1.1	1.0	1.1	1.0	1.3	1.3
.4	.4	.4	% Depr., Dep., Amort./Sales		.2	.3	.3		.6
(190) 1.0	(163) .8	(122) .9			(24) .8	(13) 1.0	(21) .8	(23) .6	(38) 1.7
1.8	1.7	1.7			1.4	1.5	1.2	1.0	2.7
2.9	2.3	2.4	% Officers', Directors' Owners' Comp/Sales	4.5	4.2	2.5	1.9	1.1	
(123) 5.4	(104) 4.6	(88) 4.5		(14)	(26) 5.9	(13) 4.4	(17) 3.8	(12) 2.5	
8.9	7.4	7.2		11.6	8.3	6.5	4.8	4.0	
6965616M	5251088M	5079210M	Net Sales ($)	11539M	81356M	73438M	213187M	471416M	4228274M
4258710M	3349234M	3072383M	Total Assets ($)	9181M	57599M	49130M	143011M	301505M	2511957M

M = $ thousand   MM = $ million
See Pages viii through xx for Explanation of Ratios and Data

Current Data Sorted by Assets   Comparative Historical Data

0-500M	500M-2MM	2-10MM	10-50MM	50-100MM	100-250MM	Type of Statement	4/1/14-3/31/15 ALL	4/1/15-3/31/16 ALL
1	1	1	3	1	4	Unqualified	18	18
	2	6	10			Reviewed	24	22
1	9	9	4			Compiled	40	45
37	33	24	4			Tax Returns	125	137
16	40	36	14	5	6	Other	115	127
	29 (4/1-9/30/18)		238 (10/1/18-3/31/19)					
55	85	76	35	6	10	**NUMBER OF STATEMENTS**	322	349
%	%	%	%	%	%	**ASSETS**	%	%
11.1	15.9	10.9	6.9		2.8	Cash & Equivalents	11.5	11.5
2.4	6.3	6.1	6.2		7.4	Trade Receivables (net)	5.5	4.6
58.5	55.8	57.4	57.8		47.2	Inventory	57.5	56.6
1.8	1.8	2.5	1.0		1.7	All Other Current	1.8	1.3
73.9	79.9	76.8	71.9		59.0	Total Current	76.3	74.0
14.4	12.2	15.0	13.2		19.9	Fixed Assets (net)	14.1	14.8
7.3	3.4	2.2	8.2		16.9	Intangibles (net)	4.9	5.6
4.4	4.6	6.0	6.7		4.2	All Other Non-Current	4.8	5.7
100.0	100.0	100.0	100.0		100.0	Total	100.0	100.0
						LIABILITIES		
17.4	11.4	12.5	9.1		18.9	Notes Payable-Short Term	10.6	12.5
1.8	1.7	1.3	.7		1.1	Cur. Mat.-L.T.D.	2.2	1.9
19.9	21.1	26.8	22.9		21.2	Trade Payables	26.0	23.6
.1	.0	.0	.1		.0	Income Taxes Payable	.1	.1
11.4	8.2	9.8	9.2		9.3	All Other Current	11.4	10.3
50.6	42.4	50.3	42.0		50.6	Total Current	50.3	48.3
24.5	16.3	10.0	9.7		26.2	Long-Term Debt	13.3	13.8
.0	.0	.0	.2		.0	Deferred Taxes	.1	.1
16.9	7.6	3.1	9.1		7.7	All Other Non-Current	5.8	6.5
7.9	33.8	36.5	39.0		15.5	Net Worth	30.4	31.2
100.0	100.0	100.0	100.0		100.0	Total Liabilities & Net Worth	100.0	100.0
						INCOME DATA		
100.0	100.0	100.0	100.0		100.0	Net Sales	100.0	100.0
40.8	40.6	36.5	31.5		38.7	Gross Profit	38.2	38.1
39.6	36.6	33.1	29.0		37.8	Operating Expenses	35.5	35.1
1.2	4.0	3.4	2.4		.9	Operating Profit	2.7	3.0
.8	.2	.6	.4		1.8	All Other Expenses (net)	.4	.5
.4	3.8	2.9	2.0		-.8	Profit Before Taxes	2.2	2.5
						RATIOS		
4.0	4.1	2.6	2.6		1.8	Current	2.5	2.7
1.8	1.8	1.7	1.6		1.0		1.6	1.7
.9	1.3	1.2	1.3		.9		1.1	1.1
.8	1.0	.6	.5		.5	Quick	.7	.7
.2	(84) .5	.3	.2		.1		(321) .2	(348) .2
.1	.1	.1	.1		.1		.1	.1
0 UND	0 UND	0 UND	0 859.0		3 126.6	Sales/Receivables	0 UND	0 UND
0 UND	0 999.8	1 522.7	4 86.9		9 40.6		1 610.0	0 999.8
0 UND	6 56.5	8 48.2	15 24.5		34 10.7		6 59.8	6 63.8
72 5.1	87 4.2	94 3.9	99 3.7		122 3.0	Cost of Sales/Inventory	89 4.1	91 4.0
114 3.2	146 2.5	146 2.5	130 2.8		174 2.1		135 2.7	135 2.7
192 1.9	203 1.8	203 1.8	203 1.8		203 1.8		192 1.9	203 1.8
0	8 43.0	31 11.6	35 10.5		51 7.2	Cost of Sales/Payables	22 16.8	20 18.6
24 14.9	33 11.0	60 6.1	49 7.4		66 5.5		49 7.4	45 8.2
78 4.7	74 4.9	107 3.4	64 5.7		104 3.5		94 3.9	91 4.0
4.8	4.5	4.5	4.7		6.4	Sales/Working Capital	5.2	4.9
10.0	7.1	7.9	7.0		179.5		8.9	9.7
-255.5	18.0	22.1	17.4		-27.8		33.7	32.3
8.7	14.8	29.6	12.8		5.0	EBIT/Interest	11.7	14.8
(40) 1.3	(70) 4.2	(67) 7.1	(33) 4.3		.4		(264) 3.4	(278) 3.8
-4.9	1.5	1.6	1.7		-3.1		1.0	1.0
						Net Profit + Depr., Dep., Amort./Cur. Mat. L/T/D	4.6	2.4
							(31) 2.7	(31) 1.5
							.7	.3
.0	.0	.1	.1		1.9	Fixed/Worth	.1	.1
.5	.2	.3	.3		27.0		.4	.4
-1.5	1.1	1.0	1.9		-.2		1.8	2.8
1.0	.7	.7	.8		9.0	Debt/Worth	.8	.7
2.9	1.9	1.6	2.2		64.8		2.1	2.3
-3.2	54.0	6.9	4.6		-5.4		11.0	15.6
56.6	39.7	29.6	26.7			% Profit Before Taxes/Tangible Net Worth	39.0	41.1
(32) 19.0	(66) 18.8	(65) 13.2	(31) 17.7				(261) 17.9	(274) 14.7
-4.7	3.5	5.0	5.9				2.4	1.9
19.0	15.3	15.3	8.9		4.0	% Profit Before Taxes/Total Assets	13.5	12.8
3.6	6.8	5.5	4.2		-1.0		5.1	4.0
-15.3	1.6	.9	1.2		-7.9		.1	.0
663.0	299.8	116.4	75.4		28.5	Sales/Net Fixed Assets	100.4	99.8
49.5	45.2	29.4	31.9		10.2		30.4	31.4
14.2	15.3	10.3	13.5		4.8		12.4	11.3
4.2	3.4	3.0	2.8		1.9	Sales/Total Assets	3.3	3.3
3.1	2.2	2.2	2.1		1.5		2.5	2.4
2.1	1.8	1.8	1.5		1.0		1.9	1.7
.6	.5	.4	.5			% Depr., Dep., Amort./Sales	.4	.3
(26) 1.0	(49) .8	(59) 1.0	(30) .8				(230) .9	(254) .8
2.5	1.6	1.7	1.3				1.8	1.7
2.8	2.7	1.5				% Officers', Directors' Owners' Comp/Sales	2.0	1.7
(29) 5.5	(51) 4.7	(42) 2.9					(156) 3.4	(170) 3.5
8.1	6.3	3.7					6.0	5.6
53721M	255387M	833253M	1752150M	716615M	2755219M	Net Sales ($)	6809179M	7754920M
15747M	92091M	331324M	787379M	436874M	1607053M	Total Assets ($)	2921163M	3541719M

M = $ thousand   MM = $ million
See Pages viii through xx for Explanation of Ratios and Data

Comparative Historical Data | Current Data Sorted by Sales

Hist 1	Hist 2	Hist 3	Type of Statement	0-1MM	1-3MM	3-5MM	5-10MM	10-25MM	25MM & OVER
12	10	11	Unqualified	2		1			8
20	19	18	Reviewed		2		1	7	8
36	24	23	Compiled	1	4	8	2	5	3
124	109	98	Tax Returns	25	36	11	11	11	4
137	105	117	Other	16	28	14	19	15	25
4/1/16-3/31/17 ALL	4/1/17-3/31/18 ALL	4/1/18-3/31/19 ALL		\<-- 29 (4/1-9/30/18) --\>			\<-- 238 (10/1/18-3/31/19) --\>		
329	267	267	**NUMBER OF STATEMENTS**	44	70	34	33	38	48
%	%	%	**ASSETS**	%	%	%	%	%	%
9.8	11.0	11.6	Cash & Equivalents	10.0	13.8	13.4	13.8	12.6	6.4
4.4	5.1	5.4	Trade Receivables (net)	3.4	2.5	5.8	7.6	8.9	6.8
59.4	57.9	56.8	Inventory	54.5	59.7	55.3	58.1	55.4	56.1
1.8	1.7	1.9	All Other Current	1.0	3.5	.6	1.4	2.3	1.5
75.4	75.7	75.8	Total Current	69.0	79.5	75.1	80.9	79.2	70.7
15.3	14.9	13.9	Fixed Assets (net)	17.2	12.9	16.5	12.7	7.5	16.1
4.2	4.3	5.2	Intangibles (net)	8.5	3.2	2.2	2.1	6.9	8.2
5.1	5.1	5.2	All Other Non-Current	5.2	4.4	6.3	4.3	6.4	5.0
100.0	100.0	100.0	Total	100.0	100.0	100.0	100.0	100.0	100.0
			LIABILITIES						
11.9	11.6	12.9	Notes Payable-Short Term	20.1	12.8	9.4	12.1	10.8	11.0
2.0	1.9	1.4	Cur. Mat.-L.T.D.	.8	1.7	2.3	1.5	1.2	.9
22.3	24.8	22.6	Trade Payables	17.6	20.0	24.0	29.8	25.1	23.2
.1	.1	.1	Income Taxes Payable	.2	.0	.0	.0	.1	.1
11.0	11.9	9.7	All Other Current	10.7	7.7	8.8	10.8	10.4	11.0
47.3	50.4	46.7	Total Current	49.3	42.3	44.6	54.2	47.6	46.2
14.4	16.3	15.8	Long-Term Debt	27.0	17.4	15.3	9.8	6.9	14.6
.1	.1	.1	Deferred Taxes	.0	.0	.0	.1	.0	.2
8.1	7.0	8.3	All Other Non-Current	18.6	7.4	8.9	.9	4.3	7.9
30.2	26.3	29.2	Net Worth	5.1	32.9	31.3	35.0	41.2	31.0
100.0	100.0	100.0	Total Liabilities & Net Worth	100.0	100.0	100.0	100.0	100.0	100.0
			INCOME DATA						
100.0	100.0	100.0	Net Sales	100.0	100.0	100.0	100.0	100.0	100.0
39.1	38.6	38.2	Gross Profit	41.1	40.7	41.1	36.1	34.4	34.2
35.6	36.0	35.3	Operating Expenses	37.8	37.2	39.1	32.8	32.2	31.9
3.5	2.6	2.8	Operating Profit	3.3	-3.5	2.0	3.2	2.2	2.3
.7	.6	.5	All Other Expenses (net)	1.3	.3	.1	.7	-.1	.7
2.7	2.0	2.3	Profit Before Taxes	2.0	3.1	1.9	2.6	2.3	1.6
			RATIOS						
3.1	2.5	2.9		4.3	4.5	2.7	2.5	3.0	2.3
1.7	1.6	1.7	Current	2.0	1.9	1.8	1.6	1.6	1.6
1.2	1.1	1.2		.9	1.3	1.4	1.2	1.2	1.0
.6	.6	.7		.8	.8	.9	.7	.8	.5
.2 (264)	.3 (266)	.3	Quick	.2 (69)	.2	.3	.4	.3	.2
.1	.1	.1		.0	.1	.1	.1	.1	.1
0 UND	0 UND	0 UND		0 UND	0 UND	0 UND	0 UND	0 999.8	1 334.5
0 999.8	1 696.1	0 995.5	Sales/Receivables	0 UND	0 UND	0 999.8	3 143.9	2 172.4	6 63.6
5 79.9	5 71.3	7 52.9		0 UND	1 251.4	5 72.9	18 20.1	15 23.7	13 27.5
96 3.8	94 3.9	91 4.0		76 4.8	101 3.6	91 4.0	78 4.7	96 3.8	99 3.7
152 2.4	135 2.7	140 2.6	Cost of Sales/Inventory	152 2.4	159 2.3	159 2.3	126 2.9	118 3.1	135 2.7
215 1.7	215 1.7	203 1.8		261 1.4	203 1.8	228 1.6	182 2.0	174 2.1	192 1.9
21 17.5	25 14.5	17 21.5		0 UND	6 57.6	26 14.2	33 11.1	22 16.7	35 10.3
46 7.9	48 7.6	48 7.6	Cost of Sales/Payables	23 15.8	29 12.7	50 7.3	58 6.3	54 6.8	53 6.9
81 4.5	91 4.0	83 4.4		89 4.1	81 4.5	126 2.9	91 4.0	83 4.4	70 5.2
4.4	4.9	4.5		-4.2	3.3	4.9	5.3	4.9	5.2
8.6	8.9	7.9	Sales/Working Capital	7.6	6.9	9.1	9.3	7.2	11.3
22.1	36.2	33.3		-21.9	18.8	16.7	22.2	24.6	196.4
13.2	13.7	14.4		9.2	13.0	10.4	70.4	17.0	11.0
(285) 3.7	(235) 3.7	(225) 4.0	EBIT/Interest	(34) 1.8	(54) 3.4	(29) 3.1	(30) 9.9	(33) 6.6	(45) 4.1
.3	.1	.9		-1.0	.4	1.4	1.2	2.0	.4
4.2	5.5	11.5	Net Profit + Depr., Dep.,						41.2
(33) 1.7	(20) 2.2	(16) 1.5	Amort./Cur. Mat. L/T/D					(10)	5.0
.3	.2	-2.5							-.8
.1	.1	.1		.1	.0	.1	.1	.0	.2
.3	.4	.3	Fixed/Worth	.6	.2	.3	.2	.2	.9
1.7	2.3	2.1		-1.0	2.6	1.0	1.0	.8	6.3
.7	.9	.8		1.0	.7	.8	.6	.6	1.0
2.2	2.4	2.3	Debt/Worth	4.4	1.8	1.8	2.5	2.0	3.2
13.9	20.8	46.5		-3.1	-28.8	19.5	8.2	5.3	41.6
36.2	35.4	33.0	% Profit Before Taxes/Tangible	57.1	28.2	38.0	36.7	31.5	31.8
(265) 13.0	(211) 13.6	(206) 15.6	Net Worth	(27) 26.9	(49) 12.6	(28) 15.1	(28) 14.8	(35) 11.0	(39) 18.8
1.8	.3	2.6		-.5	3.2	1.9	2.8	5.5	3.2
13.8	12.1	14.7	% Profit Before Taxes/Total	20.4	13.2	18.4	15.3	9.3	9.2
3.7	3.7	4.7	Assets	6.6	4.7	5.2	6.8	4.1	3.7
-1.0	-1.6	-.3		-6.5	.0	1.2	.2	1.3	-1.1
94.4	97.0	126.9		337.7	198.8	257.0	147.5	168.8	55.9
28.9	31.5	35.9	Sales/Net Fixed Assets	26.0	50.1	49.2	37.6	46.1	24.4
9.5	11.1	12.0		8.1	17.6	9.6	15.6	24.4	8.0
3.3	3.4	3.3		3.2	3.3	4.6	3.1	3.3	2.8
2.3	2.4	2.4	Sales/Total Assets	2.1	2.2	2.2	2.5	2.6	2.2
1.6	1.7	1.7		1.5	1.7	1.7	2.0	1.8	1.5
.3	.4	.5		.7	.4	.3	.4	.3	.6
(238) .8	(196) .8	(176) 1.0	% Depr., Dep., Amort./Sales	(23) 1.5	(39) .8	(24) .7	(23) .7	(26) 1.0	(41) 1.1
1.6	1.7	1.6		2.5	1.5	2.5	1.4	1.5	1.3
1.9	1.4	1.7	% Officers', Directors',	3.2	2.8	3.0	2.1	1.0	
(154) 3.6	(130) 3.2	(120) 3.6	Owners' Comp/Sales	(21) 5.6	(44) 5.1	(17) 4.2	(17) 3.2	(25) 1.9	
6.6	5.5	6.1		7.8	8.0	7.2	3.8	3.0	
6100895M	5987199M	6366345M	Net Sales ($)	29266M	131106M	131474M	238874M	587844M	5247781M
2841321M	2680718M	3270468M	Total Assets ($)	14630M	67031M	62168M	96734M	255035M	2774870M

© RMA 2019

M = $ thousand   MM = $ million
See Pages viii through xx for Explanation of Ratios and Data

Current Data Sorted by Assets   Comparative Historical Data

0-500M	500M-2MM	2-10MM	10-50MM	50-100MM	100-250MM	Type of Statement	2	3
		1				Unqualified	2	3
		2	1			Reviewed	1	2
	1	1				Compiled	3	1
7	5	3	1		1	Tax Returns	22	25
1	2	5	1	2	2	Other	16	16
	6 (4/1-9/30/18)		30 (10/1/18-3/31/19)				4/1/14-3/31/15 ALL	4/1/15-3/31/16 ALL
8	8	12	3	2	3	NUMBER OF STATEMENTS	44	47
%	%	%	%	%	%	**ASSETS**	%	%
		9.7				Cash & Equivalents	17.8	16.4
		13.5				Trade Receivables (net)	6.4	11.6
		48.0				Inventory	52.0	46.7
		6.8				All Other Current	1.6	1.5
		78.0				Total Current	77.8	76.2
		17.5				Fixed Assets (net)	14.4	13.1
		2.8				Intangibles (net)	3.3	5.0
		1.7				All Other Non-Current	4.5	5.6
		100.0				Total	100.0	100.0
						LIABILITIES		
		7.9				Notes Payable-Short Term	9.0	14.9
		1.4				Cur. Mat.-L.T.D.	2.5	3.3
		21.5				Trade Payables	17.3	14.7
		.0				Income Taxes Payable	.1	.0
		11.9				All Other Current	8.6	10.2
		42.7				Total Current	37.5	43.1
		10.3				Long-Term Debt	14.2	12.2
		.1				Deferred Taxes	.2	.0
		6.5				All Other Non-Current	6.9	6.9
		40.4				Net Worth	41.3	37.7
		100.0				Total Liabilities & Net Worth	100.0	100.0
						INCOME DATA		
		100.0				Net Sales	100.0	100.0
		34.5				Gross Profit	46.2	41.3
		31.0				Operating Expenses	41.2	36.5
		3.5				Operating Profit	5.0	4.8
		.4				All Other Expenses (net)	.4	2.0
		3.2				Profit Before Taxes	4.5	2.8
						RATIOS		
		3.3				Current	6.0	3.7
		1.9					2.6	1.9
		1.3					1.5	1.2
		1.3				Quick	2.0	1.2
		.5					.7	.6
		.4					.2	.2
		1 253.8				Sales/Receivables	0 UND	0 UND
		7 49.7					1 587.6	3 125.5
		34 10.8					15 24.6	26 14.1
		44 8.3				Cost of Sales/Inventory	63 5.8	59 6.2
		87 4.2					126 2.9	94 3.9
		146 2.5					215 1.7	192 1.9
		5 70.2				Cost of Sales/Payables	0 UND	7 55.0
		27 13.4					21 17.7	23 16.2
		42 8.6					51 7.1	47 7.8
		4.6				Sales/Working Capital	3.4	4.6
		16.9					6.2	8.9
		49.8					15.7	18.4
						EBIT/Interest	40.8	36.9
							(29) 14.0	(38) 11.8
							1.8	2.5
						Net Profit + Depr., Dep., Amort./Cur. Mat. L/T/D		
		.0				Fixed/Worth	.0	.1
		.1					.2	.3
		1.1					1.6	1.7
		.6				Debt/Worth	.4	.5
		1.4					1.1	1.2
		5.9					6.3	6.5
		61.1				% Profit Before Taxes/Tangible Net Worth	54.4	85.9
		(11) 13.0					(36) 23.2	(36) 25.3
		5.9					6.8	11.3
		32.3				% Profit Before Taxes/Total Assets	21.6	25.6
		6.5					12.5	9.8
		2.3					1.4	1.4
		270.2				Sales/Net Fixed Assets	322.7	204.2
		72.8					50.9	58.7
		4.8					12.9	12.4
		6.8				Sales/Total Assets	4.6	4.4
		4.2					2.3	2.5
		1.4					1.7	1.5
						% Depr., Dep., Amort./Sales	.3	.3
							(28) .6	(31) .7
							2.1	1.5
						% Officers', Directors' Owners' Comp/Sales	1.2	.8
							(27) 3.3	(25) 2.5
							6.9	4.2
7368M	42027M	260296M	73480M	165289M	974646M	Net Sales ($)	1217430M	2174144M
2177M	9984M	61573M	52251M	117513M	416801M	Total Assets ($)	604162M	1066948M

M = $ thousand   MM = $ million
See Pages viii through xx for Explanation of Ratios and Data

Comparative Historical Data | Current Data Sorted by Sales

4/1/16-3/31/17 ALL	4/1/17-3/31/18 ALL	4/1/18-3/31/19 ALL	Type of Statement	0-1MM	1-3MM	3-5MM	5-10MM	10-25MM	25MM & OVER
5	4	1	Unqualified					1	
1	2	3	Reviewed			1		1	1
3	1	2	Compiled		1			1	
15	13	17	Tax Returns	5	4	3	2	2	1
24	14	13	Other	1		1	2	1	8
4/1/16-3/31/17	4/1/17-3/31/18	4/1/18-3/31/19		6 (4/1-9/30/18)			30 (10/1/18-3/31/19)		
48	34	36	**NUMBER OF STATEMENTS**	6	5	5	4	6	10
%	%	%	**ASSETS**	%	%	%	%	%	%
13.6	15.6	13.6	Cash & Equivalents						10.5
6.2	5.2	6.4	Trade Receivables (net)						10.3
50.7	45.2	50.8	Inventory						46.9
2.7	3.3	3.0	All Other Current						1.9
73.1	69.4	73.8	Total Current						69.5
12.4	14.7	14.8	Fixed Assets (net)						9.0
8.2	9.9	9.2	Intangibles (net)						19.1
6.2	6.0	2.2	All Other Non-Current						2.3
100.0	100.0	100.0	Total						100.0
			LIABILITIES						
9.5	10.3	6.6	Notes Payable-Short Term						2.1
.7	1.8	2.1	Cur. Mat.-L.T.D.						6.4
18.9	17.6	19.7	Trade Payables						20.6
.0	.1	.2	Income Taxes Payable						.3
13.5	11.7	9.0	All Other Current						7.9
42.6	41.5	37.5	Total Current						37.3
6.9	17.2	10.3	Long-Term Debt						3.5
.0	.1	.0	Deferred Taxes						.0
5.3	7.6	3.1	All Other Non-Current						2.9
45.2	33.6	49.0	Net Worth						56.3
100.0	100.0	100.0	Total Liabilties & Net Worth						100.0
			INCOME DATA						
100.0	100.0	100.0	Net Sales						100.0
47.6	44.4	40.9	Gross Profit						39.7
42.3	39.8	36.2	Operating Expenses						33.8
5.3	4.6	4.7	Operating Profit						5.9
.5	.7	.6	All Other Expenses (net)						1.1
4.8	3.9	4.1	Profit Before Taxes						4.8
			RATIOS						
3.8	6.4	4.3	Current						3.6
2.0	2.3	2.2							1.8
1.1	1.1	1.2							1.3
1.2	1.1	1.4	Quick						1.3
.4	.6	.5							.5
.1	.2	.2							.3
0 UND	0 UND	0 UND	Sales/Receivables						0 999.8
0 999.8	1 479.0	1 400.9							8 46.9
11 34.0	12 29.2	14 25.7							20 18.3
62 5.9	85 4.3	56 6.5	Cost of Sales/Inventory						44 8.3
152 2.4	152 2.4	104 3.5							104 3.5
203 1.8	203 1.8	174 2.1							159 2.3
13 27.1	11 33.5	3 107.4	Cost of Sales/Payables						27 13.4
33 11.2	34 10.8	27 13.5							38 9.7
96 3.8	73 5.0	44 8.3							43 8.5
4.7	3.4	4.2	Sales/Working Capital						4.3
9.0	7.2	8.2							8.7
43.6	111.0	49.8							34.4
30.2	11.1	27.3	EBIT/Interest						
(38) 7.6	(26) 3.4	(28) 3.5							
.1	1.3	.8							
			Net Profit + Depr., Dep., Amort./Cur. Mat. L/T/D						
.0	.1	.0	Fixed/Worth						.0
.3	.4	.1							.2
1.3	NM	1.2							.7
.4	.3	.4	Debt/Worth						.4
1.0	1.8	1.0							.9
11.3	NM	6.2							4.3
72.8	59.6	49.1	% Profit Before Taxes/Tangible Net Worth						
(38) 13.4	(26) 10.7	(30) 13.0							
3.4	2.1	4.8							
24.3	13.9	27.7	% Profit Before Taxes/Total Assets						28.8
7.1	3.6	5.3							6.4
-.1	.0	.4							-2.6
268.0	162.8	263.5	Sales/Net Fixed Assets						392.5
61.3	32.5	43.0							61.4
14.8	12.5	14.5							18.6
4.5	3.8	5.2	Sales/Total Assets						6.1
2.5	2.2	2.8							2.3
1.9	1.4	1.6							1.6
.3	.1	.2	% Depr., Dep., Amort./Sales						
(26) .7	(19) .8	(22) .7							
1.2	1.3	1.9							
1.5	1.0	.7	% Officers', Directors' Owners' Comp/Sales						
(17) 4.2	(12) 2.6	(16) 1.7							
7.4	4.4	3.3							
1502171M	1348669M	1523106M	Net Sales ($)	4174M	8376M	20160M	26872M	109719M	1353805M
724507M	691650M	660299M	Total Assets ($)	2034M	3177M	10812M	24970M	25173M	594133M

© RMA 2019   M = $ thousand   MM = $ million
See Pages viii through xx for Explanation of Ratios and Data

Current Data Sorted by Assets   Comparative Historical Data

Current period groupings: 14 (4/1-9/30/18) · 60 (10/1/18-3/31/19)

0-500M	500M-2MM	2-10MM	10-50MM	50-100MM	100-250MM	Type of Statement	4/1/14-3/31/15 ALL	4/1/15-3/31/16 ALL
		1	1			Unqualified	2	1
		7	2			Reviewed	8	7
1	4	4				Compiled	10	13
3	7	4				Tax Returns	27	32
7	11	14	7	1		Other	28	21
11	22	30	10	1		**NUMBER OF STATEMENTS**	75	74
%	%	%	%	%	%	**ASSETS**	%	%
19.4	10.2	5.4	8.1		D	Cash & Equivalents	8.4	10.8
1.6	11.9	11.9	17.1		A	Trade Receivables (net)	12.7	9.0
68.6	60.2	47.9	47.9		T	Inventory	59.4	56.4
.2	.8	5.0	5.1		A	All Other Current	1.8	2.5
89.8	83.2	70.2	78.3			Total Current	82.3	78.6
5.6	12.2	22.7	6.9		N	Fixed Assets (net)	10.3	12.7
3.7	1.5	3.2	5.0		O	Intangibles (net)	1.4	2.1
.9	3.1	3.9	9.8		T	All Other Non-Current	6.0	6.7
100.0	100.0	100.0	100.0			Total	100.0	100.0
					A	**LIABILITIES**		
19.9	12.3	7.2	12.8		V	Notes Payable-Short Term	18.3	12.2
1.4	4.2	4.9	.7		A	Cur. Mat.-L.T.D.	2.9	2.1
3.4	19.4	17.5	17.0		I	Trade Payables	15.1	15.6
.0	.1	.1	.0		L	Income Taxes Payable	.1	.0
8.1	9.5	10.1	5.6		A	All Other Current	8.2	9.7
32.8	45.5	39.8	36.2		B	Total Current	44.6	39.6
12.4	13.8	15.4	3.7		L	Long-Term Debt	9.4	12.1
.0	.4	.1	.6		E	Deferred Taxes	.0	.1
1.4	6.1	9.3	19.2			All Other Non-Current	10.3	8.5
53.4	34.2	35.5	40.2			Net Worth	35.7	39.8
100.0	100.0	100.0	100.0			Total Liabilities & Net Worth	100.0	100.0
						INCOME DATA		
100.0	100.0	100.0	100.0			Net Sales	100.0	100.0
51.9	42.4	45.6	39.4			Gross Profit	40.7	40.4
42.8	38.4	41.8	34.3			Operating Expenses	37.0	35.7
9.1	4.0	3.8	5.2			Operating Profit	3.8	4.7
-1.0	.5	.1	.9			All Other Expenses (net)	-.2	-.1
10.2	3.5	3.6	4.3			Profit Before Taxes	3.9	4.7
						RATIOS		
13.1	4.9	3.3	4.8				3.4	4.4
3.4	1.6	1.8	2.6			Current	1.9	2.1
2.0	1.2	1.2	1.3				1.3	1.3
1.8	.8	.9	1.9				.9	.9
1.1	.4	.3	1.0			Quick	.4	.4
.4	.2	.2	.2				.1	.2
0 UND	3 144.4	2 162.4	5 74.6				1 283.8	2 227.4
0 UND	7 50.1	15 25.0	29 12.8			Sales/Receivables	10 37.2	9 41.8
3 117.4	23 15.6	37 9.8	74 4.9				35 10.4	23 15.8
63 5.8	130 2.8	74 4.9	87 4.2				99 3.7	104 3.5
215 1.7	159 2.3	174 2.1	192 1.9			Cost of Sales/Inventory	203 1.8	166 2.2
456 .8	243 1.5	243 1.5	281 1.3				281 1.3	261 1.4
0 UND	11 34.4	31 11.9	28 13.0				22 16.8	16 22.6
0 UND	41 8.8	63 5.8	53 6.9			Cost of Sales/Payables	33 11.0	34 10.6
13 28.7	85 4.3	87 4.2	72 5.1				52 7.0	68 5.4
2.7	2.7	3.0	1.9				3.0	2.9
3.7	6.7	4.8	4.6			Sales/Working Capital	5.0	4.9
14.2	23.3	34.9	8.2				17.5	15.8
43.0	9.0	6.6	66.3				11.8	9.3
(10) 10.5	(21) 4.1	(28) 3.4	2.7			EBIT/Interest	(65) 3.1	(63) 4.0
1.6	1.2	.0	1.0				1.3	1.7
						Net Profit + Depr., Dep., Amort./Cur. Mat. L/T/D		
.0	.1	.1	.1				.0	.0
.1	.2	.4	.2			Fixed/Worth	.2	.2
.3	.9	1.2	.5				.6	.9
.2	1.3	.8	.6				.6	.5
.8	1.7	1.6	1.9			Debt/Worth	1.6	1.3
3.2	3.6	4.1	5.1				7.1	4.9
	48.7	42.9					31.6	46.8
	(21) 24.6	(27) 11.0				% Profit Before Taxes/Tangible Net Worth	(65) 16.2	(65) 15.5
	8.9	2.2					6.1	4.1
47.8	17.1	8.1	12.2				11.7	14.0
25.0	7.1	4.6	3.0			% Profit Before Taxes/Total Assets	4.8	6.3
3.0	.8	-1.0	-.1				.7	2.3
UND	117.2	34.0	212.0				216.1	267.4
78.7	57.4	17.6	23.5			Sales/Net Fixed Assets	33.0	33.3
41.4	14.8	5.2	12.0				14.4	13.0
6.0	2.8	2.4	2.8				3.0	2.9
2.4	2.1	1.8	1.4			Sales/Total Assets	2.1	2.0
2.1	1.7	1.1	1.0				1.4	1.3
	.3	.5					.3	.3
	(12) 1.4	(24) 1.2				% Depr., Dep., Amort./Sales	(45) .8	(46) .9
	2.8	7.2					1.3	1.8
	2.4	1.5					2.2	2.0
	(14) 5.5	(15) 2.4				% Officers', Directors' Owners' Comp/Sales	(41) 3.4	(33) 3.4
	6.9	6.4					6.9	6.9
7794M	65513M	275703M	352241M	282179M		Net Sales ($)	1430901M	1442817M
2224M	27176M	148372M	198331M	99665M		Total Assets ($)	584834M	559492M

M = $ thousand   MM = $ million
See Pages viii through xx for Explanation of Ratios and Data

Comparative Historical Data | Current Data Sorted by Sales

4/1/16-3/31/17 ALL	4/1/17-3/31/18 ALL	4/1/18-3/31/19 ALL	Type of Statement	0-1MM	1-3MM	3-5MM	5-10MM	10-25MM	25MM & OVER
		2	Unqualified				1		1
8	12	9	Reviewed		1	1	2	4	1
10	6	9	Compiled	1	2	3	1	2	
23	17	14	Tax Returns	3	5	2	1	1	
35	38	40	Other	6	8	9	3	6	5
					14 (4/1-9/30/18)			60 (10/1/18-3/31/19)	
76	73	74	**NUMBER OF STATEMENTS**	10	16	15	13	13	7
%	%	%	**ASSETS**	%	%	%	%	%	%
9.6	7.8	9.2	Cash & Equivalents	19.9	7.6	9.0	6.5	7.9	
8.4	11.4	11.0	Trade Receivables (net)	1.3	16.7	8.8	9.7	13.1	
59.8	54.9	55.1	Inventory	73.7	52.8	57.9	55.7	37.3	
2.8	3.2	3.0	All Other Current	.1	.9	2.8	3.7	7.0	
80.7	77.3	78.4	Total Current	95.0	78.0	78.5	75.6	65.3	
13.5	14.9	14.7	Fixed Assets (net)	4.0	13.9	15.9	16.1	26.1	
1.7	2.3	3.0	Intangibles (net)	.0	4.2	2.5	3.9	2.5	
4.1	5.5	4.0	All Other Non-Current	1.0	3.9	3.0	4.4	6.0	
100.0	100.0	100.0	Total	100.0	100.0	100.0	100.0	100.0	
			LIABILITIES						
14.9	12.7	11.7	Notes Payable-Short Term	13.0	12.3	11.9	9.2	8.0	
3.7	3.4	3.5	Cur. Mat.-L.T.D.	1.5	2.7	4.8	6.2	3.8	
15.4	15.3	15.9	Trade Payables	5.1	13.3	16.3	17.4	21.4	
.1	.6	.1	Income Taxes Payable	.0	.2	.0	.2	.0	
7.1	9.9	9.2	All Other Current	6.0	7.1	10.7	9.1	13.9	
41.2	41.9	40.4	Total Current	25.6	35.5	43.6	42.1	47.1	
8.5	10.1	12.7	Long-Term Debt	13.6	17.5	11.0	14.0	11.4	
.2	.3	.2	Deferred Taxes	.0	.6	.0	.1	.5	
6.5	14.5	8.5	All Other Non-Current	4.4	7.4	4.8	17.7	5.2	
43.7	33.2	38.1	Net Worth	56.3	39.0	40.5	26.2	35.8	
100.0	100.0	100.0	Total Liabilties & Net Worth	100.0	100.0	100.0	100.0	100.0	
			INCOME DATA						
100.0	100.0	100.0	Net Sales	100.0	100.0	100.0	100.0	100.0	
43.8	45.8	44.6	Gross Profit	54.2	45.4	46.6	42.2	42.2	
38.3	41.6	39.9	Operating Expenses	45.8	39.9	38.2	40.1	41.5	
5.5	4.1	4.8	Operating Profit	8.5	5.4	8.4	2.1	.7	
.0	.0	.2	All Other Expenses (net)	-.9	1.4	.3	.2	-.8	
5.4	4.1	4.6	Profit Before Taxes	9.4	4.1	8.1	1.9	1.5	
			RATIOS						
4.5	3.6	4.7		16.4	6.8	5.3	2.7	2.5	
1.9	1.9	1.9	Current	3.5	2.2	1.7	1.8	1.5	
1.3	1.2	1.3		2.3	1.2	1.3	1.1	.8	
.8	.9	1.2		1.8	2.5	.6	.5	1.4	
(75) .4	.5	.4	Quick	1.1	.7	.4	.3	.4	
.2	.2	.2		.3	.3	.2	.2	.3	
0 UND	1 256.4	2 190.9		0 UND	2 186.0	3 124.2	5 67.2	2 201.9	
10 34.9	9 40.2	9 42.0	Sales/Receivables	0 UND	10 35.3	10 37.3	11 32.3	15 25.1	
24 15.2	33 11.2	29 12.5		3 117.2	122 3.0	19 19.2	23 15.7	35 10.3	
104 3.5	96 3.8	91 4.0		118 3.1	135 2.7	135 2.7	94 3.9	28 13.0	
203 1.8	174 2.1	174 2.1	Cost of Sales/Inventory	281 1.3	192 1.9	166 2.2	174 2.1	174 2.1	
304 1.2	261 1.4	243 1.5		608 .6	261 1.4	228 1.6	243 1.5	192 1.9	
14 25.7	15 25.1	13 29.0		0 UND	12 29.8	12 29.8	21 17.6	29 12.6	
36 10.1	37 9.9	43 8.4	Cost of Sales/Payables	0 UND	47 7.8	47 7.7	40 9.1	55 6.6	
73 5.0	78 4.7	76 4.8		40 9.1	74 4.9	146 2.5	83 4.4	78 4.7	
3.3	3.6	2.9		2.6	2.0	2.7	3.8	2.5	
6.0	5.7	5.3	Sales/Working Capital	3.6	4.8	6.6	4.9	8.5	
11.9	21.6	16.6		4.8	13.2	16.7	64.2	-90.8	
8.6	9.7	9.3			4.2	9.4	8.7	7.3	
(67) 3.4	(66) 4.1	(70) 3.5	EBIT/Interest		(15) 3.4	(14) 5.4	2.2	(12) 3.1	
1.4	1.4	1.0			2.2	.0	.5	-3.3	
		9.1	Net Profit + Depr., Dep.,						
	(10) 2.2		Amort./Cur. Mat. L/T/D						
		.3							
.0	.1	.1		.0	.0	.1	.1	.1	
.2	.2	.2	Fixed/Worth	.0	.3	.2	.6	.5	
.6	.9	.9		.2	.7	1.1	1.7	9.0	
.4	.8	.9		.2	1.0	.9	.9	.8	
1.5	1.7	1.6	Debt/Worth	.9	1.6	1.5	2.9	2.0	
4.1	3.7	3.6		2.1	3.2	2.5	15.3	19.6	
43.5	40.2	47.7	% Profit Before Taxes/Tangible		25.6	80.8	78.3	31.3	
(71) 16.9	(66) 15.3	(67) 17.3	Net Worth	(15)	17.3	(14) 22.8	(12) 16.3	(11) 11.9	
3.3	2.9	2.8			5.8	1.1	.5	6.3	
15.0	16.4	15.5	% Profit Before Taxes/Total	52.9	9.3	25.5	10.4	7.8	
5.8	4.7	5.2	Assets	24.8	5.7	8.4	3.1	4.5	
1.0	1.2	.5		-14.0	2.4	-.8	-1.1	-1.7	
150.1	126.1	84.4		UND	93.2	84.4	47.9	27.5	
28.7	23.0	29.8	Sales/Net Fixed Assets	111.4	24.4	61.7	21.9	15.8	
13.1	11.2	12.0		38.4	7.5	5.8	8.7	6.1	
3.2	2.9	2.8		3.6	2.6	2.5	3.1	2.6	
2.0	2.0	2.1	Sales/Total Assets	2.1	1.9	1.9	2.2	1.8	
1.3	1.4	1.5		1.9	1.0	1.1	1.4	1.4	
.4	.5	.4			.2			.5	
(40) 1.0	(44) 1.2	(52) 1.2	% Depr., Dep., Amort./Sales		(12) .4			(12) 1.2	
2.4	6.6	2.6			2.3			8.2	
2.0	2.0	2.1			3.0				
(36) 4.3	(43) 3.2	(36) 4.5	% Officers', Directors'		(13) 5.8				
8.5	5.8	6.5	Owners' Comp/Sales		7.6				
881198M	918782M	983430M	Net Sales ($)	5089M	31887M	59398M	95758M	199996M	591302M
368983M	391600M	475768M	Total Assets ($)	1958M	27139M	44988M	53489M	114797M	233397M

M = $ thousand   MM = $ million
See Pages viii through xx for Explanation of Ratios and Data

Current Data Sorted by Assets

Comparative Historical Data

Type of Statement

Type of Statement	0-500M	500M-2MM	2-10MM	10-50MM	50-100MM	100-250MM		4/1/14-3/31/15 ALL	4/1/15-3/31/16 ALL
Unqualified			1	1	3	2		5	6
Reviewed				5				10	13
Compiled	1	2	6	2				12	12
Tax Returns	12	3	5					48	43
Other	8	9	14	2	4	2		48	45
	8 (4/1-9/30/18)		74 (10/1/18-3/31/19)						
	0-500M	500M-2MM	2-10MM	10-50MM	50-100MM	100-250MM	NUMBER OF STATEMENTS	ALL	ALL
	21	14	26	10	7	4		123	119

	0-500M	500M-2MM	2-10MM	10-50MM	50-100MM	100-250MM		4/1/14-3/31/15 ALL	4/1/15-3/31/16 ALL
	%	%	%	%	%	%	**ASSETS**	%	%
	17.6	14.1	10.6	9.5			Cash & Equivalents	14.5	11.8
	8.3	6.8	11.6	7.2			Trade Receivables (net)	10.3	8.4
	49.1	47.1	47.5	50.5			Inventory	44.9	50.5
	.9	6.0	1.9	1.9			All Other Current	1.9	2.3
	75.9	73.9	71.6	69.2			Total Current	71.5	73.0
	11.8	21.4	19.1	20.8			Fixed Assets (net)	18.3	15.9
	2.5	.7	5.2	2.5			Intangibles (net)	4.0	3.6
	9.8	4.1	4.1	7.4			All Other Non-Current	6.2	7.4
	100.0	100.0	100.0	100.0			Total	100.0	100.0
							LIABILITIES		
	18.8	5.1	8.4	5.8			Notes Payable-Short Term	11.7	14.0
	1.9	2.0	1.4	1.0			Cur. Mat.-L.T.D.	2.1	1.7
	27.7	13.6	16.8	15.7			Trade Payables	20.1	17.8
	.0	.0	.5	.0			Income Taxes Payable	.1	.2
	9.6	10.1	9.9	5.1			All Other Current	9.5	12.6
	58.1	30.8	37.0	27.4			Total Current	43.5	46.2
	20.9	15.2	14.9	17.6			Long-Term Debt	14.5	15.1
	.0	.0	.4	.0			Deferred Taxes	.1	.2
	1.1	9.0	3.1	1.6			All Other Non-Current	10.9	15.4
	19.9	45.0	44.6	53.3			Net Worth	30.9	23.1
	100.0	100.0	100.0	100.0			Total Liabilities & Net Worth	100.0	100.0
							INCOME DATA		
	100.0	100.0	100.0	100.0			Net Sales	100.0	100.0
	37.8	43.1	38.8	38.5			Gross Profit	40.1	38.6
	32.3	34.9	33.7	33.5			Operating Expenses	35.4	33.9
	5.5	8.1	5.1	5.0			Operating Profit	4.7	4.7
	.4	.8	.6	.2			All Other Expenses (net)	.8	.2
	5.0	7.4	4.5	4.8			Profit Before Taxes	3.9	4.5
							RATIOS		
	5.7	6.2	3.1	3.7				3.9	4.2
	1.9	2.5	2.4	2.8			Current	1.9	2.2
	.9	1.3	1.4	1.8				1.3	1.3
	1.4	1.8	1.0	1.6				1.5	1.1
	.5	.9	.6	.4			Quick	.6 (118)	.4
	.2	.2	.4	.2				.2	.2
	0 UND	0 UND	1 521.7	0 999.8				0 UND	0 UND
	0 UND	1 256.5	12 29.8	1 637.8			Sales/Receivables	1 271.0	1 435.8
	8 44.4	8 44.9	31 11.9	10 35.7				18 20.2	14 26.2
	15 24.6	64 5.7	57 6.4	114 3.2				37 9.8	65 5.6
	56 6.5	104 3.5	101 3.6	130 2.8			Cost of Sales/Inventory	99 3.7	114 3.2
	87 4.2	203 1.8	174 2.1	174 2.1				152 2.4	182 2.0
	0 UND	6 61.6	16 23.4	17 21.0				7 50.5	10 36.3
	7 50.1	22 16.6	30 12.2	31 11.8			Cost of Sales/Payables	28 12.9	24 14.9
	35 10.3	59 6.2	48 7.6	51 7.1				45 8.1	48 7.6
	6.1	3.2	3.8	3.7				5.3	4.2
	16.1	6.1	6.7	5.4			Sales/Working Capital	9.3	8.6
	-532.8	21.7	26.3	6.6				27.2	18.0
	17.0		8.8	26.7				27.4	30.5
	(12) 4.1		(23) 4.0	11.3			EBIT/Interest	(91) 7.0	(87) 7.4
	-2.4		1.6	5.1				1.8	2.2
							Net Profit + Depr., Dep.,	18.5	12.9
							Amort./Cur. Mat. L/T/D	(10) 11.0	(14) 7.4
								3.4	.7
	.0	.0	.1	.1				.1	.1
	.2	.3	.4	.2			Fixed/Worth	.4	.3
	7.4	1.0	1.0	.6				4.1	2.3
	.5	.4	.7	.4				.6	.5
	9.3	1.7	1.4	.8			Debt/Worth	1.5	1.6
	-23.3	3.2	2.7	2.0				15.4	23.9
	260.1	47.5	38.4	47.5			% Profit Before Taxes/Tangible	53.5	56.6
	(14) 77.4	(13) 42.7	(23) 8.6	14.1			Net Worth	(97) 28.9	(93) 30.9
	36.4	29.0	2.8	9.7				8.4	10.4
	63.9	31.4	15.4	23.1			% Profit Before Taxes/Total	18.8	22.4
	25.7	11.5	5.9	8.3			Assets	8.5	8.4
	1.8	8.7	1.2	5.5				2.4	2.5
	UND	420.8	59.2	85.5				155.6	120.0
	327.6	34.9	15.3	21.8			Sales/Net Fixed Assets	27.9	34.1
	22.4	6.3	6.8	4.3				10.1	11.7
	7.9	3.9	3.7	2.9				4.8	4.1
	4.7	2.3	2.8	2.5			Sales/Total Assets	3.0	2.9
	3.6	1.4	1.6	1.7				1.9	1.8
			.6					.4	.2
		(20) .9					% Depr., Dep., Amort./Sales	(87) 1.0	(80) .8
		1.7						1.9	1.5
	5.9							1.6	1.5
	(10) 7.7						% Officers', Directors' Owners' Comp/Sales	(51) 4.0	(51) 3.2
	17.9							7.0	5.8
	38328M	47060M	338106M	473244M	1049660M	2021014M	Net Sales ($)	3580532M	4106760M
	4622M	16267M	128479M	219071M	493902M	651285M	Total Assets ($)	1170823M	1451300M

M = $ thousand   MM = $ million
See Pages viii through xx for Explanation of Ratios and Data

Comparative Historical Data

Current Data Sorted by Sales

Type of Statement

4/1/16-3/31/17 ALL	4/1/17-3/31/18 ALL	4/1/18-3/31/19 ALL	Type of Statement	0-1MM	1-3MM	3-5MM	5-10MM	10-25MM	25MM & OVER
9	5	7	Unqualified	2		1	1	2	7
8	9	5	Reviewed	8	5	2	3	3	3
7	7	11	Compiled					6	4
37	23	20	Tax Returns		9	2	10	2	
41	38	39	Other	4					8
				8 (4/1-9/30/18)			74 (10/1/18-3/31/19)		
ALL	ALL	ALL		0-1MM	1-3MM	3-5MM	5-10MM	10-25MM	25MM & OVER
102	82	82	**NUMBER OF STATEMENTS**	14	14	5	14	13	22

4/1/16-3/31/17	4/1/17-3/31/18	4/1/18-3/31/19		0-1MM	1-3MM	3-5MM	5-10MM	10-25MM	25MM & OVER
%	%	%	**ASSETS**	%	%	%	%	%	%
13.2	13.7	12.3	Cash & Equivalents	14.8	12.3		14.9	13.9	6.7
12.1	8.2	8.6	Trade Receivables (net)	8.8	6.2		17.0	3.2	9.0
49.8	51.7	48.9	Inventory	40.6	53.9		45.8	50.7	52.1
1.8	1.5	2.4	All Other Current	1.3	5.5		1.2	1.2	3.3
76.9	75.0	72.4	Total Current	65.6	77.8		78.9	69.0	71.1
14.0	16.8	17.9	Fixed Assets (net)	25.5	13.7		12.3	24.0	17.6
3.9	2.2	3.9	Intangibles (net)	.1	4.0		3.5	3.6	6.7
5.2	6.0	5.8	All Other Non-Current	8.7	4.5		5.3	3.5	4.6
100.0	100.0	100.0	Total	100.0	100.0		100.0	100.0	100.0
			LIABILITIES						
9.7	9.4	11.3	Notes Payable-Short Term	18.3	9.0		14.5	4.4	12.6
2.2	1.6	1.5	Cur. Mat.-L.T.D.	1.3	.4		.3	.9	1.1
21.6	12.7	19.1	Trade Payables	12.2	15.4		18.1	13.8	18.3
.1	.2	.2	Income Taxes Payable	.0	.0		.4	.5	.0
10.4	10.6	10.0	All Other Current	3.9	11.5		12.1	10.6	10.9
44.0	34.6	42.0	Total Current	38.7	36.3		45.4	30.2	42.8
14.2	16.7	16.3	Long-Term Debt	32.0	17.4		8.5	12.6	11.6
.2	.0	.2	Deferred Taxes	.0	.0		.5	.0	.4
6.8	4.2	4.5	All Other Non-Current	1.7	9.3		2.3	2.7	6.6
34.8	44.6	37.1	Net Worth	27.7	37.1		43.3	54.5	38.6
100.0	100.0	100.0	Total Liabilties & Net Worth	100.0	100.0		100.0	100.0	100.0
			INCOME DATA						
100.0	100.0	100.0	Net Sales	100.0	100.0		100.0	100.0	100.0
40.4	39.8	39.2	Gross Profit	43.8	43.1		33.3	42.7	36.1
36.1	36.2	33.9	Operating Expenses	35.4	35.9		29.0	37.4	33.5
4.3	3.6	5.2	Operating Profit	8.3	7.1		4.3	5.3	2.7
.3	.1	.6	All Other Expenses (net)	1.6	.8		-.1	.1	.4
4.0	3.5	4.7	Profit Before Taxes	6.7	6.3		4.4	5.2	2.3
			RATIOS						
3.5	5.8	3.5	Current	5.5	6.5		3.6	3.8	3.0
1.9	2.6	2.3		2.5	2.5		2.1	2.5	1.6
1.3	1.5	1.3		1.0	1.1		.9	1.6	1.3
1.0	1.4	1.2	Quick	1.8	1.7		1.7	.9	.8
.5	.6	.5		.9	.6		.5	.6	.3
.2	.2	.2		.2	.2		.4	.2	.1
0 UND	0 UND	0 UND	Sales/Receivables	0 UND	0 UND		1 332.4	0 UND	0 999.8
3 141.6	2 215.7	2 180.5		0 UND	0 UND		17 21.4	1 351.2	2 166.1
20 18.3	12 29.3	16 23.0		11 34.0	13 29.0		45 8.1	7 50.8	17 21.8
41 8.8	55 6.6	48 7.6	Cost of Sales/Inventory	41 9.0	52 7.0		35 10.4	68 5.4	46 7.9
104 3.5	130 2.8	101 3.6		79 4.6	101 3.6		62 5.9	122 3.0	122 3.0
174 2.1	203 1.8	166 2.2		130 2.8	228 1.6		152 2.4	152 2.4	174 2.1
12 30.0	4 95.5	12 30.6	Cost of Sales/Payables	0 UND	0 UND		12 31.7	14 26.3	24 14.9
31 11.7	24 15.5	28 12.9		17 21.3	17 21.5		19 18.8	31 11.7	29 12.6
55 6.6	38 9.5	47 7.8		39 9.4	83 4.4		37 9.8	45 8.2	47 7.8
4.9	3.9	5.0	Sales/Working Capital	4.7	3.1		4.4	4.5	5.4
8.6	6.5	8.5		10.6	7.7		6.6	6.7	9.8
30.4	15.5	24.1		NM	38.7		-748.1	22.9	15.8
18.4	13.1	15.1	EBIT/Interest	7.6			15.3	64.5	15.9
(84) 7.2	(61) 4.0	(65) 5.4		(12) 4.2			(12) 5.6	(11) 8.7	4.2
2.1	1.9	2.1		-2.2			1.8	3.2	.7
8.3			Net Profit + Depr., Dep., Amort./Cur. Mat. L/T/D						
(13) 3.1									
.7									
.1	.1	.0	Fixed/Worth	.0	.0		.0	.2	.2
.3	.3	.4		.4	.2		.3	.4	.6
1.1	.9	1.2		2.9	1.5		1.1	.8	2.8
.8	.4	.5	Debt/Worth	.5	.4		.5	.4	.7
1.9	1.5	1.7		3.2	2.5		1.4	.8	2.4
9.3	4.2	8.1		-156.1	NM		6.7	1.6	8.9
47.6	44.2	51.9	% Profit Before Taxes/Tangible Net Worth	101.4	44.1		49.7	56.7	37.8
(85) 23.1	(75) 19.4	(69) 27.2		(10) 54.3	(11) 38.4		(13) 12.8	17.1	(19) 18.4
3.7	5.8	6.6		12.6	30.7		2.9	3.4	5.1
21.6	19.8	25.3	% Profit Before Taxes/Total Assets	29.3	42.6		35.7	35.2	15.6
7.7	6.2	8.4		20.9	11.4		6.2	6.4	5.7
1.7	1.8	1.7		.0	3.6		1.2	1.9	-.3
231.3	126.9	331.6	Sales/Net Fixed Assets	UND	UND		684.1	44.8	43.9
33.5	32.0	27.9		22.4	256.0		74.6	12.1	27.0
14.4	11.0	9.1		11.7	7.9		10.4	5.1	10.5
4.6	4.4	4.3	Sales/Total Assets	4.7	4.7		4.4	4.1	3.4
2.9	2.7	3.0		3.6	3.2		3.2	2.9	2.6
1.9	1.7	1.7		1.5	1.7		1.7	1.7	1.9
.3	.4	.6	% Depr., Dep., Amort./Sales					.6	.7
(75) .8	(53) .9	(53) 1.0						(11) 1.0	(19) 1.0
1.4	1.6	1.6						1.7	1.5
1.9	1.6	1.7	% Officers', Directors' Owners' Comp/Sales						
(42) 3.4	(35) 2.7	(28) 5.4							
6.4	5.2	6.8							
4930631M	3831434M	3967412M	Net Sales ($)	8484M	26679M	18420M	108926M	221059M	3583844M
1727786M	1436322M	1513626M	Total Assets ($)	4291M	14310M	5484M	40876M	88892M	1359773M

M = $ thousand   MM = $ million
See Pages viii through xx for Explanation of Ratios and Data

Current Data Sorted by Assets   Comparative Historical Data

Type of Statement	0-500M	500M-2MM	2-10MM	10-50MM	50-100MM	100-250MM		4/1/14-3/31/15 ALL	4/1/15-3/31/16 ALL
Unqualified			1					1	1
Reviewed		2						2	1
Compiled		4						5	7
Tax Returns	11	2	2		1	1		30	24
Other	6	4	2					16	10
	4 (4/1-9/30/18)			26 (10/1/18-3/31/19)					
NUMBER OF STATEMENTS	17	8	3	1				54	43

Columns 500M-2MM through 100-250MM: DATA NOT AVAILABLE

	0-500M %						ASSETS	%	%
	24.3						Cash & Equivalents	16.6	18.7
	4.2						Trade Receivables (net)	15.1	17.6
	25.8						Inventory	20.8	19.7
	5.5						All Other Current	2.4	2.3
	59.7						Total Current	54.8	58.3
	22.2						Fixed Assets (net)	28.2	23.7
	16.1						Intangibles (net)	7.8	11.9
	2.0						All Other Non-Current	9.2	6.1
	100.0						Total	100.0	100.0
							LIABILITIES		
	12.5						Notes Payable-Short Term	17.1	13.9
	12.6						Cur. Mat.-L.T.D.	3.9	4.6
	7.4						Trade Payables	22.2	18.8
	.0						Income Taxes Payable	.2	.1
	21.5						All Other Current	10.0	10.5
	54.1						Total Current	53.3	48.0
	33.3						Long-Term Debt	30.5	24.9
	.0						Deferred Taxes	.0	.0
	13.5						All Other Non-Current	25.3	10.9
	-.9						Net Worth	-9.2	16.1
	100.0						Total Liabilties & Net Worth	100.0	100.0
							INCOME DATA		
	100.0						Net Sales	100.0	100.0
	60.2						Gross Profit	55.4	55.8
	50.2						Operating Expenses	52.2	53.7
	10.0						Operating Profit	3.2	2.1
	2.1						All Other Expenses (net)	-.3	-1.4
	7.9						Profit Before Taxes	3.6	3.5
							RATIOS		
	5.1							2.4	2.8
	2.3						Current	1.5	1.3
	.6							1.0	.8
	2.4							1.3	1.6
	(16) .6						Quick	.9	.9
	.2							.4	.4
	0 UND							0 UND	3 133.4
	0 UND						Sales/Receivables	12 30.9	13 28.6
	4 103.4							20 18.4	21 17.3
	0 UND							12 30.1	9 39.9
	29 12.7						Cost of Sales/Inventory	38 9.5	32 11.3
	122 3.0							94 3.9	76 4.8
	0 UND							1 246.1	11 31.8
	0 UND						Cost of Sales/Payables	33 11.2	29 12.8
	15 25.1							56 6.5	56 6.5
	5.2							9.6	11.0
	12.0						Sales/Working Capital	23.4	61.1
	-35.0							UND	-18.7
	35.5							15.5	12.0
	(14) 2.0						EBIT/Interest	(45) 4.8	(32) 3.2
	1.1							1.5	.8
							Net Profit + Depr., Dep., Amort./Cur. Mat. L/T/D		
	.1							.3	.4
	2.3						Fixed/Worth	1.8	1.7
	-.2							-.5	-.5
	.6							.7	.9
	8.8						Debt/Worth	3.2	2.8
	-1.8							-3.1	-3.0
	144.9							77.1	60.8
	(10) 67.6						% Profit Before Taxes/Tangible Net Worth	(35) 21.9	(26) 28.7
	34.0							11.5	2.6
	44.4							21.2	23.5
	23.8						% Profit Before Taxes/Total Assets	8.5	7.6
	2.6							2.1	2.1
	192.0							58.5	64.2
	22.4						Sales/Net Fixed Assets	24.5	16.4
	11.9							7.2	8.2
	6.5							5.6	5.2
	3.8						Sales/Total Assets	3.9	3.3
	2.2							2.6	2.4
								.9	.7
							% Depr., Dep., Amort./Sales	(43) 1.6	(34) 1.8
								3.3	3.3
	5.3							2.9	2.6
	(10) 7.2						% Officers', Directors' Owners' Comp/Sales	(26) 5.0	(24) 4.5
	11.7							8.1	8.9
Net Sales ($)	14349M	22894M	42883M	122136M	227094M			858979M	203582M
Total Assets ($)	3701M	8127M	16436M	22510M	81306M			350123M	76422M

© RMA 2019

M = $ thousand   MM = $ million

See Pages viii through xx for Explanation of Ratios and Data

Comparative Historical Data | Current Data Sorted by Sales

Type of Statement

1	2							
1	1	1					1	
2		2				1	1	
16	20	15	8	6	1	1		
7	13	12	5	2	1	1		

Type of Statement (top to bottom): Unqualified, Reviewed, Compiled, Tax Returns, Other

4/1/16-3/31/17 ALL	4/1/17-3/31/18 ALL	4/1/18-3/31/19 ALL			4 (4/1-9/30/18)	26 (10/1/18-3/31/19)		
			0-1MM	1-3MM	3-5MM	5-10MM	10-25MM	25MM & OVER

	16-17	17-18	18-19	0-1MM	1-3MM	3-5MM	5-10MM	10-25MM	25MM & OVER
NUMBER OF STATEMENTS	27	36	30	13	9	2	2	2	2
	%	%	%	%	%	%	%	%	%
ASSETS									
Cash & Equivalents	22.8	21.6	19.6	29.4					
Trade Receivables (net)	16.9	8.9	8.4	5.5					
Inventory	15.4	17.0	21.0	27.6					
All Other Current	2.5	3.8	5.0	1.4					
Total Current	57.5	51.3	54.0	63.9					
Fixed Assets (net)	30.9	29.5	24.9	14.8					
Intangibles (net)	2.8	14.4	15.5	18.7					
All Other Non-Current	8.8	5.0	5.6	2.5					
Total	100.0	100.0	100.0	100.0					
LIABILITIES									
Notes Payable-Short Term	18.7	10.4	11.9	8.4					
Cur. Mat.-L.T.D.	7.8	5.7	7.8	11.8					
Trade Payables	11.0	33.1	10.1	5.5					
Income Taxes Payable	1.1	.2	.0	.0					
All Other Current	12.5	25.0	15.9	25.3					
Total Current	51.2	74.3	45.7	51.1					
Long-Term Debt	27.7	28.5	26.3	29.4					
Deferred Taxes	.1	.0	.0	.0					
All Other Non-Current	4.8	6.2	8.5	10.3					
Net Worth	16.3	-9.1	19.4	9.2					
Total Liabilities & Net Worth	100.0	100.0	100.0	100.0					
INCOME DATA									
Net Sales	100.0	100.0	100.0	100.0					
Gross Profit	55.1	54.5	55.8	64.7					
Operating Expenses	49.7	51.1	49.7	53.7					
Operating Profit	5.3	3.3	6.1	11.0					
All Other Expenses (net)	.2	-.9	.4	1.8					
Profit Before Taxes	5.1	4.3	5.7	9.2					
RATIOS									
Current	3.2	2.9	3.8	4.3					
	1.6	1.2	1.7	2.3					
	.8	.4	.7	.8					
Quick	2.8	1.4	2.1	3.2					
	1.1	.8	(29) .7	.7					
	.4	.2	.3	.2					
Sales/Receivables	0 UND	0 UND	0 UND	0 UND					
	14 26.7	5 79.6	4 103.4	0 UND					
	24 15.0	14 26.3	16 22.9	4 84.1					
Cost of Sales/Inventory	7 50.3	10 34.9	4 97.9	0 UND					
	29 12.6	20 18.1	36 10.0	96 3.8					
	53 6.9	81 4.5	99 3.7	140 2.6					
Cost of Sales/Payables	0 UND	0 UND	0 UND	0 UND					
	18 20.6	20 18.2	11 34.5	0 UND					
	36 10.1	48 7.6	36 10.2	15 25.1					
Sales/Working Capital	7.0	8.1	7.4	4.1					
	21.4	42.3	23.3	10.7					
	-31.7	-9.2	-30.3	-41.8					
EBIT/Interest	9.1	16.7	24.0	29.7					
	(20) 4.9	(22) 2.6	(24) 3.6	(11) 1.6					
	2.1	1.0	1.0	.9					
Net Profit + Depr., Dep., Amort./Cur. Mat. L/T/D									
Fixed/Worth	.3	.2	.2	.1					
	1.1	1.2	1.1	.5					
	4.3	-.6	-3.5	-.1					
Debt/Worth	.6	.8	.6	.5					
	1.3	6.6	2.9	2.7					
	7.7	-2.2	-5.3	-1.8					
% Profit Before Taxes/Tangible Net Worth	73.2	87.8	90.5						
	(21) 26.7	(22) 29.8	(19) 49.8						
	14.8	7.2	11.1						
% Profit Before Taxes/Total Assets	23.8	22.0	38.0	53.0					
	12.6	6.5	15.7	23.8					
	6.0	.0	2.9	.5					
Sales/Net Fixed Assets	42.4	55.1	66.4	192.0					
	18.3	19.3	20.2	23.3					
	6.0	4.7	9.0	14.1					
Sales/Total Assets	4.9	5.7	5.4	5.1					
	3.7	3.2	2.8	2.6					
	2.2	2.3	2.3	2.1					
% Depr., Dep., Amort./Sales	.8	.5	.3						
	(22) 1.9	(23) 1.4	(20) 1.1						
	3.5	2.5	2.2						
% Officers', Directors' Owners' Comp/Sales	4.8	1.9	4.4						
	(19) 7.5	(14) 6.2	(18) 7.0						
	12.5	11.0	10.3						
Net Sales ($)	196104M	432630M	429356M	7633M	16622M	7985M	12072M	35814M	349230M
Total Assets ($)	56033M	140261M	132080M	2673M	5702M	1490M	4703M	13696M	103816M

© RMA 2019

M = $ thousand   MM = $ million
See Pages viii through xx for Explanation of Ratios and Data

Current Data Sorted by Assets   Comparative Historical Data

```
Type of Statement
                                                                      Unqualified          6        3
                            1            1                            Reviewed            15       11
                    1       2        3                                Compiled            23       13
            7      12       3        2                                Tax Returns         27       32
            3      13      11        7                2               Other               28       29
                9 (4/1-9/30/18)   60 (10/1/18-3/31/19)                                 4/1/14-   4/1/15-
                                                                                      3/31/15   3/31/16
         0-500M  500M-2MM  2-10MM  10-50MM  50-100MM  100-250MM                          ALL       ALL
           10      26       17       13        1         2      NUMBER OF STATEMENTS      99        88
```

	0-500M	500M-2MM	2-10MM	10-50MM	50-100MM	100-250MM		4/1/14-3/31/15 ALL	4/1/15-3/31/16 ALL
	%	%	%	%	%	%	**ASSETS**	%	%
Cash & Equivalents	30.9	10.4	6.2	6.5				13.8	14.1
Trade Receivables (net)	25.0	28.8	33.3	27.5				29.6	31.2
Inventory	14.7	37.6	21.3	26.2				25.9	25.8
All Other Current	.2	3.8	6.8	4.9				3.4	2.5
Total Current	70.7	80.6	67.7	65.1				72.6	73.7
Fixed Assets (net)	18.6	10.1	11.5	18.3				13.4	13.8
Intangibles (net)	10.2	2.2	14.8	9.1				6.6	7.1
All Other Non-Current	.5	7.1	6.1	7.5				7.4	5.5
Total	100.0	100.0	100.0	100.0				100.0	100.0
							LIABILITIES		
Notes Payable-Short Term	11.2	8.9	11.0	21.5				15.8	18.8
Cur. Mat.-L.T.D.	9.6	3.1	3.0	1.9				4.2	2.3
Trade Payables	21.2	20.6	14.9	31.2				20.1	21.0
Income Taxes Payable	.0	.1	.2	.0				.1	.0
All Other Current	63.7	11.9	16.3	9.5				13.1	10.5
Total Current	105.8	44.6	45.5	64.1				53.4	52.7
Long-Term Debt	2.4	14.0	11.1	13.8				14.7	15.2
Deferred Taxes	.0	.0	.1	.4				.2	.2
All Other Non-Current	.0	3.0	1.5	6.3				9.3	8.9
Net Worth	-8.2	38.4	41.8	15.4				22.4	23.1
Total Liabilities & Net Worth	100.0	100.0	100.0	100.0				100.0	100.0
							INCOME DATA		
Net Sales	100.0	100.0	100.0	100.0				100.0	100.0
Gross Profit	51.5	41.1	32.1	41.5				38.2	38.8
Operating Expenses	46.6	33.0	28.4	37.5				35.9	34.3
Operating Profit	4.9	8.0	3.6	4.0				2.3	4.6
All Other Expenses (net)	-.4	.2	.0	.6				.3	.1
Profit Before Taxes	5.3	7.9	3.7	3.4				2.0	4.4
							RATIOS		
Current	1.9	2.9	2.3	2.4				2.4	2.4
	1.2	2.0	1.6	1.2				1.5	1.5
	.4	1.1	1.1	.7				1.1	1.1
Quick	1.3	1.5	1.4	1.5				1.5	1.7
	.7	.7	.8	.6				.9	1.0
	.3	.5	.5	.3				.5	.6
Sales/Receivables	(1) 277.5	(9) 38.8	(22) 16.8	(30) 12.2				(16) 22.8	(16) 22.5
	(16) 23.4	(23) 16.1	(31) 11.6	(38) 9.7				(30) 12.3	(31) 11.8
	(33) 11.0	(48) 7.6	(46) 7.9	(40) 9.1				(36) 10.0	(42) 8.7
Cost of Sales/Inventory	(0) UND	(8) 43.5	(15) 24.4	(24) 14.9				(16) 23.4	(12) 30.6
	(12) 31.2	(78) 4.7	(31) 11.6	(65) 5.6				(35) 10.3	(35) 10.4
	(57) 6.4	(146) 2.5	(53) 6.9	(140) 2.6				(64) 5.7	(68) 5.4
Cost of Sales/Payables	(0) UND	(2) 155.0	(8) 47.9	(24) 15.3				(13) 28.9	(16) 22.4
	(27) 13.5	(23) 15.9	(18) 20.1	(32) 11.5				(26) 14.3	(29) 12.8
	(34) 10.6	(47) 7.8	(26) 14.2	(61) 6.0				(35) 10.5	(41) 8.9
Sales/Working Capital	14.0	4.9	8.4	8.9				7.2	7.5
	NM	9.2	16.1	35.8				16.7	15.1
	-12.3	45.5	220.7	-14.7				87.9	45.0
EBIT/Interest		42.5	38.7	6.9				17.7	20.8
		(20) 12.7	(14) 5.1	3.1				(86) 5.5	(78) 4.6
		3.2	1.3	.2				1.4	1.6
Net Profit + Depr., Dep., Amort./Cur. Mat. L/T/D								6.2	3.4
								(18) 2.3	(10) 1.4
								1.2	.0
Fixed/Worth	.1	.0	.1	.5				.1	.1
	.6	.2	.4	8.2				.4	.4
	-.4	.7	2.0	-1.9				2.7	7.7
Debt/Worth	.7	.8	.7	1.1				1.1	1.0
	1.5	1.3	2.0	43.1				2.7	2.5
	-4.1	6.6	10.2	-11.1				103.1	-111.5
% Profit Before Taxes/Tangible Net Worth		121.1	64.9					59.7	57.9
		(24) 44.8	(14) 21.7					(77) 18.1	(64) 19.5
		16.2	3.3					2.8	3.6
% Profit Before Taxes/Total Assets	67.8	28.4	15.6	7.7				17.9	12.5
	20.2	17.3	9.8	4.4				5.2	5.5
	1.4	4.0	.7	-2.2				.3	.7
Sales/Net Fixed Assets	UND	436.9	100.9	83.1				130.7	137.9
	84.6	106.2	42.7	12.6				41.3	48.7
	11.2	20.2	21.5	5.9				20.6	16.9
Sales/Total Assets	8.6	4.0	4.5	3.9				5.0	4.9
	4.6	3.3	3.4	3.5				3.9	3.9
	1.6	2.1	2.9	1.8				2.4	2.6
% Depr., Dep., Amort./Sales		.1	.3	.4				.3	.2
		(10) .4	(10) .6	(11) 1.9				(76) .7	(65) .6
		.6	.8	2.8				1.2	1.3
% Officers', Directors' Owners' Comp/Sales		2.0	1.2					1.7	1.9
		(16) 4.0	(10) 2.7					(52) 3.2	(38) 4.1
		5.2	3.3					5.8	9.9
Net Sales ($)	14362M	129195M	283876M	947130M	138240M	488401M		1604134M	1655560M
Total Assets ($)	2367M	31872M	77370M	314638M	53606M	331042M		512255M	547088M

M = $ thousand   MM = $ million
See Pages viii through xx for Explanation of Ratios and Data

Comparative Historical Data				Current Data Sorted by Sales					
			Type of Statement						
3	2	2	Unqualified					2	2
11	11	4	Reviewed		1			1	2
13	12	5	Compiled		8			2	3
34	19	22	Tax Returns	3		6	2		1
33	42	36	Other	1	9	2	5	7	12
4/1/16-3/31/17 ALL	4/1/17-3/31/18 ALL	4/1/18-3/31/19 ALL		9 (4/1-9/30/18)			60 (10/1/18-3/31/19)		
				0-1MM	1-3MM	3-5MM	5-10MM	10-25MM	25MM & OVER
94	86	69	NUMBER OF STATEMENTS	4	18	8	7	12	20
%	%	%	**ASSETS**	%	%	%	%	%	%
12.9	11.3	11.4	Cash & Equivalents		14.9			2.8	8.4
31.2	28.5	29.2	Trade Receivables (net)		27.8			34.2	29.5
23.7	24.9	27.4	Inventory		29.1			23.7	27.8
3.0	1.6	4.2	All Other Current		5.0			4.1	4.1
70.8	66.4	72.2	Total Current		76.8			64.7	69.7
16.4	18.1	13.6	Fixed Assets (net)		9.0			14.4	14.8
7.0	8.9	8.3	Intangibles (net)		7.0			14.1	7.9
5.8	6.7	6.0	All Other Non-Current		7.1			6.8	7.5
100.0	100.0	100.0	Total		100.0			100.0	100.0
			LIABILITIES						
10.8	12.0	11.7	Notes Payable-Short Term		10.6			11.7	17.7
3.6	3.7	3.8	Cur. Mat.-L.T.D.		5.7			3.5	1.7
18.9	17.9	20.8	Trade Payables		21.1			10.7	30.4
.1	.0	.1	Income Taxes Payable		.2			.0	.3
11.8	13.3	20.4	All Other Current		11.0			16.6	12.1
45.1	46.8	56.8	Total Current		48.7			42.6	62.2
17.8	16.3	12.2	Long-Term Debt		21.1			9.3	11.4
.2	.1	.2	Deferred Taxes		.0			.0	.5
14.3	6.4	3.0	All Other Non-Current		2.4			.5	5.3
22.6	30.4	27.9	Net Worth		27.8			47.6	20.6
100.0	100.0	100.0	Total Liabilities & Net Worth		100.0			100.0	100.0
			INCOME DATA						
100.0	100.0	100.0	Net Sales		100.0			100.0	100.0
39.4	42.0	40.9	Gross Profit		42.0			33.9	39.0
35.0	36.3	35.5	Operating Expenses		32.5			30.6	36.3
4.4	5.7	5.4	Operating Profit		9.5			3.4	2.7
.0	.4	.2	All Other Expenses (net)		.8			-.3	.4
4.4	5.3	5.3	Profit Before Taxes		8.7			3.7	2.3
			RATIOS						
2.9	2.7	2.5			3.1			3.3	2.4
1.6	1.6	1.6	Current		1.8			1.6	1.2
1.2	1.0	1.0			.9			1.1	.9
1.8	1.7	1.4			1.5			1.5	1.4
.9	.8	.8	Quick		.7			.7	.8
.6	.5	.4			.2			.4	.4
20 18.1	16 22.2	14 26.7		13 27.1				21 17.7	26 13.8
30 12.2	28 12.9	31 11.6	Sales/Receivables	23 16.1				32 11.3	38 9.6
40 9.1	40 9.2	46 8.0		62 5.9				51 7.2	45 8.2
12 29.7	16 22.9	12 31.4		2 150.8				1 356.4	17 21.3
33 10.9	37 9.9	44 8.3	Cost of Sales/Inventory	63 5.8				31 11.9	49 7.4
65 5.6	73 5.0	99 3.7		152 2.4				46 8.0	104 3.5
13 29.1	15 24.5	15 24.7		15 24.0				4 90.9	19 19.4
26 13.8	24 15.3	25 14.7	Cost of Sales/Payables	26 14.3				16 23.1	30 12.0
42 8.6	36 10.1	43 8.5		53 6.9				27 13.3	45 8.2
6.5	7.3	5.9			3.3			10.6	7.4
14.1	13.6	16.1	Sales/Working Capital		13.5			18.0	35.5
40.8	NM	694.9			NM			56.7	NM
17.1	19.4	28.7			37.3			28.4	6.5
(77) 5.6	(76) 5.8	(54) 5.3	EBIT/Interest	(14) 12.1				(11) 9.7	(18) 3.0
1.9	2.6	1.4			2.8			2.0	.2
7.7	5.9		Net Profit + Depr., Dep.,						
(11) 3.7	(12) 2.4		Amort./Cur. Mat. L/T/D						
1.6	.5								
.1	.2	.1			.0			.1	.2
.5	.6	.4	Fixed/Worth		.4			.3	.7
4.6	3.7	4.0			8.3			1.4	26.7
.7	.9	.8			1.1			.5	1.2
2.2	2.3	2.0	Debt/Worth		4.3			1.6	7.7
39.3	33.2	64.9			NM			3.2	292.7
78.7	88.7	87.5			119.8			85.6	54.8
(75) 37.6	(67) 29.2	(56) 35.3	% Profit Before Taxes/Tangible Net Worth	(14) 45.3				(10) 38.5	(16) 13.1
8.0	7.0	9.3			19.4			10.1	1.2
18.8	24.9	23.9			27.3			24.3	9.1
7.1	6.8	9.7	% Profit Before Taxes/Total Assets		15.6			12.9	2.8
2.3	2.7	1.5			1.9			5.5	-.4
96.0	74.7	128.9			UND			96.0	86.8
37.6	27.9	49.4	Sales/Net Fixed Assets		104.0			29.3	34.0
14.3	11.2	14.1			14.1			20.9	7.6
5.1	4.8	4.5			3.8			5.1	5.1
3.6	3.5	3.4	Sales/Total Assets		2.7			3.5	3.5
2.5	2.3	2.1			1.4			2.9	2.0
.3	.5	.3							.4
(71) .7	(53) .8	(40) .5	% Depr., Dep., Amort./Sales					(13)	1.3
1.4	2.1	1.8							2.9
2.0	1.8	1.5			2.4				
(39) 3.0	(42) 3.0	(34) 2.9	% Officers', Directors' Owners' Comp/Sales	(11) 4.0					
5.5	5.8	4.6			4.5				
1740524M	1787163M	2001204M	Net Sales ($)	780M	36925M	31013M	49864M	196677M	1685945M
643146M	632528M	810895M	Total Assets ($)	507M	17796M	7386M	15393M	59578M	710235M

© RMA 2019

M = $ thousand   MM = $ million

See Pages viii through xx for Explanation of Ratios and Data

Current Data Sorted by Assets   Comparative Historical Data

0-500M	500M-2MM	2-10MM	10-50MM	50-100MM	100-250MM	Type of Statement	ALL 4/1/14-3/31/15	ALL 4/1/15-3/31/16
1		1	1	2		Unqualified	9	4
		2	2	1		Reviewed	9	8
2	4	3	1			Compiled	15	14
20	19	9				Tax Returns	73	89
7	18	20	5	2	2	Other	78	70
	13 (4/1-9/30/18)		109 (10/1/18-3/31/19)					
30	41	35	9	5	2	NUMBER OF STATEMENTS	184	185
%	%	%	%	%	%	**ASSETS**	%	%
28.0	19.0	24.4				Cash & Equivalents	19.6	17.4
3.4	3.2	7.3				Trade Receivables (net)	4.3	5.9
50.0	42.3	33.5				Inventory	40.9	40.8
1.1	1.3	1.9				All Other Current	3.7	3.0
82.4	65.7	67.1				Total Current	68.5	67.2
12.8	25.8	24.3				Fixed Assets (net)	21.9	21.8
.8	4.1	1.9				Intangibles (net)	3.9	3.4
3.9	4.4	6.6				All Other Non-Current	5.6	7.6
100.0	100.0	100.0				Total	100.0	100.0
						LIABILITIES		
27.7	9.4	7.2				Notes Payable-Short Term	8.3	15.3
6.8	3.1	1.0				Cur. Mat.-L.T.D.	2.7	2.7
36.9	9.0	11.7				Trade Payables	13.9	14.1
.6	.1	.1				Income Taxes Payable	.1	.1
11.5	6.7	8.9				All Other Current	10.0	10.0
83.5	28.3	29.0				Total Current	35.0	42.1
11.3	21.7	13.3				Long-Term Debt	16.4	17.0
.0	.0	.0				Deferred Taxes	.2	.2
8.9	2.9	5.7				All Other Non-Current	8.0	10.2
-3.7	47.1	52.1				Net Worth	40.5	30.5
100.0	100.0	100.0				Total Liabilities & Net Worth	100.0	100.0
						INCOME DATA		
100.0	100.0	100.0				Net Sales	100.0	100.0
49.2	54.9	52.1				Gross Profit	48.8	50.0
45.1	45.6	43.5				Operating Expenses	42.3	44.7
4.1	9.3	8.6				Operating Profit	6.5	5.3
1.1	.7	.9				All Other Expenses (net)	.8	.8
3.0	8.5	7.7				Profit Before Taxes	5.7	4.5
						RATIOS		
5.6	8.0	7.7				Current	4.3	3.9
2.5	3.0	2.6					2.3	2.0
.6	1.4	1.6					1.4	1.3
2.3	2.4	3.4				Quick	2.0	1.4
1.0	.9	1.1					.6	(182) .5
.1	.2	.5					.2	.2
0 UND	0 UND	0 UND				Sales/Receivables	0 UND	0 UND
0 UND	0 UND	3 129.8					0 UND	0 UND
0 UND	6 61.9	21 17.8					4 88.7	6 57.0
40 9.1	70 5.2	69 5.3				Cost of Sales/Inventory	60 6.1	63 5.8
87 4.2	140 2.6	111 3.3					99 3.7	101 3.6
166 2.2	243 1.5	174 2.1					166 2.2	174 2.1
0 UND	0 UND	8 47.9				Cost of Sales/Payables	5 78.9	5 70.4
26 13.9	21 17.3	28 13.1					23 15.6	24 15.0
74 4.9	49 7.4	70 5.2					53 6.9	61 6.0
5.0	2.8	3.8				Sales/Working Capital	4.0	4.7
9.6	6.3	6.5					7.8	8.7
-15.4	18.7	12.2					38.8	24.7
17.0	22.3	22.2				EBIT/Interest	19.2	19.5
(19) 1.6	(30) 5.6	(26) 6.2					(141) 6.0	(144) 5.0
-1.4	1.2	2.7					1.7	1.3
						Net Profit + Depr., Dep., Amort./Cur. Mat. L/T/D	2.5	7.8
							(11) 1.3	(11) 2.4
							-12.4	.4
.0	.1	.0				Fixed/Worth	.1	.1
.1	.4	.2					.3	.4
NM	2.9	1.6					2.1	3.3
.6	.2	.3				Debt/Worth	.4	.5
1.3	1.2	.8					1.2	1.5
-2.4	8.4	2.1					4.7	8.6
91.3	74.2	46.6				% Profit Before Taxes/Tangible Net Worth	60.6	56.7
(20) 43.1	(36) 44.2	(31) 26.0					(157) 23.7	(153) 24.0
17.0	7.4	12.6					8.5	5.7
41.2	37.9	24.4				% Profit Before Taxes/Total Assets	24.4	20.5
9.9	12.0	13.6					10.2	8.1
-6.2	1.4	3.7					1.9	.4
UND	46.0	67.2				Sales/Net Fixed Assets	118.1	73.7
224.3	18.3	23.3					24.6	25.5
48.9	4.4	4.1					7.9	8.4
5.6	3.5	3.3				Sales/Total Assets	3.8	3.7
3.5	2.4	2.2					2.6	2.5
2.3	1.1	1.6					1.8	1.6
.1	.4	.6				% Depr., Dep., Amort./Sales	.4	.4
(14) .3	(28) 1.1	(28) 1.1					(127) .9	(128) 1.0
.8	2.5	1.9					2.2	2.4
4.0	3.1	1.6				% Officers', Directors' Owners' Comp/Sales	2.1	2.3
(17) 6.5	(28) 5.0	(15) 4.2					(73) 4.1	(107) 4.0
9.9	8.9	5.2					6.3	6.4
26417M	98787M	384712M	415365M	591532M	920774M	Net Sales ($)	4587854M	3768402M
7347M	43994M	173642M	206637M	336624M	421833M	Total Assets ($)	2033065M	1775873M

M = $ thousand   MM = $ million
See Pages viii through xx for Explanation of Ratios and Data

Comparative Historical Data   Current Data Sorted by Sales

4/1/16-3/31/17 ALL	4/1/17-3/31/18 ALL	4/1/18-3/31/19 ALL	Type of Statement	0-1MM	1-3MM	3-5MM	5-10MM	10-25MM	25MM & OVER
4	7	5	Unqualified	1				2	2
11	9	5	Reviewed					2	3
16	15	10	Compiled	3	1		5		1
70	56	48	Tax Returns	15	22	5	3	2	1
60	55	54	Other	10	13	5	9	8	9
				13 (4/1-9/30/18)			109 (10/1/18-3/31/19)		
161	142	122	NUMBER OF STATEMENTS	29	36	10	17	14	16
%	%	%	ASSETS	%	%	%	%	%	%
17.7	19.3	21.9	Cash & Equivalents	21.5	25.4	20.2	20.5	22.6	17.2
5.3	4.9	5.4	Trade Receivables (net)	4.6	1.2	6.0	7.7	9.4	10.4
40.8	43.3	40.5	Inventory	45.9	41.4	32.7	47.1	33.8	32.6
3.6	2.4	1.7	All Other Current	1.3	.6	1.5	1.7	4.1	3.3
67.3	70.0	69.6	Total Current	73.1	68.5	60.5	77.0	69.9	63.5
20.0	19.7	22.8	Fixed Assets (net)	19.2	27.7	24.2	12.8	22.4	28.5
4.0	4.7	2.5	Intangibles (net)	2.7	1.1	6.8	3.4	1.9	2.5
8.7	5.6	5.0	All Other Non-Current	5.0	2.6	8.5	6.9	5.8	5.6
100.0	100.0	100.0	Total	100.0	100.0	100.0	100.0	100.0	100.0
			LIABILITIES						
11.7	13.2	13.2	Notes Payable-Short Term	31.7	4.5	14.3	11.7	3.1	9.3
2.6	2.1	3.4	Cur. Mat.-L.T.D.	7.3	2.9	1.5	1.3	1.8	1.9
12.8	16.5	17.6	Trade Payables	39.4	6.7	6.9	15.7	11.5	16.3
.0	.1	.2	Income Taxes Payable	.4	.2	.0	.0	.3	.0
15.1	11.5	8.6	All Other Current	8.4	8.5	11.0	11.0	6.1	7.2
42.2	43.4	43.0	Total Current	87.2	22.9	33.8	39.8	22.8	34.7
15.0	24.4	17.3	Long-Term Debt	13.9	23.9	15.9	7.6	12.7	23.8
.1	.0	.0	Deferred Taxes	.0	.0	.0	.0	.0	.1
4.6	9.1	5.3	All Other Non-Current	6.1	9.0	.0	2.7	3.5	3.5
38.1	23.1	34.4	Net Worth	-7.3	44.2	50.3	49.9	60.9	37.9
100.0	100.0	100.0	Total Liabilities & Net Worth	100.0	100.0	100.0	100.0	100.0	100.0
			INCOME DATA						
100.0	100.0	100.0	Net Sales	100.0	100.0	100.0	100.0	100.0	100.0
49.8	51.3	52.4	Gross Profit	51.5	54.2	55.9	48.0	52.8	52.2
44.2	45.6	45.2	Operating Expenses	45.7	45.2	46.4	42.8	44.7	46.3
5.6	5.7	7.3	Operating Profit	5.8	9.0	9.5	5.3	8.1	5.9
.7	.9	1.0	All Other Expenses (net)	1.7	.6	.2	.3	1.0	1.5
4.9	4.7	6.3	Profit Before Taxes	4.0	8.4	9.3	4.9	7.1	4.5
			RATIOS						
4.3	4.2	6.4	Current	4.8	9.7	8.2	6.7	5.5	4.1
1.9	2.1	2.4		1.7	4.8	2.2	1.6	2.5	1.6
1.1	1.2	1.4		.5	2.2	1.3	1.2	2.2	1.4
1.6	1.4	2.6	Quick	2.0	3.7	2.7	1.3	3.7	2.0
.6 (139)	.6	.9		.4	1.3	.9	.5	1.2	.7
.2	.2	.3		.1	.6	.1	.4	.5	.4
0 UND	0 UND	0 UND	Sales/Receivables	0 UND	0 UND	0 UND	0 UND	0 UND	1 282.9
0 UND	0 UND	0 999.8		0 UND	0 UND	0 UND	3 113.9	1 598.0	5 75.7
7 52.6	8 47.4	10 38.1		6 56.3	3 138.1	8 45.2	20 18.7	34 10.7	29 12.5
65 5.6	63 5.8	69 5.3	Cost of Sales/Inventory	72 5.1	64 5.7	61 6.0	74 4.9	21 17.0	68 5.4
107 3.4	126 2.9	118 3.1		146 2.5	114 3.2	74 4.9	118 3.1	166 2.2	114 3.2
166 2.2	215 1.7	174 2.1		243 1.5	228 1.6	111 3.3	166 2.2	182 2.0	159 2.3
3 141.9	4 89.9	6 61.4	Cost of Sales/Payables	3 104.7	0 UND	2 168.9	6 57.6	7 49.9	33 10.9
22 16.4	29 12.8	33 11.1		49 7.5	20 18.4	11 32.3	27 13.5	58 6.3	58 6.3
53 6.9	68 5.4	64 5.7		130 2.8	40 9.1	34 10.7	68 5.4	76 4.8	70 5.2
4.8	3.4	3.8	Sales/Working Capital	3.2	2.8	5.2	3.4	3.7	6.1
9.0	9.0	7.2		11.6	5.0	10.5	9.5	5.7	8.5
99.3	23.8	18.4		-2.2	16.3	NM	21.4	7.7	15.3
26.0	18.3	17.6	EBIT/Interest	5.8	19.7		19.7	18.7	12.2
(131) 7.7	(114) 5.9	(90) 4.2		(20) 3.6	(26) 4.4		(14) 6.1	(10) 4.0	(15) 1.9
2.0	1.7	.9		.9	.4		.3	3.1	-.6
9.1			Net Profit + Depr., Dep., Amort./Cur. Mat. L/T/D						
(13) 1.9									
.4									
.1	.1	.0	Fixed/Worth	.0	.0	.0	.0	.1	.2
.3	.4	.4		.1	.4	.6	.1	.4	.8
1.4	4.4	1.9		NM	2.9	NM	.6	.6	1.0
.4	.5	.4	Debt/Worth	.7	.2	.3	.2	.4	.7
1.3	1.9	1.0		3.4	1.2	1.1	.9	.7	1.0
5.3	132.5	4.6		-2.3	26.2	NM	2.5	1.0	2.9
51.5	51.9	67.9	% Profit Before Taxes/Tangible Net Worth	82.4	76.5		49.4	31.7	32.1
(132) 22.3	(109) 23.7	(101) 26.6		(19) 28.9	(31) 54.2		(15) 25.8	18.6	(14) 19.2
7.7	7.9	9.7		10.2	16.9		.6	12.5	-3.1
22.6	21.1	30.1	% Profit Before Taxes/Total Assets	19.6	44.7	44.0	24.4	23.1	16.5
9.6	7.2	9.9		6.6	13.3	31.1	17.8	9.2	3.8
2.6	1.8	.7		-1.7	1.4	7.1	-.9	4.9	-2.1
78.8	107.6	115.3	Sales/Net Fixed Assets	928.5	117.3	315.9	91.4	45.8	25.6
25.9	28.8	21.8		87.8	19.7	21.9	46.3	11.5	10.7
9.9	8.2	7.8		9.0	4.0	3.7	20.9	7.1	5.1
4.0	3.7	3.5	Sales/Total Assets	3.7	3.7	4.4	3.6	2.8	2.9
2.6	2.4	2.4		2.3	2.2	3.2	2.9	2.3	2.2
1.6	1.4	1.5		1.0	1.0	1.9	1.8	1.8	1.6
.5	.4	.4	% Depr., Dep., Amort./Sales	.2	.4		.4	.5	1.0
(119) 1.0	(95) .9	(84) 1.1		(16) .7	(24) 1.1		(13) .9	(13) 1.1	(14) 1.3
2.3	2.4	2.0		2.6	1.8		1.3	2.3	4.1
1.8	2.2	3.0	% Officers', Directors' Owners' Comp/Sales	4.1	3.9		1.7		
(90) 4.1	(68) 4.6	(63) 4.4		(16) 6.4	(23) 5.7		(10) 3.2		
8.5	8.8	8.0		9.3	9.1		4.6		
3649835M	3343023M	2437587M	Net Sales ($)	18558M	65683M	38806M	131399M	234862M	1948279M
1469978M	1476550M	1190077M	Total Assets ($)	10979M	44940M	15428M	57758M	111318M	949654M

M = $ thousand   MM = $ million
See Pages viii through xx for Explanation of Ratios and Data

Current Data Sorted by Assets   **Comparative Historical Data**

Type of Statement

0-500M	500M-2MM	2-10MM	10-50MM	50-100MM	100-250MM		4/1/14-3/31/15 ALL	4/1/15-3/31/16 ALL
			3	2	2	Unqualified	7	11
	1	2	1			Reviewed	5	3
			1			Compiled	3	8
11	9	5	1		1	Tax Returns	24	34
4	13	8	10	1		Other	29	24
	14 (4/1-9/30/18)		61 (10/1/18-3/31/19)					
15	23	15	16	3	3	**NUMBER OF STATEMENTS**	68	80

ASSETS

0-500M %	500M-2MM %	2-10MM %	10-50MM %	50-100MM %	100-250MM %		%	%
25.1	11.0	11.5	14.7			Cash & Equivalents	16.3	18.9
6.5	11.6	14.0	11.2			Trade Receivables (net)	10.0	11.1
47.3	26.9	37.0	21.4			Inventory	31.2	27.7
5.1	4.7	7.7	1.3			All Other Current	3.8	3.6
84.0	54.3	70.2	48.6			Total Current	61.2	61.3
10.5	30.5	15.9	37.1			Fixed Assets (net)	25.1	26.6
2.2	1.1	.9	2.1			Intangibles (net)	4.3	5.6
3.3	14.1	13.0	12.2			All Other Non-Current	9.4	6.4
100.0	100.0	100.0	100.0			Total	100.0	100.0

LIABILITIES

0-500M	500M-2MM	2-10MM	10-50MM	50-100MM	100-250MM			
16.5	10.4	5.1	8.2			Notes Payable-Short Term	7.1	11.6
2.0	1.4	4.4	2.3			Cur. Mat.-L.T.D.	2.4	1.8
6.3	3.6	8.5	3.9			Trade Payables	10.7	5.3
.1	.1	.0	.1			Income Taxes Payable	.1	.1
18.2	9.6	8.8	12.9			All Other Current	8.7	9.4
43.1	25.0	26.9	27.4			Total Current	29.0	28.1
1.8	17.0	8.9	17.2			Long-Term Debt	15.3	13.6
.0	.0	.0	.1			Deferred Taxes	.2	.1
39.5	6.1	6.2	13.6			All Other Non-Current	13.3	8.6
15.5	51.8	58.0	41.7			Net Worth	42.3	49.6
100.0	100.0	100.0	100.0			Total Liabilities & Net Worth	100.0	100.0

INCOME DATA

0-500M	500M-2MM	2-10MM	10-50MM	50-100MM	100-250MM			
100.0	100.0	100.0	100.0			Net Sales	100.0	100.0
54.3	61.6	49.1	63.4			Gross Profit	53.5	58.5
49.7	51.8	43.0	55.7			Operating Expenses	49.8	55.0
4.6	9.8	6.1	7.7			Operating Profit	3.7	3.6
.9	1.7	.5	1.5			All Other Expenses (net)	.6	.3
3.7	8.2	5.6	6.2			Profit Before Taxes	3.2	3.3

RATIOS

0-500M	500M-2MM	2-10MM	10-50MM	50-100MM	100-250MM			
12.9	5.7	5.2	4.5			Current	5.6	5.4
3.4	2.1	2.8	2.0				2.5	2.2
1.9	1.3	1.5	1.2				1.3	1.2
3.5	2.3	1.9	3.8			Quick	2.8	2.8
(14) 1.3	1.1	.8	1.1				.9	1.2
.6	.4	.5	.7				.4	.3
0 UND	0 UND	0 UND	1 648.6			Sales/Receivables	0 UND	0 UND
0 UND	1 400.6	4 95.1	3 111.6				4 102.0	1 427.0
3 120.5	29 12.5	24 15.1	46 7.9				17 21.0	17 21.0
25 14.7	29 12.4	33 11.0	35 10.5			Cost of Sales/Inventory	11 31.8	10 38.1
99 3.7	72 5.1	51 7.1	69 5.3				96 3.8	58 6.3
281 1.3	215 1.7	166 2.2	174 2.1				174 2.1	203 1.8
0 UND	0 UND	3 111.1	6 61.0			Cost of Sales/Payables	0 UND	0 UND
0 UND	13 27.7	13 27.5	17 21.4				17 21.3	12 30.8
12 30.4	38 9.6	35 10.5	39 9.3				49 7.5	35 10.5
2.6	4.6	3.2	4.1			Sales/Working Capital	3.3	3.8
8.3	8.0	9.1	6.9				6.6	12.0
46.1	32.0	25.8	32.9				26.1	46.2
	51.2	106.6	4.9			EBIT/Interest	36.1	23.2
	(17) 8.6	(13) 17.3	(11) 2.2				(52) 5.9	(64) 4.0
	-.3	.2	-.2				1.3	.2
						Net Profit + Depr., Dep., Amort./Cur. Mat. L/T/D		
.0	.2	.0	.3			Fixed/Worth	.1	.1
.3	.5	.1	.9				.5	.3
-.5	.8	.7	1.7				1.3	1.5
.3	.3	.3	.4			Debt/Worth	.4	.3
1.1	.9	.4	1.2				.9	.9
-5.8	1.7	1.7	6.4				3.5	2.7
191.0	79.4	68.3	16.7			% Profit Before Taxes/Tangible Net Worth	46.9	40.7
(10) 23.9	(21) 34.5	(13) 40.7	(14) 8.9				(57) 10.2	(67) 17.7
3.6	5.7	14.7	.6				1.7	3.1
28.8	34.2	43.1	9.5			% Profit Before Taxes/Total Assets	16.3	19.5
12.1	16.5	20.7	4.4				5.9	7.1
-8.2	2.2	.7	2.1				.5	-.4
UND	30.1	124.4	19.1			Sales/Net Fixed Assets	113.4	85.5
70.2	10.4	40.5	7.7				21.8	25.1
26.8	7.3	15.9	1.4				4.6	6.4
6.4	2.7	4.6	3.8			Sales/Total Assets	3.7	5.0
4.0	1.7	2.4	1.7				2.1	2.8
1.7	1.4	1.5	.8				1.3	1.4
	.5	.2	1.1			% Depr., Dep., Amort./Sales	.3	.3
	(17) 1.3	(13) .3	2.0				(47) 1.2	(62) .9
	2.9	.9	2.9				2.7	2.3
						% Officers', Directors' Owners' Comp/Sales	3.1	2.8
							(22) 5.8	(29) 5.7
							8.0	10.0
18354M	66386M	249830M	783539M	323406M	1398027M	Net Sales ($)	1077542M	1164862M
3332M	27377M	66443M	368191M	213973M	438159M	Total Assets ($)	572709M	586650M

© RMA 2019

M = $ thousand   MM = $ million
See Pages viii through xx for Explanation of Ratios and Data

Comparative Historical Data | Current Data Sorted by Sales

			Type of Statement						
11	7	7	Unqualified					1	6
3	3	1	Reviewed					1	
4	4	4	Compiled			1	1	1	1
17	21	27	Tax Returns	8	6	5	4	1	3
34	39	36	Other	6	8	2	7	3	10
4/1/16- 3/31/17	4/1/17- 3/31/18	4/1/18- 3/31/19			14 (4/1-9/30/18)		61 (10/1/18-3/31/19)		
ALL	ALL	ALL		0-1MM	1-3MM	3-5MM	5-10MM	10-25MM	25MM & OVER
69	74	75	**NUMBER OF STATEMENTS**	14	14	8	12	7	20
%	%	%	**ASSETS**	%	%	%	%	%	%
17.0	15.3	15.6	Cash & Equivalents	11.4	19.8		14.2		17.1
9.6	6.8	10.6	Trade Receivables (net)	10.7	8.9		9.8		8.7
28.7	31.0	30.6	Inventory	53.6	19.4		18.3		26.8
4.3	4.0	4.4	All Other Current	4.4	5.2		2.9		2.2
59.5	57.2	61.2	Total Current	80.0	53.3		45.2		54.9
28.6	31.6	25.4	Fixed Assets (net)	14.3	28.7		25.4		34.0
3.8	2.6	2.2	Intangibles (net)	2.3	1.8		.1		5.2
8.1	8.6	11.2	All Other Non-Current	3.2	16.2		29.3		5.9
100.0	100.0	100.0	Total	100.0	100.0		100.0		100.0
			LIABILITIES						
10.1	10.0	9.3	Notes Payable-Short Term	16.3	6.7		2.6		7.7
3.2	2.1	2.3	Cur. Mat.-L.T.D.	1.6	1.7		6.3		2.0
6.6	5.8	5.2	Trade Payables	2.4	7.6		2.5		5.7
.0	.2	.1	Income Taxes Payable	.1	.1		.0		.0
10.9	19.6	12.3	All Other Current	1.4	26.5		16.2		12.4
30.9	37.8	29.1	Total Current	21.9	42.7		26.7		27.9
22.7	13.8	11.8	Long-Term Debt	9.4	20.5		7.7		12.4
.1	.3	.0	Deferred Taxes	.0	.0		.0		.0
4.1	7.5	14.5	All Other Non-Current	40.0	7.9		3.4		13.1
42.2	40.6	44.5	Net Worth	28.6	28.9		62.2		46.6
100.0	100.0	100.0	Total Liabilities & Net Worth	100.0	100.0		100.0		100.0
			INCOME DATA						
100.0	100.0	100.0	Net Sales	100.0	100.0		100.0		100.0
53.1	56.9	57.1	Gross Profit	50.9	62.0		74.5		49.7
47.7	50.4	50.8	Operating Expenses	44.3	52.9		62.2		48.7
5.4	6.6	6.3	Operating Profit	6.6	9.1		12.2		1.0
1.2	.5	1.1	All Other Expenses (net)	-.8	3.3		1.6		.6
4.3	6.1	5.2	Profit Before Taxes	7.4	5.8		10.6		.4
			RATIOS						
7.3	5.4	5.2		16.6	3.3		5.1		4.7
2.5	2.6	2.3	Current	6.2	1.8		2.2		1.6
1.1	1.1	1.5		2.6	.6		.8		1.2
3.1	2.5	2.5		5.2	2.0		2.4		3.7
.9 (73)	1.0 (74)	1.0	Quick	(13) 2.9	.7		1.4		.8
.3	.4	.5		.8	.0		.5		.8
0 UND	0 UND	0 UND		0 UND	0 UND		0 UND	0	799.9
1 300.9	0 UND	3 120.5	Sales/Receivables	0 UND	0 UND		3 124.4	4	89.8
11 33.8	5 68.9	23 16.2		81 4.5	7 52.0		42 8.6	12	30.7
12 30.5	22 16.5	29 12.4		81 4.5	1 257.3		33 11.1	22	16.8
70 5.2	73 5.0	64 5.7	Cost of Sales/Inventory	192 1.9	38 9.7		64 5.7	38	9.6
203 1.8	174 2.1	182 2.0		365 1.0	182 2.0		174 2.1	94	3.9
0 UND	0 UND	0 UND		0 UND	0 UND		0 UND	3	121.0
9 39.8	6 59.8	12 30.5	Cost of Sales/Payables	0 UND	15 24.9		20 18.0	10	38.0
29 12.4	34 10.8	36 10.0		14 25.7	38 9.6		41 8.8	23	15.9
3.3	4.3	4.1		1.7	7.2		4.7		6.1
7.4	9.6	8.3	Sales/Working Capital	2.7	18.2		17.0		19.9
123.3	61.1	32.0		6.1	-23.9		NM		36.4
14.2	49.2	19.0							15.7
(56) 3.9	(52) 6.6	(52) 5.6	EBIT/Interest					(14)	2.9
-.4	1.3	-.2							-.6
			Net Profit + Depr., Dep., Amort./Cur. Mat. L/T/D						
.1	.1	.1		.0	.0		.1		.3
.6	.5	.6	Fixed/Worth	.5	.6		.3		.9
4.5	1.2	1.7		-.6	NM		.8		1.5
.3	.2	.3		.2	.5		.2		.3
1.1	.9	.9	Debt/Worth	1.0	1.4		.4		1.0
6.6	2.7	1.8		-9.0	NM		1.2		6.3
65.2	78.2	59.1		51.1	94.9		59.1		31.9
(56) 16.9	(65) 24.5	(63) 22.3	% Profit Before Taxes/Tangible Net Worth	(10) 12.9	(11) 34.5		(11) 24.8	(17)	11.2
3.8	4.4	4.4		-2.9	4.4		7.0		-6.4
18.0	25.6	28.8		25.4	26.3		43.5		18.1
6.8	11.4	10.2	% Profit Before Taxes/Total Assets	10.1	14.8		21.0		5.6
-1.8	.7	-.9		-2.7	-6.0		-.6		-2.9
56.2	54.4	72.5		UND	UND		31.2		28.8
14.3	15.6	16.9	Sales/Net Fixed Assets	43.1	11.2		24.6		8.2
3.9	6.3	7.3		9.9	6.4		9.1		5.1
3.9	4.6	4.3		3.5	4.8		4.3		4.7
2.0	2.7	2.1	Sales/Total Assets	1.7	1.7		2.2		3.0
1.3	1.4	1.4		1.1	1.4		1.0		1.5
.7	.5	.5					.2		.7
(51) 1.6	(54) 1.2	(54) 1.2	% Depr., Dep., Amort./Sales				(11) .6	(18)	2.1
3.3	2.8	2.6					1.3		3.1
3.6	.9	.5							
(20) 6.5	(26) 4.9	(31) 2.3	% Officers', Directors' Owners' Comp/Sales						
9.4	6.9	7.4							
1360329M	1063442M	2839542M	Net Sales ($)	7262M	27017M	31765M	84946M	95157M	2593395M
669261M	573381M	1117475M	Total Assets ($)	5027M	13749M	13877M	66869M	71551M	946402M

© RMA 2019

M = $ thousand   MM = $ million
See Pages viii through xx for Explanation of Ratios and Data

Current Data Sorted by Assets   Comparative Historical Data

							Type of Statement		
					1		Unqualified	3	4
							Reviewed	6	5
16	4	1					Compiled	2	6
8	8	4 5		6	1		Tax Returns	41	33
	8 (4/1-9/30/18)			46 (10/1/18-3/31/19)			Other	33	32
								4/1/14-3/31/15	4/1/15-3/31/16
0-500M	500M-2MM	2-10MM	10-50MM	50-100MM	100-250MM			ALL	ALL
24	12	10	6	2		NUMBER OF STATEMENTS		85	80
%	%	%	%	%	%	ASSETS		%	%
21.7	15.9	15.9			D	Cash & Equivalents		12.0	14.2
10.0	11.1	10.4			A	Trade Receivables (net)		9.2	7.4
30.2	29.4	35.0			T	Inventory		47.9	43.1
5.8	.9	2.8			A	All Other Current		4.6	2.9
67.7	57.3	64.1				Total Current		73.7	67.6
16.8	25.2	24.7			N	Fixed Assets (net)		16.3	20.8
9.5	5.9	.9			O	Intangibles (net)		4.1	5.0
5.9	11.6	10.3			T	All Other Non-Current		5.9	6.6
100.0	100.0	100.0				Total		100.0	100.0
					A	LIABILITIES			
10.6	9.0	10.7			V	Notes Payable-Short Term		12.5	14.9
2.7	1.5	5.3			A	Cur. Mat.-L.T.D.		1.3	4.4
8.7	11.4	13.0			I	Trade Payables		24.5	19.6
.2	.0	.0			L	Income Taxes Payable		.2	.1
28.3	12.3	59.8			A	All Other Current		9.6	8.4
50.6	34.2	88.9			B	Total Current		48.2	47.4
30.8	17.1	18.6			L	Long-Term Debt		14.3	16.2
.0	.0	.9			E	Deferred Taxes		.2	.1
31.7	.4	8.9				All Other Non-Current		7.4	6.8
-13.2	48.3	-17.4				Net Worth		30.0	29.5
100.0	100.0	100.0				Total Liabilties & Net Worth		100.0	100.0
						INCOME DATA			
100.0	100.0	100.0				Net Sales		100.0	100.0
47.5	42.6	39.5				Gross Profit		38.6	38.8
46.0	38.7	39.3				Operating Expenses		34.5	34.2
1.5	3.8	.1				Operating Profit		4.1	4.6
.9	.2	.4				All Other Expenses (net)		.8	.6
.6	3.6	-.3				Profit Before Taxes		3.3	4.0
						RATIOS			
7.9	3.4	3.1						4.4	2.6
3.2	2.1	1.9				Current		2.0	1.6
1.1	.8	.7						1.2	1.2
2.0	1.2	1.2						1.6	1.0
1.0	.9	.4				Quick	(83)	.5	.4
.4	.5	.2						.2	.2
0 UND	2 170.9	0 UND					0 UND	0 UND
0 UND	9 41.6	4 91.6				Sales/Receivables	3 141.0	1 269.1
8 47.6	17 21.7	27 13.6					14 26.9	8 46.7
2 183.1	11 34.0	36 10.1					42 8.7	34 10.7
51 7.1	36 10.1	78 4.7				Cost of Sales/Inventory	58 6.3	66 5.5
94 3.9	56 6.5	89 4.1					87 4.2	87 4.2
0 UND	11 32.8	8 44.7					4 82.8	7 53.1
0 UND	15 24.1	16 22.9				Cost of Sales/Payables	23 16.0	21 17.0
16 22.5	24 15.2	34 10.8					52 7.0	40 9.2
4.2	8.8	8.3						6.5	8.1
10.5	11.9	15.9				Sales/Working Capital		15.5	17.3
109.6	-69.7	-8.3						55.5	64.2
15.1	30.1	52.4						26.0	37.5
(17) 4.8	(11) 3.2	6.0				EBIT/Interest	(66) 5.9	(63) 9.7
-.5	1.6	1.9						1.0	1.9
						Net Profit + Depr., Dep., Amort./Cur. Mat. L/T/D			
.0	.1	.4						.1	.1
.5	.4	3.5				Fixed/Worth		.5	.6
-.7	3.9	NM						3.4	2.6
1.0	.3	.6						.5	.7
-36.5	1.1	14.0				Debt/Worth		1.7	1.7
-2.2	6.8	NM						31.9	8.9
672.7	69.9							87.4	65.5
(11) 76.6	(10) 23.5					% Profit Before Taxes/Tangible Net Worth	(66) 34.0	(65) 33.8
6.3	2.6							5.5	4.4
29.0	37.8	16.9						27.8	27.3
11.9	7.4	7.5				% Profit Before Taxes/Total Assets		8.5	11.4
-5.0	1.8	3.5						.3	1.2
UND	39.2	49.5						147.7	99.8
85.6	15.7	23.7				Sales/Net Fixed Assets		43.5	24.7
13.7	7.4	4.4						15.6	11.0
6.4	5.3	4.5						6.1	6.0
5.0	3.7	2.5				Sales/Total Assets		4.3	4.1
2.3	2.3	2.1						2.7	2.7
1.3		.7						.3	.5
(11) 1.8		1.4				% Depr., Dep., Amort./Sales	(56) .6	(54) .8
2.5		2.1						1.7	1.5
								1.3	1.1
						% Officers', Directors' Owners' Comp/Sales	(30) 2.1	(30) 3.9
								4.4	6.6
23872M	48395M	153151M	309806M	256419M		Net Sales ($)		3705893M	3610397M
5631M	14180M	43379M	120181M	134572M		Total Assets ($)		936110M	729294M

M = $ thousand   MM = $ million

See Pages viii through xx for Explanation of Ratios and Data

Comparative Historical Data | | | Current Data Sorted by Sales

					Type of Statement						
4		1		1	Unqualified						1
6		1			Reviewed						
4		4		1	Compiled				1		
18		20		24	Tax Returns	7	9	4	1	1	2
23		25		28	Other	7	1	7	4	3	6
4/1/16-3/31/17 ALL		4/1/17-3/31/18 ALL		4/1/18-3/31/19 ALL		8 (4/1-9/30/18)			46 (10/1/18-3/31/19)		
						0-1MM	1-3MM	3-5MM	5-10MM	10-25MM	25MM & OVER
55		50		54	NUMBER OF STATEMENTS	14	10	11	6	4	9
%		%		%	ASSETS	%	%	%	%	%	%
11.9		17.8		18.1	Cash & Equivalents	15.5	29.3	18.5			
6.5		7.3		10.6	Trade Receivables (net)	6.2	16.0	9.6			
47.1		39.8		29.9	Inventory	39.7	25.2	24.8			
2.2		2.6		3.6	All Other Current	.2	13.6	1.0			
67.7		67.5		62.3	Total Current	61.6	84.1	54.0			
22.8		21.1		23.3	Fixed Assets (net)	17.5	7.9	33.1			
4.9		5.1		7.0	Intangibles (net)	11.6	6.4	3.8			
4.5		6.3		7.4	All Other Non-Current	9.0	1.6	9.1			
100.0		100.0		100.0	Total	100.0	100.0	100.0			
					LIABILITIES						
9.5		9.2		8.8	Notes Payable-Short Term	6.7	11.1	11.0			
3.6		4.2		3.0	Cur. Mat.-L.T.D.	2.3	.0	5.1			
17.3		12.8		10.5	Trade Payables	6.2	13.6	10.4			
.4		.2		.1	Income Taxes Payable	.2	.3	.0			
9.7		8.0		28.0	All Other Current	41.4	11.0	11.3			
40.5		34.4		50.4	Total Current	56.9	36.0	37.8			
12.2		23.2		23.3	Long-Term Debt	26.9	34.4	16.9			
.2		.1		.4	Deferred Taxes	.0	.0	.3			
9.8		13.4		16.7	All Other Non-Current	39.5	21.2	3.1			
37.3		28.8		9.2	Net Worth	-23.3	8.4	41.9			
100.0		100.0		100.0	Total Liabilities & Net Worth	100.0	100.0	100.0			
					INCOME DATA						
100.0		100.0		100.0	Net Sales	100.0	100.0	100.0			
36.0		43.6		43.7	Gross Profit	51.6	37.2	45.7			
32.9		39.3		41.8	Operating Expenses	50.9	36.0	39.6			
3.1		4.3		1.9	Operating Profit	.7	1.2	6.1			
.4		.2		.9	All Other Expenses (net)	1.3	.4	.6			
2.8		4.1		1.0	Profit Before Taxes	-.6	.8	5.5			
					RATIOS						
2.8		4.5		4.7		7.8	8.1	3.5			
1.5		2.4		2.3	Current	3.2	3.4	2.5			
1.2		1.3		1.0		1.2	1.1	.7			
1.0		1.4		1.9		3.2	2.7	1.2			
.4	(49)	.6		.9	Quick	.9	1.0	1.1			
.2		.2		.3		.2	.7	.5			
0	999.8	0	UND	0	UND	0	UND	0	UND	1	529.4
2	172.4	3	141.9	3	131.8 Sales/Receivables	0	UND	0	UND	6	61.0
5	71.9	6	57.3	20	18.5	18	19.8	22	16.4	14	26.5
51	7.1	40	9.2	22	16.6	12	30.3	0	UND	10	36.8
61	6.0	59	6.2	50	7.3 Cost of Sales/Inventory	91	4.0	26	14.0	39	9.4
96	3.8	91	4.0	85	4.3	261	1.4	48	7.6	60	6.1
13	27.9	0	UND	0	UND	0	UND	0	UND	10	36.9
21	17.1	16	23.5	11	31.9 Cost of Sales/Payables	0	UND	0	UND	14	26.9
43	8.5	27	13.3	26	14.1	29	12.8	19	19.5	22	16.6
7.3		6.7		6.1		3.1	6.5	8.8			
17.5		12.4		12.3	Sales/Working Capital	7.1	18.4	11.6			
60.9		35.8		252.6		34.8	176.1	-26.8			
53.3		35.2		15.6		15.7		38.1			
(43)	7.0	(40)	4.5	(44)	4.3 EBIT/Interest	(11)	2.0	(10)	13.2		
2.5		.9		.3		-2.8		2.1			
					Net Profit + Depr., Dep., Amort./Cur. Mat. L/T/D						
.1		.1		.1		.0	.0	.1			
.6		.3		.7	Fixed/Worth	.8	.0	.4			
1.5		1.2		-3.1		-.3	-1.0	124.3			
.7		.3		.6		.8	1.7	.2			
1.9		1.4		2.2	Debt/Worth	NM	NM	1.1			
5.3		3.1		-4.5		-1.9	-3.3	318.0			
74.4		61.8		88.1	% Profit Before Taxes/Tangible Net Worth						
(47)	28.3	(42)	26.0	(36)	28.0						
12.0		2.9		4.4							
23.0		33.2		28.2		16.2	89.5	42.0			
8.6		7.7		7.5	% Profit Before Taxes/Total Assets	-.9	21.7	13.2			
2.8		.0		-.8		-16.2	2.9	3.5			
79.3		64.0		124.4		241.6	UND	41.5			
27.8		28.4		25.0	Sales/Net Fixed Assets	34.5	UND	10.9			
6.9		11.0		7.8		9.0	32.7	6.0			
5.4		5.4		5.3		5.2	7.4	5.6			
3.7		3.7		3.6	Sales/Total Assets	2.4	5.6	3.9			
2.6		2.5		2.1		1.3	4.5	2.2			
.4		.7		.7							
(39)	1.0	(37)	1.1	(34)	1.4 % Depr., Dep., Amort./Sales						
1.7		1.9		2.2							
1.3		1.6		1.7							
(22)	1.9	(28)	3.3	(16)	4.2 % Officers', Directors' Owners' Comp/Sales						
3.9		6.4		6.2							
2021222M		933182M		791643M	Net Sales ($)	7197M	13652M	41968M	43291M	61755M	623780M
574640M		331538M		317943M	Total Assets ($)	3439M	2485M	12415M	16319M	35297M	247988M

© RMA 2019

M = $ thousand   MM = $ million
See Pages viii through xx for Explanation of Ratios and Data

Current Data Sorted by Assets　　　　　　　　　Comparative Historical Data

Type of Statement

	0-500M	500M-2MM	2-10MM	10-50MM	50-100MM	100-250MM	Type of Statement	4/1/14-3/31/15 ALL	4/1/15-3/31/16 ALL
Unqualified							Unqualified	1	
Reviewed		1	2	2		1	Reviewed	10	9
Compiled			2				Compiled	4	4
Tax Returns	2	6	2	2		1	Tax Returns	27	18
Other	1	6	6	4			Other	31	30
	0-500M	500M-2MM	2-10MM	10-50MM (35 — 10/1/18-3/31/19)	50-100MM	100-250MM			
	3 (4/1-9/30/18)								
NUMBER OF STATEMENTS	3	13	12	8		2	NUMBER OF STATEMENTS	73	61

Columns 0-500M, 10-50MM, 50-100MM and 100-250MM show "DATA NOT AVAILABLE" for the percentage/ratio data below.

0-500M	500M-2MM	2-10MM	10-50MM	50-100MM	100-250MM		4/1/14-3/31/15	4/1/15-3/31/16
%	%	%	%	%	%	**ASSETS**	%	%
	27.4	7.2				Cash & Equivalents	22.4	17.6
	12.4	19.1				Trade Receivables (net)	11.0	9.2
	26.4	38.3				Inventory	36.8	42.8
	5.6	1.3				All Other Current	4.4	4.5
	71.8	66.0				Total Current	74.6	74.1
	9.6	15.7				Fixed Assets (net)	12.5	13.8
	.0	7.0				Intangibles (net)	1.6	3.4
	18.6	11.3				All Other Non-Current	11.4	8.6
	100.0	100.0				Total	100.0	100.0
						LIABILITIES		
	9.4	5.5				Notes Payable-Short Term	9.4	14.1
	.5	4.1				Cur. Mat.-L.T.D.	.7	1.1
	18.6	15.2				Trade Payables	15.6	8.7
	.3	.0				Income Taxes Payable	.4	.8
	16.0	11.6				All Other Current	16.8	13.3
	44.8	36.4				Total Current	42.9	38.0
	3.8	19.5				Long-Term Debt	11.1	6.5
	.0	.0				Deferred Taxes	.0	.2
	.1	9.5				All Other Non-Current	10.6	9.3
	51.2	34.7				Net Worth	35.4	45.9
	100.0	100.0				Total Liabilties & Net Worth	100.0	100.0
						INCOME DATA		
	100.0	100.0				Net Sales	100.0	100.0
	55.7	54.1				Gross Profit	43.0	46.5
	40.7	40.6				Operating Expenses	35.3	37.7
	15.1	13.5				Operating Profit	7.7	8.8
	.5	.5				All Other Expenses (net)	.7	.7
	14.6	13.0				Profit Before Taxes	7.1	8.1
						RATIOS		
	7.1	4.0					5.9	5.1
	2.6	2.9				Current	1.7	2.3
	1.1	.6					1.1	1.2
	2.6	.9					1.6	1.2
	(12) 1.9	.3				Quick	.8	.6
	.5	.1					.3	.2
	0 UND	3 127.4					0 UND	0 UND
	0 999.8	14 26.3				Sales/Receivables	5 72.8	4 100.3
	33 11.2	87 4.2					22 16.5	24 15.2
	0 UND	21 17.4					19 19.5	53 6.9
	91 4.0	203 1.8				Cost of Sales/Inventory	111 3.3	135 2.7
	192 1.9	304 1.2					332 1.1	365 1.0
	0 UND	5 71.7					0 UND	0 UND
	15 24.9	30 12.1				Cost of Sales/Payables	15 23.7	15 24.6
	47 7.7	99 3.7					62 5.9	47 7.8
	3.2	2.3					2.4	2.2
	5.7	4.4				Sales/Working Capital	7.8	4.8
	54.1	-8.1					33.5	24.5
		14.2					40.5	34.7
	(10)	4.1				EBIT/Interest	(51) 8.5	(51) 8.4
		.9					2.7	1.4
						Net Profit + Depr., Dep., Amort./Cur. Mat. L/T/D		
	.0	.1					.0	.0
	.2	.3				Fixed/Worth	.1	.2
	.6	NM					.8	.6
	.2	.5					.7	.4
	.6	3.0				Debt/Worth	1.4	1.2
	3.1	-42.0					5.6	4.2
	108.4					% Profit Before Taxes/Tangible Net Worth	69.8	55.2
	(12) 44.6						(68) 25.2	(55) 24.9
	21.2						6.8	3.1
	37.7	22.6				% Profit Before Taxes/Total Assets	24.7	18.9
	26.2	5.3					9.5	9.1
	13.5	.3					2.0	1.1
	282.6	50.2					132.2	145.6
	56.7	16.6				Sales/Net Fixed Assets	40.3	28.7
	19.6	7.3					11.3	9.1
	3.6	2.1					4.0	3.2
	2.2	1.6				Sales/Total Assets	2.1	1.9
	1.5	.9					.9	.9
						% Depr., Dep., Amort./Sales	.2	.2
							(49) .6	(42) .6
							1.6	1.4
	2.7					% Officers', Directors' Owners' Comp/Sales	2.0	2.0
	(11) 3.7						(38) 3.8	(34) 4.5
	6.2						6.9	8.0
963M	35214M	69520M	209757M	382322M		Net Sales ($)	1875196M	1195208M
235M	14435M	52033M	146606M	308324M		Total Assets ($)	1457875M	1163420M

M = $ thousand　　　MM = $ million
See Pages viii through xx for Explanation of Ratios and Data

Comparative Historical Data   Current Data Sorted by Sales

	1	2	Type of Statement					1	1
2	1	5	Unqualified					1	1
2	1	5	Reviewed			1	2	1	1
4	7	3	Compiled			1	2		
16	12	10	Tax Returns	3	4	1	2		
19	21	18	Other	1	4	6	2	3	2
4/1/16-3/31/17	4/1/17-3/31/18	4/1/18-3/31/19				3 (4/1-9/30/18)	35 (10/1/18-3/31/19)		
ALL	ALL	ALL		0-1MM	1-3MM	3-5MM	5-10MM	10-25MM	25MM & OVER
41	42	38	**NUMBER OF STATEMENTS**	4	8	9	8	5	4
%	%	%	**ASSETS**	%	%	%	%	%	%
16.7	21.8	16.0	Cash & Equivalents						
15.9	8.1	13.8	Trade Receivables (net)						
39.6	35.6	33.9	Inventory						
8.0	3.7	4.6	All Other Current						
80.2	69.3	68.3	Total Current						
11.8	14.6	11.7	Fixed Assets (net)						
1.5	10.8	9.6	Intangibles (net)						
6.6	5.2	10.4	All Other Non-Current						
100.0	100.0	100.0	Total						
			LIABILITIES						
8.9	7.8	9.3	Notes Payable-Short Term						
1.0	3.4	2.5	Cur. Mat.-L.T.D.						
15.3	16.8	14.3	Trade Payables						
.9	.1	.2	Income Taxes Payable						
15.8	17.9	14.5	All Other Current						
41.9	45.0	40.7	Total Current						
9.5	11.4	12.8	Long-Term Debt						
.0	.0	.0	Deferred Taxes						
10.3	5.0	4.4	All Other Non-Current						
38.3	38.5	42.0	Net Worth						
100.0	100.0	100.0	Total Liabilties & Net Worth						
			INCOME DATA						
100.0	100.0	100.0	Net Sales						
53.9	51.2	51.8	Gross Profit						
44.9	39.4	42.1	Operating Expenses						
9.0	11.7	9.7	Operating Profit						
.9	.7	.8	All Other Expenses (net)						
8.1	11.0	8.9	Profit Before Taxes						
			RATIOS						
4.5	5.1	4.9							
2.1	2.0	2.5	Current						
1.5	.9	.7							
1.8	2.8	2.0							
.5	.6	(37) .6	Quick						
.4	.2	.2							
0 UND	0 UND	0 UND							
13 27.9	4 85.9	9 42.4	Sales/Receivables						
34 10.8	34 10.8	46 7.9							
31 11.9	11 34.2	12 30.3							
89 4.1	81 4.5	130 2.8	Cost of Sales/Inventory						
332 1.1	521 .7	243 1.5							
20 18.3	0 UND	1 326.3							
35 10.3	36 10.2	29 12.7	Cost of Sales/Payables						
64 5.7	73 5.0	58 6.3							
2.7	2.3	2.8							
6.1	10.4	5.2	Sales/Working Capital						
15.2	-31.9	-10.8							
35.9	25.6	29.7							
(33) 8.0	(29) 5.9	(29) 8.3	EBIT/Interest						
2.2	-.3	-.1							
			Net Profit + Depr., Dep., Amort./Cur. Mat. L/T/D						
.0	.0	.0							
.2	.3	.2	Fixed/Worth						
1.7	10.4	2.0							
.6	.4	.5							
1.4	2.3	1.6	Debt/Worth						
9.4	-16.8	NM							
142.1	62.2	60.1	% Profit Before Taxes/Tangible Net Worth						
(35) 24.0	(29) 11.5	(29) 35.2							
10.8	-.5	6.8							
37.8	30.4	26.0	% Profit Before Taxes/Total Assets						
11.0	7.2	10.2							
1.1	-.4	-.1							
295.9	184.5	147.7	Sales/Net Fixed Assets						
44.6	31.1	27.4							
15.8	8.0	9.8							
3.3	3.3	2.4	Sales/Total Assets						
2.2	1.6	1.8							
1.3	.9	1.0							
.2	.2	.4	% Depr., Dep., Amort./Sales						
(21) .7	(23) .5	(26) .8							
1.9	2.4	2.7							
1.4	2.3	2.5	% Officers', Directors' Owners' Comp/Sales						
(22) 5.4	(17) 4.9	(25) 4.3							
8.7	8.5	9.4							
377891M	1134370M	697776M	Net Sales ($)	1122M	16323M	34942M	53313M	69831M	522245M
212758M	528169M	521633M	Total Assets ($)	771M	10792M	31748M	45805M	62173M	370344M

© RMA 2019

M = $ thousand   MM = $ million
See Pages viii through xx for Explanation of Ratios and Data

Current Data Sorted by Assets   Comparative Historical Data

Type of Statement	0-500M	500M-2MM	2-10MM	10-50MM	50-100MM	100-250MM		4/1/14-3/31/15 ALL	4/1/15-3/31/16 ALL
Unqualified				1				3	2
Reviewed			3					5	4
Compiled	1	4	4					13	14
Tax Returns	2	7	6					20	16
Other	1	3	6	3	1	1		13	13
		8 (4/1-9/30/18)		34 (10/1/18-3/31/19)					
NUMBER OF STATEMENTS	4	14	16	6	1	1		54	49
	%	%	%	%	%	%		%	%
ASSETS									
Cash & Equivalents		24.4	19.8					16.8	16.1
Trade Receivables (net)		2.9	9.2					10.8	13.4
Inventory		56.3	50.8					41.7	45.3
All Other Current		2.1	5.5					2.5	2.6
Total Current		85.8	85.3					71.9	77.3
Fixed Assets (net)		5.1	8.1					16.1	13.9
Intangibles (net)		1.1	.4					.9	1.4
All Other Non-Current		8.0	6.1					11.2	7.3
Total		100.0	100.0					100.0	100.0
LIABILITIES									
Notes Payable-Short Term		40.9	25.3					26.4	26.6
Cur. Mat.-L.T.D.		.9	.8					2.4	2.0
Trade Payables		6.3	5.7					5.4	7.2
Income Taxes Payable		.0	.0					.2	.1
All Other Current		18.0	9.6					15.4	14.2
Total Current		66.1	41.3					49.8	50.0
Long-Term Debt		11.0	22.9					9.2	16.1
Deferred Taxes		.0	.0					.0	.1
All Other Non-Current		8.1	7.0					11.3	5.4
Net Worth		14.8	28.8					29.7	28.5
Total Liabilties & Net Worth		100.0	100.0					100.0	100.0
INCOME DATA									
Net Sales		100.0	100.0					100.0	100.0
Gross Profit		20.3	27.4					27.4	27.8
Operating Expenses		18.2	23.1					24.7	24.4
Operating Profit		2.1	4.3					2.8	3.4
All Other Expenses (net)		-.7	-1.2					.5	-.3
Profit Before Taxes		2.8	5.5					2.3	3.8
RATIOS									
Current		2.1	7.6					2.6	3.3
		1.6	2.8					1.5	1.8
		1.1	1.3					1.1	1.1
Quick		1.0	1.8					1.4	1.5
		.3	.9					.6	.5
		.1	.3					.2	.2
Sales/Receivables	0 UND	0 841.4					0 UND	1 253.8
	1 427.0	6 62.3					7 55.3	9 39.8
	4 103.3	16 22.7					36 10.1	34 10.7
Cost of Sales/Inventory	44 8.3	114 3.2					69 5.3	79 4.6
	104 3.5	152 2.4					126 2.9	118 3.1
	182 2.0	215 1.7					174 2.1	228 1.6
Cost of Sales/Payables	0 UND	0 UND					0 UND	0 UND
	3 117.4	5 77.1					5 78.1	6 62.0
	24 14.9	8 43.6					17 21.2	15 24.6
Sales/Working Capital		3.9	1.9					3.4	2.9
		10.8	3.0					7.8	7.9
		59.7	9.5					43.7	37.8
EBIT/Interest		3.4	9.0					14.1	9.5
	(11) 2.6	(15) 3.2					(48) 3.5	(42) 3.2
		.4	2.4					1.5	1.1
Net Profit + Depr., Dep., Amort./Cur. Mat. L/T/D									
Fixed/Worth		.0	.1					.1	.1
		.1	.3					.3	.3
		.4	2.4					.6	.8
Debt/Worth		1.5	.9					.7	1.0
		3.4	3.5					2.1	3.3
		20.4	442.4					5.6	9.9
% Profit Before Taxes/Tangible Net Worth		115.5	585.2					43.4	47.2
	(13) 63.8	(14) 12.5					(46) 12.2	(41) 12.4
		8.8	4.3					6.5	2.5
% Profit Before Taxes/Total Assets		27.5	11.0					10.6	10.1
		5.5	5.1					5.5	4.0
		1.8	2.0					1.4	.5
Sales/Net Fixed Assets		UND	109.9					103.4	146.2
		324.1	31.7					18.7	18.7
		33.1	8.7					8.6	9.4
Sales/Total Assets		4.1	1.9					2.6	2.5
		2.8	1.6					1.8	1.9
		1.5	.9					1.1	1.2
% Depr., Dep., Amort./Sales			.1					.4	.2
		(13) .3					(38) .8	(36) .5
			.9					1.9	1.5
% Officers', Directors' Owners' Comp/Sales								1.9	1.4
							(27) 2.8	(20) 2.6
							6.0	4.0
Net Sales ($)	3410M	56156M	95704M	149519M	153883M	24198M		605797M	504902M
Total Assets ($)	1303M	17367M	68185M	144950M	58978M	136463M		476549M	380992M

© RMA 2019

M = $ thousand   MM = $ million
See Pages viii through xx for Explanation of Ratios and Data

Comparative Historical Data / Current Data Sorted by Sales

	4/1/16-3/31/17 ALL	4/1/17-3/31/18 ALL	4/1/18-3/31/19 ALL	Type of Statement	0-1MM	1-3MM	3-5MM	5-10MM	10-25MM	25MM & OVER
	5	5	1	Unqualified						1
	4	4	3	Reviewed					3	
	6	8	9	Compiled	1	3	3	1	1	
	18	16	15	Tax Returns	2	4	3	5	1	
	13	14	14	Other	2	4	2	2	1	1
					8 (4/1-9/30/18)		34 (10/1/18-3/31/19)			25MM & OVER
	46	47	42	**NUMBER OF STATEMENTS**	5	9	8	8	10	2
	%	%	%	**ASSETS**	%	%	%	%	%	%
	16.2	16.1	20.5	Cash & Equivalents					15.0	
	11.3	12.2	8.7	Trade Receivables (net)					15.4	
	41.1	42.2	45.8	Inventory					43.2	
	2.5	2.8	3.8	All Other Current					1.6	
	71.1	73.2	78.7	Total Current					75.3	
	15.9	16.5	11.2	Fixed Assets (net)					15.7	
	.8	1.3	2.1	Intangibles (net)					2.7	
	12.2	8.9	8.0	All Other Non-Current					6.3	
	100.0	100.0	100.0	Total					100.0	
				LIABILITIES						
	17.3	26.5	30.0	Notes Payable-Short Term					25.3	
	2.2	2.4	.8	Cur. Mat.-L.T.D.					.5	
	6.9	7.3	5.4	Trade Payables					6.4	
	.0	.2	.0	Income Taxes Payable					.0	
	14.7	14.4	14.0	All Other Current					14.5	
	41.1	50.9	50.3	Total Current					46.7	
	20.1	15.6	18.2	Long-Term Debt					16.3	
	.0	.1	.1	Deferred Taxes					.2	
	5.9	7.5	7.2	All Other Non-Current					.4	
	33.0	25.9	24.2	Net Worth					36.4	
	100.0	100.0	100.0	Total Liabilities & Net Worth					100.0	
				INCOME DATA						
	100.0	100.0	100.0	Net Sales					100.0	
	30.7	27.3	28.4	Gross Profit					35.8	
	25.0	23.2	23.8	Operating Expenses					28.8	
	5.6	4.1	4.6	Operating Profit					7.1	
	1.2	.2	-.2	All Other Expenses (net)					.1	
	4.4	3.9	4.8	Profit Before Taxes					7.0	
				RATIOS						
	3.5	2.2	4.6	Current					4.6	
	1.9	1.3	1.5						1.3	
	1.2	1.0	1.1						1.2	
	1.8	1.0	1.8	Quick					1.4	
	.6	.6	.6						.8	
	.2	.2	.2						.2	
	0 UND	0 999.8	0 UND	Sales/Receivables					2 148.3	
	8 45.4	10 37.2	2 174.5						14 25.6	
	36 10.0	27 13.3	17 21.4						118 3.1	
	66 5.5	69 5.3	68 5.4	Cost of Sales/Inventory					73 5.0	
	140 2.6	111 3.3	130 2.8						166 2.2	
	243 1.5	192 1.9	228 1.6						261 1.4	
	0 UND	0 999.8	0 UND	Cost of Sales/Payables					7 56.0	
	5 72.6	6 56.3	5 77.0						13 29.0	
	33 11.0	20 18.1	14 26.0						36 10.0	
	2.2	3.5	2.7	Sales/Working Capital					2.8	
	5.2	9.2	6.3						8.4	
	16.4	64.4	33.0						24.7	
	11.2	11.4	6.9	EBIT/Interest					10.8	
	(41) 3.6	(43) 3.8	(38) 3.2						6.4	
	1.2	1.5	2.1						2.7	
				Net Profit + Depr., Dep., Amort./Cur. Mat. L/T/D						
	.1	.1	.0	Fixed/Worth					.1	
	.4	.4	.3						.4	
	1.0	1.1	2.3						UND	
	.6	.8	.7	Debt/Worth					.4	
	2.8	3.0	2.5						2.3	
	5.0	11.7	206.6						UND	
	47.5	41.7	101.5	% Profit Before Taxes/Tangible Net Worth						
	(40) 16.3	(40) 16.0	(35) 18.3							
	1.8	6.4	6.2							
	10.6	11.6	14.0	% Profit Before Taxes/Total Assets					15.0	
	4.1	4.8	5.5						5.5	
	.4	.7	2.4						3.1	
	72.5	48.1	146.3	Sales/Net Fixed Assets					74.5	
	18.4	21.8	30.8						8.2	
	4.8	6.1	8.3						3.6	
	2.3	2.6	2.6	Sales/Total Assets					2.2	
	1.6	1.9	1.6						1.4	
	.8	1.2	1.2						.8	
	.2	.4	.2	% Depr., Dep., Amort./Sales						
	(36) .6	(35) .8	(32) .8							
	3.0	2.0	2.1							
	1.3	1.0	1.2	% Officers', Directors' Owners' Comp/Sales						
	(22) 1.8	(23) 2.1	(17) 2.7							
	3.3	4.3	3.9							
	619188M	733673M	482870M	Net Sales ($)	3007M	15481M	31339M	52440M	168389M	212214M
	668056M	551925M	427246M	Total Assets ($)	7654M	17037M	14915M	27507M	262291M	97842M

© RMA 2019

M = $ thousand   MM = $ million
See Pages viii through xx for Explanation of Ratios and Data

Current Data Sorted by Assets   Comparative Historical Data

Type of Statement

	0-500M	500M-2MM	2-10MM	10-50MM	50-100MM	100-250MM		ALL 4/1/14-3/31/15	ALL 4/1/15-3/31/16
Unqualified			4	1		1		1	4
Reviewed		1	2					6	74
Compiled			2					8	8
Tax Returns	16	8	2	1				31	47
Other	11	7	7	1				22	39
		4 (4/1-9/30/18)		58 (10/1/18-3/31/19)					
NUMBER OF STATEMENTS	27	16	15	3		1		68	172

Financial Data

0-500M	500M-2MM	2-10MM	10-50MM	50-100MM	100-250MM		ALL	ALL
%	%	%	%	%	%	**ASSETS**	%	%
25.1	10.1	13.3				Cash & Equivalents	12.3	10.2
4.7	17.5	18.5				Trade Receivables (net)	10.9	5.5
39.9	38.7	29.8				Inventory	46.6	51.4
4.3	6.2	2.3				All Other Current	3.4	1.1
74.0	72.6	64.0				Total Current	73.2	68.2
11.9	20.7	11.7				Fixed Assets (net)	15.1	19.2
4.5	4.5	10.9				Intangibles (net)	5.0	5.8
9.6	2.2	13.4				All Other Non-Current	6.8	6.9
100.0	100.0	100.0				Total	100.0	100.0
						LIABILITIES		
22.2	14.8	11.0				Notes Payable-Short Term	11.1	7.3
1.3	1.7	1.2				Cur. Mat.-L.T.D.	2.3	1.6
12.6	13.7	12.8				Trade Payables	15.8	15.1
.0	.0	1.0				Income Taxes Payable	.1	.0
34.1	28.8	11.4				All Other Current	13.7	22.7
70.2	59.0	37.4				Total Current	43.0	46.7
13.1	14.1	10.7				Long-Term Debt	12.7	11.0
.0	.0	.2				Deferred Taxes	.0	.0
11.6	3.7	1.1				All Other Non-Current	4.7	2.3
5.1	23.2	50.6				Net Worth	39.7	40.0
100.0	100.0	100.0				Total Liabilities & Net Worth	100.0	100.0
						INCOME DATA		
100.0	100.0	100.0				Net Sales	100.0	100.0
45.9	43.7	38.0				Gross Profit	34.5	31.5
39.3	35.0	28.0				Operating Expenses	31.2	26.7
6.6	8.7	10.0				Operating Profit	3.3	4.9
1.4	.1	.3				All Other Expenses (net)	-.2	.7
5.2	8.6	9.7				Profit Before Taxes	3.5	4.1
						RATIOS		
2.5	4.6	6.0					3.8	3.0
1.3	1.4	1.8				Current	1.8	1.8
.9	1.0	1.2					1.3	1.1
1.2	2.5	3.0					1.3	.7
.4	.3	.9				Quick	.5	.3
.1	.2	.3					.2	.2
0 UND	1 329.0	0 UND					0 UND	0 UND
0 UND	12 30.8	7 49.8				Sales/Receivables	3 127.5	0 UND
2 187.7	40 9.2	59 6.2					14 25.5	6 59.1
0 UND	28 13.1	10 36.5					24 15.3	40 9.2
68 5.4	89 4.1	43 8.5				Cost of Sales/Inventory	70 5.2	70 5.2
135 2.7	146 2.5	74 4.9					135 2.7	114 3.2
0 UND	0 UND	5 72.0					6 63.2	5 73.3
0 UND	17 21.4	9 39.5				Cost of Sales/Payables	17 21.8	15 24.4
37 9.8	43 8.4	47 7.8					37 9.9	27 13.7
12.2	6.0	5.8					6.0	7.3
23.8	20.3	12.1				Sales/Working Capital	13.9	14.8
-131.5	142.6	38.9					34.5	60.1
23.7	57.5	58.4					21.4	22.2
(13) 2.7	(12) 10.3	(11) 9.6				EBIT/Interest	(52) 8.3	(94) 6.2
-8.3	2.7	4.4					2.1	2.1
						Net Profit + Depr., Dep., Amort./Cur. Mat. L/T/D		
.0	.1	.0					.0	.1
.1	.5	.4				Fixed/Worth	.3	.4
-1.2	NM	.9					1.4	1.3
1.0	.5	.4					.5	.6
5.7	2.5	1.3				Debt/Worth	1.5	1.4
-8.6	NM	4.5					5.1	5.2
110.3	98.1	96.8					89.8	69.5
(17) 62.0	(12) 51.3	(13) 61.7				% Profit Before Taxes/Tangible Net Worth	(60) 40.8	(150) 36.5
-20.5	33.4	11.8					6.8	10.4
56.7	39.2	36.7					25.6	23.5
16.6	21.2	19.6				% Profit Before Taxes/Total Assets	9.9	14.1
-6.1	4.8	7.1					1.9	2.5
UND	169.5	999.8					238.0	98.1
306.8	25.0	61.1				Sales/Net Fixed Assets	58.7	27.4
27.4	8.9	13.0					13.3	11.9
8.6	4.2	4.9					5.8	5.1
4.3	3.1	3.9				Sales/Total Assets	3.7	3.4
2.6	1.5	2.2					2.5	2.1
							.4	.4
						% Depr., Dep., Amort./Sales	(42) .7	(125) .7
							1.2	1.3
							1.3	1.1
						% Officers', Directors' Owners' Comp/Sales	(36) 3.1	(80) 2.1
							7.7	4.1
29531M	46142M	223531M	145431M		202220M	Net Sales ($)	906016M	1617074M
6247M	14520M	62106M	59850M		110810M	Total Assets ($)	304583M	519846M

(Middle current-data columns 10-50MM, 50-100MM, 100-250MM: **DATA NOT AVAILABLE**)

Comparative Historical Data   Current Data Sorted by Sales

			Type of Statement						
1	1	1	Unqualified						1
4	5	5	Reviewed					2	3
2	5	3	Compiled			1	1	1	
38	20	27	Tax Returns	12	9	1	2	2	1
20	18	26	Other	8	6	5	3	3	1
4/1/16-3/31/17	4/1/17-3/31/18	4/1/18-3/31/19		**4 (4/1-9/30/18)**			**58 (10/1/18-3/31/19)**		
ALL	ALL	ALL		0-1MM	1-3MM	3-5MM	5-10MM	10-25MM	25MM & OVER
65	49	62	**NUMBER OF STATEMENTS**	20	15	7	6	8	6
%	%	%	**ASSETS**	%	%	%	%	%	%
14.7	16.5	17.8	Cash & Equivalents	21.1	19.8				
8.7	10.3	12.0	Trade Receivables (net)	8.4	7.6				
44.3	42.4	36.2	Inventory	34.5	39.7				
1.9	2.6	4.1	All Other Current	1.2	11.4				
69.5	71.8	70.0	Total Current	65.2	78.4				
14.1	17.4	14.6	Fixed Assets (net)	19.0	11.2				
7.6	6.2	6.8	Intangibles (net)	3.2	8.4				
8.7	4.6	8.7	All Other Non-Current	12.7	2.0				
100.0	100.0	100.0	Total	100.0	100.0				
			LIABILITIES						
30.1	8.8	16.5	Notes Payable-Short Term	24.9	9.1				
2.1	3.1	1.5	Cur. Mat.-L.T.D.	1.1	1.8				
12.9	13.1	13.1	Trade Payables	11.5	12.8				
.1	.1	.2	Income Taxes Payable	.0	.0				
20.0	16.1	26.2	All Other Current	46.2	22.5				
65.2	41.2	57.5	Total Current	83.7	46.2				
7.8	16.6	12.7	Long-Term Debt	14.7	17.8				
.1	.1	.1	Deferred Taxes	.0	.0				
4.1	7.5	6.3	All Other Non-Current	13.2	6.4				
22.8	34.5	23.4	Net Worth	-11.7	29.6				
100.0	100.0	100.0	Total Liabilities & Net Worth	100.0	100.0				
			INCOME DATA						
100.0	100.0	100.0	Net Sales	100.0	100.0				
42.9	38.9	42.2	Gross Profit	51.9	43.4				
38.5	33.7	34.2	Operating Expenses	48.0	31.1				
4.3	5.3	8.0	Operating Profit	3.8	12.3				
.1	.5	.7	All Other Expenses (net)	.7	-.2				
4.2	4.8	7.3	Profit Before Taxes	3.2	12.5				
			RATIOS						
4.7	4.0	2.8	Current	1.9	13.2				
1.4	2.1	1.4		1.2	1.7				
1.0	1.2	1.0		.7	1.0				
1.5	1.6	1.3	Quick	1.2	3.0				
.4	.6	.4		.3	.5				
.1	.3	.2		.0	.2				
0 UND	0 UND	0 UND	Sales/Receivables	0 UND	0 UND				
2 193.5	2 170.2	2 147.7		0 UND	0 999.8				
12 30.4	19 19.1	16 22.8		14 26.4	10 35.3				
22 16.3	27 13.5	6 61.9	Cost of Sales/Inventory	0 UND	17 21.7				
64 5.7	76 4.8	59 6.2		111 3.3	91 4.0				
152 2.4	140 2.6	130 2.8		192 1.9	152 2.4				
6 58.5	1 302.9	0 UND	Cost of Sales/Payables	0 UND	0 UND				
16 23.0	16 23.0	9 40.7		3 112.0	0 UND				
35 10.5	35 10.5	38 9.7		44 8.3	45 8.1				
5.0	4.5	7.9	Sales/Working Capital	13.9	3.3				
13.2	9.9	20.2		24.1	14.7				
290.3	75.3	140.5		-18.1	-999.8				
24.4	32.3	28.6	EBIT/Interest						
(48) 5.2	(34) 11.0	(39) 9.4							
2.7	1.8	1.7							
			Net Profit + Depr., Dep., Amort./Cur. Mat. L/T/D						
.0	.0	.0	Fixed/Worth	.0	.1				
.2	.3	.3		.3	.3				
1.0	2.0	3.7		-1.3	-.4				
.5	.4	.7	Debt/Worth	2.1	.2				
2.8	1.4	2.5		13.5	3.2				
10.3	7.5	-23.4		-5.8	-2.5				
78.3	62.7	94.5	% Profit Before Taxes/Tangible Net Worth	259.6					
(55) 41.9	(39) 31.1	(46) 57.9		(12) 53.7					
9.9	11.5	18.6		-2.3					
25.9	23.3	38.8	% Profit Before Taxes/Total Assets	46.1	56.7				
10.6	11.2	17.8		7.7	38.7				
4.0	2.3	2.9		-17.3	17.0				
137.6	129.2	804.2	Sales/Net Fixed Assets	UND	200.5				
45.2	29.1	55.8		47.7	34.8				
20.7	11.2	16.4		8.2	20.5				
4.7	4.7	5.0	Sales/Total Assets	7.0	5.8				
3.1	3.2	3.9		3.0	3.2				
1.9	2.1	2.2		1.9	2.6				
.4	.4	.3	% Depr., Dep., Amort./Sales						
(47) .7	(32) 1.1	(24) .9							
1.4	2.2	2.8							
2.1	1.5	1.7	% Officers', Directors' Owners' Comp/Sales						
(34) 4.2	(19) 4.7	(20) 3.7							
9.1	6.5	6.0							
895474M	731778M	646855M	Net Sales ($)	11584M	26303M	26565M	39125M	114339M	428939M
437974M	297008M	253533M	Total Assets ($)	5028M	7299M	8671M	15412M	61025M	156098M

M = $ thousand   MM = $ million
See Pages viii through xx for Explanation of Ratios and Data

Current Data Sorted by Assets   Comparative Historical Data

0-500M	500M-2MM	2-10MM	10-50MM	50-100MM	100-250MM	Type of Statement	4/1/14-3/31/15 ALL	4/1/15-3/31/16 ALL
1			4	6		2	Unqualified	20	18
1	1		10	7	1		Reviewed	30	25
1	3		15	4		1	Compiled	32	29
36	35		14	2		1	Tax Returns	156	153
18	37		42	15	4	9	Other	147	154
	38 (4/1-9/30/18)			231 (10/1/18-3/31/19)				
56	76	85	54	5	13	**NUMBER OF STATEMENTS**	385	379
%	%	%	%	%	%	**ASSETS**	%	%
23.5	11.7	12.8	4.8		7.6	Cash & Equivalents	13.8	14.1
6.3	12.6	14.5	13.0		12.5	Trade Receivables (net)	12.4	12.8
35.7	39.4	39.2	35.9		20.1	Inventory	38.1	38.7
1.8	4.5	2.7	5.3		1.4	All Other Current	4.1	2.4
67.3	68.3	69.3	58.9		41.6	Total Current	68.4	68.1
15.9	18.0	17.5	26.8		20.1	Fixed Assets (net)	18.1	17.8
6.7	6.9	5.2	7.7		27.8	Intangibles (net)	6.7	7.3
10.1	6.8	8.0	6.6		10.5	All Other Non-Current	6.9	6.8
100.0	100.0	100.0	100.0		100.0	Total	100.0	100.0
						LIABILITIES		
14.1	12.0	8.9	16.1		2.8	Notes Payable-Short Term	11.9	12.8
4.8	3.3	2.5	3.0		1.8	Cur. Mat.-L.T.D.	2.3	2.7
11.3	12.9	15.3	14.1		10.0	Trade Payables	16.4	16.6
.2	.2	.1	.1		.1	Income Taxes Payable	.1	.3
19.4	11.5	11.8	13.4		16.7	All Other Current	10.1	11.0
49.8	39.8	38.7	46.7		31.5	Total Current	40.8	43.3
12.6	22.5	14.8	14.3		31.4	Long-Term Debt	16.0	15.5
.0	.0	.1	.2		.2	Deferred Taxes	.2	.1
14.4	7.2	5.2	6.6		6.8	All Other Non-Current	8.6	7.9
23.1	30.5	41.2	32.2		30.0	Net Worth	34.4	33.1
100.0	100.0	100.0	100.0		100.0	Total Liabilities & Net Worth	100.0	100.0
						INCOME DATA		
100.0	100.0	100.0	100.0		100.0	Net Sales	100.0	100.0
44.2	43.2	41.2	37.1		55.2	Gross Profit	40.4	41.4
40.8	38.9	37.2	33.0		46.6	Operating Expenses	35.9	36.5
3.4	4.3	4.0	4.1		8.5	Operating Profit	4.5	4.8
.3	.3	-.1	.7		5.4	All Other Expenses (net)	.6	.3
3.1	4.0	4.1	3.4		3.2	Profit Before Taxes	3.9	4.6
						RATIOS		
4.9	4.7	3.1	1.7		2.1		3.7	3.3
1.9	2.0	2.0	1.3		1.6	Current	1.8	1.8
.7	1.2	1.2	1.0		.9		1.1	1.2
2.7	2.1	1.8	.6		1.6		1.4	1.5
.6	.7	.6	.4		.7	Quick	.6	.6
.2	.3	.3	.1		.4		.3	.2
0 UND	0 UND	1 498.3	4 93.3		10 37.3		0 UND	0 999.8
0 UND	4 101.1	12 30.8	17 20.9		39 9.3	Sales/Receivables	6 60.0	7 51.1
5 68.4	21 17.2	42 8.6	41 8.8		66 5.5		25 14.7	27 13.6
1 299.3	29 12.5	44 8.3	45 8.1		74 4.9		24 15.0	30 12.0
41 8.9	73 5.0	94 3.9	85 4.3		83 4.4	Cost of Sales/Inventory	74 4.9	74 4.9
130 2.8	146 2.5	166 2.2	159 2.3		126 2.9		130 2.8	140 2.6
0 UND	3 141.8	8 46.3	14 26.4		26 13.9		4 93.3	5 77.1
2 183.9	16 22.4	24 15.0	29 12.7		51 7.1	Cost of Sales/Payables	23 15.8	23 16.1
21 17.7	35 10.5	60 6.1	62 5.9		89 4.1		49 7.5	49 7.5
8.6	6.2	4.3	9.7		5.2		5.5	5.3
21.7	11.2	6.7	18.0		19.8	Sales/Working Capital	12.1	10.7
-33.4	49.0	35.0	NM		-128.7		56.5	47.6
19.5	18.2	18.1	19.9		5.4		16.5	22.0
(36) 8.0	(60) 4.9	(71) 5.8	7.1		(12) 2.3	EBIT/Interest	(307) 6.6	(294) 6.3
-.5	1.2	1.5	1.8		-.8		2.3	1.8
						Net Profit + Depr., Dep., Amort./Cur. Mat. L/T/D	5.6	5.3
							(30) 3.3	(27) 2.6
							2.4	.9
.0	.1	.1	.2		.9		.1	.1
.3	.3	.2	.8		2.2	Fixed/Worth	.4	.4
UND	2.4	1.3	2.1		.0		2.4	1.7
.3	.4	.6	1.2		1.8		.6	.6
1.7	1.8	1.3	2.6		29.0	Debt/Worth	1.9	1.7
-6.8	17.3	3.8	6.1		-2.1		13.1	6.9
84.8	51.8	53.7	61.4			% Profit Before Taxes/Tangible Net Worth	67.1	54.9
(40) 29.1	(59) 20.7	(76) 24.9	(30) 24.8				(314) 31.9	(318) 23.2
3.4	3.5	5.9	7.5				10.8	7.6
26.8	22.9	19.4	13.9		10.3	% Profit Before Taxes/Total Assets	21.4	22.4
11.6	7.1	7.8	5.9		3.6		10.2	9.7
-4.1	.9	1.1	1.9		-3.7		3.1	2.0
556.8	119.9	80.8	36.9		54.8	Sales/Net Fixed Assets	140.0	106.9
89.6	29.9	24.4	10.9		13.7		35.4	33.0
21.4	12.0	11.9	3.6		6.7		11.3	11.0
8.4	4.8	3.2	2.9		2.2	Sales/Total Assets	4.6	4.5
4.2	3.1	2.5	1.9		1.4		3.0	2.9
2.4	1.8	1.8	1.2		.6		1.9	1.8
.2	.3	.4	.9			% Depr., Dep., Amort./Sales	.4	.4
(26) .4	(42) 1.1	(58) .8	(29) 2.2				(249) 1.0	(241) 1.1
1.4	2.4	1.9	4.8				2.3	2.2
2.4	2.3	1.0				% Officers', Directors' Owners' Comp/Sales	1.8	1.5
(26) 5.6	(38) 3.7	(37) 1.3					(167) 3.4	(182) 3.4
7.3	7.0	2.2					6.8	5.7
88604M	336742M	947883M	1402102M	536123M	3277870M	Net Sales ($)	9844788M	8391232M
14398M	86541M	350865M	681260M	363091M	1983434M	Total Assets ($)	4244491M	3868910M

© RMA 2019

M = $ thousand   MM = $ million

See Pages viii through xx for Explanation of Ratios and Data

Comparative Historical Data | Current Data Sorted by Sales

			Type of Statement						
15	14	13	Unqualified	1			3	4	5
31	16	19	Reviewed			2	5	6	6
28	20	24	Compiled		1	5	7	9	2
107	113	88	Tax Returns	18	33	11	12	12	2
111	153	125	Other	12	20	17	32	15	29
4/1/16-3/31/17 ALL	4/1/17-3/31/18 ALL	4/1/18-3/31/19 ALL		38 (4/1-9/30/18)			231 (10/1/18-3/31/19)		
				0-1MM	1-3MM	3-5MM	5-10MM	10-25MM	25MM & OVER
292	316	269	NUMBER OF STATEMENTS	31	54	35	59	46	44
%	%	%	ASSETS	%	%	%	%	%	%
12.8	14.4	13.3	Cash & Equivalents	15.4	15.1	12.7	18.1	8.5	8.5
12.8	12.0	12.0	Trade Receivables (net)	4.4	7.6	16.4	14.6	14.3	13.5
40.5	40.5	37.1	Inventory	33.5	40.8	35.6	37.7	39.9	32.4
2.7	2.6	3.3	All Other Current	7.4	1.8	1.4	2.5	2.9	5.2
68.9	69.6	65.7	Total Current	60.6	65.3	66.1	72.8	65.7	59.7
17.5	17.2	18.9	Fixed Assets (net)	17.8	19.9	21.0	15.2	20.8	19.9
7.7	6.4	7.5	Intangibles (net)	11.3	5.9	4.9	3.7	7.1	14.6
5.9	6.8	7.9	All Other Non-Current	10.2	8.9	8.0	8.3	6.4	5.8
100.0	100.0	100.0	Total	100.0	100.0	100.0	100.0	100.0	100.0
			LIABILITIES						
12.1	12.6	11.6	Notes Payable-Short Term	10.4	14.3	13.2	8.6	12.8	10.4
3.6	2.3	3.2	Cur. Mat.-L.T.D.	3.2	5.0	3.5	3.0	2.4	2.2
15.0	14.2	13.3	Trade Payables	7.4	12.2	12.4	13.2	16.8	16.1
.2	.2	.1	Income Taxes Payable	.2	.1	.3	.1	.1	.0
12.5	13.1	13.6	All Other Current	15.7	15.4	10.7	13.1	12.2	14.4
43.3	42.3	41.8	Total Current	36.8	47.0	40.0	38.0	44.2	42.9
15.9	18.0	17.3	Long-Term Debt	10.5	20.3	18.8	16.3	12.8	23.1
.2	.0	.1	Deferred Taxes	.0	.0	.1	.0	.3	.2
8.3	5.1	7.9	All Other Non-Current	21.3	11.7	3.2	3.8	6.7	4.5
32.2	34.5	32.9	Net Worth	31.3	21.0	37.9	41.9	36.0	29.4
100.0	100.0	100.0	Total Liabilities & Net Worth	100.0	100.0	100.0	100.0	100.0	100.0
			INCOME DATA						
100.0	100.0	100.0	Net Sales	100.0	100.0	100.0	100.0	100.0	100.0
41.6	40.6	42.6	Gross Profit	48.8	44.9	40.5	44.3	41.7	35.6
36.1	35.3	38.2	Operating Expenses	43.4	41.7	36.2	39.6	37.9	30.1
5.4	5.3	4.4	Operating Profit	5.4	3.2	4.3	4.7	3.7	5.5
.6	.6	.5	All Other Expenses (net)	.0	.4	.4	.1	.6	1.6
4.9	4.6	3.9	Profit Before Taxes	5.4	2.7	3.9	4.6	3.1	3.9
			RATIOS						
3.1	4.0	3.2	Current	5.5	5.6	4.3	4.3	2.3	2.1
1.8	1.8	1.8		1.4	2.3	2.1	2.4	1.3	1.6
1.1	1.1	1.1		.6	.9	1.3	1.4	1.0	1.1
1.2	1.5	1.7	Quick	2.0	2.8	2.0	2.3	.8	1.0
.6	.6	.6		.5	.6	.8	.7	.5	.5
.2	.3	.2		.2	.2	.3	.3	.2	.3
0 UND	0 UND	0 UND	Sales/Receivables	0 UND	0 UND	0 999.8	0 UND	2 198.7	4 90.3
8 46.8	7 51.6	6 61.2		0 UND	2 208.3	11 34.7	5 69.3	15 24.6	17 20.9
27 13.7	25 14.6	29 12.8		5 77.1	15 24.3	44 8.3	29 12.5	38 9.5	44 8.3
38 9.5	34 10.7	34 10.7	Cost of Sales/Inventory	7 51.6	26 13.8	55 6.6	20 18.5	52 7.0	34 10.6
79 4.6	87 4.2	78 4.7		78 4.7	83 4.4	69 5.3	76 4.8	89 4.1	64 5.7
140 2.6	159 2.3	146 2.5		281 1.3	140 2.6	111 3.3	174 2.1	140 2.6	111 3.3
6 63.8	2 146.5	3 123.0	Cost of Sales/Payables	0 UND	0 UND	4 87.2	4 93.2	10 37.9	12 30.2
21 17.3	19 19.3	19 18.8		13 29.1	14 26.9	14 25.3	20 18.4	29 12.5	29 12.6
51 7.2	42 8.6	45 8.1		28 13.2	27 13.5	40 9.1	42 8.6	72 5.1	58 6.3
5.1	5.5	5.6	Sales/Working Capital	3.9	6.1	5.0	4.6	6.4	7.4
11.1	11.2	12.1		11.8	13.4	8.5	7.3	15.7	20.0
50.7	47.6	92.5		-28.6	-31.5	30.7	26.4	-170.1	51.7
22.5	18.4	18.5	EBIT/Interest	18.9	11.6	12.0	48.1	8.7	26.8
(247) 6.1	(244) 5.7	(217) 5.0		(18) 3.3	(41) 4.3	(30) 4.4	(44) 7.0	(42) 3.9	(42) 7.1
1.8	2.1	1.2		.0	-.7	1.6	2.6	.5	2.0
6.0	17.7	14.8	Net Profit + Depr., Dep., Amort./Cur. Mat. L/T/D						
(37) 3.6	(21) 4.7	(17) 5.1							
1.0	1.0	2.8							
.1	.1	.1	Fixed/Worth	.0	.1	.1	.1	.2	.2
.5	.4	.4		.4	.5	.4	.2	.4	.8
2.5	2.1	2.2		5.2	-21.0	1.6	.6	2.1	NM
.8	.5	.6	Debt/Worth	.3	.4	.4	.4	.9	1.3
2.0	1.9	1.7		2.4	2.0	1.3	.9	2.1	3.5
14.7	17.1	11.2		-5.7	-24.0	3.3	3.0	5.7	-7.0
65.0	61.8	55.8	% Profit Before Taxes/Tangible Net Worth	48.7	79.7	31.3	55.9	65.0	74.1
(234) 31.0	(253) 25.9	(216) 23.4		(23) 11.9	(39) 21.6	(28) 12.7	(55) 27.5	(39) 23.0	(32) 27.0
10.4	7.0	4.8		1.8	1.5	3.5	10.1	5.1	9.0
21.8	21.4	20.3	% Profit Before Taxes/Total Assets	20.5	22.9	16.4	29.3	16.3	16.0
9.2	9.0	7.6		5.9	7.1	6.5	10.6	5.5	9.2
2.9	2.5	.8		-2.5	-4.0	1.2	3.4	-.2	1.4
101.5	99.0	108.1	Sales/Net Fixed Assets	677.0	187.5	78.5	126.7	67.0	98.5
31.5	33.7	28.8		37.4	35.7	19.9	47.5	20.3	21.6
9.3	11.6	10.0		8.2	9.8	11.7	14.2	9.9	6.5
4.1	4.2	4.0	Sales/Total Assets	3.1	5.6	4.0	5.0	3.5	4.1
2.6	2.8	2.6		1.6	3.1	2.8	2.6	2.9	2.1
1.6	1.7	1.6		1.3	1.8	2.0	1.9	1.5	1.5
.5	.4	.4	% Depr., Dep., Amort./Sales	.2	.3	.3	.3	.6	.4
(187) 1.0	(189) .9	(161) 1.0		(13) 1.3	(29) .9	(21) 1.7	(38) .6	(33) 1.1	(27) .9
2.2	2.1	2.4		2.6	2.0	2.5	1.4	2.9	3.3
1.7	1.6	1.4	% Officers', Directors' Owners' Comp/Sales	3.8	3.3		1.4	1.1	
(129) 3.7	(137) 3.6	(108) 2.5		(12) 6.0	(25) 5.6	(18) 4.5	(26) 2.2	(22) 1.1	
7.2	6.3	6.7		12.0	7.4	6.9	2.9	1.8	
8881678M	6617499M	6589324M	Net Sales ($)	16812M	100676M	136459M	429530M	728130M	5177717M
4239136M	3099266M	3479589M	Total Assets ($)	9750M	38515M	57905M	177104M	440710M	2755605M

M = $ thousand   MM = $ million
See Pages viii through xx for Explanation of Ratios and Data

Current Data Sorted by Assets   Comparative Historical Data

0-500M	500M-2MM	2-10MM	10-50MM	50-100MM	100-250MM	Type of Statement	4/1/14-3/31/15 ALL	4/1/15-3/31/16 ALL
1		2	10	2	9	Unqualified	35	32
	1	12	7			Reviewed	26	28
	4	8	2	1		Compiled	27	17
12	18	14				Tax Returns	64	86
7	24	51	40	14	22	Other	153	178
30 (4/1-9/30/18)			231 (10/1/18-3/31/19)					
20	47	87	59	17	31	NUMBER OF STATEMENTS	305	341
%	%	%	%	%	%	**ASSETS**	%	%
31.0	15.2	15.8	13.6	25.4	11.9	Cash & Equivalents	17.6	21.1
5.8	9.1	8.7	6.5	6.8	9.5	Trade Receivables (net)	11.1	9.5
40.6	54.6	54.7	43.2	31.4	33.3	Inventory	44.3	43.4
1.9	1.8	3.3	8.7	6.2	3.9	All Other Current	3.6	2.8
79.3	80.7	82.5	72.0	69.7	58.6	Total Current	76.6	76.9
7.5	9.0	6.7	12.8	8.7	19.5	Fixed Assets (net)	10.7	9.8
4.7	2.3	5.4	11.4	15.9	12.7	Intangibles (net)	6.9	7.0
8.5	8.0	5.4	3.8	5.7	9.3	All Other Non-Current	5.7	6.4
100.0	100.0	100.0	100.0	100.0	100.0	Total	100.0	100.0
						LIABILITIES		
17.0	22.9	14.9	9.6	2.0	9.6	Notes Payable-Short Term	11.7	14.1
3.8	5.6	2.0	1.6	.9	3.2	Cur. Mat.-L.T.D.	1.8	2.0
8.0	19.6	24.3	22.1	19.5	16.3	Trade Payables	22.9	22.6
.2	.0	.1	.0	.0	.0	Income Taxes Payable	.2	.1
13.1	16.8	9.2	17.5	14.9	15.1	All Other Current	12.3	11.7
42.0	65.0	50.5	51.0	37.4	44.2	Total Current	48.9	50.5
12.0	9.8	5.6	7.1	13.8	19.2	Long-Term Debt	12.2	9.3
.0	.0	.0	.2	.1	.2	Deferred Taxes	.4	.3
.4	4.7	4.1	7.5	1.2	7.9	All Other Non-Current	6.5	7.6
45.6	20.5	39.8	34.2	47.5	28.5	Net Worth	32.0	32.3
100.0	100.0	100.0	100.0	100.0	100.0	Total Liabilties & Net Worth	100.0	100.0
						INCOME DATA		
100.0	100.0	100.0	100.0	100.0	100.0	Net Sales	100.0	100.0
36.6	41.4	33.3	40.7	46.4	44.0	Gross Profit	37.9	38.3
28.6	37.9	28.3	38.2	45.2	41.4	Operating Expenses	34.1	33.3
8.0	3.5	5.0	2.5	1.2	2.6	Operating Profit	3.8	5.0
.5	.5	.3	.7	1.2	1.6	All Other Expenses (net)	.6	.5
7.5	3.0	4.6	1.8	.0	1.0	Profit Before Taxes	3.2	4.5
						RATIOS		
8.6	3.1	3.0	2.2	3.9	1.9		3.2	2.8
1.9	2.0	1.7	1.4	1.5	1.4	Current	1.7	1.6
1.2	1.0	1.2	1.0	1.2	1.0		1.1	1.1
5.0	1.0	1.0	.9	2.6	1.0		1.2	1.2
.6	.4	.4	.4	.8	.6	Quick	(304) .5	.5
.2	.2	.2	.1	.1	.1		.2	.2
0 UND	0 UND	0 748.9	1 390.2	1 581.7	4 86.3		1 507.1	0 999.8
0 UND	2 193.6	5 71.0	4 102.0	3 144.0	10 37.6	Sales/Receivables	6 64.6	4 90.5
7 50.5	18 20.3	14 27.0	8 44.2	6 56.9	30 12.3		17 21.9	12 30.6
10 37.6	30 12.0	41 8.9	51 7.2	16 22.9	46 7.9		31 11.9	33 10.9
35 10.3	89 4.1	79 4.6	85 4.3	59 6.2	104 3.5	Cost of Sales/Inventory	68 5.4	68 5.4
96 3.8	182 2.0	118 3.1	130 2.8	166 2.2	174 2.1		122 3.0	126 2.9
0 UND	0 UND	18 20.6	22 16.7	26 14.2	40 9.2		13 28.1	11 31.8
0 UND	12 29.4	27 13.6	32 11.5	49 7.4	55 6.6	Cost of Sales/Payables	28 12.9	29 12.7
12 30.5	41 8.8	45 8.1	72 5.1	89 4.1	69 5.3		50 7.3	52 7.0
9.5	5.8	7.2	6.9	3.1	6.5		6.0	6.1
25.4	17.0	11.4	14.7	6.4	12.8	Sales/Working Capital	12.6	13.8
81.5	385.9	32.1	227.1	26.1	77.5		59.2	62.7
38.0	36.8	32.3	17.9		9.7		40.8	43.7
(13) 10.1	(34) 6.1	(73) 9.4	(50) 4.4		(27) 1.4	EBIT/Interest	(246) 10.0	(268) 11.2
3.0	1.2	2.6	.7		-.1		1.5	2.0
			10.1				15.5	19.6
			(16) 4.1			Net Profit + Depr., Dep., Amort./Cur. Mat. L/T/D	(37) 5.0	(33) 7.6
			1.3				1.1	1.7
.0	.0	.0	.1	.1	.4		.0	.0
.0	.0	.1	.4	.2	1.5	Fixed/Worth	.2	.2
.3	.4	.3	1.9	NM	3.4		1.2	1.3
.1	.6	.7	1.1	.3	1.2		.6	.7
1.4	1.9	2.1	3.1	1.4	3.8	Debt/Worth	1.8	2.1
19.6	13.1	3.8	6.5	NM	14.5		17.2	21.9
362.7	92.8	80.1	53.9	45.0	50.8	% Profit Before Taxes/Tangible Net Worth	73.9	89.2
(16) 99.3	(39) 49.8	(78) 34.5	(50) 20.7	(13) 13.5	(24) 8.3		(244) 34.7	(273) 44.0
24.9	9.2	12.0	3.1	-36.4	-23.3		9.0	17.0
80.1	32.6	30.7	16.9	10.5	7.7	% Profit Before Taxes/Total Assets	23.5	27.9
42.8	12.6	10.7	4.5	5.3	2.2		10.2	11.4
19.2	3.4	3.4	-.1	-10.6	-2.3		1.5	3.2
UND	999.8	636.8	117.4	117.9	29.4		221.9	435.1
762.1	277.8	204.0	40.3	28.4	10.0	Sales/Net Fixed Assets	59.9	77.5
52.7	62.1	58.8	13.8	12.1	7.7		23.3	27.9
14.4	6.9	4.9	4.1	3.3	2.6		5.4	5.5
6.7	4.3	3.7	3.0	1.8	2.0	Sales/Total Assets	3.5	3.5
3.6	2.8	2.7	1.8	1.3	1.4		2.3	2.4
		.1	.1	.3	.9		.3	.2
	(15) .2	(50) .2		(45) .8	(18) 1.1	% Depr., Dep., Amort./Sales	(192) .7	(202) .6
		.5	.6	1.3	1.3		1.2	1.3
1.5		1.1	.9				.7	1.1
(10) 2.0	(22) 2.1	(25) 1.4				% Officers', Directors' Owners' Comp/Sales	(82) 2.0	(114) 2.5
4.2	4.9	3.0					4.5	4.5
43209M	356587M	1871474M	4276247M	2711631M	11139068M	Net Sales ($)	17160175M	19814073M
5562M	58944M	448250M	1385010M	1196661M	5602424M	Total Assets ($)	7359496M	8186221M

© RMA 2019

M = $ thousand   MM = $ million
See Pages viii through xx for Explanation of Ratios and Data

Comparative Historical Data | Current Data Sorted by Sales

			Type of Statement						
33	30	24	Unqualified	1				1	22
10	19	20	Reviewed			1	1	4	14
18	21	14	Compiled		1		4	2	7
54	58	45	Tax Returns	3	10	7	9	9	7
155	159	158	Other	1	13	6	21	36	81
4/1/16- 3/31/17 ALL	4/1/17- 3/31/18 ALL	4/1/18- 3/31/19 ALL			30 (4/1-9/30/18)			231 (10/1/18-3/31/19)	
				0-1MM	1-3MM	3-5MM	5-10MM	10-25MM	25MM & OVER
270	287	261	**NUMBER OF STATEMENTS**	5	24	14	35	52	131
%	%	%	**ASSETS**	%	%	%	%	%	%
16.6	18.7	16.5	Cash & Equivalents		22.9	8.8	22.8	13.1	15.9
9.0	8.1	8.0	Trade Receivables (net)		8.7	7.7	9.4	8.9	7.5
43.2	44.3	46.9	Inventory		45.2	53.1	47.7	51.6	44.4
4.1	3.7	4.4	All Other Current		1.9	2.3	2.4	4.1	5.8
72.9	74.7	75.9	Total Current		78.7	71.9	82.4	77.6	73.7
11.3	10.4	10.2	Fixed Assets (net)		11.7	10.6	5.6	7.6	12.0
10.0	9.2	7.7	Intangibles (net)		4.4	7.3	6.4	7.5	8.9
5.8	5.6	6.2	All Other Non-Current		5.2	10.3	5.6	7.2	5.4
100.0	100.0	100.0	Total		100.0	100.0	100.0	100.0	100.0
			LIABILITIES						
15.5	14.6	13.8	Notes Payable-Short Term		21.5	9.4	23.1	13.3	10.1
3.3	2.4	2.8	Cur. Mat.-L.T.D.		3.7	19.5	1.2	1.6	1.0
20.3	20.9	20.5	Trade Payables		15.3	15.8	15.2	22.1	23.3
.1	.1	.1	Income Taxes Payable		.0	.3	.0	.1	.1
13.2	12.7	13.8	All Other Current		13.8	21.8	10.6	11.8	14.9
52.3	50.7	51.0	Total Current		54.2	66.8	50.1	48.8	50.2
12.8	11.7	9.3	Long-Term Debt		13.6	12.2	5.8	6.1	10.2
.3	.1	.1	Deferred Taxes		.0	.0	.0	.1	.1
5.5	5.5	5.0	All Other Non-Current		4.2	7.3	1.7	4.2	6.2
29.1	31.9	34.7	Net Worth		27.9	13.7	42.4	40.9	33.2
100.0	100.0	100.0	Total Liabilties & Net Worth		100.0	100.0	100.0	100.0	100.0
			INCOME DATA						
100.0	100.0	100.0	Net Sales		100.0	100.0	100.0	100.0	100.0
38.9	38.4	38.8	Gross Profit		43.3	42.1	41.6	34.1	38.4
34.3	34.1	34.9	Operating Expenses		37.1	36.1	36.3	30.3	35.7
4.6	4.3	3.9	Operating Profit		6.2	5.9	5.3	3.7	2.7
1.1	.5	.7	All Other Expenses (net)		.7	.7	.2	.4	.9
3.5	3.8	3.2	Profit Before Taxes		5.5	5.2	5.1	3.3	1.8
			RATIOS						
2.6	2.9	2.9			3.2	2.6	4.6	2.5	2.5
1.5	1.5	1.5	Current		2.0	1.6	2.3	1.5	1.4
1.1	1.1	1.1			1.0	.8	1.4	1.1	1.1
1.0	1.1	1.1			1.7	.5	2.0	.8	1.0
.5	.5	.5	Quick		.6	.3	1.0	.4	.4
.2	.2	.2			.2	.1	.2	.1	.1

0	999.8	0	999.8	0	905.9		0	UND	0	UND	0	UND	0	999.8	1	292.5
4	94.2	4	102.8	4	86.3	Sales/Receivables	2	148.4	4	83.1	6	61.9	5	74.0	4	87.6
14	25.9	10	36.7	14	25.6		24	15.0	23	16.1	16	22.2	15	24.8	13	27.2
30	12.3	31	11.6	37	9.8		27	13.7	18	19.9	26	14.2	34	10.7	45	8.1
73	6.0	61	6.0	79	4.6	Cost of Sales/Inventory	96	3.8	79	4.6	76	4.8	85	4.3	72	5.1
122	3.0	114	3.2	135	2.7		192	1.9	228	1.6	122	3.0	122	3.0	130	2.8
9	41.2	9	42.7	13	29.1		0	UND	0	UND	3	145.2	13	28.6	23	16.2
30	12.2	26	13.9	29	12.4	Cost of Sales/Payables	4	85.6	17	21.9	24	15.3	28	13.2	37	9.9
54	6.7	52	7.0	58	6.3		79	4.6	32	11.4	36	10.2	60	6.1	66	5.5

6.7	8.4	6.4		5.1	4.9	6.5	7.3	7.5
14.0	14.7	13.8	Sales/Working Capital	16.9	21.1	9.2	14.2	14.4
85.0	83.6	66.3		474.7	-189.4	24.0	108.4	68.8

	36.2		27.2		19.7			32.2		9.5	42.7	40.9	12.7
(220)	8.1	(224)	8.2	(206)	6.0	EBIT/Interest	(16)	4.0	(11)	5.5	(23) 6.1	(48) 13.5	(105) 4.4
	1.3		2.6		1.1			.8		2.2	2.0	2.8	.4

	23.4		39.6		11.3	Net Profit + Depr., Dep.,				11.3
(34)	6.0	(31)	2.7	(30)	5.3	Amort./Cur. Mat. L/T/D			(26)	4.8
	1.4		1.2		1.5					1.0

.0	.0	.0		.0	.0	.0	.0	.1
.3	.2	.2	Fixed/Worth	1	.1	.0	.1	.0
2.0	1.3	1.3		4.7	NM	.2	.5	2.1
.9	.8	.7		.7	.5	.3	.9	1.0
2.4	2.3	2.4	Debt/Worth	2.7	3.7	1.0	2.5	2.6
45.3	13.9	8.0		48.2	NM	3.1	5.5	7.9

	90.5		89.0		67.7	% Profit Before Taxes/Tangible		179.6		120.5	78.2	80.4	56.0
(207)	44.1	(233)	41.5	(220)	28.8	Net Worth	(19)	32.8	(11) 63.2	(30) 35.8	(47) 38.4	(109) 17.6
	12.8		15.1		6.7			18.4		12.1	10.5	12.2	.3
	27.3		27.9		25.9	% Profit Before Taxes/Total		48.8		45.1	34.1	33.2	15.7
	10.6		11.0		7.6	Assets		13.5		16.6	13.3	16.8	4.9
	1.4		3.2		.4			2.2		-1.3	3.4	.9	-1.6
	399.3		556.8		535.8			UND		UND	999.8	997.1	173.8
	69.0		92.1		88.4	Sales/Net Fixed Assets		160.8		205.9	303.1	135.6	42.4
	18.9		24.0		19.3			25.3		26.1	83.7	30.8	12.6
	5.1		5.9		4.9			6.4		6.4	6.2	4.6	4.5
	3.5		3.6		3.2	Sales/Total Assets		3.6		3.2	3.4	3.4	3.1
	2.2		2.4		2.0			1.6		2.3	1.9	2.5	2.0

	.2		.2		.1					.1	.1	.1
(158)	.6	(167)	.6	(142)	.5	% Depr., Dep., Amort./Sales			(11) .2	(28) .4	(86) .7
	1.5		1.2		1.0					.6	1.2	1.1
	1.3		1.0		1.0	% Officers', Directors'				1.5	.9	.5
(75)	2.6	(81)	2.1	(63)	1.7	Owners' Comp/Sales			(16) 2.7	(12) 1.1	(18) .9
	4.7		4.8		3.5					3.9	1.9	2.0

19926616M	22416188M	20398216M	Net Sales ($)	3422M	42602M	54269M	258145M	866894M	19172884M
8580036M	8169167M	8696851M	Total Assets ($)	2452M	18120M	18995M	97421M	415885M	8143978M

Current Data Sorted by Assets							Comparative Historical Data	
			2	1		**Type of Statement** Unqualified	4	5
		3	2			Reviewed	6	10
	2	2				Compiled	6	8
	2	6				Tax Returns	14	29
5	5	7	2	1		Other	31	34
	7 (4/1-9/30/18)		33 (10/1/18-3/31/19)				4/1/14-3/31/15	4/1/15-3/31/16
0-500M	**500M-2MM**	**2-10MM**	**10-50MM**	**50-100MM**	**100-250MM**		**ALL**	**ALL**
5	9	18	6	2		**NUMBER OF STATEMENTS**	61	86
%	%	%	%	%	%	**ASSETS**	%	%
		20.9			DATA NOT AVAILABLE	Cash & Equivalents	17.8	17.0
		8.0				Trade Receivables (net)	5.7	5.9
		14.5				Inventory	15.6	13.8
		3.9				All Other Current	1.2	2.3
		47.2				Total Current	40.3	38.9
		35.4				Fixed Assets (net)	40.7	42.7
		8.1				Intangibles (net)	9.4	9.5
		9.2				All Other Non-Current	9.6	8.9
		100.0				Total	100.0	100.0
						LIABILITIES		
		9.1				Notes Payable-Short Term	11.4	8.8
		4.0				Cur. Mat.-L.T.D.	7.9	7.3
		17.8				Trade Payables	12.6	10.7
		.1				Income Taxes Payable	.0	.1
		8.4				All Other Current	12.4	11.9
		39.4				Total Current	44.3	38.7
		20.9				Long-Term Debt	31.1	35.3
		.2				Deferred Taxes	.4	.5
		5.1				All Other Non-Current	8.2	13.7
		34.3				Net Worth	15.9	11.9
		100.0				Total Liabilties & Net Worth	100.0	100.0
						INCOME DATA		
		100.0				Net Sales	100.0	100.0
		43.2				Gross Profit	49.9	44.0
		40.7				Operating Expenses	46.7	39.2
		2.5				Operating Profit	3.3	4.8
		-.8				All Other Expenses (net)	1.5	.7
		3.3				Profit Before Taxes	1.8	4.1
						RATIOS		
		2.7					1.8	2.0
		1.4				Current	1.1	1.2
		.6					.6	.7
		1.6					1.1	1.1
		.8				Quick	.5	.6
		.3					.2	.3
		3 119.0					**0** 965.4	**0** UND
		5 68.1				Sales/Receivables	**5** 72.7	**5** 76.9
		10 37.4					**9** 41.9	**12** 31.1
		19 19.1					**12** 29.5	**10** 36.1
		28 13.1				Cost of Sales/Inventory	**37** 9.9	**28** 13.1
		46 8.0					**63** 5.8	**42** 8.7
		17 21.1					**8** 43.2	**4** 96.2
		31 11.7				Cost of Sales/Payables	**22** 16.3	**19** 19.3
		46 8.0					**45** 8.1	**36** 10.1
		6.3					15.0	15.0
		31.8				Sales/Working Capital	96.9	47.8
		-18.3					-33.5	-35.6
		21.8					6.5	8.6
		(16) 6.4				EBIT/Interest	(56) 2.4	(81) 3.9
		1.3					.8	1.1
							5.9	4.3
						Net Profit + Depr., Dep., Amort./Cur. Mat. L/T/D	(11) 2.7	(14) 2.6
							1.9	1.6
		.5					.7	1.1
		1.1				Fixed/Worth	2.9	5.2
		-5.3					-7.6	-1.3
		.5					1.5	1.2
		2.0				Debt/Worth	10.2	14.1
		-12.7					-16.6	-3.9
		72.9					43.2	92.5
		(12) 14.3				% Profit Before Taxes/Tangible Net Worth	(39) 20.7	(51) 34.8
		6.8					2.6	7.2
		21.3					11.9	17.3
		5.5				% Profit Before Taxes/Total Assets	4.5	7.0
		2.5					-1.1	.8
		33.5					15.2	16.3
		10.0				Sales/Net Fixed Assets	6.8	6.7
		4.1					3.7	4.2
		3.9					4.0	4.0
		3.1				Sales/Total Assets	2.5	2.7
		2.1					1.4	2.0
		2.0					2.8	2.7
		(14) 3.3				% Depr., Dep., Amort./Sales	(44) 4.9	(68) 4.7
		5.3					8.0	6.2
							1.7	.6
						% Officers', Directors' Owners' Comp/Sales	(24) 3.3	(36) 1.8
							9.6	4.2
6949M	**44562M**	**298765M**	**231300M**	**190306M**		Net Sales ($)	**1188047M**	**1885764M**
1801M	**10013M**	**90508M**	**147126M**	**160639M**		Total Assets ($)	**533094M**	**896260M**

M = $ thousand   MM = $ million

See Pages viii through xx for Explanation of Ratios and Data

Comparative Historical Data | Current Data Sorted by Sales

Type of Statement

			Type of Statement	0-1MM	1-3MM	3-5MM	5-10MM	10-25MM	25MM & OVER
3	2	3	Unqualified					1	2
7	5	5	Reviewed				1	2	2
5	6	4	Compiled		1	1	3	3	2
18	11	8	Tax Returns		1	1		5	1
31	29	20	Other	2	5	5	5		3
4/1/16-3/31/17 ALL	4/1/17-3/31/18 ALL	4/1/18-3/31/19 ALL			7 (4/1-9/30/18)			33 (10/1/18-3/31/19)	25MM & OVER
64	53	40	NUMBER OF STATEMENTS	2	7	6	4	11	10

Assets / Liabilities / Income Data

Hist 16-17	Hist 17-18	Hist 18-19		0-1MM	1-3MM	3-5MM	5-10MM	10-25MM	25MM & OVER
%	%	%	**ASSETS**	%	%	%	%	%	%
15.3	15.3	20.0	Cash & Equivalents					9.4	13.6
6.5	8.2	7.0	Trade Receivables (net)					10.1	10.8
17.0	14.6	14.6	Inventory					19.7	13.9
2.2	1.9	2.7	All Other Current					4.6	1.7
41.0	40.0	44.2	Total Current					43.8	39.9
42.9	41.9	35.5	Fixed Assets (net)					36.5	30.0
8.0	13.0	10.9	Intangibles (net)					8.2	16.5
8.1	5.2	9.4	All Other Non-Current					11.5	13.6
100.0	100.0	100.0	Total					100.0	100.0
			LIABILITIES						
6.6	5.0	8.4	Notes Payable-Short Term					11.0	4.5
6.2	5.5	4.3	Cur. Mat.-L.T.D.					4.5	4.2
10.9	13.9	13.6	Trade Payables					18.9	15.1
.1	.1	.1	Income Taxes Payable					.0	.2
8.8	9.1	11.0	All Other Current					5.2	6.8
32.6	33.6	37.3	Total Current					39.6	30.7
37.9	28.3	25.6	Long-Term Debt					23.2	19.7
.2	.1	.2	Deferred Taxes					.0	.6
6.8	7.6	7.7	All Other Non-Current					10.3	2.1
22.7	30.3	29.2	Net Worth					26.8	46.8
100.0	100.0	100.0	Total Liabilities & Net Worth					100.0	100.0
			INCOME DATA						
100.0	100.0	100.0	Net Sales					100.0	100.0
50.1	44.5	42.5	Gross Profit					35.3	35.0
43.1	38.7	39.0	Operating Expenses					34.4	30.7
7.0	5.8	3.5	Operating Profit					.9	4.2
1.1	.2	-.4	All Other Expenses (net)					.5	-.2
6.0	5.6	3.9	Profit Before Taxes					.4	4.4

Ratios

Hist 16-17	Hist 17-18	Hist 18-19		0-1MM	1-3MM	3-5MM	5-10MM	10-25MM	25MM & OVER
			RATIOS						
2.6	1.8	2.5	Current					2.0	2.8
1.2	1.4	1.3						1.3	1.1
.7	.7	.6						.5	.6
1.3	1.1	1.6	Quick					.9	1.5
.5	.7	.6						.4	.7
.3	.2	.3						.1	.4
0 UND	0 UND	1 243.4	Sales/Receivables					5 75.2	5 73.2
4 85.3	5 74.3	5 73.7						6 58.7	12 31.3
11 32.1	9 40.2	11 34.0						9 38.8	25 14.6
17 21.0	18 20.0	17 21.3	Cost of Sales/Inventory					19 18.9	20 18.7
33 10.9	29 12.6	28 13.1						23 16.2	30 12.2
47 7.8	40 9.2	45 8.2						34 10.8	54 6.8
1 288.1	2 187.5	7 49.7	Cost of Sales/Payables					7 49.8	19 18.9
22 16.3	28 12.9	28 13.1						32 11.4	30 12.0
38 9.7	42 8.6	36 10.2						36 10.2	49 7.5
14.9	16.2	11.4	Sales/Working Capital					19.6	9.7
68.5	38.1	49.5						55.9	NM
-23.0	-27.3	-15.8						-8.6	-15.7
13.9	10.7	18.2	EBIT/Interest					16.2	124.6
(59) 4.0	(45) 4.5	(34) 3.6						(10) 1.8	43.8
1.3	1.7	1.0						.9	2.1
			Net Profit + Depr., Dep., Amort./Cur. Mat. L/T/D						
.8	.7	.3	Fixed/Worth					1.1	.3
1.9	2.3	1.3						14.5	.7
83.2	-18.4	-2.7						-6.4	NM
.8	.7	.6	Debt/Worth					.6	.4
3.2	4.1	4.4						23.5	2.0
180.4	-50.2	-7.7						-14.4	NM
82.2	61.5	76.2	% Profit Before Taxes/Tangible Net Worth						
(50) 27.0	(38) 27.9	(24) 27.0							
4.9	6.7	10.3							
16.6	22.3	19.3	% Profit Before Taxes/Total Assets					11.4	21.3
9.2	10.9	7.3						3.7	7.8
.8	3.0	1.5						.0	2.9
14.7	14.8	24.5	Sales/Net Fixed Assets					76.3	31.6
6.3	6.3	10.0						10.0	10.7
3.9	3.6	4.6						4.5	4.7
3.7	4.1	4.3	Sales/Total Assets					6.0	3.6
2.7	2.7	2.9						3.8	2.7
1.6	1.6	1.7						2.2	1.2
2.9	2.3	2.6	% Depr., Dep., Amort./Sales						
(44) 4.3	(35) 4.1	(28) 3.5							
7.7	6.3	5.9							
1.7	1.7	1.5	% Officers', Directors' Owners' Comp/Sales						
(28) 3.6	(17) 2.3	(14) 3.6							
8.3	8.5	7.2							
1110171M	796399M	771882M	Net Sales ($)	1042M	13820M	24248M	29195M	194523M	509054M
524494M	270203M	410087M	Total Assets ($)	613M	5811M	11418M	8348M	92314M	291583M

M = $ thousand MM = $ million
See Pages viii through xx for Explanation of Ratios and Data

Current Data Sorted by Assets   Comparative Historical Data

0-500M	500M-2MM	2-10MM	10-50MM	50-100MM	100-250MM	Type of Statement	4/1/14-3/31/15 ALL	4/1/15-3/31/16 ALL
	1	2	9	4	4	Unqualified	20	21
2	6	24	26			Reviewed	64	54
2	9	16	3		1	Compiled	36	33
6	22	16				Tax Returns	67	65
3	14	25	20	7	7	Other	78	84
	92 (4/1-9/30/18)		137 (10/1/18-3/31/19)					
13	52	83	58	11	12	NUMBER OF STATEMENTS	265	257

0-500M	500M-2MM	2-10MM	10-50MM	50-100MM	100-250MM		4/1/14-3/31/15 ALL	4/1/15-3/31/16 ALL
%	%	%	%	%	%	**ASSETS**	%	%
32.9	16.6	17.4	8.2	6.7	2.6	Cash & Equivalents	16.3	18.6
16.5	29.6	23.3	20.8	21.1	20.1	Trade Receivables (net)	28.4	20.6
16.4	13.0	12.0	9.4	16.6	7.6	Inventory	10.6	11.0
6.2	.9	2.3	1.8	4.2	2.9	All Other Current	2.7	2.7
72.2	60.2	54.9	40.2	48.6	33.1	Total Current	57.9	52.9
18.5	25.4	30.5	38.9	36.1	39.4	Fixed Assets (net)	27.4	30.7
4.0	5.0	6.6	9.7	8.4	20.2	Intangibles (net)	7.4	8.7
5.2	9.4	8.0	11.2	7.0	7.3	All Other Non-Current	7.3	7.7
100.0	100.0	100.0	100.0	100.0	100.0	Total	100.0	100.0
						LIABILITIES		
19.2	13.1	5.4	10.5	9.8	4.8	Notes Payable-Short Term	8.7	8.8
3.8	5.1	3.2	4.0	3.0	2.5	Cur. Mat.-L.T.D.	3.4	3.0
12.8	13.0	14.6	11.5	12.9	10.4	Trade Payables	16.5	12.0
.0	.7	.1	.4	.1	.6	Income Taxes Payable	.1	.3
29.2	12.1	13.4	12.0	12.8	7.6	All Other Current	14.2	16.3
65.0	43.9	36.8	38.3	38.6	25.9	Total Current	42.8	40.5
60.7	25.2	15.1	14.8	25.5	24.1	Long-Term Debt	14.3	19.2
.0	.0	.5	1.4	1.6	1.3	Deferred Taxes	.6	.8
7.9	10.2	3.5	6.2	4.5	4.3	All Other Non-Current	6.0	6.0
-33.6	20.6	44.0	39.4	29.7	44.4	Net Worth	36.2	33.4
100.0	100.0	100.0	100.0	100.0	100.0	Total Liabilities & Net Worth	100.0	100.0
						INCOME DATA		
100.0	100.0	100.0	100.0	100.0	100.0	Net Sales	100.0	100.0
27.8	27.8	27.3	23.2	17.2	28.5	Gross Profit	17.8	26.3
23.5	23.9	23.6	20.5	14.9	23.9	Operating Expenses	15.3	22.0
4.4	3.9	3.7	2.7	2.3	4.7	Operating Profit	2.5	4.3
-1.1	-.2	-.1	-.1	.5	.4	All Other Expenses (net)	-.1	.4
5.5	4.2	3.8	2.8	1.8	4.3	Profit Before Taxes	2.6	3.9
						RATIOS		
5.0	2.5	2.7	1.6	1.8	1.6		2.3	2.4
1.0	1.3	1.5	1.1	1.2	1.3	Current	1.4	1.4
.5	.9	1.0	.7	.9	.9		.9	.8
4.1	1.8	2.0	1.2	1.1	1.1		1.8	1.8
.6	1.1	1.1	.7	.6	.7	Quick	1.1	1.0
.3	.7	.7	.5	.5	.6		.6	.9
0 UND	13 27.8	12 31.0	16 23.0	12 31.3	28 13.2		11 33.0	9 38.5
7 53.8	19 19.7	21 17.5	25 14.8	20 18.4	40 9.1	Sales/Receivables	18 20.1	17 21.7
15 25.1	29 12.5	31 11.6	31 11.6	38 9.7	48 7.6		27 13.3	27 13.4
2 152.3	4 86.6	5 74.2	7 52.8	7 52.1	9 42.7		2 147.7	4 99.6
16 22.7	11 31.8	11 33.0	15 24.9	15 25.0	23 15.7	Cost of Sales/Inventory	7 51.7	11 33.7
38 9.5	25 14.8	25 14.6	29 12.7	35 10.4	42 8.6		15 23.7	24 14.9
0 UND	6 60.0	9 38.8	9 38.6	6 63.8	12 29.9		6 62.4	6 59.0
8 48.6	10 35.8	14 25.4	16 23.4	14 25.7	18 19.8	Cost of Sales/Payables	10 35.5	11 34.5
14 25.3	19 19.2	24 15.4	27 13.5	20 18.5	46 7.9		16 22.5	18 19.8
6.9	14.3	9.6	18.3	20.0	8.5		13.4	9.7
200.1	45.5	29.2	157.4	52.7	22.7	Sales/Working Capital	36.1	34.0
-18.6	-85.0	-493.4	-20.5	-105.7	-171.3		-243.8	-65.9
	22.2	20.1	11.6	4.9	13.2		17.8	21.8
	(50) 5.1	(73) 8.5	(55) 5.3	2.5	5.2	EBIT/Interest	(240) 6.2	(227) 7.0
	1.5	4.0	2.7	1.5	2.8		2.2	2.2
		5.0	6.6				6.3	8.3
		(16) 2.7	(17) 3.3			Net Profit + Depr., Dep., Amort./Cur. Mat. L/T/D	(65) 3.1	(65) 3.6
		2.1	1.7				1.5	1.7
.0	.4	.3	.6	.9	.7		.3	.3
UND	1.5	.9	1.2	1.6	2.0	Fixed/Worth	.8	1.0
-.4	7.9	2.9	3.0	12.3	22.2		3.0	3.6
.6	2.3	.5	.7	2.3	1.1		.7	.8
-20.9	5.4	1.4	2.0	3.0	2.8	Debt/Worth	1.8	2.1
-2.3	22.6	5.4	10.9	66.0	28.2		8.6	9.6
	152.2	45.9	27.8		54.3		45.1	53.1
	(43) 46.7	(70) 18.2	(47) 16.9		(10) 21.8	% Profit Before Taxes/Tangible Net Worth	(221) 23.0	(207) 25.4
	3.3	9.8	7.1		10.9		7.2	10.3
27.3	25.3	17.2	10.5	7.2	11.8		15.6	17.7
11.7	11.3	9.0	6.1	3.0	6.2	% Profit Before Taxes/Total Assets	7.4	9.0
-30.0	.7	4.6	3.2	1.4	4.3		2.2	3.0
UND	67.1	38.9	16.1	27.3	12.3		65.8	50.1
40.0	18.6	16.5	8.4	10.7	2.7	Sales/Net Fixed Assets	23.8	16.1
27.7	9.5	6.6	5.1	3.7	2.1		11.2	6.2
10.7	7.0	5.3	4.3	7.3	3.1		7.6	6.0
6.4	4.5	3.8	2.6	2.7	1.2	Sales/Total Assets	5.2	3.9
2.7	3.2	2.5	1.8	2.0	.8		3.1	2.2
	.6	1.1	1.1	.9			.5	.7
	(33) 1.9	(68) 2.2	(54) 2.0	(10) 1.8		% Depr., Dep., Amort./Sales	(236) 1.0	(211) 1.6
	3.0	3.7	3.6	2.6			2.0	3.1
	1.7	.8	.5				.6	.9
	(30) 2.7	(48) 1.9	(21) .8			% Officers', Directors', Owners' Comp/Sales	(131) 1.4	(115) 2.0
	4.7	3.8	2.4				3.3	4.1
19718M	295215M	1941526M	4143147M	3025199M	5690285M	Net Sales ($)	20932186M	15276748M
3612M	54745M	393084M	1177399M	787547M	1908100M	Total Assets ($)	4367390M	4673737M

Comparative Historical Data | Current Data Sorted by Sales

4/1/16-3/31/17 ALL	4/1/17-3/31/18 ALL	4/1/18-3/31/19 ALL	Type of Statement	0-1MM	1-3MM	3-5MM	5-10MM	10-25MM	25MM & OVER
23	19	20	Unqualified			2	1	1	16
57	56	58	Reviewed	1		2	11	15	29
40	34	31	Compiled	1	4	4	7	5	10
52	54	44	Tax Returns	2	8	7	10	13	4
83	90	76	Other	2	7	5	8	8	36
4/1/16-3/31/17 ALL	4/1/17-3/31/18 ALL	4/1/18-3/31/19 ALL			92 (4/1-9/30/18)		137 (10/1/18-3/31/19)		
255	253	229	NUMBER OF STATEMENTS	6	19	20	37	52	95
%	%	%	ASSETS	%	%	%	%	%	%
14.7	13.2	14.5	Cash & Equivalents		21.2	17.3	12.8	15.6	10.7
22.4	24.3	23.4	Trade Receivables (net)		23.9	20.4	26.1	24.7	23.3
10.7	11.4	11.8	Inventory		14.8	10.5	12.9	11.6	10.8
2.8	2.5	2.2	All Other Current		.9	3.1	1.7	1.9	2.4
50.6	51.4	51.9	Total Current		60.8	51.4	53.5	53.8	47.3
34.2	33.1	31.5	Fixed Assets (net)		26.0	32.6	31.2	31.4	33.7
7.2	7.2	7.7	Intangibles (net)		3.9	4.2	5.3	6.1	10.9
8.0	8.4	8.9	All Other Non-Current		9.3	11.8	10.0	8.8	8.1
100.0	100.0	100.0	Total		100.0	100.0	100.0	100.0	100.0
			LIABILITIES						
9.2	9.9	9.4	Notes Payable-Short Term		17.5	13.2	10.9	7.0	7.7
4.6	3.9	3.8	Cur. Mat.-L.T.D.		5.1	8.2	3.9	3.1	3.2
12.5	14.3	13.1	Trade Payables		9.1	12.3	13.5	13.4	14.0
.3	.1	.3	Income Taxes Payable		.0	.0	.8	.3	.3
14.2	14.9	13.3	All Other Current		16.8	13.8	14.9	14.1	11.6
40.7	43.2	39.9	Total Current		48.5	47.4	44.1	38.0	36.8
20.4	19.9	20.9	Long-Term Debt		57.7	26.7	20.9	16.9	15.0
.8	.8	.7	Deferred Taxes		.0	.1	.1	1.1	1.0
7.9	6.4	6.1	All Other Non-Current		10.8	6.6	9.1	3.9	5.3
30.3	29.7	32.5	Net Worth		-16.9	19.1	25.8	40.0	41.9
100.0	100.0	100.0	Total Liabilities & Net Worth		100.0	100.0	100.0	100.0	100.0
			INCOME DATA						
100.0	100.0	100.0	Net Sales		100.0	100.0	100.0	100.0	100.0
30.0	26.1	26.0	Gross Profit		36.0	34.2	31.0	26.0	20.3
26.3	23.9	22.5	Operating Expenses		31.6	29.4	27.1	22.2	17.8
3.7	2.2	3.5	Operating Profit		4.4	4.8	3.8	3.9	2.4
.5	.2	-.1	All Other Expenses (net)		-.7	-1.2	.6	-.2	.0
3.2	2.0	3.7	Profit Before Taxes		5.1	6.0	3.2	4.1	2.5
			RATIOS						
2.1	2.1	2.1	Current		3.9	2.0	2.0	2.7	1.8
1.4	1.2	1.3			1.4	1.2	1.2	1.5	1.2
.8	.8	.9			.9	.6	.7	1.0	.9
1.6	1.7	1.6	Quick		3.7	1.8	1.4	1.9	1.3
.9 (252)	.8	.9			1.1	.9	.8	1.0	.8
.5	.5	.5			.6	.5	.5	.7	.5
14 / 26.1	13 / 27.4	12 / 29.3	Sales/Receivables		12 / 30.7	15 / 24.2	15 / 23.6	14 / 26.6	13 / 28.2
24 / 15.5	24 / 15.5	21 / 17.1			24 / 15.2	20 / 18.1	22 / 16.5	22 / 16.8	23 / 16.1
36 / 10.2	35 / 10.4	31 / 11.6			41 / 8.8	28 / 13.0	30 / 12.0	31 / 11.7	32 / 11.4
6 / 60.2	4 / 88.3	5 / 69.5	Cost of Sales/Inventory		7 / 52.9	6 / 58.6	5 / 70.1	5 / 75.1	4 / 81.3
14 / 25.2	13 / 28.3	13 / 28.0			25 / 14.7	9 / 40.4	15 / 24.2	13 / 28.0	11 / 33.0
31 / 11.7	30 / 12.1	27 / 13.5			43 / 8.5	20 / 17.9	29 / 12.6	26 / 14.0	24 / 15.0
10 / 36.3	9 / 41.1	8 / 44.8	Cost of Sales/Payables		5 / 75.6	7 / 49.6	11 / 32.6	9 / 39.0	8 / 44.2
18 / 20.4	16 / 23.4	14 / 26.0			10 / 36.0	10 / 35.8	18 / 20.0	14 / 25.9	13 / 27.5
29 / 12.5	29 / 12.6	22 / 16.5			26 / 13.9	35 / 10.5	25 / 14.7	26 / 14.0	20 / 18.0
10.1	10.6	11.5	Sales/Working Capital		9.1	12.3	13.5	10.5	16.5
33.0	40.1	37.8			22.7	92.6	76.4	30.3	48.7
-30.8	-50.5	-83.4			-50.8	-20.3	-25.3	-487.5	-113.2
16.5	13.8	14.7	EBIT/Interest		10.7	37.4	13.2	13.7	17.5
(231) 4.0	(235) 4.5	(209) 5.6			3.8	(36) 6.4	(43) 5.9	(90) 5.5	5.7
1.5	1.2	2.6			1.0	1.8	1.4	3.5	2.6
6.7	7.1	4.6	Net Profit + Depr., Dep., Amort./Cur. Mat. L/T/D						7.4
(59) 2.3	(46) 2.7	(45) 2.5						(27)	2.5
1.3	1.3	1.7							1.8
.5	.4	.5	Fixed/Worth		.7	.4	.6	.3	.6
1.2	1.2	1.2			3.3	1.4	1.5	.9	1.2
0.3	12.7	6.3			-.6	4.4	27.0	9.9	3.0
.7	.8	.8	Debt/Worth		2.7	1.0	1.1	.5	.7
2.4	2.4	2.7			13.1	3.4	5.4	1.6	2.4
37.6	38.2	20.4			-2.7	46.7	234.0	12.6	8.1
37.3	34.1	55.9	% Profit Before Taxes/Tangible Net Worth		136.2	297.4	88.9	65.4	33.4
(200) 17.3	(196) 15.3	(185) 21.2			(12) 47.1	(16) 44.5	(29) 21.2	(43) 17.8	(80) 18.2
5.6	5.4	8.9			28.0	4.4	6.8	11.2	8.7
11.3	11.2	16.1	% Profit Before Taxes/Total Assets		24.6	30.3	19.9	15.3	10.9
4.7	4.9	7.4			10.4	10.9	7.8	8.3	6.3
1.2	.5	2.7			.0	1.6	.8	3.7	3.0
23.9	26.6	39.3	Sales/Net Fixed Assets		30.0	21.0	43.4	49.6	31.9
9.2	12.1	13.8			10.3	13.4	12.6	14.4	11.8
4.4	5.0	5.8			7.7	5.5	5.7	5.9	5.6
4.3	5.1	5.8	Sales/Total Assets		4.6	5.5	4.9	5.6	6.4
3.0	3.2	3.7			3.1	3.9	3.8	3.5	3.8
1.7	2.0	2.2			2.2	1.8	2.6	2.2	2.2
1.0	.9	1.0	% Depr., Dep., Amort./Sales				1.9	1.4	.9	.9
(223) 2.3	(219) 2.2	(176) 2.0					(16) 2.8	(31) 2.3	(42) 2.0	(78) 1.8
4.6	4.0	3.4					5.5	4.0	3.6	2.7
1.1	1.0	.8	% Officers', Directors' Owners' Comp/Sales		2.6	2.4	1.8	1.1	.5
(112) 2.4	(114) 2.0	(109) 2.1			(11) 4.2	(11) 4.0	(22) 2.4	(28) 2.2	(35) .8
4.8	4.6	4.6			6.9	6.7	4.5	3.7	1.8
14945752M	16391685M	15115090M	Net Sales ($)	2609M	38881M	79089M	268062M	850340M	13876109M
5099279M	4641199M	4324487M	Total Assets ($)	1357M	11966M	30860M	86221M	339153M	3854930M

M = $ thousand   MM = $ million
See Pages viii through xx for Explanation of Ratios and Data

Current Data Sorted by Assets   **Comparative Historical Data**

						Type of Statement		
1		5	3	3	3	Unqualified	19	20
	2	7	7	1		Reviewed	18	14
1	3	6	1			Compiled	24	27
29	29	13	2			Tax Returns	113	132
14	37	36	23	10	4	Other	146	121
	21 (4/1-9/30/18)		219 (10/1/18-3/31/19)				4/1/14-3/31/15	4/1/15-3/31/16
0-500M	500M-2MM	2-10MM	10-50MM	50-100MM	100-250MM		ALL	ALL
45	71	67	36	14	7	NUMBER OF STATEMENTS	320	314
%	%	%	%	%	%	**ASSETS**	%	%
25.2	19.0	13.8	11.2	15.8		Cash & Equivalents	20.1	19.6
13.9	17.4	20.2	22.2	14.2		Trade Receivables (net)	20.8	21.2
16.8	28.2	33.0	30.7	21.9		Inventory	27.7	28.1
.9	3.8	5.8	4.0	3.5		All Other Current	2.9	3.5
56.7	68.4	72.7	68.2	55.4		Total Current	71.4	72.4
27.5	15.6	14.9	11.3	23.5		Fixed Assets (net)	14.4	13.0
9.3	4.3	5.8	9.9	14.3		Intangibles (net)	5.3	6.5
6.4	11.7	6.6	10.6	6.8		All Other Non-Current	8.9	8.1
100.0	100.0	100.0	100.0	100.0		Total	100.0	100.0
						LIABILITIES		
18.6	13.5	12.4	12.6	3.7		Notes Payable-Short Term	16.2	13.2
4.4	2.4	1.8	6.6	4.5		Cur. Mat.-L.T.D.	2.8	2.4
18.0	14.5	20.8	17.7	13.6		Trade Payables	17.8	15.9
.3	.3	.2	.1	.0		Income Taxes Payable	.4	.1
26.4	11.9	14.0	22.0	17.1		All Other Current	13.5	14.3
67.8	42.7	49.1	59.1	38.9		Total Current	50.6	45.8
20.8	17.6	14.7	12.3	22.8		Long-Term Debt	12.1	12.2
.0	.0	.0	.0	.0		Deferred Taxes	.1	.1
30.5	6.5	1.4	2.9	4.7		All Other Non-Current	8.1	6.6
-18.9	33.2	34.7	25.6	33.6		Net Worth	29.0	35.4
100.0	100.0	100.0	100.0	100.0		Total Liabilities & Net Worth	100.0	100.0
						INCOME DATA		
100.0	100.0	100.0	100.0	100.0		Net Sales	100.0	100.0
51.5	43.7	39.5	33.0	52.6		Gross Profit	43.5	44.3
44.6	37.4	33.9	28.2	46.4		Operating Expenses	36.7	37.4
7.0	6.3	5.6	4.8	6.2		Operating Profit	6.7	6.9
.5	.2	.7	.8	4.5		All Other Expenses (net)	.5	.4
6.5	6.2	4.9	4.0	1.7		Profit Before Taxes	6.2	6.4
						RATIOS		
4.3	3.7	2.5	1.9	2.2			2.9	3.2
1.2	1.6	1.4	1.1	1.3		Current	1.5	1.8
.4	.9	1.0	.8	.7			1.0	1.1
3.0	1.7	1.3	.9	1.3			1.7	1.8
.6	.9	.6	.5	.9		Quick	.9	1.0
.3	.4	.3	.4	.4			.5	.4
0 UND	2 189.0	3 127.1	8 47.3	5 71.0			1 352.9	1 274.3
0 UND	16 22.2	18 20.2	28 12.9	20 18.2		Sales/Receivables	14 25.4	17 21.0
14 26.5	34 10.8	43 7.9	46 7.9	42 8.6			38 9.5	39 9.4
0 UND	8 43.8	8 47.8	15 25.0	22 16.9			9 40.3	9 42.7
19 19.0	43 8.4	63 5.8	54 6.7	73 5.0		Cost of Sales/Inventory	46 8.0	42 8.6
76 4.8	94 3.9	89 4.1	140 2.6	146 2.5			107 3.4	104 3.5
0 UND	0 UND	9 40.3	15 24.2	20 17.9			9 42.8	5 73.1
0 UND	22 16.6	32 11.4	30 12.0	35 10.4		Cost of Sales/Payables	25 14.4	24 14.9
32 11.3	47 7.8	46 8.0	60 6.1	43 8.5			49 7.4	48 7.6
10.3	6.5	6.7	9.1	6.1			5.8	5.5
53.6	13.1	15.6	41.6	24.4		Sales/Working Capital	14.4	12.5
-24.2	-275.8	-510.5	-26.0	-27.1			179.2	83.4
26.8	44.9	28.4	14.1	9.2			35.0	40.5
(30) 9.5	(58) 10.1	(57) 6.6	(30) 5.3	(11) 2.3		EBIT/Interest	(240) 10.4	(231) 10.2
1.3	1.9	1.9	1.2	.4			3.3	2.4
							4.6	6.3
						Net Profit + Depr., Dep., Amort./Cur. Mat. L/T/D	(30) 2.4	(26) 3.1
							.4	1.0
.1	.0	.1	.1	.2			.0	.0
1.3	.2	.3	.4	1.4		Fixed/Worth	.3	.2
-1.2	1.5	2.6	26.0	-.7			2.1	1.6
.3	.7	.8	1.7	.6			.7	.6
7.3	1.7	2.0	4.6	2.8		Debt/Worth	2.2	1.7
-2.4	9.9	26.5	771.9	-4.2			38.1	9.4
128.0	110.8	58.6	89.3				84.4	87.8
(25) 60.0	(60) 49.8	(56) 27.6	(28) 55.1			% Profit Before Taxes/Tangible Net Worth	(252) 45.4	(262) 43.3
31.7	13.0	8.7	5.6				15.1	15.5
55.4	33.8	22.6	19.9	17.3			36.6	34.5
17.3	14.0	8.0	7.5	5.6		% Profit Before Taxes/Total Assets	14.8	13.3
7.0	3.1	1.3	1.7	.5			3.9	3.0
231.7	999.8	84.1	247.2	33.5			279.6	378.9
27.0	77.5	50.1	58.3	15.5		Sales/Net Fixed Assets	54.0	56.5
11.3	14.8	14.5	17.4	4.2			19.4	18.9
9.0	4.4	4.8	3.8	3.2			5.2	4.8
4.9	3.1	3.3	2.6	2.2		Sales/Total Assets	3.4	3.1
2.5	2.1	2.1	1.8	1.6			2.2	2.1
.8	.2	.4	.2				.3	.3
(19) 2.7	(33) 1.2	(46) .7	(23) .6			% Depr., Dep., Amort./Sales	(164) .8	(159) .9
3.7	2.8	1.6	1.8				1.6	1.7
2.1	1.7	.9					2.0	1.9
(30) 5.2	(37) 4.2	(26) 2.4				% Officers', Directors' Owners' Comp/Sales	(135) 3.5	(133) 3.5
13.3	7.1	6.2					7.8	6.7
65531M	276096M	1140623M	2431239M	2422421M	2556476M	Net Sales ($)	12857129M	13710066M
10915M	76675M	313326M	788038M	1007144M	1136571M	Total Assets ($)	4244733M	4664621M

© RMA 2019   M = $ thousand   MM = $ million

See Pages viii through xx for Explanation of Ratios and Data

Comparative Historical Data				Current Data Sorted by Sales					
			Type of Statement						
17	13	15	Unqualified				2	1	12
17	13	17	Reviewed		1		4	4	8
16	20	11	Compiled	1			5	3	2
88	81	73	Tax Returns	18	24	11	10	8	2
151	138	124	Other	10	20	18	16	19	41
4/1/16-3/31/17	4/1/17-3/31/18	4/1/18-3/31/19			21 (4/1-9/30/18)		219 (10/1/18-3/31/19)		
ALL	ALL	ALL		0-1MM	1-3MM	3-5MM	5-10MM	10-25MM	25MM & OVER
289	265	240	**NUMBER OF STATEMENTS**	29	45	29	37	35	65
%	%	%	**ASSETS**	%	%	%	%	%	%
19.9	16.9	17.3	Cash & Equivalents	22.0	22.1	18.6	19.2	13.2	12.3
20.2	20.4	17.9	Trade Receivables (net)	12.2	13.2	20.2	21.2	17.5	20.9
28.3	30.4	27.1	Inventory	17.2	18.6	28.5	34.3	38.0	27.0
3.7	3.6	4.0	All Other Current	1.2	4.2	5.4	2.3	5.0	4.7
72.2	71.3	66.2	Total Current	52.6	58.1	72.6	77.0	73.6	65.0
14.1	16.6	17.7	Fixed Assets (net)	31.6	22.1	15.5	10.5	15.9	14.5
6.0	5.0	7.1	Intangibles (net)	8.8	7.7	7.2	4.4	2.7	9.9
7.7	7.1	8.9	All Other Non-Current	7.1	12.1	4.6	8.1	7.8	10.6
100.0	100.0	100.0	Total	100.0	100.0	100.0	100.0	100.0	100.0
			LIABILITIES						
12.2	11.8	13.4	Notes Payable-Short Term	18.2	12.9	13.6	18.9	12.6	8.6
2.4	2.5	3.4	Cur. Mat.-L.T.D.	2.4	4.0	2.9	2.0	2.1	5.1
17.4	14.8	17.2	Trade Payables	11.0	16.0	19.6	16.6	15.7	20.8
.1	.3	.2	Income Taxes Payable	.4	.1	.3	.3	.2	.1
14.2	16.1	17.2	All Other Current	17.9	19.3	10.9	12.5	16.5	21.5
46.3	45.4	51.4	Total Current	50.0	52.3	47.3	50.3	47.1	56.1
14.3	17.0	17.2	Long-Term Debt	20.5	22.0	23.5	7.8	12.6	17.3
.1	.1	.0	Deferred Taxes	.0	.0	.1	.0	.0	.0
4.6	7.2	8.8	All Other Non-Current	38.5	11.1	5.4	1.7	2.1	3.1
34.8	30.3	22.7	Net Worth	-8.9	14.7	23.7	40.2	38.2	23.5
100.0	100.0	100.0	Total Liabilties & Net Worth	100.0	100.0	100.0	100.0	100.0	100.0
			INCOME DATA						
100.0	100.0	100.0	Net Sales	100.0	100.0	100.0	100.0	100.0	100.0
43.2	42.5	43.1	Gross Profit	60.8	47.7	49.1	34.6	36.1	38.0
36.4	36.0	37.0	Operating Expenses	52.0	40.7	43.3	28.8	31.5	32.6
6.7	6.5	6.1	Operating Profit	8.8	7.0	5.7	5.8	4.6	5.3
.2	.4	.8	All Other Expenses (net)	.8	.0	.7	.6	.9	1.3
6.5	6.1	5.3	Profit Before Taxes	8.0	7.0	5.0	5.2	3.7	4.0
			RATIOS						
3.0	3.3	2.6	Current	5.6	3.0	4.1	3.6	2.9	1.9
1.7	1.7	1.4		1.5	1.3	1.8	1.6	1.6	1.1
1.0	1.1	.9		.5	.9	1.2	.9	1.1	.8
2.0	1.7	1.4	Quick	3.1	2.3	1.7	2.1	1.3	1.0
.9	.9	.7		.8	.7	1.2	.7	.6	.6
.4	.4	.3		.3	.3	.4	.4	.3	.4
1 295.7	1 462.4	1 299.5	Sales/Receivables	0 UND	2 217.5	4 100.5	0 UND	1 249.1	4 93.6
18 19.8	18 20.0	15 24.8		0 UND	12 29.7	16 22.2	21 17.0	15 24.9	24 15.2
40 9.1	44 8.3	36 10.1		16 22.4	28 13.0	38 9.6	39 9.3	35 10.3	41 8.9
11 33.4	8 45.8	7 49.6	Cost of Sales/Inventory	0 UND	0 UND	23 15.8	9 40.3	25 14.4	8 44.9
54 6.8	51 7.1	45 8.1		22 16.3	38 9.7	48 7.6	57 6.4	65 5.6	47 7.8
101 3.6	104 3.5	99 3.7		101 3.6	83 4.4	96 3.8	96 3.8	159 2.3	122 3.0
7 55.3	0 749.3	1 429.0	Cost of Sales/Payables	0 UND	0 UND	11 32.8	1 383.2	6 59.4	16 22.3
26 13.9	21 17.0	24 15.0		0 UND	19 19.5	33 11.2	18 20.6	24 15.2	33 11.1
55 6.6	42 8.6	46 7.9		38 9.5	59 6.2	55 6.6	41 8.9	42 8.7	49 7.5
5.9	6.0	7.1	Sales/Working Capital	6.4	6.7	5.7	6.4	8.8	7.8
11.9	12.7	17.5		56.9	18.9	8.5	15.1	16.4	90.0
999.8	116.9	-59.8		-17.7	-67.5	40.1	-97.4	36.9	-29.8
47.2	19.2	24.9	EBIT/Interest	21.0	44.1	18.4	42.3	37.4	13.2
(225) 10.1	(198) 7.2	(191) 8.0		(17) 4.8	(38) 9.8	(25) 8.7	(28) 7.4	(30) 7.7	(53) 5.9
2.8	1.7	1.8		.2	1.4	1.9	-.1	2.1	1.7
13.5	8.7	6.2	Net Profit + Depr., Dep., Amort./Cur. Mat. L/T/D						
(20) 4.5	(15) 3.2	(14) .7							
1.1	.9	-2.4							
.0	.1	.1	Fixed/Worth	.0	.0	.1	.1	.1	.1
.3	.3	.4		1.3	.5	.4	.2	.3	1.0
1.7	2.0	7.4		-4.0	41.5	2.4	.7	.8	-.8
.8	.7	.7	Debt/Worth	.3	.5	.7	.4	.8	1.3
2.0	2.1	2.3		4.0	2.2	1.4	1.7	1.8	4.5
11.6	12.8	226.7		-5.3	-35.0	-13.7	8.0	5.9	-4.9
105.6	84.3	87.4	% Profit Before Taxes/Tangible Net Worth	157.9	93.2	63.3	140.0	60.1	89.3
(236) 52.8	(213) 37.4	(183) 39.3		(20) 60.5	(33) 54.9	(21) 23.4	(33) 37.5	(32) 27.6	(44) 47.8
18.5	10.6	12.7		21.7	28.1	11.0	5.7	8.3	4.9
36.2	30.4	27.5	% Profit Before Taxes/Total Assets	55.4	25.4	31.4	33.2	23.2	26.6
15.6	11.1	11.3		17.3	15.4	10.9	9.4	9.0	7.7
4.6	1.9	1.7		1.4	4.6	2.4	.2	3.7	1.5
255.7	175.1	165.4	Sales/Net Fixed Assets	303.2	UND	150.6	216.5	84.1	122.4
62.3	44.6	47.0		20.3	31.5	44.7	68.2	50.1	37.4
19.4	16.0	12.3		1.9	11.3	13.9	30.5	14.5	15.5
4.7	5.1	4.8	Sales/Total Assets	5.1	3.9	4.2	6.1	5.0	4.5
3.0	3.2	3.1		2.2	2.9	3.6	3.7	3.4	2.9
2.1	2.0	2.0		1.0	1.8	2.3	2.4	2.6	2.2
.5	.4	.3	% Depr., Dep., Amort./Sales	2.5	1.2	.2	.1	.3	.3
(137) .8	(144) 1.0	(133) 1.0		(13) 3.4	(16) 1.8	(16) 1.2	(21) .4	(25) .9	(42) .7
1.9	2.4	2.3		5.5	3.5	3.0	1.4	1.6	2.1
2.3	1.7	1.6	% Officers', Directors' Owners' Comp/Sales	4.6		2.4	.9	.7	
(115) 4.2	(89) 3.5	(96) 3.8		(18) 6.8	(25) 5.1	(16) 4.1	(20) 1.8	(13) 1.5	
7.4	6.9	7.3		14.4	10.6	6.4	4.5	5.3	
12492487M	8896155M	8892386M	Net Sales ($)	16056M	82092M	111644M	267011M	586142M	7829441M
4020969M	3058085M	3332669M	Total Assets ($)	10449M	38360M	37198M	115137M	189497M	2942028M

© RMA 2019

M = $ thousand   MM = $ million
See Pages viii through xx for Explanation of Ratios and Data

TRANSPORTATION AND WAREHOUSING

Current Data Sorted by Assets							Comparative Historical Data	
						Type of Statement		
1	1	3	4	10	3	Unqualified	9	11
						Reviewed	4	3
		3				Compiled	2	1
1	1	1				Tax Returns	7	7
2	4	5	6	3	4	Other	18	28
15 (4/1-9/30/18)			37 (10/1/18-3/31/19)				4/1/14-3/31/15	4/1/15-3/31/16
0-500M	500M-2MM	2-10MM	10-50MM	50-100MM	100-250MM		ALL	ALL
4	6	12	10	13	7	**NUMBER OF STATEMENTS**	40	50
%	%	%	%	%	%	**ASSETS**	%	%
		17.8	14.7	9.2		Cash & Equivalents	11.9	18.9
		11.7	5.9	7.7		Trade Receivables (net)	11.7	15.2
		3.1	1.3	10.2		Inventory	6.5	5.2
		3.5	3.1	3.1		All Other Current	5.5	2.7
		36.0	25.1	30.2		Total Current	35.7	42.0
		51.5	49.9	55.0		Fixed Assets (net)	53.8	44.6
		6.8	15.0	6.7		Intangibles (net)	3.9	4.7
		5.7	10.0	8.1		All Other Non-Current	6.6	8.7
		100.0	100.0	100.0		Total	100.0	100.0
						LIABILITIES		
		.4	.0	3.6		Notes Payable-Short Term	3.7	8.8
		5.5	3.7	4.8		Cur. Mat.-L.T.D.	2.9	2.7
		6.4	7.1	10.9		Trade Payables	14.5	14.0
		.3	2.1	.0		Income Taxes Payable	.2	.1
		10.8	21.4	14.2		All Other Current	13.5	13.4
		23.4	34.3	33.5		Total Current	34.8	39.0
		46.5	29.1	39.1		Long-Term Debt	39.3	29.3
		1.0	2.3	.6		Deferred Taxes	1.9	.8
		16.7	13.9	5.3		All Other Non-Current	6.7	7.0
		12.5	20.4	21.5		Net Worth	17.3	23.9
		100.0	100.0	100.0		Total Liabilties & Net Worth	100.0	100.0
						INCOME DATA		
		100.0	100.0	100.0		Net Sales	100.0	100.0
						Gross Profit		
		90.2	91.8	99.0		Operating Expenses	92.4	91.1
		9.8	8.2	1.0		Operating Profit	7.6	8.9
		1.1	1.7	5.7		All Other Expenses (net)	3.3	4.9
		8.7	6.5	-4.7		Profit Before Taxes	4.3	4.0
						RATIOS		
		2.7	.9	1.9			2.3	1.8
		1.6	.7	.9		Current	1.2	1.0
		.9	.6	.5			.7	.7
		1.9	.8	.8			1.8	1.4
		1.5	.6	.5		Quick	.7	.8
		.6	.4	.3			.3	.5
		12 31.4	**0** UND	**9** 39.7			**9** 39.0	**9** 39.2
		28 12.9	**19** 19.2	**18** 20.5		Sales/Receivables	**20** 18.2	**19** 19.0
		42 8.7	**27** 13.3	**32** 11.4			**32** 11.3	**35** 10.3
						Cost of Sales/Inventory		
						Cost of Sales/Payables		
		5.0	-24.5	9.6			8.8	10.0
		14.0	-10.2	-38.2		Sales/Working Capital	32.7	-137.0
		-120.3	-6.4	-5.9			-13.5	-19.9
		33.8		5.2			5.9	6.7
		(11) 13.0		(11) .5		EBIT/Interest	(29) 3.5	(39) 3.0
		2.4		-2.8			-1.1	-.3
								6.9
						Net Profit + Depr., Dep., Amort./Cur. Mat. L/T/D		(10) 3.5
								2.4
		1.0	2.2	.9			.8	.6
		1.8	4.3	3.2		Fixed/Worth	2.1	1.5
		6.1	-13.7	NM			53.6	15.4
		.7	3.9	1.0			1.1	1.2
		2.6	5.6	3.3		Debt/Worth	3.0	3.1
		8.6	-25.3	NM			58.9	-16.5
		64.3		20.3			48.3	59.4
		(10) 31.7		(10) 5.4		% Profit Before Taxes/Tangible Net Worth	(31) 18.7	(37) 12.0
		16.0		-46.3			2.6	-1.2
		28.7	11.8	9.6			10.6	10.0
		8.3	6.7	.5		% Profit Before Taxes/Total Assets	4.6	2.4
		3.2	1.5	-17.2			-3.7	-2.1
		4.7	2.6	4.3			5.4	27.9
		2.6	1.6	2.6		Sales/Net Fixed Assets	2.4	2.7
		1.5	1.2	1.2			1.4	1.1
		2.0	1.0	2.0			2.2	2.7
		1.2	.9	1.5		Sales/Total Assets	1.2	1.5
		.9	.8	.8			.7	.7
		3.3	4.6	1.8			1.2	1.2
		(11) 5.0	(10) 5.5	5.5		% Depr., Dep., Amort./Sales	(31) 4.4	(35) 5.8
		9.6	9.9	9.4			11.6	13.7
							2.5	1.9
						% Officers', Directors' Owners' Comp/Sales	(11) 3.5	(11) 2.4
							3.9	4.5
1860M	15707M	77560M	260620M	1294022M	1275528M	Net Sales ($)	1358130M	1995839M
734M	9008M	58635M	276807M	869432M	1337317M	Total Assets ($)	999419M	1886695M

M = $ thousand MM = $ million

See Pages viii through xx for Explanation of Ratios and Data

Comparative Historical Data | Current Data Sorted by Sales

4/1/16-3/31/17 ALL	4/1/17-3/31/18 ALL	4/1/18-3/31/19 ALL	Type of Statement	0-1MM	1-3MM	3-5MM	5-10MM	10-25MM	25MM & OVER
11	11	22	Unqualified	1	2		2	4	13
3	2		Reviewed			1			
2	1	3	Compiled		1		2		
9	5	3	Tax Returns	2			1		
18	21	24	Other	2	2	1	6	4	9
					15 (4/1-9/30/18)		37 (10/1/18-3/31/19)		
43	40	52	NUMBER OF STATEMENTS	5	5	1	11	8	22
%	%	%	ASSETS	%	%	%	%	%	%
13.9	16.2	16.8	Cash & Equivalents				15.2		8.8
9.1	11.8	8.0	Trade Receivables (net)				13.9		9.0
5.1	5.9	4.3	Inventory				4.4		6.5
2.5	4.2	3.5	All Other Current				1.6		4.3
30.6	38.2	32.6	Total Current				35.1		28.5
51.6	46.0	48.7	Fixed Assets (net)				52.5		50.2
5.1	6.9	8.8	Intangibles (net)				7.9		12.3
12.6	8.9	9.9	All Other Non-Current				4.5		9.0
100.0	100.0	100.0	Total				100.0		100.0
			LIABILITIES						
10.5	1.5	4.2	Notes Payable-Short Term				1.0		2.3
3.7	4.6	5.1	Cur. Mat.-L.T.D.				6.1		4.9
7.8	10.7	7.9	Trade Payables				8.1		11.3
.1	.3	.6	Income Taxes Payable				.4		.3
12.6	8.9	14.0	All Other Current				9.4		17.0
34.7	25.9	31.8	Total Current				25.0		35.7
43.7	38.3	36.6	Long-Term Debt				52.1		36.3
.2	.8	.9	Deferred Taxes				1.0		.6
7.4	8.2	8.5	All Other Non-Current				17.9		5.4
14.0	26.8	22.2	Net Worth				4.0		22.0
100.0	100.0	100.0	Total Liabilities & Net Worth				100.0		100.0
			INCOME DATA						
100.0	100.0	100.0	Net Sales				100.0		100.0
			Gross Profit						
89.1	90.8	91.1	Operating Expenses				90.4		99.1
10.9	9.2	8.9	Operating Profit				9.6		.9
4.0	1.6	3.3	All Other Expenses (net)				1.2		4.4
6.9	7.7	5.6	Profit Before Taxes				8.4		-3.5
			RATIOS						
3.1	3.3	2.0	Current				2.8		1.1
1.1	1.3	.9					1.5		.8
.4	.7	.6					.8		.5
1.4	2.8	1.5	Quick				1.9		.7
.8	.9	.7					1.4		.4
.3	.4	.4					.6		.2
2 191.2	4 103.8	9 39.9	Sales/Receivables				21 17.7		9 41.3
17 22.1	24 15.3	19 19.4					30 12.3		22 16.4
33 11.1	40 9.1	30 12.2					42 8.6		35 10.4
			Cost of Sales/Inventory						
			Cost of Sales/Payables						
9.4	5.9	7.5	Sales/Working Capital				5.4		NM
33.2	17.7	-35.9					15.0		-17.1
-9.0	-11.7	-8.3					-12.4		-6.1
10.5	13.2	12.8	EBIT/Interest				24.3		5.8
(35) 3.6	(33) 3.7	(44) 2.9					(10) 9.8	(20) .8	
1.4	-.6	-.3					1.9		-2.4
		4.7	Net Profit + Depr., Dep., Amort./Cur. Mat. L/T/D						
	(15) 3.3								
		1.7							
.7	.8	1.0	Fixed/Worth				1.2		1.5
2.2	1.7	2.2					2.2		7.2
-15.0	8.9	108.9					7.3		-14.2
.8	.7	1.1	Debt/Worth				1.6		1.3
3.2	2.4	3.3					2.8		8.8
-22.6	14.0	133.2					10.4		-27.3
39.9	47.6	40.0	% Profit Before Taxes/Tangible Net Worth						31.2
(30) 17.8	(33) 18.1	(40) 21.6						(16) 5.4	
4.2	7.9	.2							-47.5
14.5	12.9	11.3	% Profit Before Taxes/Total Assets				33.2		8.7
6.3	5.7	5.7					6.9		1.1
1.2	-1.4	-2.1					2.9		-9.7
11.5	10.0	5.3	Sales/Net Fixed Assets				5.7		4.6
2.2	2.8	2.3					2.4		2.4
1.0	1.4	1.3					1.2		1.4
2.1	2.2	1.6	Sales/Total Assets				2.0		1.7
1.4	1.4	1.0					1.2		1.2
.7	.9	.8					.8		.9
5.0	2.1	3.4	% Depr., Dep., Amort./Sales				2.5		2.1
(30) 11.6	(28) 5.6	(36) 5.4					(10) 4.9	(14) 5.4	
16.7	8.6	9.4					9.8		7.2
2.0		2.3	% Officers', Directors' Owners' Comp/Sales						
(10) 3.0	(10) 2.5								
5.1	6.6								
2261296M	2861038M	2925297M	Net Sales ($)	1182M	11186M	4330M	74704M	152211M	2681684M
1871521M	1866596M	2551933M	Total Assets ($)	2280M	9514M	1855M	61845M	429315M	2047124M

© RMA 2019   M = $ thousand   MM = $ million
See Pages viii through xx for Explanation of Ratios and Data

Current Data Sorted by Assets   Comparative Historical Data

Type of Statement — Number of Statements (Current Data)

Type of Statement	0-500M	500M-2MM	2-10MM	10-50MM	50-100MM	100-250MM
Unqualified				2	2	
Reviewed		1	1	2		
Compiled	1	2	3	3		
Tax Returns	5	6	3	1	1	
Other	2	7	17	14		6

9 (4/1-9/30/18)   70 (10/1/18-3/31/19)

Main Data

0-500M	500M-2MM	2-10MM	10-50MM	50-100MM	100-250MM		4/1/14-3/31/15 ALL	4/1/15-3/31/16 ALL
						Type of Statement (Historical)		
						Unqualified	5	5
						Reviewed	8	10
						Compiled	13	9
						Tax Returns	16	11
						Other	44	45
8	16	24	22	3	6	**NUMBER OF STATEMENTS**	86	80
%	%	%	%	%	%	**ASSETS**	%	%
	18.6	17.7	10.5			Cash & Equivalents	15.0	14.7
	11.3	17.8	18.5			Trade Receivables (net)	15.4	14.2
	3.1	4.3	7.4			Inventory	4.5	5.2
	7.6	7.7	2.1			All Other Current	4.2	3.7
	40.6	47.5	38.4			Total Current	39.2	37.8
	40.1	35.5	47.4			Fixed Assets (net)	47.4	50.2
	3.3	7.1	7.7			Intangibles (net)	3.0	2.8
	16.0	9.9	6.5			All Other Non-Current	10.4	9.2
	100.0	100.0	100.0			Total	100.0	100.0
						LIABILITIES		
	8.0	4.9	7.3			Notes Payable-Short Term	5.5	6.0
	1.5	2.1	3.3			Cur. Mat.-L.T.D.	7.7	7.5
	16.6	12.8	9.8			Trade Payables	12.1	8.6
	.0	.1	.1			Income Taxes Payable	.0	.1
	17.7	15.0	12.8			All Other Current	14.3	19.4
	43.9	34.8	33.2			Total Current	39.6	41.6
	38.6	28.3	33.5			Long-Term Debt	48.8	38.8
	.0	.5	.2			Deferred Taxes	.5	.9
	27.0	10.6	4.1			All Other Non-Current	7.3	13.9
	-9.5	25.8	29.0			Net Worth	3.8	4.8
	100.0	100.0	100.0			Total Liabilities & Net Worth	100.0	100.0
						INCOME DATA		
	100.0	100.0	100.0			Net Sales	100.0	100.0
						Gross Profit		
	95.4	88.1	94.7			Operating Expenses	88.5	89.6
	4.6	11.9	5.3			Operating Profit	11.5	10.4
	3.5	4.3	2.5			All Other Expenses (net)	3.1	3.1
	1.1	7.5	2.8			Profit Before Taxes	8.4	7.3
						RATIOS		
	2.7	3.7	1.9				2.4	2.1
	1.0	1.4	.9			Current	1.1	1.1
	.5	.9	.6				.7	.5
	2.7	3.0	1.7				1.8	1.6
	.8	1.2	.7			Quick	.9	.8
	.3	.5	.3				.3	.3
0 UND		7 55.7	3 114.4				5 80.4	4 92.5
6 57.7		15 24.2	22 16.8			Sales/Receivables	23 16.1	20 18.6
21 17.8		36 10.1	41 8.9				39 9.3	37 9.8
						Cost of Sales/Inventory		
						Cost of Sales/Payables		
	8.6	7.4	6.8				9.2	9.6
	NM	20.7	-67.3			Sales/Working Capital	62.9	85.3
	-10.9	-50.0	-9.5				-11.0	-7.6
	19.0	18.7	19.4				11.3	16.5
(11) .6		(20) 9.9	(19) 4.5			EBIT/Interest	(72) 3.6	(70) 3.5
	-4.9	2.2	2.1				1.4	1.3
								5.9
						Net Profit + Depr., Dep., Amort./Cur. Mat. L/T/D	(14)	2.6
								1.1
	.1	.6	.6				.8	.8
	NM	1.4	2.2			Fixed/Worth	1.6	2.0
	-.5	NM	NM				-3.0	-2.5
	1.9	.9	1.1				.7	.8
	NM	2.3	2.8			Debt/Worth	3.2	3.3
	-2.6	NM	NM				-6.8	-5.7
		94.2	36.4				58.8	53.9
	(18)	22.8 (17)	21.8			% Profit Before Taxes/Tangible Net Worth	(60) 17.6	(54) 23.1
		8.5	6.3				3.7	5.2
	26.3	19.1	12.2				20.2	15.8
	4.2	8.5	6.1			% Profit Before Taxes/Total Assets	6.2	7.4
	-13.3	.1	1.3				.7	.4
	826.8	81.3	10.7				21.1	8.3
	18.5	12.6	3.2			Sales/Net Fixed Assets	3.8	3.0
	1.1	1.3	1.7				1.4	1.5
	4.1	3.5	3.0				3.1	2.5
	2.3	1.6	1.5			Sales/Total Assets	1.8	1.4
	.9	.6	1.2				.8	.8
		.5	1.5				1.3	1.8
	(13)	3.7 (20)	3.8			% Depr., Dep., Amort./Sales	(69) 4.3	(61) 5.6
		12.3	8.9				16.6	12.5
							2.2	1.6
						% Officers', Directors' Owners' Comp/Sales	(20) 2.9	(14) 2.9
							7.1	4.2
12645M	42924M	234759M	1255044M	345477M	655461M	Net Sales ($)	1542583M	1776658M
2183M	18495M	117723M	550629M	194432M	916001M	Total Assets ($)	947310M	1278990M

© RMA 2019

M = $ thousand   MM = $ million
See Pages viii through xx for Explanation of Ratios and Data

Comparative Historical Data   Current Data Sorted by Sales

Type of Statement	4/1/16-3/31/17 ALL	4/1/17-3/31/18 ALL	4/1/18-3/31/19 ALL	0-1MM	1-3MM	3-5MM	5-10MM	10-25MM	25MM & OVER
Unqualified	3	7	4		2		2	2	4
Reviewed	8	7	4		2			1	1
Compiled	6	7	9	1	2			1	2
Tax Returns	16	8	15	5	2	3	1		1
Other	46	41	47	5	4	5	8	7	18
				9 (4/1-9/30/18)			70 (10/1/18-3/31/19)		
NUMBER OF STATEMENTS	79	70	79	11	12	8	11	11	26
ASSETS	%	%	%	%	%	%	%	%	%
Cash & Equivalents	13.6	16.7	14.6	10.1	22.9		15.4	23.7	9.2
Trade Receivables (net)	15.6	17.3	15.7	9.8	7.9		30.1	24.4	15.5
Inventory	5.7	5.9	4.8	2.4	.7		7.7	3.3	7.1
All Other Current	5.3	3.5	4.8	.5	1.4		8.4	3.5	5.2
Total Current	40.1	43.4	39.9	22.8	32.2		61.6	55.0	37.1
Fixed Assets (net)	46.3	43.3	44.0	75.8	48.0		9.6	33.5	49.4
Intangibles (net)	5.0	6.0	6.9	.1	.6		13.2	8.3	6.0
All Other Non-Current	8.6	7.3	9.2	1.3	19.2		15.5	3.1	7.5
Total	100.0	100.0	100.0	100.0	100.0		100.0	100.0	100.0
LIABILITIES									
Notes Payable-Short Term	7.5	6.4	6.9	1.8	18.4		6.4	2.6	5.7
Cur. Mat.-L.T.D.	7.0	5.3	2.7	2.0	2.9		1.9	3.1	3.4
Trade Payables	14.1	13.6	15.2	14.9	15.7		24.7	11.5	11.9
Income Taxes Payable	.1	.6	.1	.0	.0		.2	.0	.1
All Other Current	11.1	20.0	13.7	6.1	12.1		21.4	12.6	13.7
Total Current	39.9	45.9	38.6	24.9	49.2		54.7	29.8	34.7
Long-Term Debt	42.2	40.2	40.1	85.5	38.4		15.9	17.5	34.9
Deferred Taxes	.9	.9	.4	.0	.4		.5	.0	.7
All Other Non-Current	12.9	17.6	13.7	4.3	38.3		21.4	6.4	3.1
Net Worth	4.2	-4.6	7.2	-14.7	-26.3		7.5	46.3	26.5
Total Liabilities & Net Worth	100.0	100.0	100.0	100.0	100.0		100.0	100.0	100.0
INCOME DATA									
Net Sales	100.0	100.0	100.0	100.0	100.0		100.0	100.0	100.0
Gross Profit									
Operating Expenses	92.6	88.6	91.6	76.1	95.9		92.7	93.3	94.5
Operating Profit	7.4	11.4	8.4	23.9	4.1		7.3	6.7	5.5
All Other Expenses (net)	3.0	2.8	3.8	10.1	6.7		.5	.5	2.1
Profit Before Taxes	4.4	8.6	4.5	13.8	-2.6		6.8	6.2	3.3
RATIOS									
Current	2.4	2.2	2.4	13.0	1.3		1.8	2.9	1.6
	1.1	1.1	1.1	1.9	.8		1.2	1.6	.9
	.5	.7	.6	.3	.2		.9	1.3	.6
Quick	2.2	2.0	1.9	13.0	1.3		1.4	2.6	1.3
	.7	.9	.8	1.9	.8		.9	1.5	.6
	.3	.3	.3	.3	.1		.5	1.1	.3
Sales/Receivables	5 75.4	5 73.2	3 139.6	0 UND	0 UND		7 51.6	12 31.0	7 53.0
	17 21.8	19 19.3	15 24.8	0 UND	5 75.6		34 10.7	32 11.3	25 14.6
	35 10.5	37 9.8	36 10.0	12 31.0	20 18.3		73 5.0	61 6.0	39 9.4
Cost of Sales/Inventory									
Cost of Sales/Payables									
Sales/Working Capital	8.4	9.2	9.4	9.8	NM		7.7	4.7	19.8
	126.7	244.8	124.2	20.3	-12.2		31.9	10.6	-49.6
	-8.5	-13.8	-9.8	-5.2	-4.3		-41.9	23.3	-9.7
EBIT/Interest	12.7	11.4	15.6				28.5	27.2	6.5
	(66) 3.0	(52) 5.0	(62) 4.4				19.0	(10) 9.1	(22) 4.4
	.9	1.0	.7				2.9	2.6	1.3
Net Profit + Depr., Dep., Amort./Cur. Mat. L/T/D	3.3		6.0						5.8
	(12) 2.0		(13) 4.2					(10) 4.0	4.0
	1.4		2.5						3.0
Fixed/Worth	.8	.5	.6	1.0	.0		.1	.3	1.1
	3.0	2.4	2.4	3.9	1.3		.7	.8	2.6
	-2.7	-5.0	-3.3	-1.1	-1.6		-.1	2.0	-29.5
Debt/Worth	1.0	1.0	1.4	2.6	.8		.9	.7	1.6
	3.4	3.7	3.7	10.4	8.4		9.6	1.4	3.3
	-5.7	-6.9	-5.2	-2.2	-3.1		-1.9	2.6	-78.5
% Profit Before Taxes/Tangible Net Worth	57.1	86.4	48.9					42.3	33.0
	(52) 16.7	(46) 31.5	(52) 21.8				(10) 25.0	(19) 16.7	
	3.3	4.6	4.8				10.0	7.9	
% Profit Before Taxes/Total Assets	14.8	21.5	14.0	12.2	31.2		20.3	20.2	10.6
	5.4	6.1	6.1	-.5	.1		12.0	11.2	6.2
	-.6	.3	-1.1	-10.3	-19.6		2.4	4.3	.7
Sales/Net Fixed Assets	17.7	25.5	39.3	2.2	UND		224.0	50.3	10.8
	3.6	5.5	4.9	.2	6.5		91.6	10.8	3.2
	1.5	1.8	1.3	.2	1.5		18.2	2.4	1.6
Sales/Total Assets	3.1	4.0	3.7	1.9	5.2		3.7	3.8	3.2
	2.0	2.3	1.7	.2	2.3		2.5	1.7	1.5
	.9	.9	.8	.2	.8		1.3	1.4	1.1
% Depr., Dep., Amort./Sales	1.5	1.1	1.3						1.1
	(57) 5.7	(45) 2.3	(54) 4.8						(23) 3.4
	15.0	8.3	10.1						6.7
% Officers', Directors' Owners' Comp/Sales	1.3	.9	1.8						
	(18) 3.0	(13) 2.6	(17) 3.0						
	5.6	8.7	8.3						
Net Sales ($)	1493936M	1898332M	2546310M	6054M	21894M	29001M	77120M	192396M	2219845M
Total Assets ($)	1035582M	1455407M	1799463M	17907M	40130M	21261M	49591M	115470M	1555104M

M = $ thousand   MM = $ million
See Pages viii through xx for Explanation of Ratios and Data

Current Data Sorted by Assets | Comparative Historical Data

Type of Statement period groups: **4 (4/1-9/30/18)** and **50 (10/1/18-3/31/19)**

0-500M	500M-2MM	2-10MM	10-50MM	50-100MM	100-250MM	Type of Statement	4/1/14-3/31/15 ALL	4/1/15-3/31/16 ALL
		1	1	2	1	Unqualified	11	9
	1	1	1	2	1	Reviewed	4	4
1	1	4	2	1	1	Compiled	7	2
3	4	2	1			Tax Returns	13	15
3	5	6	10	2	4	Other	40	40
7	11	11	16	5	4	**NUMBER OF STATEMENTS**	75	70
%	%	%	%	%	%	**ASSETS**	%	%
	17.2	26.1	17.9			Cash & Equivalents	19.7	16.7
	5.9	8.4	9.9			Trade Receivables (net)	15.7	17.0
	3.9	9.7	4.3			Inventory	3.9	2.9
	2.6	1.2	1.6			All Other Current	4.2	3.3
	29.6	45.4	33.7			Total Current	43.6	39.8
	53.1	38.3	56.2			Fixed Assets (net)	47.2	47.9
	7.2	3.4	3.4			Intangibles (net)	3.1	2.3
	10.2	12.9	6.7			All Other Non-Current	6.0	10.0
	100.0	100.0	100.0			Total	100.0	100.0
						LIABILITIES		
	11.9	3.2	.7			Notes Payable-Short Term	11.5	10.7
	4.4	11.1	3.5			Cur. Mat.-L.T.D.	9.3	5.5
	6.1	5.7	4.4			Trade Payables	11.2	11.8
	.1	.0	.3			Income Taxes Payable	1.1	.0
	7.1	15.1	11.9			All Other Current	10.3	10.3
	29.6	35.1	20.8			Total Current	43.3	38.4
	76.2	37.1	28.7			Long-Term Debt	40.2	56.7
	.0	.0	.8			Deferred Taxes	.8	.7
	5.7	3.7	2.0			All Other Non-Current	8.0	7.3
	-11.4	24.1	47.6			Net Worth	7.6	-3.1
	100.0	100.0	100.0			Total Liabilities & Net Worth	100.0	100.0
						INCOME DATA		
	100.0	100.0	100.0			Net Sales	100.0	100.0
						Gross Profit		
	89.2	85.4	80.4			Operating Expenses	87.6	90.0
	10.8	14.6	19.6			Operating Profit	12.4	10.0
	8.8	2.7	3.2			All Other Expenses (net)	3.9	4.3
	2.1	11.9	16.4			Profit Before Taxes	8.5	5.6
						RATIOS		
	2.8	1.5	3.3			Current	2.5	3.4
	1.9	1.4	2.1				1.5	1.2
	.3	1.0	1.1				.9	.5
	2.5	1.5	3.0			Quick	2.2	2.8
	1.1	.8	1.4				1.3	1.1
	.2	.5	.7				.5	.5
0	UND	1 581.0	5 78.8			Sales/Receivables	3 143.4	1 412.6
7	48.8	10 35.0	21 17.5				19 19.6	18 20.5
56	6.5	29 12.7	47 7.7				38 9.7	39 9.3
						Cost of Sales/Inventory		
						Cost of Sales/Payables		
	3.4	7.0	3.7			Sales/Working Capital	7.0	6.3
	4.5	18.5	6.5				20.3	60.9
	-5.1	211.7	37.1				-43.2	-10.7
	13.8		21.8			EBIT/Interest	12.9	15.1
	(10) 2.0		(13) 9.0				(59) 3.5	(57) 3.6
	-1.8		2.6				1.3	1.3
						Net Profit + Depr., Dep., Amort./Cur. Mat. L/T/D		
	2.5	.7	.8			Fixed/Worth	.7	.4
	7.7	1.4	1.4				1.9	2.2
	-1.6	-8.5	1.7				-18.3	-6.9
	3.1	1.0	.6			Debt/Worth	.9	1.1
	11.1	2.2	1.0				2.2	5.0
	-4.3	-30.6	2.2				-30.2	-5.2
			47.9			% Profit Before Taxes/Tangible Net Worth	62.2	67.8
			(15) 11.5				(55) 28.5	(49) 30.2
			6.5				7.9	6.8
	15.5	35.3	27.1			% Profit Before Taxes/Total Assets	21.8	17.0
	.6	6.1	4.8				7.9	6.2
	-25.8	-2.2	1.8				1.5	.2
	5.0	11.5	5.0			Sales/Net Fixed Assets	21.7	34.1
	1.4	9.2	1.8				2.8	3.4
	.5	2.4	.8				.9	1.0
	2.0	2.4	1.6			Sales/Total Assets	3.3	3.3
	.9	1.6	.9				1.5	1.5
	.2	.9	.6				.7	.8
	3.0		5.2			% Depr., Dep., Amort./Sales	1.5	1.6
	(10) 12.6		(12) 10.4				(53) 6.0	(49) 5.6
	27.9		17.0				19.8	17.7
						% Officers', Directors' Owners' Comp/Sales	2.6	1.1
							(19) 4.4	(21) 2.8
							8.7	
22538M	19111M	115286M	358466M	216684M	1564490M	Net Sales ($)	2174838M	2049878M
1674M	13923M	60415M	403565M	324938M	784424M	Total Assets ($)	1464131M	1451031M

M = $ thousand   MM = $ million
See Pages viii through xx for Explanation of Ratios and Data

Comparative Historical Data | Current Data Sorted by Sales

Type of Statement	7 2 4 11 29	7 5 6 9 32	4 5 5 10 30	0-1MM	1-3MM	3-5MM	5-10MM	10-25MM	25MM & OVER
Unqualified								2	2
Reviewed					1		1	2	1
Compiled					2			2	1
Tax Returns				5	1	1	2	1	1
Other				3	6	1	5	5	10
	4/1/16-3/31/17 ALL	4/1/17-3/31/18 ALL	4/1/18-3/31/19 ALL		4 (4/1-9/30/18)			50 (10/1/18-3/31/19)	
NUMBER OF STATEMENTS	53	59	54	8	10	2	8	12	14
	%	%	%	%	%	%	%	%	%
ASSETS									
Cash & Equivalents	13.9	17.3	19.1		30.8			15.5	13.7
Trade Receivables (net)	22.4	12.3	10.1		9.5			11.4	11.8
Inventory	4.6	5.5	5.8		4.3			9.6	9.5
All Other Current	3.9	4.4	3.7		.2			2.0	6.8
Total Current	44.8	39.6	38.7		44.8			38.5	41.8
Fixed Assets (net)	43.5	48.2	46.1		40.2			55.3	41.2
Intangibles (net)	5.2	5.2	5.6		3.7			2.2	11.1
All Other Non-Current	6.4	7.1	9.5		11.3			4.0	5.9
Total	100.0	100.0	100.0		100.0			100.0	100.0
LIABILITIES									
Notes Payable-Short Term	9.0	2.9	9.1		6.8			2.8	3.3
Cur. Mat.-L.T.D.	7.3	6.2	6.5		5.6			9.2	2.8
Trade Payables	14.3	11.7	10.2		26.2			5.6	6.4
Income Taxes Payable	.5	.2	.1		.2			.0	.0
All Other Current	11.9	9.4	20.5		59.3			6.0	11.4
Total Current	43.1	30.5	46.4		98.1			23.6	24.0
Long-Term Debt	51.5	41.6	43.9		46.3			32.2	26.8
Deferred Taxes	1.3	1.1	.8		.0			.8	1.4
All Other Non-Current	3.1	4.2	3.6		3.2			5.1	1.6
Net Worth	1.1	22.6	5.4		-47.6			38.3	46.2
Total Liabilties & Net Worth	100.0	100.0	100.0		100.0			100.0	100.0
INCOME DATA									
Net Sales	100.0	100.0	100.0		100.0			100.0	100.0
Gross Profit									
Operating Expenses	85.2	88.6	84.6		72.8			91.5	89.4
Operating Profit	14.8	11.4	15.4		27.2			8.5	10.6
All Other Expenses (net)	5.0	4.3	3.8		10.3			-.9	1.0
Profit Before Taxes	9.7	7.1	11.6		16.9			9.5	9.6
RATIOS									
Current	3.1 / 1.3 / .6	4.3 / 1.5 / .8	2.6 / 1.4 / 1.0		3.3 / 1.1 / .3			2.7 / 2.1 / 1.1	3.6 / 1.5 / 1.2
Quick	2.4 / 1.1 / .5	4.0 / 1.1 / .5	2.2 / 1.0 / .5		3.2 / 1.1 / .1			2.4 / 1.2 / .6	2.6 / 1.1 / .5
Sales/Receivables	3 104.7 / 29 12.7 / 47 7.7	3 128.1 / 14 25.3 / 41 8.8	1 377.6 / 14 25.3 / 38 9.7		0 UND / 4 94.5 / 18 20.3			11 32.2 / 25 14.8 / 37 9.8	7 50.4 / 20 18.2 / 43 8.5
Cost of Sales/Inventory									
Cost of Sales/Payables									
Sales/Working Capital	5.9 / 29.7 / -10.3	4.3 / 20.7 / -42.1	4.4 / 16.2 / NM		3.5 / NM / -3.4			4.5 / 7.1 / 38.3	4.6 / 11.0 / 27.3
EBIT/Interest	13.6 / (43) 3.8 / 1.3	9.5 / (52) 4.8 / 1.2	13.8 / (42) 3.9 / 1.0					15.9 / 3.4 / 1.2	11.2 / (11) 4.7 / .7
Net Profit + Depr., Dep., Amort./Cur. Mat. L/T/D	19.8 / (10) 3.0 / .5	3.1 / (10) 1.8 / .8							
Fixed/Worth	.4 / 1.7 / -5.7	.7 / 1.7 / -8.0	.7 / 1.5 / -183.3		.2 / .0 / -14.6			1.1 / 1.6 / 5.7	.4 / 1.2 / 2.3
Debt/Worth	.9 / 2.7 / -11.9	.8 / 2.5 / -13.5	.9 / 2.3 / -16.1		.5 / 3.9 / -5.6			.9 / 1.1 / 20.2	.7 / 1.7 / 3.6
% Profit Before Taxes/Tangible Net Worth	61.9 / (37) 36.7 / 8.9	59.5 / (42) 28.4 / 8.8	74.6 / (38) 24.9 / 7.4					47.9 / (11) 11.5 / 8.1	33.2 / (12) 23.8 / 3.9
% Profit Before Taxes/Total Assets	23.3 / 11.7 / 2.3	17.4 / 6.6 / .4	22.6 / 5.9 / -.7		302.7 / 18.5 / -7.7			21.2 / 3.9 / .6	18.6 / 7.4 / 1.1
Sales/Net Fixed Assets	54.5 / 3.6 / 1.1	8.7 / 3.7 / 1.2	11.5 / 2.8 / 1.0		UND / 5.1 / 3.4			7.6 / 1.9 / .8	14.0 / 4.1 / 1.9
Sales/Total Assets	2.6 / 1.6 / .7	2.5 / 1.6 / .6	2.3 / 1.2 / .6		6.8 / 1.8 / .8			2.2 / 1.1 / .6	2.0 / 1.2 / .8
% Depr., Dep., Amort./Sales	1.1 / (40) 8.2 / 17.3	1.6 / (46) 6.2 / 14.0	3.8 / (37) 9.7 / 17.7						
% Officers', Directors' Owners' Comp/Sales	1.5 / (11) 3.5 / 12.7	1.4 / (12) 2.2 / 7.5							
Net Sales ($)	1714140M	2465916M	2296575M	3149M	21638M	8375M	62173M	219432M	1981808M
Total Assets ($)	1011413M	1182721M	1588939M	9658M	37399M	7505M	71709M	283673M	1178995M

© RMA 2019

M = $ thousand   MM = $ million
See Pages viii through xx for Explanation of Ratios and Data

Current Data Sorted by Assets

Comparative Historical Data

	0-500M	500M-2MM	2-10MM	10-50MM	50-100MM	100-250MM		4/1/14-3/31/15 ALL	4/1/15-3/31/16 ALL
Type of Statement									
Unqualified			2	1		1		8	9
Reviewed				1	1			9	4
Compiled			1					2	3
Tax Returns		1	1	1		2		3	3
Other	1		1	7	6			24	26
		4 (4/1-9/30/18)		23 (10/1/18-3/31/19)					
NUMBER OF STATEMENTS	1	1	5	9	7	4		46	45
	%	%	%	%	%	%	**ASSETS**	%	%
							Cash & Equivalents	14.7	12.2
							Trade Receivables (net)	13.1	12.8
							Inventory	1.5	1.2
							All Other Current	1.9	4.5
							Total Current	31.1	30.8
							Fixed Assets (net)	60.2	58.6
							Intangibles (net)	4.9	5.2
							All Other Non-Current	3.8	5.4
							Total	100.0	100.0
							LIABILITIES		
							Notes Payable-Short Term	2.3	1.7
							Cur. Mat.-L.T.D.	3.5	5.6
							Trade Payables	7.7	9.7
							Income Taxes Payable	.5	.8
							All Other Current	6.9	9.3
							Total Current	20.9	27.1
							Long-Term Debt	18.6	23.0
							Deferred Taxes	3.9	4.4
							All Other Non-Current	5.6	5.9
							Net Worth	51.0	39.5
							Total Liabilities & Net Worth	100.0	100.0
							INCOME DATA		
							Net Sales	100.0	100.0
							Gross Profit		
							Operating Expenses	77.0	80.7
							Operating Profit	23.0	19.3
							All Other Expenses (net)	.6	1.2
							Profit Before Taxes	22.4	18.1
							RATIOS		
							Current	2.4	2.2
								1.6	1.3
								1.0	.6
							Quick	2.0	1.5
								1.2	1.0
								.8	.4
							Sales/Receivables	25 / 14.7	26 / 14.2
								47 / 7.8	38 / 9.6
								72 / 5.1	54 / 6.8
							Cost of Sales/Inventory		
							Cost of Sales/Payables		
							Sales/Working Capital	4.3	4.5
								9.1	16.5
								-35.5	-5.0
							EBIT/Interest	68.1	47.3
								(43) 20.5	(40) 14.5
								4.8	4.6
							Net Profit + Depr., Dep., Amort./Cur. Mat. L/T/D	22.1	12.5
								(19) 6.0	(15) 4.9
								2.9	3.0
							Fixed/Worth	.9	.8
								1.2	1.4
								2.0	3.3
							Debt/Worth	.5	.6
								.8	1.1
								2.9	4.8
							% Profit Before Taxes/Tangible Net Worth	50.3	46.2
								(44) 26.1	(40) 21.0
								10.9	9.1
							% Profit Before Taxes/Total Assets	17.7	19.6
								12.2	7.6
								5.8	3.4
							Sales/Net Fixed Assets	2.6	4.6
								.9	.9
								.5	.5
							Sales/Total Assets	1.3	1.4
								.6	.6
								.4	.4
							% Depr., Dep., Amort./Sales	4.1	3.6
								(41) 7.1	(39) 7.3
								12.0	14.6
							% Officers', Directors' Owners' Comp/Sales		
1692M	4775M	23778M	326635M	309683M	271184M	Net Sales ($)	1603615M	1575068M
241M	1039M	30110M	247356M	456743M	519091M	Total Assets ($)	2464137M	2329384M

© RMA 2019

M = $ thousand   MM = $ million
See Pages viii through xx for Explanation of Ratios and Data

Comparative Historical Data | Current Data Sorted by Sales

			Type of Statement	0-1MM	4 (4/1-9/30/18) 1-3MM	3-5MM	23 (10/1/18-3/31/19) 5-10MM	10-25MM	25MM & OVER
7	9	4	Unqualified		2				2
2	3	2	Reviewed						2
1	2	1	Compiled		1				
1	4	3	Tax Returns			1	1	2	1
22	19	17	Other		1		2	7	7
4/1/16-3/31/17 ALL	4/1/17-3/31/18 ALL	4/1/18-3/31/19 ALL							
33	37	27	**NUMBER OF STATEMENTS**		4	1	3	7	12
%	%	%	**ASSETS**	%	%	%	%	%	%
11.0	16.4	8.3	Cash & Equivalents						9.5
15.1	14.9	12.0	Trade Receivables (net)						15.4
3.4	4.7	3.6	Inventory						4.2
2.3	3.1	1.3	All Other Current						1.3
31.8	39.1	25.2	Total Current	D A T A	N O T	A V A I L A B L E			30.4
57.7	51.8	65.8	Fixed Assets (net)						59.3
4.7	4.8	3.6	Intangibles (net)						5.0
5.7	4.3	5.4	All Other Non-Current						5.3
100.0	100.0	100.0	Total						100.0
			LIABILITIES						
4.8	3.4	1.2	Notes Payable-Short Term						1.7
3.5	4.6	5.2	Cur. Mat.-L.T.D.						4.8
19.1	12.0	7.1	Trade Payables						11.0
.5	.2	.0	Income Taxes Payable						.0
7.7	7.9	4.7	All Other Current						6.2
35.7	28.0	18.1	Total Current						23.7
16.9	12.7	27.3	Long-Term Debt						20.6
4.4	2.7	5.3	Deferred Taxes						2.5
4.9	8.4	2.4	All Other Non-Current						2.8
38.2	48.1	46.9	Net Worth						50.4
100.0	100.0	100.0	Total Liabilities & Net Worth						100.0
			INCOME DATA						
100.0	100.0	100.0	Net Sales						100.0
			Gross Profit						
80.1	81.9	84.0	Operating Expenses						88.5
19.9	18.1	16.0	Operating Profit						11.5
.9	1.9	.5	All Other Expenses (net)						.8
19.1	16.2	15.5	Profit Before Taxes						10.7
			RATIOS						
2.5	2.2	2.4							1.7
1.6	1.4	1.4	Current						1.4
1.0	.9	.9							1.1
2.0	1.6	1.6							1.5
1.3	1.1	1.1	Quick						1.1
.6	.6	.8							.9
24 14.9	23 15.8	26 14.3							26 14.1
40 9.2	37 9.8	36 10.0	Sales/Receivables						37 9.8
58 6.3	59 6.2	51 7.1							60 6.1
			Cost of Sales/Inventory						
			Cost of Sales/Payables						
4.1	5.1	4.9							5.4
6.6	15.7	14.4	Sales/Working Capital						13.8
NM	-106.8	-130.2							70.8
51.9	85.0	15.2							92.7
(30) 23.5	(34) 17.6	(26) 7.7	EBIT/Interest						(11) 8.8
12.5	5.6	2.9							2.2
30.7	16.7	67.1	Net Profit + Depr., Dep.,						
(13) 9.6	(15) 5.0	(16) 6.3	Amort./Cur. Mat. L/T/D						
4.9	3.2	2.7							
.9	.8	.8							.8
1.2	1.1	1.3	Fixed/Worth						1.1
1.7	2.0	2.6							2.0
.5	.5	.5							.6
.7	.9	1.1	Debt/Worth						1.1
2.9	2.3	2.1							1.8
42.6	49.2	37.7	% Profit Before Taxes/Tangible						40.7
(30) 17.4	(32) 19.7	(25) 17.2	Net Worth						19.6
9.8	13.2	6.7							4.9
14.9	16.6	12.8	% Profit Before Taxes/Total						17.2
8.4	9.1	10.1	Assets						8.5
5.6	5.7	4.5							2.9
2.7	8.4	4.2							5.2
.9	1.3	.9	Sales/Net Fixed Assets						1.4
.7	.6	.4							.7
1.5	2.3	2.1							2.3
.6	.6	.7	Sales/Total Assets						.8
.4	.5	.3							.5
4.4	3.7	5.6							3.1
(29) 8.6	(32) 7.0	(25) 9.1	% Depr., Dep., Amort./Sales						(11) 5.7
14.0	13.2	10.9							9.4
			% Officers', Directors' Owners' Comp/Sales						
1546679M	2032888M	937747M	Net Sales ($)		9873M	4775M	22620M	127990M	772489M
1906840M	1878821M	1254580M	Total Assets ($)		21572M	1039M	29888M	331598M	870483M

M = $ thousand   MM = $ million
See Pages viii through xx for Explanation of Ratios and Data

Current Data Sorted by Assets							Comparative Historical Data	
0-500M	500M-2MM	2-10MM	10-50MM	50-100MM	100-250MM	**Type of Statement**	43	47
			4 1	5	2	Unqualified	12	14
						Reviewed		1
						Compiled	3	5
3 5 (4/1-9/30/18)		2	10 30 (10/1/18-3/31/19)	4	3	Tax Returns	2	3
1						Other	26	24
4		2	15	9	5	**NUMBER OF STATEMENTS** 4/1/14-3/31/15 ALL / 4/1/15-3/31/16 ALL	43	47
%	%	%	%	%	%	**ASSETS**	%	%
			6.2			Cash & Equivalents	10.6	10.1
			32.3			Trade Receivables (net)	15.1	16.3
			4.6			Inventory	4.9	1.9
			3.9			All Other Current	4.4	5.8
			47.1			Total Current	35.1	34.1
			46.8			Fixed Assets (net)	54.2	55.9
			3.6			Intangibles (net)	2.8	3.9
			2.5			All Other Non-Current	7.9	6.1
			100.0			Total	100.0	100.0
						LIABILITIES		
			5.2			Notes Payable-Short Term	5.5	6.0
			2.7			Cur. Mat.-L.T.D.	3.5	3.7
			13.2			Trade Payables	9.1	12.5
			.0			Income Taxes Payable	.2	.0
			11.3			All Other Current	12.7	12.3
			32.4			Total Current	31.0	34.5
			26.7			Long-Term Debt	25.2	24.6
			.0			Deferred Taxes	.3	.5
			2.7			All Other Non-Current	8.0	5.7
			38.2			Net Worth	35.5	34.7
			100.0			Total Liabilities & Net Worth	100.0	100.0
						INCOME DATA		
			100.0			Net Sales	100.0	100.0
						Gross Profit		
			84.6			Operating Expenses	87.2	86.5
			15.4			Operating Profit	12.8	13.5
			6.9			All Other Expenses (net)	2.8	8.1
			8.5			Profit Before Taxes	10.0	5.3
						RATIOS		
			2.0				2.0	2.6
			1.6			Current	1.1	1.4
			1.2				.5	.8
			1.9				1.9	2.5
			1.4			Quick	.9	1.2
			.9				.4	.4
			17 21.7				15 24.6	8 46.5
			63 5.8			Sales/Receivables	30 12.2	33 11.0
			192 1.9				46 8.0	54 6.8
						Cost of Sales/Inventory		
						Cost of Sales/Payables		
			3.4				12.5	7.2
			6.9			Sales/Working Capital	139.5	12.7
			43.2				-4.9	-24.0
			7.4				(30) 21.6	(37) 9.1
			(11) 4.0			EBIT/Interest	2.7	3.7
			1.8				1.3	.5
						Net Profit + Depr., Dep., Amort./Cur. Mat. L/T/D		
			.0				1.0	1.0
			1.4			Fixed/Worth	1.9	1.9
			2.1				5.1	3.5
			1.0				.9	.8
			2.4			Debt/Worth	1.8	1.5
			3.9				8.2	6.2
			24.1				(37) 69.6	(44) 37.3
			(14) 17.0			% Profit Before Taxes/Tangible Net Worth	11.7	10.7
			1.2				2.2	-5.6
			7.9				10.6	11.6
			5.9			% Profit Before Taxes/Total Assets	4.6	3.9
			.6				.5	-1.3
			627.8				27.9	26.3
			2.3			Sales/Net Fixed Assets	3.1	1.4
			.2				.2	.2
			2.0				3.3	2.6
			1.1			Sales/Total Assets	1.5	.8
			.1				.2	.2
			1.4				(31) 1.7	(37) 2.1
			(13) 4.9			% Depr., Dep., Amort./Sales	11.4	10.4
			28.1				19.9	24.2
						% Officers', Directors' Owners' Comp/Sales		
	11469M	22947M	621454M	276360M	138453M	Net Sales ($)	3721063M	3894613M
	5531M	15103M	495995M	610764M	889299M	Total Assets ($)	2592570M	3129668M

(Left columns 0-500M, 500M-2MM, 2-10MM: DATA NOT AVAILABLE)

© RMA 2019

M = $ thousand   MM = $ million
See Pages viii through xx for Explanation of Ratios and Data

Comparative Historical Data | Current Data Sorted by Sales

	4/1/16-3/31/17 ALL	4/1/17-3/31/18 ALL	4/1/18-3/31/19 ALL	Type of Statement	0-1MM	1-3MM	3-5MM	5-10MM	10-25MM	25MM & OVER
	19	12	11	Unqualified						1
		2	2	Reviewed		1				
	2	2		Compiled			1	2	3	5
				Tax Returns						
	21	21	22	Other	2	3		2	4	11
	42	37	35	**NUMBER OF STATEMENTS**	2	4	1	4	7	17
	%	%	%	**ASSETS**	%	%	%	%	%	%
	9.9	11.6	8.4	Cash & Equivalents						6.1
	15.9	17.3	24.0	Trade Receivables (net)						32.4
	4.4	2.6	2.8	Inventory						4.6
	4.0	4.4	4.2	All Other Current						4.1
	34.3	36.0	39.4	Total Current						47.1
	51.3	47.9	49.8	Fixed Assets (net)						44.6
	2.6	4.0	1.6	Intangibles (net)						3.3
	11.8	12.1	9.1	All Other Non-Current						5.0
	100.0	100.0	100.0	Total						100.0
				LIABILITIES						
	4.8	3.7	4.5	Notes Payable-Short Term						5.1
	5.8	2.2	3.8	Cur. Mat.-L.T.D.						5.0
	8.6	7.0	8.5	Trade Payables						11.7
	.2	.2	.0	Income Taxes Payable						.0
	9.1	9.8	11.8	All Other Current						11.2
	28.5	22.9	28.6	Total Current						33.0
	25.3	23.2	25.3	Long-Term Debt						19.5
	.6	.8	1.0	Deferred Taxes						1.7
	9.7	7.2	2.8	All Other Non-Current						3.8
	36.0	46.0	42.3	Net Worth						42.0
	100.0	100.0	100.0	Total Liabilities & Net Worth						100.0
				INCOME DATA						
	100.0	100.0	100.0	Net Sales						100.0
				Gross Profit						
	78.9	80.2	81.0	Operating Expenses						91.4
	21.1	19.8	19.0	Operating Profit						8.6
	8.8	6.7	9.5	All Other Expenses (net)						3.7
	12.4	13.1	9.5	Profit Before Taxes						4.9
				RATIOS						
	3.9	2.3	2.2	Current						2.3
	1.4	1.2	1.5							1.4
	.7	.7	.8							1.1
	2.2	2.1	2.2	Quick						2.0
	1.0	1.2	1.2							1.4
	.3	.5	.6							.7
	2 180.6	1 293.0	21 17.7	Sales/Receivables						36 10.2
	29 12.4	27 13.3	52 7.0							57 6.4
	49 7.5	60 6.1	166 2.2							130 2.8
				Cost of Sales/Inventory						
				Cost of Sales/Payables						
	4.6	4.7	2.8	Sales/Working Capital						4.1
	24.7	18.0	6.9							6.9
	-10.0	-6.0	-21.2							NM
	9.1	5.4	5.8	EBIT/Interest						7.2
	(34) 3.0	(24) 4.1	(22) 2.3						(16)	2.8
	1.3	2.4	.6							.9
				Net Profit + Depr., Dep., Amort./Cur. Mat. L/T/D						
	.1	.0	.1	Fixed/Worth						.1
	1.6	1.4	1.4							1.4
	4.2	2.1	2.2							2.1
	.7	.6	.9	Debt/Worth						1.1
	1.3	1.1	1.4							1.4
	8.5	3.2	2.7							2.7
	38.9	26.6	18.3	% Profit Before Taxes/Tangible Net Worth						21.8
	(36) 13.5	(34) 11.0	(34) 6.5						(16)	8.8
	6.4	3.9	-1.1							-.7
	9.2	7.3	7.1	% Profit Before Taxes/Total Assets						7.5
	4.1	4.7	2.2							3.7
	.9	1.1	-.4							-.1
	89.0	153.6	193.5	Sales/Net Fixed Assets						410.6
	2.2	1.5	1.0							2.3
	.2	.2	.2							.8
	1.6	1.7	1.8	Sales/Total Assets						1.9
	.7	.4	.6							1.1
	.2	.2	.2							.6
	2.3	.3	4.2	% Depr., Dep., Amort./Sales						2.8
	(30) 11.5	(27) 8.8	(29) 12.9						(15)	5.5
	25.2	21.4	24.7							9.1
				% Officers', Directors' Owners' Comp/Sales						
	2619294M	1270353M	1070683M	Net Sales ($)	1280M	7878M	3688M	28155M	114618M	915064M
	3034557M	2122226M	2016692M	Total Assets ($)	2484M	45392M	70975M	152090M	690610M	1055141M

Current data period headers: 5 (4/1-9/30/18) · 30 (10/1/18-3/31/19)

M = $ thousand   MM = $ million

See Pages viii through xx for Explanation of Ratios and Data

Current Data Sorted by Assets							Comparative Historical Data	
					3	**Type of Statement** Unqualified	14	8
			1	1		Reviewed	5	3
		2	1		2	Compiled	4	5
	1		1			Tax Returns	3	3
		5	1	4	6	Other	19	19
	5 (4/1-9/30/18)		23 (10/1/18-3/31/19)				4/1/14-3/31/15 ALL	4/1/15-3/31/16 ALL
0-500M	500M-2MM	2-10MM	10-50MM	50-100MM	100-250MM			
	1	7	4	5	11	**NUMBER OF STATEMENTS**	45	38
%	%	%	%	%	%	**ASSETS**	%	%
DATA NOT AVAILABLE					5.4	Cash & Equivalents	8.3	11.3
					7.4	Trade Receivables (net)	14.3	11.0
					.4	Inventory	1.9	1.0
					1.8	All Other Current	1.3	1.0
					14.9	Total Current	25.8	24.4
					78.4	Fixed Assets (net)	57.4	56.9
					1.3	Intangibles (net)	4.8	3.8
					5.4	All Other Non-Current	12.1	14.9
					100.0	Total	100.0	100.0
						LIABILITIES		
					1.0	Notes Payable-Short Term	1.9	6.8
					3.5	Cur. Mat.-L.T.D.	5.6	4.6
					4.5	Trade Payables	7.7	4.2
					.0	Income Taxes Payable	.0	.0
					5.4	All Other Current	6.0	9.0
					14.4	Total Current	21.1	24.6
					41.3	Long-Term Debt	29.8	28.1
					1.5	Deferred Taxes	.3	.3
					2.0	All Other Non-Current	2.2	6.2
					40.8	Net Worth	46.6	40.7
					100.0	Total Liabilties & Net Worth	100.0	100.0
						INCOME DATA		
					100.0	Net Sales	100.0	100.0
						Gross Profit		
					91.9	Operating Expenses	81.6	86.9
					8.1	Operating Profit	18.4	13.1
					5.9	All Other Expenses (net)	3.8	3.8
					2.3	Profit Before Taxes	14.6	9.3
						RATIOS		
					1.8		2.7	1.8
					.9	Current	1.2	1.0
					.5		.7	.6
					1.8		2.3	1.8
					.8	Quick	1.1	.9
					.4		.4	.5
					38 9.5		**13** 28.8	**11** 33.0
					43 8.5	Sales/Receivables	**36** 10.2	**31** 11.7
					51 7.1		**73** 5.0	**42** 8.6
						Cost of Sales/Inventory		
						Cost of Sales/Payables		
					8.9		5.3	7.2
					-104.2	Sales/Working Capital	21.5	434.6
					-4.8		-23.2	-9.7
					3.2		13.7	16.6
					1.9	EBIT/Interest	(42) 5.1	(35) 3.2
					.0		2.6	.0
						Net Profit + Depr., Dep., Amort./Cur. Mat. L/T/D		
					1.6		1.0	.8
					2.2	Fixed/Worth	1.5	1.6
					3.1		3.1	3.7
					.9		.5	.7
					1.8	Debt/Worth	1.4	1.3
					2.7		3.8	5.5
					14.3		26.8	28.3
					4.5	% Profit Before Taxes/Tangible Net Worth	(41) 14.1	(33) 13.4
					-15.3		8.5	5.3
					4.7		10.3	12.3
					1.7	% Profit Before Taxes/Total Assets	5.0	4.8
					-4.1		2.4	-.7
					1.1		10.9	5.0
					.7	Sales/Net Fixed Assets	1.0	1.3
					.4		.4	.4
					.8		1.3	1.3
					.6	Sales/Total Assets	.7	.9
					.3		.3	.3
							3.8	3.3
						% Depr., Dep., Amort./Sales	(36) 10.2	(28) 8.7
							17.6	13.8
							1.5	
						% Officers', Directors' Owners' Comp/Sales	(10) 2.1	
							5.4	
	14765M	113613M	39903M	369764M	1184497M	Net Sales ($)	2636850M	2679829M
	1942M	38677M	67461M	332363M	2092483M	Total Assets ($)	3368474M	3257530M

M = $ thousand MM = $ million

See Pages viii through xx for Explanation of Ratios and Data

Comparative Historical Data				Current Data Sorted by Sales					
Type of Statement									
Unqualified	7	10	3						3
Reviewed	4	1	2		1				1
Compiled	6	1	5		1			2	2
Tax Returns	2	4	2					2	
Other	14	23	16		1	1	2		12
	4/1/16-3/31/17 ALL	**4/1/17-3/31/18 ALL**	**4/1/18-3/31/19 ALL**	**5 (4/1-9/30/18)**		**23 (10/1/18-3/31/19)**			
				0-1MM	**1-3MM**	**3-5MM**	**5-10MM**	**10-25MM**	**25MM & OVER**
NUMBER OF STATEMENTS	33	39	28		3	1	2	4	18
	%	%	%	%	%	%	%	%	%
ASSETS									
Cash & Equivalents	11.2	9.5	7.9	D A T A					8.3
Trade Receivables (net)	18.7	15.5	15.2						13.8
Inventory	.5	.3	.2	N O T					.4
All Other Current	2.1	1.2	1.9						2.4
Total Current	32.6	26.6	25.3	A V A I L A B L E					24.9
Fixed Assets (net)	51.9	59.7	64.7						63.2
Intangibles (net)	4.8	4.6	4.1						3.9
All Other Non-Current	10.8	9.0	6.0						8.0
Total	100.0	100.0	100.0						100.0
LIABILITIES									
Notes Payable-Short Term	8.1	2.0	1.3						.7
Cur. Mat.-L.T.D.	8.0	4.0	4.5						3.0
Trade Payables	5.7	8.0	7.3						4.9
Income Taxes Payable	.0	.4	.0						.0
All Other Current	11.3	8.7	5.5						5.6
Total Current	33.1	23.1	18.6						14.2
Long-Term Debt	23.7	27.7	33.2						31.0
Deferred Taxes	.3	.1	.6						.9
All Other Non-Current	3.7	9.3	11.2						3.2
Net Worth	39.2	39.7	36.4						50.7
Total Liabilties & Net Worth	100.0	100.0	100.0						100.0
INCOME DATA									
Net Sales	100.0	100.0	100.0						100.0
Gross Profit									
Operating Expenses	84.6	84.7	90.8						91.3
Operating Profit	15.4	15.3	9.2						8.7
All Other Expenses (net)	3.2	4.2	3.1						3.8
Profit Before Taxes	12.2	11.1	6.1						4.9
RATIOS									
Current	1.6	1.8	2.3						2.6
	1.2	1.1	1.2						1.3
	.7	.6	.6						.8
Quick	1.4	1.7	2.1						2.4
	1.0	1.0	1.0						1.1
	.2	.5	.4						.4
Sales/Receivables	**3** 106.9	**10** 36.7	**21** 17.4						**27** 13.5
	30 12.1	**37** 9.8	**41** 8.8						**41** 9.0
	50 7.3	**48** 7.6	**51** 7.2						**47** 7.8
Cost of Sales/Inventory									
Cost of Sales/Payables									
Sales/Working Capital	8.6	9.0	8.9						8.3
	35.1	46.0	25.7						20.6
	-12.5	-13.8	-6.1						-36.9
EBIT/Interest	13.4	9.6	5.2						4.6
	(30) 4.4	(33) 4.5	(25) 3.2						(16) 3.0
	2.4	2.4	.7						.3
Net Profit + Depr., Dep., Amort./Cur. Mat. L/T/D									
Fixed/Worth	.8	1.0	.8						.7
	1.5	1.6	1.8						1.7
	2.5	2.1	2.7						2.6
Debt/Worth	.8	.7	.8						.3
	1.6	1.3	1.7						1.6
	6.5	2.5	2.8						2.2
% Profit Before Taxes/Tangible Net Worth	28.6	35.8	35.9						20.3
	(30) 15.8	(36) 14.6	(27) 14.3						9.8
	8.1	6.6	.8						-3.2
% Profit Before Taxes/Total Assets	11.4	9.4	9.9						10.1
	5.5	5.7	5.5						3.7
	2.8	2.8	.4						-.8
Sales/Net Fixed Assets	24.9	5.3	2.3						2.7
	1.8	1.1	1.1						.9
	.5	.3	.4						.5
Sales/Total Assets	2.0	1.7	1.3						1.1
	.9	.8	.8						.7
	.4	.3	.4						.4
% Depr., Dep., Amort./Sales	3.7	2.0	1.6						
	(24) 8.6	(28) 8.9	(18) 9.7						
	14.6	16.7	18.1						
% Officers', Directors' Owners' Comp/Sales									
Net Sales ($)	1443231M	1982955M	1722542M		7286M	3109M	16642M	70738M	1624767M
Total Assets ($)	2003079M	3264646M	2532926M		30001M	12960M	18127M	38455M	2433383M

M = $ thousand MM = $ million

See Pages viii through xx for Explanation of Ratios and Data

Current Data Sorted by Assets   Comparative Historical Data

0-500M	500M-2MM	2-10MM	10-50MM	50-100MM	100-250MM	Type of Statement	4/1/14-3/31/15 ALL	4/1/15-3/31/16 ALL
		2	4	2	9	Unqualified	18	14
1	1			3	2	Reviewed	12	14
	3	4	1			Compiled	18	3
						Tax Returns	6	9
2	5	16	15	7	14	Other	55	70
	14 (4/1-9/30/18)		82 (10/1/18-3/31/19)					
3	9	24	23	12	25	**NUMBER OF STATEMENTS**	109	110
%	%	%	%	%	%	**ASSETS**	%	%
		10.8	8.0	8.9	5.2	Cash & Equivalents	12.9	12.0
		18.9	10.3	9.1	4.9	Trade Receivables (net)	16.2	12.5
		2.7	2.4	1.1	1.9	Inventory	1.2	1.2
		2.7	2.7	2.5	1.1	All Other Current	2.5	2.1
		35.0	23.4	21.5	13.2	Total Current	32.8	27.8
		59.8	61.3	56.7	79.4	Fixed Assets (net)	55.6	63.1
		1.5	6.4	6.6	3.1	Intangibles (net)	2.1	2.9
		3.6	9.0	15.2	4.3	All Other Non-Current	9.5	6.2
		100.0	100.0	100.0	100.0	Total	100.0	100.0
						LIABILITIES		
		3.6	1.1	6.7	2.7	Notes Payable-Short Term	2.3	3.2
		6.8	8.4	2.5	4.8	Cur. Mat.-L.T.D.	5.0	5.9
		9.1	5.1	3.1	2.5	Trade Payables	6.3	4.7
		1.1	.0	.6	.0	Income Taxes Payable	.1	.1
		7.2	4.1	14.2	3.6	All Other Current	5.4	5.7
		27.7	18.6	27.1	13.6	Total Current	19.2	19.6
		40.7	36.4	20.0	41.4	Long-Term Debt	33.1	43.7
		.5	.5	1.3	.4	Deferred Taxes	.7	.7
		1.5	2.1	18.2	1.3	All Other Non-Current	2.4	2.5
		29.6	42.4	33.4	43.3	Net Worth	44.6	33.7
		100.0	100.0	100.0	100.0	Total Liabilties & Net Worth	100.0	100.0
						INCOME DATA		
		100.0	100.0	100.0	100.0	Net Sales	100.0	100.0
						Gross Profit		
		77.8	78.7	76.6	81.0	Operating Expenses	82.6	84.4
		22.2	21.3	23.4	19.0	Operating Profit	17.4	15.6
		9.4	4.4	3.8	4.4	All Other Expenses (net)	3.1	4.3
		12.8	16.9	19.7	14.6	Profit Before Taxes	14.3	11.3
						RATIOS		
		3.1	2.3	3.4	2.8		3.3	2.1
		1.3	1.5	1.4	1.4	Current	1.6	1.2
		.6	.8	.6	.8		1.0	.7
		2.5	2.0	3.0	2.2		2.7	1.9
		1.0	1.2	1.2	1.1	Quick	1.4	1.0
		.4	.5	.6	.6		.8	.6
		0 UND	0 UND	0 753.0	30 12.0		15 24.6	13 29.1
		20 18.0	31 11.8	43 8.4	36 10.2	Sales/Receivables	32 11.5	30 12.1
		63 5.8	42 8.7	60 6.1	49 7.4		45 8.1	41 9.0
						Cost of Sales/Inventory		
						Cost of Sales/Payables		
		5.9	7.5	3.0	4.4		5.3	8.4
		21.6	11.8	12.0	15.7	Sales/Working Capital	11.9	47.2
		-11.9	-25.0	-18.4	-15.7		277.5	-15.7
		10.4	13.6		4.9		18.6	10.1
		(20) 6.1	(20) 4.6		(22) 3.8	EBIT/Interest	(91) 5.1	(92) 4.6
		1.7	3.6		2.4		2.3	1.6
							5.4	14.0
						Net Profit + Depr., Dep., Amort./Cur. Mat. L/T/D	(17) 2.1	(15) 1.7
							1.3	1.3
		.6	1.1	.8	1.4		.5	.9
		2.2	2.2	1.7	2.0	Fixed/Worth	1.4	1.9
		-50.6	3.1	8.4	3.5		2.8	5.1
		.8	.4	.2	.9		.5	.8
		2.8	2.5	1.4	1.3	Debt/Worth	1.3	1.8
		-10.8	2.8	9.5	3.1		2.9	5.1
		81.6	37.1	13.4	12.6		46.7	36.4
		(16) 28.4	(21) 19.2	(10) 7.9	11.3	% Profit Before Taxes/Tangible Net Worth	(102) 21.8	(95) 14.6
		14.1	10.2	-6.0	5.7		7.4	6.0
		17.1	11.9	8.1	5.9		18.0	12.2
		6.7	8.5	4.4	4.2	% Profit Before Taxes/Total Assets	8.3	5.9
		.1	4.8	-1.2	2.0		1.7	.9
		8.0	2.3	3.8	.7		6.4	4.2
		2.9	1.3	1.0	.6	Sales/Net Fixed Assets	1.8	1.2
		.3	.8	.5	.3		.7	.4
		3.2	1.3	1.1	.5		1.9	1.8
		1.6	.9	.5	.4	Sales/Total Assets	1.0	.8
		.3	.6	.2	.3		.5	.4
		3.2	1.3	3.2	9.7		3.6	3.0
		(22) 7.9	8.4	(11) 9.6	11.2	% Depr., Dep., Amort./Sales	(88) 7.2	(88) 7.7
		39.4	19.6	14.4	31.5		12.5	19.5
							1.0	1.3
						% Officers', Directors' Owners' Comp/Sales	(16) 1.8	(14) 3.8
							3.1	8.0
890M	37630M	299905M	762582M	613014M	2122933M	Net Sales ($)	3436538M	3358359M
829M	11932M	131682M	669082M	865365M	4762519M	Total Assets ($)	4690617M	4723923M

Comparative Historical Data | Current Data Sorted by Sales

			Type of Statement	0-1MM	1-3MM	3-5MM	5-10MM	10-25MM	25MM & OVER
15	20	15	Unqualified				1	2	12
12	10	10	Reviewed		2			2	6
5	10	7	Compiled	2			2	1	2
9	2	5	Tax Returns	1	2			2	2
65	69	59	Other	6	5	2	8	11	27
4/1/16-3/31/17 ALL	4/1/17-3/31/18 ALL	4/1/18-3/31/19 ALL			14 (4/1-9/30/18)			82 (10/1/18-3/31/19)	
106	111	96	**NUMBER OF STATEMENTS**	9	9	2	11	18	47
%	%	%	**ASSETS**	%	%	%	%	%	%
11.6	10.5	10.4	Cash & Equivalents				15.2	11.1	8.0
12.3	12.2	12.3	Trade Receivables (net)				27.0	13.0	13.0
2.3	2.2	1.9	Inventory				.1	.6	3.1
2.0	2.6	2.1	All Other Current				2.1	.7	2.6
28.2	27.4	26.8	Total Current				44.4	25.5	26.8
62.3	59.8	62.2	Fixed Assets (net)				32.6	63.1	63.2
2.6	4.3	4.4	Intangibles (net)				7.1	7.7	2.2
6.9	8.5	6.5	All Other Non-Current				15.9	3.7	7.8
100.0	100.0	100.0	Total				100.0	100.0	100.0
			LIABILITIES						
2.7	3.0	5.7	Notes Payable-Short Term				12.6	2.3	3.4
6.8	6.1	5.9	Cur. Mat.-L.T.D.				1.1	8.2	3.9
8.0	4.1	6.5	Trade Payables				15.1	5.2	6.9
.1	.0	.4	Income Taxes Payable				.1	.3	.7
6.3	5.9	6.6	All Other Current				16.4	6.3	6.6
23.9	19.1	25.1	Total Current				45.4	22.3	21.5
37.4	45.0	41.7	Long-Term Debt				9.4	43.8	31.7
1.1	.8	.6	Deferred Taxes				2.0	.5	.6
1.7	3.2	4.0	All Other Non-Current				.3	.2	6.3
35.9	31.8	28.5	Net Worth				42.9	33.1	40.0
100.0	100.0	100.0	Total Liabilities & Net Worth				100.0	100.0	100.0
			INCOME DATA						
100.0	100.0	100.0	Net Sales				100.0	100.0	100.0
			Gross Profit						
79.8	80.0	77.9	Operating Expenses				81.2	73.3	86.9
20.2	20.0	22.1	Operating Profit				18.8	26.7	13.1
4.0	4.6	5.7	All Other Expenses (net)				.4	4.9	2.6
16.3	15.4	16.5	Profit Before Taxes				18.4	21.7	10.5
			RATIOS						
2.3	3.6	2.7					4.3	2.8	2.6
1.2	1.5	1.4	Current				2.3	1.3	1.5
.7	.8	.7					.8	.5	.9
1.9	3.2	2.3					4.0	2.5	2.0
1.1	1.0	1.1	Quick				1.9	1.0	1.2
.6	.6	.5					.8	.5	.7
11 32.0	14 26.8	0 UND					0 UND	0 UND	31 11.8
31 11.8	33 11.2	33 11.2	Sales/Receivables				38 9.7	13 27.8	41 8.8
47 7.7	48 7.6	48 7.6					66 5.5	41 8.9	51 7.1
			Cost of Sales/Inventory						
			Cost of Sales/Payables						
6.2	5.3	6.1					5.7	7.3	6.1
31.6	15.2	19.9	Sales/Working Capital				11.8	32.0	11.8
-10.5	-17.9	-14.4					-18.9	-10.5	-80.3
8.6	10.8	8.1						35.1	5.7
(86) 4.2	(90) 4.6	(81) 4.3	EBIT/Interest					(15) 9.3	(42) 3.8
1.9	1.9	2.4						2.3	2.4
	11.2		Net Profit + Depr., Dep.,						
	(14) 4.4		Amort./Cur. Mat. L/T/D						
	1.3								
.8	.7	1.0					.0	.9	.9
1.7	1.8	2.0	Fixed/Worth				.6	3.1	1.9
4.1	4.2	4.8					2.3	5.3	2.9
.6	.7	.7					.3	1.0	.7
1.3	1.6	2.0	Debt/Worth				.6	3.3	1.6
3.8	5.7	6.8					-6.0	5.2	2.8
32.5	24.2	32.8	% Profit Before Taxes/Tangible					79.9	16.5
(98) 13.8	(92) 11.5	(77) 14.0	Net Worth					(15) 36.5	(44) 11.8
3.4	4.4	8.2						17.7	3.7
11.6	11.8	12.4	% Profit Before Taxes/Total				25.7	19.1	8.0
5.6	5.8	5.7	Assets				12.6	10.6	4.7
2.0	1.2	2.0					7.1	2.4	2.1
4.1	4.5	3.7					174.3	3.6	2.3
1.0	1.1	1.2	Sales/Net Fixed Assets				11.7	1.8	1.0
.4	.5	.4					1.2	.3	.6
1.5	1.6	1.6					3.4	2.1	1.3
.7	.7	.7	Sales/Total Assets				2.9	1.0	.7
.3	.3	.4					.9	.3	.5
3.9	2.7	4.0						5.4	3.1
(82) 10.3	(90) 9.9	(75) 10.8	% Depr., Dep., Amort./Sales					(16) 18.0	(32) 6.9
21.6	24.6	22.4						25.3	11.4
	.6	1.7	% Officers', Directors'						
	(15) 2.2	(16) 2.2	Owners' Comp/Sales						
	4.0	4.1							
3666304M	3717324M	3836954M	Net Sales ($)	3424M	17336M	7666M	78416M	280234M	3449878M
6210005M	6422339M	6441409M	Total Assets ($)	15561M	57174M	56366M	193982M	839255M	5279071M

M = $ thousand   MM = $ million
See Pages viii through xx for Explanation of Ratios and Data

Current Data Sorted by Assets   Comparative Historical Data

Type of Statement	0-500M	500M-2MM	2-10MM	10-50MM	50-100MM	100-250MM	4/1/14-3/31/15 ALL	4/1/15-3/31/16 ALL
Unqualified	4	3	3	12	7	9	55	53
Reviewed	16	11	34	46	5	2	121	117
Compiled	86	35	63	20	1	2	172	133
Tax Returns	65	103	51	2		16	258	307
Other		126	201	83	21		450	454
	130 (4/1-9/30/18)			897 (10/1/18-3/31/19)				
NUMBER OF STATEMENTS	171	278	352	163	34	29	1056	1064
ASSETS	%	%	%	%	%	%	%	%
Cash & Equivalents	25.4	17.0	10.7	9.2	7.2	8.5	13.0	14.2
Trade Receivables (net)	15.8	23.2	27.4	23.3	21.3	18.4	24.1	23.2
Inventory	1.2	.8	1.7	1.4	1.1	1.4	1.5	1.4
All Other Current	4.4	3.8	3.6	2.6	3.3	3.8	4.2	3.1
Total Current	46.7	44.8	43.4	36.5	32.9	32.1	42.8	41.9
Fixed Assets (net)	40.2	40.4	44.7	50.4	50.4	53.3	45.5	44.5
Intangibles (net)	4.6	6.3	5.1	4.7	5.5	8.6	3.4	3.8
All Other Non-Current	8.6	8.5	6.8	8.4	11.3	6.0	8.3	9.8
Total	100.0	100.0	100.0	100.0	100.0	100.0	100.0	100.0
LIABILITIES								
Notes Payable-Short Term	13.8	6.7	6.8	4.7	7.4	3.1	9.5	8.5
Cur. Mat.-L.T.D.	8.6	6.8	6.3	9.1	8.7	8.9	7.8	7.7
Trade Payables	8.2	9.9	9.2	7.0	7.7	5.9	9.8	8.8
Income Taxes Payable	.0	.1	.3	.2	.1	.1	.1	.2
All Other Current	15.7	11.9	8.5	7.1	7.1	8.7	10.2	9.2
Total Current	46.3	35.4	31.0	28.2	31.2	26.7	37.4	34.4
Long-Term Debt	36.8	37.9	28.7	27.0	29.7	48.1	32.0	31.4
Deferred Taxes	.0	.2	.6	1.0	2.0	1.8	.6	.6
All Other Non-Current	9.7	3.5	4.1	2.7	4.0	4.1	5.6	5.1
Net Worth	7.2	23.1	35.6	41.2	33.2	19.4	24.4	28.5
Total Liabilities & Net Worth	100.0	100.0	100.0	100.0	100.0	100.0	100.0	100.0
INCOME DATA								
Net Sales	100.0	100.0	100.0	100.0	100.0	100.0	100.0	100.0
Gross Profit								
Operating Expenses	94.4	93.8	92.1	93.8	92.7	94.1	93.3	93.2
Operating Profit	5.6	6.2	7.9	6.2	7.3	5.9	6.7	6.8
All Other Expenses (net)	.2	.9	1.3	.8	.8	2.3	1.0	1.0
Profit Before Taxes	5.4	5.4	6.6	5.5	6.6	3.6	5.7	5.8
RATIOS								
Current	4.0	2.6	2.6	2.0	1.7	1.7	2.3	2.5
	1.7	1.4	1.5	1.2	1.1	1.2	1.3	1.3
	.5	.7	.9	.8	.6	.8	.7	.8
Quick	3.5	2.4	2.4	1.8	1.5	1.5	2.0	2.2
	1.6	1.2	1.3	1.1	1.0	1.0	1.1 (1062)	1.1
	.3	.6	.7	.7	.6	.5	.6	.6
Sales/Receivables	0 UND	0 UND	20 18.7	25 14.5	25 14.4	23 15.6	4 96.2	3 139.0
	0 UND	17 21.0	34 10.7	38 9.6	41 8.9	43 8.4	29 12.7	28 13.0
	20 18.7	38 9.5	46 8.0	45 8.1	47 7.7	61 6.0	44 8.3	43 8.5
Cost of Sales/Inventory								
Cost of Sales/Payables								
Sales/Working Capital	12.4	11.4	8.9	11.7	12.3	10.9	11.9	11.3
	71.2	36.7	20.3	38.1	145.4	42.0	46.3	44.7
	-21.6	-35.9	-61.1	-38.2	-14.5	-32.0	-33.7	-32.7
EBIT/Interest	13.9	16.0	17.1	13.2	10.2	6.2	12.2	13.4
	(120) 5.0	(231) 5.0	(321) 6.4	(156) 6.2	(32) 4.2	3.9	(906) 5.0	(886) 5.6
	1.0	1.1	2.1	2.3	2.2	2.4	2.1	1.8
Net Profit + Depr., Dep., Amort./Cur. Mat. L/T/D		4.0	3.9	2.3	4.7		2.5	3.0
		(16) 2.1	(58) 1.8	(43) 1.6	(14) 2.0		(156) 1.7	(149) 1.8
		1.6	1.1	1.1	.9		1.2	1.1
Fixed/Worth	.1	.4	.5	.7	1.0	1.2	.6	.6
	1.5	1.9	1.4	1.5	1.8	1.9	1.6	1.5
	-5.4	138.8	3.2	2.6	5.8	4.0	5.2	6.5
Debt/Worth	.5	.9	.9	.7	1.1	1.2	1.0	.8
	4.6	3.6	1.9	1.7	3.0	2.9	2.4	2.1
	-4.9	-166.8	5.9	3.2	7.5	5.4	11.1	12.9
% Profit Before Taxes/Tangible Net Worth	179.0	98.5	57.6	43.9	51.0	29.6	56.0	65.7
	(113) 53.9	(207) 46.4	(303) 28.9	(154) 22.8	(29) 25.0	(25) 17.2	(862) 28.8	(872) 27.3
	6.0	8.2	10.2	10.6	14.9	7.8	12.1	10.3
% Profit Before Taxes/Total Assets	40.7	26.2	19.9	15.2	11.3	8.7	18.9	19.1
	14.7	8.3	9.7	8.9	7.8	6.0	8.9	8.8
	-.6	.2	3.0	3.4	4.2	1.6	2.6	1.9
Sales/Net Fixed Assets	292.2	53.4	21.6	7.9	8.5	7.3	22.4	24.6
	18.6	10.9	5.6	3.7	2.8	2.4	6.8	6.8
	5.1	3.7	2.3	2.2	1.5	1.6	2.9	2.8
Sales/Total Assets	8.5	5.6	4.0	3.0	2.6	2.3	4.7	4.7
	5.1	3.3	2.3	2.0	1.7	1.3	2.9	2.8
	2.9	1.9	1.4	1.3	1.0	1.0	1.7	1.6
% Depr., Dep., Amort./Sales	1.5	1.4	1.4	2.4	3.0		1.9	1.8
	(90) 3.1	(154) 4.6	(279) 4.9	(150) 6.2	(24) 3.7		(760) 4.5	(751) 4.8
	8.7	10.5	10.5	10.5	9.3		8.7	9.2
% Officers', Directors' Owners' Comp/Sales	2.3	1.7	1.0	.5			1.3	1.3
	(75) 3.9	(122) 2.5	(119) 1.8	(44) 1.0			(352) 2.4	(380) 2.6
	8.6	5.3	2.8	1.5			5.2	5.7
Net Sales ($)	281046M	1385775M	5020124M	7632375M	4637451M	9193018M	26343579M	26440473M
Total Assets ($)	39556M	326411M	1774338M	3403249M	2405916M	4250790M	13071363M	12941264M

M = $ thousand   MM = $ million
See Pages viii through xx for Explanation of Ratios and Data

Comparative Historical Data				Type of Statement	Current Data Sorted by Sales					
31	39	34		Unqualified	1	2		2	1	28
112	105	102		Reviewed	7	4	2	16	24	49
125	126	135		Compiled	11	22	10	32	34	26
295	243	244		Tax Returns	44	75	42	42	31	10
449	528	512		Other	56	68	60	86	121	121
4/1/16-3/31/17 ALL	4/1/17-3/31/18 ALL	4/1/18-3/31/19 ALL			130 (4/1-9/30/18)			897 (10/1/18-3/31/19)		
					0-1MM	1-3MM	3-5MM	5-10MM	10-25MM	25MM & OVER
1012	1041	1027		NUMBER OF STATEMENTS	119	171	114	178	211	234
%	%	%		ASSETS	%	%	%	%	%	%
13.7	12.4	14.4		Cash & Equivalents	18.1	16.9	18.4	14.4	13.0	10.1
21.6	23.4	23.2		Trade Receivables (net)	10.2	15.3	19.1	25.8	29.6	29.9
1.2	1.6	1.3		Inventory	1.2	1.4	.9	1.1	1.6	1.3
4.0	3.8	3.6		All Other Current	5.0	2.3	4.1	3.5	3.7	3.6
40.5	41.2	42.5		Total Current	34.5	35.9	42.6	44.7	47.9	45.0
46.1	45.3	44.1		Fixed Assets (net)	54.4	48.8	41.9	42.6	39.8	41.7
4.3	5.4	5.4		Intangibles (net)	6.0	6.3	5.5	5.2	4.6	5.3
9.1	8.0	7.9		All Other Non-Current	5.2	9.1	10.0	7.5	7.7	8.0
100.0	100.0	100.0		Total	100.0	100.0	100.0	100.0	100.0	100.0
				LIABILITIES						
8.7	8.1	7.5		Notes Payable-Short Term	7.9	8.2	8.2	6.2	9.1	6.1
9.0	7.8	7.4		Cur. Mat.-L.T.D.	8.2	7.4	6.1	7.7	7.1	7.8
8.2	9.4	8.7		Trade Payables	4.1	7.9	7.3	9.3	10.3	10.4
.1	.1	.2		Income Taxes Payable	.0	.1	.0	.4	.2	.2
9.2	8.8	10.3		All Other Current	15.9	11.9	7.9	6.7	12.4	8.5
35.2	34.3	34.2		Total Current	36.2	35.4	29.5	30.2	39.0	33.0
34.2	33.2	32.9		Long-Term Debt	39.8	41.2	37.4	33.8	26.5	26.1
.5	.5	.5		Deferred Taxes	.2	.0	.4	.6	.6	1.0
4.4	5.2	4.6		All Other Non-Current	9.1	6.9	3.0	3.3	3.0	4.0
25.7	26.8	27.8		Net Worth	14.8	16.4	29.7	32.1	30.9	35.9
100.0	100.0	100.0		Total Liabilties & Net Worth	100.0	100.0	100.0	100.0	100.0	100.0
				INCOME DATA						
100.0	100.0	100.0		Net Sales	100.0	100.0	100.0	100.0	100.0	100.0
				Gross Profit						
93.9	93.2	93.3		Operating Expenses	83.2	92.9	94.6	94.5	95.4	95.2
6.1	6.8	6.7		Operating Profit	16.8	7.1	5.4	5.5	4.6	4.8
1.4	1.5	.9		All Other Expenses (net)	5.0	1.1	.1	.0	.2	.5
4.7	5.3	5.8		Profit Before Taxes	11.8	6.0	5.4	5.5	4.4	4.3
				RATIOS						
2.3	2.4	2.5			4.1	2.8	3.8	2.6	2.3	2.0
1.2	1.3	1.4		Current	1.1	1.2	1.6	1.6	1.4	1.3
.7	.7	.8			.2	.5	.8	.9	.8	.9
2.0	2.1	2.3			3.5	2.5	3.1	2.5	2.2	1.8
1.0 (1040)	1.1	1.2		Quick	.8	1.2	1.4	1.4	1.2	1.2
.6	.6	.6			.2	.4	.7	.8	.7	.8

0	999.8	5	68.0	4	98.4		0 UND	0 UND	0 UND	18 20.1	19 18.9	25 14.7
28	13.1	30	12.1	27	13.3	Sales/Receivables	0 UND	7 54.6	17 22.1	33 11.2	33 11.2	39 9.4
42	8.7	45	8.1	43	8.5		25 14.7	28 13.0	38 9.7	44 8.3	45 8.1	47 7.7

Comparative Historical				Current					
			Cost of Sales/Inventory						
			Cost of Sales/Payables						
11.6	10.8	10.8	Sales/Working Capital	7.8	10.9	11.3	10.1	11.3	12.3
51.2	38.0	33.6		108.6	77.7	36.7	20.4	35.1	31.5
-27.1	-29.3	-35.5		-4.3	-18.5	-44.3	-447.0	-55.1	-70.5
11.8	14.0	14.5	EBIT/Interest	9.1	13.2	14.5	18.1	14.9	17.1
(865) 4.2	(905) 4.9	(889) 5.5		(72) 3.6	(143) 4.5	(97) 5.3	(164) 5.5	(192) 6.4	(221) 6.2
1.3	1.6	1.8		.9	.7	1.9	2.0	2.0	2.4
3.5	3.7	3.7	Net Profit + Depr., Dep., Amort./Cur. Mat. L/T/D				3.9	3.7	4.7
(135) 1.8	(154) 1.9	(138) 1.8				(28) 1.9	(34) 1.9	(57) 1.8
1.1	1.1	1.2					1.1	1.2	1.2
.6	.6	.5	Fixed/Worth	.5	.6	.4	.4	.5	.6
1.0	1.0	1.5		2.2	2.3	1.6	1.3	1.4	1.3
8.8	7.2	5.4		74.0	-23.5	136.9	3.9	4.0	2.6
.9	.9	.8	Debt/Worth	.6	.9	.8	.8	.9	.8
2.4	2.4	2.1		2.7	4.9	2.8	1.8	2.0	1.9
17.5	14.0	11.4		-17.3	-17.9	-134.1	6.3	6.5	4.0
56.6	61.8	70.7	% Profit Before Taxes/Tangible Net Worth	88.1	112.9	80.9	66.8	60.8	55.1
(800) 22.0	(832) 23.9	(831) 29.5		(86) 17.5	(123) 41.4	(84) 34.7	(149) 30.3	(176) 28.9	(213) 27.0
4.6	7.2	10.0		.0	7.4	11.7	9.5	14.4	13.5
19.4	19.3	22.1	% Profit Before Taxes/Total Assets	24.0	30.0	24.5	22.1	21.1	16.5
7.3	7.8	9.1		3.9	9.7	9.1	9.6	10.7	9.4
.4	1.4	1.8		-.1	-1.3	2.4	2.8	3.1	3.7
22.4	22.4	30.2	Sales/Net Fixed Assets	16.6	26.1	63.3	29.5	47.9	21.1
6.4	6.4	6.8		4.0	7.5	8.1	6.9	8.3	6.7
2.7	2.7	2.7		1.1	2.5	3.0	3.2	3.2	2.7
4.5	4.5	4.7	Sales/Total Assets	3.3	5.4	5.1	5.1	5.2	4.2
2.7	2.7	2.8		1.6	2.8	2.8	2.8	3.1	2.8
1.6	1.5	1.5		.5	1.5	1.9	1.6	1.9	1.6
2.1	2.1	1.7	% Depr., Dep., Amort./Sales	4.4	2.5	1.5	1.7	1.0	1.4
(718) 5.5	(742) 5.1	(702) 4.8		(69) 12.0	(109) 5.5	(66) 4.6	(120) 5.0	(166) 3.9	(172) 3.5
10.0	9.8	9.7		33.1	11.7	10.8	9.0	8.5	7.6
1.5	1.1	1.0	% Officers', Directors' Owners' Comp/Sales	4.3	2.3	1.3	1.3	.9	.5
(357) 2.8	(335) 2.4	(371) 2.2		(28) 8.7	(71) 4.8	(51) 2.7	(81) 2.1	(74) 1.6	(66) 1.1
6.2	4.9	4.4		17.0	7.7	5.1	3.0	2.6	2.1
22012881M	23503622M	28149789M	Net Sales ($)	56382M	319526M	437449M	1266763M	3395802M	22673867M
10872938M	10931111M	12200260M	Total Assets ($)	108629M	214017M	196596M	587874M	1388497M	9704647M

© RMA 2019   M = $ thousand   MM = $ million
See Pages viii through xx for Explanation of Ratios and Data

Current Data Sorted by Assets | Comparative Historical Data

						Type of Statement			
5	14	6	31	32	30	Unqualified		117	124
6	42	50	115	23	10	Reviewed		221	214
62	67	89	47	4	2	Compiled		223	214
31	82	63	8	1		Tax Returns		240	198
		255	220	81	52	Other		659	626
	241 (4/1-9/30/18)		1,187 (10/1/18-3/31/19)					4/1/14- 3/31/15	4/1/15- 3/31/16
0-500M	500M-2MM	2-10MM	10-50MM	50-100MM	100-250MM			ALL	ALL
104	205	463	421	141	94	NUMBER OF STATEMENTS		1460	1376
%	%	%	%	%	%	ASSETS		%	%
30.7	14.8	10.5	9.5	6.9	6.4	Cash & Equivalents		11.7	12.1
16.9	26.4	26.5	21.4	21.6	17.8	Trade Receivables (net)		25.9	23.4
.1	1.1	1.5	1.4	1.8	2.6	Inventory		1.3	1.1
4.4	3.9	4.4	3.6	3.6	2.9	All Other Current		3.9	3.6
52.1	46.3	43.0	35.8	33.8	29.7	Total Current		42.8	40.1
36.1	39.2	44.7	54.0	57.7	56.9	Fixed Assets (net)		47.0	48.8
4.4	6.0	5.5	4.4	3.3	6.9	Intangibles (net)		3.3	3.9
7.5	8.5	6.8	5.8	5.2	6.5	All Other Non-Current		6.9	7.2
100.0	100.0	100.0	100.0	100.0	100.0	Total		100.0	100.0
						LIABILITIES			
16.7	7.2	5.5	4.5	4.9	3.5	Notes Payable-Short Term		7.9	6.5
13.4	8.6	8.5	11.2	12.0	10.8	Cur. Mat.-L.T.D.		9.3	10.0
7.5	10.2	9.4	6.5	6.8	6.7	Trade Payables		9.5	8.0
.3	.1	.2	.1	.1	.1	Income Taxes Payable		.2	.2
17.5	17.1	8.7	7.6	6.8	8.1	All Other Current		9.5	8.7
55.4	43.2	32.4	30.0	30.6	29.3	Total Current		36.3	33.4
47.9	37.8	27.6	28.1	31.3	33.0	Long-Term Debt		31.4	32.9
.2	.3	.6	1.7	2.0	2.9	Deferred Taxes		1.3	1.2
11.4	4.8	5.9	3.5	2.4	2.9	All Other Non-Current		5.2	4.5
-14.9	13.9	33.6	36.8	33.7	31.9	Net Worth		25.8	27.9
100.0	100.0	100.0	100.0	100.0	100.0	Total Liabilities & Net Worth		100.0	100.0
						INCOME DATA			
100.0	100.0	100.0	100.0	100.0	100.0	Net Sales		100.0	100.0
						Gross Profit			
93.8	92.4	91.9	93.1	93.8	93.6	Operating Expenses		94.0	93.5
6.2	7.6	8.1	6.9	6.2	6.4	Operating Profit		6.0	6.5
.3	1.8	1.3	.7	.4	1.4	All Other Expenses (net)		.6	.7
5.8	5.8	6.9	6.1	5.8	4.9	Profit Before Taxes		5.3	5.8
						RATIOS			
2.9	3.9	2.5	1.8	1.6	1.5			2.0	1.9
1.2	1.3	1.4	1.2	1.0	1.0	Current		1.2	1.2
.5	.5	.9	.8	.7	.6			.8	.8
2.8	3.2	2.1	1.6	1.4	1.3			1.8	1.7
1.1	1.2	1.2	1.0	.9	.8	Quick	(1459)	1.1	1.0
.4	.4	.7	.6	.6	.5			.7	.6
0 UND	0 UND	19 18.9	27 13.5	30 12.0	31 11.9		18	20.6	18 20.6
0 UND	18 20.5	32 11.5	35 10.5	38 9.5	38 9.7	Sales/Receivables	32	11.5	31 11.6
18 19.8	33 11.2	45 8.2	46 8.0	46 7.9	48 7.6		42	8.7	41 8.9
						Cost of Sales/Inventory			
						Cost of Sales/Payables			
20.5	13.8	9.5	11.2	14.0	14.9			13.7	13.3
82.3	43.4	24.5	34.8	999.8	506.4	Sales/Working Capital		46.4	50.3
-24.5	-24.7	-54.7	-22.0	-18.7	-12.8			-37.0	-26.7
14.3	13.1	13.6	10.1	11.1	7.6			12.4	11.9
(69) 4.5	(164) 4.2	(418) 6.2	(407) 5.2	(137) 4.5	4.0	EBIT/Interest	(1293)	5.2	(1230) 5.2
2.2	1.3	2.3	2.7	2.7	2.4			2.2	2.2
		2.1	3.2	2.7	9.0			2.8	2.7
(11) .8	(74) 1.8	(155) 1.6	(38) 1.9	(11) 4.1		Net Profit + Depr., Dep., Amort./Cur. Mat. L/T/D	(277)	1.6	(278) 1.6
.2	1.1	1.2	1.4	1.9				1.2	1.1
.0	.3	.7	1.1	1.2	1.2			.8	.7
1.3	2.0	1.5	1.6	2.2	1.8	Fixed/Worth		1.8	1.8
-1.8	-6.4	4.3	3.3	3.8	3.9			4.4	4.6
.7	.9	1.0	1.0	1.2	1.3			1.1	1.0
3.3	3.2	2.1	1.8	2.6	2.4	Debt/Worth		2.4	2.3
-3.2	-11.3	7.0	4.0	4.9	4.7			7.6	7.6
186.7	90.0	61.5	43.4	41.1	38.4			57.4	51.2
(69) 64.7	(144) 41.8	(397) 31.4	(392) 24.4	(131) 25.3	(86) 19.4	% Profit Before Taxes/Tangible Net Worth	(1232)	28.1	(1159) 26.8
23.7	8.3	11.7	11.7	13.2	10.1			12.8	11.3
53.8	29.1	19.3	13.6	13.0	10.1			16.6	16.4
19.9	9.5	9.0	7.7	7.4	6.7	% Profit Before Taxes/Total Assets		8.5	8.3
9.2	.9	2.9	3.5	3.9	2.4			2.9	2.8
991.5	65.0	22.3	5.8	4.5	4.7			21.7	18.4
28.9	15.2	5.5	3.1	2.7	2.3	Sales/Net Fixed Assets		5.3	4.5
8.4	4.7	2.7	1.9	1.8	1.7			2.5	2.2
14.8	7.2	3.8	2.5	2.2	2.2			4.6	4.2
6.4	4.2	2.5	1.8	1.7	1.4	Sales/Total Assets		2.6	2.3
3.3	2.2	1.6	1.3	1.3	1.1			1.6	1.4
.7	.9	1.6	3.6	3.1	1.2			1.9	2.2
(44) 3.5	(123) 3.5	(362) 5.1	(397) 7.2	(78) 5.6	(17) 3.2	% Depr., Dep., Amort./Sales	(1093)	4.8	(1028) 5.5
9.1	8.6	9.3	11.4	10.7	6.9			8.7	9.8
2.0	1.2	.8	.6	.5				.8	.9
(54) 4.3	(80) 2.3	(131) 1.4	(92) 1.0	(20) 1.3		% Officers', Directors' Owners' Comp/Sales	(407)	1.7	(368) 2.1
8.4	4.5	3.2	2.5	3.5				3.9	5.5
219052M	1298704M	6894740M	20035824M	20105510M	26309033M	Net Sales ($)		69631397M	72090741M
23101M	238512M	2397125M	9965138M	10066290M	14302825M	Total Assets ($)		34313941M	36659502M

M = $ thousand   MM = $ million
See Pages viii through xx for Explanation of Ratios and Data

Comparative Historical Data | **Current Data Sorted by Sales**

			Type of Statement	0-1MM	1-3MM	3-5MM	5-10MM	10-25MM	25MM & OVER
109	104	99	Unqualified				1	8	90
192	220	217	Reviewed	7	7	4	18	55	126
181	220	190	Compiled	14	18	14	42	59	43
167	208	201	Tax Returns	33	44	17	55	37	15
655	763	721	Other	28	40	54	101	162	336
4/1/16-3/31/17 ALL	4/1/17-3/31/18 ALL	4/1/18-3/31/19 ALL		241 (4/1-9/30/18)			1,187 (10/1/18-3/31/19)		
1304	1515	1428	**NUMBER OF STATEMENTS**	82	109	89	217	321	610
%	%	%	**ASSETS**	%	%	%	%	%	%
10.5	10.2	11.7	Cash & Equivalents	16.5	17.9	13.9	15.2	10.7	8.8
22.9	24.3	23.2	Trade Receivables (net)	7.2	14.0	20.5	23.0	27.5	25.3
1.6	1.3	1.4	Inventory	.2	1.0	2.2	1.2	1.3	1.7
3.6	4.3	3.9	All Other Current	3.0	2.8	5.4	4.2	4.2	3.7
38.7	40.1	40.2	Total Current	26.9	35.8	41.9	43.7	43.7	39.5
50.0	48.2	48.1	Fixed Assets (net)	59.3	48.4	46.4	43.9	44.6	50.1
4.0	5.1	5.1	Intangibles (net)	6.5	6.9	6.3	5.8	4.9	4.1
7.3	6.7	6.6	All Other Non-Current	7.4	9.0	5.5	6.6	6.7	6.2
100.0	100.0	100.0	Total	100.0	100.0	100.0	100.0	100.0	100.0
			LIABILITIES						
6.5	6.2	6.1	Notes Payable-Short Term	5.1	13.9	4.4	5.7	6.0	5.2
10.0	9.5	10.2	Cur. Mat. L.T.D.	17.0	0.6	0.5	8.0	9.1	10.7
8.5	9.1	8.1	Trade Payables	3.5	5.3	8.1	8.4	9.7	8.3
.1	.2	.2	Income Taxes Payable	.0	.4	.3	.1	.2	.1
9.1	9.3	10.0	All Other Current	7.3	9.6	10.6	10.9	8.3	10.9
34.2	34.3	34.5	Total Current	33.0	38.8	33.0	33.2	33.2	35.3
32.4	31.4	31.4	Long-Term Debt	44.4	42.4	41.5	33.2	27.0	27.9
1.3	1.2	1.1	Deferred Taxes	.2	.2	.6	.8	.9	1.7
4.0	5.2	4.9	All Other Non-Current	13.8	4.6	7.6	5.5	5.0	3.1
28.1	28.0	28.1	Net Worth	8.7	14.0	17.3	27.3	33.8	32.0
100.0	100.0	100.0	Total Liabilities & Net Worth	100.0	100.0	100.0	100.0	100.0	100.0
			INCOME DATA						
100.0	100.0	100.0	Net Sales	100.0	100.0	100.0	100.0	100.0	100.0
			Gross Profit						
94.0	93.6	92.8	Operating Expenses	73.8	87.7	92.8	93.8	94.6	94.9
6.0	6.4	7.2	Operating Profit	26.2	12.3	7.2	6.2	5.4	5.1
1.2	1.2	1.0	All Other Expenses (net)	9.6	1.8	1.0	.3	.3	.4
4.8	5.3	6.2	Profit Before Taxes	16.6	10.4	6.2	5.9	5.1	4.7
			RATIOS						
2.0	1.9	2.1	Current	2.0	4.0	4.2	2.9	2.3	1.7
1.1	1.2	1.2		.7	1.3	1.4	1.4	1.4	1.1
.7	.7	.7		.2	.5	.5	.9	.9	.8
1.7	1.7	1.8	Quick	1.8	3.2	2.9	2.5	1.9	1.6
.9	1.0	1.0		.5	1.1	1.0	1.3	1.2	.9
.6	.6	.6		.1	.3	.4	.6	.7	.6
21 17.5 / 19 18.8 / 17 21.4			Sales/Receivables	0 UND	0 UND	3 130.9	4 89.6	24 15.4	29 12.6
33 11.1 / 35 10.5 / 32 11.4				0 UND	0 999.8	24 14.9	26 14.1	34 10.8	36 10.0
41 8.8 / 47 7.8 / 43 8.5				13 29.1	31 11.9	43 8.4	39 9.4	45 8.1	46 8.0
			Cost of Sales/Inventory						
			Cost of Sales/Payables						
13.1	12.2	11.8	Sales/Working Capital	19.0	9.0	8.3	10.3	11.2	13.3
59.1	51.7	40.7		-24.0	47.8	41.9	28.8	26.6	58.4
-20.5	-26.2	-25.7		-2.0	-12.0	-15.5	-61.8	-82.2	-23.8
9.6	9.4	11.4	EBIT/Interest	8.3	9.5	10.5	12.4	12.0	11.6
(1161) 3.6	(1345) 3.9	(1289) 5.1		(53) 3.5	(85) 4.3	(78) 3.9	(186) 4.9	(298) 5.9	(589) 5.3
1.2	1.4	2.3		1.4	1.6	1.8	1.9	2.5	2.7
2.4	2.6	3.0	Net Profit + Depr., Dep., Amort./Cur. Mat. L/T/D				7.0	2.4	3.1
(231) 1.5	(285) 1.6	(289) 1.7					(20) 1.9	(69) 1.6	(179) 1.8
1.0	1.2	1.2					1.5	1.1	1.3
.9	.8	.9	Fixed/Worth	1.2	.4	.8	.6	.8	1.0
1.9	1.8	1.7		3.1	2.0	1.8	1.7	1.5	1.6
5.0	5.0	4.3		-7.0	9.1	14.9	9.4	3.3	3.6
1.0	1.0	1.0	Debt/Worth	.9	1.1	.8	.8	1.0	1.1
2.4	2.5	2.2		3.6	2.4	2.6	2.1	2.1	2.1
7.3	9.7	6.5		-5.7	14.4	191.0	17.8	5.2	4.6
40.0	44.5	55.7	% Profit Before Taxes/Tangible Net Worth	77.2	115.5	77.8	73.2	56.9	45.1
(1111) 17.0	(1253) 20.1	(1219) 27.7		(56) 28.8	(90) 34.6	(68) 29.4	(171) 33.6	(282) 28.8	(552) 25.9
4.1	6.2	12.0		8.6	8.0	8.0	11.4	13.5	12.5
12.1	13.7	17.4	% Profit Before Taxes/Total Assets	15.7	28.0	25.4	21.8	17.9	14.5
5.2	5.6	8.4		6.1	12.9	7.0	8.9	9.1	7.0
.5	1.1	3.1		1.0	1.7	1.9	2.9	3.5	3.7
14.0	14.6	16.5	Sales/Net Fixed Assets	10.6	28.2	34.1	30.5	22.7	8.6
4.0	4.2	4.4		2.7	6.1	4.6	7.4	4.9	3.6
2.0	2.2	2.2		.2	1.9	1.8	3.0	2.5	2.2
3.7	3.6	3.9	Sales/Total Assets	3.1	5.2	4.1	5.7	4.1	3.2
2.1	2.1	2.2		.9	2.5	2.0	2.8	2.4	2.0
1.3	1.4	1.4		.2	.9	1.1	1.8	1.5	1.4
2.5	2.4	2.3	% Depr., Dep., Amort./Sales	9.2	3.0	3.6	1.8	1.9	2.1
(957) 6.1	(1125) 6.1	(1021) 5.7		(48) 17.0	(71) 6.9	(54) 8.5	(151) 5.6	(265) 5.6	(432) 5.0
10.8	10.9	10.2		33.0	18.0	14.2	9.0	10.1	8.6
1.0	.8	.8	% Officers', Directors' Owners' Comp/Sales	3.6	1.7	1.8	1.2	.7	.5
(321) 2.2	(386) 1.8	(384) 1.8		(23) 8.0	(41) 3.2	(24) 2.9	(86) 2.2	(88) 1.2	(122) 1.0
5.0	4.2	4.2		15.7	6.1	4.1	4.4	2.4	2.9
65431447M	68024407M	74862863M	Net Sales ($)	35650M	206679M	349878M	1586644M	5351558M	67332454M
35888481M	36798693M	36992991M	Total Assets ($)	100366M	212409M	271666M	855312M	2694547M	32858691M

Current Data Sorted by Assets   Comparative Historical Data

0-500M	500M-2MM	2-10MM	10-50MM	50-100MM	100-250MM	Type of Statement	4/1/14-3/31/15 ALL	4/1/15-3/31/16 ALL
			8	9	2	Unqualified	22	19
		7	16	3	1	Reviewed	21	25
1		6	5	1		Compiled	22	18
5	6	5	1		1	Tax Returns	16	20
3	9	30	25	7	7	Other	48	69
	16 (4/1-9/30/18)		142 (10/1/18-3/31/19)					
9	15	48	55	20	11	**NUMBER OF STATEMENTS**	129	151
%	%	%	%	%	%	**ASSETS**	%	%
	16.4	12.8	8.9	7.1	9.7	Cash & Equivalents	9.8	10.7
	35.5	25.0	20.0	21.1	20.0	Trade Receivables (net)	27.9	22.6
	.0	.4	.8	.8	1.8	Inventory	.6	.7
	3.6	5.7	4.5	6.3	1.6	All Other Current	4.1	6.0
	55.5	43.8	34.1	35.3	33.1	Total Current	42.4	40.0
	33.9	46.6	56.3	56.6	55.1	Fixed Assets (net)	48.4	49.2
	2.7	3.4	3.5	.8	9.5	Intangibles (net)	3.0	2.7
	7.9	6.1	6.0	7.3	2.2	All Other Non-Current	6.3	8.1
	100.0	100.0	100.0	100.0	100.0	Total	100.0	100.0
						LIABILITIES		
	5.8	6.5	3.7	1.0	.2	Notes Payable-Short Term	4.9	5.3
	6.4	6.4	9.9	12.2	9.5	Cur. Mat.-L.T.D.	8.0	9.1
	12.7	9.6	5.2	6.4	10.1	Trade Payables	12.3	8.2
	.0	.0	.0	.1	.0	Income Taxes Payable	.1	.1
	8.5	5.0	5.6	8.6	9.2	All Other Current	10.1	6.5
	33.5	27.5	24.3	28.3	29.0	Total Current	35.5	29.1
	28.6	30.5	31.4	28.9	33.2	Long-Term Debt	28.8	28.3
	.0	.1	1.5	3.3	.0	Deferred Taxes	2.3	1.4
	2.3	1.2	3.7	2.8	2.6	All Other Non-Current	6.9	3.6
	35.6	40.7	39.0	36.6	35.2	Net Worth	26.6	37.6
	100.0	100.0	100.0	100.0	100.0	Total Liabilities & Net Worth	100.0	100.0
						INCOME DATA		
	100.0	100.0	100.0	100.0	100.0	Net Sales	100.0	100.0
						Gross Profit		
	92.1	87.7	92.9	96.2	94.2	Operating Expenses	92.2	92.3
	7.9	12.3	7.1	3.8	5.8	Operating Profit	7.8	7.7
	.9	3.4	1.5	-.3	.7	All Other Expenses (net)	1.7	1.0
	7.0	8.9	5.6	4.1	5.1	Profit Before Taxes	6.0	6.7
						RATIOS		
	3.8	4.2	2.4	1.9	1.9		1.8	2.0
	1.6	2.1	1.3	1.2	1.1	Current	1.2	1.3
	1.3	.9	.9	.9	.8		.9	.9
	3.4	3.9	1.9	1.5	1.7		1.7	1.6
	1.6	1.5	1.2	1.0	1.1	Quick	1.1	1.1
	1.3	.8	.7	.7	.7		.7	.7
	5 66.5	13 27.8	24 15.3	31 11.6	34 10.8		22 16.4	16 23.4
	29 12.8	32 11.3	33 11.1	38 9.6	41 8.9	Sales/Receivables	33 10.9	30 12.0
	43 8.4	42 8.6	43 8.5	42 8.7	45 8.1		45 8.1	41 8.9
						Cost of Sales/Inventory		
						Cost of Sales/Payables		
	7.0	7.4	11.0	12.0	9.2		11.8	13.2
	26.9	18.4	26.0	29.2	51.6	Sales/Working Capital	70.8	27.6
	36.0	-66.3	-115.2	-82.8	-21.8		-126.6	-129.3
	28.2	40.1	13.1	12.4	23.5		15.2	15.0
	(12) 6.0	(42) 10.8	(53) 6.4	4.3	(10) 3.9	EBIT/Interest	(116) 5.2	(133) 5.9
	1.1	1.9	2.0	2.1	2.3		2.5	2.3
			2.7				2.3	2.2
			(16) 1.7			Net Profit + Depr., Dep., Amort./Cur. Mat. L/T/D	(42) 1.6	(39) 1.5
			1.2				.9	1.0
	.1	.4	1.0	1.1	1.1		.8	.6
	.6	1.2	1.7	1.6	2.2	Fixed/Worth	1.8	1.3
	8.2	2.9	2.5	3.2	19.1		4.6	3.1
	.5	.7	.8	.6	.7		1.2	.9
	1.9	1.4	1.6	2.0	3.2	Debt/Worth	2.4	1.8
	10.9	4.0	3.3	4.0	25.0		9.3	4.3
	67.6	65.5	41.1	44.3	188.2		50.4	49.0
	(12) 51.3	(43) 34.2	(51) 21.5	21.4	(10) 29.6	% Profit Before Taxes/Tangible Net Worth	(112) 27.5	(142) 26.6
	11.3	7.0	10.5	9.6	14.4		13.6	9.6
	30.5	23.3	15.1	9.5	14.1		14.6	16.9
	14.0	12.8	8.7	7.4	6.6	% Profit Before Taxes/Total Assets	7.5	9.0
	-.9	3.1	2.4	2.9	3.8		3.2	3.0
	99.1	17.9	5.7	5.4	5.7		18.7	16.8
	19.8	6.2	3.0	3.4	2.4	Sales/Net Fixed Assets	4.7	4.3
	6.5	2.6	2.2	1.9	1.6		2.3	2.1
	5.9	4.0	2.6	3.2	2.3		5.0	4.5
	4.1	2.8	1.8	1.9	1.7	Sales/Total Assets	2.4	2.1
	3.0	2.0	1.5	1.4	1.1		1.6	1.4
	1.7	1.4	3.4	2.4			1.6	2.0
	(12) 3.1	(36) 4.8	(51) 6.6	(13) 5.0		% Depr., Dep., Amort./Sales	(99) 5.2	(113) 4.8
	12.1	12.0	8.9	10.7			7.8	8.6
		.7	.7				.7	1.0
		(15) 1.8	(14) 1.7			% Officers', Directors', Owners' Comp/Sales	(39) 2.2	(40) 2.5
		3.7	7.0				3.2	5.3
24441M	95659M	698703M	3255057M	3207982M	2781235M	Net Sales ($)	9233698M	9081847M
1851M	19810M	216860M	1265402M	1458309M	1514953M	Total Assets ($)	4043303M	4822882M

M = $ thousand   MM = $ million
See Pages viii through xx for Explanation of Ratios and Data

Comparative Historical Data   Current Data Sorted by Sales

Current Data groupings: **16 (4/1-9/30/18)** and **142 (10/1/18-3/31/19)**

	4/1/16-3/31/17 ALL	4/1/17-3/31/18 ALL	4/1/18-3/31/19 ALL	0-1MM	1-3MM	3-5MM	5-10MM	10-25MM	25MM & OVER
Type of Statement									
Unqualified	14	17	19					1	18
Reviewed	30	26	27			1	1	6	19
Compiled	11	13	13		1		2	6	4
Tax Returns	15	16	18		6	1	6	4	1
Other	60	75	81	8	4	2	11	20	36
NUMBER OF STATEMENTS	130	147	158	8	11	4	20	37	78
ASSETS	%	%	%	%	%	%	%	%	%
Cash & Equivalents	8.6	10.2	12.8		39.1		12.0	14.7	8.9
Trade Receivables (net)	23.5	25.0	22.8		6.1		30.0	24.5	24.3
Inventory	.9	1.6	.6		.0		.1	.4	1.0
All Other Current	3.1	3.4	4.5		1.9		5.5	3.5	5.9
Total Current	36.1	40.1	40.8		47.0		47.6	43.0	40.1
Fixed Assets (net)	50.3	49.9	49.6		44.7		35.7	49.2	50.9
Intangibles (net)	3.8	2.0	3.8		.0		7.8	2.8	3.6
All Other Non-Current	9.8	7.9	5.9		8.2		9.0	5.0	5.4
Total	100.0	100.0	100.0		100.0		100.0	100.0	100.0
LIABILITIES									
Notes Payable-Short Term	6.9	8.2	4.4		5.2		6.1	3.0	4.5
Cur. Mat.-L.T.D.	9.0	10.2	8.3		6.3		6.8	7.8	9.7
Trade Payables	9.8	9.4	7.7		1.0		7.0	10.0	8.1
Income Taxes Payable	.1	.1	.0		.0		.1	.0	.0
All Other Current	7.6	10.7	7.6		3.5		17.1	6.1	7.1
Total Current	33.4	38.6	28.0		16.0		37.1	26.9	29.4
Long-Term Debt	28.9	30.5	29.7		40.3		22.9	27.0	28.0
Deferred Taxes	1.5	1.5	1.0		.0		.0	.7	1.7
All Other Non-Current	3.0	2.8	2.5		.0		2.3	2.6	3.1
Net Worth	33.3	26.7	38.8		43.7		37.7	42.8	37.8
Total Liabilities & Net Worth	100.0	100.0	100.0		100.0		100.0	100.0	100.0
INCOME DATA									
Net Sales	100.0	100.0	100.0		100.0		100.0	100.0	100.0
Gross Profit									
Operating Expenses	94.5	91.5	91.9		82.8		94.6	94.5	95.5
Operating Profit	5.5	8.5	8.1		17.2		5.4	5.5	4.5
All Other Expenses (net)	1.0	1.8	1.6		4.9		.1	.3	.3
Profit Before Taxes	4.6	6.8	6.4		12.2		5.3	5.3	4.2
RATIOS									
Current	1.8	1.9	2.7		9.5		2.7	3.1	2.0
	1.1	1.3	1.5		3.8		1.4	1.7	1.4
	.7	.9	.9		1.3		.9	.9	.9
Quick	1.6	1.7	2.2		9.5		1.8	2.9	1.7
	1.0	1.1	1.3		3.4		1.2	1.5	1.2
	.6	.6	.8		1.3		.9	.8	.8
Sales/Receivables	22 16.6	25 14.5	19 19.5		0 UND		10 38.4	23 16.2	31 11.9
	33 11.2	36 10.0	33 11.0		5 66.5		34 10.6	33 11.1	36 10.1
	42 8.7	46 8.0	43 8.5		29 12.7		41 8.8	44 8.3	43 8.5
Cost of Sales/Inventory									
Cost of Sales/Payables									
Sales/Working Capital	15.6	11.9	9.9		5.6		11.4	8.0	11.4
	117.1	28.6	27.1		26.9		32.7	19.2	28.5
	-17.1	-45.6	-122.9		109.9		NM	-78.3	-209.7
EBIT/Interest	9.0	10.5	16.9				36.8	32.8	15.1
	(117) 3.5	(127) 3.8	(140) 6.0				(18) 9.8	(36) 7.4	(77) 5.8
	1.1	1.3	2.1				.7	2.4	2.2
Net Profit + Depr., Dep., Amort./Cur. Mat. L/T/D	1.9	2.8	3.7						3.0
	(31) 1.3	(37) 1.5	(37) 2.2					(25)	2.2
	.9	1.1	1.2						1.3
Fixed/Worth	.9	.8	.8		.0		.4	.7	1.0
	1.8	1.5	1.3		2.0		.8	1.3	1.4
	3.3	3.4	3.2		23.2		3.6	2.2	2.8
Debt/Worth	1.0	.9	.7		.3		.6	.7	.7
	2.1	1.6	1.7		1.4		1.1	1.3	1.7
	5.8	5.2	3.9		42.6		3.9	2.7	3.4
% Profit Before Taxes/Tangible Net Worth	34.4	28.5	55.6				62.1	62.6	51.6
	(115) 12.3	(128) 14.9	(142) 28.2				(16) 39.1	(35) 18.5	(73) 26.4
	2.1	5.0	11.2				16.0	6.6	12.8
% Profit Before Taxes/Total Assets	8.5	12.8	17.6		47.8		30.2	21.5	15.4
	4.4	5.0	8.7		22.5		13.6	8.7	8.2
	.1	.9	2.9		2.4		.5	2.5	3.8
Sales/Net Fixed Assets	11.7	13.2	15.0		UND		49.5	12.5	8.7
	4.0	4.4	4.4		3.8		12.1	4.5	3.6
	2.1	2.2	2.4		.7		3.5	2.3	2.4
Sales/Total Assets	3.8	4.2	4.0		16.8		4.5	3.4	3.7
	2.1	2.1	2.3		2.4		3.3	2.6	2.0
	1.4	1.3	1.5		.5		2.4	1.6	1.6
% Depr., Dep., Amort./Sales	1.4	2.1	2.0				1.8	3.4	2.0
	(92) 6.2	(110) 5.6	(123) 5.5				(16) 3.1	(29) 5.6	(62) 5.1
	9.7	9.8	9.1				8.2	10.6	7.7
% Officers', Directors', Owners' Comp/Sales	.9	.8	.7					.5	.7
	(37) 1.8	(40) 1.2	(40) 1.8					(14) 1.5	(14) .8
	3.5	4.5	4.1					2.7	6.9
Net Sales ($)	7712203M	6997898M	10063077M	3177M	22821M	16428M	140141M	621406M	9259104M
Total Assets ($)	4187441M	3827075M	4477185M	17886M	46495M	5604M	45991M	319127M	4042082M

M = $ thousand   MM = $ million
See Pages viii through xx for Explanation of Ratios and Data

Current Data Sorted by Assets   **Comparative Historical Data**

	0-500M	500M-2MM	2-10MM	10-50MM	50-100MM	100-250MM	Type of Statement	4/1/14-3/31/15 ALL	4/1/15-3/31/16 ALL
	1	1		1	2	2	Unqualified	11	4
	1	5	22	13	1		Reviewed	51	42
	2	15	14	3		1	Compiled	39	45
	17	19	10				Tax Returns	54	56
	14	20	45	19	5	3	Other	96	94
		20 (4/1-9/30/18)		216 (10/1/18-3/31/19)					
NUMBER OF STATEMENTS	35	60	91	36	8	6		251	241
	%	%	%	%	%	%	**ASSETS**	%	%
	32.9	23.9	8.8	7.3			Cash & Equivalents	15.0	13.5
	16.1	26.1	33.0	34.0			Trade Receivables (net)	26.9	26.6
	.1	.4	.6	3.2			Inventory	1.9	1.5
	3.5	4.0	5.5	4.6			All Other Current	4.6	6.1
	52.6	54.4	47.8	49.1			Total Current	48.3	47.7
	27.7	35.4	34.2	36.0			Fixed Assets (net)	34.6	36.9
	8.0	4.1	5.8	3.2			Intangibles (net)	5.1	4.5
	11.7	6.0	12.1	11.7			All Other Non-Current	12.0	10.9
	100.0	100.0	100.0	100.0			Total	100.0	100.0
							LIABILITIES		
	22.8	6.2	7.9	4.2			Notes Payable-Short Term	7.4	7.7
	10.0	10.4	6.7	4.5			Cur. Mat.-L.T.D.	5.0	6.3
	5.9	5.8	8.9	11.7			Trade Payables	9.7	8.2
	.4	.0	.4	.0			Income Taxes Payable	.1	.1
	38.7	19.2	11.2	12.6			All Other Current	12.7	13.5
	78.0	41.5	35.1	33.1			Total Current	34.9	35.7
	41.3	27.6	24.0	19.9			Long-Term Debt	24.8	27.5
	.0	.2	.4	.4			Deferred Taxes	.3	.4
	2.1	3.0	4.3	2.4			All Other Non-Current	2.5	3.8
	-21.3	27.6	36.3	44.3			Net Worth	37.5	32.6
	100.0	100.0	100.0	100.0			Total Liabilities & Net Worth	100.0	100.0
							INCOME DATA		
	100.0	100.0	100.0	100.0			Net Sales	100.0	100.0
							Gross Profit		
	92.1	90.8	88.6	96.1			Operating Expenses	90.9	90.7
	7.9	9.2	11.4	3.9			Operating Profit	9.1	9.3
	1.4	2.8	3.9	.0			All Other Expenses (net)	2.3	3.1
	6.5	6.4	7.5	3.8			Profit Before Taxes	6.8	6.2
							RATIOS		
	3.5	3.3	2.1	2.3			Current	2.4	2.4
	1.1	1.6	1.4	1.6				1.5	1.5
	.4	.7	.9	1.1				.9	.8
	3.5	3.2	1.9	1.8			Quick	2.3	2.2
	1.0	1.5	1.1	1.4				1.3	1.2
	.4	.7	.8	.9				.7	.7
	0 UND	0 799.2	24 15.1	35 10.3			Sales/Receivables	6 66.0	8 46.6
	0 UND	27 13.7	38 9.7	45 8.1				29 12.8	31 11.9
	16 23.5	45 8.1	54 6.8	62 5.9				50 7.3	52 7.0
							Cost of Sales/Inventory		
							Cost of Sales/Payables		
	22.5	7.5	9.9	7.9			Sales/Working Capital	10.6	9.7
	430.9	20.5	23.0	15.6				25.7	23.1
	-10.7	-26.2	-132.0	NM				-88.5	-53.8
	13.8	11.0	15.7	17.8			EBIT/Interest	13.1	23.9
	(23) 4.9	(52) 3.6	(77) 5.8	(32) 6.2				(194) 5.3	(200) 5.9
	-.7	.1	1.3	2.7				1.8	2.1
			3.7	12.3			Net Profit + Depr., Dep., Amort./Cur. Mat. L/T/D	4.2	6.1
		(21) 1.4		(13) 3.3				(46) 2.6	(49) 2.4
			.8	1.6				1.2	1.2
	.0	.4	.3	.4			Fixed/Worth	.3	.3
	1.6	.9	.7	.8				.8	.9
	-.9	166.6	2.8	1.7				2.4	5.7
	1.1	.8	.9	.7			Debt/Worth	.8	.8
	5.0	1.7	2.2	1.5				1.6	1.7
	-2.2	NM	3.7	2.6				4.2	7.6
	151.1	54.0	35.7	39.5			% Profit Before Taxes/Tangible Net Worth	42.3	46.5
	(20) 67.3	(45) 12.5	(80) 19.1	(35) 24.6				(222) 18.8	(198) 19.1
	7.7	.8	2.5	6.0				2.8	4.8
	53.6	22.5	14.2	13.8			% Profit Before Taxes/Total Assets	15.5	18.0
	22.0	5.3	5.0	8.1				7.2	7.2
	-6.5	-.7	.9	2.4				1.1	1.0
	169.5	28.5	25.6	20.5			Sales/Net Fixed Assets	40.6	29.2
	43.9	11.5	13.9	10.2				13.3	11.3
	14.6	5.4	3.6	2.7				4.5	4.8
	14.5	4.4	4.0	3.8			Sales/Total Assets	4.8	4.3
	7.2	3.2	2.9	2.2				3.3	2.9
	3.8	2.1	1.7	1.3				1.8	1.6
	.5	1.3	1.1	1.2			% Depr., Dep., Amort./Sales	1.1	1.1
	(21) 1.6	(50) 1.9	(79) 1.8	(35) 2.2				(194) 2.4	(191) 2.4
	5.9	3.5	5.9	3.5				4.4	4.5
	2.1	2.7	1.6				% Officers', Directors' Owners' Comp/Sales	2.0	1.9
	(21) 4.7	(22) 4.2	(16) 2.4					(88) 3.2	(73) 4.3
	8.6	8.0	5.1					6.1	7.8
	72752M	239086M	1202772M	1669474M	1141513M	2876894M	Net Sales ($)	5923169M	5991454M
	8548M	73677M	422642M	671498M	507389M	1389797M	Total Assets ($)	2595189M	2647623M

© RMA 2019

M = $ thousand   MM = $ million
See Pages viii through xx for Explanation of Ratios and Data

Comparative Historical Data / Current Data Sorted by Sales

Comp 1	Comp 2	Comp 3	Type of Statement	0-1MM	1-3MM	3-5MM	5-10MM	10-25MM	25MM & OVER
10	8	7	Unqualified	1			1		5
34	47	42	Reviewed	2	1	3	8	18	10
42	33	35	Compiled	2	4	7	10	10	2
36	45	46	Tax Returns	11	13	8	11	3	
119	93	106	Other	15	16	6	16	23	30
4/1/16-3/31/17 ALL	4/1/17-3/31/18 ALL	4/1/18-3/31/19 ALL		20 (4/1-9/30/18)			216 (10/1/18-3/31/19)		
241	226	236	NUMBER OF STATEMENTS	31	34	24	46	54	47
%	%	%	**ASSETS**	%	%	%	%	%	%
13.5	13.9	15.8	Cash & Equivalents	17.9	30.4	18.1	18.0	11.6	5.1
26.2	27.3	29.3	Trade Receivables (net)	7.6	11.3	26.3	33.9	38.3	43.2
1.5	.9	.9	Inventory	.0	.3	.4	.8	.7	2.6
4.5	4.2	4.8	All Other Current	2.8	2.8	6.3	4.7	6.3	5.3
45.8	46.3	50.8	Total Current	28.4	44.9	51.1	57.5	57.0	56.3
36.7	35.9	33.7	Fixed Assets (net)	58.6	28.5	39.8	30.4	27.6	28.2
5.7	7.7	5.1	Intangibles (net)	7.1	7.1	2.9	5.2	4.3	4.4
11.9	10.0	10.3	All Other Non-Current	5.9	19.6	6.3	6.9	11.1	11.1
100.0	100.0	100.0	Total	100.0	100.0	100.0	100.0	100.0	100.0
			LIABILITIES						
7.8	6.2	9.2	Notes Payable-Short Term	5.5	13.7	20.5	5.9	7.9	7.4
6.0	6.6	7.6	Cur. Mat.-L.T.D.	9.4	10.0	8.3	9.0	6.0	4.3
9.0	8.6	8.2	Trade Payables	1.2	6.2	5.7	7.4	10.6	13.8
.1	.4	.2	Income Taxes Payable	.4	.1	.0	.0	.6	.1
14.8	13.5	17.5	All Other Current	15.0	32.4	16.4	18.3	12.9	13.3
37.8	35.2	42.8	Total Current	31.6	63.0	50.9	40.6	38.0	38.9
24.6	26.7	26.4	Long-Term Debt	53.9	34.7	32.1	21.7	17.8	13.8
.3	.3	.3	Deferred Taxes	.0	.0	.4	.2	.6	.5
4.5	3.8	3.2	All Other Non-Current	1.7	2.7	4.0	3.1	4.3	3.1
32.9	34.0	27.3	Net Worth	12.8	-.4	12.6	34.3	39.3	43.7
100.0	100.0	100.0	Total Liabilities & Net Worth	100.0	100.0	100.0	100.0	100.0	100.0
			INCOME DATA						
100.0	100.0	100.0	Net Sales	100.0	100.0	100.0	100.0	100.0	100.0
			Gross Profit						
91.2	91.7	91.4	Operating Expenses	60.9	94.6	94.0	96.0	96.5	97.7
8.8	8.3	8.6	Operating Profit	39.1	5.4	6.0	4.0	3.5	2.3
1.7	2.1	2.4	All Other Expenses (net)	15.4	.7	.7	1.1	.3	-.3
7.1	6.2	6.2	Profit Before Taxes	23.7	4.8	5.3	3.0	3.2	2.5
			RATIOS						
2.3	2.3	2.4	Current	2.2	3.8	3.4	2.5	2.4	2.1
1.4	1.5	1.4		.8	1.1	2.2	1.4	1.4	1.5
.8	1.0	.9		.5	.4	1.2	1.0	1.1	1.0
2.0	2.0	2.2	Quick	2.2	3.8	3.4	2.2	2.0	1.8
1.2	1.3	1.2		.8	1.0	2.1	1.3	1.2	1.3
.6	.8	.8		.5	.4	.9	.9	.9	.9
7 55.7	7 50.7	10 38.3	Sales/Receivables	0 UND	0 UND	4 97.1	12 30.4	34 10.8	35 10.4
32 11.3	32 11.3	35 10.5		0 UND	7 51.7	31 11.6	34 10.8	44 8.3	51 7.1
54 6.8	54 6.8	52 7.0		23 15.7	21 17.3	54 6.7	51 7.2	66 5.5	66 5.5
			Cost of Sales/Inventory						
			Cost of Sales/Payables						
9.9	9.4	8.8	Sales/Working Capital	15.7	8.9	7.2	11.5	7.1	9.9
22.2	22.8	22.7		-14.6	593.8	10.9	26.5	19.9	18.0
-37.4	-390.0	-81.8		-5.5	-10.4	66.5	-825.2	110.7	71.2
15.2	13.2	13.9	EBIT/Interest	6.9	10.5	35.6	8.0	20.2	16.5
(195) 5.5	(192) 4.4	(198) 4.8		(15) 4.4	(26) 4.8	10.1	(40) 2.5	(51) 3.8	(42) 6.4
1.8	1.2	1.1		-1.0	.1	2.0	-.1	.8	3.2
4.9	4.0	4.5	Net Profit + Depr., Dep., Amort./Cur. Mat. L/T/D					2.7	11.9
(46) 2.4	(50) 2.2	(46) 2.1						(17) 1.0	(16) 4.0
1.4	1.1	.9						-.1	2.4
.4	.4	.3	Fixed/Worth	1.4	.3	.3	.3	.2	.3
.0	.9	.8		6.4	1.1	.7	.7	.6	.6
3.2	5.9	3.5		-2.2	-3.8	NM	2.9	2.1	1.1
.8	.8	.8	Debt/Worth	1.9	.4	.4	.8	.8	.8
1.7	1.9	1.8		32.0	1.9	1.3	1.7	2.1	1.5
5.1	10.4	6.9		-4.9	-6.1	NM	13.8	3.3	2.7
40.4	40.6	47.1	% Profit Before Taxes/Tangible Net Worth	52.7	76.2	59.9	35.4	41.3	32.2
(203) 18.7	(187) 15.3	(194) 18.2		(18) 20.7	(23) 29.7	(18) 27.8	(38) 12.6	(52) 16.4	(45) 16.4
5.3	2.6	3.6		6.4	.5	8.8	-.9	-2.2	4.4
14.9	11.7	18.5	% Profit Before Taxes/Total Assets	15.5	34.2	31.2	14.5	20.0	12.0
7.2	5.0	6.3		5.0	5.6	13.9	3.0	4.5	6.5
1.1	.4	.8		.9	-8.1	1.6	-.5	-.6	2.5
25.9	25.7	29.7	Sales/Net Fixed Assets	41.0	30.4	27.4	47.7	26.6	28.3
11.2	10.8	13.4		.3	16.7	12.0	13.7	18.0	12.0
4.3	3.9	4.4		.1	7.3	5.3	7.4	6.7	7.8
4.1	4.1	4.3	Sales/Total Assets	2.9	6.5	4.5	4.8	4.0	4.3
2.9	2.7	3.1		.2	3.4	2.9	3.7	2.9	3.5
1.8	1.6	1.8		.1	2.3	1.8	2.7	2.1	1.8
1.1	1.3	1.2	% Depr., Dep., Amort./Sales	7.5	.9	1.3	1.2	1.2	.9
(195) 2.4	(182) 2.7	(195) 2.0		(24) 13.0	(25) 1.9	(19) 1.9	(38) 2.0	(48) 1.8	(41) 1.8
4.1	5.2	4.6		24.0	3.8	4.6	3.5	3.4	3.1
1.5	2.0	2.2	% Officers', Directors' Owners' Comp/Sales		2.4		1.9	1.1	
(66) 3.0	(71) 3.3	(66) 3.8			(19) 5.3		(17) 2.8	(13) 2.5	
7.9	10.1	6.4			10.6		4.3	5.1	
5423052M	5837749M	7202491M	Net Sales ($)	15673M	66406M	92747M	328490M	871441M	5827734M
2587724M	2876162M	3073551M	Total Assets ($)	58152M	25868M	37938M	122440M	376641M	2452512M

© RMA 2019   M = $ thousand   MM = $ million
See Pages viii through xx for Explanation of Ratios and Data

Current Data Sorted by Assets   Comparative Historical Data

0-500M	500M-2MM	2-10MM	10-50MM	50-100MM	100-250MM	Type of Statement	4/1/14-3/31/15 ALL	4/1/15-3/31/16 ALL
	1	2	10	8	4	Unqualified	20	24
1	4	19	19	7		Reviewed	51	54
4	8	18	7	3		Compiled	45	49
21	28	20	4	1		Tax Returns	83	71
17	36	42	38	13	1	Other	138	145
	36 (4/1-9/30/18)		300 (10/1/18-3/31/19)					
43	77	101	78	32	5	**NUMBER OF STATEMENTS**	337	343
%	%	%	%	%	%	**ASSETS**	%	%
27.7	17.2	12.6	6.0	4.6		Cash & Equivalents	12.6	13.1
12.7	17.0	24.5	23.5	14.6		Trade Receivables (net)	21.7	18.3
.6	1.8	1.6	1.8	2.9		Inventory	1.5	2.0
2.0	2.4	3.6	4.1	3.3		All Other Current	3.3	2.7
43.0	38.5	42.2	35.5	25.4		Total Current	39.0	36.1
43.2	48.5	48.3	52.2	68.0		Fixed Assets (net)	48.5	51.6
4.2	5.3	2.4	2.8	3.2		Intangibles (net)	4.0	3.9
9.6	7.8	7.1	9.5	3.3		All Other Non-Current	8.5	8.4
100.0	100.0	100.0	100.0	100.0		Total	100.0	100.0
						LIABILITIES		
17.3	3.7	7.6	4.8	5.5		Notes Payable-Short Term	8.0	7.6
4.8	8.7	8.8	9.2	10.4		Cur. Mat.-L.T.D.	7.7	8.9
8.7	7.9	8.4	7.2	5.2		Trade Payables	7.9	8.1
.1	.0	.1	.1	.0		Income Taxes Payable	.2	.2
17.9	9.6	6.1	7.9	5.6		All Other Current	10.5	9.3
48.7	29.9	31.0	29.1	26.8		Total Current	34.3	34.1
41.8	44.6	30.3	27.0	30.6		Long-Term Debt	30.2	32.3
.0	.0	.3	.6	.6		Deferred Taxes	.9	.8
12.5	7.9	1.9	4.1	2.2		All Other Non-Current	4.3	4.9
-2.9	17.6	36.6	39.2	39.9		Net Worth	30.3	27.9
100.0	100.0	100.0	100.0	100.0		Total Liabilties & Net Worth	100.0	100.0
						INCOME DATA		
100.0	100.0	100.0	100.0	100.0		Net Sales	100.0	100.0
						Gross Profit		
96.1	93.3	91.0	91.7	95.0		Operating Expenses	93.0	92.7
3.9	6.7	9.0	8.3	5.0		Operating Profit	7.0	7.3
-.5	.9	1.4	.7	.6		All Other Expenses (net)	1.1	.7
4.4	5.8	7.6	7.6	4.4		Profit Before Taxes	5.9	6.6
						RATIOS		
4.2	4.3	2.7	2.0	1.7			2.2	2.4
1.1	1.4	1.4	1.2	1.1		Current	1.2	1.2
.4	.6	.9	.8	.6			.7	.6
3.6	3.9	2.4	1.6	1.6			1.9	2.2
1.0	1.3	1.3	1.0	.8		Quick	1.1	1.0
.4	.4	.7	.6	.5			.5	.5
0 UND	0 UND	18 20.6	29 12.8	27 13.5			8 43.9	10 37.7
0 UND	15 24.1	32 11.5	36 10.2	40 9.2		Sales/Receivables	28 13.0	28 13.0
20 17.9	38 9.6	43 8.4	48 7.6	48 7.6			43 8.5	40 9.1
						Cost of Sales/Inventory		
						Cost of Sales/Payables		
14.7	9.2	9.0	10.0	12.1			11.9	10.9
86.3	51.2	23.6	27.8	69.5		Sales/Working Capital	45.2	48.3
-22.2	-19.2	-58.8	-29.9	-14.0			-20.7	-21.5
20.2	12.9	12.6	14.3	13.0			15.7	15.8
(33) 2.3	(71) 3.8	(86) 6.3	(73) 6.3	4.3		EBIT/Interest	(287) 5.7	(313) 5.6
-3.5	-.7	1.7	2.9	1.3			1.9	1.5
		3.1	3.4	2.7			3.3	2.4
	(11) 1.6	(30) 1.7	(10) 2.1			Net Profit + Depr., Dep., Amort./Cur. Mat. L/T/D	(60) 1.8	(67) 1.7
		1.3	1.2	1.0			1.2	1.3
.8	.8	.7	.8	1.2			.7	.9
5.8	1.7	1.3	1.4	2.0		Fixed/Worth	1.6	1.7
-1.8	-3.8	3.1	2.7	3.6			5.5	5.0
1.0	1.1	.8	.7	.9			.7	.8
53.3	2.7	1.5	1.7	1.7		Debt/Worth	2.1	2.0
-2.9	-6.2	6.8	4.0	4.2			10.0	7.2
158.2	86.6	48.4	45.6	31.6			58.8	57.7
(24) 45.2	(53) 35.5	(90) 25.9	(72) 22.1	(30) 16.5		% Profit Before Taxes/Tangible Net Worth	(279) 25.6	(283) 26.4
-7.5	9.7	7.9	12.5	2.5			9.5	10.6
45.1	29.3	20.6	15.8	11.7			18.2	20.0
15.6	7.0	9.9	9.4	7.6		% Profit Before Taxes/Total Assets	8.1	9.0
-5.8	-3.4	2.4	4.6	.7			1.7	1.3
44.4	18.6	14.9	7.0	3.2			15.4	11.6
11.0	6.9	4.2	3.3	1.9		Sales/Net Fixed Assets	4.7	4.1
5.8	3.5	2.7	2.2	1.4			2.4	2.2
6.9	4.7	4.1	2.5	2.0			4.3	3.9
4.0	3.2	2.3	1.8	1.4		Sales/Total Assets	2.2	2.2
2.1	1.8	1.6	1.2	1.0			1.5	1.4
2.6	3.6	2.6	2.9	3.9			2.7	3.2
(23) 6.5	(51) 6.9	(74) 6.5	(75) 6.0	(21) 8.5		% Depr., Dep., Amort./Sales	(254) 5.4	(259) 6.5
11.9	12.8	12.0	9.6	11.3			8.8	10.1
3.8	1.4	.9	.6				1.2	.8
(22) 7.5	(32) 3.0	(37) 1.5	(19) 1.3			% Officers', Directors' Owners' Comp/Sales	(97) 3.1	(100) 2.3
13.5	5.9	3.5	3.0				5.9	5.3
55603M	321264M	1295570M	3398186M	3497090M	1833533M	Net Sales ($)	9775397M	9144976M
11355M	87127M	469581M	1697558M	2197270M	663714M	Total Assets ($)	4806774M	5279190M

M = $ thousand   MM = $ million
See Pages viii through xx for Explanation of Ratios and Data

Comparative Historical Data				Current Data Sorted by Sales					
			Type of Statement						
16	21	25	Unqualified		1	1	1	1	21
41	37	50	Reviewed	1		1	9	17	22
54	47	40	Compiled	3	5	8	9	7	8
69	76	74	Tax Returns	16	20	6	20	9	3
137	149	147	Other	15	24	14	15	36	43
4/1/16-3/31/17 ALL	4/1/17-3/31/18 ALL	4/1/18-3/31/19 ALL		36 (4/1-9/30/18)			300 (10/1/18-3/31/19)		
				0-1MM	1-3MM	3-5MM	5-10MM	10-25MM	25MM & OVER
317	330	336	**NUMBER OF STATEMENTS**	35	50	30	54	70	97
%	%	%	**ASSETS**	%	%	%	%	%	%
13.3	14.4	13.4	Cash & Equivalents	23.1	21.7	13.7	15.3	11.4	6.0
19.3	21.2	20.0	Trade Receivables (net)	7.8	12.3	20.5	19.8	25.7	24.1
1.7	1.5	1.7	Inventory	.2	1.4	.4	3.2	1.1	2.3
2.6	2.8	3.2	All Other Current	1.1	2.5	2.4	2.9	5.1	3.3
36.8	39.9	38.3	Total Current	32.1	37.9	37.0	41.2	43.3	35.7
50.7	49.8	50.5	Fixed Assets (net)	58.4	51.0	47.2	45.4	46.7	54.0
4.0	4.5	3.5	Intangibles (net)	2.5	2.1	6.7	3.7	3.6	3.4
8.4	5.9	7.7	All Other Non-Current	7.0	9.0	9.1	9.8	6.3	6.8
100.0	100.0	100.0	Total	100.0	100.0	100.0	100.0	100.0	100.0
			LIABILITIES						
6.1	7.0	7.0	Notes Payable-Short Term	20.2	4.8	3.5	4.7	5.5	6.8
9.0	9.8	8.5	Cur. Mat.-L.T.D.	3.1	10.3	6.0	9.8	9.0	9.3
7.8	9.4	7.7	Trade Payables	4.0	5.7	10.8	8.5	8.6	8.1
.3	.1	.1	Income Taxes Payable	.0	.0	.0	.1	.1	.1
8.5	8.5	8.8	All Other Current	16.8	6.2	14.0	8.5	5.7	8.0
31.5	34.8	32.1	Total Current	44.1	27.0	34.2	31.7	29.0	32.2
38.6	35.9	34.1	Long-Term Debt	37.7	51.5	39.1	36.6	27.1	26.0
1.0	.5	.3	Deferred Taxes	.0	.0	.2	.3	.2	.6
5.5	4.9	5.2	All Other Non-Current	5.2	13.9	3.9	3.1	3.8	3.1
23.4	23.9	28.3	Net Worth	13.0	7.5	22.6	28.4	39.9	38.0
100.0	100.0	100.0	Total Liabilties & Net Worth	100.0	100.0	100.0	100.0	100.0	100.0
			INCOME DATA						
100.0	100.0	100.0	Net Sales	100.0	100.0	100.0	100.0	100.0	100.0
			Gross Profit						
94.3	94.4	92.8	Operating Expenses	79.1	93.4	92.5	96.1	93.7	95.0
5.7	5.6	7.2	Operating Profit	20.9	6.6	7.5	3.9	6.3	5.0
1.0	.7	.8	All Other Expenses (net)	4.9	-.1	.1	.2	.5	.5
4.7	4.9	6.4	Profit Before Taxes	16.0	6.6	7.4	3.8	5.8	4.5
			RATIOS						
2.3	2.1	2.5		5.2	4.3	3.7	3.1	2.5	1.7
1.1	1.2	1.3	Current	1.0	1.3	1.3	1.4	1.7	1.1
.7	.7	.7		.3	.4	.8	.8	1.0	.8
2.1	2.0	2.0		5.0	3.5	3.5	3.0	2.0	1.5
1.0	1.1	1.1	Quick	1.0	.9	1.3	1.2	1.4	.9
.6	.6	.5		.3	.3	.7	.5	.8	.6
10 37.2	6 56.9	9 42.7		0 UND	0 UND	3 124.0	8 46.7	20 18.1	27 13.7
28 12.9	27 13.4	28 13.1	Sales/Receivables	0 UND	13 27.9	22 16.7	26 14.0	33 10.9	36 10.2
43 8.4	45 8.2	42 8.6		16 22.9	29 12.4	42 8.7	42 8.7	45 8.2	47 7.7
			Cost of Sales/Inventory						
			Cost of Sales/Payables						
10.9	12.0	10.4		6.2	5.4	9.0	9.7	9.8	13.6
52.0	50.9	37.0	Sales/Working Capital	UND	35.2	34.0	35.5	18.5	69.1
-23.3	-26.4	-29.8		-4.3	-20.1	-45.6	-39.0	NM	-30.1
11.8	13.1	13.2		18.0	17.1	13.7	10.4	13.8	13.8
(282) 4.3	(298) 4.5	(299) 5.4	EBIT/Interest	(21) 3.2	(45) 1.7	(27) 6.5	(49) 3.5	(65) 7.9	(92) 4.6
1.0	1.3	1.6		-6.2	-.6	-2.1	1.0	3.7	2.3
2.8	3.4	3.0							3.1
(62) 1.5	(46) 1.6	(56) 1.8	Net Profit + Depr., Dep., Amort./Cur. Mat. L/T/D						(36) 1.8
1.0	1.4	1.3							1.2
.8	.9	.8		.8	.8	.9	.7	.6	.9
2.0	2.0	1.5	Fixed/Worth	1.9	7.5	1.6	1.4	1.2	1.6
8.9	15.5	6.8		-21.9	-3.8	NM	3.3	2.0	2.8
.9	.8	.9		.5	1.1	1.4	1.0	.8	.9
2.6	2.6	2.0	Debt/Worth	3.5	9.9	5.0	1.5	1.3	2.0
21.5	45.5	10.1		-10.8	-6.0	NM	27.0	3.1	4.5
47.9	62.0	52.9		68.5	71.4	120.4	73.6	44.5	46.2
(255) 21.6	(257) 24.8	(274) 25.3	% Profit Before Taxes/Tangible Net Worth	(24) 20.8	(32) 46.1	(23) 25.6	(43) 29.2	(62) 26.2	(90) 22.0
5.2	8.2	10.2		7.5	1.1	-5.9	4.4	12.9	10.4
18.4	18.1	19.8		19.2	38.2	30.0	24.0	19.1	16.3
6.6	7.4	8.4	% Profit Before Taxes/Total Assets	7.1	3.5	10.0	7.2	10.7	7.9
.4	.8	1.7		-4.6	-3.7	-6.2	.0	6.2	3.4
12.3	12.7	12.6		13.7	12.3	12.0	21.4	16.9	7.2
4.3	4.8	4.7	Sales/Net Fixed Assets	3.1	6.0	6.2	6.8	4.4	3.3
2.4	2.5	2.4		.5	1.7	3.0	3.1	2.9	2.1
3.7	4.0	3.9		2.7	4.7	4.6	4.5	4.5	3.0
2.2	2.4	2.3	Sales/Total Assets	1.7	2.7	2.7	2.8	2.3	2.0
1.4	1.5	1.4		.2	1.3	1.6	1.8	1.6	1.3
3.8	3.1	3.2		10.6	4.6	2.7	3.1	3.0	2.5
(237) 6.8	(258) 5.7	(244) 6.6	% Depr., Dep., Amort./Sales	(20) 12.7	(30) 11.4	(22) 5.7	(38) 6.0	(53) 6.4	(81) 4.9
10.7	10.3	11.4		18.6	17.2	11.2	12.1	8.5	9.1
1.0	1.5	1.0		8.1	1.9	2.9	.8	.8	.5
(115) 2.3	(113) 3.1	(118) 2.1	% Officers', Directors' Owners' Comp/Sales	(11) 10.8	(18) 3.5	(17) 4.2	(27) 1.9	(22) 1.3	(23) 1.2
4.3	5.8	5.7		14.0	6.9	6.0	3.9	2.0	2.3
8024326M	9305907M	10401246M	Net Sales ($)	16046M	95941M	117359M	368425M	1134281M	8669194M
4511754M	4686456M	5126605M	Total Assets ($)	23117M	79037M	68685M	159019M	558300M	4238447M

M = $ thousand   MM = $ million
See Pages viii through xx for Explanation of Ratios and Data

Current Data Sorted by Assets   Comparative Historical Data

0-500M	500M-2MM	2-10MM	10-50MM	50-100MM	100-250MM	Type of Statement	4/1/14-3/31/15 ALL	4/1/15-3/31/16 ALL
		3	18	11	13	Unqualified	47	54
	3	8	29	5	3	Reviewed	58	56
3	5	29	9		3	Compiled	33	40
8	14	14	2			Tax Returns	34	40
6	17	52	84	31	21	Other	166	189
	58 (4/1-9/30/18)		330 (10/1/18-3/31/19)					
17	39	106	142	47	37	**NUMBER OF STATEMENTS**	338	379
%	%	%	%	%	%	**ASSETS**	%	%
19.7	20.5	12.5	10.1	7.8	4.6	Cash & Equivalents	10.5	11.9
23.1	23.3	27.3	23.6	19.8	17.0	Trade Receivables (net)	24.0	20.7
.6	2.1	.8	1.6	.8	2.8	Inventory	1.7	1.1
9.4	4.3	4.4	4.3	4.6	2.8	All Other Current	3.6	3.9
52.8	50.2	45.1	39.7	33.0	27.2	Total Current	39.8	37.5
26.4	37.5	40.8	48.8	57.2	59.0	Fixed Assets (net)	48.9	51.9
7.2	4.8	4.3	3.9	3.7	7.1	Intangibles (net)	4.6	4.0
13.6	7.6	9.8	7.5	6.1	6.6	All Other Non-Current	6.6	6.6
100.0	100.0	100.0	100.0	100.0	100.0	Total	100.0	100.0
						LIABILITIES		
5.4	15.2	7.8	4.6	2.2	4.7	Notes Payable-Short Term	6.9	5.1
15.8	8.0	7.8	9.4	12.3	10.3	Cur. Mat.-L.T.D.	8.7	9.9
19.9	10.4	8.7	6.9	8.1	5.6	Trade Payables	8.0	6.6
.0	.4	.5	.2	.0	.0	Income Taxes Payable	.1	.2
31.7	9.7	11.2	8.0	9.0	7.0	All Other Current	7.9	7.2
72.8	43.7	35.9	29.0	31.7	27.6	Total Current	31.7	29.0
27.0	35.8	32.4	30.1	28.8	33.8	Long-Term Debt	30.3	32.7
.0	.5	.3	1.0	1.6	2.0	Deferred Taxes	1.7	1.8
8.1	13.2	5.2	2.9	2.0	3.0	All Other Non-Current	4.0	3.2
-7.9	6.8	26.2	37.1	36.0	33.6	Net Worth	32.4	33.3
100.0	100.0	100.0	100.0	100.0	100.0	Total Liabilities & Net Worth	100.0	100.0
						INCOME DATA		
100.0	100.0	100.0	100.0	100.0	100.0	Net Sales	100.0	100.0
						Gross Profit		
94.7	94.7	91.8	92.3	93.1	94.9	Operating Expenses	93.8	93.8
5.3	5.3	8.2	7.7	6.9	5.1	Operating Profit	6.2	6.2
-.6	.0	1.5	1.3	1.2	1.8	All Other Expenses (net)	.8	1.1
5.9	5.3	6.7	6.4	5.6	3.3	Profit Before Taxes	5.4	5.1
						RATIOS		
3.9	4.2	2.7	2.1	1.5	1.5		2.0	2.1
.8	1.3	1.3	1.3	1.0	1.0	Current	1.2	1.2
.2	.9	.8	.9	.8	.6		.8	.8
2.7	3.8	2.5	1.9	1.3	1.4		1.9	1.8
.7	1.1	1.1	1.1	.9	.6	Quick	1.0	1.0
.0	.8	.7	.7	.7	.4		.6	.7
0 UND	0 UND	13 27.7	29 12.5	27 13.5	27 13.3		22 16.3	19 18.9
1 303.0	21 17.7	30 12.0	38 9.5	38 9.5	39 9.4	Sales/Receivables	35 10.5	31 11.6
20 18.0	32 11.5	43 8.4	49 7.4	47 7.7	45 8.2		46 7.9	39 9.3
						Cost of Sales/Inventory		
						Cost of Sales/Payables		
16.4	14.7	11.9	7.7	16.7	17.1		10.6	11.1
-251.0	44.1	36.0	23.9	425.3	-544.7	Sales/Working Capital	48.0	44.6
-6.1	-222.3	-31.2	-100.7	-26.5	-9.1		-31.0	-31.3
45.1	21.1	15.9	10.7	12.6	5.4		10.2	10.6
(12) 6.1	(33) 7.3	(94) 7.0	(136) 4.6	(46) 5.0	3.0	EBIT/Interest	(313) 4.6	(351) 4.5
-.4	-.4	1.9	2.5	1.7	2.1		2.1	1.7
		9.7	2.9	7.0		Net Profit + Depr., Dep.,	2.3	2.4
	(17) 3.2	(56) 1.6	(17) 2.7			Amort./Cur. Mat. L/T/D	(95) 1.6	(107) 1.6
	2.2	1.2	1.6				1.2	.9
.0	.3	.6	.8	1.0	1.4		.8	1.1
1.8	1.5	1.4	1.4	2.0	2.1	Fixed/Worth	1.9	1.9
-.4	-2.3	6.0	2.7	4.0	3.5		3.7	3.7
.7	.7	.9	.9	.8	1.5		1.1	1.0
11.1	2.4	2.4	1.7	2.4	2.4	Debt/Worth	2.2	2.0
-2.9	-6.7	11.7	3.5	4.2	4.0		5.5	5.0
173.6	142.5	68.0	44.2	47.4	31.5	% Profit Before Taxes/Tangible	45.3	48.6
(10) 103.7	(26) 54.7	(87) 30.2	(129) 24.0	(44) 21.6	(32) 17.2	Net Worth	(298) 25.6	(332) 23.8
-6.3	11.8	11.2	9.8	8.6	4.5		10.7	9.4
69.9	37.9	19.9	16.8	13.3	8.2	% Profit Before Taxes/Total	14.2	13.9
3.2	14.1	12.3	8.1	7.7	5.2	Assets	7.2	7.3
-5.2	-.4	3.0	3.3	2.4	1.6		2.7	1.3
UND	71.5	32.7	7.2	4.4	3.2		10.8	10.1
38.8	15.4	9.0	3.5	2.4	2.1	Sales/Net Fixed Assets	4.0	3.5
9.2	6.6	3.4	2.2	1.8	1.5		2.3	1.8
13.8	9.6	4.9	2.7	2.1	1.8		3.4	3.4
5.2	4.5	3.0	1.8	1.5	1.4	Sales/Total Assets	2.1	1.9
3.3	2.7	1.8	1.3	1.2	1.1		1.4	1.2
	.5	1.2	3.6	3.5			3.0	3.4
	(24) 2.0	(83) 3.3	(132) 7.0	(35) 6.3		% Depr., Dep., Amort./Sales	(266) 5.4	(279) 6.5
	7.0	8.9	10.2	10.2			8.5	9.7
	.9	.7	.9			% Officers', Directors'	.9	.9
	(19) 2.4	(40) 1.8	(23) 2.2			Owners' Comp/Sales	(66) 1.8	(84) 2.0
	4.3	3.0	3.9				4.8	3.7
53442M	239273M	1861461M	6500293M	6115126M	8799428M	Net Sales ($)	25531104M	23931982M
4998M	44616M	537374M	3170091M	3307341M	5423032M	Total Assets ($)	11286289M	13540176M

M = $ thousand MM = $ million
See Pages viii through xx for Explanation of Ratios and Data

Comparative Historical Data | Current Data Sorted by Sales

Type of Statement	4/1/16–3/31/17 ALL	4/1/17–3/31/18 ALL	4/1/18–3/31/19 ALL	0-1MM	1-3MM	3-5MM	5-10MM	10-25MM	25MM & OVER
Unqualified	47	45	45			1	1	7	36
Reviewed	51	59	48			2	3	8	35
Compiled	37	44	46	4	3	3	9	20	7
Tax Returns	30	42	38	4	6	4	9	11	4
Other	182	177	211	5	10	7	21	38	130
				58 (4/1-9/30/18)		330 (10/1/18-3/31/19)			
NUMBER OF STATEMENTS	347	367	388	13	19	17	43	84	212
ASSETS	%	%	%	%	%	%	%	%	%
Cash & Equivalents	11.8	11.4	11.4	15.9	16.0	14.1	14.9	12.9	9.2
Trade Receivables (net)	21.5	23.4	23.5	6.8	21.5	20.7	19.4	26.8	24.4
Inventory	1.1	1.5	1.4	.0	2.8	1.7	.9	.7	1.8
All Other Current	4.1	3.8	4.5	1.6	9.5	5.5	2.0	5.2	4.3
Total Current	38.6	40.1	40.8	24.3	49.9	42.0	37.2	45.6	39.7
Fixed Assets (net)	48.9	47.4	46.5	64.0	36.9	43.9	47.1	41.1	48.5
Intangibles (net)	5.3	5.1	4.5	6.9	3.0	8.7	3.8	4.7	4.3
All Other Non-Current	7.2	7.4	8.2	4.8	10.2	5.4	11.9	8.6	7.5
Total	100.0	100.0	100.0	100.0	100.0	100.0	100.0	100.0	100.0
LIABILITIES									
Notes Payable-Short Term	7.0	6.3	6.3	.0	3.2	9.5	6.0	10.5	5.1
Cur. Mat. L.T.D.	10.0	9.2	9.5	12.8	10.4	9.1	9.4	7.7	10.0
Trade Payables	7.5	8.6	8.3	.7	12.2	15.6	6.1	8.5	8.2
Income Taxes Payable	.3	.2	.2	.0	.0	.7	.6	.5	.1
All Other Current	8.6	10.1	10.1	5.5	23.1	8.7	7.8	8.5	10.4
Total Current	33.5	34.4	34.5	19.0	49.0	43.5	29.9	35.8	33.8
Long-Term Debt	29.4	29.7	31.3	59.6	33.6	26.7	37.1	32.1	28.3
Deferred Taxes	1.7	1.3	.9	.0	.3	.7	.3	.6	1.2
All Other Non-Current	2.8	4.5	4.7	.5	10.4	3.7	12.0	5.6	2.7
Net Worth	32.6	30.2	28.6	20.9	6.8	25.5	20.7	26.0	34.0
Total Liabilities & Net Worth	100.0	100.0	100.0	100.0	100.0	100.0	100.0	100.0	100.0
INCOME DATA									
Net Sales	100.0	100.0	100.0	100.0	100.0	100.0	100.0	100.0	100.0
Gross Profit									
Operating Expenses	94.8	94.3	92.9	57.3	89.4	91.7	95.3	93.4	94.7
Operating Profit	5.2	5.7	7.1	42.7	10.6	8.3	4.7	6.6	5.3
All Other Expenses (net)	1.1	1.4	1.2	13.7	3.7	2.3	-.7	.5	.7
Profit Before Taxes	4.1	4.3	6.0	29.0	6.8	6.0	5.4	6.0	4.5
RATIOS									
Current	1.8	2.0	2.1	3.9	7.3	1.5	2.5	3.3	1.7
	1.1	1.2	1.3	.5	1.8	1.0	1.3	1.7	1.2
	.7	.8	.8	.2	.3	.3	.7	.9	.8
Quick	1.6	1.7	1.9	2.8	5.7	1.4	2.1	2.9	1.5
	(346) 1.0	1.0	1.1	.5	1.4	.9	1.1	1.4	1.0
	.6	.6	.6	.2	.2	.1	.4	.8	.6
Sales/Receivables	20 18.3	21 17.4	20 18.4	0 UND	0 UND	0 UND	0 999.8	24 15.5	26 13.8
	32 11.4	34 10.6	35 10.5	0 UND	21 17.7	23 15.6	22 16.7	35 10.5	36 10.0
	42 8.7	45 8.2	45 8.1	6 64.0	56 6.5	47 7.7	43 8.5	47 7.8	45 8.1
Cost of Sales/Inventory									
Cost of Sales/Payables									
Sales/Working Capital	13.0	11.2	11.5	7.2	5.4	16.7	13.7	6.9	14.0
	70.6	41.2	33.3	-5.4	15.4	400.2	45.2	20.3	46.6
	-18.3	-34.2	-32.1	-2.5	-6.7	-8.3	-36.2	-120.9	-28.8
EBIT/Interest	8.9	8.1	11.2		12.5	10.7	11.6	15.2	10.1
	(311) 3.5	(333) 3.5	(358) 5.1	(12) 4.0	3.6	(41) 5.8	(79) 8.6	(204) 4.4	4.4
	.7	1.4	2.1	-1.2	-.6	1.8	2.8	2.1	2.1
Net Profit + Depr., Dep., Amort./Cur. Mat. L/T/D	2.6	2.7	4.0					3.9	3.9
	(86) 1.3	(89) 1.5	(94) 2.3				(19) 2.4	(69) 2.1	2.1
	.9	1.1	1.3					1.3	1.3
Fixed/Worth	.9	.8	.8	1.0	.3	.9	.9	.6	.9
	1.9	1.6	1.5	0.9	3.0	2.2	1.7	1.2	1.6
	4.3	3.6	3.9	NM	-4.6	NM	6.9	2.6	3.4
Debt/Worth	1.0	1.0	.9	.4	1.2	1.0	.9	.8	1.0
	2.2	1.8	2.2	4.8	6.2	2.5	1.8	1.8	2.1
	5.8	4.7	5.6	NM	-10.4	NM	27.5	6.1	3.9
% Profit Before Taxes/Tangible Net Worth	39.5	36.9	52.3	114.7	106.9	56.7	84.5	58.8	44.3
	(293) 16.2	(312) 15.7	(328) 26.1	(10) 25.2	(11) 56.9	(13) 22.2	(34) 27.5	(68) 32.5	(192) 20.9
	2.4	5.4	9.7	9.7	27.0	10.9	12.2	12.7	7.6
% Profit Before Taxes/Total Assets	10.8	11.0	17.1	40.1	28.2	14.6	32.1	19.5	14.3
	5.0	5.0	8.0	4.6	7.9	5.7	8.6	13.1	6.7
	-.3	.7	2.4	2.7	-8.4	-3.9	3.2	4.1	2.3
Sales/Net Fixed Assets	13.9	13.3	16.0	13.3	31.6	23.2	15.8	27.5	10.7
	3.4	3.9	4.5	.2	10.5	5.8	7.3	5.9	3.7
	1.8	2.1	2.2	.1	2.4	2.0	2.9	2.4	2.1
Sales/Total Assets	3.6	3.6	3.8	2.9	4.5	4.0	5.6	4.9	3.4
	1.8	1.9	2.1	.2	2.8	2.7	2.8	2.7	1.9
	1.2	1.3	1.4	.1	.6	1.3	1.6	1.4	1.4
% Depr., Dep., Amort./Sales	2.6	3.0	2.3			2.1	2.0	2.1	2.3
	(238) 6.6	(277) 6.2	(283) 5.3		(13) 7.5	(28) 7.3	(73) 4.8	(153) 5.2	5.2
	10.5	10.4	9.6			35.8	11.8	8.7	8.7
% Officers', Directors' Owners' Comp/Sales	.9	1.2	.7				1.3	.5	.5
	(77) 2.3	(95) 2.3	(98) 1.8			(17) 2.4	(34) 1.3	(38) 1.4	1.4
	5.0	5.5	3.3				2.9	2.8	2.9
Net Sales ($)	19902335M	21598633M	23569023M	6477M	38478M	67644M	331356M	1443823M	21681245M
Total Assets ($)	12271843M	12396431M	12487452M	29484M	59583M	143548M	175626M	828993M	11250218M

M = $ thousand   MM = $ million
See Pages viii through xx for Explanation of Ratios and Data

Current Data Sorted by Assets   **Comparative Historical Data**

Note: Columns 2-10MM, 10-50MM, 50-100MM, and 100-250MM are marked "DATA NOT AVAILABLE".

Period labels for Current Data: 7 (4/1-9/30/18)   24 (10/1/18-3/31/19)

0-500M	500M-2MM	2-10MM	10-50MM	50-100MM	100-250MM	Type of Statement	4/1/14-3/31/15 ALL	4/1/15-3/31/16 ALL
			1	1		Unqualified	4	6
	1	3				Reviewed	2	4
	2					Compiled	3	2
3	3	1				Tax Returns	9	9
3	5	3	4	1		Other	17	22
6	11	7	5	2		**NUMBER OF STATEMENTS**	35	43
%	%	%	%	%	%	**ASSETS**	%	%
	18.1					Cash & Equivalents	25.2	17.4
	19.6					Trade Receivables (net)	11.2	7.8
	.5					Inventory	.6	1.4
	9.3					All Other Current	5.6	6.5
	47.4					Total Current	42.5	33.2
	32.4					Fixed Assets (net)	32.5	44.7
	12.1					Intangibles (net)	8.7	11.4
	8.0					All Other Non-Current	16.3	10.6
	100.0					Total	100.0	100.0
						LIABILITIES		
	4.9					Notes Payable-Short Term	4.2	8.2
	14.1					Cur. Mat.-L.T.D.	4.1	4.8
	10.2					Trade Payables	9.5	12.0
	.2					Income Taxes Payable	.3	.0
	12.9					All Other Current	16.1	15.8
	42.2					Total Current	34.2	40.7
	8.3					Long-Term Debt	19.5	24.3
	.9					Deferred Taxes	1.0	.6
	19.6					All Other Non-Current	7.5	4.6
	29.0					Net Worth	37.8	29.8
	100.0					Total Liabilities & Net Worth	100.0	100.0
						INCOME DATA		
	100.0					Net Sales	100.0	100.0
						Gross Profit		
	95.5					Operating Expenses	90.6	88.8
	4.5					Operating Profit	9.4	11.2
	-.4					All Other Expenses (net)	2.5	2.0
	4.9					Profit Before Taxes	6.9	9.2
						RATIOS		
	4.6					Current	2.6	1.9
	1.4						1.1	.8
	1.1						.6	.4
	4.6					Quick	1.9	1.3
	1.4						.8	.6
	.3						.4	.3
	0 UND					Sales/Receivables	0 999.8	0 UND
	18 20.4						7 51.0	5 76.2
	29 12.4						29 12.5	19 19.1
						Cost of Sales/Inventory		
						Cost of Sales/Payables		
	4.9					Sales/Working Capital	12.1	15.8
	27.9						234.3	-65.6
	42.9						-14.9	-10.0
						EBIT/Interest	28.5	38.4
							(25) 9.2	(37) 8.9
							1.4	3.5
						Net Profit + Depr., Dep., Amort./Cur. Mat. L/T/D		
	.2					Fixed/Worth	.2	.7
	.9						.9	2.1
	2.1						4.9	UND
	.3					Debt/Worth	.6	.8
	.8						1.9	3.5
	-4.1						13.0	-37.3
						% Profit Before Taxes/Tangible Net Worth	99.9	88.5
							(29) 39.9	(32) 41.9
							11.0	17.8
	19.7					% Profit Before Taxes/Total Assets	25.0	23.5
	10.7						8.9	12.4
	-2.4						.5	4.4
	14.9					Sales/Net Fixed Assets	43.3	25.1
	10.7						10.2	9.0
	9.1						4.5	3.2
	4.7					Sales/Total Assets	4.8	3.8
	2.7						2.8	2.3
	2.1						1.7	1.6
						% Depr., Dep., Amort./Sales	3.4	4.0
							(23) 5.8	(31) 6.0
							10.0	13.0
						% Officers', Directors' Owners' Comp/Sales	.9	
							(11) 1.5	
							4.2	
29061M	46564M	39624M	382359M	341690M		Net Sales ($)	716474M	802138M
1755M	14942M	35623M	104758M	162893M		Total Assets ($)	328627M	341253M

M = $ thousand   MM = $ million
See Pages viii through xx for Explanation of Ratios and Data

Comparative Historical Data   Current Data Sorted by Sales

			Type of Statement	0-1MM	1-3MM	3-5MM	5-10MM	10-25MM	25MM & OVER
3	4	2	Unqualified						2
5	4	4	Reviewed		1		2	1	
1	3	2	Compiled			1		1	
14	7	7	Tax Returns	2	1	3	1		
15	23	16	Other	1	3	4	3	1	4
4/1/16-3/31/17	4/1/17-3/31/18	4/1/18-3/31/19				7 (4/1-9/30/18)	24 (10/1/18-3/31/19)		
ALL	ALL	ALL		0-1MM	1-3MM	3-5MM	5-10MM	10-25MM	25MM & OVER
38	41	31	NUMBER OF STATEMENTS	3	5	8	6	3	6
%	%	%	**ASSETS**	%	%	%	%	%	%
13.3	14.0	19.2	Cash & Equivalents						
9.4	15.2	19.8	Trade Receivables (net)						
1.7	1.3	.9	Inventory						
2.5	6.8	6.1	All Other Current						
27.0	37.3	46.0	Total Current						
44.6	35.0	29.6	Fixed Assets (net)						
15.2	11.0	12.9	Intangibles (net)						
13.2	16.7	11.5	All Other Non-Current						
100.0	100.0	100.0	Total						
			LIABILITIES						
9.9	11.7	4.6	Notes Payable-Short Term						
7.3	5.7	8.0	Cur. Mat.-L.T.D.						
7.9	10.8	12.6	Trade Payables						
.2	.7	.2	Income Taxes Payable						
23.2	18.4	15.0	All Other Current						
48.5	47.3	40.5	Total Current						
29.9	30.8	26.5	Long-Term Debt						
.7	.8	1.3	Deferred Taxes						
14.0	5.5	11.4	All Other Non-Current						
6.8	15.7	20.4	Net Worth						
100.0	100.0	100.0	Total Liabilties & Net Worth						
			INCOME DATA						
100.0	100.0	100.0	Net Sales						
			Gross Profit						
88.6	94.0	96.1	Operating Expenses						
11.4	6.0	3.9	Operating Profit						
4.4	3.0	.8	All Other Expenses (net)						
7.0	3.1	3.1	Profit Before Taxes						
			RATIOS						
1.1	2.1	2.7	Current						
.7	1.1	1.4							
.1	.5	.5							
1.0	2.0	2.1	Quick						
.5	.6	1.3							
.1	.4	.3							
0 UND	0 UND	0 UND	Sales/Receivables						
5 68.6	19 18.9	21 17.2							
23 16.2	44 8.3	39 9.3							
			Cost of Sales/Inventory						
			Cost of Sales/Payables						
91.0	10.0	8.4	Sales/Working Capital						
-28.7	70.2	37.4							
-4.1	-16.0	-58.6							
16.2	11.0	11.4	EBIT/Interest						
(32) 4.2	(39) 1.5	(23) 5.5							
1.2	-2.4	1.5							
			Net Profit + Depr., Dep., Amort./Cur. Mat. L/T/D						
1.3	.6	.3	Fixed/Worth						
2.5	1.5	1.2							
-4.0	-1.1	-.8							
1.5	1.3	.7	Debt/Worth						
5.1	2.8	3.1							
-4.4	-3.7	-2.9							
79.6	53.8	22.8	% Profit Before Taxes/Tangible Net Worth						
(24) 39.1	(26) 5.2	(20) 9.5							
9.9	-24.5	3.2							
20.0	15.8	13.4	% Profit Before Taxes/Total Assets						
4.9	1.0	5.5							
1.4	-4.7	.3							
14.6	29.8	23.3	Sales/Net Fixed Assets						
6.7	8.0	13.3							
3.0	4.1	5.3							
3.9	4.0	5.0	Sales/Total Assets						
2.6	2.6	2.7							
1.0	.9	1.5							
1.0	2.4	2.1	% Depr., Dep., Amort./Sales						
(26) 5.2	(26) 6.6	(23) 4.2							
9.4	11.4	8.3							
1.8		2.1	% Officers', Directors' Owners' Comp/Sales						
(14) 3.8		(11) 6.6							
8.2		7.9							
786957M	989767M	839298M	Net Sales ($)	2190M	10736M	33233M	39990M	49699M	703450M
417082M	541932M	319971M	Total Assets ($)	4726M	5413M	13590M	21431M	36942M	237869M

© RMA 2019   M = $ thousand   MM = $ million

See Pages viii through xx for Explanation of Ratios and Data

Current Data Sorted by Assets — Comparative Historical Data

Type of Statement

Type of Statement	0-500M	500M-2MM	2-10MM	10-50MM	50-100MM	100-250MM		4/1/14-3/31/15 ALL	4/1/15-3/31/16 ALL
Unqualified		1	1	2	1			5	4
Reviewed				3				2	5
Compiled	1	4						5	11
Tax Returns	7	7	7	1	1			18	25
Other	2	8	21	10				32	46
	7 (4/1-9/30/18)			70 (10/1/18-3/31/19)					
NUMBER OF STATEMENTS	10	20	29	16	2			62	91

(50-100MM and 100-250MM current columns: DATA NOT AVAILABLE)

ASSETS (%)

	0-500M	500M-2MM	2-10MM	10-50MM		4/1/14-3/31/15	4/1/15-3/31/16
Cash & Equivalents	30.3	17.7	9.6	5.2		14.6	18.4
Trade Receivables (net)	8.4	11.1	10.8	24.8		12.8	12.8
Inventory	.0	.3	.3	1.0		.2	1.6
All Other Current	10.2	3.8	2.6	7.7		4.0	2.4
Total Current	48.9	32.8	23.2	38.8		31.6	35.2
Fixed Assets (net)	45.6	42.5	70.2	41.3		51.1	48.2
Intangibles (net)	3.0	14.4	3.6	4.8		7.7	8.3
All Other Non-Current	2.5	10.3	2.9	15.1		9.6	8.3
Total	100.0	100.0	100.0	100.0		100.0	100.0

LIABILITIES

	0-500M	500M-2MM	2-10MM	10-50MM		4/1/14-3/31/15	4/1/15-3/31/16
Notes Payable-Short Term	7.6	3.9	7.1	6.8		11.8	10.7
Cur. Mat.-L.T.D.	7.0	12.7	9.9	10.3		12.3	10.6
Trade Payables	3.3	3.8	4.7	14.4		6.7	6.7
Income Taxes Payable	.0	.0	.0	.7		.1	.2
All Other Current	8.8	9.6	7.0	14.7		9.4	8.9
Total Current	26.7	30.1	28.7	46.9		40.3	37.1
Long-Term Debt	55.3	49.6	61.7	27.8		54.2	42.4
Deferred Taxes	.0	.0	.0	.1		.8	.4
All Other Non-Current	42.0	3.7	1.3	4.0		8.2	10.0
Net Worth	-23.9	16.6	8.3	21.3		-3.4	10.0
Total Liabilities & Net Worth	100.0	100.0	100.0	100.0		100.0	100.0

INCOME DATA

	0-500M	500M-2MM	2-10MM	10-50MM		4/1/14-3/31/15	4/1/15-3/31/16
Net Sales	100.0	100.0	100.0	100.0		100.0	100.0
Gross Profit							
Operating Expenses	98.8	92.0	94.2	94.5		92.0	93.8
Operating Profit	1.2	8.0	5.8	5.5		8.0	6.2
All Other Expenses (net)	.8	3.6	.6	1.6		2.4	.9
Profit Before Taxes	.4	4.4	5.1	3.8		5.5	5.3

RATIOS

	0-500M	500M-2MM	2-10MM	10-50MM		4/1/14-3/31/15	4/1/15-3/31/16
Current	8.6	2.9	2.1	2.0		1.5	1.7
	1.5	1.1	.9	1.3		.7	.8
	1.0	.5	.5	.9		.3	.3
Quick	8.6	2.7	2.0	1.6		1.3	1.6
	1.2	1.0	.9	.9		.5	.7
	.5	.5	.3	.3		.3	.3
Sales/Receivables	0 UND	0 UND	0 UND	21 17.7		0 UND	0 UND
	0 UND	5 81.0	17 21.1	37 9.8		8 47.6	9 39.9
	2 192.4	24 15.0	29 12.5	48 7.6		25 14.4	28 13.0
Cost of Sales/Inventory							
Cost of Sales/Payables							
Sales/Working Capital	13.9	13.5	16.2	12.2		44.9	20.5
	29.3	NM	-147.1	78.2		-22.6	-72.1
	NM	-27.8	-10.7	-60.4		-7.8	-10.5
EBIT/Interest		10.5	10.0	12.8		23.8	11.1
		(18) 4.6	(25) 3.8	(15) 4.5		(50) 3.3	(77) 4.1
		1.1	1.3	1.9		.9	.9
Net Profit + Depr., Dep., Amort./Cur. Mat. L/T/D							
Fixed/Worth	.2	1.2	2.6	.5		1.2	1.0
	1.5	1.5	23.2	1.3		16.8	8.7
	-.5	-.7	-5.7	2.4		-2.0	-1.8
Debt/Worth	.9	1.9	2.5	1.2		2.1	1.3
	1.7	4.8	47.8	2.4		UND	11.1
	-1.6	-2.5	-8.2	6.9		-3.4	-4.1
% Profit Before Taxes/Tangible Net Worth		113.4	91.4	52.4		108.2	78.8
		(12) 38.9	(16) 40.1	(14) 31.7		(31) 44.9	(51) 41.1
		4.1	13.9	15.0		19.8	7.6
% Profit Before Taxes/Total Assets	40.0	29.8	19.1	15.2		21.3	21.4
	5.8	10.2	7.3	9.8		7.3	9.2
	-43.0	-.6	.2	3.4		-.1	.1
Sales/Net Fixed Assets	58.4	17.2	3.5	8.9		14.8	19.3
	11.9	8.0	2.8	4.3		5.1	6.6
	4.1	2.5	1.5	2.1		2.6	3.3
Sales/Total Assets	6.9	5.4	2.3	3.2		4.6	4.8
	6.0	1.9	1.9	2.0		2.4	3.0
	1.9	1.2	1.3	1.3		1.7	2.0
% Depr., Dep., Amort./Sales		4.5	5.7	4.0		3.2	2.1
		(12) 5.9	(21) 9.1	(14) 4.5		(45) 7.5	(69) 6.1
		11.8	20.5	8.4		14.6	9.9
% Officers', Directors' Owners' Comp/Sales		2.0	1.2			2.5	2.4
		(11) 3.4	(12) 1.9			(26) 4.2	(39) 3.9
		7.4	4.9			5.1	6.2

	0-500M	500M-2MM	2-10MM	10-50MM	50-100MM		4/1/14-3/31/15	4/1/15-3/31/16
Net Sales ($)	10775M	79247M	250141M	596059M	392920M		1201883M	1615498M
Total Assets ($)	1930M	22760M	128015M	273911M	131467M		547385M	584211M

M = $ thousand   MM = $ million
See Pages viii through xx for Explanation of Ratios and Data

Comparative Historical Data | Current Data Sorted by Sales

			Type of Statement	0-1MM	1-3MM	3-5MM	5-10MM	10-25MM	25MM & OVER
4	2	5	Unqualified		1			2	2
2	5	3	Reviewed						3
7	6	5	Compiled	1	4			3	
15	17	22	Tax Returns	3	8	2	6	13	
44	63	42	Other	5	3	3	11		7
4/1/16-3/31/17	4/1/17-3/31/18	4/1/18-3/31/19			7 (4/1-9/30/18)		70 (10/1/18-3/31/19)		
ALL	ALL	ALL							
72	93	77	**NUMBER OF STATEMENTS**	9	16	5	17	18	12
%	%	%	**ASSETS**	%	%	%	%	%	%
11.1	12.0	13.3	Cash & Equivalents		21.3		15.8	7.2	5.7
16.2	14.1	13.8	Trade Receivables (net)		6.1		5.5	20.2	31.5
1.0	1.9	.4	Inventory		.2		.1	1.4	.1
4.5	4.5	4.9	All Other Current		11.3		1.9	2.5	8.7
32.9	32.6	32.4	Total Current		38.9		23.3	31.3	46.1
54.0	48.1	52.7	Fixed Assets (net)		43.0		65.7	55.4	31.1
6.8	9.6	7.5	Intangibles (net)		5.8		5.9	7.8	8.1
6.3	9.7	7.4	All Other Non-Current		12.3		5.1	5.5	14.7
100.0	100.0	100.0	Total		100.0		100.0	100.0	100.0
			LIABILITIES						
8.4	8.9	6.2	Notes Payable-Short Term		8.6		4.7	6.5	7.6
11.4	11.4	10.4	Cur. Mat.-L.T.D.		5.2		16.2	10.6	11.5
5.2	4.8	6.5	Trade Payables		2.0		2.5	8.4	18.8
.4	.2	.2	Income Taxes Payable		.0		.0	.0	1.0
9.7	8.7	9.7	All Other Current		9.8		5.1	8.2	20.2
35.1	34.0	32.8	Total Current		25.6		28.5	33.8	59.1
45.9	42.3	50.5	Long-Term Debt		48.7		63.6	54.7	25.9
.3	.4	.1	Deferred Taxes		.0		.0	.0	.8
6.1	11.7	8.1	All Other Non-Current		14.4		1.7	1.4	7.6
12.6	11.6	8.4	Net Worth		11.4		6.1	10.1	6.7
100.0	100.0	100.0	Total Liabilities & Net Worth		100.0		100.0	100.0	100.0
			INCOME DATA						
100.0	100.0	100.0	Net Sales		100.0		100.0	100.0	100.0
			Gross Profit						
90.5	92.0	94.3	Operating Expenses		91.4		97.3	93.5	94.9
9.5	8.0	5.7	Operating Profit		8.6		2.7	6.5	5.1
3.1	1.6	1.7	All Other Expenses (net)		3.3		-.5	.4	2.6
6.3	6.5	4.0	Profit Before Taxes		5.2		3.2	6.1	2.5
			RATIOS						
1.7	1.8	2.2	Current		5.1		2.0	1.5	1.8
.9	1.0	1.1			1.9		.9	1.1	1.1
.4	.5	.6			.8		.4	.5	.6
1.3	1.4	1.8	Quick		5.1		1.7	1.5	1.4
.7	.8	.9			1.6		.9	.9	.9
.4	.4	.4			.6		.3	.4	.3
0 999.8	0 UND	0 UND	Sales/Receivables		0 UND		0 UND	15 23.9	27 13.6
19 19.3	16 23.4	17 21.1			0 UND		3 108.7	22 16.9	37 9.8
35 10.5	29 12.4	30 12.2			25 14.7		17 21.1	28 13.1	46 7.9
			Cost of Sales/Inventory						
			Cost of Sales/Payables						
14.5	15.2	16.0	Sales/Working Capital		11.5		16.7	35.7	12.2
-229.3	-247.7	135.5			24.0		-147.1	150.1	148.5
-11.5	-16.1	-15.3			-126.0		-12.9	-12.8	-29.9
11.0	9.9	10.3	EBIT/Interest		10.5		4.4	8.2	19.7
(63) 4.8	(77) 4.9	(67) 3.3		(14)	3.0	(15)	1.8	(17) 6.4	4.6
1.5	1.1	1.5			.5		.5	2.1	1.7
		3.3	Net Profit + Depr., Dep., Amort./Cur. Mat. L/T/D						
	(10)	1.7							
		.8							
1.5	1.0	1.2	Fixed/Worth		.8		2.3	1.5	.6
3.3	3.4	2.7			1.4		56.2	4.1	1.1
-3.0	-5.4	-5.7			-47.1		-4.4	-4.9	NM
1.5	1.5	1.8	Debt/Worth		.9		3.0	2.2	1.5
5.2	5.4	3.6			2.1		98.0	6.0	3.1
-4.2	-9.0	-8.2			-55.2		-6.1	-8.2	NM
120.2	99.6	89.3	% Profit Before Taxes/Tangible Net Worth		108.0			100.7	
(48) 48.8	(59) 34.8	(49) 37.2		(11)	39.2			(12) 38.3	
22.4	11.6	11.1			1.4			14.0	
20.3	18.5	22.2	% Profit Before Taxes/Total Assets		27.2		19.1	25.3	16.6
9.8	8.8	7.7			4.7		7.3	11.5	10.3
1.2	.3	.2			-1.3		-1.6	4.5	3.4
10.6	19.1	10.4	Sales/Net Fixed Assets		13.7		7.9	6.4	130.1
4.4	4.6	4.0			6.3		2.9	3.8	8.1
2.2	2.3	2.1			2.2		2.2	2.1	4.6
4.1	3.8	3.7	Sales/Total Assets		5.5		4.3	3.5	3.8
2.3	2.3	2.0			1.8		2.2	2.3	3.0
1.5	1.4	1.3			1.2		1.4	1.3	2.1
3.5	3.2	4.4	% Depr., Dep., Amort./Sales		5.0		4.8	3.4	
(51) 7.0	(61) 6.4	(54) 6.5		(10)	6.5	(13)	6.3	(14) 7.1	
10.8	10.6	15.2			11.4		20.5	13.2	
1.1	1.6	1.4	% Officers', Directors' Owners' Comp/Sales				1.7		
(26) 2.9	(40) 2.9	(31) 2.4				(11)	2.6		
6.3	5.3	5.6					5.5		
1144197M	1563628M	1329142M	Net Sales ($)	4182M	29690M	22114M	117376M	281225M	874555M
483463M	786766M	558083M	Total Assets ($)	5796M	19015M	13892M	56869M	147537M	314974M

M = $ thousand   MM = $ million
See Pages viii through xx for Explanation of Ratios and Data

Current Data Sorted by Assets   Comparative Historical Data

0-500M	500M-2MM	2-10MM	10-50MM	50-100MM	100-250MM		4/1/14-3/31/15 ALL	4/1/15-3/31/16 ALL
						Type of Statement		
	1	2	1	1	5	Unqualified	7	17
	2	11	12			Reviewed	42	32
	2	11	3			Compiled	22	19
6	10	10	2			Tax Returns	29	29
1	10	17	15	3	10	Other	45	47
	42 (4/1-9/30/18)		93 (10/1/18-3/31/19)					
7	25	51	33	4	15	**NUMBER OF STATEMENTS**	145	144
%	%	%	%	%	%	**ASSETS**	%	%
	20.7	13.9	6.9		3.9	Cash & Equivalents	13.7	13.8
	7.9	8.4	7.5		12.8	Trade Receivables (net)	11.8	12.1
	1.6	1.5	2.2		4.0	Inventory	2.6	2.7
	1.0	2.3	2.6		3.0	All Other Current	2.5	2.8
	31.2	26.0	19.2		23.7	Total Current	30.6	31.4
	50.8	59.2	72.7		58.3	Fixed Assets (net)	57.1	56.7
	7.1	5.5	5.1		10.7	Intangibles (net)	3.4	5.5
	10.9	9.2	3.0		7.4	All Other Non-Current	9.0	6.4
	100.0	100.0	100.0		100.0	Total	100.0	100.0
						LIABILITIES		
	8.2	3.9	3.4		6.8	Notes Payable-Short Term	9.7	5.6
	12.9	10.6	12.1		6.6	Cur. Mat.-L.T.D.	10.1	10.3
	2.4	2.5	1.9		4.9	Trade Payables	3.4	3.3
	.2	.2	.1		.0	Income Taxes Payable	.2	.1
	12.5	5.2	5.6		7.8	All Other Current	5.8	7.8
	36.2	22.5	23.1		26.2	Total Current	29.2	27.2
	56.2	38.7	38.0		31.1	Long-Term Debt	29.9	34.5
	.0	.9	1.8		.5	Deferred Taxes	.9	.7
	2.6	5.3	6.7		6.9	All Other Non-Current	6.4	2.8
	5.0	32.6	30.3		35.3	Net Worth	33.6	34.8
	100.0	100.0	100.0		100.0	Total Liabilities & Net Worth	100.0	100.0
						INCOME DATA		
	100.0	100.0	100.0		100.0	Net Sales	100.0	100.0
						Gross Profit		
	90.4	91.2	90.9		95.2	Operating Expenses	94.0	92.6
	9.6	8.8	9.1		4.8	Operating Profit	6.0	7.4
	1.3	1.8	2.1		2.2	All Other Expenses (net)	.6	1.1
	8.3	7.0	6.9		2.6	Profit Before Taxes	5.5	6.3
						RATIOS		
	2.9	3.0	1.3		1.2		2.5	2.1
	1.0	1.0	.8		1.0	Current	1.1	1.0
	.2	.6	.4		.8		.5	.5
	2.6	1.6	.9		.8		1.9	1.7
	.7	.7	.6		.7	Quick	.9 (142)	.8
	.2	.4	.3		.5		.3	.4
0 UND	0 UND	9 39.0		31 11.9			4 88.8	5 71.7
5 68.6	12 30.8	24 15.1		45 8.1		Sales/Receivables	23 16.1	24 15.5
16 22.2	28 12.9	33 10.9		55 6.6			36 10.2	40 9.2
						Cost of Sales/Inventory		
						Cost of Sales/Payables		
	7.2	15.8	28.8		21.8		10.2	9.8
	-104.9	999.8	-23.9		-999.8	Sales/Working Capital	103.0	159.2
	-6.3	-11.4	-6.1		-19.6		-14.4	-15.3
	5.0	6.1	5.8		4.6		9.4	12.0
	(24) 4.2	(44) 2.8	(32) 3.2		1.9	EBIT/Interest	(137) 4.1	(130) 4.1
	.9	1.2	1.4		1.5		1.8	1.3
		1.9	1.5			Net Profit + Depr., Dep.,	2.3	2.5
		(10) 1.1	(15) 1.2			Amort./Cur. Mat. L/T/D	(43) 1.6	(43) 1.6
		1.0	1.1				1.1	1.1
	.7	1.4	1.8		1.2		.8	.9
	6.5	2.2	2.5		3.0	Fixed/Worth	1.7	1.6
	-1.9	15.2	4.5		6.9		6.5	6.2
	1.0	1.2	1.4		1.1		.8	.8
	13.3	2.0	2.2		3.3	Debt/Worth	1.8	1.6
	-4.3	15.5	4.2		7.2		8.7	6.8
	110.0	41.3	36.9		11.0	% Profit Before Taxes/Tangible	42.5	37.1
	(14) 22.7	(41) 15.5	(31) 22.6		(13) 8.5	Net Worth	(123) 18.1	(120) 19.3
	4.8	2.6	5.3		6.6		6.2	5.8
	27.2	13.9	9.9		3.9	% Profit Before Taxes/Total	13.1	14.4
	10.3	5.2	6.2		3.1	Assets	5.7	5.8
	.0	.5	1.1		1.3		1.6	.9
	7.8	5.3	1.9		1.9		5.8	5.2
	3.6	2.6	1.4		1.7	Sales/Net Fixed Assets	2.6	2.8
	1.6	1.5	1.0		1.6		1.4	1.6
	2.4	2.2	1.4		1.4		2.3	2.3
	1.6	1.6	.9		1.0	Sales/Total Assets	1.6	1.6
	1.1	1.0	.8		.9		1.0	1.0
	7.1	6.0	8.2				6.2	6.5
	(15) 13.8	(40) 11.1	(32) 13.5			% Depr., Dep., Amort./Sales	(121) 9.4	(118) 9.6
	15.4	15.7	14.5				14.5	13.5
	4.8	.7	1.5			% Officers', Directors'	1.3	2.2
	(15) 5.7	(23) 2.1	(16) 3.2			Owners' Comp/Sales	(63) 2.8	(59) 3.7
	9.8	6.0	7.5				5.8	7.2
8424M	61927M	390033M	725046M	504849M	2443011M	Net Sales ($)	2811032M	3609049M
2209M	32394M	231368M	596722M	314595M	2186939M	Total Assets ($)	2137176M	2922013M

M = $ thousand   MM = $ million
See Pages viii through xx for Explanation of Ratios and Data

Comparative Historical Data | Current Data Sorted by Sales

Type of Statement

17 ALL	18 ALL	19 ALL	Type of Statement	0-1MM	1-3MM	3-5MM	5-10MM	10-25MM	25MM & OVER
14	12	10	Unqualified	1			1	2	6
36	25	25	Reviewed		1	2	8	11	3
17	17	16	Compiled		1	6	7	2	
34	31	28	Tax Returns	1	15	3	6	2	1
49	53	56	Other	4	9	6	6	11	18
4/1/16-3/31/17	4/1/17-3/31/18	4/1/18-3/31/19			42 (4/1-9/30/18)			93 (10/1/18-3/31/19)	
150	138	135	**NUMBER OF STATEMENTS**	6	26	18	29	28	28

Financial Data

'17	'18	'19		0-1MM	1-3MM	3-5MM	5-10MM	10-25MM	25MM & OVER
%	%	%	**ASSETS**	%	%	%	%	%	%
14.2	12.3	12.2	Cash & Equivalents		16.1	16.7	15.4	9.4	6.8
11.3	10.8	8.7	Trade Receivables (net)		4.2	8.7	7.3	11.0	13.8
3.1	1.9	1.8	Inventory		.1	2.9	2.2	1.1	3.6
2.4	2.0	2.2	All Other Current		1.3	2.0	1.9	3.4	2.5
31.1	27.0	24.9	Total Current		21.6	30.3	26.7	24.9	26.6
57.5	55.3	60.9	Fixed Assets (net)		62.7	56.5	60.2	63.5	57.9
3.3	7.6	6.3	Intangibles (net)		5.4	3.4	5.5	7.5	7.2
8.1	10.1	7.9	All Other Non-Current		10.2	9.8	7.6	4.1	8.4
100.0	100.0	100.0	Total		100.0	100.0	100.0	100.0	100.0
			LIABILITIES						
6.3	6.3	4.7	Notes Payable-Short Term		7.0	2.6	4.4	3.0	6.3
12.0	10.5	10.6	Cur. Mat.-L.T.D.		9.9	12.5	10.1	13.1	8.4
3.1	3.0	2.7	Trade Payables		3.2	2.4	1.9	2.5	4.1
.2	.1	.1	Income Taxes Payable		.0	.5	.0	.0	.1
6.2	7.7	6.9	All Other Current		13.4	4.0	5.1	5.8	6.9
27.7	27.6	25.0	Total Current		33.5	21.9	21.5	24.4	25.9
38.8	37.9	41.3	Long-Term Debt		56.2	35.9	43.4	34.9	30.6
.8	.9	.8	Deferred Taxes		.1	.7	.8	2.3	.4
3.8	7.1	6.8	All Other Non-Current		9.5	2.6	4.2	5.0	9.9
28.8	26.6	26.0	Net Worth		.6	38.9	30.2	33.4	33.3
100.0	100.0	100.0	Total Liabilities & Net Worth		100.0	100.0	100.0	100.0	100.0
			INCOME DATA						
100.0	100.0	100.0	Net Sales		100.0	100.0	100.0	100.0	100.0
			Gross Profit						
91.3	92.8	91.4	Operating Expenses		94.1	90.2	93.4	90.5	94.4
8.7	7.2	8.6	Operating Profit		5.9	9.8	6.6	9.5	5.6
1.9	1.2	1.8	All Other Expenses (net)		.8	.5	1.7	2.0	1.8
6.8	6.0	6.8	Profit Before Taxes		5.0	9.3	5.0	7.6	3.9
			RATIOS						
2.5	2.5	1.8	Current		2.3	2.8	3.3	1.6	1.2
1.2	1.0	1.0			.4	1.2	.8	1.0	1.0
.6	.4	.5			.2	.7	.6	.4	.8
2.0	2.3	1.6	Quick		2.1	2.5	1.8	1.4	1.0
1.0	.9	.7			.4	.9	.7	.7	.8
.4	.3	.4			.2	.5	.5	.2	.6
3 125.1	2 189.1	3 129.1	Sales/Receivables	0 UND	5 69.1	6 56.5	6 56.3	27 13.5	
21 17.7	19 19.4	18 20.8		0 UND	13 27.6	22 16.9	23 16.0	43 8.5	
38 9.5	38 9.7	35 10.5		10 36.1	36 10.1	29 12.5	32 11.4	53 6.9	
			Cost of Sales/Inventory						
			Cost of Sales/Payables						
7.9	10.2	12.9	Sales/Working Capital		15.8	9.2	11.2	19.0	20.9
41.4	-662.1	-117.3			-20.8	29.1	-34.1	-207.8	-875.9
-14.6	-10.4	-8.8			-6.3	-18.9	-12.3	-6.1	-24.6
11.7	8.2	5.6	EBIT/Interest		6.3	10.3	4.3	7.2	5.4
(141) 4.8	(129) 3.4	(126) 3.3		(25) 4.4	(15) 4.1	(27) 2.1	(27) 3.2	(27) 3.2	
1.3	1.2	1.3			.3	1.1	.7	1.6	1.5
2.6	1.4	1.6	Net Profit + Depr., Dep., Amort./Cur. Mat. L/T/D					1.5	
(49) 1.6	(33) 1.2	(31) 1.2					(11)	1.2	
1.1	.8	1.0						1.0	
1.0	1.0	1.5	Fixed/Worth		1.7	.8	1.6	1.7	1.1
1.0	2.1	2.5			17.7	1.9	2.2	2.1	2.0
6.9	24.1	12.4			-1.6	4.3	7.6	5.3	3.3
1.0	1.0	1.2	Debt/Worth		1.5	.6	1.2	1.3	1.1
2.0	2.2	3.0			17.6	2.0	2.2	2.4	1.8
10.0	238.7	15.5			-4.0	4.9	13.0	5.1	3.7
40.9	37.7	37.9	% Profit Before Taxes/Tangible Net Worth		39.1	68.0	38.6	55.3	18.2
(121) 19.1	(106) 15.4	(105) 15.4		(14) 15.6	(16) 15.4	(24) 18.0	(24) 26.3	(25) 9.2	
6.4	2.9	5.0			5.0	2.9	-.5	13.1	6.0
16.5	11.2	13.9	% Profit Before Taxes/Total Assets		18.3	21.4	9.2	15.9	7.0
5.3	5.6	5.2			9.9	6.8	5.2	7.6	3.8
1.1	.3	.9			-2.6	1.2	-.9	1.8	1.0
6.0	6.4	4.4	Sales/Net Fixed Assets		6.2	5.7	5.0	4.0	3.0
2.9	2.4	1.9			3.3	1.9	2.7	1.9	1.7
1.5	1.5	1.4			1.5	1.3	1.0	1.3	1.6
2.3	2.2	2.0	Sales/Total Assets		2.7	2.0	2.4	2.1	1.6
1.6	1.3	1.3			1.5	1.1	1.6	1.4	1.1
1.0	1.0	.9			1.1	.9	.8	.9	.9
7.2	6.4	7.5	% Depr., Dep., Amort./Sales		7.1	8.9	8.4	8.1	4.6
(128) 10.0	(104) 11.0	(96) 11.1		(19) 9.8	(13) 10.8	(23) 13.3	(26) 11.4	(12) 7.3	
14.7	14.4	14.8			13.9	17.5	15.8	14.5	12.7
1.4	2.6	1.5	% Officers', Directors', Owners' Comp/Sales		4.8		1.2	.8	
(61) 3.9	(56) 4.5	(59) 4.0		(16) 6.1		(18) 2.8	(13) 1.8		
6.4	9.3	8.0			10.9		8.3	4.1	
3736250M	3495816M	4133290M	Net Sales ($)	2378M	48975M	69164M	216244M	447582M	3348947M
2584196M	2772148M	3364227M	Total Assets ($)	10065M	33304M	59453M	182306M	329245M	2749854M

M = $ thousand   MM = $ million
See Pages viii through xx for Explanation of Ratios and Data

Current Data Sorted by Assets   Comparative Historical Data

	0-500M	500M-2MM	2-10MM	10-50MM	50-100MM	100-250MM	Type of Statement	4/1/14-3/31/15 ALL	4/1/15-3/31/16 ALL
				1	2	2	Unqualified	9	6
		2	10	8	3		Reviewed	26	22
		5	11	8	1		Compiled	30	27
	2	10	15	1	1		Tax Returns	28	38
	3	13	41	35	3	2	Other	88	93
		25 (4/1-9/30/18)		154 (10/1/18-3/31/19)					
	5	30	77	53	10	4	NUMBER OF STATEMENTS	181	186
	%	%	%	%	%	%	**ASSETS**	%	%
		18.9	11.8	6.2	9.5		Cash & Equivalents	11.2	12.1
		16.1	7.5	7.3	9.2		Trade Receivables (net)	10.2	9.0
		3.4	2.4	1.0	2.4		Inventory	1.7	2.0
		5.7	2.6	3.3	14.4		All Other Current	3.4	2.8
		44.1	24.2	17.8	35.5		Total Current	26.5	25.9
		37.3	60.9	72.2	58.8		Fixed Assets (net)	61.7	62.5
		14.0	8.0	4.4	1.3		Intangibles (net)	4.3	4.1
		4.7	6.9	5.6	4.4		All Other Non-Current	7.5	7.5
		100.0	100.0	100.0	100.0		Total	100.0	100.0
							LIABILITIES		
		9.9	2.8	2.1	5.5		Notes Payable-Short Term	3.5	3.8
		13.6	15.5	10.9	9.4		Cur. Mat.-L.T.D.	12.1	10.0
		5.6	3.3	3.4	1.9		Trade Payables	4.8	4.5
		.0	.0	.0	.2		Income Taxes Payable	.1	.1
		13.6	6.7	7.1	9.4		All Other Current	6.8	8.4
		42.6	28.3	23.5	26.4		Total Current	27.3	26.9
		63.0	47.2	40.1	35.0		Long-Term Debt	45.6	45.7
		.0	.5	.8	3.2		Deferred Taxes	1.9	1.8
		12.6	1.9	.9	.3		All Other Non-Current	4.7	4.5
		-18.2	22.1	34.7	35.1		Net Worth	20.5	21.2
		100.0	100.0	100.0	100.0		Total Liabilities & Net Worth	100.0	100.0
							INCOME DATA		
		100.0	100.0	100.0	100.0		Net Sales	100.0	100.0
							Gross Profit		
		96.9	91.2	89.8	82.9		Operating Expenses	92.2	90.9
		3.1	8.8	10.2	17.1		Operating Profit	7.8	9.1
		.2	2.2	2.0	4.5		All Other Expenses (net)	1.4	1.5
		2.9	6.6	8.1	12.6		Profit Before Taxes	6.4	7.7
							RATIOS		
		1.9	1.5	1.1	2.3			1.5	1.8
		1.3	.7	.6	1.4		Current	.9	.9
		.8	.4	.4	.9			.4	.5
		1.8	1.2	.9	1.8			1.3	1.6
		1.1	.6	.5	.5		Quick	(180) .7	.7
		.6	.3	.2	.3			.3	.3
		0 UND	0 UND	9 38.8	3 110.4			3 130.1	2 155.5
		4 94.2	13 27.6	23 15.8	26 14.2		Sales/Receivables	16 22.7	13 28.7
		27 13.3	23 16.1	35 10.3	36 10.2			29 12.8	29 12.4
							Cost of Sales/Inventory		
							Cost of Sales/Payables		
		12.2	19.8	44.2	2.8			18.2	14.4
		55.4	-24.5	-11.2	8.4		Sales/Working Capital	-90.0	-116.4
		-26.7	-9.2	-6.9	-65.8			-12.4	-11.2
		12.5	7.0	5.7				8.3	8.7
	(28)	4.1	(71) 2.8	(51) 2.7			EBIT/Interest	(168) 3.9	(177) 4.3
		.8	.3	1.3				1.9	2.0
			2.3	1.4			Net Profit + Depr., Dep.,	1.9	2.2
		(18)	1.3	(17) 1.1			Amort./Cur. Mat. L/T/D	(49) 1.2	(45) 1.4
			.8	1.0				1.0	1.0
		.5	1.5	1.6	1.1			1.6	1.6
		4.1	3.8	2.4	2.0		Fixed/Worth	2.8	3.1
		-1.1	-27.9	4.9	2.8			20.4	21.2
		2.2	1.2	1.3	1.2			1.5	1.4
		-24.1	4.1	2.4	1.9		Debt/Worth	3.4	3.7
		-2.3	-82.8	5.9	3.4			25.7	29.4
		154.6	30.6	37.1	26.3		% Profit Before Taxes/Tangible	53.5	55.9
	(13)	69.6	(57) 14.5	(49) 14.8	19.6		Net Worth	(140) 29.4	(144) 32.3
		3.9	-4.5	6.8	9.1			9.1	12.2
		30.5	15.7	8.5	11.1		% Profit Before Taxes/Total	15.6	18.5
		16.5	5.8	4.7	4.4		Assets	7.2	8.9
		-1.0	-.8	1.0	3.4			2.9	3.6
		93.4	5.0	2.1	2.3			6.3	4.5
		12.2	2.5	1.2	1.4		Sales/Net Fixed Assets	2.3	2.0
		3.6	.9	.7	.6			1.4	1.2
		5.4	2.6	1.4	1.2			2.6	2.3
		3.8	1.5	.8	.8		Sales/Total Assets	1.5	1.4
		2.2	.7	.6	.4			1.1	.9
		2.0	6.2	7.4	6.3			5.0	6.1
	(17)	7.7	(62) 11.4	(51) 12.8	12.0		% Depr., Dep., Amort./Sales	(150) 9.3	(153) 9.8
		17.6	17.1	14.9	14.4			12.4	14.5
		1.1	1.4	1.4			% Officers', Directors'	1.8	1.9
	(14)	3.5	(35) 2.8	(12) 1.6			Owners' Comp/Sales	(67) 3.6	(69) 2.9
		6.1	6.3	3.8				5.6	5.1
	4642M	154098M	650045M	1193094M	593951M	824657M	Net Sales ($)	2787479M	3140803M
	638M	34525M	394039M	1169417M	661829M	816599M	Total Assets ($)	2091683M	2670127M

M = $ thousand   MM = $ million
See Pages viii through xx for Explanation of Ratios and Data

Comparative Historical Data / Current Data Sorted by Sales

6 23 27 26 88 (4/1/16-3/31/17)	9 23 24 33 77 (4/1/17-3/31/18)	5 23 25 29 97 (4/1/18-3/31/19)	Type of Statement	0-1MM	1-3MM	3-5MM	5-10MM	10-25MM	25MM & OVER
6	9	5	Unqualified		1			1	4
23	23	23	Reviewed			5	5	7	5
27	24	25	Compiled	1	3	3	8	7	3
26	33	29	Tax Returns	2	5	4	12	4	2
88	77	97	Other	5	14	7	25	25	21
ALL	ALL	ALL		25 (4/1-9/30/18)	25 (4/1-9/30/18)	154 (10/1/18-3/31/19)	154 (10/1/18-3/31/19)	154 (10/1/18-3/31/19)	154 (10/1/18-3/31/19)
170	166	179	NUMBER OF STATEMENTS	8	23	19	50	44	35
%	%	%	**ASSETS**	%	%	%	%	%	%
11.2	11.1	10.8	Cash & Equivalents		8.5	14.0	13.5	11.1	7.8
8.1	8.7	9.4	Trade Receivables (net)		5.2	5.9	10.8	9.1	11.8
1.3	1.6	2.1	Inventory		4.1	1.5	1.0	2.1	2.9
2.6	3.7	4.0	All Other Current		2.9	6.7	2.5	3.3	5.6
23.2	25.1	26.4	Total Current		20.7	28.0	27.8	25.6	28.0
64.2	63.5	59.8	Fixed Assets (net)		63.7	55.9	58.1	62.7	57.3
4.6	5.3	8.1	Intangibles (net)		10.8	3.6	8.8	6.9	8.8
8.0	6.1	5.8	All Other Non-Current		4.8	12.5	5.3	4.8	6.0
100.0	100.0	100.0	Total		100.0	100.0	100.0	100.0	100.0
			LIABILITIES						
3.0	3.2	4.3	Notes Payable-Short Term		8.0	3.7	4.9	1.8	3.7
12.9	11.4	13.0	Cur. Mat.-L.T.D.		9.7	14.8	15.2	14.4	10.4
4.4	3.6	3.6	Trade Payables		1.7	1.8	3.4	4.3	5.7
.2	.1	.0	Income Taxes Payable		.0	.0	.0	.0	.1
8.0	7.8	8.8	All Other Current		11.7	2.1	9.1	8.9	9.5
28.6	26.1	29.7	Total Current		31.2	22.4	32.5	29.5	29.3
53.2	45.5	46.2	Long-Term Debt		61.2	45.9	48.9	45.8	33.2
1.6	1.5	.7	Deferred Taxes		.1	.0	.7	.7	1.8
3.5	2.8	3.6	All Other Non-Current		8.6	2.1	4.6	.8	2.5
13.2	24.2	19.7	Net Worth		-1.0	29.6	13.3	23.2	33.3
100.0	100.0	100.0	Total Liabilities & Net Worth		100.0	100.0	100.0	100.0	100.0
			INCOME DATA						
100.0	100.0	100.0	Net Sales		100.0	100.0	100.0	100.0	100.0
			Gross Profit						
91.7	92.5	91.7	Operating Expenses		90.8	89.1	92.3	92.8	93.2
8.3	7.5	8.3	Operating Profit		9.2	10.9	7.7	7.2	6.8
2.0	1.5	1.9	All Other Expenses (net)		3.2	2.0	1.5	1.2	1.6
6.3	6.0	6.4	Profit Before Taxes		6.0	8.9	6.1	6.0	5.2
			RATIOS						
1.6	1.8	1.4	Current		1.6	1.8	1.4	1.2	1.8
.9	.9	.8			.6	1.2	.7	.9	.9
.4	.5	.4			.2	.6	.5	.4	.5
1.4	1.4	1.2	Quick		1.6	1.5	1.2	1.1	1.4
.7	.7	(178) .6			.4	.8	.6	.5	.6
.3	.3	.3			.1	.4	.3	.3	.3
3 123.0	3 137.3	4 102.6	Sales/Receivables	0 UND	0 UND	4 91.5	8 48.1	13 28.9	
15 24.7	15 24.4	16 22.9		0 UND	9 42.0	17 21.8	21 17.6	26 14.3	
29 12.7	29 12.8	31 11.9		13 28.4	20 18.3	28 12.9	30 12.3	36 10.1	
			Cost of Sales/Inventory						
			Cost of Sales/Payables						
15.7	12.0	18.4	Sales/Working Capital		13.9	11.1	37.5	23.3	15.3
-73.5	-60.8	-31.3			-17.1	67.0	-22.9	-34.7	-67.4
-9.7	-10.3	-9.1			-4.6	-11.7	-10.0	-8.2	-8.8
7.1	7.1	7.0	EBIT/Interest		9.4	9.0	8.9	4.8	7.2
(163) 3.6	(149) 3.3	(165) 2.8			(20) 4.5	(17) 2.3	2.8	(40) 2.6	(34) 3.1
1.2	1.2	1.1			.5	-.4	1.1	.5	1.4
2.1	2.0	1.7	Net Profit + Depr., Dep., Amort./Cur. Mat. L/T/D				1.8	1.4	1.5
(48) 1.6	(39) 1.5	(42) 1.1					(14) 1.1	(11) 1.0	(13) 1.1
1.0	1.1	1.0					.8	1.0	1.0
1.6	1.3	1.5	Fixed/Worth		1.8	1.0	1.3	1.6	1.9
3.5	2.7	2.7			7.4	1.9	2.5	2.7	2.2
-11.3	44.3	75.4			-4.1	21.7	-6.2	7.4	9.3
1.3	1.4	1.4	Debt/Worth		2.3	.9	1.4	1.3	1.5
4.0	2.7	3.5			6.4	2.2	5.3	2.7	2.1
-33.6	64.1	-86.5			-6.4	21.3	-7.3	14.3	11.1
48.3	37.0	42.3	% Profit Before Taxes/Tangible Net Worth		114.9	42.7	37.0	43.6	37.1
(125) 24.1	(130) 16.3	(134) 16.2			(15) 18.0	(16) 10.8	(33) 16.8	(35) 14.4	(29) 20.5
8.1	6.8	3.5			4.3	-16.9	6.9	-2.7	10.3
14.3	13.0	15.4	% Profit Before Taxes/Total Assets		26.6	13.5	17.4	15.4	11.0
6.2	5.5	4.7			7.5	6.3	5.7	5.3	4.4
.5	.7	.2			-.9	-.9	.7	-1.0	1.3
3.7	4.6	5.5	Sales/Net Fixed Assets		7.4	6.5	6.4	5.1	3.9
1.7	1.7	2.0			1.3	2.6	2.2	2.0	2.0
1.1	1.1	.9			.7	.9	1.0	1.0	1.5
2.0	2.0	2.6	Sales/Total Assets		3.7	2.3	2.8	2.8	2.0
1.2	1.2	1.4			1.1	1.5	1.5	1.3	1.4
.8	.8	.7			.4	.7	.7	.8	.9
7.6	7.0	6.6	% Depr., Dep., Amort./Sales		7.8	6.8	5.9	5.9	5.1
(141) 11.4	(132) 11.8	(144) 11.1			(18) 18.6	(14) 10.1	(39) 11.9	(38) 10.7	(28) 8.4
16.7	16.1	15.0			50.9	19.0	16.8	14.2	13.6
2.0	1.6	1.2	% Officers', Directors', Owners' Comp/Sales					1.4	1.0
(66) 3.0	(67) 3.0	(64) 2.5						(26) 2.2	(20) 1.4
4.6	5.2	5.0						5.9	3.4
2724117M	3456862M	3420487M	Net Sales ($)	3856M	43971M	79257M	359770M	673359M	2260274M
2597373M	3050151M	3077047M	Total Assets ($)	18524M	52026M	142396M	286977M	596410M	1980714M

M = $ thousand   MM = $ million
See Pages viii through xx for Explanation of Ratios and Data

Current Data Sorted by Assets   Comparative Historical Data

0-500M	500M-2MM	2-10MM	10-50MM	50-100MM	100-250MM	Type of Statement	4/1/14-3/31/15 ALL	4/1/15-3/31/16 ALL
		1	2	1	1	Unqualified	8	16
		2	5			Reviewed	8	8
		2		1		Compiled	11	6
3	8	4			1	Tax Returns	18	17
6	6	6	7		1	Other	51	58
	15 (4/1-9/30/18)		42 (10/1/18-3/31/19)					
9	14	15	14	2	3	**NUMBER OF STATEMENTS**	96	105
%	%	%	%	%	%	**ASSETS**	%	%
	27.3	13.2	9.5			Cash & Equivalents	12.3	17.7
	13.3	21.0	25.3			Trade Receivables (net)	19.9	20.6
	.7	1.5	.8			Inventory	.9	.6
	2.2	5.3	6.6			All Other Current	4.7	2.7
	43.4	41.0	42.2			Total Current	37.8	41.5
	31.4	48.1	42.7			Fixed Assets (net)	46.2	46.5
	8.8	4.2	5.6			Intangibles (net)	7.1	4.8
	16.3	6.8	9.6			All Other Non-Current	8.9	7.1
	100.0	100.0	100.0			Total	100.0	100.0
						LIABILITIES		
	8.6	4.6	5.3			Notes Payable-Short Term	8.2	8.9
	4.2	6.5	8.9			Cur. Mat.-L.T.D.	8.3	6.3
	9.6	4.9	11.9			Trade Payables	8.9	7.0
	.0	.0	.6			Income Taxes Payable	.2	.2
	8.8	23.3	12.6			All Other Current	10.6	13.2
	31.3	39.4	39.3			Total Current	36.3	35.6
	29.3	29.3	22.5			Long-Term Debt	36.5	29.1
	.0	1.0	.0			Deferred Taxes	.3	.6
	2.4	8.8	4.2			All Other Non-Current	3.6	6.0
	37.0	21.5	33.9			Net Worth	23.3	28.7
	100.0	100.0	100.0			Total Liabilities & Net Worth	100.0	100.0
						INCOME DATA		
	100.0	100.0	100.0			Net Sales	100.0	100.0
						Gross Profit		
	95.4	91.2	93.7			Operating Expenses	92.4	90.6
	4.6	8.8	6.3			Operating Profit	7.6	9.4
	.0	3.3	.0			All Other Expenses (net)	1.6	1.1
	4.6	5.5	6.2			Profit Before Taxes	6.0	8.3
						RATIOS		
	4.0	1.9	1.7				2.2	2.7
	1.2	1.1	1.0			Current	1.1	1.2
	.5	.6	.4				.5	.5
	3.7	1.5	1.4				1.7	2.5
	1.1	.8	.8			Quick	.9	1.0
	.5	.5	.4				.4	.4
	0 UND	4 89.9	24 14.9				4 93.1	2 161.4
	24 15.4	24 15.3	32 11.3			Sales/Receivables	22 16.6	22 16.6
	36 10.0	49 7.5	45 8.2				41 8.9	44 8.3
						Cost of Sales/Inventory		
						Cost of Sales/Payables		
	10.1	13.4	12.9				12.2	8.2
	46.6	88.3	NM			Sales/Working Capital	290.4	37.0
	-21.6	-10.5	-5.3				-16.8	-13.8
		53.0	23.1				13.4	20.0
		7.2	5.3			EBIT/Interest	(87) 4.4	(87) 6.2
		.5	3.5				1.6	2.5
							4.7	11.2
						Net Profit + Depr., Dep., Amort./Cur. Mat. L/T/D	(14) 1.7	(11) 2.8
							1.1	1.2
	.1	1.2	.5				.7	.6
	.7	1.5	1.4			Fixed/Worth	2.6	1.8
	35.9	-64.6	5.2				20.5	13.6
	.3	1.5	1.3				1.0	.8
	5.0	2.2	3.0			Debt/Worth	4.1	3.1
	47.1	-143.0	6.1				22.5	60.8
	145.6	267.7	60.8				82.4	76.0
	(12) -2.8	(11) 39.0	(13) 42.3			% Profit Before Taxes/Tangible Net Worth	(73) 34.1	(81) 48.2
	-41.0	6.8	21.4				9.7	16.3
	22.6	51.9	15.6				22.2	31.9
	-.2	13.5	8.9			% Profit Before Taxes/Total Assets	9.1	10.7
	-5.3	-.4	6.1				2.6	2.8
	191.1	6.8	26.9				16.4	20.4
	9.5	4.9	4.5			Sales/Net Fixed Assets	6.2	5.3
	3.5	2.0	1.6				2.4	2.1
	4.8	3.8	3.7				4.2	4.1
	2.7	2.6	1.6			Sales/Total Assets	2.4	2.1
	1.3	1.3	1.1				1.4	1.1
		.5	1.7				2.0	2.9
		(13) 4.1	(13) 4.6			% Depr., Dep., Amort./Sales	(79) 6.2	(81) 6.4
		7.5	9.6				9.1	12.3
							1.1	2.1
						% Officers', Directors' Owners' Comp/Sales	(20) 1.9	(21) 5.0
							4.3	6.7
9657M	49650M	272538M	862963M	100474M	585461M	Net Sales ($)	2892563M	3599246M
2499M	18115M	69972M	368720M	145961M	571350M	Total Assets ($)	1297471M	1525206M

© RMA 2019   M = $ thousand   MM = $ million

See Pages viii through xx for Explanation of Ratios and Data

Comparative Historical Data			Type of Statement	Current Data Sorted by Sales					
8	8	5	Unqualified					4	5
10	10	7	Reviewed						3
6	3	3	Compiled					2	1
12	16	16	Tax Returns						1
37	36	26	Other	2	6	2	5	2	8
				3	7	1	5		
4/1/16-	4/1/17-	4/1/18-			15 (4/1-9/30/18)			42 (10/1/18-3/31/19)	
3/31/17	3/31/18	3/31/19							
ALL	ALL	ALL		0-1MM	1-3MM	3-5MM	5-10MM	10-25MM	25MM & OVER
73	73	57	NUMBER OF STATEMENTS	5	13	3	10	8	18
%	%	%	ASSETS	%	%	%	%	%	%
15.3	15.1	20.1	Cash & Equivalents		30.2		23.8		10.1
17.2	22.3	17.2	Trade Receivables (net)		18.0		8.5		23.4
1.0	2.3	1.1	Inventory		.6		2.2		.2
3.8	2.7	3.8	All Other Current		2.7		.8		8.1
37.3	42.4	42.2	Total Current		51.4		35.2		41.8
45.4	40.7	41.3	Fixed Assets (net)		30.6		47.9		39.1
7.2	9.7	7.2	Intangibles (net)		8.9		.4		12.3
10.1	7.2	9.3	All Other Non-Current		9.2		16.5		6.8
100.0	100.0	100.0	Total		100.0		100.0		100.0
			LIABILITIES						
8.0	5.9	5.3	Notes Payable-Short Term		8.6		9.8		3.0
7.9	4.9	8.0	Cur. Mat.-L.T.D.		5.9		6.2		7.6
5.3	6.7	7.9	Trade Payables		2.9		2.2		11.0
.2	.0	.2	Income Taxes Payable		.0		.1		.5
12.9	23.6	15.3	All Other Current		19.9		12.9		18.9
34.2	41.2	36.7	Total Current		37.3		30.2		41.0
33.1	34.1	29.2	Long-Term Debt		36.5		31.4		25.6
.4	1.1	.7	Deferred Taxes		.0		1.5		1.5
6.2	5.0	6.4	All Other Non-Current		7.6		.9		11.0
26.1	18.6	26.9	Net Worth		18.6		36.0		20.9
100.0	100.0	100.0	Total Liabilities & Net Worth		100.0		100.0		100.0
			INCOME DATA						
100.0	100.0	100.0	Net Sales		100.0		100.0		100.0
			Gross Profit						
92.2	94.4	92.8	Operating Expenses		92.5		90.4		94.3
7.8	5.6	7.2	Operating Profit		7.5		9.6		5.7
.6	1.7	1.2	All Other Expenses (net)		.9		1.7		.6
7.2	3.9	6.0	Profit Before Taxes		6.6		7.9		5.1
			RATIOS						
2.4	2.9	1.9			6.7		3.1		1.5
1.2	1.1	1.1	Current		1.7		1.3		1.1
.4	.5	.6			.6		.5		.7
2.1	2.5	1.9			6.6		2.8		1.2
.9	1.0	.8	Quick		1.1		1.0		.8
.3	.5	.5			.4		.4		.5
2 147.6	11 33.8	2 152.3		0 UND		0 UND		14 25.3	
20 18.2	31 11.6	26 14.3	Sales/Receivables	20 18.7		2 154.3		31 11.7	
41 8.8	46 7.9	42 8.7		46 7.9		39 9.3		42 8.7	
			Cost of Sales/Inventory						
			Cost of Sales/Payables						
9.7	7.9	12.7			4.4		9.0		41.4
852.0	99.3	88.3	Sales/Working Capital		186.1		NM		81.3
-16.0	-12.7	-14.4			-10.0		-17.5		-16.2
13.6	7.0	24.9							28.7
(58) 4.0	(59) 2.9	(48) 5.0	EBIT/Interest						4.7
1.3	.3	.8							2.8
9.6	2.1								
(12) 1.8	(12) 1.5		Net Profit + Depr., Dep., Amort./Cur. Mat. L/T/D						
1.3	1.0								
.8	.6	.4			.2		.5		.7
2.8	3.2	1.5	Fixed/Worth		.7		1.5		3.6
-17.4	-2.7	18.4			-2.3		NM		NM
.7	1.6	1.4			.7		.5		2.7
3.7	6.2	2.7	Debt/Worth		2.6		1.7		4.5
-25.5	-5.6	27.2			-5.1		NM		NM
55.6	73.2	138.0							229.5
(53) 30.0	(44) 20.8	(45) 37.2	% Profit Before Taxes/Tangible Net Worth					(14)	53.4
6.8	2.4	6.7							23.4
22.8	15.4	26.3			61.7		28.6		17.2
8.8	5.8	8.5	% Profit Before Taxes/Total Assets		4.1		14.3		8.9
2.2	-1.8	-.9			-3.9		-3.2		4.4
16.3	18.3	20.6			42.8		32.6		40.6
6.0	6.3	6.0	Sales/Net Fixed Assets		8.3		5.8		5.5
2.3	2.5	2.1			2.7		2.2		1.5
3.8	3.7	3.9			4.0		5.4		5.1
2.2	2.3	2.6	Sales/Total Assets		2.6		2.7		1.7
1.2	1.2	1.2			1.2		1.4		.9
3.5	3.5	1.7							.4
(51) 7.0	(51) 5.8	(36) 6.5	% Depr., Dep., Amort./Sales					(14)	2.8
10.7	12.7	10.6							8.2
1.6	1.9	3.9							
(16) 4.2	(27) 6.9	(17) 6.1	% Officers', Directors' Owners' Comp/Sales						
10.3	9.8	10.1							
1788940M	1958412M	1880743M	Net Sales ($)	2665M	24006M	12122M	62844M	144357M	1634749M
972269M	1055925M	1176617M	Total Assets ($)	2545M	15939M	3882M	26044M	88364M	1039843M

M = $ thousand   MM = $ million
See Pages viii through xx for Explanation of Ratios and Data

Current Data Sorted by Assets   Comparative Historical Data

0-500M	500M-2MM	2-10MM	10-50MM	50-100MM	100-250MM	Type of Statement	4/1/14-3/31/15 ALL	4/1/15-3/31/16 ALL
			1		1	Unqualified	4	4
		1				Reviewed	3	3
	3	1	1			Compiled	4	5
4	3	1				Tax Returns		3
3	4	4	2	1	1	Other	6	15
	4 (4/1-9/30/18)		27 (10/1/18-3/31/19)					
7	10	7	4	1	2	NUMBER OF STATEMENTS	17	30
%	%	%	%	%	%	ASSETS	%	%
	28.9					Cash & Equivalents	10.1	18.1
	9.8					Trade Receivables (net)	.6	2.2
	.6					Inventory	2.2	1.8
	.3					All Other Current	1.0	7.1
	39.5					Total Current	13.8	29.3
	40.4					Fixed Assets (net)	61.9	50.4
	3.1					Intangibles (net)	13.3	8.2
	17.0					All Other Non-Current	11.0	12.1
	100.0					Total	100.0	100.0
						LIABILITIES		
	2.7					Notes Payable-Short Term	5.6	5.0
	2.7					Cur. Mat.-L.T.D.	7.4	6.5
	.4					Trade Payables	1.9	5.7
	.0					Income Taxes Payable	.2	.1
	12.0					All Other Current	16.3	20.7
	17.9					Total Current	31.4	38.0
	35.4					Long-Term Debt	50.0	41.0
	.0					Deferred Taxes	1.7	.6
	13.1					All Other Non-Current	15.0	39.7
	33.7					Net Worth	1.9	-19.3
	100.0					Total Liabilities & Net Worth	100.0	100.0
						INCOME DATA		
	100.0					Net Sales	100.0	100.0
						Gross Profit		
	82.6					Operating Expenses	95.6	88.5
	17.4					Operating Profit	4.4	11.5
	3.3					All Other Expenses (net)	1.1	3.8
	14.1					Profit Before Taxes	3.3	7.7
						RATIOS		
	13.9						2.3	2.0
	2.6					Current	.5	1.0
	1.3						.2	.5
	13.8						2.2	1.9
	2.5					Quick	.3	.7
	1.3						.1	.1
	0 UND						0 UND	0 UND
	0 UND					Sales/Receivables	1 428.0	1 429.2
	7 55.6						3 108.4	6 61.5
						Cost of Sales/Inventory		
						Cost of Sales/Payables		
	4.1						15.5	16.2
	5.9					Sales/Working Capital	-16.6	NM
	NM						-5.9	-8.3
							5.7	10.2
						EBIT/Interest	(16) 4.1	(25) 4.8
							.8	1.8
						Net Profit + Depr., Dep., Amort./Cur. Mat. L/T/D		
	.3						3.0	.9
	.8					Fixed/Worth	7.8	5.4
	4.8						-1.2	-1.2
	.3						3.0	1.2
	1.5					Debt/Worth	7.8	NM
	5.3						-2.9	-2.8
						% Profit Before Taxes/Tangible Net Worth		64.1
							(15)	26.4
								10.3
	47.6						11.6	24.8
	17.8					% Profit Before Taxes/Total Assets	8.1	8.7
	1.0						-3.2	1.8
	17.6						4.2	23.3
	3.9					Sales/Net Fixed Assets	1.8	2.9
	2.4						1.3	1.5
	2.7						2.0	4.1
	1.8					Sales/Total Assets	1.2	1.3
	.9						.8	.8
							4.7	3.1
						% Depr., Dep., Amort./Sales	(11) 5.0	(16) 4.9
							6.0	7.7
						% Officers', Directors' Owners' Comp/Sales		
3260M	18868M	49401M	86807M	30442M	264531M	Net Sales ($)	744894M	696247M
1880M	10590M	38330M	75650M	87753M	404130M	Total Assets ($)	792742M	705897M

Comparative Historical Data | | | | ## Current Data Sorted by Sales

			Type of Statement						
4	5	2	Unqualified				1		1
2	2	1	Reviewed			1			
3	2	5	Compiled		2	1	1	1	
4	7	8	Tax Returns	6	1			1	
14	5	15	Other	5	2	1	3	1	3
4/1/16-3/31/17 ALL	4/1/17-3/31/18 ALL	4/1/18-3/31/19 ALL		0-1MM	1-3MM	3-5MM	5-10MM	10-25MM	25MM & OVER
					4 (4/1-9/30/18)		27 (10/1/18-3/31/19)		
27	21	31	**NUMBER OF STATEMENTS**	11	5	3	5	3	4
%	%	%	**ASSETS**	%	%	%	%	%	%
22.4	11.4	21.2	Cash & Equivalents	26.2					
6.8	4.9	5.0	Trade Receivables (net)	.4					
1.4	5.1	1.7	Inventory	1.9					
3.0	3.2	1.5	All Other Current	2.3					
33.5	24.6	29.4	Total Current	30.8					
49.9	50.7	52.7	Fixed Assets (net)	58.5					
7.9	9.5	8.7	Intangibles (net)	3.5					
8.7	15.1	9.2	All Other Non-Current	7.1					
100.0	100.0	100.0	Total	100.0					
			LIABILITIES						
5.1	3.0	2.6	Notes Payable-Short Term	4.4					
4.4	2.0	3.4	Cur. Mat.-L.T.D.	5.7					
3.0	5.3	1.9	Trade Payables	.5					
.0	.0	.0	Income Taxes Payable	.0					
16.1	12.3	10.9	All Other Current	12.0					
28.7	22.7	18.8	Total Current	22.6					
43.4	37.7	39.7	Long-Term Debt	66.7					
1.5	1.7	.7	Deferred Taxes	.0					
9.6	11.3	11.8	All Other Non-Current	24.3					
16.8	26.5	28.9	Net Worth	-13.6					
100.0	100.0	100.0	Total Liabilities & Net Worth	100.0					
			INCOME DATA						
100.0	100.0	100.0	Net Sales	100.0					
			Gross Profit						
88.6	89.9	86.6	Operating Expenses	88.4					
11.4	10.1	13.4	Operating Profit	11.6					
1.1	4.8	2.7	All Other Expenses (net)	5.8					
10.3	5.2	10.7	Profit Before Taxes	5.8					
			RATIOS						
3.4	3.7	4.1	Current	3.0					
.8	1.2	1.7		.7					
.6	.5	.3		.3					
2.6	1.7	3.5	Quick	2.9					
.7	.8	1.5		.7					
.4	.1	.3		.3					
0 735.3	0 UND	0 UND	Sales/Receivables	0 UND					
4 96.5	4 95.8	1 460.2		0 UND					
20 18.2	17 21.4	8 45.9		0 UND					
			Cost of Sales/Inventory						
			Cost of Sales/Payables						
9.7	3.7	5.4	Sales/Working Capital	4.3					
-40.1	36.5	13.8		-37.6					
-9.2	-27.4	-9.9		-2.8					
9.6	9.9	23.1	EBIT/Interest						
(25) 4.1	(18) 3.8	(29) 5.1							
2.0	.9	2.4							
			Net Profit + Depr., Dep., Amort./Cur. Mat. L/T/D						
1.3	.7	.6	Fixed/Worth	1.0					
4.0	2.8	2.0		-6.8					
-9.9	-2.8	-4.3		-1.3					
1.7	1.2	.4	Debt/Worth	3.6					
4.0	3.2	2.3		-8.3					
-25.0	-8.2	-6.0		-2.5					
75.2	43.7	76.7	% Profit Before Taxes/Tangible Net Worth						
(20) 31.8	(14) 16.6	(21) 27.7							
9.8	2.3	12.9							
15.9	12.5	31.2	% Profit Before Taxes/Total Assets	27.0					
8.1	5.1	9.3		3.7					
3.4	.0	3.7		-.6					
15.0	7.4	4.1	Sales/Net Fixed Assets	3.9					
1.7	2.3	2.1		2.1					
1.4	1.2	1.5		1.1					
2.0	2.7	1.9	Sales/Total Assets	1.9					
1.2	1.3	1.3		1.2					
.9	.7	.8		.7					
2.5	2.9	4.0	% Depr., Dep., Amort./Sales						
(18) 4.8	(16) 4.8	(21) 6.4							
7.2	9.4	12.8							
			% Officers', Directors' Owners' Comp/Sales						
947407M	572495M	453309M	Net Sales ($)	5814M	12602M	11889M	38892M	41837M	342275M
1050542M	686998M	618333M	Total Assets ($)	5388M	5889M	7867M	33070M	36128M	529991M

M = $ thousand   MM = $ million
See Pages viii through xx for Explanation of Ratios and Data

Current Data Sorted by Assets							Comparative Historical Data	

Type of Statement

0-500M	500M-2MM	2-10MM	10-50MM	50-100MM	100-250MM		ALL	ALL
			1	6	1	Unqualified	15	10
		2	2			Reviewed	7	7
		1	1			Compiled	8	4
		3	1			Tax Returns	8	9
1 3	7	9	9	3	3	Other	36	41
	5 (4/1-9/30/18)		48 (10/1/18-3/31/19)				4/1/14-3/31/15	4/1/15-3/31/16
0-500M	500M-2MM	2-10MM	10-50MM	50-100MM	100-250MM	NUMBER OF STATEMENTS	74	71
4	7	15	14	9	4			
%	%	%	%	%	%		%	%

ASSETS

0-500M	500M-2MM	2-10MM	10-50MM	50-100MM	100-250MM		ALL	ALL
		11.3	14.6			Cash & Equivalents	11.7	10.9
		7.1	10.6			Trade Receivables (net)	16.0	15.8
		9.3	7.2			Inventory	5.2	5.9
		1.0	.9			All Other Current	2.1	2.1
		28.7	33.3			Total Current	35.1	34.6
		52.7	48.3			Fixed Assets (net)	52.3	46.4
		5.7	13.3			Intangibles (net)	4.6	8.5
		12.9	5.2			All Other Non-Current	8.0	10.5
		100.0	100.0			Total	100.0	100.0

LIABILITIES

0-500M	500M-2MM	2-10MM	10-50MM	50-100MM	100-250MM		ALL	ALL
		4.1	6.1			Notes Payable-Short Term	6.2	4.7
		2.2	3.2			Cur. Mat.-L.T.D.	2.5	4.0
		8.0	4.4			Trade Payables	8.7	12.2
		.3	.2			Income Taxes Payable	.0	.2
		8.5	8.7			All Other Current	9.0	10.2
		23.1	22.5			Total Current	26.4	31.3
		23.1	35.3			Long-Term Debt	30.3	29.2
		.5	.4			Deferred Taxes	.3	.2
		20.1	3.5			All Other Non-Current	7.6	4.9
		33.2	38.3			Net Worth	35.4	34.4
		100.0	100.0			Total Liabilties & Net Worth	100.0	100.0

INCOME DATA

0-500M	500M-2MM	2-10MM	10-50MM	50-100MM	100-250MM		ALL	ALL
		100.0	100.0			Net Sales	100.0	100.0
						Gross Profit		
		89.3	84.7			Operating Expenses	95.7	91.5
		10.7	15.3			Operating Profit	4.3	8.5
		1.6	3.5			All Other Expenses (net)	1.1	2.1
		9.0	11.8			Profit Before Taxes	3.2	6.4

RATIOS

0-500M	500M-2MM	2-10MM	10-50MM	50-100MM	100-250MM		ALL	ALL
		1.8	2.8			Current	3.1	2.2
		1.2	1.7				1.5	1.4
		.7	.8				.8	.7
		1.4	2.7			Quick	2.1	1.7
		.8	1.3				1.1	1.1
		.4	.4				.5	.4
		4 96.6	10 34.8			Sales/Receivables	8 47.7	6 62.2
		8 45.2	29 12.8				21 17.2	22 16.5
		28 13.2	41 8.9				41 8.9	46 8.0
						Cost of Sales/Inventory		
						Cost of Sales/Payables		
		7.7	4.9			Sales/Working Capital	7.3	7.6
		40.4	16.8				19.9	24.9
		-17.4	-22.2				-32.8	-53.0
		30.2	10.5			EBIT/Interest	7.9	8.6
		(14) 2.9	4.9				(64) 2.9	(56) 4.1
		2.2	3.5				-.7	1.8
						Net Profit + Depr., Dep., Amort./Cur. Mat. L/T/D	4.7	4.0
							(13) 2.6	(11) 2.1
							1.8	1.2
		1.0	1.0			Fixed/Worth	.8	.5
		1.6	1.7				1.3	1.3
		-10.6	NM				6.0	6.3
		.8	.6			Debt/Worth	.6	.5
		1.6	1.7				1.4	1.7
		-17.8	NM				13.0	7.5
		117.2	38.8			% Profit Before Taxes/Tangible Net Worth	41.6	51.7
		(11) 51.1	(11) 28.7				(61) 13.9	(61) 22.0
		5.1	7.8				-2.0	2.8
		37.6	22.2			% Profit Before Taxes/Total Assets	14.8	16.0
		9.2	10.8				5.3	7.5
		3.0	3.6				-.9	1.2
		21.7	12.8			Sales/Net Fixed Assets	9.9	18.3
		3.0	1.7				3.3	5.0
		1.7	1.2				1.0	1.4
		2.7	1.5			Sales/Total Assets	3.2	3.4
		1.5	1.0				1.5	1.6
		1.2	.9				.7	.8
		2.7	1.8			% Depr., Dep., Amort./Sales	2.2	1.6
		(11) 3.8	(13) 4.2				(61) 3.7	(51) 3.2
		5.9	6.0				5.9	10.4
						% Officers', Directors' Owners' Comp/Sales	1.0	
							(14) 2.6	
							6.6	
9436M	17678M	132406M	368337M	979943M	814850M	Net Sales ($)	2562829M	2239421M
1091M	7920M	60401M	239270M	653895M	715500M	Total Assets ($)	2344801M	1843939M

© RMA 2019

M = $ thousand   MM = $ million
See Pages viii through xx for Explanation of Ratios and Data

Comparative Historical Data / Current Data Sorted by Sales

4/1/16-3/31/17 ALL	4/1/17-3/31/18 ALL	4/1/18-3/31/19 ALL	Type of Statement	0-1MM	1-3MM	3-5MM	5-10MM	10-25MM	25MM & OVER
11	9	8	Unqualified		1		1	1	5
8	6	4	Reviewed			1		3	
3	2	2	Compiled		1			1	
6	5	5	Tax Returns	1	1	1	1		1
36	42	34	Other	1	6	5	7	6	9
					5 (4/1-9/30/18)			48 (10/1/18-3/31/19)	
64	64	53	NUMBER OF STATEMENTS	2	9	7	9	11	15
%	%	%	ASSETS	%	%	%	%	%	%
12.2	10.6	13.5	Cash & Equivalents					13.1	8.4
17.6	19.0	11.5	Trade Receivables (net)					9.8	17.5
7.7	7.9	7.7	Inventory					7.0	4.7
4.6	4.2	3.1	All Other Current					1.0	1.2
42.0	41.8	35.9	Total Current					31.0	31.9
44.4	42.3	44.9	Fixed Assets (net)					55.0	30.4
7.8	9.6	11.7	Intangibles (net)					8.0	29.8
5.8	6.3	7.6	All Other Non-Current					6.0	7.8
100.0	100.0	100.0	Total					100.0	100.0
			LIABILITIES						
7.4	5.2	8.6	Notes Payable-Short Term					5.6	4.7
3.2	3.4	2.9	Cur. Mat.-L.T.D.					3.2	2.6
18.3	9.8	7.9	Trade Payables					5.1	8.2
.1	.1	.3	Income Taxes Payable					.3	.1
11.5	12.4	10.7	All Other Current					12.3	6.3
40.6	30.9	30.4	Total Current					26.6	22.0
27.6	26.6	27.3	Long-Term Debt					29.9	17.9
.2	.4	.5	Deferred Taxes					.7	1.1
4.3	5.9	12.4	All Other Non-Current					4.8	2.6
27.4	36.1	29.4	Net Worth					37.9	56.4
100.0	100.0	100.0	Total Liabilties & Net Worth					100.0	100.0
			INCOME DATA						
100.0	100.0	100.0	Net Sales					100.0	100.0
			Gross Profit						
90.8	92.9	90.9	Operating Expenses					90.4	94.4
9.2	7.1	9.1	Operating Profit					9.6	5.6
3.3	1.7	2.2	All Other Expenses (net)					1.8	1.7
6.0	5.4	6.9	Profit Before Taxes					7.8	3.9
			RATIOS						
2.1	2.4	2.4	Current					2.1	2.6
1.4	1.4	1.3						1.0	1.3
.9	.9	.8						.7	1.0
1.6	1.6	1.7	Quick					1.3	2.6
1.1 (63)	1.1	.9						.7	1.2
.4	.4	.5						.4	.7
9 40.5	13 27.2	8 48.6	Sales/Receivables					7 52.5	12 29.2
27 13.6	24 15.0	14 25.6						21 17.3	16 22.3
46 7.9	51 7.1	31 11.9						32 11.5	52 7.0
			Cost of Sales/Inventory						
			Cost of Sales/Payables						
9.0	6.7	6.6	Sales/Working Capital					7.0	14.9
20.0	21.7	18.7						-304.3	31.6
-125.7	-66.5	-39.2						-17.4	999.8
14.1	11.4	9.6	EBIT/Interest					7.3	12.9
(56) 3.8	(54) 3.5	(47) 4.0						5.6	(12) 7.2
1.5	.8	1.7						2.6	1.6
5.9	3.0	3.6	Net Profit + Depr., Dep., Amort./Cur. Mat. L/T/D						
(12) 3.0	(13) 2.4	(15) 2.6							
1.7	.9	2.1							
.7	.6	.9	Fixed/Worth					1.1	.6
1.3	1.4	1.5						1.6	1.2
3.4	7.1	-4.9						2.7	-2.1
.7	.8	.7	Debt/Worth					.9	.7
2.2	2.4	1.8						1.3	1.6
11.2	12.0	-12.3						3.0	-4.8
58.2	46.0	72.7	% Profit Before Taxes/Tangible Net Worth						66.7
(52) 20.4	(53) 21.1	(38) 31.0						(11)	40.7
5.8	3.9	7.7							7.6
18.2	18.3	18.0	% Profit Before Taxes/Total Assets					18.6	14.1
6.6	6.2	10.2						5.6	11.3
1.8	1.0	2.4						3.2	2.1
14.7	18.6	14.9	Sales/Net Fixed Assets					5.4	16.4
4.3	4.3	3.6						1.8	6.0
1.4	1.7	1.5						1.3	1.5
3.3	2.7	2.7	Sales/Total Assets					1.8	2.7
1.7	1.4	1.5						1.2	1.3
.9	.9	.9						.9	.9
1.3	1.3	1.3	% Depr., Dep., Amort./Sales					2.4	.9
(52) 3.5	(53) 3.1	(42) 3.4						4.2	(14) 2.4
7.8	7.1	5.8						5.4	5.0
	.7		% Officers', Directors' Owners' Comp/Sales						
(11) 2.1									
4.0									
2994027M	2649358M	2322650M	Net Sales ($)	1281M	18204M	27195M	61373M	191289M	2023308M
2371967M	1780369M	1678077M	Total Assets ($)	334M	105009M	17687M	119416M	155773M	1279858M

© RMA 2019

M = $ thousand   MM = $ million
See Pages viii through xx for Explanation of Ratios and Data

Current Data Sorted by Assets   Comparative Historical Data

Date spans: **19 (4/1-9/30/18)** applies to the 500M-2MM column; **101 (10/1/18-3/31/19)** applies to the 2-10MM through 100-250MM columns.

	0-500M	500M-2MM	2-10MM	10-50MM	50-100MM	100-250MM		4/1/14-3/31/15 ALL	4/1/15-3/31/16 ALL
							Type of Statement		
Unqualified	1			3	2	4		14	19
Reviewed			4	6	2			13	12
Compiled			3	1				13	11
Tax Returns	3	4	4	3				20	13
Other	5	11	21	25	12	6		56	72
	9	15	32	38	16	10	**NUMBER OF STATEMENTS**	116	127
	%	%	%	%	%	%	**ASSETS**	%	%
		14.3	10.6	8.8	7.1	6.1	Cash & Equivalents	10.1	11.9
		40.0	31.2	19.5	22.8	27.6	Trade Receivables (net)	22.7	21.9
		17.0	20.2	21.6	20.7	6.5	Inventory	20.1	21.4
		3.9	2.4	3.3	2.2	3.5	All Other Current	5.8	4.8
		75.3	64.3	53.2	52.8	43.6	Total Current	58.7	60.0
		11.3	24.3	34.8	25.2	26.8	Fixed Assets (net)	29.0	25.6
		2.4	7.1	5.9	17.5	26.7	Intangibles (net)	5.3	7.6
		11.0	4.2	6.1	4.5	2.9	All Other Non-Current	7.0	6.9
		100.0	100.0	100.0	100.0	100.0	Total	100.0	100.0
							LIABILITIES		
		7.3	12.3	7.7	19.7	3.5	Notes Payable-Short Term	10.2	9.9
		1.3	2.1	6.8	2.8	2.5	Cur. Mat.-L.T.D.	3.4	3.8
		11.3	17.3	10.3	7.3	7.2	Trade Payables	13.3	13.4
		.0	.3	.3	.2	.2	Income Taxes Payable	.2	.2
		21.0	13.3	16.1	14.2	16.2	All Other Current	12.2	15.3
		41.0	45.3	41.2	44.1	29.5	Total Current	39.2	42.5
		14.8	20.6	18.5	16.4	24.0	Long-Term Debt	20.8	19.0
		.0	.2	.5	.8	1.5	Deferred Taxes	.2	.4
		4.3	6.8	6.5	1.2	5.5	All Other Non-Current	6.8	6.1
		40.0	27.1	33.3	37.4	39.5	Net Worth	33.0	32.0
		100.0	100.0	100.0	100.0	100.0	Total Liabilties & Net Worth	100.0	100.0
							INCOME DATA		
		100.0	100.0	100.0	100.0	100.0	Net Sales	100.0	100.0
							Gross Profit		
		90.6	93.7	90.6	85.8	91.2	Operating Expenses	93.0	92.6
		9.4	6.3	9.4	14.2	8.8	Operating Profit	7.0	7.4
		.6	.4	1.7	3.4	2.3	All Other Expenses (net)	1.3	2.3
		8.8	5.9	7.7	10.8	6.5	Profit Before Taxes	5.7	5.1
							RATIOS		
		3.2	2.7	2.8	2.4	2.2		2.5	2.5
		2.2	1.2	1.6	1.2	1.8	Current	1.6	1.5
		1.6	.9	1.2	.9	1.5		1.0	1.0
		2.6	1.9	1.5	1.2	1.7		1.4	1.3
		1.7	1.0	.8	.8	1.1	Quick	.8	.8
		.6	.5	.3	.3	.5		.5	.5
		29 12.4	26 13.8	21 17.1	34 10.6	37 9.8		15 24.9	15 24.2
		35 10.3	44 8.3	38 9.7	54 6.7	48 7.6	Sales/Receivables	33 11.1	33 11.0
		61 6.0	66 5.5	55 6.6	81 4.5	64 5.7		56 6.5	58 6.3
							Cost of Sales/Inventory		
							Cost of Sales/Payables		
		5.9	5.3	3.8	1.8	5.5		5.1	4.7
		10.1	17.1	8.3	22.7	7.9	Sales/Working Capital	13.8	11.8
		14.6	-63.1	29.8	NM	66.9		181.6	-999.8
			14.6	15.8	10.2	13.6		13.6	15.7
			(27) 7.6	(34) 5.1	5.5	6.5	EBIT/Interest	(98) 5.0	(115) 5.4
			2.1	1.3	2.6	1.9		1.6	1.9
							Net Profit + Depr., Dep.,	5.4	5.5
							Amort./Cur. Mat. L/T/D	(24) 2.5	(21) 2.5
								.8	1.6
		.0	.2	.4	.5	.7		.2	.2
		.2	1.1	.8	2.9	NM	Fixed/Worth	.8	.9
		1.1	6.0	2.5	NM	-.6		3.6	4.9
		.4	.8	.7	1.9	1.1		1.0	.8
		1.3	3.5	1.6	4.3	NM	Debt/Worth	2.5	2.5
		9.2	44.7	3.3	NM	-3.2		8.0	15.5
		85.5	86.6	39.7	46.5		% Profit Before Taxes/Tangible	66.7	57.5
		(13) 62.8	(25) 26.4	(32) 19.4	(12) 22.4		Net Worth	(100) 31.4	(100) 25.8
		15.6	.6	9.6	13.9			8.6	9.5
		65.2	24.9	13.0	15.6	17.9	% Profit Before Taxes/Total	19.3	16.9
		9.7	11.4	7.3	6.3	7.0	Assets	8.6	8.6
		4.5	1.1	1.9	2.9	1.5		2.1	1.5
		UND	57.3	14.0	32.2	17.6		52.3	50.1
		86.1	14.7	4.5	9.3	6.9	Sales/Net Fixed Assets	13.3	10.1
		12.1	4.6	2.4	1.7	2.8		3.0	3.6
		4.3	3.4	2.5	3.4	2.3		3.4	2.9
		3.3	2.2	1.5	.5	1.1	Sales/Total Assets	1.9	1.8
		2.7	1.4	.8	.4	.9		1.1	1.1
			.3	1.1	.6			.7	.9
			(23) 1.6	(31) 2.2	(14) 1.2		% Depr., Dep., Amort./Sales	(89) 1.7	(89) 2.0
			5.0	3.6	5.4			3.1	3.4
		1.3					% Officers', Directors'	1.0	1.3
		(10) 2.9					Owners' Comp/Sales	(28) 2.9	(22) 3.2
		4.5						7.9	7.1
7733M	2185M→	68083M	371441M	1250853M	1937365M	3251385M	Net Sales ($)	3652640M	4733010M
2185M		19104M	177454M	793555M	1105802M	1811496M	Total Assets ($)	2273852M	3209220M

M = $ thousand   MM = $ million
See Pages viii through xx for Explanation of Ratios and Data

Comparative Historical Data | Current Data Sorted by Sales

			Type of Statement						
11	11	10	Unqualified	1				1	8
14	13	12	Reviewed		1	4		1	6
7	9	4	Compiled			1		3	
20	19	14	Tax Returns	3	1	2	3	4	1
64	78	80	Other	5	5	8	9	22	31
4/1/16-	4/1/17-	4/1/18-							
3/31/17	3/31/18	3/31/19			19 (4/1-9/30/18)			101 (10/1/18-3/31/19)	
ALL	ALL	ALL		0-1MM	1-3MM	3-5MM	5-10MM	10-25MM	25MM & OVER
116	130	120	**NUMBER OF STATEMENTS**	9	6	11	17	31	46
%	%	%	**ASSETS**	%	%	%	%	%	%
12.8	11.6	13.3	Cash & Equivalents			10.7	8.7	12.1	7.8
21.3	25.0	25.3	Trade Receivables (net)			28.6	26.4	27.2	27.4
17.4	18.5	17.9	Inventory			19.2	15.9	24.6	17.2
3.0	3.9	3.4	All Other Current			4.6	3.3	2.5	3.1
54.6	59.1	59.9	Total Current			63.1	54.4	66.4	55.6
30.7	26.6	25.7	Fixed Assets (net)			25.1	34.5	19.6	26.6
6.2	8.9	8.7	Intangibles (net)			6.5	4.2	9.5	12.8
8.5	5.4	5.7	All Other Non-Current			5.2	6.9	4.5	5.0
100.0	100.0	100.0	Total			100.0	100.0	100.0	100.0
			LIABILITIES						
11.3	10.7	9.8	Notes Payable-Short Term			9.3	6.6	11.8	11.5
4.8	3.1	3.4	Cur. Mat.-L.T.D.			1.0	2.5	3.7	5.2
12.4	12.0	11.8	Trade Payables			17.6	12.2	13.2	10.0
.3	.2	.2	Income Taxes Payable			.0	.3	.3	.2
14.4	12.9	16.1	All Other Current			21.2	14.9	12.6	17.0
43.2	38.9	41.3	Total Current			49.2	36.5	41.6	43.9
22.5	16.4	20.8	Long-Term Debt			20.9	29.1	9.7	20.1
.7	.7	.4	Deferred Taxes			.0	.7	.5	.5
9.3	6.5	5.0	All Other Non-Current			7.8	9.1	5.6	4.1
24.3	37.5	32.4	Net Worth			22.1	24.6	42.7	31.4
100.0	100.0	100.0	Total Liabilities & Net Worth			100.0	100.0	100.0	100.0
			INCOME DATA						
100.0	100.0	100.0	Net Sales			100.0	100.0	100.0	100.0
			Gross Profit						
93.7	91.4	89.9	Operating Expenses			92.4	94.8	90.1	91.8
6.3	8.6	10.1	Operating Profit			7.6	5.2	9.9	8.2
1.8	1.4	1.4	All Other Expenses (net)			3.4	.2	.0	2.4
4.5	7.2	8.7	Profit Before Taxes			4.2	5.0	9.9	5.8
			RATIOS						
2.9	2.9	2.8				2.2	2.8	3.7	2.1
1.5	1.7	1.7	Current			1.6	1.4	2.0	1.5
.9	1.0	1.0				1.1	.8	1.0	1.1
1.7	1.9	1.9				1.5	2.0	2.0	1.4
.8	.9	1.0	Quick			1.0	.8	1.3	.9
.4	.5	.5				.3	.3	.4	.5

							Sales/Receivables						
13	28.9	21	17.5	22	16.9			6	59.6	26	14.2	32	11.3	29	12.7

(continued)

						Sales/Receivables										
13	28.9	21	17.5	22	16.9		6	59.6	26	14.2	32	11.3	29	12.7
34	10.6	41	8.8	41	8.9		34	10.6	47	7.8	44	8.3	43	8.4
59	6.2	57	6.4	61	6.0		61	6.0	62	5.9	66	5.5	64	5.7

			Cost of Sales/Inventory					
			Cost of Sales/Payables					

Hist 1	Hist 2	Hist 3	Ratio	0-1MM	1-3MM	3-5MM	5-10MM	10-25MM	25MM & OVER
4.6	4.5	4.6				4.5	5.7	3.4	5.7
13.7	10.2	8.6	Sales/Working Capital			14.6	10.3	6.1	10.0
-62.7	-847.6	112.1				27.4	-44.8	56.4	69.3

						EBIT/Interest				
	15.3		14.8		13.4				16.0		34.0		12.2
(96)	4.9	(110)	5.9	(100)	6.4		(16)	5.3	(26)	10.1	(45)	5.5
	1.5		2.5		2.1			.2		4.7		2.0

			Net Profit + Depr., Dep., Amort./Cur. Mat. L/T/D						
	8.0		6.1		10.1						10.1
(24)	3.7	(27)	3.5	(19)	3.6				(15)	3.4
	1.6		2.0		2.6					2.0

Hist 1	Hist 2	Hist 3	Ratio	0-1MM	1-3MM	3-5MM	5-10MM	10-25MM	25MM & OVER
.3	.3	.2				.1	.4	.1	.4
1.2	.9	.9	Fixed/Worth			2.4	.5	.6	1.1
4.9	5.1	8.1				-.8	NM	1.3	-2.7
.9	.7	.8				1.4	.9	.5	1.1
2.2	2.1	2.1	Debt/Worth			2.3	1.7	1.6	2.8
13.7	14.5	38.6				-6.1	NM	6.0	-8.2

						% Profit Before Taxes/Tangible Net Worth				
	67.0		51.0		56.2				45.8		74.2		50.5
(91)	28.2	(104)	23.6	(92)	22.8		(13)	14.5	(28)	28.1	(33)	28.4
	10.1		12.3		10.7			-5.9		15.8		13.6

Hist 1	Hist 2	Hist 3	Ratio	0-1MM	1-3MM	3-5MM	5-10MM	10-25MM	25MM & OVER
17.2	15.8	19.2				12.7	19.5	25.7	14.4
7.4	9.3	8.5	% Profit Before Taxes/Total Assets			4.7	7.0	11.4	6.7
.8	2.9	2.5				2.1	-1.9	8.2	2.6
36.0	38.8	55.4				130.8	18.8	77.6	20.6
10.1	10.8	11.7	Sales/Net Fixed Assets			17.3	5.2	16.2	9.5
2.6	3.9	3.0				2.2	1.6	4.5	3.0
3.4	3.4	3.4				3.4	3.1	3.4	3.3
1.8	1.8	1.9	Sales/Total Assets			2.4	1.6	1.8	1.5
.9	1.0	.9				.7	.7	1.1	1.0

						% Depr., Dep., Amort./Sales				
	1.1		.8		.6					1.0		.4		.9
(84)	2.1	(91)	2.0	(85)	1.6		(14)	3.5	(19)	1.2	(41)	2.2
	4.0		3.9		4.1			9.6		4.0		3.6

			% Officers', Directors' Owners' Comp/Sales						
	1.5		1.7		1.2						
(20)	4.4	(31)	4.2	(27)	2.0					
	7.0		9.5		7.4					

4153897M	5324721M	6886860M	Net Sales ($)	6524M	11976M	40563M	123673M	490610M	6213514M
2653743M	3448084M	3909596M	Total Assets ($)	47760M	12920M	39234M	138467M	434147M	3237068M

M = $ thousand   MM = $ million
See Pages viii through xx for Explanation of Ratios and Data

			Current Data Sorted by Assets				Comparative Historical Data	

Type of Statement	0-500M	500M-2MM	2-10MM	10-50MM	50-100MM	100-250MM	4/1/14-3/31/15 ALL	4/1/15-3/31/16 ALL
Unqualified			2	1	4		12	9
Reviewed	1		1	2			5	6
Compiled		2	4			1	3	11
Tax Returns	1	3	1				8	3
Other	1	5	6	12	6	2	31	27
		9 (4/1-9/30/18)		46 (10/1/18-3/31/19)				
NUMBER OF STATEMENTS	3	10	14	15	10	3	59	56
ASSETS	%	%	%	%	%	%	%	%
Cash & Equivalents		15.2	10.1	9.9	3.1		10.3	19.2
Trade Receivables (net)		22.9	24.5	24.1	19.8		22.6	20.0
Inventory		.0	6.8	3.6	14.5		5.4	4.8
All Other Current		7.2	5.7	1.9	4.9		3.7	3.0
Total Current		45.4	47.0	39.6	42.3		41.9	47.0
Fixed Assets (net)		32.6	45.2	49.4	50.0		45.3	44.0
Intangibles (net)		7.8	1.5	4.8	5.7		4.5	4.0
All Other Non-Current		14.3	6.3	6.2	2.0		8.2	5.0
Total		100.0	100.0	100.0	100.0		100.0	100.0
LIABILITIES								
Notes Payable-Short Term		7.5	8.5	5.6	2.3		5.1	2.9
Cur. Mat.-L.T.D.		2.7	6.6	6.9	4.1		4.7	6.2
Trade Payables		13.3	12.9	5.1	15.1		9.6	10.5
Income Taxes Payable		.4	.3	.0	.0		.1	.7
All Other Current		18.2	19.6	7.1	7.4		8.6	12.3
Total Current		42.1	47.9	24.7	28.9		28.2	32.5
Long-Term Debt		27.4	29.0	29.7	26.0		24.7	22.5
Deferred Taxes		.9	1.2	.0	1.2		1.1	2.3
All Other Non-Current		2.4	.3	8.1	1.7		7.2	2.5
Net Worth		27.2	21.5	37.5	42.2		38.8	40.2
Total Liabilities & Net Worth		100.0	100.0	100.0	100.0		100.0	100.0
INCOME DATA								
Net Sales		100.0	100.0	100.0	100.0		100.0	100.0
Gross Profit								
Operating Expenses		93.3	86.5	85.2	92.4		88.7	83.2
Operating Profit		6.7	13.5	14.8	7.6		11.3	16.8
All Other Expenses (net)		2.7	5.9	.6	.7		3.8	2.9
Profit Before Taxes		4.0	7.6	14.2	6.9		7.6	14.0
RATIOS								
Current		3.7	1.7	3.6	2.1		3.0	1.9
		.8	.9	1.3	1.5		1.6	1.4
		.3	.6	1.0	.9		.9	.9
Quick		1.9	1.4	1.8	.9		2.3	1.7
		.8	.7	1.3	.8		1.2	1.1
		.2	.5	.9	.6		.7	.6
Sales/Receivables		1 367.1	17 21.3	35 10.3	30 12.0		34 10.8	18 20.3
		6 63.3	41 8.8	60 6.1	44 8.3		42 8.6	34 10.6
		35 10.3	51 7.1	79 4.6	66 5.5		56 6.5	54 6.7
Cost of Sales/Inventory								
Cost of Sales/Payables								
Sales/Working Capital		12.9	54.0	4.1	6.5		5.2	6.8
		-28.4	-36.3	22.9	16.6		11.1	17.4
		-7.2	-6.6	447.7	-53.6		-28.6	-118.6
EBIT/Interest			29.8	13.5			52.4	31.1
			(12) 5.0	(12) 6.6			(53) 7.1	(46) 8.3
			-1.6	3.5			1.4	3.6
Net Profit + Depr., Dep., Amort./Cur. Mat. L/T/D							4.9	6.4
							(15) 2.2	(18) 2.2
							1.3	1.0
Fixed/Worth		.3	.3	.3	.9		.5	.4
		2.1	2.0	1.1	1.4		1.5	1.2
		-.8	-5.5	4.0	1.8		4.1	4.2
Debt/Worth		.4	1.6	1.4	1.1		.6	.7
		5.5	6.4	3.1	1.7		2.5	2.0
		-3.7	-7.7	9.2	2.5		5.6	4.5
% Profit Before Taxes/Tangible Net Worth				101.2	25.0		49.3	85.4
				41.4	10.6		(53) 25.2	(51) 42.6
				10.2	2.4		6.6	20.7
% Profit Before Taxes/Total Assets		33.9	19.8	12.1	7.8		19.7	32.6
		15.6	12.1	8.3	3.8		6.9	10.3
		-7.3	-11.5	5.5	.6		1.2	4.2
Sales/Net Fixed Assets		49.7	30.3	7.6	6.3		9.6	16.9
		15.4	12.3	2.9	2.5		3.5	5.0
		5.4	1.0	1.4	.9		1.0	1.5
Sales/Total Assets		4.8	4.4	1.7	2.1		2.8	3.1
		3.6	2.0	1.3	1.4		1.6	1.7
		2.2	.8	.8	.7		.5	.6
% Depr., Dep., Amort./Sales			.7	2.6			2.1	1.8
			(13) 2.8	(14) 4.9			(52) 4.7	(46) 4.5
			11.2	21.7			8.8	8.6
% Officers', Directors' Owners' Comp/Sales							1.5	.6
							(10) 2.2	(16) 2.0
							5.2	5.3
Net Sales ($)	4722M	51041M	216440M	571689M	1132369M	228473M	2213461M	1864190M
Total Assets ($)	903M	13814M	80600M	373548M	735317M	459003M	1687535M	1911349M

© RMA 2019

M = $ thousand   MM = $ million
See Pages viii through xx for Explanation of Ratios and Data

Comparative Historical Data | Current Data Sorted by Sales

Type of Statement	4/1/16-3/31/17 ALL	4/1/17-3/31/18 ALL	4/1/18-3/31/19 ALL	0-1MM	1-3MM	3-5MM	5-10MM	10-25MM	25MM & OVER
Unqualified	10	3	7		1			1	5
Reviewed	4	8	4		1			2	1
Compiled	7	8	7			1	1	2	2
Tax Returns	4	6	5	1	1		1	1	
Other	30	39	32	1	6	3	4	6	14
				9 (4/1-9/30/18)			46 (10/1/18-3/31/19)		
NUMBER OF STATEMENTS	55	64	55	2	9	4	6	12	22

ASSETS	%	%	%	%	%	%	%	%	%
Cash & Equivalents	8.2	10.6	10.6					18.0	9.9
Trade Receivables (net)	25.3	25.4	23.0					17.0	27.1
Inventory	9.7	5.7	5.3					8.0	9.0
All Other Current	6.4	4.7	4.5					2.8	2.9
Total Current	49.6	46.5	43.4					45.7	48.9
Fixed Assets (net)	40.5	41.2	44.0					40.6	39.9
Intangibles (net)	5.9	6.2	5.6					2.3	8.5
All Other Non-Current	4.0	6.0	7.0					11.4	2.7
Total	100.0	100.0	100.0					100.0	100.0

LIABILITIES									
Notes Payable-Short Term	8.5	5.8	5.6					9.3	5.5
Cur. Mat.-L.T.D.	4.0	5.0	5.6					8.9	5.1
Trade Payables	10.8	13.2	10.2					10.8	11.0
Income Taxes Payable	.4	.5	.1					.1	.0
All Other Current	11.8	10.0	12.5					8.8	9.9
Total Current	35.6	34.5	34.0					37.8	31.6
Long-Term Debt	22.7	22.3	28.5					27.9	26.4
Deferred Taxes	1.9	1.4	.9					.9	.5
All Other Non-Current	6.1	4.6	3.0					2.3	5.0
Net Worth	33.7	37.1	33.6					31.0	36.5
Total Liabilties & Net Worth	100.0	100.0	100.0					100.0	100.0

INCOME DATA									
Net Sales	100.0	100.0	100.0					100.0	100.0
Gross Profit									
Operating Expenses	89.8	90.1	89.4					91.1	93.6
Operating Profit	10.2	9.9	10.6					8.9	6.4
All Other Expenses (net)	2.9	2.4	3.1					1.1	1.8
Profit Before Taxes	7.3	7.5	7.6					7.8	4.6

RATIOS									
Current	2.7	2.1	2.3					1.2	2.3
	1.2	1.3	1.2					1.0	1.3
	.7	.8	.8					.7	.9
Quick	1.6	1.6	1.7					1.0	1.6
	.9	1.0	.9					.8	1.0
	.4	.6	.6					.5	.7
Sales/Receivables	16 22.3	18 20.3	24 15.1					23 15.7	35 10.5
	45 8.2	40 9.1	41 8.8					33 10.9	59 6.2
	68 5.4	60 6.1	68 5.4					47 7.8	70 5.2
Cost of Sales/Inventory									
Cost of Sales/Payables									
Sales/Working Capital	6.8	7.1	7.2					16.3	5.6
	17.7	21.7	34.6					400.9	23.9
	-16.0	-33.8	-23.3					-26.0	-61.3
EBIT/Interest	18.5	14.5	13.9					33.9	14.6
	(48) 4.7	(50) 4.9	(46) 4.5				(11) 4.6		(19) 6.1
	.5	1.1	1.2					2.5	1.2
Net Profit + Depr., Dep., Amort./Cur. Mat. L/T/D	3.8	2.9	6.8						
	(17) 2.3	(13) 1.3	(10) 1.7						
	1.3	.7	.9						
Fixed/Worth	.4	.4	.4					.1	.3
	1.3	1.1	1.4					1.6	1.3
	4.5	4.5	8.6					7.3	2.6
Debt/Worth	1.0	.6	.8					1.6	1.3
	2.2	2.3	2.4					2.8	2.2
	10.7	15.2	15.1					8.9	5.7
% Profit Before Taxes/Tangible Net Worth	52.4	61.5	73.5					101.2	82.8
	(45) 20.4	(55) 18.2	(44) 24.9				(11) 43.9		(19) 15.7
	1.3	2.1	8.3					18.1	3.8
% Profit Before Taxes/Total Assets	18.5	14.4	18.7					18.9	17.2
	6.9	6.2	7.0					7.7	6.0
	-.4	.8	.7					4.8	.0
Sales/Net Fixed Assets	17.2	26.0	28.4					41.2	14.2
	4.9	5.3	4.5					12.3	3.9
	1.7	1.2	1.8					1.6	2.0
Sales/Total Assets	2.5	2.9	3.2					3.5	2.2
	1.8	1.6	1.6					1.8	1.6
	.8	.6	.8					.9	.9
% Depr., Dep., Amort./Sales	2.0	2.4	.9					.4	2.5
	(44) 4.0	(47) 5.1	(45) 3.4					5.2	(18) 3.2
	9.9	15.7	9.7					17.7	5.0
% Officers', Directors' Owners' Comp/Sales		.8	2.3						
	(11) 3.6		(11) 3.5						
		15.9	5.0						
Net Sales ($)	3046199M	3255849M	2204734M	830M	19837M	16903M	43635M	203237M	1920292M
Total Assets ($)	1894835M	1823468M	1663185M	1703M	49344M	33060M	19129M	200112M	1359837M

© RMA 2019

M = $ thousand   MM = $ million
See Pages viii through xx for Explanation of Ratios and Data

Current Data Sorted by Assets   Comparative Historical Data

	0-500M	500M-2MM	2-10MM	10-50MM	50-100MM	100-250MM		9 4/1/14- 3/31/15 ALL	11 4/1/15- 3/31/16 ALL
Type of Statement									
Unqualified			1	5		4		9	11
Reviewed				1					3
Compiled	1							2	
Tax Returns	2							2	1
Other	1	1	2 / 4	1 / 5	1	3		16	19
	0-500M	500M-2MM 4 (4/1-9/30/18)	2-10MM	10-50MM 28 (10/1/18-3/31/19)	50-100MM	100-250MM			
NUMBER OF STATEMENTS	4	1	7	12	1	7		29	34
	%	%	%	%	%	%	**ASSETS**	%	%
				8.9			Cash & Equivalents	17.4	12.7
				16.3			Trade Receivables (net)	14.0	13.2
				1.8			Inventory	.4	1.6
				5.3			All Other Current	4.7	2.2
				32.4			Total Current	36.4	29.7
				54.6			Fixed Assets (net)	53.2	57.2
				2.7			Intangibles (net)	3.7	6.0
				10.4			All Other Non-Current	6.7	7.1
				100.0			Total	100.0	100.0
							LIABILITIES		
				2.8			Notes Payable-Short Term	2.5	1.6
				3.8			Cur. Mat.-L.T.D.	2.5	2.9
				3.6			Trade Payables	7.3	3.1
				.0			Income Taxes Payable	.0	.0
				12.2			All Other Current	9.2	6.0
				22.5			Total Current	21.5	13.6
				30.0			Long-Term Debt	26.4	36.1
				.0			Deferred Taxes	.8	.3
				1.5			All Other Non-Current	5.1	5.8
				45.9			Net Worth	46.3	44.2
				100.0			Total Liabilties & Net Worth	100.0	100.0
							INCOME DATA		
				100.0			Net Sales	100.0	100.0
							Gross Profit		
				77.2			Operating Expenses	84.2	85.3
				22.8			Operating Profit	15.8	14.7
				5.4			All Other Expenses (net)	2.8	3.8
				17.4			Profit Before Taxes	13.0	10.9
							RATIOS		
				2.9				4.3	3.7
				1.5			Current	2.1	2.1
				.6				1.1	1.3
				2.3				3.7	3.2
				1.2			Quick	1.7	1.9
				.4				.9	1.1
			0	UND				7 55.5	13 28.0
			30	12.0			Sales/Receivables	30 12.2	34 10.7
			52	7.0				45 8.2	51 7.2
							Cost of Sales/Inventory		
							Cost of Sales/Payables		
				4.9				2.7	4.1
				13.6			Sales/Working Capital	9.3	8.9
				-9.7				32.8	20.1
				40.0				20.8	17.1
			(11)	5.4			EBIT/Interest	(27) 8.1	(29) 6.8
				3.2				2.4	2.4
							Net Profit + Depr., Dep., Amort./Cur. Mat. L/T/D		
				.6				.7	.8
				1.4			Fixed/Worth	1.2	1.4
				2.1				2.4	3.2
				.8				.3	.3
				1.4			Debt/Worth	1.3	1.3
				2.2				2.2	5.0
				32.5			% Profit Before Taxes/Tangible	34.1	54.5
				17.7			Net Worth	(26) 17.8	(28) 15.3
				10.0				5.5	7.8
				16.9			% Profit Before Taxes/Total	17.7	14.6
				5.9			Assets	7.6	6.4
				5.1				1.7	3.3
				7.5				6.7	3.4
				2.5			Sales/Net Fixed Assets	1.7	1.6
				.2				.5	.4
				2.4				2.0	1.7
				1.3			Sales/Total Assets	1.0	.9
				.1				.4	.3
				2.6				2.4	3.8
				7.4			% Depr., Dep., Amort./Sales	(25) 7.6	(30) 6.6
				41.3				16.0	16.1
							% Officers', Directors' Owners' Comp/Sales		
5974M	84M	90577M	391142M	132517M	964559M	Net Sales ($)	800503M	1855796M
1218M	935M	38066M	348699M	84601M	1060662M	Total Assets ($)	1421778M	2108792M

M = $ thousand   MM = $ million
See Pages viii through xx for Explanation of Ratios and Data

Comparative Historical Data   **Current Data Sorted by Sales**

Type of Statement

	4/1/16-3/31/17 ALL	4/1/17-3/31/18 ALL	4/1/18-3/31/19 ALL	Type of Statement	0-1MM	1-3MM	3-5MM	5-10MM	10-25MM	25MM & OVER
	12	10	10	Unqualified			1	2	3	4
	4	2	1	Reviewed				1		
	1	1	1	Compiled				1		
	1	3	5	Tax Returns						
	21	23	15	Other	2	4 (4/1-9/30/18)		3	3	7
								28 (10/1/18-3/31/19)		
	39	39	32	**NUMBER OF STATEMENTS**	2	4	3	5	7	11

Assets / Liabilities / Income / Ratios

4/1/16-3/31/17	4/1/17-3/31/18	4/1/18-3/31/19		0-1MM	1-3MM	3-5MM	5-10MM	10-25MM	25MM & OVER
%	%	%	**ASSETS**	%	%	%	%	%	%
13.3	12.8	11.5	Cash & Equivalents						12.6
15.0	11.5	17.2	Trade Receivables (net)						22.7
1.5	.5	1.6	Inventory						2.3
4.8	7.1	3.6	All Other Current						5.8
34.6	31.9	33.8	Total Current						43.4
49.5	53.0	50.9	Fixed Assets (net)						46.2
7.1	5.8	3.3	Intangibles (net)						1.0
8.8	9.4	12.0	All Other Non-Current						9.4
100.0	100.0	100.0	Total						100.0
			LIABILITIES						
3.2	1.9	3.0	Notes Payable-Short Term						1.8
4.9	3.7	5.0	Cur. Mat.-L.T.D.						7.1
6.1	3.3	3.9	Trade Payables						3.5
.0	.0	.0	Income Taxes Payable						.0
6.9	6.9	14.7	All Other Current						14.2
21.2	15.9	26.6	Total Current						26.6
31.2	27.0	26.2	Long-Term Debt						20.3
.6	.5	.0	Deferred Taxes						.0
5.9	4.7	4.0	All Other Non-Current						4.5
41.1	51.9	43.2	Net Worth						48.7
100.0	100.0	100.0	Total Liabilities & Net Worth						100.0
			INCOME DATA						
100.0	100.0	100.0	Net Sales						100.0
			Gross Profit						
83.3	85.5	83.2	Operating Expenses						90.7
16.7	14.5	16.8	Operating Profit						9.3
4.6	2.9	5.4	All Other Expenses (net)						1.3
12.2	11.5	11.4	Profit Before Taxes						8.0
			RATIOS						
3.1	4.5	3.5	Current						3.5
1.9	2.4	1.6							1.8
1.0	1.0	.7							1.3
2.9	4.4	3.0	Quick						3.2
1.4	1.7	1.3							1.8
.8	.6	.5							1.1
(5) 73.9	(0) UND	(8) 47.6	Sales/Receivables					(33)	11.0
(34) 10.6	(26) 14.1	(33) 10.9						(43)	8.4
(56) 6.5	(51) 7.1	(45) 8.1						(55)	6.6
			Cost of Sales/Inventory						
			Cost of Sales/Payables						
4.6	3.1	3.7	Sales/Working Capital						4.5
7.7	7.7	16.4							9.3
-999.8	134.8	-19.4							17.8
9.3	10.7	21.1	EBIT/Interest						48.6
(33) 3.4	(35) 3.5	(27) 4.7							8.3
1.2	-2.4	3.1							4.1
			Net Profit + Depr., Dep., Amort./Cur. Mat. L/T/D						
.6	.7	.6	Fixed/Worth						.4
1.3	1.2	1.3							.8
3.8	2.3	2.2							1.8
.4	.3	.6	Debt/Worth						.7
1.7	.9	1.4							.9
4.4	2.3	2.5							1.7
77.0	37.0	39.6	% Profit Before Taxes/Tangible Net Worth						34.9
(36) 15.0	(35) 11.9	(29) 18.1							25.2
2.8	-1.3	8.4							10.0
9.7	12.8	16.5	% Profit Before Taxes/Total Assets						19.3
4.1	3.9	6.5							9.6
.6	-1.7	2.9							5.1
8.0	8.8	12.4	Sales/Net Fixed Assets						7.8
1.4	1.6	3.0							3.6
.2	.3	.4							1.6
2.5	2.2	2.8	Sales/Total Assets						2.7
.9	.9	1.3							1.6
.1	.2	.3							1.0
2.4	2.4	1.5	% Depr., Dep., Amort./Sales						1.5
(32) 9.3	(32) 8.5	(29) 6.8						(10)	3.0
25.0	21.1	13.1							8.2
			% Officers', Directors' Owners' Comp/Sales						
2029723M	1973599M	1584853M	Net Sales ($)	328M	7198M	10747M	36542M	123625M	1406413M
2062901M	2284471M	1534181M	Total Assets ($)	1076M	19647M	56854M	212055M	195059M	1049490M

M = $ thousand   MM = $ million
See Pages viii through xx for Explanation of Ratios and Data

Current Data Sorted by Assets   Comparative Historical Data

0-500M	500M-2MM	2-10MM	10-50MM	50-100MM	100-250MM	Type of Statement	ALL 4/1/14-3/31/15	ALL 4/1/15-3/31/16
		2	6	1	1	Unqualified	17	20
	1		7		1	Reviewed	12	12
		3				Compiled	5	2
1		1				Tax Returns	2	3
	3	5	16	7	3	Other	40	36
	9 (4/1-9/30/18)		50 (10/1/18-3/31/19)					
1	4	12	29	8	5	**NUMBER OF STATEMENTS**	76	73
%	%	%	%	%	%	**ASSETS**	%	%
		15.7	10.0			Cash & Equivalents	12.6	10.6
		26.9	22.2			Trade Receivables (net)	21.2	20.1
		.0	.8			Inventory	1.1	.9
		4.7	5.3			All Other Current	5.0	3.3
		47.3	38.2			Total Current	39.9	34.9
		39.4	51.0			Fixed Assets (net)	46.8	49.9
		1.3	5.6			Intangibles (net)	6.2	7.8
		12.0	5.1			All Other Non-Current	7.1	7.4
		100.0	100.0			Total	100.0	100.0
						LIABILITIES		
		.6	1.5			Notes Payable-Short Term	3.5	2.8
		3.6	6.3			Cur. Mat.-L.T.D.	3.4	4.0
		13.5	9.5			Trade Payables	9.6	9.8
		.0	.1			Income Taxes Payable	.3	.2
		18.6	5.1			All Other Current	9.0	10.0
		36.3	22.4			Total Current	25.8	26.8
		9.5	22.4			Long-Term Debt	24.3	26.2
		.1	.5			Deferred Taxes	.9	1.2
		6.8	4.3			All Other Non-Current	3.1	4.9
		47.3	50.3			Net Worth	45.8	40.9
		100.0	100.0			Total Liabilties & Net Worth	100.0	100.0
						INCOME DATA		
		100.0	100.0			Net Sales	100.0	100.0
						Gross Profit		
		82.8	87.8			Operating Expenses	84.8	88.4
		17.2	12.2			Operating Profit	15.2	11.6
		.8	1.4			All Other Expenses (net)	3.5	2.5
		16.3	10.8			Profit Before Taxes	11.7	9.1
						RATIOS		
		3.2	2.4			Current	2.3	2.2
		1.7	1.3				1.4	1.5
		.6	1.0				1.0	.9
		3.1	2.0			Quick	2.2	1.9
		1.6	1.1				1.3	1.2
		.5	.8				.8	.8
		41 8.9	33 10.9			Sales/Receivables	27 13.6	31 11.8
		50 7.3	42 8.6				42 8.6	44 8.3
		61 6.0	64 5.7				61 6.0	61 6.0
						Cost of Sales/Inventory		
						Cost of Sales/Payables		
		3.6	6.4			Sales/Working Capital	5.2	7.0
		15.4	20.4				13.8	20.8
		-8.9	-639.4				NM	-31.7
			21.3			EBIT/Interest	21.4	23.0
			(28) 9.6				(63) 6.5	(67) 5.9
			3.0				2.2	3.0
						Net Profit + Depr., Dep., Amort./Cur. Mat. L/T/D	2.3	4.9
							(16) 1.6	(16) 2.3
							1.4	1.6
		.1	.7			Fixed/Worth	.5	.7
		.5	1.0				1.2	1.4
		1.6	3.1				2.4	3.5
		.2	.5			Debt/Worth	.7	.8
		.7	1.3				1.4	1.8
		3.1	3.0				3.5	3.8
		72.9	57.9			% Profit Before Taxes/Tangible Net Worth	46.4	50.2
	(11) 41.5	(28) 28.3				(68) 23.3	(65) 27.5
		17.3	8.1				10.8	13.2
		32.4	17.2			% Profit Before Taxes/Total Assets	16.7	18.4
		14.9	10.6				9.2	7.3
		9.7	5.0				2.1	2.9
		122.7	8.5			Sales/Net Fixed Assets	10.2	9.4
		3.9	2.3				2.5	2.7
		1.3	1.1				.7	1.1
		3.9	2.3			Sales/Total Assets	2.2	2.2
		1.3	1.3				1.2	1.2
		.9	.8				.4	.7
			2.1			% Depr., Dep., Amort./Sales	2.5	2.9
		(28)	5.6				(62) 5.4	(62) 5.7
			8.5				11.2	10.8
						% Officers', Directors' Owners' Comp/Sales		
1281M	20051M	117535M	1159243M	518078M	1245983M	Net Sales ($)	3215409M	3980243M
132M	5277M	57715M	756555M	492358M	843574M	Total Assets ($)	3284198M	3233613M

M = $ thousand   MM = $ million
See Pages viii through xx for Explanation of Ratios and Data

Comparative Historical Data | Current Data Sorted by Sales

			Type of Statement						
19	23	10	Unqualified						5
9	9	9	Reviewed		1			1	7
4	4	3	Compiled		1			2	
3	3	3	Tax Returns		1	1			
44	41	34	Other	1	1	3	5	6	18
4/1/16-3/31/17	4/1/17-3/31/18	4/1/18-3/31/19			9 (4/1-9/30/18)			50 (10/1/18-3/31/19)	
ALL	ALL	ALL		0-1MM	1-3MM	3-5MM	5-10MM	10-25MM	25MM & OVER
79	80	59	NUMBER OF STATEMENTS	1	4	5	8	11	30
%	%	%	**ASSETS**	%	%	%	%	%	%
12.8	10.5	10.7	Cash & Equivalents					9.7	10.2
14.3	18.4	23.6	Trade Receivables (net)					22.2	25.9
1.3	1.5	1.5	Inventory					.9	2.5
3.2	2.5	4.7	All Other Current					7.2	4.8
31.6	33.0	40.5	Total Current					40.0	43.4
53.1	51.1	47.1	Fixed Assets (net)					51.3	43.2
6.8	7.7	5.2	Intangibles (net)					1.1	7.0
8.5	8.3	7.1	All Other Non-Current					7.6	6.3
100.0	100.0	100.0	Total					100.0	100.0
			LIABILITIES						
1.8	3.5	1.8	Notes Payable-Short Term					.4	3.0
5.4	4.4	5.8	Cur. Mat.-L.T.D.					4.1	6.4
5.4	9.6	10.1	Trade Payables					6.4	13.2
.2	.4	.1	Income Taxes Payable					.0	.1
9.0	6.1	10.6	All Other Current					15.0	7.4
21.8	23.9	28.3	Total Current					25.8	30.1
26.5	28.6	23.6	Long-Term Debt					28.3	27.2
1.7	.9	.5	Deferred Taxes					.7	.6
4.0	4.1	4.2	All Other Non-Current					1.8	5.7
46.1	42.4	43.5	Net Worth					43.3	36.3
100.0	100.0	100.0	Total Liabilities & Net Worth					100.0	100.0
			INCOME DATA						
100.0	100.0	100.0	Net Sales					100.0	100.0
			Gross Profit						
84.5	86.6	86.6	Operating Expenses					83.5	92.3
15.5	13.4	13.4	Operating Profit					16.5	7.7
3.6	2.9	1.9	All Other Expenses (net)					1.1	2.4
11.9	10.5	11.5	Profit Before Taxes					15.5	5.3
			RATIOS						
2.5	2.5	3.1	Current					2.2	3.3
1.4	1.4	1.3						1.3	1.4
.8	.8	.9						1.0	.8
2.1	2.1	2.3	Quick					1.2	2.2
1.2	1.2	1.1						1.1	1.2
.7	.6	.7						.9	.7
30 12.0	35 10.4	33 11.0	Sales/Receivables					31 11.9	37 9.9
41 9.0	47 7.8	42 8.6						41 8.9	44 8.3
54 6.8	59 6.2	59 6.2						59 6.2	64 5.7
			Cost of Sales/Inventory						
			Cost of Sales/Payables						
5.8	6.2	5.7	Sales/Working Capital					6.6	5.9
16.9	18.8	21.5						21.5	27.2
-16.5	-22.4	-33.7						-999.8	-39.9
23.7	17.3	27.1	EBIT/Interest						31.4
(72) 6.3	(71) 5.4	(52) 9.6						(27) 9.5	
2.3	2.5	2.1							.9
4.9	8.4	3.2	Net Profit + Depr., Dep.,						
(17) 2.2	(13) 2.3	(10) 2.4	Amort./Cur. Mat. L/T/D						
1.3	1.6	2.0							
.7	.6	.4	Fixed/Worth					.5	.4
1.4	1.3	1.0						.8	1.0
2.3	2.7	3.2						3.2	5.6
.7	.5	.4	Debt/Worth					.4	.5
1.2	1.3	1.3						2.6	1.5
2.7	3.7	3.2						3.2	16.7
45.3	42.0	70.7	% Profit Before Taxes/Tangible					62.7	72.2
(71) 20.4	(70) 19.8	(53) 29.7	Net Worth					29.3	(25) 29.7
7.0	6.1	9.4						10.6	5.1
16.6	14.8	19.6	% Profit Before Taxes/Total					15.7	17.0
6.5	7.8	10.6	Assets					9.6	10.3
2.6	2.4	3.7						7.9	2.2
7.2	9.7	12.8	Sales/Net Fixed Assets					18.9	12.7
1.5	2.1	3.0						1.6	4.9
.8	.9	1.0						.8	2.2
1.8	2.2	2.4	Sales/Total Assets					2.3	2.4
.8	1.1	1.3						.8	1.9
.4	.5	.7						.4	1.0
2.6	1.8	1.6	% Depr., Dep., Amort./Sales					.6	1.6
(68) 5.8	(63) 6.1	(51) 5.0						(10) 5.4	(26) 3.3
13.2	14.4	10.0						8.1	8.6
			% Officers', Directors' Owners' Comp/Sales						
3447560M	5529010M	3062171M	Net Sales ($)	855M	8118M	20352M	59519M	193509M	2779818M
3953115M	4757824M	2155611M	Total Assets ($)	4595M	20281M	11990M	106632M	264063M	1748050M

© RMA 2019

M = $ thousand   MM = $ million
See Pages viii through xx for Explanation of Ratios and Data

Current Data Sorted by Assets   **Comparative Historical Data**

0-500M	500M-2MM	2-10MM	10-50MM	50-100MM	100-250MM		4/1/14-3/31/15 ALL	4/1/15-3/31/16 ALL
						Type of Statement		
1			3		3	Unqualified	7	10
		4		2		Reviewed	8	9
		4	1			Compiled	13	8
	1		1			Tax Returns	10	
		8	15	5	7	Other	22	30
5 (4/1-9/30/18)			50 (10/1/18-3/31/19)					
1	1	16	20	7	10	**NUMBER OF STATEMENTS**	60	57
%	%	%	%	%	%	**ASSETS**	%	%
		9.0	8.8		2.4	Cash & Equivalents	15.2	11.6
		18.4	14.9		9.3	Trade Receivables (net)	16.8	15.6
		.6	.4		2.1	Inventory	.9	1.3
		1.2	6.9		1.6	All Other Current	1.9	3.2
		29.2	31.1		15.3	Total Current	34.8	31.7
		65.5	60.1		71.9	Fixed Assets (net)	55.2	58.6
		.2	2.8		4.0	Intangibles (net)	2.2	2.8
		5.1	6.0		8.7	All Other Non-Current	7.8	6.9
		100.0	100.0		100.0	Total	100.0	100.0
						LIABILITIES		
		3.3	1.8		1.9	Notes Payable-Short Term	3.6	3.3
		8.5	3.7		8.4	Cur. Mat.-L.T.D.	4.3	4.1
		3.7	4.2		4.2	Trade Payables	6.9	3.8
		.1	.0		.0	Income Taxes Payable	.0	.1
		10.0	4.1		5.3	All Other Current	11.1	7.8
		25.5	13.9		19.7	Total Current	26.0	19.1
		61.7	38.8		40.6	Long-Term Debt	27.4	28.6
		1.8	1.0		.0	Deferred Taxes	.9	.7
		1.3	3.5		1.4	All Other Non-Current	4.7	7.2
		9.7	42.8		38.2	Net Worth	41.0	44.4
		100.0	100.0		100.0	Total Liabilties & Net Worth	100.0	100.0
						INCOME DATA		
		100.0	100.0		100.0	Net Sales	100.0	100.0
						Gross Profit		
		80.1	76.2		93.0	Operating Expenses	83.4	81.3
		19.9	23.8		7.0	Operating Profit	16.6	18.7
		3.7	2.4		4.8	All Other Expenses (net)	2.3	1.2
		16.2	21.4		2.1	Profit Before Taxes	14.3	17.5
						RATIOS		
		2.1	3.4		1.1		3.1	2.7
		.9	2.1		1.0	Current	1.3	1.5
		.5	1.2		.5		.9	.9
		2.0	2.6		1.0		2.8	2.2
		.9	1.8		.7	Quick	1.3	1.3
		.5	1.1		.4		.8	.6
		0 UND	32 11.4		40 9.2		0 UND	15 24.4
		25 14.8	46 8.0		46 7.9	Sales/Receivables	37 9.9	41 9.0
		59 6.2	63 5.8		68 5.4		57 6.4	57 6.4
						Cost of Sales/Inventory		
						Cost of Sales/Payables		
		10.6	4.8		52.2		7.3	6.3
		-105.7	7.9		NM	Sales/Working Capital	25.4	22.5
		-20.1	18.1		-4.7		-100.2	-67.5
		15.8	24.3		3.1		40.7	24.4
		(10) 3.0	(18) 6.0		1.3	EBIT/Interest	(48) 6.8	(41) 4.5
		.8	3.2		.0		2.9	2.7
						Net Profit + Depr., Dep., Amort./Cur. Mat. L/T/D		
		1.1	.7		1.1		.5	.6
		2.2	1.8		2.3	Fixed/Worth	1.4	1.5
		NM	4.5		5.3		2.8	2.6
		1.2	.5		.9		.5	.4
		3.0	1.8		1.8	Debt/Worth	1.7	1.2
		NM	5.6		4.7		3.0	2.5
		198.1	243.9		17.7		60.1	63.1
		(12) 36.9	42.7		1.5	% Profit Before Taxes/Tangible Net Worth	(54) 24.4	(54) 15.2
		1.6	6.4		-10.5		11.7	5.2
		40.9	16.4		5.6		26.9	26.9
		14.0	10.0		.6	% Profit Before Taxes/Total Assets	9.0	7.0
		.6	4.7		-3.4		2.5	2.3
		3.5	3.1		1.4		6.9	4.8
		2.0	1.7		1.0	Sales/Net Fixed Assets	2.0	1.8
		1.2	.8		.4		1.1	1.1
		2.0	1.5		.9		2.6	1.9
		1.4	.9		.7	Sales/Total Assets	1.2	1.2
		.9	.7		.3		.6	.7
		3.4	4.1				3.0	2.9
		(11) 6.9	(19) 5.5			% Depr., Dep., Amort./Sales	(49) 6.0	(45) 7.1
		11.8	10.6				11.9	11.4
							1.5	1.7
						% Officers', Directors' Owners' Comp/Sales	(13) 2.1	(12) 7.1
							11.2	10.7
1086M	6137M	180723M	617628M	539614M	1111078M	Net Sales ($)	1778026M	2022441M
354M	894M	99235M	506987M	496778M	1803648M	Total Assets ($)	1633085M	1944840M

M = $ thousand   MM = $ million
See Pages viii through xx for Explanation of Ratios and Data

Comparative Historical Data | Current Data Sorted by Sales

4/1/16-3/31/17 ALL	4/1/17-3/31/18 ALL	4/1/18-3/31/19 ALL	Type of Statement	0-1MM	1-3MM	3-5MM	5-10MM	10-25MM	25MM & OVER
6	12	7	Unqualified		1				6
3	6	6	Reviewed				2	2	2
7	2	5	Compiled			2	2	1	
2	4	2	Tax Returns				1		1
34	31	35	Other	1	1		6	10	17
				1	5 (4/1-9/30/18)		50 (10/1/18-3/31/19)		
52	55	55	**NUMBER OF STATEMENTS**	1	2	2	11	13	26
%	%	%	**ASSETS**	%	%	%	%	%	%
9.5	11.6	7.6	Cash & Equivalents				4.2	10.0	7.4
13.3	19.3	13.5	Trade Receivables (net)				5.6	22.0	14.0
.8	1.6	1.8	Inventory				1.0	.7	3.1
2.6	4.0	3.2	All Other Current				.7	2.0	5.4
26.1	36.5	26.2	Total Current				11.5	34.8	29.9
63.7	53.3	64.1	Fixed Assets (net)				72.0	59.7	60.4
2.7	3.6	2.4	Intangibles (net)				4.4	.8	1.8
7.5	6.6	7.4	All Other Non-Current				12.0	4.8	7.8
100.0	100.0	100.0	Total				100.0	100.0	100.0
			LIABILITIES						
4.5	3.4	2.5	Notes Payable-Short Term				5.3	2.0	2.0
4.0	4.5	5.8	Cur. Mat.-L.T.D.				4.4	9.4	4.9
4.4	6.0	4.0	Trade Payables				2.0	4.2	4.8
.1	.0	.0	Income Taxes Payable				.0	.1	.0
7.0	8.3	7.7	All Other Current				9.1	7.4	8.5
19.9	22.2	20.1	Total Current				21.8	23.1	20.3
37.5	32.2	41.9	Long-Term Debt				33.9	75.2	25.8
1.0	.9	1.1	Deferred Taxes				1.4	1.7	.9
6.5	4.5	2.4	All Other Non-Current				3.4	1.4	2.3
35.0	40.2	34.4	Net Worth				39.5	-1.4	50.7
100.0	100.0	100.0	Total Liabilities & Net Worth				100.0	100.0	100.0
			INCOME DATA						
100.0	100.0	100.0	Net Sales				100.0	100.0	100.0
			Gross Profit						
80.4	78.7	82.2	Operating Expenses				83.7	77.0	84.5
19.6	21.3	17.8	Operating Profit				16.3	23.0	15.5
3.1	2.0	3.1	All Other Expenses (net)				1.7	1.9	3.0
16.5	19.3	14.8	Profit Before Taxes				14.6	21.1	12.5
			RATIOS						
2.4	2.9	2.1	Current				1.2	2.2	2.1
1.3	1.6	1.2					.6	2.0	1.1
.6	.9	.9					.4	1.2	.9
2.2	2.2	1.9	Quick				1.2	2.0	1.6
1.1	1.4	1.1					.6	1.7	1.0
.5	.9	.6					.0	1.1	.7
9 38.7	28 13.1	9 39.9	Sales/Receivables	0 UND			0 UND	37 9.8	33 11.1
39 9.4	48 7.6	43 8.4		0 UND			0 UND	48 7.6	43 8.5
51 7.1	64 5.7	55 6.6		53 6.9			53 6.9	73 5.0	54 6.8
			Cost of Sales/Inventory						
			Cost of Sales/Payables						
7.1	5.1	7.8	Sales/Working Capital				18.0	5.8	9.3
24.5	12.7	23.5					-39.4	7.9	73.4
-23.6	-234.3	-39.4					-18.6	506.8	-56.7
15.3	35.8	10.5	EBIT/Interest					6.1	45.8
(48) 5.0	(48) 5.7	(46) 3.6						(11) 4.2	(23) 3.1
1.6	2.3	1.1						2.6	.8
			Net Profit + Depr., Dep., Amort./Cur. Mat. L/T/D						
1.1	.7	1.0	Fixed/Worth				1.6	1.5	.7
1.8	1.3	2.0					2.1	2.9	1.2
4.4	2.1	4.0					4.6	62.6	2.5
.8	.7	.7	Debt/Worth				1.3	1.7	.4
1.7	1.6	1.8					1.8	4.5	.9
5.4	4.3	5.0					4.0	75.8	2.7
95.9	82.0	79.8	% Profit Before Taxes/Tangible Net Worth				63.2	902.9	35.8
(46) 15.5	(51) 25.1	(51) 27.5					(10) 23.8	(11) 68.0	11.7
4.8	9.0	2.1					6.5	36.0	.0
19.6	27.4	18.6	% Profit Before Taxes/Total Assets				24.4	52.3	18.0
4.8	8.5	8.7					9.8	14.3	5.6
1.6	4.5	.4					.0	7.2	-.1
3.3	6.0	3.0	Sales/Net Fixed Assets				2.2	3.3	4.0
1.6	2.1	1.5					1.2	1.9	1.4
.8	1.0	.8					.5	.8	.9
1.9	1.9	1.8	Sales/Total Assets				1.6	1.9	2.3
1.1	1.2	.9					1.0	1.1	.8
.6	.7	.6					.3	.7	.7
3.0	1.5	3.4	% Depr., Dep., Amort./Sales					4.2	1.9
(42) 6.2	(43) 4.6	(42) 5.5						(12) 5.4	(20) 4.9
10.6	11.5	10.9						9.6	9.5
1.1			% Officers', Directors' Owners' Comp/Sales						
(10) 2.4									
7.0									
1754643M	2437513M	2456266M	Net Sales ($)	943M	2986M	7954M	77372M	202826M	2164185M
2350118M	2832856M	2907896M	Total Assets ($)	7963M	6931M	8539M	164150M	183770M	2536543M

© RMA 2019

M = $ thousand   MM = $ million

See Pages viii through xx for Explanation of Ratios and Data

Current Data Sorted by Assets   Comparative Historical Data

							Type of Statement			
			1	2	4		Unqualified		7	9
			1	2	1		Reviewed		6	5
		1	2	2			Compiled		3	2
	3						Tax Returns		2	6
1	2	4					Other		12	14
1 (4/1-9/30/18)			30 (10/1/18-3/31/19)						4/1/14-3/31/15	4/1/15-3/31/16
0-500M	500M-2MM	2-10MM	10-50MM	50-100MM	100-250MM				ALL	ALL
1	6	6	8	8	2		NUMBER OF STATEMENTS		30	36
%	%	%	%	%	%		ASSETS		%	%
							Cash & Equivalents		21.8	18.3
							Trade Receivables (net)		19.1	15.6
							Inventory		.7	2.9
							All Other Current		4.9	4.6
							Total Current		46.5	41.5
							Fixed Assets (net)		43.2	47.5
							Intangibles (net)		2.3	5.1
							All Other Non-Current		8.0	6.0
							Total		100.0	100.0
							LIABILITIES			
							Notes Payable-Short Term		14.4	5.5
							Cur. Mat.-L.T.D.		4.0	9.8
							Trade Payables		7.5	4.9
							Income Taxes Payable		.3	.0
							All Other Current		21.3	10.1
							Total Current		47.5	30.4
							Long-Term Debt		29.2	27.4
							Deferred Taxes		.5	.7
							All Other Non-Current		8.0	2.9
							Net Worth		14.8	38.6
							Total Liabilties & Net Worth		100.0	100.0
							INCOME DATA			
							Net Sales		100.0	100.0
							Gross Profit			
							Operating Expenses		85.6	84.9
							Operating Profit		14.4	15.1
							All Other Expenses (net)		.3	3.0
							Profit Before Taxes		14.1	12.1
							RATIOS			
									2.8	2.5
							Current		1.8	1.3
									1.1	.7
									2.7	2.4
							Quick		1.5	.9
									.9	.5
								14	26.5	19	19.2
							Sales/Receivables	31	11.9	36	10.0
								47	7.7	55	6.6
							Cost of Sales/Inventory			
							Cost of Sales/Payables			
									5.7	5.5
							Sales/Working Capital		10.6	21.6
									80.2	-24.7
									38.8	12.4
							EBIT/Interest	(27)	15.5	(29)	4.8
									3.5	2.2
							Net Profit + Depr., Dep., Amort./Cur. Mat. L/T/D			
									.1	.5
							Fixed/Worth		1.0	1.7
									2.4	4.5
									.7	.6
							Debt/Worth		1.5	2.1
									6.5	8.7
									50.7	75.4
							% Profit Before Taxes/Tangible Net Worth	(26)	26.2	(32)	27.9
									13.8	14.9
									23.8	23.7
							% Profit Before Taxes/Total Assets		12.5	7.5
									4.7	4.2
									81.1	11.7
							Sales/Net Fixed Assets		3.2	4.1
									1.1	1.1
									3.6	2.2
							Sales/Total Assets		1.4	1.3
									.8	.7
									2.4	2.3
							% Depr., Dep., Amort./Sales	(24)	4.1	(27)	4.2
									8.4	9.5
							% Officers', Directors' Owners' Comp/Sales			
507M	23628M	100571M	248078M	460170M	213686M		Net Sales ($)		1028100M	1274487M
375M	8291M	32348M	219703M	602720M	409170M		Total Assets ($)		994991M	1394701M

© RMA 2019

M = $ thousand   MM = $ million
See Pages viii through xx for Explanation of Ratios and Data

Comparative Historical Data

Current Data Sorted by Sales

			Type of Statement	0-1MM	1-3MM	3-5MM	5-10MM	10-25MM	25MM & OVER
3	6	7	Unqualified				1	2	4
6	4	4	Reviewed				2	1	2
1	2	3	Compiled				2	1	
4	3	3	Tax Returns				1		
16	22	14	Other	2	2	3			8
4/1/16-3/31/17 ALL	4/1/17-3/31/18 ALL	4/1/18-3/31/19 ALL		2	1 (4/1-9/30/18)	3	30 (10/1/18-3/31/19)		
30	37	31	NUMBER OF STATEMENTS	2	2	3	4	6	14
%	%	%	ASSETS	%	%	%	%	%	%
17.7	12.8	18.1	Cash & Equivalents						13.8
19.8	14.7	22.3	Trade Receivables (net)						28.6
3.8	2.0	.5	Inventory						.6
6.3	9.5	5.6	All Other Current						6.0
47.6	39.0	46.5	Total Current						49.0
45.6	45.6	35.6	Fixed Assets (net)						36.9
1.0	5.5	5.4	Intangibles (net)						4.9
5.7	9.8	12.5	All Other Non-Current						9.2
100.0	100.0	100.0	Total						100.0
			LIABILITIES						
2.9	2.8	2.5	Notes Payable-Short Term						3.3
3.9	4.8	2.3	Cur. Mat.-L.T.D.						3.1
7.4	8.8	11.3	Trade Payables						15.2
.0	.1	.1	Income Taxes Payable						.2
11.5	11.7	10.3	All Other Current						11.8
25.7	28.2	26.6	Total Current						33.6
31.9	35.8	32.2	Long-Term Debt						33.5
.7	.5	.6	Deferred Taxes						1.1
2.0	4.5	2.6	All Other Non-Current						1.5
39.6	31.0	38.1	Net Worth						30.2
100.0	100.0	100.0	Total Liabilties & Net Worth						100.0
			INCOME DATA						
100.0	100.0	100.0	Net Sales						100.0
			Gross Profit						
88.6	88.0	89.9	Operating Expenses						91.1
11.4	12.0	10.1	Operating Profit						8.9
1.1	1.2	4.0	All Other Expenses (net)						.5
10.3	10.7	6.1	Profit Before Taxes						8.4
			RATIOS						
4.1	3.1	3.0							2.7
2.4	1.4	1.7	Current						1.4
1.1	.7	1.1							1.0
2.8	1.8	3.0							2.3
1.6	.9	1.2	Quick						1.2
.9	.4	.8							.8
20 18.2	18 20.7	31 11.8							38 9.6
37 9.9	44 8.3	45 8.2	Sales/Receivables						60 6.1
55 6.6	58 6.3	74 4.9							107 3.4
			Cost of Sales/Inventory						
			Cost of Sales/Payables						
5.6	6.3	5.0							4.9
8.8	11.9	11.2	Sales/Working Capital						10.0
30.0	-11.3	35.2							NM
28.2	29.6	17.6							
(26) 4.3	(33) 6.5	(21) 2.1	EBIT/Interest						
1.8	1.9	.3							
			Net Profit + Depr., Dep., Amort./Cur. Mat. L/T/D						
.5	.8	.1							.2
1.2	1.2	.5	Fixed/Worth						1.0
2.0	4.8	1.8							1.7
.3	.7	.7							.8
1.4	2.0	1.4	Debt/Worth						1.5
6.4	8.7	10.2							11.4
55.4	58.8	54.6	% Profit Before Taxes/Tangible Net Worth						53.9
(27) 14.3	(31) 16.1	(27) 7.0						(13)	6.9
2.2	4.5	-.8							.1
24.7	16.5	13.1	% Profit Before Taxes/Total Assets						13.1
8.8	8.3	2.9							3.6
1.0	1.6	-.9							.2
8.9	9.2	58.1							64.2
4.1	1.8	3.3	Sales/Net Fixed Assets						2.7
1.8	1.0	1.2							1.1
2.4	1.6	1.7							1.4
1.6	1.0	1.1	Sales/Total Assets						1.0
.9	.5	.5							.5
2.1	2.6	1.3							.8
(25) 3.0	(25) 8.1	(25) 6.3	% Depr., Dep., Amort./Sales						(13) 6.3
7.3	16.3	9.5							9.5
			% Officers', Directors' Owners' Comp/Sales						
1193449M	1118606M	1046640M	Net Sales ($)	862M	3986M	10550M	30605M	98566M	902071M
1087836M	1386550M	1272607M	Total Assets ($)	1432M	3239M	28531M	32889M	142157M	1064359M

M = $ thousand   MM = $ million
See Pages viii through xx for Explanation of Ratios and Data

	Current Data Sorted by Assets							Comparative Historical Data	
	0-500M	500M-2MM	2-10MM	10-50MM	50-100MM	100-250MM	**Type of Statement**		
				1		2	Unqualified	2	4
				2			Reviewed	5	5
	2	2	2				Compiled	17	16
	26	24	8				Tax Returns	53	50
	13	20	25		5	1	Other	57	46
	21 (4/1-9/30/18)			114 (10/1/18-3/31/19)				4/1/14- 3/31/15 ALL	4/1/15- 3/31/16 ALL
	41	46	37	8		3	**NUMBER OF STATEMENTS**	134	121
	%	%	%	%	%	%	**ASSETS**	%	%
	25.2	17.3	13.1				Cash & Equivalents	17.4	19.8
	16.7	8.1	10.8				Trade Receivables (net)	9.3	10.1
	3.5	.8	4.2				Inventory	3.0	4.2
	3.6	2.2	1.9				All Other Current	2.6	3.8
	48.9	28.4	30.1				Total Current	32.2	37.9
	36.6	55.6	52.8				Fixed Assets (net)	51.9	47.1
	2.5	8.6	8.1				Intangibles (net)	7.6	7.2
	12.0	7.4	9.0				All Other Non-Current	8.2	7.8
	100.0	100.0	100.0				Total	100.0	100.0
							LIABILITIES		
	11.9	7.7	3.2				Notes Payable-Short Term	10.5	7.1
	17.7	6.5	7.1				Cur. Mat.-L.T.D.	5.6	9.4
	5.5	2.7	3.6				Trade Payables	4.3	3.7
	.2	.0	.0				Income Taxes Payable	.2	.2
	9.3	4.6	7.0				All Other Current	9.6	10.1
	44.5	21.6	20.9				Total Current	30.1	30.6
	55.6	55.2	40.0				Long-Term Debt	47.9	48.0
	.0	.1	.2				Deferred Taxes	.2	.2
	11.2	4.9	2.6				All Other Non-Current	9.3	10.4
	-11.4	18.4	36.3				Net Worth	12.6	10.9
	100.0	100.0	100.0				Total Liabilities & Net Worth	100.0	100.0
							INCOME DATA		
	100.0	100.0	100.0				Net Sales	100.0	100.0
							Gross Profit		
	92.7	90.5	88.4				Operating Expenses	92.1	91.2
	7.3	9.5	11.6				Operating Profit	7.9	8.8
	.0	1.3	2.2				All Other Expenses (net)	1.3	.5
	7.3	8.3	9.4				Profit Before Taxes	6.6	8.3
							RATIOS		
	4.0	8.9	3.7					3.2	4.5
	1.8	1.2	1.6				Current	1.3	1.4
	.7	.7	.6					.5	.7
	3.7	8.7	3.5					2.8	3.9
	1.0	1.2	1.2				Quick	(133) 1.2	1.0
	.6	.5	.5					.3	.4
	0 UND	0 UND	0 UND					0 UND	0 UND
	10 35.7	6 58.6	16 22.7				Sales/Receivables	8 46.1	9 38.9
	26 14.3	22 16.4	30 12.0					23 15.9	24 15.0
							Cost of Sales/Inventory		
							Cost of Sales/Payables		
	10.0	9.1	8.5					13.2	11.6
	66.6	88.8	20.2				Sales/Working Capital	49.8	38.3
	-28.1	-41.1	-25.1					-17.3	-34.4
	7.5	14.4	19.8					14.7	13.6
	(30) 4.5	(41) 2.5	(32) 5.7				EBIT/Interest	(116) 4.2	(105) 6.6
	1.0	.4	1.2					.9	2.3
							Net Profit + Depr., Dep., Amort./Cur. Mat. L/T/D		
	.5	1.2	.6					.9	.7
	3.2	4.9	1.8				Fixed/Worth	3.5	2.5
	-1.7	-6.0	122.1					-4.4	-5.3
	1.7	1.1	.9					1.1	1.1
	6.5	7.4	1.7				Debt/Worth	4.1	3.6
	-3.2	-8.3	203.5					-5.3	-9.1
	128.1	93.9	79.9				% Profit Before Taxes/Tangible	84.2	109.8
	(24) 56.2	(32) 31.9	(29) 30.5				Net Worth	(88) 39.4	(86) 37.9
	6.6	10.3	11.6					10.1	10.0
	50.8	33.7	27.2				% Profit Before Taxes/Total	28.9	29.3
	9.4	6.5	13.8				Assets	9.6	11.6
	-.1	-.9	1.8					.1	3.0
	43.3	8.1	6.8					11.7	16.1
	15.2	4.3	3.7				Sales/Net Fixed Assets	5.0	7.1
	4.3	2.2	1.7					2.5	2.9
	7.5	3.9	2.8					4.1	4.3
	3.6	2.5	1.7				Sales/Total Assets	2.4	2.6
	2.7	1.2	.9					1.6	1.6
	1.4	5.2	3.8					3.7	2.2
	(23) 6.5	(29) 7.8	(24) 7.5				% Depr., Dep., Amort./Sales	(81) 7.2	(78) 5.5
	10.1	15.1	12.5					10.0	8.7
	5.5	2.2	2.1				% Officers', Directors'	2.6	2.3
	(20) 6.8	(22) 3.5	(10) 2.8				Owners' Comp/Sales	(72) 5.2	(71) 4.7
	11.2	6.1	3.4					9.9	10.1
	40671M	185142M	275197M	203470M		314626M	Net Sales ($)	950461M	1854585M
	10510M	58036M	144969M	195170M		503166M	Total Assets ($)	545488M	929132M

M = $ thousand   MM = $ million
See Pages viii through xx for Explanation of Ratios and Data

Comparative Historical Data　　　　　　　　　　Current Data Sorted by Sales

			Type of Statement						
1	3	3	Unqualified					1	3
3	5	4	Reviewed				2	1	1
20	17	6	Compiled		3	1	4	2	
46	48	58	Tax Returns	19	24	10	17		
55	59	64	Other	10	16	9		8	4
4/1/16-3/31/17 ALL	4/1/17-3/31/18 ALL	4/1/18-3/31/19 ALL		0-1MM	1-3MM	3-5MM	5-10MM	10-25MM	25MM & OVER
					21 (4/1-9/30/18)		114 (10/1/18-3/31/19)		
125	132	135	**NUMBER OF STATEMENTS**	29	43	20	23	12	8
%	%	%	**ASSETS**	%	%	%	%	%	%
14.7	15.2	18.2	Cash & Equivalents	20.6	18.8	19.5	16.5	15.1	
10.7	9.4	11.9	Trade Receivables (net)	13.1	7.4	14.9	16.1	12.4	
3.6	3.5	2.5	Inventory	4.6	.7	.7	2.8	8.6	
3.5	2.4	2.4	All Other Current	2.1	3.8	3.1	.8	.8	
32.6	30.4	35.1	Total Current	40.4	30.7	38.1	36.2	36.8	
52.9	57.1	49.4	Fixed Assets (net)	41.8	58.6	43.2	48.8	47.8	
5.2	6.5	6.6	Intangibles (net)	3.8	3.6	9.9	6.2	8.6	
9.4	5.9	8.9	All Other Non-Current	13.9	7.1	8.8	8.9	6.8	
100.0	100.0	100.0	Total	100.0	100.0	100.0	100.0	100.0	
			LIABILITIES						
6.7	8.9	7.7	Notes Payable-Short Term	7.5	9.3	4.1	7.5	10.6	
7.6	7.5	10.3	Cur. Mat.-L.T.D.	11.4	11.8	9.6	7.2	9.2	
5.0	3.7	3.7	Trade Payables	4.2	3.6	2.5	3.2	6.3	
.1	.2	.1	Income Taxes Payable	.0	.2	.1	.0	.3	
12.3	8.5	6.7	All Other Current	11.9	3.6	8.1	5.8	3.5	
31.7	28.8	28.5	Total Current	35.1	28.4	24.3	23.7	29.9	
48.7	50.7	49.8	Long-Term Debt	47.4	58.7	52.9	42.9	40.8	
.2	.1	.2	Deferred Taxes	.0	.0	.0	.1	.5	
8.5	12.5	5.8	All Other Non-Current	15.1	1.3	3.0	8.5	1.7	
10.9	8.0	15.7	Net Worth	2.3	11.6	19.9	24.8	27.1	
100.0	100.0	100.0	Total Liabilities & Net Worth	100.0	100.0	100.0	100.0	100.0	
			INCOME DATA						
100.0	100.0	100.0	Net Sales	100.0	100.0	100.0	100.0	100.0	
			Gross Profit						
93.5	92.1	90.9	Operating Expenses	87.1	90.1	95.6	90.4	92.2	
6.5	7.9	9.1	Operating Profit	12.9	9.9	4.4	9.6	7.8	
.5	1.2	1.1	All Other Expenses (net)	1.9	1.1	-.1	1.6	.7	
6.1	6.7	8.0	Profit Before Taxes	11.0	8.8	4.5	8.0	7.1	
			RATIOS						
3.9	3.3	4.7		3.7	8.0	7.6	4.1	1.5	
1.3	1.3	1.3	Current	1.8	2.0	1.2	1.7	1.0	
.6	.6	.7		.5	.7	.8	.8	.5	
2.5	2.8	4.1		3.4	7.5	7.1	3.5	1.2	
.9	1.0	1.2	Quick	1.0	1.7	1.2	1.7	.7	
.4	.4	.5		.4	.5	.7	.8	.4	
0 UND	0 UND	0 UND		0 UND	0 UND	0 UND	6 59.9	0 UND	
9 40.2	8 45.7	10 35.7	Sales/Receivables	0 UND	6 57.4	15 23.7	20 18.7	1 392.3	
27 13.7	24 15.2	27 13.6		24 15.4	22 16.5	30 12.2	30 12.0	28 13.1	
			Cost of Sales/Inventory						
			Cost of Sales/Payables						
10.6	10.8	9.0		9.0	9.2	8.2	8.3	11.2	
63.8	41.5	66.6	Sales/Working Capital	66.6	23.1	82.3	11.8	NM	
-26.3	-19.4	-27.8		-22.7	-27.7	-59.4	-58.9	-19.8	
15.9	11.2	10.5		7.1	9.3	4.2	28.2	17.3	
(108) 4.1	(114) 5.0	(113) 3.7	EBIT/Interest	(19) 4.1	(35) 2.7	(19) 2.2	11.6	7.4	
1.5	1.3	1.0		1.0	.5	.4	1.0	2.8	
			Net Profit + Depr., Dep., Amort./Cur. Mat. L/T/D						
1.0	1.1	.7		.5	1.1	1.1	.7	.5	
3.3	2.8	3.0	Fixed/Worth	3.3	3.2	6.5	2.0	1.5	
-3.9	-3.6	-6.2		-1.7	-9.1	-3.5	237.4	NM	
1.1	1.0	1.0		.6	.9	1.3	1.3	.9	
4.4	4.5	4.4	Debt/Worth	5.8	4.4	10.2	2.8	2.5	
-7.3	-5.5	-8.6		-3.4	-8.9	-5.3	675.5	NM	
83.7	99.8	92.2		120.2	82.7	74.0	410.0		
(78) 36.7	(85) 41.4	(93) 31.6	% Profit Before Taxes/Tangible Net Worth	(18) 39.3	(30) 27.8	(13) 23.7	(18) 56.0		
14.7	12.5	10.0		-.1	8.4	5.9	16.1		
27.5	27.9	27.5		54.8	26.7	13.7	39.5	24.1	
10.5	10.7	9.4	% Profit Before Taxes/Total Assets	6.9	8.5	5.3	22.2	12.5	
1.8	1.4	.1		-.1	.0	-.7	.1	7.3	
12.0	10.3	18.1		30.8	8.9	14.9	18.1	66.5	
4.0	4.2	4.5	Sales/Net Fixed Assets	6.2	4.1	5.0	5.4	4.3	
2.6	2.3	1.8		2.1	1.3	3.7	3.2	1.7	
3.9	4.0	3.9		4.3	3.6	4.0	3.9	4.4	
2.5	2.3	2.5	Sales/Total Assets	2.8	2.5	2.4	2.9	1.7	
1.5	1.4	1.2		1.2	1.0	1.3	2.0	1.3	
2.8	2.8	4.3		1.4	7.0	4.9	2.3		
(84) 7.8	(85) 7.8	(83) 7.7	% Depr., Dep., Amort./Sales	(19) 5.4	(24) 12.9	(12) 7.0	(16) 6.5		
12.6	11.9	13.0		9.6	17.8	8.4	12.5		
1.7	2.3	2.6		5.1	3.1	1.9			
(58) 4.3	(62) 4.3	(53) 4.1	% Officers', Directors' Owners' Comp/Sales	(10) 10.1	(19) 5.5	(12) 3.4			
7.9	7.8	7.2		12.0	7.2	5.6			
890658M	2538866M	1019106M	Net Sales ($)	16305M	76242M	75310M	162205M	189501M	499543M
445554M	1059554M	911851M	Total Assets ($)	12056M	54271M	40007M	67777M	108000M	629740M

M = $ thousand　　MM = $ million
See Pages viii through xx for Explanation of Ratios and Data

	Current Data Sorted by Assets						Type of Statement	Comparative Historical Data	
			2	4	1	3	Unqualified	12	13
		1	1	4	1	1	Reviewed	13	13
		2	4	1			Compiled	13	6
	11	5	2				Tax Returns	36	43
	7	10	12	5	3	3	Other	36	49
		8 (4/1-9/30/18)		75 (10/1/18-3/31/19)				4/1/14-3/31/15	4/1/15-3/31/16
	0-500M	500M-2MM	2-10MM	10-50MM	50-100MM	100-250MM		ALL	ALL
	18	18	21	14	5	7	NUMBER OF STATEMENTS	110	124
	%	%	%	%	%	%	ASSETS	%	%
	38.0	14.6	16.4	8.5			Cash & Equivalents	15.7	16.1
	8.4	28.7	30.7	29.7			Trade Receivables (net)	26.3	21.1
	10.1	3.1	2.2	1.6			Inventory	6.0	7.0
	4.0	5.9	5.2	2.3			All Other Current	3.9	4.0
	60.5	52.3	54.5	42.1			Total Current	52.0	48.2
	23.4	30.9	38.4	40.8			Fixed Assets (net)	30.6	37.8
	.1	5.4	3.1	10.7			Intangibles (net)	6.8	7.9
	16.0	11.3	4.1	6.4			All Other Non-Current	10.6	6.1
	100.0	100.0	100.0	100.0			Total	100.0	100.0
							LIABILITIES		
	45.4	5.8	5.4	10.6			Notes Payable-Short Term	9.4	7.2
	2.0	2.2	6.3	9.6			Cur. Mat.-L.T.D.	4.4	5.0
	4.0	12.6	13.7	12.6			Trade Payables	10.0	9.4
	.1	.0	.1	.0			Income Taxes Payable	.1	.6
	24.3	3.7	4.6	4.9			All Other Current	10.6	10.9
	75.8	24.4	30.2	37.7			Total Current	34.6	33.0
	45.1	27.0	30.3	24.1			Long-Term Debt	22.4	27.3
	.0	.5	.3	.0			Deferred Taxes	.1	.2
	4.9	15.5	1.9	1.6			All Other Non-Current	12.0	6.3
	-25.8	32.6	37.3	36.6			Net Worth	31.0	33.2
	100.0	100.0	100.0	100.0			Total Liabilities & Net Worth	100.0	100.0
							INCOME DATA		
	100.0	100.0	100.0	100.0			Net Sales	100.0	100.0
							Gross Profit		
	92.1	91.8	91.3	95.9			Operating Expenses	89.3	89.3
	7.9	8.2	8.7	4.1			Operating Profit	10.7	10.7
	.6	1.2	1.9	.5			All Other Expenses (net)	1.8	1.3
	7.3	7.1	6.8	3.5			Profit Before Taxes	8.9	9.4
							RATIOS		
	5.4	7.3	2.4	1.8				3.2	3.1
	1.0	2.3	1.8	1.3			Current	1.6	1.7
	.5	1.3	1.3	.7				.9	.8
	4.0	6.0	2.3	1.6				2.9	2.3
	.8	1.8	1.7	1.3			Quick	1.1	1.2
	.4	.8	.8	.6				.5	.5
	0 UND	8 46.7	24 15.1	25 14.7				3 139.0	3 138.9
	0 UND	35 10.5	46 7.9	47 7.7			Sales/Receivables	26 13.9	22 16.7
	0 UND	49 7.5	73 5.0	58 6.3				47 7.7	45 8.1
							Cost of Sales/Inventory		
							Cost of Sales/Payables		
	13.6	6.4	5.7	11.4				5.5	5.8
	NM	10.8	9.4	25.3			Sales/Working Capital	16.6	18.3
	-27.5	NM	20.8	-13.3				-58.5	-35.0
	67.8	48.6	19.8	7.5				27.4	17.9
	(12) 12.0	(15) 13.2	(16) 8.9	(13) 2.7			EBIT/Interest	(86) 6.6	(106) 7.4
	3.5	2.6	2.7	1.0				3.8	2.6
							Net Profit + Depr., Dep., Amort./Cur. Mat. L/T/D	7.1	6.2
								(13) 2.2	(15) 2.4
								1.0	1.2
	.0	.3	.3	.4				.1	.3
	1.7	.9	1.1	1.6			Fixed/Worth	.7	.9
	-1.5	UND	5.7	3.6				2.6	4.1
	.8	.5	.9	1.4				.5	.7
	6.7	1.3	1.9	1.7			Debt/Worth	1.8	1.9
	-2.9	UND	7.3	5.3				6.3	7.7
	233.4	105.5	103.4	48.4			% Profit Before Taxes/Tangible Net Worth	62.8	60.9
	(12) 58.3	(14) 52.1	33.4	(12) 20.0				(93) 40.7	(102) 30.1
	6.4	15.1	23.3	-.2				16.8	12.7
	90.0	30.2	18.1	11.8			% Profit Before Taxes/Total Assets	25.2	21.1
	15.7	16.7	12.2	5.2				12.3	9.1
	4.0	2.3	5.3	.0				4.1	2.8
	UND	UND	26.8	48.2			Sales/Net Fixed Assets	183.9	38.4
	75.5	19.5	6.6	6.0				13.5	6.2
	18.4	5.0	2.1	2.6				3.5	2.9
	17.8	4.3	3.2	3.4			Sales/Total Assets	4.6	3.8
	10.9	3.1	2.1	1.9				2.4	2.2
	4.0	1.7	1.1	1.3				1.4	1.3
			1.7	.9			% Depr., Dep., Amort./Sales	1.0	1.9
		(19) 3.9	(13) 3.6					(77) 3.5	(87) 4.1
		12.1	7.1					7.1	8.5
	1.7						% Officers', Directors' Owners' Comp/Sales	1.1	1.1
	(10) 3.6							(49) 3.4	(55) 3.2
	7.7							6.7	7.8
	43290M	76960M	286801M	953457M	785332M	2050927M	Net Sales ($)	2774883M	2175947M
	3474M	20782M	125514M	370028M	369156M	1036451M	Total Assets ($)	1696304M	1834809M

M = $ thousand   MM = $ million
See Pages viii through xx for Explanation of Ratios and Data

Comparative Historical Data			Type of Statement	Current Data Sorted by Sales					
8	9	10	Unqualified				1	1	9
7	12	8	Reviewed				2	1	5
13	9	7	Compiled			2		4	1
26	20	18	Tax Returns	7	5		3	3	7
33	39	40	Other	4	9	6	4	10	7
4/1/16-3/31/17 ALL	4/1/17-3/31/18 ALL	4/1/18-3/31/19 ALL		0-1MM	8 (4/1-9/30/18) 1-3MM	3-5MM	75 (10/1/18-3/31/19) 5-10MM	10-25MM	25MM & OVER
87	89	83	NUMBER OF STATEMENTS	11	14	8	10	18	22
%	%	%	ASSETS	%	%	%	%	%	%
19.0	20.9	19.0	Cash & Equivalents	34.2	26.5		14.5	15.8	14.4
18.4	22.5	23.5	Trade Receivables (net)	4.5	18.2		21.7	34.7	27.7
6.3	3.9	4.1	Inventory	15.1	2.0		1.5	1.9	2.3
3.8	5.2	4.3	All Other Current	2.5	1.9		1.8	3.9	4.1
47.6	52.4	50.9	Total Current	56.3	48.6		39.5	56.3	48.6
37.8	32.3	33.7	Fixed Assets (net)	37.1	35.9		37.0	32.5	30.8
5.0	7.7	5.5	Intangibles (net)	.1	.8		16.9	2.5	10.2
9.5	7.6	9.9	All Other Non-Current	6.4	14.7		6.6	8.7	10.5
100.0	100.0	100.0	Total	100.0	100.0		100.0	100.0	100.0
			LIABILITIES						
11.5	9.4	14.5	Notes Payable-Short Term	45.7	19.1		12.1	2.4	8.6
8.0	8.7	5.3	Cur. Mat.-L.T.D.	2.6	2.6		4.0	6.3	9.3
7.6	12.3	11.7	Trade Payables	2.3	3.6		12.6	20.0	15.0
1.0	.6	.6	Income Taxes Payable	.1	.0		.1	2.6	.2
7.6	11.0	9.1	All Other Current	27.3	10.8		2.3	3.6	7.3
35.7	42.0	41.2	Total Current	78.0	36.0		31.2	34.9	40.5
29.6	25.2	31.1	Long-Term Debt	78.1	27.2		17.4	21.7	25.8
.2	.2	.2	Deferred Taxes	.0	.0		.8	.1	.4
6.9	8.3	6.5	All Other Non-Current	.0	13.1		9.9	2.1	5.4
27.7	24.4	21.0	Net Worth	-56.2	23.7		40.8	41.2	28.0
100.0	100.0	100.0	Total Liabilities & Net Worth	100.0	100.0		100.0	100.0	100.0
			INCOME DATA						
100.0	100.0	100.0	Net Sales	100.0	100.0		100.0	100.0	100.0
			Gross Profit						
89.2	89.6	91.6	Operating Expenses	88.2	89.0		91.6	95.2	92.3
10.8	10.4	8.4	Operating Profit	11.8	11.0		8.4	4.8	7.7
1.8	2.3	1.1	All Other Expenses (net)	1.2	3.0		1.2	.1	.9
8.9	8.1	7.3	Profit Before Taxes	10.6	8.0		7.2	4.7	6.8
			RATIOS						
4.7	2.9	2.7		7.6	5.0		2.8	2.8	1.8
1.3	1.3	1.5	Current	.7	1.9		1.4	1.8	1.3
.6	.9	.8		.4	.9		.7	1.0	.8
3.1	2.1	2.5		3.8	4.9		2.7	2.6	1.6
1.0	1.1	1.4	Quick	.6	1.6		1.4	1.7	1.2
.4	.4	.6		.4	.7		.6	.9	.5
1 292.1	0 UND	1 251.3		0 UND	0 UND		0 UND	25 14.8	18 19.8
23 15.8	24 15.2	27 13.5	Sales/Receivables	0 UND	14 26.3		17 21.9	53 6.9	31 11.9
42 8.7	48 7.6	55 6.6		1 251.3	49 7.5		40 9.1	72 5.1	51 7.1
			Cost of Sales/Inventory						
			Cost of Sales/Payables						
6.0	7.2	7.3		5.2	7.9		4.5	7.0	12.1
22.2	26.9	19.7	Sales/Working Capital	-116.0	14.5		192.5	13.3	25.3
-12.2	-56.9	-67.8		-22.7	NM		-9.1	148.3	-53.7
20.2	23.0	22.8			112.1			21.3	11.3
(73) 5.1	(66) 8.8	(65) 5.2	EBIT/Interest		(10) 10.5			(15) 8.7	(18) 3.6
1.4	2.4	2.5			2.5			2.7	2.0
3.1	6.0	8.6							
(10) 2.0	(11) 3.0	(10) 2.1	Net Profit + Depr., Dep., Amort./Cur. Mat. L/T/D						
1.4	1.7	1.1							
.3	.1	.2		.0	.1		.3	.3	.0
1.2	.9	1.1	Fixed/Worth	2.8	1.3		3.4	1.1	.9
7.6	2.4	4.8		-1.3	NM		NM	1.7	6.1
.8	.8	.9		2.0	.7		.5	1.3	1.1
1.8	2.0	2.0	Debt/Worth	10.8	1.3		5.4	1.7	2.1
27.7	8.6	18.2		-2.4	NM		NM	2.8	NM
45.1	76.7	77.4			90.8			52.6	56.2
(70) 25.9	(77) 37.7	(68) 30.4	% Profit Before Taxes/Tangible Net Worth		(11) 53.2			(17) 24.2	32.3
2.9	14.3	15.1			17.2			12.4	18.1
24.0	28.7	24.4		101.3	44.3		16.2	14.9	20.3
9.1	12.5	9.6	% Profit Before Taxes/Total Assets	9.6	23.1		7.1	8.7	8.2
1.0	3.4	4.2		.7	4.0		3.0	1.4	4.2
32.8	97.7	74.4		UND	42.9		UND	48.9	197.4
5.2	10.7	13.4	Sales/Net Fixed Assets	17.1	20.5		28.8	7.4	9.3
2.0	3.3	2.9		1.2	2.1		1.8	2.8	5.2
3.2	4.4	4.6		5.6	12.0		6.9	3.2	3.7
2.0	2.2	2.9	Sales/Total Assets	4.3	2.5		3.1	2.2	2.9
.9	1.2	1.5		1.0	1.6		.3	1.7	1.4
1.6	.9	.9						2.3	.1
(60) 4.2	(51) 3.9	(53) 3.2	% Depr., Dep., Amort./Sales					(15) 3.9	(17) 1.7
8.5	10.0	7.0						6.6	3.6
1.6	1.2	.7							
(31) 4.2	(28) 4.2	(29) 2.1	% Officers', Directors' Owners' Comp/Sales						
10.8	7.9	6.1							
1620459M	2481308M	4196767M	Net Sales ($)	6611M	25234M	32466M	65264M	285267M	3781925M
1497414M	1810667M	1925405M	Total Assets ($)	8578M	11101M	16792M	173042M	174681M	1541211M

M = $ thousand   MM = $ million
See Pages viii through xx for Explanation of Ratios and Data

Current Data Sorted by Assets   Comparative Historical Data

0-500M	500M-2MM	2-10MM	10-50MM	50-100MM	100-250MM		4/1/14-3/31/15 ALL	4/1/15-3/31/16 ALL
	1	4	21	8	4	Type of Statement		
						Unqualified	39	29
2	5	28	35	3	4	Reviewed	85	85
5	17	45	8	1		Compiled	87	69
20	31	29	2			Tax Returns	135	134
18	54	117	73	25	15	Other	305	306
	77 (4/1-9/30/18)		498 (10/1/18-3/31/19)					
45	108	223	139	37	23	**NUMBER OF STATEMENTS**	651	623
%	%	%	%	%	%	**ASSETS**	%	%
20.5	16.3	13.8	9.8	8.5	16.5	Cash & Equivalents	14.8	14.8
33.5	47.7	52.1	51.7	41.6	33.8	Trade Receivables (net)	46.4	46.9
.3	1.6	1.1	.6	1.3	3.3	Inventory	1.1	.8
11.3	6.8	3.7	4.9	3.7	4.6	All Other Current	4.2	4.7
65.6	72.4	70.7	67.0	55.0	58.2	Total Current	66.5	67.1
16.9	16.3	17.7	22.8	24.9	22.7	Fixed Assets (net)	20.3	20.5
8.8	4.2	4.5	3.2	10.1	15.2	Intangibles (net)	4.9	5.4
8.7	7.2	7.1	7.0	10.0	3.9	All Other Non-Current	8.3	7.0
100.0	100.0	100.0	100.0	100.0	100.0	Total	100.0	100.0
						LIABILITIES		
13.3	8.1	9.7	9.7	7.9	6.8	Notes Payable-Short Term	9.4	9.5
1.6	2.3	3.4	4.0	4.1	3.4	Cur. Mat.-L.T.D.	2.9	2.9
27.3	28.2	29.1	28.3	24.5	23.2	Trade Payables	27.4	26.4
.6	.1	.2	.3	.1	.1	Income Taxes Payable	.2	.1
38.6	8.9	9.1	10.4	11.1	9.7	All Other Current	11.6	13.0
81.5	47.6	51.5	52.7	47.6	43.1	Total Current	51.5	51.9
10.4	17.0	14.2	13.5	14.2	20.6	Long-Term Debt	13.1	13.8
.2	.1	.1	.2	.8	1.4	Deferred Taxes	.3	.2
4.0	3.5	1.7	3.2	1.7	6.2	All Other Non-Current	5.4	4.6
4.0	31.8	32.6	30.4	35.7	28.7	Net Worth	29.6	29.4
100.0	100.0	100.0	100.0	100.0	100.0	Total Liabilities & Net Worth	100.0	100.0
						INCOME DATA		
100.0	100.0	100.0	100.0	100.0	100.0	Net Sales	100.0	100.0
						Gross Profit		
98.1	94.1	93.1	95.6	95.1	96.6	Operating Expenses	94.4	94.7
1.9	5.9	6.9	4.4	4.9	3.4	Operating Profit	5.6	5.3
-.1	1.3	1.2	.5	.0	.4	All Other Expenses (net)	1.1	.9
1.9	4.7	5.7	3.9	4.9	3.0	Profit Before Taxes	4.5	4.4
						RATIOS		
2.4	2.9	2.0	1.8	1.8	1.8		2.1	2.1
1.1	1.5	1.4	1.2	1.3	1.4	Current	1.3	1.3
.5	1.0	1.0	1.0	.9	1.1		.9	1.0
2.3	2.7	1.9	1.5	1.8	1.5		1.9	1.9
.9	1.3	1.3	1.2	1.1	1.2	Quick	1.2	1.2
.4	.9	.9	.9	.8	.5		.8	.9
0 UND	17 20.9	27 13.7	36 10.1	37 9.9	40 9.2		22 16.6	24 15.4
8 44.2	31 11.6	38 9.5	46 7.9	51 7.1	53 6.9	Sales/Receivables	38 9.6	38 9.6
30 12.3	46 8.0	56 6.5	65 5.6	62 5.9	72 5.1		54 6.8	52 7.0
						Cost of Sales/Inventory		
						Cost of Sales/Payables		
27.5	8.3	13.2	10.4	11.5	5.3		11.9	11.7
178.4	27.8	22.1	31.8	24.3	14.9	Sales/Working Capital	29.7	31.1
-26.6	-417.0	269.1	-271.8	-53.7	25.4		-149.9	-228.5
15.5	32.6	47.0	25.2	17.8	8.1		31.9	36.7
(22) 5.3	(71) 10.5	(174) 11.3	(120) 8.9	(32) 7.7	(20) 4.5	EBIT/Interest	(474) 8.7	(474) 8.7
.4	3.9	3.3	2.7	3.1	.6		3.1	2.7
		9.5	15.1	3.6			12.3	11.9
	(28) 3.9	(38) 4.9	(10) 1.7			Net Profit + Depr., Dep., Amort./Cur. Mat. L/T/D	(76) 4.5	(78) 2.8
		1.2	1.0	.8			1.4	1.3
.0	.0	.0	.1	.2	.2		.1	.1
.3	.2	.2	.6	1.2	1.0	Fixed/Worth	.4	.5
-2.2	1.8	1.6	1.9	5.0	-.7		3.0	2.6
.7	.6	.9	1.2	.9	1.4		1.0	1.1
7.0	2.1	2.3	2.7	2.6	5.0	Debt/Worth	2.7	2.5
-3.4	19.0	9.4	8.4	28.6	-7.0		13.1	10.3
115.2	119.8	71.9	78.0	57.4	55.5		71.7	76.3
(27) 59.1	(88) 50.9	(184) 36.3	(125) 37.2	(30) 23.4	(17) 25.1	% Profit Before Taxes/Tangible Net Worth	(533) 35.4	(522) 37.3
7.8	17.0	15.2	16.6	14.0	7.9		14.6	11.8
41.9	32.8	26.1	18.8	14.1	8.8		21.3	22.2
19.3	13.7	10.4	7.9	7.4	6.1	% Profit Before Taxes/Total Assets	9.3	9.3
.0	4.3	4.4	3.2	5.3	.4		2.7	2.7
UND	984.3	596.3	186.0	72.9	196.6		367.0	330.3
378.5	141.3	98.6	35.5	23.1	42.0	Sales/Net Fixed Assets	65.1	65.8
54.4	33.7	16.2	5.9	4.4	1.9		10.7	11.7
18.4	7.8	6.8	5.6	4.3	3.1		6.9	7.3
8.6	5.4	4.6	3.4	2.6	1.6	Sales/Total Assets	4.4	4.4
4.5	3.5	2.8	2.1	1.3	.9		2.4	2.4
.4	.1	.1	.2	.4	.2		.2	.2
(16) .8	(59) .3	(153) .4	(119) .7	(31) 1.2	(13) .9	% Depr., Dep., Amort./Sales	(445) .6	(424) .6
3.9	1.8	2.6	2.6	3.5	4.8		2.8	2.6
1.7	.9	.7	.7				1.1	1.1
(17) 4.6	(36) 2.3	(68) 1.3	(21) 1.3			% Officers', Directors' Owners' Comp/Sales	(196) 2.0	(188) 2.4
7.7	3.7	2.4	2.1				4.3	4.8
141504M	776879M	5585696M	11631515M	7671537M	6777328M	Net Sales ($)	33445369M	31719328M
12523M	125929M	1104635M	3163744M	2561699M	3323357M	Total Assets ($)	10586246M	9664966M

© RMA 2019

M = $ thousand   MM = $ million
See Pages viii through xx for Explanation of Ratios and Data

Comparative Historical Data | Current Data Sorted by Sales

4/1/16-3/31/17	4/1/17-3/31/18	4/1/18-3/31/19	Type of Statement	0-1MM	1-3MM	3-5MM	5-10MM	10-25MM	25MM & OVER
30	37	38	Unqualified		1		2	2	33
68	83	77	Reviewed	1	1	4	3	15	53
61	63	76	Compiled	2	9	3	10	23	29
98	91	82	Tax Returns	10	17	8	20	23	4
275	279	302	Other	9	23	18	31	70	151
ALL	ALL	ALL		77 (4/1-9/30/18)			498 (10/1/18-3/31/19)		
532	553	575	NUMBER OF STATEMENTS	22	51	33	66	133	270
%	%	%	ASSETS	%	%	%	%	%	%
12.0	13.7	13.6	Cash & Equivalents	12.7	18.6	22.1	13.0	15.9	10.7
47.5	48.0	48.3	Trade Receivables (net)	7.6	28.3	48.0	50.2	49.6	54.4
.8	1.2	1.1	Inventory	4.1	1.5	.2	1.0	.8	1.2
5.5	4.7	5.2	All Other Current	8.4	7.8	3.4	7.0	4.9	4.3
65.8	67.6	68.2	Total Current	32.7	56.2	73.7	71.3	71.1	70.5
20.4	20.3	19.3	Fixed Assets (net)	53.6	31.6	12.6	13.8	16.4	17.7
6.2	5.0	5.2	Intangibles (net)	6.8	5.2	5.0	2.9	6.1	5.3
7.6	7.1	7.3	All Other Non-Current	6.8	6.9	8.7	12.0	6.3	6.5
100.0	100.0	100.0	Total	100.0	100.0	100.0	100.0	100.0	100.0
			LIABILITIES						
12.4	12.2	9.4	Notes Payable-Short Term	4.4	9.2	6.4	8.9	9.7	10.3
3.4	3.4	3.2	Cur. Mat.-L.T.D.	2.5	2.8	1.4	2.0	4.1	3.5
20.8	26.9	28.1	Trade Payables	8.6	20.3	34.5	30.4	27.4	30.1
.2	.1	.2	Income Taxes Payable	.0	.0	.9	.2	.2	.3
11.8	11.1	11.8	All Other Current	11.1	21.8	15.1	9.5	10.5	10.8
54.6	53.8	52.8	Total Current	26.6	54.1	58.3	50.9	51.9	54.9
14.9	14.8	14.5	Long-Term Debt	30.6	33.0	11.8	11.5	12.8	11.6
.3	.2	.2	Deferred Taxes	.0	.2	.2	.2	.1	.4
4.0	2.8	2.7	All Other Non-Current	7.0	4.3	6.1	1.2	1.2	2.8
26.3	28.4	29.7	Net Worth	35.8	8.5	23.7	36.2	34.0	30.2
100.0	100.0	100.0	Total Liabilities & Net Worth	100.0	100.0	100.0	100.0	100.0	100.0
			INCOME DATA						
100.0	100.0	100.0	Net Sales	100.0	100.0	100.0	100.0	100.0	100.0
			Gross Profit						
95.1	94.7	94.5	Operating Expenses	64.0	92.3	94.7	95.0	96.0	96.6
4.9	5.3	5.5	Operating Profit	36.0	7.7	5.3	5.0	4.0	3.4
.8	1.0	.8	All Other Expenses (net)	13.3	2.8	-1.0	.3	.0	.2
4.1	4.3	4.6	Profit Before Taxes	22.7	4.9	6.3	4.7	3.9	3.2
			RATIOS						
1.9	2.0	2.1	Current	7.5	3.4	3.6	2.4	2.2	1.8
1.3	1.3	1.3		1.0	1.2	2.3	1.4	1.4	1.3
.9	1.0	1.0		.3	.6	1.2	1.0	1.0	1.0
1.7	1.8	1.9	Quick	5.7	3.0	3.5	2.2	2.0	1.7
1.1	1.2	1.2		.7	1.0	2.1	1.2	1.3	1.2
.8	.8	.9		.2	.5	1.2	.9	1.0	.9
27 13.5	23 15.8	26 14.2	Sales/Receivables	0 UND	0 UND	20 17.9	22 16.9	26 14.2	33 11.0
40 9.1	40 9.2	40 9.1		0 UND	24 15.0	48 7.6	45 8.1	35 10.4	42 8.6
59 6.2	60 6.1	56 6.5		24 14.9	44 8.3	69 5.3	78 4.7	51 7.2	57 6.4
			Cost of Sales/Inventory						
			Cost of Sales/Payables						
12.6	11.1	11.4	Sales/Working Capital	3.5	6.4	6.1	9.2	11.7	14.4
37.6	30.9	26.7		NM	81.5	9.9	27.8	24.6	27.8
-70.7	-140.5	-282.9		-3.1	-12.2	58.7	NM	190.5	-653.4
29.2	30.3	28.0	EBIT/Interest		17.2	19.0	30.1	62.4	27.0
(422) 6.5	(421) 6.9	(439) 9.1			(26) 3.8	(16) 9.0	(50) 9.2	(107) 11.4	(232) 9.3
2.1	2.2	2.9			-.7	3.4	3.2	3.8	2.9
8.6	13.1	9.5	Net Profit + Depr., Dep., Amort./Cur. Mat. L/T/D					19.5	11.0
(60) 2.7	(70) 3.3	(85) 3.5						(12) 4.7	(59) 3.6
1.3	1.1	1.0						1.2	1.0
.1	.1	.0	Fixed/Worth	.0	.1	.0	.0	.0	.1
.5	.4	.3		1.3	3.3	.0	.2	.2	.4
3.4	2.4	2.8		6.4	-7.5	.6	.9	1.3	2.7
1.2	1.0	1.0	Debt/Worth	.2	2.1	.5	.6	.9	1.1
3.2	2.7	2.5		2.2	4.9	1.1	1.1	2.0	2.9
14.7	12.1	12.3		-31.8	-19.9	NM	12.0	9.2	10.6
70.9	76.8	78.5	% Profit Before Taxes/Tangible Net Worth	22.0	97.5	56.7	82.9	68.2	83.4
(433) 32.9	(460) 36.1	(471) 37.3		(16) 10.4	(35) 24.3	(25) 32.3	(56) 34.8	(112) 41.3	(227) 41.4
11.3	12.7	14.4		7.3	2.0	5.5	12.0	17.4	17.4
18.8	20.5	23.8	% Profit Before Taxes/Total Assets	9.6	27.7	26.0	27.5	28.4	20.6
8.4	8.8	9.7		4.7	7.5	9.3	11.9	12.0	9.1
2.0	2.7	4.0		.3	-3.6	2.9	4.6	4.7	4.2
220.4	335.2	388.6	Sales/Net Fixed Assets	UND	370.0	UND	779.0	766.3	318.4
53.7	61.0	80.2		2.0	44.4	126.8	89.4	96.0	76.7
10.3	11.3	12.4		.1	6.1	13.9	24.9	17.0	14.8
6.2	6.6	6.7	Sales/Total Assets	3.0	5.7	7.7	6.9	7.4	6.8
4.1	4.4	4.3		.2	3.6	4.3	4.2	4.8	4.6
2.1	2.3	2.4		.1	1.9	1.8	2.0	3.2	2.5
.2	.2	.2	% Depr., Dep., Amort./Sales	10.1	.3	.3	.2	.2	.2
(371) .6	(367) .6	(391) .6		(10) 16.4	(31) 2.5	(14) .6	(46) .5	(81) .6	(209) .5
2.7	2.6	2.7		22.6	6.4	1.8	2.0	2.0	1.7
.9	.9	.8	% Officers', Directors' Owners' Comp/Sales		1.8	.9	1.1	.8	.6
(151) 2.1	(158) 1.6	(144) 1.5			(16) 4.7	(10) 4.2	(28) 3.1	(41) 1.4	(48) 1.0
4.8	5.3	3.7			9.8	6.2	5.3	2.2	1.8
25425221M	27733707M	32584459M	Net Sales ($)	10862M	99162M	132255M	467656M	2185558M	29688966M
8086194M	9469058M	10291887M	Total Assets ($)	37322M	79823M	52567M	188483M	767557M	9166135M

© RMA 2019

M = $ thousand   MM = $ million
See Pages viii through xx for Explanation of Ratios and Data

Current Data Sorted by Assets | Comparative Historical Data

						Type of Statement		
						Unqualified	5	5
						Reviewed	5	6
		1	3 3 1			Compiled	6	5
3	5	7	1	2		Tax Returns	18	14
2	4	13	11		1	Other	30	22
	4 (4/1-9/30/18)		52 (10/1/18-3/31/19)				4/1/14-3/31/15	4/1/15-3/31/16
0-500M	500M-2MM	2-10MM	10-50MM	50-100MM	100-250MM		ALL	ALL
5	9	21	18	2	1	NUMBER OF STATEMENTS	64	52
%	%	%	%	%	%	ASSETS	%	%
		12.5	9.8			Cash & Equivalents	15.1	16.2
		25.5	29.8			Trade Receivables (net)	34.5	29.9
		8.8	10.5			Inventory	8.0	11.8
		7.4	3.4			All Other Current	3.6	2.1
		54.3	53.6			Total Current	61.2	60.0
		30.7	32.0			Fixed Assets (net)	25.9	26.2
		10.6	7.5			Intangibles (net)	3.8	5.7
		4.4	7.0			All Other Non-Current	9.1	8.1
		100.0	100.0			Total	100.0	100.0
						LIABILITIES		
		5.9	11.1			Notes Payable-Short Term	10.0	6.6
		3.7	2.8			Cur. Mat.-L.T.D.	1.9	4.2
		23.7	17.5			Trade Payables	16.7	14.9
		.0	.0			Income Taxes Payable	.0	.0
		6.7	12.8			All Other Current	14.4	13.0
		40.0	44.2			Total Current	43.0	38.8
		30.1	13.4			Long-Term Debt	15.0	19.3
		.0	.0			Deferred Taxes	.0	.1
		6.0	11.4			All Other Non-Current	6.0	4.2
		23.8	31.0			Net Worth	36.0	37.6
		100.0	100.0			Total Liabilities & Net Worth	100.0	100.0
						INCOME DATA		
		100.0	100.0			Net Sales	100.0	100.0
						Gross Profit		
		93.5	98.0			Operating Expenses	90.6	89.3
		6.5	2.0			Operating Profit	9.4	10.7
		1.1	-1.1			All Other Expenses (net)	2.0	1.6
		5.4	3.0			Profit Before Taxes	7.4	9.2
						RATIOS		
		2.9	2.1				3.4	2.4
		1.7	1.2			Current	2.0	1.6
		1.0	.7				1.0	1.1
		2.1	1.6				2.8	2.0
		1.1	.8			Quick	1.4	1.3
		.6	.5				.9	.7
		13 29.0	33 11.1				24 14.9	22 16.4
		35 10.3	42 8.7			Sales/Receivables	38 9.6	36 10.2
		59 6.2	54 6.7				55 6.6	49 7.5
						Cost of Sales/Inventory		
						Cost of Sales/Payables		
		6.3	8.5				6.0	6.4
		18.0	85.1			Sales/Working Capital	11.9	17.7
		NM	-11.9				94.8	83.5
		24.6	9.5				76.5	31.0
		(17) 4.3	5.4			EBIT/Interest	(52) 12.0	(40) 9.1
		2.0	2.3				2.3	2.8
						Net Profit + Depr., Dep., Amort./Cur. Mat. L/T/D		
		.3	.3				.2	.2
		1.2	1.7			Fixed/Worth	.5	.5
		-21.2	NM				2.1	2.3
		.6	1.4				.4	.7
		2.7	2.3			Debt/Worth	1.8	2.1
		-88.0	NM				5.2	6.4
		56.1	65.5				80.6	111.5
		(15) 39.4	(14) 30.1			% Profit Before Taxes/Tangible Net Worth	(55) 32.6	(44) 56.3
		25.9	9.1				14.5	13.1
		24.9	10.6				28.5	34.6
		11.8	7.7			% Profit Before Taxes/Total Assets	14.9	15.1
		3.8	3.0				3.2	4.5
		58.5	28.2				96.1	50.2
		15.4	11.7			Sales/Net Fixed Assets	13.8	18.1
		5.0	4.0				4.8	5.4
		3.1	4.5				4.9	4.1
		2.3	2.4			Sales/Total Assets	2.9	2.9
		1.9	1.5				1.8	1.7
		.8	.6				.7	.7
		(16) 1.5	(17) 1.0			% Depr., Dep., Amort./Sales	(46) 1.5	(42) 1.7
		5.7	3.6				4.1	4.4
							1.6	1.3
						% Officers', Directors' Owners' Comp/Sales	(20) 3.5	(20) 3.4
							5.3	6.0
5727M	49623M	308243M	1047970M	159407M	250055M	Net Sales ($)	1040551M	993690M
745M	10698M	107345M	396404M	128144M	195692M	Total Assets ($)	412168M	517651M

M = $ thousand   MM = $ million
See Pages viii through xx for Explanation of Ratios and Data

Comparative Historical Data & Current Data Sorted by Sales

Type of Statement

	4/1/16-3/31/17	4/1/17-3/31/18	4/1/18-3/31/19	Type of Statement	0-1MM	1-3MM	3-5MM	5-10MM	10-25MM	25MM & OVER
Unqualified	12	2	3					1		3
Reviewed	6	8	5							5
Compiled	10	5	2							1
Tax Returns	23	15	15		2	1	4	4	3	1
Other		30	31		1	4	2	6	8	10
	ALL	ALL	ALL		0-1MM	1-3MM	3-5MM	5-10MM	10-25MM	25MM & OVER
NUMBER OF STATEMENTS	51	60	56		3	5	6	11	11	20

Dates period: 4 (4/1-9/30/18); 52 (10/1/18-3/31/19)

Hist 15-17 %	Hist 17-18 %	Hist 18-19 %		0-1MM %	1-3MM %	3-5MM %	5-10MM %	10-25MM %	25MM & OVER %
			ASSETS						
16.3	11.9	14.1	Cash & Equivalents				14.1	6.6	11.7
27.2	27.9	29.8	Trade Receivables (net)				37.8	26.6	31.3
11.4	9.2	11.2	Inventory				11.5	11.3	11.6
3.6	4.7	4.7	All Other Current				1.7	12.2	3.8
58.5	53.7	59.7	Total Current				65.1	56.7	58.4
25.5	27.4	26.8	Fixed Assets (net)				19.3	37.9	25.2
3.6	7.8	7.8	Intangibles (net)				10.7	.3	9.9
12.4	11.0	5.6	All Other Non-Current				4.9	5.1	6.5
100.0	100.0	100.0	Total				100.0	100.0	100.0
			LIABILITIES						
13.2	10.1	13.1	Notes Payable-Short Term				7.3	11.0	7.6
3.3	3.9	3.3	Cur. Mat.-L.T.D.				1.1	3.4	2.5
16.4	18.2	22.8	Trade Payables				32.9	16.2	20.2
.0	.1	.0	Income Taxes Payable				.0	.0	.0
16.5	15.6	12.0	All Other Current				3.5	16.1	10.3
49.4	48.0	51.2	Total Current				44.8	46.7	40.6
17.6	20.3	20.7	Long-Term Debt				17.8	19.5	12.6
.0	.2	.0	Deferred Taxes				.1	.0	.0
6.1	3.6	8.5	All Other Non-Current				10.6	5.5	10.0
26.9	28.0	19.6	Net Worth				26.8	28.3	36.8
100.0	100.0	100.0	Total Liabilities & Net Worth				100.0	100.0	100.0
			INCOME DATA						
100.0	100.0	100.0	Net Sales				100.0	100.0	100.0
			Gross Profit						
88.4	91.8	95.4	Operating Expenses				94.5	98.0	96.0
11.6	8.2	4.6	Operating Profit				5.5	2.0	4.0
1.5	2.8	.3	All Other Expenses (net)				.6	-.2	-.7
10.0	5.4	4.3	Profit Before Taxes				4.9	2.1	4.7
			RATIOS						
2.5 / 1.4 / .8	2.1 / 1.1 / .7	2.2 / 1.5 / .8	Current				3.0 / 2.1 / 1.0	2.1 / 1.6 / .5	2.2 / 1.5 / 1.0
1.5 / 1.0 / .6	1.7 / .8 / .5	2.0 / 1.0 / .5	Quick				2.2 / 2.0 / .5	1.7 / .9 / .3	1.5 / 1.1 / .8
4 102.9 / 33 11.1 / 49 7.5	10 35.4 / 39 9.3 / 59 6.2	18 20.6 / 39 9.3 / 55 6.6	Sales/Receivables				31 11.7 / 55 6.6 / 74 4.9	34 10.7 / 35 10.3 / 52 7.0	20 18.0 / 42 8.6 / 55 6.6
			Cost of Sales/Inventory						
			Cost of Sales/Payables						
7.9 / 20.9 / -55.2	11.1 / 66.6 / -14.6	8.1 / 17.2 / -26.9	Sales/Working Capital				6.0 / 18.0 / 138.6	6.5 / 13.0 / -4.8	8.3 / 15.9 / NM
45.1 / (40) 9.5 / 3.3	12.0 / (45) 4.1 / .8	14.6 / (47) 4.5 / 2.1	EBIT/Interest					80.3 / (10) 5.7 / -4.7	13.3 / (18) 4.6 / 3.1
			Net Profit + Depr., Dep., Amort./Cur. Mat. L/T/D						
.1 / .7 / 10.8	.2 / .8 / 11.6	.2 / 1.2 / -38.2	Fixed/Worth				.0 / 1.2 / -37.5	.2 / 1.5 / -7.7	.3 / 1.2 / 2.6
.9 / 2.5 / 21.3	.6 / 3.2 / NM	.9 / 2.7 / -52.3	Debt/Worth				.6 / 8.7 / -3.9	.7 / 2.2 / -17.4	1.0 / 2.2 / 7.2
109.8 / (40) 51.3 / 14.4	51.3 / (45) 22.0 / 3.1	59.8 / (39) 36.0 / 15.9	% Profit Before Taxes/Tangible Net Worth						74.8 / (18) 31.8 / 13.1
33.9 / 14.2 / 9.0	21.3 / 8.1 / .1	25.3 / 9.2 / 3.7	% Profit Before Taxes/Total Assets				31.6 / 11.8 / 3.6	24.1 / 11.9 / -11.1	11.0 / 8.3 / 4.8
102.5 / 29.2 / 5.6	43.9 / 16.6 / 4.6	57.1 / 18.5 / 5.6	Sales/Net Fixed Assets				708.0 / 55.5 / 5.7	16.0 / 8.8 / 3.5	31.9 / 20.5 / 6.4
5.5 / 3.0 / 1.7	3.5 / 2.2 / 1.3	4.9 / 2.8 / 1.6	Sales/Total Assets				3.0 / 2.3 / 1.8	3.2 / 2.2 / 1.6	5.0 / 3.2 / 1.4
.4 / (35) 1.2 / 3.4	.8 / (45) 1.8 / 4.0	.6 / (45) 1.1 / 4.0	% Depr., Dep., Amort./Sales					1.2 / (10) 2.7 / 7.2	.6 / (19) 1.0 / 2.6
1.5 / (16) 2.5 / 5.4	2.6 / (14) 4.5 / 10.3	1.2 / (16) 2.1 / 7.3	% Officers', Directors' Owners' Comp/Sales						
1292419M	1508281M	1821025M	Net Sales ($)	1330M	11182M	23450M	90150M	188002M	1506911M
545997M	685477M	839028M	Total Assets ($)	258M	10202M	7549M	39263M	92611M	689145M

M = $ thousand   MM = $ million
See Pages viii through xx for Explanation of Ratios and Data

Current Data Sorted by Assets | Comparative Historical Data

0-500M	500M-2MM	2-10MM	10-50MM	50-100MM	100-250MM		4/1/14-3/31/15 ALL	4/1/15-3/31/16 ALL
	15 (4/1-9/30/18)		104 (10/1/18-3/31/19)			**Type of Statement**		
		6	1	1		Unqualified	10	12
	1	2	9			Reviewed	7	10
2	10	6	2			Compiled	17	18
6	7	3				Tax Returns	29	31
5	19	18	17	2	2	Other	61	63
13	37	29	34	3	3	**NUMBER OF STATEMENTS**	124	134
%	%	%	%	%	%	**ASSETS**	%	%
13.6	13.5	13.0	9.7			Cash & Equivalents	15.0	15.2
19.1	33.4	33.5	32.9			Trade Receivables (net)	31.2	29.6
18.8	2.9	4.0	4.0			Inventory	3.5	3.0
9.9	6.7	3.9	3.6			All Other Current	3.8	4.6
61.4	56.4	54.5	50.1			Total Current	53.5	52.4
23.0	27.3	34.2	36.2			Fixed Assets (net)	33.3	34.1
5.5	4.9	6.2	6.8			Intangibles (net)	6.0	3.5
10.1	11.4	5.2	6.8			All Other Non-Current	7.2	10.0
100.0	100.0	100.0	100.0			Total	100.0	100.0
						LIABILITIES		
14.8	14.9	6.0	12.8			Notes Payable-Short Term	13.2	8.5
15.6	3.2	3.7	5.4			Cur. Mat.-L.T.D.	4.8	5.5
37.1	14.3	15.6	11.2			Trade Payables	21.7	15.7
.0	.0	.2	.1			Income Taxes Payable	.2	.2
15.1	7.5	14.6	12.4			All Other Current	10.2	11.7
82.6	39.9	40.1	41.9			Total Current	50.0	41.5
42.3	16.7	17.5	27.3			Long-Term Debt	28.2	23.3
.1	.1	.0	.4			Deferred Taxes	.4	.3
11.2	9.9	1.0	13.3			All Other Non-Current	7.5	8.8
-36.2	33.3	41.4	17.1			Net Worth	13.8	26.1
100.0	100.0	100.0	100.0			Total Liabilities & Net Worth	100.0	100.0
						INCOME DATA		
100.0	100.0	100.0	100.0			Net Sales	100.0	100.0
						Gross Profit		
97.3	88.8	92.1	88.8			Operating Expenses	91.5	91.3
2.7	11.2	7.9	11.2			Operating Profit	8.5	8.7
.1	4.5	1.5	2.4			All Other Expenses (net)	1.4	1.5
2.6	6.6	6.4	8.8			Profit Before Taxes	7.0	7.2
						RATIOS		
9.3	4.7	2.1	1.7			Current	2.5	3.1
1.0	1.5	1.5	1.2				1.2	1.3
.4	.5	1.0	.8				.8	.7
7.3	2.5	2.1	1.7			Quick	1.9	2.4
(12) .8	1.2	1.2	1.1				1.1	1.1
.3	.4	.8	.5				.6	.6
0 UND	0 UND	18 20.5	28 13.1			Sales/Receivables	6 62.4	3 116.6
6 60.2	24 14.9	54 6.8	39 9.3				32 11.3	31 11.6
13 28.2	36 10.0	74 4.9	53 6.9				51 7.2	53 6.9
						Cost of Sales/Inventory		
						Cost of Sales/Payables		
13.4	5.3	7.8	13.2			Sales/Working Capital	10.6	7.5
-561.7	27.3	19.8	32.0				47.6	32.5
-13.3	-21.2	NM	-39.2				-35.9	-37.8
	120.9	34.7	15.2			EBIT/Interest	26.7	40.1
(25)	8.7	(26) 7.3	(32) 5.5				(91) 7.1	(107) 7.9
	1.9	1.7	2.0				2.1	2.1
						Net Profit + Depr., Dep., Amort./Cur. Mat. L/T/D	5.5	20.3
							(13) 2.6	(16) 3.1
							.8	2.0
.0	.0	.2	.5			Fixed/Worth	.2	.2
.8	.3	.8	1.8				1.3	1.0
-.2	11.7	1.6	9.1				-14.0	3.4
1.5	.3	.5	1.4			Debt/Worth	.8	.6
-16.4	1.8	1.8	3.9				2.7	2.1
-1.9	172.0	9.0	11.8				-27.0	10.8
	86.1	72.2	61.1			% Profit Before Taxes/Tangible Net Worth	92.2	89.8
(29)	27.4	(28) 32.2	(27) 35.4				(89) 49.3	(110) 44.1
	4.1	7.9	17.6				22.9	14.5
23.2	35.2	22.5	17.8			% Profit Before Taxes/Total Assets	29.1	29.9
5.5	9.9	11.4	8.2				13.7	11.8
-4.0	1.4	.6	2.6				3.2	3.4
805.8	811.1	64.8	122.0			Sales/Net Fixed Assets	92.0	109.7
49.6	45.4	10.0	9.8				17.0	15.4
11.6	8.2	2.5	2.0				3.8	3.6
10.0	6.5	3.7	5.0			Sales/Total Assets	6.3	6.1
7.7	3.4	2.6	2.0				3.4	2.9
3.1	1.9	1.1	1.2				1.7	1.3
	.1	.5	.3			% Depr., Dep., Amort./Sales	.3	.7
(19)	1.7	(23) 1.9	(31) 2.2				(85) 1.0	(95) 2.2
	10.3	4.4	7.2				4.0	7.2
						% Officers', Directors' Owners' Comp/Sales	1.4	1.8
							(29) 2.3	(35) 3.2
							6.4	8.4
24353M	187530M	856318M	1971490M	247992M	1114152M	Net Sales ($)	4510112M	4593216M
3426M	44707M	150416M	758068M	201069M	608982M	Total Assets ($)	2179969M	2341191M

© RMA 2019

M = $ thousand   MM = $ million
See Pages viii through xx for Explanation of Ratios and Data

Comparative Historical Data | | Current Data Sorted by Sales

			Type of Statement						
10	6	8	Unqualified				1	6	8
8	12	12	Reviewed						5
20	25	20	Compiled	4	3	3	4	4	2
22	28	16	Tax Returns	3	7	2	3		1
45	44	63	Other	5	8	8	12	12	18
4/1/16-3/31/17	4/1/17-3/31/18	4/1/18-3/31/19			15 (4/1-9/30/18)			104 (10/1/18-3/31/19)	
ALL	ALL	ALL		0-1MM	1-3MM	3-5MM	5-10MM	10-25MM	25MM & OVER
105	115	119	**NUMBER OF STATEMENTS**	12	18	13	20	22	34
%	%	%	**ASSETS**	%	%	%	%	%	%
14.2	14.3	12.0	Cash & Equivalents	4.1	19.9	10.7	15.0	5.8	13.2
32.6	32.6	31.0	Trade Receivables (net)	1.8	26.0	32.6	34.7	43.2	33.3
3.0	2.6	5.2	Inventory	20.4	.1	.3	5.3	5.5	4.0
4.8	5.8	5.3	All Other Current	4.0	13.4	3.5	3.7	1.6	5.3
54.7	55.3	53.4	Total Current	30.3	59.5	47.0	58.8	56.1	56.0
32.4	33.7	32.4	Fixed Assets (net)	43.4	29.9	36.7	31.7	29.6	30.3
5.3	3.7	6.1	Intangibles (net)	5.4	3.2	5.7	5.8	8.6	6.8
7.6	7.3	8.1	All Other Non-Current	20.9	7.4	10.5	3.8	5.7	6.9
100.0	100.0	100.0	Total	100.0	100.0	100.0	100.0	100.0	100.0
			LIABILITIES						
11.5	11.3	11.4	Notes Payable-Short Term	8.8	13.6	8.4	16.5	8.3	11.4
5.4	5.7	5.5	Cur. Mat.-L.T.D.	4.5	13.4	3.1	3.8	3.9	4.5
16.9	19.1	15.8	Trade Payables	21.3	16.7	10.8	15.6	18.9	13.4
.1	.1	.1	Income Taxes Payable	.0	.0	.1	.2	.2	.0
13.2	10.1	11.3	All Other Current	8.5	11.9	7.2	5.8	16.0	13.9
47.1	46.5	44.1	Total Current	43.1	55.6	29.5	41.8	47.3	43.3
20.7	22.1	23.8	Long-Term Debt	43.2	34.1	18.2	14.4	17.2	23.3
.6	.1	.3	Deferred Taxes	.0	.2	.0	.1	.5	.5
4.5	9.7	8.4	All Other Non-Current	19.2	.0	2.9	14.0	.9	12.7
27.0	21.6	23.5	Net Worth	-5.5	10.2	49.3	29.7	34.2	20.2
100.0	100.0	100.0	Total Liabilties & Net Worth	100.0	100.0	100.0	100.0	100.0	100.0
			INCOME DATA						
100.0	100.0	100.0	Net Sales	100.0	100.0	100.0	100.0	100.0	100.0
			Gross Profit						
92.2	91.9	90.7	Operating Expenses	75.2	92.3	94.9	93.3	91.4	91.7
7.8	8.1	9.3	Operating Profit	24.8	7.7	5.1	6.7	8.6	8.3
1.2	1.6	2.7	All Other Expenses (net)	16.7	1.6	-.9	-.1	1.9	1.8
6.7	6.5	6.6	Profit Before Taxes	8.0	6.0	6.0	6.9	6.7	6.5
			RATIOS						
2.2	2.1	2.3		5.5	5.0	3.6	3.0	1.6	2.0
1.2	1.2	1.3	Current	1.4	1.0	1.5	1.7	1.2	1.4
.8	.8	.8		.1	.5	.7	1.3	1.0	.9
1.7	1.8	2.0		4.6	1.5	3.4	2.6	1.5	1.7
1.2	1.1 (118)	1.2	Quick	(11) 1.9	.8	1.2	1.6	1.0	1.2
.5	.6	.6		.2	.2	.7	.8	.7	.7
14 26.2	4 98.4	10 36.7		0 UND	0 UND	18 19.9	14 26.2	33 11.1	28 13.1
32 11.3	31 11.8	35 10.5	Sales/Receivables	0 UND	18 20.6	46 7.9	31 11.9	51 7.2	39 9.3
53 6.9	51 7.2	54 6.8		1 346.9	62 5.9	68 5.4	51 7.2	81 4.5	45 8.2
			Cost of Sales/Inventory						
			Cost of Sales/Payables						
9.0	10.9	8.6		1.4	4.2	5.4	7.1	10.3	12.7
30.4	50.5	27.3	Sales/Working Capital	NM	NM	20.2	17.9	30.4	27.6
-44.9	-40.0	-38.5		-1.9	-14.1	-37.5	68.1	NM	-48.3
21.1	29.3	17.6			8.0	16.7	189.2	18.7	15.2
(84) 8.6	(93) 7.2	(98) 6.4	EBIT/Interest	(13) 2.4	(10) 6.8	(17) 19.5	(21) 6.5	(32) 7.2
2.0	2.3	1.9			.1	2.6	4.8	2.1	1.6
13.2	4.9	12.4							34.3
(14) 3.6	(19) 2.5	(17) 3.8	Net Profit + Depr., Dep., Amort./Cur. Mat. L/T/D					(10) 4.7
1.6	1.1	1.1							1.1
.1	.1	.1		.1	.0	.1	.1	.2	.3
1.1	.8	1.0	Fixed/Worth	9.3	.7	.8	.7	1.1	1.3
3.1	6.1	5.1		NM	NM	2.8	1.5	2.5	3.9
1.0	.8	.9		.9	.7	.4	.4	1.6	1.4
2.2	2.0	2.5	Debt/Worth	11.1	4.4	1.4	1.6	2.6	3.1
15.0	23.9	13.6		-45.0	-13.5	2.8	4.0	12.5	9.8
86.5	78.2	69.1			37.9	50.3	88.5	74.6	65.1
(83) 33.3	(89) 39.3	(96) 30.3	% Profit Before Taxes/Tangible Net Worth	(12) 17.6	(11) 16.4	(17) 44.7	(20) 39.5	(28) 32.4
15.2	12.1	11.8			10.9	-2.6	16.3	20.4	11.8
22.6	22.9	23.7		6.9	18.2	19.1	37.9	24.5	18.4
10.1	10.6	8.4	% Profit Before Taxes/Total Assets	1.2	5.5	9.9	16.8	13.5	7.3
1.9	1.4	1.5		-.3	.7	1.0	5.1	6.2	1.6
172.4	194.7	126.0		165.6	480.2	91.5	322.5	374.8	122.0
15.0	14.5	19.7	Sales/Net Fixed Assets	10.0	34.8	28.3	13.7	19.9	22.0
3.9	2.7	2.7		.1	6.1	1.8	5.9	2.7	2.2
6.2	6.6	5.2		2.3	7.9	5.1	6.7	3.9	5.1
2.7	2.9	2.8	Sales/Total Assets	.2	2.6	3.0	4.0	2.3	3.0
1.5	1.3	1.3		.1	1.6	1.4	2.7	1.3	1.4
.6	.5	.5			.5		.3	.3	.6
(68) 3.1	(77) 3.5	(84) 2.3	% Depr., Dep., Amort./Sales	(10) 4.3	(13) 1.1	(18) 2.2	(29) 2.0
7.8	7.8	7.1			9.7		3.6	5.3	5.7
1.9	1.3	1.2							
(27) 3.0	(29) 4.3	(24) 1.8	% Officers', Directors' Owners' Comp/Sales						
7.8	6.0	10.0							
3702057M	4132653M	4401835M	Net Sales ($)	5535M	38722M	51284M	148470M	393922M	3763902M
1599322M	1514532M	1766668M	Total Assets ($)	19116M	30856M	27819M	69374M	218596M	1400907M

© RMA 2019   M = $ thousand   MM = $ million
See Pages viii through xx for Explanation of Ratios and Data

Current Data Sorted by Assets   Comparative Historical Data

0-500M	500M-2MM	2-10MM	10-50MM	50-100MM	100-250MM	Type of Statement	4/1/14-3/31/15 ALL	4/1/15-3/31/16 ALL
	1	2	2			Unqualified	11	4
		2	2	1		Reviewed	7	8
		6				Compiled	16	10
12	9	3				Tax Returns	12	31
3	10	14	6	3	2	Other	44	41
	7 (4/1-9/30/18)		73 (10/1/18-3/31/19)					
15	20	25	10	7	3	NUMBER OF STATEMENTS	90	94
%	%	%	%	%	%	ASSETS	%	%
26.4	12.2	18.6	12.0			Cash & Equivalents	11.9	13.0
20.3	25.8	38.9	37.6			Trade Receivables (net)	36.5	33.8
.1	.9	2.9	.1			Inventory	.5	1.0
4.2	.7	4.4	1.5			All Other Current	3.4	3.8
51.1	39.5	64.7	51.2			Total Current	52.3	51.6
24.7	22.2	23.0	34.4			Fixed Assets (net)	22.5	21.0
20.2	20.6	7.4	4.7			Intangibles (net)	15.1	18.1
4.1	17.6	4.9	9.7			All Other Non-Current	10.1	9.3
100.0	100.0	100.0	100.0			Total	100.0	100.0
						LIABILITIES		
10.6	9.0	5.7	12.1			Notes Payable-Short Term	13.9	16.1
1.6	6.6	4.3	7.2			Cur. Mat.-L.T.D.	4.7	4.1
10.1	7.9	10.0	14.5			Trade Payables	12.4	10.7
.1	.0	.1	.4			Income Taxes Payable	.5	.2
14.2	7.9	7.8	7.9			All Other Current	12.4	11.9
36.5	31.3	28.0	42.0			Total Current	43.8	43.0
48.7	42.4	15.5	19.7			Long-Term Debt	23.7	26.1
.0	.0	.0	1.1			Deferred Taxes	.8	.1
7.6	3.9	3.4	7.1			All Other Non-Current	6.9	8.5
7.3	22.4	53.0	30.1			Net Worth	24.8	22.4
100.0	100.0	100.0	100.0			Total Liabilities & Net Worth	100.0	100.0
						INCOME DATA		
100.0	100.0	100.0	100.0			Net Sales	100.0	100.0
						Gross Profit		
95.2	88.7	94.9	94.5			Operating Expenses	94.0	95.2
4.8	11.3	5.1	5.5			Operating Profit	6.0	4.8
.6	1.1	.7	1.2			All Other Expenses (net)	1.0	.4
4.2	10.2	4.3	4.3			Profit Before Taxes	5.0	4.4
						RATIOS		
7.8	2.9	5.3	1.7				2.4	2.9
1.9	1.7	2.3	1.3			Current	1.3	1.6
1.0	.7	1.2	.8				.8	.8
5.0	2.5	4.9	1.7				2.2	2.8
1.8	1.7	2.3	1.3			Quick	1.3	1.5
.8	.7	1.2	.6				.7	.7
0 UND	1 696.8	20 18.5	34 10.7				16 23.0	0 UND
0 UND	17 21.5	36 10.2	43 8.5			Sales/Receivables	34 10.8	29 12.8
24 15.5	39 9.4	43 8.5	50 7.3				47 7.8	38 9.5
						Cost of Sales/Inventory		
						Cost of Sales/Payables		
10.6	10.7	7.7	14.6				13.2	14.1
42.1	29.0	10.9	29.2			Sales/Working Capital	33.4	31.7
-716.0	-23.3	44.8	-17.3				-49.2	-62.3
26.8	13.7	69.8					20.5	24.0
(10) 3.1	(17) 5.7	(22) 13.4				EBIT/Interest	(77) 8.0	(84) 6.8
1.6	1.5	6.4					2.6	1.0
							20.5	83.6
						Net Profit + Depr., Dep., Amort./Cur. Mat. L/T/D	(11) 4.4	(10) 2.9
							1.8	1.4
.1	.3	.1	.3				.3	.2
1.1	1.4	.2	1.1			Fixed/Worth	1.5	1.6
-.5	-2.7	2.1	NM				-1.2	-.9
1.4	1.9	.3	1.4				1.3	1.2
70.0	4.1	.7	2.6			Debt/Worth	4.4	6.4
-1.9	-8.1	3.1	NM				-5.0	-3.2
	139.3	56.4					97.1	109.2
	(12) 88.7	(20) 30.0				% Profit Before Taxes/Tangible Net Worth	(58) 44.4	(57) 38.5
	21.3	12.6					22.2	17.6
27.4	31.8	28.1	9.9				29.5	34.1
18.5	10.2	14.5	6.3			% Profit Before Taxes/Total Assets	11.9	12.7
4.2	3.6	5.6	5.0				4.2	
164.6	97.5	158.9	63.0				75.9	168.9
57.3	22.0	60.2	10.8			Sales/Net Fixed Assets	32.9	36.7
16.4	10.5	6.3	2.7				10.7	14.5
11.7	6.7	6.2	4.6				7.0	7.8
5.2	3.7	4.5	2.7			Sales/Total Assets	4.6	4.7
3.2	1.7	3.1	1.5				2.5	2.6
		.2					.4	.4
	(16)	.6				% Depr., Dep., Amort./Sales	(61) 1.2	(63) 1.0
		4.2					2.8	2.9
	1.5						1.4	1.6
	(12) 2.5					% Officers', Directors' Owners' Comp/Sales	(32) 2.3	(40) 3.8
	6.3						5.0	8.9
27467M	102226M	444348M	665337M	1547436M	702904M	Net Sales ($)	4821784M	2759539M
3958M	23316M	98843M	214904M	502737M	429820M	Total Assets ($)	2367545M	929218M

© RMA 2019

M = $ thousand   MM = $ million
See Pages viii through xx for Explanation of Ratios and Data

Comparative Historical Data | Current Data Sorted by Sales

						Type of Statement										
	4		5		4	Unqualified										4
	2		9		8	Reviewed					2		1		1	4
	12		9		6	Compiled									5	1
	22		27		24	Tax Returns							4		4	
	37		53		38	Other		2		9	5		4		7	12
	4/1/16-		4/1/17-		4/1/18-			5		3	1		4		10	
	3/31/17		3/31/18		3/31/19				7 (4/1-9/30/18)				73 (10/1/18-3/31/19)			
	ALL		ALL		ALL			0-1MM	1-3MM		3-5MM	5-10MM		10-25MM		25MM & OVER
	77		103		80	NUMBER OF STATEMENTS		7	12		8	12		20		21
	%		%		%	ASSETS		%	%		%	%		%		%
	12.6		16.0		15.9	Cash & Equivalents			19.3			9.7		20.3		11.4
	33.6		29.9		30.0	Trade Receivables (net)			14.0			27.3		38.1		38.4
	1.4		.8		1.2	Inventory			.2			3.4		2.4		.2
	2.3		3.6		3.3	All Other Current			3.3			2.7		3.0		4.3
	49.9		50.3		50.5	Total Current			36.9			43.0		63.8		54.4
	22.9		26.2		25.9	Fixed Assets (net)			19.2			34.5		22.0		25.1
	19.4		13.5		15.0	Intangibles (net)			39.8			8.8		8.6		14.2
	7.8		10.0		8.6	All Other Non-Current			4.2			13.6		5.7		6.3
	100.0		100.0		100.0	Total			100.0			100.0		100.0		100.0
						LIABILITIES										
	15.8		13.3		8.0	Notes Payable-Short Term			6.9			19.3		4.0		8.7
	4.5		8.0		5.1	Cur. Mat.-L.T.D.			3.6			2.3		6.6		6.4
	10.9		8.5		9.6	Trade Payables			4.8			7.3		10.8		11.3
	.4		.2		.1	Income Taxes Payable			.1			.0		.2		.2
	12.3		9.8		9.8	All Other Current			18.2			7.2		8.2		12.4
	43.8		39.8		32.5	Total Current			33.6			36.1		29.7		39.0
	34.4		27.9		30.2	Long-Term Debt			66.2			31.7		17.7		19.0
	.3		.3		.3	Deferred Taxes			.0			.0		.4		.9
	3.8		1.5		5.0	All Other Non-Current			7.0			6.4		3.1		6.6
	17.7		30.4		32.1	Net Worth			-6.9			25.8		49.1		34.5
	100.0		100.0		100.0	Total Liabilties & Net Worth			100.0			100.0		100.0		100.0
						INCOME DATA										
	100.0		100.0		100.0	Net Sales			100.0			100.0		100.0		100.0
						Gross Profit										
	95.1		92.7		93.3	Operating Expenses			93.9			94.3		94.3		96.1
	4.9		7.3		6.7	Operating Profit			6.1			5.7		5.7		3.9
	.4		1.2		.9	All Other Expenses (net)			1.4			-.2		1.1		.8
	4.5		6.1		5.8	Profit Before Taxes			4.7			5.9		4.6		3.1
						RATIOS										
	3.5		2.8		3.4				2.4			6.4		5.8		2.3
	1.7		1.3		1.7	Current			1.5			1.6		3.1		1.3
	.7		.6		1.0				.6			.8		1.1		.9
	3.2		2.7		3.1				2.3			6.3		5.2		2.3
	1.4		1.2		1.6	Quick			1.4			1.4		2.9		1.3
	.7		.6		.7				.6			.3		.8		.7
7	55.4	1	586.0	10	37.7		0	UND		24	15.2	12	30.3	28	13.0
35	10.5	33	10.9	31	11.7	Sales/Receivables	3	125.5		32	11.4	30	12.1	41	8.8
48	7.6	42	8.7	44	8.3		30	12.1		41	8.9	45	8.2	51	7.1
						Cost of Sales/Inventory										
						Cost of Sales/Payables										
	10.6		10.9		10.1				9.6			9.1		7.6		12.9
	32.0		37.6		25.2	Sales/Working Capital			114.2			28.5		11.4		25.2
	-48.9		-22.4		-310.2				-15.9			-70.6		79.7		-65.7
	27.3		23.5		28.9				6.4					63.0		11.1
(63)	7.0	(89)	8.7	(67)	6.6	EBIT/Interest	(10)	3.9				(17)	10.4	(20)	5.8
	1.3		2.2		2.4				1.7					4.4		2.7
				14.8		Net Profit + Depr., Dep.,										
		(13)	3.1			Amort./Cur. Mat. L/T/D										
				.9												
	.2		.2		.2				2.0			.2		.1		.2
	1.0		1.2		.9	Fixed/Worth			-2.7			.8		.2		1.2
	-1.0		-2.0		-10.2				-.1			NM		NM		0.0
	1.0		.8		.8				-20.0			.7		.3		1.4
	4.5		3.3		2.3	Debt/Worth			-2.3			2.0		.9		2.9
	-3.6		-5.2		-9.4				-1.5			NM		NM		136.8
	93.3		71.3		96.6	% Profit Before Taxes/Tangible								74.8		51.8
(47)	44.6	(70)	43.8	(56)	40.5	Net Worth							(15)	28.9	(17)	33.6
	10.6		13.6		19.7									12.2		20.0
	33.8		33.3		24.6	% Profit Before Taxes/Total			18.5			23.3		45.7		12.4
	11.8		14.3		10.0	Assets			14.4			14.4		20.7		8.1
	2.4		3.3		4.7				4.4			4.1		5.5		4.6
	122.5		89.4		95.2				228.8			132.8		116.2		127.9
	46.2		24.7		42.1	Sales/Net Fixed Assets			53.4			27.1		61.6		29.1
	9.7		9.3		7.6				10.2			3.1		30.7		3.7
	6.6		6.1		6.2				5.1			7.0		6.9		6.3
	4.2		3.9		4.0	Sales/Total Assets			2.8			4.2		4.7		3.1
	2.3		2.2		2.0				1.7			1.5		3.8		1.7
	.7		.7		.4									.3		.3
(44)	1.6	(65)	2.4	(47)	1.4	% Depr., Dep., Amort./Sales							(13)	.8	(16)	1.2
	5.5		5.5		5.2									3.3		5.6
	1.7		1.2		1.5											
(30)	3.3	(44)	2.8	(30)	2.8	% Officers', Directors'									
	7.8		6.0		4.7	Owners' Comp/Sales										
	2385115M		4151021M		3489718M	Net Sales ($)		4001M	17826M		34033M	91851M		336947M		3005060M
	1018561M		1743251M		1273578M	Total Assets ($)		4031M	6891M		10263M	53228M		75949M		1123216M

© RMA 2019

M = $ thousand   MM = $ million
See Pages viii through xx for Explanation of Ratios and Data

Current Data Sorted by Assets   **Comparative Historical Data**

Date ranges: 1 (4/1-9/30/18) covers 0-500M, 500M-2MM, 2-10MM; 30 (10/1/18-3/31/19) covers 10-50MM, 50-100MM, 100-250MM. Comparative Historical Data columns: ALL 4/1/14-3/31/15; ALL 4/1/15-3/31/16.

	0-500M	500M-2MM	2-10MM	10-50MM	50-100MM	100-250MM		ALL 4/1/14–3/31/15	ALL 4/1/15–3/31/16
Type of Statement									
Unqualified		1			2	1			
Reviewed	1		1					2	2
Compiled		2							
Tax Returns	5	4	5					8	8
Other	1	4	1	3				8	12
NUMBER OF STATEMENTS	7	11	7	3	2	1		18	22
	%	%	%	%	%	%		%	%
ASSETS									
Cash & Equivalents		8.7						17.0	23.5
Trade Receivables (net)		35.0						28.3	22.5
Inventory		.0						.0	2.5
All Other Current		.3						6.1	1.6
Total Current		44.1						51.4	50.0
Fixed Assets (net)		30.3						26.8	25.1
Intangibles (net)		6.1						7.4	10.7
All Other Non-Current		19.5						14.5	14.3
Total		100.0						100.0	100.0
LIABILITIES									
Notes Payable-Short Term		8.4						14.8	8.2
Cur. Mat.-L.T.D.		3.6						2.6	7.1
Trade Payables		8.4						7.7	11.7
Income Taxes Payable		.0						.4	.1
All Other Current		12.5						14.3	31.3
Total Current		32.8						39.7	58.4
Long-Term Debt		31.8						21.4	19.0
Deferred Taxes		.0						.0	.2
All Other Non-Current		.0						9.5	8.7
Net Worth		35.4						29.4	13.8
Total Liabilities & Net Worth		100.0						100.0	100.0
INCOME DATA									
Net Sales		100.0						100.0	100.0
Gross Profit									
Operating Expenses		90.7						90.5	90.0
Operating Profit		9.3						9.5	10.0
All Other Expenses (net)		2.4						4.1	2.5
Profit Before Taxes		6.9						5.4	7.5
RATIOS									
Current		1.4						2.4	2.0
		1.0						1.2	1.0
		.7						.6	.7
Quick		1.4						2.2	2.0
		1.0						1.0	.9
		.6						.4	.6
Sales/Receivables		0 UND						0 UND	0 UND
		23 16.0						23 16.2	19 19.7
		38 9.5						37 9.8	39 9.3
Cost of Sales/Inventory									
Cost of Sales/Payables									
Sales/Working Capital		13.6						13.2	14.4
		-321.9						244.0	-332.6
		-23.3						-22.0	-19.8
EBIT/Interest								(13) 80.3	(17) 26.9
								8.9	20.6
								.0	7.9
Net Profit + Depr., Dep., Amort./Cur. Mat. L/T/D									
Fixed/Worth		.0						.1	.1
		.5						1.5	.7
		6.0						-1.8	UND
Debt/Worth		.7						.7	.8
		2.2						4.5	6.8
		6.8						-7.5	-34.7
% Profit Before Taxes/Tangible Net Worth								(13) 210.2	(16) 749.4
								58.3	95.8
								5.7	24.8
% Profit Before Taxes/Total Assets		13.7						36.3	42.5
		7.2						7.9	11.6
		.9						-4.0	10.3
Sales/Net Fixed Assets		999.8						348.2	271.4
		25.3						69.4	17.7
		4.4						5.9	9.2
Sales/Total Assets		5.7						8.5	6.3
		4.5						4.1	3.0
		1.8						2.1	2.0
% Depr., Dep., Amort./Sales								(12) .5	(11) .4
								1.5	2.1
								11.2	4.7
% Officers', Directors' Owners' Comp/Sales									(13) 1.7
									3.2
									5.6
Net Sales ($)	12833M	56690M	161230M	194148M	199527M	695122M		175722M	1169304M
Total Assets ($)	1637M	13603M	34150M	84728M	134040M	246775M		49941M	286298M

M = $ thousand   MM = $ million
See Pages viii through xx for Explanation of Ratios and Data

Comparative Historical Data | Current Data Sorted by Sales

			Type of Statement						
	1	4	Unqualified		1				3
	1	1	Reviewed						1
	3	3	Compiled		1			2	
6	10	9	Tax Returns	4	1	1	3		4
3	11	14	Other	1	2	2	3	2	4
4/1/16-3/31/17 ALL	4/1/17-3/31/18 ALL	4/1/18-3/31/19 ALL		0-1MM	1 (4/1-9/30/18) 1-3MM	3-5MM	5-10MM	30 (10/1/18-3/31/19) 10-25MM	25MM & OVER
9	26	31	NUMBER OF STATEMENTS	5	5	3	6	4	8
%	%	%	ASSETS	%	%	%	%	%	%
	14.8	7.9	Cash & Equivalents						
	25.2	25.8	Trade Receivables (net)						
	3.6	1.0	Inventory						
	2.5	1.8	All Other Current						
	46.2	36.6	Total Current						
	27.9	28.2	Fixed Assets (net)						
	9.6	17.1	Intangibles (net)						
	16.3	18.2	All Other Non-Current						
	100.0	100.0	Total						
			LIABILITIES						
	16.4	16.4	Notes Payable-Short Term						
	4.2	5.7	Cur. Mat.-L.T.D.						
	9.8	9.9	Trade Payables						
	.2	.0	Income Taxes Payable						
	16.0	16.9	All Other Current						
	46.6	49.0	Total Current						
	30.8	38.1	Long-Term Debt						
	.2	.0	Deferred Taxes						
	2.1	10.7	All Other Non-Current						
	20.3	2.2	Net Worth						
	100.0	100.0	Total Liabilities & Net Worth						
			INCOME DATA						
	100.0	100.0	Net Sales						
			Gross Profit						
	96.8	95.2	Operating Expenses						
	3.2	4.8	Operating Profit						
	.7	1.2	All Other Expenses (net)						
	2.5	3.6	Profit Before Taxes						
			RATIOS						
	1.8	1.1	Current						
	1.1	.8							
	.5	.4							
	1.7	1.0	Quick						
	1.0	.7							
	.5	.3							
	0 UND	0 UND	Sales/Receivables						
	16 22.9	16 22.6							
	38 9.5	38 9.7							
			Cost of Sales/Inventory						
			Cost of Sales/Payables						
	18.0	213.1	Sales/Working Capital						
	119.4	-87.9							
	-13.6	-15.8							
	8.6	8.3	EBIT/Interest						
	(19) 1.9	(27) 3.7							
	.9	2.4							
			Net Profit + Depr., Dep., Amort./Cur. Mat. L/T/D						
	.3	.2	Fixed/Worth						
	1.0	2.0							
	-4.7	-.4							
	1.4	1.3	Debt/Worth						
	3.4	6.8							
	-7.3	-1.7							
	133.4	67.2	% Profit Before Taxes/Tangible Net Worth						
	(19) 37.0	(18) 36.5							
	20.1	16.5							
	15.8	17.5	% Profit Before Taxes/Total Assets						
	10.1	9.5							
	-.3	3.4							
	374.0	468.7	Sales/Net Fixed Assets						
	34.9	28.4							
	8.8	6.7							
	8.0	5.7	Sales/Total Assets						
	3.9	3.6							
	2.5	1.9							
	.4	.3	% Depr., Dep., Amort./Sales						
	(13) 1.7	(22) 1.5							
	5.7	8.8							
		.9	% Officers', Directors', Owners' Comp/Sales						
		(10) 2.0							
		3.1							
67214M	829743M	1319550M	Net Sales ($)	2530M	10837M	11753M	43550M	58937M	1191943M
18431M	305193M	514933M	Total Assets ($)	1308M	4372M	4682M	7352M	17057M	480162M

M = $ thousand   MM = $ million
See Pages viii through xx for Explanation of Ratios and Data

Current Data Sorted by Assets   **Comparative Historical Data**

0-500M	500M-2MM	2-10MM	10-50MM	50-100MM	100-250MM	Type of Statement	4/1/14-3/31/15 ALL	4/1/15-3/31/16 ALL
1	2	3	11	2	3	Unqualified	29	25
	9	24	18	2	3	Reviewed	55	48
12	20	14	6	1	1	Compiled	47	38
8	33	12	2			Tax Returns	75	79
		60	43	3	7	Other	150	148
18 (4/1-9/30/18)			282 (10/1/18-3/31/19)					
21	64	113	80	8	14	**NUMBER OF STATEMENTS**	356	338
%	%	%	%	%	%	**ASSETS**	%	%
27.6	14.2	11.2	11.7		6.4	Cash & Equivalents	11.5	13.4
20.7	26.2	22.4	24.0		17.8	Trade Receivables (net)	20.1	20.7
1.8	.4	3.0	.6		6.0	Inventory	2.7	2.2
1.8	4.5	3.6	3.3		2.5	All Other Current	3.3	2.5
51.9	45.3	40.3	39.6		32.7	Total Current	37.6	38.8
29.9	39.8	47.6	45.1		60.4	Fixed Assets (net)	47.0	46.6
9.0	3.8	4.7	6.0		2.7	Intangibles (net)	5.5	6.0
9.2	11.1	7.4	9.3		4.2	All Other Non-Current	10.0	8.6
100.0	100.0	100.0	100.0		100.0	Total	100.0	100.0
						LIABILITIES		
16.1	4.5	3.2	4.8		.8	Notes Payable-Short Term	7.2	7.7
2.2	5.9	3.9	3.9		1.4	Cur. Mat.-L.T.D.	4.2	4.4
7.8	12.8	9.9	7.6		12.6	Trade Payables	9.4	8.2
.0	.1	.1	.1		.0	Income Taxes Payable	.1	.1
11.0	12.4	7.3	9.2		5.7	All Other Current	9.5	8.9
37.2	35.7	24.5	25.6		20.6	Total Current	30.4	29.3
18.5	28.8	34.8	31.4		31.5	Long-Term Debt	34.7	31.8
.0	.0	.2	.9		.5	Deferred Taxes	.4	.5
4.3	1.1	6.3	3.1		7.7	All Other Non-Current	5.9	4.1
40.0	34.3	34.2	39.1		39.7	Net Worth	28.7	34.4
100.0	100.0	100.0	100.0		100.0	Total Liabilities & Net Worth	100.0	100.0
						INCOME DATA		
100.0	100.0	100.0	100.0		100.0	Net Sales	100.0	100.0
						Gross Profit		
89.3	86.5	78.9	82.7		87.2	Operating Expenses	82.7	84.2
10.7	13.5	21.1	17.3		12.8	Operating Profit	17.3	15.8
.0	4.9	7.4	5.3		6.7	All Other Expenses (net)	5.1	4.2
10.7	8.7	13.7	12.0		6.1	Profit Before Taxes	12.2	11.6
						RATIOS		
13.9	3.6	3.0	2.7		3.8		2.5	2.6
1.4	1.6	1.8	1.6		1.9	Current	1.4	1.5
.7	.5	.9	1.0		1.2		.7	.9
13.8	3.6	2.4	2.5		2.9		2.3	2.5
1.4	(63) 1.6	1.3	1.5		1.4	Quick	1.2	1.3
.6	.4	.7	.8		.7		.6	.7
0 UND	0 UND	0 UND	24 15.1		28 12.9		0 UND	5 74.0
9 38.5	34 10.6	30 12.3	42 8.6		40 9.2	Sales/Receivables	30 12.2	34 10.7
30 12.1	48 7.6	49 7.5	57 6.4		61 6.0		49 7.4	54 6.8
						Cost of Sales/Inventory		
						Cost of Sales/Payables		
6.5	7.4	4.3	5.4		2.8		8.0	7.0
25.8	14.8	14.4	14.7		10.1	Sales/Working Capital	24.2	17.9
-37.3	-7.7	-48.9	NM		NM		-28.9	-72.8
44.0	22.4	18.8	26.8		12.4		15.7	21.9
(11) 10.5	(40) 7.5	(79) 6.7	(64) 9.5		(11) 5.0	EBIT/Interest	(250) 5.6	(259) 6.8
3.5	1.2	2.1	2.8		2.2		2.2	2.7
		12.1	7.0				3.8	7.1
	(18) 4.0	(26) 3.9				Net Profit + Depr., Dep., Amort./Cur. Mat. L/T/D	(65) 2.0	(62) 3.0
		1.6	2.2				1.2	1.6
.2	.2	.5	.6		.8		.5	.5
.6	1.0	1.5	1.4		1.4	Fixed/Worth	1.4	1.4
4.1	NM	5.8	3.4		4.7		6.8	4.8
.1	.4	.8	.8		1.0		.9	.8
2.3	2.0	2.2	1.7		1.4	Debt/Worth	2.1	2.0
11.5	NM	8.5	5.8		4.4		11.5	7.6
99.1	61.2	53.5	49.4		24.3		48.4	61.6
(17) 32.2	(48) 26.5	(97) 22.7	(72) 32.1		(13) 14.1	% Profit Before Taxes/Tangible Net Worth	(288) 24.9	(281) 26.4
8.2	2.1	9.6	13.3		4.3		8.7	12.0
62.8	29.2	16.6	18.3		5.2		17.2	18.0
27.0	5.8	7.7	8.5		3.1	% Profit Before Taxes/Total Assets	7.2	8.3
5.0	-1.6	2.9	4.3		2.1		1.8	3.2
177.4	53.9	20.7	14.2		5.0		20.2	16.5
30.6	10.5	3.8	3.6		1.1	Sales/Net Fixed Assets	4.8	5.3
3.8	2.4	.3	.8		.4		.7	.9
6.2	4.0	3.1	2.7		2.5		3.3	3.3
3.8	2.2	1.2	1.4		.7	Sales/Total Assets	1.6	1.6
1.1	.8	.3	.5		.3		.4	.6
.9	1.5	1.8	1.9		1.5		1.6	1.8
(12) 2.1	(42) 2.7	(94) 4.6	(74) 4.4		(12) 5.7	% Depr., Dep., Amort./Sales	(291) 4.4	(288) 4.1
4.3	8.0	17.3	9.3		14.4		10.9	10.1
		2.8	1.0				2.0	2.1
	(18) 3.8	(26) 2.2				% Officers', Directors', Owners' Comp/Sales	(74) 4.3	(80) 4.2
		5.6	3.5				8.6	7.0
34084M	206304M	1147475M	3133821M	1131796M	2461495M	Net Sales ($)	7419276M	8359147M
6041M	78490M	546026M	1784151M	563077M	1820365M	Total Assets ($)	4570675M	5756021M

© RMA 2019

M = $ thousand   MM = $ million
See Pages viii through xx for Explanation of Ratios and Data

Comparative Historical Data				Current Data Sorted by Sales					
			Type of Statement		1			5	13
17	15	19	Unqualified		1			5	13
63	55	50	Reviewed	5	2	2	8	14	19
29	43	31	Compiled	8	5	3	8	2	5
50	76	46	Tax Returns	22	9	6	4	4	1
142	153	154	Other	24	34	14	21	26	35
4/1/16-3/31/17	4/1/17-3/31/18	4/1/18-3/31/19		18 (4/1-9/30/18)			282 (10/1/18-3/31/19)		
ALL	ALL	ALL		0-1MM	1-3MM	3-5MM	5-10MM	10-25MM	25MM & OVER
301	342	300	**NUMBER OF STATEMENTS**	59	51	25	41	51	73
%	%	%	**ASSETS**	%	%	%	%	%	%
11.9	12.6	12.8	Cash & Equivalents	8.2	15.2	18.9	14.8	14.3	10.5
22.7	22.3	23.5	Trade Receivables (net)	5.0	15.7	21.0	28.3	32.7	35.5
2.5	2.6	1.9	Inventory	.3	1.8	3.5	2.7	1.7	2.4
3.0	2.9	3.5	All Other Current	.4	3.6	5.1	6.3	4.0	3.6
40.1	40.4	41.7	Total Current	13.8	36.4	48.4	52.0	52.7	52.1
44.0	44.9	44.3	Fixed Assets (net)	74.3	45.3	34.2	37.0	36.5	32.2
6.0	5.0	5.5	Intangibles (net)	4.1	6.5	5.1	3.5	4.2	8.1
9.9	9.7	8.6	All Other Non-Current	7.7	11.8	12.3	7.5	6.7	7.7
100.0	100.0	100.0	Total	100.0	100.0	100.0	100.0	100.0	100.0
			LIABILITIES						
6.5	7.3	4.8	Notes Payable-Short Term	.6	7.9	9.7	2.6	6.0	4.8
4.4	4.3	4.1	Cur. Mat.-L.T.D.	4.1	0.9	3.8	2.8	3.0	3.7
9.4	9.6	9.9	Trade Payables	2.5	5.6	5.2	18.2	11.7	14.8
.1	.1	.1	Income Taxes Payable	.0	.2	.0	.1	.2	.1
7.9	10.7	9.1	All Other Current	6.8	8.7	9.6	9.4	8.8	10.9
28.3	31.9	28.0	Total Current	14.0	29.2	28.3	33.0	29.6	34.3
30.7	30.8	31.1	Long-Term Debt	59.8	38.8	25.4	20.8	19.8	18.0
.5	.3	.3	Deferred Taxes	.1	.0	.0	.5	.3	.9
7.8	5.4	4.3	All Other Non-Current	1.6	1.8	3.4	4.9	7.5	6.0
32.6	31.6	36.3	Net Worth	24.4	30.2	42.9	40.8	42.8	40.9
100.0	100.0	100.0	Total Liabilities & Net Worth	100.0	100.0	100.0	100.0	100.0	100.0
			INCOME DATA						
100.0	100.0	100.0	Net Sales	100.0	100.0	100.0	100.0	100.0	100.0
			Gross Profit						
83.9	85.5	82.9	Operating Expenses	61.2	81.3	86.9	87.9	88.6	93.2
16.1	14.5	17.1	Operating Profit	38.8	18.7	13.1	12.1	11.4	6.8
4.9	4.3	5.7	All Other Expenses (net)	17.0	8.0	2.1	1.4	2.5	.7
11.2	10.2	11.5	Profit Before Taxes	21.8	10.7	11.0	10.7	8.8	6.1
			RATIOS						
2.8	2.8	3.1		3.2	3.7	3.8	3.3	3.3	2.2
1.4	1.4	1.6	Current	.9	1.6	2.6	2.0	1.8	1.6
.9	.7	.9		.2	.6	.9	1.0	1.0	1.1
2.4	2.4	2.7		2.4	3.0	3.6	3.1	3.1	2.1
1.3	1.3 (299)	1.4	Quick	.6	1.5	(24) 1.7	1.6	1.6	1.5
.7	.6	.7		.2	.5	.6	.6	1.0	.9
9 39.6	8 47.6	2 216.0		0 UND	0 UND	0 UND	21 17.0	31 11.8	37 9.9
34 10.6	36 10.1	37 9.8	Sales/Receivables	0 UND	22 16.7	38 9.7	40 9.1	47 7.7	46 7.9
49 7.5	52 7.0	53 6.9		8 46.3	41 8.9	47 7.7	54 6.7	62 5.9	57 6.4
			Cost of Sales/Inventory						
			Cost of Sales/Payables						
7.0	7.3	5.7		4.1	3.8	5.4	5.7	5.5	10.1
18.7	21.7	14.9	Sales/Working Capital	-26.0	14.9	7.9	11.6	12.5	16.1
-51.8	-25.1	-47.1		-2.7	-11.7	-57.1	-123.7	110.3	44.4
22.7	21.1	22.4		5.7	8.6	31.9	20.0	29.4	28.3
(229) 6.4	(263) 5.5	(212) 6.7	EBIT/Interest	(23) 3.5	(30) 2.7	(18) 8.2	(35) 9.4	(39) 9.7	(67) 9.8
2.2	2.0	2.3		1.6	1.2	4.1	4.2	2.0	4.1
4.2	5.3	7.3	Net Profit + Depr., Dep.,						6.9
(57) 2.1	(58) 2.8	(53) 3.8	Amort./Cur. Mat. L/T/D					(27)	3.8
1.4	1.2	1.7							1.8
.5	.4	.4		1.1	.4	.2	.2	.2	.4
1.2	1.4	1.4	Fixed/Worth	4.3	2.8	1.5	1.0	.9	.9
4.0	5.6	4.9		14.7	-17.1	3.4	2.3	3.0	2.3
.7	.6	.7		1.2	1.0	.3	.7	.4	.8
1.8	1.9	2.0	Debt/Worth	4.0	2.8	1.7	1.3	1.7	1.7
5.3	11.4	6.7		14.7	-19.2	11.3	3.5	3.7	5.2
47.8	52.4	52.0	% Profit Before Taxes/Tangible	27.2	56.7	59.8	69.2	55.0	56.3
(254) 21.2	(278) 23.5	(254) 25.3	Net Worth	(47) 11.5	(37) 19.1	(20) 28.2	(38) 40.2	(45) 29.4	(67) 32.5
7.5	8.5	10.2		2.9	5.8	7.7	17.8	10.1	16.8
16.5	18.3	20.1	% Profit Before Taxes/Total	9.0	12.3	36.0	24.2	26.8	21.0
7.4	6.0	7.6	Assets	3.2	5.5	13.1	12.5	10.0	10.6
2.2	2.1	2.6		.6	.8	2.9	5.0	4.0	4.2
18.3	17.3	22.2		.7	23.4	28.3	72.6	30.9	21.7
6.2	5.7	5.4	Sales/Net Fixed Assets	.2	3.4	6.5	7.5	10.1	10.2
.9	1.0	.8		.1	.7	3.2	1.8	1.9	4.3
3.5	3.3	3.5		.4	2.4	3.7	4.3	4.2	3.8
1.8	1.8	1.6	Sales/Total Assets	.2	1.1	2.2	2.5	2.4	2.7
.6	.6	.5		.1	.4	.9	1.0	1.1	1.5
2.0	1.7	1.7		8.7	2.2	1.8	1.6	1.4	1.2
(246) 4.4	(280) 4.0	(241) 3.8	% Depr., Dep., Amort./Sales	(49) 18.1	(36) 4.3	(20) 4.0	(30) 4.1	(44) 3.1	(62) 2.1
10.5	10.1	11.2		29.9	19.6	8.8	8.2	5.2	4.1
1.4	1.6	1.4				2.0	2.1	.8	
(70) 4.0	(80) 4.1	(61) 3.3	% Officers', Directors' Owners' Comp/Sales		(10) 3.4	(16) 3.8	(14) 2.0		
7.1	7.2	5.7				6.1	5.5	3.7	
7082819M	7299216M	8114975M	Net Sales ($)	26954M	102106M	96211M	301375M	828065M	6760264M
4442248M	4487479M	4798150M	Total Assets ($)	155809M	239648M	115726M	292313M	772573M	3222081M

© RMA 2019

M = $ thousand   MM = $ million
See Pages viii through xx for Explanation of Ratios and Data

Current Data Sorted by Assets   Comparative Historical Data

0-500M	500M-2MM	2-10MM	10-50MM	50-100MM	100-250MM	Type of Statement	4/1/14-3/31/15 ALL	4/1/15-3/31/16 ALL
1		1	4	2		Unqualified	13	12
	2	6	1	1		Reviewed	16	16
3	3	4	4			Compiled	13	15
	7	1				Tax Returns	15	15
		12	22	4	2	Other	52	60
| 14 (4/1-9/30/18) |			| 66 (10/1/18-3/31/19) |					
4	12	24	31	7	2	**NUMBER OF STATEMENTS**	109	118
%	%	%	%	%	%	**ASSETS**	%	%
	16.3	18.2	11.0			Cash & Equivalents	10.4	10.9
	24.7	18.2	13.8			Trade Receivables (net)	15.6	15.8
	6.9	1.0	4.0			Inventory	3.8	2.8
	2.4	3.4	.9			All Other Current	2.5	3.5
	50.3	40.8	29.6			Total Current	32.3	33.1
	42.9	48.0	57.4			Fixed Assets (net)	57.3	54.0
	.8	3.9	4.7			Intangibles (net)	5.1	5.8
	6.1	7.2	8.2			All Other Non-Current	5.3	7.2
	100.0	100.0	100.0			Total	100.0	100.0
						LIABILITIES		
	10.2	12.4	5.5			Notes Payable-Short Term	3.6	5.1
	1.5	4.9	3.4			Cur. Mat.-L.T.D.	4.7	4.1
	11.0	5.3	6.1			Trade Payables	7.2	7.0
	.0	.0	.1			Income Taxes Payable	.0	.1
	2.2	4.2	2.7			All Other Current	7.6	7.8
	24.9	26.8	17.8			Total Current	23.2	24.1
	13.5	34.5	43.4			Long-Term Debt	33.0	33.7
	.0	.1	.5			Deferred Taxes	.6	.4
	2.2	5.8	4.5			All Other Non-Current	6.4	5.6
	59.4	32.9	33.8			Net Worth	36.9	36.3
	100.0	100.0	100.0			Total Liabilities & Net Worth	100.0	100.0
						INCOME DATA		
	100.0	100.0	100.0			Net Sales	100.0	100.0
						Gross Profit		
	95.1	79.5	89.9			Operating Expenses	83.3	82.2
	4.9	20.5	10.1			Operating Profit	16.7	17.8
	-.6	6.1	5.1			All Other Expenses (net)	4.9	5.7
	5.5	14.4	5.0			Profit Before Taxes	11.9	12.1
						RATIOS		
	10.6	4.4	2.7				3.0	3.0
	2.6	2.0	1.6			Current	1.2	1.3
	.9	.8	1.1				.7	.7
	10.5	4.1	2.3				2.3	2.7
	2.3	1.6	1.5			Quick	1.1	1.1
	.9	.5	.9				.5	.5
	16 22.5	23 16.0	26 14.3				13 27.5	19 19.0
	30 12.3	32 11.5	36 10.1			Sales/Receivables	29 12.4	32 11.3
	63 5.8	39 9.3	43 8.4				45 8.1	45 8.2
						Cost of Sales/Inventory		
						Cost of Sales/Payables		
	5.3	3.3	5.7				6.7	5.4
	30.9	9.6	12.9			Sales/Working Capital	26.3	20.1
	-263.6	-40.9	59.8				-22.3	-20.7
		24.8	6.0				16.7	13.6
		(22) 4.2	(28) 2.4			EBIT/Interest	(87) 4.8	(98) 4.5
		2.3	1.7				1.8	1.6
							9.9	10.8
						Net Profit + Depr., Dep., Amort./Cur. Mat. L/T/D	(19) 4.2	(22) 5.8
							1.5	1.6
	.2	.5	.9				.6	.7
	.9	1.1	2.1			Fixed/Worth	1.7	1.8
	1.9	109.4	6.7				12.0	62.2
	.1	.4	1.1				.6	.7
	.5	4.0	2.9			Debt/Worth	1.5	2.1
	3.1	149.2	8.0				14.1	83.4
	48.0	82.7	31.9				34.9	45.1
	(11) 36.0	(19) 24.2	(25) 12.2			% Profit Before Taxes/Tangible Net Worth	(85) 16.5	(92) 17.8
	3.6	9.1	6.4				5.9	5.9
	34.6	22.2	8.3				12.3	13.2
	7.8	9.9	5.6			% Profit Before Taxes/Total Assets	7.0	6.9
	-.8	3.6	1.6				1.8	1.3
	76.0	5.6	3.4				9.8	7.9
	9.1	3.7	1.4			Sales/Net Fixed Assets	1.4	1.5
	4.4	1.4	.6				.4	.6
	4.1	2.3	1.9				2.5	2.0
	2.9	1.4	.9			Sales/Total Assets	.9	.8
	2.0	.8	.4				.3	.4
		2.4	1.8				2.8	3.1
		(21) 5.1	(29) 7.5			% Depr., Dep., Amort./Sales	(96) 7.1	(99) 6.4
		7.3	10.9				15.6	15.8
							1.6	1.4
						% Officers', Directors' Owners' Comp/Sales	(25) 2.8	(25) 3.9
							4.5	4.3
4209M	50581M	186767M	1002672M	341333M	102568M	Net Sales ($)	2482936M	3029042M
1251M	17530M	117540M	855574M	585568M	292077M	Total Assets ($)	2725995M	2786973M

Comparative Historical Data | | | | Current Data Sorted by Sales

			Type of Statement						
15	11	7	Unqualified			1	2	1	3
16	14	9	Reviewed			1	2	4	1
10	16	10	Compiled	1		3	3	2	1
11	7	7	Tax Returns	2	3	2			
48	45	47	Other	2	3	3	12	11	16
4/1/16-3/31/17 ALL	4/1/17-3/31/18 ALL	4/1/18-3/31/19 ALL		14 (4/1-9/30/18)			66 (10/1/18-3/31/19)		
				0-1MM	1-3MM	3-5MM	5-10MM	10-25MM	25MM & OVER
100	93	80	**NUMBER OF STATEMENTS**	5	8	10	19	18	20
%	%	%		%	%	%	%	%	%
			ASSETS						
11.5	11.8	14.2	Cash & Equivalents			19.4	17.2	14.5	12.6
16.0	17.3	18.2	Trade Receivables (net)			14.8	17.6	18.0	16.2
4.0	4.6	3.2	Inventory			8.3	.9	1.0	6.8
2.3	2.6	2.0	All Other Current			4.2	1.9	.9	1.5
33.7	36.2	37.5	Total Current			46.6	37.6	34.5	37.1
54.3	51.6	52.6	Fixed Assets (net)			34.3	51.3	58.7	54.2
5.6	6.1	3.2	Intangibles (net)			.4	4.9	5.5	2.7
6.3	6.0	6.7	All Other Non-Current			18.6	6.2	1.3	6.1
100.0	100.0	100.0	Total			100.0	100.0	100.0	100.0
			LIABILITIES						
7.5	7.4	7.4	Notes Payable-Short Term			21.5	8.2	7.2	4.8
5.1	4.0	3.6	Cur. Mat.-L.T.D.			1.8	4.4	3.7	3.7
5.7	5.0	6.2	Trade Payables			5.0	7.5	4.7	7.2
.1	.0	.1	Income Taxes Payable			.2	.0	.1	.0
7.5	10.5	3.2	All Other Current			1.6	3.7	3.5	3.3
25.8	27.0	20.5	Total Current			30.0	23.8	19.2	19.1
34.2	32.5	36.0	Long-Term Debt			18.5	34.0	44.9	36.5
.3	.2	.4	Deferred Taxes			.7	.1	.3	.8
3.5	6.1	4.0	All Other Non-Current			10.2	.7	3.1	3.5
36.2	34.2	39.2	Net Worth			40.6	41.4	32.5	40.2
100.0	100.0	100.0	Total Liabilties & Net Worth			100.0	100.0	100.0	100.0
			INCOME DATA						
100.0	100.0	100.0	Net Sales			100.0	100.0	100.0	100.0
			Gross Profit						
81.9	87.4	86.0	Operating Expenses			77.4	87.1	90.3	91.6
18.1	12.6	14.0	Operating Profit			22.6	12.9	9.7	8.4
6.1	3.4	4.5	All Other Expenses (net)			10.0	2.1	3.6	1.0
12.0	9.2	9.5	Profit Before Taxes			12.7	10.9	6.1	7.3
			RATIOS						
3.4	2.4	3.0				9.8	3.4	2.7	2.8
1.4	1.4	2.1	Current			2.7	1.7	1.5	2.1
.7	.7	1.0				.9	1.0	.9	1.3
2.7	2.1	2.9				9.7	2.9	2.7	2.6
1.2	1.2	1.6	Quick			2.7	1.5	1.4	1.9
.5	.5	.8				.4	.6	.8	.9
13 28.8	21 17.0	24 15.0				22 16.7	18 20.1	31 11.8	32 11.3
32 11.5	33 11.2	34 10.6	Sales/Receivables			37 9.8	29 12.8	35 10.4	41 9.0
43 8.5	42 8.7	45 8.2				49 7.4	48 7.6	40 9.2	52 7.0
			Cost of Sales/Inventory						
			Cost of Sales/Payables						
6.8	7.5	4.3				4.1	3.5	5.9	4.0
16.5	24.5	10.5	Sales/Working Capital			7.4	10.7	16.3	10.3
-15.3	-16.0	-471.1				-38.4	-734.4	-84.6	24.5
26.6	17.9	21.4					25.1	10.5	17.8
(81) 5.2	(75) 5.1	(69) 3.6	EBIT/Interest				(17) 2.8	(16) 3.4	4.6
1.8	1.9	1.9					2.1	-.2	2.3
5.7	5.2	6.0	Net Profit + Depr., Dep.,						
(12) 2.2	(12) 1.7	(19) 3.3	Amort./Cur. Mat. L/T/D						
1.6	1.0	2.0							
.6	.7	.5				.4	.5	.4	.7
1.5	2.0	1.4	Fixed/Worth			.9	1.7	2.3	1.0
8.9	NM	6.5				NM	7.5	-9.9	5.0
.5	.7	.4				.2	.3	.5	.8
2.1	2.2	2.3	Debt/Worth			2.0	1.6	3.2	2.4
17.0	NM	10.4				NM	11.2	-12.5	5.2
63.5	59.4	43.4	% Profit Before Taxes/Tangible				73.2	37.4	32.2
(81) 17.7	(70) 23.8	(66) 22.0	Net Worth				(16) 22.8	(13) 27.9	(19) 18.6
6.5	10.9	7.2					9.0	7.9	7.6
14.5	17.3	15.0	% Profit Before Taxes/Total			39.9	17.0	14.0	9.2
7.3	8.0	6.7	Assets			7.7	9.9	6.0	6.0
.7	2.4	2.4				.7	3.2	-1.1	2.5
10.7	13.8	10.0				55.9	6.9	13.3	7.3
1.9	2.7	2.3	Sales/Net Fixed Assets			4.6	3.5	1.3	1.7
.6	.6	.7				2.3	.7	.6	.9
2.5	3.6	2.3				2.9	2.3	2.7	2.2
.9	1.0	1.0	Sales/Total Assets			1.8	1.3	.8	1.0
.4	.5	.5				1.1	.4	.5	.6
2.8	1.5	2.1					3.1	2.5	1.8
(83) 7.1	(81) 4.3	(70) 5.9	% Depr., Dep., Amort./Sales				(16) 5.2	(16) 6.7	6.3
14.5	11.4	10.4					11.1	9.6	10.7
1.3	1.2	1.0	% Officers', Directors'						
(16) 2.5	(19) 2.2	(16) 3.4	Owners' Comp/Sales						
5.0	5.3	27.5							
2637821M	2698157M	1688130M	Net Sales ($)	2053M	16479M	38954M	133661M	299678M	1197305M
2448646M	2286490M	1869540M	Total Assets ($)	7285M	48140M	35618M	168231M	401793M	1208473M

© RMA 2019

M = $ thousand   MM = $ million
See Pages viii through xx for Explanation of Ratios and Data

Current Data Sorted by Assets   Comparative Historical Data

						Type of Statement		
1		2	7	1	1	Unqualified	13	21
		8	3			Reviewed	24	17
		1				Compiled	7	8
1	1	2	1			Tax Returns	2	8
4		9	5			Other	16	17
	18 (4/1-9/30/18)		29 (10/1/18-3/31/19)				4/1/14-3/31/15	4/1/15-3/31/16
0-500M	500M-2MM	2-10MM	10-50MM	50-100MM	100-250MM		ALL	ALL
2	5	22	16	1	1	NUMBER OF STATEMENTS	62	71
%	%	%	%	%	%	ASSETS	%	%
		10.8	6.2			Cash & Equivalents	13.7	15.6
		12.2	9.7			Trade Receivables (net)	12.5	10.8
		30.0	27.3			Inventory	22.2	21.5
		4.4	1.7			All Other Current	5.1	3.3
		57.4	44.8			Total Current	53.4	51.1
		33.9	39.9			Fixed Assets (net)	34.6	40.2
		2.1	1.1			Intangibles (net)	1.8	1.3
		6.6	14.1			All Other Non-Current	10.3	7.5
		100.0	100.0			Total	100.0	100.0
						LIABILITIES		
		17.5	16.1			Notes Payable-Short Term	11.0	10.8
		1.4	2.5			Cur. Mat.-L.T.D.	2.2	2.8
		20.6	12.0			Trade Payables	13.5	12.3
		.0	.0			Income Taxes Payable	.5	.3
		5.8	6.0			All Other Current	11.3	8.2
		45.3	36.6			Total Current	38.5	34.3
		11.6	17.6			Long-Term Debt	11.6	13.9
		.8	.1			Deferred Taxes	1.2	1.2
		2.0	6.0			All Other Non-Current	3.4	2.8
		40.4	39.7			Net Worth	45.2	47.8
		100.0	100.0			Total Liabilties & Net Worth	100.0	100.0
						INCOME DATA		
		100.0	100.0			Net Sales	100.0	100.0
						Gross Profit		
		93.1	94.7			Operating Expenses	93.0	93.7
		6.9	5.3			Operating Profit	7.0	6.3
		-.6	3.9			All Other Expenses (net)	.5	1.1
		7.5	1.4			Profit Before Taxes	6.5	5.2
						RATIOS		
		2.0	2.3				2.0	2.3
		1.5	1.3			Current	1.3	1.3
		.9	1.0				1.0	1.0
		1.7	1.0				1.2	1.2
		.6	.5			Quick	.6	.5
		.2	.2				.3	.3
		4 82.1	13 27.3				10 35.2	6 62.7
		20 17.9	18 20.7			Sales/Receivables	22 16.8	16 23.5
		38 9.7	25 14.4				42 8.6	33 11.1
						Cost of Sales/Inventory		
						Cost of Sales/Payables		
		5.8	6.9				7.1	10.0
		8.4	22.3			Sales/Working Capital	15.5	16.6
		-32.3	242.2				-240.6	-452.2
		13.5	14.3				19.8	12.7
		(20) 2.8	(15) 3.7			EBIT/Interest	(52) 6.9	(63) 4.3
		-.6	.1				2.2	.7
						Net Profit + Depr., Dep.,	6.7	16.5
						Amort./Cur. Mat. L/T/D	(22) 3.3	(17) 5.2
							1.2	1.3
		.3	.5				.4	.4
		.7	1.1			Fixed/Worth	.6	.7
		2.4	2.1				1.2	1.2
		.7	.7				.6	.4
		1.4	2.5			Debt/Worth	1.3	1.2
		5.0	3.9				2.6	2.1
		20.6	20.6			% Profit Before Taxes/Tangible	25.2	22.4
		(20) 8.0	(15) 12.0			Net Worth	(58) 15.0	(68) 8.5
		-1.3	-6.4				3.5	-.4
		8.0	9.0				11.0	9.5
		2.9	4.2			% Profit Before Taxes/Total Assets	5.6	3.8
		-1.0	-1.7				1.6	-.4
		15.0	10.4				19.1	12.8
		9.0	5.6			Sales/Net Fixed Assets	7.0	6.0
		1.7	2.2				1.4	1.7
		2.6	2.5				3.1	2.9
		1.7	1.7			Sales/Total Assets	1.4	1.7
		.8	.9				.8	.8
		1.1	1.1				.9	.9
		(20) 1.5	2.0			% Depr., Dep., Amort./Sales	(57) 1.9	(68) 2.1
		5.8	2.6				4.6	6.7
						% Officers', Directors'	.2	.4
						Owners' Comp/Sales	(11) .6	(15) .6
							4.0	5.6
394M	9991M	219594M	677860M	171131M	411122M	Net Sales ($)	2441663M	3532138M
543M	7311M	118421M	373345M	59830M	188001M	Total Assets ($)	1384871M	1882278M

Comparative Historical Data | Current Data Sorted by Sales

			Type of Statement		18 (4/1-9/30/18)		29 (10/1/18-3/31/19)		
17	7	11	Unqualified					2	9
21	15	12	Reviewed	2	1	1	4	3	1
5	3	1	Compiled				1		
5	7	5	Tax Returns	2	1	1	1		
19	17	18	Other		4	2	4	6	2
4/1/16-3/31/17 ALL	4/1/17-3/31/18 ALL	4/1/18-3/31/19 ALL		0-1MM	1-3MM	3-5MM	5-10MM	10-25MM	25MM & OVER
67	49	47	NUMBER OF STATEMENTS	4	6	4	10	11	12
%	%	%	**ASSETS**	%	%	%	%	%	%
14.8	10.6	9.4	Cash & Equivalents				3.3	12.7	8.2
15.3	13.6	11.5	Trade Receivables (net)				16.8	13.4	9.8
18.1	22.6	26.0	Inventory				32.2	30.9	31.3
3.8	3.6	5.1	All Other Current				3.1	1.9	2.8
52.1	50.3	52.0	Total Current				55.5	58.9	52.0
37.5	41.6	35.8	Fixed Assets (net)				38.3	30.5	31.2
3.0	1.4	2.4	Intangibles (net)				.9	3.5	1.5
7.4	6.5	9.9	All Other Non-Current				5.3	7.1	15.3
100.0	100.0	100.0	Total				100.0	100.0	100.0
			LIABILITIES						
11.9	20.2	15.1	Notes Payable-Short Term				11.9	18.0	15.0
3.2	6.1	1.8	Cur. Mat.-L.T.D.				1.9	1.4	3.0
11.7	15.8	16.3	Trade Payables				23.2	16.9	16.0
.3	.4	.0	Income Taxes Payable				.0	.0	.1
9.9	7.8	7.3	All Other Current				3.6	5.5	7.7
37.0	50.2	40.5	Total Current				40.6	41.7	41.8
14.5	17.0	13.2	Long-Term Debt				18.2	5.6	11.2
1.5	1.4	.4	Deferred Taxes				.0	.6	.8
2.1	2.3	3.2	All Other Non-Current				2.1	4.0	5.1
45.0	29.1	42.7	Net Worth				39.1	48.1	41.1
100.0	100.0	100.0	Total Liabilities & Net Worth				100.0	100.0	100.0
			INCOME DATA						
100.0	100.0	100.0	Net Sales				100.0	100.0	100.0
			Gross Profit						
92.1	96.1	92.5	Operating Expenses				93.3	95.9	99.7
7.9	3.9	7.5	Operating Profit				6.7	4.1	.3
.9	.1	1.0	All Other Expenses (net)				3.0	-.1	-.9
6.9	3.8	6.5	Profit Before Taxes				3.7	4.2	1.1
			RATIOS						
2.3	2.0	2.0	Current				2.0	2.3	1.5
1.3	1.4	1.4					1.7	1.5	1.2
.9	1.0	1.0					1.3	1.3	1.0
1.6	1.2	1.0	Quick				1.7	1.9	.7
.7	.5	.5					.4	.7	.5
.3	.3	.2					.1	.5	.2
6 58.0	9 41.2	8 48.5	Sales/Receivables				13 29.1	16 22.2	10 36.7
29 12.5	24 14.9	17 21.1					29 12.8	26 13.9	15 23.9
49 7.5	43 8.5	38 9.7					70 5.2	31 11.9	20 18.3
			Cost of Sales/Inventory						
			Cost of Sales/Payables						
7.4	5.9	6.6	Sales/Working Capital				5.4	7.4	12.4
18.3	15.5	11.3					6.7	8.3	34.3
-92.5	-136.8	306.7					NM	11.3	242.2
19.9	13.2	14.0	EBIT/Interest				11.9	23.4	4.4
(61) 4.8	(45) 4.7	(43) 3.2					1.7	(10) 8.0	2.9
1.0	1.3	-.2					-1.5	1.7	-.3
9.5	6.3	9.5	Net Profit + Depr., Dep., Amort./Cur. Mat. L/T/D						
(18) 2.4	(13) 4.1	(10) 3.5							
.7	2.1	1.0							
.4	.5	.4	Fixed/Worth				.4	.3	.5
.0	.0	.8					.9	.5	.7
1.5	2.0	1.7					2.6	1.4	1.4
.5	.7	.6	Debt/Worth				.7	.4	.7
1.3	1.2	1.3					1.5	1.2	2.0
3.2	3.3	4.0					7.4	3.6	3.9
20.1	20.2	20.4	% Profit Before Taxes/Tangible Net Worth				17.6	42.9	20.4
(62) 7.3	(44) 12.6	(43) 9.2					2.8	(10) 14.0	(11) 12.0
.9	1.6	-2.3					-22.0	2.2	-6.4
9.7	7.8	7.8	% Profit Before Taxes/Total Assets				9.4	10.9	6.1
3.4	3.7	3.4					1.5	6.8	3.0
.1	.0	-1.3					-2.5	.7	-2.1
12.6	12.4	11.9	Sales/Net Fixed Assets				13.0	14.7	11.6
6.5	6.0	6.3					6.0	7.4	9.7
1.7	1.5	1.7					1.4	4.4	5.2
3.3	2.5	2.5	Sales/Total Assets				2.0	2.8	3.0
1.7	1.9	1.6					1.2	2.1	2.5
.9	.8	.8					.9	1.3	1.9
1.3	1.2	1.1	% Depr., Dep., Amort./Sales				1.0		1.0
(59) 2.6	(46) 2.1	(43) 2.0					1.3		1.6
5.4	6.4	5.8					5.6		2.1
.3		.6	% Officers', Directors' Owners' Comp/Sales						
(11) 1.0	(10) 1.1	1.1							
3.8		4.1							
2975986M	970288M	1490092M	Net Sales ($)	1559M	10061M	15416M	71604M	188711M	1202741M
1735756M	749695M	747451M	Total Assets ($)	10652M	31333M	12606M	59582M	105590M	527688M

M = $ thousand   MM = $ million
See Pages viii through xx for Explanation of Ratios and Data

Current Data Sorted by Assets   Comparative Historical Data

Type of Statement	0-500M	500M-2MM	2-10MM	10-50MM	50-100MM	100-250MM		ALL 4/1/14-3/31/15	ALL 4/1/15-3/31/16
Unqualified		1	1	5				9	8
Reviewed		1		4		1		17	7
Compiled	1		2	1				9	10
Tax Returns	4	4	6	2		1		15	19
Other	5	12	10	9	3			45	43
	6 (4/1-9/30/18)			67 (10/1/18-3/31/19)					
NUMBER OF STATEMENTS	10	18	19	21	3	2		95	87
	%	%	%	%	%	%		%	%
ASSETS									
Cash & Equivalents	29.9	12.3	9.1	12.3				11.7	14.7
Trade Receivables (net)	17.9	25.5	20.5	23.9				24.5	19.7
Inventory	.5	1.7	5.8	1.0				2.5	4.6
All Other Current	8.6	.9	6.6	3.3				2.3	3.2
Total Current	56.9	40.4	42.0	40.4				41.1	42.2
Fixed Assets (net)	42.1	35.5	52.3	42.9				43.7	42.9
Intangibles (net)	.4	9.8	2.0	6.7				6.3	5.7
All Other Non-Current	.6	14.2	3.8	10.0				9.0	9.2
Total	100.0	100.0	100.0	100.0				100.0	100.0
LIABILITIES									
Notes Payable-Short Term	9.1	3.0	9.5	3.0				13.3	9.3
Cur. Mat.-L.T.D.	6.5	1.1	3.1	3.6				4.8	5.1
Trade Payables	5.4	10.7	8.6	11.5				13.7	8.3
Income Taxes Payable	.3	.0	.3	.0				.0	.0
All Other Current	13.3	10.9	4.7	8.1				7.7	13.5
Total Current	34.6	25.7	26.2	26.3				39.5	36.2
Long-Term Debt	73.5	27.2	37.1	27.3				30.4	25.7
Deferred Taxes	.0	.0	.9	.9				.4	.2
All Other Non-Current	17.5	5.2	3.5	1.0				4.5	17.5
Net Worth	-25.6	42.0	32.2	44.6				25.2	20.4
Total Liabilities & Net Worth	100.0	100.0	100.0	100.0				100.0	100.0
INCOME DATA									
Net Sales	100.0	100.0	100.0	100.0				100.0	100.0
Gross Profit									
Operating Expenses	84.7	84.2	73.5	87.5				85.0	84.0
Operating Profit	15.3	15.8	26.5	12.5				15.0	16.0
All Other Expenses (net)	1.6	1.3	9.6	3.4				4.4	3.0
Profit Before Taxes	13.7	14.5	16.9	9.1				10.6	13.1
RATIOS									
Current	11.7	7.8	3.6	2.6				2.3	3.4
	1.5	1.3	1.4	1.4				1.4	1.6
	.8	.7	.9	1.1				.7	.7
Quick	10.9	7.8	2.6	2.5				2.1	2.9
	1.0	1.0	1.0	1.3				1.1	1.2
	.3	.7	.3	.9				.6	.5
Sales/Receivables	0 UND	11 34.1	0 UND	34 10.7				3 129.3	4 90.0
	0 UND	37 9.8	34 10.6	41 8.9				34 10.8	33 10.9
	9 39.1	87 4.2	63 5.8	60 6.1				56 6.5	48 7.6
Cost of Sales/Inventory									
Cost of Sales/Payables									
Sales/Working Capital	10.6	3.1	6.5	4.2				6.8	7.6
	75.2	241.9	16.2	16.9				20.4	16.8
	NM	-21.2	-41.0	NM				-19.3	-24.4
EBIT/Interest		14.7	15.2	34.5				16.8	15.9
		(11) 6.1	(11) 6.1	(18) 5.7				(76) 5.0	(65) 5.2
		-1.7	-2.1	1.5				1.4	1.4
Net Profit + Depr., Dep., Amort./Cur. Mat. L/T/D								5.7	2.4
								(16) 3.1	(12) 1.4
								1.6	1.0
Fixed/Worth	.2	.2	.3	.5				.5	.3
	58.4	1.5	2.2	1.3				1.3	1.4
	-.3	-1.7	13.0	10.9				15.6	-179.3
Debt/Worth	.2	.1	.9	.4				.7	.4
	127.9	.9	4.1	1.7				2.5	1.9
	-2.5	-6.5	43.2	10.7				32.3	-184.0
% Profit Before Taxes/Tangible Net Worth		51.0	77.8	37.2				47.0	57.6
		(10) 31.2	(16) 37.3	(17) 18.1				(73) 24.4	(65) 28.2
		10.5	18.8	6.1				10.8	11.2
% Profit Before Taxes/Total Assets	83.7	26.6	19.8	16.0				18.8	28.6
	37.5	15.0	8.1	5.5				5.8	11.7
	5.6	-.5	1.4	1.9				1.1	2.3
Sales/Net Fixed Assets	183.4	15.5	27.7	9.3				26.0	41.9
	25.5	9.2	3.6	3.6				5.7	6.6
	2.5	2.1	.2	1.2				1.0	1.2
Sales/Total Assets	11.7	2.9	2.7	2.7				3.6	3.9
	5.9	1.4	.6	1.4				1.8	1.9
	1.8	1.1	.2	.7				.5	.7
% Depr., Dep., Amort./Sales		2.1	.4	1.6				1.8	1.5
		(12) 5.3	(14) 3.0	(20) 3.8				(70) 5.4	(64) 3.9
		8.3	12.0	8.8				10.8	9.4
% Officers', Directors' Owners' Comp/Sales								2.9	3.7
								(16) 9.4	(18) 5.0
								12.6	11.0
Net Sales ($)	25177M	40478M	166668M	739936M	148085M	108776M		2025520M	1448435M
Total Assets ($)	3385M	21410M	80398M	366924M	237974M	335198M		1308139M	882622M

M = $ thousand   MM = $ million
See Pages viii through xx for Explanation of Ratios and Data

Comparative Historical Data | Current Data Sorted by Sales

	Hist	Hist	Hist			6 (4/1-9/30/18)		67 (10/1/18-3/31/19)	
Type of Statement				0-1MM	1-3MM	3-5MM	5-10MM	10-25MM	25MM & OVER
Unqualified	5	8	7		1			4	2
Reviewed	7	8	6			1	1		4
Compiled	10	6	4	1				3	
Tax Returns	9	16	16	6	5	3	1	1	
Other	25	36	40	10	7	2	5	7	9
	4/1/16-3/31/17 ALL	4/1/17-3/31/18 ALL	4/1/18-3/31/19 ALL						
NUMBER OF STATEMENTS	56	74	73	17	13	6	7	15	15
	%	%	%	%	%	%	%	%	%
ASSETS									
Cash & Equivalents	14.1	16.4	13.9	12.1	13.5			14.1	14.0
Trade Receivables (net)	22.5	17.6	21.5	7.6	13.7			23.6	33.6
Inventory	4.3	1.7	2.3	.0	.0			7.7	1.1
All Other Current	3.2	2.7	4.1	2.5	6.5			1.7	4.1
Total Current	44.1	38.4	41.8	22.2	33.7			47.0	52.8
Fixed Assets (net)	39.5	39.7	44.1	67.9	50.1			29.7	34.3
Intangibles (net)	8.4	5.0	5.6	8.6	3.4			10.6	3.3
All Other Non-Current	8.0	17.0	8.5	1.3	12.8			12.7	9.6
Total	100.0	100.0	100.0	100.0	100.0			100.0	100.0
LIABILITIES									
Notes Payable-Short Term	9.9	10.2	5.3	4.5	5.6			5.5	4.2
Cur. Mat.-L.T.D.	2.5	5.5	3.2	2.1	5.6			3.0	3.2
Trade Payables	10.9	9.7	9.2	3.4	2.0			10.7	16.9
Income Taxes Payable	.0	.1	.2	.0	.2			.1	.5
All Other Current	13.0	15.6	8.1	8.2	3.7			4.1	9.7
Total Current	36.4	41.2	26.0	18.2	17.1			23.4	34.4
Long-Term Debt	24.1	26.8	35.7	45.8	51.4			21.4	13.9
Deferred Taxes	.8	.3	.5	.0	1.2			1.0	.0
All Other Non-Current	9.7	6.0	5.5	12.8	1.5			4.7	3.5
Net Worth	29.0	25.8	32.3	23.2	28.8			49.6	48.2
Total Liabilities & Net Worth	100.0	100.0	100.0	100.0	100.0			100.0	100.0
INCOME DATA									
Net Sales	100.0	100.0	100.0	100.0	100.0			100.0	100.0
Gross Profit									
Operating Expenses	84.3	88.9	82.8	66.7	73.3			90.1	93.2
Operating Profit	15.7	11.1	17.2	33.3	26.7			9.9	6.8
All Other Expenses (net)	3.1	2.5	3.9	12.1	2.0			.7	1.1
Profit Before Taxes	12.6	8.6	13.4	21.2	24.6			9.2	5.8
RATIOS									
Current	2.5	2.8	3.7	3.4	23.3			3.6	3.6
	1.6	1.2	1.4	1.0	2.1			2.0	1.4
	.9	.6	.9	.4	.7			1.1	.9
Quick	2.3	2.8	3.6	3.1	23.2			3.4	3.6
	1.3	1.0	1.3	.8	2.1			1.9	1.3
	.6	.4	.6	.2	.4			.9	.6
Sales/Receivables	13 27.7	0 UND	5 72.2	0 UND	0 UND			33 10.9	36 10.2
	37 9.8	33 11.2	35 10.4	4 88.5	8 43.6			59 6.2	41 8.9
	49 7.5	49 7.4	59 6.2	22 16.7	91 4.0			63 5.8	54 6.8
Cost of Sales/Inventory									
Cost of Sales/Payables									
Sales/Working Capital	6.8	7.3	4.8	6.8	2.7			4.0	5.7
	12.4	31.8	16.9	851.0	11.3			7.4	19.6
	-59.5	-13.9	-47.8	-8.3	-26.5			26.2	-87.1
EBIT/Interest	15.0	14.7	15.4	15.0				25.7	30.4
	(42) 5.5	(55) 4.9	(49) 5.8	(10) 5.3				(13) 4.5	(12) 8.0
	2.5	1.5	1.3	-.9				-2.0	2.6
Net Profit + Depr., Dep., Amort./Cur. Mat. L/T/D	5.1	6.5							
	(10) 3.4	(10) 3.9							
	1.5	1.5							
Fixed/Worth	.4	.3	.3	1.8	.1			.3	.3
	1.2	1.2	1.4	6.4	.8			.9	1.0
	3.8	9.8	-45.9	-8.6	8.4			-1.2	1.8
Debt/Worth	.5	.5	.3	1.0	.0			.2	.5
	2.7	2.4	1.2	5.6	.2			.8	.9
	9.9	18.0	-117.8	-43.7	28.8			-10.1	2.8
% Profit Before Taxes/Tangible Net Worth	67.3	55.4	51.0	54.8	52.2			43.4	39.0
	(47) 35.2	(59) 27.4	(54) 26.3	(11) 26.5	(11) 35.2			(11) 17.7	(13) 20.9
	12.5	6.8	10.5	13.5	11.0			4.6	7.8
% Profit Before Taxes/Total Assets	27.0	26.3	24.5	25.1	38.9			19.8	17.2
	8.7	8.4	7.9	6.8	10.3			6.9	10.9
	3.5	.9	2.3	1.8	4.0			1.4	4.0
Sales/Net Fixed Assets	34.8	36.9	21.2	7.2	19.0			16.9	27.7
	7.3	7.6	5.6	.6	2.1			5.6	8.9
	1.1	2.0	.7	.2	.7			1.6	3.6
Sales/Total Assets	3.3	3.1	3.0	1.4	1.4			2.7	4.1
	1.9	1.9	1.4	.5	1.2			1.2	2.6
	.6	.8	.5	.2	.4			.8	1.5
% Depr., Dep., Amort./Sales	.8	1.3	1.5	6.6				1.2	.7
	(44) 4.3	(58) 2.8	(58) 5.2	(11) 11.2				(14) 3.8	(14) 2.4
	9.8	12.9	9.9	14.5				9.5	6.1
% Officers', Directors' Owners' Comp/Sales	1.6	2.4	1.6						
	(14) 4.2	(19) 5.3	(10) 3.5						
	9.9	12.6	5.7						
Net Sales ($)	1304053M	1728264M	1229120M	9529M	20126M	23006M	46277M	237270M	892912M
Total Assets ($)	675218M	1069537M	1045289M	25420M	46636M	5464M	35947M	442146M	489676M

M = $ thousand   MM = $ million
See Pages viii through xx for Explanation of Ratios and Data

INFORMATION

INFORMATION—Newspaper Publishers NAICS 511110

Current Data Sorted by Assets

Comparative Historical Data

0-500M	500M-2MM	2-10MM	10-50MM	50-100MM	100-250MM	Type of Statement	4/1/14-3/31/15 ALL	4/1/15-3/31/16 ALL
		1			1	Unqualified	8	7
		1	2			Reviewed	9	10
		1				Compiled	3	4
	2	2	5	2		Tax Returns	8	11
1	2	5				Other	25	13
		3 (4/1-9/30/18)	22 (10/1/18-3/31/19)					
1	4	10	7	2	1	NUMBER OF STATEMENTS	53	45
%	%	%	%	%	%		%	%
						ASSETS		
		18.6				Cash & Equivalents	13.1	11.6
		32.1				Trade Receivables (net)	21.9	20.9
		11.5				Inventory	3.6	1.9
		1.7				All Other Current	8.4	1.8
		64.0				Total Current	47.0	36.2
		14.7				Fixed Assets (net)	22.5	24.9
		17.0				Intangibles (net)	20.9	22.2
		4.3				All Other Non-Current	9.6	16.7
		100.0				Total	100.0	100.0
						LIABILITIES		
		9.5				Notes Payable-Short Term	4.9	3.5
		5.2				Cur. Mat.-L.T.D.	4.3	3.1
		17.4				Trade Payables	8.0	8.2
		.1				Income Taxes Payable	.1	.4
		28.9				All Other Current	14.7	23.2
		61.2				Total Current	32.0	38.4
		11.2				Long-Term Debt	20.8	21.1
		.0				Deferred Taxes	.5	.3
		34.5				All Other Non-Current	21.2	3.6
		-6.9				Net Worth	25.5	36.6
		100.0				Total Liabilties & Net Worth	100.0	100.0
						INCOME DATA		
		100.0				Net Sales	100.0	100.0
		58.8				Gross Profit	55.5	57.0
		51.5				Operating Expenses	48.2	51.0
		7.3				Operating Profit	7.3	6.0
		1.9				All Other Expenses (net)	2.3	.2
		5.4				Profit Before Taxes	5.0	5.8
						RATIOS		
		2.1				Current	2.9	2.2
		1.3					1.4	1.4
		.8					.9	.6
		2.0				Quick	2.5	2.1
		.8					1.0	1.2
		.6					.7	.5
		29 12.8				Sales/Receivables	31 11.9	34 10.8
		41 8.8					36 10.0	39 9.4
		85 4.3					45 8.2	47 7.7
		0 UND				Cost of Sales/Inventory	0 UND	0 UND
		0 UND					7 54.6	5 74.4
		69 5.3					19 19.7	14 25.4
		21 17.2				Cost of Sales/Payables	12 30.6	11 33.6
		46 7.9					28 12.9	28 12.9
		159 2.3					46 8.0	63 5.8
		5.5				Sales/Working Capital	5.4	9.3
		12.5					19.3	30.1
		-53.9					-50.3	-13.4
						EBIT/Interest	7.0	14.4
							(44) 4.0	(38) 4.7
							1.2	1.4
						Net Profit + Depr., Dep., Amort./Cur. Mat. L/T/D	3.0	
							(12) 1.3	
							.2	
		.1				Fixed/Worth	.2	.1
		1.0					.9	1.1
		-.2					-1.7	-4.9
		1.7				Debt/Worth	.7	.6
		NM					2.6	2.1
		-2.5					-5.1	-9.3
						% Profit Before Taxes/Tangible Net Worth	75.0	45.2
							(33) 10.5	(32) 16.5
							.1	1.4
		16.9				% Profit Before Taxes/Total Assets	13.5	16.0
		9.7					6.5	5.7
		1.8					.3	.4
		151.9				Sales/Net Fixed Assets	58.2	97.1
		50.3					9.2	6.7
		7.2					3.5	2.8
		3.6				Sales/Total Assets	3.1	2.6
		1.6					1.6	1.3
		1.2					.9	.8
						% Depr., Dep., Amort./Sales	1.6	1.0
							(37) 3.7	(33) 3.3
							4.8	4.4
						% Officers', Directors' Owners' Comp/Sales	2.9	
							(12) 6.1	
							15.8	
4011M	16310M	133283M	159345M	352350M	104052M	Net Sales ($)	1650160M	1233149M
402M	5628M	55539M	120810M	192604M	123600M	Total Assets ($)	1504023M	1497075M

© RMA 2019

M = $ thousand   MM = $ million
See Pages viii through xx for Explanation of Ratios and Data

Comparative Historical Data | Current Data Sorted by Sales

Type of Statement

	4/1/16-3/31/17		4/1/17-3/31/18		4/1/18-3/31/19		0-1MM	1-3MM	3-5MM	5-10MM	10-25MM	25MM & OVER
	8		7		2	Unqualified				1	1	2
	5		5		3	Reviewed						1
	4		1		1	Compiled				1		
	9		2		5	Tax Returns			1	3		
	6		13		14	Other		1	2	5	3	4
	ALL		ALL		ALL			3 (4/1-9/30/18)		22 (10/1/18-3/31/19)		
	32		28		25	NUMBER OF STATEMENTS		1	3	10	4	7

	4/1/16-3/31/17 %		4/1/17-3/31/18 %		4/1/18-3/31/19 %		0-1MM %	1-3MM %	3-5MM %	5-10MM %	10-25MM %	25MM & OVER %
						ASSETS						
	18.9		21.6		18.3	Cash & Equivalents				24.5		
	25.7		16.8		25.1	Trade Receivables (net)				24.7		
	1.9		2.1		6.2	Inventory				13.2		
	2.7		2.3		1.3	All Other Current				1.3		
	49.4		42.8		50.9	Total Current				63.8		
	20.8		25.2		25.1	Fixed Assets (net)				18.9		
	17.3		22.0		18.3	Intangibles (net)				15.0		
	12.5		10.0		5.7	All Other Non-Current				2.3		
	100.0		100.0		100.0	Total				100.0		
						LIABILITIES						
	9.0		3.3		5.7	Notes Payable-Short Term				9.9		
	2.9		3.7		4.0	Cur. Mat.-L.T.D.				1.3		
	11.8		8.0		11.1	Trade Payables				18.3		
	.2		.2		.2	Income Taxes Payable				.3		
	11.2		12.6		20.5	All Other Current				13.2		
	35.2		27.8		41.5	Total Current				42.9		
	31.9		22.1		18.7	Long-Term Debt				20.6		
	.4		.2		.4	Deferred Taxes				.0		
	22.4		5.7		15.7	All Other Non-Current				5.1		
	10.1		44.2		23.7	Net Worth				31.4		
	100.0		100.0		100.0	Total Liabilities & Net Worth				100.0		
						INCOME DATA						
	100.0		100.0		100.0	Net Sales				100.0		
	57.8		53.1		62.2	Gross Profit				66.4		
	53.2		47.7		57.5	Operating Expenses				60.9		
	4.6		5.3		4.7	Operating Profit				5.5		
	.8		1.6		1.6	All Other Expenses (net)				3.0		
	3.8		3.8		3.0	Profit Before Taxes				2.5		
						RATIOS						
	2.6		3.4		2.0	Current				2.6		
	1.4		1.8		1.1					1.8		
	.8		.8		.8					1.1		
	1.8		3.1		2.0	Quick				2.1		
	1.1		1.7		.9					1.8		
	.7		.7		.7					.7		
28	13.0	29	12.4	27	13.6	Sales/Receivables				28 13.2		
39	9.4	38	9.5	32	11.3					42 8.6		
56	6.5	54	6.7	51	7.2					114 3.2		
0	UND	0	UND	0	UND	Cost of Sales/Inventory				0 UND		
6	64.3	8	48.6	4	99.2					6 59.6		
17	21.5	22	16.3	41	9.0					332 1.1		
11	32.1	9	39.3	17	21.6	Cost of Sales/Payables				39 9.3		
30	12.1	25	14.5	32	11.3					104 3.5		
74	4.9	81	4.5	118	3.1					243 1.5		
	5.5		3.7		6.6	Sales/Working Capital				3.9		
	19.7		15.0		40.8					7.0		
	-36.5		-20.0		-35.3					19.8		
	8.6		8.1		10.7	EBIT/Interest						
(28)	2.5	(20)	1.9	(20)	4.7							
	.6		.1		-.4							
						Net Profit + Depr., Dep., Amort./Cur. Mat. L/T/D						
	.3		.1		.2	Fixed/Worth				.1		
	1.9		.8		1.4					.6		
	-.8		-3.2		-1.2					-.8		
	1.3		.5		1.0	Debt/Worth				1.0		
	NM		2.7		2.3					2.0		
	-3.0		-5.0		-3.1					-2.9		
	38.6		30.3		43.2	% Profit Before Taxes/Tangible Net Worth						
(16)	11.7	(17)	5.4	(17)	19.0							
	-1.2		-2.5		-1.9							
	16.3		17.5		17.7	% Profit Before Taxes/Total Assets				15.2		
	4.2		3.3		5.1					6.7		
	-1.1		-1.1		-.7					-3.2		
	93.0		35.6		59.9	Sales/Net Fixed Assets				77.0		
	10.6		4.9		8.2					27.5		
	4.1		2.4		3.4					3.4		
	3.9		1.8		3.0	Sales/Total Assets				2.0		
	1.6		1.1		1.6					1.4		
	1.0		.8		1.0					.8		
	.7		1.4		1.9	% Depr., Dep., Amort./Sales						
(26)	2.7	(24)	3.4	(18)	2.6							
	4.1		4.8		5.2							
	2.0					% Officers', Directors', Owners' Comp/Sales						
(11)	2.8											
	5.2											
	981659M		936996M		769351M	Net Sales ($)		2849M	11920M	72150M	62531M	619901M
	897374M		856743M		498583M	Total Assets ($)		531M	3581M	67246M	42632M	384593M

(Right-side columns 0-1MM through 3-5MM marked **DATA NOT AVAILABLE** for Assets, Liabilities, Income Data and Ratios.)

M = $ thousand   MM = $ million
See Pages viii through xx for Explanation of Ratios and Data

Current Data Sorted by Assets

Comparative Historical Data

						Type of Statement		
		1	2	2	3	Unqualified	18	16
		1	3			Reviewed	10	10
	2	1	1			Compiled	4	5
4	3	1				Tax Returns	6	12
2	2	8	4	2	2	Other	35	36
	5 (4/1-9/30/18)		38 (10/1/18-3/31/19)				4/1/14-3/31/15	4/1/15-3/31/16
0-500M	500M-2MM	2-10MM	10-50MM	50-100MM	100-250MM		ALL	ALL
6	7	11	10	4	5	NUMBER OF STATEMENTS	73	79
%	%	%	%	%	%	ASSETS	%	%
		15.2	9.4			Cash & Equivalents	16.3	16.2
		24.4	32.4			Trade Receivables (net)	24.6	21.7
		3.7	5.5			Inventory	4.8	5.4
		2.8	3.4			All Other Current	3.5	3.1
		46.1	50.8			Total Current	49.2	46.3
		8.9	18.3			Fixed Assets (net)	12.7	14.2
		32.4	23.2			Intangibles (net)	27.4	27.7
		12.5	7.6			All Other Non-Current	10.7	11.8
		100.0	100.0			Total	100.0	100.0
						LIABILITIES		
		3.7	7.0			Notes Payable-Short Term	3.4	6.4
		5.1	2.7			Cur. Mat.-L.T.D.	2.9	3.8
		13.8	16.8			Trade Payables	11.7	11.6
		.0	.2			Income Taxes Payable	.3	.7
		24.3	18.9			All Other Current	24.3	24.2
		46.9	45.6			Total Current	42.6	46.8
		7.5	10.0			Long-Term Debt	15.9	20.4
		.0	2.1			Deferred Taxes	.6	.3
		3.4	12.2			All Other Non-Current	18.3	19.4
		42.2	30.1			Net Worth	22.6	13.1
		100.0	100.0			Total Liabilities & Net Worth	100.0	100.0
						INCOME DATA		
		100.0	100.0			Net Sales	100.0	100.0
		54.3	41.1			Gross Profit	48.6	52.0
		49.9	32.4			Operating Expenses	41.5	46.3
		4.3	8.7			Operating Profit	7.1	5.7
		.5	5.9			All Other Expenses (net)	1.6	1.2
		3.8	2.8			Profit Before Taxes	5.5	4.5
						RATIOS		
		1.8	2.0				2.0	1.5
		.9	1.1			Current	1.2	1.1
		.7	.8				.8	.7
		1.8	1.8				2.0	1.3
		.8	.9			Quick	.9	.9
		.3	.6				.6	.5
		26 14.0	26 14.3				28 13.1	27 13.4
		29 12.8	53 6.9			Sales/Receivables	37 9.8	37 9.8
		54 6.8	66 5.5				57 6.4	63 5.8
		0 UND	0 UND				0 UND	0 UND
		0 UND	0 UND			Cost of Sales/Inventory	3 120.8	1 361.2
		10 36.7	34 10.6				19 18.9	16 22.2
		22 16.8	24 15.0				12 31.1	13 27.9
		38 9.7	47 7.7			Cost of Sales/Payables	29 12.7	36 10.1
		59 6.2	73 5.0				56 6.5	70 5.2
		12.5	7.3				8.3	11.1
		-54.9	38.6			Sales/Working Capital	25.0	50.9
		-16.2	-16.6				-21.3	-15.5
							38.3	30.8
						EBIT/Interest	(53) 8.1	(64) 5.7
							1.4	.9
						Net Profit + Depr., Dep.,	19.4	15.7
						Amort./Cur. Mat. L/T/D	(17) 3.7	(20) 3.0
							.7	1.5
		.0	.2				.2	.2
		.2	3.6			Fixed/Worth	1.6	1.8
		-.4	-.5				-.3	-.2
		.8	1.0				.9	1.7
		4.1	4.9			Debt/Worth	12.6	12.7
		-2.5	-5.6				-2.9	-2.4
						% Profit Before Taxes/Tangible	121.9	185.8
						Net Worth	(41) 47.3	(42) 58.3
							4.7	8.3
		52.4	31.6				26.4	23.5
		5.6	10.6			% Profit Before Taxes/Total	7.7	5.5
		-3.7	-5.5			Assets	1.0	.2
		349.3	48.8				88.4	75.7
		79.3	26.0			Sales/Net Fixed Assets	28.4	29.1
		55.5	7.0				9.2	8.8
		5.7	3.0				2.6	3.1
		2.1	2.0			Sales/Total Assets	2.0	1.9
		1.4	1.3				1.1	1.1
							.8	.8
						% Depr., Dep., Amort./Sales	(46) 1.7	(52) 1.6
							4.4	4.7
							3.0	3.6
						% Officers', Directors'	(13) 6.0	(16) 5.7
						Owners' Comp/Sales	9.0	14.3
14865M	29272M	149513M	554455M	443767M	886984M	Net Sales ($)	4059072M	3234922M
1938M	10296M	55194M	264644M	292744M	808192M	Total Assets ($)	2306285M	2623017M

M = $ thousand   MM = $ million
See Pages viii through xx for Explanation of Ratios and Data

Comparative Historical Data | Current Data Sorted by Sales

	4/1/16-3/31/17 ALL	4/1/17-3/31/18 ALL	4/1/18-3/31/19 ALL	Type of Statement	0-1MM	1-3MM	3-5MM	5-10MM	10-25MM	25MM & OVER
				Unqualified					1	7
				Reviewed					2	2
				Compiled			1	1	1	
				Tax Returns		4	2	2		
				Other	1	3	1	1	7	7
	9 9 4 10 40	8 6 4 10 28	8 4 3 8 20			5 (4/1-9/30/18)			38 (10/1/18-3/31/19)	
NUMBER OF STATEMENTS	72	56	43		1	7	4	4	11	16
ASSETS	%	%	%		%	%	%	%	%	%
Cash & Equivalents	11.8	16.6	18.2						13.9	16.9
Trade Receivables (net)	30.9	28.1	27.1						32.6	23.9
Inventory	5.4	3.2	3.0						6.1	2.4
All Other Current	3.2	3.8	2.6						3.3	2.8
Total Current	51.3	51.7	50.9						55.8	46.1
Fixed Assets (net)	11.7	12.0	12.7						13.9	12.4
Intangibles (net)	21.3	23.2	26.8						21.8	25.2
All Other Non-Current	15.7	13.0	9.6						8.4	16.3
Total	100.0	100.0	100.0						100.0	100.0
LIABILITIES										
Notes Payable-Short Term	7.5	15.3	5.4						3.9	2.8
Cur. Mat. L.T.D.	3.7	3.3	2.8						5.2	1.7
Trade Payables	13.0	11.8	12.1						14.4	14.0
Income Taxes Payable	.4	.1	.1						.0	.3
All Other Current	30.4	25.0	22.3						19.5	26.4
Total Current	55.1	55.6	42.7						43.0	45.3
Long-Term Debt	22.2	16.9	14.6						5.3	11.0
Deferred Taxes	.3	.3	.5						.4	1.1
All Other Non-Current	17.8	18.9	7.9						3.4	15.9
Net Worth	4.7	8.5	34.2						47.9	26.7
Total Liabilities & Net Worth	100.0	100.0	100.0						100.0	100.0
INCOME DATA										
Net Sales	100.0	100.0	100.0						100.0	100.0
Gross Profit	53.3	55.3	53.5						48.3	44.9
Operating Expenses	47.8	47.8	45.7						36.5	36.3
Operating Profit	5.5	7.5	7.8						11.8	8.6
All Other Expenses (net)	1.1	2.8	2.0						.3	3.9
Profit Before Taxes	4.4	4.6	5.8						11.4	4.7
RATIOS										
Current	1.5	1.9	1.9						2.0	1.7
	1.0	1.2	1.1						1.6	1.0
	.6	.7	.7						.9	.6
Quick	1.3	1.7	1.8						2.0	1.6
	.9	1.0	.9						.9	.8
	.5	.6	.6						.7	.6
Sales/Receivables	24 15.4	26 13.9	26 14.0						27 13.6	26 14.2
	39 9.3	40 9.1	45 8.1						54 6.8	48 7.6
	66 5.5	64 5.7	58 6.3						65 5.6	62 5.9
Cost of Sales/Inventory	0 UND	0 UND	0 UND						0 UND	0 UND
	0 UND	0 UND	0 UND						4 91.0	0 UND
	21 17.7	13 29.0	16 23.3						44 8.3	15 24.3
Cost of Sales/Payables	14 26.5	15 24.8	13 27.6						22 16.8	9 38.8
	31 11.6	34 10.7	38 9.7						35 10.5	51 7.1
	68 5.4	59 6.2	72 5.1						55 6.6	89 4.1
Sales/Working Capital	21.0	11.0	9.8						9.8	10.4
	137.3	29.2	45.3						18.7	NM
	-12.9	-21.9	-18.8						-34.4	-12.0
EBIT/Interest	31.1	35.5	17.5							9.9
	(55) 5.4	(45) 5.9	(29) 3.9						(12) 4.8	
	.7	-1.7	-.2							.2
Net Profit + Depr., Dep., Amort./Cur. Mat. L/T/D	9.9									
	(10) 3.2									
	.5									
Fixed/Worth	.2	.1	.1						.1	.4
	0.1	.7	0						.2	4.0
	-.2	-.3	-.4						1.4	-.2
Debt/Worth	1.5	1.3	1.0						.8	4.1
	-153.2	7.0	4.9						1.8	8.1
	-3.4	-2.7	-2.5						4.1	-4.2
% Profit Before Taxes/Tangible Net Worth	235.5	161.1	134.2						158.9	
	(35) 75.0	(33) 65.0	(27) 42.6						(10) 100.6	
	26.9	11.0	-3.3						8.1	
% Profit Before Taxes/Total Assets	31.1	32.9	32.4						52.4	28.0
	8.6	6.5	9.5						19.0	8.3
	-1.3	-1.1	-1.0						.0	.5
Sales/Net Fixed Assets	135.2	149.3	291.0						139.0	43.7
	39.2	45.3	37.7						58.1	33.2
	14.6	14.7	14.7						8.0	14.5
Sales/Total Assets	3.8	3.7	3.6						2.7	2.7
	2.4	2.3	2.0						2.0	1.6
	1.5	1.2	1.2						1.7	.9
% Depr., Dep., Amort./Sales	.4	.4	.4							.7
	(49) .8	(42) .9	(24) 1.2						(10) 2.1	
	2.9	2.7	3.0							3.6
% Officers', Directors' Owners' Comp/Sales	3.7	1.9	3.5							
	(20) 7.2	(14) 4.7	(13) 5.4							
	11.7	10.4	13.9							
Net Sales ($)	3371767M	2300911M	2078856M		708M	13604M	13897M	24652M	192007M	1833988M
Total Assets ($)	2127592M	1765500M	1433008M		183M	9379M	6253M	4574M	95686M	1316933M

M = $ thousand   MM = $ million
See Pages viii through xx for Explanation of Ratios and Data

INFORMATION—Book Publishers NAICS 511130

Current Data Sorted by Assets | **Comparative Historical Data**

Type of Statement

0-500M	500M-2MM	2-10MM	10-50MM	50-100MM	100-250MM	Type of Statement	4/1/14-3/31/15 ALL	4/1/15-3/31/16 ALL
	1	1	2	6	1	Unqualified	21	12
	1	3	5			Reviewed	18	18
1	1	1				Compiled	6	4
2	4	2			1	Tax Returns	12	10
1	5	8	9	2	2	Other	42	43

Periods: 17 (4/1-9/30/18) · 42 (10/1/18-3/31/19)

Data

0-500M	500M-2MM	2-10MM	10-50MM	50-100MM	100-250MM		4/1/14-3/31/15 ALL	4/1/15-3/31/16 ALL
4	12	15	16	9	3	**NUMBER OF STATEMENTS**	99	87
%	%	%	%	%	%	**ASSETS**	%	%
	11.5	12.3	13.9			Cash & Equivalents	14.6	17.8
	20.4	21.4	20.8			Trade Receivables (net)	20.7	22.7
	46.5	20.8	19.8			Inventory	27.8	21.5
	.1	6.8	10.5			All Other Current	6.9	4.7
	78.5	61.3	65.0			Total Current	70.0	66.7
	6.4	14.3	14.9			Fixed Assets (net)	9.1	9.8
	10.3	12.8	11.0			Intangibles (net)	11.0	13.9
	4.8	11.6	9.1			All Other Non-Current	9.9	9.6
	100.0	100.0	100.0			Total	100.0	100.0
						LIABILITIES		
	13.7	9.6	4.5			Notes Payable-Short Term	6.4	5.0
	1.9	1.6	2.1			Cur. Mat.-L.T.D.	2.0	1.2
	4.3	6.2	8.2			Trade Payables	12.0	11.6
	.0	.1	.0			Income Taxes Payable	.4	.4
	24.9	27.9	17.2			All Other Current	13.8	16.7
	44.8	45.3	32.0			Total Current	34.6	34.9
	2.2	14.7	5.8			Long-Term Debt	8.1	10.9
	.0	.0	.0			Deferred Taxes	.4	.6
	26.1	10.2	6.1			All Other Non-Current	11.2	5.2
	26.9	29.7	56.2			Net Worth	45.7	48.3
	100.0	100.0	100.0			Total Liabilities & Net Worth	100.0	100.0
						INCOME DATA		
	100.0	100.0	100.0			Net Sales	100.0	100.0
	60.9	59.5	56.2			Gross Profit	53.7	56.7
	54.0	54.4	48.3			Operating Expenses	46.1	49.2
	6.9	5.1	7.9			Operating Profit	7.6	7.4
	.1	2.3	4.0			All Other Expenses (net)	.4	1.0
	6.8	2.8	3.9			Profit Before Taxes	7.2	6.5
						RATIOS		
	5.2	2.4	3.4				3.6	4.0
	2.8	1.4	2.2			Current	2.3	2.2
	2.3	.7	1.3				1.5	1.2
	3.0	1.4	1.8				2.0	2.4
	1.1	.7	1.0			Quick	1.1	1.2
	.2	.5	.7				.6	.6
6 57.5	29 12.6	35 10.5					32 11.4 / 31 11.6	
41 8.8	54 6.8	60 6.1				Sales/Receivables	57 6.4 / 56 6.5	
57 6.4	69 5.3	81 4.5					85 4.3 / 76 4.8	
146 2.5	62 5.9	89 4.1					79 4.6 / 53 6.9	
192 1.9	107 3.4	130 2.8				Cost of Sales/Inventory	140 2.6 / 130 2.8	
730 .5	243 1.5	192 1.9					261 1.4 / 203 1.8	
0 UND	8 46.0	29 12.7					22 16.6 / 18 19.9	
3 109.3	21 17.1	42 8.7				Cost of Sales/Payables	47 7.7 / 48 7.6	
33 10.9	60 6.1	66 5.5					114 3.2 / 89 4.1	
	1.8	3.7	2.4				2.3	2.3
	4.5	5.5	4.0			Sales/Working Capital	3.8	4.6
	9.8	-19.0	12.0				7.1	20.9
		3.5	26.5				32.5	24.3
	(14) 1.3	(12) 2.6				EBIT/Interest	(78) 4.9	(65) 5.6
		-.6	-2.1				1.8	1.1
							6.5	3.8
						Net Profit + Depr., Dep., Amort./Cur. Mat. L/T/D	(13) 2.4	(14) 2.6
							.5	.4
	.0	.1	.0				.0	.0
	.0	.5	.2			Fixed/Worth	.1	.1
	.3	-2.4	1.2				.7	.7
	.4	.8	.3				.5	.4
	.5	2.2	.8			Debt/Worth	1.2	1.1
	1.8	-6.3	2.2				3.2	5.7
	37.8	37.9	18.0				39.9	36.1
	(10) 9.8	(10) 1.4	(15) 7.1			% Profit Before Taxes/Tangible Net Worth	(87) 14.2	(73) 12.5
	-.2	-2.1	-2.3				2.0	4.0
	17.5	10.7	10.0				12.1	15.0
	7.0	1.0	3.8			% Profit Before Taxes/Total Assets	5.6	5.2
	-.4	-1.1	-4.0				.8	1.2
	UND	132.0	66.0				76.5	181.9
	588.5	41.7	19.1			Sales/Net Fixed Assets	34.8	37.2
	26.3	5.0	4.8				13.3	11.2
	3.2	2.1	1.6				1.7	2.0
	2.2	1.9	1.3			Sales/Total Assets	1.3	1.3
	.8	1.2	1.3				.9	1.0
		.4	.6				.5	.4
	(13) 1.4	(10) 2.1				% Depr., Dep., Amort./Sales	(64) 1.3	(55) 1.2
		1.7	10.4				2.8	2.7
							2.9	2.0
	(25) 5.2	(22) 5.0				% Officers', Directors' Owners' Comp/Sales		
							8.2	7.5
5252M	41325M	148313M	486621M	522953M	518383M	Net Sales ($)	3837812M	3307356M
1805M	17274M	85357M	345545M	619092M	588076M	Total Assets ($)	3513496M	3070523M

M = $ thousand   MM = $ million
See Pages viii through xx for Explanation of Ratios and Data

Comparative Historical Data | Current Data Sorted by Sales

							Type of Statement	0-1MM	1-3MM	3-5MM	5-10MM	10-25MM	25MM & OVER
	11		17		11		Unqualified		1			1	9
	10		11		9		Reviewed	1			1	5	2
	5		4		3		Compiled	1			2		
	8		7		9		Tax Returns		3	1	4		1
	40		32		27		Other	2	2	4	5	8	6
	4/1/16-3/31/17		4/1/17-3/31/18		4/1/18-3/31/19				17 (4/1-9/30/18)			42 (10/1/18-3/31/19)	
	ALL		ALL		ALL								
	74		71		59		**NUMBER OF STATEMENTS**	4	6	5	12	14	18
	%		%		%		**ASSETS**	%	%	%	%	%	%
	14.5		13.9		15.4		Cash & Equivalents				12.0	12.4	16.1
	20.9		20.6		20.6		Trade Receivables (net)				23.1	23.2	20.1
	25.5		23.1		23.0		Inventory				28.8	22.0	12.4
	4.0		7.0		5.5		All Other Current				7.0	5.2	4.6
	64.9		64.7		64.4		Total Current				70.9	62.8	53.1
	8.8		9.8		10.6		Fixed Assets (net)				13.0	10.6	10.7
	14.9		16.2		14.6		Intangibles (net)				7.7	14.5	23.0
	11.4		9.3		10.4		All Other Non-Current				8.4	12.1	13.2
	100.0		100.0		100.0		Total				100.0	100.0	100.0
							LIABILITIES						
	5.5		6.2		7.5		Notes Payable-Short Term				8.8	5.1	2.7
	2.0		1.8		1.7		Cur. Mat.-L.T.D.				1.7	1.8	2.3
	13.6		12.6		7.3		Trade Payables				5.8	8.4	10.7
	.7		.1		.1		Income Taxes Payable				.1	.0	.2
	19.6		16.0		22.9		All Other Current				23.1	24.9	19.0
	41.4		36.8		39.5		Total Current				39.4	40.2	34.9
	11.1		10.3		7.8		Long-Term Debt				10.4	9.8	7.5
	.4		.5		.2		Deferred Taxes				.0	.0	.7
	4.1		8.7		11.1		All Other Non-Current				25.0	10.9	7.2
	43.1		43.7		41.3		Net Worth				25.1	39.1	49.7
	100.0		100.0		100.0		Total Liabilties & Net Worth				100.0	100.0	100.0
							INCOME DATA						
	100.0		100.0		100.0		Net Sales				100.0	100.0	100.0
	58.0		55.8		58.7		Gross Profit				55.8	57.1	55.2
	50.8		50.4		51.8		Operating Expenses				51.0	54.7	45.7
	7.2		5.4		7.0		Operating Profit				4.8	2.4	9.5
	1.6		1.1		1.7		All Other Expenses (net)				-.1	2.1	.5
	5.7		4.4		5.2		Profit Before Taxes				4.9	.4	9.0
							RATIOS						
	2.8		4.5		3.1						5.1	2.3	3.0
	2.0		2.0		2.3		Current				2.2	1.8	2.0
	1.1		1.1		1.3						1.1	1.1	1.0
	1.6		2.2		2.2						3.0	1.3	2.3
	.9		.9		1.0		Quick				.9	.9	1.2
	.5		.5		.6						.4	.7	.6
26	14.3	32	11.4	29	12.6			8	48.6	36	10.1	31	11.9
54	6.8	53	6.9	54	6.8		Sales/Receivables	36	10.2	65	5.6	57	6.4
79	4.6	78	4.7	76	4.8			58	6.3	76	4.8	111	3.3
68	5.4	54	6.7	54	6.7			41	8.8	39	9.4	32	11.3
152	2.4	126	2.9	118	3.1		Cost of Sales/Inventory	130	2.8	122	3.0	99	3.7
228	1.6	203	1.8	192	1.9			192	1.9	159	2.3	130	2.8
24	15.0	23	16.2	16	22.7			0	762.7	27	13.6	27	13.5
54	6.7	49	7.4	34	10.7		Cost of Sales/Payables	20	18.0	49	7.4	46	7.9
122	3.0	96	3.8	65	5.6			52	7.0	69	5.3	130	2.8
	3.1		2.3		3.0						4.3	3.0	2.9
	6.1		4.8		4.6		Sales/Working Capital				5.8	4.9	4.8
	36.5		24.8		15.8						113.4	NM	NM
	14.8		16.2		16.1							3.8	33.0
(60)	4.2	(59)	3.9	(44)	3.1		EBIT/Interest				(12) 2.7	(12) 4.5
	1.0		1.0		.3						-1.6	-.5
			4.9										
		(10)	3.1				Net Profit + Depr., Dep., Amort./Cur. Mat. L/T/D						
			2.2										
	.0		.0		.0						.0	.0	.1
	.2		.1		.2		Fixed/Worth				.2	.2	.8
	.7		.7		2.0						NM	NM	-.1
	.7		.3		.4						.4	.7	.4
	1.3		1.1		.9		Debt/Worth				1.3	1.1	1.2
	10.2		12.3		375.4						NM	NM	-3.5
	31.5		28.2		35.4		% Profit Before Taxes/Tangible Net Worth					8.6	56.5
(61)	12.5	(54)	10.6	(45)	7.1						(11) 3.7	(12) 19.0
	2.9		1.4		.0							-12.5	6.8
	11.8		12.3		11.7		% Profit Before Taxes/Total Assets				17.5	6.9	20.8
	4.4		4.2		4.9						8.3	1.0	5.7
	.7		-.1		.0						1.1	-2.0	.0
	105.0		156.5		217.9						535.4	149.5	54.7
	34.5		44.6		38.2		Sales/Net Fixed Assets				54.7	20.8	24.2
	16.0		10.5		9.2						12.5	11.0	7.2
	1.8		2.0		2.1						3.2	2.1	1.4
	1.3		1.4		1.4		Sales/Total Assets				2.7	1.5	1.0
	.9		.8		1.0						1.6	1.3	.6
	.3		.6		.5							.4	1.2
(36)	.8	(37)	1.6	(33)	1.4		% Depr., Dep., Amort./Sales				(10)	1.0	(10) 1.8
	2.3		3.5		2.0							5.9	5.4
	2.5		1.9		2.3								
(17)	4.6	(13)	3.8	(12)	3.1		% Officers', Directors' Owners' Comp/Sales						
	6.8		8.3		4.9								
	3050793M		2530392M		1722847M		Net Sales ($)	2275M	10014M	21997M	79958M	233231M	1375372M
	2869147M		2751514M		1657149M		Total Assets ($)	2994M	4910M	41878M	40146M	154890M	1412331M

© RMA 2019   **M = $ thousand   MM = $ million**
See Pages viii through xx for Explanation of Ratios and Data

Current Data Sorted by Assets

Comparative Historical Data

0-500M	500M-2MM	2-10MM	10-50MM	50-100MM	100-250MM	Type of Statement	4/1/14-3/31/15 ALL	4/1/15-3/31/16 ALL
		1	2	4	2	Unqualified	5	10
	1		1			Reviewed	5	4
						Compiled	7	6
1	1	1	3	1	2	Tax Returns	9	5
						Other	17	20
	4 (4/1-9/30/18)		21 (10/1/18-3/31/19)					
1	3	6	6	5	4	NUMBER OF STATEMENTS	43	45
%	%	%	%	%	%	**ASSETS**	%	%
						Cash & Equivalents	19.5	12.2
						Trade Receivables (net)	20.9	25.1
						Inventory	15.5	12.2
						All Other Current	4.3	3.8
						Total Current	60.3	53.3
						Fixed Assets (net)	12.4	14.3
						Intangibles (net)	15.6	16.8
						All Other Non-Current	11.8	15.6
						Total	100.0	100.0
						LIABILITIES		
						Notes Payable-Short Term	7.8	6.7
						Cur. Mat.-L.T.D.	2.2	3.1
						Trade Payables	12.2	16.5
						Income Taxes Payable	.1	.3
						All Other Current	11.8	18.5
						Total Current	34.1	45.1
						Long-Term Debt	15.9	15.3
						Deferred Taxes	.3	.4
						All Other Non-Current	19.8	6.7
						Net Worth	29.9	32.5
						Total Liabilties & Net Worth	100.0	100.0
						INCOME DATA		
						Net Sales	100.0	100.0
						Gross Profit	48.6	51.2
						Operating Expenses	40.1	44.6
						Operating Profit	8.5	6.6
						All Other Expenses (net)	1.4	1.3
						Profit Before Taxes	7.1	5.3
						RATIOS		
						Current	3.4	2.4
							1.7	1.4
							1.0	.8
						Quick	2.1	1.8
							1.1	.9
							.7	.7
						Sales/Receivables	17 — 21.1	18 — 20.0
							33 — 10.9	39 — 9.4
							54 — 6.7	49 — 7.4
						Cost of Sales/Inventory	0 — UND	0 — UND
							19 — 19.2	16 — 22.7
							61 — 6.0	42 — 8.7
						Cost of Sales/Payables	13 — 28.9	12 — 31.6
							24 — 15.0	32 — 11.5
							55 — 6.6	76 — 4.8
						Sales/Working Capital	3.6	5.8
							16.8	17.4
							-142.8	-45.9
						EBIT/Interest	41.5	26.1
							(35) 7.0	(42) 6.1
							1.6	1.0
						Net Profit + Depr., Dep., Amort./Cur. Mat. L/T/D		
						Fixed/Worth	.1	.1
							.4	.8
							-3.1	-.9
						Debt/Worth	.4	.6
							2.1	3.0
							-8.2	-4.0
						% Profit Before Taxes/Tangible Net Worth	73.5	79.2
							(31) 30.8	(31) 25.7
							13.9	1.0
						% Profit Before Taxes/Total Assets	24.0	22.5
							9.3	5.6
							3.8	.3
						Sales/Net Fixed Assets	176.9	114.6
							41.9	27.4
							9.1	10.5
						Sales/Total Assets	3.9	3.7
							2.0	2.1
							1.3	1.4
						% Depr., Dep., Amort./Sales	.4	.6
							(28) 1.1	(33) 1.7
							3.1	3.5
						% Officers', Directors' Owners' Comp/Sales	1.8	2.3
							(13) 4.6	(10) 5.2
							9.6	11.7
990M	26490M	70809M	247548M	355508M	576686M	Net Sales ($)	1181966M	1530166M
150M	4279M	26736M	201260M	301133M	712762M	Total Assets ($)	909491M	953069M

© RMA 2019

M = $ thousand   MM = $ million
See Pages viii through xx for Explanation of Ratios and Data

Comparative Historical Data / Current Data Sorted by Sales

Type of Statement

	4/1/16-3/31/17 ALL	4/1/17-3/31/18 ALL	4/1/18-3/31/19 ALL		0-1MM	1-3MM	3-5MM	5-10MM	10-25MM	25MM & OVER
						4 (4/1-9/30/18)		**21 (10/1/18-3/31/19)**		
Unqualified	4	8	9						2	7
Reviewed	5	2	2					1	1	
Compiled	2									
Tax Returns	7	4	3							
Other	21	16	11		1	1	1	1	5	5
NUMBER OF STATEMENTS	39	30	25		1	1	1	2	8	12
	%	%	%		%	%	%	%	%	%
ASSETS										
Cash & Equivalents	22.6	25.0	15.4							17.2
Trade Receivables (net)	21.1	17.8	24.9							17.7
Inventory	14.5	15.5	7.2							5.5
All Other Current	5.2	2.7	1.8							1.6
Total Current	63.5	61.1	49.3							42.1
Fixed Assets (net)	14.0	15.3	14.4							17.1
Intangibles (net)	11.4	14.7	22.5							26.7
All Other Non-Current	11.1	8.8	13.7							14.1
Total	100.0	100.0	100.0							100.0
LIABILITIES										
Notes Payable-Short Term	13.5	4.8	4.4							1.8
Cur. Mat.-L.T.D.	4.9	3.0	2.3							2.3
Trade Payables	18.9	18.3	15.3							12.7
Income Taxes Payable	.0	.1	.1							.2
All Other Current	21.9	29.0	23.6							15.7
Total Current	59.3	55.3	45.7							32.8
Long-Term Debt	12.4	18.8	16.3							18.5
Deferred Taxes	.1	.2	.2							.5
All Other Non-Current	7.9	3.4	7.7							1.9
Net Worth	20.3	22.3	30.0							46.3
Total Liabilties & Net Worth	100.0	100.0	100.0							100.0
INCOME DATA										
Net Sales	100.0	100.0	100.0							100.0
Gross Profit	49.4	55.3	49.2							52.3
Operating Expenses	43.0	47.2	46.8							51.6
Operating Profit	6.4	8.1	2.4							.7
All Other Expenses (net)	2.3	1.1	.3							-.1
Profit Before Taxes	4.2	7.0	2.1							.8
RATIOS										
Current	2.0	1.9	2.0							1.9
	1.1	1.2	1.4							1.5
	.8	.7	.9							.8
Quick	1.3	1.5	1.7							1.8
	.8	.9	1.2							1.5
	.4	.4	.6							.7
Sales/Receivables	6 56.5	16 23.1	20 18.3							20 18.2
	33 11.0	34 10.6	31 11.7							33 11.0
	47 7.8	49 7.4	66 5.5							72 5.1
Cost of Sales/Inventory	0 UND	0 UND	0 UND							0 UND
	9 41.4	13 27.2	5 73.0							4 103.9
	66 5.5	104 3.5	35 10.4							40 9.1
Cost of Sales/Payables	11 33.5	18 20.7	18 20.5							28 13.1
	33 10.9	48 7.6	40 9.2							46 8.0
	78 4.7	85 4.3	83 4.4							159 2.3
Sales/Working Capital	6.7	7.6	7.2							6.1
	42.6	19.4	17.7							8.2
	-31.4	-16.5	-57.9							-35.0
EBIT/Interest	12.1	46.5	18.1							
	(32) 4.7	(25) 6.1	(19) 5.5							
	-.1	1.3	.3							
Net Profit + Depr., Dep., Amort./Cur. Mat. L/T/D										
Fixed/Worth	.0	.1	.1							.2
	.4	.7	1.1							1.4
	2.3	-1.5	-.7							NM
Debt/Worth	.6	1.1	1.3							.9
	3.2	4.1	2.6							2.6
	-8.8	-3.1	-2.9							NM
% Profit Before Taxes/Tangible Net Worth	103.7	106.5	73.7							
	(29) 20.5	(19) 38.5	(17) 13.5							
	-2.8	2.8	-2.4							
% Profit Before Taxes/Total Assets	18.8	30.8	18.8							7.5
	7.1	9.9	7.0							4.3
	-1.7	1.3	-1.4							-1.8
Sales/Net Fixed Assets	283.7	78.3	84.2							47.1
	40.7	28.4	23.1							10.4
	9.5	10.2	7.8							4.1
Sales/Total Assets	4.9	3.8	2.9							1.6
	2.2	1.7	1.5							1.2
	1.3	1.2	1.0							.7
% Depr., Dep., Amort./Sales	.6	1.3	.6							
	(22) 1.8	(19) 2.0	(16) 1.8							
	4.0	3.9	3.8							
% Officers', Directors' Owners' Comp/Sales	5.8									
	(11) 7.0									
	15.5									
Net Sales ($)	1254164M	934575M	1278031M		990M	2175M	4750M	13754M	133844M	1122518M
Total Assets ($)	829278M	717960M	1246320M		150M	2034M	3352M	2808M	113510M	1124466M

© RMA 2019

M = $ thousand   MM = $ million
See Pages viii through xx for Explanation of Ratios and Data

Current Data Sorted by Assets | Comparative Historical Data

Type of Statement	0-500M	500M-2MM	2-10MM	10-50MM	50-100MM	100-250MM		4/1/14-3/31/15 ALL	4/1/15-3/31/16 ALL
Unqualified		2	8	19	12	16		51	55
Reviewed			9	4	1			17	8
Compiled		2	2	2		1		10	6
Tax Returns	3	5	5	2				26	26
Other	10	18	59	73	53	54		230	228
	62 (4/1-9/30/18)			298 (10/1/18-3/31/19)					
NUMBER OF STATEMENTS	13	27	83	100	66	71		334	323
ASSETS	%	%	%	%	%	%		%	%
Cash & Equivalents	29.3	27.0	29.8	24.6	19.9	20.6		23.9	24.0
Trade Receivables (net)	32.4	39.6	32.2	26.5	15.8	11.8		22.7	21.6
Inventory	6.9	3.0	1.3	1.8	1.2	.3		1.8	1.4
All Other Current	4.7	4.2	7.1	6.1	5.5	4.4		5.1	5.0
Total Current	73.2	73.7	70.5	59.0	42.4	37.1		53.4	51.9
Fixed Assets (net)	2.2	5.6	8.7	8.8	5.5	4.8		10.2	9.2
Intangibles (net)	9.8	3.7	10.1	23.1	43.0	49.5		27.2	29.7
All Other Non-Current	14.5	16.9	10.7	9.0	9.0	8.6		9.2	9.2
Total	100.0	100.0	100.0	100.0	100.0	100.0		100.0	100.0
LIABILITIES									
Notes Payable-Short Term	7.9	6.7	7.0	5.1	2.0	.5		5.2	3.8
Cur. Mat.-L.T.D.	.5	2.0	3.8	3.1	3.3	1.2		2.6	2.7
Trade Payables	23.2	10.9	9.1	6.8	4.5	2.4		6.9	6.6
Income Taxes Payable	.0	.0	.2	.2	.4	.1		.4	.4
All Other Current	57.2	31.0	40.3	45.8	33.7	23.0		28.5	31.2
Total Current	88.8	50.6	60.3	60.9	43.9	27.1		43.7	44.7
Long-Term Debt	9.7	4.9	15.8	28.8	34.4	29.1		20.5	21.7
Deferred Taxes	.0	.0	.2	.4	.9	1.4		.8	.9
All Other Non-Current	33.5	6.1	12.0	10.4	12.1	11.6		12.8	12.4
Net Worth	-32.0	38.4	11.7	-.5	8.7	30.8		22.2	20.3
Total Liabilties & Net Worth	100.0	100.0	100.0	100.0	100.0	100.0		100.0	100.0
INCOME DATA									
Net Sales	100.0	100.0	100.0	100.0	100.0	100.0		100.0	100.0
Gross Profit									
Operating Expenses	90.1	95.5	93.7	100.6	100.7	105.3		95.4	96.8
Operating Profit	9.9	4.5	6.3	-.6	-.7	-5.3		4.6	3.2
All Other Expenses (net)	2.1	-.2	1.3	3.7	6.8	8.0		3.1	4.1
Profit Before Taxes	7.7	4.6	5.0	-4.3	-7.5	-13.3		1.5	-.8
RATIOS									
Current	2.6	3.6	3.5	2.2	1.5	2.3		2.4	2.4
	1.4	1.7	1.3	1.0	.9	1.2		1.2	1.1
	.4	1.1	.7	.6	.7	.7		.8	.7
Quick	2.2	3.6	2.7	1.9	1.4	2.1		2.1	2.0
	1.2	1.6	1.2	.9	.8	1.0		1.0	.9
	.3	.7	.6	.5	.5	.6		.7	.6
Sales/Receivables	0 UND	13 29.0	24 14.9	35 10.3	35 10.4	40 9.2		33 10.9	30 12.0
	20 18.6	42 8.7	52 7.0	62 5.9	53 6.9	64 5.7		54 6.7	54 6.8
	50 7.3	70 5.2	74 4.9	89 4.1	76 4.8	101 3.6		79 4.6	81 4.5
Cost of Sales/Inventory									
Cost of Sales/Payables									
Sales/Working Capital	7.7	4.8	3.9	4.9	5.5	4.2		4.7	4.7
	72.0	8.9	13.4	259.1	-31.6	10.4		17.8	31.9
	-11.8	103.1	-13.3	-4.0	-5.4	-7.6		-15.5	-9.2
EBIT/Interest		128.2	42.7	8.9	5.2	.4		21.1	11.7
	(18) 16.9	(51) 4.2	(79) .5	(49) -1.0	(56) -.6			(248) 2.8	(229) .6
		3.5	-5.0	-9.8	-5.0	-4.0		-2.1	-3.8
Net Profit + Depr., Dep., Amort./Cur. Mat. L/T/D				21.5				6.5	8.3
			(11) 2.7					(41) 1.0	(35) 2.4
				.2				-.4	-2.1
Fixed/Worth	.0	.0	.0	.1	.3	.2		.1	.2
	.0	.1	.3	-2.3	-.1	-.4		1.7	-5.3
	UND	.4	-.3	-.1	.0	-.1		-.1	-.1
Debt/Worth	2.1	.4	.8	1.2	3.7	3.6		1.0	1.1
	UND	.8	3.4	-8.6	-2.2	-2.6		89.8	-16.6
	-1.5	16.4	-3.3	-1.9	-1.4	-1.4		-2.0	-1.8
% Profit Before Taxes/Tangible Net Worth		90.7	134.6	60.8	54.3	38.1		65.7	71.8
	(21) 38.9	(52) 40.4	(43) 19.8	(21) 15.6	(24) -9.9			(168) 24.8	(157) 27.5
		24.7	4.9	-3.9	-13.5	-38.5		-9.6	-10.5
% Profit Before Taxes/Total Assets	80.3	30.3	26.9	14.4	7.0	-.9		16.6	12.5
	32.7	19.3	6.1	.7	-4.0	-6.3		5.0	1.1
	-18.6	3.6	-3.3	-19.0	-14.6	-12.7		-7.2	-10.5
Sales/Net Fixed Assets	UND	999.8	396.1	85.7	79.5	32.9		60.8	58.7
	UND	203.6	67.1	35.7	24.7	20.1		26.4	25.9
	156.4	39.3	20.8	14.9	15.4	10.5		12.1	11.3
Sales/Total Assets	9.7	3.8	3.6	1.9	1.3	.8		2.1	2.3
	5.5	2.9	2.4	1.3	.8	.5		1.2	1.2
	4.1	2.3	1.3	.9	.4	.3		.7	.7
% Depr., Dep., Amort./Sales			.4	.6	2.1	2.5		.8	.7
		(42) .7	(54) 1.7	(24) 3.1	(20) 3.8			(166) 1.8	(134) 1.9
		2.4	2.9	6.3	5.7			4.6	4.7
% Officers', Directors' Owners' Comp/Sales								4.3	5.3
								(40) 8.2	(34) 9.2
								14.4	16.7
Net Sales ($)	19823M	108506M	992219M	3972645M	4554127M	7048454M		16410018M	17891267M
Total Assets ($)	3198M	32885M	417886M	2589929M	4857974M	11427620M		19011024M	20308758M

© RMA 2019

M = $ thousand   MM = $ million
See Pages viii through xx for Explanation of Ratios and Data

Comparative Historical Data / Current Data Sorted by Sales

53	51	57	Type of Statement						
						62 (4/1-9/30/18)		298 (10/1/18-3/31/19)	
				0-1MM	1-3MM	3-5MM	5-10MM	10-25MM	25MM & OVER
53	51	57	Unqualified			2	2	15	38
9	14	14	Reviewed		2		4	5	3
9	11	7	Compiled	1			1	4	1
21	20	15	Tax Returns	2	2		4	3	4
242	248	267	Other	3	20	11			152
4/1/16-3/31/17 ALL	4/1/17-3/31/18 ALL	4/1/18-3/31/19 ALL							
334	344	360	NUMBER OF STATEMENTS	6	24	17	39	80	194
%	%	%	**ASSETS**	%	%	%	%	%	%
24.2	22.6	24.5	Cash & Equivalents		23.4	33.8	33.6	22.3	22.8
22.2	22.7	24.2	Trade Receivables (net)		32.5	33.9	30.9	25.1	20.5
.9	.8	1.6	Inventory		6.0	1.4	.5	1.4	1.3
5.3	5.2	5.7	All Other Current		6.2	2.3	7.2	6.3	5.6
52.6	51.3	55.9	Total Current		68.2	71.4	72.2	55.1	50.3
8.4	8.1	6.9	Fixed Assets (net)		3.8	5.3	5.7	8.0	6.6
31.1	30.7	27.0	Intangibles (net)		7.7	6.0	11.9	29.7	33.6
7.9	9.9	10.1	All Other Non-Current		20.3	17.3	10.2	7.2	9.5
100.0	100.0	100.0	Total		100.0	100.0	100.0	100.0	100.0
			LIABILITIES						
2.2	5.3	4.3	Notes Payable-Short Term		9.0	5.7	5.8	6.0	2.6
3.8	2.6	2.7	Cur. Mat.-L.T.D.		2.0	2.9	2.4	3.2	2.8
6.7	6.7	6.9	Trade Payables		5.1	17.0	6.6	8.1	5.2
.3	.3	.2	Income Taxes Payable		.0	.0	.1	.1	.3
33.2	32.8	37.1	All Other Current		43.7	30.6	48.7	40.7	33.2
46.2	47.6	51.2	Total Current		59.9	56.2	63.6	58.1	44.1
27.2	26.7	24.4	Long-Term Debt		10.8	6.0	9.3	28.5	28.9
.9	.7	.6	Deferred Taxes		.0	.2	.3	.6	.8
14.0	14.1	11.8	All Other Non-Current		19.2	11.5	13.3	10.4	11.6
11.6	10.8	12.0	Net Worth		10.1	26.1	13.5	2.3	14.7
100.0	100.0	100.0	Total Liabilities & Net Worth		100.0	100.0	100.0	100.0	100.0
			INCOME DATA						
100.0	100.0	100.0	Net Sales		100.0	100.0	100.0	100.0	100.0
			Gross Profit						
97.6	98.6	99.2	Operating Expenses		97.0	95.1	96.8	101.3	100.3
2.4	1.4	.8	Operating Profit		3.0	4.9	3.2	-1.3	-.3
4.0	4.6	4.2	All Other Expenses (net)		.7	.4	1.5	4.1	5.4
-1.6	-3.1	-3.4	Profit Before Taxes		2.3	4.5	1.8	-5.4	-5.7
			RATIOS						
2.1	2.0	2.3	Current		2.7	3.8	3.9	2.3	2.1
1.2	1.1	1.1			1.5	1.6	1.3	1.0	1.1
.7	.7	.7			1.1	.6	.7	.6	.7
1.8	1.8	2.1	Quick		2.6	3.6	2.9	2.1	1.8
1.0	1.0	1.0			1.1	1.4	1.1	.9	1.0
.6	.5	.5			.6	.5	.6	.4	.5
30 12.0	29 12.4	31 11.7	Sales/Receivables		0 UND	17 21.2	42 8.7	29 12.4	35 10.4
53 6.9	54 6.8	55 6.6			50 7.3	45 8.2	60 6.1	54 6.8	60 6.1
76 4.8	81 4.5	87 4.2			94 3.9	68 5.4	85 4.3	83 4.4	91 4.0
			Cost of Sales/Inventory						
			Cost of Sales/Payables						
5.3	5.4	4.6	Sales/Working Capital		6.0	3.8	3.6	5.4	4.6
25.6	36.6	27.2			16.1	7.4	11.4	NM	27.8
-9.6	-6.7	-6.5			84.1	-12.5	-5.4	-4.6	-7.2
14.7	10.4	10.3	EBIT/Interest		16.8	132.0	42.0	7.2	8.0
(254) 1.6	(252) .2	(260) .2		(15) 3.5	(13) 16.7	(26) 4.0	(60) -.8	(145) -.2	
-3.1	-3.6	-5.2			-3.9	3.2	-5.3	-9.7	-4.4
5.5	6.9	4.7	Net Profit + Depr., Dep., Amort./Cur. Mat. L/T/D						4.7
(36) 1.7	(25) 1.1	(33) 1.9						(20) 1.0	
-5.0	-2.8	-.6							-.9
.2	.1	.1	Fixed/Worth		.0	.0	.0	.1	.1
-1.1	2.5	4.1			.1	.1	.2	-.5	-.9
-.1	-.1	-.1			.4	-.4	-.2	.0	-.1
1.5	1.4	1.3	Debt/Worth		.5	.7	.7	1.7	1.9
-6.1	-14.7	-12.0			2.7	2.3	5.3	-3.9	-6.2
-1.7	-1.5	-1.8			-3.0	-17.9	-2.4	-1.7	-1.7
67.6	80.9	92.0	% Profit Before Taxes/Tangible Net Worth		101.2	112.7	140.6	116.3	72.9
(146) 23.9	(166) 26.7	(168) 29.3		(17) 32.8	(11) 53.5	(23) 37.7	(31) 19.8	(82) 21.9	
-13.2	-13.6	-4.7			-4.8	33.9	5.3	1.2	-13.5
13.5	14.8	15.6	% Profit Before Taxes/Total Assets		32.1	30.3	23.8	11.7	12.0
1.5	-.1	.5			9.4	21.7	5.9	-1.1	-3.5
-10.7	-12.0	-12.7			-6.4	-1.3	-2.7	-21.2	-13.2
67.4	79.2	105.4	Sales/Net Fixed Assets		UND	999.8	204.8	103.9	76.5
26.1	29.2	36.5			148.0	257.9	65.6	41.7	25.9
13.6	14.8	16.0			35.6	65.0	20.8	16.7	13.8
2.4	2.3	2.4	Sales/Total Assets		4.4	3.8	2.6	2.8	1.5
1.2	1.1	1.2			2.5	3.1	1.8	1.3	.9
.7	.6	.6			1.5	2.3	1.1	.7	.5
.8	.7	.6	% Depr., Dep., Amort./Sales				.5	.5	1.2
(137) 1.8	(144) 1.7	(152) 1.7				(21) .7	(36) 1.0	(80) 2.6	
4.0	3.6	3.5					1.5	2.9	4.3
2.7	4.5	2.2	% Officers', Directors' Owners' Comp/Sales					1.4	
(39) 5.7	(35) 6.6	(29) 4.3						(11) 2.5	
12.3	13.1	7.3						9.9	
16302979M	16471060M	16695774M	Net Sales ($)	3222M	50791M	66512M	288619M	1390889M	14895741M
19312052M	18683446M	19329492M	Total Assets ($)	7227M	33410M	36239M	211524M	1812514M	17228578M

© RMA 2019

M = $ thousand   MM = $ million

See Pages viii through xx for Explanation of Ratios and Data

Current Data Sorted by Assets

Comparative Historical Data

Type of Statement							16	10
Unqualified							16	10
Reviewed							12	8
Compiled							11	11
Tax Returns							47	34
Other							106	95

		1	3 7	2 1	2 1	6	4/1/14- 3/31/15	4/1/15- 3/31/16
		2	2	1		3	ALL	ALL
	6	6	5	1	1			
	9	17	22	20	2	15		
		22 (4/1-9/30/18)		113 (10/1/18-3/31/19)				
	0-500M	500M-2MM	2-10MM	10-50MM	50-100MM	100-250MM		
NUMBER OF STATEMENTS	15	26	39	25	6	24	192	158
ASSETS	%	%	%	%	%	%	%	%
Cash & Equivalents	35.6	21.5	16.1	18.7		9.8	23.0	21.2
Trade Receivables (net)	15.9	32.7	27.2	28.2		13.9	22.1	22.8
Inventory	6.0	.2	4.1	2.8		3.3	2.5	2.7
All Other Current	4.6	4.0	4.3	6.3		6.7	5.7	4.8
Total Current	62.1	58.5	51.7	56.0		33.8	53.4	51.5
Fixed Assets (net)	21.5	24.0	23.7	21.7		22.3	24.1	25.0
Intangibles (net)	6.0	7.9	11.3	7.6		14.4	8.6	10.5
All Other Non-Current	10.4	9.6	13.4	14.7		29.5	13.9	13.0
Total	100.0	100.0	100.0	100.0		100.0	100.0	100.0
LIABILITIES								
Notes Payable-Short Term	35.4	10.7	5.1	5.6		3.2	14.5	14.0
Cur. Mat.-L.T.D.	11.2	5.0	3.1	5.6		1.3	2.8	3.7
Trade Payables	10.4	12.8	11.0	7.0		3.5	9.2	8.0
Income Taxes Payable	.0	.2	.5	.0		.0	1.2	.4
All Other Current	50.9	17.7	23.6	19.2		16.7	16.8	13.9
Total Current	107.9	46.4	43.3	37.4		24.6	44.6	40.0
Long-Term Debt	9.6	23.2	23.2	18.6		51.3	18.6	19.1
Deferred Taxes	.0	.0	.2	.3		.5	.2	.5
All Other Non-Current	.9	8.3	7.6	5.9		7.1	11.8	9.6
Net Worth	-18.4	22.0	25.7	37.7		16.5	24.7	30.8
Total Liabilities & Net Worth	100.0	100.0	100.0	100.0		100.0	100.0	100.0
INCOME DATA								
Net Sales	100.0	100.0	100.0	100.0		100.0	100.0	100.0
Gross Profit								
Operating Expenses	95.8	88.7	83.8	85.0		88.6	89.2	91.3
Operating Profit	4.2	11.3	16.2	15.0		11.4	10.8	8.7
All Other Expenses (net)	1.4	1.0	4.5	5.4		7.9	1.7	2.2
Profit Before Taxes	2.8	10.3	11.7	9.7		3.5	9.1	6.5
RATIOS								
Current	3.9	3.9	4.3	3.4		5.0	3.4	2.7
	.9	1.1	1.1	1.3		1.3	1.5	1.3
	.4	.8	.7	.9		1.0	.8	.8
Quick	3.9	3.2	3.5	3.4		3.3	2.6	2.5
	.4	1.1	1.0	1.0		1.2	1.2 (157)	1.1
	.1	.8	.4	.7		.9	.6	.6
Sales/Receivables	0 UND	0 UND	9 41.7	39 9.3		33 10.9	1 278.0	2 190.7
	0 UND	33 10.9	38 9.7	55 6.6		50 7.3	23 16.0	29 12.4
	12 30.0	49 7.4	74 4.9	69 5.3		146 2.5	56 6.5	62 5.9
Cost of Sales/Inventory								
Cost of Sales/Payables								
Sales/Working Capital	6.6	7.7	5.2	4.0		4.0	7.1	7.0
	-172.7	64.2	20.7	26.5		11.3	20.7	24.5
	-14.5	-42.9	-6.6	-22.3		NM	-30.4	-37.6
EBIT/Interest		43.3	74.5	34.9		7.3	35.7	29.1
	(19) 8.7	(29) 6.0	(18) 11.2			(18) 1.0	(143) 6.7	(123) 8.2
	1.5	2.4	2.1			-1.4	.7	1.1
Net Profit + Depr., Dep., Amort./Cur. Mat. L/T/D							6.8	6.5
							(20) 1.7	(12) 3.7
							.5	1.7
Fixed/Worth	.1	.1	.1	.0		.0	.1	.1
	.8	1.1	.5	.6		.7	.5	.6
	-.3	-3.9	10.1	3.8		NM	4.7	3.8
Debt/Worth	.7	.3	.9	.6		1.4	.5	.6
	3.8	2.5	2.9	1.8		5.5	1.9	1.8
	-2.5	-5.4	126.7	8.6		-4.4	-75.7	-11.7
% Profit Before Taxes/Tangible Net Worth	171.0	101.2	78.0	79.6		63.3	94.1	74.3
	(10) 72.1	(17) 62.0	(30) 33.3	(21) 21.4		(16) 24.1	(142) 37.8	(116) 39.5
	18.2	4.8	2.8	5.7		-12.2	9.6	8.0
% Profit Before Taxes/Total Assets	73.5	44.7	31.2	22.4		10.9	32.8	30.7
	15.8	21.9	8.4	10.3		1.3	9.6	12.4
	-16.8	3.9	1.0	2.7		-5.2	.1	1.5
Sales/Net Fixed Assets	242.4	142.4	81.6	137.3		UND	155.0	143.2
	40.1	50.5	16.8	16.5		70.9	21.8	21.0
	19.6	9.8	9.5	3.3		1.3	6.2	5.7
Sales/Total Assets	11.9	5.6	3.2	2.0		.7	4.6	4.6
	4.4	4.2	1.9	1.3		.6	2.5	2.4
	3.0	2.1	.9	1.0		.4	1.2	1.0
% Depr., Dep., Amort./Sales			.9	1.7			.7	1.0
			(23) 1.9	(13) 4.4			(115) 2.0	(83) 2.3
			9.8	10.9			6.2	6.9
% Officers', Directors' Owners' Comp/Sales		2.8	1.2				3.3	3.5
		(11) 5.5	(11) 3.6				(72) 7.5	(59) 8.0
		8.3	4.5				12.0	13.4
Net Sales ($)	21897M	127922M	458222M	784314M	452921M	2200620M	3834912M	3101071M
Total Assets ($)	3785M	29983M	204052M	540648M	479589M	3908931M	3729214M	3241221M

M = $ thousand   MM = $ million
See Pages viii through xx for Explanation of Ratios and Data

Comparative Historical Data | Current Data Sorted by Sales

4/1/16-3/31/17 ALL	4/1/17-3/31/18 ALL	4/1/18-3/31/19 ALL	Type of Statement	0-1MM	1-3MM	3-5MM	5-10MM	10-25MM	25MM & OVER
6	5	13	Unqualified			2		2	9
18	10	10	Reviewed		1	2	2	3	4
7	6	8	Compiled		2	1	1	1	4
26	19	19	Tax Returns	4	2	4	2	2	1
85	70	85	Other	9	6	6	10	22	29
				22 (4/1-9/30/18)		113 (10/1/18-3/31/19)			
142	110	135	**NUMBER OF STATEMENTS**	13	15	15	15	30	47
%	%	%	**ASSETS**	%	%	%	%	%	%
17.2	21.3	18.4	Cash & Equivalents	9.0	37.4	21.9	21.6	14.1	15.5
21.9	18.0	24.0	Trade Receivables (net)	4.2	14.2	34.2	36.1	33.3	19.5
2.5	2.1	3.0	Inventory	6.9	.0	1.6	1.2	4.0	3.3
5.6	7.8	5.6	All Other Current	.0	5.5	3.9	8.6	4.0	7.7
47.1	49.3	51.0	Total Current	20.1	57.1	61.5	67.5	55.4	46.0
27.1	26.9	22.9	Fixed Assets (net)	57.4	20.3	16.5	18.8	16.3	21.7
11.7	7.2	10.0	Intangibles (net)	14.2	6.1	8.8	4.6	12.2	10.7
14.1	16.5	16.2	All Other Non-Current	8.3	16.4	13.2	9.1	16.1	21.5
100.0	100.0	100.0	Total	100.0	100.0	100.0	100.0	100.0	100.0
			LIABILITIES						
11.2	18.5	9.6	Notes Payable-Short Term	17.6	28.9	4.2	4.1	5.6	7.3
4.1	3.5	4.4	Cur. Mat.-L.T.D.	7.3	8.8	4.4	0.1	3.5	2.3
9.3	9.2	9.0	Trade Payables	5.6	9.0	7.6	21.8	9.8	5.6
.4	.4	.2	Income Taxes Payable	.0	.1	.1	.4	.5	.0
18.6	13.0	22.9	All Other Current	16.2	51.0	16.6	11.4	32.8	15.2
43.6	44.5	46.1	Total Current	46.6	97.9	32.8	43.9	52.3	30.4
26.5	21.8	27.2	Long-Term Debt	31.3	21.6	26.2	21.3	14.5	38.2
.2	.3	.2	Deferred Taxes	.0	.0	.3	.0	.4	.3
9.7	15.0	6.4	All Other Non-Current	.0	2.4	9.1	8.8	8.4	6.4
19.9	18.6	20.1	Net Worth	22.1	-21.9	31.6	26.1	24.4	24.6
100.0	100.0	100.0	Total Liabilties & Net Worth	100.0	100.0	100.0	100.0	100.0	100.0
			INCOME DATA						
100.0	100.0	100.0	Net Sales	100.0	100.0	100.0	100.0	100.0	100.0
			Gross Profit						
91.6	90.6	87.1	Operating Expenses	73.9	92.5	92.4	81.5	87.9	88.6
8.4	9.4	12.9	Operating Profit	26.1	7.5	7.6	18.5	12.1	11.4
2.5	3.2	4.1	All Other Expenses (net)	12.1	1.5	.9	1.1	2.4	5.7
5.9	6.1	8.8	Profit Before Taxes	14.1	6.0	6.7	17.4	9.6	5.7
			RATIOS						
3.0	2.5	3.7	Current	1.4	4.4	6.8	4.5	2.2	3.4
1.3	1.3	1.2		.3	.9	3.4	1.3	1.1	1.3
.6	.7	.8		.1	.5	1.1	1.0	.7	1.0
2.2	2.0	3.2	Quick	.9	4.4	6.5	4.2	2.1	3.2
1.0	1.0	1.1		.3	.9	2.6	1.2	1.0	1.1
.5	.4	.5		.1	.4	.9	.9	.4	.8
4 87.3	0 UND	6 61.1	Sales/Receivables	0 UND	0 UND	24 15.2	16 23.2	27 13.4	24 15.4
30 12.2	26 14.1	38 9.7		0 UND	0 UND	41 8.8	33 10.9	42 8.6	48 7.6
65 5.6	49 7.5	64 5.7		17 22.0	17 21.8	76 4.8	104 3.5	73 5.0	81 4.5
			Cost of Sales/Inventory						
			Cost of Sales/Payables						
6.4	7.2	5.3	Sales/Working Capital	21.0	5.1	4.8	6.8	5.6	3.7
22.1	32.8	22.7		-6.0	-172.7	13.4	19.4	86.5	10.3
-15.4	-19.8	-21.5		-1.6	-21.5	57.4	-451.2	-11.1	-160.6
13.2	15.5	20.5	EBIT/Interest			40.2	185.0	41.4	14.3
(106) 5.4	(84) 4.1	(98) 4.7		(10)	(12) 7.3	(23) 14.2	(37) 7.5	3.5	
1.1	-2.0	1.0			.9	5.7	1.2	.4	
4.4	10.9	4.3	Net Profit + Depr., Dep.,						
(13) 2.1	(11) 3.9	(11) 2.2	Amort./Cur. Mat. L/T/D						
.9	1.2	1.3							
.2	.1	.1	Fixed/Worth	.5	.1	.0	.2	.0	.0
.9	.8	.7		2.0	1.1	.3	.6	.5	.7
-6.4	NM	12.3		10.6	-.2	-.2	12.3	5.6	-.8
.9	.7	.9	Debt/Worth	1.3	.3	.2	.3	1.0	1.3
4.1	2.3	3.3		3.3	1.3	2.0	2.3	2.8	4.2
-6.8	-7.6	-8.4		NM	-2.5	-6.0	-22.7	NM	-12.0
83.7	98.5	82.9	% Profit Before Taxes/Tangible	90.8		111.4	108.7	108.3	68.0
(94) 30.0	(78) 18.3	(96) 32.8	Net Worth	(10) 7.0	(10)	(11) 61.9	(23) 66.5	(33) 32.4	25.4
6.0	.3	3.3		-4.2		14.1	7.6	2.8	1.9
20.8	25.7	31.0	% Profit Before Taxes/Total	24.0	61.6	35.5	59.4	26.5	15.7
6.3	5.5	8.8	Assets	3.5	29.5	7.7	32.3	10.4	8.4
.2	-3.4	.5		-.3	1.6	-.1	6.5	3.2	-1.3
68.7	162.4	147.3	Sales/Net Fixed Assets	19.8	210.8	UND	71.2	146.0	285.3
15.9	22.0	32.8		2.0	40.1	55.6	21.2	41.2	33.8
4.7	3.9	5.9		.2	11.0	15.8	10.2	13.2	3.1
3.6	4.5	3.6	Sales/Total Assets	2.1	7.9	4.4	5.4	4.1	1.7
1.8	2.1	1.5		1.2	3.6	1.8	4.1	2.2	.8
.8	.9	.8		.1	2.6	1.0	1.0	1.1	.6
1.1	1.0	.9	% Depr., Dep., Amort./Sales					.2	1.6
(70) 2.1	(58) 3.3	(51) 1.9						(15) 1.5	(14) 3.5
5.7	7.3	9.8						4.6	8.3
2.5	3.8	3.3	% Officers', Directors'						
(45) 7.4	(39) 6.6	(35) 5.4	Owners' Comp/Sales						
10.6	11.1	10.2							
4026598M	2388328M	4045896M	Net Sales ($)	6238M	30540M	57862M	102967M	477363M	3370926M
4334584M	3143849M	5166988M	Total Assets ($)	19871M	8274M	40293M	51319M	404816M	4642415M

M = $ thousand   MM = $ million
See Pages viii through xx for Explanation of Ratios and Data

	Current Data Sorted by Assets						Comparative Historical Data	
Type of Statement								
Unqualified			1	2	6	6	12	15
Reviewed			2	4	1		14	15
Compiled			1	1	1		12	5
Tax Returns	2	2	10	3			23	12
Other	5	8	21	17	3	8	64	66
		7 (4/1-9/30/18)		97 (10/1/18-3/31/19)			4/1/14-3/31/15	4/1/15-3/31/16
	0-500M	500M-2MM	2-10MM	10-50MM	50-100MM	100-250MM	ALL	ALL
NUMBER OF STATEMENTS	7	10	35	27	11	14	125	113
ASSETS	%	%	%	%	%	%	%	%
Cash & Equivalents		33.3	12.8	13.3	14.1	6.2	11.8	14.1
Trade Receivables (net)		1.3	1.7	2.4	3.5	2.1	1.7	2.9
Inventory		.9	.7	.9	.6	.9	1.2	.9
All Other Current		10.7	.7	2.4	.9	1.6	2.0	2.5
Total Current		46.2	15.8	19.0	19.0	10.7	16.7	20.4
Fixed Assets (net)		37.7	72.7	68.6	68.2	76.4	68.9	67.2
Intangibles (net)		6.8	5.0	5.8	10.5	9.6	6.8	7.1
All Other Non-Current		9.3	6.5	6.7	2.2	3.3	7.6	5.3
Total		100.0	100.0	100.0	100.0	100.0	100.0	100.0
LIABILITIES								
Notes Payable-Short Term		6.4	1.1	2.4	.1	.9	2.3	1.7
Cur. Mat.-L.T.D.		2.1	3.7	5.7	3.2	2.9	5.8	4.7
Trade Payables		14.1	4.1	7.0	6.3	5.0	6.4	7.9
Income Taxes Payable		.0	.3	.0	.0	.3	.2	.3
All Other Current		19.5	7.5	8.0	12.6	7.1	12.8	14.6
Total Current		42.1	16.6	23.1	22.2	16.2	27.5	29.2
Long-Term Debt		23.7	48.1	40.2	38.1	41.4	42.0	42.9
Deferred Taxes		.0	.0	.3	.0	.0	.3	.3
All Other Non-Current		3.3	3.2	4.9	21.3	24.6	10.8	12.3
Net Worth		30.9	32.1	31.5	18.3	17.8	19.3	15.4
Total Liabilties & Net Worth		100.0	100.0	100.0	100.0	100.0	100.0	100.0
INCOME DATA								
Net Sales		100.0	100.0	100.0	100.0	100.0	100.0	100.0
Gross Profit								
Operating Expenses		88.0	84.3	86.9	91.7	97.7	87.4	89.2
Operating Profit		12.0	15.7	13.1	8.3	2.3	12.6	10.8
All Other Expenses (net)		-.5	4.8	2.6	2.8	3.7	4.8	3.1
Profit Before Taxes		12.5	10.9	10.5	5.5	-1.3	7.9	7.8
RATIOS								
Current		1.9	1.8	1.1	1.5	1.0	1.5	1.3
		1.1	1.2	.7	.6	.7	.6	.6
		.4	.5	.3	.3	.4	.2	.3
Quick		1.9	1.6	1.0	1.4	.9	1.4	1.0
		.6	1.2	.6	.5	.4	(123) .5	.5
		.2	.4	.2	.2	.3	.2	.2
Sales/Receivables		0 UND	0 UND	0 UND	1 623.2	0 UND	0 UND	0 UND
		0 UND	0 999.8	3 126.5	5 70.2	8 48.2	0 999.8	1 325.1
		3 127.9	7 54.2	4 83.2	10 37.9	12 30.0	4 91.8	6 56.6
Cost of Sales/Inventory								
Cost of Sales/Payables								
Sales/Working Capital		10.8	15.2	46.0	24.8	NM	29.6	41.1
		UND	50.1	-18.2	-25.0	-18.7	-19.7	-14.6
		-28.0	-13.3	-8.4	-9.4	-7.5	-6.4	-6.8
EBIT/Interest			14.2	12.2	5.5	3.4	7.3	8.8
			(27) 3.3	(24) 4.8	(10) 2.6	1.0	(101) 3.2	(103) 3.5
			.8	3.2	1.7	-2.3	1.2	1.4
Net Profit + Depr., Dep., Amort./Cur. Mat. L/T/D							3.3	4.0
							(16) 2.8	(20) 2.1
							1.4	1.3
Fixed/Worth		.3	1.1	1.2	2.0	2.2	1.5	1.4
		1.1	2.9	2.4	4.9	9.0	4.2	3.5
		UND	UND	9.3	-2.7	-7.0	-8.7	-11.2
Debt/Worth		.4	.5	1.3	1.2	1.4	1.4	1.4
		4.1	2.1	2.4	5.3	9.4	4.0	2.9
		-46.7	UND	10.7	-4.2	-9.8	-10.7	-13.4
% Profit Before Taxes/Tangible Net Worth			88.2	61.0			45.9	43.1
			(27) 19.3	(23) 35.0			(87) 27.6	(80) 22.9
			-2.0	3.5			11.0	11.2
% Profit Before Taxes/Total Assets		123.1	16.5	18.2	12.6	6.9	12.4	12.3
		16.4	6.1	10.1	4.9	.0	6.1	5.7
		2.1	-.2	2.6	3.9	-7.5	.7	1.5
Sales/Net Fixed Assets		UND	2.7	3.1	3.5	1.9	3.6	3.7
		6.6	1.4	1.3	1.3	1.0	1.5	1.4
		1.2	.6	.6	.7	.4	.8	.8
Sales/Total Assets		7.7	2.0	1.6	2.1	1.3	2.1	1.9
		2.9	1.0	1.0	.9	.8	1.0	1.0
		.9	.4	.6	.6	.4	.6	.7
% Depr., Dep., Amort./Sales			4.0	4.4	5.2		4.3	3.9
			(30) 7.9	(24) 6.7	(10) 6.2		(115) 6.7	(95) 7.1
			20.6	9.7	9.9		11.0	9.3
% Officers', Directors' Owners' Comp/Sales							1.9	1.9
							(22) 2.8	(14) 3.0
							6.9	5.1
Net Sales ($)	7908M	77428M	194306M	764661M	936288M	1816488M	3275562M	3820263M
Total Assets ($)	1371M	11324M	157609M	641093M	776421M	2115869M	2779625M	3382318M

M = $ thousand MM = $ million

See Pages viii through xx for Explanation of Ratios and Data

Comparative Historical Data · Current Data Sorted by Sales

4/1/16-3/31/17 ALL	4/1/17-3/31/18 ALL	4/1/18-3/31/19 ALL		0-1MM	1-3MM	3-5MM	5-10MM	10-25MM	25MM & OVER
			Type of Statement		7 (4/1-9/30/18)		97 (10/1/18-3/31/19)		
20	11	15	Unqualified		1				14
11	13	7	Reviewed				1	3	3
6	22	3	Compiled		1				2
13	22	17	Tax Returns	4	6	2	2	2	1
54	63	62	Other	8	8	6	10	12	18
104	131	104	**NUMBER OF STATEMENTS**	12	16	8	13	17	38
%	%	%	**ASSETS**	%	%	%	%	%	%
17.5	15.3	15.4	Cash & Equivalents	3.4	20.6		15.5	19.2	15.9
1.9	2.1	2.1	Trade Receivables (net)	1.2	1.2		2.0	1.7	3.1
.9	.8	.8	Inventory	.3	.7		.3	1.4	1.0
1.9	2.4	2.2	All Other Current	5.3	.1		5.8	1.7	1.4
22.2	20.7	20.5	Total Current	10.3	22.6		23.7	24.0	21.4
65.3	67.0	66.8	Fixed Assets (net)	82.0	64.3		54.3	65.2	65.8
5.8	6.3	6.5	Intangibles (net)	5.3	7.9		2.2	2.6	9.9
6.7	6.0	6.2	All Other Non-Current	2.4	5.3		19.9	8.2	2.9
100.0	100.0	100.0	Total	100.0	100.0		100.0	100.0	100.0
			LIABILITIES						
2.3	1.7	2.1	Notes Payable-Short Term	5.6	1.3		6.5	1.4	.5
5.7	5.0	4.4	Cur. Mat.-L.T.D.	2.6	.1		2.9	7.2	3.8
6.0	5.1	7.3	Trade Payables	1.4	11.6		4.7	10.1	7.6
.3	.4	.1	Income Taxes Payable	.0	.2		.0	.3	.1
13.4	13.6	9.6	All Other Current	1.6	7.7		5.5	11.3	13.1
27.7	25.7	23.5	Total Current	11.2	27.9		19.5	30.2	25.1
36.2	41.0	41.7	Long-Term Debt	53.0	56.5		32.4	32.0	35.2
.2	.0	.1	Deferred Taxes	.0	.0		.0	.0	.2
5.0	9.3	10.7	All Other Non-Current	2.8	17.1		4.2	3.5	16.6
31.0	24.0	24.0	Net Worth	32.8	-1.5		43.9	34.3	22.8
100.0	100.0	100.0	Total Liabilities & Net Worth	100.0	100.0		100.0	100.0	100.0
			INCOME DATA						
100.0	100.0	100.0	Net Sales	100.0	100.0		100.0	100.0	100.0
			Gross Profit						
88.6	86.9	89.0	Operating Expenses	73.0	92.3		95.9	79.6	93.4
11.4	13.1	11.0	Operating Profit	27.0	7.7		4.1	20.4	6.6
2.2	3.9	3.0	All Other Expenses (net)	8.7	4.3		-2.0	2.5	2.7
9.2	9.3	8.0	Profit Before Taxes	18.3	3.4		6.0	17.8	3.9
			RATIOS						
1.5	1.7	1.5		1.4	1.8		1.7	1.6	1.1
.9	.7	.8	Current	.4	1.2		1.1	.7	.8
.5	.4	.4		.1	.5		.6	.2	.4
1.5	1.3	1.4		1.2	1.8		1.5	1.3	1.0
.7	.6	.7	Quick	.3	1.2		.8	.4	.6
.4	.3	.3		.0	.5		.2	.2	.3
0 UND	0 UND	0 UND		0 UND	0 UND		1 389.6	0 999.8	0 UND
2 233.5	1 322.4	3 141.8	Sales/Receivables	0 UND	0 UND		3 105.0	3 134.9	4 83.5
6 56.8	7 52.4	7 53.2		0 UND	2 214.1		6 62.8	6 62.9	10 38.2
			Cost of Sales/Inventory						
			Cost of Sales/Payables						
15.9	16.3	25.3		19.1	11.2		25.0	15.5	47.2
-49.7	-34.5	-32.0	Sales/Working Capital	-30.6	49.5		89.0	-22.0	-26.1
-7.2	-5.8	-9.9		-3.6	-15.3		-15.8	-8.4	-9.4
13.5	10.0	9.0			4.1			23.9	5.5
(89) 5.2	(108) 4.3	(86) 3.6	EBIT/Interest		(13) 1.3			(13) 9.4	(36) 2.9
2.3	1.6	.8			-1.3			4.6	.8
3.8	4.1	3.3	Net Profit + Depr., Dep.,						
(12) 2.9	(12) 3.0	(12) 1.8	Amort./Cur. Mat. L/T/D						
1.8	1.3	1.5							
1.1	1.4	1.2		1.2	1.3		.2	.8	1.5
2.4	0.0	2.9	Fixed/Worth	2.8	NM		1.2	1.9	3.9
6.9	-73.7	UND		-7.1	-2.0		3.5	4.0	-8.6
.8	1.1	1.2		.5	1.5		.4	.6	1.4
2.2	2.4	2.9	Debt/Worth	3.4	NM		1.3	1.4	4.4
7.8	-117.0	-26.8		-8.7	-3.1		3.1	9.2	-11.8
61.1	56.1	66.7	% Profit Before Taxes/Tangible				40.2	113.1	64.2
(89) 25.8	(98) 26.7	(77) 20.3	Net Worth				(12) 17.6	(15) 65.9	(28) 18.5
10.2	7.8	1.2					-7.7	39.9	2.4
18.0	15.8	15.1	% Profit Before Taxes/Total	6.1	9.7		14.9	42.1	13.3
8.2	7.5	5.9	Assets	3.6	1.8		9.1	27.9	5.0
2.3	.7	-.1		-.3	-4.3		-1.0	13.8	-.5
3.6	3.5	3.1		1.2	8.0		19.7	4.8	3.1
1.5	1.6	1.6	Sales/Net Fixed Assets	.5	.9		1.9	2.1	1.8
.7	.7	.7		.2	.6		.9	.9	.9
2.1	2.0	2.0		1.0	5.3		2.3	2.4	1.8
1.0	1.2	1.0	Sales/Total Assets	.2	.8		1.3	1.3	1.2
.6	.6	.6		.1	.4		.7	.8	.7
3.5	3.5	4.1			3.2		1.1	4.2	4.4
(89) 6.0	(111) 6.1	(80) 6.2	% Depr., Dep., Amort./Sales		(13) 5.3		(11) 6.8	(13) 5.8	(28) 5.6
8.7	10.2	10.8			19.2		13.9	8.0	9.2
.9	1.0	.7	% Officers', Directors'						
(13) 2.2	(16) 3.0	(14) 2.2	Owners' Comp/Sales						
5.5	8.2	5.2							
2757250M	3509335M	3797079M	Net Sales ($)	5944M	28560M	32485M	92450M	261804M	3375836M
2492106M	3324228M	3703687M	Total Assets ($)	28933M	50227M	39038M	112354M	244806M	3228329M

M = $ thousand   MM = $ million
See Pages viii through xx for Explanation of Ratios and Data

Current Data Sorted by Assets   Comparative Historical Data

						Type of Statement		
		1	7		1	Unqualified	13	19
		2	1		1	Reviewed	6	7
	1	3				Compiled	6	3
2	6	6	8	3	3	Tax Returns	9	13
	7 (4/1-9/30/18)		37 (10/1/18-3/31/19)			Other	47	38
							4/1/14-	4/1/15-
							3/31/15	3/31/16
0-500M	500M-2MM	2-10MM	10-50MM	50-100MM	100-250MM		ALL	ALL
2	7	12	16	3	4	NUMBER OF STATEMENTS	81	80
%	%	%	%	%	%	ASSETS	%	%
		15.6	6.2			Cash & Equivalents	9.4	10.0
		13.4	9.1			Trade Receivables (net)	12.1	12.1
		.0	.6			Inventory	.2	.1
		.6	6.9			All Other Current	2.4	2.5
		29.6	22.7			Total Current	24.1	24.6
		20.0	20.3			Fixed Assets (net)	26.3	25.8
		33.1	46.1			Intangibles (net)	38.8	39.6
		17.3	11.0			All Other Non-Current	10.8	9.9
		100.0	100.0			Total	100.0	100.0
						LIABILITIES		
		3.0	3.2			Notes Payable-Short Term	5.9	4.0
		5.9	3.6			Cur. Mat.-L.T.D.	12.8	6.3
		3.1	1.9			Trade Payables	2.0	2.2
		.1	.1			Income Taxes Payable	.2	.0
		3.3	2.8			All Other Current	7.1	4.9
		15.4	11.5			Total Current	27.9	17.5
		39.4	25.3			Long-Term Debt	37.9	33.1
		.0	2.1			Deferred Taxes	.9	1.0
		8.2	11.6			All Other Non-Current	18.4	12.1
		37.0	49.4			Net Worth	14.9	36.4
		100.0	100.0			Total Liabilties & Net Worth	100.0	100.0
						INCOME DATA		
		100.0	100.0			Net Sales	100.0	100.0
						Gross Profit		
		93.2	85.5			Operating Expenses	86.5	87.3
		6.8	14.5			Operating Profit	13.5	12.7
		.4	3.5			All Other Expenses (net)	4.8	3.9
		6.3	11.0			Profit Before Taxes	8.7	8.7
						RATIOS		
		5.4	4.3				3.1	2.7
		1.1	2.3			Current	1.7	1.8
		.7	1.0				.7	1.0
		5.1	3.5				2.7	2.6
		1.1	2.2			Quick	1.4	1.6
		.6	.8				.6	.9
		26 14.3	39 9.3				32 11.3	39 9.4
		48 7.6	54 6.7			Sales/Receivables	50 7.3	51 7.1
		55 6.6	65 5.6				62 5.9	61 6.0
						Cost of Sales/Inventory		
						Cost of Sales/Payables		
		4.3	5.0				4.8	4.9
		UND	8.7			Sales/Working Capital	10.3	10.6
		-9.7	NM				-23.1	NM
		9.5	5.1				7.0	9.3
		(10) 2.2	(12) 3.7			EBIT/Interest	(68) 2.8	(70) 3.4
		1.1	1.9				.9	1.0
						Net Profit + Depr., Dep., Amort./Cur. Mat. L/T/D		
		.2	1.3				.7	.6
		-1.6	-6.4			Fixed/Worth	208.6	16.5
		-.4	-1.0				-.4	-.3
		.2	1.6				.9	.5
		-8.1	-10.5			Debt/Worth	-9.2	63.0
		-1.9	-3.1				-1.9	-1.7
						% Profit Before Taxes/Tangible Net Worth	83.3	55.6
							(40) 25.4	(41) 19.1
							8.0	.6
		7.1	9.1				13.5	10.3
		3.5	6.4			% Profit Before Taxes/Total Assets	5.3	3.9
		.9	3.7				1.3	-.1
		15.1	6.1				7.7	9.1
		6.0	3.2			Sales/Net Fixed Assets	3.9	4.1
		1.6	2.3				2.0	2.0
		1.8	.8				1.3	1.1
		.9	.7			Sales/Total Assets	.6	.7
		.4	.5				.5	.5
		2.7					2.3	3.1
		5.1				% Depr., Dep., Amort./Sales	(67) 4.3	(66) 5.0
		6.7					7.1	7.3
						% Officers', Directors' Owners' Comp/Sales	2.9	2.4
							(14) 8.7	(14) 7.9
							12.0	14.0
831M	9765M	66204M	241852M	75992M	298906M	Net Sales ($)	1256903M	1053419M
532M	6926M	57533M	395683M	197900M	612398M	Total Assets ($)	2019314M	1944747M

M = $ thousand   MM = $ million
See Pages viii through xx for Explanation of Ratios and Data

Comparative Historical Data | Current Data Sorted by Sales

			Type of Statement						
15	16	9	Unqualified				2	6	1
2	4	1	Reviewed					1	
5	1	3	Compiled		2	1			
13	3	3	Tax Returns		1	1	1		
32	32	28	Other	5	4	5	2	7	5
4/1/16-3/31/17 ALL	4/1/17-3/31/18 ALL	4/1/18-3/31/19 ALL			7 (4/1-9/30/18)			37 (10/1/18-3/31/19)	
				0-1MM	1-3MM	3-5MM	5-10MM	10-25MM	25MM & OVER
67	56	44	NUMBER OF STATEMENTS	5	7	7	4	15	6
%	%	%	ASSETS	%	%	%	%	%	%
9.1	9.8	11.2	Cash & Equivalents					9.7	
8.6	10.8	10.2	Trade Receivables (net)					11.6	
.1	.4	.2	Inventory					.6	
1.9	2.8	7.6	All Other Current					1.1	
19.7	23.8	29.3	Total Current					23.1	
31.2	30.8	19.0	Fixed Assets (net)					17.9	
38.3	33.7	41.6	Intangibles (net)					50.9	
10.9	11.8	10.1	All Other Non-Current					8.1	
100.0	100.0	100.0	Total					100.0	
			LIABILITIES						
2.3	2.9	4.1	Notes Payable Short Term					3.6	
6.1	6.7	3.8	Cur. Mat.-L.T.D.					4.1	
2.2	2.9	2.2	Trade Payables					2.4	
.0	.3	.0	Income Taxes Payable					.1	
6.3	15.8	6.7	All Other Current					3.3	
17.0	28.7	16.9	Total Current					13.5	
35.7	40.4	33.7	Long-Term Debt					27.5	
.6	.8	1.0	Deferred Taxes					1.0	
20.4	10.2	8.2	All Other Non-Current					9.8	
26.3	19.8	40.3	Net Worth					48.1	
100.0	100.0	100.0	Total Liabilties & Net Worth					100.0	
			INCOME DATA						
100.0	100.0	100.0	Net Sales					100.0	
			Gross Profit						
90.8	92.0	87.1	Operating Expenses					83.3	
9.2	8.0	12.9	Operating Profit					16.7	
3.3	5.3	2.4	All Other Expenses (net)					3.1	
5.8	2.7	10.6	Profit Before Taxes					13.5	
			RATIOS						
2.6	4.3	5.0	Current					4.5	
1.5	1.4	1.8						1.6	
.9	.7	.9						.8	
2.4	4.2	3.5	Quick					3.9	
1.4	1.4	1.4						1.4	
.8	.6	.7						.8	
24 15.3	32 11.4	35 10.5	Sales/Receivables					39 9.3	
47 7.7	46 8.0	51 7.2						57 6.4	
61 6.0	64 5.7	64 5.7						66 5.5	
			Cost of Sales/Inventory						
			Cost of Sales/Payables						
5.7	4.4	4.1	Sales/Working Capital					4.5	
13.2	18.2	8.7						8.7	
-145.6	-14.0	-30.6						-24.5	
7.0	5.2	5.6	EBIT/Interest					12.5	
(56) 2.6	(45) 2.2	(33) 2.7						(13) 4.3	
-.6	.7	1.1						2.1	
			Net Profit + Depr., Dep., Amort./Cur. Mat. L/T/D						
.6	.5	.3	Fixed/Worth					3.6	
31.1	-4.0	-6.4						-5.0	
-.3	-.8	-.3						-.4	
.6	.4	.4	Debt/Worth					5.6	
43.1	-6.8	-10.0						-11.0	
-1.7	-2.4	-1.8						-2.7	
72.4	12.5	62.5	% Profit Before Taxes/Tangible Net Worth						
(34) 7.9	(25) 5.6	(19) 12.3							
1.0	-3.0	3.8							
10.3	6.0	9.6	% Profit Before Taxes/Total Assets					12.6	
3.7	3.4	6.3						8.1	
-2.3	-1.5	1.3						5.7	
7.6	7.0	9.9	Sales/Net Fixed Assets					8.1	
4.7	3.0	4.4						3.3	
1.8	1.6	2.4						2.7	
1.1	1.1	1.0	Sales/Total Assets					.9	
.7	.6	.7						.7	
.5	.5	.4						.5	
2.4	2.6	2.8	% Depr., Dep., Amort./Sales					2.5	
(55) 5.0	(49) 5.6	(34) 5.7						(13) 4.5	
8.1	9.4	7.3						6.5	
			% Officers', Directors' Owners' Comp/Sales						
680549M	597681M	693550M	Net Sales ($)	1785M	12154M	27040M	31890M	259136M	361545M
1228462M	1125580M	1270972M	Total Assets ($)	3433M	20306M	57930M	42079M	419418M	727806M

© RMA 2019

M = $ thousand   MM = $ million

See Pages viii through xx for Explanation of Ratios and Data

Current Data Sorted by Assets   Comparative Historical Data

	0-500M	500M-2MM	2-10MM	10-50MM	50-100MM	100-250MM		4/1/14-3/31/15 ALL	4/1/15-3/31/16 ALL
Type of Statement									
Unqualified			6	4	8	7		34	34
Reviewed									1
Compiled			5					2	12
Tax Returns		1	1					5	9
Other	4	1	4	13	2	4		41	35
	4	2	20 (4/1-9/30/18)	40 (10/1/18-3/31/19)					
NUMBER OF STATEMENTS	4	2	16	17	10	11		82	91
	%	%	%	%	%	%		%	%
ASSETS									
Cash & Equivalents			17.6	15.1	10.8	7.8		12.3	13.0
Trade Receivables (net)			12.0	11.6	9.3	11.9		11.0	10.8
Inventory			.1	.3	.2	3.8		.9	.4
All Other Current			2.0	4.0	4.8	6.5		5.0	4.9
Total Current			31.7	31.1	25.1	30.1		29.2	29.1
Fixed Assets (net)			46.2	29.0	22.4	21.4		33.6	33.3
Intangibles (net)			13.6	30.4	32.1	36.9		21.2	21.4
All Other Non-Current			8.4	9.6	20.4	11.6		16.0	16.2
Total			100.0	100.0	100.0	100.0		100.0	100.0
LIABILITIES									
Notes Payable-Short Term			.8	.8	.0	1.2		3.6	2.7
Cur. Mat.-L.T.D.			7.8	3.5	2.1	3.1		3.3	4.1
Trade Payables			6.3	5.7	2.5	5.0		4.3	4.2
Income Taxes Payable			.0	.3	.2	.4		.2	.3
All Other Current			8.9	6.7	4.4	5.3		11.7	16.0
Total Current			23.7	17.0	9.2	15.0		23.2	27.4
Long-Term Debt			36.9	20.4	21.5	87.1		35.6	41.8
Deferred Taxes			.0	.4	.3	3.5		.7	.5
All Other Non-Current			8.5	7.2	6.5	7.0		9.0	8.3
Net Worth			30.8	55.0	62.5	-12.5		31.5	22.1
Total Liabilities & Net Worth			100.0	100.0	100.0	100.0		100.0	100.0
INCOME DATA									
Net Sales			100.0	100.0	100.0	100.0		100.0	100.0
Gross Profit									
Operating Expenses			86.3	89.0	85.0	79.2		87.7	85.1
Operating Profit			13.7	11.0	15.0	20.8		12.3	14.9
All Other Expenses (net)			1.6	4.3	4.0	2.7		2.5	3.5
Profit Before Taxes			12.2	6.7	11.0	18.1		9.7	11.4
RATIOS									
Current			3.2	3.7	3.6	3.0		2.9	2.5
			1.3	2.1	2.5	1.5		1.5	1.5
			.7	1.1	1.5	1.2		.7	.6
Quick			3.2	3.0	2.7	2.1		2.1	2.0
			1.3	2.1	2.3	1.2		1.3	1.2
			.4	.9	1.3	.7		.5	.5
Sales/Receivables			4 100.4	14 25.4	35 10.3	31 11.7		7 54.0	10 36.6
			20 18.1	43 8.5	57 6.4	60 6.1		36 10.2	41 8.8
			51 7.1	65 5.6	83 4.4	64 5.7		59 6.2	64 5.7
Cost of Sales/Inventory									
Cost of Sales/Payables									
Sales/Working Capital			4.9	3.3	3.0	3.7		4.6	4.5
			506.1	5.4	3.7	12.1		13.0	14.2
			-18.6	79.5	9.3	18.1		-14.6	-10.2
EBIT/Interest			19.3	12.9		25.5		12.7	12.7
			(12) 7.3	(13) 1.0		3.9		(65) 3.7	(77) 3.4
			-.2	-3.3		1.8		.1	-.2
Net Profit + Depr., Dep., Amort./Cur. Mat. L/T/D									11.6
								(15) 2.4	
									1.8
Fixed/Worth			1.0	.5	.3	1.1		.5	.4
			3.0	1.2	1.3	-1.6		1.3	1.5
			-1.0	NM	-.3	-.3		-1.4	-.9
Debt/Worth			.5	.4	.2	1.4		.6	.5
			2.3	2.4	2.6	-3.9		2.6	3.8
			-4.3	-3.1	-3.7	-2.1		-2.8	-2.3
% Profit Before Taxes/Tangible Net Worth			85.0	78.5				63.9	47.6
			(10) 25.3	(12) .5				(57) 9.0	(59) 11.3
			-1.5	-7.9				-6.8	-1.8
% Profit Before Taxes/Total Assets			41.2	20.5	16.5	20.1		17.7	17.4
			16.5	.8	6.7	8.9		6.3	4.8
			2.7	-4.7	3.1	4.6		-2.7	-.8
Sales/Net Fixed Assets			54.5	16.9	14.6	6.8		11.3	18.1
			2.2	3.4	3.6	5.1		3.5	3.2
			.7	1.5	2.0	1.9		1.3	1.5
Sales/Total Assets			2.5	1.1	.9	1.0		1.5	1.2
			.7	.7	.5	.7		.8	.8
			.6	.3	.4	.4		.6	.5
% Depr., Dep., Amort./Sales			2.0					3.2	2.8
			(13) 6.5					(59) 7.4	(71) 5.8
			13.5					14.9	12.3
% Officers', Directors' Owners' Comp/Sales									
Net Sales ($)	6996M	3736M	102604M	412409M	399841M	1742016M		2769272M	3123381M
Total Assets ($)	1025M	2797M	76331M	433750M	710248M	1914565M		3065923M	3804228M

Comparative Historical Data · Current Data Sorted by Sales

31	30	25	Type of Statement					3		6	15
1			Unqualified								
7	2	5	Reviewed								
			Compiled		1			1	1		
3	2	2	Tax Returns	2	1	2	1	1			
36	33	28	Other	1	4	4	3	8			8

4/1/16-3/31/17 ALL	4/1/17-3/31/18 ALL	4/1/18-3/31/19 ALL		0-1MM	1-3MM (20, 4/1-9/30/18)	3-5MM	5-10MM (40, 10/1/18-3/31/19)	10-25MM	25MM & OVER
78	67	60	**NUMBER OF STATEMENTS**	3	8	6	5	15	23
%	%	%	**ASSETS**	%	%	%	%	%	%
11.8	12.5	16.8	Cash & Equivalents					16.5	10.9
11.6	10.7	10.5	Trade Receivables (net)					10.7	13.6
.2	.7	.8	Inventory					.1	2.1
4.4	5.9	4.5	All Other Current					2.7	6.7
28.0	29.9	32.5	Total Current					30.0	33.3
31.9	28.4	30.5	Fixed Assets (net)					20.0	21.6
21.1	28.4	25.0	Intangibles (net)					37.3	30.0
19.0	13.3	11.9	All Other Non-Current					12.7	15.1
100.0	100.0	100.0	Total					100.0	100.0
			LIABILITIES						
1.7	6.6	4.0	Notes Payable-Short Term					.7	.6
3.7	6.1	4.1	Cur. Mat.-L.T.D.					5.1	2.6
7.2	7.6	4.7	Trade Payables					5.4	5.7
.1	.1	.2	Income Taxes Payable					.0	.5
12.3	12.3	10.9	All Other Current					9.7	5.9
25.0	32.7	24.0	Total Current					21.0	15.3
42.6	39.0	38.9	Long-Term Debt					23.1	51.6
.5	.7	.8	Deferred Taxes					.0	2.1
8.3	7.0	6.7	All Other Non-Current					8.3	9.3
23.5	20.6	29.6	Net Worth					47.6	21.7
100.0	100.0	100.0	Total Liabilities & Net Worth					100.0	100.0
			INCOME DATA						
100.0	100.0	100.0	Net Sales					100.0	100.0
			Gross Profit						
88.1	86.3	83.7	Operating Expenses					84.3	82.2
11.9	13.7	16.3	Operating Profit					15.7	17.8
2.8	3.2	3.3	All Other Expenses (net)					4.5	2.9
9.1	10.5	13.0	Profit Before Taxes					11.2	14.9
			RATIOS						
2.3	2.6	3.5	Current					3.5	3.5
1.2	1.4	1.8						1.8	2.3
.7	.5	.9						1.0	1.3
2.2	1.8	2.9	Quick					3.0	2.5
1.1	1.0	1.6						1.7	1.3
.6	.4	.7						1.0	.9
9 42.3	9 42.3	9 39.7	Sales/Receivables					20 18.5	34 10.7
38 9.5	34 10.8	37 9.8						57 6.4	46 8.0
64 5.7	56 6.5	63 5.8						66 5.5	69 5.3
			Cost of Sales/Inventory						
			Cost of Sales/Payables						
4.5	4.0	3.6	Sales/Working Capital					3.4	3.4
21.4	13.5	7.2						6.4	7.0
-16.0	-8.6	-189.6						139.4	18.1
10.5	12.3	23.6	EBIT/Interest					18.3	40.9
(64) 2.4	(56) 3.2	(48) 4.9						(12) 6.7	(20) 10.3
-1.1	-.3	1.2						-2.5	2.6
10.2	4.6		Net Profit + Depr., Dep., Amort./Cur. Mat. L/T/D						
(11) 3.5	(14) 2.0								
1.5	.7								
.5	.5	.6	Fixed/Worth					.7	.5
1.7	7.6	1.8						1.8	1.9
-.6	-.2	-.4						-.2	-.3
.5	.6	.4	Debt/Worth					.7	.4
4.8	-6.9	3.2						3.8	5.5
-2.4	-1.9	-2.7						-1.6	-2.7
30.0	33.8	78.5	% Profit Before Taxes/Tangible Net Worth						58.7
(44) 5.2	(32) 10.5	(36) 22.5							(13) 23.3
-6.2	-2.5	1.0							10.3
16.2	13.1	27.0	% Profit Before Taxes/Total Assets					28.9	17.5
3.5	5.1	8.8						16.2	8.3
-1.4	-2.5	1.5						-5.4	4.6
16.7	12.1	11.9	Sales/Net Fixed Assets					23.6	8.4
3.7	5.7	4.5						4.5	5.1
1.7	1.6	1.6						2.0	2.0
1.2	1.2	1.6	Sales/Total Assets					1.0	1.1
.8	.7	.7						.7	.7
.5	.5	.5						.3	.5
3.8	3.2	2.8	% Depr., Dep., Amort./Sales						3.1
(55) 7.0	(50) 6.0	(40) 6.3							(18) 4.6
13.0	9.3	11.6							6.8
			% Officers', Directors' Owners' Comp/Sales						
3181340M	2890990M	2667602M	Net Sales ($)	1769M	17395M	22036M	35776M	239064M	2351562M
3580754M	3257204M	3138716M	Total Assets ($)	5431M	31433M	32753M	43773M	392326M	2633000M

M = $ thousand   MM = $ million
See Pages viii through xx for Explanation of Ratios and Data

Current Data Sorted by Assets   **Comparative Historical Data**

0-500M	500M-2MM	2-10MM	10-50MM	50-100MM	100-250MM	Type of Statement	4/1/14-3/31/15 ALL	4/1/15-3/31/16 ALL
1		1	2	1	8	Unqualified	19	17
1		1	1			Reviewed	4	5
1		1	1			Compiled	6	2
1		1	1			Tax Returns	2	2
1						Other	20	21
	11 (4/1-9/30/18)	4	29 (10/1/18-3/31/19) 6	5	6			
2		7	11	6	14	**NUMBER OF STATEMENTS**	51	47
%	%	%	%	%	%	**ASSETS**	%	%
			8.1		20.0	Cash & Equivalents	14.8	11.7
			13.1		11.6	Trade Receivables (net)	14.8	16.5
			.8		3.0	Inventory	1.6	4.8
			7.6		1.9	All Other Current	2.9	3.6
			29.6		36.5	Total Current	34.1	36.6
			40.7		31.3	Fixed Assets (net)	45.1	39.6
			3.4		24.4	Intangibles (net)	13.7	15.7
			26.3		7.7	All Other Non-Current	7.2	8.1
			100.0		100.0	Total	100.0	100.0
						LIABILITIES		
			2.7		.1	Notes Payable-Short Term	5.1	4.7
			3.9		3.0	Cur. Mat.-L.T.D.	3.5	4.9
			4.9		5.9	Trade Payables	7.1	6.2
			.1		.6	Income Taxes Payable	.5	.5
			15.6		8.1	All Other Current	8.0	13.4
			27.2		17.6	Total Current	24.1	29.6
			35.1		68.1	Long-Term Debt	44.5	33.5
			.6		2.4	Deferred Taxes	1.5	1.7
			.3		6.9	All Other Non-Current	8.3	3.3
			36.7		5.0	Net Worth	21.5	31.9
			100.0		100.0	Total Liabilties & Net Worth	100.0	100.0
						INCOME DATA		
			100.0		100.0	Net Sales	100.0	100.0
						Gross Profit		
			78.3		79.2	Operating Expenses	86.9	88.8
			21.7		20.8	Operating Profit	13.1	11.2
			2.8		2.6	All Other Expenses (net)	4.1	3.4
			18.9		18.2	Profit Before Taxes	9.0	7.8
						RATIOS		
			1.4		2.8		2.0	2.0
			1.0		1.4	Current	1.2	1.1
			.5		.9		.5	.5
			.8		2.7		1.9	1.4
			.7		1.1	Quick	.8	.8
			.5		.8		.4	.4
		17	22.0	18	19.9		9 38.9	12 30.2
		33	11.2	28	13.2	Sales/Receivables	28 13.1	29 12.5
		78	4.7	64	5.7		46 8.0	54 6.7
						Cost of Sales/Inventory		
						Cost of Sales/Payables		
			6.3		2.6		7.9	7.0
			129.1		14.2	Sales/Working Capital	39.9	84.9
			-5.9		-49.2		-8.3	-9.6
			9.9		27.0		9.2	17.1
		(10)	6.0	(13)	11.1	EBIT/Interest	(43) 3.6	(40) 4.8
			3.3		2.7		1.7	1.6
						Net Profit + Depr., Dep.,	9.8	17.2
						Amort./Cur. Mat. L/T/D	(12) 3.3	(11) 4.8
							2.5	2.5
			.4		.4		.7	.4
			1.1		2.4	Fixed/Worth	2.7	1.7
			2.4		-31.6		-1.5	-4.0
			.4		1.6		.8	.8
			.7		3.1	Debt/Worth	3.1	3.4
			5.5		-46.2		-3.1	-6.1
			46.4		118.8	% Profit Before Taxes/Tangible	80.4	89.2
		(10)	18.2	(10)	86.0	Net Worth	(33) 22.1	(32) 31.7
			9.7		28.6		8.3	8.3
			16.2		37.9	% Profit Before Taxes/Total	18.7	21.9
			8.3		18.2	Assets	6.3	7.7
			4.8		5.3		2.0	1.9
			6.1		16.7		23.6	12.2
			1.2		2.4	Sales/Net Fixed Assets	2.7	4.8
			.6		2.3		1.3	1.4
			3.4		1.3		2.5	2.6
			.5		1.1	Sales/Total Assets	1.2	1.1
			.4		.7		.7	.7
							2.4	2.2
						% Depr., Dep., Amort./Sales	(34) 8.1	(27) 7.4
							19.1	15.5
								1.5
						% Officers', Directors'		(10) 1.8
						Owners' Comp/Sales		4.2
2446M		61438M	348625M	352029M	2676116M	Net Sales ($)	2518732M	2370161M
238M		38517M	260663M	412150M	2474764M	Total Assets ($)	2453638M	2339863M

(Columns 0-500M, 500M-2MM and 2-10MM: **DATA NOT AVAILABLE**)

M = $ thousand   MM = $ million
See Pages viii through xx for Explanation of Ratios and Data

Comparative Historical Data / Current Data Sorted by Sales

Hist 4/1/16-3/31/17 ALL	Hist 4/1/17-3/31/18 ALL	Hist 4/1/18-3/31/19 ALL		0-1MM	1-3MM	3-5MM	5-10MM	10-25MM	25MM & OVER
			Type of Statement						
12	11	12	Unqualified				1	1	10
3	1	3	Reviewed	1			1	1	1
4		2	Compiled					1	
	4	2	Tax Returns		1		1		1
15	18	21	Other	1	3	1	2	2	12
					11 (4/1-9/30/18)			29 (10/1/18-3/31/19)	
34	34	40	**NUMBER OF STATEMENTS**	2	5	1	5	4	23
%	%	%		%	%	%	%	%	%
			ASSETS						
14.3	13.0	11.8	Cash & Equivalents						15.0
17.0	19.9	16.6	Trade Receivables (net)						14.5
4.4	4.2	2.7	Inventory						2.2
3.6	3.2	3.8	All Other Current						5.1
39.3	40.3	34.9	Total Current						36.7
36.1	34.7	34.7	Fixed Assets (net)						35.1
15.0	15.4	17.9	Intangibles (net)						19.8
9.6	9.6	12.6	All Other Non-Current						8.4
100.0	100.0	100.0	Total						100.0
			LIABILITIES						
5.7	5.1	4.2	Notes Payable-Short Term						.1
3.6	11.3	3.1	Cur. Mat.-L.T.D.						2.8
10.5	12.9	8.9	Trade Payables						6.1
.4	.3	.3	Income Taxes Payable						.4
13.3	17.6	15.5	All Other Current						12.5
33.4	47.2	31.9	Total Current						21.9
24.9	40.9	45.1	Long-Term Debt						56.5
1.4	1.0	1.3	Deferred Taxes						1.7
10.0	17.0	9.8	All Other Non-Current						6.1
30.4	-5.8	11.9	Net Worth						13.8
100.0	100.0	100.0	Total Liabilties & Net Worth						100.0
			INCOME DATA						
100.0	100.0	100.0	Net Sales						100.0
			Gross Profit						
87.0	89.2	82.0	Operating Expenses						83.0
13.0	10.8	18.0	Operating Profit						17.0
2.7	2.9	3.2	All Other Expenses (net)						2.6
10.3	7.9	14.8	Profit Before Taxes						14.4
			RATIOS						
2.3	1.8	2.4	Current						2.0
1.3	.9	1.1							1.4
.8	.4	.7							.9
1.8	1.3	1.8	Quick						1.5
.8	.8	.8							.9
.4	.4	.6							.7
7 49.3	12 30.4	20 18.7	Sales/Receivables						19 19.1
30 12.0	35 10.3	33 11.1							33 11.0
53 6.9	53 6.9	61 6.0							50 7.3
			Cost of Sales/Inventory						
			Cost of Sales/Payables						
8.5	8.4	6.5	Sales/Working Capital						5.4
19.8	-152.9	68.6							21.0
-14.1	-5.7	-16.3							-58.0
29.6	8.8	17.6	EBIT/Interest						20.1
(29) 5.6	(29) 2.4	(34) 4.8						(21)	6.0
2.7	-1.2	2.4							2.5
			Net Profit + Depr., Dep., Amort./Cur. Mat. L/T/D						
.4	.2	.4	Fixed/Worth						.6
1.4	4.3	1.8							2.4
-4.5	-2.7	-54.2							115.9
.7	.5	.6	Debt/Worth						.9
1.5	8.2	3.1							3.4
-12.8	-3.1	-20.1							168.1
149.0	140.4	87.0	% Profit Before Taxes/Tangible Net Worth						100.2
(24) 31.4	(20) 24.6	(28) 26.6						(18)	44.7
6.1	14.6	12.1							16.2
21.4	13.1	17.4	% Profit Before Taxes/Total Assets						27.9
7.2	4.9	8.2							9.6
2.0	-2.2	3.4							4.8
14.3	23.5	10.8	Sales/Net Fixed Assets						10.2
7.1	6.9	2.4							2.7
1.7	1.3	.9							2.2
2.6	3.1	2.2	Sales/Total Assets						2.1
1.3	1.5	.8							1.1
.7	.6	.5							.7
1.5	1.6	1.9	% Depr., Dep., Amort./Sales						1.6
(24) 2.4	(24) 2.0	(25) 4.7						(11)	2.4
11.2	13.7	12.2							6.0
			% Officers', Directors' Owners' Comp/Sales						
1942257M	2422009M	3440654M	Net Sales ($)	617M	8928M	3164M	38788M	80884M	3308273M
1799107M	1887515M	3186332M	Total Assets ($)	9150M	24794M	17557M	147067M	76671M	2911093M

© RMA 2019   M = $ thousand   MM = $ million
See Pages viii through xx for Explanation of Ratios and Data

Current Data Sorted by Assets   Comparative Historical Data

Type of Statement	0-500M	500M-2MM	2-10MM	10-50MM	50-100MM	100-250MM		4/1/14-3/31/15 ALL	4/1/15-3/31/16 ALL
Unqualified			6	19	10	8		93	98
Reviewed			3	4	1	1		12	14
Compiled		2	1					14	5
Tax Returns	2	6						25	23
Other	1	4	19	26	4	9		104	94
		21 (4/1-9/30/18)		105 (10/1/18-3/31/19)					
NUMBER OF STATEMENTS	3	12	29	49	15	18		248	234
	%	%	%	%	%	%		%	%
ASSETS									
Cash & Equivalents		11.5	18.8	12.5	5.4	7.0		13.1	15.7
Trade Receivables (net)		28.5	22.0	10.8	12.3	11.5		14.4	13.2
Inventory		15.2	10.4	2.2	2.9	2.5		4.1	3.2
All Other Current		.3	3.3	3.1	3.0	3.5		4.7	3.0
Total Current		55.6	54.5	28.7	23.5	24.4		36.3	35.2
Fixed Assets (net)		29.3	32.4	51.2	54.5	51.8		45.7	45.6
Intangibles (net)		3.8	3.7	9.7	15.0	15.5		9.7	8.3
All Other Non-Current		11.2	9.3	10.4	7.0	8.3		8.3	10.9
Total		100.0	100.0	100.0	100.0	100.0		100.0	100.0
LIABILITIES									
Notes Payable-Short Term		7.9	10.1	4.3	2.0	3.5		6.2	3.7
Cur. Mat.-L.T.D.		3.2	5.6	3.4	2.7	2.0		3.3	4.0
Trade Payables		20.3	11.5	6.3	4.9	3.4		9.1	8.8
Income Taxes Payable		.2	.0	.1	.2	.3		.2	.2
All Other Current		14.1	11.5	10.2	8.3	10.2		11.3	14.0
Total Current		45.7	38.9	24.4	18.0	19.4		30.1	30.7
Long-Term Debt		28.5	23.0	24.1	26.5	27.8		24.0	22.0
Deferred Taxes		.8	.8	2.2	3.8	1.6		1.4	1.4
All Other Non-Current		3.1	5.1	7.7	13.0	8.5		9.9	9.8
Net Worth		21.8	32.2	41.5	38.6	42.7		34.6	36.1
Total Liabilities & Net Worth		100.0	100.0	100.0	100.0	100.0		100.0	100.0
INCOME DATA									
Net Sales		100.0	100.0	100.0	100.0	100.0		100.0	100.0
Gross Profit									
Operating Expenses		86.0	96.5	89.7	87.2	89.7		91.0	90.2
Operating Profit		14.0	3.5	10.3	12.8	10.3		9.0	9.8
All Other Expenses (net)		2.6	2.2	2.0	1.9	2.9		3.0	1.9
Profit Before Taxes		11.4	1.3	8.3	10.9	7.3		6.0	7.9
RATIOS									
Current		2.8	2.8	2.2	1.9	2.1		2.3	2.5
		1.2	1.9	1.3	1.1	1.4		1.3	1.3
		.8	.8	.6	.5	.9		.7	.7
Quick		1.9	2.2	1.9	1.5	1.6		1.6	2.1
		.9	1.2	1.1	.7	1.1		.9	1.0
		.5	.5	.5	.3	.7		.5	.5
Sales/Receivables		10 34.9	19 19.5	12 30.5	19 19.1	12 29.2		15 24.1	11 32.6
		29 12.6	31 11.8	28 13.1	28 13.0	24 14.9		30 12.3	26 14.3
		69 5.3	46 7.9	43 8.5	42 8.6	70 5.2		42 8.7	43 8.5
Cost of Sales/Inventory									
Cost of Sales/Payables									
Sales/Working Capital		8.2	4.5	5.0	4.1	2.8		6.4	4.8
		23.8	7.5	22.5	28.4	15.7		22.4	20.7
		-31.7	-84.3	-6.9	-8.1	-65.1		-17.6	-21.4
EBIT/Interest		15.9	13.3	7.6	8.2	12.9		18.1	16.8
		6.6	(24) 5.0	(44) 3.8	(14) 3.2	(16) 4.5		(205) 4.7	(199) 4.3
		4.3	.0	1.7	1.6	1.4		1.0	1.1
Net Profit + Depr., Dep., Amort./Cur. Mat. L/T/D				7.1				4.4	9.3
			(21) 2.7					(66) 2.4	(67) 3.2
				1.7				1.7	1.8
Fixed/Worth		.1	.2	.8	1.2	1.2		.6	.6
		.9	1.1	2.2	2.6	2.0		1.5	1.4
		3.3	2.4	5.9	-1.4	6.4		9.7	9.6
Debt/Worth		.9	.5	.7	.7	1.0		.6	.6
		2.3	1.1	2.1	3.1	2.3		1.9	1.6
		10.6	14.7	7.7	-6.0	9.7		16.0	18.2
% Profit Before Taxes/Tangible Net Worth		93.4	59.1	38.4	27.4	34.7		44.9	41.5
	(10) 45.2	(24) 22.4	(42) 14.6	(10) 14.5	(15) 18.1			(193) 10.5	(183) 14.5
		27.8	5.7	3.1	5.7	6.5		1.7	2.9
% Profit Before Taxes/Total Assets		20.2	20.4	11.1	7.2	9.1		13.0	13.8
		16.5	6.8	4.1	4.5	4.7		4.1	4.4
		7.5	-5.4	1.0	.9	1.2		-.3	.3
Sales/Net Fixed Assets		561.6	113.6	7.3	7.8	1.5		18.3	21.4
		15.1	13.7	1.1	.8	.8		2.1	1.5
		4.2	2.2	.6	.5	.7		.6	.7
Sales/Total Assets		4.1	4.0	1.6	.9	.9		2.7	2.3
		2.9	2.3	.6	.5	.5		.8	.8
		1.7	.8	.4	.4	.3		.4	.4
% Depr., Dep., Amort./Sales			.7	3.2	13.9			2.5	4.5
		(24) 2.6	(44) 10.2	(11) 19.7				(185) 11.6	(169) 11.9
			13.9	18.5	22.1			21.6	20.2
% Officers', Directors' Owners' Comp/Sales								1.8	2.9
							(35) 3.8	(32) 6.1
								6.9	12.5
Net Sales ($)	4444M	53649M	410962M	1313056M	857496M	2576383M		10554784M	8889453M
Total Assets ($)	887M	15018M	174022M	1144571M	1047366M	3142989M		11759375M	10634228M

M = $ thousand   MM = $ million
See Pages viii through xx for Explanation of Ratios and Data

Comparative Historical Data | Current Data Sorted by Sales

					Type of Statement						
64		54		43	Unqualified		1	3	8	10	21
15		11		9	Reviewed			1	3	2	3
8		0		2	Compiled			2			
10		13		9	Tax Returns			1			
76		69		63	Other	1	4	2	1	1	1
						2	4	2	13	17	25
4/1/16-3/31/17		4/1/17-3/31/18		4/1/18-3/31/19		21 (4/1-9/30/18)			105 (10/1/18-3/31/19)		
ALL		ALL		ALL		0-1MM	1-3MM	3-5MM	5-10MM	10-25MM	25MM & OVER
173		153		126	NUMBER OF STATEMENTS	3	9	9	25	30	50
%		%		%	ASSETS	%	%	%	%	%	%
15.0		13.9		12.5	Cash & Equivalents				17.6	11.7	10.2
12.3		11.9		15.4	Trade Receivables (net)				12.9	14.3	18.4
4.3		4.2		6.1	Inventory				3.3	7.8	4.2
3.1		3.0		2.9	All Other Current				3.5	2.0	4.1
34.7		33.0		36.9	Total Current				37.3	35.8	36.9
46.4		48.2		44.2	Fixed Assets (net)				46.5	46.4	43.4
8.7		8.5		9.0	Intangibles (net)				5.2	12.2	11.9
10.2		10.3		9.8	All Other Non-Current				11.0	5.6	7.7
100.0		100.0		100.0	Total				100.0	100.0	100.0
					LIABILITIES						
9.1		11.8		5.5	Notes Payable-Short Term				2.7	7.2	4.3
3.5		3.5		3.7	Cur. Mat.-L.T.D.				3.1	6.4	2.7
7.6		6.0		8.5	Trade Payables				4.5	11.5	8.8
.2		.2		.1	Income Taxes Payable				.1	.0	.2
12.3		12.0		10.8	All Other Current				6.2	13.0	12.8
32.6		34.4		28.6	Total Current				16.6	38.0	28.8
21.0		23.0		25.7	Long-Term Debt				25.7	30.3	20.9
1.8		2.0		1.8	Deferred Taxes				2.1	2.4	1.7
9.9		9.1		7.2	All Other Non-Current				4.9	6.1	8.3
34.8		31.5		36.6	Net Worth				50.7	23.3	40.2
100.0		100.0		100.0	Total Liabilties & Net Worth				100.0	100.0	100.0
					INCOME DATA						
100.0		100.0		100.0	Net Sales				100.0	100.0	100.0
					Gross Profit						
90.2		91.6		90.7	Operating Expenses				93.0	89.9	91.0
9.8		8.4		9.3	Operating Profit				7.0	10.1	9.0
1.9		1.8		2.2	All Other Expenses (net)				2.1	3.9	1.0
7.9		6.6		7.1	Profit Before Taxes				4.9	6.1	8.0
					RATIOS						
2.2		2.4		2.3					4.5	2.3	1.9
1.1		1.1		1.4	Current				2.1	1.3	1.2
.7		.6		.7					1.0	.6	.9
1.7		1.6		1.8					3.0	2.0	1.5
.9		.9		1.1	Quick				1.7	.8	1.0
.5		.4		.5					.7	.4	.6
9	38.6	11	33.4	16	22.2	Sales/Receivables	7	50.3	18	20.6	17	21.0
23	16.0	22	16.4	28	13.0		31	11.8	32	11.5	27	13.7
37	9.8	41	8.8	46	7.9		53	6.9	45	8.1	48	7.6
					Cost of Sales/Inventory						
					Cost of Sales/Payables						
6.0		5.5		4.6	Sales/Working Capital				3.8	4.2	7.1
56.0		87.5		18.8					6.4	9.7	28.1
-12.6		-9.2		-26.4					NM	-9.5	-50.0
20.3		13.4		10.7	EBIT/Interest				6.7	10.8	13.8
(154)	5.6	(134)	6.1	(112)	4.2		(21)	4.2	(28)	2.4	(44)	6.4
1.2		1.0		1.4					1.7	.7	2.0
13.8		9.6		6.1	Net Profit + Depr., Dep., Amort./Cur. Mat. L/T/D				7.8	5.9
(53)	4.8	(39)	4.6	(39)	3.1				(14)	2.0	(13)	5.4
2.7		3.0		1.7						1.1	3.2
.6		.7		.7	Fixed/Worth				.3	.9	.9
1.5		1.5		1.6					1.1	2.3	1.9
0.9		4.6		5.9					2.5	-5.2	5.8
.6		.7		.7	Debt/Worth				.4	.9	.9
1.9		1.6		2.0					1.0	2.8	2.7
12.9		9.6		10.9					2.4	-8.8	9.7
47.3		38.4		46.0	% Profit Before Taxes/Tangible Net Worth				28.5	35.4	68.1
(138)	18.4	(122)	14.8	(102)	18.3		(23)	10.1	(21)	12.8	(41)	26.5
4.1		2.6		5.4					3.4	3.9	10.5
15.2		13.9		14.0	% Profit Before Taxes/Total Assets				11.0	8.4	15.0
6.2		6.6		5.5					4.3	2.8	7.6
1.0		.1		.9					.6	-3.8	3.0
13.4		16.2		19.9	Sales/Net Fixed Assets				21.4	10.6	21.9
2.3		1.9		2.5					1.2	1.6	2.7
.7		.7		.7					.5	.7	.8
2.6		2.2		2.5	Sales/Total Assets				2.0	2.3	2.7
.9		.9		.9					.6	.7	1.1
.4		.4		.5					.4	.4	.5
3.5		3.0		1.9	% Depr., Dep., Amort./Sales				2.4	3.1	.8
(128)	11.3	(109)	11.1	(92)	8.5		(22)	10.4	(23)	14.5	(31)	3.7
20.4		20.1		18.0					18.4	20.7	13.1
2.1		3.0		1.3	% Officers', Directors' Owners' Comp/Sales						
(21)	5.1	(14)	6.3	(15)	5.6						
8.7		8.7		8.8							
6763438M		6440463M		5215990M	Net Sales ($)	1918M	18013M	31409M	178795M	483688M	4502167M
7259679M		7203010M		5524853M	Total Assets ($)	3153M	49086M	67483M	330960M	757225M	4316946M

© RMA 2019

M = $ thousand   MM = $ million

See Pages viii through xx for Explanation of Ratios and Data

Current Data Sorted by Assets / Comparative Historical Data

Type of Statement	0-500M	500M-2MM	2-10MM	10-50MM	50-100MM	100-250MM		ALL 4/1/14-3/31/15	ALL 4/1/15-3/31/16
Unqualified			1	5	6	2		24	30
Reviewed			3	1				6	2
Compiled		1	1	1				13	12
Tax Returns	2	1	2	1				12	18
Other	1	11	12	9	5	5		50	52
		15 (4/1-9/30/18)		54 (10/1/18-3/31/19)					
NUMBER OF STATEMENTS	4	13	18	16	11	7		105	114
ASSETS	%	%	%	%	%	%		%	%
Cash & Equivalents		21.7	15.5	15.1	11.6			17.3	16.7
Trade Receivables (net)		14.4	23.4	16.7	8.0			17.8	20.8
Inventory		11.2	17.2	7.9	5.4			10.8	11.8
All Other Current		4.0	5.6	6.6	1.1			3.8	6.4
Total Current		51.2	61.8	46.4	26.1			49.7	55.7
Fixed Assets (net)		36.6	24.5	36.0	45.7			30.1	27.2
Intangibles (net)		5.9	5.3	9.4	19.1			8.9	9.6
All Other Non-Current		6.2	8.5	8.2	9.2			11.3	7.4
Total		100.0	100.0	100.0	100.0			100.0	100.0
LIABILITIES									
Notes Payable-Short Term		10.8	11.4	2.2	.0			5.1	3.5
Cur. Mat.-L.T.D.		5.3	1.9	4.1	3.7			2.4	2.7
Trade Payables		17.9	18.1	14.6	7.9			17.7	19.1
Income Taxes Payable		.0	.0	.0	.0			.1	.1
All Other Current		25.0	12.1	5.6	7.7			16.2	11.0
Total Current		59.0	43.6	26.6	19.3			41.4	36.5
Long-Term Debt		12.6	15.6	17.8	30.0			16.9	19.5
Deferred Taxes		.0	.0	.1	.7			.7	.3
All Other Non-Current		2.6	5.4	4.9	5.2			13.1	5.0
Net Worth		25.8	35.5	50.6	44.8			27.8	38.7
Total Liabilities & Net Worth		100.0	100.0	100.0	100.0			100.0	100.0
INCOME DATA									
Net Sales		100.0	100.0	100.0	100.0			100.0	100.0
Gross Profit									
Operating Expenses		91.8	93.5	89.8	82.5			92.0	89.4
Operating Profit		8.2	6.5	10.2	17.5			8.1	10.6
All Other Expenses (net)		.7	.4	1.3	5.9			1.4	2.2
Profit Before Taxes		7.6	6.1	8.9	11.6			6.7	8.4
RATIOS									
Current		4.5	2.4	2.1	2.6			2.5	3.6
		1.1	1.4	1.4	1.6			1.4	1.7
		.5	.9	1.2	1.0			.8	1.0
Quick		4.2	1.7	1.8	1.6			1.9	2.3
		.6	.8	1.1	1.3			.9	1.1
		.3	.5	.5	.5			.5	.6
Sales/Receivables		0 UND	9 41.6	23 15.7	9 41.3			8 43.7	8 44.1
		3 130.6	34 10.8	34 10.6	12 30.9			26 13.9	30 12.3
		39 9.3	63 5.8	51 7.2	33 10.9			42 8.6	49 7.5
Cost of Sales/Inventory									
Cost of Sales/Payables									
Sales/Working Capital		16.6	3.9	4.5	4.0			6.0	5.6
		204.5	20.1	11.5	13.9			24.1	13.0
		-16.3	-67.0	23.6	-142.9			-52.9	-253.7
EBIT/Interest			37.4	43.2	14.9			26.1	33.7
			(16) 12.7	(11) 11.4	(10) 10.1			(76) 8.7	(81) 9.9
			3.0	3.1	2.2			1.1	1.8
Net Profit + Depr., Dep., Amort./Cur. Mat. L/T/D								19.4	
								(11) 3.4	
								.5	
Fixed/Worth		.3	.1	.2	1.0			.3	.2
		.8	.8	.7	1.5			.8	.7
		-10.0	2.2	1.5	-2.1			2.7	6.9
Debt/Worth		.2	.8	.6	.6			.5	.4
		2.9	2.1	1.2	.9			1.6	1.9
		-17.2	9.0	5.1	-4.4			10.9	47.8
% Profit Before Taxes/Tangible Net Worth			87.9	39.6				82.8	84.5
			(15) 34.8	(14) 24.8				(83) 29.2	(90) 31.6
			13.7	2.2				7.5	12.8
% Profit Before Taxes/Total Assets		39.9	24.2	20.6	6.3			22.7	25.1
		19.2	10.4	7.1	4.9			10.4	11.9
		11.3	4.9	1.2	.8			.4	1.6
Sales/Net Fixed Assets		46.4	114.4	34.5	52.4			53.3	66.9
		11.4	16.1	5.0	1.4			11.1	16.1
		3.9	5.6	2.5	.6			1.7	3.0
Sales/Total Assets		6.5	3.1	2.3	1.2			4.1	4.1
		3.1	2.3	1.3	.6			1.8	2.0
		2.0	1.6	.6	.3			.9	.8
% Depr., Dep., Amort./Sales			1.7	1.1				.4	.5
			(10) 4.7	(14) 8.6				(79) 2.0	(75) 2.6
			6.3	13.6				8.9	9.7
% Officers', Directors' Owners' Comp/Sales								1.4	.6
								(19) 4.5	(24) 2.7
								9.0	5.4
Net Sales ($)	3491M	90345M	248378M	586366M	924643M	1122892M		4558920M	6860520M
Total Assets ($)	962M	18588M	99544M	380266M	839008M	1080927M		3371673M	4173445M

M = $ thousand   MM = $ million
See Pages viii through xx for Explanation of Ratios and Data

Comparative Historical Data | Current Data Sorted by Sales

4/1/16-3/31/17 ALL	4/1/17-3/31/18 ALL	4/1/18-3/31/19 ALL	Type of Statement	0-1MM	1-3MM	3-5MM	5-10MM	10-25MM	25MM & OVER
19	15	14	Unqualified				2	3	9
3	4	4	Reviewed				2	1	1
4	8	3	Compiled	1			1	1	
12	8	5	Tax Returns	1			1	1	
41	31	43	Other	2	2	4	8	10	17
					15 (4/1-9/30/18)		54 (10/1/18-3/31/19)		
79	66	69	**NUMBER OF STATEMENTS**	4	4	6	15	13	27
%	%	%	**ASSETS**	%	%	%	%	%	%
14.1	16.6	15.0	Cash & Equivalents				18.1	19.6	11.0
20.5	16.4	17.6	Trade Receivables (net)				17.9	14.0	20.8
10.2	11.3	10.5	Inventory				6.5	24.5	9.0
3.6	5.1	4.0	All Other Current				3.5	5.2	4.4
48.5	49.4	47.2	Total Current				46.0	63.4	45.2
27.4	28.7	33.9	Fixed Assets (net)				37.5	15.6	32.3
15.0	11.3	10.6	Intangibles (net)				11.0	7.7	15.8
9.1	10.6	8.4	All Other Non-Current				5.4	13.3	6.7
100.0	100.0	100.0	Total				100.0	100.0	100.0
			LIABILITIES						
4.6	5.1	7.4	Notes Payable-Short Term				6.8	11.8	1.5
3.4	2.7	3.4	Cur. Mat.-L.T.D.				5.0	.9	3.7
17.9	14.9	15.5	Trade Payables				10.7	22.3	20.8
.1	.0	.0	Income Taxes Payable				.0	.0	.0
11.6	11.3	11.3	All Other Current				9.0	6.9	9.0
37.6	34.0	37.7	Total Current				31.4	41.9	35.0
16.3	20.3	17.4	Long-Term Debt				30.3	10.7	18.3
.5	.2	.1	Deferred Taxes				.0	.0	.3
4.0	8.7	4.1	All Other Non-Current				6.7	.0	6.3
41.7	36.8	40.8	Net Worth				31.6	47.3	40.0
100.0	100.0	100.0	Total Liabilties & Net Worth				100.0	100.0	100.0
			INCOME DATA						
100.0	100.0	100.0	Net Sales				100.0	100.0	100.0
			Gross Profit						
91.2	87.9	90.6	Operating Expenses				93.0	88.5	93.0
8.8	12.1	9.4	Operating Profit				7.0	11.5	7.0
2.6	4.1	2.3	All Other Expenses (net)				5.7	1.6	2.3
6.2	8.0	7.1	Profit Before Taxes				1.3	9.9	4.7
			RATIOS						
2.2	3.6	2.5					5.0	2.7	2.1
1.2	1.3	1.3	Current				1.3	1.6	1.3
.9	.8	.9					.9	1.0	1.0
1.6	2.0	1.7					5.0	2.0	1.4
.9	.9	.9	Quick				1.0	.6	.9
.5	.5	.5					.7	.4	.5
10 37.2	9 41.2	8 47.2					11 32.7	0 UND	20 18.7
29 12.4	23 16.0	32 11.5	Sales/Receivables				41 8.9	9 39.1	32 11.4
50 7.3	42 8.7	48 7.6					64 5.7	43 8.5	47 7.8
			Cost of Sales/Inventory						
			Cost of Sales/Payables						
6.9	5.2	5.1					2.0	4.4	10.4
37.3	21.8	21.1	Sales/Working Capital				16.2	23.9	21.1
-47.2	-41.1	-71.0					-66.7	NM	-142.9
39.5	50.7	23.4					21.7		23.5
(62) 9.2	(53) 6.7	(51) 11.6	EBIT/Interest		(11) 12.3			(24) 11.2	
1.4	2.2	2.6					2.6		2.6
			Net Profit + Depr., Dep., Amort./Cur. Mat. L/T/D						
.2	.2	.2					.1	.1	.5
.9	1.1	1.0	Fixed/Worth				1.9	.6	1.0
9.9	NM	4.1					-2.1	1.4	1.6
.7	.7	.5					1.0	.4	.9
2.2	2.6	2.0	Debt/Worth				2.9	2.1	3.3
69.7	NM	9.2					5.4	7.3	8.0
68.5	78.1	63.1	% Profit Before Taxes/Tangible Net Worth				73.1	136.6	73.6
(60) 30.8	(50) 38.4	(54) 32.3		(10) 12.6	(11) 43.1				(22) 32.4
5.6	11.4	8.0					-1.1	25.0	3.0
21.4	20.8	25.8	% Profit Before Taxes/Total Assets				14.4	26.5	19.6
11.1	7.6	9.0					5.9	19.2	5.4
1.8	3.7	2.6					.7	5.0	.8
102.3	82.3	46.4	Sales/Net Fixed Assets				17.0	153.7	37.4
16.6	11.0	9.8					11.4	47.5	9.4
1.7	1.3	2.0					1.6	8.7	1.5
4.4	3.9	3.0	Sales/Total Assets				2.8	5.8	2.9
2.1	1.7	2.0					1.7	2.6	1.7
.8	.6	.8					.5	1.5	.8
.5	.9	1.3					2.2		.7
(48) 3.0	(44) 3.4	(45) 6.4	% Depr., Dep., Amort./Sales		(12) 5.3			(18) 7.8	
11.7	14.9	12.7					18.7		12.0
1.2	.6	2.1	% Officers', Directors' Owners' Comp/Sales						
(20) 3.2	(16) 1.8	(11) 3.8							
5.4	7.9	4.3							
5098683M	4217800M	2976115M	Net Sales ($)	2763M	8174M	26323M	110351M	211162M	2617342M
3450588M	2430434M	2419295M	Total Assets ($)	2112M	4111M	95913M	189290M	325144M	1802725M

© RMA 2019

M = $ thousand   MM = $ million
See Pages viii through xx for Explanation of Ratios and Data

Current Data Sorted by Assets   Comparative Historical Data

						Type of Statement		
		1	5	4	3	Unqualified	12	10
		4	1			Reviewed	7	7
	1	1	2			Compiled	5	7
2	3	3				Tax Returns	10	7
1	4	12	9	7	6	Other	44	57
	7 (4/1-9/30/18)		62 (10/1/18-3/31/19)				4/1/14-3/31/15	4/1/15-3/31/16
0-500M	500M-2MM	2-10MM	10-50MM	50-100MM	100-250MM		ALL	ALL
3	8	21	17	11	9	NUMBER OF STATEMENTS	78	88
%	%	%	%	%	%	ASSETS	%	%
		22.1	13.9	7.9		Cash & Equivalents	16.5	18.8
		35.9	23.4	15.4		Trade Receivables (net)	27.9	22.1
		6.8	6.3	5.4		Inventory	11.5	12.6
		4.0	5.6	3.7		All Other Current	7.6	5.8
		68.7	49.3	32.5		Total Current	63.6	59.3
		18.0	24.1	43.7		Fixed Assets (net)	19.8	18.9
		7.0	15.3	11.7		Intangibles (net)	8.5	11.5
		6.2	11.3	12.1		All Other Non-Current	8.2	10.4
		100.0	100.0	100.0		Total	100.0	100.0
						LIABILITIES		
		6.8	4.8	6.7		Notes Payable-Short Term	4.9	6.2
		2.0	2.8	2.2		Cur. Mat.-L.T.D.	2.6	2.2
		23.8	15.7	13.8		Trade Payables	23.0	20.7
		.2	.0	.3		Income Taxes Payable	.3	.3
		14.8	14.1	16.5		All Other Current	22.8	18.1
		47.6	37.3	39.6		Total Current	53.5	47.5
		15.5	23.6	26.7		Long-Term Debt	12.2	15.4
		.8	.4	2.5		Deferred Taxes	.7	.9
		5.4	3.2	6.7		All Other Non-Current	9.2	6.8
		30.7	35.4	24.5		Net Worth	24.3	29.4
		100.0	100.0	100.0		Total Liabilties & Net Worth	100.0	100.0
						INCOME DATA		
		100.0	100.0	100.0		Net Sales	100.0	100.0
						Gross Profit		
		94.1	91.4	92.2		Operating Expenses	95.2	91.4
		5.9	8.6	7.8		Operating Profit	4.8	8.6
		1.5	-.1	3.0		All Other Expenses (net)	1.1	1.1
		4.4	8.7	4.9		Profit Before Taxes	3.7	7.5
						RATIOS		
		3.2	2.4	1.1		Current	1.9	2.3
		1.7	1.3	.6			1.2	1.3
		.7	.8	.5			.9	.9
		2.4	1.4	.9		Quick	1.4	1.6
		1.4	1.0	.5			.9	.9
		.6	.6	.3			.6	.6
		17 21.9	26 13.9	10 35.6		Sales/Receivables	14 26.1	6 58.3
		33 11.1	34 10.6	13 27.9			29 12.5	22 16.6
		45 8.1	51 7.2	35 10.5			47 7.7	45 8.2
						Cost of Sales/Inventory		
						Cost of Sales/Payables		
		5.9	5.8	49.7		Sales/Working Capital	9.7	9.8
		16.5	15.9	-26.8			46.1	29.6
		-18.8	-26.7	-7.4			-55.1	-46.7
		97.3	21.0	8.2		EBIT/Interest	25.8	25.9
		(14) 6.8	(12) 8.7	(10) 2.3			(61) 6.7	(63) 6.8
		2.8	2.6	1.7			1.4	1.9
						Net Profit + Depr., Dep., Amort./Cur. Mat. L/T/D	7.5	5.8
							(11) 3.0	(17) 4.7
							.6	1.6
		.2	.3	2.3		Fixed/Worth	.3	.2
		.4	.8	2.6			.8	.6
		-5.3	5.9	-1.9			-8.3	-1.0
		.7	.6	2.0		Debt/Worth	1.6	1.1
		2.2	2.9	5.3			4.3	3.2
		-22.8	9.8	-4.9			-33.2	-8.7
		77.5	81.3			% Profit Before Taxes/Tangible Net Worth	101.1	82.6
		(15) 53.1	(14) 32.3				(57) 36.3	(59) 49.2
		17.2	8.2				5.9	14.6
		30.9	25.4	11.2		% Profit Before Taxes/Total Assets	19.8	26.6
		7.5	10.8	5.1			6.7	11.1
		3.3	4.2	2.2			1.1	2.3
		105.6	55.8	19.7		Sales/Net Fixed Assets	91.8	101.1
		43.9	25.6	2.0			31.5	39.0
		19.4	1.6	.7			11.0	12.1
		5.8	3.2	3.3		Sales/Total Assets	6.0	5.2
		3.5	1.9	1.4			3.3	2.9
		2.6	.8	.4			1.7	1.3
		.3	.7			% Depr., Dep., Amort./Sales	.3	.3
		(16) 1.2	(13) 1.4				(51) 1.0	(63) .8
		3.8	16.6				1.9	2.0
						% Officers', Directors' Owners' Comp/Sales	1.3	1.7
							(17) 3.0	(12) 3.9
							8.3	11.2
20319M	91381M	410939M	802508M	1421646M	1549756M	Net Sales ($)	7027273M	9094203M
738M	12358M	107956M	389089M	742425M	1458852M	Total Assets ($)	2670655M	3691046M

Comparative Historical Data   Current Data Sorted by Sales

ALL 4/1/16-3/31/17	ALL 4/1/17-3/31/18	ALL 4/1/18-3/31/19	Type of Statement	0-1MM	1-3MM	3-5MM	5-10MM	10-25MM	25MM & OVER
12	8	13	Unqualified		1		1	3	8
7	8	5	Reviewed				1	2	2
8	5	4	Compiled					1	3
8	12	8	Tax Returns			1	4	3	
51	50	39	Other	2	1	2	3	6	25
					7 (4/1-9/30/18)			62 (10/1/18-3/31/19)	
86	83	69	**NUMBER OF STATEMENTS**	2	2	3	9	15	38
%	%	%	**ASSETS**	%	%	%	%	%	%
17.9	17.4	20.3	Cash & Equivalents					23.5	14.6
24.5	22.4	24.7	Trade Receivables (net)					30.2	24.2
9.8	5.6	5.6	Inventory					7.6	4.8
5.6	7.1	5.4	All Other Current					7.8	5.6
57.9	52.5	56.1	Total Current					69.1	49.2
24.7	27.5	23.9	Fixed Assets (net)					20.6	23.9
8.8	11.7	10.1	Intangibles (net)					5.2	14.3
8.6	8.3	9.9	All Other Non-Current					5.1	12.6
100.0	100.0	100.0	Total					100.0	100.0
			LIABILITIES						
10.2	7.7	6.8	Notes Payable-Short Term					3.2	7.1
3.4	3.4	3.7	Cur. Mat.-L.T.D.					2.2	2.1
19.7	18.1	16.7	Trade Payables					17.1	19.2
.1	.1	.1	Income Taxes Payable					.1	.2
18.5	15.2	15.4	All Other Current					21.7	14.1
51.9	44.5	42.8	Total Current					44.3	42.7
13.4	18.3	18.7	Long-Term Debt					14.3	19.7
.8	.7	1.1	Deferred Taxes					.6	1.2
8.2	8.7	5.1	All Other Non-Current					3.6	5.4
25.7	27.9	32.3	Net Worth					37.3	31.0
100.0	100.0	100.0	Total Liabilties & Net Worth					100.0	100.0
			INCOME DATA						
100.0	100.0	100.0	Net Sales					100.0	100.0
			Gross Profit						
94.5	92.2	91.5	Operating Expenses					93.6	91.3
5.5	7.8	8.5	Operating Profit					6.4	8.7
1.0	1.3	1.0	All Other Expenses (net)					.4	.8
4.5	6.5	7.4	Profit Before Taxes					5.9	7.9
			RATIOS						
1.8	1.5	2.9	Current					2.4	2.5
1.1	1.1	1.2						1.7	1.0
.8	.8	.8						1.1	.6
1.2	1.2	2.3	Quick					2.1	1.5
.9	.8	1.0						1.4	.7
.5	.5	.5						.8	.5
12 31.3	9 39.8	12 30.1	Sales/Receivables					12 30.1	14 26.7
26 14.2	27 13.5	30 12.1						31 11.7	29 12.4
42 8.6	41 9.0	45 8.1						46 7.9	40 9.2
			Cost of Sales/Inventory						
			Cost of Sales/Payables						
9.0	12.3	5.8	Sales/Working Capital					6.1	9.9
115.3	92.7	33.9						11.8	NM
-38.0	-25.5	-25.7						118.0	-18.1
34.7	17.1	22.9	EBIT/Interest					169.0	21.7
(70) 10.1	(60) 6.2	(50) 6.4						(11) 9.8	(28) 7.4
1.6	1.6	2.5						3.4	2.6
15.1	54.6	16.5	Net Profit + Depr., Dep.,						11.6
(14) 5.1	(12) 9.0	(15) 3.2	Amort./Cur. Mat. L/T/D						(10) 4.0
.9	2.1	2.6							2.6
.4	.3	.2	Fixed/Worth					.1	.3
.9	1.0	.8						.4	1.0
-0.3	-2.1	NM						1.1	-4.5
1.1	.8	.7	Debt/Worth					.8	1.0
3.5	2.6	2.3						1.6	3.5
-37.6	-18.2	NM						4.3	-20.5
110.1	64.0	74.0	% Profit Before Taxes/Tangible					81.1	79.4
(63) 38.4	(59) 26.3	(52) 42.5	Net Worth					(14) 70.0	(26) 47.7
5.3	8.1	10.1						35.4	10.6
21.2	14.4	23.9	% Profit Before Taxes/Total					44.1	21.5
8.5	5.9	11.0	Assets					20.1	10.9
1.6	2.4	4.2						3.4	5.4
60.6	97.7	86.4	Sales/Net Fixed Assets					100.9	70.0
21.1	28.7	29.8						40.8	20.2
6.1	3.3	2.7						25.2	2.1
5.2	5.7	5.5	Sales/Total Assets					7.4	5.1
2.6	2.3	2.6						4.1	2.0
1.3	.8	.8						2.6	.9
.6	.3	.5	% Depr., Dep., Amort./Sales					.3	.5
(60) 1.6	(58) 1.6	(43) 1.6						(11) 1.0	(23) 1.6
3.6	9.3	14.0						3.9	4.9
1.4	.3	.5	% Officers', Directors'						
(18) 3.1	(21) .6	(12) 1.1	Owners' Comp/Sales						
3.9	3.5	4.2							
5681323M	4750700M	4296549M	Net Sales ($)	1008M	4852M	13411M	65177M	254769M	3957332M
2581002M	3643500M	2711418M	Total Assets ($)	2462M	7856M	25196M	68364M	134467M	2473073M

M = $ thousand   MM = $ million
See Pages viii through xx for Explanation of Ratios and Data

Current Data Sorted by Assets   Comparative Historical Data

0-500M	500M-2MM	2-10MM	10-50MM	50-100MM	100-250MM		4/1/14-3/31/15 ALL	4/1/15-3/31/16 ALL
						Type of Statement		
		3	5	9	3	Unqualified	28	33
		4	4			Reviewed	13	15
	1	3	1			Compiled	13	11
3	6	2				Tax Returns	32	23
3	12	12	27	5	7	Other	96	95
	12 (4/1-9/30/18)		98 (10/1/18-3/31/19)					
6	19	24	37	14	10	**NUMBER OF STATEMENTS**	182	177
%	%	%	%	%	%	**ASSETS**	%	%
	20.9	17.1	12.6	6.7	3.8	Cash & Equivalents	15.2	15.9
	31.7	31.1	22.2	22.5	13.5	Trade Receivables (net)	27.5	25.8
	6.0	4.3	2.4	4.2	4.2	Inventory	8.1	6.7
	5.6	8.4	7.3	2.5	2.1	All Other Current	4.7	4.0
	64.3	60.9	44.5	35.9	23.6	Total Current	55.5	52.4
	19.1	26.1	21.5	41.6	54.0	Fixed Assets (net)	23.7	24.8
	5.4	9.2	21.2	15.2	5.7	Intangibles (net)	9.6	12.6
	11.2	3.8	12.8	7.4	16.6	All Other Non-Current	11.3	10.2
	100.0	100.0	100.0	100.0	100.0	Total	100.0	100.0
						LIABILITIES		
	10.7	5.8	7.9	10.8	5.3	Notes Payable-Short Term	7.4	9.2
	.9	4.4	2.2	4.1	3.0	Cur. Mat.-L.T.D.	3.1	4.3
	11.6	12.6	13.6	9.4	7.3	Trade Payables	14.9	15.5
	.3	.4	.0	.1	2.7	Income Taxes Payable	.4	.1
	17.1	16.5	9.7	9.9	11.7	All Other Current	12.6	14.3
	40.5	39.7	33.5	34.2	30.0	Total Current	38.4	43.4
	16.5	13.8	20.7	40.1	22.3	Long-Term Debt	18.4	15.6
	.0	.5	.3	.5	1.0	Deferred Taxes	.4	.8
	5.9	5.3	9.8	7.9	10.8	All Other Non-Current	10.5	10.1
	37.1	40.7	35.7	17.3	35.9	Net Worth	32.3	30.1
	100.0	100.0	100.0	100.0	100.0	Total Liabilities & Net Worth	100.0	100.0
						INCOME DATA		
	100.0	100.0	100.0	100.0	100.0	Net Sales	100.0	100.0
						Gross Profit		
	90.4	88.6	92.1	85.5	96.7	Operating Expenses	92.1	93.1
	9.6	11.4	7.9	14.5	3.3	Operating Profit	7.9	6.9
	.7	2.1	3.5	8.9	3.3	All Other Expenses (net)	1.8	1.4
	8.9	9.3	4.4	5.6	.0	Profit Before Taxes	6.1	5.5
						RATIOS		
	2.8	3.2	1.9	1.6	1.0		3.0	2.3
	1.7	1.8	1.1	.9	.7	Current	1.4	1.3
	1.0	1.3	.7	.4	.3		.9	.7
	2.2	2.7	1.4	1.3	.8		2.4	1.8
	1.4	1.5	.8	.7	.6	Quick	1.0	1.0
	.8	1.0	.6	.3	.1		.6	.4
	10 38.4	3 112.5	24 15.4	14 26.3	20 18.1		15 23.6	13 27.1
	22 16.4	27 13.3	40 9.2	46 8.0	38 9.7	Sales/Receivables	40 9.2	38 9.5
	63 5.8	63 5.8	89 4.1	87 4.2	69 5.3		65 5.6	63 5.8
						Cost of Sales/Inventory		
						Cost of Sales/Payables		
	7.4	4.0	5.4	8.0	NM		5.6	7.5
	15.9	9.9	44.9	-36.9	-15.2	Sales/Working Capital	22.5	25.4
	141.4	26.3	-12.8	-3.4	-2.1		-54.3	-15.2
	82.5	53.2	12.6	14.3			29.9	24.5
	(16) 14.4	(21) 9.1	(32) 3.4	(11) 4.8		EBIT/Interest	(145) 7.5	(141) 5.0
	7.0	.3	1.4	1.6			1.2	1.1
						Net Profit + Depr., Dep.,		13.6	5.1
						Amort./Cur. Mat. L/T/D	(15) 4.0	(21) 2.5
							1.7	1.5
	.3	.1	.1	1.4	.9		.1	.2
	.5	.6	1.1	NM	2.0	Fixed/Worth	.8	1.0
	-1.7	3.1	-1.0	-.4	4.0		UND	-5.3
	.6	.5	.7	1.2	1.3		.5	.7
	1.2	1.9	2.8	NM	2.1	Debt/Worth	1.9	2.5
	-11.7	8.2	-5.6	-3.4	4.4		-26.5	-14.6
	86.4	57.4	37.9			% Profit Before Taxes/Tangible	63.0	56.8
	(13) 44.6	(19) 29.2	(23) 27.8			Net Worth	(135) 33.2	(124) 21.7
	11.5	3.4	13.4				6.1	2.6
	63.5	29.8	11.7	14.7	8.2	% Profit Before Taxes/Total	22.8	20.4
	23.2	9.1	4.3	5.7	4.0	Assets	6.4	8.1
	7.4	1.1	-1.1	-1.6	-.5		.3	.4
	114.3	82.7	48.1	45.6	6.4		79.7	69.0
	27.2	14.0	12.6	1.3	.9	Sales/Net Fixed Assets	18.6	18.8
	16.4	4.1	3.2	.4	.5		5.0	4.7
	5.2	4.7	1.9	2.1	1.5		3.8	3.9
	4.2	2.3	1.0	.8	.5	Sales/Total Assets	2.0	2.4
	2.8	1.5	.7	.3	.3		.8	.8
	.4	1.1	1.3	7.4			.7	.9
	(12) .9	(13) 2.4	(26) 4.6	(11) 13.1		% Depr., Dep., Amort./Sales	(107) 1.9	(112) 2.4
	2.4	5.2	15.7	17.9			6.1	9.4
						% Officers', Directors'	2.0	1.3
						Owners' Comp/Sales	(41) 3.5	(34) 3.9
							5.8	10.2
8709M	120445M	284525M	1517690M	1039184M	1207802M	Net Sales ($)	5777514M	6576577M
1939M	27535M	105697M	926411M	1010380M	1611537M	Total Assets ($)	5080203M	5191562M

M = $ thousand   MM = $ million
See Pages viii through xx for Explanation of Ratios and Data

Comparative Historical Data / Current Data Sorted by Sales

	4/1/16-3/31/17 ALL	4/1/17-3/31/18 ALL	4/1/18-3/31/19 ALL	0-1MM	1-3MM	3-5MM	5-10MM	10-25MM	25MM & OVER
Type of Statement					12 (4/1-9/30/18)		98 (10/1/18-3/31/19)		
Unqualified	27	26	20	1		1	3	5	11
Reviewed	15	8	8					5	2
Compiled	8	5	5			3	3	5	2
Tax Returns	14	14	11			3	3	3	
Other	62	73	66	2	6	6	11	14	27
NUMBER OF STATEMENTS	126	126	110	5	6	10	20	29	40
ASSETS	%	%	%	%	%	%	%	%	%
Cash & Equivalents	15.9	16.6	14.7			22.1	12.7	17.2	10.2
Trade Receivables (net)	26.3	22.4	24.9			29.3	17.2	32.2	24.9
Inventory	4.7	5.6	4.1			5.8	4.0	3.4	4.3
All Other Current	8.6	6.6	5.8			7.4	5.7	5.9	6.0
Total Current	55.5	51.1	49.5			64.5	39.6	58.7	45.4
Fixed Assets (net)	25.9	25.6	27.4			22.5	30.1	22.6	28.7
Intangibles (net)	12.1	15.9	13.2			6.2	18.1	10.0	15.9
All Other Non-Current	6.4	7.3	9.8			6.8	12.2	8.7	9.9
Total	100.0	100.0	100.0			100.0	100.0	100.0	100.0
LIABILITIES									
Notes Payable-Short Term	8.5	9.2	8.3			7.2	5.5	11.8	7.2
Cur. Mat.-L.T.D.	3.9	3.3	2.7			1.4	2.0	3.2	3.4
Trade Payables	19.5	13.4	11.4			9.2	9.1	14.0	13.1
Income Taxes Payable	.2	.2	.4			.0	.1	.3	.7
All Other Current	16.8	15.7	12.8			14.1	11.2	14.4	13.8
Total Current	48.9	41.9	35.5			31.9	27.9	43.8	38.2
Long-Term Debt	19.2	17.4	20.5			17.1	17.9	18.4	22.2
Deferred Taxes	.3	.4	.4			.8	.1	.5	.4
All Other Non-Current	6.8	11.1	8.8			4.9	11.4	5.4	8.3
Net Worth	24.8	29.3	34.8			45.4	42.6	31.9	30.8
Total Liabilities & Net Worth	100.0	100.0	100.0			100.0	100.0	100.0	100.0
INCOME DATA									
Net Sales	100.0	100.0	100.0			100.0	100.0	100.0	100.0
Gross Profit									
Operating Expenses	92.7	90.2	90.1			92.5	91.1	94.4	91.5
Operating Profit	7.3	9.8	9.9			7.5	8.9	5.6	8.5
All Other Expenses (net)	2.2	2.9	3.0			.3	5.2	4.1	1.5
Profit Before Taxes	5.0	6.9	6.9			7.1	3.7	1.5	7.0
RATIOS									
Current	2.3	2.3	2.4			3.9	2.3	1.9	1.8
	1.3	1.5	1.3			2.6	1.5	1.3	1.0
	.8	.8	.7			.8	.7	.9	.7
Quick	1.8	2.0	1.8			2.9	1.8	1.6	1.2
	.9	1.1	1.0			2.2	.9	1.1	.8
	.5	.5	.6			.8	.4	.6	.6
Sales/Receivables	17 21.8	11 33.6	15 24.7			0 UND	8 46.8	17 21.4	27 13.7
	35 10.4	33 11.1	35 10.5			32 11.3	21 17.0	40 9.2	43 8.5
	59 6.2	54 6.7	70 5.2			57 6.4	62 5.9	94 3.9	87 4.2
Cost of Sales/Inventory									
Cost of Sales/Payables									
Sales/Working Capital	7.6	5.6	6.6			5.1	9.6	5.0	7.8
	28.2	17.1	20.9			6.5	23.6	18.2	109.3
	-14.9	-26.9	-15.5			-87.9	-15.9	-19.1	-12.8
EBIT/Interest	21.3	27.4	27.2				68.9	89.6	13.9
	(106) 5.1	(97) 5.3	(90) 7.4		(14)		5.1	(25) 9.1	(36) 5.4
	.6	.9	1.5				1.1	1.6	1.4
Net Profit + Depr., Dep., Amort./Cur. Mat. L/T/D	8.3	10.6	6.6						
	(16) 4.0	(14) 4.3	(14) 4.6						
	1.6	2.0	2.6						
Fixed/Worth	.2	.1	.2			.1	.5	.1	.3
	1.5	1.0	1.0			.4	1.6	.4	1.7
	-2.4	-1.9	-2.1			NM	-1.4	-3.2	-.7
Debt/Worth	1.1	.8	.6			.5	.7	.5	1.1
	3.6	2.5	2.1			.8	2.4	2.2	2.5
	-12.2	-8.1	8.0			NM	-5.7	-4.8	-8.4
% Profit Before Taxes/Tangible Net Worth	77.8	75.4	57.4				52.0	41.0	75.2
	(87) 22.6	(90) 23.0	(75) 29.4			(12) 12.2	(20) 18.8	(28) 30.2	
	5.7	2.8	11.7				.6	11.0	16.1
% Profit Before Taxes/Total Assets	17.9	24.0	23.7			43.2	25.1	20.7	16.9
	6.0	6.2	7.5			16.9	2.9	8.5	6.5
	-.3	.7	1.0			-15.0	-2.8	-2.8	2.8
Sales/Net Fixed Assets	46.2	55.2	62.4			118.6	26.6	105.2	47.4
	15.5	20.3	13.5			24.1	8.4	27.6	10.8
	4.3	3.7	2.5			8.9	2.2	5.9	1.4
Sales/Total Assets	3.9	3.4	3.2			4.4	3.7	4.9	2.3
	2.2	2.1	1.8			3.2	2.0	1.8	1.6
	.9	.9	.7			1.7	.5	.7	.8
% Depr., Dep., Amort./Sales	.6	.5	1.2				1.6	1.0	1.4
	(86) 1.7	(61) 2.2	(70) 2.8		(14)		4.4	(17) 2.7	(25) 4.7
	4.9	9.0	11.5				19.2	15.4	12.1
% Officers', Directors' Owners' Comp/Sales	2.7	1.6	1.9						
	(13) 3.8	(25) 2.9	(18) 3.8						
	5.8	8.2	7.8						
Net Sales ($)	4937744M	5017686M	4178355M	2610M	14292M	42495M	138532M	434329M	3546097M
Total Assets ($)	3444541M	4290277M	3683499M	4444M	25114M	21465M	245738M	686997M	2699741M

M = $ thousand   MM = $ million
See Pages viii through xx for Explanation of Ratios and Data

Current Data Sorted by Assets   Comparative Historical Data

0-500M	500M-2MM	2-10MM	10-50MM	50-100MM	100-250MM	Type of Statement	4/1/14-3/31/15 ALL	4/1/15-3/31/16 ALL
	2	13	13	12	9	Unqualified	52	58
		8	4			Reviewed	27	22
1		5	1			Compiled	16	16
13	5	4	1			Tax Returns	47	41
20	16	41	27	12	19	Other	170	170
	31 (4/1-9/30/18)		195 (10/1/18-3/31/19)					
34	23	71	46	24	28	**NUMBER OF STATEMENTS**	312	307
%	%	%	%	%	%	**ASSETS**	%	%
42.0	13.2	20.6	15.5	15.3	13.2	Cash & Equivalents	21.3	19.2
19.6	38.3	39.6	33.7	18.8	12.6	Trade Receivables (net)	27.0	24.9
2.9	.8	1.5	1.5	1.4	2.3	Inventory	2.2	2.5
4.5	7.1	3.9	6.6	4.0	4.1	All Other Current	4.1	3.9
69.1	59.4	65.6	57.2	39.6	32.1	Total Current	54.6	50.5
18.5	22.9	18.9	23.6	20.3	26.4	Fixed Assets (net)	22.1	25.0
3.2	7.5	8.5	6.7	35.1	36.3	Intangibles (net)	14.1	14.0
9.3	10.3	7.1	12.4	5.1	5.3	All Other Non-Current	9.2	10.5
100.0	100.0	100.0	100.0	100.0	100.0	Total	100.0	100.0
						LIABILITIES		
31.8	19.8	9.9	7.0	.9	.1	Notes Payable-Short Term	9.9	9.1
7.1	2.9	7.1	4.1	1.6	3.0	Cur. Mat.-L.T.D.	3.0	3.5
8.6	20.7	14.1	12.9	6.8	8.5	Trade Payables	11.9	11.5
.1	.0	.0	.2	.1	.4	Income Taxes Payable	.2	.3
49.3	11.1	22.3	23.4	11.4	15.6	All Other Current	17.8	16.1
96.9	54.6	53.4	47.6	20.8	27.7	Total Current	42.8	40.5
32.4	17.5	14.9	20.9	32.5	33.2	Long-Term Debt	17.1	17.1
.4	.0	.3	.2	.2	1.6	Deferred Taxes	.6	.6
22.4	15.7	12.2	8.9	5.4	7.6	All Other Non-Current	9.3	9.7
-52.5	12.3	19.2	22.3	41.1	29.9	Net Worth	30.2	32.1
100.0	100.0	100.0	100.0	100.0	100.0	Total Liabilities & Net Worth	100.0	100.0
						INCOME DATA		
100.0	100.0	100.0	100.0	100.0	100.0	Net Sales	100.0	100.0
						Gross Profit		
94.9	90.0	92.7	92.8	95.6	93.7	Operating Expenses	93.9	93.4
5.1	10.0	7.3	7.2	4.4	6.3	Operating Profit	6.1	6.6
1.1	2.3	1.6	2.4	4.8	7.2	All Other Expenses (net)	2.1	2.3
4.0	7.7	5.7	4.9	-.4	-.9	Profit Before Taxes	4.1	4.3
						RATIOS		
6.3	1.9	2.6	2.8	2.7	1.8		2.4	2.7
.8	1.1	1.6	1.3	1.9	1.1	Current	1.3	1.4
.3	.8	.8	.9	1.3	.9		.8	.9
5.4	1.5	2.4	2.7	2.1	1.5		2.2	2.3
.7	1.0	1.4	1.1	1.7	1.0	Quick	1.2	1.1
.3	.4	.7	.5	1.1	.6		.7	.6
0 UND	7 50.4	23 15.6	34 10.8	30 12.1	27 13.5		15 25.1	14 26.4
0 UND	42 8.7	51 7.1	56 6.5	43 8.4	48 7.6	Sales/Receivables	36 10.1	38 9.6
20 17.9	65 5.6	63 5.8	81 4.5	57 6.4	79 4.6		61 6.0	60 6.1
						Cost of Sales/Inventory		
						Cost of Sales/Payables		
10.4	12.0	6.2	3.8	4.7	6.3		6.3	6.6
-70.9	60.1	14.7	13.3	8.4	19.7	Sales/Working Capital	20.2	20.2
-13.4	-34.8	-27.0	-27.8	16.1	-14.4		-26.0	-43.1
18.0	32.5	57.9	34.9	39.5	4.2		22.9	23.4
(22) 7.3	(20) 9.5	(50) 7.1	(36) 10.4	(20) 1.5	(23) 2.3	EBIT/Interest	(233) 5.8	(234) 5.4
-.6	4.9	1.3	2.2	-1.3	-1.2		.9	.6
		120.5				Net Profit + Depr., Dep.,	7.0	7.9
		(11) 12.5				Amort./Cur. Mat. L/T/D	(40) 3.5	(42) 3.7
		2.7					1.2	1.6
.0	.0	.1	.2	.4	.4		.2	.1
.1	1.2	.6	1.1	1.4	2.8	Fixed/Worth	.9	.8
UND	-1.3	12.1	NM	-.3	-.2		-2.5	5.1
.5	.8	.6	.7	.7	1.5		.7	.7
UND	2.8	1.7	1.9	3.4	56.6	Debt/Worth	3.0	2.7
-1.7	-7.7	-8.2	NM	-1.7	-2.0		-11.3	58.9
267.9	102.1	81.7	65.9	38.9	27.1	% Profit Before Taxes/Tangible	77.8	72.6
(18) 84.1	(16) 44.7	(52) 32.1	(35) 25.4	(15) 12.0	(15) 7.8	Net Worth	(219) 31.3	(232) 29.8
3.6	16.6	6.6	9.0	-69.3	-8.4		7.5	6.5
99.1	38.7	24.2	22.3	19.6	5.9	% Profit Before Taxes/Total	20.3	19.3
33.7	22.0	11.2	6.4	2.6	2.7	Assets	8.3	6.9
-1.8	8.4	1.9	1.4	-6.0	-5.9		.0	-.8
UND	210.4	150.5	47.4	17.4	32.0		77.0	67.1
999.8	97.0	26.4	19.3	7.8	9.1	Sales/Net Fixed Assets	17.3	14.6
24.6	5.5	8.6	6.9	4.1	1.1		6.0	4.6
14.6	5.3	3.6	3.1	2.3	.9		4.0	3.6
6.1	3.9	3.0	1.7	1.3	.6	Sales/Total Assets	2.3	2.0
2.9	2.1	2.0	1.1	.5	.3		1.1	.9
	.2	.6	1.1	2.0	.9		.8	1.0
	(14) 2.2	(47) 1.6	(40) 2.0	(13) 3.3	(13) 3.8	% Depr., Dep., Amort./Sales	(186) 2.3	(191) 2.8
	11.0	4.6	4.6	10.6	23.4		6.3	8.9
5.5		1.5				% Officers', Directors'	3.0	3.0
(18) 7.7		(13) 2.7				Owners' Comp/Sales	(69) 6.4	(72) 5.9
12.7		5.9					12.5	11.5
51514M	95375M	975471M	2068535M	2261363M	3254668M	Net Sales ($)	10421466M	13074931M
5774M	25708M	345135M	1073128M	1668262M	4348390M	Total Assets ($)	8932307M	9084541M

M = $ thousand   MM = $ million
See Pages viii through xx for Explanation of Ratios and Data

Comparative Historical Data | Current Data Sorted by Sales

56 / 44 / 49 etc.			Type of Statement						
56	44	49	Unqualified	1	1	1	5	14	27
26	21	12	Reviewed				2	8	2
6	5	7	Compiled		1	1	3		2
30	36	23	Tax Returns	3	11	1	7	1	
149	168	135	Other	17	9	12	15	27	55
4/1/16-3/31/17 ALL	4/1/17-3/31/18 ALL	4/1/18-3/31/19 ALL		0-1MM	1-3MM	3-5MM	5-10MM	10-25MM	25MM & OVER
				31 (4/1-9/30/18)			195 (10/1/18-3/31/19)		
267	274	226	NUMBER OF STATEMENTS	21	22	15	32	50	86
%	%	%	ASSETS	%	%	%	%	%	%
23.0	20.8	20.5	Cash & Equivalents	26.2	39.6	15.3	20.6	16.5	17.5
27.1	24.4	29.7	Trade Receivables (net)	21.9	15.6	37.2	35.5	38.3	26.7
2.0	2.0	1.7	Inventory	2.7	.8	.9	1.7	1.4	2.1
5.1	4.8	4.9	All Other Current	2.1	9.9	3.8	2.5	6.0	4.8
57.2	51.9	56.9	Total Current	52.8	65.8	57.3	60.3	62.1	51.2
20.8	25.1	21.2	Fixed Assets (net)	41.6	20.5	19.0	21.8	19.3	17.8
13.6	14.9	13.5	Intangibles (net)	3.2	2.3	13.5	5.1	12.6	22.5
8.4	8.1	8.4	All Other Non-Current	2.6	11.3	10.2	12.8	6.0	8.5
100.0	100.0	100.0	Total	100.0	100.0	100.0	100.0	100.0	100.0
			LIABILITIES						
5.5	8.2	11.4	Notes Payable-Short Term	7.9	34.3	13.6	17.7	11.2	3.9
3.7	4.6	5.0	Cur. Mat.-L.T.D.	3.3	10.8	.7	2.2	7.4	4.3
12.1	10.5	12.2	Trade Payables	12.0	9.5	15.0	11.9	14.2	11.5
.3	.1	.1	Income Taxes Payable	.1	.1	.0	.0	.0	.3
18.5	19.3	23.4	All Other Current	44.0	38.6	5.2	21.4	23.1	18.7
40.1	42.8	52.2	Total Current	67.3	93.4	34.5	53.3	55.9	38.6
17.4	23.3	23.1	Long-Term Debt	33.7	44.8	12.7	12.3	9.3	28.9
.5	.6	.4	Deferred Taxes	.7	.0	.1	.3	.2	.7
9.2	9.3	12.1	All Other Non-Current	20.7	18.2	5.4	14.9	12.1	8.7
32.8	24.0	12.0	Net Worth	-23.0	-56.4	47.2	19.2	22.5	23.2
100.0	100.0	100.0	Total Liabilties & Net Worth	100.0	100.0	100.0	100.0	100.0	100.0
			INCOME DATA						
100.0	100.0	100.0	Net Sales	100.0	100.0	100.0	100.0	100.0	100.0
			Gross Profit						
92.5	91.1	93.2	Operating Expenses	84.6	93.5	91.1	93.7	95.8	93.9
7.5	8.9	6.8	Operating Profit	15.4	6.5	8.9	6.3	4.2	6.1
2.1	2.6	2.8	All Other Expenses (net)	8.2	1.3	3.1	.6	1.9	3.1
5.4	6.3	4.0	Profit Before Taxes	7.2	5.2	5.8	5.7	2.3	3.0
			RATIOS						
2.5	2.5	2.4	Current	6.6	1.7	6.1	2.6	2.1	2.2
1.5	1.5	1.3		1.0	.8	1.4	1.4	1.5	1.5
.9	.8	.8		.3	.5	1.1	.8	.9	.9
2.2	2.3	2.1	Quick	6.3	1.6	5.7	2.3	2.1	2.0
1.3	1.3	1.1		.5	.7	1.3	1.3	1.4	1.1
.7	.6	.6		.2	.3	1.1	.7	.7	.7
19 19.4	13 28.6	17 21.3	Sales/Receivables	0 UND	0 UND	18 20.3	17 21.5	35 10.3	29 12.4
41 8.8	38 9.6	45 8.1		11 33.0	0 UND	44 8.3	51 7.2	53 6.9	48 7.6
63 5.8	66 5.5	65 5.6		47 7.8	33 11.0	68 5.4	76 4.8	74 4.9	69 5.3
			Cost of Sales/Inventory						
			Cost of Sales/Payables						
5.9	5.5	6.0	Sales/Working Capital	4.0	39.8	5.0	5.6	6.0	5.6
15.0	13.6	16.6		UND	-66.7	16.2	16.3	12.1	14.2
-70.6	-22.4	-27.3		-2.7	-23.4	86.7	-25.0	-71.9	-72.2
25.6	26.6	29.0	EBIT/Interest		18.0	28.5	70.1	29.0	33.8
(210) 6.8	(202) 3.8	(171) 6.2		(18) 6.8	(14) 12.9	(23) 7.2	(35) 14.6	(73) 4.2	
1.6	.3	.9		.3	2.4	1.0	1.1	.4	
16.1	13.1	12.5	Net Profit + Depr., Dep., Amort./Cur. Mat. L/T/D						5.2
(33) 4.4	(30) 3.6	(27) 3.7						(13) 3.5	
1.7	1.2	2.1							1.9
.1	.2	.1	Fixed/Worth	.0	.0	.0	.1	.1	.3
.8	1.0	.8		1.7	1.8	.8	.4	.6	1.7
6.5	-2.0	-1.8		UND	-.2	-3.4	2.8	2.4	-.4
.8	.6	.7	Debt/Worth	.5	.9	.3	.7	.7	.9
2.8	2.8	2.7		15.5	-5.6	1.9	1.9	1.6	4.1
-40.3	-5.3	-4.3		-3.1	-1.9	-8.2	101.2	18.2	-2.9
69.5	62.6	76.9	% Profit Before Taxes/Tangible Net Worth	84.1	267.9	112.6	83.6	72.2	63.4
(196) 37.1	(184) 26.7	(151) 27.9		(13) 43.1	(10) 93.3	(11) 38.5	(25) 31.3	(40) 23.6	(52) 26.1
10.0	3.9	7.8		.1	17.4	13.3	4.0	4.9	8.1
23.2	19.5	26.4	% Profit Before Taxes/Total Assets	37.6	105.8	36.4	46.1	19.2	15.9
8.0	7.1	8.0		1.7	24.2	17.0	10.9	10.4	5.1
1.6	-.9	0		.0	-1.8	1.9	1.2	.0	-1.7
76.2	79.1	156.7	Sales/Net Fixed Assets	UND	UND	999.8	193.0	89.4	59.2
17.4	16.2	21.4		12.5	202.6	46.3	24.5	22.7	16.1
5.9	4.0	6.5		.5	24.5	9.8	5.0	8.4	7.0
3.7	3.3	3.9	Sales/Total Assets	3.9	14.6	4.3	3.8	3.4	3.0
2.1	1.8	2.4		2.3	6.8	3.2	2.6	2.8	1.6
1.0	.8	1.1		.4	4.4	1.3	1.6	1.3	.8
.7	.9	.5	% Depr., Dep., Amort./Sales				.6	.6	.5
(159) 2.0	(166) 2.7	(135) 2.0					(22) 1.6	(33) 2.6	(55) 1.9
5.9	7.8	6.0					7.4	4.6	4.2
2.0	2.5	1.8	% Officers', Directors' Owners' Comp/Sales		5.1		1.5		
(49) 5.1	(49) 4.6	(43) 5.1			(13) 7.5		(10) 3.0		
8.5	8.8	8.1			12.1		5.3		
10407510M	9363791M	8706926M	Net Sales ($)	8986M	47726M	56223M	232691M	793250M	7568050M
8474703M	8790925M	7466397M	Total Assets ($)	60582M	10966M	173115M	126581M	772065M	6323088M

M = $ thousand   MM = $ million
See Pages viii through xx for Explanation of Ratios and Data

Current Data Sorted by Assets							Comparative Historical Data	

Type of Statement

0-500M	500M-2MM	2-10MM	10-50MM	50-100MM	100-250MM	Type of Statement	4/1/14-3/31/15 ALL	4/1/15-3/31/16 ALL
		2	1		1	Unqualified	6	8
		1				Reviewed	2	2
		2		2		Compiled	6	2
		2				Tax Returns	6	6
1	6	5	7	5	3	Other	40	35
	8 (4/1-9/30/18)		33 (10/1/18-3/31/19)					
6	6	10	8	7	4	NUMBER OF STATEMENTS	60	53
%	%	%	%	%	%	ASSETS	%	%
		18.1				Cash & Equivalents	28.6	30.9
		34.4				Trade Receivables (net)	25.7	27.4
		1.0				Inventory	1.6	1.5
		2.8				All Other Current	5.4	4.0
		56.4				Total Current	61.3	63.7
		11.4				Fixed Assets (net)	14.0	15.9
		17.9				Intangibles (net)	15.0	11.7
		14.3				All Other Non-Current	9.7	8.6
		100.0				Total	100.0	100.0
						LIABILITIES		
		2.2				Notes Payable-Short Term	8.1	12.2
		2.0				Cur. Mat.-L.T.D.	3.8	.8
		13.3				Trade Payables	12.2	8.0
		.1				Income Taxes Payable	.0	.0
		9.5				All Other Current	21.0	33.6
		27.1				Total Current	45.2	54.7
		13.0				Long-Term Debt	11.5	13.0
		.0				Deferred Taxes	.3	.2
		3.6				All Other Non-Current	8.7	14.3
		56.3				Net Worth	34.4	17.9
		100.0				Total Liabilities & Net Worth	100.0	100.0
						INCOME DATA		
		100.0				Net Sales	100.0	100.0
						Gross Profit		
		90.8				Operating Expenses	94.5	93.6
		9.2				Operating Profit	5.5	6.4
		-.3				All Other Expenses (net)	2.3	1.9
		9.5				Profit Before Taxes	3.3	4.5
						RATIOS		
		5.6				Current	2.5	3.5
		1.7					1.4	1.5
		1.3					.9	.9
		4.8				Quick	2.4	3.5
		1.7					1.3	1.4
		1.2					.7	.8
	0 UND					Sales/Receivables	2 166.7	0 UND
	46 8.0						37 9.8	45 8.2
	65 5.6						61 6.0	64 5.7
						Cost of Sales/Inventory		
						Cost of Sales/Payables		
		8.3				Sales/Working Capital	4.9	5.6
		18.6					12.8	13.8
		NM					-33.9	-45.0
						EBIT/Interest	32.6	35.3
							(37) 3.0	(29) 3.1
							-1.7	-5.3
						Net Profit + Depr., Dep., Amort./Cur. Mat. L/T/D		
		.0				Fixed/Worth	.1	.1
		.4					.4	.2
		NM					-.9	6.2
		.2				Debt/Worth	.6	.5
		1.7					3.5	2.1
		NM					-9.7	-21.5
						% Profit Before Taxes/Tangible Net Worth	102.2	102.2
							(41) 49.0	(39) 38.0
							-9.1	1.9
		68.8				% Profit Before Taxes/Total Assets	36.5	29.6
		20.2					6.2	6.1
		5.9					-8.5	-6.9
		376.5				Sales/Net Fixed Assets	153.2	143.7
		91.4					34.6	38.8
		11.8					12.1	10.4
		5.8				Sales/Total Assets	3.8	4.5
		2.7					2.2	2.3
		2.0					1.3	1.3
						% Depr., Dep., Amort./Sales	.3	.3
							(22) 1.2	(34) 1.1
							3.3	2.4
						% Officers', Directors' Owners' Comp/Sales		
12549M	39692M	174804M	304742M	1076159M	660135M	Net Sales ($)	4728864M	3143946M
1536M	7115M	49698M	185734M	578069M	602090M	Total Assets ($)	2859843M	1595122M

© RMA 2019

M = $ thousand   MM = $ million
See Pages viii through xx for Explanation of Ratios and Data

Comparative Historical Data   Current Data Sorted by Sales

			Type of Statement	0-1MM	1-3MM	3-5MM	5-10MM	10-25MM	25MM & OVER
8	7	4	Unqualified					1	2
1	3	1	Reviewed					1	
	1	2	Compiled						2
9	6	3	Tax Returns	1			2		
39	30	31	Other		6	3	1	8	13
4/1/16-3/31/17 ALL	4/1/17-3/31/18 ALL	4/1/18-3/31/19 ALL			8 (4/1-9/30/18)			33 (10/1/18-3/31/19)	
57	47	41	NUMBER OF STATEMENTS	1	6	3	4	10	17
%	%	%	**ASSETS**	%	%	%	%	%	%
25.6	28.3	25.8	Cash & Equivalents					21.0	17.7
22.6	23.1	29.0	Trade Receivables (net)					23.9	26.9
2.7	2.4	.5	Inventory					.2	.6
5.1	7.2	4.1	All Other Current					3.9	4.4
56.0	60.9	59.4	Total Current					49.1	49.7
15.6	14.4	11.6	Fixed Assets (net)					8.1	17.8
19.4	17.0	18.8	Intangibles (net)					23.3	25.1
9.0	7.7	10.3	All Other Non-Current					19.5	7.5
100.0	100.0	100.0	Total					100.0	100.0
			LIABILITIES						
9.6	6.3	8.4	Notes Payable-Short Term					1.6	3.2
.8	1.6	4.4	Cur. Mat.-L.T.D.					3.4	2.8
11.5	10.7	11.9	Trade Payables					7.4	13.3
.6	.8	.1	Income Taxes Payable					.1	.0
28.5	30.8	21.4	All Other Current					17.6	30.8
51.0	50.2	46.1	Total Current					30.0	50.1
15.7	13.7	21.5	Long-Term Debt					8.4	28.8
.5	.4	.3	Deferred Taxes					.0	.8
17.3	11.1	12.9	All Other Non-Current					7.7	14.8
15.6	24.6	19.1	Net Worth					54.0	5.5
100.0	100.0	100.0	Total Liabilties & Net Worth					100.0	100.0
			INCOME DATA						
100.0	100.0	100.0	Net Sales					100.0	100.0
			Gross Profit						
91.3	97.0	94.9	Operating Expenses					92.9	100.8
8.7	3.0	5.1	Operating Profit					7.1	-.8
2.8	1.6	2.8	All Other Expenses (net)					2.0	4.1
5.9	1.4	2.3	Profit Before Taxes					5.0	-4.9
			RATIOS						
2.6	2.8	3.3						3.8	2.9
1.3	1.7	1.7	Current					1.7	1.6
.8	.8	.7						.7	.5
2.4	2.4	2.9						3.5	2.4
1.0	1.2	1.6	Quick					1.6	1.6
.6	.4	.7						.6	.5
4 88.9	0 UND	6 60.0						0 UND	14 25.5
36 10.2	40 9.2	44 8.3	Sales/Receivables					43 8.5	61 6.0
66 5.5	59 6.2	66 5.5						56 6.5	79 4.6
			Cost of Sales/Inventory						
			Cost of Sales/Payables						
7.4	4.9	6.6						3.6	7.1
23.4	17.9	20.6	Sales/Working Capital					11.5	22.1
-14.9	-27.4	-20.7						-54.2	-5.7
21.1	30.6	11.1							4.2
(38) 7.1	(29) 4.6	(26) 2.1	EBIT/Interest					(13) -5.4	
-.1	-2.6	-13.6							-30.6
			Net Profit + Depr., Dep., Amort./Cur. Mat. L/T/D						
.0	.0	.1						.0	.5
.9	.8	.9	Fixed/Worth					.5	-6.0
-.4	-2.0	-.3						NM	-.1
.7	.7	.5						.4	1.8
3.6	3.0	5.4	Debt/Worth					2.7	-12.2
-2.8	-5.8	-4.0						NM	-2.0
128.9	73.0	167.1	% Profit Before Taxes/Tangible Net Worth						
(33) 39.5	(31) 12.5	(23) 31.3							
15.5	-10.7	-82.6							
23.7	21.3	27.2	% Profit Before Taxes/Total Assets					24.1	15.3
12.2	7.4	9.8						16.1	-4.7
.4	-6.1	-17.0						-2.9	-55.2
200.3	143.7	176.2	Sales/Net Fixed Assets					211.6	135.5
39.5	47.6	39.5						47.5	26.8
9.7	10.3	11.6						9.9	8.9
5.0	4.1	4.4	Sales/Total Assets					3.8	2.4
2.4	2.1	2.2						1.6	2.2
1.2	1.2	1.4						1.0	1.3
.3	.5	.1	% Depr., Dep., Amort./Sales						
(21) .9	(26) .9	(19) .9							
3.6	3.0	3.3							
	3.2		% Officers', Directors' Owners' Comp/Sales						
	(14) 5.3								
	17.9								
3150928M	2712248M	2268081M	Net Sales ($)	319M	10711M	12351M	26933M	167214M	2050553M
2425993M	1912720M	1424242M	Total Assets ($)	29M	3691M	4052M	9251M	134864M	1272355M

M = $ thousand   MM = $ million
See Pages viii through xx for Explanation of Ratios and Data

Current Data Sorted by Assets

Comparative Historical Data

						Type of Statement		
		2	5	2	1	Unqualified	10	20
	1		1			Reviewed	5	8
		1				Compiled	6	4
5	1	2				Tax Returns	24	25
5	10	22	13	1	3	Other	71	64
	9 (4/1-9/30/18)		66 (10/1/18-3/31/19)				4/1/14-3/31/15	4/1/15-3/31/16
0-500M	500M-2MM	2-10MM	10-50MM	50-100MM	100-250MM		ALL	ALL
10	12	27	19	3	4	NUMBER OF STATEMENTS	116	121
%	%	%	%	%	%	ASSETS	%	%
30.4	16.6	18.1	18.1			Cash & Equivalents	25.4	24.9
16.6	35.5	29.8	23.4			Trade Receivables (net)	29.2	23.2
.5	.1	2.3	6.0			Inventory	2.4	3.2
6.0	2.8	6.5	7.0			All Other Current	2.6	3.7
53.5	55.0	56.6	54.4			Total Current	59.5	55.0
20.4	26.5	18.3	17.2			Fixed Assets (net)	19.4	20.4
18.2	.2	9.5	22.8			Intangibles (net)	10.8	15.2
7.9	18.2	15.5	5.6			All Other Non-Current	10.3	9.5
100.0	100.0	100.0	100.0			Total	100.0	100.0
						LIABILITIES		
11.9	17.1	5.4	5.4			Notes Payable-Short Term	11.7	10.9
.4	3.2	4.7	2.2			Cur. Mat.-L.T.D.	3.1	2.5
15.3	6.2	12.4	12.1			Trade Payables	12.7	9.7
.0	.0	.0	.0			Income Taxes Payable	.2	.2
6.8	21.6	18.8	38.4			All Other Current	16.7	22.8
34.4	48.1	41.4	58.2			Total Current	44.5	46.2
31.5	16.1	13.1	21.4			Long-Term Debt	20.1	15.9
.0	.1	.5	.2			Deferred Taxes	.3	.5
4.8	9.2	7.7	7.0			All Other Non-Current	11.9	11.5
29.4	26.5	37.2	13.2			Net Worth	23.2	25.9
100.0	100.0	100.0	100.0			Total Liabilities & Net Worth	100.0	100.0
						INCOME DATA		
100.0	100.0	100.0	100.0			Net Sales	100.0	100.0
						Gross Profit		
92.0	81.0	87.2	92.8			Operating Expenses	89.2	92.8
8.0	19.0	12.8	7.2			Operating Profit	10.8	7.2
.0	5.2	3.4	4.0			All Other Expenses (net)	1.9	2.3
8.0	13.7	9.3	3.3			Profit Before Taxes	8.9	4.9
						RATIOS		
4.2	6.4	2.7	1.8				2.8	3.9
1.7	1.3	1.5	.7			Current	1.4	1.7
1.1	.4	.9	.5				1.0	.7
4.1	5.9	2.7	1.1				2.5	3.3
1.5	1.1	1.1	.6			Quick	1.3	1.3
.8	.3	.8	.4				.8	.5

0	UND	17	20.9	18	20.5	22	16.6			Sales/Receivables	12	29.6	4	85.6
1	511.8	43	8.5	44	8.3	41	8.9				36	10.1	34	10.6
28	13.1	58	6.3	60	6.1	59	6.2				62	5.9	63	5.8

						Cost of Sales/Inventory		

						Cost of Sales/Payables		

8.3	5.5	6.2	10.1				7.1	5.5
23.2	29.2	12.2	-28.7			Sales/Working Capital	22.8	16.3
NM	-9.3	-112.0	-7.4				-112.4	-23.7

			30.0		10.7			EBIT/Interest		38.9	26.6
		(18)	6.7	(14)	2.0				(82)	7.3	(81)	7.8
			3.7		-.3					3.2		1.8

						Net Profit + Depr., Dep., Amort./Cur. Mat. L/T/D		5.3
							(12)	3.8
								1.3

.1	.0	.0	.2				.1	.1
.3	.6	.7	11.7			Fixed/Worth	.6	.8
5.9	13.0	-2.3	.0				3.4	-5.4
.3	.7	.6	3.3				.6	.6
1.0	2.7	1.7	11.8			Debt/Worth	2.0	2.4
NM	13.4	-11.8	-1.9				25.6	-8.5

			106.0		88.5		74.5	% Profit Before Taxes/Tangible Net Worth		99.4	123.3
	(10)	41.7	(19)	31.9	(11)	29.4			(92)	44.4	(85)	47.6
		8.3		9.9		6.3				9.4		15.6

101.1	80.0	34.7	8.4			% Profit Before Taxes/Total Assets	29.1	36.0
33.3	8.8	7.3	2.4				12.5	10.5
.5	.7	2.8	-2.6				3.2	.8
UND	701.5	485.5	121.8				94.9	156.7
39.4	70.7	46.4	59.1			Sales/Net Fixed Assets	30.8	23.1
26.2	2.8	5.4	13.8				10.2	7.3
13.1	4.6	3.7	3.5				4.4	4.2
7.5	3.3	2.6	1.7			Sales/Total Assets	2.7	2.4
3.0	.6	1.2	.6				1.6	1.1

			1.3		.2			% Depr., Dep., Amort./Sales		.7	.7
		(10)	2.8	(13)	1.0				(66)	2.0	(60)	3.9
			5.4		2.8					4.1		9.0

						% Officers', Directors' Owners' Comp/Sales		4.1	2.0
							(31)	6.6	(29)	7.1
								15.8		14.7

14849M	30548M	357075M	942749M	138734M	523917M	Net Sales ($)	3023591M	3764456M
1618M	12898M	153022M	456309M	217220M	731281M	Total Assets ($)	2182977M	3426218M

M = $ thousand   MM = $ million
See Pages viii through xx for Explanation of Ratios and Data

Comparative Historical Data				Current Data Sorted by Sales					
			Type of Statement						
11	12	10	Unqualified					1	5
3	4	2	Reviewed				1	4	1
1	1	1	Compiled			1			
15	15	8	Tax Returns	1	3	1	1	2	
39	60	54	Other	9	9	2		14	15
4/1/16-3/31/17 ALL	4/1/17-3/31/18 ALL	4/1/18-3/31/19 ALL		9 (4/1-9/30/18)			66 (10/1/18-3/31/19)		
				0-1MM	1-3MM	3-5MM	5-10MM	10-25MM	25MM & OVER
69	92	75	**NUMBER OF STATEMENTS**	10	12	4	7	21	21
%	%	%	**ASSETS**	%	%	%	%	%	%
23.9	23.4	18.9	Cash & Equivalents	12.6	14.5			20.7	17.7
24.5	29.9	25.3	Trade Receivables (net)	12.7	21.2			27.7	27.3
3.8	2.4	2.4	Inventory	.5	.1			1.7	5.5
3.8	3.9	6.1	All Other Current	8.0	1.2			6.9	9.6
56.0	59.6	52.8	Total Current	33.8	37.1			57.1	60.1
18.9	15.1	19.5	Fixed Assets (net)	39.0	31.3			17.6	9.1
15.7	12.8	16.6	Intangibles (net)	9.0	9.1			14.0	25.5
9.4	12.5	11.2	All Other Non-Current	18.2	22.5			11.4	5.3
100.0	100.0	100.0	Total	100.0	100.0			100.0	100.0
			LIABILITIES						
10.9	13.5	7.7	Notes Payable-Short Term	16.0	9.7			6.7	5.1
3.8	3.7	3.0	Cur. Mat.-L.T.D.	2.3	2.3			6.5	1.1
11.0	12.1	10.9	Trade Payables	12.6	7.3			11.6	14.1
.4	.1	.0	Income Taxes Payable	.0	.0			.1	.0
25.1	24.1	22.4	All Other Current	3.8	21.1			22.5	37.4
51.3	53.5	44.0	Total Current	34.6	40.5			47.5	57.7
20.8	12.4	20.0	Long-Term Debt	22.5	39.4			12.8	21.6
.4	.3	.4	Deferred Taxes	.0	.1			.3	.7
7.3	5.9	7.4	All Other Non-Current	13.8	9.1			7.3	5.8
20.3	27.8	28.2	Net Worth	29.1	10.9			32.2	14.1
100.0	100.0	100.0	Total Liabilities & Net Worth	100.0	100.0			100.0	100.0
			INCOME DATA						
100.0	100.0	100.0	Net Sales	100.0	100.0			100.0	100.0
			Gross Profit						
93.6	92.7	89.5	Operating Expenses	74.9	85.4			92.5	98.0
6.4	7.3	10.5	Operating Profit	25.1	14.6			7.5	2.0
3.8	1.4	3.5	All Other Expenses (net)	11.1	5.8			1.1	2.1
2.6	5.9	7.1	Profit Before Taxes	14.0	8.7			6.4	-.1
			RATIOS						
3.2	2.5	2.5	Current	4.5	1.6			2.9	1.7
1.4	1.3	1.3		1.6	1.3			1.6	1.0
.8	.8	.7		.2	.5			.6	.8
3.1	2.4	1.9	Quick	4.1	1.5			2.9	1.0
1.2	1.2	1.0		.6	1.3			1.1	.8
.7	.7	.4		.2	.5			.4	.5
2 195.9	6 57.4	15 23.8	Sales/Receivables	0 UND	0 UND		17 21.2	24 15.1
37 9.8	44 8.3	40 9.2		0 UND	24 15.3		37 9.9	46 8.0
63 5.8	62 5.9	59 6.2		38 9.7	62 5.9		60 6.1	60 6.1
			Cost of Sales/Inventory						
			Cost of Sales/Payables						
7.0	6.9	6.7	Sales/Working Capital	5.6	14.9			5.8	7.9
15.3	23.0	24.6		16.5	49.8			12.2	274.5
-30.6	-23.4	-25.4		-.6	-36.6			-17.4	-24.5
23.5	22.5	30.2	EBIT/Interest					31.2	9.1
(53) 4.2	(68) 6.9	(53) 4.4					(17) 3.9	(16) 1.6	
-5.4	-.1	.8						.6	-.5
8.0	28.1		Net Profit + Depr., Dep., Amort./Cur. Mat. L/T/D						
(11) 5.0	(10) 2.1								
1.3	-.6								
.1	.0	.0	Fixed/Worth	.1	.1			.0	.1
.9	.4	.9		2.4	.8			.8	1.3
-1.5	4.9	-.6		17.1	9.2			-.4	-.1
.9	.8	.7	Debt/Worth	1.0	.8			.6	2.2
4.9	2.5	4.2		6.8	2.7			6.3	-30.4
-5.8	-67.5	-5.2		104.4	NM			-6.6	-1.8
92.1	76.0	95.2	% Profit Before Taxes/Tangible Net Worth					88.8	109.0
(46) 31.0	(68) 43.3	(50) 34.9					(14) 26.8	(10) 37.6	
1.3	6.8	9.4						5.0	11.9
21.2	34.7	22.4	% Profit Before Taxes/Total Assets	23.5	61.2			17.6	13.9
5.3	10.3	6.0		3.5	10.6			4.8	2.3
-5.9	.1	.0		-.3	1.6			.3	-4.0
188.1	340.1	195.2	Sales/Net Fixed Assets	UND	228.1			315.7	158.9
30.9	64.8	47.5		22.8	24.0			46.4	68.7
8.9	14.3	9.0		.2	3.0			6.4	24.4
4.6	4.9	3.9	Sales/Total Assets	3.8	8.4			3.5	3.9
2.3	3.0	2.3		1.4	3.3			2.0	2.3
1.1	1.2	.9		.1	.6			1.1	.9
.7	.3	.4	% Depr., Dep., Amort./Sales						.2
(34) 2.1	(40) 1.1	(30) 1.3						(11) .8	
5.3	4.6	3.8							1.9
6.3	1.5	1.9	% Officers', Directors' Owners' Comp/Sales						
(15) 10.6	(26) 3.5	(14) 5.6							
18.8	4.6	4.6							
2000262M	2832400M	2007872M	Net Sales ($)	2999M	23763M	14717M	49185M	322586M	1594622M
1399149M	1912093M	1572348M	Total Assets ($)	15968M	28733M	12431M	31998M	300521M	1182697M

M = $ thousand   MM = $ million
See Pages viii through xx for Explanation of Ratios and Data

FINANCE AND INSURANCE

Current Data Sorted by Assets   Comparative Historical Data

Type of Statement	0-500M	500M-2MM	2-10MM	10-50MM	50-100MM	100-250MM		4/1/14-3/31/15 ALL	4/1/15-3/31/16 ALL
Unqualified			8	31	12	16		79	73
Reviewed			7	8	1			35	36
Compiled		2	6					16	15
Tax Returns	5	5	8	1				27	36
Other	4	9	28	42	18	19		169	138
		21 (4/1-9/30/18)		209 (10/1/18-3/31/19)					
NUMBER OF STATEMENTS	9	16	57	82	31	35		326	298

ASSETS	0-500M	500M-2MM %	2-10MM %	10-50MM %	50-100MM %	100-250MM %		%	%
Cash & Equivalents		12.1	7.9	4.5	6.8	3.9		5.2	5.1
Trade Receivables (net)		28.6	49.3	56.9	62.2	47.1		61.1	54.8
Inventory		.0	3.4	3.0	.7	3.5		4.5	4.3
All Other Current		19.1	9.5	9.4	7.2	4.8		5.2	5.7
Total Current		59.7	70.1	73.9	77.0	59.4		75.9	69.9
Fixed Assets (net)		30.0	15.0	6.2	12.4	10.7		8.6	10.5
Intangibles (net)		1.1	2.0	1.2	2.3	1.2		2.4	1.9
All Other Non-Current		9.1	13.0	18.8	8.4	28.7		13.1	17.7
Total		100.0	100.0	100.0	100.0	100.0		100.0	100.0

LIABILITIES	0-500M	500M-2MM	2-10MM	10-50MM	50-100MM	100-250MM			
Notes Payable-Short Term		21.1	21.0	34.4	32.8	32.4		34.2	32.2
Cur. Mat.-L.T.D.		5.5	3.9	5.2	6.1	5.9		4.1	4.3
Trade Payables		.8	2.4	2.4	3.4	2.2		2.4	1.5
Income Taxes Payable		.0	.0	.0	.0	.4		.2	.2
All Other Current		8.4	13.7	7.7	8.4	6.4		8.6	8.1
Total Current		35.8	40.9	49.7	50.7	47.3		49.4	46.3
Long-Term Debt		21.7	21.0	12.7	18.5	21.9		14.0	20.4
Deferred Taxes		.0	.0	.1	.0	1.5		.3	.3
All Other Non-Current		5.5	11.7	9.8	4.3	5.2		9.4	8.2
Net Worth		36.9	26.4	27.7	26.6	24.2		27.1	24.8
Total Liabilities & Net Worth		100.0	100.0	100.0	100.0	100.0		100.0	100.0

INCOME DATA	0-500M	500M-2MM	2-10MM	10-50MM	50-100MM	100-250MM			
Net Sales		100.0	100.0	100.0	100.0	100.0		100.0	100.0
Gross Profit									
Operating Expenses		60.5	72.6	71.6	71.5	64.0		71.1	70.4
Operating Profit		39.5	27.4	28.4	28.5	36.0		28.9	29.6
All Other Expenses (net)		7.2	11.6	12.9	12.9	13.3		10.3	11.9
Profit Before Taxes		32.3	15.8	15.5	15.7	22.6		18.6	17.7

RATIOS	0-500M	500M-2MM	2-10MM	10-50MM	50-100MM	100-250MM			
Current		4.4	4.5	2.0	2.3	1.5		2.5	2.5
		1.7	1.8	1.5	1.6	1.2		1.4	1.4
		.6	1.2	1.2	1.1	.6		1.2	1.1
Quick		4.2	2.5	1.8	2.0	1.4		2.0	1.9
		1.2	1.2	1.3	1.4	1.0		1.3	1.3
		.2	.6	1.0	1.0	.4		1.0	.7
Sales/Receivables		0 UND	12 31.2	34 10.6	63 5.8	16 22.2		118 3.1	28 13.2
		0 UND	332 1.1	608 .6	1217 .3	406 .9		608 .6	456 .8
		730 .5	912 .4	1217 .3	1825 .2	1825 .2		1217 .3	1217 .3
Cost of Sales/Inventory									
Cost of Sales/Payables									
Sales/Working Capital		.9	.5	.6	.7	1.0		.6	.6
		1.9	1.8	1.1	1.1	2.3		1.4	1.4
		NM	12.4	6.9	3.6	-5.0		6.5	19.1
EBIT/Interest		14.9	5.8	3.9	3.8	5.8		5.2	5.9
		(14) 5.0	(39) 2.5	(53) 2.3	(22) 2.7	(22) 3.0		(245) 3.0	(219) 3.1
		1.9	1.7	1.7	1.6	1.6		1.8	1.7
Net Profit + Depr., Dep., Amort./Cur. Mat. L/T/D								11.9	5.5
								(20) 1.6	(24) 1.2
								.1	.1
Fixed/Worth		.0	.0	.0	.0	.0		.0	.0
		.0	.0	.0	.0	.1		.0	.0
		1.9	1.9	.2	.3	.3		.3	.2
Debt/Worth		.7	1.4	1.8	1.4	2.3		1.8	1.5
		1.9	3.3	3.4	4.5	4.4		3.7	3.4
		6.8	12.7	7.5	7.9	6.9		8.2	8.6
% Profit Before Taxes/Tangible Net Worth		102.7	59.3	27.8	44.0	33.2		39.8	34.1
		(15) 36.3	(50) 17.5	(78) 15.7	13.8	(34) 19.4		(308) 20.5	(277) 18.2
		15.4	4.7	8.2	6.0	10.3		9.0	8.9
% Profit Before Taxes/Total Assets		19.5	7.7	6.3	7.7	6.3		8.4	8.3
		9.0	4.0	3.3	3.1	3.7		4.1	4.0
		3.6	1.5	1.1	1.1	1.9		1.8	1.4
Sales/Net Fixed Assets		UND	UND	365.2	140.6	210.3		336.7	816.4
		UND	153.1	53.0	51.5	48.9		55.6	56.8
		.7	7.2	14.2	3.5	2.1		13.0	10.1
Sales/Total Assets		.6	1.0	.5	.3	.5		.6	.5
		.4	.4	.3	.3	.2		.3	.3
		.3	.2	.2	.1	.1		.2	.2
% Depr., Dep., Amort./Sales			.3	.4	.6	.3		.4	.4
			(27) 1.3	(54) .9	(18) 1.9	(18) .7		(189) .8	(164) .9
			19.1	2.3	9.2	1.5		2.1	3.8
% Officers', Directors' Owners' Comp/Sales			1.8	1.8				2.5	2.8
			(13) 6.6	(20) 6.4				(46) 7.3	(48) 6.9
			12.5	14.0				14.7	12.7

	0-500M	500M-2MM	2-10MM	10-50MM	50-100MM	100-250MM		4/1/14-3/31/15 ALL	4/1/15-3/31/16 ALL
Net Sales ($)	10620M	14729M	222226M	1125259M	630112M	2166985M		5472452M	5431230M
Total Assets ($)	2033M	17852M	332382M	2021592M	2190983M	5228915M		13525224M	13382950M

Comparative Historical Data | | | Current Data Sorted by Sales

Type of Statement								
64	65	67	Unqualified		10	8	14	12	23
32	35	16	Reviewed		3	4	2	7	
6	8	8	Compiled	1	5	1		1	
24	15	19	Tax Returns	13	4		1	1	
155	138	120	Other	21	21	19	16	29	14
4/1/16-	4/1/17-	4/1/18-			21 (4/1-9/30/18)		209 (10/1/18-3/31/19)		
3/31/17	3/31/18	3/31/19							
ALL	ALL	ALL		0-1MM	1-3MM	3-5MM	5-10MM	10-25MM	25MM & OVER
281	261	230	**NUMBER OF STATEMENTS**	35	43	32	33	50	37
%	%	%	**ASSETS**	%	%	%	%	%	%
5.2	6.0	7.4	Cash & Equivalents	9.0	9.7	3.2	13.3	4.5	5.8
55.7	52.2	50.6	Trade Receivables (net)	44.3	47.5	65.3	43.5	50.6	53.7
4.1	4.3	2.8	Inventory	3.6	.4	.4	.8	3.5	7.8
8.1	8.2	9.1	All Other Current	11.3	10.6	6.0	10.7	11.8	2.9
73.1	70.7	70.0	Total Current	68.2	68.1	75.0	68.3	70.4	70.3
8.5	10.6	12.2	Fixed Assets (net)	19.5	10.5	6.7	10.6	10.1	16.3
1.5	1.5	1.5	Intangibles (net)	1.4	2.4	.7	2.0	1.1	1.5
16.9	17.2	16.3	All Other Non-Current	10.8	19.0	17.7	19.2	18.4	11.9
100.0	100.0	100.0	Total	100.0	100.0	100.0	100.0	100.0	100.0
			LIABILITIES						
30.1	30.2	29.2	Notes Payable-Short Term	14.9	30.3	37.3	23.2	32.8	34.8
4.4	4.0	5.6	Cur. Mat.-L.T.D.	3.0	10.0	2.0	8.7	4.9	3.9
2.1	2.0	2.3	Trade Payables	2.0	1.3	.8	3.8	2.4	3.6
.1	.1	.1	Income Taxes Payable	.0	.0	.0	.0	.3	.1
8.8	8.2	9.8	All Other Current	12.4	7.3	11.5	13.1	10.2	5.3
45.5	44.5	46.9	Total Current	32.3	48.9	51.7	48.7	50.5	47.8
17.6	18.0	20.2	Long-Term Debt	30.3	25.3	11.1	20.6	16.9	16.7
.4	.2	.3	Deferred Taxes	.0	.1	.0	.1	.7	.6
8.8	9.0	8.4	All Other Non-Current	9.9	8.6	14.6	4.9	8.0	5.4
27.6	28.2	24.2	Net Worth	27.5	17.1	22.7	25.7	23.9	29.5
100.0	100.0	100.0	Total Liabilities & Net Worth	100.0	100.0	100.0	100.0	100.0	100.0
			INCOME DATA						
100.0	100.0	100.0	Net Sales	100.0	100.0	100.0	100.0	100.0	100.0
			Gross Profit						
72.4	74.0	70.6	Operating Expenses	61.6	62.4	74.5	71.6	72.2	82.0
27.6	26.0	29.4	Operating Profit	38.4	37.6	25.5	28.4	27.8	18.0
11.6	10.3	11.8	All Other Expenses (net)	15.4	14.2	12.3	12.5	11.4	5.1
16.1	15.8	17.6	Profit Before Taxes	23.0	23.3	13.1	15.9	16.4	12.9
			RATIOS						
2.6	2.8	2.4		12.7	2.4	3.1	2.1	2.0	1.8
1.5	1.5	1.4	Current	1.9	1.3	1.5	1.4	1.3	1.4
1.2	1.1	1.1		1.2	1.0	1.1	1.1	.8	1.2
2.0	2.1	1.8		8.9	2.0	2.0	1.6	1.5	1.6
1.3	1.3	1.2	Quick	1.5	1.2	1.4	1.2	1.1	1.2
.9	.9	.6		1.0	1.0	1.0	.8	.8	.9
27 13.3	14 25.8	13 28.6		0 UND	9 38.9	22 16.7	4 91.9	9 40.6	24 15.2
521 .7	456 .8	456 .8	Sales/Receivables	332 1.1	730 .5	1217 .3	243 1.5	281 1.3	304 1.2
1217 .3	1217 .3	1217 .3		1825 .2	1217 .3	1825 .2	1217 .3	1217 .3	608 .6
			Cost of Sales/Inventory						
			Cost of Sales/Payables						
.6	.6	.7		.3	.4	.6	.9	.8	1.2
1.5	1.6	1.7	Sales/Working Capital	1.0	1.4	.9	2.0	2.3	3.5
8.9	15.6	14.5		11.0	89.3	3.0	12.0	-6.1	14.7
5.3	5.4	5.0		12.5	5.0	2.9	7.1	3.4	5.8
(206) 2.8	(185) 2.5	(155) 2.6	EBIT/Interest	(21) 5.3	(22) 2.0	(21) 2.0	(19) 2.5	(38) 2.3	(34) 3.1
1.6	1.5	1.7		2.3	1.7	1.3	1.8	1.5	1.7
10.1	41.5	8.8							
(17) 2.1	(13) 5.0	(15) 1.5	Net Profit + Depr., Dep., Amort./Cur. Mat. L/T/D						
.3	.4	.4							
.0	.0	.0		.0	.0	.0	.0	.0	.0
.0	.0	.0	Fixed/Worth	.0	.0	.0	.1	.1	.1
.2	.3	.4		1.1	.1	.1	.3	1.0	.7
1.6	1.3	1.6		1.0	1.5	2.1	1.0	2.1	1.3
3.4	2.8	3.6	Debt/Worth	2.1	2.7	4.0	4.6	4.2	2.7
8.2	6.7	8.0		8.4	9.4	12.2	11.9	7.0	7.1
33.7	28.4	37.1		39.4	38.5	27.5	26.6	39.7	42.6
(265) 16.4	(242) 14.5	(214) 16.6	% Profit Before Taxes/Tangible Net Worth	(32) 14.4	(40) 16.5	(29) 15.4	(30) 16.5	(47) 14.3	(36) 22.1
6.5	5.7	8.0		5.9	5.7	2.6	10.8	9.6	9.6
7.6	7.4	7.6		9.3	7.8	6.0	7.4	6.9	10.8
3.8	3.4	3.9	% Profit Before Taxes/Total Assets	4.3	3.9	2.0	3.0	3.0	5.3
1.2	1.2	1.4		1.8	1.5	.3	1.3	1.2	2.9
999.8	332.1	897.6		UND	UND	999.8	385.5	141.3	111.4
61.5	51.3	56.3	Sales/Net Fixed Assets	UND	198.1	122.2	51.5	33.6	44.8
13.3	10.3	7.2		1.4	7.0	20.6	14.1	5.1	4.8
.6	.5	.6		.5	.4	.4	.7	.7	1.0
.3	.3	.3	Sales/Total Assets	.2	.3	.2	.3	.3	.7
.2	.2	.2		.1	.1	.1	.2	.1	.4
.4	.3	.4			.2	.4	.3	.6	.3
(148) 1.0	(150) .7	(123) 1.0	% Depr., Dep., Amort./Sales	(22) .9	(16) .9	(24) .9	(34) 1.3	(21) .7	
3.1	2.1	7.1			17.1	3.8	2.3	6.9	1.8
2.3	2.9	1.8		1.8	2.3				
(49) 5.9	(42) 7.4	(40) 5.9	% Officers', Directors' Owners' Comp/Sales	(11) 9.1	(10) 5.8				
16.8	14.5	12.7		13.4	14.4				
5684060M	5972446M	4169931M	Net Sales ($)	16450M	86109M	124657M	236387M	814119M	2892209M
13310072M	12762749M	9793757M	Total Assets ($)	109779M	519500M	684706M	1095436M	3623440M	3760896M

© RMA 2019

M = $ thousand   MM = $ million
See Pages viii through xx for Explanation of Ratios and Data

Current Data Sorted by Assets   Comparative Historical Data

0-500M	500M-2MM	2-10MM	10-50MM	50-100MM	100-250MM	Type of Statement	4/1/14-3/31/15 ALL	4/1/15-3/31/16 ALL
		2	21	8	14	Unqualified	54	48
	1	1	3		1	Reviewed	11	9
		2	2			Compiled	34	23
1	2	3	4		1	Tax Returns	19	20
1	2	12	24	4	9	Other	148	132
	19 (4/1-9/30/18)		98 (10/1/18-3/31/19)					
2	5	20	54	12	24	NUMBER OF STATEMENTS	266	232
%	%	%	%	%	%	ASSETS	%	%
		5.3	11.3	9.0	6.7	Cash & Equivalents	7.2	7.8
		66.9	69.6	46.3	58.1	Trade Receivables (net)	69.9	67.1
		.9	2.5	.0	1.5	Inventory	1.5	.8
		9.6	3.0	15.5	10.5	All Other Current	6.0	4.8
		82.7	86.3	70.9	76.8	Total Current	84.5	80.6
		7.0	2.1	9.1	6.1	Fixed Assets (net)	4.0	5.7
		3.5	2.3	.1	1.3	Intangibles (net)	3.1	3.0
		6.8	9.3	19.9	15.8	All Other Non-Current	8.4	10.7
		100.0	100.0	100.0	100.0	Total	100.0	100.0
						LIABILITIES		
		25.6	30.1	21.0	28.1	Notes Payable-Short Term	34.2	35.1
		2.8	1.2	3.5	5.3	Cur. Mat.-L.T.D.	1.3	2.0
		5.0	2.4	1.5	2.7	Trade Payables	1.4	1.6
		.2	.2	.0	.0	Income Taxes Payable	.1	.2
		9.4	7.6	9.1	11.3	All Other Current	8.9	5.9
		42.9	41.5	35.1	47.3	Total Current	45.8	44.8
		13.9	15.8	27.1	24.9	Long-Term Debt	8.0	10.0
		.0	.0	.0	.0	Deferred Taxes	.1	.4
		12.9	7.6	3.3	4.3	All Other Non-Current	14.3	12.2
		30.3	35.0	34.5	23.4	Net Worth	31.8	32.6
		100.0	100.0	100.0	100.0	Total Liabilities & Net Worth	100.0	100.0
						INCOME DATA		
		100.0	100.0	100.0	100.0	Net Sales	100.0	100.0
						Gross Profit		
		72.6	69.5	62.2	79.5	Operating Expenses	71.4	73.1
		27.4	30.5	37.8	20.5	Operating Profit	28.6	26.9
		11.9	10.8	15.0	9.1	All Other Expenses (net)	9.8	10.5
		15.5	19.7	22.8	11.5	Profit Before Taxes	18.8	16.4
						RATIOS		
		6.2	5.5	5.8	3.8		3.4	3.0
		1.7	1.9	2.3	1.4	Current	1.8	1.7
		1.1	1.4	1.4	1.1		1.3	1.3
		6.2	5.5	4.9	3.3		3.1	2.9
		1.6	1.9	1.7	1.3	Quick	(265) 1.6	1.6
		.9	1.3	1.2	1.0		1.2	1.3
		35 10.4	192 1.9	28 13.0	58 6.3		261 1.4	203 1.8
		228 1.6	912 .4	730 .5	456 .8	Sales/Receivables	730 .5	730 .5
		1217 .3	1825 .2	1217 .3	1217 .3		1217 .3	1217 .3
						Cost of Sales/Inventory		
						Cost of Sales/Payables		
		.6	.4	.4	.8		.5	.6
		1.4	.8	.6	1.1	Sales/Working Capital	1.2	1.1
		58.2	2.0	1.2	6.3		2.7	2.8
		23.1	5.6		3.9		6.2	6.3
		(14) 4.2	(38) 2.7		(15) 2.6	EBIT/Interest	(206) 3.4	(174) 3.0
		2.6	1.8		1.4		1.9	1.6
						Net Profit + Depr., Dep.,	15.9	
						Amort./Cur. Mat. L/T/D	(11) 7.7	
							1.3	
		.0	.0	.0	.0		.0	.0
		.1	.0	.0	.0	Fixed/Worth	.0	.1
		2.2	.2	.1	.3		.2	.2
		1.0	1.0	1.1	2.4		1.1	1.2
		10.1	2.6	2.2	3.8	Debt/Worth	3.0	2.7
		60.0	7.2	2.9	7.8		8.0	7.0
		81.7	50.2	24.5	34.4	% Profit Before Taxes/Tangible	44.6	35.4
		(16) 33.2	(50) 15.1	15.5	(23) 9.2	Net Worth	(244) 22.7	(215) 17.7
		5.1	4.8	4.3	4.0		9.5	6.9
		15.1	8.1	7.2	5.9	% Profit Before Taxes/Total	10.9	9.9
		4.3	4.0	5.1	2.9	Assets	5.1	4.7
		1.2	2.0	1.7	.5		2.4	1.2
		941.5	311.6	217.5	408.0		235.8	196.9
		98.5	48.4	57.9	43.4	Sales/Net Fixed Assets	42.1	38.6
		16.3	16.9	4.8	18.3		14.3	12.4
		1.4	.4	.3	.7		.6	.6
		.4	.3	.2	.3	Sales/Total Assets	.4	.3
		.2	.2	.1	.2		.2	.2
		.1	.4		.3		.5	.4
		(11) .8	(35) .6		(19) 1.2	% Depr., Dep., Amort./Sales	(166) .9	(149) .9
		1.5	1.5		2.2		2.0	1.9
						% Officers', Directors'	3.4	2.5
						Owners' Comp/Sales	(53) 7.1	(45) 7.8
							18.3	15.8
224M	3869M	149159M	556287M	227509M	2055226M	Net Sales ($)	3828457M	4565559M
839M	5359M	107438M	1405896M	931122M	3713069M	Total Assets ($)	9328079M	9929096M

M = $ thousand   MM = $ million
See Pages viii through xx for Explanation of Ratios and Data

Comparative Historical Data   Current Data Sorted by Sales

			Type of Statement						
47	40	45	Unqualified		7	3	10	13	12
12	7	5	Reviewed	1	1	2		1	
17	4	5	Compiled			2		2	1
13	12	10	Tax Returns	4	3	2		1	
117	87	52	Other	7	8	1	10	15	11
4/1/16-3/31/17 ALL	4/1/17-3/31/18 ALL	4/1/18-3/31/19 ALL		19 (4/1-9/30/18)			98 (10/1/18-3/31/19)		
				0-1MM	1-3MM	3-5MM	5-10MM	10-25MM	25MM & OVER
206	150	117	NUMBER OF STATEMENTS	12	19	10	20	32	24
%	%	%	ASSETS	%	%	%	%	%	%
7.5	7.4	10.0	Cash & Equivalents	15.6	7.8	5.2	7.4	11.2	11.6
70.6	65.2	63.0	Trade Receivables (net)	45.5	68.1	81.8	59.5	69.7	53.8
.7	.9	1.6	Inventory	.0	.3	1.0	5.3	.9	1.6
5.2	4.7	7.6	All Other Current	15.0	5.0	1.3	8.4	4.8	11.7
83.9	78.3	82.3	Total Current	76.0	81.2	89.3	80.7	86.7	78.7
4.9	5.5	4.5	Fixed Assets (net)	9.1	1.4	3.3	2.3	5.0	6.5
2.8	2.5	1.9	Intangibles (net)	.9	2.6	4.7	.2	2.7	1.1
8.3	13.7	11.3	All Other Non-Current	13.9	14.8	2.7	16.8	5.7	13.6
100.0	100.0	100.0	Total	100.0	100.0	100.0	100.0	100.0	100.0
			LIABILITIES						
36.1	35.7	27.2	Notes Payable-Short Term	13.0	34.4	28.6	28.4	27.8	26.3
1.7	1.4	2.5	Cur. Mat.-L.T.D.	2.5	.0	.1	2.7	1.3	6.8
2.4	1.7	2.8	Trade Payables	1.8	1.4	2.7	.5	5.0	3.6
.0	.1	.1	Income Taxes Payable	.0	.0	.4	.4	.0	.0
6.7	9.4	9.6	All Other Current	17.4	12.5	2.9	9.4	9.8	6.1
46.9	48.4	42.3	Total Current	34.7	48.4	34.7	41.5	43.9	42.8
8.5	9.7	18.4	Long-Term Debt	23.6	2.0	22.7	19.9	19.8	24.1
.0	.0	.0	Deferred Taxes	.0	.0	.0	.0	.0	.0
10.4	9.4	7.0	All Other Non-Current	6.8	8.8	13.4	2.4	7.9	5.5
34.1	32.5	32.3	Net Worth	34.9	40.8	29.1	36.2	28.4	27.6
100.0	100.0	100.0	Total Liabilities & Net Worth	100.0	100.0	100.0	100.0	100.0	100.0
			INCOME DATA						
100.0	100.0	100.0	Net Sales	100.0	100.0	100.0	100.0	100.0	100.0
			Gross Profit						
74.8	73.6	71.7	Operating Expenses	67.7	62.1	74.3	67.9	68.5	87.8
25.2	26.4	28.3	Operating Profit	32.3	37.9	25.7	32.1	31.5	12.2
9.9	10.4	10.6	All Other Expenses (net)	11.2	15.9	9.8	12.0	12.3	3.2
15.3	16.0	17.6	Profit Before Taxes	21.1	22.0	15.9	20.2	19.2	9.0
			RATIOS						
3.0	2.9	5.3	Current	7.2	9.6	32.7	5.7	3.8	5.4
1.7	1.6	1.7		1.8	1.6	2.7	2.0	1.7	1.6
1.3	1.3	1.3		1.1	1.2	1.5	1.3	1.3	1.1
2.8	2.7	4.2	Quick	5.9	9.6	32.3	5.5	3.8	3.7
1.6	1.6	1.7		1.6	1.6	2.1	1.6	1.6	1.6
1.3	1.2	1.2		.3	1.2	1.5	1.2	1.2	1.1
243 1.5	99 3.7	76 4.8	Sales/Receivables	0 UND	107 3.4	406 .9	54 6.7	203 1.8	35 10.4
912 .4	730 .5	730 .5		406 .9	1825 .2	912 .4	730 .5	912 .4	111 3.3
1217 .3	1825 .2	1217 .3		1825 .2	2000 .1	1825 .2	1217 .3	1217 .3	730 .5
			Cost of Sales/Inventory						
			Cost of Sales/Payables						
.5	.5	.4	Sales/Working Capital	.5	.3	.3	.4	.5	.8
1.2	1.0	.9		.6	.4	.8	1.1	.9	3.1
2.6	3.3	2.7		UND	1.2	1.3	1.6	2.0	15.5
6.3	5.3	5.5	EBIT/Interest				6.2	5.4	5.1
(164) 2.9	(106) 2.9	(80) 3.1				(13) 3.6	(26) 3.1	(19) 3.2	
1.5	1.5	1.8					2.1	1.9	1.3
20.4			Net Profit + Depr., Dep., Amort./Cur. Mat. L/T/D						
(13) 1.1									
.2									
.0	.0	.0	Fixed/Worth	.0	.0	.0	.0	.0	.0
.0	.0	.0		.0	.0	.0	.0	.1	.0
.2	.1	.2		.2	.0	NM	.1	.2	.4
1.0	1.1	1.3	Debt/Worth	.8	.2	1.4	1.1	1.8	1.8
2.5	2.6	2.8		1.9	2.3	11.6	2.0	2.9	3.1
6.7	6.2	8.0		25.0	16.9	NM	6.1	7.2	7.3
34.2	33.0	39.0	% Profit Before Taxes/Tangible Net Worth	163.9	33.8		24.5	64.1	35.2
(192) 14.5	(142) 11.6	(108) 17.0		21.6	(16) 9.4		16.3	(30) 25.7	(22) 10.8
4.7	3.2	5.0		4.4	3.6		3.6	10.3	6.4
9.1	8.6	7.6	% Profit Before Taxes/Total Assets	10.2	4.8	13.9	8.4	10.8	7.3
3.7	3.8	4.1		3.1	3.0	4.9	3.6	6.4	4.8
1.2	.8	1.4		1.0	1.2	.9	.7	2.9	1.7
624.0	UND	455.3	Sales/Net Fixed Assets	UND	UND	UND	258.4	211.8	387.6
63.3	68.3	64.2		514.5	117.5	39.1	67.2	35.5	67.7
18.3	17.5	16.8		17.5	17.0	8.2	9.1	12.4	21.4
.7	.5	.5	Sales/Total Assets	.5	.3	.5	.4	.5	1.9
.3	.3	.3		.2	.1	.3	.2	.3	.6
.2	.2	.2		.2	.1	.2	.1	.2	.3
.4	.5	.3	% Depr., Dep., Amort./Sales				.2	.4	.2
(128) 1.0	(75) .9	(73) .8				(16) .5	(22) .9	(18) .7	
2.1	2.0	1.6					1.6	1.9	1.6
3.1	1.8	3.2	% Officers', Directors' Owners' Comp/Sales						
(33) 6.2	(23) 7.0	(16) 7.8							
12.1	17.0	16.9							
4193767M	3367864M	2992274M	Net Sales ($)	6616M	32212M	39137M	140618M	521306M	2252385M
8463002M	7917852M	6163723M	Total Assets ($)	25944M	277440M	131542M	877708M	1869305M	2981784M

© RMA 2019   M = $ thousand   MM = $ million
See Pages viii through xx for Explanation of Ratios and Data

Current Data Sorted by Assets   Comparative Historical Data

0-500M	500M-2MM	2-10MM	10-50MM	50-100MM	100-250MM	**Type of Statement**	4/1/14-3/31/15 ALL	4/1/15-3/31/16 ALL
2	2	42	141	56	84	Unqualified	282	338
			3	1	2	Reviewed	12	6
	1	2	1	1		Compiled	10	10
3	2	6	6			Tax Returns	23	23
9	5	20	46	20	14	Other	173	208
	47 (4/1-9/30/18)		422 (10/1/18-3/31/19)					
14	10	70	197	78	100	**NUMBER OF STATEMENTS**	500	585
%	%	%	%	%	%	**ASSETS**	%	%
31.5	40.4	26.5	16.1	11.6	7.7	Cash & Equivalents	20.3	19.1
14.4	.5	7.8	13.3	15.8	14.6	Trade Receivables (net)	13.4	15.3
7.7	6.9	21.0	31.7	26.0	25.6	Inventory	31.9	29.3
14.3	4.0	14.2	20.3	23.0	26.5	All Other Current	8.6	15.5
67.8	51.8	69.5	81.4	76.4	74.4	Total Current	74.2	79.2
14.4	36.7	13.6	3.3	1.4	1.4	Fixed Assets (net)	9.1	5.5
2.6	8.9	5.0	.7	2.1	2.0	Intangibles (net)	1.7	1.7
15.9	2.5	11.8	14.7	20.1	22.2	All Other Non-Current	15.0	13.6
100.0	100.0	100.0	100.0	100.0	100.0	Total	100.0	100.0
						LIABILITIES		
20.5	9.0	27.7	46.4	38.4	48.0	Notes Payable-Short Term	45.0	43.8
.7	2.3	1.2	2.1	2.2	4.6	Cur. Mat.-L.T.D.	.7	2.1
12.0	1.5	3.2	6.9	12.5	9.1	Trade Payables	1.9	5.8
.0	.0	.0	.1	.1	.2	Income Taxes Payable	.2	.2
13.9	1.7	5.1	9.1	7.9	7.8	All Other Current	6.0	8.3
47.1	14.5	37.3	64.6	61.0	69.7	Total Current	53.8	60.2
34.5	18.8	14.9	4.8	5.5	8.2	Long-Term Debt	8.1	7.6
.2	.0	.1	.1	.0	.1	Deferred Taxes	.2	.2
1.3	.0	1.6	.9	2.7	2.1	All Other Non-Current	2.1	1.5
17.6	66.7	46.0	29.6	30.7	20.0	Net Worth	35.7	30.5
100.0	100.0	100.0	100.0	100.0	100.0	Total Liabilities & Net Worth	100.0	100.0
						INCOME DATA		
100.0	100.0	100.0	100.0	100.0	100.0	Net Sales	100.0	100.0
						Gross Profit		
81.9	87.6	77.2	85.8	86.3	86.6	Operating Expenses	82.5	78.7
18.1	12.4	22.8	14.2	13.7	13.4	Operating Profit	17.5	21.3
6.7	7.4	8.7	5.9	4.9	6.6	All Other Expenses (net)	6.8	5.6
11.4	5.0	14.1	8.3	8.8	6.8	Profit Before Taxes	10.7	15.6
						RATIOS		
4.0	20.9	2.9	1.4	1.4	1.2		2.1	1.6
1.6	5.2	1.8	1.2	1.1	1.1	Current	1.2	1.2
.9	1.0	1.3	1.1	1.1	1.0		1.1	1.1
4.0	20.9	2.1	1.0	1.1	1.0		1.4	1.2
1.5	3.3	1.0	.2	.2	.1	Quick	.4	.3
.2	.3	.5	.1	.1	.1		.1	.1
0 UND	0 UND	0 UND	0 UND	0 791.7	4 81.9		0 UND	0 UND
0 UND	0 UND	0 999.8	4 94.7	13 27.8	18 20.6	Sales/Receivables	4 87.4	4 86.8
17 21.8	8 45.2	30 12.0	29 12.6	62 5.9	61 6.0		33 10.9	37 9.8
						Cost of Sales/Inventory		
						Cost of Sales/Payables		
3.3	.8	.8	2.1	2.6	3.8		1.6	2.1
12.9	4.5	1.9	3.9	6.0	8.2	Sales/Working Capital	4.2	4.4
UND	NM	4.7	7.5	13.2	15.9		9.4	9.2
		9.9	3.8	4.9	2.2		5.3	7.6
		(37) 2.6	(131) 1.5	(43) 1.5	(50) 1.0	EBIT/Interest	(323) 2.7	(321) 4.2
		1.6	.8	1.0	-.1		1.2	2.2
			16.1			Net Profit + Depr., Dep.,	14.7	23.0
			(23) .9			Amort./Cur. Mat. L/T/D	(30) 4.0	(32) 11.5
			-1.0				-1.5	.2
.0	.0	.0	.0	.0	.0		.0	.0
.0	.3	.0	.0	.0	.1	Fixed/Worth	.1	.1
.7	1.5	.4	.1	.1	.2		.2	.1
.9	.1	.7	1.6	1.6	3.7		1.0	1.5
1.8	.4	1.3	3.3	4.2	5.9	Debt/Worth	3.0	4.0
9.5	2.0	2.8	5.3	7.1	9.8		6.2	6.9
76.8	35.8	24.5	20.4	14.1	21.8	% Profit Before Taxes/Tangible	30.5	52.3
(12) 9.6	10.4	(64) 6.6	(196) 5.9	(77) 5.0	(98) 6.4	Net Worth	(488) 12.9	(571) 26.1
-16.8	.5	-1.7	-4.0	-5.6	-10.2		2.3	9.7
39.0	22.3	9.4	5.5	4.0	3.9	% Profit Before Taxes/Total	7.7	10.6
2.6	2.9	2.6	1.4	.8	1.1	Assets	3.3	5.4
-4.8	.3	-.7	-.8	-.7	-1.1		.5	2.0
UND	190.5	553.5	114.7	161.8	125.7		103.5	150.7
UND	18.8	46.7	59.6	70.9	65.0	Sales/Net Fixed Assets	36.2	53.3
6.2	.2	3.4	23.5	39.8	30.3		11.2	17.9
3.7	1.8	.8	.8	.8	.7		.7	.7
1.5	.8	.5	.6	.6	.4	Sales/Total Assets	.4	.5
.3	.1	.1	.3	.3	.2		.2	.3
		.4	.4	.3	.4		.4	.3
		(41) 1.1	(150) .6	(58) .6	(73) .8	% Depr., Dep., Amort./Sales	(328) .9	(393) .6
		3.5	1.0	1.0	1.4		1.7	1.1
			2.6				3.7	3.9
			(10) 4.8			% Officers', Directors'	(46) 9.2	(52) 10.0
			12.8			Owners' Comp/Sales	18.3	19.2
8129M	15499M	219580M	3244242M	3173413M	6827122M	Net Sales ($)	9602659M	12284759M
3024M	14361M	397682M	5301013M	5481092M	15403096M	Total Assets ($)	19892522M	27703977M

© RMA 2019   **M = $ thousand   MM = $ million**
See Pages viii through xx for Explanation of Ratios and Data

Comparative Historical Data | | | | Current Data Sorted by Sales

			Type of Statement						
331	287	327	Unqualified	6	26	21	45	86	143
11	8	6	Reviewed		1	1		2	2
7	4	5	Compiled	2	2		1		
17	11	17	Tax Returns	10	2	3		1	
195	119	114	Other	22	15	10	17	26	24
4/1/16-3/31/17	4/1/17-3/31/18	4/1/18-3/31/19		47 (4/1-9/30/18)	422 (10/1/18-3/31/19)				
ALL	ALL	ALL		0-1MM	1-3MM	3-5MM	5-10MM	10-25MM	25MM & OVER
561	429	469	**NUMBER OF STATEMENTS**	40	46	35	64	115	169
%	%	%	**ASSETS**	%	%	%	%	%	%
20.9	15.0	16.1	Cash & Equivalents	17.8	23.7	28.7	20.7	14.8	10.1
14.2	13.4	12.9	Trade Receivables (net)	10.3	19.6	14.8	6.6	10.4	15.4
27.2	28.4	26.6	Inventory	4.6	10.3	27.7	25.2	35.4	30.5
17.5	18.7	20.7	All Other Current	16.3	11.8	14.7	11.8	20.5	28.8
79.8	75.5	76.3	Total Current	49.0	65.5	85.9	64.2	81.1	84.9
5.6	6.1	5.1	Fixed Assets (net)	26.1	8.7	3.8	3.3	2.3	2.1
1.8	2.4	2.1	Intangibles (net)	8.1	1.9	.4	.6	1.3	2.1
12.8	16.1	16.5	All Other Non-Current	17.1	23.9	9.9	31.9	15.3	10.9
100.0	100.0	100.0	Total	100.0	100.0	100.0	100.0	100.0	100.0
			LIABILITIES						
43.3	45.4	41.0	Notes Payable-Short Term	18.6	18.7	35.5	39.7	46.4	50.4
2.6	2.4	2.5	Cur. Mat. L.T.D.	2.5	1.8	2.0	.4	2.2	3.8
5.3	6.0	7.8	Trade Payables	3.1	3.4	4.2	2.7	8.3	12.4
.2	.1	.1	Income Taxes Payable	.0	.0	.0	.1	.0	.2
8.2	6.7	8.0	All Other Current	8.7	5.8	4.0	4.8	9.0	9.9
59.6	60.7	59.4	Total Current	32.9	29.7	45.6	47.7	66.0	76.6
5.6	9.5	8.3	Long-Term Debt	26.8	16.0	13.1	13.6	4.6	1.4
.2	.1	.1	Deferred Taxes	.1	.0	.2	.3	.1	.0
2.3	1.8	1.6	All Other Non-Current	1.9	1.8	1.6	2.6	1.7	.9
32.3	27.9	30.6	Net Worth	38.6	52.5	39.6	35.8	27.5	21.1
100.0	100.0	100.0	Total Liabilties & Net Worth	100.0	100.0	100.0	100.0	100.0	100.0
			INCOME DATA						
100.0	100.0	100.0	Net Sales	100.0	100.0	100.0	100.0	100.0	100.0
			Gross Profit						
77.0	80.2	84.7	Operating Expenses	67.3	67.3	78.9	78.8	85.5	96.4
23.0	19.8	15.3	Operating Profit	32.7	32.7	21.1	21.2	14.5	3.6
5.3	6.3	6.3	All Other Expenses (net)	16.9	11.9	9.1	6.8	5.1	2.5
17.7	13.5	9.0	Profit Before Taxes	15.9	20.8	12.1	14.3	9.4	1.1
			RATIOS						
1.7	1.6	1.6		4.3	20.7	3.9	2.0	1.3	1.2
1.2	1.2	1.2	Current	1.4	2.3	1.7	1.4	1.2	1.1
1.1	1.1	1.1		.5	1.3	1.2	1.2	1.1	1.0
1.3	1.1	1.1		3.3	14.2	2.0	1.5	.7	.4
.3	.3	.3	Quick	.9	1.4	1.0	.5	.2	.2
.1	.1	.1		.2	.4	.3	.2	.2	.2
0 UND	0 UND	0 UND		0 UND	0 UND	0 UND	0 UND	0 904.6	2 166.8
7 53.8	5 66.9	7 53.8	Sales/Receivables	0 UND	7 49.6	2 202.1	2 190.4	6 62.7	11 32.0
45 8.1	34 10.8	44 8.3		66 5.5	730 .5	28 13.1	41 8.8	29 12.4	46 8.0
			Cost of Sales/Inventory						
			Cost of Sales/Payables						
2.0	1.8	1.8		.4	.3	.8	1.4	2.5	4.8
4.5	4.3	4.7	Sales/Working Capital	6.2	1.0	1.8	2.5	4.2	8.4
8.7	9.0	10.5		-7.1	4.3	3.7	5.6	7.0	15.0
8.5	6.6	3.9		17.1	7.6	10.2	5.3	3.6	2.2
(317) 4.3	(264) 3.3	(272) 1.7	EBIT/Interest	(12) 4.5	(25) 2.6	(25) 2.3	(42) 2.3	(73) 1.7	(95) 1.1
2.5	1.4	.8		2.1	1.3	1.0	1.1	.9	.1
46.9	52.7	21.9						23.8	21.9
(38) 4.2	(34) 15.6	(38) 1.8	Net Profit + Depr., Dep., Amort./Cur. Mat. L/T/D				(11) 3.0	(19) 3.0	.3
.1	.1	-.3						-.3	-.5
.0	.0	.0		.0	.0	.0	.0	.0	.0
.0	.0	.0	Fixed/Worth	.2	.0	.0	.0	.0	.1
.1	.1	.1		1.3	.2	.1	.1	.1	.2
1.3	1.7	1.4		.8	.3	.5	1.1	2.0	3.3
3.6	3.6	3.4	Debt/Worth	2.1	1.0	1.1	1.8	3.8	5.4
6.5	6.5	6.3		7.7	2.9	3.5	3.3	5.5	8.7
56.5	34.1	21.0		22.6	17.4	20.7	20.8	25.9	20.7
(551) 28.0	(412) 13.7	(457) 6.0	% Profit Before Taxes/Tangible Net Worth	(35) 5.6	(44) 4.3	(34) 7.6	(114) 6.4	(166) 7.5	2.8
11.3	4.3	-3.8		-9.4	-1.0	.4	2.1	-.8	-21.7
12.8	7.6	5.2		4.9	8.2	9.5	6.4	6.8	3.6
6.4	3.7	1.4	% Profit Before Taxes/Total Assets	1.8	2.5	2.6	2.5	1.6	.6
2.4	.8	-.9		-2.2	-.1	.4	.2	-.1	-3.9
192.4	183.1	180.5		UND	UND	851.4	379.0	100.0	109.2
62.4	60.3	59.6	Sales/Net Fixed Assets	6.6	96.7	65.6	96.6	61.4	49.4
24.9	19.9	22.8		.3	8.2	16.3	25.6	26.2	30.1
.9	.7	.8		.3	.5	.8	.7	.7	.8
.6	.5	.5	Sales/Total Assets	.1	.2	.5	.4	.6	.7
.3	.3	.3		.1	.1	.2	.1	.4	.5
.3	.3	.4		7.0	.4	.3	.3	.4	.4
(360) .6	(295) .6	(329) .7	% Depr., Dep., Amort./Sales	(17) 11.1	(18) 1.1	(19) .8	(47) .6	(93) .6	(135) .7
1.0	1.0	1.3		28.0	1.8	.9	1.1	1.0	1.2
3.8	4.5	2.7							
(37) 6.7	(30) 11.2	(27) 6.8	% Officers', Directors' Owners' Comp/Sales						
16.5	18.9	18.7							
13401076M	11633518M	13487985M	Net Sales ($)	18325M	89037M	144209M	448921M	1896644M	10890849M
26290177M	24884447M	26600268M	Total Assets ($)	163499M	805394M	566335M	2371693M	5171124M	17522223M

© RMA 2019   M = $ thousand   MM = $ million
See Pages viii through xx for Explanation of Ratios and Data

Current Data Sorted by Assets   Comparative Historical Data

Type of Statement

0-500M	500M-2MM	2-10MM	10-50MM	50-100MM	100-250MM	Type of Statement	4/1/14-3/31/15 ALL	4/1/15-3/31/16 ALL
	1	12	38	18	29	Unqualified	86	96
	2	6	8			Reviewed	14	15
	4	6	4		1	Compiled	15	14
1	5	7	1		1	Tax Returns	24	14
4	17	28	58	23	36	Other	161	151
0-500M	35 (4/1-9/30/18) 500M-2MM	2-10MM	275 (10/1/18-3/31/19) 10-50MM	50-100MM	100-250MM			
5	29	59	109	41	67	NUMBER OF STATEMENTS	300	290
%	%	%	%	%	%	ASSETS	%	%
	16.8	11.2	9.4	7.3	6.1	Cash & Equivalents	9.9	9.8
	43.4	44.8	61.3	62.3	53.6	Trade Receivables (net)	55.9	56.5
	11.2	5.9	1.3	.1	1.1	Inventory	3.8	3.1
	5.2	7.1	9.1	4.5	9.4	All Other Current	6.3	7.3
	76.6	68.9	81.1	74.1	70.3	Total Current	75.9	76.6
	11.5	13.4	1.4	2.0	1.5	Fixed Assets (net)	6.1	4.6
	3.6	5.1	2.6	3.8	4.4	Intangibles (net)	2.2	1.9
	8.4	12.5	14.9	20.1	23.8	All Other Non-Current	15.8	16.9
	100.0	100.0	100.0	100.0	100.0	Total	100.0	100.0
						LIABILITIES		
	14.7	16.1	29.7	34.5	24.5	Notes Payable-Short Term	28.2	28.3
	1.0	2.5	1.0	.7	1.2	Cur. Mat.-L.T.D.	2.4	2.6
	6.9	4.9	3.3	3.3	3.5	Trade Payables	3.1	3.6
	.0	.1	.1	.1	.0	Income Taxes Payable	.1	.1
	8.8	6.2	7.9	7.7	7.3	All Other Current	8.7	8.0
	31.4	29.6	41.9	46.2	36.5	Total Current	42.5	42.6
	9.5	17.5	15.2	23.3	26.5	Long-Term Debt	17.1	17.6
	.0	.0	.0	.0	.5	Deferred Taxes	.1	.1
	11.8	9.0	8.8	5.7	6.8	All Other Non-Current	9.1	8.3
	47.3	43.9	34.1	24.8	29.8	Net Worth	31.2	31.4
	100.0	100.0	100.0	100.0	100.0	Total Liabilities & Net Worth	100.0	100.0
						INCOME DATA		
	100.0	100.0	100.0	100.0	100.0	Net Sales	100.0	100.0
						Gross Profit		
	74.2	68.4	63.6	68.6	63.1	Operating Expenses	66.7	64.9
	25.8	31.6	36.4	31.4	36.9	Operating Profit	33.3	35.1
	10.4	11.5	13.5	10.9	13.3	All Other Expenses (net)	9.3	10.7
	15.4	20.1	22.8	20.5	23.6	Profit Before Taxes	23.9	24.4
						RATIOS		
	21.5	4.4	5.6	5.5	8.7		4.1	4.8
	3.8	1.9	1.7	1.4	1.5	Current	1.7	1.8
	1.6	1.6	1.3	1.2	1.2		1.2	1.3
	8.7	3.2	4.2	4.2	3.5		3.0	3.6
	3.5	1.6	1.6	1.4	1.4	Quick	1.5	1.6
	1.4	1.0	1.2	1.2	1.1		1.1	1.1
	1 / 551.9	16 / 23.4	43 / 8.5	41 / 8.9	20 / 17.9		24 / 15.1	33 / 10.9
	96 / 3.8	91 / 4.0	1217 / .3	912 / .4	912 / .4	Sales/Receivables	730 / .5	912 / .4
	730 / .5	1217 / .3	1825 / .2	1825 / .2	1825 / .2		1825 / .2	1825 / .2
						Cost of Sales/Inventory		
						Cost of Sales/Payables		
	.5	.4	.4	.3	.3		.4	.4
	2.2	1.6	.8	1.0	.8	Sales/Working Capital	1.1	.9
	7.2	7.0	1.9	3.4	3.7		4.7	2.6
	13.9	12.9	5.5	2.4	3.3		6.8	6.8
	(18) 3.5	(34) 6.8	(62) 2.9	(22) 1.8	(32) 2.3	EBIT/Interest	(180) 3.8	(181) 3.7
	1.3	2.6	1.7	1.0	1.6		1.9	2.0
						Net Profit + Depr., Dep., Amort./Cur. Mat. L/T/D	7.8	119.8
							(19) 1.4	(10) 6.8
							.6	.7
	.0	.0	.0	.0	.0		.0	.0
	.0	.0	.0	.0	.0	Fixed/Worth	.0	.0
	.3	.3	.0	.1	.0		.1	.1
	.3	.5	1.1	2.2	1.7		1.1	1.2
	1.1	1.4	2.4	4.0	2.8	Debt/Worth	2.8	2.5
	5.1	4.6	7.0	7.0	5.2		6.4	5.9
	32.4	48.5	33.6	31.4	30.1		42.3	34.4
	(27) 12.2	(55) 14.4	(103) 17.0	(39) 11.7	(64) 11.3	% Profit Before Taxes/Tangible Net Worth	(276) 17.5	(272) 15.1
	1.0	4.2	6.8	3.9	3.7		6.8	7.2
	14.7	14.5	9.2	5.8	5.5		9.3	10.1
	5.5	4.9	4.3	3.0	2.9	% Profit Before Taxes/Total Assets	4.1	4.2
	.3	1.7	1.4	1.0	.9		1.7	1.9
	UND	UND	UND	342.8	UND		UND	UND
	100.8	103.1	176.9	86.7	141.1	Sales/Net Fixed Assets	71.7	90.4
	14.0	10.6	39.0	14.5	23.5		19.7	22.1
	1.7	.9	.4	.3	.3		.6	.5
	1.0	.4	.2	.2	.1	Sales/Total Assets	.2	.2
	.2	.1	.1	.1	.1		.1	.1
	.2	.3	.3	.3	.2		.3	.4
	(12) .7	(33) 1.1	(53) .5	(24) .6	(33) .7	% Depr., Dep., Amort./Sales	(153) .8	(136) .9
	1.6	4.0	1.4	1.2	1.8		1.7	2.1
		1.3	1.8				2.8	2.7
	(14)	2.6	(15) 5.8			% Officers', Directors' Owners' Comp/Sales	(45) 9.8	(39) 9.4
		12.3	11.4				19.2	17.4
3187M	66664M	236048M	1193742M	854664M	4448832M	Net Sales ($)	6240582M	5475293M
1151M	39296M	314384M	2780778M	3014028M	10243259M	Total Assets ($)	15069234M	15674955M

© RMA 2019

M = $ thousand   MM = $ million
See Pages viii through xx for Explanation of Ratios and Data

Comparative Historical Data | Current Data Sorted by Sales

Type of Statement					35 (4/1-9/30/18)		275 (10/1/18-3/31/19)		
				0-1MM	1-3MM	3-5MM	5-10MM	10-25MM	25MM & OVER
Unqualified	78	81	98	8	13	9	22	29	17
Reviewed	12	22	16	6	4	2	3	1	
Compiled	10	11	15	4	3	1	1	3	3
Tax Returns	24	24	15	5	4	4	2		
Other	187	180	166	23	29	12	39	35	28
	4/1/16-3/31/17 ALL	4/1/17-3/31/18 ALL	4/1/18-3/31/19 ALL						
NUMBER OF STATEMENTS	311	318	310	46	53	28	65	70	48
ASSETS	%	%	%	%	%	%	%	%	%
Cash & Equivalents	10.2	9.2	9.8	11.9	13.5	9.9	6.6	9.9	7.8
Trade Receivables (net)	53.4	54.1	54.4	41.5	50.2	52.7	63.8	59.5	52.5
Inventory	3.2	3.1	2.9	3.4	5.8	4.9	1.1	1.3	2.7
All Other Current	8.6	8.5	7.7	8.6	3.9	6.2	8.9	5.7	13.1
Total Current	75.4	75.0	74.8	65.4	73.3	73.7	80.4	76.4	76.1
Fixed Assets (net)	4.2	4.9	5.0	15.8	2.0	3.0	3.8	3.7	2.5
Intangibles (net)	2.6	3.1	3.7	1.3	5.6	3.8	1.8	3.4	6.7
All Other Non-Current	17.8	17.0	16.6	17.5	19.1	19.5	13.9	16.5	14.8
Total	100.0	100.0	100.0	100.0	100.0	100.0	100.0	100.0	100.0
LIABILITIES									
Notes Payable-Short Term	25.5	27.1	24.9	15.7	23.2	23.9	29.8	26.1	28.1
Cur. Mat.-L.T.D.	1.5	1.6	1.3	2.4	.7	.8	1.1	1.4	1.5
Trade Payables	3.5	3.3	3.9	2.1	6.1	2.8	3.9	3.4	4.7
Income Taxes Payable	.1	.0	.1	.0	.2	.1	.0	.1	.0
All Other Current	8.4	7.5	7.4	8.0	7.0	2.7	5.9	8.3	10.9
Total Current	39.0	39.6	37.7	28.2	37.2	30.4	40.6	39.3	45.1
Long-Term Debt	18.3	18.8	19.0	22.8	10.3	15.4	20.5	23.3	19.0
Deferred Taxes	.1	.0	.1	.0	.0	.0	.0	.4	.2
All Other Non-Current	10.7	8.7	8.1	8.8	11.5	10.2	7.3	5.4	7.7
Net Worth	31.9	32.9	35.1	40.2	40.9	44.1	31.6	31.7	28.0
Total Liabilities & Net Worth	100.0	100.0	100.0	100.0	100.0	100.0	100.0	100.0	100.0
INCOME DATA									
Net Sales	100.0	100.0	100.0	100.0	100.0	100.0	100.0	100.0	100.0
Gross Profit									
Operating Expenses	67.4	67.3	66.2	56.9	68.1	61.3	64.0	66.4	78.7
Operating Profit	32.6	32.7	33.8	43.1	31.9	38.7	36.0	33.6	21.3
All Other Expenses (net)	11.0	11.7	12.3	21.1	12.0	10.6	10.4	12.4	7.8
Profit Before Taxes	21.6	21.0	21.4	22.0	19.9	28.1	25.5	21.2	13.5
RATIOS									
Current	6.9	6.6	6.7	7.8	4.8	11.3	7.9	6.1	3.2
	1.8	1.7	1.8	2.1	2.0	4.1	1.6	1.7	1.5
	1.3	1.3	1.3	1.2	1.5	1.4	1.3	1.2	1.1
Quick	5.1	4.5	4.4	5.5	4.2	10.0	4.9	6.0	2.1
	1.5	1.5	1.6	1.6	1.7	2.8	1.5	1.5	1.4
	1.1	1.1	1.2	.8	1.3	1.2	1.2	1.2	.9
Sales/Receivables	23 16.1	31 11.8	23 16.0	0 UND	1 246.2	26 14.1	56 6.5	31 11.6	7 53.2
	730 .5	912 .4	608 .6	332 1.1	912 .4	608 .6	1217 .3	912 .4	89 4.1
	1825 .2	1825 .2	1825 .2	1825 .2	1825 .2	1825 .2	1825 .2	1825 .2	608 .6
Cost of Sales/Inventory									
Cost of Sales/Payables									
Sales/Working Capital	.4	.3	.4	.3	.3	.4	.4	.3	1.3
	1.0	.9	.9	.7	.9	.7	.6	.9	3.6
	3.8	3.1	3.3	2.3	3.3	2.4	1.5	2.7	22.5
EBIT/Interest	7.4	6.7	5.7	8.4	8.1	60.8	5.7	4.1	4.3
	(168) 3.3	(173) 3.3	(170) 2.7	(20) 3.5	(26) 3.7	(17) 3.6	(35) 3.5	(37) 2.1	(35) 2.3
	1.7	1.8	1.6	1.2	1.4	2.5	1.7	1.1	1.6
Net Profit + Depr., Dep., Amort./Cur. Mat. L/T/D	73.7		23.0						
	(12) 2.1	(10)	.4						
	.2		.0						
Fixed/Worth	.0	.0	.0	.0	.0	.0	.0	.0	.0
	.0	.0	.0	.0	.0	.0	.0	.0	.0
	.1	.1	.1	.3	.1	.0	.0	.1	.1
Debt/Worth	.9	1.0	1.1	.6	.6	.3	1.5	1.4	2.0
	2.8	2.8	2.4	1.7	1.6	1.6	2.4	3.0	2.8
	7.4	6.2	6.2	6.0	6.8	5.9	5.6	6.3	7.2
% Profit Before Taxes/Tangible Net Worth	31.4	28.8	33.4	20.0	32.7	43.5	29.7	31.9	66.5
	(290) 14.2	(298) 13.7	(292) 14.8	(45) 5.9	(49) 10.0	(26) 15.3	(62) 16.1	(66) 16.6	(44) 31.2
	6.3	5.2	4.3	.9	2.6	7.2	8.4	3.9	11.8
% Profit Before Taxes/Total Assets	8.3	7.3	8.4	6.7	7.0	11.4	8.7	7.6	11.3
	3.7	3.6	4.2	2.5	3.2	5.2	3.9	4.0	5.5
	1.5	1.5	1.1	.3	1.0	3.1	1.4	.2	1.6
Sales/Net Fixed Assets	UND	UND	UND	UND	UND	999.8	999.8	558.9	999.8
	86.1	91.5	130.1	UND	133.0	116.2	141.6	89.0	58.6
	23.6	18.9	22.1	1.7	22.7	38.4	35.4	14.3	23.8
Sales/Total Assets	.5	.4	.5	.3	.6	.5	.3	.4	2.0
	.2	.2	.2	.1	.2	.3	.2	.2	.6
	.1	.1	.1	.1	.1	.2	.1	.1	.3
% Depr., Dep., Amort./Sales	.4	.3	.3	.6	.3	.4	.3	.2	.0
	(154) .9	(159) .8	(156) .7	(13) 4.3	(27) .7	(17) .6	(30) .7	(43) .5	(26) .5
	1.8	1.9	1.8	12.8	1.5	1.6	1.3	3.2	1.6
% Officers', Directors' Owners' Comp/Sales	2.3	2.2	1.8		1.9				
	(45) 7.7	(48) 11.3	(47) 9.4		(15) 10.3				
	15.5	25.3	19.0		20.8				
Net Sales ($)	6329660M	6218436M	6803137M	21467M	110779M	107486M	448041M	1127864M	4987500M
Total Assets ($)	16965261M	17895849M	16392896M	213725M	839898M	770886M	2866982M	6483394M	5218011M

M = $ thousand   MM = $ million
See Pages viii through xx for Explanation of Ratios and Data

Current Data Sorted by Assets

Comparative Historical Data

Type of Statement	0-500M	500M-2MM	2-10MM	10-50MM	50-100MM	100-250MM		4/1/14-3/31/15 ALL	4/1/15-3/31/16 ALL
Unqualified	1	6	21	39	13	18		52	47
Reviewed	2		3	4				4	10
Compiled	3	2	1	2	1			8	10
Tax Returns	1	2	2	1				7	7
Other	16	12	25		8	15		98	79
		18 (4/1-9/30/18)		198 (10/1/18-3/31/19)					
NUMBER OF STATEMENTS	23	22	52	64	22	33		169	153
	%	%	%	%	%	%		%	%
ASSETS									
Cash & Equivalents	62.4	42.7	31.3	14.2	13.7	14.5		26.4	27.1
Trade Receivables (net)	2.8	.9	21.4	14.8	25.9	23.2		11.0	13.6
Inventory	.0	18.9	17.3	24.0	21.2	21.2		18.3	18.1
All Other Current	6.8	15.0	9.0	16.6	13.5	15.4		21.1	16.8
Total Current	72.0	77.4	79.0	69.7	74.2	74.3		76.8	75.5
Fixed Assets (net)	11.9	16.1	6.8	6.1	1.2	1.7		6.7	6.5
Intangibles (net)	5.5	2.0	3.3	3.7	3.2	5.1		2.6	3.3
All Other Non-Current	10.6	4.4	10.9	20.4	21.3	18.9		13.8	14.7
Total	100.0	100.0	100.0	100.0	100.0	100.0		100.0	100.0
LIABILITIES									
Notes Payable-Short Term	24.7	33.1	32.0	43.4	50.8	45.9		40.7	41.0
Cur. Mat.-L.T.D.	.0	.6	.8	1.3	1.2	3.0		1.0	.9
Trade Payables	7.5	2.3	3.9	4.8	2.5	2.3		3.0	3.2
Income Taxes Payable	.0	.0	.0	.0	.0	.1		.4	.3
All Other Current	9.3	4.9	7.9	7.7	6.0	7.8		8.6	13.0
Total Current	41.5	40.8	44.5	57.2	60.5	59.0		53.7	58.5
Long-Term Debt	2.0	6.5	3.6	11.4	6.7	4.8		5.2	5.0
Deferred Taxes	.0	.0	.1	.1	.7	.1		.2	.3
All Other Non-Current	.7	1.7	.3	3.0	2.2	2.5		2.8	1.6
Net Worth	55.8	50.9	51.4	28.3	29.9	33.7		38.1	34.6
Total Liabilities & Net Worth	100.0	100.0	100.0	100.0	100.0	100.0		100.0	100.0
INCOME DATA									
Net Sales	100.0	100.0	100.0	100.0	100.0	100.0		100.0	100.0
Gross Profit									
Operating Expenses	83.6	90.6	86.0	85.2	92.4	78.5		84.6	82.1
Operating Profit	16.4	9.4	14.0	14.8	7.6	21.5		15.4	17.9
All Other Expenses (net)	-.2	1.0	2.2	6.5	2.4	5.9		2.3	2.8
Profit Before Taxes	16.6	8.5	11.8	8.3	5.2	15.6		13.1	15.1
RATIOS									
Current	20.9	5.5	4.1	1.5	1.8	1.2		2.8	2.5
	10.3	1.9	1.6	1.2	1.1	1.1		1.3	1.2
	1.5	1.2	1.3	1.1	1.1	1.1		1.1	1.1
Quick	20.9	5.5	2.6	1.2	1.2	1.2		2.4	2.0
	8.6	1.2	1.2	.3	.6	.5		.5	.5
	1.1	.4	.5	.1	.1	.1		.1	.1
Sales/Receivables	0 UND	0 UND	0 UND	0 UND	3 127.6	3 136.4		0 UND	0 UND
	0 UND	0 UND	12 29.4	4 82.7	22 16.5	15 24.3		4 81.2	5 68.6
	0 UND	3 138.3	152 2.4	46 7.9	365 1.0	406 .9		31 11.6	30 12.3
Cost of Sales/Inventory									
Cost of Sales/Payables									
Sales/Working Capital	4.7	4.0	1.2	2.3	1.9	1.9		1.8	2.2
	12.1	7.1	2.1	4.6	4.2	4.9		3.7	4.7
	41.9	13.8	4.6	18.3	11.0	8.4		10.2	17.3
EBIT/Interest			12.1	5.3	17.1	5.8		14.7	11.1
		(35) 3.7	(37) 2.3	(14) 1.9	(16) 2.0			(114) 3.9	(108) 4.6
			1.0	.4	-.6	1.0		1.4	2.3
Net Profit + Depr., Dep., Amort./Cur. Mat. L/T/D									
Fixed/Worth	.0	.0	.0	.0	.0	.0		.0	.0
	.1	.0	.0	.1	.1	.0		.0	.0
	.3	.5	.1	.4	.1	.2		.2	.1
Debt/Worth	.0	.2	.4	2.1	2.1	1.2		.7	.8
	.1	1.1	1.4	3.4	3.4	4.8		2.3	2.8
	1.8	3.9	2.2	5.4	6.4	6.6		5.4	6.9
% Profit Before Taxes/Tangible Net Worth	169.6	73.8	40.9	21.7	21.3	22.6		54.8	64.4
	(21) 48.1	20.6	(51) 13.2	(62) 7.1	(21) 2.8	(32) 8.7		(164) 20.3	(144) 31.8
	6.9	-3.2	1.1	-4.1	-11.8	-1.2		6.2	12.6
% Profit Before Taxes/Total Assets	119.7	21.5	15.0	5.9	4.9	6.3		15.5	17.1
	20.2	7.4	7.1	1.8	.3	2.7		5.5	8.1
	1.3	-2.4	.9	-.6	-2.4	-.3		1.1	3.3
Sales/Net Fixed Assets	988.0	257.0	493.7	151.7	186.7	145.2		141.0	184.4
	82.8	103.6	80.8	46.5	57.8	53.0		48.1	71.9
	16.6	7.8	23.2	10.6	39.9	27.4		19.0	24.8
Sales/Total Assets	10.4	3.2	1.2	.8	.8	.7		1.1	1.3
	4.5	2.0	.8	.6	.6	.3		.5	.7
	1.7	.8	.4	.3	.3	.2		.4	.4
% Depr., Dep., Amort./Sales			.2	.3	.4	.4		.3	.2
		(29) .7	(44) .7	(15) .7	(20) .8			(116) .8	(109) .5
			1.1	1.4	1.5	1.6		1.4	1.0
% Officers', Directors' Owners' Comp/Sales								5.4	4.3
								(27) 9.8	(27) 8.2
								18.1	24.7
Net Sales ($)	21244M	65157M	328252M	1206361M	897616M	2290492M		3408042M	3958303M
Total Assets ($)	4324M	28533M	286494M	1748825M	1580948M	5278281M		6411635M	6283022M

M = $ thousand   MM = $ million
See Pages viii through xx for Explanation of Ratios and Data

Comparative Historical Data & Current Data Sorted by Sales

			Type of Statement						
57	62	98	Unqualified	3	7	12	16	21	39
4	3	9	Reviewed		2	4	1	1	1
2	6	9	Compiled	3	1	2	3		
12	9	6	Tax Returns	2	1		2	1	
32	55	94	Other	19	15	15	11	13	21
4/1/16- 3/31/17 ALL	4/1/17- 3/31/18 ALL	4/1/18- 3/31/19 ALL		0-1MM	1-3MM	3-5MM	5-10MM	10-25MM	25MM & OVER
					18 (4/1-9/30/18)		198 (10/1/18-3/31/19)		
107	135	216	NUMBER OF STATEMENTS	27	26	33	33	36	61
%	%	%	ASSETS	%	%	%	%	%	%
21.5	23.7	26.3	Cash & Equivalents	47.3	33.6	34.4	21.5	16.3	18.2
19.0	11.3	16.1	Trade Receivables (net)	10.5	18.3	11.6	18.5	15.8	19.1
12.8	19.9	18.6	Inventory	12.2	11.6	10.4	15.7	32.7	22.2
17.6	19.8	13.1	All Other Current	5.7	6.9	15.4	16.7	7.8	18.8
70.9	74.7	74.1	Total Current	75.7	70.4	71.7	72.3	72.5	78.2
8.7	6.9	6.8	Fixed Assets (net)	10.3	4.0	9.4	8.8	8.2	3.0
3.9	2.8	3.8	Intangibles (net)	9.0	3.6	.9	2.2	4.1	3.8
16.5	15.6	15.3	All Other Non-Current	4.9	22.0	18.0	16.7	15.1	15.0
100.0	100.0	100.0	Total	100.0	100.0	100.0	100.0	100.0	100.0
			LIABILITIES						
38.2	41.9	38.8	Notes Payable-Short Term	18.2	24.9	44.0	34.8	37.5	53.8
1.2	2.1	1.2	Cur. Mat.-L.T.D.	.2	.0	.6	1.4	2.1	1.8
3.2	3.5	4.0	Trade Payables	4.6	2.6	3.6	1.7	7.3	3.7
.2	.0	.0	Income Taxes Payable	.0	.0	.0	.0	.0	.0
6.9	9.6	7.5	All Other Current	2.5	16.2	3.2	9.8	6.8	7.4
49.7	57.2	51.4	Total Current	25.5	43.8	51.4	47.7	53.8	66.8
10.5	6.2	6.5	Long-Term Debt	5.2	7.7	7.2	11.0	8.8	2.5
.2	.2	.1	Deferred Taxes	.0	.0	.0	.0	.3	.3
2.8	2.4	1.8	All Other Non-Current	.6	2.6	1.2	3.2	1.7	1.7
36.7	34.0	40.1	Net Worth	68.7	45.9	40.3	38.1	35.4	28.7
100.0	100.0	100.0	Total Liabilities & Net Worth	100.0	100.0	100.0	100.0	100.0	100.0
			INCOME DATA						
100.0	100.0	100.0	Net Sales	100.0	100.0	100.0	100.0	100.0	100.0
			Gross Profit						
78.6	82.9	85.5	Operating Expenses	83.4	72.1	84.7	86.2	85.3	92.3
21.4	17.1	14.5	Operating Profit	16.6	27.9	15.3	13.8	14.7	7.7
4.9	4.0	3.7	All Other Expenses (net)	1.1	7.2	5.4	2.3	4.8	2.5
16.4	13.1	10.8	Profit Before Taxes	15.6	20.7	9.9	11.5	9.9	5.3
			RATIOS						
2.9	1.7	2.7		20.9	5.0	4.6	2.2	1.9	1.3
1.3	1.2	1.3	Current	7.5	1.5	1.9	1.5	1.2	1.1
1.1	1.1	1.1		1.5	1.2	1.2	1.2	1.1	1.1
2.1	1.1	1.8		20.9	4.0	4.2	1.8	1.6	1.1
1.0	.4	1.0	Quick	6.9	1.3	1.2	.9	.3	.3
.2	.2	.2		1.1	.4	.4	.4	.1	.1
0 UND	0 UND	0 UND		0 UND	0 UND	0 UND	1 347.5	0 UND	2 178.4
7 55.0	4 102.7	4 91.4	Sales/Receivables	0 UND	0 UND	0 UND	14 26.0	12 31.4	10 36.6
70 5.2	23 15.8	37 9.9		19 19.6	174 2.1	12 31.6	304 1.2	41 9.0	74 4.9
			Cost of Sales/Inventory						
			Cost of Sales/Payables						
1.7	1.6	1.9		.8	1.6	1.3	1.6	2.6	3.1
3.8	4.7	4.5	Sales/Working Capital	4.7	4.8	4.2	3.3	4.6	5.5
11.1	20.8	12.1		15.2	14.7	8.6	7.4	13.2	11.2
11.5	10.2	8.6			22.7	8.2	16.8	10.6	5.0
(65) 4.9	(94) 3.5	(118) 2.5	EBIT/Interest	(13) 6.2	(21) 2.3	(20) 4.8	(21) 2.4	(36) 1.9	
2.5	1.7	.8			.5	-.3	1.2	1.2	.5
		7.3	Net Profit + Depr., Dep.,						
	(13) 1.6		Amort./Cur. Mat. L/T/D						
		-.5							
.0	.0	.0		.0	.0	.0	.0	.0	.0
.0	.0	.0	Fixed/Worth	.0	.0	.0	.0	.1	.1
.1	.2	.2		.3	.1	.1	.3	.7	.2
1.0	1.1	.6		.1	.4	.3	1.1	1.1	2.0
2.5	3.1	2.3	Debt/Worth	.2	1.7	1.5	2.5	3.1	3.9
5.1	6.0	5.0		1.8	6.0	2.7	4.1	5.7	6.1
51.0	41.3	37.0	% Profit Before Taxes/Tangible	68.3	86.7	29.5	31.9	24.9	25.7
(102) 34.1	(131) 19.8	(209) 10.8	Net Worth	11.5	(24) 34.5	(32) 13.2	(32) 10.6	(35) 8.0	(59) 8.0
14.8	5.6	.0		1.6	3.1	1.9	-1.9	.5	-11.6
14.6	10.5	10.6	% Profit Before Taxes/Total	26.9	23.7	13.9	8.3	6.9	5.9
8.4	4.6	2.8	Assets	7.2	6.2	4.7	4.5	1.7	1.5
3.2	.9	-.3		.7	.7	.3	.1	.1	-1.9
347.2	228.9	246.6		UND	346.5	419.2	406.5	81.6	100.4
86.3	58.8	61.4	Sales/Net Fixed Assets	128.3	99.5	102.6	67.1	40.3	50.8
27.7	25.6	20.1		11.5	27.4	31.4	8.2	6.8	28.8
.9	.9	1.2		3.9	2.5	2.3	.9	1.1	.9
.6	.6	.7	Sales/Total Assets	1.2	.5	.8	.6	.6	.7
.3	.4	.3		.3	.3	.4	.3	.3	.4
.3	.3	.3			.2	.1	.2	.4	.4
(66) .5	(96) .6	(124) .7	% Depr., Dep., Amort./Sales	(12) .5	(19) .3	(23) .9	(25) .8	(40) .7	
1.4	.9	1.4			1.7	.7	1.4	1.9	1.3
4.3	9.5	4.6	% Officers', Directors'						
(22) 11.9	(14) 13.4	(29) 7.3	Owners' Comp/Sales						
26.6	22.9	19.7							
2662729M	2773060M	4809122M	Net Sales ($)	13745M	45497M	125852M	240004M	540936M	3843088M
4831093M	4980908M	8927405M	Total Assets ($)	33079M	144930M	367998M	624438M	1451545M	6305415M

M = $ thousand   MM = $ million
See Pages viii through xx for Explanation of Ratios and Data

Current Data Sorted by Assets | Comparative Historical Data

Type of Statement

0-500M	500M-2MM	2-10MM	10-50MM	50-100MM	100-250MM		4/1/14-3/31/15 ALL	4/1/15-3/31/16 ALL
	2	4	13	9	11	Unqualified	50	49
	1	2				Reviewed	6	3
			2		1	Compiled	8	8
3	1	1	1			Tax Returns	7	8
5	9	19	20	11	12	Other	73	71
	10 (4/1-9/30/18)		117 (10/1/18-3/31/19)					
8	13	26	36	20	24	**NUMBER OF STATEMENTS**	144	139

0-500M	500M-2MM	2-10MM	10-50MM	50-100MM	100-250MM		4/1/14-3/31/15 ALL	4/1/15-3/31/16 ALL
%	%	%	%	%	%	**ASSETS**	%	%
	45.3	31.9	27.2	24.1	22.4	Cash & Equivalents	34.6	31.1
	10.6	15.1	19.1	11.9	12.9	Trade Receivables (net)	20.2	20.1
	.0	.2	1.2	2.9	2.2	Inventory	1.7	1.9
	17.1	11.7	11.3	15.4	11.9	All Other Current	11.6	9.5
	73.0	59.0	58.9	54.2	49.4	Total Current	68.1	62.6
	5.4	16.8	12.7	4.6	4.6	Fixed Assets (net)	11.0	11.1
	5.6	14.2	17.0	31.1	35.5	Intangibles (net)	9.4	12.7
	16.0	10.1	11.4	10.1	10.6	All Other Non-Current	11.5	13.6
	100.0	100.0	100.0	100.0	100.0	Total	100.0	100.0
						LIABILITIES		
	10.7	6.4	5.0	2.9	6.5	Notes Payable-Short Term	11.7	5.7
	.2	3.1	2.6	1.1	1.8	Cur. Mat.-L.T.D.	5.1	6.1
	5.7	10.0	12.7	6.9	12.9	Trade Payables	12.4	11.6
	.0	.3	.3	.0	.1	Income Taxes Payable	.1	.1
	2.2	26.0	23.6	34.9	26.9	All Other Current	24.0	23.8
	18.7	45.8	44.3	45.9	48.2	Total Current	53.3	47.4
	27.7	15.9	15.8	25.3	15.7	Long-Term Debt	19.7	23.0
	.0	.0	.0	.4	.3	Deferred Taxes	.2	.2
	11.7	4.6	7.9	6.7	3.4	All Other Non-Current	8.6	7.6
	41.9	33.7	31.9	21.8	32.4	Net Worth	18.2	21.8
	100.0	100.0	100.0	100.0	100.0	Total Liabilities & Net Worth	100.0	100.0
						INCOME DATA		
	100.0	100.0	100.0	100.0	100.0	Net Sales	100.0	100.0
						Gross Profit		
	83.4	83.9	85.8	93.0	93.0	Operating Expenses	86.6	90.1
	16.6	16.1	14.2	7.0	7.0	Operating Profit	13.4	9.9
	2.6	1.0	2.5	3.2	2.9	All Other Expenses (net)	1.7	2.7
	14.0	15.2	11.6	3.8	4.0	Profit Before Taxes	11.7	7.2

RATIOS

0-500M	500M-2MM	2-10MM	10-50MM	50-100MM	100-250MM		4/1/14-3/31/15	4/1/15-3/31/16
	16.1	3.6	2.7	1.5	1.2	Current	2.5	3.0
	5.3	1.2	1.6	1.3	.9		1.3	1.3
	3.2	.7	1.0	1.0	.7		1.0	.9
	7.9	3.1	2.2	1.2	.9	Quick	2.0	2.2
	4.0	1.1	1.0	1.0	.7		1.1	1.1
	2.0	.5	.6	.6	.4		.7	.6
0 UND	0 999.8 / 1 510.1	6 56.7	17 21.0	15 24.8		Sales/Receivables	4 95.8	8 47.0
0 999.8	12 31.3	25 14.4	32 11.3	34 10.7			23 16.0	26 13.9
32 11.3	37 9.9	54 6.7	60 6.1	61 6.0			56 6.5	45 8.1
						Cost of Sales/Inventory		
						Cost of Sales/Payables		
	1.7	6.2	4.2	3.8	4.6	Sales/Working Capital	4.6	4.1
	6.6	47.1	9.5	10.3	-40.4		10.8	14.6
	13.7	-19.4	NM	42.2	-16.0		-78.4	-55.5
	50.9	41.8	17.2	49.7	9.0	EBIT/Interest	53.9	51.2
	(10) 4.6	(20) 11.4	(24) 5.2	(17) 2.2	(21) .8		(104) 7.0	(101) 8.8
	1.6	3.0	2.0	-1.3	.4		1.7	1.2
			40.4			Net Profit + Depr., Dep., Amort./Cur. Mat. L/T/D	19.1	20.5
			(10) 6.0				(22) 4.6	(17) 4.2
			2.0				1.9	1.7
	.0	.2	.0	.1	.1	Fixed/Worth	.1	.1
	.1	.5	.3	.4	-2.9		.4	.4
	NM	-.6	1.1	-.4	.0		UND	-1.4
	.3	.5	.5	1.6	4.1	Debt/Worth	.8	.7
	1.3	2.5	3.2	11.2	-27.6		3.4	2.9
	NM	-3.6	-13.0	-1.8	-1.8		-23.4	-14.1
	285.0	117.1	115.9	85.1	57.9	% Profit Before Taxes/Tangible Net Worth	90.2	83.5
	(10) 80.4	(16) 65.8	(26) 41.7	(12) 46.5	(10) 41.4		(106) 40.7	(95) 34.6
	7.5	38.0	6.2	13.2	1.8		10.7	9.1
	64.0	47.7	20.4	18.6	11.1	% Profit Before Taxes/Total Assets	36.9	28.7
	21.4	21.0	5.2	1.7	.2		11.6	9.1
	2.7	4.9	.7	-6.9	-2.2		1.1	.0
	UND	143.2	133.1	54.0	100.2	Sales/Net Fixed Assets	70.2	80.7
	75.1	28.2	27.3	31.3	43.4		24.1	29.8
	34.9	10.5	10.0	17.4	20.9		12.0	12.7
	4.2	4.3	2.5	1.4	1.3	Sales/Total Assets	3.5	3.0
	2.5	2.6	1.6	.7	1.0		1.7	1.5
	1.3	1.5	.8	.5	.6		.7	.8
		.4	.8		.6	% Depr., Dep., Amort./Sales	.8	.7
	(16) 1.1	(26) 2.4			(10) 2.3		(90) 2.0	(76) 1.8
	1.6	6.1			4.2		3.2	3.1
						% Officers', Directors' Owners' Comp/Sales	3.1	1.9
							(23) 8.6	(24) 5.7
							16.7	12.3
37499M	42646M	456806M	1392496M	1502969M	4095262M	Net Sales ($)	6506646M	7354610M
2208M	13566M	121378M	809200M	1476031M	4151275M	Total Assets ($)	5127537M	5777075M

Comparative Historical Data

Current Data Sorted by Sales

				0-1MM	1-3MM	3-5MM	5-10MM	10-25MM	25MM & OVER
			Type of Statement						
45	38	39	Unqualified	1		1	4	4	29
1	2	3	Reviewed			1		2	
3	5	3	Compiled			1			2
7	11	6	Tax Returns	3		1	2		
79	83	76	Other	4	9	5	9	13	36
4/1/16-3/31/17 ALL	4/1/17-3/31/18 ALL	4/1/18-3/31/19 ALL		10 (4/1-9/30/18)			117 (10/1/18-3/31/19)		
135	139	127	**NUMBER OF STATEMENTS**	8	9	9	15	19	67
%	%	%	**ASSETS**	%	%	%	%	%	%
33.0	33.3	29.0	Cash & Equivalents				15.7	33.8	25.1
18.8	15.2	14.6	Trade Receivables (net)				20.9	13.5	15.4
1.1	1.2	1.3	Inventory				.0	.2	2.3
8.8	10.2	12.1	All Other Current				22.7	9.6	10.4
61.7	59.9	56.9	Total Current				59.3	57.2	53.2
9.6	10.8	10.8	Fixed Assets (net)				12.7	12.0	10.1
16.0	19.0	20.3	Intangibles (net)				8.4	15.1	27.3
12.7	10.4	12.0	All Other Non-Current				19.6	15.7	9.5
100.0	100.0	100.0	Total				100.0	100.0	100.0
			LIABILITIES						
6.3	5.8	7.3	Notes Payable-Short Term				8.7	3.2	5.5
6.2	3.2	1.9	Cur. Mat.-L.T.D.				2.3	.5	2.4
10.6	9.6	11.2	Trade Payables				4.1	18.0	11.7
.1	.1	.2	Income Taxes Payable				.0	.6	.2
24.9	25.7	24.2	All Other Current				46.1	19.6	25.3
48.2	44.3	44.7	Total Current				61.2	41.7	45.0
18.2	16.7	18.2	Long-Term Debt				10.2	18.4	18.3
.2	.1	.1	Deferred Taxes				.0	.1	.2
5.4	8.2	6.4	All Other Non-Current				8.7	16.7	3.1
28.1	30.6	30.6	Net Worth				19.9	23.1	33.4
100.0	100.0	100.0	Total Liabilties & Net Worth				100.0	100.0	100.0
			INCOME DATA						
100.0	100.0	100.0	Net Sales				100.0	100.0	100.0
			Gross Profit						
87.9	89.5	88.5	Operating Expenses				86.3	85.2	92.9
12.1	10.5	11.5	Operating Profit				13.7	14.8	7.1
3.4	2.5	2.3	All Other Expenses (net)				.7	3.3	2.3
8.6	8.0	9.2	Profit Before Taxes				13.0	11.5	4.8
			RATIOS						
2.3	2.7	2.7					1.8	6.4	2.0
1.3	1.5	1.3	Current				1.0	2.5	1.2
.9	.9	.9					.6	.9	.8
2.1	2.3	2.2					1.8	3.4	1.4
1.1	1.1	1.0	Quick				.7	1.4	.8
.6	.6	.6					.1	.5	.5
6 57.6	4 103.8	4 99.0					5 74.6	0 UND	11 31.9
27 13.3	21 17.5	25 14.7	Sales/Receivables				35 10.4	31 11.8	27 13.6
43 8.4	53 6.9	45 8.2					46 8.0	53 6.9	45 8.2
			Cost of Sales/Inventory						
			Cost of Sales/Payables						
4.9	4.3	4.4					4.4	3.4	7.1
14.2	13.2	15.3	Sales/Working Capital				12.7	8.7	25.3
-67.1	-38.0	-26.7					-12.2	-24.5	-26.6
20.7	35.5	26.2					104.1	100.0	24.9
(91) 4.9	(97) 5.9	(97) 4.0	EBIT/Interest				(11) 17.3	(10) 6.5	(59) 2.3
.8	.7	.5					5.7	-.5	.3
29.8	54.0	16.5							7.5
(13) 3.1	(17) 2.4	(16) 3.8	Net Profit + Depr., Dep., Amort./Cur. Mat. L/T/D						(12) 3.0
1.9	-1.6	.7							-2.0
.1	.1	.1					.1	.0	.1
.4	.7	.4	Fixed/Worth				.3	.3	.8
-4.4	-.3	-1.3					-6.9	.8	-.2
.9	.8	.9					1.0	.3	1.6
5.0	3.1	5.8	Debt/Worth				8.0	.9	7.0
-13.1	-5.1	-5.7					-15.6	-5.7	-3.7
91.5	117.4	105.2					84.6	144.3	96.2
(94) 46.0	(94) 40.8	(78) 46.1	% Profit Before Taxes/Tangible Net Worth				(11) 48.6	(14) 45.6	(37) 45.4
17.6	1.7	13.7					16.1	19.4	10.1
24.4	25.1	25.2					49.3	30.0	18.0
11.0	7.1	7.2	% Profit Before Taxes/Total Assets				12.4	13.5	3.0
1.0	-.3	-1.7					1.7	.7	-2.6
107.0	100.5	106.4					221.0	135.3	67.4
32.3	32.4	36.1	Sales/Net Fixed Assets				68.1	28.0	30.5
15.5	13.5	13.3					12.3	9.5	14.5
3.2	2.8	2.9					3.2	3.0	2.8
1.7	1.4	1.6	Sales/Total Assets				1.9	1.6	1.4
.7	.7	.7					.6	.9	.7
.7	.7	.7					.7	.6	.7
(74) 1.3	(75) 1.8	(70) 1.4	% Depr., Dep., Amort./Sales				(10) 1.2	(10) 1.7	(40) 1.8
2.9	3.6	3.5					3.7	7.2	3.0
1.8	1.9	2.9							
(23) 3.1	(19) 6.8	(17) 7.6	% Officers', Directors' Owners' Comp/Sales						
15.6	13.0	14.6							
9286968M	8986887M	7527678M	Net Sales ($)	5176M	17815M	33739M	103302M	312584M	7055062M
7082666M	7784026M	6573658M	Total Assets ($)	27993M	18013M	78883M	239491M	315159M	5894119M

M = $ thousand   MM = $ million
See Pages viii through xx for Explanation of Ratios and Data

Current Data Sorted by Assets | | | | | | | Comparative Historical Data

0-500M	500M-2MM	2-10MM	10-50MM	50-100MM	100-250MM	Type of Statement	4/1/14-3/31/15 ALL	4/1/15-3/31/16 ALL
	3	7	15	6	13	Unqualified	47	44
		1		1		Reviewed		2
2	1	3	1			Compiled	2	3
1	1					Tax Returns	5	12
2	5	7	8	2	6	Other	31	30
	7 (4/1-9/30/18)	78 (10/1/18-3/31/19)						
5	10	18	24	9	19	NUMBER OF STATEMENTS	85	91
%	%	%	%	%	%	**ASSETS**	%	%
	60.5	38.6	19.7		17.9	Cash & Equivalents	22.0	22.4
	2.4	24.4	15.6		20.2	Trade Receivables (net)	22.7	20.4
	.1	.5	.6		.8	Inventory	2.6	2.9
	5.2	10.1	21.1		27.9	All Other Current	22.0	23.7
	68.3	73.6	57.1		66.8	Total Current	69.3	69.3
	15.5	7.6	12.3		7.5	Fixed Assets (net)	9.1	11.7
	13.7	8.5	6.8		15.2	Intangibles (net)	6.6	5.8
	2.5	10.4	23.9		10.6	All Other Non-Current	14.9	13.2
	100.0	100.0	100.0		100.0	Total	100.0	100.0
						LIABILITIES		
	22.0	25.3	19.2		25.1	Notes Payable-Short Term	27.9	33.0
	1.4	.7	2.1		.5	Cur. Mat.-L.T.D.	3.9	3.2
	7.7	7.1	7.5		7.9	Trade Payables	7.1	10.2
	.1	.4	.0		.2	Income Taxes Payable	.3	.3
	7.6	4.9	12.7		12.1	All Other Current	10.7	8.3
	38.8	38.4	41.5		45.8	Total Current	49.8	54.9
	8.8	2.4	13.5		16.8	Long-Term Debt	10.8	13.4
	.0	.0	.0		.6	Deferred Taxes	.4	.4
	11.7	6.3	3.4		2.5	All Other Non-Current	7.2	6.7
	40.7	52.8	41.6		34.2	Net Worth	31.8	24.6
	100.0	100.0	100.0		100.0	Total Liabilties & Net Worth	100.0	100.0
						INCOME DATA		
	100.0	100.0	100.0		100.0	Net Sales	100.0	100.0
						Gross Profit		
	79.5	79.2	84.3		85.8	Operating Expenses	82.4	81.1
	20.5	20.8	15.7		14.2	Operating Profit	17.6	18.9
	4.2	5.4	4.1		3.9	All Other Expenses (net)	3.8	3.7
	16.3	15.4	11.6		10.3	Profit Before Taxes	13.8	15.3
						RATIOS		
	3.5	3.1	2.8		2.3	Current	2.2	2.8
	1.2	2.1	1.2		1.2		1.2	1.2
	1.1	1.1	1.0		1.0		1.0	1.0
	3.5	2.9	2.2		1.6	Quick	2.1	1.9
	1.1	1.6	1.0		.9		1.0	.9
	1.0	1.1	.3		.1		.1	.2
	0 UND	0 UND	1 384.6		22 16.3	Sales/Receivables	0 999.8	0 UND
	0 UND	8 47.9	35 10.4		51 7.1		15 23.6	17 21.8
	9 42.4	107 3.4	101 3.6		87 4.2		101 3.6	76 4.8
						Cost of Sales/Inventory		
						Cost of Sales/Payables		
	2.5	.9	3.1		2.1	Sales/Working Capital	2.0	2.7
	7.5	4.4	9.9		6.1		7.3	6.6
	23.3	10.2	56.8		19.0		359.0	79.9
		5.8	6.7		7.8	EBIT/Interest	8.5	10.3
		(14) 2.1	(12) 1.9		(12) 4.4		(47) 3.7	(55) 3.6
		-.1	.2		1.7		1.7	1.5
						Net Profit + Depr., Dep., Amort./Cur. Mat. L/T/D		
	.1	.0	.0		.1	Fixed/Worth	.0	.0
	.3	.1	.2		.1		.1	.1
	4.5	.5	.6		4.5		.5	.6
	.8	.4	.6		2.0	Debt/Worth	1.2	1.0
	3.3	.7	1.8		3.2		3.3	4.3
	9.9	6.2	6.6		9.9		8.4	10.6
		43.3	37.8		47.6	% Profit Before Taxes/Tangible Net Worth	43.5	66.7
		12.2	(22) 15.9		(15) 4.7		(75) 18.5	(79) 23.1
		-3.9	-.2		-1.7		4.6	4.0
	19.9	17.2	12.9		9.6	% Profit Before Taxes/Total Assets	12.3	18.3
	7.2	3.6	2.7		2.7		4.1	3.9
	.5	-1.0	-.4		.3		.8	1.1
	56.4	85.1	121.6		45.9	Sales/Net Fixed Assets	98.9	130.3
	36.1	24.7	27.6		23.2		45.3	41.7
	6.1	5.0	5.7		9.6		15.6	11.8
	1.8	2.3	1.3		1.3	Sales/Total Assets	1.5	2.0
	1.0	.9	.8		.6		.6	.6
	.5	.2	.3		.3		.3	.3
		.6	.5		1.1	% Depr., Dep., Amort./Sales	.4	.5
		(15) 1.2	(15) 1.3		(14) 1.7		(55) 1.1	(64) 1.2
		2.3	3.5		2.6		1.9	3.1
						% Officers', Directors' Owners' Comp/Sales		2.9
							(17)	9.3
								26.1
4427M	16135M	107636M	763758M	420291M	2229511M	Net Sales ($)	3041888M	3172406M
1269M	13138M	105004M	744519M	650411M	3181569M	Total Assets ($)	4644547M	4549430M

M = $ thousand   MM = $ million
See Pages viii through xx for Explanation of Ratios and Data

Comparative Historical Data — Current Data Sorted by Sales

			Type of Statement	0-1MM	1-3MM	3-5MM	5-10MM	10-25MM	25MM & OVER
38	43	44	Unqualified		4	4	4	9	23
1		2	Reviewed	1					1
7	3	7	Compiled	2	1	1	1	2	
2	1	2	Tax Returns	2					
27	20	30	Other	5	5	5	3	3	9
4/1/16-3/31/17 ALL	4/1/17-3/31/18 ALL	4/1/18-3/31/19 ALL		7 (4/1-9/30/18)			78 (10/1/18-3/31/19)		
75	67	85	**NUMBER OF STATEMENTS**	10	10	10	8	14	33
%	%	%	**ASSETS**	%	%	%	%	%	%
27.4	25.2	29.6	Cash & Equivalents	34.7	45.9	40.6		22.2	22.6
21.9	19.0	17.7	Trade Receivables (net)	26.9	19.8	3.5		19.6	16.0
2.0	1.4	.9	Inventory	4.1	.1	1.1		.9	.4
22.4	26.7	19.4	All Other Current	.2	4.6	16.9		19.5	33.4
73.8	72.3	67.7	Total Current	65.9	70.4	62.0		62.2	72.3
9.7	9.0	9.0	Fixed Assets (net)	16.0	2.3	15.1		11.1	7.5
6.3	5.6	9.7	Intangibles (net)	10.7	5.6	3.0		14.0	10.9
10.2	13.1	13.6	All Other Non-Current	7.4	21.7	19.8		12.7	9.3
100.0	100.0	100.0	Total	100.0	100.0	100.0		100.0	100.0
			LIABILITIES						
26.1	26.0	22.1	Notes Payable-Short Term	22.4	29.0	18.1		24.2	24.3
1.8	2.1	1.9	Cur. Mat.-L.T.D.	1.3	.1	2.3		.6	2.7
10.9	9.1	7.5	Trade Payables	6.6	8.2	9.4		7.7	8.5
.3	.1	.2	Income Taxes Payable	.1	.1	.0		.5	.1
15.2	17.6	10.0	All Other Current	3.9	2.7	7.3		5.6	16.5
54.2	54.9	41.7	Total Current	34.3	40.1	37.1		38.6	52.2
7.1	7.9	11.0	Long-Term Debt	17.5	1.0	6.5		15.2	8.6
.2	.1	.2	Deferred Taxes	.0	.0	.0		.0	.5
2.4	6.0	5.5	All Other Non-Current	15.9	6.8	7.0		5.6	2.3
36.1	31.2	41.6	Net Worth	32.3	52.0	49.4		40.5	36.4
100.0	100.0	100.0	Total Liabilities & Net Worth	100.0	100.0	100.0		100.0	100.0
			INCOME DATA						
100.0	100.0	100.0	Net Sales	100.0	100.0	100.0		100.0	100.0
			Gross Profit						
86.2	84.3	81.8	Operating Expenses	56.5	69.6	83.6		92.8	90.5
13.8	15.7	18.2	Operating Profit	43.5	30.4	16.4		7.2	9.5
3.8	3.5	3.9	All Other Expenses (net)	7.6	5.0	5.3		5.1	1.0
10.0	12.2	14.3	Profit Before Taxes	35.8	25.4	11.1		2.0	8.5
			RATIOS						
2.9	2.5	3.0		6.3	3.1	3.9		2.9	2.0
1.2	1.3	1.2	Current	1.5	1.3	1.7		1.7	1.2
1.1	1.1	1.1		1.1	1.0	.9		1.1	1.1
2.3	2.4	2.5		6.3	2.9	2.8		2.9	1.6
1.0	.9	1.1	Quick	1.2	1.2	1.1		1.4	.9
.3	.2	.5		1.0	.9	.4		1.0	.9
0 UND	0 999.8	0 UND		0 UND	0 UND	0 UND		1 316.7	3 109.0
21 17.4	24 15.2	15 23.9	Sales/Receivables	0 UND	10 37.3	1 546.7		46 7.9	23 15.8
111 3.3	63 5.8	81 4.5		146 2.5	45 8.1	11 32.5		89 4.1	74 4.9
			Cost of Sales/Inventory						
			Cost of Sales/Payables						
3.3	3.2	2.5		.8	1.2	1.6		4.4	2.7
5.9	6.1	6.0	Sales/Working Capital	4.0	7.5	6.6		6.0	6.1
22.0	22.3	18.8		11.2	NM	NM		15.4	18.7
10.7	33.1	15.0							36.3
(41) 3.7	(35) 4.5	(55) 4.6	EBIT/Interest					(18) 6.0	
1.5	1.5	.4							2.2
			Net Profit + Depr., Dep., Amort./Cur. Mat. L/T/D						
.0	.0	.0		.0	.0	.0		.0	.0
.1	.1	.1	Fixed/Worth	1.0	.0	.1		.1	.1
.6	.2	.5		-.6	.3	.6		1.2	.4
.8	.7	.7		.3	.2	.5		1.1	1.8
3.2	2.3	2.5	Debt/Worth	11.6	1.9	.8		2.3	3.3
8.0	5.1	5.9		-6.4	5.1	3.2		8.1	5.3
65.5	50.3	41.0			95.6	24.1		46.6	44.4
(68) 22.2	(63) 21.9	(76) 15.7	% Profit Before Taxes/Tangible Net Worth		17.3	8.5		(13) 3.2	(29) 15.9
4.7	5.1	-.9			-13.9	-1.2		-7.6	-1.9
19.3	23.2	13.7		58.4	34.0	8.0		5.4	11.4
5.6	6.4	3.2	% Profit Before Taxes/Total Assets	10.6	6.9	4.3		.2	4.7
.7	.8	-.1		1.9	-.6	-.4		-2.1	-.1
107.7	91.5	99.9		UND	UND	63.2		123.0	53.7
38.9	35.9	29.8	Sales/Net Fixed Assets	7.6	58.4	24.4		75.8	27.7
15.5	14.9	9.0		1.9	14.1	4.9		7.2	14.8
2.8	1.9	1.4		1.5	1.5	1.6		2.3	1.4
1.0	.8	.8	Sales/Total Assets	.6	.8	.7		1.1	.7
.4	.5	.4		.1	.2	.3		.5	.5
.5	.7	.6						.5	.9
(55) .9	(47) 1.1	(58) 1.2	% Depr., Dep., Amort./Sales					(10) .6	(24) 1.5
2.2	1.8	2.3						2.8	2.2
2.8		3.1							
(16) 4.4		(15) 6.8	% Officers', Directors' Owners' Comp/Sales						
9.0		13.2							
3420868M	3764485M	3541758M	Net Sales ($)	4843M	19144M	39889M	63886M	242733M	3171263M
4012774M	3834779M	4695910M	Total Assets ($)	19087M	50562M	119914M	338639M	412131M	3755577M

M = $ thousand   MM = $ million
See Pages viii through xx for Explanation of Ratios and Data

FINANCE—Investment Banking and Securities Dealing NAICS 523110

Current Data Sorted by Assets | Comparative Historical Data

0-500M	500M-2MM	2-10MM	10-50MM	50-100MM	100-250MM	Type of Statement	4/1/14-3/31/15 ALL	4/1/15-3/31/16 ALL
	2	3	5	5	1	Unqualified	22	18
		2				Reviewed	2	2
		1				Compiled		3
2		1	1			Tax Returns	11	13
2	6	5	7	2		Other	12	22
	3 (4/1-9/30/18)		43 (10/1/18-3/31/19)					
4	10	12	12	7	1	NUMBER OF STATEMENTS	47	58
%	%	%	%	%	%	ASSETS	%	%
	23.5	21.7	38.1			Cash & Equivalents	38.5	28.5
	22.0	7.2	18.2			Trade Receivables (net)	15.5	16.3
	3.6	4.2	5.6			Inventory	7.3	2.9
	11.2	10.7	14.3			All Other Current	6.4	9.5
	60.2	43.9	76.2			Total Current	67.6	57.2
	6.8	40.8	2.8			Fixed Assets (net)	12.8	16.8
	21.5	5.7	7.0			Intangibles (net)	9.6	11.5
	11.4	9.7	14.0			All Other Non-Current	10.0	14.5
	100.0	100.0	100.0			Total	100.0	100.0
						LIABILITIES		
	12.4	13.7	7.5			Notes Payable-Short Term	5.2	8.7
	3.4	1.9	1.3			Cur. Mat.-L.T.D.	1.1	5.5
	16.1	2.8	3.9			Trade Payables	6.2	7.9
	.2	.1	.0			Income Taxes Payable	.4	.2
	53.8	4.6	18.1			All Other Current	13.0	10.5
	85.9	23.1	30.7			Total Current	26.0	32.9
	5.7	33.9	8.2			Long-Term Debt	15.6	22.1
	1.0	.7	.4			Deferred Taxes	.4	.5
	.0	3.5	13.9			All Other Non-Current	7.2	14.9
	7.4	38.7	46.8			Net Worth	50.8	29.7
	100.0	100.0	100.0			Total Liabilities & Net Worth	100.0	100.0
						INCOME DATA		
	100.0	100.0	100.0			Net Sales	100.0	100.0
						Gross Profit		
	76.3	53.5	73.6			Operating Expenses	74.4	74.5
	23.7	46.5	26.4			Operating Profit	25.6	25.5
	1.9	15.7	3.3			All Other Expenses (net)	2.1	4.8
	21.8	30.7	23.1			Profit Before Taxes	23.6	20.7
						RATIOS		
	3.1	8.5	7.5				5.6	4.5
	1.6	1.5	3.8			Current	2.5	1.5
	1.0	.4	1.9				1.4	1.0
	2.3	2.5	5.9				5.5	3.7
	1.3	1.0	1.8			Quick	2.1	1.3
	.6	.2	1.2				1.2	.8
0 UND	0 UND	6 63.5					0 UND	0 UND
21 17.5	2 206.3	18 20.1				Sales/Receivables	14 25.2	7 54.2
76 4.8	83 4.4	38 9.6					48 7.6	60 6.1
						Cost of Sales/Inventory		
						Cost of Sales/Payables		
	4.4	2.3	2.1				2.6	3.0
	10.2	13.1	3.7			Sales/Working Capital	4.8	5.9
	NM	-4.3	10.8				12.7	NM
							210.1	21.1
						EBIT/Interest	(22) 27.6	(33) 6.1
							3.0	2.2
						Net Profit + Depr., Dep., Amort./Cur. Mat. L/T/D		
	.0	.0	.0				.0	.0
	.2	.1	.1			Fixed/Worth	.1	.1
	-.4	15.3	.1				.5	3.3
	.4	.4	.6				.4	.5
	1.6	2.3	1.1			Debt/Worth	.7	2.1
	-4.4	17.4	5.3				5.2	11.8
		98.3	74.8				122.4	54.5
	(10) 39.0	(11) 38.7				% Profit Before Taxes/Tangible Net Worth	(40) 26.1	(46) 26.2
	12.3	11.2					4.3	5.9
	46.3	54.0	26.1				61.0	27.5
	19.7	4.9	19.3			% Profit Before Taxes/Total Assets	10.6	8.7
	-.1	2.4	6.2				1.0	1.4
	718.6	216.1	UND				233.3	654.4
	117.9	16.0	429.5			Sales/Net Fixed Assets	66.0	57.8
	22.8	.2	30.1				22.0	12.5
	3.1	1.8	2.2				2.5	2.5
	2.4	.3	1.5			Sales/Total Assets	1.3	1.4
	.7	.1	1.1				.6	.5
							.2	.3
						% Depr., Dep., Amort./Sales	(32) .5	(29) 1.0
							1.4	3.2
							4.1	3.9
						% Officers', Directors' Owners' Comp/Sales	(13) 10.6	(17) 11.8
							15.3	18.4
2649M	27336M	64460M	576658M	329013M	112750M	Net Sales ($)	1614024M	1845285M
264M	11746M	63593M	343019M	428909M	245842M	Total Assets ($)	1403408M	2127751M

© RMA 2019

M = $ thousand   MM = $ million
See Pages viii through xx for Explanation of Ratios and Data

Comparative Historical Data | Current Data Sorted by Sales

			Type of Statement						
22	15	16	Unqualified	1	2	2	1	1	9
2	2	2	Reviewed	1				1	
3	2	1	Compiled	1					
9	8	5	Tax Returns	3	1		1		
17	16	22	Other	5	3	3	3	3	5
4/1/16-3/31/17 ALL	4/1/17-3/31/18 ALL	4/1/18-3/31/19 ALL		0-1MM	3 (4/1-9/30/18) 1-3MM	3-5MM	43 (10/1/18-3/31/19) 5-10MM	10-25MM	25MM & OVER
53	43	46	**NUMBER OF STATEMENTS**	11	6	5	5	5	14
%	%	%	**ASSETS**	%	%	%	%	%	%
30.0	37.4	32.7	Cash & Equivalents	17.8					49.1
16.1	12.7	14.3	Trade Receivables (net)	13.3					12.8
2.7	1.0	4.2	Inventory	.0					7.5
3.8	5.3	9.4	All Other Current	3.6					6.9
52.5	56.4	60.6	Total Current	34.7					76.2
11.3	13.4	13.7	Fixed Assets (net)	43.3					4.4
7.1	8.7	12.0	Intangibles (net)	15.5					11.9
29.1	21.5	13.8	All Other Non-Current	6.5					7.5
100.0	100.0	100.0	Total	100.0					100.0
			LIABILITIES						
4.9	7.7	21.0	Notes Payable-Short Term	57.5					8.4
2.0	1.0	1.6	Cur. Mat.-L.T.D.	3.3					1.1
8.1	9.1	5.8	Trade Payables	.7					4.7
.0	.1	.1	Income Taxes Payable	.0					.0
21.1	23.1	21.8	All Other Current	1.2					23.7
36.1	41.0	50.3	Total Current	62.8					37.8
18.6	13.0	14.8	Long-Term Debt	37.0					7.6
.5	.2	.6	Deferred Taxes	.0					.6
8.0	6.1	4.6	All Other Non-Current	1.6					6.1
36.8	39.7	29.7	Net Worth	-1.3					47.8
100.0	100.0	100.0	Total Liabilities & Net Worth	100.0					100.0
			INCOME DATA						
100.0	100.0	100.0	Net Sales	100.0					100.0
			Gross Profit						
71.6	74.7	68.6	Operating Expenses	43.5					84.9
28.4	25.3	31.4	Operating Profit	56.5					15.1
4.9	3.5	5.9	All Other Expenses (net)	17.0					-.1
23.5	21.8	25.5	Profit Before Taxes	39.5					15.2
			RATIOS						
3.0	4.7	5.6		2.4					5.2
1.4	1.5	1.9	Current	1.0					1.9
.8	.9	1.1		.2					1.4
2.8	4.3	4.6		2.0					5.1
1.2	1.3	1.6	Quick	.5					1.8
.5	.7	.7		.2					.8
0 UND	0 UND	0 UND		0 UND				7	48.9
13 27.4	4 87.6	13 27.1	Sales/Receivables	0 UND				19	19.3
45 8.1	43 8.5	43 8.5		126 2.9				39	9.3
			Cost of Sales/Inventory						
			Cost of Sales/Payables						
2.5	2.5	1.9		4.0					2.4
9.7	9.1	6.0	Sales/Working Capital	-140.8					3.7
-21.2	-62.3	35.8		-1.5					17.5
24.3	70.2	14.5							14.1
(28) 6.2	(21) 5.6	(26) 4.8	EBIT/Interest					(11)	8.8
3.2	1.7	2.0							3.1
			Net Profit + Depr., Dep., Amort./Cur. Mat. L/T/D						
.0	.0	.0		.0					.0
.1	.1	.1	Fixed/Worth	.1					.1
.5	1.1	.4		19.0					.2
.5	.3	.5		1.0					.8
1.7	1.3	1.4	Debt/Worth	3.2					1.6
8.1	5.7	7.1		-15.1					4.7
91.1	94.6	79.8							74.8
(44) 19.8	(37) 34.5	(39) 38.7	% Profit Before Taxes/Tangible Net Worth					(13)	41.1
3.9	9.8	9.9							15.6
37.7	45.9	27.7		267.1					25.5
6.9	9.6	11.4	% Profit Before Taxes/Total Assets	10.1					10.2
.9	1.7	3.6		3.3					6.3
413.5	275.3	UND		UND					380.7
72.4	50.0	172.4	Sales/Net Fixed Assets	8.7					67.5
23.7	11.4	23.2		.2					26.6
2.9	4.0	2.9		4.2					2.4
1.0	1.7	1.3	Sales/Total Assets	.2					1.5
.3	.4	.4		.1					1.1
.3	.4	.2							
(30) .8	(25) 1.4	(23) .7	% Depr., Dep., Amort./Sales						
2.9	2.3	2.7							
3.6		2.5							
(12) 5.1		(12) 6.4	% Officers', Directors' Owners' Comp/Sales						
36.2		12.7							
1710426M	1462349M	1112866M	Net Sales ($)	5387M	11019M	19273M	32290M	91025M	953872M
2127865M	1371524M	1093373M	Total Assets ($)	30145M	8220M	125194M	98389M	106095M	725330M

M = $ thousand   MM = $ million
See Pages viii through xx for Explanation of Ratios and Data

Current Data Sorted by Assets   Comparative Historical Data

						Type of Statement		
		1	6	7	5	4	Unqualified	28	30
			1				Reviewed	2	4
1			1				Compiled	1	3
8	4		1	3		1	Tax Returns	15	17
4	1	12 (4/1-9/30/18)	6	56 (10/1/18-3/31/19)	3	2	Other	33	33
								4/1/14-	4/1/15-
0-500M	500M-2MM	2-10MM	10-50MM	50-100MM	100-250MM		3/31/15	3/31/16
							ALL	ALL
13	6	15	19	8	7	NUMBER OF STATEMENTS	79	87
%	%	%	%	%	%	**ASSETS**	%	%
51.8		34.3	39.5			Cash & Equivalents	41.9	42.6
1.6		19.8	24.9			Trade Receivables (net)	13.1	14.2
.0		1.3	.0			Inventory	.0	.7
1.3		9.0	4.5			All Other Current	7.2	7.0
54.7		64.5	68.9			Total Current	62.2	64.6
25.3		4.7	7.5			Fixed Assets (net)	11.6	9.7
8.9		12.7	15.8			Intangibles (net)	6.2	7.4
11.1		18.1	7.9			All Other Non-Current	20.1	18.3
100.0		100.0	100.0			Total	100.0	100.0
						LIABILITIES		
24.8		10.1	5.9			Notes Payable-Short Term	7.8	12.7
3.7		1.4	8.6			Cur. Mat.-L.T.D.	1.3	2.2
11.6		12.5	8.9			Trade Payables	13.8	10.2
.0		1.0	.1			Income Taxes Payable	.3	.2
88.2		13.7	19.1			All Other Current	13.5	18.6
128.3		38.7	42.7			Total Current	36.7	43.9
97.3		13.8	16.4			Long-Term Debt	9.7	6.3
.0		.0	.0			Deferred Taxes	.1	.0
28.4		1.3	8.4			All Other Non-Current	5.3	6.4
-154.0		46.2	32.5			Net Worth	48.2	43.2
100.0		100.0	100.0			Total Liabilties & Net Worth	100.0	100.0
						INCOME DATA		
100.0		100.0	100.0			Net Sales	100.0	100.0
						Gross Profit		
77.3		85.6	80.7			Operating Expenses	86.1	85.9
22.7		14.4	19.3			Operating Profit	13.9	14.1
1.5		.2	3.0			All Other Expenses (net)	.2	1.0
21.2		14.2	16.3			Profit Before Taxes	13.8	13.1
						RATIOS		
2.4		5.8	3.6				3.6	2.7
.8		1.8	2.5			Current	2.1	1.8
.1		1.2	1.2				1.1	1.2
2.2		5.8	3.6				3.0	2.4
.8		1.3	2.5			Quick	1.7	1.7
.1		.8	1.1				1.0	.9
0 UND	0 UND	0 UND					0 UND	0 UND
0 UND	17 21.8	22 16.5				Sales/Receivables	4 88.2	6 58.9
0 UND	70 5.2	215 1.7					34 10.7	29 12.5
						Cost of Sales/Inventory		
						Cost of Sales/Payables		
51.7		3.3	1.1				3.2	4.3
-51.4		6.5	4.1			Sales/Working Capital	9.8	10.5
-16.6		23.8	9.5				71.7	65.1
			56.9				152.2	175.3
		(12) 9.0				EBIT/Interest	(44) 23.0	(46) 8.6
			2.0				3.8	1.8
						Net Profit + Depr., Dep., Amort./Cur. Mat. L/T/D		
.0		.0	.0				.0	.0
4.5		.0	.1			Fixed/Worth	.1	.1
-.2		.2	.3				.5	.4
2.4		.2	.5				.3	.5
-4.3		1.7	1.7			Debt/Worth	1.0	1.0
-1.2		28.6	4.8				3.6	3.9
		35.2	55.2			% Profit Before Taxes/Tangible	98.7	85.5
		(12) 18.1	(16) 25.8			Net Worth	(73) 32.7	(77) 21.7
		2.3	3.8				6.0	3.9
432.5		16.6	19.3				42.1	39.6
90.5		8.0	9.6			% Profit Before Taxes/Total Assets	15.8	10.9
26.5		.4	2.8				3.1	2.2
UND		UND	UND				368.3	999.8
115.9		62.0	74.8			Sales/Net Fixed Assets	57.8	77.2
34.1		22.5	18.0				22.2	32.2
38.8		3.8	3.3				4.9	6.1
15.5		1.2	.8			Sales/Total Assets	2.2	2.9
7.0		.7	.3				.7	1.1
			.7				.4	.3
		(10) .8				% Depr., Dep., Amort./Sales	(42) .8	(45) .7
			4.1				1.6	1.4
						% Officers', Directors'	4.8	1.5
						Owners' Comp/Sales	(18) 12.6	(17) 12.9
							22.5	21.7
29727M	44238M	193197M	891156M	584026M	2606799M	Net Sales ($)	3020766M	3556167M
2359M	7329M	85151M	452834M	532965M	1190184M	Total Assets ($)	2286099M	1934176M

© RMA 2019   M = $ thousand   MM = $ million
See Pages viii through xx for Explanation of Ratios and Data

Comparative Historical Data   Current Data Sorted by Sales

Type of Statement									
	18	22	23	Unqualified	2	1	2	3	15
	2	3	1	Reviewed			1		
	2	1	2	Compiled		1		1	
	9	14	17	Tax Returns	4	6	1	3	1	2
	27	25	25	Other	2	2	1	5	5	9
	4/1/16-3/31/17 ALL	4/1/17-3/31/18 ALL	4/1/18-3/31/19 ALL		0-1MM	1-3MM	3-5MM	5-10MM	10-25MM	25MM & OVER

Middle periods: 12 (4/1-9/30/18) · 56 (10/1/18-3/31/19)

	4/1/16-3/31/17 ALL	4/1/17-3/31/18 ALL	4/1/18-3/31/19 ALL	0-1MM	1-3MM	3-5MM	5-10MM	10-25MM	25MM & OVER
NUMBER OF STATEMENTS	58	65	68	6	11	4	11	10	26
ASSETS	%	%	%	%	%	%	%	%	%
Cash & Equivalents	36.1	41.2	41.7		47.5		43.1	42.6	46.3
Trade Receivables (net)	11.9	13.0	16.8		2.2		26.0	18.7	18.6
Inventory	2.6	.0	1.2		.0		5.5	.0	.0
All Other Current	9.6	12.0	6.2		3.0		2.1	16.0	5.1
Total Current	60.2	66.2	65.8		52.7		76.7	77.3	70.0
Fixed Assets (net)	10.6	10.8	9.3		18.0		5.5	5.3	4.9
Intangibles (net)	8.3	11.2	13.2		19.8		7.9	8.5	15.9
All Other Non-Current	20.9	11.8	11.7		9.5		9.9	8.9	9.1
Total	100.0	100.0	100.0		100.0		100.0	100.0	100.0
LIABILITIES									
Notes Payable-Short Term	4.5	13.2	9.6		22.0		16.1	3.1	2.8
Cur. Mat.-L.T.D.	2.6	3.2	3.6		5.0		1.2	.6	6.3
Trade Payables	12.0	10.0	12.5		11.3		12.4	11.6	16.2
Income Taxes Payable	.4	.4	.3		.0		.1	.0	.3
All Other Current	18.3	19.1	31.8		100.0		5.7	19.4	21.0
Total Current	37.7	45.9	57.8		138.3		35.6	34.6	46.6
Long-Term Debt	6.8	21.5	28.7		65.2		64.9	3.6	13.9
Deferred Taxes	.1	.1	.0		.0		.0	.0	.1
All Other Non-Current	13.8	7.2	9.0		4.5		6.2	3.7	3.0
Net Worth	41.6	25.3	4.5		-108.0		-6.7	58.1	36.3
Total Liabilities & Net Worth	100.0	100.0	100.0		100.0		100.0	100.0	100.0
INCOME DATA									
Net Sales	100.0	100.0	100.0		100.0		100.0	100.0	100.0
Gross Profit									
Operating Expenses	85.5	86.9	85.2		73.2		82.3	93.6	93.5
Operating Profit	14.5	13.1	14.8		26.8		17.7	6.4	6.5
All Other Expenses (net)	.4	.7	1.3		4.2		.8	2.6	-.7
Profit Before Taxes	14.1	12.4	13.5		22.6		16.9	3.7	7.1
RATIOS									
Current	2.3	3.1	3.5		2.8		7.7	5.5	3.0
	1.5	1.9	1.7		.9		2.0	3.9	1.5
	1.2	1.3	1.1		.2		1.2	1.4	1.2
Quick	2.1	2.3	3.5		2.8		5.0	5.4	2.9
	1.3	1.5	1.4		.8		2.0	3.6	1.4
	.6	.9	.9		.2		1.2	1.2	1.1
Sales/Receivables	0 UND	0 UND	0 UND	0 UND		0 UND	0 UND		
	7 54.2	5 67.4	8 46.9	0 UND		17 21.8	12 30.1	23 15.9	
	36 10.0	26 14.3	43 8.4	0 UND		261 1.4	56 6.5	41 8.9	
Cost of Sales/Inventory									
Cost of Sales/Payables									
Sales/Working Capital	2.1	2.8	2.8		7.6		1.5	1.6	4.2
	10.5	9.2	8.4		-51.4		8.2	2.7	9.1
	182.1	33.8	86.9		-17.5		140.8	7.8	23.0
EBIT/Interest	224.3	73.5	34.8						67.8
	(31) 38.5	(36) 14.7	(41) 11.6					(20)	25.6
	2.5	2.3	1.9						-.1
Net Profit + Depr., Dep., Amort./Cur. Mat. L/T/D									
Fixed/Worth	.0	.0	.0		.0		.0	.0	.0
	.0	.1	.0		.0		.0	.1	.1
	.9	.8	1.1		.4		-.1	.2	.0
Debt/Worth	.4	.5	.7		3.8		.2	.2	.9
	1.3	1.6	2.1		-2.9		2.2	1.2	1.5
	3.9	8.7	NM		-1.2		-4.8	2.8	3.8
% Profit Before Taxes/Tangible Net Worth	78.2	66.4	60.9					108.2	62.0
	(50) 22.7	(50) 26.0	(51) 24.5					13.0	(21) 33.4
	4.1	5.6	3.6					-22.8	3.7
% Profit Before Taxes/Total Assets	38.2	37.0	35.1		425.0		35.3	33.9	26.7
	9.3	13.4	14.8		45.1		19.3	6.4	13.4
	2.3	3.0	2.3		4.3		5.8	-4.8	1.4
Sales/Net Fixed Assets	997.2	676.7	UND		UND		UND	517.9	UND
	135.9	82.7	110.6		999.8		313.4	40.1	92.4
	27.2	32.4	26.9		13.9		74.8	13.7	30.7
Sales/Total Assets	4.7	4.8	5.3		16.9		7.1	5.8	4.3
	1.8	2.4	1.8		9.9		1.2	.9	2.0
	.6	1.1	.6		.5		.6	.6	.9
% Depr., Dep., Amort./Sales	.2	.2	.5						.3
	(32) .7	(39) .6	(32) .8					(13)	.7
	2.0	1.2	1.3						.9
% Officers', Directors' Owners' Comp/Sales	2.5	7.2	6.0						
	(16) 7.8	(20) 14.0	(15) 12.0						
	17.3	31.3	23.4						
Net Sales ($)	2291517M	2879630M	4349143M	2250M	19601M	14008M	73957M	149879M	4089448M
Total Assets ($)	1523492M	1372264M	2270822M	11669M	36987M	37560M	93175M	330678M	1760753M

M = $ thousand   MM = $ million
See Pages viii through xx for Explanation of Ratios and Data

Current Data Sorted by Assets

0-500M	500M-2MM	2-10MM	10-50MM	50-100MM	100-250MM
	1	2	1	5	
	1	1	3		
		1	1		
2	1				
	1				
	5 (4/1-9/30/18)		3	4	1	2
			25 (10/1/18-3/31/19)		
2	4	7	9	6	2
%	%	%	%	%	%

Comparative Historical Data

Type of Statement		
Unqualified	14	11
Reviewed	2	2
Compiled	2	3
Tax Returns	5	3
Other	21	14
	4/1/14- 3/31/15 ALL	4/1/15- 3/31/16 ALL
NUMBER OF STATEMENTS	44	33

	%	%
ASSETS		
Cash & Equivalents	26.9	29.9
Trade Receivables (net)	26.2	27.6
Inventory	7.8	14.3
All Other Current	9.3	9.0
Total Current	70.2	80.8
Fixed Assets (net)	11.3	7.9
Intangibles (net)	6.8	4.4
All Other Non-Current	11.7	6.9
Total	100.0	100.0
LIABILITIES		
Notes Payable-Short Term	15.9	7.9
Cur. Mat.-L.T.D.	2.5	1.4
Trade Payables	20.6	14.7
Income Taxes Payable	.1	.1
All Other Current	9.9	17.2
Total Current	49.0	41.2
Long-Term Debt	8.3	8.0
Deferred Taxes	.2	.2
All Other Non-Current	2.2	1.2
Net Worth	40.3	49.4
Total Liabilities & Net Worth	100.0	100.0
INCOME DATA		
Net Sales	100.0	100.0
Gross Profit		
Operating Expenses	81.2	83.9
Operating Profit	18.8	16.1
All Other Expenses (net)	4.2	1.2
Profit Before Taxes	14.6	14.9
RATIOS		
Current	3.3	4.5
	1.5	2.0
	1.1	1.3
Quick	1.5	3.3
	1.1	1.4
	.6	.8
Sales/Receivables	3 108.0	11 32.3
	27 13.7	30 12.3
	54 6.7	47 7.7
Cost of Sales/Inventory		
Cost of Sales/Payables		
Sales/Working Capital	1.9	2.6
	5.1	6.0
	57.0	19.6
EBIT/Interest	78.9	171.2
	(30) 10.1	(22) 12.3
	1.5	1.3
Net Profit + Depr., Dep., Amort./Cur. Mat. L/T/D		
Fixed/Worth	.0	.0
	.1	.1
	.7	.4
Debt/Worth	.6	.4
	1.9	1.1
	9.2	6.3
% Profit Before Taxes/Tangible Net Worth	60.5	53.9
	(40) 21.1	(32) 27.2
	8.5	10.4
% Profit Before Taxes/Total Assets	25.8	27.4
	8.0	12.4
	.7	1.7
Sales/Net Fixed Assets	UND	428.0
	44.7	44.7
	19.7	22.4
Sales/Total Assets	6.3	4.9
	1.4	1.9
	.3	.5
% Depr., Dep., Amort./Sales	.4	.0
	(26) 1.0	(25) 1.0
	4.4	1.6
% Officers', Directors' Owners' Comp/Sales		1.7
		(11) 5.5
		9.4

0-500M	500M-2MM	2-10MM	10-50MM	50-100MM	100-250MM		4/1/14-3/31/15	4/1/15-3/31/16
11596M	18798M	615981M	406525M	198672M	2900460M	Net Sales ($)	6491598M	3493025M
372M	4596M	38449M	204741M	438777M	342478M	Total Assets ($)	1704731M	1213774M

M = $ thousand   MM = $ million
See Pages viii through xx for Explanation of Ratios and Data

Comparative Historical Data / Current Data Sorted by Sales

	4/1/16-3/31/17 ALL	4/1/17-3/31/18 ALL	4/1/18-3/31/19 ALL	Type of Statement	0-1MM	1-3MM	3-5MM	5-10MM	10-25MM	25MM & OVER
	13	9	9	Unqualified	1			1	1	6
	3	4	5	Reviewed		1				4
	1	4	2	Compiled			2			
	6	5	3	Tax Returns						
	16	13	11	Other	1	1	1	1	2	5
					5 (4/1-9/30/18)			25 (10/1/18-3/31/19)		
	39	35	30	NUMBER OF STATEMENTS	1	4	4	3	3	15
	%	%	%	**ASSETS**	%	%	%	%	%	%
	29.1	36.6	39.1	Cash & Equivalents						33.0
	28.9	21.8	32.2	Trade Receivables (net)						41.3
	7.3	10.3	7.1	Inventory						8.9
	15.3	12.6	6.0	All Other Current						8.8
	80.5	81.3	84.4	Total Current						92.0
	10.9	6.0	6.0	Fixed Assets (net)						3.9
	2.3	6.3	4.0	Intangibles (net)						.8
	6.3	6.3	5.6	All Other Non-Current						3.3
	100.0	100.0	100.0	Total						100.0
				LIABILITIES						
	11.9	8.8	10.7	Notes Payable-Short Term						17.1
	4.3	.6	.6	Cur. Mat.-L.T.D.						.5
	18.4	18.8	30.9	Trade Payables						30.3
	.0	.2	.2	Income Taxes Payable						.1
	15.1	17.8	12.6	All Other Current						10.7
	49.7	46.3	55.0	Total Current						58.6
	6.4	1.5	3.2	Long-Term Debt						.7
	.5	.0	.1	Deferred Taxes						.1
	3.5	4.0	2.3	All Other Non-Current						3.7
	39.8	48.1	39.5	Net Worth						36.9
	100.0	100.0	100.0	Total Liabilities & Net Worth						100.0
				INCOME DATA						
	100.0	100.0	100.0	Net Sales						100.0
				Gross Profit						
	84.0	88.2	89.7	Operating Expenses						90.8
	16.0	11.8	10.3	Operating Profit						9.2
	1.5	.1	.5	All Other Expenses (net)						.6
	14.5	11.7	9.8	Profit Before Taxes						8.6
				RATIOS						
	3.8	7.2	4.6							2.1
	1.8	1.5	1.3	Current						1.3
	1.1	1.1	1.1							1.1
	2.1	6.1	2.5							2.0
	1.2	1.3	1.0	Quick						1.1
	.8	.8	.9							.8
1	314.2	0 999.8	5 77.8						13	29.0
24	15.4	13 28.5	33 11.2	Sales/Receivables					40	9.1
50	7.3	43 8.4	94 3.9						89	4.1
				Cost of Sales/Inventory						
				Cost of Sales/Payables						
	3.0	1.2	2.6							4.4
	11.5	9.1	8.2	Sales/Working Capital						11.3
	44.2	401.0	67.2							70.0
	36.3	40.6	53.0							87.6
(23)	9.0	(19) 8.8	(19) 9.3	EBIT/Interest					(13)	14.3
	-.4	1.4	4.4							5.3
				Net Profit + Depr., Dep., Amort./Cur. Mat. L/T/D						
	.0	.0	.0							.0
	.1	.0	.0	Fixed/Worth						.0
	.7	.4	.4							.3
	.4	.2	1.0							1.0
	1.2	1.5	2.5	Debt/Worth						2.4
	5.3	10.9	7.0							7.3
	88.6	53.8	55.5	% Profit Before Taxes/Tangible Net Worth						51.1
(34)	36.6	(31) 20.8	29.3							41.2
	8.6	5.7	7.5							10.5
	32.5	19.0	15.1	% Profit Before Taxes/Total Assets						15.9
	8.6	9.7	8.6							9.0
	-.2	1.0	1.7							7.3
	529.1	UND	784.6	Sales/Net Fixed Assets						743.6
	86.1	135.1	120.7							106.0
	22.0	36.7	30.8							39.5
	5.9	9.6	6.6	Sales/Total Assets						7.5
	3.3	3.1	1.7							3.2
	.7	.6	.6							.8
	.1	.1	.1							.0
(28)	.9	(16) .3	(18) .3	% Depr., Dep., Amort./Sales					(11)	.3
	1.8	1.3	1.0							.7
				% Officers', Directors' Owners' Comp/Sales						
	3900461M	2829393M	4152032M	Net Sales ($)	919M	8049M	14842M	24496M	48153M	4055573M
	1073161M	921651M	1029413M	Total Assets ($)	1121M	22459M	23759M	51522M	157169M	773383M

© RMA 2019

M = $ thousand   MM = $ million
See Pages viii through xx for Explanation of Ratios and Data

Current Data Sorted by Assets   Comparative Historical Data

0-500M	500M-2MM	2-10MM	10-50MM	50-100MM	100-250MM	Type of Statement	ALL 4/1/14-3/31/15	ALL 4/1/15-3/31/16
		3	5	2	2	Unqualified	27	20
		3		1		Reviewed	8	4
	1	1	2			Compiled	4	9
4	4	7	5			Tax Returns	36	29
4	13	19	17	10	7	Other	107	105
6 (4/1-9/30/18)			104 (10/1/18-3/31/19)					
8	18	33	29	13	9	**NUMBER OF STATEMENTS**	182	167
%	%	%	%	%	%	**ASSETS**	%	%
	10.7	13.8	17.7	18.5		Cash & Equivalents	13.7	15.1
	5.2	9.1	13.5	15.5		Trade Receivables (net)	23.0	15.9
	8.5	1.7	3.9	.0		Inventory	3.0	3.3
	6.1	4.5	10.5	2.5		All Other Current	6.4	5.6
	30.5	29.1	45.6	36.5		Total Current	46.1	39.9
	53.5	40.9	21.0	16.3		Fixed Assets (net)	28.3	29.8
	7.8	10.9	6.5	22.7		Intangibles (net)	5.1	5.5
	8.3	19.2	26.8	24.5		All Other Non-Current	20.4	24.8
	100.0	100.0	100.0	100.0		Total	100.0	100.0
						LIABILITIES		
	12.0	7.8	10.8	3.5		Notes Payable-Short Term	17.4	14.2
	2.0	2.7	3.2	.7		Cur. Mat.-L.T.D.	2.2	1.6
	2.6	2.8	7.5	4.6		Trade Payables	4.0	3.4
	.0	.0	.0	.2		Income Taxes Payable	.1	.0
	10.1	15.3	10.2	13.8		All Other Current	9.5	7.7
	26.7	28.6	31.7	22.8		Total Current	33.2	27.0
	40.2	31.4	13.7	17.6		Long-Term Debt	22.0	22.2
	.0	.2	.1	.1		Deferred Taxes	.0	.0
	10.1	3.7	4.9	6.9		All Other Non-Current	6.6	3.9
	23.1	36.1	49.6	52.7		Net Worth	38.2	46.9
	100.0	100.0	100.0	100.0		Total Liabilities & Net Worth	100.0	100.0
						INCOME DATA		
	100.0	100.0	100.0	100.0		Net Sales	100.0	100.0
						Gross Profit		
	65.2	70.2	62.1	55.2		Operating Expenses	59.9	61.7
	34.8	29.8	37.9	44.8		Operating Profit	40.1	38.3
	8.0	8.3	8.9	9.2		All Other Expenses (net)	12.4	11.4
	26.7	21.5	29.0	35.6		Profit Before Taxes	27.8	26.9
						RATIOS		
	5.2	1.9	2.9	3.5			3.1	4.2
	1.1	.7	1.6	1.6		Current	1.4	1.6
	.4	.2	1.0	1.0			.6	.5
	4.8	1.4	2.3	3.0			2.3	3.3
	.5	.6	1.1	1.6		Quick	1.1	1.1
	.1	.2	.4	1.0			.3	.3
0 UND	0 UND	0 UND	0 UND	0 UND			0 UND	0 UND
0 UND	0 UND	0 UND	2 203.0	7 53.2		Sales/Receivables	3 104.9	0 UND
16 23.5	36 10.1	40 9.2	89 4.1				89 4.1	39 9.4
						Cost of Sales/Inventory		
						Cost of Sales/Payables		
	6.7	10.8	.5	3.2			1.5	1.5
	NM	-20.8	6.1	6.1		Sales/Working Capital	12.2	15.3
	-5.3	-5.6	136.6	NM			-11.0	-12.1
	32.2	8.2	11.4	151.7			22.2	18.5
	(12) 3.2	(21) 3.1	(15) 3.0	(11) 33.4		EBIT/Interest	(89) 7.3	(94) 4.8
	2.1	1.3	-.5	4.2			3.4	1.8
						Net Profit + Depr., Dep., Amort./Cur. Mat. L/T/D		
	.7	.0	.0	.0			.0	.0
	2.4	1.9	.1	.0		Fixed/Worth	.2	.1
	-9.4	11.3	1.8	6.2			2.5	2.2
	1.0	.8	.1	.4			.5	.3
	3.1	2.9	1.1	1.3		Debt/Worth	1.8	1.3
	-11.4	NM	11.8	NM			10.0	5.2
	83.5	79.6	43.4	147.3			57.1	56.2
	(12) 27.2	(25) 20.4	(23) 6.5	(10) 35.1		% Profit Before Taxes/Tangible Net Worth	(153) 14.9	(147) 12.6
	14.0	.9	2.3	4.3			5.0	3.1
	19.8	19.5	8.8	27.7			19.0	13.2
	5.7	6.0	3.8	8.6		% Profit Before Taxes/Total Assets	5.6	5.3
	1.7	.2	.8	1.8			1.9	1.1
	22.9	282.8	UND	177.4			UND	UND
	.6	8.7	64.8	50.4		Sales/Net Fixed Assets	35.7	36.9
	.3	.2	3.6	16.6			.6	.4
	3.2	2.1	1.9	1.1			1.5	1.9
	.4	.8	.2	.4		Sales/Total Assets	.2	.2
	.2	.1	.1	.2			.1	.1
	.9	3.0	.4				.6	.9
	(12) 8.2	(21) 5.2	(11) 4.6			% Depr., Dep., Amort./Sales	(92) 2.7	(77) 2.4
	14.7	22.7	14.4				13.4	18.7
							3.0	1.8
						% Officers', Directors' Owners' Comp/Sales	(28) 13.2	(23) 12.3
							24.2	20.7
17806M	39084M	258825M	598510M	694601M	527834M	Net Sales ($)	3232599M	2646192M
1705M	22267M	135394M	561890M	855216M	1303668M	Total Assets ($)	5958718M	5900934M

M = $ thousand   MM = $ million
See Pages viii through xx for Explanation of Ratios and Data

Comparative Historical Data				Current Data Sorted by Sales					
34	19	12	**Type of Statement** / Unqualified	2	.3		1	1	5
2	4	4	Reviewed			1		2	1
5	7	4	Compiled	3					1
26	24	20	Tax Returns	12	2	2	1	1	2
103	84	70	Other	18	9	13	6	9	15
4/1/16-3/31/17 ALL	4/1/17-3/31/18 ALL	4/1/18-3/31/19 ALL		6 (4/1-9/30/18)			104 (10/1/18-3/31/19)		
				0-1MM	1-3MM	3-5MM	5-10MM	10-25MM	25MM & OVER
170	138	110	**NUMBER OF STATEMENTS**	35	14	16	8	13	24
%	%	%	**ASSETS**	%	%	%	%	%	%
16.2	16.6	16.0	Cash & Equivalents	12.4	10.3	20.8		20.1	18.2
19.8	16.5	9.7	Trade Receivables (net)	.3	6.8	14.9		7.8	23.5
3.7	3.2	2.9	Inventory	.0	9.8	4.7		3.7	2.6
7.7	7.4	7.6	All Other Current	8.8	9.9	2.8		12.9	5.9
47.4	43.7	36.3	Total Current	21.5	36.8	43.2		44.6	50.2
25.8	30.3	31.6	Fixed Assets (net)	55.2	29.9	20.4		14.0	15.7
5.4	5.7	9.6	Intangibles (net)	.4	11.5	11.8		18.4	13.6
21.4	20.3	22.5	All Other Non-Current	22.9	21.7	24.6		23.0	20.5
100.0	100.0	100.0	Total	100.0	100.0	100.0		100.0	100.0
			LIABILITIES						
20.7	14.6	9.6	Notes Payable-Short Term	5.2	25.9	5.7		14.6	5.6
2.8	3.0	2.1	Cur. Mat.-L.T.D.	2.0	6.0	.9		1.4	1.6
3.4	6.0	4.1	Trade Payables	1.0	4.3	2.1		7.4	9.2
.1	.0	.0	Income Taxes Payable	.0	.0	.0		.0	.0
10.9	7.3	12.0	All Other Current	4.3	7.9	23.3		23.4	13.8
37.9	30.9	27.7	Total Current	12.6	44.1	32.0		46.8	30.3
21.3	24.4	28.5	Long-Term Debt	45.4	23.4	11.6		19.6	21.5
.1	.1	.1	Deferred Taxes	.0	.0	.0		.4	.2
5.9	3.4	5.2	All Other Non-Current	4.3	6.1	8.1		.0	8.1
34.7	41.2	38.4	Net Worth	37.8	26.4	48.3		33.2	40.0
100.0	100.0	100.0	Total Liabilties & Net Worth	100.0	100.0	100.0		100.0	100.0
			INCOME DATA						
100.0	100.0	100.0	Net Sales	100.0	100.0	100.0		100.0	100.0
			Gross Profit						
60.5	61.3	65.0	Operating Expenses	43.3	75.0	79.7		89.6	72.0
39.5	38.7	35.0	Operating Profit	56.7	25.0	20.3		10.4	28.0
11.6	12.6	8.4	All Other Expenses (net)	14.9	7.3	5.2		3.4	4.6
27.9	26.1	26.6	Profit Before Taxes	41.7	17.6	15.1		7.0	23.4
			RATIOS						
3.6	3.5	3.0		9.9	1.8	3.3		1.5	4.4
1.5	1.4	1.2	Current	1.1	.7	1.8		.9	1.6
.5	.6	.5		.4	.3	.8		.4	1.0
2.6	3.0	2.1		8.8	.7	3.1		.9	4.1
1.1	1.2	.9	Quick	1.0	.2	1.3		.4	1.5
.3	.2	.3		.2	.1	.7		.1	.5
0 UND	0 UND	0 UND		0 UND	0 UND	0 UND		0 UND	1 342.2
5 79.6	1 296.5	0 UND	Sales/Receivables	0 UND	0 UND	8 47.6		0 999.8	28 12.9
72 5.1	52 7.0	33 11.2		0 UND	21 17.8	58 6.3		45 8.2	68 5.4
			Cost of Sales/Inventory						
			Cost of Sales/Payables						
1.2	1.5	3.0		1.2	1.5	3.9		32.1	3.6
10.8	13.0	25.4	Sales/Working Capital	41.5	-55.5	15.1		-15.0	8.1
-5.4	-10.1	-7.3		-5.5	-5.3	-26.8		-4.3	188.4
15.1	28.0	29.7		9.9				3.3	70.2
(91) 4.8	(69) 6.3	(68) 3.9	EBIT/Interest	(18) 3.6			(10) 1.3	(18) 11.8	
2.1	1.9	1.6		2.6				-3.6	1.5
			Net Profit + Depr., Dep., Amort./Cur. Mat. L/T/D						
.0	.0	.0		.0	.0	.0		.0	.0
.1	.1	.8	Fixed/Worth	1.8	.7	.9		.1	.1
2.4	2.5	6.7		3.5	NM	10.2		-4.3	4.9
.4	.4	.5		.2	1.0	.4		1.5	.6
1.3	1.6	2.2	Debt/Worth	1.6	2.3	2.2		4.5	2.3
6.0	6.3	19.9		4.2	-3.5	20.4		-6.0	7.7
46.8	42.3	74.4		27.2	146.6	60.2			200.1
(142) 10.7	(117) 13.2	(84) 19.0	% Profit Before Taxes/Tangible Net Worth	(29) 12.4	(10) 19.0	(13) 23.6			(19) 75.9
3.9	3.7	4.4		2.0	4.6	-2.1			27.4
13.3	13.0	19.5		8.4	38.4	14.9		2.7	35.6
4.9	4.8	5.9	% Profit Before Taxes/Total Assets	5.2	5.5	4.4		1.0	15.0
1.2	1.3	1.1		1.3	1.1	.2		-7.1	3.4
UND	UND	650.6		UND	UND	562.6		UND	200.9
48.0	45.3	20.4	Sales/Net Fixed Assets	.4	18.8	32.5		44.4	55.1
.8	.7	.5		.1	1.7	5.1		8.9	10.1
1.3	1.8	2.1		.3	3.0	1.9		4.9	3.1
.2	.2	.4	Sales/Total Assets	.1	.5	1.3		1.9	1.9
.1	.1	.1		.1	.1	.3		.3	.6
1.0	.6	.4		10.8					.1
(75) 6.6	(66) 11.3	(57) 4.3	% Depr., Dep., Amort./Sales	(18) 20.1				(16) .4	
18.5	24.8	15.2		23.8					2.4
2.2	3.7	2.0							
(22) 11.1	(19) 8.6	(19) 7.7	% Officers', Directors' Owners' Comp/Sales						
31.6	32.4	20.7							
3155361M	2883482M	2136660M	Net Sales ($)	15637M	25846M	62826M	57800M	206468M	1768083M
6519309M	4995558M	2880140M	Total Assets ($)	191983M	112335M	225808M	351412M	548956M	1449646M

© RMA 2019

M = $ thousand   MM = $ million
See Pages viii through xx for Explanation of Ratios and Data

	Current Data Sorted by Assets							Comparative Historical Data	
2		5	11	7	15	Type of Statement			
		3	1		1	Unqualified		30	35
		3	2			Reviewed		4	6
9	2	2	2			Compiled		5	7
7	14	33	30	9	13	Tax Returns		21	22
	17 (4/1-9/30/18)		154 (10/1/18-3/31/19)			Other		81	76
								4/1/14-3/31/15	4/1/15-3/31/16
0-500M	500M-2MM	2-10MM	10-50MM	50-100MM	100-250MM			ALL	ALL
18	16	46	46	16	29	**NUMBER OF STATEMENTS**		141	146
%	%	%	%	%	%	**ASSETS**		%	%
33.9	19.8	26.8	24.5	32.5	22.8	Cash & Equivalents		26.3	27.2
2.2	8.3	12.1	15.9	5.1	9.8	Trade Receivables (net)		13.4	10.9
.1	.0	2.7	.1	.0	.4	Inventory		1.7	.4
6.6	1.0	7.3	9.1	7.1	5.8	All Other Current		6.0	6.3
42.8	29.1	48.9	49.7	44.7	38.9	Total Current		47.4	44.8
28.4	36.2	19.4	12.0	9.4	9.5	Fixed Assets (net)		17.3	20.6
12.0	13.6	11.3	9.6	5.4	5.8	Intangibles (net)		12.8	11.0
16.8	21.1	20.5	28.8	40.5	45.9	All Other Non-Current		22.5	23.6
100.0	100.0	100.0	100.0	100.0	100.0	Total		100.0	100.0
						LIABILITIES			
2.6	7.1	5.0	8.7	4.2	11.9	Notes Payable-Short Term		10.8	11.3
5.5	6.6	1.5	1.5	.1	.8	Cur. Mat.-L.T.D.		2.2	2.8
5.2	5.1	4.0	4.0	1.8	2.2	Trade Payables		3.7	4.8
.0	.0	.1	.0	.3	.3	Income Taxes Payable		.1	.1
28.2	9.2	14.9	18.6	14.5	5.8	All Other Current		12.4	14.4
41.4	28.0	25.4	32.8	20.9	21.0	Total Current		29.2	33.3
34.2	50.2	24.5	27.1	8.6	13.9	Long-Term Debt		21.0	20.1
.0	.0	.0	.1	.3	.2	Deferred Taxes		.3	.4
9.1	7.5	2.8	3.2	12.1	7.1	All Other Non-Current		5.4	4.5
15.4	14.3	47.2	36.9	58.2	57.8	Net Worth		44.2	41.6
100.0	100.0	100.0	100.0	100.0	100.0	Total Liabilities & Net Worth		100.0	100.0
						INCOME DATA			
100.0	100.0	100.0	100.0	100.0	100.0	Net Sales		100.0	100.0
						Gross Profit			
78.5	56.2	76.1	64.9	48.3	43.6	Operating Expenses		68.1	73.8
21.5	43.8	23.9	35.1	51.7	56.4	Operating Profit		31.9	26.2
.6	10.0	4.6	7.8	20.0	15.3	All Other Expenses (net)		4.8	5.8
20.9	33.8	19.2	27.3	31.7	41.1	Profit Before Taxes		27.1	20.5
						RATIOS			
3.7	2.7	4.5	4.4	18.0	3.1			5.3	4.3
1.3	.9	1.7	1.8	2.1	1.2	Current		2.3	2.0
.2	.2	.9	.9	.4	.3			1.0	.8
3.4	2.7	4.5	2.9	17.4	2.6			4.7	3.8
1.3	.8	1.3	1.5	1.7	.9	Quick		1.5	1.6
.2	.2	.7	.6	.3	.3			.6	.5
0 UND	0 UND	0 UND	0 UND	0 UND	0 UND			0 UND	0 UND
0 UND	0 UND	2 219.1	12 29.5	0 UND	23 15.9	Sales/Receivables		5 67.3	2 161.7
0 UND	16 23.1	31 11.8	56 6.5	32 11.4	43 8.4			61 6.0	37 9.9
						Cost of Sales/Inventory			
						Cost of Sales/Payables			
15.1	6.5	3.5	3.2	.6	1.9			2.7	2.9
97.2	UND	10.9	7.9	4.2	7.6	Sales/Working Capital		8.9	8.0
-31.7	-7.4	-39.0	-106.8	-3.0	-2.1			UND	-34.7
		69.9	136.2	90.9	92.2			56.5	94.0
		(27) 6.7	(27) 11.2	(10) 21.5	(15) 17.0	EBIT/Interest		(88) 15.8	(94) 10.0
		2.9	3.7	4.1	5.4			4.6	1.2
								6.2	11.7
						Net Profit + Depr., Dep., Amort./Cur. Mat. L/T/D		(10) 3.5	(13) 4.5
								.1	2.1
.0	.0	.0	.0	.0	.0			.0	.0
.7	.6	.1	.1	.0	.0	Fixed/Worth		.2	.2
NM	11.3	1.5	.8	.7	.1			1.4	3.0
.2	.8	.5	.3	.1	.2			.3	.5
2.1	4.4	1.4	1.4	.4	.6	Debt/Worth		1.0	1.2
-2.0	-267.8	4.8	10.7	1.8	2.1			5.6	11.0
464.8	94.2	179.2	102.2	35.4	25.1	% Profit Before Taxes/Tangible Net Worth		134.7	123.9
(12) 126.4	(11) 67.9	(40) 58.0	(36) 30.8	(14) 10.4	(26) 10.3			(116) 48.1	(115) 20.7
27.7	25.1	8.0	4.1	.8	4.1			8.0	3.2
167.1	77.1	67.6	56.0	14.6	18.0	% Profit Before Taxes/Total Assets		55.9	36.3
72.8	45.4	15.6	13.4	6.5	5.8			14.5	9.1
19.3	8.7	2.6	2.7	.7	2.5			3.2	1.2
UND	225.3	730.2	849.3	UND	UND			289.8	146.8
51.2	37.6	50.9	66.6	UND	262.9	Sales/Net Fixed Assets		41.4	25.8
27.6	.2	7.7	14.9	9.5	6.3			8.5	6.2
12.9	3.7	3.6	2.1	1.1	.5			2.8	3.0
6.8	1.8	2.0	.9	.1	.1	Sales/Total Assets		1.2	1.1
2.8	.2	.4	.1	.1	.1			.3	.3
.4		.2	.5		.4			.6	.7
(11) 1.2	(26) .7	(22) .9		(10) 1.6		% Depr., Dep., Amort./Sales		(77) 1.1	(89) 1.2
2.1	5.7	2.2		6.9				3.4	3.6
9.4								1.7	7.3
(10) 16.9						% Officers', Directors' Owners' Comp/Sales		(32) 16.3	(34) 14.8
21.9								34.8	32.8
28731M	50232M	548503M	1401802M	689882M	2160016M	Net Sales ($)		4575470M	6679913M
3938M	20505M	241572M	1226083M	1130294M	4745981M	Total Assets ($)		5463250M	6546221M

M = $ thousand   MM = $ million
See Pages viii through xx for Explanation of Ratios and Data

Comparative Historical Data　　　　　　　Current Data Sorted by Sales

			Type of Statement						
35	43	40	Unqualified	2	2	3	2	13	18
7	7	5	Reviewed		1		2	2	
4	5	5	Compiled	2				1	2
17	19	15	Tax Returns	9	4			1	1
81	100	106	Other	10	26	9	12	24	25
4/1/16-3/31/17	4/1/17-3/31/18	4/1/18-3/31/19			17 (4/1-9/30/18)		154 (10/1/18-3/31/19)		
ALL	ALL	ALL		0-1MM	1-3MM	3-5MM	5-10MM	10-25MM	25MM & OVER
144	174	171	NUMBER OF STATEMENTS	23	33	12	16	41	46
%	%	%	**ASSETS**	%	%	%	%	%	%
27.1	29.1	26.1	Cash & Equivalents	15.0	20.1	33.8	33.4	26.1	31.5
11.3	10.8	10.7	Trade Receivables (net)	3.7	5.5	15.6	4.6	10.7	18.7
1.5	.5	.8	Inventory	.0	2.4	.0	.0	.0	1.4
9.6	6.4	6.8	All Other Current	5.8	7.6	1.9	.9	7.2	9.9
49.5	46.8	44.5	Total Current	24.5	35.7	51.3	38.9	43.9	61.5
14.2	15.6	17.3	Fixed Assets (net)	48.6	15.9	11.8	14.8	12.1	9.6
10.3	9.6	9.6	Intangibles (net)	3.5	16.0	19.7	9.2	4.4	10.3
25.9	28.0	28.6	All Other Non-Current	23.5	32.5	17.2	37.1	39.6	18.5
100.0	100.0	100.0	Total	100.0	100.0	100.0	100.0	100.0	100.0
			LIABILITIES						
6.7	8.6	7.0	Notes Payable-Short Term	4.2	9.6	7.4	8.2	5.5	7.4
2.5	2.4	2.1	Cur. Mat.-L.T.D.	.6	4.0	3.7	4.6	.7	1.6
4.7	3.9	3.7	Trade Payables	4.3	1.1	.8	3.9	2.3	7.3
.3	.1	.1	Income Taxes Payable	.0	.0	.0	.0	.0	.3
13.3	13.7	15.2	All Other Current	8.5	10.3	15.0	18.6	18.2	18.1
27.6	28.5	28.2	Total Current	17.6	25.0	26.8	35.4	26.7	34.9
23.7	16.0	25.3	Long-Term Debt	25.6	41.0	32.3	18.0	15.4	23.5
.3	.2	.1	Deferred Taxes	.0	.0	.0	.0	.1	.3
6.0	7.6	5.6	All Other Non-Current	5.2	2.2	7.8	2.9	6.7	7.6
42.3	47.7	40.8	Net Worth	51.7	31.9	33.0	43.8	51.0	33.8
100.0	100.0	100.0	Total Liabilities & Net Worth	100.0	100.0	100.0	100.0	100.0	100.0
			INCOME DATA						
100.0	100.0	100.0	Net Sales	100.0	100.0	100.0	100.0	100.0	100.0
			Gross Profit						
69.3	61.1	63.4	Operating Expenses	58.9	69.1	47.6	61.0	59.3	70.1
30.7	38.9	36.6	Operating Profit	41.1	30.9	52.4	39.0	40.7	29.9
4.2	4.8	8.8	All Other Expenses (net)	16.5	10.1	27.9	3.8	8.5	1.1
26.4	34.0	27.8	Profit Before Taxes	24.6	20.8	24.6	35.2	32.2	28.9
			RATIOS						
6.8	3.8	4.4		3.8	3.2	24.8	4.2	2.7	4.8
2.3	1.9	1.6	Current	1.8	1.0	4.4	2.0	1.3	2.0
.9	.7	.7		.4	.5	.3	.3	.5	1.1
4.4	3.5	3.7		3.8	2.2	24.7	4.1	2.6	4.6
1.4	1.6	1.3	Quick	1.8	.9	3.7	2.0	1.1	1.7
.4	.5	.5		.3	.3	.3	.2	.4	.7
0 UND	0 UND	0 UND		0 UND	0 UND	0 UND	0 UND	0 UND	0 UND
0 UND	1 357.5	0 999.8	Sales/Receivables	0 UND	0 UND	1 513.6	0 UND	3 142.5	32 11.3
31 11.9	38 9.7	37 9.9		0 UND	22 16.6	57 6.4	4 90.0	31 11.9	62 5.9
			Cost of Sales/Inventory						
			Cost of Sales/Payables						
1.9	3.3	3.3		1.6	11.6	.1	4.0	5.3	2.9
7.1	10.9	12.7	Sales/Working Capital	7.4	-135.6	1.5	8.8	17.4	6.6
-50.1	-37.6	-20.2		-28.3	-9.2	-16.4	-11.2	-8.2	NM
110.4	119.5	72.3			25.2		96.0	70.5	174.3
(83) 16.3	(99) 24.9	(94) 13.6	EBIT/Interest		(21) 5.7		(10) 19.1	(22) 27.6	(30) 49.4
5.8	5.4	4.0			3.1		6.0	5.3	10.9
		35.5	Net Profit + Depr., Dep.,						
	(11) 0.5		Amort./Cur. Mat. L/T/D						
		1.8							
.0	.0	.0		.0	.0	.0	.0	.0	.0
.1	.1	.1	Fixed/Worth	1.0	.1	.0	.0	.0	.1
1.4	.8	1.2		3.4	.7	.2	NM	1.2	1.4
.3	.2	.2		.3	.2	.1	.5	.2	.3
1.0	1.0	1.2	Debt/Worth	.8	1.7	.4	1.4	.9	1.7
5.9	5.1	8.5		7.6	-8.4	NM	NM	2.6	31.8
90.2	155.1	100.0	% Profit Before Taxes/Tangible	81.9	84.7		78.1	143.9	232.8
(116) 23.8	(142) 44.9	(139) 28.6	Net Worth	(22) 19.7	(23) 28.3		(12) 26.7	(37) 26.0	(36) 90.4
4.8	5.3	4.6		4.6	1.9		11.4	6.6	25.5
52.0	66.9	63.1	% Profit Before Taxes/Total	20.3	53.6	8.4	35.6	65.4	102.4
11.7	15.5	14.0	Assets	4.8	0.0	1.0	19.7	9.9	28.0
3.0	3.5	3.6		.9	1.4	.7	7.3	3.5	13.5
286.7	UND	UND		UND	UND	UND	UND	UND	246.7
39.2	61.3	65.4	Sales/Net Fixed Assets	5.8	53.4	UND	74.4	140.6	58.4
10.3	14.7	9.2		.1	2.6	32.0	33.2	22.8	16.9
2.7	3.2	2.8		1.8	3.1	.8	4.0	3.1	2.6
1.1	1.3	1.0	Sales/Total Assets	.2	.4	.1	1.1	1.7	1.9
.3	.2	.1		.1	.1	.1	.1	.1	.8
.5	.4	.4		1.8	.6			.2	.4
(82) 1.2	(89) 1.0	(85) .9	% Depr., Dep., Amort./Sales	(11) 9.8	(17) 1.2			(20) .4	(28) .7
3.7	2.9	2.6		24.2	9.3			1.2	1.7
4.0	6.2	4.0	% Officers', Directors'						
(23) 12.1	(22) 12.3	(31) 10.7	Owners' Comp/Sales						
31.8	18.4	20.6							
4237965M	4809213M	4879166M	Net Sales ($)	8256M	66538M	49504M	121550M	665545M	3967773M
6215583M	6987382M	7368373M	Total Assets ($)	54852M	597031M	517363M	375781M	2634599M	3188747M

M = $ thousand　　MM = $ million
See Pages viii through xx for Explanation of Ratios and Data

Current Data Sorted by Assets   **Comparative Historical Data**

	0-500M	500M-2MM	2-10MM	10-50MM	50-100MM	100-250MM	Type of Statement	ALL 4/1/14-3/31/15	ALL 4/1/15-3/31/16
	1	1	9	13	2	8	Unqualified	32	40
	2	2	4	3			Reviewed	4	1
	4	2	3	1		2	Compiled	13	18
	19	10	5	1			Tax Returns	34	50
	25	23	22	22	2	5	Other	81	93
	18 (4/1-9/30/18)			171 (10/1/18-3/31/19)					
	49	38	43	40	4	15	NUMBER OF STATEMENTS	164	202
	%	%	%	%	%	%	ASSETS	%	%
	56.5	29.6	30.7	20.5		10.2	Cash & Equivalents	27.3	30.1
	1.4	6.8	16.6	26.8		17.0	Trade Receivables (net)	13.8	13.4
	.0	.0	.0	1.1		.4	Inventory	.8	.1
	3.6	2.5	5.2	9.5		25.4	All Other Current	9.7	7.2
	61.5	38.9	52.6	57.9		53.1	Total Current	51.7	50.8
	19.0	16.7	13.7	10.4		4.0	Fixed Assets (net)	19.5	14.6
	12.2	28.5	21.9	16.7		26.5	Intangibles (net)	13.5	15.8
	7.2	15.9	11.8	14.9		16.4	All Other Non-Current	15.3	18.8
	100.0	100.0	100.0	100.0		100.0	Total	100.0	100.0
							LIABILITIES		
	26.9	8.8	8.8	8.4		25.2	Notes Payable-Short Term	16.4	15.7
	7.0	4.1	4.0	1.6		1.8	Cur. Mat.-L.T.D.	2.8	2.5
	4.3	2.8	4.3	9.4		2.1	Trade Payables	6.6	4.5
	.0	.1	.1	.0		.2	Income Taxes Payable	.3	.3
	27.7	15.7	20.8	15.7		14.9	All Other Current	21.9	23.2
	65.9	31.5	38.0	35.1		44.2	Total Current	48.0	46.3
	31.3	36.2	22.3	34.7		19.7	Long-Term Debt	23.5	22.0
	.0	.0	.0	.0		1.9	Deferred Taxes	.3	.4
	5.3	11.0	10.6	15.3		7.5	All Other Non-Current	11.4	6.3
	-2.5	21.4	29.1	14.7		26.7	Net Worth	16.9	24.9
	100.0	100.0	100.0	100.0		100.0	Total Liabilities & Net Worth	100.0	100.0
							INCOME DATA		
	100.0	100.0	100.0	100.0		100.0	Net Sales	100.0	100.0
							Gross Profit		
	78.2	82.6	77.5	69.2		76.8	Operating Expenses	78.3	76.0
	21.8	17.4	22.5	30.8		23.2	Operating Profit	21.7	24.0
	1.0	1.8	3.1	3.6		3.1	All Other Expenses (net)	3.2	2.2
	20.8	15.6	19.4	27.3		20.1	Profit Before Taxes	18.5	21.8
							RATIOS		
	4.1	6.0	4.9	4.1		1.8		3.2	3.4
	1.4	1.6	1.5	2.1		1.2	Current	1.2	1.4
	.5	.3	.9	1.3		1.0		.5	.5
	3.8	4.5	3.7	3.4		1.3		2.5	2.9
	1.4	1.4	1.5	1.8		1.0	Quick	(163) 1.2	(201) 1.2
	.4	.2	.9	.9		.1		.3	.3
	0 UND	0 UND	0 UND	1 515.0		4 95.3		0 UND	0 UND
	0 UND	0 UND	7 53.7	40 9.2		21 17.1	Sales/Receivables	0 UND	0 999.8
	0 UND	0 UND	39 9.4	76 4.8		57 6.4		28 12.9	29 12.5
							Cost of Sales/Inventory		
							Cost of Sales/Payables		
	19.3	9.6	5.9	3.3		2.7		7.6	6.9
	84.2	29.3	18.5	6.2		10.0	Sales/Working Capital	36.0	21.7
	-35.8	-12.4	-38.2	31.5		88.6		-11.1	-28.7
	108.0	29.5	38.4	70.6				59.9	76.9
	(31) 32.4	(25) 15.0	(27) 22.0	(20) 12.9			EBIT/Interest	(105) 17.2	(129) 23.3
	4.6	3.8	5.4	4.8				4.6	6.4
							Net Profit + Depr., Dep., Amort./Cur. Mat. L/T/D	50.1	14.3
								(14) 2.2	(16) 4.5
								.9	1.7
	.0	.0	.1	.0		.0		.1	.0
	.4	.3	.6	.2		.3	Fixed/Worth	.4	.3
	-1.2	-4.7	-.4	-.4		-.3		-2.1	4.4
	.5	.8	.9	.3		5.5		.5	.4
	2.5	NM	6.5	1.3		10.6	Debt/Worth	3.0	2.6
	-3.0	-1.7	-2.4	-3.3		-2.0		-4.8	-13.5
	700.0	93.5	198.2	173.8			% Profit Before Taxes/Tangible Net Worth	207.5	283.4
	(31) 340.0	(19) 57.3	(26) 72.8	(26) 48.3				(110) 75.6	(149) 101.8
	84.1	10.9	10.8	23.9				22.7	27.3
	342.1	68.9	64.5	91.6		19.9	% Profit Before Taxes/Total Assets	67.5	105.3
	109.1	34.4	29.5	24.1		8.4		25.2	31.4
	26.5	3.3	7.5	9.0		.8		3.9	8.4
	UND	UND	537.6	216.1		203.5		183.9	260.1
	197.9	164.6	67.7	70.3		25.5	Sales/Net Fixed Assets	46.5	52.1
	34.3	23.9	27.2	20.6		16.0		16.2	19.2
	19.3	5.8	3.5	3.0		.8		5.9	5.8
	9.6	3.5	2.6	1.7		.8	Sales/Total Assets	2.7	2.8
	4.5	2.5	1.5	1.1		.5		.8	1.0
	.3	.4	.2	.3		.4		.5	.3
	(21) .6	(13) 1.3	(20) .7	(24) .9		(11) .5	% Depr., Dep., Amort./Sales	(91) 1.2	(117) .8
	.9	2.4	3.8	1.8		4.1		2.2	1.7
	13.6	10.5	5.9				% Officers', Directors' Owners' Comp/Sales	11.7	11.2
	(29) 17.6	(18) 19.0	(12) 9.0					(47) 16.2	(64) 18.2
	23.4	26.4	15.2					26.3	29.1
	106464M	158164M	744132M	2187425M	121387M	1898177M	Net Sales ($)	6095307M	6297009M
	9464M	40688M	195079M	1016661M	267372M	2309611M	Total Assets ($)	4080625M	4996742M

© RMA 2019   M = $ thousand   MM = $ million
See Pages viii through xx for Explanation of Ratios and Data

Comparative Historical Data | | | | Current Data Sorted by Sales

3/31/17 ALL	3/31/18 ALL	3/31/19 ALL	Type of Statement	0-1MM	1-3MM	3-5MM	5-10MM	10-25MM	25MM & OVER
49	35	34	Unqualified	1		2	3	7	21
2	5	9	Reviewed		2	2	2	2	1
15	19	12	Compiled		4	1	1	3	3
42	42	35	Tax Returns	11	11	7	3	3	
99	102	99	Other	14	21	10	19	9	26
4/1/16-3/31/17 ALL	4/1/17-3/31/18 ALL	4/1/18-3/31/19 ALL		18 (4/1-9/30/18)		171 (10/1/18-3/31/19)			
207	203	189	NUMBER OF STATEMENTS	26	38	22	28	24	51
%	%	%	ASSETS	%	%	%	%	%	%
29.0	31.5	32.9	Cash & Equivalents	42.2	40.1	33.9	33.6	33.7	21.5
14.1	12.4	12.6	Trade Receivables (net)	.2	4.3	9.2	12.5	22.4	22.0
.3	.2	.3	Inventory	.0	.0	.0	.0	.0	1.0
5.8	6.8	6.7	All Other Current	5.1	2.8	2.1	3.4	3.2	15.9
49.3	51.0	52.4	Total Current	47.6	47.2	45.1	49.6	59.3	60.4
13.4	15.2	14.0	Fixed Assets (net)	26.9	17.4	18.6	13.2	7.3	6.3
19.6	17.2	20.0	Intangibles (net)	18.9	22.2	20.4	25.4	15.2	18.1
17.7	16.7	13.6	All Other Non-Current	6.7	13.2	15.8	11.8	18.3	15.2
100.0	100.0	100.0	Total	100.0	100.0	100.0	100.0	100.0	100.0
			LIABILITIES						
14.2	13.8	14.5	Notes Payable-Short Term	21.7	11.9	19.5	13.5	10.4	13.1
2.3	2.7	4.1	Cur. Mat.-L.T.D.	5.1	5.3	2.5	6.3	4.1	2.1
4.1	4.8	4.8	Trade Payables	2.8	3.6	2.2	4.3	4.9	8.1
.1	.2	.0	Income Taxes Payable	.0	.0	.0	.2	.0	.1
19.7	19.3	19.9	All Other Current	18.3	17.8	29.5	11.7	19.8	22.6
40.4	40.7	43.4	Total Current	48.0	38.7	53.8	36.0	39.2	46.0
24.7	25.0	29.8	Long-Term Debt	38.1	24.5	20.2	42.7	27.8	27.4
.3	.2	.2	Deferred Taxes	.0	.0	.0	.0	.0	.6
7.2	7.9	10.0	All Other Non-Current	.6	8.9	9.0	9.3	4.5	19.0
27.4	26.1	16.7	Net Worth	13.4	27.9	17.0	12.0	28.6	7.0
100.0	100.0	100.0	Total Liabilties & Net Worth	100.0	100.0	100.0	100.0	100.0	100.0
			INCOME DATA						
100.0	100.0	100.0	Net Sales	100.0	100.0	100.0	100.0	100.0	100.0
			Gross Profit						
78.1	78.3	76.8	Operating Expenses	70.6	67.1	88.1	85.3	75.7	78.0
21.9	21.7	23.2	Operating Profit	29.4	32.9	11.9	14.7	24.3	22.0
2.2	1.8	2.5	All Other Expenses (net)	4.1	4.2	-.1	.6	2.4	2.4
19.7	19.8	20.8	Profit Before Taxes	25.2	28.7	11.9	14.0	21.9	19.6
			RATIOS						
3.8	3.8	4.1	Current	6.9	6.7	6.0	6.4	3.6	2.9
1.6	1.5	1.6		1.2	2.4	1.6	1.3	2.1	1.6
.8	.7	.9		.3	.8	.1	.7	1.0	1.0
3.3	3.3	3.4	Quick	4.3	4.8	5.9	4.0	3.2	1.9
1.4	1.3	1.4		1.2	2.4	1.6	1.3	1.8	1.2
.6	.4	.5		.2	.8	.1	.7	.5	.5
0 UND	0 UND	0 UND	Sales/Receivables	0 UND	0 UND	0 UND	0 UND	0 UND	5 67.5
2 156.5	0 UND	0 UND		0 UND	0 UND	0 UND	0 UND	17 21.3	24 15.1
36 10.0	32 11.5	29 12.5		0 UND	0 UND	5 71.6	33 10.9	49 7.4	64 5.7
			Cost of Sales/Inventory						
			Cost of Sales/Payables						
6.3	6.1	6.8	Sales/Working Capital	7.7	8.9	7.3	8.1	5.3	5.5
24.7	22.2	22.8		87.2	30.3	78.4	35.3	14.1	10.1
-48.3	-32.3	-84.0		-9.9	-15.3	-12.4	-31.7	NM	51.8
54.3	68.8	55.3	EBIT/Interest	48.0	73.3	28.6	60.0	244.2	34.0
(127) 19.1	(121) 16.8	(116) 15.7		(15) 14.0	(23) 29.4	(15) 15.0	(19) 14.0	(13) 37.7	(31) 11.0
3.9	3.0	4.7		4.0	7.0	1.7	5.6	6.3	3.5
6.7	14.8	15.0	Net Profit + Depr., Dep., Amort./Cur. Mat. L/T/D						15.9
(10) 2.0	(17) 6.7	(17) 3.6							(11) 7.6
.3	2.6	2.1							3.4
.0	.0	.0	Fixed/Worth	.0	.0	.0	.0	.0	.1
.2	.3	.3		.9	.5	.4	.3	.0	.3
-1.3	-1.7	-.4		5.6	-.9	-1.8	-.3	.5	-.1
.5	.5	.7	Debt/Worth	.7	.4	.5	.8	.4	1.2
2.3	2.0	3.6		3.9	2.5	2.5	-37.6	1.5	6.4
-4.9	-3.2	-2.3		-1.5	-3.1	-2.7	-1.6	-15.8	-1.7
167.3	244.5	315.4	% Profit Before Taxes/Tangible Net Worth	447.2	657.6	84.8	48.7	496.1	210.3
(140) 54.8	(133) 85.8	(114) 71.3		(17) 154.2	(23) 307.2	(13) 56.1	(13) 7.6	(17) 85.9	(31) 47.7
15.8	19.4	18.6		25.2	44.4	9.0	1.1	38.8	17.8
58.0	79.8	98.9	% Profit Before Taxes/Total Assets	176.4	222.8	57.6	83.7	108.8	89.7
22.1	29.5	29.5		43.9	68.5	10.0	23.7	40.9	19.8
4.0	4.3	7.3		4.5	12.6	2.0	2.5	15.6	4.5
341.1	264.3	620.8	Sales/Net Fixed Assets	UND	UND	UND	999.8	999.8	139.6
69.8	59.8	83.8		109.8	78.5	170.4	100.0	214.5	51.7
21.5	20.1	25.3		16.7	23.0	29.8	26.2	50.9	20.4
5.9	5.6	5.8	Sales/Total Assets	6.4	9.7	13.1	6.8	4.4	3.1
2.4	2.7	2.8		2.7	3.5	3.8	3.8	2.8	2.1
.9	1.1	1.2		1.1	.9	2.9	2.2	1.2	.8
.3	.4	.4	% Depr., Dep., Amort./Sales		.4	.4		.2	.4
(99) .8	(99) .8	(91) .7			(15) .8	(11) .7		(12) .5	(35) .7
1.9	1.9	1.9			2.4	1.9		1.7	1.8
9.5	6.7	9.5	% Officers', Directors' Owners' Comp/Sales	15.7	10.1				
(65) 15.7	(71) 13.3	(64) 15.5		(16) 19.6	(23) 15.3				
31.3	26.1	23.0		26.8	20.3				
6398548M	5033603M	5215749M	Net Sales ($)	14794M	72046M	82168M	195108M	419031M	4432602M
5676412M	4359076M	3838875M	Total Assets ($)	14173M	103975M	84253M	93341M	302653M	3240480M

© RMA 2019   M = $ thousand   MM = $ million
See Pages viii through xx for Explanation of Ratios and Data

Current Data Sorted by Assets   Comparative Historical Data

0-500M	500M-2MM	2-10MM	10-50MM	50-100MM	100-250MM	Type of Statement	4/1/14-3/31/15 ALL	4/1/15-3/31/16 ALL
		5	3	1	4	Unqualified	12	12
		1				Reviewed	1	3
						Compiled	2	2
1						Tax Returns	5	9
1	4	4	12	3	3	Other	24	19
	9 (4/1-9/30/18)		33 (10/1/18-3/31/19)					
2	4	10	15	4	7	NUMBER OF STATEMENTS	44	45
%	%	%	%	%	%	ASSETS	%	%
		43.1	27.7			Cash & Equivalents	35.2	36.9
		19.6	14.9			Trade Receivables (net)	8.6	11.9
		3.7	.0			Inventory	.8	.2
		8.1	11.0			All Other Current	2.1	4.3
		74.4	53.6			Total Current	46.7	53.4
		10.0	18.9			Fixed Assets (net)	19.6	20.1
		2.7	3.3			Intangibles (net)	12.2	6.0
		12.9	24.2			All Other Non-Current	21.2	20.6
		100.0	100.0			Total	100.0	100.0
						LIABILITIES		
		11.1	1.0			Notes Payable-Short Term	1.2	2.8
		.7	.9			Cur. Mat.-L.T.D.	1.2	.9
		9.3	10.5			Trade Payables	2.7	6.0
		.5	.5			Income Taxes Payable	.0	.4
		10.5	25.3			All Other Current	16.6	12.8
		32.1	38.2			Total Current	21.7	22.8
		12.9	9.2			Long-Term Debt	15.0	10.6
		.4	.0			Deferred Taxes	.5	.1
		5.6	4.0			All Other Non-Current	10.6	3.2
		49.0	48.7			Net Worth	52.2	63.3
		100.0	100.0			Total Liabilities & Net Worth	100.0	100.0
						INCOME DATA		
		100.0	100.0			Net Sales	100.0	100.0
						Gross Profit		
		82.0	73.8			Operating Expenses	75.8	77.0
		18.0	26.2			Operating Profit	24.2	23.0
		1.1	2.3			All Other Expenses (net)	6.1	2.9
		17.0	23.9			Profit Before Taxes	18.1	20.1
						RATIOS		
		5.1	3.3			Current	9.8	8.3
		3.4	1.4				2.6	2.8
		.9	.6				.9	1.2
		4.2	2.1			Quick	9.1	6.1
		3.1	.9				2.5	2.6
		.8	.0				.7	1.1
		8 43.3	0 UND			Sales/Receivables	0 UND	0 UND
		34 10.8	20 18.6				6 58.2	6 58.3
		46 8.0	50 7.3				35 10.5	34 10.6
						Cost of Sales/Inventory		
						Cost of Sales/Payables		
		1.9	7.1			Sales/Working Capital	.9	1.3
		4.8	15.2				4.8	6.2
		-50.4	-6.4				-20.7	29.2
						EBIT/Interest	111.3	350.0
							(20) 14.8	(19) 16.7
							1.5	6.3
						Net Profit + Depr., Dep., Amort./Cur. Mat. L/T/D		
		.0	.1			Fixed/Worth	.0	.0
		.2	.5				.2	.2
		1.8	1.2				1.7	.9
		.4				Debt/Worth	.3	.2
		.9	1.0				1.0	.5
		9.2	1.4				8.9	1.4
			54.0			% Profit Before Taxes/Tangible Net Worth	16.7	61.3
		(12)	13.3				(35) 9.6	(41) 15.0
			.5				.7	4.8
		37.5	16.6			% Profit Before Taxes/Total Assets	8.9	24.8
		21.7	6.5				3.7	8.9
		2.3	-.1				.4	2.9
		118.0	46.0			Sales/Net Fixed Assets	142.4	454.3
		51.9	13.2				29.8	44.5
		11.3	.6				4.0	6.1
		3.1	2.8			Sales/Total Assets	1.6	3.4
		1.5	1.5				.5	1.6
		.6	.1				.1	.2
						% Depr., Dep., Amort./Sales	.8	.6
							(21) 2.8	(28) 1.2
							8.0	8.3
						% Officers', Directors', Owners' Comp/Sales		5.1
								(11) 6.9
								17.6
3366M	11808M	117118M	450327M	97526M	1257184M	Net Sales ($)	921013M	1050562M
422M	5044M	63690M	341483M	253147M	1183276M	Total Assets ($)	1709825M	1054940M

M = $ thousand   MM = $ million
See Pages viii through xx for Explanation of Ratios and Data

Comparative Historical Data | Current Data Sorted by Sales

			Type of Statement	0-1MM	1-3MM	3-5MM	5-10MM	10-25MM	25MM & OVER
8	8	13	Unqualified	1		1	3	3	5
2	2	1	Reviewed					1	
	2		Compiled						
			Tax Returns						
4	5	1	Other	1	7	2	3	3	11
17	26	27			9 (4/1-9/30/18)			33 (10/1/18-3/31/19)	
4/1/16-3/31/17 ALL	4/1/17-3/31/18 ALL	4/1/18-3/31/19 ALL							
31	43	42	**NUMBER OF STATEMENTS**	3	7	3	6	7	16
%	%	%	**ASSETS**	%	%	%	%	%	%
31.5	32.2	38.0	Cash & Equivalents						22.5
8.2	12.1	13.3	Trade Receivables (net)						20.6
.2	1.1	.9	Inventory						1.4
5.4	8.5	9.2	All Other Current						15.7
45.3	54.0	61.4	Total Current						60.2
21.4	16.5	15.5	Fixed Assets (net)						9.4
18.1	13.0	6.9	Intangibles (net)						15.9
15.3	16.5	16.3	All Other Non-Current						14.6
100.0	100.0	100.0	Total						100.0
			LIABILITIES						
2.9	2.6	3.5	Notes Payable-Short Term						2.3
1.1	.8	.7	Cur. Mat.-L.T.D.						.4
3.1	5.4	8.5	Trade Payables						18.2
.3	.1	.5	Income Taxes Payable						1.0
15.5	11.4	19.2	All Other Current						20.6
23.0	20.3	32.4	Total Current						42.4
16.9	21.5	14.2	Long-Term Debt						9.4
.9	.1	.1	Deferred Taxes						.1
5.1	4.8	4.2	All Other Non-Current						4.2
54.1	53.4	49.0	Net Worth						43.9
100.0	100.0	100.0	Total Liabilties & Net Worth						100.0
			INCOME DATA						
100.0	100.0	100.0	Net Sales						100.0
			Gross Profit						
77.7	72.6	79.4	Operating Expenses						90.1
22.3	27.4	20.6	Operating Profit						9.9
7.4	4.8	3.2	All Other Expenses (net)						1.9
14.9	22.6	17.4	Profit Before Taxes						8.0
			RATIOS						
5.2	7.2	6.1							3.2
2.4	3.8	2.1	Current						1.6
.8	1.3	1.0							.9
5.2	6.3	5.3							2.0
1.4	2.4	1.7	Quick						1.0
.5	1.0	.5							.4
0 UND	0 UND	0 UND						0	UND
0 972.0	1 283.9	11 33.0	Sales/Receivables					17	22.1
43 8.4	39 9.4	42 8.7						53	6.9
			Cost of Sales/Inventory						
			Cost of Sales/Payables						
1.4	.7	2.5							3.1
3.3	2.9	8.6	Sales/Working Capital						10.6
-20.8	13.4	-52.4							-116.3
17.2	27.6	25.7							
(14) 10.8	(18) 10.0	(18) 9.5	EBIT/Interest						
2.5	2.7	.7							
			Net Profit + Depr., Dep., Amort./Cur. Mat. L/T/D						
.0	.0	.0							.1
.2	.1	.2	Fixed/Worth						.2
2.6	1.8	1.8							NM
.4	.2	.4							.9
1.3	1.0	1.0	Debt/Worth						1.4
12.3	4.8	12.1							NM
79.1	35.9	56.4	% Profit Before Taxes/Tangible Net Worth						74.3
(26) 8.5	(36) 11.1	(35) 12.4						(12)	9.6
1.8	3.0	.1							-.1
18.1	15.9	33.8	% Profit Before Taxes/Total Assets						45.1
6.0	5.9	6.1							2.4
.8	2.0	.1							-2.6
UND	UND	265.3							100.9
27.7	37.0	33.8	Sales/Net Fixed Assets						33.8
1.2	6.5	6.9							10.6
1.5	2.3	2.9							4.2
.5	.5	1.0	Sales/Total Assets						1.5
.2	.2	.3							.6
1.0	.7	.7							.6
(19) 3.6	(18) 3.2	(21) 2.0	% Depr., Dep., Amort./Sales					(10)	1.5
17.7	14.6	4.7							4.1
			% Officers', Directors' Owners' Comp/Sales						
647021M	957231M	1937329M	Net Sales ($)	393M	15209M	12780M	43635M	127005M	1738307M
1414651M	2193020M	1847062M	Total Assets ($)	4659M	166992M	21192M	93767M	296094M	1264358M

M = $ thousand   MM = $ million
See Pages viii through xx for Explanation of Ratios and Data

Current Data Sorted by Assets							Comparative Historical Data	

© RMA 2019   M = $ thousand   MM = $ million   See Pages viii through xx for Explanation of Ratios and Data

0-500M	500M-2MM	2-10MM	10-50MM	50-100MM	100-250MM	Type of Statement	4/1/14-3/31/15 ALL	4/1/15-3/31/16 ALL
1			1	7	11	Unqualified	33	29
1			3	1		Reviewed	3	
1		1				Compiled	4	3
6	8	4				Tax Returns	15	30
11	10	26	16	13	5	Other	54	75
	11 (4/1-9/30/18)		116 (10/1/18-3/31/19)					
19	18	33	20	21	16	**NUMBER OF STATEMENTS**	109	137
%	%	%	%	%	%	**ASSETS**	%	%
39.6	25.0	22.4	15.9	21.9	36.2	Cash & Equivalents	21.9	30.7
3.8	10.0	9.2	11.3	12.3	10.4	Trade Receivables (net)	11.0	9.6
.4	4.8	3.8	.0	.1	.0	Inventory	1.4	2.7
3.9	6.4	4.1	14.6	5.9	8.6	All Other Current	9.7	8.2
47.8	46.1	39.5	41.8	40.3	55.2	Total Current	44.0	51.3
26.7	25.4	18.8	12.3	5.6	6.7	Fixed Assets (net)	17.0	15.2
7.5	8.8	11.6	2.4	4.9	3.8	Intangibles (net)	6.4	8.2
18.0	19.7	30.1	43.4	49.2	34.3	All Other Non-Current	32.6	25.3
100.0	100.0	100.0	100.0	100.0	100.0	Total	100.0	100.0
						LIABILITIES		
9.0	5.1	9.8	8.0	5.2	7.4	Notes Payable-Short Term	11.3	10.6
2.1	1.6	.8	1.2	1.2	2.5	Cur. Mat.-L.T.D.	1.6	1.7
13.1	1.1	3.0	1.0	6.1	2.6	Trade Payables	2.9	4.5
.1	.0	.0	.1	.1	.3	Income Taxes Payable	.1	.3
46.6	9.3	11.7	8.2	8.5	16.5	All Other Current	9.1	11.8
70.9	17.2	25.3	18.5	21.0	29.3	Total Current	25.0	28.9
13.0	65.2	28.4	24.3	19.6	27.1	Long-Term Debt	22.0	23.9
.0	.0	.0	.0	.0	.0	Deferred Taxes	.3	.0
16.7	5.1	4.3	4.0	.4	2.6	All Other Non-Current	10.4	8.9
-.6	12.5	42.1	53.2	59.0	41.0	Net Worth	42.3	38.4
100.0	100.0	100.0	100.0	100.0	100.0	Total Liabilities & Net Worth	100.0	100.0
						INCOME DATA		
100.0	100.0	100.0	100.0	100.0	100.0	Net Sales	100.0	100.0
						Gross Profit		
76.0	72.1	57.8	46.3	41.2	48.9	Operating Expenses	59.8	65.8
24.0	27.9	42.2	53.7	58.8	51.1	Operating Profit	40.2	34.2
-.4	7.5	12.5	14.8	16.9	19.4	All Other Expenses (net)	12.6	8.5
24.4	20.3	29.7	39.0	42.0	31.7	Profit Before Taxes	27.6	25.7
						RATIOS		
2.5	13.2	7.9	7.2	17.8	8.5	Current	6.9	4.4
1.2	2.1	2.0	2.5	2.4	2.6	Current	1.8	2.2
.1	1.1	1.1	1.2	1.0	1.2	Current	1.0	.8
2.2	5.5	7.5	2.6	7.9	8.5	Quick	4.2	4.2
1.0	2.0	1.8	1.1	2.2	2.1	Quick	1.4	1.7
.1	1.1	.6	.2	.6	.6	Quick	.5	.5
0 UND	0 UND	0 UND	0 UND	0 UND	0 UND	Sales/Receivables	0 UND	0 UND
0 UND	0 UND	0 UND	0 770.9	0 UND	42 8.7	Sales/Receivables	1 318.5	0 UND
3 141.6	28 13.2	16 23.4	25 14.6	53 6.9	87 4.2	Sales/Receivables	51 7.2	35 10.3
						Cost of Sales/Inventory		
						Cost of Sales/Payables		
22.5	4.5	.9	.4	.2	.5	Sales/Working Capital	1.1	1.2
165.5	15.1	10.8	3.0	3.9	2.5	Sales/Working Capital	6.1	11.3
-7.1	253.9	86.3	13.9	NM	12.7	Sales/Working Capital	NM	-375.1
79.6		50.9	718.5			EBIT/Interest	25.8	33.2
(10) 14.7		(17) 8.5	(13) 5.4			EBIT/Interest	(59) 6.2	(71) 8.6
4.7		3.1	3.0			EBIT/Interest	2.6	4.0
						Net Profit + Depr., Dep., Amort./Cur. Mat. L/T/D		
.0	.0	.0	.0	.0	.0	Fixed/Worth	.0	.0
.3	.3	.0	.0	.0	.0	Fixed/Worth	.0	.0
4.2	-.5	.6	.6	.1	.3	Fixed/Worth	.8	.8
.7	.2	.6	.1	.0	.2	Debt/Worth	.4	.3
2.9	1.6	1.3	1.1	.3	1.8	Debt/Worth	1.2	1.1
22.8	-4.8	15.9	3.8	4.7	6.8	Debt/Worth	3.9	7.9
999.8	104.5	107.1	35.8	27.9	18.9	% Profit Before Taxes/Tangible Net Worth	59.0	63.5
(15) 609.5	(12) 32.5	(26) 28.5	(18) 9.5	(19) 7.1	(14) 6.9	% Profit Before Taxes/Tangible Net Worth	(98) 14.3	(112) 16.8
58.3	1.0	1.1	1.8	1.6	1.5	% Profit Before Taxes/Tangible Net Worth	2.9	5.2
392.2	75.6	43.6	18.7	17.0	22.0	% Profit Before Taxes/Total Assets	24.4	34.0
139.6	19.2	5.9	5.2	3.6	2.4	% Profit Before Taxes/Total Assets	4.5	7.0
15.7	.4	.3	1.6	.8	1.2	% Profit Before Taxes/Total Assets	1.0	1.8
UND	UND	UND	948.6	UND	UND	Sales/Net Fixed Assets	UND	UND
108.2	39.2	190.1	61.6	UND	UND	Sales/Net Fixed Assets	67.9	73.5
14.4	6.2	4.9	5.1	27.0	47.8	Sales/Net Fixed Assets	5.1	11.3
14.2	5.1	1.0	1.0	.5	.8	Sales/Total Assets	1.9	2.9
6.7	2.8	.2	.1	.1	.1	Sales/Total Assets	.3	.7
3.1	.9	.1	.1	.0	.1	Sales/Total Assets	.1	.1
		1.3	.2			% Depr., Dep., Amort./Sales	.2	.5
		(10) 9.3	(10) .9			% Depr., Dep., Amort./Sales	(45) 1.0	(52) 1.3
		19.6	8.3			% Depr., Dep., Amort./Sales	3.9	5.3
						% Officers', Directors' Owners' Comp/Sales	6.1	3.6
						% Officers', Directors' Owners' Comp/Sales	(21) 21.2	(27) 14.5
						% Officers', Directors' Owners' Comp/Sales	28.5	25.6
18741M	47924M	144799M	435343M	591471M	1050457M	Net Sales ($)	2008725M	2102343M
3321M	15372M	203609M	501409M	1578338M	2386784M	Total Assets ($)	4766469M	3327583M

Comparative Historical Data | | Type of Statement | ## Current Data Sorted by Sales

			Type of Statement						
24	24	21	Unqualified	1	2	3	3	5	7
3	4	5	Reviewed	1	2	2			
3	5	2	Compiled				1		
17	16	18	Tax Returns	13	2	1	2		
75	64	81	Other	23	23	8	6	8	13
4/1/16-3/31/17 ALL	4/1/17-3/31/18 ALL	4/1/18-3/31/19 ALL		11 (4/1-9/30/18)			116 (10/1/18-3/31/19)		
				0-1MM	1-3MM	3-5MM	5-10MM	10-25MM	25MM & OVER
122	113	127	**NUMBER OF STATEMENTS**	38	30	14	12	13	20
%	%	%	**ASSETS**	%	%	%	%	%	%
25.1	24.2	26.0	Cash & Equivalents	23.7	23.1	36.3	42.0	11.6	27.1
14.3	12.3	9.5	Trade Receivables (net)	5.5	5.6	7.3	14.5	12.7	19.3
3.1	.8	1.7	Inventory	2.4	3.0	.1	.2	2.6	.1
9.9	7.6	6.9	All Other Current	.8	8.5	8.0	6.0	15.0	10.6
52.4	45.0	44.1	Total Current	32.4	40.3	51.7	62.7	42.0	57.2
17.3	18.5	16.2	Fixed Assets (net)	27.6	18.1	9.3	3.8	15.8	4.1
7.1	9.4	7.1	Intangibles (net)	7.8	13.1	.0	4.7	.5	7.3
23.2	27.1	32.6	All Other Non-Current	32.2	28.6	39.0	28.8	41.7	31.4
100.0	100.0	100.0	Total	100.0	100.0	100.0	100.0	100.0	100.0
			LIABILITIES						
12.2	10.3	7.7	Notes Payable-Short Term	7.8	12.1	10.8	2.0	7.2	2.4
2.8	2.0	1.4	Cur. Mat.-L.T.D.	1.7	1.5	.0	.0	3.2	1.5
3.2	6.2	4.4	Trade Payables	4.7	3.2	3.6	8.0	3.4	4.6
.0	.0	.1	Income Taxes Payable	.1	.0	.0	.0	.0	.3
11.2	9.8	16.1	All Other Current	21.4	8.0	9.5	21.6	13.6	21.3
29.4	27.3	29.7	Total Current	35.7	24.9	23.8	31.5	27.3	30.1
23.4	18.6	29.0	Long-Term Debt	38.9	32.7	8.7	19.3	20.8	30.2
.1	.1	.0	Deferred Taxes	.0	.0	.0	.0	.0	.0
7.9	6.1	5.4	All Other Non-Current	1.9	5.4	20.8	.3	1.9	6.3
39.2	48.0	35.9	Net Worth	23.5	37.0	46.7	48.8	50.0	33.5
100.0	100.0	100.0	Total Liabilties & Net Worth	100.0	100.0	100.0	100.0	100.0	100.0
			INCOME DATA						
100.0	100.0	100.0	Net Sales	100.0	100.0	100.0	100.0	100.0	100.0
			Gross Profit						
64.7	64.5	56.9	Operating Expenses	49.9	60.3	52.3	59.8	54.6	67.8
35.3	35.5	43.1	Operating Profit	50.1	39.7	47.7	40.2	45.4	32.2
11.3	8.3	11.8	All Other Expenses (net)	20.0	6.4	12.3	16.5	9.0	3.1
24.0	27.1	31.3	Profit Before Taxes	30.1	33.3	35.4	23.7	36.4	29.1
			RATIOS						
4.9	5.3	6.9		7.3	6.2	26.8	10.9	8.4	2.8
1.6	1.9	2.0	Current	1.9	1.7	5.3	1.6	2.1	2.2
.9	.8	1.1		.3	1.0	.9	1.2	1.0	1.3
3.2	3.5	4.3		5.3	4.0	11.3	5.9	8.1	2.7
1.3	1.4	1.6	Quick	1.7	1.1	2.6	1.6	1.6	1.5
.5	.5	.4		.1	.4	.2	1.1	.4	1.0
0 UND	0 UND	0 UND		0 UND	0 UND	0 UND	0 UND	0 UND	0 UND
6 60.9	0 UND	0 UND	Sales/Receivables	0 UND	0 UND	0 UND	0 UND	9 40.4	23 15.6
50 7.3	38 9.6	39 9.4		7 49.3	1 402.4	14 26.1	60 6.1	55 6.6	87 4.2
			Cost of Sales/Inventory						
			Cost of Sales/Payables						
1.4	1.5	1.4		.6	1.3	.2	.8	2.2	2.7
5.8	6.8	11.1	Sales/Working Capital	12.7	17.6	2.5	11.4	4.5	6.5
-222.6	-77.6	165.5		-6.5	UND	NM	64.1	NM	81.5
43.0	43.8	54.4		34.6	36.0				999.8
(69) 5.8	(63) 7.7	(65) 8.6	EBIT/Interest	(16) 7.2	(13) 5.4			(15)	9.0
2.3	4.0	2.8		2.6	1.4				2.6
			Net Profit + Depr., Dep., Amort./Cur. Mat. L/T/D						
.0	.0	.0		.0	.0	.0	.0	.0	.0
.1	.0	.0	Fixed/Worth	.0	.0	.0	.0	.1	.1
1.1	1.7	.9		3.1	1.7	.0	.2	.4	NM
.5	.2	.2		.3	.2	.1	.2	.3	.5
1.6	.9	1.5	Debt/Worth	2.0	1.7	.2	1.0	1.0	3.5
6.9	10.3	6.6		NM	50.1	2.6	4.1	5.1	NM
53.4	62.9	93.8	% Profit Before Taxes/Tangible Net Worth	70.0	471.3	33.5	160.8	51.5	146.4
(103) 20.4	(94) 17.4	(104) 17.0		(29) 7.6	(24) 30.8	(13) 8.2	(11) 10.5	(12) 16.1	(15) 38.4
2.9	2.7	1.9		.2	3.6	2.8	-1.4	5.5	9.6
29.9	24.1	40.9	% Profit Before Taxes/Total Assets	27.0	69.6	28.3	53.8	19.5	44.3
5.6	7.3	7.6		3.5	5.8	4.9	6.7	10.4	24.6
1.0	1.4	1.0		.1	.8	1.4	-.9	2.4	14.3
UND	UND	UND	Sales/Net Fixed Assets	UND	UND	UND	UND	UND	965.5
86.3	85.5	108.2		56.7	515.7	195.9	262.7	42.8	90.4
10.9	4.6	14.4		.5	17.1	21.4	47.7	7.6	27.0
2.1	1.8	1.9	Sales/Total Assets	3.2	2.9	2.1	4.6	1.1	1.6
.6	.5	.5		.1	.6	.1	.9	.3	.9
.1	.1	.1		.0	.1	.1	.1	.1	.6
.6	.5	.5	% Depr., Dep., Amort./Sales	1.2					.0
(55) 1.8	(48) 1.3	(43) 1.4		(12) 11.0				(11)	.5
14.0	15.1	7.9		24.9					2.3
2.9	6.5	5.9	% Officers', Directors' Owners' Comp/Sales						
(17) 7.8	(18) 9.0	(20) 12.6							
14.7	11.3	20.2							
3957060M	4265845M	2288735M	Net Sales ($)	17236M	57162M	54965M	87299M	200884M	1871189M
4791589M	4678059M	4688833M	Total Assets ($)	296137M	471704M	475747M	573255M	935828M	1936162M

M = $ thousand   MM = $ million
See Pages viii through xx for Explanation of Ratios and Data

Current Data Sorted by Assets | Comparative Historical Data

0-500M	500M-2MM	2-10MM	10-50MM	50-100MM	100-250MM	Type of Statement	4/1/14-3/31/15 ALL	4/1/15-3/31/16 ALL
		2		1	3	Unqualified	7	11
			2			Reviewed		
	1	2				Compiled	1	2
1			2	1		Tax Returns	1	3
2			3	2	7	Other	16	21
	8 (4/1-9/30/18)		21 (10/1/18-3/31/19)					
3	1	4	7	4	10	**NUMBER OF STATEMENTS**	25	37
%	%	%	%	%	%	**ASSETS**	%	%
					56.9	Cash & Equivalents	49.3	46.5
					2.6	Trade Receivables (net)	7.9	10.3
					.0	Inventory	.0	.0
					10.4	All Other Current	3.7	3.4
					70.0	Total Current	60.9	60.2
					2.3	Fixed Assets (net)	4.4	9.4
					3.8	Intangibles (net)	9.9	9.0
					23.9	All Other Non-Current	24.8	21.5
					100.0	Total	100.0	100.0
						LIABILITIES		
					.2	Notes Payable-Short Term	3.8	7.9
					.0	Cur. Mat.-L.T.D.	.9	1.3
					11.8	Trade Payables	15.2	8.4
					.0	Income Taxes Payable	.5	.3
					36.0	All Other Current	49.2	26.4
					48.0	Total Current	69.6	44.3
					1.2	Long-Term Debt	14.1	14.0
					.5	Deferred Taxes	.1	.1
					18.5	All Other Non-Current	5.9	9.8
					31.9	Net Worth	10.2	31.8
					100.0	Total Liabilties & Net Worth	100.0	100.0
						INCOME DATA		
					100.0	Net Sales	100.0	100.0
						Gross Profit		
					86.1	Operating Expenses	85.9	90.8
					13.9	Operating Profit	14.1	9.2
					5.9	All Other Expenses (net)	1.0	1.5
					8.0	Profit Before Taxes	13.0	7.8
						RATIOS		
					1.7	Current	2.1	3.3
					1.2		1.3	1.4
					1.0		.9	.9
					1.5	Quick	2.0	3.2
					1.0		1.3	1.3
					.9		.6	.7
					0 UND	Sales/Receivables	0 UND	0 UND
					0 UND		0 UND	2 155.7
					261 1.4		26 14.1	47 7.8
						Cost of Sales/Inventory		
						Cost of Sales/Payables		
					.5	Sales/Working Capital	1.7	1.4
					1.7		8.4	7.6
					NM		-5.9	-124.1
						EBIT/Interest	36.5	21.3
							(12) 5.4	(21) 8.6
							-7.8	2.5
						Net Profit + Depr., Dep., Amort./Cur. Mat. L/T/D		
					.0	Fixed/Worth	.0	.0
					.0		.0	.1
					.0		.3	.8
					1.5	Debt/Worth	1.1	.8
					4.2		2.3	2.1
					17.0		12.0	9.9
					16.2	% Profit Before Taxes/Tangible Net Worth	27.1	19.0
					6.5		(20) 8.9	(31) 6.6
					1.3		1.9	1.0
					4.7	% Profit Before Taxes/Total Assets	9.5	13.0
					.8		3.1	2.5
					.1		.0	.4
					UND	Sales/Net Fixed Assets	UND	UND
					UND		67.2	48.3
					7.7		26.0	14.8
					.5	Sales/Total Assets	1.7	1.8
					.1		.7	.7
					.1		.2	.2
						% Depr., Dep., Amort./Sales		.5
							(15) 1.7	1.7
								4.6
						% Officers', Directors' Owners' Comp/Sales		
696M	2880M	2949M	97317M	527403M	572728M	Net Sales ($)	1093921M	1476444M
625M	1636M	13649M	189669M	343773M	1645261M	Total Assets ($)	1556137M	2660571M

M = $ thousand   MM = $ million
See Pages viii through xx for Explanation of Ratios and Data

Comparative Historical Data   Current Data Sorted by Sales

Type of Statement

	18 4/1/16-3/31/17 ALL	17 4/1/17-3/31/18 ALL	16 4/1/18-3/31/19 ALL		0-1MM	1-3MM	3-5MM	5-10MM	10-25MM	25MM & OVER
Unqualified	7	7	6					4	2	
Reviewed	2	1	2						2	
Compiled	1		3		1	2				
Tax Returns	1	2	2		1					1
Other	18	17	16		4		1	1	6	4

8 (4/1-9/30/18) spans 0-1MM, 1-3MM, 3-5MM; *21 (10/1/18-3/31/19)* spans 5-10MM, 10-25MM, 25MM & OVER.

	4/1/16-3/31/17 ALL	4/1/17-3/31/18 ALL	4/1/18-3/31/19 ALL	0-1MM	1-3MM	3-5MM	5-10MM	10-25MM	25MM & OVER
NUMBER OF STATEMENTS	29	27	29	6	2	1	5	10	5
ASSETS	%	%	%	%	%	%	%	%	%
Cash & Equivalents	40.1	43.9	43.1					59.0	
Trade Receivables (net)	14.8	6.8	7.1					3.3	
Inventory	.0	.0	.0					.0	
All Other Current	4.8	2.1	6.7					1.2	
Total Current	59.6	52.8	56.9					63.5	
Fixed Assets (net)	3.6	6.6	5.9					2.7	
Intangibles (net)	14.5	15.6	12.8					7.1	
All Other Non-Current	22.3	25.0	24.4					26.7	
Total	100.0	100.0	100.0					100.0	
LIABILITIES									
Notes Payable-Short Term	11.3	6.3	5.7					.1	
Cur. Mat.-L.T.D.	5.7	.9	1.4					1.5	
Trade Payables	11.2	5.8	10.1					14.9	
Income Taxes Payable	.4	.4	.7					.8	
All Other Current	30.9	29.1	32.6					23.2	
Total Current	59.5	42.4	50.4					40.5	
Long-Term Debt	13.4	8.9	14.4					11.8	
Deferred Taxes	.0	.5	.2					.0	
All Other Non-Current	7.1	4.6	7.4					5.8	
Net Worth	19.9	43.5	27.6					41.9	
Total Liabilties & Net Worth	100.0	100.0	100.0					100.0	
INCOME DATA									
Net Sales	100.0	100.0	100.0					100.0	
Gross Profit									
Operating Expenses	82.7	86.9	79.1					84.0	
Operating Profit	17.3	13.1	20.9					16.0	
All Other Expenses (net)	2.8	-.2	6.8					2.4	
Profit Before Taxes	14.5	13.3	14.1					13.6	
RATIOS									
Current	2.2	1.8	2.0					2.6	
	1.1	1.1	1.2					1.2	
	.7	.7	1.0					1.0	
Quick	2.2	1.8	1.9					2.5	
	1.1	1.1	1.1					1.2	
	.6	.6	.5					1.0	
Sales/Receivables	0 UND	0 UND	0 UND					0 UND	
	29 12.6	2 233.2	0 UND					9 41.2	
	94 3.9	22 16.4	96 3.8					83 4.4	
Cost of Sales/Inventory									
Cost of Sales/Payables									
Sales/Working Capital	1.6	1.4	.8					.6	
	8.8	10.3	5.2					5.6	
	-7.6	-14.3	-17.0					NM	
EBIT/Interest	42.0	69.9	11.3						
	(19) 8.8	(15) 11.7	(16) 6.7						
	1.5	3.7	1.4						
Net Profit + Depr., Dep., Amort./Cur. Mat. L/T/D									
Fixed/Worth	.0	.0	.0					.0	
	.0	.0	.0					.0	
	NM	.3	.2					.1	
Debt/Worth	.7	.8	.6					.6	
	5.1	2.5	2.2					1.8	
	-3.8	5.5	17.8					4.8	
% Profit Before Taxes/Tangible Net Worth	63.5	65.7	23.0					36.5	
	(20) 9.4	(24) 17.7	(24) 6.8					8.7	
	-.3	3.8	2.3					3.5	
% Profit Before Taxes/Total Assets	30.7	11.9	11.5					9.9	
	4.1	6.1	2.9					2.3	
	-.1	2.4	.4					1.1	
Sales/Net Fixed Assets	UND	UND	UND					UND	
	137.4	131.4	UND					109.9	
	16.6	16.1	16.7					10.2	
Sales/Total Assets	1.9	1.4	1.1					.6	
	.6	.8	.3					.2	
	.4	.2	.1					.2	
% Depr., Dep., Amort./Sales		.8							
		(10) 1.4							
		3.9							
% Officers', Directors' Owners' Comp/Sales									
Net Sales ($)	1522067M	1097404M	1203973M	1753M	4772M	3399M	40810M	172082M	981157M
Total Assets ($)	1502363M	1270755M	2194613M	11778M	4132M	20860M	697020M	812780M	648043M

© RMA 2019   M = $ thousand   MM = $ million
See Pages viii through xx for Explanation of Ratios and Data

Current Data Sorted by Assets   Comparative Historical Data

0-500M	500M-2MM	2-10MM	10-50MM	50-100MM	100-250MM	Type of Statement	4/1/14-3/31/15 ALL	4/1/15-3/31/16 ALL
1			2	11	8	Unqualified	39	38
		1				Reviewed	1	
						Compiled		3
						Tax Returns	2	1
3	6	2	14	9	9	Other	40	31
							4/1/14-3/31/15	4/1/15-3/31/16
8 (4/1-9/30/18)			58 (10/1/18-3/31/19)				ALL	ALL
4	6	3	16	20	17	**NUMBER OF STATEMENTS**	82	73
%	%	%	%	%	%	**ASSETS**	%	%
			56.0	49.9	33.1	Cash & Equivalents	43.5	40.2
			13.6	10.2	10.3	Trade Receivables (net)	13.4	13.5
			.0	.0	.2	Inventory	.1	.0
			6.8	7.8	6.2	All Other Current	7.8	8.2
			76.4	67.8	49.7	Total Current	64.8	61.9
			8.6	5.1	7.9	Fixed Assets (net)	8.7	7.7
			7.6	9.1	17.8	Intangibles (net)	8.6	8.0
			7.4	18.0	24.6	All Other Non-Current	17.8	22.4
			100.0	100.0	100.0	Total	100.0	100.0
						LIABILITIES		
			.5	.3	.2	Notes Payable-Short Term	1.3	2.5
			.5	.2	.4	Cur. Mat.-L.T.D.	1.2	2.3
			10.0	7.9	14.2	Trade Payables	12.9	13.3
			.2	.3	.7	Income Taxes Payable	.2	.3
			33.6	16.9	26.9	All Other Current	27.9	24.3
			44.9	25.6	42.4	Total Current	43.6	42.7
			10.2	6.4	5.4	Long-Term Debt	14.8	10.2
			.1	.3	1.2	Deferred Taxes	.1	.4
			3.6	10.7	6.9	All Other Non-Current	9.9	5.2
			41.3	56.9	44.1	Net Worth	31.6	41.6
			100.0	100.0	100.0	Total Liabilities & Net Worth	100.0	100.0
						INCOME DATA		
			100.0	100.0	100.0	Net Sales	100.0	100.0
						Gross Profit		
			90.3	95.6	96.8	Operating Expenses	95.9	95.2
			9.7	4.4	3.2	Operating Profit	4.1	4.8
			-.8	.0	-.2	All Other Expenses (net)	.8	.9
			10.5	4.4	3.4	Profit Before Taxes	3.3	3.9
						RATIOS		
			2.3	5.0	1.7		2.3	2.9
			1.7	2.6	1.1	Current	1.4	1.5
			1.1	1.7	.8		1.0	1.0
			2.0	5.0	1.5		2.0	2.5
			1.6	1.9	.9	Quick	1.2	1.2
			1.1	1.4	.7		.8	.8
			0 UND	9 41.2	6 59.7		3 110.5	3 107.9
			33 11.1	18 20.8	20 18.3	Sales/Receivables	15 23.6	14 26.0
			48 7.6	29 12.7	42 8.6		34 10.7	35 10.4
						Cost of Sales/Inventory		
						Cost of Sales/Payables		
			2.1	2.6	12.8		5.9	4.0
			8.3	5.5	49.8	Sales/Working Capital	13.0	17.0
			27.6	9.2	-12.5		-146.3	NM
			158.5				53.7	56.6
			(10) 13.4			EBIT/Interest	(39) 14.2	(35) 9.9
			3.5				-.7	-1.1
						Net Profit + Depr., Dep.,	8.1	5.5
						Amort./Cur. Mat. L/T/D	(15) 2.0	(12) 3.9
							-1.0	3.2
			.0	.0	.0		.0	.0
			.0	.1	.5	Fixed/Worth	.1	.1
			.4	.4	-1.3		1.1	.4
			.7	.4	.5		.9	.6
			2.1	.7	2.2	Debt/Worth	1.8	1.3
			5.8	3.0	-11.3		9.4	4.3
			87.1	41.4	40.0	% Profit Before Taxes/Tangible	42.2	34.5
			(15) 20.8	(19) 11.6	(12) 11.9	Net Worth	(67) 10.4	(65) 10.8
			13.2	-1.2	-5.3		-12.5	-1.4
			17.6	8.4	8.8	% Profit Before Taxes/Total	11.3	13.5
			7.4	5.1	5.4	Assets	4.0	5.1
			3.2	-.6	-.3		-6.6	-2.0
			UND	912.7	558.4		999.8	UND
			999.8	43.0	28.9	Sales/Net Fixed Assets	75.6	73.9
			33.3	28.1	12.5		21.7	18.3
			2.5	2.8	2.7		3.8	4.2
			1.1	1.7	2.4	Sales/Total Assets	2.1	2.2
			.9	.9	1.2		1.0	1.1
				.3			.2	.3
				(12) .6		% Depr., Dep., Amort./Sales	(46) .5	(42) .7
				1.2			1.8	1.8
						% Officers', Directors' Owners' Comp/Sales		
6805M	68393M	43515M	615938M	2918333M	7042284M	Net Sales ($)	15462263M	13701829M
583M	7602M	10627M	405051M	1458651M	3147809M	Total Assets ($)	5869236M	5338139M

© RMA 2019

M = $ thousand   MM = $ million
See Pages viii through xx for Explanation of Ratios and Data

Comparative Historical Data | Current Data Sorted by Sales

			Type of Statement						
15	16 1 1	22 1	Unqualified	1			2		19
1 1 31	1 1 42	1 1 43	Reviewed Compiled Tax Returns				1		
4/1/16- 3/31/17 ALL	4/1/17- 3/31/18 ALL	4/1/18- 3/31/19 ALL	Other	3 0-1MM	3 8 (4/1-9/30/18) 1-3MM	2 3-5MM	3 58 (10/1/18-3/31/19) 5-10MM	3 10-25MM	29 25MM & OVER
48	61	66	**NUMBER OF STATEMENTS**	4	3	2	4	5	48
%	%	%	**ASSETS**	%	%	%	%	%	%
43.8	43.0	45.1	Cash & Equivalents						45.2
14.4	15.1	10.4	Trade Receivables (net)						10.7
.2	.1	.0	Inventory						.1
9.2	6.5	6.8	All Other Current						7.4
67.6	64.6	62.3	Total Current						63.4
8.5	6.7	7.1	Fixed Assets (net)						5.8
8.1	12.2	12.1	Intangibles (net)						11.9
15.8	16.5	18.5	All Other Non-Current						18.9
100.0	100.0	100.0	Total						100.0
			LIABILITIES						
.4	3.6	3.4	Notes Payable-Short Term						.4
.7	.3	.4	Cur. Mat.-L.T.D.						.4
12.7	14.6	10.2	Trade Payables						11.4
.5	.3	.4	Income Taxes Payable						.4
35.1	25.2	22.9	All Other Current						24.9
49.5	43.9	37.2	Total Current						37.5
10.6	4.5	6.6	Long-Term Debt						6.1
.9	.8	.4	Deferred Taxes						.5
3.8	7.3	6.4	All Other Non-Current						5.9
35.2	43.5	49.4	Net Worth						50.0
100.0	100.0	100.0	Total Liabilties & Net Worth						100.0
			INCOME DATA						
100.0	100.0	100.0	Net Sales						100.0
			Gross Profit						
95.5	95.4	91.9	Operating Expenses						94.7
4.5	4.6	8.1	Operating Profit						5.3
.1	-.3	-.2	All Other Expenses (net)						.0
4.4	4.9	8.2	Profit Before Taxes						5.4
			RATIOS						
2.6	2.0	2.9							2.8
1.7	1.5	1.6	Current						1.6
1.0	1.0	1.1							1.1
2.2	1.9	2.8							2.3
1.4	1.1	1.5	Quick						1.5
.8	.8	.9							.9
5 79.6	5 69.7	4 91.5						6	63.4
17 21.9	17 21.5	16 22.9	Sales/Receivables					16	22.9
49 7.5	35 10.5	34 10.7						29	12.4
			Cost of Sales/Inventory						
			Cost of Sales/Payables						
5.3	5.8	3.1							3.4
10.7	12.4	13.0	Sales/Working Capital						11.5
62.4	-327.7	81.8							59.0
57.2	81.4	55.6							43.3
(17) 7.1	(25) 19.8	(30) 10.2	EBIT/Interest					(19)	7.9
2.6	3.0	4.3							2.7
			Net Profit + Depr., Dep., Amort./Cur. Mat. L/T/D						
.0	.0	.0							.0
.1	.1	.1	Fixed/Worth						.1
.5	.6	.6							.7
.6	.8	.4							.4
1.3	1.9	1.6	Debt/Worth						1.1
4.7	4.6	6.8							8.4
55.8	51.3	60.2	% Profit Before Taxes/Tangible						50.0
(41) 21.1	(56) 15.7	(57) 17.6	Net Worth					(41)	13.4
3.5	1.9	.6							-.5
17.1	14.5	12.9	% Profit Before Taxes/Total						10.5
7.8	6.7	6.9	Assets						6.6
.9	.4	1.0							.2
999.8	999.8	UND							999.8
64.5	62.4	95.2	Sales/Net Fixed Assets						44.3
21.6	27.4	27.6							26.5
4.2	3.7	2.9							2.9
2.2	2.2	1.8	Sales/Total Assets						2.1
1.1	1.3	1.0							1.1
.2	.3	.3							.3
(25) .5	(37) .7	(30) 1.0	% Depr., Dep., Amort./Sales					(24)	.6
2.0	1.4	1.6							1.5
			% Officers', Directors' Owners' Comp/Sales						
11092785M	10222950M	10695268M	Net Sales ($)	1949M	7226M	8912M	27987M	96552M	10552642M
3638269M	4351868M	5030323M	Total Assets ($)	1171M	4534M	13713M	20076M	162488M	4828341M

M = $ thousand   MM = $ million
See Pages viii through xx for Explanation of Ratios and Data

Current Data Sorted by Assets | **Comparative Historical Data**

	0-500M	500M-2MM	2-10MM	10-50MM	50-100MM	100-250MM	Type of Statement	4/1/14-3/31/15 ALL	4/1/15-3/31/16 ALL
				1	2	9	Unqualified	23	22
				1			Reviewed	2	2
	2			2	2		Compiled	3	2
							Tax Returns	12	6
	2	4 (4/1-9/30/18)	3	14 (55, 10/1/18-3/31/19)	6	11	Other	46	48
	4	4	3	18	10	20	**NUMBER OF STATEMENTS**	86	80
	%	%	%	%	%	%	**ASSETS**	%	%
				54.8	82.1	63.5	Cash & Equivalents	52.1	49.2
				9.6	3.9	7.9	Trade Receivables (net)	9.3	12.5
				2.0	.0	.0	Inventory	.7	.9
				2.8	2.9	5.0	All Other Current	5.8	5.7
				69.3	88.9	76.3	Total Current	67.8	68.3
				7.4	1.6	1.1	Fixed Assets (net)	5.4	2.9
				1.4	.1	4.6	Intangibles (net)	5.8	7.3
				22.0	9.4	17.9	All Other Non-Current	21.0	21.5
				100.0	100.0	100.0	Total	100.0	100.0
							LIABILITIES		
				2.2	.0	1.1	Notes Payable-Short Term	3.3	1.5
				.8	.0	.2	Cur. Mat.-L.T.D.	1.8	1.7
				5.1	3.0	6.7	Trade Payables	12.9	9.7
				.3	.3	.2	Income Taxes Payable	.2	.6
				32.4	47.8	37.9	All Other Current	33.0	36.0
				40.7	51.1	46.1	Total Current	51.2	49.3
				11.9	.2	1.2	Long-Term Debt	7.8	4.1
				.5	.0	.2	Deferred Taxes	.1	.1
				10.8	8.1	13.2	All Other Non-Current	7.8	6.3
				36.0	40.6	39.3	Net Worth	33.1	40.1
				100.0	100.0	100.0	Total Liabilities & Net Worth	100.0	100.0
							INCOME DATA		
				100.0	100.0	100.0	Net Sales	100.0	100.0
							Gross Profit		
				86.5	91.0	95.7	Operating Expenses	89.6	90.4
				13.5	9.0	4.3	Operating Profit	10.4	9.6
				-1.9	-3.6	-3.4	All Other Expenses (net)	-.2	-1.6
				15.3	12.6	7.6	Profit Before Taxes	10.6	11.2
							RATIOS		
				2.3	2.1	2.3	Current	2.0	1.9
				1.6	1.8	1.7		1.4	1.5
				1.2	1.3	1.3		.9	.9
				2.0	2.1	2.3	Quick	2.0	1.9
				1.5	1.6	1.6		1.2	1.2
				1.0	1.3	1.1		.7	.7
		0	UND	0 UND	21 17.2		Sales/Receivables	0 UND	0 999.8
		21	17.6	26 14.2	74 4.9			22 16.9	34 10.6
		54	6.7	101 3.6	130 2.8			74 4.9	85 4.3
							Cost of Sales/Inventory		
							Cost of Sales/Payables		
				1.4	.4	.7	Sales/Working Capital	1.5	1.3
				2.5	1.0	1.0		7.0	3.4
				17.0	2.1	3.8		-21.0	-30.5
							EBIT/Interest	105.6	52.1
								(30) 22.1	(32) 13.5
								1.3	2.1
							Net Profit + Depr., Dep., Amort./Cur. Mat. L/T/D		
				.0	.0	.0	Fixed/Worth	.0	.0
				.0	.0	.0		.0	.0
				.2	.0	.0		.4	.1
				.9	.9	.9	Debt/Worth	.9	.8
				1.5	1.3	1.7		1.7	1.6
				1.9	3.0	5.7		6.1	7.5
				19.0	16.7	12.7	% Profit Before Taxes/Tangible Net Worth	56.4	50.6
			(17)	12.2	5.5	(18) 7.2		(73) 15.5	(70) 17.1
				6.2	2.4	-.2		5.3	4.6
				8.3	8.8	6.1	% Profit Before Taxes/Total Assets	14.8	13.2
				5.0	1.9	1.1		5.4	5.9
				2.4	1.0	-.7		1.1	1.1
				UND	UND	UND	Sales/Net Fixed Assets	UND	UND
				335.0	UND	625.5		68.4	114.2
				23.8	12.5	51.3		18.5	20.9
				.7	.5	.5	Sales/Total Assets	1.5	1.2
				.6	.3	.4		.7	.6
				.3	.2	.2		.3	.4
							% Depr., Dep., Amort./Sales	.3	.3
			(37)					(37) .9	(40) .7
								1.8	1.3
							% Officers', Directors' Owners' Comp/Sales	1.2	1.2
			(17)					(17) 5.5	(13) 6.3
								11.9	19.0
	4177M	7549M	15372M	449490M	259843M	1173039M	Net Sales ($)	3166628M	3168765M
	823M	4056M	18438M	558339M	743708M	3275451M	Total Assets ($)	5142404M	5407092M

M = $ thousand   MM = $ million
See Pages viii through xx for Explanation of Ratios and Data

Comparative Historical Data | Current Data Sorted by Sales

	4/1/16-3/31/17 ALL	4/1/17-3/31/18 ALL	4/1/18-3/31/19 ALL	Type of Statement	0-1MM	1-3MM	3-5MM	5-10MM	10-25MM	25MM & OVER
	19	17	16	Unqualified		1			6	9
	1	1	1	Reviewed		1			1	
	2		2	Compiled						2
	3	3	2	Tax Returns	1	1				
	41	42	38	Other	4	3		6	6	19
					4 (4/1-9/30/18)			55 (10/1/18-3/31/19)		
	66	63	59	NUMBER OF STATEMENTS	5	5		6	13	30
	%	%	%	ASSETS	%	%	%	%	%	%
Cash & Equivalents	49.0	48.9	58.9						66.9	64.7
Trade Receivables (net)	8.4	12.3	9.7						9.9	7.5
Inventory	.0	.3	.6						.0	1.2
All Other Current	6.6	6.1	5.2						10.7	4.1
Total Current	64.0	67.6	74.4						87.5	77.6
Fixed Assets (net)	5.4	7.0	3.2						5.5	3.3
Intangibles (net)	10.9	6.7	7.2						.3	3.1
All Other Non-Current	19.7	18.8	15.2						6.7	16.0
Total	100.0	100.0	100.0						100.0	100.0
				LIABILITIES						
Notes Payable-Short Term	3.2	4.2	1.4						2.0	1.3
Cur. Mat.-L.T.D.	2.1	2.3	2.2						.0	.5
Trade Payables	10.1	7.9	8.1						5.0	4.5
Income Taxes Payable	.4	.3	.2						.1	.2
All Other Current	33.9	33.5	32.5						35.8	41.1
Total Current	49.8	48.3	44.4						42.9	47.6
Long-Term Debt	8.8	4.1	11.7						1.3	6.6
Deferred Taxes	.0	.1	.4						.0	.4
All Other Non-Current	9.2	7.8	12.4						8.5	10.4
Net Worth	32.2	39.6	31.0						47.3	35.0
Total Liabilities & Net Worth	100.0	100.0	100.0						100.0	100.0
				INCOME DATA						
Net Sales	100.0	100.0	100.0						100.0	100.0
Gross Profit										
Operating Expenses	96.0	92.9	88.1						86.0	98.4
Operating Profit	4.0	7.1	11.9						14.0	1.6
All Other Expenses (net)	-.9	-1.5	-1.7						-5.7	-2.6
Profit Before Taxes	4.8	8.7	13.6						19.7	4.3
				RATIOS						
	2.1	2.2	2.3						2.4	2.1
Current	1.4	1.5	1.6						2.0	1.6
	.9	.9	1.2						1.6	1.3
	2.0	2.0	2.1						2.2	2.0
Quick	1.3	1.4	1.5						1.7	1.5
	.7	.8	.9						1.4	1.1
	0 UND	0 UND	0 UND						0 UND	0 999.8
Sales/Receivables	20 18.7	30 12.3	30 12.1						55 6.6	46 8.0
	61 6.0	83 4.4	91 4.0						135 2.7	85 4.3
				Cost of Sales/Inventory						
				Cost of Sales/Payables						
	1.3	1.1	.9						.4	.9
Sales/Working Capital	7.3	2.9	2.0						1.2	1.8
	-21.0	-72.4	10.1						1.9	5.7
	62.3	79.4	39.3							
EBIT/Interest	(27) 8.9	(20) 14.5	(22) 12.6							
	.6	2.0	1.5							
				Net Profit + Depr., Dep., Amort./Cur. Mat. L/T/D						
	.0	.0	.0						.0	.0
Fixed/Worth	.0	.0	.0						.0	.0
	.4	.3	.1						.2	.0
	1.1	.8	.9						.7	.9
Debt/Worth	2.6	2.0	1.6						.9	1.4
	9.9	5.5	9.0						1.6	3.3
% Profit Before Taxes/Tangible	35.0	23.0	18.1						20.1	12.2
Net Worth	(54) 13.2	(54) 10.9	(48) 10.4						14.8	(27) 7.0
	-8.4	-2.6	2.9						5.5	-1.8
% Profit Before Taxes/Total	16.1	7.8	9.0						9.8	5.4
Assets	4.5	3.9	3.7						7.3	1.4
	-2.3	-1.2	.5						3.0	-1.3
	UND	UND	UND						UND	UND
Sales/Net Fixed Assets	193.3	199.0	644.5						132.0	475.4
	19.2	15.7	38.2						4.4	57.9
	1.5	1.0	.7						.7	.6
Sales/Total Assets	.5	.6	.5						.5	.5
	.3	.3	.3						.2	.4
	.3	.3	.2							.1
% Depr., Dep., Amort./Sales	(24) .7	(19) .9	(18) .6						(12)	.4
	1.9	2.3	1.7							1.7
				% Officers', Directors' Owners' Comp/Sales						
Net Sales ($)	2293354M	2416197M	1909470M	3698M	7774M		38984M	205358M	1653656M
Total Assets ($)	4022321M	4463762M	4600815M	23036M	14038M		341892M	622984M	3598865M

M = $ thousand   MM = $ million
See Pages viii through xx for Explanation of Ratios and Data

Current Data Sorted by Assets   Comparative Historical Data

0-500M	500M-2MM	2-10MM	10-50MM	50-100MM	100-250MM	Type of Statement	4/1/14-3/31/15 ALL	4/1/15-3/31/16 ALL
		5	1		1	Unqualified	11	12
		2				Reviewed	1	
	1	1				Compiled	2	3
1	2	1				Tax Returns	3	6
4	1	2	2		1	Other	11	11
	1 (4/1-9/30/18)		23 (10/1/18-3/31/19)					
5	4	10	3	1	1	**NUMBER OF STATEMENTS**	28	32
%	%	%	%	%	%		%	%
						ASSETS		
		41.1				Cash & Equivalents	35.0	40.4
		13.1				Trade Receivables (net)	10.1	7.3
		.0				Inventory	.5	.9
		10.2				All Other Current	5.1	3.7
		64.4				Total Current	50.7	52.3
		3.3				Fixed Assets (net)	18.6	10.7
		17.8				Intangibles (net)	6.1	13.1
		14.5				All Other Non-Current	24.6	23.9
		100.0				Total	100.0	100.0
						LIABILITIES		
		.3				Notes Payable-Short Term	6.4	3.6
		2.3				Cur. Mat.-L.T.D.	1.8	3.4
		4.4				Trade Payables	14.1	11.1
		.1				Income Taxes Payable	.1	.2
		17.7				All Other Current	8.8	16.3
		24.9				Total Current	31.2	34.7
		16.1				Long-Term Debt	7.6	8.3
		.0				Deferred Taxes	.1	.4
		6.2				All Other Non-Current	8.2	3.5
		52.7				Net Worth	52.9	53.2
		100.0				Total Liabilities & Net Worth	100.0	100.0
						INCOME DATA		
		100.0				Net Sales	100.0	100.0
						Gross Profit		
		93.3				Operating Expenses	92.7	90.0
		6.7				Operating Profit	7.3	10.0
		1.8				All Other Expenses (net)	.2	-.2
		4.9				Profit Before Taxes	7.0	10.2
						RATIOS		
		8.1				Current	2.8	2.9
		2.0					1.7	1.6
		1.6					.9	1.0
		2.7				Quick	2.7	2.9
		2.0					1.4	1.6
		1.6					.8	.6
		4 82.6				Sales/Receivables	0 UND	0 UND
		9 41.7					5 77.2	5 80.9
		37 9.9					27 13.4	19 19.7
						Cost of Sales/Inventory		
						Cost of Sales/Payables		
		4.4				Sales/Working Capital	6.2	6.5
		10.6					24.0	19.4
		12.3					-308.8	153.0
						EBIT/Interest	57.2	74.9
							(13) 4.2	(14) 19.2
							-2.6	2.7
						Net Profit + Depr., Dep., Amort./Cur. Mat. L/T/D		
		.1				Fixed/Worth	.0	.0
		.1					.2	.1
		.2					1.2	.3
		.5				Debt/Worth	.4	.4
		1.1					.7	.8
		5.5					1.9	4.5
						% Profit Before Taxes/Tangible Net Worth	54.8	81.3
							(25) 11.8	(29) 28.5
							-2.5	11.2
		23.0				% Profit Before Taxes/Total Assets	34.8	24.7
		10.4					6.6	11.9
		.3					-1.1	5.3
		UND				Sales/Net Fixed Assets	174.3	168.3
		149.9					39.7	47.3
		40.5					20.6	23.3
		3.4				Sales/Total Assets	5.1	3.9
		2.7					2.7	2.3
		1.7					1.2	1.3
						% Depr., Dep., Amort./Sales	.4	.4
							(20) 1.1	(21) .6
							1.5	1.7
						% Officers', Directors' Owners' Comp/Sales		
4282M	10030M	125530M	284116M	36109M	138125M	Net Sales ($)	880586M	1544409M
976M	5701M	46353M	92542M	94757M	244268M	Total Assets ($)	702670M	1047169M

M = $ thousand   MM = $ million
See Pages viii through xx for Explanation of Ratios and Data

Comparative Historical Data   **Current Data Sorted by Sales**

			Type of Statement	0-1MM	1-3MM	3-5MM	5-10MM	10-25MM	25MM & OVER
12	13	7	Unqualified			1	1	4	1
			Reviewed						
2	4	3	Compiled		1		1	1	
3	5	4	Tax Returns	2	1		1		
11	9	10	Other	3	1	1		2	3
4/1/16-3/31/17 ALL	4/1/17-3/31/18 ALL	4/1/18-3/31/19 ALL		1 (4/1-9/30/18)		23 (10/1/18-3/31/19)			
28	31	24	**NUMBER OF STATEMENTS**	5	3	2	3	7	4
%	%	%	**ASSETS**	%	%	%	%	%	%
49.5	45.4	40.3	Cash & Equivalents						
4.2	5.6	7.3	Trade Receivables (net)						
.6	.0	.0	Inventory						
1.1	2.1	6.9	All Other Current						
55.5	53.0	54.5	Total Current						
7.7	11.7	6.3	Fixed Assets (net)						
13.4	13.9	15.0	Intangibles (net)						
23.3	21.4	24.2	All Other Non-Current						
100.0	100.0	100.0	Total						
			LIABILITIES						
6.0	.7	.5	Notes Payable-Short Term						
2.9	3.2	1.1	Cur. Mat.-L.T.D.						
9.2	12.3	4.3	Trade Payables						
.3	.7	.3	Income Taxes Payable						
13.1	14.9	20.6	All Other Current						
31.5	31.7	26.7	Total Current						
5.6	11.3	7.8	Long-Term Debt						
.8	1.0	.1	Deferred Taxes						
16.0	8.4	7.5	All Other Non-Current						
46.1	47.6	57.9	Net Worth						
100.0	100.0	100.0	Total Liabilities & Net Worth						
			INCOME DATA						
100.0	100.0	100.0	Net Sales						
			Gross Profit						
81.4	90.3	84.7	Operating Expenses						
18.6	9.7	15.3	Operating Profit						
-1.4	-1.2	-.4	All Other Expenses (net)						
19.9	10.9	15.7	Profit Before Taxes						
			RATIOS						
5.4	3.4	3.3	Current						
2.3	2.1	2.3							
1.1	.7	1.1							
5.4	3.4	3.0	Quick						
2.3	2.0	2.0							
.9	.7	1.1							
0 UND	0 UND	0 UND	Sales/Receivables						
3 144.1	5 73.2	5 76.2							
20 18.3	23 15.7	31 11.9							
			Cost of Sales/Inventory						
			Cost of Sales/Payables						
2.4	2.2	4.8	Sales/Working Capital						
6.2	7.4	11.2							
NM	-142.1	260.3							
192.7	138.5		EBIT/Interest						
(12) 53.7	(10) 11.4								
4.7	-1.3								
			Net Profit + Depr., Dep., Amort./Cur. Mat. L/T/D						
.0	.0	.0	Fixed/Worth						
.1	.1	.1							
.2	1.8	.2							
.3	.4	.4	Debt/Worth						
.5	.8	.8							
2.4	92.8	2.5							
75.8	46.7	125.4	% Profit Before Taxes/Tangible Net Worth						
(23) 38.6	(24) 18.6	(22) 52.8							
17.7	9.7	12.3							
52.5	17.2	62.0	% Profit Before Taxes/Total Assets						
17.1	9.6	18.4							
8.6	.0	7.3							
157.8	284.8	904.6	Sales/Net Fixed Assets						
56.7	44.6	125.8							
14.3	17.3	29.4							
3.5	3.0	3.8	Sales/Total Assets						
1.8	1.7	2.7							
.8	.6	1.0							
.4	.3	.2	% Depr., Dep., Amort./Sales						
(14) .6	(14) .5	(11) .4							
1.1	1.4	1.0							
			% Officers', Directors' Owners' Comp/Sales						
943710M	982327M	598192M	Net Sales ($)	2065M	6057M	7791M	21599M	111188M	449492M
1136885M	1244869M	484597M	Total Assets ($)	2911M	2193M	7068M	24418M	35416M	412591M

M = $ thousand   MM = $ million
See Pages viii through xx for Explanation of Ratios and Data

Current Data Sorted by Assets							Comparative Historical Data	

		2 1	6	4	1	**Type of Statement**		
	1					Unqualified	25	18
	1					Reviewed		
1	1	2	2	2	5	Compiled	2	1
	7 (4/1-9/30/18)		21 (10/1/18-3/31/19)			Tax Returns	2	3
0-500M	500M-2MM	2-10MM	10-50MM	50-100MM	100-250MM	Other	14	23
							4/1/14- 3/31/15	4/1/15- 3/31/16
1	2	5	8	6	6		ALL	ALL
						NUMBER OF STATEMENTS	43	45
%	%	%	%	%	%	**ASSETS**	%	%
						Cash & Equivalents	47.7	39.0
						Trade Receivables (net)	10.3	10.4
						Inventory	.1	.1
						All Other Current	5.4	7.4
						Total Current	63.5	56.9
						Fixed Assets (net)	3.5	3.6
						Intangibles (net)	7.0	16.9
						All Other Non-Current	26.0	22.5
						Total	100.0	100.0
						LIABILITIES		
						Notes Payable-Short Term	2.6	4.0
						Cur. Mat.-L.T.D.	1.7	2.3
						Trade Payables	12.2	8.2
						Income Taxes Payable	.4	.3
						All Other Current	21.2	20.8
						Total Current	38.0	35.8
						Long-Term Debt	2.3	8.2
						Deferred Taxes	.6	1.3
						All Other Non-Current	19.6	17.8
						Net Worth	39.5	37.0
						Total Liabilties & Net Worth	100.0	100.0
						INCOME DATA		
						Net Sales	100.0	100.0
						Gross Profit		
						Operating Expenses	83.6	79.6
						Operating Profit	16.4	20.4
						All Other Expenses (net)	-1.3	1.1
						Profit Before Taxes	17.7	19.2
						RATIOS		
							4.6	2.6
						Current	1.4	1.5
							1.0	1.0
							4.5	2.0
						Quick	1.4	1.3
							.6	.8
							8 46.5	5 80.0
						Sales/Receivables	28 13.0	23 16.2
							89 4.1	58 6.3
						Cost of Sales/Inventory		
						Cost of Sales/Payables		
							1.0	1.4
						Sales/Working Capital	2.3	6.2
							999.8	-61.9
							569.1	94.7
						EBIT/Interest	(16) 73.2	(25) 18.7
							4.8	2.2
						Net Profit + Depr., Dep., Amort./Cur. Mat. L/T/D		
							.0	.0
						Fixed/Worth	.1	2.1
							.3	2.1
							.9	.6
						Debt/Worth	2.4	2.2
							9.2	NM
						% Profit Before Taxes/Tangible Net Worth	46.0	97.0
							(37) 14.5	(34) 21.4
							3.4	4.7
						% Profit Before Taxes/Total Assets	9.8	21.1
							5.5	5.1
							1.5	1.9
							UND	UND
						Sales/Net Fixed Assets	58.4	138.5
							13.6	30.1
							1.0	1.6
						Sales/Total Assets	.5	.5
							.2	.3
							.6	.6
						% Depr., Dep., Amort./Sales	(17) .8	(11) 1.1
							2.2	2.9
						% Officers', Directors' Owners' Comp/Sales		
883M	16316M	12347M	175193M	230861M	426877M	Net Sales ($)	1314104M	1517094M
36M	1898M	22656M	222404M	432995M	937664M	Total Assets ($)	2512552M	2942101M

M = $ thousand   MM = $ million
See Pages viii through xx for Explanation of Ratios and Data

Comparative Historical Data   ## Current Data Sorted by Sales

			Type of Statement						
15	15	13	Unqualified		2		3	5	3
		1	Reviewed			1			
1			Compiled						
2	3	1	Tax Returns					1	
22	18	13	Other	2		2	1		8
4/1/16-	4/1/17-	4/1/18-			7 (4/1-9/30/18)		21 (10/1/18-3/31/19)		
3/31/17	3/31/18	3/31/19		0-1MM	1-3MM	3-5MM	5-10MM	10-25MM	25MM & OVER
ALL	ALL	ALL							
40	36	28	NUMBER OF STATEMENTS	2	2	3	4	6	11
%	%	%	ASSETS	%	%	%	%	%	%
46.3	43.3	52.0	Cash & Equivalents						42.9
8.2	6.3	5.6	Trade Receivables (net)						8.6
.1	.0	1.0	Inventory						2.5
8.6	8.0	11.1	All Other Current						7.2
63.1	57.6	69.6	Total Current						61.3
6.3	4.2	1.7	Fixed Assets (net)						1.6
11.6	11.7	5.1	Intangibles (net)						10.0
19.0	26.5	23.6	All Other Non-Current						27.1
100.0	100.0	100.0	Total						100.0
			LIABILITIES						
5.0	7.1	14.5	Notes Payable-Short Term						4.2
.9	3.3	3.4	Cur. Mat.-L.T.D.						.4
9.5	6.1	13.7	Trade Payables						13.8
.1	.5	.1	Income Taxes Payable						.1
19.3	20.1	27.8	All Other Current						16.7
34.9	37.2	59.5	Total Current						35.1
12.9	9.2	5.4	Long-Term Debt						4.4
.1	.2	.3	Deferred Taxes						.8
19.7	23.2	19.3	All Other Non-Current						16.5
32.4	30.3	15.4	Net Worth						43.2
100.0	100.0	100.0	Total Liabilities & Net Worth						100.0
			INCOME DATA						
100.0	100.0	100.0	Net Sales						100.0
			Gross Profit						
78.1	79.1	85.5	Operating Expenses						92.8
21.9	20.9	14.5	Operating Profit						7.2
.9	.1	-1.0	All Other Expenses (net)						-1.6
21.0	20.8	15.5	Profit Before Taxes						8.8
			RATIOS						
3.5	3.1	2.3							2.4
1.5	1.6	1.5	Current						1.6
1.0	1.0	1.0							1.1
3.4	2.7	2.1							2.4
1.3	1.3	1.2	Quick						1.2
.6	.4	.7							.8
3 128.2	1 263.7	0 UND						7	49.4
39 9.3	18 20.6	12 29.7	Sales/Receivables					42	8.6
83 4.4	68 5.4	48 7.6						70	5.2
			Cost of Sales/Inventory						
			Cost of Sales/Payables						
1.0	1.4	1.1							1.0
3.8	6.9	2.7	Sales/Working Capital						2.9
NM	-15.3	NM							54.4
24.0	39.4	96.6							
(21) 6.4	(19) 9.5	(10) 13.1	EBIT/Interest						
2.1	4.2	-7.3							
			Net Profit + Depr., Dep., Amort./Cur. Mat. L/T/D						
.0	.0	.0							.0
.0	.0	.0	Fixed/Worth						.0
.5	.3	.1							.1
.7	.7	.7							.6
2.0	2.8	1.7	Debt/Worth						.7
-6.1	-10.1	-121.3							7.3
45.9	145.9	30.1	% Profit Before Taxes/Tangible Net Worth						
(29) 16.7	(25) 28.7	(20) 14.5							
1.3	6.0	6.0							
17.1	18.7	14.0	% Profit Before Taxes/Total Assets						14.6
7.1	9.7	5.2							5.6
.8	3.2	1.2							1.3
UND	UND	UND							UND
167.2	412.8	UND	Sales/Net Fixed Assets						66.4
19.8	42.0	31.4							38.8
.9	1.1	1.3							1.5
.5	.5	.4	Sales/Total Assets						.4
.3	.3	.3							.4
.7	.3								
(13) 1.8	(11) .8		% Depr., Dep., Amort./Sales						
3.0	2.0								
			% Officers', Directors' Owners' Comp/Sales						
1566222M	1256942M	862477M	Net Sales ($)	1743M	3545M	12035M	28856M	101070M	715228M
2816523M	2456341M	1617653M	Total Assets ($)	5632M	8712M	9509M	125159M	293410M	1175231M

Current Data Sorted by Assets   Comparative Historical Data

0-500M	500M-2MM	2-10MM	10-50MM	50-100MM	100-250MM		4/1/14-3/31/15 ALL	4/1/15-3/31/16 ALL
	7 (4/1-9/30/18)		23 (10/1/18-3/31/19)			**Type of Statement**	18 (4/1/14-3/31/15)	28 (4/1/15-3/31/16)
	2	1	2	4	1	Unqualified	9	19
		1				Reviewed		
						Compiled		
						Tax Returns		1
	1	7	8	1	2	Other	18	28
	3	9	10	5	3	**NUMBER OF STATEMENTS**	27	48
	%	%	%	%	%	**ASSETS**	%	%
			60.2			Cash & Equivalents	75.8	65.1
			11.5			Trade Receivables (net)	4.5	9.6
			.0			Inventory	.0	.0
			4.2			All Other Current	9.4	11.8
			75.8			Total Current	89.7	86.6
			.0			Fixed Assets (net)	.1	.3
			.0			Intangibles (net)	.3	.2
			24.2			All Other Non-Current	9.9	12.9
			100.0			Total	100.0	100.0
						LIABILITIES		
			.0			Notes Payable-Short Term	4.1	7.0
			49.5			Cur. Mat.-L.T.D.	29.7	30.0
			1.5			Trade Payables	4.9	5.9
			.7			Income Taxes Payable	.2	.3
			6.5			All Other Current	16.0	15.8
			58.3			Total Current	55.0	58.9
			.0			Long-Term Debt	.5	2.1
			.0			Deferred Taxes	.0	.0
			12.3			All Other Non-Current	2.9	4.6
			29.4			Net Worth	41.7	34.3
			100.0			Total Liabilties & Net Worth	100.0	100.0
						INCOME DATA		
			100.0			Net Sales	100.0	100.0
						Gross Profit		
			88.1			Operating Expenses	88.3	81.0
			11.9			Operating Profit	11.7	19.0
			-2.9			All Other Expenses (net)	-2.2	-1.9
			14.9			Profit Before Taxes	13.9	20.9
						RATIOS		
			2.8				2.5	2.2
			1.4			Current	1.5	1.4
			.9				1.3	1.1
			2.8				2.5	2.0
			1.3			Quick	1.4	1.3
			.7				1.1	1.0
			0 UND				0 UND	0 UND
			1 548.0			Sales/Receivables	0 UND	1 318.6
			135 2.7				72 5.1	96 3.8
						Cost of Sales/Inventory		
						Cost of Sales/Payables		
			.6				.6	.6
			4.2			Sales/Working Capital	1.3	1.8
			NM				4.0	3.0
						EBIT/Interest		
						Net Profit + Depr., Dep., Amort./Cur. Mat. L/T/D		
			.0				.0	.0
			.0			Fixed/Worth	.0	.0
			.0				.0	.0
			1.1				.7	.9
			2.8			Debt/Worth	1.9	2.3
			9.2				3.6	4.7
			34.1				34.6	49.3
			12.3			% Profit Before Taxes/Tangible Net Worth	(26) 20.1	(47) 19.5
			-76.4				3.7	6.0
			16.8				10.5	12.9
			5.4			% Profit Before Taxes/Total Assets	5.9	8.2
			-6.6				1.0	.3
			UND				UND	UND
			UND			Sales/Net Fixed Assets	UND	UND
			UND				UND	UND
			.5				.9	.6
			.4			Sales/Total Assets	.4	.3
			.2				.2	.3
						% Depr., Dep., Amort./Sales		
						% Officers', Directors' Owners' Comp/Sales		
	1210M	28451M	108626M	130877M	98795M	Net Sales ($)	241990M	438137M
	2742M	49662M	263271M	426063M	502022M	Total Assets ($)	809482M	1287822M

(The first columns, 0-500M through 2-10MM and 50-100MM / 100-250MM, are marked **DATA NOT AVAILABLE**.)

M = $ thousand   MM = $ million
See Pages viii through xx for Explanation of Ratios and Data

Comparative Historical Data | Current Data Sorted by Sales

9 1 1 _ 23	7 _ 1 1 10	10 _ 1 _ 19	Type of Statement	0-1MM	1-3MM	3-5MM	5-10MM	10-25MM	25MM & OVER
			Unqualified	2	2		3	3	
			Reviewed						
			Compiled			1			
			Tax Returns						
			Other	2	5	3	3	4	2
4/1/16- 3/31/17 ALL	4/1/17- 3/31/18 ALL	4/1/18- 3/31/19 ALL			7 (4/1-9/30/18)			23 (10/1/18-3/31/19)	
34	19	30	**NUMBER OF STATEMENTS**	4	5	3	4	7	5
%	%	%	**ASSETS**	%	%	%	%	%	%
60.6	68.2	66.0	Cash & Equivalents						
3.2	5.2	8.4	Trade Receivables (net)						
.0	.0	.0	Inventory						
16.9	13.5	11.2	All Other Current						
80.7	86.9	85.7	Total Current						
1.1	2.0	.0	Fixed Assets (net)						
.2	.5	.0	Intangibles (net)						
17.9	10.7	14.3	All Other Non-Current						
100.0	100.0	100.0	Total						
			LIABILITIES						
6.1	11.2	5.4	Notes Payable-Short Term						
23.5	25.2	32.2	Cur. Mat.-L.T.D.						
5.1	8.6	6.6	Trade Payables						
.2	.1	2.7	Income Taxes Payable						
23.6	20.7	8.6	All Other Current						
58.5	65.8	55.4	Total Current						
.6	.4	2.1	Long-Term Debt						
.0	.0	.0	Deferred Taxes						
7.3	2.9	4.6	All Other Non-Current						
33.6	30.9	37.9	Net Worth						
100.0	100.0	100.0	Total Liabilties & Net Worth						
			INCOME DATA						
100.0	100.0	100.0	Net Sales						
			Gross Profit						
77.1	82.3	79.6	Operating Expenses						
22.9	17.7	20.4	Operating Profit						
-2.6	-1.7	-2.1	All Other Expenses (net)						
25.6	19.3	22.5	Profit Before Taxes						
			RATIOS						
1.9	2.0	2.8							
1.4	1.3	1.4	Current						
1.0	1.0	1.1							
1.8	1.4	2.3							
1.2	1.1	1.2	Quick						
.6	.7	.8							
0 UND	0 UND	0 UND							
0 UND	17 22.1	8 44.2	Sales/Receivables						
38 9.6	140 2.6	122 3.0							
			Cost of Sales/Inventory						
			Cost of Sales/Payables						
.6	.6	.5							
1.8	1.8	1.3	Sales/Working Capital						
10.0	3.4	6.0							
			EBIT/Interest						
			Net Profit + Depr., Dep., Amort./Cur. Mat. L/T/D						
.0	.0	0							
.0	.0	.0	Fixed/Worth						
.0	.0	.0							
1.3	1.3	.9							
2.4	2.6	2.2	Debt/Worth						
7.5	4.6	3.8							
37.5	24.0	34.1							
16.2	(17) 10.5	15.0	% Profit Before Taxes/Tangible Net Worth						
1.6	1.3	.4							
10.5	12.8	13.9							
5.9	2.6	7.0	% Profit Before Taxes/Total Assets						
.3	.0	.4							
UND	UND	UND							
UND	UND	UND	Sales/Net Fixed Assets						
UND	UND	UND							
.5	.5	.5							
.4	.4	.4	Sales/Total Assets						
.2	.2	.2							
			% Depr., Dep., Amort./Sales						
			% Officers', Directors' Owners' Comp/Sales						
431212M	216861M	367959M	Net Sales ($)	1643M	7999M	18729M	33284M	118607M	187697M
1484752M	889585M	1243760M	Total Assets ($)	5374M	126256M	39398M	109636M	311690M	651406M

© RMA 2019

M = $ thousand   MM = $ million
See Pages viii through xx for Explanation of Ratios and Data

Current Data Sorted by Assets | Comparative Historical Data

0-500M	500M-2MM	2-10MM	10-50MM	50-100MM	100-250MM	Type of Statement	4/1/14-3/31/15 ALL	4/1/15-3/31/16 ALL
1	1	2	24	10	10	Unqualified	81	77
1	1	13	13	2	1	Reviewed	59	46
9	15	12	9	2		Compiled	66	67
87	69	24	5		1	Tax Returns	298	348
60	67	47	61	15	19	Other	312	310
	48 (4/1-9/30/18)		533 (10/1/18-3/31/19)					
158	153	98	112	29	31	NUMBER OF STATEMENTS	816	848
%	%	%	%	%	%	ASSETS	%	%
44.9	25.7	28.7	30.2	38.0	26.2	Cash & Equivalents	31.5	33.3
4.7	10.2	14.7	19.4	17.7	15.5	Trade Receivables (net)	14.3	13.9
.0	.0	.8	.2	.1	.0	Inventory	.2	.1
3.4	4.9	3.1	8.5	8.4	7.5	All Other Current	4.8	4.5
53.1	40.8	47.3	58.2	64.1	49.2	Total Current	50.8	51.8
20.3	15.9	12.8	8.8	7.5	6.0	Fixed Assets (net)	13.1	13.6
15.8	29.5	22.4	13.3	14.8	29.6	Intangibles (net)	21.1	20.2
10.8	13.8	17.5	19.6	13.6	15.2	All Other Non-Current	15.0	14.4
100.0	100.0	100.0	100.0	100.0	100.0	Total	100.0	100.0
						LIABILITIES		
21.5	9.7	5.4	3.7	1.7	1.0	Notes Payable-Short Term	10.5	11.0
3.5	2.7	3.4	1.7	1.1	2.2	Cur. Mat.-L.T.D.	3.7	3.4
6.4	11.3	16.2	19.4	13.4	16.9	Trade Payables	16.9	18.6
.5	.0	.1	.2	.6	.1	Income Taxes Payable	.2	.3
16.3	12.0	15.7	25.0	30.6	21.7	All Other Current	17.6	16.4
48.0	35.6	40.7	49.9	47.4	41.8	Total Current	48.8	49.7
29.0	27.0	26.1	18.2	16.6	24.3	Long-Term Debt	21.2	23.0
.0	.0	.1	.0	.2	.4	Deferred Taxes	.2	.2
9.1	2.4	7.5	5.1	3.9	7.4	All Other Non-Current	7.3	6.0
13.8	34.9	25.5	26.7	31.9	26.1	Net Worth	22.5	21.1
100.0	100.0	100.0	100.0	100.0	100.0	Total Liabilities & Net Worth	100.0	100.0
						INCOME DATA		
100.0	100.0	100.0	100.0	100.0	100.0	Net Sales	100.0	100.0
						Gross Profit		
79.4	81.9	83.7	85.2	89.0	87.0	Operating Expenses	85.8	85.8
20.6	18.1	16.3	14.8	11.0	13.0	Operating Profit	14.2	14.2
.8	3.2	1.7	1.4	.7	2.8	All Other Expenses (net)	1.4	1.4
19.7	14.8	14.6	13.4	10.3	10.1	Profit Before Taxes	12.8	12.8
						RATIOS		
6.5	2.7	2.1	1.5	2.1	1.6	Current	1.9	1.9
1.6	1.2	1.2	1.2	1.2	1.1		1.1	1.1
.5	.4	.8	.9	.9	.9		.7	.6
6.3	2.5	2.0	1.4	2.0	1.3	Quick	1.7	1.7
1.3	1.0	1.1	1.0	1.0	1.0		1.0	1.0
.4	.4	.6	.6	.8	.8		.5	.5
0 UND	0 UND	0 UND	2 221.5	17 20.9	20 18.2	Sales/Receivables	0 UND	0 UND
0 UND	0 UND	12 30.2	30 12.0	55 6.6	66 5.5		6 60.6	5 75.6
0 UND	11 32.1	45 8.1	96 3.8	99 3.7	101 3.6		43 8.4	41 9.0
						Cost of Sales/Inventory		
						Cost of Sales/Payables		
11.4	7.7	7.1	5.4	1.9	7.5	Sales/Working Capital	8.6	9.5
34.8	54.3	18.9	14.2	11.0	26.2		56.1	70.0
-25.6	-13.6	-23.8	-17.0	-71.9	-22.5		-15.3	-14.9
44.6	40.3	41.0	24.5	39.7	30.4	EBIT/Interest	40.8	39.1
(82) 18.7	(101) 9.7	(77) 8.1	(69) 10.8	(17) 5.1	(24) 4.7		(573) 11.0	(564) 10.6
4.4	3.2	2.9	3.8	2.3	3.8		3.9	3.4
			21.3			Net Profit + Depr., Dep., Amort./Cur. Mat. L/T/D	13.8	14.1
			(10) 4.6				(59) 4.3	(46) 3.2
			2.0				1.4	1.2
.0	.0	.0	.1	.0	.1	Fixed/Worth	.0	.0
.3	.6	.6	.4	.1	-1.7		.5	.4
UND	-.8	-.8	2.0	NM	-.1		-1.6	-1.0
.3	.7	1.5	1.5	.9	2.2	Debt/Worth	1.2	1.1
1.7	5.8	6.2	3.8	3.5	-23.1		6.0	6.3
-3.2	-2.0	-5.2	NM	NM	-2.0		-4.0	-3.7
354.2	159.8	240.0	78.7	60.6	105.9	% Profit Before Taxes/Tangible Net Worth	185.2	189.1
(103) 169.7	(89) 69.8	(62) 61.0	(84) 28.5	(22) 28.8	(13) 61.4		(524) 62.9	(536) 57.9
53.7	21.1	18.7	7.3	4.6	16.7		18.4	12.3
177.4	49.6	26.5	20.2	14.4	17.7	% Profit Before Taxes/Total Assets	41.9	43.9
65.5	17.6	14.5	8.6	6.3	7.0		13.6	13.7
21.7	6.0	2.4	2.4	.9	3.8		4.6	3.6
UND	476.7	193.8	89.2	336.6	66.5	Sales/Net Fixed Assets	205.0	230.5
61.7	57.3	41.6	30.3	37.3	20.0		47.4	45.5
14.8	20.8	16.8	10.6	11.9	14.3		17.3	15.5
9.3	4.2	2.3	1.6	1.2	1.3	Sales/Total Assets	4.1	4.3
4.2	1.9	1.3	1.0	.7	.9		1.9	1.9
2.4	.8	.6	.5	.4	.6		1.0	.9
.3	.3	.5	.7	.7	1.2	% Depr., Dep., Amort./Sales	.5	.5
(56) 1.3	(56) 1.5	(51) 1.3	(72) 1.6	(14) 2.1	(14) 2.1		(399) 1.1	(418) 1.1
2.2	3.0	2.6	2.8	3.5	2.5		2.3	2.4
9.0	5.8	2.9	5.5			% Officers', Directors' Owners' Comp/Sales	6.8	6.7
(92) 13.4	(76) 10.0	(45) 6.8	(17) 8.5				(395) 11.9	(404) 12.4
21.5	17.6	14.7	34.0				20.6	20.1
190467M	549681M	1385172M	3682691M	1678809M	6915047M	Net Sales ($)	18651341M	21904767M
33189M	165005M	460690M	2627342M	1975575M	5312777M	Total Assets ($)	12329307M	12908854M

M = $ thousand   MM = $ million
See Pages viii through xx for Explanation of Ratios and Data

Comparative Historical Data / Current Data Sorted by Sales

			Type of Statement						
62	73	48	Unqualified	1	2	1	4	12	28
47	31	31	Reviewed		2	3	8	8	10
48	42	47	Compiled	5	12	4	9	10	7
209	227	186	Tax Returns	90	52	16	16	7	5
277	267	269	Other	60	55	25	34	38	57
4/1/16-3/31/17	4/1/17-3/31/18	4/1/18-3/31/19			48 (4/1-9/30/18)		533 (10/1/18-3/31/19)		
ALL	ALL	ALL		0-1MM	1-3MM	3-5MM	5-10MM	10-25MM	25MM & OVER
643	640	581	**NUMBER OF STATEMENTS**	156	123	49	71	75	107
%	%	%	**ASSETS**	%	%	%	%	%	%
32.0	32.0	32.9	Cash & Equivalents	33.1	32.6	29.1	37.5	30.4	33.6
13.4	12.7	11.9	Trade Receivables (net)	4.5	11.6	14.6	12.5	16.5	18.2
.0	.1	.2	Inventory	.5	.0	.0	.0	.3	.0
5.3	5.0	5.2	All Other Current	1.7	5.4	6.5	5.9	7.3	7.5
50.7	49.9	50.2	Total Current	39.8	49.5	50.2	55.9	54.4	59.4
13.8	14.6	14.3	Fixed Assets (net)	25.3	11.5	11.3	7.4	9.0	11.0
21.1	21.2	20.7	Intangibles (net)	23.1	26.7	20.2	15.6	16.0	17.4
14.4	14.3	14.8	All Other Non-Current	11.8	12.2	18.3	21.2	20.6	12.2
100.0	100.0	100.0	Total	100.0	100.0	100.0	100.0	100.0	100.0
			LIABILITIES						
11.8	10.4	10.1	Notes Payable-Short Term	17.9	10.3	10.2	9.5	4.0	3.4
3.9	2.9	2.7	Cur. Mat.-L.T.D.	3.0	3.6	2.4	2.0	1.8	2.5
17.2	15.2	12.8	Trade Payables	3.0	13.7	19.1	13.6	22.5	15.5
.2	.5	.2	Income Taxes Payable	.5	.0	.0	.0	.4	.2
16.7	18.9	17.7	All Other Current	12.5	13.1	14.6	25.5	20.7	24.7
49.9	47.9	43.5	Total Current	36.9	40.8	46.3	50.6	49.3	46.4
27.8	27.1	25.1	Long-Term Debt	36.3	26.7	12.5	16.3	17.6	23.6
.1	.2	.1	Deferred Taxes	.0	.0	.0	.1	.1	.1
4.8	5.8	5.9	All Other Non-Current	8.5	4.3	1.4	6.8	5.2	6.1
17.4	19.1	25.4	Net Worth	18.3	28.2	39.8	26.2	27.7	23.7
100.0	100.0	100.0	Total Liabilities & Net Worth	100.0	100.0	100.0	100.0	100.0	100.0
			INCOME DATA						
100.0	100.0	100.0	Net Sales	100.0	100.0	100.0	100.0	100.0	100.0
			Gross Profit						
85.3	84.7	82.8	Operating Expenses	76.1	80.5	86.1	86.0	85.7	89.5
14.7	15.3	17.2	Operating Profit	23.9	19.5	13.9	14.0	14.3	10.5
1.5	2.0	1.8	All Other Expenses (net)	4.1	1.3	.4	.6	.8	1.3
13.2	13.3	15.4	Profit Before Taxes	19.8	18.2	13.5	13.4	13.5	9.1
			RATIOS						
2.0	2.2	2.3	Current	3.9	4.0	2.1	2.1	1.5	2.0
1.1	1.1	1.2		1.3	1.4	1.1	1.3	1.1	1.2
.6	.5	.7		.3	.7	.7	.8	.8	.9
1.8	1.9	2.2	Quick	3.8	3.2	1.6	2.1	1.4	1.7
(642) 1.0	1.0	1.1		1.2	1.2	.9	1.1	1.0	1.0
.5	.5	.5		.3	.5	.5	.5	.6	.8
0 UND	0 UND	0 UND	Sales/Receivables	0 UND	0 UND	0 UND	0 UND	0 999.8	10 36.6
6 58.8	2 156.5	1 518.0		0 UND	0 UND	1 648.2	7 52.0	23 15.7	35 10.3
47 7.8	40 9.2	37 9.9		0 UND	18 20.4	47 7.7	38 9.7	91 4.0	83 4.4
			Cost of Sales/Inventory						
			Cost of Sales/Payables						
7.8	7.4	7.1	Sales/Working Capital	4.6	6.8	12.2	7.2	6.7	7.5
93.0	49.4	26.3		33.7	21.0	54.6	19.7	29.6	20.4
-13.8	-14.6	-21.1		-12.0	-23.6	-11.7	-24.8	-21.8	-61.7
45.2	31.5	39.6	EBIT/Interest	27.8	37.8	48.7	32.3	116.0	39.2
(438) 9.5	(414) 9.1	(370) 10.9		(80) 8.0	(85) 9.7	(36) 10.6	(47) 12.1	(43) 20.6	(79) 7.2
3.0	3.0	3.5		2.2	3.4	4.5	3.0	5.3	3.5
6.8	31.5	8.2	Net Profit + Depr., Dep., Amort./Cur. Mat. L/T/D						40.7
(43) 2.8	(52) 4.7	(32) 2.9							(16) 3.7
.9	1.7	1.4							1.6
.1	.0	.0	Fixed/Worth	.0	.0	.1	.0	.0	.1
.5	.5	.4		.4	.4	.4	.2	.4	.6
-.7	-1.0	-1.8		-3.8	-.7	-2.9	-6.2	2.8	-.4
1.1	1.1	.9	Debt/Worth	.5	.6	.5	.6	1.4	1.1
5.3	6.0	4.4		4.5	4.3	5.5	2.7	4.4	4.6
-3.2	-3.4	-4.2		-2.2	-2.9	-7.1	-26.3	-11.6	-4.1
164.0	146.3	201.9	% Profit Before Taxes/Tangible Net Worth	222.8	277.1	296.7	164.5	149.5	96.1
(408) 54.4	(402) 52.0	(373) 65.0		(97) 71.7	(72) 98.2	(34) 95.2	(50) 52.7	(54) 63.4	(66) 41.9
13.9	14.7	18.0		17.5	26.8	34.2	11.4	18.1	13.1
39.9	40.8	52.5	% Profit Before Taxes/Total Assets	71.4	72.1	49.6	45.2	37.1	22.4
13.2	13.2	17.2		25.5	23.8	18.0	15.7	13.1	10.9
3.7	3.3	4.2		5.1	6.0	5.5	3.0	2.6	3.7
172.0	217.2	314.9	Sales/Net Fixed Assets	UND	653.5	195.3	999.8	178.8	73.2
43.9	41.2	41.0		38.0	56.8	49.0	89.3	41.3	28.0
16.7	14.8	14.9		6.3	21.3	19.5	23.0	20.0	13.7
4.3	4.2	4.0	Sales/Total Assets	4.0	4.8	4.2	5.8	2.2	2.9
1.8	1.8	1.7		1.8	2.2	2.5	2.1	1.2	1.3
.9	.9	.8		.7	1.1	1.0	.8	.7	.9
.6	.6	.5	% Depr., Dep., Amort./Sales	1.2	.2	.4	.3	.6	.5
(324) 1.2	(311) 1.4	(263) 1.5		(56) 2.2	(42) 1.4	(24) 1.4	(36) .6	1.4	(69) 1.6
2.4	2.8	2.7		11.7	2.8	2.6	2.5	2.2	2.5
6.5	6.3	5.8	% Officers', Directors', Owners' Comp/Sales	9.1	6.1	4.9	3.1	2.9	1.9
(272) 10.9	(275) 12.0	(236) 10.0		(84) 14.5	(57) 11.2	(29) 7.7	(28) 5.9	(22) 7.0	(16) 8.9
18.6	21.2	20.1		23.2	17.2	14.7	14.5	13.2	29.4
14602229M	12774734M	14401867M	Net Sales ($)	74927M	227624M	193076M	499558M	1228979M	12177703M
10430654M	11938367M	10574578M	Total Assets ($)	109529M	226881M	171318M	564274M	1394169M	8108407M

© RMA 2019

M = $ thousand   MM = $ million

See Pages viii through xx for Explanation of Ratios and Data

Current Data Sorted by Assets							Comparative Historical Data	

0-500M	500M-2MM	2-10MM	10-50MM	50-100MM	100-250MM	Type of Statement	4/1/14-3/31/15 ALL	4/1/15-3/31/16 ALL
		1			1	Unqualified	7	10
		1	1			Reviewed	2	1
		1		1		Compiled		1
5	1	2	3	2		Tax Returns	8	9
4	1	5				Other	11	15
						NUMBER OF STATEMENTS		
9	2	10	5	3	1		28	36
%	%	%	%	%	%	**ASSETS**	%	%
		37.7				Cash & Equivalents	22.4	21.0
		29.4				Trade Receivables (net)	23.8	22.7
		.0				Inventory	.0	.0
		.9				All Other Current	10.0	8.9
		68.0				Total Current	56.3	52.6
		6.4				Fixed Assets (net)	19.9	21.1
		16.4				Intangibles (net)	10.0	15.6
		9.2				All Other Non-Current	13.9	10.7
		100.0				Total	100.0	100.0
						LIABILITIES		
		1.7				Notes Payable-Short Term	5.6	7.3
		1.9				Cur. Mat.-L.T.D.	10.2	4.3
		6.6				Trade Payables	5.9	3.9
		.0				Income Taxes Payable	.2	.7
		8.2				All Other Current	29.4	20.7
		18.4				Total Current	51.2	37.0
		19.0				Long-Term Debt	20.6	25.3
		.5				Deferred Taxes	.5	.5
		8.2				All Other Non-Current	9.9	14.1
		53.9				Net Worth	17.9	23.2
		100.0				Total Liabilities & Net Worth	100.0	100.0
						INCOME DATA		
		100.0				Net Sales	100.0	100.0
						Gross Profit		
		80.9				Operating Expenses	88.3	87.1
		19.1				Operating Profit	11.7	12.9
		5.0				All Other Expenses (net)	1.6	1.6
		14.2				Profit Before Taxes	10.2	11.3
						RATIOS		
		21.2					4.1	5.0
		6.2				Current	1.3	2.1
		1.2					.6	.8
		21.2					3.2	4.3
		6.1				Quick	1.1	1.6
		1.1					.4	.4
	0 UND	0 UND					0 UND	0 UND
		34 10.6				Sales/Receivables	24 15.2	23 16.0
		47 7.8					44 8.3	48 7.6
						Cost of Sales/Inventory		
						Cost of Sales/Payables		
		3.3					5.7	5.9
		4.8				Sales/Working Capital	22.0	22.1
		80.2					-46.7	-33.1
							31.7	87.0
						EBIT/Interest	(20) 8.0	(26) 10.0
							3.5	2.0
						Net Profit + Depr., Dep., Amort./Cur. Mat. L/T/D		
		.0					.1	.3
		.1				Fixed/Worth	.4	.6
		NM					7.0	NM
		.2					.4	.5
		1.1				Debt/Worth	4.9	6.0
		NM					NM	-4.8
							217.7	173.3
						% Profit Before Taxes/Tangible Net Worth	(21) 75.3	(25) 94.6
							25.1	18.2
		55.6					53.5	70.0
		24.1				% Profit Before Taxes/Total Assets	19.4	19.0
		4.2					9.6	5.7
		999.8					253.4	132.5
		376.6				Sales/Net Fixed Assets	42.7	25.6
		43.9					11.3	10.4
		3.8					6.9	4.8
		2.5				Sales/Total Assets	3.2	3.1
		1.8					.9	1.1
							.4	.3
						% Depr., Dep., Amort./Sales	(18) 1.2	(23) 1.5
							2.2	2.2
							5.2	7.3
						% Officers', Directors' Owners' Comp/Sales	(12) 5.5	(15) 12.1
							8.6	15.0
25055M	18722M	166350M	618448M	676936M	205575M	Net Sales ($)	763601M	1260896M
1498M	2190M	47232M	100932M	235838M	112215M	Total Assets ($)	383285M	784847M

© RMA 2019   M = $ thousand   MM = $ million

See Pages viii through xx for Explanation of Ratios and Data

Comparative Historical Data

Current Data Sorted by Sales

			Type of Statement						
7	3	2	Unqualified						2
2	4	2	Reviewed						1
2	4	2	Compiled				1		1
7	7	9	Tax Returns	1	1		2		1
20	14	15	Other	2	1	2	2	5	5
4/1/16-	4/1/17-	4/1/18-		2					
3/31/17	3/31/18	3/31/19			2 (4/1-9/30/18)		28 (10/1/18-3/31/19)		
ALL	ALL	ALL		0-1MM	1-3MM	3-5MM	5-10MM	10-25MM	25MM & OVER
38	32	30	NUMBER OF STATEMENTS	5	2	2	5	6	10
%	%	%	ASSETS	%	%	%	%	%	%
18.0	24.6	39.0	Cash & Equivalents						26.3
29.0	28.5	24.8	Trade Receivables (net)						29.5
.5	.0	.7	Inventory						.0
5.9	15.2	4.9	All Other Current						4.5
53.3	68.3	69.5	Total Current						60.2
13.7	11.0	9.2	Fixed Assets (net)						16.7
16.0	8.8	11.8	Intangibles (net)						8.6
17.0	11.9	9.6	All Other Non-Current						14.4
100.0	100.0	100.0	Total						100.0
			LIABILITIES						
10.4	19.7	9.4	Notes Payable-Short Term						5.7
2.7	1.3	3.1	Cur. Mat.-L.T.D.						4.2
13.5	7.8	10.4	Trade Payables						5.7
.0	.3	.0	Income Taxes Payable						.1
16.9	39.8	14.4	All Other Current						18.0
43.5	68.7	37.3	Total Current						33.7
25.0	16.0	20.8	Long-Term Debt						26.0
1.2	1.7	.2	Deferred Taxes						.7
8.6	7.6	3.2	All Other Non-Current						9.1
21.8	6.2	38.5	Net Worth						30.5
100.0	100.0	100.0	Total Liabilties & Net Worth						100.0
			INCOME DATA						
100.0	100.0	100.0	Net Sales						100.0
			Gross Profit						
88.1	87.8	82.9	Operating Expenses						87.4
11.9	12.2	17.1	Operating Profit						12.6
.5	.7	2.3	All Other Expenses (net)						.4
11.5	11.5	14.8	Profit Before Taxes						12.3
			RATIOS						
2.8	2.3	6.6							2.2
1.3	1.5	1.9	Current						1.6
.9	.8	1.2							1.2
2.3	2.2	6.6							2.1
1.2	1.2	1.7	Quick						1.5
.6	.2	1.1							1.2
16 23.3	0 UND	0 UND						1	259.7
34 10.6	31 11.8	30 12.3	Sales/Receivables					33	11.1
62 5.9	51 7.2	39 9.4						45	8.2
			Cost of Sales/Inventory						
			Cost of Sales/Payables						
6.9	6.4	4.6							6.9
20.9	14.3	10.3	Sales/Working Capital						16.1
-39.6	-232.9	74.3							45.7
27.2	80.2	97.5							
(27) 7.2	(25) 20.0	(20) 18.6	EBIT/Interest						
3.8	7.3	2.4							
			Net Profit + Depr., Dep., Amort./Cur. Mat. l./T/D						
.1	.0	.0							.1
1.6	.2	.1	Fixed/Worth						.4
-.6	1.7	NM							-4.5
1.2	.8	.3							.9
6.1	2.9	1.2	Debt/Worth						1.7
-3.1	-12.2	-30.0							-14.3
97.6	141.9	144.3	% Profit Before Taxes/Tangible Net Worth						
(23) 39.3	(22) 86.6	(22) 57.7							
10.1	40.4	.6							
37.9	48.5	62.1	% Profit Before Taxes/Total Assets						67.7
11.3	26.7	20.0							19.6
1.8	4.8	1.6							.8
177.6	561.3	UND							55.1
36.9	100.3	179.7	Sales/Net Fixed Assets						40.5
11.5	18.8	37.0							12.6
4.4	5.6	8.2							6.1
2.4	3.4	3.3	Sales/Total Assets						3.3
1.1	1.7	1.8							2.1
.3	.1	.3							
(20) .7	(14) .4	(13) 1.3	% Depr., Dep., Amort./Sales						
2.0	1.6	2.2							
2.7	1.4	1.9							
(13) 8.4	(13) 4.5	(14) 5.9	% Officers', Directors' Owners' Comp/Sales						
15.8	11.0	15.1							
2299801M	1292852M	1711086M	Net Sales ($)	2282M	4198M	7529M	32149M	71288M	1593640M
1168175M	415783M	499905M	Total Assets ($)	4856M	760M	2074M	76898M	18761M	396556M

M = $ thousand   MM = $ million
See Pages viii through xx for Explanation of Ratios and Data

Current Data Sorted by Assets   Comparative Historical Data

0-500M	500M-2MM	2-10MM	10-50MM	50-100MM	100-250MM	Type of Statement	4/1/14-3/31/15 ALL	4/1/15-3/31/16 ALL
1	2	5	12	2	6	Unqualified	28	31
1		1	2		1	Reviewed	3	3
		2				Compiled	3	3
4	3	2				Tax Returns	10	7
4	1	5	12	3	3	Other	47	56
	9 (4/1-9/30/18)		63 (10/1/18-3/31/19)					
10	6	15	26	5	10	**NUMBER OF STATEMENTS**	91	100
%	%	%	%	%	%	**ASSETS**	%	%
35.6		19.1	32.6		27.2	Cash & Equivalents	31.0	32.0
11.9		28.7	15.8		19.1	Trade Receivables (net)	13.9	15.4
.0		.0	.0		.0	Inventory	.7	.1
6.5		4.7	9.3		6.9	All Other Current	8.1	7.7
54.1		52.5	57.7		53.2	Total Current	53.8	55.3
23.1		20.3	12.9		15.7	Fixed Assets (net)	14.5	14.8
16.3		11.0	12.2		14.7	Intangibles (net)	20.7	17.5
6.6		16.1	17.2		16.4	All Other Non-Current	11.0	12.5
100.0		100.0	100.0		100.0	Total	100.0	100.0
						LIABILITIES		
21.6		5.1	1.2		2.8	Notes Payable-Short Term	4.5	6.3
2.6		2.1	1.7		1.7	Cur. Mat.-L.T.D.	3.1	3.4
8.3		11.8	7.8		27.4	Trade Payables	12.4	11.1
.0		.3	.3		.1	Income Taxes Payable	.9	.9
65.3		13.2	40.7		23.6	All Other Current	23.4	28.1
97.8		32.5	51.7		55.6	Total Current	44.3	49.7
1.4		13.2	10.3		16.0	Long-Term Debt	9.9	12.5
.0		.5	.6		.1	Deferred Taxes	1.0	1.4
.0		8.9	2.5		5.7	All Other Non-Current	6.1	9.7
.9		44.8	34.9		22.5	Net Worth	38.7	26.6
100.0		100.0	100.0		100.0	Total Liabilities & Net Worth	100.0	100.0
						INCOME DATA		
100.0		100.0	100.0		100.0	Net Sales	100.0	100.0
						Gross Profit		
92.9		91.7	89.1		88.1	Operating Expenses	88.5	88.9
7.1		8.3	10.9		11.9	Operating Profit	11.5	11.1
-.1		3.2	2.3		-.4	All Other Expenses (net)	.2	.7
7.2		5.1	8.6		12.3	Profit Before Taxes	11.3	10.4
						RATIOS		
2.1		4.0	1.8		1.3	Current	2.0	2.0
1.0		1.3	1.2		.8		1.3	1.2
.1		.9	.9		.6		1.0	.8
2.1		4.0	1.6		1.3	Quick	1.8	1.6
.5		1.3	1.2		.8		1.1	1.1
.1		.7	.6		.4		.6	.6
0 UND		11 31.9	14 25.4		0 UND	Sales/Receivables	2 234.8	5 76.5
0 UND		33 10.9	33 11.2		72 5.1		19 18.8	22 16.7
6 64.0		65 5.6	51 7.2		203 1.8		36 10.1	40 9.1
						Cost of Sales/Inventory		
						Cost of Sales/Payables		
12.4		5.2	4.1		15.5	Sales/Working Capital	7.0	8.6
NM		12.2	28.3		-16.0		19.4	22.6
-13.4		-56.1	-33.7		-3.5		-149.3	-26.6
			228.5			EBIT/Interest	51.6	84.6
			(15) 21.9				(56) 13.5	(58) 24.7
			3.5				4.3	1.6
						Net Profit + Depr., Dep., Amort./Cur. Mat. L/T/D	25.6	18.1
							(14) 3.6	(12) 5.2
							1.7	1.8
.0		.1	.1		.1	Fixed/Worth	.1	.1
.2		.2	.5		1.7		.6	.5
-15.6		3.5	-.7		-1.9		24.9	-2.5
.9		.7	.7		1.6	Debt/Worth	1.1	1.3
2.0		1.5	2.5		NM		3.4	5.8
-1.9		4.0	-69.5		-5.8		-30.4	-10.2
		35.2	57.4			% Profit Before Taxes/Tangible Net Worth	91.9	155.5
		(12) 3.4	(18) 22.5				(67) 49.2	(70) 66.5
		-41.1	12.1				9.6	18.5
96.0		16.2	17.6		13.6	% Profit Before Taxes/Total Assets	32.8	39.8
25.6		6.1	5.8		6.8		11.6	11.8
11.3		-15.2	1.8		-1.0		3.4	1.7
UND		68.2	95.6		26.9	Sales/Net Fixed Assets	76.1	82.7
111.6		42.1	23.2		7.8		35.8	28.6
58.1		8.9	10.4		3.8		11.2	13.4
21.1		3.9	2.8		1.9	Sales/Total Assets	3.5	4.3
10.7		1.7	1.5		.7		1.8	1.6
4.6		.6	.6		.5		.9	.7
			1.1			% Depr., Dep., Amort./Sales	.7	.6
		(17) 2.9					(57) 1.6	(65) 1.2
			4.8				3.7	2.9
						% Officers', Directors' Owners' Comp/Sales	1.9	4.0
							(10) 8.7	(10) 10.7
							13.7	20.7
40736M	27621M	188159M	1265072M	938984M	1762681M	Net Sales ($)	4894528M	4009394M
2465M	7769M	78076M	710774M	402183M	1732758M	Total Assets ($)	3649168M	3889235M

Comparative Historical Data | Current Data Sorted by Sales

			Type of Statement	0-1MM	1-3MM	3-5MM	5-10MM	10-25MM	25MM & OVER
30	32	28	Unqualified		3	1	5	5	14
1	5	5	Reviewed		1			1	2
5	2	2	Compiled				2		
8	11	9	Tax Returns	3	1	3	3		16
38	36	28	Other		2	3	5	2	
4/1/16- 3/31/17	4/1/17- 3/31/18	4/1/18- 3/31/19			9 (4/1-9/30/18)		63 (10/1/18-3/31/19)		
ALL	ALL	ALL							
82	86	72	**NUMBER OF STATEMENTS**	3	7	7	15	8	32
%	%	%	**ASSETS**	%	%	%	%	%	%
34.1	26.8	28.6	Cash & Equivalents				29.3		22.7
15.7	17.2	17.4	Trade Receivables (net)				16.4		22.9
.1	.2	.1	Inventory				.0		.2
8.0	4.7	7.5	All Other Current				9.0		9.2
57.9	48.9	53.6	Total Current				54.7		55.0
11.9	15.4	15.7	Fixed Assets (net)				8.2		12.9
16.3	20.3	17.7	Intangibles (net)				24.2		17.9
13.9	15.4	13.0	All Other Non-Current				12.8		14.2
100.0	100.0	100.0	Total				100.0		100.0
			LIABILITIES						
7.5	3.8	5.7	Notes Payable-Short Term				1.3		3.2
1.5	2.9	1.7	Cur. Mat.-L.T.D.				1.6		1.6
11.3	10.0	10.0	Trade Payables				6.0		13.5
.8	.5	.3	Income Taxes Payable				.2		.4
28.0	29.7	33.5	All Other Current				47.1		32.5
49.2	47.0	52.1	Total Current				56.1		51.1
10.2	12.8	10.4	Long-Term Debt				5.4		13.9
1.0	.8	.4	Deferred Taxes				.0		.6
6.5	5.3	6.3	All Other Non-Current				4.8		3.6
33.1	34.1	30.8	Net Worth				33.7		30.9
100.0	100.0	100.0	Total Liabilties & Net Worth				100.0		100.0
			INCOME DATA						
100.0	100.0	100.0	Net Sales				100.0		100.0
			Gross Profit						
88.1	87.7	90.8	Operating Expenses				89.6		93.2
11.9	12.3	9.2	Operating Profit				10.4		6.8
.7	1.7	1.7	All Other Expenses (net)				3.2		1.2
11.2	10.6	7.5	Profit Before Taxes				7.1		5.6
			RATIOS						
2.4	1.7	2.0					5.4		1.5
1.3	1.2	1.2	Current				1.3		1.0
.8	.7	.7					1.0		.8
2.1	1.6	1.8					5.4		1.3
1.1	1.0	1.1	Quick				1.3		.9
.7	.6	.5					.5		.6
4 103.6	2 202.2	0 UND					2 180.9		13 28.1
25 14.5	23 16.1	26 14.1	Sales/Receivables				41 8.9		34 10.8
39 9.4	43 8.5	51 7.1					79 4.6		54 6.8
			Cost of Sales/Inventory						
			Cost of Sales/Payables						
3.7	7.1	7.0					4.6		15.2
27.5	42.6	29.8	Sales/Working Capital				8.3		72.0
-22.0	-21.1	-16.4					-56.1		-11.9
80.7	98.5	62.0							62.0
(48) 9.4	(54) 12.3	(44) 7.3	EBIT/Interest					(24)	17.7
1.6	1.8	1.0							1.3
	74.1	3.4							
	(11) 10.2	(11) 1.8	Net Profit + Depr., Dep., Amort./Cur. Mat. L/T/D						
	1.6	.5							
.0	.1	.1					.1		.1
.3	.6	.5	Fixed/Worth				.?		.0
UND	1.2	-1.1					-.5		-1.1
.7	.8	.8					.3		1.5
3.5	4.5	2.5	Debt/Worth				1.4		3.8
-16.4	-5.3	-6.9					-6.6		-6.3
82.2	86.0	62.8	% Profit Before Taxes/Tangible Net Worth						74.1
(60) 38.4	(58) 44.5	(47) 33.3						(20)	31.5
11.4	16.0	5.0							15.8
19.0	21.0	20.3					23.3		15.2
8.9	10.8	8.4	% Profit Before Taxes/Total Assets				10.9		8.1
2.5	.5	.2					-.5		.2
152.9	167.6	128.0					68.2		81.6
34.8	30.9	32.6	Sales/Net Fixed Assets				32.9		19.7
14.9	11.0	10.2					14.2		10.2
3.1	3.0	3.7					3.5		3.6
1.7	1.7	1.8	Sales/Total Assets				.8		1.9
.8	.6	.7					.4		.8
.6	.6	.7					.4		.8
(55) 1.3	(46) 1.4	(41) 1.2	% Depr., Dep., Amort./Sales				(10) .8		(19) 1.2
2.7	3.1	3.9					3.6		4.2
8.4	3.3	3.5	% Officers', Directors' Owners' Comp/Sales						
(10) 11.0	(16) 8.4	(12) 5.3							
18.3	13.4	17.1							
4764011M	3724514M	4223253M	Net Sales ($)	820M	13545M	26297M	116013M	143256M	3923322M
4184421M	2963478M	2934025M	Total Assets ($)	3079M	14844M	31384M	172963M	222497M	2489258M

M = $ thousand   MM = $ million
See Pages viii through xx for Explanation of Ratios and Data

Current Data Sorted by Assets | Comparative Historical Data

Type of Statement

0-500M	500M-2MM	2-10MM	10-50MM	50-100MM	100-250MM	Type of Statement	4/1/14-3/31/15 ALL	4/1/15-3/31/16 ALL
			6	7	2	Unqualified	18	26
	2	1	1			Reviewed	1	5
1		4				Compiled	8	11
3	6	1				Tax Returns	11	18
5	8	11	11	3	8	Other	42	43
	7 (4/1-9/30/18)		73 (10/1/18-3/31/19)					
9	16	17	18	10	10	NUMBER OF STATEMENTS	80	103

Data

0-500M	500M-2MM	2-10MM	10-50MM	50-100MM	100-250MM		ALL	ALL
%	%	%	%	%	%	**ASSETS**	%	%
	33.9	25.9	28.4	40.8	18.4	Cash & Equivalents	24.4	30.9
	15.0	40.7	21.7	6.4	19.2	Trade Receivables (net)	23.4	18.8
	.0	.0	.0	.0	.0	Inventory	.9	.0
	14.3	1.6	3.1	8.2	13.5	All Other Current	6.7	4.1
	63.3	68.2	53.3	55.4	51.2	Total Current	55.6	53.8
	10.0	9.9	16.1	3.2	1.5	Fixed Assets (net)	13.5	13.4
	13.7	7.8	12.3	22.5	21.3	Intangibles (net)	14.7	12.4
	13.1	14.1	18.4	18.9	26.0	All Other Non-Current	16.2	20.4
	100.0	100.0	100.0	100.0	100.0	Total	100.0	100.0
						LIABILITIES		
	7.0	6.2	1.7	.0	6.3	Notes Payable-Short Term	6.7	6.4
	1.5	2.8	.6	1.3	.0	Cur. Mat.-L.T.D.	1.9	1.7
	6.8	4.8	8.3	7.4	15.7	Trade Payables	10.5	11.2
	.0	.1	.8	.5	.9	Income Taxes Payable	.2	.2
	25.8	12.8	26.8	30.2	23.9	All Other Current	19.9	24.1
	41.1	26.8	38.3	39.4	46.8	Total Current	39.1	43.6
	10.7	17.6	12.5	37.6	3.1	Long-Term Debt	17.6	17.1
	.0	.0	.3	.8	3.3	Deferred Taxes	.5	.5
	5.7	9.7	13.5	6.1	3.5	All Other Non-Current	9.6	8.0
	42.5	46.0	35.3	16.0	43.4	Net Worth	33.2	30.7
	100.0	100.0	100.0	100.0	100.0	Total Liabilties & Net Worth	100.0	100.0
						INCOME DATA		
	100.0	100.0	100.0	100.0	100.0	Net Sales	100.0	100.0
						Gross Profit		
	76.3	69.6	89.1	77.9	69.1	Operating Expenses	87.3	86.6
	23.7	30.4	10.9	22.1	30.9	Operating Profit	12.7	13.4
	3.6	2.5	2.3	2.5	-.1	All Other Expenses (net)	1.6	1.4
	20.0	27.9	8.6	19.5	31.0	Profit Before Taxes	11.1	12.0
						RATIOS		
	10.7	4.9	3.1	1.9	1.5	Current	2.3	3.1
	1.6	2.6	1.5	1.3	1.0		1.5	1.4
	1.1	1.2	1.1	.8	.7		.9	.7
	9.2	4.9	3.1	1.7	1.3	Quick	2.1	2.8
	1.6	2.0	1.4	1.2	.9		1.3	1.2
	1.1	1.2	.9	.5	.2		.7	.5
	0 UND	9 41.7	10 37.4	5 75.2	12 30.8	Sales/Receivables	1 361.0	0 UND
	0 UND	42 8.6	32 11.3	10 37.7	126 2.9		29 12.5	23 16.1
	23 15.9	730 .5	57 6.4	39 9.3	228 1.6		60 6.1	62 5.9
						Cost of Sales/Inventory		
						Cost of Sales/Payables		
	2.9	.7	4.1	2.6	4.7	Sales/Working Capital	5.2	4.5
	18.0	5.0	12.7	9.3	34.8		13.3	15.3
	51.7	NM	NM	-33.2	-.6		-220.6	-16.0
		66.9				EBIT/Interest	41.8	74.7
		(11) 7.4					(45) 10.8	(58) 14.0
		3.7					2.9	2.1
						Net Profit + Depr., Dep., Amort./Cur. Mat. L/T/D		
	.0	.0	.1	.0	.0	Fixed/Worth	.0	.0
	.1	.0	.5	.1	.1		.2	.2
	1.5	.4	-13.5	.0	.7		2.1	1.7
	.2	.2	.8	1.8	1.5	Debt/Worth	.8	.8
	1.5	.9	3.6	5.6	1.7		2.0	2.2
	NM	2.9	-55.3	-1.8	304.2		UND	28.3
	174.6	63.2	269.5			% Profit Before Taxes/Tangible Net Worth	67.0	92.0
	(12) 97.6	(15) 19.6	(13) 24.4				(60) 28.3	(84) 32.9
	28.2	9.5	4.5				8.8	5.4
	108.2	40.4	38.7	26.2	25.3	% Profit Before Taxes/Total Assets	28.6	31.1
	33.9	8.1	8.0	6.1	8.5		9.0	10.7
	5.5	5.0	.5	-.9	-.1		2.7	1.6
	UND	891.3	80.0	UND	261.3	Sales/Net Fixed Assets	196.4	230.2
	401.0	134.7	48.4	79.0	59.2		52.5	40.2
	44.0	28.9	12.0	21.6	27.1		17.1	16.5
	6.4	4.8	3.4	2.0	1.1	Sales/Total Assets	4.1	3.6
	2.9	1.3	1.7	.9	.3		1.8	1.3
	1.0	.3	.6	.2	.1		.5	.6
			.8			% Depr., Dep., Amort./Sales	.7	.7
		(12)	1.7				(42) 1.1	(53) 1.1
			6.5				2.0	2.1
						% Officers', Directors' Owners' Comp/Sales	4.1	5.1
							(17) 6.0	(20) 9.3
							20.3	17.0
14475M	74047M	236400M	921413M	839660M	914748M	Net Sales ($)	3724904M	3851513M
1199M	20462M	94052M	486158M	761534M	1322003M	Total Assets ($)	2127040M	2841819M

© RMA 2019

M = $ thousand   MM = $ million
See Pages viii through xx for Explanation of Ratios and Data

Comparative Historical Data | Current Data Sorted by Sales

	4/1/16-3/31/17 ALL	4/1/17-3/31/18 ALL	4/1/18-3/31/19 ALL	0-1MM	1-3MM	3-5MM	5-10MM	10-25MM	25MM & OVER
Type of Statement									
Unqualified	19	16	15		1		1	2	12
Reviewed	4	5	4		1		2	2	1
Compiled	4	4	5	1	2			2	
Tax Returns	19	11	10	4	3		2	1	
Other	43	56	46	6	7	3	5	8	17
				7 (4/1-9/30/18)			73 (10/1/18-3/31/19)		
NUMBER OF STATEMENTS	89	92	80	11	13	3	10	13	30
	%	%	%	%	%	%	%	%	%
ASSETS									
Cash & Equivalents	35.3	30.2	32.0	45.0	33.8		30.8	27.8	28.6
Trade Receivables (net)	18.3	23.7	19.8	10.0	23.4		15.3	25.3	21.6
Inventory	1.3	.5	.0	.0	.0		.4	.0	.0
All Other Current	7.8	4.9	6.8	.1	8.2		20.4	4.8	4.9
Total Current	62.7	59.2	58.6	55.0	65.3		66.9	57.9	55.1
Fixed Assets (net)	12.2	12.7	11.4	31.9	2.1		14.8	2.4	8.9
Intangibles (net)	10.9	14.3	14.4	2.5	22.2		6.7	18.4	17.6
All Other Non-Current	14.1	13.7	15.6	10.5	10.4		11.6	21.3	18.3
Total	100.0	100.0	100.0	100.0	100.0		100.0	100.0	100.0
LIABILITIES									
Notes Payable-Short Term	10.4	6.8	4.9	8.6	6.1		10.6	2.6	2.3
Cur. Mat.-L.T.D.	2.3	2.7	1.2	.3	1.3		1.2	.7	1.5
Trade Payables	10.1	9.4	7.7	.4	8.2		15.6	7.3	8.4
Income Taxes Payable	.4	.9	.4	.0	.2		.0	.4	.8
All Other Current	21.6	20.9	28.3	40.5	22.9		31.1	24.0	29.8
Total Current	44.8	40.6	42.5	49.8	38.7		58.5	35.0	42.9
Long-Term Debt	12.2	17.1	14.2	11.1	11.1		2.2	4.5	26.2
Deferred Taxes	.4	.3	.6	.0	.0			1.7	.8
All Other Non-Current	9.0	7.2	9.1	9.4	2.6		13.2	16.2	6.6
Net Worth	33.6	34.8	33.7	29.7	47.6		26.1	42.6	23.4
Total Liabilties & Net Worth	100.0	100.0	100.0	100.0	100.0		100.0	100.0	100.0
INCOME DATA									
Net Sales	100.0	100.0	100.0	100.0	100.0		100.0	100.0	100.0
Gross Profit									
Operating Expenses	82.1	82.1	77.5	61.4	71.7		83.0	73.8	87.1
Operating Profit	17.9	17.9	22.5	38.6	28.3		17.0	26.2	12.9
All Other Expenses (net)	1.3	1.3	2.4	4.0	2.9		4.0	1.9	1.6
Profit Before Taxes	16.6	16.6	20.1	34.6	25.4		13.0	24.4	11.3
RATIOS									
Current	3.3	3.1	4.1	23.3	19.5		7.0	2.7	1.8
	1.7	1.5	1.5	1.8	1.5		1.9	1.6	1.4
	.8	.9	1.0	.2	.8		.7	1.0	.8
Quick	2.7	2.8	4.0	23.2	12.9		6.2	2.7	1.6
	1.3	1.3	1.4	1.8	1.5		1.8	1.2	1.3
	.6	.8	.8	.2	.7		.1	.9	.5
Sales/Receivables	0 UND	0 UND	0 UND	0 UND	0 UND		0 UND	18 20.2	5 68.4
	15 24.1	26 14.0	22 16.9	0 UND	0 UND		19 19.3	30 12.0	32 11.3
	53 6.9	64 5.7	58 6.3	12 30.0	114 3.2		49 7.5	70 5.2	64 5.7
Cost of Sales/Inventory									
Cost of Sales/Payables									
Sales/Working Capital	2.8	3.4	3.7	1.1	1.7		4.8	2.8	6.7
	10.7	15.7	13.6	2.8	17.6		23.2	14.0	15.8
	-40.2	-93.8	NM	-3.9	NM		-15.0	78.8	-35.8
EBIT/Interest	85.3	41.4	58.0						50.5
	(48) 24.0	(49) 10.7	(42) 15.7					(21) 15.0	
	4.5	2.0	3.4						.2
Net Profit + Depr., Dep., Amort./Cur. Mat. L/T/D									
Fixed/Worth	.0	.0	.0	.0	.0		.0	.0	.1
	.1	.3	.1	.0	.0		.3	.0	.5
	1.1	UND	2.9	1.8	NM		NM	.1	-.3
Debt/Worth	.6	.6	.8	.3	.2		.2	.9	1.4
	1.7	1.7	1.7	1.0	1.3		1.2	1.7	5.8
	168.4	-28.3	768.0	4.0	-2.7		NM	7.9	-2.8
% Profit Before Taxes/Tangible Net Worth	108.2	72.2	155.9	228.7				95.1	163.5
	(69) 40.5	(67) 25.7	(61) 30.3	(10) 26.6				(12) 30.4	(19) 26.2
	7.3	4.7	10.1	4.4				14.5	4.0
% Profit Before Taxes/Total Assets	44.9	26.0	56.9	189.2	80.1		117.0	30.3	50.4
	11.9	11.6	11.0	10.4	25.4		19.1	11.5	9.9
	2.6	2.3	2.9	5.0	4.5		.0	2.5	.5
Sales/Net Fixed Assets	UND	590.8	753.9	UND	UND		744.7	UND	106.7
	45.9	48.3	78.2	96.6	475.0		63.4	163.0	48.3
	22.8	17.3	24.1	.1	64.7		35.8	67.2	15.8
Sales/Total Assets	5.2	4.1	3.8	4.6	7.6		9.1	5.4	3.7
	1.9	1.4	1.5	.2	1.0		3.6	.5	1.8
	.4	.4	.4	.1	.6		1.1	.2	.8
% Depr., Dep., Amort./Sales	.4	.5	.4						.4
	(46) .9	(42) .8	(37) 1.0						(18) 1.3
	2.2	1.7	4.0						4.3
% Officers', Directors' Owners' Comp/Sales	3.5	3.7	2.6						
	(20) 8.6	(15) 7.6	(17) 5.9						
	20.2	20.1	11.2						
Net Sales ($)	3357371M	4529877M	3000743M	4644M	24152M	11002M	70428M	221504M	2669013M
Total Assets ($)	2726641M	2825921M	2685408M	21223M	28539M	31102M	160745M	710465M	1733334M

M = $ thousand   MM = $ million
See Pages viii through xx for Explanation of Ratios and Data

Current Data Sorted by Assets   Comparative Historical Data

0-500M	500M-2MM	2-10MM	10-50MM	50-100MM	100-250MM		4/1/14-3/31/15 ALL	4/1/15-3/31/16 ALL
						Type of Statement		
		1	3	2	7	Unqualified	12	15
						Reviewed	2	
1	1	1				Compiled	6	2
1						Tax Returns	4	6
2	2	4	3	2	3	Other	17	17
	6 (4/1-9/30/18)		27 (10/1/18-3/31/19)					
4	3	6	6	4	10	**NUMBER OF STATEMENTS**	41	40
%	%	%	%	%	%	**ASSETS**	%	%
					23.8	Cash & Equivalents	31.3	26.1
					28.3	Trade Receivables (net)	7.6	5.4
					.0	Inventory	.0	.0
					7.9	All Other Current	5.7	4.0
					59.9	Total Current	44.6	35.6
					11.2	Fixed Assets (net)	14.0	20.3
					1.2	Intangibles (net)	4.4	6.3
					27.7	All Other Non-Current	37.0	37.8
					100.0	Total	100.0	100.0
						LIABILITIES		
					14.0	Notes Payable-Short Term	6.0	15.7
					7.5	Cur. Mat.-L.T.D.	2.5	2.6
					8.7	Trade Payables	4.4	6.8
					.0	Income Taxes Payable	.1	.1
					12.3	All Other Current	10.9	20.6
					42.5	Total Current	23.8	45.8
					12.3	Long-Term Debt	12.3	16.9
					1.0	Deferred Taxes	.5	.0
					4.2	All Other Non-Current	1.0	4.7
					39.9	Net Worth	62.4	32.6
					100.0	Total Liabilities & Net Worth	100.0	100.0
						INCOME DATA		
					100.0	Net Sales	100.0	100.0
						Gross Profit		
					78.3	Operating Expenses	66.7	70.7
					21.7	Operating Profit	33.3	29.3
					16.9	All Other Expenses (net)	7.6	8.8
					4.8	Profit Before Taxes	25.7	20.4
						RATIOS		
					6.3	Current	9.0	6.2
					1.3		2.9	.6
					.9		.7	.2
					4.4	Quick	8.2	5.2
					1.2		2.9	.5
					.8		.5	.2
					20 18.2	Sales/Receivables	0 UND	0 UND
					49 7.5		3 145.4	0 UND
					521 .7		39 9.4	31 11.7
						Cost of Sales/Inventory		
						Cost of Sales/Payables		
					1.2	Sales/Working Capital	1.3	2.2
					3.7		5.1	-15.0
					-37.9		-12.1	-1.8
						EBIT/Interest	49.3	25.1
							(22) 11.6	(23) 6.9
							2.5	3.1
						Net Profit + Depr., Dep., Amort./Cur. Mat. L/T/D		
					.0	Fixed/Worth	.0	.0
					.0		.0	.0
					1.8		.5	2.1
					.4	Debt/Worth	.1	.3
					2.0		.6	1.2
					9.7		1.7	5.1
						% Profit Before Taxes/Tangible Net Worth	27.7	49.7
							(37) 8.0	(32) 6.9
							.9	2.3
					6.8	% Profit Before Taxes/Total Assets	21.9	14.5
					.7		6.9	4.2
					-3.2		.3	.8
					UND	Sales/Net Fixed Assets	UND	UND
					70.0		64.5	73.1
					35.6		17.9	4.7
					2.0	Sales/Total Assets	1.2	1.4
					.2		.5	.3
					.1		.1	.1
						% Depr., Dep., Amort./Sales	.5	.7
							(21) 1.3	(16) 1.3
							2.2	7.1
						% Officers', Directors' Owners' Comp/Sales		
6099M	9112M	76205M	71959M	52366M	2613268M	Net Sales ($)	1253317M	1067852M
898M	3874M	44599M	140902M	237808M	1884989M	Total Assets ($)	3250316M	2935612M

M = $ thousand   MM = $ million
See Pages viii through xx for Explanation of Ratios and Data

Comparative Historical Data / Current Data Sorted by Sales

	14	14	13	Type of Statement		2		2	2	7
		3		Unqualified						
	1	1	3	Reviewed	2	1				
	2		1	Compiled		6				
	15	20	16	Tax Returns	2	1				
	4/1/16-3/31/17 ALL	4/1/17-3/31/18 ALL	4/1/18-3/31/19 ALL	Other	2	6		1		3
					0-1MM	1-3MM	3-5MM	5-10MM	10-25MM	25MM & OVER
					\[6 (4/1-9/30/18)\]			\[27 (10/1/18-3/31/19)\]		
	32	38	33	**NUMBER OF STATEMENTS**	4	10		3	6	10
	%	%	%	**ASSETS**	%	%	%	%	%	%
	26.0	27.7	32.3	Cash & Equivalents		38.2				28.4
	4.1	9.4	15.0	Trade Receivables (net)		2.4				32.4
	.1	3.5	.0	Inventory		.0				.0
	8.3	6.3	5.8	All Other Current		2.9	D			7.8
	38.6	47.0	53.1	Total Current		43.5	A			68.6
	17.2	13.6	8.1	Fixed Assets (net)		2.4	T			16.0
	5.6	4.7	1.0	Intangibles (net)		.5	A			2.2
	38.6	34.7	37.8	All Other Non-Current		53.6				13.2
	100.0	100.0	100.0	Total		100.0	N			100.0
				LIABILITIES			O			
	8.6	16.5	8.8	Notes Payable-Short Term		11.1	T			6.6
	.4	1.3	2.5	Cur. Mat.-L.T.D.		.0				7.5
	2.9	5.3	4.9	Trade Payables		2.4	A			8.9
	.1	.0	.0	Income Taxes Payable		.0	V			.0
	10.4	12.6	19.1	All Other Current		16.2	A			16.2
	22.4	35.7	35.3	Total Current		29.7	I			38.2
	14.5	9.3	4.9	Long-Term Debt		2.6	L			8.6
	.5	.3	.3	Deferred Taxes		.0	A			.4
	5.9	6.1	4.9	All Other Non-Current		6.1	B			1.2
	56.8	48.5	54.6	Net Worth		61.5	L			51.6
	100.0	100.0	100.0	Total Liabilties & Net Worth		100.0	E			100.0
				INCOME DATA						
	100.0	100.0	100.0	Net Sales		100.0				100.0
				Gross Profit						
	60.0	65.8	68.7	Operating Expenses		57.3				74.5
	40.0	34.2	31.3	Operating Profit		42.7				25.5
	7.0	6.6	9.4	All Other Expenses (net)		16.9				9.0
	33.0	27.6	21.9	Profit Before Taxes		25.8				16.4
				RATIOS						
	9.5	6.5	9.9			30.3				6.3
	3.0	1.7	3.0	Current		3.0				3.1
	.9	.6	.9			.6				1.1
	9.3	6.0	8.4			26.0				5.7
	2.8	1.0	2.0	Quick		2.4				3.1
	.5	.3	.7			.6				1.1
	0 UND	0 UND	0 UND		0 UND				14	25.9
	0 UND	11 32.2	9 38.5	Sales/Receivables	0 UND				35	10.3
	31 11.6	76 4.8	60 6.1		10 35.3				203	1.8
				Cost of Sales/Inventory						
				Cost of Sales/Payables						
	1.0	1.1	1.2			.4				1.3
	3.8	7.0	4.2	Sales/Working Capital		7.6				2.8
	-33.7	-14.4	-38.8			-2.0				13.6
	18.1	18.6	114.4							
(19)	5.3	(23) 7.2	(15) 8.6	EBIT/Interest						
	2.4	3.8	-1.9							
				Net Profit + Depr., Dep., Amort./Cur. Mat. L/T/D						
	.0	.0	.0			.0				.0
	.0	.0	.0	Fixed/Worth		.0				.2
	1.3	.4	.3			.1				1.8
	.1	.2	.1			.0				.2
	.5	1.0	.6	Debt/Worth		.4				.7
	2.3	3.3	2.2			2.9				9.7
	16.9	22.3	63.3							
(27)	9.9	(33) 10.9	(30) 11.2	% Profit Before Taxes/Tangible Net Worth						
	4.3	2.9	-.2							
	14.5	11.8	25.7			28.6				67.7
	3.8	5.7	6.6	% Profit Before Taxes/Total Assets		11.9				6.7
	1.2	.5	-.3			.9				-3.2
	UND	UND	UND			UND				202.9
	171.6	66.4	104.7	Sales/Net Fixed Assets		133.5				56.8
	4.1	11.7	35.4			65.1				7.8
	1.0	1.1	2.7			2.2				4.2
	.2	.2	.5	Sales/Total Assets		.3				.8
	.1	.1	.1			.0				.2
	.9	.3	.1							
(11)	1.7	(15) 1.0	(13) .4	% Depr., Dep., Amort./Sales						
	8.8	2.9	1.8							
				% Officers', Directors' Owners' Comp/Sales						
	1343496M	1506863M	2829009M	Net Sales ($)	2202M	21372M		24540M	84773M	2696122M
	2342241M	3239053M	2313070M	Total Assets ($)	27444M	282322M		198820M	264869M	1539615M

© RMA 2019

M = $ thousand   MM = $ million
See Pages viii through xx for Explanation of Ratios and Data

Current Data Sorted by Assets

Comparative Historical Data

						Type of Statement		
		1				Unqualified	2	2
				1		Reviewed		
2	1		4	1	4	Compiled	4	4
1	4	3 (4/1-9/30/18)	4	19 (10/1/18-3/31/19)		Tax Returns	1	3
						Other	10	10
0-500M	500M-2MM	2-10MM	10-50MM	50-100MM	100-250MM		4/1/14- 3/31/15 ALL	4/1/15- 3/31/16 ALL
3	5	5	3	2	4	NUMBER OF STATEMENTS	17	19
%	%	%	%	%	%	ASSETS	%	%
						Cash & Equivalents	22.7	18.8
						Trade Receivables (net)	6.9	6.1
						Inventory	1.4	.0
						All Other Current	2.3	7.0
						Total Current	33.3	31.9
						Fixed Assets (net)	39.5	40.1
						Intangibles (net)	.5	.2
						All Other Non-Current	26.7	27.8
						Total	100.0	100.0
						LIABILITIES		
						Notes Payable-Short Term	3.2	6.0
						Cur. Mat.-L.T.D.	1.1	3.6
						Trade Payables	1.8	.7
						Income Taxes Payable	.1	.0
						All Other Current	4.5	9.9
						Total Current	10.7	20.3
						Long-Term Debt	21.3	31.2
						Deferred Taxes	.0	.0
						All Other Non-Current	2.0	3.1
						Net Worth	66.1	45.4
						Total Liabilties & Net Worth	100.0	100.0
						INCOME DATA		
						Net Sales	100.0	100.0
						Gross Profit		
						Operating Expenses	56.0	57.9
						Operating Profit	44.0	42.1
						All Other Expenses (net)	13.0	25.3
						Profit Before Taxes	31.0	16.7
						RATIOS		
							10.3	7.3
						Current	2.2	1.6
							1.1	.7
							10.3	7.1
						Quick	1.9	1.6
							1.1	.3
							0 UND	0 UND
						Sales/Receivables	0 999.8	0 UND
							14 26.1	12 31.0
						Cost of Sales/Inventory		
						Cost of Sales/Payables		
							.6	.6
						Sales/Working Capital	3.2	3.1
							NM	-4.8
						EBIT/Interest		
						Net Profit + Depr., Dep., Amort./Cur. Mat. L/T/D		
							.0	.1
						Fixed/Worth	.4	.7
							2.2	UND
							.1	.1
						Debt/Worth	.3	1.0
							1.7	UND
							19.0	16.3
						% Profit Before Taxes/Tangible Net Worth	6.8 (15)	4.3
							-.3	.0
							9.1	7.0
						% Profit Before Taxes/Total Assets	1.8	2.8
							-.3	.0
							27.6	15.0
						Sales/Net Fixed Assets	2.9	.5
							.2	.2
							1.3	.4
						Sales/Total Assets	.2	.2
							.1	.1
						% Depr., Dep., Amort./Sales		
						% Officers', Directors' Owners' Comp/Sales		
1643M	4585M	20753M	13259M	19822M	35048M	Net Sales ($)	131660M	54552M
545M	4147M	21803M	76406M	154645M	523662M	Total Assets ($)	519331M	350555M

Comparative Historical Data | Current Data Sorted by Sales

			Type of Statement						
3			Unqualified		1				
4	2	1	Reviewed						
6	6	1	Compiled		1				
10	16	3	Tax Returns	3					
		17	Other	7					
4/1/16-3/31/17	4/1/17-3/31/18	4/1/18-3/31/19		0-1MM	3 (4/1-9/30/18) 1-3MM	3-5MM	5-10MM	19 (10/1/18-3/31/19) 10-25MM	25MM & OVER
ALL	ALL	ALL							
23	24	22	**NUMBER OF STATEMENTS**	10	5	2	2	3	
%	%	%	**ASSETS**	%	%	%	%	%	%
18.0	16.5	29.7	Cash & Equivalents	33.3					
11.5	2.9	.2	Trade Receivables (net)	.4					
7.6	.1	.0	Inventory	.0					
3.9	5.5	6.4	All Other Current	2.5					
41.0	25.1	36.3	Total Current	36.2					
45.1	52.6	30.6	Fixed Assets (net)	43.0					
.7	8.1	2.2	Intangibles (net)	3.4					
13.2	14.2	30.9	All Other Non-Current	17.4					
100.0	100.0	100.0	Total	100.0					
			LIABILITIES						
5.8	5.1	3.5	Notes Payable-Short Term	4.6					
1.3	.8	2.1	Cur. Mat.-L.T.D.	.7					
4.8	2.8	4.7	Trade Payables	.0					
1.2	1.0	.3	Income Taxes Payable	.2					
6.4	7.4	11.1	All Other Current	23.2					
19.5	17.2	21.7	Total Current	28.7					
33.6	31.2	19.9	Long-Term Debt	32.1					
.2	.0	.0	Deferred Taxes	.0					
7.2	7.2	12.6	All Other Non-Current	7.1					
39.4	44.4	45.8	Net Worth	32.1					
100.0	100.0	100.0	Total Liabilities & Net Worth	100.0					
			INCOME DATA						
100.0	100.0	100.0	Net Sales	100.0					
			Gross Profit						
62.4	56.9	45.2	Operating Expenses	38.4					
37.6	43.1	54.8	Operating Profit	61.6					
13.6	15.6	11.4	All Other Expenses (net)	10.5					
24.0	27.4	43.4	Profit Before Taxes	51.1					
			RATIOS						
5.9	4.5	9.7		6.7					
2.2	1.5	1.3	Current	1.3					
.6	.8	.9		1.1					
5.9	4.4	6.4		6.7					
1.7	1.5	1.1	Quick	1.3					
.6	.3	.6		1.0					
0 UND	0 UND	0 UND		0 UND					
6 62.5	0 UND	0 UND	Sales/Receivables	0 UND					
50 7.3	20 17.9	0 UND		0 UND					
			Cost of Sales/Inventory						
			Cost of Sales/Payables						
.9	1.0	1.4		2.0					
7.2	6.1	18.0	Sales/Working Capital	7.2					
-8.8	-20.7	-86.1		UND					
22.3		22.0							
(14) 8.1		(12) 10.8	EBIT/Interest						
3.0		4.6							
			Net Profit + Depr., Dep., Amort./Cur. Mat. L/T/D						
.3	.4	.0		.6					
1.1	2.7	.6	Fixed/Worth	1.5					
4.5	28.8	2.8		UND					
.4	.3	.1		1.2					
1.5	1.8	1.3	Debt/Worth	2.3					
8.5	30.3	23.4		UND					
28.0	25.6	19.9							
(19) 5.1	(20) 4.2	(20) 9.7	% Profit Before Taxes/Tangible Net Worth						
.9	1.2	3.5							
17.0	4.7	23.3		78.7					
4.7	2.5	5.1	% Profit Before Taxes/Total Assets	8.8					
.5	.0	2.8		3.4					
14.8	8.8	UND		UND					
3.5	.3	6.0	Sales/Net Fixed Assets	.8					
.2	.1	.2		.2					
2.2	.7	.8		3.1					
.2	.1	.2	Sales/Total Assets	.3					
.1	.1	.1		.1					
1.3	3.8								
(16) 6.3	(13) 18.3		% Depr., Dep., Amort./Sales						
13.1	29.8								
			% Officers', Directors' Owners' Comp/Sales						
235783M	232419M	95110M	Net Sales ($)	3728M	11502M	8808M	18016M	53056M	
566793M	895939M	781208M	Total Assets ($)	16097M	223505M	115388M	202648M	223570M	

(Rightmost column "25MM & OVER": DATA NOT AVAILABLE)

Current Data Sorted by Assets   Comparative Historical Data

0-500M	500M-2MM	2-10MM	10-50MM	50-100MM	100-250MM	Type of Statement	4/1/14-3/31/15 ALL	4/1/15-3/31/16 ALL
		4	8	15	12	Unqualified	37	48
		4	2			Reviewed	1	4
	1	1	1		2	Compiled	9	10
3	8	4	2	2		Tax Returns	23	19
3	8	5	23	8	13	Other	68	49
18 (4/1-9/30/18)			111 (10/1/18-3/31/19)					
6	17	18	36	25	27	**NUMBER OF STATEMENTS**	138	130
%	%	%	%	%	%	**ASSETS**	%	%
	19.0	7.7	15.2	21.2	15.4	Cash & Equivalents	20.5	14.3
	16.3	14.8	7.6	9.3	24.2	Trade Receivables (net)	11.4	10.6
	.2	.8	2.9	1.7	.6	Inventory	1.6	1.5
	12.4	4.0	9.6	8.0	8.0	All Other Current	7.9	8.7
	47.9	27.3	35.3	40.2	48.2	Total Current	41.4	35.0
	19.3	26.3	16.7	5.5	11.2	Fixed Assets (net)	22.1	22.0
	5.5	2.5	9.3	7.3	7.1	Intangibles (net)	5.9	6.8
	27.3	43.9	38.7	47.0	33.5	All Other Non-Current	30.6	36.2
	100.0	100.0	100.0	100.0	100.0	Total	100.0	100.0
						LIABILITIES		
	23.8	10.2	10.5	8.4	13.8	Notes Payable-Short Term	15.6	13.0
	6.6	4.9	2.3	4.3	2.0	Cur. Mat.-L.T.D.	2.0	3.5
	9.7	.5	3.6	2.8	1.8	Trade Payables	2.6	2.5
	.0	.0	.0	.0	.1	Income Taxes Payable	.2	.1
	37.3	14.6	11.8	6.7	7.8	All Other Current	10.6	7.3
	77.5	30.2	28.1	22.1	25.6	Total Current	31.0	26.4
	18.4	24.8	16.8	27.1	23.7	Long-Term Debt	22.5	21.7
	.0	.0	.0	.0	.2	Deferred Taxes	.1	.4
	8.9	15.0	7.2	5.4	1.9	All Other Non-Current	4.8	5.2
	-4.8	30.0	47.9	45.4	48.6	Net Worth	41.6	46.4
	100.0	100.0	100.0	100.0	100.0	Total Liabilities & Net Worth	100.0	100.0
						INCOME DATA		
	100.0	100.0	100.0	100.0	100.0	Net Sales	100.0	100.0
						Gross Profit		
	59.3	54.2	55.0	54.9	58.3	Operating Expenses	60.9	56.0
	40.7	45.8	45.0	45.1	41.7	Operating Profit	39.1	44.0
	11.1	32.1	12.6	13.0	20.0	All Other Expenses (net)	10.2	14.5
	29.6	13.7	32.3	32.0	21.7	Profit Before Taxes	28.9	29.6
						RATIOS		
	4.1	3.2	2.7	10.1	3.5		5.8	4.7
	1.2	.7	1.3	1.6	1.6	Current	2.2	1.4
	.2	.2	.5	.3	.6		.7	.5
	3.9	1.6	2.4	4.1	3.3		4.2	3.0
	1.1	.6	.9	1.5	1.3	Quick	1.4	.9
	.1	.0	.2	.2	.1		.3	.3
0 UND	0 UND	0 UND	0 UND	0 UND			0 UND	0 UND
0 UND	0 UND	10 37.7	4 89.7	0 UND	10 36.5	Sales/Receivables	4 102.0	3 111.6
59 6.2	608 .6	37 9.9	39 9.3	81 4.5			63 5.8	45 8.1
						Cost of Sales/Inventory		
						Cost of Sales/Payables		
	1.4	4.2	1.0	.5	.2		1.1	1.9
	3.7	-14.1	7.2	3.2	3.9	Sales/Working Capital	5.8	21.7
	-8.1	-1.4	-4.4	-1.4	-3.2		-17.7	-4.5
			36.3	40.1	7.1		20.9	18.5
		(26) 7.4	(16) 11.2	(20) 5.5		EBIT/Interest	(83) 5.9	(80) 6.2
			4.0	2.5	.8		2.7	2.5
						Net Profit + Depr., Dep., Amort./Cur. Mat. L/T/D		
	.0	.0	.0	.0	.0		.0	.0
	.0	.1	.0	.0	.0	Fixed/Worth	.0	.0
	1.6	7.2	.8	.1	.1		1.3	1.5
	.2	.5	.2	.1	.3		.2	.3
	5.1	5.5	1.0	1.8	.7	Debt/Worth	1.2	1.1
	NM	18.1	2.1	7.4	6.3		10.9	6.0
	85.0	53.0	35.0	22.7	21.5		70.3	33.2
(13) 29.1	(16) 7.2	(32) 11.8	(22) 9.4	(22) 5.6		% Profit Before Taxes/Tangible Net Worth	(122) 17.8	(112) 15.1
	6.8	-.9	4.1	1.8	-1.1		3.2	2.4
	37.6	4.5	13.6	15.3	10.1		14.4	13.7
	5.0	1.8	6.6	3.4	2.0	% Profit Before Taxes/Total Assets	5.7	5.7
	.8	-.5	2.1	.3	-1.5		1.7	1.3
	UND	UND	UND	UND	UND		UND	UND
	904.6	37.1	112.1	UND	UND	Sales/Net Fixed Assets	67.5	59.5
	4.5	.4	3.1	24.0	39.1		1.1	.9
	1.9	1.2	.8	.6	.3		1.2	.8
	.6	.2	.1	.2	.1	Sales/Total Assets	.3	.2
	.1	.1	.1	.1	.1		.1	.1
			2.0				.8	.4
		(15) 11.0				% Depr., Dep., Amort./Sales	(56) 3.5	(62) 3.1
		27.0					12.8	17.2
							2.0	2.3
						% Officers', Directors' Owners' Comp/Sales	(31) 10.9	(15) 9.2
							24.7	35.0
1561M	64411M	103126M	455334M	769537M	1838529M	Net Sales ($)	2534257M	2946277M
689M	20329M	93569M	894244M	1740014M	4669516M	Total Assets ($)	6468398M	6538734M

M = $ thousand   MM = $ million
See Pages viii through xx for Explanation of Ratios and Data

Comparative Historical Data | Current Data Sorted by Sales

			Type of Statement						
40	36	39	Unqualified	3	6	4	5	8	13
3	4	6	Reviewed	3	3				
8	9	5	Compiled	3			1		1
13	22	19	Tax Returns	12	3	2	2		
60	64	60	Other	8	17	3	4	12	16
4/1/16-3/31/17 ALL	4/1/17-3/31/18 ALL	4/1/18-3/31/19 ALL		18 (4/1-9/30/18) 0-1MM	1-3MM	3-5MM	111 (10/1/18-3/31/19) 5-10MM	10-25MM	25MM & OVER
124	135	129	**NUMBER OF STATEMENTS**	29	29	9	12	20	30
%	%	%	**ASSETS**	%	%	%	%	%	%
16.6	15.3	17.0	Cash & Equivalents	15.6	16.2		18.4	16.2	20.8
8.3	15.0	13.2	Trade Receivables (net)	12.6	9.6		8.1	23.7	16.0
1.1	1.7	1.4	Inventory	.2	2.9		.0	1.2	1.9
10.3	10.0	9.6	All Other Current	12.8	10.0		1.2	4.5	9.4
36.3	41.9	41.2	Total Current	41.2	38.8		27.7	45.6	48.1
25.2	22.2	14.4	Fixed Assets (net)	16.4	15.3		19.8	12.9	6.0
7.3	7.7	7.6	Intangibles (net)	4.8	3.4		3.0	7.5	18.3
31.1	28.2	36.8	All Other Non-Current	37.3	42.6		49.4	34.0	27.5
100.0	100.0	100.0	Total	100.0	100.0		100.0	100.0	100.0
			LIABILITIES						
7.7	10.2	12.9	Notes Payable-Short Term	16.9	20.0		7.5	7.4	9.7
3.3	2.6	3.5	Cur. Mat.-L.T.D.	1.6	3.4		6.6	1.8	3.7
3.0	3.5	3.3	Trade Payables	1.1	.7		.9	1.6	10.8
.0	.1	.0	Income Taxes Payable	.0	.0		.0	.0	.1
8.5	13.4	13.9	All Other Current	8.7	20.2		2.4	6.3	24.9
22.6	29.7	33.6	Total Current	28.3	44.3		17.4	17.2	49.1
22.5	23.9	22.3	Long-Term Debt	27.0	17.6		29.7	26.6	16.9
.2	.1	.1	Deferred Taxes	.0	.0		.0	.0	.2
6.7	7.2	6.7	All Other Non-Current	5.7	6.9		1.8	.7	15.5
48.1	39.1	37.3	Net Worth	39.0	31.2		51.2	55.6	18.2
100.0	100.0	100.0	Total Liabilities & Net Worth	100.0	100.0		100.0	100.0	100.0
			INCOME DATA						
100.0	100.0	100.0	Net Sales	100.0	100.0		100.0	100.0	100.0
			Gross Profit						
63.7	62.0	56.9	Operating Expenses	54.2	48.4		52.1	57.0	70.4
36.3	38.0	43.1	Operating Profit	45.8	51.6		47.9	43.0	29.6
12.3	13.9	16.2	All Other Expenses (net)	21.2	17.6		18.0	17.2	10.2
24.0	24.1	26.8	Profit Before Taxes	24.6	34.0		29.8	25.8	19.4
			RATIOS						
6.3	6.8	4.1		7.0	5.3		2.5	5.7	3.0
1.3	1.5	1.3	Current	1.2	1.3		1.5	2.4	1.3
.6	.4	.4		.5	.2		.2	.8	.4
3.9	5.6	2.8		3.3	3.8		2.5	4.4	2.2
.9	.9	1.1	Quick	1.0	.8		.9	1.7	1.3
.3	.3	.1		.1	.1		.1	.5	.1
0 UND	0 UND	0 UND		0 UND	0 UND		0 UND	0 UND	0 UND
11 33.4	10 35.3	2 159.7	Sales/Receivables	0 UND	0 UND		0 UND	13 28.7	23 16.2
52 7.0	87 4.2	56 6.5		104 3.5	50 7.3		1 326.4	85 4.3	68 5.4
			Cost of Sales/Inventory						
			Cost of Sales/Payables						
1.6	.6	1.0		1.1	.3		.4	1.0	2.4
9.4	8.6	8.2	Sales/Working Capital	2.5	4.0		19.4	5.9	13.7
-9.3	-4.9	-3.7		-3.0	-2.0		-3.0	-108.4	-13.1
15.0	12.8	16.8		15.7	16.0			58.8	38.8
(75) 4.1	(79) 5.4	(83) 6.6	EBIT/Interest	(13) 11.5	(21) 4.0		(14) 7.2	(24) 6.7	
1.5	1.5	2.3		2.3	1.7			4.9	1.5
			Net Profit + Depr., Dep., Amort./Cur. Mat. L/T/D						
.0	.0	.0		.0	.0		.0	.0	.0
.1	.1	.0	Fixed/Worth	.0	.0		.0	.0	.1
2.0	2.7	.8		.8	.2		.8	.5	-.3
.4	.3	.2		.2	.2		.2	.1	.7
1.2	1.9	1.5	Debt/Worth	2.6	1.1		1.1	.7	6.0
4.4	15.3	7.7		13.4	5.1		5.3	2.4	-2.2
36.8	55.5	34.5		42.6	14.7		41.5	25.2	96.1
(107) 9.4	(111) 10.9	(109) 11.3	% Profit Before Taxes/Tangible Net Worth	(25) 7.8	(27) 8.6		6.5	(18) 12.2	(18) 26.4
2.1	1.3	2.2		-.2	2.6		-1.2	2.6	12.9
11.4	11.2	12.7		10.0	6.6		6.1	17.7	19.1
3.6	3.6	4.3	% Profit Before Taxes/Total Assets	3.8	2.2		2.1	7.3	8.9
.9	.2	.4		.1	.9		-.0	1.8	-1.7
UND	UND	UND		UND	UND		UND	UND	UND
40.3	106.2	227.0	Sales/Net Fixed Assets	227.0	UND		UND	143.4	51.1
.5	3.1	7.9		5.4	5.7		.5	11.5	22.0
.9	.7	.8		.5	.2		.1	.9	1.7
.2	.2	.2	Sales/Total Assets	.1	.1		.1	.2	.7
.1	.1	.1		.1	.0		.1	.1	.3
.6	.6	.9							.7
(65) 3.9	(58) 2.9	(42) 2.5	% Depr., Dep., Amort./Sales					(15) 1.4	
24.5	19.1	21.0							2.0
.8	1.1	1.6	% Officers', Directors', Owners' Comp/Sales						
(14) 16.2	(18) 8.5	(20) 12.8							
29.0	31.9	31.0							
2312597M	2818764M	3232498M	Net Sales ($)	11457M	54823M	37354M	82630M	350139M	2696095M
6924407M	7521416M	7418361M	Total Assets ($)	213939M	865104M	325623M	800522M	1802797M	3410376M

© RMA 2019

M = $ thousand   MM = $ million
See Pages viii through xx for Explanation of Ratios and Data

REAL ESTATE AND RENTAL AND LEASING

Current Data Sorted by Assets							Comparative Historical Data		
						Type of Statement			
5	20	63	49	19	21	Unqualified	258		227
	5	6	10		2	Reviewed	50		35
6	28	44	7	3	2	Compiled	154		105
161	427	326	50	7	2	Tax Returns	1411		1369
92	280	402	145	30	17	Other	1026		914
	126 (4/1-9/30/18)		2,103 (10/1/18-3/31/19)				4/1/14-3/31/15 ALL		4/1/15-3/31/16 ALL
0-500M	500M-2MM	2-10MM	10-50MM	50-100MM	100-250MM	**NUMBER OF STATEMENTS**	2899		2650
264	760	841	261	59	44				
%	%	%	%	%	%	**ASSETS**	%		%
18.3	6.8	6.2	7.7	8.5	6.2	Cash & Equivalents	7.5		7.4
1.5	1.4	1.3	3.3	9.0	3.2	Trade Receivables (net)	1.3		1.4
1.5	1.0	1.6	2.2	1.4	2.7	Inventory	1.0		.9
6.6	2.2	2.2	2.6	5.9	8.3	All Other Current	2.0		2.1
27.9	11.4	11.3	15.7	24.8	20.4	Total Current	11.8		11.9
63.7	80.4	79.9	69.6	47.4	48.9	Fixed Assets (net)	79.1		79.2
1.8	2.0	2.0	2.6	3.6	2.8	Intangibles (net)	1.8		2.0
6.5	6.2	6.8	12.1	24.2	27.9	All Other Non-Current	7.3		7.0
100.0	100.0	100.0	100.0	100.0	100.0	Total	100.0		100.0
						LIABILITIES			
4.9	4.1	3.3	4.3	4.6	5.1	Notes Payable-Short Term	3.4		4.2
4.6	3.6	2.9	1.7	2.0	1.9	Cur. Mat.-L.T.D.	3.4		3.5
2.3	.8	.9	1.5	4.8	3.0	Trade Payables	1.1		1.2
.0	.0	.0	.0	.0	.1	Income Taxes Payable	.0		.0
15.2	4.4	5.4	5.1	7.9	4.5	All Other Current	5.7		6.3
27.0	13.0	12.6	12.6	19.4	14.6	Total Current	13.7		15.1
74.2	70.8	64.5	53.6	40.6	46.1	Long-Term Debt	68.2		68.2
.0	.0	.0	.0	.0	.2	Deferred Taxes	.1		.0
8.2	5.2	4.0	4.9	8.4	11.3	All Other Non-Current	4.0		4.2
-9.4	11.0	18.9	28.8	31.6	27.8	Net Worth	14.1		12.4
100.0	100.0	100.0	100.0	100.0	100.0	Total Liabilities & Net Worth	100.0		100.0
						INCOME DATA			
100.0	100.0	100.0	100.0	100.0	100.0	Net Sales	100.0		100.0
						Gross Profit			
68.3	66.7	67.9	72.4	78.0	78.7	Operating Expenses	68.5		67.9
31.7	33.3	32.1	27.6	22.0	21.3	Operating Profit	31.5		32.1
14.7	16.8	17.5	16.3	12.0	14.6	All Other Expenses (net)	17.8		18.3
17.0	16.5	14.7	11.3	10.0	6.6	Profit Before Taxes	13.8		13.8
						RATIOS			
3.5	2.3	2.4	3.7	4.5	3.9		2.0		2.2
1.0	.9	.9	1.2	1.4	1.6	Current	.8		.8
.3	.2	.3	.4	.6	.6		.2		.2
2.4	1.9	1.8	2.6	2.4	2.0		1.6		1.8
.8	.7	.6	.9	1.0	.7	Quick	.6 (2647)		.6
.2	.2	.2	.2	.2	.3		.1		.2
0 UND	0 UND	0 UND	0 UND	1 547.1	0 UND		0 UND	0	UND
0 UND	0 UND	0 UND	0 UND	7 49.9	8 48.0	Sales/Receivables	0 UND	0	UND
0 UND	0 UND	1 377.0	7 54.0	64 5.7	31 11.6		1 453.0	0	753.0
						Cost of Sales/Inventory			
						Cost of Sales/Payables			
6.6	6.0	4.9	2.8	1.9	1.0		7.2		6.3
UND	-51.9	-49.7	29.6	7.9	7.6	Sales/Working Capital	-20.5		-24.7
-5.4	-3.9	-3.9	-5.2	-6.8	-5.3		-3.7		-3.5
6.3	4.6	4.8	4.4	7.3	4.1		4.6		4.8
(125) 3.3	(407) 2.7	(432) 2.6	(122) 2.2	(33) 2.3	(22) 1.3	EBIT/Interest	(1437) 2.7	(1329)	2.6
1.4	1.4	1.4	1.0	1.0	-.2		1.3		1.3
		4.2					3.2		3.1
	(19)	2.5				Net Profit + Depr., Dep.,	(80) 1.8	(68)	1.7
		1.0				Amort./Cur. Mat. L/T/D	1.1		.8
1.0	2.0	1.8	1.2	.3	.2		1.8		1.8
4.7	4.6	4.2	2.9	1.8	1.4	Fixed/Worth	4.3		4.4
-7.4	-22.4	-299.1	10.0	6.8	5.5		-63.8		-34.1
.8	1.5	1.3	1.0	1.1	1.0		1.4		1.5
6.3	4.3	3.9	2.9	2.7	3.5	Debt/Worth	4.3		4.7
-6.1	-23.0	-277.7	11.4	11.1	11.9		-55.0		-32.9
81.6	27.3	24.1	14.3	12.6	16.2	% Profit Before Taxes/Tangible	29.6		27.6
(170) 17.3	(537) 9.3	(623) 8.5	(215) 4.5	(49) 5.6	(38) 3.6	Net Worth	(2110) 9.5	(1900)	9.1
2.4	.8	.2	-.7	.2	-.8		.0		.1
27.6	7.7	6.4	4.4	5.9	2.8	% Profit Before Taxes/Total	6.7		6.8
4.9	3.0	2.4	1.4	1.8	1.1	Assets	2.4		2.6
-.2	.2	.0	-.3	-.1	-1.0		-.2		.0
5.2	.5	.4	.8	12.3	3.5		.5		.5
.5	.2	.2	.2	.6	.4	Sales/Net Fixed Assets	.2		.2
.2	.1	.1	.1	.2	.1		.1		.1
1.5	.4	.3	.3	.5	.3		.3		.3
.3	.2	.2	.1	.2	.1	Sales/Total Assets	.2		.2
.2	.1	.1	.1	.1	.1		.1		.1
9.3	12.1	13.5	9.0	2.2	3.1		11.7		11.9
(177) 15.9	(624) 19.0	(637) 21.4	(200) 19.6	(37) 7.4	(32) 15.0	% Depr., Dep., Amort./Sales	(2305) 19.6	(2151)	19.3
24.8	25.6	31.0	32.3	20.2	26.2		28.3		28.0
6.6	2.1	1.7	2.9				3.2		2.9
(21) 10.5	(58) 4.7	(55) 5.7	(25) 5.4			% Officers', Directors' Owners' Comp/Sales	(237) 6.0	(215)	6.4
14.0	10.1	11.7	9.8				11.5		13.0
103232M	411149M	1261499M	1724451M	1864158M	1986564M	Net Sales ($)	10331590M		8986311M
71184M	906222M	3794049M	5528417M	4175150M	7392981M	Total Assets ($)	22004927M		20052396M

M = $ thousand   MM = $ million

See Pages viii through xx for Explanation of Ratios and Data

Comparative Historical Data   Current Data Sorted by Sales

			Type of Statement						
248	257	177	Unqualified	66	34	15	12	24	26
45	42	23	Reviewed	7	4	2	2	3	5
116	102	90	Compiled	58	19	5	3	3	2
1242	1190	973	Tax Returns	784	135	30	16	7	1
960	956	966	Other	618	184	44	47	49	24
4/1/16-3/31/17 ALL	4/1/17-3/31/18 ALL	4/1/18-3/31/19 ALL		126 (4/1-9/30/18)			2,103 (10/1/18-3/31/19)		
				0-1MM	1-3MM	3-5MM	5-10MM	10-25MM	25MM & OVER
2611	2547	2229	NUMBER OF STATEMENTS	1533	376	96	80	86	58
%	%	%	ASSETS	%	%	%	%	%	%
8.5	8.0	8.1	Cash & Equivalents	6.6	10.1	11.8	11.0	16.6	10.7
1.4	1.5	1.8	Trade Receivables (net)	.5	1.5	5.1	7.3	10.1	13.6
.9	1.0	1.5	Inventory	.8	1.4	4.5	5.4	5.5	3.1
2.1	2.1	3.0	All Other Current	2.5	2.7	2.4	3.4	8.5	8.5
12.9	12.5	14.3	Total Current	10.4	15.7	23.8	27.1	40.7	35.9
77.5	76.9	75.5	Fixed Assets (net)	82.4	73.1	57.7	48.3	33.7	35.8
2.0	2.2	2.1	Intangibles (net)	1.6	2.3	2.9	4.6	4.2	5.4
7.6	8.3	8.1	All Other Non-Current	5.5	8.9	15.6	20.0	21.5	22.9
100.0	100.0	100.0	Total	100.0	100.0	100.0	100.0	100.0	100.0
			LIABILITIES						
3.7	2.9	4.0	Notes Payable-Short Term	3.6	3.7	5.9	7.2	4.7	6.8
3.4	3.4	3.2	Cur. Mat.-L.T.D.	3.3	3.5	1.9	2.0	2.7	2.2
1.2	1.2	1.3	Trade Payables	.6	1.3	1.8	4.5	4.1	8.9
.0	.0	.0	Income Taxes Payable	.0	.0	.0	.0	.1	.1
6.0	5.7	6.2	All Other Current	5.2	7.2	6.4	8.3	13.0	13.9
14.2	13.2	14.7	Total Current	12.7	15.7	15.9	21.9	24.6	32.0
65.4	65.7	65.6	Long-Term Debt	68.3	71.5	65.2	49.3	31.4	27.5
.1	.0	.0	Deferred Taxes	.0	.0	.1	.2	.0	.1
4.2	4.1	5.3	All Other Non-Current	4.8	4.8	3.0	5.9	12.2	12.0
16.1	16.9	14.5	Net Worth	14.1	8.0	15.8	22.7	31.8	28.5
100.0	100.0	100.0	Total Liabilties & Net Worth	100.0	100.0	100.0	100.0	100.0	100.0
			INCOME DATA						
100.0	100.0	100.0	Net Sales	100.0	100.0	100.0	100.0	100.0	100.0
			Gross Profit						
68.4	68.5	68.5	Operating Expenses	65.6	69.7	76.3	78.0	84.2	89.7
31.6	31.5	31.5	Operating Profit	34.4	30.3	23.7	22.0	15.8	10.3
16.1	16.5	16.6	All Other Expenses (net)	18.8	15.1	9.8	9.6	6.5	4.4
15.5	15.0	14.9	Profit Before Taxes	15.7	15.2	13.9	12.4	9.3	5.9
			RATIOS						
2.2	2.3	2.6		2.4	2.7	4.8	4.0	5.3	1.9
.9	.9	1.0	Current	.8	1.0	1.3	1.5	1.7	1.1
.3	.3	.3		.2	.3	.5	.6	.9	.6
1.8	1.9	2.0		1.8	2.0	3.7	3.2	3.8	1.6
(2609) .7	(2545) .7	.7	Quick	.6	.7	1.1	1.0	1.1	.8
.2	.2	.2		.2	.2	.3	.3	.5	.4
0 UND	0 UND	0 UND		0 UND	0 UND	0 UND	0 UND	0 UND	6 61.8
0 UND	0 UND	0 UND	Sales/Receivables	0 UND	0 UND	0 835.5	1 265.3	5 76.5	20 18.2
1 568.8	1 289.0	1 342.3		0 UND	2 197.3	7 51.2	23 15.6	57 6.4	56 6.5
			Cost of Sales/Inventory						
			Cost of Sales/Payables						
5.7	5.2	4.7		5.2	5.6	3.1	3.0	1.9	5.9
-52.0	-57.5	-211.5	Sales/Working Capital	-40.0	-335.4	26.5	13.0	8.4	22.4
-4.1	-4.4	-4.2		-3.6	-5.4	-6.4	-24.1	-47.8	-6.6
5.2	4.8	4.9		4.4	5.4	4.7	6.0	20.4	7.1
(1412) 2.7	(1344) 2.7	(1141) 2.6	EBIT/Interest	(721) 2.6	(210) 2.7	(63) 2.6	(48) 2.1	(58) 3.7	(41) 2.3
1.4	1.4	1.3		1.3	1.3	1.4	.8	.8	.8
3.3	5.6	8.5		3.1					
(59) 1.9	(56) 2.6	(38) 3.0	Net Profit + Depr., Dep., Amort./Cur. Mat. L/T/D	(14) 2.3					
1.1	1.2	1.3		.7					
1.8	1.7	1.6		2.0	1.4	.4	.3	.0	.2
4.2	4.0	4.0	Fixed/Worth	4.2	5.0	2.9	1.7	1.3	1.2
-58.3	-196.3	-83.3		UND	-6.3	NM	214.9	7.7	129.7
1.4	1.4	1.3		1.4	1.3	1.2	.9	.9	.7
4.0	4.1	3.9	Debt/Worth	3.9	6.1	3.0	2.6	2.8	3.2
-52.5	-137.2	-57.0		-342.1	-6.9	-38.8	NM	16.8	185.1
28.0	28.2	25.8		23.8	36.5	27.9	16.4	41.2	30.1
(1904) 9.5	(1889) 9.3	(1632) 8.6	% Profit Before Taxes/Tangible Net Worth	(1141) 8.2	(246) 10.0	(71) 9.8	(60) 4.8	(69) 8.4	(45) 15.0
.4	.2	.4		.1	.8	1.8	-.7	.7	1.7
7.3	7.3	7.1		6.3	9.1	8.6	9.0	15.8	9.2
2.7	2.9	2.6	% Profit Before Taxes/Total Assets	2.4	3.3	3.6	2.2	3.2	2.6
.0	.0	.0		-.2	.2	.5	-.2	.0	-.3
.5	.5	.5		.3	.8	17.0	13.1	57.8	18.9
.2	.2	.2	Sales/Net Fixed Assets	.2	.3	.6	1.4	8.6	3.7
.1	.1	.1		.1	.2	.2	.2	.4	.6
.3	.3	.4		.3	.5	.8	1.5	2.0	1.6
.2	.2	.2	Sales/Total Assets	.2	.2	.4	.3	.5	.8
.1	.1	.1		.1	.1	.2	.2	.2	.3
11.6	11.2	11.7		14.4	9.8	3.4	1.7	.8	.6
(2111) 19.1	(2050) 18.8	(1707) 19.2	% Depr., Dep., Amort./Sales	(1210) 20.9	(272) 18.3	(68) 11.6	(58) 9.5	(56) 5.1	(43) 2.5
27.2	27.6	27.8		28.7	28.5	19.7	20.4	17.3	12.4
2.8	2.9	2.4		2.7	3.2	2.1	.9	.8	
(203) 6.6	(198) 5.8	(170) 5.7	% Officers', Directors' Owners' Comp/Sales	(79) 8.7	(40) 5.7	(18) 5.0	(14) 3.4	(13) 1.7	
15.5	10.3	10.9		15.6	10.9	7.2	4.7	4.3	
8549434M	8165042M	7351053M	Net Sales ($)	542704M	629468M	372186M	567382M	1378914M	3860399M
22118683M	22205099M	21868003M	Total Assets ($)	3569273M	3439311M	1734003M	2333251M	4984452M	5807713M

© RMA 2019

M = $ thousand   MM = $ million
See Pages viii through xx for Explanation of Ratios and Data

Current Data Sorted by Assets   Comparative Historical Data

0-500M	500M-2MM	2-10MM	10-50MM	50-100MM	100-250MM	Type of Statement		
1	10	31	55	10	31	Unqualified	183	174
3	26	78	52	15	6	Reviewed	257	297
26	152	262	82	8	2	Compiled	789	626
398	2048	1961	217	2	6	Tax Returns	6452	6307
214	1136	1960	602	96	69	Other	4241	3834
	301 (4/1-9/30/18)		9,258 (10/1/18-3/31/19)				4/1/14-3/31/15 ALL	4/1/15-3/31/16 ALL
642	3372	4292	1008	131	114	**NUMBER OF STATEMENTS**	11922	11238
%	%	%	%	%	%	**ASSETS**	%	%
14.0	5.3	4.8	5.8	6.9	7.3	Cash & Equivalents	5.2	5.4
1.4	.8	.9	2.1	4.5	4.0	Trade Receivables (net)	.9	1.0
1.3	.3	.4	2.0	1.4	3.4	Inventory	.6	.5
3.6	1.0	1.3	1.8	1.8	3.0	All Other Current	1.3	1.2
20.3	7.3	7.4	11.7	14.7	17.8	Total Current	8.0	8.2
73.2	87.0	85.5	75.8	66.5	64.3	Fixed Assets (net)	84.9	84.8
2.1	1.7	2.4	4.1	3.8	4.4	Intangibles (net)	2.1	2.0
4.3	4.0	4.8	8.4	15.0	13.6	All Other Non-Current	5.0	5.0
100.0	100.0	100.0	100.0	100.0	100.0	Total	100.0	100.0
						LIABILITIES		
5.5	2.7	2.2	3.1	3.5	3.2	Notes Payable-Short Term	2.4	3.0
5.0	4.1	3.5	2.7	2.5	2.7	Cur. Mat.-L.T.D.	4.1	4.1
1.5	.4	.5	1.5	3.5	2.9	Trade Payables	.7	.7
.0	.0	.0	.0	.1	.2	Income Taxes Payable	.0	.0
13.9	3.6	3.3	4.8	4.0	4.8	All Other Current	3.9	3.9
25.9	10.8	9.5	12.1	13.6	13.8	Total Current	11.1	11.7
64.5	66.6	63.2	53.5	51.9	43.4	Long-Term Debt	66.3	65.1
.0	.0	.0	.1	.1	.4	Deferred Taxes	.0	.0
4.4	2.8	3.4	3.9	3.2	5.3	All Other Non-Current	3.3	3.3
5.2	19.7	23.8	30.5	31.3	37.1	Net Worth	19.3	19.9
100.0	100.0	100.0	100.0	100.0	100.0	Total Liabilities & Net Worth	100.0	100.0
						INCOME DATA		
100.0	100.0	100.0	100.0	100.0	100.0	Net Sales	100.0	100.0
						Gross Profit		
50.8	46.1	47.4	54.2	64.6	69.8	Operating Expenses	48.1	48.2
49.2	53.9	52.6	45.8	35.4	30.2	Operating Profit	51.9	51.8
17.4	21.6	22.7	19.4	15.9	13.6	All Other Expenses (net)	23.3	22.4
31.8	32.3	30.0	26.3	19.4	16.5	Profit Before Taxes	28.6	29.5
						RATIOS		
2.1	1.7	2.1	2.3	2.4	3.7		1.8	1.8
.8	.6	.7	.9	.9	1.5	Current	.6	.6
.2	.2	.2	.3	.4	.6		.2	.2
1.9	1.5	1.8	1.7	1.8	2.6		1.4	1.5
.6 (3371)	.5 (4291)	.6	.6	.7	1.0	Quick	.5 (11919)	.5 (11237)
.1	.2	.2	.2	.2	.4		.1	.1
0 UND	0 UND	0 UND	0 UND	0 UND	0 865.9		0 UND	0 UND
0 UND	0 UND	0 UND	0 UND	4 102.0	10 37.5	Sales/Receivables	0 UND	0 UND
0 UND	0 UND	0 UND	7 53.6	19 19.7	32 11.5		0 UND	0 UND
						Cost of Sales/Inventory		
						Cost of Sales/Payables		
9.7	8.8	5.4	4.5	3.9	2.4		8.1	8.0
-26.0	-9.3	-13.1	-42.4	-46.7	8.6	Sales/Working Capital	-9.4	-9.4
-2.9	-2.8	-3.0	-2.8	-4.0	-2.9		-2.7	-2.5
8.1	7.3	6.3	7.2	6.5	6.5		6.9	7.0
(269) 4.8	(1489) 4.5	(1755) 4.0	(460) 4.2	(70) 4.0	(70) 3.1	EBIT/Interest	(4683) 4.3	(4698) 4.3
2.8	3.1	2.7	2.3	1.8	1.7		2.6	2.7
	3.5	3.1	4.8	2.9	4.5	Net Profit + Depr., Dep.,	3.5	3.4
	(53) 2.0	(136) 1.8	(71) 2.3	(11) 2.4	(17) 2.8	Amort./Cur. Mat. L/T/D	(347) 2.0	(347) 1.9
	1.3	1.1	1.2	1.1	1.2		1.2	1.1
1.4	2.1	2.1	1.5	1.1	1.0		2.1	2.1
3.9	4.0	3.9	3.2	2.8	2.0	Fixed/Worth	4.3	4.3
-52.0	22.5	21.6	12.1	9.1	4.0		31.7	26.5
1.0	1.4	1.4	1.0	.8	.9		1.5	1.5
4.1	3.5	3.3	2.8	2.4	2.1	Debt/Worth	3.8	3.8
-16.1	23.9	22.9	13.6	9.1	5.4		38.6	30.6
74.2	35.4	30.7	26.3	22.6	16.5	% Profit Before Taxes/Tangible	32.7	34.6
(461) 24.6	(2667) 17.3	(3445) 14.3	(836) 11.2	(109) 10.8	(103) 6.9	Net Worth	(9335) 15.5	(8908) 15.9
9.1	7.9	5.9	3.9	2.7	1.7		6.0	6.2
21.0	9.8	7.7	6.6	6.2	5.9	% Profit Before Taxes/Total	8.0	8.2
7.7	5.2	4.1	3.6	3.7	2.6	Assets	4.0	4.2
2.5	1.9	1.5	1.0	.9	.5		1.4	1.5
1.1	.3	.2	.3	.7	.7		.3	.3
.3	.2	.2	.2	.2	.2	Sales/Net Fixed Assets	.2	.2
.2	.1	.1	.1	.1	.1		.1	.1
.8	.2	.2	.2	.3	.3		.2	.2
.2	.2	.1	.1	.1	.1	Sales/Total Assets	.1	.1
.1	.1	.1	.1	.1	.1		.1	.1
8.9	12.5	13.9	12.1	5.6	8.0	% Depr., Dep., Amort./Sales	13.0	12.9
(480) 15.1	(2893) 18.2	(3521) 19.8	(807) 19.9	(111) 16.2	(83) 17.2		(10247) 18.8	(9689) 18.8
23.1	25.7	27.1	30.5	29.5	26.8		25.6	25.6
5.0	2.6	1.9	1.8	.5		% Officers', Directors'	2.5	2.4
(39) 10.4	(103) 5.0	(136) 4.6	(89) 3.5	(14) 1.5		Owners' Comp/Sales	(554) 5.7	(552) 5.2
17.4	10.8	10.7	11.0	7.3			11.7	11.7
185788M	1068981M	4152603M	6872251M	4209683M	6046572M	Net Sales ($)	22468234M	20097342M
198347M	4129075M	18606964M	19930119M	9029350M	17895072M	Total Assets ($)	71279615M	67584006M

M = $ thousand   MM = $ million
See Pages viii through xx for Explanation of Ratios and Data

Comparative Historical Data | | | Type of Statement | ## Current Data Sorted by Sales

Comparative Historical Data			Type of Statement	Current Data Sorted by Sales					
150	145	138	Unqualified	32	22	11	19	18	36
221	204	180	Reviewed	77	40	13	12	22	16
613	565	532	Compiled	375	97	27	15	8	10
5748	5243	4632	Tax Returns	4076	467	44	29	12	4
3900	4170	4077	Other	2872	738	143	131	104	89
4/1/16-3/31/17 ALL	4/1/17-3/31/18 ALL	4/1/18-3/31/19 ALL		301 (4/1-9/30/18)			9,258 (10/1/18-3/31/19)		
				0-1MM	1-3MM	3-5MM	5-10MM	10-25MM	25MM & OVER
10632	10327	9559	**NUMBER OF STATEMENTS**	7432	1364	238	206	164	155
%	%	%	**ASSETS**	%	%	%	%	%	%
5.7	5.9	5.8	Cash & Equivalents	5.1	7.2	8.1	9.8	10.5	12.7
1.1	1.1	1.1	Trade Receivables (net)	.5	1.0	3.0	4.5	9.1	15.7
.6	.5	.6	Inventory	.2	.8	1.3	2.3	5.8	13.2
1.4	1.3	1.4	All Other Current	1.2	1.6	2.3	1.5	4.7	4.2
8.7	8.9	8.9	Total Current	6.9	10.7	14.8	18.1	30.1	45.8
84.4	83.9	83.6	Fixed Assets (net)	87.2	78.1	71.8	63.6	50.8	39.7
2.0	2.3	2.3	Intangibles (net)	1.8	4.0	4.1	5.8	5.1	3.8
4.9	4.9	5.1	All Other Non-Current	4.1	7.3	9.4	12.4	13.9	10.8
100.0	100.0	100.0	Total	100.0	100.0	100.0	100.0	100.0	100.0
			LIABILITIES						
2.6	2.4	2.7	Notes Payable-Short Term	2.5	3.1	3.8	3.0	5.8	6.5
3.9	4.0	3.7	Cur. Mat.-L.T.D.	3.9	3.3	3.1	2.8	2.7	2.9
.7	.7	.7	Trade Payables	.3	.8	1.1	2.8	5.0	10.9
.0	.0	.0	Income Taxes Payable	.0	.0	.1	.0	.1	.2
3.8	4.0	4.3	All Other Current	3.9	4.9	4.9	6.1	8.6	10.6
11.1	11.1	11.5	Total Current	10.5	12.2	13.1	14.6	22.3	31.1
64.5	63.8	63.1	Long-Term Debt	65.2	61.7	53.7	51.8	40.5	28.5
.0	.0	.0	Deferred Taxes	.0	.1	.1	.1	.3	.3
3.4	3.4	3.4	All Other Non-Current	3.2	3.6	3.6	5.1	5.8	5.6
20.9	21.7	22.1	Net Worth	21.1	22.5	29.6	28.3	31.2	34.6
100.0	100.0	100.0	Total Liabilities & Net Worth	100.0	100.0	100.0	100.0	100.0	100.0
			INCOME DATA						
100.0	100.0	100.0	Net Sales	100.0	100.0	100.0	100.0	100.0	100.0
			Gross Profit						
48.4	48.5	48.4	Operating Expenses	45.5	51.4	60.3	67.8	74.2	87.6
51.6	51.5	51.6	Operating Profit	54.5	48.6	39.7	32.2	25.8	12.4
21.1	21.2	21.4	All Other Expenses (net)	23.4	16.9	13.3	11.4	9.6	3.9
30.5	30.4	30.2	Profit Before Taxes	31.1	31.8	26.4	20.8	16.2	8.5
			RATIOS						
1.9	2.0	2.0	Current	1.8	2.6	2.6	2.8	3.0	3.0
.7	.7	.7		.6	.9	.9	1.1	1.2	1.6
.2	.2	.2		.2	.3	.3	.4	.6	1.1
1.6	1.7	1.7	Quick	1.5	2.2	2.1	2.2	2.2	2.1
(10630) .5 (10326) .6 (9557) .6				(7430) .5	.7	.7	.8	.8	1.1
.1	.2	.2		.1	.2	.2	.3	.3	.5
0 UND	0 UND	0 UND	Sales/Receivables	0 UND	0 UND	0 UND	0 UND	0 UND	4 88.0
0 UND	0 UND	0 UND		0 UND	0 UND	0 UND	2 185.4	7 48.8	22 16.5
0 UND	0 UND	0 UND		0 UND	3 133.7	8 45.5	18 20.4	31 11.7	46 8.0
			Cost of Sales/Inventory						
			Cost of Sales/Payables						
6.4	6.0	6.4	Sales/Working Capital	7.4	4.7	4.9	4.3	4.8	4.4
-10.7	-14.0	-13.2		-9.2	-58.0	-82.9	45.0	24.5	11.4
-2.8	-2.8	-2.9		-2.6	-3.9	-4.6	-5.3	-8.5	72.4
6.8	6.9	6.8	EBIT/Interest	6.5	6.6	9.8	8.1	12.8	15.9
(4705) 4.3 (4564) 4.3 (4113) 4.2				(2838) 4.3	(757) 4.0	(145) 4.4	(139) 3.7	(109) 4.5	(125) 4.9
2.8	2.8	2.7		2.9	2.6	2.3	1.7	1.8	2.0
3.7	3.9	3.6	Net Profit + Depr., Dep., Amort./Cur. Mat. L/T/D	3.0	4.0	4.1		5.9	7.0
(355) 2.0 (335) 2.2 (294) 2.0				(164) 1.8	(51) 1.9	(19) 2.3	(19)	2.9	(32) 4.6
1.1	1.2	1.1		1.1	1.1	1.0		2.1	2.0
2.0	2.0	2.0	Fixed/Worth	2.1	1.7	1.3	1.1	.4	.2
3.9	3.0	3.0		4.0	3.8	2.7	2.5	2.0	1.3
20.3	24.4	21.1		20.9	40.9	27.4	10.1	7.2	3.0
1.4	1.3	1.3	Debt/Worth	1.4	1.2	.7	.7	.9	.8
3.5	3.3	3.3		3.3	3.4	2.3	2.5	2.6	2.1
22.5	27.2	23.3		22.7	87.7	34.6	13.5	9.5	6.3
33.3	32.5	32.7	% Profit Before Taxes/Tangible Net Worth	31.3	39.6	37.1	34.3	41.0	41.9
(8530) 15.8 (8204) 15.3 (7621) 15.2				(5959) 14.8	(1042) 17.9	(187) 14.5	(162) 14.1	(137) 15.3	(134) 17.6
6.4	6.2	6.1		6.1	7.5	5.1	2.9	2.8	8.9
8.5	8.5	8.6	% Profit Before Taxes/Total Assets	8.2	10.4	11.2	9.7	13.2	11.2
4.4	4.4	4.5		4.3	5.5	5.3	4.4	4.4	5.9
1.6	1.6	1.6		1.5	2.3	1.9	.7	.6	2.2
.3	.3	.3	Sales/Net Fixed Assets	.2	.4	.7	2.7	24.0	38.7
.2	.2	.2		.2	.2	.2	.3	.7	4.8
.1	.1	.1		.1	.1	.2	.2	.2	.7
.2	.2	.2	Sales/Total Assets	.2	.3	.4	.7	1.9	3.0
.1	.1	.1		.1	.2	.2	.2	.3	1.4
.1	.1	.1		.1	.1	.1	.1	.1	.4
12.8	12.9	12.8	% Depr., Dep., Amort./Sales	13.8	11.3	8.5	5.4	1.5	.7
(9116) 18.6 (8730) 19.0 (7895) 19.0				(6237) 19.8	(1064) 17.1	(179) 16.5	(162) 14.9	(133) 10.2	(120) 1.7
25.7	26.4	26.7		27.3	24.7	24.6	24.3	22.6	6.9
2.1	2.4	2.3	% Officers', Directors' Owners' Comp/Sales	2.9	2.3	1.8	2.0	.9	.4
(479) 5.0 (443) 6.3 (387) 4.9				(182) 5.4	(102) 4.9	(31) 7.9	(28) 3.1	(20) 3.0	(24) 1.4
12.3	14.5	11.6		12.6	11.9	15.3	10.6	9.5	2.3
21367435M	22749156M	22535878M	Net Sales ($)	2551409M	2222973M	907189M	1454522M	2669205M	12730580M
67694791M	71415622M	69788927M	Total Assets ($)	19106176M	14133661M	5329817M	7944150M	10339971M	12935152M

M = $ thousand   MM = $ million
See Pages viii through xx for Explanation of Ratios and Data

Current Data Sorted by Assets   Comparative Historical Data

Date ranges: Column "500M-2MM" — 13 (4/1-9/30/18); Column "10-50MM" — 390 (10/1/18-3/31/19). Historical columns: 4/1/14-3/31/15 ALL and 4/1/15-3/31/16 ALL.

Type of Statement	0-500M	500M-2MM	2-10MM	10-50MM	50-100MM	100-250MM	4/1/14-3/31/15 ALL	4/1/15-3/31/16 ALL
Unqualified		1		1	1	4	4	8
Reviewed			2	2		1	10	6
Compiled	2	2	8	9			34	23
Tax Returns	25	73	82	16	2	6	283	216
Other	20	58	88				212	177
NUMBER OF STATEMENTS	47	134	180	28	3	11	543	430

ASSETS	0-500M %	500M-2MM %	2-10MM %	10-50MM %	50-100MM %	100-250MM %	4/1/14-3/31/15 ALL %	4/1/15-3/31/16 ALL %
Cash & Equivalents	37.8	8.1	5.9	6.9		10.4	8.5	9.5
Trade Receivables (net)	2.3	1.4	.8	1.2		9.1	1.2	1.2
Inventory	1.4	.6	.2	1.6		1.4	.8	.6
All Other Current	4.1	2.2	.5	.5		1.1	1.2	1.4
Total Current	45.5	12.3	7.5	10.2		22.0	11.7	12.8
Fixed Assets (net)	35.4	80.2	84.1	79.1		67.8	80.5	79.4
Intangibles (net)	8.2	3.6	3.9	5.1		7.0	2.8	3.0
All Other Non-Current	10.9	3.9	4.5	5.7		3.1	5.1	4.8
Total	100.0	100.0	100.0	100.0		100.0	100.0	100.0

LIABILITIES	0-500M	500M-2MM	2-10MM	10-50MM	50-100MM	100-250MM	Hist 1	Hist 2
Notes Payable-Short Term	2.5	2.7	2.2	2.8		1.3	2.7	4.0
Cur. Mat.-L.T.D.	3.0	2.7	3.0	2.0		.2	3.7	3.1
Trade Payables	.6	.5	.8	1.4		7.7	1.4	1.9
Income Taxes Payable	.0	.0	.0	.0		.0	.0	.1
All Other Current	16.4	4.9	1.4	8.0		3.4	7.0	6.3
Total Current	22.5	10.9	7.5	14.2		12.6	14.7	15.4
Long-Term Debt	32.6	68.9	71.6	49.5		54.3	67.6	65.4
Deferred Taxes	.0	.0	.0	.5		.0	.0	.0
All Other Non-Current	20.4	3.7	3.4	4.4		1.5	5.5	4.5
Net Worth	24.4	16.6	17.5	31.3		31.6	12.1	14.7
Total Liabilities & Net Worth	100.0	100.0	100.0	100.0		100.0	100.0	100.0

INCOME DATA	0-500M	500M-2MM	2-10MM	10-50MM	50-100MM	100-250MM	Hist 1	Hist 2
Net Sales	100.0	100.0	100.0	100.0		100.0	100.0	100.0
Gross Profit								
Operating Expenses	75.1	55.3	55.5	71.3		85.8	60.6	58.7
Operating Profit	24.9	44.7	44.5	28.7		14.2	39.4	41.3
All Other Expenses (net)	3.7	15.0	17.5	12.1		24.2	16.4	14.8
Profit Before Taxes	21.2	29.6	27.0	16.5		-10.0	23.0	26.5

RATIOS	0-500M	500M-2MM	2-10MM	10-50MM	50-100MM	100-250MM	Hist 1	Hist 2
Current	7.4	3.7	2.9	4.4		3.6	2.4	3.0
	2.3	1.2	1.1	1.0		1.2	.8	1.0
	1.0	.4	.4	.2		1.0	.3	.3
Quick	5.5	3.2	2.9	4.2		3.0	2.2	2.6
	1.8	.9	1.0	.8		1.0	.7	.9
	.6	.3	.3	.2		.7	.2	.3
Sales/Receivables	0 UND	0 UND	0 UND	0 UND		5 68.9	0 UND	0 UND
	0 UND	0 UND	0 UND	1 306.8		8 47.7	0 UND	0 UND
	0 UND	0 UND	0 UND	12 31.1		42 8.6	0 UND	0 UND
Cost of Sales/Inventory								
Cost of Sales/Payables								
Sales/Working Capital	8.3	4.5	5.3	2.8		3.3	7.9	6.0
	17.0	63.2	91.6	NM		12.3	-48.9	219.5
	73.8	-7.2	-8.3	-3.7		-999.8	-4.9	-6.6
EBIT/Interest	29.9	7.8	5.7	4.9			6.3	6.8
	(18) 5.4	(78) 4.5	(109) 3.6	(21) 3.1			(300) 3.4	(259) 3.9
	2.8	2.5	2.6	2.4			2.2	2.5
Net Profit + Depr., Dep., Amort./Cur. Mat. L/T/D								
Fixed/Worth	.0	1.5	2.1	1.4		1.3	2.1	2.0
	.6	5.2	6.2	3.7		3.4	4.9	5.1
	5.8	-8.9	-17.8	17.4		4.5	-18.7	-18.5
Debt/Worth	.2	.8	1.6	1.0		2.1	1.6	1.5
	1.7	4.5	5.8	3.3		2.6	4.8	5.0
	-100.6	-11.9	-21.5	21.1		7.3	-19.2	-21.5
% Profit Before Taxes/Tangible Net Worth	144.2	59.1	50.9	29.1		.4	45.3	63.4
	(35) 63.3	(94) 19.8	(124) 18.2	(25) 14.3		(10) -5.3	(380) 19.6	(303) 23.0
	8.3	8.9	4.8	-1.1		-14.1	8.8	10.3
% Profit Before Taxes/Total Assets	75.3	16.1	11.1	7.6		.7	10.7	12.9
	19.6	7.5	6.0	4.7		-1.6	4.7	6.3
	3.9	2.9	1.7	.0		-4.4	2.1	2.4
Sales/Net Fixed Assets	UND	.6	.4	.5		1.8	.5	.5
	19.6	.3	.2	.2		.2	.3	.3
	2.2	.2	.1	.1		.1	.2	.2
Sales/Total Assets	6.7	.5	.3	.4		.8	.4	.4
	2.2	.3	.2	.2		.1	.2	.2
	.6	.2	.1	.1		.1	.1	.2
% Depr., Dep., Amort./Sales	2.6	6.6	9.0	8.7			8.7	8.0
	(17) 6.5	(110) 14.3	(129) 15.0	(25) 12.3			(440) 14.3	(321) 12.4
	15.2	20.9	24.5	14.6			20.0	18.4
% Officers', Directors', Owners' Comp/Sales		4.6					2.7	3.8
		(19) 7.2					(53) 6.3	(41) 6.0
		13.9					10.2	8.5
Net Sales ($)	24086M	71169M	201160M	204511M	32506M	886255M	774559M	696861M
Total Assets ($)	10020M	163157M	793976M	600080M	201650M	1691070M	2361893M	2283606M

M = $ thousand   MM = $ million
See Pages viii through xx for Explanation of Ratios and Data

Comparative Historical Data

Current Data Sorted by Sales

			Type of Statement						
5	5	7	Unqualified	1				4	2
4	4	5	Reviewed	1			1	2	1
27	20	12	Compiled	6	4	2			
245	195	189	Tax Returns	141	39	6	2	1	
155	161	190	Other	137	30	9	3	8	3
4/1/16-3/31/17	4/1/17-3/31/18	4/1/18-3/31/19		13 (4/1-9/30/18)			390 (10/1/18-3/31/19)		
ALL	ALL	ALL		0-1MM	1-3MM	3-5MM	5-10MM	10-25MM	25MM & OVER
436	385	403	**NUMBER OF STATEMENTS**	286	73	17	6	15	6
%	%	%	**ASSETS**	%	%	%	%	%	%
9.1	10.3	10.7	Cash & Equivalents	9.4	12.7	19.1		5.4	
.7	1.2	1.4	Trade Receivables (net)	.6	2.1	2.7		5.9	
.5	.5	.6	Inventory	.7	.3	.2		.4	
2.3	1.2	1.5	All Other Current	1.8	.5			1.0	
12.6	13.2	14.2	Total Current	12.4	15.5	22.5		12.7	
77.2	78.3	76.1	Fixed Assets (net)	78.9	72.5	61.9		80.2	
3.0	3.3	4.5	Intangibles (net)	3.9	6.4	6.3		2.4	
7.1	5.3	5.2	All Other Non-Current	4.7	5.7	9.3		4.8	
100.0	100.0	100.0	Total	100.0	100.0	100.0		100.0	
			LIABILITIES						
2.4	2.2	2.4	Notes Payable-Short Term	1.9	2.5	10.6		1.2	
3.6	3.2	2.8	Cur. Mat.-L.T.D.	2.9	3.0	3.0		1.1	
1.4	.7	.9	Trade Payables	.4	.7	.6		6.3	
.0	.0	.0	Income Taxes Payable	.0	.0	.0		.0	
4.9	4.0	4.8	All Other Current	5.3	1.2	3.6		11.4	
12.3	10.1	11.0	Total Current	10.5	7.4	17.8		19.9	
62.9	69.9	64.1	Long-Term Debt	63.6	71.8	76.9		50.9	
.0	.0	.0	Deferred Taxes	.0	.0	.0		.0	
5.1	4.7	5.5	All Other Non-Current	6.3	4.0	2.7		2.5	
19.7	15.3	19.4	Net Worth	19.7	16.8	2.6		26.7	
100.0	100.0	100.0	Total Liabilities & Net Worth	100.0	100.0	100.0		100.0	
			INCOME DATA						
100.0	100.0	100.0	Net Sales	100.0	100.0	100.0		100.0	
			Gross Profit						
57.8	58.7	59.5	Operating Expenses	57.3	58.5	66.4		76.7	
42.2	41.3	40.5	Operating Profit	42.7	41.5	33.6		23.3	
13.4	13.4	14.9	All Other Expenses (net)	16.2	11.8	9.0		18.8	
28.8	27.9	25.6	Profit Before Taxes	26.5	29.7	24.6		4.5	
			RATIOS						
2.8	4.2	3.7	Current	3.1	6.7	6.4		2.6	
1.0	1.4	1.2		1.1	2.0	1.5		1.1	
.3	.4	.4		.4	.6	.6		.3	
2.5	3.8	3.0	Quick	2.9	6.0	6.3		2.6	
.8	1.2	1.0		.9	2.0	1.4		.6	
.2	.3	.3		.3	.6	.6		.2	
0 UND	0 UND	0 UND	Sales/Receivables	0 UND	0 UND	0 UND		2 165.2	
0 UND	0 UND	0 UND		0 UND	0 UND	1 331.7		5 68.9	
0 UND	0 UND	1 451.0		0 UND	1 509.8	28 13.1		10 37.8	
			Cost of Sales/Inventory						
			Cost of Sales/Payables						
6.6	5.1	5.0	Sales/Working Capital	5.4	4.5	3.9		5.8	
-353.8	29.4	36.2		95.7	14.1	13.1		39.1	
-6.1	-7.9	-9.0		-6.8	-21.2	-27.8		-11.4	
6.9	6.4	6.6	EBIT/Interest	5.7	8.5	14.0			
(287) 3.9	(253) 4.0	(232) 4.1		(151) 3.8	(51) 4.9	(13) 3.8			
2.7	2.5	2.6		2.5	3.0	2.3			
			Net Profit + Depr., Dep., Amort./Cur. Mat. L/T/D						
1.7	1.8	1.5	Fixed/Worth	1.6	1.4	1.3		2.7	
3.0	4.6	4.5		4.4	7.8	5.5		3.4	
615.9	-45.6	-22.8		-83.9	-5.8	-1.2		4.9	
1.1	1.1	1.1	Debt/Worth	1.1	1.1	1.1		2.1	
3.5	4.0	4.7		4.4	8.0	4.7		3.0	
820.8	-48.6	-24.7		-31.3	-7.2	-3.2		5.3	
71.0	53.5	57.9	% Profit Before Taxes/Tangible Net Worth	54.3	88.3	145.5		37.0	
(331) 26.3	(278) 23.8	(289) 18.4		(209) 16.5	(45) 38.8	(11) 20.9		(13) -3.4	
9.9	8.9	5.2		5.5	13.0	15.7		-6.6	
15.8	15.2	12.8	% Profit Before Taxes/Total Assets	12.0	20.0	38.1		9.6	
7.3	7.1	6.6		6.0	9.8	10.9		4.3	
3.0	2.8	1.8		1.7	4.2	4.0		-1.6	
.6	.6	.6	Sales/Net Fixed Assets	.5	1.4	17.3		1.2	
.3	.3	.3		.2	.4	.5		.3	
.2	.2	.2		.1	.2	.3		.1	
.4	.5	.4	Sales/Total Assets	.4	.6	1.6		1.0	
.2	.3	.2		.2	.3	.4		.2	
.2	.2	.1		.1	.2	.3		.1	
7.7	7.9	8.2	% Depr., Dep., Amort./Sales	9.3	4.5	5.1		5.3	
(337) 12.3	(294) 12.2	(291) 14.0		(199) 15.5	(59) 9.0	(14) 9.2		(12) 13.2	
17.2	17.9	21.5		24.0	15.5	13.9		24.6	
3.3	3.3	4.1	% Officers', Directors' Owners' Comp/Sales	4.4					
(45) 7.1	(42) 7.1	(38) 6.6		(22) 7.9					
12.5	12.4	12.9		14.0					
1699063M	999937M	1419687M	Net Sales ($)	131732M	114596M	63672M	44217M	248579M	816891M
2617684M	2424103M	3459953M	Total Assets ($)	678534M	464537M	167321M	129680M	1202091M	817790M

© RMA 2019 M = $ thousand   MM = $ million
See Pages viii through xx for Explanation of Ratios and Data

Current Data Sorted by Assets   Comparative Historical Data

Type of Statement

	0-500M	500M-2MM	2-10MM	10-50MM	50-100MM	100-250MM		Hist ALL	Hist ALL
Unqualified	1		10	16	4	7		63	53
Reviewed	2	1	23	10	2	4		45	46
Compiled	3	23	32	10	2			143	115
Tax Returns	64	189	189	28	2	1		719	680
Other	41	130	238	80	15	11		591	471
		48 (4/1-9/30/18)		1,090 (10/1/18-3/31/19)				4/1/14-3/31/15	4/1/15-3/31/16
NUMBER OF STATEMENTS	111	343	492	144	25	23		1561	1365
ASSETS	%	%	%	%	%	%		%	%
Cash & Equivalents	17.4	7.4	5.3	6.9	5.6	12.2		6.8	6.6
Trade Receivables (net)	3.6	1.3	1.3	2.0	.4	2.4		1.6	1.6
Inventory	4.3	1.1	.7	2.7	2.0	2.2		1.2	1.4
All Other Current	5.3	1.1	1.5	2.9	1.7	2.4		2.0	1.3
Total Current	30.6	10.9	8.7	14.5	9.7	19.1		11.6	10.9
Fixed Assets (net)	60.9	79.3	82.1	73.6	65.6	59.0		79.4	79.6
Intangibles (net)	3.6	2.7	2.6	4.0	3.3	5.7		2.6	2.4
All Other Non-Current	4.8	7.1	6.6	7.9	21.3	16.2		6.4	7.0
Total	100.0	100.0	100.0	100.0	100.0	100.0		100.0	100.0
LIABILITIES									
Notes Payable-Short Term	7.0	4.0	2.3	1.6	.9	4.4		4.2	4.0
Cur. Mat.-L.T.D.	6.8	3.8	3.3	3.6	1.5	1.1		4.1	4.1
Trade Payables	5.2	1.4	.7	2.0	.8	1.7		1.1	1.3
Income Taxes Payable	.4	.0	.0	.0	.0	.5		.0	.2
All Other Current	21.3	5.0	4.5	5.6	2.2	5.1		5.2	4.9
Total Current	40.7	14.2	10.9	12.7	5.4	12.9		14.6	14.6
Long-Term Debt	57.6	57.7	57.5	55.5	49.2	34.3		58.6	59.6
Deferred Taxes	.0	.0	.0	.2	.2	.8		.1	.0
All Other Non-Current	6.1	4.5	3.1	4.5	2.1	11.4		4.9	4.1
Net Worth	-4.2	23.5	28.5	27.0	43.0	40.6		21.9	21.7
Total Liabilties & Net Worth	100.0	100.0	100.0	100.0	100.0	100.0		100.0	100.0
INCOME DATA									
Net Sales	100.0	100.0	100.0	100.0	100.0	100.0		100.0	100.0
Gross Profit									
Operating Expenses	60.6	53.0	51.5	54.1	60.1	65.8		53.1	51.7
Operating Profit	39.4	47.0	48.5	45.9	39.9	34.2		46.9	48.3
All Other Expenses (net)	11.8	20.2	20.0	19.5	14.7	10.7		19.7	19.5
Profit Before Taxes	27.6	26.8	28.5	26.4	25.3	23.5		27.2	28.8
RATIOS									
Current	2.0	2.4	2.2	2.5	4.7	5.2		2.4	2.3
	.6	.8	.7	1.1	1.8	1.4		.8	.7
	.2	.2	.2	.3	.5	.6		.2	.2
Quick	1.5	2.0	1.9	1.7	3.5	3.3		1.8	1.9
	.5	.7	.6	(143) .7	1.0	.9		(1560) .6	.6
	.1	.2	.2	.2	.1	.3		.1	.1
Sales/Receivables	0 UND	0 UND	0 UND	0 UND	0 UND	0 UND		0 UND	0 UND
	0 UND	0 UND	0 UND	0 UND	0 UND	8 45.7		0 UND	0 UND
	0 UND	0 UND	0 UND	6 61.8	10 34.8	13 27.2		0 UND	1 564.1
Cost of Sales/Inventory									
Cost of Sales/Payables									
Sales/Working Capital	24.0	5.2	5.6	3.0	2.6	1.5		5.0	6.0
	-18.2	-39.0	-18.3	73.1	10.5	7.0		-20.0	-18.7
	-3.0	-2.9	-2.6	-2.9	-5.6	-3.6		-2.8	-2.7
EBIT/Interest	10.0	6.9	6.8	7.0	11.6	7.8		7.8	7.6
	(55) 5.1	(156) 3.9	(210) 3.8	(64) 4.0	(18) 5.3	(15) 3.3		(728) 4.2	(656) 4.4
	2.3	2.5	2.5	2.4	2.2	2.0		2.3	2.7
Net Profit + Depr., Dep., Amort./Cur. Mat. L/T/D			3.7	4.1				4.3	3.9
			(16) 1.5	(15) 2.1				(70) 2.2	(59) 1.9
			1.0	1.2				1.1	1.0
Fixed/Worth	1.0	1.7	1.6	1.5	.7	.7		1.6	1.6
	3.2	3.4	3.2	2.6	2.4	1.3		3.7	3.4
	UND	26.1	15.0	20.4	7.0	4.7		31.4	18.5
Debt/Worth	.8	1.2	1.0	.9	.2	.4		1.0	1.1
	4.5	3.1	2.6	2.7	1.5	1.4		3.3	3.0
	-5.9	39.7	15.5	30.8	8.5	4.1		41.9	22.6
% Profit Before Taxes/Tangible Net Worth	152.9	37.1	28.0	26.5	16.4	16.7		30.5	28.7
	(79) 18.3	(276) 16.8	(406) 11.5	(113) 11.2	(21) 8.1	(20) 6.9		(1218) 14.1	(1093) 14.1
	8.5	4.9	3.8	4.3	2.7	3.3		4.7	5.4
% Profit Before Taxes/Total Assets	39.8	9.6	7.6	7.0	7.1	4.9		8.8	8.8
	10.0	4.5	3.5	3.6	3.5	3.8		4.3	4.5
	2.3	1.2	1.3	1.0	1.2	1.3		1.1	1.4
Sales/Net Fixed Assets	31.3	.4	.3	.4	.7	1.4		.3	.4
	1.2	.2	.2	.2	.3	.3		.2	.2
	.2	.1	.1	.1	.1	.2		.1	.1
Sales/Total Assets	4.4	.3	.2	.2	.3	.3		.3	.3
	.5	.2	.1	.1	.1	.2		.2	.2
	.2	.1	.1	.1	.1	.1		.1	.1
% Depr., Dep., Amort./Sales	2.5	9.4	11.8	8.6	3.1	6.2		10.4	10.1
	(61) 12.2	(274) 18.0	(384) 19.1	(120) 18.9	(20) 12.1	(19) 15.2		(1300) 18.0	(1138) 17.3
	20.2	25.4	27.0	25.3	21.0	20.2		25.6	24.1
% Officers', Directors' Owners' Comp/Sales	3.1	5.1	1.7	3.1				1.7	2.0
	(15) 6.1	(20) 6.7	(24) 7.3	(14) 5.3				(97) 5.3	(105) 5.0
	14.3	13.4	14.9	15.0				9.0	10.9
Net Sales ($)	69335M	208161M	722595M	928647M	427594M	1405359M		4574808M	4943632M
Total Assets ($)	29367M	412218M	2214446M	2826403M	1818296M	3551100M		12696887M	12140548M

© RMA 2019

M = $ thousand   MM = $ million
See Pages viii through xx for Explanation of Ratios and Data

Comparative Historical Data | | Current Data Sorted by Sales

					Type of Statement						
42		45		38	Unqualified	7	7	5	3	5	11
42		43		42	Reviewed	19	8	1	4	6	4
87		81		70	Compiled	43	14	6	3	2	2
612		555		473	Tax Returns	396	62	7	6	1	1
507		563		515	Other	327	99	28	31	16	14
4/1/16-3/31/17 ALL		4/1/17-3/31/18 ALL		4/1/18-3/31/19 ALL		48 (4/1-9/30/18)			1,090 (10/1/18-3/31/19)		
						0-1MM	1-3MM	3-5MM	5-10MM	10-25MM	25MM & OVER
1290		1277		1138	**NUMBER OF STATEMENTS**	792	190	47	47	30	32
%		%		%	**ASSETS**	%	%	%	%	%	%
6.2		7.7		7.5	Cash & Equivalents	5.8	9.1	15.5	11.8	14.5	14.1
1.2		2.0		1.6	Trade Receivables (net)	.6	2.2	6.1	4.2	9.3	5.4
1.3		1.4		1.5	Inventory	.3	1.6	5.6	5.2	10.3	10.5
1.7		1.8		1.9	All Other Current	1.6	1.5	3.5	3.8	2.7	7.3
10.3		12.9		12.5	Total Current	8.3	14.5	30.7	25.1	36.7	37.3
80.3		77.8		77.3	Fixed Assets (net)	83.4	73.9	54.8	49.6	47.3	46.8
2.7		2.8		3.0	Intangibles (net)	2.3	3.6	4.1	5.9	6.5	7.5
6.7		6.5		7.2	All Other Non-Current	6.0	8.1	10.4	19.4	9.5	8.4
100.0		100.0		100.0	Total	100.0	100.0	100.0	100.0	100.0	100.0
					LIABILITIES						
3.4		3.3		3.2	Notes Payable-Short Term	2.9	1.9	5.7	9.4	8.8	1.6
3.6		3.5		3.7	Cur. Mat.-L.T.D.	3.9	3.9	2.1	3.9	2.6	3.5
1.0		1.3		1.5	Trade Payables	.6	1.6	4.8	7.0	6.1	6.9
.1		.1		.1	Income Taxes Payable	.0	.1	.0	.8	.4	.0
5.8		5.5		6.4	All Other Current	5.2	7.7	15.7	7.2	6.8	13.7
13.8		13.6		15.0	Total Current	12.5	15.2	28.3	28.3	24.7	25.7
58.7		57.5		56.7	Long-Term Debt	59.9	56.5	42.8	33.4	53.1	34.8
.0		.0		.1	Deferred Taxes	.0	.0	.1	.2	.2	1.1
4.7		5.3		4.1	All Other Non-Current	3.8	4.1	2.9	7.0	4.4	9.1
22.9		23.5		24.2	Net Worth	23.7	24.2	26.0	31.1	17.6	29.3
100.0		100.0		100.0	Total Liabilties & Net Worth	100.0	100.0	100.0	100.0	100.0	100.0
					INCOME DATA						
100.0		100.0		100.0	Net Sales	100.0	100.0	100.0	100.0	100.0	100.0
					Gross Profit						
52.0		53.6		53.7	Operating Expenses	49.1	56.7	73.6	66.3	70.0	84.4
48.0		46.4		46.3	Operating Profit	50.9	43.3	26.4	33.7	30.0	15.6
19.1		19.0		18.9	All Other Expenses (net)	21.7	16.3	9.6	9.0	6.7	3.4
28.9		27.4		27.5	Profit Before Taxes	29.2	27.0	16.8	24.7	23.3	12.2
					RATIOS						
2.2		2.4		2.3		2.1	2.3	2.2	2.4	3.8	4.2
.7		.8		.8	Current	.7	1.0	1.0	1.1	1.8	2.0
.2		.2		.2		.2	.3	.4	.6	1.1	1.1
1.8		2.0		1.9		1.8	2.1	1.5	1.8	2.9	2.4
(1289) .5		.6 (1137)		.6	Quick	.5 (189)	.7	.6	.7	1.1	1.4
.1		.2		.2		.1	.2	.2	.1	.4	1.1
0 UND		0 UND		0 UND		0 UND	0 UND	0 UND	0 UND	0 UND	0 826.5
0 UND		0 UND		0 UND	Sales/Receivables	0 UND	0 UND	0 UND	0 UND	3 111.4	10 36.8
1 476.2		0 UND		0 UND		0 UND	3 142.1	7 51.6	11 32.4	16 23.1	22 16.6
					Cost of Sales/Inventory						
					Cost of Sales/Payables						
5.6		5.4		5.2		5.6	5.8	4.4	5.5	2.7	2.8
-15.7		-26.2		-32.6	Sales/Working Capital	-13.0	UND	96.3	46.7	9.3	8.5
-2.5		-2.9		-2.8		-2.3	-3.7	-4.0	-11.1	90.1	210.8
7.7		8.0		7.5		6.0	8.4	22.1	20.1	10.9	9.9
(613) 4.1		(597) 4.2 (518)		4.0	EBIT/Interest	(310) 3.9 (97)	4.6 (32)	3.5 (28)	5.9 (25)	4.8 (26)	3.9
2.5		2.2		2.5		2.6	2.4	.5	2.3	2.6	2.0
4.5		3.6		4.2		3.8					
(50) 2.6		(52) 2.2 (37)		2.4	Net Profit + Depr., Dep., Amort./Cur. Mat. L/T/D	(15) 1.4					
1.1		1.2		1.2		1.0					
1.7		1.5		1.5		1.7	1.4	.5	.1	.6	.8
3.6		3.2		3.1	Fixed/Worth	3.4	3.7	2.2	1.9	1.3	1.3
18.3		20.6		21.1		15.9	NM	28.5	4.7	-3.8	5.1
1.1		1.0		1.0		1.1	1.0	.8	.5	.5	.7
3.0		2.8		2.9	Debt/Worth	2.8	4.0	2.9	1.7	2.2	2.3
22.3		26.7		25.7		18.5	-137.4	81.1	13.7	-5.5	11.3
31.0		30.6		32.0		28.3	39.7	68.1	33.8	25.4	48.0
(1027) 13.9		(1006) 13.4 (915)		13.2	% Profit Before Taxes/Tangible Net Worth	(653) 11.5 (142)	15.5 (37)	29.6 (36)	21.3 (20)	14.1 (27)	15.4
4.5		4.5		4.1		3.5	7.3	5.1	6.3	6.1	4.8
8.5		9.5		8.9		7.6	11.9	20.8	18.0	15.6	10.3
4.4		4.1		4.1	% Profit Before Taxes/Total Assets	3.6	5.0	5.2	5.6	6.5	4.7
1.2		1.3		1.3		1.0	2.1	.4	2.2	2.7	1.2
.3		.4		.4		.2	.7	16.0	54.6	12.0	17.0
.2		.2		.2	Sales/Net Fixed Assets	.2	.2	.4	2.2	1.0	2.1
.1		.1		.1		.1	.1	.2	.2	.4	.4
.2		.3		.3		.2	.4	2.7	2.8	1.8	2.8
.1		.2		.1	Sales/Total Assets	.1	.2	.3	.3	.4	1.0
.1		.1		.1		.1	.1	.2	.1	.2	.3
10.9		9.9		10.0		12.2	8.8	2.2	1.1	1.1	1.5
(1065) 18.2		(998) 17.9 (878)		18.1	% Depr., Dep., Amort./Sales	(611) 19.6 (144)	16.9 (35)	13.2 (34)	8.2 (26)	5.4 (28)	4.7
25.8		26.0		25.6		27.1	23.9	25.2	19.2	17.3	10.8
2.9		1.7		2.7		5.0	1.1	2.6			
(81) 7.0		(100) 6.3 (76)		6.2	% Officers', Directors' Owners' Comp/Sales	(37) 11.1 (14)	3.9 (10)	3.8			
13.0		10.9		13.7		17.6	7.5	8.8			
3220831M		5431734M		3761691M	Net Sales ($)	273810M	307103M	179706M	343628M	459296M	2198148M
10468655M		11009251M		10851830M	Total Assets ($)	2226308M	1727632M	686537M	1833180M	1487338M	2890835M

M = $ thousand   MM = $ million
See Pages viii through xx for Explanation of Ratios and Data

Current Data Sorted by Assets   Comparative Historical Data

Type of Statement	0-500M	500M-2MM	2-10MM	10-50MM	50-100MM	100-250MM	ALL 4/1/14-3/31/15	ALL 4/1/15-3/31/16
Unqualified	1	2	2	7	5	5	33	32
Reviewed		1	4	8			26	27
Compiled	5	17	12	1			58	50
Tax Returns	96	78	31	6	2	2	269	283
Other	77	86	69	39	15	9	293	272
	40 (4/1-9/30/18)			540 (10/1/18-3/31/19)				
NUMBER OF STATEMENTS	179	184	118	61	22	16	679	664
ASSETS	%	%	%	%	%	%	%	%
Cash & Equivalents	50.4	25.3	17.8	18.2	26.2	24.0	25.7	31.9
Trade Receivables (net)	2.6	4.9	4.0	9.1	8.3	8.4	5.2	6.0
Inventory	.7	1.8	2.4	2.4	3.5	6.3	2.3	1.8
All Other Current	3.5	5.5	7.9	9.3	6.8	1.5	5.7	5.2
Total Current	57.3	37.4	32.1	39.0	44.9	40.2	38.9	44.9
Fixed Assets (net)	23.1	43.2	47.9	33.6	36.3	26.0	39.1	33.1
Intangibles (net)	4.6	7.0	8.5	9.9	6.8	15.2	4.8	5.3
All Other Non-Current	15.1	12.4	11.5	17.5	12.1	18.5	17.2	16.8
Total	100.0	100.0	100.0	100.0	100.0	100.0	100.0	100.0
LIABILITIES								
Notes Payable-Short Term	15.9	7.4	4.7	6.8	10.0	12.3	8.4	9.4
Cur. Mat.-L.T.D.	2.1	2.2	2.1	2.8	.7	1.5	2.7	2.5
Trade Payables	3.3	4.0	2.9	2.9	4.7	9.0	4.4	4.7
Income Taxes Payable	.2	.1	.0	.1	.1	.1	.1	.4
All Other Current	24.5	17.3	12.2	20.6	13.6	14.7	17.7	16.4
Total Current	46.0	31.0	22.0	33.1	29.0	37.6	33.2	33.4
Long-Term Debt	16.7	32.4	39.7	23.8	30.1	17.9	29.7	25.2
Deferred Taxes	.0	.0	.0	.0	.1	.2	.1	.0
All Other Non-Current	5.7	7.9	6.6	5.2	4.2	3.8	10.0	9.8
Net Worth	31.7	28.6	31.7	37.9	36.6	40.5	27.1	31.6
Total Liabilties & Net Worth	100.0	100.0	100.0	100.0	100.0	100.0	100.0	100.0
INCOME DATA								
Net Sales	100.0	100.0	100.0	100.0	100.0	100.0	100.0	100.0
Gross Profit								
Operating Expenses	78.6	79.1	74.2	75.6	88.0	82.7	77.8	80.0
Operating Profit	21.4	20.9	25.8	24.4	12.0	17.3	22.2	20.0
All Other Expenses (net)	2.8	6.8	8.1	6.5	4.5	3.6	6.9	4.7
Profit Before Taxes	18.6	14.0	17.7	17.9	7.5	13.7	15.4	15.3
RATIOS								
Current	7.8	2.9	3.4	2.1	3.4	1.6	3.3	3.5
	1.5	1.2	1.3	1.2	1.8	1.1	1.3	1.4
	.6	.3	.6	.6	.9	.5	.5	.6
Quick	7.1	2.6	2.4	1.9	3.0	1.3	2.6	2.9
	1.5	.8	.9	.9	1.2	.8	1.0	1.1
	.6	.2	.3	.4	.5	.3	.3	.4
Sales/Receivables	0 UND	0 UND	0 UND	0 UND	0 UND	0 UND	0 UND	0 UND
	0 UND	0 UND	0 UND	4 103.2	1 466.4	11 32.2	0 UND	0 UND
	0 UND	2 243.1	3 112.6	31 11.8	14 26.4	40 9.1	4 96.5	3 118.5
Cost of Sales/Inventory								
Cost of Sales/Payables								
Sales/Working Capital	11.6	13.0	4.8	4.8	3.4	5.8	7.8	8.5
	67.7	140.3	39.9	26.6	15.0	274.2	47.4	43.6
	-61.5	-8.2	-20.1	-10.1	-101.0	-1.7	-18.7	-26.0
EBIT/Interest	73.0	26.6	23.7	30.2	8.2	72.5	31.0	43.3
	(71) 18.8	(97) 7.3	(77) 5.5	(38) 10.4	(10) 3.8	(14) 6.9	(390) 8.5	(384) 9.6
	3.4	2.1	2.3	4.1	2.8	.2	2.7	2.7
Net Profit + Depr., Dep., Amort./Cur. Mat. L/T/D							10.6	3.1
							(24) 3.9	(15) 1.4
							1.5	1.0
Fixed/Worth	.0	.2	.6	.1	.1	.0	.1	.1
	.2	1.3	2.2	.7	.5	.5	.9	.6
	1.5	-39.6	6.7	3.2	2.0	6.8	7.9	4.1
Debt/Worth	.1	.6	1.0	1.0	.4	.9	.6	.5
	.8	2.4	2.7	1.9	1.0	3.5	2.5	1.7
	54.5	-48.0	10.2	4.9	2.3	8.3	27.5	9.5
% Profit Before Taxes/Tangible Net Worth	331.6	110.5	83.0	70.7	20.0	42.2	106.3	130.8
	(140) 114.9	(132) 43.4	(98) 28.8	(53) 34.8	(20) 7.3	(13) 24.8	(535) 35.6	(534) 45.0
	27.9	13.3	8.5	8.4	3.0	8.4	9.7	14.8
% Profit Before Taxes/Total Assets	166.9	32.2	28.0	19.4	7.6	10.8	37.3	52.1
	61.1	12.4	6.4	8.0	3.2	4.8	11.5	14.8
	9.0	2.6	2.8	3.5	1.6	1.0	2.8	2.9
Sales/Net Fixed Assets	UND	110.9	49.4	56.7	51.6	46.2	111.5	131.3
	105.4	16.3	5.5	14.0	8.9	20.0	16.1	27.5
	17.3	.4	.2	.2	1.1	1.5	.4	2.2
Sales/Total Assets	16.2	8.6	3.9	2.6	2.1	1.8	6.3	7.6
	5.8	2.0	.7	.9	1.0	1.2	1.9	2.6
	2.7	.3	.2	.2	.5	.2	.3	.5
% Depr., Dep., Amort./Sales	.4	.4	.6	.9	.8	.8	.5	.5
	(64) 1.1	(117) 2.0	(82) 5.4	(40) 2.1	(19) 2.4	(11) .8	(449) 1.9	(402) 1.4
	4.8	14.7	16.7	6.3	4.9	17.9	16.2	10.7
% Officers', Directors' Owners' Comp/Sales	5.8	1.4	1.5				2.6	2.1
	(80) 11.6	(52) 3.5	(20) 5.2				(203) 6.1	(226) 5.9
	22.6	9.7	7.1				15.2	14.4
Net Sales ($)	312950M	1061117M	1509201M	2514728M	6630083M	3694680M	9212879M	11592144M
Total Assets ($)	36422M	197691M	577894M	1374954M	1617528M	2673463M	6026941M	6500925M

M = $ thousand   MM = $ million
See Pages viii through xx for Explanation of Ratios and Data

Comparative Historical Data   Current Data Sorted by Sales

Hist 1	Hist 2	Hist 3	Type of Statement	0-1MM	1-3MM	3-5MM	5-10MM	10-25MM	25MM & OVER
20	24	21	Unqualified		1	2	2	5	11
23	19	14	Reviewed	1	4	3	5		1
37	34	35	Compiled	15	3	2	5	6	4
228	213	215	Tax Returns	106	48	17	21	16	7
250	263	295	Other	88	62	22	28	43	52
4/1/16-3/31/17 ALL	4/1/17-3/31/18 ALL	4/1/18-3/31/19 ALL		40 (4/1-9/30/18)			540 (10/1/18-3/31/19)		
558	553	580	**NUMBER OF STATEMENTS**	210	118	43	59	75	75
%	%	%	**ASSETS**	%	%	%	%	%	%
28.5	30.1	30.8	Cash & Equivalents	24.6	36.7	35.0	34.9	34.4	29.6
5.9	5.8	4.7	Trade Receivables (net)	1.3	4.4	7.4	6.3	6.3	10.0
1.8	1.9	1.8	Inventory	.6	5.4	1.0	.7	1.3	1.6
5.8	5.5	5.7	All Other Current	3.1	4.6	9.3	2.1	12.7	8.6
42.0	43.4	43.0	Total Current	29.6	51.0	52.7	44.0	54.6	49.8
35.6	36.6	36.2	Fixed Assets (net)	55.4	27.6	27.8	29.7	19.7	22.3
5.6	6.5	7.1	Intangibles (net)	3.4	6.1	2.9	12.5	8.2	15.8
16.8	13.5	13.8	All Other Non-Current	11.6	15.3	16.6	13.7	17.5	12.1
100.0	100.0	100.0	Total	100.0	100.0	100.0	100.0	100.0	100.0
			LIABILITIES						
8.7	9.4	9.7	Notes Payable-Short Term	10.0	13.9	7.4	6.0	7.8	7.9
2.6	2.7	2.1	Cur. Mat.-L.T.D	2.4	2.0	2.0	2.4	1.5	2.1
5.5	4.6	3.6	Trade Payables	2.3	3.5	2.1	4.7	4.1	6.8
.1	.3	.1	Income Taxes Payable	.2	.0	.0	.4	.1	.1
17.1	18.7	18.6	All Other Current	13.2	22.5	25.1	18.2	19.7	23.1
33.9	35.7	34.1	Total Current	28.1	42.0	36.5	31.7	33.2	40.1
24.9	27.5	27.6	Long-Term Debt	40.1	24.7	19.5	25.9	12.2	18.7
.1	.0	.0	Deferred Taxes	.0	.1	.0	.0	.0	.0
7.8	5.5	6.4	All Other Non-Current	4.1	6.9	3.4	14.8	5.7	7.9
33.3	31.3	31.8	Net Worth	27.6	26.4	40.5	27.6	48.9	33.2
100.0	100.0	100.0	Total Liabilities & Net Worth	100.0	100.0	100.0	100.0	100.0	100.0
			INCOME DATA						
100.0	100.0	100.0	Net Sales	100.0	100.0	100.0	100.0	100.0	100.0
			Gross Profit						
78.1	80.0	78.0	Operating Expenses	62.0	81.4	77.0	91.2	91.5	94.4
21.9	20.0	22.0	Operating Profit	38.0	18.6	23.0	8.8	8.5	5.6
4.7	4.9	5.6	All Other Expenses (net)	12.8	2.1	3.5	1.1	.0	1.2
17.2	15.1	16.3	Profit Before Taxes	25.1	16.4	19.5	7.7	8.5	4.4
			RATIOS						
3.4	3.0	3.6		3.2	6.6	6.6	3.6	3.7	2.0
1.4	1.3	1.3	Current	1.0	1.6	1.5	1.3	1.7	1.3
.6	.6	.6		.3	.6	.9	.6	1.2	.8
2.9	2.7	2.9		2.4	4.4	4.9	3.6	3.5	1.7
1.1	1.1	1.1	Quick	.8	1.2	1.3	1.3	1.3	1.0
.4	.4	.4		.2	.4	.3	.5	.5	.5
0 UND	0 UND	0 UND		0 UND	0 UND	0 UND	0 UND	0 UND	0 999.8
0 UND	0 UND	0 UND	Sales/Receivables	0 UND	0 UND	0 999.8	0 965.1	0 999.8	2 173.8
5 81.1	4 103.1	2 173.9		0 UND	1 255.8	9 39.5	4 83.3	3 141.4	15 24.1
			Cost of Sales/Inventory						
			Cost of Sales/Payables						
7.3	10.1	7.9		5.7	6.7	4.8	15.5	11.9	14.4
50.4	57.9	67.7	Sales/Working Capital	UND	42.1	19.8	161.0	34.7	68.9
-19.6	-20.7	-18.0		-3.8	-43.2	-41.4	-38.0	161.0	-110.9
34.7	32.8	32.5		23.8	21.3	23.3	48.3	84.0	44.8
(309) 7.9	(299) 7.5	(307) 8.6	EBIT/Interest	(85) 5.9	(68) 6.8	(25) 6.3	(33) 8.4	(43) 22.3	(53) 10.7
2.8	2.6	2.8		3.1	2.0	2.2	2.7	5.5	1.9
9.2	4.4	8.5	Net Profit + Depr., Dep.,						
(17) 4.5	(21) 1.9	(17) 1.8	Amort./Cur. Mat. L/T/D						
1.9	1.1	-.2							
.1	.1	.1		.1	.0	.0	.1	.1	.2
.8	.8	.8	Fixed/Worth	1.8	.6	.2	.0	.0	.0
5.1	4.9	5.1		7.8	5.2	2.3	-30.7	1.2	2.7
.5	.6	.5		.5	.4	.3	.4	.5	.9
1.8	1.9	1.9	Debt/Worth	2.2	2.2	1.3	1.9	1.1	1.8
13.4	12.5	22.0		89.6	-52.9	5.2	-8.7	3.6	9.0
116.1	122.9	130.9	% Profit Before Taxes/Tangible	97.6	189.4	122.4	198.7	126.0	125.4
(454) 42.2	(447) 37.9	(456) 45.1	Net Worth	(165) 24.6	(85) 59.4	(38) 35.7	(41) 80.6	(67) 66.6	(60) 45.9
11.8	9.7	10.2		8.6	14.5	8.5	16.0	24.8	11.4
46.8	46.7	50.5	% Profit Before Taxes/Total	38.1	93.0	51.0	91.8	54.7	29.6
12.1	11.1	12.4	Assets	6.6	18.5	8.7	20.5	26.8	13.2
3.8	2.6	3.2		2.7	3.6	2.9	4.3	5.7	2.8
142.3	161.6	169.8		75.8	714.3	328.7	133.8	187.8	157.5
26.0	27.6	22.6	Sales/Net Fixed Assets	.6	35.8	31.6	32.4	79.0	32.2
.7	.7	.8		.2	6.7	.9	13.0	19.0	10.9
7.0	8.6	7.7		2.7	9.2	7.3	12.5	17.0	10.2
2.1	2.4	2.2	Sales/Total Assets	.3	3.1	2.1	7.3	5.2	3.4
.3	.3	.4		.1	1.1	.4	2.2	1.8	1.4
.4	.4	.5		4.6	.4	.4	.4	.2	.3
(355) 1.5	(345) 1.4	(333) 2.2	% Depr., Dep., Amort./Sales	(119) 14.9	(57) 1.1	(22) .8	(40) .7	(43) .5	(52) 1.0
13.2	12.5	13.2		20.8	6.4	3.5	2.4	1.4	2.6
2.3	2.8	2.9		7.5	4.3	1.7	2.5	.6	.6
(184) 6.2	(167) 6.1	(160) 7.2	% Officers', Directors' Owners' Comp/Sales	(60) 15.5	(38) 7.0	(15) 5.3	(19) 3.5	(17) 1.5	(11) 2.2
13.1	12.9	17.4		28.4	12.7	9.5	9.3	5.2	7.2
11163560M	8059937M	15722759M	Net Sales ($)	78296M	217016M	169710M	423388M	1253036M	13581313M
4260485M	4640181M	6477952M	Total Assets ($)	306153M	280823M	445628M	358175M	1142079M	3945094M

M = $ thousand   MM = $ million
See Pages viii through xx for Explanation of Ratios and Data

Current Data Sorted by Assets   Comparative Historical Data

						Type of Statement		
1	6	7	8	1	2	Unqualified	31	33
1	3	5	5			Reviewed	10	10
3	4	4	1			Compiled	31	14
30	48	40	3		1	Tax Returns	137	167
31	54	79	21	4	5	Other	170	178
	31 (4/1-9/30/18)		336 (10/1/18-3/31/19)				4/1/14-3/31/15 ALL	4/1/15-3/31/16 ALL
0-500M	500M-2MM	2-10MM	10-50MM	50-100MM	100-250MM			
66	115	135	38	5	8	**NUMBER OF STATEMENTS**	379	402
%	%	%	%	%	%	**ASSETS**	%	%
47.9	23.4	19.7	17.3			Cash & Equivalents	20.3	23.7
4.8	9.6	9.6	10.8			Trade Receivables (net)	6.6	7.5
.1	.9	.5	.2			Inventory	1.1	.9
5.7	4.6	5.2	3.3			All Other Current	5.4	5.1
58.5	38.5	35.0	31.7			Total Current	33.4	37.3
21.3	39.3	48.9	39.6			Fixed Assets (net)	46.3	43.0
10.9	8.3	5.3	8.0			Intangibles (net)	7.3	6.2
9.3	14.0	10.8	20.7			All Other Non-Current	13.0	13.6
100.0	100.0	100.0	100.0			Total	100.0	100.0
						LIABILITIES		
8.4	7.2	8.2	1.8			Notes Payable-Short Term	7.9	8.8
3.9	3.3	2.6	1.6			Cur. Mat.-L.T.D.	3.1	2.2
7.6	4.4	3.7	8.3			Trade Payables	4.1	3.2
.1	.0	.0	.0			Income Taxes Payable	.1	.1
24.0	14.3	16.1	13.8			All Other Current	17.2	14.7
44.0	29.2	30.7	25.5			Total Current	32.4	29.0
27.8	33.5	34.1	31.7			Long-Term Debt	37.9	31.1
.0	.0	.0	.0			Deferred Taxes	.0	.1
20.5	3.3	3.9	7.1			All Other Non-Current	6.8	7.2
7.7	34.0	31.4	35.7			Net Worth	22.9	32.6
100.0	100.0	100.0	100.0			Total Liabilties & Net Worth	100.0	100.0
						INCOME DATA		
100.0	100.0	100.0	100.0			Net Sales	100.0	100.0
						Gross Profit		
82.3	76.6	74.9	80.8			Operating Expenses	78.8	76.0
17.7	23.4	25.1	19.2			Operating Profit	21.2	24.0
1.9	8.2	10.2	7.0			All Other Expenses (net)	8.0	8.7
15.8	15.3	14.9	12.2			Profit Before Taxes	13.2	15.3
						RATIOS		
6.0	3.5	2.3	2.3				2.9	3.7
1.7	1.1	1.0	1.1			Current	1.1	1.3
.5	.3	.4	.7				.4	.5
5.6	2.6	2.2	1.7				2.3	3.2
1.3	1.0	.9	1.0			Quick	(377) 1.0	1.1
.4	.3	.3	.6				.2	.3
0 UND	0 UND	0 UND	0 UND				0 UND	0 UND
0 UND	0 UND	0 999.8	9 40.4			Sales/Receivables	0 UND	0 UND
0 999.8	7 49.0	24 15.0	41 9.0				10 37.7	9 38.8
						Cost of Sales/Inventory		
						Cost of Sales/Payables		
5.2	5.4	7.4	5.4				7.1	5.0
40.8	57.0	53.0	149.8			Sales/Working Capital	86.0	35.8
-16.8	-8.1	-6.9	-12.7				-8.9	-11.1
38.1	47.1	32.9	20.2				17.5	32.0
(36) 9.2	(57) 7.9	(68) 5.7	(25) 4.3			EBIT/Interest	(211) 4.6	(190) 7.8
2.0	2.8	2.2	.6				1.8	2.4
							13.6	23.1
						Net Profit + Depr., Dep.,	(13) 4.4	(12) 3.8
						Amort./Cur. Mat. L/T/D	1.7	1.8
.0	.1	.1	.2				.2	.1
.3	1.1	1.9	1.5			Fixed/Worth	1.7	1.1
13.5	7.0	5.9	4.8				16.4	6.4
.4	.6	.7	.8				.7	.5
3.3	2.4	2.7	2.0			Debt/Worth	3.1	2.1
-4.6	24.6	26.8	9.5				211.9	16.6
283.3	99.8	56.6	51.2				84.7	89.9
(43) 69.1	(92) 24.6	(109) 22.7	(32) 13.1			% Profit Before Taxes/Tangible Net Worth	(288) 21.4	(322) 21.5
13.5	4.8	5.0	-1.4				4.5	4.8
84.1	33.7	21.1	18.8				23.4	30.0
33.3	11.1	5.1	3.9			% Profit Before Taxes/Total Assets	5.7	7.1
1.4	1.6	1.1	-.9				.9	1.1
UND	115.3	61.2	20.9				74.8	81.5
91.6	14.3	.9	7.4			Sales/Net Fixed Assets	5.7	8.9
18.9	.3	.2	.2				.2	.2
10.7	3.4	2.2	1.8				3.4	3.1
3.9	1.4	.5	.5			Sales/Total Assets	.8	1.0
1.2	.2	.2	.2				.2	.2
.7	1.1	.6	.5				1.4	1.3
(22) 1.2	(67) 7.8	(87) 13.3	(31) 3.5			% Depr., Dep., Amort./Sales	(243) 6.5	(253) 5.9
4.9	20.3	26.1	18.5				19.6	20.1
4.2	2.6	2.7					2.9	3.8
(19) 5.9	(35) 5.5	(32) 6.4				% Officers', Directors' Owners' Comp/Sales	(85) 5.9	(101) 8.0
13.0	13.0	13.4					14.3	14.9
63722M	322708M	788114M	932337M	1017837M	989928M	Net Sales ($)	4221575M	2955239M
13495M	127919M	569520M	709939M	406814M	1166314M	Total Assets ($)	2366077M	2924975M

M = $ thousand   MM = $ million
See Pages viii through xx for Explanation of Ratios and Data

Comparative Historical Data | | | Current Data Sorted by Sales

			Type of Statement						
35	30	25	Unqualified	1	9	2	4		9
15	20	14	Reviewed	3	2	1		4	4
17	14	12	Compiled	5	2		3	2	
116	149	122	Tax Returns	70	22	14	7	8	1
165	204	194	Other	74	44	22	18	20	16
4/1/16-3/31/17 ALL	4/1/17-3/31/18 ALL	4/1/18-3/31/19 ALL		31 (4/1-9/30/18)			336 (10/1/18-3/31/19)		
				0-1MM	1-3MM	3-5MM	5-10MM	10-25MM	25MM & OVER
348	417	367	NUMBER OF STATEMENTS	153	79	39	32	34	30
%	%	%	ASSETS	%	%	%	%	%	%
21.4	22.6	25.6	Cash & Equivalents	19.7	30.3	31.1	32.1	31.3	22.9
7.2	7.3	8.8	Trade Receivables (net)	2.2	5.3	14.4	14.7	21.2	23.2
1.7	1.3	.5	Inventory	.3	1.3	.3	.1	.8	.1
5.8	5.7	5.2	All Other Current	2.9	4.3	11.6	5.3	7.7	8.1
36.1	36.9	40.1	Total Current	25.0	41.3	57.3	52.2	61.0	54.3
43.5	42.2	39.3	Fixed Assets (net)	61.3	33.8	21.2	17.6	14.6	16.9
7.9	8.4	7.9	Intangibles (net)	5.8	8.7	8.4	5.1	12.1	14.5
12.5	12.5	12.7	All Other Non-Current	7.9	16.2	13.1	25.1	12.3	14.3
100.0	100.0	100.0	Total	100.0	100.0	100.0	100.0	100.0	100.0
			LIABILITIES						
7.2	8.4	7.0	Notes Payable-Short Term	5.6	8.4	10.9	4.8	10.5	3.7
2.6	3.1	2.9	Cur. Mat.-L.T.D.	3.0	3.3	4.1	1.9	2.0	1.9
4.9	4.4	5.1	Trade Payables	1.0	4.0	11.6	5.0	10.2	14.5
.0	.0	.0	Income Taxes Payable	.0	.0	.0	.0	.0	.2
13.3	15.9	16.9	All Other Current	14.4	17.2	15.2	19.0	19.8	25.2
28.0	31.9	31.9	Total Current	24.0	32.9	41.9	30.8	42.5	45.5
34.2	30.7	32.7	Long-Term Debt	49.7	25.2	16.3	16.3	17.8	21.1
.1	.0	.0	Deferred Taxes	.0	.0	.0	.0	.0	.0
5.8	4.8	7.2	All Other Non-Current	8.5	1.4	14.5	6.6	9.6	3.5
31.9	32.6	28.3	Net Worth	17.7	40.5	27.4	46.3	30.1	30.0
100.0	100.0	100.0	Total Liabilties & Net Worth	100.0	100.0	100.0	100.0	100.0	100.0
			INCOME DATA						
100.0	100.0	100.0	Net Sales	100.0	100.0	100.0	100.0	100.0	100.0
			Gross Profit						
79.0	76.0	77.5	Operating Expenses	67.2	81.8	86.5	82.9	86.9	90.1
21.0	24.0	22.5	Operating Profit	32.8	18.2	13.5	17.1	13.1	9.9
6.9	7.7	7.6	All Other Expenses (net)	14.6	4.0	.8	2.1	2.3	2.4
14.1	16.3	14.9	Profit Before Taxes	18.1	14.2	12.7	14.9	10.8	7.6
			RATIOS						
3.5	3.8	3.1		3.2	3.6	4.2	3.9	2.8	1.7
1.2	1.2	1.2	Current	.9	1.1	1.6	1.8	1.6	1.1
.5	.5	.4		.3	.3	.9	.9	.9	.6
2.8	3.2	2.6		2.4	3.2	3.0	3.4	2.5	1.3
.9	1.0	1.0	Quick	.8	1.0	1.4	1.4	1.5	.9
.3	.3	.3		.2	.3	.8	.8	.7	.5
0 UND	0 UND	0 UND		0 UND	0 UND	0 UND	0 UND	0 UND	9 41.9
0 UND	0 UND	0 UND	Sales/Receivables	0 UND	0 UND	4 99.9	6 57.0	11 32.8	21 17.1
13 28.1	12 29.6	13 27.6		0 UND	10 38.0	22 16.3	35 10.4	31 11.8	44 8.3
			Cost of Sales/Inventory						
			Cost of Sales/Payables						
5.0	5.4	6.2		4.7	6.2	5.2	3.8	8.4	14.9
40.5	44.1	53.0	Sales/Working Capital	-38.6	184.6	16.7	18.8	30.0	156.1
-12.9	-8.8	-9.0		-3.7	-3.9	-51.3	-33.9	-62.4	-14.5
25.1	29.3	35.2		12.1	20.2	88.4	84.3	65.8	50.9
(189) 5.3	(211) 7.2	(194) 6.0	EBIT/Interest	(62) 3.6	(36) 6.7	(28) 9.9	(24) 11.0	(20) 30.6	(24) 13.1
2.2	2.4	2.1		1.6	2.5	2.8	3.6	3.7	1.1
9.8	16.4		Net Profit + Depr., Dep.,						
(13) 3.4	(10) 3.8		Amort./Cur. Mat. L/T/D						
2.1	.9								
.1	.1	.1		.6	.0	.0	.0	.1	.1
1.3	1.2	1.3	Fixed/Worth	2.0	.5	.3	.1	.3	.3
14.2	6.5	6.9		14.8	3.8	8.1	1.6	3.1	-7.8
.6	.5	.6		1.2	.4	.5	.4	.5	1.1
2.4	2.5	2.4	Debt/Worth	3.5	1.6	1.3	1.1	2.1	2.2
80.2	31.5	86.4		UND	24.6	-51.8	5.0	NM	-33.1
85.6	81.9	79.0		36.0	151.8	125.3	78.4	91.5	89.1
(272) 22.3	(333) 22.1	(284) 27.7	% Profit Before Taxes/Tangible Net Worth	(115) 12.1	(65) 33.5	(28) 50.0	(28) 42.0	(26) 47.3	(22) 54.5
3.7	4.2	5.3		3.7	5.5	3.4	15.5	23.1	12.9
25.2	25.2	30.4		14.0	26.3	58.0	44.8	64.6	25.6
6.9	5.8	7.6	% Profit Before Taxes/Total Assets	3.5	7.1	22.5	23.3	28.4	11.6
1.2	.8	1.2		.3	.2	2.3	3.8	10.1	4.0
72.1	74.6	115.4		19.3	208.3	115.4	145.4	177.9	140.7
6.7	9.3	16.0	Sales/Net Fixed Assets	.3	23.5	42.1	54.3	58.5	28.3
.3	.2	.3		.1	.7	14.3	9.9	23.4	15.0
2.8	2.9	3.3		.9	2.9	4.4	3.5	7.4	4.5
.9	.8	1.0	Sales/Total Assets	.2	1.1	2.3	2.3	3.6	2.3
.2	.2	.2		.1	.4	.7	.7	2.5	1.0
1.3	1.3	.7		9.2	.8	.3	.1	.3	.1
(223) 7.4	(243) 7.8	(213) 5.9	% Depr., Dep., Amort./Sales	(96) 20.1	(39) 3.3	(20) 1.0	(17) .6	(20) .6	(21) .7
21.9	19.7	20.5		28.6	18.1	2.0	4.3	1.1	2.9
3.7	2.3	2.9		4.5	3.7	3.9	1.2	1.1	
(75) 7.1	(96) 5.8	(91) 5.7	% Officers', Directors' Owners' Comp/Sales	(27) 8.5	(19) 5.5	(15) 5.9	(13) 1.7	(14) 3.6	
15.1	12.2	13.0		15.3	7.6	11.2	7.8	13.3	
5657901M	4613321M	4114646M	Net Sales ($)	59374M	147595M	151933M	234512M	508058M	3013174M
3240546M	3821796M	2994001M	Total Assets ($)	293575M	256471M	142733M	252661M	517480M	1531081M

© RMA 2019

M = $ thousand   MM = $ million
See Pages viii through xx for Explanation of Ratios and Data

Current Data Sorted by Assets

Comparative Historical Data

Type of Statement

Type of Statement	0-500M	500M-2MM	2-10MM	10-50MM	50-100MM	100-250MM		4/1/14-3/31/15 ALL	4/1/15-3/31/16 ALL
Unqualified		1	2	4	1	2		21	25
Reviewed		4	5	5	2			23	15
Compiled	2		10	2				33	28
Tax Returns	20	38	33	6				172	126
Other	22	60	81	24	3	2		204	234
	21 (4/1-9/30/18)		308 (10/1/18-3/31/19)						

Main Data

	0-500M	500M-2MM	2-10MM	10-50MM	50-100MM	100-250MM		4/1/14-3/31/15 ALL	4/1/15-3/31/16 ALL
NUMBER OF STATEMENTS	44	103	131	41	6	4		453	428
	%	%	%	%	%	%		%	%
ASSETS									
Cash & Equivalents	27.5	13.5	9.4	8.7				12.0	13.4
Trade Receivables (net)	8.3	3.6	4.7	5.3				5.4	7.0
Inventory	.7	1.8	.4	3.6				1.0	1.0
All Other Current	3.1	4.9	4.4	2.1				3.0	3.0
Total Current	39.5	23.8	18.9	19.7				21.5	24.5
Fixed Assets (net)	43.0	64.6	68.5	55.2				63.9	60.2
Intangibles (net)	6.6	4.9	2.9	9.2				2.9	3.8
All Other Non-Current	10.9	6.7	9.6	15.9				11.8	11.6
Total	100.0	100.0	100.0	100.0				100.0	100.0
LIABILITIES									
Notes Payable-Short Term	9.9	5.4	4.3	3.9				6.8	6.5
Cur. Mat.-L.T.D.	1.0	2.1	2.1	1.5				2.6	2.7
Trade Payables	6.3	2.4	2.6	2.3				3.3	3.2
Income Taxes Payable	.0	.0	.0	.0				.3	.2
All Other Current	15.5	8.9	6.6	14.7				9.9	8.7
Total Current	32.7	18.7	15.6	22.4				23.0	21.4
Long-Term Debt	27.9	45.1	52.8	30.8				47.0	44.5
Deferred Taxes	.0	.0	.0	.4				.1	.1
All Other Non-Current	14.7	5.0	6.2	5.2				6.5	5.2
Net Worth	24.7	31.1	25.4	41.3				23.3	28.9
Total Liabilities & Net Worth	100.0	100.0	100.0	100.0				100.0	100.0
INCOME DATA									
Net Sales	100.0	100.0	100.0	100.0				100.0	100.0
Gross Profit									
Operating Expenses	75.3	55.2	58.9	62.8				63.2	64.3
Operating Profit	24.7	44.8	41.1	37.2				36.8	35.7
All Other Expenses (net)	6.0	14.2	15.5	11.2				14.8	13.3
Profit Before Taxes	18.7	30.6	25.6	26.0				22.0	22.4
RATIOS									
Current	4.0	3.4	2.8	2.4				2.7	3.1
	1.1	1.0	1.0	1.0				.9	1.0
	.3	.3	.2	.2				.2	.3
Quick	4.0	2.5	2.1	1.7				2.4	2.6
	1.0	(102) .8	.8	.7				.6	.7
	.3	.2	.1	.2				.1	.2
Sales/Receivables	0 UND	0 UND	0 UND	0 UND				0 UND	0 UND
	0 UND	0 UND	0 UND	1 453.3				0 UND	0 UND
	7 53.5	0 UND	6 61.6	34 10.6				7 52.6	11 32.3
Cost of Sales/Inventory									
Cost of Sales/Payables									
Sales/Working Capital	9.8	6.0	3.8	4.0				7.4	5.3
	84.9	-239.0	-524.3	127.0				-47.0	-261.4
	-10.5	-4.4	-4.0	-2.1				-3.1	-3.0
EBIT/Interest	8.1	16.7	7.9	20.8				14.1	15.6
	(26) 3.1	(55) 6.3	(59) 4.3	(23) 6.8				(216) 4.5	(217) 4.2
	1.6	2.8	2.4	1.8				2.1	2.0
Net Profit + Depr., Dep., Amort./Cur. Mat. L/T/D								14.6	11.2
								(17) 2.0	(18) 3.3
								.9	1.3
Fixed/Worth	.2	.7	1.3	.5				.8	.5
	1.5	2.4	2.8	1.8				3.0	2.6
	23.8	6.2	32.4	5.7				46.2	18.2
Debt/Worth	.3	.8	1.0	.5				1.0	.7
	1.5	2.4	2.9	1.6				3.1	2.6
	23.9	7.9	43.9	6.8				UND	29.1
% Profit Before Taxes/Tangible Net Worth	84.3	59.1	32.2	41.9				51.6	51.3
	(35) 32.7	(91) 21.7	(102) 14.5	(35) 14.2				(341) 17.2	(337) 16.7
	6.7	10.0	5.9	5.1				4.6	3.9
% Profit Before Taxes/Total Assets	39.5	16.3	7.5	8.1				11.0	12.4
	6.9	6.5	4.2	5.4				4.7	5.6
	1.3	2.6	1.8	.1				1.2	1.2
Sales/Net Fixed Assets	115.5	7.9	.8	2.2				8.4	21.4
	15.8	.3	.2	.4				.3	.3
	.3	.1	.1	.1				.1	.1
Sales/Total Assets	6.0	1.5	.3	.7				.9	1.1
	2.5	.2	.1	.2				.2	.2
	.2	.1	.1	.1				.1	.1
% Depr., Dep., Amort./Sales	.4	6.3	8.9	1.8				5.2	4.3
	(30) 3.4	(68) 13.3	(98) 19.0	(30) 8.8				(343) 15.0	(313) 15.1
	15.3	22.7	26.4	21.5				22.5	22.6
% Officers', Directors' Owners' Comp/Sales	9.2	3.2						3.2	2.3
	(11) 17.5	(12) 10.3						(56) 9.3	(47) 7.6
	24.9	17.9						17.5	15.5
Net Sales ($)	38085M	135774M	401540M	376425M	294069M	1056266M		3829350M	2502348M
Total Assets ($)	12851M	123266M	604484M	822955M	409324M	587476M		4612851M	4353998M

M = $ thousand   MM = $ million
See Pages viii through xx for Explanation of Ratios and Data

Comparative Historical Data   Current Data Sorted by Sales

4/1/16-3/31/17 ALL	4/1/17-3/31/18 ALL	4/1/18-3/31/19 ALL	Type of Statement	0-1MM	1-3MM	3-5MM	5-10MM	10-25MM	25MM & OVER
21	12	8	Unqualified	2	1	2		2	1
14	10	14	Reviewed	2	1	4	2		5
17	11	18	Compiled	8	6		1	3	
123	130	97	Tax Returns	72	17	5	1	1	1
211	188	192	Other	113	36	12	12	12	7
				21 (4/1-9/30/18)			308 (10/1/18-3/31/19)		
386	351	329	NUMBER OF STATEMENTS	197	61	23	16	18	14
%	%	%	ASSETS	%	%	%	%	%	%
13.4	12.3	12.9	Cash & Equivalents	8.4	18.3	23.3	11.2	33.7	11.3
6.1	6.7	5.0	Trade Receivables (net)	1.2	5.8	9.4	10.2	21.1	21.3
1.1	1.0	1.4	Inventory	.1	2.4	2.8	1.3	2.9	10.0
4.4	3.0	4.1	All Other Current	2.9	5.8	5.7	6.5	9.0	2.8
25.1	22.9	23.4	Total Current	12.5	32.4	41.3	29.2	66.7	45.4
58.5	61.4	61.9	Fixed Assets (net)	77.9	46.5	33.0	37.0	14.4	41.5
4.3	4.5	5.1	Intangibles (net)	2.6	9.6	11.7	10.8	1.4	7.0
12.2	11.2	9.7	All Other Non-Current	7.0	11.6	14.0	22.9	17.5	6.1
100.0	100.0	100.0	Total	100.0	100.0	100.0	100.0	100.0	100.0
			LIABILITIES						
6.2	5.9	5.3	Notes Payable-Short Term	4.2	6.9	8.0	4.0	6.6	9.1
2.2	3.0	1.0	Cur. Mat.-L.T.D.	2.3	1.8	1.2	.6	.6	1.3
2.6	2.4	3.0	Trade Payables	.6	5.6	5.9	4.1	8.2	13.1
.8	.0	.0	Income Taxes Payable	.0	.0	.1	.0	.0	.3
11.5	10.2	9.6	All Other Current	6.5	10.0	14.4	10.9	19.4	31.0
23.3	21.5	19.9	Total Current	13.6	24.1	29.5	19.5	34.8	54.9
45.6	45.9	43.6	Long-Term Debt	50.2	49.5	14.9	43.2	8.1	19.0
.1	.0	.1	Deferred Taxes	.1	.0	.1	.0	.0	.3
5.7	3.9	6.9	All Other Non-Current	6.7	9.7	4.0	13.1	.8	3.6
25.3	28.7	29.5	Net Worth	29.4	16.8	51.5	24.2	56.4	22.2
100.0	100.0	100.0	Total Liabilities & Net Worth	100.0	100.0	100.0	100.0	100.0	100.0
			INCOME DATA						
100.0	100.0	100.0	Net Sales	100.0	100.0	100.0	100.0	100.0	100.0
			Gross Profit						
64.9	62.4	60.7	Operating Expenses	49.4	70.1	81.1	74.1	89.0	92.8
35.1	37.6	39.3	Operating Profit	50.6	29.9	18.9	25.9	11.0	7.2
11.7	14.0	13.1	All Other Expenses (net)	18.9	7.2	3.3	5.1	-.5	-.1
23.4	23.6	26.2	Profit Before Taxes	31.7	22.8	15.6	20.8	11.5	7.3
			RATIOS						
2.8	3.1	3.0	Current	2.6	3.8	6.0	2.8	3.5	2.6
1.1	1.0	1.1		.9	1.3	1.6	1.4	2.4	1.6
.3	.2	.3		.1	.3	.6	.8	1.3	.6
2.2	2.4	2.1	Quick	2.1	2.9	4.6	1.8	3.2	1.7
.8	.7 (328)	.8		.6 (60)	.9	1.0	1.0	1.8	.7
.2	.1	.2		.1	.2	.4	.3	1.0	.2
0 UND	0 UND	0 UND	Sales/Receivables	0 UND	0 UND	0 UND	0 UND	0 UND	4 90.8
0 UND	0 UND	0 UND		0 UND	0 UND	1 251.9	7 52.9	29 12.8	11 33.1
10 35.7	5 78.3	6 57.5		0 UND	5 79.1	26 13.9	33 11.1	62 5.9	38 9.7
			Cost of Sales/Inventory						
			Cost of Sales/Payables						
5.7	5.8	5.1	Sales/Working Capital	4.9	5.5	5.9	2.6	4.6	5.3
97.6	244.0	99.8		-39.5	24.9	38.9	16.8	10.1	24.7
-4.1	-3.4	-4.3		-2.6	-8.7	-42.4	-15.8	NM	-7.7
23.7	10.5	12.1	EBIT/Interest	9.3	6.9	81.4	20.8	55.4	79.4
(211) 5.0	(191) 4.3	(170) 5.0		(88) 5.0	(35) 3.0	(14) 7.7	(11) 2.9	(11) 7.9	(11) 10.7
2.9	2.5	2.5		2.8	1.6	2.6	.2	3.2	2.5
60.3	10.8	13.4	Net Profit + Depr., Dep., Amort./Cur. Mat. L/T/D						
(14) 8.3	(19) 5.5	(12) 5.4							
4.0	2.8	1.2							
.5	.7	.8	Fixed/Worth	1.6	.4	.1	.1	.0	.5
2.3	2.5	2.5		2.9	3.3	.8	1.9	.2	.9
16.5	10.9	9.1		8.8	-4.8	1.5	3.2	.9	-2.0
.7	.8	.7	Debt/Worth	1.0	.7	.1	1.0	.3	.6
2.9	2.5	2.4		2.8	4.9	.8	1.7	.5	1.8
32.2	15.6	15.6		9.3	-5.8	6.8	10.1	2.2	-3.8
49.3	48.0	50.4	% Profit Before Taxes/Tangible Net Worth	42.2	94.7	65.6	40.4	72.7	76.4
(305) 19.0	(287) 18.6	(271) 17.1		(171) 14.0	(41) 30.2	(19) 30.9	(13) 9.9	(17) 31.3	(10) 29.7
8.0	5.8	7.2		6.2	8.3	14.6	-5.3	17.9	13.1
13.4	13.2	14.3	% Profit Before Taxes/Total Assets	8.2	22.1	30.7	18.8	35.3	24.3
5.7	5.6	5.3		4.2	5.3	16.9	6.1	20.6	8.1
2.0	1.7	1.9		1.6	2.2	2.6	.1	7.3	.8
16.1	13.5	8.1	Sales/Net Fixed Assets	.3	51.7	58.3	37.6	322.2	37.3
.4	.3	.3		.2	3.3	9.5	1.1	83.8	7.9
.2	.1	.1		.2	.2	.6	.4	6.5	2.0
1.5	1.1	1.0	Sales/Total Assets	.2	3.2	3.5	1.1	5.7	6.0
.2	.2	.2		.1	.7	1.6	.4	2.6	3.0
.1	.1	.1		.1	.2	.3	.1	1.0	1.1
3.8	3.6	3.5	% Depr., Dep., Amort./Sales	12.1	1.1	.6	.4		.7
(257) 12.8	(250) 13.7	(235) 14.2		(145) 19.2	(38) 8.7	(17) 3.0	(12) 4.7		1.5
22.0	23.8	23.2		25.7	19.4	11.6	10.2		4.0
4.1	3.8	2.9	% Officers', Directors' Owners' Comp/Sales	2.2	4.8				
(48) 8.4	(39) 7.1	(39) 10.2		(14) 14.9	(10) 9.0				
14.7	14.1	18.2		27.3	16.1				
3654673M	3786308M	2302159M	Net Sales ($)	70408M	111337M	87871M	111325M	246667M	1674551M
4445094M	4139034M	2560356M	Total Assets ($)	559018M	376719M	241804M	484810M	144616M	753389M

M = $ thousand   MM = $ million
See Pages viii through xx for Explanation of Ratios and Data

Current Data Sorted by Assets   **Comparative Historical Data**

0-500M	500M-2MM	2-10MM	10-50MM	50-100MM	100-250MM	Type of Statement	4/1/14-3/31/15 ALL	4/1/15-3/31/16 ALL
		2				Unqualified	2	1
	1	1				Reviewed		1
3	5	1				Compiled	2	
3	5	1	5	1	1	Tax Returns	10	8
	1 (4/1-9/30/18)		29 (10/1/18-3/31/19)		2	Other	8	10
6	11	9	1	1	2	**NUMBER OF STATEMENTS**	22	20
%	%	%	%	%	%	**ASSETS**	%	%
	20.1					Cash & Equivalents	23.1	27.7
	11.8					Trade Receivables (net)	25.2	25.3
	1.1					Inventory	.0	.0
	.4					All Other Current	.9	8.2
	33.3					Total Current	49.1	61.1
	32.4					Fixed Assets (net)	25.7	22.5
	2.9					Intangibles (net)	6.9	8.0
	31.4					All Other Non-Current	18.5	8.4
	100.0					Total	100.0	100.0
						LIABILITIES		
	7.5					Notes Payable-Short Term	16.3	18.7
	4.1					Cur. Mat.-L.T.D.	1.4	1.6
	7.6					Trade Payables	23.0	8.5
	.0					Income Taxes Payable	.4	.1
	5.3					All Other Current	16.5	10.1
	24.5					Total Current	57.5	39.0
	37.4					Long-Term Debt	15.0	13.8
	.0					Deferred Taxes	.0	.0
	2.6					All Other Non-Current	20.5	7.7
	35.6					Net Worth	7.0	39.5
	100.0					Total Liabilties & Net Worth	100.0	100.0
						INCOME DATA		
	100.0					Net Sales	100.0	100.0
						Gross Profit		
	74.2					Operating Expenses	94.0	87.3
	25.8					Operating Profit	6.0	12.7
	9.6					All Other Expenses (net)	.9	3.3
	16.2					Profit Before Taxes	5.2	9.4
						RATIOS		
	6.0					Current	4.4	4.2
	1.3						1.2	1.5
	.5						.8	1.1
	6.0					Quick	4.4	2.8
	.8						1.2	1.2
	.5						.8	.9
0	UND					Sales/Receivables	0 UND	0 UND
2	196.1						24 15.4	12 29.9
22	16.6						33 11.2	42 8.6
						Cost of Sales/Inventory		
						Cost of Sales/Payables		
	5.8					Sales/Working Capital	9.0	10.2
	57.3						56.2	37.6
	-2.7						-84.8	355.3
						EBIT/Interest	25.3	
							(16) 5.7	
							-1.4	
						Net Profit + Depr., Dep., Amort./Cur. Mat. L/T/D		
	.0					Fixed/Worth	.1	.0
	.1						.4	.2
	77.6						-1.6	23.6
	.2					Debt/Worth	.4	.2
	9.8						1.3	1.2
	90.7						-24.2	24.5
						% Profit Before Taxes/Tangible Net Worth	142.2	236.3
							(16) 19.2	(16) 76.7
							3.5	3.5
	24.2					% Profit Before Taxes/Total Assets	25.6	131.1
	8.5						6.0	39.7
	.1						-1.5	-1.3
	UND					Sales/Net Fixed Assets	191.4	UND
	59.1						62.5	44.4
	.3						14.7	21.6
	5.6					Sales/Total Assets	7.6	11.5
	.7						4.5	5.5
	.2						2.9	2.1
						% Depr., Dep., Amort./Sales	.6	.2
							(12) 1.0	(10) .8
							2.0	5.8
						% Officers', Directors' Owners' Comp/Sales		
12389M	33147M	143451M	2262M	90638M	1110784M	Net Sales ($)	309286M	590729M
1755M	13019M	41648M	20088M	92491M	352723M	Total Assets ($)	156667M	323311M

© RMA 2019

M = $ thousand   MM = $ million
See Pages viii through xx for Explanation of Ratios and Data

Comparative Historical Data   ## Current Data Sorted by Sales

4/1/16-3/31/17 ALL	4/1/17-3/31/18 ALL	4/1/18-3/31/19 ALL	Type of Statement	0-1MM	1-3MM	3-5MM	5-10MM	10-25MM	25MM & OVER
1	1	2	Unqualified					1	1
1	1	1	Reviewed					1	
1		1	Compiled	1					
6	5	9	Tax Returns	8	1				
20	17	17	Other	1	3	4	3	2	4
				0-1MM	1 (4/1-9/30/18) 1-3MM	3-5MM	29 (10/1/18-3/31/19) 5-10MM	10-25MM	25MM & OVER
29	24	30	**NUMBER OF STATEMENTS**	10	4	4	3	4	5
%	%	%	**ASSETS**	%	%	%	%	%	%
37.5	23.5	23.0	Cash & Equivalents	22.4					
21.8	23.1	19.4	Trade Receivables (net)	1.3					
.0	.0	1.1	Inventory	.0					
6.4	3.7	2.2	All Other Current	.4					
65.7	50.3	45.7	Total Current	24.1					
15.9	15.4	24.9	Fixed Assets (net)	52.0					
13.8	9.4	8.8	Intangibles (net)	.8					
4.6	24.9	20.6	All Other Non-Current	23.2					
100.0	100.0	100.0	Total	100.0					
			LIABILITIES						
24.5	16.9	8.1	Notes Payable-Short Term	2.5					
4.8	2.1	3.3	Cur. Mat.-L.T.D.	5.8					
29.5	11.6	10.9	Trade Payables	.1					
.0	.2	.0	Income Taxes Payable	.0					
34.3	10.9	9.6	All Other Current	17.1					
93.3	41.7	31.9	Total Current	25.4					
9.5	9.9	22.9	Long-Term Debt	59.1					
.1	.0	.0	Deferred Taxes	.0					
18.0	6.8	10.6	All Other Non-Current	1.5					
-20.8	41.6	34.6	Net Worth	13.9					
100.0	100.0	100.0	Total Liabilities & Net Worth	100.0					
			INCOME DATA						
100.0	100.0	100.0	Net Sales	100.0					
			Gross Profit						
94.5	81.3	83.5	Operating Expenses	64.2					
5.5	18.7	16.5	Operating Profit	35.8					
1.5	1.2	5.4	All Other Expenses (net)	12.6					
4.0	17.5	11.1	Profit Before Taxes	23.2					
			RATIOS						
3.0	5.7	6.3	Current	5.2					
1.2	1.4	1.3		.4					
.5	.5	.5		.1					
3.0	5.5	6.1	Quick	5.2					
1.1	1.3	1.0		.4					
.4	.5	.5		.1					
0 UND	0 UND	0 UND	Sales/Receivables	0 UND					
23 16.2	10 37.0	10 37.2		0 UND					
37 9.9	31 11.6	32 11.5		0 UND					
			Cost of Sales/Inventory						
			Cost of Sales/Payables						
10.8	7.8	6.1	Sales/Working Capital	14.5					
128.0	26.7	55.9		-6.1					
-16.2	-17.8	-15.9		-.7					
50.8	82.4	6.4	EBIT/Interest						
(17) 2.0	(16) 46.5	(18) 1.5							
.3	8.9	-5.0							
			Net Profit + Depr., Dep., Amort./Cur. Mat. L/T/D						
.0	.0	.0	Fixed/Worth	2.2					
.3	.2	7		50.4					
-.6	2.1	-118.4		-109.3					
.7	.2	.4	Debt/Worth	7.9					
23.2	1.2	4.3		56.7					
-2.2	UND	-70.2		-333.8					
177.4	134.7	98.5	% Profit Before Taxes/Tangible Net Worth						
(16) 48.7	(19) 82.4	(21) 42.2							
17.0	21.6	-1.0							
38.0	70.9	33.4	% Profit Before Taxes/Total Assets	12.5					
14.0	34.9	2.9		2.9					
-1.4	12.8	-3.5		.8					
880.4	728.1	UND	Sales/Net Fixed Assets	UND					
78.3	137.9	78.0		.8					
42.8	26.2	1.9		.2					
12.4	5.8	5.6	Sales/Total Assets	1.0					
6.7	4.0	4.3		.2					
2.8	1.6	.3		.1					
.3		.6	% Depr., Dep., Amort./Sales						
(11) 1.1	(12) 1.7								
2.2		21.7							
			% Officers', Directors' Owners' Comp/Sales						
847917M	604019M	1392671M	Net Sales ($)	3338M	7107M	16451M	23127M	81093M	1261555M
457367M	207285M	521724M	Total Assets ($)	20346M	23284M	2426M	4790M	16776M	454102M

© RMA 2019

M = $ thousand   MM = $ million
See Pages viii through xx for Explanation of Ratios and Data

Current Data Sorted by Assets | Comparative Historical Data

	0-500M	500M-2MM	2-10MM	10-50MM	50-100MM	100-250MM		4/1/14-3/31/15 ALL	4/1/15-3/31/16 ALL
Type of Statement									
Unqualified		4	17	27	14	21		79	69
Reviewed	3	4	8	12	4	1		50	47
Compiled	3	6	30	13	2	2		94	72
Tax Returns	74	169	205	36	2	1		641	756
Other	72	156	230	130	18	17		626	606
		51 (4/1-9/30/18)		1,230 (10/1/18-3/31/19)					
NUMBER OF STATEMENTS	152	339	490	218	40	42		1490	1550
	%	%	%	%	%	%	ASSETS	%	%
Cash & Equivalents	31.8	10.6	8.0	9.9	12.9	11.3		12.2	11.8
Trade Receivables (net)	3.9	4.5	4.5	4.6	13.9	12.9		5.2	4.7
Inventory	5.0	6.2	5.3	10.8	5.7	14.3		6.0	6.8
All Other Current	4.8	3.9	3.2	7.3	3.7	4.4		4.2	4.1
Total Current	45.5	25.2	21.1	32.6	36.1	43.0		27.6	27.3
Fixed Assets (net)	36.4	63.2	65.4	43.8	32.8	18.9		56.0	57.6
Intangibles (net)	4.6	3.1	3.4	5.0	5.4	7.1		3.3	3.3
All Other Non-Current	13.4	8.5	10.1	18.6	25.7	31.0		13.1	11.7
Total	100.0	100.0	100.0	100.0	100.0	100.0		100.0	100.0
							LIABILITIES		
Notes Payable-Short Term	16.7	8.9	6.2	9.8	3.7	5.0		8.9	10.8
Cur. Mat.-L.T.D.	3.8	3.9	2.8	2.8	1.5	6.1		2.8	2.7
Trade Payables	4.1	2.1	1.5	3.2	6.9	6.5		3.0	2.7
Income Taxes Payable	.1	.1	.0	.1	.0	.1		.1	.0
All Other Current	21.5	10.9	7.7	9.2	7.7	11.3		9.6	10.6
Total Current	46.1	26.0	18.2	25.0	19.8	28.9		24.4	26.8
Long-Term Debt	25.5	47.2	49.7	34.7	31.0	32.4		40.5	42.7
Deferred Taxes	.0	.0	.0	.0	.2	.2		.0	.0
All Other Non-Current	5.3	4.8	4.6	7.1	6.7	6.2		5.7	5.6
Net Worth	23.1	22.0	27.4	33.1	42.3	32.2		29.3	24.9
Total Liabilities & Net Worth	100.0	100.0	100.0	100.0	100.0	100.0		100.0	100.0
							INCOME DATA		
Net Sales	100.0	100.0	100.0	100.0	100.0	100.0		100.0	100.0
Gross Profit									
Operating Expenses	73.2	62.8	60.8	67.3	65.9	82.6		66.6	67.3
Operating Profit	26.8	37.2	39.2	32.7	34.1	17.4		33.4	32.7
All Other Expenses (net)	5.8	15.4	17.7	15.3	8.4	5.1		13.8	14.6
Profit Before Taxes	21.0	21.9	21.6	17.4	25.7	12.3		19.5	18.1
							RATIOS		
	4.3	3.0	3.3	2.9	4.3	3.2		3.1	3.0
Current	1.2	.8	1.1	1.3	1.7	1.3		1.1	1.0
	.2	.2	.3	.6	1.0	.7		.3	.2
	3.5	1.9	2.4	1.8	3.0	1.5		2.1	2.0
Quick	.7	.5	.8	.6	1.4	.8		.7 (1549)	.6
	.2	.1	.2	.1	.4	.1		.1	.1
	0 UND	0 UND	0 UND	0 UND	0 UND	3 142.2		0 UND	0 UND
Sales/Receivables	0 UND	0 UND	0 UND	0 929.5	15 23.9	12 29.7		0 UND	0 UND
	0 UND	0 UND	7 54.1	21 17.3	56 6.5	65 5.6		6 64.3	4 94.4
							Cost of Sales/Inventory		
							Cost of Sales/Payables		
	11.4	5.6	3.7	2.5	1.1	1.0		4.2	4.2
Sales/Working Capital	51.6	-81.0	65.1	9.8	3.7	6.4		77.0	276.7
	-6.3	-3.1	-3.2	-5.6	756.5	-7.5		-4.1	-3.0
	14.5	11.9	11.0	8.4	59.7	6.4		17.1	10.6
EBIT/Interest	(63) 4.4	(146) 4.9	(231) 4.5	(111) 3.1	(23) 7.6	(33) 2.4	(720)	4.8 (752)	4.2
	1.0	2.2	2.4	1.6	2.6	1.2		1.8	1.9
			4.0				Net Profit + Depr., Dep.,	5.0	10.6
		(18)	2.2				Amort./Cur. Mat. L/T/D	(53) 2.0 (45)	3.9
			1.3					1.0	1.1
	.0	.6	.8	.1	.0	.0		.2	.3
Fixed/Worth	.8	3.2	2.9	1.3	.7	.2		2.2	2.3
	5.1	53.9	10.9	8.2	2.8	3.3		9.4	10.7
	.3	1.0	1.1	.9	.5	.7		.7	.9
Debt/Worth	1.3	3.5	3.1	3.2	2.5	2.3		2.5	2.8
	UND	UND	21.7	17.5	5.5	12.5		17.6	21.6
	156.3	55.1	40.2	25.3	36.3	22.5	% Profit Before Taxes/Tangible	45.6	38.6
	(116) 47.6	(255) 18.8	(399) 14.4	(183) 11.7	(37) 11.0	(34) 7.8	Net Worth	(1207) 16.3 (1246)	13.3
	9.4	5.1	3.8	2.6	2.9	2.2		3.6	2.8
	71.3	13.2	8.5	8.0	10.2	9.6	% Profit Before Taxes/Total	12.4	9.8
	17.5	4.5	3.9	3.0	4.0	2.8	Assets	4.4	3.9
	1.4	.8	.9	.5	1.0	.4		.7	.4
	UND	14.7	3.4	50.7	60.3	744.6		30.7	23.8
Sales/Net Fixed Assets	50.7	.3	.2	1.1	2.6	47.7		.4	.3
	1.4	.1	.1	.2	.3	1.2		.1	.1
	7.7	1.0	.5	.7	.5	.9		1.2	.9
Sales/Total Assets	2.7	.2	.2	.2	.2	.4		.2	.2
	.4	.1	.1	.1	.1	.2		.1	.1
	1.0	8.5	7.6	1.1		.5		2.0	3.5
% Depr., Dep., Amort./Sales	(61) 7.2	(207) 17.3	(346) 17.5	(144) 8.5	(29) 3.0	(25) 2.1	(976)	14.0 (1052)	15.3
	18.4	25.0	26.2	22.9	13.4	5.9		23.3	24.6
	3.9	2.7	2.3	1.2			% Officers', Directors'	1.9	2.5
	(38) 8.0	(34) 4.8	(39) 4.5	(12) 2.0			Owners' Comp/Sales	(179) 5.9 (190)	5.2
	15.8	10.4	9.2	12.5				12.8	13.0
Net Sales ($)	143363M	423787M	1373256M	2747497M	1257083M	4259508M		10633949M	10258650M
Total Assets ($)	34415M	397312M	2327726M	4503020M	2958638M	6376127M		14687751M	15697068M

M = $ thousand   MM = $ million
See Pages viii through xx for Explanation of Ratios and Data

Comparative Historical Data | Current Data Sorted by Sales

			Type of Statement						
58	60	83	Unqualified	10	4	6	7	18	38
30	46	32	Reviewed	6	9	2	5	3	7
69	75	56	Compiled	25	14	4	5	7	1
628	568	487	Tax Returns	344	87	23	18	10	5
567	604	623	Other	298	136	50	57	44	38
4/1/16-3/31/17 ALL	4/1/17-3/31/18 ALL	4/1/18-3/31/19 ALL		51 (4/1-9/30/18) 0-1MM	1-3MM	3-5MM	1,230 (10/1/18-3/31/19) 5-10MM	10-25MM	25MM & OVER
1352	1353	1281	**NUMBER OF STATEMENTS**	683	250	85	92	82	89
%	%	%	**ASSETS**	%	%	%	%	%	%
12.3	11.7	12.1	Cash & Equivalents	9.2	14.5	19.2	15.0	15.3	15.3
5.1	5.3	5.0	Trade Receivables (net)	1.4	3.7	10.3	11.5	14.0	16.8
6.6	5.2	6.7	Inventory	3.4	6.7	11.9	10.2	12.4	19.2
4.7	3.8	4.3	All Other Current	2.5	5.2	10.3	8.3	6.1	4.6
28.6	26.0	28.2	Total Current	16.4	30.0	51.7	45.0	47.8	56.0
53.8	56.8	55.2	Fixed Assets (net)	73.2	50.5	26.4	24.2	24.5	17.1
4.1	4.6	3.9	Intangibles (net)	2.6	4.5	5.7	6.5	5.6	6.8
13.5	12.6	12.7	All Other Non-Current	7.7	15.0	16.3	24.3	22.1	20.1
100.0	100.0	100.0	Total	100.0	100.0	100.0	100.0	100.0	100.0
			LIABILITIES						
9.1	7.5	8.6	Notes Payable-Short Term	7.3	8.1	14.7	10.0	10.4	11.7
2.8	2.7	3.3	Cur. Mat.-L.T.D.	3.1	4.5	1.7	2.7	1.4	5.3
2.8	3.1	2.6	Trade Payables	1.0	2.4	2.3	5.5	5.4	10.1
.1	.1	.1	Income Taxes Payable	.1	.0	.0	.1	.3	.1
11.3	10.9	10.5	All Other Current	8.6	10.9	8.7	15.5	18.9	13.7
26.1	24.3	25.1	Total Current	20.0	26.0	27.5	33.7	36.4	41.0
41.9	42.7	42.5	Long-Term Debt	51.7	46.7	22.2	20.8	23.8	19.1
.0	.0	.0	Deferred Taxes	.0	.0	.0	.1	.0	.1
5.2	5.4	5.3	All Other Non-Current	3.8	5.2	15.6	8.0	3.5	5.8
26.7	27.5	27.1	Net Worth	24.5	22.1	34.8	37.5	36.2	34.1
100.0	100.0	100.0	Total Liabilities & Net Worth	100.0	100.0	100.0	100.0	100.0	100.0
			INCOME DATA						
100.0	100.0	100.0	Net Sales	100.0	100.0	100.0	100.0	100.0	100.0
			Gross Profit						
65.4	65.0	64.8	Operating Expenses	55.2	67.7	76.8	78.2	81.4	89.4
34.6	35.0	35.2	Operating Profit	44.8	32.3	23.2	21.8	18.6	10.6
13.5	14.1	14.6	All Other Expenses (net)	20.9	12.1	6.5	3.7	3.1	1.9
21.1	20.9	20.7	Profit Before Taxes	23.9	20.2	16.7	18.2	15.5	8.8
			RATIOS						
3.3	2.9	3.3		2.6	4.1	5.8	4.2	3.0	2.3
1.1	1.0	1.1	Current	.7	1.3	2.6	1.5	1.4	1.3
.3	.3	.3		.2	.4	1.2	.8	.6	.9
2.1	2.0	2.2		1.8	2.8	4.0	2.9	2.1	1.6
(1350) .6	.7	.7	Quick	.5	.9	1.3	.9	.7	.8
.1	.1	.1		.1	.2	.3	.1	.2	.3
0 UND	0 UND	0 UND		0 UND	0 UND	0 UND	0 UND	0 UND	2 150.9
0 UND	0 UND	0 UND	Sales/Receivables	0 UND	0 UND	0 999.8	1 276.5	7 49.4	15 24.4
4 89.4	7 50.0	7 49.0		0 UND	8 48.4	29 12.4	27 13.4	44 8.3	53 6.9
			Cost of Sales/Inventory						
			Cost of Sales/Payables						
3.8	4.3	3.5		5.0	3.7	1.5	2.8	2.5	3.7
102.0	327.0	50.3	Sales/Working Capital	-19.6	35.4	5.7	7.4	8.6	12.0
-4.0	-4.0	-3.9		-2.1	-5.9	40.7	-25.1	-21.4	-45.3
14.8	15.1	11.3		6.7	13.8	27.0	33.7	29.6	13.1
(664) 4.5	(693) 4.6	(607) 4.4	EBIT/Interest	(230) 4.0	(134) 4.0	(55) 8.1	(54) 7.9	(61) 4.7	(73) 4.8
2.0	2.1	2.0		2.1	1.5	3.2	2.6	2.0	1.8
5.3	4.6	5.4		3.9					7.9
(38) 2.1	(44) 1.7	(41) 2.3	Net Profit + Depr., Dep., Amort./Cur. Mat. L/T/D	(12) 2.3				(13) 2.3
.9	.6	.8		.9					.4
.2	.3	.2		1.2	.1	.0	.0	.0	.0
1.0	2.0	2.2	Fixed/Worth	3.5	2.2	.3	.3	.3	.3
9.0	10.4	10.8		15.2	41.1	4.7	1.5	3.1	1.8
.8	.8	.8		1.1	.7	.6	.4	.6	.8
3.0	2.9	3.0	Debt/Worth	3.4	3.4	1.7	1.9	2.5	2.3
24.8	22.4	29.6		38.7	194.1	16.9	5.8	10.3	6.3
48.1	45.8	45.9		35.0	56.4	67.1	93.7	78.2	43.2
(1079) 16.8	(1090) 15.9	(1024) 16.2	% Profit Before Taxes/Tangible Net Worth	(540) 12.3	(193) 18.2	(69) 26.3	(77) 30.1	(69) 22.6	(76) 17.1
4.8	4.6	4.1		2.5	4.9	10.7	5.4	4.5	5.4
11.3	12.2	11.3		7.1	14.7	23.1	22.1	20.7	14.2
4.4	4.3	4.1	% Profit Before Taxes/Total Assets	3.2	5.4	7.6	8.2	8.0	5.9
1.0	1.1	.8		.5	.7	1.1	1.4	1.0	2.2
51.9	28.8	39.0		.4	46.2	236.6	221.0	405.6	148.6
.4	.3	.4	Sales/Net Fixed Assets	.2	.7	29.0	24.0	26.3	41.1
.1	.1	.1		.1	.2	.6	2.8	2.1	3.8
1.0	1.1	1.0		.2	1.3	2.9	2.2	2.2	2.4
.2	.2	.2	Sales/Total Assets	.1	.3	.8	.8	1.1	1.3
.1	.1	.1		.1	.1	.2	.3	.3	.6
3.0	2.7	2.6		13.1	2.3	.3	.3	.5	.3
(839) 15.2	(887) 15.5	(812) 14.6	% Depr., Dep., Amort./Sales	(455) 20.8	(150) 13.1	(45) 1.4	(49) 1.3	(48) 1.3	(65) .8
24.3	23.8	24.6		27.4	22.3	11.7	5.7	4.4	2.6
1.9	2.9	2.4		4.9	2.9	2.0	2.7	1.1	1.3
(156) 5.3	(160) 5.8	(130) 5.4	% Officers', Directors' Owners' Comp/Sales	(36) 9.2	(38) 6.6	(16) 4.5	(15) 5.6	(15) 2.1	(10) 2.5
11.2	11.6	12.3		17.6	14.3	9.5	7.3	3.6	7.2
11328831M	10655038M	10204494M	Net Sales ($)	246274M	440706M	342662M	669450M	1289952M	7215450M
15136861M	15451803M	16597238M	Total Assets ($)	1882590M	2071606M	983709M	2050531M	2565536M	7043266M

M = $ thousand   MM = $ million
See Pages viii through xx for Explanation of Ratios and Data

Current Data Sorted by Assets   Comparative Historical Data

0-500M	500M-2MM	2-10MM	10-50MM	50-100MM	100-250MM	Type of Statement	4/1/14-3/31/15 ALL	4/1/15-3/31/16 ALL
		1	4	4		Unqualified	19	15
	1	7	7	2		Reviewed	24	26
	1	4	1			Compiled	10	15
3	7	10				Tax Returns	25	16
3	9	14	16	2	5	Other	54	49
	19 (4/1-9/30/18)		82 (10/1/18-3/31/19)					
6	18	36	28	8	5	**NUMBER OF STATEMENTS**	132	121
%	%	%	%	%	%	**ASSETS**	%	%
	14.2	9.5	5.8			Cash & Equivalents	11.1	12.2
	10.0	5.6	5.7			Trade Receivables (net)	6.3	5.6
	3.0	11.5	13.7			Inventory	10.9	12.2
	.9	3.0	1.9			All Other Current	1.6	2.4
	28.1	29.6	27.1			Total Current	30.0	32.4
	61.8	61.7	66.9			Fixed Assets (net)	62.6	58.2
	4.2	3.9	3.5			Intangibles (net)	3.9	3.9
	5.9	4.9	2.5			All Other Non-Current	3.5	5.6
	100.0	100.0	100.0			Total	100.0	100.0
						LIABILITIES		
	3.7	26.1	26.4			Notes Payable-Short Term	15.5	20.4
	5.3	3.8	4.2			Cur. Mat.-L.T.D.	4.7	2.9
	15.3	4.3	3.6			Trade Payables	4.9	4.7
	.0	.1	.3			Income Taxes Payable	.1	.0
	10.9	1.8	2.6			All Other Current	7.5	10.2
	35.1	36.1	37.1			Total Current	32.7	38.2
	53.2	27.5	37.3			Long-Term Debt	39.9	32.7
	.0	1.2	1.0			Deferred Taxes	.5	.7
	17.6	5.8	1.5			All Other Non-Current	4.3	5.0
	-5.9	29.4	23.0			Net Worth	22.6	23.3
	100.0	100.0	100.0			Total Liabilities & Net Worth	100.0	100.0
						INCOME DATA		
	100.0	100.0	100.0			Net Sales	100.0	100.0
						Gross Profit		
	96.2	90.4	93.1			Operating Expenses	90.7	89.6
	3.8	9.6	6.9			Operating Profit	9.3	10.4
	4.2	1.9	3.9			All Other Expenses (net)	1.6	1.8
	-.5	7.7	3.0			Profit Before Taxes	7.8	8.6
						RATIOS		
	2.5	4.0	1.2				2.5	2.1
	1.1	1.1	.6			Current	1.1	1.1
	.3	.3	.3				.3	.5
	1.7	2.6	.8				1.9	1.7
	.8	.6	.3			Quick	.8	.6
	.2	.1	.1				.2	.1
	0 UND	2 179.5	12 31.4				1 401.1	0 UND
	1 618.4	9 38.5	22 16.6			Sales/Receivables	9 39.9	6 57.6
	30 12.3	26 13.8	46 8.0				25 14.6	22 16.8
						Cost of Sales/Inventory		
						Cost of Sales/Payables		
	9.1	4.2	7.3				7.2	6.2
	129.2	92.9	-13.0			Sales/Working Capital	56.0	73.3
	-3.7	-2.6	-2.6				-6.9	-6.5
	3.6	4.9	1.7				4.9	6.3
	(15) 1.2	(34) 2.2	(25) 1.3			EBIT/Interest	(118) 2.3	(111) 2.5
	-1.5	1.4	.8				1.3	1.1
						Net Profit + Depr., Dep., Amort./Cur. Mat. L/T/D		
	3.2	.9	1.2				1.1	.8
	8.4	2.2	6.1			Fixed/Worth	4.5	3.5
	-1.5	8.1	13.7				12.0	9.0
	4.2	1.5	4.0				2.3	2.1
	9.5	4.3	8.2			Debt/Worth	5.5	4.5
	-3.0	10.4	14.0				15.1	12.2
	92.9	29.3	37.7			% Profit Before Taxes/Tangible Net Worth	56.8	54.9
	(10) 32.5	(32) 16.4	(25) 9.3				(111) 22.6	(106) 23.1
	4.7	7.3	-2.7				9.1	5.1
	9.2	8.7	3.1			% Profit Before Taxes/Total Assets	9.3	11.3
	1.0	3.9	.9				3.9	3.8
	-11.2	1.0	-.6				1.2	.4
	11.9	6.6	1.2				9.8	11.6
	1.4	1.1	.8			Sales/Net Fixed Assets	1.2	1.3
	.9	.6	.5				.6	.7
	3.4	1.1	.8				1.5	1.4
	1.1	.6	.5			Sales/Total Assets	.7	.7
	.5	.4	.4				.5	.5
	13.5	20.3	17.6				16.1	15.4
	(15) 29.5	(28) 30.8	(21) 28.9			% Depr., Dep., Amort./Sales	(95) 26.6	(83) 24.5
	46.9	50.5	39.7				38.4	35.8
		2.5	.9			% Officers', Directors' Owners' Comp/Sales	1.2	1.3
	(20)	5.4	(10) 2.3				(48) 2.6	(44) 2.8
		9.3	4.1				5.3	8.2
4756M	43470M	192346M	412506M	372371M	864933M	Net Sales ($)	2313195M	1733976M
1266M	22375M	168830M	621093M	511291M	1021396M	Total Assets ($)	2883968M	2124469M

Comparative Historical Data / Current Data Sorted by Sales

			Type of Statement	0-1MM	1-3MM	3-5MM	5-10MM	10-25MM	25MM & OVER
10	10	9	Unqualified				2	4	3
15	19	17	Reviewed		5	4	2	6	
10	8	6	Compiled		3		1		
18	18	20	Tax Returns	2	3	2	2		
45	43	49	Other	8	6	4	8	13	10
4/1/16-3/31/17	4/1/17-3/31/18	4/1/18-3/31/19			19 (4/1-9/30/18)		82 (10/1/18-3/31/19)		
ALL	ALL	ALL							
98	98	101	NUMBER OF STATEMENTS	18	22	10	15	23	13
%	%	%	**ASSETS**	%	%	%	%	%	%
9.0	8.8	9.8	Cash & Equivalents	15.3	10.1	10.7	11.7	5.7	6.0
4.1	5.8	7.5	Trade Receivables (net)	4.2	8.6	12.5	5.9	5.5	12.1
17.1	12.3	12.8	Inventory	.2	11.5	21.2	5.7	13.9	32.0
1.5	3.7	3.0	All Other Current	2.9	2.2	.5	1.7	2.1	9.7
31.7	30.6	33.1	Total Current	22.6	32.4	44.9	25.0	27.0	59.7
60.1	61.3	58.7	Fixed Assets (net)	66.5	62.2	49.4	63.5	65.9	31.1
4.0	4.4	3.7	Intangibles (net)	4.8	1.4	4.5	4.6	4.4	3.2
4.2	3.7	4.5	All Other Non-Current	6.2	4.0	1.1	6.8	2.7	6.0
100.0	100.0	100.0	Total	100.0	100.0	100.0	100.0	100.0	100.0
			LIABILITIES						
20.3	20.6	20.4	Notes Payable-Short Term	12.9	23.2	22.7	19.4	29.1	9.9
3.9	5.1	4.3	Cur. Mat.-L.T.D.	4.9	5.2	1.8	2.8	5.1	4.5
3.7	3.8	8.0	Trade Payables	3.3	12.6	18.8	7.8	3.4	7.0
.2	.0	.1	Income Taxes Payable	.0	.0	.3	.0	.1	.6
15.2	10.1	5.3	All Other Current	6.0	4.7	7.3	2.9	5.7	5.8
43.3	39.6	38.1	Total Current	27.0	45.6	50.9	32.9	43.4	27.7
32.7	35.1	35.7	Long-Term Debt	56.0	37.7	30.6	32.0	27.3	27.6
.8	.8	1.1	Deferred Taxes	.0	.9	.4	2.2	2.2	.2
3.8	5.4	6.9	All Other Non-Current	5.4	4.2	12.5	20.9	2.2	1.3
19.4	19.1	18.2	Net Worth	11.5	11.6	5.7	11.9	24.9	43.2
100.0	100.0	100.0	Total Liabilities & Net Worth	100.0	100.0	100.0	100.0	100.0	100.0
			INCOME DATA						
100.0	100.0	100.0	Net Sales	100.0	100.0	100.0	100.0	100.0	100.0
			Gross Profit						
93.3	93.0	92.2	Operating Expenses	89.8	90.7	99.3	92.0	93.0	91.8
6.7	7.0	7.8	Operating Profit	10.2	9.3	.7	8.0	7.0	8.2
.8	3.0	2.6	All Other Expenses (net)	4.6	1.5	1.3	3.0	3.9	.1
5.9	4.1	5.2	Profit Before Taxes	5.7	7.9	-.6	5.0	3.1	8.1
			RATIOS						
2.8	1.9	2.2	Current	3.5	5.9	2.4	8.4	1.1	6.2
1.1	1.1	1.1		1.0	1.2	.9	1.2	.6	1.4
.4	.3	.3		.1	.3	.3	.6	.3	1.1
1.6	1.3	1.4	Quick	1.8	4.8	.8	8.2	.6	1.0
.5	.4	.5		1.0	.8	.4	.7	.3	.8
.1	.1	.2		.1	.2	.0	.4	.2	.3
0 855.1	2 170.7	3 135.8	Sales/Receivables	0 UND	2 155.4	0 UND	7 49.1	16 23.5	11 32.8
7 50.0	8 46.4	16 22.5		0 UND	11 34.1	8 47.3	15 24.3	28 12.9	28 13.2
23 15.8	34 10.7	41 8.8		30 12.3	41 8.8	60 6.1	36 10.1	51 7.1	40 9.1
			Cost of Sales/Inventory						
			Cost of Sales/Payables						
5.0	7.2	5.5	Sales/Working Capital	9.9	7.1	6.6	4.1	18.0	1.9
36.2	78.7	83.1		NM	34.2	NM	72.1	-6.0	8.6
-4.3	-2.6	-3.5		-1.3	-3.9	-2.6	-8.6	-2.5	95.6
4.2	3.2	3.5	EBIT/Interest	5.1	3.5		4.4	1.8	4.7
(87) 1.8	(87) 1.6	(90) 1.7		(12) 2.0	2.1		(14) 2.1	(22) 1.5	(11) 3.4
.8	.8	1.2		1.1	1.4		1.0	1.0	2.7
	13.1		Net Profit + Depr., Dep., Amort./Cur. Mat. L/T/D						
	(10) 1.4								
	.8								
.8	1.1	.9	Fixed/Worth	1.2	.8	.3	1.8	1.1	.2
2.9	5.4	4.2		26.6	5.2	9.0	6.0	4.5	.2
9.8	18.8	14.2		-1.8	9.0	-3.4	339.9	11.7	2.1
1.7	2.3	1.5	Debt/Worth	1.2	2.1	2.4	1.5	2.5	.4
4.8	6.9	5.8		26.7	5.9	8.4	6.3	6.9	1.7
13.0	41.0	15.4		-3.1	12.8	-4.9	348.6	11.6	11.1
31.0	31.2	38.6	% Profit Before Taxes/Tangible Net Worth	21.1	68.0		24.7	30.7	63.0
(83) 12.5	(81) 11.4	(82) 14.9		(11) 6.7	(19) 29.9		(12) 13.8	(22) 9.8	(12) 45.2
.6	-1.5	6.4		3.6	9.8		6.9	.0	10.1
7.4	6.5	6.3	% Profit Before Taxes/Total Assets	14.7	7.2	3.8	9.4	2.9	21.4
2.5	1.8	2.7		1.2	3.9	.0	2.9	1.1	5.0
-.6	-.7	.4		-.5	1.5	-6.6	.4	-.5	4.6
9.4	5.4	15.5	Sales/Net Fixed Assets	1.7	8.1	381.4	7.0	2.2	31.0
1.1	1.0	1.1		.8	1.4	5.5	1.0	.8	23.4
.6	.7	.6		.3	.7	.6	.6	.6	3.8
1.1	1.1	1.1	Sales/Total Assets	1.2	1.1	3.4	1.2	.8	3.0
.7	.7	.7		.4	.7	.9	.7	.6	1.1
.4	.5	.4		.2	.5	.5	.4	.4	.6
12.9	13.8	16.0	% Depr., Dep., Amort./Sales	16.2	25.5		13.9	13.9	
(70) 26.6	(73) 26.1	(69) 29.5		(14) 41.6	(18) 30.4		(12) 30.8	(16) 26.6	
37.3	38.5	41.6		65.3	49.2		32.2	35.9	
1.4	1.0	1.7	% Officers', Directors' Owners' Comp/Sales			3.3			.8
(37) 3.0	(36) 2.9	(38) 4.6				(13) 7.9		(10) 1.7	
7.7	7.0	8.5				8.7		3.6	
1589164M	1591837M	1890382M	Net Sales ($)	9138M	44827M	37761M	115693M	378501M	1304462M
2008087M	1908709M	2346251M	Total Assets ($)	25518M	64842M	48702M	171837M	696541M	1338811M

M = $ thousand   MM = $ million
See Pages viii through xx for Explanation of Ratios and Data

Current Data Sorted by Assets   Comparative Historical Data

0-500M	500M-2MM	2-10MM	10-50MM	50-100MM	100-250MM		4/1/14-3/31/15 ALL	4/1/15-3/31/16 ALL
		2	2	8	2	Type of Statement — Unqualified	21	13
	4	21	1	1		Reviewed	22	22
	2	2	1			Compiled	10	8
	6	2	1		1	Tax Returns	15	13
1	5	5	10	11	5	Other	40	39
	21 (4/1-9/30/18)		71 (10/1/18-3/31/19)					
1	11	15	36	20	9	**NUMBER OF STATEMENTS**	108	95
%	%	%	%	%	%	**ASSETS**	%	%
	12.4	6.4	5.3	5.0		Cash & Equivalents	6.8	6.9
	21.2	15.3	11.0	6.5		Trade Receivables (net)	9.3	9.1
	10.2	11.8	8.3	9.2		Inventory	7.4	7.4
	2.5	.4	4.5	2.1		All Other Current	7.3	3.9
	46.3	34.0	29.1	22.7		Total Current	30.8	27.3
	42.5	43.2	40.6	46.2		Fixed Assets (net)	52.6	48.5
	2.3	2.6	1.4	.3		Intangibles (net)	1.4	.7
	9.0	20.3	29.0	30.8		All Other Non-Current	15.3	23.5
	100.0	100.0	100.0	100.0		Total	100.0	100.0
						LIABILITIES		
	7.9	20.2	4.3	14.0		Notes Payable-Short Term	12.4	10.0
	9.6	4.3	8.4	12.8		Cur. Mat.-L.T.D.	5.2	6.5
	6.4	3.0	1.3	1.3		Trade Payables	2.3	1.4
	.1	.1	.2	.5		Income Taxes Payable	.2	.1
	17.8	11.7	1.7	2.3		All Other Current	4.8	4.2
	41.8	39.3	15.9	30.8		Total Current	24.9	22.2
	31.3	44.9	63.5	43.1		Long-Term Debt	52.0	56.8
	.0	2.2	1.9	1.4		Deferred Taxes	1.1	1.3
	6.1	.5	2.1	5.1		All Other Non-Current	3.8	2.7
	20.8	13.1	16.6	19.6		Net Worth	18.3	16.9
	100.0	100.0	100.0	100.0		Total Liabilities & Net Worth	100.0	100.0
						INCOME DATA		
	100.0	100.0	100.0	100.0		Net Sales	100.0	100.0
						Gross Profit		
	81.4	76.3	87.1	87.0		Operating Expenses	88.2	87.9
	18.6	23.7	12.9	13.0		Operating Profit	11.8	12.1
	.5	11.4	7.7	6.9		All Other Expenses (net)	4.2	5.3
	18.2	12.3	5.2	6.0		Profit Before Taxes	7.6	6.8
						RATIOS		
	2.8	5.1	6.0	9.7			5.3	9.5
	1.6	1.1	3.2	.7		Current	1.4	1.7
	.3	.2	.9	.2			.4	.3
	2.8	5.0	3.5	4.3			3.2	5.9
	.7	.3	1.4	.4		Quick	.9	.9
	.3	.1	.3	.1			.2	.2
	0 UND	5 74.5	3 122.7	2 163.5			4 102.3	1 248.4
	7 55.3	29 12.6	12 29.2	14 26.9		Sales/Receivables	11 32.7	10 36.8
	41 9.0	51 7.2	58 6.3	26 13.9			32 11.5	31 11.7
						Cost of Sales/Inventory		
						Cost of Sales/Payables		
	5.6	2.4	1.0	4.8			2.9	2.3
	40.2	12.1	8.7	NM		Sales/Working Capital	16.0	15.6
	-4.0	-2.1	NM	-1.1			-3.4	-3.6
	13.2	4.9	1.9	2.6			3.5	3.8
	(10) 4.5	(11) 2.4	(28) 1.4	(16) 2.1		EBIT/Interest	(92) 1.8	(86) 2.0
	3.2	1.3	1.1	1.2			1.3	1.4
						Net Profit + Depr., Dep., Amort./Cur. Mat. L/T/D	27.5	
							(10) 1.3	
							.9	
	.0	.0	.1	.1			.1	.3
	1.3	2.2	2.7	1.6		Fixed/Worth	2.8	2.5
	8.0	3.2	5.7	6.0			8.1	6.3
	.7	2.3	4.5	3.3			2.5	2.8
	1.4	5.1	7.4	7.7		Debt/Worth	6.4	5.9
	298.0	12.2	14.6	9.2			14.7	14.0
		37.7	13.8	20.5		% Profit Before Taxes/Tangible Net Worth	25.8	27.0
		(13) 22.5	(34) 11.0	13.7			(95) 15.2	(85) 12.8
		6.9	4.5	6.1			9.5	7.1
	24.9	6.4	2.1	3.7		% Profit Before Taxes/Total Assets	5.0	3.8
	4.2	1.4	1.4	1.7			2.2	2.4
	3.6	.6	.4	.7			1.0	1.1
	999.8	UND	17.1	262.1			27.3	16.8
	5.2	1.4	.7	1.7		Sales/Net Fixed Assets	.8	1.2
	.6	.8	.5	.4			.4	.5
	2.2	.9	.5	.5			.6	.7
	.9	.5	.3	.3		Sales/Total Assets	.4	.4
	.4	.2	.2	.3			.3	.3
		13.3	11.1			% Depr., Dep., Amort./Sales	7.0	3.5
		(10) 38.0	(29) 46.9				(68) 35.4	(59) 25.6
		48.9	71.2				65.7	59.7
						% Officers', Directors' Owners' Comp/Sales	1.9	1.6
							(28) 4.1	(25) 3.3
							7.8	7.2
841M	40901M	47842M	391296M	956409M	617247M	Net Sales ($)	2323396M	2354105M
471M	11478M	83041M	1057831M	1391256M	1383616M	Total Assets ($)	4713550M	4505204M

M = $ thousand   MM = $ million
See Pages viii through xx for Explanation of Ratios and Data

Comparative Historical Data | Current Data Sorted by Sales

11	11	14	Type of Statement						
17	22	27	Unqualified	2	1	8	2	5	6
5	2	5	Reviewed		1		6	6	4
13	8	9	Compiled		1	1	2		1
36	30	37	Tax Returns	3	4		1	1	
4/1/16- 3/31/17 ALL	4/1/17- 3/31/18 ALL	4/1/18- 3/31/19 ALL	Other	7	1	4	7	9	9
					21 (4/1-9/30/18)		**71 (10/1/18-3/31/19)**		
				0-1MM	1-3MM	3-5MM	5-10MM	10-25MM	25MM & OVER
81	73	92	**NUMBER OF STATEMENTS**	12	8	13	18	21	20
%	%	%	**ASSETS**	%	%	%	%	%	%
5.4	5.9	6.7	Cash & Equivalents	11.6	3.8	3.8	6.8	6.2
11.6	13.7	12.8	Trade Receivables (net)	8.2	13.3	7.8	11.1	17.2
5.9	5.5	8.5	Inventory	6.2	2.2	5.5	24.3	3.3
5.4	5.6	3.0	All Other Current	3.5	4.4	3.8	.7	3.4
28.3	30.7	31.0	Total Current	29.6	23.7	20.9	42.9	30.0
48.9	46.2	43.1	Fixed Assets (net)	45.6	53.6	46.0	34.2	43.1
.7	1.1	1.3	Intangibles (net)	2.0	1.8	1.4	.9	.4
22.1	22.0	24.6	All Other Non-Current	22.8	20.9	31.7	22.0	26.5
100.0	100.0	100.0	Total	100.0	100.0	100.0	100.0	100.0
			LIABILITIES					
10.5	7.8	9.9	Notes Payable-Short Term	7.7	5.6	4.6	9.6	12.6
9.7	9.9	8.3	Cur. Mat.-L.T.D.	12.1	6.0	10.3	11.3	4.6
2.9	1.5	2.1	Trade Payables	.2	.8	3.1	4.2	1.8
.1	.1	.2	Income Taxes Payable	.0	.1	.0	.7	.1
3.2	4.2	5.3	All Other Current	2.4	2.4	9.3	3.2	1.1
26.4	23.6	25.8	Total Current	22.4	14.9	27.2	29.0	20.2
51.7	50.2	51.9	Long-Term Debt	31.3	63.6	64.9	44.2	55.9
1.6	1.6	1.6	Deferred Taxes	2.3	2.0	1.0	1.4	1.8
2.8	4.0	2.8	All Other Non-Current	4.1	7.9	.4	2.8	.8
17.5	20.6	17.8	Net Worth	40.0	11.7	6.5	22.6	21.2
100.0	100.0	100.0	Total Liabilties & Net Worth	100.0	100.0	100.0	100.0	100.0
			INCOME DATA					
100.0	100.0	100.0	Net Sales	100.0	100.0	100.0	100.0	100.0
			Gross Profit					
87.0	87.0	84.8	Operating Expenses	61.1	82.0	87.9	91.0	91.4
13.0	13.0	15.2	Operating Profit	38.9	18.0	12.1	9.0	8.6
7.3	6.6	6.9	All Other Expenses (net)	6.6	14.3	9.0	3.5	3.8
5.7	6.3	8.3	Profit Before Taxes	32.3	3.6	3.1	5.5	4.8
			RATIOS					
5.7	6.7	5.9		4.3	5.0	8.1	4.7	11.2
1.3	1.5	2.2	Current	1.6	4.0	2.0	2.2	3.6
.3	.4	.4		.3	.4	.2	.3	1.1
3.9	3.7	4.3		4.1	3.1	3.9	3.2	9.4
.6	.8	1.1	Quick	.3	1.3	.8	.7	3.0
.2	.2	.2		.2	.3	.1	.1	.6
3 136.6	3 117.6	3 144.4		0 UND	2 153.0	2 219.5	2 153.8	10 37.1
13 27.1	14 26.7	14 25.4	Sales/Receivables	0 UND	11 31.9	12 30.4	7 55.3	24 15.2
55 6.6	51 7.2	40 9.1		37 9.8	34 10.6	58 6.3	27 13.3	60 6.1
			Cost of Sales/Inventory					
			Cost of Sales/Payables					
2.0	2.5	2.7		1.5	2.1	4.4	.8	2.7
15.4	8.2	9.5	Sales/Working Capital	5.5	12.5	20.5	13.0	5.8
-2.9	-2.2	-3.2		-2.1	-1.9	-2.5	-2.2	33.6
3.3	3.6	3.4		1.5		2.1	3.4	2.3
(69) 1.7	(62) 1.8	(75) 1.7	EBIT/Interest		(13) 1.2	(19) 2.0	1.6
1.1	1.1	1.2			1.0	1.2	1.3
			Net Profit + Depr., Dep., Amort./Cur. Mat. L/T/D					
.1	.3	.1		.0	1.3	.9	.0	.1
2.8	1.0	2.3	Fixed/Worth	.9	2.9	4.4	.7	.9
6.4	6.1	4.9		3.0	47.2	8.3	5.1	4.1
2.7	2.3	2.6		.6	2.4	4.9	2.6	3.7
5.9	5.3	6.1	Debt/Worth	2.2	8.3	9.7	7.0	5.5
11.1	11.7	9.8		7.3	168.9	34.7	7.9	7.6
20.2	20.0	21.3	% Profit Before Taxes/Tangible	66.0	25.9	13.5	18.8	19.0
(73) 9.7	(69) 11.6	(86) 11.8	Net Worth	30.5	(11) 12.8	(16) 10.3	12.8	10.4
3.9	5.5	5.6		3.0	4.3	2.9	6.2	5.8
3.5	3.2	3.7	% Profit Before Taxes/Total	22.4	1.5	1.7	3.7	2.9
1.5	1.8	1.5	Assets	7.9	1.4	1.0	2.3	1.4
.4	.5	.7		1.9	-.2	.0	1.0	1.2
19.3	12.4	35.2		UND	3.8	14.6	709.3	71.9
.8	1.0	1.3	Sales/Net Fixed Assets	4.6	.5	.7	5.2	2.6
.4	.4	.5		.3	.4	.5	.5	.4
.6	.5	.7		.7	.4	.5	.6	.8
.3	.3	.4	Sales/Total Assets	.3	.3	.3	.4	.6
.2	.2	.2		.2	.1	.2	.3	.3
6.0	4.2	2.2			20.8	23.4		
(47) 45.6	(44) 31.1	(54) 31.2	% Depr., Dep., Amort./Sales	(12) 45.1	(16) 46.0		
67.0	64.3	60.0			65.8	79.7		
1.9	3.3	2.2	% Officers', Directors'					
(15) 4.1	(12) 4.2	(18) 3.2	Owners' Comp/Sales					
7.9	6.7	5.6						
1217742M	1213431M	2054536M	Net Sales ($)	7054M	15676M	53281M	144541M	384503M	1449481M
3362807M	3125621M	3927693M	Total Assets ($)	35161M	35023M	274954M	493591M	951721M	2137243M

M = $ thousand   MM = $ million
See Pages viii through xx for Explanation of Ratios and Data

Current Data Sorted by Assets   Comparative Historical Data

						Type of Statement		
1	2 2 7	3 15 10	12 48 5	5 5	15 5	Unqualified Reviewed Compiled	53 80 24	47 70 24
10 9	8 11	10 29	5 60	23	30	Tax Returns Other	38 119	42 150
	44 (4/1-9/30/18)		286 (10/1/18-3/31/19)				4/1/14- 3/31/15	4/1/15- 3/31/16
0-500M	500M-2MM	2-10MM	10-50MM	50-100MM	100-250MM		ALL	ALL
20	30	67	130	33	50	NUMBER OF STATEMENTS	314	333
%	%	%	%	%	%	ASSETS	%	%
27.4	10.1	8.3	5.9	4.6	5.6	Cash & Equivalents	9.8	8.9
6.3	18.1	12.1	11.3	8.0	10.2	Trade Receivables (net)	10.8	9.3
3.2	12.6	12.6	11.3	9.1	5.7	Inventory	9.4	8.8
5.3	1.9	4.5	1.9	3.4	4.5	All Other Current	2.7	2.9
42.2	42.7	37.5	30.4	25.2	26.0	Total Current	32.7	29.9
39.5	43.2	51.9	56.3	66.9	60.4	Fixed Assets (net)	53.7	59.1
4.8	4.4	3.3	2.0	2.6	.4	Intangibles (net)	1.9	2.4
13.5	9.7	7.2	11.3	5.4	13.2	All Other Non-Current	11.7	8.6
100.0	100.0	100.0	100.0	100.0	100.0	Total	100.0	100.0
						LIABILITIES		
8.1	20.4	15.9	8.6	10.5	9.9	Notes Payable-Short Term	11.8	8.7
5.5	9.6	9.4	11.1	10.4	7.9	Cur. Mat.-L.T.D.	10.0	11.2
1.6	7.9	3.9	4.1	4.8	3.8	Trade Payables	3.5	3.5
.1	.0	.2	.3	.1	.6	Income Taxes Payable	.2	.2
30.4	25.9	11.1	5.4	4.7	3.6	All Other Current	5.6	6.3
45.8	63.8	40.5	29.4	30.5	25.9	Total Current	31.1	29.9
20.6	47.4	33.1	38.4	45.3	45.2	Long-Term Debt	38.8	42.2
.0	.0	.5	.6	1.1	2.4	Deferred Taxes	1.0	1.4
7.3	1.1	7.2	1.9	2.5	1.9	All Other Non-Current	4.8	4.6
26.3	-12.4	18.6	29.6	20.5	24.6	Net Worth	24.3	21.9
100.0	100.0	100.0	100.0	100.0	100.0	Total Liabilities & Net Worth	100.0	100.0
						INCOME DATA		
100.0	100.0	100.0	100.0	100.0	100.0	Net Sales	100.0	100.0
						Gross Profit		
73.2	91.3	86.3	87.9	89.8	79.1	Operating Expenses	84.8	84.3
26.8	8.7	13.7	12.1	10.2	20.9	Operating Profit	15.2	15.7
1.5	4.0	3.7	3.4	2.7	7.9	All Other Expenses (net)	2.8	3.3
25.3	4.7	10.1	8.8	7.5	13.0	Profit Before Taxes	12.5	12.4
						RATIOS		
5.1	2.0	2.0	1.4	1.2	1.3		1.6	1.7
2.2	1.0	1.1	.9	.9	1.1	Current	1.0	1.0
.3	.2	.5	.4	.6	.6		.5	.4
4.8	1.8	1.4	.9	.8	1.0		1.1	1.1
1.9	.4	.4	.4	.5	.6	Quick	.5	.6
.2	.2	.2	.2	.2	.3		.2	.2
0 UND	0 UND	0 999.8	9 39.9	13 27.8	18 19.8		3 127.7	1 626.5
0 UND	16 22.5	11 32.8	25 14.6	28 13.0	27 13.4	Sales/Receivables	23 16.1	22 16.7
1 315.2	41 8.9	39 9.4	47 7.8	53 6.9	56 6.5		42 8.6	44 8.3
						Cost of Sales/Inventory		
						Cost of Sales/Payables		
3.2	8.4	6.6	11.8	21.2	8.3		8.7	10.0
10.8	NM	41.1	-30.5	-67.5	73.7	Sales/Working Capital	-81.5	-97.3
-59.2	-3.1	-3.7	-3.7	-6.0	-4.8		-5.2	-3.9
25.8	12.3	8.9	5.6	3.7	4.3		7.0	7.2
(13) 9.8	(26) 2.8	(60) 2.5	(120) 2.6	(30) 2.7	(41) 3.1	EBIT/Interest	(270) 3.6	(295) 3.3
2.3	.1	.8	1.4	1.9	2.1		1.8	1.6
			2.6				2.5	1.7
		(26) 1.3				Net Profit + Depr., Dep., Amort./Cur. Mat. L/T/D	(48) 1.4	(49) 1.4
		.8					.9	1.0
.1	.2	.9	.8	1.8	1.1		.8	1.1
1.0	2.0	1.8	2.1	3.5	2.9	Fixed/Worth	2.2	2.7
NM	-8.2	30.4	5.4	6.6	4.3		5.2	7.3
.5	1.3	1.5	1.5	2.1	2.2		1.4	1.7
2.3	2.8	3.8	2.9	3.9	3.4	Debt/Worth	3.3	3.5
NM	-10.0	75.8	7.1	6.8	7.4		10.3	12.7
170.2	62.7	54.0	22.5	25.1	24.7	% Profit Before Taxes/Tangible	43.0	42.1
(15) 67.4	(21) 17.4	(51) 22.2	(118) 14.9	(31) 15.5	(49) 14.2	Net Worth	(274) 23.4	(279) 21.3
27.0	5.2	7.2	7.9	9.0	8.3		11.8	10.4
43.3	19.4	12.9	7.3	6.6	7.2	% Profit Before Taxes/Total	10.4	11.2
22.8	4.4	4.1	3.8	3.8	4.0	Assets	5.8	4.9
6.6	-3.9	.2	1.4	2.0	1.8		2.1	1.5
446.7	58.9	10.9	7.0	2.2	4.1		7.8	6.0
8.6	4.7	1.4	1.2	.8	.8	Sales/Net Fixed Assets	1.4	1.2
3.1	.8	.6	.5	.5	.4		.5	.5
4.0	3.8	1.9	2.0	1.4	.8		1.7	1.6
2.2	1.2	.8	.6	.7	.5	Sales/Total Assets	.7	.6
.4	.5	.4	.4	.4	.2		.4	.4
2.1	.5	2.3	4.7	4.9	1.4		3.1	4.4
(10) 12.3	(21) 15.6	(58) 13.4	(115) 19.3	(18) 10.3	(10) 5.8	% Depr., Dep., Amort./Sales	(236) 13.6	(239) 19.0
55.0	65.9	52.5	46.8	21.8	20.8		43.7	42.6
		1.6	1.5				1.3	2.0
		(13) 2.9	(13) 1.8			% Officers', Directors' Owners' Comp/Sales	(52) 4.2	(55) 3.5
		5.6					8.2	5.3
21181M	95698M	612202M	3810805M	2335272M	5106665M	Net Sales ($)	11914645M	14348701M
5107M	34089M	375456M	3347663M	2435869M	7555680M	Total Assets ($)	11993293M	14772512M

© RMA 2019   M = $ thousand   MM = $ million
See Pages viii through xx for Explanation of Ratios and Data

Comparative Historical Data

Current Data Sorted by Sales

			Type of Statement						
45	45	37	Unqualified	1	2	3	2	6	23
56	66	76	Reviewed	3	5	7	17	21	23
23	29	22	Compiled	3	3	4	4	4	4
35	40	33	Tax Returns	8	13	4	4	2	2
155	164	162	Other	19	15	7	24	30	67
4/1/16-3/31/17 ALL	4/1/17-3/31/18 ALL	4/1/18-3/31/19 ALL		44 (4/1-9/30/18) 0-1MM	1-3MM	3-5MM	286 (10/1/18-3/31/19) 5-10MM	10-25MM	25MM & OVER
314	344	330	**NUMBER OF STATEMENTS**	34	38	25	51	63	119
%	%	%	**ASSETS**	%	%	%	%	%	%
9.7	9.7	7.9	Cash & Equivalents	12.7	11.9	8.0	6.2	5.0	7.4
8.8	9.9	11.3	Trade Receivables (net)	9.8	5.5	12.1	15.4	11.2	11.7
8.8	8.7	10.1	Inventory	1.3	6.3	7.4	8.8	7.8	16.2
3.5	2.8	3.2	All Other Current	4.6	3.6	2.2	3.6	2.3	3.2
30.8	31.0	32.5	Total Current	28.4	27.4	29.7	34.0	26.3	38.5
57.6	56.6	54.9	Fixed Assets (net)	54.1	55.0	57.7	52.8	57.5	54.0
2.3	3.2	2.5	Intangibles (net)	5.9	2.2	3.8	.9	2.0	2.2
9.3	9.2	10.1	All Other Non-Current	11.5	15.5	8.9	12.4	14.2	5.2
100.0	100.0	100.0	Total	100.0	100.0	100.0	100.0	100.0	100.0
			LIABILITIES						
10.0	8.9	11.5	Notes Payable-Short Term	12.3	5.3	4.8	10.6	11.2	15.2
10.8	11.5	9.7	Cur. Mat.-L.T.D.	12.2	11.2	9.4	9.2	10.1	8.6
3.9	4.6	4.3	Trade Payables	1.4	1.4	5.8	4.1	3.6	6.1
.3	.2	.3	Income Taxes Payable	.1	.0	1.0	.1	.2	.3
6.2	5.7	9.6	All Other Current	9.9	10.1	15.9	18.1	5.3	6.7
31.3	30.9	35.4	Total Current	35.8	28.0	36.9	42.2	30.4	36.9
39.3	39.9	38.8	Long-Term Debt	41.7	44.2	34.5	44.7	39.0	34.5
1.4	1.0	.8	Deferred Taxes	.2	.4	.3	.4	.7	1.5
4.5	3.9	3.3	All Other Non-Current	4.5	1.8	3.1	2.8	2.8	4.0
23.5	24.3	21.7	Net Worth	17.8	25.6	25.2	9.9	27.1	23.1
100.0	100.0	100.0	Total Liabilties & Net Worth	100.0	100.0	100.0	100.0	100.0	100.0
			INCOME DATA						
100.0	100.0	100.0	Net Sales	100.0	100.0	100.0	100.0	100.0	100.0
			Gross Profit						
85.1	85.6	85.8	Operating Expenses	73.7	82.7	84.4	81.6	85.7	92.5
14.9	14.4	14.2	Operating Profit	26.3	17.3	15.6	18.4	14.3	7.5
4.7	4.4	4.0	All Other Expenses (net)	6.9	5.6	2.6	5.4	4.5	2.1
10.3	10.1	10.2	Profit Before Taxes	19.4	11.7	13.1	13.0	9.8	5.4
			RATIOS						
1.7	1.9	1.6		4.4	3.7	1.8	1.5	1.4	1.4
.9	.9	1.0	Current	1.2	1.2	.7	.9	.7	1.1
.4	.4	.4		.1	.3	.3	.4	.3	.8
1.1	1.2	1.1		3.5	3.1	.9	1.2	1.0	.9
.5	.5	.4	Quick	.5	.6	.4	.5	.3	.5
.2	.2	.2		.1	.2	.2	.2	.2	.3
2 191.7	1 495.0	4 94.4		0 UND	0 UND	1 633.6	2 186.2	11 33.4	13 27.4
18 20.5	21 17.0	21 17.0	Sales/Receivables	0 UND	2 182.2	22 16.8	24 15.5	34 10.7	24 15.3
39 9.3	44 8.3	46 7.9		41 8.8	24 15.2	47 7.7	65 5.6	51 7.2	39 9.4
			Cost of Sales/Inventory						
			Cost of Sales/Payables						
8.4	8.8	9.2		2.9	5.0	9.3	5.9	13.3	14.7
-98.9	-96.4	-150.3	Sales/Working Capital	UND	30.6	-7.0	-119.5	-10.2	121.5
-3.7	-2.9	-3.9		-1.2	-2.9	-2.1	-4.1	-3.4	-15.7
5.8	5.7	6.6		9.7	12.8	8.1	5.3	5.7	6.2
(283) 2.9	(310) 2.7	(290) 2.7	EBIT/Interest	(23) 2.4	(34) 3.5	(20) 2.5	(44) 2.3	(56) 2.5	(113) 2.9
1.2	1.3	1.5		.1	.2	1.6	1.2	1.6	2.0
2.6	2.4	2.6						1.3	2.7
(43) 1.3	(48) 1.4	(40) 1.2	Net Profit + Depr., Dep., Amort./Cur. Mat. L/T/D				(10) .8	(20) 1.3	
.8	.9	.8						.8	.8
1.1	.9	.9		.4	.7	.5	.7	.9	1.2
2.6	2.6	2.3	Fixed/Worth	3.4	1.9	2.7	1.9	2.3	2.4
5.8	6.7	6.7		-16.8	-20.1	7.2	5.1	7.0	4.3
1.4	1.3	1.6		1.8	.8	1.2	1.5	1.2	1.8
3.1	3.2	3.3	Debt/Worth	5.5	2.6	3.4	3.8	3.6	3.0
10.7	10.4	9.2		-18.8	27.0	11.1	7.3	9.7	6.6
32.9	40.1	31.2		87.4	59.5	50.7	26.5	22.7	31.0
(270) 16.5	(299) 17.8	(285) 16.1	% Profit Before Taxes/Tangible Net Worth	(25) 27.0	(27) 22.4	(21) 14.9	(45) 14.8	(58) 15.7	(109) 15.8
4.6	7.1	8.6		5.5	7.6	9.1	4.8	7.6	10.1
9.4	9.1	9.2		20.7	18.5	11.7	10.9	8.1	7.5
3.7	3.7	4.1	% Profit Before Taxes/Total Assets	6.1	2.9	4.6	4.1	4.4	4.0
.5	1.0	1.2		-1.5	-1.6	1.0	.0	1.2	2.3
6.7	6.7	8.7		8.6	4.0	64.9	35.9	8.1	8.3
1.1	1.3	1.3	Sales/Net Fixed Assets	.9	1.0	.6	1.1	.8	2.8
.5	.5	.5		.4	.4	.4	.5	.5	.8
1.6	1.6	1.9		1.1	1.2	.9	1.5	1.1	2.4
.6	.7	.7	Sales/Total Assets	.4	.5	.4	.4	.5	1.3
.4	.4	.4		.2	.3	.3	.3	.3	.6
4.5	4.1	3.3		6.9	15.7	8.8	6.6	5.6	1.0
(216) 19.6	(230) 19.1	(232) 13.3	% Depr., Dep., Amort./Sales	(23) 52.1	(29) 43.3	(22) 39.4	(41) 28.0	(50) 22.7	(67) 4.5
45.1	47.7	46.6		75.7	66.6	65.1	58.8	39.5	7.5
1.2	1.0	1.3						1.3	
(51) 2.6	(47) 2.4	(49) 2.9	% Officers', Directors' Owners' Comp/Sales					(14) 3.0	
3.8	7.2	5.3						6.5	
10824804M	14428358M	11981823M	Net Sales ($)	16552M	69567M	104043M	385227M	1020707M	10385727M
12387322M	14390192M	13753864M	Total Assets ($)	58471M	193712M	280021M	1216662M	2367902M	9637096M

M = $ thousand   MM = $ million
See Pages viii through xx for Explanation of Ratios and Data

Current Data Sorted by Assets   **Comparative Historical Data**

						Type of Statement		
	1	2		3	1	Unqualified	12	6
1	4	1				Reviewed	6	12
2	1	2	1			Compiled	7	9
5	5	14	2		2	Tax Returns	21	16
6	2 (4/1-9/30/18)		46 (10/1/18-3/31/19)	2		Other	27	35
0-500M	500M-2MM	2-10MM	10-50MM	50-100MM	100-250MM		4/1/14-3/31/15 ALL	4/1/15-3/31/16 ALL
9	11	19	6	3		NUMBER OF STATEMENTS	73	78
%	%	%	%	%	%	ASSETS	%	%
	5.9	11.4				Cash & Equivalents	8.1	8.2
	.6	4.9				Trade Receivables (net)	6.9	6.2
	28.7	37.7				Inventory	22.4	24.6
	2.1	.8				All Other Current	1.1	1.1
	37.4	54.7				Total Current	38.5	40.2
	46.2	34.9				Fixed Assets (net)	37.1	31.5
	8.7	6.7				Intangibles (net)	9.7	8.3
	7.8	3.6				All Other Non-Current	14.7	20.1
	100.0	100.0				Total	100.0	100.0
						LIABILITIES		
	25.9	27.3				Notes Payable-Short Term	24.7	18.9
	6.3	11.4				Cur. Mat.-L.T.D.	7.3	14.4
	7.0	6.8				Trade Payables	5.9	7.2
	.0	.1				Income Taxes Payable	.0	.4
	11.2	6.3				All Other Current	10.1	13.7
	50.3	51.8				Total Current	48.0	54.5
	15.6	14.6				Long-Term Debt	33.0	22.6
	.0	.8				Deferred Taxes	.1	.1
	11.2	9.4				All Other Non-Current	7.3	7.2
	22.9	23.4				Net Worth	11.6	15.6
	100.0	100.0				Total Liabilties & Net Worth	100.0	100.0
						INCOME DATA		
	100.0	100.0				Net Sales	100.0	100.0
						Gross Profit		
	86.8	91.0				Operating Expenses	89.4	89.3
	13.2	9.0				Operating Profit	10.6	10.7
	2.6	2.9				All Other Expenses (net)	2.8	3.9
	10.7	6.1				Profit Before Taxes	7.8	6.8
						RATIOS		
	1.5	1.5					2.5	1.7
	.9	1.1				Current	.9	.7
	.2	.6					.3	.2
	1.0	1.4					.9	.7
	.0	.2				Quick	.2	.2
	.0	.1					.0	.0
	0 UND	0 UND					0 UND	0 UND
	0 UND	1 249.0				Sales/Receivables	0 999.8	0 970.4
	1 272.0	13 29.1					20 18.7	5 74.5
						Cost of Sales/Inventory		
						Cost of Sales/Payables		
	10.7	16.3					4.6	8.8
	-18.0	33.7				Sales/Working Capital	-257.8	-18.4
	-3.3	-16.0					-4.3	-4.2
		14.6					12.5	19.6
		3.9				EBIT/Interest	(63) 4.4	(66) 6.8
		.5					1.4	1.6
						Net Profit + Depr., Dep., Amort./Cur. Mat. L/T/D		
	.8	.4					1.0	.5
	2.1	1.2				Fixed/Worth	2.6	1.8
	-2.7	-3.4					-1.9	-3.5
	1.1	.7					2.0	1.3
	2.6	2.6				Debt/Worth	8.3	4.0
	-3.9	-11.5					-6.0	-9.8
		83.3				% Profit Before Taxes/Tangible Net Worth	119.7	99.5
		(14) 55.4					(48) 45.8	(54) 38.4
		29.9					11.9	9.8
	13.9	23.7				% Profit Before Taxes/Total Assets	17.2	16.4
	5.7	9.9					7.4	8.0
	1.1	-2.7					1.6	1.4
	23.2	34.3				Sales/Net Fixed Assets	18.1	21.6
	3.2	14.2					9.0	9.0
	1.2	2.8					2.8	2.7
	2.2	2.3				Sales/Total Assets	2.5	2.5
	1.2	1.9					1.8	1.8
	.5	1.6					1.1	1.0
		1.9				% Depr., Dep., Amort./Sales	4.3	2.1
		(10) 7.4					(38) 7.5	(39) 8.2
		26.4					25.5	28.1
						% Officers', Directors' Owners' Comp/Sales	2.0	2.3
							(23) 4.1	(24) 3.7
							7.8	7.6
13557M	17447M	167130M	167406M	376040M		Net Sales ($)	1114811M	1798446M
3219M	11860M	84447M	116385M	217431M		Total Assets ($)	723592M	1169158M

(In the 100-250MM column, the notation "DATA NOT AVAILABLE" is printed vertically across the Assets and Liabilities sections.)

M = $ thousand   MM = $ million
See Pages viii through xx for Explanation of Ratios and Data

Comparative Historical Data | | | | Current Data Sorted by Sales

			Type of Statement	0-1MM	1-3MM	3-5MM	5-10MM	10-25MM	25MM & OVER
5	3	4	Unqualified		1			2	3
3	8	3	Reviewed		1				
8	5	6	Compiled	3	1	1	1		
15	17	6	Tax Returns	2	1		1	1	
38	21	29	Other	5	4	2	8	7	3
4/1/16- 3/31/17 ALL	4/1/17- 3/31/18 ALL	4/1/18- 3/31/19 ALL		*2 (4/1-9/30/18)*			46 (10/1/18-3/31/19)		
69	54	48	**NUMBER OF STATEMENTS**	10	9	3	10	10	6
%	%	%	**ASSETS**	%	%	%	%	%	%
9.3	9.4	10.7	Cash & Equivalents	7.7			12.6	8.9	
6.0	3.5	3.8	Trade Receivables (net)	.7			4.4	5.3	
23.3	22.6	29.2	Inventory	15.6			42.0	22.9	
3.3	5.2	3.5	All Other Current	.6			.6	8.3	
41.9	40.7	47.2	Total Current	24.6			59.6	45.5	
39.0	42.9	39.8	Fixed Assets (net)	63.2			29.0	46.0	
7.1	6.7	8.1	Intangibles (net)	10.3			8.0	7.0	
11.9	9.7	4.9	All Other Non-Current	1.8			3.5	1.5	
100.0	100.0	100.0	Total	100.0			100.0	100.0	
			LIABILITIES						
20.2	38.5	28.5	Notes Payable-Short Term	36.7			34.5	20.6	
5.7	6.7	9.6	Cur. Mat.-L.T.D.	10.7			3.0	12.2	
5.9	5.2	6.9	Trade Payables	3.2			7.3	5.3	
.1	.2	.1	Income Taxes Payable	.0			.3	.0	
8.0	6.4	7.8	All Other Current	10.4			7.2	8.1	
39.9	57.1	52.8	Total Current	61.0			52.3	46.3	
25.6	25.5	18.8	Long-Term Debt	29.0			14.0	13.5	
.0	.4	.3	Deferred Taxes	.0			.0	1.5	
7.8	3.2	11.8	All Other Non-Current	27.8			15.6	2.2	
26.7	13.9	16.2	Net Worth	-17.8			18.1	36.5	
100.0	100.0	100.0	Total Liabilities & Net Worth	100.0			100.0	100.0	
			INCOME DATA						
100.0	100.0	100.0	Net Sales	100.0			100.0	100.0	
			Gross Profit						
91.1	90.4	89.5	Operating Expenses	79.8			89.7	92.4	
8.9	9.6	10.5	Operating Profit	20.2			10.3	7.6	
2.8	4.2	2.8	All Other Expenses (net)	4.3			2.4	1.8	
6.1	5.4	7.8	Profit Before Taxes	15.9			7.9	5.8	
			RATIOS						
2.7	1.6	2.1		7.8			1.9	1.8	
1.1	.6	1.1	Current	.4			1.1	1.1	
.3	.2	.4		.2			.5	.5	
1.1	.4	1.1		6.7			.6	1.4	
.2	.1	.2	Quick	.1			.2	.3	
.1	.0	.0		.0			.0	.1	
0 UND	0 UND	0 UND		0 UND			0 UND	0 UND	
0 999.8	0 851.6	0 999.8	Sales/Receivables	0 UND			0 879.1	3 111.7	
15 24.7	10 37.7	5 73.7		2 154.0			3 120.1	21 17.7	
			Cost of Sales/Inventory						
			Cost of Sales/Payables						
4.6	7.1	8.0		2.2			15.0	16.3	
50.2	-17.4	263.8	Sales/Working Capital	-12.1			516.8	27.7	
-6.5	-3.7	-9.1		-2.0			-14.1	-8.5	
17.8	7.2	11.8					44.1		
(66) 4.4	(49) 2.7	(43) 3.8	EBIT/Interest				5.9		
1.2	.9	.6					2.0		
			Net Profit + Depr., Dep., Amort./Cur. Mat. L/T/D						
.4	.6	.4		1.8			.2	.5	
1.8	3.4	1.3	Fixed/Worth	2.7			1.1	1.6	
-7.7	-2.2	-2.7		-.4			-.9	NM	
1.0	1.5	.8		1.0			.6	.5	
3.1	4.3	2.6	Debt/Worth	-3.8			3.5	2.2	
-26.0	-5.4	-4.6		-2.1			-9.2	NM	
68.1	79.5	70.3	% Profit Before Taxes/Tangible Net Worth						
(49) 30.6	(35) 16.9	(32) 33.7							
7.6	4.5	14.0							
21.1	11.8	25.9	% Profit Before Taxes/Total Assets	32.5			35.3	21.7	
8.5	5.5	9.3		4.4			17.3	8.2	
1.2	-.2	-.3		-12.8			1.4	-2.7	
16.1	19.9	26.0		6.2			53.9	17.5	
6.9	5.5	10.8	Sales/Net Fixed Assets	1.6			29.6	2.9	
2.6	2.3	2.5		.1			4.0	2.4	
2.4	2.6	2.5		1.8			3.1	2.2	
1.8	1.9	1.9	Sales/Total Assets	1.0			2.1	1.7	
1.1	1.1	1.2		.1			1.8	1.6	
4.6	6.5	3.1	% Depr., Dep., Amort./Sales						
(38) 22.1	(27) 15.7	(25) 13.6							
29.3	23.8	25.3							
2.9	2.9	1.8	% Officers', Directors' Owners' Comp/Sales						
(23) 5.8	(20) 4.9	(11) 8.6							
6.9	11.1	11.3							
1378155M	749384M	741580M	Net Sales ($)	4212M	15948M	13177M	67065M	135103M	506075M
966985M	564938M	433342M	Total Assets ($)	6246M	31036M	5695M	29660M	76111M	284594M

M = $ thousand   MM = $ million
See Pages viii through xx for Explanation of Ratios and Data

Current Data Sorted by Assets | Comparative Historical Data

0-500M	500M-2MM	2-10MM	10-50MM	50-100MM	100-250MM	Type of Statement	4/1/14-3/31/15 ALL	4/1/15-3/31/16 ALL
		3	2	2	1	Unqualified	3	6
	1	1	1			Reviewed	5	5
	1	1	1			Compiled	4	7
	3	3				Tax Returns	7	10
3	4	6	3	1		Other	39	30
	4 (4/1-9/30/18)		29 (10/1/18-3/31/19)					
3	5	14	6	3	2	**NUMBER OF STATEMENTS**	58	58
%	%	%	%	%	%	**ASSETS**	%	%
		9.4				Cash & Equivalents	8.4	11.0
		23.7				Trade Receivables (net)	25.9	23.3
		10.2				Inventory	7.9	7.6
		1.7				All Other Current	3.3	1.9
		45.0				Total Current	45.6	43.9
		35.1				Fixed Assets (net)	36.7	40.8
		11.4				Intangibles (net)	8.3	6.6
		8.5				All Other Non-Current	9.4	8.7
		100.0				Total	100.0	100.0
						LIABILITIES		
		5.7				Notes Payable-Short Term	4.7	7.7
		3.4				Cur. Mat.-L.T.D.	8.7	6.3
		7.4				Trade Payables	12.1	10.6
		.0				Income Taxes Payable	.1	.0
		6.7				All Other Current	5.6	11.0
		23.2				Total Current	31.4	35.6
		24.8				Long-Term Debt	27.3	34.2
		.0				Deferred Taxes	.3	.9
		6.6				All Other Non-Current	10.3	5.6
		45.4				Net Worth	30.6	23.7
		100.0				Total Liabilties & Net Worth	100.0	100.0
						INCOME DATA		
		100.0				Net Sales	100.0	100.0
						Gross Profit		
		88.0				Operating Expenses	93.6	88.1
		12.0				Operating Profit	6.4	11.9
		2.7				All Other Expenses (net)	2.2	1.4
		9.3				Profit Before Taxes	4.3	10.5
						RATIOS		
		6.2					3.3	2.0
		2.5				Current	1.4	1.2
		.8					.9	.7
		4.8					2.5	1.7
		1.2				Quick	.9	.9
		.6					.6	.6
		26 14.3					5 68.7	3 108.5
		39 9.3				Sales/Receivables	58 6.3	51 7.1
		72 5.1					79 4.6	74 4.9
						Cost of Sales/Inventory		
						Cost of Sales/Payables		
		3.4					6.7	6.9
		8.9				Sales/Working Capital	18.4	22.8
		-28.2					-71.3	-16.4
		19.3					16.4	20.2
		(10) 5.7				EBIT/Interest	(53) 3.6	(53) 4.9
		.6					1.0	2.5
							4.5	4.3
						Net Profit + Depr., Dep., Amort./Cur. Mat. L/T/D	(10) 1.6	(10) 2.0
							1.5	1.2
		.3					.4	.5
		.8				Fixed/Worth	1.5	1.3
		NM					NM	-11.0
		.4					.8	.6
		1.7				Debt/Worth	2.2	1.9
		NM					NM	-10.2
		48.4					49.1	51.6
		(11) 4.3				% Profit Before Taxes/Tangible Net Worth	(44) 22.2	(42) 31.4
		-2.6					2.1	8.3
		22.0					20.9	22.0
		5.1				% Profit Before Taxes/Total Assets	5.5	8.3
		-.3					.1	2.6
		18.3					16.5	11.5
		6.8				Sales/Net Fixed Assets	5.2	4.9
		3.2					3.3	2.4
		2.6					2.7	2.2
		1.6				Sales/Total Assets	1.9	1.5
		1.1					1.3	1.1
		3.6					4.2	3.0
		(10) 5.8				% Depr., Dep., Amort./Sales	(36) 7.4	(40) 6.4
		13.1					9.7	15.2
							1.6	2.2
						% Officers', Directors' Owners' Comp/Sales	(11) 4.2	(10) 5.2
							6.1	7.7
4940M	6882M	135697M	244360M	179415M	189354M	Net Sales ($)	1018077M	2242593M
674M	6551M	76322M	156768M	208981M	459487M	Total Assets ($)	768162M	1260373M

M = $ thousand   MM = $ million
See Pages viii through xx for Explanation of Ratios and Data

Comparative Historical Data | Current Data Sorted by Sales

16 4/1/16-3/31/17 ALL	21 4/1/17-3/31/18 ALL	17 4/1/18-3/31/19 ALL	Type of Statement	0-1MM	1-3MM (4 4/1-9/30/18)	3-5MM	5-10MM (29 10/1/18-3/31/19)	10-25MM	25MM & OVER
3	6	8	Unqualified		1		1	1	5
4	4	2	Reviewed					1	1
3	3	2	Compiled					1	1
5	7	4	Tax Returns	2			1	1	
16	21	17	Other	6		3	2	2	4
31	41	33	NUMBER OF STATEMENTS	8	8	3	4	6	11
%	%	%	ASSETS	%	%	%	%	%	%
7.7	10.7	10.7	Cash & Equivalents						8.1
27.1	29.6	18.5	Trade Receivables (net)						27.6
10.7	6.3	10.5	Inventory						14.3
1.6	1.6	1.5	All Other Current						1.4
47.0	48.1	41.2	Total Current						51.5
40.6	36.9	40.1	Fixed Assets (net)						27.4
4.7	8.6	12.5	Intangibles (net)						18.0
7.7	6.4	6.1	All Other Non-Current						3.1
100.0	100.0	100.0	Total						100.0
			LIABILITIES						
8.9	9.5	4.1	Notes Payable-Short Term						4.7
12.0	6.4	14.3	Cur. Mat.-L.T.D.						5.4
10.8	8.7	6.1	Trade Payables						7.5
.0	.0	.0	Income Taxes Payable						.1
5.4	12.6	6.4	All Other Current						8.3
36.9	37.3	30.9	Total Current						25.9
32.2	19.6	27.2	Long-Term Debt						15.2
1.7	.8	.4	Deferred Taxes						.6
3.7	3.5	6.1	All Other Non-Current						3.6
25.6	38.8	35.4	Net Worth						54.6
100.0	100.0	100.0	Total Liabilities & Net Worth						100.0
			INCOME DATA						
100.0	100.0	100.0	Net Sales						100.0
			Gross Profit						
89.8	90.2	84.6	Operating Expenses						88.4
10.2	9.8	15.4	Operating Profit						11.6
3.0	1.1	3.9	All Other Expenses (net)						1.9
7.2	8.7	11.4	Profit Before Taxes						9.8
			RATIOS						
2.6	2.4	3.4	Current						3.5
1.4	1.2	1.7							1.7
.9	.9	.8							1.1
1.8	1.7	2.3	Quick						1.7
1.0	1.0	1.1							1.2
.6	.6	.6							.8
26 13.9	34 10.8	13 27.4	Sales/Receivables						38 9.5
60 6.1	57 6.4	38 9.5							52 7.0
81 4.5	83 4.4	64 5.7							81 4.5
			Cost of Sales/Inventory						
			Cost of Sales/Payables						
5.6	5.8	4.0	Sales/Working Capital						3.6
15.5	40.0	10.9							8.8
-21.9	-32.7	-24.3							46.7
10.1	15.2	25.8	EBIT/Interest						49.6
(27) 5.6	(35) 4.3	(24) 4.6							(10) 11.5
2.0	-.1	1.1							1.8
	4.7		Net Profit + Depr., Dep., Amort./Cur. Mat. L/T/D						
	(10) 1.3								
	.7								
.3	.4	.4	Fixed/Worth						.3
1.5	1.2	1.4							.9
3.1	3.8	-15.6							2.8
1.3	.6	.4	Debt/Worth						.4
2.3	1.6	1.9							1.1
4.2	9.0	-29.5							4.6
39.0	131.2	47.6	% Profit Before Taxes/Tangible Net Worth						65.0
(24) 25.3	(36) 25.2	(24) 23.1							(10) 26.6
4.8	-2.1	2.0							16.3
13.8	25.6	21.3	% Profit Before Taxes/Total Assets						20.3
7.4	6.9	5.4							9.8
1.8	-.5	.5							2.4
13.6	18.4	20.1	Sales/Net Fixed Assets						30.3
4.7	6.1	4.3							4.5
2.4	2.0	1.5							2.1
2.4	3.0	2.4	Sales/Total Assets						2.4
1.5	1.8	1.4							1.3
1.0	1.2	.6							1.0
3.4	2.8	3.2	% Depr., Dep., Amort./Sales						
(21) 4.8	(27) 6.2	(24) 6.0							
20.0	10.8	12.4							
	3.8		% Officers', Directors' Owners' Comp/Sales						
	(10) 5.5								
	10.3								
765279M	1239852M	760648M	Net Sales ($)	4010M	1225M	12572M	31117M	90685M	621039M
645407M	1077511M	908783M	Total Assets ($)	11028M	6049M	4163M	17298M	92217M	778028M

M = $ thousand   MM = $ million
See Pages viii through xx for Explanation of Ratios and Data

Current Data Sorted by Assets

Comparative Historical Data

	0-500M	500M-2MM	2-10MM	10-50MM	50-100MM	100-250MM	Type of Statement		4/1/14-3/31/15 ALL	4/1/15-3/31/16 ALL
		1	2 4	3 1	2	1	Unqualified		7	4
		4	7	1	1	1	Reviewed		7	9
	8	14	2				Compiled		12	11
	3	20	16			3	Tax Returns		31	41
		6 (4/1-9/30/18)		91 (10/1/18-3/31/19)			Other		45	54
	11	39	31	8	3	5	NUMBER OF STATEMENTS		102	119
	%	%	%	%	%	%	ASSETS		%	%
	22.0	22.6	9.0				Cash & Equivalents		14.2	13.1
	13.9	11.9	11.0				Trade Receivables (net)		10.7	8.7
	15.0	6.5	13.7				Inventory		6.6	9.6
	.3	.5	3.2				All Other Current		2.3	1.8
	51.1	41.5	36.9				Total Current		33.8	33.2
	33.1	47.9	50.3				Fixed Assets (net)		50.6	52.0
	4.7	6.3	4.2				Intangibles (net)		5.0	5.8
	11.1	4.3	8.6				All Other Non-Current		10.6	9.0
	100.0	100.0	100.0				Total		100.0	100.0
							LIABILITIES			
	13.1	15.2	9.6				Notes Payable-Short Term		10.1	13.9
	25.5	3.5	5.0				Cur. Mat.-L.T.D.		5.5	4.8
	7.3	5.8	8.0				Trade Payables		5.7	5.6
	.9	.0	.0				Income Taxes Payable		.4	.1
	64.1	15.7	8.7				All Other Current		8.1	9.4
	110.9	40.2	31.3				Total Current		29.9	33.7
	25.3	31.7	36.2				Long-Term Debt		31.8	34.1
	.0	.0	.7				Deferred Taxes		.4	.4
	3.9	4.1	12.2				All Other Non-Current		6.4	8.1
	-40.1	24.0	19.6				Net Worth		31.5	23.8
	100.0	100.0	100.0				Total Liabilties & Net Worth		100.0	100.0
							INCOME DATA			
	100.0	100.0	100.0				Net Sales		100.0	100.0
							Gross Profit			
	89.2	87.1	92.2				Operating Expenses		88.7	89.0
	10.8	12.9	7.8				Operating Profit		11.3	11.0
	.6	3.4	3.7				All Other Expenses (net)		3.1	2.4
	10.3	9.5	4.0				Profit Before Taxes		8.2	8.6
							RATIOS			
	2.9	2.5	2.6						2.6	2.4
	.6	1.3	1.1				Current		1.0	1.0
	.3	.6	.3						.4	.4
	.9	2.1	1.7						2.1	1.8
	.4	1.1	.6				Quick		.6	.6
	.1	.5	.2						.2	.2
	0 UND	0 UND	1 316.3						0 UND	0 UND
	5 71.7	14 27.0	15 24.6				Sales/Receivables		11 33.4	9 38.8
	21 17.1	22 16.8	24 14.9						30 12.2	24 15.0
							Cost of Sales/Inventory			
							Cost of Sales/Payables			
	18.9	8.9	5.3						9.1	10.9
	-10.2	52.0	32.3				Sales/Working Capital		NM	711.8
	-2.2	-11.4	-10.1						-10.4	-6.8
		18.7	10.0						13.4	14.5
	(31)	8.3 (28)	2.9				EBIT/Interest	(88)	4.6 (99)	4.7
		1.0	.7						1.5	1.7
							Net Profit + Depr., Dep.,		4.0	5.8
							Amort./Cur. Mat. L/T/D	(14)	2.0 (14)	2.2
									1.5	1.3
	.3	.9	.9						.7	.8
	-3.1	3.5	5.6				Fixed/Worth		1.9	2.3
	-.9	10.4	999.8						9.9	27.8
	1.5	1.3	1.3						.9	.9
	-11.0	5.5	6.6				Debt/Worth		2.3	2.8
	-2.8	352.0	999.8						15.5	428.1
		104.1	67.0						64.9	86.8
	(31)	44.9 (24)	26.4				% Profit Before Taxes/Tangible Net Worth	(80)	36.0 (90)	40.5
		8.1	-4.1						7.9	11.9
	114.3	29.1	13.6						23.4	21.6
	22.2	8.9	5.9				% Profit Before Taxes/Total Assets		10.6	8.6
	.7	1.7	-.8						1.8	.9
	46.0	16.4	8.1						11.8	13.2
	29.1	4.6	4.3				Sales/Net Fixed Assets		4.2	4.7
	4.7	2.1	2.3						2.1	1.6
	8.2	3.9	2.5						3.0	3.2
	3.2	1.9	2.0				Sales/Total Assets		1.9	1.7
	1.9	1.3	1.1						1.1	1.1
		6.1	6.0						4.8	4.0
	(22)	11.2 (18)	7.8				% Depr., Dep., Amort./Sales	(65)	7.1 (73)	9.5
		17.2	13.3						12.5	15.2
		2.7	1.5						3.0	3.4
	(19)	7.1 (10)	3.3				% Officers', Directors' Owners' Comp/Sales	(44)	5.4 (52)	5.7
		8.0	5.9						9.4	8.9
	9835M	109160M	245041M	236551M	162475M	784673M	Net Sales ($)		982949M	1539250M
	2163M	44045M	137055M	204770M	206684M	732984M	Total Assets ($)		737695M	1313418M

M = $ thousand   MM = $ million
See Pages viii through xx for Explanation of Ratios and Data

Comparative Historical Data   Current Data Sorted by Sales

8	6	8	Type of Statement						
10	6	8	Unqualified				1	2	5
8	9	12	Reviewed		1	1	1	1	4
26	17	24	Compiled	1	3	2	6		
43	46	45	Tax Returns	9	8	3	2	2	
			Other	8	13	9	5	6	4
4/1/16-3/31/17	4/1/17-3/31/18	4/1/18-3/31/19			6 (4/1-9/30/18)		91 (10/1/18-3/31/19)		
ALL	ALL	ALL		0-1MM	1-3MM	3-5MM	5-10MM	10-25MM	25MM & OVER
95	84	97	NUMBER OF STATEMENTS	18	25	15	15	11	13
%	%	%	**ASSETS**	%	%	%	%	%	%
13.1	13.6	15.2	Cash & Equivalents	16.4	18.4	18.6	15.0	14.1	4.8
8.8	13.5	11.7	Trade Receivables (net)	8.0	13.5	9.5	14.6	11.9	12.2
10.8	10.2	9.7	Inventory	5.7	8.4	18.4	9.0	10.1	8.1
2.5	2.7	1.4	All Other Current	.0	.8	1.2	1.2	5.7	.9
35.2	40.0	38.0	Total Current	30.1	41.2	47.8	39.9	41.8	26.0
49.6	46.2	46.3	Fixed Assets (net)	58.8	42.6	42.9	47.4	43.6	40.8
9.2	8.7	8.0	Intangibles (net)	2.6	9.1	2.7	5.5	10.0	21.0
6.0	5.0	7.7	All Other Non-Current	8.5	7.0	6.6	7.2	4.6	12.1
100.0	100.0	100.0	Total	100.0	100.0	100.0	100.0	100.0	100.0
			LIABILITIES						
8.7	13.1	12.5	Notes Payable-Short Term	12.9	7.6	6.9	11.0	32.6	13.1
6.0	6.5	7.2	Cur. Mat.-L.T.D.	15.9	5.1	6.5	4.4	1.3	7.9
6.9	7.4	6.7	Trade Payables	4.4	4.6	3.1	14.5	10.4	6.2
.1	.2	.1	Income Taxes Payable	.0	.4	.0	.0	.0	.0
8.5	11.2	17.6	All Other Current	39.7	17.1	8.8	8.0	18.8	7.8
30.1	38.5	44.1	Total Current	72.8	34.8	25.3	38.0	63.1	35.0
36.9	35.7	33.3	Long-Term Debt	35.2	41.7	32.0	29.2	16.6	34.7
.6	.4	.4	Deferred Taxes	.0	.0	.0	1.4	.0	1.2
9.7	6.8	7.1	All Other Non-Current	.0	3.6	9.5	9.5	6.2	18.7
22.7	18.6	15.1	Net Worth	-8.1	19.8	33.1	22.0	14.1	10.3
100.0	100.0	100.0	Total Liabilties & Net Worth	100.0	100.0	100.0	100.0	100.0	100.0
			INCOME DATA						
100.0	100.0	100.0	Net Sales	100.0	100.0	100.0	100.0	100.0	100.0
			Gross Profit						
87.8	91.5	90.1	Operating Expenses	81.9	87.3	90.8	95.1	95.5	95.6
12.2	8.5	9.9	Operating Profit	18.1	12.7	9.2	4.9	4.5	4.4
3.7	3.3	3.2	All Other Expenses (net)	5.1	5.6	-.1	1.3	.9	3.7
8.5	5.1	6.7	Profit Before Taxes	12.9	7.1	9.4	3.6	3.6	.7
			RATIOS						
2.7	2.2	2.5		1.9	2.9	3.3	1.8	3.2	1.6
1.1	1.3	1.1	Current	.6	1.3	1.8	1.0	.8	1.0
.7	.5	.4		.3	.7	.6	.4	.3	.3
1.6	1.4	1.6		1.4	2.6	2.1	1.7	1.3	1.1
.7	.8	.8	Quick	.5	1.1	.9	.8	.5	.7
.3	.3	.3		.2	.4	.4	.3	.2	.2
0 UND	2 162.5	0 999.8		0 UND	0 UND	0 999.8	0 999.8	1 680.3	16 23.4
14 26.6	17 21.3	15 24.1	Sales/Receivables	7 52.8	13 28.8	14 26.0	12 31.2	19 19.7	26 14.3
27 13.3	35 10.4	26 13.8		26 14.0	30 12.2	20 18.6	21 17.2	45 8.1	39 9.4
			Cost of Sales/Inventory						
			Cost of Sales/Payables						
10.4	6.7	8.3		16.0	8.2	5.3	6.7	5.8	15.9
102.0	43.7	67.2	Sales/Working Capital	-10.0	39.6	15.2	67.2	-20.9	286.9
-11.6	-10.4	-9.8		-2.1	-13.5	-11.6	-14.8	-4.9	-4.7
12.7	12.2	13.3		21.5	14.1	16.3	10.7	61.4	2.9
(80) 4.9	(71) 4.2	(83) 3.3	EBIT/Interest	(10) 9.5	(21) 2.2	(13) 3.9	2.9	4.8	.4
1.3	.9	.7		.1	.9	.5	1.0	.7	-1.1
3.9	5.4		Net Profit + Depr., Dep.,						
(15) 2.2	(10) 1.9		Amort./Cur. Mat. L/T/D						
1.6	1.6								
1.1	.8	.9		1.0	1.2	.4	.8	.4	2.3
2.8	2.8	4.9	Fixed/Worth	4.4	6.2	1.0	3.5	7.1	6.8
-3.9	NM	-66.5		-2.5	-16.3	1.5	6.7	19.6	-1.4
1.2	1.4	1.7		.9	3.0	1.1	1.6	3.0	2.8
3.0	5.9	6.6	Debt/Worth	4.9	10.4	2.3	6.7	7.4	14.5
-7.7	NM	-60.5		-5.3	-11.7	3.4	16.6	28.3	-3.2
62.8	92.7	94.7	% Profit Before Taxes/Tangible	36.0	121.4	98.8	117.2		
(67) 27.7	(63) 33.1	(71) 28.4	Net Worth	(11) 17.6	(17) 44.8	(13) 47.5	(14) 46.1		
11.0	9.8	-5.2		1.4	-4.3	9.0	-1.8		
24.3	19.1	22.6	% Profit Before Taxes/Total	37.2	35.5	29.1	14.1	24.3	7.7
9.6	7.8	7.1	Assets	10.0	8.1	13.6	6.3	14.8	-3.9
.8	.1	.5		.6	-.2	4.7	.0	-1.6	-6.8
18.3	15.2	14.2		12.9	16.6	17.5	12.4	11.1	16.8
3.9	4.5	4.7	Sales/Net Fixed Assets	3.0	3.8	7.3	5.5	5.6	4.6
2.2	1.8	2.2		.1	2.0	2.8	3.7	2.4	1.8
2.9	2.9	2.7		3.2	2.0	5.6	3.2	3.2	2.0
1.9	1.7	1.8	Sales/Total Assets	1.6	1.7	2.0	2.5	2.2	1.0
1.0	1.0	1.0		.1	1.0	1.2	2.0	1.7	.7
2.7	4.3	6.0		3.5	6.1		6.8		
(63) 8.4	(45) 9.5	(51) 9.7	% Depr., Dep., Amort./Sales	(10) 14.5	(15) 12.3		(10) 8.2		
13.4	18.8	16.0		25.0	18.6		10.4		
3.0	1.9	2.7			6.4				
(39) 6.0	(29) 4.9	(35) 5.5	% Officers', Directors'		(11) 7.1				
11.1	7.9	7.9	Owners' Comp/Sales		8.0				
1968181M	1371714M	1547735M	Net Sales ($)	6639M	49569M	60214M	106234M	169578M	1155501M
1571220M	1139223M	1327701M	Total Assets ($)	20432M	36610M	46950M	43755M	96747M	1083207M

M = $ thousand   MM = $ million
See Pages viii through xx for Explanation of Ratios and Data

Current Data Sorted by Assets   Comparative Historical Data

						Type of Statement		
		2		1	1	2	Unqualified		
	1		3	2	2		Reviewed	8	8
2	4		5	1			Compiled	6	12
7	19		6	1			Tax Returns	20	17
5	12		13	7	2	1	Other	46	46
	6 (4/1-9/30/18)			93 (10/1/18-3/31/19)				39	40
0-500M	500M-2MM		2-10MM	10-50MM	50-100MM	100-250MM		4/1/14-3/31/15 ALL	4/1/15-3/31/16 ALL
14	38		27	12	5	3	NUMBER OF STATEMENTS	119	123
%	%		%	%	%	%	**ASSETS**	%	%
42.8	11.5		7.7	6.5			Cash & Equivalents	10.2	12.1
9.2	4.5		7.1	4.3			Trade Receivables (net)	9.3	6.7
9.8	12.5		10.9	7.0			Inventory	10.9	11.5
.2	.4		4.3	7.3			All Other Current	1.6	1.6
62.0	28.8		30.0	25.2			Total Current	32.0	32.0
22.7	60.2		57.7	70.0			Fixed Assets (net)	56.7	54.7
6.8	6.3		5.7	2.6			Intangibles (net)	2.8	5.3
8.5	4.7		6.7	2.2			All Other Non-Current	8.6	8.1
100.0	100.0		100.0	100.0			Total	100.0	100.0
							LIABILITIES		
1.5	12.7		17.2	26.2			Notes Payable-Short Term	14.2	15.6
3.5	6.6		9.5	6.1			Cur. Mat.-L.T.D.	6.8	7.4
2.2	5.5		5.1	2.5			Trade Payables	5.4	4.4
.0	.2		.0	.0			Income Taxes Payable	.2	.1
26.4	10.9		6.3	6.4			All Other Current	5.3	6.1
33.7	35.8		38.2	41.3			Total Current	32.0	33.5
22.6	43.1		20.4	31.8			Long-Term Debt	42.3	43.3
.0	.0		.9	.0			Deferred Taxes	.4	.2
8.2	5.4		5.4	2.2			All Other Non-Current	6.2	8.7
35.5	15.7		35.1	24.7			Net Worth	19.2	14.3
100.0	100.0		100.0	100.0			Total Liabilties & Net Worth	100.0	100.0
							INCOME DATA		
100.0	100.0		100.0	100.0			Net Sales	100.0	100.0
							Gross Profit		
97.6	86.1		87.8	84.7			Operating Expenses	83.2	81.5
2.4	13.9		12.2	15.3			Operating Profit	16.8	18.5
-.5	6.4		4.0	9.9			All Other Expenses (net)	5.2	4.4
2.9	7.5		8.1	5.4			Profit Before Taxes	11.6	14.1
							RATIOS		
8.0	2.1		1.2	1.0				2.7	2.0
2.8	.8		.8	.6			Current	1.2	1.1
1.5	.1		.3	.1				.5	.4
4.3	1.3		1.1	.6				1.7	1.6
2.3	.2		.3	.2			Quick	.7	.7
1.4	.1		.0	.1				.2	.2
0 UND	0 UND		0 UND	2 240.1				0 UND	0 UND
5 68.2	2 179.6		7 54.9	26 14.2			Sales/Receivables	9 39.7	7 54.4
10 37.0	15 25.0		38 9.5	28 12.9				41 9.0	25 14.8
							Cost of Sales/Inventory		
							Cost of Sales/Payables		
4.9	9.4		27.3	58.8				6.1	8.6
8.0	-24.0		-17.1	-15.1			Sales/Working Capital	57.7	29.5
31.1	-3.1		-7.0	-1.8				-10.8	-7.2
14.3	6.9		24.0	5.0				9.7	14.1
(10) 4.6	(31) 3.1		(23) 4.3	(11) 2.6			EBIT/Interest	(95) 4.0	(96) 3.9
1.4	1.0		1.7	.9				1.4	1.8
							Net Profit + Depr., Dep., Amort./Cur. Mat. L/T/D		
.2	1.1		1.2	1.2				.8	.8
.6	2.8		2.4	2.3			Fixed/Worth	1.9	2.3
-10.8	-5.9		8.4	698.1				12.6	29.9
.5	1.3		1.1	1.4				.9	.8
1.3	3.7		3.4	3.5			Debt/Worth	2.3	3.3
-61.1	-7.6		44.8	751.2				20.3	428.1
45.6	53.4		57.6	24.9				45.5	52.0
(10) 24.6	(26) 20.5		(23) 25.0	(10) 10.2			% Profit Before Taxes/Tangible Net Worth	(93) 21.9	(93) 26.4
-1.0	-.1		11.2	-12.6				7.8	9.3
18.8	15.0		21.5	6.2				17.9	17.4
14.0	4.9		7.4	3.2			% Profit Before Taxes/Total Assets	6.3	7.9
-2.6	.0		2.6	-1.5				1.0	2.7
38.1	8.2		10.2	3.0				8.8	13.7
18.6	2.8		2.1	1.3			Sales/Net Fixed Assets	2.9	2.7
10.2	.8		1.1	.5				.8	.7
4.3	2.4		1.7	1.5				2.3	2.4
3.2	1.7		1.3	.9			Sales/Total Assets	1.4	1.2
2.1	.4		.9	.5				.4	.5
	7.1		9.2					4.5	5.4
	(25) 11.5		(20) 14.8				% Depr., Dep., Amort./Sales	(79) 11.6	(78) 10.0
	25.3		22.0					17.8	20.2
	2.5		2.0					2.3	2.7
	(16) 5.1		(12) 3.9				% Officers', Directors' Owners' Comp/Sales	(42) 5.5	(45) 5.9
	8.5		5.8					7.2	9.7
12672M	76412M		186627M	182108M	366402M	214065M	Net Sales ($)	1539688M	1458866M
3877M	42115M		150035M	174483M	398204M	589706M	Total Assets ($)	1485069M	1653632M

M = $ thousand   MM = $ million
See Pages viii through xx for Explanation of Ratios and Data

Comparative Historical Data | Current Data Sorted by Sales

			Type of Statement						
9	7	6	Unqualified	1	1		1	1	2
7	11	8	Reviewed		1		2	2	3
10	10	12	Compiled	1	4	4	1	2	
45	41	33	Tax Returns	16	9	4	3	1	
54	39	40	Other	6	11	3	9	8	3
4/1/16- 3/31/17	4/1/17- 3/31/18	4/1/18- 3/31/19		6 (4/1-9/30/18)		93 (10/1/18-3/31/19)			
ALL	ALL	ALL		0-1MM	1-3MM	3-5MM	5-10MM	10-25MM	25MM & OVER
125	108	99	NUMBER OF STATEMENTS	24	26	11	16	14	8
%	%	%	ASSETS	%	%	%	%	%	%
10.8	12.8	13.7	Cash & Equivalents	17.3	13.2	22.3	8.5	11.2	
6.5	7.1	5.9	Trade Receivables (net)	1.4	8.2	8.0	5.7	8.4	
11.7	12.1	11.1	Inventory	5.3	17.8	9.6	5.2	15.2	
1.7	1.7	2.3	All Other Current	.1	.2	.6	6.7	7.2	
30.7	33.7	33.0	Total Current	24.1	39.4	40.6	26.2	41.9	
57.9	52.9	55.3	Fixed Assets (net)	62.5	49.7	52.9	66.9	40.4	
3.6	7.2	5.4	Intangibles (net)	4.7	7.7	3.8	5.5	5.1	
7.7	6.1	6.3	All Other Non-Current	8.7	3.2	2.7	1.4	12.6	
100.0	100.0	100.0	Total	100.0	100.0	100.0	100.0	100.0	
			LIABILITIES						
18.2	14.7	14.4	Notes Payable-Short Term	4.7	16.1	13.5	14.7	24.6	
6.1	6.0	6.5	Cur. Mat.-L.T.D.	6.5	3.6	10.4	12.5	5.1	
4.3	5.1	4.6	Trade Payables	2.7	4.9	3.6	5.1	6.9	
.0	.1	.1	Income Taxes Payable	.0	.0	.6	.0	.0	
7.5	7.3	10.6	All Other Current	23.4	8.3	5.7	5.1	7.2	
36.1	33.3	36.2	Total Current	37.3	33.0	33.8	37.4	43.7	
51.1	35.9	31.4	Long-Term Debt	40.9	40.4	24.7	26.7	15.6	
.2	.5	.3	Deferred Taxes	.0	.0	.0	.8	.8	
6.8	7.0	5.0	All Other Non-Current	3.5	3.4	17.9	5.0	3.0	
5.9	23.4	27.1	Net Worth	18.3	23.2	23.6	30.2	37.0	
100.0	100.0	100.0	Total Liabilties & Net Worth	100.0	100.0	100.0	100.0	100.0	
			INCOME DATA						
100.0	100.0	100.0	Net Sales	100.0	100.0	100.0	100.0	100.0	
			Gross Profit						
81.4	87.3	87.4	Operating Expenses	80.7	90.7	87.6	90.6	91.5	
18.6	12.7	12.6	Operating Profit	19.3	9.3	12.4	9.4	8.5	
5.2	3.9	5.1	All Other Expenses (net)	11.9	4.8	1.0	2.1	1.3	
13.4	8.8	7.5	Profit Before Taxes	7.5	4.6	11.4	7.3	7.1	
			RATIOS						
1.9	2.7	2.3		2.1	4.0	4.6	1.3	1.5	
.9	1.1	.9	Current	.2	1.0	.9	.6	1.1	
.4	.4	.2		.0	.3	.4	.3	.7	
1.3	1.7	1.5		1.6	2.0	3.3	1.0	1.1	
.5	.6	.5	Quick	.1	.5	.8	.5	.7	
.1	.2	.1		.0	.0	.1	.1	.1	
0 UND	0 UND	0 UND		0 UND	0 UND	0 999.8	0 UND	0 UND	
4 89.0	11 34.3	6 58.0	Sales/Receivables	0 UND	6 56.7	16 23.3	10 38.0	19 19.5	
20 18.1	27 13.3	27 13.6		7 54.5	22 16.3	29 12.7	41 8.9	39 9.3	
			Cost of Sales/Inventory						
			Cost of Sales/Payables						
8.0	7.9	8.8		9.3	5.9	4.9	61.7	18.9	
-30.6	220.8	-23.3	Sales/Working Capital	-5.9	NM	-21.7	-18.5	54.0	
-7.1	-7.7	-6.7		-.9	-11.9	-4.2	-7.0	-10.3	
11.1	12.2	13.4		4.5	12.3	14.3	11.6	68.5	
(100) 3.8	(91) 4.2	(81) 3.7	EBIT/Interest	(12) 2.8	(24) 3.3	(10) 5.4	3.0	(12) 3.7	
1.4	1.6	1.5		1.0	1.2	2.5	1.7	1.1	
			Net Profit + Depr., Dep., Amort./Cur. Mat. L/T/D						
1.0	.8	1.0		.6	.8	1.2	1.5	.5	
2.8	2.1	2.2	Fixed/Worth	6.1	2.1	3.0	2.8	1.4	
-12.3	UND	14.2		-3.9	-13.8	8.4	72.2	4.9	
1.2	.8	1.1		1.4	1.0	1.3	1.3	.7	
4.1	3.1	3.0	Debt/Worth	6.9	2.3	2.3	3.8	2.7	
-14.8	UND	100.0		6.9	-63.0	22.3	93.0	28.8	
62.2	54.9	44.0	% Profit Before Taxes/Tangible Net Worth	35.4	52.8		45.0	43.3	
(87) 29.5	(82) 30.2	(77) 20.3		(15) 16.8	(19) 27.9		(13) 11.7	(13) 22.5	
10.0	12.3	5.3		-11.3	2.3		6.8	4.9	
22.1	18.3	15.7	% Profit Before Taxes/Total Assets	13.1	15.5	23.8	15.1	16.4	
7.8	7.7	5.5		2.1	5.5	17.1	5.1	5.5	
1.9	2.3	1.2		-4.0	.9	5.5	1.5	1.6	
10.7	15.6	11.9		10.2	18.0	8.9	8.1	26.1	
2.8	3.2	2.9	Sales/Net Fixed Assets	.7	5.0	2.9	1.5	7.9	
.9	1.4	1.1		.1	2.2	2.0	1.1	1.5	
2.6	2.4	2.2		1.7	3.0	2.4	2.7	1.8	
1.5	1.5	1.4	Sales/Total Assets	.4	2.1	1.8	1.1	1.4	
.6	.9	.9		.1	1.5	1.3	.9	.9	
5.7	6.9	7.5		5.9	5.4		9.4		
(67) 13.9	(67) 11.5	(63) 13.8	% Depr., Dep., Amort./Sales	(22) 13.9	(11) 9.0		(13) 15.1		
19.7	21.3	22.7		25.1	29.3		22.7		
2.5	2.4	2.2			3.8	2.0			
(48) 4.9	(48) 4.5	(37) 4.3	% Officers', Directors' Owners' Comp/Sales	(12) 6.6	(10) 3.0				
9.5	8.3	7.9			10.4	4.5			
2183240M	1131045M	1038286M	Net Sales ($)	10591M	43176M	44938M	110531M	194374M	634676M
1573232M	1259331M	1358420M	Total Assets ($)	34960M	40039M	34749M	95914M	332714M	820044M

© RMA 2019   M = $ thousand   MM = $ million
See Pages viii through xx for Explanation of Ratios and Data

Current Data Sorted by Assets

Comparative Historical Data

						Type of Statement		
			1	7	1	13		
			8	8	1		Unqualified	19	25
			6				Reviewed	11	15
1			9	3			Compiled	15	8
9	10		20	13	7	13	Tax Returns	46	54
4	8						Other	73	78
	13 (4/1-9/30/18)			121 (10/1/18-3/31/19)				4/1/14- 3/31/15	4/1/15- 3/31/16
0-500M	500M-2MM	2-10MM	10-50MM	50-100MM	100-250MM		ALL	ALL
14	18	36	31	9	26	NUMBER OF STATEMENTS	164	180
%	%	%	%	%	%	ASSETS	%	%
28.5	18.6	10.5	6.5		3.8	Cash & Equivalents	14.6	12.5
10.1	8.1	9.8	6.7		2.2	Trade Receivables (net)	9.7	6.4
.0	3.4	6.2	5.1		1.1	Inventory	2.7	3.3
4.5	3.7	3.2	2.2		2.0	All Other Current	4.3	1.5
43.0	33.8	29.7	20.5		9.1	Total Current	31.2	23.7
46.7	62.2	63.1	72.7		82.5	Fixed Assets (net)	56.9	66.4
2.1	2.4	2.1	.8		3.2	Intangibles (net)	3.4	3.0
8.2	1.6	5.2	6.1		5.2	All Other Non-Current	8.5	6.8
100.0	100.0	100.0	100.0		100.0	Total	100.0	100.0
						LIABILITIES		
1.7	8.8	4.1	1.9		9.0	Notes Payable-Short Term	6.1	4.4
30.3	9.4	10.3	7.3		3.0	Cur. Mat.-L.T.D.	7.9	8.6
6.3	2.0	8.1	3.0		3.4	Trade Payables	5.5	2.8
.0	.0	.1	.0		.4	Income Taxes Payable	.0	.1
17.3	1.9	3.1	2.1		5.8	All Other Current	8.4	10.1
55.5	22.0	25.7	14.2		21.7	Total Current	28.0	26.1
101.0	57.5	44.6	37.9		43.3	Long-Term Debt	47.5	51.5
.0	.0	.3	2.0		2.0	Deferred Taxes	.7	.8
.0	.7	3.6	1.4		.5	All Other Non-Current	5.7	4.9
-56.6	19.7	25.8	44.4		32.5	Net Worth	18.1	16.8
100.0	100.0	100.0	100.0		100.0	Total Liabilties & Net Worth	100.0	100.0
						INCOME DATA		
100.0	100.0	100.0	100.0		100.0	Net Sales	100.0	100.0
						Gross Profit		
80.8	81.4	75.8	75.0		66.6	Operating Expenses	71.1	72.1
19.2	18.6	24.2	25.0		33.4	Operating Profit	28.9	27.9
5.2	6.4	5.5	7.5		22.9	All Other Expenses (net)	8.0	6.7
14.0	12.2	18.7	17.5		10.5	Profit Before Taxes	20.9	21.2
						RATIOS		
1.6	9.1	2.9	3.1		1.7		3.1	2.1
.7	1.3	.8	1.5		.8	Current	1.1	1.0
.2	.1	.4	.5		.3		.5	.4
1.3	4.5	1.3	2.1		1.2		2.1	1.8
.6	(17) 1.1	.7	.9		.5	Quick	.9	.7
.2	.1	.3	.4		.3		.3	.3
0 UND	0 UND	0 UND	6 60.6		6 63.3		0 UND	0 UND
0 UND	0 UND	38 9.6	21 17.6		34 10.7	Sales/Receivables	11 33.2	3 137.3
4 87.5	32 11.5	57 6.4	41 8.9		47 7.7		44 8.3	36 10.2
						Cost of Sales/Inventory		
						Cost of Sales/Payables		
5.6	3.0	4.8	3.3		8.8		3.6	4.7
-30.9	14.7	-26.5	23.8		-5.8	Sales/Working Capital	50.7	-291.0
-2.6	-1.8	-3.6	-6.9		-2.2		-4.3	-4.1
20.5	7.7	9.4	8.2		4.5		11.0	11.2
(10) 6.2	(12) 1.0	(30) 4.8	(26) 4.1		(10) 2.9	EBIT/Interest	(125) 5.3	(135) 4.3
2.1	-2.2	2.0	2.5		1.6		1.9	1.7
						Net Profit + Depr., Dep., Amort./Cur. Mat. L/T/D	4.4	8.0
							(12) 2.6	(16) 2.0
							1.2	1.0
.2	.7	1.2	1.2		2.6		.8	1.2
1.9	4.4	2.0	1.7		3.5	Fixed/Worth	2.2	2.5
-.4	12.5	12.0	2.8		4.5		25.7	20.1
1.5	.9	1.1	.7		1.8		.7	1.0
NM	3.4	2.7	1.1		3.1	Debt/Worth	2.6	2.9
-1.5	11.9	27.5	2.4		4.3		95.8	59.5
	72.9	69.3	27.5		16.3	% Profit Before Taxes/Tangible Net Worth	45.5	66.7
(15)	14.7	(30) 31.5	9.7	(24)	4.7		(127) 20.2	(140) 25.0
	-.3	19.3	4.8		1.6		7.6	11.8
57.3	12.1	20.1	8.0		5.6	% Profit Before Taxes/Total Assets	16.3	16.9
24.7	1.5	9.8	4.3		1.0		6.2	6.3
-1.1	-.9	2.7	2.4		.3		1.5	.9
UND	3.1	2.5	2.5		.3		5.9	2.6
3.8	.6	1.1	.3		.2	Sales/Net Fixed Assets	.9	.7
1.4	.2	.4	.2		.1		.2	.3
3.7	1.4	1.3	1.2		.3		1.8	1.1
1.5	.5	.6	.3		.1	Sales/Total Assets	.5	.5
.6	.1	.3	.2		.1		.2	.2
		13.1	8.7		11.9	% Depr., Dep., Amort./Sales	5.0	7.2
	(27)	23.6	(26) 28.6	(14)	23.8		(120) 15.8	(137) 23.5
		43.2	41.9		33.3		33.8	42.9
						% Officers', Directors' Owners' Comp/Sales	2.7	2.2
							(27) 4.7	(20) 5.1
							9.6	8.9
10895M	18703M	144853M	573527M	227890M	1282721M	Net Sales ($)	2130487M	2286608M
3229M	21939M	175450M	777523M	601697M	4661748M	Total Assets ($)	4358804M	4858415M

Comparative Historical Data | | | | Current Data Sorted by Sales

			Type of Statement	0-1MM	1-3MM	3-5MM	5-10MM	10-25MM	25MM & OVER
15	18	22	Unqualified			1	4	5	12
13	7	9	Reviewed		1	3		1	4
9	7	7	Compiled	2	2	1	2		
41	39	31	Tax Returns	17	4	5	4	1	
89	88	65	Other	9	15	9	12	6	14
4/1/16-3/31/17 ALL	4/1/17-3/31/18 ALL	4/1/18-3/31/19 ALL			13 (4/1-9/30/18)		121 (10/1/18-3/31/19)		
167	159	134	**NUMBER OF STATEMENTS**	28	22	19	22	13	30
%	%	%	**ASSETS**	%	%	%	%	%	%
9.6	13.0	10.8	Cash & Equivalents	20.7	11.9	7.3	11.5	4.6	5.3
6.2	7.3	7.0	Trade Receivables (net)	2.9	7.1	8.8	9.2	8.5	7.4
3.8	3.6	3.7	Inventory	.1	4.1	7.7	4.7	.9	4.5
2.8	2.6	2.7	All Other Current	1.5	5.5	2.3	2.2	2.3	2.7
22.3	26.5	24.2	Total Current	25.3	28.6	26.1	27.6	16.3	19.9
66.8	63.4	68.8	Fixed Assets (net)	69.0	59.6	69.3	69.7	75.2	71.6
3.1	3.5	1.9	Intangibles (net)	2.2	2.7	1.4	.5	2.1	2.2
7.8	6.5	5.0	All Other Non-Current	3.5	9.1	3.1	2.2	6.3	6.3
100.0	100.0	100.0	Total	100.0	100.0	100.0	100.0	100.0	100.0
			LIABILITIES						
4.5	3.8	4.6	Notes Payable-Short Term	5.2	.4	3.4	4.2	6.2	7.7
8.0	7.9	9.8	Cur. Mat.-L.T.D.	20.2	12.1	8.4	4.8	6.2	4.8
3.5	3.9	4.6	Trade Payables	1.9	8.0	3.2	4.9	5.3	4.9
.0	.0	.1	Income Taxes Payable	.0	.1	.0	.0	.0	.4
9.7	7.8	4.6	All Other Current	4.0	4.2	2.0	6.6	5.5	5.2
25.8	23.4	23.8	Total Current	31.3	24.8	17.0	20.6	23.1	22.9
42.4	41.7	50.7	Long-Term Debt	78.9	58.3	44.4	39.7	44.6	33.3
.9	.8	1.3	Deferred Taxes	.0	.5	1.9	.7	2.7	2.4
3.9	4.5	1.5	All Other Non-Current	.9	3.1	.4	2.2	.3	1.7
27.1	29.6	22.8	Net Worth	-11.2	13.3	36.3	36.8	29.3	39.8
100.0	100.0	100.0	Total Liabilities & Net Worth	100.0	100.0	100.0	100.0	100.0	100.0
			INCOME DATA						
100.0	100.0	100.0	Net Sales	100.0	100.0	100.0	100.0	100.0	100.0
			Gross Profit						
72.8	68.0	74.6	Operating Expenses	69.8	80.5	73.2	71.3	66.0	81.9
27.2	32.0	25.4	Operating Profit	30.2	19.5	26.8	28.7	34.0	18.1
7.8	8.2	10.1	All Other Expenses (net)	9.4	8.3	3.7	12.2	20.6	10.0
19.4	23.7	15.3	Profit Before Taxes	20.9	11.3	23.2	16.5	13.4	8.1
			RATIOS						
2.4	2.7	2.4	Current	2.4	3.9	2.4	5.0	2.0	1.9
.9	1.1	1.0		.9	.7	1.0	1.5	.7	1.1
.3	.4	.4		.1	.3	.5	.5	.6	.7
1.6	2.2	1.5	Quick	1.7	2.0	1.2	3.9	1.5	1.5
.6	.9 (133)	.8		.6 (21)	.7	.8	1.0	.6	.8
.2	.3	.3		.1	.3	.4	.4	.3	.3
0 UND	0 UND	0 UND	Sales/Receivables	0 UND	0 UND	1 424.5	1 319.3	5 68.5	15 24.6
6 66.1	13 28.7	19 18.8		0 UND	12 29.9	32 11.3	29 12.7	37 9.9	36 10.0
45 8.2	38 9.5	48 7.6		0 UND	42 8.7	56 6.5	57 6.4	83 4.4	47 7.8
			Cost of Sales/Inventory						
			Cost of Sales/Payables						
5.1	5.0	4.9	Sales/Working Capital	3.2	4.4	3.3	2.8	4.8	8.6
-34.4	42.6	NM		NM	-12.5	-69.4	6.3	-14.4	201.5
-2.6	-4.6	-3.3		-2.0	-1.7	-5.7	-5.9	-2.8	-6.1
9.1	12.4	8.5	EBIT/Interest	8.7	8.9	8.9	8.2		9.1
(136) 4.3	(122) 4.8	(94) 3.8		(16) 3.0	(18) 2.6	4.6	(14) 3.4	(23) 4.5	4.5
1.4	2.3	2.0		1.0	-.3	3.2	2.0		2.2
3.9		3.4	Net Profit + Depr., Dep., Amort./Cur. Mat. L/T/D						
(10) 2.0		(17) 2.1							
1.6		1.4							
1.2	1.0	1.2	Fixed/Worth	1.1	1.1	1.4	.9	2.0	1.3
2.3	2.0	2.4		4.5	3.6	1.7	1.8	3.6	2.3
8.7	4.8	5.0		13.1	20.7	3.0	3.1	6.6	3.7
.8	.9	1.0	Debt/Worth	1.3	1.5	.8	.4	1.7	.9
2.2	1.9	2.3		4.4	4.7	1.4	1.8	3.1	1.8
27.6	6.1	8.5		NM	44.3	2.4	NM	6.4	3.1
51.4	55.1	37.8	% Profit Before Taxes/Tangible Net Worth	68.2	75.9	52.9	30.7	35.1	17.5
(135) 17.7	(134) 24.8	(115) 13.4		(21) 14.9	(18) 26.1	(18) 19.2	(17) 8.9	(12) 12.1	(29) 12.7
6.2	8.3	4.3		.4	3.4	9.3	4.7	.0	3.6
13.2	20.9	12.3	% Profit Before Taxes/Total Assets	27.1	17.0	11.6	11.4	10.9	9.8
5.4	7.9	4.2		3.2	3.4	6.4	3.7	2.0	5.6
1.0	2.8	.9		.0	-1.0	4.3	1.9	-.2	1.0
2.0	3.6	2.2	Sales/Net Fixed Assets	2.6	2.1	2.2	3.1	2.4	2.0
.6	.8	.5		.6	.7	.4	.6	.1	.7
.2	.2	.2		.2	.3	.2	.1	.1	.2
1.0	1.1	1.1	Sales/Total Assets	.9	.7	1.1	1.4	1.6	1.3
.4	.4	.4		.5	.4	.3	.5	.1	.5
.2	.2	.1		.1	.2	.2	.1	.1	.2
10.7	7.0	11.8	% Depr., Dep., Amort./Sales	22.3	27.3	16.4	8.9	13.8	5.3
(129) 22.7	(97) 18.5	(87) 26.7		(14) 35.4	(15) 40.9	(12) 38.1	(19) 26.7	(10) 24.5	(17) 9.5
37.9	35.3	40.9		58.1	74.0	50.3	30.1	36.5	16.5
1.5	2.7	1.7	% Officers', Directors' Owners' Comp/Sales						
(31) 3.4	(20) 6.4	(15) 4.7							
7.2	11.9	11.0							
2696419M	2705113M	2258589M	Net Sales ($)	9106M	36864M	75904M	151460M	196268M	1788987M
5515033M	5656252M	6241586M	Total Assets ($)	34410M	130282M	251094M	761580M	1488317M	3575903M

© RMA 2019

M = $ thousand   MM = $ million
See Pages viii through xx for Explanation of Ratios and Data

Current Data Sorted by Assets   Comparative Historical Data

0-500M	500M-2MM	2-10MM	10-50MM	50-100MM	100-250MM	Type of Statement	4/1/14-3/31/15 ALL	4/1/15-3/31/16 ALL
	1	3	22	20	22	Unqualified	48	60
1	2	25	29	6	2	Reviewed	73	69
1	3	17	6	3	1	Compiled	48	45
10	16	13	1	1		Tax Returns	43	49
4	18	52	82	22	44	Other	190	199
62 (4/1-9/30/18)		365 (10/1/18-3/31/19)						
16	40	110	140	52	69	**NUMBER OF STATEMENTS**	402	422
%	%	%	%	%	%	**ASSETS**	%	%
28.4	12.4	9.9	6.7	3.5	3.4	Cash & Equivalents	8.2	7.6
10.9	14.3	14.3	13.2	13.5	9.8	Trade Receivables (net)	13.5	13.2
9.9	7.6	14.6	18.3	20.7	9.7	Inventory	10.6	11.7
4.6	.7	2.3	2.3	1.6	3.0	All Other Current	3.0	2.5
53.8	35.0	41.1	40.5	39.3	26.0	Total Current	35.3	34.9
27.3	56.0	50.8	51.7	50.7	64.5	Fixed Assets (net)	54.7	55.9
1.6	2.9	2.5	2.7	2.9	2.5	Intangibles (net)	3.7	2.6
17.3	6.1	5.6	5.1	7.1	7.1	All Other Non-Current	6.3	6.6
100.0	100.0	100.0	100.0	100.0	100.0	Total	100.0	100.0
						LIABILITIES		
27.6	8.9	7.9	12.6	14.0	20.4	Notes Payable-Short Term	10.5	10.8
14.7	6.9	10.0	8.8	7.0	7.2	Cur. Mat.-L.T.D.	8.4	7.5
7.7	5.4	5.6	6.8	5.3	4.3	Trade Payables	6.0	5.4
.2	.2	.1	.3	.5	.4	Income Taxes Payable	.2	.3
24.1	9.9	5.8	4.8	3.4	3.2	All Other Current	4.7	5.2
74.4	31.3	29.3	33.2	30.2	35.4	Total Current	29.9	29.3
39.2	43.7	25.6	27.4	28.3	28.2	Long-Term Debt	32.0	31.9
.1	.3	.5	.8	1.1	2.2	Deferred Taxes	1.3	1.1
6.7	8.6	2.4	3.7	3.0	3.1	All Other Non-Current	3.9	4.2
-20.3	16.2	42.1	34.8	37.5	31.2	Net Worth	32.9	33.5
100.0	100.0	100.0	100.0	100.0	100.0	Total Liabilities & Net Worth	100.0	100.0
						INCOME DATA		
100.0	100.0	100.0	100.0	100.0	100.0	Net Sales	100.0	100.0
						Gross Profit		
83.7	77.6	85.4	90.4	89.0	86.9	Operating Expenses	86.1	87.4
16.3	22.4	14.6	9.6	11.0	13.1	Operating Profit	13.9	12.6
1.9	4.3	1.4	2.2	2.1	5.5	All Other Expenses (net)	2.3	2.5
14.4	18.1	13.1	7.4	8.8	7.6	Profit Before Taxes	11.6	10.1
						RATIOS		
3.6	3.2	2.3	1.8	2.2	1.5		2.0	2.2
1.2	1.4	1.4	1.2	1.1	.9	Current	1.2	1.2
.2	.2	.7	.7	.8	.4		.7	.7
2.8	3.1	1.5	1.3	1.1	.9		1.5	1.6
.4	1.1	.9	.6	.7	.4	Quick	.8	.8
.1	.1	.4	.3	.3	.2		.3	.3
0 UND	0 UND	12 31.7	28 13.2	32 11.5	33 11.0		20 18.7	18 20.2
0 UND	15 23.7	41 9.0	46 8.0	49 7.4	58 6.3	Sales/Receivables	45 8.1	43 8.5
15 24.4	54 6.8	68 5.4	69 5.3	74 4.9	76 4.8		66 5.5	64 5.7
						Cost of Sales/Inventory		
						Cost of Sales/Payables		
4.8	8.4	5.3	5.8	4.4	9.2		5.4	5.4
NM	33.9	10.9	15.4	16.7	-15.1	Sales/Working Capital	22.7	18.9
-1.9	-2.6	-11.5	-13.0	-19.7	-1.5		-8.4	-8.8
6.8	13.6	13.1	9.9	10.4	4.5		10.7	10.0
(14) 2.4	(34) 7.5	(98) 5.8	(134) 3.2	(49) 3.6	(66) 3.0	EBIT/Interest	(377) 4.8	(389) 4.4
-1.9	1.2	2.2	1.5	2.1	1.3		2.2	1.8
		4.0	3.7	3.0			5.1	4.7
		(12) 1.9	(36) 2.1	(13) 1.6		Net Profit + Depr., Dep., Amort./Cur. Mat. L/T/D	(66) 2.6	(73) 2.2
		1.0	1.0	1.2			1.1	1.2
.0	.7	.7	.8	.5	1.6		.8	.9
1.5	3.0	1.4	1.4	1.6	2.3	Fixed/Worth	1.8	1.8
-2.2	-45.4	2.4	3.0	3.1	3.9		3.8	4.1
2.8	.9	.7	.9	.9	1.7		1.0	.9
131.9	3.8	1.6	2.0	2.0	2.2	Debt/Worth	2.2	2.1
-2.8	-46.4	3.0	5.2	3.9	3.9		4.9	5.4
999.8	85.5	49.1	32.5	32.1	23.0		42.8	39.6
(10) 143.0	(27) 37.4	(107) 22.8	(129) 16.9	(49) 19.5	(66) 11.9	% Profit Before Taxes/Tangible Net Worth	(360) 21.7	(385) 19.7
18.2	14.2	7.5	7.5	8.8	4.4		10.3	7.4
37.9	24.7	17.3	11.1	11.7	5.9		12.1	12.4
11.7	11.2	7.6	4.7	5.6	3.6	% Profit Before Taxes/Total Assets	6.7	5.9
-6.8	.6	2.8	1.7	2.8	.7		2.5	1.4
UND	21.4	7.9	6.2	7.2	1.1		4.7	5.0
49.4	1.9	2.1	1.7	1.4	.8	Sales/Net Fixed Assets	1.5	1.5
2.6	.5	.9	.8	.8	.5		.8	.8
3.6	2.4	1.6	1.3	1.1	.6		1.4	1.4
2.0	1.0	1.1	.9	.8	.5	Sales/Total Assets	.8	.8
.7	.3	.7	.6	.6	.4		.5	.5
	6.1	5.9	4.9	9.6	8.9		5.7	5.4
	(28) 17.8	(82) 12.0	(120) 13.3	(31) 13.0	(10) 12.2	% Depr., Dep., Amort./Sales	(287) 13.2	(303) 13.5
	39.6	24.3	21.6	16.2	16.2		23.1	24.4
		1.5	1.2	.4			2.0	1.5
		(28) 3.1	(15) 2.6	(10) 1.2		% Officers', Directors' Owners' Comp/Sales	(77) 3.6	(88) 3.5
		5.8	9.9	2.5			6.4	5.5
13774M	80000M	720660M	3797354M	3259006M	6672978M	Net Sales ($)	11569329M	13742439M
4196M	50817M	587184M	3461072M	3780343M	11342988M	Total Assets ($)	15062893M	17206301M

M = $ thousand   MM = $ million
See Pages viii through xx for Explanation of Ratios and Data

Comparative Historical Data / Current Data Sorted by Sales

4/1/16-3/31/17 ALL	4/1/17-3/31/18 ALL	4/1/18-3/31/19 ALL	Type of Statement	0-1MM	1-3MM	3-5MM	5-10MM	10-25MM	25MM & OVER
42	51	68	Unqualified	1	1		1	16	49
65	64	65	Reviewed	4	5	4	11	26	15
32	47	31	Compiled	4	3	5	9	5	5
48	37	41	Tax Returns	11	10	9	7	3	1
193	218	222	Other	16	21	16	29	45	95
				62 (4/1-9/30/18)			365 (10/1/18-3/31/19)		
380	417	427	NUMBER OF STATEMENTS	36	40	34	57	95	165
%	%	%	**ASSETS**	%	%	%	%	%	%
7.7	7.4	8.0	Cash & Equivalents	16.0	10.7	10.5	9.3	8.1	4.5
11.4	12.7	13.0	Trade Receivables (net)	8.7	10.4	10.4	17.2	13.8	13.1
12.2	14.1	14.9	Inventory	1.3	10.4	13.4	14.2	14.8	19.6
2.5	2.1	2.3	All Other Current	.8	1.6	1.9	1.8	2.3	3.0
33.9	36.3	38.2	Total Current	26.8	33.2	36.3	42.5	39.1	40.2
56.1	54.5	52.9	Fixed Assets (net)	56.2	58.5	54.7	51.1	52.1	51.5
2.9	3.6	2.6	Intangibles (net)	2.8	.4	6.0	1.6	2.3	2.9
7.2	5.6	6.3	All Other Non-Current	14.3	8.0	3.0	4.8	6.5	5.3
100.0	100.0	100.0	Total	100.0	100.0	100.0	100.0	100.0	100.0
			LIABILITIES						
11.3	12.8	13.0	Notes Payable-Short Term	7.7	10.7	12.3	8.3	10.1	18.2
8.7	8.9	8.7	Cur. Mat.-L.T.D.	7.9	10.4	10.1	9.7	9.2	7.5
5.5	5.5	5.8	Trade Payables	1.6	4.9	5.7	6.7	5.1	7.1
.2	.2	.3	Income Taxes Payable	.0	.3	.1	.2	.1	.4
4.9	4.5	5.8	All Other Current	17.6	6.5	4.9	4.6	5.2	4.1
30.6	31.9	33.6	Total Current	34.9	32.8	33.0	29.6	29.7	37.2
31.8	29.5	29.2	Long-Term Debt	33.5	32.6	43.8	24.8	31.1	24.8
1.2	1.1	.9	Deferred Taxes	.3	.1	1.1	.5	1.0	1.4
3.4	4.0	3.7	All Other Non-Current	9.2	2.9	3.8	1.8	3.7	3.4
33.0	33.5	32.6	Net Worth	22.1	31.6	18.3	43.4	34.5	33.3
100.0	100.0	100.0	Total Liabilities & Net Worth	100.0	100.0	100.0	100.0	100.0	100.0
			INCOME DATA						
100.0	100.0	100.0	Net Sales	100.0	100.0	100.0	100.0	100.0	100.0
			Gross Profit						
87.3	87.4	86.9	Operating Expenses	65.5	81.0	90.0	87.1	90.9	90.1
12.7	12.6	13.1	Operating Profit	34.5	19.0	10.0	12.9	9.1	9.9
2.5	2.8	2.7	All Other Expenses (net)	8.0	2.5	.2	1.1	2.7	2.8
10.2	9.7	10.3	Profit Before Taxes	26.6	16.5	9.8	11.8	6.4	7.1
			RATIOS						
1.9	2.0	1.9	Current	4.3	1.9	2.3	2.2	2.0	1.7
1.2	1.2	1.2		.7	1.3	1.1	1.5	1.3	1.1
.6	.6	.6		.1	.3	.5	.9	.7	.7
1.4	1.4	1.3	Quick	3.9	1.4	1.6	1.5	1.5	1.0
.6	(416) .6	.7		.4	.9	.7	1.1	.8	.6
.2	.3	.3		.1	.2	.3	.4	.4	.2
17 21.7	20 18.3	20 18.3	Sales/Receivables	0 UND	0 UND	0 UND	22 16.4	29 12.6	32 11.5
39 9.4	44 8.3	44 8.3		0 UND	28 13.2	33 11.0	41 8.8	49 7.4	47 7.8
64 5.7	68 5.4	69 5.3		29 12.5	60 6.1	60 6.1	79 4.6	72 5.1	73 5.0
			Cost of Sales/Inventory						
			Cost of Sales/Payables						
6.0	5.4	5.9	Sales/Working Capital	3.7	6.3	7.8	4.3	5.2	7.0
21.9	20.8	17.1		-5.9	18.1	78.2	10.1	11.2	26.8
-7.1	-6.1	-7.3		-.8	-4.3	-9.8	-19.9	-12.4	-8.1
9.9	8.8	8.8	EBIT/Interest	7.8	15.1	7.8	13.5	6.9	6.2
(349) 3.6	(392) 3.4	(395) 3.8		(27) 3.4	(35) 7.6	(32) 4.6	(52) 6.1	(91) 2.9	(158) 3.4
1.3	1.6	1.7		1.1	2.3	2.1	2.1	1.4	1.7
2.7	3.4	4.0	Net Profit + Depr., Dep., Amort./Cur. Mat. L/T/D					2.9	5.9
(70) 1.7	(67) 1.8	(69) 1.9					(28) 1.6	(26) 2.4	
.8	1.1	1.2						1.0	1.5
.9	.8	.8	Fixed/Worth	.3	.7	.9	.7	.8	.8
1.8	1.8	1.6		1.9	2.1	1.9	1.2	1.5	1.8
4.1	4.5	3.5		9.8	5.7	10.5	2.1	3.9	3.1
.9	1.0	1.0	Debt/Worth	.7	.9	.9	.7	1.2	1.3
2.2	2.3	2.1		3.0	2.1	1.9	1.3	2.0	2.2
5.1	6.4	5.2		NM	8.0	18.6	3.3	4.9	4.2
36.6	31.7	37.4	% Profit Before Taxes/Tangible Net Worth	87.1	82.1	41.0	56.1	33.5	28.9
(334) 15.5	(364) 16.7	(388) 18.8		(27) 18.8	(36) 30.7	(27) 21.1	(55) 24.8	(89) 16.1	(154) 17.0
3.7	5.3	7.2		4.1	11.2	5.8	6.6	4.7	8.1
12.2	11.2	12.1	% Profit Before Taxes/Total Assets	14.0	25.1	20.3	16.5	11.1	8.9
4.5	4.6	5.5		3.7	9.7	7.8	8.5	5.0	4.8
.8	1.2	1.9		.3	2.2	2.0	2.4	1.2	1.9
4.2	5.3	7.5	Sales/Net Fixed Assets	4.2	5.7	27.7	10.7	5.3	8.6
1.3	1.5	1.5		.5	1.2	1.9	1.9	1.7	1.5
.7	.7	.7		.2	.7	.8	.9	.8	.8
1.2	1.4	1.4	Sales/Total Assets	.7	1.5	2.0	1.8	1.4	1.3
.8	.8	.8		.3	.9	.9	1.1	.9	.8
.5	.5	.5		.1	.6	.6	.7	.6	.5
6.9	6.9	6.0	% Depr., Dep., Amort./Sales	13.5	11.2	9.0	4.4	6.3	3.5
(270) 15.9	(286) 14.8	(276) 13.1		(25) 26.9	(31) 24.0	(19) 15.1	(44) 12.4	(76) 14.1	(81) 9.9
29.6	26.2	22.9		61.6	34.8	34.9	20.5	22.6	13.9
1.2	1.0	1.2	% Officers', Directors' Owners' Comp/Sales				1.7	1.5	1.0
(80) 3.1	(76) 3.2	(70) 2.5			(11) 3.2	(13) 3.6	(10) 2.5		(25) 1.3
5.8	6.8	5.7				8.5	5.3	5.3	2.4
10807354M	12019166M	14543772M	Net Sales ($)	13602M	77534M	144123M	412084M	1541337M	12355092M
14603720M	15157528M	19226600M	Total Assets ($)	70046M	111420M	175195M	488715M	2265229M	16115995M

© RMA 2019

M = $ thousand   MM = $ million
See Pages viii through xx for Explanation of Ratios and Data

Current Data Sorted by Assets   Comparative Historical Data

0-500M	500M-2MM 17 (4/1-9/30/18)	2-10MM	10-50MM 81 (10/1/18-3/31/19)	50-100MM	100-250MM	Type of Statement	4/1/14-3/31/15 ALL	4/1/15-3/31/16 ALL
		2	5	1	9	Unqualified	16	12
	1	4	9			Reviewed	13	12
	2	1	2			Compiled	12	11
5	7	1	5			Tax Returns	26	31
6	5	11	10	4	9	Other	44	47
11	15	23	26	5	18	**NUMBER OF STATEMENTS**	111	113
%	%	%	%	%	%	**ASSETS**	%	%
17.8	20.5	11.4	7.1		2.5	Cash & Equivalents	10.0	10.3
7.8	8.4	21.1	15.0		13.9	Trade Receivables (net)	15.2	13.9
.2	5.8	5.3	12.0		3.1	Inventory	6.3	6.3
4.9	2.0	2.1	5.8		2.5	All Other Current	3.3	3.5
30.6	36.7	40.0	39.9		22.0	Total Current	34.8	33.9
59.7	38.9	44.7	36.6		29.6	Fixed Assets (net)	45.8	48.3
8.8	13.1	7.5	6.1		8.6	Intangibles (net)	2.4	2.5
1.0	11.3	7.7	17.4		39.8	All Other Non-Current	16.9	15.3
100.0	100.0	100.0	100.0		100.0	Total	100.0	100.0
						LIABILITIES		
9.2	9.0	6.1	8.6		8.7	Notes Payable-Short Term	12.5	9.6
30.7	11.8	8.7	12.9		9.2	Cur. Mat.-L.T.D.	7.0	11.9
6.0	4.6	7.1	9.1		4.7	Trade Payables	4.9	4.0
.0	.0	.0	.0		.4	Income Taxes Payable	.0	.1
35.5	3.1	25.7	7.8		7.4	All Other Current	10.3	8.8
81.3	28.5	47.7	38.4		30.3	Total Current	34.7	34.3
43.9	39.9	28.5	20.7		32.5	Long-Term Debt	33.4	37.8
.0	.0	.2	.0		1.7	Deferred Taxes	.4	.4
28.1	13.2	5.3	8.2		7.8	All Other Non-Current	4.5	6.3
-53.4	18.4	18.2	32.7		27.6	Net Worth	26.9	21.1
100.0	100.0	100.0	100.0		100.0	Total Liabilities & Net Worth	100.0	100.0
						INCOME DATA		
100.0	100.0	100.0	100.0		100.0	Net Sales	100.0	100.0
						Gross Profit		
71.1	84.0	83.4	87.3		79.0	Operating Expenses	82.7	82.0
28.9	16.0	16.6	12.7		21.0	Operating Profit	17.3	18.0
3.1	2.5	3.5	3.1		6.2	All Other Expenses (net)	5.0	4.9
25.8	13.5	13.1	9.6		14.8	Profit Before Taxes	12.2	13.1
						RATIOS		
.8	5.1	1.4	1.4		2.0		2.6	2.4
.3	1.8	.7	1.1		.7	Current	1.1	1.1
.0	.7	.3	.7		.2		.4	.3
.8	4.8	1.0	1.2		1.0		1.6	1.6
.3	1.3	.5	.6		.6	Quick	.8	.7
.0	.2	.1	.4		.2		.2	.2
0 UND	0 UND	13 27.7	12 29.3		24 15.4		0 UND	0 UND
0 UND	4 95.5	46 7.9	35 10.5		36 10.0	Sales/Receivables	29 12.7	24 15.5
0 UND	24 15.1	73 5.0	51 7.1		51 7.1		51 7.1	54 6.7
						Cost of Sales/Inventory		
						Cost of Sales/Payables		
-36.8	5.0	15.5	9.8		7.5		3.9	4.8
-3.0	11.4	-9.3	38.3		-5.5	Sales/Working Capital	27.7	51.1
-1.8	-9.9	-1.9	-9.0		-1.3		-5.6	-4.5
	7.7	13.6	7.9		4.4		7.0	8.9
	(13) 3.9	(21) 4.8	(24) 4.4		3.3	EBIT/Interest	(89) 3.6	(92) 3.4
	.2	2.1	2.4		1.5		1.4	1.4
						Net Profit + Depr., Dep., Amort./Cur. Mat. L/T/D	105.0 (10) 6.1 .7	5.0 (11) 2.0 .3
1.4	.3	.7	.3		.0		.2	.7
-1.7	2.6	2.6	1.2		1.1	Fixed/Worth	1.5	2.0
-.2	-3.9	-1.7	3.0		3.2		3.8	13.2
.9	1.0	2.0	1.4		2.5		1.0	1.0
-2.8	134.6	6.2	3.6		3.0	Debt/Worth	2.9	4.5
-1.5	-5.2	-19.6	12.8		5.8		15.9	28.0
		48.4	56.2		49.2		49.8	54.3
	(16)	22.1 (25)	25.6		(16) 19.5	% Profit Before Taxes/Tangible Net Worth	(96) 17.9	(89) 24.5
		12.2	6.4		8.7		5.7	5.9
168.7	24.9	10.5	11.6		8.3		11.2	16.3
19.9	10.9	4.9	6.7		5.0	% Profit Before Taxes/Total Assets	4.7	6.2
-.9	.3	1.2	2.0		1.8		.9	.4
9.7	99.4	67.3	17.8		39.9		24.8	15.3
2.7	4.6	4.6	5.5		9.3	Sales/Net Fixed Assets	2.9	1.7
.9	.9	.7	1.0		1.1		.6	.6
5.1	3.0	2.4	2.0		.9		1.7	1.9
1.8	.8	1.3	.7		.4	Sales/Total Assets	.7	.6
.5	.6	.6	.4		.3		.3	.3
		1.6	2.2				1.7	3.0
	(18)	19.4 (21)	10.7			% Depr., Dep., Amort./Sales	(78) 18.0	(82) 21.1
		64.1	37.0				58.0	58.0
							2.0	1.7
						% Officers', Directors' Owners' Comp/Sales	(26) 4.5	(23) 4.1
							13.8	10.5
7726M	34472M	146811M	769063M	234962M	1618757M	Net Sales ($)	1867375M	1374304M
3213M	17126M	107949M	579270M	399311M	3015650M	Total Assets ($)	3595023M	2905492M

M = $ thousand   MM = $ million
See Pages viii through xx for Explanation of Ratios and Data

Comparative Historical Data | Current Data Sorted by Sales

	Comparative Historical Data			Current Data Sorted by Sales					
Type of Statement									
Unqualified	18	25	17				7	1	9
Reviewed	13	10	14		2	3	2	4	3
Compiled	10	6	5	2			1	1	1
Tax Returns	31	28	17	12	2		2	1	
Other	61	40	45	6	6	3	9	7	14
	4/1/16-3/31/17 ALL	4/1/17-3/31/18 ALL	4/1/18-3/31/19 ALL	0-1MM	17 (4/1-9/30/18) 1-3MM	3-5MM	81 (10/1/18-3/31/19) 5-10MM	10-25MM	25MM & OVER
NUMBER OF STATEMENTS	133	109	98	20	10	6	21	14	27
	%	%	%	%	%	%	%	%	%
ASSETS									
Cash & Equivalents	9.7	10.4	10.3	13.0	16.3		14.0	10.2	4.4
Trade Receivables (net)	15.3	13.3	14.1	1.9	18.4		18.3	19.5	15.1
Inventory	9.4	5.9	6.0	.1	4.7		6.3	5.7	10.8
All Other Current	4.5	5.8	3.8	3.3	3.1		2.7	5.7	3.0
Total Current	38.9	35.5	34.2	18.4	42.4		41.2	41.1	33.3
Fixed Assets (net)	39.3	43.5	38.3	63.7	46.2		35.8	21.7	26.3
Intangibles (net)	4.2	5.4	7.9	12.7	3.2		6.9	9.4	7.7
All Other Non-Current	17.6	15.7	19.6	5.2	8.3		16.0	27.7	32.6
Total	100.0	100.0	100.0	100.0	100.0		100.0	100.0	100.0
LIABILITIES									
Notes Payable-Short Term	7.6	11.6	7.8	7.1	4.3		11.8	6.6	6.7
Cur. Mat.-L.T.D.	10.8	10.0	12.7	10.8	41.1		6.9	6.3	10.9
Trade Payables	5.3	6.0	6.8	1.0	11.6		7.6	5.7	10.0
Income Taxes Payable	.4	.2	.1	.0	.0		.0	.1	.3
All Other Current	12.0	11.2	14.0	16.8	11.8		24.2	7.6	10.3
Total Current	36.1	39.0	41.3	35.7	68.9		50.5	26.3	38.2
Long-Term Debt	30.9	36.3	32.6	41.4	56.5		23.3	33.8	24.4
Deferred Taxes	.5	.4	.4	.0	.0		.0	.4	1.1
All Other Non-Current	7.8	8.6	10.3	21.4	6.0		3.3	7.6	9.2
Net Worth	24.6	15.6	15.4	1.5	-31.4		22.9	31.8	27.1
Total Liabilities & Net Worth	100.0	100.0	100.0	100.0	100.0		100.0	100.0	100.0
INCOME DATA									
Net Sales	100.0	100.0	100.0	100.0	100.0		100.0	100.0	100.0
Gross Profit									
Operating Expenses	79.0	81.4	81.4	68.3	78.0		85.9	83.0	86.9
Operating Profit	21.0	18.6	18.6	31.7	22.0		14.1	17.0	13.1
All Other Expenses (net)	5.2	6.2	4.7	6.4	2.7		4.9	5.7	4.6
Profit Before Taxes	15.9	12.3	13.9	25.4	19.3		9.2	11.3	8.5
RATIOS									
Current	2.3	1.7	1.8	1.8	2.6		1.2	3.2	1.7
	1.1	1.0	1.0	.6	.7		.8	1.5	1.0
	.5	.3	.3	.0	.3		.5	1.1	.3
Quick	1.5	1.4	1.2	1.7	2.4		1.0	2.2	1.0
	.6	.5	.6	.4	.5		.6	1.1	.6
	.2	.2	.2	.0	.2		.3	.5	.2
Sales/Receivables	0 UND	0 UND	2 179.3	0 UND	0 UND		5 79.1	9 42.4	24 15.1
	24 15.2	19 19.0	24 15.2	0 UND	22 16.3		29 12.7	27 13.3	38 9.5
	48 7.6	48 7.6	47 7.7	0 UND	114 3.2		57 6.4	58 6.3	47 7.7
Cost of Sales/Inventory									
Cost of Sales/Payables									
Sales/Working Capital	4.0	6.0	8.0	5.3	NM		13.5	4.0	8.0
	45.0	-999.8	-638.7	-8.2	-6.6		-30.3	11.9	157.0
	-4.5	-3.5	-2.9	-1.9	-1.9		-5.7	24.1	-3.9
EBIT/Interest	10.1	8.3	7.9	13.3			10.9	5.4	4.7
	(105) 4.5	(91) 3.9	(85) 3.9	(15) 4.0			(18) 4.9	(12) 4.3	(26) 3.4
	2.3	1.3	1.8	2.3			1.7	3.0	1.5
Net Profit + Depr., Dep., Amort./Cur. Mat. L/T/D	2.8								
	(15) 1.6								
	.2								
Fixed/Worth	.2	.2	.2	1.0	.9		.4	.0	.1
	1.3	1.9	1.9	7.2	6.6		2.0	.6	1.8
	5.2	64.5	93.5	-2.0	-.1		-10.5	3.1	3.6
Debt/Worth	1.2	1.8	2.0	1.5	1.7		1.4	1.8	2.7
	3.7	5.1	4.9	202.0	12.1		10.7	2.7	3.1
	11.9	NM	374.5	-2.7	-2.7		-35.8	60.2	12.3
% Profit Before Taxes/Tangible Net Worth	69.8	53.9	52.7	30.6			41.5	46.6	56.5
	(112) 31.1	(82) 23.8	(75) 22.9	(11) 13.6			(15) 29.7	(12) 27.0	(25) 20.4
	13.5	5.3	9.4	-1.1			9.4	15.6	6.0
% Profit Before Taxes/Total Assets	17.3	14.5	12.1	24.1	96.8		16.4	10.5	8.3
	6.2	4.9	5.4	11.7	3.6		5.3	7.7	4.8
	2.1	.7	1.2	.6	1.0		1.1	2.0	1.8
Sales/Net Fixed Assets	30.4	26.7	43.0	2.8	55.7		82.9	100.9	39.5
	4.4	4.3	5.5	1.1	4.9		13.8	20.0	13.1
	.9	.7	1.0	.5	.7		1.0	2.0	2.4
Sales/Total Assets	1.9	2.0	2.1	.9	5.3		2.7	2.2	2.0
	.7	.7	.7	.6	.8		1.1	.8	.8
	.3	.3	.4	.5			.4	.4	.4
% Depr., Dep., Amort./Sales	1.4	2.5	2.4	20.9			1.7		1.7
	(85) 14.4	(63) 13.8	(58) 14.2	(15) 38.5			(13) 18.9		(10) 4.9
	54.7	52.9	50.0	53.1			55.1		9.1
% Officers', Directors' Owners' Comp/Sales	1.9	3.2	2.9						
	(28) 5.5	(23) 5.9	(13) 7.8						
	10.3	16.2	16.2						
Net Sales ($)	2687881M	2264351M	2811791M	9167M	19034M	24118M	154757M	245889M	2358826M
Total Assets ($)	3932378M	3827322M	4122519M	25112M	30342M	58384M	310122M	524801M	3173758M

© RMA 2019   M = $ thousand   MM = $ million
See Pages viii through xx for Explanation of Ratios and Data

Current Data Sorted by Assets

Comparative Historical Data

	0-500M	500M-2MM	2-10MM	10-50MM	50-100MM	100-250MM		4/1/14-3/31/15 ALL	4/1/15-3/31/16 ALL
Type of Statement									
Unqualified		1	5	20	14	33		66	54
Reviewed	2	3	19	21	4	2		78	67
Compiled	21	7	14	10	1	2		62	54
Tax Returns	23	32	21	6	1	1		154	127
Other		45	101	70	31	24		311	296
	61 (4/1-9/30/18)		472 (10/1/18-3/31/19)						
NUMBER OF STATEMENTS	46	88	160	127	50	62		671	598
	%	%	%	%	%	%		%	%
ASSETS									
Cash & Equivalents	30.0	16.3	12.7	9.4	4.1	3.8		9.8	11.2
Trade Receivables (net)	5.5	11.9	15.1	14.5	18.6	11.9		13.6	12.7
Inventory	5.4	4.1	8.6	10.0	12.3	8.6		7.8	7.9
All Other Current	2.3	2.0	3.8	4.3	3.3	6.2		4.3	3.4
Total Current	43.3	34.4	40.2	38.2	38.3	30.5		35.5	35.1
Fixed Assets (net)	44.9	49.2	49.6	46.8	42.9	53.6		50.3	49.9
Intangibles (net)	4.6	7.8	2.2	3.6	6.9	1.7		3.5	4.1
All Other Non-Current	7.2	8.7	8.1	11.4	11.9	14.2		10.7	10.9
Total	100.0	100.0	100.0	100.0	100.0	100.0		100.0	100.0
LIABILITIES									
Notes Payable-Short Term	17.6	11.9	10.6	8.2	14.2	11.6		10.0	10.5
Cur. Mat.-L.T.D.	10.2	5.8	6.7	9.1	5.8	8.4		7.0	9.1
Trade Payables	2.9	8.0	6.4	4.7	4.6	4.1		5.3	5.3
Income Taxes Payable	.1	.3	.1	.1	.2	.0		.2	.2
All Other Current	9.7	14.3	8.9	5.3	5.5	5.6		6.3	7.5
Total Current	40.6	40.2	32.8	27.5	30.3	29.8		28.8	32.6
Long-Term Debt	37.8	45.5	31.6	25.5	32.2	36.7		39.1	39.4
Deferred Taxes	.0	.0	.2	1.2	1.5	2.1		.8	.9
All Other Non-Current	17.8	4.8	5.5	5.0	3.5	4.1		6.0	4.2
Net Worth	3.7	9.4	30.0	40.8	32.4	27.3		25.3	22.9
Total Liabilities & Net Worth	100.0	100.0	100.0	100.0	100.0	100.0		100.0	100.0
INCOME DATA									
Net Sales	100.0	100.0	100.0	100.0	100.0	100.0		100.0	100.0
Gross Profit									
Operating Expenses	74.6	80.1	84.2	86.4	84.6	79.4		77.5	77.6
Operating Profit	25.4	19.9	15.8	13.6	15.4	20.6		22.5	22.4
All Other Expenses (net)	3.1	4.1	3.0	3.5	9.6	10.9		5.6	5.7
Profit Before Taxes	22.3	15.8	12.8	10.2	5.8	9.7		16.9	16.7
RATIOS									
Current	4.3	2.3	2.2	2.8	2.4	1.6		2.7	2.1
	1.1	1.1	1.2	1.3	1.4	1.0		1.3	1.2
	.3	.3	.6	.8	.7	.5		.7	.5
Quick	3.5	2.1	1.8	2.2	1.7	1.1		1.7	1.5
	1.0	.7	.8	.9	1.0	.4		(670) .8	(597) .8
	.2	.2	.3	.4	.3	.2		.3	.3
Sales/Receivables	0 UND	0 UND	0 790.0	20 18.5	30 12.3	15 23.9		0 UND	0 UND
	0 UND	5 67.0	33 11.1	46 7.9	48 7.6	33 11.1		23 15.6	25 14.5
	13 27.8	38 9.7	61 6.0	64 5.7	79 4.6	65 5.6		54 6.8	55 6.6
Cost of Sales/Inventory									
Cost of Sales/Payables									
Sales/Working Capital	6.6	8.7	5.2	3.9	2.1	4.2		4.2	4.5
	114.9	80.1	16.6	10.4	9.6	96.7		17.1	24.0
	-6.6	-5.0	-10.7	-14.5	-8.5	-4.9		-11.2	-6.8
EBIT/Interest	27.5	24.8	16.1	11.0	7.4	4.4		13.4	13.1
	(30) 4.8	(71) 6.6	(140) 4.8	(118) 3.5	(42) 2.7	(47) 2.7		(530) 4.6	(474) 4.6
	1.0	1.1	1.4	1.5	1.4	1.8		1.8	1.8
Net Profit + Depr., Dep., Amort./Cur. Mat. L/T/D			3.6	3.5				6.7	4.3
		(18) 2.2	(29) 1.6					(98) 2.4	(78) 2.2
			1.3	.6				1.1	1.1
Fixed/Worth	.4	.8	.5	.3	.7	.4		.5	.5
	1.7	2.4	1.6	1.2	1.4	2.3		1.7	1.8
	-4.8	-3.6	5.0	2.7	3.7	3.9		5.5	6.3
Debt/Worth	.8	.9	.8	.7	1.0	1.8		1.0	1.0
	4.0	4.9	1.9	1.7	3.5	3.6		2.6	2.8
	-4.9	-6.0	7.0	4.8	8.8	5.6		10.2	12.7
% Profit Before Taxes/Tangible Net Worth	217.9	86.1	58.0	38.3	29.5	24.7		47.5	54.8
	(28) 65.2	(56) 33.9	(135) 30.1	(122) 20.3	(45) 17.2	(60) 15.0		(550) 22.3	(491) 23.3
	28.9	8.1	6.6	5.4	.3	5.8		7.6	7.9
% Profit Before Taxes/Total Assets	60.0	39.2	20.0	13.8	9.2	5.5		16.0	15.9
	21.3	12.3	7.7	5.8	3.5	3.2		6.8	6.8
	1.6	.3	1.1	1.1	.0	1.4		1.6	1.7
Sales/Net Fixed Assets	44.9	12.7	10.7	8.6	8.5	7.5		10.3	9.9
	7.5	3.5	2.2	2.1	1.5	1.1		2.0	1.9
	1.3	1.1	.7	.8	.8	.5		.6	.6
Sales/Total Assets	4.4	3.0	1.9	1.3	1.1	.9		1.8	1.6
	2.1	1.5	1.0	.7	.6	.4		.8	.7
	.8	.6	.4	.4	.3	.2		.3	.3
% Depr., Dep., Amort./Sales	6.0	3.0	5.1	6.6	5.6	5.4		4.4	4.9
	(23) 17.4	(50) 13.7	(120) 15.9	(101) 13.6	(28) 12.5	(19) 10.9		(496) 12.0	(418) 13.7
	43.8	32.0	44.9	23.7	22.6	25.6		24.0	27.5
% Officers', Directors' Owners' Comp/Sales	4.1	3.1	1.6	1.9				2.2	1.6
	(12) 7.7	(29) 5.6	(40) 3.3	(20) 3.5				(129) 4.2	(100) 4.0
	19.2	9.2	6.7	5.0				8.6	7.0
Net Sales ($)	49592M	211556M	1139856M	2763205M	2627743M	7337623M		10405498M	9773936M
Total Assets ($)	11749M	99802M	832536M	3021695M	3514177M	9671916M		14166663M	13450508M

© RMA 2019

M = $ thousand   MM = $ million
See Pages viii through xx for Explanation of Ratios and Data

Comparative Historical Data | Current Data Sorted by Sales

					Type of Statement						
52		52		73	Unqualified		6	1	9	17	40
57		56		49	Reviewed	1	8	6	6	16	12
48		40		36	Compiled	4	7	10	4	4	7
107		97		81	Tax Returns	28	19	13	13	5	3
308		284		294	Other	49	45	31	48	55	66
4/1/16-3/31/17 ALL		4/1/17-3/31/18 ALL		4/1/18-3/31/19 ALL			61 (4/1-9/30/18)		472 (10/1/18-3/31/19)		
						0-1MM	1-3MM	3-5MM	5-10MM	10-25MM	25MM & OVER
572		529		533	NUMBER OF STATEMENTS	82	85	61	80	97	128
%		%		%	ASSETS	%	%	%	%	%	%
11.2		11.3		12.2	Cash & Equivalents	14.1	19.3	12.5	13.6	9.0	7.5
13.9		14.6		13.6	Trade Receivables (net)	4.7	11.9	16.7	16.1	18.5	13.6
7.8		8.3		8.2	Inventory	1.0	5.5	6.3	11.4	7.1	14.7
3.1		3.4		3.7	All Other Current	2.2	4.0	1.3	3.0	7.6	3.2
36.0		37.7		37.7	Total Current	21.9	40.7	36.8	44.0	42.1	39.0
49.5		48.2		48.3	Fixed Assets (net)	62.5	48.0	49.3	40.0	43.2	48.0
4.2		4.6		4.0	Intangibles (net)	5.6	3.5	3.4	2.4	4.6	4.2
10.2		9.4		10.0	All Other Non-Current	9.9	7.8	10.6	13.6	10.1	8.8
100.0		100.0		100.0	Total	100.0	100.0	100.0	100.0	100.0	100.0
					LIABILITIES						
8.8		10.0		11.3	Notes Payable-Short Term	10.2	6.1	11.9	15.8	12.8	11.3
7.7		8.1		7.5	Cur. Mat.-L.T.D.	8.7	6.7	7.6	7.3	8.1	7.1
5.5		5.7		5.5	Trade Payables	5.0	3.6	4.9	6.0	6.3	6.5
.1		.2		.1	Income Taxes Payable	.3	.1	.3	.1	.1	.1
6.7		6.9		8.3	All Other Current	6.3	8.2	15.4	7.2	8.3	7.0
28.8		30.9		32.8	Total Current	30.5	24.7	40.1	36.3	35.6	32.0
36.9		35.5		33.6	Long-Term Debt	43.7	42.0	35.0	32.5	25.0	28.2
.8		.9		.7	Deferred Taxes	.0	.1	.3	.7	.9	1.8
5.4		6.3		6.0	All Other Non-Current	4.7	10.4	5.6	5.0	6.2	4.5
28.0		26.4		26.8	Net Worth	21.0	22.9	19.0	25.5	32.3	33.4
100.0		100.0		100.0	Total Liabilties & Net Worth	100.0	100.0	100.0	100.0	100.0	100.0
					INCOME DATA						
100.0		100.0		100.0	Net Sales	100.0	100.0	100.0	100.0	100.0	100.0
					Gross Profit						
79.3		83.4		82.7	Operating Expenses	66.5	80.3	88.6	85.0	85.4	88.2
20.7		16.6		17.3	Operating Profit	33.5	19.7	11.4	15.0	14.6	11.8
5.3		4.3		4.9	All Other Expenses (net)	7.9	3.5	3.8	3.2	5.5	4.9
15.4		12.3		12.5	Profit Before Taxes	25.6	16.2	7.6	11.8	9.0	6.9
					RATIOS						
2.6		2.3		2.5		1.8	5.8	2.1	2.4	2.2	2.2
1.2		1.2		1.2	Current	.7	1.9	1.0	1.4	1.3	1.2
.5		.7		.6		.1	.7	.4	.7	.9	.7
2.0		1.7		1.8		1.5	5.0	1.7	1.8	1.6	1.3
.9		.8		.8	Quick	.5	1.3	.8	.9	.9	.8
.3		.3		.3		.1	.4	.3	.4	.4	.3

0	UND	2	164.9	2	147.8		0	UND	0	UND	5	77.5	8	44.5	15	24.4	25	14.7
27	13.4	30	12.1	31	11.6	Sales/Receivables	0	UND	8	47.6	33	11.1	35	10.4	43	8.5	40	9.2
61	6.0	60	6.1	58	6.3		23	16.0	53	6.9	54	6.7	62	5.9	70	5.2	60	6.1

(Cost of Sales/Inventory — no data)

(Cost of Sales/Payables — no data)

4.0		4.6		5.1	Sales/Working Capital	9.0	2.9	5.4	3.3	5.4	6.0
21.7		29.9		17.3		-12.4	9.4	308.8	8.9	14.2	25.0
-9.1		-11.2		-7.8		-1.6	-18.3	-4.2	-17.0	-38.8	-8.3

	11.0		12.2		11.9			13.1		12.1		7.8		19.9		12.6		7.1
(462)	4.7	(438)	3.7	(448)	4.0	EBIT/Interest	(54)	4.1	(68)	5.1	(56)	3.3	(75)	5.4	(78)	4.5	(117)	3.3
	1.3		1.5		1.5			1.1		1.1		1.1		2.0		1.5		1.7

	3.7		6.0		4.5	Net Profit + Depr., Dep., Amort./Cur. Mat. L/T/D					3.3		8.5		5.9
(77)	2.0	(71)	2.4	(63)	2.0				(10)	1.2	(20)	2.2	(17)	2.5
	1.1		1.4		1.1					.2		1.1		1.4

.5		.5		.5	Fixed/Worth	1.0	.3	.5	.1	.6	.6
1.7		1.7		1.6		2.5	1.6	1.8	.9	1.3	1.9
7.0		5.1		5.1		-17.8	16.2	31.8	4.5	2.8	3.7

.8		.9		.9	Debt/Worth	.7	.9	1.1	.6	1.0	1.1
2.5		2.3		2.3		2.4	3.1	2.1	2.0	2.4	2.5
12.5		10.4		8.6		-13.8	-28.2	85.9	6.2	6.2	6.2

	43.7		48.5		48.6	% Profit Before Taxes/Tangible Net Worth		65.3		68.6		51.7		48.2		42.3		36.2
(463)	19.1	(436)	20.9	(446)	21.6		(58)	28.2	(61)	32.3	(48)	24.4	(70)	17.3	(92)	21.9	(117)	20.3
	5.1		6.0		6.5			7.5		6.3		4.8		6.8		3.3		7.1

14.4		15.2		16.4	% Profit Before Taxes/Total Assets	25.5	22.9	14.0	20.0	14.5	11.4
5.9		5.6		5.8		9.2	7.8	4.3	7.7	4.1	5.2
.7		.9		1.1		.0	.2	-.5	1.2	.7	1.9

9.3		11.3		10.9	Sales/Net Fixed Assets	3.6	14.9	14.7	15.9	13.4	8.5
2.0		2.5		2.2		.8	2.0	2.9	3.6	2.7	2.3
.6		.7		.7		.2	.7	.9	1.6	1.0	.8

1.7		1.8		1.7	Sales/Total Assets	1.3	2.4	2.2	1.9	1.9	1.7
.7		1.0		.8		.5	.8	.9	1.1	1.0	.9
.3		.4		.4		.2	.3	.4	.5	.5	.6

	4.8		3.9		5.4	% Depr., Dep., Amort./Sales		14.1		11.7		2.8		3.0		4.4		4.1
(386)	14.0	(351)	12.2	(341)	13.6		(56)	29.8	(50)	39.4	(44)	14.1	(55)	10.4	(74)	10.4	(62)	8.9
	29.1		26.2		31.3			61.7		56.1		49.3		21.7		21.3		13.8

	2.2		1.4		1.8	% Officers', Directors' Owners' Comp/Sales		5.4		3.6		2.4		2.0		1.8		.4
(118)	4.3	(114)	3.6	(111)	3.7		(13)	11.2	(21)	5.8	(18)	3.8	(25)	3.2	(21)	3.3	(13)	.0
	8.1		6.7		6.7			18.8		14.5		7.0		4.2		5.2		1.7

7967680M		11205317M		14129575M	Net Sales ($)	36385M	159678M	234864M	579176M	1543329M	11576143M
12191020M		14328359M		17151875M	Total Assets ($)	112372M	404648M	456230M	1153789M	3497644M	11527192M

© RMA 2019 M = $ thousand MM = $ million
See Pages viii through xx for Explanation of Ratios and Data

Current Data Sorted by Assets   Comparative Historical Data

0-500M	500M-2MM	2-10MM	10-50MM	50-100MM	100-250MM	Type of Statement	4/1/14-3/31/15	4/1/15-3/31/16
1	1	1	3		2	Unqualified	27	16
	1				1	Reviewed	1	
		1				Compiled	1	2
2	2	1				Tax Returns	15	17
5	4	5	5			Other	26	35
	5 (4/1-9/30/18)		30 (10/1/18-3/31/19)				ALL	ALL
8	8	8	8		3	NUMBER OF STATEMENTS	70	70
%	%	%	%	%	%	ASSETS	%	%
						Cash & Equivalents	14.2	15.9
						Trade Receivables (net)	9.3	10.8
						Inventory	1.3	2.2
						All Other Current	4.4	4.3
						Total Current	29.2	33.2
						Fixed Assets (net)	42.2	35.7
						Intangibles (net)	13.2	15.8
						All Other Non-Current	15.5	15.3
						Total	100.0	100.0
						LIABILITIES		
						Notes Payable-Short Term	3.0	10.3
						Cur. Mat.-L.T.D.	1.9	1.9
						Trade Payables	4.1	4.4
						Income Taxes Payable	.1	.1
						All Other Current	16.3	14.2
						Total Current	25.4	30.8
						Long-Term Debt	30.6	23.0
						Deferred Taxes	1.0	.8
						All Other Non-Current	7.7	6.9
						Net Worth	35.4	38.4
						Total Liabilties & Net Worth	100.0	100.0
						INCOME DATA		
						Net Sales	100.0	100.0
						Gross Profit		
						Operating Expenses	65.9	68.4
						Operating Profit	34.1	31.6
						All Other Expenses (net)	10.4	8.7
						Profit Before Taxes	23.7	22.9
						RATIOS		
						Current	2.9	3.4
							1.1	1.3
							.4	.5
						Quick	2.8	2.9
							1.0	1.1
							.3	.3
						Sales/Receivables	0 UND	0 UND
							5 71.0	9 41.0
							41 8.8	33 11.1
						Cost of Sales/Inventory		
						Cost of Sales/Payables		
						Sales/Working Capital	4.1	3.4
							53.1	27.5
							-4.4	-7.3
						EBIT/Interest	18.0	12.7
							(35) 6.1	(33) 4.5
							2.0	2.5
						Net Profit + Depr., Dep., Amort./Cur. Mat. L/T/D		
						Fixed/Worth	.0	.0
							2.7	1.3
							28.3	14.2
						Debt/Worth	.8	.5
							3.9	1.8
							-622.3	-12.2
						% Profit Before Taxes/Tangible Net Worth	46.4	66.9
							(52) 17.6	(51) 15.3
							7.4	6.5
						% Profit Before Taxes/Total Assets	11.8	18.8
							5.8	5.9
							1.4	3.1
						Sales/Net Fixed Assets	155.2	186.7
							6.7	17.9
							.2	.3
						Sales/Total Assets	1.1	1.7
							.3	.6
							.2	.2
						% Depr., Dep., Amort./Sales	1.2	.9
							(44) 5.0	(39) 4.8
							19.7	23.2
						% Officers', Directors' Owners' Comp/Sales		
7239M	13797M	36617M	162399M		313901M	Net Sales ($)	1094378M	1156680M
1885M	8907M	28435M	242354M		415947M	Total Assets ($)	1580422M	1847301M

Data Not Available

Comparative Historical Data | **Current Data Sorted by Sales**

	4/1/16-3/31/17 ALL	4/1/17-3/31/18 ALL	4/1/18-3/31/19 ALL	0-1MM	1-3MM	3-5MM	5-10MM	10-25MM	25MM & OVER
Type of Statement									
Unqualified	12	16	8	1	1		3		3
Reviewed	1		2		1			1	
Compiled	3	2	1			1			
Tax Returns	12	8	5	2	2		1		
Other	22	23	19	8	3	2	4	1	1
				5 (4/1-9/30/18)		30 (10/1/18-3/31/19)			
NUMBER OF STATEMENTS	50	49	35	11	7	3	8	2	4
	%	%	%	%	%	%	%	%	%
ASSETS									
Cash & Equivalents	17.0	18.8	23.1	13.6					
Trade Receivables (net)	11.2	9.7	8.5	5.0					
Inventory	2.4	2.2	5.0	6.7					
All Other Current	9.4	5.1	6.7	5.1					
Total Current	40.1	35.9	43.3	30.4					
Fixed Assets (net)	36.7	29.5	23.5	29.9					
Intangibles (net)	12.4	14.5	15.0	31.4					
All Other Non-Current	10.8	20.1	18.1	8.0					
Total	100.0	100.0	100.0	100.0					
LIABILITIES									
Notes Payable-Short Term	4.5	3.7	8.7	7.5					
Cur. Mat.-L.T.D.	2.3	2.4	1.6	2.4					
Trade Payables	4.5	4.5	5.7	3.7					
Income Taxes Payable	.3	.6	.0	.0					
All Other Current	16.3	14.0	22.9	28.0					
Total Current	27.9	25.2	38.9	41.6					
Long-Term Debt	41.2	34.7	23.0	32.8					
Deferred Taxes	.8	.1	.7	.0					
All Other Non-Current	4.0	2.1	6.7	.6					
Net Worth	26.0	38.0	30.7	25.0					
Total Liabilties & Net Worth	100.0	100.0	100.0	100.0					
INCOME DATA									
Net Sales	100.0	100.0	100.0	100.0					
Gross Profit									
Operating Expenses	66.1	66.0	75.6	72.6					
Operating Profit	33.9	34.0	24.4	27.4					
All Other Expenses (net)	9.5	8.5	8.3	4.9					
Profit Before Taxes	24.3	25.5	16.1	22.5					
RATIOS									
Current	2.5 / 1.3 / .6	3.7 / 1.4 / .5	2.5 / 1.1 / .5	2.1 / .5 / .4					
Quick	1.6 / .8 / .3	3.3 / .9 / .4	2.1 / .6 / .2	2.1 / .4 / .1					
Sales/Receivables	0 UND / 6 62.1 / 36 10.0	0 UND / 8 44.5 / 42 8.7	0 UND / 2 147.1 / 38 9.7	0 UND / 0 UND / 42 8.6					
Cost of Sales/Inventory									
Cost of Sales/Payables									
Sales/Working Capital	4.0 / 22.7 / -6.3	3.3 / 14.4 / -4.8	5.4 / 58.9 / -8.1	6.0 / -8.1 / -2.8					
EBIT/Interest	10.7 / (26) 5.1 / 2.6	42.8 / (24) 5.9 / 3.3	22.6 / (24) 4.1 / 1.0						
Net Profit + Depr., Dep., Amort./Cur. Mat. L/T/D									
Fixed/Worth	.0 / 1.0 / 12.4	.0 / .2 / 2.9	.0 / .1 / 2.2	.0 / 1.9 / -1.5					
Debt/Worth	.5 / 2.7 / -18.8	.5 / 1.5 / NM	.8 / 1.4 / -13.0	.9 / 4.7 / -1.7					
% Profit Before Taxes/Tangible Net Worth	64.1 / (37) 25.9 / 7.5	79.7 / (37) 27.3 / 4.6	79.7 / (24) 22.3 / 5.9						
% Profit Before Taxes/Total Assets	22.0 / 7.1 / 3.7	30.4 / 14.4 / 3.2	25.4 / 7.8 / .1	14.0 / 5.3 / .0					
Sales/Net Fixed Assets	453.4 / 12.4 / .2	UND / 47.0 / .5	UND / 68.3 / 5.7	UND / 45.1 / .4					
Sales/Total Assets	1.7 / .5 / .1	2.2 / .5 / .2	2.9 / 1.2 / .3	2.8 / .6 / .2					
% Depr., Dep., Amort./Sales	1.2 / (29) 7.2 / 23.3	.5 / (25) 3.0 / 20.6	.3 / (19) 1.1 / 13.3						
% Officers', Directors' Owners' Comp/Sales									
Net Sales ($)	771079M	310959M	533953M	5487M	11897M	11030M	59494M	26356M	419689M
Total Assets ($)	978115M	528869M	697528M	27588M	7122M	36731M	119983M	186124M	319980M

M = $ thousand   MM = $ million
See Pages viii through xx for Explanation of Ratios and Data

PROFESSIONAL, SCIENTIFIC, AND TECHNICAL SERVICES

Current Data Sorted by Assets   Comparative Historical Data

						Type of Statement		
3	1	14	31	14	11	Unqualified	97	97
3	13	63	48	8	5	Reviewed	168	151
29	28	47	13		1	Compiled	185	170
224	143	69	17	7		Tax Returns	696	752
263	277	279	134	51	26	Other	1052	1080
	95 (4/1-9/30/18)		1,727 (10/1/18-3/31/19)				4/1/14-3/31/15 ALL	4/1/15-3/31/16 ALL
0-500M	500M-2MM	2-10MM	10-50MM	50-100MM	100-250MM	NUMBER OF STATEMENTS		
522	462	472	243	80	43		2198	2250
%	%	%	%	%	%	**ASSETS**	%	%
46.8	38.9	32.4	32.4	39.1	39.1	Cash & Equivalents	36.9	38.1
4.7	10.5	18.3	19.5	11.9	19.4	Trade Receivables (net)	12.5	12.5
.4	.6	1.2	2.1	.0	.5	Inventory	.9	.8
13.6	15.0	15.1	13.5	11.0	8.7	All Other Current	11.8	11.4
65.5	65.0	67.0	67.5	62.0	67.7	Total Current	62.1	62.8
16.6	15.4	15.1	14.1	23.1	18.8	Fixed Assets (net)	19.1	18.9
4.3	3.5	4.4	2.6	2.7	1.7	Intangibles (net)	3.0	2.9
13.6	16.1	13.4	15.8	12.2	11.8	All Other Non-Current	15.8	15.5
100.0	100.0	100.0	100.0	100.0	100.0	Total	100.0	100.0
						LIABILITIES		
42.5	19.5	11.1	7.7	5.1	5.5	Notes Payable-Short Term	24.1	21.5
4.6	2.3	2.0	3.6	8.4	3.2	Cur. Mat.-L.T.D.	3.6	2.7
3.0	1.9	3.1	3.6	2.3	1.5	Trade Payables	3.0	3.1
.4	.1	.2	.0	.2	.6	Income Taxes Payable	.4	.4
42.6	35.9	30.7	27.7	23.7	18.1	All Other Current	31.3	31.4
93.0	59.7	47.0	40.9	39.8	28.9	Total Current	62.4	59.0
12.7	12.0	10.5	7.5	6.7	11.3	Long-Term Debt	12.3	11.6
.0	.1	.2	.5	.2	.1	Deferred Taxes	.1	.1
7.5	4.6	5.7	6.8	2.7	3.3	All Other Non-Current	6.7	6.1
-13.2	23.7	36.5	44.3	50.5	56.5	Net Worth	18.5	23.2
100.0	100.0	100.0	100.0	100.0	100.0	Total Liabilities & Net Worth	100.0	100.0
						INCOME DATA		
100.0	100.0	100.0	100.0	100.0	100.0	Net Sales	100.0	100.0
						Gross Profit		
82.2	80.5	78.4	75.2	71.1	66.5	Operating Expenses	79.4	78.9
17.8	19.5	21.6	24.8	28.9	33.5	Operating Profit	20.6	21.1
.7	1.3	1.8	.3	1.7	.9	All Other Expenses (net)	1.8	1.5
17.1	18.2	19.8	24.5	27.2	32.6	Profit Before Taxes	18.8	19.6
						RATIOS		
2.1	2.7	3.8	4.4	4.6	6.6		3.0	3.1
1.0	1.1	1.5	1.8	1.8	3.7	Current	1.2	1.2
.4	.7	.9	1.1	1.1	1.5		.6	.7
1.7	2.2	3.1	3.5	4.3	6.6		2.5	2.5
(521) .7	(461) 1.0	1.1	1.3	1.5	2.9	Quick	(2195) 1.0	(2249) 1.0
.2	.3	.5	.6	.7	1.1		.4	.4
0 UND	0 UND	0 UND	0 UND	0 UND	2 185.8		0 UND	0 UND
0 UND	0 UND	0 UND	6 57.8	4 88.8	8 43.0	Sales/Receivables	0 UND	0 UND
0 UND	1 254.3	37 9.9	57 6.4	13 28.5	61 6.0		10 38.2	9 42.0
						Cost of Sales/Inventory		
						Cost of Sales/Payables		
28.5	10.9	6.1	5.1	5.6	4.0		9.1	9.0
-999.8	68.4	19.7	11.7	16.0	7.0	Sales/Working Capital	63.3	54.5
-22.5	-28.8	-86.3	107.1	63.1	20.7		-30.7	-34.6
91.2	108.5	162.2	257.7	650.7	530.0		159.3	170.6
(341) 19.7	(339) 19.8	(364) 27.6	(196) 65.6	(62) 144.5	(36) 174.8	EBIT/Interest	(1594) 27.0	(1626) 31.0
3.0	4.6	4.8	6.2	26.7	19.3		4.0	4.0
	4.4	11.7	17.8	50.7			7.0	7.6
	(16) 1.5	(38) 4.7	(31) 6.8	(11) 6.4		Net Profit + Depr., Dep., Amort./Cur. Mat. L/T/D	(124) 1.8	(107) 2.1
	1.1	1.0	.8	1.1			.7	.8
.0	.0	.1	.1	.2	.1		.1	.1
.4	.3	.2	.2	.4	.3	Fixed/Worth	.4	.4
-1.8	7.1	1.6	.7	.7	.4		6.4	2.6
.7	.7	.5	.4	.3	.2		.5	.5
5.8	2.9	1.8	1.4	.7	.5	Debt/Worth	2.4	2.2
-2.9	UND	16.6	4.7	2.2	1.0		-80.1	48.8
887.7	393.7	299.7	298.7	362.2	254.7		355.2	381.9
(314) 235.8	(348) 119.7	(388) 107.3	(220) 145.3	(77) 173.1	(41) 132.4	% Profit Before Taxes/Tangible Net Worth	(1631) 129.8	(1757) 126.4
58.6	38.8	12.0	22.8	25.8	49.2		24.8	22.5
243.1	104.8	101.1	141.2	174.6	158.8		148.7	145.2
66.5	32.4	30.0	53.8	107.1	96.6	% Profit Before Taxes/Total Assets	39.2	39.9
10.5	6.9	3.7	5.0	5.1	12.1		4.3	4.3
UND	512.1	238.5	78.5	40.9	26.7		251.9	251.6
189.5	113.9	63.3	35.6	20.7	17.0	Sales/Net Fixed Assets	58.2	57.3
43.8	32.1	25.3	18.9	14.6	12.6		21.2	20.7
22.5	9.1	5.8	4.5	6.0	3.6		9.1	8.9
9.9	4.6	3.3	3.0	4.3	3.1	Sales/Total Assets	4.5	4.2
4.4	2.2	1.8	1.8	2.0	2.3		2.3	2.1
.2	.2	.3	.5	.7	.9		.4	.3
(183) .4	(202) .4	(276) .6	(183) .8	(67) 1.0	(29) 1.2	% Depr., Dep., Amort./Sales	(1223) .8	(1219) .8
1.0	.9	1.2	1.3	1.5	1.6		1.5	1.4
8.0	6.8	4.4	5.8	12.2	11.7		8.7	8.4
(295) 17.3	(254) 16.3	(202) 16.5	(87) 15.5	(29) 25.6	(12) 20.2	% Officers', Directors' Owners' Comp/Sales	(1058) 19.2	(1099) 18.2
30.2	31.4	32.7	33.1	37.6	31.1		33.3	31.6
1601540M	3380524M	10537437M	18532719M	29497834M	22342925M	Net Sales ($)	80339790M	89218953M
119448M	509293M	2173808M	5233447M	5598005M	7184982M	Total Assets ($)	21144722M	21855647M

M = $ thousand   MM = $ million
See Pages viii through xx for Explanation of Ratios and Data

Comparative Historical Data

Current Data Sorted by Sales

			Type of Statement						
62	80	74	Unqualified	1	4	2		14	53
146	166	140	Reviewed	1	1	3	10	36	89
149	148	118	Compiled	11	15	8	23	41	20
552	597	460	Tax Returns	81	136	63	89	56	35
1046	1020	1030	Other	127	178	107	177	187	254

4/1/16- 3/31/17 ALL	4/1/17- 3/31/18 ALL	4/1/18- 3/31/19 ALL		95 (4/1-9/30/18)			1,727 (10/1/18-3/31/19)		
				0-1MM	1-3MM	3-5MM	5-10MM	10-25MM	25MM & OVER
1955	2011	1822	NUMBER OF STATEMENTS	221	334	183	299	334	451
%	%	%	ASSETS	%	%	%	%	%	%
37.7	37.0	38.6	Cash & Equivalents	44.0	43.4	36.5	36.7	35.6	36.9
13.7	12.6	12.3	Trade Receivables (net)	5.1	7.7	9.9	15.0	16.1	15.6
.8	.6	.9	Inventory	.2	.3	1.4	1.3	1.7	.6
13.4	14.3	14.1	All Other Current	7.7	14.8	17.3	16.4	16.5	12.2
65.6	64.4	65.9	Total Current	57.1	66.2	65.0	69.3	69.9	65.3
16.6	16.9	15.9	Fixed Assets (net)	24.2	13.9	13.8	12.8	12.6	18.7
3.0	3.8	3.8	Intangibles (net)	5.2	4.5	4.6	2.9	3.9	2.6
14.8	14.9	14.4	All Other Non-Current	13.5	15.5	16.6	15.0	13.5	13.4
100.0	100.0	100.0	Total	100.0	100.0	100.0	100.0	100.0	100.0
			LIABILITIES						
23.0	22.5	21.4	Notes Payable-Short Term	28.1	34.3	33.7	23.4	12.8	8.5
3.2	3.1	3.1	Cur. Mat.-L.T.D.	1.9	2.5	4.7	3.4	2.0	4.1
2.9	2.8	2.7	Trade Payables	3.2	1.9	3.7	2.1	3.5	2.6
.3	.2	.2	Income Taxes Payable	.2	.1	.7	.3	.1	.1
31.9	34.4	34.4	All Other Current	34.0	34.7	34.2	43.0	37.6	26.5
61.2	63.0	61.8	Total Current	67.4	73.5	77.0	72.2	56.0	41.8
11.9	11.9	10.9	Long-Term Debt	18.0	15.1	8.6	10.6	7.4	8.3
.2	.1	.2	Deferred Taxes	.0	.0	.3	.1	.2	.3
6.0	6.1	5.9	All Other Non-Current	9.0	4.2	5.1	5.9	7.0	5.1
20.8	18.8	21.1	Net Worth	5.6	7.1	8.9	11.2	29.4	44.6
100.0	100.0	100.0	Total Liabilties & Net Worth	100.0	100.0	100.0	100.0	100.0	100.0
			INCOME DATA						
100.0	100.0	100.0	Net Sales	100.0	100.0	100.0	100.0	100.0	100.0
			Gross Profit						
78.4	79.9	79.0	Operating Expenses	72.0	80.3	83.3	82.2	81.2	75.9
21.6	20.1	21.0	Operating Profit	28.0	19.7	16.7	17.8	18.8	24.1
1.2	1.1	1.1	All Other Expenses (net)	4.1	.8	1.1	.3	.7	.9
20.3	19.0	19.9	Profit Before Taxes	23.9	18.9	15.6	17.5	18.2	23.3
			RATIOS						
3.2	3.0	3.3		2.9	3.0	2.0	2.8	3.5	4.8
1.3	1.2	1.3	Current	1.0	1.1	1.0	1.1	1.4	1.9
.7	.7	.7		.4	.6	.5	.6	.9	1.0
2.6	2.4	2.7		2.6	2.4	1.4	2.2	2.6	4.3
1.0 (2010)	1.0 (1820)	1.0	Quick	1.0 (333)	.9	.7 (298)	1.0	1.0	1.4
.4	.3	.4		.3	.3	.3	.3	.5	.7
0 UND	0 UND	0 UND		0 UND	0 UND	0 UND	0 UND	0 UND	0 UND
0 UND	0 UND	0 UND	Sales/Receivables	0 UND	0 UND	0 UND	0 UND	0 UND	3 130.7
13 28.9	9 40.9	8 43.0		0 UND	0 UND	0 UND	14 27.0	31 11.6	15 23.6
			Cost of Sales/Inventory						
			Cost of Sales/Payables						
7.5	9.2	8.1		6.9	9.8	10.6	11.2	7.3	7.1
40.0	45.8	44.1	Sales/Working Capital	141.5	112.7	778.0	85.6	35.4	19.5
-35.7	-31.9	-37.4		-7.4	-22.5	-23.9	-29.5	-153.2	348.5
162.0	163.4	161.3		55.3	93.0	76.5	169.9	187.4	341.7
(1452) 33.9	(1470) 26.6	(1338) 27.8	EBIT/Interest	(110) 11.9	(230) 22.7	(139) 18.7	(242) 32.5	(256) 27.2	(361) 74.9
4.7	3.4	4.5		3.5	4.2	2.0	6.6	4.2	6.9
6.1	15.8	15.3						7.0	23.0
(112) 2.9	(143) 3.3	(105) 2.6	Net Profit + Depr., Dep., Amort./Cur. Mat. L/T/D				(25) 2.0	(66) 2.0	5.3
1.7	1.0	1.1						.8	1.1
.0	.0	.0		.0	.0	.0	.0	.1	.1
.3	.3	.3	Fixed/Worth	.3	.2	.3	.3	.2	.3
3.3	5.9	2.2		5.4	22.9	2.5	-3.2	1.6	.9
.5	.6	.5		.7	.6	.9	.8	.5	.3
2.4	2.6	2.2	Debt/Worth	2.8	3.5	4.6	4.8	2.0	1.0
999.8	-67.7	130.1		-10.4	-7.4	-10.0	-12.0	22.5	3.9
389.0	400.0	392.8		409.1	423.5	469.8	470.7	336.4	356.5
(1481) 144.4	(1483) 142.8	(1388) 145.3	% Profit Before Taxes/Tangible Net Worth	(155) 100.0	(230) 154.6	(128) 127.9	(207) 154.9	(268) 108.5	(400) 172.6
28.6	25.0	28.3		22.8	51.7	24.1	47.1	11.8	33.5
150.1	142.0	148.8		107.9	152.2	106.9	140.8	125.6	173.5
44.0	41.7	45.8	% Profit Before Taxes/Total Assets	28.9	46.7	30.5	45.0	37.1	88.8
5.2	4.2	5.4		4.7	9.4	2.4	7.3	3.0	6.0
313.3	387.7	368.9		UND	UND	902.8	832.5	297.2	94.0
64.8	70.6	74.4	Sales/Net Fixed Assets	53.3	153.8	114.0	134.2	82.2	37.4
23.5	23.7	24.9		9.1	32.2	29.7	44.3	31.0	18.9
8.3	9.4	9.4		5.2	10.9	9.8	13.1	11.5	7.7
4.3	4.4	4.4	Sales/Total Assets	2.5	4.4	4.9	5.3	4.8	4.5
2.3	2.4	2.3		1.0	2.0	2.1	2.9	2.3	3.0
.3	.3	.3		.4	.2	.1	.1	.2	.5
(1043) .7	(1055) .7	(940) .6	% Depr., Dep., Amort./Sales	(77) 1.5	(117) .5	(74) .4	(132) .4	(196) .5	(344) .8
1.3	1.3	1.2		10.4	1.1	1.0	.7	1.1	1.2
8.6	9.3	6.9		9.8	9.0	6.9	3.8	4.1	7.1
(959) 19.9	(959) 19.2	(879) 17.2	% Officers', Directors' Owners' Comp/Sales	(90) 17.2	(200) 16.6	(94) 16.3	(161) 15.2	(156) 15.5	(178) 23.4
33.8	32.3	31.6		27.1	28.3	32.0	32.5	32.2	36.0
84704548M	98750767M	85892979M	Net Sales ($)	115276M	615454M	693312M	2157678M	5394862M	76916397M
21389090M	22558527M	20818983M	Total Assets ($)	137262M	280143M	234346M	647889M	1972803M	17546540M

M = $ thousand   MM = $ million
See Pages viii through xx for Explanation of Ratios and Data

Current Data Sorted by Assets

Comparative Historical Data

							Type of Statement		
	1		1	3	1	1	Unqualified	8	12
		2	1				Reviewed	1	4
	1						Compiled	6	4
5	5						Tax Returns	14	26
7	5	4	4	1			Other	45	43
	6 (4/1-9/30/18)		36 (10/1/18-3/31/19)					4/1/14-3/31/15	4/1/15-3/31/16
0-500M	500M-2MM	2-10MM	10-50MM	50-100MM	100-250MM			ALL	ALL
12	12	7	8	2	1		NUMBER OF STATEMENTS	74	89
%	%	%	%	%	%		ASSETS	%	%
52.8	30.2						Cash & Equivalents	32.3	31.7
.5	4.8						Trade Receivables (net)	13.2	14.9
.0	.0						Inventory	.5	.3
15.3	8.7						All Other Current	9.2	7.0
68.6	43.7						Total Current	55.2	53.9
14.0	12.8						Fixed Assets (net)	16.4	18.9
4.8	24.8						Intangibles (net)	11.0	8.7
12.6	18.8						All Other Non-Current	17.4	18.5
100.0	100.0						Total	100.0	100.0
							LIABILITIES		
22.1	5.5						Notes Payable-Short Term	14.0	8.6
2.1	2.3						Cur. Mat.-L.T.D.	1.2	1.3
3.8	2.6						Trade Payables	4.6	6.1
.0	.0						Income Taxes Payable	.0	.3
41.7	22.5						All Other Current	20.6	28.6
69.7	32.8						Total Current	40.4	45.0
5.1	16.3						Long-Term Debt	12.7	13.2
.0	.0						Deferred Taxes	.6	.3
12.7	18.1						All Other Non-Current	10.3	5.4
12.6	32.8						Net Worth	36.0	36.0
100.0	100.0						Total Liabilties & Net Worth	100.0	100.0
							INCOME DATA		
100.0	100.0						Net Sales	100.0	100.0
							Gross Profit		
96.7	91.1						Operating Expenses	89.5	87.9
3.3	8.9						Operating Profit	10.5	12.1
-.3	1.2						All Other Expenses (net)	1.9	1.6
3.7	7.7						Profit Before Taxes	8.6	10.5
							RATIOS		
3.7	2.4							3.8	3.7
1.1	1.0						Current	1.6	1.3
.6	.1							.9	.9
3.7	1.7							3.6	3.1
1.1	.7						Quick	1.3	1.2
.3	.1							.6	.5
0 UND	0 UND							0 UND	0 UND
0 UND	0 UND						Sales/Receivables	3 144.8	0 999.8
0 UND	0 UND							33 10.9	29 12.8
							Cost of Sales/Inventory		
							Cost of Sales/Payables		
24.9	7.1							7.2	8.6
441.3	NM						Sales/Working Capital	14.1	28.7
38.6	-23.7							-542.5	-47.7
								96.5	52.9
							EBIT/Interest	(55) 32.6	(59) 20.0
								6.0	4.3
							Net Profit + Depr., Dep., Amort./Cur. Mat. L/T/D		
.0	.1							.1	.1
.1	.4						Fixed/Worth	.2	.4
.7	-11.7							.8	21.5
.4	.8							.4	.5
5.9	2.5						Debt/Worth	1.2	1.8
-3.4	-2.0							41.0	72.0
							% Profit Before Taxes/Tangible Net Worth	147.5	168.9
								(60) 58.9	(70) 64.6
								19.7	21.4
88.1	46.3						% Profit Before Taxes/Total Assets	41.3	52.6
21.4	4.1							15.0	15.8
-92.2	-.1							2.6	5.3
UND	234.3						Sales/Net Fixed Assets	131.8	146.0
UND	90.0							39.8	46.4
39.0	16.9							15.6	11.6
17.9	6.1						Sales/Total Assets	5.1	5.5
9.2	2.0							2.8	2.8
6.3	1.3							1.5	1.7
							% Depr., Dep., Amort./Sales	.4	.3
								(41) 1.1	(52) 1.0
								1.7	1.9
							% Officers', Directors' Owners' Comp/Sales	3.3	6.2
								(22) 5.6	(26) 9.3
								9.8	13.6
21887M	47567M	71440M	406442M	178166M	69231M		Net Sales ($)	1661482M	2377187M
2428M	11973M	27133M	164208M	153013M	135651M		Total Assets ($)	1020070M	1071030M

M = $ thousand   MM = $ million
See Pages viii through xx for Explanation of Ratios and Data

Comparative Historical Data | Current Data Sorted by Sales

4/1/16-3/31/17 ALL	4/1/17-3/31/18 ALL	4/1/18-3/31/19 ALL	Type of Statement	0-1MM	1-3MM	3-5MM	5-10MM	10-25MM	25MM & OVER
6	8	7	Unqualified					2	5
2		3	Reviewed				2	2	1
3	4	1	Compiled		1				
17	18	10	Tax Returns	3	5	1	1		
50	33	21	Other	5	3	2	5	1	5
				6 (4/1-9/30/18)			36 (10/1/18-3/31/19)		
78	63	42	**NUMBER OF STATEMENTS**	8	9	3	8	3	11
%	%	%	**ASSETS**	%	%	%	%	%	%
36.1	37.4	38.6	Cash & Equivalents						31.8
10.0	8.3	5.8	Trade Receivables (net)						12.6
.1	.0	.0	Inventory						.0
4.6	6.5	9.3	All Other Current						6.9
50.8	52.3	53.8	Total Current						51.3
19.6	13.8	11.8	Fixed Assets (net)						13.3
12.0	14.1	18.1	Intangibles (net)						26.7
17.6	19.8	16.3	All Other Non-Current						8.6
100.0	100.0	100.0	Total						100.0
			LIABILITIES						
6.8	8.3	8.4	Notes Payable-Short Term						1.9
2.0	2.0	2.5	Cur. Mat.-L.T.D.						3.6
4.1	6.4	4.0	Trade Payables						4.5
.3	.1	.0	Income Taxes Payable						.0
19.4	19.1	25.5	All Other Current						13.8
32.5	36.0	40.3	Total Current						23.9
18.4	14.1	11.0	Long-Term Debt						10.6
.1	.1	.1	Deferred Taxes						.2
5.7	7.6	10.9	All Other Non-Current						3.0
43.4	42.2	37.7	Net Worth						62.2
100.0	100.0	100.0	Total Liabilties & Net Worth						100.0
			INCOME DATA						
100.0	100.0	100.0	Net Sales						100.0
			Gross Profit						
83.7	89.6	91.8	Operating Expenses						90.9
16.3	10.4	8.2	Operating Profit						9.1
3.4	.8	.3	All Other Expenses (net)						-1.7
12.9	9.6	8.0	Profit Before Taxes						10.9
			RATIOS						
4.5	3.5	3.6							4.1
1.6	1.5	1.6	Current						1.9
1.0	.9	.6							1.2
3.9	3.2	3.6							3.9
1.5	1.4	1.2	Quick						1.9
.8	.7	.5							1.1
0 UND	0 UND	0 UND							3 124.0
0 UND	0 UND	0 UND	Sales/Receivables						9 39.2
19 19.3	15 24.8	9 40.8							35 10.3
			Cost of Sales/Inventory						
			Cost of Sales/Payables						
8.3	8.2	8.6							5.5
14.3	14.8	19.4	Sales/Working Capital						9.4
NM	-123.8	-66.4							14.7
62.3	58.7	60.1							124.5
(49) 19.0	(42) 16.6	(28) 19.8	EBIT/Interest					(10)	26.5
8.5	5.9	2.5							6.8
			Net Profit + Depr., Dep., Amort./Cur. Mat. L/T/D						
.1	.0	.0							.2
.3	.3	.2	Fixed/Worth						.4
1.6	UND	.7							1.3
.5	.3	.5							.5
1.3	1.5	1.6	Debt/Worth						.8
18.9	-35.0	-4.1							25.3
126.4	102.6	118.8							
(61) 67.7	(46) 43.5	(29) 35.5	% Profit Before Taxes/Tangible Net Worth						
27.2	19.9	6.6							
48.8	44.7	52.5							23.0
22.6	21.2	15.9	% Profit Before Taxes/Total Assets						16.4
6.4	3.9	.4							9.6
97.1	176.0	352.7							104.3
39.1	49.4	74.3	Sales/Net Fixed Assets						16.7
12.2	17.2	17.2							13.0
5.3	7.7	6.5							3.2
2.6	3.1	2.6	Sales/Total Assets						2.3
1.1	1.2	1.6							1.3
.7	.4	.5							
(41) 1.2	(32) 1.2	(16) 1.1	% Depr., Dep., Amort./Sales						
1.9	1.8	1.9							
5.3	3.1	5.6							
(20) 8.2	(22) 5.9	(11) 6.6	% Officers', Directors', Owners' Comp/Sales						
15.1	9.8	8.6							
2044388M	1575018M	794733M	Net Sales ($)	4563M	17013M	11282M	59768M	48268M	653839M
1663369M	936136M	494406M	Total Assets ($)	3237M	4568M	3649M	21184M	8896M	452872M

M = $ thousand   MM = $ million
See Pages viii through xx for Explanation of Ratios and Data

		Current Data Sorted by Assets					Comparative Historical Data	

Type of Statement

0-500M	500M-2MM	2-10MM	10-50MM	50-100MM	100-250MM	Type of Statement	4/1/14-3/31/15 ALL	4/1/15-3/31/16 ALL
		2	2		1	Unqualified	7	8
		3	1			Reviewed	3	3
	1	1				Compiled	2	4
4	1	1				Tax Returns	8	10
13	13	10	3	1	1	Other	34	24
	2 (4/1-9/30/18)		56 (10/1/18-3/31/19)					
17	15	16	7	1	2	NUMBER OF STATEMENTS	54	49
%	%	%	%	%	%	**ASSETS**	%	%
50.6	37.3	34.3				Cash & Equivalents	26.6	32.2
10.5	11.4	36.0				Trade Receivables (net)	29.5	20.3
1.7	2.9	.2				Inventory	1.8	1.5
3.2	16.2	3.0				All Other Current	8.7	3.4
66.0	67.8	73.5				Total Current	66.6	57.4
15.5	19.9	19.4				Fixed Assets (net)	18.5	21.4
2.0	.2	2.8				Intangibles (net)	6.6	10.0
16.6	12.1	4.3				All Other Non-Current	8.2	11.3
100.0	100.0	100.0				Total	100.0	100.0
						LIABILITIES		
28.0	19.4	20.1				Notes Payable-Short Term	11.5	14.0
.5	2.9	1.4				Cur. Mat.-L.T.D.	3.2	3.4
.0	10.4	6.2				Trade Payables	3.1	4.7
.0	.0	.2				Income Taxes Payable	.5	.4
46.7	33.7	18.0				All Other Current	15.2	27.8
75.2	66.4	45.9				Total Current	33.5	50.4
49.7	6.0	10.1				Long-Term Debt	17.3	11.3
.0	.0	.0				Deferred Taxes	.1	.3
20.7	.0	1.2				All Other Non-Current	8.0	12.7
-45.6	27.7	42.7				Net Worth	41.2	25.3
100.0	100.0	100.0				Total Liabilties & Net Worth	100.0	100.0
						INCOME DATA		
100.0	100.0	100.0				Net Sales	100.0	100.0
						Gross Profit		
71.4	87.8	86.9				Operating Expenses	79.3	88.7
28.6	12.2	13.1				Operating Profit	20.7	11.3
.9	.4	1.9				All Other Expenses (net)	2.4	1.1
27.6	11.7	11.2				Profit Before Taxes	18.3	10.2
						RATIOS		
3.5	1.5	4.3				Current	6.0	5.7
1.5	1.0	1.9					2.6	1.8
.4	.6	1.4					1.2	.8
3.0	1.1	3.7				Quick	5.3	5.3
1.4	.7	1.7					2.4	1.8
.4	.4	1.3					1.2	.6
0 UND	0 UND	2 193.1				Sales/Receivables	0 UND	0 UND
0 UND	0 UND	38 9.6					38 9.5	4 87.8
0 UND	4 84.7	111 3.3					99 3.7	64 5.7
						Cost of Sales/Inventory		
						Cost of Sales/Payables		
19.9	15.6	3.9				Sales/Working Capital	3.4	5.4
32.7	999.8	12.5					8.4	12.3
-45.3	-21.0	32.6					29.6	-112.0
55.9	19.8	37.8				EBIT/Interest	95.9	66.8
(11) 27.0	(12) 7.9	(11) 14.9					(40) 13.9	(34) 10.3
15.2	-.2	1.9					2.8	.8
						Net Profit + Depr., Dep., Amort./Cur. Mat. L/T/D		
.1	.0	.0				Fixed/Worth	.1	.1
.2	.3	.2					.3	.5
-.6	4.5	1.0					1.9	-12.1
1.0	.9	.4				Debt/Worth	.3	.3
8.8	3.6	1.3					.9	1.8
-2.4	13.8	2.7					5.3	-16.2
999.8	225.8	55.7				% Profit Before Taxes/Tangible Net Worth	150.0	187.1
(11) 586.2	(12) 39.2	(15) 25.3					(44) 59.6	(35) 46.3
61.9	20.1	16.4					9.5	.8
698.5	35.5	17.9				% Profit Before Taxes/Total Assets	58.9	72.1
201.5	15.1	10.0					20.6	10.5
21.4	2.9	3.3					4.5	-2.2
682.4	364.8	272.4				Sales/Net Fixed Assets	95.8	228.1
83.4	31.1	28.5					32.7	48.6
33.2	14.0	7.8					8.6	10.5
23.2	6.3	5.2				Sales/Total Assets	4.4	5.8
11.8	3.6	2.6					2.2	2.7
4.3	2.5	1.7					1.2	1.3
						% Depr., Dep., Amort./Sales	.6	.4
							(35) 1.0	(26) 1.5
							2.3	2.4
						% Officers', Directors' Owners' Comp/Sales	1.2	1.5
							(15) 4.3	(14) 7.4
							26.5	17.8
37499M	84856M	239396M	309813M	67288M	179516M	Net Sales ($)	1270229M	879107M
2578M	17704M	80579M	174311M	97604M	232885M	Total Assets ($)	785444M	649076M

M = $ thousand   MM = $ million
See Pages viii through xx for Explanation of Ratios and Data

Comparative Historical Data / Current Data Sorted by Sales

				Type of Statement						
				Unqualified					1	4
				Reviewed					3	1
				Compiled				1	1	
				Tax Returns	2	1	1	2	2	
6	9	5		Other	9	9	2	10	5	6
2	5	4								
6	5	2								
7	9	6								
39	44	41				2 (4/1-9/30/18)		56 (10/1/18-3/31/19)		
4/1/16- 3/31/17	4/1/17- 3/31/18	4/1/18- 3/31/19			0-1MM	1-3MM	3-5MM	5-10MM	10-25MM	25MM & OVER
ALL	ALL	ALL								
60	72	58		NUMBER OF STATEMENTS	11	10	3	13	10	11
%	%	%		ASSETS	%	%	%	%	%	%
27.4	28.8	37.7		Cash & Equivalents	46.6	40.2		36.9	40.2	30.9
26.5	21.5	20.4		Trade Receivables (net)	14.1	2.9		20.0	32.8	23.3
.3	.3	1.5		Inventory	2.6	.0		3.3	3.5	.9
7.4	10.2	7.5		All Other Current	5.7	16.3		5.2	3.5	9.1
61.7	60.8	67.0		Total Current	68.9	59.3		65.4	76.8	64.1
15.0	13.2	16.1		Fixed Assets (net)	26.2	15.8		19.4	11.8	8.9
10.4	9.4	5.1		Intangibles (net)	3.1	.0		1.6	2.0	19.3
12.9	16.7	11.8		All Other Non-Current	1.8	24.9		13.6	9.5	7.7
100.0	100.0	100.0		Total	100.0	100.0		100.0	100.0	100.0
				LIABILITIES						
14.2	10.7	19.9		Notes Payable-Short Term	29.4	25.6		19.6	8.4	7.2
2.3	2.4	1.8		Cur. Mat.-L.T.D.	.5	.7		4.2	.7	2.6
7.2	5.2	5.4		Trade Payables	.0	.7		11.8	6.9	6.6
.2	.2	.1		Income Taxes Payable	.0	.0		.0	.4	.2
19.6	24.1	32.5		All Other Current	63.6	45.4		15.4	24.0	22.1
43.5	42.6	59.8		Total Current	93.5	72.3		51.0	40.4	38.6
21.1	20.6	22.5		Long-Term Debt	22.3	62.3		10.0	6.8	20.8
.0	.0	.0		Deferred Taxes	.0	.0		.0	.0	.0
8.1	5.2	7.0		All Other Non-Current	24.4	.0		7.5	.9	3.0
27.3	31.6	10.7		Net Worth	-40.2	-34.6		31.6	51.8	37.7
100.0	100.0	100.0		Total Liabilities & Net Worth	100.0	100.0		100.0	100.0	100.0
				INCOME DATA						
100.0	100.0	100.0		Net Sales	100.0	100.0		100.0	100.0	100.0
				Gross Profit						
87.3	85.5	82.8		Operating Expenses	71.8	74.7		85.0	84.5	89.5
12.7	14.5	17.2		Operating Profit	28.2	25.3		15.0	15.5	10.5
1.7	2.2	1.7		All Other Expenses (net)	2.8	1.1		.6	.6	3.5
11.0	12.3	15.5		Profit Before Taxes	25.3	24.2		14.4	14.9	6.9
				RATIOS						
3.0	4.3	2.7			1.7	1.3		2.0	4.2	3.2
1.6	1.7	1.5		Current	1.4	.9		1.5	2.1	2.2
1.1	.9	.8			.4	.5		.8	1.4	1.4
2.4	3.8	2.6			1.7	1.3		2.0	3.8	2.9
1.5	1.3	1.4		Quick	1.4	.5		1.0	2.1	1.7
.8	.6	.6			.4	.2		.6	1.4	1.1
0 UND	0 UND	0 UND			0 UND	0 UND		0 UND	0 UND	2 188.3
37 9.8	10 37.9	2 186.9		Sales/Receivables	0 UND	0 UND		0 UND	28 13.1	35 10.3
61 6.0	63 5.8	54 6.8			13 28.9	0 UND		55 6.6	70 5.2	64 5.7
				Cost of Sales/Inventory						
				Cost of Sales/Payables						
7.4	6.6	7.8			12.1	30.4		8.3	4.8	3.4
22.0	15.7	23.3		Sales/Working Capital	26.0	NM		24.0	15.4	7.5
95.8	-40.1	-62.3			-11.2	-16.7		-57.4	27.0	11.9
41.4	82.2	41.9				89.9				
(40) 9.1	(52) 19.4	(42) 17.7		EBIT/Interest		25.6				
1.9	1.7	1.5				8.1				
				Net Profit + Depr., Dep., Amort./Cur. Mat. L/T/D						
.1	.0	.1			.2	.1		.0	.1	.1
.3	.2	.3		Fixed/Worth	.3	1.0		.2	.2	.5
-1.5	4.0	2.5			-.3	-6.2		1.7	.4	.0
.7	.4	.8			1.1	1.4		.8	.4	.4
2.2	1.6	2.5		Debt/Worth	3.4	7.5		3.6	1.3	2.3
-7.3	-46.6	NM			-1.7	-5.0		11.3	2.4	-4.2
194.2	287.9	297.7						297.7	82.3	
(42) 66.6	(53) 43.5	(44) 35.5		% Profit Before Taxes/Tangible Net Worth				(12) 52.1	30.1	
21.4	7.0	17.9						19.0	24.0	
52.8	52.3	85.5			266.7	433.5		102.1	52.0	34.9
17.6	13.0	15.3		% Profit Before Taxes/Total Assets	66.7	49.9		9.3	11.9	6.5
3.8	1.1	4.0			12.7	14.4		2.7	6.8	-5.8
220.0	999.8	271.0			143.0	UND		682.3	227.9	169.6
43.7	63.5	61.2		Sales/Net Fixed Assets	34.6	153.6		31.1	58.4	65.8
16.5	15.0	18.3			30.6	24.8		12.6	16.3	28.8
5.8	5.1	7.1			7.3	22.2		11.5	9.2	3.0
2.8	2.9	3.4		Sales/Total Assets	4.3	4.2		5.8	3.6	1.9
1.7	1.5	1.7			1.2	2.3		3.0	2.1	.9
.4	.2	.4								
(32) 1.0	(31) .6	(26) 1.0		% Depr., Dep., Amort./Sales						
2.2	1.6	1.5								
2.4	2.4	10.8								
(20) 9.1	(20) 6.2	(17) 24.8		% Officers', Directors' Owners' Comp/Sales						
16.5	13.7	31.5								
1659748M	1403685M	918368M		Net Sales ($)	4822M	20017M	11557M	95305M	170731M	615936M
1062372M	977847M	605661M		Total Assets ($)	5625M	5322M	6108M	28205M	52284M	508117M

M = $ thousand   MM = $ million
See Pages viii through xx for Explanation of Ratios and Data

Current Data Sorted by Assets   Comparative Historical Data

						Type of Statement		
1	1	1	3			Unqualified	4	6
		1	1			Reviewed	3	4
3	6	10	5		1	Compiled	48	46
84	38	11	4			Tax Returns	169	251
104	101	134	59	8	10	Other	457	454
0-500M	500M-2MM	2-10MM	10-50MM	50-100MM	100-250MM		4/1/14-3/31/15 ALL	4/1/15-3/31/16 ALL
	131 (4/1-9/30/18)		455 (10/1/18-3/31/19)					
192	146	157	72	8	11	**NUMBER OF STATEMENTS**	681	761
%	%	%	%	%	%	**ASSETS**	%	%
37.9	14.6	11.0	17.9		14.3	Cash & Equivalents	20.4	21.3
14.9	25.2	36.2	31.8		34.5	Trade Receivables (net)	27.9	26.3
.2	1.8	3.4	6.2		2.8	Inventory	2.8	3.0
3.1	5.5	7.3	8.4		7.3	All Other Current	6.4	4.6
56.0	47.1	57.9	64.3		58.9	Total Current	57.4	55.2
14.1	17.9	17.1	9.7		14.1	Fixed Assets (net)	17.1	15.8
18.1	25.6	17.6	15.7		17.1	Intangibles (net)	15.4	17.6
11.7	9.3	7.3	10.3		9.9	All Other Non-Current	10.2	11.4
100.0	100.0	100.0	100.0		100.0	Total	100.0	100.0
						LIABILITIES		
35.0	9.4	9.1	7.5		7.7	Notes Payable-Short Term	16.3	21.8
6.9	2.6	2.9	2.8		2.7	Cur. Mat.-L.T.D.	3.2	3.6
2.4	1.6	2.2	3.7		7.1	Trade Payables	2.6	2.3
.1	.1	.1	.0		.1	Income Taxes Payable	.2	.2
23.7	13.7	15.7	18.8		14.6	All Other Current	17.6	17.3
68.1	27.4	30.0	32.9		32.3	Total Current	39.8	45.1
12.9	22.4	16.8	10.7		15.1	Long-Term Debt	17.0	17.9
.0	.2	.0	.2		.0	Deferred Taxes	.2	.1
5.0	7.6	8.0	8.3		7.0	All Other Non-Current	6.6	8.0
13.9	42.5	45.2	47.9		45.5	Net Worth	36.5	28.8
100.0	100.0	100.0	100.0		100.0	Total Liabilties & Net Worth	100.0	100.0
						INCOME DATA		
100.0	100.0	100.0	100.0		100.0	Net Sales	100.0	100.0
						Gross Profit		
83.0	81.1	83.4	80.6		79.3	Operating Expenses	82.2	83.5
17.0	18.9	16.6	19.4		20.7	Operating Profit	17.8	16.5
1.2	2.4	3.7	2.9		1.2	All Other Expenses (net)	2.8	2.2
15.9	16.5	13.0	16.5		19.4	Profit Before Taxes	15.0	14.2
						RATIOS		
4.3	3.9	3.4	4.0		3.6		4.0	3.7
1.2	1.7	2.0	1.8		1.7	Current	1.8	1.6
.4	.6	1.2	1.3		1.1		.9	.7
4.3	3.1	2.8	2.8		3.4		3.3	3.2
(191) 1.1	1.4	1.7	1.4		1.2	Quick	1.5	1.3
.4	.5	1.0	1.0		.9		.7	.6
0 UND	0 UND	33 11.2	32 11.4		42 8.7		0 UND	0 UND
0 UND	33 11.0	46 7.9	45 8.2		51 7.1	Sales/Receivables	35 10.3	29 12.6
20 18.3	57 6.4	68 5.4	62 5.9		73 5.0		60 6.1	59 6.2
						Cost of Sales/Inventory		
						Cost of Sales/Payables		
10.4	6.3	5.2	5.5		5.0		5.8	6.3
139.2	11.6	10.7	8.1		12.3	Sales/Working Capital	13.8	18.5
-19.4	-28.1	32.0	16.9		43.9		-114.3	-38.0
53.8	36.0	49.0	75.2				73.8	73.7
(122) 15.3	(115) 14.1	(132) 12.8	(59) 22.2			EBIT/Interest	(517) 15.0	(600) 13.7
4.5	4.3	4.5	4.1				3.3	3.3
							12.1	6.9
						Net Profit + Depr., Dep., Amort./Cur. Mat. L/T/D	(26) 2.4	(28) 2.1
							.3	1.6
.0	.0	.1	.1		.2		.1	.1
.2	.4	.4	.3		.8	Fixed/Worth	.3	.3
5.6	38.1	20.6	1.7		.9		2.6	62.0
.3	.6	.6	.5		.6		.5	.6
4.8	3.8	1.9	1.7		2.3	Debt/Worth	1.7	2.7
-2.6	-6.6	53.3	11.5		6.2		UND	-8.0
491.8	171.0	129.3	182.5				181.0	199.8
(120) 130.7	(100) 53.3	(119) 53.3	(59) 102.3			% Profit Before Taxes/Tangible Net Worth	(511) 72.7	(526) 73.9
34.7	20.2	24.2	21.5				18.6	19.1
137.4	55.4	42.2	67.6		96.4		71.0	76.5
52.4	19.3	17.7	25.3		69.3	% Profit Before Taxes/Total Assets	25.9	26.0
14.1	5.0	4.9	4.8		4.9		4.2	4.2
UND	427.5	75.7	101.7		24.1		194.9	255.1
163.1	60.6	34.4	37.5		19.7	Sales/Net Fixed Assets	42.7	46.9
31.3	16.8	16.1	20.8		8.5		18.8	20.4
10.5	3.9	3.4	3.3		3.3		5.1	5.8
5.9	2.5	2.5	2.6		2.1	Sales/Total Assets	3.0	3.2
3.2	1.4	1.8	1.8		1.2		1.9	2.0
.5	.6	.7	.8				.8	.7
(53) .8	(65) 1.3	(116) 1.3	(52) 1.3			% Depr., Dep., Amort./Sales	(377) 1.3	(424) 1.3
1.6	2.7	2.0	1.9				2.1	2.1
12.8	8.0	13.3	7.8				13.5	11.9
(131) 19.7	(78) 14.3	(67) 21.4	(33) 15.8			% Officers', Directors' Owners' Comp/Sales	(361) 21.6	(436) 20.7
27.2	23.2	31.1	23.3				30.9	30.4
232829M	458483M	2276668M	3452954M	1146224M	3521469M	Net Sales ($)	11905422M	15264863M
36862M	156477M	720713M	1371334M	549615M	1498369M	Total Assets ($)	4003468M	5080881M

© RMA 2019

M = $ thousand   MM = $ million
See Pages viii through xx for Explanation of Ratios and Data

Comparative Historical Data

Current Data Sorted by Sales

			Type of Statement						
5	6	6	Unqualified	1	1		1	3	1
2	4	2	Reviewed					1	
35	28	25	Compiled	1	3	7	1	6	7
171	132	137	Tax Returns	60	42	11	11	8	5
429	424	416	Other	91	79	41	62	65	78
4/1/16- 3/31/17 ALL	4/1/17- 3/31/18 ALL	4/1/18- 3/31/19 ALL		131 (4/1-9/30/18)			455 (10/1/18-3/31/19)		
				0-1MM	1-3MM	3-5MM	5-10MM	10-25MM	25MM & OVER
642	594	586	NUMBER OF STATEMENTS	153	125	59	75	83	91
%	%	%	ASSETS	%	%	%	%	%	%
20.0	19.3	21.7	Cash & Equivalents	29.1	25.3	16.6	18.5	12.5	18.4
26.8	27.8	25.8	Trade Receivables (net)	12.5	23.1	29.8	33.5	35.8	33.8
3.6	3.0	2.3	Inventory	.2	.7	4.0	2.6	2.8	5.8
6.1	6.5	5.9	All Other Current	2.0	4.7	6.3	8.1	7.7	10.1
56.5	56.6	55.6	Total Current	43.8	53.9	56.7	62.8	58.9	68.1
14.3	15.3	15.3	Fixed Assets (net)	24.0	13.0	12.0	13.1	12.1	10.8
19.9	19.0	19.4	Intangibles (net)	20.8	22.7	24.0	14.7	20.4	12.7
9.3	9.1	9.7	All Other Non-Current	11.5	10.4	7.3	9.5	8.6	8.4
100.0	100.0	100.0	Total	100.0	100.0	100.0	100.0	100.0	100.0
			LIABILITIES						
17.7	16.6	17.5	Notes Payable-Short Term	28.4	16.3	21.2	15.1	9.8	7.3
3.3	3.9	4.1	Cur. Mat.-L.T.D.	3.5	.6	3.6	3.0	2.9	2.8
2.7	2.2	2.5	Trade Payables	2.1	2.4	1.4	1.2	3.0	4.4
.2	.1	.1	Income Taxes Payable	.1	.0	.2	.1	.1	.0
18.3	17.4	18.2	All Other Current	20.8	14.6	16.2	16.6	20.8	19.0
42.3	40.2	42.4	Total Current	55.0	40.8	42.6	36.0	36.5	33.6
19.3	18.1	16.1	Long-Term Debt	21.0	18.9	14.1	12.0	15.4	9.3
.2	.1	.1	Deferred Taxes	.0	.1	.1	.0	.1	.2
8.7	6.9	6.9	All Other Non-Current	5.5	4.6	8.7	10.6	7.7	7.5
29.6	34.6	34.6	Net Worth	18.5	35.6	34.5	41.4	40.3	49.4
100.0	100.0	100.0	Total Liabilties & Net Worth	100.0	100.0	100.0	100.0	100.0	100.0
			INCOME DATA						
100.0	100.0	100.0	Net Sales	100.0	100.0	100.0	100.0	100.0	100.0
			Gross Profit						
84.2	83.5	82.2	Operating Expenses	76.0	81.7	87.8	88.5	86.6	80.7
15.8	16.5	17.8	Operating Profit	24.0	18.3	12.2	11.5	13.4	19.3
1.7	2.0	2.3	All Other Expenses (net)	4.6	.4	1.1	1.1	2.1	3.2
14.2	14.5	15.4	Profit Before Taxes	19.4	17.9	11.1	10.5	11.3	16.1
			RATIOS						
3.7	4.0	3.8		4.0	5.1	3.0	4.6	3.3	3.6
1.7	1.7	1.7	Current	1.2	1.6	2.0	2.1	1.8	2.2
.8	.9	.9		.3	.7	.7	1.1	1.0	1.4
3.2	3.2	3.1		3.6	4.5	2.5	3.9	2.5	2.7
1.3	1.3	(585) 1.4	Quick	(152) 1.0	1.4	1.6	1.7	1.4	1.5
.6	.7	.7		.3	.6	.5	.9	.9	1.0
0 UND	0 UND	0 UND		0 UND	0 UND	0 999.8	14 26.6	32 11.3	32 11.4
33 10.9	36 10.1	33 10.9	Sales/Receivables	0 UND	19 18.9	40 9.2	44 8.3	45 8.2	46 8.0
59 6.2	61 6.0	56 6.5		26 13.9	56 6.5	73 5.0	65 5.6	60 6.1	63 5.8
			Cost of Sales/Inventory						
			Cost of Sales/Payables						
5.9	5.9	6.2		8.8	7.3	4.6	5.4	6.1	5.6
14.9	15.3	13.8	Sales/Working Capital	157.8	15.5	11.7	11.4	13.7	8.2
-56.1	-76.3	-60.9		-10.1	-44.9	-31.3	67.8	567.9	15.7
49.9	47.7	51.1		28.3	69.4	32.7	42.1	42.5	97.2
(506) 12.8	(459) 11.5	(444) 14.2	EBIT/Interest	(90) 7.4	(93) 23.2	(50) 9.8	(65) 13.6	(73) 14.5	(73) 26.0
2.8	2.8	4.5		4.5	9.0	1.3	3.2	2.8	4.0
3.1	3.0	8.3	Net Profit + Depr., Dep.,						11.4
(23) 1.9	(26) 1.8	(28) 3.4	Amort./Cur. Mat. L/T/D					(12) 3.8	
.1	1.1	.8							.8
.1	.1	.0		.0	.0	.0	.0	.1	.1
.4	.3	.3	Fixed/Worth	.3	.3	.3	.2	.5	.3
-11.9	150.4	6.6		7.0	2.2	-1.3	2.9	-1.3	.8
.6	.6	.5		.4	.5	.7	.4	.8	.5
2.8	2.4	2.4	Debt/Worth	4.2	3.9	4.8	1.7	2.2	1.3
-6.3	-7.3	-9.4		-2.4	-5.8	-3.3	999.8	-16.2	5.3
173.8	179.2	194.0	% Profit Before Taxes/Tangible Net Worth	178.6	309.6	155.5	198.4	133.7	183.2
(436) 66.1	(412) 75.3	(413) 80.6		(100) 57.6	(86) 97.4	(35) 76.3	(57) 52.8	(57) 75.9	(78) 100.5
17.7	19.5	24.8		20.5	36.2	10.0	23.5	27.1	24.8
63.5	68.1	70.6	% Profit Before Taxes/Total Assets	88.9	111.0	45.6	52.0	46.2	73.1
25.6	25.4	27.0		30.1	41.9	10.2	17.3	19.7	39.2
4.4	5.1	7.0		6.9	13.8	1.4	6.0	3.9	5.8
194.3	211.8	373.8		UND	UND	405.5	199.7	83.6	65.9
49.3	52.5	48.6	Sales/Net Fixed Assets	56.0	92.4	50.8	56.1	41.8	31.9
19.8	19.2	20.0		12.4	28.6	23.0	19.5	23.1	19.7
4.7	5.0	5.0		6.9	7.5	5.4	5.0	4.0	3.6
2.9	3.0	3.0	Sales/Total Assets	2.8	3.4	2.7	3.1	2.8	2.8
2.0	1.9	1.9		.9	2.0	1.8	2.4	2.2	2.0
.7	.6	.6		.7	.6	.5	.5	.6	.8
(337) 1.3	(295) 1.2	(300) 1.3	% Depr., Dep., Amort./Sales	(56) 1.8	(37) 1.5	(31) .8	(50) 1.2	(59) 1.1	(67) 1.4
2.0	2.0	2.0		18.5	2.8	2.2	1.7	1.6	1.8
10.4	11.6	10.7		11.0	10.6	8.0	10.0	11.3	11.6
(378) 19.2	(339) 19.0	(313) 18.5	% Officers', Directors' Owners' Comp/Sales	(79) 17.0	(80) 18.5	(38) 17.3	(43) 21.9	(37) 21.6	(36) 16.1
27.8	27.0	26.5		23.2	26.2	26.1	31.1	30.1	23.4
10282683M	14418712M	11088627M	Net Sales ($)	77701M	222473M	230243M	541079M	1351428M	8665703M
3820572M	4792011M	4333370M	Total Assets ($)	74277M	103430M	92584M	196452M	506065M	3360562M

M = $ thousand   MM = $ million
See Pages viii through xx for Explanation of Ratios and Data

Current Data Sorted by Assets   **Comparative Historical Data**

Type of Statement	0-500M	500M-2MM	2-10MM	10-50MM	50-100MM	100-250MM		4/1/14-3/31/15 ALL	4/1/15-3/31/16 ALL
Unqualified			3	1		1		3	3
Reviewed						1			
Compiled	16	5	2	5	2	2		4	1
Tax Returns	12	10	5					13	16
Other								15	22
			8 (4/1-9/30/18)	57 (10/1/18-3/31/19)					
NUMBER OF STATEMENTS	28	15	10	6	2	4		35	42

	0-500M	500M-2MM	2-10MM	10-50MM	50-100MM	100-250MM		4/1/14-3/31/15	4/1/15-3/31/16
ASSETS	%	%	%	%	%	%		%	%
Cash & Equivalents	43.3	14.2	26.6					19.1	28.0
Trade Receivables (net)	7.6	8.8	16.7					12.6	13.1
Inventory	.0	.0	1.3					1.8	1.0
All Other Current	1.1	5.5	15.0					10.3	6.6
Total Current	52.0	28.5	59.6					43.7	48.7
Fixed Assets (net)	22.4	11.3	6.6					20.0	17.6
Intangibles (net)	11.6	43.1	20.6					21.8	22.5
All Other Non-Current	13.7	17.1	13.2					14.6	11.3
Total	100.0	100.0	100.0					100.0	100.0
LIABILITIES									
Notes Payable-Short Term	35.3	14.1	6.2					9.1	19.4
Cur. Mat.-L.T.D.	1.8	2.6	3.2					3.2	1.7
Trade Payables	11.8	1.4	3.6					4.0	12.4
Income Taxes Payable	.0	.0	.1					.2	.1
All Other Current	42.5	17.7	25.9					33.2	27.9
Total Current	91.4	35.9	38.9					49.6	61.4
Long-Term Debt	9.9	33.7	22.7					41.0	16.4
Deferred Taxes	.0	.0	.0					.1	.1
All Other Non-Current	.3	.9	5.4					2.7	7.1
Net Worth	-1.7	29.5	32.9					6.5	15.0
Total Liabilities & Net Worth	100.0	100.0	100.0					100.0	100.0
INCOME DATA									
Net Sales	100.0	100.0	100.0					100.0	100.0
Gross Profit									
Operating Expenses	79.1	82.6	85.0					86.0	80.5
Operating Profit	20.9	17.4	15.0					14.0	19.5
All Other Expenses (net)	.1	2.2	.7					2.8	1.7
Profit Before Taxes	20.7	15.2	14.4					11.2	17.8
RATIOS									
Current	3.6	3.9	2.7					3.2	2.4
	1.3	1.2	2.0					1.6	1.1
	.4	.2	.5					.4	.5
Quick	3.5	2.3	2.1					2.4	2.0
	1.2	(14) .9	1.0					.9	1.0
	.4	.2	.4					.2	.2
Sales/Receivables	0 UND	0 UND	0 UND					0 UND	0 UND
	0 UND	0 UND	2 161.3					5 67.9	0 999.8
	0 UND	36 10.2	60 6.1					46 8.0	55 6.6
Cost of Sales/Inventory									
Cost of Sales/Payables									
Sales/Working Capital	25.5	12.9	3.8					6.1	4.7
	54.7	47.9	7.4					91.2	550.5
	-38.7	-8.7	-6.7					-23.4	-19.1
EBIT/Interest	45.4	13.3						26.2	24.0
	(17) 13.5	(13) 7.4						(28) 8.1	(32) 11.7
	6.6	2.8						1.6	5.1
Net Profit + Depr., Dep., Amort./Cur. Mat. L/T/D									
Fixed/Worth	.0	.0	.0					.2	.1
	.8	1.0	.5					.7	1.1
	UND	-.3	-.1					-1.4	-2.3
Debt/Worth	.3	2.5	.4					.8	.9
	2.7	-13.3	10.8					3.1	10.9
	-8.2	-1.2	-1.8					-3.0	-2.2
% Profit Before Taxes/Tangible Net Worth	999.8							106.3	854.5
	(19) 230.8							(20) 40.7	(26) 161.5
	80.9							7.2	67.1
% Profit Before Taxes/Total Assets	347.0	28.0	61.4					57.1	144.4
	105.2	19.3	17.7					15.9	33.5
	37.6	6.0	7.3					.0	10.6
Sales/Net Fixed Assets	UND	552.0	94.4					123.2	170.6
	368.8	46.0	51.1					25.7	37.4
	14.3	9.3	15.7					4.1	14.6
Sales/Total Assets	36.0	2.0	2.8					5.6	5.3
	6.5	1.3	1.8					2.5	2.4
	2.8	.8	1.0					1.2	1.3
% Depr., Dep., Amort./Sales								1.2	1.1
								(18) 3.7	(17) 1.4
								6.3	3.2
% Officers', Directors' Owners' Comp/Sales	7.6							8.5	10.0
	(17) 11.4							(17) 19.6	(19) 12.8
	19.3							26.1	21.0
Net Sales ($)	19506M	27615M	95779M	210959M	934866M	670197M		630518M	543390M
Total Assets ($)	3014M	16157M	40745M	104729M	175809M	767050M		466928M	375514M

© RMA 2019

M = $ thousand   MM = $ million
See Pages viii through xx for Explanation of Ratios and Data

Comparative Historical Data | | | Current Data Sorted by Sales

			Type of Statement	0-1MM	1-3MM	3-5MM	5-10MM	10-25MM	25MM & OVER
2	4	5	Unqualified				1	1	3
			Reviewed						1
1	2	1	Compiled						
25	19	23	Tax Returns	16	6		1	2	5
23	25	36	Other	10	10	4	2	5	5
4/1/16-3/31/17	4/1/17-3/31/18	4/1/18-3/31/19			8 (4/1-9/30/18)		57 (10/1/18-3/31/19)		
ALL	ALL	ALL							
51	50	65	**NUMBER OF STATEMENTS**	26	16	4	4	6	9
%	%	%	**ASSETS**	%	%	%	%	%	%
29.1	29.2	28.8	Cash & Equivalents	39.9	18.6				
11.6	11.1	11.6	Trade Receivables (net)	8.9	4.1				
.0	.8	.6	Inventory	.0	.0				
5.7	6.1	6.9	All Other Current	2.9	5.7				
46.4	47.2	47.9	Total Current	51.8	28.4				
11.0	14.9	17.4	Fixed Assets (net)	19.6	12.2				
29.1	25.2	21.8	Intangibles (net)	14.3	43.1				
13.6	12.7	12.9	All Other Non-Current	14.0	16.4				
100.0	100.0	100.0	Total	100.0	100.0				
			LIABILITIES						
22.6	9.8	20.3	Notes Payable-Short Term	10.6	19.8				
2.7	3.6	2.8	Cur. Mat.-L.T.D.	1.8	3.7				
2.4	2.0	7.1	Trade Payables	12.5	2.3				
.0	.1	.1	Income Taxes Payable	.0	.0				
13.0	12.9	28.6	All Other Current	26.8	38.0				
40.7	28.3	58.9	Total Current	51.8	63.8				
14.5	20.4	21.8	Long-Term Debt	18.3	22.4				
.1	.1	.1	Deferred Taxes	.0	.0				
.9	4.3	3.0	All Other Non-Current	.7	2.2				
43.6	46.9	16.3	Net Worth	29.2	11.6				
100.0	100.0	100.0	Total Liabilities & Net Worth	100.0	100.0				
			INCOME DATA						
100.0	100.0	100.0	Net Sales	100.0	100.0				
			Gross Profit						
78.3	79.9	82.8	Operating Expenses	79.6	83.0				
21.7	20.1	17.2	Operating Profit	20.4	17.0				
.9	3.3	1.5	All Other Expenses (net)	1.0	1.1				
20.9	16.9	15.7	Profit Before Taxes	19.4	15.9				
			RATIOS						
4.6	8.8	3.3		4.2	2.3				
1.7	2.1	1.5	Current	2.1	1.1				
.3	.8	.6		.9	.1				
4.4	8.4	3.0		3.9	1.6				
1.0	(64) 1.6	1.1	Quick	(25) 1.4	.7				
.3	.4	.5		.8	.1				
0 UND	0 UND	0 UND		0 UND	0 UND				
0 UND	0 UND	0 UND	Sales/Receivables	0 UND	0 UND				
30 12.1	22 16.3	41 8.9		8 43.0	0 UND				
			Cost of Sales/Inventory						
			Cost of Sales/Payables						
3.7	5.0	6.5		10.2	22.3				
31.4	14.1	28.1	Sales/Working Capital	53.3	NM				
-12.2	-37.5	-39.8		UND	-4.0				
38.9	31.8	33.5		39.2	13.3				
(32) 15.4	(37) 10.0	(48) 8.2	EBIT/Interest	(17) 12.5	(13) 6.2				
6.4	3.2	3.6		6.5	4.0				
			Net Profit + Depr., Dep., Amort./Cur. Mat. L/T/D						
.0	.0	.0		.0	.0				
.2	.4	.8	Fixed/Worth	.8	1.0				
UND	-3.6	-.5		UND	-.5				
.3	.1	.7		.3	3.0				
1.6	1.4	3.6	Debt/Worth	1.4	-10.6				
-2.4	-2.0	-2.1		-11.3	-1.2				
296.4	141.5	488.1		999.8					
(35) 98.3	(33) 51.2	(40) 88.8	% Profit Before Taxes/Tangible Net Worth	(19) 173.6					
35.6	24.8	15.5		50.9					
66.5	45.0	118.4		154.2	35.6				
33.2	18.3	27.7	% Profit Before Taxes/Total Assets	50.4	21.7				
14.5	7.3	6.3		10.8	10.1				
176.3	192.1	534.0		UND	UND				
65.0	32.0	46.0	Sales/Net Fixed Assets	199.0	82.8				
17.0	10.5	9.0		8.9	17.4				
3.6	4.0	5.9		34.1	5.6				
2.3	2.0	2.3	Sales/Total Assets	4.3	1.6				
1.5	.9	1.1		2.0	1.0				
.5	.8	.7							
(23) 1.0	(17) 1.2	(22) 1.9	% Depr., Dep., Amort./Sales						
2.0	3.8	3.6							
4.7	7.0	7.3		7.5					
(22) 9.7	(25) 15.0	(29) 12.5	% Officers', Directors' Owners' Comp/Sales	(17) 12.5					
16.8	27.8	22.6		23.4					
713031M	564687M	1958922M	Net Sales ($)	12158M	24446M	17127M	26312M	92827M	1786052M
433781M	501069M	1107504M	Total Assets ($)	5247M	16495M	8714M	11857M	123127M	942064M

M = $ thousand   MM = $ million
See Pages viii through xx for Explanation of Ratios and Data

Current Data Sorted by Assets   Comparative Historical Data

0-500M	500M-2MM	2-10MM	10-50MM	50-100MM	100-250MM	Type of Statement	4/1/14-3/31/15 ALL	4/1/15-3/31/16 ALL
1	2	5	4		1	Unqualified	16	12
		1	2		1	Reviewed	5	8
		1				Compiled	3	5
5	3	4	11	1	2	Tax Returns	16	14
4	16	7				Other	51	45
	17 (4/1-9/30/18)		54 (10/1/18-3/31/19)					
10	21	18	17	1	4	NUMBER OF STATEMENTS	91	84
%	%	%	%	%	%	ASSETS	%	%
65.4	44.8	33.1	21.2			Cash & Equivalents	41.5	36.7
.2	9.6	22.2	14.3			Trade Receivables (net)	12.3	14.3
.0	.0	.0	.1			Inventory	.0	.1
9.2	5.6	18.8	16.7			All Other Current	17.2	14.2
74.8	60.0	74.1	52.3			Total Current	71.1	65.4
14.3	12.8	5.9	8.7			Fixed Assets (net)	6.8	5.7
2.1	4.5	11.5	7.9			Intangibles (net)	9.1	13.9
9.0	22.6	8.5	31.1			All Other Non-Current	13.1	15.0
100.0	100.0	100.0	100.0			Total	100.0	100.0
						LIABILITIES		
45.4	7.2	5.4	3.4			Notes Payable-Short Term	7.9	6.7
5.2	.2	6.1	1.1			Cur. Mat.-L.T.D.	.8	3.6
3.0	4.5	12.3	2.8			Trade Payables	5.8	5.1
.0	.1	.2	.1			Income Taxes Payable	.0	1.2
78.3	35.8	38.9	49.4			All Other Current	48.7	44.8
131.9	47.8	63.0	56.8			Total Current	63.3	61.4
56.1	3.4	4.1	3.8			Long-Term Debt	7.2	12.1
.0	.0	.2	.1			Deferred Taxes	.3	.2
5.2	8.9	2.0	16.1			All Other Non-Current	5.3	7.1
-93.2	39.9	30.7	23.2			Net Worth	23.9	19.1
100.0	100.0	100.0	100.0			Total Liabilties & Net Worth	100.0	100.0
						INCOME DATA		
100.0	100.0	100.0	100.0			Net Sales	100.0	100.0
						Gross Profit		
92.2	79.5	93.4	84.9			Operating Expenses	89.8	92.2
7.8	20.5	6.6	15.1			Operating Profit	10.2	7.8
.3	2.2	-.3	1.0			All Other Expenses (net)	.9	.4
7.5	18.3	6.9	14.1			Profit Before Taxes	9.3	7.4
						RATIOS		
1.5	7.0	2.9	1.3			Current	2.0	1.8
.8	1.2	1.0	1.1				1.0	1.1
.2	.7	1.0	.9				.9	.8
1.4	5.8	2.1	1.2			Quick	1.5	1.4
.5	1.2	1.0	.9				.9	.9
.1	.7	.3	.1				.5	.3
0 UND	0 UND	0 UND	5 80.1			Sales/Receivables	0 UND	0 UND
0 UND	2 204.6	1 288.2	8 48.4				2 146.3	2 150.9
0 UND	9 40.5	11 32.3	47 7.7				30 12.1	29 12.7
						Cost of Sales/Inventory		
						Cost of Sales/Payables		
340.3	6.6	26.5	3.9			Sales/Working Capital	9.7	12.3
UND	111.1	163.5	11.2				90.2	152.4
-15.9	-5.6	-47.9	NM				-28.7	-13.6
		152.0	65.6			EBIT/Interest	33.0	33.8
	(13) 41.1	(11) 15.3					(53) 14.7	(49) 14.5
		5.1	3.3				1.8	3.3
						Net Profit + Depr., Dep., Amort./Cur. Mat. L/T/D		
.0	.0	.0	.0			Fixed/Worth	.0	.0
2.2	.0	.3	.4				.3	.2
-.1	.3	-2.9	NM				-1.3	5.7
2.6	.2	.7	2.4			Debt/Worth	1.8	2.1
UND	3.1	13.2	5.7				16.0	12.6
-1.6	11.4	-166.2	NM				-13.5	-12.3
	110.7	235.2	68.9			% Profit Before Taxes/Tangible Net Worth	166.5	117.2
	(18) 55.9	(12) 41.0	(13) 42.6				(61) 56.6	(56) 47.2
	10.2	2.9	17.7				20.9	14.8
288.7	36.5	16.6	12.3			% Profit Before Taxes/Total Assets	22.3	21.6
17.0	13.8	7.1	6.0				6.9	6.5
-5.4	.9	2.1	3.8				1.1	.7
UND	UND	999.8	102.8			Sales/Net Fixed Assets	999.8	999.8
UND	999.8	200.9	63.9				101.8	105.1
115.2	28.3	65.2	17.3				24.5	22.4
85.3	16.3	14.6	.9			Sales/Total Assets	11.6	9.8
12.8	2.4	6.3	.5				2.9	1.6
3.7	.3	.5	.2				.4	.3
		.0	.1			% Depr., Dep., Amort./Sales	.2	.2
	(12) .2	(12) .6					(44) .6	(41) .6
		.8	2.9				2.1	1.6
						% Officers', Directors' Owners' Comp/Sales	1.0	1.5
							(28) 6.9	(19) 7.4
							13.2	17.3
68293M	245674M	757136M	2485329M	34361M	222758M	Net Sales ($)	3712765M	4052864M
1495M	22728M	86467M	475660M	75249M	849801M	Total Assets ($)	1731048M	2137487M

M = $ thousand   MM = $ million
See Pages viii through xx for Explanation of Ratios and Data

Comparative Historical Data / **Current Data Sorted by Sales**

Hist 15	Hist 14	Hist 13		0-1MM	1-3MM	3-5MM	5-10MM	10-25MM	25MM & OVER
			Type of Statement						
15	14	13	Unqualified		1		2	4	6
11	5	4	Reviewed			1		1	2
2	3	1	Compiled					1	
10	9	12	Tax Returns	6	3	1	2		
56	53	41	Other	8	5	3	3	10	12
4/1/16- 3/31/17	4/1/17- 3/31/18	4/1/18- 3/31/19			17 (4/1-9/30/18)			54 (10/1/18-3/31/19)	
ALL	ALL	ALL							
94	84	71	**NUMBER OF STATEMENTS**	14	9	5	7	16	20
%	%	%	**ASSETS**	%	%	%	%	%	%
36.8	35.0	37.0	Cash & Equivalents	58.4				25.6	30.8
18.4	10.5	12.0	Trade Receivables (net)	.1				15.5	19.6
.8	.1	.0	Inventory	.0				.1	.0
14.6	17.5	12.7	All Other Current	5.9				14.1	24.3
70.7	63.2	61.8	Total Current	64.4				55.3	74.8
6.3	7.6	9.5	Fixed Assets (net)	14.1				8.0	5.4
9.4	9.1	7.2	Intangibles (net)	.3				6.8	7.8
13.7	20.1	21.5	All Other Non-Current	21.3				29.9	12.1
100.0	100.0	100.0	Total	100.0				100.0	100.0
			LIABILITIES						
8.9	5.3	10.7	Notes Payable-Short Term	12.3				4.0	4.0
1.9	1.5	2.0	Cur. Mat.-L.T.D.	1.7				.7	.8
7.5	6.4	5.6	Trade Payables	.9				3.3	4.0
.0	.6	.1	Income Taxes Payable	.2				.1	.3
42.6	51.7	47.3	All Other Current	76.7				46.1	53.1
61.0	65.3	66.4	Total Current	91.8				54.2	62.8
5.1	5.1	10.9	Long-Term Debt	9.0				3.0	3.9
.1	.1	.1	Deferred Taxes	.0				.0	.2
7.0	7.2	9.2	All Other Non-Current	6.0				12.5	.3
26.8	22.3	13.4	Net Worth	-6.8				30.2	32.8
100.0	100.0	100.0	Total Liabilities & Net Worth	100.0				100.0	100.0
			INCOME DATA						
100.0	100.0	100.0	Net Sales	100.0				100.0	100.0
			Gross Profit						
92.1	91.3	86.8	Operating Expenses	78.5				85.6	97.5
7.9	8.7	13.2	Operating Profit	21.5				14.4	2.5
.9	.5	1.1	All Other Expenses (net)	3.4				1.1	.0
7.0	8.2	12.1	Profit Before Taxes	18.1				13.3	2.5
			RATIOS						
1.7	1.7	2.9	Current	1.0				2.4	1.6
1.1	1.1	1.0		.9				1.1	1.0
.9	.7	.7		.2				.8	1.0
1.6	1.5	2.8	Quick	1.0				2.1	1.1
1.0	.9	1.0		.7				1.1	.7
.4	.2	.3		.2				.1	.3
0 999.8	0 UND	0 UND	Sales/Receivables	0 UND				2 172.1	1 339.9
3 123.1	3 137.7	2 176.3		0 UND				8 45.9	3 131.1
24 14.9	28 13.1	15 24.8		0 UND				47 7.7	16 22.6
			Cost of Sales/Inventory						
			Cost of Sales/Payables						
12.4	9.2	11.8	Sales/Working Capital	UND				5.0	86.9
121.4	114.3	205.1		-15.5				21.2	249.0
-105.2	-17.4	-16.4		-2.8				NM	NM
32.4	21.8	99.0	EBIT/Interest					246.0	157.0
(53) 9.3	(46) 6.1	(39) 15.3						(10) 15.4	(11) 15.3
2.1	1.6	2.7						1.8	7.5
			Net Profit + Depr., Dep., Amort./Cur. Mat. L/T/D						
.0	.0	.0	Fixed/Worth	.0				.1	.0
.2	.2	.2		.0				.3	.1
.8	2.1	4.3		UND				NM	1.1
1.5	1.5	1.1	Debt/Worth	3.4				1.7	1.1
8.2	8.4	5.9		47.5				3.7	5.1
-43.2	UND	-800.3		-168.7				NM	14.9
120.2	101.8	98.9	% Profit Before Taxes/Tangible Net Worth					99.6	49.7
(69) 37.3	(63) 32.4	(53) 41.8						(12) 50.8	(18) 26.2
15.0	10.1	11.6						20.1	3.6
20.6	17.4	18.7	% Profit Before Taxes/Total Assets	16.4				18.2	15.2
7.3	4.3	7.1		4.0				10.6	4.8
.4	1.2	1.9		.0				2.7	1.4
999.8	999.8	999.8	Sales/Net Fixed Assets	UND				113.8	999.8
254.9	98.3	117.4		UND				48.4	947.8
32.4	21.5	26.7		14.1				8.0	61.2
17.5	9.1	12.8	Sales/Total Assets	3.1				5.2	33.3
3.4	1.6	1.1		.3				.7	13.3
.4	.3	.3		.2				.3	5.2
.0	.1	.0	% Depr., Dep., Amort./Sales					.5	.0
(43) .5	(35) .4	(34) .5						(11) 2.4	(13) .0
1.4	1.9	3.0						3.0	.2
1.6	5.3	5.6	% Officers', Directors', Owners' Comp/Sales						
(21) 9.5	(12) 14.1	(18) 15.1							
17.1	24.9	35.3							
4226634M	2731514M	3813551M	Net Sales ($)	5287M	14226M	18079M	47750M	250723M	3477486M
1964110M	1901864M	1511400M	Total Assets ($)	16280M	16526M	21068M	81711M	572407M	803408M

Current Data Sorted by Assets

Comparative Historical Data

			1	1	2	1	**Type of Statement**		
		1	4	2			Unqualified	11	10
	1	1	2	1			Reviewed	6	6
	25	9	2				Compiled	7	8
	29	19	26	12	5	1	Tax Returns	63	62
		17 (4/1-9/30/18)		128 (10/1/18-3/31/19)			Other	109	131
	0-500M	500M-2MM	2-10MM	10-50MM	50-100MM	100-250MM		4/1/14-3/31/15 ALL	4/1/15-3/31/16 ALL
	55	30	35	16	7	2	**NUMBER OF STATEMENTS**	196	217
	%	%	%	%	%	%	**ASSETS**	%	%
	41.8	27.7	21.9	22.1			Cash & Equivalents	29.9	22.4
	17.7	23.1	33.4	19.1			Trade Receivables (net)	20.2	23.9
	.1	1.1	2.3	1.1			Inventory	1.2	2.2
	4.0	7.7	4.2	6.7			All Other Current	7.0	5.7
	63.5	59.5	61.8	49.0			Total Current	58.3	54.1
	10.6	15.5	8.6	15.7			Fixed Assets (net)	17.2	17.7
	12.8	18.2	11.2	25.0			Intangibles (net)	12.4	13.2
	13.0	6.8	18.4	10.3			All Other Non-Current	12.2	14.9
	100.0	100.0	100.0	100.0			Total	100.0	100.0
							LIABILITIES		
	22.2	11.4	13.7	6.0			Notes Payable-Short Term	18.4	19.5
	2.2	1.0	2.4	2.3			Cur. Mat.-L.T.D.	2.3	2.5
	4.7	4.3	3.0	7.7			Trade Payables	7.2	6.5
	.5	.1	.2	.0			Income Taxes Payable	.0	.2
	39.7	25.7	21.8	25.2			All Other Current	19.3	18.4
	69.3	42.6	40.9	41.2			Total Current	47.3	47.1
	10.9	11.9	16.1	15.9			Long-Term Debt	15.5	15.1
	.0	.0	.3	.1			Deferred Taxes	.1	.4
	4.2	5.4	3.2	6.5			All Other Non-Current	9.8	10.2
	15.6	40.1	39.4	36.3			Net Worth	27.2	27.2
	100.0	100.0	100.0	100.0			Total Liabilties & Net Worth	100.0	100.0
							INCOME DATA		
	100.0	100.0	100.0	100.0			Net Sales	100.0	100.0
							Gross Profit		
	79.1	80.3	88.7	83.1			Operating Expenses	84.2	84.2
	20.9	19.7	11.3	16.9			Operating Profit	15.8	15.8
	1.3	2.5	2.4	3.9			All Other Expenses (net)	2.1	1.4
	19.6	17.2	8.8	13.1			Profit Before Taxes	13.7	14.3
							RATIOS		
	3.2	6.6	4.2	3.1				5.4	3.6
	1.3	2.6	1.8	1.2			Current	1.7	1.5
	.7	.7	.9	.4				.7	.7
	3.2	5.1	3.2	2.6				4.4	3.0
	1.1	2.0	1.4	1.1			Quick	1.3	1.3
	.5	.6	.8	.4				.5	.5
0	UND	0 UND	24 15.4	5 74.8				0 UND	0 UND
0	UND	33 10.9	59 6.2	49 7.4			Sales/Receivables	10 35.7	15 23.6
20	18.0	52 7.0	83 4.4	58 6.3				53 6.9	54 6.8
							Cost of Sales/Inventory		
							Cost of Sales/Payables		
	15.4	4.6	5.4	3.9				5.7	6.9
	100.2	11.4	8.2	31.9			Sales/Working Capital	15.3	21.0
	-31.3	-56.0	-77.9	-4.8				-35.3	-23.8
	62.5	213.5	25.0	63.1				33.7	40.8
(34)	23.6	(19) 37.0	(24) 10.5	(11) 17.0			EBIT/Interest	(125) 8.8	(151) 10.9
	8.1	2.7	2.5	6.0				1.1	3.1
							Net Profit + Depr., Dep.,		7.3	
							Amort./Cur. Mat. L/T/D	(12) 3.8	
								.9	
	.0	.0	.0	.2				.0	.0
	.0	.2	.1	1.6			Fixed/Worth	.2	.4
	.9	NM	.2	-.4				-2.6	-15.0
	.3	.2	.2	.9				.3	.4
	3.3	1.4	1.1	6.6			Debt/Worth	2.9	1.6
	-4.0	-10.1	7.3	-2.9				-5.4	-9.9
	614.3	135.1	72.8	146.2			% Profit Before Taxes/Tangible	174.3	176.2
(35)	150.0	(20) 87.1	(30) 26.5	(10) 74.9			Net Worth	(133) 65.5	(155) 71.8
	46.2	11.8	7.2	42.9				15.3	22.2
	160.8	57.8	39.4	41.6			% Profit Before Taxes/Total	58.1	69.7
	81.8	25.1	14.0	12.9			Assets	22.1	22.2
	27.2	6.3	2.3	7.0				1.4	4.1
	UND	856.0	274.8	31.2				377.2	394.9
	UND	136.0	65.7	15.8			Sales/Net Fixed Assets	52.1	43.4
	97.7	26.9	23.6	7.4				15.6	15.2
	13.1	4.4	3.8	2.5				6.9	6.0
	7.2	2.7	2.7	1.8			Sales/Total Assets	3.0	3.0
	3.8	1.2	.9	.7				1.5	1.7
		.2	.2	.9				.7	.7
	(10)	.8	(19) .6	(13) 1.5			% Depr., Dep., Amort./Sales	(94) 1.4	(90) 1.3
		2.1	1.3	3.0				3.3	2.2
	5.3	2.9	8.0				% Officers', Directors'	5.8	5.7
(27)	15.1	(10) 7.6	(16) 13.9				Owners' Comp/Sales	(91) 15.2	(114) 12.6
	20.9	22.4	17.0					29.0	22.8
	81617M	144168M	456599M	593901M	782573M	218118M	Net Sales ($)	2101907M	2575010M
	8592M	32067M	165629M	369135M	462756M	322030M	Total Assets ($)	1301026M	1213684M

© RMA 2019

M = $ thousand   MM = $ million
See Pages viii through xx for Explanation of Ratios and Data

Comparative Historical Data | Current Data Sorted by Sales

						Type of Statement						
	10		8		5	Unqualified					2	3
	7		8		7	Reviewed			1		5	1
	10		7		5	Compiled		3				2
	41		45		36	Tax Returns	19	6	5	5	1	
	102		101		92	Other	20	23	10	11	11	17
	4/1/16- 3/31/17 ALL		4/1/17- 3/31/18 ALL		4/1/18- 3/31/19 ALL		17 (4/1-9/30/18)		128 (10/1/18-3/31/19)			
							0-1MM	1-3MM	3-5MM	5-10MM	10-25MM	25MM & OVER
	170		169		145	NUMBER OF STATEMENTS	39	32	16	16	19	23
	%		%		%	ASSETS	%	%	%	%	%	%
	25.4		31.1		29.6	Cash & Equivalents	35.3	33.2	31.0	27.3	29.7	15.3
	22.1		22.8		22.9	Trade Receivables (net)	18.3	19.3	16.8	35.5	30.9	24.5
	1.2		1.2		.9	Inventory	.0	1.0	.2	3.3	1.4	.8
	4.4		7.9		5.3	All Other Current	2.0	6.0	3.8	4.4	8.2	9.3
	53.2		63.0		58.7	Total Current	55.5	59.5	51.8	70.6	70.2	49.8
	15.7		14.8		11.7	Fixed Assets (net)	14.3	10.4	10.9	10.4	5.2	15.7
	16.3		11.1		17.4	Intangibles (net)	19.1	10.9	23.8	9.5	13.4	27.7
	14.7		11.1		12.3	All Other Non-Current	11.0	19.2	13.4	9.5	11.2	6.8
	100.0		100.0		100.0	Total	100.0	100.0	100.0	100.0	100.0	100.0
						LIABILITIES						
	12.1		11.1		15.0	Notes Payable-Short Term	22.7	10.7	24.7	9.7	8.4	10.5
	2.1		2.8		2.0	Cur. Mat. L.T.D.	1.1	2.0	2.4	1.2	2.3	3.7
	6.9		6.7		4.4	Trade Payables	3.4	6.0	1.3	3.0	2.6	8.7
	.2		.0		.3	Income Taxes Payable	.7	.0	.3	.0	.0	.2
	20.1		20.5		29.5	All Other Current	28.8	45.1	27.4	29.0	17.6	20.7
	41.4		41.1		51.2	Total Current	56.7	63.7	56.1	42.9	30.9	43.8
	16.3		11.3		14.7	Long-Term Debt	16.1	7.1	7.4	8.6	22.5	25.4
	.1		.2		.1	Deferred Taxes	.1	.0	.0	.0	.6	.2
	9.1		6.5		4.7	All Other Non-Current	4.0	2.2	10.3	6.3	.9	7.8
	33.1		40.9		29.3	Net Worth	23.1	27.0	26.2	42.2	45.0	22.9
	100.0		100.0		100.0	Total Liabilities & Net Worth	100.0	100.0	100.0	100.0	100.0	100.0
						INCOME DATA						
	100.0		100.0		100.0	Net Sales	100.0	100.0	100.0	100.0	100.0	100.0
						Gross Profit						
	86.6		84.8		82.9	Operating Expenses	68.5	86.6	88.5	89.1	88.1	89.9
	13.4		15.2		17.1	Operating Profit	31.5	13.4	11.5	10.9	11.9	10.1
	1.7		1.6		2.3	All Other Expenses (net)	2.9	1.6	1.1	3.7	1.5	2.7
	11.8		13.7		14.8	Profit Before Taxes	28.6	11.8	10.4	7.2	10.4	7.3
						RATIOS						
	3.7		3.6		3.8		3.9	4.7	2.2	5.8	4.6	1.9
	1.7		1.7		1.4	Current	1.1	1.3	1.2	2.3	2.7	1.2
	.8		1.0		.7		.7	.5	.4	1.2	1.8	.7
	3.4		3.0		3.2		3.9	4.7	2.2	4.7	3.6	1.7
	1.5		1.5		1.4	Quick	1.0	1.2	1.2	2.0	2.2	1.2
	.7		.7		.6		.6	.4	.4	1.2	1.4	.5
0	UND	0	UND	0	UND		0 UND	0 UND	0 UND	0 UND	26 14.0	1 299.7
25	14.5	17	22.1	25	14.6	Sales/Receivables	0 892.0	11 32.3	6 64.0	43 8.4	47 7.7	50 7.3
52	7.0	53	6.9	58	6.3		26 14.3	74 4.9	58 6.3	60 6.1	63 5.8	63 5.8
						Cost of Sales/Inventory						
						Cost of Sales/Payables						
	6.7		6.4		6.9		10.5	6.4	12.9	5.0	5.0	11.9
	13.9		16.5		32.7	Sales/Working Capital	148.0	28.4	101.6	10.3	7.3	46.8
	-81.7		659.2		-30.4		-26.0	-17.4	-8.8	97.2	11.5	-15.3
	41.4		56.5		54.8		55.0	192.3	69.1	46.2	110.5	39.0
(112)	9.9	(99)	14.4	(96)	19.2	EBIT/Interest	(24) 13.1	(19) 31.7	(13) 22.2	(10) 16.2	(11) 10.7	(19) 6.0
	1.5		2.5		3.4		3.8	14.3	8.1	-3.6	6.9	2.4
	15.6		36.5		23.1	Net Profit + Depr., Dep.,						
(14)	8.7	(12)	8.1	(10)	10.5	Amort./Cur. Mat. L/T/D						
	3.1		5.6		3.0							
	.0		.0		.0		.0	.0	.0	.0	.0	.3
	.3		.7		.1	Fixed/Worth	.0	.0	.5	.2	.1	-43.2
	UND		1.8		4.5		1.1	.7	NM	.9	4.8	-.3
	.4		.4		.3		.3	.1	.4	.4	.2	1.6
	1.8		1.2		2.3	Debt/Worth	4.3	1.0	6.1	1.0	.7	-25.0
	-7.8		24.7		-3.6		-2.3	NM	-2.2	4.9	13.4	-2.0
	132.0		190.3		172.4	% Profit Before Taxes/Tangible	708.6	147.8	109.1	108.8	65.5	200.5
(122)	45.0	(135)	61.4	(96)	64.0	Net Worth	(24) 237.6	(24) 58.8	(10) 77.0	(13) 39.7	(15) 26.9	(10) 86.2
	13.6		13.5		16.6		40.0	8.4	49.2	-10.1	16.3	42.3
	44.9		71.1		91.6	% Profit Before Taxes/Total	163.2	114.4	57.5	49.6	43.6	42.8
	15.0		23.7		29.9	Assets	78.2	35.0	23.5	22.3	15.6	9.3
	1.9		4.5		6.4		10.8	2.9	6.5	-5.0	7.0	4.6
	340.6		462.3		UND		UND	UND	956.2	207.3	274.8	103.4
	41.8		47.7		106.5	Sales/Net Fixed Assets	UND	133.6	172.8	59.8	64.0	15.9
	14.1		17.3		18.9		29.9	25.8	16.5	27.2	35.9	8.5
	4.7		6.2		6.5		8.5	10.0	7.7	5.6	4.2	5.1
	2.7		3.4		3.3	Sales/Total Assets	3.8	3.3	4.1	3.5	3.0	2.5
	1.5		1.7		1.5		1.3	1.3	1.0	2.6	1.9	1.2
	.6		.4		.4						.2	1.3
(82)	1.2	(90)	1.1	(52)	1.1	% Depr., Dep., Amort./Sales					(13) .6	(13) 1.6
	3.1		2.0		2.5						1.8	4.0
	7.2		5.4		4.6	% Officers', Directors'	8.8	10.1				
(80)	13.3	(74)	13.3	(56)	12.7	Owners' Comp/Sales	(15) 17.3	(11) 15.1				
	25.1		21.2		20.4		23.6	20.4				
	3922483M		2418299M		2276976M	Net Sales ($)	15163M	58664M	61407M	117820M	310359M	1713563M
	2362266M		1590694M		1360209M	Total Assets ($)	47060M	41423M	42906M	38967M	170689M	1019164M

© RMA 2019   M = $ thousand   MM = $ million
See Pages viii through xx for Explanation of Ratios and Data

Current Data Sorted by Assets | Comparative Historical Data

	0-500M	500M-2MM	2-10MM	10-50MM	50-100MM	100-250MM		23	27
Type of Statement									
Unqualified			4					23	27
Reviewed		1	33	23	2			76	75
Compiled	3	11	22	2				54	51
Tax Returns	50	30	16	1				131	147
Other	44	64	75	41	4	2		237	220
		37 (4/1-9/30/18)		407 (10/1/18-3/31/19)				4/1/14-3/31/15 ALL	4/1/15-3/31/16 ALL
NUMBER OF STATEMENTS	97	106	150	74	10	7		521	520
	%	%	%	%	%	%		%	%
ASSETS									
Cash & Equivalents	37.8	24.5	12.8	13.4	12.6			20.2	21.9
Trade Receivables (net)	11.3	38.1	55.7	50.6	40.8			38.4	36.7
Inventory	.4	3.9	2.1	1.9	.0			2.1	1.8
All Other Current	3.1	3.4	6.7	10.1	12.2			4.8	5.1
Total Current	52.6	69.8	77.3	76.0	65.6			65.6	65.6
Fixed Assets (net)	31.0	16.7	13.4	11.9	11.6			21.1	19.7
Intangibles (net)	5.0	4.0	3.3	4.0	15.9			3.4	3.3
All Other Non-Current	11.4	9.5	6.1	8.1	6.9			9.9	11.5
Total	100.0	100.0	100.0	100.0	100.0			100.0	100.0
LIABILITIES									
Notes Payable-Short Term	24.5	6.4	6.4	4.8	3.7			16.1	13.6
Cur. Mat.-L.T.D.	4.1	1.7	2.0	2.9	3.0			3.1	3.4
Trade Payables	5.2	14.9	18.9	17.3	9.3			13.1	11.8
Income Taxes Payable	.2	.3	.9	.7	.2			1.1	1.1
All Other Current	30.2	13.5	14.4	19.7	26.3			19.4	20.1
Total Current	64.1	36.8	42.7	45.3	42.4			52.9	49.9
Long-Term Debt	16.4	10.1	8.9	7.8	10.9			12.0	10.3
Deferred Taxes	.0	.2	1.3	1.2	1.3			.7	.6
All Other Non-Current	5.5	3.9	5.0	8.3	2.6			6.7	6.7
Net Worth	14.0	49.1	42.1	37.4	42.8			27.7	32.5
Total Liabilities & Net Worth	100.0	100.0	100.0	100.0	100.0			100.0	100.0
INCOME DATA									
Net Sales	100.0	100.0	100.0	100.0	100.0			100.0	100.0
Gross Profit									
Operating Expenses	90.2	86.1	90.8	91.8	93.5			89.7	90.2
Operating Profit	9.8	13.9	9.2	8.2	6.5			10.3	9.8
All Other Expenses (net)	.5	1.2	1.5	2.2	1.7			1.6	1.7
Profit Before Taxes	9.3	12.7	7.7	6.0	4.8			8.7	8.1
RATIOS									
Current	4.0	4.9	2.9	2.1	2.0			3.1	3.1
	1.0	2.4	1.9	1.7	1.6			1.6	1.6
	.3	1.2	1.4	1.3	1.2			.9	1.0
Quick	3.9	4.4	2.5	2.0	1.7			2.7	3.0
	1.0	1.9	1.7	1.4	1.3			1.4	1.4
		.9	1.1	1.1	1.0			.8	.8
Sales/Receivables	0 UND	0 UND	59 6.2	69 5.3	83 4.4			0 UND	0 UND
	0 UND	47 7.7	78 4.7	89 4.1	101 3.6			56 6.5	58 6.3
	1 688.4	79 4.6	104 3.5	111 3.3	122 3.0			89 4.1	85 4.3
Cost of Sales/Inventory									
Cost of Sales/Payables									
Sales/Working Capital	18.6	4.4	4.6	4.6	5.1			5.6	5.3
	999.8	8.7	8.0	6.5	7.7			12.9	11.9
	-22.8	49.9	14.5	12.7	17.9			-191.7	371.0
EBIT/Interest	55.3	79.0	77.8	44.5	110.4			50.4	59.6
	(60) 17.1	(71) 19.3	(117) 20.3	(62) 17.7	20.1		(389)	14.0	(372) 14.9
	1.2	3.8	3.1	4.1	3.0			2.7	3.7
Net Profit + Depr., Dep., Amort./Cur. Mat. L/T/D			7.4	6.9				6.5	8.3
		(25) 4.5	(32) 3.1				(78)	3.0	(79) 3.0
		2.0	1.6					1.4	1.5
Fixed/Worth	.1	.0	.1	.1	.1			.1	.1
	.9	.2	.2	.3	.5			.4	.3
	UND	1.2	.6	.6	1.3			1.6	1.5
Debt/Worth	.3	.3	.7	.9	1.1			.5	.5
	1.9	1.1	1.2	1.7	2.9			1.7	1.5
	-16.1	3.2	3.6	3.0	5.7			7.0	6.1
% Profit Before Taxes/Tangible Net Worth	315.0	108.9	62.0	40.4				74.1	92.3
	(68) 76.2	(92) 50.8	(137) 25.3	(69) 21.9			(427)	35.2	(438) 35.8
	.1	19.7	5.7	14.3				10.1	9.2
% Profit Before Taxes/Total Assets	143.5	50.5	31.7	17.5	11.6			37.6	40.2
	44.1	23.9	11.5	7.4	5.3			12.7	12.7
	.0	7.0	2.1	4.4	3.4			2.5	2.3
Sales/Net Fixed Assets	395.4	113.3	72.0	42.6	25.9			58.9	71.7
	59.3	38.1	29.4	28.4	22.5			28.8	33.2
	16.2	17.6	18.6	15.4	13.9			14.6	16.2
Sales/Total Assets	20.7	4.5	3.2	2.5	2.0			4.7	4.8
	8.3	3.0	2.6	2.0	1.6			2.8	2.9
	3.5	2.1	2.1	1.6	.9			2.0	2.0
% Depr., Dep., Amort./Sales	.4	.4	.7	.7	.8			.7	.5
	(41) 1.0	(61) .9	(108) 1.1	(66) 1.0	1.2		(360)	1.2	(351) 1.1
	1.8	1.5	1.5	1.8	1.9			1.9	1.8
% Officers', Directors' Owners' Comp/Sales	6.4	4.7	4.2	2.5				4.6	4.8
	(58) 11.6	(50) 7.6	(36) 7.5	(11) 5.5			(208)	9.4	(215) 9.4
	20.5	11.9	10.8	11.8				17.4	17.0
Net Sales ($)	205153M	411995M	2230704M	3503356M	1044738M	1527088M		14783041M	12316542M
Total Assets ($)	20063M	117286M	764271M	1774022M	637569M	861218M		4500555M	4633241M

M = $ thousand   MM = $ million
See Pages viii through xx for Explanation of Ratios and Data

Comparative Historical Data & Current Data Sorted by Sales

21	20	19	Type of Statement					5	14
55	68	60	Unqualified		1	1	4	26	28
44	37	38	Reviewed	1	4	7	8	12	6
97	97	97	Compiled	21	35	12	19	7	3
194	200	230	Tax Returns	28	40	30	46	42	44
4/1/16-3/31/17	4/1/17-3/31/18	4/1/18-3/31/19	Other						
ALL	ALL	ALL		0-1MM	1-3MM	3-5MM	5-10MM	10-25MM	25MM & OVER
					37 (4/1-9/30/18)		407 (10/1/18-3/31/19)		
411	422	444	NUMBER OF STATEMENTS	50	80	50	77	92	95
%	%	%	**ASSETS**	%	%	%	%	%	%
20.6	19.8	21.0	Cash & Equivalents	28.8	31.8	25.5	20.9	12.7	13.6
40.4	40.0	40.4	Trade Receivables (net)	17.5	24.3	35.3	46.2	54.6	50.1
1.9	1.8	2.1	Inventory	.6	3.0	3.9	2.1	2.0	1.2
5.7	5.9	6.0	All Other Current	2.4	2.0	4.6	5.5	7.8	10.5
68.6	67.5	69.4	Total Current	49.3	61.2	69.3	74.7	77.1	75.5
17.9	17.0	17.9	Fixed Assets (net)	34.6	23.4	16.8	16.3	11.3	12.6
3.6	5.5	4.3	Intangibles (net)	2.7	4.7	5.8	3.1	4.4	4.9
9.9	10.0	8.4	All Other Non-Current	13.4	10.7	8.1	6.0	7.3	7.0
100.0	100.0	100.0	Total	100.0	100.0	100.0	100.0	100.0	100.0
			LIABILITIES						
11.4	12.1	10.0	Notes Payable-Short Term	14.5	17.1	14.1	7.6	6.4	4.8
2.7	3.3	2.6	Cur. Mat.-L.T.D.	2.3	3.3	1.1	2.0	3.1	2.8
14.0	13.9	14.4	Trade Payables	5.6	8.8	14.6	15.9	19.8	17.0
.8	.9	.6	Income Taxes Payable	.0	.1	1.0	1.0	.3	.9
20.0	21.1	19.1	All Other Current	25.0	17.7	21.7	15.3	16.4	21.4
48.8	51.2	46.5	Total Current	47.4	47.0	52.6	41.8	46.0	46.9
11.9	10.9	10.7	Long-Term Debt	25.1	14.9	6.1	7.9	7.9	7.1
1.0	.8	.7	Deferred Taxes	.0	.1	.0	.3	2.0	1.2
6.6	4.8	5.4	All Other Non-Current	2.8	5.2	7.2	5.0	6.6	4.9
31.8	32.3	36.6	Net Worth	24.7	32.9	34.0	45.0	37.5	39.9
100.0	100.0	100.0	Total Liabilties & Net Worth	100.0	100.0	100.0	100.0	100.0	100.0
			INCOME DATA						
100.0	100.0	100.0	Net Sales	100.0	100.0	100.0	100.0	100.0	100.0
			Gross Profit						
91.1	92.2	89.9	Operating Expenses	77.9	88.3	92.4	90.8	92.3	93.0
8.9	7.8	10.1	Operating Profit	22.1	11.7	7.6	9.2	7.7	7.0
1.1	1.1	1.3	All Other Expenses (net)	4.9	.9	.1	.2	1.0	1.7
7.8	6.7	8.8	Profit Before Taxes	17.3	10.8	7.5	9.1	6.7	5.2
			RATIOS						
3.2	3.0	3.0		4.3	5.8	3.5	4.3	2.4	2.0
1.7	1.7	1.7	Current	1.4	1.5	1.6	2.6	1.8	1.6
1.1	1.0	1.1		.2	.5	1.0	1.3	1.3	1.3
2.9	2.6	2.6		4.0	4.9	3.2	4.0	2.3	1.9
1.5	1.4	1.5	Quick	1.2	1.4	1.5	2.3	1.6	1.4
.9	.8	.9		.2	.5	.9	1.1	1.0	1.1
2 159.4	0 999.8	0 939.4		0 UND	0 UND	0 UND	1 524.3	64 5.7	61 6.0
59 6.2	61 6.0	64 5.7	Sales/Receivables	0 UND	0 UND	41 9.0	72 5.1	79 4.6	81 4.5
89 4.1	89 4.1	91 4.0		31 11.9	61 6.0	79 4.6	101 3.6	104 3.5	101 3.6
			Cost of Sales/Inventory						
			Cost of Sales/Payables						
5.5	5.4	5.1		4.0	5.1	5.2	4.3	5.2	5.6
11.3	10.6	9.4	Sales/Working Capital	44.7	23.3	9.6	8.7	8.1	8.5
87.4	407.5	63.1		-7.0	-35.0	-374.5	27.8	22.0	13.2
77.4	59.1	55.2		16.9	98.0	63.3	177.2	49.7	51.2
(305) 16.1	(325) 12.6	(327) 18.2	EBIT/Interest	(26) 5.6	(53) 17.8	(33) 26.7	(57) 35.7	(75) 16.0	(83) 18.2
3.3	2.0	3.4		-.3	1.0	4.5	6.0	3.0	5.3
8.0	6.9	7.0						8.3	6.9
(65) 3.1	(67) 2.9	(71) 3.9	Net Profit + Depr., Dep., Amort./Cur. Mat. L/T/D				(23) 3.8	(39) 3.1
1.5	1.1	1.5						1.3	1.5
.1	.1	.1		.0	.1	.0	.1	.1	.1
.3	.3	.3	Fixed/Worth	.7	.4	.2	.2	.3	.3
1.2	1.1	1.1		5.1	UND	1.0	.9	.8	.6
.5	.6	.6		.5	.3	.4	.3	.9	.9
1.7	1.5	1.4	Debt/Worth	1.5	1.4	1.0	.8	1.4	1.8
5.6	7.3	4.4		10.9	-14.9	4.6	3.0	4.3	3.4
78.7	81.6	78.2		155.8	187.4	91.5	76.0	74.0	43.9
(347) 37.0	(351) 35.2	(382) 33.3	% Profit Before Taxes/Tangible Net Worth	(42) 34.3	(58) 50.8	(41) 40.4	(67) 43.4	(84) 24.7	(90) 22.2
11.5	6.7	11.8		7.1	.0	13.5	15.4	5.8	14.9
37.1	35.0	39.2		64.7	82.3	54.3	47.2	32.5	17.8
13.0	12.0	14.6	% Profit Before Taxes/Total Assets	8.9	33.4	20.0	22.8	11.6	7.2
2.8	1.4	3.0		-.1	1.1	2.7	7.4	2.1	4.0
70.3	82.3	90.7		177.7	178.9	214.7	111.2	80.9	48.5
32.9	31.9	32.8	Sales/Net Fixed Assets	20.2	43.8	44.4	35.6	30.7	25.9
16.5	16.0	16.7		1.5	13.6	18.7	20.8	19.0	15.0
4.7	4.6	4.4		6.5	9.0	6.1	4.9	3.2	2.9
2.8	2.9	2.7	Sales/Total Assets	2.0	3.9	3.1	3.0	2.6	2.3
2.1	1.9	1.9		.5	2.5	2.3	2.3	2.1	1.7
.6	.6	.6		2.6	.4	.3	.6	.6	.7
(273) 1.0	(287) 1.0	(292) 1.1	% Depr., Dep., Amort./Sales	(17) 14.1	(41) .8	(30) .6	(46) 1.0	(74) 1.0	(84) 1.1
1.5	1.7	1.7		23.8	1.6	1.4	1.4	1.5	1.8
5.2	5.5	5.0		5.2	6.3	3.5	7.3	2.5	3.7
(166) 8.4	(173) 9.5	(158) 8.2	% Officers', Directors' Owners' Comp/Sales	(17) 10.5	(49) 11.8	(25) 6.4	(27) 9.1	(23) 6.0	(17) 5.7
14.5	15.0	13.6		22.6	15.9	9.1	11.6	9.1	17.0
7559370M	8814422M	8923034M	Net Sales ($)	23574M	149853M	198384M	547853M	1480510M	6522860M
3558840M	4302430M	4174429M	Total Assets ($)	32787M	51319M	70587M	183135M	655037M	3181564M

© RMA 2019

M = $ thousand   MM = $ million
See Pages viii through xx for Explanation of Ratios and Data

Current Data Sorted by Assets   Comparative Historical Data

Type of Statement	0-500M	500M-2MM	2-10MM	10-50MM	50-100MM	100-250MM	4/1/14-3/31/15 ALL	4/1/15-3/31/16 ALL
Unqualified			5	4			6	7
Reviewed		2	10	2			24	14
Compiled	1	4	6	1			13	12
Tax Returns	24	13	8	1		1	53	49
Other	10	25	26	7	1	1	69	66
	11 (4/1-9/30/18)			140 (10/1/18-3/31/19)				
NUMBER OF STATEMENTS	35	44	55	14	1	2	165	148
ASSETS	%	%	%	%	%	%	%	%
Cash & Equivalents	26.5	17.0	10.5	8.7			15.3	16.0
Trade Receivables (net)	18.8	22.1	35.1	32.8			27.8	28.7
Inventory	4.7	4.1	4.6	6.0			4.8	4.7
All Other Current	5.9	3.9	4.8	8.5			3.9	3.2
Total Current	55.9	47.1	54.9	56.1			51.7	52.6
Fixed Assets (net)	30.5	31.8	31.8	35.2			33.3	34.3
Intangibles (net)	6.2	6.2	4.9	5.7			6.0	4.4
All Other Non-Current	7.4	14.9	8.4	3.1			9.0	8.6
Total	100.0	100.0	100.0	100.0			100.0	100.0
LIABILITIES								
Notes Payable-Short Term	24.5	12.9	7.2	4.7			15.1	11.0
Cur. Mat.-L.T.D.	8.2	3.6	5.6	6.3			4.7	5.0
Trade Payables	4.2	13.8	11.9	17.3			10.6	12.6
Income Taxes Payable	.0	.0	.0	.0			.4	.3
All Other Current	15.2	5.6	11.4	11.4			12.5	11.0
Total Current	52.1	35.8	36.1	39.6			43.3	39.8
Long-Term Debt	25.9	30.9	24.1	16.7			23.4	31.8
Deferred Taxes	.0	.1	1.2	.0			.4	.3
All Other Non-Current	.7	7.7	3.5	4.0			7.8	3.9
Net Worth	21.3	25.4	35.0	39.7			25.1	24.2
Total Liabilties & Net Worth	100.0	100.0	100.0	100.0			100.0	100.0
INCOME DATA								
Net Sales	100.0	100.0	100.0	100.0			100.0	100.0
Gross Profit								
Operating Expenses	92.2	90.3	89.7	93.4			91.8	93.5
Operating Profit	7.8	9.7	10.3	6.6			8.2	6.5
All Other Expenses (net)	.5	.6	1.8	.7			1.1	.9
Profit Before Taxes	7.3	9.1	8.4	5.9			7.1	5.6
RATIOS								
Current	3.4	6.0	2.3	1.7			2.9	2.6
	1.2	1.4	1.5	1.5			1.4	1.5
	.5	.5	1.0	1.2			.8	.9
Quick	3.1	3.9	2.0	1.3			2.4	2.2
	1.1	.9	1.1	1.1			1.2	1.3
	.4	.3	.7	.7			.6	.6
Sales/Receivables	0 UND	0 UND	22 16.3	34 10.8			0 UND	2 230.7
	0 UND	10 36.0	40 9.2	46 7.9			28 13.0	30 12.3
	27 13.5	55 6.6	78 4.7	78 4.7			61 6.0	56 6.5
Cost of Sales/Inventory								
Cost of Sales/Payables								
Sales/Working Capital	15.2	8.3	7.8	8.6			7.9	7.1
	67.2	23.9	14.8	10.4			27.0	22.4
	-29.8	-15.4	-119.1	35.1			-42.4	-103.7
EBIT/Interest	22.0	21.0	31.1	30.9			23.0	24.8
	(22) 12.5	(35) 5.5	(52) 9.0	(13) 11.8			(132) 6.8	(127) 7.5
	4.3	1.1	2.7	5.7			1.8	2.6
Net Profit + Depr., Dep., Amort./Cur. Mat. L/T/D							7.3	5.4
							(17) 1.8	(18) 2.4
							1.2	1.3
Fixed/Worth	.1	.1	.2	.4			.4	.4
	1.3	1.0	.9	1.0			1.1	1.0
	-2.3	8.9	2.9	2.2			-37.8	5.8
Debt/Worth	.5	.6	1.0	1.2			.7	.9
	6.5	2.9	1.8	2.0			1.9	2.4
	-4.5	NM	4.2	3.4			-42.4	19.1
% Profit Before Taxes/Tangible Net Worth	209.5	118.2	76.4	52.0			98.9	76.9
	(23) 109.4	(33) 38.6	(49) 42.3	(12) 30.1			(122) 39.3	(118) 45.0
	36.8	8.9	12.8	19.2			10.4	14.7
% Profit Before Taxes/Total Assets	65.0	44.2	21.6	20.6			34.7	27.0
	31.8	8.9	12.6	8.7			14.2	11.4
	11.1	2.3	3.9	6.2			2.0	4.0
Sales/Net Fixed Assets	124.3	66.4	33.7	18.2			43.3	38.5
	27.8	17.6	11.4	8.4			13.0	15.0
	20.4	4.3	5.5	3.6			5.8	5.9
Sales/Total Assets	10.9	3.8	3.5	2.7			5.0	5.1
	7.3	2.9	2.6	2.2			3.1	3.3
	4.2	2.0	1.6	1.6			2.1	2.3
% Depr., Dep., Amort./Sales	.4	1.3	1.2	1.7			1.1	1.1
	(18) 1.5	(23) 2.7	(44) 2.6	(13) 2.8			(105) 2.1	(82) 2.7
	2.6	6.9	3.9	3.9			3.9	4.6
% Officers', Directors' Owners' Comp/Sales	3.8	3.8	2.1				3.4	3.1
	(29) 6.2	(19) 5.4	(18) 3.4				(77) 5.3	(73) 4.7
	13.7	9.2	7.2				8.6	9.8
Net Sales ($)	59411M	156901M	596496M	592100M	60230M	1224344M	1459717M	1781083M
Total Assets ($)	7737M	46895M	237764M	275679M	65979M	231500M	488795M	597938M

M = $ thousand   MM = $ million
See Pages viii through xx for Explanation of Ratios and Data

Comparative Historical Data | Current Data Sorted by Sales

Type of Statement

Category	4/1/16-3/31/17 ALL	4/1/17-3/31/18 ALL	4/1/18-3/31/19 ALL	0-1MM	1-3MM	3-5MM	5-10MM	10-25MM	25MM & OVER
Unqualified	4	6	9		1		1	5	2
Reviewed	20	12	14		1		5	4	3
Compiled	15	13	12		3	1	5	3	1
Tax Returns	42	45	46	13	14	7	9	2	1
Other	61	68	70	9	17	11	13	13	7
				11 (4/1-9/30/18)			140 (10/1/18-3/31/19)		
NUMBER OF STATEMENTS	142	144	151	22	36	19	33	27	14
	%	%	%	%	%	%	%	%	%
ASSETS									
Cash & Equivalents	16.4	16.2	16.3	15.2	25.3	15.4	14.3	9.5	14.2
Trade Receivables (net)	28.4	31.2	27.0	10.9	18.9	25.4	35.3	37.3	35.6
Inventory	5.5	4.8	4.6	2.8	3.9	6.4	5.3	4.0	6.0
All Other Current	4.2	4.2	5.2	8.7	2.2	6.9	5.4	2.8	9.2
Total Current	54.5	56.4	53.1	37.6	50.3	54.2	60.3	53.5	64.9
Fixed Assets (net)	31.5	32.7	31.5	50.5	31.1	23.5	25.1	32.6	26.9
Intangibles (net)	4.9	3.5	6.0	3.9	7.1	7.8	4.6	6.9	5.1
All Other Non-Current	9.1	7.4	9.4	8.0	11.5	14.5	9.9	7.0	3.1
Total	100.0	100.0	100.0	100.0	100.0	100.0	100.0	100.0	100.0
LIABILITIES									
Notes Payable-Short Term	17.3	11.6	12.6	9.4	22.6	12.8	10.2	8.2	5.5
Cur. Mat.-L.T.D.	5.2	6.8	5.6	7.1	6.9	1.8	4.3	7.0	4.8
Trade Payables	11.9	10.9	11.0	.9	8.5	10.4	16.9	12.8	17.0
Income Taxes Payable	.5	.3	.0	.0	.0	.0	.0	.0	.0
All Other Current	14.2	7.2	10.5	10.5	11.6	6.4	9.2	12.5	12.0
Total Current	49.1	36.7	39.6	27.9	49.6	31.5	40.6	40.5	39.3
Long-Term Debt	30.2	28.5	26.0	29.4	30.6	26.2	25.6	21.1	18.6
Deferred Taxes	.3	.5	.5	.0	.0	.3	1.8	.0	1.3
All Other Non-Current	4.3	2.8	4.1	1.2	3.4	8.0	3.8	5.3	3.5
Net Worth	16.2	31.5	29.8	41.5	16.5	33.9	28.2	33.2	37.3
Total Liabilities & Net Worth	100.0	100.0	100.0	100.0	100.0	100.0	100.0	100.0	100.0
INCOME DATA									
Net Sales	100.0	100.0	100.0	100.0	100.0	100.0	100.0	100.0	100.0
Gross Profit									
Operating Expenses	92.9	91.1	90.9	75.1	92.1	94.2	95.1	92.5	94.7
Operating Profit	7.1	8.9	9.1	24.9	7.9	5.8	4.9	7.5	5.3
All Other Expenses (net)	1.2	.5	1.0	3.4	1.2	.3	.5	.3	.3
Profit Before Taxes	5.9	8.4	8.1	21.5	6.7	5.5	4.4	7.2	5.0
RATIOS									
Current	2.2	3.2	2.7	4.8	3.3	8.4	2.6	2.0	2.2
	1.3	1.6	1.4	1.1	.8	1.8	1.5	1.3	1.6
	.7	.9	.8	.5	.4	.9	1.1	1.0	1.2
Quick	1.9	2.8	2.2	2.9	2.9	4.2	2.4	1.9	1.6
	(141) 1.0	1.4	1.1	.9	.7	1.6	1.3	1.1	1.1
	.5	.6	.6	.4	.4	.6	.7	.8	.7
Sales/Receivables	0 UND	2 183.8	0 UND	0 UND	0 UND	0 UND	12 29.9	26 13.9	37 9.8
	28 13.2	34 10.8	29 12.7	0 UND	8 46.6	21 17.6	37 9.8	39 9.4	52 7.0
	61 6.0	62 5.9	60 6.1	29 12.5	35 10.4	60 6.1	91 4.0	70 5.2	81 4.5
Cost of Sales/Inventory									
Cost of Sales/Payables									
Sales/Working Capital	8.8	6.4	8.5	12.9	10.5	6.3	7.6	9.0	7.2
	49.8	19.7	24.0	133.3	-110.8	10.2	12.9	24.3	10.4
	-27.0	-216.6	-37.6	-19.0	-11.2	-92.8	62.4	-119.1	35.1
EBIT/Interest	28.3	34.2	26.7	22.8	18.4	20.0	20.3	48.8	49.5
	(122) 8.3	(117) 7.6	(124) 9.8	(14) 7.0	(28) 5.6	(15) 9.4	(27) 6.8	16.2	(13) 11.8
	2.2	2.7	2.4	4.3	.0	3.0	1.6	4.7	4.8
Net Profit + Depr., Dep., Amort./Cur. Mat. L/T/D			5.9						
			(12) 2.5						
			1.1						
Fixed/Worth	.3	.2	.2	.2	.1	.0	.1	.4	.1
	1.2	.9	1.0	1.2	1.3	.2	1.0	.9	.8
	-6.5	7.7	4.1	4.7	-2.4	3.1	2.7	4.1	2.2
Debt/Worth	1.0	.6	.8	.3	.6	.8	.8	1.0	1.2
	2.7	1.8	2.2	1.1	9.6	2.6	2.2	1.6	2.2
	-12.1	11.9	17.2	29.6	-4.6	5.5	4.5	5.1	3.4
% Profit Before Taxes/Tangible Net Worth	91.8	81.4	109.4	177.8	168.2	76.1	91.4	92.0	51.8
	(99) 44.0	(114) 41.7	(119) 46.6	(18) 68.5	(22) 78.5	(16) 37.7	(28) 39.9	(23) 48.2	(12) 30.1
	11.1	15.4	16.2	16.2	2.4	12.6	10.1	19.6	21.6
% Profit Before Taxes/Total Assets	31.6	35.6	37.0	49.2	56.7	20.2	26.3	40.0	19.3
	13.6	14.5	15.1	16.8	19.6	9.3	11.0	17.8	7.6
	2.3	5.3	4.8	8.4	.5	3.3	1.1	7.7	6.2
Sales/Net Fixed Assets	43.5	44.8	52.3	24.3	80.7	264.2	55.7	29.0	51.3
	16.3	16.8	17.6	7.1	22.6	27.8	19.9	11.4	8.9
	6.5	6.7	6.2	1.6	6.1	17.8	5.2	8.1	4.2
Sales/Total Assets	4.9	5.0	4.6	4.7	7.2	8.3	3.7	4.6	3.1
	3.4	3.1	2.9	2.4	3.5	3.5	2.7	3.5	2.5
	2.5	2.2	1.9	.9	2.5	2.2	1.9	2.2	1.8
% Depr., Dep., Amort./Sales	.8	1.0	1.1	2.4	.5		1.5	1.0	1.7
	(93) 1.8	(84) 2.1	(99) 2.4	(11) 7.2	(21) 1.4		(23) 2.3	(24) 2.8	(11) 2.8
	4.1	4.4	3.9	19.3	3.0		4.0	3.4	4.5
% Officers', Directors' Owners' Comp/Sales	2.5	2.7	2.8	5.8	3.8	1.3	2.7		
	(77) 4.0	(70) 5.2	(70) 4.8	(11) 7.8	(23) 4.9	(11) 3.9	(16) 4.3		
	8.5	7.2	8.5	17.9	13.1	13.1	6.6		
Net Sales ($)	1901042M	1205931M	2689482M	13022M	68141M	77596M	238348M	442427M	1849948M
Total Assets ($)	655114M	491353M	865554M	18041M	31327M	25360M	118618M	146301M	525907M

© RMA 2019

M = $ thousand   MM = $ million
See Pages viii through xx for Explanation of Ratios and Data

Current Data Sorted by Assets — Comparative Historical Data

Type of Statement	0-500M	500M-2MM	2-10MM	10-50MM	50-100MM	100-250MM	4/1/14-3/31/15 ALL	4/1/15-3/31/16 ALL
Unqualified	1	4	38	86	20	16	189	158
Reviewed	3	19	111	105	7	1	284	283
Compiled	7	36	65	17	2	2	208	193
Tax Returns	87	85	63	4	3	2	375	319
Other	66	145	284	183	40	36	797	830
		143 (4/1-9/30/18)		1,393 (10/1/18-3/31/19)				
NUMBER OF STATEMENTS	164	289	561	395	72	55	1853	1783
ASSETS	%	%	%	%	%	%	%	%
Cash & Equivalents	39.8	23.5	14.6	13.5	16.3	8.4	18.4	17.9
Trade Receivables (net)	16.8	33.7	47.2	47.4	37.7	32.1	40.7	40.7
Inventory	2.1	4.8	4.8	3.1	1.2	3.3	4.0	4.2
All Other Current	3.8	4.1	6.6	9.3	10.5	11.4	6.7	6.0
Total Current	62.5	66.1	73.1	73.4	65.6	55.3	69.8	68.8
Fixed Assets (net)	24.8	19.9	16.1	12.8	15.0	13.1	18.0	18.4
Intangibles (net)	4.0	4.3	3.8	6.2	12.7	23.2	4.1	4.6
All Other Non-Current	8.7	9.7	7.0	7.6	6.7	8.5	8.1	8.1
Total	100.0	100.0	100.0	100.0	100.0	100.0	100.0	100.0
LIABILITIES								
Notes Payable-Short Term	27.6	11.3	7.5	6.6	3.9	1.9	11.0	11.7
Cur. Mat.-L.T.D.	4.1	3.3	2.4	2.7	2.9	1.8	3.3	2.8
Trade Payables	7.3	8.2	11.4	12.8	8.8	14.0	10.2	9.6
Income Taxes Payable	.1	.1	.3	.8	1.1	.3	1.4	1.3
All Other Current	21.3	14.4	16.3	18.2	21.4	17.4	16.9	16.0
Total Current	60.4	37.3	37.9	41.2	38.1	35.4	42.7	41.3
Long-Term Debt	25.1	16.5	9.9	10.0	15.0	17.0	12.9	13.3
Deferred Taxes	.1	.2	.6	1.1	1.2	.6	.7	.7
All Other Non-Current	5.4	5.0	4.7	6.2	3.8	8.0	6.2	5.7
Net Worth	8.9	41.0	46.9	41.5	41.9	39.0	37.5	39.0
Total Liabilties & Net Worth	100.0	100.0	100.0	100.0	100.0	100.0	100.0	100.0
INCOME DATA								
Net Sales	100.0	100.0	100.0	100.0	100.0	100.0	100.0	100.0
Gross Profit								
Operating Expenses	87.4	88.1	90.2	93.3	91.9	94.6	91.8	91.2
Operating Profit	12.6	11.9	9.8	6.7	8.1	5.4	8.2	8.8
All Other Expenses (net)	.9	1.6	1.2	.8	2.6	2.6	1.2	1.5
Profit Before Taxes	11.7	10.3	8.6	5.9	5.5	2.8	7.0	7.3
RATIOS								
Current	5.2	5.5	3.9	2.7	2.5	2.1	3.3	3.4
	1.5	2.2	2.1	1.9	1.8	1.6	1.9	1.9
	.6	1.0	1.3	1.3	1.4	1.3	1.2	1.2
Quick	5.0	4.7	3.4	2.3	2.1	1.6	2.9	3.0
	1.5	1.8	1.7	1.6	1.6	1.2	1.5 (1782)	1.6
	.5	.8	1.0	1.0	1.0	.8	.9	1.0
Sales/Receivables	0 UND	0 UND	45 8.1	56 6.5	53 6.9	54 6.8	32 11.5	30 12.3
	0 UND	38 9.5	66 5.5	74 4.9	70 5.2	74 4.9	62 5.9	61 6.0
	27 13.3	72 5.1	91 4.0	94 3.9	91 4.0	99 3.7	87 4.2	89 4.1
Cost of Sales/Inventory								
Cost of Sales/Payables								
Sales/Working Capital	9.7	4.7	4.1	4.5	4.4	4.5	4.8	4.6
	52.3	12.2	6.8	7.0	6.6	8.0	8.5	8.5
	-57.8	999.8	18.7	15.1	14.3	15.7	33.0	27.9
EBIT/Interest	48.4	57.5	70.0	57.3	30.6	21.5	44.7	51.0
	(106) 17.7	(218) 12.1	(444) 17.0	(335) 12.6	(61) 10.6	(49) 7.7	(1459) 12.5	(1394) 13.3
	6.0	2.3	4.9	4.3	3.1	2.1	3.0	3.8
Net Profit + Depr., Dep., Amort./Cur. Mat. L/T/D		9.3	8.6	6.6	6.3	9.9	5.8	8.3
		(17) 3.1	(85) 3.4	(107) 3.5	(29) 4.5	(17) 5.1	(300) 2.5	(292) 3.1
		1.5	1.9	1.7	1.8	2.6	1.2	1.6
Fixed/Worth	.0	.1	.1	.1	.2	.3	.1	.1
	.5	.3	.2	.3	.5	.5	.3	.3
	8.1	2.1	.7	.7	1.1	-.6	1.1	.9
Debt/Worth	.4	.3	.4	.7	.8	1.3	.5	.5
	2.0	1.2	1.1	1.4	1.8	3.4	1.3	1.2
	-19.6	6.6	2.7	3.3	10.4	-14.5	4.4	4.1
% Profit Before Taxes/Tangible Net Worth	422.1	109.6	60.1	51.8	47.6	39.6	60.5	61.8
	(118) 127.9	(235) 50.5	(512) 33.9	(353) 24.9	(60) 16.1	(40) 21.3	(1589) 27.9	(1541) 28.5
	42.3	14.9	14.3	12.2	7.0	4.5	9.1	10.2
% Profit Before Taxes/Total Assets	145.7	49.7	28.4	17.6	15.6	8.3	26.5	26.2
	57.4	19.4	14.0	9.6	6.2	5.5	10.7	11.7
	12.5	3.8	4.8	4.3	1.7	.8	2.6	3.1
Sales/Net Fixed Assets	850.9	129.1	89.0	62.6	33.5	57.1	75.0	77.3
	71.8	38.9	30.0	26.3	18.0	20.4	28.3	28.1
	22.0	14.0	10.8	12.8	7.7	11.4	12.0	11.9
Sales/Total Assets	14.2	5.4	3.4	2.9	2.4	2.1	3.8	3.7
	6.9	3.2	2.5	2.2	1.9	1.5	2.5	2.5
	4.0	2.0	1.8	1.7	1.5	.9	1.9	1.8
% Depr., Dep., Amort./Sales	.5	.5	.5	.6	.9	1.0	.6	.6
	(73) 1.0	(156) 1.1	(398) 1.1	(338) 1.2	(61) 1.7	(36) 1.4	(1334) 1.3	(1310) 1.2
	1.7	2.9	2.4	2.1	3.1	2.6	2.3	2.3
% Officers', Directors' Owners' Comp/Sales	4.9	3.8	1.7	1.6			3.1	3.3
	(107) 10.2	(104) 7.2	(148) 3.6	(41) 2.7			(547) 6.6	(536) 7.1
	14.7	12.8	7.1	6.9			14.5	12.7
Net Sales ($)	383069M	1284796M	7632113M	19754177M	10091432M	14077763M	51569276M	50675716M
Total Assets ($)	39780M	346368M	2818105M	8466037M	4940029M	8713468M	24010865M	23723027M

© RMA 2019

M = $ thousand   MM = $ million
See Pages viii through xx for Explanation of Ratios and Data

Comparative Historical Data | Current Data Sorted by Sales

			Type of Statement						
156	150	165	Unqualified	1	3	1	9	29	122
286	259	246	Reviewed	6	8	11	33	89	101
147	143	127	Compiled	9	11	15	32	41	19
292	298	244	Tax Returns	37	65	36	56	41	9
779	730	754	Other	39	96	78	125	167	249
4/1/16-3/31/17	4/1/17-3/31/18	4/1/18-3/31/19		143 (4/1-9/30/18)			1,393 (10/1/18-3/31/19)		
ALL	ALL	ALL		0-1MM	1-3MM	3-5MM	5-10MM	10-25MM	25MM & OVER
1660	1580	1536	**NUMBER OF STATEMENTS**	92	181	141	255	367	500
%	%	%	**ASSETS**	%	%	%	%	%	%
17.9	17.6	18.6	Cash & Equivalents	23.0	27.5	21.4	21.1	17.3	13.4
39.6	41.6	40.5	Trade Receivables (net)	16.6	27.5	35.9	38.4	46.0	47.8
4.3	4.0	3.8	Inventory	2.5	4.1	5.5	5.5	3.9	2.7
7.1	7.1	6.9	All Other Current	2.9	4.1	5.6	5.3	6.8	9.9
69.0	70.4	69.8	Total Current	44.9	63.2	68.4	70.3	73.9	73.7
17.7	16.8	16.7	Fixed Assets (net)	44.2	23.1	15.6	16.6	13.7	12.0
5.1	5.2	5.6	Intangibles (net)	4.5	3.4	3.6	5.4	4.8	8.0
8.3	7.6	7.9	All Other Non-Current	6.5	10.2	12.4	7.8	7.5	6.3
100.0	100.0	100.0	Total	100.0	100.0	100.0	100.0	100.0	100.0
			LIABILITIES						
12.1	10.5	9.8	Notes Payable-Short Term	11.4	19.7	16.6	9.2	7.6	5.8
2.9	2.9	2.8	Cur. Mat.-L.T.D.	3.5	3.7	3.3	2.2	2.9	2.6
10.0	10.6	10.7	Trade Payables	5.1	8.7	7.3	9.6	11.3	13.6
.9	.6	.4	Income Taxes Payable	.1	.1	.0	.3	.2	.8
17.1	17.0	17.2	All Other Current	14.8	16.6	15.6	15.2	17.2	19.4
42.9	41.7	41.0	Total Current	35.0	48.8	42.9	36.6	39.2	42.2
13.7	13.4	13.3	Long-Term Debt	34.9	18.9	16.6	11.6	9.2	10.2
.8	.8	.7	Deferred Taxes	.2	.0	.7	.3	.8	1.0
4.7	5.7	5.3	All Other Non-Current	3.7	8.3	4.3	3.7	5.6	5.4
37.8	38.4	39.8	Net Worth	26.2	23.9	35.5	47.9	45.2	41.2
100.0	100.0	100.0	Total Liabilities & Net Worth	100.0	100.0	100.0	100.0	100.0	100.0
			INCOME DATA						
100.0	100.0	100.0	Net Sales	100.0	100.0	100.0	100.0	100.0	100.0
			Gross Profit						
91.6	91.4	90.5	Operating Expenses	67.6	88.8	91.0	91.6	91.9	93.7
8.4	8.6	9.5	Operating Profit	32.4	11.2	9.0	8.4	8.1	6.3
1.4	1.4	1.3	All Other Expenses (net)	7.8	1.3	1.2	.6	.7	.8
7.0	7.2	8.2	Profit Before Taxes	24.6	9.9	7.9	7.9	7.4	5.5
			RATIOS						
3.4	3.4	3.6		5.8	4.2	5.4	4.9	3.7	2.6
1.9	1.9	1.9	Current	1.4	1.7	2.2	2.5	2.1	1.8
1.2	1.2	1.2		.6	.7	1.0	1.2	1.3	1.3
2.9	2.9	3.1		5.8	3.9	4.4	4.5	3.2	2.1
(1659) 1.6	(1579) 1.5	1.6	Quick	1.3	1.5	1.6	2.0	1.8	1.5
.9	1.0	.9		.4	.6	.8	1.0	1.1	1.0
30 12.1	33 11.0	33 11.1		0 UND	0 UND	0 UND	21 17.5	44 8.3	54 6.8
60 6.1	63 5.8	62 5.9	Sales/Receivables	0 UND	35 10.4	59 6.2	54 6.7	63 5.8	72 5.1
87 4.2	89 4.1	87 4.2		52 7.0	74 4.9	94 3.9	87 4.2	89 4.1	91 4.0
			Cost of Sales/Inventory						
			Cost of Sales/Payables						
4.5	4.6	4.5		4.4	4.5	3.5	4.5	4.4	4.9
8.5	8.1	8.2	Sales/Working Capital	21.4	17.3	7.4	7.7	7.4	7.6
32.6	31.1	27.8		-10.1	-38.6	NM	29.7	20.7	15.5
41.2	49.8	55.5		33.6	37.2	42.5	68.5	67.0	52.7
(1306) 11.6	(1242) 13.8	(1213) 13.4	EBIT/Interest	(42) 7.9	(130) 11.3	(114) 9.4	(194) 15.8	(308) 16.9	(425) 13.3
2.4	3.3	4.1		3.1	2.5	1.9	4.4	5.1	4.6
9.7	9.8	6.9				11.2	6.1	7.5	7.6
(262) 3.6	(260) 3.8	(259) 3.6	Net Profit + Depr., Dep., Amort./Cur. Mat. L/T/D		(14) 4.0	(29) 2.3	(67) 3.3	(145) 3.9	
1.6	1.7	1.8				1.7	.3	2.0	1.9
.1	.1	.1		.1	.0	.1	.1	.1	.1
.3	.3	.3	Fixed/Worth	1.1	.3	.2	.2	.2	.3
1.1	1.0	1.0		6.8	4.6	1.5	1.1	.7	.7
.5	.5	.5		.3	.3	.3	.3	.5	.8
1.3	1.3	1.3	Debt/Worth	1.9	1.7	1.3	.9	1.1	1.6
4.8	4.6	4.3		16.3	-29.9	12.2	3.2	3.0	3.7
65.8	66.9	71.7	% Profit Before Taxes/Tangible Net Worth	133.2	110.0	106.7	82.6	62.4	60.4
(1408) 29.1	(1365) 30.5	(1318) 34.2		(73) 37.9	(134) 51.3	(114) 42.2	(224) 37.8	(332) 36.9	(441) 28.7
9.3	10.0	13.2		8.0	18.1	8.9	16.1	14.8	12.5
26.6	26.9	32.7	% Profit Before Taxes/Total Assets	75.4	61.6	47.9	38.7	31.0	18.9
10.4	11.6	12.8		8.2	23.9	14.7	18.9	13.3	9.5
2.5	3.2	4.3		2.7	4.7	1.4	5.9	5.0	4.5
84.2	92.4	91.7		142.3	208.0	141.2	120.6	86.5	69.8
28.8	28.6	30.0	Sales/Net Fixed Assets	7.7	28.8	36.0	37.0	35.3	26.9
12.1	13.1	12.7		.2	10.9	14.0	14.0	14.3	14.3
3.7	3.7	3.7		3.6	5.7	5.3	4.2	3.6	3.2
2.6	2.6	2.5	Sales/Total Assets	1.4	2.9	2.5	2.9	2.6	2.4
1.8	1.8	1.8		.2	1.7	1.7	2.0	2.0	1.8
.6	.6	.5		1.2	.6	.5	.4	.4	.6
(1168) 1.3	(1133) 1.2	(1062) 1.2	% Depr., Dep., Amort./Sales	(54) 11.5	(83) 1.5	(83) 1.1	(148) 1.0	(281) 1.0	(413) 1.2
2.4	2.3	2.3		24.4	4.5	2.1	2.2	1.9	2.1
3.3	3.5	2.6		8.3	6.1	3.8	2.6	1.1	1.4
(471) 6.9	(465) 6.9	(415) 5.7	% Officers', Directors' Owners' Comp/Sales	(26) 12.0	(85) 9.7	(54) 6.0	(105) 5.2	(90) 3.1	(55) 3.6
13.5	13.4	11.1		23.0	14.4	10.4	8.6	7.2	
46570735M	50277684M	53223350M	Net Sales ($)	46626M	336820M	545926M	1856128M	5762570M	44675280M
21279673M	23036057M	25323787M	Total Assets ($)	105744M	243227M	345604M	849286M	2573812M	21206114M

M = $ thousand   MM = $ million
See Pages viii through xx for Explanation of Ratios and Data

Current Data Sorted by Assets   Comparative Historical Data

Type of Statement	0-500M	500M-2MM	2-10MM	10-50MM	50-100MM	100-250MM		4/1/14-3/31/15 ALL	4/1/15-3/31/16 ALL
Unqualified			2						2
Reviewed			3	1				5	6
Compiled		3	4					8	5
Tax Returns	12	6	4					27	25
Other	9	15	10	6				29	34
		4 (4/1-9/30/18)		71 (10/1/18-3/31/19)					
NUMBER OF STATEMENTS	21	24	23	7				69	72

Columns 50-100MM and 100-250MM: DATA NOT AVAILABLE

	0-500M %	500M-2MM %	2-10MM %	10-50MM %	50-100MM %	100-250MM %		%	%
ASSETS									
Cash & Equivalents	33.1	28.7	7.5					20.9	17.6
Trade Receivables (net)	15.3	31.2	40.9					26.9	33.0
Inventory	1.3	.1	.4					1.4	1.2
All Other Current	1.4	3.8	6.3					6.2	5.9
Total Current	51.0	63.9	55.2					55.3	57.7
Fixed Assets (net)	19.3	20.9	33.2					29.4	22.4
Intangibles (net)	1.8	10.2	1.7					7.9	6.8
All Other Non-Current	27.7	5.1	9.9					7.4	13.2
Total	100.0	100.0	100.0					100.0	100.0
LIABILITIES									
Notes Payable-Short Term	14.0	8.8	5.1					12.2	12.2
Cur. Mat.-L.T.D.	4.4	.9	4.5					3.6	3.6
Trade Payables	21.4	4.6	7.3					5.6	5.5
Income Taxes Payable	.0	.0	.6					.6	.3
All Other Current	14.3	12.0	13.7					10.8	17.6
Total Current	54.1	26.2	31.3					32.7	39.2
Long-Term Debt	47.2	13.9	12.4					31.1	18.3
Deferred Taxes	.0	.0	1.6					1.6	1.7
All Other Non-Current	18.5	3.1	2.7					7.5	3.5
Net Worth	-19.6	56.8	52.0					27.1	37.3
Total Liabilities & Net Worth	100.0	100.0	100.0					100.0	100.0
INCOME DATA									
Net Sales	100.0	100.0	100.0					100.0	100.0
Gross Profit									
Operating Expenses	92.2	83.8	90.6					90.6	91.7
Operating Profit	7.8	16.2	9.4					9.4	8.3
All Other Expenses (net)	3.9	3.8	1.4					2.8	1.0
Profit Before Taxes	3.9	12.4	8.1					6.6	7.2
RATIOS									
Current	4.1	9.4	3.3					6.1	4.5
	1.3	2.9	1.8					1.8	2.4
	.3	1.5	1.4					.8	1.1
Quick	3.6	9.1	3.3					4.0	4.4
	1.3	2.9	1.6					1.7	2.1
	.3	1.1	1.1					.8	1.1
Sales/Receivables	0 UND	0 UND	51 7.2					0 UND	0 788.8
	0 UND	33 10.9	62 5.9					51 7.2	54 6.7
	31 11.9	74 4.9	85 4.3					70 5.2	81 4.5
Cost of Sales/Inventory									
Cost of Sales/Payables									
Sales/Working Capital	17.1	4.6	5.0					4.5	4.5
	28.3	10.5	10.9					13.3	7.9
	-21.9	16.4	22.9					-84.3	226.1
EBIT/Interest	55.6	287.4	41.9					29.0	44.0
	(16) 7.3	(22) 55.1	(20) 16.7					(55) 7.0	(61) 6.1
	-1.1	5.5	2.3					.6	.5
Net Profit + Depr., Dep., Amort./Cur. Mat. L/T/D									
Fixed/Worth	.0	.1	.4					.2	.2
	.4	.3	.7					.7	.5
	-1.9	.8	.9					15.5	2.1
Debt/Worth	.6	.3	.5					.3	.4
	5.9	.5	.9					1.7	1.5
	-2.3	2.5	1.7					54.9	6.5
% Profit Before Taxes/Tangible Net Worth	999.8	116.0	64.0					84.7	96.9
	(14) 106.2	(20) 76.4	(22) 33.7					(53) 33.4	(57) 41.5
	58.6	31.8	9.1					4.6	4.1
% Profit Before Taxes/Total Assets	60.8	83.4	31.7					39.9	38.8
	29.8	39.2	16.7					12.8	15.1
	-21.2	3.4	1.5					.1	.8
Sales/Net Fixed Assets	555.8	74.5	11.3					51.1	40.4
	68.6	26.6	6.9					14.8	21.7
	13.0	8.8	4.2					6.6	7.4
Sales/Total Assets	9.2	4.6	2.7					5.0	3.7
	4.5	3.4	2.2					2.6	2.5
	2.8	2.0	1.7					1.4	1.5
% Depr., Dep., Amort./Sales			2.3					1.3	1.0
		(21) 3.4						(44) 3.2	(43) 2.2
			6.6					6.6	3.7
% Officers', Directors' Owners' Comp/Sales	8.6	4.3	3.1					5.7	4.3
	(13) 14.2	(11) 7.4	(11) 5.9					(30) 9.9	(34) 7.9
	28.6	11.9	6.8					15.9	14.8
Net Sales ($)	23769M	84491M	234076M	161728M				631111M	774692M
Total Assets ($)	4198M	26177M	97606M	104727M				601269M	667866M

M = $ thousand   MM = $ million
See Pages viii through xx for Explanation of Ratios and Data

Comparative Historical Data | Current Data Sorted by Sales

Type of Statement	4/1/16-3/31/17 ALL	4/1/17-3/31/18 ALL	4/1/18-3/31/19 ALL	0-1MM	1-3MM	3-5MM	5-10MM	10-25MM	25MM & OVER
Unqualified	4		2					1	1
Reviewed	3	1	4				2	1	1
Compiled	5	5	7		1	2	4	2	
Tax Returns	25	21	22	8	7	4	1	2	
Other	29	34	40	6	10	5	9	8	2
	4 (4/1-9/30/18)						71 (10/1/18-3/31/19)		
NUMBER OF STATEMENTS	66	61	75	14	18	11	16	12	4
ASSETS	%	%	%	%	%	%	%	%	%
Cash & Equivalents	17.8	18.0	22.2	22.8	27.5	30.9	21.6	11.7	
Trade Receivables (net)	27.7	28.2	30.5	20.7	22.1	24.2	42.2	35.5	
Inventory	.6	1.4	.6	1.9	.2	.0	.6	.0	
All Other Current	7.3	3.4	3.8	1.2	1.9	7.4	3.7	6.8	
Total Current	53.3	50.9	57.2	46.6	51.6	62.5	68.2	54.0	
Fixed Assets (net)	31.7	31.4	23.8	36.3	14.2	21.4	24.7	28.2	
Intangibles (net)	6.9	8.8	5.3	1.8	8.5	9.7	1.1	5.2	
All Other Non-Current	8.0	8.9	13.7	15.0	25.7	6.4	6.0	12.6	
Total	100.0	100.0	100.0	100.0	100.0	100.0	100.0	100.0	
LIABILITIES									
Notes Payable-Short Term	13.0	12.2	9.3	19.2	7.2	3.7	8.0	4.9	
Cur. Mat.-L.T.D.	6.1	5.3	3.4	4.3	2.6	2.0	3.6	2.9	
Trade Payables	7.0	4.7	10.4	28.4	4.6	6.7	6.1	6.0	
Income Taxes Payable	.2	.1	.2	.0	.0	.0	.0	1.2	
All Other Current	10.6	11.0	13.0	11.2	18.0	8.2	8.5	15.2	
Total Current	36.8	33.2	36.4	63.1	32.4	20.7	26.2	30.2	
Long-Term Debt	23.7	23.6	22.8	48.2	29.8	13.3	11.1	11.7	
Deferred Taxes	1.2	.2	.6	.0	.0	1.2	1.4	.2	
All Other Non-Current	5.4	6.7	7.1	18.7	11.2	.4	.4	4.6	
Net Worth	32.9	36.4	33.1	-29.7	26.6	64.5	61.0	53.3	
Total Liabilties & Net Worth	100.0	100.0	100.0	100.0	100.0	100.0	100.0	100.0	
INCOME DATA									
Net Sales	100.0	100.0	100.0	100.0	100.0	100.0	100.0	100.0	
Gross Profit									
Operating Expenses	93.2	90.0	88.8	92.5	87.0	85.2	87.3	88.1	
Operating Profit	6.8	10.0	11.2	7.5	13.0	14.8	12.7	11.9	
All Other Expenses (net)	1.0	1.2	2.9	8.5	1.4	2.6	1.8	.6	
Profit Before Taxes	5.8	8.7	8.3	-1.0	11.6	12.2	10.9	11.3	
RATIOS									
Current	4.6	4.9	4.6	4.0	3.3	10.1	5.4	5.4	
	1.9	1.7	2.0	.9	1.9	4.3	2.9	1.7	
	.8	.7	1.0	.1	.7	1.4	1.6	1.4	
Quick	4.0	4.8	4.3	3.5	3.2	7.1	5.1	5.1	
	1.5	1.6	1.9	.9	1.9	3.7	2.9	1.5	
	.6	.7	.9	.1	.6	1.2	1.3	.8	
Sales/Receivables	0 UND	0 UND	0 UND	0 UND	0 UND	0 UND	35 10.4	45 8.1	
	41 8.9	49 7.4	45 8.1	13 28.4	0 UND	30 12.0	70 5.2	81 4.5	
	72 5.1	64 5.7	81 4.5	45 8.2	48 7.6	62 5.9	87 4.2	87 4.2	
Cost of Sales/Inventory									
Cost of Sales/Payables									
Sales/Working Capital	5.1	5.2	5.3	16.6	7.1	3.3	4.5	4.1	
	12.4	13.6	13.9	NM	19.7	11.7	7.0	10.9	
	-19.2	-74.7	235.1	-2.4	-142.6	19.4	12.4	182.0	
EBIT/Interest	37.9	31.7	77.2		145.8	129.4	116.2	107.7	
	(53) 11.2	(55) 11.4	(64) 15.4		(17) 9.5	(10) 16.5	(15) 36.3	(10) 25.1	
	2.3	2.5	2.7		.8	5.2	13.3	3.4	
Net Profit + Depr., Dep., Amort./Cur. Mat. L/T/D									
Fixed/Worth	.3	.3	.1	.1	.1	.1	.1	.3	
	.8	.9	.5	3.9	.4	.4	.4	.8	
	-3.0	12.3	1.5	-2.3	NM	.6	.7	.9	
Debt/Worth	.5	.4	.4	.9	.4	.1	.4	.4	
	1.3	1.5	.9	67.2	1.0	.6	.6	.9	
	-14.4	27.8	7.4	-2.5	NM	1.7	1.0	3.2	
% Profit Before Taxes/Tangible Net Worth	83.9	91.8	112.2		214.4	90.8	105.5	77.1	
	(48) 42.5	(47) 43.3	(61) 62.7		(14) 80.7	(10) 48.3	40.2	(11) 48.6	
	6.8	15.8	27.3		36.6	23.7	16.5	38.3	
% Profit Before Taxes/Total Assets	45.5	54.4	49.9	26.3	65.3	69.7	50.6	42.9	
	12.9	17.4	24.4	-1.8	33.7	26.7	27.4	26.2	
	.5	3.4	.9	-42.4	3.3	2.8	9.0	2.9	
Sales/Net Fixed Assets	34.8	43.7	68.6	274.6	102.5	33.5	33.9	22.2	
	11.0	14.6	14.0	18.6	46.1	21.3	9.5	8.2	
	5.2	5.6	6.9	3.4	9.7	5.8	5.7	5.2	
Sales/Total Assets	4.8	4.1	4.4	5.5	5.2	4.9	4.3	2.8	
	2.5	2.7	2.7	3.0	3.4	3.6	2.6	2.4	
	1.5	2.1	1.7	1.6	2.3	1.7	2.1	1.7	
% Depr., Dep., Amort./Sales	1.3	1.5	1.4				2.0		
	(41) 2.8	(38) 3.1	(41) 3.4				(11) 3.8		
	5.4	4.2	5.8				5.8		
% Officers', Directors' Owners' Comp/Sales	5.9	5.6	3.5		4.9				
	(37) 8.0	(31) 10.8	(39) 7.0		(13) 8.8				
	12.8	20.0	14.3		14.3				
Net Sales ($)	574956M	441094M	504064M	5665M	34724M	42327M	104412M	195350M	121586M
Total Assets ($)	406996M	229553M	232708M	4783M	11669M	15670M	41285M	100613M	58688M

M = $ thousand   MM = $ million
See Pages viii through xx for Explanation of Ratios and Data

Current Data Sorted by Assets   Comparative Historical Data

Type of Statement	0-500M	500M-2MM	2-10MM	10-50MM	50-100MM	100-250MM		4/1/14-3/31/15 ALL	4/1/15-3/31/16 ALL
Unqualified	1		1	7	3	2		15	21
Reviewed		1	6	7	1			14	19
Compiled	4	6	10	1	1	1		33	23
Tax Returns	4	13	6		1			59	42
Other	14	18	45	26	6	1		108	123
		26 (4/1-9/30/18)		159 (10/1/18-3/31/19)					
NUMBER OF STATEMENTS	23	38	68	41	11	4		229	228
ASSETS	%	%	%	%	%	%		%	%
Cash & Equivalents	29.6	17.5	14.7	12.2	10.2			18.6	14.9
Trade Receivables (net)	19.9	31.1	30.7	23.8	25.2			25.9	29.3
Inventory	1.8	4.4	4.1	2.7	5.4			3.0	3.1
All Other Current	1.3	4.1	3.3	2.9	3.8			3.0	2.1
Total Current	52.4	57.0	52.9	41.5	44.7			50.5	49.4
Fixed Assets (net)	33.1	32.7	36.7	38.7	35.6			34.4	34.0
Intangibles (net)	9.4	3.0	5.4	12.7	6.8			7.5	9.3
All Other Non-Current	5.0	7.3	4.9	7.1	12.9			7.6	7.3
Total	100.0	100.0	100.0	100.0	100.0			100.0	100.0
LIABILITIES									
Notes Payable-Short Term	39.7	4.0	5.8	3.3	4.7			7.0	7.0
Cur. Mat.-L.T.D.	3.8	4.9	3.5	2.4	1.1			3.5	3.6
Trade Payables	9.3	7.3	7.3	6.6	4.0			6.2	7.7
Income Taxes Payable	.1	.8	.2	.0	.3			.5	.5
All Other Current	7.7	8.0	7.4	13.3	13.1			10.4	12.1
Total Current	60.7	25.0	24.1	25.7	23.1			27.6	31.0
Long-Term Debt	25.3	35.3	20.0	15.7	18.3			23.4	26.8
Deferred Taxes	.0	.2	.5	.9	1.5			.8	.9
All Other Non-Current	40.0	9.3	2.4	5.5	4.4			6.2	8.4
Net Worth	-25.9	30.3	53.0	52.2	52.6			42.1	32.8
Total Liabilities & Net Worth	100.0	100.0	100.0	100.0	100.0			100.0	100.0
INCOME DATA									
Net Sales	100.0	100.0	100.0	100.0	100.0			100.0	100.0
Gross Profit									
Operating Expenses	87.7	81.5	87.2	90.5	88.2			87.4	87.5
Operating Profit	12.3	18.5	12.8	9.5	11.8			12.6	12.5
All Other Expenses (net)	4.6	4.2	2.3	1.2	5.6			2.3	1.7
Profit Before Taxes	7.6	14.3	10.5	8.3	6.1			10.3	10.8
RATIOS									
Current	8.8	7.0	3.7	2.7	2.1			4.0	3.3
	1.3	2.3	2.4	1.6	1.9			2.2	1.7
	.2	1.4	1.4	1.2	1.5			1.2	1.0
Quick	8.8	6.8	3.2	2.3	1.7			3.6	3.0
	1.3	2.0	2.1	1.4	1.6			1.9	1.5
	.2	1.1	1.1	.9	.9			1.0	.9
Sales/Receivables	0 UND	19 19.4	41 9.0	42 8.6	47 7.7		26 13.8	27 13.5
	12 30.6	39 9.3	55 6.6	53 6.9	68 5.4		48 7.6	51 7.1
	43 8.5	74 4.9	74 4.9	68 5.4	74 4.9		70 5.2	72 5.1
Cost of Sales/Inventory									
Cost of Sales/Payables									
Sales/Working Capital	8.5	4.2	3.9	5.0	5.8			4.4	5.5
	37.5	9.1	6.9	10.7	7.1			8.9	11.3
	-9.2	19.4	18.5	34.2	10.9			40.3	182.8
EBIT/Interest	71.2	42.9	24.3	21.8				37.3	38.7
	(17) 13.4	(30) 16.7	(57) 8.7	(35) 7.0			(177) 9.5	(183) 10.0
	1.4	2.8	2.1	3.2				2.4	3.2
Net Profit + Depr., Dep., Amort./Cur. Mat. L/T/D			8.8	10.1				9.6	7.1
		(16) 3.5	(15) 5.5				(48) 3.7	(45) 2.5
		1.2	1.7					2.1	1.2
Fixed/Worth	.3	.3	.3	.6	.2			.3	.4
	1.0	1.0	.6	1.0	.7			.7	1.0
	-2.7	8.5	1.7	3.0	1.1			2.4	7.0
Debt/Worth	.6	.6	.3	.5	.6			.4	.4
	3.4	1.3	.8	1.4	.9			1.1	1.6
	-1.8	43.2	2.6	3.3	2.0			5.5	19.5
% Profit Before Taxes/Tangible Net Worth	88.6	147.3	57.6	41.9	37.9			64.6	70.0
	(15) 37.8	(31) 62.1	(63) 24.1	(38) 27.3	14.0		(194) 27.6	(177) 33.6
	.0	20.2	7.0	4.6	6.2			9.0	11.5
% Profit Before Taxes/Total Assets	39.3	34.6	27.6	17.3	15.4			25.5	27.8
	9.2	20.2	12.4	7.2	4.4			10.1	13.2
	.0	2.2	2.0	3.7	2.7			2.3	3.9
Sales/Net Fixed Assets	55.0	21.7	11.5	9.5	11.7			19.7	14.1
	17.9	11.0	5.7	4.4	3.7			8.1	7.0
	5.3	5.7	3.2	2.7	2.4			3.6	4.4
Sales/Total Assets	6.6	3.9	2.5	2.0	2.0			3.3	3.0
	3.7	2.6	1.8	1.6	1.3			2.0	2.0
	2.1	1.9	1.3	1.0	1.1			1.2	1.3
% Depr., Dep., Amort./Sales	.4	1.1	2.1	2.6				1.5	2.1
	(12) 2.4	(29) 2.8	(57) 3.9	5.1			(178) 3.6	(169) 3.8
	7.8	4.6	8.3	6.4				5.5	5.7
% Officers', Directors' Owners' Comp/Sales		2.4	2.8					3.1	2.6
	(22) 7.8	(18) 4.9					(85) 6.9	(70) 5.2
	13.2	7.3						11.9	8.8
Net Sales ($)	35235M	128976M	594178M	1481231M	1137881M	456283M		5655008M	5902465M
Total Assets ($)	7281M	43490M	309210M	949279M	773006M	710611M		3896733M	4295919M

Comparative Historical Data | | | | Current Data Sorted by Sales

			Type of Statement						
8	19	14	Unqualified	1				2	11
23	15	15	Reviewed		1	3		7	4
18	24	23	Compiled	1	3	4	10	3	2
39	43	23	Tax Returns	4	8	5	3	3	
109	106	110	Other	12	19	10	24	22	23
4/1/16-3/31/17 ALL	4/1/17-3/31/18 ALL	4/1/18-3/31/19 ALL		26 (4/1-9/30/18)			159 (10/1/18-3/31/19)		
				0-1MM	1-3MM	3-5MM	5-10MM	10-25MM	25MM & OVER
197	207	185	NUMBER OF STATEMENTS	18	31	22	37	37	40
%	%	%	ASSETS	%	%	%	%	%	%
15.8	15.4	16.2	Cash & Equivalents	14.8	21.7	21.8	14.8	13.6	13.2
29.4	29.7	27.2	Trade Receivables (net)	9.7	31.1	21.0	35.1	27.7	27.6
3.7	3.3	3.6	Inventory	1.6	.7	8.7	5.3	2.5	3.2
3.6	3.3	3.1	All Other Current	.2	2.6	3.3	1.8	5.0	4.2
52.5	51.6	50.1	Total Current	26.3	56.2	54.9	56.9	48.8	48.2
32.0	33.1	35.5	Fixed Assets (net)	60.0	31.0	34.3	33.1	34.7	31.7
9.9	8.6	8.0	Intangibles (net)	5.3	7.8	6.3	4.5	9.9	11.9
5.6	6.6	6.4	All Other Non-Current	8.3	5.0	4.5	5.5	6.7	8.1
100.0	100.0	100.0	Total	100.0	100.0	100.0	100.0	100.0	100.0
			LIABILITIES						
9.7	9.1	8.9	Notes Payable-Short Term	36.2	9.2	4.3	7.7	5.0	3.8
4.0	4.1	3.4	Cur. Mat.-L.T.D.	5.3	3.2	3.6	4.6	2.8	2.0
7.6	8.8	7.2	Trade Payables	2.8	6.2	9.3	11.2	5.2	6.8
.6	.3	.3	Income Taxes Payable	.1	.8	.1	.4	.0	.1
9.5	11.8	9.1	All Other Current	5.8	7.8	7.2	7.9	9.3	13.5
31.4	34.0	28.8	Total Current	50.2	27.2	24.5	31.8	22.3	26.2
21.8	26.2	23.0	Long-Term Debt	39.7	32.3	20.9	24.6	16.7	13.6
.8	.7	.5	Deferred Taxes	.7	.0	.0	.4	.7	1.1
7.0	8.2	9.4	All Other Non-Current	3.0	37.0	1.8	4.7	4.1	4.6
38.9	30.9	38.3	Net Worth	6.5	3.6	52.9	38.6	56.1	54.6
100.0	100.0	100.0	Total Liabilities & Net Worth	100.0	100.0	100.0	100.0	100.0	100.0
			INCOME DATA						
100.0	100.0	100.0	Net Sales	100.0	100.0	100.0	100.0	100.0	100.0
			Gross Profit						
89.5	87.1	87.1	Operating Expenses	55.1	86.9	94.0	88.8	91.2	92.4
10.5	12.9	12.9	Operating Profit	44.9	13.1	6.0	11.2	8.8	7.6
1.9	2.2	3.0	All Other Expenses (net)	18.4	1.6	2.2	1.3	1.0	1.0
8.5	10.7	9.9	Profit Before Taxes	26.5	11.5	3.8	9.9	7.9	6.6
			RATIOS						
3.2	3.4	3.5	Current	2.0	7.3	8.4	3.8	3.3	2.7
1.8	1.9	2.0		.7	2.5	2.6	2.1	2.2	1.9
1.1	1.0	1.2		.2	1.3	1.4	1.1	1.3	1.4
2.9	3.2	3.0	Quick	1.6	7.2	7.2	3.2	2.9	2.1
1.6	1.5	1.7		.7	2.3	1.9	1.8	2.0	1.6
.9	.8	1.0		.2	1.2	1.1	.9	1.2	1.1
31 11.6	29 12.4	34 10.6	Sales/Receivables	0 UND	5 74.8	0 UND	40 9.2	41 8.8	46 8.0
50 7.3	50 7.3	49 7.5		26 13.9	43 8.5	41 8.8	50 7.3	57 6.4	54 6.8
70 5.2	69 5.3	72 5.1		79 4.6	74 4.9	60 6.1	74 4.9	76 4.8	72 5.1
			Cost of Sales/Inventory						
			Cost of Sales/Payables						
5.5	5.1	4.4	Sales/Working Capital	7.0	3.9	4.5	4.2	4.8	4.8
9.9	10.1	8.4		-13.4	7.2	7.6	7.9	8.3	7.5
80.0	-206.7	29.4		-2.7	40.7	18.8	52.0	18.1	18.0
27.3	22.2	31.1	EBIT/Interest	17.8	47.5	27.9	25.9	34.1	37.6
(153) 8.1	(154) 11.0	(152) 10.2		(10) 14.4	(22) 9.7	(19) 4.5	(33) 14.9	(34) 6.7	(34) 10.6
1.6	3.1	2.4		4.0	1.7	-.6	2.4	3.3	2.4
10.7	11.0	9.5	Net Profit + Depr., Dep., Amort./Cur. Mat. L/T/D					8.2	33.4
(38) 4.4	(41) 4.3	(43) 3.9						(11) 5.5	(14) 8.8
1.3	1.4	1.2						2.5	2.5
.3	.4	.4	Fixed/Worth	.7	.3	.4	.3	.3	.4
.9	.8	.8		2.9	.9	.0	.7	.8	.7
3.2	3.8	2.3		7.2	-2.7	1.4	2.1	1.8	1.1
.5	.5	.5	Debt/Worth	1.0	.3	.4	.4	.3	.5
1.2	1.4	1.0		2.7	2.3	1.0	1.0	.8	.8
7.8	12.5	4.6		7.7	-3.8	2.4	6.6	2.5	2.0
69.0	73.6	63.5	% Profit Before Taxes/Tangible Net Worth	79.8	174.9	67.4	65.0	66.8	43.0
(163) 31.5	(165) 32.9	(160) 28.2		(16) 19.6	(20) 39.2	24.3	(30) 24.1	(35) 29.4	(37) 27.3
7.3	10.6	6.3		10.1	12.8	-19.8	8.4	5.2	6.6
25.5	29.6	27.6	% Profit Before Taxes/Total Assets	26.9	36.9	32.4	29.0	25.1	19.8
10.1	10.7	11.0		5.7	14.4	15.2	14.6	6.5	8.7
2.0	3.1	2.0		1.9	3.9	-7.2	1.9	2.7	2.5
18.8	28.8	14.8	Sales/Net Fixed Assets	8.8	28.2	35.3	16.7	10.5	12.3
7.7	8.1	6.6		.6	13.2	6.5	6.9	6.4	5.5
4.4	3.6	3.2		.1	4.1	4.3	4.5	2.8	3.1
3.1	3.3	2.9	Sales/Total Assets	1.3	3.7	3.9	3.1	2.6	2.3
2.2	2.3	1.9		.3	2.3	2.3	2.3	1.7	1.7
1.4	1.4	1.2		.1	1.8	1.5	1.6	1.0	1.2
2.2	1.7	2.1	% Depr., Dep., Amort./Sales	4.7	.8	1.4	1.8	2.7	2.3
(138) 3.8	(145) 3.2	(151) 3.5		(14) 19.7	(20) 2.4	(17) 3.0	(31) 3.5	(31) 4.0	(38) 3.8
5.8	5.9	6.6		26.2	6.7	8.1	6.5	5.7	5.5
3.5	3.0	2.9	% Officers', Directors' Owners' Comp/Sales		7.6			2.8	
(65) 6.4	(73) 6.1	(51) 6.4			(1G) 9.3			(13) 4.6	
10.4	10.8	12.2			14.8			10.1	
3726295M	3750320M	3833784M	Net Sales ($)	7182M	52847M	89823M	256705M	571605M	2855622M
2529189M	2389555M	2792877M	Total Assets ($)	25002M	38688M	42751M	189776M	433161M	2063499M

M = $ thousand   MM = $ million
See Pages viii through xx for Explanation of Ratios and Data

	Current Data Sorted by Assets							Comparative Historical Data	

Type of Statement

Type of Statement	0-500M	500M-2MM	2-10MM	10-50MM	50-100MM	100-250MM	4/1/14-3/31/15 ALL	4/1/15-3/31/16 ALL
Unqualified				1		1	4	6
Reviewed		1	4	4			6	9
Compiled	1	1	2	1			9	7
Tax Returns	15	10	2	2	1		51	55
Other	21	21	13	6		1	68	48
	10 (4/1-9/30/18)			97 (10/1/18-3/31/19)				
NUMBER OF STATEMENTS	37	33	21	13	1	2	138	125

	0-500M %	500M-2MM %	2-10MM %	10-50MM %	50-100MM %	100-250MM %	ALL %	ALL %
ASSETS								
Cash & Equivalents	34.4	26.8	12.8	14.5			22.1	23.2
Trade Receivables (net)	20.4	31.5	42.6	38.9			26.2	22.9
Inventory	9.9	5.8	16.2	15.2			18.6	14.6
All Other Current	6.9	3.7	5.6	5.9			5.5	4.8
Total Current	71.5	67.7	77.2	74.5			72.4	65.5
Fixed Assets (net)	14.7	19.7	10.3	15.6			15.8	18.5
Intangibles (net)	3.0	3.5	5.2	5.9			3.3	4.0
All Other Non-Current	10.8	9.1	7.2	4.0			8.4	12.0
Total	100.0	100.0	100.0	100.0			100.0	100.0
LIABILITIES								
Notes Payable-Short Term	37.9	9.3	11.6	5.6			9.7	14.2
Cur. Mat.-L.T.D.	1.8	1.1	.9	1.3			1.6	2.3
Trade Payables	14.1	14.5	16.2	16.5			13.1	10.9
Income Taxes Payable	.4	.0	.1	.3			.4	.3
All Other Current	21.9	23.9	11.7	31.7			28.0	23.4
Total Current	76.0	48.8	40.6	55.5			52.8	51.0
Long-Term Debt	12.0	10.1	4.9	5.1			13.0	10.3
Deferred Taxes	.0	.0	.0	.2			.2	.1
All Other Non-Current	7.1	11.1	3.2	2.2			8.2	11.5
Net Worth	5.0	30.0	51.3	37.1			25.7	27.1
Total Liabilities & Net Worth	100.0	100.0	100.0	100.0			100.0	100.0
INCOME DATA								
Net Sales	100.0	100.0	100.0	100.0			100.0	100.0
Gross Profit								
Operating Expenses	89.4	91.5	88.2	93.2			92.2	90.4
Operating Profit	10.6	8.5	11.8	6.8			7.8	9.6
All Other Expenses (net)	1.1	.0	.1	.1			1.3	1.5
Profit Before Taxes	9.5	8.4	11.7	6.7			6.6	8.2
RATIOS								
Current	2.4	4.1	3.2	1.8			2.7	2.7
	1.3	1.6	2.4	1.4			1.5	1.5
	.6	.8	1.7	1.1			1.0	.9
Quick	1.7	3.3	2.7	1.1			1.8	2.1
	.7	1.1	1.9	1.0			1.0	.9
	.4	.5	.6	.8			.4	.5
Sales/Receivables	0 UND	6 60.4	17 21.6	30 12.1			0 UND	0 UND
	0 UND	33 10.9	48 7.6	41 8.9			28 13.0	20 17.9
	21 17.0	89 4.1	81 4.5	74 4.9			49 7.5	50 7.3
Cost of Sales/Inventory								
Cost of Sales/Payables								
Sales/Working Capital	14.1	4.3	4.9	10.0			7.3	7.4
	174.9	11.0	6.4	13.8			16.3	19.7
	-13.7	-51.9	16.8	60.1			-715.6	-97.8
EBIT/Interest	42.5	40.2	79.4				35.9	60.8
	(23) 13.7	(22) 15.5	(18) 34.8				(90) 8.4	(87) 18.8
	1.1	1.8	8.7				1.8	3.4
Net Profit + Depr., Dep., Amort./Cur. Mat. L/T/D								
Fixed/Worth	.0	.1	.1	.3			.1	.0
	.4	.5	.2	.5			.4	.3
	-.6	4.2	.5	1.1			5.2	2.4
Debt/Worth	.4	.5	.4	1.0			.6	.7
	2.4	1.6	.9	1.8			2.2	2.0
	-3.7	7.6	1.5	5.4			150.0	14.6
% Profit Before Taxes/Tangible Net Worth	144.6	124.6	104.3	120.9			98.1	108.4
	(21) 100.0	(26) 55.0	(19) 51.8	52.0			(108) 45.6	(98) 50.7
	24.0	16.8	18.4	17.2			12.6	19.6
% Profit Before Taxes/Total Assets	74.2	42.9	41.0	24.8			30.9	44.4
	27.8	22.5	20.5	13.6			12.8	16.0
	4.4	5.2	10.8	7.6			2.7	4.0
Sales/Net Fixed Assets	613.0	99.0	89.3	49.2			142.4	241.4
	128.8	34.8	37.4	15.8			44.6	45.9
	29.1	11.2	17.5	9.7			18.9	16.4
Sales/Total Assets	9.8	3.9	4.2	3.7			5.2	5.6
	6.1	3.2	3.3	3.3			3.6	3.1
	3.8	2.2	1.9	2.5			2.1	1.9
% Depr., Dep., Amort./Sales	.2	.2	.4	.6			.3	.4
	(14) .6	(17) .4	(11) 1.1	(12) .9			(75) .8	(73) .8
	1.4	1.1	1.1	1.3			1.5	1.8
% Officers', Directors' Owners' Comp/Sales	4.3	3.0					2.8	3.0
	(21) 7.0	(22) 5.7					(60) 5.7	(54) 5.2
	9.7	7.5					9.9	10.1
Net Sales ($)	66661M	105039M	304369M	617575M	245333M	337594M	1973122M	1683318M
Total Assets ($)	8260M	33632M	97452M	209405M	58037M	267993M	635510M	700391M

Comparative Historical Data | | Current Data Sorted by Sales

			Type of Statement	0-1MM	1-3MM	3-5MM	5-10MM	10-25MM	25MM & OVER
3	3	2	Unqualified		1				1
8	11	8	Reviewed				1	3	4
9	3	5	Compiled	1			2	1	1
39	39	29	Tax Returns	7	6	8	6	1	1
57	61	63	Other	17	14	10	8	4	10
4/1/16-3/31/17 ALL	4/1/17-3/31/18 ALL	4/1/18-3/31/19 ALL			10 (4/1-9/30/18)		97 (10/1/18-3/31/19)		
116	117	107	**NUMBER OF STATEMENTS**	25	21	18	17	9	17
%	%	%	**ASSETS**	%	%	%	%	%	%
24.9	17.4	24.4	Cash & Equivalents	28.9	30.4	30.4	16.4		12.9
23.4	27.3	31.1	Trade Receivables (net)	13.5	36.7	33.7	37.6		39.9
16.5	17.2	10.3	Inventory	12.6	7.7	1.7	14.3		13.2
5.1	6.8	5.4	All Other Current	9.9	4.4	.2	5.3		4.8
69.9	68.8	71.3	Total Current	64.9	79.1	65.9	73.6		70.8
16.8	14.0	15.2	Fixed Assets (net)	23.2	7.8	20.3	8.7		12.6
4.6	7.4	5.0	Intangibles (net)	2.5	3.1	2.3	10.9		9.6
8.7	9.8	8.6	All Other Non-Current	9.5	10.0	11.4	6.8		6.9
100.0	100.0	100.0	Total	100.0	100.0	100.0	100.0		100.0
			LIABILITIES						
12.2	10.9	19.2	Notes Payable-Short Term	33.8	15.5	26.2	13.6		5.7
4.2	4.1	1.4	Cur. Mat.-L.T.D.	.7	3.2	.7	1.4		1.1
11.9	12.6	14.8	Trade Payables	5.3	18.0	19.5	18.9		16.0
.3	.2	.2	Income Taxes Payable	.5	.0	.0	.2		.2
27.6	29.3	21.4	All Other Current	18.5	19.0	24.1	27.7		25.7
56.3	57.1	57.0	Total Current	58.8	55.8	70.4	61.8		48.7
12.5	13.4	9.4	Long-Term Debt	11.7	5.3	17.6	6.8		6.7
.3	.0	.0	Deferred Taxes	.0	.0	.0	.0		.2
6.5	9.0	7.1	All Other Non-Current	9.3	7.6	10.5	6.0		3.2
24.5	20.5	26.5	Net Worth	20.4	31.3	1.4	25.3		41.3
100.0	100.0	100.0	Total Liabilties & Net Worth	100.0	100.0	100.0	100.0		100.0
			INCOME DATA						
100.0	100.0	100.0	Net Sales	100.0	100.0	100.0	100.0		100.0
			Gross Profit						
92.3	90.1	90.4	Operating Expenses	83.3	94.8	91.1	92.2		91.8
7.7	9.9	9.6	Operating Profit	16.7	5.2	8.9	7.8		8.2
.5	1.0	.5	All Other Expenses (net)	1.0	1.1	.4	-.3		.5
7.2	8.9	9.1	Profit Before Taxes	15.7	4.1	8.5	8.1		7.7
			RATIOS						
2.7	2.4	3.0	Current	3.1	5.0	3.8	2.3		2.0
1.3	1.4	1.6		1.6	1.5	.8	1.7		1.4
.9	.9	.8		.6	.8	.4	.7		1.1
2.0	1.4	2.3	Quick	2.5	4.3	3.8	2.2		1.8
.9	.8	1.0		.6	1.1	.8	1.1		1.0
.4	.4	.5		.4	.7	.4	.4		.8
0 UND	6 62.9	1 361.3	Sales/Receivables	0 UND	1 598.3	6 61.4	14 26.8	30	12.1
18 20.7	30 12.2	28 12.9		0 UND	33 10.9	17 21.1	37 9.8	48	7.6
55 6.6	58 6.3	63 5.8		25 14.4	101 3.6	47 7.7	74 4.9	70	5.2
			Cost of Sales/Inventory						
			Cost of Sales/Payables						
8.0	6.5	6.1	Sales/Working Capital	7.5	4.2	6.2	5.0		10.0
23.4	17.3	16.9		20.6	11.3	-59.2	10.4		14.4
-44.9	-72.1	-43.3		-8.4	-40.4	-12.6	-25.2		60.1
54.0	82.0	44.3	EBIT/Interest	45.0	20.6	68.6	140.7		43.1
(87) 11.3	(99) 13.7	(75) 16.7		(13) 14.8	(14) 4.8	(14) 17.6	(14) 51.0	(12)	21.6
2.7	3.3	2.3		3.4	-4.8	2.6	.8		3.3
			Net Profit + Depr., Dep., Amort./Cur. Mat. L/T/D						
.1	.1	.1	Fixed/Worth	.0	.1	.1	.1		.1
.5	.4	.4		.3	.1	1.9	.2		.4
5.8	NM	3.4		NM	2.1	-.4	-.4		.9
.6	1.1	.7	Debt/Worth	.3	.4	.8	1.0		1.0
2.5	2.9	1.5		1.3	1.8	4.5	1.4		1.8
UND	-35.7	-52.6		-4.2	10.2	-3.3	-6.2		5.4
98.4	115.9	123.3	% Profit Before Taxes/Tangible Net Worth	124.4	125.9	215.7	133.3		111.4
(87) 41.0	(85) 51.2	(80) 63.9		(18) 60.2	(17) 40.9	(10) 90.5	(11) 104.3	(15)	52.0
12.4	16.7	18.2		17.4	13.0	48.6	29.9		17.0
38.1	29.2	51.3	% Profit Before Taxes/Total Assets	76.4	34.1	57.7	48.9		27.8
13.9	11.6	20.5		27.8	11.6	30.5	24.6		11.7
2.3	2.8	7.2		7.9	-3.6	9.5	4.0		7.2
102.7	149.0	162.3	Sales/Net Fixed Assets	UND	144.7	196.5	120.2		125.4
39.9	39.9	50.7		50.7	69.5	34.0	66.5		41.8
20.7	15.5	17.1		13.7	29.7	8.2	33.8		13.6
5.6	4.5	5.5	Sales/Total Assets	7.2	4.7	9.2	4.3		4.3
3.6	2.8	3.5		4.3	2.5	4.1	3.4		3.4
2.1	1.6	2.4		1.2	2.2	3.2	2.3		2.5
.2	.4	.2	% Depr., Dep., Amort./Sales	.2	.2				.4
(62) .6	(74) .6	(55) .7		(10) .7	(10) .5			(13)	.8
1.2	1.7	1.1		2.2	1.1				1.2
3.6	2.1	2.6	% Officers', Directors' Owners' Comp/Sales	5.9	4.0	2.7	1.7		
(59) 5.6	(64) 5.3	(57) 4.6		(13) 8.3	(14) 5.7	(11) 4.1	(12) 4.2		
9.2	7.4	8.0		12.6	9.3	14.8	5.5		
1343577M	1847276M	1676571M	Net Sales ($)	12428M	40191M	66226M	126360M	144180M	1287186M
451431M	1008750M	674779M	Total Assets ($)	5594M	17487M	17930M	46728M	43180M	543860M

© RMA 2019

M = $ thousand   MM = $ million
See Pages viii through xx for Explanation of Ratios and Data

Current Data Sorted by Assets   Comparative Historical Data

Date sub-periods: 3 (4/1–9/30/18)   27 (10/1/18–3/31/19)

Type of Statement	0-500M	500M-2MM	2-10MM	10-50MM	50-100MM	100-250MM	4/1/14-3/31/15 ALL	4/1/15-3/31/16 ALL
Unqualified						1		1
Reviewed			2				1	1
Compiled			3				1	5
Tax Returns			2	3			7	4
Other			9				15	10
	9	9		4		1		
NUMBER OF STATEMENTS	9	9	16	4		1	24	21
	%	%	%	%	%	%	%	%
ASSETS								
Cash & Equivalents	D	D	20.6	D			16.4	15.7
Trade Receivables (net)	A	A	37.5	A			35.0	36.7
Inventory	T	T	5.9	T			3.3	6.7
All Other Current	A	A	5.0	A			7.5	5.3
Total Current			68.9				62.2	64.3
Fixed Assets (net)	N	N	22.3	N			24.1	24.1
Intangibles (net)	O	O	1.9	O			1.7	7.2
All Other Non-Current	T	T	6.8	T			12.0	4.4
Total			100.0				100.0	100.0
LIABILITIES	A	A		A				
Notes Payable-Short Term	V	V	5.3	V			7.2	8.2
Cur. Mat.-L.T.D.	A	A	.9	A			1.6	2.8
Trade Payables	I	I	12.2	I			6.6	8.8
Income Taxes Payable	L	L	.1	L			.4	.2
All Other Current	A	A	24.9	A			13.9	8.2
Total Current	B	B	43.4	B			29.7	28.1
Long-Term Debt	L	L	13.8	L			10.8	8.5
Deferred Taxes	E	E	.0	E			.4	1.1
All Other Non-Current			1.2				3.7	4.8
Net Worth			41.6				55.4	57.4
Total Liabilties & Net Worth			100.0				100.0	100.0
INCOME DATA								
Net Sales			100.0				100.0	100.0
Gross Profit								
Operating Expenses			86.3				88.2	87.9
Operating Profit			13.7				11.8	12.1
All Other Expenses (net)			2.6				.6	2.4
Profit Before Taxes			11.1				11.2	9.7
RATIOS								
Current			3.4				4.2	5.3
			2.1				1.9	2.5
			1.4				1.1	1.4
Quick			2.8				3.2	4.3
			1.5				1.8	1.7
			1.1				1.0	1.1
Sales/Receivables			34 10.7				32 11.4	30 12.2
			51 7.1				49 7.4	60 6.1
			66 5.5				96 3.8	83 4.4
Cost of Sales/Inventory								
Cost of Sales/Payables								
Sales/Working Capital			5.4				3.4	3.2
			8.8				7.1	5.5
			17.5				45.1	27.4
EBIT/Interest			153.0				(18) 200.5	(17) 99.7
			(10) 44.9				27.6	20.2
			5.1				2.1	2.5
Net Profit + Depr., Dep., Amort./Cur. Mat. L/T/D								
Fixed/Worth			.1				.1	.1
			.2				.3	.3
			1.6				1.1	1.0
Debt/Worth			.5				.4	.3
			1.4				.9	.7
			6.0				1.6	1.6
% Profit Before Taxes/Tangible Net Worth			94.0				(23) 56.5	(20) 92.5
			(14) 33.0				26.9	28.1
			18.8				4.1	3.3
% Profit Before Taxes/Total Assets			30.7				31.0	27.9
			14.5				8.5	13.6
			4.4				1.3	1.4
Sales/Net Fixed Assets			61.3				100.1	38.8
			26.8				22.6	17.5
			8.0				5.9	5.0
Sales/Total Assets			3.4				3.0	3.1
			2.4				2.5	1.9
			1.5				1.6	1.6
% Depr., Dep., Amort./Sales							(20) .6	(14) .6
							1.2	1.7
							3.4	3.0
% Officers', Directors' Owners' Comp/Sales								
Net Sales ($)		47260M	163525M	192872M		351969M	641304M	578602M
Total Assets ($)		9353M	71085M	115917M		200498M	404967M	408212M

Comparative Historical Data | Current Data Sorted by Sales

4/1/16-3/31/17 ALL	4/1/17-3/31/18 ALL	4/1/18-3/31/19 ALL	Type of Statement	0-1MM	1-3MM	3-5MM	5-10MM	10-25MM	25MM & OVER
2	1	1	Unqualified						1
3	4	2	Reviewed					2	
2	2	3	Compiled				2	1	
6	5	2	Tax Returns					1	
9	8	22	Other	1	4	1 4	5	5	3
						3 (4/1-9/30/18)		27 (10/1/18-3/31/19)	
22	20	30	**NUMBER OF STATEMENTS**	1	4	5	7	9	4
%	%	%	**ASSETS**	%	%	%	%	%	%
14.7	15.6	18.9	Cash & Equivalents						
29.5	38.7	32.8	Trade Receivables (net)						
6.7	12.9	9.9	Inventory						
2.9	3.8	4.3	All Other Current						
53.8	71.0	65.9	Total Current						
31.7	19.4	21.3	Fixed Assets (net)						
6.7	3.3	4.5	Intangibles (net)						
7.8	6.2	8.3	All Other Non-Current						
100.0	100.0	100.0	Total						
			LIABILITIES						
8.5	14.8	9.3	Notes Payable-Short Term						
5.0	2.8	.9	Cur. Mat.-L.T.D.						
11.1	15.9	10.5	Trade Payables						
.4	.2	.6	Income Taxes Payable						
8.8	17.9	19.6	All Other Current						
33.8	51.5	40.9	Total Current						
23.2	9.6	14.8	Long-Term Debt						
.5	.8	.0	Deferred Taxes						
2.2	4.1	3.7	All Other Non-Current						
40.3	34.1	40.6	Net Worth						
100.0	100.0	100.0	Total Liabilities & Net Worth						
			INCOME DATA						
100.0	100.0	100.0	Net Sales						
			Gross Profit						
91.0	91.0	87.4	Operating Expenses						
9.0	9.0	12.6	Operating Profit						
3.3	1.5	1.7	All Other Expenses (net)						
5.8	7.4	11.0	Profit Before Taxes						
			RATIOS						
2.3	2.9	3.7							
1.9	2.0	1.8	Current						
.9	.7	1.1							
2.3	2.7	2.8							
1.4	1.3	1.2	Quick						
.8	.6	.8							
19 19.3	28 13.1	26 14.3							
52 7.0	45 8.1	51 7.2	Sales/Receivables						
68 5.4	79 4.6	69 5.3							
			Cost of Sales/Inventory						
			Cost of Sales/Payables						
6.6	6.1	5.3							
10.1	9.0	9.1	Sales/Working Capital						
-95.8	-13.3	NM							
137.5	81.7	141.6							
(20) 11.0	(13) 19.0	(20) 21.2	EBIT/Interest						
1.6	3.6	4.1							
			Net Profit + Depr., Dep., Amort./Cur. Mat. L/T/D						
.3	.1	.1							
1.1	.2	.3	Fixed/Worth						
2.4	1.6	1.7							
.6	.4	.4							
1.4	.9	1.4	Debt/Worth						
5.2	4.2	4.8							
80.0	57.1	78.3							
(19) 34.5	(16) 37.9	(25) 40.8	% Profit Before Taxes/Tangible Net Worth						
5.8	22.7	18.2							
34.9	35.6	37.9							
14.6	19.2	14.5	% Profit Before Taxes/Total Assets						
.8	4.3	3.3							
19.8	96.1	63.5							
12.8	29.9	25.3	Sales/Net Fixed Assets						
3.4	14.5	8.4							
3.4	3.6	3.8							
2.4	3.1	2.4	Sales/Total Assets						
1.6	1.7	1.5							
1.3	.6	.9							
(18) 2.1	(15) 1.5	(13) 1.5	% Depr., Dep., Amort./Sales						
5.7	2.9	2.0							
			% Officers', Directors' Owners' Comp/Sales						
436786M	318992M	755626M	Net Sales ($)	345M	8634M	20768M	52278M	142362M	531239M
340259M	150430M	396853M	Total Assets ($)	3876M	6628M	10484M	18920M	51620M	305325M

M = $ thousand   MM = $ million
See Pages viii through xx for Explanation of Ratios and Data

Current Data Sorted by Assets   Comparative Historical Data

0-500M	500M-2MM	2-10MM	10-50MM	50-100MM	100-250MM	Type of Statement	7	7
		2	1	1	1	Unqualified	7	7
	2	7	3			Reviewed	13	12
	2	5				Compiled	13	18
14	8	2				Tax Returns	40	43
13	19	24	7			Other	78	78
	10 (4/1-9/30/18)		101 (10/1/18-3/31/19)				4/1/14-3/31/15 ALL	4/1/15-3/31/16 ALL
27	31	40	11	1	1	NUMBER OF STATEMENTS	151	158
%	%	%	%	%	%	**ASSETS**	%	%
30.6	16.3	17.6	8.2			Cash & Equivalents	20.4	19.0
16.5	34.8	24.5	36.9			Trade Receivables (net)	28.5	32.4
1.6	4.4	8.0	7.7			Inventory	6.7	6.2
5.2	4.7	5.8	4.0			All Other Current	3.2	2.9
53.9	60.1	55.8	56.9			Total Current	58.8	60.6
19.5	22.7	30.7	24.6			Fixed Assets (net)	27.4	24.6
8.4	7.0	7.7	10.6			Intangibles (net)	6.3	6.6
18.2	10.3	5.8	8.0			All Other Non-Current	7.5	8.3
100.0	100.0	100.0	100.0			Total	100.0	100.0
						LIABILITIES		
33.0	13.8	7.6	8.5			Notes Payable-Short Term	16.4	11.6
8.2	3.8	5.1	5.9			Cur. Mat.-L.T.D.	2.3	3.0
11.3	10.1	7.5	10.9			Trade Payables	12.1	9.7
.0	.0	.3	.0			Income Taxes Payable	.3	.3
24.6	17.2	9.6	13.1			All Other Current	14.3	12.5
77.1	44.8	30.1	38.4			Total Current	45.3	37.1
22.8	14.4	19.9	15.1			Long-Term Debt	21.1	19.4
.0	.4	.0	.6			Deferred Taxes	.4	.2
7.2	4.9	5.6	6.9			All Other Non-Current	15.1	7.6
-7.1	35.6	44.4	39.0			Net Worth	18.1	35.7
100.0	100.0	100.0	100.0			Total Liabilties & Net Worth	100.0	100.0
						INCOME DATA		
100.0	100.0	100.0	100.0			Net Sales	100.0	100.0
						Gross Profit		
90.0	86.8	89.2	93.6			Operating Expenses	90.8	89.8
10.0	13.2	10.8	6.4			Operating Profit	9.2	10.2
.5	2.2	3.1	1.9			All Other Expenses (net)	1.9	1.8
9.5	11.0	7.6	4.5			Profit Before Taxes	7.3	8.4
						RATIOS		
1.8	4.2	2.6	2.5			Current	3.5	3.7
1.0	1.4	1.8	1.5				1.5	1.7
.3	.8	1.1	.9				.9	1.1
1.8	4.0	2.5	1.9			Quick	3.5	3.2
.7	1.1	1.3	1.3				1.3	1.4
.3	.6	.7	.8				.6	.8
0 UND	15 25.1	10 37.0	42 8.6			Sales/Receivables	1 530.5	17 20.9
0 UND	35 10.3	37 9.9	49 7.5				38 9.6	44 8.3
17 20.9	68 5.4	57 6.4	91 4.0				58 6.3	64 5.7
						Cost of Sales/Inventory		
						Cost of Sales/Payables		
33.1	4.5	4.9	6.4			Sales/Working Capital	6.9	5.1
118.8	17.9	11.2	11.7				14.4	12.3
-8.9	-50.4	106.4	-22.9				-114.4	94.0
32.4	23.0	33.1	48.4			EBIT/Interest	23.6	35.4
(20) 14.8	(21) 6.5	(34) 5.5	3.5				(107) 4.3	(123) 10.4
.4	2.0	1.8	1.9				1.1	2.4
						Net Profit + Depr., Dep., Amort./Cur. Mat. L/T/D	11.7	10.2
							(17) 4.0	(18) 2.5
							1.9	.9
.1	.1	.1	.3			Fixed/Worth	.2	.2
1.1	.6	.8	.9				.8	.5
-.4	3.7	2.1	3.0				24.3	2.6
1.1	.5	.5	.5			Debt/Worth	.7	.7
3.0	2.5	1.0	.9				2.0	1.6
-2.2	22.0	4.3	12.3				-124.6	10.5
347.6	87.4	64.7				% Profit Before Taxes/Tangible Net Worth	109.4	75.8
(17) 129.9	(25) 25.6	(32) 18.6					(112) 33.3	(130) 38.4
66.3	5.3	9.5					6.6	13.5
81.9	46.0	23.8	18.9			% Profit Before Taxes/Total Assets	32.9	27.7
44.3	21.0	8.1	9.0				10.4	12.9
10.0	2.4	1.4	2.3				1.1	3.9
270.4	80.1	73.8	20.5			Sales/Net Fixed Assets	113.5	55.6
44.4	17.7	13.5	14.3				21.1	20.4
16.9	8.5	3.6	6.7				6.8	6.6
9.4	5.2	3.4	3.0			Sales/Total Assets	5.2	3.8
6.0	3.1	2.4	1.9				3.0	2.6
2.9	1.3	1.3	1.6				1.9	1.8
.9	.6	.7	1.5			% Depr., Dep., Amort./Sales	.9	.7
(14) 1.8	(14) 1.3	(28) 2.2	(10) 2.9				(98) 1.9	(112) 1.6
4.8	4.0	5.4	5.6				3.9	4.0
7.4	2.9	3.0				% Officers', Directors' Owners' Comp/Sales	3.2	3.5
(18) 11.2	(15) 7.6	(15) 5.4					(64) 6.0	(66) 8.2
15.5	13.9	13.7					10.4	12.8
44439M	104490M	444517M	450404M	33257M	193748M	Net Sales ($)	1929607M	3123511M
5936M	34456M	182531M	208920M	57537M	141495M	Total Assets ($)	893831M	1142552M

M = $ thousand   MM = $ million
See Pages viii through xx for Explanation of Ratios and Data

Comparative Historical Data   Current Data Sorted by Sales

4/1/16-3/31/17 ALL	4/1/17-3/31/18 ALL	4/1/18-3/31/19 ALL	Type of Statement	0-1MM	1-3MM	3-5MM	5-10MM	10-25MM	25MM & OVER
5	10	5	Unqualified		1		3	3	2
9	8	12	Reviewed				3	6	2
8	10	7	Compiled	2			3	2	
33	32	24	Tax Returns	10	7	2	4	4	1
56	60	63	Other	9	16	9	14	9	6
				10 (4/1-9/30/18)			101 (10/1/18-3/31/19)		
111	120	111	NUMBER OF STATEMENTS	21	24	11	24	20	11
%	%	%	**ASSETS**	%	%	%	%	%	%
16.9	17.2	19.4	Cash & Equivalents	18.8	21.6	24.0	24.2	9.8	17.8
31.1	32.8	26.4	Trade Receivables (net)	13.2	20.6	21.5	36.2	37.1	28.5
6.4	6.2	5.3	Inventory	3.5	3.8	2.8	2.3	13.7	6.0
3.0	3.3	5.1	All Other Current	5.4	5.1	6.5	3.7	4.6	7.2
57.3	59.5	56.2	Total Current	40.9	51.1	54.8	66.3	65.1	59.6
25.6	23.6	25.2	Fixed Assets (net)	37.4	26.4	24.2	18.6	19.8	25.0
5.9	9.3	8.4	Intangibles (net)	10.0	10.7	3.9	7.1	5.3	13.2
11.2	7.6	10.2	All Other Non-Current	11.7	11.8	17.1	8.0	9.8	2.2
100.0	100.0	100.0	Total	100.0	100.0	100.0	100.0	100.0	100.0
			LIABILITIES						
14.7	14.5	15.6	Notes Payable-Short Term	14.0	25.2	13.3	17.5	11.4	3.3
4.0	2.3	5.5	Cur. Mat.-L.T.D.	7.4	5.4	1.2	8.1	3.4	4.9
14.7	11.6	9.5	Trade Payables	8.6	9.1	8.8	9.1	11.6	10.0
.3	.3	.1	Income Taxes Payable	.0	.0	.0	.5	.1	.0
19.1	16.0	15.6	All Other Current	20.2	13.5	26.8	10.4	15.7	11.8
52.8	44.6	46.4	Total Current	50.1	53.2	50.2	45.5	42.2	30.0
17.3	16.6	18.9	Long-Term Debt	27.1	24.5	16.4	10.4	14.0	20.7
.2	.2	.2	Deferred Taxes	.0	.5	.0	.0	.0	.5
13.9	5.6	5.9	All Other Non-Current	8.1	4.7	.3	6.1	8.1	5.1
15.9	33.2	28.7	Net Worth	14.7	17.2	33.2	37.9	35.7	43.7
100.0	100.0	100.0	Total Liabilities & Net Worth	100.0	100.0	100.0	100.0	100.0	100.0
			INCOME DATA						
100.0	100.0	100.0	Net Sales	100.0	100.0	100.0	100.0	100.0	100.0
			Gross Profit						
90.3	91.3	89.3	Operating Expenses	79.0	89.4	89.0	92.2	95.1	92.1
9.7	8.7	10.7	Operating Profit	21.0	10.6	11.0	7.8	4.9	7.9
1.8	2.1	2.1	All Other Expenses (net)	6.3	1.0	1.1	1.1	.8	1.4
7.8	6.5	8.6	Profit Before Taxes	14.7	9.5	9.9	6.7	4.1	6.5
			RATIOS						
2.6	3.4	2.5		1.7	2.4	4.2	4.7	2.1	4.6
1.4	1.5	1.5	Current	1.1	1.2	1.7	1.8	1.6	2.5
.8	1.0	.8		.3	.6	.4	1.1	1.1	.8
2.3	3.2	2.4		1.7	2.2	2.7	4.0	1.9	4.3
1.1	1.2	1.2	Quick	.8	.9	1.3	1.4	1.1	1.6
.6	.7	.6		.2	.5	.4	1.0	.7	.6
11 32.0	23 16.1	0 UND		0 UND	0 UND	2 234.9	27 13.7	34 10.6	35 10.5
38 9.5	38 9.6	34 10.7	Sales/Receivables	0 UND	9 42.6	25 14.8	37 9.9	44 8.3	46 7.9
59 6.2	60 6.1	54 6.8		28 13.1	64 5.7	47 7.8	49 7.5	66 5.5	54 6.8
			Cost of Sales/Inventory						
			Cost of Sales/Payables						
8.0	6.9	6.3		5.7	6.4	3.9	5.4	6.9	4.5
17.7	16.8	19.4	Sales/Working Capital	55.3	76.0	37.1	12.1	13.2	8.9
-30.7	-177.2	-33.2		-5.1	-13.7	-16.2	44.9	70.6	-22.9
50.7	25.4	28.6		18.2	25.4		18.1	17.1	65.3
(87) 9.5	(95) 6.7	(88) 5.9	EBIT/Interest	(12) 2.7	(20) 6.2		(17) 6.0	(19) 3.5	23.4
1.0	1.6	2.0		-.2	.8		2.4	.6	2.3
12.5	6.1	7.2	Net Profit + Depr., Dep.,						
(15) 3.5	(17) 1.7	(11) 2.4	Amort./Cur. Mat. L/T/D						
1.2	-.5	.4							
.2	.2	.1		.5	.1	.1	.1	.2	.2
.8	.5	.8	Fixed/Worth	2.0	.8	.0	.4	.8	.3
-6.3	9.1	3.7		-.5	2.9	14.9	2.9	1.9	-.7
.7	.6	.6		1.1	.7	.5	.4	.9	.4
1.8	1.7	1.8	Debt/Worth	3.4	1.3	2.0	1.8	1.3	.7
-14.9	35.6	55.9		-4.2	-6.0	55.9	6.5	11.8	-3.1
81.9	67.6	92.5	% Profit Before Taxes/Tangible	69.7	152.1		85.7	36.5	
(78) 37.8	(91) 28.0	(84) 26.2	Net Worth	(15) 15.0	(16) 72.3		(20) 50.0	(16) 14.7	
13.9	10.5	9.3		4.5	10.4		10.2	4.6	
34.1	29.8	44.3	% Profit Before Taxes/Total	38.1	52.3	60.2	48.9	21.2	28.8
13.0	9.4	15.1	Assets	4.3	30.5	21.2	19.8	4.7	10.8
2.4	1.6	2.2		1.1	1.0	14.8	3.2	-.9	3.6
72.4	70.8	75.4		41.4	435.4	85.7	82.7	73.5	20.5
20.9	18.9	19.2	Sales/Net Fixed Assets	13.4	21.0	24.7	50.5	15.5	13.1
8.2	7.9	8.0		1.4	7.7	9.9	11.6	9.0	6.7
4.7	3.8	4.9		3.4	5.9	8.3	5.7	3.6	3.3
2.8	2.9	2.9	Sales/Total Assets	2.0	3.6	3.4	3.3	2.8	2.9
2.0	1.9	1.5		.4	1.4	1.8	2.1	1.9	1.4
.7	.7	.8		2.1	.8		.5	.8	
(74) 1.6	(86) 1.8	(67) 2.2	% Depr., Dep., Amort./Sales	(13) 4.9	(11) 2.1		(15) .7	(16) 2.2	
3.4	3.9	4.9		26.8	5.4		4.2	3.2	
4.1	3.4	4.8	% Officers', Directors'	8.9	5.3		2.8		
(53) 6.8	(48) 7.4	(48) 8.0	Owners' Comp/Sales	(10) 13.1	(15) 7.6		(13) 5.4		
10.6	12.8	13.8		18.5	13.5		14.5		
1110729M	1760440M	1270855M	Net Sales ($)	10373M	45013M	40536M	166561M	317127M	691245M
601408M	896237M	630875M	Total Assets ($)	13587M	31123M	15833M	62404M	138853M	369075M

© RMA 2019
M = $ thousand   MM = $ million
See Pages viii through xx for Explanation of Ratios and Data

Current Data Sorted by Assets   Comparative Historical Data

	0-500M	500M-2MM	2-10MM	10-50MM	50-100MM	100-250MM	Type of Statement	4/1/14-3/31/15 ALL	4/1/15-3/31/16 ALL
				1	1	2	Unqualified	3	3
	2						Reviewed	4	4
1	1	4	1				Compiled	3	2
10	1	2					Tax Returns	21	19
10	7	3	5	2		Other	21	42
		6					5 (4/1-9/30/18)	54 (10/1/18-3/31/19)	
21	**11**	**15**	**7**	**3**	**2**	**NUMBER OF STATEMENTS**	**52**	**70**
%	%	%	%	%	%	**ASSETS**	%	%
30.3	21.6	5.9				Cash & Equivalents	17.3	18.4
17.4	37.0	39.0				Trade Receivables (net)	31.2	26.2
3.8	1.7	24.2				Inventory	8.3	8.9
2.3	4.0	4.7				All Other Current	6.1	2.1
53.8	64.3	73.8				Total Current	63.0	55.6
23.8	29.6	14.2				Fixed Assets (net)	21.2	28.6
12.1	4.4	5.1				Intangibles (net)	7.4	9.8
10.3	1.7	6.8				All Other Non-Current	8.3	6.1
100.0	100.0	100.0				Total	100.0	100.0
						LIABILITIES		
9.7	12.7	8.0				Notes Payable-Short Term	21.3	19.0
3.9	8.8	.7				Cur. Mat.-L.T.D.	1.9	2.2
6.4	9.6	12.3				Trade Payables	19.0	8.9
.0	.1	.2				Income Taxes Payable	.8	.4
13.4	6.4	15.3				All Other Current	16.3	12.5
33.5	37.6	36.4				Total Current	59.3	43.1
15.6	35.3	15.3				Long-Term Debt	10.7	15.8
.0	.0	.1				Deferred Taxes	.5	.3
14.2	2.8	1.8				All Other Non-Current	4.1	8.7
36.7	24.2	46.4				Net Worth	25.4	32.0
100.0	100.0	100.0				Total Liabilities & Net Worth	100.0	100.0
						INCOME DATA		
100.0	100.0	100.0				Net Sales	100.0	100.0
						Gross Profit		
89.7	82.9	91.7				Operating Expenses	87.9	90.4
10.3	17.1	8.3				Operating Profit	12.1	9.6
2.3	4.1	.2				All Other Expenses (net)	1.5	2.0
8.0	13.1	8.1				Profit Before Taxes	10.6	7.6
						RATIOS		
5.1	8.4	3.0					2.2	2.9
2.4	2.1	1.8				Current	1.4	1.6
.8	1.3	1.3					.8	.7
4.7	8.4	1.8					2.1	2.3
2.3	2.0	.8				Quick	1.2	1.2
.4	1.2	.5					.5	.6
0 UND	0 UND	15 25.0					8 47.1	1 287.8
0 UND	44 8.3	56 6.5				Sales/Receivables	46 7.9	27 13.5
40 9.2	54 6.8	79 4.6					63 5.8	57 6.4
						Cost of Sales/Inventory		
						Cost of Sales/Payables		
6.9	4.4	3.6					5.4	4.9
28.0	8.5	7.8				Sales/Working Capital	16.0	20.3
NM	32.4	15.6					-48.5	-32.9
68.0		23.2					37.0	61.9
(11) 6.6		(14) 9.8				EBIT/Interest	(40) 10.1	(54) 12.8
-.2		1.4					4.0	3.1
								18.5
						Net Profit + Depr., Dep., Amort./Cur. Mat. L/T/D	(11) 4.8	
								1.6
.0	.1	.1					.1	.2
.3	.4	.2				Fixed/Worth	.7	.9
-23.2	18.8	1.3					6.1	126.5
.3	.1	.4					1.0	.5
.9	.7	.8				Debt/Worth	3.6	1.9
-36.1	132.2	5.2					33.9	299.3
195.8		72.0					151.3	100.4
(15) 69.8		(13) 27.8				% Profit Before Taxes/Tangible Net Worth	(41) 65.6	(56) 44.2
40.6		18.4					28.2	23.4
84.5	68.8	21.3					35.1	37.1
30.8	27.8	13.3				% Profit Before Taxes/Total Assets	15.2	15.8
13.9	2.9	4.3					5.8	5.8
UND	98.0	178.8					64.7	49.8
66.1	31.9	30.3				Sales/Net Fixed Assets	25.7	18.9
15.4	7.5	7.4					8.8	7.0
14.1	6.8	3.2					4.2	6.0
4.0	3.6	2.1				Sales/Total Assets	3.0	3.2
2.4	2.1	1.7					1.9	1.6
		.2					.6	.5
		(12) 1.1				% Depr., Dep., Amort./Sales	(36) 1.1	(45) 1.8
		2.4					3.9	3.7
3.2							3.4	4.3
(11) 6.7						% Officers', Directors' Owners' Comp/Sales	(25) 4.2	(26) 5.8
11.2							7.7	12.8
44299M	42269M	200908M	322605M	783485M	379225M	Net Sales ($)	720715M	757283M
5218M	11459M	82768M	148127M	288006M	211907M	Total Assets ($)	414891M	443961M

© RMA 2019

M = $ thousand   MM = $ million
See Pages viii through xx for Explanation of Ratios and Data

Comparative Historical Data

Current Data Sorted by Sales

			Type of Statement						
2	3	4	Unqualified						4
6	7	7	Reviewed		2		1		2
4	4	4	Compiled	1	1		1		1
13	16	14	Tax Returns	5	1	1	4		
25	35	30	Other	5	6	4	5	5	5
4/1/16- 3/31/17 ALL	4/1/17- 3/31/18 ALL	4/1/18- 3/31/19 ALL		0-1MM	5 (4/1-9/30/18) 1-3MM	3-5MM	54 (10/1/18-3/31/19) 5-10MM	10-25MM	25MM & OVER
50	65	59	**NUMBER OF STATEMENTS**	11	10	8	10	8	12
%	%	%	**ASSETS**	%	%	%	%	%	%
23.3	19.8	18.6	Cash & Equivalents	18.2	32.7		3.9		13.3
27.7	30.8	29.4	Trade Receivables (net)	21.5	21.8		22.1		35.3
9.0	12.3	9.7	Inventory	.8	8.6		16.0		8.0
3.6	5.2	5.2	All Other Current	.9	1.7		10.4		8.9
63.6	68.2	62.9	Total Current	41.3	64.8		52.5		65.5
16.7	16.4	20.8	Fixed Assets (net)	42.8	16.5		27.4		14.6
12.4	8.0	9.4	Intangibles (net)	15.5	2.0		15.1		14.5
7.3	7.4	6.9	All Other Non-Current	.4	16.7		4.9		5.3
100.0	100.0	100.0	Total	100.0	100.0		100.0		100.0
			LIABILITIES						
12.0	11.4	10.8	Notes Payable-Short Term	5.5	12.6		10.6		9.3
3.5	2.4	3.7	Cur. Mat.-L.T.D.	5.3	2.5		7.9		2.2
13.2	14.4	9.8	Trade Payables	3.9	6.4		14.8		14.9
.1	.6	.1	Income Taxes Payable	.0	.0		.3		.0
13.4	14.9	15.7	All Other Current	3.9	23.9		7.4		24.5
42.1	43.7	40.0	Total Current	18.7	45.4		41.1		50.9
12.5	15.0	17.9	Long-Term Debt	31.9	4.5		39.8		8.9
1.0	.2	.1	Deferred Taxes	.0	.0		.1		.2
2.8	11.1	6.9	All Other Non-Current	5.7	23.5		1.5		4.0
41.6	29.9	35.2	Net Worth	43.7	26.6		17.5		36.0
100.0	100.0	100.0	Total Liabilties & Net Worth	100.0	100.0		100.0		100.0
			INCOME DATA						
100.0	100.0	100.0	Net Sales	100.0	100.0		100.0		100.0
			Gross Profit						
93.3	92.1	89.8	Operating Expenses	80.5	91.6		97.9		94.4
6.7	7.9	10.2	Operating Profit	19.5	8.4		2.1		5.6
1.3	1.2	1.9	All Other Expenses (net)	8.2	.3		-.2		.9
5.4	6.7	8.2	Profit Before Taxes	11.3	8.1		2.3		4.7
			RATIOS						
3.4	3.8	3.1		3.3	13.1		2.4		2.7
1.6	1.7	1.9	Current	2.1	3.5		1.8		1.6
.9	.8	1.1		1.0	.5		.7		.9
3.2	2.6	2.7		3.0	13.1		1.2		1.8
(49) 1.3	1.1	1.2	Quick	2.0	3.0		.7		1.1
.8	.6	.5		.7	.2		.2		.6
11 32.8	2 182.7	0 UND		0 UND	0 UND		0 UND	27 13.3	
49 7.4	38 9.7	33 11.2	Sales/Receivables	0 UND	0 UND		21 17.5	51 7.2	
70 5.2	74 4.9	63 5.8		65 5.6	44 8.3		58 6.3	63 5.8	
			Cost of Sales/Inventory						
			Cost of Sales/Payables						
5.1	4.0	5.2		5.1	4.7		6.8		5.3
14.7	10.3	12.6	Sales/Working Capital	6.8	26.5		22.2		8.9
-85.9	-53.0	129.7		574.0	-11.6		-33.3		NM
32.1	96.9	49.1							213.8
(40) 6.6	(48) 12.0	(45) 7.7	EBIT/Interest						7.1
-.2	2.6	2.4							2.1
			Net Profit + Depr., Dep., Amort./Cur. Mat. L/T/D						
.1	.0	.1		.2	.1		.2		.1
.5	.2	.4	Fixed/Worth	1.7	.3		.8		.3
2.4	2.6	-46.0		-46.0	-.4		NM		-1.2
.5	.3	.4		.4	.1		.5		.5
1.7	1.5	.9	Debt/Worth	1.6	.6		1.4		1.3
NM	50.6	-69.0		-69.0	-3.2		NM		-13.4
93.5	116.1	121.5	% Profit Before Taxes/Tangible Net Worth						
(38) 40.2	(50) 29.5	(44) 54.7							
12.6	16.4	24.1							
32.8	41.8	54.3	% Profit Before Taxes/Total Assets	54.3	75.2		32.6		22.2
10.7	12.6	18.6		21.7	45.6		17.3		8.7
.0	4.3	4.3		.8	1.2		1.5		4.2
73.9	420.8	98.1		90.6	75.3		59.1		90.5
27.5	45.6	31.5	Sales/Net Fixed Assets	11.0	62.8		15.0		38.3
12.4	12.1	10.8		1.9	25.5		7.0		15.6
3.8	4.8	4.7		3.5	13.3		8.1		3.3
2.5	2.9	2.7	Sales/Total Assets	2.1	6.5		2.4		2.6
1.6	1.6	1.8		1.2	3.2		1.5		1.6
.5	.4	.3							
(31) 1.0	(33) 1.2	(33) 1.0	% Depr., Dep., Amort./Sales						
3.0	2.7	3.2							
3.6	2.6	2.7	% Officers', Directors' Owners' Comp/Sales						
(19) 8.0	(22) 5.4	(19) 6.0							
17.1	10.2	10.0							
657842M	941578M	1772791M	Net Sales ($)	5142M	17296M	33575M	76510M	140060M	1500208M
411258M	607182M	747485M	Total Assets ($)	3894M	3889M	10338M	32023M	55820M	641521M

M = $ thousand   MM = $ million
See Pages viii through xx for Explanation of Ratios and Data

Current Data Sorted by Assets | Comparative Historical Data

						Type of Statement		
1	2	19	28	9	16	Unqualified	106	82
	7	31	20	1		Reviewed	71	61
3	15	27	5			Compiled	59	72
26	48	17	2		1	Tax Returns	142	157
32	75	158	101	30	27	Other	457	467
	52 (4/1-9/30/18)			649 (10/1/18-3/31/19)			4/1/14-3/31/15	4/1/15-3/31/16
0-500M	500M-2MM	2-10MM	10-50MM	50-100MM	100-250MM		ALL	ALL
62	147	252	156	40	44	NUMBER OF STATEMENTS	835	839
%	%	%	%	%	%	ASSETS	%	%
45.6	27.8	19.5	22.9	17.3	21.0	Cash & Equivalents	24.7	24.6
20.8	39.4	45.8	38.9	25.6	23.7	Trade Receivables (net)	38.2	38.2
.9	1.8	1.6	2.1	1.9	2.1	Inventory	2.0	1.7
3.4	3.8	5.8	6.5	3.8	5.6	All Other Current	4.2	4.5
70.7	72.7	72.8	70.4	48.6	52.5	Total Current	69.0	69.1
10.6	11.0	8.1	8.2	7.4	6.2	Fixed Assets (net)	11.8	11.8
2.9	6.1	9.8	13.8	35.8	32.0	Intangibles (net)	9.2	9.0
15.8	10.3	9.3	7.7	8.2	9.3	All Other Non-Current	9.9	10.1
100.0	100.0	100.0	100.0	100.0	100.0	Total	100.0	100.0
						LIABILITIES		
32.1	12.0	10.1	5.4	2.0	2.3	Notes Payable-Short Term	10.6	10.9
1.4	2.6	2.8	2.4	1.5	1.0	Cur. Mat.-L.T.D.	2.4	2.9
7.0	11.1	11.6	11.8	10.6	7.5	Trade Payables	12.3	11.7
.0	.3	.1	.5	.2	.4	Income Taxes Payable	.3	.3
38.2	19.9	26.0	31.8	29.5	26.2	All Other Current	22.6	25.3
78.6	45.9	50.6	51.8	43.8	37.3	Total Current	48.2	51.1
13.1	12.8	14.6	17.4	17.2	17.8	Long-Term Debt	11.4	12.4
.0	.0	.1	.2	.7	.8	Deferred Taxes	.3	.3
11.3	7.5	5.1	7.5	9.4	8.8	All Other Non-Current	9.4	11.1
-3.1	33.7	29.6	23.0	28.9	35.2	Net Worth	30.7	25.2
100.0	100.0	100.0	100.0	100.0	100.0	Total Liabilties & Net Worth	100.0	100.0
						INCOME DATA		
100.0	100.0	100.0	100.0	100.0	100.0	Net Sales	100.0	100.0
						Gross Profit		
91.2	91.4	92.8	96.9	98.2	96.3	Operating Expenses	93.1	93.1
8.8	8.6	7.2	3.1	1.8	3.7	Operating Profit	6.9	6.9
.0	.6	.7	1.7	3.8	3.3	All Other Expenses (net)	1.4	1.2
8.8	8.0	6.5	1.4	-2.1	.5	Profit Before Taxes	5.6	5.7
						RATIOS		
4.9	4.4	2.9	2.4	2.0	1.9		2.9	2.9
1.3	1.7	1.7	1.5	1.1	1.4	Current	1.6	1.6
.5	1.0	1.0	1.0	.7	1.0		1.0	1.0
4.9	4.3	2.5	2.2	1.7	1.8		2.8	2.7
1.3	1.7	1.5	1.3	1.1	1.2	Quick	(834) 1.4	1.4
.4	.9	.9	.9	.6	.8		.9	.8
0 UND	12 31.5	36 10.1	40 9.2	47 7.8	55 6.6		27 13.6	23 15.7
0 UND	36 10.2	54 6.8	61 6.0	70 5.2	76 4.8	Sales/Receivables	47 7.7	47 7.8
28 13.1	55 6.6	73 5.0	83 4.4	85 4.3	94 3.9		68 5.4	69 5.3
						Cost of Sales/Inventory		
						Cost of Sales/Payables		
10.1	6.3	6.0	5.4	5.4	4.5		5.9	6.6
49.4	13.2	11.7	10.2	15.1	11.5	Sales/Working Capital	14.5	15.7
-22.2	274.2	82.7	76.9	-8.6	80.1		-999.8	-189.0
58.1	73.4	46.4	30.2	8.8	13.6		66.0	57.3
(33) 13.9	(96) 13.9	(185) 9.4	(113) 6.2	(28) 2.5	(30) 3.2	EBIT/Interest	(599) 13.2	(587) 11.9
1.6	2.1	2.0	-2.4	-1.6	.1		2.3	1.8
		7.6	11.3				14.7	22.2
	(20) 3.0	(26) 3.5				Net Profit + Depr., Dep., Amort./Cur. Mat. L/T/D	(74) 3.6	(75) 5.6
		.2	-.1				.8	1.0
.0	.0	.0	.1	.2	.1		.1	.0
.1	.1	.2	.2	2.4	.6	Fixed/Worth	.2	.2
NM	1.0	2.2	3.4	-.1	-.1		2.8	2.8
.3	.4	.6	.7	1.6	1.3		.7	.7
4.1	1.2	2.1	2.4	18.6	7.4	Debt/Worth	2.2	2.0
-6.7	10.2	71.6	NM	-1.8	-2.7		51.7	48.1
301.2	92.4	101.7	78.4	51.4	57.6	% Profit Before Taxes/Tangible Net Worth	95.7	94.0
(40) 138.9	(118) 41.3	(193) 46.9	(117) 34.9	(21) 16.7	(26) 12.9		(638) 44.2	(636) 45.1
39.6	13.5	20.0	9.0	-6.4	-17.6		16.1	16.9
117.8	47.0	30.6	19.9	9.1	8.1	% Profit Before Taxes/Total Assets	32.0	32.2
49.7	23.4	13.1	7.3	2.1	2.4		13.3	13.8
6.3	4.7	3.3	-7.8	-6.7	-4.8		2.3	3.2
UND	999.8	441.2	155.9	83.8	60.6		197.9	274.7
278.0	180.5	97.4	60.4	38.3	22.4	Sales/Net Fixed Assets	53.3	60.3
36.6	34.7	36.8	19.8	16.2	13.4		20.2	21.3
12.9	5.8	4.2	3.0	1.8	1.5		4.7	5.0
7.7	4.1	3.0	2.2	1.2	1.0	Sales/Total Assets	3.0	3.2
3.2	2.2	1.9	1.4	.5	.5		1.6	1.8
.2	.2	.3	.4	.2	.8		.4	.3
(17) .5	(62) .5	(127) .6	(92) 1.0	(16) 1.0	(27) 1.6	% Depr., Dep., Amort./Sales	(459) .9	(459) .8
1.4	1.8	1.6	2.3	2.9	3.3		2.1	1.8
4.1	2.3	1.8	.4			% Officers', Directors' Owners' Comp/Sales	2.2	2.0
(30) 10.3	(52) 5.0	(50) 3.6	(12) 2.1				(218) 5.1	(242) 4.5
25.2	9.1	7.4	5.4				10.3	9.9
150862M	791818M	3708187M	7945013M	3734228M	7774232M	Net Sales ($)	26939588M	25110934M
15620M	177056M	1260264M	3517432M	2860818M	7087270M	Total Assets ($)	14780376M	13292327M

M = $ thousand   MM = $ million
See Pages viii through xx for Explanation of Ratios and Data

Comparative Historical Data | | | | Current Data Sorted by Sales

4/1/16-3/31/17 ALL	4/1/17-3/31/18 ALL	4/1/18-3/31/19 ALL	Type of Statement	0-1MM	1-3MM	3-5MM	5-10MM	10-25MM	25MM & OVER
73	68	75	Unqualified	2	1	2	5	14	51
60	53	59	Reviewed		1	3	9	26	20
59	44	50	Compiled	4	3	5	7	23	8
122	117	94	Tax Returns	11	26	15	23	14	5
410	449	423	Other	12	44	36	68	120	143
					52 (4/1-9/30/18)		649 (10/1/18-3/31/19)		
724	731	701	**NUMBER OF STATEMENTS**	29	75	61	112	197	227
%	%	%	**ASSETS**	%	%	%	%	%	%
26.2	25.0	24.3	Cash & Equivalents	40.3	34.1	24.0	24.9	22.1	20.6
38.1	36.5	38.2	Trade Receivables (net)	20.5	23.3	34.6	42.2	42.0	40.9
1.2	1.7	1.7	Inventory	.7	1.7	2.4	.9	1.7	2.2
4.9	5.8	5.2	All Other Current	3.6	2.8	5.0	6.1	5.2	5.8
70.5	69.0	69.4	Total Current	65.2	61.9	65.9	74.2	71.0	69.6
10.2	11.2	8.8	Fixed Assets (net)	24.6	13.4	8.3	6.9	8.2	6.8
10.3	9.8	12.2	Intangibles (net)	4.4	9.5	11.6	9.9	11.5	15.9
9.0	10.0	9.7	All Other Non-Current	5.9	15.2	14.2	9.1	9.2	7.7
100.0	100.0	100.0	Total	100.0	100.0	100.0	100.0	100.0	100.0
			LIABILITIES						
11.0	10.5	10.5	Notes Payable-Short Term	11.5	20.4	13.2	13.7	9.6	5.4
2.4	2.4	2.4	Cur. Mat.-L.T.D.	2.0	2.8	2.3	3.2	2.4	1.8
11.3	10.3	10.8	Trade Payables	4.0	9.0	6.7	10.3	11.8	12.8
.3	.3	.2	Income Taxes Payable	.0	.0	.2	.2	.2	.4
24.5	25.9	27.3	All Other Current	29.0	21.8	22.7	27.9	27.6	29.6
49.5	49.4	51.1	Total Current	46.5	54.0	45.1	55.2	51.6	50.1
13.2	13.6	15.1	Long-Term Debt	13.3	22.0	11.8	16.0	12.4	15.7
.7	.3	.2	Deferred Taxes	.0	.0	.0	.0	.2	.4
8.8	8.2	7.2	All Other Non-Current	6.9	13.4	5.7	4.3	7.6	6.7
27.8	28.5	26.4	Net Worth	33.2	10.7	37.4	24.4	28.3	27.2
100.0	100.0	100.0	Total Liabilties & Net Worth	100.0	100.0	100.0	100.0	100.0	100.0
			INCOME DATA						
100.0	100.0	100.0	Net Sales	100.0	100.0	100.0	100.0	100.0	100.0
			Gross Profit						
93.6	93.6	93.8	Operating Expenses	76.1	91.2	88.2	95.7	96.2	95.4
6.4	6.4	6.2	Operating Profit	23.9	8.8	11.8	4.3	3.8	4.6
1.2	1.3	1.2	All Other Expenses (net)	3.9	-.1	.6	.6	.8	2.0
5.3	5.1	5.0	Profit Before Taxes	19.9	8.9	11.2	3.7	3.0	2.6
			RATIOS						
3.4	3.1	2.7		6.3	4.4	5.5	3.3	2.4	2.3
1.7	1.5	1.6	Current	2.7	1.4	1.9	1.7	1.5	1.5
1.0	1.0	1.0		.8	.5	1.1	.9	1.0	1.1
3.1	2.9	2.4		6.3	4.4	4.4	2.8	2.1	2.1
1.5 (730)	1.4	1.4	Quick	2.4	1.3	1.7	1.7	1.3	1.3
.9	.8	.8		.6	.5	1.0	.8	.9	.9
27 13.3	21 17.7	28 13.0		0 UND	0 UND	19 18.8	25 14.8	32 11.5	43 8.5
49 7.5	49 7.5	52 7.0	Sales/Receivables	0 UND	24 15.1	46 7.9	44 8.3	52 7.0	61 6.0
69 5.3	72 5.1	74 4.9		54 6.7	54 6.8	74 4.9	69 5.3	72 5.1	81 4.5
			Cost of Sales/Inventory						
			Cost of Sales/Payables						
5.6	5.8	6.1		3.5	4.7	5.0	7.3	6.6	6.2
12.9	14.7	12.9	Sales/Working Capital	10.1	20.9	8.9	13.3	16.2	12.1
154.2	429.0	NM		-11.0	-32.0	65.3	-65.1	96.8	79.1
43.5	43.6	37.0		19.2	44.8	34.6	42.4	48.5	30.2
(501) 11.0	(500) 9.9	(485) 7.8	EBIT/Interest	(11) 7.2	(51) 11.7	(35) 8.4	(77) 7.3	(150) 7.6	(161) 7.2
.9	1.2	.6		1.6	2.2	1.5	-1.4	1.4	.2
10.6	9.5	11.0						4.3	12.2
(69) 3.1	(59) 3.4	(65) 3.3	Net Profit + Depr., Dep., Amort./Cur. Mat. L/T/D					(15) 1.9	(37) 3.6
1.0	.2	.2						.1	1.5
.0	.0	.0		.0	.0	.0	.0	.0	.1
.2	.1	.2	Fixed/Worth	.2	.4	.1	.1	.2	.2
2.4	2.7	6.4		6.9	-2.1	1.2	3.6	2.0	-3.8
.5	.6	.7		.2	.7	.3	.5	.7	.8
1.8	2.0	2.3	Debt/Worth	3.0	2.7	1.2	1.7	2.3	2.7
-107.0	157.0	-25.6		229.9	-7.7	-23.9	-10.9	59.9	-15.3
89.7	91.4	97.3		257.7	131.1	116.2	127.2	89.6	80.0
(541) 41.7	(553) 43.0	(515) 42.4	% Profit Before Taxes/Tangible Net Worth	(23) 38.0	(50) 64.9	(45) 42.4	(81) 47.4	(151) 42.0	(165) 38.2
12.9	12.4	13.3		21.6	34.3	11.7	11.5	12.6	12.6
31.5	34.3	32.1		56.6	53.5	47.3	40.1	30.6	23.0
12.7	12.5	11.8	% Profit Before Taxes/Total Assets	18.0	25.0	20.0	13.7	11.2	7.6
1.4	1.5	.8		3.3	6.2	6.1	-.5	.5	-2.3
272.5	343.7	373.9		UND	UND	838.7	805.0	341.7	155.8
70.2	77.1	74.7	Sales/Net Fixed Assets	31.6	77.3	168.2	124.1	79.1	61.4
21.8	23.5	26.3		3.8	21.3	30.6	50.4	27.6	20.9
4.6	4.5	4.4		3.7	5.9	4.7	5.4	4.6	3.6
2.9	2.9	2.7	Sales/Total Assets	2.1	2.6	2.7	3.6	3.0	2.4
1.7	1.6	1.5		.6	1.6	1.2	2.1	1.7	1.3
.3	.2	.3		.4	.6	.2	.2	.4	.3
(374) .8	(363) .7	(341) .7	% Depr., Dep., Amort./Sales	(12) 4.7	(23) 1.7	(25) .4	(53) .4	(98) .8	(130) .8
2.1	1.9	2.1		16.0	3.3	2.0	.8	1.9	2.2
2.0	2.4	1.9		14.8	3.6	3.4	2.2	1.5	.5
(173) 4.8	(171) 5.1	(150) 4.5	% Officers', Directors' Owners' Comp/Sales	(12) 27.3	(29) 5.8	(15) 6.2	(38) 4.0	(37) 2.5	(19) 1.5
10.0	10.1	9.9		29.7	11.5	9.2	7.5	5.6	5.4
26786592M	23785984M	24104340M	Net Sales ($)	14221M	153539M	237604M	807837M	3107288M	19783851M
14637962M	13023389M	14918460M	Total Assets ($)	15126M	75379M	135030M	410679M	1683444M	12598802M

Current Data Sorted by Assets   Comparative Historical Data

	0-500M	500M-2MM	2-10MM	10-50MM	50-100MM	100-250MM		4/1/14-3/31/15 ALL	4/1/15-3/31/16 ALL
Type of Statement									
Unqualified	2		29	46	17	12		133	137
Reviewed		4	37	28	1			101	87
Compiled	5	18	41	9				56	62
Tax Returns	34	47	32	2				154	134
Other	115	273	348	180	43	35		570	579
		219 (4/1-9/30/18)		1,139 (10/1/18-3/31/19)					
NUMBER OF STATEMENTS	156	342	487	265	61	47		1014	999
	%	%	%	%	%	%		%	%
ASSETS									
Cash & Equivalents	37.8	22.4	20.2	19.9	14.0	11.5		21.1	20.0
Trade Receivables (net)	28.7	42.4	47.8	45.3	35.5	34.7		41.7	44.0
Inventory	3.7	4.8	4.5	5.0	6.7	5.1		3.5	2.9
All Other Current	7.4	5.8	5.8	7.0	5.0	8.7		5.1	5.2
Total Current	77.5	75.3	78.4	77.2	61.2	59.9		71.3	72.1
Fixed Assets (net)	12.0	13.3	8.9	6.9	6.3	5.1		11.2	10.7
Intangibles (net)	4.6	3.4	6.3	10.2	22.1	25.4		8.9	10.1
All Other Non-Current	5.9	8.0	6.4	5.6	10.4	9.6		8.5	7.1
Total	100.0	100.0	100.0	100.0	100.0	100.0		100.0	100.0
LIABILITIES									
Notes Payable-Short Term	27.2	12.2	8.6	6.3	4.2	3.6		10.2	9.9
Cur. Mat.-L.T.D.	4.0	1.4	1.5	1.4	3.2	1.5		2.0	1.9
Trade Payables	16.9	22.9	23.4	24.5	18.7	22.1		18.1	18.8
Income Taxes Payable	.0	.3	.3	.3	.5	.1		.4	.4
All Other Current	28.2	17.2	18.1	20.9	22.3	20.1		18.8	17.6
Total Current	76.3	54.0	51.9	53.5	48.9	47.5		49.6	48.7
Long-Term Debt	14.3	9.1	8.3	5.6	19.7	18.5		10.8	9.6
Deferred Taxes	.1	.0	.1	.2	.3	1.0		.3	.3
All Other Non-Current	5.3	5.4	5.0	7.5	9.7	6.5		7.9	6.8
Net Worth	4.0	31.6	34.7	33.3	21.3	26.5		31.4	34.6
Total Liabilities & Net Worth	100.0	100.0	100.0	100.0	100.0	100.0		100.0	100.0
INCOME DATA									
Net Sales	100.0	100.0	100.0	100.0	100.0	100.0		100.0	100.0
Gross Profit									
Operating Expenses	93.8	92.2	93.7	95.7	95.8	95.6		93.4	93.4
Operating Profit	6.2	7.8	6.3	4.3	4.2	4.4		6.6	6.6
All Other Expenses (net)	.9	.9	.9	.5	2.9	2.2		1.1	1.1
Profit Before Taxes	5.2	6.9	5.4	3.9	1.3	2.3		5.5	5.6
RATIOS									
Current	3.8	2.6	2.4	2.1	2.0	1.7		2.7	2.5
	1.4	1.4	1.5	1.4	1.2	1.3		1.5	1.5
	.8	1.0	1.1	1.1	1.0	1.1		1.1	1.1
Quick	2.8	2.2	2.0	1.7	1.6	1.3		2.4	2.3
	1.2	1.3	1.3	1.2	1.0	1.0		1.3	1.3
	.6	.8	.9	.8	.7	.7		.9	.9
Sales/Receivables	0 UND	18 20.3	31 11.6	41 9.0	47 7.8	46 8.0		28 13.2	31 11.7
	14 25.2	34 10.7	49 7.4	57 6.4	60 6.1	63 5.8		49 7.5	49 7.5
	34 10.6	53 6.9	69 5.3	79 4.6	76 4.8	91 4.0		69 5.3	69 5.3
Cost of Sales/Inventory									
Cost of Sales/Payables									
Sales/Working Capital	11.3	8.4	6.9	6.1	5.1	6.6		6.5	6.9
	33.5	19.1	14.4	13.6	22.4	11.5		15.2	15.2
	-47.7	-168.1	52.4	74.9	-566.0	73.9		88.9	94.2
EBIT/Interest	23.9	34.8	70.1	77.8	15.4	15.7		47.9	56.2
	(89) 6.3	(224) 10.0	(358) 15.5	(193) 16.7	(52) 5.0	(43) 4.8		(744) 11.2	(709) 13.8
	1.4	2.0	3.8	3.2	.4	-.6		2.3	2.2
Net Profit + Depr., Dep., Amort./Cur. Mat. L/T/D			16.8	16.6	26.1			12.9	15.4
		(29) 3.7	(43) 4.5	(15) 6.1				(103) 3.3	(83) 5.0
		1.7	1.0	1.9				1.4	1.9
Fixed/Worth	.0	.0	.0	.0	.1	.1		.0	.0
	.2	.2	.1	.2	.5	.4		.2	.2
	3.2	1.5	.7	.8	-.1	-.1		1.9	1.5
Debt/Worth	.4	.6	.7	1.0	2.0	2.2		.7	.7
	3.6	2.0	1.9	2.4	6.7	7.1		2.3	2.1
	-5.7	9.7	7.4	13.5	-2.9	-3.6		14.7	10.1
% Profit Before Taxes/Tangible Net Worth	168.5	100.1	88.8	74.7	88.2	55.0		81.0	86.7
	(106) 64.8	(280) 44.6	(414) 45.5	(221) 36.5	(36) 30.9	(26) 34.7		(811) 37.6	(799) 45.3
	25.8	11.0	15.4	22.3	2.9	7.8		13.5	14.4
% Profit Before Taxes/Total Assets	64.1	36.6	26.7	19.3	13.0	11.5		26.6	29.0
	24.3	13.6	13.1	10.7	5.9	5.7		11.5	12.9
	2.7	2.4	4.4	2.9	-2.1	-4.6		2.6	2.4
Sales/Net Fixed Assets	UND	863.1	495.4	250.7	111.9	148.3		296.3	279.5
	131.2	95.1	111.3	99.8	54.4	67.1		78.1	87.1
	37.7	26.7	33.6	27.8	27.2	25.7		24.8	29.6
Sales/Total Assets	10.3	5.7	4.7	4.1	3.0	2.9		4.8	5.0
	6.2	4.4	3.4	2.8	1.8	1.4		3.2	3.3
	3.9	2.8	2.3	1.6	1.1	.9		1.9	2.0
% Depr., Dep., Amort./Sales	.2	.2	.2	.2	.4	.2		.2	.2
	(43) .5	(130) .7	(282) .4	(186) .4	(37) .9	(23) .7		(609) .6	(580) .5
	1.3	1.9	1.3	1.2	2.0	2.3		1.6	1.3
% Officers', Directors' Owners' Comp/Sales	5.9	2.4	1.1	.6				2.4	2.0
	(40) 9.0	(81) 4.3	(80) 2.3	(27) 1.3				(240) 5.2	(220) 4.7
	15.1	6.8	5.1	2.6				10.0	9.4
Net Sales ($)	304719M	1727686M	8166623M	17368267M	8712073M	14851675M		42297737M	46502956M
Total Assets ($)	39160M	387685M	2308566M	5959378M	4201283M	7835053M		20388549M	20321797M

© RMA 2019

M = $ thousand   MM = $ million
See Pages viii through xx for Explanation of Ratios and Data

Comparative Historical Data | | | | | Current Data Sorted by Sales | | | | |

4/1/16-3/31/17 ALL	4/1/17-3/31/18 ALL	4/1/18-3/31/19 ALL	Type of Statement	0-1MM	1-3MM	3-5MM	5-10MM	10-25MM	25MM & OVER
104	96	106	Unqualified	2	1	1	2	31	69
96	97	70	Reviewed		2	2	16	17	33
44	65	73	Compiled	5	6	8	13	28	13
120	95	115	Tax Returns	22	29	16	31	15	2
551	934	994	Other	47	126	107	191	237	286
				219 (4/1-9/30/18)			1,139 (10/1/18-3/31/19)		
915	1287	1358	**NUMBER OF STATEMENTS**	76	164	134	253	328	403
%	%	%	**ASSETS**	%	%	%	%	%	%
20.0	21.0	22.1	Cash & Equivalents	23.5	30.2	24.8	22.9	22.1	17.3
44.9	44.2	42.8	Trade Receivables (net)	17.5	32.0	35.6	45.4	47.1	49.1
3.3	4.4	4.7	Inventory	3.8	5.7	5.1	4.8	3.9	5.0
5.5	6.4	6.3	All Other Current	9.7	5.9	5.8	6.3	4.8	7.1
73.6	76.0	75.9	Total Current	54.5	73.8	71.4	79.4	77.8	78.5
10.0	9.7	9.7	Fixed Assets (net)	32.2	13.9	9.2	9.1	8.2	5.6
9.1	7.7	7.5	Intangibles (net)	6.8	4.6	9.7	4.9	7.6	9.7
7.3	6.6	6.9	All Other Non-Current	6.4	7.7	9.7	6.7	6.5	6.2
100.0	100.0	100.0	Total	100.0	100.0	100.0	100.0	100.0	100.0
			LIABILITIES						
10.3	9.4	10.8	Notes Payable-Short Term	23.7	16.1	13.1	11.7	8.4	6.9
2.3	1.7	1.8	Cur. Mat.-L.T.D.	3.1	2.2	.6	2.5	1.3	1.8
20.0	23.7	22.5	Trade Payables	8.2	16.8	20.7	23.5	22.0	27.9
.3	.3	.3	Income Taxes Payable	.0	.6	.3	.1	.2	.3
19.4	18.5	19.9	All Other Current	28.1	22.2	17.1	18.8	17.5	20.9
52.3	53.6	55.3	Total Current	63.0	57.9	51.9	56.7	49.3	57.8
10.7	9.0	9.5	Long-Term Debt	27.9	12.9	9.4	6.5	7.7	8.0
.4	.2	.1	Deferred Taxes	.2	.0	.0	.1	.1	.2
7.7	6.6	5.9	All Other Non-Current	7.0	5.4	6.6	4.7	5.3	7.0
28.9	30.6	29.2	Net Worth	2.0	23.9	32.1	32.0	37.6	27.0
100.0	100.0	100.0	Total Liabilities & Net Worth	100.0	100.0	100.0	100.0	100.0	100.0
			INCOME DATA						
100.0	100.0	100.0	Net Sales	100.0	100.0	100.0	100.0	100.0	100.0
			Gross Profit						
94.1	94.0	93.9	Operating Expenses	76.8	94.6	94.3	95.0	94.0	95.9
5.9	6.0	6.1	Operating Profit	23.3	5.4	5.7	5.0	6.0	4.1
1.0	.9	.9	All Other Expenses (net)	5.9	.7	.8	.4	.6	.7
4.9	5.1	5.2	Profit Before Taxes	17.4	4.7	4.9	4.6	5.4	3.3
			RATIOS						
2.4	2.3	2.4	Current	3.3	3.5	3.0	2.6	2.5	1.9
1.5	1.5	1.4		1.0	1.5	1.4	1.5	1.6	1.3
1.1	1.1	1.0		.5	.9	.9	1.1	1.1	1.1
2.2	2.0	2.0	Quick	2.1	2.5	2.5	2.2	2.3	1.6
1.3	1.2	1.2		.8	1.2	1.2	1.3	1.4	1.1
.9	.9	.8		.2	.7	.7	.9	1.0	.8
33 11.2	28 13.0	26 14.2	Sales/Receivables	0 UND	10 36.5	14 25.9	23 15.6	33 11.2	41 8.9
51 7.1	46 8.0	45 8.1		8 46.1	29 12.7	36 10.2	39 9.3	50 7.3	55 6.6
69 5.3	66 5.5	65 5.6		39 9.3	49 7.4	56 6.5	60 6.1	70 5.2	74 4.9
			Cost of Sales/Inventory						
			Cost of Sales/Payables						
6.9	7.6	7.3	Sales/Working Capital	4.6	7.4	7.3	8.0	6.4	8.3
15.2	15.8	16.4		UND	23.8	17.3	16.3	13.8	17.4
82.3	71.1	133.2		-4.6	-60.7	-72.5	68.5	46.3	83.4
42.5	60.0	51.7	EBIT/Interest	7.6	25.5	36.5	44.8	96.4	57.8
(661) 10.6	(894) 11.8	(959) 11.6		(35) 5.3	(106) 9.2	(95) 8.2	(171) 10.9	(235) 23.1	(317) 11.5
2.3	2.3	2.4		1.7	1.4	.6	2.1	4.7	2.7
17.3	10.0	16.1	Net Profit + Depr., Dep., Amort./Cur. Mat. L/T/D					19.3	16.9
(86) 6.7	(97) 4.4	(101) 4.9					(30) 5.9	(57) 5.5	
2.5	1.1	1.6						1.7	1.6
.0	.0	.0	Fixed/Worth	.0	.0	.0	.0	.0	.0
?	?	?		1.2	.3	.2	.1	.1	.2
2.1	1.1	1.4		63.6	1.9	2.9	.6	.7	1.3
.8	.8	.8	Debt/Worth	.5	.5	.5	.7	.7	1.3
2.3	2.2	2.2		4.7	1.9	1.9	2.0	1.6	3.0
19.7	17.7	14.5		-7.4	-22.6	29.2	6.5	6.5	22.0
80.9	84.3	92.9	% Profit Before Taxes/Tangible Net Worth	81.8	123.6	106.1	96.2	93.7	83.0
(720) 36.4	(1028) 38.2	(1083) 43.7		(52) 29.6	(121) 42.7	(104) 58.2	(212) 42.8	(277) 45.6	(317) 44.2
13.5	13.5	15.3		14.3	11.8	10.6	7.0	17.1	21.8
24.4	25.3	28.1	% Profit Before Taxes/Total Assets	26.6	37.3	38.4	33.4	28.6	20.8
10.9	11.0	11.9		9.0	12.1	14.9	12.0	14.0	10.8
2.3	2.2	2.8		1.4	2.1	.8	2.6	4.7	3.0
328.0	383.7	409.3	Sales/Net Fixed Assets	UND	981.0	389.7	822.7	419.8	322.1
81.6	94.4	96.1		24.9	60.1	85.8	112.9	107.8	106.5
26.0	29.7	29.2		.5	19.2	27.8	36.4	30.4	38.8
4.7	5.1	5.2	Sales/Total Assets	3.8	6.3	5.5	5.7	4.9	4.6
3.3	3.6	3.5		1.4	3.9	3.5	4.2	3.4	3.3
2.0	2.2	2.1		.3	2.3	2.2	2.6	2.2	2.0
.2	.2	.2	% Depr., Dep., Amort./Sales	1.0	.2	.3	.2	.2	.1
(523) .5	(663) .5	(701) .5		(31) 6.1	(55) .7	(48) 1.0	(119) .5	(186) .5	(262) .3
1.5	1.3	1.3		15.4	1.3	2.0	1.4	1.7	.9
1.8	1.7	1.4	% Officers', Directors' Owners' Comp/Sales	8.5	4.8	3.2	2.0	1.0	.4
(190) 4.8	(233) 3.6	(233) 3.7		(12) 16.6	(39) 6.5	(38) 4.7	(62) 4.3	(51) 2.1	(33) .9
9.0	7.6	7.3		21.9	11.2	7.7	6.2	4.4	1.7
44954614M	50277174M	51131043M	Net Sales ($)	32580M	325942M	524231M	1813014M	5311042M	43124234M
19843538M	22644463M	20731125M	Total Assets ($)	57454M	120181M	223121M	648548M	2259089M	17422732M

M = $ thousand   MM = $ million
See Pages viii through xx for Explanation of Ratios and Data

Current Data Sorted by Assets   Comparative Historical Data

						Type of Statement		
		2	6	1	2	Unqualified	6	5
		6			1	Reviewed	1	3
		5				Compiled	4	4
2	2	3				Tax Returns	11	14
4	1	10	2		2	Other	34	32
	3 (4/1-9/30/18)		46 (10/1/18-3/31/19)				4/1/14-3/31/15 ALL	4/1/15-3/31/16 ALL
0-500M	500M-2MM	2-10MM	10-50MM	50-100MM	100-250MM	NUMBER OF STATEMENTS	56	58
6	3	26	8	1	5			
%	%	%	%	%	%	ASSETS	%	%
		19.1				Cash & Equivalents	17.6	17.9
		42.6				Trade Receivables (net)	36.1	38.8
		3.8				Inventory	2.7	3.0
		7.4				All Other Current	7.7	4.8
		73.0				Total Current	64.2	64.5
		11.5				Fixed Assets (net)	15.0	16.9
		7.6				Intangibles (net)	10.5	8.1
		7.9				All Other Non-Current	10.4	10.5
		100.0				Total	100.0	100.0
						LIABILITIES		
		11.9				Notes Payable-Short Term	13.5	13.4
		1.4				Cur. Mat.-L.T.D.	4.3	1.9
		18.4				Trade Payables	17.0	14.9
		.2				Income Taxes Payable	.4	1.2
		10.2				All Other Current	22.6	20.2
		42.1				Total Current	57.9	51.7
		8.8				Long-Term Debt	14.7	19.0
		.3				Deferred Taxes	.5	.1
		3.8				All Other Non-Current	16.5	11.6
		45.1				Net Worth	10.4	17.7
		100.0				Total Liabilties & Net Worth	100.0	100.0
						INCOME DATA		
		100.0				Net Sales	100.0	100.0
		42.4				Gross Profit	46.1	47.1
		34.7				Operating Expenses	40.6	39.8
		7.8				Operating Profit	5.4	7.4
		.5				All Other Expenses (net)	.9	.7
		7.3				Profit Before Taxes	4.5	6.7
						RATIOS		
		3.7					2.3	2.4
		2.1				Current	1.4	1.2
		1.1					.7	.8
		3.0					1.8	2.3
		1.8				Quick	1.1	1.1
		.9					.5	.6
		31 11.9					14 25.4	20 18.0
		45 8.1				Sales/Receivables	39 9.4	39 9.3
		74 4.9					68 5.4	58 6.3
		0 UND					0 UND	0 UND
		0 UND				Cost of Sales/Inventory	0 UND	0 UND
		6 58.3					2 159.2	2 146.7
		15 24.4					9 42.8	7 51.3
		27 13.4				Cost of Sales/Payables	19 18.8	24 15.2
		42 8.7					40 9.2	44 8.3
		4.8					8.0	7.7
		10.2				Sales/Working Capital	32.0	34.2
		NM					-16.3	-34.1
		30.6					43.0	35.7
		(22) 14.8				EBIT/Interest	(42) 13.5	(47) 15.1
		2.6					-.1	1.2
						Net Profit + Depr., Dep., Amort./Cur. Mat. L/T/D		
		.0					.1	.1
		.2				Fixed/Worth	.4	.6
		.9					-1.7	UND
		.4					.8	1.1
		2.0				Debt/Worth	3.4	3.1
		3.6					-7.1	-57.3
		91.2				% Profit Before Taxes/Tangible Net Worth	116.2	111.0
		(24) 49.5					(37) 57.0	(42) 66.7
		18.5					29.0	12.0
		32.1				% Profit Before Taxes/Total Assets	35.5	31.6
		20.6					14.0	13.4
		5.7					-.8	2.2
		457.4					147.3	155.9
		54.6				Sales/Net Fixed Assets	54.9	43.0
		18.7					14.4	12.4
		4.4					6.0	5.5
		3.3				Sales/Total Assets	3.9	3.5
		2.1					2.1	2.1
		.3					.2	.2
		(12) .9				% Depr., Dep., Amort./Sales	(35) .7	(30) .7
		1.6					1.8	2.3
						% Officers', Directors' Owners' Comp/Sales	1.6	3.0
							(20) 3.9	(16) 5.9
							5.4	12.4
10502M	22568M	409913M	443079M	116216M	2143061M	Net Sales ($)	2986568M	2604304M
1761M	3494M	127947M	159738M	92520M	942244M	Total Assets ($)	1190055M	1233147M

© RMA 2019

M = $ thousand   MM = $ million
See Pages viii through xx for Explanation of Ratios and Data

Comparative Historical Data   Current Data Sorted by Sales

Type of Statement	5 4 5 3 26	9 6 5 8 31	11 6 6 7 19				3 2 5 3	2 2 5 2	9 1 1
Unqualified Reviewed Compiled Tax Returns Other				1 1	1 2	3	3 4	2 5	4
	4/1/16- 3/31/17 ALL	4/1/17- 3/31/18 ALL	4/1/18- 3/31/19 ALL	0-1MM	1-3MM	3 (4/1-9/30/18) 3-5MM	5-10MM	46 (10/1/18-3/31/19) 10-25MM	25MM & OVER
NUMBER OF STATEMENTS	43	58	49	2	3	3	10	16	15
	%	%	%	%	%	%	%	%	%
ASSETS									
Cash & Equivalents	17.2	16.3	13.7				15.8	19.6	11.7
Trade Receivables (net)	35.4	43.1	44.5				32.4	46.0	49.7
Inventory	5.3	3.4	3.0				.1	6.1	2.9
All Other Current	4.8	4.5	5.6				6.7	2.9	4.4
Total Current	62.7	67.3	66.8				55.0	74.7	68.7
Fixed Assets (net)	12.4	13.5	16.4				25.9	10.9	17.2
Intangibles (net)	15.0	11.1	10.8				4.0	8.1	12.4
All Other Non-Current	10.0	8.1	6.0				15.1	6.2	1.7
Total	100.0	100.0	100.0				100.0	100.0	100.0
LIABILITIES									
Notes Payable-Short Term	13.8	16.4	11.7				19.7	9.7	8.6
Cur. Mat.-L.T.D.	2.6	1.8	6.2				.3	1.5	1.2
Trade Payables	22.2	17.7	19.6				8.5	20.3	26.0
Income Taxes Payable	1.6	.5	.3				.0	.3	.2
All Other Current	14.6	13.1	11.2				10.2	10.3	14.1
Total Current	54.8	49.6	49.0				38.7	42.0	50.1
Long-Term Debt	12.0	13.9	20.6				6.7	7.8	10.5
Deferred Taxes	.7	.2	.3				.7	.3	.1
All Other Non-Current	15.8	6.8	3.9				2.1	5.0	2.7
Net Worth	16.8	29.5	26.3				51.8	44.8	36.6
Total Liabilities & Net Worth	100.0	100.0	100.0				100.0	100.0	100.0
INCOME DATA									
Net Sales	100.0	100.0	100.0				100.0	100.0	100.0
Gross Profit	37.0	43.0	40.6				54.1	36.8	27.2
Operating Expenses	32.2	38.3	34.4				48.1	29.0	23.7
Operating Profit	4.8	4.7	6.2				6.0	7.8	3.5
All Other Expenses (net)	.8	.4	.7				.0	.7	1.0
Profit Before Taxes	4.0	4.3	5.5				6.1	7.1	2.6
RATIOS									
Current	2.1 1.3 .9	3.1 1.3 1.0	2.6 1.3 1.0				3.7 2.3 .8	3.1 1.8 1.2	1.7 1.2 1.1
Quick	1.6 1.0 .7	2.4 1.2 .9	2.1 1.2 .9				3.6 2.0 .6	2.3 1.6 1.1	1.5 1.0 1.0
Sales/Receivables	18 20.2 49 7.5 63 5.8	30 12.0 49 7.5 64 5.7	30 12.0 49 7.4 72 5.1				7 50.0 35 10.3 99 3.7	30 12.0 46 7.9 85 4.3	40 9.1 54 6.7 61 6.0
Cost of Sales/Inventory	0 UND 0 UND 10 34.8	0 UND 0 UND 7 49.8	0 UND 0 UND 6 65.2				0 UND 0 UND 0 UND	0 UND 0 893.3 13 27.1	0 UND 0 UND 9 39.1
Cost of Sales/Payables	9 42.0 27 13.3 49 7.5	8 46.0 29 12.6 53 6.9	16 22.8 27 13.3 55 6.6				0 UND 5 80.3 30 12.3	17 21.2 28 13.1 43 8.4	22 16.4 35 10.3 61 6.0
Sales/Working Capital	8.6 29.9 -161.2	7.7 19.0 659.5	7.2 22.2 NM				2.5 61.8 -29.5	7.1 15.3 26.1	10.3 21.2 39.8
EBIT/Interest	27.9 (36) 9.4 1.7	39.1 (50) 10.2 1.2	36.9 (44) 14.2 2.9					30.6 (14) 14.9 7.1	288.5 (14) 10.3 2.5
Net Profit + Depr., Dep., Amort./Cur. Mat. L/T/D		13.7 (13) 4.3 1.2							
Fixed/Worth	.1 .6 2.8	.0 .2 2.2	.1 .4 1.6				.1 .4 2.0	.0 .2 .9	.2 .4 3.3
Debt/Worth	1.5 3.8 -19.6	.6 2.7 NM	.6 2.8 10.1				.3 1.2 2.8	.6 2.6 5.6	1.0 3.0 10.0
% Profit Before Taxes/Tangible Net Worth	112.9 (32) 71.1 26.5	80.3 (44) 35.6 5.3	109.3 (41) 59.1 20.7				72.2 26.4 .2	99.9 (14) 60.9 22.7	99.3 (13) 63.0 18.8
% Profit Before Taxes/Total Assets	21.2 11.3 4.7	28.4 9.8 .8	32.5 16.5 5.7				32.9 17.9 .7	33.0 20.8 5.7	21.1 9.2 5.8
Sales/Net Fixed Assets	200.2 48.7 21.2	525.7 76.4 18.1	306.4 55.3 15.2				38.1 16.2 7.2	993.1 67.1 16.0	214.0 39.3 23.2
Sales/Total Assets	5.1 3.5 1.7	5.1 3.4 2.2	4.7 3.4 2.4				4.9 2.8 1.4	4.7 3.6 2.8	4.2 3.3 2.6
% Depr., Dep., Amort./Sales	.3 (27) .6 2.4	.4 (35) .7 3.1	.3 (25) .7 1.7						
% Officers', Directors' Owners' Comp/Sales		1.8 (23) 7.7 14.8	5.1 (10) 8.9 13.6						
Net Sales ($)	1766068M	2427231M	3145339M	1390M	5366M	12082M	74892M	274218M	2777391M
Total Assets ($)	862078M	1148372M	1327704M	357M	1067M	5768M	35860M	106877M	1177775M

© RMA 2019   M = $ thousand   MM = $ million
See Pages viii through xx for Explanation of Ratios and Data

Current Data Sorted by Assets | Comparative Historical Data

Type of Statement	0-500M	500M-2MM	2-10MM	10-50MM	50-100MM	100-250MM	4/1/14-3/31/15 ALL	4/1/15-3/31/16 ALL
Unqualified	1		11	13	4	5	43	46
Reviewed		1	23	11			63	48
Compiled	3	5	12	2			47	39
Tax Returns	41	42	23	4	1		175	197
Other	46	87	119	56	9	9	335	388
		59 (4/1-9/30/18)		469 (10/1/18-3/31/19)				
NUMBER OF STATEMENTS	91	135	188	86	14	14	663	718
	%	%	%	%	%	%	%	%
ASSETS								
Cash & Equivalents	39.6	22.7	18.3	16.5	27.4	16.5	23.2	24.2
Trade Receivables (net)	20.6	40.2	48.5	41.5	18.8	27.6	38.5	38.5
Inventory	1.3	4.1	3.7	1.3	3.8	2.9	3.1	3.4
All Other Current	5.5	2.6	3.8	6.1	6.5	7.6	3.8	3.9
Total Current	67.0	69.6	74.4	65.4	56.4	54.7	68.6	69.9
Fixed Assets (net)	16.8	17.1	10.2	12.1	11.1	2.7	14.3	13.1
Intangibles (net)	5.2	5.4	8.1	15.6	23.0	34.6	7.1	7.9
All Other Non-Current	11.1	7.9	7.2	7.0	9.5	8.0	10.0	9.0
Total	100.0	100.0	100.0	100.0	100.0	100.0	100.0	100.0
LIABILITIES								
Notes Payable-Short Term	26.3	13.9	8.3	6.2	1.3	3.2	14.4	15.3
Cur. Mat.-L.T.D.	1.1	2.7	1.6	2.8	1.5	1.2	1.8	2.0
Trade Payables	10.7	14.0	17.8	14.7	6.4	20.0	15.3	15.2
Income Taxes Payable	.1	.0	.2	.2	.3	.7	.3	.3
All Other Current	27.4	19.2	20.4	17.7	25.9	26.0	18.5	18.0
Total Current	65.6	49.9	48.3	41.6	35.4	51.1	50.4	50.9
Long-Term Debt	20.3	11.4	10.7	15.8	11.1	12.8	11.3	11.4
Deferred Taxes	.0	.0	.1	.2	.2	.9	.2	.3
All Other Non-Current	7.2	12.7	5.4	6.5	18.9	7.0	8.0	8.5
Net Worth	6.9	26.0	35.4	35.9	34.3	28.2	30.1	29.0
Total Liabilities & Net Worth	100.0	100.0	100.0	100.0	100.0	100.0	100.0	100.0
INCOME DATA								
Net Sales	100.0	100.0	100.0	100.0	100.0	100.0	100.0	100.0
Gross Profit								
Operating Expenses	89.3	90.7	93.8	91.6	98.2	93.1	92.2	91.3
Operating Profit	10.7	9.3	6.2	8.4	1.8	6.9	7.8	8.7
All Other Expenses (net)	.7	1.4	1.3	1.5	.8	2.0	1.3	1.2
Profit Before Taxes	10.0	7.9	4.9	6.9	1.0	4.9	6.5	7.4
RATIOS								
Current	4.0	3.2	2.7	2.9	2.9	1.4	3.0	3.1
	1.7	1.6	1.7	1.5	1.3	1.1	1.6	1.6
	.5	1.0	1.1	1.0	.9	.9	1.0	1.0
Quick	3.6	3.2	2.5	2.7	2.9	1.2	2.6	2.9
	1.4	1.4	1.5	1.3	1.0	.8	1.3	1.4
	.5	.8	.9	.9	.6	.7	.8	.8
Sales/Receivables	0 UND	23 15.9	37 9.8	48 7.6	27 13.7	47 7.7	17 21.4	14 25.5
	0 UND	34 10.7	56 6.5	63 5.8	45 8.1	76 4.8	43 8.5	42 8.6
	30 12.3	54 6.8	79 4.6	85 4.3	62 5.9	96 3.8	65 5.6	64 5.7
Cost of Sales/Inventory								
Cost of Sales/Payables								
Sales/Working Capital	12.6	8.5	5.6	4.6	4.0	7.8	6.9	6.7
	40.1	16.3	10.8	10.3	10.2	39.8	16.3	15.6
	-34.9	-115.6	52.4	NM	-205.3	-17.0	-214.8	575.4
EBIT/Interest	75.3	46.5	54.3	53.0	122.3	103.6	61.4	55.3
	(53) 10.4	(94) 11.7	(137) 15.1	(65) 10.1	(10) .4	(12) 5.0	(463) 12.8	(503) 13.2
	2.0	2.1	3.0	1.3	-42.9	1.9	3.2	2.9
Net Profit + Depr., Dep., Amort./Cur. Mat. L/T/D			20.8	29.1			6.1	15.7
		(11) 3.4	(10) 3.8				(36) 3.1	(38) 3.6
			1.2	.8			.8	1.0
Fixed/Worth	.0	.0	.0	.0	.0	.2	.0	.0
	.1	.3	.2	.3	.4	-.5	.2	.2
	2.8	2.2	1.0	-2.2	-.2	-.1	1.5	2.3
Debt/Worth	.4	.5	.7		1.1	3.1	.6	.6
	2.1	1.7	1.6	2.4	2.4	-18.5	1.7	1.9
	-9.5	21.6	9.8	-17.5	-3.1	-2.2	14.8	25.1
% Profit Before Taxes/Tangible Net Worth	218.8	111.5	81.4	63.4			95.4	93.6
	(64) 91.4	(105) 51.6	(154) 40.6	(62) 39.5			(529) 45.0	(553) 46.2
	40.3	22.2	15.8	15.3			18.0	18.8
% Profit Before Taxes/Total Assets	86.4	41.0	25.3	24.7	12.0	9.7	35.9	38.6
	46.2	22.4	13.3	10.4	1.8	4.6	14.8	15.8
	10.9	5.1	4.1	.6	-6.9	2.5	3.5	3.7
Sales/Net Fixed Assets	UND	531.4	395.3	184.6	150.6	180.9	347.0	411.4
	247.0	76.6	109.9	49.1	38.8	71.8	67.8	71.6
	34.8	16.9	25.0	17.3	12.9	39.2	19.1	23.0
Sales/Total Assets	15.0	5.7	3.9	3.3	2.1	2.2	5.3	5.2
	7.4	4.0	2.9	2.1	1.2	.9	3.5	3.5
	3.9	2.5	2.2	1.2	.7	.5	2.2	2.3
% Depr., Dep., Amort./Sales	.3	.2	.2	.3			.2	.2
	(30) .6	(65) .6	(96) .7	(59) .9			(348) .8	(357) .8
	1.6	1.9	1.7	2.3			2.1	2.0
% Officers', Directors' Owners' Comp/Sales	4.6	2.6	1.4				2.5	2.2
	(38) 8.4	(51) 5.4	(49) 3.1				(233) 5.6	(264) 5.1
	13.8	11.0	6.2				10.7	9.7
Net Sales ($)	227567M	684371M	2831187M	3989273M	1787362M	3241808M	14252224M	14944175M
Total Assets ($)	22393M	155015M	875069M	1873132M	1033598M	2342480M	7064159M	6787313M

© RMA 2019

M = $ thousand   MM = $ million
See Pages viii through xx for Explanation of Ratios and Data

Comparative Historical Data | Current Data Sorted by Sales

			Type of Statement						
43	49	34	Unqualified	1	2	2	1	7	21
50	40	35	Reviewed				7	16	12
29	24	22	Compiled	2	3	2	5	8	2
138	136	111	Tax Returns	19	30	20	20	17	5
320	325	326	Other	26	42	26	77	86	69
4/1/16-3/31/17 ALL	4/1/17-3/31/18 ALL	4/1/18-3/31/19 ALL		59 (4/1-9/30/18)			469 (10/1/18-3/31/19)		
				0-1MM	1-3MM	3-5MM	5-10MM	10-25MM	25MM & OVER
580	574	528	**NUMBER OF STATEMENTS**	48	77	50	110	134	109
%	%	%	**ASSETS**	%	%	%	%	%	%
22.0	23.2	23.0	Cash & Equivalents	30.1	25.7	31.4	22.4	20.7	17.6
39.6	39.5	39.1	Trade Receivables (net)	12.2	30.4	26.7	43.9	48.0	46.8
3.1	3.7	3.0	Inventory	1.0	4.4	3.7	3.4	3.3	1.9
4.5	4.1	4.4	All Other Current	2.0	3.4	5.2	5.0	4.0	5.4
69.1	70.5	69.4	Total Current	45.2	63.9	67.0	74.7	76.0	71.8
12.4	12.0	13.2	Fixed Assets (net)	33.5	17.7	17.2	11.4	8.2	7.4
9.8	9.5	9.2	Intangibles (net)	6.1	10.0	7.2	5.5	10.1	13.6
8.7	8.0	8.1	All Other Non-Current	15.2	8.4	8.5	8.4	5.8	7.1
100.0	100.0	100.0	Total	100.0	100.0	100.0	100.0	100.0	100.0
			LIABILITIES						
14.2	12.3	12.2	Notes Payable-Short Term	24.0	19.5	18.0	9.0	9.2	6.0
3.0	2.3	2.0	Cur. Mat.-L.T.D.	1.3	3.4	2.2	1.7	1.5	2.0
14.9	15.0	14.8	Trade Payables	5.1	8.9	13.9	14.8	17.9	20.1
.2	.2	.2	Income Taxes Payable	.1	.1	.1	.2	.2	.3
20.2	20.7	21.2	All Other Current	23.2	17.8	16.4	21.7	24.1	20.7
52.6	50.5	50.3	Total Current	53.7	49.7	50.5	47.3	52.9	49.1
11.4	13.4	13.5	Long-Term Debt	19.8	21.1	17.4	10.0	9.4	11.9
.3	.1	.1	Deferred Taxes	.0	.0	.0	.2	.1	.2
6.7	7.6	8.2	All Other Non-Current	23.3	6.6	2.0	8.4	6.8	6.7
29.0	28.3	27.9	Net Worth	3.1	22.5	30.0	34.1	30.8	32.1
100.0	100.0	100.0	Total Liabilties & Net Worth	100.0	100.0	100.0	100.0	100.0	100.0
			INCOME DATA						
100.0	100.0	100.0	Net Sales	100.0	100.0	100.0	100.0	100.0	100.0
			Gross Profit						
93.6	93.2	92.0	Operating Expenses	77.9	91.5	93.4	92.9	94.8	93.5
6.4	6.8	8.0	Operating Profit	22.1	8.5	6.6	7.1	5.2	6.5
1.1	1.0	1.3	All Other Expenses (net)	5.2	1.0	.4	.9	.8	1.0
5.3	5.9	6.8	Profit Before Taxes	16.9	7.4	6.2	6.2	4.5	5.5
			RATIOS						
2.6	3.0	2.9		4.4	2.8	5.0	3.8	2.4	2.3
1.4	1.4	1.6	Current	1.2	1.4	1.5	2.0	1.7	1.4
.9	1.0	1.0		.5	.8	.7	1.2	1.1	1.0
2.4	2.7	2.7		3.6	2.7	5.0	3.6	2.2	2.2
1.2	1.3	1.4	Quick	1.1	1.3	1.4	1.7	1.4	1.2
.8	.8	.8		.4	.6	.6	.9	.9	.8
19 19.7	24 15.5	22 16.4		0 UND	14 25.8	0 UND	27 13.3	35 10.3	44 8.3
43 8.5	44 8.3	46 7.9	Sales/Receivables	0 UND	32 11.3	26 14.0	43 8.4	54 6.7	60 6.1
65 5.6	66 5.5	70 5.2		30 12.3	58 6.3	49 7.5	66 5.5	78 4.7	83 4.4
			Cost of Sales/Inventory						
			Cost of Sales/Payables						
7.5	6.9	6.7		6.0	8.5	12.3	6.2	6.5	6.7
19.1	17.3	15.3	Sales/Working Capital	34.9	16.2	23.3	12.1	11.5	13.3
-94.9	-200.1	-112.9		-14.5	-38.4	-17.0	38.9	81.5	108.7
48.3	44.5	52.8		8.5	26.8	56.8	50.2	50.5	112.8
(411) 11.7	(406) 8.4	(371) 11.6	EBIT/Interest	(19) 3.3	(58) 9.0	(36) 8.8	(75) 15.7	(100) 16.0	(83) 12.8
2.3	2.0	1.9		-.7	1.6	1.0	4.0	2.2	2.5
5.4	6.8	20.2	Net Profit + Depr., Dep.,						
(37) 2.9	(35) 2.9	(25) 3.3	Amort./Cur. Mat. L/T/D						
1.0	.8	1.1							
.0	.0	.0		.0	.0	.0	.0	.0	.0
.2	.2	.2	Fixed/Worth	.1	.3	.3	.1	.1	.3
12.6	4.0	2.3		2.8	-7.5	NM	.6	1.3	-.5
.6	.6	.6		.4	.6	.4	.5	.9	.8
2.3	2.3	1.9	Debt/Worth	2.8	2.2	1.8	1.1	1.8	2.8
UND	UND	64.7		53.8	-9.4	-6.8	4.5	77.3	-11.1
101.5	93.8	96.7	% Profit Before Taxes/Tangible	162.3	151.8	103.9	91.6	86.5	79.8
(435) 47.5	(432) 45.7	(400) 48.0	Net Worth	(37) 75.6	(52) 75.9	(35) 40.6	(96) 45.3	(103) 42.4	(77) 43.2
19.2	15.2	18.2		7.8	28.7	17.8	20.9	16.9	22.2
34.6	32.8	36.5	% Profit Before Taxes/Total	80.5	63.3	54.2	32.0	29.4	26.0
15.2	13.6	15.8	Assets	18.2	25.4	20.3	16.7	13.2	12.8
2.6	2.9	3.3		2.7	3.1	3.0	6.4	1.9	3.2
313.4	353.2	531.2		UND	523.0	478.3	846.6	450.9	250.8
79.9	90.9	86.2	Sales/Net Fixed Assets	34.9	60.1	91.0	89.7	109.0	89.3
24.1	23.3	21.4		5.8	15.8	12.5	21.2	36.3	28.6
5.4	5.0	4.9		4.6	5.0	7.6	5.5	4.6	4.1
3.6	3.4	3.2	Sales/Total Assets	3.2	3.6	4.1	3.5	3.1	2.8
2.3	2.1	2.0		.7	2.2	2.0	2.5	2.2	1.7
.2	.2	.3		.1	.3	.3	.3	.2	.2
(314) .7	(298) .6	(265) .7	% Depr., Dep., Amort./Sales	(17) 4.6	(39) .5	(25) .8	(48) .8	(66) .7	(70) .7
1.7	1.8	2.0		16.8	1.7	2.3	1.6	1.8	1.5
2.4	2.5	2.1	% Officers', Directors'	8.5	4.9	3.0	1.7	1.2	
(195) 5.0	(163) 4.9	(146) 4.8	Owners' Comp/Sales	(12) 14.0	(35) 7.6	(21) 5.4	(38) 4.3	(31) 1.9	
8.9	9.7	9.4		19.3	11.5	8.2	7.2	4.7	
15141643M	13776899M	12761568M	Net Sales ($)	23037M	152122M	197518M	770699M	2160516M	9457676M
6747933M	6186706M	6301687M	Total Assets ($)	24461M	73250M	73362M	304336M	1066648M	4759630M

Current Data Sorted by Assets   **Comparative Historical Data**

						Type of Statement		
2	3	31	30	13	12	Unqualified	107	121
4	11	28	15	1	1	Reviewed	71	56
52	11	16	4			Compiled	53	54
56	32	15	3			Tax Returns	161	162
	78	128	87	25	17	Other	413	427
	92 (4/1-9/30/18)		583 (10/1/18-3/31/19)				4/1/14-3/31/15 ALL	4/1/15-3/31/16 ALL
0-500M	500M-2MM	2-10MM	10-50MM	50-100MM	100-250MM			
114	135	218	139	39	30	NUMBER OF STATEMENTS	805	820
%	%	%	%	%	%	**ASSETS**	%	%
51.2	26.3	18.6	18.7	14.9	10.0	Cash & Equivalents	24.2	24.4
10.6	36.2	42.3	37.1	25.2	23.3	Trade Receivables (net)	33.0	32.2
.4	1.3	1.2	1.6	4.9	.8	Inventory	1.5	1.3
2.1	6.8	6.3	7.2	7.7	6.2	All Other Current	7.0	6.4
64.3	70.7	68.3	64.7	52.7	40.3	Total Current	65.9	64.3
15.2	9.8	12.7	10.6	12.1	9.5	Fixed Assets (net)	13.6	14.0
5.3	5.4	6.4	13.2	21.4	40.5	Intangibles (net)	8.9	9.5
15.3	14.1	12.5	11.5	13.8	9.7	All Other Non-Current	11.6	12.1
100.0	100.0	100.0	100.0	100.0	100.0	Total	100.0	100.0
						LIABILITIES		
26.7	12.3	8.4	5.4	8.7	5.1	Notes Payable-Short Term	11.9	11.0
3.0	2.0	2.1	3.6	2.6	4.7	Cur. Mat.-L.T.D.	2.4	2.4
4.8	8.9	12.1	10.9	7.0	4.5	Trade Payables	10.7	10.9
.4	.2	.3	.7	.9	.2	Income Taxes Payable	.4	.4
36.2	20.6	21.1	21.5	16.1	14.7	All Other Current	22.1	22.6
71.2	44.0	43.9	42.1	35.3	29.2	Total Current	47.5	47.3
15.8	9.6	14.5	18.9	16.8	21.7	Long-Term Debt	12.1	13.4
.0	.1	.2	.4	.1	2.3	Deferred Taxes	.3	.3
11.4	5.4	9.2	7.8	7.9	3.6	All Other Non-Current	7.5	7.2
1.7	40.9	32.2	30.9	40.0	43.2	Net Worth	32.6	31.8
100.0	100.0	100.0	100.0	100.0	100.0	Total Liabilties & Net Worth	100.0	100.0
						INCOME DATA		
100.0	100.0	100.0	100.0	100.0	100.0	Net Sales	100.0	100.0
						Gross Profit		
85.9	90.4	89.9	88.4	93.3	89.8	Operating Expenses	88.8	88.5
14.1	9.6	10.1	11.6	6.7	10.2	Operating Profit	11.2	11.5
1.0	.8	1.9	2.2	3.0	3.4	All Other Expenses (net)	1.2	1.6
13.2	8.8	8.2	9.4	3.7	6.8	Profit Before Taxes	9.9	10.0
						RATIOS		
5.0	4.2	3.3	2.9	2.2	1.9		3.2	3.4
1.7	2.1	1.6	1.6	1.4	1.4	Current	1.6	1.6
.5	1.1	1.1	1.1	1.1	1.0		1.0	.9
5.0	3.7	2.7	2.6	1.6	1.7		2.7	3.0
1.4	1.7	1.5	1.3	1.2	1.2	Quick	1.3	1.3
.4	.9	.9	.8	.8	.7		.8	.7
0 UND	2 237.6	30 12.2	25 14.7	15 24.0	43 8.5		2 151.5	1 515.4
0 UND	31 11.8	49 7.4	55 6.6	42 8.7	62 5.9	Sales/Receivables	38 9.5	38 9.5
3 111.5	54 6.7	69 5.3	81 4.5	76 4.8	89 4.1		65 5.6	66 5.5
						Cost of Sales/Inventory		
						Cost of Sales/Payables		
10.8	6.1	5.1	4.4	3.9	5.1		6.1	5.8
70.6	14.0	11.1	9.9	9.6	11.5	Sales/Working Capital	15.4	13.2
-32.6	91.8	63.6	61.3	68.9	NM		-478.5	-101.0
116.9	54.3	52.5	45.5	9.0	7.8		55.4	52.0
(50) 37.7	(90) 13.1	(157) 12.4	(105) 11.6	(35) 4.3	(26) 3.5	EBIT/Interest	(553) 13.3	(542) 12.6
5.6	2.4	2.8	2.6	1.4	.8		2.9	2.0
		27.5	14.7	7.9			5.8	12.8
	(15)	8.8	(27) 4.2	(10) 3.6		Net Profit + Depr., Dep., Amort./Cur. Mat. L/T/D	(72) 2.7	(45) 4.8
		2.4	1.3	-.4			1.1	1.7
.0	.0	.0	.0	.1	.2		.0	.0
.1	.1	.1	.3	.5	-.7	Fixed/Worth	.2	.2
UND	.6	.9	-5.9	-2.5	-.1		2.4	3.1
.2	.4	.6	.5	1.1	1.4		.6	.5
1.9	1.2	1.4	2.0	4.3	-9.7	Debt/Worth	2.0	1.9
-6.6	6.7	5.9	-26.5	-13.0	-2.4		26.6	44.0
432.0	115.5	80.1	74.2	52.1	58.3		105.0	96.9
(77) 150.3	(113) 58.2	(185) 44.7	(104) 36.2	(27) 15.0	(13) 11.8	% Profit Before Taxes/Tangible Net Worth	(625) 49.9	(631) 45.5
42.6	15.4	11.8	14.5	-.7	1.2		15.1	14.1
156.8	51.8	29.9	28.5	8.6	10.3		40.8	37.9
58.3	22.5	14.4	14.3	3.8	7.1	% Profit Before Taxes/Total Assets	16.6	15.1
5.9	4.5	3.4	2.9	.8	.3		3.2	2.6
UND	674.2	405.5	223.8	65.8	61.6		259.3	388.6
320.5	101.2	65.1	60.0	23.5	32.4	Sales/Net Fixed Assets	66.4	70.9
38.5	31.6	19.0	16.6	9.3	10.1		20.5	19.0
18.0	6.2	4.1	3.2	2.5	1.3		4.9	4.6
8.1	4.3	2.9	2.3	1.3	1.1	Sales/Total Assets	3.0	2.9
4.2	2.5	1.7	1.4	.7	.7		1.7	1.5
.3	.2	.3	.3	.6	1.0		.3	.3
(36) .7	(70) .4	(125) .7	(101) .7	(26) .9	(13) 2.2	% Depr., Dep., Amort./Sales	(487) .7	(430) .9
1.7	1.2	2.0	2.4	4.5	4.6		1.9	2.6
5.7	3.5	2.2	.6				3.5	3.4
(54) 10.6	(45) 5.5	(41) 4.3	(13) 2.2			% Officers', Directors' Owners' Comp/Sales	(196) 8.4	(206) 8.3
17.5	13.8	10.7	6.6				16.9	17.1
237649M	753061M	3287723M	7893598M	4225577M	5372481M	Net Sales ($)	27975815M	26378580M
23954M	155464M	1114317M	3033800M	2829752M	4685089M	Total Assets ($)	13770911M	13607949M

© RMA 2019

M = $ thousand   MM = $ million
See Pages viii through xx for Explanation of Ratios and Data

Comparative Historical Data | Current Data Sorted by Sales

96	90	89	Type of Statement	1	5	2	6	23	52
61	50	58	Unqualified / Reviewed	2	2	5	7	20	16
32	43	35	Compiled	4	5	3	8	13	2
138	113	102	Tax Returns	25	34	16	19	5	3
387	434	391	Other	32	60	29	59	84	127
4/1/16-3/31/17	4/1/17-3/31/18	4/1/18-3/31/19		92 (4/1-9/30/18)		583 (10/1/18-3/31/19)			
ALL	ALL	ALL		0-1MM	1-3MM	3-5MM	5-10MM	10-25MM	25MM & OVER
714	730	675	NUMBER OF STATEMENTS	64	106	55	99	151	200
%	%	%	ASSETS	%	%	%	%	%	%
26.2	23.9	25.1	Cash & Equivalents	37.4	35.2	25.9	29.0	22.1	15.9
32.8	33.4	32.8	Trade Receivables (net)	5.8	22.3	29.5	30.5	41.7	42.4
1.0	1.4	1.4	Inventory	1.0	.8	1.5	.5	1.4	2.1
7.1	7.1	6.0	All Other Current	3.0	4.8	7.2	6.1	6.4	6.8
67.1	65.8	65.2	Total Current	47.2	63.2	64.1	66.0	71.6	67.1
13.4	13.0	11.9	Fixed Assets (net)	20.5	15.5	13.4	8.5	11.8	8.7
8.0	10.3	9.8	Intangibles (net)	8.8	4.1	6.9	8.1	8.8	15.6
11.6	11.0	13.0	All Other Non-Current	23.5	17.3	15.7	17.4	7.8	8.5
100.0	100.0	100.0	Total	100.0	100.0	100.0	100.0	100.0	100.0
			LIABILITIES						
12.9	11.5	11.5	Notes Payable-Short Term	16.2	18.9	15.9	9.6	8.1	8.4
2.5	2.8	2.7	Cur. Mat.-L.T.D.	3.0	1.6	4.0	2.0	2.6	3.1
9.2	9.3	9.4	Trade Payables	4.3	6.3	7.3	6.8	12.6	12.0
.3	.3	.4	Income Taxes Payable	.1	.5	.0	.1	.3	.7
20.8	21.0	23.1	All Other Current	39.1	19.5	21.0	21.3	21.9	22.2
45.8	44.8	47.0	Total Current	62.7	46.7	48.3	39.8	45.5	46.5
13.9	13.8	15.1	Long-Term Debt	19.9	15.1	14.6	11.8	13.2	16.8
.2	.2	.3	Deferred Taxes	.0	.1	.1	.0	.3	.5
7.7	8.2	8.2	All Other Non-Current	11.6	7.4	10.0	4.0	8.6	8.8
32.5	33.0	29.4	Net Worth	5.8	30.7	27.1	44.4	32.3	27.4
100.0	100.0	100.0	Total Liabilities & Net Worth	100.0	100.0	100.0	100.0	100.0	100.0
			INCOME DATA						
100.0	100.0	100.0	Net Sales	100.0	100.0	100.0	100.0	100.0	100.0
			Gross Profit						
88.9	88.2	89.2	Operating Expenses	79.7	85.5	90.3	91.5	91.6	91.0
11.1	11.8	10.8	Operating Profit	20.3	14.5	9.7	8.5	8.4	9.0
1.6	1.8	1.7	All Other Expenses (net)	5.6	1.6	.4	1.4	1.1	1.5
9.5	10.0	9.1	Profit Before Taxes	14.7	12.9	9.3	7.1	7.3	7.5
			RATIOS						
3.5	3.5	3.3	Current	6.2	5.2	4.6	4.4	3.3	2.2
1.7	1.7	1.6		1.2	1.9	2.0	2.2	1.7	1.5
1.0	1.0	1.0		.2	.7	.9	1.1	1.2	1.1
3.1	3.2	3.0	Quick	3.5	5.0	3.4	4.2	3.0	1.9
1.5	1.5	1.5		1.0	1.7	1.5	1.9	1.5	1.3
.9	.8	.8		.2	.4	.8	.9	.9	.9
3 134.2	2 226.6	2 174.4	Sales/Receivables	0 UND	0 UND	0 UND	1 243.4	28 12.9	33 10.9
39 9.3	42 8.6	40 9.2		0 UND	7 52.7	41 8.9	35 10.3	48 7.6	59 6.2
65 5.6	69 5.3	66 5.5		1 313.8	54 6.7	56 6.5	59 6.2	66 5.5	79 4.6
			Cost of Sales/Inventory						
			Cost of Sales/Payables						
6.1	5.3	5.9	Sales/Working Capital	4.4	5.1	6.2	6.1	6.2	5.9
12.1	12.0	13.3		110.1	15.7	13.3	12.1	11.8	11.5
228.5	281.2	372.9		-6.9	-30.6	-65.4	89.1	42.3	53.0
57.4	47.9	52.0	EBIT/Interest	71.6	59.7	27.1	61.6	81.2	30.3
(491) 11.6	(504) 10.1	(463) 10.3		(21) 3.2	(60) 13.8	(38) 7.9	(71) 12.8	(115) 19.0	(158) 8.0
2.2	2.2	2.3		.4	2.2	2.3	1.8	2.9	2.5
6.9	12.3	14.9	Net Profit + Depr., Dep., Amort./Cur. Mat. L/T/D					30.2	15.2
(65) 2.5	(58) 3.5	(63) 4.3						(11) 4.2	(45) 4.7
1.3	2.0	1.1						.9	1.5
.0	.0	.0	Fixed/Worth	.0	.0	.0	.0	.0	.1
.2	.2	.2		.2	.1	.2	.1	.2	.3
1.6	2.2	1.7		11.3	1.2	1.6	.5	1.0	-.7
.5	.5	.5	Debt/Worth	.2	.3	.7	.6	.6	.8
1.6	1.5	1.7		4.0	.9	1.9	.8	1.5	3.4
20.6	28.1	27.2		-17.3	5.6	-79.3	5.7	7.1	-8.2
98.1	94.7	105.0	% Profit Before Taxes/Tangible Net Worth	146.3	172.5	152.8	112.4	93.2	88.1
(564) 43.2	(564) 45.4	(519) 48.3		(46) 34.4	(89) 58.0	(40) 60.1	(84) 45.5	(123) 55.0	(137) 39.6
12.0	14.5	12.7		1.2	11.5	16.2	9.7	25.4	14.3
36.1	36.9	40.0	% Profit Before Taxes/Total Assets	70.5	75.3	53.8	47.2	38.5	24.4
14.3	13.6	15.2		5.6	23.5	24.9	12.1	18.4	11.5
2.5	2.9	3.1		.0	4.2	6.3	3.0	4.9	3.5
372.7	489.6	407.4	Sales/Net Fixed Assets	UND	UND	873.4	877.1	399.3	209.1
66.4	75.0	73.3		120.9	82.6	52.7	101.2	87.7	58.3
19.5	19.9	21.3		8.7	18.8	22.3	31.7	22.3	19.8
4.8	4.9	5.0	Sales/Total Assets	7.5	7.7	6.2	6.4	4.7	3.7
2.9	2.9	3.0		2.3	3.4	3.6	3.2	3.2	2.6
1.7	1.5	1.6		.4	1.5	1.9	1.8	2.1	1.5
.3	.3	.2	% Depr., Dep., Amort./Sales	.6	.3	.7	.2	.2	.2
(399) .8	(386) .8	(371) .7		(26) 2.4	(44) .5	(25) 1.6	(49) .6	(87) .7	(140) .7
2.2	2.1	2.2		14.8	2.4	4.0	1.8	1.7	1.9
3.3	2.8	3.0	% Officers', Directors' Owners' Comp/Sales	6.4	4.9	3.9	3.6	1.9	.6
(185) 7.2	(182) 7.4	(157) 6.8		(20) 15.2	(38) 9.9	(20) 7.4	(31) 6.4	(30) 4.2	(18) 2.1
16.3	15.6	14.9		27.0	16.0	12.4	11.2	12.1	9.7
23379349M	27169841M	21770089M	Net Sales ($)	31439M	207726M	214920M	697986M	2476474M	18141544M
11743843M	13366342M	11842376M	Total Assets ($)	79911M	242021M	100791M	502138M	1074983M	9842532M

Current Data Sorted by Assets   **Comparative Historical Data**

Type of Statement	0-500M	500M-2MM	2-10MM	10-50MM	50-100MM	100-250MM		4/1/14-3/31/15 ALL	4/1/15-3/31/16 ALL
Unqualified		1	4	6	3	1		18	21
Reviewed		1	2	1				11	9
Compiled	1		3	1				4	12
Tax Returns	4		1					17	11
Other	7	15	15	16	8	1		58	74
		17 (4/1-9/30/18)		76 (10/1/18-3/31/19)					
NUMBER OF STATEMENTS	12	20	25	23	11	2		108	127
	%	%	%	%	%	%		%	%
ASSETS									
Cash & Equivalents	50.9	24.1	21.4	21.8	14.1			28.1	22.0
Trade Receivables (net)	18.3	31.4	38.2	36.0	33.4			35.8	39.7
Inventory	.0	4.4	.1	1.7	.0			.1	.6
All Other Current	6.3	7.1	5.7	5.0	13.1			3.9	6.3
Total Current	75.5	67.0	65.4	64.5	60.7			67.9	68.6
Fixed Assets (net)	3.7	9.4	8.1	11.1	10.3			12.8	12.5
Intangibles (net)	6.2	4.1	7.7	15.9	12.3			9.9	11.1
All Other Non-Current	14.6	19.6	18.8	8.4	16.7			9.4	7.8
Total	100.0	100.0	100.0	100.0	100.0			100.0	100.0
LIABILITIES									
Notes Payable-Short Term	6.6	18.8	5.5	4.4	1.5			12.1	10.1
Cur. Mat.-L.T.D.	.0	1.9	.8	1.8	2.6			1.4	2.0
Trade Payables	4.2	7.4	11.4	7.7	18.6			6.9	7.7
Income Taxes Payable	.3	.1	.4	.4	.3			.4	1.4
All Other Current	31.7	23.0	32.7	24.4	32.2			26.9	24.1
Total Current	42.8	51.1	50.8	38.7	55.3			47.8	45.3
Long-Term Debt	.0	8.1	3.4	9.4	8.8			9.0	12.5
Deferred Taxes	.9	.0	.3	.2	.0			.2	.5
All Other Non-Current	.4	25.4	3.8	4.6	13.5			16.5	7.1
Net Worth	55.9	15.4	41.7	47.1	22.4			26.4	34.5
Total Liabilities & Net Worth	100.0	100.0	100.0	100.0	100.0			100.0	100.0
INCOME DATA									
Net Sales	100.0	100.0	100.0	100.0	100.0			100.0	100.0
Gross Profit									
Operating Expenses	91.9	91.7	98.2	94.9	91.9			92.2	92.2
Operating Profit	8.1	8.3	1.8	5.1	8.1			7.8	7.8
All Other Expenses (net)	.5	.8	-.8	2.7	.8			1.4	1.4
Profit Before Taxes	7.6	7.5	2.6	2.4	7.3			6.4	6.4
RATIOS									
Current	4.5	7.3	3.7	2.4	1.8			4.2	2.8
	1.9	2.2	1.7	1.7	1.1			1.8	1.6
	1.1	.8	1.0	1.4	.7			1.0	1.1
Quick	4.5	7.3	3.0	2.3	1.4			4.1	2.7
	1.5	1.6	1.3	1.5	.7			1.5	1.3
	1.1	.7	.9	1.1	.5			.9	.9
Sales/Receivables	0 UND	3 143.8	11 34.5	20 18.0	6 62.7			1 245.5	12 29.3
	0 UND	13 27.3	37 9.8	42 8.7	51 7.1			33 11.0	42 8.7
	34 10.6	35 10.4	44 8.3	60 6.1	69 5.3			60 6.1	63 5.8
Cost of Sales/Inventory									
Cost of Sales/Payables									
Sales/Working Capital	5.5	8.8	11.8	7.3	11.0			6.6	6.5
	14.9	31.4	21.2	15.1	75.7			13.7	16.0
	393.7	-72.5	NM	32.0	-16.9			694.8	166.1
EBIT/Interest			43.8	59.7	133.8			36.6	30.0
		(12) 10.2	(18) 17.5	(18) 12.4				(64) 8.2	(92) 10.5
		3.5	-.6	1.3				1.3	1.6
Net Profit + Depr., Dep., Amort./Cur. Mat. L/T/D									6.6
								(11) 4.6	
								3.3	
Fixed/Worth	.0	.0	.0	.0	.0			.0	.0
	.0	.2	.1	.1	.6			.2	.2
	.2	-1.2	.6	1.4	-.9			8.3	3.7
Debt/Worth	.2	.3	.3	.7	1.3			.4	.6
	.8	.9	1.2	1.5	11.5			2.0	2.2
	5.1	-14.9	8.3	5.0	-12.7			-48.2	65.0
% Profit Before Taxes/Tangible Net Worth	105.2	132.1	59.6	51.3				76.4	83.3
	(11) 33.9	(14) 65.1	(22) 24.5	(20) 30.3				(80) 27.8	(97) 33.1
	6.3	13.3	4.9	1.1				7.0	6.9
% Profit Before Taxes/Total Assets	79.2	60.5	28.5	26.6	9.3			23.9	25.6
	17.6	16.2	11.5	11.7	6.6			8.1	11.9
	1.4	7.2	-.4	-1.6	2.4			1.0	1.6
Sales/Net Fixed Assets	UND	701.0	999.8	654.5	248.7			908.1	416.9
	UND	131.5	186.7	139.5	34.2			106.5	91.9
	319.0	39.2	46.5	31.4	22.4			20.6	29.2
Sales/Total Assets	18.5	11.4	8.2	5.8	4.8			7.2	6.2
	6.8	5.7	3.9	3.7	1.8			3.7	3.6
	4.3	3.3	2.3	1.2	1.1			1.4	1.5
% Depr., Dep., Amort./Sales			.1	.1				.2	.2
		(13) .4	(13) .6					(50) .5	(65) .4
		1.7	2.0					2.1	2.0
% Officers', Directors' Owners' Comp/Sales								1.9	2.1
								(39) 5.3	(28) 4.8
								8.8	9.4
Net Sales ($)	56898M	186269M	847816M	2491171M	2771252M	201505M		3565222M	5863646M
Total Assets ($)	2985M	20912M	124290M	533279M	809806M	346117M		1443480M	1985634M

M = $ thousand   MM = $ million
See Pages viii through xx for Explanation of Ratios and Data

Comparative Historical Data | Current Data Sorted by Sales

				17 (4/1-9/30/18)			76 (10/1/18-3/31/19)		
			Type of Statement	0-1MM	1-3MM	3-5MM	5-10MM	10-25MM	25MM & OVER
11	15	15	Unqualified		1			7	7
10	2	4	Reviewed		1			1	2
3	6	4	Compiled			1			3
15	7	8	Tax Returns	1	1	1	3	2	
56	62	62	Other	3	7	4	9	10	29
4/1/16-3/31/17 ALL	4/1/17-3/31/18 ALL	4/1/18-3/31/19 ALL							
95	97	93	**NUMBER OF STATEMENTS**	4	10	6	12	20	41
%	%	%	**ASSETS**	%	%	%	%	%	%
22.4	23.6	24.7	Cash & Equivalents		42.7		31.0	21.0	19.7
42.1	39.1	32.6	Trade Receivables (net)		15.4		33.7	30.5	37.2
.3	.4	1.4	Inventory		.0		7.3	.2	.9
4.9	7.2	6.9	All Other Current		8.4		3.5	5.2	7.5
69.7	70.3	65.6	Total Current		66.5		75.5	56.9	65.4
10.0	10.4	8.7	Fixed Assets (net)		9.8		4.2	12.7	8.1
12.2	10.5	10.0	Intangibles (net)		9.3		4.6	14.3	11.7
8.1	8.8	15.7	All Other Non-Current		14.4		15.7	16.1	14.7
100.0	100.0	100.0	Total		100.0		100.0	100.0	100.0
			LIABILITIES						
15.0	15.1	7.6	Notes Payable-Short Term		7.6		14.5	3.2	4.7
1.9	2.5	1.4	Cur. Mat.-L.T.D.		2.4		1.0	.6	1.9
8.3	9.9	9.3	Trade Payables		3.3		5.0	14.8	9.1
.4	.8	.3	Income Taxes Payable		.0		.1	.2	.5
27.2	25.9	28.4	All Other Current		14.2		37.8	25.5	32.1
52.8	54.1	47.0	Total Current		27.4		58.4	44.3	48.4
11.5	11.4	6.6	Long-Term Debt		5.2		4.1	12.3	5.0
.4	.6	.3	Deferred Taxes		.0		.0	.2	.3
10.0	6.8	9.3	All Other Non-Current		3.3		42.3	4.0	6.0
25.4	27.1	36.8	Net Worth		64.0		-4.7	39.3	40.3
100.0	100.0	100.0	Total Liabilities & Net Worth		100.0		100.0	100.0	100.0
			INCOME DATA						
100.0	100.0	100.0	Net Sales		100.0		100.0	100.0	100.0
			Gross Profit						
95.7	94.7	94.1	Operating Expenses		81.5		98.5	95.6	95.4
4.3	5.3	5.9	Operating Profit		18.5		1.5	4.4	4.6
1.3	1.0	.9	All Other Expenses (net)		2.0		.4	1.1	.8
3.0	4.4	5.0	Profit Before Taxes		16.5		1.1	3.3	3.8
			RATIOS						
2.5	2.8	2.6			7.3		10.6	3.8	2.3
1.6	1.6	1.7	Current		2.3		2.1	1.8	1.6
1.1	1.0	1.0			.8		1.1	1.0	.9
2.4	2.7	2.4			7.1		7.9	3.0	2.2
1.5	1.4	1.3	Quick		1.5		1.9	1.7	1.2
1.0	.9	.8			.8		1.1	.8	.7
(9) 39.3	(9) 39.9	(5) 70.6			(0) UND		(3) 117.1	(9) 39.3	(6) 57.0
(41) 8.9	(39) 9.4	(36) 10.2	Sales/Receivables		(3) 110.6		(20) 18.7	(36) 10.0	(41) 9.0
(62) 5.9	(60) 6.1	(47) 7.7			(39) 9.3		(47) 7.8	(60) 6.1	(51) 7.1
			Cost of Sales/Inventory						
			Cost of Sales/Payables						
8.2	6.9	9.3			5.5		9.4	4.6	11.6
20.0	14.4	19.9	Sales/Working Capital		8.3		15.7	21.9	21.2
372.5	229.1	NM			-56.8		237.0	NM	-273.7
28.4	46.4	55.1						46.8	114.7
(70) 6.2	(77) 13.3	(61) 11.5	EBIT/Interest					(13) 5.8	(30) 20.3
1.7	1.9	1.0						-1.4	2.8
6.0			Net Profit + Depr., Dep.,						
(10) 2.7			Amort./Cur. Mat. L/T/D						
.4									
.1	.0	.0			.0		.0	.0	.0
.3	.2	.1	Fixed/Worth		.1		.1	.3	.2
0.1	5.2	1.0			NM		-.3	2.1	.9
.9	.6	.4			.2		.3	.4	.7
2.7	2.1	1.5	Debt/Worth		.6		2.5	1.6	1.8
UND	NM	11.8			NM		-6.8	19.5	11.5
88.8	98.6	72.3	% Profit Before Taxes/Tangible					111.4	62.0
(72) 41.9	(73) 35.8	(75) 29.8	Net Worth					(16) 19.4	(34) 40.7
15.7	12.5	11.4						-4.3	21.0
24.2	29.2	27.9	% Profit Before Taxes/Total		85.4		16.3	30.1	29.0
10.8	12.8	11.5	Assets		44.3		8.2	8.5	12.2
1.6	2.7	2.4			5.3		-.3	-3.2	4.1
506.5	613.5	999.8			UND		732.1	856.7	921.4
76.1	148.4	142.2	Sales/Net Fixed Assets		211.9		154.7	78.4	146.5
28.2	32.9	34.2			10.9		127.0	23.7	32.0
6.9	6.7	7.2			5.3		11.4	4.6	10.6
3.7	3.7	3.9	Sales/Total Assets		2.6		5.7	1.9	4.7
2.0	1.8	1.7			1.3		3.8	1.1	2.8
.2	.1	.1						.2	.1
(52) .6	(51) .4	(46) .4	% Depr., Dep., Amort./Sales					(12) 1.1	(23) .6
1.6	1.9	2.0						2.1	2.1
6.4	4.1	2.2							
(24) 10.6	(19) 6.5	(17) 4.0	% Officers', Directors' Owners' Comp/Sales						
15.8	15.6	7.5							
4299633M	5833815M	6554911M	Net Sales ($)	1780M	21361M	22852M	88167M	324614M	6096137M
1832600M	1604592M	1837389M	Total Assets ($)	422M	10069M	5962M	18300M	302053M	1500583M

M = $ thousand   MM = $ million
See Pages viii through xx for Explanation of Ratios and Data

Current Data Sorted by Assets   Comparative Historical Data

Type of Statement

Type of Statement	0-500M	500M-2MM	2-10MM	10-50MM	50-100MM	100-250MM	4/1/14-3/31/15 ALL	4/1/15-3/31/16 ALL
Unqualified			6	10	6		32	27
Reviewed	1	1	10	12	1		28	25
Compiled	2	4	12	2			22	31
Tax Returns	21	9	6	4			54	61
Other	23	40	53	36	13	10	168	176
		25 (4/1-9/30/18)		257 (10/1/18-3/31/19)				

Main Data

	0-500M	500M-2MM	2-10MM	10-50MM	50-100MM	100-250MM		4/1/14-3/31/15 ALL	4/1/15-3/31/16 ALL
NUMBER OF STATEMENTS	47	54	87	64	20	10		304	320
	%	%	%	%	%	%	**ASSETS**	%	%
	37.6	25.2	18.1	14.8	9.5	15.1	Cash & Equivalents	21.2	24.8
	18.3	30.0	42.6	39.3	29.8	29.2	Trade Receivables (net)	32.4	32.6
	.0	1.8	4.3	4.3	3.9	.3	Inventory	3.8	3.5
	3.1	7.5	4.5	5.7	8.6	3.8	All Other Current	6.8	5.5
	59.1	64.5	69.4	64.0	51.9	48.5	Total Current	64.3	66.4
	18.0	14.3	11.8	9.2	8.4	10.6	Fixed Assets (net)	14.2	13.1
	5.8	9.4	10.1	16.4	33.3	32.9	Intangibles (net)	10.3	8.0
	17.1	11.8	8.6	10.3	6.3	8.0	All Other Non-Current	11.3	12.5
	100.0	100.0	100.0	100.0	100.0	100.0	Total	100.0	100.0
							LIABILITIES		
	34.7	11.3	10.1	6.4	3.3	3.4	Notes Payable-Short Term	14.6	14.3
	1.7	2.5	1.9	3.1	2.0	4.3	Cur. Mat.-L.T.D.	2.9	3.3
	6.0	7.2	16.6	14.3	15.3	9.0	Trade Payables	14.2	15.9
	.0	.1	.2	.2	.5	.0	Income Taxes Payable	.3	.3
	37.5	14.9	25.6	30.1	24.4	17.0	All Other Current	21.1	18.8
	79.9	36.1	54.4	54.1	45.5	33.7	Total Current	53.2	52.6
	25.8	15.9	11.3	12.1	27.9	24.3	Long-Term Debt	12.5	14.9
	.0	.0	.0	.1	.7	.0	Deferred Taxes	.1	.1
	2.0	3.2	11.1	12.3	3.3	3.5	All Other Non-Current	8.1	7.6
	-7.7	44.8	23.3	21.3	22.6	38.5	Net Worth	26.2	24.9
	100.0	100.0	100.0	100.0	100.0	100.0	Total Liabilities & Net Worth	100.0	100.0
							INCOME DATA		
	100.0	100.0	100.0	100.0	100.0	100.0	Net Sales	100.0	100.0
							Gross Profit		
	89.0	91.1	93.1	91.1	92.3	95.9	Operating Expenses	91.3	91.6
	11.0	8.9	6.9	8.9	7.7	4.1	Operating Profit	8.7	8.4
	.4	1.5	1.0	2.2	3.7	5.2	All Other Expenses (net)	1.0	1.1
	10.6	7.4	6.0	6.6	4.0	-1.1	Profit Before Taxes	7.7	7.2
							RATIOS		
	5.8	7.8	2.1	2.0	1.5	3.1		2.7	2.6
	1.0	2.5	1.3	1.4	1.2	1.7	Current	1.4	1.4
	.4	1.0	1.0	.8	.9	.9		.9	.9
	3.4	5.7	2.0	1.6	1.2	3.0		2.3	2.3
	1.0	2.2	1.1	1.0	1.0	1.5	Quick	1.1	1.2
	.4	.7	.7	.7	.6	.8		.6	.7
	0 UND	0 UND	21 17.1	48 7.6	46 7.9	37 9.8		11 33.5	7 55.8
	0 UND	35 10.3	50 7.3	66 5.5	70 5.2	72 5.1	Sales/Receivables	42 8.6	41 8.9
	32 11.4	55 6.6	66 5.5	89 4.1	85 4.3	85 4.3		68 5.4	68 5.4
							Cost of Sales/Inventory		
							Cost of Sales/Payables		
	9.9	4.4	8.8	8.0	7.2	4.5		6.2	7.1
	345.0	12.4	20.0	16.0	21.5	9.4	Sales/Working Capital	18.0	18.1
	-22.1	NM	-109.2	-19.7	-140.2	-47.2		-53.7	-88.4
	41.7	46.6	70.0	34.2	41.5	15.3		46.8	55.7
	(25) 9.5	(34) 9.8	(67) 12.2	(51) 11.4	(18) 3.6	4.5	EBIT/Interest	(207) 12.3	(233) 12.8
	2.3	.9	2.3	3.6	.7	-2.9		1.7	2.1
				4.9				16.1	40.2
				(16) 2.6			Net Profit + Depr., Dep., Amort./Cur. Mat. L/T/D	(43) 4.0	(44) 5.5
				1.0				1.7	2.0
	.0	.0	.0	.1	.3	.2		.1	.0
	.2	.1	.3	.9	NM	.6	Fixed/Worth	.3	.3
	3.6	2.5	1.9	-.3	-.1	.0		17.6	2.4
	.2	.3	1.0	1.0	2.0	1.1		.6	.7
	.9	.8	2.8	6.0	NM	NM	Debt/Worth	2.7	2.7
	-2.3	8.3	33.0	-4.8	-1.6	-2.1		-22.3	-74.1
	256.4	120.2	152.6	95.5	118.4			115.7	110.4
	(32) 110.9	(43) 39.6	(68) 70.9	(41) 50.0	(10) 75.7		% Profit Before Taxes/Tangible Net Worth	(223) 52.9	(239) 49.0
	47.7	9.2	27.8	20.8	20.0			14.3	17.6
	136.3	46.8	40.4	28.2	18.3	21.9		36.9	32.2
	52.3	13.4	15.5	12.9	6.9	8.0	% Profit Before Taxes/Total Assets	13.8	13.5
	9.9	1.6	2.1	2.5	.2	-8.5		1.8	2.5
	UND	436.0	197.5	134.3	86.6	149.4		168.0	278.8
	135.8	54.7	70.3	57.9	23.2	62.3	Sales/Net Fixed Assets	55.1	60.7
	30.2	28.2	22.1	17.6	9.7	13.2		16.2	19.0
	18.8	4.8	4.4	3.6	2.4	2.7		4.8	5.0
	6.3	3.0	3.3	2.3	1.6	1.6	Sales/Total Assets	3.0	3.2
	3.2	2.1	2.1	1.2	.8	.4		1.8	2.0
	.4	.1	.3	.3	1.3			.4	.4
	(14) 1.0	(25) .7	(53) .7	(42) 1.0	(13) 2.1		% Depr., Dep., Amort./Sales	(172) .8	(182) 1.0
	2.6	3.3	1.9	1.7	5.1			2.5	2.3
	4.6	2.8	2.0	.8				2.7	3.0
	(25) 8.1	(28) 4.5	(16) 4.8	(12) 2.4			% Officers', Directors' Owners' Comp/Sales	(95) 5.0	(101) 5.1
	20.0	8.2	7.2	4.9				11.6	7.8
	99893M	233325M	1546662M	3406753M	2654510M	4113096M	Net Sales ($)	10377849M	9393219M
	9816M	58139M	443241M	1516338M	1448175M	1525555M	Total Assets ($)	5550002M	4426576M

M = $ thousand   MM = $ million
See Pages viii through xx for Explanation of Ratios and Data

Comparative Historical Data | Current Data Sorted by Sales

			Type of Statement						
26	29	23	Unqualified		2			5	16
23	28	23	Reviewed					5	15
21	21	21	Compiled	1	3	3	4	6	4
44	50	40	Tax Returns	10	8	7	5	7	3
157	146	175	Other	15	31	9	27	34	59
4/1/16-3/31/17 ALL	4/1/17-3/31/18 ALL	4/1/18-3/31/19 ALL		25 (4/1-9/30/18)			257 (10/1/18-3/31/19)		
				0-1MM	1-3MM	3-5MM	5-10MM	10-25MM	25MM & OVER
271	274	282	NUMBER OF STATEMENTS	26	44	19	39	57	97
%	%	%	ASSETS	%	%	%	%	%	%
23.3	19.5	21.2	Cash & Equivalents	32.2	22.9	34.7	22.9	20.9	14.4
31.9	33.2	34.0	Trade Receivables (net)	18.2	27.5	26.0	37.0	35.2	40.8
3.5	2.9	2.9	Inventory	.1	2.3	.5	2.4	4.5	3.7
5.3	5.8	5.4	All Other Current	4.5	2.4	7.9	6.5	5.6	5.9
64.0	61.3	63.6	Total Current	54.9	55.1	69.0	68.9	66.3	64.9
12.9	14.4	12.5	Fixed Assets (net)	19.2	17.2	12.7	11.5	10.5	9.9
13.9	14.4	13.2	Intangibles (net)	5.8	14.6	7.4	8.8	13.9	16.9
9.2	9.9	10.8	All Other Non-Current	20.1	13.0	10.8	10.8	9.3	8.3
100.0	100.0	100.0	Total	100.0	100.0	100.0	100.0	100.0	100.0
			LIABILITIES						
12.7	13.8	12.9	Notes Payable-Short Term	27.8	13.4	31.5	12.9	11.6	5.7
3.0	3.1	2.3	Cur. Mat.-L.T.D.	1.8	2.4	3.2	.7	2.1	3.0
14.6	14.0	12.1	Trade Payables	4.9	5.2	12.0	12.0	14.4	16.0
.2	.2	.2	Income Taxes Payable	.0	.1	.0	.0	.3	.3
21.7	22.2	26.2	All Other Current	41.9	19.5	25.6	31.1	25.6	23.4
52.3	53.4	53.7	Total Current	76.4	40.6	72.3	56.7	54.1	48.5
14.9	17.0	16.4	Long-Term Debt	35.4	14.3	10.8	18.0	12.1	15.3
.1	.1	.1	Deferred Taxes	.0	.0	.0	.0	.0	.2
6.9	8.7	7.5	All Other Non-Current	1.1	6.7	3.6	4.1	9.3	10.8
25.8	20.9	22.3	Net Worth	-13.0	38.4	13.3	21.3	24.5	25.3
100.0	100.0	100.0	Total Liabilities & Net Worth	100.0	100.0	100.0	100.0	100.0	100.0
			INCOME DATA						
100.0	100.0	100.0	Net Sales	100.0	100.0	100.0	100.0	100.0	100.0
			Gross Profit						
91.8	91.0	91.6	Operating Expenses	90.5	87.7	89.5	92.2	93.6	92.7
8.2	9.0	8.4	Operating Profit	9.5	12.3	10.5	7.8	6.4	7.3
1.3	2.0	1.6	All Other Expenses (net)	2.0	2.9	.6	.9	.9	1.9
6.9	7.0	6.8	Profit Before Taxes	7.5	9.4	9.9	7.0	5.5	5.4
			RATIOS						
2.4	2.1	2.7	Current	3.1	10.4	5.1	3.7	2.0	2.0
1.3	1.3	1.4		.9	1.9	1.4	1.5	1.2	1.4
.9	.8	.9		.4	.7	.7	.9	.8	1.0
2.0	1.9	2.3	Quick	2.5	10.3	4.7	3.7	1.6	1.8
1.2	1.0	1.2		.9	1.3	1.3	1.3	1.0	1.1
.7	.7	.6		.3	.4	.6	.6	.6	.8
15 24.6	13 28.7	11 32.3	Sales/Receivables	0 UND	0 UND	0 UND	21 17.4	11 32.3	40 9.2
47 7.7	44 8.3	48 7.6		0 UND	24 15.0	27 13.4	50 7.3	50 7.3	60 6.1
72 5.1	69 5.3	73 5.0		41 8.8	63 5.8	49 7.5	78 4.7	68 5.4	81 4.5
			Cost of Sales/Inventory						
			Cost of Sales/Payables						
6.4	7.8	7.3	Sales/Working Capital	5.1	5.5	6.0	6.3	12.0	7.8
20.8	23.1	20.6		-146.3	20.5	21.5	13.1	36.1	16.7
-55.7	-26.3	-41.9		-16.9	-28.4	-22.3	-207.0	-32.2	-255.1
49.0	40.7	43.6	EBIT/Interest	8.8	82.3	82.4	41.4	32.3	48.0
(195) 9.6	(203) 8.1	(205) 9.9		(12) 6.2	(25) 7.8	(14) 14.1	(29) 13.9	(41) 10.2	(84) 9.8
1.9	1.3	1.5		-.8	1.4	.7	2.9	.7	1.9
11.3	10.1	19.6	Net Profit + Depr., Dep., Amort./Cur. Mat. L/T/D						12.6
(25) 4.8	(25) 6.1	(28) 4.2						(23) 3.9	
1.8	2.8	1.0							1.8
.1	.1	.0	Fixed/Worth	.0	.0	.0	.1	.1	.1
.5	.4	.3		.1	.1	.3	.1	.7	.8
1.0	37.0	8.7		NM	1.6	17.8	2.1	-.4	-.2
.8	.9	.7	Debt/Worth	.5	.2	.3	.6	1.0	1.1
4.2	3.2	2.7		1.6	.8	2.4	1.8	3.5	3.6
-7.7	-9.3	-7.3		-2.2	18.0	112.0	33.0	-4.2	-4.5
129.3	122.6	142.6	% Profit Before Taxes/Tangible Net Worth	119.0	191.7	161.6	144.2	160.0	110.1
(186) 52.8	(188) 50.4	(199) 57.3		(17) 19.4	(34) 53.8	(16) 107.3	(30) 56.2	(38) 65.9	(64) 53.6
20.2	14.6	22.1		4.0	22.0	41.6	21.3	20.3	25.4
34.1	34.3	40.6	% Profit Before Taxes/Total Assets	79.1	55.4	60.6	48.8	42.4	28.3
11.5	13.6	14.5		6.4	19.7	23.2	35.8	14.7	12.7
1.9	1.6	2.3		-2.8	2.7	7.0	2.0	-.2	2.5
204.4	172.9	240.3	Sales/Net Fixed Assets	UND	UND	459.9	206.7	198.7	138.2
47.8	54.0	64.9		133.9	73.3	58.3	64.5	78.5	43.2
16.1	17.1	19.6		8.7	25.2	27.4	38.6	27.6	15.3
4.3	4.5	4.6	Sales/Total Assets	9.7	4.7	9.3	4.7	4.6	4.1
2.7	2.8	3.0		2.9	3.0	4.4	3.3	3.4	2.7
1.5	1.6	1.7		1.6	1.5	2.3	2.7	1.6	1.6
.3	.4	.3	% Depr., Dep., Amort./Sales		.4	.2	.2	.4	.3
(150) 1.1	(149) .9	(148) 1.0		(10)	1.1	(10) .3	(22) .8	(32) .8	(65) 1.1
2.2	2.2	2.1			3.6	2.0	1.3	1.7	2.1
2.6	3.2	3.1	% Officers', Directors' Owners' Comp/Sales	7.9	4.3	3.6	1.6	1.7	
(74) 5.0	(79) 6.7	(81) 5.2		(10) 19.4	(22) 7.3	(10) 6.3	(16) 3.6	(14) 3.7	
10.5	12.9	9.2		32.3	10.9	7.3	6.6	7.2	
11965618M	7715102M	12054239M	Net Sales ($)	12724M	85288M	78239M	292341M	987356M	10598291M
5445751M	4473755M	5001264M	Total Assets ($)	6974M	76959M	28466M	115638M	588189M	4185038M

© RMA 2019

M = $ thousand   MM = $ million
See Pages viii through xx for Explanation of Ratios and Data

Current Data Sorted by Assets   Comparative Historical Data

0-500M	500M-2MM	2-10MM	10-50MM	50-100MM	100-250MM	Type of Statement	4/1/14-3/31/15 ALL	4/1/15-3/31/16 ALL
	1	4	12	3	4	Unqualified	35	30
3	1	12	11	2		Reviewed	23	29
3	3	14	3	1		Compiled	19	19
4	6	5				Tax Returns	24	29
9	16	36	26	7	3	Other	120	121
	27 (4/1-9/30/18)		162 (10/1/18-3/31/19)					
19	27	71	52	13	7	**NUMBER OF STATEMENTS**	221	228
%	%	%	%	%	%	**ASSETS**	%	%
21.9	22.7	12.4	11.8	14.3		Cash & Equivalents	15.6	17.3
35.0	41.6	48.8	45.1	30.1		Trade Receivables (net)	39.1	36.2
5.3	3.2	4.1	2.0	14.4		Inventory	3.6	4.1
2.5	.9	4.6	6.4	10.4		All Other Current	5.0	5.6
64.6	68.4	69.8	65.3	69.1		Total Current	63.3	63.2
16.0	15.2	14.6	23.5	17.1		Fixed Assets (net)	19.8	17.8
6.8	4.9	5.9	5.6	8.8		Intangibles (net)	7.9	9.7
12.7	11.5	9.6	5.6	4.9		All Other Non-Current	8.9	9.3
100.0	100.0	100.0	100.0	100.0		Total	100.0	100.0
						LIABILITIES		
11.3	8.1	8.6	7.6	14.1		Notes Payable-Short Term	11.4	10.4
.8	2.5	2.2	2.3	2.9		Cur. Mat.-L.T.D.	2.8	2.4
20.7	26.6	18.9	24.0	17.1		Trade Payables	19.7	17.3
.0	.0	.2	.1	.0		Income Taxes Payable	.3	.3
60.2	9.3	11.9	14.7	17.9		All Other Current	15.8	16.4
93.0	46.5	41.8	48.7	52.0		Total Current	49.9	46.7
4.0	12.1	7.4	11.6	11.0		Long-Term Debt	15.3	14.9
.0	.0	.1	.4	.1		Deferred Taxes	.7	.3
5.6	4.9	4.6	3.5	6.2		All Other Non-Current	8.9	6.1
-2.6	36.5	46.1	35.8	30.7		Net Worth	25.2	32.0
100.0	100.0	100.0	100.0	100.0		Total Liabilties & Net Worth	100.0	100.0
						INCOME DATA		
100.0	100.0	100.0	100.0	100.0		Net Sales	100.0	100.0
						Gross Profit		
96.8	92.2	90.9	93.8	97.4		Operating Expenses	92.9	93.5
3.2	7.8	9.1	6.2	2.6		Operating Profit	7.1	6.5
-.1	1.6	1.7	.6	1.0		All Other Expenses (net)	1.3	.8
3.3	6.2	7.5	5.7	1.5		Profit Before Taxes	5.8	5.7
						RATIOS		
2.1	3.2	2.9	2.0	2.5			2.3	2.5
.9	1.6	1.5	1.3	1.1		Current	1.3	1.3
.5	.8	1.1	1.0	1.0			.9	.9
2.1	3.1	2.7	1.8	1.3			1.9	2.2
.9	1.4	1.3	1.2	1.0		Quick	1.1	1.1
.4	.8	1.0	.8	.5			.7	.7
0 UND	15 24.8	34 10.6	36 10.0	33 11.1			25 14.6	21 17.8
3 111.6	28 13.1	47 7.8	49 7.4	40 9.1		Sales/Receivables	43 8.5	38 9.6
47 7.8	43 8.5	73 5.0	63 5.8	79 4.6			63 5.8	60 6.1
						Cost of Sales/Inventory		
						Cost of Sales/Payables		
18.3	7.0	6.5	8.7	5.4			8.2	7.2
-176.0	22.0	13.6	22.1	19.6		Sales/Working Capital	25.4	25.1
-23.7	-36.3	75.5	774.0	295.2			-75.2	-65.6
	48.0	60.0	36.6	24.0			36.2	32.1
	(19) 16.6	(58) 17.8	(45) 8.3	(12) 5.9		EBIT/Interest	(172) 7.7	(184) 9.1
	9.0	7.5	3.2	1.5			2.6	2.4
			15.1			Net Profit + Depr., Dep.,	8.3	21.0
			(18) 4.4			Amort./Cur. Mat. L/T/D	(36) 2.5	(29) 7.6
			2.5				.6	2.4
.0	.0	.0	.2	.1			.1	.1
.2	.4	.1	.6	.4		Fixed/Worth	.6	.5
1.2	4.5	.9	1.4	3.6			5.7	4.5
.6	.5	.5	1.1	.7			.8	.8
2.5	1.9	1.2	1.7	5.3		Debt/Worth	2.7	2.6
-7.3	23.1	4.5	4.9	19.4			122.6	28.2
287.8	176.5	82.8	47.3	94.4		% Profit Before Taxes/Tangible	71.9	75.5
(12) 109.0	(21) 59.6	(66) 48.0	(48) 29.4	(11) 13.4		Net Worth	(170) 34.7	(176) 30.9
-.6	24.0	19.0	14.4	8.3			13.3	12.1
173.8	52.7	34.0	19.1	7.7		% Profit Before Taxes/Total	22.5	23.6
32.7	24.1	15.8	8.3	4.9		Assets	10.1	9.6
-10.7	5.5	8.4	4.0	.9			2.7	2.4
UND	999.8	170.7	81.2	157.1			163.5	225.2
UND	145.0	73.7	19.9	41.8		Sales/Net Fixed Assets	38.8	42.7
55.7	15.1	17.3	5.7	4.1			9.9	11.1
28.2	7.3	5.1	4.2	3.7			5.2	5.1
7.2	4.2	3.4	2.9	2.2		Sales/Total Assets	2.9	2.8
5.0	3.1	2.2	2.1	1.1			1.7	1.7
	.3	.2	.3	.1			.4	.3
	(15) .7	(51) .5	(47) 1.3	(10) .7		% Depr., Dep., Amort./Sales	(160) 1.0	(156) 1.1
	1.6	2.4	4.0	3.8			2.7	2.6
		.7					1.9	1.2
		(18) 2.9				% Officers', Directors'	(41) 4.7	(57) 2.9
		3.5				Owners' Comp/Sales	10.0	5.0
59826M	163327M	1398383M	3692073M	2646523M	1861071M	Net Sales ($)	10680873M	12493669M
3646M	31763M	373779M	1157327M	1038190M	985404M	Total Assets ($)	5016658M	5160336M

M = $ thousand   MM = $ million
See Pages viii through xx for Explanation of Ratios and Data

Comparative Historical Data | Current Data Sorted by Sales

			Type of Statement						
26	28	24	Unqualified			1	1	4	18
17	26	29	Reviewed	2	1		4	7	15
11	18	24	Compiled	1	2	1	4	8	8
16	20	15	Tax Returns	2	5	2	2	4	
103	105	97	Other	6	6	7	17	22	39
4/1/16-3/31/17 ALL	4/1/17-3/31/18 ALL	4/1/18-3/31/19 ALL		27 (4/1-9/30/18)			162 (10/1/18-3/31/19)		
				0-1MM	1-3MM	3-5MM	5-10MM	10-25MM	25MM & OVER
173	197	189	NUMBER OF STATEMENTS	11	14	11	28	45	80
%	%	%	ASSETS	%	%	%	%	%	%
16.0	16.1	14.4	Cash & Equivalents	17.0	14.5	37.3	15.1	13.9	11.0
40.2	43.3	43.0	Trade Receivables (net)	16.3	36.6	35.1	43.6	44.9	47.6
4.5	3.9	4.3	Inventory	9.1	.8	.1	5.7	2.9	5.0
3.5	4.8	4.7	All Other Current	.1	2.3	.5	2.0	6.8	6.0
64.2	68.1	66.4	Total Current	42.4	54.2	73.0	66.5	68.5	69.6
18.2	16.4	17.8	Fixed Assets (net)	37.7	26.4	11.1	14.1	15.4	17.2
9.3	8.1	7.3	Intangibles (net)	7.6	.6	11.2	6.1	7.7	8.0
8.3	7.4	8.5	All Other Non-Current	12.3	18.9	4.7	13.3	8.3	5.2
100.0	100.0	100.0	Total	100.0	100.0	100.0	100.0	100.0	100.0
			LIABILITIES						
10.7	11.3	8.7	Notes Payable-Short Term	9.1	10.7	8.9	5.9	9.5	8.9
2.7	2.1	2.2	Cur. Mat.-L.T.D.	3.1	.4	2.8	2.2	2.2	2.4
18.6	20.4	21.4	Trade Payables	7.4	24.0	29.2	16.5	19.0	24.9
.3	.2	.1	Income Taxes Payable	.0	.0	.0	.0	.3	.1
13.2	17.4	17.3	All Other Current	92.3	10.1	11.9	10.9	14.0	13.1
45.5	51.4	49.8	Total Current	111.9	45.2	52.7	35.4	45.0	49.4
14.5	10.2	10.2	Long-Term Debt	22.4	14.0	6.7	5.8	6.6	12.0
.4	.4	.2	Deferred Taxes	.0	.0	.0	.0	.4	.1
7.1	4.9	4.4	All Other Non-Current	.0	11.4	3.0	7.5	3.1	3.6
32.5	33.2	35.4	Net Worth	-34.3	29.5	37.7	51.3	44.9	34.9
100.0	100.0	100.0	Total Liabilities & Net Worth	100.0	100.0	100.0	100.0	100.0	100.0
			INCOME DATA						
100.0	100.0	100.0	Net Sales	100.0	100.0	100.0	100.0	100.0	100.0
			Gross Profit						
92.8	93.7	93.2	Operating Expenses	84.5	85.6	94.7	92.1	95.0	94.8
7.2	6.3	6.8	Operating Profit	15.5	14.4	5.3	7.9	5.0	5.2
1.6	1.2	1.2	All Other Expenses (net)	13.1	1.3	.2	.2	.2	.6
5.6	5.1	5.6	Profit Before Taxes	2.4	13.1	5.1	7.7	4.8	4.6
			RATIOS						
2.4	2.3	2.7		.8	3.2	3.1	3.5	2.1	2.1
1.4	1.4	1.3	Current	.4	1.0	1.6	2.4	1.5	1.3
1.0	.9	1.0		.1	.7	.8	1.2	1.0	1.1
2.2	2.2	2.2		.8	3.2	2.9	3.3	2.1	1.8
1.2	1.2	1.2	Quick	.4	1.0	1.6	2.0	1.2	1.2
.8	.7	.8		.0	.5	.8	1.1	.8	.8
33 11.0	27 13.6	29 12.6		0 UND	5 67.0	0 UND	35 10.4	26 14.0	33 10.9
47 7.8	43 8.5	45 8.2	Sales/Receivables	0 UND	33 11.2	20 18.0	46 8.0	45 8.1	49 7.5
66 5.5	64 5.7	61 6.0		29 12.7	51 7.2	47 7.7	89 4.1	63 5.8	63 5.8
			Cost of Sales/Inventory						
			Cost of Sales/Payables						
7.3	7.2	8.3		-176.0	7.1	10.7	4.4	8.9	8.7
18.4	19.4	22.0	Sales/Working Capital	-7.5	NM	22.0	9.7	16.6	22.7
-601.2	-149.9	-523.0		-2.4	-45.0	-20.0	25.3	279.0	90.9
28.4	42.3	42.1					65.8	44.1	35.6
(140) 7.8	(141) 10.0	(148) 13.4	EBIT/Interest				(22) 19.0	(37) 14.4	(72) 7.7
2.0	1.5	4.1					11.0	3.9	2.6
9.1	11.4	13.5	Net Profit + Depr., Dep.,						17.7
(28) 2.4	(25) 4.1	(30) 4.0	Amort./Cur. Mat. L/T/D						(21) 4.8
1.3	1.6	2.3							2.5
.1	.1	.1		.0	.0	.0	.0	.1	.1
.5	.3	.4	Fixed/Worth	.5	.8	.1	.2	.3	.4
4.2	2.5	1.5		3.7	6.0	4.6	.5	1.0	1.6
.8	.7	.7		1.6	.5	.5	.5	.8	.9
2.4	2.5	1.9	Debt/Worth	3.0	2.5	1.3	.9	1.7	2.1
29.4	19.6	6.8		-3.6	NM	-3.6	4.0	4.6	9.3
77.3	75.7	89.5	% Profit Before Taxes/Tangible		193.2		73.5	67.7	66.2
(133) 27.7	(157) 38.6	(161) 38.5	Net Worth		(11) 57.2		(27) 31.5	(41) 44.2	(67) 29.7
9.0	11.6	14.9			12.5		15.4	30.2	13.4
18.5	24.1	28.7	% Profit Before Taxes/Total	30.8	70.8	65.6	27.5	30.9	19.1
7.0	9.3	12.8	Assets	.4	22.0	52.7	15.9	14.8	8.3
1.7	2.2	4.3		-.4	2.3	12.0	8.5	5.6	3.6
209.1	277.6	243.0		UND	UND	UND	208.7	236.5	134.0
40.2	61.8	56.7	Sales/Net Fixed Assets	8.6	205.3	734.7	46.7	81.2	41.8
10.7	13.5	12.9		.1	6.4	33.0	13.4	16.8	10.3
4.6	5.2	5.2		7.2	6.8	7.4	3.5	5.4	4.6
2.9	3.2	3.4	Sales/Total Assets	1.1	4.5	6.9	2.8	3.6	3.5
1.6	1.8	2.2		.1	.9	3.3	1.9	2.3	2.3
.4	.2	.3					.4	.2	.2
(111) 1.1	(119) .9	(128) .7	% Depr., Dep., Amort./Sales				(20) .9	(29) .7	(65) .5
2.8	2.4	2.5					2.7	3.0	1.7
1.0	1.0	.8						2.1	.3
(31) 2.6	(37) 3.2	(39) 3.0	% Officers', Directors' Owners' Comp/Sales					(13) 3.0	(11) .6
5.2	7.0	6.1						10.7	2.8
12861999M	9110780M	9821203M	Net Sales ($)	4087M	26664M	43717M	212044M	758803M	8775888M
5216334M	3862697M	3590109M	Total Assets ($)	11917M	36911M	8672M	91187M	262887M	3178535M

M = $ thousand   MM = $ million
See Pages viii through xx for Explanation of Ratios and Data

Current Data Sorted by Assets   Comparative Historical Data

Type of Statement	0-500M	500M-2MM	2-10MM	10-50MM	50-100MM	100-250MM	4/1/14-3/31/15 ALL	4/1/15-3/31/16 ALL
Unqualified	1	6	8	21	9	7	51	45
Reviewed		4	14	9	1		45	44
Compiled		4	10	2		2	39	30
Tax Returns	16	14	13	1		2	60	62
Other	22	48	72	36	5	13	242	228
		26 (4/1-9/30/18)		312 (10/1/18-3/31/19)				
NUMBER OF STATEMENTS	39	76	117	69	15	22	437	409
ASSETS	%	%	%	%	%	%	%	%
Cash & Equivalents	37.8	23.6	18.3	21.8	14.2	8.5	23.8	22.9
Trade Receivables (net)	23.7	39.6	41.4	39.4	26.5	27.3	37.5	35.5
Inventory	1.7	3.3	2.6	2.5	9.1	2.5	2.4	2.1
All Other Current	6.6	3.9	6.7	7.4	10.2	7.6	4.8	6.0
Total Current	69.8	70.5	69.0	71.1	59.9	46.0	68.6	66.5
Fixed Assets (net)	12.1	19.4	11.8	9.9	7.3	15.6	14.5	15.2
Intangibles (net)	4.4	2.8	10.1	10.8	27.9	32.6	6.1	7.9
All Other Non-Current	13.7	7.3	9.2	8.2	4.9	5.8	10.8	10.4
Total	100.0	100.0	100.0	100.0	100.0	100.0	100.0	100.0
LIABILITIES								
Notes Payable-Short Term	30.3	12.2	11.0	8.5	8.6	1.2	12.4	11.9
Cur. Mat.-L.T.D.	4.1	2.4	1.7	3.1	1.5	3.5	1.9	1.9
Trade Payables	4.6	11.2	10.0	10.4	14.0	6.6	10.4	9.7
Income Taxes Payable	.0	.2	.0	.2	.2	.0	.2	.3
All Other Current	26.1	21.0	18.4	22.4	13.3	17.1	17.5	20.5
Total Current	65.2	46.9	41.1	44.7	37.4	28.4	42.4	44.3
Long-Term Debt	13.9	17.2	12.3	8.2	20.1	25.8	11.2	12.8
Deferred Taxes	.0	.1	.2	.2	.0	.6	.2	.3
All Other Non-Current	9.8	4.1	5.0	8.8	11.2	7.8	7.5	6.3
Net Worth	11.2	31.7	41.4	38.0	31.2	37.4	38.7	36.3
Total Liabilities & Net Worth	100.0	100.0	100.0	100.0	100.0	100.0	100.0	100.0
INCOME DATA								
Net Sales	100.0	100.0	100.0	100.0	100.0	100.0	100.0	100.0
Gross Profit								
Operating Expenses	85.7	89.3	88.9	89.4	101.3	86.1	87.6	88.4
Operating Profit	14.3	10.7	11.1	10.6	-1.3	13.9	12.4	11.6
All Other Expenses (net)	1.5	2.1	1.1	2.2	2.2	5.4	1.9	2.4
Profit Before Taxes	12.8	8.6	9.9	8.4	-3.5	8.5	10.5	9.2
RATIOS								
Current	3.7	3.8	3.6	3.6	2.5	2.1	3.7	3.8
	1.8	1.6	1.8	1.9	1.5	1.7	1.8	1.9
	.5	.7	1.2	1.2	.9	1.2	1.0	1.1
Quick	3.0	3.5	3.0	3.1	2.2	1.8	3.4	3.5
	1.6	1.4	1.6	1.6	1.1	1.3	1.6	1.6
	.4	.6	.9	1.0	.5	.7	.9	.9
Sales/Receivables	0 UND	1 249.6	27 13.6	28 12.9	46 8.0	41 8.8	8 46.1	7 56.0
	1 611.0	35 10.5	47 7.7	57 6.4	68 5.4	72 5.1	43 8.4	43 8.4
	35 10.5	54 6.7	76 4.8	83 4.4	78 4.7	83 4.4	73 5.0	70 5.2
Cost of Sales/Inventory								
Cost of Sales/Payables								
Sales/Working Capital	8.6	7.2	5.0	4.3	4.3	5.2	5.4	5.0
	30.5	17.1	10.3	8.0	9.8	8.0	12.0	10.7
	-9.7	-41.1	42.6	25.6	-24.7	26.8	231.6	82.4
EBIT/Interest	43.5	30.7	46.6	32.9	12.0	4.3	64.0	53.1
	(21) 9.0	(51) 10.6	(79) 9.7	(51) 8.2	(13) 4.9	(19) 3.3	(293) 16.1	(282) 14.0
	3.0	2.6	2.9	2.6	.6	2.1	3.1	2.4
Net Profit + Depr., Dep., Amort./Cur. Mat. L/T/D				7.1			18.9	13.0
				(10) 4.0			(32) 3.7	(33) 3.3
				1.2			1.6	1.1
Fixed/Worth	.0	.0	.0	.0	.1	.4	.0	.0
	.2	.2	.1	.1	2.8	-1.9	.2	.2
	-3.8	2.0	1.6	.9	-.2	-.2	1.0	1.5
Debt/Worth	.7	.4	.5	.6	1.0	1.4	.5	.5
	1.7	1.6	1.2	1.7	69.4	-9.5	1.4	1.4
	-3.7	13.3	10.9	7.2	-1.8	-3.0	8.0	7.0
% Profit Before Taxes/Tangible Net Worth	318.5	143.2	78.3	63.1		55.9	106.6	78.9
	(27) 127.6	(59) 56.1	(97) 45.5	(58) 31.5		(10) 21.6	(374) 47.5	(337) 34.9
	58.8	21.6	12.3	14.3		11.8	13.0	5.4
% Profit Before Taxes/Total Assets	108.6	45.6	37.3	27.9	5.1	9.1	44.3	38.4
	43.6	22.1	14.4	12.4	1.8	4.9	16.5	13.6
	10.5	7.1	4.1	4.8	-2.8	2.7	3.6	1.6
Sales/Net Fixed Assets	UND	983.3	591.1	164.4	140.9	41.6	302.1	305.5
	263.5	72.1	87.9	47.1	20.1	20.4	60.1	66.9
	72.8	15.9	24.3	22.2	17.4	6.0	19.0	17.8
Sales/Total Assets	11.3	6.3	4.2	3.3	2.7	1.9	5.2	5.0
	5.6	4.4	3.0	2.2	1.5	1.2	3.1	3.0
	2.2	2.3	2.2	1.6	1.0	.8	1.8	1.6
% Depr., Dep., Amort./Sales		.2	.2	.4	.3	1.1	.3	.3
	(30) .6	(67) .7	(49) .8	(11) .7		(11) 2.1	(250) .8	(252) .7
		3.4	1.8	2.5	2.0	4.0	1.9	1.6
% Officers', Directors' Owners' Comp/Sales	6.9	3.8	2.1	1.3			2.5	2.3
	(14) 12.0	(22) 5.6	(26) 3.7	(12) 4.4			(113) 6.0	(116) 5.5
	18.6	11.5	8.1	8.8			14.1	13.6
Net Sales ($)	64287M	542302M	1908959M	3204743M	1626625M	4625228M	14483438M	12726345M
Total Assets ($)	9113M	87169M	583668M	1435052M	1028395M	3594280M	6631368M	6198950M

© RMA 2019

M = $ thousand   MM = $ million
See Pages viii through xx for Explanation of Ratios and Data

Comparative Historical Data | Current Data Sorted by Sales

34	42	52	Type of Statement						

34	42	52	Unqualified		2	4	2	12	32
35	41	28	Reviewed			1	6	13	8
17	25	18	Compiled			1	6	6	5
61	53	44	Tax Returns	15	8	4	10	5	2
215	227	196	Other	21	21	11	28	58	57
4/1/16-3/31/17 ALL	4/1/17-3/31/18 ALL	4/1/18-3/31/19 ALL		0-1MM	26 (4/1-9/30/18) 1-3MM	3-5MM	312 (10/1/18-3/31/19) 5-10MM	10-25MM	25MM & OVER
362	388	338	NUMBER OF STATEMENTS	36	32	20	52	94	104
%	%	%	ASSETS	%	%	%	%	%	%
24.1	23.3	21.6	Cash & Equivalents	19.9	39.4	18.7	19.3	21.5	18.6
35.1	36.5	37.0	Trade Receivables (net)	15.4	29.4	35.2	44.7	41.5	39.1
1.5	2.1	2.9	Inventory	2.7	3.5	5.0	2.9	1.9	3.4
4.8	7.2	6.4	All Other Current	4.0	7.0	3.9	4.2	7.4	7.8
65.5	69.1	68.0	Total Current	42.0	79.3	62.7	71.1	72.3	69.0
15.2	12.4	13.2	Fixed Assets (net)	38.2	11.8	14.6	12.2	8.6	9.4
10.1	9.9	10.2	Intangibles (net)	5.3	3.1	8.2	8.9	11.0	14.3
9.1	8.6	8.7	All Other Non-Current	14.5	5.8	14.5	7.8	8.2	7.3
100.0	100.0	100.0	Total	100.0	100.0	100.0	100.0	100.0	100.0
			LIABILITIES						
15.1	13.2	12.2	Notes Payable-Short Term	16.8	18.5	17.3	10.4	11.8	9.0
2.4	2.1	2.5	Cur. Mat.-L.T.D.	4.9	1.8	3.6	1.9	2.0	2.6
9.6	10.9	9.7	Trade Payables	4.6	9.2	7.7	10.3	9.0	12.3
.1	.4	.1	Income Taxes Payable	.0	.0	.4	.1	.1	.1
18.8	21.8	20.4	All Other Current	14.3	26.6	14.9	19.5	19.4	22.8
46.0	48.4	44.9	Total Current	40.6	56.1	43.9	42.2	42.5	46.7
14.8	15.2	14.0	Long-Term Debt	33.3	7.9	14.0	11.3	10.7	13.5
.2	.1	.2	Deferred Taxes	.2	.0	.5	.1	.2	.3
6.2	8.0	6.6	All Other Non-Current	8.7	5.1	13.4	6.9	3.1	7.9
32.8	28.3	34.3	Net Worth	17.2	30.9	28.2	39.5	43.5	31.6
100.0	100.0	100.0	Total Liabilties & Net Worth	100.0	100.0	100.0	100.0	100.0	100.0
			INCOME DATA						
100.0	100.0	100.0	Net Sales	100.0	100.0	100.0	100.0	100.0	100.0
			Gross Profit						
88.7	89.4	89.1	Operating Expenses	72.4	87.6	93.8	90.5	90.6	92.4
11.3	10.6	10.9	Operating Profit	27.6	12.4	6.2	9.5	9.4	7.6
2.0	1.7	1.9	All Other Expenses (net)	5.0	2.3	.9	1.1	1.2	2.0
9.3	9.0	9.0	Profit Before Taxes	22.6	10.1	5.4	8.4	8.2	5.6
			RATIOS						
3.0	3.0	3.3		2.4	3.8	5.4	4.9	3.9	2.3
1.6	1.7	1.7	Current	1.2	2.3	1.5	1.8	1.9	1.6
1.0	1.0	1.1		.2	1.2	.7	1.1	1.2	1.1
2.9	2.7	3.0		2.1	3.1	5.0	4.8	3.2	2.1
1.4	1.4	1.5	Quick	.6	2.2	1.3	1.5	1.8	1.3
.9	.9	.8		.1	.8	.7	.7	1.1	.9
9 42.1	8 47.3	13 28.9		0 UND	0 UND	12 31.6	14 25.4	30 12.1	36 10.0
42 8.7	44 8.3	44 8.3	Sales/Receivables	0 UND	22 16.7	26 14.1	38 9.7	49 7.5	58 6.3
68 5.4	72 5.1	73 5.0		46 8.0	69 5.3	56 6.5	61 6.0	76 4.8	78 4.7
			Cost of Sales/Inventory						
			Cost of Sales/Payables						
6.0	5.5	5.1		2.4	4.9	6.9	7.8	4.6	5.3
13.4	12.7	12.0	Sales/Working Capital	NM	8.5	15.2	14.5	9.6	11.7
-325.1	253.3	144.8		-2.5	39.3	-32.4	140.0	30.7	42.9
50.0	41.1	33.5		19.9	58.9	11.6	42.2	53.5	31.0
(249) 10.1	(240) 9.6	(234) 8.1	EBIT/Interest	(19) 3.6	(18) 15.1	(14) 5.6	(36) 12.5	(66) 8.5	(81) 6.3
1.4	2.0	2.5		3.0	3.8	.8	3.0	2.3	2.6
10.6	6.8	6.9							10.7
(30) 3.8	(29) 3.0	(27) 3.8	Net Profit + Depr., Dep., Amort./Cur. Mat. L/T/D					(17)	3.9
.6	1.0	.8							1.1
.0	.0	.0		.0	.0	.0	.0	.0	.1
.2	.2	.2	Fixed/Worth	1.9	.2	.3	.2	.1	.3
1.6	5.1	4.4		UND	2.7	NM	2.4	.0	2.1
.6	.6	.6		1.1	.4	.5	.3	.4	.9
1.6	1.9	1.6	Debt/Worth	4.6	1.0	2.4	1.6	1.1	2.2
18.4	174.1	78.5		-10.7	25.9	-9.5	13.2	7.3	-13.8
88.4	105.1	97.2		209.6	127.5	145.8	95.0	89.6	76.5
(284) 41.2	(292) 35.5	(259) 43.9	% Profit Before Taxes/Tangible Net Worth	(25) 51.6	(25) 75.2	(14) 55.5	(40) 54.7	(81) 43.8	(74) 32.3
8.1	11.6	14.4		11.1	27.6	13.8	22.2	7.9	13.0
34.4	35.8	36.4		33.9	75.7	34.8	52.6	32.9	24.2
11.6	11.6	14.1	% Profit Before Taxes/Total Assets	9.9	29.7	14.6	27.6	14.1	9.1
2.1	2.0	4.0		4.6	1.1	6.0	6.7	2.2	3.7
266.2	413.7	507.9		UND	897.7	983.3	853.8	752.1	199.3
68.7	72.8	69.3	Sales/Net Fixed Assets	12.5	81.6	69.2	81.7	105.1	41.7
18.3	18.8	19.5		.4	22.9	16.6	23.5	32.0	19.8
4.8	4.9	4.7		4.5	5.5	5.9	6.5	4.2	3.8
3.1	2.9	2.9	Sales/Total Assets	.7	4.0	3.9	4.4	2.9	2.6
1.6	1.6	1.8		.2	2.5	2.2	2.2	2.0	1.5
.3	.2	.3		3.8	.4		.3	.2	.3
(202) .8	(211) .7	(175) .8	% Depr., Dep., Amort./Sales	(12) 10.4	(11) 1.2		(21) .7	(54) .7	(68) .7
2.1	1.9	2.2		23.5	3.2		4.7	1.5	2.0
2.6	2.8	2.5			7.5		2.5	2.0	.9
(95) 4.7	(102) 7.3	(77) 5.4	% Officers', Directors' Owners' Comp/Sales		(10) 11.8		(17) 4.3	(21) 4.5	(14) 3.2
11.3	13.1	11.3			16.1			8.4	6.6
13141820M	18009724M	11972144M	Net Sales ($)	16703M	65595M	75763M	384035M	1516148M	9913900M
6949168M	6977089M	6737677M	Total Assets ($)	40364M	24570M	28391M	176656M	1034524M	5433172M

M = $ thousand   MM = $ million
See Pages viii through xx for Explanation of Ratios and Data

Current Data Sorted by Assets | Comparative Historical Data

0-500M	500M-2MM	2-10MM	10-50MM	50-100MM	100-250MM	Type of Statement	4/1/14-3/31/15 ALL	4/1/15-3/31/16 ALL
	1	8	9		1	Unqualified	21	22
1		14	8		1	Reviewed	26	29
2	2	10				Compiled	16	12
11	14	4	1			Tax Returns	39	33
9	27	34	19	3	3	Other	73	96
	17 (4/1-9/30/18)		165 (10/1/18-3/31/19)					
23	44	70	37	3	5	**NUMBER OF STATEMENTS**	175	192
%	%	%	%	%	%	**ASSETS**	%	%
24.3	14.1	13.0	7.6			Cash & Equivalents	15.9	16.6
24.9	40.8	45.6	45.9			Trade Receivables (net)	39.0	42.1
1.9	.9	1.2	1.8			Inventory	2.6	2.3
5.9	2.9	8.5	9.4			All Other Current	7.1	5.4
56.9	58.7	68.3	64.6			Total Current	64.6	66.5
31.1	28.6	18.0	15.9			Fixed Assets (net)	23.3	19.7
5.4	2.9	3.7	13.1			Intangibles (net)	5.6	6.0
6.7	9.8	10.0	6.4			All Other Non-Current	6.5	7.8
100.0	100.0	100.0	100.0			Total	100.0	100.0
						LIABILITIES		
17.2	12.6	7.9	4.3			Notes Payable-Short Term	11.1	10.5
7.1	3.7	3.6	2.8			Cur. Mat.-L.T.D.	3.8	3.1
12.3	11.5	13.9	12.5			Trade Payables	11.1	12.0
.1	.0	.6	.5			Income Taxes Payable	.5	.7
16.7	10.3	11.4	13.7			All Other Current	12.0	15.3
53.4	38.2	37.4	33.9			Total Current	38.7	41.7
34.2	19.7	14.8	12.6			Long-Term Debt	14.6	15.4
.5	.7	.6	1.0			Deferred Taxes	.3	.5
3.6	8.4	3.5	2.7			All Other Non-Current	4.6	4.5
8.4	33.0	43.8	49.8			Net Worth	41.8	38.0
100.0	100.0	100.0	100.0			Total Liabilities & Net Worth	100.0	100.0
						INCOME DATA		
100.0	100.0	100.0	100.0			Net Sales	100.0	100.0
						Gross Profit		
86.4	89.1	93.2	91.0			Operating Expenses	92.9	91.5
13.6	10.9	6.8	9.0			Operating Profit	7.1	8.5
2.9	3.7	.8	1.3			All Other Expenses (net)	1.3	1.6
10.7	7.2	6.0	7.7			Profit Before Taxes	5.9	6.9
						RATIOS		
2.8	3.2	3.2	2.6				3.5	3.0
1.3	1.8	1.9	2.0			Current	1.8	1.9
.7	.8	1.2	1.6				1.1	1.2
2.5	3.2	2.9	2.2				3.1	2.8
1.3	1.8	1.6	1.7			Quick	1.5	1.6
.3	.6	1.0	1.3				.9	1.0
0 UND	11 32.7	42 8.6	50 7.3				33 11.1	35 10.3
0 UND	49 7.4	73 5.0	85 4.3			Sales/Receivables	61 6.0	60 6.1
63 5.8	68 5.4	99 3.7	99 3.7				89 4.1	87 4.2
						Cost of Sales/Inventory		
						Cost of Sales/Payables		
12.3	6.9	4.4	4.7				4.8	5.3
61.9	13.0	7.0	6.0			Sales/Working Capital	8.8	9.1
-35.5	NM	20.5	10.3				30.4	39.3
61.8	27.4	38.6	42.6				45.8	51.2
(14) 9.6	(28) 9.1	(60) 13.5	(33) 14.8			EBIT/Interest	(143) 10.8	(158) 13.8
-.1	4.1	2.4	4.1				1.9	2.9
			21.7				6.0	9.3
			(10) 5.8			Net Profit + Depr., Dep., Amort./Cur. Mat. L/T/D	(24) 1.9	(25) 4.3
			1.5				.4	1.7
.1	.1	.1	.1				.1	.1
3.0	.4	.4	.3			Fixed/Worth	.4	.3
UND	3.3	.8	1.3				1.5	1.3
1.7	.6	.5	.6				.5	.5
6.6	2.0	1.2	1.5			Debt/Worth	1.2	1.3
-6.4	8.1	2.8	2.5				3.8	4.5
570.1	104.2	51.5	53.9				61.5	61.1
(17) 100.0	(37) 43.0	(63) 24.3	(32) 25.1			% Profit Before Taxes/Tangible Net Worth	(151) 28.4	(162) 29.6
25.5	15.0	8.7	9.1				6.2	8.9
76.9	35.8	23.3	19.0				27.0	25.9
23.3	14.9	12.0	8.8			% Profit Before Taxes/Total Assets	10.4	11.9
-.4	3.6	3.0	2.9				1.3	2.0
343.6	115.5	58.3	73.2				47.9	75.3
17.7	24.7	17.6	24.2			Sales/Net Fixed Assets	20.4	25.1
6.4	7.6	7.6	3.7				6.8	7.4
6.6	4.5	3.2	2.6				3.7	3.8
3.6	3.1	2.5	1.9			Sales/Total Assets	2.4	2.5
1.8	1.8	1.7	1.3				1.7	1.6
.7	.4	.7	.3				.8	.7
(12) 4.1	(26) 2.2	(56) 1.7	(33) .9			% Depr., Dep., Amort./Sales	(133) 1.5	(128) 1.8
8.4	8.6	3.7	3.8				3.0	3.8
7.2	3.6	5.1					3.5	3.4
(13) 14.4	(18) 6.6	(18) 7.1				% Officers', Directors' Owners' Comp/Sales	(65) 6.3	(56) 6.3
21.2	9.8	9.8					14.8	13.7
23005M	157390M	885584M	1661986M	400722M	953029M	Net Sales ($)	3832344M	3590863M
5831M	48131M	350828M	882129M	254539M	863399M	Total Assets ($)	1718566M	1952704M

M = $ thousand   MM = $ million
See Pages viii through xx for Explanation of Ratios and Data

Comparative Historical Data | Current Data Sorted by Sales

				Type of Statement	17 (4/1-9/30/18)			165 (10/1/18-3/31/19)		
	17	13	19	Unqualified	1			4	4	10
	28	24	24	Reviewed		1		6	8	9
	9	7	14	Compiled		3	1	7	3	
	32	22	30	Tax Returns	10	9	5	3	2	1
	72	82	95	Other	9	16	12	17	18	23
	4/1/16-3/31/17 ALL	4/1/17-3/31/18 ALL	4/1/18-3/31/19 ALL		0-1MM	1-3MM	3-5MM	5-10MM	10-25MM	25MM & OVER
	158	148	182	**NUMBER OF STATEMENTS**	20	29	18	37	35	43
	%	%	%	**ASSETS**	%	%	%	%	%	%
	16.3	16.2	13.2	Cash & Equivalents	12.3	19.1	17.5	14.5	8.9	10.3
	38.2	40.4	41.2	Trade Receivables (net)	24.5	28.4	36.2	45.2	54.7	45.4
	2.4	1.9	1.6	Inventory	2.1	.3	1.6	1.0	2.1	2.1
	5.3	6.7	7.3	All Other Current	4.4	7.6	4.0	4.8	7.7	11.8
	62.3	65.2	63.3	Total Current	43.3	55.4	59.3	65.6	73.4	69.6
	22.3	21.0	21.3	Fixed Assets (net)	44.5	24.2	22.2	21.6	16.7	11.7
	6.4	6.0	6.9	Intangibles (net)	5.5	4.0	4.1	5.9	4.2	13.8
	9.0	7.7	8.5	All Other Non-Current	6.9	16.4	14.5	7.0	5.8	4.8
	100.0	100.0	100.0	Total	100.0	100.0	100.0	100.0	100.0	100.0
				LIABILITIES						
	9.5	10.5	9.1	Notes Payable-Short Term	9.6	11.3	24.3	8.6	5.6	4.5
	4.0	5.0	3.8	Cur. Mat.-L.T.D.	9.2	3.2	.5	3.6	4.8	2.3
	11.0	12.1	12.6	Trade Payables	11.4	8.3	5.6	14.5	16.9	13.7
	.7	.7	.4	Income Taxes Payable	.1	.0	.9	.3	.3	.7
	12.7	15.5	12.9	All Other Current	6.2	13.3	15.7	9.2	12.0	18.5
	38.0	43.8	38.8	Total Current	36.5	36.2	47.0	36.3	39.6	39.7
	17.3	17.4	18.2	Long-Term Debt	42.8	22.5	9.9	21.6	8.4	12.2
	.5	.5	.7	Deferred Taxes	.6	1.0	.0	.1	1.0	1.0
	2.5	6.8	4.4	All Other Non-Current	4.5	7.2	8.5	4.1	2.8	2.4
	41.7	31.5	38.0	Net Worth	15.9	33.1	34.6	37.8	48.3	44.7
	100.0	100.0	100.0	Total Liabilties & Net Worth	100.0	100.0	100.0	100.0	100.0	100.0
				INCOME DATA						
	100.0	100.0	100.0	Net Sales	100.0	100.0	100.0	100.0	100.0	100.0
				Gross Profit						
	92.6	91.9	91.0	Operating Expenses	75.9	93.8	91.7	90.2	93.4	94.3
	7.4	8.1	9.0	Operating Profit	24.1	6.2	8.3	9.8	6.6	5.7
	1.5	1.5	1.9	All Other Expenses (net)	10.6	.2	1.3	.9	.5	1.3
	5.9	6.6	7.1	Profit Before Taxes	13.5	6.0	7.0	8.9	6.0	4.4
				RATIOS						
	3.2	3.1	2.8		1.8	5.2	2.8	4.4	3.0	2.4
	1.8	1.8	1.8	Current	1.0	1.6	2.2	1.9	1.9	1.8
	1.2	1.2	1.1		.2	.9	1.5	1.1	1.3	1.5
	2.8	2.8	2.5		1.8	4.9	2.7	4.2	2.6	2.0
	1.5	1.5	1.6	Quick	.8	1.6	1.9	1.7	1.7	1.5
	.9	1.0	1.0		.2	.4	1.1	1.0	1.1	1.2
33	11.0	37	9.9	34	10.7	Sales/Receivables	0	UND	0	UND	0	UND	43	8.5	48	7.6	39	9.3

	Comp	Comp	Comp		0-1MM	1-3MM	3-5MM	5-10MM	10-25MM	25MM & OVER
Sales/Receivables	62 / 5.9	60 / 6.1	64 / 5.7		0 / UND	49 / 7.4	49 / 7.4	68 / 5.4	89 / 4.1	74 / 4.9
	87 / 4.2	87 / 4.2	94 / 3.9		63 / 5.8	72 / 5.1	83 / 4.4	104 / 3.5	99 / 3.7	99 / 3.7
Cost of Sales/Inventory										
Cost of Sales/Payables										
Sales/Working Capital	5.2	4.8	4.9		13.3	6.1	4.4	4.1	4.7	5.1
	9.6	8.5	8.5		-443.0	10.7	7.7	7.8	7.0	7.3
	32.7	35.6	49.8		-3.8	-64.8	28.4	55.8	15.6	14.2
EBIT/Interest	32.8	30.0	40.1			15.6	27.4	32.7	55.6	36.9
	(127) 10.9	(122) 6.9	(143) 12.0			(21) 5.2	(12) 9.6	(31) 9.1	(34) 24.9	(37) 13.7
	2.4	2.8	2.7			-1.0	4.8	3.2	4.3	2.8
Net Profit + Depr., Dep., Amort./Cur. Mat. L/T/D	4.3	18.2	16.8							23.5
	(19) 3.0	(22) 4.0	(25) 5.3						(13)	5.4
	1.8	2.5	1.6							1.5
Fixed/Worth	.1	.1	.1		.5	.1	.1	.1	.1	.1
	.4	.4	.4		4.5	.6	.2	.5	.3	.3
	1.7	2.0	2.4		UND	3.1	NM	2.7	.0	1.0
Debt/Worth	.6	.6	.6		2.0	.5	.5	.8	.5	.9
	1.4	1.3	1.9		5.4	1.7	1.0	1.8	1.1	2.0
	5.3	5.4	5.7		UND	15.3	NM	6.9	3.2	2.7
% Profit Before Taxes/Tangible Net Worth	60.2	57.7	71.7		355.6	91.0	56.7	69.7	65.2	58.4
	(136) 30.6	(128) 25.8	(154) 32.7		(16) 46.2	(23) 42.6	(14) 30.5	(31) 32.8	(34) 23.8	(36) 32.9
	9.5	7.4	10.8		.0	6.7	6.2	7.9	12.1	11.1
% Profit Before Taxes/Total Assets	27.0	23.9	24.5		27.4	29.3	52.2	24.3	23.4	20.9
	11.1	9.3	12.3		5.6	16.3	12.2	15.2	12.0	11.4
	2.0	2.2	3.2		-.4	.2	4.4	4.1	3.8	2.9
Sales/Net Fixed Assets	68.8	65.0	67.0		53.7	58.4	81.4	63.2	57.0	83.1
	21.3	25.3	22.0		10.1	17.7	27.6	14.0	17.6	29.4
	6.2	7.8	7.7		.2	6.9	9.5	5.1	8.8	17.2
Sales/Total Assets	4.4	3.6	3.6		3.5	3.7	5.2	3.0	3.3	3.7
	2.3	2.3	2.4		1.8	2.8	3.3	2.1	2.5	2.3
	1.5	1.6	1.5		.2	1.4	2.1	1.5	1.4	1.5
% Depr., Dep., Amort./Sales	.6	.6	.6		1.5	.5		.9	.5	.4
	(106) 1.6	(102) 1.7	(132) 1.6		(13) 17.8	(17) 2.6		(31) 2.5	(29) 1.5	(34) .9
	3.5	4.2	4.4		24.1	6.6		4.4	3.3	2.0
% Officers', Directors' Owners' Comp/Sales	3.9	4.4	3.9			5.0		5.9	2.3	
	(50) 5.6	(40) 7.3	(55) 7.1			(13) 6.9		(11) 7.1	(11) 5.1	
	10.4	12.8	11.3			16.1		9.0	11.3	
Net Sales ($)	3260822M	3387938M	4081716M		8752M	59770M	64680M	266927M	586101M	3095486M
Total Assets ($)	1812855M	1936505M	2404857M		9825M	54779M	37251M	147481M	278748M	1876773M

M = $ thousand   MM = $ million

See Pages viii through xx for Explanation of Ratios and Data

Current Data Sorted by Assets   Comparative Historical Data

Type of Statement	0-500M	500M-2MM	2-10MM	10-50MM	50-100MM	100-250MM		4/1/14-3/31/15 ALL	4/1/15-3/31/16 ALL
Unqualified	2	12	16	4		6		44	40
Reviewed	1	16	7			1		23	26
Compiled	3	11	2					21	23
Tax Returns	21	11	6	1				63	54
Other	15	49	65	32	8	6		166	170
		25 (4/1-9/30/18)		270 (10/1/18-3/31/19)					
NUMBER OF STATEMENTS	36	66	110	58	12	13		317	313
ASSETS	%	%	%	%	%	%		%	%
Cash & Equivalents	39.3	26.4	18.7	16.7	7.3	17.2		24.2	23.6
Trade Receivables (net)	24.6	44.8	50.8	42.9	22.5	29.7		36.2	37.3
Inventory	.9	2.4	2.3	4.4	6.5	2.0		3.1	2.3
All Other Current	5.0	3.0	6.2	7.5	14.2	8.2		5.2	4.9
Total Current	69.8	76.5	78.0	71.4	50.5	57.1		68.7	68.0
Fixed Assets (net)	20.9	13.5	7.9	8.1	16.9	7.7		15.2	16.1
Intangibles (net)	4.7	3.2	5.6	10.8	22.3	26.5		6.3	7.2
All Other Non-Current	4.5	6.7	8.6	9.7	10.3	8.8		9.8	8.7
Total	100.0	100.0	100.0	100.0	100.0	100.0		100.0	100.0
LIABILITIES									
Notes Payable-Short Term	22.8	11.9	9.1	5.6	.1	4.5		11.4	9.8
Cur. Mat.-L.T.D.	9.3	3.2	1.7	3.5	2.1	.5		2.1	2.3
Trade Payables	9.3	12.4	12.3	14.6	11.4	13.3		12.4	10.2
Income Taxes Payable	.0	.2	.1	.1	.0	.1		.4	.3
All Other Current	10.6	25.0	23.2	20.1	20.8	18.4		20.2	15.6
Total Current	52.0	52.7	46.4	43.9	34.4	36.7		46.4	38.1
Long-Term Debt	31.4	12.3	12.1	4.8	21.4	13.1		13.5	13.3
Deferred Taxes	.0	.0	.2	.0	.2	.2		.3	.3
All Other Non-Current	12.6	2.6	5.9	9.8	7.3	5.0		8.9	6.2
Net Worth	4.0	32.3	35.4	41.5	36.7	44.9		30.9	42.1
Total Liabilties & Net Worth	100.0	100.0	100.0	100.0	100.0	100.0		100.0	100.0
INCOME DATA									
Net Sales	100.0	100.0	100.0	100.0	100.0	100.0		100.0	100.0
Gross Profit									
Operating Expenses	87.3	91.7	92.1	92.3	89.3	97.1		90.2	89.3
Operating Profit	12.7	8.3	7.9	7.7	10.7	2.9		9.8	10.7
All Other Expenses (net)	1.5	1.1	.3	.6	6.2	.4		1.3	1.3
Profit Before Taxes	11.2	7.1	7.5	7.1	4.6	2.5		8.5	9.5
RATIOS									
Current	3.5	4.1	3.3	2.9	2.1	2.2		3.5	4.0
	1.7	2.2	2.1	1.7	1.6	1.5		1.8	1.9
	.9	.9	1.1	1.1	1.0	1.2		1.1	1.1
Quick	3.3	3.9	3.1	2.6	1.3	2.0		3.2	3.1
	1.4	2.1	1.9	1.4	.9	1.2		1.5	1.7
	.8	.7	.9	.8	.4	.9		.9	1.0
Sales/Receivables	0 UND	19 19.3	41 9.0	49 7.5	32 11.5	40 9.1		20 18.4	20 18.0
	0 UND	41 8.8	64 5.7	63 5.8	60 6.1	63 5.8		46 8.0	51 7.1
	36 10.2	70 5.2	85 4.3	83 4.4	68 5.4	76 4.8		69 5.3	72 5.1
Cost of Sales/Inventory									
Cost of Sales/Payables									
Sales/Working Capital	8.4	5.1	5.1	4.4	4.9	7.0		5.4	5.2
	30.2	10.6	7.7	10.4	7.9	13.0		10.4	10.6
	-235.9	-83.2	90.2	67.5	NM	24.6		82.2	46.3
EBIT/Interest	66.6	44.2	126.3	36.3		26.8		73.2	57.0
	(25) 19.5	(40) 12.1	(81) 29.5	(39) 15.3		(11) 4.5		(220) 13.3	(213) 7.4
	6.1	2.2	5.0	1.5		.9		1.6	1.5
Net Profit + Depr., Dep., Amort./Cur. Mat. L/T/D			128.6					18.8	8.0
			(10) 14.2					(31) 4.1	(30) 2.6
			5.3					.3	2.0
Fixed/Worth	.0	.0	.0	.0	.1	.2		.0	.0
	.7	.1	.1	.2	1.9	.6		.2	.2
	-.5	NM	.6	2.1	-.2	-.4		1.4	1.3
Debt/Worth	.4	.4	.4	.5	.9	1.1		.6	.4
	2.4	1.2	1.1	1.5	3.8	14.9		1.6	1.2
	-3.9	NM	8.3	11.8	-3.3	-6.4		11.5	4.2
% Profit Before Taxes/Tangible Net Worth	238.0	92.8	82.2	74.9				103.6	83.5
	(23) 188.2	(50) 51.5	(90) 42.9	(46) 36.7				(253) 45.8	(262) 35.6
	69.6	11.9	17.3	14.9				14.1	9.1
% Profit Before Taxes/Total Assets	135.1	54.8	35.0	27.1	11.6	9.3		40.7	41.0
	71.5	23.6	18.1	10.6	5.3	4.1		14.5	12.8
	15.7	1.8	5.4	1.3	-.7	.1		2.5	2.4
Sales/Net Fixed Assets	999.8	982.3	527.9	254.2	66.7	89.4		204.0	174.7
	129.9	83.8	79.5	63.1	33.7	53.4		56.5	47.6
	24.2	20.3	32.5	22.6	9.6	7.6		14.5	14.7
Sales/Total Assets	12.9	5.3	3.8	3.2	2.0	2.3		4.5	4.5
	7.9	3.6	3.0	2.4	1.5	1.7		3.0	2.9
	4.1	2.5	2.0	1.7	1.0	.8		1.7	1.6
% Depr., Dep., Amort./Sales	.3	.4	.2	.2				.3	.3
	(13) .6	(31) .9	(65) .4	(40) .6				(195) .8	(193) .8
	1.4	2.2	1.1	2.5				2.3	2.8
% Officers', Directors' Owners' Comp/Sales	3.6	2.8	2.0					3.4	3.0
	(19) 8.4	(18) 4.9	(20) 3.3					(93) 5.3	(93) 7.0
	14.3	7.0	6.4					11.0	11.6
Net Sales ($)	73563M	342507M	1637331M	3967377M	1074357M	3356906M		8569794M	8068788M
Total Assets ($)	8574M	81437M	566239M	1372910M	772367M	2050999M		4633682M	4952130M

Comparative Historical Data / Current Data Sorted by Sales

			Type of Statement	0-1MM	1-3MM	3-5MM	5-10MM	10-25MM	25MM & OVER
	31	43	40	Unqualified	1		3	3	8	25
	22	26	25	Reviewed	1	1	1	5	11	6
	19	20	16	Compiled		1		4	8	3
	51	44	39	Tax Returns	9	12	10	6	1	1
	164	190	175	Other	3	24	24	30	39	55
	4/1/16- 3/31/17	4/1/17- 3/31/18	4/1/18- 3/31/19		25 (4/1-9/30/18)			270 (10/1/18-3/31/19)		
	ALL	ALL	ALL		0-1MM	1-3MM	3-5MM	5-10MM	10-25MM	25MM & OVER
	287	323	295	**NUMBER OF STATEMENTS**	14	38	38	48	67	90
	%	%	%	**ASSETS**	%	%	%	%	%	%
	23.3	21.3	22.0	Cash & Equivalents	26.1	33.9	23.2	25.3	20.6	15.1
	39.3	40.2	42.6	Trade Receivables (net)	22.3	29.7	42.3	39.9	53.2	44.9
	2.5	2.7	2.7	Inventory	.0	1.0	7.1	1.5	1.0	4.0
	4.7	5.3	6.0	All Other Current	6.5	3.3	3.4	5.1	5.7	8.9
	69.8	69.4	73.3	Total Current	54.9	67.9	76.0	71.8	80.5	72.8
	12.7	11.5	11.1	Fixed Assets (net)	38.3	17.9	10.2	12.5	6.2	7.4
	9.3	9.1	7.6	Intangibles (net)	2.7	6.6	6.2	6.5	4.6	12.1
	8.3	10.0	8.0	All Other Non-Current	3.9	7.6	7.5	9.3	8.8	7.6
	100.0	100.0	100.0	Total	100.0	100.0	100.0	100.0	100.0	100.0
				LIABILITIES						
	12.2	10.4	10.2	Notes Payable-Short Term	20.1	19.0	11.7	7.8	11.0	4.9
	2.8	2.6	3.3	Cur. Mat.-L.T.D.	11.2	3.2	5.5	2.9	1.1	3.0
	10.6	10.9	12.4	Trade Payables	2.5	12.0	14.1	10.2	11.6	15.1
	.2	.2	.1	Income Taxes Payable	.0	.2	.1	.1	.2	.1
	17.2	20.3	21.1	All Other Current	10.1	15.9	20.8	27.6	20.1	22.5
	42.9	44.4	47.1	Total Current	43.8	50.2	52.2	48.5	44.0	45.7
	13.6	11.8	13.5	Long-Term Debt	32.4	15.7	16.2	17.3	6.7	11.5
	.2	.3	.1	Deferred Taxes	.0	.0	.0	.0	.3	.1
	7.6	6.5	6.8	All Other Non-Current	22.5	5.0	4.0	4.0	2.9	10.6
	35.7	37.0	32.5	Net Worth	1.4	29.0	27.5	30.2	46.1	32.2
	100.0	100.0	100.0	Total Liabilties & Net Worth	100.0	100.0	100.0	100.0	100.0	100.0
				INCOME DATA						
	100.0	100.0	100.0	Net Sales	100.0	100.0	100.0	100.0	100.0	100.0
				Gross Profit						
	89.0	89.8	91.6	Operating Expenses	76.5	91.0	91.8	90.9	92.3	93.9
	11.0	10.2	8.4	Operating Profit	23.5	9.0	8.2	9.1	7.7	6.1
	1.5	1.2	.9	All Other Expenses (net)	4.2	.9	1.8	.5	.5	.7
	9.5	9.0	7.5	Profit Before Taxes	19.3	8.0	6.5	8.6	7.2	5.4
				RATIOS						
	3.6	3.4	3.2		8.9	3.6	3.8	4.9	3.8	2.7
	2.0	1.8	1.8	Current	2.2	1.8	2.4	1.6	2.2	1.7
	1.1	1.1	1.0		.7	.8	.8	.9	1.2	1.1
	3.2	3.0	3.0		8.9	3.5	3.3	4.9	3.2	2.5
	1.7	1.6	1.6	Quick	1.3	1.6	2.3	1.6	2.1	1.3
	.9	.9	.8		.5	.5	.7	.9	1.0	.8
23 / 15.9	26 / 14.0	29 / 12.4		0 UND	0 UND	13 27.2	18 20.2	44 8.3	43 8.4	
47 / 7.8	53 / 6.9	56 / 6.5	Sales/Receivables	0 UND	30 12.1	44 8.3	55 6.6	63 5.8	63 5.8	
70 / 5.2	74 / 4.9	78 / 4.7		45 8.1	64 5.7	78 4.7	81 4.5	81 4.5	76 4.8	
			Cost of Sales/Inventory						
			Cost of Sales/Payables						
	5.4	4.8	5.2		2.7	5.3	5.5	5.2	4.8	6.1
	10.3	11.0	9.2	Sales/Working Capital	15.7	16.7	11.1	10.0	7.2	9.4
	101.1	68.9	-999.8		-124.6	-71.0	-33.9	-78.4	28.9	33.0
	68.7	74.2	70.7			57.9	53.6	93.2	75.8	109.9
(198) 14.5	(224) 13.7	(205) 15.3	EBIT/Interest	(24) 15.4	(25) 8.7	(30) 16.2	(49) 20.7	(70) 13.3	
	2.5	2.8	3.3		2.6	2.1	1.3	4.4	1.8	
	12.0	19.8	56.9	Net Profit + Depr., Dep.,						
(21) 3.3	(27) 4.0	(20) 6.8	Amort./Cur. Mat. L/T/D						
	1.1	1.6	.9							
	.0	.0	.0		.0	.0	.0	.0	.0	.0
	.2	.1	.2	Fixed/Worth	.5	.3	.2	.3	.1	.2
	2.6	1.1	6.7		NM	-23.6	-.5	112.3	.2	-1.0
	.4	.4	.5		.4	.3	.4	.3	.4	.6
	1.5	1.5	1.2	Debt/Worth	1.0	1.5	1.3	1.5	.8	1.8
	17.1	15.9	195.7		NM	-6.8	-4.6	961.1	4.2	-19.2
	99.0	86.8	92.2	% Profit Before Taxes/Tangible	150.0	200.3	94.1	117.9	76.8	82.0
(226) 42.0	(258) 44.0	(224) 48.9	Net Worth	(11) 23.8	(27) 84.9	(26) 51.2	(37) 71.7	(57) 42.1	(66) 42.3
	12.2	14.8	17.6		5.0	13.5	.5	25.1	19.4	20.3
	42.0	30.9	41.7	% Profit Before Taxes/Total	80.4	82.4	53.7	57.7	38.9	26.9
	16.1	13.7	16.4	Assets	25.9	26.8	19.5	25.6	17.7	11.0
	2.9	4.7	3.9		6.0	.4	1.7	4.9	8.9	2.2
	401.6	349.7	469.5		UND	801.2	999.8	520.3	469.5	271.3
	94.4	84.4	77.6	Sales/Net Fixed Assets	19.8	63.5	114.3	66.2	80.5	75.1
	22.4	22.1	25.6		2.6	17.4	30.9	22.7	42.0	25.0
	4.7	4.3	4.4		7.7	7.3	5.5	4.9	4.0	4.0
	3.0	2.8	3.0	Sales/Total Assets	2.6	3.3	3.3	3.5	3.0	2.6
	1.7	1.7	1.9		.4	2.4	2.2	1.8	2.2	1.8
	.2	.2	.2			.3	.2	.4	.1	.2
(155) .7	(189) .6	(163) .6	% Depr., Dep., Amort./Sales	(19) .8	(14) .9	(26) .6	(44) .4	(53) .7	
	2.2	1.6	1.6			1.9	1.9	2.2	.9	1.5
	3.1	2.5	2.8	% Officers', Directors'		5.6	2.3	2.6	2.5	
(69) 5.4	(76) 4.1	(66) 4.5	Owners' Comp/Sales	(14) 7.7	(10) 4.4	(15) 3.2	(13) 3.6		
	9.9	8.2	9.5			15.6	6.0	9.2	6.1	
8169504M	11349058M	10452041M	Net Sales ($)	6401M	73265M	153424M	348832M	1041796M	8828323M
4128862M	5677988M	4852526M	Total Assets ($)	13601M	39754M	285787M	164203M	428616M	3920565M

© RMA 2019   M = $ thousand   MM = $ million
See Pages viii through xx for Explanation of Ratios and Data

Current Data Sorted by Assets

Comparative Historical Data

0-500M	500M-2MM	2-10MM	10-50MM	50-100MM	100-250MM	Type of Statement	4/1/14-3/31/15 ALL	4/1/15-3/31/16 ALL
		2	4	4	1	Unqualified	12	10
	1	2	3			Reviewed	6	4
	1	2				Compiled	4	3
	2	2	1			Tax Returns	11	11
5	3	15	9	3		Other	42	59
	15 (4/1-9/30/18)		45 (10/1/18-3/31/19)					
5	7	23	17	7	1	**NUMBER OF STATEMENTS**	75	87
%	%	%	%	%	%	**ASSETS**	%	%
		37.9	20.6			Cash & Equivalents	24.3	23.2
		17.0	22.2			Trade Receivables (net)	20.9	23.5
		6.7	8.2			Inventory	5.4	6.6
		3.0	3.1			All Other Current	6.6	4.8
		64.6	54.1			Total Current	57.2	58.0
		22.1	18.7			Fixed Assets (net)	25.4	23.1
		8.4	15.4			Intangibles (net)	8.0	8.6
		4.9	11.8			All Other Non-Current	9.3	10.2
		100.0	100.0			Total	100.0	100.0
						LIABILITIES		
		1.7	1.0			Notes Payable-Short Term	5.1	7.1
		2.5	1.4			Cur. Mat.-L.T.D.	6.4	4.4
		10.9	12.1			Trade Payables	9.9	8.7
		.2	.2			Income Taxes Payable	.4	.4
		11.3	14.1			All Other Current	16.8	16.2
		26.6	28.9			Total Current	38.6	36.9
		14.1	5.8			Long-Term Debt	16.2	17.8
		.0	.0			Deferred Taxes	.4	.4
		16.6	3.9			All Other Non-Current	8.0	11.6
		42.7	61.4			Net Worth	36.7	33.3
		100.0	100.0			Total Liabilities & Net Worth	100.0	100.0
						INCOME DATA		
		100.0	100.0			Net Sales	100.0	100.0
						Gross Profit		
		87.6	85.5			Operating Expenses	90.1	88.4
		12.4	14.5			Operating Profit	9.9	11.6
		-.1	2.0			All Other Expenses (net)	1.8	2.4
		12.5	12.5			Profit Before Taxes	8.1	9.2
						RATIOS		
		7.6	3.7			Current	3.9	3.3
		3.2	1.8				1.8	1.7
		1.8	1.2				1.0	1.1
		7.6	3.3			Quick	3.4	3.0
		3.2	1.7				1.3	1.3
		1.2	.7				.6	.7
		14 25.3	47 7.8			Sales/Receivables	14 25.6	31 11.6
		24 15.4	68 5.4				44 8.3	51 7.1
		51 7.1	101 3.6				72 5.1	69 5.3
						Cost of Sales/Inventory		
						Cost of Sales/Payables		
		2.9	2.1			Sales/Working Capital	3.0	2.9
		5.0	3.7				8.7	8.4
		11.8	23.8				-85.8	270.9
		171.1	57.0			EBIT/Interest	31.0	22.6
		(15) 39.1	(12) 16.8				(50) 5.8	(63) 6.2
		5.8	3.6				-.8	1.2
						Net Profit + Depr., Dep., Amort./Cur. Mat. L/T/D	33.4	14.7
							(11) 6.4	(16) 3.6
							1.2	1.2
		.1	.2			Fixed/Worth	.2	.2
		.4	.5				.8	.6
		1.1	1.0				4.3	2.2
		.3	.2			Debt/Worth	.5	.6
		.7	1.2				1.3	1.5
		2.8	2.9				9.9	14.0
		49.2	61.6			% Profit Before Taxes/Tangible Net Worth	58.8	53.4
		(19) 26.5	(16) 26.2				(61) 29.6	(68) 20.4
		12.2	11.2				1.3	2.9
		27.3	21.0			% Profit Before Taxes/Total Assets	21.6	23.5
		14.0	16.1				8.1	6.9
		7.0	4.1				-3.9	.2
		30.3	17.7			Sales/Net Fixed Assets	29.9	36.7
		10.1	9.2				12.0	14.1
		7.0	4.5				2.9	5.1
		2.6	1.6			Sales/Total Assets	2.4	2.8
		1.8	1.3				1.5	1.5
		1.2	.8				.9	.8
		.6	1.0			% Depr., Dep., Amort./Sales	.8	1.0
		(18) 1.4	(15) 2.0				(54) 1.9	(59) 2.7
		2.9	6.7				5.1	6.0
						% Officers', Directors' Owners' Comp/Sales	2.5	3.8
							(16) 4.7	(15) 5.7
							12.3	8.6
4744M	21337M	224263M	450433M	270091M	113342M	Net Sales ($)	2265830M	3356509M
1415M	6444M	120163M	413794M	543283M	246313M	Total Assets ($)	2254278M	3040898M

M = $ thousand   MM = $ million
See Pages viii through xx for Explanation of Ratios and Data

Comparative Historical Data | Current Data Sorted by Sales

			Type of Statement	0-1MM	1-3MM	3-5MM	5-10MM	10-25MM	25MM & OVER
12	6	11	Unqualified		1		1	5	4
4	8	6	Reviewed		1		1	3	2
4	5	3	Compiled			1	1	1	
9	9	5	Tax Returns		2	1	1	1	
31	44	35	Other	4	5	4	4	9	8
4/1/16-3/31/17 ALL	4/1/17-3/31/18 ALL	4/1/18-3/31/19 ALL			15 (4/1-9/30/18)			45 (10/1/18-3/31/19)	
60	72	60	**NUMBER OF STATEMENTS**	4	9	6	8	19	14

%	%	%	**ASSETS**	%	%	%	%	%	%
25.2	28.6	25.9	Cash & Equivalents					25.5	20.3
25.6	21.5	18.2	Trade Receivables (net)					20.4	19.1
8.5	8.3	7.2	Inventory					5.3	11.0
4.2	3.1	3.0	All Other Current					3.5	4.3
63.5	61.4	54.4	Total Current					54.7	54.7
25.1	23.9	22.5	Fixed Assets (net)					23.4	14.0
5.7	7.0	10.8	Intangibles (net)					14.1	11.6
5.8	7.7	12.3	All Other Non-Current					7.9	19.7
100.0	100.0	100.0	Total					100.0	100.0
			LIABILITIES						
3.8	3.3	4.2	Notes Payable-Short Term					.9	1.2
2.7	3.2	2.0	Cur. Mat.-L.T.D.					1.5	1.9
9.6	8.0	11.4	Trade Payables					11.3	9.8
.1	.3	.1	Income Taxes Payable					.5	.0
16.9	17.1	20.8	All Other Current					10.4	19.6
33.0	31.9	38.6	Total Current					24.6	32.6
19.9	18.0	10.4	Long-Term Debt					4.1	10.1
.1	.1	.1	Deferred Taxes					.0	.4
6.3	10.3	8.7	All Other Non-Current					9.3	5.5
40.6	39.7	42.2	Net Worth					62.0	51.5
100.0	100.0	100.0	Total Liabilities & Net Worth					100.0	100.0
			INCOME DATA						
100.0	100.0	100.0	Net Sales					100.0	100.0
			Gross Profit						
88.5	85.9	90.4	Operating Expenses					91.1	89.7
11.5	14.1	9.6	Operating Profit					8.9	10.3
2.3	2.1	1.1	All Other Expenses (net)					.1	2.3
9.3	11.9	8.4	Profit Before Taxes					8.8	8.0
			RATIOS						
4.0	5.0	4.4	Current					3.8	3.7
1.9	1.9	2.2						2.4	1.6
1.2	1.3	1.0						1.1	1.2
3.0	3.8	3.5	Quick					3.7	2.9
1.4	1.6	1.6						1.8	1.1
.9	.8	.7						.9	.6
32 11.3	10 34.8	17 21.9	Sales/Receivables					24 15.4	43 8.4
49 7.5	47 7.8	46 7.9						51 7.1	62 5.9
73 5.0	79 4.6	68 5.4						66 5.5	73 5.0
			Cost of Sales/Inventory						
			Cost of Sales/Payables						
2.8	3.4	2.7	Sales/Working Capital					2.9	2.5
5.4	6.3	7.7						5.0	7.5
27.6	19.4	NM						24.0	267.6
39.9	50.3	52.3	EBIT/Interest					187.9	71.7
(45) 9.6	(56) 11.8	(39) 15.6						(13) 49.7	(10) 16.8
3.0	2.0	2.0						.9	2.3
		11.4	Net Profit + Depr., Dep., Amort./Cur. Mat. L/T/D						
	(13) 3.7								
		.7							
.1	.1	.2	Fixed/Worth					.2	.2
.7	.5	.5						.4	.4
2.0	2.4	2.0						.7	.0
.6	.4	.3	Debt/Worth					.3	.2
1.3	1.1	1.2						.6	1.5
6.2	4.8	9.7						2.3	7.3
82.9	59.2	51.6	% Profit Before Taxes/Tangible Net Worth					51.5	56.0
(51) 27.5	(59) 32.2	(48) 25.1						(17) 26.8	(12) 32.5
6.6	11.0	2.0						10.5	4.8
35.8	27.9	22.0	% Profit Before Taxes/Total Assets					27.3	20.5
11.3	14.3	10.2						16.1	13.1
2.8	2.5	.9						3.0	2.7
30.3	37.2	24.3	Sales/Net Fixed Assets					21.5	23.7
10.0	13.3	9.9						9.2	10.1
3.4	3.4	5.0						5.2	4.6
2.7	2.5	2.4	Sales/Total Assets					2.3	1.7
1.6	1.6	1.5						1.4	1.4
.8	.9	.9						.8	.7
1.1	.8	1.0	% Depr., Dep., Amort./Sales					.6	1.2
(43) 3.2	(53) 2.7	(43) 2.0						(15) 2.3	(13) 2.1
6.1	5.5	6.1						8.0	6.5
2.2	2.2	2.2	% Officers', Directors' Owners' Comp/Sales						
(15) 4.5	(13) 3.6	(11) 3.6							
8.8	10.5	7.7							
2262335M	2544980M	1084210M	Net Sales ($)	2485M	17868M	22853M	58845M	323299M	658860M
2051521M	2151845M	1331412M	Total Assets ($)	1487M	21032M	12746M	87011M	454281M	754855M

© RMA 2019

M = $ thousand   MM = $ million

See Pages viii through xx for Explanation of Ratios and Data

Current Data Sorted by Assets | Comparative Historical Data

	0-500M	500M-2MM	2-10MM	10-50MM	50-100MM	100-250MM	Type of Statement	4/1/14-3/31/15 ALL	4/1/15-3/31/16 ALL
		1	2	15	6	5	Unqualified	53	46
		4	4	4	1		Reviewed	11	15
		1	4	2	1		Compiled	8	12
	1	4	1				Tax Returns	10	14
	4	9	31	13	6	9	Other	76	86
		24 (4/1-9/30/18)		99 (10/1/18-3/31/19)					
NUMBER OF STATEMENTS	5	15	42	34	13	14		158	173
	%	%	%	%	%	%	**ASSETS**	%	%
		30.0	23.0	19.7	27.6	21.6	Cash & Equivalents	16.7	19.3
		33.7	33.2	27.8	21.0	19.5	Trade Receivables (net)	28.9	28.4
		5.4	8.2	3.7	1.2	1.6	Inventory	3.9	4.8
		2.0	3.7	6.7	8.2	3.8	All Other Current	7.2	5.8
		71.0	68.1	57.9	58.0	46.5	Total Current	56.7	58.2
		13.2	23.0	19.9	20.6	22.5	Fixed Assets (net)	22.1	23.5
		12.2	4.5	11.3	9.8	28.4	Intangibles (net)	8.1	6.1
		3.5	4.4	10.9	11.6	2.5	All Other Non-Current	13.1	12.2
		100.0	100.0	100.0	100.0	100.0	Total	100.0	100.0
							LIABILITIES		
		30.2	4.7	6.9	1.0	2.6	Notes Payable-Short Term	6.9	6.1
		.1	2.2	1.3	1.5	1.5	Cur. Mat.-L.T.D.	2.4	2.8
		5.2	17.9	10.4	6.1	5.3	Trade Payables	9.0	10.9
		.1	.0	.5	.0	.0	Income Taxes Payable	.2	.2
		16.0	25.9	16.1	25.9	16.4	All Other Current	19.7	15.9
		51.6	50.8	35.2	34.5	25.7	Total Current	38.2	36.0
		10.8	12.5	8.9	13.6	17.8	Long-Term Debt	14.3	12.8
		.0	.0	.8	.0	1.2	Deferred Taxes	.4	.2
		5.5	9.2	7.2	4.2	11.7	All Other Non-Current	7.6	7.2
		32.0	27.5	47.9	47.7	43.6	Net Worth	39.5	43.9
		100.0	100.0	100.0	100.0	100.0	Total Liabilities & Net Worth	100.0	100.0
							INCOME DATA		
		100.0	100.0	100.0	100.0	100.0	Net Sales	100.0	100.0
							Gross Profit		
		93.0	94.3	93.6	97.4	96.4	Operating Expenses	94.6	93.0
		7.0	5.7	6.4	2.6	3.6	Operating Profit	5.4	7.0
		-.3	1.3	.4	1.7	4.3	All Other Expenses (net)	.7	1.1
		7.4	4.5	6.0	.9	-.7	Profit Before Taxes	4.7	5.9
							RATIOS		
		7.4	4.0	4.0	3.7	3.4	Current	3.2	3.5
		3.2	1.5	1.8	1.7	1.8		1.6	1.9
		.9	1.0	1.3	1.0	1.1		.9	1.1
		7.4	3.5	2.8	3.2	3.3	Quick	2.5	2.8
		2.4	1.3	1.5	1.6	1.5		1.2	1.5
		.9	.6	.9	.8	.9		.7	.9
		(12) 31.7	(29) 12.7	(40) 9.1	(49) 7.5	(51) 7.1	Sales/Receivables	(30) 12.0	(26) 13.8
		(26) 13.9	(42) 8.7	(53) 6.9	(60) 6.1	(58) 6.3		(53) 6.9	(51) 7.2
		(63) 5.8	(96) 3.8	(85) 4.3	(85) 4.3	(87) 4.2		(76) 4.8	(73) 5.0
							Cost of Sales/Inventory		
							Cost of Sales/Payables		
		3.8	2.6	2.9	2.7	2.6	Sales/Working Capital	3.7	3.6
		10.5	8.8	6.7	4.3	8.2		9.4	7.8
		-28.6	304.5	19.0	NM	46.3		-133.1	55.3
		51.8	36.3	13.4		10.8	EBIT/Interest	42.2	56.5
		(10) 13.1	(30) 6.6	(21) 6.1		(12) 3.8		(114) 6.3	(119) 10.6
		7.1	.5	1.8		-4.3		-.5	.5
							Net Profit + Depr., Dep.,	11.5	5.2
							Amort./Cur. Mat. L/T/D	(19) 4.6 / (20) 2.3	
								.3	-.5
		.0	.1	.1	.1	.2	Fixed/Worth	.1	.1
		.2	.3	.3	.7	.8		.5	.4
		4.5	NM	1.2	NM	8.4		1.8	1.3
		.4	.5	.5	.6	.7	Debt/Worth	.4	.3
		2.1	1.5	.9	.7	4.5		1.3	.9
		103.1	NM	2.5	NM	NM		6.0	4.5
		183.3	72.1	35.5	10.8	57.0	% Profit Before Taxes/Tangible Net Worth	43.2	51.2
		(12) 57.8	(32) 28.0	(29) 8.5	(10) 1.5	(11) 13.7		(133) 16.2	(144) 15.2
		2.0	4.6	2.5	-3.3	-6.3		.2	-.5
		57.4	22.8	9.6	5.9	7.0	% Profit Before Taxes/Total Assets	15.2	20.9
		33.8	6.5	4.8	1.4	2.3		6.2	7.1
		5.9	-2.3	1.0	-1.5	-5.6		-1.4	-1.0
		729.0	59.0	84.7	19.4	48.4	Sales/Net Fixed Assets	50.5	56.1
		75.8	17.6	16.3	7.7	19.8		18.1	19.3
		11.7	5.3	3.0	3.7	1.8		3.8	3.1
		5.0	2.6	2.3	1.6	1.6	Sales/Total Assets	2.8	2.9
		2.9	1.6	1.2	1.2	.9		1.6	1.5
		2.2	1.2	.7	.6	.4		.9	1.0
			1.0	.4	.8	1.4	% Depr., Dep., Amort./Sales	.8	.7
		(31) 1.8	(25) 2.3	2.8	(10) 2.1			(119) 1.9	(132) 1.8
		4.3	4.1	7.5	5.8			4.8	4.7
							% Officers', Directors' Owners' Comp/Sales	4.2	3.5
								(19) 9.7	(24) 5.5
								15.2	9.6
	7378M	49979M	388391M	1436343M	962254M	2282943M	Net Sales ($)	6775936M	7133667M
	1102M	14276M	199288M	826524M	812085M	2019178M	Total Assets ($)	5915497M	5512091M

M = $ thousand   MM = $ million
See Pages viii through xx for Explanation of Ratios and Data

Comparative Historical Data | | | | Current Data Sorted by Sales

Hist 4/1/16-3/31/17 ALL	Hist 4/1/17-3/31/18 ALL	Hist 4/1/18-3/31/19 ALL	Type of Statement	0-1MM	1-3MM	3-5MM	5-10MM	10-25MM	25MM & OVER
					24 (4/1-9/30/18)		99 (10/1/18-3/31/19)		
35	35	29	Unqualified	1		2		10	16
4	3	9	Reviewed			1	1	5	2
11	6	7	Compiled			1	1	3	2
11	15	6	Tax Returns	2	3			1	
77	76	72	Other	4	8	7	21	13	19
138	135	123	**NUMBER OF STATEMENTS**	7	11	11	23	32	39
%	%	%	**ASSETS**	%	%	%	%	%	%
19.6	22.3	24.8	Cash & Equivalents		30.1	37.1	26.5	15.2	24.7
29.6	29.2	28.1	Trade Receivables (net)		32.0	20.8	37.1	27.0	29.5
5.4	5.5	4.8	Inventory		5.1	10.0	7.0	3.8	2.1
4.4	4.8	4.8	All Other Current		1.7	3.8	2.8	4.6	7.4
59.0	61.8	62.5	Total Current		68.8	71.7	73.4	50.6	63.8
23.6	19.8	20.6	Fixed Assets (net)		16.5	22.8	16.8	24.0	16.5
8.1	9.5	10.5	Intangibles (net)		12.4	2.3	5.1	12.4	14.2
9.2	8.9	6.5	All Other Non-Current		2.3	3.2	4.7	12.9	5.4
100.0	100.0	100.0	Total		100.0	100.0	100.0	100.0	100.0
			LIABILITIES						
13.1	11.6	10.7	Notes Payable-Short Term		9.3	32.0	5.4	7.8	2.9
2.6	2.0	1.7	Cur. Mat.-L.T.D.		2.3	.0	2.7	1.9	1.2
10.3	10.0	10.9	Trade Payables		3.3	17.8	19.6	6.7	10.9
.2	.3	.2	Income Taxes Payable		.1	.0	.1	.1	.4
16.2	17.0	20.6	All Other Current		20.3	17.6	28.2	17.7	21.9
42.4	40.9	44.1	Total Current		35.2	67.5	56.1	34.2	37.4
15.5	12.2	12.0	Long-Term Debt		16.6	7.6	10.2	14.6	9.6
.2	.3	.3	Deferred Taxes		.0	.0	.0	.4	.8
6.7	7.1	7.6	All Other Non-Current		3.3	20.9	6.9	5.9	7.3
35.3	39.5	36.0	Net Worth		44.9	4.0	26.9	44.9	45.0
100.0	100.0	100.0	Total Liabilities & Net Worth		100.0	100.0	100.0	100.0	100.0
			INCOME DATA						
100.0	100.0	100.0	Net Sales		100.0	100.0	100.0	100.0	100.0
			Gross Profit						
94.3	92.4	95.1	Operating Expenses		96.6	101.3	93.7	92.0	95.8
5.7	7.6	4.9	Operating Profit		3.4	-1.3	6.3	8.0	4.2
1.2	.7	1.1	All Other Expenses (net)		-1.7	.6	.6	2.1	.9
4.5	6.9	3.8	Profit Before Taxes		5.1	-1.9	5.6	5.9	3.2
			RATIOS						
3.3 / 1.7 / 1.1	3.1 / 1.9 / 1.2	4.0 / 1.6 / 1.0	Current		7.4 / 1.8 / .9	5.4 / 3.3 / .6	4.1 / 1.6 / 1.0	4.7 / 1.5 / .9	3.0 / 1.7 / 1.3
2.5 / 1.3 / .9	2.6 / 1.6 / .9	3.4 / 1.4 / .8	Quick		7.4 / 1.8 / .9	3.6 / 2.4 / .4	3.6 / 1.3 / .7	3.9 / 1.3 / .6	2.5 / 1.6 / .9
31 11.9 / 52 7.0 / 72 5.1	25 14.5 / 53 6.9 / 73 5.0	29 12.5 / 53 6.9 / 81 4.5	Sales/Receivables		0 UND / 25 14.8 / 74 4.9	27 13.5 / 58 6.3 / 101 3.6	31 11.6 / 39 9.4 / 94 3.9	33 11.1 / 50 7.3 / 101 3.6	51 7.2 / 57 6.4 / 70 5.2
			Cost of Sales/Inventory						
			Cost of Sales/Payables						
3.5 / 8.6 / NM	4.1 / 9.0 / 40.2	3.0 / 8.0 / 72.7	Sales/Working Capital		4.7 / 26.9 / -28.6	2.1 / 3.1 / -3.4	2.8 / 8.4 / 72.7	2.5 / 9.4 / -59.6	3.2 / 7.8 / 19.2
26.8 / (99) 6.4 / -1.2	32.7 / (97) 9.0 / 2.4	17.1 / (87) 6.2 / .7	EBIT/Interest		24.8 / (10) 12.2 / -22.7			20.8 / (17) 6.8 / .1	15.9 / (22) 3.8 / 1.0	19.3 / (29) 6.7 / 2.4
5.4 / (16) 3.1 / 1.2	9.8 / (20) 4.9 / 3.3	24.5 / (14) 6.1 / 2.9	Net Profit + Depr., Dep., Amort./Cur. Mat. L/T/D						
.1 / .5 / 2.0	.1 / .4 / 1.3	.1 / .4 / 4.5	Fixed/Worth		.0 / 1.2 / -5.1	.1 / 1.5 / -.2	.1 / .1 / 9.7	.1 / .6 / 1.2	.1 / .3 / 1.8
.5 / 1.5 / 9.1	.4 / 1.3 / 9.1	.6 / 1.4 / 29.9	Debt/Worth		.4 / 2.0 / -21.3	.2 / 1.2 / -3.1	.6 / 1.5 / 30.3	.4 / .8 / 10.0	.6 / 1.1 / 6.3
41.0 / (110) 17.2 / -1.4	60.2 / (109) 22.0 / 5.7	50.5 / (96) 11.9 / 1.4	% Profit Before Taxes/Tangible Net Worth					74.4 / (18) 16.4 / 5.0	46.0 / (27) 8.1 / 1.4	42.9 / (32) 12.4 / 5.7
15.4 / 7.0 / -3.9	17.8 / 8.8 / .9	17.0 / 5.5 / -1.3	% Profit Before Taxes/Total Assets		57.4 / 33.8 / -29.1	14.9 / 5.9 / -26.3	20.6 / 5.0 / -1.9	20.4 / 2.5 / -.3	13.4 / 6.1 / 1.4
60.6 / 14.2 / 3.5	89.3 / 25.2 / 6.3	72.8 / 17.7 / 5.1	Sales/Net Fixed Assets		729.0 / 60.7 / 11.5	24.5 / 13.6 / 4.0	94.4 / 22.2 / 9.9	37.2 / 11.9 / 1.9	91.0 / 24.9 / 6.7
3.2 / 1.7 / .9	3.4 / 1.9 / 1.0	2.7 / 1.5 / .8	Sales/Total Assets		5.4 / 3.0 / 2.8	1.7 / 1.2 / .8	2.8 / 2.1 / 1.4	2.2 / 1.1 / .6	2.7 / 1.5 / .9
.8 / (102) 2.2 / 5.3	.7 / (85) 2.2 / 4.3	.8 / (89) 1.9 / 4.5	% Depr., Dep., Amort./Sales					.7 / (16) 1.5 / 4.6	1.0 / (23) 2.8 / 7.5	.5 / (33) 1.5 / 2.9
4.7 / (18) 9.1 / 12.8	1.8 / (19) 7.1 / 13.2	1.7 / (11) 6.8 / 10.1	% Officers', Directors' Owners' Comp/Sales						
7142298M	6605602M	5127288M	Net Sales ($)	4256M	23239M	46158M	173820M	536111M	4343704M
4954949M	4736265M	3872453M	Total Assets ($)	11978M	6419M	38901M	101774M	843091M	2870290M

M = $ thousand   MM = $ million
See Pages viii through xx for Explanation of Ratios and Data

Current Data Sorted by Assets   **Comparative Historical Data**

						Type of Statement		
3	3	8	3	5		Unqualified	34	27
	2	1				Reviewed	6	2
3	1	1				Compiled	2	5
1	3	1				Tax Returns	6	6
2	1	6	1	3		Other	6	5
							25	25
	24 (4/1-9/30/18)		33 (10/1/18-3/31/19)				4/1/14-	4/1/15-
							3/31/15	3/31/16
0-500M	500M-2MM	2-10MM	10-50MM	50-100MM	100-250MM		ALL	ALL
3	10	13	19	4	8	NUMBER OF STATEMENTS	73	65
%	%	%	%	%	%	**ASSETS**	%	%
	19.8	24.7	24.8			Cash & Equivalents	26.0	26.4
	32.3	34.7	33.3			Trade Receivables (net)	27.7	24.9
	.3	.9	2.2			Inventory	1.5	.6
	8.4	2.9	5.1			All Other Current	6.8	5.9
	60.7	63.3	65.5			Total Current	62.0	57.8
	24.4	32.2	22.5			Fixed Assets (net)	21.8	22.5
	2.5	1.1	6.2			Intangibles (net)	4.7	6.3
	12.5	3.4	5.8			All Other Non-Current	11.5	13.5
	100.0	100.0	100.0			Total	100.0	100.0
						LIABILITIES		
	11.4	4.5	1.8			Notes Payable-Short Term	6.6	9.8
	1.7	1.8	1.6			Cur. Mat.-L.T.D.	2.1	1.2
	2.3	7.8	10.7			Trade Payables	8.9	5.2
	.0	.5	.1			Income Taxes Payable	.3	.4
	16.4	19.9	15.2			All Other Current	20.2	19.3
	31.9	34.5	29.3			Total Current	38.1	35.9
	16.5	20.0	8.6			Long-Term Debt	13.0	11.4
	.0	.0	.1			Deferred Taxes	.3	.1
	10.5	2.9	14.9			All Other Non-Current	9.3	8.4
	41.0	42.7	47.1			Net Worth	39.4	44.2
	100.0	100.0	100.0			Total Liabilties & Net Worth	100.0	100.0
						INCOME DATA		
	100.0	100.0	100.0			Net Sales	100.0	100.0
						Gross Profit		
	94.7	95.6	98.4			Operating Expenses	92.9	93.3
	5.3	4.4	1.6			Operating Profit	7.1	6.7
	3.4	-.5	.1			All Other Expenses (net)	2.2	2.5
	1.9	4.9	1.4			Profit Before Taxes	4.9	4.2
						RATIOS		
	5.9	3.2	5.4				3.9	5.2
	2.0	1.7	2.9			Current	1.7	1.9
	1.0	1.2	1.5				1.1	1.2
	5.9	3.1	5.4				3.1	3.8
	1.4	1.7	2.9			Quick	1.5	1.7
	.8	1.2	1.0				.9	1.0
0 UND	8 45.9	26 13.9					10 36.5	5 79.5
64 5.7	34 10.6	56 6.5				Sales/Receivables	48 7.6	48 7.6
101 3.6	74 4.9	81 4.5					69 5.3	78 4.7
						Cost of Sales/Inventory		
						Cost of Sales/Payables		
	3.8	4.7	2.6				3.7	3.0
	10.2	8.8	3.9			Sales/Working Capital	9.8	7.1
	NM	46.6	14.1				NM	75.7
			10.8				39.3	22.9
	(12)	4.6				EBIT/Interest	(43) 8.7	(42) 2.8
		1.4					3.1	-2.0
						Net Profit + Depr., Dep., Amort./Cur. Mat. L/T/D		
	.0	.1	.0				.1	.1
	.5	.5	.2			Fixed/Worth	.3	.4
	3.0	1.4	1.3				.9	1.1
	.9	.5	.5				.4	.3
	1.6	1.2	.5			Debt/Worth	1.2	.9
	3.4	1.7	23.4				4.1	3.5
		40.4	15.7				69.5	28.3
	(12)	24.9	(16) 5.1			% Profit Before Taxes/Tangible Net Worth	(63) 14.1	(56) 6.0
		11.1	2.0				2.5	-2.3
	14.8	22.9	5.9				24.1	15.8
	.3	11.2	2.3			% Profit Before Taxes/Total Assets	6.4	3.5
	-8.1	6.3	-1.4				1.4	-1.4
	412.0	292.7	161.9				98.2	130.1
	41.2	14.2	28.6			Sales/Net Fixed Assets	16.2	15.3
	5.0	2.3	3.0				3.5	1.9
	3.7	3.3	2.6				3.7	2.7
	1.4	2.8	1.8			Sales/Total Assets	1.9	1.5
	1.0	1.1	1.0				.9	.5
			1.2				.9	.6
		(14)	2.7			% Depr., Dep., Amort./Sales	(57) 1.9	(49) 2.1
			3.1				4.6	4.0
							2.6	4.9
						% Officers', Directors' Owners' Comp/Sales	(13) 7.5	(12) 15.8
							15.7	29.3
6984M	26305M	151550M	766692M	274353M	1801367M	Net Sales ($)	6260367M	5800738M
411M	12776M	66250M	384541M	301502M	1536515M	Total Assets ($)	1871755M	2067275M

M = $ thousand MM = $ million
See Pages viii through xx for Explanation of Ratios and Data

Comparative Historical Data | | | Current Data Sorted by Sales

			Type of Statement						
28	17	22	Unqualified	1	3	1		7	10
	3	3	Reviewed				1	1	1
2	1	5	Compiled		1		2		2
1	3	5	Tax Returns	3		1		1	
29	22	22	Other	1	2	1	3	6	9
4/1/16-3/31/17	4/1/17-3/31/18	4/1/18-3/31/19		24 (4/1-9/30/18)			33 (10/1/18-3/31/19)		
ALL	ALL	ALL		0-1MM	1-3MM	3-5MM	5-10MM	10-25MM	25MM & OVER
60	46	57	**NUMBER OF STATEMENTS**	5	6	3	6	15	22
%	%	%	**ASSETS**	%	%	%	%	%	%
28.2	21.7	23.9	Cash & Equivalents					27.9	15.5
28.6	25.2	28.4	Trade Receivables (net)					31.3	31.5
.5	.9	1.0	Inventory					.2	2.0
4.5	5.4	6.1	All Other Current					1.7	7.0
61.8	53.1	59.4	Total Current					61.1	56.1
18.3	20.7	25.2	Fixed Assets (net)					27.2	20.8
9.6	13.7	5.8	Intangibles (net)					5.3	9.4
10.4	12.5	9.6	All Other Non-Current					6.5	13.8
100.0	100.0	100.0	Total					100.0	100.0
			LIABILITIES						
7.2	9.7	4.4	Notes Payable-Short Term					2.9	2.2
3.1	2.2	1.9	Cur. Mat.-L.T.D.					.8	2.8
7.0	9.2	6.6	Trade Payables					5.5	10.8
.5	.0	.1	Income Taxes Payable					.4	.1
20.6	17.5	15.9	All Other Current					13.3	19.7
38.4	38.6	29.0	Total Current					23.1	35.6
14.4	18.2	17.0	Long-Term Debt					14.7	17.8
.1	.0	.0	Deferred Taxes					.0	.1
9.2	7.9	8.6	All Other Non-Current					2.3	9.4
37.9	35.3	45.4	Net Worth					59.9	37.2
100.0	100.0	100.0	Total Liabilities & Net Worth					100.0	100.0
			INCOME DATA						
100.0	100.0	100.0	Net Sales					100.0	100.0
			Gross Profit						
92.8	93.9	96.6	Operating Expenses					96.8	96.4
7.2	6.1	3.4	Operating Profit					3.2	3.6
2.6	2.4	1.6	All Other Expenses (net)					1.7	2.3
4.6	3.7	1.8	Profit Before Taxes					1.5	1.2
			RATIOS						
3.8	3.8	4.9						5.4	2.8
1.9	1.5	2.1	Current					2.9	1.3
1.0	1.0	1.1						1.7	.9
3.6	3.7	4.7						5.4	2.3
1.6	1.2	1.6	Quick					2.9	1.1
1.0	.8	1.0						1.6	.8
21 17.2	**2** 170.4	**19** 19.4						**34** 10.6	**23** 16.2
52 7.0	**34** 10.7	**54** 6.7	Sales/Receivables					**66** 5.5	**49** 7.4
74 4.9	**63** 5.8	**78** 4.7						**99** 3.7	**72** 5.1
			Cost of Sales/Inventory						
			Cost of Sales/Payables						
3.0	4.1	3.6						1.1	3.9
7.3	10.0	8.8	Sales/Working Capital					4.7	17.5
170.7	-319.5	54.9						9.9	-115.8
24.8	20.0	12.2							19.8
(41) 3.3	**(34)** 3.6	**(41)** 5.6	EBIT/Interest					**(17)** 4.1	
-1.4	.0	.0							-.8
			Net Profit + Depr., Dep., Amort./Cur. Mat. L/T/D						
.1	.1	.0						.0	.1
.3	.4	.4	Fixed/Worth					.3	.5
1.6	1.9	1.4						.9	NM
.4	.5	.5						.4	.5
1.2	1.6	1.3	Debt/Worth					.6	2.2
15.7	NM	3.0						1.4	NM
31.2	44.9	40.3	% Profit Before Taxes/Tangible Net Worth					25.5	29.0
(48) 9.4	**(35)** 10.1	**(49)** 10.0						14.3	**(17)** 10.8
-3.7	4.7	1.9						2.2	.2
11.8	11.0	14.2	% Profit Before Taxes/Total Assets					15.2	11.6
2.8	4.1	3.3						3.3	3.2
-2.9	-.6	-1.2						1.3	-5.2
124.4	135.8	140.4						148.1	73.2
28.1	30.1	15.9	Sales/Net Fixed Assets					10.6	23.2
3.0	1.4	2.1						1.7	4.0
2.8	3.3	3.3						2.8	2.9
1.5	1.5	1.8	Sales/Total Assets					1.7	2.0
.5	.7	.7						.6	1.2
.5	.6	1.2						1.7	1.0
(41) 1.7	**(30)** 2.0	**(38)** 2.5	% Depr., Dep., Amort./Sales					**(11)** 2.8	**(16)** 1.7
3.6	4.7	5.0						7.1	3.0
		.5	% Officers', Directors' Owners' Comp/Sales						
	(12) 2.2	11.0							
3853843M	3613485M	3027251M	Net Sales ($)	3254M	12300M	11503M	39806M	226175M	2734213M
2487885M	2335607M	2301995M	Total Assets ($)	4343M	16434M	2328M	38595M	326392M	1913903M

M = $ thousand   MM = $ million
See Pages viii through xx for Explanation of Ratios and Data

Current Data Sorted by Assets   Comparative Historical Data

	0-500M	500M-2MM	2-10MM	10-50MM	50-100MM	100-250MM	Type of Statement	4/1/14-3/31/15 ALL	4/1/15-3/31/16 ALL
			2	9	4	3	Unqualified	25	25
	1	4	18	15	1		Reviewed	49	48
	1	9	13	5			Compiled	48	42
	32	26	14	2			Tax Returns	108	124
	19	34	68	33	2	4	Other	202	209
		21 (4/1-9/30/18)		298 (10/1/18-3/31/19)					
NUMBER OF STATEMENTS	53	73	115	64	7	7		432	448
ASSETS	%	%	%	%	%	%		%	%
Cash & Equivalents	36.2	25.4	18.1	23.0				27.0	24.9
Trade Receivables (net)	19.2	39.2	47.1	40.2				37.6	37.2
Inventory	.6	3.8	2.4	2.8				2.5	2.5
All Other Current	5.4	1.7	4.2	6.3				4.7	3.8
Total Current	61.3	70.0	71.6	72.4				71.8	68.4
Fixed Assets (net)	14.6	14.8	15.7	7.8				12.6	14.4
Intangibles (net)	8.3	6.9	5.6	12.8				6.7	7.0
All Other Non-Current	15.7	8.3	7.0	7.0				8.9	10.3
Total	100.0	100.0	100.0	100.0				100.0	100.0
LIABILITIES									
Notes Payable-Short Term	44.2	12.7	6.9	3.2				12.5	13.7
Cur. Mat.-L.T.D.	3.5	1.5	1.0	2.1				1.9	1.9
Trade Payables	23.6	18.8	25.5	29.3				24.9	25.6
Income Taxes Payable	.0	.0	.1	.2				.3	.3
All Other Current	40.3	22.6	23.4	23.7				18.9	20.5
Total Current	111.6	55.6	56.8	58.4				58.5	62.0
Long-Term Debt	16.7	13.8	9.8	9.7				7.7	13.0
Deferred Taxes	.0	.0	.0	.2				.2	.2
All Other Non-Current	3.8	1.7	6.9	6.0				7.9	7.1
Net Worth	-32.1	28.9	26.4	25.6				25.7	17.8
Total Liabilities & Net Worth	100.0	100.0	100.0	100.0				100.0	100.0
INCOME DATA									
Net Sales	100.0	100.0	100.0	100.0				100.0	100.0
Gross Profit									
Operating Expenses	94.9	94.2	92.4	93.7				91.3	92.4
Operating Profit	5.1	5.8	7.6	6.3				8.7	7.6
All Other Expenses (net)	.4	1.4	1.5	.7				.8	1.1
Profit Before Taxes	4.7	4.4	6.1	5.6				7.9	6.5
RATIOS									
	1.7	2.3	2.0	1.8				2.3	1.9
Current	.6	1.2	1.3	1.2				1.2	1.2
	.3	.8	.9	1.0				.9	.8
	1.7	2.2	1.9	1.4				2.1	1.7
Quick	.6	1.1	1.1	1.0				1.1	1.1
	.2	.7	.8	.8				.8	.7
	0 UND	12 30.2	38 9.5	40 9.1				18 20.0	16 22.3
Sales/Receivables	0 UND	34 10.7	56 6.5	57 6.4				42 8.6	39 9.4
	26 13.9	51 7.2	79 4.6	78 4.7				68 5.4	64 5.7
Cost of Sales/Inventory									
Cost of Sales/Payables									
	25.0	10.9	8.0	8.5				8.2	9.7
Sales/Working Capital	-62.7	30.0	19.4	21.1				24.7	36.8
	-9.0	-28.0	-54.2	-104.3				-85.9	-34.7
	28.3	30.9	53.6	76.8				66.3	57.8
EBIT/Interest	(34) 8.6	(55) 7.3	(83) 8.0	(42) 10.8				(291) 15.2	(310) 10.2
	.5	2.1	1.3	1.3				3.0	1.8
				10.1			Net Profit + Depr., Dep.,	6.8	6.1
				(15) 4.6			Amort./Cur. Mat. L/T/D	(34) 3.1	(36) 2.3
				.1				.9	1.0
	.0	.1	.1	.1				.1	.1
Fixed/Worth	.5	.3	.5	.5				.3	.4
	-1.2	-5.3	-2.3	NM				3.2	-10.6
	1.0	.7	.9	1.4				.9	1.1
Debt/Worth	155.0	2.7	3.2	8.1				3.7	4.7
	-2.0	-17.6	-21.1	-143.3				853.1	-16.8
	584.0	107.3	99.3	95.9			% Profit Before Taxes/Tangible	157.1	137.0
	(29) 109.2	(52) 43.2	(81) 51.6	(47) 34.5			Net Worth	(326) 54.9	(316) 59.1
	13.3	12.5	22.4	8.3				14.1	15.0
	95.5	30.7	27.5	16.9			% Profit Before Taxes/Total	34.1	33.1
	31.7	12.0	10.1	6.9			Assets	13.3	11.5
	-.6	1.9	1.3	1.6				2.1	.9
	UND	484.7	146.3	229.6				320.7	231.9
Sales/Net Fixed Assets	359.4	72.8	47.4	56.8				63.4	53.1
	50.4	21.1	18.0	17.9				20.7	18.6
	12.9	6.1	4.2	3.9				5.2	5.5
Sales/Total Assets	7.8	4.1	3.1	2.4				3.5	3.4
	4.7	2.9	2.2	1.5				2.0	1.9
	.2	.3	.4	.2				.3	.4
% Depr., Dep., Amort./Sales	(22) .5	(43) .7	(81) .9	(48) .7				(254) .7	(281) .7
	1.3	2.1	2.0	1.8				1.6	1.9
	4.1	2.9	2.4	.8			% Officers', Directors'	2.2	2.4
	(34) 8.3	(35) 5.6	(31) 5.3	(13) 1.3			Owners' Comp/Sales	(172) 5.4	(175) 6.1
	12.7	9.8	8.7	3.9				10.8	11.3
Net Sales ($)	123664M	403664M	1797218M	3781905M	1165713M	1058794M		12036308M	12154172M
Total Assets ($)	12217M	85205M	602502M	1361258M	472028M	1232463M		5691560M	5672967M

© RMA 2019   M = $ thousand   MM = $ million
See Pages viii through xx for Explanation of Ratios and Data

Comparative Historical Data / Current Data Sorted by Sales

Type of Statement									
25	22	18	Unqualified					3	15
45	39	39	Reviewed		4	2	5	12	16
31	10	28	Compiled	1	2	1	9	10	5
73	74	74	Tax Returns	15	14	14	16	11	4
185	207	160	Other	12	20	13	28	41	46
4/1/16-3/31/17 ALL	4/1/17-3/31/18 ALL	4/1/18-3/31/19 ALL		0-1MM	21 (4/1-9/30/18) 1-3MM	3-5MM	298 (10/1/18-3/31/19) 5-10MM	10-25MM	25MM & OVER
359	361	319	**NUMBER OF STATEMENTS**	28	40	30	58	77	86
%	%	%	**ASSETS**	%	%	%	%	%	%
24.8	24.3	23.6	Cash & Equivalents	24.5	24.0	25.8	28.1	23.3	19.6
38.0	37.1	38.6	Trade Receivables (net)	17.0	21.4	35.0	40.7	48.6	44.4
2.0	2.7	2.5	Inventory	.4	2.5	3.8	2.6	2.1	3.0
3.9	4.2	4.3	All Other Current	1.4	1.6	5.5	3.4	4.6	6.3
68.8	68.3	69.0	Total Current	43.2	49.6	70.1	74.8	78.6	73.4
12.7	13.1	13.3	Fixed Assets (net)	31.1	21.9	16.1	9.9	10.2	7.7
10.0	9.6	9.1	Intangibles (net)	11.2	12.0	5.1	5.6	6.5	13.2
8.5	8.9	8.6	All Other Non-Current	14.2	16.6	8.7	9.7	4.8	5.7
100.0	100.0	100.0	Total	100.0	100.0	100.0	100.0	100.0	100.0
			LIABILITIES						
9.6	13.9	13.5	Notes Payable-Short Term	22.2	28.0	20.0	13.7	10.7	4.1
2.0	2.3	1.9	Cur. Mat.-L.T.D.	4.8	2.2	1.6	1.2	.8	2.5
24.4	25.0	24.5	Trade Payables	7.3	17.9	19.2	28.4	25.4	31.6
.3	.3	.1	Income Taxes Payable	.0	.0	.0	.0	.1	.2
20.9	20.6	25.8	All Other Current	20.5	24.8	42.9	27.0	22.4	24.4
57.2	62.0	65.9	Total Current	54.8	73.0	83.7	70.4	59.4	62.6
13.1	14.5	12.1	Long-Term Debt	29.4	19.1	18.8	8.4	4.8	9.9
.2	.2	.1	Deferred Taxes	.0	.0	.0	.0	.0	.1
7.4	6.8	5.2	All Other Non-Current	4.9	4.3	2.2	4.6	5.7	6.8
22.0	16.5	16.8	Net Worth	10.8	3.6	-4.7	16.6	30.1	20.5
100.0	100.0	100.0	Total Liabilties & Net Worth	100.0	100.0	100.0	100.0	100.0	100.0
			INCOME DATA						
100.0	100.0	100.0	Net Sales	100.0	100.0	100.0	100.0	100.0	100.0
			Gross Profit						
91.3	92.5	93.7	Operating Expenses	86.7	92.5	94.8	94.6	93.5	95.7
8.7	7.5	6.3	Operating Profit	13.3	7.5	5.2	5.4	6.5	4.3
1.2	1.1	1.2	All Other Expenses (net)	6.6	1.1	.3	.6	.4	.9
7.5	6.4	5.1	Profit Before Taxes	6.6	6.4	4.9	4.8	6.2	3.4
			RATIOS						
2.2	2.0	1.9		7.5	1.4	2.2	2.3	2.0	1.6
1.2	1.2	1.2	Current	1.4	.7	1.1	1.3	1.4	1.1
.8	.9	.8		.2	.4	.6	.8	1.0	.9
2.2	1.8	1.8		7.5	1.4	1.6	2.3	2.0	1.3
1.1	1.0	1.0	Quick	.7	.7	1.0	1.1	1.2	1.0
.7	.7	.7		.2	.3	.4	.7	.9	.8
20 18.2	21 17.7	20 18.0		0 UND	0 UND	0 UND	14 26.1	36 10.2	37 9.8
41 8.8	44 8.3	46 8.0	Sales/Receivables	0 UND	21 17.6	32 11.5	43 8.4	56 6.5	53 6.9
64 5.7	72 5.1	68 5.4		47 7.8	48 7.6	62 5.9	60 6.1	79 4.6	73 5.0
			Cost of Sales/Inventory						
			Cost of Sales/Payables						
8.1	8.9	9.4		6.5	18.2	8.8	8.4	8.5	11.3
33.6	35.9	33.4	Sales/Working Capital	108.8	-43.5	99.9	38.1	16.1	38.0
-31.2	-30.6	-26.1		-2.9	-9.2	-14.6	-20.8	NM	-56.8
85.4	41.6	37.1		13.5	13.6	28.0	40.9	129.0	27.6
(229) 14.1	(257) 11.3	(226) 8.2	EBIT/Interest	(14) 4.6	(28) 1.8	(23) 12.9	(46) 8.6	(55) 17.8	(60) 6.4
2.4	1.5	1.3		.4	-1.7	2.5	1.9	4.1	.7
7.6	10.7	10.1							7.6
(29) 2.5	(35) 3.3	(23) 3.9	Net Profit + Depr., Dep., Amort./Cur. Mat. L/T/D					(16)	4.2
1.2	.4	.1							.2
.1	.1	.1		.0	.0	.1	.0	.1	.1
.6	.5	.4	Fixed/Worth	1.7	1.2	.3	.4	.3	.6
-1.4	-2.3	-2.3		UND	-.9	-2.0	-1.6	3.2	-.8
.9	1.0	1.1		1.3	.9	.6	.7	.8	2.3
4.3	4.8	5.3	Debt/Worth	5.3	8.8	4.0	3.8	3.0	11.3
-15.2	-11.8	-12.4		-4.5	-2.6	-3.3	-9.6	37.7	-10.5
105.2	117.0	110.3		463.6	133.8	124.3	112.8	101.4	128.6
(237) 54.4	(243) 47.4	(214) 51.6	% Profit Before Taxes/Tangible Net Worth	(19) 26.3	(23) 25.2	(20) 40.6	(37) 61.4	(59) 52.8	(56) 52.5
14.9	15.6	14.6		4.6	1.8	4.7	26.2	25.5	14.3
32.3	27.3	28.1		40.6	34.0	38.1	44.6	30.9	19.6
11.4	9.8	9.6	% Profit Before Taxes/Total Assets	5.2	4.0	11.9	12.9	13.9	6.2
1.9	.8	1.3		.7	-3.0	3.0	2.9	4.8	.0
255.9	224.1	280.6		UND	532.6	416.9	482.4	187.2	221.4
60.2	59.9	62.4	Sales/Net Fixed Assets	57.8	58.0	53.5	75.5	58.7	63.0
19.5	19.1	19.6		.5	8.8	22.8	23.2	22.1	20.6
5.1	4.9	5.2		7.1	6.0	8.5	6.0	4.5	4.4
3.3	3.3	3.4	Sales/Total Assets	2.4	3.1	4.6	3.9	3.1	3.0
1.8	1.9	2.2		.3	1.8	3.1	2.6	2.3	2.0
.3	.3	.3		.3	.6	.3	.2	.4	.2
(217) .8	(215) .9	(198) .8	% Depr., Dep., Amort./Sales	(17) 1.8	(18) 1.8	(15) .8	(35) .7	(52) .8	(61) .6
1.7	2.0	1.9		27.1	2.8	1.5	1.5	1.5	1.6
2.2	2.6	2.7		7.2	4.1	2.8	2.9	1.5	.8
(126) 5.1	(121) 5.1	(114) 5.3	% Officers', Directors' Owners' Comp/Sales	(14) 11.9	(22) 9.0	(16) 5.4	(26) 4.7	(21) 3.0	(15) 1.4
11.1	9.8	10.9		18.0	13.3	8.9	7.2	6.9	5.7
10465279M	11678797M	8330958M	Net Sales ($)	16784M	72329M	113579M	416108M	1220431M	6491727M
4981843M	5638459M	3765673M	Total Assets ($)	34132M	61269M	33280M	134975M	488141M	3013876M

M = $ thousand   MM = $ million
See Pages viii through xx for Explanation of Ratios and Data

Current Data Sorted by Assets   Comparative Historical Data

0-500M	500M-2MM	2-10MM	10-50MM	50-100MM	100-250MM	Type of Statement	4/1/14-3/31/15 ALL	4/1/15-3/31/16 ALL
			4			Unqualified	10	10
	1	2		1		Reviewed	6	9
1	4					Compiled	8	5
8	3	1	7		2	Tax Returns	14	16
7	11	14				Other	55	47
	10 (4/1-9/30/18)		56 (10/1/18-3/31/19)					
16	19	17	11	1	2	**NUMBER OF STATEMENTS**	93	87
%	%	%	%	%	%	**ASSETS**	%	%
47.6	19.4	24.5	30.4			Cash & Equivalents	26.7	30.8
8.9	37.2	41.4	25.8			Trade Receivables (net)	37.5	30.5
.0	.5	1.3	3.8			Inventory	1.4	.9
1.6	7.2	4.1	9.6			All Other Current	4.4	4.8
58.1	64.3	71.4	69.6			Total Current	70.0	67.0
11.2	20.7	8.4	9.0			Fixed Assets (net)	14.7	15.8
2.7	7.3	13.8	15.1			Intangibles (net)	4.6	6.3
28.0	7.7	6.4	6.2			All Other Non-Current	10.7	10.9
100.0	100.0	100.0	100.0			Total	100.0	100.0
						LIABILITIES		
35.7	15.5	8.7	6.6			Notes Payable-Short Term	16.5	12.7
3.3	3.8	3.0	1.5			Cur. Mat.-L.T.D.	1.9	1.7
.3	6.4	11.8	14.1			Trade Payables	12.4	10.2
.0	.0	.0	.1			Income Taxes Payable	.3	.1
24.9	16.3	25.1	22.3			All Other Current	23.1	24.7
64.1	41.9	48.5	44.5			Total Current	54.2	49.3
25.0	16.2	7.6	7.7			Long-Term Debt	9.8	9.6
.0	1.2	.0	.1			Deferred Taxes	.4	.1
4.7	5.7	17.0	7.4			All Other Non-Current	8.7	11.3
6.2	34.9	27.0	40.3			Net Worth	26.9	29.6
100.0	100.0	100.0	100.0			Total Liabilities & Net Worth	100.0	100.0
						INCOME DATA		
100.0	100.0	100.0	100.0			Net Sales	100.0	100.0
						Gross Profit		
81.8	84.4	90.2	93.7			Operating Expenses	88.5	90.7
18.2	15.6	9.8	6.3			Operating Profit	11.5	9.3
1.0	6.1	.7	.6			All Other Expenses (net)	2.1	2.4
17.1	9.5	9.0	5.7			Profit Before Taxes	9.4	7.0
						RATIOS		
8.0	4.8	4.1	4.0				2.7	3.1
.6	1.8	1.3	1.4			Current	1.4	1.4
.2	1.1	.8	1.1				.8	.9
6.8	4.8	3.9	3.8				2.6	2.4
.6	1.8	1.3	1.4			Quick	1.3	1.3
.2	.9	.7	.5				.8	.8
0 UND	2 146.2	41 8.9	20 18.3				5 77.2	0 UND
0 UND	43 8.4	54 6.8	37 9.9			Sales/Receivables	42 8.6	40 9.2
0 UND	60 6.1	74 4.9	64 5.7				64 5.7	59 6.2
						Cost of Sales/Inventory		
						Cost of Sales/Payables		
43.6	4.8	4.3	3.3				8.2	7.5
-106.9	18.8	26.1	7.2			Sales/Working Capital	17.1	22.9
-22.9	28.7	-20.4	26.8				-40.3	-91.0
79.0	41.5	80.3					63.9	67.1
(10) 13.6	(14) 10.5	(11) 24.7				EBIT/Interest	(62) 12.5	(60) 15.5
3.4	2.1	1.9					1.5	1.8
						Net Profit + Depr., Dep.,	9.6	13.7
						Amort./Cur. Mat. L/T/D	(10) 3.4	(12) 3.9
							.7	2.3
.0	.1	.1	.1				.0	.1
.1	.3	.3	.3			Fixed/Worth	.4	.3
7.4	8.4	-.2	1.2				2.6	2.8
.2	.3	.7	.5				.6	.4
1.9	3.7	3.4	2.3			Debt/Worth	2.4	2.4
-4.9	9.4	-3.1	9.3				10.9	22.8
600.0	126.3	165.5				% Profit Before Taxes/Tangible	166.7	105.7
(11) 180.0	(15) 46.2	(11) 47.9				Net Worth	(75) 63.4	(69) 48.2
95.0	13.4	17.4					18.6	13.1
408.2	54.2	43.2	20.2			% Profit Before Taxes/Total	53.5	42.2
118.4	11.0	14.8	6.7			Assets	16.8	11.7
22.7	2.6	4.1	1.0				4.3	1.5
UND	143.5	194.6	105.0				169.0	153.7
999.8	33.7	57.0	36.6			Sales/Net Fixed Assets	38.3	38.4
232.8	18.8	22.4	17.8				18.6	17.9
25.0	4.9	3.6	3.0				5.8	5.5
19.0	3.1	3.0	2.0			Sales/Total Assets	3.3	3.3
10.9	2.5	2.0	1.4				2.1	1.9
		.4					.5	.6
	(13) .8					% Depr., Dep., Amort./Sales	(57) 1.0	(51) 1.2
	1.5						1.9	2.2
							6.6	6.5
						% Officers', Directors'	(26) 9.7	(33) 13.9
						Owners' Comp/Sales	18.3	23.0
38922M	83124M	221715M	584835M	151142M	301241M	Net Sales ($)	2232208M	1596908M
2447M	25210M	77775M	277635M	71031M	455825M	Total Assets ($)	1008310M	755069M

© RMA 2019

M = $ thousand   MM = $ million
See Pages viii through xx for Explanation of Ratios and Data

Comparative Historical Data / Current Data Sorted by Sales

	8	6	4	Type of Statement					1	3
	4	3	4	Unqualified						
	6	6	5	Reviewed				1	2	1
	10	10	12	Compiled			3	2		
	38	30	41	Tax Returns	3	4	3	2		
	4/1/16-3/31/17 ALL	4/1/17-3/31/18 ALL	4/1/18-3/31/19 ALL	Other	2	6	8	11	6	8
					10 (4/1-9/30/18)			56 (10/1/18-3/31/19)		
					0-1MM	1-3MM	3-5MM	5-10MM	10-25MM	25MM & OVER
NUMBER OF STATEMENTS	66	55	66		5	10	14	16	9	12
ASSETS	%	%	%		%	%	%	%	%	%
Cash & Equivalents	27.2	27.3	29.8			55.3	21.6	23.3		20.4
Trade Receivables (net)	31.6	30.1	28.9			15.0	29.6	39.5		32.5
Inventory	.1	1.0	1.1			1.9	.0	.9		3.4
All Other Current	4.5	4.9	5.2			4.8	2.4	7.4		9.1
Total Current	63.4	63.3	64.9			76.9	53.5	71.1		65.4
Fixed Assets (net)	14.6	16.7	12.9			2.2	14.5	10.5		10.8
Intangibles (net)	6.7	10.8	10.3			5.8	8.7	11.9		17.9
All Other Non-Current	15.4	9.2	11.9			15.1	23.4	6.5		6.0
Total	100.0	100.0	100.0			100.0	100.0	100.0		100.0
LIABILITIES										
Notes Payable-Short Term	17.6	11.3	16.4			23.8	15.2	22.8		6.2
Cur. Mat.-L.T.D.	4.6	3.0	3.0			1.5	6.9	2.0		2.0
Trade Payables	15.1	10.0	7.5			2.8	4.4	7.1		14.3
Income Taxes Payable	.7	.4	.0			.0	.0	.0		.1
All Other Current	22.7	19.2	21.5			28.8	21.7	20.0		17.7
Total Current	60.6	43.9	48.5			57.0	48.1	51.9		40.2
Long-Term Debt	8.4	12.0	14.3			40.0	4.3	7.0		9.2
Deferred Taxes	.6	.3	.4			.0	1.7	.0		.1
All Other Non-Current	7.6	7.7	8.8			7.5	7.3	15.2		10.5
Net Worth	22.8	36.0	28.0			-4.4	38.6	25.9		40.0
Total Liabilities & Net Worth	100.0	100.0	100.0			100.0	100.0	100.0		100.0
INCOME DATA										
Net Sales	100.0	100.0	100.0			100.0	100.0	100.0		100.0
Gross Profit										
Operating Expenses	90.0	88.6	86.5			76.2	92.5	94.0		88.4
Operating Profit	10.0	11.4	13.5			23.8	7.5	6.0		11.6
All Other Expenses (net)	1.3	2.0	2.6			2.8	1.0	.8		2.1
Profit Before Taxes	8.7	9.4	11.0			21.0	6.5	5.2		9.5
RATIOS										
Current	2.3	2.9	4.6			10.5	12.8	4.0		3.0
	1.2	1.8	1.4			1.2	1.3	1.7		1.6
	.6	1.0	.8			.6	.2	.9		1.1
Quick	2.0	2.7	4.5			9.5	11.2	3.3		3.0
	1.1	1.6	1.3			1.0	1.2	1.6		1.6
	.6	.9	.7			.6	.2	.8		.6
Sales/Receivables	4 86.7	0 999.8	0 UND			0 UND	0 UND	29 12.8		38 9.5
	39 9.4	34 10.7	40 9.1			0 UND	35 10.4	49 7.5		57 6.4
	57 6.4	58 6.3	58 6.3			45 8.1	62 5.9	74 4.9		85 4.3
Cost of Sales/Inventory										
Cost of Sales/Payables										
Sales/Working Capital	9.8	6.8	6.0			25.0	4.3	5.0		4.3
	39.3	16.6	21.3			80.7	25.5	18.2		11.1
	-13.4	-214.1	-36.2			-19.4	-85.2	-50.9		24.5
EBIT/Interest	54.2	73.9	41.2					38.7		85.8
	(41) 9.9	(38) 11.4	(44) 11.2				(11) 3.8			(10) 11.2
	.3	2.1	2.2					2.3		1.4
Net Profit + Depr., Dep., Amort./Cur. Mat. L/T/D	16.4									
	(12) 5.9									
	1.6									
Fixed/Worth	.0	.1	.1			.0	.0	.2		.1
	.2	.4	.3			.0	.2	.3		.4
	5.1	UND	NM			NM	NM	NM		NM
Debt/Worth	.7	.7	.4			.1	.2	.3		.8
	2.2	2.3	2.4			6.5	1.3	3.8		2.4
	-25.2	-25.9	-13.9			-4.7	NM	NM		NM
% Profit Before Taxes/Tangible Net Worth	121.3	148.0	160.9				140.5	106.3		
	(48) 50.1	(40) 67.0	(48) 48.1				(11) 57.4	(12) 22.5		
	6.0	20.4	18.7				6.4	6.4		
% Profit Before Taxes/Total Assets	56.3	45.5	76.5			568.1	51.7	71.9		26.5
	11.9	18.2	16.3			83.8	18.4	7.7		16.3
	-.8	4.8	3.5			9.8	.8	.7		1.9
Sales/Net Fixed Assets	163.1	303.1	515.1			UND	999.8	116.8		94.3
	50.3	42.0	63.0			UND	118.9	28.4		35.0
	19.7	17.4	23.5			72.8	24.2	20.5		8.7
Sales/Total Assets	5.6	5.6	8.5			22.0	10.9	6.2		3.1
	3.7	3.5	3.2			13.9	3.3	3.1		2.1
	1.9	1.8	2.1			3.0	2.5	1.5		1.4
% Depr., Dep., Amort./Sales	.3	.7	.5					.6		
	(39) .8	(29) .9	(36) .9					(12) 1.0		
	2.2	1.9	1.6					1.6		
% Officers', Directors' Owners' Comp/Sales	4.9	6.4	8.9							
	(20) 11.5	(17) 12.7	(17) 16.4							
	20.4	27.7	26.5							
Net Sales ($)	1158170M	1102046M	1380979M		2595M	20953M	54982M	116022M	149874M	1036553M
Total Assets ($)	523147M	831482M	909923M		2752M	4943M	14702M	68799M	51309M	767418M

© RMA 2019

M = $ thousand   MM = $ million
See Pages viii through xx for Explanation of Ratios and Data

Current Data Sorted by Assets   Comparative Historical Data

Type of Statement

	0-500M	500M-2MM	2-10MM	10-50MM	50-100MM	100-250MM		4/1/14-3/31/15 ALL	4/1/15-3/31/16 ALL
Unqualified			1			3		6	6
Reviewed				5				7	9
Compiled		2	3	1				10	5
Tax Returns	6	9	2	1				10	17
Other	6	9	11	8	3			38	43
		8 (4/1-9/30/18)		62 (10/1/18-3/31/19)				4/1/14-3/31/15 ALL	4/1/15-3/31/16 ALL
NUMBER OF STATEMENTS	12	20	17	15	3	3		71	80
	%	%	%	%	%	%		%	%
ASSETS									
Cash & Equivalents	29.6	17.8	10.9	13.6				13.6	12.1
Trade Receivables (net)	13.5	22.9	24.7	16.4				22.1	23.1
Inventory	1.7	3.1	1.2	.4				5.3	6.1
All Other Current	1.5	2.7	7.9	3.7				3.7	2.8
Total Current	46.3	46.4	44.7	34.0				44.8	44.1
Fixed Assets (net)	39.3	45.8	42.3	41.4				35.2	39.2
Intangibles (net)	6.4	1.0	5.5	14.1				10.4	8.3
All Other Non-Current	8.0	6.9	7.5	10.4				9.6	8.4
Total	100.0	100.0	100.0	100.0				100.0	100.0
LIABILITIES									
Notes Payable-Short Term	24.4	7.1	4.9	2.1				15.9	12.3
Cur. Mat.-L.T.D.	8.2	4.4	6.3	3.8				4.4	4.1
Trade Payables	9.4	8.1	12.2	5.2				9.4	10.6
Income Taxes Payable	.4	.0	.1	.0				.5	.0
All Other Current	3.3	12.1	13.5	7.9				11.2	12.5
Total Current	45.5	31.7	37.1	19.0				41.5	39.5
Long-Term Debt	54.0	42.2	38.3	32.9				33.2	31.0
Deferred Taxes	.0	.0	.0	.2				.4	.4
All Other Non-Current	2.8	3.9	6.3	5.7				8.2	3.9
Net Worth	-2.2	22.2	18.3	42.2				16.7	25.1
Total Liabilities & Net Worth	100.0	100.0	100.0	100.0				100.0	100.0
INCOME DATA									
Net Sales	100.0	100.0	100.0	100.0				100.0	100.0
Gross Profit									
Operating Expenses	76.5	76.9	86.4	86.9				83.6	89.6
Operating Profit	23.5	23.1	13.6	13.1				16.4	10.4
All Other Expenses (net)	4.6	5.6	5.1	2.4				3.1	4.2
Profit Before Taxes	18.9	17.4	8.5	10.7				13.3	6.2
RATIOS									
Current	8.9	3.0	2.3	4.1				2.7	2.4
	1.7	1.0	1.2	1.9				1.3	1.2
	.5	.5	.5	1.1				.6	.7
Quick	8.9	2.9	1.9	4.0				2.0	2.1
	1.5	.9	.8	1.8				.9	.9
	.5	.5	.4	.7				.4	.6
Sales/Receivables	0 UND	0 UND	12 30.6	33 11.1				5 73.7	18 20.6
	19 18.8	27 13.7	46 8.0	60 6.1				37 9.9	48 7.6
	39 9.3	35 10.5	69 5.3	73 5.0				65 5.6	68 5.4
Cost of Sales/Inventory									
Cost of Sales/Payables									
Sales/Working Capital	2.5	5.8	4.5	3.3				5.8	6.0
	12.4	-615.4	31.0	7.0				23.0	30.2
	-25.3	-10.3	-8.2	91.7				-11.4	-13.7
EBIT/Interest	11.0	22.8	33.9	39.4				38.8	18.7
	(11) 3.0	(16) 8.7	(12) 6.3	(13) 5.8				(54) 10.3	(69) 3.5
	1.3	3.5	1.1	.2				2.6	.4
Net Profit + Depr., Dep., Amort./Cur. Mat. L/T/D									12.5
								(10)	2.2
									.0
Fixed/Worth	.3	.2	.1	.7				.3	.6
	1.9	1.5	4.5	1.6				1.5	1.1
	-3.1	7.6	-2.3	31.8				-2.5	-28.7
Debt/Worth	1.7	.9	.6	.7				.7	.8
	3.8	4.1	4.9	1.9				2.5	2.5
	-4.7	171.8	-4.5	39.6				-10.9	-28.1
% Profit Before Taxes/Tangible Net Worth		108.5	59.5	40.5				129.1	54.6
		(17) 62.8	(10) 29.6	(12) 26.6				(49) 48.7	(57) 32.1
		24.7	9.1	.5				18.6	6.9
% Profit Before Taxes/Total Assets	32.6	36.9	18.3	19.5				35.1	19.8
	21.8	17.9	11.7	10.5				14.6	7.8
	2.2	3.1	3.3	-1.9				4.8	-.5
Sales/Net Fixed Assets	35.3	495.4	60.3	6.7				41.1	22.5
	6.5	5.3	2.2	1.8				6.7	3.8
	.9	.6	.8	1.1				1.6	1.1
Sales/Total Assets	3.5	4.7	2.9	1.1				3.0	2.6
	1.6	2.0	1.2	.7				1.9	1.7
	.6	.5	.5	.6				.7	.7
% Depr., Dep., Amort./Sales		4.3	1.3	3.2				1.4	1.1
		(12) 12.1	(15) 11.0	(14) 6.0				(44) 4.9	(60) 4.9
		25.0	14.1	12.3				13.0	13.4
% Officers', Directors' Owners' Comp/Sales			1.6					2.5	2.8
			(10) 7.3					(25) 4.9	(28) 4.9
			13.1					9.3	10.6
Net Sales ($)	6518M	58805M	155986M	254540M	291674M	370653M		1521384M	2246605M
Total Assets ($)	2914M	21078M	77513M	297302M	177549M	485527M		1198927M	1612770M

M = $ thousand   MM = $ million
See Pages viii through xx for Explanation of Ratios and Data

Comparative Historical Data | Current Data Sorted by Sales

Type of Statement	4/1/16-3/31/17 ALL	4/1/17-3/31/18 ALL	4/1/18-3/31/19 ALL		0-1MM	1-3MM	3-5MM	5-10MM	10-25MM	25MM & OVER
Unqualified	4	5	4							4
Reviewed	8	5	5					1	2	2
Compiled	6	8	6				1	2	3	
Tax Returns	12	13	18		9	3	2	3	1	
Other	40	45	37		11	7	4	3	9	3
					8 (4/1-9/30/18)			62 (10/1/18-3/31/19)		
NUMBER OF STATEMENTS	70	76	70		20	10	7	9	15	9
	%	%	%		%	%	%	%	%	%
ASSETS										
Cash & Equivalents	8.8	14.3	16.2		18.4	11.9			12.2	
Trade Receivables (net)	18.4	20.7	20.3		5.3	17.1			23.6	
Inventory	4.9	4.6	1.6		.0	2.0			1.4	
All Other Current	3.4	3.5	4.1		.9	6.8			5.5	
Total Current	35.4	43.1	42.2		24.7	37.9			42.7	
Fixed Assets (net)	44.0	36.9	43.0		63.8	48.9			32.0	
Intangibles (net)	11.3	12.2	7.1		3.5	9.1			17.3	
All Other Non-Current	9.2	7.7	7.8		8.0	4.1			8.1	
Total	100.0	100.0	100.0		100.0	100.0			100.0	
LIABILITIES										
Notes Payable-Short Term	10.8	10.8	8.0		10.9	9.5			3.5	
Cur. Mat.-L.T.D.	4.6	6.0	5.3		8.2	4.3			2.9	
Trade Payables	8.6	12.4	9.7		5.2	4.2			8.9	
Income Taxes Payable	.0	.0	.1		.2	.0			.1	
All Other Current	9.6	12.1	9.9		2.2	5.0			12.7	
Total Current	33.5	41.4	33.0		26.7	23.0			28.0	
Long-Term Debt	42.3	47.5	51.6		71.2	49.6			19.5	
Deferred Taxes	.2	.6	.1		.0	.0			.2	
All Other Non-Current	8.1	7.7	4.5		9.0	.1			5.8	
Net Worth	16.0	2.8	10.9		-6.8	27.4			46.4	
Total Liabilities & Net Worth	100.0	100.0	100.0		100.0	100.0			100.0	
INCOME DATA										
Net Sales	100.0	100.0	100.0		100.0	100.0			100.0	
Gross Profit										
Operating Expenses	83.4	82.2	81.2		64.4	84.4			87.5	
Operating Profit	16.6	17.8	18.8		35.6	15.6			12.5	
All Other Expenses (net)	6.4	4.8	5.2		9.1	4.9			.8	
Profit Before Taxes	10.2	13.0	13.6		26.5	10.8			11.7	
RATIOS										
Current	2.2	2.5	2.6		2.2	3.1			2.7	
	1.1	1.2	1.3		.5	1.7			1.6	
	.5	.7	.6		.4	.6			.8	
Quick	1.8	1.8	2.1		2.1	2.3			2.3	
	.8	.9	1.1		.5	1.1			1.2	
	.4	.6	.5		.4	.6			.8	
Sales/Receivables	7 53.2	14 26.3	10 36.5		0 UND	21 17.6			40 9.1	
	38 9.5	38 9.7	34 10.6		0 UND	34 10.6			63 5.8	
	69 5.3	59 6.2	59 6.2		32 11.3	42 8.6			87 4.2	
Cost of Sales/Inventory										
Cost of Sales/Payables										
Sales/Working Capital	6.9	6.6	4.4		4.3	4.6			3.6	
	86.5	25.7	16.3		-17.9	12.2			8.2	
	-7.5	-13.4	-12.4		-6.2	-53.9			-26.0	
EBIT/Interest	23.3	9.2	14.5		10.6				40.9	
	(61) 3.9	(68) 4.0	(58) 5.0		(17) 3.7				(13) 14.2	
	1.3	1.1	1.4		2.1				1.5	
Net Profit + Depr., Dep., Amort./Cur. Mat. L/T/D										
Fixed/Worth	.9	1.0	.6		1.8	.7			.1	
	2.9	8.6	1.9		7.2	1.6			1.3	
	-6.7	-.7	-7.0		-1.7	-2.5			999.8	
Debt/Worth	1.2	1.4	1.1		1.8	.6			.6	
	4.3	29.4	4.1		151.3	3.4			2.3	
	-14.0	-2.8	-13.7		-3.8	-8.1			999.8	
% Profit Before Taxes/Tangible Net Worth	66.7	117.8	83.6		100.0				114.7	
	(46) 31.5	(43) 33.6	(48) 39.8		(11) 57.1				(12) 28.8	
	10.6	10.9	18.4		24.7				15.7	
% Profit Before Taxes/Total Assets	19.7	23.7	23.4		31.9	21.3			18.9	
	8.5	8.9	12.6		17.3	11.3			12.9	
	1.4	.4	1.6		2.7	.7			3.0	
Sales/Net Fixed Assets	20.0	19.5	26.2		2.1	41.6			31.7	
	2.3	7.4	2.0		1.0	1.3			2.8	
	.8	1.1	1.0		.4	.7			1.2	
Sales/Total Assets	2.7	2.6	2.9		1.2	3.8			2.2	
	.9	1.1	.9		.6	.7			1.0	
	.5	.7	.6		.3	.5			.6	
% Depr., Dep., Amort./Sales	1.1	1.3	2.2		11.3				1.4	
	(53) 4.0	(55) 5.6	(49) 9.8		(13) 17.2				(14) 6.0	
	15.8	11.9	16.1		30.6				16.1	
% Officers', Directors' Owners' Comp/Sales	2.4	1.4	2.8							
	(18) 4.9	(22) 3.9	(24) 5.2							
	8.9	9.4	9.5							
Net Sales ($)	1779294M	1753106M	1138176M		7551M	16666M	30485M	64026M	241422M	778026M
Total Assets ($)	1400877M	1426012M	1061883M		13673M	21504M	30215M	36501M	306798M	653192M

© RMA 2019

M = $ thousand   MM = $ million
See Pages viii through xx for Explanation of Ratios and Data

Current Data Sorted by Assets | Comparative Historical Data

Period counts: **7 (4/1-9/30/18)** · **54 (10/1/18-3/31/19)**

M = $ thousand   MM = $ million

Type of Statement	0-500M	500M-2MM	2-10MM	10-50MM	50-100MM	100-250MM	4/1/14-3/31/15 ALL	4/1/15-3/31/16 ALL
Unqualified			1	3		1	12	10
Reviewed		1	6	3	3		15	12
Compiled		2	2				6	8
Tax Returns		4	7				13	8
Other	4	5	6	7	1	5	47	30
NUMBER OF STATEMENTS	**4**	**12**	**22**	**13**	**4**	**6**	**93**	**68**
	%	%	%	%	%	%	%	%
ASSETS								
Cash & Equivalents		21.3	13.1	7.9			15.5	13.2
Trade Receivables (net)		26.5	28.9	28.6			31.7	25.7
Inventory		1.3	3.1	5.6			3.8	4.4
All Other Current		2.2	.4	2.6			3.5	2.6
Total Current		51.3	45.5	44.6			54.5	45.8
Fixed Assets (net)		16.8	45.3	32.3			30.1	32.3
Intangibles (net)		3.4	4.0	12.5			8.9	10.9
All Other Non-Current		28.5	5.1	10.6			6.5	11.0
Total		100.0	100.0	100.0			100.0	100.0
LIABILITIES								
Notes Payable-Short Term		3.5	7.0	6.9			7.0	11.1
Cur. Mat.-L.T.D.		3.3	5.1	4.6			4.7	4.5
Trade Payables		17.0	15.4	17.8			18.5	17.5
Income Taxes Payable		.0	.2	.1			.1	.1
All Other Current		28.5	15.1	12.6			19.8	16.7
Total Current		52.3	42.8	42.0			50.1	49.9
Long-Term Debt		17.4	28.8	14.1			24.9	31.4
Deferred Taxes		.0	.7	5.7			.5	.7
All Other Non-Current		3.6	11.3	9.7			7.8	8.1
Net Worth		26.6	16.5	28.5			16.7	9.8
Total Liabilties & Net Worth		100.0	100.0	100.0			100.0	100.0
INCOME DATA								
Net Sales		100.0	100.0	100.0			100.0	100.0
Gross Profit								
Operating Expenses		90.4	87.9	99.2			92.7	92.9
Operating Profit		9.6	12.1	.8			7.3	7.1
All Other Expenses (net)		3.8	5.0	.6			1.7	1.9
Profit Before Taxes		5.8	7.1	.3			5.5	5.2
RATIOS								
Current		2.2	1.6	2.0			1.8	1.7
		1.2	.8	1.0			1.1	1.0
		.4	.6	.8			.8	.7
Quick		2.2	1.5	1.5			1.6	1.4
		1.1	.8	1.0			.9	.9
		.3	.4	.6			.6	.5
Sales/Receivables		0 UND	15 23.8	33 11.0			22 16.8	15 24.6
		6 56.8	32 11.3	46 7.9			42 8.7	34 10.8
		51 7.2	51 7.1	81 4.5			59 6.2	54 6.7
Cost of Sales/Inventory								
Cost of Sales/Payables								
Sales/Working Capital		11.8	20.1	11.5			9.2	13.8
		NM	-51.6	-334.4			59.1	-175.0
		-13.4	-8.9	-15.3			-17.1	-18.7
EBIT/Interest			32.0	13.5			16.7	15.6
			(18) 2.2	5.1			(81) 5.5	(66) 4.5
			-1.2	-3.1			1.0	.9
Net Profit + Depr., Dep., Amort./Cur. Mat. L/T/D							3.7	4.7
							(20) 2.6	(15) 2.9
							1.4	.7
Fixed/Worth		.1	.6	.7			.6	.5
		.2	3.0	2.4			1.7	2.3
		7.4	-4.5	-.5			-7.5	-1.4
Debt/Worth		.5	1.9	1.0			1.6	1.8
		2.0	2.9	2.7			4.4	5.8
		38.5	-18.6	-5.8			-27.8	-5.8
% Profit Before Taxes/Tangible Net Worth		363.9	65.1				77.9	77.2
		(10) 49.1	(16) 36.3				(64) 33.8	(43) 35.2
		4.9	4.2				15.0	9.6
% Profit Before Taxes/Total Assets		78.5	19.4	16.0			15.8	18.1
		37.1	4.9	4.9			8.8	6.2
		10.2	-1.1	-11.8			.4	.1
Sales/Net Fixed Assets		652.9	19.0	32.1			30.1	35.6
		68.6	5.3	4.9			13.3	11.8
		18.6	3.1	2.9			4.4	4.8
Sales/Total Assets		8.9	3.8	2.4			4.1	4.6
		4.1	2.6	1.9			2.4	2.6
		3.8	1.3	1.4			1.6	1.5
% Depr., Dep., Amort./Sales			2.0	1.2			1.4	1.2
			(20) 4.3	(11) 3.5			(69) 2.5	(55) 2.9
			9.8	6.0			5.2	5.3
% Officers', Directors' Owners' Comp/Sales							2.5	2.1
							(29) 3.6	(24) 3.4
							8.3	7.4
Net Sales ($)	7832M	69321M	359697M	433843M	461950M	1035636M	2873656M	3017435M
Total Assets ($)	1335M	13327M	130357M	230575M	274547M	839997M	1577121M	1705881M

M = $ thousand   MM = $ million
See Pages viii through xx for Explanation of Ratios and Data

Comparative Historical Data / Current Data Sorted by Sales

			Type of Statement	0-1MM	1-3MM	3-5MM	5-10MM	10-25MM	25MM & OVER
8	6	8	Unqualified					1	7
14	18	10	Reviewed			1	1	7	1
5	4	4	Compiled		1	1	1	2	2
10	11	11	Tax Returns	3		1	4	2	1
32	28	28	Other	2	3	3	2	5	13
4/1/16-3/31/17 ALL	4/1/17-3/31/18 ALL	4/1/18-3/31/19 ALL			7 (4/1-9/30/18)			54 (10/1/18-3/31/19)	
69	67	61	**NUMBER OF STATEMENTS**	5	4	6	7	17	22
%	%	%	**ASSETS**	%	%	%	%	%	%
12.1	13.7	13.5	Cash & Equivalents					16.1	8.7
30.4	31.6	27.5	Trade Receivables (net)					34.0	27.6
4.3	2.9	3.7	Inventory					1.5	7.2
2.2	3.4	1.6	All Other Current					1.2	2.3
49.0	51.6	46.3	Total Current					52.8	45.8
31.8	26.2	29.6	Fixed Assets (net)					30.3	26.6
11.9	11.1	12.3	Intangibles (net)					11.0	15.5
7.3	11.1	11.9	All Other Non-Current					5.9	12.1
100.0	100.0	100.0	Total					100.0	100.0
			LIABILITIES						
6.9	7.5	5.0	Notes Payable-Short Term					5.5	6.7
	5.0	4.8	Cur. Mat.-L.T.D.					5.8	2.5
14.6	14.9	15.3	Trade Payables					15.6	17.7
.0	.1	.1	Income Taxes Payable					.3	.1
15.1	22.1	17.2	All Other Current					17.3	14.4
42.1	49.7	42.4	Total Current					44.5	41.3
26.6	21.8	25.2	Long-Term Debt					12.5	24.6
.6	1.0	1.7	Deferred Taxes					2.1	3.1
5.6	8.8	10.7	All Other Non-Current					4.0	24.6
25.1	18.6	20.0	Net Worth					36.9	6.4
100.0	100.0	100.0	Total Liabilities & Net Worth					100.0	100.0
			INCOME DATA						
100.0	100.0	100.0	Net Sales					100.0	100.0
			Gross Profit						
92.1	95.7	92.7	Operating Expenses					97.2	98.9
7.9	4.3	7.3	Operating Profit					2.8	1.1
1.0	.7	3.3	All Other Expenses (net)					.5	1.7
6.9	3.6	4.0	Profit Before Taxes					2.4	-.7
			RATIOS						
2.0	2.1	1.8	Current					2.0	1.9
1.4	1.3	1.0						1.0	1.1
.8	.7	.7						.8	.7
1.9	1.9	1.6	Quick					1.9	1.4
1.1	1.2	.9						1.0	.9
.7	.6	.6						.7	.6
18 20.4	19 19.0	16 23.5	Sales/Receivables					25 14.5	33 10.9
38 9.5	45 8.2	39 9.3						45 8.2	46 8.0
62 5.9	61 6.0	59 6.2						85 4.3	66 5.5
			Cost of Sales/Inventory						
			Cost of Sales/Payables						
12.0	10.1	12.5	Sales/Working Capital					8.2	12.4
27.5	22.9	-125.1						-334.4	57.6
-27.3	-20.6	-14.3						-22.1	-16.7
46.6	25.6	31.6	EBIT/Interest					24.5	12.7
(64) 12.8	(56) 3.5	(53) 5.1						(16) 5.1	2.6
3.3	-.1	.3						-2.1	-1.2
4.8	5.2		Net Profit + Depr., Dep., Amort./Cur. Mat. L/T/D						
(11) 2.0	(13) 3.1	1.0							
1.5	1.0								
.4	.2	.4	Fixed/Worth					.6	.7
1.4	1.4	1.9						1.8	2.8
15.2	-2.5	-1.3						-3.2	-.5
1.2	.8	1.2	Debt/Worth					1.2	1.3
2.3	5.4	3.8						2.4	20.5
NM	-5.3	-5.8						-15.5	-2.0
116.5	68.1	73.2	% Profit Before Taxes/Tangible Net Worth					53.3	70.8
(52) 46.1	(42) 33.9	(40) 27.1						(12) 27.1	(12) 11.9
26.7	7.6	4.2						.8	-14.8
27.9	25.3	25.9	% Profit Before Taxes/Total Assets					20.2	9.5
14.0	6.2	5.2						6.6	2.5
5.0	-1.2	-1.2						-1.2	-8.0
36.8	85.6	47.4	Sales/Net Fixed Assets					59.3	22.6
14.0	16.8	16.7						12.5	15.8
4.5	5.7	4.5						3.8	5.1
4.6	3.8	4.0	Sales/Total Assets					3.5	3.6
2.8	2.8	2.3						2.6	2.2
1.7	1.8	1.4						1.5	1.4
1.2	.5	1.2	% Depr., Dep., Amort./Sales					1.6	1.2
(53) 3.0	(47) 2.2	(43) 3.0						(14) 4.3	(17) 2.6
5.0	5.4	6.0						7.8	4.5
2.6	2.7	2.5	% Officers', Directors' Owners' Comp/Sales						
(23) 4.6	(25) 4.5	(19) 3.5							
6.6	9.2	5.0							
3153775M	2504154M	2368279M	Net Sales ($)	1765M	6901M	25054M	54648M	316702M	1963209M
1750214M	1481863M	1490138M	Total Assets ($)	11878M	2445M	7855M	21477M	158910M	1287573M

M = $ thousand   MM = $ million
See Pages viii through xx for Explanation of Ratios and Data

Current Data Sorted by Assets

Comparative Historical Data

	0-500M	500M-2MM	2-10MM	10-50MM	50-100MM	100-250MM		4/1/14-3/31/15 ALL	4/1/15-3/31/16 ALL
			2	7	3	1	Type of Statement		
			2	7			Unqualified	16	20
		1	4	2			Reviewed	16	9
	6	7	6				Compiled	17	17
	9	9	20	14			Tax Returns	49	36
		9 (4/1-9/30/18)		97 (10/1/18-3/31/19)	1	5	Other	72	86
	15	17	34	30	4	6	NUMBER OF STATEMENTS	170	168
	%	%	%	%	%	%	ASSETS	%	%
	21.2	29.0	12.5	13.2			Cash & Equivalents	22.8	19.1
	20.2	27.0	36.9	33.1			Trade Receivables (net)	32.6	36.1
	1.2	13.8	11.5	15.2			Inventory	9.7	9.4
	6.9	3.7	1.5	2.1			All Other Current	3.5	2.3
	49.5	73.4	62.5	63.7			Total Current	68.6	67.0
	13.3	15.7	15.2	17.1			Fixed Assets (net)	13.2	14.4
	4.2	5.3	10.7	14.2			Intangibles (net)	9.4	10.4
	33.1	5.5	11.6	5.1			All Other Non-Current	8.7	8.2
	100.0	100.0	100.0	100.0			Total	100.0	100.0
							LIABILITIES		
	60.9	17.3	14.7	16.3			Notes Payable-Short Term	15.9	10.0
	7.3	1.8	1.6	4.7			Cur. Mat.-L.T.D.	2.1	2.0
	8.9	17.5	17.6	16.1			Trade Payables	20.0	16.9
	.1	.0	.3	.1			Income Taxes Payable	.2	.2
	15.8	13.3	13.8	11.7			All Other Current	17.9	16.3
	93.0	49.9	48.1	49.0			Total Current	56.2	45.4
	18.6	14.3	12.2	14.0			Long-Term Debt	12.4	14.7
	.0	.0	.0	.2			Deferred Taxes	.2	.3
	11.5	1.9	6.2	8.7			All Other Non-Current	9.8	9.0
	-23.2	33.9	33.5	28.2			Net Worth	21.4	30.6
	100.0	100.0	100.0	100.0			Total Liabilities & Net Worth	100.0	100.0
							INCOME DATA		
	100.0	100.0	100.0	100.0			Net Sales	100.0	100.0
							Gross Profit		
	89.2	90.0	91.4	92.6			Operating Expenses	92.7	91.3
	10.8	10.0	8.6	7.4			Operating Profit	7.3	8.7
	1.1	-.1	.7	1.0			All Other Expenses (net)	2.0	2.8
	9.7	10.2	7.9	6.3			Profit Before Taxes	5.3	5.9
							RATIOS		
	4.2	3.9	1.9	2.2				2.5	3.2
	1.0	2.0	1.2	1.6			Current	1.3	1.5
	.3	.5	.9	1.2				.9	1.0
	4.0	3.2	1.3	2.0				1.8	2.5
	.9	1.5	.9	1.1			Quick	1.0	1.2
	.3	.3	.6	.7				.6	.7
	0 UND	0 UND	22 16.4	31 11.9				8 45.9	18 19.8
	0 999.8	33 10.9	42 8.6	42 8.7			Sales/Receivables	33 10.9	38 9.6
	26 14.3	49 7.5	51 7.1	68 5.4				59 6.2	63 5.8
							Cost of Sales/Inventory		
							Cost of Sales/Payables		
	12.1	4.1	11.0	5.2				7.9	7.4
	UND	6.6	35.5	10.0			Sales/Working Capital	22.6	16.8
	-33.7	-14.4	-124.6	17.4				-50.1	606.9
	76.0	22.2	14.0	30.3				26.4	39.5
	(12) 11.8	(11) 6.5	(26) 5.8	(24) 3.2			EBIT/Interest	(124) 6.7	(121) 9.1
	.9	2.2	.1	.9				1.9	1.6
				10.7				11.5	
			(10) 2.2				Net Profit + Depr., Dep., Amort./Cur. Mat. L/T/D	(10) 1.7	
				.6				-.9	
	.0	.0	.1	.2				.1	.0
	.1	.2	.3	.4			Fixed/Worth	.3	.3
	-3.0	-2.8	NM	-2.8				29.5	UND
	.1	.3	.9	1.0				1.0	.8
	1.8	.9	2.7	2.6			Debt/Worth	3.7	3.1
	-3.3	-4.2	NM	-6.2				-101.5	-20.8
		123.4	108.0	43.2				102.8	95.5
		(11) 55.6	(26) 66.5	(21) 28.6			% Profit Before Taxes/Tangible Net Worth	(126) 38.2	(122) 48.8
		13.5	19.2	5.8				11.7	12.1
	82.1	57.2	31.3	15.2				24.1	29.2
	38.6	31.5	15.1	4.9			% Profit Before Taxes/Total Assets	9.6	11.2
	2.6	8.7	.9	1.2				2.3	1.9
	999.8	542.7	193.4	94.9				315.4	243.4
	110.4	87.7	59.3	20.5			Sales/Net Fixed Assets	64.2	63.5
	19.0	13.4	24.6	10.8				24.9	19.1
	10.9	5.7	4.8	3.0				5.4	5.0
	7.0	3.2	3.6	2.1			Sales/Total Assets	3.2	3.1
	2.8	2.2	1.9	1.5				2.2	1.8
			.2	.4				.2	.3
		(23) .5	(24) 1.6				% Depr., Dep., Amort./Sales	(103) .7	(101) .8
			1.0	2.9				1.8	2.2
			.7					2.1	1.7
		(10) 1.5					% Officers', Directors' Owners' Comp/Sales	(63) 4.0	(61) 2.9
			1.9					7.6	7.2
	69088M	68794M	464529M	1410077M	345664M	1819908M	Net Sales ($)	4579448M	5504434M
	4246M	17012M	146553M	687447M	286444M	1057471M	Total Assets ($)	2212955M	2749361M

M = $ thousand   MM = $ million
See Pages viii through xx for Explanation of Ratios and Data

Comparative Historical Data

Current Data Sorted by Sales

Hist 1	Hist 2	Hist 3	Type of Statement	0-1MM	1-3MM	3-5MM	5-10MM	10-25MM	25MM & OVER
15	15	13	Unqualified					2	11
9	7	9	Reviewed	1				2	6
12	10	7	Compiled					2	3
27	29	19	Tax Returns	2	2			3	8
55	57	58	Other	5	8	4	4	10/11	20
4/1/16-3/31/17 ALL	4/1/17-3/31/18 ALL	4/1/18-3/31/19 ALL		9 (4/1-9/30/18)			97 (10/1/18-3/31/19)		
118	118	106	**NUMBER OF STATEMENTS**	8	12	8	15	26	37
%	%	%	**ASSETS**	%	%	%	%	%	%
21.2	21.0	16.3	Cash & Equivalents		20.8		18.6	18.5	12.0
31.8	29.1	31.3	Trade Receivables (net)		32.3		33.7	31.2	36.9
9.0	11.0	11.3	Inventory		11.6		8.0	9.6	15.3
3.2	3.1	2.9	All Other Current		.4		4.0	1.4	2.5
65.2	64.2	61.7	Total Current		65.0		64.3	60.8	66.7
16.6	16.0	15.2	Fixed Assets (net)		19.5		9.2	17.6	10.4
9.8	11.2	11.7	Intangibles (net)		10.8		16.9	6.4	16.9
8.3	8.6	11.3	All Other Non-Current		4.7		9.6	15.2	6.0
100.0	100.0	100.0	Total		100.0		100.0	100.0	100.0
			LIABILITIES						
10.6	14.8	21.2	Notes Payable-Short Term		10.4		15.9	26.3	15.5
3.8	4.5	3.4	Cur. Mat.-L.T.D.		1.3		2.2	1.8	4.1
15.5	15.7	15.7	Trade Payables		5.3		24.6	13.1	17.8
.1	.1	.2	Income Taxes Payable		.0		.0	.5	.3
17.3	16.8	14.1	All Other Current		13.4		18.8	12.6	15.9
47.3	51.9	54.6	Total Current		30.3		61.5	54.4	53.5
13.2	16.6	14.9	Long-Term Debt		16.5		8.9	13.2	14.0
.2	.1	.1	Deferred Taxes		.0		.0	.1	.1
7.5	6.5	7.5	All Other Non-Current		4.4		4.3	9.6	10.1
31.8	24.9	22.9	Net Worth		48.8		25.4	22.7	22.3
100.0	100.0	100.0	Total Liabilties & Net Worth		100.0		100.0	100.0	100.0
			INCOME DATA						
100.0	100.0	100.0	Net Sales		100.0		100.0	100.0	100.0
			Gross Profit						
92.8	92.1	91.4	Operating Expenses		84.3		90.0	93.5	95.3
7.2	7.9	8.6	Operating Profit		15.7		10.0	6.5	4.7
1.4	1.7	1.0	All Other Expenses (net)		-.6		.7	-.2	2.0
5.8	6.2	7.7	Profit Before Taxes		16.3		9.3	6.7	2.7
			RATIOS						
2.3	2.8	2.3			6.4		1.9	2.5	2.0
1.4	1.4	1.3	Current		3.7		1.0	1.2	1.4
1.0	1.0	.9			1.3		.7	.9	1.1
1.9	2.5	2.0			6.4		1.8	1.8	1.6
1.1	1.1	1.0	Quick		3.1		.8	1.0	1.0
.8	.6	.6			.6		.5	.6	.6
17 22.1	9 39.8	17 21.4			22 16.6		15 24.1	7 53.0	38 9.5
36 10.1	39 9.4	41 9.0	Sales/Receivables		34 10.6		34 10.7	29 12.8	56 6.5
57 6.4	54 6.8	57 6.4			43 8.4		53 6.9	49 7.4	74 4.9
			Cost of Sales/Inventory						
			Cost of Sales/Payables						
7.1	5.0	5.9			3.8		16.9	8.5	5.8
17.1	18.0	15.6	Sales/Working Capital		5.2		82.7	28.7	12.2
-217.1	-799.5	-170.3			51.7		-19.0	-170.3	30.1
53.0	27.6	17.8					47.3	15.2	12.9
(95) 12.2	(88) 6.2	(83) 5.4	EBIT/Interest				(11) 11.0	(21) 2.2	(33) 5.6
3.3	1.0	1.1					1.8	-1.5	1.2
	3.9	11.6	Net Profit + Depr., Dep.,						
	(16) 3.0	(13) 2.9	Amort./Cur. Mat. L/T/D						
	.4	1.2							
.1	.1	.1			.1		.0	.1	.2
.7	.4	.3	Fixed/Worth		.3		.2	.3	.4
-8.2	-2.8	-3.1			NM		-.3	1.6	-1.9
.9	.9	.8			.3		.3	.8	1.6
2.2	3.2	2.7	Debt/Worth		.7		26.9	1.7	3.4
-26.9	-8.1	-5.5			NM		-3.3	69.5	-4.1
107.6	93.7	100.5	% Profit Before Taxes/Tangible					134.6	51.5
(85) 60.5	(82) 46.2	(73) 43.7	Net Worth					(21) 59.8	(26) 35.7
19.5	9.1	14.3						2.7	11.3
35.1	28.5	31.2	% Profit Before Taxes/Total		49.6		45.7	38.1	17.3
13.3	8.6	11.3	Assets		28.5		23.2	9.6	7.2
2.6	1.2	1.7			5.1		4.9	-2.0	1.8
125.0	190.4	209.1			104.7		613.8	367.0	81.0
42.5	41.1	44.0	Sales/Net Fixed Assets		21.3		136.7	97.4	34.4
14.9	12.8	12.7			7.8		34.5	13.6	12.6
5.0	4.6	4.6			4.7		5.7	5.5	3.6
3.4	3.1	2.9	Sales/Total Assets		2.7		3.1	4.2	2.3
2.0	2.0	1.8			1.7		1.8	2.0	1.4
.4	.3	.3						.3	.5
(73) .8	(70) .9	(66) .9	% Depr., Dep., Amort./Sales					(17) .6	(30) 1.4
2.2	2.1	2.3						2.3	2.4
1.5	1.9	.9						.7	
(45) 3.3	(36) 3.8	(27) 2.3	% Officers', Directors'					(11) 1.7	
5.4	9.7	7.7	Owners' Comp/Sales					2.6	
3752192M	4043391M	4178060M	Net Sales ($)	4024M	23187M	31430M	111957M	400939M	3606523M
1885356M	2115914M	2199173M	Total Assets ($)	14645M	36992M	10478M	43027M	133006M	1961025M

M = $ thousand   MM = $ million
See Pages viii through xx for Explanation of Ratios and Data

Current Data Sorted by Assets — Comparative Historical Data

0-500M	500M-2MM	2-10MM	10-50MM	50-100MM	100-250MM	Type of Statement	ALL 4/1/14-3/31/15	ALL 4/1/15-3/31/16
		2	5		2	Unqualified	8	7
		1	2			Reviewed	10	10
	1	1				Compiled	10	7
6	6	3	1			Tax Returns	17	17
3	12	14	12	4	2	Other	67	56
	9 (4/1-9/30/18)		68 (10/1/18-3/31/19)					
9	19	21	20	4	4	**NUMBER OF STATEMENTS**	112	97
%	%	%	%	%	%	**ASSETS**	%	%
	30.1	20.2	19.3			Cash & Equivalents	23.6	21.6
	40.7	35.6	30.4			Trade Receivables (net)	35.8	35.8
	1.5	.2	.1			Inventory	.9	.7
	4.4	8.7	6.9			All Other Current	5.9	3.8
	76.7	64.8	56.8			Total Current	66.3	61.9
	8.3	17.5	10.5			Fixed Assets (net)	14.8	16.9
	6.0	7.8	15.0			Intangibles (net)	8.4	8.6
	9.0	9.9	17.6			All Other Non-Current	10.6	12.6
	100.0	100.0	100.0			Total	100.0	100.0
						LIABILITIES		
	8.7	4.0	2.0			Notes Payable-Short Term	12.8	9.5
	11.7	1.3	4.4			Cur. Mat.-L.T.D.	2.1	1.5
	15.8	5.7	11.5			Trade Payables	10.3	10.3
	.1	.2	.1			Income Taxes Payable	.3	.7
	29.9	24.6	38.1			All Other Current	21.8	25.1
	66.2	35.8	56.1			Total Current	47.2	47.0
	19.9	5.5	16.6			Long-Term Debt	12.2	14.0
	.0	.1	.5			Deferred Taxes	.0	.1
	24.1	14.5	9.1			All Other Non-Current	7.2	8.6
	-10.2	44.1	17.7			Net Worth	33.3	30.3
	100.0	100.0	100.0			Total Liabilties & Net Worth	100.0	100.0
						INCOME DATA		
	100.0	100.0	100.0			Net Sales	100.0	100.0
						Gross Profit		
	95.1	86.2	88.8			Operating Expenses	91.2	91.8
	4.9	13.8	11.2			Operating Profit	8.8	8.2
	.4	1.3	3.5			All Other Expenses (net)	1.8	1.8
	4.5	12.5	7.6			Profit Before Taxes	7.0	6.5
						RATIOS		
	11.2	6.8	2.0				2.9	3.1
	1.7	2.7	1.1			Current	1.5	1.6
	.7	1.3	.9				.9	.9
	11.2	6.5	1.6				2.5	2.9
	1.6	2.7	1.0			Quick	1.4	1.5
	.7	1.0	.7				.8	.9
	4 102.5	34 10.6	51 7.2				12 30.8	19 19.5
	42 8.7	46 7.9	61 6.0			Sales/Receivables	51 7.2	47 7.7
	62 5.9	78 4.7	83 4.4				74 4.9	78 4.7
						Cost of Sales/Inventory		
						Cost of Sales/Payables		
	5.7	4.1	5.1				7.4	6.1
	11.2	6.2	40.8			Sales/Working Capital	13.6	13.3
	-116.6	17.8	-67.6				-185.4	-141.6
	36.3	240.5	13.8				32.6	56.5
	(11) 1.7	(14) 17.1	(14) 2.7			EBIT/Interest	(80) 11.0	(68) 18.0
	-7.8	7.1	-.9				2.5	1.7
						Net Profit + Depr., Dep., Amort./Cur. Mat. L/T/D	6.9	45.0
							(16) 3.0	(17) 5.5
							1.2	1.1
	.0	.1	.1				.0	.1
	.5	.2	1.5			Fixed/Worth	.3	.3
	-.2	NM	-.4				2.2	2.5
	.5	.4	1.0				.5	.6
	2.0	1.2	12.6			Debt/Worth	1.7	1.7
	-2.0	NM	-2.7				25.1	11.7
	116.1	115.1	168.0				85.9	100.8
	(13) 44.5	(16) 39.8	(11) 77.9			% Profit Before Taxes/Tangible Net Worth	(88) 40.9	(76) 44.5
	12.0	2.5	15.4				10.9	13.7
	42.2	29.8	25.2				39.0	40.5
	17.0	16.0	9.8			% Profit Before Taxes/Total Assets	15.0	14.1
	-18.6	4.5	-.5				2.7	1.1
	419.8	121.4	107.5				229.2	117.0
	303.7	42.1	19.6			Sales/Net Fixed Assets	36.1	38.7
	75.7	18.0	15.0				12.6	12.2
	7.2	3.7	3.0				4.5	4.7
	3.5	2.7	1.8			Sales/Total Assets	3.0	2.8
	2.5	1.9	1.1				1.8	1.6
		.8	.5				.5	.5
		(14) .9	(12) 1.3			% Depr., Dep., Amort./Sales	(70) 1.3	(73) 1.1
		1.6	3.9				2.3	2.1
							2.2	3.4
						% Officers', Directors' Owners' Comp/Sales	(35) 5.8	(30) 8.2
							13.9	16.4
16497M	133488M	304918M	937791M	514695M	878541M	Net Sales ($)	2426013M	2097538M
1864M	22726M	109508M	515219M	222502M	576466M	Total Assets ($)	1198402M	1017873M

M = $ thousand   MM = $ million
See Pages viii through xx for Explanation of Ratios and Data

Comparative Historical Data | Current Data Sorted by Sales

Hist 4/1/16-3/31/17 ALL	Hist 4/1/17-3/31/18 ALL	Hist 4/1/18-3/31/19 ALL	Type of Statement	0-1MM	1-3MM	3-5MM	5-10MM	10-25MM	25MM & OVER
8	8	9	Unqualified					2	7
8	5	3	Reviewed					1	2
4	5	2	Compiled					2	
19	10	16	Tax Returns	4	2	2	7	1	
58	44	47	Other	3	3	6	9	8	18
					9 (4/1-9/30/18)			68 (10/1/18-3/31/19)	
97	72	77	NUMBER OF STATEMENTS	7	5	8	16	14	27
%	%	%	**ASSETS**	%	%	%	%	%	%
20.9	22.7	25.1	Cash & Equivalents				26.8	19.8	20.7
33.8	34.0	31.4	Trade Receivables (net)				36.0	39.3	32.7
1.4	1.6	.5	Inventory				.0	.0	.3
6.1	5.4	6.5	All Other Current				10.0	2.4	10.0
62.3	63.7	63.4	Total Current				72.9	61.5	63.7
15.6	14.0	12.2	Fixed Assets (net)				6.2	12.3	10.9
12.4	11.0	12.3	Intangibles (net)				8.8	12.5	15.3
9.7	11.3	12.1	All Other Non-Current				12.1	13.6	10.2
100.0	100.0	100.0	Total				100.0	100.0	100.0
			LIABILITIES						
11.5	14.5	7.2	Notes Payable-Short Term				8.1	3.3	5.2
2.5	2.4	5.0	Cur. Mat.-L.T.D.				.4	6.0	4.3
10.8	9.3	11.0	Trade Payables				13.3	3.7	12.9
1.9	.5	.1	Income Taxes Payable				.0	.2	.1
21.6	30.3	31.4	All Other Current				16.4	21.8	44.2
48.3	57.1	54.6	Total Current				38.2	35.1	66.8
16.9	20.7	14.8	Long-Term Debt				15.9	7.3	18.9
.1	.3	.3	Deferred Taxes				.0	.2	.7
6.9	6.3	14.3	All Other Non-Current				3.2	37.3	8.9
27.8	15.6	16.1	Net Worth				42.6	20.2	4.7
100.0	100.0	100.0	Total Liabilities & Net Worth				100.0	100.0	100.0
			INCOME DATA						
100.0	100.0	100.0	Net Sales				100.0	100.0	100.0
			Gross Profit						
92.8	92.6	90.6	Operating Expenses				81.6	92.6	91.6
7.2	7.4	9.4	Operating Profit				18.4	7.4	8.4
2.6	2.2	1.5	All Other Expenses (net)				.9	2.2	2.7
4.6	5.2	7.9	Profit Before Taxes				17.5	5.1	5.7
			RATIOS						
2.2	2.6	3.5	Current				12.4	6.6	1.3
1.4	1.4	1.3					2.5	3.0	1.1
.9	.8	1.0					1.5	1.1	.7
1.9	2.3	3.3	Quick				12.4	6.5	1.2
1.2	1.1	1.2					2.5	2.6	.9
.7	.7	.7					1.1	1.1	.5
9 39.9	6 64.7	18 19.8	Sales/Receivables				34 10.6	41 9.0	34 10.6
47 7.8	48 7.6	51 7.1					53 6.9	66 5.5	53 6.9
73 5.0	79 4.6	72 5.1					73 5.0	89 4.1	72 5.1
			Cost of Sales/Inventory						
			Cost of Sales/Payables						
7.6	6.4	5.8	Sales/Working Capital				4.3	4.9	11.2
20.5	20.7	19.0					9.2	8.0	65.0
-49.6	-25.8	-279.3					20.0	43.8	-58.1
51.5	65.2	35.8	EBIT/Interest				172.0	240.5	25.0
(74) 8.6	(49) 6.3	(52) 9.8					(12) 35.0	(10) 12.5	(21) 2.7
.7	1.0	1.0					8.7	-1.2	1.5
27.1			Net Profit + Depr., Dep.,						
(16) 5.8			Amort./Cur. Mat. L/T/D						
1.2									
.1	.0	.1	Fixed/Worth				.0	.1	.4
.5	.4	.4					.2	.2	-1.7
194.9	-.5	-.4					UND	NM	-.3
.9	.6	.6	Debt/Worth				.4	.5	4.1
2.3	2.7	4.1					1.3	1.0	-10.8
-8.2	-3.1	-3.1					UND	NM	-2.6
108.4	75.6	149.8	% Profit Before Taxes/Tangible				200.0	138.4	242.8
(70) 49.1	(45) 41.1	(49) 44.5	Net Worth				(12) 49.9	(11) 35.5	(12) 98.0
5.8	6.1	10.0					15.4	.1	33.5
39.3	31.1	30.1	% Profit Before Taxes/Total				57.2	30.1	26.5
12.3	9.2	15.3	Assets				29.3	12.0	10.9
-.4	-.2	.4					11.0	-.6	3.0
126.4	276.2	306.8	Sales/Net Fixed Assets				765.2	167.3	118.5
34.1	43.6	72.8					88.3	33.5	26.0
14.1	14.4	15.9					30.5	15.4	13.7
4.2	4.8	4.0	Sales/Total Assets				6.3	4.2	3.4
3.0	2.7	2.6					3.3	2.1	2.3
1.8	1.7	1.6					1.5	1.8	1.6
.4	.5	.4	% Depr., Dep., Amort./Sales						.7
(57) 1.1	(42) 1.0	(42) 1.0						(19)	1.4
2.1	2.2	3.1							3.8
2.8	3.0	1.9	% Officers', Directors'						
(31) 8.6	(21) 7.3	(20) 5.1	Owners' Comp/Sales						
15.0	11.1	8.5							
3273421M	2340003M	2785930M	Net Sales ($)	2770M	10364M	28317M	117428M	201977M	2425074M
2065389M	1620640M	1448285M	Total Assets ($)	13237M	4985M	7525M	92077M	112270M	1218191M

© RMA 2019

M = $ thousand   MM = $ million
See Pages viii through xx for Explanation of Ratios and Data

Current Data Sorted by Assets

Comparative Historical Data

						Type of Statement		
				1		Unqualified	1	2
		1				Reviewed	1	2
		2	1			Compiled	4	3
1		3				Tax Returns	19	15
4	2	4			1	Other	16	18
1	5				1		4/1/14-3/31/15	4/1/15-3/31/16
	5 (4/1-9/30/18)			22 (10/1/18-3/31/19)			ALL	ALL
0-500M	500M-2MM	2-10MM	10-50MM	50-100MM	100-250MM	NUMBER OF STATEMENTS	41	40
6	7	10	2		2			
%	%	%	%	%	%		%	%
						ASSETS		
		19.6				Cash & Equivalents	28.1	31.7
		23.4		D		Trade Receivables (net)	10.0	6.1
		6.5		A		Inventory	3.8	4.4
		5.3		T		All Other Current	1.6	2.3
		54.9		A		Total Current	43.5	44.4
		23.7				Fixed Assets (net)	32.5	36.3
		11.2		N		Intangibles (net)	8.2	8.3
		10.2		O		All Other Non-Current	15.8	10.9
		100.0		T		Total	100.0	100.0
				A		**LIABILITIES**		
		7.5		V		Notes Payable-Short Term	9.9	15.1
		1.5		A		Cur. Mat.-L.T.D.	4.2	2.0
		5.8		I		Trade Payables	18.2	17.5
		.2		L		Income Taxes Payable	.0	.1
		8.8		A		All Other Current	10.9	24.0
		23.9		B		Total Current	43.2	58.7
		13.1		L		Long-Term Debt	29.2	31.5
		.0		E		Deferred Taxes	.6	.5
		7.0				All Other Non-Current	8.3	16.2
		56.0				Net Worth	18.6	-6.8
		100.0				Total Liabilities & Net Worth	100.0	100.0
						INCOME DATA		
		100.0				Net Sales	100.0	100.0
						Gross Profit		
		87.1				Operating Expenses	88.1	93.2
		12.9				Operating Profit	11.9	6.8
		1.2				All Other Expenses (net)	1.5	1.7
		11.7				Profit Before Taxes	10.4	5.1
						RATIOS		
		5.4					2.7	2.9
		3.2				Current	1.6	1.3
		1.4					.4	.5
		4.1					2.6	2.5
		2.3				Quick	1.5	1.0
		.8					.4	.2
	3	116.5					0 UND	0 UND
	43	8.4				Sales/Receivables	1 464.0	0 UND
	73	5.0					24 15.5	3 109.9
						Cost of Sales/Inventory		
						Cost of Sales/Payables		
		2.8					9.1	13.4
		4.0				Sales/Working Capital	40.7	112.9
		NM					-34.7	-20.9
							22.0	18.9
						EBIT/Interest	(30) 7.2	(24) 5.0
							3.5	.8
						Net Profit + Depr., Dep., Amort./Cur. Mat. L/T/D		
		.2					.1	.2
		.3				Fixed/Worth	1.9	2.5
		1.4					-1.9	-1.2
		.4					.7	.5
		.7				Debt/Worth	2.0	4.4
		2.0					-12.6	-2.3
							185.6	91.6
						% Profit Before Taxes/Tangible Net Worth	(29) 57.5	(25) 25.5
							19.8	-32.5
		33.8					48.2	38.1
		10.9				% Profit Before Taxes/Total Assets	20.4	10.4
		5.9					5.9	-3.1
		31.6					94.1	40.3
		14.9				Sales/Net Fixed Assets	18.2	16.1
		5.2					4.9	8.7
		3.6					7.8	9.1
		1.6				Sales/Total Assets	3.8	4.3
		1.2					1.4	1.9
							.9	.9
						% Depr., Dep., Amort./Sales	(23) 2.9	(24) 3.5
							4.1	4.4
							5.4	2.8
						% Officers', Directors' Owners' Comp/Sales	(20) 8.6	(21) 8.9
							10.7	19.5
10285M	23480M	114438M	23188M		321372M	Net Sales ($)	328521M	666241M
1287M	5790M	47461M	54101M		310318M	Total Assets ($)	178401M	242913M

M = $ thousand   MM = $ million
See Pages viii through xx for Explanation of Ratios and Data

Comparative Historical Data | Current Data Sorted by Sales

	4/1/16-3/31/17 ALL	4/1/17-3/31/18 ALL	4/1/18-3/31/19 ALL	0-1MM	1-3MM	3-5MM	5-10MM	10-25MM	25MM & OVER
Type of Statement				5 (4/1-9/30/18)			22 (10/1/18-3/31/19)		
Unqualified	1		1			1			
Reviewed	3		1			1			
Compiled	4	2	4			1	1	2	
Tax Returns	10	6	10	4	1	2	1	1	2
Other	13	8	11	1	2	5	1		1
NUMBER OF STATEMENTS	31	16	27	5	3	10	3	3	3
	%	%	%	%	%	%	%	%	%
ASSETS									
Cash & Equivalents	24.2	40.6	32.8			31.2			
Trade Receivables (net)	10.8	6.5	9.4			7.4			
Inventory	5.1	1.5	5.6			7.6			
All Other Current	8.8	.9	6.2			7.7			
Total Current	48.9	49.4	54.0			53.9			
Fixed Assets (net)	37.1	23.5	25.4			27.6			
Intangibles (net)	4.6	12.7	5.2			8.5			
All Other Non-Current	9.5	14.3	15.4			10.1			
Total	100.0	100.0	100.0			100.0			
LIABILITIES									
Notes Payable-Short Term	14.0	5.6	8.6			5.2			
Cur. Mat.-L.T.D.	3.1	.4	1.1			.9			
Trade Payables	17.3	5.1	13.6			13.9			
Income Taxes Payable	.7	.1	.1			.1			
All Other Current	24.5	12.3	17.1			33.0			
Total Current	59.6	23.5	40.5			53.0			
Long-Term Debt	17.1	17.1	21.3			12.8			
Deferred Taxes	.2	.8	.1			.0			
All Other Non-Current	7.2	10.7	4.3			.0			
Net Worth	16.1	48.0	33.7			34.1			
Total Liabilities & Net Worth	100.0	100.0	100.0			100.0			
INCOME DATA									
Net Sales	100.0	100.0	100.0			100.0			
Gross Profit									
Operating Expenses	93.2	94.2	90.4			90.4			
Operating Profit	6.8	5.8	9.6			9.6			
All Other Expenses (net)	3.1	.8	1.4			.7			
Profit Before Taxes	3.7	4.9	8.2			8.8			
RATIOS									
Current	5.9	7.8	7.7			8.8			
	1.3	2.2	2.6			6.5			
	.2	.7	.9			.7			
Quick	3.6	7.2	6.6			8.3			
	.7	1.8	1.7			4.8			
	.1	.4	.4			.5			
Sales/Receivables	0 UND	0 UND	0 UND			0 UND			
	2 209.6	0 UND	2 183.9			4 101.8			
	26 13.8	3 107.1	38 9.5			54 6.8			
Cost of Sales/Inventory									
Cost of Sales/Payables									
Sales/Working Capital	7.1	5.8	3.9			2.1			
	94.3	10.7	8.7			4.7			
	-11.4	NM	-385.0			-45.6			
EBIT/Interest	12.4	4.2	16.3						
	(22) 2.0	(10) 1.7	(20) 2.4						
	-2.9	-1.3	-1.0						
Net Profit + Depr., Dep., Amort./Cur. Mat. L/T/D									
Fixed/Worth	.1	.1	.2			.2			
	.8	.3	.4			.5			
	-3.1	NM	1.5			NM			
Debt/Worth	.2	.3	.3			.2			
	.8	.9	.8			.4			
	-5.4	NM	4.3			NM			
% Profit Before Taxes/Tangible Net Worth	55.0	78.9	81.0						
	(20) 27.0	(12) 27.5	(23) 57.1						
	4.4	2.5	3.4						
% Profit Before Taxes/Total Assets	27.2	36.1	51.4			55.7			
	9.4	5.5	10.0			15.4			
	-1.1	-.1	-1.0			-1.1			
Sales/Net Fixed Assets	128.6	87.6	47.5			41.1			
	16.4	21.7	19.1			16.2			
	4.8	5.5	8.3			5.2			
Sales/Total Assets	6.7	3.8	4.5			5.7			
	3.8	1.9	2.8			2.2			
	1.3	.9	1.3			1.2			
% Depr., Dep., Amort./Sales	1.3		.9						
	(17) 2.5		(18) 2.7						
	5.0		4.3						
% Officers', Directors' Owners' Comp/Sales	4.5		2.3						
	(13) 7.5		(10) 4.9						
	14.5		13.1						
Net Sales ($)	196486M	190328M	492763M	2987M	5174M	39765M	26700M	50347M	367790M
Total Assets ($)	108331M	203315M	418957M	4943M	1791M	62007M	11006M	20484M	318726M

© RMA 2019

M = $ thousand   MM = $ million
See Pages viii through xx for Explanation of Ratios and Data

Current Data Sorted by Assets | Comparative Historical Data

0-500M	500M-2MM	2-10MM	10-50MM	50-100MM	100-250MM		4/1/14-3/31/15 ALL	4/1/15-3/31/16 ALL
						Type of Statement		
		1			1	Unqualified	2	4
	1	2	1			Reviewed	7	5
1	2	1				Compiled	3	3
7			1			Tax Returns	7	8
4	3	3			1	Other	15	15
	3 (4/1-9/30/18)		26 (10/1/18-3/31/19)					
12	6	7	2		2	**NUMBER OF STATEMENTS**	34	35
%	%	%	%	%	%	**ASSETS**	%	%
47.3						Cash & Equivalents	16.2	20.8
28.5						Trade Receivables (net)	15.6	22.9
4.8			D			Inventory	5.5	7.6
.6			A			All Other Current	6.6	2.2
81.1			T			Total Current	43.9	53.5
9.7			A			Fixed Assets (net)	33.2	28.0
6.8						Intangibles (net)	7.9	5.9
2.4			N			All Other Non-Current	14.9	12.7
100.0			O			Total	100.0	100.0
			T			**LIABILITIES**		
13.9						Notes Payable-Short Term	11.4	17.3
1.6			A			Cur. Mat.-L.T.D.	4.8	5.5
2.2			V			Trade Payables	11.0	14.2
.0			A			Income Taxes Payable	.1	.2
22.2			I			All Other Current	14.1	20.3
39.9			L			Total Current	41.5	57.6
11.1			A			Long-Term Debt	27.7	18.4
.0			B			Deferred Taxes	.2	.6
18.2			L			All Other Non-Current	4.2	9.3
30.8			E			Net Worth	26.4	14.0
100.0						Total Liabilties & Net Worth	100.0	100.0
						INCOME DATA		
100.0						Net Sales	100.0	100.0
						Gross Profit		
87.4						Operating Expenses	87.8	92.1
12.6						Operating Profit	12.2	7.9
.6						All Other Expenses (net)	3.4	.5
12.0						Profit Before Taxes	8.8	7.4
						RATIOS		
9.4							2.9	2.9
2.3						Current	1.1	1.3
1.2							.5	.6
8.4							2.5	2.5
1.9						Quick	.8	1.0
1.0							.3	.4
0 UND							0 UND	2 170.8
0 UND						Sales/Receivables	15 24.5	26 14.2
41 9.0							55 6.6	61 6.0
						Cost of Sales/Inventory		
						Cost of Sales/Payables		
10.9							5.8	6.4
18.8						Sales/Working Capital	384.1	18.3
41.0							-14.1	-21.5
							21.7	7.5
						EBIT/Interest	(26) 7.7	(28) 2.0
							2.4	-3.9
								5.8
						Net Profit + Depr., Dep., Amort./Cur. Mat. L/T/D		(11) 3.1
								2.1
.0							.4	.4
.2						Fixed/Worth	2.0	1.3
UND							-2.2	-3.2
.4							.8	.8
1.3						Debt/Worth	3.0	3.9
-9.8							-14.3	-10.6
							42.0	61.4
						% Profit Before Taxes/Tangible Net Worth	(24) 29.6	(24) 26.3
							16.0	8.7
129.8							24.2	31.0
65.9						% Profit Before Taxes/Total Assets	11.7	5.5
4.1							3.1	-6.2
UND							26.6	30.8
UND						Sales/Net Fixed Assets	15.1	14.4
41.7							5.8	7.2
10.5							4.3	6.1
6.9						Sales/Total Assets	2.5	2.9
3.6							1.1	1.8
							1.5	1.7
						% Depr., Dep., Amort./Sales	(26) 3.0	(27) 3.1
							5.8	4.7
							1.8	2.1
						% Officers', Directors' Owners' Comp/Sales	(12) 6.2	(10) 7.1
							9.1	10.8
15093M	28949M	63751M	177877M		216107M	Net Sales ($)	581371M	678319M
2364M	6144M	35097M	32906M		286957M	Total Assets ($)	378466M	327619M

(Middle columns labeled: DATA NOT AVAILABLE)

© RMA 2019

M = $ thousand   MM = $ million
See Pages viii through xx for Explanation of Ratios and Data

Comparative Historical Data | Current Data Sorted by Sales

			Type of Statement						
4	2	1	Unqualified						1
2	2	1	Reviewed					1	
3	6	4	Compiled			1	3		
5	3	10	Tax Returns						
12	19	13	Other	7	2	1	2		3
				3					3
4/1/16- 3/31/17	4/1/17- 3/31/18	4/1/18- 3/31/19		0-1MM	3 (4/1-9/30/18) 1-3MM	3-5MM	26 (10/1/18-3/31/19) 5-10MM	10-25MM	25MM & OVER
ALL	ALL	ALL							
26	32	29	NUMBER OF STATEMENTS	10	3	3	5	3	4
%	%	%	ASSETS	%	%	%	%	%	%
15.4	17.5	28.2	Cash & Equivalents	29.8					
12.9	16.7	23.9	Trade Receivables (net)	30.9					
6.6	10.1	4.4	Inventory	3.0					
4.5	3.9	1.5	All Other Current	1.3					
39.3	48.3	58.1	Total Current	65.0					
40.4	32.4	22.5	Fixed Assets (net)	24.4					
8.9	8.2	11.6	Intangibles (net)	8.2					
11.4	11.1	7.8	All Other Non-Current	2.4					
100.0	100.0	100.0	Total	100.0					
			LIABILITIES						
7.1	10.0	8.2	Notes Payable-Short Term	13.3					
6.6	3.6	6.4	Cur. Mat.-L.T.D.	2.7					
8.9	16.1	14.7	Trade Payables	2.8					
.2	1.9	.0	Income Taxes Payable	.0					
15.1	17.2	22.7	All Other Current	21.1					
37.9	48.7	52.1	Total Current	39.9					
34.4	35.3	22.1	Long-Term Debt	17.6					
1.2	.5	.8	Deferred Taxes	.0					
18.5	9.3	12.4	All Other Non-Current	21.8					
7.9	6.2	12.6	Net Worth	20.6					
100.0	100.0	100.0	Total Liabilties & Net Worth	100.0					
			INCOME DATA						
100.0	100.0	100.0	Net Sales	100.0					
			Gross Profit						
92.9	91.3	89.2	Operating Expenses	82.6					
7.1	8.7	10.8	Operating Profit	17.4					
1.2	1.8	2.7	All Other Expenses (net)	4.0					
5.9	6.9	8.1	Profit Before Taxes	13.4					
			RATIOS						
3.0	3.7	2.8		5.1					
1.4	1.7	1.8	Current	1.4					
.6	1.0	.9		.7					
1.6	2.0	2.8		4.8					
1.2	1.4	1.5	Quick	1.3					
.3	.4	.8		.6					
0 UND	2 228.1	0 UND		0 UND					
12 30.9	20 18.5	19 18.8	Sales/Receivables	2 217.1					
32 11.4	41 8.8	54 6.7		47 7.7					
			Cost of Sales/Inventory						
			Cost of Sales/Payables						
8.5	5.3	10.3		10.1					
22.5	10.9	20.0	Sales/Working Capital	29.9					
-18.4	233.6	-374.7		-83.2					
6.8	14.1	15.1							
(22) 3.4	(28) 5.2	(19) 2.8	EBIT/Interest						
-2.6	1.9	-.3							
			Net Profit + Depr., Dep., Amort./Cur. Mat. L/T/D						
.4	.5	.1		.0					
1.7	1.6	1.0	Fixed/Worth	.6					
-1.0	-1.6	-3.7		UND					
.8	.8	.7		1.1					
1.8	3.1	2.3	Debt/Worth	2.8					
-4.1	-4.8	-2.5		-3.5					
50.1	81.8	119.8	% Profit Before Taxes/Tangible						
(18) 11.6	(23) 34.1	(19) 65.2	Net Worth						
-3.7	10.9	18.5							
11.6	36.1	52.7	% Profit Before Taxes/Total	96.1					
4.3	8.4	9.6	Assets	8.4					
-5.8	-.2	.4		2.4					
16.1	24.8	646.4		UND					
7.6	11.0	37.6	Sales/Net Fixed Assets	UND					
2.0	5.0	7.5		6.5					
3.9	4.5	7.0		7.1					
1.6	2.6	4.7	Sales/Total Assets	4.0					
1.0	1.4	1.6		1.1					
2.5	1.7	1.4							
(21) 4.5	(24) 3.0	(12) 3.5	% Depr., Dep., Amort./Sales						
8.1	7.8	5.4							
	1.4	2.8	% Officers', Directors'						
	(13) 4.3	(14) 9.5	Owners' Comp/Sales						
	9.1	14.5							
564200M	625885M	501777M	Net Sales ($)	5620M	5454M	11399M	36666M	48654M	393984M
470631M	694092M	363468M	Total Assets ($)	6334M	1173M	1500M	19336M	15262M	319863M

M = $ thousand   MM = $ million
See Pages viii through xx for Explanation of Ratios and Data

Current Data Sorted by Assets

Comparative Historical Data

							Type of Statement		
			1		2		Unqualified	3	2
							Reviewed		1
							Compiled	3	1
1	3	3	8				Tax Returns	4	3
4	4	6	32 (10/1/18-3/31/19)				Other	12	20
	0 (4/1-9/30/18)							4/1/14-3/31/15	4/1/15-3/31/16
0-500M	500M-2MM	2-10MM	10-50MM	50-100MM	100-250MM			ALL	ALL
5	7	9	9		2		NUMBER OF STATEMENTS	22	27
%	%	%	%	%	%		ASSETS	%	%
							Cash & Equivalents	17.7	18.0
							Trade Receivables (net)	50.3	44.1
							Inventory	.0	1.8
							All Other Current	5.0	5.6
							Total Current	73.0	69.6
							Fixed Assets (net)	10.2	10.7
							Intangibles (net)	10.1	8.7
							All Other Non-Current	6.6	11.0
							Total	100.0	100.0
							LIABILITIES		
							Notes Payable-Short Term	9.8	8.8
							Cur. Mat.-L.T.D.	1.2	1.0
							Trade Payables	10.1	11.5
							Income Taxes Payable	.3	.9
							All Other Current	21.3	19.2
							Total Current	42.7	41.3
							Long-Term Debt	11.7	9.2
							Deferred Taxes	.4	.1
							All Other Non-Current	1.9	2.7
							Net Worth	43.4	46.6
							Total Liabilties & Net Worth	100.0	100.0
							INCOME DATA		
							Net Sales	100.0	100.0
							Gross Profit		
							Operating Expenses	92.3	93.9
							Operating Profit	7.7	6.1
							All Other Expenses (net)	.6	1.3
							Profit Before Taxes	7.1	4.8
							RATIOS		
								3.5	3.4
							Current	2.2	2.0
								1.3	1.4
								3.4	3.4
							Quick	1.8	1.6
								1.1	1.2
								45 8.1	31 11.9
							Sales/Receivables	60 6.1	53 6.9
								81 4.5	87 4.2
							Cost of Sales/Inventory		
							Cost of Sales/Payables		
								3.9	3.8
							Sales/Working Capital	10.2	12.8
								24.3	27.2
								190.4	130.5
							EBIT/Interest	(17) 32.4	(20) 18.7
								4.5	3.3
							Net Profit + Depr., Dep., Amort./Cur. Mat. L/T/D		
								.1	.0
							Fixed/Worth	.2	.1
								1.1	.4
								.3	.6
							Debt/Worth	1.1	1.1
								8.7	2.5
								65.5	99.0
							% Profit Before Taxes/Tangible Net Worth	(19) 42.9	(24) 42.5
								28.3	15.5
								38.7	28.3
							% Profit Before Taxes/Total Assets	23.3	17.5
								8.1	2.7
								89.9	205.3
							Sales/Net Fixed Assets	43.9	63.8
								20.5	31.1
								5.0	5.3
							Sales/Total Assets	3.0	3.4
								2.3	2.3
								.6	.2
							% Depr., Dep., Amort./Sales	(14) .9	(15) .5
								2.6	1.8
							% Officers', Directors' Owners' Comp/Sales		
20290M	32232M	133450M	508879M		358769M		Net Sales ($)	1309802M	841809M
1692M	6629M	44357M	240635M		351980M		Total Assets ($)	585506M	254137M

(Left-side Current Data columns marked: DATA NOT AVAILABLE)

M = $ thousand   MM = $ million
See Pages viii through xx for Explanation of Ratios and Data

Comparative Historical Data | Current Data Sorted by Sales

Type of Statement	4/1/16-3/31/17 ALL	4/1/17-3/31/18 ALL	4/1/18-3/31/19 ALL	0-1MM	1-3MM	3-5MM	5-10MM	10-25MM	25MM & OVER
Unqualified	3	2	3				1		2
Reviewed	1								
Compiled	2								
Tax Returns	3	1	7	1		1	3	1	1
Other	13	23	22	2	1	6	1	5	7
				0 (4/1-9/30/18)			32 (10/1/18-3/31/19)		
NUMBER OF STATEMENTS	22	26	32	3	1	7	5	6	10
	%	%	%	%	%	%	%	%	%
ASSETS									
Cash & Equivalents	12.6	11.5	15.7						11.9
Trade Receivables (net)	45.0	48.2	40.7						37.3
Inventory	.9	.8	.5						.0
All Other Current	8.4	7.9	3.5						5.2
Total Current	66.9	68.4	60.5						54.4
Fixed Assets (net)	12.3	12.1	18.1						19.7
Intangibles (net)	14.6	15.6	13.8						21.5
All Other Non-Current	6.2	4.0	7.7						4.3
Total	100.0	100.0	100.0						100.0
LIABILITIES									
Notes Payable-Short Term	15.2	12.9	12.2						13.5
Cur. Mat.-L.T.D.	3.3	1.9	3.7						3.2
Trade Payables	13.5	14.0	15.1						8.3
Income Taxes Payable	.1	.1	.0						.0
All Other Current	12.4	12.2	10.1						16.7
Total Current	44.5	41.2	41.1						41.7
Long-Term Debt	8.1	20.6	20.3						21.6
Deferred Taxes	.1	.2	.1						.2
All Other Non-Current	3.5	3.2	3.1						6.3
Net Worth	43.8	34.8	35.4						30.2
Total Liabilties & Net Worth	100.0	100.0	100.0						100.0
INCOME DATA									
Net Sales	100.0	100.0	100.0						100.0
Gross Profit									
Operating Expenses	99.7	97.1	91.4						100.9
Operating Profit	.3	2.9	8.6						-.9
All Other Expenses (net)	1.3	1.3	3.8						3.0
Profit Before Taxes	-1.0	1.6	4.8						-3.9
RATIOS									
Current	2.4	2.4	2.3						1.7
	1.6	1.4	1.4						1.1
	.9	1.0	.9						.9
Quick	2.1	2.1	2.2						1.6
	1.2	1.2	1.2						1.0
	.8	.9	.8						.8
Sales/Receivables	37 9.8	38 9.6	21 17.3						46 8.0
	59 6.2	64 5.7	46 7.9						57 6.4
	78 4.7	91 4.0	65 5.6						68 5.4
Cost of Sales/Inventory									
Cost of Sales/Payables									
Sales/Working Capital	7.8	8.7	7.5						9.2
	10.7	16.8	30.7						NM
	-40.3	-776.8	-66.4						-42.4
EBIT/Interest	13.7	74.9	29.1						
	(15) 1.7	(22) 1.3	(25) 18.2						
	.8	-6.2	.1						
Net Profit + Depr., Dep., Amort./Cur. Mat. L/T/D									
Fixed/Worth	.1	.1	.1						.2
	.3	.5	.4						2.0
	NM	-.3	NM						-.3
Debt/Worth	.5	.6	.8						1.4
	1.9	3.6	3.7						4.0
	-8.4	-6.1	NM						-2.1
% Profit Before Taxes/Tangible Net Worth	34.1	71.1	155.8						
	(16) 22.9	(16) 24.5	(24) 58.0						
	-2.8	-7.9	4.2						
% Profit Before Taxes/Total Assets	17.4	27.0	33.4						10.6
	4.1	1.7	9.2						-5.8
	-1.2	-7.7	-4.7						-17.3
Sales/Net Fixed Assets	75.4	107.0	149.1						28.8
	30.2	54.3	60.1						14.7
	15.4	22.0	12.1						7.6
Sales/Total Assets	4.4	4.4	5.7						3.4
	2.8	2.7	3.2						2.4
	2.0	1.8	1.6						1.5
% Depr., Dep., Amort./Sales	.4	.3	.4						
	(13) .9	(14) .9	(17) 1.1						
	2.2	3.9	4.5						
% Officers', Directors' Owners' Comp/Sales									
Net Sales ($)	669156M	1402767M	1053620M	1423M	2472M	27581M	36990M	120224M	864930M
Total Assets ($)	327383M	776287M	645293M	6950M	248M	5383M	25104M	65909M	541699M

M = $ thousand   MM = $ million
See Pages viii through xx for Explanation of Ratios and Data

Current Data Sorted by Assets   Comparative Historical Data

	0-500M	500M-2MM	2-10MM	10-50MM	50-100MM	100-250MM		4/1/14-3/31/15 ALL	4/1/15-3/31/16 ALL
Type of Statement									
Unqualified	2	1		5	2	3		14	9
Reviewed			1	3	1			8	6
Compiled	12	9	12					83	62
Tax Returns	153	105	25	3		1		332	355
Other	75	82	24			4		222	242
	16 (4/1-9/30/18)			507 (10/1/18-3/31/19)					
NUMBER OF STATEMENTS	242	197	62	11	3	8		659	674
	%	%	%	%	%	%		%	%
ASSETS									
Cash & Equivalents	35.9	24.0	12.7	10.7				24.3	26.8
Trade Receivables (net)	2.1	2.8	2.5	10.7				3.4	3.4
Inventory	10.4	5.6	4.9	9.2				8.9	8.8
All Other Current	1.8	3.1	1.9	2.1				2.0	1.8
Total Current	50.2	35.5	21.9	32.6				38.6	40.9
Fixed Assets (net)	28.4	31.9	50.4	45.6				36.8	34.8
Intangibles (net)	11.6	26.1	20.2	19.2				14.4	14.3
All Other Non-Current	9.7	6.5	7.5	2.5				10.3	10.0
Total	100.0	100.0	100.0	100.0				100.0	100.0
LIABILITIES									
Notes Payable-Short Term	17.9	6.7	3.0	6.4				10.6	12.4
Cur. Mat.-L.T.D.	5.6	3.8	4.5	3.5				4.8	5.0
Trade Payables	6.9	4.0	3.6	8.3				8.1	6.7
Income Taxes Payable	.1	.0	.1	.7				.1	.0
All Other Current	12.9	6.9	5.0	6.4				12.8	13.0
Total Current	43.4	21.5	16.3	25.2				36.4	37.2
Long-Term Debt	40.0	48.2	52.8	26.5				37.9	37.3
Deferred Taxes	.0	.0	.0	.1				.1	.0
All Other Non-Current	4.5	3.0	4.2	3.2				6.4	4.9
Net Worth	12.0	27.3	26.7	44.9				19.2	20.6
Total Liabilities & Net Worth	100.0	100.0	100.0	100.0				100.0	100.0
INCOME DATA									
Net Sales	100.0	100.0	100.0	100.0				100.0	100.0
Gross Profit									
Operating Expenses	89.3	84.2	82.1	91.8				87.0	86.8
Operating Profit	10.7	15.8	17.9	8.2				13.0	13.2
All Other Expenses (net)	.9	3.1	5.3	.4				2.8	2.7
Profit Before Taxes	9.7	12.7	12.5	7.8				10.2	10.6
RATIOS									
Current	4.5	6.3	2.9	1.9				3.3	3.8
	1.7	2.2	1.6	1.3				1.4	1.5
	.6	.9	.5	1.0				.6	.6
Quick	3.6	5.2	2.1	1.7				2.5	3.0
	1.1	1.5	1.1	.8				.9	1.0
	.3	.4	.3	.4				.3	.4
Sales/Receivables	0 UND	0 UND	0 UND	2 162.3				0 UND	0 UND
	0 UND	0 UND	0 UND	5 66.5				0 UND	0 UND
	0 999.8	2 149.8	4 96.2	33 11.0				2 152.7	2 156.3
Cost of Sales/Inventory									
Cost of Sales/Payables									
Sales/Working Capital	15.5	7.8	12.4	14.1				14.1	12.1
	51.6	21.7	35.9	30.5				62.7	44.6
	-39.5	-69.3	-20.6	-464.5				-27.3	-34.7
EBIT/Interest	45.8	23.6	20.3	24.6				31.9	37.4
	(159) 13.8	(159) 7.7	(45) 3.9	(10) 8.0				(484) 8.0	(486) 11.2
	3.6	2.7	1.6	5.1				2.2	3.4
Net Profit + Depr., Dep., Amort./Cur. Mat. L/T/D								9.9	6.0
								(20) 5.0	(20) 3.5
								1.5	2.1
Fixed/Worth	.1	.3	1.0	.7				.4	.3
	1.3	1.7	4.0	1.7				2.3	1.9
	-.9	-.8	-2.8	2.2				-1.8	-2.1
Debt/Worth	.4	.7	1.6	.6				.7	.6
	3.5	5.1	6.5	1.5				5.2	3.9
	-3.3	-1.9	-3.3	4.1				-3.8	-4.7
% Profit Before Taxes/Tangible Net Worth	320.5	158.4	111.4	119.4				169.9	199.9
	(150) 144.1	(116) 81.3	(37) 51.0	(10) 59.3				(422) 81.4	(433) 81.5
	59.1	37.0	18.7	30.6				28.2	29.6
% Profit Before Taxes/Total Assets	107.7	48.2	21.6	18.3				53.7	61.1
	43.5	21.9	10.6	11.3				22.4	25.9
	13.6	6.4	3.3	6.6				4.5	7.1
Sales/Net Fixed Assets	140.6	71.0	14.6	9.5				52.8	68.8
	35.5	18.9	4.8	3.9				17.7	20.5
	15.5	5.3	1.1	2.9				5.4	6.9
Sales/Total Assets	11.1	4.2	2.6	2.5				7.5	8.0
	6.7	2.6	1.3	2.0				3.8	4.1
	3.9	1.7	.9	1.4				1.9	2.1
% Depr., Dep., Amort./Sales	.7	1.1	1.5	1.1				1.1	.8
	(117) 1.5	(88) 2.6	(43) 3.1	1.9				(402) 2.4	(388) 1.9
	3.0	5.5	9.0	3.6				4.8	4.1
% Officers', Directors', Owners' Comp/Sales	5.6	3.5	2.8					5.1	5.1
	(181) 9.0	(122) 5.8	(28) 3.7					(371) 8.3	(406) 8.1
	12.9	9.3	9.2					11.9	11.6
Net Sales ($)	416965M	593236M	433732M	405668M	343489M	3438307M		8080552M	9249976M
Total Assets ($)	59917M	196858M	229002M	192993M	193227M	1267254M		2157753M	2638506M

M = $ thousand   MM = $ million

See Pages viii through xx for Explanation of Ratios and Data

Comparative Historical Data | | | | Current Data Sorted by Sales

7	11	13	Type of Statement						
			Type of Statement		3	1		3	7
7	11	13	Unqualified		3	1		3	7
5	7	5	Reviewed						4
68	52	33	Compiled	8	10	6	4	4	1
288	254	284	Tax Returns	61	145	48	21	7	2
198	181	188	Other	38	92	26	20	5	7
4/1/16-3/31/17 ALL	4/1/17-3/31/18 ALL	4/1/18-3/31/19 ALL		16 (4/1-9/30/18)			507 (10/1/18-3/31/19)		
				0-1MM	1-3MM	3-5MM	5-10MM	10-25MM	25MM & OVER
566	505	523	**NUMBER OF STATEMENTS**	107	250	81	45	19	21
%	%	%	**ASSETS**	%	%	%	%	%	%
27.2	27.6	27.7	Cash & Equivalents	25.7	27.3	34.1	30.1	25.0	15.0
3.2	3.3	2.6	Trade Receivables (net)	1.0	2.3	3.1	5.0	3.7	7.5
8.5	9.2	7.9	Inventory	5.6	9.3	6.7	8.5	3.9	10.3
1.8	1.8	2.3	All Other Current	1.6	2.1	3.0	4.0	1.8	1.4
40.7	41.9	40.5	Total Current	33.9	41.0	46.8	47.5	34.5	34.1
33.7	32.1	32.5	Fixed Assets (net)	43.8	29.6	26.9	26.6	45.8	30.1
15.5	16.6	19.1	Intangibles (net)	13.9	21.0	18.1	18.1	14.4	31.7
10.1	9.5	8.0	All Other Non-Current	8.4	8.3	8.1	7.7	5.3	4.1
100.0	100.0	100.0	Total	100.0	100.0	100.0	100.0	100.0	100.0
			LIABILITIES						
9.8	10.9	11.4	Notes Payable-Short Term	12.6	8.9	16.3	18.7	3.4	6.8
4.6	5.3	4.7	Cur. Mat.-L.T.D.	5.2	5.3	3.1	4.4	3.0	3.8
5.4	7.3	5.4	Trade Payables	3.7	5.7	6.0	5.8	4.0	9.1
.1	.1	.1	Income Taxes Payable	.1	.0	.0	.1	.0	.4
10.9	13.3	9.5	All Other Current	9.3	9.0	11.4	10.1	8.4	8.8
30.8	36.8	31.1	Total Current	30.8	29.0	36.8	39.1	18.8	28.9
42.9	39.2	44.2	Long-Term Debt	60.0	45.7	30.0	31.4	38.8	32.4
.1	.0	.0	Deferred Taxes	.0	.0	.0	.0	.0	.0
5.9	5.0	3.8	All Other Non-Current	4.5	3.7	2.3	5.7	5.9	2.0
20.3	19.0	20.9	Net Worth	4.7	21.6	30.9	23.8	36.3	36.7
100.0	100.0	100.0	Total Liabilties & Net Worth	100.0	100.0	100.0	100.0	100.0	100.0
			INCOME DATA						
100.0	100.0	100.0	Net Sales	100.0	100.0	100.0	100.0	100.0	100.0
			Gross Profit						
86.6	87.1	86.8	Operating Expenses	74.8	89.3	89.7	91.2	88.4	95.8
13.4	12.9	13.2	Operating Profit	25.2	10.7	10.3	8.8	11.6	4.2
2.6	2.0	2.3	All Other Expenses (net)	7.6	1.0	.9	.4	.3	1.4
10.8	10.9	10.9	Profit Before Taxes	17.6	9.7	9.4	8.4	11.3	2.8
			RATIOS						
4.6	3.6	4.5	Current	3.7	5.5	4.4	4.6	2.7	2.0
1.7	1.4	1.8		1.0	2.0	2.1	2.1	2.0	1.1
.6	.6	.6		.3	.7	.7	1.2	1.3	.5
3.6	2.7	3.6	Quick	2.9	4.3	3.5	3.5	2.4	1.5
1.2	1.0	1.2		.7	1.4	1.6	1.7	1.5	.7
.4	.4	.4		.3	.4	.4	.6	.5	.4
0 UND	0 UND	0 UND	Sales/Receivables	0 UND	0 UND	0 UND	0 UND	0 UND	3 131.4
0 UND	0 UND	0 UND		0 UND	0 UND	0 UND	0 UND	1 327.9	5 75.3
2 230.2	2 163.3	2 183.3		0 UND	1 306.5	2 175.8	5 80.0	4 97.5	22 16.8
			Cost of Sales/Inventory						
			Cost of Sales/Payables						
10.8	12.9	12.4	Sales/Working Capital	12.2	11.4	11.2	14.4	16.6	13.9
35.0	51.4	38.1		-158.0	28.9	26.2	28.4	28.7	118.6
-34.7	-39.6	-45.3		-7.3	-57.9	-66.9	101.4	56.1	-20.2
30.2	42.1	28.7	EBIT/Interest	14.3	22.1	66.5	96.8	78.7	12.3
(396) 8.6	(374) 10.0	(384) 8.7		(66) 4.9	(182) 9.0	(61) 16.1	(38) 29.1	(16) 8.2	5.9
3.0	3.1	2.7		1.4	2.4	3.8	5.2	3.6	.3
7.2	10.7	7.2	Net Profit + Depr., Dep., Amort./Cur. Mat. L/T/D						
(10) 4.3	(12) 5.2	(11) 4.6							
1.8	3.0	2.7							
.4	.4	.3	Fixed/Worth	.6	.2	.1	.1	.7	.0
1.9	2.0	1.7		4.0	2.4	1.0	.8	1.6	1.7
-1.7	-1.2	-1.0		-1.0	-.6	-1.1	3.3	-10.6	-1.4
.6	.7	.6	Debt/Worth	.9	.5	.4	.6	.7	1.4
5.0	4.9	4.7		8.9	7.2	1.7	2.0	2.1	3.8
-4.0	-3.6	-2.7		-2.5	-2.1	-3.0	-6.6	-12.2	-3.0
216.5	244.9	248.0	% Profit Before Taxes/Tangible Net Worth	150.0	281.6	275.9	247.6	539.0	85.2
(355) 90.7	(304) 100.0	(319) 96.0		(63) 62.3	(143) 116.2	(53) 103.5	(32) 111.4	(14) 161.7	(14) 39.5
31.7	33.6	37.5		23.8	49.3	34.4	59.4	77.6	6.5
64.1	72.6	59.4	% Profit Before Taxes/Total Assets	50.0	60.4	95.1	61.5	108.4	22.4
24.4	28.5	26.5		14.2	32.2	37.5	29.8	17.9	6.6
6.2	7.4	6.8		1.1	9.9	8.7	16.1	11.1	-3.9
69.3	75.6	93.4	Sales/Net Fixed Assets	54.8	117.7	175.7	103.1	21.4	15.6
18.6	24.6	21.4		12.3	24.7	28.6	33.2	7.9	7.5
6.6	6.9	6.6		.8	10.4	8.3	10.0	3.6	4.7
7.1	8.5	7.4	Sales/Total Assets	4.8	6.9	10.0	8.4	7.0	3.2
3.9	4.4	3.6		2.2	3.9	5.1	5.0	3.8	2.0
1.9	1.9	1.9		.5	2.2	2.5	2.4	1.4	1.1
.9	.7	.9	% Depr., Dep., Amort./Sales	2.0	.8	.6	.3	.6	1.5
(320) 2.1	(273) 1.6	(265) 1.9		(57) 5.0	(113) 1.7	(42) 1.7	(20) 1.1	(17) 1.7	(16) 2.2
4.1	3.8	4.2		17.0	3.4	3.1	2.5	4.4	3.1
4.9	4.5	4.1	% Officers', Directors' Owners' Comp/Sales	7.2	4.6	4.3	2.4	1.4	
(348) 7.8	(313) 7.4	(335) 7.4		(53) 11.3	(183) 7.1	(56) 7.3	(29) 4.1	(10) 2.6	
12.5	11.6	11.3		17.1	10.3	11.5	8.3	5.6	
4810469M	6139236M	5631397M	Net Sales ($)	61816M	471978M	306985M	313679M	273363M	4203576M
1725839M	2067877M	2139251M	Total Assets ($)	66699M	156758M	92829M	95553M	110429M	1616983M

M = $ thousand   MM = $ million
See Pages viii through xx for Explanation of Ratios and Data

Current Data Sorted by Assets | **Comparative Historical Data**

Type of Statement

Type of Statement	0-500M	500M-2MM	2-10MM	10-50MM	50-100MM	100-250MM	ALL 4/1/14-3/31/15	ALL 4/1/15-3/31/16
Unqualified	1	2	16	21	6	7	78	74
Reviewed	1	6	32	8		1	78	85
Compiled	6	14	20	2			107	90
Tax Returns	125	77	33	5	3	3	395	439
Other	106	119	133	59	9	10	593	622
		60 (4/1-9/30/18)		765 (10/1/18-3/31/19)				
NUMBER OF STATEMENTS	239	218	234	95	18	21	1251	1310

	0-500M %	500M-2MM %	2-10MM %	10-50MM %	50-100MM %	100-250MM %	ALL %	ALL %
ASSETS								
Cash & Equivalents	40.7	23.6	19.4	15.3	18.0	21.3	24.2	25.6
Trade Receivables (net)	14.1	32.7	39.5	34.3	20.9	15.8	28.0	27.9
Inventory	3.5	5.0	4.9	4.6	3.6	1.1	5.4	4.8
All Other Current	2.0	3.4	5.6	6.3	7.2	5.6	3.6	3.7
Total Current	60.3	64.8	69.5	60.5	49.8	43.9	61.2	62.0
Fixed Assets (net)	21.1	16.3	14.2	19.4	15.0	23.2	20.6	20.6
Intangibles (net)	6.9	8.0	5.5	11.3	24.5	25.8	6.6	6.4
All Other Non-Current	11.7	10.9	10.8	8.8	10.7	7.1	11.7	10.9
Total	100.0	100.0	100.0	100.0	100.0	100.0	100.0	100.0
LIABILITIES								
Notes Payable-Short Term	24.1	12.3	9.7	8.3	11.2	2.8	13.8	14.2
Cur. Mat.-L.T.D.	4.4	2.0	2.2	3.2	4.9	2.1	2.6	3.3
Trade Payables	7.7	10.4	11.5	12.1	10.3	7.5	10.7	10.3
Income Taxes Payable	.1	.1	.1	.2	.0	.3	.2	.3
All Other Current	23.2	15.6	17.6	19.2	15.0	7.1	16.1	17.2
Total Current	59.4	40.4	41.1	43.0	41.5	19.8	43.4	45.3
Long-Term Debt	19.8	15.2	11.8	18.8	44.7	36.5	15.8	17.5
Deferred Taxes	.0	.0	.1	.1	.8	.1	.2	.2
All Other Non-Current	7.7	4.8	5.9	4.1	2.6	11.0	8.1	7.0
Net Worth	13.1	39.6	41.1	33.9	10.4	32.7	32.6	30.0
Total Liabilities & Net Worth	100.0	100.0	100.0	100.0	100.0	100.0	100.0	100.0
INCOME DATA								
Net Sales	100.0	100.0	100.0	100.0	100.0	100.0	100.0	100.0
Gross Profit								
Operating Expenses	88.8	89.6	88.3	88.2	92.4	90.2	90.2	89.0
Operating Profit	11.2	10.4	11.7	11.8	7.6	9.8	9.8	11.0
All Other Expenses (net)	.6	1.0	1.2	2.9	2.0	6.1	1.2	1.5
Profit Before Taxes	10.6	9.4	10.5	8.9	5.5	3.7	8.6	9.5

RATIOS

Ratio	0-500M	500M-2MM	2-10MM	10-50MM	50-100MM	100-250MM	ALL 4/1/14-3/31/15	ALL 4/1/15-3/31/16
Current	4.1	3.8	3.6	2.4	2.3	4.2	3.7	4.1
	1.5	2.0	1.8	1.5	1.3	2.7	1.7	1.7
	.6	1.0	1.2	.9	.7	1.1	.9	.9
Quick	3.7	3.5	3.2	2.0	1.7	3.6	3.1	3.5
	1.4	1.7	1.6	1.2	.7	1.5	(1250) 1.4	1.5
	.5	.7	.9	.6	.4	.9	.7	.7
Sales/Receivables	0 UND	0 UND	28 12.9	38 9.6	9 42.7	0 UND	0 UND	0 UND
	0 UND	31 11.6	46 7.9	51 7.2	42 8.7	42 8.6	28 13.0	28 13.1
	18 20.7	58 6.3	74 4.9	79 4.6	56 6.5	74 4.9	58 6.3	56 6.5
Cost of Sales/Inventory								
Cost of Sales/Payables								
Sales/Working Capital	9.8	6.3	5.0	4.1	7.5	3.9	6.5	6.2
	63.4	13.7	9.9	12.7	15.8	8.0	15.4	16.2
	-36.2	332.1	30.2	-101.6	-14.5	29.8	-222.8	-163.4
EBIT/Interest	37.5	37.0	87.4	34.9	14.6	8.3	45.6	50.0
	(143) 10.6	(164) 11.4	(170) 16.7	(74) 10.1	(15) 3.7	(16) 2.9	(882) 10.3	(903) 11.0
	2.8	2.8	3.9	1.5	.9	-1.1	2.1	2.0
Net Profit + Depr., Dep., Amort./Cur. Mat. L/T/D			19.2	14.9			7.0	13.3
		(18) 6.0	(10) 1.7				(71) 2.8	(75) 4.5
			3.2	1.0			1.3	1.5
Fixed/Worth	.0	.0	.0	.0	.2	.2	.0	.0
	.3	.2	.2	.4	2.6	.5	.3	.3
	7.2	1.2	.9	2.4	-.1	-.4	2.7	2.6
Debt/Worth	.4	.4	.4	.8	.6	.6	.5	.4
	2.4	1.3	1.1	2.1	5.7	4.3	1.5	1.5
	-5.1	8.5	5.1	16.1	-1.7	-2.6	14.4	12.8
% Profit Before Taxes/Tangible Net Worth	258.1	139.1	87.3	76.6	89.7	85.7	97.5	106.5
	(163) 97.4	(179) 51.7	(203) 47.3	(77) 36.7	(10) 64.8	(12) 20.9	(988) 42.2	(1035) 46.5
	41.7	17.7	17.2	13.9	8.3	-5.1	11.4	13.0
% Profit Before Taxes/Total Assets	85.5	44.7	39.1	26.3	29.8	14.3	43.6	43.2
	37.9	19.4	17.4	12.5	6.6	8.9	14.7	16.5
	5.8	4.7	6.1	1.7	.6	-3.0	2.6	2.8
Sales/Net Fixed Assets	UND	469.1	257.9	216.0	136.2	91.7	255.7	237.6
	86.7	52.7	55.4	26.1	31.8	11.4	41.6	42.9
	17.1	14.4	14.7	6.4	6.0	1.7	10.1	11.0
Sales/Total Assets	10.8	5.6	4.0	3.1	3.4	2.6	5.6	5.9
	6.0	3.3	2.8	1.9	1.4	.8	3.2	3.3
	3.4	2.1	1.7	.9	1.0	.6	1.8	1.8
% Depr., Dep., Amort./Sales	.4	.2	.3	.5	.4		.4	.4
	(72) 1.5	(92) .7	(123) .7	(60) 1.3	(12) 1.5		(692) 1.3	(713) 1.2
	3.7	2.7	1.8	3.5	4.7		3.3	3.4
% Officers', Directors' Owners' Comp/Sales	4.5	2.8	1.4	1.1			2.8	2.9
	(120) 7.5	(89) 5.4	(67) 2.7	(10) 6.0			(515) 6.6	(520) 6.2
	16.5	7.7	4.8	8.0			12.2	13.4
Net Sales ($)	417906M	1026860M	2932662M	4646923M	3709645M	6712925M	18734086M	23519363M
Total Assets ($)	49841M	249966M	1024452M	2032348M	1338453M	2971690M	9794083M	10090687M

© RMA 2019

M = $ thousand   MM = $ million
See Pages viii through xx for Explanation of Ratios and Data

Comparative Historical Data | Current Data Sorted by Sales

Type of Statement	4/1/16-3/31/17 ALL	4/1/17-3/31/18 ALL	4/1/18-3/31/19 ALL	0-1MM	1-3MM	3-5MM	5-10MM	10-25MM	25MM & OVER
Unqualified	58	56	53	1	2	2	2	14	32
Reviewed	71	42	48		2	6	11	17	12
Compiled	67	71	42	2	11	5	8	12	4
Tax Returns	302	271	246	69	65	40	37	26	9
Other	478	496	436	69	93	48	84	82	60
				60 (4/1-9/30/18)			765 (10/1/18-3/31/19)		
NUMBER OF STATEMENTS	976	936	825	141	173	101	142	151	117
ASSETS	%	%	%	%	%	%	%	%	%
Cash & Equivalents	23.3	22.8	26.2	31.0	32.9	25.2	24.1	23.3	18.0
Trade Receivables (net)	28.4	30.0	28.7	15.4	17.7	31.2	35.0	39.4	37.8
Inventory	5.4	4.8	4.4	3.7	5.3	5.2	5.5	3.1	3.7
All Other Current	4.7	4.6	4.1	1.4	3.5	4.1	4.6	5.2	6.1
Total Current	61.9	62.2	63.5	51.4	59.4	65.7	69.1	71.0	65.5
Fixed Assets (net)	19.8	19.1	17.6	25.7	20.6	18.7	14.2	11.2	14.8
Intangibles (net)	7.8	8.4	8.2	9.6	7.5	6.7	6.1	7.5	12.2
All Other Non-Current	10.5	10.3	10.8	13.3	12.5	8.9	10.6	10.3	7.5
Total	100.0	100.0	100.0	100.0	100.0	100.0	100.0	100.0	100.0
LIABILITIES									
Notes Payable-Short Term	14.4	12.3	14.2	16.5	18.0	14.9	16.2	9.5	9.2
Cur. Mat.-L.T.D.	3.8	3.0	2.9	2.6	2.2	6.5	2.5	2.0	3.2
Trade Payables	10.3	11.0	10.0	8.0	8.2	9.3	10.5	11.3	13.5
Income Taxes Payable	.4	.2	.1	.1	.1	.0	.1	.1	.2
All Other Current	18.8	19.0	18.6	18.8	21.0	17.8	17.1	16.8	19.4
Total Current	47.7	45.5	45.9	46.0	49.5	48.5	46.3	39.8	45.6
Long-Term Debt	17.0	18.0	17.2	19.4	15.4	21.2	13.4	12.1	24.8
Deferred Taxes	.1	.1	.1	.0	.1	.0	.1	.2	.1
All Other Non-Current	6.3	7.2	6.0	7.3	6.8	6.1	6.1	5.0	4.2
Net Worth	28.9	29.2	30.9	27.3	28.3	24.2	34.1	43.0	25.3
Total Liabilities & Net Worth	100.0	100.0	100.0	100.0	100.0	100.0	100.0	100.0	100.0
INCOME DATA									
Net Sales	100.0	100.0	100.0	100.0	100.0	100.0	100.0	100.0	100.0
Gross Profit									
Operating Expenses	90.2	90.3	88.9	81.2	89.8	90.0	91.1	90.8	90.8
Operating Profit	9.8	9.7	11.1	18.8	10.2	10.0	8.9	9.2	9.2
All Other Expenses (net)	1.5	1.2	1.3	2.5	.5	1.3	.7	.9	2.3
Profit Before Taxes	8.3	8.5	9.8	16.3	9.6	8.7	8.3	8.3	6.9
RATIOS									
Current	3.7	3.3	3.6	4.9	4.5	3.3	3.4	3.4	2.6
	1.7	1.7	1.8	1.8	1.6	1.9	1.7	1.9	1.6
	.9	.9	1.0	.7	.7	1.0	1.1	1.1	1.0
Quick	3.0	2.9	3.2	4.2	3.8	3.1	3.1	3.2	2.2
	(975) 1.3	(934) 1.4	1.5	1.8	1.3	1.6	1.4	1.7	1.3
	.6	.7	.7	.5	.5	.7	.8	.9	.8
Sales/Receivables	0 UND	0 UND	0 UND	0 UND	0 UND	0 UND	10 37.6	24 15.4	32 11.3
	32 11.4	33 11.2	31 11.6	0 UND	5 77.6	32 11.4	41 8.9	43 8.5	48 7.6
	60 6.1	60 6.1	57 6.4	26 14.1	39 9.3	65 5.6	72 5.1	62 5.9	73 5.0
Cost of Sales/Inventory									
Cost of Sales/Payables									
Sales/Working Capital	6.0	6.1	6.1	7.1	5.8	6.7	5.7	6.1	6.7
	15.6	17.0	14.5	19.8	32.6	13.5	11.9	12.4	16.0
	-97.4	-118.4	-290.8	-21.1	-34.1	583.7	103.1	94.8	228.4
EBIT/Interest	40.7	42.8	49.3	22.3	49.3	34.9	40.9	94.7	43.3
	(692) 10.6	(677) 10.5	(582) 10.8	(69) 6.6	(122) 12.3	(82) 11.1	(109) 11.2	(107) 26.1	(93) 10.0
	1.9	2.2	2.5	1.9	2.0	1.7	3.4	3.4	3.4
Net Profit + Depr., Dep., Amort./Cur. Mat. L/T/D	6.5	7.3	12.3					12.5	18.2
	(51) 2.2	(44) 4.2	(41) 3.3				(15)	6.5	(14) 1.8
	.5	1.2	1.5					3.3	1.0
Fixed/Worth	.1	.0	.0	.0	.0	.0	.0	.0	.0
	.3	.2	.2	.3	.2	.4	.2	.1	.4
	2.8	3.2	2.1	2.8	2.3	11.6	1.1	.8	4.7
Debt/Worth	.5	.5	.4	.4	.3	.5	.5	.5	.7
	1.5	1.6	1.6	1.4	1.8	2.3	1.3	1.3	2.1
	20.0	69.4	32.9	UND	-509.3	-8.3	6.7	4.3	74.0
% Profit Before Taxes/Tangible Net Worth	101.5	100.0	122.7	144.5	127.1	203.0	98.2	93.1	103.9
	(769) 41.7	(716) 43.4	(644) 55.6	(109) 59.4	(129) 54.9	(72) 82.6	(113) 55.3	(131) 47.3	(90) 55.4
	11.2	11.3	20.4	19.9	23.3	20.8	17.3	14.9	22.7
% Profit Before Taxes/Total Assets	41.0	37.6	47.0	59.0	52.7	57.2	43.5	47.0	31.7
	14.7	15.0	19.1	20.2	23.8	22.0	19.0	18.0	14.3
	2.1	2.9	4.4	2.2	5.7	2.8	5.7	3.5	5.7
Sales/Net Fixed Assets	235.4	254.2	484.4	UND	801.0	493.6	282.3	569.5	283.0
	40.2	48.2	54.5	31.9	44.0	51.4	52.3	99.4	45.9
	11.6	12.1	12.9	5.2	13.0	16.4	11.9	28.2	11.5
Sales/Total Assets	5.7	5.3	5.6	5.5	6.9	8.2	4.3	5.3	4.7
	3.0	3.1	3.2	3.0	3.6	3.7	3.1	3.8	3.0
	1.7	1.8	1.8	1.3	1.9	2.2	2.1	2.3	1.6
% Depr., Dep., Amort./Sales	.3	.3	.3	1.0	.4	.3	.3	.2	.2
	(529) 1.0	(490) 1.1	(368) 1.0	(46) 2.5	(58) 1.6	(43) .9	(72) .7	(72) .5	(77) .7
	3.1	2.8	3.1	5.6	4.3	3.0	1.8	1.5	2.6
% Officers', Directors' Owners' Comp/Sales	2.8	3.0	2.6	8.1	4.4	2.3	2.4	1.1	1.2
	(368) 5.5	(334) 6.4	(292) 5.7	(53) 14.7	(82) 7.0	(39) 4.6	(56) 3.9	(45) 2.1	(17) 2.1
	11.7	12.0	10.3	22.1	10.4	7.2	5.7	5.4	10.1
Net Sales ($)	20182874M	20286778M	19446921M	69868M	334001M	397786M	1009974M	2340193M	15295099M
Total Assets ($)	8375720M	8294002M	7666750M	77774M	196366M	185828M	435200M	1189200M	5582382M

M = $ thousand   MM = $ million
See Pages viii through xx for Explanation of Ratios and Data

MANAGEMENT OF COMPANIES AND ENTERPRISES

Current Data Sorted by Assets   Comparative Historical Data

	0-500M	500M-2MM	2-10MM	10-50MM	50-100MM	100-250MM	Type of Statement	4/1/14-3/31/15 ALL	4/1/15-3/31/16 ALL
	1		6	24	15	17	Unqualified	77	80
	1	1	15	20	1	2	Reviewed	43	40
	3	2	15	4		2	Compiled	46	43
	12	42	39	13		1	Tax Returns	130	159
	32	42	83	68	27	30	Other	253	280
		52 (4/1-9/30/18)		466 (10/1/18-3/31/19)					
	49	87	158	129	43	52	NUMBER OF STATEMENTS	549	602
	%	%	%	%	%	%	ASSETS	%	%
	27.9	9.8	8.7	13.8	14.8	7.1	Cash & Equivalents	11.3	12.4
	4.8	3.4	10.1	15.4	13.8	19.5	Trade Receivables (net)	11.9	10.9
	5.2	5.0	7.1	7.9	11.1	7.0	Inventory	6.8	6.1
	6.8	3.2	4.2	6.2	3.5	6.3	All Other Current	3.9	3.3
	44.7	21.4	30.1	43.3	43.3	39.9	Total Current	33.8	32.7
	35.6	61.5	50.2	34.6	32.4	24.3	Fixed Assets (net)	44.7	44.3
	3.7	3.1	6.8	9.1	12.6	20.6	Intangibles (net)	6.9	7.3
	16.0	14.0	12.9	12.9	11.7	15.2	All Other Non-Current	14.5	15.7
	100.0	100.0	100.0	100.0	100.0	100.0	Total	100.0	100.0
							LIABILITIES		
	9.5	8.6	9.0	6.5	8.7	3.6	Notes Payable-Short Term	6.9	8.4
	4.2	2.5	2.1	3.1	4.1	2.0	Cur. Mat.-L.T.D.	3.8	5.1
	4.6	3.0	5.2	8.9	6.8	11.9	Trade Payables	7.1	6.8
	.0	.0	.0	.2	.1	.2	Income Taxes Payable	.3	.2
	39.3	11.2	9.6	9.1	11.8	10.6	All Other Current	11.9	10.6
	57.7	25.3	26.0	27.9	31.5	28.4	Total Current	30.0	30.9
	23.2	45.0	35.9	29.9	20.7	32.3	Long-Term Debt	33.5	31.0
	.0	.0	.1	.4	1.4	.6	Deferred Taxes	.4	.4
	7.6	4.3	4.8	5.8	3.4	8.7	All Other Non-Current	7.4	6.7
	11.6	25.5	33.2	36.0	43.0	29.9	Net Worth	28.7	30.9
	100.0	100.0	100.0	100.0	100.0	100.0	Total Liabilities & Net Worth	100.0	100.0
							INCOME DATA		
	100.0	100.0	100.0	100.0	100.0	100.0	Net Sales	100.0	100.0
							Gross Profit		
	78.4	62.4	64.8	80.9	82.9	88.6	Operating Expenses	73.2	71.9
	21.6	37.6	35.2	19.1	17.1	11.4	Operating Profit	26.8	28.1
	2.8	14.0	13.1	6.1	3.6	4.4	All Other Expenses (net)	9.4	8.5
	18.8	23.6	22.1	12.9	13.5	7.0	Profit Before Taxes	17.4	19.5
							RATIOS		
	2.4	2.3	3.3	2.6	2.1	2.5		2.5	2.4
	.9	.6	1.2	1.4	1.4	1.3	Current	1.2	1.2
	.3	.1	.2	.9	1.0	.9		.5	.4
	1.8	2.0	2.2	1.9	1.5	1.5		1.8	1.9
	.4	.5	.7	1.0	1.0	.9	Quick	.8 (601)	.9
	.2	.1	.1	.4	.4	.5		.3	.3
	0 UND	0 UND	0 UND	0 999.8	3 137.2	16 22.4		0 UND	0 UND
	0 UND	0 UND	0 UND	25 14.5	38 9.6	46 7.9	Sales/Receivables	5 79.5	5 81.0
	0 UND	2 154.5	27 13.4	51 7.2	53 6.9	78 4.7		42 8.6	41 8.9
							Cost of Sales/Inventory		
							Cost of Sales/Payables		
	14.3	7.4	5.8	4.4	4.0	2.9		5.5	5.9
	-131.8	-22.4	46.8	14.0	12.8	10.1	Sales/Working Capital	33.1	38.0
	-6.5	-2.7	-2.5	-63.1	-41.7	-211.2		-6.5	-6.0
	18.4	17.9	29.8	15.9	25.7	7.3		17.8	18.6
	(21) 4.8	(42) 6.3	(83) 7.4	(92) 5.1	(39) 4.5	(47) 2.1	EBIT/Interest	(377) 5.7	(389) 5.8
	1.7	2.0	2.5	2.0	1.6	.7		2.2	2.0
				7.2		14.9	Net Profit + Depr., Dep.,	10.0	11.8
				(20) 2.6		(16) 1.9	Amort./Cur. Mat. L/T/D	(60) 3.6	(57) 2.9
				1.5		.0		1.6	1.4
	.0	.8	.3	.3	.4	.4		.3	.3
	1.0	3.7	2.2	1.2	1.2	1.8	Fixed/Worth	1.6	1.5
	4.4	24.5	18.5	6.4	4.7	-1.0		8.5	9.6
	.7	.6	.9	.7	.7	1.4		.9	.7
	3.1	3.8	2.7	2.3	2.2	7.1	Debt/Worth	2.3	2.3
	-4.4	49.3	17.9	17.3	7.5	-4.0		16.4	18.2
	129.5	64.2	54.6	36.2	39.8	45.9	% Profit Before Taxes/Tangible	50.4	51.4
	(35) 34.7	(69) 22.5	(125) 22.0	(104) 15.0	(36) 18.0	(34) 16.2	Net Worth	(435) 21.4	(473) 20.6
	5.1	7.9	6.5	5.2	5.8	1.4		6.1	5.8
	63.1	21.4	15.0	14.8	10.8	7.2	% Profit Before Taxes/Total	14.1	14.7
	12.5	4.0	6.0	5.4	6.5	1.7	Assets	6.1	6.3
	1.4	1.4	1.4	.9	1.6	-1.1		1.5	1.5
	UND	16.4	35.7	25.6	28.5	25.8		29.5	26.9
	28.5	.3	1.1	5.1	7.1	8.3	Sales/Net Fixed Assets	4.0	3.6
	1.0	.1	.1	1.5	1.2	2.0		.2	.2
	7.2	2.0	2.3	2.0	1.9	1.6		2.2	2.1
	2.2	.2	.3	1.3	1.0	.8	Sales/Total Assets	.8	.8
	.5	.1	.1	.3	.4	.4		.2	.2
	.5	5.9	2.0	1.3	1.1	1.0		1.4	1.4
	(19) 11.2	(54) 18.9	(106) 12.0	(102) 3.4	(36) 3.3	(33) 2.9	% Depr., Dep., Amort./Sales	(404) 5.2	(425) 5.2
	19.2	27.7	25.4	8.6	9.8	5.7		17.7	17.9
	8.5	3.0	.9	.7			% Officers', Directors'	2.0	1.6
	(11) 10.6	(16) 5.8	(20) 3.4	(17) 1.4			Owners' Comp/Sales	(77) 4.4	(88) 4.6
	12.4	15.9	5.7	4.0				13.0	13.8
	45847M	136468M	1111133M	4810433M	3865678M	10569380M	Net Sales ($)	18347738M	21309031M
	12916M	106453M	766231M	3186001M	3088252M	8555918M	Total Assets ($)	13093824M	16275123M

© RMA 2019

M = $ thousand   MM = $ million
See Pages viii through xx for Explanation of Ratios and Data

Comparative Historical Data / Current Data Sorted by Sales

				Type of Statement						
56	69	63	Unqualified	1	2		5	8	47
32	36	40	Reviewed	5	2	2	5	13	13
34	33	26	Compiled	12	3		1	8	2
115	123	107	Tax Returns	59	12	11	7	9	9
243	298	282	Other	95	34	11	23	38	81
4/1/16-3/31/17	4/1/17-3/31/18	4/1/18-3/31/19		52 (4/1-9/30/18)		466 (10/1/18-3/31/19)			
ALL	ALL	ALL		0-1MM	1-3MM	3-5MM	5-10MM	10-25MM	25MM & OVER
480	559	518	**NUMBER OF STATEMENTS**	172	53	24	41	76	152
%	%	%	**ASSETS**	%	%	%	%	%	%
12.3	13.1	12.3	Cash & Equivalents	7.3	21.4	14.7	16.4	16.0	11.4
10.7	10.3	11.0	Trade Receivables (net)	.9	5.8	7.3	7.5	21.0	21.0
4.6	6.3	7.1	Inventory	2.3	4.0	7.7	8.9	10.6	11.2
5.0	5.0	4.9	All Other Current	3.4	7.0	3.4		6.5	5.8
32.5	34.8	35.4	Total Current	13.9	38.1	33.1	36.3	54.1	49.5
44.0	42.9	42.8	Fixed Assets (net)	70.4	41.9	27.3	40.2	23.6	24.6
7.7	10.6	8.3	Intangibles (net)	1.7	4.6	17.3	6.6	8.8	16.0
15.9	11.8	13.5	All Other Non-Current	14.1	15.3	22.2	16.8	13.4	10.0
100.0	100.0	100.0	Total	100.0	100.0	100.0	100.0	100.0	100.0
			LIABILITIES						
6.2	5.8	7.8	Notes Payable-Short Term	7.0	6.9	8.0	13.3	7.3	7.8
3.2	3.1	2.8	Cur. Mat.-L.T.D.	2.3	3.4	3.2	1.6	2.2	3.7
6.6	6.7	6.5	Trade Payables	.6	3.2	8.6	5.2	11.1	12.0
.1	.1	.1	Income Taxes Payable	.0	.0	.0	.2	.3	.1
10.7	11.9	12.8	All Other Current	8.5	30.6	16.8	9.5	12.0	12.2
26.8	27.6	30.0	Total Current	18.4	44.1	36.7	29.7	33.0	35.9
31.4	31.9	33.1	Long-Term Debt	44.9	41.0	32.9	30.3	17.0	25.9
.3	.2	.3	Deferred Taxes	.0	.0	.0	.1	.2	.8
6.0	5.8	5.5	All Other Non-Current	3.8	8.9	5.3	2.7	7.1	6.3
35.5	34.4	31.0	Net Worth	32.9	5.9	25.1	37.2	42.8	31.1
100.0	100.0	100.0	Total Liabilties & Net Worth	100.0	100.0	100.0	100.0	100.0	100.0
			INCOME DATA						
100.0	100.0	100.0	Net Sales	100.0	100.0	100.0	100.0	100.0	100.0
			Gross Profit						
73.3	72.7	73.6	Operating Expenses	52.2	67.9	73.4	73.3	87.4	92.9
26.7	27.3	26.4	Operating Profit	47.8	32.1	26.6	26.7	12.6	7.1
9.4	8.4	8.9	All Other Expenses (net)	19.7	10.8	4.5	5.2	.7	1.7
17.3	19.0	17.5	Profit Before Taxes	28.1	21.3	22.1	21.4	11.9	5.3
			RATIOS						
2.8	2.7	2.7	Current	3.0	3.0	2.8	4.1	4.1	2.0
1.3	1.3	1.2		.6	1.1	1.0	1.4	1.8	1.4
.6	.5	.5		.1	.2	.3	.4	1.0	1.0
1.9	1.8	1.9	Quick	1.9	2.4	1.8	3.0	3.0	1.4
.9	(558) .9	.7		.4	.7	.5	1.0	1.3	.9
.3	.3	.2		.1	.2	.1	.2	.4	.5
0 UND	0 UND	0 UND	Sales/Receivables	0 UND	0 UND	0 UND	0 UND	4 101.1	15 23.9
5 79.0	3 127.8	3 112.1		0 UND	0 UND	0 UND	2 236.7	31 11.6	39 9.3
40 9.2	41 8.9	42 8.7		0 UND	25 14.8	18 20.8	35 10.4	61 6.0	57 6.4
			Cost of Sales/Inventory						
			Cost of Sales/Payables						
4.5	4.8	5.5	Sales/Working Capital	6.1	4.7	8.7	3.6	3.3	7.6
27.3	20.7	24.0		-9.1	782.0	NM	12.2	7.3	16.9
-8.9	-9.8	-7.9		-1.6	-4.5	-6.7	-17.2	-338.7	NM
14.4	14.2	18.4	EBIT/Interest	10.6	20.1	19.7	20.1	55.7	13.3
(304) 4.7	(357) 4.3	(324) 4.9		(58) 4.1	(28) 9.0	(16) 5.9	(26) 7.2	(57) 12.2	(139) 4.7
1.6	1.6	1.7		2.2	1.9	1.2	2.4	2.1	1.2
4.4	5.8	5.4	Net Profit + Depr., Dep., Amort./Cur. Mat. L/T/D						5.7
(35) 1.7	(46) 2.5	(54) 2.3							(34) 2.2
.7	.8	1.5							1.0
.3	.3	.3	Fixed/Worth	1.0	.2	.2	.1	.1	.4
1.6	1.6	1.7		3.0	1.6	9.7	.9	.4	1.4
9.3	12.8	15.7		9.2	-4.3	-.3	3.6	2.4	-13.8
.7	.7	.8	Debt/Worth	.7	1.0	.2	.6	.4	1.4
2.3	2.3	2.9		2.7	5.4	9.1	1.8	1.4	4.1
17.8	27.9	34.9		17.5	-7.7	-2.8	6.6	16.8	-21.9
50.5	49.3	48.0	% Profit Before Taxes/Tangible Net Worth	34.7	89.2	62.3	73.7	51.3	54.7
(385) 14.6	(437) 20.2	(403) 19.6		(147) 14.3	(36) 20.8	(14) 15.1	(35) 40.8	(60) 21.0	(111) 25.7
3.1	5.9	6.1		5.1	4.7	6.1	9.1	9.7	9.6
13.0	14.5	15.1	% Profit Before Taxes/Total Assets	8.7	39.3	13.5	22.8	21.5	14.2
5.2	5.0	5.7		3.2	7.5	5.6	8.2	10.0	6.2
.6	1.1	1.1		.9	1.1	.9	1.5	1.8	.6
25.3	32.7	29.8	Sales/Net Fixed Assets	.5	187.2	143.6	24.1	61.6	34.7
4.0	3.9	4.6		.2	7.5	21.3	4.9	12.1	13.7
.2	.2	.2		.1	.3	3.0	.6	3.3	3.8
2.1	2.0	2.2	Sales/Total Assets	.2	4.3	4.0	2.3	2.6	2.8
.7	.8	.9		.1	.7	1.2	1.1	1.6	1.7
.1	.2	.2		.1	.1	.2	.2	.8	.9
1.8	1.7	1.6	% Depr., Dep., Amort./Sales	15.5	1.9	.9	.9	1.4	.6
(319) 5.4	(365) 6.2	(350) 5.2		(112) 20.9	(26) 8.2	(16) 2.3	(28) 2.5	(54) 3.1	(114) 1.8
19.0	18.6	18.7		30.0	28.4	9.9	13.9	5.8	4.4
1.3	2.4	1.1	% Officers', Directors', Owners' Comp/Sales		5.9		1.3	1.0	.4
(67) 4.3	(75) 5.2	(72) 3.1		(14) 9.4		(10) 2.7	(13) 2.9	(20) .7	
11.2	12.5	9.5			11.3		4.6	5.6	2.0
16589614M	21492926M	20538939M	Net Sales ($)	63317M	87849M	90361M	308622M	1249573M	18739217M
13827825M	17563954M	15715771M	Total Assets ($)	477844M	420163M	228779M	949189M	2022397M	11617399M

© RMA 2019

M = $ thousand   MM = $ million
See Pages viii through xx for Explanation of Ratios and Data

Current Data Sorted by Assets   Comparative Historical Data

0-500M	500M-2MM	2-10MM	10-50MM	50-100MM	100-250MM	Type of Statement	4/1/14-3/31/15 ALL	4/1/15-3/31/16 ALL
		1	4	4	8	Unqualified	18	20
		1	2	1	1	Reviewed	5	1
2	2	1				Compiled	5	4
1	2	1	1			Tax Returns	12	8
2	6	12	21	6	7	Other	41	47
	14 (4/1-9/30/18)		72 (10/1/18-3/31/19)					
5	10	16	28	11	16	NUMBER OF STATEMENTS	81	80
%	%	%	%	%	%	ASSETS	%	%
	26.2	17.3	11.2	7.3	11.9	Cash & Equivalents	18.3	15.3
	13.5	13.9	13.9	19.9	15.3	Trade Receivables (net)	14.8	18.0
	8.5	4.6	6.7	9.9	12.2	Inventory	6.2	7.1
	5.0	1.2	7.9	3.1	8.5	All Other Current	7.5	8.0
	53.2	37.0	39.7	40.1	47.8	Total Current	46.8	48.3
	12.5	39.2	29.4	31.7	35.9	Fixed Assets (net)	28.8	30.1
	7.4	11.5	15.8	12.0	11.0	Intangibles (net)	4.5	6.4
	26.8	12.3	15.1	16.1	5.4	All Other Non-Current	19.9	15.1
	100.0	100.0	100.0	100.0	100.0	Total	100.0	100.0
						LIABILITIES		
	1.9	6.6	10.8	3.5	5.8	Notes Payable-Short Term	10.6	4.7
	1.3	6.8	3.3	1.1	2.1	Cur. Mat.-L.T.D.	2.1	3.3
	10.7	7.3	9.0	6.4	9.8	Trade Payables	8.1	10.7
	.0	.0	.0	.1	.1	Income Taxes Payable	.2	.0
	17.8	14.7	14.3	7.4	10.3	All Other Current	8.1	11.8
	31.6	35.4	37.4	18.5	28.1	Total Current	29.1	30.6
	9.9	21.2	22.8	16.9	24.7	Long-Term Debt	19.0	26.3
	.0	.1	.8	.0	.7	Deferred Taxes	.3	.3
	11.1	5.9	5.2	2.4	6.9	All Other Non-Current	11.9	10.8
	47.4	37.4	33.8	62.2	39.6	Net Worth	39.7	32.0
	100.0	100.0	100.0	100.0	100.0	Total Liabilties & Net Worth	100.0	100.0
						INCOME DATA		
	100.0	100.0	100.0	100.0	100.0	Net Sales	100.0	100.0
						Gross Profit		
	86.2	76.0	80.1	91.8	96.0	Operating Expenses	85.3	84.9
	13.8	24.0	19.9	8.2	4.0	Operating Profit	14.7	15.1
	.8	7.8	6.1	3.3	1.5	All Other Expenses (net)	4.3	4.5
	13.0	16.2	13.8	4.9	2.5	Profit Before Taxes	10.5	10.6
						RATIOS		
	6.6	2.7	1.8	3.5	2.4	Current	4.0	3.4
	3.0	.9	1.1	2.3	1.7		1.6	1.7
	1.1	.7	.7	1.6	1.3		.8	.9
	3.9	2.4	1.3	3.4	1.4	Quick	2.5	2.5
	1.3	.8	.7	1.6	1.0		(80) 1.2 (79) 1.1	
	.7	.3	.3	.9	.5		.7	.6
0 UND	0 UND	0 768.3	27 13.5	17 22.1		Sales/Receivables	1 486.1 0 UND	
0 UND	1 362.1	18 20.0	51 7.1	31 11.9			20 18.4 21 17.4	
21 17.0	22 16.3	39 9.4	78 4.7	51 7.1			47 7.8 51 7.1	
						Cost of Sales/Inventory		
						Cost of Sales/Payables		
	2.9	12.9	7.6	2.5	4.2	Sales/Working Capital	4.0	4.9
	14.1	NM	26.6	4.0	9.1		10.1	11.4
	NM	-8.7	-13.3	11.0	28.9		-22.3	-42.9
		78.8	11.2		12.0	EBIT/Interest	24.2	19.2
		(11) 4.5	(22) 3.6		(15) 4.1		(55) 5.0	(54) 4.7
		-.3	1.7		1.4		2.0	.8
						Net Profit + Depr., Dep.,	15.0	18.4
						Amort./Cur. Mat. L/T/D	(18) 3.0 (18) 3.1	
							1.3	1.5
	.0	.2	.4	.2	.3	Fixed/Worth	.1	.1
	.2	2.1	.8	.5	1.1		.6	.8
	NM	5.4	-6.0	.9	6.5		3.1	5.3
	.2	1.2	1.4	.4	.7	Debt/Worth	.4	.5
	.9	3.9	5.8	.5	1.6		1.4	1.6
	-31.7	13.8	-14.4	1.3	8.6		7.4	26.4
		152.5	54.3	18.0	14.8	% Profit Before Taxes/Tangible	39.5	57.4
		(14) 14.2	(17) 20.9	(10) 10.9	(13) 9.3	Net Worth	(65) 17.1 (64) 18.1	
		-6.9	14.0	-1.7	5.6		5.8	4.3
	55.2	32.8	11.6	10.6	8.7	% Profit Before Taxes/Total	19.7	20.9
	10.5	5.8	6.7	5.1	4.4	Assets	6.1	5.9
	7.3	-1.4	1.3	-1.2	1.9		1.2	.1
	UND	29.1	51.5	64.9	17.7	Sales/Net Fixed Assets	64.8	62.9
	39.9	14.8	10.1	5.4	5.0		12.8	12.1
	12.2	.1	3.6	.2	2.6		1.9	2.4
	6.1	2.8	2.7	1.7	2.1	Sales/Total Assets	2.5	3.0
	2.1	1.8	1.3	1.3	1.5		1.2	1.5
	.5	.1	.3	.2	1.0		.3	.6
		.8	.7			% Depr., Dep., Amort./Sales	1.0	.7
		(11) 2.9	(21) 2.4				(61) 2.2 (60) 2.3	
		21.8	8.2				13.6	4.0
						% Officers', Directors'	2.8	2.1
						Owners' Comp/Sales	(16) 7.0 (13) 7.4	
							21.7	9.6
2911M	53432M	342092M	1463482M	925317M	3751163M	Net Sales ($)	4576248M	5198680M
502M	10377M	82489M	772508M	860565M	2363228M	Total Assets ($)	3049761M	3029992M

M = $ thousand   MM = $ million
See Pages viii through xx for Explanation of Ratios and Data

Comparative Historical Data				Current Data Sorted by Sales					
			Type of Statement						
18	16	17	Unqualified				3		14
3	5	6	Reviewed	1	2		1		4
1	5	5	Compiled	2	1				1
8	14	5	Tax Returns	2					
30	57	54	Other	10	3	4	10	5	22
4/1/16-3/31/17 ALL	4/1/17-3/31/18 ALL	4/1/18-3/31/19 ALL		0-1MM	14 (4/1-9/30/18) 1-3MM	3-5MM	72 (10/1/18-3/31/19) 5-10MM	10-25MM	25MM & OVER
60	97	86	NUMBER OF STATEMENTS	15	6	4	11	9	41
%	%	%	ASSETS	%	%	%	%	%	%
14.5	16.4	14.2	Cash & Equivalents	9.9			9.6		15.0
12.9	15.2	15.8	Trade Receivables (net)	4.9			12.7		20.4
4.8	5.9	7.6	Inventory	.4			.2		11.5
7.2	6.5	5.6	All Other Current	13.3			.1		5.8
39.4	44.0	43.1	Total Current	28.5			22.6		52.7
31.8	27.3	30.0	Fixed Assets (net)	32.0			59.1		28.2
8.7	14.5	11.7	Intangibles (net)	12.0			8.9		10.9
20.0	14.3	15.2	All Other Non-Current	27.4			9.4		8.3
100.0	100.0	100.0	Total	100.0			100.0		100.0
			LIABILITIES						
5.2	5.6	7.3	Notes Payable-Short Term	7.0			1.8		4.4
3.9	3.2	3.2	Cur. Mat.-L.T.D.	5.4			4.4		2.9
9.2	9.6	9.0	Trade Payables	1.0			5.4		12.1
.2	.2	.0	Income Taxes Payable	.0			.0		.1
10.7	21.7	13.4	All Other Current	14.6			4.2		13.9
29.1	40.3	33.0	Total Current	28.0			15.8		33.3
23.1	20.3	19.7	Long-Term Debt	23.4			38.1		17.2
.9	.2	.4	Deferred Taxes	.0			.0		.5
4.8	5.1	6.3	All Other Non-Current	4.3			1.7		5.8
42.1	34.1	40.6	Net Worth	44.2			44.4		43.1
100.0	100.0	100.0	Total Liabilities & Net Worth	100.0			100.0		100.0
			INCOME DATA						
100.0	100.0	100.0	Net Sales	100.0			100.0		100.0
			Gross Profit						
83.5	84.5	84.5	Operating Expenses	58.6			83.3		96.0
16.5	15.5	15.5	Operating Profit	41.4			16.7		4.0
1.6	3.8	4.2	All Other Expenses (net)	16.7			5.5		.6
14.9	11.7	11.2	Profit Before Taxes	24.7			11.2		3.3
			RATIOS						
2.4	2.5	2.5	Current	3.3			3.5		2.3
1.6	1.3	1.4		1.1			1.3		1.7
.4	.5	.8		.3			.6		1.2
1.8	1.7	1.7	Quick	2.7			3.5		1.7
.9	.8	.9		.4			1.3		1.1
.4	.4	.5		.1			.5		.7
0 796.8	0 814.8	1 602.2	Sales/Receivables	0 UND			0 UND		17 21.9
16 22.7	17 20.9	19 19.0		0 UND			6 62.8		38 9.7
42 8.6	39 9.3	46 8.0		28 12.9			27 13.5		55 6.6
			Cost of Sales/Inventory						
			Cost of Sales/Payables						
5.0	5.2	5.3	Sales/Working Capital	1.8			5.6		5.1
13.4	30.9	16.5		60.2			24.8		10.6
-24.6	-11.8	-26.6		-1.5			-13.9		119.1
23.1	20.0	17.6	EBIT/Interest						19.3
(41) 6.5	(67) 5.9	(62) 4.1						(37) 5.7	
2.1	.7	1.3							1.7
4.9	6.0	15.2	Net Profit + Depr., Dep., Amort./Cur. Mat. L/T/D						17.1
(14) 2.9	(14) 3.0	(13) 2.7						(12) 3.1	
.5	.2	.6							1.0
.0	.1	.2	Fixed/Worth	.0			.9		.4
.8	.7	.8		.0			2.1		.7
5.3	4.0	7.7		3.2			15.2		5.1
.5	.7	.6	Debt/Worth	.4			.3		.6
1.3	1.6	1.9		2.5			7.4		1.4
7.3	NM	NM		-39.9			15.5		6.5
49.0	40.8	51.0	% Profit Before Taxes/Tangible Net Worth	17.9			197.4		24.8
(50) 25.3	(73) 18.5	(65) 15.5		(11) 10.4		(10) 32.2		(32) 15.0	
3.9	5.8	5.6		.1			-17.1		9.0
19.4	19.8	12.6	% Profit Before Taxes/Total Assets	12.5			6.6		11.5
10.1	7.0	6.7		3.5			3.5		6.7
1.7	.5	1.6		1.3			-1.9		2.0
71.6	90.4	56.3	Sales/Net Fixed Assets	UND			23.1		24.2
14.0	17.0	12.2		UND			.4		9.2
2.6	4.0	3.2		.1			.2		3.9
3.0	3.4	2.7	Sales/Total Assets	.5			2.9		2.8
1.7	1.8	1.5		.2			.4		1.7
.9	.7	.5		.1			.2		1.3
.8	.9	.9	% Depr., Dep., Amort./Sales						.8
(39) 2.0	(66) 1.7	(57) 2.9						(33) 1.9	
3.9	5.0	8.2							3.6
	.6		% Officers', Directors' Owners' Comp/Sales						
	(17) 1.4								
	5.8								
4063037M	4681273M	6538397M	Net Sales ($)	7300M	10869M	14881M	91671M	160398M	6253278M
2628697M	2919704M	4089669M	Total Assets ($)	84561M	29355M	30855M	321981M	164675M	3458242M

© RMA 2019   M = $ thousand   MM = $ million
See Pages viii through xx for Explanation of Ratios and Data

ADMINISTRATIVE AND SUPPORT AND WASTE MANAGEMENT AND REMEDIATION SERVICES

Current Data Sorted by Assets | Comparative Historical Data

	0-500M	500M-2MM	2-10MM	10-50MM	50-100MM	100-250MM	Type of Statement	4/1/14-3/31/15 ALL	4/1/15-3/31/16 ALL
		4	5	9	4	6	Unqualified	39	39
		3	1	3			Reviewed	22	13
	2	3	7				Compiled	24	19
	21	8	10	4			Tax Returns	76	69
	19	26	42	29	8	12	Other	154	162
		27 (4/1-9/30/18)		199 (10/1/18-3/31/19)					
NUMBER OF STATEMENTS	42	44	65	45	12	18		315	302
	%	%	%	%	%	%	**ASSETS**	%	%
Cash & Equivalents	38.4	19.9	22.0	15.1	10.9	10.4		26.1	25.6
Trade Receivables (net)	18.2	20.5	18.2	31.9	19.0	18.1		18.6	20.4
Inventory	.5	.4	1.0	1.6	7.5	1.8		2.3	2.1
All Other Current	6.3	5.9	10.4	4.5	6.6	8.8		4.8	6.5
Total Current	63.4	46.7	51.6	53.1	44.0	39.0		51.8	54.6
Fixed Assets (net)	10.8	28.7	27.8	23.2	7.2	22.0		22.3	22.8
Intangibles (net)	12.3	9.2	5.0	12.4	33.6	23.7		9.5	6.6
All Other Non-Current	13.6	15.4	15.6	11.2	15.2	15.3		16.4	15.9
Total	100.0	100.0	100.0	100.0	100.0	100.0		100.0	100.0
							LIABILITIES		
Notes Payable-Short Term	8.1	10.5	4.9	7.0	4.8	1.9		7.6	9.7
Cur. Mat.-L.T.D.	3.9	1.9	2.0	2.3	2.4	1.6		2.2	2.4
Trade Payables	15.2	10.9	7.6	7.0	7.6	8.7		8.3	9.3
Income Taxes Payable	.1	.3	.1	.2	.1	.1		.2	.2
All Other Current	44.8	22.8	16.4	20.0	14.1	21.4		19.9	21.4
Total Current	71.9	46.4	31.0	36.5	28.9	33.7		38.1	43.1
Long-Term Debt	15.4	18.2	22.0	23.4	30.4	27.8		16.4	18.6
Deferred Taxes	.0	.0	.1	.4	.3	1.1		.2	.3
All Other Non-Current	14.0	15.5	6.3	7.5	6.2	14.5		8.0	6.6
Net Worth	-1.3	20.0	40.5	32.3	34.3	22.9		37.3	31.4
Total Liabilities & Net Worth	100.0	100.0	100.0	100.0	100.0	100.0		100.0	100.0
							INCOME DATA		
Net Sales	100.0	100.0	100.0	100.0	100.0	100.0		100.0	100.0
Gross Profit									
Operating Expenses	93.1	87.8	83.4	88.7	93.5	94.8		84.9	87.9
Operating Profit	6.9	12.2	16.6	11.3	6.5	5.2		15.1	12.1
All Other Expenses (net)	.6	4.0	3.7	1.5	4.9	.2		2.1	2.2
Profit Before Taxes	6.3	8.2	12.8	9.8	1.6	5.0		13.0	9.9
							RATIOS		
	5.1	2.4	4.7	2.6	2.4	2.5		4.1	3.4
Current	1.2	1.1	1.6	1.5	1.6	1.5		1.5	1.5
	.5	.5	.8	.9	1.3	.8		.8	.8
	5.1	2.3	3.5	2.2	1.6	2.0		3.6	2.8
Quick	1.1	.9	1.5	1.4	1.4	1.0		1.3	1.2
	.3	.3	.4	.8	.9	.5		.7	.5
	0 UND	0 UND	0 UND	15 24.7	37 9.8	20 18.7		0 UND	0 UND
Sales/Receivables	0 UND	10 36.3	10 37.8	51 7.1	56 6.5	42 8.6		7 50.4	11 32.4
	10 36.0	42 8.6	49 7.5	94 3.9	76 4.8	62 5.9		43 8.4	51 7.1
Cost of Sales/Inventory									
Cost of Sales/Payables									
	15.0	9.2	3.5	4.7	3.6	5.8		6.8	6.4
Sales/Working Capital	96.3	93.1	14.4	14.3	9.3	8.1		20.4	22.6
	-19.7	-12.5	-28.6	-33.1	12.6	-28.2		-65.3	-39.8
	31.1	54.9	50.4	12.1	8.4	3.4		36.1	40.3
EBIT/Interest	(15) 8.4	(24) 6.9	(47) 12.1	(35) 4.2	(10) 1.3	(14) 2.4		(186) 10.1	(177) 9.9
	1.7	1.1	1.5	.9	.0	.8		2.6	2.4
							Net Profit + Depr., Dep.,	11.4	17.5
							Amort./Cur. Mat. L/T/D	(25) 5.1	(20) 3.4
								2.9	2.1
	.0	.1	.0	.4	.1	.9		.0	.0
Fixed/Worth	.1	1.0	.8	1.0	3.2	3.1		.3	.4
	-2.2	-2.7	3.7	-1.7	-.2	-.3		3.1	5.2
	.2	.7	.5	.7	2.4	4.5		.4	.5
Debt/Worth	5.6	4.8	1.9	3.0	30.9	NM		1.7	1.9
	-2.5	-7.6	11.4	-18.7	-1.8	-3.1		21.1	173.8
	258.9	112.2	96.5	49.0			% Profit Before Taxes/Tangible	102.9	92.9
	(26) 38.1	(28) 63.5	(54) 32.1	(29) 33.2			Net Worth	(248) 42.1	(230) 37.9
	9.9	9.9	3.4	.9				13.6	10.7
	56.2	58.3	47.5	19.9	6.7	7.7	% Profit Before Taxes/Total	35.9	35.1
	15.3	11.0	11.0	9.7	.4	3.4	Assets	13.2	10.5
	.0	-2.0	.8	.1	-5.2	-1.9		3.2	1.2
	UND	74.6	278.5	55.6	30.3	51.4		230.7	261.9
Sales/Net Fixed Assets	371.8	21.1	20.7	10.7	18.2	11.2		38.3	33.4
	36.8	6.7	2.1	2.9	9.3	3.1		7.5	6.2
	15.8	4.9	4.3	2.7	2.0	1.6		5.2	5.0
Sales/Total Assets	6.9	3.0	2.3	1.6	.9	1.3		2.6	2.6
	3.8	1.2	.5	.7	.5	.5		1.1	1.2
	.4	.4	.4	.8		1.1	% Depr., Dep., Amort./Sales	.6	.4
	(14) 1.0	(24) 1.0	(47) 1.4	(35) 1.3		(10) 1.6		(187) 1.5	(186) 1.5
	1.5	4.1	5.4	5.2		3.3		4.5	5.0
	5.4	5.0	.5				% Officers', Directors'	2.0	1.9
	(16) 13.3	(11) 8.9	(17) 1.6				Owners' Comp/Sales	(69) 8.4	(67) 8.6
	25.0	18.8	8.2					19.2	21.5
Net Sales ($)	66775M	200325M	859347M	1832917M	1018376M	4312821M		9925688M	9153374M
Total Assets ($)	8795M	57180M	312302M	984425M	873968M	3162250M		6187497M	5495080M

© RMA 2019

M = $ thousand   MM = $ million
See Pages viii through xx for Explanation of Ratios and Data

Comparative Historical Data   Current Data Sorted by Sales

				Type of Statement						
33		40	28	Unqualified	1	1	2	4	2	18
11		10	7	Reviewed				3	2	2
13		12	12	Compiled	2	3		2	5	
46		56	43	Tax Returns	11	13	8	5	4	2
142		139	136	Other	23	19	11	19	23	41
4/1/16-		4/1/17-	4/1/18-			27 (4/1-9/30/18)		199 (10/1/18-3/31/19)		
3/31/17		3/31/18	3/31/19							
ALL		ALL	ALL		0-1MM	1-3MM	3-5MM	5-10MM	10-25MM	25MM & OVER
245		257	226	**NUMBER OF STATEMENTS**	37	36	21	33	36	63
%		%	%	**ASSETS**	%	%	%	%	%	%
23.5		21.5	21.7	Cash & Equivalents	28.2	28.7	19.5	21.2	24.0	13.8
18.7		21.0	21.4	Trade Receivables (net)	7.8	13.9	28.8	27.8	20.8	28.2
1.9		2.1	1.3	Inventory	.1	.5	.7	.3	1.5	3.1
5.9		5.9	7.3	All Other Current	6.1	5.3	3.8	15.6	4.6	7.4
50.1		50.5	51.7	Total Current	42.2	48.5	52.8	64.9	50.8	52.5
23.9		23.8	22.4	Fixed Assets (net)	29.2	28.8	21.2	18.2	22.7	17.0
10.3		11.2	11.7	Intangibles (net)	11.2	5.4	9.9	6.2	9.6	20.1
15.6		14.6	14.3	All Other Non-Current	17.5	17.3	16.0	10.7	16.8	10.4
100.0		100.0	100.0	Total	100.0	100.0	100.0	100.0	100.0	100.0
				LIABILITIES						
5.0		7.8	6.8	Notes Payable-Short Term	1.3	11.8	10.2	7.7	5.7	6.0
3.1		2.6	2.4	Cur. Mat.-L.T.D.	2.6	3.5	.4	2.7	1.9	2.3
9.0		9.9	9.6	Trade Payables	12.1	9.0	5.4	11.9	11.0	8.0
.1		.1	.1	Income Taxes Payable	.1	.3	.0	.0	.0	.2
24.6		18.0	23.9	All Other Current	25.4	35.2	19.3	22.0	20.0	21.4
41.8		38.4	42.8	Total Current	41.5	59.8	35.4	44.2	38.6	38.0
18.8		22.9	21.2	Long-Term Debt	24.5	19.0	22.2	13.3	21.0	24.5
.2		.1	.2	Deferred Taxes	.0	.1	.0	.1	.3	.4
7.7		8.8	10.4	All Other Non-Current	14.5	18.2	6.7	2.9	8.1	10.0
31.4		29.8	25.4	Net Worth	19.5	2.8	35.7	39.5	32.0	27.0
100.0		100.0	100.0	Total Liabilities & Net Worth	100.0	100.0	100.0	100.0	100.0	100.0
				INCOME DATA						
100.0		100.0	100.0	Net Sales	100.0	100.0	100.0	100.0	100.0	100.0
				Gross Profit						
85.2		87.1	88.6	Operating Expenses	81.8	89.6	81.3	86.2	92.5	93.4
14.8		12.9	11.4	Operating Profit	18.2	10.4	18.7	13.8	7.5	6.6
2.7		3.0	2.5	All Other Expenses (net)	8.8	.8	3.3	.9	.7	1.4
12.1		9.8	8.9	Profit Before Taxes	9.4	9.5	15.4	12.8	6.7	5.2
				RATIOS						
3.0		2.8	2.9		6.0	3.4	6.7	2.8	3.5	2.4
1.3		1.4	1.5	Current	1.4	1.1	1.2	1.6	1.4	1.6
.7		.8	.7		.4	.5	.7	1.0	.5	.9
2.4		2.3	2.5		5.3	2.8	5.8	2.5	3.1	2.0
1.1		1.2	1.2	Quick	1.4	.8	1.2	1.0	1.2	1.4
.5		.7	.5		.3	.3	.6	.7	.4	.7

0	UND	0	UND	0	UND		0	UND	0	UND	0	UND	1	616.2	1	679.2	23	16.1

15	24.8	16	23.4	17	21.3	Sales/Receivables	0	UND	2	236.6	10	37.7	30	12.0	19	19.4	51	7.1
50	7.3	53	6.9	54	6.8		9	40.1	22	16.6	60	6.1	52	7.0	49	7.5	73	5.0

				Cost of Sales/Inventory						
				Cost of Sales/Payables						
6.3		7.7	6.7		4.4	7.3	5.7	5.3	7.4	5.8
26.3		23.7	20.3	Sales/Working Capital	32.3	207.3	37.4	16.4	18.2	12.2
-27.3		-43.0	-27.7		-11.1	-5.4	-18.9	-370.8	-17.1	-127.6

	34.6		32.9		27.8			17.2		27.0		63.4		99.5		38.0		12.3
(153)	6.1	(174)	7.2	(145)	4.7	EBIT/Interest	(11)	4.5	(20)	3.0	(12)	6.1	(23)	9.3	(29)	8.5	(50)	2.6
	1.3		1.7		1.0			-2.4		1.3		1.4		3.2		1.2		.5

	7.5		5.3		6.8	Net Profit + Depr., Dep.,									6.8
(18)	4.1	(25)	3.9	(25)	5.2	Amort./Cur. Mat. L/T/D								(16)	5.3
	1.4		1.4		1.8										2.5

.1		.1	.1		.0	.0	.0	.0	.2	.3
.5		.6	.9	Fixed/Worth	.2	1.2	.9	.5	.9	3.0
5.3		-34.0	-2.7		65.5	NM	6.1	1.5	-5.7	-.4
.6		.8	.6		.3	.6	.2	.6	.8	1.3
2.1		3.1	3.0	Debt/Worth	2.2	2.8	3.0	1.6	2.6	74.7
UND		-30.7	-8.7		-5.6	-9.2	12.2	17.2	-28.9	-3.6

	84.9		82.1		100.0	% Profit Before Taxes/Tangible		46.1		199.4		83.5		106.6		97.7		88.0
(184)	45.9	(184)	30.7	(153)	34.3	Net Worth	(25)	13.3	(25)	63.8	(17)	36.8	(27)	33.0	(25)	50.4	(34)	39.4
	4.3		4.9		4.0			.0		6.6		7.6		6.3		.9		5.1

34.8		27.3	33.4		21.3	60.4	50.8	54.0	42.5	23.3
10.5		8.6	7.8	% Profit Before Taxes/Total Assets	3.3	9.9	9.7	11.0	13.1	6.9
.2		.7	-.3		-1.1	.4	-3.8	.7	.3	-1.2
186.9		125.4	183.4		UND	197.3	UND	752.8	118.7	58.9
30.2		26.1	28.3	Sales/Net Fixed Assets	36.9	27.2	22.1	42.3	17.5	27.0
5.6		5.7	6.0		.3	2.7	6.9	12.9	4.0	7.3
3.9		4.5	4.8		5.9	5.5	3.8	5.7	5.4	3.5
2.2		2.5	2.3	Sales/Total Assets	1.3	2.7	2.4	3.3	2.9	1.7
1.0		.9	.9		.1	.4	1.0	1.4	1.3	1.1

	.4		.6		.5			1.3		.7				.2		.4		.4
(155)	1.7	(161)	1.7	(136)	1.2	% Depr., Dep., Amort./Sales	(13)	14.1	(22)	1.2		(21)	.9	(28)	1.6	(43)	1.3
	5.8		4.5		4.6			38.3		5.6				3.9		3.8		4.1

	4.1		1.7		1.6	% Officers', Directors'			9.1							
(42)	9.6	(54)	5.0	(50)	6.6	Owners' Comp/Sales		(14)	11.7							
	25.0		14.8		16.5				23.6							

6813066M		9284851M	8290561M	Net Sales ($)	16923M	67028M	85248M	231576M	615687M	7274099M
4821282M		5759132M	5398920M	Total Assets ($)	61725M	87920M	74179M	155043M	344382M	4675671M

M = $ thousand   MM = $ million
See Pages viii through xx for Explanation of Ratios and Data

Current Data Sorted by Assets   Comparative Historical Data

						Type of Statement		
				8	1	4	Unqualified	25	22
			2	3	1		Reviewed	11	12
	1		4				Compiled	2	1
	5	4	3				Tax Returns	19	14
	7	8	4	15			Other	56	61
		11 (4/1-9/30/18)	18	81 (10/1/18-3/31/19)	3	1		4/1/14- 3/31/15	4/1/15- 3/31/16
	0-500M	500M-2MM	2-10MM	10-50MM	50-100MM	100-250MM		ALL	ALL
	13	12	31	26	5	5	NUMBER OF STATEMENTS	113	110
	%	%	%	%	%	%	ASSETS	%	%
	42.5	21.3	12.0	12.7			Cash & Equivalents	16.1	16.8
	22.2	35.8	42.1	51.8			Trade Receivables (net)	38.3	40.9
	1.6	.0	1.2	.5			Inventory	2.0	1.5
	1.0	1.9	5.7	5.6			All Other Current	4.2	3.9
	67.3	59.0	61.0	70.6			Total Current	60.7	63.1
	25.4	21.4	25.7	13.7			Fixed Assets (net)	21.4	21.9
	3.0	4.6	6.2	5.8			Intangibles (net)	8.7	6.0
	4.3	15.1	7.1	9.9			All Other Non-Current	9.2	9.0
	100.0	100.0	100.0	100.0			Total	100.0	100.0
							LIABILITIES		
	45.5	22.8	14.1	10.6			Notes Payable-Short Term	8.2	10.2
	7.4	2.3	3.4	3.1			Cur. Mat.-L.T.D.	3.1	3.2
	1.6	5.0	9.2	14.4			Trade Payables	13.8	15.1
	.0	1.4	.7	.1			Income Taxes Payable	.3	.1
	22.2	26.3	20.0	19.9			All Other Current	16.2	16.9
	76.7	57.9	47.3	48.1			Total Current	41.6	45.4
	25.9	21.3	21.0	9.0			Long-Term Debt	15.9	11.7
	.0	.0	.1	.3			Deferred Taxes	.3	.4
	5.5	.6	5.5	13.1			All Other Non-Current	8.7	7.5
	-8.2	20.2	26.1	29.5			Net Worth	33.6	35.0
	100.0	100.0	100.0	100.0			Total Liabilities & Net Worth	100.0	100.0
							INCOME DATA		
	100.0	100.0	100.0	100.0			Net Sales	100.0	100.0
							Gross Profit		
	90.9	89.9	89.8	95.4			Operating Expenses	94.9	94.6
	9.1	10.1	10.2	4.6			Operating Profit	5.1	5.4
	1.0	.0	4.4	.5			All Other Expenses (net)	.9	.2
	8.0	10.1	5.8	4.1			Profit Before Taxes	4.2	5.2
							RATIOS		
	15.0	4.5	3.3	2.0				3.1	2.7
	3.0	1.1	1.3	1.5			Current	1.4	1.6
	.5	.4	.9	1.1				.9	1.0
	15.0	4.3	2.8	1.8				2.9	2.6
	3.0	1.1	1.2	1.3			Quick	1.3	1.4
	.5	.3	.8	1.0				.8	.9
0	UND	0 UND	26 13.9	37 9.8				18 20.4	23 15.8
0	UND	36 10.1	44 8.3	52 7.0			Sales/Receivables	45 8.2	45 8.1
32	11.3	53 6.9	62 5.9	72 5.1				63 5.8	61 6.0
							Cost of Sales/Inventory		
							Cost of Sales/Payables		
	10.2	8.3	7.8	9.1				5.6	8.8
	28.4	NM	26.6	17.7			Sales/Working Capital	17.7	17.2
	-17.9	-16.6	-53.5	82.1				-72.7	NM
		93.0	54.3	47.3				42.1	47.8
		13.1	(25) 14.7	(23) 8.7			EBIT/Interest	(82) 6.7	(88) 12.5
		5.9	3.2	1.1				1.4	1.8
								15.2	18.0
							Net Profit + Depr., Dep.,	(17) 4.1	(18) 4.4
							Amort./Cur. Mat. L/T/D	.9	2.2
	.1	.1	.1	.1				.1	.1
	1.0	.2	.8	.2			Fixed/Worth	.4	.5
	-.8	3.5	7.0	1.2				4.8	1.7
	.4	.6	.4	1.0				.5	.6
	3.5	2.0	3.4	2.1			Debt/Worth	1.7	1.6
	-2.7	441.4	32.9	19.0				78.3	8.7
		225.5	86.7	62.8				57.2	69.2
	(10)	117.1	(25) 49.2	(21) 35.3			% Profit Before Taxes/Tangible	(87) 30.3	(91) 27.4
		29.0	19.2	15.2			Net Worth	7.7	4.6
	85.3	68.1	23.4	14.4				22.0	21.8
	14.1	28.6	9.8	10.6			% Profit Before Taxes/Total	6.9	11.2
	-32.7	7.5	2.4	3.2			Assets	.4	1.1
	UND	103.1	134.2	267.4				92.3	122.4
	47.5	42.9	64.2	65.0			Sales/Net Fixed Assets	34.9	37.8
	11.1	15.0	4.6	19.2				11.7	8.7
	18.6	5.4	4.7	5.1				5.0	5.2
	7.8	3.8	3.6	3.3			Sales/Total Assets	3.2	3.5
	4.2	3.0	1.8	2.3				1.7	2.2
			.3	.1				.3	.4
		(19)	.9	(21) .6			% Depr., Dep., Amort./Sales	(80) .9	(70) 1.0
			2.7	1.8				2.6	2.8
								.6	1.6
							% Officers', Directors'	(21) 2.7	(17) 2.5
							Owners' Comp/Sales	5.3	5.7
	30605M	48461M	546148M	1839224M	997890M	1116450M	Net Sales ($)	5176504M	5666800M
	3267M	12080M	177877M	529651M	325680M	776752M	Total Assets ($)	2276102M	1971931M

© RMA 2019   M = $ thousand   MM = $ million
See Pages viii through xx for Explanation of Ratios and Data

Comparative Historical Data | Current Data Sorted by Sales

			Type of Statement						
14	19	15	Unqualified				1	1	13
10	10	8	Reviewed				1	1	6
/	6	4	Compiled	2				2	
11	11	13	Tax Returns	1	6	5	1		
66	62	52	Other	4	3	4	8	10	23
4/1/16-3/31/17 ALL	4/1/17-3/31/18 ALL	4/1/18-3/31/19 ALL		0-1MM	1-3MM	3-5MM	5-10MM	10-25MM	25MM & OVER
						11 (4/1-9/30/18)		81 (10/1/18-3/31/19)	
108	108	92	NUMBER OF STATEMENTS	7	9	9	11	14	42
%	%	%	ASSETS	%	%	%	%	%	%
19.7	17.8	17.4	Cash & Equivalents				10.4	16.0	11.3
36.8	38.0	40.5	Trade Receivables (net)				35.1	51.1	51.1
1.3	1.7	1.1	Inventory				.7	1.8	1.2
5.3	5.3	5.2	All Other Current				6.4	5.7	7.4
63.1	62.8	64.3	Total Current				52.5	74.6	71.0
21.1	18.8	21.8	Fixed Assets (net)				26.3	11.3	14.6
5.0	7.6	6.0	Intangibles (net)				6.5	5.7	7.6
10.8	10.8	8.0	All Other Non-Current				14.7	8.3	6.8
100.0	100.0	100.0	Total				100.0	100.0	100.0
			LIABILITIES						
8.9	10.2	17.7	Notes Payable-Short Term				20.8	14.0	10.1
2.1	2.6	3.7	Cur. Mat.-L.T.D.				1.5	3.2	3.6
11.7	12.9	9.7	Trade Payables				11.6	8.8	14.0
.1	.4	.5	Income Taxes Payable				.3	.2	.6
16.1	17.9	20.9	All Other Current				12.1	25.3	19.3
38.8	44.0	52.5	Total Current				46.4	51.5	47.6
14.2	14.1	17.7	Long-Term Debt				15.4	11.6	8.5
.4	.4	.1	Deferred Taxes				.0	.2	.2
8.5	4.9	8.4	All Other Non-Current				18.5	5.5	9.8
38.2	36.6	21.3	Net Worth				19.7	31.3	34.0
100.0	100.0	100.0	Total Liabilties & Net Worth				100.0	100.0	100.0
			INCOME DATA						
100.0	100.0	100.0	Net Sales				100.0	100.0	100.0
			Gross Profit						
92.7	91.9	91.8	Operating Expenses				94.2	95.5	94.7
7.3	8.1	8.2	Operating Profit				5.8	4.5	5.3
.9	1.5	2.1	All Other Expenses (net)				1.3	1.0	.9
6.4	6.6	6.1	Profit Before Taxes				4.5	3.5	4.4
			RATIOS						
3.4	2.8	2.7					3.7	2.6	2.1
1.5	1.5	1.4	Current				1.0	1.4	1.5
1.0	.9	1.0					.8	.9	1.1
2.9	2.6	2.4					3.0	2.6	1.8
(107) 1.4	1.3	1.2	Quick				.9	1.4	1.2
1.0	.8	.8					.7	.8	.9
23 15.7	22 16.7	26 13.9					18 20.8	33 11.2	38 9.5
40 9.2	41 9.0	45 8.2	Sales/Receivables				32 11.5	47 7.8	53 6.9
54 6.7	57 6.4	62 5.9					62 5.9	60 6.1	68 5.4
			Cost of Sales/Inventory						
			Cost of Sales/Payables						
7.6	8.2	8.0					9.1	7.7	7.3
17.4	20.9	20.9	Sales/Working Capital				-167.8	17.1	17.7
272.0	-181.8	-122.1					-25.4	-144.5	62.4
55.5	41.5	50.8					60.0	87.7	47.6
(90) 14.9	(90) 10.7	(76) 11.0	EBIT/Interest		(10) 8.7			(13) 16.1	(37) 8.7
2.5	2.2	1.9					4.3	3.2	1.8
13.2	17.2	12.8							15.0
(15) 4.0	(15) 3.6	(15) 2.7	Net Profit + Depr., Dep., Amort./Cur. Mat. L/T/D						(10) 5.1
.9	.5	.9							.5
.1	.1	.1					.2	.1	.1
.4	.4	.6	Fixed/Worth				.3	.4	.6
1.4	1.5	5.3					-6.9	3.0	1.2
.4	.8	.7					.4	.6	.8
1.4	2.0	2.2	Debt/Worth				1.8	2.1	2.1
5.5	9.6	27.8					-13.5	38.2	5.8
82.4	100.0	96.8						79.7	76.1
(96) 39.5	(91) 44.4	(74) 45.4	% Profit Before Taxes/Tangible Net Worth					(12) 47.7	(36) 36.5
10.2	10.0	18.9						25.4	15.0
28.5	30.9	24.0					40.6	26.6	19.2
11.3	11.1	11.8	% Profit Before Taxes/Total Assets				13.5	17.8	10.8
2.6	3.1	2.0					.7	3.8	3.9
140.3	146.2	152.4					100.4	642.5	165.7
34.2	46.3	48.6	Sales/Net Fixed Assets				28.5	112.7	51.8
9.7	14.1	9.4					4.6	74.6	12.0
4.8	5.8	5.1					4.1	5.1	4.6
3.4	3.8	3.5	Sales/Total Assets				3.6	4.2	3.3
1.8	2.3	2.4					2.1	2.5	2.3
.4	.3	.2							.2
(75) .9	(65) 1.1	(55) .9	% Depr., Dep., Amort./Sales						(33) .9
2.7	2.8	2.3							2.2
1.8	1.1	1.3							
(18) 3.6	(19) 4.0	(20) 4.5	% Officers', Directors' Owners' Comp/Sales						
7.8	6.7	8.7							
4614144M	4358873M	4578778M	Net Sales ($)	2411M	19582M	34870M	84545M	245737M	4191633M
1814276M	1656621M	1825307M	Total Assets ($)	8455M	18614M	11011M	35460M	77473M	1674294M

© RMA 2019

M = $ thousand   MM = $ million

See Pages viii through xx for Explanation of Ratios and Data

Current Data Sorted by Assets   Comparative Historical Data

						Type of Statement		
1	3	10	7	10	5	Unqualified	34	37
1	6	22	14			Reviewed	53	45
1	12	15	3			Compiled	45	44
21	20	10	1			Tax Returns	67	78
30	58	97	49	11	7	Other	316	283
	59 (4/1-9/30/18)		355 (10/1/18-3/31/19)				4/1/14-3/31/15	4/1/15-3/31/16
0-500M	500M-2MM	2-10MM	10-50MM	50-100MM	100-250MM		ALL	ALL
54	99	154	74	21	12	**NUMBER OF STATEMENTS**	515	487
%	%	%	%	%	%	**ASSETS**	%	%
38.0	18.9	14.7	10.1	9.4	2.0	Cash & Equivalents	17.1	17.1
27.3	51.2	60.5	63.3	44.1	30.9	Trade Receivables (net)	55.3	54.0
.0	.1	.1	.1	.0	.5	Inventory	.1	.2
8.8	4.9	6.9	4.7	10.9	3.7	All Other Current	7.2	5.2
74.1	75.2	82.3	78.2	64.4	37.1	Total Current	79.8	76.5
8.8	11.2	4.9	4.6	6.0	12.1	Fixed Assets (net)	6.4	7.5
6.9	5.4	4.7	9.0	23.3	44.6	Intangibles (net)	5.9	7.3
10.3	8.2	8.2	8.2	6.4	6.3	All Other Non-Current	7.9	8.7
100.0	100.0	100.0	100.0	100.0	100.0	Total	100.0	100.0
						LIABILITIES		
49.5	17.9	19.4	18.9	4.9	6.7	Notes Payable-Short Term	25.2	22.4
5.5	2.1	1.0	.9	1.2	2.7	Cur. Mat.-L.T.D.	1.6	2.2
6.3	10.2	8.1	10.9	15.4	5.8	Trade Payables	7.8	8.0
.0	.2	.3	.3	.0	.4	Income Taxes Payable	.3	.5
30.0	21.4	17.4	18.3	17.5	14.0	All Other Current	19.1	18.6
91.3	51.8	46.1	49.3	39.0	29.5	Total Current	54.0	51.7
10.7	11.2	4.1	6.2	25.6	34.8	Long-Term Debt	9.1	8.3
.0	.1	.1	.1	.6	1.3	Deferred Taxes	.1	.1
2.1	6.1	3.0	5.8	4.6	.9	All Other Non-Current	6.4	5.1
-4.0	30.8	46.6	38.6	30.2	33.5	Net Worth	30.4	34.8
100.0	100.0	100.0	100.0	100.0	100.0	Total Liabilties & Net Worth	100.0	100.0
						INCOME DATA		
100.0	100.0	100.0	100.0	100.0	100.0	Net Sales	100.0	100.0
						Gross Profit		
95.8	92.6	94.5	96.1	95.3	93.9	Operating Expenses	95.3	95.1
4.2	7.4	5.5	3.9	4.7	6.1	Operating Profit	4.7	4.9
.7	2.2	.3	.5	1.4	3.5	All Other Expenses (net)	.6	.7
3.5	5.3	5.2	3.3	3.2	2.6	Profit Before Taxes	4.0	4.3
						RATIOS		
3.9	3.0	3.6	2.4	2.2	2.4		3.0	2.6
1.2	1.7	1.8	1.6	1.9	1.7	Current	1.6	1.6
.5	1.0	1.2	1.2	1.1	1.2		1.1	1.1
3.0	3.0	3.3	2.3	2.0	2.4		2.7	2.5
1.0	1.5	1.7	1.4	1.6	1.5	Quick	1.4	1.5
.4	.8	1.1	1.1	1.0	.9		1.0	1.0
0 UND	15 24.9	32 11.3	38 9.7	40 9.1	34 10.6		27 13.6	25 14.4
0 UND	32 11.5	42 8.7	51 7.1	51 7.1	49 7.4	Sales/Receivables	42 8.7	41 8.9
27 13.7	49 7.4	58 6.3	66 5.5	62 5.9	61 6.0		55 6.6	58 6.3
						Cost of Sales/Inventory		
						Cost of Sales/Payables		
14.1	11.7	8.2	8.5	7.1	9.3		9.7	9.6
148.8	25.2	15.2	15.8	10.4	19.7	Sales/Working Capital	20.4	19.6
-25.1	999.8	41.7	48.5	96.1	29.4		103.1	156.9
47.1	35.0	38.7	23.7	26.2	3.5		33.9	37.8
(33) 10.9	(67) 7.8	(124) 10.7	(64) 7.6	(19) 6.6	(11) 1.7	EBIT/Interest	(423) 9.3	(383) 9.4
2.2	1.6	3.6	2.5	2.0	.7		2.9	2.8
			71.7				19.5	18.4
		(14) 7.0				Net Profit + Depr., Dep.,	(36) 5.5	(34) 7.0
		2.7				Amort./Cur. Mat. L/T/D	1.0	1.6
.0	.0	.0	.0	.1	13.5		.0	.0
.0	.1	.1	.1	1.8	-.3	Fixed/Worth	.1	.1
1.1	.6	.2	.4	-.2	-.1		.5	.7
.4	.6	.4	.7	.9	18.9		.6	.7
3.9	1.9	1.2	2.4	21.2	-5.5	Debt/Worth	2.1	1.8
-4.5	9.0	4.0	8.0	-3.5	-2.1		10.0	9.7
210.2	135.6	71.1	51.4	79.1			87.2	88.1
(34) 50.3	(81) 35.0	(141) 37.3	(64) 31.5	(13) 32.4		% Profit Before Taxes/Tangible Net Worth	(416) 42.1	(399) 40.9
1.5	12.7	16.8	10.1	11.0			17.6	15.4
76.3	42.9	32.4	19.2	13.2	10.8		28.4	31.8
24.2	17.4	14.8	9.3	9.5	3.8	% Profit Before Taxes/Total Assets	12.9	13.0
-9.8	2.3	5.5	2.8	1.5	-.9		4.1	3.1
UND	999.8	670.1	470.4	281.6	129.2		906.6	999.8
UND	224.7	204.6	133.9	78.3	100.1	Sales/Net Fixed Assets	215.7	224.3
201.7	49.2	93.0	61.6	42.5	25.7		80.0	77.4
23.7	8.6	7.1	5.9	4.7	3.1		7.1	7.4
8.9	6.4	5.0	4.4	2.7	2.6	Sales/Total Assets	5.2	5.1
4.8	4.1	3.6	3.5	1.7	.6		3.7	3.5
.1	.1	.1	.1	.1	.2		.1	.1
(17) .3	(42) .3	(102) .2	(56) .3	(15) .5		% Depr., Dep., Amort./Sales	(304) .2	(273) .2
1.2	.8	.3	.5	1.1			.5	.4
1.0	1.6	1.0	.5				1.0	1.5
(19) 5.3	(32) 2.7	(37) 2.2	(11) .9			% Officers', Directors' Owners' Comp/Sales	(132) 3.1	(123) 3.2
12.8	4.3	3.7	2.7				6.2	7.0
176692M	977502M	4412131M	7144752M	5025762M	3702936M	Net Sales ($)	21083087M	22191964M
14192M	117626M	763287M	1626663M	1539832M	1506942M	Total Assets ($)	4734177M	5472427M

M = $ thousand   MM = $ million
See Pages viii through xx for Explanation of Ratios and Data

Comparative Historical Data | **Current Data Sorted by Sales**

4/1/16-3/31/17 ALL	4/1/17-3/31/18 ALL	4/1/18-3/31/19 ALL		0-1MM	1-3MM	3-5MM	5-10MM	10-25MM	25MM & OVER
			Type of Statement						
38	37	36	Unqualified	1		2	4	3	26
43	42	43	Reviewed		1	2	3	9	28
36	36	31	Compiled	1	1	2	5	12	10
57	56	52	Tax Returns	9	9	5	12	15	2
272	245	252	Other	11	15	25	30	55	116
				59 (4/1-9/30/18)			355 (10/1/18-3/31/19)		
446	416	414	**NUMBER OF STATEMENTS**	22	26	36	54	94	182
%	%	%	**ASSETS**	%	%	%	%	%	%
15.0	16.1	17.3	Cash & Equivalents	27.9	23.7	23.6	23.2	21.0	10.2
54.3	54.6	52.8	Trade Receivables (net)	6.9	38.9	51.9	43.1	57.3	61.0
.2	.2	.1	Inventory	.0	.0	.1	.0	.3	.1
4.8	5.8	6.4	All Other Current	10.1	10.9	5.6	7.5	4.1	6.3
74.2	76.7	76.6	Total Current	44.9	73.5	81.2	73.8	82.7	77.5
7.7	6.1	7.1	Fixed Assets (net)	35.2	8.5	4.9	10.0	4.2	4.6
9.4	8.8	8.0	Intangibles (net)	11.3	5.8	9.3	4.0	4.7	10.5
8.7	8.4	8.3	All Other Non-Current	8.6	12.1	4.6	12.1	8.4	7.3
100.0	100.0	100.0	Total	100.0	100.0	100.0	100.0	100.0	100.0
			LIABILITIES						
22.3	24.6	21.8	Notes Payable-Short Term	12.3	25.9	30.0	29.9	22.2	18.1
2.1	1.5	1.9	Cur. Mat.-L.T.D.	1.5	.7	5.9	1.5	2.3	1.2
6.8	6.8	9.2	Trade Payables	6.5	6.6	11.7	8.9	7.8	10.1
.2	.2	.2	Income Taxes Payable	.0	.6	.2	.1	.1	.3
19.1	18.0	20.1	All Other Current	46.0	17.2	27.3	16.2	18.5	17.8
50.3	51.1	53.1	Total Current	66.3	51.1	75.1	56.7	51.0	47.5
11.2	7.7	9.0	Long-Term Debt	18.2	9.2	15.2	7.8	6.6	8.3
.2	.1	.2	Deferred Taxes	.0	.0	.1	.1	.2	.2
7.5	7.6	4.1	All Other Non-Current	.3	1.5	4.4	3.5	6.0	4.1
30.7	33.5	33.6	Net Worth	15.3	38.3	5.2	31.9	36.2	39.9
100.0	100.0	100.0	Total Liabilties & Net Worth	100.0	100.0	100.0	100.0	100.0	100.0
			INCOME DATA						
100.0	100.0	100.0	Net Sales	100.0	100.0	100.0	100.0	100.0	100.0
			Gross Profit						
95.5	95.6	94.5	Operating Expenses	83.1	86.4	94.0	95.6	96.1	96.0
4.5	4.4	5.5	Operating Profit	16.9	13.6	6.0	4.4	3.9	4.0
.9	.9	1.0	All Other Expenses (net)	8.4	1.7	.2	.4	.1	.8
3.6	3.5	4.5	Profit Before Taxes	8.5	11.9	5.8	4.0	3.7	3.2
			RATIOS						
2.8	3.1	3.0		3.9	7.2	3.4	3.2	3.5	2.5
1.5	1.6	1.7	Current	1.1	1.7	1.3	1.7	2.1	1.7
1.1	1.1	1.1		.2	.8	.7	1.0	1.2	1.2
2.5	2.8	2.9		3.0	5.7	3.3	3.1	3.3	2.3
1.4	1.5	1.5	Quick	.9	1.4	1.2	1.4	1.9	1.5
1.0	1.0	1.0		.2	.6	.6	.8	1.1	1.1
29 12.6	27 13.3	24 15.0		0 UND	0 UND	11 32.7	5 75.3	27 13.7	34 10.8
42 8.7	41 8.8	39 9.3	Sales/Receivables	0 UND	30 12.3	32 11.5	30 12.0	38 9.6	46 7.9
57 6.4	58 6.3	57 6.4		21 17.4	61 6.0	50 7.3	49 7.4	56 6.5	59 6.2
			Cost of Sales/Inventory						
			Cost of Sales/Payables						
9.5	9.6	9.1		4.1	5.4	10.1	10.3	8.5	9.9
20.8	19.6	18.5	Sales/Working Capital	71.5	14.2	48.5	25.9	17.2	17.2
112.9	195.9	123.1		-2.2	-97.4	-49.8	-583.8	49.4	50.4
27.6	31.4	31.2			66.9	28.1	22.4	42.5	26.3
(361) 7.0	(326) 7.0	(318) 8.4	EBIT/Interest		(16) 19.9	(20) 6.5	(46) 7.0	(72) 9.6	(158) 8.2
2.1	1.7	2.6			5.5	.1	2.0	2.8	2.7
19.5	31.2	14.8							36.4
(33) 5.1	(22) 7.4	(25) 6.9	Net Profit + Depr., Dep., Amort./Cur. Mat. L/T/D						(21) 7.1
1.5	1.8	2.0							2.2
.0	.0	.0		.0	.0	.0	.0	.0	.0
.1	.1	.1	Fixed/Worth	.4	.0	.2	.1	.1	.1
1.0	.6	.5		4.6	.2	-.1	.5	.2	.5
.7	.5	.6		.3	.3	.8	.6	.4	.8
2.2	2.1	1.9	Debt/Worth	3.1	1.0	6.8	2.2	1.1	2.2
16.4	17.9	9.6		-9.5	10.8	-3.9	16.8	4.7	9.4
74.3	78.0	80.3		24.8	143.5	368.7	95.5	84.0	67.1
(348) 37.4	(325) 40.8	(337) 35.7	% Profit Before Taxes/Tangible Net Worth	(16) 16.4	(21) 57.5	(22) 30.0	(45) 39.2	(82) 48.5	(151) 35.6
14.7	11.6	13.8		-25.1	11.7	-20.0	12.5	15.5	16.7
25.1	31.8	32.8		11.1	70.6	59.4	35.1	38.7	24.7
10.9	10.8	12.5	% Profit Before Taxes/Total Assets	2.8	29.1	13.0	14.5	19.1	11.1
2.5	1.6	2.6		-25.8	10.2	-10.6	2.9	3.7	3.5
696.3	999.8	999.8		UND	UND	UND	921.7	999.8	482.9
204.8	235.7	208.0	Sales/Net Fixed Assets	46.3	UND	407.2	145.4	264.9	164.6
71.9	80.9	71.8		.2	40.0	70.8	44.9	113.2	76.8
6.9	7.5	7.6		4.2	9.1	8.0	9.1	8.3	6.9
4.9	5.3	5.1	Sales/Total Assets	1.5	4.7	6.6	5.7	5.6	5.0
3.5	3.6	3.6		.2	2.5	3.9	3.5	3.9	3.7
.1	.1	.1		1.2		.1	.1	.1	.1
(262) .2	(206) .2	(236) .2	% Depr., Dep., Amort./Sales	(12) 12.5		(12) .2	(24) .2	(55) .2	(127) .2
.4	.4	.5		25.3		.7	.9	.4	.4
1.6	1.5	1.0				.2	1.7	1.0	.7
(109) 3.1	(100) 2.8	(103) 2.4	% Officers', Directors' Owners' Comp/Sales			(11) 3.7	(18) 2.7	(34) 2.4	(28) 1.1
6.1	7.2	4.3				9.4	4.3	3.9	2.5
21506162M	19930852M	21439775M	Net Sales ($)	9058M	55131M	145074M	396295M	1521186M	19313031M
5664961M	5654676M	5568542M	Total Assets ($)	15200M	21983M	29438M	219176M	300400M	4982345M

M = $ thousand MM = $ million

See Pages viii through xx for Explanation of Ratios and Data

Current Data Sorted by Assets							Comparative Historical Data	

0-500M	500M-2MM	2-10MM	10-50MM	50-100MM	100-250MM	Type of Statement	4/1/14-3/31/15 ALL	4/1/15-3/31/16 ALL
	2		1		1	Unqualified	3	3
1		1	2			Reviewed	3	3
	2	1				Compiled		
4	1	1				Tax Returns	4	3
2	4	7	4			Other	6	9
	4 (4/1-9/30/18)		30 (10/1/18-3/31/19)					
6	10	10	7		1	NUMBER OF STATEMENTS	16	18
%	%	%	%	%	%	**ASSETS**	%	%
	20.5	24.3				Cash & Equivalents	20.6	31.7
	38.6	48.8				Trade Receivables (net)	48.7	36.7
	.0	.0				Inventory	.2	.0
	3.5	6.1	D	A		All Other Current	1.2	4.8
	62.6	79.2	A	T		Total Current	70.7	73.2
	8.4	4.9	A	N		Fixed Assets (net)	10.2	6.1
	20.2	1.8	O	T		Intangibles (net)	1.1	10.3
	8.9	14.2				All Other Non-Current	18.0	10.3
	100.0	100.0	A	V		Total	100.0	100.0
			A	I		**LIABILITIES**		
	26.7	10.9	L	A		Notes Payable-Short Term	18.4	20.1
	4.1	.3	B	L		Cur. Mat.-L.T.D.	3.5	3.7
	3.2	5.2	E			Trade Payables	5.7	4.6
	.2	.0				Income Taxes Payable	1.1	.9
	10.8	7.5				All Other Current	13.0	25.1
	45.0	23.9				Total Current	41.7	54.5
	2.4	7.9				Long-Term Debt	13.4	7.0
	.0	.0				Deferred Taxes	.0	.0
	6.8	2.2				All Other Non-Current	4.6	6.8
	45.8	66.1				Net Worth	40.2	31.7
	100.0	100.0				Total Liabilities & Net Worth	100.0	100.0
						INCOME DATA		
	100.0	100.0				Net Sales	100.0	100.0
						Gross Profit		
	89.0	90.3				Operating Expenses	93.5	93.0
	11.0	9.7				Operating Profit	6.5	7.0
	.7	-.6				All Other Expenses (net)	.0	.0
	10.3	10.3				Profit Before Taxes	6.5	7.0
						RATIOS		
	5.5	23.0					4.8	3.0
	3.4	6.5				Current	2.0	2.0
	1.3	1.7					1.0	1.1
	5.5	21.1					4.8	3.0
	3.2	5.5				Quick	1.9	2.0
	1.1	1.4					1.0	1.0
	0 UND	30 12.1					30 12.3	0 UND
	21 17.2	43 8.4				Sales/Receivables	43 8.5	39 9.4
	46 7.9	65 5.6					56 6.5	55 6.6
						Cost of Sales/Inventory		
						Cost of Sales/Payables		
	5.6	3.5					8.4	10.0
	13.2	6.2				Sales/Working Capital	15.9	19.4
	NM	26.3					NM	222.9
							57.8	52.2
						EBIT/Interest	(15) 12.7	(14) 19.9
							1.7	3.8
						Net Profit + Depr., Dep., Amort./Cur. Mat. L/T/D		
	.0	.0					.0	.0
	.1	.0				Fixed/Worth	.1	.1
	-1.1	.1					1.1	.4
	.2	.1					.4	.6
	.6	.5				Debt/Worth	1.3	1.9
	-2.3	1.4					7.1	18.6
		95.0					67.6	132.8
		39.1				% Profit Before Taxes/Tangible Net Worth	(14) 19.4	(15) 57.8
		21.5					1.4	2.1
	74.5	65.2					37.1	57.0
	37.7	25.6				% Profit Before Taxes/Total Assets	9.0	25.5
	18.8	11.4					2.8	3.4
	UND	448.2					399.4	890.4
	211.3	349.6				Sales/Net Fixed Assets	123.2	180.8
	76.9	56.7					35.0	41.8
	10.9	5.6					8.1	9.4
	5.5	4.0				Sales/Total Assets	5.1	4.7
	3.9	2.6					3.2	3.4
							.1	.1
						% Depr., Dep., Amort./Sales	(12) .4	(10) .4
							1.0	.8
						% Officers', Directors' Owners' Comp/Sales		
11482M	100419M	203088M	973431M		269923M	Net Sales ($)	661152M	216232M
1343M	12910M	43669M	205756M		109496M	Total Assets ($)	301648M	53400M

M = $ thousand   MM = $ million
See Pages viii through xx for Explanation of Ratios and Data

Comparative Historical Data | Current Data Sorted by Sales

4/1/16-3/31/17 ALL	4/1/17-3/31/18 ALL	4/1/18-3/31/19 ALL	Type of Statement	0-1MM	1-3MM	3-5MM	5-10MM	10-25MM	25MM & OVER
2	3	4	Unqualified				1	1	2
3	2	4	Reviewed					2	2
1	3	3	Compiled			1		2	
10	6	6	Tax Returns	2	2	1	2		
13	21	17	Other	1	1	1	2	5	7
				4 (4/1-9/30/18)				30 (10/1/18-3/31/19)	
29	**35**	**34**	**NUMBER OF STATEMENTS**	**2**	**3**	**4**	**4**	**10**	**11**
%	%	%	**ASSETS**	%	%	%	%	%	%
40.5	18.8	23.6	Cash & Equivalents					20.2	11.1
38.6	56.6	43.0	Trade Receivables (net)					53.9	63.7
.2	.0	.0	Inventory					.0	.0
2.9	2.9	3.6	All Other Current					4.5	4.5
82.2	78.3	70.2	Total Current					78.6	79.2
6.3	8.8	8.1	Fixed Assets (net)					4.5	6.8
2.3	3.4	7.9	Intangibles (net)					8.5	.2
9.2	9.5	13.8	All Other Non-Current					8.4	13.8
100.0	100.0	100.0	Total					100.0	100.0
			LIABILITIES						
8.3	15.8	24.2	Notes Payable-Short Term					25.0	19.3
3.2	.8	2.1	Cur. Mat.-L.T.D.					.0	2.7
7.7	8.9	4.8	Trade Payables					4.4	10.0
.9	.3	.3	Income Taxes Payable					.2	.6
18.0	12.8	10.7	All Other Current					11.0	15.8
38.1	38.6	42.1	Total Current					40.5	48.5
4.9	7.1	5.9	Long-Term Debt					.0	9.9
.5	.6	.0	Deferred Taxes					.0	.0
2.2	4.1	4.4	All Other Non-Current					3.8	5.3
54.4	49.6	47.7	Net Worth					55.6	36.3
100.0	100.0	100.0	Total Liabilties & Net Worth					100.0	100.0
			INCOME DATA						
100.0	100.0	100.0	Net Sales					100.0	100.0
			Gross Profit						
90.4	92.1	89.5	Operating Expenses					89.3	95.8
9.6	7.9	10.5	Operating Profit					10.7	4.2
.1	.5	.1	All Other Expenses (net)					-.1	.3
9.5	7.4	10.4	Profit Before Taxes					10.8	3.9
			RATIOS						
7.3	4.0	6.7						14.4	2.2
2.2	2.1	2.5	Current					3.8	1.8
1.4	1.3	1.4						1.5	1.3
7.3	3.7	5.9						13.9	2.1
2.1	2.0	2.5	Quick					3.7	1.4
1.4	1.3	1.3						1.4	1.2
0 UND	28 13.1	1 320.5						14 25.3	39 9.4
40 9.1	46 8.0	41 9.0	Sales/Receivables					38 9.6	47 7.8
61 6.0	58 6.3	57 6.4						65 5.6	66 5.5
			Cost of Sales/Inventory						
			Cost of Sales/Payables						
6.5	8.4	6.0						5.3	9.7
12.6	14.5	11.4	Sales/Working Capital					10.6	13.9
27.8	39.8	49.9						41.5	46.9
110.9	67.2	64.7							16.6
(20) 16.4	(29) 12.9	(25) 19.5	EBIT/Interest					(10) 6.1	
6.4	7.3	3.5							2.9
			Net Profit + Depr., Dep., Amort./Cur. Mat. L/T/D						
.0	.0	.0						.0	.0
.0	.1	.1	Fixed/Worth					.1	.1
.3	.5	.3						.1	.3
.1	.3	.2						.1	1.4
1.0	.8	1.1	Debt/Worth					.3	2.3
2.7	2.9	2.4						.7	2.8
129.9	98.3	109.9							55.0
(26) 67.6	(32) 49.4	(30) 47.5	% Profit Before Taxes/Tangible Net Worth						45.5
33.0	27.6	22.2							12.4
86.1	36.2	57.6						65.2	17.0
32.2	23.7	22.8	% Profit Before Taxes/Total Assets					38.3	14.1
11.9	12.7	11.4						21.8	3.7
UND	475.4	448.2						448.2	354.6
367.7	136.4	133.4	Sales/Net Fixed Assets					246.6	112.6
82.1	38.1	48.0						110.9	46.1
10.1	8.0	8.2						10.9	5.7
5.1	4.9	4.3	Sales/Total Assets					5.3	4.4
2.8	3.8	3.2						3.7	3.1
.1	.2	.1							
(12) .3	(22) .3	(18) .1	% Depr., Dep., Amort./Sales						
.5	.6	.3							
2.4	2.0	2.2							
(13) 8.9	(11) 5.7	(13) 6.0	% Officers', Directors' Owners' Comp/Sales						
26.7	25.5	16.3							
360647M	1103857M	1558343M	Net Sales ($)	1136M	4413M	12730M	26678M	157727M	1355659M
92228M	279612M	373174M	Total Assets ($)	1019M	885M	1662M	8949M	29157M	331502M

M = $ thousand   MM = $ million
See Pages viii through xx for Explanation of Ratios and Data

Current Data Sorted by Assets   **Comparative Historical Data**

Type of Statement								
Unqualified	1	2	15	17	5	7	43	48
Reviewed		4	32	18			59	52
Compiled		8	20				53	46
Tax Returns	12	22	9				46	48
Other	16	35	78	59	18	9	246	268
		49 (4/1-9/30/18)		338 (10/1/18-3/31/19)			4/1/14-3/31/15	4/1/15-3/31/16
	0-500M	500M-2MM	2-10MM	10-50MM	50-100MM	100-250MM	ALL	ALL
NUMBER OF STATEMENTS	29	71	154	94	23	16	447	462
ASSETS	%	%	%	%	%	%	%	%
Cash & Equivalents	31.9	17.0	13.2	11.2	6.3	7.1	13.4	14.1
Trade Receivables (net)	32.7	54.0	60.0	56.1	47.1	41.3	57.3	55.5
Inventory	.0	.0	.5	.0	.0	.0	.2	.2
All Other Current	9.5	6.3	6.4	5.7	7.9	7.7	5.7	5.3
Total Current	74.1	77.3	80.1	72.9	61.3	56.1	76.7	75.2
Fixed Assets (net)	11.7	8.3	6.6	6.6	7.0	5.5	6.6	7.1
Intangibles (net)	9.9	4.4	7.0	12.5	27.0	31.6	6.4	7.8
All Other Non-Current	4.4	10.1	6.4	7.9	4.7	6.9	10.4	9.8
Total	100.0	100.0	100.0	100.0	100.0	100.0	100.0	100.0
LIABILITIES								
Notes Payable-Short Term	13.5	23.9	19.3	15.3	10.5	7.1	20.5	20.0
Cur. Mat.-L.T.D.	1.3	2.3	1.3	1.1	3.1	2.2	1.6	1.3
Trade Payables	3.9	5.1	7.9	7.9	5.1	6.0	7.7	7.9
Income Taxes Payable	.0	.0	.0	.3	.1	.1	.3	.3
All Other Current	40.1	16.8	17.0	16.8	18.3	12.9	21.1	17.7
Total Current	58.8	48.0	45.5	41.4	37.0	28.4	51.2	47.3
Long-Term Debt	13.2	7.9	3.7	9.0	14.5	30.0	6.5	7.2
Deferred Taxes	.0	.0	.0	.0	.1	.1	.1	.2
All Other Non-Current	26.0	2.9	3.4	6.5	5.7	3.1	7.2	7.6
Net Worth	2.0	41.2	47.4	43.1	42.7	38.4	34.9	37.6
Total Liabilties & Net Worth	100.0	100.0	100.0	100.0	100.0	100.0	100.0	100.0
INCOME DATA								
Net Sales	100.0	100.0	100.0	100.0	100.0	100.0	100.0	100.0
Gross Profit								
Operating Expenses	95.0	94.4	95.8	95.2	95.6	96.3	96.5	95.9
Operating Profit	5.0	5.6	4.2	4.8	4.4	3.7	3.5	4.1
All Other Expenses (net)	1.2	.5	.4	.4	.7	1.4	.4	.2
Profit Before Taxes	3.9	5.2	3.8	4.4	3.6	2.3	3.1	3.9
RATIOS								
Current	3.9	5.7	3.2	3.0	2.3	3.2	2.6	2.8
	1.5	2.2	1.8	1.7	1.8	2.1	1.6	1.7
	.7	1.0	1.3	1.2	1.2	1.4	1.1	1.2
Quick	3.6	5.7	2.8	2.7	2.2	3.0	2.5	2.7
	1.3	2.1	1.6	1.7	1.5	1.7	1.5	1.5
	.7	.9	1.1	1.1	1.1	1.3	1.0	1.1
Sales/Receivables	0 UND	22 16.4	27 13.5	36 10.1	37 9.8	42 8.6	28 13.2	27 13.3
	10 36.0	34 10.8	44 8.3	49 7.5	51 7.1	49 7.5	41 8.8	42 8.6
	34 10.7	45 8.1	59 6.2	62 5.9	68 5.4	55 6.6	56 6.5	57 6.4
Cost of Sales/Inventory								
Cost of Sales/Payables								
Sales/Working Capital	12.7	8.4	9.0	8.7	8.2	7.8	10.7	10.0
	31.6	17.7	15.0	14.1	12.2	11.1	18.5	16.8
	-67.6	-242.6	37.5	37.8	52.9	15.9	76.7	47.2
EBIT/Interest	23.6	85.8	37.7	34.3	17.4	8.5	37.0	44.9
	(16) 5.6	(55) 11.2	(131) 11.5	(76) 8.6	(22) 6.6	(15) 6.3	(373) 12.1	(391) 14.2
	-1.9	2.0	3.1	4.4	3.1	2.5	2.9	3.4
Net Profit + Depr., Dep., Amort./Cur. Mat. L/T/D			11.6	73.3			56.9	25.6
		(14) 1.8	(11) 10.4			(43) 6.9	(40) 6.3	
			-1.8	2.2			2.4	1.3
Fixed/Worth	.0	.0	.0	.0	.1	.3	.0	.0
	.0	.0	.1	.1	.4	.7	.1	.1
	1.1	.7	.3	.4	-.3	-.1	.4	.4
Debt/Worth	.4	.2	.6	.7	1.9	2.6	.6	.6
	3.1	.9	1.2	1.6	3.2	6.1	1.7	1.5
	-2.7	18.1	4.5	5.0	-6.2	-3.5	5.8	6.0
% Profit Before Taxes/Tangible Net Worth	163.2	83.5	80.1	70.5	62.3	145.8	72.3	74.2
	(19) 58.8	(55) 37.1	(139) 40.8	(78) 39.3	(15) 44.0	(11) 47.2	(379) 40.9	(387) 38.4
	25.6	13.5	17.7	19.0	19.8	37.2	16.7	15.0
% Profit Before Taxes/Total Assets	40.9	46.9	30.1	25.8	14.3	18.7	27.3	30.4
	20.0	17.6	15.2	13.8	8.6	9.7	13.2	12.9
	.0	3.4	6.2	7.4	4.5	6.6	3.3	4.8
Sales/Net Fixed Assets	UND	UND	999.8	542.7	201.9	151.9	672.6	614.8
	615.6	348.1	270.3	146.1	89.8	67.6	203.6	175.1
	58.8	72.5	90.1	72.6	57.5	31.9	76.4	68.7
Sales/Total Assets	16.0	9.0	6.8	5.7	4.4	4.1	7.5	7.2
	7.8	6.6	5.5	4.2	2.5	2.7	5.5	5.2
	4.2	5.0	4.0	3.2	2.0	2.1	3.9	3.5
% Depr., Dep., Amort./Sales	.1	.1	.1	.1	.1	.4	.1	.1
	(12) .4	(34) .2	(95) .2	(67) .2	(12) .5	(10) .7	(283) .2	(296) .2
	1.0	.4	.4	.5	.8	1.2	.4	.4
% Officers', Directors' Owners' Comp/Sales			1.1	.5	.4		1.2	1.1
		(20) 2.7	(36) 1.5	(11) 1.0			(111) 2.3	(124) 2.6
			3.8	4.0	2.9		4.9	4.1
Net Sales ($)	82424M	634938M	4751644M	10196099M	5448825M	7717878M	28831576M	30498357M
Total Assets ($)	6472M	84478M	790957M	2186106M	1690543M	2655115M	6403206M	7910886M

M = $ thousand   MM = $ million
See Pages viii through xx for Explanation of Ratios and Data

Comparative Historical Data				Current Data Sorted by Sales					
			Type of Statement						
35	40	46	Unqualified	1	1		1	7	36
66	57	55	Reviewed	1			2	17	35
34	36	28	Compiled				8	10	10
46	47	43	Tax Returns	5	9	2	10	14	3
266	245	215	Other	8	8	13	16	39	131
4/1/16-3/31/17 ALL	**4/1/17-3/31/18 ALL**	**4/1/18-3/31/19 ALL**			**49 (4/1-9/30/18)**		**338 (10/1/18-3/31/19)**		
				0-1MM	**1-3MM**	**3-5MM**	**5-10MM**	**10-25MM**	**25MM & OVER**
447	425	387	**NUMBER OF STATEMENTS**	15	18	15	37	87	215
%	%	%	**ASSETS**	%	%	%	%	%	%
13.1	13.9	14.1	Cash & Equivalents	29.9	21.6	17.0	15.6	14.0	12.0
56.6	55.3	54.4	Trade Receivables (net)	16.5	38.5	53.6	63.6	60.6	54.3
.4	.4	.2	Inventory	.0	.0	.0	.0	.3	.2
6.5	5.0	6.6	All Other Current	8.7	7.5	12.4	5.8	4.5	6.9
76.5	74.6	75.3	Total Current	55.2	67.7	83.0	85.0	79.4	73.4
6.8	7.8	7.2	Fixed Assets (net)	21.0	17.6	8.5	5.2	6.6	5.9
7.8	9.2	10.3	Intangibles (net)	8.3	9.1	3.8	4.6	8.0	12.8
9.0	8.4	7.2	All Other Non-Current	15.5	5.6	4.8	5.1	6.0	7.8
100.0	100.0	100.0	Total	100.0	100.0	100.0	100.0	100.0	100.0
			LIABILITIES						
19.6	17.1	17.7	Notes Payable-Short Term	5.9	13.7	14.7	32.2	19.5	15.9
2.0	1.2	1.6	Cur. Mat.-L.T.D.	.7	1.8	.3	.7	2.7	1.4
7.6	6.9	6.9	Trade Payables	1.1	2.2	6.8	7.9	8.4	6.9
.3	.3	.1	Income Taxes Payable	.0	.1	.0	.0	.0	.1
18.7	20.4	18.5	All Other Current	29.0	41.0	14.0	17.1	14.6	18.1
48.1	46.0	44.8	Total Current	36.7	58.7	35.8	57.9	45.2	42.4
7.0	5.8	8.2	Long-Term Debt	5.4	25.7	.8	1.7	8.5	8.4
.1	.2	.0	Deferred Taxes	.0	.0	.0	.0	.0	.0
7.7	6.0	5.9	All Other Non-Current	25.5	21.2	3.7	3.0	2.8	5.2
37.0	42.0	41.2	Net Worth	32.4	-5.6	59.8	37.4	43.5	44.1
100.0	100.0	100.0	Total Liabilties & Net Worth	100.0	100.0	100.0	100.0	100.0	100.0
			INCOME DATA						
100.0	100.0	100.0	Net Sales	100.0	100.0	100.0	100.0	100.0	100.0
			Gross Profit						
95.7	95.8	95.3	Operating Expenses	82.1	96.6	96.4	97.0	94.6	96.1
4.3	4.2	4.7	Operating Profit	17.9	3.4	3.6	3.0	5.4	3.9
.5	.5	.5	All Other Expenses (net)	3.3	.8	-.5	.4	.6	.4
3.8	3.7	4.1	Profit Before Taxes	14.6	2.6	4.1	2.6	4.8	3.5
			RATIOS						
3.0	3.2	3.6		10.8	6.2	5.6	3.8	3.7	3.0
1.8	1.7	1.8	Current	1.7	1.8	3.5	1.8	1.9	1.8
1.3	1.2	1.2		.9	.6	1.5	1.0	1.3	1.2
2.8	3.0	3.2		8.1	6.2	3.9	3.6	3.6	2.7
1.6	1.6	1.7	Quick	1.5	1.8	2.3	1.5	1.9	1.6
1.1	1.1	1.1		.9	.5	1.2	.9	1.2	1.1
29 12.4	**27** 13.3	**28** 13.1		**0** UND	**0** UND	**28** 13.1	**32** 11.4	**26** 14.1	**32** 11.4
41 8.8	**42** 8.6	**42** 8.7	Sales/Receivables	**0** UND	**25** 14.5	**36** 10.1	**40** 9.1	**47** 7.8	**44** 8.3
55 6.6	**58** 6.3	**57** 6.4		**74** 4.9	**42** 8.6	**45** 8.1	**52** 7.0	**61** 6.0	**58** 6.3
			Cost of Sales/Inventory						
			Cost of Sales/Payables						
9.1	9.2	8.8		4.3	7.5	6.3	7.7	9.1	9.4
15.6	17.4	15.1	Sales/Working Capital	17.4	23.3	12.6	22.6	14.5	15.0
42.3	47.6	44.0		-71.2	-49.9	22.5	-189.7	37.3	39.2
51.1	40.8	34.1			7.3	123.8	38.0	37.0	34.0
(367) 12.1	(340) 9.8	(315) 8.5	EBIT/Interest		(11) 2.7	(10) 22.8	(30) 7.8	(78) 10.4	(180) 8.7
3.5	2.7	3.2			-2.5	5.7	1.3	3.4	4.0
24.4	17.2	11.9							15.6
(36) 6.1	(30) 6.5	(33) 4.7	Net Profit + Depr., Dep., Amort./Cur. Mat. L/T/D						(25) 5.4
1.3	1.6	1.0							1.3
.0	.0	.0		.0	.0	.0	.0	.0	.0
.1	.1	.1	Fixed/Worth	.0	.0	.0	.0	.1	.1
.3	.4	.6		1.2	-.6	.2	1.4	.3	.6
.5	.4	.6		.2	.3	.1	.3	.4	.7
1.4	1.5	1.5	Debt/Worth	1.1	6.0	.3	1.3	1.2	1.8
5.3	4.9	7.3		-5.5	-2.0	2.0	-282.0	6.0	5.7
73.3	61.5	79.8		100.0	73.7	74.7	83.2	93.9	70.7
(376) 37.9	(356) 30.8	(317) 41.6	% Profit Before Taxes/Tangible Net Worth	(11) 38.4	(11) 25.6	(14) 34.8	(27) 33.6	(74) 46.0	(180) 42.2
14.7	11.6	18.0		.0	3.1	9.5	6.9	17.9	19.8
31.6	26.6	30.6		38.2	34.8	38.5	34.8	39.5	25.9
14.7	12.0	14.3	% Profit Before Taxes/Total Assets	12.3	17.4	25.4	10.9	17.7	13.0
4.0	3.6	6.0		-1.1	-.7	3.4	.7	6.6	6.6
727.9	718.0	904.3		UND	999.8	UND	UND	999.8	574.8
203.8	205.0	213.9	Sales/Net Fixed Assets	UND	197.4	489.0	568.4	229.4	169.8
74.6	64.3	73.1		8.9	24.3	38.3	83.0	73.3	76.2
6.9	7.0	6.8		6.4	11.9	7.5	7.4	7.4	6.5
5.4	5.1	5.2	Sales/Total Assets	1.9	5.6	5.2	5.4	5.5	4.9
3.8	3.6	3.5		.2	4.2	3.7	4.2	3.7	3.5
.1	.1	.1					.1	.1	.1
(277) .2	(265) .2	(230) .2	% Depr., Dep., Amort./Sales				(17) .2	(50) .2	(143) .2
.4	.5	.5					.4	.4	.4
.9	1.1	.8					1.5	.9	.4
(119) 2.2	(90) 2.5	(80) 1.7	% Officers', Directors' Owners' Comp/Sales				(11) 2.3	(23) 2.2	(36) 1.1
3.6	5.0	4.0					4.2	3.8	2.8
29476028M	**27179630M**	**28831808M**	Net Sales ($)	**5457M**	**34725M**	**61304M**	**263728M**	**1471974M**	**26994620M**
7088065M	**6618267M**	**7413671M**	Total Assets ($)	**8170M**	**16118M**	**14366M**	**54160M**	**343314M**	**6977543M**

M = $ thousand MM = $ million

See Pages viii through xx for Explanation of Ratios and Data

Current Data Sorted by Assets | Comparative Historical Data

0-500M	500M-2MM	2-10MM	10-50MM	50-100MM	100-250MM	Type of Statement	4/1/14-3/31/15 ALL	4/1/15-3/31/16 ALL
2	3	2	16	5	1	Unqualified	34	23
	1	4	3			Reviewed	7	11
	1	3	1			Compiled	7	7
3	3	6	1			Tax Returns	18	14
6	16	30	12	3	5	Other	51	56
	14 (4/1-9/30/18)		113 (10/1/18-3/31/19)					
11	24	45	33	8	6	**NUMBER OF STATEMENTS**	117	111
%	%	%	%	%	%	**ASSETS**	%	%
42.8	34.7	21.2	21.7			Cash & Equivalents	27.1	27.7
29.2	41.6	43.5	31.3			Trade Receivables (net)	35.2	37.6
.0	.0	.0	.0			Inventory	.1	.3
6.1	7.3	8.9	17.4			All Other Current	9.0	7.8
78.1	83.6	73.5	70.5			Total Current	71.4	73.4
4.8	7.0	5.5	3.9			Fixed Assets (net)	7.6	8.0
7.9	1.1	9.2	11.6			Intangibles (net)	8.2	8.3
9.2	8.3	11.8	14.0			All Other Non-Current	12.9	10.3
100.0	100.0	100.0	100.0			Total	100.0	100.0
						LIABILITIES		
21.9	17.4	11.1	7.4			Notes Payable-Short Term	10.4	12.8
.0	.0	.6	1.3			Cur. Mat.-L.T.D.	1.3	3.0
9.5	8.3	11.4	4.4			Trade Payables	10.0	7.6
.0	.0	1.5	.5			Income Taxes Payable	.4	.4
52.1	27.5	24.6	40.5			All Other Current	35.4	32.1
83.6	53.1	49.1	54.2			Total Current	57.6	55.8
3.9	3.6	4.4	5.7			Long-Term Debt	9.1	7.0
.0	.0	.2	.1			Deferred Taxes	.2	.2
.0	2.3	7.8	6.4			All Other Non-Current	7.8	6.5
12.6	41.1	38.5	33.6			Net Worth	25.4	30.5
100.0	100.0	100.0	100.0			Total Liabilties & Net Worth	100.0	100.0
						INCOME DATA		
100.0	100.0	100.0	100.0			Net Sales	100.0	100.0
						Gross Profit		
95.9	95.0	97.2	97.3			Operating Expenses	96.3	94.8
4.1	5.0	2.8	2.7			Operating Profit	3.7	5.2
.0	.6	-.1	.4			All Other Expenses (net)	.3	.1
4.0	4.4	2.9	2.2			Profit Before Taxes	3.4	5.1
						RATIOS		
5.1	5.3	2.4	2.3			Current	2.2	2.2
2.0	1.5	1.4	1.2				1.3	1.4
.7	1.1	1.0	.9				1.0	1.1
4.6	4.7	2.4	2.0			Quick	1.9	2.1
2.0	1.5	1.3	.9				1.1	1.2
.7	1.0	.9	.6				.9	.9
1 283.7	1 403.8	1 319.4	1 351.2			Sales/Receivables	2 154.4	4 103.0
2 168.9	17 21.3	27 13.6	19 18.9				17 22.0	21 17.7
27 13.6	48 7.6	44 8.3	47 7.8				44 8.3	43 8.4
						Cost of Sales/Inventory		
						Cost of Sales/Payables		
16.3	8.9	12.1	17.3			Sales/Working Capital	15.8	12.1
72.2	20.0	30.7	84.6				52.4	44.1
-69.8	384.0	-999.8	-100.6				-890.7	315.4
	74.6	65.2	88.0			EBIT/Interest	46.5	39.0
	(14) 16.7	(34) 22.2	(21) 8.5				(84) 12.0	(70) 14.3
	2.7	4.4	2.4				3.5	3.0
						Net Profit + Depr., Dep., Amort./Cur. Mat. L/T/D	4.7	
							(10) 3.4	
							.8	
.0	.0	.0	.0			Fixed/Worth	.0	.0
.0	.1	.1	.1				.1	.1
.3	.2	.3	.7				1.7	.8
.2	.5	.7	1.2			Debt/Worth	1.1	.9
.6	1.4	1.9	3.5				3.2	2.3
-218.0	4.3	5.4	29.0				61.2	19.9
	99.6	117.5	131.9			% Profit Before Taxes/Tangible Net Worth	105.3	86.2
	(23) 65.3	(40) 46.2	(29) 46.8				(96) 45.5	(90) 40.5
	13.3	19.2	18.6				12.7	10.5
55.6	40.6	31.4	18.7			% Profit Before Taxes/Total Assets	22.5	29.8
46.8	15.6	15.0	10.1				11.0	14.5
9.7	2.4	3.5	5.4				1.4	3.6
UND	UND	999.8	999.8			Sales/Net Fixed Assets	999.8	999.8
999.8	916.9	293.7	598.9				249.6	406.7
193.3	152.9	134.1	86.9				71.9	69.7
55.4	21.5	11.0	14.7			Sales/Total Assets	14.0	11.7
13.3	7.5	6.2	5.1				6.3	6.3
7.3	4.2	3.8	3.4				3.3	3.3
		.0	.0			% Depr., Dep., Amort./Sales	.1	.1
	(26)	.1	(21) .2				(59) .2	(58) .2
		.3	.5				.5	.8
						% Officers', Directors' Owners' Comp/Sales	1.4	2.8
							(25) 2.8	(23) 5.9
							7.5	9.5
95218M	486960M	2506547M	8558323M	4205159M	1278308M	Net Sales ($)	9035258M	9312562M
2967M	30402M	196702M	848540M	601060M	797347M	Total Assets ($)	1555130M	1313750M

M = $ thousand   MM = $ million
See Pages viii through xx for Explanation of Ratios and Data

Comparative Historical Data				Current Data Sorted by Sales					
23	27	29	Type of Statement — Unqualified					2	27
7	9	8	Reviewed					4	4
4	6	5	Compiled				1	1	3
11	10	13	Tax Returns				1	6	1
51	58	72	Other	1	5	2	9	20	35
4/1/16-3/31/17 ALL	4/1/17-3/31/18 ALL	4/1/18-3/31/19 ALL		14 (4/1-9/30/18)			113 (10/1/18-3/31/19)		
				0-1MM	1-3MM	3-5MM	5-10MM	10-25MM	25MM & OVER
96	110	127	**NUMBER OF STATEMENTS**	1	8	4	11	33	70
%	%	%	**ASSETS**	%	%	%	%	%	%
27.9	31.5	26.8	Cash & Equivalents				24.6	22.7	27.0
35.4	36.4	37.0	Trade Receivables (net)				46.5	45.9	32.7
.1	.1	.1	Inventory				.0	.0	.1
11.2	9.8	11.7	All Other Current				10.5	6.8	15.7
74.6	77.8	75.7	Total Current				81.6	75.4	75.4
6.6	4.4	5.3	Fixed Assets (net)				3.3	5.6	4.4
9.1	10.7	7.8	Intangibles (net)				7.9	6.1	8.5
9.7	7.1	11.3	All Other Non-Current				7.2	12.9	11.7
100.0	100.0	100.0	Total				100.0	100.0	100.0
			LIABILITIES						
10.2	10.5	11.8	Notes Payable-Short Term				17.6	12.9	5.9
2.0	.7	.7	Cur. Mat.-L.T.D.				.4	.5	.9
7.6	8.4	8.5	Trade Payables				16.4	7.7	7.4
1.0	.7	.7	Income Taxes Payable				.0	.5	1.1
30.2	35.8	33.7	All Other Current				10.6	20.1	42.5
51.0	56.1	55.5	Total Current				45.0	41.7	57.9
8.3	5.5	4.4	Long-Term Debt				2.8	4.6	4.1
.4	.1	.1	Deferred Taxes				.0	.2	.1
7.5	5.7	5.8	All Other Non-Current				8.0	9.0	5.0
32.8	32.7	34.2	Net Worth				44.3	44.5	32.9
100.0	100.0	100.0	Total Liabilties & Net Worth				100.0	100.0	100.0
			INCOME DATA						
100.0	100.0	100.0	Net Sales				100.0	100.0	100.0
			Gross Profit						
91.9	95.3	96.6	Operating Expenses				95.6	96.1	97.7
8.1	4.7	3.4	Operating Profit				4.4	3.9	2.3
.6	.3	.1	All Other Expenses (net)				-.6	-.4	.2
7.5	4.4	3.3	Profit Before Taxes				5.0	4.4	2.1
			RATIOS						
2.6	2.4	2.6	Current				2.9	4.3	1.7
1.4	1.3	1.4					2.0	1.5	1.2
1.1	1.1	1.0					1.1	1.2	1.0
2.5	2.3	2.6	Quick				2.9	3.4	1.6
1.3	1.2	1.1					1.6	1.5	1.0
.8	.9	.7					.9	1.0	.7
1 257.0	1 244.2	1 283.7	Sales/Receivables				16 22.3	2 241.2	1 371.4
15 24.9	25 14.6	19 18.9					47 7.7	31 11.9	9 39.7
47 7.7	47 7.7	45 8.1					54 6.7	45 8.2	41 8.8
			Cost of Sales/Inventory						
			Cost of Sales/Payables						
8.7	10.4	11.7	Sales/Working Capital				6.2	12.5	16.0
38.2	37.7	39.8					10.8	23.8	94.1
225.0	253.3	999.8					16.2	78.4	-999.8
70.8	51.4	65.3	EBIT/Interest					24.4	124.4
(59) 14.6	(69) 15.9	(81) 19.8					(21) 9.6	(45) 31.3	
5.6	4.2	3.6						3.2	7.2
			Net Profit + Depr., Dep., Amort./Cur. Mat. L/T/D						
.0	.0	.0	Fixed/Worth				.0	.0	.0
.1	.1	.1					.1	.0	.1
.5	.4	.3					.4	.2	.5
.7	1.0	.7	Debt/Worth				.5	.5	1.4
2.0	2.9	2.1					2.0	1.1	3.5
13.0	16.2	10.7					5.5	3.8	15.3
105.3	100.4	99.6	% Profit Before Taxes/Tangible Net Worth				73.4	92.2	132.7
(80) 56.1	(93) 57.7	(111) 46.8			(10) 48.3			(30) 40.8	(61) 57.3
22.8	20.4	16.9					12.2	11.5	19.4
40.7	25.9	31.0	% Profit Before Taxes/Total Assets				34.5	39.8	22.5
15.8	12.7	12.1					11.8	17.6	10.9
5.0	3.3	3.7					1.2	3.6	5.0
999.8	999.8	999.8	Sales/Net Fixed Assets				999.8	UND	999.8
225.8	369.9	419.3					125.1	367.2	548.9
121.3	115.1	118.9					84.3	152.2	129.6
13.2	13.1	16.5	Sales/Total Assets				5.7	9.5	21.2
5.8	6.4	5.9					3.7	6.9	6.3
2.7	3.2	3.6					2.0	4.0	4.1
.0	.1	.0	% Depr., Dep., Amort./Sales					.1	.0
(41) .2	(51) .2	(69) .1					(12) .2	(48) .1	
.4	.4	.4						.4	.4
1.1	.3	.6	% Officers', Directors' Owners' Comp/Sales						
(13) 2.4	(13) 1.8	(16) 1.7							
4.0	5.0	3.8							
7556746M	13359846M	17130515M	Net Sales ($)	73M	14193M	15223M	81009M	564664M	16455353M
1398901M	2360546M	2477018M	Total Assets ($)	1532M	3483M	3579M	31162M	218112M	2219150M

M = $ thousand   MM = $ million
See Pages viii through xx for Explanation of Ratios and Data

Current Data Sorted by Assets

Comparative Historical Data

						Type of Statement		
			1		1	Unqualified	1	2
			1			Reviewed	2	1
			1			Compiled	3	1
		2				Tax Returns	4	1
2	1	5	5			Other	7	16
	2						4/1/14-	4/1/15-
	3 (4/1-9/30/18)		18 (10/1/18-3/31/19)				3/31/15	3/31/16
0-500M	500M-2MM	2-10MM	10-50MM	50-100MM	100-250MM		ALL	ALL
2	3	7	8		1	NUMBER OF STATEMENTS	17	21
%	%	%	%	%	%		%	%
						ASSETS		
						Cash & Equivalents	14.5	15.2
						Trade Receivables (net)	33.1	33.3
						Inventory	1.2	1.0
						All Other Current	3.6	9.7
						Total Current	52.4	59.2
						Fixed Assets (net)	30.5	17.7
						Intangibles (net)	7.8	18.5
						All Other Non-Current	9.3	4.6
						Total	100.0	100.0
						LIABILITIES		
						Notes Payable-Short Term	12.7	14.0
						Cur. Mat.-L.T.D.	5.6	6.0
						Trade Payables	10.0	9.4
						Income Taxes Payable	1.4	1.1
						All Other Current	16.8	16.8
						Total Current	46.5	47.2
						Long-Term Debt	49.6	38.3
						Deferred Taxes	.7	.4
						All Other Non-Current	3.6	10.0
						Net Worth	-.4	4.1
						Total Liabilities & Net Worth	100.0	100.0
						INCOME DATA		
						Net Sales	100.0	100.0
						Gross Profit		
						Operating Expenses	89.1	92.5
						Operating Profit	10.9	7.5
						All Other Expenses (net)	3.7	2.7
						Profit Before Taxes	7.3	4.7
						RATIOS		
							2.1	3.0
						Current	1.6	1.7
							.9	.9
							2.1	2.5
						Quick	1.5	1.2
							.7	.6
							21 17.4	27 13.7
						Sales/Receivables	32 11.4	42 8.6
							61 6.0	65 5.6
						Cost of Sales/Inventory		
						Cost of Sales/Payables		
							10.6	6.3
						Sales/Working Capital	30.5	13.8
							NM	-75.5
							58.6	24.8
						EBIT/Interest	(13) 6.6	(19) 8.8
							1.8	.3
						Net Profit + Depr., Dep., Amort./Cur. Mat. L/T/D		
							.3	.3
						Fixed/Worth	1.0	.8
							-2.7	-.8
							.5	.8
						Debt/Worth	.9	3.0
							-5.7	-4.0
							125.6	98.4
						% Profit Before Taxes/Tangible Net Worth	(12) 42.1	(14) 34.1
							12.7	3.2
							45.6	23.0
						% Profit Before Taxes/Total Assets	14.1	8.9
							2.5	-2.9
							56.7	58.4
						Sales/Net Fixed Assets	10.9	17.9
							5.4	7.9
							4.6	3.4
						Sales/Total Assets	2.6	2.3
							2.2	1.3
							.9	1.1
						% Depr., Dep., Amort./Sales	(12) 1.8	(17) 2.2
							4.1	5.1
						% Officers', Directors' Owners' Comp/Sales		
2591M	18742M	86390M	515405M		487090M	Net Sales ($)	1107371M	1011523M
822M	4102M	26222M	222515M		241254M	Total Assets ($)	424037M	456059M

(Left data columns marked "DATA NOT AVAILABLE")

M = $ thousand   MM = $ million
See Pages viii through xx for Explanation of Ratios and Data

Comparative Historical Data				Current Data Sorted by Sales					

				Type of Statement							
1		1	2	Unqualified							2
1			1	Reviewed							1
2		3	1	Compiled							1
5		4	3	Tax Returns							
14		16	14	Other				1	1	1	6
4/1/16-3/31/17 ALL		4/1/17-3/31/18 ALL	4/1/18-3/31/19 ALL			0-1MM	3 (4/1-9/30/18) 1-3MM	3-5MM	18 (10/1/18-3/31/19) 5-10MM	10-25MM	25MM & OVER
23		24	21	**NUMBER OF STATEMENTS**			3	3	3	2	10
%		%	%	**ASSETS**		%	%	%	%	%	%
7.3		11.0	14.0	Cash & Equivalents							14.0
22.1		31.4	21.6	Trade Receivables (net)	D						35.0
.5		1.1	.7	Inventory	A						1.3
9.0		2.5	8.9	All Other Current	T						8.8
38.9		46.1	45.3	Total Current	A						59.0
24.1		15.1	14.4	Fixed Assets (net)							13.5
28.9		25.9	28.5	Intangibles (net)	N						24.9
8.1		12.9	11.8	All Other Non-Current	O						2.6
100.0		100.0	100.0	Total	T						100.0
				LIABILITIES	A						
6.9		12.4	7.9	Notes Payable-Short Term	V						6.6
7.6		3.4	4.7	Cur. Mat.-L.T.D.	A						7.6
8.4		18.2	12.8	Trade Payables	I						15.8
1.2		.0	.0	Income Taxes Payable	L						.1
16.1		10.3	17.2	All Other Current	A						13.1
40.2		44.3	42.7	Total Current	B						43.1
27.8		20.4	20.5	Long-Term Debt	L						22.6
.4		.0	.0	Deferred Taxes	E						.0
9.4		7.5	8.2	All Other Non-Current							10.7
22.3		27.8	28.6	Net Worth							23.6
100.0		100.0	100.0	Total Liabilties & Net Worth							100.0
				INCOME DATA							
100.0		100.0	100.0	Net Sales							100.0
				Gross Profit							
90.3		95.9	91.1	Operating Expenses							92.4
9.7		4.1	8.9	Operating Profit							7.6
3.2		1.3	.5	All Other Expenses (net)							.2
6.5		2.8	8.5	Profit Before Taxes							7.4
				RATIOS							
2.6		3.3	3.0	Current							3.4
1.1		1.2	1.6								1.4
.3		.8	.5								.5
1.7		3.1	2.5	Quick							2.6
.8		1.0	1.2								1.1
.3		.7	.5								.5
17 21.1	20	18.2	0 UND	Sales/Receivables						29	12.4
36 10.2	38	9.6	29 12.4							39	9.4
54 6.8	52	7.0	40 9.1							74	4.9
				Cost of Sales/Inventory							
				Cost of Sales/Payables							
9.1		8.0	10.4	Sales/Working Capital							6.0
26.1		61.7	34.7								23.0
-8.1		-28.5	-12.8								-14.6
18.7		33.9	93.5	EBIT/Interest							139.3
(20) 4.9	(19)	5.4	(16) 8.5								33.1
.2		1.0	2.0								2.3
				Net Profit + Depr., Dep., Amort./Cur. Mat. L/T/D							
.4		.2	.2	Fixed/Worth							.3
6.9		.6	.6								1.4
-1.1		-.1	-.1								-.1
1.6		.6	.5	Debt/Worth							.3
8.2		2.7	1.9								4.6
-4.8		-1.6	-1.9								-2.0
77.0		57.9	90.0	% Profit Before Taxes/Tangible Net Worth							
(13) 37.8	(13)	49.9	(13) 45.2								
-.6		13.1	31.6								
21.2		30.2	39.4	% Profit Before Taxes/Total Assets							29.7
5.9		8.9	19.4								22.4
-3.3		.4	7.5								4.9
38.2		74.9	117.3	Sales/Net Fixed Assets							34.9
13.0		29.9	21.9								19.8
7.5		14.6	17.9								16.5
4.5		5.2	3.7	Sales/Total Assets							3.4
1.7		2.9	2.9								3.0
1.1		1.2	1.9								1.8
1.1		.1	.2	% Depr., Dep., Amort./Sales							
(18) 2.0	(12)	1.0	(10) 2.2								
6.0		2.2	2.5								
				% Officers', Directors' Owners' Comp/Sales							
916357M		538533M	1110218M	Net Sales ($)		5323M	13246M	24353M	36271M		1031025M
558878M		349456M	494915M	Total Assets ($)		1912M	9261M	5498M	11387M		466857M

M = $ thousand   MM = $ million
See Pages viii through xx for Explanation of Ratios and Data

Current Data Sorted by Assets							Comparative Historical Data	
						Type of Statement		
		3	2	1	2	Unqualified	5	11
	1					Reviewed	3	4
		3			1	Compiled	2	4
	1	1				Tax Returns	4	4
2	3	11	4	4	2	Other	19	24
	10 (4/1-9/30/18)		32 (10/1/18-3/31/19)				4/1/14-3/31/15	4/1/15-3/31/16
0-500M	500M-2MM	2-10MM	10-50MM	50-100MM	100-250MM	**NUMBER OF STATEMENTS**	ALL	ALL
2	5	18	7	5	5		33	47
%	%	%	%	%	%	**ASSETS**	%	%
		12.3				Cash & Equivalents	10.2	15.8
		41.7				Trade Receivables (net)	44.1	41.4
		3.0				Inventory	.4	.8
		5.0				All Other Current	5.6	5.3
		62.1				Total Current	60.2	63.3
		18.4				Fixed Assets (net)	16.4	17.3
		13.0				Intangibles (net)	15.0	12.9
		6.5				All Other Non-Current	8.4	6.5
		100.0				Total	100.0	100.0
						LIABILITIES		
		11.4				Notes Payable-Short Term	14.2	11.1
		1.8				Cur. Mat.-L.T.D.	2.0	2.9
		11.5				Trade Payables	13.5	12.0
		.4				Income Taxes Payable	.1	.2
		10.0				All Other Current	23.7	26.5
		35.1				Total Current	53.6	52.7
		12.5				Long-Term Debt	19.6	14.1
		.7				Deferred Taxes	.5	.4
		.8				All Other Non-Current	8.9	8.2
		50.9				Net Worth	17.4	24.5
		100.0				Total Liabilities & Net Worth	100.0	100.0
						INCOME DATA		
		100.0				Net Sales	100.0	100.0
						Gross Profit		
		87.3				Operating Expenses	95.0	96.2
		12.7				Operating Profit	5.0	3.8
		1.4				All Other Expenses (net)	1.1	1.0
		11.3				Profit Before Taxes	3.9	2.8
						RATIOS		
		3.6					2.1	3.0
		2.0				Current	1.5	1.5
		1.0					.9	.9
		3.4					1.9	2.9
		1.7				Quick	1.4	1.4
		.8					.8	.8
	33	11.0					45 8.1	37 9.8
	50	7.3				Sales/Receivables	54 6.8	54 6.8
	66	5.5					68 5.4	63 5.8
						Cost of Sales/Inventory		
						Cost of Sales/Payables		
		4.0					7.5	7.6
		10.4				Sales/Working Capital	14.9	18.8
		NM					-68.2	-78.3
		9.2					28.5	10.1
	(11)	5.7				EBIT/Interest	(29) 4.8	(40) 3.6
		-9.9					1.9	1.0
							15.8	11.2
						Net Profit + Depr., Dep., Amort./Cur. Mat. L/T/D	(10) 4.3	(16) 5.1
							1.4	2.1
		.0					.4	.3
		.3				Fixed/Worth	1.1	1.1
		1.0					-.9	-10.8
		.4					.9	.7
		1.2				Debt/Worth	4.6	5.9
		3.8					-9.8	-25.5
		124.1					56.0	84.5
	(15)	25.8				% Profit Before Taxes/Tangible Net Worth	(20) 35.9	(33) 45.7
		17.3					11.7	6.6
		23.4					26.2	19.4
		11.6				% Profit Before Taxes/Total Assets	10.8	8.5
		3.3					.9	.3
		391.4					40.9	39.6
		24.3				Sales/Net Fixed Assets	25.3	15.9
		11.2					14.4	10.2
		5.2					4.4	4.0
		2.9				Sales/Total Assets	3.3	3.1
		1.4					2.0	2.0
		1.2					1.0	1.1
	(13)	1.8				% Depr., Dep., Amort./Sales	(27) 1.5	(40) 1.8
		2.6					2.2	3.5
						% Officers', Directors' Owners' Comp/Sales		
1920M	61225M	217549M	437781M	1014414M	1473231M	Net Sales ($)	2487650M	3310149M
192M	5837M	74290M	127096M	363921M	1022333M	Total Assets ($)	1107799M	1706298M

M = $ thousand   MM = $ million
See Pages viii through xx for Explanation of Ratios and Data

Comparative Historical Data

Current Data Sorted by Sales

4/1/16-3/31/17 ALL	4/1/17-3/31/18 ALL	4/1/18-3/31/19 ALL	Type of Statement	0-1MM	1-3MM	3-5MM	5-10MM	10-25MM	25MM & OVER
5	9	8	Unqualified		1			2	5
3	2	1	Reviewed			1			
2	3	4	Compiled					3	1
2	3	3	Tax Returns		1				2
23	21	26	Other	2	2	1	5	7	9
					10 (4/1-9/30/18)			32 (10/1/18-3/31/19)	
35	38	42	NUMBER OF STATEMENTS	2	4	2	5	12	17
%	%	%	**ASSETS**	%	%	%	%	%	%
10.3	11.7	12.0	Cash & Equivalents					7.4	10.9
42.2	39.3	41.0	Trade Receivables (net)					50.6	37.9
1.5	1.1	1.4	Inventory					4.6	.2
6.8	7.2	5.5	All Other Current					5.6	4.7
60.8	59.2	59.9	Total Current					68.1	53.7
18.3	19.9	17.7	Fixed Assets (net)					14.2	17.5
14.2	13.9	15.5	Intangibles (net)					12.4	21.6
6.7	7.0	6.8	All Other Non-Current					5.3	7.2
100.0	100.0	100.0	Total					100.0	100.0
			LIABILITIES						
12.9	13.1	14.8	Notes Payable-Short Term					18.7	12.1
4.2	3.8	2.1	Cur. Mat.-L.T.D.					2.5	3.0
13.7	9.8	19.9	Trade Payables					19.7	7.9
.2	.2	.4	Income Taxes Payable					.9	.2
18.0	12.5	10.2	All Other Current					9.4	13.1
49.0	39.4	47.3	Total Current					51.3	36.2
15.1	20.8	13.0	Long-Term Debt					9.1	17.6
.7	.2	.5	Deferred Taxes					.0	.4
4.5	8.1	1.5	All Other Non-Current					1.1	2.0
30.8	31.5	37.8	Net Worth					38.5	43.8
100.0	100.0	100.0	Total Liabilties & Net Worth					100.0	100.0
			INCOME DATA						
100.0	100.0	100.0	Net Sales					100.0	100.0
			Gross Profit						
94.5	94.6	93.5	Operating Expenses					95.6	95.3
5.5	5.4	6.5	Operating Profit					4.4	4.7
1.5	.8	1.2	All Other Expenses (net)					.2	1.4
4.1	4.7	5.3	Profit Before Taxes					4.2	3.3
			RATIOS						
2.1	2.1	3.1	Current					2.7	2.6
1.4	1.4	1.6						1.4	1.6
.9	1.1	.9						1.0	1.0
1.9	1.9	3.0	Quick					1.8	2.6
1.2	1.2	1.5						1.3	1.5
.8	1.0	.7						.7	.8
32 11.5	28 13.2	34 10.8	Sales/Receivables					33 10.9	41 9.0
46 8.0	53 6.9	49 7.5						42 8.6	53 6.9
61 6.0	66 5.5	65 5.6						53 6.9	87 4.2
			Cost of Sales/Inventory						
			Cost of Sales/Payables						
10.2	8.5	6.6	Sales/Working Capital					10.3	6.6
16.6	21.3	18.9						32.9	18.2
-87.5	124.1	-156.2						NM	NM
14.4	14.1	9.3	EBIT/Interest					12.6	14.6
(32) 3.8	(32) 4.0	(29) 2.6						(10) -1.8	(14) 1.0
.9	.0	-6.5						-33.6	.2
	6.6		Net Profit + Depr., Dep., Amort./Cur. Mat. L/T/D						
	(11) 4.9								
	-.3								
.3	.3	.2	Fixed/Worth					.0	.2
.7	.9	.6						.6	1.3
-1.6	NM	NM						.9	-1.4
1.2	1.4	.6	Debt/Worth					1.2	.6
5.4	2.3	2.2						2.2	2.8
-9.2	-58.4	-36.2						8.1	-11.5
59.0	96.3	45.6	% Profit Before Taxes/Tangible Net Worth					192.4	38.8
(23) 36.0	(28) 42.2	(31) 24.7						(10) 75.2	(11) 24.7
3.2	-6.6	6.7						-66.3	6.7
14.9	22.3	22.1	% Profit Before Taxes/Total Assets					64.1	19.0
5.9	8.3	7.0						6.6	4.3
-.7	-1.9	2.2						-27.3	-1.6
87.5	34.2	72.1	Sales/Net Fixed Assets					UND	38.3
24.2	20.9	25.7						40.3	16.7
12.5	9.9	11.4						22.6	9.5
4.3	4.3	5.2	Sales/Total Assets					6.0	3.5
3.2	3.1	3.1						4.3	2.7
2.2	2.0	1.8						2.8	1.6
.5	1.0	.6	% Depr., Dep., Amort./Sales						.9
(27) 1.6	(28) 1.8	(28) 1.6							(10) 2.0
2.3	3.6	2.6							2.9
			% Officers', Directors' Owners' Comp/Sales						
2535084M	2560849M	3206120M	Net Sales ($)	1392M	7760M	8246M	35701M	213431M	2939590M
932558M	1250158M	1593669M	Total Assets ($)	2485M	10374M	2834M	15155M	59070M	1503751M

© RMA 2019   M = $ thousand   MM = $ million
See Pages viii through xx for Explanation of Ratios and Data

Current Data Sorted by Assets							Comparative Historical Data	
				2		Type of Statement Unqualified	1	3
		1	1			Reviewed	5	5
1	1	1				Compiled	9	7
4	2					Tax Returns	23	15
5	3	2		1		Other	28	22
	2 (4/1-9/30/18)		22 (10/1/18-3/31/19)				4/1/14-3/31/15	4/1/15-3/31/16
0-500M	500M-2MM	2-10MM	10-50MM	50-100MM	100-250MM		ALL	ALL
10	6	4	1	3		NUMBER OF STATEMENTS	66	52
%	%	%	%	%	%	ASSETS	%	%
17.6					DATA NOT AVAILABLE	Cash & Equivalents	14.6	13.3
25.6						Trade Receivables (net)	31.0	30.9
7.2						Inventory	5.3	5.6
4.8						All Other Current	2.5	2.9
55.2						Total Current	53.4	52.7
33.4						Fixed Assets (net)	29.5	21.2
10.5						Intangibles (net)	8.8	16.9
1.0						All Other Non-Current	8.4	9.3
100.0						Total	100.0	100.0
						LIABILITIES		
29.8						Notes Payable-Short Term	9.6	14.2
9.3						Cur. Mat.-L.T.D.	2.4	4.1
4.6						Trade Payables	12.5	10.3
.2						Income Taxes Payable	.1	.1
6.1						All Other Current	13.5	18.4
49.9						Total Current	38.1	47.1
43.5						Long-Term Debt	19.3	23.0
.0						Deferred Taxes	.5	.0
27.5						All Other Non-Current	5.3	27.9
-20.8						Net Worth	36.8	2.0
100.0						Total Liabilties & Net Worth	100.0	100.0
						INCOME DATA		
100.0						Net Sales	100.0	100.0
						Gross Profit		
89.3						Operating Expenses	92.4	94.5
10.7						Operating Profit	7.6	5.5
1.6						All Other Expenses (net)	1.7	1.2
9.1						Profit Before Taxes	5.9	4.4
						RATIOS		
5.1							3.1	2.0
1.4						Current	1.4	1.2
.5							1.0	.8
4.8							2.9	1.7
.8						Quick	1.1	1.0
.3							.8	.6
0 UND							18 20.7	8 46.6
19 18.8						Sales/Receivables	39 9.4	30 12.1
31 11.6							51 7.1	52 7.0
						Cost of Sales/Inventory		
						Cost of Sales/Payables		
8.1							9.0	12.1
518.1						Sales/Working Capital	25.0	38.7
-11.1							-493.0	-41.6
							15.2	7.2
						EBIT/Interest	(49) 4.5	(39) 2.1
							2.0	-.4
						Net Profit + Depr., Dep., Amort./Cur. Mat. L/T/D		
1.2							.4	.4
NM						Fixed/Worth	1.0	1.7
-.1							3.3	-.4
1.3							.9	1.2
NM						Debt/Worth	2.1	3.7
-2.4							30.8	-4.5
							80.0	85.9
						% Profit Before Taxes/Tangible Net Worth	(51) 28.1	(32) 25.8
							1.7	2.2
67.2							29.4	17.8
19.6						% Profit Before Taxes/Total Assets	8.1	3.3
12.5							.9	-2.8
76.5							41.9	56.8
38.2						Sales/Net Fixed Assets	13.7	23.2
4.5							6.5	9.7
8.5							5.0	5.0
4.6						Sales/Total Assets	3.0	3.0
1.6							1.9	2.0
							1.3	.8
						% Depr., Dep., Amort./Sales	(47) 2.5	(32) 2.0
							6.4	4.2
							2.5	1.6
						% Officers', Directors' Owners' Comp/Sales	(32) 5.0	(28) 5.6
							10.5	10.4
11395M	23504M	32368M	200412M	560359M		Net Sales ($)	751679M	1334970M
2704M	4882M	18601M	11436M	199548M		Total Assets ($)	369329M	608511M

M = $ thousand MM = $ million

See Pages viii through xx for Explanation of Ratios and Data

Comparative Historical Data | Current Data Sorted by Sales

Type of Statement									
	4/1/16-3/31/17 ALL	4/1/17-3/31/18 ALL	4/1/18-3/31/19 ALL	0-1MM	1-3MM	3-5MM	5-10MM	10-25MM	25MM & OVER
Unqualified		1	2						2
Reviewed	1	4	2		1			1	1
Compiled	4	4	3			1	1		
Tax Returns	14	12	6	4		2			
Other	12	17	11	4	5			1	1
NUMBER OF STATEMENTS	31	38	24	8	6	3	1	2	4
	%	%	%	%	%	%	%	%	%
ASSETS									
Cash & Equivalents	13.0	16.5	11.5						
Trade Receivables (net)	26.4	18.2	28.8						
Inventory	9.0	7.7	5.8						
All Other Current	2.4	5.4	3.3						
Total Current	50.9	47.7	49.4						
Fixed Assets (net)	27.5	26.8	32.5						
Intangibles (net)	13.5	14.9	12.6						
All Other Non-Current	8.2	10.6	5.5						
Total	100.0	100.0	100.0						
LIABILITIES									
Notes Payable-Short Term	15.4	20.0	17.1						
Cur. Mat.-L.T.D.	3.3	5.5	6.1						
Trade Payables	12.2	8.3	6.0						
Income Taxes Payable	.2	.1	.1						
All Other Current	15.8	16.4	8.9						
Total Current	46.9	50.3	38.1						
Long-Term Debt	18.1	36.9	37.7						
Deferred Taxes	.1	.1	.2						
All Other Non-Current	20.2	11.8	13.5						
Net Worth	14.7	.9	10.5						
Total Liabilities & Net Worth	100.0	100.0	100.0						
INCOME DATA									
Net Sales	100.0	100.0	100.0						
Gross Profit									
Operating Expenses	95.4	93.0	89.1						
Operating Profit	4.6	7.0	10.9						
All Other Expenses (net)	-.1	1.5	2.6						
Profit Before Taxes	4.7	5.5	8.4						
RATIOS									
Current	1.8	2.7	3.8						
	1.2	1.4	1.3						
	.8	.5	1.0						
Quick	1.6	2.0	3.0						
	.8	.8	1.1						
	.4	.2	.5						
Sales/Receivables	2 167.7	3 105.8	5 74.9						
	29 12.8	23 15.7	29 12.4						
	47 7.8	42 8.7	45 8.1						
Cost of Sales/Inventory									
Cost of Sales/Payables									
Sales/Working Capital	12.0	8.0	7.9						
	50.2	32.4	37.5						
	-27.7	-22.4	NM						
EBIT/Interest	10.3	14.0	15.8						
	(20) 3.7	(31) 6.6	(19) 5.0						
	.5	1.3	2.2						
Net Profit + Depr., Dep., Amort./Cur. Mat. L/T/D									
Fixed/Worth	.5	.2	1.0						
	1.1	2.2	2.3						
	3.9	-.4	-.7						
Debt/Worth	1.3	1.4	1.1						
	2.2	5.1	4.8						
	7.6	-2.9	-2.9						
% Profit Before Taxes/Tangible Net Worth	79.2	124.3	76.2						
	(25) 28.0	(22) 18.3	(15) 49.2						
	9.2	-1.5	2.4						
% Profit Before Taxes/Total Assets	25.6	22.9	22.5						
	7.8	10.5	13.1						
	-1.1	-.6	4.9						
Sales/Net Fixed Assets	45.0	66.4	69.4						
	12.9	19.5	14.1						
	6.2	6.6	4.8						
Sales/Total Assets	4.5	6.3	6.7						
	2.9	2.8	3.1						
	1.9	1.6	1.8						
% Depr., Dep., Amort./Sales	1.1	.9	.5						
	(20) 3.6	(25) 2.2	(14) 3.0						
	5.6	4.4	6.8						
% Officers', Directors' Owners' Comp/Sales	3.8	4.4	2.8						
	(14) 5.9	(16) 8.8	(12) 4.2						
	19.0	16.4	10.8						
Net Sales ($)	763443M	378424M	828038M	5561M	8291M	12076M	9554M	31785M	760771M
Total Assets ($)	291264M	143931M	237171M	5392M	7756M	2495M	3914M	6630M	210984M

M = $ thousand   MM = $ million
See Pages viii through xx for Explanation of Ratios and Data

Current Data Sorted by Assets   **Comparative Historical Data**

						Type of Statement		
1	1	10	19	4	1	Unqualified	46	28
	3	6	6			Reviewed	17	14
	3	1				Compiled	10	9
	6	3				Tax Returns	20	16
5	9	19	15	6	7	Other	68	62
	11 (4/1-9/30/18)		114 (10/1/18-3/31/19)				4/1/14-3/31/15 ALL	4/1/15-3/31/16 ALL
0-500M	500M-2MM	2-10MM	10-50MM	50-100MM	100-250MM			
6	22	39	40	10	8	NUMBER OF STATEMENTS	161	129
%	%	%	%	%	%	**ASSETS**	%	%
	22.5	22.9	18.1	7.2		Cash & Equivalents	26.5	27.3
	25.2	26.9	28.1	14.8		Trade Receivables (net)	24.8	26.5
	.0	.0	1.7	.8		Inventory	.6	.7
	8.3	12.1	8.3	2.9		All Other Current	8.7	4.4
	56.0	61.8	56.3	24.9		Total Current	60.6	59.0
	24.1	11.0	14.5	8.2		Fixed Assets (net)	12.8	13.1
	2.1	11.5	10.8	44.9		Intangibles (net)	13.5	17.4
	17.8	15.7	18.4	22.0		All Other Non-Current	13.1	10.5
	100.0	100.0	100.0	100.0		Total	100.0	100.0
						LIABILITIES		
	7.8	7.3	8.2	1.3		Notes Payable-Short Term	7.5	6.6
	2.8	2.0	7.1	2.8		Cur. Mat.-L.T.D.	2.9	2.9
	7.7	6.1	6.7	5.9		Trade Payables	11.6	11.0
	.4	.1	.1	.0		Income Taxes Payable	.4	.1
	21.0	25.3	18.7	10.8		All Other Current	17.7	18.5
	39.7	40.9	40.9	20.8		Total Current	40.1	39.1
	23.1	8.1	16.7	46.6		Long-Term Debt	15.4	12.7
	.0	.3	.1	.0		Deferred Taxes	.6	.6
	6.4	4.6	5.6	11.4		All Other Non-Current	6.9	6.4
	30.9	46.2	36.8	21.1		Net Worth	37.0	41.1
	100.0	100.0	100.0	100.0		Total Liabilities & Net Worth	100.0	100.0
						INCOME DATA		
	100.0	100.0	100.0	100.0		Net Sales	100.0	100.0
						Gross Profit		
	81.7	90.8	80.2	95.7		Operating Expenses	89.6	89.7
	18.3	9.2	19.8	4.3		Operating Profit	10.4	10.3
	5.2	1.3	2.2	4.4		All Other Expenses (net)	1.5	1.7
	13.1	7.9	17.6	-.2		Profit Before Taxes	8.9	8.6
						RATIOS		
	2.6	3.5	2.9	2.3			2.5	2.9
	1.4	1.7	1.3	1.0		Current	1.5	1.6
	.8	1.0	.9	.8			1.0	1.0
	1.9	2.7	2.7	2.0			2.1	2.8
	.9	1.2	1.1	.9		Quick	1.2	1.4
	.3	.7	.5	.8			.8	1.4
0 UND	5 68.6	14 25.7	27 13.6				11 33.1	10 35.9
3 108.0	32 11.4	35 10.3	30 12.0			Sales/Receivables	26 14.1	31 11.9
47 7.7	51 7.1	52 7.0	72 5.1				51 7.1	49 7.4
						Cost of Sales/Inventory		
						Cost of Sales/Payables		
	9.0	4.9	4.1	7.1			5.8	6.9
	152.7	11.3	14.8	-333.3		Sales/Working Capital	14.9	13.6
	-50.1	-129.6	-45.8	-32.4			-112.9	NM
	25.2	61.4	93.2	2.2			58.9	63.5
	(16) 9.5	(25) 10.9	(32) 19.5	.7		EBIT/Interest	(126) 12.7	(99) 12.8
	-1.7	1.8	3.7	.7			2.4	1.9
			34.1				23.7	43.0
		(11) 9.4				Net Profit + Depr., Dep., Amort./Cur. Mat. L/T/D	(21) 6.3	(21) 7.9
		2.5					1.4	2.8
	.1	.0	.1	.7			.1	.1
	.2	.1	.3	-.2		Fixed/Worth	.3	.4
	21.7	1.0	2.2	-.1			3.1	NM
	.6	.4	.7	2.2			.7	.5
	2.3	1.5	2.1	-1.9		Debt/Worth	1.8	1.5
	85.2	4.7	9.6	-1.7			51.2	-16.1
	65.6	69.1	113.1				134.3	103.7
	(18) 29.3	(33) 26.4	(33) 46.6			% Profit Before Taxes/Tangible Net Worth	(126) 52.2	(95) 57.1
	-.5	4.2	23.2				13.3	15.8
	20.9	33.9	33.1	5.2			36.1	39.1
	9.1	10.3	17.4	-1.7		% Profit Before Taxes/Total Assets	15.0	14.7
	-1.3	1.8	5.6	-2.5			2.6	3.3
	239.7	519.9	68.2	21.4			102.9	107.1
	34.3	52.7	28.4	15.4		Sales/Net Fixed Assets	35.7	31.5
	13.7	24.6	12.2	14.9			17.7	16.2
	6.1	3.4	3.1	2.0			4.2	4.4
	3.2	2.6	1.7	1.2		Sales/Total Assets	2.6	3.0
	.8	1.4	1.1	.8			1.3	1.3
	.1	.3	1.1				.7	.9
	(16) .9	(22) 1.1	(31) 1.8			% Depr., Dep., Amort./Sales	(100) 1.4	(82) 1.4
	2.3	2.0	3.1				2.6	2.2
	6.4	.7					3.5	3.2
	(10) 8.1	(10) 2.9				% Officers', Directors' Owners' Comp/Sales	(36) 7.6	(25) 6.5
	10.5	5.6					12.3	13.5
16448M	234537M	638067M	1664875M	909725M	911509M	Net Sales ($)	4737002M	4477984M
1179M	29165M	205453M	852848M	710192M	976245M	Total Assets ($)	3941897M	3095620M

M = $ thousand   MM = $ million
See Pages viii through xx for Explanation of Ratios and Data

Comparative Historical Data   Current Data Sorted by Sales

			Type of Statement	0-1MM	1-3MM	3-5MM	5-10MM	10-25MM	25MM & OVER
52	36	35	Unqualified		3	1		9	22
15	26	16	Reviewed			2	4	3	7
7	6	4	Compiled		2		1	1	
18	21	9	Tax Returns	1	2	1	4		1
43	49	61	Other	6	6	5	8	14	22
4/1/16-3/31/17 ALL	4/1/17-3/31/18 ALL	4/1/18-3/31/19 ALL			11 (4/1-9/30/18)		114 (10/1/18-3/31/19)		
135	138	125	**NUMBER OF STATEMENTS**	7	13	9	17	27	52
%	%	%	**ASSETS**	%	%	%	%	%	%
26.7	24.6	19.5	Cash & Equivalents		27.8		28.2	16.2	17.5
27.1	26.1	26.7	Trade Receivables (net)		16.4		29.6	24.4	31.8
.7	.5	.5	Inventory		.0		.0	.0	.0
6.9	6.6	8.9	All Other Current		8.8		12.2	15.7	5.1
61.4	57.8	55.6	Total Current		53.0		69.9	56.3	54.4
11.8	13.9	14.0	Fixed Assets (net)		4.2		12.9	11.4	12.3
13.3	15.0	13.4	Intangibles (net)		8.1		2.9	18.4	18.6
13.5	13.3	16.9	All Other Non-Current		34.6		14.3	13.9	14.7
100.0	100.0	100.0	Total		100.0		100.0	100.0	100.0
			LIABILITIES						
7.4	8.3	8.5	Notes Payable-Short Term		21.4		9.9	5.3	3.7
5.1	3.1	4.2	Cur. Mat.-L.T.D.		3.2		1.5	1.8	5.4
7.9	8.6	6.5	Trade Payables		5.4		7.3	6.0	7.6
.4	.4	.2	Income Taxes Payable		.0		.3	.1	.3
19.8	20.1	21.3	All Other Current		26.3		27.7	25.8	18.9
40.7	40.5	40.7	Total Current		56.4		46.7	39.0	35.9
17.0	13.2	18.6	Long-Term Debt		8.3		8.4	6.2	27.1
.5	.2	.3	Deferred Taxes		.0		.0	.2	.6
6.3	6.4	5.8	All Other Non-Current		7.4		8.2	8.6	4.4
35.5	39.7	34.7	Net Worth		27.9		36.7	46.1	32.0
100.0	100.0	100.0	Total Liabilties & Net Worth		100.0		100.0	100.0	100.0
			INCOME DATA						
100.0	100.0	100.0	Net Sales		100.0		100.0	100.0	100.0
			Gross Profit						
89.5	89.2	86.0	Operating Expenses		84.6		94.8	94.1	88.2
10.5	10.8	14.0	Operating Profit		15.4		5.2	5.9	11.8
1.8	2.7	3.1	All Other Expenses (net)		3.4		.5	.7	3.0
8.7	8.1	10.8	Profit Before Taxes		12.0		4.7	5.2	8.8
			RATIOS						
2.5	2.6	2.8	Current		3.9		3.4	2.9	2.4
1.5	1.4	1.4			1.0		2.1	1.4	1.4
1.0	.9	.8			.4		1.0	.9	.9
2.3	2.2	2.2	Quick		3.5		2.9	1.7	2.1
1.4	1.3	1.0			.9		1.4	.9	1.2
.7	.8	.7			.1		.8	.4	.8
10 36.9	10 36.8	7 52.1	Sales/Receivables	0 UND		0 UND		15 24.6	27 13.6
34 10.8	30 12.3	31 11.8		3 109.0		42 8.6		32 11.4	35 10.4
47 7.8	46 8.0	51 7.1		53 6.9		49 7.4		52 7.0	58 6.3
			Cost of Sales/Inventory						
			Cost of Sales/Payables						
6.1	6.2	5.2	Sales/Working Capital		1.2		4.7	8.1	6.7
15.6	18.8	17.5			999.8		8.2	17.5	21.9
-137.6	-80.6	-46.5			-9.0		-250.0	-47.2	-135.0
46.9	58.2	64.5	EBIT/Interest				90.8	89.1	85.9
(104) 7.9	(104) 8.1	(96) 7.0			(10) 5.6		(20) 16.7	(46) 8.7	
2.2	1.4	.9			-1.1		2.1	.7	
19.1	28.8	33.9	Net Profit + Depr., Dep., Amort./Cur. Mat. L/T/D						34.0
(25) 3.9	(18) 10.2	(21) 3.5						(16) 4.3	
1.2	4.1	1.3						1.6	
.1	.1	.1	Fixed/Worth		.0		.1	.0	.1
.4	.4	.3			.0		.2	.2	.5
3.0	2.5	5.3			NM		2.9	1.0	-.7
.7	.7	.7	Debt/Worth		.7		.3	.7	1.1
1.7	1.9	2.3			3.0		1.0	1.6	2.4
21.7	21.2	43.6			NM		37.9	24.2	-4.4
116.2	116.8	91.9	% Profit Before Taxes/Tangible Net Worth		41.9		54.6	114.4	147.9
(105) 55.4	(112) 48.8	(97) 33.1		(10) 18.3		(15) 20.1		(21) 33.1	(38) 57.0
13.1	12.1	7.9			4.2		1.7	-6.1	11.6
36.9	28.5	29.1	% Profit Before Taxes/Total Assets		9.2		31.6	22.4	37.9
14.1	10.8	9.6			2.8		11.2	10.3	16.4
3.2	1.8	1.7			-2.6		1.0	-4.4	-1.4
126.9	120.1	148.5	Sales/Net Fixed Assets		UND		583.5	263.3	54.7
33.1	30.6	32.1			124.3		43.7	38.4	24.5
16.7	13.6	15.4			34.3		31.0	16.8	14.4
4.4	4.2	3.5	Sales/Total Assets		3.1		5.4	3.8	3.7
2.8	2.5	2.0			.9		3.0	2.3	2.0
1.5	1.3	1.0			.3		2.5	1.4	1.1
.8	.5	.5	% Depr., Dep., Amort./Sales				.4	.7	1.0
(91) 1.3	(87) 1.2	(79) 1.5					(12) .5	(15) 1.3	(40) 1.7
2.1	2.6	2.6					1.1	3.0	2.6
3.4	2.7	2.6	% Officers', Directors' Owners' Comp/Sales						
(32) 6.9	(34) 5.5	(27) 4.7							
11.4	10.2	9.2							
4616970M	3466221M	4375161M	Net Sales ($)	1883M	24621M	34080M	124420M	429778M	3760379M
3848130M	2519502M	2775082M	Total Assets ($)	11662M	56417M	53248M	41493M	275261M	2337001M

M = $ thousand   MM = $ million
See Pages viii through xx for Explanation of Ratios and Data

Current Data Sorted by Assets

Comparative Historical Data

	0-500M	500M-2MM	2-10MM	10-50MM	50-100MM	100-250MM	Type of Statement	4/1/14-3/31/15 ALL	4/1/15-3/31/16 ALL
		1	7	7	2	11	Unqualified	61	60
		2	10	11	2	1	Reviewed	41	32
	1	5	3	2		1	Compiled	44	35
	14	8	13	1			Tax Returns	80	78
	16	33	48	36	6	7	Other	189	159
		32 (4/1-9/30/18)		215 (10/1/18-3/31/19)					
	31	49	81	57	10	19	NUMBER OF STATEMENTS	415	364
	%	%	%	%	%	%	ASSETS	%	%
Cash & Equivalents	34.7	26.0	20.2	14.9	25.3	12.8		20.7	20.3
Trade Receivables (net)	10.0	17.9	27.8	34.2	31.1	21.9		26.1	24.0
Inventory	3.4	2.8	5.3	5.8	8.0	2.2		5.8	4.5
All Other Current	3.2	5.1	7.9	8.7	1.7	8.5		5.3	5.2
Total Current	51.3	51.8	.61.2	63.6	66.1	45.5		57.9	54.0
Fixed Assets (net)	22.9	29.1	20.9	14.7	17.0	9.5		22.6	24.3
Intangibles (net)	5.4	9.2	11.1	11.8	13.0	31.1		8.2	9.9
All Other Non-Current	20.4	10.0	6.8	9.9	3.9	14.0		11.3	11.8
Total	100.0	100.0	100.0	100.0	100.0	100.0		100.0	100.0
							LIABILITIES		
Notes Payable-Short Term	14.0	5.2	4.9	8.3	8.1	5.4		10.3	12.1
Cur. Mat.-L.T.D.	6.4	1.2	1.9	2.1	.5	1.4		3.2	3.2
Trade Payables	9.4	9.8	12.6	10.6	22.6	6.6		10.4	11.7
Income Taxes Payable	.0	.0	.1	.1	.0	.0		.3	.2
All Other Current	26.3	17.6	16.9	22.7	75.2	19.7		16.1	18.5
Total Current	56.1	33.9	36.3	43.7	106.4	33.1		40.3	45.7
Long-Term Debt	60.0	24.2	13.5	14.1	12.6	11.3		17.3	19.8
Deferred Taxes	.0	.7	.6	.4	.5	.8		.3	.6
All Other Non-Current	3.9	5.7	4.7	6.9	2.2	2.4		6.5	7.6
Net Worth	-19.9	35.5	44.8	34.9	-21.8	52.4		35.6	26.2
Total Liabilties & Net Worth	100.0	100.0	100.0	100.0	100.0	100.0		100.0	100.0
							INCOME DATA		
Net Sales	100.0	100.0	100.0	100.0	100.0	100.0		100.0	100.0
Gross Profit									
Operating Expenses	87.3	81.4	88.0	89.6	91.8	89.1		87.9	88.8
Operating Profit	12.7	18.6	12.0	10.4	8.2	10.9		12.1	11.2
All Other Expenses (net)	1.2	5.8	2.2	3.0	1.7	2.6		2.0	3.3
Profit Before Taxes	11.5	12.8	9.8	7.3	6.6	8.2		10.1	7.9
							RATIOS		
	2.9	8.2	3.6	2.3	2.0	2.0		3.2	2.7
Current	1.0	1.4	1.7	1.4	1.3	1.4		1.6	1.3
	.4	.6	1.1	1.1	1.0	1.1		1.0	.8
	2.9	6.1	2.6	1.8	1.9	1.8		2.6	2.2
Quick	.8	1.3	1.5	1.1	1.1	1.2		1.3	1.0
	.3	.4	.7	.7	.8	.8		.7	.6
	0 UND	0 UND	3 107.0	26 14.2	16 23.0	10 35.7		1 513.4	0 UND
Sales/Receivables	0 UND	2 154.7	32 11.4	49 7.5	50 7.3	36 10.2		29 12.5	29 12.4
	5 68.8	31 11.8	54 6.8	87 4.2	60 6.1	87 4.2		55 6.6	54 6.7
							Cost of Sales/Inventory		
							Cost of Sales/Payables		
	15.0	7.2	5.3	5.9	9.7	4.0		6.0	6.7
Sales/Working Capital	359.5	71.7	11.9	11.2	18.2	8.4		17.3	29.0
	-15.5	-16.1	53.4	63.3	NM	24.2		-338.0	-31.8
	41.6	86.0	72.8	49.7		31.8		37.5	28.2
EBIT/Interest	(20) 5.2	(28) 11.9	(56) 13.1	(42) 6.4		(13) 7.6		(300) 9.7	(253) 6.0
	2.9	2.2	3.6	2.5		1.9		2.7	1.9
			34.5	43.1				7.9	5.9
Net Profit + Depr., Dep., Amort./Cur. Mat. L/T/D		(12)	4.4	(14) 2.9				(36) 2.9	(43) 2.6
			1.5	1.1				1.3	1.8
	.0	.0	.1	.1	.1	.1		.1	.1
Fixed/Worth	.4	.4	.3	.3	.9	.3		.4	.7
	-2.7	6.1	1.7	2.8	-.2	8.4		2.4	6.8
	1.6	.3	.3	1.1	1.5	.8		.6	.7
Debt/Worth	4.3	1.4	1.6	2.9	10.9	2.1		1.7	2.4
	-3.7	19.2	4.9	11.2	-2.7	39.6		9.1	56.7
	322.1	99.6	94.5	80.7		48.1		93.2	72.9
% Profit Before Taxes/Tangible Net Worth	(20) 61.2	(38) 46.1	(68) 39.8	(48) 33.6		(16) 23.3		(341) 40.7	(277) 29.9
	13.1	15.2	12.9	10.9		5.1		12.4	8.9
	72.7	46.8	38.1	22.2	20.2	9.6		30.8	22.3
% Profit Before Taxes/Total Assets	15.2	15.3	11.6	10.1	16.7	4.7		11.5	8.0
	3.1	3.8	3.2	1.3	-1.4	.4		3.3	1.9
	999.8	417.7	336.2	122.7	226.7	52.7		119.2	120.6
Sales/Net Fixed Assets	67.1	27.5	37.7	50.5	27.9	25.5		27.2	24.9
	9.4	2.7	8.7	9.2	10.0	10.9		6.8	6.7
	10.2	5.4	4.4	3.0	3.9	1.9		4.8	4.4
Sales/Total Assets	4.8	3.2	2.4	1.8	2.0	.7		2.5	2.5
	2.4	.8	1.2	1.1	1.0	.3		1.3	1.1
	.4	.5	.4	.3		1.0		.4	.4
% Depr., Dep., Amort./Sales	(10) .9	(23) 2.1	(53) 1.5	(43) 1.1		(10) 2.0		(280) 1.4	(234) 1.3
	4.3	9.4	4.6	3.0		2.5		3.6	4.0
	4.2	2.1	1.6					2.0	2.6
% Officers', Directors' Owners' Comp/Sales	(12) 7.1	(11) 3.8	(18) 4.7					(122) 5.2	(99) 5.1
	19.3	9.5	14.1					9.3	12.9
Net Sales ($)	37166M	251778M	1214696M	3103254M	1972037M	5110777M		18072563M	17209832M
Total Assets ($)	6697M	50696M	388850M	1397836M	730968M	3288085M		7277398M	7189908M

M = $ thousand   MM = $ million
See Pages viii through xx for Explanation of Ratios and Data

Comparative Historical Data | | | | Current Data Sorted by Sales

			Type of Statement						
46	36	28	Unqualified	1			3	3	21
31	26	26	Reviewed	1			2	11	12
21	15	11	Compiled	2	3	1	1	1	3
57	47	36	Tax Returns	14	10	3	3	6	
156	131	146	Other	18	18	13	24	25	48
4/1/16-3/31/17 ALL	4/1/17-3/31/18 ALL	4/1/18-3/31/19 ALL		32 (4/1-9/30/18)			215 (10/1/18-3/31/19)		
				0-1MM	1-3MM	3-5MM	5-10MM	10-25MM	25MM & OVER
311	255	247	NUMBER OF STATEMENTS	36	31	17	33	46	84
%	%	%	**ASSETS**	%	%	%	%	%	%
22.5	22.9	21.6	Cash & Equivalents	17.2	33.9	25.8	23.2	23.8	16.3
24.2	25.7	24.8	Trade Receivables (net)	2.6	14.0	16.2	22.5	33.7	36.0
4.7	4.3	4.5	Inventory	.7	4.5	7.4	3.6	6.9	4.7
5.8	7.7	6.7	All Other Current	3.2	4.3	7.0	11.1	8.3	6.5
57.1	60.5	57.7	Total Current	23.8	56.6	56.4	60.4	72.7	63.5
21.8	20.6	20.3	Fixed Assets (net)	50.5	26.4	12.9	16.7	12.4	12.3
12.3	10.3	11.8	Intangibles (net)	5.1	3.1	23.9	16.1	9.3	15.0
8.8	8.6	10.3	All Other Non-Current	20.6	13.9	6.7	6.8	5.6	9.2
100.0	100.0	100.0	Total	100.0	100.0	100.0	100.0	100.0	100.0
			LIABILITIES						
8.6	9.8	7.0	Notes Payable-Short Term	6.5	8.9	6.7	6.7	6.9	6.9
2.8	3.7	2.3	Cur. Mat.-L.T.D.	1.9	6.1	1.3	.6	1.9	2.1
9.7	11.7	11.1	Trade Payables	6.1	6.5	10.6	6.6	18.4	12.9
.2	.3	.1	Income Taxes Payable	.0	.0	.0	.3	.0	.0
21.5	24.0	22.1	All Other Current	9.1	28.7	14.5	21.1	21.2	27.7
42.8	49.5	42.6	Total Current	23.6	50.2	33.1	35.3	48.4	49.7
19.6	18.0	21.4	Long-Term Debt	61.9	34.3	25.5	11.6	5.1	11.2
.4	.3	.5	Deferred Taxes	.0	1.0	.0	1.6	.0	.5
6.2	8.4	5.0	All Other Non-Current	6.4	6.6	2.7	3.4	7.0	4.0
31.0	23.8	30.4	Net Worth	8.1	7.9	38.8	48.2	39.6	34.7
100.0	100.0	100.0	Total Liabilities & Net Worth	100.0	100.0	100.0	100.0	100.0	100.0
			INCOME DATA						
100.0	100.0	100.0	Net Sales	100.0	100.0	100.0	100.0	100.0	100.0
			Gross Profit						
87.3	88.0	87.2	Operating Expenses	63.3	89.7	86.0	90.9	92.6	92.4
12.7	12.0	12.8	Operating Profit	36.7	10.3	14.0	9.1	7.4	7.6
3.7	2.5	3.0	All Other Expenses (net)	14.1	1.7	1.0	1.8	.2	1.1
9.0	9.6	9.8	Profit Before Taxes	22.6	8.6	13.0	7.3	7.2	6.5
			RATIOS						
3.0	2.9	2.9	Current	3.5	5.9	4.7	4.8	3.1	2.2
1.4	1.4	1.5		1.0	1.2	2.2	1.7	1.6	1.5
.8	.9	.9		.2	.7	1.4	.9	1.1	1.1
2.4	2.3	2.3	Quick	2.7	4.9	3.3	4.8	2.4	1.9
1.1	1.1	1.2		.7	1.1	1.7	1.7	1.3	1.2
.6	.6	.6		.2	.4	.7	.8	.8	.7
0 907.0	0 UND	1 666.8	Sales/Receivables	0 UND	0 UND	0 UND	3 109.6	8 43.4	24 15.5
28 13.1	26 13.9	28 13.2		0 UND	5 69.5	10 35.7	38 9.5	34 10.6	49 7.5
55 6.6	57 6.4	54 6.7		0 UND	29 12.8	40 9.2	52 7.0	57 6.4	73 5.0
			Cost of Sales/Inventory						
			Cost of Sales/Payables						
6.6	6.3	6.0	Sales/Working Capital	6.1	4.9	6.2	4.7	5.8	6.7
19.4	17.4	15.0		NM	22.8	17.4	10.8	12.0	13.8
-36.3	-106.7	-139.1		-6.9	-25.6	52.2	-66.5	57.1	55.4
34.4	28.0	47.8	EBIT/Interest	7.9	56.1	45.8	74.9	80.3	84.4
(201) 6.6	(166) 6.9	(166) 9.2		(15) 4.3	(22) 6.4	(12) 24.5	(22) 6.1	(31) 13.2	(64) 10.2
1.5	1.9	2.4		1.4	1.7	5.4	.4	5.3	2.5
6.2	9.7	40.8	Net Profit + Depr., Dep., Amort./Cur. Mat. L/T/D						60.2
(20) 2.8	(24) 4.5	(29) 5.8							(15) 14.2
1.1	3.1	1.5							1.5
.1	.0	.1	Fixed/Worth	.1	.0	.0	.1	.0	.1
.5	.4	.3		3.1	.4	.2	.3	.2	.3
-260.7	2.7	4.4		9.8	3.3	NM	-1.7	.9	2.3
.6	.7	.6	Debt/Worth	1.7	.5	.4	.3	.5	.9
3.3	2.8	2.3		4.8	1.9	2.0	1.4	1.9	2.2
-21.4	-15.8	19.1		-6.7	30.7	-5.7	-23.7	4.2	17.3
95.2	91.0	93.1	% Profit Before Taxes/Tangible Net Worth	51.7	80.0	306.5	96.1	116.6	82.5
(223) 34.1	(187) 36.0	(196) 38.4		(25) 17.9	(26) 33.6	(12) 80.9	(24) 39.0	(39) 46.7	(70) 36.6
9.1	9.3	12.9		3.5	9.2	48.1	14.1	19.3	16.1
27.4	25.9	32.6	% Profit Before Taxes/Total Assets	13.3	48.0	59.4	30.7	43.6	21.8
8.3	8.8	11.4		3.7	15.2	24.2	10.9	18.9	9.9
1.0	1.4	2.8		.9	3.3	10.5	1.4	7.1	2.0
163.2	207.7	206.6	Sales/Net Fixed Assets	96.5	206.6	UND	112.2	551.9	168.4
33.8	39.0	34.4		5.5	50.3	97.3	34.8	45.6	45.9
6.5	8.6	8.2		.2	5.4	17.8	8.4	16.4	12.8
4.3	4.6	4.5	Sales/Total Assets	2.2	7.4	4.3	4.7	4.9	4.0
2.3	2.4	2.3		.6	3.1	3.2	2.4	3.2	2.0
1.0	1.3	1.1		.1	.9	1.5	1.2	1.8	1.4
.5	.4	.4	% Depr., Dep., Amort./Sales	6.9	.5		.3	.2	.3
(192) 1.4	(150) 1.1	(145) 1.3		(19) 14.5	(14) 1.2		(19) 1.6	(31) .8	(57) 1.2
4.9	3.9	4.0		22.4	4.8		4.6	2.0	2.2
2.1	1.7	1.7	% Officers', Directors' Owners' Comp/Sales		4.6			.9	
(70) 4.3	(63) 4.2	(48) 4.4			(10) 6.7			(13) 1.7	
11.4	12.3	11.9			16.5			9.1	
16812116M	11632102M	11689708M	Net Sales ($)	16675M	54382M	66255M	239634M	710902M	10601860M
6389290M	5349589M	5863132M	Total Assets ($)	71823M	36573M	29689M	167344M	392739M	5164964M

© RMA 2019

M = $ thousand   MM = $ million
See Pages viii through xx for Explanation of Ratios and Data

Current Data Sorted by Assets   Comparative Historical Data

Type of Statement

Type of Statement	0-500M	500M-2MM	2-10MM	10-50MM	50-100MM	100-250MM		4/1/14-3/31/15 ALL	4/1/15-3/31/16 ALL
Unqualified		2	3	5	1	1		16	13
Reviewed	1	1	5	3	1			14	11
Compiled	1	1	4	7				14	11
Tax Returns	3	3	10	2				33	29
Other	6	3	10	12	1	4		60	50

Current data periods: 17 (4/1-9/30/18), 72 (10/1/18-3/31/19)

	0-500M	500M-2MM	2-10MM	10-50MM	50-100MM	100-250MM		4/1/14-3/31/15 ALL	4/1/15-3/31/16 ALL
NUMBER OF STATEMENTS	10	10	32	29	3	5		137	114
	%	%	%	%	%	%		%	%
ASSETS									
Cash & Equivalents	48.1	50.9	33.7	35.8				39.7	39.2
Trade Receivables (net)	2.2	20.1	20.4	16.0				17.4	15.7
Inventory	.0	.0	1.0	1.3				.3	.6
All Other Current	1.7	13.1	8.8	14.9				10.9	10.4
Total Current	52.0	84.1	63.9	68.0				68.3	65.9
Fixed Assets (net)	12.5	4.2	10.7	7.8				9.5	8.8
Intangibles (net)	22.8	1.7	14.4	10.3				10.9	8.9
All Other Non-Current	12.5	10.0	11.0	13.9				11.3	16.3
Total	100.0	100.0	100.0	100.0				100.0	100.0
LIABILITIES									
Notes Payable-Short Term	16.8	9.7	3.3	1.5				4.9	6.1
Cur. Mat.-L.T.D.	.2	.0	.5	2.0				1.2	.6
Trade Payables	24.1	22.7	19.8	19.0				16.5	18.7
Income Taxes Payable	.0	.5	.3	.2				.7	.3
All Other Current	13.9	40.4	32.4	41.3				32.3	34.4
Total Current	55.1	73.3	56.3	64.0				55.6	60.1
Long-Term Debt	.4	8.1	7.6	20.3				8.8	7.6
Deferred Taxes	1.1	.0	.1	.6				.2	.2
All Other Non-Current	39.8	1.8	5.7	2.7				8.6	9.1
Net Worth	3.5	16.8	30.3	12.3				26.8	23.0
Total Liabilties & Net Worth	100.0	100.0	100.0	100.0				100.0	100.0
INCOME DATA									
Net Sales	100.0	100.0	100.0	100.0				100.0	100.0
Gross Profit									
Operating Expenses	91.5	95.4	93.9	94.5				95.6	94.8
Operating Profit	8.5	4.6	6.1	5.5				4.4	5.2
All Other Expenses (net)	-.2	.4	-.2	.5				.1	.3
Profit Before Taxes	8.7	4.3	6.3	5.1				4.3	4.9
RATIOS									
Current	4.2	2.7	2.8	1.6				2.1	1.7
	1.8	1.2	1.2	1.1				1.2	1.1
	.7	.8	.7	.8				.9	.7
Quick	4.2	2.7	2.5	1.1				2.0	1.4
	1.4	1.0	1.0	.8				1.1	1.0
	.7	.4	.5	.6				.6	.5
Sales/Receivables	0 UND	0 UND	1 583.3	2 194.9				0 999.8	0 999.8
	0 UND	2 208.1	17 22.1	17 22.1				5 78.6	5 75.8
	3 110.3	73 5.0	64 5.7	31 11.6				30 12.1	26 14.1
Cost of Sales/Inventory									
Cost of Sales/Payables									
Sales/Working Capital	6.8	12.2	5.5	14.9				10.3	14.2
	165.0	63.9	77.2	62.5				41.5	138.0
	-29.4	-30.8	-18.1	-19.0				-46.6	-32.7
EBIT/Interest			55.9	96.5				68.6	79.0
			(19) 15.4	(15) 23.2				(61) 11.1	(54) 18.0
			3.2	1.4				1.9	2.5
Net Profit + Depr., Dep., Amort./Cur. Mat. L/T/D								16.0	15.2
								(10) 4.1	(11) 11.5
								3.0	6.3
Fixed/Worth	.0	.0	.1	.1				.0	.0
	.2	.1	.4	.6				.3	.3
	.0	NM	5.5	3.3				2.9	1.6
Debt/Worth	.2	.6	.7	1.3				1.0	1.5
	1.3	5.2	2.2	5.2				4.1	5.6
	-2.4	-401.8	759.7	194.6				-39.3	999.8
% Profit Before Taxes/Tangible Net Worth			60.1	144.7				81.2	130.3
			(25) 36.9	(24) 43.5				(100) 37.4	(87) 48.3
			13.6	8.1				12.2	14.5
% Profit Before Taxes/Total Assets	59.1	17.8	23.0	18.7				21.2	23.6
	41.4	11.8	7.8	8.5				8.1	9.4
	3.9	.1	2.7	2.6				1.2	4.0
Sales/Net Fixed Assets	UND	UND	280.7	245.5				601.1	846.5
	352.1	166.9	60.0	63.3				107.8	163.2
	46.6	85.7	13.7	17.4				24.6	34.7
Sales/Total Assets	33.2	8.1	4.8	3.9				8.0	9.8
	3.9	4.2	2.5	2.2				3.0	3.3
	3.0	1.9	1.3	1.3				1.4	1.9
% Depr., Dep., Amort./Sales			.3	.1				.2	.1
			(21) .9	(21) .5				(75) .5	(69) .3
			2.4	1.5				1.1	.9
% Officers', Directors' Owners' Comp/Sales			.8					1.1	.7
			(11) 3.8					(46) 2.9	(38) 2.0
			9.8					6.9	3.8
Net Sales ($)	50011M	71429M	588567M	2387365M	209105M	1168769M		11560971M	5340534M
Total Assets ($)	2597M	11034M	148922M	642249M	165980M	902042M		2599038M	1795560M

Comparative Historical Data   Current Data Sorted by Sales

			Type of Statement	0-1MM	1-3MM	3-5MM	5-10MM	10-25MM	25MM & OVER
13	15	12	Unqualified		1	2		1	8
8	11	10	Reviewed		1			4	5
9	8	13	Compiled		2		1	3	6
26	25	18	Tax Returns	1	5	1	3	7	1
54	50	36	Other	3	2	3	6		16
4/1/16-3/31/17 ALL	4/1/17-3/31/18 ALL	4/1/18-3/31/19 ALL			17 (4/1-9/30/18)		72 (10/1/18-3/31/19)		
110	109	89	**NUMBER OF STATEMENTS**	4	11	7	10	21	36
%	%	%	**ASSETS**	%	%	%	%	%	%
37.2	37.4	37.6	Cash & Equivalents		41.0		33.9	44.4	31.5
15.8	17.5	16.4	Trade Receivables (net)		13.7		27.1	11.7	18.1
1.0	.7	.9	Inventory		.0		.2	1.6	1.2
13.0	11.0	10.2	All Other Current		2.2		2.5	13.6	12.0
67.1	66.6	65.0	Total Current		56.8		63.7	71.3	62.7
11.1	10.3	10.9	Fixed Assets (net)		3.2		10.5	12.2	12.0
9.5	9.6	12.6	Intangibles (net)		17.8		15.5	8.7	13.0
12.2	13.5	11.4	All Other Non-Current		22.2		10.2	7.8	12.3
100.0	100.0	100.0	Total		100.0		100.0	100.0	100.0
			LIABILITIES						
4.2	3.9	4.6	Notes Payable-Short Term		23.9		1.6	2.2	2.4
1.3	.4	1.0	Cur. Mat.-L.T.D.		.1		.0	.3	2.1
13.5	17.7	19.5	Trade Payables		14.4		11.5	23.1	23.9
.3	.5	.3	Income Taxes Payable		.2		.0	.5	.3
37.7	35.3	33.0	All Other Current		39.4		37.1	36.3	30.1
57.0	57.8	58.4	Total Current		78.0		50.2	62.4	58.8
4.5	5.4	10.9	Long-Term Debt		7.5		10.8	4.9	17.2
.3	.2	.4	Deferred Taxes		.1		.0	.7	.2
7.7	8.6	8.1	All Other Non-Current		18.1		2.1	12.9	6.2
30.5	28.0	22.2	Net Worth		-3.6		36.9	19.1	17.6
100.0	100.0	100.0	Total Liabilities & Net Worth		100.0		100.0	100.0	100.0
			INCOME DATA						
100.0	100.0	100.0	Net Sales		100.0		100.0	100.0	100.0
			Gross Profit						
93.2	94.8	93.5	Operating Expenses		87.6		93.9	93.8	94.7
6.8	5.2	6.5	Operating Profit		12.4		6.1	6.2	5.3
.3	.4	.3	All Other Expenses (net)		.0		-.2	.7	.7
6.5	4.8	6.2	Profit Before Taxes		12.4		6.4	5.6	4.7
			RATIOS						
2.0	1.7	2.3	Current		2.8		2.0	2.4	2.0
1.1	1.1	1.1			.8		1.1	1.1	1.1
.9	.8	.8			.3		.7	.8	.8
1.6	1.5	1.9	Quick		2.7		2.0	1.6	1.7
.9	.9	.9			.8		1.1	.8	.9
.5	.6	.5			.3		.6	.5	.6
0 896.9	1 604.3	0 999.8	Sales/Receivables		0 911.5		1 717.0	0 849.2	1 254.0
5 73.5	10 38.0	13 29.0			8 46.2		27 13.3	6 59.2	15 24.0
30 12.0	32 11.3	38 9.5			48 7.6		78 4.7	73 5.0	25 14.8
			Cost of Sales/Inventory						
			Cost of Sales/Payables						
8.7	9.0	6.9	Sales/Working Capital		4.5		5.8	8.1	9.8
65.6	89.7	75.4			-27.8		NM	153.5	56.2
-49.9	-29.2	-19.8			-3.2		-15.8	-27.3	-23.3
54.6	44.8	40.3	EBIT/Interest					30.9	106.0
(48) 10.4	(49) 15.7	(46) 11.5						(11) 10.5	(22) 17.9
3.3	5.1	2.2						2.3	1.7
37.7			Net Profit + Depr., Dep., Amort./Cur. Mat. L/T/D						
(13) 6.0									
2.7									
.0	.0	.0	Fixed/Worth		.0		.0	.1	.0
.3	.4	.4			6.0		.4	.5	.4
3.0	2.5	3.3			.0		1.8	NM	3.0
.9	1.1	.6	Debt/Worth		1.2		.9	.7	.6
4.1	3.4	2.5			-3.5		2.1	2.7	2.4
NM	59.5	194.6			-2.3		68.4	NM	19.9
86.9	93.5	68.8	% Profit Before Taxes/Tangible Net Worth					127.5	48.5
(83) 36.2	(85) 35.6	(70) 35.7						(16) 37.1	(30) 30.4
14.0	13.4	7.5						14.4	8.2
22.2	17.3	21.7	% Profit Before Taxes/Total Assets		46.0		22.9	34.1	18.3
8.8	7.6	8.0			16.1		7.7	6.9	10.3
2.7	2.3	2.7			6.3		4.1	2.5	4.3
626.3	493.2	316.8	Sales/Net Fixed Assets		482.7		184.6	217.8	419.2
72.9	108.1	82.9			109.3		48.8	39.5	94.5
19.5	21.0	16.3			35.6		10.0	18.0	15.6
6.5	6.3	4.4	Sales/Total Assets		3.4		3.3	5.7	5.0
3.3	2.6	2.4			2.3		2.1	2.1	2.8
1.5	1.3	1.3			.7		1.4	1.2	1.6
.1	.2	.1	% Depr., Dep., Amort./Sales					.1	.1
(62) .4	(61) .6	(56) .6						(14) .6	(23) .7
1.4	1.8	1.8						1.7	1.9
.7	.7	.8	% Officers', Directors' Owners' Comp/Sales						
(35) 1.8	(29) 2.6	(27) 2.6							
4.4	6.0	6.4							
5662784M	7371704M	4475246M	Net Sales ($)	1347M	17742M	29666M	72225M	341692M	4012574M
2325746M	2409244M	1872824M	Total Assets ($)	2445M	13644M	17449M	44547M	191755M	1602984M

© RMA 2019

M = $ thousand   MM = $ million

See Pages viii through xx for Explanation of Ratios and Data

Current Data Sorted by Assets   Comparative Historical Data

Type of Statement	0-500M	500M-2MM	2-10MM	10-50MM	50-100MM	100-250MM		4/1/14-3/31/15 ALL	4/1/15-3/31/16 ALL
Unqualified			1	3	1	1		7	10
Reviewed			2	2				5	4
Compiled	1		1	1		1		8	6
Tax Returns	2		2		1			8	16
Other	5	2	11	8	6	1		43	31
		6 (4/1-9/30/18)		48 (10/1/18-3/31/19)					
NUMBER OF STATEMENTS	8	7	15	14	8	2		71	67
	%	%	%	%	%	%		%	%
ASSETS									
Cash & Equivalents			26.4	22.4				32.4	42.6
Trade Receivables (net)			9.2	13.0				7.3	10.8
Inventory			2.4	.5				.6	.9
All Other Current			7.9	9.4				8.9	8.1
Total Current			45.9	45.3				49.2	62.4
Fixed Assets (net)			28.7	18.9				25.8	17.8
Intangibles (net)			7.7	12.3				6.0	4.1
All Other Non-Current			17.7	23.5				19.0	15.6
Total			100.0	100.0				100.0	100.0
LIABILITIES									
Notes Payable-Short Term			3.0	1.7				3.5	2.7
Cur. Mat.-L.T.D.			3.4	1.5				3.1	2.3
Trade Payables			5.0	8.7				9.8	10.0
Income Taxes Payable			.0	.1				.1	.1
All Other Current			37.1	27.7				40.7	38.6
Total Current			48.4	39.8				57.2	53.6
Long-Term Debt			14.2	9.8				15.0	14.5
Deferred Taxes			.0	.3				.8	.3
All Other Non-Current			4.4	8.8				9.7	6.9
Net Worth			33.0	41.3				17.4	24.6
Total Liabilities & Net Worth			100.0	100.0				100.0	100.0
INCOME DATA									
Net Sales			100.0	100.0				100.0	100.0
Gross Profit									
Operating Expenses			93.4	88.4				94.1	93.4
Operating Profit			6.6	11.6				5.9	6.6
All Other Expenses (net)			1.5	.0				1.4	.3
Profit Before Taxes			5.1	11.5				4.5	6.3
RATIOS									
Current			3.2	2.7				1.5	2.2
			1.2	1.2				.9	1.3
			.4	.7				.3	.7
Quick			1.2	2.2				1.2	2.0
			.7	.8				.8	.9
			.3	.4				.2	.5
Sales/Receivables	0	UND	0	UND				0 UND	0 UND
	0	UND	11	32.1				1 415.5	2 190.3
	17	21.4	41	9.0				13 28.2	14 25.2
Cost of Sales/Inventory									
Cost of Sales/Payables									
Sales/Working Capital			8.7	4.4				14.5	8.9
			55.8	107.6				-111.3	18.6
			-9.7	-19.0				-6.2	-12.9
EBIT/Interest			74.0					23.3	44.0
		(10)	4.6					(41) 3.1	(36) 8.3
			1.6					1.2	1.6
Net Profit + Depr., Dep., Amort./Cur. Mat. L/T/D									
Fixed/Worth			.2	.0				.0	.0
			1.2	.2				.6	.3
			-4.0	2.7				5.6	-999.8
Debt/Worth			1.0	1.0				1.3	1.3
			3.8	1.7				3.1	3.6
			-32.6	5.6				-13.6	-161.4
% Profit Before Taxes/Tangible Net Worth			47.6	45.0				104.0	113.4
		(11)	33.8	(13) 17.4				(50) 43.6	(49) 37.4
			17.0	9.3				15.3	11.0
% Profit Before Taxes/Total Assets			16.6	13.1				21.3	24.0
			6.2	4.3				6.9	7.5
			2.0	1.2				1.5	2.2
Sales/Net Fixed Assets			277.6	422.8				538.5	812.8
			17.2	39.8				28.8	76.0
			1.7	2.7				2.8	15.2
Sales/Total Assets			5.5	3.5				3.1	4.8
			2.2	1.7				2.1	2.6
			1.4	.8				1.1	1.5
% Depr., Dep., Amort./Sales			.3	.2				.3	.1
		(12)	2.7	(11) 1.3				(47) 2.7	(39) .9
			12.3	9.3				8.0	4.4
% Officers', Directors' Owners' Comp/Sales								2.3	1.0
								(13) 3.2	(17) 3.3
								5.0	8.0
Net Sales ($)	22939M	32470M	256443M	589099M	739982M	404119M		2981396M	3638703M
Total Assets ($)	2720M	10559M	85099M	267515M	580003M	257531M		1669746M	1732546M

M = $ thousand   MM = $ million
See Pages viii through xx for Explanation of Ratios and Data

Comparative Historical Data / Current Data Sorted by Sales

Type of Statement	4/1/16-3/31/17 ALL	4/1/17-3/31/18 ALL	4/1/18-3/31/19 ALL		0-1MM	1-3MM	3-5MM	5-10MM	10-25MM	25MM & OVER
Unqualified	7	6	6			1			3	2
Reviewed	4	6	4						1	3
Compiled	7	4	4							3
Tax Returns	18	7	4				1	1	2	1
Other	35	36	36		1	9	2			15
						6 (4/1-9/30/18)		48 (10/1/18-3/31/19)		
NUMBER OF STATEMENTS	71	59	54		1	10	4	6	10	23
ASSETS	%	%	%		%	%	%	%	%	%
Cash & Equivalents	35.3	36.0	25.3		6.2				25.8	31.2
Trade Receivables (net)	9.4	7.1	11.0		7.8				6.5	13.0
Inventory	1.0	.9	.9		.4				3.9	.2
All Other Current	9.2	15.7	9.8		13.8				6.2	11.2
Total Current	54.9	59.7	47.0		28.1				42.5	55.6
Fixed Assets (net)	29.1	25.1	24.2		23.8				32.5	14.1
Intangibles (net)	5.6	4.6	12.2		25.4				13.3	10.7
All Other Non-Current	10.4	10.7	16.7		22.7				11.7	19.6
Total	100.0	100.0	100.0		100.0				100.0	100.0
LIABILITIES										
Notes Payable-Short Term	11.4	1.3	7.0		24.4				2.4	.4
Cur. Mat.-L.T.D.	4.8	2.4	2.8		2.6				2.7	1.1
Trade Payables	9.7	11.1	8.0		3.2				3.7	11.5
Income Taxes Payable	.1	.5	.4		.0				.0	.9
All Other Current	33.3	49.2	33.5		31.1				22.0	38.9
Total Current	59.3	64.5	51.6		61.4				30.8	52.8
Long-Term Debt	15.7	8.9	14.7		12.4				17.7	8.2
Deferred Taxes	.2	.2	.4		.0				.2	.8
All Other Non-Current	5.7	6.5	4.5		10.5				1.0	4.8
Net Worth	19.1	20.0	28.8		15.7				50.4	33.4
Total Liabilties & Net Worth	100.0	100.0	100.0		100.0				100.0	100.0
INCOME DATA										
Net Sales	100.0	100.0	100.0		100.0				100.0	100.0
Gross Profit										
Operating Expenses	93.2	93.1	92.8		84.2				93.0	95.9
Operating Profit	6.8	6.9	7.2		15.8				7.0	4.1
All Other Expenses (net)	.3	-.7	.4		1.0				.1	.2
Profit Before Taxes	6.5	7.6	6.7		14.8				6.9	3.9
RATIOS										
Current	1.8	1.3	1.9		3.5				3.6	1.8
	1.0	1.0	1.1		1.5				1.2	1.1
	.5	.6	.5		.1				.8	.8
Quick	1.5	1.1	1.2		1.4				3.5	1.1
	.8	.7	.8		.3				.9	.8
	.3	.3	.3		.0				.4	.5
Sales/Receivables	0 UND	0 999.8	0 UND		0 UND				0 UND	0 UND
	2 234.8	4 89.8	1 380.0		0 UND				13 27.8	1 278.9
	18 19.8	22 16.8	30 12.3		1 356.0				43 8.5	21 17.8
Cost of Sales/Inventory										
Cost of Sales/Payables										
Sales/Working Capital	7.5	11.7	10.3		3.6				10.1	8.7
	400.0	132.7	158.0		22.4				48.8	191.3
	-13.5	-11.9	-13.3		-4.3				-9.4	-19.3
EBIT/Interest	24.3	40.1	24.6							241.3
	(41) 4.2	(28) 9.3	(33) 4.0							(11) 11.4
	1.4	4.7	1.3							2.2
Net Profit + Depr., Dep., Amort./Cur. Mat. L/T/D										
Fixed/Worth	.1	.0	.0		.1				.1	.0
	.8	.9	1.1		1.1				1.1	.8
	5.5	3.0	-15.9		-.5				6.4	-.7
Debt/Worth	1.0	1.0	1.0		.8				.2	1.5
	3.1	3.1	3.5		2.3				1.4	3.1
	-64.3	35.7	-32.6		-2.3				6.3	-32.5
% Profit Before Taxes/Tangible Net Worth	99.9	109.8	91.4							80.6
	(53) 34.2	(47) 40.4	(40) 32.2							(16) 25.1
	10.7	8.5	17.1							17.3
% Profit Before Taxes/Total Assets	24.8	19.3	18.0		38.6				17.5	14.0
	7.6	7.8	5.6		4.7				8.6	5.1
	1.2	2.5	1.2		-.2				1.1	3.9
Sales/Net Fixed Assets	228.2	443.4	422.8		131.0				40.4	688.4
	26.8	26.1	21.8		16.6				10.2	39.9
	2.7	3.4	3.5		1.9				1.4	14.5
Sales/Total Assets	4.3	3.2	4.1		4.7				2.7	4.2
	2.4	1.9	2.0		2.5				1.5	2.9
	1.4	1.0	1.2		.6				.8	1.2
% Depr., Dep., Amort./Sales	.3	.4	.3							.2
	(51) 1.8	(38) 2.0	(35) 1.3							(16) .6
	8.6	6.5	7.5							2.3
% Officers', Directors' Owners' Comp/Sales	1.6	.9	1.2							
	(18) 4.1	(13) 2.5	(12) 2.3							
	8.2	6.4	4.8							
Net Sales ($)	3591345M	6129475M	2045052M		917M	17592M	14545M	42573M	162217M	1807208M
Total Assets ($)	1604758M	2102242M	1203427M		459M	35464M	5836M	21419M	137424M	1002825M

Current Data Sorted by Assets **Comparative Historical Data**

Type of Statement	0-500M	500M-2MM	2-10MM	10-50MM	50-100MM	100-250MM		4/1/14-3/31/15 ALL	4/1/15-3/31/16 ALL
Unqualified		2	3	4	1	2		22	20
Reviewed		1			1			4	1
Compiled			2					1	5
Tax Returns	1		4					11	9
Other	5	2	9	9	6	7		34	41
			13 (4/1-9/30/18)	46 (10/1/18-3/31/19)					
NUMBER OF STATEMENTS	6	5	18	13	8	9		72	76
	%	%	%	%	%	%		%	%
ASSETS									
Cash & Equivalents			32.3	44.8				32.9	36.7
Trade Receivables (net)			17.2	10.7				14.0	15.2
Inventory			12.0	15.1				8.3	7.9
All Other Current			11.6	10.2				7.8	9.0
Total Current			73.2	80.8				63.0	68.7
Fixed Assets (net)			15.2	5.3				13.9	11.7
Intangibles (net)			6.7	8.4				9.4	9.8
All Other Non-Current			4.9	5.5				13.7	9.8
Total			100.0	100.0				100.0	100.0
LIABILITIES									
Notes Payable-Short Term			4.2	3.7				3.6	9.3
Cur. Mat.-L.T.D.			.3	.0				1.3	1.5
Trade Payables			19.5	24.5				16.8	17.4
Income Taxes Payable			.1	.0				.4	.7
All Other Current			32.7	23.1				27.0	25.1
Total Current			56.9	51.2				49.2	54.1
Long-Term Debt			7.4	.7				10.4	11.5
Deferred Taxes			.0	.1				.3	.3
All Other Non-Current			8.3	1.7				6.8	7.0
Net Worth			27.5	46.2				33.3	27.0
Total Liabilities & Net Worth			100.0	100.0				100.0	100.0
INCOME DATA									
Net Sales			100.0	100.0				100.0	100.0
Gross Profit									
Operating Expenses			95.9	100.9				93.4	93.6
Operating Profit			4.1	-.9				6.6	6.4
All Other Expenses (net)			.2	-.5				.4	.6
Profit Before Taxes			3.9	-.3				6.2	5.7
RATIOS									
			4.2	3.5				2.5	2.7
Current			1.6	1.6				1.4	1.4
			1.0	1.2				.8	.9
			2.4	1.6				2.0	1.8
Quick			.9	1.2				.9	1.0
			.6	.5				.4	.5
			0 UND	1 471.9				1 529.2	2 235.1
Sales/Receivables			7 53.5	13 27.2				11 33.5	13 28.7
			35 10.4	24 15.1				40 9.1	38 9.5
Cost of Sales/Inventory									
Cost of Sales/Payables									
			6.8	3.3				5.0	5.2
Sales/Working Capital			11.6	11.7				21.8	18.6
			-197.7	42.7				-24.0	-38.1
			167.5					41.2	76.1
EBIT/Interest			(12) 21.7					(40) 14.2	(49) 11.9
			1.6					1.6	3.3
Net Profit + Depr., Dep., Amort./Cur. Mat. L/T/D									
			.0	.0				.0	.0
Fixed/Worth			.2	.2				.2	.3
			1.2	.4				1.2	11.3
			.4	.5				.8	.7
Debt/Worth			3.0	1.1				1.8	2.4
			14.6	6.6				64.9	-8.0
			73.2	54.6				62.3	94.3
% Profit Before Taxes/Tangible Net Worth			(15) 26.8	(11) 11.7				(57) 32.3	(56) 31.8
			.3	-23.2				8.1	7.1
			26.2	20.2				17.6	24.3
% Profit Before Taxes/Total Assets			10.9	3.6				8.4	7.2
			-.9	-6.9				1.3	1.7
			UND	990.6				434.9	459.2
Sales/Net Fixed Assets			177.8	88.3				35.5	41.0
			19.2	16.8				6.5	7.3
			4.0	3.9				3.9	4.3
Sales/Total Assets			3.0	2.5				1.8	2.2
			2.1	1.4				1.0	1.0
			.2					.4	.2
% Depr., Dep., Amort./Sales			(10) 1.2					(42) 1.7	(43) .8
			5.8					2.7	2.6
								1.2	1.1
% Officers', Directors' Owners' Comp/Sales								(12) 2.4	(10) 2.5
								4.3	3.8
Net Sales ($)	28542M	38128M	259954M	845915M	1482350M	1372693M		6225303M	4331517M
Total Assets ($)	1567M	7087M	81438M	275848M	626118M	1324763M		2592232M	2534345M

M = $ thousand   MM = $ million
See Pages viii through xx for Explanation of Ratios and Data

Comparative Historical Data   **Current Data Sorted by Sales**

4/1/16-3/31/17 ALL	4/1/17-3/31/18 ALL	4/1/18-3/31/19 ALL	Type of Statement	0-1MM	1-3MM	3-5MM	5-10MM	10-25MM	25MM & OVER
17	13	12	Unqualified			1	2	1	8
2	1	2	Reviewed				1		1
4	3	2	Compiled			1	1		1
12	7	5	Tax Returns	1			1	3	
32	41	38	Other	2	3	1	46	3	23
					13 (4/1-9/30/18)		46 (10/1/18-3/31/19)		
67	65	59	NUMBER OF STATEMENTS	3	3	3	11	7	32
%	%	%	ASSETS	%	%	%	%	%	%
36.9	37.6	32.7	Cash & Equivalents				30.1		32.7
14.4	15.6	13.7	Trade Receivables (net)				17.1		13.4
9.3	10.0	10.0	Inventory				7.9		11.1
7.3	7.4	11.6	All Other Current				12.8		11.5
67.8	70.7	67.9	Total Current				67.9		68.7
12.1	10.2	9.7	Fixed Assets (net)				10.2		6.1
6.9	10.6	12.3	Intangibles (net)				14.2		14.6
13.1	8.5	10.0	All Other Non-Current				7.7		10.7
100.0	100.0	100.0	Total				100.0		100.0
			LIABILITIES						
3.3	3.7	7.9	Notes Payable-Short Term				5.1		3.1
1.5	.8	.8	Cur. Mat.-L.T.D.				.8		.4
18.2	18.8	20.5	Trade Payables				24.0		23.1
.7	.2	.0	Income Taxes Payable				.1		.0
31.6	31.4	25.8	All Other Current				35.2		24.6
55.3	54.9	55.0	Total Current				65.3		51.2
11.1	7.9	6.8	Long-Term Debt				9.1		5.5
.3	.5	.1	Deferred Taxes				.0		.2
8.6	5.7	7.9	All Other Non-Current				9.2		6.9
24.8	31.0	30.2	Net Worth				16.4		36.1
100.0	100.0	100.0	Total Liabilities & Net Worth				100.0		100.0
			INCOME DATA						
100.0	100.0	100.0	Net Sales				100.0		100.0
			Gross Profit						
94.0	96.1	97.6	Operating Expenses				96.9		98.1
6.0	3.9	2.4	Operating Profit				3.1		1.9
1.0	-.3	.8	All Other Expenses (net)				-.7		1.3
5.0	4.2	1.6	Profit Before Taxes				3.8		.6
			RATIOS						
2.3	2.3	2.8					5.8		2.4
1.1	1.5	1.5	Current				1.2		1.5
.8	.9	1.0					1.0		1.1
1.9	1.9	1.7					1.7		1.5
1.0	1.0	1.0	Quick				.8		1.1
.5	.5	.5					.5		.4
0 854.1	4 90.6	1 418.5					0 UND		10 37.2
10 36.8	15 25.1	13 27.2	Sales/Receivables				6 63.1		18 19.9
27 13.3	38 9.5	33 11.0					36 10.1		41 8.9
			Cost of Sales/Inventory						
			Cost of Sales/Payables						
5.4	4.5	5.8					6.5		4.8
25.9	11.4	13.9	Sales/Working Capital				56.7		11.0
-25.0	-38.2	-221.1					-127.6		45.3
85.2	45.3	99.0							234.6
(41) 10.0	(40) 16.2	(36) 16.7	EBIT/Interest					(18)	20.1
1.9	2.8	.9							.9
			Net Profit + Depr., Dep., Amort./Cur. Mat. L/T/D						
.0	.0	.0					.0		.0
.3	.2	.2	Fixed/Worth				.2		.2
-11.6	2.7	1.4					2.2		1.4
.6	.8	.7					1.5		.8
3.1	2.5	3.0	Debt/Worth				5.1		3.2
-77.3	45.2	22.0					26.4		18.9
58.3	55.3	63.3	% Profit Before Taxes/Tangible Net Worth						55.8
(49) 21.3	(52) 18.6	(47) 20.4						(25)	11.7
2.4	7.3	.3							-1.9
23.7	18.4	18.1	% Profit Before Taxes/Total Assets				24.2		12.9
7.1	6.6	5.4					5.4		4.2
-.1	2.4	-.5					.1		-.8
520.2	496.7	617.8	Sales/Net Fixed Assets				UND		617.8
56.6	63.4	82.6					66.8		76.7
6.9	8.6	13.0					22.1		11.1
4.4	4.3	4.2	Sales/Total Assets				4.5		3.7
2.4	2.2	2.5					2.6		2.0
1.2	.8	1.2					2.1		.8
.3	.2	.1	% Depr., Dep., Amort./Sales						.1
(40) .9	(37) .8	(36) 1.2						(21)	1.6
2.9	2.2	3.0							4.4
1.4	1.2	1.4	% Officers', Directors' Owners' Comp/Sales						
(12) 2.7	(11) 2.0	(12) 2.0							
8.5	4.0	5.5							
3461624M	4154837M	4027582M	Net Sales ($)	1589M	6260M	12494M	87952M	133547M	3785740M
1880503M	3015147M	2316821M	Total Assets ($)	2674M	1032M	6924M	33315M	29733M	2243143M

M = $ thousand   MM = $ million
See Pages viii through xx for Explanation of Ratios and Data

Current Data Sorted by Assets

Comparative Historical Data

								Type of Statement		
			1	2	2			Unqualified	11	14
			3	2				Reviewed	9	17
1	5		4	1				Compiled	16	10
8	1		3	1				Tax Returns	10	20
5	7		25	16	1	1		Other	77	55
	8 (4/1-9/30/18)			81 (10/1/18-3/31/19)					4/1/14-3/31/15	4/1/15-3/31/16
0-500M	500M-2MM	2-10MM		10-50MM	50-100MM	100-250MM			ALL	ALL
14	13	36		22	3	1		NUMBER OF STATEMENTS	123	116
%	%	%		%	%	%		ASSETS	%	%
21.8	21.2	13.0		5.0				Cash & Equivalents	11.2	13.6
35.9	47.6	54.7		61.7				Trade Receivables (net)	50.4	50.0
.0	.1	1.7		.1				Inventory	1.1	.4
2.6	2.2	8.3		4.2				All Other Current	5.6	4.8
60.3	71.1	77.6		70.9				Total Current	68.3	68.8
12.9	14.0	12.4		6.6				Fixed Assets (net)	15.1	12.2
23.3	7.4	3.9		11.1				Intangibles (net)	7.5	8.8
3.5	7.4	6.1		11.3				All Other Non-Current	9.1	10.2
100.0	100.0	100.0		100.0				Total	100.0	100.0
								LIABILITIES		
20.7	11.2	13.1		17.5				Notes Payable-Short Term	17.4	19.7
3.1	3.5	2.6		1.2				Cur. Mat.-L.T.D.	2.1	2.1
1.3	3.2	6.6		9.4				Trade Payables	10.1	7.6
.0	.0	.1		.6				Income Taxes Payable	.7	.2
32.1	17.0	22.6		24.2				All Other Current	28.2	17.9
57.2	34.9	45.0		52.9				Total Current	58.5	47.5
33.9	16.5	8.2		8.3				Long-Term Debt	10.6	14.7
.0	.0	.0		.1				Deferred Taxes	.2	.2
8.7	4.2	5.3		8.0				All Other Non-Current	9.7	3.8
.1	44.4	41.5		30.8				Net Worth	21.0	33.7
100.0	100.0	100.0		100.0				Total Liabilities & Net Worth	100.0	100.0
								INCOME DATA		
100.0	100.0	100.0		100.0				Net Sales	100.0	100.0
								Gross Profit		
98.6	95.7	96.2		96.5				Operating Expenses	95.7	95.8
1.4	4.3	3.8		3.5				Operating Profit	4.3	4.2
.4	.5	.7		.7				All Other Expenses (net)	.9	.4
1.0	3.8	3.1		2.8				Profit Before Taxes	3.4	3.8
								RATIOS		
2.1	6.3	3.0		2.1					2.2	2.7
1.2	2.0	1.7		1.3				Current	1.4	1.6
.4	1.1	1.2		.9					1.0	1.1
2.1	4.8	2.8		2.0					2.0	2.4
.9	2.0	1.4		1.2				Quick	1.3	1.5
.4	1.1	1.0		.9					.9	1.1

	0	UND	29	12.5	34	10.7	47	7.7			Sales/Receivables	27	13.3	29	12.4
	5	68.0	34	10.8	42	8.6	62	5.9				41	8.9	44	8.3
	42	8.6	49	7.5	60	6.1	70	5.2				56	6.5	59	6.2

								Cost of Sales/Inventory		
								Cost of Sales/Payables		
20.8	7.3	7.6		8.7				Sales/Working Capital	11.3	10.2
163.4	15.1	15.5		23.8					23.9	19.8
-37.2	NM	32.2		-120.8					435.8	82.3

	43.4		36.8		56.4		43.0		EBIT/Interest		30.5		28.5
(13)	9.0	(12)	15.3	(33)	12.2	(21)	12.4			(106)	9.3	(100)	8.2
	-8.4		1.0		1.9		2.8				1.9		2.8

								Net Profit + Depr., Dep., Amort./Cur. Mat. L/T/D		23.4		5.5
									(18)	13.4	(18)	3.0
										2.7		1.2

.0	.1	.1		.1				Fixed/Worth	.1	.1
.2	.4	.2		.1					.3	.3
-6.4	.8	.7		NM					4.8	1.3
1.0	.5	.5		1.0				Debt/Worth	1.0	.8
NM	1.1	1.2		2.6					2.6	1.9
-1.7	10.7	3.6		NM					-47.6	13.4

			132.0		68.6		75.0		% Profit Before Taxes/Tangible Net Worth		81.4		77.9
		(11)	16.5	(32)	45.4	(17)	34.8			(89)	35.7	(93)	36.1
			-7.5		16.5		8.7				11.0		15.6

69.0	32.0	27.7		19.4				% Profit Before Taxes/Total Assets	26.1	24.8
12.6	7.1	13.6		9.2					10.6	12.5
-54.8	-2.0	2.2		2.5					1.4	4.0
UND	234.7	207.2		208.0				Sales/Net Fixed Assets	162.2	164.6
256.7	56.5	47.8		97.8					65.5	67.7
53.0	19.0	32.5		29.6					24.8	31.7
20.5	7.0	6.5		4.7				Sales/Total Assets	6.3	5.7
10.5	4.6	4.5		3.8					4.6	4.7
4.1	3.2	2.9		2.9					3.2	3.3

				.3		.2		% Depr., Dep., Amort./Sales		.2		.3
		(27)	.6	(20)	.3				(85)	.6	(74)	.6
			1.5		.5					1.5		1.0

				.8				% Officers', Directors' Owners' Comp/Sales		1.6		1.4
		(16)	2.6						(38)	3.4	(47)	2.6
			4.1							5.9		5.7

33609M	87419M	745132M		2035000M	895753M	323408M		Net Sales ($)	5454949M	5935847M
3249M	17122M	161911M		551641M	228958M	104571M		Total Assets ($)	1468153M	1758146M

© RMA 2019

M = $ thousand   MM = $ million
See Pages viii through xx for Explanation of Ratios and Data

Comparative Historical Data | **Current Data Sorted by Sales**

	Hist 4/1/16-3/31/17 ALL	Hist 4/1/17-3/31/18 ALL	Hist 4/1/18-3/31/19 ALL	0-1MM	1-3MM	3-5MM	5-10MM	10-25MM	25MM & OVER
Type of Statement									
Unqualified	12	9	5						5
Reviewed	10	8	5					2	3
Compiled	10	10	11	1		2	3	3	2
Tax Returns	11	21	13	2	3	3	2	1	2
Other	61	57	55	2	4	3	8	17	21
				8 (4/1-9/30/18)			81 (10/1/18-3/31/19)		
NUMBER OF STATEMENTS	104	105	89	5	7	8	13	23	33
	%	%	%	%	%	%	%	%	%
ASSETS									
Cash & Equivalents	15.2	14.4	13.6				13.6	18.6	7.8
Trade Receivables (net)	48.7	48.6	52.5				53.2	51.5	63.9
Inventory	.9	.5	.8				2.9	.8	.3
All Other Current	4.5	4.6	5.7				3.8	7.1	6.4
Total Current	69.3	68.1	72.6				73.5	78.0	78.4
Fixed Assets (net)	14.1	15.2	11.0				17.3	8.8	7.1
Intangibles (net)	8.5	8.6	9.2				2.2	6.9	5.0
All Other Non-Current	8.1	8.1	7.2				7.0	6.4	9.5
Total	100.0	100.0	100.0				100.0	100.0	100.0
LIABILITIES									
Notes Payable-Short Term	15.5	17.8	14.6				10.1	12.6	16.7
Cur. Mat.-L.T.D.	3.5	3.2	2.4				2.1	3.8	1.1
Trade Payables	6.3	5.8	6.2				5.4	8.2	8.2
Income Taxes Payable	.6	.1	.2				.0	.1	.4
All Other Current	23.8	20.0	24.6				20.1	20.0	28.1
Total Current	49.6	47.0	48.0				37.8	44.7	54.6
Long-Term Debt	16.7	19.0	13.5				21.7	6.4	6.1
Deferred Taxes	.1	.0	.0				.0	.0	.1
All Other Non-Current	4.4	10.0	6.2				9.5	9.5	2.6
Net Worth	29.1	24.0	32.3				31.0	39.4	36.6
Total Liabilities & Net Worth	100.0	100.0	100.0				100.0	100.0	100.0
INCOME DATA									
Net Sales	100.0	100.0	100.0				100.0	100.0	100.0
Gross Profit									
Operating Expenses	95.5	94.9	96.5				95.4	95.0	96.6
Operating Profit	4.5	5.1	3.5				4.6	5.0	3.4
All Other Expenses (net)	.3	.7	.6				.6	.7	.1
Profit Before Taxes	4.2	4.4	2.9				4.0	4.3	3.3
RATIOS									
Current	2.5	3.1	2.6				4.3	4.9	2.2
	1.4	1.5	1.4				2.1	1.8	1.4
	1.1	1.1	1.1				1.2	1.2	1.1
Quick	2.4	2.5	2.5				4.2	4.7	2.0
	1.3	1.5	1.3				2.1	1.3	1.3
	1.0	1.0	.9				1.1	1.1	.9
Sales/Receivables	31 11.8	34 10.8	31 11.8				31 11.9	38 9.7	41 8.8
	43 8.5	43 8.5	47 7.8				47 7.8	42 8.6	53 6.9
	65 5.6	54 6.7	61 6.0				56 6.5	62 5.9	64 5.7
Cost of Sales/Inventory									
Cost of Sales/Payables									
Sales/Working Capital	11.1	8.5	8.7				7.3	7.6	9.3
	21.1	18.9	19.0				14.6	16.8	18.6
	114.2	122.8	163.4				64.0	33.2	200.9
EBIT/Interest	35.4	35.6	43.9				32.8	122.4	49.4
	(86) 10.7	(90) 9.5	(83) 12.2				15.0	(22) 21.4	(30) 9.7
	2.4	2.4	2.0				1.9	3.8	3.3
Net Profit + Depr., Dep., Amort./Cur. Mat. L/T/D	11.1	97.0							
	(12) 3.1	(10) 18.6							
	1.0	1.7							
Fixed/Worth	.1	.1	.1				.1	.1	.1
	.3	.3	.2				.5	.2	.1
	2.5	4.7	1.1				1.5	.6	.6
Debt/Worth	.6	.6	.7				.5	.5	.8
	1.9	2.2	2.2				1.1	1.3	2.3
	20.4	27.9	7.5				14.3	3.6	5.6
% Profit Before Taxes/Tangible Net Worth	99.0	75.9	83.2				153.6	99.0	59.7
	(80) 36.0	(82) 39.5	(71) 40.0				(11) 70.8	(20) 56.3	(28) 35.7
	18.7	15.9	6.1				4.8	20.9	11.6
% Profit Before Taxes/Total Assets	28.4	24.1	27.5				32.0	37.5	23.9
	13.6	12.3	10.9				12.7	17.5	9.6
	3.1	3.3	1.2				1.9	9.2	2.8
Sales/Net Fixed Assets	174.1	195.6	251.7				377.9	189.8	246.1
	72.1	74.4	96.2				41.5	42.3	140.5
	32.3	25.9	31.6				11.5	38.2	39.7
Sales/Total Assets	6.3	5.9	6.7				7.0	6.7	5.7
	4.4	4.5	4.5				4.5	4.5	4.3
	3.0	3.0	3.0				3.0	3.8	3.1
% Depr., Dep., Amort./Sales	.2	.2	.2					.3	.2
	(63) .5	(63) .4	(60) .5					(18) .9	(29) .3
	1.0	1.0	1.1					1.5	.5
% Officers', Directors' Owners' Comp/Sales	1.0	1.1	1.0					.9	
	(37) 2.5	(32) 3.5	(33) 2.8					(10) 3.0	
	5.5	6.0	5.8					4.5	
Net Sales ($)	5304512M	5022547M	4120321M	1748M	14544M	33103M	100127M	379491M	3591308M
Total Assets ($)	1438222M	1287334M	1067452M	707M	8840M	9620M	23487M	108696M	916102M

M = $ thousand   MM = $ million
See Pages viii through xx for Explanation of Ratios and Data

Current Data Sorted by Assets   Comparative Historical Data

						Type of Statement		
2		1	7	2	5	Unqualified	21	17
	3	14	6			Reviewed	38	33
1	4	6	1			Compiled	17	17
7	13	4	1			Tax Returns	41	51
11	24	38	24	8	15	Other	120	141
	22 (4/1-9/30/18)		175 (10/1/18-3/31/19)				4/1/14-3/31/15 ALL	4/1/15-3/31/16 ALL
0-500M	500M-2MM	2-10MM	10-50MM	50-100MM	100-250MM			
21	44	63	39	10	20	NUMBER OF STATEMENTS	237	259
%	%	%	%	%	%	ASSETS	%	%
26.6	14.1	12.8	8.5	6.4	6.9	Cash & Equivalents	12.3	12.5
23.8	31.9	38.9	28.4	14.6	10.1	Trade Receivables (net)	31.0	29.6
4.8	11.8	11.6	10.5	6.7	7.0	Inventory	10.5	8.6
.8	1.7	5.1	8.6	5.0	2.7	All Other Current	5.1	4.6
56.0	59.5	68.4	55.9	32.7	26.8	Total Current	58.9	55.3
24.5	22.3	14.0	12.2	10.9	8.9	Fixed Assets (net)	13.9	13.5
16.0	9.0	11.3	23.3	49.3	55.3	Intangibles (net)	18.2	21.4
3.6	9.2	6.3	8.5	7.1	9.1	All Other Non-Current	8.9	9.7
100.0	100.0	100.0	100.0	100.0	100.0	Total	100.0	100.0
						LIABILITIES		
20.0	21.1	8.6	8.9	.1	.2	Notes Payable-Short Term	12.9	10.3
3.3	2.5	1.7	1.8	.7	1.8	Cur. Mat.-L.T.D.	3.3	3.3
8.5	13.1	17.8	13.3	8.2	7.0	Trade Payables	13.3	13.5
.2	.0	.2	.0	.0	.0	Income Taxes Payable	.3	.2
13.3	17.4	15.6	20.6	25.1	19.7	All Other Current	21.2	22.4
45.2	54.2	43.9	44.6	34.2	28.7	Total Current	50.9	49.7
22.0	19.0	16.3	35.6	60.8	104.3	Long-Term Debt	26.3	35.6
.0	.2	.1	.1	.0	.3	Deferred Taxes	.4	.2
11.6	12.2	9.1	10.0	5.7	11.6	All Other Non-Current	10.3	10.6
21.4	14.4	30.5	9.6	-.7	-45.0	Net Worth	12.1	3.8
100.0	100.0	100.0	100.0	100.0	100.0	Total Liabilities & Net Worth	100.0	100.0
						INCOME DATA		
100.0	100.0	100.0	100.0	100.0	100.0	Net Sales	100.0	100.0
						Gross Profit		
95.5	91.5	93.9	91.2	94.9	98.0	Operating Expenses	94.7	93.8
4.5	8.5	6.1	8.8	5.1	2.0	Operating Profit	5.3	6.2
3.0	2.0	1.2	2.6	2.8	12.4	All Other Expenses (net)	1.8	2.3
1.5	6.5	4.9	6.2	2.2	-10.4	Profit Before Taxes	3.5	3.9
						RATIOS		
2.9	2.2	2.7	2.1	1.3	1.2		2.2	2.2
1.4	1.5	1.6	1.3	1.1	.8	Current	1.3	1.3
.7	1.0	1.1	.9	.5	.5		.8	.8
2.9	1.6	2.2	1.5	1.0	.7		1.7	1.9
1.3	.9	1.1	.9	.7	.5	Quick	.9	1.0
.5	.8	.7	.6	.1	.3		.5	.5
(0) UND	(11) 31.9	(35) 10.5	(35) 10.3	(0) UND	(7) 52.8		(26) 13.8	(23) 15.6
(7) 52.2	(39) 9.4	(45) 8.1	(49) 7.4	(26) 14.2	(19) 19.5	Sales/Receivables	(46) 8.0	(41) 8.9
(37) 9.9	(66) 5.5	(65) 5.6	(65) 5.6	(50) 7.3	(41) 9.0		(63) 5.8	(63) 5.8
						Cost of Sales/Inventory		
						Cost of Sales/Payables		
19.2	6.4	5.7	7.1	18.5	35.0		6.3	6.7
53.3	16.8	10.4	12.1	54.3	-26.8	Sales/Working Capital	18.8	20.5
-14.8	-534.8	58.6	-74.5	-8.1	-9.5		-31.6	-22.2
15.1	29.4	35.5	59.0		5.6		25.4	24.6
(17) 4.2	(40) 6.2	(58) 9.3	(28) 5.1		(15) .4	EBIT/Interest	(205) 5.8	(223) 5.9
-.6	2.4	2.5	1.4		-.5		1.5	1.2
						Net Profit + Depr., Dep.,	7.5	7.9
						Amort./Cur. Mat. L/T/D	(40) 4.5	(35) 3.0
							1.1	1.2
.3	.2	.1	.2	1.3	-.4		.2	.1
1.8	.8	.5	-2.5	-.2	-.1	Fixed/Worth	.8	.8
-.5	25.4	8.3	-.2	-.1	.0		-.5	-.3
.7	1.4	.9	1.0	7.1	-2.4		1.4	1.3
7.9	2.9	1.7	-19.9	-1.9	-1.4	Debt/Worth	4.7	6.7
-2.8	NM	85.6	-2.6	-1.3	-1.1		-2.6	-2.3
200.2	76.6	92.3	71.3			% Profit Before Taxes/Tangible	74.9	74.2
(14) 122.7	(33) 34.8	(49) 34.2	(18) 43.6			Net Worth	(152) 33.5	(148) 39.1
58.2	15.6	15.3	26.0				12.0	10.8
56.9	28.8	22.5	25.8	22.1	3.8	% Profit Before Taxes/Total	21.3	24.9
16.7	11.1	13.1	12.6	11.5	-2.5	Assets	8.2	8.6
-1.5	3.3	1.9	1.1	-2.0	-12.0		.8	.8
397.8	73.6	119.0	77.8	22.0	26.9		63.9	71.2
33.1	26.6	29.0	18.6	13.8	16.7	Sales/Net Fixed Assets	24.1	25.7
7.7	14.7	12.2	12.7	9.2	11.0		13.5	11.6
9.8	4.3	3.8	2.6	2.1	1.3		3.6	3.6
6.4	2.8	2.7	2.0	1.3	1.0	Sales/Total Assets	2.4	2.4
2.8	1.8	1.8	1.3	.7	.5		1.4	1.3
	.7	.5	.6				.7	.8
	(23) 1.5	(45) 1.2	(29) 2.0			% Depr., Dep., Amort./Sales	(160) 1.7	(160) 1.5
	2.5	2.2	3.7				3.4	3.1
2.9	3.5	2.0					2.2	3.2
(12) 6.6	(22) 4.6	(13) 3.6				% Officers', Directors'	(59) 4.2	(77) 5.3
11.0	7.0	6.7				Owners' Comp/Sales	9.5	8.9
44834M	158753M	835116M	2078587M	896713M	4042294M	Net Sales ($)	6787983M	7035097M
5630M	50061M	297462M	984089M	656952M	3000741M	Total Assets ($)	4531671M	5029905M

M = $ thousand   MM = $ million
See Pages viii through xx for Explanation of Ratios and Data

Comparative Historical Data

Current Data Sorted by Sales

					22 (4/1-9/30/18)		175 (10/1/18-3/31/19)			
4/1/16-3/31/17 ALL	4/1/17-3/31/18 ALL	4/1/18-3/31/19 ALL	**Type of Statement**	0-1MM	1-3MM	3-5MM	5-10MM	10-25MM	25MM & OVER
20	17	17	Unqualified	2				3	12
30	24	23	Reviewed		2		4	11	6
20	18	12	Compiled	1	3	2		5	1
41	21	25	Tax Returns	3	5	6	8	2	1
128	110	120	Other	10	12	18	13	24	43
239	190	197	**NUMBER OF STATEMENTS**	16	20	28	25	45	63
%	%	%	**ASSETS**	%	%	%	%	%	%
11.6	12.2	12.8	Cash & Equivalents	20.1	13.0	11.1	16.3	14.7	8.8
26.7	31.4	29.5	Trade Receivables (net)	13.1	29.2	34.2	33.3	36.7	25.0
8.5	10.1	10.0	Inventory	8.3	10.0	9.7	9.8	11.4	9.6
4.5	3.8	4.3	All Other Current	1.7	1.6	1.6	2.6	5.8	6.7
51.3	57.5	56.6	Total Current	43.3	53.8	56.6	62.1	68.6	50.0
16.6	12.8	15.9	Fixed Assets (net)	33.9	22.9	19.0	16.3	9.7	12.1
22.0	21.1	20.0	Intangibles (net)	16.5	16.5	13.2	12.6	17.1	30.1
10.2	8.5	7.4	All Other Non-Current	6.2	6.8	11.2	9.0	4.6	7.7
100.0	100.0	100.0	Total	100.0	100.0	100.0	100.0	100.0	100.0
			LIABILITIES						
8.9	8.7	11.4	Notes Payable-Short Term	13.0	13.9	30.7	7.5	12.1	2.6
2.7	2.3	2.1	Cur. Mat.-L.T.D.	3.4	.8	3.4	2.0	1.8	1.8
11.3	13.3	13.3	Trade Payables	5.6	15.8	10.9	13.7	16.2	13.3
.3	.1	.1	Income Taxes Payable	.2	.0	.0	.0	.2	.0
18.2	18.4	17.7	All Other Current	13.5	19.7	13.8	13.3	16.5	22.3
41.4	42.8	44.5	Total Current	35.7	50.2	58.7	36.5	46.7	40.1
34.7	29.9	32.5	Long-Term Debt	23.2	23.4	21.6	30.1	12.6	57.8
.3	.2	.1	Deferred Taxes	.0	.0	.3	.1	.1	.2
10.4	8.9	10.3	All Other Non-Current	4.7	13.4	16.3	6.1	9.9	10.0
13.3	18.2	12.6	Net Worth	36.7	12.9	3.1	27.1	30.7	-8.2
100.0	100.0	100.0	Total Liabilties & Net Worth	100.0	100.0	100.0	100.0	100.0	100.0
			INCOME DATA						
100.0	100.0	100.0	Net Sales	100.0	100.0	100.0	100.0	100.0	100.0
			Gross Profit						
93.0	93.3	93.5	Operating Expenses	88.1	94.0	94.9	94.1	93.0	94.1
7.0	6.7	6.5	Operating Profit	11.9	6.0	5.1	5.9	7.0	5.9
3.1	2.5	3.1	All Other Expenses (net)	5.2	3.0	1.0	2.0	1.2	5.2
4.0	4.2	3.5	Profit Before Taxes	6.7	2.9	4.1	3.9	5.8	.7
			RATIOS						
2.1	2.1	2.2		4.2	2.3	2.0	2.7	2.8	1.7
1.2	1.3	1.3	Current	1.3	1.9	1.2	1.8	1.6	1.2
.8	.8	.9		.8	.9	.8	1.0	1.1	.8
1.6	1.6	1.7		3.5	1.8	1.3	2.3	2.2	1.1
.9	1.0	.9	Quick	.8	1.0	.9	1.0	1.3	.7
.5	.6	.6		.4	.4	.5	.8	.7	.5
22 16.8	27 13.3	19 19.6		0 UND	0 UND	29 12.7	14 26.0	29 12.7	18 20.4
41 8.8	47 7.8	41 9.0	Sales/Receivables	30 12.1	33 11.2	41 8.8	41 9.0	46 8.0	44 8.3
61 6.0	70 5.2	62 5.9		51 7.1	63 5.8	66 5.5	61 6.0	66 5.5	58 6.3
			Cost of Sales/Inventory						
			Cost of Sales/Payables						
7.3	7.3	7.3		7.1	6.2	9.9	5.9	7.2	9.7
24.0	19.4	21.5	Sales/Working Capital	19.4	34.6	27.1	19.5	10.5	38.5
-20.4	-44.4	-71.0		-14.2	-253.1	-69.4	NM	42.5	-27.3
23.3	26.3	23.9		8.3	50.7	15.3	23.5	40.5	24.4
(205) 5.2	(159) 7.8	(166) 5.6	EBIT/Interest	(10) 4.0	(19) 4.2	(26) 4.2	(23) 7.8	(40) 9.4	(48) 5.4
1.2	2.0	1.4		-2.9	1.2	1.9	2.3	2.0	.4
12.8	11.8	9.0	Net Profit + Depr., Dep.,						
(27) 6.8	(22) 4.7	(15) 3.6	Amort./Cur. Mat. L/T/D						
2.1	1.4	.6							
.2	.1	.2		.1	.0	.6	.2	.1	.2
1.6	.6	1.1	Fixed/Worth	3.6	1.3	1.2	.6	.4	.6
-.3	-.4	-.3		-.7	NM	-2.4	NM	-1.7	-.1
1.3	1.3	1.3		.3	1.4	1.4	1.1	.9	1.5
6.2	4.3	5.2	Debt/Worth	3.3	7.8	4.9	2.1	2.5	-3.7
-2.4	-3.0	-2.6		-4.0	-2.3	-21.7	NM	-12.3	-1.5
76.7	79.3	102.7		123.5	139.5	115.4	128.9	94.7	101.9
(137) 33.0	(117) 46.1	(120) 42.8	% Profit Before Taxes/Tangible Net Worth	(10) 58.7	(14) 40.5	(18) 35.3	(19) 34.8	(32) 46.4	(27) 47.2
12.3	20.3	17.7		18.2	-1.1	13.0	10.1	16.8	27.8
22.5	23.2	26.2		42.3	32.5	30.2	31.0	22.0	25.8
8.4	10.7	11.2	% Profit Before Taxes/Total Assets	6.0	13.9	8.3	14.7	10.3	11.4
.4	1.8	.6		-1.5	.3	3.7	1.7	1.5	-1.6
56.1	62.3	77.7		27.3	318.5	49.3	116.7	119.1	33.1
20.2	26.9	24.5	Sales/Net Fixed Assets	9.9	54.4	23.2	25.4	35.1	18.5
9.6	14.1	12.0		.9	9.9	8.8	14.1	15.9	11.9
3.3	3.4	3.8		2.9	6.4	4.1	5.9	3.8	2.9
2.3	2.3	2.5	Sales/Total Assets	.9	3.1	2.8	2.9	2.8	1.9
1.1	1.1	1.3		.4	1.5	1.8	1.9	1.8	1.0
.7	.6	.6				1.2	.2	.4	.7
(164) 1.5	(115) 1.4	(113) 1.5	% Depr., Dep., Amort./Sales			(17) 2.4	(14) 1.0	(32) 1.2	(39) 1.9
4.4	2.7	3.4				3.6	1.9	2.1	4.9
2.3	2.5	2.2			2.8	2.2	2.8		
(66) 5.4	(55) 5.9	(52) 4.5	% Officers', Directors' Owners' Comp/Sales		(10) 4.5	(11) 3.8	(11) 4.8		
9.2	9.2	7.5			6.2	4.7	6.9		
8003971M	5790968M	8056297M	Net Sales ($)	8106M	38894M	110175M	176176M	728596M	6994350M
5558287M	4105655M	4994935M	Total Assets ($)	11542M	17923M	56620M	76044M	355429M	4477377M

M = $ thousand   MM = $ million
See Pages viii through xx for Explanation of Ratios and Data

Current Data Sorted by Assets | Comparative Historical Data

0-500M	500M-2MM	2-10MM	10-50MM	50-100MM	100-250MM	Type of Statement	4/1/14-3/31/15 ALL	4/1/15-3/31/16 ALL
		1	1	1	1	Unqualified	3	4
		2	2			Reviewed	9	7
14	20	7				Compiled	12	8
7	10	16	6	1		Tax Returns	36	39
	5 (4/1-9/30/18)		84 (10/1/18-3/31/19)			Other	45	67
21	30	26	9	2	1	NUMBER OF STATEMENTS	105	125

0-500M %	500M-2MM %	2-10MM %	10-50MM %	50-100MM %	100-250MM %		%	%
						ASSETS		
43.0	31.5	22.9				Cash & Equivalents	27.7	25.9
12.9	17.6	19.9				Trade Receivables (net)	16.1	13.6
2.3	.9	3.0				Inventory	3.6	3.0
1.4	.8	6.1				All Other Current	3.0	2.7
59.5	50.8	51.9				Total Current	50.4	45.2
28.2	26.4	27.1				Fixed Assets (net)	26.6	31.5
2.8	16.0	11.0				Intangibles (net)	11.8	12.6
9.4	6.8	10.0				All Other Non-Current	11.2	10.7
100.0	100.0	100.0				Total	100.0	100.0
						LIABILITIES		
38.0	3.2	2.9				Notes Payable-Short Term	8.1	12.8
1.8	7.3	3.8				Cur. Mat.-L.T.D.	4.9	4.4
3.8	2.8	8.1				Trade Payables	9.6	6.9
.0	.0	.0				Income Taxes Payable	.1	.4
5.0	23.6	15.5				All Other Current	20.5	14.8
48.6	37.0	30.2				Total Current	43.3	39.3
37.7	31.7	26.8				Long-Term Debt	27.4	33.4
.0	.0	.0				Deferred Taxes	.0	.0
6.6	8.1	11.0				All Other Non-Current	7.4	6.4
7.1	23.2	31.9				Net Worth	21.9	20.9
100.0	100.0	100.0				Total Liabilities & Net Worth	100.0	100.0
						INCOME DATA		
100.0	100.0	100.0				Net Sales	100.0	100.0
						Gross Profit		
85.0	88.9	87.2				Operating Expenses	89.5	86.9
15.0	11.1	12.8				Operating Profit	10.5	13.1
4.1	.7	2.5				All Other Expenses (net)	1.0	2.8
10.9	10.4	10.2				Profit Before Taxes	9.5	10.3
						RATIOS		
16.3	5.1	3.2					2.7	4.0
3.9	2.6	2.1				Current	1.3	1.4
.6	.7	.8					.6	.5
15.4	4.9	3.2					2.3	3.9
3.2	2.6	1.8				Quick	1.0	1.2
.6	.7	.5					.5	.5
0 UND	0 UND	8 45.5					0 UND	0 UND
0 UND	3 120.7	21 17.6				Sales/Receivables	11 33.9	10 35.4
14 27.0	23 15.8	27 13.4					25 14.6	21 17.4
						Cost of Sales/Inventory		
						Cost of Sales/Payables		
8.1	9.6	6.9					11.7	10.5
22.7	16.9	12.5				Sales/Working Capital	55.3	43.1
-61.2	-49.7	-32.8					-24.1	-36.6
36.4	50.6	193.1					83.1	45.0
(14) 13.0	(24) 15.5	(19) 8.0				EBIT/Interest	(86) 23.0	(99) 12.4
4.7	5.0	3.0					5.0	3.8
						Net Profit + Depr., Dep.,	40.4	
						Amort./Cur. Mat. L/T/D	(10) 5.4	
							1.6	
.1	.0	.2					.2	.3
.8	.7	.8				Fixed/Worth	.7	1.1
-2.7	-1.2	-3.1					-3.4	-1.9
.2	.5	.5					.6	.8
1.9	1.0	2.4				Debt/Worth	1.9	2.6
-4.5	-2.5	-6.1					-6.8	-5.3
301.1	101.1	99.4				% Profit Before Taxes/Tangible	99.1	114.1
(14) 107.2	(20) 65.0	(19) 45.4				Net Worth	(74) 56.0	(86) 55.6
21.3	25.3	20.7					28.3	25.8
82.2	60.2	45.4				% Profit Before Taxes/Total	52.2	53.3
61.2	30.0	18.6				Assets	21.8	18.6
8.9	7.0	4.3					6.7	8.2
137.6	186.3	21.8					106.0	50.0
41.4	23.0	12.3				Sales/Net Fixed Assets	22.4	15.2
14.3	9.1	7.7					10.0	8.1
11.2	7.2	4.6					6.4	5.9
6.7	4.8	3.0				Sales/Total Assets	3.8	3.6
3.9	2.4	1.5					2.6	2.4
.7	.6	1.0					.7	.7
(10) 1.9	(17) 2.5	(20) 2.3				% Depr., Dep., Amort./Sales	(65) 1.8	(70) 2.2
5.4	4.2	4.5					3.1	3.9
	1.5	2.8					3.8	3.0
	(20) 3.6	(10) 3.7				% Officers', Directors'	(45) 5.7	(61) 4.6
	6.8	6.0				Owners' Comp/Sales	7.7	8.2
33525M	165642M	278592M	474040M	336642M	237693M	Net Sales ($)	1871635M	2137780M
4495M	32433M	91429M	254173M	163905M	119265M	Total Assets ($)	723362M	880410M

M = $ thousand   MM = $ million
See Pages viii through xx for Explanation of Ratios and Data

Comparative Historical Data | Current Data Sorted by Sales

			Type of Statement						
4	3	4	Unqualified		1				3
7	3	2	Reviewed					1	1
9	8	2	Compiled					1	1
28	42	41	Tax Returns	7	13	5	8	8	
43	48	40	Other	5	8	6	8	7	6
4/1/16-3/31/17	4/1/17-3/31/18	4/1/18-3/31/19			5 (4/1-9/30/18)		84 (10/1/18-3/31/19)		
ALL	ALL	ALL		0-1MM	1-3MM	3-5MM	5-10MM	10-25MM	25MM & OVER
91	104	89	NUMBER OF STATEMENTS	12	22	11	16	17	11
%	%	%	ASSETS	%	%	%	%	%	%
23.6	22.6	29.7	Cash & Equivalents	32.6	30.3	34.9	27.4	31.5	20.8
10.4	14.2	16.1	Trade Receivables (net)	7.1	17.8	14.8	12.9	26.1	12.5
1.6	3.1	2.5	Inventory	3.2	1.8	.6	1.3	5.2	2.5
3.0	2.2	3.1	All Other Current	1.3	.5	9.1	1.0	5.2	4.2
38.7	42.1	51.4	Total Current	44.2	50.4	59.4	42.7	68.1	40.1
28.9	34.8	28.2	Fixed Assets (net)	42.7	26.3	25.9	27.1	16.5	37.9
17.3	13.6	11.5	Intangibles (net)	5.2	15.1	5.9	14.1	7.9	18.7
15.1	9.5	8.9	All Other Non-Current	7.9	8.2	8.8	16.1	7.4	3.4
100.0	100.0	100.0	Total	100.0	100.0	100.0	100.0	100.0	100.0
			LIABILITIES						
9.9	6.8	11.1	Notes Payable-Short Term	56.1	7.4	2.1	3.2	4.6	.0
6.1	5.5	4.4	Cur. Mat.-L.T.D.	3.6	2.4	5.0	7.6	5.2	3.1
5.8	5.1	5.4	Trade Payables	4.4	1.5	6.0	2.6	12.8	6.0
.0	.0	.0	Income Taxes Payable	.0	.0	.0	.0	.0	.1
12.9	19.8	16.2	All Other Current	3.6	9.2	44.7	6.0	19.0	26.1
34.8	37.2	37.2	Total Current	67.6	20.5	57.9	19.4	41.6	35.4
33.4	36.3	31.3	Long-Term Debt	27.2	46.7	38.4	31.5	16.1	21.2
.1	.0	.0	Deferred Taxes	.0	.0	.0	.0	.0	.0
8.4	8.7	7.6	All Other Non-Current	2.3	14.9	.0	9.5	9.5	.3
23.3	17.8	24.0	Net Worth	2.9	17.8	3.7	39.5	32.9	43.1
100.0	100.0	100.0	Total Liabilties & Net Worth	100.0	100.0	100.0	100.0	100.0	100.0
			INCOME DATA						
100.0	100.0	100.0	Net Sales	100.0	100.0	100.0	100.0	100.0	100.0
			Gross Profit						
89.4	89.5	87.3	Operating Expenses	70.6	87.7	84.8	90.0	94.9	91.8
10.6	10.5	12.7	Operating Profit	29.4	12.3	15.2	10.0	5.1	8.2
.8	1.5	2.1	All Other Expenses (net)	11.3	1.8	.9	.6	.2	-.8
9.7	9.0	10.6	Profit Before Taxes	18.0	10.5	14.3	9.5	4.9	9.0
			RATIOS						
2.9	3.1	4.6		12.5	12.7	11.1	3.5	3.8	2.4
1.1	1.4	2.4	Current	1.2	3.0	3.3	2.5	2.4	1.4
.6	.6	.7		.3	.9	.9	1.1	.7	.5
2.6	2.9	4.0		7.8	12.7	11.0	3.5	3.7	2.2
1.0	1.2	2.2	Quick	1.2	3.0	3.3	2.4	2.2	1.2
.5	.4	.5		.3	.7	.7	1.1	.4	.5
0 UND	0 UND	0 UND		0 UND	0 UND	0 999.8	0 UND	10 36.6	12 30.1
5 73.0	12 30.6	15 23.7	Sales/Receivables	0 UND	9 40.2	20 18.0	0 UND	22 16.3	19 18.9
20 18.4	19 18.9	24 15.2		5 72.9	24 15.5	27 13.7	24 15.2	24 14.9	20 18.4
			Cost of Sales/Inventory						
			Cost of Sales/Payables						
14.1	10.0	8.7		6.4	7.5	7.8	11.1	8.1	9.4
123.1	48.4	19.0	Sales/Working Capital	NM	12.3	12.4	21.9	19.0	23.5
-30.6	-25.1	-34.3		-5.8	89.8	-93.7	147.3	-20.2	-12.7
43.1	32.6	42.0			31.2		112.9	181.6	
(72) 12.8	(88) 12.1	(66) 9.3	EBIT/Interest	(16) 15.1		(14) 21.4	(12) 8.0		
5.6	3.4	3.3			5.5		7.4	2.4	
			Net Profit + Depr., Dep., Amort./Cur. Mat. L/T/D						
.4	.4	.2		.2	.2	.1	.1	.0	.6
1.6	2.2	.8	Fixed/Worth	1.2	4.0	.7	.7	.3	1.2
-1.3	-2.9	-2.7		NM	-.6	4.7	2.6	NM	-3.9
.8	.8	.4		.2	.8	.5	.5	.4	.4
3.3	3.3	1.9	Debt/Worth	1.3	7.1	1.0	1.1	.6	2.5
-3.8	-6.2	-4.0		NM	-2.9	4.8	NM	NM	-7.2
184.7	173.4	101.8	% Profit Before Taxes/Tangible Net Worth		189.2		149.8	99.5	
(57) 56.1	(71) 72.0	(63) 55.3		(12) 46.5		(12) 76.1	(13) 71.6		
24.1	19.7	23.1			7.4		57.1	31.5	
39.1	54.4	61.7	% Profit Before Taxes/Total Assets	76.8	68.6	71.0	61.0	71.4	24.7
19.1	18.1	21.8		17.1	22.8	12.1	44.5	21.8	13.7
9.6	7.2	5.7		4.6	2.1	5.0	19.9	3.9	11.4
41.9	26.6	66.4	Sales/Net Fixed Assets	34.3	78.9	36.7	249.9	681.7	13.0
14.6	12.0	15.3		14.3	23.9	15.3	17.3	39.8	8.2
8.4	6.9	8.1		2.5	5.6	7.9	9.0	11.6	4.0
4.9	5.2	6.7	Sales/Total Assets	6.2	7.3	7.2	7.9	6.8	3.4
3.6	3.5	3.5		3.4	3.1	3.0	5.1	4.8	2.5
2.0	2.3	2.1		1.3	1.6	1.8	2.9	3.2	1.4
1.0	1.6	1.0	% Depr., Dep., Amort./Sales		.8		1.2	.0	
(52) 2.9	(67) 3.4	(56) 2.4		(10) 2.5		(10) 1.9	(12) 1.0		
5.2	5.7	4.6			4.8		2.5	4.3	
2.9	2.7	2.1	% Officers', Directors' Owners' Comp/Sales		1.2				
(35) 6.2	(54) 5.0	(43) 3.7			2.7		(11)		
11.3	8.4	6.1			4.1				
1703327M	1447645M	1526134M	Net Sales ($)	6726M	40512M	46126M	112207M	232010M	1088553M
707806M	622805M	665700M	Total Assets ($)	5340M	31434M	17054M	35961M	64495M	511416M

© RMA 2019   M = $ thousand   MM = $ million
See Pages viii through xx for Explanation of Ratios and Data

Current Data Sorted by Assets / Comparative Historical Data

	0-500M	500M-2MM	2-10MM	10-50MM	50-100MM	100-250MM	Type of Statement	4/1/14-3/31/15 ALL	4/1/15-3/31/16 ALL
	2	3	4	10	5	7	Unqualified	37	28
		1	9	7			Reviewed	34	38
	2	7	12				Compiled	29	46
	29	28	10				Tax Returns	87	106
	35	48	55	21	4	8	Other	152	141
		25 (4/1-9/30/18)		282 (10/1/18-3/31/19)					
NUMBER OF STATEMENTS	68	87	90	38	9	15		339	359
	%	%	%	%	%	%	**ASSETS**	%	%
Cash & Equivalents	28.9	21.2	12.5	14.3		5.4	Cash & Equivalents	17.5	16.7
Trade Receivables (net)	22.1	36.6	46.9	45.9		34.8	Trade Receivables (net)	37.3	36.3
Inventory	2.5	2.7	2.4	1.0		.3	Inventory	1.8	1.7
All Other Current	3.3	3.8	4.8	4.8		5.5	All Other Current	4.5	4.5
Total Current	56.9	64.3	66.5	65.9		45.9	Total Current	61.1	59.2
Fixed Assets (net)	24.3	17.0	15.6	15.5		13.9	Fixed Assets (net)	19.8	21.1
Intangibles (net)	9.1	11.9	9.6	12.1		32.6	Intangibles (net)	10.5	11.7
All Other Non-Current	9.7	6.8	8.4	6.4		7.6	All Other Non-Current	8.6	8.0
Total	100.0	100.0	100.0	100.0		100.0	Total	100.0	100.0
							LIABILITIES		
Notes Payable-Short Term	20.1	9.7	12.2	14.3		1.9	Notes Payable-Short Term	14.3	15.1
Cur. Mat.-L.T.D.	4.6	3.3	2.5	2.5		1.9	Cur. Mat.-L.T.D.	3.2	4.1
Trade Payables	7.6	11.6	12.2	8.6		7.3	Trade Payables	12.3	10.1
Income Taxes Payable	.1	.1	.9	.4		.0	Income Taxes Payable	.2	.3
All Other Current	27.2	14.8	17.6	19.4		15.3	All Other Current	16.7	13.4
Total Current	59.6	39.5	45.3	45.1		26.4	Total Current	46.6	43.0
Long-Term Debt	25.1	21.9	12.0	9.7		22.6	Long-Term Debt	18.0	20.8
Deferred Taxes	.0	.1	.2	.0		.8	Deferred Taxes	.2	.3
All Other Non-Current	13.3	3.0	1.5	5.3		8.4	All Other Non-Current	5.9	4.6
Net Worth	2.0	35.5	41.0	39.9		41.8	Net Worth	29.3	31.3
Total Liabilities & Net Worth	100.0	100.0	100.0	100.0		100.0	Total Liabilities & Net Worth	100.0	100.0
							INCOME DATA		
Net Sales	100.0	100.0	100.0	100.0		100.0	Net Sales	100.0	100.0
Gross Profit							Gross Profit		
Operating Expenses	94.0	92.2	94.3	91.3		96.1	Operating Expenses	94.4	93.2
Operating Profit	6.0	7.8	5.7	8.7		3.9	Operating Profit	5.6	6.8
All Other Expenses (net)	.3	.3	.5	.9		2.2	All Other Expenses (net)	.7	1.1
Profit Before Taxes	5.8	7.4	5.1	7.8		1.7	Profit Before Taxes	5.0	5.8
							RATIOS		
	3.5	3.5	2.2	2.2		2.0		2.5	2.7
Current	1.2	1.8	1.4	1.4		1.6	Current	1.4	1.4
	.5	.9	1.0	1.1		1.5		1.0	1.0
	3.2	2.8	2.2	2.0		1.9		2.3	2.2
Quick	1.1	1.6	1.2	1.4		1.5	Quick	1.3	1.3
	.4	.7	.8	1.0		1.0		.8	.8
	0 UND	14 25.8	29 12.4	40 9.1		54 6.7		16 22.3	14 25.8
Sales/Receivables	5 69.4	26 14.0	38 9.6	51 7.1		59 6.2	Sales/Receivables	33 11.2	32 11.4
	26 14.2	42 8.6	59 6.2	65 5.6		83 4.4		51 7.2	52 7.0
							Cost of Sales/Inventory		
							Cost of Sales/Payables		
	17.1	8.5	8.4	7.2		8.5		10.0	10.0
Sales/Working Capital	67.7	18.3	23.2	16.1		10.2	Sales/Working Capital	26.4	25.0
	-30.2	-149.3	-341.8	55.4		15.3		-320.1	-325.9
	28.9	22.4	57.1	62.0		39.4		23.8	28.8
EBIT/Interest	(50) 9.3	(72) 8.9	(80) 13.2	(33) 13.1		1.6	EBIT/Interest	(274) 8.1	(295) 8.3
	2.5	3.8	4.3	5.6		-.3		2.2	2.2
			6.6	26.5			Net Profit + Depr., Dep., Amort./Cur. Mat. L/T/D	15.9	23.8
		(11) 3.1	(10) 9.2					(41) 6.7	(42) 3.7
			2.1	3.8				1.9	2.0
	.1	.2	.1	.2		.1		.2	.1
Fixed/Worth	.5	.5	.3	.4		-4.1	Fixed/Worth	.7	.7
	NM	-2.3	1.6	1.4		-.5		7.7	20.5
	.6	.6	.7	.8		1.6		.8	.8
Debt/Worth	2.5	3.4	1.8	2.2		-10.1	Debt/Worth	2.7	2.3
	-6.4	-11.9	5.6	6.3		-3.5		44.2	-216.5
	253.4	97.0	69.0	89.7			% Profit Before Taxes/Tangible Net Worth	85.5	84.0
	(47) 72.7	(61) 51.8	(77) 41.9	(33) 60.2				(261) 42.9	(269) 48.6
	34.5	16.7	24.4	32.4				18.4	18.3
	65.3	38.1	22.9	29.0		17.5	% Profit Before Taxes/Total Assets	26.3	30.5
	23.7	15.9	14.2	16.2		2.1		12.1	14.0
	4.8	4.5	9.0	8.4		-6.5		3.2	3.4
	853.6	147.4	104.8	66.9		74.9	Sales/Net Fixed Assets	110.8	112.1
	44.4	39.3	39.3	46.8		24.9		38.8	40.3
	15.2	15.6	17.2	11.9		5.3		14.6	15.9
	11.1	7.6	5.6	4.9		3.0	Sales/Total Assets	6.6	6.3
	6.6	4.1	4.1	3.3		1.8		4.2	4.1
	3.9	2.6	2.7	1.9		1.1		2.6	2.7
	.8	.5	.3	.5			% Depr., Dep., Amort./Sales	.4	.5
	(29) 1.4	(47) 1.3	(68) .8	(34) .9				(224) .9	(256) .9
	2.9	2.0	1.5	1.7				2.0	1.8
	3.8	2.2	1.5	.9			% Officers', Directors' Owners' Comp/Sales	1.8	1.8
	(36) 5.7	(38) 3.1	(34) 3.6	(14) 1.1				(144) 4.1	(143) 3.9
	10.9	5.2	4.8	2.5				7.8	7.4
Net Sales ($)	148052M	525897M	1789918M	2917597M	2589663M	4564330M	Net Sales ($)	10763822M	11114567M
Total Assets ($)	16334M	100374M	432785M	773279M	573050M	2342480M	Total Assets ($)	3411201M	3485211M

Comparative Historical Data | **Current Data Sorted by Sales**

			Type of Statement						
28	28	31	Unqualified	1	2			4	24
28	21	17	Reviewed					7	10
26	37	21	Compiled	1	4	2	3	11	
77	88	67	Tax Returns	10	24	8	9	12	4
154	149	171	Other	13	33	20	28	36	41
4/1/16-3/31/17 ALL	4/1/17-3/31/18 ALL	4/1/18-3/31/19 ALL		25 (4/1-9/30/18)			282 (10/1/18-3/31/19)		
				0-1MM	1-3MM	3-5MM	5-10MM	10-25MM	25MM & OVER
313	323	307	**NUMBER OF STATEMENTS**	25	63	30	40	70	79
%	%	%	**ASSETS**	%	%	%	%	%	%
16.1	14.8	18.5	Cash & Equivalents	25.5	26.0	22.8	12.9	17.9	11.9
35.1	38.5	37.7	Trade Receivables (net)	24.1	21.0	33.7	40.6	45.7	48.1
1.6	1.6	2.2	Inventory	.5	3.0	5.8	1.0	2.8	.7
4.3	3.9	4.2	All Other Current	4.2	3.5	.9	3.7	5.1	5.5
57.1	58.9	62.5	Total Current	54.3	53.5	63.2	58.2	71.4	66.2
18.4	19.7	17.8	Fixed Assets (net)	26.0	22.8	21.2	17.3	14.9	12.8
14.2	12.0	11.6	Intangibles (net)	11.9	13.7	11.2	14.0	5.9	13.9
10.3	9.4	8.1	All Other Non-Current	7.7	10.0	4.4	10.5	7.7	7.1
100.0	100.0	100.0	Total	100.0	100.0	100.0	100.0	100.0	100.0
			LIABILITIES						
13.9	16.1	12.9	Notes Payable-Short Term	15.0	15.2	10.0	10.3	13.8	11.9
3.3	3.6	3.2	Cur. Mat.-L.T.D.	4.3	3.1	7.0	3.3	2.5	2.0
11.0	10.4	10.2	Trade Payables	5.9	8.6	12.4	11.9	11.7	10.0
.3	.4	.4	Income Taxes Payable	.3	.0	.1	.0	.8	.5
17.6	17.6	19.1	All Other Current	24.9	23.7	13.2	12.7	18.6	19.5
46.0	48.2	45.7	Total Current	50.4	50.6	42.6	38.3	47.3	43.9
15.9	15.3	18.2	Long-Term Debt	23.7	31.2	23.0	21.5	8.6	11.1
.2	.1	.1	Deferred Taxes	.0	.0	.3	.1	.1	.2
4.4	3.2	5.5	All Other Non-Current	4.4	11.9	5.8	3.6	2.5	4.2
33.5	33.2	30.5	Net Worth	21.5	6.3	28.3	36.6	41.5	40.6
100.0	100.0	100.0	Total Liabilities & Net Worth	100.0	100.0	100.0	100.0	100.0	100.0
			INCOME DATA						
100.0	100.0	100.0	Net Sales	100.0	100.0	100.0	100.0	100.0	100.0
			Gross Profit						
93.9	94.1	93.3	Operating Expenses	87.7	93.6	89.2	92.9	95.0	95.1
6.1	5.9	6.7	Operating Profit	12.3	6.4	10.8	7.1	5.0	4.9
.8	.5	.5	All Other Expenses (net)	.5	.4	.6	.9	.2	.7
5.3	5.4	6.1	Profit Before Taxes	11.9	6.0	10.2	6.1	4.8	4.1
			RATIOS						
2.5	2.4	2.6	Current	3.2	3.6	4.2	2.6	3.8	2.0
1.4	1.4	1.6		1.1	1.5	2.1	1.6	1.5	1.5
.8	.9	.9		.4	.7	1.0	1.1	.9	1.2
2.3	2.2	2.4	Quick	3.1	3.0	4.2	2.4	2.6	1.9
1.2	1.2	1.4		1.0	1.1	2.1	1.5	1.3	1.4
.7	.8	.8		.3	.6	.6	.9	.8	1.0
15 24.3	18 20.4	16 22.2	Sales/Receivables	0 UND	0 UND	0 UND	15 24.5	17 21.6	34 10.7
30 12.3	33 11.0	33 10.9		21 17.8	19 19.3	30 12.1	31 11.8	34 10.8	46 8.0
51 7.2	50 7.3	54 6.7		64 5.7	36 10.2	52 7.0	59 6.2	52 7.0	63 5.8
			Cost of Sales/Inventory						
			Cost of Sales/Payables						
10.3	11.1	9.0	Sales/Working Capital	7.0	11.4	6.1	10.6	8.7	9.9
27.7	31.8	22.2		27.0	37.8	9.6	21.3	30.5	17.4
-57.4	-76.7	-149.3		-11.9	-45.1	NM	197.4	-92.1	42.4
40.5	40.5	36.3	EBIT/Interest	32.5	18.6	18.8	30.2	87.8	45.8
(261) 10.6	(264) 11.9	(259) 10.8		(16) 7.1	(50) 7.8	(26) 6.9	(35) 9.1	(60) 17.8	(72) 13.3
2.8	3.0	3.7		4.1	3.1	.8	3.0	7.4	2.7
15.3	21.3	11.9	Net Profit + Depr., Dep., Amort./Cur. Mat. L/T/D					6.6	31.3
(35) 5.7	(36) 6.0	(31) 4.8						(11) 3.6	(17) 8.4
2.5	2.6	2.1						1.6	2.3
.1	.1	.2	Fixed/Worth	.2	.2	.2	.3	.1	.2
.6	.6	.5		.7	.7	.6	.6	.3	.4
-10.2	3.9	5.4		5.4	-.8	-2.8	2.8	1.6	1.4
.7	.8	.7	Debt/Worth	.8	.5	.9	.9	.4	1.0
2.5	2.0	2.3		2.6	5.9	4.2	1.9	1.9	1.9
-21.2	30.4	315.0		NM	-2.9	-24.6	10.0	6.0	7.0
95.7	94.0	95.3	% Profit Before Taxes/Tangible Net Worth	167.4	122.8	131.7	104.6	104.5	88.0
(229) 43.1	(251) 42.4	(232) 53.9		(19) 71.4	(38) 48.6	(20) 62.4	(32) 55.2	(58) 52.2	(65) 51.3
20.6	19.7	26.7		28.6	18.6	-12.2	9.3	28.9	33.1
32.1	32.0	31.7	% Profit Before Taxes/Total Assets	55.1	39.1	35.5	31.1	34.1	26.8
12.7	13.7	16.1		19.2	18.2	15.4	12.7	15.9	14.7
4.5	4.9	6.8		4.4	3.6	1.2	4.9	10.7	5.2
116.1	110.5	105.9	Sales/Net Fixed Assets	40.6	134.1	307.4	91.6	164.6	77.5
43.5	33.6	40.7		15.8	34.1	42.1	36.0	60.9	47.4
16.4	15.1	15.6		7.0	11.5	14.1	15.1	23.6	22.0
6.3	6.2	6.6	Sales/Total Assets	6.7	6.9	6.2	7.5	8.8	5.4
4.2	4.0	4.1		3.2	4.1	3.6	4.0	4.9	4.0
2.6	2.5	2.6		1.1	2.6	2.5	2.3	3.4	2.3
.4	.5	.5	% Depr., Dep., Amort./Sales	1.4	.9	.7	.3	.3	.5
(198) .9	(208) -1.0	(190) .9		(14) 2.6	(34) 1.3	(13) 2.0	(25) .8	(44) .6	(60) .8
1.7	1.9	1.8		6.3	2.6	5.5	1.9	1.2	1.3
1.9	1.8	1.8	% Officers', Directors' Owners' Comp/Sales	4.1	3.3	2.1	1.9	1.3	.9
(113) 3.6	(129) 3.4	(124) 3.7		(12) 9.1	(31) 4.7	(14) 3.7	(15) 4.3	(31) 2.0	(21) 2.4
7.8	6.9	5.8		14.5	7.8	5.8	5.1	3.7	4.3
9854537M	10895791M	12535457M	Net Sales ($)	14451M	119582M	114562M	282496M	1124428M	10879938M
3116522M	3236204M	4238302M	Total Assets ($)	8951M	37126M	69417M	101656M	268632M	3752520M

M = $ thousand   MM = $ million
See Pages viii through xx for Explanation of Ratios and Data

Current Data Sorted by Assets — Comparative Historical Data

0-500M	500M-2MM	2-10MM	10-50MM	50-100MM	100-250MM	Type of Statement			
						Unqualified		25	23
1	5	7	11	4	7	Reviewed		70	72
4	14	40	10			Compiled		64	57
101	78	13	1			Tax Returns		230	241
56	103	27	1	1	1	Other		257	274
	53 (4/1-9/30/18)	101	39	5	6			4/1/14-3/31/15	4/1/15-3/31/16
			583 (10/1/18-3/31/19)					ALL	ALL
162	200	188	62	10	14	NUMBER OF STATEMENTS		646	667
%	%	%	%	%	%	**ASSETS**		%	%
23.1	13.8	9.3	11.6	14.7	15.0	Cash & Equivalents		14.6	14.7
11.7	18.0	29.8	35.0	35.4	31.8	Trade Receivables (net)		23.3	23.6
2.4	3.7	4.1	3.5	1.1	.6	Inventory		4.5	4.8
2.5	2.3	3.8	5.3	7.7	8.7	All Other Current		3.3	3.8
39.7	37.8	47.0	55.4	58.9	56.2	Total Current		45.7	46.8
46.6	44.7	39.9	31.4	26.1	29.3	Fixed Assets (net)		40.9	39.5
5.2	7.7	6.1	7.9	13.5	7.1	Intangibles (net)		5.2	5.3
8.4	9.8	6.9	5.3	1.5	7.5	All Other Non-Current		8.1	8.5
100.0	100.0	100.0	100.0	100.0	100.0	Total		100.0	100.0
						LIABILITIES			
18.7	8.2	7.7	4.7	8.3	.8	Notes Payable-Short Term		11.6	10.9
11.6	6.5	6.1	6.0	6.3	3.9	Cur. Mat.-L.T.D.		6.9	6.8
7.8	7.2	11.6	11.7	8.6	8.9	Trade Payables		9.6	9.5
.2	.1	.1	.2	.2	.4	Income Taxes Payable		.3	.2
9.6	8.0	7.4	12.9	12.8	15.6	All Other Current		9.8	9.5
48.0	30.0	32.9	35.6	36.2	29.6	Total Current		38.2	36.9
59.0	38.9	27.1	23.5	16.1	20.6	Long-Term Debt		33.8	34.8
.0	.1	.5	.4	1.8	.0	Deferred Taxes		.3	.2
3.6	2.7	2.3	5.4	14.5	9.9	All Other Non-Current		6.3	4.9
-10.7	28.4	37.2	35.0	31.5	39.9	Net Worth		21.4	23.2
100.0	100.0	100.0	100.0	100.0	100.0	Total Liabilties & Net Worth		100.0	100.0
						INCOME DATA			
100.0	100.0	100.0	100.0	100.0	100.0	Net Sales		100.0	100.0
						Gross Profit			
92.2	89.3	92.5	93.1	93.0	93.7	Operating Expenses		92.6	92.7
7.8	10.7	7.5	6.9	7.0	6.3	Operating Profit		7.4	7.3
1.4	3.1	.9	.7	1.0	.6	All Other Expenses (net)		.9	1.0
6.4	7.7	6.5	6.1	6.0	5.7	Profit Before Taxes		6.5	6.3
						RATIOS			
2.9	2.7	2.6	1.8	2.4	3.2			2.5	2.7
1.0	1.3	1.5	1.5	2.0	1.5	Current		1.3	1.4
.4	.6	1.0	1.2	1.3	1.4			.8	.8
2.6	2.2	2.2	1.7	2.3	2.2			2.1	2.2
.8	1.1	1.3	1.2	1.7	1.4	Quick	(645) 1.1 (666)	1.2	
.3	.5	.7	.9	.7	1.3			.6	.6
0 UND	0 UND	27 13.5	41 8.9	45 8.2	48 7.6		1 615.8	1	377.8
0 UND	18 20.4	41 8.9	54 6.8	65 5.6	51 7.1	Sales/Receivables	24 15.1	25	14.6
12 29.8	32 11.4	63 5.8	65 5.6	83 4.4	57 6.4		47 7.8	46	7.9
						Cost of Sales/Inventory			
						Cost of Sales/Payables			
20.4	11.6	7.9	8.7	3.5	4.0			9.8	9.5
UND	46.5	18.2	13.0	9.2	16.6	Sales/Working Capital		34.7	24.2
-14.9	-24.8	-458.7	28.4	NM	25.5			-44.1	-53.7
15.3	16.8	24.0	31.5	83.5	36.9			22.0	23.6
(133) 6.0	(165) 5.6	(172) 8.5	(60) 10.4	9.6	13.3	EBIT/Interest	(566) 7.6	(586)	8.0
.9	1.7	2.4	3.8	1.9	9.8			2.4	2.5
		4.3	6.1					6.7	6.0
		(21) 2.2	(13) 3.1			Net Profit + Depr., Dep., Amort./Cur. Mat. L/T/D	(50) 2.7	(49)	2.4
		1.4	1.6					1.4	1.5
1.0	.7	.7	.5	.3	.3			.6	.6
5.1	2.0	1.3	1.1	.9	1.1	Fixed/Worth		1.5	1.4
-1.7	-215.6	4.1	3.2	-.6	1.5			8.6	24.0
1.4	.9	.9	1.1	.3	.8			1.0	.8
13.1	3.0	2.0	2.2	1.3	1.7	Debt/Worth		2.4	2.5
-3.5	-117.9	6.9	7.7	-2.3	2.3			23.6	74.6
223.6	103.4	64.6	57.6		38.9	% Profit Before Taxes/Tangible Net Worth		100.0	91.5
(97) 88.9	(148) 48.4	(164) 37.2	(54) 37.9	(12) 27.9			(503) 42.4	(516)	43.3
20.9	12.7	10.7	20.1	23.5				15.0	15.9
42.2	26.9	24.3	22.2	19.6	13.8	% Profit Before Taxes/Total Assets		32.2	30.9
16.3	12.0	13.4	12.4	11.1	11.7			14.1	14.0
.2	2.0	2.0	7.9	3.4	9.9			3.6	3.7
40.9	23.4	11.6	13.6	16.0	15.5			19.5	22.3
13.8	7.4	6.7	8.9	8.0	9.1	Sales/Net Fixed Assets		8.9	10.0
4.7	3.5	3.9	5.0	6.0	7.4			4.7	4.7
8.3	4.6	3.5	3.0	2.6	3.3			4.9	4.7
4.8	2.9	2.5	2.2	2.2	2.7	Sales/Total Assets		3.0	3.1
2.8	1.7	1.7	1.7	1.0	2.0			2.0	2.1
1.8	2.0	2.2	2.0					1.7	1.9
(81) 5.4	(118) 4.3	(143) 3.9	(57) 3.1			% Depr., Dep., Amort./Sales	(451) 3.1	(444)	3.4
9.6	7.8	6.5	4.9					5.8	6.0
3.3	2.4	1.2	.6					2.3	2.4
(102) 6.2	(117) 3.9	(74) 2.1	(14) 1.1			% Officers', Directors' Owners' Comp/Sales	(332) 4.3	(348)	4.5
9.4	5.9	3.5	3.2					8.2	8.4
214823M	688148M	2246927M	3039691M	2073230M	6418838M	Net Sales ($)		10272603M	15650192M
39790M	216765M	871845M	1336031M	757020M	2448936M	Total Assets ($)		3700201M	5265002M

M = $ thousand   MM = $ million
See Pages viii through xx for Explanation of Ratios and Data

Comparative Historical Data / Current Data Sorted by Sales

			Type of Statement	0-1MM	1-3MM	3-5MM	5-10MM	10-25MM	25MM & OVER
29	27	29	Unqualified			1	1	6	21
69	70	56	Reviewed	2	1	2	16	23	12
56	47	32	Compiled	2	7	11	7	5	
216	234	209	Tax Returns	62	71	31	28	14	3
269	321	310	Other	42	68	44	48	56	52
4/1/16-3/31/17 ALL	4/1/17-3/31/18 ALL	4/1/18-3/31/19 ALL			53 (4/1-9/30/18)		583 (10/1/18-3/31/19)		
639	699	636	**NUMBER OF STATEMENTS**	108	147	89	100	104	88
%	%	%	**ASSETS**	%	%	%	%	%	%
14.3	15.1	14.7	Cash & Equivalents	17.4	17.7	16.4	12.0	11.1	11.8
23.3	23.6	22.1	Trade Receivables (net)	7.3	13.5	23.0	24.2	34.8	36.5
4.3	3.4	3.4	Inventory	.3	4.9	3.6	5.2	3.1	2.5
3.1	3.1	3.3	All Other Current	2.4	2.7	2.6	2.2	4.3	6.2
45.0	45.3	43.5	Total Current	27.5	38.8	45.5	43.6	53.2	57.1
39.6	40.1	41.8	Fixed Assets (net)	61.0	43.4	35.7	42.6	35.2	28.9
5.1	6.5	6.7	Intangibles (net)	4.6	7.8	8.3	5.8	5.3	8.5
10.3	8.1	8.0	All Other Non-Current	6.9	10.0	10.5	8.0	6.3	5.5
100.0	100.0	100.0	Total	100.0	100.0	100.0	100.0	100.0	100.0
			LIABILITIES						
10.5	11.2	10.2	Notes Payable-Short Term	13.7	12.5	12.0	8.3	8.1	5.0
7.0	8.1	7.6	Cur. Mat.-L.T.D.	5.6	10.3	7.7	8.3	6.6	5.8
9.1	9.3	9.2	Trade Payables	2.4	8.4	9.2	9.4	14.3	12.3
.1	.1	.1	Income Taxes Payable	.2	.1	.0	.1	.1	.3
10.6	10.4	9.0	All Other Current	9.1	8.6	8.3	7.7	7.6	13.1
37.4	39.1	36.1	Total Current	31.0	39.9	37.2	33.9	36.8	36.4
33.6	36.1	38.3	Long-Term Debt	52.0	48.3	40.6	37.9	22.9	20.9
.3	.3	.2	Deferred Taxes	.0	.0	.4	.5	.2	.5
4.3	3.9	3.4	All Other Non-Current	5.4	2.9	2.1	1.5	2.3	6.7
24.5	20.5	22.0	Net Worth	11.5	8.9	19.7	26.3	37.7	35.5
100.0	100.0	100.0	Total Liabilities & Net Worth	100.0	100.0	100.0	100.0	100.0	100.0
			INCOME DATA						
100.0	100.0	100.0	Net Sales	100.0	100.0	100.0	100.0	100.0	100.0
			Gross Profit						
91.8	91.5	91.5	Operating Expenses	79.7	94.4	93.9	93.2	94.4	93.4
8.2	8.5	8.5	Operating Profit	20.3	5.6	6.1	6.8	5.6	6.6
.8	1.3	1.7	All Other Expenses (net)	7.6	.6	.5	.4	.3	.7
7.3	7.2	6.8	Profit Before Taxes	12.7	5.0	5.6	6.4	5.4	5.9
			RATIOS						
2.6	2.5	2.5	Current	2.5	3.0	3.0	2.6	2.3	2.1
1.4	1.4	1.4		1.0	1.3	1.4	1.5	1.4	1.5
.7	.8	.7		.3	.5	.7	.8	1.1	1.2
2.1	2.2	2.2	Quick	2.3	2.3	2.5	2.3	2.0	1.9
(638) 1.1	(698) 1.2	1.1		.8	.9	1.1	1.2	1.3	1.3
.6	.6	.6		.2	.4	.6	.6	.8	.9
2 156.6	0 UND	0 UND	Sales/Receivables	0 UND	0 UND	1 268.5	9 39.0	27 13.5	41 8.8
27 13.7	27 13.3	26 13.9		0 UND	8 45.2	25 14.6	31 11.8	39 9.3	50 7.3
48 7.6	50 7.3	48 7.6		10 35.7	26 13.9	46 7.9	46 8.0	63 5.8	60 6.1
			Cost of Sales/Inventory						
			Cost of Sales/Payables						
9.3	9.8	10.0	Sales/Working Capital	16.5	13.7	8.7	8.6	9.4	7.3
29.5	26.5	27.6		UND	49.3	42.8	23.2	19.6	13.1
-37.8	-38.4	-40.4		-8.9	-18.8	-59.7	-50.0	161.0	28.0
21.8	20.7	19.3	EBIT/Interest	13.8	18.9	14.0	21.4	25.4	33.5
(562) 8.2	(615) 8.3	(554) 8.0		(75) 4.0	(130) 6.2	(78) 5.3	(92) 11.0	(95) 8.4	(84) 10.6
3.2	2.2	1.8		1.2	1.5	.9	1.6	3.0	4.3
5.0	5.1	6.2	Net Profit + Depr., Dep., Amort./Cur. Mat. L/T/D					5.3	38.3
(55) 2.2	(65) 2.6	(52) 2.5						(13) 2.5	(24) 4.2
1.5	1.3	1.5						1.9	1.5
.6	.6	.7	Fixed/Worth	1.3	.9	.5	.7	.5	.4
1.3	1.5	1.6		4.6	2.8	1.5	1.3	.0	1.1
12.5	24.8	62.4		-6.6	-3.9	108.0	6.1	4.0	2.2
.9	1.0	1.0	Debt/Worth	1.3	1.2	1.0	1.0	.8	1.1
2.2	2.6	2.7		6.6	5.7	3.3	2.5	2.0	1.7
30.7	137.0	999.8		-10.7	-5.3	261.0	15.8	7.6	5.6
88.5	96.1	92.5	% Profit Before Taxes/Tangible Net Worth	117.3	179.8	103.8	96.3	68.7	57.7
(491) 42.1	(534) 44.7	(482) 41.1		(72) 27.1	(97) 61.2	(69) 52.1	(79) 50.0	(92) 36.6	(73) 36.4
15.1	14.1	14.4		3.9	23.4	6.4	21.8	8.3	22.4
31.6	31.8	28.0	% Profit Before Taxes/Total Assets	33.3	31.1	26.2	30.9	27.6	22.4
14.4	13.8	12.8		8.9	14.5	12.8	17.8	11.4	12.5
3.7	2.9	2.2		1.6	1.9	-.3	2.0	3.4	8.3
22.4	20.7	20.3	Sales/Net Fixed Assets	11.4	25.1	31.1	14.1	18.5	15.9
9.0	8.6	8.4		4.1	8.7	10.9	6.9	9.7	9.8
4.9	4.3	4.2		.9	4.1	5.7	4.3	4.7	7.0
4.6	4.4	4.4	Sales/Total Assets	4.6	5.2	5.4	4.6	4.3	3.4
3.0	2.9	2.8		2.2	3.3	3.2	2.8	2.8	2.6
1.9	2.0	1.8		.3	2.0	2.2	1.8	2.2	2.1
1.9	2.2	2.0	% Depr., Dep., Amort./Sales	5.1	2.2	1.2	2.9	1.5	.7
(432) 3.5	(446) 4.1	(415) 4.0		(68) 9.6	(74) 5.0	(48) 2.8	(68) 4.3	(85) 3.1	(72) 3.0
6.3	6.9	6.8		19.2	8.5	4.3	6.5	5.4	4.3
2.1	2.0	2.1	% Officers', Directors' Owners' Comp/Sales	5.1	2.8	2.4	1.7	1.2	.7
(332) 4.2	(334) 4.3	(311) 3.7		(43) 7.5	(102) 4.8	(51) 3.7	(55) 2.5	(43) 1.8	(17) 1.3
7.9	7.8	7.1		14.1	8.1	5.6	4.6	3.7	4.1
15774653M	20191991M	14681657M	Net Sales ($)	52363M	255172M	348915M	702604M	1591755M	11730848M
5426639M	6163312M	5670387M	Total Assets ($)	54635M	101125M	135391M	270937M	581750M	4526549M

M = $ thousand   MM = $ million
See Pages viii through xx for Explanation of Ratios and Data

Current Data Sorted by Assets   **Comparative Historical Data**

Type of Statement counts — current: 3 (4/1-9/30/18); 55 (10/1/18-3/31/19). Columns for 10-50MM, 50-100MM, 100-250MM marked DATA NOT AVAILABLE.

Type of Statement	0-500M	500M-2MM	2-10MM	10-50MM	50-100MM	100-250MM	4/1/14-3/31/15 ALL	4/1/15-3/31/16 ALL
Unqualified							1	2
Reviewed			1				4	4
Compiled		1	3				5	3
Tax Returns	9	6	1				21	19
Other	8	16	10	1		2	34	30
NUMBER OF STATEMENTS	17	23	15	1		2	65	58
	%	%	%	%	%	%	%	%
ASSETS								
Cash & Equivalents	32.6	18.3	6.8				15.8	15.0
Trade Receivables (net)	11.0	25.2	27.8				20.2	22.5
Inventory	2.8	1.7	3.9				3.7	2.5
All Other Current	3.6	1.3	7.2				2.3	3.5
Total Current	49.9	46.6	45.7				42.0	43.5
Fixed Assets (net)	29.9	34.9	39.1				39.5	36.0
Intangibles (net)	17.0	11.2	7.8				9.1	9.8
All Other Non-Current	3.2	7.4	7.4				9.3	10.7
Total	100.0	100.0	100.0				100.0	100.0
LIABILITIES								
Notes Payable-Short Term	23.9	8.5	8.8				11.5	12.6
Cur. Mat.-L.T.D.	3.1	3.5	3.9				5.2	6.7
Trade Payables	49.6	7.3	8.3				6.5	10.0
Income Taxes Payable	.8	.1	.0				.0	.0
All Other Current	41.9	5.7	5.8				9.9	6.2
Total Current	119.2	25.1	26.8				33.1	35.4
Long-Term Debt	47.2	22.6	29.3				29.7	33.8
Deferred Taxes	.0	.0	.0				.6	.3
All Other Non-Current	1.3	4.7	6.6				8.5	4.8
Net Worth	-67.7	47.6	37.3				28.1	25.7
Total Liabilities & Net Worth	100.0	100.0	100.0				100.0	100.0
INCOME DATA								
Net Sales	100.0	100.0	100.0				100.0	100.0
Gross Profit								
Operating Expenses	89.3	90.6	81.1				89.3	89.1
Operating Profit	10.7	9.4	18.9				10.7	10.9
All Other Expenses (net)	.3	1.2	5.8				1.2	1.5
Profit Before Taxes	10.4	8.1	13.1				9.5	9.4
RATIOS								
Current	3.3	3.5	2.1				2.7	2.9
	.9	2.3	1.7				1.6	1.6
	.2	.8	1.1				.7	.8
Quick	3.3	3.3	1.9				2.6	2.3
	.4	2.0	1.3				1.2	1.3
	.1	.8	.6				.5	.7
Sales/Receivables	0 UND	2 189.8	0 UND				0 UND	0 UND
	3 127.9	25 14.7	16 22.7				18 20.4	21 17.0
	17 20.9	41 8.9	83 4.4				42 8.6	50 7.3
Cost of Sales/Inventory								
Cost of Sales/Payables								
Sales/Working Capital	15.3	7.2	6.9				10.1	8.0
	-37.0	13.7	11.4				23.5	23.4
	-8.2	-53.5	581.0				-25.9	-43.1
EBIT/Interest	33.1	33.8	21.4				42.2	36.2
	(13) 6.5	(22) 9.3	(12) 9.7				(54) 6.6	(50) 8.7
	3.5	3.0	1.7				2.2	1.4
Net Profit + Depr., Dep., Amort./Cur. Mat. L/T/D								
Fixed/Worth	.3	.4	.5				.4	.6
	1.4	.8	1.0				1.6	1.8
	-.2	1.5	-13.7				32.5	-18.4
Debt/Worth	1.0	.6	.5				.6	.7
	-11.2	1.3	1.8				2.3	3.4
	-1.3	3.1	-74.1				217.9	-30.4
% Profit Before Taxes/Tangible Net Worth		84.2	82.0				76.0	95.5
	(21) 56.4	(11) 30.3					(50) 39.3	(43) 40.6
	30.2	14.1					20.5	6.0
% Profit Before Taxes/Total Assets	172.3	48.9	30.6				31.3	33.4
	78.0	19.3	6.8				12.9	10.2
	9.1	3.7	2.2				3.7	-1.0
Sales/Net Fixed Assets	180.5	14.5	18.8				24.9	18.4
	22.9	10.3	11.1				9.4	11.0
	8.8	7.6	.6				4.0	6.8
Sales/Total Assets	14.0	4.3	2.9				4.0	5.1
	5.0	3.2	2.2				3.0	3.2
	3.1	2.0	.2				1.9	2.0
% Depr., Dep., Amort./Sales		.9	1.5				.9	1.5
	(13) 1.6	(13) 3.3					(44) 2.2	(37) 3.1
	3.9	18.5					4.0	4.6
% Officers', Directors' Owners' Comp/Sales	4.4	2.4					2.2	3.0
	(10) 8.4	(10) 5.2					(28) 7.2	(22) 6.9
	13.6	12.9					11.8	12.2
Net Sales ($)	15937M	81273M	114519M	52072M		115772M	1132488M	809435M
Total Assets ($)	2489M	26312M	60384M	11625M		283956M	503709M	492775M

© RMA 2019

M = $ thousand   MM = $ million

See Pages viii through xx for Explanation of Ratios and Data

Comparative Historical Data **Current Data Sorted by Sales**

			Type of Statement						
2	3	1 4	Unqualified	1	1		1	2	
2	2		Reviewed						
23	24	17	Compiled						1
27	36	36	Tax Returns	8	5	3	1		1
4/1/16-3/31/17	4/1/17-3/31/18	4/1/18-3/31/19	Other	8	8	7	9	3	1
ALL	ALL	ALL		0-1MM	3 (4/1-9/30/18) 1-3MM	3-5MM	55 (10/1/18-3/31/19) 5-10MM	10-25MM	25MM & OVER
54	65	58	**NUMBER OF STATEMENTS**	17	13	11	10	5	2
%	%	%	**ASSETS**	%	%	%	%	%	%
14.6	19.5	20.6	Cash & Equivalents	27.7	13.8	32.1	6.6		
20.7	18.9	21.0	Trade Receivables (net)	8.4	16.9	22.1	44.1		
2.5	3.5	2.8	Inventory	2.8	1.7	.0	1.8		
3.8	2.9	4.0	All Other Current	2.2	2.1	4.1	3.3		
41.7	44.8	48.4	Total Current	41.1	34.5	58.3	55.8		
36.0	34.8	33.1	Fixed Assets (net)	43.3	31.5	31.3	30.3		
15.0	12.8	12.2	Intangibles (net)	11.4	23.3	6.2	8.0		
7.3	7.6	6.3	All Other Non-Current	4.2	10.7	4.2	5.9		
100.0	100.0	100.0	Total	100.0	100.0	100.0	100.0		
			LIABILITIES						
15.3	10.7	13.0	Notes Payable-Short Term	16.3	8.7	17.8	8.6		
8.5	7.8	3.5	Cur. Mat.-L.T.D.	3.3	4.6	1.4	5.2		
6.7	9.6	20.3	Trade Payables	44.7	8.9	6.0	12.8		
.1	.0	.3	Income Taxes Payable	.8	.0	.2	.0		
5.7	10.5	16.6	All Other Current	7.1	31.5	24.9	8.3		
36.4	38.6	53.5	Total Current	72.1	53.7	50.2	34.9		
45.9	52.0	32.0	Long-Term Debt	53.8	34.6	14.8	18.8		
.2	.1	.0	Deferred Taxes	.0	.0	.0	.0		
2.3	3.4	4.0	All Other Non-Current	3.4	.6	8.0	4.1		
15.2	6.0	10.5	Net Worth	-29.3	11.1	27.0	42.2		
100.0	100.0	100.0	Total Liabilities & Net Worth	100.0	100.0	100.0	100.0		
			INCOME DATA						
100.0	100.0	100.0	Net Sales	100.0	100.0	100.0	100.0		
			Gross Profit						
87.3	85.4	87.6	Operating Expenses	78.8	89.8	90.9	92.4		
12.7	14.6	12.4	Operating Profit	21.2	10.2	9.1	7.6		
1.5	3.7	2.1	All Other Expenses (net)	5.8	.9	.7	.2		
11.2	10.9	10.3	Profit Before Taxes	15.4	9.4	8.3	7.4		
			RATIOS						
2.6	2.0	3.2		2.8	2.9	4.8	3.2		
1.4	1.2	1.6	Current	1.0	.8	2.7	1.7		
.6	.6	.7		.4	.1	1.7	.9		
2.4	1.6	3.1		2.8	2.6	4.8	3.0		
1.2	1.0	1.4	Quick	1.0	.8	2.7	1.5		
.4	.4	.4		.3	.1	1.1	.8		
0 UND	0 UND	0 UND		0 UND	0 UND	0 UND	23 16.1		
10 35.8	7 51.1	17 21.3	Sales/Receivables	0 UND	3 127.9	17 21.0	34 10.7		
40 9.2	43 8.5	44 8.3		16 23.1	47 7.8	58 6.3	66 5.5		
			Cost of Sales/Inventory						
			Cost of Sales/Payables						
11.0	14.3	7.6		15.3	8.3	4.1	7.6		
36.8	44.8	16.6	Sales/Working Capital	UND	-52.8	8.4	17.2		
-32.7	-15.8	-33.9		-6.2	-7.9	23.5	-54.8		
20.6	20.3	28.0		10.9	45.0	35.5	55.2		
(44) 10.1	(52) 7.3	(48) 8.7	EBIT/Interest	(10) 4.8	6.0	(10) 21.4	9.3		
1.5	2.4	2.9		3.2	2.3	4.9	-1.1		
			Net Profit + Depr., Dep., Amort./Cur. Mat. L/T/D						
.6	.5	.4		.7	.2	.4	.4		
1.9	2.8	.9	Fixed/Worth	2.5	.8	.7	.9		
-1.8	-3.7	-12.8		-4.0	-2.2	1.0	1.6		
1.0	1.1	.8		1.0	.4	.5	.9		
4.4	5.6	2.2	Debt/Worth	2.6	3.5	.8	1.3		
-4.0	-6.2	-12.5		-6.4	-2.7	5.4	2.5		
123.5	146.1	91.8	% Profit Before Taxes/Tangible Net Worth	141.5					
(34) 58.4	(40) 39.0	(42) 56.5		(11) 34.1					
14.7	3.3	23.6		17.3					
41.5	47.9	51.9	% Profit Before Taxes/Total Assets	136.3	79.1	51.2	45.7		
23.5	11.0	18.4		9.1	21.5	27.2	17.2		
2.0	1.4	4.4		4.5	9.0	-7.9	-1.7		
31.8	36.0	37.6		45.0	43.8	23.4	17.1		
12.7	11.2	13.0	Sales/Net Fixed Assets	6.3	14.1	10.3	11.2		
6.6	4.5	5.6		.8	3.5	7.6	9.3		
4.7	5.0	4.4		6.3	4.6	4.4	5.0		
3.5	3.0	3.1	Sales/Total Assets	2.7	2.5	3.3	3.3		
2.4	1.2	2.0		.6	2.0	2.2	2.9		
.8	1.0	1.2							
(34) 2.8	(37) 2.6	(31) 3.1	% Depr., Dep., Amort./Sales						
4.3	11.3	6.9							
2.3	3.2	2.5							
(26) 5.1	(24) 5.2	(27) 5.1	% Officers', Directors' Owners' Comp/Sales						
9.7	10.8	12.2							
257246M	425477M	379573M	Net Sales ($)	7478M	26127M	44145M	68474M	90277M	143072M
179226M	265797M	384766M	Total Assets ($)	19226M	9568M	16204M	21303M	188840M	129625M

M = $ thousand   MM = $ million
See Pages viii through xx for Explanation of Ratios and Data

Current Data Sorted by Assets   Comparative Historical Data

0-500M	500M-2MM	2-10MM	10-50MM	50-100MM	100-250MM	Type of Statement	6	6
		1	4		1	Unqualified	6	6
		9	2	1		Reviewed	13	14
2	3	3	2		1	Compiled	13	9
20	16	8	1			Tax Returns	77	58
21	36	22	8	1		Other	64	86
	10 (4/1-9/30/18)		149 (10/1/18-3/31/19)				4/1/14- 3/31/15	4/1/15- 3/31/16
							ALL	ALL
43	55	43	15	1	2	NUMBER OF STATEMENTS	173	173
%	%	%	%	%	%	**ASSETS**	%	%
27.7	19.9	10.7	4.8			Cash & Equivalents	17.7	15.4
16.0	32.4	36.2	35.1			Trade Receivables (net)	26.6	31.5
4.9	1.9	3.8	23.1			Inventory	4.8	4.4
5.3	3.9	6.5	2.1			All Other Current	2.7	1.9
53.9	58.1	57.2	65.2			Total Current	51.9	53.3
22.1	24.4	25.8	15.5			Fixed Assets (net)	28.0	27.9
10.7	9.6	8.3	12.5			Intangibles (net)	8.0	8.4
13.2	7.9	8.8	6.8			All Other Non-Current	12.1	10.4
100.0	100.0	100.0	100.0			Total	100.0	100.0
						LIABILITIES		
19.6	10.1	9.0	23.6			Notes Payable-Short Term	13.7	14.1
7.0	3.2	4.0	6.3			Cur. Mat.-L.T.D.	4.4	5.4
5.1	8.2	10.9	13.1			Trade Payables	9.4	11.4
.1	.3	.1	.0			Income Taxes Payable	.1	.1
21.4	13.6	13.0	9.5			All Other Current	14.3	11.4
53.2	35.5	36.9	52.5			Total Current	41.9	42.5
38.8	24.1	14.6	10.8			Long-Term Debt	26.3	29.3
.0	.0	.5	.9			Deferred Taxes	.1	.2
4.9	6.5	3.8	2.5			All Other Non-Current	8.7	4.2
3.1	33.9	44.2	33.3			Net Worth	23.0	23.8
100.0	100.0	100.0	100.0			Total Liabilties & Net Worth	100.0	100.0
						INCOME DATA		
100.0	100.0	100.0	100.0			Net Sales	100.0	100.0
						Gross Profit		
90.7	92.2	88.7	98.0			Operating Expenses	90.5	90.9
9.3	7.8	11.3	2.0			Operating Profit	9.5	9.1
.5	.4	.7	1.2			All Other Expenses (net)	1.6	1.3
8.8	7.4	10.6	.7			Profit Before Taxes	7.9	7.8
						RATIOS		
3.3	4.9	2.9	1.5				2.7	3.0
1.3	1.8	1.6	1.2			Current	1.4	1.5
.5	1.1	1.1	1.0				.8	.8
3.0	4.6	2.5	1.3				2.4	2.8
1.1	1.6	1.3	1.1			Quick	1.3	1.3
.3	.8	.8	.4				.6	.7
0 UND	12 30.9	27 13.3	39 9.3				0 UND	2 162.9
0 UND	30 12.0	49 7.4	62 5.9			Sales/Receivables	22 16.4	33 11.1
25 14.4	48 7.6	72 5.1	114 3.2				52 7.0	59 6.2
						Cost of Sales/Inventory		
						Cost of Sales/Payables		
11.9	7.7	6.7	10.8				9.5	8.8
67.5	13.0	13.2	14.9			Sales/Working Capital	24.7	21.3
-35.2	212.2	107.3	-723.1				-49.7	-42.2
39.4	61.8	41.8	6.4				30.0	36.2
(29) 13.2	(46) 16.4	(40) 12.9	2.7			EBIT/Interest	(133) 9.4	(140) 10.5
2.3	1.5	1.9	.3				3.0	2.2
							4.6	5.4
						Net Profit + Depr., Dep., Amort./Cur. Mat. L/T/D	(14) 3.1	(14) 3.7
							1.8	2.0
.0	.3	.2	.1				.1	.2
1.3	.7	.6	.6			Fixed/Worth	.7	.9
-.6	-17.4	1.4	3.1				6.4	NM
.7	.7	.5	1.5				.7	.9
6.3	1.8	1.4	3.6			Debt/Worth	2.0	1.8
-2.4	-19.2	5.3	15.2				29.1	-31.1
287.8	128.0	66.8	31.1				106.0	113.4
(25) 100.0	(40) 76.9	(39) 34.1	(14) 15.9			% Profit Before Taxes/Tangible Net Worth	(135) 48.5	(127) 50.7
24.7	2.8	10.5	-47.5				15.4	18.2
83.9	48.0	30.2	7.6				42.1	41.4
34.7	30.2	10.7	5.4			% Profit Before Taxes/Total Assets	15.7	17.1
1.8	1.5	2.5	-6.1				4.2	3.6
511.5	162.9	39.5	78.9				93.8	62.8
47.6	22.8	18.6	45.5			Sales/Net Fixed Assets	23.4	17.2
17.5	9.6	5.3	5.8				6.3	7.4
10.3	5.7	3.8	2.4				5.9	5.5
5.7	3.6	2.5	1.6			Sales/Total Assets	3.3	3.2
3.4	2.5	1.8	1.4				1.9	1.9
.5	.4	1.1	.4				.6	1.0
(12) .8	(21) 1.5	(25) 2.4	(11) 2.5			% Depr., Dep., Amort./Sales	(101) 1.9	(90) 2.2
2.4	2.5	4.0	6.8				4.8	6.0
6.1	3.0	1.3					2.7	2.9
(19) 7.7	(20) 5.6	(11) 2.7				% Officers', Directors' Owners' Comp/Sales	(84) 7.1	(77) 5.5
17.7	8.3	3.9					10.7	9.5
66434M	214956M	576383M	576015M	242278M	337493M	Net Sales ($)	1391141M	3426315M
10117M	54587M	207771M	295208M	80695M	305491M	Total Assets ($)	603240M	1171046M

© RMA 2019   M = $ thousand   MM = $ million

See Pages viii through xx for Explanation of Ratios and Data

Comparative Historical Data   **Current Data Sorted by Sales**

			Type of Statement						
			Unqualified						6
4	7	6	Reviewed				2	7	3
12	11	12	Compiled	2	2	2	1	1	
9	8	8	Tax Returns	9	13	12	7	3	1
66	64	45	Other	11	27	15	14	14	7
68	77	88				10 (4/1-9/30/18)	149 (10/1/18-3/31/19)		
4/1/16-3/31/17	4/1/17-3/31/18	4/1/18-3/31/19							
ALL	ALL	ALL		0-1MM	1-3MM	3-5MM	5-10MM	10-25MM	25MM & OVER
159	167	159	NUMBER OF STATEMENTS	22	42	29	24	25	17
%	%	%	ASSETS	%	%	%	%	%	%
15.8	17.6	18.0	Cash & Equivalents	23.4	20.8	18.9	20.2	13.1	6.5
24.7	29.7	28.9	Trade Receivables (net)	12.8	30.4	23.3	30.9	39.1	37.8
5.1	5.7	5.3	Inventory	1.1	3.6	3.6	6.4	4.8	17.2
3.3	2.9	4.8	All Other Current	6.0	5.2	6.4	3.1	4.4	2.3
49.0	55.9	57.0	Total Current	43.3	60.0	52.2	60.6	61.4	63.8
31.3	26.6	23.1	Fixed Assets (net)	27.3	25.9	25.6	20.7	18.2	17.0
8.7	8.9	10.4	Intangibles (net)	19.2	8.5	8.7	4.8	10.7	14.2
11.0	8.5	9.5	All Other Non-Current	10.3	5.6	13.5	13.9	9.7	5.0
100.0	100.0	100.0	Total	100.0	100.0	100.0	100.0	100.0	100.0
			LIABILITIES						
13.1	12.8	13.5	Notes Payable-Short Term	22.4	12.4	9.9	13.1	10.2	16.0
4.7	3.2	4.7	Cur. Mat.-L.T.D.	10.1	2.2	2.7	6.4	4.2	5.4
10.3	9.4	8.7	Trade Payables	7.6	4.9	7.0	8.7	12.2	16.9
.1	.1	.2	Income Taxes Payable	.1	.5	.0	.1	.0	.0
11.2	13.3	15.0	All Other Current	14.8	14.2	19.8	15.4	14.3	9.9
39.4	38.7	42.0	Total Current	55.0	34.2	39.4	43.7	40.8	48.2
28.8	21.9	24.4	Long-Term Debt	41.4	22.1	33.3	22.9	12.3	13.3
.3	.2	.2	Deferred Taxes	.0	.0	.1	.5	.2	.8
6.7	6.9	4.9	All Other Non-Current	7.0	6.3	6.2	2.2	3.2	2.7
24.7	32.3	28.4	Net Worth	-3.4	37.4	21.0	30.6	43.5	35.0
100.0	100.0	100.0	Total Liabilities & Net Worth	100.0	100.0	100.0	100.0	100.0	100.0
			INCOME DATA						
100.0	100.0	100.0	Net Sales	100.0	100.0	100.0	100.0	100.0	100.0
			Gross Profit						
91.2	91.9	91.5	Operating Expenses	85.4	91.7	89.3	92.7	94.1	97.3
8.8	8.1	8.5	Operating Profit	14.6	8.3	10.7	7.3	5.9	2.7
1.4	.5	.7	All Other Expenses (net)	1.3	.5	.1	.8	.3	2.0
7.3	7.7	7.8	Profit Before Taxes	13.3	7.8	10.7	6.5	5.5	.7
			RATIOS						
2.5	3.0	3.1		3.9	6.0	4.8	3.2	2.5	1.8
1.3	1.5	1.4	Current	1.1	2.2	1.8	1.4	1.4	1.2
.7	.8	.9		.4	1.1	.8	.9	1.1	.9
2.1	2.8	2.7		3.9	5.3	3.3	2.7	2.0	1.5
1.2	1.2	1.2	Quick	1.0	2.1	.9	1.3	1.2	1.0
.4	.6	.6		.2	.9	.5	.5	.9	.4
0 UND	3 140.3	3 145.8		0 UND	12 30.4	0 999.8	2 195.2	19 18.8	26 13.9
28 13.1	33 11.1	31 11.7	Sales/Receivables	0 UND	32 11.4	17 21.0	25 14.5	59 6.2	42 8.6
54 6.8	54 6.7	59 6.2		21 17.8	64 5.7	35 10.3	64 5.7	81 4.5	66 5.5
			Cost of Sales/Inventory						
			Cost of Sales/Payables						
8.5	8.4	8.4		10.4	7.1	8.6	6.7	7.5	12.4
31.1	20.1	17.5	Sales/Working Capital	NM	12.5	27.8	25.3	13.2	31.3
-30.6	-40.3	-108.7		-10.8	70.6	-72.3	-207.1	136.7	-76.2
30.3	21.3	39.9		18.5	41.6	78.7	53.1	41.8	11.0
(130) 7.9	(133) 7.8	(132) 10.7	EBIT/Interest	(13) 9.9	(33) 10.4	(22) 15.2	28.7	(24) 9.0	(16) 3.7
2.0	2.6	1.7		3.0	.7	1.6	6.2	1.5	.6
2.7	4.2	5.7							
(13) 1.5	(11) 2.6	(11) 2.9	Net Profit + Depr., Dep., Amort./Cur. Mat. L/T/D						
1.1	1.4	1.4							
.3	.2	.1		.0	.1	.1	.2	.2	.2
1.0	.9	.7	Fixed/Worth	1.3	.8	.9	.5	.5	.6
999.8	5.0	5.9		-.4	-9.8	-2.7	2.9	1.2	2.8
.9	.8	.7		.8	.6	.4	1.0	.7	1.4
2.5	2.0	2.3	Debt/Worth	NM	1.6	1.9	2.3	1.4	3.2
-27.2	13.6	94.5		-1.7	-14.4	-11.7	13.2	5.2	7.5
88.8	108.9	102.3		127.8	103.1	191.9	119.9	82.4	37.8
(116) 36.6	(130) 52.3	(120) 47.6	% Profit Before Taxes/Tangible Net Worth	(11) 19.9	(29) 63.5	(21) 98.8	(21) 70.4	(23) 34.1	(15) 23.0
11.9	16.3	7.8		-3.0	7.5	3.7	12.3	5.8	2.9
29.3	40.7	45.3		65.6	55.1	66.5	43.8	36.3	9.6
11.0	14.2	17.0	% Profit Before Taxes/Total Assets	18.6	20.7	42.9	31.5	12.7	7.4
2.4	4.6	1.7		-2.9	1.0	.8	3.8	1.7	-1.4
52.2	71.8	97.2		UND	181.0	212.2	90.0	67.7	65.4
15.6	18.5	23.6	Sales/Net Fixed Assets	37.2	19.4	23.6	27.1	22.8	27.2
6.2	7.4	9.1		14.4	7.7	9.0	18.3	9.9	7.2
5.0	5.2	5.4		8.6	5.3	7.4	7.7	3.9	4.6
2.9	3.2	3.3	Sales/Total Assets	3.4	3.5	4.5	3.8	2.6	2.4
1.7	2.0	2.1		1.7	2.0	2.6	2.4	1.8	1.6
.8	.6	.5			.5		.4	1.0	.4
(106) 1.8	(91) 1.6	(70) 1.9	% Depr., Dep., Amort./Sales	(13) .9		(13) 1.5	(15) 2.4	(12) 1.2	
5.0	4.8	3.4		3.1		3.2	4.2	4.5	
3.1	2.9	2.7			5.9	2.9			
(79) 5.7	(75) 5.5	(52) 6.3	% Officers', Directors' Owners' Comp/Sales	(14) 7.9	(13) 3.9				
9.1	10.5	10.3		13.3	6.8				
2321991M	1545555M	2013559M	Net Sales ($)	13367M	78327M	110366M	174819M	395666M	1241014M
891687M	846864M	953869M	Total Assets ($)	8212M	38621M	32456M	60309M	169289M	644982M

© RMA 2019

M = $ thousand   MM = $ million
See Pages viii through xx for Explanation of Ratios and Data

ADMIN & WASTE MANAGEMENT SERVICES—Packaging and Labeling Services NAICS 561910

Current Data Sorted by Assets							Comparative Historical Data	

			2	8	2	2	Type of Statement		
			10	10	1		Unqualified	12	12
		2	7				Reviewed	23	20
8	7	13	1				Compiled	16	10
5	14	25	17	5	2		Tax Returns	23	33
							Other	62	68
	13 (4/1-9/30/18)		128 (10/1/18-3/31/19)					4/1/14-3/31/15	4/1/15-3/31/16
0-500M	500M-2MM	2-10MM	10-50MM	50-100MM	100-250MM			ALL	ALL
13	23	57	36	8	4		NUMBER OF STATEMENTS	136	143
%	%	%	%	%	%		ASSETS	%	%
25.7	8.2	8.6	6.9				Cash & Equivalents	9.2	13.2
30.9	35.6	33.8	28.3				Trade Receivables (net)	27.5	27.0
3.5	13.9	18.9	19.6				Inventory	19.1	17.0
1.9	2.6	3.8	4.0				All Other Current	1.7	1.3
62.0	60.2	65.0	58.9				Total Current	57.5	58.5
27.5	29.3	24.9	30.4				Fixed Assets (net)	28.7	29.6
4.5	5.5	6.4	7.6				Intangibles (net)	7.7	5.7
6.1	5.0	3.6	3.1				All Other Non-Current	6.2	6.1
100.0	100.0	100.0	100.0				Total	100.0	100.0
							LIABILITIES		
13.5	11.0	11.1	12.8				Notes Payable-Short Term	12.0	12.3
6.7	1.8	3.3	3.7				Cur. Mat.-L.T.D.	3.6	3.6
7.0	19.1	20.4	20.4				Trade Payables	18.5	17.8
.2	.2	.0	.0				Income Taxes Payable	.2	.2
53.5	11.2	9.5	6.8				All Other Current	10.5	8.6
80.8	43.2	44.3	43.7				Total Current	44.9	42.6
31.2	18.7	12.2	14.8				Long-Term Debt	19.1	17.1
.0	.0	.3	.1				Deferred Taxes	.4	.1
5.6	7.5	6.9	5.4				All Other Non-Current	5.5	5.3
-17.4	30.5	36.3	36.2				Net Worth	30.2	34.9
100.0	100.0	100.0	100.0				Total Liabilities & Net Worth	100.0	100.0
							INCOME DATA		
100.0	100.0	100.0	100.0				Net Sales	100.0	100.0
							Gross Profit		
91.3	90.2	92.8	94.1				Operating Expenses	93.7	93.2
8.7	9.8	7.2	5.9				Operating Profit	6.3	6.8
3.5	2.6	1.4	1.2				All Other Expenses (net)	1.9	1.5
5.2	7.2	5.8	4.7				Profit Before Taxes	4.4	5.3
							RATIOS		
3.7	2.2	2.4	1.8					2.2	2.2
1.9	1.3	1.5	1.2				Current	1.3	1.4
.9	.9	1.0	.9					1.0	1.0
3.7	1.6	1.4	1.2					1.6	1.8
1.9	.9	.8	.6				Quick	.8	.9
.7	.5	.6	.6					.5	.5
0 UND	18 20.6	25 14.5	34 10.6					25 14.6	20 18.1
33 11.2	34 10.7	39 9.3	45 8.1				Sales/Receivables	40 9.2	36 10.0
54 6.7	47 7.7	52 7.0	59 6.2					49 7.4	51 7.2
							Cost of Sales/Inventory		
							Cost of Sales/Payables		
9.6	9.3	8.4	8.0					7.8	8.5
35.0	22.0	14.4	24.9				Sales/Working Capital	17.6	21.7
-76.3	-54.3	358.8	NM					-89.6	-225.0
	38.4	19.0	19.8					15.1	15.8
	(19) 7.8	(48) 9.4	(34) 4.8				EBIT/Interest	(118) 5.2	(115) 4.3
	2.8	3.1	1.8					1.2	1.1
								6.5	12.7
							Net Profit + Depr., Dep., Amort./Cur. Mat. L/T/D	(14) 2.6	(17) 2.7
								1.6	1.4
.4	.2	.1	.4					.2	.2
3.5	.7	.6	1.1				Fixed/Worth	.9	.7
-1.8	2.8	1.9	4.6					4.6	3.1
.5	.9	1.1	.9					.9	.8
8.8	2.7	1.8	2.2				Debt/Worth	2.7	2.1
-16.1	5.1	8.6	13.5					15.0	8.4
	125.1	88.6	45.4					56.8	60.6
	(19) 70.9	(50) 42.4	(30) 25.5				% Profit Before Taxes/Tangible Net Worth	(109) 26.4	(124) 27.7
	21.7	11.7	9.5					6.7	9.5
50.2	38.7	23.9	13.2					15.2	20.5
22.0	24.3	8.9	7.5				% Profit Before Taxes/Total Assets	6.5	9.1
4.4	2.8	3.6	2.0					1.4	2.0
529.1	53.1	70.4	22.3					57.7	57.9
31.2	26.3	14.3	7.5				Sales/Net Fixed Assets	12.4	14.9
4.6	4.9	6.8	4.5					4.6	4.9
9.5	4.9	3.8	2.8					3.6	4.4
3.5	3.3	2.7	2.0				Sales/Total Assets	2.5	2.9
2.5	1.7	2.1	1.6					1.7	1.7
	.8	.7	1.5					.6	.6
	(17) 2.7	(44) 1.8	(30) 2.9				% Depr., Dep., Amort./Sales	(110) 2.4	(105) 2.2
	13.2	3.8	4.0					4.5	4.3
		1.0						1.5	2.0
	(21) 2.2						% Officers', Directors' Owners' Comp/Sales	(50) 3.8	(51) 3.2
		4.1						5.7	6.5
17221M	114014M	951741M	1820636M	1563148M	1039603M		Net Sales ($)	4747823M	5278014M
3418M	28936M	310203M	849786M	570519M	526051M		Total Assets ($)	2442633M	2254428M

M = $ thousand   MM = $ million
See Pages viii through xx for Explanation of Ratios and Data

Comparative Historical Data — Current Data Sorted by Sales

	4/1/16-3/31/17 ALL	4/1/17-3/31/18 ALL	4/1/18-3/31/19 ALL	0-1MM	1-3MM	3-5MM	5-10MM	10-25MM	25MM & OVER
					13 (4/1-9/30/18)		128 (10/1/18-3/31/19)		
Type of Statement									
Unqualified	13	13	14				1	2	11
Reviewed	16	13	21	1			3	3	14
Compiled	12	7	9		1	1	3	4	
Tax Returns	36	31	29	5	7	2	7	6	2
Other	55	57	68	6	6	3	9	19	25
NUMBER OF STATEMENTS	132	121	141	12	14	6	23	34	52
	%	%	%	%	%	%	%	%	%
ASSETS									
Cash & Equivalents	13.4	10.3	9.2	11.5	16.4		11.5	8.1	5.3
Trade Receivables (net)	27.2	27.5	31.5	16.4	27.1		34.3	34.1	33.4
Inventory	16.8	17.3	16.7	.4	10.3		12.5	23.1	19.0
All Other Current	1.9	2.2	3.9	.9	4.0		6.3	2.3	4.9
Total Current	59.3	57.2	61.3	29.3	57.8		64.6	67.6	62.6
Fixed Assets (net)	27.7	26.2	27.8	65.4	25.1		25.0	24.3	24.5
Intangibles (net)	7.5	11.6	7.2	2.2	10.9		6.6	5.2	9.7
All Other Non-Current	5.5	5.1	3.7	3.1	6.2		3.8	3.0	3.3
Total	100.0	100.0	100.0	100.0	100.0		100.0	100.0	100.0
LIABILITIES									
Notes Payable-Short Term	9.7	8.6	11.2	9.2	19.3		10.8	9.9	10.6
Cur. Mat.-L.T.D.	8.2	3.8	3.5	3.7	4.9		2.8	3.1	3.5
Trade Payables	18.2	16.9	18.8	1.4	8.3		14.8	22.0	24.8
Income Taxes Payable	.2	.2	.1	.0	.4		.0	.0	.0
All Other Current	8.6	10.6	13.2	48.8	14.0		16.0	6.8	9.2
Total Current	45.0	40.2	46.8	63.1	46.9		44.4	41.8	48.1
Long-Term Debt	27.0	16.3	16.5	41.2	18.0		14.8	10.2	13.6
Deferred Taxes	.4	.1	.2	.0	.0		.0	.4	.2
All Other Non-Current	3.4	3.5	5.9	10.2	1.3		11.9	6.5	2.8
Net Worth	24.3	39.9	30.6	-14.5	33.8		28.9	41.1	35.3
Total Liabilities & Net Worth	100.0	100.0	100.0	100.0	100.0		100.0	100.0	100.0
INCOME DATA									
Net Sales	100.0	100.0	100.0	100.0	100.0		100.0	100.0	100.0
Gross Profit									
Operating Expenses	92.8	92.5	92.9	76.8	88.1		94.7	94.9	95.3
Operating Profit	7.2	7.5	7.1	23.2	11.9		5.3	5.1	4.7
All Other Expenses (net)	1.7	.6	1.7	9.8	4.7		1.0	.1	.7
Profit Before Taxes	5.5	6.8	5.4	13.5	7.3		4.3	4.9	4.1
RATIOS									
Current	2.5	2.6	2.2	6.6	2.1		2.2	3.0	1.7
	1.5	1.3	1.3	1.0	1.2		1.3	1.5	1.2
	1.1	1.1	1.0	.1	.9		.8	1.1	1.0
Quick	2.0	1.9	1.5	6.5	2.1		1.6	1.6	1.1
	1.0	.8	.8	.8	.8		.9	.9	.7
	.5	.6	.6	.1	.6		.5	.7	.5
Sales/Receivables	19 19.6	27 13.7	28 13.1	0 UND	0 UND		31 11.6	30 12.0	35 10.4
	35 10.4	39 9.3	40 9.1	0 UND	34 10.6		46 8.0	39 9.4	46 8.0
	47 7.7	55 6.6	54 6.7	30 12.1	55 6.6		57 6.4	53 6.9	56 6.5
Cost of Sales/Inventory									
Cost of Sales/Payables									
Sales/Working Capital	7.2	6.9	8.5	6.3	8.4		8.4	9.2	8.5
	15.0	16.4	19.6	UND	38.3		12.5	13.9	22.2
	84.4	75.2	513.8	-1.6	-79.1		-24.2	58.0	216.2
EBIT/Interest	21.6	22.4	19.3		22.2		18.2	30.2	20.2
	(106) 5.7	(99) 9.2	(122) 6.2		(11) 7.8		(19) 5.9	(29) 9.6	(49) 5.1
	1.8	3.2	1.9		3.4		1.9	2.7	1.9
Net Profit + Depr., Dep., Amort./Cur. Mat. L/T/D	4.6	10.9	6.7						8.7
	(26) 2.6	(21) 5.2	(17) 3.0					(11) 2.8	2.8
	1.1	2.1	1.7						1.3
Fixed/Worth	.2	.3	.2	1.8	.6		.1	.2	.4
	.8	.9	.9	2.8	1.8		.3	.7	.9
	4.0	2.6	3.5	-11.3	-10.9		4.7	1.3	3.0
Debt/Worth	.7	.8	1.0	.9	1.4		1.1	.8	1.0
	1.9	1.9	2.3	2.7	3.2		2.7	1.6	2.3
	11.3	7.3	8.7	-19.9	-156.5		10.3	5.6	7.9
% Profit Before Taxes/Tangible Net Worth	67.2	69.3	84.6		95.1		123.8	86.0	50.5
	(106) 28.5	(101) 26.4	(117) 33.7		(10) 41.0		(20) 65.5	(30) 33.0	(45) 28.2
	6.6	13.8	9.9		1.9		10.8	16.5	9.2
% Profit Before Taxes/Total Assets	26.3	25.5	24.8	19.6	41.4		28.6	29.6	17.3
	9.3	9.6	8.2	6.9	16.1		11.6	11.8	7.0
	1.8	4.3	2.6	1.5	1.5		1.6	4.6	1.8
Sales/Net Fixed Assets	67.8	46.9	51.3	5.2	46.6		439.2	52.5	57.1
	12.5	14.1	12.8	1.4	20.0		26.9	12.7	11.9
	4.5	4.4	5.3	.2	5.8		6.5	6.9	4.8
Sales/Total Assets	4.0	3.5	3.8	2.5	4.5		3.4	4.6	3.2
	2.7	2.4	2.7	1.0	3.2		2.7	3.1	2.4
	1.7	1.7	1.7	.2	1.7		2.1	2.0	1.6
% Depr., Dep., Amort./Sales	1.2	.7	1.2				1.0	.7	1.3
	(88) 2.4	(90) 2.3	(103) 2.4				(15) 1.7	(27) 1.8	(42) 2.4
	4.8	4.3	4.2				3.6	3.9	4.1
% Officers', Directors' Owners' Comp/Sales	1.9	1.4	1.1					.8	
	(44) 3.6	(42) 3.3	(42) 2.6					(13) 2.0	
	7.1	5.2	5.0					3.4	
Net Sales ($)	4859417M	4598722M	5506363M	6781M	24942M	23089M	165738M	596402M	4689411M
Total Assets ($)	2548532M	2450172M	2288913M	16747M	16252M	14430M	88959M	220124M	1932401M

M = $ thousand   MM = $ million
See Pages viii through xx for Explanation of Ratios and Data

Current Data Sorted by Assets | Comparative Historical Data

		1	3	3		1	Type of Statement		
		1		4			Unqualified	6	8
		1	5				Reviewed	7	5
3	6	11	3	1			Compiled	4	8
6	11		18	6	4	3	Tax Returns	14	11
	11 (4/1-9/30/18)			68 (10/1/18-3/31/19)			Other	26	35
								4/1/14-3/31/15	4/1/15-3/31/16
0-500M	500M-2MM	2-10MM	10-50MM	50-100MM	100-250MM			ALL	ALL
9	18	30	14	4	4	**NUMBER OF STATEMENTS**	57	67

0-500M	500M-2MM	2-10MM	10-50MM	50-100MM	100-250MM		4/1/14-3/31/15 ALL	4/1/15-3/31/16 ALL
%	%	%	%	%	%	**ASSETS**	%	%
	15.7	21.0	27.0			Cash & Equivalents	20.8	22.2
	29.0	38.0	33.8			Trade Receivables (net)	29.1	29.2
	.7	4.0	2.8			Inventory	5.3	2.6
	5.5	4.2	11.6			All Other Current	7.4	5.4
	50.9	67.2	75.2			Total Current	62.6	59.4
	27.0	18.9	15.3			Fixed Assets (net)	17.1	22.7
	10.8	7.7	4.2			Intangibles (net)	9.5	6.5
	11.3	6.2	5.2			All Other Non-Current	10.8	11.4
	100.0	100.0	100.0			Total	100.0	100.0
						LIABILITIES		
	11.5	9.2	6.0			Notes Payable-Short Term	9.7	9.3
	4.7	1.6	1.6			Cur. Mat.-L.T.D.	2.5	2.0
	14.5	10.0	12.4			Trade Payables	14.6	14.2
	.0	.4	.0			Income Taxes Payable	.1	.1
	22.3	25.6	47.9			All Other Current	26.3	26.5
	52.9	46.8	68.1			Total Current	53.2	52.1
	33.1	11.2	8.7			Long-Term Debt	10.8	20.1
	.0	.1	.2			Deferred Taxes	.5	.3
	3.0	12.1	2.4			All Other Non-Current	19.0	3.7
	11.0	29.9	20.6			Net Worth	16.5	23.9
	100.0	100.0	100.0			Total Liabilties & Net Worth	100.0	100.0
						INCOME DATA		
	100.0	100.0	100.0			Net Sales	100.0	100.0
						Gross Profit		
	88.0	94.0	93.6			Operating Expenses	94.1	91.1
	12.0	6.0	6.4			Operating Profit	5.9	8.9
	1.4	1.9	.5			All Other Expenses (net)	.6	3.1
	10.6	4.1	5.9			Profit Before Taxes	5.3	5.8
						RATIOS		
	2.3	2.4	1.4				1.9	1.7
	1.1	1.4	1.1			Current	1.1	1.1
	.6	.8	.9				.7	.8
	2.1	2.2	1.1				1.4	1.5
	1.1	1.1	.9			Quick	.9	.9
	.6	.8	.8				.6	.6
	0 UND	16 23.4	26 13.8				12 31.5	9 41.5
	15 24.3	38 9.7	43 8.4			Sales/Receivables	22 16.7	25 14.4
	41 9.0	69 5.3	70 5.2				46 7.9	49 7.5
						Cost of Sales/Inventory		
						Cost of Sales/Payables		
	9.4	6.2	13.9				10.7	11.8
	529.8	20.8	22.5			Sales/Working Capital	83.1	64.4
	-22.8	-25.6	-31.9				-21.8	-34.2
	40.6	27.7	182.5				23.0	45.6
	(14) 4.2	(22) 8.5	(10) 5.0			EBIT/Interest	(41) 9.1	(48) 9.7
	-6.3	1.7	-7.0				3.3	2.5
						Net Profit + Depr., Dep., Amort./Cur. Mat. L/T/D		
	.3	.2	.1				.3	.2
	1.1	.4	.5			Fixed/Worth	1.2	.7
	-1.7	4.1	2.6				-.6	6.8
	.6	1.0	2.5				1.3	.9
	3.5	2.7	4.2			Debt/Worth	6.3	2.8
	-8.0	NM	8.0				-6.4	13.4
	128.7	140.4	57.2			% Profit Before Taxes/Tangible	88.1	80.9
	(11) 43.3	(23) 41.1	(12) 17.9			Net Worth	(35) 46.4	(53) 36.9
	4.3	17.7	-16.6				14.3	8.2
	39.2	33.1	12.4			% Profit Before Taxes/Total	24.7	21.8
	10.4	8.6	7.1			Assets	12.3	9.9
	-1.7	3.2	-1.1				5.2	2.7
	102.5	78.5	186.2				121.0	107.4
	31.9	40.2	34.1			Sales/Net Fixed Assets	37.0	31.5
	10.0	10.8	8.6				14.2	7.8
	7.5	5.0	3.5				5.1	5.3
	4.3	2.8	2.9			Sales/Total Assets	3.1	3.3
	2.2	1.9	1.7				1.7	1.6
		.6	.3				.4	.6
		(23) 1.1	(12) .8			% Depr., Dep., Amort./Sales	(34) .7	(42) 1.8
		3.7	2.5				2.2	3.1
		1.6					3.3	2.6
		(10) 3.9				% Officers', Directors' Owners' Comp/Sales	(18) 4.5	(21) 4.6
		5.4					10.1	9.2
11400M	92619M	480923M	760819M	547475M	597761M	Net Sales ($)	1564545M	1748397M
2830M	20314M	149574M	291398M	243695M	539378M	Total Assets ($)	851111M	965357M

M = $ thousand   MM = $ million
See Pages viii through xx for Explanation of Ratios and Data

Comparative Historical Data | Current Data Sorted by Sales

Type of Statement	4/1/16-3/31/17 ALL	4/1/17-3/31/18 ALL	4/1/18-3/31/19 ALL	0-1MM	1-3MM	3-5MM	5-10MM	10-25MM	25MM & OVER
Unqualified	4	3	8		1		1	3	3
Reviewed	9	7	5					1	4
Compiled	3	1	5			1		2	2
Tax Returns	11	17	13					2	2
Other	39	44	48	3	9	2	9	7	18
					11 (4/1-9/30/18)		68 (10/1/18-3/31/19)		
NUMBER OF STATEMENTS	66	72	79	6	13	4	14	15	27
ASSETS	%	%	%	%	%	%	%	%	%
Cash & Equivalents	19.1	20.5	21.7		24.6		23.5	23.9	16.9
Trade Receivables (net)	30.1	28.4	30.2		10.8		34.7	38.7	36.5
Inventory	4.5	2.6	3.6		7.3		.0	2.9	4.8
All Other Current	6.1	7.3	5.2		3.4		7.8	3.5	7.7
Total Current	60.0	58.8	60.6		46.1		65.9	69.0	65.8
Fixed Assets (net)	23.7	23.7	20.9		38.2		15.1	14.2	11.7
Intangibles (net)	5.6	8.6	9.2		10.6		5.2	7.4	11.0
All Other Non-Current	10.8	8.9	9.2		5.0		13.8	9.3	11.5
Total	100.0	100.0	100.0		100.0		100.0	100.0	100.0
LIABILITIES									
Notes Payable-Short Term	11.7	13.2	7.9		6.6		10.0	6.3	8.8
Cur. Mat.-L.T.D.	2.3	4.4	2.2		.6		4.9	2.2	1.6
Trade Payables	13.6	18.1	10.1		2.5		16.8	10.7	12.2
Income Taxes Payable	.1	.0	.2		.2		.0	.5	.1
All Other Current	29.3	32.5	30.7		12.2		27.6	27.7	44.9
Total Current	57.0	68.2	51.1		22.2		59.2	47.4	67.5
Long-Term Debt	24.3	23.3	21.6		45.1		26.0	9.6	9.4
Deferred Taxes	.2	.1	.2		.0		.0	.3	.3
All Other Non-Current	6.4	11.4	8.7		16.0		20.4	6.4	3.3
Net Worth	12.1	-3.0	18.4		16.7		-5.6	36.4	19.5
Total Liabilties & Net Worth	100.0	100.0	100.0		100.0		100.0	100.0	100.0
INCOME DATA									
Net Sales	100.0	100.0	100.0		100.0		100.0	100.0	100.0
Gross Profit									
Operating Expenses	89.8	88.2	91.7		95.6		94.3	91.7	94.3
Operating Profit	10.2	11.8	8.3		4.4		5.7	8.3	5.7
All Other Expenses (net)	2.8	3.1	1.3		.5		.0	.8	.7
Profit Before Taxes	7.3	8.6	7.0		3.8		5.7	7.5	4.9
RATIOS									
Current	1.8	1.7	2.2		5.8		3.8	2.2	1.3
	1.1	1.0	1.2		2.5		1.1	1.4	1.1
	.6	.5	.8		.8		.7	1.0	.7
Quick	1.4	1.4	2.0		3.1		3.0	2.0	1.1
	.9	.9	.9		2.0		.9	1.4	.8
	.5	.4	.7		.6		.7	1.0	.5
Sales/Receivables	9 40.8	9 39.1	10 38.1	0 UND		0 UND	18 20.0	23 16.1	
	28 13.1	24 15.0	33 10.9	13 27.7		33 10.9	35 10.4	38 9.5	
	55 6.6	51 7.1	55 6.6	43 8.4		56 6.5	62 5.9	68 5.4	
Cost of Sales/Inventory									
Cost of Sales/Payables									
Sales/Working Capital	10.3	11.1	8.6		5.1		8.4	6.4	18.1
	56.5	-344.6	27.6		7.3		442.5	21.7	62.5
	24.6	-11.9	-23.6		-66.3		-21.1	-300.1	-12.1
EBIT/Interest	37.7	29.7	32.7				22.9	48.0	40.1
	(50) 7.1	(49) 7.3	(58) 6.2				(10) 3.8	(13) 12.0	(20) 5.1
	3.0	1.5	.8				-5.2	3.6	1.3
Net Profit + Depr., Dep., Amort./Cur. Mat. L/T/D			14.1						
		(14) 3.3							
			.4						
Fixed/Worth	.3	.2	.2		.1		.2	.2	.3
	1.0	1.2	.9		.3		.7	.4	2.0
	-3.8	-.8	-4.7		NM		-1.3	2.9	-1.0
Debt/Worth	1.3	1.9	1.1		.4		2.1	1.0	2.6
	4.9	5.5	4.1		.6		6.4	2.3	5.4
	-33.2	-5.7	-12.2		-4.9		-4.0	14.4	-9.8
% Profit Before Taxes/Tangible Net Worth	111.3	133.0	85.3					105.5	109.4
	(48) 38.8	(46) 58.1	(54) 30.8				(12) 41.2	(17) 25.3	
	12.8	20.6	8.7					18.3	3.7
% Profit Before Taxes/Total Assets	28.2	35.8	31.2		39.0		64.6	43.0	21.4
	9.0	13.2	8.8		14.5		10.2	11.0	8.7
	2.5	1.7	2.1		.1		.0	5.2	2.5
Sales/Net Fixed Assets	94.0	169.7	77.7		47.8		126.7	70.6	69.1
	32.2	49.8	34.6		10.2		50.3	40.8	42.4
	6.8	9.8	10.2		5.2		20.5	11.7	15.2
Sales/Total Assets	4.8	5.3	4.8		5.2		7.4	4.8	4.5
	2.9	3.2	3.2		3.2		3.8	2.8	3.3
	1.3	1.5	1.7		1.2		2.2	1.6	1.5
% Depr., Dep., Amort./Sales	.5	.5	.5					.6	.4
	(39) 1.1	(47) 1.2	(50) 1.3				(10) 1.1	(20) 1.0	
	3.0	4.1	4.6					2.4	2.6
% Officers', Directors' Owners' Comp/Sales	1.6	1.5	3.6						
	(25) 3.0	(24) 3.5	(24) 5.1						
	7.7	7.1	8.3						
Net Sales ($)	1646396M	2009203M	2490997M	2771M	25241M	16793M	99916M	236202M	2110074M
Total Assets ($)	791220M	1038858M	1247189M	7603M	19328M	4672M	30344M	93349M	1091893M

© RMA 2019

M = $ thousand   MM = $ million
See Pages viii through xx for Explanation of Ratios and Data

Current Data Sorted by Assets   Comparative Historical Data

Type of Statement

Type of Statement	4/1/14-3/31/15 ALL	4/1/15-3/31/16 ALL
Unqualified	33	25
Reviewed	26	24
Compiled	28	18
Tax Returns	54	55
Other	123	123

Current Data — Type of Statement counts by asset size

Type of Statement	0-500M	500M-2MM	2-10MM	10-50MM	50-100MM	100-250MM
Unqualified		1	9	5	4	8
Reviewed		9	10	5		
Compiled		9	2	1		
Tax Returns	13	14	8		7	3
Other	8	26	44	25		

22 (4/1-9/30/18)   180 (10/1/18-3/31/19)

Main Data

	0-500M	500M-2MM	2-10MM	10-50MM	50-100MM	100-250MM	4/1/14-3/31/15 ALL	4/1/15-3/31/16 ALL
NUMBER OF STATEMENTS	21	50	73	36	11	11	264	245
	%	%	%	%	%	%	%	%
ASSETS								
Cash & Equivalents	23.7	22.8	13.9	14.1	9.4	19.6	17.8	18.9
Trade Receivables (net)	10.7	25.5	24.6	24.2	25.8	24.8	23.3	22.7
Inventory	8.9	6.3	5.3	8.5	9.3	3.8	8.5	6.4
All Other Current	13.3	5.4	5.8	4.5	5.2	14.2	5.5	4.1
Total Current	56.6	60.1	49.5	51.3	49.6	62.4	55.1	52.2
Fixed Assets (net)	30.9	22.9	33.6	34.9	25.7	7.2	26.9	30.2
Intangibles (net)	1.8	6.8	8.0	7.0	21.4	24.5	8.0	8.1
All Other Non-Current	10.7	10.3	8.8	6.8	3.3	5.9	10.0	9.5
Total	100.0	100.0	100.0	100.0	100.0	100.0	100.0	100.0
LIABILITIES								
Notes Payable-Short Term	51.1	8.5	5.6	7.9	6.5	10.5	12.9	9.7
Cur. Mat.-L.T.D.	4.1	3.7	2.6	3.2	3.0	.7	3.2	3.9
Trade Payables	8.6	8.0	9.5	13.2	9.1	15.5	10.1	12.8
Income Taxes Payable	.0	.2	.3	.0	.9	.3	.2	.1
All Other Current	20.8	17.3	11.7	21.2	14.6	17.0	17.9	12.9
Total Current	84.6	37.5	29.6	45.5	34.0	44.0	44.1	39.5
Long-Term Debt	24.7	28.5	26.1	19.2	22.1	12.2	19.2	21.5
Deferred Taxes	.1	.1	.3	.2	.2	.3	.2	.3
All Other Non-Current	2.5	10.3	5.3	6.3	1.6	5.5	7.3	8.6
Net Worth	-11.6	23.5	38.8	28.9	42.0	37.9	29.2	30.1
Total Liabilities & Net Worth	100.0	100.0	100.0	100.0	100.0	100.0	100.0	100.0
INCOME DATA								
Net Sales	100.0	100.0	100.0	100.0	100.0	100.0	100.0	100.0
Gross Profit								
Operating Expenses	84.7	87.9	87.2	92.3	84.8	94.7	89.7	88.0
Operating Profit	15.3	12.1	12.8	7.7	15.2	5.3	10.3	12.0
All Other Expenses (net)	4.5	1.8	3.7	1.1	3.9	1.4	2.5	2.8
Profit Before Taxes	10.8	10.3	9.0	6.6	11.3	3.9	7.8	9.1
RATIOS								
Current	3.0	3.8	3.1	1.8	1.7	2.0	3.0	2.9
	.9	2.1	1.5	1.3	1.4	1.3	1.3	1.4
	.4	.9	.9	.9	1.1	1.0	.9	.9
Quick	3.0	2.6	2.4	1.6	1.3	2.0	2.0	2.5
	.5	1.5	1.2	.9	.9	1.0	1.1 (244)	1.2
	.2	.7	.6	.6	.6	.8	.5	.5
Sales/Receivables	0 UND	1 418.7	5 66.7	20 18.1	41 8.9	51 7.1	1 334.2	0 UND
	0 UND	23 15.9	25 14.4	41 8.9	54 6.7	62 5.9	26 13.9	29 12.6
	0 UND	47 7.8	56 6.5	73 5.0	85 4.3	74 4.9	51 7.1	50 7.3
Cost of Sales/Inventory								
Cost of Sales/Payables								
Sales/Working Capital	11.7	5.2	6.5	6.0	7.8	6.2	6.7	6.5
	-160.0	19.6	14.9	17.6	15.9	15.0	21.6	16.6
	-11.9	-400.4	-56.9	-72.4	41.7	170.8	-78.3	-106.4
EBIT/Interest	26.3	19.5	19.6	42.6	132.5		27.5	27.3
	(13) 4.1	(36) 8.4	(56) 8.4	(27) 6.8	(10) 43.8		(201) 8.9	(183) 7.0
	.7	1.5	1.5	1.5	8.4		2.3	2.1
Net Profit + Depr., Dep., Amort./Cur. Mat. L/T/D							15.0	25.1
							(38) 4.1	(27) 4.5
							1.4	1.6
Fixed/Worth	.3	.1	.1	.3	.2	.1	.1	.1
	2.6	.6	1.0	1.1	.8	.5	.7	.7
	UND	61.2	6.5	6.7	1.5	-.5	4.8	5.4
Debt/Worth	.7	.7	.7	1.0	1.3	.9	.7	.7
	6.0	2.2	2.0	2.5	2.5	10.7	2.3	2.4
	-7.2	NM	13.8	13.4	4.1	-4.2	14.5	12.9
% Profit Before Taxes/Tangible Net Worth	212.0	115.1	75.0	48.5			77.4	69.2
	(14) 120.8	(38) 51.0	(59) 38.4	(28) 24.7			(207) 35.8	(200) 29.0
	35.0	16.9	9.2	12.6			10.8	9.1
% Profit Before Taxes/Total Assets	46.5	40.9	26.1	13.8	26.6	7.5	26.2	28.5
	10.9	25.3	7.3	5.9	16.6	5.5	10.0	7.8
	1.8	4.9	1.1	1.2	3.1	-7.8	2.3	2.1
Sales/Net Fixed Assets	UND	197.7	99.3	31.6	44.0	96.0	88.2	108.7
	30.1	41.3	12.4	8.7	7.2	43.3	18.1	17.1
	4.2	8.7	1.5	3.0	5.7	15.6	4.5	3.4
Sales/Total Assets	10.1	4.6	3.8	3.1	2.1	1.8	3.9	4.3
	3.9	3.1	2.1	1.9	1.9	1.6	2.3	2.1
	2.3	1.7	.8	1.0	1.3	.7	1.1	1.0
% Depr., Dep., Amort./Sales	.6	.3	.7	.7			.6	.5
	(14) 4.2	(25) 1.8	(46) 2.7	(31) 2.9			(172) 2.0	(161) 1.8
	20.7	6.0	6.7	5.3			6.6	6.4
% Officers', Directors' Owners' Comp/Sales		2.0	1.9				2.3	2.4
		(19) 4.6	(18) 3.5				(68) 5.4	(70) 5.2
		10.8	6.9				12.0	9.8
Net Sales ($)	21545M	231008M	898624M	1989513M	1452935M	2356780M	9748585M	8871120M
Total Assets ($)	4776M	55690M	364049M	818329M	860253M	1683104M	3999996M	4203914M

© RMA 2019

M = $ thousand   MM = $ million
See Pages viii through xx for Explanation of Ratios and Data

Comparative Historical Data | | | | Current Data Sorted by Sales

4/1/16-3/31/17 ALL	4/1/17-3/31/18 ALL	4/1/18-3/31/19 ALL	Type of Statement	0-1MM	1-3MM	3-5MM	5-10MM	10-25MM	25MM & OVER
27	32	27	Unqualified	1	2	1		4	19
19	9	15	Reviewed			1	3	3	8
20	19	11	Compiled		3	3	3	1	
45	43	36	Tax Returns	1			1	1	2
102	105	113	Other	15	11	6	1	3	25
				22 (4/1-9/30/18)			180 (10/1/18-3/31/19)		
213	208	202	NUMBER OF STATEMENTS	25	37	24	25	37	54
%	%	%	ASSETS	%	%	%	%	%	%
17.0	21.4	17.2	Cash & Equivalents	9.5	22.5	19.8	18.5	18.4	14.6
22.2	22.0	23.4	Trade Receivables (net)	3.5	16.9	24.6	25.5	27.9	32.4
5.0	5.8	6.7	Inventory	5.8	3.0	4.9	7.4	10.2	7.5
6.7	6.3	6.7	All Other Current	14.4	2.0	5.9	2.0	8.1	7.7
50.8	55.6	53.9	Total Current	33.3	44.5	55.3	53.4	64.6	62.2
26.7	27.6	29.0	Fixed Assets (net)	49.8	38.2	26.4	23.9	20.5	22.5
12.2	8.5	8.5	Intangibles (net)	11.1	5.5	6.9	14.1	6.4	9.0
10.3	8.3	8.5	All Other Non-Current	5.8	11.7	11.4	8.6	8.5	6.4
100.0	100.0	100.0	Total	100.0	100.0	100.0	100.0	100.0	100.0
			LIABILITIES						
11.3	8.3	11.7	Notes Payable-Short Term	15.9	19.0	14.0	7.4	6.3	9.6
4.1	3.8	3.0	Cur. Mat.-L.T.D.	3.2	4.0	4.9	3.1	1.3	2.6
11.2	11.9	10.0	Trade Payables	3.4	7.9	5.0	5.8	13.7	16.0
.1	.0	.2	Income Taxes Payable	.0	.0	.0	.0	.6	.4
15.2	16.3	16.2	All Other Current	7.4	19.2	8.5	12.9	21.8	19.2
41.9	40.4	41.1	Total Current	29.9	50.0	32.4	29.3	43.7	47.9
22.0	24.5	24.3	Long-Term Debt	48.0	38.3	17.2	18.1	17.3	14.8
.4	.1	.2	Deferred Taxes	.0	.0	.1	.9	.0	.3
7.8	8.0	6.2	All Other Non-Current	3.5	6.9	11.3	4.4	10.4	2.8
27.9	27.0	28.1	Net Worth	19.0	4.8	39.1	47.4	28.6	34.3
100.0	100.0	100.0	Total Liabilities & Net Worth	100.0	100.0	100.0	100.0	100.0	100.0
			INCOME DATA						
100.0	100.0	100.0	Net Sales	100.0	100.0	100.0	100.0	100.0	100.0
			Gross Profit						
89.4	88.9	88.3	Operating Expenses	62.7	87.7	94.4	84.7	94.6	95.2
10.6	11.1	11.7	Operating Profit	37.3	12.3	5.6	15.3	5.4	4.8
3.2	2.6	2.8	All Other Expenses (net)	13.3	2.8	.1	1.6	1.1	.7
7.4	8.5	8.9	Profit Before Taxes	24.0	9.5	5.4	13.7	4.3	4.1
			RATIOS						
2.2	3.0	2.6	Current	3.3	3.5	2.7	5.0	3.0	1.7
1.3	1.3	1.4		.9	1.1	2.2	1.9	1.5	1.3
.8	.8	.9		.3	.5	1.3	1.1	1.0	1.1
1.7	2.3	2.3	Quick	2.5	3.5	2.6	3.1	2.2	1.4
1.1	1.0	1.0		.3	1.0	1.6	1.4	1.0	1.0
.5	.5	.6		.1	.4	.7	.8	.6	.6
5 79.3	1 552.2	4 96.7	Sales/Receivables	0 UND	0 UND	1 388.4	6 57.9	15 24.5	25 14.6
29 12.5	27 13.5	27 13.4		0 UND	14 25.8	42 8.6	23 16.0	35 10.5	48 7.6
50 7.3	49 7.4	61 6.0		0 UND	37 9.9	68 5.4	74 4.9	55 6.6	69 5.3
			Cost of Sales/Inventory						
			Cost of Sales/Payables						
8.6	7.1	6.4	Sales/Working Capital	5.9	5.4	5.1	3.6	6.9	8.1
26.4	22.9	19.7		-47.5	308.7	9.0	10.9	11.8	21.0
-23.5	-63.3	-54.5		-4.4	-10.2	62.2	52.2	376.8	122.3
(161) 13.4	(158) 25.1	(150) 25.6	EBIT/Interest	(13) 10.0	(25) 11.4	(17) 25.8	(20) 45.6	(30) 21.8	(45) 41.6
5.2	6.1	7.7		4.1	2.2	9.1	11.1	9.4	8.3
1.1	1.2	1.5		1.7	.4	.6	4.4	1.0	2.2
(22) 9.8	(18) 13.7	(22) 5.2	Net Profit + Depr., Dep., Amort./Cur. Mat. L/T/D					(12) 10.8	
6.0	4.2	2.8						3.8	
3.2	2.7	1.5						1.8	
.1	.1	.2	Fixed/Worth	1.0	.2	.0	.1	.1	.2
.9	.7	.8		5.7	1.7	.7	.5	.8	.8
10.6	8.7	7.6		UND	-11.9	2.8	2.1	NM	2.7
.8	.8	.9	Debt/Worth	1.2	.8	.6	.3	.9	1.0
2.6	2.5	2.3		5.3	2.9	1.2	1.7	2.8	2.0
-44.6	792.4	305.9		UND	-10.5	5.1	9.6	NM	8.3
65.5	83.0	95.0	% Profit Before Taxes/Tangible Net Worth	125.0	69.8	85.8	110.3	194.7	71.4
(158) 25.4	(157) 26.1	(154) 40.2		(19) 37.7	(23) 26.9	(20) 30.7	(20) 50.4	(28) 55.3	(44) 36.9
5.5	4.0	13.3		18.7	4.7	2.2	15.1	17.1	15.4
18.1	25.9	27.0	% Profit Before Taxes/Total Assets	17.2	30.0	37.1	35.4	27.4	25.1
7.0	6.6	10.2		6.0	10.9	23.3	14.6	11.7	8.2
.2	.8	2.1		2.4	-.7	1.3	5.4	-1.5	3.0
93.4	107.0	96.2	Sales/Net Fixed Assets	113.2	101.9	197.8	199.3	111.2	67.0
18.6	22.5	18.5		1.1	10.7	34.1	27.9	26.4	18.5
3.8	5.3	3.9		.1	1.1	6.5	6.4	5.8	7.1
3.4	4.2	3.9	Sales/Total Assets	2.3	3.9	3.4	3.7	4.6	4.3
2.0	2.4	2.2		.3	1.7	2.9	2.2	3.2	2.4
1.1	1.4	1.1		.1	.8	1.5	1.1	1.7	1.6
(134) .9	(133) .7	(129) .7	% Depr., Dep., Amort./Sales	(17) 7.9	(22) 1.4	(12) .3	(13) .5	(22) .7	(43) .6
2.5	1.8	2.4		19.6	2.9	1.5	2.5	1.9	1.9
6.8	5.1	6.4		26.2	12.9	4.4	3.7	4.5	3.9
1.9	2.4	2.2	% Officers', Directors', Owners' Comp/Sales		4.1			1.4	
(51) 4.8	(67) 5.1	(50) 4.6		(14)	8.1			(13) 2.2	
9.1	9.5	10.1			11.9			5.6	
5779741M	6495853M	6950405M	Net Sales ($)	10430M	65763M	99724M	189614M	560813M	6024061M
3256255M	3151666M	3786201M	Total Assets ($)	42177M	82371M	89821M	291376M	252438M	3028018M

M = $ thousand   MM = $ million
See Pages viii through xx for Explanation of Ratios and Data

Current Data Sorted by Assets   Comparative Historical Data

0-500M	500M-2MM	2-10MM	10-50MM	50-100MM	100-250MM		4/1/14-3/31/15 ALL	4/1/15-3/31/16 ALL
	4	5	14	8	6	Type of Statement — Unqualified	22	28
4	4	15	14		1	Reviewed	33	32
	3	22		1	1	Compiled	24	27
15	14	15	1	1	1	Tax Returns	53	56
7	24	34	43	16	15	Other	112	106
	45 (4/1-9/30/18)		237 (10/1/18-3/31/19)					
22	49	91	72	26	22	NUMBER OF STATEMENTS	244	249
%	%	%	%	%	%	ASSETS	%	%
23.8	14.2	10.6	11.0	9.6	3.2	Cash & Equivalents	10.5	12.7
14.0	16.1	15.5	15.2	12.4	10.2	Trade Receivables (net)	16.8	16.7
.1	.0	1.0	1.3	.5	1.4	Inventory	1.3	1.0
2.1	2.3	3.8	2.2	2.6	3.1	All Other Current	2.7	3.1
39.9	32.6	30.9	29.6	25.1	17.8	Total Current	31.4	33.5
46.1	44.0	54.5	54.0	56.0	54.1	Fixed Assets (net)	49.0	47.4
5.5	14.8	8.3	6.6	12.1	23.6	Intangibles (net)	10.9	8.9
8.5	8.5	6.3	9.8	6.9	4.5	All Other Non-Current	8.8	10.2
100.0	100.0	100.0	100.0	100.0	100.0	Total	100.0	100.0
						LIABILITIES		
13.2	13.0	3.1	3.1	5.0	7.7	Notes Payable-Short Term	5.2	5.6
7.1	9.5	7.7	6.0	4.2	2.8	Cur. Mat.-L.T.D.	8.6	7.5
6.8	13.0	10.0	7.2	5.6	8.2	Trade Payables	9.8	10.4
.0	.0	.0	.0	.0	.0	Income Taxes Payable	.1	.2
14.2	7.8	5.4	10.3	8.0	4.7	All Other Current	7.7	7.7
41.3	43.3	26.3	26.6	22.8	23.4	Total Current	31.4	31.4
64.5	54.3	37.2	28.6	40.0	43.1	Long-Term Debt	41.4	39.5
.0	.0	.7	.7	1.0	.8	Deferred Taxes	.6	.9
2.8	8.0	4.5	4.8	4.3	6.0	All Other Non-Current	10.0	6.4
-8.6	-5.6	31.4	39.3	31.8	26.7	Net Worth	16.6	21.8
100.0	100.0	100.0	100.0	100.0	100.0	Total Liabilities & Net Worth	100.0	100.0
						INCOME DATA		
100.0	100.0	100.0	100.0	100.0	100.0	Net Sales	100.0	100.0
						Gross Profit		
87.8	94.5	90.3	89.2	93.3	97.2	Operating Expenses	92.9	91.7
12.2	5.5	9.7	10.8	6.7	2.8	Operating Profit	7.1	8.3
.4	1.3	1.6	1.0	1.6	3.8	All Other Expenses (net)	1.8	1.5
11.9	4.2	8.1	9.8	5.1	-1.1	Profit Before Taxes	5.3	6.8
						RATIOS		
3.8	1.6	2.2	1.8	1.7	1.2	Current	1.8	2.1
1.2	.8	1.1	1.2	1.2	.8		.9	1.1
.4	.3	.7	.8	.8	.5		.5	.6
3.3	1.5	1.9	1.6	1.6	.9	Quick	1.6	1.7
1.2	(48) .7	.9	1.1	1.0	.7		.7	.9
.4	.3	.6	.7	.7	.5		.4	.5
0 UND	0 UND	14 25.8	27 13.7	31 11.8	24 15.1	Sales/Receivables	18 20.3	17 21.6
0 UND	17 21.0	29 12.8	38 9.5	41 8.9	38 9.6		30 12.3	31 11.6
38 9.5	32 11.4	39 9.4	50 7.3	50 7.3	49 7.4		41 8.9	45 8.2
						Cost of Sales/Inventory		
						Cost of Sales/Payables		
9.4	28.3	10.3	7.8	9.8	37.1	Sales/Working Capital	12.8	10.4
555.1	-44.8	75.0	28.0	27.8	-32.2		-174.9	80.5
-32.7	-11.1	-24.0	-18.5	-21.8	-10.9		-11.3	-16.2
39.6	16.1	13.2	19.8	9.0	3.8	EBIT/Interest	12.5	14.3
(18) 7.7	(41) 3.6	(84) 3.8	(66) 5.5	(25) 4.0	2.5		(234) 4.6	(229) 5.4
1.5	.3	1.3	2.2	2.0	-.2		1.6	1.7
		6.0	8.7	9.6		Net Profit + Depr., Dep., Amort./Cur. Mat. L/T/D	3.5	4.5
		(17) 2.1	(23) 3.7	(11) 4.1			(33) 1.8	(39) 2.3
		1.1	2.1	3.5			1.3	1.3
.4	1.0	1.0	1.0	1.9	2.5	Fixed/Worth	1.2	1.0
3.7	13.5	2.5	1.6	2.3	7.5		3.7	2.3
-1.7	-1.0	27.5	4.0	6.5	-2.1		-4.4	-10.2
.7	2.1	.7	.7	2.1	2.5	Debt/Worth	1.5	1.2
5.8	25.3	2.8	1.7	2.6	9.5		5.2	3.3
-3.7	-2.3	39.0	5.7	8.3	-4.1		-8.3	-20.2
219.6	98.6	67.2	40.7	33.2	47.1	% Profit Before Taxes/Tangible Net Worth	74.8	62.5
(14) 51.2	(26) 50.3	(71) 21.8	(60) 26.0	(23) 21.5	(13) 21.0		(163) 29.7	(180) 30.7
27.7	2.9	2.1	8.4	12.5	8.4		10.3	14.7
49.8	32.2	17.1	18.5	7.8	4.7	% Profit Before Taxes/Total Assets	17.1	19.6
24.3	11.2	6.6	9.0	5.5	1.9		7.4	8.7
7.5	-1.4	.5	2.7	2.6	-7.5		1.3	1.3
24.4	19.0	6.4	3.5	2.4	2.4	Sales/Net Fixed Assets	8.4	9.5
11.1	8.2	3.6	2.4	1.9	2.1		3.4	3.7
8.6	3.1	1.8	1.5	1.6	1.4		1.9	2.0
10.0	4.9	2.8	1.7	1.2	1.3	Sales/Total Assets	2.8	2.9
4.9	2.9	1.6	1.4	1.0	.9		1.7	1.7
2.3	1.6	1.1	1.0	.9	.8		1.1	1.1
1.0	2.8	5.0	5.0	5.9		% Depr., Dep., Amort./Sales	4.1	4.2
(13) 4.9	(29) 7.3	(74) 7.9	(69) 6.7	(17) 8.0			(186) 7.4	(185) 7.3
8.2	10.7	12.4	9.5	11.1			10.5	10.3
	1.3	1.5	1.8			% Officers', Directors' Owners' Comp/Sales	1.9	1.6
	(22) 2.5	(35) 2.9	(14) 2.9				(97) 2.9	(91) 3.1
	4.6	5.4	5.6				5.2	6.3
37434M	220440M	876151M	2135416M	2186773M	3876153M	Net Sales ($)	5723260M	6174361M
6168M	56428M	462346M	1615708M	1869245M	3677418M	Total Assets ($)	4938220M	5187616M

Comparative Historical Data / Current Data Sorted by Sales

Comparative Historical Data date columns (left to right): 4/1/16-3/31/17 ALL · 4/1/17-3/31/18 ALL · 4/1/18-3/31/19 ALL

Current Data span headers: 45 (4/1-9/30/18) covers 0-1MM, 1-3MM, 3-5MM · 237 (10/1/18-3/31/19) covers 5-10MM, 10-25MM, 25MM & OVER

'17 ALL	'18 ALL	'19 ALL	Type of Statement	0-1MM	1-3MM	3-5MM	5-10MM	10-25MM	25MM & OVER
21	25	37	Unqualified		2	2	4	7	22
32	27	33	Reviewed	2	2	1	4	15	9
28	31	26	Compiled	3	1	5	10	5	2
53	54	47	Tax Returns	9	10	7	12	5	4
109	109	139	Other	7	21	13	19	22	57
243	246	282	**NUMBER OF STATEMENTS**	21	36	28	49	54	94
%	%	%	**ASSETS**	%	%	%	%	%	%
13.1	12.1	11.7	Cash & Equivalents	11.8	15.2	15.9	11.3	12.4	8.8
15.1	14.4	14.7	Trade Receivables (net)	12.6	8.9	8.2	19.0	18.7	14.9
.8	.8	.8	Inventory	.1	.1	.0	.9	.8	1.5
1.8	3.4	2.8	All Other Current	1.9	2.8	2.7	3.5	2.7	2.8
30.8	30.7	30.0	Total Current	26.4	27.0	26.9	34.7	34.5	27.9
53.2	53.9	52.0	Fixed Assets (net)	55.3	50.9	47.8	50.5	51.6	53.9
8.4	8.5	10.3	Intangibles (net)	9.7	12.1	10.5	8.4	8.2	12.0
7.6	7.0	7.6	All Other Non-Current	8.5	10.0	14.8	6.3	5.7	6.2
100.0	100.0	100.0	Total	100.0	100.0	100.0	100.0	100.0	100.0
			LIABILITIES						
6.3	3.6	6.2	Notes Payable-Short Term	4.7	12.5	3.0	5.0	3.7	7.0
8.3	7.2	6.8	Cur. Mat.-L.T.D.	5.7	5.4	10.3	9.0	6.9	5.4
9.0	8.1	9.0	Trade Payables	5.4	5.9	4.1	12.8	12.3	8.6
.0	.1	.0	Income Taxes Payable	.0	.0	.0	.0	.0	.0
8.7	8.6	7.9	All Other Current	11.3	8.8	12.3	5.4	5.1	8.5
32.5	27.6	29.9	Total Current	27.0	32.7	29.7	32.2	28.0	29.5
38.7	43.0	40.8	Long-Term Debt	36.9	56.8	45.1	46.5	33.9	35.4
.6	.4	.5	Deferred Taxes	.0	.0	.1	.4	.9	.9
6.1	5.5	5.1	All Other Non-Current	2.8	4.5	4.3	7.8	6.1	4.2
22.1	23.5	23.6	Net Worth	33.3	6.0	20.9	13.1	31.2	30.0
100.0	100.0	100.0	Total Liabilities & Net Worth	100.0	100.0	100.0	100.0	100.0	100.0
			INCOME DATA						
100.0	100.0	100.0	Net Sales	100.0	100.0	100.0	100.0	100.0	100.0
			Gross Profit						
91.7	90.1	91.4	Operating Expenses	77.6	87.6	89.0	93.2	94.2	94.0
8.3	9.9	8.6	Operating Profit	22.4	12.4	11.0	6.8	5.8	6.0
1.1	1.9	1.5	All Other Expenses (net)	4.9	1.8	.4	1.1	1.0	1.4
7.1	8.0	7.2	Profit Before Taxes	17.5	10.7	10.5	5.7	4.8	4.6
			RATIOS						
1.9	2.1	1.8	Current	2.6	2.1	1.5	2.1	2.0	1.5
1.1	1.2	1.1		.9	1.1	.8	1.2	1.2	1.1
.6	.7	.6		.2	.3	.4	.7	.8	.7
1.6	1.9	1.6	Quick	2.6	2.1	1.4	1.9	1.8	1.3
1.0	1.0	(281) .9		.5	1.0	(27) .8	.9	1.1	.9
.5	.5	.5		.2	.3	.5	.6	.7	.6
10 37.2	8 44.3	16 23.0	Sales/Receivables	0 UND	0 UND	0 UND	8 43.3	21 17.6	28 12.9
29 12.8	29 12.4	30 12.1		9 42.6	16 22.7	13 27.3	30 12.0	30 12.0	38 9.6
41 8.9	42 8.6	44 8.3		51 7.2	29 12.4	35 10.5	44 8.3	42 8.6	49 7.4
			Cost of Sales/Inventory						
			Cost of Sales/Payables						
11.1	10.2	10.9	Sales/Working Capital	9.3	9.9	43.6	10.5	7.4	11.7
96.5	53.5	117.5		-50.3	NM	-40.3	49.9	37.3	57.2
-14.2	-20.9	-18.3		-2.3	-10.3	-9.6	-31.6	-33.3	-18.8
15.2	17.6	12.5	EBIT/Interest	37.0	14.2	13.6	18.5	18.8	8.4
(228) 6.0	(228) 5.4	(256) 3.9		(15) 3.7	(29) 6.3	(27) 3.2	(45) 4.0	(52) 3.7	(88) 3.8
1.9	2.0	1.1		.1	1.4	.3	1.4	.7	1.2
3.5	4.4	9.3	Net Profit + Depr., Dep., Amort./Cur. Mat. L/T/D					34.1	17.4
(42) 2.3	(45) 3.1	(56) 3.7						(13) 4.7	(29) 4.0
1.5	1.6	2.0						1.5	2.6
1.0	1.1	1.1	Fixed/Worth	.8	.8	1.0	.9	1.1	1.3
2.3	2.3	2.7		3.8	2.7	1.1	3.1	2.2	2.5
-21.6	28.2	-35.3		-46.8	-3.9	-10.2	-2.1	15.4	12.4
1.1	.9	1.1	Debt/Worth	1.0	.6	1.3	.8	.9	1.4
3.0	2.6	3.2		4.3	2.4	4.5	3.8	2.8	2.8
-34.8	54.2	-45.3		-56.2	-6.3	-13.4	-8.2	16.4	28.4
71.3	70.3	56.6	% Profit Before Taxes/Tangible Net Worth	111.4	92.4	99.4	64.9	43.8	41.5
(175) 34.7	(189) 32.0	(207) 27.4		(15) 41.7	(26) 39.0	(20) 40.4	(30) 25.4	(44) 20.6	(72) 26.6
13.6	13.0	8.0		19.0	9.7	3.3	4.1	-5.1	14.4
20.3	22.2	19.2	% Profit Before Taxes/Total Assets	25.0	28.7	31.5	22.3	13.6	13.1
10.0	8.1	6.7		6.7	11.2	7.1	8.6	6.7	5.7
1.9	2.7	.6		1.5	1.8	-2.2	.8	-1.3	1.6
8.2	7.7	6.9	Sales/Net Fixed Assets	11.0	9.5	10.2	12.0	7.0	3.3
3.3	2.9	2.9		2.9	3.7	4.4	4.3	3.8	2.3
1.9	1.7	1.8		.6	2.0	1.8	2.0	2.1	1.7
2.8	2.9	2.6	Sales/Total Assets	3.4	3.1	2.9	4.5	3.3	1.7
1.7	1.6	1.5		1.0	1.9	1.9	2.1	1.7	1.2
1.2	1.0	1.0		.3	1.0	.7	1.2	1.2	1.0
5.0	5.3	4.7	% Depr., Dep., Amort./Sales	3.2	4.2	5.4	4.1	3.5	5.0
(190) 7.5	(184) 7.5	(206) 7.1		(16) 13.8	(25) 6.6	(21) 8.5	(38) 6.7	(41) 6.4	(65) 7.0
11.3	10.8	10.9		22.9	10.0	11.7	12.0	9.1	9.3
1.8	1.4	1.5	% Officers', Directors' Owners' Comp/Sales	3.3	1.1	1.2	1.7	1.1	
(105) 3.1	(84) 2.8	(83) 2.9		(18) 5.1	(13) 1.9	(17) 2.2	(20) 2.9	(14) 2.5	
7.5	5.2	5.8		8.2	4.2	3.4	3.9	6.5	
5823713M	6271108M	9332367M	Net Sales ($)	13238M	66340M	117479M	358867M	894181M	7882262M
4876114M	5646013M	7687313M	Total Assets ($)	31356M	77926M	104268M	219970M	588035M	6665758M

© RMA 2019

M = $ thousand   MM = $ million
See Pages viii through xx for Explanation of Ratios and Data

Current Data Sorted by Assets   **Comparative Historical Data**

Type of Statement

	0-500M	500M-2MM	2-10MM	10-50MM	50-100MM	100-250MM	4/1/14-3/31/15 ALL	4/1/15-3/31/16 ALL
Unqualified					1	1	7	3
Reviewed					1	1	1	6
Compiled			6				3	5
Tax Returns	2	3	2				9	11
Other	1	7	17	4	1	1	23	27
		3 (4/1-9/30/18)		46 (10/1/18-3/31/19)				
NUMBER OF STATEMENTS	3	10	25	5	3	3	43	52

	0-500M %	500M-2MM %	2-10MM %	10-50MM %	50-100MM %	100-250MM %	4/1/14-3/31/15 ALL %	4/1/15-3/31/16 ALL %
ASSETS								
Cash & Equivalents		12.3	11.0				12.6	9.6
Trade Receivables (net)		12.2	23.8				21.2	24.1
Inventory		.1	1.7				1.8	.5
All Other Current		2.5	3.6				3.9	3.4
Total Current		27.2	40.1				39.4	37.5
Fixed Assets (net)		52.8	48.7				43.6	44.3
Intangibles (net)		7.2	6.7				7.1	6.4
All Other Non-Current		12.7	4.5				9.9	11.8
Total		100.0	100.0				100.0	100.0
LIABILITIES								
Notes Payable-Short Term		9.7	2.7				2.9	7.9
Cur. Mat.-L.T.D.		4.1	8.7				5.0	4.7
Trade Payables		3.6	10.4				9.7	9.9
Income Taxes Payable		.0	.0				.0	.0
All Other Current		1.4	6.1				24.0	11.7
Total Current		18.9	27.9				41.8	34.2
Long-Term Debt		36.6	33.4				30.5	31.0
Deferred Taxes		.0	.5				.0	.2
All Other Non-Current		1.8	2.5				4.1	8.8
Net Worth		42.7	35.8				23.6	25.8
Total Liabilities & Net Worth		100.0	100.0				100.0	100.0
INCOME DATA								
Net Sales		100.0	100.0				100.0	100.0
Gross Profit								
Operating Expenses		90.8	92.5				87.6	90.5
Operating Profit		9.2	7.5				12.4	9.5
All Other Expenses (net)		.4	1.2				1.5	2.1
Profit Before Taxes		8.8	6.3				10.9	7.4
RATIOS								
Current		3.2	2.5				2.2	2.6
		1.5	1.3				1.2	1.3
		.6	.9				.7	.6
Quick			1.9				2.1	2.5
			1.1				1.0	1.2
			.7				.5	.4
Sales/Receivables	0 UND	23 16.1					18 19.8	27 13.7
	0 UND	28 13.0					39 9.4	42 8.6
	41 8.9	49 7.4					59 6.2	55 6.6
Cost of Sales/Inventory								
Cost of Sales/Payables								
Sales/Working Capital		13.4	8.0				9.4	7.5
		96.8	23.0				67.2	29.0
		-52.9	-95.0				-10.7	-14.0
EBIT/Interest			14.9				14.1	18.4
			(23) 9.0				(36) 4.3	(43) 7.6
			1.7				2.5	1.0
Net Profit + Depr., Dep., Amort./Cur. Mat. L/T/D								
Fixed/Worth		.4	.6				.5	.8
		1.3	1.5				2.5	1.9
		NM	4.7				39.8	14.7
Debt/Worth		.5	1.1				1.3	.8
		.9	2.6				3.6	2.9
		NM	5.8				-15.4	15.6
% Profit Before Taxes/Tangible Net Worth			66.8				71.1	54.5
			(22) 32.9				(32) 45.8	(42) 26.8
			12.7				20.6	5.7
% Profit Before Taxes/Total Assets		56.1	23.6				19.3	18.6
		40.3	14.6				11.1	6.9
		10.5	1.9				4.9	.2
Sales/Net Fixed Assets		17.0	8.6				10.7	10.5
		6.9	4.1				3.8	4.0
		3.4	2.5				2.0	2.1
Sales/Total Assets		4.7	2.6				2.7	2.8
		3.3	1.9				1.8	1.7
		2.5	1.4				.9	1.1
% Depr., Dep., Amort./Sales			4.2				3.1	2.1
			(19) 6.4				(34) 6.8	(36) 7.2
			10.0				8.8	12.0
% Officers', Directors' Owners' Comp/Sales			.9				.1	2.8
			(11) 1.4				(14) 2.9	(16) 6.7
			4.0				8.6	11.9
Net Sales ($)	1589M	40756M	213026M	178626M	174233M	407960M	1064646M	1861955M
Total Assets ($)	739M	11903M	105739M	112959M	203648M	377268M	706132M	1187064M

© RMA 2019

M = $ thousand   MM = $ million
See Pages viii through xx for Explanation of Ratios and Data

Comparative Historical Data | | Current Data Sorted by Sales

			Type of Statement						
3	3	2	Unqualified				3	2	2
7	11	2	Reviewed						2
2	4	6	Compiled			1	1		
9	15	8	Tax Returns	1	2	2		1	1
26	23	31	Other	1	4	4	11	7	4
4/1/16- 3/31/17 ALL	4/1/17- 3/31/18 ALL	4/1/18- 3/31/19 ALL		0-1MM	1-3MM	3-5MM	5-10MM	10-25MM	25MM & OVER
					3 (4/1-9/30/18)		46 (10/1/18-3/31/19)		
4/	56	49	**NUMBER OF STATEMENTS**	2	6	7	15	10	9
%	%	%	**ASSETS**	%	%	%	%	%	%
14.4	14.9	11.1	Cash & Equivalents				12.9	13.6	
23.2	17.7	19.0	Trade Receivables (net)				23.4	31.9	
.7	2.5	1.9	Inventory				1.3	1.2	
2.8	2.7	2.8	All Other Current				1.5	6.4	
41.1	37.7	34.8	Total Current				39.0	53.1	
42.3	47.3	49.3	Fixed Assets (net)				50.0	35.8	
6.8	7.4	8.5	Intangibles (net)				6.1	7.7	
9.8	7.5	7.2	All Other Non-Current				4.9	3.4	
100.0	100.0	100.0	Total				100.0	100.0	
			LIABILITIES						
2.2	5.0	6.0	Notes Payable-Short Term				4.4	8.0	
5.1	7.3	6.7	Cur. Mat.-L.T.D.				9.6	5.8	
17.9	9.4	8.5	Trade Payables				9.2	13.8	
.0	.0	.0	Income Taxes Payable				.0	.0	
7.1	5.4	4.5	All Other Current				3.1	9.8	
32.4	27.2	25.8	Total Current				26.2	37.4	
32.1	33.2	35.2	Long-Term Debt				28.6	23.8	
.3	.1	.4	Deferred Taxes				.4	.0	
6.0	5.3	3.1	All Other Non-Current				2.6	4.7	
29.2	34.3	35.2	Net Worth				42.3	34.1	
100.0	100.0	100.0	Total Liabilities & Net Worth				100.0	100.0	
			INCOME DATA						
100.0	100.0	100.0	Net Sales				100.0	100.0	
			Gross Profit						
82.6	88.6	91.4	Operating Expenses				90.4	93.6	
17.4	11.4	8.6	Operating Profit				9.6	6.4	
1.3	1.8	2.4	All Other Expenses (net)				.7	1.4	
16.1	9.7	6.2	Profit Before Taxes				8.9	5.0	
			RATIOS						
3.1	3.5	2.3	Current				3.0	2.0	
1.3	1.3	1.1					1.1	1.1	
.8	.6	.7					.6	.9	
2.9	3.5	1.7	Quick				2.8	1.8	
1.3	1.1	(48) 1.0					1.0	1.0	
.5	.4	.6					.6	.6	
16 22.7	9 39.6	18 20.7	Sales/Receivables				16 22.4	23 16.0	
38 9.6	32 11.3	29 12.5					29 12.7	32 11.3	
64 5.7	53 6.9	52 7.0					51 7.1	72 5.1	
			Cost of Sales/Inventory						
			Cost of Sales/Payables						
6.2	8.4	9.8	Sales/Working Capital				9.5	8.8	
31.1	35.3	35.2					83.9	29.1	
-39.2	-15.7	-42.3					-69.9	-147.6	
29.4	17.8	19.2	EBIT/Interest				33.4		
(39) 12.3	(46) 6.4	(44) 9.4					(14) 10.4		
2.1	1.7	.9					3.6		
			Net Profit + Depr., Dep., Amort./Cur. Mat. L/T/D						
.4	.8	.8	Fixed/Worth				.5	.3	
1.6	1.6	1.5					1.3	1.8	
UND	UND	44.0					3.6	NM	
.8	.7	.9	Debt/Worth				.9	1.2	
2.8	2.5	2.6					1.2	3.0	
UND	UND	45.6					4.7	NM	
136.4	76.3	100.7	% Profit Before Taxes/Tangible Net Worth				108.0		
(36) 34.8	(44) 35.6	(40) 42.4					(14) 52.5		
19.2	8.7	15.4					21.5		
26.7	23.4	24.9	% Profit Before Taxes/Total Assets				41.9	21.3	
15.5	10.7	14.6					20.6	13.1	
7.6	2.1	.9					8.2	1.0	
17.0	11.9	9.0	Sales/Net Fixed Assets				8.6	UND	
3.2	4.5	4.1					5.3	4.6	
2.4	1.9	2.1					3.2	3.1	
2.5	3.0	3.1	Sales/Total Assets				3.0	3.5	
1.6	1.7	1.9					2.2	2.3	
1.0	1.2	1.2					1.8	1.5	
2.3	1.8	4.2	% Depr., Dep., Amort./Sales						
(30) 6.3	(35) 4.7	(31) 7.4							
12.4	10.9	11.5							
.8	1.7	1.1	% Officers', Directors' Owners' Comp/Sales						
(13) 3.4	(22) 3.9	(17) 4.0							
10.7	7.2	5.1							
1246273M	1601379M	1016190M	Net Sales ($)	86M	11847M	26999M	103922M	154441M	718895M
1077690M	1114527M	812256M	Total Assets ($)	346M	9018M	17403M	47200M	97142M	641147M

© RMA 2019

M = $ thousand   MM = $ million
See Pages viii through xx for Explanation of Ratios and Data

Current Data Sorted by Assets   Comparative Historical Data

	0-500M	500M-2MM	2-10MM	10-50MM	50-100MM	100-250MM		4/1/14-3/31/15 ALL	4/1/15-3/31/16 ALL
Type of Statement									
Unqualified				3	1	1		9	7
Reviewed			1	4				13	13
Compiled		1	3	1		1		4	7
Tax Returns	1	5						6	10
Other	2	1	4	6	3	2		26	27
		3 (4/1-9/30/18)		37 (10/1/18-3/31/19)					
NUMBER OF STATEMENTS	3	7	8	14	4	4		58	64
	%	%	%	%	%	%		%	%
ASSETS									
Cash & Equivalents				9.0				12.8	13.5
Trade Receivables (net)				18.6				27.2	23.8
Inventory				3.9				2.6	1.4
All Other Current				3.2				5.5	3.4
Total Current				34.8				48.2	42.1
Fixed Assets (net)				38.9				36.7	40.4
Intangibles (net)				15.3				7.8	9.0
All Other Non-Current				11.0				7.3	8.4
Total				100.0				100.0	100.0
LIABILITIES									
Notes Payable-Short Term				4.1				5.3	5.5
Cur. Mat.-L.T.D.				5.3				6.5	4.9
Trade Payables				9.9				12.8	9.5
Income Taxes Payable				.0				.3	.3
All Other Current				5.1				6.9	6.0
Total Current				24.5				31.7	26.1
Long-Term Debt				32.7				22.3	30.0
Deferred Taxes				.2				.4	2.2
All Other Non-Current				8.2				5.3	2.9
Net Worth				34.5				40.2	38.7
Total Liabilties & Net Worth				100.0				100.0	100.0
INCOME DATA									
Net Sales				100.0				100.0	100.0
Gross Profit									
Operating Expenses				87.1				92.6	90.7
Operating Profit				12.9				7.4	9.3
All Other Expenses (net)				2.7				1.2	2.0
Profit Before Taxes				10.2				6.2	7.3
RATIOS									
Current				2.0				3.1	2.9
				1.5				1.5	1.6
				.9				1.0	.8
Quick				1.7				2.7	2.6
				1.1				1.2	1.4
				.7				.7	.7
Sales/Receivables			32	11.4				35 10.3	29 12.5
			53	6.9				54 6.7	53 6.9
			72	5.1				73 5.0	70 5.2
Cost of Sales/Inventory									
Cost of Sales/Payables									
Sales/Working Capital				5.9				4.6	5.0
				13.6				13.1	11.0
				-100.9				147.9	-82.9
EBIT/Interest				40.9				21.1	21.8
			(12)	6.5				(49) 7.4	(50) 5.6
				.7				2.3	.8
Net Profit + Depr., Dep., Amort./Cur. Mat. L/T/D								2.4	16.2
								(10) 1.7	(10) 3.3
								1.2	1.1
Fixed/Worth				.7				.3	.4
				3.5				.7	1.1
				-9.9				1.7	3.4
Debt/Worth				.9				.6	.6
				4.2				1.4	1.6
				-24.1				3.9	5.5
% Profit Before Taxes/Tangible Net Worth				138.6				40.0	58.9
			(10)	39.4				(54) 22.9	(56) 19.8
				.0				4.9	2.8
% Profit Before Taxes/Total Assets				21.8				15.4	19.6
				9.2				8.0	7.5
				-.7				2.1	.0
Sales/Net Fixed Assets				11.4				14.5	10.1
				2.8				5.4	4.0
				2.2				2.2	2.1
Sales/Total Assets				2.2				2.7	2.5
				1.2				1.9	1.5
				.6				1.1	.9
% Depr., Dep., Amort./Sales				2.9				1.7	2.4
			(13)	5.5				(49) 4.3	(50) 4.9
				10.1				7.5	7.5
% Officers', Directors' Owners' Comp/Sales								5.0	1.4
								(16) 7.8	(17) 5.8
								11.2	8.8
Net Sales ($)	11665M	22647M	74721M	408314M	275401M	774581M		1866856M	1838513M
Total Assets ($)	964M	7871M	34358M	304924M	291761M	784419M		1148984M	1339521M

© RMA 2019

M = $ thousand   MM = $ million
See Pages viii through xx for Explanation of Ratios and Data

Comparative Historical Data   Current Data Sorted by Sales

				Type of Statement		0-1MM	1-3MM	3-5MM	5-10MM	10-25MM	25MM & OVER
7		3	5	Unqualified							5
11		8	6	Reviewed					1	2	2
4		5	6	Compiled			2	2	2	1	1
7		6	6	Tax Returns			1	1	1		
25		27	18	Other		4	4	4	2	2	8
4/1/16-		4/1/17-	4/1/18-			2					
3/31/17		3/31/18	3/31/19				3 (4/1-9/30/18)		37 (10/1/18-3/31/19)		
ALL		ALL	ALL								
54		49	40	NUMBER OF STATEMENTS		6	6	7	6	5	16
%		%	%	ASSETS	%	%	%	%	%	%	%
12.4		8.8	10.7	Cash & Equivalents	D						4.6
28.6		28.6	23.5	Trade Receivables (net)	A						23.3
2.3		1.6	2.7	Inventory	T						3.7
4.1		4.4	2.8	All Other Current	A						2.5
47.4		43.5	39.7	Total Current							34.0
36.6		41.2	35.3	Fixed Assets (net)	N						37.0
8.7		7.4	14.6	Intangibles (net)	O						23.6
7.3		8.0	10.5	All Other Non-Current	T						5.4
100.0		100.0	100.0	Total							100.0
				LIABILITIES	A						
4.7		6.0	7.2	Notes Payable-Short Term	V						5.4
12.4		4.6	7.0	Cur. Mat.-L.T.D.	A						4.5
10.9		11.9	12.7	Trade Payables	I						9.6
.3		.1	.2	Income Taxes Payable	L						.0
13.0		8.1	9.3	All Other Current	A						10.0
41.3		30.7	36.4	Total Current	B						29.6
25.3		29.0	34.2	Long-Term Debt	L						33.9
.5		.7	.8	Deferred Taxes	E						1.6
4.5		4.9	9.5	All Other Non-Current							5.2
28.4		34.6	19.1	Net Worth							29.8
100.0		100.0	100.0	Total Liabilities & Net Worth							100.0
				INCOME DATA							
100.0		100.0	100.0	Net Sales							100.0
				Gross Profit							
92.5		93.5	92.8	Operating Expenses							91.3
7.5		6.5	7.2	Operating Profit							8.7
1.4		1.5	1.9	All Other Expenses (net)							1.8
6.2		5.0	5.3	Profit Before Taxes							6.9
				RATIOS							
2.2		2.2	1.8								1.7
1.6		1.3	1.3	Current							1.2
.9		.9	.8								.9
1.9		1.9	1.7								1.6
1.4		1.1	1.1	Quick							1.0
.9		.8	.6								.6
38 9.5		39 9.3	29 12.7							39	9.3
61 6.0		55 6.6	53 6.9	Sales/Receivables						76	4.8
78 4.7		72 5.1	79 4.6							104	3.5
				Cost of Sales/Inventory							
				Cost of Sales/Payables							
5.4		6.2	7.8								8.5
11.4		17.8	28.7	Sales/Working Capital							18.3
-54.5		-82.0	-36.0								-40.1
15.1		25.4	8.3								7.7
(47) 6.8		(45) 5.3	(38) 1.8	EBIT/Interest							2.3
2.8		1.4	.4								.6
				Net Profit + Depr., Dep., Amort./Cur. Mat. L/T/D							
.5		.6	.7								1.4
1.1		1.2	6.6	Fixed/Worth							8.0
7.1		-15.3	-3.1								-3.3
.8		.8	1.0								2.1
1.7		1.9	8.1	Debt/Worth							11.8
8.2		-36.9	-7.6								-8.1
52.4		48.8	83.2								
(43) 22.8		(36) 15.9	(23) 25.6	% Profit Before Taxes/Tangible Net Worth							
12.6		3.7	.6								
17.2		18.1	15.4								19.2
8.8		7.6	2.2	% Profit Before Taxes/Total Assets							3.2
2.8		.7	-1.8								-1.3
8.7		9.0	14.2								3.7
4.6		3.9	3.4	Sales/Net Fixed Assets							3.3
2.6		2.1	2.5								2.5
2.4		2.6	3.1								1.6
1.5		1.4	1.5	Sales/Total Assets							1.0
1.0		.9	.9								.9
2.1		2.1	2.5								3.0
(38) 4.0		(42) 4.6	(31) 5.0	% Depr., Dep., Amort./Sales						(12)	5.2
7.6		8.9	9.3								7.7
3.0		2.2	.4								
(15) 3.6		(14) 5.2	(10) 2.3	% Officers', Directors' Owners' Comp/Sales							
10.8		8.6	6.0								
1651242M		1683040M	1567329M	Net Sales ($)		13456M	27808M	46975M	87791M		1391299M
1324550M		1279709M	1424297M	Total Assets ($)		7784M	39332M	43014M	37947M		1296220M

Current Data Sorted by Assets | Comparative Historical Data

Type of Statement

0-500M	500M-2MM	2-10MM	10-50MM	50-100MM	100-250MM	Type of Statement	4/1/14-3/31/15 ALL	4/1/15-3/31/16 ALL
		2	7		2	Unqualified	15	15
		2	6			Reviewed	6	11
						Compiled	6	8
	4					Tax Returns	5	3
2	4	12	14	11	6	Other	28	30
	13 (4/1-9/30/18)		59 (10/1/18-3/31/19)					
2	8	16	27	11	8	NUMBER OF STATEMENTS	60	67
%	%	%	%	%	%	ASSETS	%	%
		15.3	11.5	10.3		Cash & Equivalents	13.6	13.4
		20.5	13.6	7.9		Trade Receivables (net)	10.1	13.9
		3.0	3.0	.6		Inventory	2.2	2.0
		3.5	1.5	2.7		All Other Current	1.6	3.1
		42.3	29.6	21.6		Total Current	27.5	32.3
		47.0	45.6	58.2		Fixed Assets (net)	48.2	45.7
		2.4	9.7	10.8		Intangibles (net)	7.1	9.5
		8.3	15.1	9.4		All Other Non-Current	17.2	12.5
		100.0	100.0	100.0		Total	100.0	100.0
						LIABILITIES		
		3.2	3.0	2.2		Notes Payable-Short Term	4.4	2.7
		3.5	6.0	4.4		Cur. Mat.-L.T.D.	4.0	5.3
		10.6	5.2	3.8		Trade Payables	4.2	7.8
		.0	.1	.5		Income Taxes Payable	.1	.1
		9.3	4.8	12.1		All Other Current	8.1	7.0
		26.7	19.1	23.1		Total Current	20.9	22.9
		32.6	31.5	37.2		Long-Term Debt	27.3	28.7
		.0	1.2	.3		Deferred Taxes	.3	.3
		4.2	12.8	5.3		All Other Non-Current	10.4	7.8
		36.5	35.3	34.1		Net Worth	41.0	40.2
		100.0	100.0	100.0		Total Liabilities & Net Worth	100.0	100.0
						INCOME DATA		
		100.0	100.0	100.0		Net Sales	100.0	100.0
						Gross Profit		
		90.1	85.5	100.5		Operating Expenses	87.9	89.2
		9.9	14.5	-.5		Operating Profit	12.1	10.8
		-.2	1.3	2.2		All Other Expenses (net)	1.3	1.8
		10.1	13.2	-2.7		Profit Before Taxes	10.8	8.9
						RATIOS		
		4.0	2.9	3.4			2.6	3.0
		2.3	2.1	1.3		Current	1.2	1.5
		.8	.9	.5			.7	.8
		3.4	2.7	2.9			2.4	2.6
		2.0	1.9	.7		Quick	.8	1.2
		.8	.5	.5			.6	.6
		29 12.6	24 15.0	27 13.7			25 14.6	26 14.3
		39 9.4	39 9.3	35 10.5		Sales/Receivables	33 11.1	33 10.9
		54 6.7	61 6.0	46 7.9			46 7.9	47 7.8
						Cost of Sales/Inventory		
						Cost of Sales/Payables		
		4.4	4.0	4.5			7.1	5.2
		9.2	8.9	16.1		Sales/Working Capital	44.8	16.1
		-49.7	-16.4	-4.9			-11.9	-20.7
		34.4	16.5	12.4			21.6	24.4
		(15) 5.2	9.6	(10) 2.2		EBIT/Interest	(54) 6.8	(62) 5.2
		.6	2.9	-.5			1.7	2.0
						Net Profit + Depr., Dep.,	9.6	3.7
						Amort./Cur. Mat. L/T/D	(11) 2.4	(11) 1.4
							1.1	.7
		.7	.9	1.3			.6	.6
		1.2	1.2	2.7		Fixed/Worth	1.4	1.3
		2.5	3.7	4.6			4.0	10.0
		.7	.9	1.1			.5	.5
		1.7	1.5	2.6		Debt/Worth	1.5	1.3
		3.2	4.7	5.6			4.5	14.1
		42.7	61.8	21.1		% Profit Before Taxes/Tangible	47.5	54.7
		(15) 23.9	(23) 35.1	(10) 10.6		Net Worth	(49) 19.0	(52) 25.7
		.2	8.1	-4.5			7.4	4.7
		21.2	19.3	5.9		% Profit Before Taxes/Total	16.4	17.4
		8.5	8.6	1.3		Assets	9.2	5.9
		-.5	3.3	-1.6			2.8	1.3
		8.4	3.5	1.9			4.1	5.4
		3.5	2.2	1.6		Sales/Net Fixed Assets	2.2	2.3
		2.6	1.6	1.2			1.2	1.2
		2.3	1.6	1.1			1.6	1.8
		1.9	1.1	1.0		Sales/Total Assets	1.0	1.1
		1.2	.6	.3			.5	.7
		4.2	6.0				3.2	3.1
		(14) 5.3	(23) 7.5			% Depr., Dep., Amort./Sales	(48) 7.2	(55) 7.1
		7.0	10.2				11.8	12.9
						% Officers', Directors'	1.6	1.6
						Owners' Comp/Sales	(13) 2.2	(10) 2.9
							4.4	13.3
899M	26399M	187648M	635474M	719026M	1063909M	Net Sales ($)	1592233M	1651483M
567M	10060M	92636M	593222M	908634M	1289796M	Total Assets ($)	1829053M	1917782M

M = $ thousand   MM = $ million
See Pages viii through xx for Explanation of Ratios and Data

Comparative Historical Data | Current Data Sorted by Sales

	4/1/16-3/31/17 ALL	4/1/17-3/31/18 ALL	4/1/18-3/31/19 ALL	Type of Statement	0-1MM	1-3MM	3-5MM	5-10MM	10-25MM	25MM & OVER
	10	16	9	Unqualified				2	2	5
	10	6	8	Reviewed				1	2	5
	7	5		Compiled						
	6	3	6	Tax Returns		2	3			
	24	39	49	Other	3	4	2	8	16	17
		13 (4/1-9/30/18)						59 (10/1/18-3/31/19)		
	57	69	72	NUMBER OF STATEMENTS	3	6	5	11	20	27
	%	%	%	**ASSETS**	%	%	%	%	%	%
	15.7	9.0	11.4	Cash & Equivalents				17.2	12.5	7.7
	13.6	15.5	12.7	Trade Receivables (net)				8.9	17.7	12.2
	.6	1.3	2.6	Inventory				4.6	1.8	3.1
	3.3	1.4	2.5	All Other Current				2.8	2.7	2.0
	33.2	27.2	29.2	Total Current				33.4	34.8	24.9
	48.4	56.7	48.9	Fixed Assets (net)				50.8	47.2	52.2
	7.6	9.2	10.8	Intangibles (net)				7.3	7.7	13.2
	10.7	6.9	11.1	All Other Non-Current				8.5	10.4	9.7
	100.0	100.0	100.0	Total				100.0	100.0	100.0
				LIABILITIES						
	1.5	2.6	4.6	Notes Payable-Short Term				2.2	1.7	3.7
	8.5	8.7	4.8	Cur. Mat.-L.T.D.				8.3	4.7	4.5
	8.2	7.3	6.7	Trade Payables				4.2	8.7	6.1
	.1	.0	.1	Income Taxes Payable				.1	.1	.2
	11.2	4.8	6.5	All Other Current				4.2	6.2	7.9
	29.5	23.4	22.7	Total Current				19.1	21.4	22.5
	28.3	33.5	35.3	Long-Term Debt				32.6	35.0	36.6
	.1	.5	.8	Deferred Taxes				.9	1.1	1.0
	9.2	11.4	7.7	All Other Non-Current				11.3	9.9	7.7
	32.9	31.1	33.5	Net Worth				36.1	32.5	32.2
	100.0	100.0	100.0	Total Liabilties & Net Worth				100.0	100.0	100.0
				INCOME DATA						
	100.0	100.0	100.0	Net Sales				100.0	100.0	100.0
				Gross Profit						
	87.1	87.9	90.4	Operating Expenses				91.2	85.5	94.0
	12.9	12.1	9.6	Operating Profit				8.8	14.5	6.0
	.9	1.9	1.7	All Other Expenses (net)				.8	.9	2.4
	12.0	10.1	7.8	Profit Before Taxes				8.1	13.7	3.5
				RATIOS						
	2.4	2.8	2.9					4.2	2.8	2.0
	1.2	1.5	1.5	Current				2.2	2.1	1.3
	.7	.8	.7					.9	.9	.7
	1.9	2.3	2.6					4.0	2.5	1.6
	1.1	1.3	1.0	Quick				1.6	2.1	.9
	.6	.7	.5					.3	.8	.5
26	14.2	27 13.3	24 15.2	Sales/Receivables	8 46.3	22 16.7	29 12.8			
38	9.7	41 8.8	34 10.6		41 8.9	35 10.3	37 9.9			
50	7.3	58 6.3	51 7.1		45 8.1	64 5.7	51 7.1			
				Cost of Sales/Inventory						
				Cost of Sales/Payables						
	5.7	4.9	4.8					2.0	4.6	7.4
	32.4	15.2	17.0	Sales/Working Capital				15.0	6.9	18.4
	-11.7	-31.0	-18.6					-145.7	NM	-15.4
	19.8	15.7	13.7					22.3	29.0	9.1
	(50) 5.2	(64) 6.1	(68) 4.0	EBIT/Interest				5.2	(19) 10.7	(26) 2.9
	1.9	1.9	1.4					1.4	3.5	1.2
		4.7	5.2	Net Profit + Depr., Dep.,						
		(10) 2.4	(12) 3.7	Amort./Cur. Mat. L/T/D						
		1.0	1.9							
	.8	1.1	.9					.7	.9	1.1
	1.4	1.9	1.6	Fixed/Worth				1.0	1.3	2.2
	4.0	18.8	6.6					12.2	3.4	-33.1
	.7	1.2	.9					.6	1.3	1.1
	1.7	2.2	2.2	Debt/Worth				1.1	2.2	2.2
	6.8	19.3	10.0					15.8	3.9	-63.2
	53.5	50.7	46.8	% Profit Before Taxes/Tangible					61.8	37.6
	(47) 27.0	(56) 28.3	(58) 20.5	Net Worth					(19) 37.2	(20) 16.0
	7.9	9.3	3.2						20.0	3.6
	20.8	15.0	17.5	% Profit Before Taxes/Total				22.0	21.9	9.3
	9.3	7.3	5.8	Assets				6.2	11.3	2.0
	3.3	1.8	.2					.1	3.5	.4
	4.4	3.6	3.8					4.6	4.3	3.3
	2.3	2.0	2.3	Sales/Net Fixed Assets				2.6	3.1	1.9
	1.5	1.2	1.6					.7	1.9	1.6
	1.8	1.9	1.8					1.8	2.1	1.5
	1.2	1.1	1.1	Sales/Total Assets				1.0	1.5	1.1
	.6	.7	.6					.3	.7	.8
	3.6	5.6	4.7	% Depr., Dep., Amort./Sales					5.7	3.9
	(43) 8.9	(56) 8.3	(50) 6.6						(17) 6.6	(16) 6.9
	13.2	12.3	9.8						9.2	10.4
	1.7	1.6	1.5	% Officers', Directors'						
	(10) 3.8	(12) 2.2	(13) 2.4	Owners' Comp/Sales						
	4.5	7.7	4.2							
	1606284M	2184003M	2633355M	Net Sales ($)	1144M	10987M	18593M	81179M	321694M	2199758M
	1587749M	2217130M	2894915M	Total Assets ($)	1303M	15313M	97378M	110761M	363058M	2307102M

M = $ thousand   MM = $ million
See Pages viii through xx for Explanation of Ratios and Data

Current Data Sorted by Assets   Comparative Historical Data

	0-500M	500M-2MM	2-10MM	10-50MM	50-100MM	100-250MM	Type of Statement		
				1	1	2	Unqualified	10	7
		1	1	5	1		Reviewed	10	12
		1	5	2			Compiled	5	3
			5				Tax Returns	9	10
		6	10	10	7	4	3 Other	43	49
		10 (4/1-9/30/18)	45 (10/1/18-3/31/19)					4/1/14-3/31/15 ALL	4/1/15-3/31/16 ALL
	0-500M	500M-2MM	2-10MM	10-50MM	50-100MM	100-250MM	NUMBER OF STATEMENTS	77	81
		8	21	15	6	5			

0-500M	500M-2MM	2-10MM	10-50MM	50-100MM	100-250MM		4/1/14-3/31/15 ALL	4/1/15-3/31/16 ALL
%	%	%	%	%	%	**ASSETS**	%	%
D		14.1	7.8			Cash & Equivalents	7.1	8.8
A		19.7	13.0			Trade Receivables (net)	15.9	15.7
T		.5	3.2			Inventory	2.9	5.4
A		2.1	.5			All Other Current	2.6	2.2
		36.4	24.5			Total Current	28.5	32.2
N		49.8	61.9			Fixed Assets (net)	55.7	49.9
O		3.2	7.6			Intangibles (net)	6.4	9.3
T		10.5	6.0			All Other Non-Current	9.4	8.6
		100.0	100.0			Total	100.0	100.0
A						**LIABILITIES**		
V		1.7	2.2			Notes Payable-Short Term	7.9	5.9
A		8.0	8.0			Cur. Mat.-L.T.D.	6.0	5.6
I		12.4	6.4			Trade Payables	11.7	9.4
L		.0	.2			Income Taxes Payable	.2	.1
A		7.6	3.0			All Other Current	7.8	4.9
B		29.7	19.7			Total Current	33.6	26.0
L		43.2	35.0			Long-Term Debt	42.1	34.1
E		.3	.3			Deferred Taxes	.4	.3
		8.2	8.5			All Other Non-Current	9.7	4.2
		18.6	36.5			Net Worth	14.2	35.4
		100.0	100.0			Total Liabilities & Net Worth	100.0	100.0
						INCOME DATA		
		100.0	100.0			Net Sales	100.0	100.0
						Gross Profit		
		88.7	89.7			Operating Expenses	90.0	90.3
		11.3	10.3			Operating Profit	10.0	9.7
		1.8	3.1			All Other Expenses (net)	2.6	1.8
		9.5	7.1			Profit Before Taxes	7.4	7.9
						RATIOS		
		2.5	2.2				2.6	2.2
		1.4	1.2			Current	1.0	1.2
		.9	.6				.5	.6
		2.0	2.2				1.7	1.6
		1.1	.9			Quick	.8	1.0
		.7	.5				.4	.5
		22 16.4	34 10.6				11 33.8	11 32.9
		38 9.5	42 8.6			Sales/Receivables	29 12.5	33 11.0
		52 7.0	55 6.6				47 7.7	51 7.2
						Cost of Sales/Inventory		
						Cost of Sales/Payables		
		7.9	6.2				8.4	11.3
		21.7	36.2			Sales/Working Capital	-115.4	41.5
		-60.2	-11.5				-10.9	-20.3
		13.0	9.1				15.7	17.0
		(19) 6.0	4.1			EBIT/Interest	(70) 5.0	(72) 5.1
		3.0	1.0				.9	1.9
							4.6	5.8
						Net Profit + Depr., Dep., Amort./Cur. Mat. L/T/D	(12) 2.2	(10) 1.5
							1.1	.9
		.7	.9				1.1	1.0
		1.9	2.3			Fixed/Worth	2.5	1.5
		-23.8	9.6				-3.9	NM
		.8	.6				1.0	.8
		2.6	3.7			Debt/Worth	5.5	2.1
		-30.6	9.4				-5.9	NM
		56.7	50.8				47.5	51.3
		(15) 34.6	(13) 23.4			% Profit Before Taxes/Tangible Net Worth	(53) 27.0	(61) 21.3
		12.4	2.8				2.0	5.6
		26.7	17.1				21.0	19.7
		13.0	6.7			% Profit Before Taxes/Total Assets	7.1	7.2
		3.2	.3				-.3	1.2
		16.0	2.9				7.2	8.1
		3.6	1.6			Sales/Net Fixed Assets	2.5	3.2
		1.3	1.2				1.2	1.6
		2.4	1.3				2.8	2.5
		1.4	.9			Sales/Total Assets	1.4	1.3
		.9	.7				.8	.8
		4.1	8.7				2.6	2.4
		(13) 6.9	10.3			% Depr., Dep., Amort./Sales	(56) 5.8	(56) 5.5
		11.6	14.7				13.0	10.3
							2.1	2.6
						% Officers', Directors' Owners' Comp/Sales	(21) 2.8	(18) 4.1
							5.0	8.2
	9962M	167326M	281179M	587988M	614329M	Net Sales ($)	1678157M	2633576M
	9417M	89800M	314431M	431593M	823365M	Total Assets ($)	1608254M	2534675M

M = $ thousand   MM = $ million
See Pages viii through xx for Explanation of Ratios and Data

Comparative Historical Data   ## Current Data Sorted by Sales

4/1/16-3/31/17 ALL	4/1/17-3/31/18 ALL	4/1/18-3/31/19 ALL	Type of Statement	0-1MM	1-3MM	3-5MM	5-10MM	10-25MM	25MM & OVER
5	4	4	Unqualified				1	4	4
6	2	8	Reviewed	1			2		2
8	6	8	Compiled	1	3		2	2	2
4	12	5	Tax Returns			1	2	2	
49	35	30	Other	3	7	3	3	9	8
4/1/16-3/31/17 ALL	4/1/17-3/31/18 ALL	4/1/18-3/31/19 ALL			10 (4/1-9/30/18)			45 (10/1/18-3/31/19)	
72	59	55	**NUMBER OF STATEMENTS**	5	7	4	8	15	16
%	%	%	**ASSETS**	%	%	%	%	%	%
9.6	11.0	10.1	Cash & Equivalents					10.6	9.2
14.8	12.9	14.8	Trade Receivables (net)					23.6	13.9
2.3	5.5	2.4	Inventory					1.0	3.4
1.6	1.5	1.2	All Other Current					1.1	.9
28.2	30.8	28.5	Total Current					36.3	27.4
55.8	53.4	53.7	Fixed Assets (net)					53.6	51.6
6.9	8.3	9.4	Intangibles (net)					5.8	16.7
9.0	7.5	8.4	All Other Non-Current					4.3	4.3
100.0	100.0	100.0	Total					100.0	100.0
			LIABILITIES						
5.9	4.6	2.3	Notes Payable-Short Term					1.8	2.8
6.8	7.9	6.7	Cur. Mat.-L.T.D.					7.6	5.0
7.2	7.8	8.0	Trade Payables					13.6	6.4
.1	.1	.1	Income Taxes Payable					.0	.2
6.8	5.9	11.9	All Other Current					8.1	6.4
26.7	26.3	28.9	Total Current					30.9	20.8
36.7	39.1	39.2	Long-Term Debt					41.2	40.6
.2	.3	.3	Deferred Taxes					.0	.6
3.1	5.1	6.5	All Other Non-Current					10.5	6.9
33.2	29.2	25.0	Net Worth					17.4	31.0
100.0	100.0	100.0	Total Liabilties & Net Worth					100.0	100.0
			INCOME DATA						
100.0	100.0	100.0	Net Sales					100.0	100.0
			Gross Profit						
87.8	91.7	88.5	Operating Expenses					89.3	90.1
12.2	8.3	11.5	Operating Profit					10.7	9.9
3.1	3.0	3.0	All Other Expenses (net)					2.2	3.1
9.1	5.3	8.6	Profit Before Taxes					8.5	6.8
			RATIOS						
2.1	2.2	2.2						1.9	2.8
1.1	1.0	1.1	Current					1.5	1.0
.5	.5	.6						.9	.6
2.0	1.4	1.9						1.9	2.3
.9	.8	.9	Quick					1.2	.8
.4	.4	.5						.7	.5
24 15.2	16 23.4	24 14.9						33 10.9	29 12.7
41 8.9	33 11.0	41 8.9	Sales/Receivables					42 8.7	40 9.2
54 6.7	49 7.4	54 6.8						53 6.9	65 5.6
			Cost of Sales/Inventory						
			Cost of Sales/Payables						
7.4	10.8	7.5						6.3	5.3
74.7	248.6	160.3	Sales/Working Capital					21.7	NM
-8.0	-9.5	-11.8						-82.8	-13.2
13.2	13.3	11.2						9.8	10.7
(65) 7.4	(53) 3.5	(50) 4.8	EBIT/Interest					6.0	(15) 3.7
.9	.9	1.6						3.4	1.0
3.1			Net Profit + Depr., Dep.,						
(12) 1.8			Amort./Cur. Mat. L/T/D						
1.2									
1.1	1.0	.9						1.0	1.2
2.2	1.9	2.1	Fixed/Worth					2.8	2.2
36.6	-7.1	-31.2						-2.1	NM
.8	.8	1.0						.7	2.0
2.4	2.1	2.6	Debt/Worth					2.7	3.5
60.8	-15.3	-36.6						-4.2	NM
61.6	68.7	57.9	% Profit Before Taxes/Tangible					68.7	85.5
(56) 27.1	(40) 18.6	(41) 29.4	Net Worth					(11) 39.5	(12) 24.4
5.1	5.8	11.2						12.2	13.7
19.7	23.6	15.6	% Profit Before Taxes/Total					29.6	12.4
8.8	5.3	7.5	Assets					15.6	3.9
.5	.1	1.1						6.7	.6
4.5	5.2	3.9						8.7	3.3
2.1	2.9	2.2	Sales/Net Fixed Assets					2.2	1.9
1.3	1.4	1.2						1.3	1.4
1.8	2.2	1.8						2.5	1.3
1.1	1.3	1.1	Sales/Total Assets					1.3	1.1
.8	.8	.8						.8	.8
5.4	4.9	6.2						6.2	7.4
(54) 9.2	(41) 9.3	(37) 9.8	% Depr., Dep., Amort./Sales					(11) 10.1	(10) 9.3
13.1	15.4	14.3						14.7	13.4
2.5	3.5	2.9	% Officers', Directors'						
(15) 5.0	(24) 4.7	(14) 6.6	Owners' Comp/Sales						
11.1	10.1	10.7							
2363535M	1402962M	1660784M	Net Sales ($)	2510M	15247M	15825M	54787M	224469M	1347946M
2187477M	1392847M	1668606M	Total Assets ($)	6030M	24112M	17503M	36655M	193166M	1391140M

© RMA 2019

M = $ thousand   MM = $ million
See Pages viii through xx for Explanation of Ratios and Data

Current Data Sorted by Assets

Comparative Historical Data

Type of Statement	0-500M	500M-2MM	2-10MM	10-50MM	50-100MM	100-250MM	4/1/14-3/31/15 ALL	4/1/15-3/31/16 ALL
Unqualified			2	5	2	2	17	18
Reviewed	1	5	20	9			41	43
Compiled	1	2	4	1			13	6
Tax Returns	4	4	3				14	29
Other	7	14	32	18	3	2	60	69
		8 (4/1-9/30/18)		133 (10/1/18-3/31/19)				
NUMBER OF STATEMENTS	13	25	61	33	5	4	145	165
ASSETS	%	%	%	%	%	%	%	%
Cash & Equivalents	24.8	13.6	8.7	10.8			12.5	14.0
Trade Receivables (net)	30.9	37.5	47.9	42.5			39.2	37.4
Inventory	.6	4.6	1.5	1.9			2.0	2.7
All Other Current	3.9	9.2	3.7	11.1			5.3	5.6
Total Current	60.2	64.9	61.9	66.3			59.0	59.8
Fixed Assets (net)	32.2	24.2	25.9	22.0			27.2	26.1
Intangibles (net)	3.1	8.6	4.4	9.2			7.0	6.8
All Other Non-Current	4.6	2.3	7.8	2.4			6.8	7.3
Total	100.0	100.0	100.0	100.0			100.0	100.0
LIABILITIES								
Notes Payable-Short Term	18.3	20.6	9.8	6.2			8.0	9.7
Cur. Mat.-L.T.D.	6.5	11.9	3.5	2.7			4.1	5.3
Trade Payables	6.0	14.8	12.3	14.1			12.8	14.9
Income Taxes Payable	.1	.0	.4	.1			.3	.3
All Other Current	5.8	6.4	8.9	15.8			10.7	12.6
Total Current	36.7	53.8	34.9	38.9			35.8	42.8
Long-Term Debt	22.9	20.7	15.3	13.7			15.2	17.1
Deferred Taxes	.0	.0	.1	.0			.6	.2
All Other Non-Current	1.6	3.1	3.1	3.1			4.7	4.3
Net Worth	39.2	22.4	46.8	44.2			43.6	35.5
Total Liabilities & Net Worth	100.0	100.0	100.0	100.0			100.0	100.0
INCOME DATA								
Net Sales	100.0	100.0	100.0	100.0			100.0	100.0
Gross Profit								
Operating Expenses	91.6	95.6	92.7	92.0			93.3	93.5
Operating Profit	8.4	4.4	7.3	8.0			6.7	6.5
All Other Expenses (net)	3.6	.2	.3	1.6			.6	1.1
Profit Before Taxes	4.8	4.2	7.0	6.3			6.1	5.4
RATIOS								
Current	7.2	3.2	3.3	2.6			2.9	2.6
	1.9	1.5	1.9	1.7			1.7	1.6
	1.2	.9	1.2	1.3			1.1	1.1
Quick	7.2	2.8	2.9	2.2			2.5	2.3
	1.8	1.4	1.6	1.4			1.5	1.4
	1.1	.7	1.0	1.0			.9	.8
Sales/Receivables	0 UND	2 155.0	52 7.0	55 6.6			49 7.5	34 10.6
	33 11.0	41 8.8	85 4.3	76 4.8			69 5.3	58 6.3
	83 4.4	73 5.0	101 3.6	99 3.7			91 4.0	94 3.9
Cost of Sales/Inventory								
Cost of Sales/Payables								
Sales/Working Capital	7.7	6.7	4.6	4.6			5.4	5.4
	9.4	20.1	7.9	7.3			10.9	12.5
	96.0	-109.4	21.2	19.5			41.8	66.3
EBIT/Interest		17.1	28.6	22.5			24.4	26.8
		(23) 5.6	(57) 11.7	(31) 11.4			(126) 8.0	(140) 9.1
		2.0	3.1	.9			1.7	1.5
Net Profit + Depr., Dep., Amort./Cur. Mat. L/T/D							5.9	5.5
							(29) 2.4	(32) 2.9
							1.4	1.2
Fixed/Worth	.3	.2	.2	.2			.3	.3
	.6	1.3	.5	.6			.6	.6
	1.2	NM	1.1	1.4			1.9	2.3
Debt/Worth	.3	1.0	.6	.8			.6	.7
	.8	2.3	1.3	1.5			1.6	1.8
	3.3	NM	2.6	3.9			4.8	4.9
% Profit Before Taxes/Tangible Net Worth	210.9	86.6	62.4	50.4			60.6	62.8
	(12) 41.7	(19) 52.3	(56) 28.1	(28) 33.0			(128) 32.2	(138) 31.6
	-5.6	13.1	14.1	3.8			7.8	7.7
% Profit Before Taxes/Total Assets	130.8	29.7	23.7	25.8			25.2	22.7
	13.6	13.8	14.0	12.8			11.4	9.6
	-3.1	2.3	5.7	.0			1.4	1.1
Sales/Net Fixed Assets	49.6	63.0	25.0	27.7			24.5	28.4
	20.4	14.5	9.5	10.3			9.8	11.3
	15.5	7.8	5.0	5.8			5.0	5.1
Sales/Total Assets	10.3	5.5	2.8	2.7			2.9	3.3
	5.2	3.7	2.0	1.8			2.1	2.3
	2.6	1.8	1.5	1.6			1.5	1.5
% Depr., Dep., Amort./Sales		.5	1.0	.6			1.1	1.0
		(14) 1.5	(45) 2.5	(29) 1.4			(111) 2.6	(129) 2.3
		4.2	4.5	3.5			4.4	4.4
% Officers', Directors' Owners' Comp/Sales		3.8	1.5				1.4	2.6
		(13) 5.5	(18) 3.1				(44) 2.4	(67) 4.6
		9.5	4.6				6.3	9.9
Net Sales ($)	23286M	93802M	643689M	1616955M	590995M	854911M	3872307M	4205479M
Total Assets ($)	3194M	24940M	293992M	768694M	339084M	655488M	2472879M	2401262M

M = $ thousand   MM = $ million
See Pages viii through xx for Explanation of Ratios and Data

Comparative Historical Data | Current Data Sorted by Sales

			Type of Statement						
17	15	11	Unqualified		3	4	8	3	8
44	39	35	Reviewed	1	3		8	12	7
14	6	8	Compiled	1		1	3	2	1
13	13	11	Tax Returns		5	2	1	3	
76	68	76	Other	4	9	10	17	17	19
4/1/16- 3/31/17 ALL	4/1/17- 3/31/18 ALL	4/1/18- 3/31/19 ALL			8 (4/1-9/30/18)			133 (10/1/18-3/31/19)	
				0-1MM	1-3MM	3-5MM	5-10MM	10-25MM	25MM & OVER
164	141	141	NUMBER OF STATEMENTS	6	17	17	29	37	35
%	%	%	ASSETS	%	%	%	%	%	%
12.0	11.6	11.6	Cash & Equivalents		20.1	9.4	10.6	11.3	9.3
37.7	41.6	42.5	Trade Receivables (net)		33.6	41.6	39.7	48.9	42.9
2.5	2.7	2.1	Inventory		6.0	1.9	2.0	1.0	2.1
6.1	4.1	6.7	All Other Current		7.1	4.0	3.2	8.4	9.7
58.2	60.0	63.0	Total Current		66.8	56.8	55.5	69.5	64.0
26.4	25.3	24.5	Fixed Assets (net)		27.7	33.1	28.8	20.5	19.3
8.1	9.0	7.6	Intangibles (net)		2.1	7.4	5.8	4.8	14.0
7.3	5.7	5.0	All Other Non-Current		3.4	2.7	9.9	5.2	2.7
100.0	100.0	100.0	Total		100.0	100.0	100.0	100.0	100.0
			LIABILITIES						
8.6	9.0	11.3	Notes Payable-Short Term		23.1	17.2	11.4	9.5	4.9
4.1	3.7	4.9	Cur. Mat.-L.T.D.		4.4	11.1	3.9	5.0	2.6
11.6	15.7	12.7	Trade Payables		8.1	14.6	7.2	16.1	15.4
.6	.3	.2	Income Taxes Payable		.0	.0	.7	.2	.1
8.8	10.5	10.3	All Other Current		5.6	8.2	8.1	9.0	17.4
33.6	39.3	39.4	Total Current		41.2	51.2	31.2	39.8	40.4
18.2	14.8	16.8	Long-Term Debt		19.6	27.7	18.1	10.3	16.6
.4	.3	.0	Deferred Taxes		.0	.0	.0	.0	.2
4.1	5.8	3.1	All Other Non-Current		1.2	.0	7.2	3.5	2.2
43.6	39.8	40.7	Net Worth		38.1	21.1	43.5	46.3	40.7
100.0	100.0	100.0	Total Liabilties & Net Worth		100.0	100.0	100.0	100.0	100.0
			INCOME DATA						
100.0	100.0	100.0	Net Sales		100.0	100.0	100.0	100.0	100.0
			Gross Profit						
91.8	92.2	93.1	Operating Expenses		93.6	96.9	91.6	91.3	94.3
8.2	7.8	6.9	Operating Profit		6.4	3.1	8.4	8.7	5.7
1.4	.9	1.0	All Other Expenses (net)		2.6	.0	.7	.5	1.1
6.9	7.0	6.0	Profit Before Taxes		3.8	3.1	7.7	8.2	4.6
			RATIOS						
3.2	3.3	3.0			6.9	3.8	3.9	2.8	2.2
1.8	1.7	1.7	Current		2.4	1.6	1.7	2.0	1.6
1.1	1.2	1.2			1.1	.8	1.1	1.3	1.3
2.8	3.1	2.7			5.3	3.5	3.9	2.7	1.8
1.4	1.5	1.4	Quick		1.5	1.6	1.3	1.6	1.3
.9	1.0	1.0			.9	.8	1.0	1.0	.9
41 8.8	43 8.4	42 8.6	Sales/Receivables	0 UND	27 13.4	37 9.9	50 7.3	56 6.5	
69 5.3	74 4.9	73 5.0		41 8.8	68 5.4	78 4.7	79 4.6	76 4.8	
91 4.0	96 3.8	96 3.8		56 6.5	96 3.8	99 3.7	99 3.7	101 3.6	
			Cost of Sales/Inventory						
			Cost of Sales/Payables						
4.9	4.9	5.1			6.3	4.4	4.6	4.3	6.0
9.5	9.5	8.9	Sales/Working Capital		9.4	13.8	9.4	7.9	8.8
57.8	34.5	36.3			56.4	-19.7	115.3	16.6	23.7
35.6	37.9	24.8			38.4	18.2	22.3	34.0	22.9
(140) 10.5	(123) 10.2	(128) 9.3	EBIT/Interest	(14) 6.2	4.7 (28)	8.8 (33)	16.3 (34)	10.3	
2.0	2.0	1.5			.7	-2.0	3.0	4.6	-.9
7.9	14.8	13.4	Net Profit + Depr., Dep.,						
(30) 4.0	(20) 5.3	(19) 3.2	Amort./Cur. Mat. L/T/D						
1.4	2.4	2.0							
.2	.2	.2			.2	.3	.2	.2	.3
.5	.5	.6	Fixed/Worth		.7	1.1	.6	.4	.6
1.9	1.5	1.4			1.3	NM	1.3	.9	5.9
.5	.6	.6			.3	.5	.6	.6	.8
1.4	1.2	1.4	Debt/Worth		.8	2.3	1.4	1.4	2.3
4.2	4.4	4.5			8.4	NM	3.8	2.7	15.5
61.5	68.9	62.7	% Profit Before Taxes/Tangible		154.2	66.7	63.3	68.3	45.1
(141) 32.1	(120) 37.0	(121) 30.8	Net Worth	(16) 44.9	14.0 (13)	27.9 (26)	33.7 (34)	30.4 (27)	
10.2	12.1	12.2			-5.5	-39.9	18.4	17.1	-3.9
25.1	29.0	24.2	% Profit Before Taxes/Total		39.5	23.6	22.7	29.7	20.1
10.0	11.4	13.4	Assets		14.0	4.7	14.0	16.9	10.6
2.5	2.2	1.9			-1.7	-10.2	4.9	6.1	-2.5
27.2	26.1	30.7			57.8	21.2	26.8	42.2	28.3
11.2	12.2	13.1	Sales/Net Fixed Assets		20.4	8.3	10.8	14.4	13.6
5.4	5.5	6.2			11.7	4.4	3.8	6.8	7.3
2.9	3.1	3.1			6.2	5.0	2.7	3.2	2.7
2.1	2.1	2.2	Sales/Total Assets		4.1	2.1	1.8	2.6	1.9
1.5	1.6	1.6			2.3	1.7	1.4	1.8	1.5
1.2	1.1	.8			.3	.8	1.2	.8	.6
(127) 2.0	(107) 2.3	(104) 1.9	% Depr., Dep., Amort./Sales	(12) 1.1	2.5 (11)	2.5 (18)	2.2 (27)	1.5 (32)	
4.8	4.0	3.8			2.2	7.5	6.5	3.8	3.6
1.9	1.3	1.7					2.5	1.2	
(53) 5.0	(46) 2.9	(45) 3.6	% Officers', Directors'			(12)	4.2 (12)	1.4	
9.3	6.6	6.1	Owners' Comp/Sales				5.4	2.7	
4008007M	3190738M	3823638M	Net Sales ($)	2455M	34326M	65534M	190945M	601857M	2928521M
2352753M	1815638M	2085392M	Total Assets ($)	1810M	10429M	28407M	107366M	277990M	1659390M

© RMA 2019

M = $ thousand   MM = $ million
See Pages viii through xx for Explanation of Ratios and Data

Current Data Sorted by Assets   Comparative Historical Data

0-500M	500M-2MM	2-10MM	10-50MM	50-100MM	100-250MM	Type of Statement	4/1/14-3/31/15 ALL	4/1/15-3/31/16 ALL
		1	3	5	3	Unqualified	15	12
		7	6			Reviewed	15	15
	1	3	1			Compiled	13	11
1	2	6	1			Tax Returns	13	8
3	9	15	8	5	3	Other	34	56
2	7 (4/1-9/30/18)	78 (10/1/18-3/31/19)						
6	12	32	19	10	6	**NUMBER OF STATEMENTS**	90	102

0-500M	500M-2MM	2-10MM	10-50MM	50-100MM	100-250MM		4/1/14-3/31/15 ALL	4/1/15-3/31/16 ALL
%	%	%	%	%	%	**ASSETS**	%	%
	13.7	13.2	8.9	9.6		Cash & Equivalents	11.6	10.2
	19.8	19.7	19.5	12.0		Trade Receivables (net)	24.4	20.4
	11.8	10.3	7.7	2.3		Inventory	9.7	8.2
	5.9	2.2	2.1	1.6		All Other Current	3.3	3.1
	51.2	45.4	38.2	25.6		Total Current	48.9	41.8
	34.6	41.3	44.7	56.2		Fixed Assets (net)	39.0	45.8
	9.4	6.5	8.7	10.4		Intangibles (net)	5.2	7.0
	4.8	6.8	8.4	7.9		All Other Non-Current	6.9	5.4
	100.0	100.0	100.0	100.0		Total	100.0	100.0
						LIABILITIES		
	4.3	3.2	3.8	.9		Notes Payable-Short Term	7.5	6.6
	3.6	4.5	4.7	3.7		Cur. Mat.-L.T.D.	6.5	5.3
	17.4	14.8	9.9	5.5		Trade Payables	21.5	16.4
	.0	.0	.0	.3		Income Taxes Payable	.1	.3
	2.2	8.4	4.8	6.9		All Other Current	8.4	10.6
	27.5	30.9	23.1	17.4		Total Current	44.0	39.2
	26.6	21.7	35.1	33.7		Long-Term Debt	22.6	25.1
	.0	.2	.6	.3		Deferred Taxes	.5	.8
	5.4	4.1	6.5	5.2		All Other Non-Current	4.2	3.7
	40.5	43.2	34.7	43.3		Net Worth	28.7	31.3
	100.0	100.0	100.0	100.0		Total Liabilities & Net Worth	100.0	100.0
						INCOME DATA		
	100.0	100.0	100.0	100.0		Net Sales	100.0	100.0
						Gross Profit		
	93.6	90.6	93.4	92.0		Operating Expenses	91.5	95.3
	6.4	9.4	6.6	8.0		Operating Profit	8.5	4.7
	2.3	1.5	1.7	1.1		All Other Expenses (net)	2.1	1.3
	4.1	8.0	4.9	7.0		Profit Before Taxes	6.4	3.4
						RATIOS		
	3.8	3.5	3.3	3.2			2.6	2.2
	2.0	1.3	1.9	2.2		Current	1.3	1.2
	.9	.8	.9	.7			.7	.7
	2.7	2.4	2.7	2.7			2.0	1.6
	1.5	1.1	1.3	1.9		Quick	1.0	.9
	.5	.5	.7	.7			.5	.5
	8 48.2	21 17.0	27 13.6	31 11.6			21 17.8	19 19.0
	16 22.9	30 12.0	42 8.6	41 8.9		Sales/Receivables	34 10.7	33 11.0
	54 6.8	51 7.2	50 7.3	63 5.8			47 7.8	49 7.4
						Cost of Sales/Inventory		
						Cost of Sales/Payables		
	4.0	9.3	6.3	5.4			6.9	7.7
	13.1	17.9	11.1	9.8		Sales/Working Capital	24.8	39.2
	NM	-26.1	-42.0	-11.1			-20.3	-19.6
		20.4	24.6				25.2	12.8
		(29) 7.2	(18) 5.2			EBIT/Interest	(77) 8.2	(92) 4.0
		1.6	.8				1.4	.1
							5.6	5.5
						Net Profit + Depr., Dep., Amort./Cur. Mat. L/T/D	(13) 2.0	(21) 2.1
							1.3	1.3
	.1	.4	.6	1.0			.5	.9
	.6	1.3	1.3	2.1		Fixed/Worth	1.1	1.6
	17.6	2.6	4.1	4.2			3.5	8.5
	.4	.5	1.0	.4			.6	.9
	1.9	1.3	3.9	2.4		Debt/Worth	1.7	2.6
	NM	3.9	11.8	4.6			7.9	15.5
		66.2	47.8				48.0	56.6
		(26) 30.3	(17) 29.5			% Profit Before Taxes/Tangible Net Worth	(78) 24.2	(84) 16.8
		7.9	2.7				11.0	.3
	18.5	26.2	30.1	14.3			20.0	12.2
	2.6	9.9	5.8	11.0		% Profit Before Taxes/Total Assets	7.5	4.7
	-.2	1.8	.0	7.1			1.4	-2.7
	23.1	15.4	7.7	2.5			24.7	12.9
	12.3	6.0	3.6	1.7		Sales/Net Fixed Assets	7.1	4.1
	3.7	2.1	1.5	1.1			3.1	2.1
	3.2	3.0	3.0	1.3			4.1	2.0
	2.5	2.5	1.5	1.0		Sales/Total Assets	2.3	2.0
	1.0	1.1	.9	.7			1.5	1.2
		2.4	2.4				1.3	2.0
		(26) 4.3	(17) 5.6			% Depr., Dep., Amort./Sales	(74) 2.6	(87) 4.1
		9.5	11.4				5.0	7.5
		.6					1.0	1.1
		(11) 1.0				% Officers', Directors' Owners' Comp/Sales	(32) 1.4	(24) 2.4
		3.6					3.1	5.7
12179M	31279M	441671M	967028M	779220M	1433112M	Net Sales ($)	3542450M	3970503M
1338M	14024M	161609M	509369M	702771M	956075M	Total Assets ($)	1966503M	2316110M

Comparative Historical Data   Current Data Sorted by Sales

4/1/16-3/31/17 ALL	4/1/17-3/31/18 ALL	4/1/18-3/31/19 ALL	Type of Statement	0-1MM	1-3MM	3-5MM	5-10MM	10-25MM	25MM & OVER
10	11	12	Unqualified					2	10
19	20	13	Reviewed	2			3	3	6
12	10	6	Compiled		1	1	2	2	
14	17	12	Tax Returns	2	3	2	1	1	3
44	55	42	Other	2	5	6	7	5	17
						7 (4/1-9/30/18)		78 (10/1/18-3/31/19)	
99	113	85	**NUMBER OF STATEMENTS**	6	9	9	13	13	35
%	%	%	**ASSETS**	%	%	%	%	%	%
9.4	11.1	12.6	Cash & Equivalents				13.0	12.9	10.7
23.8	19.0	18.3	Trade Receivables (net)				15.6	22.5	19.7
8.7	9.3	8.9	Inventory				8.9	6.5	10.2
2.6	2.4	2.5	All Other Current				1.3	4.2	2.0
44.5	41.9	42.3	Total Current				38.9	46.1	42.6
44.2	47.2	41.9	Fixed Assets (net)				48.4	38.9	41.2
4.3	6.1	8.6	Intangibles (net)				4.2	10.7	8.3
6.9	4.9	7.2	All Other Non-Current				8.6	4.3	7.9
100.0	100.0	100.0	Total				100.0	100.0	100.0
			LIABILITIES						
8.8	6.7	6.8	Notes Payable-Short Term				7.5	2.7	4.9
7.2	5.4	4.2	Cur. Mat.-L.T.D.				4.7	4.9	3.6
16.8	15.0	11.7	Trade Payables				16.6	15.2	10.0
.2	.0	.1	Income Taxes Payable				.0	.1	.1
10.1	8.1	10.6	All Other Current				2.1	8.1	6.3
43.1	35.3	33.3	Total Current				30.9	31.0	24.9
22.8	28.2	26.9	Long-Term Debt				19.4	22.3	28.8
.4	.5	.4	Deferred Taxes				.0	1.4	.6
6.2	7.5	5.3	All Other Non-Current				3.5	2.5	7.3
27.4	28.5	34.0	Net Worth				46.3	42.8	38.4
100.0	100.0	100.0	Total Liabilities & Net Worth				100.0	100.0	100.0
			INCOME DATA						
100.0	100.0	100.0	Net Sales				100.0	100.0	100.0
			Gross Profit						
92.6	89.8	93.0	Operating Expenses				93.8	94.4	93.6
7.4	10.2	7.0	Operating Profit				6.2	5.6	6.4
1.8	2.4	1.6	All Other Expenses (net)				1.1	.6	1.2
5.6	7.9	5.4	Profit Before Taxes				5.1	5.0	5.2
			RATIOS						
1.9	2.3	3.2					1.6	3.4	3.5
1.2	1.2	1.5	Current				1.1	1.4	1.9
.7	.8	.8					.7	.8	1.2
1.5	1.8	2.3					1.3	3.3	2.4
.9	.9	1.2	Quick				.8	1.1	1.6
.5	.5	.6					.5	.7	.8
22 16.6	16 22.6	18 20.5					7 49.2	22 16.7	27 13.6
35 10.3	32 11.3	34 10.7	Sales/Receivables				34 10.7	31 11.8	41 8.9
48 7.6	45 8.2	51 7.2					51 7.1	51 7.1	51 7.2
			Cost of Sales/Inventory						
			Cost of Sales/Payables						
9.9	7.9	7.0					14.3	9.6	6.3
35.7	40.5	15.0	Sales/Working Capital				166.4	13.0	10.7
-25.5	-24.6	-26.3					20.0	-29.3	41.1
10.7	17.2	17.0					17.4	27.7	18.5
(90) 4.1	(96) 5.7	(73) 4.5	EBIT/Interest		(12) 6.1		(12) 6.2	(31) 7.4	
.0	1.8	1.0					.5	1.3	.3
3.3	5.6	11.9							
(14) 2.2	(20) 3.1	(12) 2.9	Net Profit + Depr., Dep., Amort./Cur. Mat. L/T/D						
1.2	2.0	1.5							
.7	.9	.4					.5	.7	.4
1.8	1.6	1.3	Fixed/Worth				1.0	1.3	1.2
7.2	13.7	4.0					2.1	2.9	4.1
1.0	.9	.7					.4	1.0	.9
2.7	2.5	2.1	Debt/Worth				1.2	2.1	1.8
18.1	28.6	10.9					2.7	4.1	8.4
62.6	57.0	45.4					32.9	94.5	47.8
(82) 21.9	(90) 26.1	(69) 25.4	% Profit Before Taxes/Tangible Net Worth		(11) 17.1		(12) 29.9	(31) 37.3	
1.3	9.5	4.3					3.2	3.9	5.3
13.5	16.9	19.7					24.7	50.3	20.7
5.4	6.9	7.1	% Profit Before Taxes/Total Assets				6.5	11.0	9.0
-1.0	1.4	.1					-.6	.7	.0
12.6	11.3	16.2					29.3	12.0	17.9
5.7	5.5	5.1	Sales/Net Fixed Assets				5.8	6.4	3.7
2.4	2.0	1.9					1.9	4.2	1.8
3.4	3.2	3.0					2.7	2.9	3.2
2.1	2.2	2.1	Sales/Total Assets				2.3	2.7	1.5
1.2	1.1	1.0					1.1	1.7	1.0
2.0	2.6	2.2						3.0	1.0
(77) 4.0	(86) 4.4	(65) 4.3	% Depr., Dep., Amort./Sales				(12)	(12) 4.9	(27) 2.9
7.7	8.9	10.6						10.6	8.9
1.4	1.0	.6							
(41) 2.9	(33) 2.1	(20) 2.1	% Officers', Directors' Owners' Comp/Sales						
5.3	5.2	5.4							
3561112M	4213966M	3664489M	Net Sales ($)	1982M	17252M	32327M	85592M	201734M	3325602M
2140996M	2277948M	2345186M	Total Assets ($)	10813M	11005M	31758M	56637M	134104M	2100869M

M = $ thousand   MM = $ million
See Pages viii through xx for Explanation of Ratios and Data

Current Data Sorted by Assets

Comparative Historical Data

						Type of Statement		
						Unqualified		
						Reviewed	1	2
						Compiled	8	3
						Tax Returns	9	13
2	1	2				Other	10	14
4	10	1 1					4/1/14-	4/1/15-
5	5	1 8	2				3/31/15	3/31/16
	1 (4/1-9/30/18)		40 (10/1/18-3/31/19)				ALL	ALL
0-500M	500M-2MM	2-10MM	10-50MM	50-100MM	100-250MM			
11	16	12	2			NUMBER OF STATEMENTS	28	32
%	%	%	%	%	%	ASSETS	%	%
21.2	16.4	14.5		D	D	Cash & Equivalents	13.6	11.0
22.4	9.5	23.4		A	A	Trade Receivables (net)	19.8	18.7
.2	.5	.6		T	T	Inventory	1.0	2.1
.8	.8	.6		A	A	All Other Current	.9	3.6
44.6	27.3	39.1				Total Current	35.3	35.5
43.5	57.3	50.3		N	N	Fixed Assets (net)	51.8	46.5
4.7	12.6	6.3		O	O	Intangibles (net)	8.9	8.3
7.2	2.8	4.3		T	T	All Other Non-Current	4.0	9.6
100.0	100.0	100.0				Total	100.0	100.0
				A	A	LIABILITIES		
22.6	1.2	3.5		V	V	Notes Payable-Short Term	2.8	11.9
7.7	7.6	5.6		A	A	Cur. Mat.-L.T.D.	7.3	3.4
11.5	3.5	2.6		I	I	Trade Payables	7.3	8.6
.0	.0	.0		L	L	Income Taxes Payable	.1	.4
7.1	11.8	2.4		A	A	All Other Current	3.8	6.2
48.9	24.1	14.1		B	B	Total Current	21.2	30.5
34.3	36.4	28.0		L	L	Long-Term Debt	34.3	32.4
.0	.0	.1		E	E	Deferred Taxes	.5	.6
2.8	2.2	1.1				All Other Non-Current	11.1	7.6
13.9	37.3	56.6				Net Worth	32.8	29.0
100.0	100.0	100.0				Total Liabilities & Net Worth	100.0	100.0
						INCOME DATA		
100.0	100.0	100.0				Net Sales	100.0	100.0
						Gross Profit		
92.9	91.0	82.6				Operating Expenses	87.2	90.5
7.1	9.0	17.4				Operating Profit	12.8	9.5
.4	.5	4.6				All Other Expenses (net)	3.5	.4
6.8	8.5	12.8				Profit Before Taxes	9.2	9.2
						RATIOS		
3.3	4.2	10.0					5.0	2.9
1.4	1.5	1.9				Current	1.7	1.3
.6	.9	1.3					1.0	.5
3.1	4.0	9.5					5.0	2.7
1.4	1.3	1.8				Quick	1.7	1.1
.6	.7	1.3					.8	.4

1	473.0	0	UND	22	16.4		Sales/Receivables	0	UND	0	UND
17	21.1	3	135.6	40	9.1			33	11.0	25	14.7
47	7.8	43	8.4	64	5.7			46	8.0	42	8.7

						Cost of Sales/Inventory		
						Cost of Sales/Payables		
8.4	7.2	3.1					8.0	6.8
44.7	28.4	13.6				Sales/Working Capital	14.7	29.8
-16.0	-53.3	29.5					NM	-29.6
44.6	16.3						13.8	15.6
6.4	(15) 4.8					EBIT/Interest	(25) 7.3	(31) 6.8
-2.5	-.4						2.7	1.7
						Net Profit + Depr., Dep., Amort./Cur. Mat. L/T/D		
.5	1.0	.4					.9	.8
2.1	1.8	1.0				Fixed/Worth	2.5	1.4
-7.6	-4.6	3.5					-16.9	NM
.7	.6	.2					.8	.9
2.6	3.0	.9				Debt/Worth	2.5	2.1
-15.1	-9.4	3.4					-38.2	NM
	42.6	50.7				% Profit Before Taxes/Tangible Net Worth	82.1	75.1
(11)	25.5	(10) 26.7					(19) 38.4	(24) 46.6
	-1.4	19.5					17.2	15.2
68.6	24.3	28.7				% Profit Before Taxes/Total Assets	25.3	27.4
18.0	11.3	16.1					12.0	17.5
-15.9	-3.4	6.8					3.8	1.8
26.2	7.0	5.0				Sales/Net Fixed Assets	9.9	8.2
12.1	3.3	3.3					4.5	4.8
5.3	1.4	2.1					2.2	2.9
8.7	2.7	2.2				Sales/Total Assets	3.4	2.4
3.0	1.4	1.6					2.3	2.0
2.5	1.0	.9					1.4	1.6
	7.2	4.2				% Depr., Dep., Amort./Sales	3.7	2.1
(11)	10.3	(10) 6.2					(20) 7.4	(30) 5.5
	11.8	14.5					11.1	11.0
	2.8					% Officers', Directors' Owners' Comp/Sales	3.5	2.4
(12)	5.8						(16) 4.7	(19) 4.7
	6.5						6.2	6.9
14746M	32960M	96693M	48962M			Net Sales ($)	146250M	404902M
3051M	18785M	61015M	58537M			Total Assets ($)	71188M	190396M

M = $ thousand   MM = $ million
See Pages viii through xx for Explanation of Ratios and Data

Comparative Historical Data

Current Data Sorted by Sales

				Type of Statement						
1		2		Unqualified						
2		3		Reviewed			1	1		
4		6		Compiled			1	1		
11		12		Tax Returns	3	3	1	1		
19		14		Other	5	10	2	1	5	1
4/1/16-		4/1/17-				6				
3/31/17		3/31/18				1 (4/1-9/30/18)		40 (10/1/18-3/31/19)		
ALL		ALL			0-1MM	1-3MM	3-5MM	5-10MM	10-25MM	25MM & OVER

1 ALL 4/1/16-3/31/17	2 ALL 4/1/17-3/31/18	2 ALL 4/1/18-3/31/19		0-1MM	1-3MM	3-5MM	5-10MM	10-25MM	25MM & OVER
37	37	41	NUMBER OF STATEMENTS	8	19	3	4	6	1
%	%	%	ASSETS	%	%	%	%	%	%
14.2	16.3	16.6	Cash & Equivalents		18.2				
21.1	16.4	17.5	Trade Receivables (net)		11.7				
.8	.4	.5	Inventory		.5				
3.1	.9	.8	All Other Current		1.1				
39.2	34.1	35.3	Total Current		31.5				
49.4	48.6	51.2	Fixed Assets (net)		50.3				
6.0	13.1	9.1	Intangibles (net)		12.6				
5.4	4.2	4.4	All Other Non-Current		5.6				
100.0	100.0	100.0	Total		100.0				
			LIABILITIES						
7.2	5.0	7.9	Notes Payable-Short Term		11.1				
5.5	8.7	6.9	Cur. Mat.-L.T.D.		7.4				
5.1	4.6	5.7	Trade Payables		7.2				
.1	.0	.0	Income Taxes Payable		.0				
6.8	4.6	7.5	All Other Current		5.0				
24.7	22.9	27.9	Total Current		30.8				
32.4	44.3	33.5	Long-Term Debt		36.4				
.2	.5	.1	Deferred Taxes		.0				
3.6	2.1	1.9	All Other Non-Current		2.1				
39.1	30.2	36.6	Net Worth		30.7				
100.0	100.0	100.0	Total Liabilities & Net Worth		100.0				
			INCOME DATA						
100.0	100.0	100.0	Net Sales		100.0				
			Gross Profit						
87.3	90.5	88.9	Operating Expenses		90.0				
12.7	9.5	11.1	Operating Profit		10.0				
1.2	2.9	1.9	All Other Expenses (net)		.9				
11.4	6.6	9.3	Profit Before Taxes		9.2				
			RATIOS						
4.0	3.1	4.1			3.8				
2.2	1.6	1.5	Current		1.5				
.7	.6	.8			.9				
3.6	2.8	4.0			3.8				
1.9	1.6	1.5	Quick		1.5				
.6	.6	.7			.7				
0 UND	0 UND	0 UND			0 UND				
27 13.3	32 11.4	21 17.2	Sales/Receivables		12 31.6				
55 6.6	51 7.2	49 7.4			46 7.9				
			Cost of Sales/Inventory						
			Cost of Sales/Payables						
6.6	7.2	7.3			7.8				
22.5	25.7	25.3	Sales/Working Capital		27.0				
-31.6	-26.1	-34.3			-44.9				
17.3	13.1	33.0			31.4				
(32) 9.1	(33) 4.9	(37) 6.4	EBIT/Interest		(18) 7.2				
7.4	1.2	1.3			2.1				
			Net Profit + Depr., Dep., Amort./Cur. Mat. L/T/D						
.8	.9	.7			.7				
1.3	1.8	1.4	Fixed/Worth		2.2				
4.8	-3.4	-9.3			-3.8				
.4	.8	.6			.6				
1.5	1.6	1.8	Debt/Worth		3.7				
12.3	-6.8	-19.3			-7.5				
93.1	84.9	61.7			109.5				
(31) 51.7	(26) 27.2	(30) 32.4	% Profit Before Taxes/Tangible Net Worth		(13) 42.0				
29.7	9.9	16.6			24.5				
32.5	30.3	27.6			26.0				
21.9	10.3	12.3	% Profit Before Taxes/Total Assets		10.4				
11.7	1.1	2.0			5.0				
14.1	10.9	9.6			12.6				
5.4	4.4	4.2	Sales/Net Fixed Assets		7.0				
2.6	2.4	1.8			1.7				
3.5	3.4	3.0			4.3				
2.5	2.0	1.8	Sales/Total Assets		1.8				
1.8	1.2	1.3			1.3				
3.9	2.5	3.9			1.9				
(21) 5.1	(28) 7.5	(29) 7.2	% Depr., Dep., Amort./Sales		(17) 4.8				
13.0	9.5	11.3			10.5				
2.9	4.0	2.9			3.5				
(20) 7.2	(18) 7.7	(24) 5.0	% Officers', Directors' Owners' Comp/Sales		(13) 5.9				
9.8	12.0	6.9			7.4				
183367M	550193M	193361M	Net Sales ($)	4701M	35670M	9653M	28069M	84793M	30475M
86180M	382441M	141388M	Total Assets ($)	10739M	23513M	4656M	13591M	56754M	32135M

© RMA 2019

M = $ thousand   MM = $ million
See Pages viii through xx for Explanation of Ratios and Data

Current Data Sorted by Assets | Comparative Historical Data

0-500M	500M-2MM	2-10MM	10-50MM	50-100MM	100-250MM	Type of Statement		
	2 2 2 3 10	2 2 5 3 20	5 3 3 13	3	3	Unqualified	11	10
						Reviewed	18	15
						Compiled	16	14
6	13 (4/1-9/30/18)		82 (10/1/18-3/31/19)	1	5	Tax Returns	46	31
4			13			Other	51	50
							4/1/14- 3/31/15 ALL	4/1/15- 3/31/16 ALL
10	17	32	24	4	6	NUMBER OF STATEMENTS	142	120
%	%	%	%	%	%	ASSETS	%	%
31.2	15.2	10.6	10.7			Cash & Equivalents	17.0	14.7
14.0	28.8	25.4	24.1			Trade Receivables (net)	22.8	19.9
.0	2.5	6.7	2.8			Inventory	4.9	3.4
2.0	.3	4.9	2.4			All Other Current	2.3	2.6
47.1	46.8	47.6	40.1			Total Current	47.0	40.7
37.7	38.6	39.0	36.9			Fixed Assets (net)	38.3	41.7
13.2	7.6	6.9	14.8			Intangibles (net)	6.0	8.3
2.0	7.0	6.5	8.1			All Other Non-Current	8.7	9.3
100.0	100.0	100.0	100.0			Total	100.0	100.0
						LIABILITIES		
5.1	4.5	9.0	8.3			Notes Payable-Short Term	8.7	7.0
4.4	9.9	5.5	5.9			Cur. Mat.-L.T.D.	6.3	5.3
19.4	11.0	10.2	9.3			Trade Payables	9.6	8.6
.0	.1	.0	.0			Income Taxes Payable	.1	.0
8.4	7.6	9.3	6.3			All Other Current	7.0	5.2
37.3	33.1	34.1	29.8			Total Current	31.7	26.1
70.9	24.8	17.5	26.4			Long-Term Debt	23.6	25.3
.0	.0	.5	.9			Deferred Taxes	.3	.3
.0	8.0	3.7	6.4			All Other Non-Current	4.3	8.3
-8.3	34.1	44.1	36.5			Net Worth	40.0	40.0
100.0	100.0	100.0	100.0			Total Liabilities & Net Worth	100.0	100.0
						INCOME DATA		
100.0	100.0	100.0	100.0			Net Sales	100.0	100.0
						Gross Profit		
86.8	89.9	89.9	94.8			Operating Expenses	90.2	91.8
13.2	10.1	10.1	5.2			Operating Profit	9.8	8.2
1.0	1.3	1.5	1.2			All Other Expenses (net)	1.2	1.5
12.3	8.8	8.7	4.0			Profit Before Taxes	8.6	6.7
						RATIOS		
14.9	3.2	2.2	2.4				3.5	3.8
8.8	2.0	1.3	1.3			Current	1.6	1.7
.3	.8	.8	.9				.9	1.0
14.1	3.2	2.0	2.1				3.0	3.4
8.3	1.7	(31) 1.0	1.0			Quick	1.3	1.3
.3	.5	.6	.7				.7	.8
0 UND	0 UND	32 11.5	45 8.1				14 26.8	8 43.4
1 335.2	30 12.3	51 7.2	63 5.8			Sales/Receivables	36 10.1	37 9.8
66 5.5	58 6.3	66 5.5	74 4.9				53 6.9	59 6.2
						Cost of Sales/Inventory		
						Cost of Sales/Payables		
3.1	8.5	7.0	7.2				5.7	6.0
6.4	16.3	16.3	14.8			Sales/Working Capital	16.8	14.0
-26.7	NM	-185.1	-27.0				-52.9	-162.5
	27.0	28.2	10.4				23.3	18.5
	(11) 11.5	(27) 7.9	(22) 5.8			EBIT/Interest	(121) 6.6	(103) 7.7
	.2	2.0	.6				1.7	2.0
							4.6	6.4
						Net Profit + Depr., Dep., Amort./Cur. Mat. L/T/D	(18) 2.1	(15) 2.6
							1.2	1.4
.1	.7	.5	1.0				.4	.4
-7.8	1.1	1.0	2.1			Fixed/Worth	1.2	1.3
-1.3	5.5	2.1	7.9				3.7	3.7
.1	.6	.9	1.3				.4	.5
-14.4	2.0	1.3	3.5			Debt/Worth	1.4	1.7
-3.2	25.7	3.3	14.5				7.8	4.8
	85.8	82.2	64.2				54.5	57.3
	(14) 65.9	(29) 27.1	(21) 14.7			% Profit Before Taxes/Tangible Net Worth	(120) 25.5	(100) 30.4
	23.6	9.2	3.5				12.1	8.3
100.1	44.6	29.2	13.4				22.8	25.8
17.2	25.5	10.3	7.8			% Profit Before Taxes/Total Assets	10.1	10.6
-8.5	6.1	2.8	.2				2.7	3.1
269.8	37.7	15.9	9.2				18.3	11.9
13.1	10.0	4.6	3.4			Sales/Net Fixed Assets	7.2	5.1
3.7	5.2	2.8	2.4				3.1	2.8
4.2	4.2	2.5	2.0				3.4	3.1
2.3	3.8	1.9	1.3			Sales/Total Assets	2.3	2.1
.8	2.8	1.3	1.0				1.5	1.4
	2.7	2.3	1.5				2.2	2.1
	(10) 3.1	(26) 4.9	(21) 4.2			% Depr., Dep., Amort./Sales	(97) 4.7	(89) 5.3
	14.5	7.5	10.0				7.7	9.6
		1.9					2.4	2.9
		(10) 4.4				% Officers', Directors' Owners' Comp/Sales	(49) 4.7	(33) 5.4
		9.4					8.4	10.4
20049M	68851M	286749M	746254M	532732M	1373287M	Net Sales ($)	2849280M	2379614M
2989M	18431M	134308M	515813M	267946M	1436129M	Total Assets ($)	1782776M	1729148M

M = $ thousand   MM = $ million
See Pages viii through xx for Explanation of Ratios and Data

Comparative Historical Data   Current Data Sorted by Sales

4/1/16-3/31/17 ALL	4/1/17-3/31/18 ALL	4/1/18-3/31/19 ALL	Type of Statement	0-1MM	1-3MM	3-5MM	5-10MM	10-25MM	25MM & OVER
8	9	13	Unqualified					2	11
15	11	7	Reviewed		1	1	2	1	2
7	5	10	Compiled			2	3	4	1
23	31	12	Tax Returns	3	4	2	2	1	
53	46	53	Other	6	7	7	13	7	13
				13 (4/1-9/30/18)			82 (10/1/18-3/31/19)		
106	102	95	**NUMBER OF STATEMENTS**	9	12	12	20	15	27
%	%	%	**ASSETS**	%	%	%	%	%	%
15.8	13.4	12.4	Cash & Equivalents		16.2	19.8	11.2	15.9	4.8
22.2	22.4	23.7	Trade Receivables (net)		16.3	16.7	30.5	26.2	26.4
2.9	2.1	3.9	Inventory		8.9	3.8	1.6	5.5	3.8
2.9	2.0	2.9	All Other Current		1.1	.7	5.1	4.1	2.6
43.7	39.9	42.8	Total Current		42.6	41.0	48.4	51.7	37.6
39.7	41.5	36.5	Fixed Assets (net)		45.0	52.0	33.4	30.3	29.6
8.4	11.5	13.6	Intangibles (net)		6.8	4.0	8.2	15.1	22.1
8.2	7.1	7.1	All Other Non-Current		5.7	3.0	10.0	2.9	10.8
100.0	100.0	100.0	Total		100.0	100.0	100.0	100.0	100.0
			LIABILITIES						
5.3	5.1	7.0	Notes Payable-Short Term		5.5	8.3	3.8	9.3	8.6
5.0	7.2	6.1	Cur. Mat.-L.T.D.		15.1	3.0	5.4	7.6	4.7
9.5	9.5	10.8	Trade Payables		5.4	10.7	9.5	22.3	10.7
.1	.0	.0	Income Taxes Payable		.1	.0	.0	.0	.1
6.4	8.6	7.7	All Other Current		4.1	7.1	9.1	8.0	7.0
26.3	30.4	31.6	Total Current		30.3	29.2	27.8	47.1	31.0
24.9	32.9	29.3	Long-Term Debt		37.2	20.8	17.3	35.8	28.2
.6	.7	.6	Deferred Taxes		.0	.9	.3	.0	1.5
6.5	3.5	4.7	All Other Non-Current		2.2	9.7	1.9	6.3	6.2
41.7	32.5	33.8	Net Worth		30.4	39.4	52.7	10.8	33.1
100.0	100.0	100.0	Total Liabilities & Net Worth		100.0	100.0	100.0	100.0	100.0
			INCOME DATA						
100.0	100.0	100.0	Net Sales		100.0	100.0	100.0	100.0	100.0
			Gross Profit						
91.9	89.3	91.6	Operating Expenses		85.9	90.0	93.2	90.8	96.0
8.1	10.7	8.4	Operating Profit		14.1	10.0	6.8	9.2	4.0
1.4	1.6	1.6	All Other Expenses (net)		1.6	2.7	-.2	1.2	2.4
6.6	9.2	6.8	Profit Before Taxes		12.5	7.3	7.0	8.0	1.6
			RATIOS						
3.3	2.7	2.4			5.9	3.1	2.5	2.1	2.1
1.6	1.3	1.4	Current		1.6	1.2	1.7	1.4	1.1
.9	.9	.9			.6	.8	1.2	.9	1.0
2.9	2.4	2.1			4.3	3.1	2.5	1.9	1.7
1.4	1.1	(94) 1.1	Quick		1.5	.9	(19) 1.5	1.3	1.0
.8	.7	.7			.3	.7	1.0	.6	.7
23 16.2	16 22.3	28 12.9		0 UND	15 24.8	22 16.8	30 12.1	45 8.2	
42 8.7	40 9.1	50 7.3	Sales/Receivables	45 8.1	45 8.2	54 6.8	52 7.0	60 6.1	
65 5.6	63 5.8	68 5.4		63 5.8	58 6.3	72 5.1	76 4.8	72 5.1	
			Cost of Sales/Inventory						
			Cost of Sales/Payables						
5.7	7.6	7.3			6.1	5.9	7.1	7.1	8.4
18.5	29.3	16.3	Sales/Working Capital		106.6	21.2	11.7	14.1	27.4
-71.7	-68.7	-65.7			-5.4	-156.2	45.3	-29.3	-163.6
16.1	18.6	17.1					30.5	34.9	7.4
(90) 5.0	(91) 6.3	(78) 4.2	EBIT/Interest			(16) 8.5	8.5	(14) 17.9	(26) 3.0
.8	1.5	.6					.6	3.3	.3
4.8	5.8	7.9							
(14) 2.2	(14) 2.2	(14) 2.7	Net Profit + Depr., Dep., Amort./Cur. Mat. L/T/D						
.4	1.4	1.4							
.4	.6	.6			.7	.5	.5	.5	1.1
1.2	1.3	1.4	Fixed/Worth		2.4	1.4	.8	1.6	2.7
6.3	NM	11.0			NM	3.2	1.1	-1.7	-2.4
.6	.6	.8			.5	.6	.4	1.1	2.1
1.7	1.8	2.3	Debt/Worth		2.5	1.2	1.1	7.2	5.4
8.8	-29.0	29.4			NM	3.1	2.3	-3.8	-4.6
56.0	54.6	88.3				56.0	63.0	90.6	108.5
(85) 29.9	(76) 30.8	(73) 35.3	% Profit Before Taxes/Tangible Net Worth			(11) 11.5	(19) 22.2	(11) 72.9	(19) 26.8
13.7	8.1	10.0				.7	1.3	8.7	13.2
25.2	23.3	27.6			39.1	26.2	30.9	29.3	10.2
8.5	9.3	8.1	% Profit Before Taxes/Total Assets		17.5	9.9	13.0	14.4	4.7
.4	1.6	.6			3.4	.9	2.0	5.7	-1.4
14.6	13.7	17.2			22.2	7.8	18.7	19.9	11.0
5.1	5.1	6.0	Sales/Net Fixed Assets		6.9	3.2	7.9	9.0	6.0
2.6	2.2	2.7			1.9	1.7	3.4	2.5	2.8
2.7	3.2	2.9			3.9	3.1	3.3	2.5	2.1
1.8	1.8	1.8	Sales/Total Assets		2.1	1.6	2.6	1.9	1.5
1.2	1.2	1.1			.9	1.2	1.7	1.2	1.1
3.3	3.2	2.5					2.7	2.0	1.2
(74) 4.8	(77) 5.5	(68) 4.9	% Depr., Dep., Amort./Sales			(17) 3.8	(12) 4.6	(19) 4.2	
9.7	8.7	8.3					8.2	11.0	8.1
2.1	1.8	2.0							
(31) 3.4	(32) 3.7	(22) 3.5	% Officers', Directors' Owners' Comp/Sales						
6.4	9.3	10.2							
2806783M	3015639M	3027922M	Net Sales ($)	4195M	25717M	46470M	147064M	237489M	2566987M
1928464M	2265046M	2375616M	Total Assets ($)	5327M	25450M	36388M	82811M	200668M	2024972M

© RMA 2019   M = $ thousand   MM = $ million
See Pages viii through xx for Explanation of Ratios and Data

EDUCATIONAL SERVICES

Current Data Sorted by Assets   Comparative Historical Data

						Type of Statement		
11	39	221	501	205	205	Unqualified	1426	1510
1	6	23	24	5	1	Reviewed	78	74
8	9	18	5			Compiled	43	41
21	33	20	5			Tax Returns	112	107
24	44	135	117	29	30	Other	401	419
	1,599 (4/1-9/30/18)		141 (10/1/18-3/31/19)				4/1/14-3/31/15	4/1/15-3/31/16
0-500M	500M-2MM	2-10MM	10-50MM	50-100MM	100-250MM		ALL	ALL
65	131	417	652	239	236	NUMBER OF STATEMENTS	2060	2151
%	%	%	%	%	%	**ASSETS**	%	%
50.7	33.1	27.5	21.7	21.3	19.0	Cash & Equivalents	24.5	24.7
9.1	7.7	6.2	4.1	3.2	4.1	Trade Receivables (net)	6.3	5.6
.1	.1	.1	.1	.1	.1	Inventory	.1	.2
4.9	4.3	3.0	2.5	2.8	2.4	All Other Current	3.2	2.9
64.8	45.2	36.8	28.4	27.5	25.5	Total Current	34.2	33.3
23.4	43.3	52.9	55.6	52.7	52.8	Fixed Assets (net)	55.0	52.6
2.0	2.6	.4	1.5	.9	2.4	Intangibles (net)	1.2	1.8
9.8	8.8	10.0	14.5	18.9	19.3	All Other Non-Current	9.6	12.4
100.0	100.0	100.0	100.0	100.0	100.0	Total	100.0	100.0
						LIABILITIES		
4.3	6.1	1.5	.8	1.4	.6	Notes Payable-Short Term	2.2	2.0
1.5	2.9	2.5	1.7	2.1	2.1	Cur. Mat.-L.T.D.	2.4	2.3
6.2	6.6	3.1	2.0	1.8	1.3	Trade Payables	3.3	3.3
.1	.0	.0	.0	.0	.1	Income Taxes Payable	.1	.1
23.1	13.1	10.5	8.1	6.3	4.8	All Other Current	10.4	9.3
35.2	28.7	17.7	12.6	11.5	8.9	Total Current	18.4	17.0
7.7	23.9	28.4	28.3	28.7	30.2	Long-Term Debt	30.4	29.2
.0	.0	.0	.0	.1	.0	Deferred Taxes	.0	.0
11.2	11.5	16.4	17.2	34.0	43.3	All Other Non-Current	6.5	20.1
45.8	35.9	37.4	41.9	25.8	17.6	Net Worth	44.8	33.6
100.0	100.0	100.0	100.0	100.0	100.0	Total Liabilities & Net Worth	100.0	100.0
						INCOME DATA		
100.0	100.0	100.0	100.0	100.0	100.0	Net Sales	100.0	100.0
						Gross Profit		
96.0	91.5	93.8	94.1	92.4	93.4	Operating Expenses	93.2	93.8
4.0	8.5	6.2	5.9	7.6	6.6	Operating Profit	6.8	6.2
.6	2.7	2.1	1.4	1.9	1.4	All Other Expenses (net)	1.6	2.1
3.4	5.7	4.1	4.4	5.7	5.3	Profit Before Taxes	5.2	4.0
						RATIOS		
11.3	6.3	5.7	5.4	5.2	5.2		4.9	5.1
3.6	2.1	2.5	2.5	2.5	2.7	Current	2.3	2.3
1.4	.9	1.0	1.3	1.2	1.5		1.2	1.2
11.3	5.7	5.3	5.1	4.6	4.9		4.5	4.6
3.2	2.0	2.2	2.4	2.2	2.3	Quick	2.0	2.0
1.4	.8	.8	1.1	1.0	1.2		1.0	1.0
0 UND	0 UND	0 UND	1 471.7	0 999.8	1 376.3		1 627.4	0 976.3
0 UND	2 160.0	5 68.8	6 59.2	6 63.8	9 38.7	Sales/Receivables	8 48.0	7 54.9
2 199.7	14 26.5	21 17.8	27 13.3	20 18.0	41 8.8		30 12.2	25 14.8
						Cost of Sales/Inventory		
						Cost of Sales/Payables		
8.5	6.0	2.7	2.2	1.8	1.8		2.7	2.7
19.8	15.8	6.5	5.1	4.3	3.6	Sales/Working Capital	6.2	6.2
47.5	-82.2	527.1	15.3	29.5	13.4		33.5	36.1
19.6	9.7	5.5	6.7	9.0	7.3		6.7	6.1
(25) 1.8	(71) 3.1	(287) 2.1	(549) 2.5	(209) 3.1	(216) 2.3	EBIT/Interest	(1571) 2.3	(1610) 2.3
-10.5	.8	.4	.4	.8	.7		.7	.6
							8.1	
						Net Profit + Depr., Dep.,	(11) 2.1	
						Amort./Cur. Mat. L/T/D	.4	
.0	.2	.6	.7	.6	.9		.6	.6
.2	1.0	1.3	1.1	1.3	2.6	Fixed/Worth	1.2	1.4
.8	4.4	3.0	2.7	-14.9	-4.4		2.4	4.7
.1	.2	.5	.4	.4	.7		.4	.4
.4	1.1	1.1	1.0	1.2	3.0	Debt/Worth	1.0	1.3
1.7	5.8	4.1	3.1	-12.2	-8.9		2.7	6.7
105.4	37.8	17.2	10.4	9.9	10.3		14.5	14.8
(55) 21.2	(105) 13.4	(363) 6.2	(559) 4.1	(173) 4.6	(151) 5.3	% Profit Before Taxes/Tangible	(1903) 5.4	(1743) 4.5
.0	-1.7	-1.6	-.1	1.5	1.1	Net Worth	-.4	-.6
60.8	18.1	8.3	4.7	4.5	4.0		6.5	5.7
11.0	6.1	2.4	2.0	2.0	1.4	% Profit Before Taxes/Total	2.4	1.8
-6.4	-2.0	-1.3	-.7	-.2	-.4	Assets	-.4	-.6
UND	86.3	6.9	1.4	1.3	1.2		3.0	2.8
57.0	8.1	1.4	.9	.8	.8	Sales/Net Fixed Assets	1.0	1.0
15.2	1.3	.7	.6	.6	.6		.6	.7
12.0	3.8	1.5	.7	.7	.6		1.3	1.2
5.7	2.3	.8	.5	.4	.4	Sales/Total Assets	.6	.6
3.4	.9	.5	.4	.3	.3		.4	.4
.4	.8	2.1	4.0	3.9	3.5		2.9	2.9
(29) .7	(81) 2.4	(333) 4.1	(571) 6.0	(215) 5.9	(210) 5.1	% Depr., Dep., Amort./Sales	(1763) 4.9	(1739) 5.0
2.2	4.1	6.5	7.9	8.3	7.2		7.1	7.3
5.6	2.9	3.2	3.7	1.3	1.2		3.2	3.1
(15) 8.6	(21) 7.3	(35) 6.1	(44) 7.0	(16) 2.3	(14) 2.6	% Officers', Directors' Owners' Comp/Sales	(227) 6.1	(219) 6.0
10.9	12.2	9.5	13.1	9.1	4.3		10.0	9.9
85708M	423810M	2447897M	10537538M	11500477M	18715316M	Net Sales ($)	50532293M	56234877M
14093M	153229M	2227645M	16294711M	17359192M	37093052M	Total Assets ($)	72636350M	86011672M

M = $ thousand   MM = $ million
See Pages viii through xx for Explanation of Ratios and Data

Comparative Historical Data

Current Data Sorted by Sales

			Type of Statement						
1446	1292	1182	Unqualified	8	79	96	231	353	415
62	66	60	Reviewed	4	13	10	21	11	1
43	45	40	Compiled	4	15	12	6	2	1
72	78	79	Tax Returns	22	34	7	11	4	1
395	417	379	Other	28	77	48	82	87	57
4/1/16-3/31/17	4/1/17-3/31/18	4/1/18-3/31/19			1,599 (4/1-9/30/18)		141 (10/1/18-3/31/19)		
ALL	ALL	ALL		0-1MM	1-3MM	3-5MM	5-10MM	10-25MM	25MM & OVER
2018	1898	1740	**NUMBER OF STATEMENTS**	66	218	173	351	457	475
%	%	%	**ASSETS**	%	%	%	%	%	%
23.6	24.0	24.6	Cash & Equivalents	30.8	26.4	26.9	22.3	24.8	23.6
4.9	5.2	4.9	Trade Receivables (net)	4.5	5.2	5.1	6.0	4.4	4.5
.2	.1	.1	Inventory	.1	.1	.0	.0	.1	.1
2.7	2.8	2.9	All Other Current	1.7	1.8	2.6	3.4	2.8	3.4
31.4	32.1	32.5	Total Current	37.0	33.5	34.7	31.8	32.1	31.6
53.6	52.3	52.0	Fixed Assets (net)	53.6	56.1	55.1	53.7	50.4	49.1
1.5	1.8	1.4	Intangibles (net)	3.2	1.4	.7	1.1	.8	2.1
13.5	13.8	14.1	All Other Non-Current	6.2	9.1	9.5	13.4	16.6	17.1
100.0	100.0	100.0	Total	100.0	100.0	100.0	100.0	100.0	100.0
			LIABILITIES						
1.6	1.7	1.6	Notes Payable-Short Term	3.1	2.7	2.4	2.0	1.0	.8
2.1	2.2	2.1	Cur. Mat.-L.T.D.	1.6	3.2	2.0	1.9	1.9	2.0
2.6	2.8	2.6	Trade Payables	2.0	3.2	3.2	3.2	2.1	2.3
.0	.2	.0	Income Taxes Payable	.1	.0	.0	.0	.0	.0
9.2	8.7	8.9	All Other Current	15.1	9.5	9.0	10.7	8.6	6.8
15.6	15.5	15.2	Total Current	21.8	18.5	16.6	17.7	13.7	11.9
29.8	28.2	27.5	Long-Term Debt	35.9	28.2	31.2	26.0	23.3	29.9
.0	.0	.0	Deferred Taxes	.0	.0	.0	.0	.0	.0
19.4	17.2	22.2	All Other Non-Current	9.5	10.8	20.8	12.1	16.1	43.1
35.2	39.0	35.0	Net Worth	32.8	42.5	31.4	44.2	46.9	15.0
100.0	100.0	100.0	Total Liabilities & Net Worth	100.0	100.0	100.0	100.0	100.0	100.0
			INCOME DATA						
100.0	100.0	100.0	Net Sales	100.0	100.0	100.0	100.0	100.0	100.0
			Gross Profit						
93.7	94.2	93.6	Operating Expenses	84.2	92.9	94.9	94.8	93.1	94.3
6.3	5.8	6.4	Operating Profit	15.8	7.1	5.1	5.2	6.9	5.7
3.0	1.6	1.7	All Other Expenses (net)	7.1	2.2	2.7	1.4	.6	1.6
3.3	4.2	4.7	Profit Before Taxes	8.8	4.8	2.4	3.8	6.2	4.1
			RATIOS						
5.0	5.4	5.6	Current	7.1	7.4	5.6	5.3	6.0	5.0
2.3	2.4	2.6		3.1	2.6	2.5	2.3	2.8	2.6
1.2	1.2	1.2		.7	.9	1.3	1.1	1.3	1.5
4.6	5.0	5.2	Quick	7.1	7.3	5.3	4.9	5.4	4.5
2.1	2.2	2.3		2.6	2.5	2.4	2.0	2.4	2.3
1.0	1.0	1.0		.5	.9	1.1	.9	1.1	1.2
0 751.1	0 999.8	0 999.8	Sales/Receivables	0 UND	0 UND	0 UND	1 521.7	1 332.9	0 861.7
7 50.7	6 58.8	5 68.4		0 UND	2 170.4	4 93.5	5 72.2	8 46.0	8 48.6
26 14.3	24 15.1	24 15.5		4 95.5	14 26.4	21 17.6	24 15.4	26 13.9	30 12.1
			Cost of Sales/Inventory						
			Cost of Sales/Payables						
2.6	2.5	2.3	Sales/Working Capital	3.9	3.2	2.6	2.6	2.0	2.2
5.8	5.8	5.8		11.4	9.5	6.0	6.8	4.3	5.1
29.2	30.8	29.4		-21.8	-104.2	24.1	116.0	13.2	16.8
6.1	6.7	7.0	EBIT/Interest	2.9	5.5	5.5	5.3	10.4	8.1
(1576) 2.0	(1490) 2.2	(1357) 2.5		(28) 1.7	(147) 2.3	(130) 2.1	(265) 1.9	(366) 3.3	(421) 2.6
.2	.4	.5		-.4	.3	.2	.2	1.0	.6
2.4	12.2		Net Profit + Depr., Dep., Amort./Cur. Mat. L/T/D						
(11) .8	(16) 4.3								
-1.7	1.4								
.7	.6	.6	Fixed/Worth	.1	.6	.7	.6	.6	.7
1.4	1.3	1.2		1.3	1.4	1.4	1.1	.9	2.1
5.0	3.9	4.8		5.1	2.9	4.6	2.5	1.8	-4.4
.4	.4	.4	Debt/Worth	.4	.4	.5	.4	.3	.7
1.2	1.1	1.1		1.2	1.0	1.2	.9	.8	2.7
6.8	7.5	7.6		9.4	3.6	5.3	3.0	2.1	-7.8
14.2	12.4	14.2	% Profit Before Taxes/Tangible Net Worth	27.0	26.6	15.1	12.0	11.5	12.9
(1654) 4.4	(1583) 4.7	(1406) 5.1		(53) 4.1	(190) 8.1	(142) 6.0	(304) 3.4	(404) 5.0	(313) 6.1
-1.2	-.1	.0		-1.9	-1.5	-.3	-1.7	.9	1.1
5.3	5.3	5.9	% Profit Before Taxes/Total Assets	11.6	11.1	6.2	5.3	5.6	5.2
1.7	1.9	2.1		2.5	3.1	2.0	1.5	2.6	1.9
-1.0	-.7	-.8		-1.9	-1.3	-1.9	-1.4	.0	-.6
2.1	2.7	2.5	Sales/Net Fixed Assets	63.8	10.3	4.3	2.4	1.6	2.2
.9	1.0	1.0		1.8	1.1	1.1	.9	.9	1.0
.6	.7	.7		.4	.6	.6	.7	.6	.7
1.0	1.1	1.1	Sales/Total Assets	3.3	2.3	1.4	1.0	.8	1.0
.6	.6	.6		1.0	.8	.7	.6	.5	.6
.4	.4	.4		.3	.4	.4	.4	.4	.4
3.2	3.1	3.1	% Depr., Dep., Amort./Sales	2.0	2.0	2.5	3.5	3.7	3.2
(1699) 5.4	(1596) 5.2	(1439) 5.1		(35) 4.4	(159) 4.2	(145) 4.4	(305) 5.6	(393) 6.1	(402) 4.5
7.8	7.5	7.4		16.3	7.4	7.2	7.9	8.1	6.5
3.3	3.2	2.9	% Officers', Directors' Owners' Comp/Sales	6.3	5.5	5.8	2.3	3.1	1.8
(170) 5.8	(163) 5.7	(145) 6.1		(11) 9.3	(29) 7.9	(12) 8.0	(30) 3.9	(23) 5.5	(40) 3.9
10.7	11.7	10.6		12.9	10.7	12.1	11.5	11.9	7.5
50734966M	48036398M	43710746M	Net Sales ($)	39543M	426631M	674445M	2535376M	7354950M	32679801M
86787691M	78490745M	73141922M	Total Assets ($)	97939M	785279M	1139940M	4685544M	15969363M	50463857M

M = $ thousand   MM = $ million
See Pages viii through xx for Explanation of Ratios and Data

Current Data Sorted by Assets							Comparative Historical Data	

Type of Statement

						Type of Statement		
	1		3	11	12	15	Unqualified	48	58
							Reviewed		2
							Compiled	1	1
							Tax Returns	4	2
6	1	2	3	1	2	Other	14	12
	48 (4/1-9/30/18)		9 (10/1/18-3/31/19)				4/1/14-3/31/15	4/1/15-3/31/16
0-500M	500M-2MM	2-10MM	10-50MM	50-100MM	100-250MM		ALL	ALL
6	2	5	14	13	17	NUMBER OF STATEMENTS	67	75

%	%	%	%	%	%	ASSETS	%	%
			22.9	21.8	19.0	Cash & Equivalents	21.6	26.8
			6.9	8.1	5.1	Trade Receivables (net)	11.8	8.7
			.1	.4	.1	Inventory	.5	.9
			10.8	.4	4.2	All Other Current	3.4	3.1
			40.8	30.7	28.5	Total Current	37.3	39.5
			46.4	56.1	57.0	Fixed Assets (net)	48.9	48.6
			.5	.6	.7	Intangibles (net)	2.9	.4
			12.4	12.6	13.9	All Other Non-Current	10.9	11.4
			100.0	100.0	100.0	Total	100.0	100.0

						LIABILITIES		
			3.5	2.0	.2	Notes Payable-Short Term	1.1	1.6
			.9	1.1	2.2	Cur. Mat.-L.T.D.	2.4	1.7
			2.5	2.8	2.2	Trade Payables	2.5	4.3
			.0	.0	.0	Income Taxes Payable	.3	.4
			5.3	8.7	6.6	All Other Current	8.3	13.2
			12.2	14.6	11.1	Total Current	14.6	21.1
			40.0	14.2	19.0	Long-Term Debt	24.8	21.4
			.0	.0	.0	Deferred Taxes	.3	.2
			19.4	42.7	27.1	All Other Non-Current	9.2	15.4
			28.4	28.4	42.7	Net Worth	51.1	41.9
			100.0	100.0	100.0	Total Liabilties & Net Worth	100.0	100.0

						INCOME DATA		
			100.0	100.0	100.0	Net Sales	100.0	100.0
						Gross Profit		
			89.8	102.4	97.7	Operating Expenses	92.3	94.1
			10.2	-2.4	2.3	Operating Profit	7.7	5.9
			5.2	-.9	.7	All Other Expenses (net)	2.1	1.5
			5.0	-1.5	1.6	Profit Before Taxes	5.6	4.3

						RATIOS		
			9.2	4.3	4.2		5.6	5.8
			4.9	2.0	2.4	Current	2.8	2.7
			3.1	1.7	1.7		1.6	1.6
			8.5	4.2	3.8		4.9	5.1
			4.1	2.0	2.1	Quick	2.3	2.5
			2.9	1.5	1.4		1.3	1.3
		4	84.2	19	19.3	8	47.2	Sales/Receivables	15	23.8	6	61.9
		26	13.8	32	11.5	29	12.5		38	9.7	24	15.5
		68	5.4	52	7.0	42	8.6		63	5.8	49	7.5

						Cost of Sales/Inventory		

						Cost of Sales/Payables		

			.6	2.3	1.9	Sales/Working Capital	2.2	2.2
			1.8	4.3	4.3		3.9	4.2
			3.3	11.3	6.8		9.3	9.3
			14.5	3.8	8.2	EBIT/Interest	20.1	7.2
		(10)	1.7	(12) -1.4	(14) 2.9		(52) 4.5	(55) 2.6
			-4.1	-7.1	-1.4		1.2	1.2

						Net Profit + Depr., Dep., Amort./Cur. Mat. L/T/D		

			.2	1.3	1.1	Fixed/Worth	.5	.6
			1.7	2.0	1.7		.9	1.2
			NM	13.2	2.5		1.8	1.9
			.7	1.5	1.0	Debt/Worth	.4	.6
			2.5	2.4	1.9		.7	1.1
			NM	17.5	2.8		2.4	2.3
			7.7	1.2	7.9	% Profit Before Taxes/Tangible Net Worth	14.4	14.5
		(11)	2.6	(11) -3.1	2.3		(64) 4.8	(68) 2.9
			-2.6	-17.0	-7.8		.2	-2.0
			3.1	1.1	3.1	% Profit Before Taxes/Total Assets	6.6	5.9
			2.0	-.8	1.0		2.6	1.3
			-1.0	-4.1	-2.7		-.1	-.7
			3.8	1.9	1.4	Sales/Net Fixed Assets	6.0	2.8
			.9	.9	.8		1.3	1.1
			.2	.8	.5		.7	.7
			.7	.8	.6	Sales/Total Assets	1.2	1.1
			.3	.5	.5		.7	.6
			.2	.5	.3		.4	.4
			5.6	3.8	4.1	% Depr., Dep., Amort./Sales	2.5	2.9
		(13)	7.5	5.0	(14) 5.5		(62) 4.2	(67) 4.8
			18.1	6.2	8.6		7.4	7.0

						% Officers', Directors' Owners' Comp/Sales		

2703M	5291M	15409M	188838M	727592M	1299399M	Net Sales ($)	2381726M	2432861M
971M	3431M	22896M	399339M	946109M	2633537M	Total Assets ($)	3768524M	3694340M

M = $ thousand   MM = $ million
See Pages viii through xx for Explanation of Ratios and Data

Comparative Historical Data | | | | ## Current Data Sorted by Sales

			Type of Statement						
62	37	42	Unqualified	1	1	4	1	7	28
			Reviewed						
			Compiled						
			Tax Returns						
15	12	15	Other	6	5		1		3
					48 (4/1-9/30/18)		9 (10/1/18-3/31/19)		
4/1/16-3/31/17 ALL	4/1/17-3/31/18 ALL	4/1/18-3/31/19 ALL		0-1MM	1-3MM	3-5MM	5-10MM	10-25MM	25MM & OVER
77	49	57	**NUMBER OF STATEMENTS**	7	6	4	2	7	31
%	%	%	**ASSETS**	%	%	%	%	%	%
24.3	25.3	29.2	Cash & Equivalents						20.7
9.3	8.4	7.3	Trade Receivables (net)						6.7
1.1	.5	.2	Inventory						.2
4.2	4.8	4.3	All Other Current						4.0
38.9	39.0	41.0	Total Current						31.6
46.7	48.5	44.3	Fixed Assets (net)						56.2
1.9	1.8	1.3	Intangibles (net)						.7
12.5	10.7	13.4	All Other Non-Current						11.6
100.0	100.0	100.0	Total						100.0
			LIABILITIES						
1.5	1.7	4.4	Notes Payable-Short Term						1.2
2.3	1.5	1.2	Cur. Mat.-L.T.D.						1.7
4.0	2.5	2.2	Trade Payables						3.0
.3	.2	.0	Income Taxes Payable						.0
10.4	5.0	7.9	All Other Current						8.1
18.5	10.9	15.8	Total Current						13.9
26.1	26.5	21.0	Long-Term Debt						16.4
.2	.3	.0	Deferred Taxes						.0
10.3	13.1	22.9	All Other Non-Current						37.9
44.8	49.2	40.3	Net Worth						31.8
100.0	100.0	100.0	Total Liabilties & Net Worth						100.0
			INCOME DATA						
100.0	100.0	100.0	Net Sales						100.0
			Gross Profit						
92.9	94.8	96.4	Operating Expenses						99.7
7.1	5.2	3.6	Operating Profit						.3
5.6	3.9	1.4	All Other Expenses (net)						.0
1.5	1.2	2.2	Profit Before Taxes						.2
			RATIOS						
5.6	9.2	6.1							4.1
3.1	4.5	3.1	Current						2.2
1.5	1.9	1.8							1.7
5.0	7.9	6.0							3.4
2.7	4.2	2.9	Quick						2.0
1.2	1.3	1.6							1.4
12 29.6	8 44.2	6 63.0							15 24.0
31 11.7	32 11.5	25 14.4	Sales/Receivables						29 12.5
53 6.9	68 5.4	46 7.9							46 7.9
			Cost of Sales/Inventory						
			Cost of Sales/Payables						
1.6	1.2	1.7							2.4
3.0	2.3	3.3	Sales/Working Capital						4.3
11.0	9.5	6.8							8.3
7.1	7.2	5.9							5.1
(51) 2.5	(32) 1.9	(39) 2.1	EBIT/Interest						(27) 1.3
.1	-2.1	-1.6							-1.7
			Net Profit + Depr., Dep., Amort./Cur. Mat. L/T/D						
.6	.6	.2							1.4
1.1	1.0	1.5	Fixed/Worth						1.8
1.7	1.9	2.8							2.9
.5	.2	.5							1.1
1.1	1.1	1.7	Debt/Worth						2.2
2.7	2.1	4.0							4.1
12.9	9.4	6.2							4.9
(68) 3.5	(43) .0	(50) 1.7	% Profit Before Taxes/Tangible Net Worth						(28) .6
-2.4	-4.2	-7.6							-8.9
6.2	4.9	3.1							3.0
1.5	.1	1.0	% Profit Before Taxes/Total Assets						.2
-1.4	-2.2	-2.7							-2.7
5.5	3.4	5.8							1.4
1.1	1.2	1.0	Sales/Net Fixed Assets						.9
.6	.5	.7							.7
1.4	1.4	1.0							.7
.6	.5	.5	Sales/Total Assets						.5
.3	.3	.4							.4
2.8	3.5	3.9							4.0
(67) 5.3	(39) 5.8	(46) 5.5	% Depr., Dep., Amort./Sales						(28) 5.1
8.3	13.3	8.0							7.0
			% Officers', Directors' Owners' Comp/Sales						
2830381M	1846469M	2239232M	Net Sales ($)	3579M	11684M	14414M	12040M	134591M	2062924M
4594016M	3084975M	4006283M	Total Assets ($)	8856M	71224M	39299M	37468M	330067M	3519369M

© RMA 2019

M = $ thousand   MM = $ million
See Pages viii through xx for Explanation of Ratios and Data

Current Data Sorted by Assets   **Comparative Historical Data**

Type of Statement	0-500M	500M-2MM	2-10MM	10-50MM	50-100MM	100-250MM		4/1/14-3/31/15 ALL	4/1/15-3/31/16 ALL
Unqualified	2	3	19	69	118	188		484	524
Reviewed								4	
Compiled	1		1			1		6	2
Tax Returns	1		3	1				6	7
Other	2		13	28	25	35		108	113
		444 (4/1-9/30/18)		70 (10/1/18-3/31/19)					
NUMBER OF STATEMENTS	6	7	36	98	143	224		608	646
	%	%	%	%	%	%		%	%
ASSETS									
Cash & Equivalents			15.5	18.1	13.3	13.9		14.7	15.4
Trade Receivables (net)			9.0	6.9	3.7	3.8		4.7	4.6
Inventory			.6	.3	.2	.2		.4	.4
All Other Current			3.3	3.6	2.3	2.7		2.9	2.7
Total Current			28.4	28.9	19.6	20.6		22.8	23.1
Fixed Assets (net)			57.4	50.2	50.4	49.5		51.9	50.1
Intangibles (net)			2.2	3.0	2.1	1.1		1.8	1.8
All Other Non-Current			12.0	17.9	27.8	28.8		23.5	25.0
Total			100.0	100.0	100.0	100.0		100.0	100.0
LIABILITIES									
Notes Payable-Short Term			1.2	2.9	1.1	1.0		1.8	1.3
Cur. Mat.-L.T.D.			2.7	3.0	1.7	1.1		1.9	1.7
Trade Payables			3.7	3.4	1.9	2.2		2.8	2.5
Income Taxes Payable			.0	.1	.0	.0		.1	.0
All Other Current			11.9	10.1	5.5	4.7		6.7	5.9
Total Current			19.5	19.5	10.2	9.1		13.3	11.5
Long-Term Debt			29.7	38.9	25.1	22.8		27.5	25.9
Deferred Taxes			.1	.1	.1	.0		.1	.1
All Other Non-Current			9.8	4.8	5.6	5.9		5.2	5.6
Net Worth			41.0	36.7	59.0	62.2		53.8	57.0
Total Liabilties & Net Worth			100.0	100.0	100.0	100.0		100.0	100.0
INCOME DATA									
Net Sales			100.0	100.0	100.0	100.0		100.0	100.0
Gross Profit									
Operating Expenses			89.8	89.9	96.1	96.6		93.2	94.4
Operating Profit			10.2	10.1	3.9	3.4		6.8	5.6
All Other Expenses (net)			4.0	4.2	-.2	-1.1		1.0	2.8
Profit Before Taxes			6.2	5.9	4.2	4.5		5.8	2.8
RATIOS									
			3.5	2.7	3.2	4.4		3.3	3.5
Current			1.8	1.8	1.9	1.9		1.7	1.8
			.8	.8	1.0	1.1		.9	1.1
			3.0	2.5	2.9	3.6		2.9	3.2
Quick			1.5	1.3	1.5	1.5		(607) 1.5	1.5
			.8	.6	.6	.8		.6	.8
			5 79.8	5 76.0	7 52.0	10 38.1		7 55.9	7 52.7
Sales/Receivables			10 36.3	12 29.7	17 21.7	19 19.6		15 25.0	16 22.3
			33 11.2	36 10.2	38 9.7	36 10.1		31 11.7	33 11.1
Cost of Sales/Inventory									
Cost of Sales/Payables									
			4.2	3.1	3.3	2.4		3.3	2.8
Sales/Working Capital			8.0	8.6	6.3	6.5		9.7	7.5
			-30.4	-20.9	-615.6	48.7		-32.3	77.1
			7.2	7.1	5.5	6.7		7.8	5.0
EBIT/Interest			(28) 2.2	(73) 2.2	(130) 2.2	(204) 2.9		(499) 3.2	(549) 1.9
			1.1	-.2	.2	.7		1.0	-.2
								22.2	6.1
Net Profit + Depr., Dep., Amort./Cur. Mat. L/T/D								(26) 3.1	(24) 1.8
								1.2	.7
			.8	.6	.6	.5		.6	.5
Fixed/Worth			1.5	1.1	.9	.8		.9	.8
			3.2	2.2	1.3	1.1		1.5	1.4
			.6	.6	.3	.3		.4	.3
Debt/Worth			1.2	1.1	.6	.5		.7	.6
			4.4	2.5	1.1	.8		1.4	1.3
			26.6	14.2	5.6	5.4		9.7	6.3
% Profit Before Taxes/Tangible Net Worth			(30) 2.9	(87) 3.2	(135) 2.0	(217) 2.1		(567) 4.5	(607) 1.9
			.2	-1.2	-1.7	-.4		.2	-1.5
			5.8	6.4	3.7	3.5		5.5	3.5
% Profit Before Taxes/Total Assets			1.8	2.2	1.4	1.4		2.4	1.0
			-.1	-.9	-1.0	-.2		-.3	-1.0
			4.7	4.7	1.0	1.0		1.5	1.4
Sales/Net Fixed Assets			1.1	1.0	.8	.8		.9	.8
			.5	.6	.6	.6		.6	.6
			1.1	.9	.5	.5		.7	.7
Sales/Total Assets			.8	.6	.4	.4		.5	.4
			.4	.4	.3	.3		.3	.3
			2.1	3.7	5.1	5.1		4.5	4.8
% Depr., Dep., Amort./Sales			(32) 4.3	(82) 5.6	(141) 6.9	(211) 7.2		(567) 6.2	(605) 6.4
			8.0	8.5	9.0	8.8		8.3	8.5
						2.7		3.6	4.5
% Officers', Directors' Owners' Comp/Sales						(19) 11.7		(41) 9.8	(49) 9.4
						19.7		21.1	21.2
Net Sales ($)	2376M	14216M	196259M	2351177M	5092870M	17088820M		26573564M	28296977M
Total Assets ($)	623M	7534M	211218M	2740586M	10893117M	37081932M		52975260M	61304790M

Comparative Historical Data				Current Data Sorted by Sales					
			Type of Statement						
524	427	399	Unqualified	5	13	11	15	72	283
4	2		Reviewed						
3	3	3	Compiled	1		1			1
3	1	5	Tax Returns	2	1		1	1	
126	123	107	Other	6	6	7	8	21	59
4/1/16-3/31/17	4/1/17-3/31/18	4/1/18-3/31/19		444 (4/1-9/30/18)			70 (10/1/18-3/31/19)		
ALL	ALL	ALL		0-1MM	1-3MM	3-5MM	5-10MM	10-25MM	25MM & OVER
660	556	514	**NUMBER OF STATEMENTS**	14	20	19	24	94	343
%	%	%	**ASSETS**	%	%	%	%	%	%
15.3	14.7	15.0	Cash & Equivalents	14.8	15.7	13.0	16.3	11.5	16.0
4.6	4.7	4.9	Trade Receivables (net)	5.3	3.0	7.8	7.6	5.0	4.6
.3	.3	.3	Inventory	.9	.5	.7	.3	.3	.2
2.6	2.7	2.7	All Other Current	1.1	.7	2.2	2.0	3.0	2.9
22.8	22.5	23.0	Total Current	22.1	20.0	23.7	26.2	19.8	23.8
50.3	50.8	50.2	Fixed Assets (net)	60.2	53.3	52.0	58.7	51.2	48.6
1.6	1.9	2.1	Intangibles (net)	6.1	4.3	3.2	2.2	3.3	1.4
25.2	24.8	24.7	All Other Non-Current	11.6	22.5	21.2	12.9	25.7	26.2
100.0	100.0	100.0	Total	100.0	100.0	100.0	100.0	100.0	100.0
			LIABILITIES						
1.8	1.2	1.5	Notes Payable-Short Term	2.7	.6	2.3	1.4	2.8	1.1
1.6	1.7	1.8	Cur. Mat.-L.T.D.	4.3	2.1	2.8	5.1	1.9	1.4
2.5	2.6	2.6	Trade Payables	3.8	4.3	2.4	2.8	2.5	2.5
.0	.0	.0	Income Taxes Payable	.0	.3	.0	.0	.1	.0
6.7	6.3	6.7	All Other Current	1.7	9.0	9.0	10.8	5.7	6.6
12.6	11.7	12.6	Total Current	12.5	16.3	16.6	20.1	13.2	11.6
26.9	26.4	26.8	Long-Term Debt	29.2	36.8	54.0	47.2	24.8	23.7
.1	.0	.0	Deferred Taxes	.0	.0	.0	.1	.0	.1
5.0	5.5	5.7	All Other Non-Current	2.6	4.2	5.5	10.1	3.5	6.2
55.5	56.4	54.8	Net Worth	55.6	42.7	24.0	22.4	58.5	58.5
100.0	100.0	100.0	Total Liabilities & Net Worth	100.0	100.0	100.0	100.0	100.0	100.0
			INCOME DATA						
100.0	100.0	100.0	Net Sales	100.0	100.0	100.0	100.0	100.0	100.0
			Gross Profit						
96.1	94.9	94.4	Operating Expenses	71.9	78.0	86.0	97.9	94.8	96.5
3.9	5.1	5.6	Operating Profit	28.1	22.0	14.0	2.1	5.2	3.5
4.2	.4	.6	All Other Expenses (net)	10.5	10.1	8.2	3.6	.7	-1.1
-.3	4.7	5.0	Profit Before Taxes	17.6	11.9	5.8	-1.4	4.5	4.6
			RATIOS						
3.7	3.5	3.5		8.7	3.8	6.0	2.2	2.9	3.6
1.7	1.8	1.8	Current	1.8	1.9	2.0	1.5	1.4	2.0
1.0	1.0	1.0		.6	.8	1.0	.5	.8	1.1
3.1	3.0	3.1		5.0	3.7	4.5	2.0	2.7	3.2
1.4	1.4	1.5	Quick	1.5	1.7	1.6	1.1	1.2	1.5
.7	.8	.7		.5	.6	.8	.4	.5	.8
8 45.8	8 48.0	7 54.7		0 UND	0 UND	1 408.7	4 83.2	7 54.5	9 42.2
17 21.5	18 20.4	16 22.8	Sales/Receivables	6 58.6	9 40.0	6 65.1	11 33.2	17 21.1	17 21.5
33 11.1	34 10.8	35 10.3		31 11.8	21 17.8	35 10.3	34 10.8	46 7.9	33 11.1
			Cost of Sales/Inventory						
			Cost of Sales/Payables						
2.8	2.8	3.0		3.4	1.8	2.8	4.0	3.5	2.6
7.1	7.9	7.0	Sales/Working Capital	11.3	5.3	7.6	10.2	10.1	6.4
74.1	NM	-93.4		-9.4	-13.0	999.8	-7.0	-19.5	41.4
4.2	6.9	6.7			8.5	3.8	5.4	5.0	7.2
(559) 1.1	(474) 2.8	(442) 2.6	EBIT/Interest		(12) 6.1	(12) 1.6	(17) -.4	(83) 1.8	(310) 3.0
-1.4	.8	.5			1.8	.9	-3.4	.0	.8
8.6	9.9	12.0	Net Profit + Depr., Dep.,						
(31) 2.2	(17) 3.9	(16) 4.1	Amort./Cur. Mat. L/T/D						
1.0	2.6	.4							
.6	.6	.6		.4	.2	.4	.9	.6	.5
.8	.9	.9	Fixed/Worth	1.1	1.3	1.7	1.5	.8	.8
1.4	1.4	1.4		1.6	4.5	-1.0	NM	1.4	1.2
.3	.3	.3		.5	.4	.4	.8	.3	.3
.6	.6	.6	Debt/Worth	.7	2.2	1.3	1.7	.7	.6
1.3	1.2	1.3		1.3	7.1	-5.8	NM	1.2	1.0
4.7	8.2	7.0		26.5	11.5	3.4	16.1	6.6	7.0
(623) .2	(527) 2.3	(481) 2.2	% Profit Before Taxes/Tangible Net Worth	(13) .7	(18) 3.0	(13) 2.2	(18) -2.7	(90) 2.2	(329) 2.5
-3.6	-.5	-1.0		-6.5	-.8	-3.3	-14.9	-1.6	-.4
2.5	4.4	4.3		12.1	6.4	2.8	5.0	4.0	4.2
.1	1.5	1.6	% Profit Before Taxes/Total Assets	1.4	2.6	.9	.3	1.4	1.6
-2.2	-.3	-.6		-2.8	-.2	-.4	-6.2	-1.0	-.2
1.3	1.3	1.3		28.6	6.1	3.2	2.2	1.0	1.2
.8	.8	.8	Sales/Net Fixed Assets	.8	.8	.7	.8	.7	.9
.6	.6	.6		.3	.3	.4	.5	.6	.7
.6	.7	.6		1.2	.8	.7	.9	.6	.6
.4	.4	.4	Sales/Total Assets	.5	.3	.4	.6	.4	.4
.3	.3	.3		.2	.1	.3	.2	.3	.3
4.7	4.7	4.8		3.1	3.8	3.6	2.7	4.8	4.8
(620) 6.6	(519) 6.7	(476) 6.8	% Depr., Dep., Amort./Sales	(10) 8.9	(14) 6.6	(17) 8.5	(22) 6.0	(90) 7.0	(323) 6.7
8.7	8.9	8.8		12.7	26.7	11.3	14.7	9.3	8.4
6.1	2.3	3.0							2.6
(44) 10.5	(36) 7.6	(37) 8.4	% Officers', Directors' Owners' Comp/Sales					(26) 10.0	
22.2	16.6	19.8							21.3
27654101M	27010240M	24745718M	Net Sales ($)	6568M	35623M	80815M	174142M	1756751M	22691819M
61458573M	54239756M	50935010M	Total Assets ($)	32765M	175372M	302864M	578398M	5096257M	44749354M

M = $ thousand   MM = $ million
See Pages viii through xx for Explanation of Ratios and Data

Current Data Sorted by Assets   Comparative Historical Data

						Type of Statement		
1	2	5	6	1	1	Unqualified	20	18
	1	1				Reviewed	3	8
		1				Compiled	3	
3	2	4				Tax Returns	9	8
3	5	5	3		1	Other	29	31
	15 (4/1-9/30/18)		30 (10/1/18-3/31/19)				4/1/14-3/31/15	4/1/15-3/31/16
0-500M	500M-2MM	2-10MM	10-50MM	50-100MM	100-250MM		ALL	ALL
7	10	16	9	1	2	NUMBER OF STATEMENTS	64	65
%	%	%	%	%	%	ASSETS	%	%
	25.8	20.1				Cash & Equivalents	27.0	32.0
	36.8	26.4				Trade Receivables (net)	23.5	22.0
	6.1	.2				Inventory	2.0	1.2
	7.0	3.6				All Other Current	5.6	4.1
	75.7	50.3				Total Current	58.1	59.3
	12.8	36.7				Fixed Assets (net)	27.4	22.5
	1.3	6.2				Intangibles (net)	8.6	10.6
	10.2	6.8				All Other Non-Current	5.9	7.6
	100.0	100.0				Total	100.0	100.0
						LIABILITIES		
	9.7	5.4				Notes Payable-Short Term	9.4	8.2
	.9	4.8				Cur. Mat.-L.T.D.	2.7	2.0
	3.7	11.7				Trade Payables	7.9	8.9
	1.2	.0				Income Taxes Payable	.1	.1
	22.7	11.3				All Other Current	26.9	22.5
	38.2	33.1				Total Current	47.1	41.7
	12.4	23.5				Long-Term Debt	18.1	19.2
	.0	.0				Deferred Taxes	.3	.4
	8.6	2.1				All Other Non-Current	12.7	10.0
	40.8	41.3				Net Worth	21.9	28.7
	100.0	100.0				Total Liabilties & Net Worth	100.0	100.0
						INCOME DATA		
	100.0	100.0				Net Sales	100.0	100.0
						Gross Profit		
	88.0	94.1				Operating Expenses	91.9	91.1
	12.0	5.9				Operating Profit	8.1	8.9
	4.7	2.0				All Other Expenses (net)	1.5	2.3
	7.4	3.9				Profit Before Taxes	6.7	6.6
						RATIOS		
	8.0	3.9					2.9	3.1
	3.0	1.8				Current	1.4	1.8
	2.1	1.1					.8	.9
	4.9	3.6					2.6	2.9
	2.7	1.8				Quick	1.1	1.7
	1.8	.9					.6	.8
3	117.4	4 102.6					3 109.2	7 50.1
36	10.1	33 11.2				Sales/Receivables	20 18.2	29 12.8
85	4.3	66 5.5					55 6.6	54 6.7
						Cost of Sales/Inventory		
						Cost of Sales/Payables		
	2.4	4.0					6.5	3.2
	4.6	11.7				Sales/Working Capital	29.6	9.7
	11.0	734.0					-17.4	-31.1
		25.0					42.0	40.4
	(12)	8.8				EBIT/Interest	(43) 4.7	(51) 7.8
		5.2					.3	.7
						Net Profit + Depr., Dep., Amort./Cur. Mat. L/T/D		
	.1	.2					.0	.1
	.1	.9				Fixed/Worth	.7	.7
	NM	5.0					2.7	165.0
	.1	.6					.5	.5
	.4	1.0				Debt/Worth	1.5	1.3
	NM	6.7					8.2	UND
		53.3					71.9	51.7
	(14)	12.7				% Profit Before Taxes/Tangible Net Worth	(51) 14.5	(49) 23.3
		-7.5					.7	2.4
	21.5	16.8					22.4	22.2
	4.3	6.6				% Profit Before Taxes/Total Assets	6.3	7.1
	1.5	.1					-.4	-.7
	200.5	98.4					151.0	94.2
	69.0	6.9				Sales/Net Fixed Assets	24.3	23.5
	14.7	1.6					3.3	5.1
	5.3	3.0					4.3	3.4
	2.6	1.6				Sales/Total Assets	1.7	2.0
	1.3	.7					1.1	1.0
		.9					.6	.4
	(10)	1.5				% Depr., Dep., Amort./Sales	(40) 2.4	(30) 1.5
		2.0					4.0	3.3
						% Officers', Directors' Owners' Comp/Sales	4.2	3.2
							(14) 9.7	(11) 4.7
							16.6	12.3
10428M	40967M	109209M	314292M	45907M	400035M	Net Sales ($)	2779627M	1754101M
1512M	10329M	62594M	258531M	75527M	325452M	Total Assets ($)	1533609M	1221928M

M = $ thousand   MM = $ million
See Pages viii through xx for Explanation of Ratios and Data

Comparative Historical Data

Current Data Sorted by Sales

				Type of Statement						
11	14	16	Unqualified	1	2		6	1	6
5	4	2	Reviewed				1	1	
2	1	1	Compiled		1				
6	8	9	Tax Returns	2	4		3		
33	31	17	Other	4	4	2	1	3	3
4/1/16-3/31/17 ALL	4/1/17-3/31/18 ALL	4/1/18-3/31/19 ALL		15 (4/1-9/30/18)			30 (10/1/18-3/31/19)		
				0-1MM	1-3MM	3-5MM	5-10MM	10-25MM	25MM & OVER
57	58	45	NUMBER OF STATEMENTS	7	11	2	11	5	9
%	%	%	ASSETS	%	%	%	%	%	%
31.4	29.3	29.5	Cash & Equivalents		36.3		30.2		
18.7	23.6	21.4	Trade Receivables (net)		17.0		21.9		
1.2	1.6	1.5	Inventory		1.4		4.3		
3.3	5.2	4.9	All Other Current		6.0		4.3		
54.7	59.7	57.2	Total Current		60.7		60.7		
16.1	17.0	21.2	Fixed Assets (net)		20.2		25.6		
17.5	15.4	13.5	Intangibles (net)		8.2		8.6		
11.7	7.9	8.1	All Other Non-Current		11.0		5.2		
100.0	100.0	100.0	Total		100.0		100.0		
			LIABILITIES						
9.6	7.0	11.4	Notes Payable-Short Term		26.2		4.3		
1.8	2.9	3.3	Cur. Mat.-L.T.D.		5.1		6.0		
6.8	10.2	7.3	Trade Payables		1.1		10.3		
.2	.1	.3	Income Taxes Payable		1.0		.0		
17.4	33.7	21.4	All Other Current		7.7		16.2		
35.9	54.0	43.6	Total Current		41.1		36.8		
22.2	18.8	23.5	Long-Term Debt		20.1		22.1		
.3	.2	.2	Deferred Taxes		.0		.0		
9.4	9.4	10.6	All Other Non-Current		5.6		2.0		
32.2	17.6	22.1	Net Worth		33.2		39.1		
100.0	100.0	100.0	Total Liabilities & Net Worth		100.0		100.0		
			INCOME DATA						
100.0	100.0	100.0	Net Sales		100.0		100.0		
			Gross Profit						
93.9	92.4	94.0	Operating Expenses		88.1		95.6		
6.1	7.6	6.0	Operating Profit		11.9		4.4		
1.8	.4	2.9	All Other Expenses (net)		4.6		-1.1		
4.3	7.3	3.1	Profit Before Taxes		7.3		5.6		
			RATIOS						
3.0	3.4	4.2			7.8		4.0		
1.8	1.5	1.7	Current		2.1		2.9		
.9	.6	.7			.8		.7		
2.8	2.9	3.7			4.0		3.8		
1.6	1.4	1.6	Quick		2.1		2.1		
.8	.5	.6			.7		.7		
5 70.3	4 100.7	2 184.6		0 UND			5 76.0		
28 12.9	26 14.3	17 21.1	Sales/Receivables	3 108.6			17 21.1		
54 6.7	56 6.5	59 6.2		83 4.4			62 5.9		
			Cost of Sales/Inventory						
			Cost of Sales/Payables						
5.5	3.5	4.0			2.6		3.3		
13.8	14.9	11.8	Sales/Working Capital		4.6		11.5		
-39.6	-13.1	-16.3			-45.2		-7.1		
25.3	36.2	14.7					14.7		
(38) 5.2	(36) 8.9	(31) 5.8	EBIT/Interest				(10) 7.8		
.1	-.5	1.2					1.2		
			Net Profit + Depr., Dep., Amort./Cur. Mat. L/T/D						
.0	.2	.1			.1		.3		
.4	2.3	.9	Fixed/Worth		.2		.7		
-1.1	-.3	-.2			UND		-.2		
.4	.7	.4			.1		.5		
1.2	8.8	1.6	Debt/Worth		.5		.9		
-3.7	-2.4	-2.1			UND		-3.8		
84.8	66.5	55.8							
(40) 16.2	(33) 22.2	(31) 14.8	% Profit Before Taxes/Tangible Net Worth						
-1.0	-2.4	.7							
30.8	39.8	19.9			33.3		18.0		
6.5	8.5	5.6	% Profit Before Taxes/Total Assets		10.2		7.7		
-2.3	-4.8	-2.7			2.7		4.5		
171.7	92.8	121.6			71.0		110.6		
25.9	32.6	41.7	Sales/Net Fixed Assets		57.3		13.4		
6.1	9.6	6.9			15.1		3.1		
4.2	3.9	4.0			3.0		3.1		
2.0	2.2	2.2	Sales/Total Assets		2.2		2.3		
.9	1.1	.8			.8		1.0		
1.1	.4	.7							
(29) 2.2	(32) 1.0	(23) 1.1	% Depr., Dep., Amort./Sales						
6.7	4.6	1.9							
3.1	2.0	2.8							
(15) 4.5	(12) 3.6	(12) 5.0	% Officers', Directors' Owners' Comp/Sales						
15.5	6.8	9.9							
1037354M	1252642M	920838M	Net Sales ($)	4699M	21362M	7591M	90328M	67757M	729101M
1325292M	1041913M	733945M	Total Assets ($)	9932M	15049M	5018M	70358M	60294M	573294M

M = $ thousand   MM = $ million
See Pages viii through xx for Explanation of Ratios and Data

Current Data Sorted by Assets   Comparative Historical Data

0-500M	500M-2MM	2-10MM	10-50MM	50-100MM	100-250MM		23 4/1/14-3/31/15 ALL	22 4/1/15-3/31/16 ALL
						Type of Statement		
1	2	5				Unqualified	10	4
	1					Reviewed	1	1
2	2	1				Compiled	1	
1	6	9				Tax Returns	1	4
			2			Other	23	22
		10 (4/1-9/30/18)	22 (10/1/18-3/31/19)					
4	11	15	2			**NUMBER OF STATEMENTS**	36	31
%	%	%	%	%	%	**ASSETS**	%	%
	35.6	19.0		D	D	Cash & Equivalents	18.1	18.3
	14.3	25.6		A	A	Trade Receivables (net)	28.5	20.7
	2.1	1.8		T	T	Inventory	2.2	3.1
	8.7	2.2		A	A	All Other Current	1.7	5.5
	60.8	48.6				Total Current	50.5	47.5
	20.6	34.4		N	N	Fixed Assets (net)	29.5	39.2
	5.0	5.6		O	O	Intangibles (net)	10.5	7.1
	13.5	11.4		T	T	All Other Non-Current	9.5	6.2
	100.0	100.0				Total	100.0	100.0
				A	A	**LIABILITIES**		
	9.6	1.4		V	V	Notes Payable-Short Term	5.3	4.3
	2.2	1.3		A	A	Cur. Mat.-L.T.D.	3.2	3.5
	2.3	4.4		I	I	Trade Payables	2.1	3.2
	.0	.3		L	L	Income Taxes Payable	.1	.0
	20.4	35.6		A	A	All Other Current	31.9	31.1
	34.5	43.0		B	B	Total Current	42.6	42.1
	9.9	5.8		L	L	Long-Term Debt	9.7	14.2
	.0	.2		E	E	Deferred Taxes	.2	.5
	6.1	9.6				All Other Non-Current	10.6	11.3
	49.4	41.5				Net Worth	36.9	31.9
	100.0	100.0				Total Liabilties & Net Worth	100.0	100.0
						INCOME DATA		
	100.0	100.0				Net Sales	100.0	100.0
						Gross Profit		
	87.1	91.6				Operating Expenses	94.2	96.5
	12.9	8.4				Operating Profit	5.8	3.5
	.5	1.2				All Other Expenses (net)	.6	1.2
	12.4	7.2				Profit Before Taxes	5.2	2.3
						RATIOS		
	5.5	1.3					1.8	1.6
	2.3	1.1				Current	1.1	1.2
	1.0	1.0					.8	.7
	5.4	1.2					1.7	1.5
	1.5	1.0				Quick	.9	1.0
	.9	.9					.7	.4
	0 UND	16 22.6					20 18.4	5 68.7
	13 28.5	62 5.9				Sales/Receivables	85 4.3	41 8.8
	32 11.5	126 2.9					140 2.6	114 3.2
						Cost of Sales/Inventory		
						Cost of Sales/Payables		
	3.1	14.7					3.6	5.7
	6.9	42.5				Sales/Working Capital	50.0	20.7
	-63.0	999.8					-12.1	-16.3
		80.1					34.7	40.7
	(13)	3.5				EBIT/Interest	(29) 15.5	(27) 6.5
		-10.9					-.5	.1
						Net Profit + Depr., Dep., Amort./Cur. Mat. L/T/D		
	.2	.3					.5	.6
	.5	.8				Fixed/Worth	.8	1.5
	.7	1.6					1.9	4.1
	.2	1.0					.9	1.1
	1.1	1.7				Debt/Worth	2.0	2.5
	4.0	2.7					4.1	8.7
	102.4	28.7					51.2	34.2
	(10) 47.5	(14) 11.5				% Profit Before Taxes/Tangible Net Worth	(32) 17.8	(26) 15.6
	31.7	-10.9					-5.5	-1.0
	34.6	8.0					16.1	13.5
	29.0	4.4				% Profit Before Taxes/Total Assets	7.6	6.5
	19.8	-5.8					-1.6	-1.3
	24.6	7.5					8.0	6.9
	10.9	4.4				Sales/Net Fixed Assets	6.0	3.3
	7.3	2.9					3.2	2.6
	2.5	2.0					1.9	1.9
	1.8	1.3				Sales/Total Assets	1.3	1.3
	1.5	.8					.9	.9
		1.4					2.6	2.8
	(11)	2.7				% Depr., Dep., Amort./Sales	(31) 4.0	(30) 4.8
		4.1					6.2	6.6
						% Officers', Directors' Owners' Comp/Sales		
4681M	23140M	80050M	51830M			Net Sales ($)	374048M	355702M
1152M	12258M	57182M	32181M			Total Assets ($)	356963M	218560M

Note: Columns 50-100MM and 100-250MM — DATA NOT AVAILABLE

Comparative Historical Data

Current Data Sorted by Sales

7	6	8	Type of Statement	1	3		2	2	
1			Unqualified						
	2	1	Reviewed						
2	2	5	Compiled		1				
13	13	18	Tax Returns		4	1			
			Other	1	7	5	4		1
4/1/16-3/31/17 ALL	4/1/17-3/31/18 ALL	4/1/18-3/31/19 ALL		0-1MM	1-3MM [10 (4/1-9/30/18)]	3-5MM	5-10MM [22 (10/1/18-3/31/19)]	10-25MM	25MM & OVER
23	23	32	**NUMBER OF STATEMENTS**	2	15	6	6	2	1
%	%	%	**ASSETS**	%	%	%	%	%	%
28.9	21.1	31.9	Cash & Equivalents		33.6				
25.0	34.7	19.3	Trade Receivables (net)		16.1				
2.1	1.5	2.8	Inventory		2.9				
2.6	2.8	4.1	All Other Current		6.2				
58.6	60.1	58.1	Total Current		58.9				
32.1	30.5	25.7	Fixed Assets (net)		21.6				
4.7	4.7	4.4	Intangibles (net)		6.3				
4.6	4.8	11.7	All Other Non-Current		13.2				
100.0	100.0	100.0	Total		100.0				
			LIABILITIES						
6.8	7.2	4.0	Notes Payable-Short Term		7.0				
3.1	1.4	1.4	Cur. Mat.-L.T.D.		2.0				
3.3	2.1	3.2	Trade Payables		1.6				
.0	.2	.4	Income Taxes Payable		.2				
31.4	26.7	27.6	All Other Current		22.3				
44.6	37.6	36.6	Total Current		33.1				
7.7	7.3	6.7	Long-Term Debt		10.3				
.1	.0	.1	Deferred Taxes		.0				
10.0	6.7	10.2	All Other Non-Current		9.4				
37.6	48.3	46.5	Net Worth		47.3				
100.0	100.0	100.0	Total Liabilities & Net Worth		100.0				
			INCOME DATA						
100.0	100.0	100.0	Net Sales		100.0				
			Gross Profit						
93.0	92.6	89.2	Operating Expenses		88.2				
7.0	7.4	10.8	Operating Profit		11.8				
1.6	.0	.8	All Other Expenses (net)		.6				
5.4	7.4	10.0	Profit Before Taxes		11.1				
			RATIOS						
2.2	2.3	3.8	Current		4.8				
1.3	1.4	1.3			2.3				
.8	1.1	1.0			1.0				
2.0	1.8	3.4	Quick		4.8				
1.2	1.3	1.2			1.5				
.6	1.0	.9			.9				
19 18.9	32 11.5	3 129.7	Sales/Receivables		0 UND				
49 7.5	101 3.6	30 12.0			30 12.3				
135 2.7	182 2.0	68 5.4			49 7.5				
			Cost of Sales/Inventory						
			Cost of Sales/Payables						
3.0	2.3	4.7	Sales/Working Capital		3.3				
10.5	10.8	15.4			12.0				
-14.0	24.2	420.2			-63.0				
60.8	20.9	79.7	EBIT/Interest		80.5				
(20) 9.4	(18) 6.2	(23) 12.9			(11) 22.4				
.8	.2	2.3			2.4				
			Net Profit + Depr., Dep., Amort./Cur. Mat. L/T/D						
.5	.3	.3	Fixed/Worth		.2				
.7	.7	.6			.5				
1.2	1.2	1.0			.7				
.9	.5	.7	Debt/Worth		.6				
2.0	1.3	1.3			1.1				
3.5	1.9	2.7			4.0				
72.1	39.2	76.7	% Profit Before Taxes/Tangible Net Worth		100.9				
(22) 19.1	13.7	(30) 31.5			(13) 50.9				
-14.2	.2	8.1			22.3				
18.3	21.0	29.0	% Profit Before Taxes/Total Assets		34.6				
9.5	7.8	17.4			24.5				
-2.0	.1	2.5			4.3				
11.2	8.2	20.6	Sales/Net Fixed Assets		25.4				
4.6	4.3	7.8			12.1				
3.2	3.2	4.0			4.2				
1.5	1.6	2.5	Sales/Total Assets		2.5				
1.3	1.1	1.6			1.6				
1.0	1.0	1.2			1.3				
2.3	1.1	1.3	% Depr., Dep., Amort./Sales						
(21) 3.6	(18) 2.9	(22) 2.6							
5.1	4.4	4.2							
		2.6	% Officers', Directors' Owners' Comp/Sales						
	(10)	6.6							
		9.2							
192130M	94986M	159701M	Net Sales ($)	1340M	26489M	21364M	45214M	22747M	42547M
143509M	79351M	102773M	Total Assets ($)	3295M	19433M	14835M	39574M	9606M	16030M

M = $ thousand   MM = $ million
See Pages viii through xx for Explanation of Ratios and Data

Current Data Sorted by Assets   Comparative Historical Data

0-500M	500M-2MM	2-10MM	10-50MM	50-100MM	100-250MM	Type of Statement	4/1/14-3/31/15 ALL	4/1/15-3/31/16 ALL
	7	8	8	4	8	Unqualified	69	52
		5				Reviewed	3	3
	2	1				Compiled	5	1
6	4	2				Tax Returns	9	15
2	2	11	3	1	3	Other	52	55
	27 (4/1-9/30/18)		50 (10/1/18-3/31/19)					
8	15	27	11	5	11	**NUMBER OF STATEMENTS**	138	126
%	%	%	%	%	%	**ASSETS**	%	%
	30.1	14.9	29.9		17.9	Cash & Equivalents	22.5	23.0
	17.5	21.5	8.5		14.0	Trade Receivables (net)	16.5	18.7
	2.4	.9	3.1		.1	Inventory	2.4	1.2
	2.0	5.3	1.6		.8	All Other Current	4.4	3.3
	52.0	42.7	43.1		32.8	Total Current	45.8	46.1
	36.5	46.5	19.1		42.8	Fixed Assets (net)	38.7	37.6
	8.0	.5	27.8		7.8	Intangibles (net)	6.3	5.7
	3.5	10.3	10.0		16.5	All Other Non-Current	9.3	10.6
	100.0	100.0	100.0		100.0	Total	100.0	100.0
						LIABILITIES		
	1.8	2.1	.0		.0	Notes Payable-Short Term	7.8	4.6
	2.5	2.7	1.7		1.8	Cur. Mat.-L.T.D.	2.4	2.2
	3.2	7.0	8.7		3.1	Trade Payables	5.3	4.9
	.0	.2	.1		.1	Income Taxes Payable	.2	.0
	23.8	11.4	15.2		24.3	All Other Current	18.9	20.6
	31.4	23.4	25.7		29.3	Total Current	34.6	32.3
	13.8	19.7	8.9		12.6	Long-Term Debt	17.5	18.4
	.0	1.7	.0		.2	Deferred Taxes	.8	.7
	5.9	3.6	13.7		21.1	All Other Non-Current	9.9	12.6
	48.8	51.5	51.7		36.8	Net Worth	37.3	36.0
	100.0	100.0	100.0		100.0	Total Liabilities & Net Worth	100.0	100.0
						INCOME DATA		
	100.0	100.0	100.0		100.0	Net Sales	100.0	100.0
						Gross Profit		
	84.6	88.4	92.8		89.4	Operating Expenses	92.1	93.7
	15.4	11.6	7.2		10.6	Operating Profit	7.9	6.3
	3.5	4.5	-.7		2.1	All Other Expenses (net)	1.0	1.9
	11.9	7.1	7.9		8.5	Profit Before Taxes	6.9	4.4
						RATIOS		
	5.7	4.0	9.3		1.7		2.7	2.7
	1.5	1.7	1.6		1.2	Current	1.4	1.4
	.7	.8	1.2		1.0		1.0	.9
	5.4	2.7	5.9		1.6		2.4	2.5
	1.4	1.4	1.6		1.2	Quick	1.2	1.3
	.6	.5	.9		1.0		.8	.8
	0 UND	13 29.0	4 94.9		18 20.2		4 83.5	5 71.0
	11 34.5	30 12.0	17 21.6		47 7.8	Sales/Receivables	21 17.4	24 15.2
	47 7.8	47 7.8	31 11.8		72 5.1		55 6.6	76 4.8
						Cost of Sales/Inventory		
						Cost of Sales/Payables		
	3.8	2.9	3.2		7.9		5.8	4.6
	35.8	13.1	6.9		13.0	Sales/Working Capital	13.0	10.2
	-62.7	-28.3	33.6		-195.8		-301.2	-86.4
		19.7					19.3	21.3
		(21) 4.0				EBIT/Interest	(108) 5.4	(96) 3.8
		-2.0					1.5	-1.1
							5.9	6.6
						Net Profit + Depr., Dep., Amort./Cur. Mat. L/T/D	(21) 1.9	(19) 1.4
							.9	.3
	.2	.3	.1		.7		.5	.4
	.5	.8	.3		1.0	Fixed/Worth	1.0	1.1
	3.1	1.9	5.2		1.6		2.6	3.1
	.3	.3	.2		.5		.6	.7
	1.4	.9	2.0		.9	Debt/Worth	1.5	1.8
	5.6	1.6	5.9		4.3		5.6	8.3
	65.0	32.0					47.1	43.6
	(13) 31.7	(24) 8.5				% Profit Before Taxes/Tangible Net Worth	(117) 14.0	(102) 10.3
	2.0	-1.5					3.3	-3.3
	32.4	11.2	19.2		20.8		15.5	14.5
	8.5	3.6	5.6		5.4	% Profit Before Taxes/Total Assets	5.6	3.9
	2.2	-1.8	-.9		2.2		.7	-2.4
	24.9	12.2	49.9		4.5		13.5	15.7
	12.4	3.6	16.1		2.5	Sales/Net Fixed Assets	4.9	5.3
	4.5	.9	1.0		1.2		1.9	1.6
	3.8	2.2	1.9		1.5		2.2	2.1
	2.6	1.4	1.6		.9	Sales/Total Assets	1.4	1.3
	1.4	.5	.4		.4		.9	.8
	1.1	1.6					1.6	1.6
	(13) 2.7	(26) 3.7				% Depr., Dep., Amort./Sales	(115) 3.3	(96) 3.0
	5.1	6.9					4.9	5.3
							3.0	3.7
						% Officers', Directors' Owners' Comp/Sales	(24) 5.3	(25) 5.5
							11.7	15.4
16472M	41900M	294293M	483304M	287984M	1410556M	Net Sales ($)	4457602M	3713784M
1228M	18255M	155656M	289498M	337633M	1455733M	Total Assets ($)	3444506M	3347037M

M = $ thousand   MM = $ million
See Pages viii through xx for Explanation of Ratios and Data

Comparative Historical Data / Current Data Sorted by Sales

			Type of Statement						
41	33	35	Unqualified		7	3	3	7	15
8	5	5	Reviewed		1		2	2	
1	1	3	Compiled	2		1			
15	14	12	Tax Returns	4	5	1	2		
51	31	22	Other	1	4	3	4	4	6
4/1/16-3/31/17 ALL	4/1/17-3/31/18 ALL	4/1/18-3/31/19 ALL		0-1MM	27 (4/1-9/30/18) 1-3MM	3-5MM	50 (10/1/18-3/31/19) 5-10MM	10-25MM	25MM & OVER
116	84	77	NUMBER OF STATEMENTS	7	17	8	11	13	21
%	%	%	ASSETS	%	%	%	%	%	%
20.7	25.6	22.6	Cash & Equivalents		24.5		31.5	21.3	20.7
18.3	20.0	15.0	Trade Receivables (net)		12.6		15.5	18.4	16.7
3.0	1.6	1.4	Inventory		1.7		.2	1.6	1.8
5.3	4.2	2.9	All Other Current		2.3		8.8	1.5	2.0
47.3	51.3	41.9	Total Current		41.0		56.0	42.8	41.2
36.6	30.2	37.8	Fixed Assets (net)		42.6		34.9	27.1	29.4
6.5	7.1	9.0	Intangibles (net)		4.9		.8	16.7	13.5
9.6	11.3	11.2	All Other Non-Current		11.5		8.4	13.4	16.0
100.0	100.0	100.0	Total		100.0		100.0	100.0	100.0
			LIABILITIES						
6.1	4.4	1.8	Notes Payable-Short Term		5.5		1.5	.0	.1
2.7	1.8	3.2	Cur. Mat.-L.T.D.		1.2		12.0	1.3	1.7
6.1	5.6	6.2	Trade Payables		6.0		3.4	9.9	7.2
.1	.5	.1	Income Taxes Payable		.0		.0	.3	.1
18.2	21.3	17.5	All Other Current		17.2		6.2	13.7	25.1
33.2	33.6	28.8	Total Current		29.9		23.2	25.2	34.1
20.7	12.4	16.5	Long-Term Debt		10.5		10.5	19.3	10.6
.7	.5	.8	Deferred Taxes		.8		2.3	.6	.2
13.2	15.8	10.7	All Other Non-Current		2.5		6.9	6.9	24.7
32.2	37.7	43.0	Net Worth		56.2		57.1	48.0	30.4
100.0	100.0	100.0	Total Liabilities & Net Worth		100.0		100.0	100.0	100.0
			INCOME DATA						
100.0	100.0	100.0	Net Sales		100.0		100.0	100.0	100.0
			Gross Profit						
92.3	92.6	88.8	Operating Expenses		90.2		94.3	92.7	90.2
7.7	7.4	11.2	Operating Profit		9.8		5.7	7.3	9.8
2.2	.5	2.7	All Other Expenses (net)		.2		-.5	.3	1.9
5.5	6.9	8.5	Profit Before Taxes		9.7		6.3	6.9	7.9
			RATIOS						
3.1	3.2	3.7			7.5		7.4	5.9	1.7
1.6	1.5	1.5	Current		1.7		3.7	2.4	1.3
1.0	1.1	.8			.4		1.1	1.0	1.0
2.5	2.5	2.5			5.7		7.1	5.6	1.6
1.3	1.2	1.3	Quick		1.4		1.8	2.1	1.2
.6	.8	.7			.4		1.1	.9	.9
3 110.5	0 852.6	0 906.2			0 UND		0 UND	17 22.1	17 20.9
24 15.3	30 12.3	26 14.1	Sales/Receivables		2 149.7		30 12.3	29 12.8	42 8.6
66 5.5	66 5.5	47 7.8			47 7.8		44 8.3	52 7.0	59 6.2
			Cost of Sales/Inventory						
			Cost of Sales/Payables						
4.1	4.3	4.8			3.9		2.9	2.4	8.5
10.5	13.4	16.6	Sales/Working Capital		14.7		5.1	11.1	17.6
UND	149.4	-90.6			-21.9		35.8	NM	NM
12.8	18.5	14.7						24.8	15.0
(88) 3.1	(59) 3.5	(52) 5.7	EBIT/Interest				(10) 7.7	(16) 7.7	
-.1	-.5	-.9						-.4	-1.8
7.5	12.6								
(20) 1.7	(12) 5.3		Net Profit + Depr., Dep., Amort./Cur. Mat. L/T/D						
.5	.8								
.4	.2	.3			.2		.2	.3	.4
1.2	.9	.8	Fixed/Worth		.5		.6	.8	.8
5.4	2.7	2.2			2.0		1.1	4.4	NM
.6	.5	.3			.2		.1	.4	.6
2.2	1.6	1.3	Debt/Worth		.7		.5	1.8	1.1
10.5	8.0	5.7			1.7		1.6	9.1	NM
37.3	83.4	54.7			65.3		57.3	59.4	48.3
(92) 9.1	(70) 16.4	(63) 15.4	% Profit Before Taxes/Tangible Net Worth	(16) 29.0		(10) 11.0	(11) 17.9	(16) 37.0
.8	1.0	3.2			-.8		-6.3	5.4	8.1
13.4	29.7	20.0			34.6		33.3	10.9	20.0
3.1	6.9	6.3	% Profit Before Taxes/Total Assets		11.2		4.8	4.4	8.0
-.7	-.3	.0			-.4		-4.4	1.4	-2.7
21.5	29.7	20.2			37.0		14.8	30.0	15.3
5.6	8.1	6.0	Sales/Net Fixed Assets		6.0		6.3	12.2	6.3
1.4	3.0	1.8			1.0		3.9	3.4	1.9
2.7	3.0	2.6			7.2		2.2	3.0	1.8
1.2	1.8	1.5	Sales/Total Assets		1.5		1.6	1.6	1.2
.7	.9	.7			.6		1.0	.5	.8
1.5	1.4	1.6			1.0			1.5	2.1
(95) 3.6	(63) 3.0	(65) 3.5	% Depr., Dep., Amort./Sales	(15) 3.5		(11) 1.9	(17) 3.2	
5.5	5.3	6.5			6.9			4.3	5.5
3.0	1.8	2.8							
(20) 5.6	(12) 6.2	(12) 4.5	% Officers', Directors' Owners' Comp/Sales						
8.1	25.3	8.4							
2911368M	2510680M	2534509M	Net Sales ($)	2283M	36577M	32279M	78265M	221051M	2164054M
2687183M	1992489M	2258003M	Total Assets ($)	16534M	41274M	19322M	62111M	251966M	1866796M

© RMA 2019   M = $ thousand   MM = $ million
See Pages viii through xx for Explanation of Ratios and Data

Current Data Sorted by Assets   Comparative Historical Data

	0-500M	500M-2MM	2-10MM	10-50MM	50-100MM	100-250MM		4/1/14-3/31/15 ALL	4/1/15-3/31/16 ALL
Type of Statement									
Unqualified			7	6	3	2		26	29
Reviewed	1	2						2	1
Compiled	6							1	3
Tax Returns	12	12	4	2		2		15	9
Other								19	20
	30 (4/1-9/30/18)			29 (10/1/18-3/31/19)					
NUMBER OF STATEMENTS	19	14	11	8	3	4		63	62
	%	%	%	%	%	%		%	%
ASSETS									
Cash & Equivalents	47.1	17.0	7.6					23.8	27.1
Trade Receivables (net)	1.6	5.4	7.1					6.2	5.2
Inventory	4.8	.5	.4					.6	.3
All Other Current	4.9	6.2	4.4					2.0	1.3
Total Current	58.4	29.0	19.5					32.7	33.9
Fixed Assets (net)	21.3	56.8	46.6					47.7	49.3
Intangibles (net)	8.9	.2	.9					3.0	3.2
All Other Non-Current	11.3	14.0	32.9					16.6	13.5
Total	100.0	100.0	100.0					100.0	100.0
LIABILITIES									
Notes Payable-Short Term	10.9	8.4	2.5					2.2	4.6
Cur. Mat.-L.T.D.	5.0	.5	.8					2.5	1.5
Trade Payables	3.1	5.9	2.2					3.3	1.9
Income Taxes Payable	.0	.0	.0					.2	.1
All Other Current	14.4	13.3	8.9					7.8	7.1
Total Current	33.4	28.1	14.5					16.0	15.2
Long-Term Debt	7.7	25.2	31.4					18.9	26.3
Deferred Taxes	.0	.0	.0					.0	.0
All Other Non-Current	7.9	.0	5.3					7.3	4.5
Net Worth	51.0	46.7	48.8					57.8	53.8
Total Liabilties & Net Worth	100.0	100.0	100.0					100.0	100.0
INCOME DATA									
Net Sales	100.0	100.0	100.0					100.0	100.0
Gross Profit									
Operating Expenses	92.0	84.7	92.4					93.1	90.5
Operating Profit	8.0	15.3	7.6					6.9	9.5
All Other Expenses (net)	.4	4.5	2.3					.4	1.2
Profit Before Taxes	7.6	10.8	5.3					6.5	8.3
RATIOS									
Current	4.4	10.9	1.8					8.4	7.1
	2.8	.9	1.1					2.1	2.6
	.8	.1	.8					.9	.6
Quick	4.4	10.9	1.8					8.2	6.7
	2.0	.5	.7					1.8	2.6
	.4	.0	.5					.8	.5
Sales/Receivables	0 UND	0 UND	1 279.0					0 UND	0 UND
	0 UND	0 UND	13 28.3					6 58.9	3 115.9
	0 UND	5 79.2	23 16.0					33 11.0	31 11.9
Cost of Sales/Inventory									
Cost of Sales/Payables									
Sales/Working Capital	5.9	4.2	7.6					4.0	3.0
	21.0	NM	47.6					12.4	9.1
	-35.3	-2.8	-18.7					-56.0	-23.7
EBIT/Interest								15.0	9.9
								(42) 4.9	(41) 2.3
								.1	-.1
Net Profit + Depr., Dep., Amort./Cur. Mat. L/T/D									
Fixed/Worth	.1	.3	.3					.4	.4
	.3	1.5	.7					.9	.9
	.9	5.4	3.4					1.6	2.0
Debt/Worth	.3	.2	.2					.2	.2
	1.0	2.0	.4					.7	.7
	4.2	5.1	3.6					1.9	2.3
% Profit Before Taxes/Tangible Net Worth	133.2	60.6	22.0					39.5	28.6
	(17) 43.8	(13) 18.4	(10) -.4					(60) 10.3	(59) 6.5
	-9.1	-2.7	-8.9					1.1	.0
% Profit Before Taxes/Total Assets	67.9	14.3	7.0					17.8	15.2
	21.3	4.7	.1					5.2	4.3
	-2.1	-2.6	-7.2					.3	-.1
Sales/Net Fixed Assets	452.4	9.3	9.5					11.9	10.2
	20.7	1.9	1.9					1.3	1.3
	7.3	.7	.5					.8	.7
Sales/Total Assets	8.2	2.2	1.4					2.7	2.0
	3.2	.9	.9					.9	.8
	2.0	.5	.3					.4	.3
% Depr., Dep., Amort./Sales			2.4					1.8	3.2
			2.6					(52) 4.6	(45) 5.2
			15.1					7.0	8.2
% Officers', Directors' Owners' Comp/Sales	2.3							5.0	6.5
	(10) 6.6							(14) 8.6	(16) 9.3
	11.1							14.9	14.2
Net Sales ($)	17261M	17278M	65018M	101014M	76010M	594263M		858032M	991453M
Total Assets ($)	3811M	14047M	73406M	186777M	177651M	498291M		1307229M	1254293M

M = $ thousand   MM = $ million
See Pages viii through xx for Explanation of Ratios and Data

Comparative Historical Data | Current Data Sorted by Sales

18	18	18	Type of Statement						
					1	1	6	6	4
2		2	Unqualified						
2	2	1	Reviewed						
8	11	8	Compiled	1		2			
22	19	32	Tax Returns	7	1				
			Other	17	7	2	4		2
4/1/16-3/31/17 ALL	4/1/17-3/31/18 ALL	4/1/18-3/31/19 ALL		0-1MM	30 (4/1-9/30/18) 1-3MM	3-5MM	29 (10/1/18-3/31/19) 5-10MM	10-25MM	25MM & OVER
52	50	59	NUMBER OF STATEMENTS	25	8	4	10	6	6
%	%	%	**ASSETS**	%	%	%	%	%	%
26.1	23.8	23.6	Cash & Equivalents	31.9			9.9		
6.7	6.0	4.1	Trade Receivables (net)	.9			8.2		
2.9	.1	1.8	Inventory	3.6			.3		
3.9	3.6	4.5	All Other Current	3.2			5.2		
39.6	33.5	34.0	Total Current	39.6			23.6		
42.8	47.5	42.2	Fixed Assets (net)	43.2			45.3		
3.8	3.5	5.0	Intangibles (net)	4.6			.7		
13.8	15.5	18.9	All Other Non-Current	12.6			30.4		
100.0	100.0	100.0	Total	100.0			100.0		
			LIABILITIES						
8.4	2.4	7.0	Notes Payable-Short Term	11.1			2.8		
1.9	3.2	2.1	Cur. Mat.-L.T.D.	.7			.5		
5.3	3.0	4.1	Trade Payables	2.2			2.4		
.1	.0	.0	Income Taxes Payable	.0			.0		
8.7	7.7	12.2	All Other Current	13.5			9.4		
24.4	16.3	25.3	Total Current	27.5			15.2		
17.7	30.3	18.6	Long-Term Debt	21.0			27.5		
.0	.0	.0	Deferred Taxes	.0					
6.2	4.8	4.6	All Other Non-Current	1.7			5.4		
51.8	48.6	51.4	Net Worth	49.9			51.9		
100.0	100.0	100.0	Total Liabilities & Net Worth	100.0			100.0		
			INCOME DATA						
100.0	100.0	100.0	Net Sales	100.0			100.0		
			Gross Profit						
94.7	92.3	92.5	Operating Expenses	85.8			98.9		
5.3	7.7	7.5	Operating Profit	14.2			1.1		
1.9	2.1	1.5	All Other Expenses (net)	3.6			-3.1		
3.4	5.6	6.0	Profit Before Taxes	10.6			4.2		
			RATIOS						
7.0	5.6	4.0	Current	4.2			5.9		
2.2	2.3	1.3		1.3			1.8		
.8	1.0	.6		.4			.8		
5.8	5.3	3.7	Quick	4.2			4.0		
1.9	1.7	1.1		1.0			1.8		
.5	.7	.4		.2			.6		
0 UND	0 UND	0 UND	Sales/Receivables	0 UND			15 24.2		
3 133.6	1 244.6	2 155.2		0 UND			18 20.0		
24 14.9	30 12.3	17 21.2		0 UND			38 9.6		
			Cost of Sales/Inventory						
			Cost of Sales/Payables						
3.6	3.6	5.6	Sales/Working Capital	4.8			4.6		
8.7	11.2	26.4		31.0			7.9		
UND	UND	-12.9		-12.0			-23.2		
12.2	10.2	5.1	EBIT/Interest						
(27) 2.0	(34) 3.0	(30) 1.6							
-4.4	-.9	-4.4							
			Net Profit + Depr., Dep., Amort./Cur. Mat. L/T/D						
.2	.3	.3	Fixed/Worth	.3			.5		
.8	.8	.8		.8			.7		
1.8	2.5	2.7		3.5			1.5		
.1	.2	.3	Debt/Worth	.3			.1		
.5	.7	.9		1.5			.4		
1.9	2.5	3.2		4.7			1.7		
31.1	30.4	44.0	% Profit Before Taxes/Tangible Net Worth	68.1			5.8		
(46) 4.1	(46) 6.8	(53) 3.2		(24) 28.4			1.4		
-8.5	-1.0	-3.0		-7.1			-3.3		
15.4	15.4	18.0	% Profit Before Taxes/Total Assets	26.3			5.8		
1.2	4.1	2.9		6.0			1.4		
4.8	-1.2	-2.1		-2.4			-3.3		
40.1	13.0	17.1	Sales/Net Fixed Assets	24.7			5.6		
2.0	1.6	3.1		6.6			1.9		
.9	.7	.8		1.1			.8		
3.4	3.5	2.4	Sales/Total Assets	3.1			1.3		
1.0	1.0	1.0		1.4			.8		
.4	.4	.5		.6			.6		
2.4	1.7	2.2	% Depr., Dep., Amort./Sales	1.0					
(32) 5.3	(43) 4.2	(41) 3.3		(14) 2.4					
7.6	7.1	6.6		4.7					
	4.2	3.9	% Officers', Directors' Owners' Comp/Sales						
	(15) 7.3	(13) 7.5							
	14.6	12.9							
304986M	668128M	870844M	Net Sales ($)	12844M	13727M	16493M	73375M	99859M	654546M
756636M	1118194M	953983M	Total Assets ($)	14388M	20019M	18198M	109432M	231209M	560737M

© RMA 2019
M = $ thousand   MM = $ million
See Pages viii through xx for Explanation of Ratios and Data

Current Data Sorted by Assets   Comparative Historical Data

Type of Statement (current data periods: 4 (4/1-9/30/18) and 68 (10/1/18-3/31/19); columns 10-50MM, 50-100MM, 100-250MM: DATA NOT AVAILABLE)

0-500M	500M-2MM	2-10MM	10-50MM	50-100MM	100-250MM	Type of Statement	4/1/14-3/31/15 ALL	4/1/15-3/31/16 ALL
	1	1		1		Unqualified	10	6
1	1	2	1			Reviewed	2	1
16	6	1				Compiled	7	5
19	12	2	4			Tax Returns	35	31
						Other	22	30
36	20	10	5	1		**NUMBER OF STATEMENTS**	76	73
%	%	%	%	%	%	**ASSETS**	%	%
40.0	28.0	10.1				Cash & Equivalents	23.1	23.2
2.3	8.3	4.7				Trade Receivables (net)	3.9	4.9
2.7	1.3	11.6				Inventory	2.8	4.2
3.8	4.2	2.5				All Other Current	1.1	3.9
48.8	41.8	28.9				Total Current	30.9	36.2
39.9	46.8	47.2				Fixed Assets (net)	51.6	45.9
4.9	5.0	2.5				Intangibles (net)	7.5	4.7
6.4	6.4	21.4				All Other Non-Current	9.9	13.3
100.0	100.0	100.0				Total	100.0	100.0
						LIABILITIES		
18.0	6.7	1.6				Notes Payable-Short Term	7.6	17.7
4.2	1.4	1.8				Cur. Mat.-L.T.D.	5.1	2.9
2.3	2.9	2.7				Trade Payables	5.1	5.2
.1	2.5	.0				Income Taxes Payable	.0	.0
11.7	21.0	12.8				All Other Current	9.8	15.3
36.4	34.4	18.9				Total Current	27.6	41.0
23.1	33.3	24.5				Long-Term Debt	35.9	21.0
.0	.0	.0				Deferred Taxes	.0	.0
1.1	.3	10.1				All Other Non-Current	6.0	8.0
39.3	32.0	46.6				Net Worth	30.5	30.0
100.0	100.0	100.0				Total Liabilities & Net Worth	100.0	100.0
						INCOME DATA		
100.0	100.0	100.0				Net Sales	100.0	100.0
						Gross Profit		
89.1	89.2	91.0				Operating Expenses	90.2	88.8
10.9	10.8	9.0				Operating Profit	9.8	11.2
1.2	3.1	4.0				All Other Expenses (net)	3.0	3.6
9.7	7.7	5.0				Profit Before Taxes	6.8	7.5
						RATIOS		
8.5	17.7	4.9					6.5	4.4
2.1	1.5	2.5				Current	1.2	.9
.5	.5	.3					.3	.3
8.5	17.7	2.2					5.9	2.9
1.6	1.2	.8				Quick	.9	.6
.3	.4	.3					.3	.2
0 UND	0 UND	0 UND					0 UND	0 UND
0 UND	0 UND	4 100.2				Sales/Receivables	0 UND	G UND
0 UND	10 36.0	24 15.3					9 41.3	1 394.9
						Cost of Sales/Inventory		
						Cost of Sales/Payables		
7.9	5.4	2.8					7.8	7.3
22.6	37.7	12.1				Sales/Working Capital	83.0	-291.1
-41.0	-12.1	-9.3					-17.1	-7.7
19.2	20.5	24.8					8.4	21.9
(22) 8.4	(13) 2.8	3.0				EBIT/Interest	(45) 3.0	(43) 5.5
1.2	.6	-.4					1.1	2.6
						Net Profit + Depr., Dep., Amort./Cur. Mat. L/T/D		
.2	.2	.4					.6	.3
1.0	.6	.8				Fixed/Worth	1.9	1.3
4.9	-8.5	NM					-13.7	UND
.2	.2	.4					.4	.5
1.0	1.5	.9				Debt/Worth	1.7	2.0
24.3	-10.1	NM					-33.5	UND
215.5	51.2						58.4	92.2
(30) 73.6	(14) 14.7					% Profit Before Taxes/Tangible Net Worth	(56) 13.3	(55) 39.5
29.6	-.8						2.1	8.4
77.2	22.9	22.1					24.4	34.6
46.1	11.9	8.4				% Profit Before Taxes/Total Assets	9.3	9.8
3.6	.3	-1.3					.7	.8
54.5	36.9	9.6					38.1	43.3
17.6	4.4	2.6				Sales/Net Fixed Assets	5.9	13.3
6.2	1.4	.5					1.1	1.2
6.7	2.4	2.0					5.2	5.6
4.6	1.7	1.0				Sales/Total Assets	2.1	2.8
2.1	1.0	.4					.6	.8
.7	.7						.9	.7
(14) 1.1	(12) 3.4					% Depr., Dep., Amort./Sales	(56) 2.5	(49) 2.6
3.2	9.4						5.6	7.3
4.5							5.2	4.3
(18) 6.8						% Officers', Directors' Owners' Comp/Sales	(31) 8.2	(26) 8.2
9.0							13.0	20.1
36414M	58437M	53326M	75604M	27263M		Net Sales ($)	349264M	404330M
8459M	21840M	45260M	83276M	50952M		Total Assets ($)	458262M	204789M

(Columns 10-50MM, 50-100MM, 100-250MM in the Current Data section: DATA NOT AVAILABLE)

M = $ thousand   MM = $ million
See Pages viii through xx for Explanation of Ratios and Data

Comparative Historical Data			Type of Statement	Current Data Sorted by Sales					
4	4	3	Unqualified					2	1
	1	2	Reviewed		1		1		
4	3	3	Compiled	1	2				
36	30	24	Tax Returns	11	11	1		1	
39	34	40	Other	13	16	4	3	3	1
4/1/16- 3/31/17	4/1/17- 3/31/18	4/1/18- 3/31/19			4 (4/1-9/30/18)		68 (10/1/18-3/31/19)		
ALL	ALL	ALL		0-1MM	1-3MM	3-5MM	5-10MM	10-25MM	25MM & OVER
83	72	72	NUMBER OF STATEMENTS	25	30	5	4	6	2
%	%	%	ASSETS	%	%	%	%	%	%
26.3	23.1	30.1	Cash & Equivalents	30.6	36.1				
5.9	2.7	4.4	Trade Receivables (net)	2.2	4.1				
2.7	5.2	3.6	Inventory	3.4	.9				
5.3	3.3	3.6	All Other Current	2.0	4.2				
40.3	34.4	41.7	Total Current	38.2	45.2				
42.4	47.5	45.1	Fixed Assets (net)	54.0	40.5				
7.9	11.1	4.6	Intangibles (net)	6.0	4.2				
9.4	7.1	8.5	All Other Non-Current	1.9	10.1				
100.0	100.0	100.0	Total	100.0	100.0				
			LIABILITIES						
10.9	7.4	11.4	Notes Payable-Short Term	24.6	3.7				
2.4	1.9	3.2	Cur. Mat.-L.T.D.	4.9	2.2				
3.6	2.3	2.5	Trade Payables	1.3	3.0				
.1	.1	.8	Income Taxes Payable	.0	.2				
19.3	13.0	14.1	All Other Current	13.6	9.9				
36.4	24.6	31.8	Total Current	44.4	18.9				
24.5	19.9	26.6	Long-Term Debt	21.8	34.4				
.8	.0	.0	Deferred Taxes	.0	.0				
8.6	8.1	3.4	All Other Non-Current	.7	.2				
29.8	47.3	38.2	Net Worth	33.1	46.5				
100.0	100.0	100.0	Total Liabilties & Net Worth	100.0	100.0				
			INCOME DATA						
100.0	100.0	100.0	Net Sales	100.0	100.0				
			Gross Profit						
88.1	89.1	88.9	Operating Expenses	89.9	86.7				
11.9	10.9	11.1	Operating Profit	10.1	13.3				
2.8	2.1	2.8	All Other Expenses (net)	3.3	1.7				
9.1	8.7	8.3	Profit Before Taxes	6.8	11.6				
			RATIOS						
4.2	7.2	7.4		5.6	12.9				
1.2	1.9	1.7	Current	1.2	3.1				
.6	.5	.5		.3	.8				
2.9	5.3	7.3		4.7	12.8				
.9	1.2	1.2	Quick	1.0	2.5				
.5	.4	.4		.2	.7				
0 UND	0 UND	0 UND		0 UND	0 UND				
0 UND	0 UND	0 UND	Sales/Receivables	0 UND	0 UND				
4 84.0	3 122.1	5 77.1		0 UND	5 70.0				
			Cost of Sales/Inventory						
			Cost of Sales/Payables						
6.9	5.0	7.0		7.4	7.0				
66.2	27.4	21.0	Sales/Working Capital	56.9	12.9				
-28.4	-17.6	-16.1		-8.5	-39.8				
15.2	19.4	15.3		13.0	32.8				
(58) 5.1	(47) 7.2	(51) 4.9	EBIT/Interest	(17) 6.8	(18) 3.6				
.8	2.6	.4		-.6	1.3				
			Net Profit + Depr., Dep., Amort./Cur. Mat. L/T/D						
.4	.4	.2		.6	.2				
1.5	1.2	1.0	Fixed/Worth	1.6	.6				
-2.2	6.3	6.9		39.2	2.6				
.4	.3	.2		.2	.2				
2.5	1.2	1.3	Debt/Worth	1.4	.9				
-8.7	6.4	22.5		55.4	4.2				
99.7	69.3	93.3	% Profit Before Taxes/Tangible	151.9	114.1				
(56) 37.1	(57) 23.1	(58) 39.6	Net Worth	(20) 39.4	(24) 58.6				
2.6	2.8	3.1		4.7	10.0				
50.6	30.0	57.5	% Profit Before Taxes/Total	66.7	67.6				
13.2	11.3	17.9	Assets	22.5	22.2				
.4	2.8	1.7		.4	6.5				
44.3	27.9	31.5		20.9	45.2				
12.0	7.8	7.2	Sales/Net Fixed Assets	6.9	9.2				
2.0	1.4	1.9		1.3	2.4				
5.6	5.3	5.1		5.2	5.2				
3.1	1.7	2.2	Sales/Total Assets	2.0	2.3				
1.0	.9	1.0		1.0	1.5				
.8	1.0	1.0		1.0	1.1				
(49) 2.2	(47) 3.0	(40) 2.9	% Depr., Dep., Amort./Sales	(10) 2.8	(15) 3.1				
3.5	5.4	5.4		11.5	7.8				
6.4	4.9	3.7	% Officers', Directors'	3.7					
(35) 10.2	(28) 6.6	(27) 6.1	Owners' Comp/Sales	(11) 7.3					
15.3	9.5	8.6		10.9					
1792805M	246976M	251044M	Net Sales ($)	12926M	50760M	20746M	27521M	81902M	57189M
516798M	282964M	209787M	Total Assets ($)	13897M	30249M	12556M	36699M	38448M	77938M

© RMA 2019

M = $ thousand   MM = $ million
See Pages viii through xx for Explanation of Ratios and Data

Current Data Sorted by Assets   Comparative Historical Data

						Type of Statement		
1	6	15	27	4	8	Unqualified	99	99
		1	1			Reviewed	8	10
3	4	7				Compiled	13	14
17	9	1	2	3		Tax Returns	44	37
12	13	25	18			Other	96	87
	81 (4/1-9/30/18)		96 (10/1/18-3/31/19)				4/1/14-3/31/15 ALL	4/1/15-3/31/16 ALL
0-500M	500M-2MM	2-10MM	10-50MM	50-100MM	100-250MM			
33	32	49	48	7	8	NUMBER OF STATEMENTS	260	247
%	%	%	%	%	%	ASSETS	%	%
47.8	36.9	21.5	26.1			Cash & Equivalents	25.5	26.8
9.6	7.3	12.7	6.7			Trade Receivables (net)	9.5	9.7
.9	2.6	2.1	.6			Inventory	2.0	1.6
.0	2.2	2.9	5.1			All Other Current	4.0	3.3
58.2	48.9	39.2	38.5			Total Current	41.0	41.5
27.3	33.7	49.8	40.4			Fixed Assets (net)	41.5	40.7
8.6	1.5	3.4	7.6			Intangibles (net)	5.0	5.2
5.7	15.9	7.7	13.6			All Other Non-Current	12.5	12.6
100.0	100.0	100.0	100.0			Total	100.0	100.0
						LIABILITIES		
9.3	2.6	2.2	1.3			Notes Payable-Short Term	5.7	5.5
2.8	8.6	2.2	1.6			Cur. Mat.-L.T.D.	2.6	1.9
3.0	4.0	3.3	2.8			Trade Payables	4.0	5.0
.0	.4	.0	.1			Income Taxes Payable	.0	.0
30.6	13.6	15.6	14.2			All Other Current	16.0	11.2
45.7	29.2	23.3	20.0			Total Current	28.4	23.7
30.7	14.9	23.2	22.6			Long-Term Debt	21.9	25.0
.0	.0	.0	.1			Deferred Taxes	.1	.1
4.7	14.3	4.5	11.4			All Other Non-Current	8.8	8.7
18.9	41.6	49.0	46.0			Net Worth	40.8	42.5
100.0	100.0	100.0	100.0			Total Liabilities & Net Worth	100.0	100.0
						INCOME DATA		
100.0	100.0	100.0	100.0			Net Sales	100.0	100.0
						Gross Profit		
90.1	90.0	90.5	92.6			Operating Expenses	90.1	91.5
9.9	10.0	9.5	7.4			Operating Profit	9.9	8.5
.0	1.5	1.3	2.1			All Other Expenses (net)	2.6	2.6
9.8	8.5	8.2	5.4			Profit Before Taxes	7.3	5.9
						RATIOS		
10.9	7.2	5.8	5.5				5.8	7.4
2.2	2.2	1.7	2.5			Current	1.9	2.4
.8	1.1	.9	1.2				.8	1.0
10.9	6.6	5.1	4.7				4.9	6.3
2.2	2.1	1.4	1.9			Quick	1.6	1.8
.6	.9	.4	.8				.6	.8
0 UND	0 UND	0 UND	2 149.3				0 UND	0 UND
0 UND	5 79.4	13 28.6	16 22.4			Sales/Receivables	7 51.2	8 46.6
1 430.2	16 23.0	45 8.1	28 13.2				31 11.7	34 10.7
						Cost of Sales/Inventory		
						Cost of Sales/Payables		
7.1	3.9	3.7	2.5				4.5	3.1
22.0	12.0	9.6	4.8			Sales/Working Capital	13.7	9.4
-83.7	176.6	-46.8	39.4				-30.8	999.8
33.3	54.8	8.6	21.7				14.9	15.7
(15) 21.0	(16) 10.5	(31) 3.4	(34) 7.2			EBIT/Interest	(165) 3.1	(152) 4.0
-1.2	3.3	1.1	2.0				1.0	1.4
						Net Profit + Depr., Dep., Amort./Cur. Mat. L/T/D		
.0	.1	.4	.5				.3	.3
.3	.6	1.3	.9			Fixed/Worth	.9	.8
3.1	1.2	2.2	2.9				3.0	2.2
.1	.1	.2	.3				.3	.2
.8	.4	1.3	1.1			Debt/Worth	1.1	.8
-6.0	4.2	3.0	4.2				5.3	4.2
139.7	58.7	44.6	23.3				43.7	29.3
(24) 62.8	(27) 19.1	(46) 13.2	(42) 7.4			% Profit Before Taxes/Tangible Net Worth	(227) 10.9	(220) 8.2
23.3	-6.2	-.1	-.4				1.4	.4
132.4	41.3	12.4	8.9				21.4	12.6
44.2	19.2	5.9	4.8			% Profit Before Taxes/Total Assets	5.3	4.0
2.9	-3.1	-.1	.0				.3	.0
285.5	41.3	10.9	8.7				30.5	23.5
38.5	13.8	1.6	1.7			Sales/Net Fixed Assets	6.4	5.2
11.6	4.8	.7	.9				1.0	.9
9.9	3.5	1.7	1.4				3.1	2.5
5.4	2.2	.9	.7			Sales/Total Assets	1.4	1.2
3.1	1.3	.5	.4				.5	.5
.4	.7	1.4	1.5				1.1	1.3
(21) 1.2	(19) 1.6	(31) 3.9	(40) 2.6			% Depr., Dep., Amort./Sales	(183) 3.1	(184) 3.7
3.3	2.5	5.6	7.2				6.0	6.6
3.8	3.4						3.6	3.1
(15) 9.7	(10) 6.2					% Officers', Directors' Owners' Comp/Sales	(53) 7.6	(40) 7.5
11.0	7.8						14.7	17.8
35731M	78276M	420376M	1290447M	261059M	1261123M	Net Sales ($)	4724218M	3638303M
6094M	31182M	242034M	1033114M	432881M	1119035M	Total Assets ($)	4478043M	4148123M

M = $ thousand   MM = $ million
See Pages viii through xx for Explanation of Ratios and Data

	Comparative Historical Data			Type of Statement	Current Data Sorted by Sales					
	70	63	61	Unqualified	4	5	4	14	16	18
	3	8	2	Reviewed		2				
	4	6	14	Compiled		8	2	4		
	34	40	29	Tax Returns	10	13	4	1		1
	48	71	71	Other	14	19	4	11	17	6
	4/1/16-3/31/17	4/1/17-3/31/18	4/1/18-3/31/19		81 (4/1-9/30/18)			96 (10/1/18-3/31/19)		
	ALL	ALL	ALL		0-1MM	1-3MM	3-5MM	5-10MM	10-25MM	25MM & OVER
	159	188	177	**NUMBER OF STATEMENTS**	28	47	14	30	33	25
	%	%	%	**ASSETS**	%	%	%	%	%	%
	26.5	30.5	30.5	Cash & Equivalents	43.6	34.6	30.4	21.2	23.0	29.0
	8.0	9.3	9.1	Trade Receivables (net)	6.1	6.3	16.7	9.2	10.5	11.6
	1.4	1.3	1.4	Inventory	4.0	.3	1.9	.6	1.6	.7
	5.0	4.1	2.8	All Other Current	.1	1.2	2.1	3.7	3.5	7.1
	41.0	45.3	43.8	Total Current	53.8	42.5	51.1	34.8	38.6	48.4
	39.6	38.2	39.0	Fixed Assets (net)	36.4	41.9	36.9	46.8	42.9	23.1
	6.3	5.4	5.6	Intangibles (net)	5.8	3.6	1.6	7.4	5.3	9.3
	13.2	11.1	11.7	All Other Non-Current	3.9	12.0	10.3	11.0	13.2	19.2
	100.0	100.0	100.0	Total	100.0	100.0	100.0	100.0	100.0	100.0
				LIABILITIES						
	4.9	6.4	3.2	Notes Payable-Short Term	7.1	4.0	5.1	.6	2.4	.7
	2.2	3.4	3.2	Cur. Mat.-L.T.D.	.9	6.9	4.1	2.5	1.5	1.2
	5.2	4.4	3.3	Trade Payables	3.9	1.9	4.5	3.2	3.6	4.2
	.1	.1	.1	Income Taxes Payable	.0	.3	.0	.1	.1	.0
	13.8	18.3	17.4	All Other Current	13.8	22.1	9.2	13.3	13.4	27.2
	26.3	32.6	27.2	Total Current	25.7	35.1	22.9	19.7	21.0	33.3
	20.5	23.0	22.9	Long-Term Debt	12.9	31.7	31.8	16.7	24.9	17.0
	.0	.0	.0	Deferred Taxes	.0	.0	.0	.0	.0	.2
	7.9	9.9	11.0	All Other Non-Current	3.9	8.2	11.1	3.8	16.9	25.3
	45.2	34.5	38.9	Net Worth	57.5	25.0	34.2	59.8	37.2	24.1
	100.0	100.0	100.0	Total Liabilities & Net Worth	100.0	100.0	100.0	100.0	100.0	100.0
				INCOME DATA						
	100.0	100.0	100.0	Net Sales	100.0	100.0	100.0	100.0	100.0	100.0
				Gross Profit						
	91.4	90.7	92.1	Operating Expenses	85.5	92.1	89.2	94.6	92.0	98.4
	8.6	9.3	7.9	Operating Profit	14.5	7.9	10.8	5.4	8.0	1.6
	2.7	2.4	1.2	All Other Expenses (net)	.1	1.6	1.2	.3	2.0	1.8
	5.9	6.8	6.7	Profit Before Taxes	14.4	6.4	9.6	5.1	6.0	-.2
				RATIOS						
	5.4	5.4	6.0	Current	15.0	6.7	6.6	5.9	5.2	2.9
	2.2	2.0	1.9		3.9	1.9	1.6	2.2	1.9	1.9
	.9	.9	1.0		1.0	.4	.9	1.0	1.1	1.0
	5.3	5.3	5.0	Quick	15.0	5.1	6.6	5.4	4.6	2.8
	1.7	1.8	1.8		3.5	1.9	1.6	1.9	1.8	1.6
	.7	.8	.8		.7	.4	.7	.9	.6	.9
	0 UND	0 UND	0 UND	Sales/Receivables	0 UND	0 UND	2 183.4	1 403.9	11 33.4	2 199.9
	10 35.9	5 74.6	7 48.9		0 UND	0 UND	21 17.1	11 32.9	22 16.6	20 17.9
	34 10.6	28 13.2	31 11.8		7 50.8	5 71.8	35 10.3	47 7.8	37 9.9	54 6.8
				Cost of Sales/Inventory						
				Cost of Sales/Payables						
	3.7	4.1	3.3	Sales/Working Capital	3.3	4.4	2.8	3.2	2.9	3.5
	8.7	10.3	8.4		9.7	13.3	12.2	9.5	5.3	7.6
	-85.1	-253.9	UND		UND	-18.6	NM	-66.9	314.6	NM
	13.7	26.3	23.1	EBIT/Interest		16.7		25.5	18.2	14.5
	(91) 3.7	(114) 4.8	(106) 4.6		(32) 5.6		(16) 2.5	(26) 4.4	(14) 3.8	
	.1	1.3	.7			-1.2		-1.0	1.7	-.9
				Net Profit + Depr., Dep., Amort./Cur. Mat. L/T/D						
	.2	.1	.2	Fixed/Worth	.0	.1	.3	.6	.5	.2
	.9	.8	.8		.4	.8	.9	1.0	.8	.7
	2.3	3.2	2.5		1.5	2.5	7.7	1.8	3.5	2.7
	.2	.3	.2	Debt/Worth	.1	.1	.5	.2	.3	.4
	.7	1.3	1.0		.4	.8	1.0	1.1	1.1	2.5
	3.2	7.9	4.1		3.7	2.8	9.2	2.2	4.3	-6.5
	46.4	60.0	47.0	% Profit Before Taxes/Tangible Net Worth	83.8	48.0	147.2	55.4	30.6	28.4
	(138) 10.7	(155) 21.0	(149) 13.1		(25) 36.4	(38) 13.9	(12) 27.6	(28) 5.2	(28) 14.9	(18) 8.2
	-.6	3.2	-.9		2.6	-2.3	7.6	-1.0	-2.5	-5.6
	21.7	23.5	25.4	% Profit Before Taxes/Total Assets	82.8	37.7	43.4	15.9	10.7	7.4
	4.2	6.4	6.0		19.2	8.2	14.9	3.5	4.9	4.3
	-1.2	.3	-.9		2.3	-3.3	3.5	-.5	-1.4	-8.7
	23.9	53.6	27.4	Sales/Net Fixed Assets	70.5	41.5	21.8	7.3	8.6	31.7
	4.5	7.1	4.6		14.5	7.7	5.7	2.4	1.7	7.9
	.9	1.1	1.1		1.6	1.0	.9	.9	.9	3.2
	2.7	3.8	2.9	Sales/Total Assets	6.0	3.9	3.7	2.3	1.4	2.3
	1.2	1.5	1.4		1.9	2.2	.9	1.1	.9	1.4
	.5	.7	.6		.9	.7	.4	.4	.5	1.1
	1.0	.9	1.2	% Depr., Dep., Amort./Sales	.9	.5	1.1	1.9	1.4	.5
	(123) 3.3	(138) 2.6	(121) 2.4		(14) 3.4	(30) 1.4	(10) 2.9	(21) 4.9	(30) 3.3	(16) 2.0
	6.4	6.5	5.9			4.0	14.8	7.4	6.9	4.3
	3.6	4.9	3.5	% Officers', Directors' Owners' Comp/Sales	7.2	3.0				
	(34) 8.9	(43) 9.6	(34) 6.5		(11) 10.3	(11) 4.5				
	14.4	13.8	10.4		12.7	7.1				
	3005249M	3377686M	3347012M	Net Sales ($)	15744M	82341M	53686M	218452M	502718M	2474071M
	3918042M	3122806M	2864340M	Total Assets ($)	20456M	79957M	77664M	321151M	730206M	1634906M

© RMA 2019

M = $ thousand   MM = $ million
See Pages viii through xx for Explanation of Ratios and Data

Current Data Sorted by Assets · Comparative Historical Data

Type of Statement	0-500M	500M-2MM	2-10MM	10-50MM	50-100MM	100-250MM		4/1/14-3/31/15 ALL	4/1/15-3/31/16 ALL
Unqualified	1	9	35	43	31	22		171	174
Reviewed		2	2	4				8	7
Compiled	8	6	7	1				13	18
Tax Returns	9	17	25	33	11	8		34	30
Other								80	82
	171 (4/1-9/30/18)			106 (10/1/18-3/31/19)					
NUMBER OF STATEMENTS	18	34	71	82	42	30		306	311
	%	%	%	%	%	%		%	%
ASSETS									
Cash & Equivalents	47.5	28.2	34.5	30.9	21.1	23.0		28.9	30.1
Trade Receivables (net)	9.1	24.2	15.3	13.0	9.2	3.2		15.4	13.9
Inventory	.3	.8	1.8	2.4	1.0	.3		1.2	1.0
All Other Current	2.1	8.1	6.0	5.0	5.4	3.8		3.9	3.7
Total Current	59.0	61.4	57.6	51.3	36.7	30.4		49.3	48.7
Fixed Assets (net)	25.1	20.6	27.4	29.0	39.9	45.6		33.1	32.6
Intangibles (net)	8.0	7.2	3.5	5.1	3.5	5.9		4.2	4.0
All Other Non-Current	7.9	10.8	11.5	14.6	19.9	18.1		13.3	14.7
Total	100.0	100.0	100.0	100.0	100.0	100.0		100.0	100.0
LIABILITIES									
Notes Payable-Short Term	17.3	15.4	4.8	1.5	.4	1.6		5.7	5.1
Cur. Mat.-L.T.D.	.7	1.0	1.4	1.9	2.4	1.9		1.8	2.2
Trade Payables	3.0	10.1	4.4	5.9	3.3	2.3		6.6	6.4
Income Taxes Payable	.0	.0	.0	.0	.0	.0		.3	.1
All Other Current	26.5	25.2	11.9	14.4	9.4	7.6		13.5	16.7
Total Current	47.5	51.7	22.6	23.8	15.5	13.5		27.9	30.4
Long-Term Debt	16.4	14.4	16.6	24.3	23.2	34.8		20.5	19.8
Deferred Taxes	.0	.0	.0	.0	.1	.0		.1	.1
All Other Non-Current	.8	7.4	4.3	11.2	38.2	27.0		6.9	11.1
Net Worth	35.3	26.5	56.5	40.7	23.1	24.8		44.6	38.6
Total Liabilities & Net Worth	100.0	100.0	100.0	100.0	100.0	100.0		100.0	100.0
INCOME DATA									
Net Sales	100.0	100.0	100.0	100.0	100.0	100.0		100.0	100.0
Gross Profit									
Operating Expenses	92.6	94.5	85.4	91.3	94.2	88.2		91.9	91.8
Operating Profit	7.4	5.5	14.6	8.7	5.8	11.8		8.1	8.2
All Other Expenses (net)	-.3	1.0	5.3	1.2	3.4	7.0		2.8	3.4
Profit Before Taxes	7.7	4.4	9.3	7.5	2.4	4.8		5.3	4.9
RATIOS									
Current	18.0	4.7	6.8	9.1	9.2	5.5		6.0	5.7
	1.5	1.5	2.8	3.0	2.6	2.4		2.3	2.2
	.5	.9	1.4	1.2	1.2	1.3		1.1	1.0
Quick	18.0	4.2	5.5	6.9	7.1	4.7		5.8	5.2
	1.5	1.5	2.6	2.4	2.3	2.0		2.0	1.9
	.5	.7	1.2	1.2	1.1	1.0		1.0	.8
Sales/Receivables	0 UND	0 UND	0 UND	1 471.4	0 UND	0 UND		0 987.7	1 306.4
	0 UND	13 28.8	12 29.5	18 19.9	9 41.4	7 53.3		25 14.4	19 18.9
	11 33.5	46 7.9	43 8.4	48 7.6	41 8.8	31 11.9		52 7.0	49 7.4
Cost of Sales/Inventory									
Cost of Sales/Payables									
Sales/Working Capital	6.9	3.4	1.7	2.0	1.4	2.2		2.6	2.3
	73.0	19.1	5.1	4.7	4.5	3.8		7.2	6.7
	-14.7	-206.9	23.0	18.2	17.7	14.3		45.7	-268.9
EBIT/Interest	20.0	66.7	39.7	18.8	9.4	6.4		19.9	18.4
	(15) 5.2	(18) 7.7	(38) 8.2	(51) 4.0	(32) 2.1	(18) 2.0		(190) 4.5	(184) 3.1
	-7.0	-17.6	.6	1.0	-1.4	.3		.4	.7
Net Profit + Depr., Dep., Amort./Cur. Mat. L/T/D								27.2	11.2
								(18) 3.4	(11) 5.0
								2.0	1.4
Fixed/Worth	.0	.0	.0	.1	.6	.6		.1	.1
	.8	.8	.2	.8	.9	1.9		.6	.7
	6.9	4.1	1.0	1.8	-11.6	-4.7		1.8	2.3
Debt/Worth	.4	.6	.2	.2	.6	.9		.3	.3
	2.3	1.5	.6	.8	1.4	2.5		1.0	1.1
	-6.1	12.0	1.9	3.8	-54.2	-7.8		4.7	5.2
% Profit Before Taxes/Tangible Net Worth	74.3	82.8	45.8	26.5	11.8	11.6		31.7	22.4
	(13) 18.8	(28) 14.9	(65) 11.7	(67) 6.7	(31) 2.8	(22) 5.1		(269) 6.7	(255) 5.7
	-11.7	-5.3	-.3	.4	.5	-2.0		-.7	-.6
% Profit Before Taxes/Total Assets	54.2	37.3	18.4	11.4	4.0	3.6		11.3	8.9
	3.7	10.4	6.2	4.7	.7	.9		3.0	2.4
	-7.2	-3.1	.0	.0	-4.1	-1.1		-.6	-.7
Sales/Net Fixed Assets	UND	426.9	256.3	31.4	6.0	4.6		42.1	47.2
	36.2	57.7	20.5	5.8	1.5	1.1		8.4	7.4
	13.6	12.3	3.6	1.8	.6	.5		1.0	1.2
Sales/Total Assets	8.0	5.3	2.7	2.3	1.1	1.0		2.6	2.5
	4.6	2.8	1.4	1.2	.6	.5		1.2	1.1
	2.5	1.9	.8	.6	.3	.2		.5	.5
% Depr., Dep., Amort./Sales		.3	.6	.9	2.1	2.8		1.0	.9
		(18) .6	(42) 1.4	(66) 2.0	(32) 3.7	(23) 4.3		(224) 2.3	(237) 2.6
		1.3	3.3	4.1	7.1	16.2		5.6	5.4
% Officers', Directors' Owners' Comp/Sales		1.7	2.5					1.8	2.5
		(10) 4.1	(11) 5.1					(58) 4.0	(40) 5.3
		5.4	7.1					9.4	8.6
Net Sales ($)	15784M	149254M	685089M	3094211M	2892528M	3425399M		8460134M	8786644M
Total Assets ($)	3666M	39845M	377009M	2095679M	3160660M	4943291M		9443230M	9183492M

Comparative Historical Data

Current Data Sorted by Sales

4/1/16-3/31/17 ALL	4/1/17-3/31/18 ALL	4/1/18-3/31/19 ALL	Type of Statement	0-1MM	1-3MM	3-5MM	5-10MM	10-25MM	25MM & OVER
118	122	141	Unqualified	5	10	6	19	33	68
6	8	6	Reviewed				1	2	3
7	7	5	Compiled	1	1		1	1	1
17	21	22	Tax Returns	8	3	3	4	3	1
80	90	103	Other	11	12	11	15	23	31
					171 (4/1-9/30/18)			106 (10/1/18-3/31/19)	
228	248	277	**NUMBER OF STATEMENTS**	25	26	20	40	62	104
%	%	%	**ASSETS**	%	%	%	%	%	%
32.5	31.7	30.2	Cash & Equivalents	34.0	34.2	26.5	34.8	31.4	26.6
15.3	12.2	13.1	Trade Receivables (net)	3.8	13.2	22.5	16.1	13.2	12.3
1.6	1.3	1.5	Inventory	.2	.3	.5	2.7	.5	2.3
3.8	5.6	5.4	All Other Current	4.5	3.2	7.2	4.6	4.7	6.6
53.2	50.8	50.2	Total Current	42.5	50.9	56.7	58.2	49.8	47.7
25.7	29.0	30.8	Fixed Assets (net)	36.5	35.3	14.4	26.0	32.6	32.1
4.5	4.9	5.0	Intangibles (net)	9.4	2.6	9.7	2.9	5.0	4.4
16.7	15.2	14.1	All Other Non-Current	11.6	11.2	19.2	12.9	12.6	15.8
100.0	100.0	100.0	Total	100.0	100.0	100.0	100.0	100.0	100.0
			LIABILITIES						
7.9	4.0	4.9	Notes Payable-Short Term	7.2	7.5	15.7	5.2	4.5	1.8
2.4	2.3	1.7	Cur. Mat.-L.T.D.	1.4	1.5	.7	.7	1.5	2.4
6.7	5.3	5.1	Trade Payables	1.7	7.0	7.6	3.5	4.4	5.9
.1	.0	.0	Income Taxes Payable	.0	.0	.0	.0	.0	.1
17.5	18.2	14.4	All Other Current	8.4	27.5	19.7	11.6	10.2	15.1
34.6	29.7	26.1	Total Current	18.7	43.4	43.7	21.1	20.5	25.3
15.8	15.6	21.6	Long-Term Debt	33.7	14.9	21.7	18.0	15.6	25.2
.1	.0	.0	Deferred Taxes	.0	.0	.0	.0	.0	.0
9.6	10.3	14.1	All Other Non-Current	2.2	1.6	10.4	4.8	3.3	30.8
40.0	44.4	38.3	Net Worth	45.4	40.1	24.1	56.1	60.5	18.6
100.0	100.0	100.0	Total Liabilties & Net Worth	100.0	100.0	100.0	100.0	100.0	100.0
			INCOME DATA						
100.0	100.0	100.0	Net Sales	100.0	100.0	100.0	100.0	100.0	100.0
			Gross Profit						
92.9	92.5	90.4	Operating Expenses	77.2	90.7	87.8	88.9	88.5	95.6
7.1	7.5	9.6	Operating Profit	22.8	9.3	12.2	11.1	11.5	4.4
2.1	1.9	3.1	All Other Expenses (net)	14.7	1.3	1.2	3.8	1.9	1.6
4.9	5.6	6.5	Profit Before Taxes	8.1	8.0	11.0	7.3	9.6	2.8
			RATIOS						
5.3	6.4	7.3		9.7	7.1	5.6	21.6	6.7	6.3
2.1	2.4	2.7	Current	3.3	2.3	1.6	3.7	2.7	2.4
1.0	1.1	1.2		1.2	.4	.9	1.3	1.6	1.2
4.7	5.0	5.6		9.7	7.1	5.0	19.2	5.3	4.5
1.8	2.0	2.2	Quick	2.8	2.2	1.5	2.7	2.6	1.7
.7	.9	1.0		1.1	.3	.7	1.2	1.3	1.0
2 194.6	0 999.8	0 UND		0 UND	0 UND	0 UND	2 188.7	0 UND	0 UND
21 17.3	16 23.2	12 31.0	Sales/Receivables	0 UND	7 48.7	20 18.6	12 31.3	20 18.5	16 23.2
43 8.4	41 9.0	41 8.9		4 94.6	32 11.4	46 8.0	59 6.2	45 8.2	41 8.9
			Cost of Sales/Inventory						
			Cost of Sales/Payables						
2.9	2.3	2.2		1.7	2.6	3.2	1.2	1.9	2.4
8.0	5.7	5.3	Sales/Working Capital	5.9	13.7	7.5	3.2	4.8	5.7
-278.9	38.7	34.3		73.0	-6.4	-80.3	20.5	16.6	20.7
19.4	18.0	19.7		13.3	18.8	31.9	11.1	27.2	16.6
(134) 3.8	(143) 4.1	(172) 3.8	EBIT/Interest	(13) 1.6	(15) 6.1	(12) 8.0	(25) 3.5	(37) 9.4	(70) 2.9
-.6	.8	-.9		-4.0	-10.5	-1.9	-3.3	1.9	-1.0
	6.0	4.4	Net Profit + Depr., Dep.,						
	(10) .2	(12) 2.3	Amort./Cur. Mat. L/T/D						
		-1.5	.5						
.1	.1	.1		.0	.0	.0	.0	.1	.3
.4	.6	.8	Fixed/Worth	.8	.8	.8	.4	.6	1.1
2.0	1.6	2.2		1.8	2.3	NM	1.2	1.0	-4.7
.3	.3	.3		.4	.3	.6	.2	.2	.7
1.0	.8	1.0	Debt/Worth	1.4	.7	1.8	.5	.6	2.1
4.4	3.5	4.4		13.5	7.8	NM	2.4	1.5	-10.5
28.1	24.3	27.5	% Profit Before Taxes/Tangible	74.3	21.1	55.8	23.5	40.8	19.3
(194) 7.6	(219) 7.1	(226) 8.5	Net Worth	(21) .7	(21) 8.4	(15) 10.8	(36) 9.2	(59) 10.6	(74) 6.3
-1.7	-1.2	-.5		-6.3	-5.6	-23.3	-.9	2.4	-1.8
11.3	11.0	11.4	% Profit Before Taxes/Total	10.6	12.6	31.3	11.9	17.5	8.0
3.3	2.8	3.6	Assets	.7	5.6	10.9	5.0	4.9	2.9
-1.6	-1.1	-1.3		-2.4	5.9	7.4	-1.6	.9	-2.3
68.3	38.8	56.6		UND	423.8	365.2	105.4	78.2	25.4
10.7	8.3	8.0	Sales/Net Fixed Assets	15.4	13.0	50.2	12.3	5.6	5.0
2.2	1.7	1.6		.6	1.5	7.2	1.5	1.6	1.2
2.7	2.5	2.7		4.6	2.9	3.5	2.2	2.7	2.4
1.4	1.2	1.2	Sales/Total Assets	.9	1.6	2.3	1.2	1.3	1.1
.7	.6	.5		.1	.3	.9	.4	.6	.6
.8	.9	.8			.4		.6	.7	1.1
(159) 1.8	(179) 2.2	(187) 2.0	% Depr., Dep., Amort./Sales		(13) .9		(28) 1.6	(46) 1.9	(82) 2.4
4.8	4.7	4.8			7.9		7.3	4.6	4.4
3.3	2.3	2.2	% Officers', Directors'						
(31) 4.9	(36) 6.5	(37) 4.6	Owners' Comp/Sales						
13.5	12.2	14.7							
7306664M	8317913M	10262265M	Net Sales ($)	12299M	52368M	79496M	297248M	993768M	8827086M
7194643M	8176056M	10620150M	Total Assets ($)	38769M	121189M	117329M	644207M	1838391M	7860265M

M = $ thousand   MM = $ million
See Pages viii through xx for Explanation of Ratios and Data

HEALTH CARE AND SOCIAL
ASSISTANCE

Current Data Sorted by Assets — Comparative Historical Data

Type of Statement	0-500M	500M-2MM	2-10MM	10-50MM	50-100MM	100-250MM	4/1/14-3/31/15 ALL	4/1/15-3/31/16 ALL
Unqualified	2	2	23	75	33	26	169	199
Reviewed	1	16	43	34		1	117	120
Compiled	98	131	73	10			629	524
Tax Returns	503	291	156	17	2	2	1614	1891
Other	494	541	389	144	29	26	1871	1910
	253 (4/1-9/30/18)			2,909 (10/1/18-3/31/19)				
NUMBER OF STATEMENTS	1098	981	684	280	64	55	4400	4644
ASSETS	%	%	%	%	%	%	%	%
Cash & Equivalents	45.0	32.0	23.4	15.3	19.1	16.6	32.0	33.5
Trade Receivables (net)	2.7	5.0	13.0	21.3	18.4	16.3	7.9	7.1
Inventory	1.2	1.7	1.8	2.2	1.3	.8	1.2	1.2
All Other Current	4.2	4.4	3.1	4.4	7.8	5.6	3.8	3.0
Total Current	53.1	43.1	41.3	43.2	46.6	39.3	44.9	44.8
Fixed Assets (net)	27.8	35.5	41.5	40.0	32.2	33.7	37.0	36.0
Intangibles (net)	6.4	8.1	6.5	6.5	6.4	12.0	4.8	5.2
All Other Non-Current	12.7	13.3	10.6	10.3	14.8	15.0	13.3	14.0
Total	100.0	100.0	100.0	100.0	100.0	100.0	100.0	100.0
LIABILITIES								
Notes Payable-Short Term	32.3	15.7	7.5	3.7	1.2	2.3	18.4	18.5
Cur. Mat.-L.T.D.	6.3	4.9	5.5	4.3	3.1	2.6	5.2	6.0
Trade Payables	2.1	3.6	5.6	6.6	6.5	4.5	3.5	3.4
Income Taxes Payable	.1	.1	.1	.3	.5	.1	.3	.3
All Other Current	39.6	23.8	21.7	18.1	16.8	16.9	25.0	26.7
Total Current	80.4	48.0	40.4	32.9	28.0	26.5	52.4	54.8
Long-Term Debt	28.1	28.0	28.6	25.0	21.6	23.3	26.7	25.2
Deferred Taxes	.0	.1	.3	.4	.9	.4	.1	.1
All Other Non-Current	7.4	4.2	2.6	4.6	8.8	6.9	5.9	5.7
Net Worth	-16.0	19.7	28.0	37.1	40.7	43.0	14.9	14.2
Total Liabilties & Net Worth	100.0	100.0	100.0	100.0	100.0	100.0	100.0	100.0
INCOME DATA								
Net Sales	100.0	100.0	100.0	100.0	100.0	100.0	100.0	100.0
Gross Profit								
Operating Expenses	87.9	84.9	83.9	87.8	91.4	92.0	84.9	85.2
Operating Profit	12.1	15.1	16.1	12.2	8.6	8.0	15.1	14.8
All Other Expenses (net)	.4	2.0	3.8	2.3	2.1	1.4	2.4	2.2
Profit Before Taxes	11.7	13.1	12.3	10.0	6.5	6.6	12.7	12.5
RATIOS								
Current	3.0	2.8	2.4	3.0	3.5	2.4	2.6	2.5
	1.0	1.0	1.0	1.4	1.7	1.6	1.0	1.0
	.3	.4	.5	.9	1.1	1.0	.4	.4
Quick	2.7	2.2	2.2	2.4	2.7	2.0	2.3	2.3
	(1097) .8	.8	.9	1.2	1.3	1.3	(4396) .9	(4638) .9
	.3	.3	.4	.7	.9	.8	.3	.3
Sales/Receivables	0 UND	0 UND	0 UND	1 476.5	19 19.7	21 17.5	0 UND	0 UND
	0 UND	0 UND	0 UND	26 14.0	30 12.2	34 10.6	0 UND	0 UND
	0 UND	0 UND	20 17.9	43 8.4	41 8.8	46 8.0	0 999.8	0 UND
Cost of Sales/Inventory								
Cost of Sales/Payables								
Sales/Working Capital	29.3	18.0	12.6	6.0	4.6	6.0	17.5	18.8
	-999.8	-999.8	-999.8	21.4	12.4	18.8	999.8	-999.8
	-24.2	-24.5	-22.8	-75.0	69.4	296.5	-23.8	-22.1
EBIT/Interest	52.0	58.5	54.6	26.7	33.4	22.9	49.0	50.0
	(677) 12.0	(725) 11.5	(511) 9.2	(216) 8.7	(51) 10.8	(46) 5.9	(2907) 10.0	(3095) 9.1
	1.0	2.1	2.0	1.9	3.1	.6	1.6	1.3
Net Profit + Depr., Dep., Amort./Cur. Mat. L/T/D	3.1	5.0	5.5	5.2	11.0		5.4	4.7
	(10) 1.7	(27) 2.2	(54) 2.6	(34) 1.6	(16) 2.7		(217) 2.0	(219) 2.0
	.0	1.1	1.3	1.2	1.6		1.0	.8
Fixed/Worth	.1	.2	.4	.4	.3	.4	.2	.2
	.9	1.8	1.8	1.1	.6	1.1	1.4	1.4
	-1.0	-3.6	26.3	4.7	1.8	2.2	-16.2	-8.9
Debt/Worth	.6	.7	.9	.6	.4	.8	.7	.7
	7.6	4.3	3.1	1.8	1.3	1.8	3.3	3.6
	-2.7	-7.0	124.4	9.3	3.2	6.8	-11.7	-9.9
% Profit Before Taxes/Tangible Net Worth	513.6	230.5	151.2	72.3	26.1	48.5	242.1	251.0
	(632) 147.6	(634) 79.7	(523) 39.5	(240) 18.4	(55) 13.0	(46) 9.1	(3055) 69.4	(3162) 73.0
	45.9	23.2	8.6	4.6	3.5	.0	13.4	12.9
% Profit Before Taxes/Total Assets	167.1	68.0	40.9	21.5	12.4	11.3	80.4	81.1
	49.3	21.8	10.9	5.9	4.5	2.9	17.7	18.7
	1.8	2.7	1.6	1.1	1.4	-.3	1.5	1.1
Sales/Net Fixed Assets	721.8	115.6	47.8	24.3	20.8	26.1	121.6	138.6
	76.5	31.8	17.3	7.7	8.7	6.6	26.5	30.6
	23.2	10.3	3.8	2.5	2.6	2.6	7.7	8.5
Sales/Total Assets	22.7	13.3	8.1	4.4	3.3	2.6	13.0	13.7
	11.1	6.4	4.1	2.1	2.1	1.7	5.9	6.2
	5.5	2.6	1.4	1.1	1.1	1.0	2.4	2.5
% Depr., Dep., Amort./Sales	.3	.5	.7	1.2	1.1	1.1	.6	.6
	(477) .6	(545) 1.1	(503) 1.7	(245) 2.2	(54) 2.0	(34) 2.4	(2736) 1.6	(2901) 1.4
	1.5	2.8	4.5	3.9	3.3	3.2	3.9	3.4
% Officers', Directors' Owners' Comp/Sales	10.4	6.8	5.8	3.9	7.4	6.9	10.0	9.6
	(670) 18.5	(520) 15.0	(258) 17.5	(66) 12.2	(11) 28.6	(14) 30.3	(2200) 20.0	(2413) 18.3
	28.1	29.2	30.8	24.7	40.3	36.8	31.1	30.4
Net Sales ($)	4015606M	9812490M	17099588M	22322438M	12423906M	22180546M	89586410M	102210764M
Total Assets ($)	255771M	1039373M	3106688M	6477013M	4581148M	8722655M	24130218M	25853768M

M = $ thousand   MM = $ million
See Pages viii through xx for Explanation of Ratios and Data

Comparative Historical Data | Current Data Sorted by Sales

			Type of Statement						
169	168	161	Unqualified	3	5	2	5	25	121
104	81	95	Reviewed	2	7	3	5	22	56
382	412	312	Compiled	26	57	46	75	58	50
1176	1072	971	Tax Returns	234	238	117	151	151	80
1607	1719	1623	Other	219	334	178	237	295	360
4/1/16-3/31/17 ALL	4/1/17-3/31/18 ALL	4/1/18-3/31/19 ALL		253 (4/1-9/30/18)			2,909 (10/1/18-3/31/19)		
				0-1MM	1-3MM	3-5MM	5-10MM	10-25MM	25MM & OVER
3448	3452	3162	NUMBER OF STATEMENTS	484	641	346	473	551	667
%	%	%	ASSETS	%	%	%	%	%	%
31.0	31.9	32.7	Cash & Equivalents	26.6	34.8	36.5	37.5	34.2	28.3
8.8	8.4	7.8	Trade Receivables (net)	2.1	4.3	5.6	5.6	11.3	15.4
1.6	1.4	1.6	Inventory	.4	1.6	2.1	1.6	1.9	1.8
4.0	3.9	4.1	All Other Current	3.9	5.3	3.1	3.4	3.7	4.6
45.4	45.7	46.2	Total Current	33.0	46.0	47.2	48.1	51.1	50.1
36.0	35.8	34.5	Fixed Assets (net)	47.9	32.0	31.8	31.8	32.1	32.3
5.6	6.8	7.0	Intangibles (net)	6.0	7.2	9.1	7.6	7.0	6.2
13.0	11.7	12.3	All Other Non-Current	13.2	14.8	11.9	12.5	9.8	11.5
100.0	100.0	100.0	Total	100.0	100.0	100.0	100.0	100.0	100.0
			LIABILITIES						
17.6	17.7	18.1	Notes Payable-Short Term	17.8	22.9	20.6	24.2	17.0	9.0
6.1	5.3	5.4	Cur. Mat.-L.T.D.	4.9	5.2	4.5	7.0	5.1	5.4
3.3	3.6	3.9	Trade Payables	1.2	2.2	3.4	2.8	4.6	7.7
.2	.2	.1	Income Taxes Payable	.1	.0	.1	.1	.1	.2
26.3	27.6	28.1	All Other Current	21.8	21.9	26.4	31.6	34.1	31.9
53.5	54.3	55.5	Total Current	45.7	52.3	54.9	65.7	61.0	54.3
26.7	26.6	27.7	Long-Term Debt	38.2	33.5	32.1	24.9	22.1	18.9
.2	.3	.2	Deferred Taxes	.0	.0	.1	.1	.3	.4
4.8	4.8	5.1	All Other Non-Current	5.9	6.3	5.7	2.8	3.7	6.0
14.8	14.1	11.5	Net Worth	10.1	7.9	7.3	6.5	12.9	20.4
100.0	100.0	100.0	Total Liabilties & Net Worth	100.0	100.0	100.0	100.0	100.0	100.0
			INCOME DATA						
100.0	100.0	100.0	Net Sales	100.0	100.0	100.0	100.0	100.0	100.0
			Gross Profit						
86.0	85.9	86.2	Operating Expenses	67.5	84.1	88.0	89.4	92.1	93.9
14.0	14.1	13.8	Operating Profit	32.5	15.9	12.0	10.6	7.9	6.1
2.0	2.1	1.9	All Other Expenses (net)	8.9	1.4	.5	.4	.1	.4
11.9	12.0	11.9	Profit Before Taxes	23.6	14.6	11.4	10.2	7.8	5.7
			RATIOS						
2.5	2.5	2.8		3.4	4.3	3.3	2.5	2.4	2.0
1.0	1.0	1.0	Current	.8	1.3	1.1	1.0	1.1	1.1
.4	.4	.4		.2	.4	.5	.4	.5	.6
2.2	2.2	2.4		3.0	3.7	3.0	2.3	2.0	1.8
.9 (3446)	.9 (3161)	.9	Quick	.7	1.0 (345)	1.0	.9	.9	.9
.3	.3	.3		.2	.3	.4	.3	.4	.5
0 UND	0 UND	0 UND		0 UND	0 UND	0 UND	0 UND	0 UND	0 UND
0 UND	0 UND	0 UND	Sales/Receivables	0 UND	0 UND	0 UND	0 UND	0 UND	1 613.3
1 285.4	1 547.7	1 694.8		0 UND	0 UND	0 UND	0 UND	18 20.6	32 11.5
			Cost of Sales/Inventory						
			Cost of Sales/Payables						
16.6	17.3	16.3		9.0	13.5	19.1	28.2	18.1	17.0
747.3	999.8	489.6	Sales/Working Capital	-58.5	102.9	265.9	-999.8	474.4	457.1
-25.6	-26.0	-26.0		-5.2	-19.2	-32.0	-27.2	-35.9	-47.9
45.8	46.6	49.0		21.1	40.0	59.7	91.3	57.6	39.4
(2444) 9.0	(2392) 8.6	(2226) 10.7	EBIT/Interest	(220) 5.5	(423) 12.2	(243) 13.9	(366) 16.6	(440) 10.6	(534) 8.7
1.2	1.3	1.7		2.4	2.6	2.0	1.0	1.2	1.4
6.1	4.0	5.0					5.8	4.8	5.0
(206) 1.8	(167) 1.9	(145) 2.0	Net Profit + Depr., Dep., Amort./Cur. Mat. L/T/D		(16) 2.6	(33) 2.0	(82) 2.0		
.9	.9	1.2					1.3	.9	1.2
.3	.3	.2		.2	.1	.2	.2	.3	.4
1.5	1.6	1.3	Fixed/Worth	2.3	.9	1.1	1.4	1.2	1.2
7.0	4.0	5.0		UND	4.3	1.7	2.2	4.4	136.7
.7	.7	.7		.7	.4	.5	.7	.8	.9
3.8	4.0	3.6	Debt/Worth	3.3	3.8	3.8	4.4	3.8	3.3
-10.3	-7.1	-7.3		-9.4	-4.7	-4.1	-5.1	-8.4	-22.0
223.6	224.5	239.2		147.6	323.8	271.1	391.0	279.0	153.3
(2352) 63.4	(2292) 66.1	(2130) 66.8	% Profit Before Taxes/Tangible Net Worth	(338) 38.6	(414) 101.7	(224) 89.6	(302) 98.3	(372) 72.7	(480) 32.5
12.0	12.2	12.7		13.3	35.2	22.7	24.4	7.9	4.9
66.4	72.8	78.9		66.5	108.8	103.8	112.2	58.1	35.9
16.5	16.7	18.6	% Profit Before Taxes/Total Assets	11.9	38.4	36.1	31.5	14.6	7.5
.9	.9	1.7		2.7	6.0	4.5	.4	.5	.3
123.8	126.4	143.8		98.4	208.8	182.0	204.3	125.7	97.2
27.5	26.8	30.2	Sales/Net Fixed Assets	8.8	31.0	38.8	46.0	34.5	27.9
7.8	8.5	9.2		.2	8.9	12.4	17.8	13.0	10.0
13.0	13.3	13.5		5.2	10.2	14.7	18.3	17.4	15.3
5.7	6.1	6.1	Sales/Total Assets	1.7	5.2	7.4	9.8	8.2	6.6
2.3	2.4	2.5		.2	2.4	3.4	5.1	3.8	2.8
.6	.5	.5		1.3	.5	.3	.4	.4	.6
(2198) 1.4	(2101) 1.4	(1858) 1.3	% Depr., Dep., Amort./Sales	(256) 13.2	(282) 1.4	(175) .8	(264) .9	(373) 1.1	(508) 1.3
3.4	3.1	2.9		20.0	3.8	2.0	2.2	2.2	2.2
9.4	9.0	7.9		10.9	8.9	8.2	6.4	7.0	7.2
(1730) 18.7	(1703) 18.7	(1539) 17.5	% Officers', Directors' Owners' Comp/Sales	(162) 21.5	(344) 14.2	(201) 16.9	(263) 19.8	(310) 18.6	(259) 22.4
30.3	29.9	29.1		29.0	22.2	25.6	25.6	31.8	32.2
87749948M	90963466M	87854574M	Net Sales ($)	250501M	1186444M	1356581M	3351992M	8893122M	72815934M
25260633M	25958955M	24182648M	Total Assets ($)	532293M	708971M	541625M	872072M	2152002M	19375685M

M = $ thousand   MM = $ million
See Pages viii through xx for Explanation of Ratios and Data

Current Data Sorted by Assets   Comparative Historical Data

Type of Statement	0-500M	500M-2MM	2-10MM	10-50MM	50-100MM	100-250MM		4/1/14-3/31/15 ALL	4/1/15-3/31/16 ALL
Unqualified			5	3	2	1		16	17
Reviewed			2					6	2
Compiled	28	9	4					12	15
Tax Returns	19	11	10	10	2	3		41	68
Other								48	46
	18 (4/1-9/30/18)		93 (10/1/18-3/31/19)						
NUMBER OF STATEMENTS	49	20	21	13	4	4		123	148
ASSETS	%	%	%	%	%	%		%	%
Cash & Equivalents	47.0	21.6	29.1	19.2				29.3	36.2
Trade Receivables (net)	1.1	11.0	22.9	10.0				11.0	10.4
Inventory	.1	.8	1.9	.5				1.2	1.2
All Other Current	3.8	8.1	6.6	4.5				5.4	3.9
Total Current	51.9	41.4	60.5	34.2				47.0	51.7
Fixed Assets (net)	24.9	29.7	29.7	34.0				36.9	28.8
Intangibles (net)	4.5	9.3	3.1	21.5				4.8	4.1
All Other Non-Current	18.7	19.6	6.7	10.3				11.3	15.4
Total	100.0	100.0	100.0	100.0				100.0	100.0
LIABILITIES									
Notes Payable-Short Term	31.9	13.5	6.0	.6				20.4	19.7
Cur. Mat.-L.T.D.	2.7	8.5	3.8	6.6				4.3	5.6
Trade Payables	.8	11.0	5.4	10.6				3.7	5.2
Income Taxes Payable	.0	.0	2.0	.0				.8	.4
All Other Current	30.5	16.1	26.7	9.1				19.0	25.6
Total Current	65.9	49.1	43.9	26.9				48.3	56.5
Long-Term Debt	25.1	21.1	24.6	24.0				24.2	30.1
Deferred Taxes	.0	.0	.8	.1				.2	.1
All Other Non-Current	7.9	3.0	1.8	9.4				5.2	7.3
Net Worth	1.0	26.8	28.9	39.6				22.2	5.9
Total Liabilities & Net Worth	100.0	100.0	100.0	100.0				100.0	100.0
INCOME DATA									
Net Sales	100.0	100.0	100.0	100.0				100.0	100.0
Gross Profit									
Operating Expenses	84.6	78.7	92.5	97.7				87.6	85.1
Operating Profit	15.4	21.3	7.5	2.3				12.4	14.9
All Other Expenses (net)	1.7	5.2	4.3	.6				1.8	2.0
Profit Before Taxes	13.6	16.1	3.2	1.6				10.6	12.8
RATIOS									
Current	4.5	2.9	4.2	2.5				3.1	3.9
	1.5	.5	1.2	1.2				1.4	1.2
	.3	.3	.8	.5				.5	.5
Quick	4.5	1.1	3.5	2.3				2.6	3.1
	1.4	.4	1.1	1.0				1.2	1.2
	.2	.2	.8	.5				.3	.4
Sales/Receivables	0 UND	0 UND	0 UND	0 UND				0 UND	0 UND
	0 UND	0 UND	27 13.6	19 18.9				0 UND	0 UND
	0 UND	11 32.2	54 6.8	42 8.6				29 12.7	19 19.1
Cost of Sales/Inventory									
Cost of Sales/Payables									
Sales/Working Capital	18.5	34.5	4.6	4.7				8.7	8.6
	64.4	-30.3	36.8	14.8				56.4	75.9
	-36.6	-8.0	-54.8	-14.2				-27.2	-33.5
EBIT/Interest	70.9	48.7	55.2	26.3				35.4	26.6
	(28) 12.1	(14) 8.8	(14) 3.3	(12) 2.4				(90) 9.8	(88) 8.3
	5.4	-3.6	-5.1	-8.0				2.0	1.0
Net Profit + Depr., Dep., Amort./Cur. Mat. L/T/D									
Fixed/Worth	.0	.0	.0	.6				.3	.1
	.5	.9	1.2	1.6				1.1	.8
	UND	-4.1	4.6	-1.4				6.9	10.4
Debt/Worth	.3	.5	.9	.8				.7	.5
	4.7	3.7	2.1	3.0				1.8	2.8
	-4.3	-6.5	29.2	-4.7				73.0	-11.2
% Profit Before Taxes/Tangible Net Worth	447.2	216.3	50.8					140.4	323.8
	(32) 247.7	(11) 109.3	(18) 14.2					(97) 50.5	(106) 64.6
	115.6	44.0	-9.2					5.7	11.6
% Profit Before Taxes/Total Assets	175.4	82.5	12.3	8.9				63.7	112.0
	96.2	33.2	3.8	1.8				18.3	30.0
	29.7	-3.3	-7.1	-6.4				1.7	1.9
Sales/Net Fixed Assets	UND	51.1	451.9	22.7				106.0	380.8
	95.9	34.2	19.2	3.9				20.8	35.9
	31.4	9.0	5.7	1.8				4.9	8.4
Sales/Total Assets	18.6	6.7	4.8	2.6				7.9	12.2
	11.1	4.5	2.8	1.2				4.3	5.0
	6.3	1.4	1.9	.7				1.5	2.2
% Depr., Dep., Amort./Sales	.4	.8	.2	1.0				.8	.6
	(15) .8	(10) 1.6	(15) 2.2	(10) 2.0				(83) 2.0	(91) 1.3
	1.5	10.2	2.9	5.1				3.9	2.8
% Officers', Directors' Owners' Comp/Sales	10.2							5.3	6.4
	(28) 13.3							(48) 10.7	(75) 12.6
	26.3							23.3	26.1
Net Sales ($)	117378M	115333M	377241M	515537M	774470M	849523M		2570823M	1722285M
Total Assets ($)	8933M	23356M	109428M	298817M	321326M	645432M		1197343M	720343M

M = $ thousand   MM = $ million
See Pages viii through xx for Explanation of Ratios and Data

Comparative Historical Data | Current Data Sorted by Sales

H1	H2	H3	Type of Statement	0-1MM	1-3MM	3-5MM	5-10MM	10-25MM	25MM & OVER
22	21	11	Unqualified					6	5
3	4		Reviewed						
11	7	4	Compiled	1	1			1	1
47	32	41	Tax Returns	18	8	5	4	6	12
53	68	55	Other	10	10	5	6	12	12
4/1/16-3/31/17 ALL	4/1/17-3/31/18 ALL	4/1/18-3/31/19 ALL		18 (4/1-9/30/18)			93 (10/1/18-3/31/19)		
136	132	111	NUMBER OF STATEMENTS	29	19	10	10	25	18
%	%	%	ASSETS	%	%	%	%	%	%
30.3	32.8	33.4	Cash & Equivalents	35.7	42.7	36.7	38.0	27.0	24.2
14.1	14.2	9.2	Trade Receivables (net)	1.2	4.2	8.9	11.2	16.0	17.0
.9	.7	.7	Inventory	.1	.0	3.0	.1	1.2	.5
6.3	4.2	5.5	All Other Current	3.2	5.2	3.7	.6	9.7	7.7
51.7	52.0	48.8	Total Current	40.3	52.1	52.2	49.9	53.9	49.3
31.1	26.9	28.7	Fixed Assets (net)	29.2	29.4	24.4	23.5	28.3	32.8
4.8	6.2	7.8	Intangibles (net)	10.0	5.6	.0	14.4	6.0	9.6
12.4	15.0	14.8	All Other Non-Current	20.5	12.9	23.4	12.3	11.8	8.3
100.0	100.0	100.0	Total	100.0	100.0	100.0	100.0	100.0	100.0
			LIABILITIES						
13.9	17.6	18.0	Notes Payable-Short Term	20.9	36.0	27.2	18.2	7.9	3.0
3.3	3.9	4.4	Cur. Mat.-L.T.D.	1.3	4.4	1.4	8.5	8.4	3.3
4.3	6.1	5.2	Trade Payables	1.1	.9	1.1	1.5	12.4	10.5
.4	.3	.4	Income Taxes Payable	.0	.0	.0	.0	1.7	.0
26.2	20.0	23.6	All Other Current	33.7	15.5	16.5	4.4	31.9	18.8
48.1	47.9	51.5	Total Current	56.9	56.8	46.3	32.6	62.3	35.6
18.2	26.3	23.7	Long-Term Debt	20.1	29.5	18.9	34.4	24.4	18.9
.2	.1	.2	Deferred Taxes	.0	.0	.0	.0	.0	.9
6.8	4.0	6.2	All Other Non-Current	8.2	1.5	2.8	16.6	5.7	4.6
26.7	21.6	18.5	Net Worth	14.7	12.1	32.1	16.5	7.5	40.0
100.0	100.0	100.0	Total Liabilities & Net Worth	100.0	100.0	100.0	100.0	100.0	100.0
			INCOME DATA						
100.0	100.0	100.0	Net Sales	100.0	100.0	100.0	100.0	100.0	100.0
			Gross Profit						
88.5	86.1	87.0	Operating Expenses	70.4	87.6	90.2	91.6	100.0	90.8
11.5	13.9	13.0	Operating Profit	29.6	12.4	9.8	8.4	.0	9.2
1.6	1.3	2.7	All Other Expenses (net)	7.0	.4	1.0	5.8	-.4	1.4
10.0	12.5	10.3	Profit Before Taxes	22.6	12.0	8.8	2.6	.4	7.8
			RATIOS						
2.8	4.0	3.7		4.3	3.7	7.9	23.8	1.5	2.8
1.1	1.3	1.1	Current	1.1	1.0	2.6	2.6	.9	1.9
.5	.6	.4		.1	.4	.3	.5	.6	1.0
2.2	3.1	2.8		4.3	3.6	7.0	23.8	1.3	2.4
1.0	1.2	1.0	Quick	1.0	1.0	1.7	2.6	.8	1.2
.3	.5	.3		.1	.3	.3	.3	.4	.6
0 UND	0 UND	0 UND		0 UND	0 UND	0 UND	0 UND	0 UND	0 UND
0 UND	0 UND	0 UND	Sales/Receivables	0 UND	0 UND	0 UND	0 UND	18 20.7	24 15.3
37 9.9	31 11.6	23 15.6		0 UND	0 UND	0 UND	14 26.3	51 7.2	39 9.4
			Cost of Sales/Inventory						
			Cost of Sales/Payables						
9.2	8.7	10.6		18.3	17.6	12.7	5.0	11.5	5.5
142.2	59.4	126.3	Sales/Working Capital	215.0	999.8	62.8	48.2	-999.8	10.1
-28.6	-33.7	-26.1		-6.7	-27.1	-54.8	-28.9	-21.9	-820.7
37.1	38.2	46.3			45.9			61.7	35.4
(94) 12.0	(82) 12.1	(76) 8.2	EBIT/Interest		(14) 15.9			(21) 3.0	(16) 7.9
2.8	2.7	.3			4.6			-11.9	1.8
			Net Profit + Depr., Dep., Amort./Cur. Mat. L/T/D						
.1	.1	.0		.0	.0	.0	.1	.4	.5
.9	.8	.9	Fixed/Worth	.3	1.0	.5	1.1	2.8	.9
9.8	7.1	-12.3		UND	-3.1	NM	-.7	-.7	1.8
.6	.5	.4		.3	.4	.1	.2	1.3	1.0
2.2	1.3	3.0	Debt/Worth	2.7	4.7	.8	2.9	6.8	1.7
46.8	-20.5	-8.0		-9.2	-8.0	NM	-2.1	-3.8	27.4
261.3	206.4	276.5	% Profit Before Taxes/Tangible Net Worth	375.4	348.9			143.0	24.9
(107) 65.5	(98) 78.4	(76) 101.3		(21) 160.3	(10) 214.9			(14) 25.1	(16) 7.5
10.9	12.1	9.0		79.6	101.7			5.8	2.0
61.1	86.2	103.2	% Profit Before Taxes/Total Assets	144.6	158.3	143.0	100.6	14.1	12.7
18.5	29.0	19.9		48.1	82.0	43.6	38.1	4.6	3.3
1.9	2.9	.3		4.0	26.2	-11.0	-2.8	-12.3	.4
153.7	255.9	454.7	Sales/Net Fixed Assets	UND	999.8	654.0	282.8	182.9	26.6
23.7	40.7	40.4		71.2	46.0	78.3	42.8	45.3	9.5
4.7	8.4	8.3		9.1	11.6	28.0	23.3	5.7	2.9
8.2	10.9	11.1	Sales/Total Assets	13.9	15.8	11.8	22.4	9.5	4.9
4.1	4.7	4.6		4.6	7.4	7.3	4.9	3.5	2.2
1.4	2.1	2.0		1.9	4.3	5.7	1.6	2.0	1.1
.4	.3	.6	% Depr., Dep., Amort./Sales					.2	1.3
(84) 1.2	(71) 1.1	(58) 1.5						(18) 1.6	(16) 2.0
3.4	2.6	3.0						3.3	2.8
3.3	6.7	7.8	% Officers', Directors' Owners' Comp/Sales	7.8	11.1				
(56) 10.7	(47) 11.9	(46) 13.3		(15) 11.3	(11) 15.0				
24.7	26.9	29.3		29.7	24.5				
2676692M	2827149M	2749482M	Net Sales ($)	15604M	38236M	37357M	71898M	404646M	2181741M
2007531M	1430626M	1407292M	Total Assets ($)	14424M	7925M	6540M	57973M	151290M	1169140M

Current Data Sorted by Assets

Comparative Historical Data

Type of Statement	0-500M	500M-2MM	2-10MM	10-50MM	50-100MM	100-250MM		4/1/14-3/31/15	4/1/15-3/31/16
Unqualified	1	2	1	6	2	3		19	17
Reviewed	9	19	10	1				4	9
Compiled	80	58	15	1				282	246
Tax Returns	570	403	38			1		1277	1970
Other	415	346	72	19	4	6		788	831
		66 (4/1-9/30/18)		2,016 (10/1/18-3/31/19)				ALL	ALL
NUMBER OF STATEMENTS	1075	828	136	27	6	10		2370	3073

	0-500M %	500M-2MM %	2-10MM %	10-50MM %	50-100MM %	100-250MM %		%	%
ASSETS									
Cash & Equivalents	33.4	18.6	11.2	8.1		6.1		25.7	27.5
Trade Receivables (net)	1.8	2.1	6.8	12.6		7.5		3.1	2.5
Inventory	.3	.2	.4	1.3		1.2		.4	.3
All Other Current	2.1	3.6	4.0	3.4		3.9		2.3	1.9
Total Current	37.6	24.5	22.3	25.3		18.7		31.4	32.3
Fixed Assets (net)	32.4	29.4	39.2	31.7		31.2		37.4	34.7
Intangibles (net)	21.5	37.0	26.6	32.9		49.4		19.3	19.8
All Other Non-Current	8.4	9.1	11.9	10.0		.7		11.9	13.3
Total	100.0	100.0	100.0	100.0		100.0		100.0	100.0
LIABILITIES									
Notes Payable-Short Term	23.4	6.7	4.3	6.0		12.7		15.3	17.5
Cur. Mat.-L.T.D.	7.1	5.4	5.2	10.9		4.0		6.0	6.3
Trade Payables	1.2	1.1	2.2	10.4		4.8		1.3	1.5
Income Taxes Payable	.2	.0	.0	.1		.0		.1	.0
All Other Current	15.7	6.1	8.3	18.2		15.8		14.2	13.1
Total Current	47.7	19.4	20.1	45.5		37.4		36.9	38.3
Long-Term Debt	54.7	61.5	48.8	38.5		37.6		56.8	56.1
Deferred Taxes	.0	.0	.1	.0		1.5		.0	.0
All Other Non-Current	5.0	2.4	3.2	3.1		20.6		6.9	4.3
Net Worth	-7.3	16.7	27.8	12.8		3.0		-.6	1.2
Total Liabilities & Net Worth	100.0	100.0	100.0	100.0		100.0		100.0	100.0
INCOME DATA									
Net Sales	100.0	100.0	100.0	100.0		100.0		100.0	100.0
Gross Profit									
Operating Expenses	85.3	83.5	81.2	95.3		101.2		84.7	86.0
Operating Profit	14.7	16.5	18.8	4.7		-1.2		15.3	14.0
All Other Expenses (net)	1.4	2.8	4.2	2.5		4.1		2.5	2.1
Profit Before Taxes	13.3	13.7	14.6	2.2		-5.2		12.8	11.9
RATIOS									
Current	3.7	4.2	3.6	1.4		1.8		3.8	3.6
	1.1	1.4	1.0	.9		.8		1.1	1.1
	.3	.4	.4	.5		.1		.3	.3
Quick	3.4	3.6	2.6	1.4		1.3		3.4	3.3
	(1074) 1.0	(827) 1.1	.8	.6		.5		(2368) 1.0	(3072) 1.0
	.3	.3	.2	.2		.1		.3	.3
Sales/Receivables	0 UND	0 UND	0 UND	11 32.6		0 UND		0 UND	0 UND
	0 UND	0 UND	0 UND	22 16.4		11 33.7		0 UND	0 UND
	0 UND	0 UND	4 89.3	38 9.5		47 7.8		0 UND	0 UND
Cost of Sales/Inventory									
Cost of Sales/Payables									
Sales/Working Capital	19.2	11.3	11.5	18.2		10.5		15.8	16.4
	368.9	58.5	-589.3	-97.8		-31.8		155.2	354.3
	-22.6	-20.2	-14.2	-10.1		-13.0		-19.3	-18.9
EBIT/Interest	36.8	18.7	19.5	6.9		20.2		22.4	22.0
	(763) 11.5	(723) 6.4	(118) 7.8	(26) 1.8		.2		(1802) 7.1	(2358) 6.6
	3.1	2.6	3.3	-.3		-7.5		2.0	1.8
Net Profit + Depr., Dep., Amort./Cur. Mat. L/T/D								7.5	6.0
								(21) 3.1	(22) 1.6
								.7	1.0
Fixed/Worth	.3	.7	1.2	1.9		1.5		.6	.6
	12.5	-4.6	10.3	-49.7		-.5		12.5	21.9
	-.5	-.3	-.8	-.2		-.1		-.6	-.6
Debt/Worth	1.0	2.6	1.2	2.0		1.4		1.2	1.4
	-9.0	-3.8	NM	-84.9		-1.8		-180.8	-23.5
	-1.8	-1.5	-2.7	-1.6		-1.3		-2.0	-2.0
% Profit Before Taxes/Tangible Net Worth	559.4	217.1	145.9	142.4				360.4	364.3
	(496) 176.2	(323) 94.3	(68) 55.3	(13) 26.3				(1180) 113.2	(1455) 127.2
	67.1	42.6	22.3	2.8				34.5	39.6
% Profit Before Taxes/Total Assets	118.8	45.1	30.0	10.4		10.7		69.8	71.2
	48.6	21.1	15.4	4.3		-.8		26.8	26.3
	11.0	6.3	6.0	-4.2		-11.9		4.8	4.3
Sales/Net Fixed Assets	110.8	37.2	19.1	12.0		16.2		49.0	63.0
	26.4	12.7	6.8	5.7		8.6		14.4	16.2
	9.7	5.0	3.2	4.4		4.8		5.8	6.1
Sales/Total Assets	10.7	3.2	3.0	2.1		5.7		7.1	7.1
	5.2	1.9	1.7	1.6		1.4		3.5	3.5
	2.9	1.3	1.1	1.3		.6		1.9	1.8
% Depr., Dep., Amort./Sales	.7	1.8	1.8	2.3				1.4	1.3
	(490) 1.8	(412) 4.0	(87) 4.2	(22) 3.9				(1316) 3.0	(1736) 3.2
	4.6	7.9	7.0	6.4				6.0	6.1
% Officers', Directors' Owners' Comp/Sales	9.6	7.5	4.6					10.2	10.0
	(726) 15.2	(545) 11.4	(74) 7.7					(1586) 15.6	(2134) 15.8
	22.0	18.6	15.3					22.9	23.1
Net Sales ($)	1535078M	1959592M	1402446M	1122130M	745240M	5427796M		18130849M	12637264M
Total Assets ($)	260964M	764908M	490541M	633184M	439780M	1682290M		4536641M	4914159M

Comparative Historical Data / Current Data Sorted by Sales

			Type of Statement						
12	14	15	Unqualified		2	1	4	8	
9	2	39	Reviewed	6	14	12	1	5	1
220	144	164	Compiled	38	65	27	17	6	1
963	935	1012	Tax Returns	349	533	77	39	10	4
735	822	862	Other	259	408	86	54	33	22
4/1/16-3/31/17 ALL	4/1/17-3/31/18 ALL	4/1/18-3/31/19 ALL		66 (4/1-9/30/18) 0-1MM	1-3MM	3-5MM	2,016 (10/1/18-3/31/19) 5-10MM	10-25MM	25MM & OVER
1939	1917	2082	NUMBER OF STATEMENTS	652	1022	203	111	58	36
%	%	%	ASSETS	%	%	%	%	%	%
25.7	25.0	25.5	Cash & Equivalents	24.1	26.4	30.4	27.1	13.6	11.3
3.1	2.8	2.4	Trade Receivables (net)	1.1	2.2	3.1	3.9	10.3	11.0
.3	.2	.3	Inventory	.2	.3	.5	.2	.4	1.3
2.1	2.2	2.9	All Other Current	1.9	3.2	3.5	2.9	5.1	3.6
31.2	30.2	31.1	Total Current	27.2	32.2	37.4	34.1	29.3	27.2
35.1	34.5	31.6	Fixed Assets (net)	35.2	28.2	32.2	34.4	42.7	35.6
22.0	25.6	28.4	Intangibles (net)	28.9	30.7	20.8	22.4	20.3	28.9
11.8	9.7	8.9	All Other Non-Current	8.7	9.0	9.6	9.1	7.7	8.2
100.0	100.0	100.0	Total	100.0	100.0	100.0	100.0	100.0	100.0
			LIABILITIES						
12.6	14.3	15.2	Notes Payable-Short Term	17.7	13.4	18.8	14.9	10.5	9.1
7.5	7.4	6.3	Cur. Mat.-L.T.D.	6.0	6.4	5.4	7.1	8.6	10.2
1.5	1.5	1.4	Trade Payables	.9	1.2	2.3	1.1	3.7	8.9
.1	.0	.1	Income Taxes Payable	.1	.1	.3	.0	.0	.1
13.0	12.5	11.4	All Other Current	9.1	11.1	11.9	21.1	17.5	20.5
34.6	35.7	34.5	Total Current	33.8	32.2	38.6	44.2	40.4	48.7
56.4	57.2	56.6	Long-Term Debt	61.7	57.9	45.2	49.4	44.7	34.7
.0	.0	.0	Deferred Taxes	.0	.0	.0	.0	.3	.5
5.1	4.0	4.0	All Other Non-Current	4.3	3.4	3.3	4.5	6.2	12.8
3.9	3.1	4.9	Net Worth	.2	6.5	12.8	2.0	8.4	3.3
100.0	100.0	100.0	Total Liabilties & Net Worth	100.0	100.0	100.0	100.0	100.0	100.0
			INCOME DATA						
100.0	100.0	100.0	Net Sales	100.0	100.0	100.0	100.0	100.0	100.0
			Gross Profit						
84.4	84.6	84.5	Operating Expenses	83.4	84.0	85.7	86.4	92.1	96.1
15.6	15.4	15.5	Operating Profit	16.6	16.0	14.3	13.6	7.9	3.9
2.3	2.3	2.2	All Other Expenses (net)	3.9	1.6	.6	.9	1.1	2.4
13.2	13.1	13.3	Profit Before Taxes	12.7	14.4	13.7	12.7	6.8	1.5
			RATIOS						
3.2	3.1	3.7		4.0	4.3	3.1	3.2	2.7	1.4
1.0	1.0	1.2	Current	1.0	1.4	1.3	1.0	.9	.9
.3	.3	.3		.3	.4	.4	.5	.3	.4
2.9	2.8	3.3		3.5	3.9	2.8	2.4	2.3	1.3
(1937) .9	(1913) .9	(2080) 1.0	Quick	.8 (1020)	1.2	1.1	1.0	.7	.6
.3	.3	.3		.2	.3	.3	.4	.2	.3
0 UND	0 UND	0 UND		0 UND	0 UND	0 UND	0 UND	0 UND	0 UND
0 UND	0 UND	0 UND	Sales/Receivables	0 UND	0 UND	0 UND	0 UND	0 UND	16 23.0
0 UND	0 UND	0 UND		0 UND	0 UND	0 UND	0 UND	27 13.7	33 11.0
			Cost of Sales/Inventory						
			Cost of Sales/Payables						
14.9	17.3	14.9		14.0	13.5	21.2	21.4	13.4	19.2
607.3	999.8	137.1	Sales/Working Capital	-856.5	73.3	108.2	999.8	-408.7	-108.6
-18.0	-17.7	-20.3		-11.0	-25.0	-30.5	-33.2	-14.6	-12.0
26.0	25.2	25.6		13.4	33.2	52.6	46.5	20.7	15.1
(1525) 7.6	(1498) 7.5	(1645) 8.1	EBIT/Interest	(456) 4.9	(838) 9.9	(162) 14.6	(99) 13.3	(55) 5.4	(35) 3.9
2.1	2.4	2.6		1.4	3.6	3.8	3.4	.9	-.2
5.3	4.3	5.8	Net Profit + Depr., Dep.,						
(30) 3.3	(26) 1.9	(18) 2.0	Amort./Cur. Mat. L/T/D						
.8	.8	.9							
.7	.7	.5		.5	.5	.5	.9	1.3	1.6
136.0	-11.9	-45.0	Fixed/Worth	47.4	-8.7	4.2	-11.0	-5.0	-3.3
-.5	-.4	-.4		-.3	-.3	-.7	-.6	-.5	-.5
1.5	1.6	1.4		1.5	1.4	1.0	1.5	1.3	2.3
-17.8	-7.0	-6.1	Debt/Worth	-5.6	-4.3	26.9	-10.3	-9.5	-5.2
2.0	-1.8	-1.6		-1.5	-1.6	-2.3	-2.5	-2.1	-1.7
346.8	361.6	333.5		260.2	393.0	432.1	677.3	150.1	157.8
(902) 118.8	(833) 124.8	(904) 123.3	% Profit Before Taxes/Tangible Net Worth	(284) 83.4	(424) 140.6	(108) 177.4	(49) 178.2	(23) 86.7	(16) 28.6
45.4	43.0	45.1		23.8	65.8	51.9	63.4	26.4	6.6
71.4	74.0	73.9		53.9	83.3	111.2	105.1	52.4	14.5
27.6	27.7	28.8	% Profit Before Taxes/Total Assets	19.0	34.2	40.8	38.6	14.0	6.4
5.5	6.3	7.0		2.4	12.9	11.6	6.3	.0	-4.9
50.1	50.7	64.2		64.6	68.8	75.5	57.6	24.2	18.5
14.6	14.9	17.1	Sales/Net Fixed Assets	10.9	19.2	23.7	24.4	10.3	8.2
5.7	5.8	6.4		3.8	8.1	9.0	10.0	5.4	4.9
6.3	6.2	6.2		4.5	6.2	10.8	10.2	6.5	5.0
3.1	3.1	3.1	Sales/Total Assets	2.2	3.2	5.2	5.2	3.3	2.1
1.7	1.6	1.7		1.2	1.8	2.7	3.2	2.0	1.5
1.2	1.2	1.1		1.6	.9	.7	.9	.9	2.1
(1041) 2.9	(992) 3.2	(1019) 3.0	% Depr., Dep., Amort./Sales	(302) 4.9	(474) 2.8	(109) 1.9	(70) 1.9	(40) 2.5	(24) 3.6
5.9	6.4	6.3		10.0	5.8	3.9	3.7	4.3	5.0
9.4	8.9	8.0		9.5	8.6	6.0	3.1	2.5	
(1300) 15.2	(1259) 14.2	(1349) 13.5	% Officers', Directors' Owners' Comp/Sales	(379) 14.8	(717) 13.1	(140) 10.9	(75) 9.0	(29) 9.7	
22.6	21.9	20.6		21.7	19.4	25.8	21.9	25.1	
16080039M	15729575M	12192282M	Net Sales ($)	406700M	1745353M	772034M	753318M	899602M	7615275M
3860279M	3971163M	4271667M	Total Assets ($)	285814M	647639M	207840M	289479M	433795M	2407100M

© RMA 2019   M = $ thousand   MM = $ million
See Pages viii through xx for Explanation of Ratios and Data

Current Data Sorted by Assets   Comparative Historical Data

Type of Statement	0-500M	500M-2MM	2-10MM	10-50MM	50-100MM	100-250MM		4/1/14-3/31/15 ALL	4/1/15-3/31/16 ALL
Unqualified								1	1
Reviewed			2						
Compiled	5	1						10	20
Tax Returns	78	16	1					102	144
Other	60	10	10			1		71	52
		4 (4/1-9/30/18)		184 (10/1/18-3/31/19)					

0-500M	500M-2MM	2-10MM	10-50MM	50-100MM	100-250MM		ALL	ALL
143	27	11	6	1	1	**NUMBER OF STATEMENTS**	184	217
%	%	%	%	%	%	**ASSETS**	%	%
36.4	20.3	18.7				Cash & Equivalents	33.0	32.8
4.0	7.8	15.4				Trade Receivables (net)	3.7	3.0
1.7	1.3	.0				Inventory	.6	1.3
2.5	2.2	9.6				All Other Current	3.4	2.2
44.6	31.5	43.8				Total Current	40.7	39.4
34.3	31.3	37.2	DATA			Fixed Assets (net)	34.7	35.2
11.3	22.0	9.8	NOT			Intangibles (net)	11.4	11.1
9.8	15.1	9.2	AVAILABLE			All Other Non-Current	13.2	14.3
100.0	100.0	100.0				Total	100.0	100.0
						LIABILITIES		
19.3	1.6	4.3				Notes Payable-Short Term	16.1	18.7
5.3	3.2	1.6				Cur. Mat.-L.T.D.	3.0	5.8
1.4	.4	.7				Trade Payables	2.2	1.7
.0	.0	.0				Income Taxes Payable	.3	.6
15.0	9.1	15.6				All Other Current	13.6	16.1
41.0	14.3	22.2				Total Current	35.3	42.8
34.1	42.6	22.3				Long-Term Debt	31.2	34.9
.0	.0	.0				Deferred Taxes	.0	.0
10.7	1.3	4.6				All Other Non-Current	7.2	5.7
14.2	41.8	50.9				Net Worth	26.4	16.5
100.0	100.0	100.0				Total Liabilties & Net Worth	100.0	100.0
						INCOME DATA		
100.0	100.0	100.0				Net Sales	100.0	100.0
						Gross Profit		
81.7	78.8	74.1				Operating Expenses	80.7	81.7
18.3	21.2	25.9				Operating Profit	19.3	18.3
.6	1.8	4.3				All Other Expenses (net)	1.6	2.5
17.7	19.3	21.6				Profit Before Taxes	17.7	15.8
						RATIOS		
4.6	11.0	3.5					5.3	4.4
1.2	1.9	2.7				Current	1.6	1.1
.5	.9	.4					.4	.2
4.5	11.0	3.3					5.0	4.1
1.2	1.9	1.0				Quick	1.4	.9
.4	.7	.3					.3	.2
0 UND	0 UND	0 UND					0 UND	0 UND
0 UND	0 UND	0 UND				Sales/Receivables	0 UND	0 UND
0 UND	0 UND	50 7.3					0 UND	0 UND
						Cost of Sales/Inventory		
						Cost of Sales/Payables		
13.1	8.5	2.8					15.7	12.7
76.0	24.6	7.5				Sales/Working Capital	60.2	552.0
-24.0	-422.5	-8.3					-28.2	-15.6
40.0	20.6						46.2	45.0
(94) 17.0	(23) 10.0					EBIT/Interest	(109) 16.7	(142) 12.0
4.9	6.5						4.8	3.9
						Net Profit + Depr., Dep., Amort./Cur. Mat. L/T/D		
.2	.3	.1					.2	.3
1.0	2.3	.9				Fixed/Worth	1.1	1.2
-5.2	-1.5	2.8					-7.5	-5.9
.4	.6	.3					.4	.5
1.9	2.8	2.0				Debt/Worth	2.0	3.5
-3.4	-3.6	5.6					-6.8	-4.5
390.0	189.9	122.5					299.3	350.0
(97) 163.0	(18) 91.5	(10) 49.8				% Profit Before Taxes/Tangible Net Worth	(128) 103.1	(147) 118.8
65.3	26.9	22.4					48.1	50.5
146.6	45.0	65.0					137.4	113.6
62.8	23.8	17.6				% Profit Before Taxes/Total Assets	45.7	46.2
23.2	10.8	10.2					18.2	9.6
81.2	36.7	60.2					109.9	79.7
20.3	9.3	10.6				Sales/Net Fixed Assets	23.9	20.2
7.6	2.2	1.0					6.3	7.8
8.6	2.7	2.7					11.0	8.9
5.5	1.5	.8				Sales/Total Assets	4.4	4.1
3.0	.8	.5					1.9	2.0
.5	.6						.8	.9
(68) 1.4	(11) 1.2					% Depr., Dep., Amort./Sales	(83) 2.2	(109) 2.1
2.7	6.8						4.6	4.9
8.4	4.3						7.6	7.1
(89) 13.7	(17) 7.9					% Officers', Directors' Owners' Comp/Sales	(112) 13.0	(154) 12.4
19.2	12.7						20.6	19.1
118082M	48554M	58302M	280448M	192338M		Net Sales ($)	1367094M	5268254M
24798M	23784M	33915M	188627M	106599M		Total Assets ($)	438291M	772988M

© RMA 2019

M = $ thousand   MM = $ million
See Pages viii through xx for Explanation of Ratios and Data

Comparative Historical Data

Current Data Sorted by Sales

			Type of Statement						2
2	2	2	Unqualified						
			Reviewed						
11	25	6	Compiled	5		1			
84	100	95	Tax Returns	73	19	1	1	1	
72	70	85	Other	47	22	7	2	3	4
4/1/16-3/31/17 ALL	4/1/17-3/31/18 ALL	4/1/18-3/31/19 ALL		4 (4/1-9/30/18)		184 (10/1/18-3/31/19)			
				0-1MM	1-3MM	3-5MM	5-10MM	10-25MM	25MM & OVER
169	197	188	NUMBER OF STATEMENTS	125	41	9	3	4	6
%	%	%	ASSETS	%	%	%	%	%	%
33.7	35.2	32.4	Cash & Equivalents	33.3	28.0				
5.4	5.0	6.3	Trade Receivables (net)	5.0	5.8				
1.2	1.3	1.5	Inventory	1.9	.7				
3.0	2.2	2.8	All Other Current	3.3	2.2				
43.4	43.7	42.9	Total Current	43.5	36.7				
29.2	32.5	33.7	Fixed Assets (net)	34.6	37.1				
14.3	15.5	12.9	Intangibles (net)	14.0	10.7				
13.1	8.4	10.4	All Other Non-Current	7.7	15.5				
100.0	100.0	100.0	Total	100.0	100.0				
			LIABILITIES						
21.9	14.8	15.2	Notes Payable-Short Term	17.6	12.1				
4.3	5.0	4.8	Cur. Mat.-L.T.D.	4.8	6.0				
2.5	1.7	1.2	Trade Payables	1.4	.8				
.3	.1	.0	Income Taxes Payable	.0	.0				
13.3	13.0	13.9	All Other Current	10.8	19.7				
42.3	34.5	35.2	Total Current	34.7	38.7				
29.4	38.4	33.8	Long-Term Debt	37.6	30.4				
.0	.0	.0	Deferred Taxes	.0	.0				
4.2	4.5	9.3	All Other Non-Current	11.9	2.7				
24.1	22.5	21.7	Net Worth	15.9	28.2				
100.0	100.0	100.0	Total Liabilties & Net Worth	100.0	100.0				
			INCOME DATA						
100.0	100.0	100.0	Net Sales	100.0	100.0				
			Gross Profit						
79.2	79.8	81.0	Operating Expenses	80.0	83.7				
20.8	20.2	19.0	Operating Profit	20.0	16.3				
2.0	2.3	1.0	All Other Expenses (net)	1.2	1.0				
18.7	17.9	18.0	Profit Before Taxes	18.8	15.3				
			RATIOS						
4.5	5.4	4.9	Current	4.6	5.6				
1.6	1.6	1.5		1.4	1.0				
.4	.4	.6		.6	.2				
3.9	4.8	4.6	Quick	4.5	5.0				
1.3	1.4	1.2		1.2	1.0				
.3	.3	.4		.4	.2				
0 UND	0 UND	0 UND	Sales/Receivables	0 UND	0 UND				
0 UND	0 UND	0 UND		0 UND	0 UND				
0 UND	0 UND	0 UND		0 UND	0 UND				
			Cost of Sales/Inventory						
			Cost of Sales/Payables						
10.4	11.7	10.6	Sales/Working Capital	10.4	12.5				
42.2	48.7	50.0		60.4	999.8				
-24.9	-25.3	-28.8		-32.2	20.1				
54.3	34.7	39.2	EBIT/Interest	39.0	26.0				
(110) 12.5	(128) 11.0	(130) 14.5		(83) 14.9	(31) 10.4				
3.0	4.1	5.0		5.0	3.7				
			Net Profit + Depr., Dep., Amort./Cur. Mat. L/T/D						
.2	.1	.2	Fixed/Worth	.2	.3				
1.0	1.0	1.1		1.1	.0				
-4.9	-4.8	-5.8		-1.7	-4.9				
.4	.3	.4	Debt/Worth	.5	.3				
2.5	2.5	2.0		3.0	1.2				
-5.2	-3.0	-4.8		-3.2	-9.4				
544.1	266.3	297.1	% Profit Before Taxes/Tangible Net Worth	290.5	301.5				
(114) 172.9	(125) 100.0	(130) 129.0		(83) 131.8	(29) 128.5				
62.0	47.5	39.8		58.3	32.8				
130.6	120.7	123.5	% Profit Before Taxes/Total Assets	134.9	89.2				
54.0	48.6	51.3		53.5	35.7				
11.8	15.7	17.1		19.7	10.8				
93.5	88.7	62.0	Sales/Net Fixed Assets	71.0	39.1				
24.6	22.7	17.4		18.9	15.0				
8.9	7.4	6.5		5.4	7.6				
7.8	7.9	7.5	Sales/Total Assets	7.7	7.4				
3.7	3.9	4.2		4.1	4.8				
1.6	1.8	1.7		1.6	2.6				
.7	.7	.5	% Depr., Dep., Amort./Sales	.6	.5				
(72) 1.6	(99) 1.7	(89) 1.5		(56) 1.5	(22) 1.3				
3.2	4.3	2.8		3.3	2.5				
7.4	8.8	7.1	% Officers', Directors' Owners' Comp/Sales	9.1	5.2				
(109) 14.4	(120) 15.3	(114) 12.1		(76) 14.3	(29) 7.9				
23.6	22.2	19.2		19.5	15.8				
814591M	1487460M	697724M	Net Sales ($)	64428M	67192M	35159M	19446M	58509M	452990M
415350M	336938M	377723M	Total Assets ($)	31533M	23398M	10704M	5528M	53167M	253393M

M = $ thousand   MM = $ million
See Pages viii through xx for Explanation of Ratios and Data

	Current Data Sorted by Assets						Type of Statement	Comparative Historical Data	
	1	1		2		2	Unqualified		
		1		5			Reviewed	3	5
	14	11	2				Compiled	11	10
	64	37	3				Tax Returns	34	23
	49	40	19	7		5	Other	153	193
		12 (4/1-9/30/18)		253 (10/1/18-3/31/19)				134	133
	0-500M	500M-2MM	2-10MM	10-50MM	50-100MM	100-250MM		4/1/14-3/31/15 ALL	4/1/15-3/31/16 ALL
	128	90	26	14		7	**NUMBER OF STATEMENTS**	335	364
	%	%	%	%	%	%	**ASSETS**	%	%
	30.1	19.2	18.1	17.8			Cash & Equivalents	23.0	23.7
	3.5	6.1	9.6	21.5			Trade Receivables (net)	6.3	7.1
	16.3	9.0	7.3	6.6			Inventory	11.5	11.8
	1.1	3.6	2.1	2.8			All Other Current	1.8	1.0
	51.0	37.8	37.1	48.7			Total Current	42.7	43.7
	31.6	39.5	39.0	29.0			Fixed Assets (net)	36.6	35.2
	9.2	15.8	13.6	18.1			Intangibles (net)	11.6	9.6
	8.2	7.0	10.3	4.2			All Other Non-Current	9.3	11.4
	100.0	100.0	100.0	100.0			Total	100.0	100.0
							LIABILITIES		
	17.1	8.3	6.0	5.3			Notes Payable-Short Term	12.2	13.8
	8.6	4.9	8.1	6.1			Cur. Mat.-L.T.D.	8.7	9.5
	2.0	2.7	12.8	8.6			Trade Payables	4.9	5.9
	.4	.0	.0	.1			Income Taxes Payable	.1	.1
	15.2	13.4	9.6	16.1			All Other Current	16.9	16.6
	43.3	29.4	36.6	36.2			Total Current	42.9	45.9
	47.1	44.0	34.4	29.7			Long-Term Debt	41.5	36.0
	.0	.0	.0	.0			Deferred Taxes	.0	.0
	5.9	4.4	1.5	3.7			All Other Non-Current	6.5	5.9
	3.7	22.2	27.5	30.4			Net Worth	9.1	12.2
	100.0	100.0	100.0	100.0			Total Liabilties & Net Worth	100.0	100.0
							INCOME DATA		
	100.0	100.0	100.0	100.0			Net Sales	100.0	100.0
							Gross Profit		
	86.3	84.9	87.7	90.6			Operating Expenses	88.3	88.3
	13.7	15.1	12.3	9.4			Operating Profit	11.7	11.7
	.9	2.0	1.4	2.9			All Other Expenses (net)	1.8	1.4
	12.8	13.0	10.9	6.5			Profit Before Taxes	9.9	10.4
							RATIOS		
	4.4	3.3	1.4	3.4				2.9	3.0
	1.6	1.4	1.1	1.1			Current	1.1	1.2
	.6	.6	.7	.7				.6	.5
	3.2	2.5	1.2	3.3				2.1	2.1
	.9	1.0	.8	.8			Quick	(333) .8	.8
	.4	.3	.4	.4				.2	.3
	0 UND	0 UND	0 UND	9 40.3				0 UND	0 UND
	0 UND	0 UND	1 539.7	22 16.5			Sales/Receivables	0 UND	0 UND
	0 UND	5 75.2	19 19.2	35 10.3				7 53.9	5 75.9
							Cost of Sales/Inventory		
							Cost of Sales/Payables		
	9.3	11.5	32.4	8.6				15.4	13.1
	37.9	34.6	187.3	131.8			Sales/Working Capital	159.5	94.6
	-47.2	-34.6	-26.4	-14.0				-26.7	-25.6
	37.0	39.6	45.2	7.0				35.5	34.7
	(95) 9.7	(76) 9.6	(23) 6.8	(13) 4.3			EBIT/Interest	(267) 8.3	(281) 9.0
	3.0	1.9	1.5	-2.1				2.2	2.9
								3.5	
							Net Profit + Depr., Dep., Amort./Cur. Mat. L/T/D	(15) 1.3	
								.4	
	.2	.4	.9	.9				.6	.5
	4.1	3.9	2.0	NM			Fixed/Worth	3.1	2.7
	-.4	-1.5	-7.1	-.8				-1.1	-2.0
	.5	.7	1.1	1.1				1.1	.8
	14.9	13.3	4.6	NM			Debt/Worth	5.9	6.1
	-2.5	-3.9	-17.0	-3.5				-3.7	-4.3
	347.5	181.0	179.2					219.7	208.2
	(71) 113.1	(50) 66.0	(19) 63.3				% Profit Before Taxes/Tangible Net Worth	(202) 82.6	(228) 77.0
	56.7	19.8	.5					21.5	24.3
	121.4	56.2	39.2	15.5				67.4	64.8
	53.4	27.3	14.8	6.7			% Profit Before Taxes/Total Assets	21.5	22.5
	12.2	4.3	.1	-2.2				3.5	4.7
	171.7	66.5	28.7	17.3				46.8	52.1
	26.6	17.1	10.6	12.2			Sales/Net Fixed Assets	18.2	18.2
	11.5	5.1	6.6	5.6				7.7	8.5
	10.4	7.5	6.9	3.6				8.2	8.3
	5.3	3.3	4.1	2.5			Sales/Total Assets	4.7	4.7
	3.1	1.9	1.4	.8				2.5	2.6
	.5	1.1	1.4	1.7				1.1	1.1
	(69) 1.6	(48) 2.0	(19) 2.8	(11) 3.6			% Depr., Dep., Amort./Sales	(192) 2.3	(218) 2.2
	3.9	4.2	5.1	4.7				4.7	4.2
	7.3	4.1	5.2					7.6	8.1
	(91) 10.3	(54) 7.7	(15) 8.8				% Officers', Directors' Owners' Comp/Sales	(209) 12.3	(212) 12.8
	16.2	14.2	18.5					19.4	20.1
	221443M	618561M	543687M	617781M		1360388M	Net Sales ($)	2480060M	2340738M
	31975M	90039M	112109M	246366M		1084939M	Total Assets ($)	1053160M	842696M

© RMA 2019

M = $ thousand   MM = $ million
See Pages viii through xx for Explanation of Ratios and Data

Comparative Historical Data   Current Data Sorted by Sales

Type of Statement	4/1/16-3/31/17 ALL	4/1/17-3/31/18 ALL	4/1/18-3/31/19 ALL		0-1MM	1-3MM	3-5MM	5-10MM	10-25MM	25MM & OVER
Unqualified	2	3	5				1			4
Reviewed	7	8	9		1			1	2	5
Compiled	24	32	27		5	11	3	4	4	
Tax Returns	137	139	104		25	48	11	14	5	1
Other	115	126	120		28	42	15	10	8	17
					12 (4/1-9/30/18)			253 (10/1/18-3/31/19)		
NUMBER OF STATEMENTS	285	308	265		59	101	30	29	19	27
ASSETS	%	%	%		%	%	%	%	%	%
Cash & Equivalents	22.6	21.8	23.9		22.9	26.2	21.9	27.6	20.5	18.5
Trade Receivables (net)	8.2	7.4	6.0		2.4	4.9	3.1	10.8	12.3	11.2
Inventory	12.0	14.1	12.1		13.0	13.9	13.5	9.2	6.7	8.6
All Other Current	1.5	1.1	2.1		1.3	.8	4.6	3.6	2.6	4.0
Total Current	44.3	44.4	44.1		39.5	45.9	43.0	51.2	42.1	42.3
Fixed Assets (net)	35.6	35.8	34.4		42.8	33.0	37.0	27.4	39.1	22.6
Intangibles (net)	8.8	9.6	13.9		11.6	13.4	7.2	13.7	10.9	30.4
All Other Non-Current	11.4	10.2	7.6		6.0	7.6	12.9	7.7	7.8	4.7
Total	100.0	100.0	100.0		100.0	100.0	100.0	100.0	100.0	100.0
LIABILITIES										
Notes Payable-Short Term	11.3	15.1	12.0		15.7	11.3	19.7	9.5	6.1	4.4
Cur. Mat.-L.T.D.	9.1	6.2	7.0		5.0	6.4	8.3	11.7	9.8	5.4
Trade Payables	5.7	5.1	3.8		1.0	1.8	2.3	3.1	8.9	16.1
Income Taxes Payable	.3	.0	.2		.6	.2	.0	.1	.0	.1
All Other Current	15.3	15.3	13.8		10.9	10.0	10.5	23.3	18.4	24.5
Total Current	41.8	41.9	36.8		33.2	29.7	40.7	47.6	43.2	50.5
Long-Term Debt	33.1	37.8	43.7		49.9	41.8	62.9	45.2	28.9	24.8
Deferred Taxes	.0	.0	.0		.0	.0	.0	.0	.0	.1
All Other Non-Current	7.9	3.7	4.8		6.4	6.0	4.3	1.7	.8	3.1
Net Worth	17.2	16.6	14.7		10.5	22.4	-7.9	5.5	27.2	21.5
Total Liabilties & Net Worth	100.0	100.0	100.0		100.0	100.0	100.0	100.0	100.0	100.0
INCOME DATA										
Net Sales	100.0	100.0	100.0		100.0	100.0	100.0	100.0	100.0	100.0
Gross Profit										
Operating Expenses	87.1	86.3	86.4		79.9	84.9	90.6	86.9	94.8	95.1
Operating Profit	12.9	13.7	13.6		20.1	15.1	9.4	13.1	5.2	4.9
All Other Expenses (net)	1.8	2.1	1.6		4.6	1.0	.6	-.3	-.2	1.3
Profit Before Taxes	11.1	11.6	12.1		15.6	14.1	8.8	13.4	5.3	3.6
RATIOS										
Current	3.4	3.8	3.5		3.6	5.7	3.2	2.7	1.4	1.4
	1.3	1.4	1.4		1.5	1.9	1.5	1.5	1.1	1.0
	.6	.6	.6		.6	.8	.5	.7	.4	.7
Quick	2.4	2.3	2.6		2.0	4.3	1.9	2.3	1.4	1.1
	.9	(307) .9	.8		.9	1.2	.7	1.1	.7	.8
	.3	.3	.3		.3	.4	.1	.4	.2	.4
Sales/Receivables	0 UND	0 UND	0 UND		0 UND	0 UND	0 UND	0 UND	0 UND	0 999.8
	0 UND	0 UND	0 UND		0 UND	0 UND	0 UND	0 UND	0 UND	18 20.6
	12 31.5	9 41.6	5 74.9		0 UND	2 176.0	0 UND	14 25.2	17 21.7	30 12.2
Cost of Sales/Inventory										
Cost of Sales/Payables										
Sales/Working Capital	12.8	13.5	11.1		8.7	7.8	16.1	12.8	27.2	37.7
	49.7	66.3	48.4		25.2	23.9	65.0	77.4	230.6	-649.5
	-32.6	-31.2	-39.2		-26.1	-44.6	-27.2	-40.0	-29.8	-33.5
EBIT/Interest	34.2	38.9	35.1		12.3	51.5	33.1	77.4	45.5	10.3
	(214) 10.5	(233) 9.7	(213) 8.7		(40) 3.4	(77) 15.3	(28) 11.7	(27) 16.2	(18) 2.0	(23) 4.2
	2.7	1.9	2.3		1.4	5.1	2.3	1.6	-.5	.1
Net Profit + Depr., Dep., Amort./Cur. Mat. L/T/D	4.6	2.5	12.4							
	(11) 2.9	(14) 1.7	(14) 1.8							
	1.6	.5	1.0							
Fixed/Worth	.4	.5	.5		.5	.2	.8	.6	.4	1.9
	2.2	2.2	4.1		3.6	2.0	6.3	-6.5	2.8	-1.2
	7.2	-1.4	-.7		-.6	-1.7	-1.0	-.3	-3.0	-.4
Debt/Worth	.8	.8	.8		.7	.4	2.9	.9	1.0	4.0
	3.7	4.9	14.3		14.3	5.7	9.5	-29.5	4.6	-5.0
	-11.9	-4.4	-3.3		-2.7	-3.8	-3.0	-2.3	-5.5	-.4
% Profit Before Taxes/Tangible Net Worth	177.2	211.5	219.5		132.9	229.0	496.2	409.0	169.0	357.8
	(200) 64.9	(193) 83.5	(148) 80.0		(34) 74.8	(61) 82.4	(18) 77.3	(12) 146.1	(12) 17.3	(11) 40.8
	13.8	31.0	30.3		27.6	47.8	41.4	31.3	-8.1	-4.8
% Profit Before Taxes/Total Assets	61.8	69.5	79.8		58.5	104.6	78.1	150.9	50.1	25.2
	23.6	25.9	32.5		20.9	51.0	38.1	38.9	3.9	5.7
	4.0	3.6	4.8		2.0	21.3	7.1	6.9	-2.5	-2.2
Sales/Net Fixed Assets	48.5	48.4	73.8		55.8	97.5	152.2	103.7	45.5	55.4
	17.2	19.8	19.1		8.3	19.3	20.9	35.9	22.2	17.6
	7.4	7.8	7.6		2.7	8.4	5.6	18.3	10.5	10.7
Sales/Total Assets	8.2	7.9	7.9		4.5	6.4	11.6	15.4	13.5	9.3
	4.2	4.6	4.2		2.4	4.0	6.1	7.8	6.5	3.9
	2.4	2.4	2.2		1.3	2.6	2.2	5.1	3.9	2.0
% Depr., Dep., Amort./Sales	1.1	.9	.9		1.8	.8	.5	.6	1.1	1.1
	(172) 2.4	(180) 1.7	(152) 1.9		(35) 5.1	(51) 1.8	(15) 1.7	(18) 1.0	(14) 2.0	(19) 1.7
	4.4	4.0	4.4		9.7	3.6	4.2	2.5	3.2	4.6
% Officers', Directors' Owners' Comp/Sales	7.5	7.8	5.3		6.8	4.5	7.8	6.2	3.1	
	(178) 11.4	(189) 12.6	(164) 9.3		(34) 12.1	(70) 7.9	(20) 10.9	(19) 12.8	(12) 10.0	
	18.9	17.8	15.7		16.1	10.7	17.5	24.7	24.9	
Net Sales ($)	4144472M	3102863M	3361860M		30740M	182615M	113054M	204935M	327198M	2503318M
Total Assets ($)	1149963M	1108252M	1565428M		22386M	77165M	46101M	43125M	75285M	1301366M

M = $ thousand   MM = $ million
See Pages viii through xx for Explanation of Ratios and Data

Current Data Sorted by Assets | **Comparative Historical Data**

0-500M	500M-2MM	2-10MM	10-50MM	50-100MM	100-250MM	Type of Statement	4/1/14-3/31/15 ALL	4/1/15-3/31/16 ALL
1		4	11	2		Unqualified	22	18
1	1					Reviewed		3
		1				Compiled	8	4
22	3	4		1		Tax Returns	30	35
10	6	11	8	2		Other	31	41
19 (4/1-9/30/18)			69 (10/1/18-3/31/19)					
34	10	20	19	5		**NUMBER OF STATEMENTS**	91	101
%	%	%	%	%	%	**ASSETS**	%	%
63.6	25.8	20.5	17.2		DATA NOT AVAILABLE	Cash & Equivalents	35.9	34.4
1.2	23.9	19.8	17.6			Trade Receivables (net)	13.6	13.4
1.0	.0	.0	.2			Inventory	.1	.2
2.0	.0	10.4	11.7			All Other Current	4.7	8.1
67.7	49.7	50.7	46.7			Total Current	54.3	56.0
19.7	33.5	36.0	30.8			Fixed Assets (net)	30.0	26.5
4.9	13.9	3.7	6.3			Intangibles (net)	2.3	3.7
7.7	3.0	9.6	16.2			All Other Non-Current	13.4	13.7
100.0	100.0	100.0	100.0			Total	100.0	100.0
						LIABILITIES		
12.9	7.9	6.4	2.5			Notes Payable-Short Term	17.8	19.1
4.9	.2	1.5	2.3			Cur. Mat.-L.T.D.	3.0	2.3
1.1	1.6	3.2	4.8			Trade Payables	2.8	2.8
.0	.0	.0	.5			Income Taxes Payable	.8	.9
15.0	8.7	10.7	12.2			All Other Current	15.7	12.5
33.9	18.5	21.9	22.4			Total Current	40.1	37.6
25.7	7.8	21.2	12.7			Long-Term Debt	16.6	16.7
.0	.0	.7	1.3			Deferred Taxes	.1	.1
4.0	.5	12.7	4.9			All Other Non-Current	4.4	3.0
36.4	73.3	43.5	58.7			Net Worth	39.0	42.6
100.0	100.0	100.0	100.0			Total Liabilties & Net Worth	100.0	100.0
						INCOME DATA		
100.0	100.0	100.0	100.0			Net Sales	100.0	100.0
						Gross Profit		
79.0	85.6	88.9	98.5			Operating Expenses	89.1	89.9
21.0	14.4	11.1	1.5			Operating Profit	10.9	10.1
.5	2.1	4.8	.1			All Other Expenses (net)	.8	1.7
20.5	12.3	6.3	1.4			Profit Before Taxes	10.1	8.4
						RATIOS		
19.0	12.3	4.9	3.0				4.6	5.1
2.0	2.9	3.1	1.8			Current	2.0	2.1
1.0	1.2	1.1	1.3				1.0	1.1
18.1	12.3	4.8	2.4				4.3	3.9
1.9	2.9	2.0	1.4			Quick	1.9	1.7
1.0	1.2	1.0	1.0				.7	.8
0 UND	**0** UND	**1** 446.6	**17** 21.1				**0** UND	**0** UND
0 UND	**20** 18.7	**26** 14.2	**29** 12.5			Sales/Receivables	**1** 555.8	**0** UND
0 UND	**33** 11.2	**40** 9.1	**42** 8.7				**37** 9.9	**33** 10.9
						Cost of Sales/Inventory		
						Cost of Sales/Payables		
9.3	3.6	4.1	6.3				6.6	6.6
26.5	24.0	14.7	9.7			Sales/Working Capital	19.1	13.2
UND	NM	110.2	21.5				-204.6	248.0
109.8		20.7	24.1				32.0	42.5
(18) 19.8		(13) 4.3	8.2			EBIT/Interest	(54) 6.8	(67) 7.2
4.0		1.4	4.1				.6	1.0
						Net Profit + Depr., Dep., Amort./Cur. Mat. L/T/D		
.0	.2	.1	.3				.1	.0
.3	.6	.8	.5			Fixed/Worth	.6	.5
1.4	NM	1.8	.8				1.8	1.5
.1	.1	.5	.6				.3	.3
.7	.4	1.2	.8			Debt/Worth	.8	1.0
9.4	NM	3.8	1.0				2.3	3.5
415.8		34.7	20.5				184.4	84.8
(29) 146.0		(17) 10.2	11.0			% Profit Before Taxes/Tangible Net Worth	(81) 26.8	(88) 25.5
78.4		7.2	2.5				5.0	1.7
179.5	85.3	15.0	9.1				92.2	56.5
94.3	64.7	5.8	5.2			% Profit Before Taxes/Total Assets	14.7	13.7
32.5	7.9	1.7	1.9				1.9	.5
UND	44.9	83.2	25.0				128.0	269.4
92.4	20.8	16.8	9.3			Sales/Net Fixed Assets	27.8	37.5
30.6	12.8	3.6	3.6				4.9	6.4
12.4	11.2	3.6	3.0				8.9	8.5
7.9	6.9	2.5	2.2			Sales/Total Assets	3.6	3.8
4.4	2.3	1.0	1.0				1.7	1.6
.3		.8	1.2				.7	.7
(12) .5		(13) 1.3	(17) 1.7			% Depr., Dep., Amort./Sales	(61) 1.6	(64) 1.3
1.2		3.3	2.9				3.3	2.7
5.3							5.7	4.3
(19) 9.1						% Officers', Directors' Owners' Comp/Sales	(36) 14.0	(37) 7.6
12.9							20.3	15.3
48686M	67857M	235455M	729489M	1576574M		Net Sales ($)	1114070M	1764036M
6168M	11475M	81331M	378112M	344068M		Total Assets ($)	748966M	1095167M

M = $ thousand MM = $ million

See Pages viii through xx for Explanation of Ratios and Data

Comparative Historical Data

Current Data Sorted by Sales

				Type of Statement						
14		19	18	Unqualified		1	2		4	11
4		3	2	Reviewed		1		1		
3		2	1	Compiled					1	
27		25	30	Tax Returns	13	5	4	2	5	1
37		46	37	Other	7	6	6	3	6	9
4/1/16-3/31/17 ALL		4/1/17-3/31/18 ALL	4/1/18-3/31/19 ALL		0-1MM	19 (4/1-9/30/18) 1-3MM	3-5MM	69 (10/1/18-3/31/19) 5-10MM	10-25MM	25MM & OVER
85		95	88	NUMBER OF STATEMENTS	20	13	12	6	16	21
%		%	%	ASSETS	%	%	%	%	%	%
36.0		29.9	38.3	Cash & Equivalents	73.1	46.9	27.3		18.8	25.8
17.8		17.7	12.1	Trade Receivables (net)	.1	3.2	15.4		21.6	17.0
.1		.0	.4	Inventory	.0	1.4	1.4		.1	.1
6.3		8.2	5.8	All Other Current	.2	4.7	1.2		7.0	11.3
60.3		55.9	56.7	Total Current	73.3	56.3	45.3		47.5	54.2
26.4		25.8	27.8	Fixed Assets (net)	17.4	37.4	29.8		28.6	30.1
4.0		7.5	6.1	Intangibles (net)	5.3	5.7	6.9		12.3	3.8
9.4		10.9	9.4	All Other Non-Current	4.0	.6	18.0		11.6	11.9
100.0		100.0	100.0	Total	100.0	100.0	100.0		100.0	100.0
				LIABILITIES						
9.4		20.8	8.0	Notes Payable-Short Term	10.3	10.5	7.6		7.1	2.1
1.4		2.9	2.9	Cur. Mat.-L.T.D.	3.3	2.8	5.9		1.5	2.4
3.2		5.0	2.5	Trade Payables	1.0	1.3	2.7		3.1	4.9
.6		.0	.1	Income Taxes Payable	.0	.0	.0		.0	.4
21.2		19.3	12.6	All Other Current	19.0	7.2	3.7		17.5	12.8
35.8		48.0	26.1	Total Current	33.6	21.8	20.0		29.2	22.6
17.9		13.6	18.6	Long-Term Debt	28.7	16.2	35.1		9.3	11.1
.4		.5	.4	Deferred Taxes	.0	.0	.0		.9	1.2
4.7		5.4	5.8	All Other Non-Current	5.3	14.5	.1		6.5	4.2
41.1		32.5	49.0	Net Worth	32.4	47.5	44.9		54.2	60.9
100.0		100.0	100.0	Total Liabilties & Net Worth	100.0	100.0	100.0		100.0	100.0
				INCOME DATA						
100.0		100.0	100.0	Net Sales	100.0	100.0	100.0		100.0	100.0
				Gross Profit						
90.3		92.6	87.2	Operating Expenses	70.2	79.3	90.9		97.3	97.5
9.7		7.4	12.8	Operating Profit	29.8	20.7	9.1		2.7	2.5
.7		.8	1.6	All Other Expenses (net)	3.8	2.4	1.4		.5	.2
9.0		6.6	11.2	Profit Before Taxes	26.0	18.3	7.7		2.2	2.3
				RATIOS						
4.1		4.5	5.1		8.5	33.8	9.8		3.1	3.7
2.2		2.2	2.2	Current	1.9	3.2	2.8		1.5	2.7
1.1		1.2	1.2		1.0	.9	.9		.8	1.4
3.5		3.8	4.8		8.4	28.4	9.4		2.1	3.2
1.9		1.9	1.8	Quick	1.9	3.2	2.7		1.3	2.0
1.0		.9	1.0		1.0	.7	.3		.8	1.1
0 UND	0	UND	0 UND		0 UND	0 UND	0 UND		11 34.5	5 69.8
6 60.7	15	24.6	3 110.6	Sales/Receivables	0 UND	0 UND	0 UND		24 15.5	25 14.4
46 8.0	41	8.8	30 12.3		0 UND	1 543.3	33 11.0		41 8.8	42 8.7
				Cost of Sales/Inventory						
				Cost of Sales/Payables						
6.3		6.5	6.0		3.7	8.2	4.4		12.1	5.4
12.5		17.4	15.3	Sales/Working Capital	20.3	13.7	36.2		31.8	8.7
195.9		98.0	110.2		UND	NM	NM		-69.9	21.4
32.7		34.0	71.9				223.9		26.1	37.5
(55) 10.9	(62)	7.8	(61) 11.1	EBIT/Interest		(10) 10.1	10.1	(12)	10.4	(20) 10.8
3.7		1.8	3.6				1.7		1.6	4.2
				Net Profit + Depr., Dep., Amort./Cur. Mat. L/T/D						
.0		.1	.1		.0	.1	.1		.4	.3
.5		.5	.5	Fixed/Worth	.2	.3	.8		.7	.5
1.5		1.3	1.2		2.4	NM	1.5		1.7	.8
.5		.4	.3		.2	.0	.1		.5	.6
1.0		1.2	.8	Debt/Worth	1.2	.6	.8		1.0	.7
4.1		4.2	1.9		6.4	NM	4.2		4.5	1.0
132.9		121.4	115.8		572.7	413.7	137.2		65.6	26.1
(73) 34.9	(80)	36.8	(78) 29.3	% Profit Before Taxes/Tangible Net Worth	(18) 110.5	(10) 186.2	(10) 23.5	(14)	8.3	14.2
4.7		5.6	7.9		69.3	55.6	13.0		3.8	4.7
62.2		49.9	79.7		197.8	163.5	74.5		18.5	13.4
16.6		15.6	13.5	% Profit Before Taxes/Total Assets	83.2	47.8	17.9		4.3	7.7
2.3		2.9	3.6		39.1	7.7	4.6		1.5	2.6
367.0		155.7	122.2		UND	543.2	212.5		51.3	28.7
38.2		29.3	25.2	Sales/Net Fixed Assets	152.8	13.7	38.5		26.3	9.8
5.4		7.8	7.8		37.2	7.2	12.2		4.3	4.0
7.4		7.7	8.5		12.4	8.1	9.0		8.2	3.8
3.8		3.8	3.3	Sales/Total Assets	7.2	5.7	6.0		2.6	2.8
1.8		1.9	1.9		2.2	3.0	1.7		1.6	1.8
.4		.4	.6						.8	1.2
(55) 1.3	(68)	1.1	(52) 1.3	% Depr., Dep., Amort./Sales				(12)	1.3	(19) 1.7
2.4		2.7	2.7						3.0	2.6
5.1		5.8	5.1							
(29) 10.0	(36)	8.8	(29) 9.1	% Officers', Directors' Owners' Comp/Sales						
25.5		19.3	14.3							
1296883M		1739999M	2658061M	Net Sales ($)	8403M	21329M	47934M	36551M	257884M	2285960M
744019M		800857M	821154M	Total Assets ($)	5471M	9842M	16230M	15890M	144268M	629453M

© RMA 2019

M = $ thousand   MM = $ million
See Pages viii through xx for Explanation of Ratios and Data

Current Data Sorted by Assets   Comparative Historical Data

Type of Statement	0-500M	500M-2MM	2-10MM	10-50MM	50-100MM	100-250MM		4/1/14-3/31/15 ALL	4/1/15-3/31/16 ALL
Unqualified		2	5	4		2		19	19
Reviewed		1	2	1				13	7
Compiled	5	2	5	1				35	28
Tax Returns	53	16	2					127	149
Other	43	30	31	11	1	4		120	144
		15 (4/1-9/30/18)		206 (10/1/18-3/31/19)					
NUMBER OF STATEMENTS	101	51	45	17	1	6		314	347
	%	%	%	%	%	%		%	%
ASSETS									
Cash & Equivalents	48.1	26.8	16.7	13.9				26.8	31.0
Trade Receivables (net)	4.1	18.6	44.6	46.4				18.0	17.2
Inventory	.3	.4	.2	.0				.3	.3
All Other Current	3.0	4.2	4.3	7.2				2.8	3.2
Total Current	55.5	50.0	65.7	67.5				47.9	51.7
Fixed Assets (net)	21.1	24.5	20.1	17.6				31.0	28.6
Intangibles (net)	13.9	9.4	6.1	8.0				7.6	7.5
All Other Non-Current	9.5	16.2	8.2	6.9				13.5	12.1
Total	100.0	100.0	100.0	100.0				100.0	100.0
LIABILITIES									
Notes Payable-Short Term	21.4	11.7	12.0	2.7				22.3	19.0
Cur. Mat.-L.T.D.	4.4	2.7	1.1	8.7				3.2	3.6
Trade Payables	2.2	5.9	5.1	4.9				3.7	2.6
Income Taxes Payable	.1	.6	.0	.0				.1	.2
All Other Current	17.1	8.1	19.7	18.6				18.2	14.3
Total Current	45.1	29.0	37.9	34.9				47.5	39.7
Long-Term Debt	29.0	32.1	16.8	11.7				24.0	24.3
Deferred Taxes	.0	.0	.0	.0				.0	.0
All Other Non-Current	4.1	8.3	13.4	7.6				10.3	9.6
Net Worth	21.8	30.5	31.9	45.8				18.2	26.4
Total Liabilties & Net Worth	100.0	100.0	100.0	100.0				100.0	100.0
INCOME DATA									
Net Sales	100.0	100.0	100.0	100.0				100.0	100.0
Gross Profit									
Operating Expenses	85.4	86.7	91.1	93.2				87.9	87.3
Operating Profit	14.6	13.3	8.9	6.8				12.1	12.7
All Other Expenses (net)	.9	2.1	2.1	.3				2.6	2.2
Profit Before Taxes	13.7	11.2	6.7	6.5				9.5	10.5
RATIOS									
Current	6.7	9.0	4.3	3.7				4.7	5.5
	2.0	1.8	2.3	2.2				1.6	1.9
	.6	.9	1.0	1.2				.5	.7
Quick	6.7	9.0	4.2	3.2				4.5	5.0
	1.7	1.7	2.1	1.7				1.4 (346)	1.8
	.5	.7	.9	1.2				.4	.6
Sales/Receivables	0 UND	0 UND	25 14.6	41 8.9				0 UND	0 UND
	0 UND	0 UND	40 9.2	56 6.5				0 UND	0 UND
	0 UND	30 12.0	68 5.4	68 5.4				41 9.0	33 11.0
Cost of Sales/Inventory									
Cost of Sales/Payables									
Sales/Working Capital	12.6	8.3	5.8	4.6				8.9	7.7
	49.7	16.1	9.5	11.4				41.7	30.1
	-59.2	-64.6	-142.1	36.8				-21.2	-55.5
EBIT/Interest	59.6	26.4	88.4	127.1				34.2	42.5
	(56) 18.7	(33) 5.7	(33) 5.0	(15) 22.4				(218) 9.2	(242) 10.5
	2.8	.1	-1.3	2.4				1.5	2.1
Net Profit + Depr., Dep., Amort./Cur. Mat. L/T/D								6.6	
								(12) 2.4	
								1.2	
Fixed/Worth	.0	.0	.0	.0				.1	.1
	.3	.9	.4	.4				.9	.8
	6.9	-5.8	3.0	1.6				-8.3	15.8
Debt/Worth	.2	.3	.3	.5				.4	.3
	1.3	1.8	.8	1.0				2.8	1.7
	-4.8	-9.5	8.6	3.0				-13.9	-52.6
% Profit Before Taxes/Tangible Net Worth	286.3	116.8	73.3	66.3				160.0	138.7
	(67) 132.5	(36) 52.8	(37) 30.2	(14) 38.1				(219) 57.0	(259) 63.4
	60.6	21.6	-1.1	13.5				12.9	16.5
% Profit Before Taxes/Total Assets	148.7	54.8	46.1	38.0				58.9	62.7
	66.9	20.0	15.1	15.6				17.7	23.6
	21.2	.1	-1.5	3.3				1.7	3.9
Sales/Net Fixed Assets	999.8	173.7	240.6	120.9				138.7	151.0
	72.5	33.9	37.8	29.8				29.7	31.1
	23.0	7.0	12.8	8.9				8.7	11.0
Sales/Total Assets	14.7	6.4	4.6	4.1				8.6	8.5
	7.0	3.4	3.3	3.6				4.2	4.7
	4.1	1.7	1.9	1.5				1.9	2.1
% Depr., Dep., Amort./Sales	.3	.4	.1	.3				.4	.5
	(38) .8	(31) .9	(31) 1.0	(16) 1.6				(196) 1.2	(203) 1.1
	1.8	2.3	2.2	3.2				2.9	2.8
% Officers', Directors' Owners' Comp/Sales	5.8	3.3	1.1					4.0	4.9
	(64) 8.5	(15) 6.0	(10) 3.7					(127) 8.7	(161) 9.8
	14.9	11.8	6.0					14.3	15.9
Net Sales ($)	158325M	217921M	706322M	1095517M	32515M	1684254M		5222908M	3320485M
Total Assets ($)	20002M	56228M	215960M	360829M	63632M	1016222M		2245663M	1509393M

M = $ thousand   MM = $ million
See Pages viii through xx for Explanation of Ratios and Data

Comparative Historical Data			Type of Statement	Current Data Sorted by Sales					
10	9	13	Unqualified			1	1	5	6
12	8	4	Reviewed					3	1
25	18	13	Compiled	2	4	3	1	2	1
103	91	71	Tax Returns	28	24	13	4	1	1
119	123	120	Other	26	33	10	14	17	20
4/1/16-3/31/17 ALL	4/1/17-3/31/18 ALL	4/1/18-3/31/19 ALL		15 (4/1-9/30/18)			206 (10/1/18-3/31/19)		
				0-1MM	1-3MM	3-5MM	5-10MM	10-25MM	25MM & OVER
269	249	221	**NUMBER OF STATEMENTS**	56	61	27	20	28	29
%	%	%	**ASSETS**	%	%	%	%	%	%
30.3	30.7	32.9	Cash & Equivalents	42.7	40.0	32.5	31.9	20.0	12.1
17.4	18.5	19.6	Trade Receivables (net)	1.7	10.6	18.1	20.8	44.1	49.9
.8	.7	.3	Inventory	.4	.4	.1	.6	.1	.0
4.4	4.0	4.0	All Other Current	2.3	4.6	2.9	1.0	4.5	8.7
52.9	54.0	56.7	Total Current	47.1	55.6	53.6	54.3	68.7	70.7
25.0	26.3	21.0	Fixed Assets (net)	23.5	23.2	26.9	23.0	15.5	9.9
9.1	8.8	11.9	Intangibles (net)	17.0	10.2	9.1	13.0	5.4	14.1
13.2	11.0	10.4	All Other Non-Current	12.4	11.0	10.4	9.7	10.4	5.4
100.0	100.0	100.0	Total	100.0	100.0	100.0	100.0	100.0	100.0
			LIABILITIES						
22.1	18.6	15.4	Notes Payable-Short Term	10.2	12.7	46.0	10.8	13.2	8.3
3.3	3.4	3.5	Cur. Mat.-L.T.D.	3.0	4.2	4.0	2.0	2.0	5.3
3.3	4.3	3.9	Trade Payables	1.0	3.4	3.0	10.3	5.1	6.1
.1	.2	.2	Income Taxes Payable	.1	.0	.6	.5	.1	.0
16.3	18.4	15.4	All Other Current	14.0	18.3	5.6	14.7	15.5	21.4
45.0	44.9	38.5	Total Current	28.4	38.5	59.3	38.2	35.9	41.1
24.2	21.8	26.0	Long-Term Debt	33.5	27.9	36.9	14.2	7.7	23.2
.0	.0	.0	Deferred Taxes	.0	.0	.0	.0	.0	.1
7.4	8.9	7.2	All Other Non-Current	7.0	1.4	7.1	7.7	5.7	20.7
23.3	24.4	28.3	Net Worth	31.2	32.1	-3.3	39.8	50.7	14.8
100.0	100.0	100.0	Total Liabilties & Net Worth	100.0	100.0	100.0	100.0	100.0	100.0
			INCOME DATA						
100.0	100.0	100.0	Net Sales	100.0	100.0	100.0	100.0	100.0	100.0
			Gross Profit						
86.3	89.1	87.7	Operating Expenses	78.6	88.9	93.4	90.7	90.6	92.9
13.7	10.9	12.3	Operating Profit	21.4	11.1	6.6	9.3	9.4	7.1
1.5	1.3	1.4	All Other Expenses (net)	3.3	.6	.8	1.6	.5	.9
12.2	9.6	10.9	Profit Before Taxes	18.1	10.5	5.8	7.8	8.9	6.2
			RATIOS						
4.1	6.2	6.5		8.6	7.0	7.6	11.2	4.0	3.5
1.6	1.8	2.2	Current	1.7	2.5	1.7	1.6	2.6	2.3
.6	.7	.9		.6	.8	.3	.6	1.0	1.3
3.8	4.9	6.5		8.6	6.9	7.6	10.8	4.0	3.0
1.4	1.6	1.8	Quick	1.5	2.2	1.6	1.6	2.1	2.0
.5	.6	.7		.5	.7	.3	.6	1.0	.8
0 UND	0 UND	0 UND		0 UND	0 UND	0 UND	0 UND	29 12.8	39 9.4
0 UND	0 UND	0 UND	Sales/Receivables	0 UND	0 UND	0 UND	19 19.4	42 8.7	56 6.5
35 10.5	37 9.8	41 8.9		0 UND	1 704.4	37 9.8	41 8.9	72 5.1	68 5.4
			Cost of Sales/Inventory						
			Cost of Sales/Payables						
8.2	8.2	7.8		8.2	9.1	10.7	6.7	5.3	5.7
26.1	28.2	21.5	Sales/Working Capital	52.2	29.5	31.6	64.1	9.6	9.3
-34.2	-55.0	-93.7		-52.6	-81.3	-56.0	-42.5	NM	25.8
42.5	41.8	55.6		99.8	38.2	44.9	54.5	190.6	98.0
(180) 10.1	(163) 9.3	(144) 11.3	EBIT/Interest	(22) 17.0	(40) 11.3	(23) 2.4	(12) 12.8	(22) 17.7	(25) 11.4
2.8	2.0	1.5		2.6	2.3	-.8	-3.2	.8	2.1
11.5		4.3	Net Profit + Depr., Dep.,						
(11) 2.8		(10) 3.1	Amort./Cur. Mat. L/T/D						
1.6		.3							
.0	.1	.0		.0	.1	.1	.1	.0	.0
.5	.5	.4	Fixed/Worth	.2	.6	.6	.5	.4	.3
16.0	10.0	9.9		2.6	-5.8	-.5	NM	1.4	-.6
.4	.3	.3		.1	.4	.2	.1	.4	.5
1.7	1.6	1.3	Debt/Worth	1.0	1.6	3.7	1.3	.7	1.3
-15.2	UND	-12.8		-21.4	-6.3	-2.7	NM	7.1	-3.4
204.7	175.3	167.2		204.1	232.1	217.1	86.7	72.9	70.9
(197) 81.0	(187) 60.9	(157) 66.1	% Profit Before Taxes/Tangible Net Worth	(41) 77.8	(41) 91.6	(16) 47.7	(15) 67.7	(24) 32.0	(20) 41.8
25.3	20.7	22.2		10.3	43.6	-5.2	-.4	6.9	15.2
73.8	69.4	76.8		141.1	109.8	62.5	69.1	50.1	47.4
27.9	24.6	31.3	% Profit Before Taxes/Total Assets	49.5	53.1	21.2	20.5	19.5	15.5
5.1	3.9	3.4		9.2	7.9	-3.2	-8.0	3.0	2.7
245.2	163.3	372.8		UND	143.9	999.8	190.2	408.2	197.7
41.5	42.2	45.3	Sales/Net Fixed Assets	44.8	42.2	57.6	36.8	48.6	93.1
13.2	13.1	15.4		9.1	18.6	12.1	10.7	15.1	19.2
9.2	8.8	7.8		11.0	9.7	13.9	7.5	5.2	4.7
5.0	4.6	4.3	Sales/Total Assets	3.4	5.3	4.9	3.6	3.5	3.8
2.4	2.6	2.6		2.1	3.0	2.8	2.1	2.5	2.3
.3	.3	.3		.5	.2	.5	.3	.6	.1
(144) 1.1	(124) .8	(119) .9	% Depr., Dep., Amort./Sales	(23) 1.1	(29) .7	(15) 1.2	(10) 1.0	(18) 1.1	(24) .4
2.7	2.1	2.2		8.7	1.2	3.1	2.3	1.7	1.9
5.7	4.0	4.6		8.3	5.0	3.0			
(135) 10.9	(121) 9.0	(92) 8.2	% Officers', Directors' Owners' Comp/Sales	(27) 13.0	(34) 8.1	(14) 5.1			
17.0	14.7	12.7		19.7	10.4	7.2			
3090247M	3570180M	3894854M	Net Sales ($)	30219M	117442M	112587M	139577M	456807M	3038222M
1423115M	1649713M	1732873M	Total Assets ($)	22260M	36560M	24434M	50835M	176795M	1421989M

© RMA 2019

M = $ thousand   MM = $ million
See Pages viii through xx for Explanation of Ratios and Data

Current Data Sorted by Assets   Comparative Historical Data

						Type of Statement		
						Unqualified		
						Reviewed		
3	1					Compiled	8	3
12	7					Tax Returns	37	40
12	8					Other	28	25
	0 (4/1-9/30/18)		43 (10/1/18-3/31/19)				4/1/14-3/31/15	4/1/15-3/31/16
0-500M	500M-2MM	2-10MM	10-50MM	50-100MM	100-250MM		ALL	ALL
27	16					NUMBER OF STATEMENTS	73	68
%	%	%	%	%	%	ASSETS	%	%
47.8	25.7	D	D	D	D	Cash & Equivalents	39.1	32.7
.0	3.6	A	A	A	A	Trade Receivables (net)	4.5	2.0
1.8	1.4	T	T	T	T	Inventory	1.2	.4
6.1	5.3	A	A	A	A	All Other Current	2.9	5.4
55.8	36.0					Total Current	47.6	40.4
25.9	31.7	N	N	N	N	Fixed Assets (net)	27.4	36.2
14.0	28.5	O	O	O	O	Intangibles (net)	9.3	10.6
4.4	3.7	T	T	T	T	All Other Non-Current	15.7	12.9
100.0	100.0					Total	100.0	100.0
		A	A	A	A	LIABILITIES		
40.4	23.4	V	V	V	V	Notes Payable-Short Term	27.5	19.8
1.9	7.2	A	A	A	A	Cur. Mat.-L.T.D.	5.9	12.3
2.1	1.1	I	I	I	I	Trade Payables	2.0	.4
.1	.0	L	L	L	L	Income Taxes Payable	.0	.0
35.7	10.9	A	A	A	A	All Other Current	15.7	21.6
80.3	42.7	B	B	B	B	Total Current	51.0	54.2
33.3	41.3	L	L	L	L	Long-Term Debt	18.6	39.2
.0	.0	E	E	E	E	Deferred Taxes	.0	.0
2.1	3.5					All Other Non-Current	10.0	12.3
-15.7	12.6					Net Worth	20.4	-5.7
100.0	100.0					Total Liabilties & Net Worth	100.0	100.0
						INCOME DATA		
100.0	100.0					Net Sales	100.0	100.0
						Gross Profit		
84.0	90.7					Operating Expenses	83.7	87.7
16.0	9.3					Operating Profit	16.3	12.3
.1	1.0					All Other Expenses (net)	1.2	1.3
16.0	8.3					Profit Before Taxes	15.1	11.0
						RATIOS		
6.0	3.0						3.5	5.2
1.6	1.0					Current	1.0	1.1
.3	.2						.4	.3
5.7	3.0						3.5	3.9
1.6	.9					Quick	1.0 (67)	1.0
.2	.1						.4	.2
0 UND	0 UND						0 UND	0 UND
0 UND	0 UND					Sales/Receivables	0 UND	0 UND
0 UND	0 UND						0 UND	0 UND
						Cost of Sales/Inventory		
						Cost of Sales/Payables		
18.8	19.4						13.4	11.5
43.2	603.2					Sales/Working Capital	UND	632.8
-18.0	-11.2						-21.2	-17.3
139.0	12.0						72.1	40.7
(19) 42.3	(13) 2.9					EBIT/Interest	(52) 19.5	(45) 9.1
1.6	.8						5.0	.7
						Net Profit + Depr., Dep., Amort./Cur. Mat. L/T/D		
.1	1.9						.1	.3
.6	-6.5					Fixed/Worth	.8	1.9
-.3	-.3						UND	-.6
.5	2.2						.6	.5
3.0	-8.2					Debt/Worth	1.7	4.1
-1.9	-2.2						-10.9	-2.5
945.1							303.1	166.1
(15) 193.9						% Profit Before Taxes/Tangible Net Worth	(53) 86.8	(42) 85.0
116.7							52.2	15.6
261.2	64.9						85.4	82.1
89.2	14.5					% Profit Before Taxes/Total Assets	43.3	16.3
24.0	2.9						7.8	-.6
999.8	231.8						190.9	68.6
78.5	21.6					Sales/Net Fixed Assets	31.9	27.4
19.7	8.7						10.7	7.5
17.4	7.3						12.3	14.2
11.4	5.0					Sales/Total Assets	4.5	5.5
5.9	3.1						2.3	2.5
.2							.6	.7
(13) 1.1						% Depr., Dep., Amort./Sales	(36) 1.2	(37) 1.1
1.3							2.7	2.7
6.1	6.9						10.9	12.0
(15) 12.5	(10) 13.1					% Officers', Directors' Owners' Comp/Sales	(44) 17.6	(41) 21.5
28.9	21.9						27.3	27.7
57122M	71038M					Net Sales ($)	1108663M	482598M
4867M	13059M					Total Assets ($)	138336M	46026M

M = $ thousand   MM = $ million
See Pages viii through xx for Explanation of Ratios and Data

Comparative Historical Data

Current Data Sorted by Sales

			Type of Statement						
1	1		Unqualified						
			Reviewed						
	2	4	Compiled		3	1			
24	22	19	Tax Returns	5	9	5			
19	18	20	Other	4	7	3	4	2	
4/1/16- 3/31/17	4/1/17- 3/31/18	4/1/18- 3/31/19			0 (4/1-9/30/18)		43 (10/1/18-3/31/19)		
ALL	ALL	ALL		0-1MM	1-3MM	3-5MM	5-10MM	10-25MM	25MM & OVER
44	43	43	NUMBER OF STATEMENTS	9	19	9	4	2	
%	%	%	ASSETS	%	%	%	%	%	%
27.3	35.2	39.6	Cash & Equivalents		42.9				D
9.3	1.7	1.4	Trade Receivables (net)		3.1				A
.6	2.2	1.6	Inventory		1.5				T
3.9	2.4	5.8	All Other Current		.0				A
41.1	41.5	48.4	Total Current		47.5				
30.9	38.6	28.1	Fixed Assets (net)		23.5				N
12.0	6.2	19.4	Intangibles (net)		23.3				O
16.1	13.7	4.1	All Other Non-Current		5.7				T
100.0	100.0	100.0	Total		100.0				
			LIABILITIES						A
24.5	22.2	34.1	Notes Payable-Short Term		25.5				V
6.9	5.5	3.9	Cur. Mat.-L.T.D.		3.7				A
3.5	2.8	1.8	Trade Payables		.2				I
.1	.0	.1	Income Taxes Payable		.2				L
17.5	20.8	26.4	All Other Current		26.5				A
52.4	51.3	66.3	Total Current		56.0				B
26.1	33.4	36.3	Long-Term Debt		39.3				L
.0	.0	.0	Deferred Taxes		.0				E
4.6	3.5	2.6	All Other Non-Current		3.9				
16.9	11.7	-5.2	Net Worth		.8				
100.0	100.0	100.0	Total Liabilties & Net Worth		100.0				
			INCOME DATA						
100.0	100.0	100.0	Net Sales		100.0				
			Gross Profit						
85.2	85.7	86.5	Operating Expenses		85.8				
14.8	14.3	13.5	Operating Profit		14.2				
1.1	1.2	.4	All Other Expenses (net)		-.7				
13.8	13.1	13.1	Profit Before Taxes		14.8				
			RATIOS						
4.4	3.5	4.0			8.6				
.9	.9	1.4	Current		1.6				
.3	.3	.3			.3				
4.1	3.0	3.9			8.6				
.9	.8	1.3	Quick		1.6				
.3	.2	.2			.2				
0 UND	0 UND	0 UND			0 UND				
0 UND	0 UND	0 UND	Sales/Receivables		0 UND				
0 UND	0 UND	0 UND			0 UND				
			Cost of Sales/Inventory						
			Cost of Sales/Payables						
15.6	21.9	18.8			21.3				
-138.1	-127.8	64.4	Sales/Working Capital		43.2				
-21.4	-24.2	-17.0			-23.2				
25.0	64.9	115.3			250.4				
(29) 4.1	(30) 8.8	(32) 6.1	EBIT/Interest	(14) 46.2					
-.2	1.1	1.7			4.6				
			Net Profit + Depr., Dep., Amort./Cur. Mat. L/T/D						
.2	.4	.2			.2				
1.2	1.1	2.0	Fixed/Worth		.8				
-2.1	-28.3	-.3			-.3				
.6	.4	.7			.6				
5.5	1.5	-77.4	Debt/Worth		-7.5				
-5.6	-32.3	-2.0			-1.7				
273.3	612.5	763.9	% Profit Before Taxes/Tangible Net Worth						
(27) 89.1	(32) 103.7	(21) 185.5							
7.9	34.8	84.0							
63.4	147.9	126.2	% Profit Before Taxes/Total Assets		307.8				
27.9	46.7	38.9			77.0				
-4.4	4.6	8.2			15.1				
119.9	104.8	298.3			349.7				
49.1	32.7	56.9	Sales/Net Fixed Assets		74.6				
12.5	8.4	14.7			21.4				
15.1	13.1	14.8			17.4				
7.0	6.9	7.9	Sales/Total Assets		13.5				
2.5	3.6	4.1			4.6				
.6	.5	.5			.2				
(23) 1.3	(25) .8	(22) 1.3	% Depr., Dep., Amort./Sales	(10) .6					
3.8	1.9	2.5			1.3				
14.0	11.7	6.8	% Officers', Directors' Owners' Comp/Sales		6.0				
(26) 26.7	(31) 22.7	(25) 12.5		(14) 9.8					
34.6	30.7	24.8			27.3				
164664M	119865M	128160M	Net Sales ($)	3672M	39661M	33934M	28301M	22592M	
45295M	20009M	17926M	Total Assets ($)	1780M	5414M	5720M	4124M	888M	

M = $ thousand   MM = $ million
                    See Pages viii through xx for Explanation of Ratios and Data

Current Data Sorted by Assets | Comparative Historical Data

0-500M	500M-2MM	2-10MM	10-50MM	50-100MM	100-250MM		4/1/14-3/31/15 ALL	4/1/15-3/31/16 ALL
						Type of Statement		
2	2	6	5	4	1	Unqualified	18	26
1	1	4	1			Reviewed	8	6
2	5	5				Compiled	28	24
53	24	8		2		Tax Returns	126	143
40	37	26	18		3	Other	155	166
	18 (4/1-9/30/18)		232 (10/1/18-3/31/19)					
98	69	49	24	6	4	NUMBER OF STATEMENTS	335	365
%	%	%	%	%	%	**ASSETS**	%	%
45.7	35.6	16.2	15.4			Cash & Equivalents	26.7	29.2
5.7	10.9	31.1	23.2			Trade Receivables (net)	16.5	13.4
4.2	2.0	3.3	2.4			Inventory	2.1	2.7
3.5	4.7	3.9	2.4			All Other Current	3.5	3.3
59.0	53.3	54.5	43.3			Total Current	48.8	48.6
25.4	25.7	29.1	33.3			Fixed Assets (net)	32.5	29.1
6.5	11.7	5.7	8.8			Intangibles (net)	6.9	7.9
9.0	9.3	10.6	14.7			All Other Non-Current	11.8	14.4
100.0	100.0	100.0	100.0			Total	100.0	100.0
						LIABILITIES		
17.6	8.3	7.0	3.3			Notes Payable-Short Term	11.5	15.5
4.3	3.2	2.5	2.3			Cur. Mat.-L.T.D.	4.4	3.1
5.3	5.0	9.7	9.0			Trade Payables	6.4	4.5
.3	.1	.1	.0			Income Taxes Payable	.2	.1
23.2	12.0	17.2	14.0			All Other Current	17.4	16.9
50.7	28.6	36.5	28.7			Total Current	39.9	40.0
34.8	26.7	16.4	17.7			Long-Term Debt	27.3	18.8
.0	.0	.1	.0			Deferred Taxes	.1	.2
10.7	2.8	7.9	2.3			All Other Non-Current	7.8	9.3
3.8	41.9	39.1	51.2			Net Worth	25.0	31.7
100.0	100.0	100.0	100.0			Total Liabilties & Net Worth	100.0	100.0
						INCOME DATA		
100.0	100.0	100.0	100.0			Net Sales	100.0	100.0
						Gross Profit		
86.9	81.7	90.1	90.3			Operating Expenses	86.8	86.9
13.1	18.3	9.9	9.7			Operating Profit	13.2	13.1
.7	1.1	1.8	2.5			All Other Expenses (net)	1.5	1.3
12.4	17.2	8.1	7.3			Profit Before Taxes	11.7	11.8
						RATIOS		
4.2	8.3	5.0	3.4				3.6	3.6
1.6	1.7	1.4	1.9			Current	1.3	1.7
.4	.6	.8	.9				.6	.6
4.2	6.6	4.4	3.0				3.0	3.2
1.2	1.5	1.3	1.5			Quick	1.2	1.4
.3	.5	.7	.8				.5	.5
0 UND	0 UND	0 UND	14 25.4				0 UND	0 UND
0 UND	0 UND	32 11.3	34 10.7			Sales/Receivables	0 UND	0 UND
0 UND	0 999.8	52 7.0	58 6.3				37 9.8	32 11.5
						Cost of Sales/Inventory		
						Cost of Sales/Payables		
10.5	7.3	6.6	5.8				9.2	8.4
52.6	27.6	13.6	10.0			Sales/Working Capital	48.1	29.3
-32.3	-58.5	-33.3	-49.1				-31.5	-32.3
55.5	87.4	122.7	31.7				40.0	47.9
(54) 9.1	(49) 18.9	(36) 16.9	(19) 3.3			EBIT/Interest	(227) 10.1	(234) 10.7
.0	4.3	4.9	1.1				2.7	2.1
						Net Profit + Depr., Dep.,	7.4	9.3
						Amort./Cur. Mat. L/T/D	(15) 2.9	(16) 3.7
							2.1	1.3
.0	.1	.1	.3				.2	.1
.5	.5	.7	.7			Fixed/Worth	1.0	.8
-4.6	20.0	4.7	1.9				-44.3	8.1
.3	.3	.5	.4				.5	.4
2.6	1.1	2.1	1.1			Debt/Worth	2.1	1.4
-2.5	NM	7.2	5.2				-15.2	UND
445.2	295.8	81.9	54.3			% Profit Before Taxes/Tangible	171.2	189.7
(61) 107.1	(52) 107.2	(40) 52.9	(21) 22.5			Net Worth	(242) 58.4	(274) 55.6
42.9	48.4	11.4	2.3				19.7	9.4
146.5	111.4	38.4	19.9			% Profit Before Taxes/Total	56.4	74.1
55.7	50.1	12.9	5.3			Assets	18.9	19.7
2.7	16.0	3.2	.1				3.1	3.0
UND	143.4	95.3	18.3				77.8	140.4
74.9	38.7	24.8	7.9			Sales/Net Fixed Assets	18.9	24.5
17.3	9.5	3.7	2.9				6.0	6.4
12.4	7.6	4.5	3.0				6.6	7.7
7.5	4.8	3.1	1.8			Sales/Total Assets	3.4	3.7
4.4	3.1	1.5	.9				1.7	1.7
.4	.2	.5	1.3				.8	.6
(36) .9	(39) .8	(38) 1.4	(21) 1.9			% Depr., Dep., Amort./Sales	(193) 2.0	(216) 1.6
2.4	2.1	3.8	4.2				3.8	3.4
7.0	3.4	2.7				% Officers', Directors'	5.2	7.2
(48) 10.7	(26) 7.9	(11) 3.3				Owners' Comp/Sales	(137) 10.7	(159) 13.5
18.2	18.1	6.2					22.3	23.8
168794M	566365M	826479M	1526266M	1607163M	575887M	Net Sales ($)	3932981M	6106377M
19769M	72515M	242045M	637751M	436548M	548604M	Total Assets ($)	1995382M	3242778M

© RMA 2019

M = $ thousand   MM = $ million
See Pages viii through xx for Explanation of Ratios and Data

Comparative Historical Data | Current Data Sorted by Sales

17	23	20	Type of Statement	2	1		2	8	7
6	4	7	Unqualified	1			2	3	1
15	16	12	Reviewed				2	5	
92	99	87	Compiled		4	1	2		
148	129	124	Tax Returns	30	27	10	10	2	8
4/1/16-	4/1/17-	4/1/18-	Other	21	24	16	23	17	23
3/31/17	3/31/18	3/31/19			18 (4/1-9/30/18)		232 (10/1/18-3/31/19)		
ALL	ALL	ALL		0-1MM	1-3MM	3-5MM	5-10MM	10-25MM	25MM & OVER
278	271	250	NUMBER OF STATEMENTS	54	56	27	39	35	39
%	%	%	ASSETS	%	%	%	%	%	%
29.4	27.1	33.2	Cash & Equivalents	43.1	38.5	25.9	34.0	21.2	26.9
15.9	15.8	14.3	Trade Receivables (net)	5.1	5.8	7.3	16.2	36.6	22.4
2.7	2.7	3.2	Inventory	4.3	3.6	2.5	1.1	3.6	3.3
5.8	3.9	3.8	All Other Current	3.9	5.3	4.8	1.8	3.9	2.5
53.9	49.4	54.5	Total Current	56.5	53.1	40.5	53.1	65.2	55.1
24.8	29.2	26.8	Fixed Assets (net)	31.7	28.9	32.6	25.1	17.3	23.0
8.4	12.0	8.6	Intangibles (net)	4.6	8.1	12.6	8.5	11.1	10.0
12.9	9.5	10.2	All Other Non-Current	7.2	10.0	14.3	13.4	6.4	11.9
100.0	100.0	100.0	Total	100.0	100.0	100.0	100.0	100.0	100.0
			LIABILITIES						
14.5	15.8	11.0	Notes Payable-Short Term	11.0	14.7	10.7	12.1	8.6	6.8
3.3	5.0	3.4	Cur. Mat.-L.T.D.	3.8	4.9	4.3	2.8	1.5	2.7
4.7	5.0	6.5	Trade Payables	3.9	3.4	2.3	10.8	9.7	10.3
.1	.1	.2	Income Taxes Payable	.0	.6	.0	.0	.1	.0
18.5	19.1	17.5	All Other Current	12.0	22.1	20.6	12.3	22.5	17.1
41.0	44.9	38.6	Total Current	30.7	45.6	37.9	38.1	42.4	36.9
20.8	28.2	26.6	Long-Term Debt	31.5	43.9	28.1	21.3	7.6	16.3
.1	.1	.0	Deferred Taxes	.0	.0	.0	.0	.2	.0
7.1	8.9	6.8	All Other Non-Current	3.9	12.2	4.7	7.7	5.7	4.5
30.9	17.9	28.0	Net Worth	33.9	-1.8	29.3	32.9	44.1	42.3
100.0	100.0	100.0	Total Liabilties & Net Worth	100.0	100.0	100.0	100.0	100.0	100.0
			INCOME DATA						
100.0	100.0	100.0	Net Sales	100.0	100.0	100.0	100.0	100.0	100.0
			Gross Profit						
87.0	86.4	86.6	Operating Expenses	76.7	89.1	87.4	86.3	93.1	90.9
13.0	13.6	13.4	Operating Profit	23.3	10.9	12.6	13.7	6.9	9.1
1.0	1.5	1.3	All Other Expenses (net)	4.3	.1	1.7	-.5	.4	1.0
11.9	12.1	12.1	Profit Before Taxes	19.1	10.8	11.0	14.2	6.5	8.1
			RATIOS						
3.9	2.9	5.1		14.1	4.3	6.1	5.1	4.2	3.7
1.6	1.3	1.7	Current	3.2	1.6	1.1	1.7	2.2	2.0
.7	.5	.7		.5	.5	.4	.5	.9	1.0
3.7	2.4	4.2		7.7	3.9	2.1	4.9	4.2	3.5
(277) 1.3	(270) 1.1	1.5	Quick	2.4	1.1	.7	1.6	1.7	1.5
.4	.4	.5		.3	.3	.2	.5	.9	.8
0 UND	0 UND	0 UND		0 UND	0 UND	0 UND	0 UND	17 21.1	0 UND
0 UND	0 UND	0 UND	Sales/Receivables	0 UND	0 UND	0 UND	0 UND	35 10.4	21 17.0
35 10.5	34 10.6	28 13.1		0 UND	0 UND	0 UND	41 8.9	52 7.0	61 6.0
			Cost of Sales/Inventory						
			Cost of Sales/Payables						
7.4	11.3	7.3		5.7	9.0	11.0	8.2	6.6	6.5
30.3	54.7	29.0	Sales/Working Capital	15.9	44.7	259.6	26.7	11.7	20.9
-42.0	-23.2	-47.3		-10.1	-27.6	-19.1	-43.3	-194.6	580.3
51.8	44.1	75.0		25.2	56.0	76.8	79.4	255.0	76.8
(177) 12.1	(203) 10.5	(167) 11.4	EBIT/Interest	(24) 6.9	(40) 9.0	(22) 7.1	(26) 25.8	(25) 20.4	(30) 12.5
2.9	2.0	2.4		-.3	2.7	2.0	7.5	3.6	1.0
		21.2	Net Profit + Depr., Dep.,						
	(16) 2.6		Amort./Cur. Mat. L/T/D						
		1.2							
.1	.1	.1		.0	.1	.3	.1	.1	.2
.5	.8	.6	Fixed/Worth	.5	1.2	1.8	.9	.4	.6
3.2	-5.6	18.9		5.6	-.8	-3.0	1.9	4.7	1.6
.4	.6	.4		.2	.4	.9	.5	.4	.4
1.6	3.2	1.6	Debt/Worth	.9	5.5	2.1	1.1	1.7	1.1
27.4	-4.7	-16.8		-83.0	-2.5	-13.5	7.6	6.3	11.5
177.8	234.4	219.5	% Profit Before Taxes/Tangible	408.5	254.1	342.2	251.8	92.2	134.4
(219) 62.8	(182) 72.1	(182) 72.9	Net Worth	(40) 72.9	(33) 107.7	(19) 107.1	(32) 83.4	(27) 59.2	(31) 43.5
15.6	19.1	16.1		10.9	32.4	4.8	19.2	11.2	9.6
69.9	84.6	87.1	% Profit Before Taxes/Total	104.7	87.7	98.4	133.2	58.5	70.1
22.4	22.3	31.5	Assets	40.4	45.2	29.5	38.4	13.4	17.6
4.3	3.9	3.7		-.2	10.0	3.7	5.6	5.9	1.6
201.9	152.6	142.8		UND	266.7	73.9	135.4	163.4	115.2
26.0	23.3	33.8	Sales/Net Fixed Assets	27.8	41.8	26.4	75.9	40.7	14.3
7.4	7.0	8.1		4.4	10.1	6.8	10.4	9.5	8.5
7.0	7.7	8.9		9.2	10.8	10.2	8.2	6.2	11.0
3.6	3.8	4.5	Sales/Total Assets	3.5	5.3	5.2	6.0	3.7	3.2
1.7	1.7	2.2		1.5	3.4	3.7	3.1	2.1	1.7
.5	.6	.4		.5	.7	.6	.2	.4	.3
(163) 1.3	(152) 1.7	(141) 1.2	% Depr., Dep., Amort./Sales	(18) 1.9	(29) 1.4	(14) 1.4	(24) .8	(23) 1.1	(33) 1.0
3.4	3.9	2.9		11.3	3.1	3.5	2.9	1.8	2.0
4.6	4.5	4.5	% Officers', Directors'	8.2	5.1	2.8	2.4	3.2	
(119) 10.8	(115) 10.0	(89) 9.5	Owners' Comp/Sales	(18) 15.4	(31) 8.6	(10) 4.7	(13) 7.9	(10) 5.6	
17.4	19.3	17.7		25.7	15.7	17.8	18.3	19.2	
4488629M	4377405M	5270954M	Net Sales ($)	29479M	106176M	106468M	262972M	607287M	4158572M
2373580M	2230798M	1957232M	Total Assets ($)	23186M	28252M	73285M	105622M	272984M	1453903M

M = $ thousand   MM = $ million
See Pages viii through xx for Explanation of Ratios and Data

Current Data Sorted by Assets   Comparative Historical Data

0-500M	500M-2MM	2-10MM	10-50MM	50-100MM	100-250MM	Type of Statement	20	21
	2	1	4	2		Unqualified	20	21
	1					Reviewed	1	
	1	1				Compiled	1	3
		1				Tax Returns	3	2
2	4	8	3	5	1	Other	6	12
	17 (4/1-9/30/18)		18 (10/1/18-3/31/19)				4/1/14-3/31/15 ALL	4/1/15-3/31/16 ALL
2	7	11	7	7	1	NUMBER OF STATEMENTS	31	38
%	%	%	%	%	%		%	%
						ASSETS		
		19.8				Cash & Equivalents	24.5	31.6
		16.0				Trade Receivables (net)	10.8	7.0
		.1				Inventory	1.3	1.1
		1.1				All Other Current	1.2	2.0
		37.1				Total Current	37.8	41.7
		29.1				Fixed Assets (net)	49.9	46.2
		3.0				Intangibles (net)	.3	3.4
		30.9				All Other Non-Current	12.0	8.7
		100.0				Total	100.0	100.0
						LIABILITIES		
		8.3				Notes Payable-Short Term	3.9	5.6
		3.0				Cur. Mat.-L.T.D.	2.1	1.7
		9.1				Trade Payables	6.2	2.4
		.1				Income Taxes Payable	.1	.0
		18.1				All Other Current	5.0	6.0
		38.7				Total Current	17.3	15.8
		11.1				Long-Term Debt	19.1	12.9
		.2				Deferred Taxes	1.2	.0
		3.7				All Other Non-Current	1.1	1.2
		46.3				Net Worth	61.3	70.1
		100.0				Total Liabilities & Net Worth	100.0	100.0
						INCOME DATA		
		100.0				Net Sales	100.0	100.0
						Gross Profit		
		89.2				Operating Expenses	97.4	92.9
		10.8				Operating Profit	2.6	7.1
		6.4				All Other Expenses (net)	-1.5	-.6
		4.4				Profit Before Taxes	4.1	7.7
						RATIOS		
		3.1				Current	5.1	6.0
		1.4					2.8	3.1
		.1					1.4	1.5
		3.0				Quick	4.8	5.6
		1.4					2.5	3.1
		.1					1.0	1.3
	0	UND				Sales/Receivables	0 UND	0 UND
	13	27.2					22 16.3	18 20.1
	34	10.6					34 10.7	41 8.9
						Cost of Sales/Inventory		
						Cost of Sales/Payables		
		6.3				Sales/Working Capital	3.1	2.4
		16.1					7.9	6.1
		-9.7					19.9	22.8
		31.3				EBIT/Interest	52.2	44.9
	(10)	2.3					(30) 9.1	(30) 7.0
		.7					2.1	1.5
						Net Profit + Depr., Dep., Amort./Cur. Mat. L/T/D		
		.4				Fixed/Worth	.5	.4
		.6					.7	.6
		2.5					1.8	1.2
		.3				Debt/Worth	.2	.1
		1.5					.5	.3
		6.9					1.1	.7
		22.1				% Profit Before Taxes/Tangible Net Worth	13.1	43.1
		6.7					(29) 10.0	(37) 7.0
		.3					2.1	2.6
		15.3				% Profit Before Taxes/Total Assets	10.5	16.8
		.8					7.4	5.4
		.0					.8	1.9
		30.9				Sales/Net Fixed Assets	5.3	4.7
		6.3					2.5	2.7
		4.0					1.8	1.5
		2.6				Sales/Total Assets	2.8	2.1
		1.8					1.4	1.1
		1.1					.7	.7
						% Depr., Dep., Amort./Sales	2.3	2.4
							3.1 (32)	3.5
							5.1	4.7
						% Officers', Directors' Owners' Comp/Sales		
9941M	25133M	89941M	195483M	334331M	67449M	Net Sales ($)	654514M	698196M
481M	8380M	46077M	177455M	467355M	106042M	Total Assets ($)	641659M	704069M

Comparative Historical Data | Current Data Sorted by Sales

			Type of Statement						
15	11	9	Unqualified	1			1	4	3
1	1		Reviewed						
2	3	2	Compiled			1		1	
	1	1	Tax Returns			1			
23	21	23	Other	5	1	2	5	4	6
4/1/16-3/31/17 ALL	4/1/17-3/31/18 ALL	4/1/18-3/31/19 ALL		0-1MM	17 (4/1-9/30/18) 1-3MM	3-5MM	18 (10/1/18-3/31/19) 5-10MM	10-25MM	25MM & OVER
41	37	35	**NUMBER OF STATEMENTS**	5	2	3	7	9	9
%	%	%	**ASSETS**	%	%	%	%	%	%
29.1	28.4	31.4	Cash & Equivalents						
11.5	13.7	8.2	Trade Receivables (net)						
1.9	2.2	.7	Inventory						
4.0	4.6	2.4	All Other Current						
46.6	48.9	42.7	Total Current						
45.7	36.5	31.4	Fixed Assets (net)						
1.1	5.6	5.9	Intangibles (net)						
6.6	9.1	20.0	All Other Non-Current						
100.0	100.0	100.0	Total						
			LIABILITIES						
4.3	21.1	10.3	Notes Payable-Short Term						
1.5	1.6	1.6	Cur. Mat.-L.T.D.						
3.5	7.3	6.1	Trade Payables						
.0	.0	.0	Income Taxes Payable						
5.6	22.6	10.2	All Other Current						
14.9	52.7	28.2	Total Current						
14.3	9.3	8.8	Long-Term Debt						
.0	.1	.1	Deferred Taxes						
2.4	3.0	2.2	All Other Non-Current						
68.4	35.1	60.7	Net Worth						
100.0	100.0	100.0	Total Liabilities & Net Worth						
			INCOME DATA						
100.0	100.0	100.0	Net Sales						
			Gross Profit						
93.6	90.3	88.3	Operating Expenses						
6.4	9.7	11.7	Operating Profit						
.2	-1.0	.9	All Other Expenses (net)						
6.1	10.7	10.8	Profit Before Taxes						
			RATIOS						
7.9	6.1	8.8	Current						
3.3	2.5	3.0							
2.0	1.0	.6							
6.5	5.7	8.4	Quick						
3.1	2.2	2.9							
1.4	.9	.6							
0 UND	3 111.8	0 UND	Sales/Receivables						
17 22.1	15 24.5	13 27.2							
45 8.2	40 9.2	27 13.6							
			Cost of Sales/Inventory						
			Cost of Sales/Payables						
2.4	2.8	1.9	Sales/Working Capital						
4.7	7.9	6.3							
16.9	-314.7	-45.9							
11.9	84.2	41.1	EBIT/Interest						
(32) 5.6	(26) 22.4	(26) 15.9							
-.7	7.9	1.6							
			Net Profit + Depr., Dep., Amort./Cur. Mat. L/T/D						
.4	.4	.3	Fixed/Worth						
.6	.7	.4							
1.1	1.1	.9							
.2	.1	.1	Debt/Worth						
.4	.4	.3							
.8	2.7	2.7							
21.4	74.0	20.6	% Profit Before Taxes/Tangible Net Worth						
(40) 5.9	(32) 14.4	(32) 13.5							
-1.8	8.4	3.3							
13.0	32.4	20.0	% Profit Before Taxes/Total Assets						
3.2	10.6	6.5							
-.8	4.8	2.2							
7.6	25.0	25.2	Sales/Net Fixed Assets						
3.4	5.3	4.9							
1.5	2.0	2.2							
2.4	4.0	2.6	Sales/Total Assets						
1.4	1.7	1.2							
.7	.7	.6							
1.5	1.1	1.6	% Depr., Dep., Amort./Sales						
(34) 3.6	(26) 2.5	(24) 2.4							
5.2	4.0	3.7							
			% Officers', Directors' Owners' Comp/Sales						
611218M	744556M	722278M	Net Sales ($)	2964M	4352M	11868M	55585M	131694M	515815M
650594M	743871M	805790M	Total Assets ($)	7265M	2899M	5889M	87088M	130975M	571674M

M = $ thousand   MM = $ million
See Pages viii through xx for Explanation of Ratios and Data

Current Data Sorted by Assets   **Comparative Historical Data**

0-500M	500M-2MM	2-10MM	10-50MM	50-100MM	100-250MM	Type of Statement	4/1/14-3/31/15 ALL	4/1/15-3/31/16 ALL
	6	33	53	6	5	Unqualified	125	115
		3				Reviewed	4	9
	2	1				Compiled	3	7
7	6	4	1			Tax Returns	16	19
8	13	27	21	7	2	Other	74	90
	120 (4/1-9/30/18)		85 (10/1/18-3/31/19)					
15	27	68	75	13	7	NUMBER OF STATEMENTS	222	240
%	%	%	%	%	%	ASSETS	%	%
52.2	27.2	19.2	24.6	20.1		Cash & Equivalents	23.0	25.3
2.2	26.1	22.0	17.2	10.4		Trade Receivables (net)	19.6	20.2
.2	.0	.1	.4	.3		Inventory	.2	.3
1.1	1.1	5.1	3.5	2.6		All Other Current	4.0	3.4
55.6	54.4	46.4	45.7	33.5		Total Current	46.8	49.1
29.7	33.4	38.4	42.2	39.0		Fixed Assets (net)	42.5	37.0
4.0	7.7	4.1	5.2	19.0		Intangibles (net)	3.5	5.6
10.7	4.5	11.1	6.8	8.6		All Other Non-Current	7.2	8.3
100.0	100.0	100.0	100.0	100.0		Total	100.0	100.0
						LIABILITIES		
32.9	6.2	3.5	2.6	10.4		Notes Payable-Short Term	4.0	3.9
5.9	2.1	2.7	2.3	1.1		Cur. Mat.-L.T.D.	2.2	2.4
5.7	5.1	5.9	5.6	2.6		Trade Payables	5.5	5.7
.1	.0	.0	.0	.4		Income Taxes Payable	.0	.1
20.2	12.2	9.4	11.2	8.3		All Other Current	13.0	11.9
64.9	25.7	21.4	21.6	22.7		Total Current	24.8	24.0
14.0	17.3	16.9	17.4	16.2		Long-Term Debt	20.9	20.4
.0	.0	.0	.0	.0		Deferred Taxes	.1	.2
5.5	.8	3.8	4.6	6.8		All Other Non-Current	3.0	3.1
15.5	56.2	57.8	56.4	54.2		Net Worth	51.2	52.2
100.0	100.0	100.0	100.0	100.0		Total Liabilties & Net Worth	100.0	100.0
						INCOME DATA		
100.0	100.0	100.0	100.0	100.0		Net Sales	100.0	100.0
						Gross Profit		
90.7	88.4	93.9	97.5	94.9		Operating Expenses	92.9	92.6
9.3	11.6	6.1	2.5	5.1		Operating Profit	7.1	7.4
.2	2.5	2.7	.2	1.5		All Other Expenses (net)	1.2	1.2
9.1	9.1	3.4	2.3	3.6		Profit Before Taxes	5.9	6.2
						RATIOS		
7.7	9.8	5.0	4.4	5.0		Current	3.5	4.1
2.2	2.4	2.6	2.4	2.3			2.2	2.2
1.0	.8	1.4	1.3	1.7			1.4	1.3
7.7	9.8	4.4	4.1	4.6		Quick	3.3	3.6
2.2	2.4	2.3	2.0	2.1			2.0 (238)	2.0
1.0	.7	1.2	1.3	1.5			1.2	1.2
0 UND	0 UND	15 24.7	17 21.7	30 12.1		Sales/Receivables	12 30.7	13 27.4
0 UND	24 15.0	33 11.0	29 12.7	36 10.1			34 10.6	31 11.6
0 UND	59 6.2	54 6.8	59 6.2	47 7.7			53 6.9	44 8.3
						Cost of Sales/Inventory		
						Cost of Sales/Payables		
12.0	4.3	4.7	3.7	3.0		Sales/Working Capital	4.6	4.2
19.0	10.1	8.5	8.3	4.8			9.4	8.5
UND	-31.5	25.6	20.2	16.4			23.6	32.3
	33.7	7.2	9.4			EBIT/Interest	20.1	24.5
	(15) 4.3	(45) 2.3	(69) 4.0				(162) 4.8	(177) 6.7
	-.3	.4	-.3				1.2	1.2
						Net Profit + Depr., Dep., Amort./Cur. Mat. L/T/D		12.0
								(13) 3.8
								1.6
.0	.1	.2	.4	.5		Fixed/Worth	.4	.3
.4	.6	.6	.8	.8			.8	.7
1.0	2.4	1.3	1.4	3.3			1.7	1.5
.2	.1	.2	.4	.2		Debt/Worth	.3	.3
.8	.7	.7	.9	.7			.8	.8
5.0	3.6	1.6	1.6	4.2			2.0	2.4
211.9	76.9	18.0	9.6	12.0		% Profit Before Taxes/Tangible Net Worth	25.0	31.7
(12) 52.7	(23) 24.1	(65) 2.6	(72) 5.6	(11) 7.1			(205) 8.0	(215) 9.0
-7.9	-3.1	-1.0	-2.7	-1.5			.1	.0
159.2	38.5	9.1	5.3	10.5		% Profit Before Taxes/Total Assets	12.3	16.9
26.1	11.7	1.8	2.9	5.2			4.5	4.7
-5.0	-3.0	-.4	-.7	-1.3			.0	.4
999.8	59.2	17.4	8.4	4.8		Sales/Net Fixed Assets	12.8	25.7
59.8	16.4	6.8	4.3	2.5			4.3	5.8
15.9	3.3	2.5	1.7	1.6			2.0	2.2
14.7	5.2	3.0	2.3	1.3		Sales/Total Assets	2.9	3.5
7.8	3.0	1.7	1.3	1.1			1.6	1.7
2.3	1.5	1.3	.9	.8			1.0	1.0
	.5	.9	1.5	2.2		% Depr., Dep., Amort./Sales	1.5	.9
	(18) 1.4	(60) 1.6	(71) 2.4	(11) 3.2			(192) 2.3	(204) 2.2
	3.1	3.0	3.5	4.7			3.4	3.6
						% Officers', Directors' Owners' Comp/Sales	3.2	1.5
							(25) 7.1	(32) 3.8
							20.5	10.9
24442M	107350M	871264M	2835172M	994210M	1237297M	Net Sales ($)	5297998M	6144484M
2792M	30245M	388111M	1774220M	912558M	1194196M	Total Assets ($)	3569108M	4160831M

M = $ thousand   MM = $ million
See Pages viii through xx for Explanation of Ratios and Data

Comparative Historical Data / Current Data Sorted by Sales

			Type of Statement						
88	99	103	Unqualified	1	6	3	10	40	43
1	1	3	Reviewed		1		1	1	
3	8	3	Compiled		1			2	
24	25	18	Tax Returns	5	5	1	5	1	1
82	83	78	Other	10	9	5	9	20	25
4/1/16-3/31/17 ALL	4/1/17-3/31/18 ALL	4/1/18-3/31/19 ALL		0-1MM	120 (4/1-9/30/18) 1-3MM	3-5MM	5-10MM	85 (10/1/18-3/31/19) 10-25MM	25MM & OVER
198	216	205	NUMBER OF STATEMENTS	16	22	9	25	64	69
%	%	%	ASSETS	%	%	%	%	%	%
26.6	25.9	24.5	Cash & Equivalents	33.1	32.9		21.4	22.4	23.4
18.5	16.6	18.2	Trade Receivables (net)	3.2	15.2		18.8	21.3	19.4
.2	.2	.2	Inventory	.1	.0		.1	.3	.2
3.5	3.5	3.4	All Other Current	.3	2.7		2.3	4.8	3.7
48.8	46.3	46.3	Total Current	36.7	50.8		42.6	48.8	46.7
40.4	41.8	38.7	Fixed Assets (net)	47.1	41.5		44.3	34.1	37.4
3.9	5.5	6.8	Intangibles (net)	8.1	3.1		4.3	6.1	9.5
7.0	6.4	8.3	All Other Non-Current	8.1	4.5		8.8	11.1	6.5
100.0	100.0	100.0	Total	100.0	100.0		100.0	100.0	100.0
			LIABILITIES						
3.3	5.1	6.0	Notes Payable-Short Term	.4	4.3		21.9	3.2	4.5
2.8	1.8	2.6	Cur. Mat.-L.T.D.	1.9	1.6		7.5	1.6	2.3
5.1	4.3	5.3	Trade Payables	3.5	4.6		4.9	5.6	6.0
.0	.0	.1	Income Taxes Payable	.0	.0		.0	.0	.1
11.7	12.1	11.2	All Other Current	17.1	5.3		8.2	10.5	13.4
22.9	23.3	25.1	Total Current	22.8	15.9		42.5	20.8	26.4
19.9	17.3	17.4	Long-Term Debt	31.2	16.2		18.0	15.6	16.1
.1	.1	.0	Deferred Taxes	.0	.0		.0	.0	.0
5.2	6.0	3.9	All Other Non-Current	.0	5.6		.8	5.9	3.5
51.9	53.2	53.6	Net Worth	46.0	62.3		38.7	57.6	53.9
100.0	100.0	100.0	Total Liabilties & Net Worth	100.0	100.0		100.0	100.0	100.0
			INCOME DATA						
100.0	100.0	100.0	Net Sales	100.0	100.0		100.0	100.0	100.0
			Gross Profit						
93.5	93.0	94.4	Operating Expenses	77.3	90.1		93.3	96.7	98.1
6.5	7.0	5.6	Operating Profit	22.7	9.9		6.7	3.3	1.9
1.3	1.7	1.5	All Other Expenses (net)	12.7	1.1		1.1	.2	.6
5.2	5.3	4.0	Profit Before Taxes	9.9	8.8		5.7	3.1	1.3
			RATIOS						
4.8	5.3	4.7		3.0	10.4		4.5	6.1	3.7
2.6	2.4	2.4	Current	1.6	3.9		2.8	2.7	2.0
1.4	1.3	1.3		1.0	1.4		1.0	1.4	1.3
4.5	5.0	4.4		2.8	10.4		4.5	5.2	3.4
2.4	2.1	2.1	Quick	1.6	3.8		2.4	2.3	1.9
1.3	1.2	1.1		1.0	1.4		1.0	1.4	1.1
9 38.5	5 78.9	10 37.5		0 UND	0 UND		0 UND	18 20.0	19 19.7
29 12.4	26 14.1	29 12.7	Sales/Receivables	0 UND	0 UND		28 12.9	33 11.1	32 11.4
48 7.6	46 7.9	54 6.8		19 18.8	60 6.1		54 6.7	56 6.5	50 7.3
			Cost of Sales/Inventory						
			Cost of Sales/Payables						
3.4	3.6	4.1		4.0	3.4		5.9	3.6	3.9
7.2	8.1	9.1	Sales/Working Capital	9.8	9.2		8.5	8.8	9.7
25.9	36.6	35.2		UND	NM		572.9	24.5	37.6
23.5	25.3	9.7			33.7		15.2	10.6	9.9
(149) 5.0	(155) 4.2	(148) 3.3	EBIT/Interest	(11) 1.3		(16) 3.0	(49) 3.8	(62) 2.9	
.6	.4	-.1		-1.6		.9	.4	-.6	
			Net Profit + Depr., Dep., Amort./Cur. Mat. L/T/D						
.4	.4	.3		.1	.2		.2	.2	.5
.8	.8	.7	Fixed/Worth	1.0	.6		.8	.6	.8
1.6	1.6	1.5		2.5	1.5		1.9	1.4	1.4
.3	.2	.3		.4	.1		.1	.3	.4
.7	.7	.8	Debt/Worth	1.5	.4		.4	.8	.9
2.0	1.8	2.0		4.5	1.0		2.3	1.6	2.2
25.3	23.0	15.5		14.4	70.1		45.9	17.8	11.0
(181) 6.9	(194) 8.1	(188) 5.6	% Profit Before Taxes/Tangible Net Worth	(13) .0	(20) 9.5	(23) 3.9	(62) 6.8	(62) 4.3	
-.6	-1.0	-2.9		-9.9	-2.0		1.5	-3.1	-4.7
12.7	12.2	9.2		6.3	63.2		32.1	8.0	6.5
3.8	4.1	2.9	% Profit Before Taxes/Total Assets	.8	5.2		9.6	3.0	2.1
-1.4	-1.5	-1.4		-4.2	-1.5		.6	-1.3	-2.0
17.5	22.0	18.4		UND	49.6		30.5	16.6	12.1
5.3	5.1	5.6	Sales/Net Fixed Assets	2.7	7.1		6.0	7.0	4.9
2.1	2.1	2.1		.2	1.7		1.3	2.7	2.3
2.9	3.3	2.9		2.3	5.0		3.7	2.7	2.6
1.7	1.7	1.6	Sales/Total Assets	.5	2.1		1.6	1.7	1.4
1.0	1.0	1.0		.1	.8		.9	1.2	1.1
1.0	1.1	1.2			.8		.4	1.1	1.3
(172) 2.1	(184) 2.1	(169) 2.1	% Depr., Dep., Amort./Sales	(16) 2.1		(22) 1.6	(57) 1.9	(61) 2.3	
3.3	3.5	3.3		3.1		4.0	3.0	3.2	
3.5	5.2	3.7							
(29) 7.4	(25) 8.0	(23) 7.2	% Officers', Directors' Owners' Comp/Sales						
14.3	19.6	23.5							
4791310M	5329526M	6069735M	Net Sales ($)	5251M	43357M	32584M	183169M	1053972M	4751402M
3586709M	3764429M	4302122M	Total Assets ($)	15579M	51374M	19753M	128258M	762837M	3324321M

M = $ thousand   MM = $ million
See Pages viii through xx for Explanation of Ratios and Data

Current Data Sorted by Assets   Comparative Historical Data

0-500M	500M-2MM	2-10MM	10-50MM	50-100MM	100-250MM	Type of Statement	4/1/14-3/31/15 ALL	4/1/15-3/31/16 ALL
			1	1	3	Unqualified	5	6
			1			Reviewed	1	1
2	1	3				Compiled	8	4
2	6	2				Tax Returns	19	12
5	17	16	9	1	1	Other	38	43
	8 (4/1-9/30/18)		63 (10/1/18-3/31/19)					
9	24	21	11	2	4	NUMBER OF STATEMENTS	71	66
%	%	%	%	%	%	**ASSETS**	%	%
	20.5	13.1	14.4			Cash & Equivalents	20.4	17.5
	23.9	20.0	24.1			Trade Receivables (net)	19.4	17.9
	1.9	.4	4.7			Inventory	1.9	2.4
	7.3	4.0	3.4			All Other Current	6.0	2.5
	53.5	37.6	46.6			Total Current	47.8	40.4
	33.3	41.8	28.5			Fixed Assets (net)	29.4	34.2
	10.5	6.8	20.5			Intangibles (net)	8.9	14.0
	2.8	13.8	4.4			All Other Non-Current	13.9	11.5
	100.0	100.0	100.0			Total	100.0	100.0
						LIABILITIES		
	25.7	13.1	3.4			Notes Payable-Short Term	16.8	14.6
	6.7	4.6	4.0			Cur. Mat.-L.T.D.	5.1	7.7
	10.1	2.8	8.0			Trade Payables	6.6	7.4
	.0	.3	.9			Income Taxes Payable	.2	.1
	18.8	23.7	13.9			All Other Current	16.5	17.4
	61.3	44.6	30.3			Total Current	45.2	47.2
	18.3	23.4	23.4			Long-Term Debt	21.4	26.7
	.0	.0	.3			Deferred Taxes	.2	.1
	.0	3.4	9.4			All Other Non-Current	5.8	6.2
	20.5	28.6	36.6			Net Worth	27.5	19.9
	100.0	100.0	100.0			Total Liabilities & Net Worth	100.0	100.0
						INCOME DATA		
	100.0	100.0	100.0			Net Sales	100.0	100.0
						Gross Profit		
	86.2	83.6	82.4			Operating Expenses	81.5	85.8
	13.8	16.4	17.6			Operating Profit	18.5	14.2
	2.7	4.2	1.1			All Other Expenses (net)	1.4	3.6
	11.1	12.2	16.5			Profit Before Taxes	17.2	10.6
						RATIOS		
	1.4	3.7	3.1				3.4	2.6
	.9	1.3	1.6			Current	1.3	1.1
	.6	.3	.9				.6	.6
	1.4	3.3	2.5				2.7	1.9
	.8	1.0	1.2			Quick	1.1	1.0
	.4	.2	.7				.5	.6
	0 934.8	0 UND	37 9.8				0 UND	0 UND
	31 11.6	41 9.0	57 6.4			Sales/Receivables	36 10.2	42 8.6
	42 8.6	55 6.6	63 5.8				56 6.5	57 6.4
						Cost of Sales/Inventory		
						Cost of Sales/Payables		
	24.1	5.4	5.6				5.7	6.8
	-82.3	26.8	11.1			Sales/Working Capital	31.6	517.9
	-11.7	-6.1	-58.2				-15.7	-21.6
	89.1	30.7	50.3				49.6	26.4
	(19) 27.8	(16) 6.2	7.4			EBIT/Interest	(53) 9.6	(56) 6.3
	1.3	-.6	2.8				2.8	-1.0
						Net Profit + Depr., Dep., Amort./Cur. Mat. L/T/D		
	.5	.4	.5				.3	.6
	1.6	1.2	1.6			Fixed/Worth	.8	3.1
	-1.9	-2.1	7.3				-4.3	-.7
	1.5	.6	.6				.5	.9
	3.9	3.0	4.6			Debt/Worth	1.9	8.2
	-4.4	-4.3	-6.5				-6.6	-4.1
	406.3	78.3				% Profit Before Taxes/Tangible Net Worth	177.5	119.5
	(16) 144.4	(14) 53.5					(49) 62.0	(41) 45.6
	44.0	39.8					21.5	-.4
	73.0	28.1	29.9			% Profit Before Taxes/Total Assets	44.5	33.1
	42.6	17.2	13.2				21.2	12.4
	1.2	3.3	4.0				4.8	-1.1
	30.7	16.2	10.7			Sales/Net Fixed Assets	66.2	26.2
	13.0	7.3	6.8				11.7	9.4
	7.1	1.8	3.4				5.5	4.1
	6.4	2.7	2.6			Sales/Total Assets	5.6	3.5
	3.7	1.5	1.9				2.1	2.0
	2.8	.8	.6				1.3	1.3
	2.0	1.9	2.3			% Depr., Dep., Amort./Sales	1.4	1.6
	(20) 2.7	(16) 3.3	(10) 2.5				(50) 2.5	(55) 2.8
	5.0	6.5	4.7				4.0	6.1
						% Officers', Directors' Owners' Comp/Sales	3.1	5.4
							(19) 10.0	(20) 9.2
							36.1	13.7
29681M	132503M	156937M	465468M	110075M	573668M	Net Sales ($)	1350364M	1986222M
2998M	32376M	78820M	281607M	134046M	565267M	Total Assets ($)	991820M	1059948M

M = $ thousand   MM = $ million
See Pages viii through xx for Explanation of Ratios and Data

Comparative Historical Data | Current Data Sorted by Sales

	4/1/16-3/31/17 ALL	4/1/17-3/31/18 ALL	4/1/18-3/31/19 ALL	0-1MM	1-3MM	3-5MM	5-10MM	10-25MM	25MM & OVER
				(8) 4/1-9/30/18		(63) 10/1/18-3/31/19			
Type of Statement									
Unqualified	4	7	5					1	4
Reviewed	1	2	1						1
Compiled	3	2	6	1	2		1	2	
Tax Returns	18	34	10		1	3	4	2	
Other	32	55	49	5	4	15	13		9
NUMBER OF STATEMENTS	58	100	71	6	7	18	18	8	14
ASSETS	%	%	%	%	%	%	%	%	%
Cash & Equivalents	17.4	19.2	16.5			21.7	13.2		11.7
Trade Receivables (net)	16.9	19.9	23.2			25.5	25.2		23.8
Inventory	2.8	1.5	1.8			2.7	.8		4.0
All Other Current	2.0	5.9	5.2			8.5	8.3		3.8
Total Current	39.0	46.5	46.7			58.4	47.5		43.3
Fixed Assets (net)	33.3	40.0	32.8			24.1	37.0		33.2
Intangibles (net)	12.3	7.4	11.0			15.6	6.2		12.4
All Other Non-Current	15.4	6.1	9.5			2.0	9.3		11.2
Total	100.0	100.0	100.0			100.0	100.0		100.0
LIABILITIES									
Notes Payable-Short Term	11.2	12.4	14.2			16.7	18.3		4.2
Cur. Mat.-L.T.D.	7.0	10.6	5.1			7.0	6.8		2.7
Trade Payables	5.9	7.1	8.7			9.5	8.1		7.4
Income Taxes Payable	.0	.0	.2			.0	.0		.7
All Other Current	16.9	24.2	20.1			17.0	26.0		16.7
Total Current	40.9	54.3	48.3			50.1	59.2		31.8
Long-Term Debt	25.3	28.0	18.6			23.2	8.2		17.8
Deferred Taxes	.0	.0	.0			.0	.0		.1
All Other Non-Current	2.0	2.5	4.1			3.3	.5		6.8
Net Worth	31.7	15.1	28.9			23.4	32.1		43.6
Total Liabilities & Net Worth	100.0	100.0	100.0			100.0	100.0		100.0
INCOME DATA									
Net Sales	100.0	100.0	100.0			100.0	100.0		100.0
Gross Profit									
Operating Expenses	84.8	83.7	83.4			82.9	83.2		91.0
Operating Profit	15.2	16.3	16.6			17.1	16.8		9.0
All Other Expenses (net)	1.7	2.4	2.4			1.9	.8		.8
Profit Before Taxes	13.6	13.9	14.2			15.2	16.1		8.2
RATIOS									
Current	2.8	1.9	2.2			2.8	2.1		2.5
	1.1	1.0	1.2			1.1	1.2		1.7
	.5	.5	.6			.8	.5		1.0
Quick	2.6	1.8	1.9			2.0	1.7		2.0
	1.1	.9	1.0			1.0	1.0		1.4
	.4	.4	.5			.6	.4		.8
Sales/Receivables	0 999.8	0 UND	0 999.8			13 27.9	0 UND		43 8.5
	39 9.4	38 9.7	40 9.2			32 11.3	36 10.2		52 7.0
	61 6.0	58 6.3	54 6.7			43 8.4	42 8.6		59 6.2
Cost of Sales/Inventory									
Cost of Sales/Payables									
Sales/Working Capital	6.4	10.0	8.8			10.8	10.3		6.7
	36.9	129.4	47.8			158.1	89.0		11.2
	-9.7	-7.4	-17.4			-27.8	-8.2		-157.2
EBIT/Interest	36.8	36.4	52.2			93.2	62.4		62.2
	(51) 11.4	(77) 15.5	(57) 12.9			(14) 26.8	(15) 30.1		6.4
	2.6	.3	1.2			8.0	6.9		.0
Net Profit + Depr., Dep., Amort./Cur. Mat. L/T/D									
Fixed/Worth	.3	.5	.4			.4	.1		.5
	.9	1.5	1.0			1.5	.8		.8
	20.3	-2.6	-3.8			-1.8	NM		3.8
Debt/Worth	.6	.7	.6			1.1	.5		.4
	1.5	3.4	3.0			7.1	1.6		1.1
	NM	-4.2	-6.1			-3.5	-5.9		8.1
% Profit Before Taxes/Tangible Net Worth	111.1	140.4	150.0			457.6	144.4		135.2
	(44) 63.8	(61) 78.2	(49) 74.1			(11) 236.3	(13) 56.0	(12)	39.7
	4.0	27.3	16.3			89.1	41.9		-4.3
% Profit Before Taxes/Total Assets	51.0	50.6	56.3			77.7	63.2		32.4
	17.0	26.4	23.0			42.6	32.9		11.6
	.2	.4	2.8			17.1	12.6		-1.0
Sales/Net Fixed Assets	28.2	19.7	32.2			85.8	80.1		9.4
	5.7	7.4	9.9			14.8	12.3		5.7
	2.8	2.1	3.5			7.1	5.8		3.2
Sales/Total Assets	3.1	3.6	4.2			5.3	5.4		2.7
	1.7	2.2	2.3			3.3	3.1		1.9
	.8	1.1	1.3			2.2	1.8		.8
% Depr., Dep., Amort./Sales	1.7	1.0	1.9			1.3	1.9		2.2
	(49) 3.1	(85) 3.4	(55) 2.7			(14) 3.0	(15) 2.7		2.5
	5.1	8.4	5.3			5.4	4.4		5.0
% Officers', Directors' Owners' Comp/Sales	2.2	2.5	2.3						
	(13) 7.7	(14) 5.8	(16) 5.7						
	14.0	26.0	12.7						
Net Sales ($)	1809840M	2011675M	1468332M	2359M	12697M	73908M	124909M	109066M	1145393M
Total Assets ($)	1087952M	956226M	1095114M	11350M	15257M	38075M	93066M	71387M	865979M

© RMA 2019

M = $ thousand   MM = $ million
See Pages viii through xx for Explanation of Ratios and Data

Current Data Sorted by Assets　　　　Comparative Historical Data

			13	7	1	2	Type of Statement		
		3	9	1	1		Unqualified	29	23
	3	8	12	4			Reviewed	24	20
	12	19	24	5	1		Compiled	41	39
	10	35	93	33	6	4	Tax Returns	91	94
		28 (4/1-9/30/18)		278 (10/1/18-3/31/19)			Other	154	144
								4/1/14-3/31/15	4/1/15-3/31/16
	0-500M	500M-2MM	2-10MM	10-50MM	50-100MM	100-250MM		ALL	ALL
	25	65	151	50	9	6	NUMBER OF STATEMENTS	339	320
	%	%	%	%	%	%	ASSETS	%	%
	34.1	27.4	16.9	9.7			Cash & Equivalents	22.3	23.7
	.0	17.3	20.3	22.3			Trade Receivables (net)	18.0	16.9
	.6	3.1	4.5	2.3			Inventory	2.9	2.6
	16.5	1.7	1.4	2.0			All Other Current	2.9	2.3
	51.2	49.5	43.1	36.4			Total Current	46.1	45.5
	31.0	35.0	44.3	37.3			Fixed Assets (net)	38.9	38.5
	8.4	10.1	8.6	20.0			Intangibles (net)	8.7	9.3
	9.5	5.4	4.1	6.3			All Other Non-Current	6.4	6.7
	100.0	100.0	100.0	100.0			Total	100.0	100.0
							LIABILITIES		
	37.0	6.0	3.1	4.7			Notes Payable-Short Term	8.7	8.3
	10.1	5.4	4.6	3.8			Cur. Mat.-L.T.D.	7.6	6.3
	1.5	4.8	6.4	7.9			Trade Payables	7.0	6.9
	.4	.0	.0	.0			Income Taxes Payable	.1	.1
	40.5	13.9	9.5	8.5			All Other Current	13.0	9.8
	89.5	30.1	23.6	24.9			Total Current	36.3	31.5
	35.6	29.0	25.8	21.6			Long-Term Debt	28.5	27.3
	.0	.0	.0	.0			Deferred Taxes	.0	.0
	1.8	6.2	2.6	6.5			All Other Non-Current	2.9	2.4
	-26.9	34.6	48.0	47.0			Net Worth	32.3	38.9
	100.0	100.0	100.0	100.0			Total Liabilities & Net Worth	100.0	100.0
							INCOME DATA		
	100.0	100.0	100.0	100.0			Net Sales	100.0	100.0
							Gross Profit		
	86.2	81.4	74.6	80.8			Operating Expenses	76.7	76.2
	13.8	18.6	25.4	19.2			Operating Profit	23.3	23.8
	1.1	1.2	3.2	2.2			All Other Expenses (net)	2.3	1.8
	12.7	17.4	22.2	17.0			Profit Before Taxes	21.1	22.0
							RATIOS		
	3.0	3.9	3.8	2.5				3.7	4.0
	.6	1.9	1.9	1.6			Current	1.9	2.0
	.3	.7	1.1	.9				.8	.9
	2.2	3.6	3.5	2.4				3.2	3.5
	.4	1.8	1.6	1.3			Quick	1.6	1.8
	.1	.5	.9	.8				.7	.8
	0　UND	0　UND	7　50.2	32　11.5				0　UND	0　UND
	0　UND	0　UND	34　10.6	43　8.4			Sales/Receivables	24　15.5	26　14.3
	0　UND	33　10.9	49　7.4	52　7.0				46　7.9	46　8.0
							Cost of Sales/Inventory		
							Cost of Sales/Payables		
	22.7	9.4	5.2	6.4				7.1	6.5
	-45.6	20.4	11.7	13.6			Sales/Working Capital	15.3	15.8
	-14.2	-45.7	117.4	-56.4				-82.3	-265.2
	64.5	172.5	97.1	64.6				90.1	112.5
	(18)　4.7	(49)　21.6	(131)　25.3	(45)　17.4			EBIT/Interest	(272)　26.6	(260)　30.9
	1.3	1.3	5.1	3.6				7.1	7.9
			11.6	21.1				30.2	12.0
		(17)　5.1	(14)　8.7				Net Profit + Depr., Dep., Amort./Cur. Mat. L/T/D	(24)　6.9	(30)　5.3
			1.9	2.9				2.6	2.4
	.1	.2	.4	.6				.4	.4
	2.2	.7	1.1	1.4			Fixed/Worth	1.0	1.0
	-.4	4.4	2.9	2.5				5.9	3.3
	.8	.4	.5	.9				.4	.4
	5.8	.9	1.1	1.7			Debt/Worth	1.3	1.2
	-2.0	6.4	3.9	2.8				13.6	5.8
	559.4	226.9	173.0	139.7			% Profit Before Taxes/Tangible Net Worth	229.6	237.8
	(15)　246.2	(53)　100.1	(127)　96.9	(45)　93.6				(265)　96.9	(261)　103.4
	56.1	26.5	36.2	34.6				33.8	33.3
	356.7	135.6	79.6	39.7			% Profit Before Taxes/Total Assets	111.8	110.4
	64.3	43.4	34.7	21.5				36.6	41.1
	2.0	6.6	7.7	3.4				10.8	10.6
	310.7	44.6	13.6	11.6				28.4	26.4
	43.9	15.3	5.9	4.8			Sales/Net Fixed Assets	8.9	10.1
	12.4	5.6	2.4	2.5				3.6	3.6
	15.5	5.3	2.9	2.2				4.7	4.4
	10.0	3.5	2.0	1.6			Sales/Total Assets	2.7	2.7
	4.2	2.1	1.1	.9				1.5	1.4
	.5	1.2	2.1	2.2				1.7	1.6
	(14)　1.4	(39)　2.6	(140)　3.5	(48)　3.6			% Depr., Dep., Amort./Sales	(268)　3.1	(254)　3.0
	4.8	5.6	6.4	6.3				5.6	6.0
	1.6		3.1					1.9	2.7
	(11)　6.6		(10)　5.6				% Officers', Directors' Owners' Comp/Sales	(52)　8.5	(51)　9.3
	14.6		14.0					22.3	24.1
	73674M	317132M	1506808M	1661834M	1183479M	512374M	Net Sales ($)	5296911M	5901722M
	6822M	78200M	731810M	992965M	642232M	780314M	Total Assets ($)	2917635M	3809963M

© RMA 2019

M = $ thousand　　MM = $ million
See Pages viii through xx for Explanation of Ratios and Data

Comparative Historical Data | Current Data Sorted by Sales

			Type of Statement	0-1MM	1-3MM	3-5MM	5-10MM	10-25MM	25MM & OVER
25	27	23	Unqualified		2	2	4	7	8
18	14	14	Reviewed		1	3	3	4	3
31	21	27	Compiled	3	4	3	8	8	1
80	48	61	Tax Returns	10	9	10	17	8	7
167	181	181	Other	11	25	19	53	50	23
4/1/16-3/31/17 ALL	4/1/17-3/31/18 ALL	4/1/18-3/31/19 ALL			28 (4/1-9/30/18)			278 (10/1/18-3/31/19)	
321	291	306	NUMBER OF STATEMENTS	24	41	37	85	77	42
%	%	%	ASSETS	%	%	%	%	%	%
20.5	22.7	18.8	Cash & Equivalents	6.6	18.3	24.4	18.6	23.3	13.9
17.3	18.2	18.2	Trade Receivables (net)	2.6	12.5	11.8	21.5	21.3	26.1
2.9	3.0	3.3	Inventory	.2	1.4	4.5	4.6	3.7	2.8
1.9	2.6	2.8	All Other Current	13.2	3.7	2.4	.9	1.7	2.2
42.6	46.4	43.2	Total Current	22.6	35.9	43.1	45.5	50.0	44.9
40.5	35.3	38.9	Fixed Assets (net)	65.2	48.5	39.9	35.4	33.4	30.7
11.3	11.1	12.5	Intangibles (net)	7.5	9.9	9.5	14.6	12.5	16.3
5.6	7.2	5.4	All Other Non-Current	4.8	5.8	7.4	4.5	4.1	8.1
100.0	100.0	100.0	Total	100.0	100.0	100.0	100.0	100.0	100.0
			LIABILITIES						
6.1	6.2	6.7	Notes Payable-Short Term	13.8	18.0	4.6	5.2	3.0	3.2
5.5	4.3	5.0	Cur. Mat.-L.T.D.	4.9	5.1	7.9	5.2	4.5	3.1
6.3	6.8	5.8	Trade Payables	1.8	4.3	4.8	5.7	6.9	8.3
.1	.0	.0	Income Taxes Payable	.2	.1	.0	.0	.0	.0
11.5	14.3	12.7	All Other Current	32.9	10.4	9.1	11.3	11.5	11.6
29.6	31.6	30.2	Total Current	53.5	37.9	26.4	27.4	26.0	26.1
29.5	24.8	26.6	Long-Term Debt	50.2	42.3	29.8	23.1	17.0	19.5
.0	.0	.0	Deferred Taxes	.0	.0	.0	.0	.0	.0
2.1	4.4	3.8	All Other Non-Current	.7	4.3	1.7	6.6	2.6	3.8
38.8	39.2	39.4	Net Worth	-4.4	15.5	42.2	43.0	54.4	50.6
100.0	100.0	100.0	Total Liabilties & Net Worth	100.0	100.0	100.0	100.0	100.0	100.0
			INCOME DATA						
100.0	100.0	100.0	Net Sales	100.0	100.0	100.0	100.0	100.0	100.0
			Gross Profit						
76.9	78.9	78.0	Operating Expenses	61.8	83.8	83.3	81.5	73.2	79.1
23.1	21.1	22.0	Operating Profit	38.2	16.2	16.7	18.5	26.8	20.9
2.3	3.0	2.4	All Other Expenses (net)	16.4	3.1	.8	1.1	.8	.8
20.8	18.1	19.6	Profit Before Taxes	21.8	13.1	15.9	17.4	26.0	20.1
			RATIOS						
3.2	3.9	3.5		1.6	4.3	2.8	3.9	3.8	3.0
2.0	2.0	1.8	Current	.6	1.2	1.6	1.8	2.1	1.9
1.0	1.0	.9		.2	.4	.8	.9	1.5	1.1
3.0	3.5	3.2		1.1	3.6	2.4	3.6	3.5	2.8
1.8	1.6	1.6	Quick	.3	1.1	1.3	1.5	1.9	1.6
.8	.8	.7		.0	.3	.6	.8	1.1	1.0
0 UND	0 UND	0 UND		0 UND	0 UND	0 UND	0 UND	24 15.2	17 21.8
26 13.8	31 11.8	31 11.7	Sales/Receivables	0 UND	0 UND	12 31.5	34 10.6	36 10.0	43 8.4
49 7.4	49 7.5	49 7.5		0 UND	49 7.4	45 8.2	51 7.1	48 7.6	58 6.3
			Cost of Sales/Inventory						
			Cost of Sales/Payables						
6.8	5.9	6.3		3.4	5.8	8.6	6.3	5.9	6.5
17.8	12.5	15.4	Sales/Working Capital	-9.4	71.8	23.2	13.6	11.0	15.9
-486.0	-672.0	-72.9		-1.9	-13.3	-37.0	-151.5	22.2	134.4
109.6	125.7	106.2		4.4	14.6	88.5	114.3	151.7	160.3
(264) 36.1	(226) 30.7	(255) 19.3	EBIT/Interest	(16) 2.3	(31) 4.4	(30) 7.8	(73) 19.3	(68) 59.8	(37) 45.5
6.9	3.9	3.9		.5	.1	2.5	4.7	14.2	7.0
13.0	9.1	14.3						17.5	
(22) 4.7	(26) 3.8	(33) 7.5	Net Profit + Depr., Dep., Amort./Cur. Mat. L/T/D				(17) 7.6		
2.0	1.6	2.0						4.2	
.4	.3	.4		1.3	.4	.3	.4	.3	.5
.9	.8	1.1	Fixed/Worth	3.4	1.9	1.0	1.2	.8	.7
4.8	3.0	3.8		-8.4	-10.0	2.6	5.3	1.7	3.4
.5	.4	.5		.9	.8	.4	.4	.5	.6
1.1	1.1	1.3	Debt/Worth	3.7	2.2	.9	1.4	1.0	1.4
8.3	6.2	5.1		-8.9	-12.9	2.3	8.4	2.1	5.0
251.7	180.2	190.7		49.8	223.0	173.0	184.1	190.9	222.2
(256) 105.5	(241) 81.5	(251) 98.8	% Profit Before Taxes/Tangible Net Worth	(15) 12.6	(30) 43.6	(31) 71.9	(69) 87.5	(72) 137.7	(34) 119.8
38.3	23.9	36.2		1.6	15.7	20.6	38.6	76.0	41.0
103.1	84.3	81.4		8.3	64.2	83.4	72.2	113.8	95.0
34.8	24.7	29.3	% Profit Before Taxes/Total Assets	2.3	10.6	19.7	35.5	64.7	25.3
9.4	4.6	6.7			-1.6	5.6	8.9	25.6	10.6
22.7	34.0	19.9		16.6	15.3	27.7	21.6	24.9	19.9
8.1	8.9	6.9	Sales/Net Fixed Assets	.5	5.2	9.5	6.8	7.5	10.3
3.4	3.7	2.9		.1	1.3	2.6	3.5	3.9	4.7
4.2	4.1	3.8		1.4	4.6	4.6	3.8	3.9	3.3
2.5	2.4	2.2	Sales/Total Assets	.2	1.5	2.9	2.3	2.3	2.2
1.3	1.1	1.2		.1	.7	1.3	1.3	1.5	1.4
1.7	1.4	1.9		4.0	1.1	1.3	2.1	2.1	1.5
(245) 3.3	(217) 2.9	(250) 3.3	% Depr., Dep., Amort./Sales	(18) 16.2	(27) 5.3	(27) 3.7	(73) 3.5	(70) 3.1	(35) 2.5
5.8	5.0	5.9		23.6	12.5	6.1	5.4	4.6	3.9
1.3	2.0	1.6							
(37) 6.0	(26) 4.8	(27) 5.1	% Officers', Directors' Owners' Comp/Sales						
26.0	14.1	14.6							
7330497M	7391484M	5255301M	Net Sales ($)	11815M	83107M	148568M	644751M	1221533M	3145527M
4394530M	4586803M	3232343M	Total Assets ($)	54639M	108653M	79302M	398592M	710814M	1880343M

© RMA 2019

M = $ thousand   MM = $ million
See Pages viii through xx for Explanation of Ratios and Data

Current Data Sorted by Assets | | | | | | | Comparative Historical Data

0-500M	500M-2MM	2-10MM	10-50MM	50-100MM	100-250MM	Type of Statement	4/1/14-3/31/15 ALL	4/1/15-3/31/16 ALL
1	1	20	32	16	7	Unqualified	90	87
		2	4	2		Reviewed	10	9
	1	7				Compiled	34	23
19	18	13	1	1		Tax Returns	48	54
21	24	43	30	6	7	Other	141	145
	73 (4/1-9/30/18)		203 (10/1/18-3/31/19)					
41	44	85	67	25	14	NUMBER OF STATEMENTS	323	318
%	%	%	%	%	%	**ASSETS**	%	%
41.3	28.5	17.5	19.1	25.4	10.7	Cash & Equivalents	21.6	21.7
3.5	17.2	14.8	20.9	14.9	9.9	Trade Receivables (net)	15.5	15.7
3.0	1.5	1.4	2.1	1.0	.2	Inventory	1.3	1.6
1.7	9.0	5.2	3.8	2.8	4.3	All Other Current	3.5	3.0
49.6	56.3	38.9	45.9	44.1	25.1	Total Current	41.9	42.0
27.2	31.0	43.4	39.8	38.1	34.8	Fixed Assets (net)	38.8	39.5
8.7	7.5	10.8	5.9	10.6	30.2	Intangibles (net)	8.6	8.3
14.4	5.2	6.9	8.4	7.2	9.9	All Other Non-Current	10.7	10.2
100.0	100.0	100.0	100.0	100.0	100.0	Total	100.0	100.0
						LIABILITIES		
15.1	11.0	4.4	3.6	.1	.8	Notes Payable-Short Term	6.2	7.6
5.9	5.9	2.8	2.4	1.2	1.9	Cur. Mat.-L.T.D.	4.8	3.8
8.7	5.9	6.1	6.9	6.0	5.0	Trade Payables	7.9	6.0
.0	.0	.1	.0	.0	.0	Income Taxes Payable	.1	.0
39.8	13.7	10.3	12.3	11.6	6.2	All Other Current	11.9	13.0
69.5	36.5	23.8	25.1	18.9	13.9	Total Current	31.0	30.4
24.0	44.1	25.0	19.3	20.6	30.3	Long-Term Debt	25.7	24.6
.0	.0	.0	.0	.0	.5	Deferred Taxes	.1	.0
4.9	7.0	3.6	2.7	6.9	5.6	All Other Non-Current	7.6	4.0
1.6	12.4	47.6	52.9	53.5	49.8	Net Worth	35.7	40.9
100.0	100.0	100.0	100.0	100.0	100.0	Total Liabilties & Net Worth	100.0	100.0
						INCOME DATA		
100.0	100.0	100.0	100.0	100.0	100.0	Net Sales	100.0	100.0
						Gross Profit		
88.7	85.2	85.6	93.6	94.5	96.9	Operating Expenses	86.9	86.1
11.3	14.8	14.4	6.4	5.5	3.1	Operating Profit	13.1	13.9
.1	2.3	2.1	1.1	-.3	3.8	All Other Expenses (net)	1.5	1.8
11.2	12.4	12.4	5.4	5.8	-.7	Profit Before Taxes	11.6	12.1
						RATIOS		
6.5	4.4	3.1	3.9	5.4	2.3		3.6	3.6
1.6	1.9	1.7	2.1	3.3	1.9	Current	2.0	1.8
.4	.8	.9	1.4	1.8	1.3		1.0	1.0
4.7	3.9	2.7	3.5	4.9	2.1		3.2	3.1
1.6	1.8	1.5	1.8	3.0	1.4	Quick	1.6 (317)	1.6
.3	.5	.5	1.2	1.6	1.1		.9	.8
0 UND	0 UND	0 UND	23 16.0	24 15.4	23 15.8		0 UND	0 UND
0 UND	0 UND	18 19.9	37 9.9	40 9.1	36 10.0	Sales/Receivables	28 13.0	27 13.3
0 UND	47 7.8	38 9.6	56 6.5	51 7.1	59 6.2		47 7.7	47 7.7
						Cost of Sales/Inventory		
						Cost of Sales/Payables		
12.2	7.6	6.4	3.7	2.9	7.1		5.8	5.5
60.0	19.4	16.6	8.0	4.2	13.8	Sales/Working Capital	13.3	13.3
-24.8	-72.1	-114.9	19.9	9.7	22.5		UND	-539.4
29.8	106.1	49.6	26.2	42.3	6.7		35.0	51.6
(18) 12.8	(30) 11.7	(65) 11.6	(60) 7.9	(18) 4.8	(12) 1.6	EBIT/Interest	(243) 6.6	(257) 10.9
-1.5	.7	2.2	.9	.5	-.7		1.6	2.0
							5.2	8.5
						Net Profit + Depr., Dep., Amort./Cur. Mat. L/T/D	(22) 3.2	(21) 4.2
							1.7	1.1
.0	.2	.4	.4	.4	.9		.4	.4
.6	.7	.9	.9	.7	1.4	Fixed/Worth	1.1	.9
UND	-6.0	3.0	1.4	1.2	-.4		2.9	3.1
.2	.3	.4	.4	.3	.9		.4	.3
1.2	1.0	1.2	.8	.6	1.5	Debt/Worth	1.2	1.2
-6.1	-7.3	4.1	1.7	1.9	-1.6		13.2	5.6
435.7	126.4	132.0	35.8	21.3	16.0		100.0	108.2
(28) 95.9	(30) 58.4	(70) 30.7	(62) 9.0	(22) 6.3	(10) 6.4	% Profit Before Taxes/Tangible Net Worth	(257) 25.0	(261) 25.8
8.1	21.2	6.4	.3	-1.6	-.6		3.7	6.0
109.0	68.4	51.6	17.6	11.9	5.1		38.6	41.6
20.5	23.3	14.2	4.2	3.6	2.5	% Profit Before Taxes/Total Assets	9.9	11.7
-3.7	.9	2.6	-.7	-1.2	-2.3		.8	1.8
999.8	73.8	15.4	8.6	8.9	8.5		18.2	20.6
46.6	19.0	5.4	3.6	2.3	3.3	Sales/Net Fixed Assets	5.6	6.2
12.1	6.0	2.4	2.1	1.5	2.1		2.3	2.3
13.8	5.5	3.2	2.2	1.9	1.4		3.3	3.6
6.3	3.8	2.0	1.6	1.1	.9	Sales/Total Assets	1.8	1.9
4.1	2.4	1.2	1.0	.8	.6		1.0	1.0
.3	.4	1.6	1.6	1.5			1.6	1.3
(20) 1.4	(24) 1.0	(73) 2.8	(61) 2.7	(23) 2.5		% Depr., Dep., Amort./Sales	(252) 2.8	(255) 2.7
3.4	3.1	5.2	3.7	6.3			5.1	4.7
3.6	1.2	.8					2.5	2.5
(13) 8.6	(12) 3.7	(13) 5.8				% Officers', Directors' Owners' Comp/Sales	(57) 6.7	(57) 7.0
11.8	7.6	13.4					14.8	14.8
72912M	218504M	897252M	2955518M	2826951M	2237130M	Net Sales ($)	8622006M	8191320M
9467M	44576M	420979M	1697536M	1723151M	2283168M	Total Assets ($)	6482558M	6233904M

M = $ thousand   MM = $ million
See Pages viii through xx for Explanation of Ratios and Data

Comparative Historical Data | Current Data Sorted by Sales

Type of Statement									
	70	75	77	Unqualified	1	2		15	18	41
	7	4	0	Reviewed		1			3	4
	16	7	8	Compiled	2	2	1		3	1
	44	40	52	Tax Returns	7	17	10	10	6	1
	130	143	131	Other	11	21	13	23	26	37

	4/1/16-3/31/17 ALL	4/1/17-3/31/18 ALL	4/1/18-3/31/19 ALL	73 (4/1-9/30/18) 0-1MM	1-3MM	3-5MM	203 (10/1/18-3/31/19) 5-10MM	10-25MM	25MM & OVER
NUMBER OF STATEMENTS	267	269	276	21	43	24	48	55	85
ASSETS	%	%	%	%	%	%	%	%	%
Cash & Equivalents	24.6	24.4	23.5	22.7	30.4	32.2	25.5	20.0	19.0
Trade Receivables (net)	15.5	16.0	14.8	3.3	9.5	16.9	11.5	15.6	20.9
Inventory	1.4	1.6	1.7	2.0	1.8	2.5	1.5	1.7	1.5
All Other Current	2.6	3.9	4.7	3.3	3.8	8.9	6.5	3.2	4.3
Total Current	44.0	45.9	44.7	31.2	45.5	60.5	45.0	40.6	45.8
Fixed Assets (net)	36.5	37.4	37.2	54.8	29.3	23.2	40.8	43.4	34.8
Intangibles (net)	9.9	7.9	9.7	4.6	12.5	6.0	9.6	9.0	11.2
All Other Non-Current	9.5	8.8	8.3	9.2	12.7	10.3	4.6	6.9	8.2
Total	100.0	100.0	100.0	100.0	100.0	100.0	100.0	100.0	100.0
LIABILITIES									
Notes Payable-Short Term	6.8	5.9	6.3	15.6	10.2	7.0	4.9	5.6	3.0
Cur. Mat.-L.T.D.	4.3	5.0	3.5	1.8	2.7	8.5	3.1	5.2	1.9
Trade Payables	5.5	5.8	6.6	11.9	3.2	9.0	5.8	5.6	7.4
Income Taxes Payable	.0	.1	.0	.0	.0	.0	.0	.2	.0
All Other Current	14.0	15.3	15.6	16.0	31.3	13.8	12.8	7.8	14.8
Total Current	30.7	32.2	32.0	45.3	47.4	38.3	26.6	24.4	27.0
Long-Term Debt	25.3	24.5	26.4	39.0	41.3	26.0	18.4	27.3	19.7
Deferred Taxes	.0	.1	.0	.0	.0	.0	.0	.0	.1
All Other Non-Current	6.2	7.4	4.5	12.2	1.5	13.8	2.4	3.4	3.4
Net Worth	37.7	35.8	37.1	3.3	9.8	21.9	52.6	44.9	49.8
Total Liabilities & Net Worth	100.0	100.0	100.0	100.0	100.0	100.0	100.0	100.0	100.0
INCOME DATA									
Net Sales	100.0	100.0	100.0	100.0	100.0	100.0	100.0	100.0	100.0
Gross Profit									
Operating Expenses	88.3	89.8	89.3	75.1	89.7	86.6	90.4	87.1	94.2
Operating Profit	11.7	10.2	10.7	24.9	10.3	13.4	9.6	12.9	5.8
All Other Expenses (net)	1.1	1.3	1.4	10.8	1.7	-.1	.2	.6	.7
Profit Before Taxes	10.6	8.9	9.2	14.1	8.6	13.5	9.4	12.3	5.1
RATIOS									
Current	3.7	3.5	4.0	4.7	5.7	7.0	3.2	4.4	3.3
	2.0	1.8	1.9	.5	1.9	2.5	1.8	2.1	1.9
	1.1	1.0	1.1	.2	.5	.6	1.1	1.4	1.3
Quick	3.4	3.1	3.6	4.5	4.3	6.2	2.7	3.8	2.9
	1.9	(268) 1.5	1.7	.4	1.9	1.8	1.5	2.0	1.7
	1.0	.8	.9	.2	.4	.6	.9	1.1	1.2
Sales/Receivables	0 UND	0 UND	0 UND	0 UND	0 UND	0 UND	0 UND	16 22.7	22 16.4
	27 13.6	25 14.8	23 16.0	0 UND	0 UND	0 UND	16 23.5	30 12.2	39 9.4
	50 7.3	43 8.4	46 8.0	0 UND	12 31.1	41 8.8	30 12.2	44 8.3	56 6.5
Cost of Sales/Inventory									
Cost of Sales/Payables									
Sales/Working Capital	5.3	5.4	5.3	17.5	9.7	5.5	5.4	3.9	4.5
	11.9	13.9	13.8	-10.5	30.5	9.4	19.4	11.3	9.7
	117.0	382.1	125.6	-2.3	-20.8	-54.7	111.0	26.0	22.5
EBIT/Interest	45.5	27.5	41.9		27.3	72.5	62.6	48.1	20.8
	(213) 10.1	(208) 8.1	(203) 8.4	(27) 5.8	(17) 24.9	(36) 16.0	(45) 14.9	(71) 6.4	
	1.7	1.3	.9		-2.8	2.3	3.8	1.8	.4
Net Profit + Depr., Dep., Amort./Cur. Mat. L/T/D	8.1	7.3	29.2						
	(18) 5.0	(14) 4.4	(20) 11.8						
	1.5	2.1	3.7						
Fixed/Worth	.4	.4	.3	.3	.2	.1	.3	.4	.5
	.8	.0	.9	8.0	.8	.5	.8	.9	.9
	2.3	2.9	2.6	-3.6	-3.3	-.8	1.8	1.8	1.4
Debt/Worth	.4	.4	.4	.2	.3	.1	.3	.3	.6
	1.1	1.1	1.0	15.0	1.5	.9	.9	.9	.8
	5.7	5.8	4.8	-3.7	-9.5	-4.2	2.7	2.2	2.2
% Profit Before Taxes/Tangible Net Worth	69.8	60.6	91.3	222.7	183.8	119.5	130.5	87.0	34.7
	(216) 17.7	(221) 16.2	(222) 18.0	(11) 42.9	(31) 52.1	(16) 67.7	(43) 23.5	(47) 25.1	(74) 8.5
	5.4	2.4	3.4	11.1	-3.8	19.7	5.6	3.0	.9
% Profit Before Taxes/Total Assets	35.9	27.2	34.5	61.4	90.9	60.1	49.1	53.1	13.7
	8.9	7.1	8.7	9.5	10.9	27.4	9.5	12.8	4.1
	1.5	.3	.0	-1.7	-4.5	14.0	4.0	1.0	-1.2
Sales/Net Fixed Assets	26.6	24.4	25.7	15.6	142.7	109.1	19.6	7.0	15.8
	6.7	6.1	6.4	2.9	18.2	30.9	7.2	3.6	5.2
	2.4	2.3	2.6	.2	6.3	12.4	3.0	2.1	2.4
Sales/Total Assets	3.6	3.6	3.9	3.7	6.8	5.8	3.8	3.2	2.7
	1.8	2.0	2.1	1.1	4.2	4.0	2.2	1.5	1.7
	1.0	1.1	1.1	.2	2.0	2.0	1.3	1.1	1.0
% Depr., Dep., Amort./Sales	1.4	1.4	1.4	2.2	.3	.2	1.8	1.7	1.4
	(205) 2.5	(219) 2.7	(210) 2.4	(12) 3.7	(21) 3.2	(16) .5	(39) 3.0	(50) 2.5	(72) 2.4
	4.0	3.7	3.9	24.4	8.1	1.7	4.2	5.9	3.2
% Officers', Directors' Owners' Comp/Sales	4.0	3.2	2.4		4.9				
	(43) 7.2	(45) 8.4	(47) 5.8	(11) 8.0					
	12.8	13.5	10.7		11.4				
Net Sales ($)	8505565M	10413685M	9208267M	10097M	82360M	95131M	359461M	898946M	7762272M
Total Assets ($)	5923583M	7121512M	6178877M	22268M	58709M	34181M	203918M	744670M	5115131M

© RMA 2019

M = $ thousand   MM = $ million
See Pages viii through xx for Explanation of Ratios and Data

Current Data Sorted by Assets   Comparative Historical Data

0-500M	500M-2MM	2-10MM	10-50MM	50-100MM	100-250MM	Type of Statement	4/1/14-3/31/15 ALL	4/1/15-3/31/16 ALL
1	1	2	8	3	5	Unqualified	21	26
1		1	5			Reviewed	11	7
	2	3	1			Compiled	31	19
10	9	3	2			Tax Returns	51	40
10	15	20	16	4	4	Other	100	131
	15 (4/1-9/30/18)		111 (10/1/18-3/31/19)					
22	27	29	32	7	9	NUMBER OF STATEMENTS	214	223
%	%	%	%	%	%	ASSETS	%	%
46.7	25.7	17.8	14.0			Cash & Equivalents	22.5	25.3
5.6	23.7	26.6	37.7			Trade Receivables (net)	21.7	22.7
1.0	.2	4.6	4.3			Inventory	2.4	2.4
4.5	5.7	3.5	3.0			All Other Current	3.1	3.5
57.7	55.2	52.6	59.0			Total Current	49.7	53.9
28.1	24.3	26.4	23.0			Fixed Assets (net)	29.2	28.3
5.2	4.2	16.5	9.7			Intangibles (net)	11.0	8.3
9.0	16.3	4.5	8.3			All Other Non-Current	10.1	9.5
100.0	100.0	100.0	100.0			Total	100.0	100.0
						LIABILITIES		
38.8	19.9	3.2	4.4			Notes Payable-Short Term	8.1	7.4
2.4	5.9	3.0	10.9			Cur. Mat.-L.T.D.	5.8	4.6
4.0	16.3	7.8	11.4			Trade Payables	7.0	7.1
.0	.0	.0	.2			Income Taxes Payable	.3	.2
66.0	18.1	12.8	19.7			All Other Current	13.9	19.4
111.3	60.1	26.7	46.7			Total Current	35.1	38.8
31.0	35.2	19.7	20.0			Long-Term Debt	23.1	18.9
.0	1.1	.0	.4			Deferred Taxes	.3	.3
13.9	10.1	13.3	5.5			All Other Non-Current	4.9	7.5
-56.1	-6.5	40.3	27.4			Net Worth	36.7	34.5
100.0	100.0	100.0	100.0			Total Liabilities & Net Worth	100.0	100.0
						INCOME DATA		
100.0	100.0	100.0	100.0			Net Sales	100.0	100.0
						Gross Profit		
91.2	85.5	84.6	91.9			Operating Expenses	86.0	86.3
8.8	14.5	15.4	8.1			Operating Profit	14.0	13.7
.2	.8	2.8	3.3			All Other Expenses (net)	1.6	1.8
8.6	13.7	12.6	4.8			Profit Before Taxes	12.4	11.9
						RATIOS		
2.2	2.5	5.5	3.0				3.4	3.8
1.0	1.3	2.5	1.5			Current	1.7	2.0
.3	.3	1.6	.7				.7	.9
2.1	2.4	5.1	2.6				2.8	3.4
.9	1.3	2.2	1.3			Quick	1.5	1.5
.2	.3	.8	.6				.6	.7
0 UND	0 UND	0	844.3	41	8.8		0 UND	0 UND
0 UND	0 UND	39	9.4	55	6.6	Sales/Receivables	28 13.0	32 11.4
0 UND	42 8.7	79	4.6	83	4.4		58 6.3	54 6.7
						Cost of Sales/Inventory		
						Cost of Sales/Payables		
33.0	4.4	4.3	3.9				6.0	5.1
-746.6	77.0	7.5	14.7			Sales/Working Capital	15.7	22.0
-17.0	-5.0	21.5	-11.0				-47.3	-99.1
32.6	131.3	103.4	19.3				57.1	51.5
(10) 9.7	(20) 18.5	(21) 34.8	(30) 4.0			EBIT/Interest	(163) 10.6	(159) 12.0
-7.3	.9	5.4	-.2				1.9	1.4
						Net Profit + Depr., Dep.,	10.4	14.2
						Amort./Cur. Mat. L/T/D	(27) 3.3	(23) 5.3
							2.1	2.0
.2	.1	.2	.4				.2	.2
7.7	.4	.8	1.2			Fixed/Worth	.6	.7
-.9	-.6	4.6	-2.5				6.1	4.9
.7	.5	.5	.7				.5	.4
NM	2.8	1.5	6.2			Debt/Worth	1.5	1.2
-1.9	-2.3	5.4	-13.3				UND	14.6
999.8	320.8	197.9	62.9			% Profit Before Taxes/Tangible	132.2	149.1
(11) 78.4	(16) 54.0	(24) 52.3	(21) 20.5			Net Worth	(162) 47.9	(181) 48.9
10.5	25.1	24.9	-9.6				14.2	14.3
85.8	102.1	35.2	23.1			% Profit Before Taxes/Total	57.4	58.3
26.2	19.4	21.9	10.3			Assets	16.3	17.4
-8.6	4.9	10.5	-3.4				1.4	2.3
651.6	85.2	26.8	26.8				50.7	57.5
110.8	22.1	10.6	11.9			Sales/Net Fixed Assets	11.3	13.9
14.3	14.0	5.4	5.3				5.1	5.7
30.8	4.8	2.7	2.9				5.0	5.2
10.7	3.3	2.0	2.1			Sales/Total Assets	2.6	2.9
6.5	2.2	1.4	1.4				1.5	1.5
	.5	1.1	.8				1.0	1.3
	(14) 3.0	(21) 2.6	(27) 1.8			% Depr., Dep., Amort./Sales	(146) 2.8	(142) 2.6
	6.1	3.4	4.9				5.2	5.3
	3.5						3.7	2.3
	(11) 4.7					% Officers', Directors'	(59) 8.1	(56) 7.4
	10.8					Owners' Comp/Sales	15.5	11.1
89874M	121100M	378450M	1468603M	953245M	1737857M	Net Sales ($)	7135119M	6714169M
5433M	28749M	159570M	678524M	484955M	1590902M	Total Assets ($)	4723107M	4392044M

M = $ thousand   MM = $ million

See Pages viii through xx for Explanation of Ratios and Data

Comparative Historical Data / Current Data Sorted by Sales

Current data periods: 0-1MM & 1-3MM = 15 (4/1-9/30/18); 3-5MM through 25MM & OVER = 111 (10/1/18-3/31/19)

4/1/16-3/31/17 ALL	4/1/17-3/31/18 ALL	4/1/18-3/31/19 ALL		0-1MM	1-3MM	3-5MM	5-10MM	10-25MM	25MM & OVER
			Type of Statement						
17	18	20	Unqualified		2			2	16
6	9	7	Reviewed		1		2	1	4
15	14	6	Compiled				2	1	2
28	27	24	Tax Returns	3	8	4	6	2	1
89	82	69	Other	4	7	13	8	18	19
155	150	126	**NUMBER OF STATEMENTS**	7	18	17	18	24	42
%	%	%	**ASSETS**	%	%	%	%	%	%
17.8	20.7	23.5	Cash & Equivalents		19.9	29.8	36.4	19.7	18.3
27.9	25.1	24.0	Trade Receivables (net)		29.9	8.4	21.4	25.6	32.1
2.4	3.0	3.0	Inventory		1.1	.0	2.5	4.2	4.7
4.4	4.2	4.2	All Other Current		.9	12.6	1.1	3.9	4.5
52.5	53.1	54.8	Total Current		51.8	50.8	61.3	53.3	59.6
27.1	26.0	24.6	Fixed Assets (net)		27.5	21.7	26.5	22.9	19.9
10.7	12.3	11.3	Intangibles (net)		7.7	5.8	10.4	17.1	14.0
9.7	8.6	9.2	All Other Non-Current		13.0	21.6	1.7	6.6	6.5
100.0	100.0	100.0	Total		100.0	100.0	100.0	100.0	100.0
			LIABILITIES						
8.7	5.4	13.2	Notes Payable-Short Term		33.1	30.0	12.5	3.9	3.5
5.3	4.2	5.3	Cur. Mat.-L.T.D.		5.2	4.5	4.1	2.0	9.0
8.5	9.8	9.6	Trade Payables		19.5	4.4	7.9	7.0	11.3
.2	.1	.1	Income Taxes Payable		.0	.0	.0	.2	.3
15.1	19.4	25.7	All Other Current		29.4	30.2	25.8	27.6	18.6
37.7	38.9	54.0	Total Current		87.1	69.1	50.3	40.7	42.6
25.3	21.7	25.2	Long-Term Debt		36.1	23.3	16.0	10.9	22.4
.2	.3	.4	Deferred Taxes		.0	.0	.0	1.4	.3
11.1	5.4	9.5	All Other Non-Current		21.5	11.3	20.0	2.0	5.1
25.6	33.7	10.9	Net Worth		-44.7	-3.7	13.6	44.9	29.5
100.0	100.0	100.0	Total Liabilties & Net Worth		100.0	100.0	100.0	100.0	100.0
			INCOME DATA						
100.0	100.0	100.0	Net Sales		100.0	100.0	100.0	100.0	100.0
			Gross Profit						
87.4	87.4	88.4	Operating Expenses		100.6	75.3	91.1	88.2	88.7
12.6	12.6	11.6	Operating Profit		-.6	24.7	8.9	11.8	11.3
2.8	1.5	2.0	All Other Expenses (net)		1.1	.4	3.0	1.3	2.3
9.8	11.1	9.7	Profit Before Taxes		-1.7	24.3	5.9	10.4	9.0
			RATIOS						
3.3	3.5	3.0	Current		4.9	2.0	2.5	3.8	2.7
1.6	1.7	1.7			1.3	.9	1.9	2.3	2.0
.9	.8	.7			.3	.4	.9	.6	1.0
2.7	3.3	2.6	Quick		4.9	1.5	2.5	3.6	2.5
1.4	1.3	1.4			1.3	.9	1.3	1.9	1.7
.7	.7	.5			.2	.1	.7	.7	.7
4 89.1	0 UND	0 UND	Sales/Receivables		0 UND	0 UND	1 525.4	38 9.7	
41 9.0	38 9.5	38 9.7			14 26.2	0 UND	12 29.3	45 8.2	47 7.7
59 6.2	63 5.9	58 6.3			65 5.6	1 683.6	46 8.0	85 4.3	66 5.5
			Cost of Sales/Inventory						
			Cost of Sales/Payables						
6.1	5.1	4.7	Sales/Working Capital		4.0	15.0	6.9	4.0	5.6
18.4	13.2	16.0			75.8	-493.4	29.7	6.4	11.6
-66.8	-166.5	-19.8			-4.4	-7.1	-165.9	-26.1	-769.9
47.3	38.6	73.2	EBIT/Interest		18.0	131.4	49.5	145.0	41.3
(117) 8.9	(109) 5.7	(93) 8.8			(11) .0	(12) 40.1	(13) 9.7	(18) 29.0	(37) 6.5
1.2	.1	.1			-15.2	8.7	3.6	-6.6	.7
5.4	27.7	7.0	Net Profit + Depr., Dep., Amort./Cur. Mat. L/T/D						
(15) 3.3	(15) 4.5	(15) 3.0							
1.6	1.0	.6							
.2	.2	.2	Fixed/Worth		.2	.1	.2	.2	.3
.7	.7	.9			1.3	2.3	1.0	.7	.9
-10.7	UND	-1.7			-.8	-.5	-1.8	2.5	-1.6
.4	.4	.6	Debt/Worth		.3	1.0	.7	.3	.6
1.5	1.3	2.6			NM	12.3	2.7	1.1	2.0
-34.8	-40.2	-6.2			-1.6	-2.4	-6.4	12.1	-11.2
107.1	106.3	117.2	% Profit Before Taxes/Tangible Net Worth			996.6	154.8	93.9	124.2
(111) 38.4	(111) 33.2	(84) 41.6				(10) 332.1	(13) 33.6	(20) 36.1	(28) 44.4
9.1	1.8	16.1				71.5	13.4	-1.7	13.2
40.7	37.3	37.9	% Profit Before Taxes/Total Assets		21.0	181.3	25.6	44.2	32.1
11.8	10.7	17.1			5.8	74.4	11.8	21.4	13.8
.4	.0	.9			-24.6	19.6	4.0	-.4	
41.9	42.9	49.1	Sales/Net Fixed Assets		112.1	49.1	195.1	34.3	30.7
12.6	12.4	16.8			15.6	30.3	19.2	12.9	13.1
5.0	5.1	7.3			4.8	18.4	7.4	5.6	6.7
4.3	4.3	5.0	Sales/Total Assets		6.8	7.5	24.6	2.6	3.3
2.2	2.1	2.5			2.3	3.6	3.5	1.9	2.3
1.5	1.1	1.5			1.3	2.5	1.7	1.3	1.5
1.1	1.0	.9	% Depr., Dep., Amort./Sales		.9		.2	.9	.8
(100) 2.4	(94) 2.6	(84) 2.1			(10) 1.8		(15) 1.8	(16) 2.6	(35) 1.7
5.0	6.2	4.8			13.2		3.2	7.2	4.4
2.4	3.3	3.3	% Officers', Directors', Owners' Comp/Sales		3.5				
(36) 9.2	(29) 6.3	(34) 4.8			(11) 6.0				
16.5	14.0	12.7			8.2				
6065869M	4344845M	4749129M	Net Sales ($)	5538M	32385M	68912M	124967M	403593M	4113734M
4616298M	3863540M	2948133M	Total Assets ($)	6838M	17584M	19248M	45077M	284283M	2575103M

Current Data Sorted by Assets | Comparative Historical Data

0-500M	500M-2MM	2-10MM	10-50MM	50-100MM	100-250MM	Type of Statement	ALL 4/1/14-3/31/15	ALL 4/1/15-3/31/16
	1	3	7	3	3	Unqualified	20	11
	3	4	8			Reviewed	14	29
1	11	7	3			Compiled	28	25
3	18	7	2			Tax Returns	47	63
6	19	39	41	7	4	Other	149	143
	23 (4/1-9/30/18)		177 (10/1/18-3/31/19)					
10	52	60	61	10	7	NUMBER OF STATEMENTS	258	271
%	%	%	%	%	%	**ASSETS**	%	%
25.1	29.8	18.2	11.9	11.0		Cash & Equivalents	17.5	18.4
12.5	10.1	18.6	20.8	18.0		Trade Receivables (net)	15.5	15.4
.4	1.0	.2	.1	.3		Inventory	.5	.5
.2	6.4	3.8	2.7	1.0		All Other Current	5.1	2.8
38.2	47.4	40.8	35.5	30.2		Total Current	38.5	37.1
47.4	42.9	41.9	39.9	23.8		Fixed Assets (net)	41.5	44.0
9.2	5.4	9.6	13.4	41.8		Intangibles (net)	8.6	10.8
5.3	4.3	7.7	11.2	4.1		All Other Non-Current	11.4	8.2
100.0	100.0	100.0	100.0	100.0		Total	100.0	100.0
						LIABILITIES		
45.9	14.5	6.5	3.3	2.4		Notes Payable-Short Term	8.4	11.0
3.9	7.7	7.2	6.6	7.8		Cur. Mat.-L.T.D.	8.0	7.1
11.0	3.4	3.0	4.0	4.3		Trade Payables	5.3	6.4
.0	.0	.3	.0	.1		Income Taxes Payable	.2	.2
36.9	23.4	17.4	10.8	4.7		All Other Current	13.9	13.3
97.7	49.0	34.4	24.7	19.3		Total Current	35.7	38.0
19.6	26.3	25.8	24.4	42.4		Long-Term Debt	29.5	30.6
.0	.2	.1	.7	1.4		Deferred Taxes	.2	.1
.0	10.1	4.5	4.6	.7		All Other Non-Current	7.2	4.7
-17.3	14.4	35.2	45.7	36.2		Net Worth	27.4	26.6
100.0	100.0	100.0	100.0	100.0		Total Liabilities & Net Worth	100.0	100.0
						INCOME DATA		
100.0	100.0	100.0	100.0	100.0		Net Sales	100.0	100.0
						Gross Profit		
94.7	85.7	80.2	82.1	84.1		Operating Expenses	83.1	84.0
5.3	14.3	19.8	17.9	15.9		Operating Profit	16.9	16.0
-.7	1.0	1.3	1.2	4.2		All Other Expenses (net)	1.6	2.2
6.0	13.3	18.4	16.7	11.7		Profit Before Taxes	15.3	13.8
						RATIOS		
1.6	3.9	3.3	2.6	2.5			2.7	2.5
.6	1.2	1.3	1.4	1.4		Current	1.4	1.3
.2	.3	.6	.9	1.0			.7	.6
1.6	3.3	3.0	2.5	2.4			2.1	2.3
.6	1.0	1.0	1.4	1.4		Quick	1.2	1.2
.2	.2	.3	.8	1.0			.5	.5
0 UND	0 UND	0 UND	22 16.7	26 14.2			0 UND	0 UND
0 UND	0 UND	18 20.0	35 10.3	36 10.2		Sales/Receivables	21 17.4	10 35.8
7 52.2	30 12.0	47 7.7	58 6.3	62 5.9			47 7.7	51 7.2
						Cost of Sales/Inventory		
						Cost of Sales/Payables		
UND	6.6	7.2	5.1	10.2			7.4	8.6
-37.0	67.0	42.9	17.1	14.2		Sales/Working Capital	26.9	28.0
-12.4	-18.2	-31.2	-131.8	326.4			-25.8	-32.4
	18.1	71.1	39.3	15.0			47.9	48.2
(40) 6.5	(49) 17.2	(56) 15.8	2.7			EBIT/Interest	(216) 10.7	(226) 10.0
	.0	2.1	3.3	.9			3.1	2.0
							9.9	7.6
						Net Profit + Depr., Dep., Amort./Cur. Mat. L/T/D	(25) 5.8	(24) 3.1
							1.1	1.4
.9	.4	.6	.5	.8			.5	.6
4.9	1.3	1.2	1.4	26.4		Fixed/Worth	1.3	1.5
-.3	UND	9.5	4.1	-.4			6.2	46.1
.8	.6	.6	.8	1.8			.6	.8
6.0	3.1	1.5	1.3	41.1		Debt/Worth	2.1	2.3
-1.8	-10.8	78.9	7.6	-2.2			21.5	-64.2
	127.9	124.4	137.4				142.2	149.4
	(38) 56.3	(46) 43.7	(56) 61.5			% Profit Before Taxes/Tangible Net Worth	(200) 53.7	(200) 59.1
	14.8	14.1	14.3				16.8	15.1
97.6	41.5	49.3	34.6	23.7			43.8	51.2
61.1	19.8	20.9	16.6	4.4		% Profit Before Taxes/Total Assets	15.2	16.5
-27.2	-.7	3.0	4.4	-.6			3.8	1.7
137.8	78.6	17.4	6.9	9.4			17.9	15.3
21.3	8.1	5.9	3.9	5.2		Sales/Net Fixed Assets	5.7	5.8
6.3	3.6	3.6	2.5	2.5			3.4	2.8
15.4	7.1	3.9	2.2	1.5			3.7	4.0
6.3	3.1	2.6	1.5	1.1		Sales/Total Assets	2.1	2.3
3.8	1.7	1.6	.8	.6			1.2	1.3
	2.1	3.1	3.5				2.8	2.7
	(35) 3.2	(42) 5.3	(54) 5.2			% Depr., Dep., Amort./Sales	(194) 5.3	(213) 5.2
	7.8	8.3	8.4				9.8	7.8
	3.3	3.7	12.5				3.1	3.1
	(13) 9.0	(12) 12.3	(13) 26.8			% Officers', Directors' Owners' Comp/Sales	(51) 10.4	(61) 17.1
	30.8	31.7	37.3				26.5	28.8
14042M	449106M	1118115M	2484461M	877356M	1012797M	Net Sales ($)	4358836M	5122414M
2328M	64569M	257731M	1393459M	807506M	1145423M	Total Assets ($)	2600444M	3053417M

© RMA 2019

M = $ thousand   MM = $ million
See Pages viii through xx for Explanation of Ratios and Data

Comparative Historical Data / Current Data Sorted by Sales

			Type of Statement	0-1MM	1-3MM	3-5MM	5-10MM	10-25MM	25MM & OVER
17	19	17	Unqualified					5	12
22	16	15	Reviewed		1	1	2	5	6
34	21	22	Compiled	3	4	4	2	5	3
40	29	30	Tax Returns	3	9	4	4	5	5
152	137	116	Other	6	11	10	26	25	38
4/1/16-3/31/17	4/1/17-3/31/18	4/1/18-3/31/19			23 (4/1-9/30/18)		177 (10/1/18-3/31/19)		
ALL	ALL	ALL							
265	222	200	NUMBER OF STATEMENTS	12	25	19	34	46	64
%	%	%	**ASSETS**	%	%	%	%	%	%
19.1	16.9	19.0	Cash & Equivalents	12.6	22.6	22.8	18.7	21.1	16.4
15.4	15.4	16.5	Trade Receivables (net)	3.1	11.9	17.7	18.6	19.8	17.0
.4	.2	.4	Inventory	.0	.8	2.1	.2	.1	.1
3.6	3.8	3.7	All Other Current	2.9	.9	4.9	9.4	1.8	3.0
38.5	36.3	39.7	Total Current	18.6	36.2	47.5	46.9	42.8	36.6
39.6	46.6	40.4	Fixed Assets (net)	73.0	48.1	40.7	32.7	39.1	36.2
12.5	10.6	12.2	Intangibles (net)	3.3	9.5	7.9	8.5	11.7	18.5
9.4	6.5	7.8	All Other Non-Current	5.1	6.2	3.9	11.9	6.4	8.8
100.0	100.0	100.0	Total	100.0	100.0	100.0	100.0	100.0	100.0
			LIABILITIES						
6.3	7.6	9.1	Notes Payable-Short Term	3.3	23.3	8.6	5.0	6.1	9.2
7.4	8.4	6.9	Cur. Mat.-L.T.D.	6.5	4.6	14.6	5.7	6.0	6.8
4.4	7.4	3.9	Trade Payables	1.1	6.2	7.2	2.9	3.3	3.4
.1	.1	.1	Income Taxes Payable	.0	.0	.0	.0	.0	.3
17.9	15.4	16.8	All Other Current	8.1	16.5	7.6	20.9	18.5	18.0
36.1	38.9	36.8	Total Current	19.0	50.6	38.1	34.5	34.0	37.7
30.5	32.0	26.6	Long-Term Debt	33.2	26.5	35.6	21.1	22.2	28.8
.2	.3	.3	Deferred Taxes	.0	.0	.0	.4	.0	.9
6.8	7.3	5.5	All Other Non-Current	.0	12.1	12.3	6.4	5.2	1.6
26.3	21.4	30.8	Net Worth	47.8	10.8	14.0	37.5	38.7	31.0
100.0	100.0	100.0	Total Liabilities & Net Worth	100.0	100.0	100.0	100.0	100.0	100.0
			INCOME DATA						
100.0	100.0	100.0	Net Sales	100.0	100.0	100.0	100.0	100.0	100.0
			Gross Profit						
82.9	82.3	83.3	Operating Expenses	56.8	88.6	82.6	80.7	83.8	87.3
17.1	17.7	16.7	Operating Profit	43.2	11.4	17.4	19.3	16.2	12.7
1.7	1.9	1.2	All Other Expenses (net)	6.9	1.7	1.0	.2	1.0	.8
15.4	15.7	15.5	Profit Before Taxes	36.3	9.8	16.4	19.1	15.2	11.9
			RATIOS						
2.4	2.3	3.2		1.4	3.4	3.9	5.1	3.2	1.7
1.2	1.2	1.4	Current	.8	1.5	1.1	2.6	1.3	1.4
.7	.6	.6		.2	.3	.4	1.2	.8	.8
2.1	1.9	2.8		1.3	3.1	3.4	4.0	3.2	1.6
1.0	1.1	1.2	Quick	.6	1.0	.9	2.0	1.1	1.2
.6	.5	.5		.1	.3	.4	.8	.7	.6
0 UND	0 UND	0 UND		0 UND	0 UND	0 UND	0 UND	0 UND	0 UND
22 16.8	17 21.9	27 13.4	Sales/Receivables	0 UND	0 UND	31 11.9	26 13.8	36 10.1	29 12.8
49 7.4	47 7.8	47 7.7		0 UND	9 40.9	51 7.2	54 6.7	53 6.9	49 7.5
			Cost of Sales/Inventory						
			Cost of Sales/Payables						
7.7	9.3	7.0		NM	5.5	3.7	4.9	7.2	12.0
50.5	56.0	24.4	Sales/Working Capital	-7.6	24.5	70.5	8.7	21.7	29.5
-27.7	-20.4	-31.2		-4.0	-28.6	-15.3	109.9	-27.8	-80.5
38.7	34.8	37.7			27.6	43.0	106.3	57.4	31.4
(225) 8.9	(190) 10.7	(169) 12.4	EBIT/Interest	(20) 6.9	(16) 15.5	(28) 17.7	(40) 15.2	(57) 12.7	
2.6	2.3	2.0		-.9	2.0	4.3	3.6	1.0	
11.4	7.0	17.3							
(23) 4.3	(24) 3.3	(20) 4.9	Net Profit + Depr., Dep., Amort./Cur. Mat. L/T/D						
1.6	1.7	2.0							
.5	.8	.6		1.2	.7	.6	.2	.7	.5
1.5	1.6	1.4	Fixed/Worth	1.9	1.7	2.8	.8	1.3	1.8
16.4	72.8	12.3		4.2	-2.6	-.7	1.4	4.3	-23.4
.8	.9	.7		.6	.5	.5	.3	.9	1.1
2.4	2.6	1.9	Debt/Worth	1.6	2.3	3.5	1.1	1.6	3.0
-50.3	-64.0	69.0		3.3	-4.5	-3.0	4.5	14.9	-16.2
134.8	134.3	137.7		47.4	86.2	181.2	123.3	172.4	145.1
(196) 49.1	(164) 55.5	(156) 58.8	% Profit Before Taxes/Tangible Net Worth	18.4 (17) 33.1	(11) 56.8	(31) 62.4	(41) 90.1	(44) 81.6	
15.1	16.9	15.8		7.8	-13.6	28.9	24.4	25.4	14.3
40.9	39.5	41.5		14.0	39.9	57.0	58.9	59.8	30.9
16.2	17.2	18.7	% Profit Before Taxes/Total Assets	7.8	5.8	37.4	27.5	22.9	14.5
3.1	2.9	2.5		2.7	-5.5	3.6	5.6	7.8	-.1
15.4	11.9	16.9		1.3	21.4	28.2	15.6	17.1	18.7
5.9	4.9	5.5	Sales/Net Fixed Assets	.3	4.2	6.1	6.2	5.5	5.9
3.2	2.7	3.0		.1	2.4	3.3	3.6	2.9	3.5
3.9	4.0	3.7		.5	5.0	3.8	3.1	4.1	4.4
2.1	2.1	2.1	Sales/Total Assets	.2	2.5	2.7	2.5	2.3	2.0
1.2	1.3	1.2		.1	1.1	1.7	1.1	1.3	1.2
2.3	2.3	2.7			2.1	2.4	2.2	3.2	2.5
(203) 4.4	(180) 4.6	(148) 5.1	% Depr., Dep., Amort./Sales	(17) 3.6	(16) 3.2	(23) 5.5	(36) 4.6	(47) 5.2	
7.9	8.6	8.5			10.8	8.2	8.5	7.8	9.2
4.4	3.8	3.4						4.4	8.1
(47) 14.9	(36) 16.4	(40) 14.6	% Officers', Directors' Owners' Comp/Sales					(11) 25.2	(15) 25.0
24.3	31.2	31.9						33.0	41.7
6829251M	5492885M	5955877M	Net Sales ($)	5609M	46476M	72386M	247940M	770500M	4812966M
3926069M	3287751M	3671016M	Total Assets ($)	20933M	50391M	31362M	247460M	421984M	2898886M

M = $ thousand   MM = $ million
See Pages viii through xx for Explanation of Ratios and Data

Current Data Sorted by Assets

Comparative Historical Data

						Type of Statement		
1	7	13	28	12	10	Unqualified	85	109
	1	5	5			Reviewed	30	23
2	9	9				Compiled	35	51
44	32	7	1	9	1	Tax Returns	131	133
58	58	60	35	9	11	Other	313	308
	59 (4/1-9/30/18)		359 (10/1/18-3/31/19)				4/1/14-3/31/15	4/1/15-3/31/16
							ALL	ALL
0-500M	500M-2MM	2-10MM	10-50MM	50-100MM	100-250MM	NUMBER OF STATEMENTS		
105	107	94	69	21	22		594	624
%	%	%	%	%	%	ASSETS	%	%
43.7	24.8	20.5	23.2	17.5	12.1	Cash & Equivalents	22.2	22.6
19.2	31.4	35.6	24.7	23.4	12.8	Trade Receivables (net)	29.0	31.1
.8	1.2	1.6	.6	2.7	1.1	Inventory	1.3	1.7
4.5	3.1	3.7	2.2	1.2	7.0	All Other Current	3.3	3.9
68.2	60.6	61.5	50.7	44.8	33.0	Total Current	55.8	59.2
12.0	13.4	14.6	17.0	18.6	16.7	Fixed Assets (net)	19.5	17.5
10.4	12.1	12.6	17.9	23.3	37.6	Intangibles (net)	11.2	11.8
9.4	13.9	11.4	14.3	13.2	12.7	All Other Non-Current	13.5	11.4
100.0	100.0	100.0	100.0	100.0	100.0	Total	100.0	100.0
						LIABILITIES		
18.8	9.5	10.6	4.5	1.7	1.2	Notes Payable-Short Term	9.7	10.6
4.0	3.4	2.1	3.5	5.3	1.3	Cur. Mat.-L.T.D.	2.8	2.9
4.9	4.6	8.5	6.0	8.1	6.6	Trade Payables	7.6	8.5
.1	.0	.3	.0	.0	.0	Income Taxes Payable	.2	.3
31.0	16.9	18.9	14.3	12.1	9.1	All Other Current	20.0	18.4
58.8	34.3	40.4	28.3	27.1	18.2	Total Current	40.4	40.7
15.2	20.0	15.6	16.5	20.5	35.0	Long-Term Debt	16.1	16.3
.0	.0	.2	.0	.3	.2	Deferred Taxes	.2	.2
9.1	4.5	6.7	3.1	2.8	2.9	All Other Non-Current	7.9	6.7
17.0	41.1	37.1	52.1	49.3	43.7	Net Worth	35.5	36.0
100.0	100.0	100.0	100.0	100.0	100.0	Total Liabilties & Net Worth	100.0	100.0
						INCOME DATA		
100.0	100.0	100.0	100.0	100.0	100.0	Net Sales	100.0	100.0
						Gross Profit		
94.3	92.1	91.3	96.1	94.5	98.2	Operating Expenses	92.7	92.7
5.7	7.9	8.7	3.9	5.5	1.8	Operating Profit	7.3	7.3
.7	.9	1.8	1.3	.3	2.8	All Other Expenses (net)	1.2	1.4
5.0	6.9	6.9	2.5	5.1	-1.0	Profit Before Taxes	6.1	5.9
						RATIOS		
9.4	4.9	3.6	3.5	3.2	3.3		3.5	3.7
2.3	1.6	1.9	2.1	1.6	2.1	Current	1.8	1.9
.6	.9	1.1	1.2	1.0	1.1		.9	1.0
8.3	4.9	3.4	3.2	3.2	3.0		3.3	3.5
2.1	1.4	1.7	2.0	1.6	1.9	Quick	1.6 (623)	1.7
.4	.8	.9	1.0	.8	.8		.8	.9
0 UND	0 UND	24 15.5	29 12.8	31 11.7	28 12.9		0 UND	5 76.2
0 UND	21 17.7	38 9.6	42 8.6	53 6.9	40 9.1	Sales/Receivables	35 10.3	36 10.0
26 13.8	49 7.4	52 7.0	53 6.9	73 5.0	52 7.0		55 6.6	54 6.8
						Cost of Sales/Inventory		
						Cost of Sales/Payables		
12.6	9.0	5.6	4.2	3.6	4.3		7.1	6.6
36.7	26.2	13.2	9.6	15.1	8.4	Sales/Working Capital	16.4	14.8
-47.5	-84.7	89.3	30.8	NM	77.9		-172.3	336.4
45.2	35.3	43.0	22.3	26.8	14.0		44.2	48.0
(50) 8.4	(66) 11.2	(72) 7.0	(54) 7.0	(19) 10.8	(19) 1.8	EBIT/Interest	(416) 9.8	(440) 10.4
-.8	2.5	.9	-1.0	1.3	-1.8		1.5	1.6
						Net Profit + Depr., Dep., Amort./Cur. Mat. L/T/D	10.5	11.3
							(37) 4.1	(32) 3.3
							.7	.9
.0	.0	.0	.1	.3	.5		.1	.1
.1	.1	.2	.3	.6	NM	Fixed/Worth	.4	.3
.9	5.0	2.2	.9	NM	-.1		2.9	2.3
.2	.4	.5	.3	.6	.5		.4	.4
1.3	1.6	1.2	.7	1.6	NM	Debt/Worth	1.4	1.2
-4.6	-40.8	-28.9	NM	NM	-1.8		21.2	24.3
244.8	129.7	70.7	49.4	45.3	77.2	% Profit Before Taxes/Tangible Net Worth	88.2	94.5
(69) 75.6	(79) 65.3	(70) 37.4	(52) 18.6	(16) 10.8	(11) 12.8		(455) 32.2	(481) 36.5
30.6	23.4	9.6	.4	1.6	-3.9		5.1	7.5
90.4	51.7	29.4	19.5	7.9	11.4	% Profit Before Taxes/Total Assets	35.2	36.5
34.3	28.1	13.7	4.3	6.0	1.4		10.8	12.7
-2.9	6.4	1.4	-3.7	.9	-5.1		.9	1.8
UND	576.5	369.6	124.3	40.2	54.5	Sales/Net Fixed Assets	232.8	256.3
355.0	164.9	68.1	17.3	10.6	13.4		50.8	63.1
83.7	35.2	21.2	4.3	3.5	3.8		9.0	14.0
15.2	6.7	4.9	2.8	2.6	1.5		6.0	6.4
7.7	4.5	3.0	1.8	1.2	1.1	Sales/Total Assets	3.1	3.4
4.0	3.2	1.6	.9	.8	.7		1.7	1.7
.2	.1	.3	.5	1.1	.5		.4	.3
(34) .4	(45) .5	(52) .9	(51) 1.3	(16) 2.3	(13) 1.3	% Depr., Dep., Amort./Sales	(356) 1.0	(381) .8
1.6	1.5	1.9	2.5	3.4	3.6		2.4	2.0
2.7	2.1	1.3				% Officers', Directors' Owners' Comp/Sales	2.7	2.1
(48) 5.5	(41) 4.6	(21) 2.5					(169) 4.5	(164) 4.3
7.9	7.7	5.4					8.7	8.0
193280M	586378M	1477768M	3089827M	2270754M	6342630M	Net Sales ($)	16083805M	17489156M
21351M	113737M	466108M	1602817M	1441121M	3096570M	Total Assets ($)	7848406M	8656633M

M = $ thousand   MM = $ million
See Pages viii through xx for Explanation of Ratios and Data

Comparative Historical Data | Current Data Sorted by Sales

			Type of Statement					
88	86	71	Unqualified		3	2	11	16	39
17	12	11	Reviewed			3	3	4	4
33	33	20	Compiled		4	4	7	3	2
95	108	85	Tax Returns	17	28	14	16	8	2
251	237	231	Other	27	42	31	29	42	60
4/1/16-	4/1/17-	4/1/18-			59 (4/1-9/30/18)		359 (10/1/18-3/31/19)		
3/31/17	3/31/18	3/31/19							
ALL	ALL	ALL		0-1MM	1-3MM	3-5MM	5-10MM	10-25MM	25MM & OVER
484	476	418	**NUMBER OF STATEMENTS**	44	77	51	66	73	107
%	%	%	**ASSETS**	%	%	%	%	%	%
20.3	25.8	27.3	Cash & Equivalents	37.2	39.1	21.5	25.2	26.5	19.2
29.6	28.1	26.8	Trade Receivables (net)	12.6	19.4	32.1	32.9	30.2	29.3
1.6	.8	1.2	Inventory	.6	.5	1.8	1.4	1.2	1.5
4.1	3.7	3.6	All Other Current	7.4	2.7	4.3	3.0	2.1	3.6
55.6	58.4	58.8	Total Current	57.8	61.8	59.7	62.4	60.1	53.6
18.8	17.7	14.3	Fixed Assets (net)	21.4	12.5	13.9	11.8	16.2	13.3
14.3	13.0	14.7	Intangibles (net)	14.9	12.7	13.6	11.8	9.8	21.5
11.3	10.9	12.2	All Other Non-Current	6.1	13.1	12.8	13.9	13.9	11.6
100.0	100.0	100.0	Total	100.0	100.0	100.0	100.0	100.0	100.0
			LIABILITIES						
9.4	11.6	10.4	Notes Payable-Short Term	23.8	11.0	10.9	10.5	8.3	5.6
3.5	3.0	3.2	Cur. Mat.-L.T.D.	3.3	2.4	6.6	4.0	1.5	3.0
8.5	6.5	6.1	Trade Payables	4.4	3.3	5.9	6.0	7.0	8.3
.3	.1	.1	Income Taxes Payable	.1	.0	.0	.4	.0	.1
16.7	18.6	19.8	All Other Current	42.0	18.2	18.3	20.0	15.1	15.7
38.4	39.8	39.6	Total Current	73.6	34.9	41.7	40.9	31.9	32.6
20.0	18.6	18.1	Long-Term Debt	20.1	21.1	19.8	16.6	11.0	20.0
.1	.1	.1	Deferred Taxes	.0	.0	.1	.1	.0	.2
9.9	8.0	5.8	All Other Non-Current	5.7	10.6	6.7	6.9	1.7	3.9
31.6	33.5	36.5	Net Worth	.6	33.4	31.8	35.6	55.4	43.4
100.0	100.0	100.0	Total Liabilities & Net Worth	100.0	100.0	100.0	100.0	100.0	100.0
			INCOME DATA						
100.0	100.0	100.0	Net Sales	100.0	100.0	100.0	100.0	100.0	100.0
			Gross Profit						
92.8	93.8	93.6	Operating Expenses	92.3	89.8	93.9	93.7	95.3	95.4
7.2	6.2	6.4	Operating Profit	7.7	10.2	6.1	6.3	4.7	4.6
1.2	.9	1.2	All Other Expenses (net)	3.8	1.1	.7	.6	.2	1.4
6.0	5.4	5.2	Profit Before Taxes	3.9	9.0	5.4	5.7	4.5	3.1
			RATIOS						
3.7	4.3	4.0		8.5	8.0	3.2	4.9	4.7	3.1
1.7	1.9	2.0	Current	1.0	2.5	1.7	1.7	2.4	2.0
.9	1.0	1.0		.3	.9	1.0	1.0	1.1	1.1
3.3	3.9	3.8		6.8	7.5	2.9	4.9	4.4	2.8
1.5	1.7	1.8	Quick	.7	2.3	1.4	1.6	2.3	2.0
.8	.9	.8		.3	.8	.8	.9	1.1	1.0

6	60.0	0	UND	0	UND		Sales/Receivables	0	UND	0	UND	0	UND	0	UND	26	13.9	28	13.2
35	10.5	31	11.8	31	11.9			0	UND	0	UND	21	17.1	29	12.6	38	9.5	41	8.9
55	6.6	51	7.1	49	7.5			29	12.4	33	11.2	57	6.4	52	7.0	46	7.9	54	6.8

			Cost of Sales/Inventory						

			Cost of Sales/Payables						

6.6	6.5	6.6	Sales/Working Capital	11.1	6.6	12.7	8.6	4.5	5.5
18.3	16.2	17.0		NM	17.4	29.0	23.2	12.1	13.3
-105.9	500.1	-295.4		-5.7	-544.3	136.0	-143.3	92.6	61.5

	31.3		34.7		31.1		EBIT/Interest		18.2		43.3		17.0		92.0		27.8		37.4
(354)	8.3	(335)	8.4	(280)	7.4			(19)	.2	(36)	4.3	(31)	8.5	(47)	14.3	(56)	10.3	(91)	8.1
	1.3		1.7		.6				-4.7		.1		2.1		3.4		.3		1.1
	9.2		6.2		11.8		Net Profit + Depr., Dep.,												80.3
(27)	5.7	(28)	4.2	(20)	3.5	Amort./Cur. Mat. L/T/D											(13)	4.7
	1.0		2.1		.9														1.3
	.0		.0		.0		Fixed/Worth		.0		.0		.0		.0		.1		.1
	.4		.4		.2				.1		.1		.2		.2		.3		.4
	3.5		2.8		2.5				7.3		1.5		5.1		-8.8		.7		-1.1
	.4		.4		.4		Debt/Worth		.1		.2		.5		.3		.3		.5
	1.6		1.4		1.3				20.7		.8		3.2		1.5		.7		1.5
	-20.6		-55.4		-9.8				-1.8		NM		-8.7		-18.5		3.2		-3.9
	101.0		111.3		110.6	% Profit Before Taxes/Tangible		103.3		143.6		151.4		131.2		74.0		74.1
(354)	30.7	(352)	34.7	(297)	44.1	Net Worth	(23)	50.0	(58)	59.5	(35)	45.8	(46)	62.1	(62)	19.7	(73)	33.9
	6.5		7.0		8.4				.0		24.5		16.9		11.7		-1.0		8.5
	31.3		40.1		43.4	% Profit Before Taxes/Total		49.0		61.1		45.8		53.8		29.3		25.6
	10.0		11.0		15.7	Assets		7.7		28.0		21.6		23.2		8.7		6.9
	1.2		1.1		.5				-9.4		3.5		3.8		4.5		-.9		.6
	297.0		402.0		520.6	Sales/Net Fixed Assets		UND		UND		841.3		578.1		212.9		147.8
	57.2		66.0		89.3				368.0		168.1		179.0		153.1		41.4		41.5
	10.1		13.3		17.4				17.5		33.0		38.7		42.9		5.7		7.8
	5.4		6.4		6.4	Sales/Total Assets		7.3		10.0		9.3		8.2		5.4		4.0
	2.8		3.5		3.6				3.5		4.1		5.0		4.8		2.7		2.3
	1.5		1.8		1.6				1.5		2.9		3.0		3.2		1.4		1.1
	.3		.3		.3	% Depr., Dep., Amort./Sales		.8		.2		.2		.1		.7		.3
(261)	1.1	(271)	.9	(211)	.9		(13)	2.4	(29)	.9	(18)	.5	(34)	.4	(44)	1.5	(73)	1.0
	2.6		2.0		2.1				14.6		2.1		1.5		1.2		2.5		2.2
	2.7		2.1		2.2	% Officers', Directors'		2.3		3.3		2.7		1.9		.9		
(119)	5.5	(121)	4.7	(113)	4.6	Owners' Comp/Sales	(15)	5.8	(32)	5.2	(21)	6.0	(22)	2.4	(14)	1.7		
	10.2		8.9		7.7				11.1		7.7		8.4		5.9		4.2		

12185082M	20190956M	13960637M	Net Sales ($)	21874M	140396M	199835M	471504M	1222670M	11904358M
7044054M	7948229M	6741704M	Total Assets ($)	12026M	73177M	57461M	163987M	755056M	5679997M

M = $ thousand   MM = $ million
See Pages viii through xx for Explanation of Ratios and Data

Current Data Sorted by Assets | Comparative Historical Data

Type of Statement	0-500M	500M-2MM	2-10MM	10-50MM	50-100MM	100-250MM		4/1/14-3/31/15 ALL	4/1/15-3/31/16 ALL
Unqualified		2	8	3	2	2		21	20
Reviewed			6	6				19	15
Compiled		1	1	3				15	13
Tax Returns	5	7	6		1	2		27	25
Other	10	15	18	12				68	54
		22 (4/1-9/30/18)		88 (10/1/18-3/31/19)					
NUMBER OF STATEMENTS	15	25	39	24	3	4		150	127
	%	%	%	%	%	%	**ASSETS**	%	%
	44.0	16.6	17.1	19.5			Cash & Equivalents	17.1	20.6
	6.7	11.7	33.2	32.3			Trade Receivables (net)	28.9	23.5
	.9	1.9	.5	.6			Inventory	1.7	1.7
	3.0	5.1	2.8	2.6			All Other Current	3.2	3.1
	54.6	35.4	53.6	55.0			Total Current	51.0	49.0
	33.1	53.0	34.4	32.8			Fixed Assets (net)	36.2	38.3
	6.1	3.1	4.2	4.6			Intangibles (net)	4.7	4.8
	6.2	8.5	7.8	7.7			All Other Non-Current	8.1	8.0
	100.0	100.0	100.0	100.0			Total	100.0	100.0
							LIABILITIES		
	17.5	6.2	5.1	1.0			Notes Payable-Short Term	9.9	9.4
	9.6	8.3	7.9	4.5			Cur. Mat.-L.T.D.	4.4	5.1
	7.8	2.9	5.6	4.6			Trade Payables	6.4	4.8
	.0	.0	.0	.1			Income Taxes Payable	.4	.1
	15.7	11.4	8.6	9.4			All Other Current	9.0	8.2
	50.6	28.8	27.2	19.6			Total Current	30.2	27.6
	78.4	30.9	20.4	15.3			Long-Term Debt	24.3	28.6
	.0	.0	.3	1.0			Deferred Taxes	.5	.1
	1.1	7.4	14.2	1.7			All Other Non-Current	7.3	6.7
	-30.3	33.0	37.9	62.4			Net Worth	37.7	37.1
	100.0	100.0	100.0	100.0			Total Liabilities & Net Worth	100.0	100.0
							INCOME DATA		
	100.0	100.0	100.0	100.0			Net Sales	100.0	100.0
							Gross Profit		
	83.8	89.3	90.8	93.6			Operating Expenses	92.2	92.0
	16.2	10.7	9.2	6.4			Operating Profit	7.8	8.0
	1.6	3.9	1.1	-.5			All Other Expenses (net)	.8	1.0
	14.7	6.8	8.1	6.8			Profit Before Taxes	6.9	7.1
							RATIOS		
	7.9	5.2	3.9	5.1				4.5	4.5
	1.3	2.1	1.9	2.9			Current	2.2	2.2
	.8	.5	1.0	1.8				1.1	1.1
	7.9	4.1	3.8	4.9				4.4	4.2
	1.3	1.3	1.7	2.5			Quick	1.8	2.1
	.8	.3	1.0	1.7				1.0	1.0
	0 UND	0 UND	8 44.7	53 6.9				0 734.2	0 UND
	0 UND	0 UND	51 7.2	68 5.4			Sales/Receivables	55 6.6	43 8.4
	0 UND	31 11.9	79 4.6	85 4.3				81 4.5	73 5.0
							Cost of Sales/Inventory		
							Cost of Sales/Payables		
	18.2	8.3	4.0	3.1				4.3	4.0
	53.6	28.4	10.0	4.5			Sales/Working Capital	8.7	10.8
	-226.3	-13.8	999.8	7.7				60.0	147.8
	97.0	24.6	24.2	40.2				18.2	19.1
	(10) 22.1	(20) 2.1	(36) 8.3	(20) 6.4			EBIT/Interest	(130) 6.2	(104) 8.3
	3.9	-3.3	.9	1.1				2.0	3.1
								3.3	3.4
							Net Profit + Depr., Dep., Amort./Cur. Mat. L/T/D	(20) 2.5	(18) 2.6
								1.6	1.8
	.4	.7	.4	.4				.4	.4
	UND	1.6	.9	.6			Fixed/Worth	.9	1.0
	-.3	NM	1.8	.8				1.9	1.9
	.1	.4	.5	.3				.5	.3
	UND	1.7	1.3	.5			Debt/Worth	1.6	1.4
	-3.7	NM	3.6	1.7				5.1	3.7
		54.4	38.5	25.5				70.4	82.7
		(19) 7.2	(33) 17.3	16.9			% Profit Before Taxes/Tangible Net Worth	(131) 19.2	(111) 28.6
		-11.4	-.8	3.3				3.2	11.7
	154.4	38.7	21.8	16.3				21.9	29.2
	58.4	2.1	9.3	5.6			% Profit Before Taxes/Total Assets	8.3	11.8
	.0	-11.2	-1.5	2.0				1.3	4.4
	511.9	11.7	15.3	9.5				15.4	18.3
	24.5	6.9	7.2	4.4			Sales/Net Fixed Assets	7.6	7.8
	7.8	1.4	3.4	2.8				4.1	3.0
	13.2	4.7	3.3	2.3				3.4	3.8
	7.7	2.6	2.2	1.5			Sales/Total Assets	2.4	2.3
	2.4	.9	1.6	1.2				1.4	1.2
		3.5	2.4	3.4				2.4	2.5
		(18) 5.5	(29) 3.9	(22) 4.9			% Depr., Dep., Amort./Sales	(119) 3.8	(95) 3.8
		8.6	5.3	6.2				6.1	5.8
			1.2					1.3	1.8
		(12) 2.5					% Officers', Directors' Owners' Comp/Sales	(50) 3.5	(35) 2.6
		7.4						6.5	9.0
	31773M	97148M	459384M	1121056M	280684M	588157M	Net Sales ($)	3031762M	2658053M
	4063M	32308M	202371M	605436M	220900M	572015M	Total Assets ($)	2108659M	1654311M

M = $ thousand   MM = $ million
See Pages viii through xx for Explanation of Ratios and Data

Comparative Historical Data   Current Data Sorted by Sales

4/1/16-3/31/17 ALL	4/1/17-3/31/18 ALL	4/1/18-3/31/19 ALL	Type of Statement	0-1MM	1-3MM	3-5MM	5-10MM	10-25MM	25MM & OVER
15	21	17	Unqualified		2	2	4	4	5
17	13	12	Reviewed	1			2	3	6
15	16	5	Compiled			1		3	1
17	18	18	Tax Returns	2	5	3	6	2	
51	52	58	Other	9	9	4	6	15	15
					22 (4/1-9/30/18)		88 (10/1/18-3/31/19)		
115	120	110	NUMBER OF STATEMENTS	12	16	10	18	27	27
%	%	%	ASSETS	%	%	%	%	%	%
17.2	18.8	20.7	Cash & Equivalents	6.6	37.6	36.9	18.6	16.6	16.7
26.1	24.0	23.5	Trade Receivables (net)	5.9	8.9	22.4	20.0	36.5	29.7
1.1	1.3	1.2	Inventory	3.0	.0	1.1	.9	.6	1.9
2.0	2.7	3.2	All Other Current	.6	2.9	1.6	8.6	2.1	2.6
46.4	46.8	48.6	Total Current	16.1	49.3	61.9	48.1	55.8	50.9
40.7	39.2	38.7	Fixed Assets (net)	71.6	38.9	27.0	38.6	32.1	34.9
6.5	6.3	5.2	Intangibles (net)	7.4	.9	7.8	4.7	3.6	-7.7
6.4	7.8	7.5	All Other Non-Current	4.9	10.8	3.3	8.6	8.6	6.4
100.0	100.0	100.0	Total	100.0	100.0	100.0	100.0	100.0	100.0
			LIABILITIES						
5.0	10.7	6.2	Notes Payable-Short Term	1.8	11.4	11.9	7.9	5.7	2.3
7.7	6.7	7.5	Cur. Mat.-L.T.D.	6.1	6.5	3.9	12.8	8.2	6.0
3.7	4.4	4.9	Trade Payables	1.9	1.8	4.4	7.4	6.3	5.3
.2	.0	.0	Income Taxes Payable	.0	.0	.1	.0	.0	.1
9.7	11.5	10.4	All Other Current	1.2	8.1	21.8	13.4	10.3	9.8
26.4	33.3	29.1	Total Current	11.0	27.7	42.1	41.6	30.4	23.6
31.1	29.4	29.9	Long-Term Debt	74.7	40.0	16.2	29.7	20.3	18.9
.5	.5	.3	Deferred Taxes	.0	.0	.4	.0	.2	.9
6.2	4.7	7.4	All Other Non-Current	4.5	5.4	3.6	6.6	16.5	2.8
35.8	32.1	33.2	Net Worth	9.6	26.9	37.8	22.2	32.5	53.8
100.0	100.0	100.0	Total Liabilities & Net Worth	100.0	100.0	100.0	100.0	100.0	100.0
			INCOME DATA						
100.0	100.0	100.0	Net Sales	100.0	100.0	100.0	100.0	100.0	100.0
			Gross Profit						
90.9	90.2	90.3	Operating Expenses	77.9	84.6	85.5	94.3	94.1	94.5
9.1	9.8	9.7	Operating Profit	22.1	15.4	14.5	5.7	5.9	5.5
1.3	.9	1.5	All Other Expenses (net)	10.5	.0	.4	.7	.6	.2
7.8	8.9	8.2	Profit Before Taxes	11.6	15.4	14.2	5.0	5.4	5.3
			RATIOS						
4.3	4.5	4.6	Current	3.0	41.0	42.2	4.7	4.3	4.6
2.3	2.1	2.0		1.1	2.7	1.7	1.7	2.1	2.4
1.3	.9	1.1		.5	1.1	.7	1.0	1.2	1.5
3.9	4.2	4.3	Quick	1.3	34.9	42.2	4.0	4.2	4.5
2.1	1.8	1.7		.6	2.7	1.4	1.7	2.1	2.3
1.1	.7	.9		.1	1.0	.7	.5	1.1	1.1
6 64.5	0 UND	0 UND	Sales/Receivables	0 UND	0 UND	0 UND	0 UND	36 10.0	42 8.6
52 7.0	48 7.6	43 8.4		0 UND	0 UND	6 66.3	12 30.8	54 6.8	58 6.3
85 4.3	74 4.9	69 5.3		0 UND	0 UND	89 4.1	69 5.3	74 4.9	76 4.8
			Cost of Sales/Inventory						
			Cost of Sales/Payables						
4.3	4.1	4.2	Sales/Working Capital	9.7	4.7	3.8	5.6	4.1	3.5
9.0	10.3	12.2		UND	19.6	26.8	18.2	10.4	7.6
39.9	-91.8	297.8		-11.2	342.0	-27.2	NM	31.7	14.5
18.9	14.3	26.9	EBIT/Interest		68.5		26.3	35.0	19.3
(102) 6.8	(100) 5.9	(93) 6.6			(11) 11.2		(16) 6.8	(25) 4.6	(25) 5.8
2.0	.4	.2			-3.3		-1.0	-.4	.8
3.1	7.3	5.0	Net Profit + Depr., Dep., Amort./Cur. Mat. L/T/D						
(16) 2.0	(15) 2.8	(12) 1.8							
1.1	1.6	1.2							
.5	.5	.4	Fixed/Worth	1.0	.5	.2	.6	.3	.4
1.1	.9	1.0		1.8	1.2	1.1	1.1	.9	.8
2.7	2.6	2.7		UND	54.5	UND	-1.6	3.5	1.8
.4	.4	.4	Debt/Worth	.2	.4	.4	.4	.2	.4
1.3	1.1	1.4		1.3	1.5	2.0	1.4	1.4	1.1
4.4	4.4	5.0		UND	79.5	UND	-6.4	12.7	2.7
48.7	70.9	41.0	% Profit Before Taxes/Tangible Net Worth	47.2	109.2		48.5	39.6	23.7
(96) 23.1	(102) 20.2	(90) 17.4		(10) .7	(13) 26.5		(13) 18.9	(21) 17.3	(25) 19.0
8.5	3.1	-.7		-8.7	-21.1		4.8	-6.7	6.8
25.0	24.3	23.2	% Profit Before Taxes/Total Assets	8.9	108.2	98.7	26.0	25.6	10.5
10.1	8.8	7.6		.5	14.1	12.7	7.6	10.1	5.3
2.5	.5	-1.5		-2.2	-8.6	1.8	-3.0	-2.2	-.3
10.7	13.3	14.0	Sales/Net Fixed Assets	2.0	61.7	72.6	18.8	19.3	10.8
6.0	5.9	7.1		.8	8.5	11.7	6.8	9.1	4.7
2.6	2.5	2.8		.2	2.4	6.7	3.7	5.0	2.4
3.2	3.0	3.6	Sales/Total Assets	1.8	7.0	7.7	4.8	3.8	2.6
2.1	2.2	2.1		.4	2.6	2.5	2.4	2.5	1.4
1.1	1.2	1.2		.1	.8	1.9	1.7	1.7	1.0
2.7	3.1	3.3	% Depr., Dep., Amort./Sales				3.6	2.5	3.4
(93) 4.3	(91) 4.4	(81) 4.5					(13) 4.7	(23) 3.8	(24) 4.9
6.5	7.2	7.3					6.6	4.8	6.9
2.5	1.6	1.3	% Officers', Directors', Owners' Comp/Sales						
(29) 4.0	(32) 3.4	(29) 2.6							
8.9	5.7	6.8							
3074191M	2869500M	2578202M	Net Sales ($)	4509M	31578M	37922M	132779M	428737M	1942677M
2264389M	1736629M	1637093M	Total Assets ($)	10017M	26790M	19832M	59338M	178092M	1343024M

M = $ thousand   MM = $ million
See Pages viii through xx for Explanation of Ratios and Data

Current Data Sorted by Assets   Comparative Historical Data

						Type of Statement		
	2	15	2	4		Unqualified	31	24
						Reviewed	3	2
	2					Compiled		
	1	4	5	3		Tax Returns		1
	13 (4/1-9/30/18)	27 (10/1/18-3/31/19)				Other	15	15
0-500M	500M-2MM	2-10MM	10-50MM	50-100MM	100-250MM		4/1/14-3/31/15 ALL	4/1/15-3/31/16 ALL
	2	5	19	7	7	NUMBER OF STATEMENTS	49	42
%	%	%	%	%	%	ASSETS	%	%
			29.4			Cash & Equivalents	25.4	23.3
			15.7			Trade Receivables (net)	15.1	15.4
			8.3			Inventory	3.5	3.0
			1.4			All Other Current	3.7	4.4
			54.8			Total Current	47.7	46.0
			28.3			Fixed Assets (net)	34.4	31.0
			2.7			Intangibles (net)	4.4	7.3
			14.2			All Other Non-Current	13.5	15.7
			100.0			Total	100.0	100.0
						LIABILITIES		
			1.0			Notes Payable-Short Term	1.1	.3
			1.5			Cur. Mat.-L.T.D.	1.6	2.2
			8.0			Trade Payables	6.2	10.4
			.7			Income Taxes Payable	.3	.1
			7.1			All Other Current	9.1	8.4
			18.4			Total Current	18.3	21.4
			6.8			Long-Term Debt	13.5	13.1
			.1			Deferred Taxes	.6	.5
			7.0			All Other Non-Current	1.2	2.7
			67.7			Net Worth	66.4	62.4
			100.0			Total Liabilties & Net Worth	100.0	100.0
						INCOME DATA		
			100.0			Net Sales	100.0	100.0
						Gross Profit		
			95.3			Operating Expenses	94.6	97.0
			4.7			Operating Profit	5.4	3.0
			-1.0			All Other Expenses (net)	-.5	.5
			5.7			Profit Before Taxes	5.9	2.5
						RATIOS		
			6.8				6.0	4.8
			3.0			Current	2.8	2.3
			2.2				1.6	1.2
			6.1				5.4	4.4
			2.7			Quick	2.4	1.8
			2.0				1.2	.8
		38	9.6				33 11.0	34 10.6
		51	7.1			Sales/Receivables	41 9.0	39 9.3
		58	6.3				49 7.4	59 6.2
						Cost of Sales/Inventory		
						Cost of Sales/Payables		
			2.1				2.5	2.9
			3.1			Sales/Working Capital	5.3	6.4
			5.6				14.5	38.9
			37.1				38.1	15.3
		(12)	8.9			EBIT/Interest	(39) 10.9	(34) 3.4
			2.2				4.7	-5.7
						Net Profit + Depr., Dep., Amort./Cur. Mat. L/T/D		
			.3				.3	.3
			.4			Fixed/Worth	.5	.6
			.7				.8	1.2
			.1				.2	.2
			.3			Debt/Worth	.4	.5
			.6				1.1	1.5
			21.0				12.9	5.5
		(17)	6.4			% Profit Before Taxes/Tangible Net Worth	(47) 7.2	(37) 1.7
			1.5				2.5	-6.4
			11.3				7.7	4.7
			5.6			% Profit Before Taxes/Total Assets	5.0	1.6
			.6				1.6	-2.7
			19.6				9.3	8.2
			3.5			Sales/Net Fixed Assets	3.7	3.6
			1.8				2.0	2.1
			1.3				1.4	1.4
			1.1			Sales/Total Assets	1.1	1.0
			.8				.8	.8
			1.3				2.3	1.9
		(18)	3.1			% Depr., Dep., Amort./Sales	(42) 3.5	(36) 3.5
			4.4				4.4	4.1
						% Officers', Directors' Owners' Comp/Sales		
	7220M	89872M	536083M	463487M	891072M	Net Sales ($)	2484616M	2230496M
	2659M	23586M	462901M	478101M	882473M	Total Assets ($)	2297403M	2302586M

(Left-most three columns region: DATA NOT AVAILABLE)

M = $ thousand   MM = $ million
See Pages viii through xx for Explanation of Ratios and Data

Comparative Historical Data   Current Data Sorted by Sales

	27 3 2 7 4/1/16-3/31/17 ALL	20 1 12 4/1/17-3/31/18 ALL	23 2 15 4/1/18-3/31/19 ALL	Type of Statement	0-1MM	1-3MM 13 (4/1-9/30/18)	3-5MM	5-10MM	10-25MM 27 (10/1/18-3/31/19)	25MM & OVER
	27	20	23	Unqualified		1		1	7	15
	3			Reviewed		1				
				Compiled						
				Tax Returns						
	2 7	1 12	2 15	Other				2		9
	39	33	40	**NUMBER OF STATEMENTS**	2	13		3	11	24
	%	%	%	**ASSETS**	%	%	%	%	%	%
	22.6	24.5	25.2	Cash & Equivalents	D	D			33.3	20.5
	15.6	15.8	14.8	Trade Receivables (net)	A	A			11.4	17.2
	5.4	4.9	7.2	Inventory	T	T			8.3	7.9
	3.8	2.2	2.6	All Other Current	A	A			2.8	3.0
	47.4	47.5	49.8	Total Current					55.8	48.5
	31.5	27.7	29.8	Fixed Assets (net)	N	N			31.2	26.6
	6.6	4.8	4.1	Intangibles (net)	O	O			1.1	5.3
	14.5	20.0	16.3	All Other Non-Current	T	T			12.0	19.6
	100.0	100.0	100.0	Total					100.0	100.0
				LIABILITIES	A	A				
	4.9	2.2	1.7	Notes Payable-Short Term	V	V			2.5	1.3
	2.1	1.3	1.9	Cur. Mat.-L.T.D.	A	A			.3	1.9
	7.4	7.8	9.0	Trade Payables	I	I			7.8	11.1
	.5	.0	.5	Income Taxes Payable	L	L			1.3	.3
	11.0	10.1	10.2	All Other Current	A	A			5.7	13.7
	25.8	21.3	23.2	Total Current	B	B			17.5	28.3
	16.0	18.0	21.4	Long-Term Debt	L	L			6.9	14.0
	.4	.0	.0	Deferred Taxes	E	E			.1	.0
	4.3	5.3	3.8	All Other Non-Current					1.6	5.5
	53.5	55.4	51.6	Net Worth					73.9	52.1
	100.0	100.0	100.0	Total Liabilties & Net Worth					100.0	100.0
				INCOME DATA						
	100.0	100.0	100.0	Net Sales					100.0	100.0
				Gross Profit						
	97.7	97.7	96.5	Operating Expenses					97.1	97.7
	2.3	2.3	3.5	Operating Profit					2.9	2.3
	-.3	-.1	.5	All Other Expenses (net)					-2.2	-.4
	2.5	2.4	2.9	Profit Before Taxes					5.0	2.7
				RATIOS						
	4.3	4.0	5.2	Current					7.4	3.0
	2.8	2.4	2.7						5.3	2.1
	1.2	1.1	1.6						2.5	1.6
	3.8	3.7	4.8	Quick					7.1	2.7
	2.2	1.7	2.0						4.9	1.5
	.9	.8	1.0						1.7	.9
34	10.6	38 9.6	36 10.1	Sales/Receivables					33 11.0	41 8.8
47	7.8	48 7.6	52 7.0						41 8.9	53 6.9
60	6.1	62 5.9	58 6.3						51 7.1	64 5.7
				Cost of Sales/Inventory						
				Cost of Sales/Payables						
	2.6	2.4	2.2	Sales/Working Capital					1.8	2.3
	5.0	5.2	4.8						3.1	6.0
	39.5	30.7	11.3						8.4	13.4
	23.3	42.0	30.5	EBIT/Interest						23.8
(32)	7.5	(25) 7.3	(27) 4.6						(16) 4.8	
	1.4	-.5	.9							-3.1
				Net Profit + Depr., Dep., Amort./Cur. Mat. L/T/D						
	.3	.2	.3	Fixed/Worth					.3	.3
	.6	.5	.5						.3	.5
	1.1	.7	.8						.7	1.1
	.3	.2	.2	Debt/Worth					.1	.3
	.5	.5	.4						.2	.5
	1.6	1.0	1.4						.6	1.4
	12.9	13.5	13.4	% Profit Before Taxes/Tangible Net Worth					33.7	14.1
(35)	6.1	(29) 7.5	(35) 5.3						6.4	(20) 6.0
	2.3	-1.9	.6						.6	1.2
	8.2	8.6	6.8	% Profit Before Taxes/Total Assets					14.1	6.8
	4.2	4.0	2.9						5.6	2.9
	1.0	-1.3	-.1						.6	-3.4
	13.4	13.3	11.9	Sales/Net Fixed Assets					12.8	14.6
	3.7	3.5	3.9						3.5	3.9
	2.2	2.4	2.3						1.6	2.8
	1.5	1.4	1.4	Sales/Total Assets					1.3	1.4
	1.2	1.1	1.2						1.1	1.2
	.9	.9	.7						.8	.7
	2.3	2.3	2.2	% Depr., Dep., Amort./Sales					2.4	1.5
(36)	3.4	(28) 3.0	(34) 3.1						(10) 3.7	(20) 2.9
	4.8	4.4	4.3						4.7	3.3
				% Officers', Directors' Owners' Comp/Sales						
	2007758M	2004318M	1987734M	Net Sales ($)	3317M			21665M	201064M	1761688M
	1847360M	1717846M	1849720M	Total Assets ($)	3778M			17937M	197601M	1630404M

M = $ thousand   MM = $ million
See Pages viii through xx for Explanation of Ratios and Data

Current Data Sorted by Assets   **Comparative Historical Data**

0-500M	500M-2MM	2-10MM	10-50MM	50-100MM	100-250MM	Type of Statement		
	1	14	14	3	4	Unqualified	42	47
5	1	3	2	1		Reviewed	8	7
2	4	2	1			Compiled	16	13
7	2	2	1	11	9	Tax Returns	25	25
	11	18	22			Other	96	112
	34 (4/1-9/30/18)		106 (10/1/18-3/31/19)				4/1/14-3/31/15 ALL	4/1/15-3/31/16 ALL
14	19	39	40	15	13	**NUMBER OF STATEMENTS**	187	204
%	%	%	%	%	%	**ASSETS**	%	%
43.2	26.0	25.0	18.7	16.6	10.7	Cash & Equivalents	19.2	19.6
17.3	11.2	23.0	25.2	27.7	11.0	Trade Receivables (net)	25.0	22.5
.1	10.5	2.4	4.7	2.8	1.1	Inventory	2.5	2.6
7.9	1.3	4.1	4.8	1.9	2.0	All Other Current	4.9	3.6
68.6	49.1	54.5	53.4	49.1	24.8	Total Current	51.7	48.3
21.7	33.8	26.7	19.4	13.3	23.9	Fixed Assets (net)	29.5	29.6
3.9	14.9	8.9	16.8	28.1	35.4	Intangibles (net)	8.9	11.3
5.8	2.2	9.9	10.4	9.5	15.9	All Other Non-Current	9.8	10.8
100.0	100.0	100.0	100.0	100.0	100.0	Total	100.0	100.0
						LIABILITIES		
18.2	14.7	3.5	5.8	5.1	2.0	Notes Payable-Short Term	10.1	9.5
3.7	3.0	4.6	2.6	1.5	2.5	Cur. Mat.-L.T.D.	3.4	3.5
3.0	5.8	7.1	12.1	16.4	4.6	Trade Payables	10.0	7.2
10.2	1.8	.0	.2	.0	.0	Income Taxes Payable	.4	.3
17.0	17.1	18.4	10.9	9.8	8.8	All Other Current	15.0	12.5
52.1	42.5	33.7	31.6	32.8	17.9	Total Current	38.9	33.0
29.7	46.5	14.6	16.8	26.3	35.0	Long-Term Debt	20.1	23.7
.0	.0	.0	.7	1.2	.4	Deferred Taxes	.2	.3
7.0	3.9	1.9	3.4	4.6	1.0	All Other Non-Current	9.6	4.6
11.3	7.2	49.8	47.6	35.2	45.6	Net Worth	31.1	38.4
100.0	100.0	100.0	100.0	100.0	100.0	Total Liabilities & Net Worth	100.0	100.0
						INCOME DATA		
100.0	100.0	100.0	100.0	100.0	100.0	Net Sales	100.0	100.0
						Gross Profit		
89.4	87.0	92.8	93.2	91.0	96.1	Operating Expenses	88.0	89.7
10.6	13.0	7.2	6.8	9.0	3.9	Operating Profit	12.0	10.3
3.7	5.9	1.6	1.9	2.8	2.9	All Other Expenses (net)	2.1	2.1
6.9	7.1	5.6	4.9	6.2	.9	Profit Before Taxes	9.9	8.1
						RATIOS		
3.2	1.8	3.9	2.9	2.8	2.0		2.8	3.3
1.4	1.0	2.1	1.6	1.7	1.6	Current	1.6	1.7
.8	.5	1.4	.9	.9	1.2		.9	.9
2.7	1.6	3.5	2.4	2.8	1.8		2.6	3.0
1.0	.6	1.8	1.3	1.6	1.3	Quick	1.3	1.4
.6	.4	1.1	.7	.8	.9		.7	.7
0 UND	0 UND	11 33.4	25 14.8	38 9.5	26 14.0		0 UND	0 999.8
0 UND	0 UND	33 11.0	49 7.4	56 6.5	54 6.7	Sales/Receivables	36 10.2	38 9.7
45 8.1	0 UND	51 7.2	66 5.5	87 4.2	64 5.7		63 5.8	59 6.2
						Cost of Sales/Inventory		
						Cost of Sales/Payables		
12.2	15.4	4.5	4.2	5.0	5.8		5.9	6.0
119.7	328.5	9.9	12.8	9.1	11.7	Sales/Working Capital	18.6	16.4
-106.2	-56.3	66.5	-53.0	-45.3	41.7		-185.5	-76.6
	89.2	26.2	11.6		7.9		35.3	26.5
	(13) 1.5	(24) 5.0	(29) 5.9		3.3	EBIT/Interest	(128) 6.9	(151) 5.3
	-4.0	.5	-2.8		.0		1.3	.5
							12.5	12.3
						Net Profit + Depr., Dep., Amort./Cur. Mat. L/T/D	(16) 4.5	(25) 2.4
							1.4	.3
.0	.2	.2	.1	.0	.6		.3	.3
.4	1.0	.6	.4	1.2	7.7	Fixed/Worth	1.0	.9
-43.1	-3.6	2.2	4.3	-.1	-.2		6.3	4.6
.3	.6	.3	.3	.6	.4		.5	.5
14.4	3.5	.9	1.4	-12.9	8.6	Debt/Worth	2.0	1.8
-37.0	-5.0	3.4	NM	-1.8	-1.6		42.0	26.8
	123.6	63.0	33.0			% Profit Before Taxes/Tangible Net Worth	123.5	87.3
	(13) 87.5	(33) 5.8	(30) 13.1				(146) 31.8	(161) 21.5
	10.3	-3.3	.0				4.8	1.6
28.0	62.7	29.0	19.5	9.8	5.1	% Profit Before Taxes/Total Assets	37.8	28.1
5.9	3.6	5.4	4.0	6.0	3.2		10.3	6.3
-.3	-.1	-1.3	-2.9	4.0	-2.5		.6	-.2
UND	216.3	62.4	148.0	418.4	34.2		42.8	49.1
102.7	23.0	17.2	28.6	40.3	5.4	Sales/Net Fixed Assets	14.3	11.4
12.0	9.5	4.2	3.1	5.6	2.4		5.2	3.3
18.0	8.2	4.2	2.7	2.3	1.5		4.8	3.8
7.4	4.5	2.4	1.5	1.3	.9	Sales/Total Assets	2.6	1.8
3.0	2.4	1.4	.9	.6	.4		1.3	1.0
	.4	.4	.8				.7	1.1
	(12) 1.0	(30) 1.5	(26) 2.9			% Depr., Dep., Amort./Sales	(130) 1.9	(142) 2.7
	13.0	3.1	4.6				4.1	5.8
							4.1	2.0
						% Officers', Directors' Owners' Comp/Sales	(38) 7.2	(37) 7.3
							15.3	14.7
43021M	196204M	1187186M	2338839M	1630086M	2235637M	Net Sales ($)	8379921M	10245900M
4410M	24468M	204443M	1076975M	1040933M	2023025M	Total Assets ($)	4326969M	5904325M

M = $ thousand   MM = $ million
See Pages viii through xx for Explanation of Ratios and Data

Comparative Historical Data | Current Data Sorted by Sales

					Type of Statement						
	42		39	36	Unqualified	1	1	5	4	11	14
	7		4	7	Reviewed				1	2	4
	6		5	12	Compiled	5		1	3	2	1
	13		15	7	Tax Returns	1	2	1		2	1
	98		93	78	Other	1	8	6	6	17	40
	4/1/16-3/31/17		4/1/17-3/31/18	4/1/18-3/31/19			34 (4/1-9/30/18)		106 (10/1/18-3/31/19)		
	ALL		ALL	ALL		0-1MM	1-3MM	3-5MM	5-10MM	10-25MM	25MM & OVER
	166		156	140	NUMBER OF STATEMENTS	8	11	13	14	34	60
	%		%	%	ASSETS	%	%	%	%	%	%
	21.2		21.6	22.9	Cash & Equivalents	27.3	27.6	38.9	30.8	14.6
	24.6		19.6	20.8	Trade Receivables (net)	24.8	8.7	22.7	17.6	26.5
	2.7		3.4	3.8	Inventory	10.6	5.9	.2	4.0	3.4
	3.9		4.9	3.9	All Other Current	1.9	7.4	1.1	3.6	4.7
	52.4		49.6	51.5	Total Current	64.6	49.6	63.0	56.0	49.2
	26.5		26.6	23.4	Fixed Assets (net)	20.9	25.5	16.9	27.0	16.4
	12.4		14.8	16.0	Intangibles (net)	9.8	8.2	10.7	12.0	23.5
	8.7		8.9	9.1	All Other Non-Current	4.8	16.8	9.4	5.0	10.9
	100.0		100.0	100.0	Total	100.0	100.0	100.0	100.0	100.0
					LIABILITIES						
	5.3		8.9	7.2	Notes Payable-Short Term	22.4	2.2	5.4	5.2	5.6
	2.5		2.9	3.2	Cur. Mat.-L.T.D.	3.2	1.3	8.7	3.7	1.7
	9.1		9.6	8.7	Trade Payables	6.3	3.4	6.4	4.9	14.0
	.4		.3	1.3	Income Taxes Payable	.1	.1	10.2	1.0	.1
	17.0		17.6	14.1	All Other Current	16.2	9.0	18.9	15.9	14.2
	34.3		39.4	34.5	Total Current	48.1	15.9	49.5	30.8	35.6
	23.6		23.4	24.2	Long-Term Debt	70.2	12.6	9.7	15.4	22.0
	.3		.6	.4	Deferred Taxes	.0	.0	.5	.0	.7
	6.3		5.0	3.3	All Other Non-Current	11.6	.1	.6	1.1	4.1
	35.6		31.6	37.6	Net Worth	-29.9	71.4	39.8	52.7	37.7
	100.0		100.0	100.0	Total Liabilties & Net Worth	100.0	100.0	100.0	100.0	100.0
					INCOME DATA						
	100.0		100.0	100.0	Net Sales	100.0	100.0	100.0	100.0	100.0
					Gross Profit						
	91.0		92.4	91.9	Operating Expenses	93.1	93.4	95.2	93.2	93.2
	9.0		7.6	8.1	Operating Profit	6.9	6.6	4.8	6.8	6.8
	2.5		1.8	2.7	All Other Expenses (net)	.8	.7	1.7	.9	2.4
	6.4		5.8	5.4	Profit Before Taxes	6.1	5.9	3.2	5.9	4.4
					RATIOS						
	3.9		3.0	3.0		2.6	10.4	3.0	3.8	2.3
	1.8		1.6	1.7	Current	1.7	3.3	1.7	2.1	1.6
	.9		.9	.9		1.0	1.3	.8	1.1	.9
	3.4		2.6	2.6		2.6	10.2	2.9	3.5	1.9
	1.4		1.3	1.3	Quick	1.7	2.1	1.4	1.7	1.3
	.8		.6	.7		.4	.9	.8	.9	.7

3	126.5	0	999.8	5	75.7		0	UND	0	UND	0	UND	10	35.9	22	16.5
38	9.7	34	10.7	38	9.6	Sales/Receivables	0	899.0	14	26.0	27	13.7	36	10.2	54	6.8
60	6.1	58	6.3	61	6.0		64	5.7	47	7.7	51	7.1	52	7.0	65	5.6

					Cost of Sales/Inventory						
					Cost of Sales/Payables						

5.9		5.3	5.9		5.9	3.5	6.3	5.0	6.2
15.8		18.3	15.6	Sales/Working Capital	20.4	7.6	18.7	12.0	18.9
-82.3		-47.7	-200.1		224.2	129.1	-153.7	NM	-268.4

	28.9		17.0		17.0					26.2		16.6
(116)	4.5	(115)	3.6	(96)	3.3	EBIT/Interest			(28)	5.0	(45)	4.9
	.5		-.4		.5					.3		1.3

	9.9		8.8		4.4	Net Profit + Depr., Dep., Amort./Cur. Mat. L/T/D	
(17)	3.9	(17)	2.8	(13)	.7		
	1.8		1.3		-8.4		

.2		.2	.2		.0	.1	.0	.2	.2
.7		1.1	.6	Fixed/Worth	.5	.3	.8	.6	.7
4.9		-1.6	-195.6		-.2	.6	-37.3	2.0	-.4

.4		.6	.3		.3	.0	.2	.2	.6
1.8		2.7	1.8	Debt/Worth	23.1	.3	2.0	.9	4.3
38.6		-4.9	-15.9		-1.7	1.0	-71.2	6.5	-2.9

	86.5		54.8		63.3	% Profit Before Taxes/Tangible Net Worth		24.9			53.6		58.4
(129)	21.8	(103)	15.3	(99)	13.5		(12)	6.4	(29)	4.3	(38)	17.0
	2.9		.4		.5			-3.0			-3.1		2.7

30.4		23.4	20.8	% Profit Before Taxes/Total Assets	38.8	16.6	64.0	33.3	18.6
6.3		5.5	4.4		4.5	4.4	3.1	3.1	6.0
-.6		-2.8	-.4		-7.4	-1.7	-1.1	-1.3	.8

80.5		88.0	111.6	Sales/Net Fixed Assets	UND	84.0	UND	93.1	207.2
18.7		21.1	27.1		41.2	15.9	39.3	15.3	33.8
3.7		3.6	4.2		5.2	2.6	11.0	3.9	5.4

4.2		4.3	4.2	Sales/Total Assets	6.3	4.3	9.6	3.5	4.0
2.4		1.8	2.1		3.1	1.4	4.3	2.3	1.8
1.1		1.0	1.0		1.3	1.0	1.4	1.2	.9

	.8		.6		.6	% Depr., Dep., Amort./Sales		1.0			.6		.5
(113)	2.1	(101)	1.9	(89)	1.8		(10)	1.8	(24)	2.0	(33)	1.6
	5.4		5.0		4.1			4.4			3.4		3.8

	4.7		3.4		1.6	% Officers', Directors' Owners' Comp/Sales	
(22)	10.7	(15)	12.0	(14)	8.5		
	18.6		17.7		15.0		

8017401M		6976168M	7630973M	Net Sales ($)	2868M	23497M	53688M	105174M	574832M	6870914M
4893481M		4304552M	4374254M	Total Assets ($)	14146M	10820M	43082M	88588M	356065M	3861553M

M = $ thousand   MM = $ million
See Pages viii through xx for Explanation of Ratios and Data

Current Data Sorted by Assets   Comparative Historical Data

0-500M	500M-2MM	2-10MM	10-50MM	50-100MM	100-250MM	Type of Statement	ALL 4/1/14-3/31/15	ALL 4/1/15-3/31/16
	2	11	49	43	70	Unqualified	200	205
		2	2	2		Reviewed	9	6
2	1	2	1		1	Compiled	13	15
5	7	6	5	1		Tax Returns	19	19
4	12	24	54	38	31	Other	229	209
	156 (4/1-9/30/18)		219 (10/1/18-3/31/19)					
11	22	45	111	84	102	**NUMBER OF STATEMENTS**	470	454
%	%	%	%	%	%	**ASSETS**	%	%
55.2	28.3	16.7	15.4	17.0	16.4	Cash & Equivalents	14.8	15.0
15.8	12.0	17.8	20.3	15.7	12.7	Trade Receivables (net)	16.3	16.6
4.6	2.4	4.8	2.6	1.8	1.5	Inventory	2.4	2.2
1.6	.4	2.0	5.1	3.4	3.8	All Other Current	3.5	3.5
77.3	43.2	41.2	43.5	37.9	34.4	Total Current	37.0	37.3
9.9	33.2	42.5	40.4	41.5	40.9	Fixed Assets (net)	43.4	42.5
.5	12.2	9.6	5.0	3.4	4.2	Intangibles (net)	4.8	4.1
12.3	11.4	6.6	11.1	17.2	20.4	All Other Non-Current	14.8	16.0
100.0	100.0	100.0	100.0	100.0	100.0	Total	100.0	100.0
						LIABILITIES		
46.1	4.1	2.5	2.1	.8	.5	Notes Payable-Short Term	4.7	3.2
14.0	1.6	4.2	4.1	3.0	1.7	Cur. Mat.-L.T.D.	3.7	3.5
9.5	7.1	8.1	10.0	6.3	5.5	Trade Payables	7.4	6.6
.0	.1	.0	.1	.0	.0	Income Taxes Payable	.0	.0
5.7	12.8	9.4	13.1	8.3	8.6	All Other Current	10.4	11.4
75.3	25.7	24.2	29.4	18.4	16.3	Total Current	26.2	24.7
10.7	26.0	22.0	26.5	22.8	25.0	Long-Term Debt	29.4	28.4
.0	.0	.0	.1	.0	.1	Deferred Taxes	.1	.1
9.6	.4	1.0	5.7	7.3	6.6	All Other Non-Current	5.3	6.4
4.4	47.8	52.8	38.3	51.4	51.9	Net Worth	39.0	40.4
100.0	100.0	100.0	100.0	100.0	100.0	Total Liabilties & Net Worth	100.0	100.0
						INCOME DATA		
100.0	100.0	100.0	100.0	100.0	100.0	Net Sales	100.0	100.0
						Gross Profit		
92.8	83.6	81.2	91.8	96.0	95.6	Operating Expenses	91.3	92.0
7.2	16.4	18.8	8.2	4.0	4.4	Operating Profit	8.7	8.0
-.2	3.9	.9	1.1	1.1	1.1	All Other Expenses (net)	1.8	1.9
7.4	12.5	17.9	7.1	2.9	3.3	Profit Before Taxes	6.9	6.0
						RATIOS		
6.0	6.1	2.9	3.3	3.3	3.3		2.7	2.9
1.0	2.9	1.8	1.7	2.3	2.1	Current	1.7	1.8
.7	1.2	1.1	1.0	1.4	1.5		1.1	1.1
5.2	5.6	2.4	2.6	3.0	2.8		2.2	2.5
1.0	2.8	1.5	1.3	1.9	1.8	Quick	1.4	1.5
.7	1.1	.9	.8	1.1	1.2		.8	.9
0 UND	0 UND	10 37.2	34 10.6	41 8.8	36 10.0		31 11.9	33 11.1
0 UND	0 UND	33 11.1	46 8.0	47 7.7	45 8.2	Sales/Receivables	43 8.5	45 8.1
0 UND	29 12.6	43 8.4	61 6.0	56 6.5	54 6.8		56 6.5	56 6.5
						Cost of Sales/Inventory		
						Cost of Sales/Payables		
4.4	7.2	5.6	3.8	2.9	3.5		4.8	4.7
27.9	12.3	10.9	9.2	6.0	6.8	Sales/Working Capital	10.3	9.1
-15.8	46.9	NM	-379.2	15.5	13.2		77.1	61.4
	20.8	51.5	22.2	10.9	5.3		14.2	12.2
	(13) 6.3	(34) 9.5	(95) 4.0	(81) 3.7	(92) 2.1	EBIT/Interest	(414) 4.1	(393) 3.7
	1.0	-.5	.0	.6	.5		.6	.8
			6.7				4.3	4.0
		(11) 2.3				Net Profit + Depr., Dep., Amort./Cur. Mat. L/T/D	(24) 2.9	(12) 3.2
		1.5					.8	1.3
.0	.1	.5	.5	.6	.5		.6	.6
.2	.6	.8	1.2	.8	.8	Fixed/Worth	1.0	.9
3.4	4.8	1.4	2.6	1.2	1.5		2.9	2.3
.5	.3	.5	.6	.4	.5		.5	.6
13.5	.9	.8	1.6	.8	.9	Debt/Worth	1.3	1.3
-26.3	8.1	1.7	5.8	1.4	2.6		4.6	3.7
	186.5	149.5	44.7	12.5	9.7		33.5	30.8
	(18) 65.3	(42) 39.3	(93) 10.7	(79) 5.6	(99) 3.0	% Profit Before Taxes/Tangible Net Worth	(407) 8.0	(393) 8.4
	28.0	-.4	1.0	-.6	-1.6		.4	.0
102.0	62.5	51.9	12.7	7.7	4.5		10.6	10.4
14.5	31.3	13.2	4.3	2.8	1.9	% Profit Before Taxes/Total Assets	3.9	3.3
-3.6	5.2	-.4	-1.0	-.1	-.5		-.6	-.3
UND	106.7	14.0	7.9	4.0	3.4		6.2	5.6
90.3	17.2	6.5	3.8	2.5	2.3	Sales/Net Fixed Assets	2.6	2.6
24.8	2.7	2.7	2.1	1.6	1.6		1.7	1.8
12.4	6.0	2.8	1.9	1.4	1.2		1.9	1.8
5.4	3.0	1.9	1.2	1.0	.9	Sales/Total Assets	1.1	1.1
1.7	1.3	1.1	.9	.7	.7		.8	.8
	1.9	2.3	2.4	3.6	3.0		3.0	3.2
	(13) 4.0	(41) 3.5	(106) 3.7	(81) 5.2	(84) 4.3	% Depr., Dep., Amort./Sales	(398) 4.7	(378) 4.7
	14.8	5.7	5.2	6.5	6.2		6.6	6.6
					4.7		8.4	5.8
				(10)	13.7	% Officers', Directors' Owners' Comp/Sales	(40) 17.0	(38) 16.3
					34.7		37.1	30.4
15907M	125433M	477095M	4570336M	6826740M	16423928M	Net Sales ($)	33397934M	36659619M
2738M	21556M	244136M	3118682M	6247243M	16405916M	Total Assets ($)	30796684M	33251870M

M = $ thousand   MM = $ million
See Pages viii through xx for Explanation of Ratios and Data

Comparative Historical Data | Current Data Sorted by Sales

'16-'17	'17-'18	'18-'19	Type of Statement	0-1MM	1-3MM	3-5MM	5-10MM	10-25MM	25MM & OVER
161	172	175	Unqualified	2	1	3		26	143
7	9	6	Reviewed				1	1	4
7	7	7	Compiled	2	2	1			2
21	25	24	Tax Returns	6	5	3	4	3	3
198	195	163	Other	8	5	9	11	18	112
4/1/16- 3/31/17 ALL	4/1/17- 3/31/18 ALL	4/1/18- 3/31/19 ALL		156 (4/1-9/30/18)			219 (10/1/18-3/31/19)		
394	408	375	NUMBER OF STATEMENTS	16	14	13	20	48	264
%	%	%	**ASSETS**	%	%	%	%	%	%
14.6	16.1	18.1	Cash & Equivalents	14.7	31.1	29.2	22.8	20.1	16.4
16.5	16.8	16.3	Trade Receivables (net)	14.5	3.5	4.1	16.7	18.8	17.2
2.6	2.8	2.4	Inventory	3.8	1.1	1.7	4.6	3.0	2.2
4.1	3.4	3.6	All Other Current	.3	.2	1.6	3.2	4.1	4.0
37.9	39.1	40.5	Total Current	33.2	35.9	36.6	47.3	46.0	39.8
43.3	41.7	39.7	Fixed Assets (net)	45.3	52.2	24.0	34.2	37.1	40.4
4.5	4.2	5.3	Intangibles (net)	8.3	6.1	11.5	14.5	8.2	3.5
14.4	15.0	14.5	All Other Non-Current	13.2	5.9	27.9	4.0	8.7	16.3
100.0	100.0	100.0	Total	100.0	100.0	100.0	100.0	100.0	100.0
			LIABILITIES						
4.2	2.4	2.8	Notes Payable-Short Term	9.1	25.5	.6	3.4	2.8	1.3
3.7	3.7	3.4	Cur. Mat.-L.T.D.	11.2	5.7	1.2	3.4	5.9	2.4
7.9	7.5	7.6	Trade Payables	.6	1.3	9.1	7.7	11.0	7.6
.0	.0	.0	Income Taxes Payable	.0	.0	.0	.1	.0	.0
11.0	11.0	10.1	All Other Current	4.2	7.6	15.0	5.7	11.1	10.6
26.8	24.6	23.9	Total Current	25.0	40.1	25.8	20.3	30.7	21.9
28.1	26.4	24.2	Long-Term Debt	43.8	34.2	19.2	21.8	22.8	23.2
.1	.0	.1	Deferred Taxes	.0	.0	.0	.0	.0	.1
8.6	5.6	5.6	All Other Non-Current	1.2	.5	6.9	.7	3.7	6.7
36.4	43.4	46.2	Net Worth	29.9	25.1	48.1	57.2	42.7	48.1
100.0	100.0	100.0	Total Liabilities & Net Worth	100.0	100.0	100.0	100.0	100.0	100.0
			INCOME DATA						
100.0	100.0	100.0	Net Sales	100.0	100.0	100.0	100.0	100.0	100.0
			Gross Profit						
91.3	91.5	92.1	Operating Expenses	70.2	90.5	75.2	77.4	93.2	95.2
8.7	8.5	7.9	Operating Profit	29.8	9.5	24.8	22.6	6.8	4.8
2.0	1.0	1.2	All Other Expenses (net)	9.5	1.0	6.5	.9	.1	.7
6.7	7.5	6.7	Profit Before Taxes	20.3	8.5	18.3	21.6	6.7	4.1
			RATIOS						
3.0	3.2	3.3		8.4	3.4	4.2	5.1	3.5	3.1
1.7	1.8	2.0	Current	1.2	1.2	1.1	2.4	2.0	2.0
1.0	1.1	1.2		.5	.7	.5	1.3	1.2	1.3
2.5	2.8	2.9		6.9	3.4	3.5	3.4	3.2	2.8
1.4	1.6	1.7	Quick	1.2	1.1	1.1	2.0	1.8	1.7
.9	.9	1.0		.5	.6	.4	1.0	1.0	1.0
31 11.9	30 12.1	31 11.6		0 UND	0 UND	0 UND	0 UND	27 13.3	38 9.6
45 8.2	43 8.5	43 8.4	Sales/Receivables	0 UND	0 UND	0 UND	27 13.6	43 8.4	46 8.0
57 6.4	57 6.4	54 6.7		59 6.2	23 15.6	28 13.2	40 9.1	58 6.3	56 6.5
			Cost of Sales/Inventory						
			Cost of Sales/Payables						
4.6	4.2	4.1		4.2	7.4	8.7	4.5	3.1	3.8
10.3	8.7	7.8	Sales/Working Capital	17.8	25.6	16.0	7.5	7.2	7.5
152.5	42.7	33.6		-15.0	-15.8	-7.9	38.2	24.1	19.6
14.4	12.7	13.8		6.3	12.9		57.8	34.7	12.5
(347) 3.8	(353) 4.1	(323) 3.4	EBIT/Interest	(11) 3.0	(12) 3.6		(15) 30.3	(38) 2.8	(243) 3.2
.6	.5	.5		-1.5	-3.7		5.4	-.3	.5
17.3	11.2	11.5	Net Profit + Depr., Dep.,						8.4
(11) 8.6	(21) 6.3	(27) 5.1	Amort./Cur. Mat. L/T/D					(18)	3.6
6.0	1.5	1.6							1.6
.6	.5	.5		.2	.5	.0	.3	.5	.5
1.0	.9	.8	Fixed/Worth	2.5	1.3	.1	.7	.9	.8
2.4	1.9	1.7		NM	3.7	NM	1.9	2.3	1.5
.5	.5	.5		.5	.5	.2	.3	.7	.5
1.1	1.0	1.0	Debt/Worth	4.4	.7	1.2	.8	1.5	1.0
3.9	3.1	3.0		-11.1	NM	-89.7	2.4	4.0	2.2
29.5	37.9	33.2	% Profit Before Taxes/Tangible	52.0	119.1		300.1	38.7	17.9
(336) 6.9	(360) 7.1	(337) 7.3	Net Worth	(11) 27.5	(11) 9.6		(19) 91.0	(43) 7.0	(244) 5.4
-.2	-.4	.1		9.3	-11.1		46.6	-3.3	.1
10.7	10.4	12.1	% Profit Before Taxes/Total	14.0	43.6	65.1	64.1	13.8	8.8
3.2	3.4	3.3	Assets	7.7	6.7	14.2	39.5	1.9	2.8
-.5	-.7	-.6		-1.1	-10.9	2.2	15.1	-2.1	-.4
6.1	6.5	6.9		47.8	40.8	UND	16.5	10.4	4.5
2.6	2.9	3.0	Sales/Net Fixed Assets	2.3	2.5	69.5	8.3	4.1	2.6
1.7	1.8	1.8		.2	.4	5.9	3.3	2.4	1.8
1.8	1.9	1.8		1.3	5.1	4.9	3.0	2.2	1.6
1.1	1.2	1.1	Sales/Total Assets	.8	1.5	3.0	2.0	1.3	1.1
.7	.8	.8		.2	.3	.2	1.2	.7	.8
3.0	2.9	2.8		5.7	2.6		2.2	2.8	2.9
(340) 4.6	(361) 4.4	(329) 4.1	% Depr., Dep., Amort./Sales	(10) 11.7	(11) 6.0		(17) 2.8	(43) 4.2	(241) 4.1
6.5	6.3	5.9		20.0	18.1		5.8	5.4	5.8
4.6	5.3	5.3							5.3
(30) 17.4	(34) 13.6	(32) 12.9	% Officers', Directors' Owners' Comp/Sales					(16)	13.7
42.5	33.2	31.3							36.6
28948383M	29154096M	28439439M	Net Sales ($)	8865M	23293M	47836M	150726M	810114M	27398605M
26322787M	25355956M	26040271M	Total Assets ($)	35263M	46242M	227557M	124231M	882638M	24724340M

© RMA 2019

M = $ thousand   MM = $ million
See Pages viii through xx for Explanation of Ratios and Data

Current Data Sorted by Assets   Comparative Historical Data

0-500M	500M-2MM	2-10MM	10-50MM	50-100MM	100-250MM		4/1/14-3/31/15 ALL	4/1/15-3/31/16 ALL
						Type of Statement		
2	1		17	21	21	Unqualified	109	81
					1	Reviewed	2	1
						Compiled		2
						Tax Returns		1
	2	1	14	12	20	Other	47	37
	79 (4/1-9/30/18)		33 (10/1/18-3/31/19)					
2	3	1	31	33	42	**NUMBER OF STATEMENTS**	158	122
%	%	%	%	%	%	**ASSETS**	%	%
			15.2	17.5	16.3	Cash & Equivalents	15.3	17.7
			14.2	12.4	10.0	Trade Receivables (net)	14.4	14.4
			2.2	2.2	1.4	Inventory	1.9	1.8
			1.4	1.1	3.6	All Other Current	3.2	2.3
			33.0	33.1	31.3	Total Current	34.7	36.2
			44.9	42.8	41.4	Fixed Assets (net)	45.2	45.3
			.9	.7	2.0	Intangibles (net)	.7	.6
			21.3	23.4	25.3	All Other Non-Current	19.3	18.0
			100.0	100.0	100.0	Total	100.0	100.0
						LIABILITIES		
			.4	.5	.1	Notes Payable-Short Term	.6	.7
			1.9	2.3	1.1	Cur. Mat.-L.T.D.	2.4	2.2
			8.3	5.5	4.5	Trade Payables	6.3	5.6
			.0	.0	.0	Income Taxes Payable	.0	.0
			24.3	7.8	7.8	All Other Current	9.3	10.1
			34.9	16.1	13.4	Total Current	18.6	18.6
			31.7	22.9	22.6	Long-Term Debt	26.1	24.7
			.0	.0	.0	Deferred Taxes	.0	.1
			6.9	5.9	6.2	All Other Non-Current	4.4	4.4
			26.5	55.1	57.8	Net Worth	50.9	52.2
			100.0	100.0	100.0	Total Liabilities & Net Worth	100.0	100.0
						INCOME DATA		
			100.0	100.0	100.0	Net Sales	100.0	100.0
						Gross Profit		
			102.0	100.2	99.2	Operating Expenses	97.9	95.7
			-2.0	-.2	.8	Operating Profit	2.1	4.3
			-.9	-1.6	.3	All Other Expenses (net)	-.4	1.0
			-1.1	1.4	.5	Profit Before Taxes	2.5	3.3
						RATIOS		
			3.3	2.9	3.2		3.1	2.9
			1.4	2.1	1.8	Current	2.0	2.0
			1.0	1.4	1.4		1.3	1.5
			3.1	2.8	2.9		2.6	2.6
			1.3	1.9	1.6	Quick	1.7	1.8
			.8	1.3	1.2		1.0	1.2
			34 10.8	34 10.6	36 10.2		39 9.4	35 10.4
			41 8.9	45 8.1	39 9.3	Sales/Receivables	45 8.2	43 8.5
			50 7.3	53 6.9	48 7.6		54 6.7	54 6.7
						Cost of Sales/Inventory		
						Cost of Sales/Payables		
			5.9	3.1	3.4		3.6	4.1
			15.6	6.5	7.8	Sales/Working Capital	7.0	6.7
			-206.5	14.7	19.4		16.8	13.2
			8.5	6.0	4.0		7.0	9.1
			(30) 1.9	(32) 3.2	(39) 1.5	EBIT/Interest	(153) 3.1	(116) 3.8
			-.7	-.7	-.5		.5	.9
						Net Profit + Depr., Dep., Amort./Cur. Mat. L/T/D		
			.5	.6	.5		.6	.6
			1.0	.8	.7	Fixed/Worth	.9	.8
			3.9	1.2	1.0		1.3	1.3
			.5	.4	.4		.5	.5
			1.5	.8	.8	Debt/Worth	.9	.8
			4.6	1.5	1.1		1.6	1.4
			9.7	7.8	8.5	% Profit Before Taxes/Tangible	10.0	10.5
			(26) 1.6	(32) 2.0	(41) 1.1	Net Worth	(152) 4.4	(119) 4.6
			-2.0	-2.2	-1.6		-.9	.0
			4.8	4.3	4.9	% Profit Before Taxes/Total	5.2	5.6
			.6	1.3	.6	Assets	2.2	2.7
			-3.4	-1.4	-1.2		-.7	-.1
			4.4	3.2	3.2		3.2	3.5
			2.7	2.3	2.2	Sales/Net Fixed Assets	2.3	2.5
			1.6	1.8	1.5		1.8	1.8
			1.6	1.2	1.2		1.3	1.5
			1.1	1.0	.9	Sales/Total Assets	1.0	1.0
			.8	.7	.7		.8	.8
			3.1	4.7	3.9		4.3	3.8
			(30) 4.3	5.3	(34) 5.7	% Depr., Dep., Amort./Sales	(146) 5.3	(111) 4.9
			6.5	6.2	7.0		6.6	6.1
						% Officers', Directors' Owners' Comp/Sales	9.0	
							(10) 11.6	
							32.9	
199M	3045M	3976M	1003086M	2589907M	8547842M	Net Sales ($)	13117115M	10967033M
264M	3547M	8040M	837693M	2602310M	6944160M	Total Assets ($)	13208710M	10457090M

M = $ thousand   MM = $ million
See Pages viii through xx for Explanation of Ratios and Data

Comparative Historical Data / Current Data Sorted by Sales

91	70	62	Type of Statement	2	1			8	51
	2	1	Unqualified						
1		1	Reviewed						1
			Compiled						
			Tax Returns						
			Other	2	1		1	5	40
45	59	49		0-1MM	79 (4/1-9/30/18)		33 (10/1/18-3/31/19)		25MM & OVER
4/1/16-	4/1/17-	4/1/18-			1-3MM	3-5MM	5-10MM	10-25MM	
3/31/17	3/31/18	3/31/19							
ALL	ALL	ALL							
137	132	112	**NUMBER OF STATEMENTS**	4	1	1	1	13	92
%	%	%	**ASSETS**	%	%	%	%	%	%
17.5	15.5	16.7	Cash & Equivalents					19.2	16.1
13.7	13.3	11.8	Trade Receivables (net)					11.0	12.2
1.8	1.8	1.8	Inventory					1.8	1.9
3.6	3.2	2.2	All Other Current					1.6	2.2
36.6	33.8	32.5	Total Current					33.6	32.4
45.2	43.1	42.4	Fixed Assets (net)					46.1	42.5
.5	1.2	1.7	Intangibles (net)					1.0	1.4
17.6	22.0	23.3	All Other Non-Current					19.3	23.8
100.0	100.0	100.0	Total					100.0	100.0
			LIABILITIES						
.7	.5	.3	Notes Payable-Short Term					.4	.3
1.9	2.6	1.7	Cur. Mat.-L.T.D.					2.0	1.7
6.0	6.3	5.8	Trade Payables					7.1	5.8
.0	.0	.0	Income Taxes Payable					.0	.0
9.8	12.1	12.5	All Other Current					10.0	13.1
18.5	21.5	20.2	Total Current					19.6	20.8
27.3	24.8	25.2	Long-Term Debt					39.3	23.5
.0	.0	.0	Deferred Taxes					.0	.0
7.5	8.0	6.3	All Other Non-Current					2.9	6.8
46.7	45.7	48.3	Net Worth					38.2	49.0
100.0	100.0	100.0	Total Liabilties & Net Worth					100.0	100.0
			INCOME DATA						
100.0	100.0	100.0	Net Sales					100.0	100.0
			Gross Profit						
97.5	99.1	100.3	Operating Expenses					100.4	100.4
2.5	.9	-.3	Operating Profit					-.4	-.4
1.3	-1.6	-.7	All Other Expenses (net)					1.5	-.9
1.2	2.5	.4	Profit Before Taxes					-1.9	.6
			RATIOS						
3.6	2.9	3.1						4.0	2.9
2.2	1.9	1.9	Current					2.2	1.8
1.3	1.3	1.3						.9	1.3
2.9	2.7	2.9						3.6	2.7
1.8	1.6	1.6	Quick					2.1	1.6
1.1	1.0	1.1						.7	1.1
35 10.4	35 10.5	35 10.5						33 11.1	36 10.2
43 8.4	43 8.5	41 8.8	Sales/Receivables					38 9.5	41 8.9
54 6.8	54 6.7	50 7.3						55 6.6	49 7.5
			Cost of Sales/Inventory						
			Cost of Sales/Payables						
3.1	3.6	3.4						2.4	3.6
6.7	7.1	8.1	Sales/Working Capital					6.4	8.7
18.3	17.0	22.3						NM	22.5
5.7	6.3	5.6						11.4	5.4
(132) 2.4	(127) 2.6	(106) 1.9	EBIT/Interest					(12) .3	(88) 2.3
-.8	.3	-.6						-1.0	-.5
			Net Profit + Depr., Dep., Amort./Cur. Mat. L/T/D						
.6	.6	.5						.4	.5
.9	.8	.8	Fixed/Worth					.9	.8
1.6	1.4	1.3						42.7	1.2
.5	.5	.4						.4	.4
1.0	.9	.9	Debt/Worth					.9	.9
2.1	1.8	1.5						74.3	1.5
9.3	10.6	7.8	% Profit Before Taxes/Tangible					6.8	9.3
(127) 3.8	(120) 4.3	(104) 1.9	Net Worth					(11) .5	(87) 1.9
-3.4	-1.0	-1.8						-82.0	-1.3
4.2	5.1	4.4	% Profit Before Taxes/Total					2.6	4.7
1.6	2.0	1.0	Assets					-1.0	1.1
-1.9	-.9	-1.3						-5.2	-1.2
3.4	3.5	3.4						3.6	3.5
2.3	2.3	2.3	Sales/Net Fixed Assets					1.7	2.3
1.7	1.6	1.5						1.4	1.6
1.4	1.3	1.2						1.1	1.3
1.0	1.0	1.0	Sales/Total Assets					.9	1.0
.8	.7	.7						.7	.7
3.4	3.7	4.0						2.6	4.1
(128) 5.0	(121) 4.9	(103) 5.2	% Depr., Dep., Amort./Sales					6.0	(83) 5.2
6.1	6.1	6.3						6.8	6.2
			% Officers', Directors' Owners' Comp/Sales						
12271971M	12330541M	12148055M	Net Sales ($)	1572M	1672M	3976M	5042M	262199M	11873594M
12034139M	12484911M	10396014M	Total Assets ($)	2055M	1756M	8040M	10122M	307657M	10066384M

M = $ thousand   MM = $ million
See Pages viii through xx for Explanation of Ratios and Data

Current Data Sorted by Assets | Comparative Historical Data

	0-500M	500M-2MM	2-10MM	10-50MM	50-100MM	100-250MM		4/1/14-3/31/15 ALL	4/1/15-3/31/16 ALL
Type of Statement									
Unqualified		1	3	14	6	3		37	31
Reviewed		1	2					3	1
Compiled			2					2	1
Tax Returns	1							6	4
Other		4	5	11	2	1		32	37
	0-500M	500M-2MM	30 (4/1-9/30/18) 2-10MM	26 (10/1/18-3/31/19) 10-50MM	50-100MM	100-250MM			
NUMBER OF STATEMENTS	1	6	12	25	8	4		80	74
	%	%	%	%	%	%		%	%
ASSETS									
Cash & Equivalents			12.1	19.0				17.1	18.2
Trade Receivables (net)			19.9	22.5				19.1	18.5
Inventory			.2	.4				.7	.2
All Other Current			1.6	2.6				3.3	4.8
Total Current			33.7	44.6				40.3	41.8
Fixed Assets (net)			49.8	40.4				39.7	41.2
Intangibles (net)			3.3	6.1				7.1	7.1
All Other Non-Current			13.3	8.9				12.8	9.9
Total			100.0	100.0				100.0	100.0
LIABILITIES									
Notes Payable-Short Term			15.4	5.7				4.5	3.8
Cur. Mat.-L.T.D.			5.1	2.3				4.6	1.9
Trade Payables			7.0	4.5				7.5	6.1
Income Taxes Payable			.0	.0				.1	.0
All Other Current			9.9	9.7				11.2	8.2
Total Current			37.4	22.1				28.0	20.1
Long-Term Debt			16.7	16.5				21.9	27.8
Deferred Taxes			.4	.1				.2	.2
All Other Non-Current			20.9	5.6				9.7	7.2
Net Worth			24.5	55.6				40.1	44.6
Total Liabilties & Net Worth			100.0	100.0				100.0	100.0
INCOME DATA									
Net Sales			100.0	100.0				100.0	100.0
Gross Profit									
Operating Expenses			94.3	96.9				96.3	92.3
Operating Profit			5.7	3.1				3.7	7.7
All Other Expenses (net)			6.5	.6				1.2	1.8
Profit Before Taxes			-.8	2.6				2.4	5.9
RATIOS									
Current			1.9	4.1				2.8	3.4
			1.0	1.8				1.7	2.0
			.6	1.3				1.1	1.2
Quick			1.9	3.9				2.5	3.1
			1.0	1.8				1.6	1.8
			.5	1.2				.9	.9
Sales/Receivables			21 17.7	30 12.0				21 17.7	22 16.6
			29 12.4	49 7.4				37 9.9	42 8.6
			45 8.1	58 6.3				52 7.0	57 6.4
Cost of Sales/Inventory									
Cost of Sales/Payables									
Sales/Working Capital			8.5	3.3				5.5	4.6
			NM	11.2				11.7	10.6
			-10.8	17.9				73.8	47.2
EBIT/Interest				8.6				9.5	17.9
			(18)	1.0				(64) 2.9	(63) 4.3
				-2.6				-1.0	1.1
Net Profit + Depr., Dep., Amort./Cur. Mat. L/T/D								14.0	
								(10) 3.4	
								1.1	
Fixed/Worth			.6	.5				.6	.5
			1.2	.9				1.0	1.1
			2.5	1.7				3.0	3.6
Debt/Worth			.4	.3				.5	.4
			1.4	.6				1.3	1.1
			7.3	3.1				6.6	5.6
% Profit Before Taxes/Tangible Net Worth			24.5	14.2				24.4	29.1
			(10) 5.3	(23) 3.5				(69) 8.2	(63) 10.6
			-2.4	-1.8				-2.3	-.1
% Profit Before Taxes/Total Assets			9.1	8.8				9.5	10.9
			.7	1.1				4.2	5.2
			-6.4	-4.2				-2.2	.1
Sales/Net Fixed Assets			17.3	10.9				12.7	9.3
			2.5	3.6				4.0	3.2
			1.4	1.9				2.5	1.9
Sales/Total Assets			2.9	2.1				2.7	2.4
			1.4	1.6				1.5	1.4
			1.1	.9				1.0	.7
% Depr., Dep., Amort./Sales			1.8	1.7				1.1	1.6
			(11) 2.8	(23) 2.6				(73) 2.2	(65) 2.7
			3.4	4.8				3.6	4.0
% Officers', Directors', Owners' Comp/Sales								.7	2.3
								(11) 3.0	(10) 6.2
								5.3	11.9
Net Sales ($)	560M	35409M	90615M	998070M	639398M	841624M		3502042M	3424828M
Total Assets ($)	6M	8387M	57904M	612235M	558533M	706557M		2346171M	2519434M

M = $ thousand   MM = $ million
See Pages viii through xx for Explanation of Ratios and Data

Comparative Historical Data				Current Data Sorted by Sales					
			Type of Statement						
27	24	27	Unqualified			1	4	5	17
4	3	3	Reviewed				2	1	
3			Compiled						
1		3	Tax Returns	2		1			
38	40	23	Other		3		5	4	11
4/1/16-3/31/17 ALL	4/1/17-3/31/18 ALL	4/1/18-3/31/19 ALL		0-1MM	1-3MM 30 (4/1-9/30/18)	3-5MM	5-10MM 26 (10/1/18-3/31/19)	10-25MM	25MM & OVER
73	67	56	**NUMBER OF STATEMENTS**	2	3	2	11	10	28
%	%	%	**ASSETS**	%	%	%	%	%	%
14.5	15.4	18.6	Cash & Equivalents				20.2	18.0	15.0
17.4	24.4	20.8	Trade Receivables (net)				15.4	24.6	23.7
.3	.7	.3	Inventory				.2	.4	.4
5.2	4.6	1.8	All Other Current				1.9	1.1	2.0
37.5	45.1	41.4	Total Current				37.6	44.1	41.1
43.9	39.3	41.3	Fixed Assets (net)				48.9	41.2	38.9
8.8	5.0	6.6	Intangibles (net)				.0	3.9	10.7
9.9	10.7	10.7	All Other Non-Current				13.5	10.8	9.3
100.0	100.0	100.0	Total				100.0	100.0	100.0
			LIABILITIES						
3.2	4.0	6.2	Notes Payable-Short Term				2.5	3.2	4.8
2.5	1.9	2.8	Cur. Mat.-L.T.D.				4.9	1.6	2.3
5.7	7.2	5.2	Trade Payables				7.6	4.6	5.7
.1	.1	.0	Income Taxes Payable				.0	.0	.0
8.7	14.0	15.5	All Other Current				9.0	12.7	9.5
20.2	27.3	29.6	Total Current				24.0	22.2	22.2
33.5	25.4	23.7	Long-Term Debt				17.6	30.0	24.1
.1	.4	.2	Deferred Taxes				.3	.3	.1
4.6	4.9	8.0	All Other Non-Current				19.8	11.8	3.9
41.5	42.1	38.6	Net Worth				38.4	35.7	49.6
100.0	100.0	100.0	Total Liabilities & Net Worth				100.0	100.0	100.0
			INCOME DATA						
100.0	100.0	100.0	Net Sales				100.0	100.0	100.0
			Gross Profit						
92.3	96.0	95.6	Operating Expenses				93.9	99.0	96.8
7.7	4.0	4.4	Operating Profit				6.1	1.0	3.2
1.9	.8	2.0	All Other Expenses (net)				.0	.8	1.0
5.8	3.3	2.5	Profit Before Taxes				6.1	.1	2.2
			RATIOS						
2.8	2.9	3.3					2.9	5.5	3.3
1.8	1.9	1.8	Current				1.5	1.7	1.8
1.3	1.1	1.1					.7	1.3	1.3
2.7	2.9	3.1					2.9	5.2	3.1
1.6	1.5	1.7	Quick				1.3	1.7	1.8
1.0	.8	1.0					.4	1.2	1.2
24 15.1	33 10.9	24 15.4					19 18.9	23 16.2	37 9.8
45 8.2	51 7.2	45 8.2	Sales/Receivables				29 12.8	51 7.2	49 7.5
61 6.0	63 5.8	58 6.3					32 11.5	76 4.8	60 6.1
			Cost of Sales/Inventory						
			Cost of Sales/Payables						
5.1	4.7	4.9					6.4	3.0	4.3
10.0	9.3	12.9	Sales/Working Capital				45.2	12.9	11.0
33.5	60.0	75.8					-19.9	31.1	27.3
11.2	9.7	9.1							8.6
(66) 3.9	(54) 2.7	(43) 1.7	EBIT/Interest					(25) 1.5	
.1	-.2	.0							.1
			Net Profit + Depr., Dep., Amort./Cur. Mat. L/T/D						
.6	.5	.5					.3	.4	.6
1.1	1.0	.9	Fixed/Worth				.7	1.1	.9
3.9	3.3	2.2					2.2	NM	2.2
.7	.6	.4					.2	.2	.6
1.3	1.2	1.0	Debt/Worth				.7	1.0	1.2
6.5	6.6	6.1					1.6	NM	3.3
31.1	36.3	22.8					36.4		14.6
(61) 13.6	(60) 9.4	(49) 5.5	% Profit Before Taxes/Tangible Net Worth				(10) 7.4		(26) 4.8
-1.3	-4.6	-1.6					1.6		-1.7
14.6	7.8	11.6					19.2	12.1	8.4
5.0	2.8	1.7	% Profit Before Taxes/Total Assets				3.4	.4	1.2
-.6	-3.0	-1.6					-.2	-23.4	-1.0
9.2	14.6	12.4					20.8	24.0	10.3
3.0	4.0	3.4	Sales/Net Fixed Assets				2.4	3.2	3.6
1.4	2.4	1.7					1.2	1.6	2.1
1.9	2.4	2.1					3.0	2.8	2.1
1.4	1.7	1.5	Sales/Total Assets				1.3	1.6	1.5
.8	1.1	1.0					1.0	.8	1.0
1.9	1.6	1.8					1.3		1.7
(65) 2.8	(53) 2.4	(49) 2.7	% Depr., Dep., Amort./Sales				2.8		(26) 2.6
4.2	3.2	4.0					3.4		3.5
			% Officers', Directors' Owners' Comp/Sales						
4400984M	4919690M	2605676M	Net Sales ($)	817M	5333M	7710M	81922M	177329M	2332565M
3236086M	2724822M	1943622M	Total Assets ($)	4815M	2936M	5782M	98667M	125342M	1706080M

© RMA 2019

M = $ thousand   MM = $ million
See Pages viii through xx for Explanation of Ratios and Data

Current Data Sorted by Assets

Comparative Historical Data

		2	17	7	7	Type of Statement		
		2				Unqualified	44	35
	1	1	1			Reviewed	1	2
	1	1	1			Compiled	2	1
1	1	1	1		1	Tax Returns	4	1
	11	5	24	13	6	Other	55	50
	22 (4/1-9/30/18)		80 (10/1/18-3/31/19)				4/1/14-3/31/15	4/1/15-3/31/16
0-500M	500M-2MM	2-10MM	10-50MM	50-100MM	100-250MM		ALL	ALL
1	13	11	43	20	14	NUMBER OF STATEMENTS	106	89
%	%	%	%	%	%	ASSETS	%	%
	24.5	15.3	15.4	16.0	12.0	Cash & Equivalents	18.8	17.7
	16.4	39.6	24.9	22.9	11.9	Trade Receivables (net)	19.0	20.7
	.0	1.4	1.7	1.0	1.3	Inventory	2.9	2.5
	8.5	1.4	3.9	2.7	1.0	All Other Current	2.9	3.2
	49.4	57.8	45.9	42.7	26.2	Total Current	43.6	44.0
	40.1	28.1	33.9	32.0	37.4	Fixed Assets (net)	39.1	38.9
	2.0	1.9	12.8	10.7	16.7	Intangibles (net)	5.8	5.3
	8.6	12.2	7.3	14.6	19.8	All Other Non-Current	11.5	11.8
	100.0	100.0	100.0	100.0	100.0	Total	100.0	100.0
						LIABILITIES		
	9.7	1.1	1.6	.4	.2	Notes Payable-Short Term	5.4	2.5
	12.2	4.0	3.9	1.9	8.1	Cur. Mat.-L.T.D.	4.1	3.1
	5.8	13.2	8.3	5.5	4.3	Trade Payables	8.3	8.5
	.0	.0	.0	.0	1.6	Income Taxes Payable	.0	.0
	10.6	29.3	17.3	16.4	5.9	All Other Current	11.1	16.7
	38.3	47.7	31.1	24.3	20.2	Total Current	28.9	30.9
	42.8	24.8	24.6	22.4	21.9	Long-Term Debt	28.4	29.2
	.0	.0	.0	.0	.0	Deferred Taxes	.0	.3
	1.9	.3	6.7	1.1	4.1	All Other Non-Current	8.6	3.3
	17.0	27.2	37.6	52.2	53.8	Net Worth	34.0	36.3
	100.0	100.0	100.0	100.0	100.0	Total Liabilties & Net Worth	100.0	100.0
						INCOME DATA		
	100.0	100.0	100.0	100.0	100.0	Net Sales	100.0	100.0
						Gross Profit		
	81.5	91.5	85.5	81.6	91.8	Operating Expenses	90.3	85.7
	18.5	8.5	14.5	18.4	8.2	Operating Profit	9.7	14.3
	.8	.8	3.2	1.1	-.1	All Other Expenses (net)	1.3	3.2
	17.7	7.7	11.3	17.3	8.3	Profit Before Taxes	8.5	11.2
						RATIOS		
	3.8	2.5	3.0	4.4	3.5		3.3	3.5
	1.2	1.2	1.8	1.9	1.6	Current	1.9	2.0
	.7	.7	1.0	1.2	.9		1.0	1.1
	3.6	2.3	2.8	3.6	3.3		3.0	3.2
	1.2	1.1	1.3	1.8	1.4	Quick	1.7	1.7
	.3	.7	.9	1.1	.8		.9	.9

	0	UND	25	14.4	30	12.0	46	7.9	36	10.2		25	14.5	36	10.2
	0	UND	45	8.1	51	7.2	66	5.5	45	8.1	Sales/Receivables	41	9.0	47	7.8
	36	10.1	63	5.8	72	5.1	87	4.2	62	5.9		58	6.3	65	5.6

						Cost of Sales/Inventory		
						Cost of Sales/Payables		
	15.1	11.7	4.4	2.0	3.2		4.4	4.2
	46.3	29.1	8.8	7.8	14.5	Sales/Working Capital	8.9	7.5
	-30.4	-29.2	-999.8	15.6	-63.5		NM	74.5

										EBIT/Interest				
	34.1			30.4		40.6		11.6			43.9		55.0
(11)	6.7		(32)	9.1	(15)	22.1		7.2			(89)	8.0	(77)	7.2
	4.1			1.6		3.4		3.1			1.2		2.0

						Net Profit + Depr., Dep., Amort./Cur. Mat. L/T/D		
							3.5	
							(11) 1.2	
							.0	
	.4	.6	.5	.3	.6		.5	.4
	1.1	1.2	1.1	.7	1.1	Fixed/Worth	.9	.9
	UND	-4.5	3.7	2.3	2.1		9.0	2.8
	.9	.9	.6	.2	.5		.4	.5
	2.1	1.8	1.4	.8	1.4	Debt/Worth	1.9	1.3
	UND	-14.1	6.2	4.7	3.2		22.1	4.6

									% Profit Before Taxes/Tangible Net Worth				
	491.7			104.2		145.8		104.6		60.5		81.4
(10)	215.5		(33)	12.6	(17)	34.7	(13)	11.3		(83) 15.5	(74)	17.1
	72.0			2.5		4.2		4.0		4.7		2.6

	108.2	44.4	27.0	40.5	16.6	% Profit Before Taxes/Total Assets	23.4	25.4
	45.2	12.8	6.3	9.8	5.7		7.1	6.5
	14.3	3.2	1.4	1.5	2.3		.3	.9
	32.6	153.3	11.8	15.2	6.8	Sales/Net Fixed Assets	13.4	12.1
	18.8	16.6	6.5	4.4	1.9		3.7	3.3
	3.6	5.2	2.7	1.4	1.2		1.6	1.5
	8.1	4.4	2.3	1.9	1.5	Sales/Total Assets	2.9	2.3
	4.8	3.6	1.3	.9	.9		1.2	1.2
	2.5	2.4	.8	.6	.5		.8	.6

									% Depr., Dep., Amort./Sales				
	.6		1.9	1.2	1.7		2.0		2.2
(12)	1.2		3.2	2.4	(12) 4.7		(94) 3.5	(81)	3.7
	6.7		5.1	5.4	5.9		5.9		5.6

						% Officers', Directors' Owners' Comp/Sales		
							5.4	3.6
							(14) 13.2	(11) 7.5
							36.8	18.7

2649M	80645M	242586M	1816366M	1640167M	3867966M	Net Sales ($)	5098030M	5183027M
342M	15292M	61247M	1066707M	1373170M	2252649M	Total Assets ($)	4317559M	4869737M

M = $ thousand   MM = $ million
See Pages viii through xx for Explanation of Ratios and Data

Comparative Historical Data   Current Data Sorted by Sales

	4/1/16-3/31/17 ALL	4/1/17-3/31/18 ALL	4/1/18-3/31/19 ALL		0-1MM	1-3MM	3-5MM	5-10MM	10-25MM	25MM & OVER
Type of Statement						22 (4/1-9/30/18)			80 (10/1/18-3/31/19)	
Unqualified	43	34	33			2			5	26
Reviewed	6	3	2						2	
Compiled	1	1	3			1			1	1
Tax Returns	2	4	5			2			1	2
Other	66	42	59			5	1	6	18	29
NUMBER OF STATEMENTS	118	84	102			10	1	6	27	58
ASSETS	%	%	%		%	%	%	%	%	%
Cash & Equivalents	14.4	14.1	16.1	D		8.0			21.4	13.9
Trade Receivables (net)	23.7	22.9	23.0	A		5.7			21.4	26.4
Inventory	1.8	1.8	1.3	T		.0			.6	1.9
All Other Current	3.7	3.7	3.5	A		.5			8.1	1.9
Total Current	43.6	42.5	43.9			14.2			51.5	44.2
Fixed Assets (net)	32.9	35.9	34.7	N		73.4			27.8	32.0
Intangibles (net)	8.9	12.2	10.3	O		.3			11.9	10.8
All Other Non-Current	14.6	9.4	11.2	T		12.1			8.7	13.0
Total	100.0	100.0	100.0			100.0			100.0	100.0
LIABILITIES				A						
Notes Payable-Short Term	3.7	3.9	2.1	V		.5			3.0	.9
Cur. Mat.-L.T.D.	3.8	6.0	5.3	A		10.1			4.5	4.4
Trade Payables	9.5	9.1	7.4	I		1.0			7.2	8.2
Income Taxes Payable	.2	.0	.2	L		.0			.0	.4
All Other Current	18.7	18.0	16.4	A		8.0			23.8	15.3
Total Current	36.0	37.0	31.4	B		19.6			38.5	29.2
Long-Term Debt	26.2	24.9	26.8	L		64.7			26.5	18.9
Deferred Taxes	.0	.0	.0	E		.0			.0	.0
All Other Non-Current	3.6	4.1	3.9			.0			1.0	5.9
Net Worth	34.2	34.0	37.9			15.7			34.0	46.0
Total Liabilities & Net Worth	100.0	100.0	100.0			100.0			100.0	100.0
INCOME DATA										
Net Sales	100.0	100.0	100.0			100.0			100.0	100.0
Gross Profit										
Operating Expenses	87.9	88.8	85.8			66.7			89.2	89.5
Operating Profit	12.1	11.2	14.2			33.3			10.8	10.5
All Other Expenses (net)	2.8	1.5	1.7			11.5			.9	.1
Profit Before Taxes	9.2	9.6	12.4			21.8			10.0	10.4
RATIOS										
Current	3.3	3.1	3.2			2.8			3.1	3.2
	1.5	1.6	1.6			.7			1.6	1.8
	1.0	.9	.9			.3			.8	1.0
Quick	3.0	3.0	2.8			2.8			2.5	3.1
	1.3	1.4	1.4			.7			1.3	1.7
	.8	.8	.8			.2			.7	.9
Sales/Receivables	36 10.1	37 9.8	26 13.8			0 UND			20 18.1	42 8.7
	49 7.5	50 7.3	46 8.0			0 UND			45 8.1	51 7.1
	64 5.7	64 5.7	72 5.1			14 25.9			72 5.1	73 5.0
Cost of Sales/Inventory										
Cost of Sales/Payables										
Sales/Working Capital	4.8	3.9	4.9			15.3			4.4	4.7
	12.7	13.0	14.3			-13.3			11.9	10.1
	-230.7	-36.8	-59.3			-5.2			-45.1	-999.8
EBIT/Interest	52.1	45.8	30.5						36.3	29.1
	(103) 9.4	(68) 9.4	(80) 7.9						(20) 6.9	(50) 8.7
	.6	.6	3.1						2.1	2.8
Net Profit + Depr., Dep., Amort./Cur. Mat. L/T/D	8.8	15.7	24.1							
	(12) 3.6	(11) 7.3	(10) 9.1							
	2.0	-.4	1.1							
Fixed/Worth	.4	.5	.4			1.9			.5	.4
	.7	1.1	1.0			2.7			1.1	.9
	NM	3.4	3.3			UND			-1.6	1.6
Debt/Worth	.5	.5	.5			1.5			.9	.4
	1.2	1.2	1.5			2.0			1.6	1.1
	-67.6	7.3	5.8			UND			-7.5	4.2
% Profit Before Taxes/Tangible Net Worth	82.2	130.2	136.6						139.7	121.9
	(88) 25.5	(67) 20.1	(81) 22.9						(19) 13.6	(49) 20.9
	-.2	2.9	5.9						-1.6	5.9
% Profit Before Taxes/Total Assets	28.5	38.2	34.4			30.6			36.4	27.8
	9.7	6.6	10.9			10.8			10.1	9.7
	-1.1	-.3	2.5			4.9			.9	2.1
Sales/Net Fixed Assets	14.2	10.2	16.6			5.1			18.9	13.4
	6.4	4.9	6.6			2.4			7.4	6.6
	2.1	1.6	2.5			.1			3.4	2.2
Sales/Total Assets	2.8	2.6	3.0			3.6			4.1	2.4
	1.5	1.4	1.6			1.3			1.9	1.5
	.8	.6	.8			.1			.8	.8
% Depr., Dep., Amort./Sales	1.7	1.8	1.5			1.6			1.1	1.6
	(109) 3.3	(79) 3.1	(96) 2.9			11.3			(25) 2.2	(55) 2.9
	5.3	5.5	5.2			24.3			4.4	4.4
% Officers', Directors' Owners' Comp/Sales	2.2		3.9							
	(11) 11.0		(11) 11.0							
	17.2		30.2							
Net Sales ($)	5628086M	4189849M	7650379M			19891M	3300M	46373M	435647M	7145168M
Total Assets ($)	4903965M	3709705M	4769407M			64243M	1117M	81399M	400045M	4222603M

Current Data Sorted by Assets							Comparative Historical Data	

						Type of Statement		
2	13	60	96	35	32	Unqualified	277	359
	8	60	17	8	2	Reviewed	108	103
3	18	33	6	2	3	Compiled	102	76
16	14	9	1			Tax Returns	108	91
37	125	254	197	57	59	Other	746	767
	278 (4/1-9/30/18)			889 (10/1/18-3/31/19)			4/1/14-3/31/15	4/1/15-3/31/16
0-500M	500M-2MM	2-10MM	10-50MM	50-100MM	100-250MM		ALL	ALL
58	178	416	317	102	96	NUMBER OF STATEMENTS	1341	1396
%	%	%	%	%	%	**ASSETS**	%	%
31.1	14.1	12.0	11.1	7.6	7.9	Cash & Equivalents	11.5	11.6
23.1	43.4	28.6	14.8	15.3	12.6	Trade Receivables (net)	23.6	23.4
.3	.3	.1	.3	.3	.2	Inventory	.3	.2
4.2	3.0	3.5	2.3	3.6	3.1	All Other Current	3.2	2.6
58.7	60.8	44.3	28.5	26.9	23.9	Total Current	38.5	37.8
28.6	24.2	37.8	51.2	53.5	51.1	Fixed Assets (net)	41.2	41.9
2.0	4.6	6.1	7.2	8.2	9.3	Intangibles (net)	6.3	6.5
10.7	10.4	11.8	13.1	11.5	15.8	All Other Non-Current	13.9	13.9
100.0	100.0	100.0	100.0	100.0	100.0	Total	100.0	100.0
						LIABILITIES		
8.4	7.3	4.8	2.6	3.0	3.2	Notes Payable-Short Term	4.1	4.9
3.1	1.6	3.8	4.1	1.8	2.9	Cur. Mat.-L.T.D.	3.1	2.6
21.9	20.5	12.3	7.0	6.8	5.7	Trade Payables	10.8	9.9
.2	.1	.0	.0	.1	.1	Income Taxes Payable	.1	.1
73.2	47.1	21.0	12.6	11.8	10.7	All Other Current	22.2	20.0
106.8	76.6	42.0	26.3	23.4	22.6	Total Current	40.2	37.4
23.6	13.5	30.0	47.3	48.5	46.6	Long-Term Debt	34.2	34.2
.0	.0	.0	.1	.0	.0	Deferred Taxes	.0	.1
5.8	8.7	6.5	4.9	9.5	9.0	All Other Non-Current	8.5	8.9
-36.3	1.2	21.6	21.5	18.6	21.7	Net Worth	17.0	19.4
100.0	100.0	100.0	100.0	100.0	100.0	Total Liabilities & Net Worth	100.0	100.0
						INCOME DATA		
100.0	100.0	100.0	100.0	100.0	100.0	Net Sales	100.0	100.0
						Gross Profit		
96.2	94.4	88.3	87.9	92.1	94.7	Operating Expenses	89.0	89.2
3.8	5.6	11.7	12.1	7.9	5.3	Operating Profit	11.0	10.8
.8	1.8	5.3	7.4	5.3	3.9	All Other Expenses (net)	3.9	4.0
3.0	3.9	6.3	4.7	2.6	1.4	Profit Before Taxes	7.1	6.8
						RATIOS		
2.2	2.1	2.1	2.3	1.9	1.7	Current	2.3	2.1
.8	1.1	1.2	1.2	1.2	1.1		1.3	1.2
.3	.5	.6	.6	.8	.6		.7	.7
1.6	2.0	1.9	2.1	1.6	1.5	Quick	2.1	2.0
.8	1.0	1.1	1.1	1.0	1.0		(1338) 1.2	1.1
.3	.4	.5	.5	.6	.6		.6	.6
0 UND	22 16.7	23 15.9	22 16.9	29 12.6	29 12.6	Sales/Receivables	19 19.3	17 21.1
4 86.5	33 11.1	39 9.4	35 10.4	38 9.5	39 9.3		35 10.5	34 10.6
26 14.2	45 8.2	54 6.8	52 7.0	49 7.5	50 7.3		49 7.4	49 7.5
						Cost of Sales/Inventory		
						Cost of Sales/Payables		
15.9	14.1	9.3	6.0	8.3	8.7	Sales/Working Capital	8.0	9.4
-91.9	140.6	36.1	25.7	38.8	98.2		27.8	38.8
-10.6	-11.5	-10.1	-11.5	-19.5	-14.8		-17.3	-17.5
43.9	24.1	19.9	5.2	3.9	2.5	EBIT/Interest	12.7	16.8
(28) 1.8	(94) 1.5	(296) 3.3	(253) 2.0	(93) 1.8	(87) 1.5		(1001) 3.8	(1047) 3.8
-5.3	-13.0	.0	.8	.6	.5		1.2	1.0
		19.8	6.5		5.7	Net Profit + Depr., Dep., Amort./Cur. Mat. L/T/D	5.4	6.3
		(17) 3.3	(16) 2.8		(10) 2.5		(66) 3.1	(77) 3.3
		.3	1.3		1.9		1.7	1.3
.1	.3	.4	.9	1.9	1.6	Fixed/Worth	.6	.6
1.5	1.0	2.0	4.2	5.4	4.1		2.3	2.5
-.6	-.6	-4.2	-8.3	-3.7	-7.5		-5.7	-6.1
1.2	.8	.9	1.3	2.1	1.9	Debt/Worth	.9	1.0
3.2	5.4	3.9	7.2	6.2	5.8		4.1	4.2
-2.6	-3.9	-9.3	-12.2	-9.6	-17.3		-12.9	-11.3
109.4	76.9	52.9	28.3	30.5	20.4	% Profit Before Taxes/Tangible Net Worth	63.2	66.3
(33) 25.5	(108) 33.5	(268) 23.3	(205) 9.1	(67) 6.7	(66) 5.3		(921) 23.6	(963) 24.4
.0	-4.9	3.2	-.7	-3.0	-.5		4.8	4.1
38.7	26.0	16.8	6.3	6.2	3.8	% Profit Before Taxes/Total Assets	14.6	16.0
3.6	4.0	4.4	2.6	1.4	1.2		5.7	5.6
-24.7	-15.2	-1.1	-.6	-1.0	-.7		.7	.1
429.7	82.9	27.1	4.6	3.4	3.5	Sales/Net Fixed Assets	23.7	22.0
46.2	31.7	9.1	1.6	1.3	1.4		4.4	4.2
8.9	14.8	1.8	.9	.7	.8		1.2	1.2
11.5	6.0	3.5	1.4	1.3	1.3	Sales/Total Assets	3.5	3.5
7.9	4.6	2.2	.9	.8	.7		1.6	1.5
4.0	3.1	1.0	.5	.5	.5		.7	.7
.3	.4	.8	1.9	2.6	2.0	% Depr., Dep., Amort./Sales	.8	.9
(33) 1.2	(145) .7	(372) 1.6	(296) 3.9	(96) 4.4	(77) 4.9		(1220) 2.3	(1248) 2.4
3.8	1.3	4.3	7.5	7.0	7.1		5.4	5.4
3.6	2.0	2.2	1.8		3.0	% Officers', Directors' Owners' Comp/Sales	2.0	2.0
(16) 6.9	(19) 4.9	(44) 4.8	(27) 3.8		(14) 5.0		(141) 4.3	(134) 5.0
10.0	7.2	10.7	9.5		14.8		9.3	12.3
109779M	987859M	4449108M	9063075M	8831580M	16130378M	Net Sales ($)	40440547M	42549890M
13108M	221736M	2138415M	7021632M	7035191M	14920452M	Total Assets ($)	29776583M	31266891M

M = $ thousand   MM = $ million
See Pages viii through xx for Explanation of Ratios and Data

Comparative Historical Data			Type of Statement	Current Data Sorted by Sales					
306	268	238	Unqualified	10	17	13	25	86	87
100	103	95	Reviewed	4	4	4	22	38	23
71	67	65	Compiled	3	8	9	19	19	7
63	65	40	Tax Returns	9	12	7	10	2	
699	673	729	Other	56	66	49	204	176	178
4/1/16-3/31/17	4/1/17-3/31/18	4/1/18-3/31/19		278 (4/1-9/30/18)			889 (10/1/18-3/31/19)		
ALL	ALL	ALL		0-1MM	1-3MM	3-5MM	5-10MM	10-25MM	25MM & OVER
1239	1176	1167	NUMBER OF STATEMENTS	82	107	82	280	321	295
%	%	%	ASSETS	%	%	%	%	%	%
10.7	11.7	12.3	Cash & Equivalents	11.0	14.1	16.3	12.1	13.8	9.6
26.2	23.1	24.4	Trade Receivables (net)	1.8	10.4	27.7	34.5	26.3	23.1
.2	.2	.2	Inventory	.0	.2	.3	.2	.1	.4
3.5	3.8	3.1	All Other Current	2.1	3.6	2.7	3.2	2.6	3.8
40.6	38.9	40.0	Total Current	15.0	28.3	47.0	50.0	42.8	36.9
39.4	41.7	41.4	Fixed Assets (net)	67.8	52.7	35.5	32.7	39.1	42.2
7.1	5.7	6.4	Intangibles (net)	8.7	7.7	3.3	5.3	5.5	8.3
12.9	13.7	12.2	All Other Non-Current	8.6	11.3	14.2	12.0	12.6	12.6
100.0	100.0	100.0	Total	100.0	100.0	100.0	100.0	100.0	100.0
			LIABILITIES						
5.6	5.0	4.5	Notes Payable-Short Term	3.3	2.8	5.7	6.6	3.5	4.1
2.7	3.4	3.3	Cur. Mat.-L.T.D.	5.3	5.9	3.2	1.7	3.5	3.0
10.9	9.6	11.5	Trade Payables	2.7	10.9	13.4	14.8	12.0	10.2
.1	.1	.0	Income Taxes Payable	.0	.1	.2	.0	.0	.1
21.3	21.6	23.7	All Other Current	12.8	35.9	45.5	28.5	19.0	16.6
40.5	39.6	43.0	Total Current	24.1	55.5	68.1	51.6	38.0	34.0
30.6	34.9	34.8	Long-Term Debt	67.9	45.1	31.1	22.5	31.7	38.0
.1	.0	.0	Deferred Taxes	.0	.0	.1	.0	.0	.1
9.9	8.0	6.8	All Other Non-Current	6.6	4.7	5.3	9.2	5.3	7.4
19.0	17.4	15.3	Net Worth	1.4	-5.4	-4.5	16.7	24.9	20.5
100.0	100.0	100.0	Total Liabilities & Net Worth	100.0	100.0	100.0	100.0	100.0	100.0
			INCOME DATA						
100.0	100.0	100.0	Net Sales	100.0	100.0	100.0	100.0	100.0	100.0
			Gross Profit						
90.6	90.1	90.4	Operating Expenses	55.8	71.5	93.5	95.7	96.1	94.7
9.4	9.9	9.6	Operating Profit	44.2	28.5	6.5	4.3	3.9	5.3
3.4	3.5	5.0	All Other Expenses (net)	24.8	15.3	3.7	2.2	1.6	2.6
6.0	6.5	4.6	Profit Before Taxes	19.4	13.3	2.8	2.1	2.4	2.7
			RATIOS						
2.1	2.1	2.1		1.5	2.2	2.4	2.1	2.2	1.9
1.2	1.2	1.2	Current	.3	.6	1.1	1.2	1.3	1.2
.7	.7	.6		.0	.2	.4	.6	.8	.8
1.9	1.9	1.9		1.2	1.8	2.2	2.0	2.1	1.7
1.1	(1175) 1.1	1.0	Quick	.2	.5	1.0	1.1	1.2	1.1
.6	.6	.5		.0	.1	.4	.5	.7	.7
22 16.9	22 16.8	22 16.9		0 UND	0 UND	3 122.2	28 13.1	29 12.6	32 11.3
38 9.7	35 10.4	36 10.0	Sales/Receivables	0 UND	0 UND	28 13.0	39 9.3	40 9.1	41 8.9
51 7.1	48 7.6	51 7.2		0 UND	19 19.5	45 8.2	53 6.9	54 6.7	52 7.0
			Cost of Sales/Inventory						
			Cost of Sales/Payables						
8.8	8.8	9.0		6.6	12.6	10.0	8.8	8.4	8.4
32.4	31.9	44.6	Sales/Working Capital	-5.2	-19.1	135.7	32.8	24.7	35.9
-17.1	-16.6	-12.5		-1.2	-2.6	-6.1	-13.1	-23.3	-21.8
12.6	8.9	8.4		7.3	15.2	5.2	12.8	9.5	5.7
(953) 3.3	(908) 3.1	(851) 2.0	EBIT/Interest	(22) 4.1	(43) 3.9	(47) .5	(200) 2.4	(275) 2.0	(264) 2.0
.7	.8	.3		1.3	-1.3	-7.1	-1.4	.2	.9
5.8	4.7	8.6						12.9	8.1
(59) 2.9	(48) 2.5	(53) 3.3	Net Profit + Depr., Dep., Amort./Cur. Mat. L/T/D				(16) 2.4	(24) 4.4	
1.3	1.7	1.6						.1	2.0
.5	.5	.5		2.1	.7	.4	.4	.4	.9
2.2	2.3	2.9	Fixed/Worth	13.3	17.0	2.3	1.8	1.8	3.5
-5.6	-7.3	-4.8		-3.5	-3.0	-1.6	-3.7	-9.5	-5.6
1.0	1.0	1.1		2.5	1.4	.5	1.0	.9	1.4
4.0	4.0	5.3	Debt/Worth	136.2	-70.1	4.6	5.1	3.5	5.5
-10.6	-13.4	-9.0		-4.0	-4.4	-3.1	-7.9	-28.2	-11.7
60.5	48.8	45.9	% Profit Before Taxes/Tangible Net Worth	41.6	94.3	45.3	50.8	42.4	39.9
(857) 21.2	(797) 16.9	(747) 15.2		(42) 23.8	(51) 32.8	(48) 19.1	(179) 15.1	(230) 12.6	(197) 12.1
3.1	1.9	-.1		6.4	4.0	-4.0	-5.6	-1.4	1.0
14.3	13.2	11.1	% Profit Before Taxes/Total Assets	8.9	19.4	17.1	13.7	10.9	7.9
4.7	4.4	2.9		2.7	3.4	1.1	3.0	3.3	2.8
-.3	-.1	-1.3		.1	-.7	6.9	-6.1	-1.2	.3
25.0	23.0	24.0	Sales/Net Fixed Assets	1.2	34.1	58.7	39.2	23.0	17.2
6.1	4.1	4.5		.2	1.3	11.7	15.0	4.6	3.2
1.3	1.2	1.1		.1	.2	2.0	2.2	1.4	1.3
3.4	3.5	3.7	Sales/Total Assets	.5	4.5	5.1	4.6	3.4	3.0
1.6	1.5	1.6		.2	.7	2.4	2.8	1.7	1.1
.7	.7	.7		.1	.1	.8	1.1	.9	.7
.8	.9	.9		10.0	1.5	.6	.5	1.0	1.1
(1094) 2.3	(1053) 2.5	(1019) 2.4	% Depr., Dep., Amort./Sales	(71) 26.9	(78) 10.8	(67) 1.3	(242) 1.2	(300) 2.4	(261) 2.7
5.6	5.7	5.9		41.2	31.5	4.8	3.2	4.4	5.4
1.8	1.9	2.1			3.6	1.8	2.3	1.4	3.6
(121) 4.4	(123) 4.1	(128) 5.1	% Officers', Directors' Owners' Comp/Sales		(17) 6.9	(17) 5.8	(30) 4.9	(28) 3.1	(31) 5.0
12.0	7.6	9.6			9.8	7.9	8.8	14.8	11.0
43076538M	39978811M	39571779M	Net Sales ($)	44927M	189638M	334720M	2079083M	5142845M	31780566M
31972517M	31297223M	31350534M	Total Assets ($)	333892M	696156M	372660M	1952201M	5131627M	22863998M

© RMA 2019

M = $ thousand   MM = $ million
See Pages viii through xx for Explanation of Ratios and Data

	Current Data Sorted by Assets					Type of Statement	Comparative Historical Data	
2	9	31	29	12	4	Unqualified	113	117
		4	1			Reviewed	1	4
1	1	1				Compiled	4	5
2	4	2	2	1		Tax Returns	13	10
1	4	25	24	2	3	Other	75	55
	99 (4/1-9/30/18)		65 (10/1/18-3/31/19)				4/1/14-3/31/15	4/1/15-3/31/16
0-500M	500M-2MM	2-10MM	10-50MM	50-100MM	100-250MM		ALL	ALL
6	18	63	55	15	7	**NUMBER OF STATEMENTS**	206	191
%	%	%	%	%	%	**ASSETS**	%	%
	19.6	21.1	27.3	7.4		Cash & Equivalents	19.1	19.0
	13.6	16.2	15.2	19.5		Trade Receivables (net)	15.0	14.3
	.0	.3	.4	.2		Inventory	.2	.3
	1.9	1.9	1.3	.5		All Other Current	2.2	1.6
	35.0	39.5	44.2	27.6		Total Current	36.5	35.3
	49.6	48.1	45.6	46.2		Fixed Assets (net)	50.9	50.1
	6.8	.5	1.0	15.0		Intangibles (net)	3.4	3.7
	8.6	11.9	9.2	11.1		All Other Non-Current	9.2	10.9
	100.0	100.0	100.0	100.0		Total	100.0	100.0
						LIABILITIES		
	1.2	1.0	1.1	2.0		Notes Payable-Short Term	2.9	2.4
	4.3	2.1	1.9	3.8		Cur. Mat.-L.T.D.	2.5	2.6
	3.4	3.9	3.7	3.4		Trade Payables	4.1	3.7
	.0	.1	.0	.0		Income Taxes Payable	.1	.1
	19.0	11.5	14.0	11.0		All Other Current	11.9	10.8
	27.9	18.5	20.6	20.2		Total Current	21.5	19.5
	22.2	17.5	17.8	38.3		Long-Term Debt	26.6	26.6
	.0	.2	.0	.0		Deferred Taxes	.2	.1
	1.2	2.9	1.6	12.7		All Other Non-Current	3.1	3.4
	48.7	60.9	59.9	28.8		Net Worth	48.7	50.5
	100.0	100.0	100.0	100.0		Total Liabilties & Net Worth	100.0	100.0
						INCOME DATA		
	100.0	100.0	100.0	100.0		Net Sales	100.0	100.0
						Gross Profit		
	93.7	95.5	96.9	94.5		Operating Expenses	93.0	93.3
	6.3	4.5	3.1	5.5		Operating Profit	7.0	6.7
	1.2	.4	.1	3.6		All Other Expenses (net)	1.7	1.9
	5.1	4.1	3.1	2.0		Profit Before Taxes	5.3	4.8
						RATIOS		
	2.0	4.1	3.2	2.0			3.0	3.1
	1.3	2.7	2.5	1.1		Current	1.7	1.9
	.6	1.4	1.7	.9			1.0	1.1
	1.9	3.7	3.2	2.0			2.7	2.9
	1.1	2.5	2.4	1.1		Quick	1.5	1.7
	.6	1.3	1.5	.9			1.0	1.0
	0 UND	17 21.0	22 16.5	31 11.8			15 23.7	20 18.6
	1 250.2	30 12.2	35 10.3	38 9.5		Sales/Receivables	31 11.8	31 11.8
	21 17.0	38 9.5	42 8.6	42 8.6			40 9.2	40 9.2
						Cost of Sales/Inventory		
						Cost of Sales/Payables		
	13.5	4.3	3.1	13.9			6.3	5.8
	53.2	8.3	6.7	77.0		Sales/Working Capital	14.5	12.0
	-9.5	27.5	12.0	-51.3			-999.8	81.7
	20.0	14.2	17.3	5.7			9.5	7.2
	(12) 7.5	(53) 2.7	(49) 4.8	(14) 2.7		EBIT/Interest	(170) 2.9	(168) 2.9
	.0	-1.6	1.8	1.1			1.2	.9
						Net Profit + Depr., Dep., Amort./Cur. Mat. L/T/D		4.2
							(10)	1.7
								1.1
	.6	.4	.5	1.0			.6	.6
	1.1	.8	.7	1.7		Fixed/Worth	1.2	1.1
	3.7	1.3	1.1	-2.0			2.2	2.0
	.4	.3	.4	1.1			.4	.4
	1.1	.5	.6	2.0		Debt/Worth	1.1	1.0
	6.2	1.2	1.1	-3.9			2.7	2.5
	74.9	17.4	12.7				20.5	12.7
	(15) 12.9	(61) 5.7	(53) 7.1			% Profit Before Taxes/Tangible Net Worth	(197) 8.1	(179) 5.7
	-1.5	-6.5	2.3				1.0	-.2
	17.1	10.4	8.0	7.6			8.4	6.4
	6.4	3.6	4.1	2.6		% Profit Before Taxes/Total Assets	3.6	2.6
	-1.3	-3.1	1.4	.4			.2	.0
	18.7	9.1	4.9	19.0			6.0	5.9
	6.6	3.4	2.9	3.4		Sales/Net Fixed Assets	3.0	3.1
	.4	2.0	1.9	2.2			1.7	1.7
	5.2	2.3	1.9	2.0			2.4	2.2
	2.8	1.6	1.3	1.6		Sales/Total Assets	1.5	1.5
	.3	.8	1.0	1.4			.9	.9
	.9	1.2	1.8	2.0			1.6	1.5
	2.8	(61) 2.1	(50) 2.8	(12) 2.5		% Depr., Dep., Amort./Sales	(186) 2.5	(177) 2.6
	19.1	4.2	3.7	3.1			3.9	3.7
								2.4	2.3
						% Officers', Directors' Owners' Comp/Sales	(17) 5.6	(13) 6.1
							9.6	8.5
8273M	66536M	673554M	1757683M	1941067M	859619M	Net Sales ($)	5460661M	4270715M
1339M	23887M	362575M	1024382M	1135489M	1097786M	Total Assets ($)	4514411M	3335007M

Comparative Historical Data / Current Data Sorted by Sales

	4/1/16-3/31/17 ALL	4/1/17-3/31/18 ALL	4/1/18-3/31/19 ALL	99 (4/1-9/30/18) 0-1MM	1-3MM	3-5MM	65 (10/1/18-3/31/19) 5-10MM	10-25MM	25MM & OVER
Type of Statement									
Unqualified	106	109	87	4	3	9	20	22	29
Reviewed	4	5	5		1		2	2	
Compiled	10	10	3	2			1		
Tax Returns	8	13	10	1	2	2	2	2	1
Other	60	71	59	5	7	2	7	20	18
NUMBER OF STATEMENTS	188	208	164	12	13	13	32	46	48
	%	%	%	%	%	%	%	%	%
ASSETS									
Cash & Equivalents	20.1	20.1	21.7	10.4	32.8	22.7	25.2	24.0	16.6
Trade Receivables (net)	15.1	15.9	15.3	.8	4.3	13.6	11.5	16.2	23.9
Inventory	.5	.2	.3	.0	.1	.0	.0	.5	.4
All Other Current	2.2	2.0	1.5	1.8	.1	1.2	2.7	1.2	1.3
Total Current	37.9	38.2	38.7	13.0	37.2	37.5	39.5	41.9	42.2
Fixed Assets (net)	46.4	46.6	46.7	77.4	33.2	55.2	48.7	45.9	39.9
Intangibles (net)	3.8	3.6	3.0	5.1	8.1	.0	.8	.7	5.5
All Other Non-Current	11.9	11.6	11.6	4.5	21.5	7.3	11.0	11.5	12.4
Total	100.0	100.0	100.0	100.0	100.0	100.0	100.0	100.0	100.0
LIABILITIES									
Notes Payable-Short Term	2.7	3.4	1.8	3.9	.6	5.8	.5	1.3	1.9
Cur. Mat.-L.T.D.	2.6	2.8	2.6	6.6	.5	4.1	2.6	2.0	2.4
Trade Payables	3.4	3.9	3.8	.2	1.8	3.5	3.1	3.7	5.8
Income Taxes Payable	.0	.0	.0	.0	.0	.0	.1	.1	.0
All Other Current	12.5	12.8	13.6	5.8	9.1	20.1	12.3	13.3	16.2
Total Current	21.2	22.9	21.9	16.5	12.0	33.5	18.5	20.2	26.4
Long-Term Debt	26.3	23.5	21.5	45.6	8.3	18.9	17.8	19.4	24.3
Deferred Taxes	.0	.1	.1	.0	.0	.0	.0	.0	.1
All Other Non-Current	3.2	4.1	3.7	3.4	.6	.0	3.3	3.3	6.1
Net Worth	49.3	49.4	52.9	34.5	79.1	47.5	60.1	57.0	43.0
Total Liabilties & Net Worth	100.0	100.0	100.0	100.0	100.0	100.0	100.0	100.0	100.0
INCOME DATA									
Net Sales	100.0	100.0	100.0	100.0	100.0	100.0	100.0	100.0	100.0
Gross Profit									
Operating Expenses	93.4	94.2	95.5	85.9	93.5	96.0	95.2	97.5	96.7
Operating Profit	6.6	5.8	4.5	14.1	6.5	4.0	4.8	2.5	3.3
All Other Expenses (net)	1.7	1.4	.8	3.0	-1.8	.3	1.1	.8	.9
Profit Before Taxes	4.9	4.4	3.7	11.1	8.4	3.7	3.7	1.7	2.4
RATIOS									
Current	2.8	2.9	3.2	2.2	11.1	3.7	4.1	3.1	2.5
	1.8	1.8	2.1	.5	3.5	1.8	2.7	2.4	1.6
	1.0	1.0	1.1	.2	1.5	.7	1.1	1.4	1.0
Quick	2.7	2.8	3.1	2.0	11.1	3.3	3.7	3.0	2.5
	1.7	1.7	2.0	.4	3.0	1.8	2.6	2.2	1.6
	.9	.9	1.0	.1	1.5	.7	1.0	1.4	1.0
Sales/Receivables	18 20.0	21 17.2	17 22.0	0 UND	0 UND	8 44.0	14 25.8	22 16.8	31 11.9
	32 11.5	30 12.1	31 11.8	0 UND	5 80.3	21 17.2	29 12.4	33 11.1	38 9.7
	41 8.9	39 9.3	40 9.1	0 UND	22 16.3	42 8.7	39 9.4	40 9.1	45 8.2
Cost of Sales/Inventory									
Cost of Sales/Payables									
Sales/Working Capital	5.2	4.9	4.9	10.6	2.1	5.0	4.3	4.3	6.5
	13.3	14.1	11.1	-10.6	11.6	14.9	7.9	8.0	13.0
	UND	NM	74.4	-2.2	43.6	-34.6	49.6	17.0	393.9
EBIT/Interest	8.0	8.2	13.8			20.9	14.9	13.9	9.7
	(158) 3.2	(172) 3.1	(138) 4.0		(11) 6.9	(27) 4.8	(41) 3.5	(45) 4.0	
	.5	.8	.3			-.7	-2.4	.4	1.8
Net Profit + Depr., Dep., Amort./Cur. Mat. L/T/D									
Fixed/Worth	.6	.6	.5	1.2	.0	.6	.5	.5	.6
	1.0	1.0	.9	2.6	.7	.9	.7	.7	.9
	2.1	2.1	1.7	-11.0	1.3	3.0	1.2	1.5	1.7
Debt/Worth	.4	.4	.4	.5	.1	.3	.2	.3	.7
	1.0	.9	.7	1.7	.1	.6	.5	.5	1.1
	2.6	2.6	1.9	-13.7	.6	4.8	1.8	1.5	2.0
% Profit Before Taxes/Tangible Net Worth	16.4	16.3	15.8		28.9	13.4	17.1	13.3	16.8
	(175) 6.4	(188) 6.7	(147) 7.4		(11) 8.8	(12) 3.9	(30) 7.4	(44) 5.3	(42) 10.4
	-.8	.3	-.5		3.8	-6.6	-1.2	-.9	3.3
% Profit Before Taxes/Total Assets	8.3	7.6	8.5	10.8	19.1	10.0	11.6	6.2	8.1
	3.3	3.1	3.8	.2	8.1	2.6	4.6	2.8	4.2
	-.4	-.2	-.6	-1.4	1.6	-4.0	-1.4	-.6	1.0
Sales/Net Fixed Assets	7.4	7.9	7.3	.5	435.5	6.7	6.3	6.3	10.2
	3.2	3.3	3.4	.2	4.4	2.3	2.9	3.3	4.0
	2.0	2.1	2.0	.2	1.8	1.4	2.2	2.0	3.0
Sales/Total Assets	2.2	2.3	2.3	.3	2.2	3.0	2.3	2.2	2.4
	1.5	1.5	1.5	.2	.8	1.6	1.5	1.6	1.8
	1.0	.9	.9	.1	.4	.9	.9	1.1	1.2
% Depr., Dep., Amort./Sales	1.3	1.5	1.5	12.0	.7	2.0	1.1	1.7	1.5
	(178) 2.4	(192) 2.4	(152) 2.5	21.7	(10) 4.1	(12) 3.1	(31) 2.5	(45) 2.6	(42) 2.3
	3.9	3.9	3.9	44.4	9.2	7.2	3.5	3.3	3.0
% Officers', Directors' Owners' Comp/Sales	2.4	2.5							
	(14) 6.7	(17) 5.3							
	12.8	13.0							
Net Sales ($)	5103044M	8862720M	5306732M	4411M	25873M	53238M	237793M	741991M	4243426M
Total Assets ($)	4108164M	4856760M	3645458M	27579M	43913M	42037M	232643M	721556M	2577730M

M = $ thousand   MM = $ million
See Pages viii through xx for Explanation of Ratios and Data

Current Data Sorted by Assets   Comparative Historical Data

Type of Statement	0-500M	500M-2MM	2-10MM	10-50MM	50-100MM	100-250MM		4/1/14-3/31/15 ALL	4/1/15-3/31/16 ALL
Unqualified		5	21	37	7	3		123	103
Reviewed		2	6					14	5
Compiled				1				7	7
Tax Returns	5	9	4					8	8
Other	8	11	23	22	5	5		77	81
		79 (4/1-9/30/18)		95 (10/1/18-3/31/19)					
NUMBER OF STATEMENTS	13	27	54	60	12	8		229	204
	%	%	%	%	%	%	**ASSETS**	%	%
	34.0	28.6	14.4	16.3	12.8		Cash & Equivalents	18.0	17.9
	10.9	21.6	22.6	20.3	15.6		Trade Receivables (net)	15.8	20.0
	.3	.0	.1	.3	.0		Inventory	.1	.1
	6.4	1.2	2.1	3.5	2.3		All Other Current	3.0	3.2
	51.5	51.5	39.1	40.5	30.8		Total Current	37.0	41.3
	33.2	34.0	47.0	48.2	49.2		Fixed Assets (net)	48.8	45.8
	4.8	6.1	6.5	2.6	7.2		Intangibles (net)	3.5	3.2
	10.5	8.4	7.4	8.7	12.8		All Other Non-Current	10.7	9.7
	100.0	100.0	100.0	100.0	100.0		Total	100.0	100.0
							LIABILITIES		
	16.6	10.3	1.9	1.9	1.7		Notes Payable-Short Term	2.5	3.6
	.5	2.1	2.9	1.4	2.4		Cur. Mat.-L.T.D.	2.7	2.1
	1.9	13.2	4.6	6.0	2.5		Trade Payables	4.9	4.4
	.0	.0	.0	.0	.3		Income Taxes Payable	.1	.1
	13.3	20.6	17.8	11.6	9.1		All Other Current	14.6	12.8
	32.2	46.3	27.2	21.0	16.0		Total Current	24.8	23.0
	15.4	17.4	28.9	23.0	40.8		Long-Term Debt	27.9	24.8
	.0	.0	.0	.1	.3		Deferred Taxes	.1	.1
	31.5	9.9	4.0	5.1	5.4		All Other Non-Current	5.2	5.9
	20.9	26.4	39.9	50.8	37.6		Net Worth	42.2	46.2
	100.0	100.0	100.0	100.0	100.0		Total Liabilities & Net Worth	100.0	100.0
							INCOME DATA		
	100.0	100.0	100.0	100.0	100.0		Net Sales	100.0	100.0
							Gross Profit		
	93.3	91.5	90.8	96.3	94.2		Operating Expenses	92.5	90.9
	6.7	8.5	9.2	3.7	5.8		Operating Profit	7.5	9.1
	2.1	1.5	3.0	.3	4.5		All Other Expenses (net)	1.3	1.7
	4.6	7.0	6.2	3.4	1.2		Profit Before Taxes	6.3	7.3
							RATIOS		
	5.3	7.2	3.6	3.2	3.2			3.7	3.4
	1.6	2.0	1.8	2.2	2.0		Current	2.0	1.9
	.9	.6	.9	1.4	1.3			1.1	1.2
	5.3	7.2	3.0	3.1	3.0			3.5	3.2
	1.2	1.7	1.6	1.9	1.6		Quick	1.8	1.8
	.7	.6	.9	1.2	1.1			1.0	1.1
	0 UND	0 UND	19 19.0	31 11.9	24 15.0			16 22.8	15 24.5
	0 UND	27 13.7	41 9.0	42 8.6	40 9.2		Sales/Receivables	33 11.2	35 10.5
	14 26.1	40 9.2	59 6.2	63 5.8	56 6.5			45 8.2	55 6.6
							Cost of Sales/Inventory		
							Cost of Sales/Payables		
	16.9	7.0	5.3	4.1	4.6			5.2	4.3
	39.4	15.5	13.7	6.8	11.5		Sales/Working Capital	11.1	9.4
	-510.8	-25.3	-49.3	14.6	24.4			60.2	36.2
		52.0	13.0	11.1	4.7			8.7	16.0
		(19) 5.7	(42) 3.0	(49) 3.6	(11) 1.4		EBIT/Interest	(188) 3.6	(166) 4.0
		1.7	-3.0	1.1	-.8			1.1	1.3
								27.4	
							Net Profit + Depr., Dep., Amort./Cur. Mat. L/T/D	(10) 5.8	
								2.0	
	.3	.1	.7	.6	.6			.6	.5
	.8	1.1	1.2	.9	1.0		Fixed/Worth	1.1	.9
	-2.5	-54.0	NM	1.4	NM			2.4	2.1
	.4	.3	.4	.4	.4			.4	.4
	.7	1.2	1.4	.7	1.2		Debt/Worth	1.0	1.0
	-12.0	-20.6	NM	2.4	NM			3.0	2.9
		103.9	25.6	13.1				26.3	25.2
	(19) 45.0	(41) 7.6	(55) 6.0				% Profit Before Taxes/Tangible Net Worth	(205) 8.1	(186) 9.0
		16.2	-5.9	1.0				1.6	1.2
	118.6	47.4	15.2	5.7	9.4			10.8	10.2
	51.9	15.1	3.1	2.5	.6		% Profit Before Taxes/Total Assets	3.9	4.1
	-45.2	1.9	-4.2	.2	-3.6			.0	.3
	51.7	50.6	10.1	6.3	3.4			7.6	10.0
	30.8	21.7	4.3	3.0	2.5		Sales/Net Fixed Assets	2.7	3.1
	14.9	9.3	1.2	1.1	1.2			1.5	1.6
	13.8	6.5	2.5	2.0	1.8			2.4	2.4
	6.8	4.3	1.4	1.1	1.0		Sales/Total Assets	1.3	1.4
	4.7	1.9	.8	.8	.8			.8	.9
		.6	1.2	1.3	1.7			1.6	1.3
	(20) 1.0	(48) 3.1	(55) 2.5	(10) 2.4			% Depr., Dep., Amort./Sales	(207) 2.7	(182) 2.5
		2.3	5.3	4.6	4.4			4.2	4.0
		1.3						1.7	3.1
	(10) 5.6						% Officers', Directors' Owners' Comp/Sales	(29) 4.7	(11) 5.6
		9.6						10.6	9.3
	28801M	158750M	514249M	1760387M	1054528M	856717M	Net Sales ($)	4408500M	4497466M
	3383M	27873M	298033M	1315489M	900194M	1305509M	Total Assets ($)	3716731M	3551461M

Comparative Historical Data | Current Data Sorted by Sales

Type of Statement	4/1/16-3/31/17	4/1/17-3/31/18	4/1/18-3/31/19	0-1MM	1-3MM	3-5MM	5-10MM	10-25MM	25MM & OVER
Unqualified	100	95	73	1	7	3	12	27	23
Reviewed	7	4	8	1	1		4	2	
Compiled	2	4	1						1
Tax Returns	7	12	18	3	5	2	7	1	
Other	72	111	74	5	7	6	19	16	21
	ALL	ALL	ALL	79 (4/1-9/30/18)		95 (10/1/18-3/31/19)			
NUMBER OF STATEMENTS	188	226	174	9	20	12	42	46	45

ASSETS

	%	%	%	%	%	%	%	%	%
Cash & Equivalents	19.1	19.5	18.2		25.0	15.7	24.8	17.0	13.2
Trade Receivables (net)	20.7	18.4	19.7		15.1	20.4	14.0	24.3	24.6
Inventory	.1	.2	.2		.2	.0	.0	.1	.6
All Other Current	3.3	2.8	2.8		1.9	.9	1.9	2.5	3.8
Total Current	43.2	41.0	40.9		42.2	37.0	40.7	43.9	42.2
Fixed Assets (net)	45.2	42.9	43.9		39.3	37.5	47.4	45.0	38.3
Intangibles (net)	2.8	8.1	6.4		5.6	13.6	5.4	1.5	10.8
All Other Non-Current	8.8	8.0	8.7		12.8	11.8	6.5	9.6	8.7
Total	100.0	100.0	100.0		100.0	100.0	100.0	100.0	100.0

LIABILITIES

Notes Payable-Short Term	2.2	3.5	4.2		11.7	3.8	2.1	5.3	2.4
Cur. Mat.-L.T.D.	2.1	2.1	2.0		4.5	2.1	1.6	1.3	2.0
Trade Payables	4.2	4.9	6.0		2.7	3.3	8.7	4.2	7.3
Income Taxes Payable	.1	.2	.0		.0	.0	.0	.0	.1
All Other Current	14.6	17.7	14.6		7.4	12.1	13.4	22.5	12.7
Total Current	23.2	28.3	26.8		26.3	21.3	25.8	33.4	24.6
Long-Term Debt	25.0	24.5	25.3		32.5	25.8	21.6	21.2	25.8
Deferred Taxes	.1	.1	.1		.0	.0	.1	.0	.3
All Other Non-Current	4.2	4.6	7.4		1.0	25.4	.9	5.0	7.4
Net Worth	47.5	42.6	40.4		40.1	27.6	51.7	40.4	41.9
Total Liabilities & Net Worth	100.0	100.0	100.0		100.0	100.0	100.0	100.0	100.0

INCOME DATA

Net Sales	100.0	100.0	100.0		100.0	100.0	100.0	100.0	100.0
Gross Profit									
Operating Expenses	93.2	94.1	93.2		80.8	94.1	93.6	97.4	95.8
Operating Profit	6.8	5.9	6.8		19.2	5.9	6.4	2.6	4.2
All Other Expenses (net)	1.1	1.7	2.0		4.9	-.2	.5	.8	2.9
Profit Before Taxes	5.7	4.2	4.8		14.3	6.1	5.9	1.8	1.4

RATIOS

Current	3.7	3.5	3.6		8.5	6.4	5.7	3.1	2.8
	2.1	1.9	1.9		2.1	1.3	3.1	1.7	1.9
	1.2	1.1	1.1		1.2	.7	1.5	.9	1.3
Quick	3.4	3.2	3.3		8.0	6.4	5.7	2.8	2.6
	1.9	1.8	1.7		1.8	1.2	2.6	1.6	1.7
	1.1	.9	.9		1.2	.7	1.0	.9	1.0
Sales/Receivables	25 14.5	11 32.5	15 24.8		0 UND	0 UND	0 UND	27 13.7	34 10.8
	40 9.2	34 10.7	38 9.7		13 28.8	40 9.1	36 10.0	42 8.7	43 8.5
	53 6.9	49 7.4	57 6.4		35 10.4	65 5.6	57 6.4	63 5.8	60 6.1
Cost of Sales/Inventory									
Cost of Sales/Payables									
Sales/Working Capital	4.5	5.2	5.5		5.8	6.5	4.1	4.4	6.0
	9.2	11.0	11.3		11.7	65.4	7.7	13.5	9.6
	28.0	216.7	312.0		52.6	-17.9	24.7	-96.8	27.8
EBIT/Interest	11.7	13.1	13.9		22.9	50.8	46.0	9.4	10.1
	(148) 3.6	(174) 2.8	(134) 3.3		(13) 5.7	(10) 5.8	(34) 7.2	(32) 1.3	(39) 2.7
	1.0	-1.4	.1		2.1	.5	-.4	-5.1	.2
Net Profit + Depr., Dep., Amort./Cur. Mat. L/T/D		14.1							
		(10) 3.4							
		1.4							
Fixed/Worth	.4	.5	.6		.3	.8	.5	.6	.7
	1.0	1.0	1.0		.8	2.7	.9	1.0	1.0
	1.7	3.3	3.9		3.9	-4.4	1.7	2.9	3.4
Debt/Worth	.4	.4	.4		.2	.5	.2	.5	.6
	.9	1.1	1.0		.9	6.6	.6	1.1	1.4
	2.0	5.0	6.1		NM	-8.2	2.0	5.0	4.1
% Profit Before Taxes/Tangible Net Worth	25.8	29.8	30.5		83.3		51.6	12.9	18.9
	(170) 8.4	(188) 9.8	(138) 8.6		(15) 16.2		(36) 18.8	(38) 3.8	(37) 7.7
	.1	-2.1	.0		2.7		1.6	-7.7	.0
% Profit Before Taxes/Total Assets	13.2	12.6	13.4		34.1	99.0	32.9	5.7	7.8
	3.9	3.8	3.3		12.5	7.7	7.6	1.0	1.9
	.0	-1.7	-.9		1.2	1.7	-.1	-2.6	-.7
Sales/Net Fixed Assets	9.5	15.6	15.5		21.1	38.7	13.1	14.0	8.4
	3.0	3.7	4.2		11.9	24.4	2.5	3.5	4.4
	1.5	1.5	1.3		1.0	1.6	1.1	1.4	2.5
Sales/Total Assets	2.5	2.7	2.9		4.7	7.1	3.6	2.6	2.5
	1.3	1.5	1.5		1.8	2.7	1.4	1.3	1.5
	.8	.8	.8		.5	.8	.8	.9	.9
% Depr., Dep., Amort./Sales	1.3	1.2	1.2		1.0	.7	1.5	1.2	1.2
	(173) 2.4	(186) 2.6	(141) 2.4		(13) 3.4	(10) 2.3	(32) 3.6	(41) 2.1	(38) 1.6
	3.9	4.9	4.4		6.9	6.3	4.7	3.7	2.8
% Officers', Directors' Owners' Comp/Sales	4.1	4.5	3.2						
	(16) 6.2	(23) 6.6	(24) 5.9						
	9.2	11.7	12.0						
Net Sales ($)	4615597M	5374627M	4373432M	4345M	36077M	47654M	307285M	798536M	3179535M
Total Assets ($)	3507098M	4624176M	3850481M	11026M	40955M	50760M	277405M	784546M	2685789M

© RMA 2019

M = $ thousand   MM = $ million

See Pages viii through xx for Explanation of Ratios and Data

Current Data Sorted by Assets / Comparative Historical Data

						Type of Statement		
1	15	30	52	58	80	Unqualified	245	267
	2	9	2		1	Reviewed	25	25
3	6	2	1	1		Compiled	13	22
3	12	7				Tax Returns	56	33
11	16	30	73	58	41	Other	213	212
	179 (4/1-9/30/18)		335 (10/1/18-3/31/19)				4/1/14-	4/1/15-
							3/31/15	3/31/16
0-500M	500M-2MM	2-10MM	10-50MM	50-100MM	100-250MM		ALL	ALL
18	51	78	128	117	122	**NUMBER OF STATEMENTS**	552	559
%	%	%	%	%	%	**ASSETS**	%	%
39.8	24.2	13.7	12.7	13.5	13.6	Cash & Equivalents	15.2	15.5
19.1	14.7	4.1	4.5	2.6	3.2	Trade Receivables (net)	6.5	5.3
.2	.6	.1	.1	.0	.1	Inventory	.2	.2
6.1	1.9	1.9	1.7	.9	1.4	All Other Current	1.7	1.9
65.2	41.5	19.7	19.1	17.0	18.3	Total Current	23.6	22.8
19.9	49.1	66.0	63.7	64.4	59.2	Fixed Assets (net)	57.6	59.0
.1	1.8	1.7	1.5	1.1	1.6	Intangibles (net)	2.7	2.9
14.8	7.6	12.6	15.8	17.5	20.8	All Other Non-Current	16.2	15.3
100.0	100.0	100.0	100.0	100.0	100.0	Total	100.0	100.0
						LIABILITIES		
10.6	1.3	1.3	1.2	.4	.9	Notes Payable-Short Term	2.8	4.2
5.3	2.7	3.7	2.2	1.5	1.5	Cur. Mat.-L.T.D.	3.2	3.2
13.4	7.6	2.3	2.3	1.9	2.1	Trade Payables	4.8	3.3
.6	.0	.0	.0	.0	.0	Income Taxes Payable	.0	.0
69.5	21.2	8.4	7.8	5.2	7.7	All Other Current	11.9	11.4
99.5	32.8	15.6	13.6	8.9	12.2	Total Current	22.7	22.1
8.6	36.5	65.3	49.9	44.9	38.9	Long-Term Debt	44.2	45.2
.0	.0	.1	.0	.0	.0	Deferred Taxes	.1	.0
15.3	10.6	8.6	18.6	32.5	37.6	All Other Non-Current	21.1	24.4
-23.3	20.0	10.4	17.8	13.7	11.4	Net Worth	11.9	8.3
100.0	100.0	100.0	100.0	100.0	100.0	Total Liabilities & Net Worth	100.0	100.0
						INCOME DATA		
100.0	100.0	100.0	100.0	100.0	100.0	Net Sales	100.0	100.0
						Gross Profit		
91.2	86.0	84.7	92.9	95.4	95.7	Operating Expenses	92.4	92.8
8.8	14.0	15.3	7.1	4.6	4.3	Operating Profit	7.6	7.2
-.7	2.2	5.4	6.0	4.7	5.1	All Other Expenses (net)	3.5	5.8
9.5	11.9	9.8	1.1	-.1	-.8	Profit Before Taxes	4.1	1.4
						RATIOS		
1.8	2.1	2.6	3.0	4.4	3.5		2.7	3.0
.7	1.1	1.2	1.7	1.7	1.7	Current	1.4	1.4
.4	.3	.4	.8	.9	.8		.6	.6
1.1	2.0	2.5	2.9	4.0	3.3		2.4	2.7
.6	1.0	1.0	1.5	1.6	1.4	Quick	1.2	1.2
.4	.3	.4	.6	.7	.7		.5	.5
0 UND	0 UND	0 844.9	3 124.0	12 30.3	10 35.2		3 109.8	3 144.6
5 75.4	3 113.2	3 109.3	19 19.0	19 19.4	18 20.6	Sales/Receivables	18 20.1	17 21.6
14 26.8	19 19.2	12 31.0	30 12.3	31 11.9	27 13.6		32 11.4	30 12.2
						Cost of Sales/Inventory		
						Cost of Sales/Payables		
28.7	12.3	7.2	4.0	1.9	2.1		4.2	3.6
-49.0	74.9	40.9	11.2	7.4	6.7	Sales/Working Capital	22.3	18.8
-14.6	-14.1	-17.3	-18.9	-43.7	-20.6		-16.3	-14.7
	16.2	4.3	2.8	2.3	2.3		4.5	3.1
(31)	5.3 (65)	2.2 (108)	1.2 (110)	1.1 (111)	1.1	EBIT/Interest	(455) 1.8 (463)	1.3
	2.3	1.0	-.4	.1	-.4		.6	.1
						Net Profit + Depr., Dep.,	9.7	7.1
						Amort./Cur. Mat. L/T/D	(18) 5.3 (21)	4.0
							2.8	2.8
.0	.1	1.2	1.4	1.7	1.8		1.2	1.4
2.1	1.3	4.9	4.1	4.0	4.7	Fixed/Worth	4.1	5.6
-.4	-2.9	-3.0	-13.8	-10.5	-12.8		-6.5	-6.1
1.9	.3	1.2	1.1	1.5	2.6		1.5	1.8
-155.7	1.8	5.3	4.3	5.0	6.0	Debt/Worth	5.7	8.1
-2.4	-5.7	-4.7	-18.7	-16.4	-19.1		-8.9	-8.9
	110.2	35.9	10.1	9.0	11.4	% Profit Before Taxes/Tangible	29.3	29.4
(38)	33.8 (49)	15.1 (88)	2.6 (81)	1.5 (87)	1.4	Net Worth	(364) 8.1 (364)	5.0
	8.3	-1.7	-6.0	-3.7	-6.0		.2	-4.3
158.7	29.2	9.7	2.8	1.7	1.9		5.9	4.5
63.7	13.1	4.5	.3	.1	.0	% Profit Before Taxes/Total	1.8	.8
15.7	1.9	.0	-2.1	-1.8	-2.5	Assets	-.9	-1.8
UND	194.0	2.0	1.4	.7	.7		2.2	1.9
74.8	4.9	1.0	.8	.5	.4	Sales/Net Fixed Assets	.8	.7
16.6	1.0	.5	.4	.4	.3		.4	.4
20.7	5.1	1.1	.7	.4	.4		1.0	.9
10.5	2.1	.7	.5	.3	.3	Sales/Total Assets	.5	.4
4.0	.9	.5	.3	.2	.2		.3	.3
.2	1.2	4.4	6.6	8.4	9.4		4.7	5.4
(13) .4	(36) 4.8 (71)	7.4 (122)	8.5 (114)	11.8 (118)	13.4	% Depr., Dep., Amort./Sales	(502) 8.9 (515)	9.7
.8	8.7	12.3	12.9	15.4	17.2		14.2	14.3
			6.9				3.5	2.8
		(11)	10.2			% Officers', Directors'	(47) 6.6 (41)	7.0
			12.9			Owners' Comp/Sales	13.3	11.9
42920M	185375M	383826M	2084205M	3081228M	7808655M	Net Sales ($)	12114975M	13839595M
4640M	57414M	381328M	3642464M	8702579M	18718229M	Total Assets ($)	27126143M	31067289M

M = $ thousand   MM = $ million
See Pages viii through xx for Explanation of Ratios and Data

Comparative Historical Data | | | Current Data Sorted by Sales

			Type of Statement						
273	242	236	Unqualified	10	20	18	13	74	101
19	13	14	Reviewed	1	3	4	5		1
15	17	13	Compiled	2	10				1
26	19	22	Tax Returns	2	7	8	4	1	
229	242	229	Other	10	20	18	30	73	78
4/1/16-3/31/17	4/1/17-3/31/18	4/1/18-3/31/19			179 (4/1-9/30/18)			335 (10/1/18-3/31/19)	
ALL	ALL	ALL		0-1MM	1-3MM	3-5MM	5-10MM	10-25MM	25MM & OVER
562	533	514	**NUMBER OF STATEMENTS**	25	60	48	52	148	181
%	%	%	**ASSETS**	%	%	%	%	%	%
13.8	14.1	15.4	Cash & Equivalents	15.4	16.4	21.2	16.3	12.6	15.4
5.4	5.0	5.2	Trade Receivables (net)	1.0	5.3	4.4	10.1	5.3	4.5
.2	.1	.1	Inventory	.0	.1	.6	.1	.1	.1
1.6	1.7	1.7	All Other Current	5.1	1.9	.7	2.4	1.3	1.5
21.1	20.9	22.4	Total Current	21.6	23.6	27.0	28.9	19.3	21.5
60.8	61.4	60.1	Fixed Assets (net)	68.1	67.4	54.6	56.4	62.1	57.6
1.9	1.9	1.4	Intangibles (net)	1.1	.7	2.0	1.2	1.4	1.7
16.2	15.8	16.0	All Other Non-Current	9.1	8.2	16.5	13.5	17.2	19.2
100.0	100.0	100.0	Total	100.0	100.0	100.0	100.0	100.0	100.0
			LIABILITIES						
3.0	1.2	1.3	Notes Payable-Short Term	6.6	.8	2.8	.4	.6	1.1
2.5	5.0	2.3	Cur. Mat.-L.T.D.	3.7	4.0	3.4	1.7	1.9	1.7
3.0	2.9	3.1	Trade Payables	3.4	4.2	4.7	4.5	2.4	2.3
.0	.0	.0	Income Taxes Payable	.4	.0	.0	.0	.0	.0
9.3	9.0	10.8	All Other Current	10.9	17.7	12.3	16.4	7.8	8.9
17.8	18.1	17.4	Total Current	25.0	26.6	23.1	23.0	12.8	14.0
49.0	44.7	45.7	Long-Term Debt	51.8	50.9	66.0	46.4	43.4	39.6
.0	.1	.0	Deferred Taxes	.0	.0	.1	.0	.0	.0
24.6	23.7	23.8	All Other Non-Current	6.0	5.1	15.5	9.3	34.5	30.2
8.6	13.5	13.0	Net Worth	17.3	17.4	-4.7	21.3	9.4	16.3
100.0	100.0	100.0	Total Liabilties & Net Worth	100.0	100.0	100.0	100.0	100.0	100.0
			INCOME DATA						
100.0	100.0	100.0	Net Sales	100.0	100.0	100.0	100.0	100.0	100.0
			Gross Profit						
92.6	92.4	92.1	Operating Expenses	75.6	80.4	85.4	94.5	97.1	95.3
7.4	7.6	7.9	Operating Profit	24.4	19.6	14.6	5.5	2.9	4.7
5.3	2.8	4.8	All Other Expenses (net)	7.5	6.9	5.6	5.3	3.7	4.3
2.1	4.7	3.1	Profit Before Taxes	16.9	12.7	8.9	.2	-.8	.4
			RATIOS						
3.1	2.8	3.4		1.4	2.1	2.5	3.3	3.7	3.6
1.5	1.4	1.5	Current	.4	.8	1.3	1.6	1.7	1.8
.7	.7	.7		.2	.3	.6	.9	.8	.9
2.8	2.5	3.0		1.0	1.9	2.4	3.0	3.4	3.4
1.3	1.2	1.3	Quick	.4	.7	1.2	1.5	1.5	1.7
.6	.6	.6		.2	.3	.6	.6	.8	.7
4 82.1	4 81.5	4 98.9	Sales/Receivables	0 UND	0 UND	0 999.8	2 148.4	11 34.4	14 25.5
17 20.9	17 21.8	15 24.0		0 776.0	3 144.2	2 180.1	11 33.4	18 20.1	22 16.9
30 12.0	31 11.9	27 13.6		4 92.2	8 44.5	6 61.4	38 9.6	26 13.9	33 11.2
			Cost of Sales/Inventory						
			Cost of Sales/Payables						
3.2	3.8	3.0	Sales/Working Capital	NM	9.0	8.5	3.8	2.6	2.2
13.0	16.8	14.5		-11.4	-73.9	29.3	16.7	10.0	7.2
-21.0	-14.9	-18.3		-4.3	-12.6	-19.5	-63.5	-17.9	-55.0
3.6	4.4	3.0	EBIT/Interest	13.1	11.5	4.4	2.9	2.4	2.5
(481) 1.5	(457) 2.0	(433) 1.4		(17) 4.0	(41) 3.5	(32) 2.2	(42) 1.0	(136) 1.1	(165) 1.1
.2	.6	.0		1.3	1.7	1.2	-.5	-.3	-.1
5.6	6.4	4.6	Net Profit + Depr., Dep., Amort./Cur. Mat. L/T/D						
(15) 3.8	(12) 4.0	(16) 3.2							
2.1	2.0	1.4							
1.5	1.4	1.3	Fixed/Worth	1.1	1.1	.6	.9	1.7	1.4
5.2	4.0	4.0		5.1	4.2	8.1	3.3	5.0	3.5
-6.4	-9.3	-8.1		-5.9	-3.9	-2.1	-20.3	-8.9	-14.1
1.7	1.6	1.4	Debt/Worth	.8	.5	1.1	1.1	1.6	1.6
6.5	4.9	5.0		7.7	4.8	11.8	3.4	6.7	4.6
-10.1	-13.5	-10.8		-4.6	-5.0	-3.7	-24.5	-12.6	-20.0
23.0	19.3	15.6	% Profit Before Taxes/Tangible Net Worth	34.5	44.4	93.8	52.9	11.5	11.5
(367) 5.8	(362) 8.4	(351) 4.8		(16) 12.7	(42) 16.4	(26) 16.2	(36) 3.8	(99) 3.3	(132) 1.6
-2.4	.2	-4.0		2.2	3.0	-.4	-6.3	-6.6	-4.5
3.8	4.7	4.5	% Profit Before Taxes/Total Assets	14.4	20.1	19.1	7.0	2.2	2.3
1.1	1.9	1.0		5.5	8.0	5.3	1.5	.1	.2
-1.4	-1.0	-1.5		.5	1.3	.3	-2.8	-2.2	-1.9
1.4	1.3	1.4	Sales/Net Fixed Assets	1.3	4.3	15.3	8.8	.9	1.1
.6	.6	.7		.9	.9	1.2	.9	.5	.6
.4	.4	.4		.3	.5	.6	.4	.4	.4
.8	.7	.8	Sales/Total Assets	.9	1.3	2.9	1.6	.5	.6
.4	.4	.4		.6	.8	.9	.5	.3	.4
.3	.3	.3		.1	.4	.5	.2	.2	.3
6.3	6.3	6.5	% Depr., Dep., Amort./Sales	7.0	3.9	3.7	2.6	7.8	6.8
(528) 10.1	(499) 9.9	(474) 10.0		(22) 9.3	(53) 8.2	(36) 6.6	(45) 7.4	(142) 10.9	(176) 11.0
14.4	14.8	14.8		24.2	12.2	12.0	12.2	15.6	14.8
3.9	4.9	3.1	% Officers', Directors' Owners' Comp/Sales					6.4	1.8
(42) 8.2	(35) 10.0	(43) 6.1					(12)	11.4 (10)	3.9
11.8	19.0	11.1						25.0	7.8
13680798M	13079427M	13586209M	Net Sales ($)	15856M	110888M	188075M	375096M	2537594M	10358700M
32439944M	31548964M	31506654M	Total Assets ($)	49433M	313870M	477203M	966723M	8000749M	21698676M

M = $ thousand MM = $ million
See Pages viii through xx for Explanation of Ratios and Data

Current Data Sorted by Assets

Comparative Historical Data

						Type of Statement		
5	5	11	29	10	12	Unqualified	61	63
1	2	8	2			Reviewed	17	17
6	11	11	3			Compiled	17	20
22	15	9	2			Tax Returns	61	39
32	39	75	50	17	8	Other	111	151
	56 (4/1-9/30/18)		329 (10/1/18-3/31/19)				4/1/14-3/31/15	4/1/15-3/31/16
0-500M	500M-2MM	2-10MM	10-50MM	50-100MM	100-250MM		ALL	ALL
66	72	114	86	27	20	NUMBER OF STATEMENTS	267	290
%	%	%	%	%	%	ASSETS	%	%
32.9	18.9	9.7	9.2	6.1	10.2	Cash & Equivalents	14.7	15.0
10.6	8.1	3.7	3.5	4.7	3.2	Trade Receivables (net)	5.4	6.5
.3	.3	.1	.5	.5	.0	Inventory	.1	.2
1.5	5.1	1.4	2.4	2.9	.5	All Other Current	3.3	2.5
45.4	32.4	15.0	15.5	14.2	13.9	Total Current	23.5	24.2
35.7	45.1	72.3	69.7	70.1	67.0	Fixed Assets (net)	61.1	57.9
8.0	9.5	3.7	4.8	.6	1.4	Intangibles (net)	5.3	5.7
10.9	12.9	9.1	10.0	15.1	17.7	All Other Non-Current	10.1	12.2
100.0	100.0	100.0	100.0	100.0	100.0	Total	100.0	100.0
						LIABILITIES		
7.8	4.6	4.9	1.3	.6	.1	Notes Payable-Short Term	5.0	3.4
1.9	2.5	2.5	1.5	2.3	1.5	Cur. Mat.-L.T.D.	3.8	2.6
16.1	9.5	2.9	2.5	2.9	2.5	Trade Payables	4.2	4.7
.0	.0	.0	.0	.0	.0	Income Taxes Payable	.0	.0
73.9	24.0	9.1	6.4	12.8	5.3	All Other Current	16.3	12.3
99.8	40.5	19.4	11.7	18.6	9.3	Total Current	29.2	23.0
18.5	50.5	76.3	63.1	52.2	52.3	Long-Term Debt	61.3	51.1
.0	.0	.0	.0	.2	.0	Deferred Taxes	.0	.0
12.0	10.9	2.6	10.8	10.8	25.3	All Other Non-Current	9.8	14.3
-30.3	-1.9	1.6	14.4	18.2	13.1	Net Worth	-.4	11.5
100.0	100.0	100.0	100.0	100.0	100.0	Total Liabilties & Net Worth	100.0	100.0
						INCOME DATA		
100.0	100.0	100.0	100.0	100.0	100.0	Net Sales	100.0	100.0
						Gross Profit		
92.9	84.1	81.2	87.2	88.3	93.4	Operating Expenses	85.2	87.0
7.1	15.9	18.8	12.8	11.7	6.6	Operating Profit	14.8	13.0
1.0	4.3	11.0	9.7	6.6	8.7	All Other Expenses (net)	7.4	6.1
6.1	11.6	7.8	3.1	5.1	-2.1	Profit Before Taxes	7.4	6.9
						RATIOS		
2.2	2.9	2.2	2.4	2.7	2.6		2.4	2.6
.7	1.2	.9	1.1	1.0	1.0	Current	1.2	1.3
.3	.5	.4	.6	.2	.6		.4	.5
2.2	2.0	2.0	2.1	1.7	2.4		1.9	2.3
.6	1.0	.9	.9	.8	.9	Quick	1.0	1.1
.3	.3	.3	.5	.2	.5	(266)	.3	.4
0 UND	0 UND	0 UND	1 352.9	2 205.4	7 55.5		0 UND	0 UND
0 UND	2 176.1	2 147.4	8 47.6	16 22.7	15 23.9	Sales/Receivables	3 124.0	4 98.4
6 60.3	10 37.6	12 30.2	20 18.5	47 7.7	35 10.5		20 17.9	24 14.9
						Cost of Sales/Inventory		
						Cost of Sales/Payables		
31.1	10.7	8.6	5.9	4.2	5.1		9.5	8.1
-52.3	111.4	-171.8	76.9	UND	UND	Sales/Working Capital	79.7	35.2
-13.0	-12.5	-8.1	-11.7	-4.6	-7.8		-9.0	-14.9
50.6	10.0	3.6	2.3	3.5	1.8		5.4	7.5
(32) 5.0	(48) 4.0	(89) 1.9	(67) 1.5	(20) 2.0	(17) 1.0	EBIT/Interest	(175) 2.5	(222) 2.6
1.2	1.5	.9	.1	.8	.1		.9	1.0
						Net Profit + Depr., Dep., Amort./Cur. Mat. L/T/D		24.9
							(12)	6.1
								1.2
.3	.5	2.5	1.9	1.6	1.9		1.2	1.0
1.5	NM	8.3	6.6	3.1	3.2	Fixed/Worth	11.6	5.2
-.6	-1.3	-2.9	-26.5	8.1	-18.5		-2.5	-4.2
.4	1.2	2.4	1.8	1.6	1.9		1.5	1.2
8.7	-17.9	9.2	6.0	2.3	3.9	Debt/Worth	15.4	8.6
-1.9	-3.1	-4.2	-29.5	7.8	-29.2		-3.9	-6.3
108.9	95.3	58.0	21.5	15.8	5.0		65.5	72.2
(37) 79.8	(33) 42.1	(70) 21.3	(60) 3.6	(24) 4.0	(14) -.1	% Profit Before Taxes/Tangible Net Worth	(149) 21.7	(179) 20.1
22.2	29.2	1.1	-7.5	-1.1	-12.6		-.3	1.0
61.7	28.0	9.4	5.0	6.2	1.3		13.9	16.2
18.5	13.3	2.8	1.4	2.0	-.3	% Profit Before Taxes/Total Assets	5.1	3.9
1.9	4.2	-.6	-2.0	-.4	-2.0		-.2	.0
104.0	49.7	1.2	1.1	1.1	1.1		7.5	12.0
27.2	6.7	.7	.5	.7	.5	Sales/Net Fixed Assets	1.0	1.2
8.4	1.2	.4	.3	.3	.3		.5	.5
13.9	4.5	.8	.6	.6	.5		2.2	2.4
6.4	2.0	.5	.4	.4	.3	Sales/Total Assets	.7	.7
3.1	1.0	.3	.2	.2	.2		.3	.3
.2	1.5	6.0	4.6	3.4	5.2		3.8	3.3
(32) .9	(48) 3.5	(90) 9.5	(76) 8.1	(20) 6.8	(16) 10.4	% Depr., Dep., Amort./Sales	(225) 7.8	(241) 6.9
1.6	6.8	12.2	15.6	9.6	16.2		12.6	12.0
3.8	3.6	3.3	4.0				3.0	4.1
(20) 7.5	(24) 5.9	(18) 4.8	(10) 5.1			% Officers', Directors' Owners' Comp/Sales	(44) 5.2	(48) 5.5
16.6	7.3	6.0	16.2				10.7	10.3
128081M	219889M	411407M	1181611M	1129665M	1309097M	Net Sales ($)	2026551M	3500223M
15745M	81253M	565908M	2070989M	1922264M	2865278M	Total Assets ($)	3426364M	5988632M

M = $ thousand   MM = $ million
See Pages viii through xx for Explanation of Ratios and Data

Comparative Historical Data | Current Data Sorted by Sales

			Type of Statement	0-1MM	1-3MM	3-5MM	5-10MM	10-25MM	25MM & OVER
68	61	72	Unqualified	1	6	7	21	14	23
27	44	13	Reviewed		6	1	4	2	
11	38	31	Compiled	9	16	4	1	1	
52	83	48	Tax Returns	20	16	9	3		
183	202	221	Other	27	83	38	18	18	24
4/1/16-3/31/17 ALL	4/1/17-3/31/18 ALL	4/1/18-3/31/19 ALL		56 (4/1-9/30/18)			329 (10/1/18-3/31/19)		
341	428	385	**NUMBER OF STATEMENTS**	57	127	59	60	35	47
%	%	%	**ASSETS**	%	%	%	%	%	%
15.3	18.9	15.0	Cash & Equivalents	15.4	16.1	16.1	15.8	11.9	11.9
5.7	8.1	5.7	Trade Receivables (net)	3.1	4.6	5.2	9.9	4.8	7.9
.2	.1	.3	Inventory	.0	.2	.1	.9	.1	.3
2.5	3.0	2.4	All Other Current	2.7	2.4	.9	3.5	.9	3.6
23.6	30.1	23.5	Total Current	21.1	23.3	22.4	30.1	17.8	23.7
60.1	53.9	60.0	Fixed Assets (net)	62.5	62.4	61.8	51.8	64.0	55.2
4.4	5.4	5.4	Intangibles (net)	8.8	4.9	7.1	5.7	1.1	3.7
11.9	10.6	11.2	All Other Non-Current	7.6	9.4	8.8	12.4	17.1	17.4
100.0	100.0	100.0	Total	100.0	100.0	100.0	100.0	100.0	100.0
			LIABILITIES						
4.1	4.2	4.0	Notes Payable-Short Term	7.8	2.7	4.6	4.8	2.6	2.2
3.0	4.4	2.1	Cur. Mat.-L.T.D.	4.6	1.8	1.5	1.2	1.5	2.2
5.2	7.1	6.3	Trade Payables	2.4	5.7	9.6	9.4	4.7	5.6
.0	.0	.0	Income Taxes Payable	.0	.0	.0	.0	.0	.0
15.3	18.2	22.4	All Other Current	26.6	25.0	22.3	27.5	9.6	13.7
27.6	33.9	34.8	Total Current	41.4	35.2	38.0	42.9	18.5	23.8
52.6	46.6	55.7	Long-Term Debt	59.8	62.7	62.3	39.5	49.0	49.2
.0	.0	.0	Deferred Taxes	.0	.0	.0	.0	.0	.1
14.1	8.1	9.4	All Other Non-Current	9.5	7.0	8.0	2.2	14.5	22.5
5.7	11.4	.1	Net Worth	-10.7	-4.9	-8.4	15.4	18.1	4.5
100.0	100.0	100.0	Total Liabilities & Net Worth	100.0	100.0	100.0	100.0	100.0	100.0
			INCOME DATA						
100.0	100.0	100.0	Net Sales	100.0	100.0	100.0	100.0	100.0	100.0
			Gross Profit						
89.0	87.1	86.2	Operating Expenses	66.4	87.3	87.6	92.2	90.3	95.1
11.0	12.9	13.8	Operating Profit	33.6	12.7	12.4	7.8	9.7	4.9
6.2	5.5	7.3	All Other Expenses (net)	15.2	6.2	7.1	5.6	5.1	4.9
4.8	7.4	6.5	Profit Before Taxes	18.5	6.5	5.3	2.2	4.6	.0
			RATIOS						
2.4	2.7	2.4	Current	3.0	3.0	1.5	1.9	1.8	2.8
1.0	1.3	1.0		.6	1.5	.7	.8	.9	1.2
.4	.5	.4		.2	.5	.3	.4	.5	.6
2.2	2.3	2.0	Quick	1.7	2.3	1.5	1.8	1.7	2.2
.9	1.1	.8		.5	1.3	.6	.6	.7	1.0
.3	.4	.3		.1	.4	.3	.2	.2	.5
0 UND	0 UND	0 UND	Sales/Receivables	0 UND	0 UND	0 999.8	1 282.0	1 250.1	12 29.4
3 105.7	4 89.1	3 122.3		0 UND	2 155.1	3 142.3	6 58.6	9 40.0	19 18.8
18 19.8	21 17.7	16 23.1		0 UND	10 37.0	15 25.1	20 18.7	23 15.8	41 9.0
			Cost of Sales/Inventory						
			Cost of Sales/Payables						
9.7	7.5	10.1	Sales/Working Capital	13.5	8.9	17.4	10.6	10.8	4.2
999.8	44.2	485.8		-40.0	31.0	-56.3	-44.4	-68.0	42.3
-11.8	-13.1	-10.1		-4.8	-14.9	-10.0	-6.7	-5.5	-14.0
4.6	7.1	4.1	EBIT/Interest	10.0	4.1	8.1	3.7	11.7	2.5
(248) 1.8	(301) 2.3	(273) 2.0		(29) 3.4	(88) 2.1	(46) 2.0	(42) 1.4	(25) 1.8	(43) 1.2
.7	.9	.6		2.4	1.1	.9	-.1	.1	.5
			Net Profit + Depr., Dep., Amort./Cur. Mat. L/T/D						
1.2	.7	1.3	Fixed/Worth	1.3	1.6	1.8	.5	1.3	1.5
6.9	4.8	5.4		14.6	8.4	9.0	3.0	3.2	3.0
-4.3	-5.0	-3.4		-2.4	-2.4	-2.4	-7.6	12.1	-3.5
1.3	1.1	1.6	Debt/Worth	1.3	1.6	2.3	.8	1.5	1.9
7.7	7.0	7.0		19.1	8.7	12.1	4.4	4.3	3.8
-6.0	-7.2	-4.6		-3.9	-3.9	-3.5	-12.3	40.0	-4.7
74.2	66.1	62.5	% Profit Before Taxes/Tangible Net Worth	87.4	86.7	82.6	38.7	32.8	4.3
(207) 17.3	(271) 20.3	(238) 16.2		(32) 41.5	(75) 26.2	(32) 34.1	(38) 5.9	(28) 9.4	(33) -.4
-.4	3.8	.5		16.7	7.6	-6.9	-7.1	2.5	-11.3
12.2	15.8	12.8	% Profit Before Taxes/Total Assets	27.6	14.1	14.7	11.4	6.2	.0
3.1	4.4	3.3		7.7	4.4	4.0	1.9	2.1	.0
-.7	-.4	-.7		2.4	.4	1.2	-2.2	-1.6	-2.1
11.7	28.0	9.9	Sales/Net Fixed Assets	9.2	11.4	20.4	46.7	2.0	2.8
1.0	1.3	1.0		.9	1.1	1.0	1.2	.5	1.1
.4	.5	.4		.2	.5	.4	.3	.3	.6
2.8	4.0	2.5	Sales/Total Assets	2.9	2.5	3.9	3.3	.9	1.7
.7	.8	.7		.7	.7	.8	.6	.4	.6
.3	.4	.3		.2	.4	.4	.3	.2	.4
3.0	1.5	3.1	% Depr., Dep., Amort./Sales	1.9	3.4	5.0	.9	4.2	2.1
(275) 7.2	(336) 6.7	(282) 6.9		(37) 7.7	(92) 6.7	(41) 8.2	(46) 5.1	(23) 7.6	(43) 6.0
12.6	11.4	11.5		25.8	11.0	14.7	11.6	10.3	9.6
2.6	2.5	3.5	% Officers', Directors' Owners' Comp/Sales	2.2	4.4	3.1			
(68) 5.0	(69) 5.5	(74) 5.5		(12) 8.9	(37) 5.8	(14) 5.1			
7.6	15.5	9.4		16.6	7.0	28.7			
4415235M	3666456M	4379750M	Net Sales ($)	32387M	234157M	235024M	420718M	541726M	2915738M
6013826M	6245636M	7521437M	Total Assets ($)	90931M	467502M	439505M	1029383M	1578990M	3915126M

© RMA 2019

M = $ thousand   MM = $ million
See Pages viii through xx for Explanation of Ratios and Data

Current Data Sorted by Assets | | | | | | Comparative Historical Data

0-500M	500M-2MM	2-10MM	10-50MM	50-100MM	100-250MM	Type of Statement	93	80
2	2	18	22	5	4	Unqualified	93	80
		1	1			Reviewed	5	2
1	1	2			1	Compiled	4	7
4	4					Tax Returns	23	27
6	9	20	10	6	5	Other	75	64
	55 (4/1-9/30/18)		69 (10/1/18-3/31/19)				4/1/14-3/31/15 ALL	4/1/15-3/31/16 ALL
13	16	41	33	11	10	**NUMBER OF STATEMENTS**	200	180
%	%	%	%	%	%	**ASSETS**	%	%
24.8	11.5	14.7	18.0	10.3	4.9	Cash & Equivalents	20.3	19.0
22.0	16.6	9.4	14.6	9.7	10.2	Trade Receivables (net)	12.3	11.2
.1	.8	1.7	.0	.0	.0	Inventory	.4	.1
2.3	5.3	3.7	2.5	1.5	1.4	All Other Current	2.8	2.2
49.1	34.3	29.5	35.1	21.5	16.5	Total Current	35.8	32.6
28.8	39.3	64.0	48.3	61.2	45.5	Fixed Assets (net)	50.0	50.7
7.2	11.1	.2	4.6	6.0	13.2	Intangibles (net)	2.4	2.1
14.8	15.4	6.2	12.0	11.3	24.7	All Other Non-Current	11.8	14.5
100.0	100.0	100.0	100.0	100.0	100.0	Total	100.0	100.0
						LIABILITIES		
13.5	2.3	3.3	2.4	.2	.4	Notes Payable-Short Term	3.6	4.8
2.6	.9	2.3	2.7	2.3	1.5	Cur. Mat.-L.T.D.	2.0	2.0
15.4	17.9	4.8	3.3	1.7	2.4	Trade Payables	6.7	4.9
.0	.0	.1	.1	.0	.0	Income Taxes Payable	.2	.1
21.1	23.5	7.7	9.0	9.6	6.5	All Other Current	12.3	10.3
52.6	44.7	18.2	17.5	13.8	10.8	Total Current	24.9	22.0
3.5	31.9	41.8	24.3	57.7	29.4	Long-Term Debt	31.0	29.3
.0	.0	.0	.0	.3	.0	Deferred Taxes	.2	.2
17.2	3.0	2.7	5.6	5.0	7.4	All Other Non-Current	8.5	6.4
26.7	20.4	37.3	52.5	23.2	52.3	Net Worth	35.5	42.1
100.0	100.0	100.0	100.0	100.0	100.0	Total Liabilties & Net Worth	100.0	100.0
						INCOME DATA		
100.0	100.0	100.0	100.0	100.0	100.0	Net Sales	100.0	100.0
						Gross Profit		
97.9	92.6	93.5	94.9	89.6	95.2	Operating Expenses	93.9	91.7
2.1	7.4	6.5	5.1	10.4	4.8	Operating Profit	6.1	8.3
.2	.1	4.0	1.6	6.3	.1	All Other Expenses (net)	2.9	2.9
1.9	7.3	2.5	3.5	4.1	4.8	Profit Before Taxes	3.2	5.4
						RATIOS		
2.9	3.2	3.8	4.1	2.5	2.9		2.8	3.2
.8	1.6	2.0	2.0	1.4	1.8	Current	1.6	1.8
.5	.4	.7	1.2	.5	1.1		.9	.9
2.9	2.7	3.6	3.6	2.3	2.6		2.7	3.2
.8	1.2	1.5	1.8	1.4	1.5	Quick	1.5	1.7
.5	.3	.5	1.1	.4	1.0		.8	.8
0 UND	0 UND	3 112.8	21 17.8	5 68.5	29 12.5		5 76.7	1 361.3
17 21.0	14 27.0	23 15.6	36 10.0	34 10.7	45 8.2	Sales/Receivables	24 15.4	24 15.1
33 11.0	40 9.2	38 9.7	49 7.5	63 5.8	54 6.7		39 9.4	39 9.3
						Cost of Sales/Inventory		
						Cost of Sales/Payables		
20.2	10.5	4.2	3.6	5.8	4.1		5.7	5.3
-72.3	29.3	11.0	9.4	9.6	14.1	Sales/Working Capital	15.3	15.2
-25.1	-5.6	-18.9	25.2	-9.3	NM		-106.7	-81.5
		9.1	11.6	11.2	6.8		6.8	9.4
(12) 4.9	(32) 2.9	(30) 3.8	(10) 1.6			EBIT/Interest	(145) 2.5	(126) 2.5
	-.3	-.4	1.2	-.1			.8	.5
						Net Profit + Depr., Dep., Amort./Cur. Mat. L/T/D		
.4	.2	.7	.6	.7	.6		.6	.5
1.0	1.4	1.3	.9	3.4	1.3	Fixed/Worth	1.1	1.0
NM	-.7	8.2	3.2	-2.1	2.9		3.3	3.4
.4	.5	.4	.2	.6	.5		.5	.3
4.3	1.1	.8	1.0	5.0	1.5	Debt/Worth	1.4	.9
-6.6	-2.3	9.6	3.2	-4.1	3.0		4.3	3.9
	28.1	21.2	18.2				21.2	25.5
(11) 15.4	(35) 4.8	(29) 7.8				% Profit Before Taxes/Tangible Net Worth	(168) 7.3	(152) 4.8
	-13.3	-8.6	1.9				-.6	-.3
71.3	20.1	8.7	8.4	9.4	5.3		8.4	11.7
2.4	6.4	3.3	5.1	3.6	1.9	% Profit Before Taxes/Total Assets	3.0	2.6
-21.1	-1.9	-2.5	.8	-.7	-1.4		-.6	-.4
155.3	77.5	3.5	5.8	2.6	3.2		13.6	6.6
15.0	10.4	1.8	1.9	.8	2.3	Sales/Net Fixed Assets	2.7	2.6
6.3	2.5	.7	1.4	.5	1.2		1.1	1.1
19.9	4.7	1.9	1.8	1.4	1.2		3.0	2.7
4.3	2.3	1.1	1.0	.6	.8	Sales/Total Assets	1.4	1.3
2.4	1.3	.5	.6	.2	.3		.6	.6
	.5	1.5	1.9	3.0	2.1		1.5	1.6
(13) 2.5	(34) 3.4	(30) 3.7	6.0	3.8		% Depr., Dep., Amort./Sales	(178) 3.0	(156) 3.1
	3.1	8.9	5.3	7.6	5.8		5.7	5.5
							2.7	3.6
						% Officers', Directors' Owners' Comp/Sales	(26) 5.2	(26) 6.9
							7.6	13.6
17907M	53547M	290861M	853971M	614340M	1121121M	Net Sales ($)	3319868M	3635152M
2727M	17857M	218254M	663850M	795762M	1379221M	Total Assets ($)	2918893M	3038641M

© RMA 2019

M = $ thousand   MM = $ million
See Pages viii through xx for Explanation of Ratios and Data

Comparative Historical Data | Current Data Sorted by Sales

			Type of Statement						
71	63	53	Unqualified	4	2	5	10	16	16
2	2	2	Reviewed			1	1		1
12	8	5	Compiled	2	2				
16	7	8	Tax Returns	3	4			1	
62	70	56	Other	8	7	7	10	9	15
4/1/16-3/31/17 ALL	4/1/17-3/31/18 ALL	4/1/18-3/31/19 ALL		0-1MM	1-3MM	3-5MM	5-10MM	10-25MM	25MM & OVER
					55 (4/1-9/30/18)		69 (10/1/18-3/31/19)		
163	150	124	NUMBER OF STATEMENTS	17	15	13	21	26	32
%	%	%	**ASSETS**	%	%	%	%	%	%
18.3	17.9	15.0	Cash & Equivalents	15.4	11.9	14.2	19.9	17.3	11.6
11.9	13.5	13.1	Trade Receivables (net)	12.4	8.6	9.5	11.2	15.3	16.6
.3	.5	.7	Inventory	.0	1.4	.6	.1	.0	1.7
3.0	3.2	3.1	All Other Current	1.5	2.2	5.5	4.9	3.6	1.7
33.5	35.1	31.9	Total Current	29.3	24.0	29.8	36.0	36.3	31.6
49.4	47.9	51.2	Fixed Assets (net)	52.6	58.1	64.0	51.7	45.5	46.3
3.2	4.9	5.1	Intangibles (net)	5.2	7.6	.4	3.5	4.8	7.0
13.9	12.1	11.8	All Other Non-Current	13.0	10.3	5.8	8.7	13.4	15.0
100.0	100.0	100.0	Total	100.0	100.0	100.0	100.0	100.0	100.0
			LIABILITIES						
3.1	5.0	3.5	Notes Payable-Short Term	.7	10.9	1.2	6.1	2.3	1.8
1.6	2.3	2.2	Cur. Mat.-L.T.D.	2.7	2.2	2.2	1.2	1.4	3.2
5.0	4.4	6.7	Trade Payables	11.4	1.2	2.8	13.7	5.0	5.3
.2	.1	.0	Income Taxes Payable	.0	.0	.0	.0	.0	.2
11.7	12.5	11.6	All Other Current	8.2	23.4	5.7	11.5	8.4	12.7
21.6	24.3	24.1	Total Current	23.0	37.8	12.0	32.5	17.1	23.1
28.7	30.6	32.3	Long-Term Debt	22.5	43.3	48.5	24.3	25.7	36.2
.1	.1	.0	Deferred Taxes	.0	.0	.0	.0	.0	.1
6.0	4.5	5.6	All Other Non-Current	4.7	10.9	4.4	3.4	2.7	8.0
43.6	40.4	38.0	Net Worth	49.8	8.1	35.1	39.8	54.5	32.5
100.0	100.0	100.0	Total Liabilities & Net Worth	100.0	100.0	100.0	100.0	100.0	100.0
			INCOME DATA						
100.0	100.0	100.0	Net Sales	100.0	100.0	100.0	100.0	100.0	100.0
			Gross Profit						
94.8	92.2	94.0	Operating Expenses	92.0	96.3	87.9	96.1	93.8	95.3
5.2	7.8	6.0	Operating Profit	8.0	3.7	12.1	3.9	6.2	4.7
2.6	1.3	2.4	All Other Expenses (net)	5.5	2.3	4.0	.7	1.5	1.8
2.6	6.4	3.7	Profit Before Taxes	2.4	1.4	8.1	3.2	4.8	2.9
			RATIOS						
3.4	3.7	3.6	Current	3.5	1.9	3.9	5.5	4.7	2.2
1.7	1.9	1.7		1.2	1.4	1.9	3.5	3.2	1.5
.9	1.0	.7		.7	.5	.6	.8	1.7	.9
3.0	3.5	3.5	Quick	3.5	1.9	3.1	4.9	4.0	2.0
1.6	1.8	1.5		1.2	.6	1.5	2.3	2.7	1.3
.7	.9	.6		.6	.1	.5	.3	1.1	.8
4 87.9	5 79.7	8 47.3	Sales/Receivables	0 UND	0 UND	2 210.1	6 63.2	22 16.3	23 16.1
26 14.1	24 14.9	29 12.4		18 20.3	4 98.0	22 16.4	21 17.2	36 10.0	39 9.4
41 8.9	41 9.0	44 8.3		54 6.7	24 14.9	32 11.3	44 8.3	46 8.0	51 7.1
			Cost of Sales/Inventory						
			Cost of Sales/Payables						
5.4	5.6	4.6	Sales/Working Capital	6.1	15.1	3.6	2.9	3.7	8.4
14.9	12.8	14.1		356.0	40.6	11.0	6.7	5.9	18.3
-78.9	670.4	-27.5		-10.8	-12.0	-18.4	-59.5	18.0	NM
10.5	15.7	9.7	EBIT/Interest	9.4	4.6	8.1	13.5	19.9	7.6
(128) 2.3	(115) 4.2	(100) 3.1		(11) 2.0	(12) 1.1	(11) 3.5	(18) 5.9	(20) 6.7	(28) 2.4
.6	1.2	.3		-2.8	-5.6	1.6	-1.2	1.0	.7
			Net Profit + Depr., Dep., Amort./Cur. Mat. L/T/D						
.5	.5	.6	Fixed/Worth	.6	1.0	.6	.7	.5	.7
1.0	1.0	1.3		1.1	21.5	1.3	.9	.8	1.6
3.0	2.7	7.0		6.8	-2.0	NM	3.8	1.8	NM
.3	.3	.4	Debt/Worth	.4	.8	.5	.3	.2	.8
1.0	1.2	1.2		.7	52.2	1.2	.5	.7	1.7
3.8	3.1	10.7		8.0	-2.8	NM	4.4	2.7	NM
20.9	30.8	19.7	% Profit Before Taxes/Tangible Net Worth	28.0		26.6	16.3	10.1	20.9
(137) 4.8	(127) 7.0	(100) 5.0		(16) 3.9		(10) 10.9	(17) 4.8	(24) 2.9	(24) 8.2
-1.1	1.7	-3.0		-19.3		1.9	-2.9	-3.7	.8
9.2	12.7	8.9	% Profit Before Taxes/Total Assets	17.2	16.2	13.4	7.8	9.0	8.8
1.8	3.6	3.6		2.5	-.3	6.5	3.2	3.0	4.5
-.8	.4	-1.4		-2.4	-15.1	3.2	-7.3	-1.2	.4
10.3	9.5	6.5	Sales/Net Fixed Assets	18.4	10.6	8.8	4.1	6.5	5.8
2.5	2.5	2.3		4.1	2.9	1.3	1.9	2.9	2.3
1.2	1.4	1.2		.2	1.2	.6	1.5	1.6	1.6
2.5	2.7	2.4	Sales/Total Assets	2.4	4.7	2.3	2.3	1.9	2.2
1.3	1.3	1.3		.9	2.0	1.1	1.3	1.2	1.2
.6	.7	.6		.1	.8	.4	.6	.8	.6
1.4	1.4	1.6	% Depr., Dep., Amort./Sales	.5	1.7	1.2	1.1	1.7	2.0
(146) 3.0	(130) 3.0	(107) 3.1		(14) 10.6	(13) 2.9	(10) 4.7	(18) 2.4	(24) 3.1	(28) 3.8
5.4	5.4	5.7		39.1	5.6	15.1	4.2	4.5	5.8
2.4	3.2	2.4	% Officers', Directors' Owners' Comp/Sales						
(25) 4.6	(23) 3.9	(16) 3.6							
7.8	7.6	7.3							
3263305M	2934038M	2951747M	Net Sales ($)	11220M	31220M	48460M	138790M	414411M	2307646M
2871288M	2700335M	3077671M	Total Assets ($)	39975M	29995M	72689M	141800M	627617M	2165595M

Current Data Sorted by Assets   Comparative Historical Data

Type of Statement	0-500M	500M-2MM	2-10MM	10-50MM	50-100MM	100-250MM		4/1/14-3/31/15 ALL	4/1/15-3/31/16 ALL
Unqualified	2	13	43	62	11	5		218	214
Reviewed		1	1	1				3	4
Compiled			2	2				13	8
Tax Returns	3	3	2	2	5	2		17	20
Other	9	16	40	22	5	2		104	95
		176 (4/1-9/30/18)		67 (10/1/18-3/31/19)					
NUMBER OF STATEMENTS	14	33	88	85	16	7		355	341

	%	%	%	%	%	%		%	%
ASSETS									
Cash & Equivalents	44.8	33.0	25.3	17.2	18.3			22.2	24.2
Trade Receivables (net)	11.4	22.4	20.0	17.6	15.6			18.8	16.7
Inventory	.1	.1	.1	.1	.5			.3	.3
All Other Current	.8	2.4	3.8	2.8	.6			2.2	2.8
Total Current	57.1	57.9	49.3	37.7	35.0			43.4	44.0
Fixed Assets (net)	26.3	34.7	40.1	42.9	29.5			41.2	39.8
Intangibles (net)	5.8	1.2	2.0	1.8	7.8			2.2	1.9
All Other Non-Current	10.8	6.2	8.6	17.7	27.6			13.1	14.3
Total	100.0	100.0	100.0	100.0	100.0			100.0	100.0
LIABILITIES									
Notes Payable-Short Term	20.6	4.6	2.2	2.6	1.3			3.2	3.5
Cur. Mat.-L.T.D.	1.2	1.2	1.6	1.1	1.4			1.7	1.3
Trade Payables	12.4	5.5	8.4	5.7	4.7			6.3	8.1
Income Taxes Payable	.0	.1	.3	.0	.0			.0	.1
All Other Current	22.7	10.4	10.3	7.9	9.6			10.4	10.3
Total Current	57.0	21.8	22.9	17.3	17.0			21.6	23.4
Long-Term Debt	60.0	8.6	17.1	17.1	18.3			17.1	16.1
Deferred Taxes	.0	.0	.0	.0	.0			.0	.0
All Other Non-Current	43.0	3.3	4.1	3.3	7.1			4.3	4.3
Net Worth	-60.0	66.4	55.9	62.3	57.6			57.0	56.2
Total Liabilities & Net Worth	100.0	100.0	100.0	100.0	100.0			100.0	100.0
INCOME DATA									
Net Sales	100.0	100.0	100.0	100.0	100.0			100.0	100.0
Gross Profit									
Operating Expenses	96.2	95.0	95.0	98.7	101.8			95.7	97.2
Operating Profit	3.8	5.0	5.0	1.3	-1.8			4.3	2.8
All Other Expenses (net)	.5	-1.7	.9	-.5	-1.6			.5	.8
Profit Before Taxes	3.3	6.7	4.0	1.8	-.2			3.7	2.0
RATIOS									
Current	6.0	8.0	5.8	4.2	3.7			4.4	4.2
	1.1	3.4	3.0	2.3	1.8			2.1	2.3
	.5	1.7	1.4	1.5	1.3			1.3	1.2
Quick	6.0	7.9	5.4	4.0	3.7			4.1	3.9
	1.1	3.4	2.5	2.1	1.7			2.0	2.0
	.3	1.6	1.2	1.3	1.2			1.2	1.1
Sales/Receivables	0 UND	6 65.5	7 48.7	28 13.1	39 9.4			16 22.3	10 35.4
	0 UND	23 16.0	30 12.1	41 8.8	50 7.3			36 10.1	31 11.6
	10 37.3	36 10.1	50 7.3	63 5.8	72 5.1			52 7.0	50 7.3
Cost of Sales/Inventory									
Cost of Sales/Payables									
Sales/Working Capital	7.4	3.7	2.8	3.0	4.0			3.7	3.5
	NM	6.4	6.3	7.4	5.8			9.4	9.2
	-26.9	13.3	29.3	17.9	26.1			29.8	35.8
EBIT/Interest		9.5	8.8	8.9	4.5			9.8	7.7
	(16) 7.1	(54) 2.6	(69) 1.9	1.5			(253) 2.4	(235) 1.9
		2.4	1.1	-1.5	.0			.1	-.9
Net Profit + Depr., Dep., Amort./Cur. Mat. L/T/D									
Fixed/Worth	.1	.1	.2	.4	.3			.3	.3
	2.9	.5	.6	.7	.8			.7	.7
	NM	1.0	1.2	1.0	1.5			1.2	1.2
Debt/Worth	1.1	.1	.3	.2	.4			.2	.2
	11.0	.5	.5	.5	.7			.6	.6
	-2.7	1.2	1.9	1.1	2.1			1.5	1.6
% Profit Before Taxes/Tangible Net Worth	466.5	31.7	14.4	8.7	2.8			12.3	11.2
	(10) 113.8	16.9	(82) 4.7	(82) 1.9	(14) .6			(330) 3.7	(320) 2.2
	7.2	3.4	.0	-2.2	-1.1			-1.1	-2.8
% Profit Before Taxes/Total Assets	124.2	19.7	7.0	4.8	1.9			7.6	6.4
	29.4	8.0	2.1	.9	.3			1.9	1.3
	-17.4	2.2	-.2	-1.6	-.5			-1.1	-1.7
Sales/Net Fixed Assets	154.3	57.7	17.4	5.5	15.6			14.1	19.4
	51.1	16.6	4.4	2.5	3.3			4.0	4.0
	5.9	2.6	1.3	1.3	1.9			1.5	1.6
Sales/Total Assets	16.4	4.6	3.0	1.9	1.6			2.8	2.8
	4.6	2.4	1.4	1.1	.9			1.4	1.5
	2.2	1.2	.6	.6	.4			.7	.7
% Depr., Dep., Amort./Sales		.7	.8	1.5	1.6			1.1	1.1
	(25) 2.0	(70) 2.4	(79) 2.6	(15) 3.2			(303) 2.3	(288) 2.1
		3.6	5.9	3.9	4.2			4.3	4.1
% Officers', Directors' Owners' Comp/Sales								3.5	4.6
							(38)	6.0 (43)	6.7
								13.7	16.3
Net Sales ($)	23894M	128539M	936689M	2832325M	1122875M	690279M		6999192M	6928196M
Total Assets ($)	3603M	44772M	476712M	1918756M	1089895M	897194M		5866587M	6127370M

M = $ thousand   MM = $ million
See Pages viii through xx for Explanation of Ratios and Data

Comparative Historical Data

Current Data Sorted by Sales

			Type of Statement						
194	156	136	Unqualified	4	15	9	22	43	43
7	4	3	Reviewed	1	1			1	
4	2	2	Compiled	1		1			
16	20	8	Tax Returns			3	1		
110	112	94	Other	10	11	19	18	17	19
4/1/16-3/31/17 ALL	4/1/17-3/31/18 ALL	4/1/18-3/31/19 ALL		0-1MM	176 (4/1-9/30/18) 1-3MM	3-5MM	67 (10/1/18-3/31/19) 5-10MM	10-25MM	25MM & OVER
331	294	243	**NUMBER OF STATEMENTS**	20	27	32	41	61	62
%	%	%	**ASSETS**	%	%	%	%	%	%
22.6	23.4	23.8	Cash & Equivalents	29.9	26.2	29.2	26.9	22.7	17.0
17.8	18.0	18.4	Trade Receivables (net)	9.8	10.4	11.8	17.0	21.2	26.4
.1	.1	.1	Inventory	.0	.0	.0	.1	.1	.3
3.1	3.4	2.9	All Other Current	.7	2.5	3.0	4.3	2.2	3.4
43.6	44.9	45.3	Total Current	40.5	39.1	44.0	48.4	46.2	47.1
39.6	39.5	38.8	Fixed Assets (net)	44.9	48.4	43.8	38.7	36.1	32.7
1.7	1.6	2.7	Intangibles (net)	4.1	.5	3.0	2.7	.3	5.3
15.1	14.0	13.3	All Other Non-Current	10.5	11.9	9.1	10.3	17.4	14.8
100.0	100.0	100.0	Total	100.0	100.0	100.0	100.0	100.0	100.0
			LIABILITIES						
3.7	4.1	3.7	Notes Payable-Short Term	2.9	2.7	8.9	3.4	2.4	3.1
1.5	1.3	1.3	Cur. Mat.-L.T.D.	1.7	.6	.9	1.3	1.6	1.5
6.0	7.2	6.9	Trade Payables	2.8	4.0	3.3	5.8	7.1	12.0
.4	.0	.1	Income Taxes Payable	.2	.0	.0	.4	.0	.1
9.3	9.6	10.0	All Other Current	18.0	5.1	3.9	8.1	10.9	13.2
20.9	22.2	22.1	Total Current	25.7	12.4	17.0	19.1	21.9	29.9
14.5	15.1	18.5	Long-Term Debt	22.2	27.4	29.3	11.1	13.7	17.6
.0	.0	.0	Deferred Taxes	.0	.0	.0	.0	.0	.0
4.6	4.7	6.2	All Other Non-Current	11.4	16.0	3.2	2.7	2.4	7.8
59.9	58.0	53.2	Net Worth	40.7	44.1	50.6	67.1	61.9	44.7
100.0	100.0	100.0	Total Liabilities & Net Worth	100.0	100.0	100.0	100.0	100.0	100.0
			INCOME DATA						
100.0	100.0	100.0	Net Sales	100.0	100.0	100.0	100.0	100.0	100.0
			Gross Profit						
96.0	97.2	97.1	Operating Expenses	87.8	95.7	93.0	97.7	99.6	100.0
4.0	2.8	2.9	Operating Profit	12.2	4.3	7.0	2.3	.4	.0
.8	-.5	-.1	All Other Expenses (net)	1.6	.9	-.4	-.8	-.3	-.2
3.2	3.3	3.0	Profit Before Taxes	10.6	3.3	7.4	3.1	.7	.2
			RATIOS						
5.0	5.2	5.3	Current	7.0	9.3	10.0	8.1	4.1	2.5
2.3	2.2	2.6		3.6	3.6	4.5	3.3	2.5	1.7
1.3	1.2	1.4		.6	2.3	2.3	1.8	1.4	1.2
4.5	4.9	4.8	Quick	6.9	9.3	9.2	6.3	4.0	2.4
2.1	1.9	2.3		3.6	3.4	3.7	3.1	2.4	1.6
1.1	1.1	1.2		.3	2.0	2.0	1.7	1.2	1.1
12 30.2	13 27.9	10 35.5	Sales/Receivables	0 UND	1 501.5	7 53.2	3 115.2	27 13.3	35 10.5
33 11.0	31 11.7	35 10.5		4 83.6	13 28.3	23 15.6	25 14.8	40 9.2	43 8.4
56 6.5	51 7.1	55 6.6		36 10.0	31 11.8	45 8.1	50 7.3	59 6.2	62 5.9
			Cost of Sales/Inventory						
			Cost of Sales/Payables						
3.5	3.9	3.1	Sales/Working Capital	1.7	2.5	2.9	2.4	3.2	6.8
8.1	8.8	7.1		7.3	4.6	5.2	4.9	7.0	12.9
28.0	63.5	25.0		-20.9	9.0	16.4	13.0	23.2	40.3
8.8	14.6	9.0	EBIT/Interest		7.5	5.8	22.4	8.3	9.3
(220) 3.0	(200) 3.3	(168) 2.4		(19) 2.4	(18) 3.3	(27) 1.9	(46) 2.6	(54) 1.9	
-1.5	.1	.2			1.1	1.0	.0	-.6	.2
			Net Profit + Depr., Dep., Amort./Cur. Mat. L/T/D						
.2	.3	.3	Fixed/Worth	.2	.4	.2	.2	.3	.4
.7	.7	.7		.7	.7	.8	.5	.6	.8
1.1	1.2	1.2		3.7	1.2	1.5	.9	.9	1.2
.2	.2	.2	Debt/Worth	.1	.1	.1	.1	.2	.5
.5	.5	.6		.8	.4	.5	.4	.5	1.0
1.3	1.5	1.7		20.8	1.7	1.5	1.1	1.2	2.6
13.5	16.0	14.7	% Profit Before Taxes/Tangible Net Worth	89.3	17.0	29.3	11.0	13.8	10.0
(317) 3.7	(277) 4.5	(227) 4.3		(18) 19.2	(26) 3.9	(30) 10.6	(40) .8	(59) 1.6	(54) 4.3
-1.4	-.8	-.7		2.7	-.1	.7	-3.1	-2.2	-.6
9.1	8.1	7.5	% Profit Before Taxes/Total Assets	24.1	8.1	20.8	8.1	4.8	5.8
2.0	2.5	1.9		6.9	1.8	4.9	.6	1.2	1.7
-1.1	-.9	-.7		.5	.3	.2	-1.7	-1.5	-.8
16.3	23.4	17.3	Sales/Net Fixed Assets	52.0	4.2	36.0	24.3	14.5	29.1
3.5	4.2	3.3		3.6	1.4	2.1	2.8	3.0	5.2
1.5	1.6	1.5		.3	.7	.9	1.2	1.7	2.7
2.7	2.9	2.8	Sales/Total Assets	2.3	1.5	2.4	3.2	2.5	3.6
1.4	1.4	1.3		1.0	.8	1.2	1.4	1.3	1.8
.6	.8	.7		.1	.3	.5	.6	.7	1.1
1.2	1.0	1.1	% Depr., Dep., Amort./Sales	2.1	2.4	1.0	.7	.9	1.0
(282) 2.3	(245) 2.1	(201) 2.5		(12) 7.4	(23) 4.0	(24) 3.1	(31) 2.8	(55) 2.7	(56) 1.9
4.5	3.7	4.1		21.8	7.8	6.4	6.5	3.9	2.6
2.2	3.0	2.2	% Officers', Directors' Owners' Comp/Sales						
(31) 5.9	(33) 5.4	(21) 3.9							
10.5	11.6	6.5							
8044536M	5711741M	5734601M	Net Sales ($)	12967M	51306M	126498M	294903M	1009425M	4239502M
6194166M	4646759M	4430932M	Total Assets ($)	49884M	97086M	178210M	382866M	1182832M	2540054M

© RMA 2019

M = $ thousand   MM = $ million
See Pages viii through xx for Explanation of Ratios and Data

Current Data Sorted by Assets   Comparative Historical Data

0-500M	500M-2MM	2-10MM	10-50MM	50-100MM	100-250MM	Type of Statement	4/1/14-3/31/15 ALL	4/1/15-3/31/16 ALL
2	7	75	56	7	6	Unqualified	166	175
2	1	1	2	1		Reviewed	6	8
1	1	2	1			Compiled	8	6
15	4					Tax Returns	16	16
20	13	40	32	6	1	Other	68	72
	180 (4/1-9/30/18)		115 (10/1/18-3/31/19)					
40	26	118	91	13	7	NUMBER OF STATEMENTS	264	277
%	%	%	%	%	%	ASSETS	%	%
30.3	29.7	22.6	19.5	28.7		Cash & Equivalents	23.6	22.9
21.2	21.2	17.0	16.2	11.1		Trade Receivables (net)	17.9	16.4
.0	1.0	.5	.5	2.4		Inventory	.7	.7
1.5	4.4	4.3	2.1	6.3		All Other Current	3.5	4.2
53.0	56.3	44.3	38.4	48.5		Total Current	45.6	44.2
26.9	35.5	44.0	43.9	36.5		Fixed Assets (net)	39.4	41.3
8.5	2.1	.8	3.0	.1		Intangibles (net)	2.6	2.4
11.6	6.1	10.9	14.8	15.0		All Other Non-Current	12.3	12.1
100.0	100.0	100.0	100.0	100.0		Total	100.0	100.0
						LIABILITIES		
15.3	2.1	2.5	2.0	1.1		Notes Payable-Short Term	4.4	4.1
6.5	2.3	1.7	2.1	1.7		Cur. Mat.-L.T.D.	1.9	2.2
4.0	5.4	5.9	5.6	4.3		Trade Payables	7.0	6.6
.0	.0	.1	.0	.0		Income Taxes Payable	.1	.0
24.2	26.0	14.8	10.5	9.9		All Other Current	13.7	13.7
50.1	35.9	25.0	20.1	17.0		Total Current	27.2	26.7
17.9	24.5	17.5	21.7	20.4		Long-Term Debt	21.6	23.1
.0	.0	.0	.0	.0		Deferred Taxes	.1	.0
8.2	4.1	9.1	3.2	.7		All Other Non-Current	5.0	4.8
23.8	35.5	48.3	54.9	61.8		Net Worth	46.2	45.4
100.0	100.0	100.0	100.0	100.0		Total Liabilities & Net Worth	100.0	100.0
						INCOME DATA		
100.0	100.0	100.0	100.0	100.0		Net Sales	100.0	100.0
						Gross Profit		
92.6	92.9	96.5	97.1	87.9		Operating Expenses	96.3	95.8
7.4	7.1	3.5	2.9	12.1		Operating Profit	3.7	4.2
.2	2.7	1.5	.0	6.0		All Other Expenses (net)	1.1	1.3
7.2	4.4	2.0	2.9	6.1		Profit Before Taxes	2.6	2.9
						RATIOS		
6.1	7.2	3.4	3.4	5.5			3.6	4.1
1.2	2.5	2.1	1.9	2.3		Current	1.9	2.0
.4	1.5	1.3	1.2	1.6			1.0	1.1
6.1	7.1	3.2	3.1	4.8			3.3	3.9
1.2	2.2	1.8	1.7	1.3		Quick	1.6	1.6
.3	1.4	1.1	1.1	1.0			.9	.9
0 UND	11 31.8	12 30.8	22 16.5	19 19.2			15 23.7	14 27.0
5 79.0	28 13.0	30 12.3	33 11.0	30 12.0		Sales/Receivables	31 11.8	29 12.5
30 12.1	36 10.1	43 8.5	45 8.2	46 7.9			42 8.6	41 8.9
						Cost of Sales/Inventory		
						Cost of Sales/Payables		
10.2	4.5	4.6	3.5	1.8			4.1	3.7
56.9	7.9	8.6	9.8	8.2		Sales/Working Capital	10.6	10.6
-47.7	39.6	26.7	36.8	11.0			196.3	109.0
35.5	94.0	14.3	9.9				9.7	9.2
(23) 11.9	(17) 2.8	(91) 3.4	(78) 4.2			EBIT/Interest	(192) 2.4	(200) 2.5
2.9	-2.8	.2	1.1				.1	-.5
						Net Profit + Depr., Dep., Amort./Cur. Mat. L/T/D		
.1	.2	.5	.4	.3			.3	.3
.6	.6	.8	.8	.5		Fixed/Worth	.8	.8
-5.1	NM	1.3	1.5	1.1			1.7	1.6
.3	.3	.3	.3	.3			.4	.3
1.4	.7	.7	.8	.5		Debt/Worth	.8	.8
-15.9	NM	1.3	2.1	1.6			2.4	2.3
227.1	48.3	14.3	19.0	13.6			16.5	16.6
(29) 99.2	(20) 9.3	(110) 4.7	(86) 5.7	5.9		% Profit Before Taxes/Tangible Net Worth	(242) 5.0	(246) 4.1
7.2	-1.5	-2.1	-.9	1.6			-2.0	-1.0
104.4	27.2	8.4	7.2	7.7			8.7	8.5
34.6	1.1	2.5	3.4	3.1		% Profit Before Taxes/Total Assets	2.8	2.1
1.2	-5.3	-1.5	-.6	1.0			-1.4	-.9
257.0	47.2	12.8	6.5	7.6			16.7	15.6
25.9	17.6	3.6	3.0	4.7		Sales/Net Fixed Assets	4.4	3.7
14.5	4.3	2.1	1.5	1.3			2.1	1.9
10.7	4.3	2.6	1.8	2.0			3.1	2.6
7.1	3.0	1.7	1.4	.9		Sales/Total Assets	1.6	1.5
3.6	1.5	1.0	.7	.5			1.0	.9
.5	.6	1.2	1.5	1.6			1.1	1.1
(20) .9	(18) 1.9	(110) 2.1	(86) 2.6	(12) 2.0		% Depr., Dep., Amort./Sales	(232) 2.3	(248) 2.3
3.0	3.3	3.7	4.1	4.6			3.9	4.1
2.6							1.6	1.5
(15) 3.6						% Officers', Directors' Owners' Comp/Sales	(32) 3.3	(23) 3.0
9.2							8.6	5.9
79070M	94566M	1282336M	3426816M	1243524M	2923660M	Net Sales ($)	6590472M	6247009M
9786M	30119M	638010M	2046911M	891269M	1143974M	Total Assets ($)	4469729M	4869787M

© RMA 2019

M = $ thousand   MM = $ million
See Pages viii through xx for Explanation of Ratios and Data

Comparative Historical Data / Current Data Sorted by Sales

			Type of Statement						
138	152	153	Unqualified	3	14	11	35	50	40
6	7	6	Reviewed	1	1	1	1	2	
7	7	5	Compiled		2		1	2	
19	19	20	Tax Returns	5	9	2	3		1
79	108	111	Other	15	15	11	17	29	24
4/1/16-3/31/17 ALL	4/1/17-3/31/18 ALL	4/1/18-3/31/19 ALL		180 (4/1-9/30/18) 0-1MM	1-3MM	3-5MM	115 (10/1/18-3/31/19) 5-10MM	10-25MM	25MM & OVER
249	293	295	NUMBER OF STATEMENTS	24	41	25	57	83	65
%	%	%	ASSETS	%	%	%	%	%	%
23.0	22.1	23.8	Cash & Equivalents	26.8	24.7	23.5	27.2	17.6	27.1
18.5	17.6	17.4	Trade Receivables (net)	15.8	15.0	16.8	14.2	17.6	22.4
.7	.7	.6	Inventory	.0	.1	.2	.9	.2	1.4
3.0	4.2	3.3	All Other Current	.3	3.7	2.7	4.9	3.3	3.0
45.3	44.6	45.1	Total Current	42.9	43.4	43.3	47.1	38.6	54.0
38.5	40.3	40.1	Fixed Assets (net)	36.9	42.9	38.1	39.0	48.4	30.7
3.5	3.3	2.6	Intangibles (net)	11.4	2.3	2.8	.0	1.3	3.5
12.6	11.8	12.2	All Other Non-Current	8.7	11.4	15.8	13.8	11.7	11.9
100.0	100.0	100.0	Total	100.0	100.0	100.0	100.0	100.0	100.0
			LIABILITIES						
4.6	3.9	4.0	Notes Payable-Short Term	21.1	2.8	2.3	2.5	2.3	2.7
1.9	1.8	2.5	Cur. Mat.-L.T.D.	4.9	3.0	3.5	2.2	1.6	2.3
7.0	6.0	5.5	Trade Payables	2.4	3.8	3.8	5.1	5.1	9.3
.0	.3	.0	Income Taxes Payable	.0	.0	.0	.0	.1	.0
13.8	16.3	15.4	All Other Current	25.1	10.8	11.9	18.2	12.3	17.4
27.4	28.4	27.5	Total Current	53.4	20.4	21.5	27.9	21.5	31.8
21.2	20.1	19.6	Long-Term Debt	34.4	19.4	10.9	15.7	25.3	13.6
.0	.0	.0	Deferred Taxes	.0	.0	.0	.0	.0	.0
4.5	5.2	6.2	All Other Non-Current	12.3	6.7	17.6	7.5	1.6	4.1
46.9	46.2	46.8	Net Worth	-.1	53.5	50.0	48.8	51.7	50.5
100.0	100.0	100.0	Total Liabilties & Net Worth	100.0	100.0	100.0	100.0	100.0	100.0
			INCOME DATA						
100.0	100.0	100.0	Net Sales	100.0	100.0	100.0	100.0	100.0	100.0
			Gross Profit						
95.8	95.7	95.4	Operating Expenses	85.6	91.5	92.3	98.0	97.7	97.6
4.2	4.3	4.6	Operating Profit	14.4	8.5	7.7	2.0	2.3	2.4
.6	.5	1.1	All Other Expenses (net)	5.8	3.3	3.3	.4	-.2	-.5
3.6	3.8	3.5	Profit Before Taxes	8.5	5.2	4.4	1.6	2.6	2.9
			RATIOS						
4.3	3.9	3.6	Current	9.8	6.0	5.0	3.7	3.1	3.3
1.8	1.9	2.1		2.3	2.5	1.9	2.8	1.9	1.8
1.1	1.1	1.2		.1	1.0	.9	1.3	1.1	1.3
3.9	3.3	3.3	Quick	9.8	5.2	4.1	3.6	2.6	3.0
1.6	1.7	1.8		2.1	2.5	1.9	2.1	1.7	1.7
.9	1.0	1.0		.1	.6	.8	1.0	1.1	1.1
18 20.7	13 28.8	10 35.7	Sales/Receivables	0 UND	0 UND	6 64.4	10 36.9	24 15.3	23 15.9
31 11.6	29 12.4	30 12.3		5 69.9	26 14.2	18 19.8	25 14.8	33 11.1	34 10.8
43 8.4	41 9.0	42 8.7		41 9.0	47 7.7	39 9.3	40 9.1	42 8.6	49 7.4
			Cost of Sales/Inventory						
			Cost of Sales/Payables						
3.9	4.5	4.5	Sales/Working Capital	3.2	4.4	4.2	3.9	5.5	4.4
11.5	11.5	10.2		9.8	8.9	11.3	6.6	10.2	11.2
98.1	67.0	48.9		-12.9	-308.0	-651.6	31.6	82.5	28.7
16.1	13.8	16.0	EBIT/Interest		34.2	28.7	20.6	8.8	17.2
(183) 4.2	(210) 3.4	(224) 4.1		(32) 3.2	(16) 7.4	(43) 3.3	(70) 4.3	(55) 5.2	
.2	1.0	.5			-1.1	.6	-.8	1.5	1.4
			Net Profit + Depr., Dep., Amort./Cur. Mat. L/T/D						
.3	.3	.4	Fixed/Worth	.2	.3	.2	.3	.6	.3
.7	.8	.7		5.7	.9	.7	.7	1.0	.5
1.6	1.5	1.5		-.5	1.9	1.5	1.0	2.2	1.1
.3	.4	.3	Debt/Worth	.2	.3	.1	.3	.4	.4
.8	.7	.7		5.8	.6	.5	.6	.9	.8
2.1	1.9	1.8		-2.2	1.8	1.3	1.1	2.1	2.0
19.4	18.5	22.3	% Profit Before Taxes/Tangible Net Worth	83.0	75.1	25.8	16.7	19.9	21.3
(220) 6.3	(262) 7.3	(265) 6.0		(14) 17.1	(37) 5.7	(23) .0	(51) 4.9	(81) 6.0	(59) 6.1
-1.8	.1	-1.6		-1.2	-3.2	-2.7	-1.8	-.7	.7
11.3	10.9	11.5	% Profit Before Taxes/Total Assets	45.5	34.6	24.5	11.3	7.7	10.5
3.6	4.0	3.1		5.1	3.0	1.7	2.1	3.3	3.8
-.8	.1	1.0		-1.1	-2.7	-2.3	-2.9	.5	.3
15.9	18.6	17.9	Sales/Net Fixed Assets	29.6	41.5	60.9	20.8	6.0	18.4
4.5	4.5	4.6		17.9	7.8	4.3	4.3	3.1	5.7
1.9	1.9	2.1		2.0	.8	1.9	1.8	2.1	3.5
2.9	3.4	3.3	Sales/Total Assets	6.6	5.8	5.7	2.9	2.4	3.4
1.7	1.6	1.7		2.9	1.7	1.6	1.8	1.6	1.8
.9	1.0	1.0		.8	.6	.6	1.0	1.0	1.3
1.2	1.0	1.2	% Depr., Dep., Amort./Sales	.7	1.6	1.1	1.2	1.5	.8
(211) 2.2	(261) 2.1	(252) 2.2		(14) 2.4	(30) 2.8	(16) 2.2	(51) 2.1	(80) 2.6	(61) 1.8
3.7	3.3	3.7		11.6	5.9	6.0	3.9	3.4	2.6
1.7	1.6	2.6	% Officers', Directors' Owners' Comp/Sales		2.0				
(27) 5.3	(33) 4.7	(39) 6.2			(12) 3.6				
14.2	12.8	12.2			7.0				
6363790M	7509006M	9049972M	Net Sales ($)	13276M	82904M	101424M	401608M	1355689M	7095071M
4604250M	5278696M	4760069M	Total Assets ($)	16657M	113670M	157274M	334591M	1263669M	2874208M

© RMA 2019
M = $ thousand   MM = $ million
See Pages viii through xx for Explanation of Ratios and Data

Current Data Sorted by Assets   Comparative Historical Data

	0-500M	500M-2MM	2-10MM	10-50MM	50-100MM	100-250MM	Type of Statement	4/1/14-3/31/15 ALL	4/1/15-3/31/16 ALL
	3	16	130	104	21	16	Unqualified	417	425
		1	3				Reviewed	8	7
	1	4	1				Compiled	9	9
	11	3	5				Tax Returns	30	28
	20	31	71	49	9	2	Other	173	141
		348 (4/1-9/30/18)		153 (10/1/18-3/31/19)					
	35	55	210	153	30	18	NUMBER OF STATEMENTS	637	610
	%	%	%	%	%	%	**ASSETS**	%	%
	46.7	28.8	24.2	18.9	20.8	16.9	Cash & Equivalents	22.5	22.3
	16.3	21.3	18.3	12.1	14.3	16.1	Trade Receivables (net)	17.2	16.6
	.7	1.4	.4	.5	1.1	.1	Inventory	1.1	.7
	2.4	5.0	3.9	3.2	2.4	3.7	All Other Current	3.7	3.0
	66.1	56.4	46.9	34.7	38.6	36.8	Total Current	44.4	42.7
	18.6	32.7	41.0	46.6	38.1	35.8	Fixed Assets (net)	41.6	42.2
	1.7	1.9	.7	1.8	2.4	1.8	Intangibles (net)	1.1	1.1
	13.6	9.0	11.3	17.0	21.0	25.6	All Other Non-Current	12.9	14.0
	100.0	100.0	100.0	100.0	100.0	100.0	Total	100.0	100.0
							LIABILITIES		
	25.7	6.1	3.7	1.6	.8	5.9	Notes Payable-Short Term	4.2	4.0
	1.2	2.8	1.9	1.8	2.5	2.9	Cur. Mat.-L.T.D.	1.7	1.6
	14.5	12.1	5.6	4.5	4.7	6.0	Trade Payables	6.6	7.2
	.0	.1	.0	.0	.0	.0	Income Taxes Payable	.1	.1
	24.1	10.9	10.1	8.8	6.7	8.4	All Other Current	11.0	10.6
	65.6	32.0	21.3	16.7	14.8	23.2	Total Current	23.5	23.5
	10.7	15.1	15.3	20.5	26.3	22.4	Long-Term Debt	16.9	17.5
	.0	.1	.0	.0	.1	.0	Deferred Taxes	.1	.1
	.3	2.5	2.7	3.1	10.0	6.0	All Other Non-Current	3.9	4.2
	23.4	50.3	60.7	59.6	48.9	48.4	Net Worth	55.6	54.7
	100.0	100.0	100.0	100.0	100.0	100.0	Total Liabilities & Net Worth	100.0	100.0
							INCOME DATA		
	100.0	100.0	100.0	100.0	100.0	100.0	Net Sales	100.0	100.0
							Gross Profit		
	88.9	97.8	97.5	97.4	96.9	97.3	Operating Expenses	96.5	96.0
	11.1	2.2	2.5	2.6	3.1	2.7	Operating Profit	3.5	4.0
	.3	.3	-.1	.2	-.2	.0	All Other Expenses (net)	-.1	1.0
	10.8	1.9	2.7	2.4	3.4	2.7	Profit Before Taxes	3.6	3.1
							RATIOS		
	7.0	4.2	5.4	3.8	4.3	2.7		4.3	4.6
	1.9	2.2	2.3	2.4	2.3	1.7	Current	2.3	2.2
	.6	1.3	1.4	1.2	1.5	1.1		1.3	1.2
	6.8	4.1	5.2	3.4	3.5	2.4		3.8	3.8
	1.9	1.8	2.1	2.1	1.9	1.6	Quick	2.0	2.0
	.5	1.0	1.2	1.1	1.3	.9		1.1	1.1
	0 UND	0 UND	13 27.6	17 22.1	23 15.6	39 9.3		11 34.0	12 30.7
	0 UND	29 12.5	33 11.0	35 10.3	41 8.9	57 6.4	Sales/Receivables	31 11.6	31 11.6
	16 23.4	42 8.6	51 7.2	51 7.1	62 5.9	79 4.6		51 7.1	54 6.7
							Cost of Sales/Inventory		
							Cost of Sales/Payables		
	7.2	4.5	3.2	3.4	2.5	1.7		3.9	3.5
	32.9	9.1	7.0	7.6	5.2	4.1	Sales/Working Capital	7.9	8.6
	-16.8	36.2	19.5	20.7	11.3	285.5		31.8	31.0
	15.9	11.0	15.0	10.6	4.5	9.4		12.6	10.3
	(11) 5.4	(29) 1.6	(150) 4.2	(122) 2.6	(26) 2.4	2.8	EBIT/Interest	(442) 3.1	(424) 2.4
	-46.0	-6.3	-1.0	.4	-.6	.4		-.5	-.8
							Net Profit + Depr., Dep., Amort./Cur. Mat. L/T/D		
	.0	.1	.3	.4	.5	.2		.3	.3
	.1	.3	.6	.7	.9	.8	Fixed/Worth	.7	.7
	1.0	1.3	1.1	1.3	1.4	1.3		1.3	1.3
	.2	.2	.2	.2	.6	.7		.3	.2
	.9	.7	.5	.6	1.0	.8	Debt/Worth	.6	.6
	6.0	2.3	1.2	1.4	2.1	2.4		1.5	1.5
	208.0	22.0	12.7	7.6	5.4	10.8		13.4	13.3
	(29) 50.9	(51) 5.4	(203) 4.0	(149) 2.7	(28) 3.2	(17) 2.7	% Profit Before Taxes/Tangible Net Worth	(601) 4.2	(574) 3.6
	.4	-1.6	-2.1	-1.4	-1.1	-2.2		-2.2	-1.9
	81.8	11.2	7.5	5.4	2.7	4.2		7.7	7.4
	22.1	3.0	2.0	1.6	1.4	1.5	% Profit Before Taxes/Total Assets	2.7	1.7
	-2.8	-1.3	-1.6	-.8	-.8	-.8		-1.4	-1.2
	UND	44.1	15.1	4.5	6.5	7.0		13.9	11.9
	237.8	10.4	4.1	2.4	2.0	2.8	Sales/Net Fixed Assets	4.0	3.7
	9.8	3.9	1.6	1.3	.9	1.6		1.7	1.5
	8.1	3.8	2.7	1.6	1.1	1.3		2.6	2.4
	4.4	2.3	1.5	1.0	.7	.7	Sales/Total Assets	1.5	1.3
	2.2	1.3	.8	.6	.4	.3		.8	.7
	.3	.5	.9	1.8	1.3	1.7		1.0	1.1
	(12) 1.8	(40) 1.3	(183) 1.7	(147) 2.7	(29) 3.5	2.6	% Depr., Dep., Amort./Sales	(559) 2.0	(542) 2.1
	3.3	1.9	3.3	4.1	5.4	5.1		3.8	3.9
			2.7					2.3	1.8
		(10)	5.6				% Officers', Directors' Owners' Comp/Sales	(50) 5.7	(46) 4.2
			15.4					11.9	10.9
	34354M	179213M	2085614M	4045334M	1763776M	2394099M	Net Sales ($)	14297175M	12056937M
	7160M	68299M	1123119M	3579457M	2165999M	2590904M	Total Assets ($)	10279521M	11129677M

© RMA 2019

M = $ thousand   MM = $ million
See Pages viii through xx for Explanation of Ratios and Data

Comparative Historical Data | Current Data Sorted by Sales

			Type of Statement						
359	325	290	Unqualified	3	27	30	45	101	84
2	3	4	Reviewed	1	1		1	1	
4	6	6	Compiled	3	1	1			
19	19	19	Tax Returns	10	3	4	1	1	25
155	200	182	Other	24	37	26	26	44	
4/1/16- 3/31/17 ALL	4/1/17- 3/31/18 ALL	4/1/18- 3/31/19 ALL			348 (4/1-9/30/18)			153 (10/1/18-3/31/19)	
				0-1MM	1-3MM	3-5MM	5-10MM	10-25MM	25MM & OVER
539	553	501	NUMBER OF STATEMENTS	41	69	61	74	147	109
%	%	%	ASSETS	%	%	%	%	%	%
22.0	22.8	24.2	Cash & Equivalents	39.0	25.8	24.4	23.6	21.7	21.3
16.0	17.9	16.3	Trade Receivables (net)	5.4	14.7	13.7	18.6	18.2	18.7
1.1	.8	.6	Inventory	1.2	.7	.3	.5	.6	.6
3.1	3.5	3.6	All Other Current	3.6	3.8	2.5	3.7	4.5	2.9
42.3	45.0	44.7	Total Current	49.2	45.0	40.8	46.4	45.0	43.5
42.9	39.5	39.9	Fixed Assets (net)	38.5	39.5	41.4	39.8	38.9	41.1
1.4	1.7	1.4	Intangibles (net)	.1	1.3	1.5	.8	1.4	2.2
13.4	13.7	14.1	All Other Non-Current	12.3	14.2	16.3	13.0	14.8	13.1
100.0	100.0	100.0	Total	100.0	100.0	100.0	100.0	100.0	100.0
			LIABILITIES						
4.1	3.3	4.8	Notes Payable-Short Term	3.7	14.7	2.0	4.9	2.4	3.6
2.0	1.7	2.0	Cur. Mat.-L.T.D.	2.1	1.8	1.9	2.7	1.8	1.8
5.7	6.7	6.6	Trade Payables	7.5	8.9	4.3	4.5	6.3	7.8
.1	.0	.0	Income Taxes Payable	.0	.0	.0	.1	.0	.0
8.9	10.6	10.5	All Other Current	11.0	9.9	7.9	8.3	12.1	11.7
20.8	22.2	23.9	Total Current	24.4	35.3	16.1	20.4	22.6	24.8
18.5	17.0	17.5	Long-Term Debt	19.3	13.4	22.5	14.7	17.1	18.8
.1	.0	.0	Deferred Taxes	.0	.0	.0	.1	.0	.0
3.7	4.3	3.2	All Other Non-Current	2.1	2.2	1.6	2.4	2.7	6.5
57.0	56.5	55.4	Net Worth	54.3	49.1	59.8	62.4	57.6	49.8
100.0	100.0	100.0	Total Liabilities & Net Worth	100.0	100.0	100.0	100.0	100.0	100.0
			INCOME DATA						
100.0	100.0	100.0	Net Sales	100.0	100.0	100.0	100.0	100.0	100.0
			Gross Profit						
96.5	96.0	96.9	Operating Expenses	88.4	97.8	96.5	96.8	97.8	98.5
3.5	4.0	3.1	Operating Profit	11.6	2.2	3.5	3.2	2.2	1.5
.9	-.1	.0	All Other Expenses (net)	4.9	-.7	.1	-.6	-.5	-.2
2.6	4.0	3.1	Profit Before Taxes	6.7	2.9	3.5	3.8	2.7	1.7
			RATIOS						
4.7	4.9	4.5		7.3	7.1	5.4	6.1	3.8	3.0
2.4	2.4	2.3	Current	3.2	3.1	2.8	2.7	2.1	1.9
1.3	1.2	1.3		1.1	1.0	1.8	1.4	1.2	1.2
4.0	4.4	4.1		6.6	6.5	5.1	5.7	3.1	2.8
2.1	2.1	2.1	Quick	2.6	2.7	2.4	2.3	1.7	1.8
1.1	1.1	1.1		.8	.8	1.5	1.2	1.1	1.1
11 31.8	13 28.3	11 33.3		0 UND	1 370.2	13 28.5	16 22.7	17 20.9	22 16.5
33 11.2	34 10.6	33 11.1	Sales/Receivables	0 UND	28 13.1	31 11.8	33 10.9	37 9.8	41 8.9
53 6.9	55 6.6	51 7.2		16 22.6	43 8.5	55 6.6	53 6.9	51 7.1	55 6.6
			Cost of Sales/Inventory						
			Cost of Sales/Payables						
3.4	3.2	3.5		2.3	2.0	3.2	3.0	3.8	4.9
7.6	7.0	7.5	Sales/Working Capital	6.9	5.7	6.0	6.4	8.3	9.8
27.3	30.1	24.8		80.5	124.8	12.7	20.5	26.0	33.9
11.5	12.3	11.1		13.0	13.6	10.5	14.9	12.4	9.1
(397) 2.9	(380) 3.3	(356) 2.6	EBIT/Interest	(16) 1.6	(40) 2.5	(44) 3.4	(47) 2.4	(118) 3.7	(91) 2.6
-1.1	.4	-.5		-7.8	-6.9	.8	-1.2	-.1	.4
			Net Profit + Depr., Dep., Amort./Cur. Mat. L/T/D						
.3	.3	.3		.0	.2	.3	.2	.3	.4
.7	.6	.7	Fixed/Worth	.4	.6	.7	.6	.6	.8
1.3	1.3	1.2		1.3	1.1	1.3	1.1	1.1	1.4
.3	.2	.2		.2	.1	.2	.2	.3	.5
.6	.6	.6	Debt/Worth	.6	.4	.6	.5	.6	.8
1.3	1.8	1.6		2.7	1.1	1.2	1.6	1.6	2.1
11.5	11.9	12.5	% Profit Before Taxes/Tangible Net Worth	82.4	14.7	17.8	14.2	9.9	10.8
(513) 3.4	(525) 4.5	(477) 3.5		(39) 4.1	(62) 3.4	(59) 5.4	(73) 3.2	(143) 3.1	(101) 3.3
-2.6	-.8	-1.5		-3.4	-5.2	-.4	-2.1	-1.5	-1.0
7.0	7.7	7.3	% Profit Before Taxes/Total Assets	39.5	8.3	8.3	7.5	6.1	5.2
2.0	2.6	2.0		4.0	2.0	2.8	2.0	2.0	1.6
-1.7	-.6	-1.1		-1.0	-5.4	-1.6	-1.6	-.8	-1.0
10.0	12.7	13.2		UND	33.5	11.4	19.5	10.0	7.3
3.1	3.5	3.7	Sales/Net Fixed Assets	6.7	3.5	2.8	4.0	3.4	4.2
1.4	1.6	1.6		.4	1.2	1.0	1.7	1.7	1.9
2.3	2.3	2.4		3.2	2.9	2.0	2.2	2.6	2.2
1.2	1.3	1.3	Sales/Total Assets	.8	1.1	.9	1.4	1.3	1.4
.7	.7	.7		.2	.5	.5	.9	.8	1.0
1.3	1.2	1.2		2.5	.7	1.4	.9	1.1	1.2
(467) 2.3	(469) 2.2	(429) 2.0	% Depr., Dep., Amort./Sales	(17) 6.4	(49) 1.9	(54) 2.3	(67) 1.7	(138) 2.1	(104) 2.0
4.2	3.7	3.7		16.4	4.4	4.6	3.6	3.5	3.5
1.4	3.1	5.1	% Officers', Directors' Owners' Comp/Sales						
(33) 5.5	(35) 7.4	(30) 9.2							
13.6	12.7	19.9							
12046514M	12523030M	10502390M	Net Sales ($)	19082M	142695M	245079M	539923M	2387656M	7167955M
10223265M	11153410M	9534938M	Total Assets ($)	55142M	204732M	404439M	571505M	2787098M	5512022M

M = $ thousand   MM = $ million
See Pages viii through xx for Explanation of Ratios and Data

Current Data Sorted by Assets   Comparative Historical Data

						Type of Statement		
	1	9	28	4	1	Unqualified	29	43
	1					Reviewed		
						Compiled		
			1			Tax Returns	2	2
			9			Other	10	16
1	4	10	15 (10/1/18-3/31/19)				10	16
54 (4/1-9/30/18)							4/1/14-3/31/15	4/1/15-3/31/16
0-500M	500M-2MM	2-10MM	10-50MM	50-100MM	100-250MM		ALL	ALL
1	6	19	38	4	1	**NUMBER OF STATEMENTS**	41	61
%	%	%	%	%	%		%	%
		20.2	22.2			**ASSETS** Cash & Equivalents	26.5	24.4
		7.1	4.6			Trade Receivables (net)	6.1	6.1
		14.0	10.7			Inventory	9.7	10.2
		2.4	2.0			All Other Current	4.7	4.0
		43.8	39.5			Total Current	46.9	44.7
		45.6	44.4			Fixed Assets (net)	41.1	39.7
		.0	.6			Intangibles (net)	1.3	2.2
		10.5	15.5			All Other Non-Current	10.6	13.4
		100.0	100.0			Total	100.0	100.0
		.6	.5			**LIABILITIES** Notes Payable-Short Term	.4	1.1
		.9	.7			Cur. Mat.-L.T.D.	.4	.3
		3.4	2.9			Trade Payables	4.5	4.5
		.0	.0			Income Taxes Payable	.0	.0
		4.4	2.5			All Other Current	2.7	2.3
		9.4	6.6			Total Current	7.9	8.2
		12.4	11.9			Long-Term Debt	13.1	10.7
		.0	.0			Deferred Taxes	.0	.0
		.5	.6			All Other Non-Current	1.9	2.0
		77.8	80.8			Net Worth	77.2	79.0
		100.0	100.0			Total Liabilities & Net Worth	100.0	100.0
		100.0	100.0			**INCOME DATA** Net Sales	100.0	100.0
						Gross Profit		
		92.0	93.4			Operating Expenses	93.4	93.6
		8.0	6.6			Operating Profit	6.6	6.4
		6.2	1.8			All Other Expenses (net)	3.9	3.5
		1.7	4.8			Profit Before Taxes	2.8	2.9
		9.1	13.8			**RATIOS**	14.3	15.9
		5.5	7.4			Current	6.0	7.8
		3.2	3.3				3.7	3.3
		6.3	10.7				6.2	8.5
		3.6	4.1			Quick	4.3	4.1
		1.6	2.2				2.8	1.9
	0 999.8		4 98.0				2 227.9	3 141.0
	3 145.9		8 43.4			Sales/Receivables	10 36.8	8 47.6
	29 12.4		29 12.8				22 16.6	24 15.1
						Cost of Sales/Inventory		
						Cost of Sales/Payables		
		2.8	1.9				2.6	2.2
		4.4	4.0			Sales/Working Capital	4.5	5.1
		14.9	11.5				7.6	10.7
		14.4	76.9				12.6	75.0
	(12) 3.2	(26) 6.7				EBIT/Interest	(21) 1.3	(31) 2.2
		.1	.4				-3.6	-13.1
						Net Profit + Depr., Dep., Amort./Cur. Mat. L/T/D		
		.3	.4				.3	.2
		.6	.6			Fixed/Worth	.5	.5
		.8	.8				.8	.8
		.1	.0				.1	.1
		.2	.2			Debt/Worth	.2	.2
		.3	.5				.6	.4
		13.5	9.8				8.5	11.5
		7.6	2.4			% Profit Before Taxes/Tangible Net Worth	2.8 (59)	4.9
		-2.6	-.1				-2.7	-3.3
		10.0	7.5				7.0	9.2
		5.7	2.1			% Profit Before Taxes/Total Assets	2.4	4.0
		-2.5	-.1				-1.4	-1.4
		36.9	6.4				9.6	9.6
		3.0	2.5			Sales/Net Fixed Assets	5.4	4.8
		1.6	1.1				1.8	1.9
		4.7	2.8				3.2	3.0
		1.4	1.2			Sales/Total Assets	1.8	1.3
		.9	.5				.8	.5
		.5	1.1				.7	.7
	(14) 2.8	2.0				% Depr., Dep., Amort./Sales	(40) 1.3	(57) 1.4
		4.8	4.4				3.7	3.6
						% Officers', Directors' Owners' Comp/Sales		
457M	13191M	287651M	1329423M	351674M	340975M	Net Sales ($)	1319097M	1572101M
481M	7885M	101063M	867480M	325674M	118773M	Total Assets ($)	701446M	1058748M

M = $ thousand   MM = $ million
See Pages viii through xx for Explanation of Ratios and Data

Comparative Historical Data   Current Data Sorted by Sales

28	31	43	Type of Statement		6	7	11	19
		1	Unqualified	1				
1			Reviewed					
1		1	Compiled				1	
14	17	24	Tax Returns	2	4	2	3	4	9
			Other					
4/1/16-3/31/17	4/1/17-3/31/18	4/1/18-3/31/19		54 (4/1-9/30/18)			15 (10/1/18-3/31/19)		
ALL	ALL	ALL		0-1MM	1-3MM	3-5MM	5-10MM	10-25MM	25MM & OVER
44	48	69	**NUMBER OF STATEMENTS**	3	4	8	10	16	28

28 %	31 %	43 %		0-1MM %	1-3MM %	3-5MM %	5-10MM %	10-25MM %	25MM %
			ASSETS						
24.0	25.5	23.5	Cash & Equivalents				24.7	23.7	20.9
6.2	7.7	5.5	Trade Receivables (net)				6.5	4.3	5.3
9.6	11.0	11.0	Inventory				11.0	6.8	14.6
2.1	3.1	2.1	All Other Current				.6	3.9	2.3
41.9	47.2	42.1	Total Current				42.8	38.7	43.1
37.6	39.2	44.4	Fixed Assets (net)				44.3	46.2	42.1
2.8	.9	.4	Intangibles (net)				.0	1.4	.0
17.7	12.6	13.2	All Other Non-Current				12.9	13.7	14.8
100.0	100.0	100.0	Total				100.0	100.0	100.0
			LIABILITIES						
1.1	.4	.5	Notes Payable-Short Term				.9	.9	.4
1.3	.5	.7	Cur. Mat.-L.T.D.				.7	1.4	.3
3.5	6.6	2.8	Trade Payables				2.6	3.5	2.8
.0	.0	.0	Income Taxes Payable				.0	.0	.0
2.8	2.9	2.8	All Other Current				1.9	2.9	3.6
8.8	10.4	6.9	Total Current				6.2	8.8	7.1
12.7	9.6	11.4	Long-Term Debt				13.6	12.5	10.3
.0	.0	.0	Deferred Taxes				.0	.0	.0
.9	1.7	.5	All Other Non-Current				.8	.2	.7
77.7	78.3	81.2	Net Worth				79.3	78.5	81.9
100.0	100.0	100.0	Total Liabilties & Net Worth				100.0	100.0	100.0
			INCOME DATA						
100.0	100.0	100.0	Net Sales				100.0	100.0	100.0
			Gross Profit						
96.7	95.9	93.1	Operating Expenses				89.9	90.5	98.0
3.3	4.1	6.9	Operating Profit				10.1	9.5	2.0
-.6	-.1	2.6	All Other Expenses (net)				8.4	2.5	-1.7
3.9	4.2	4.2	Profit Before Taxes				1.7	7.0	3.7
			RATIOS						
14.1	13.5	13.5	Current				19.4	10.1	13.0
6.2	7.4	7.7					5.2	5.0	7.7
2.9	3.4	3.7					2.9	3.2	3.6
7.8	8.1	9.6	Quick				17.2	5.2	9.0
3.7	4.4	4.2					3.1	3.9	3.6
2.1	2.4	2.2					1.6	2.7	1.9
5 72.0	3 143.0	2 207.8	Sales/Receivables				0 UND	4 86.9	1 273.1
14 26.3	13 27.9	7 51.9					23 16.0	16 22.8	4 99.8
38 9.7	35 10.5	29 12.8					47 7.8	37 9.8	8 44.8
			Cost of Sales/Inventory						
			Cost of Sales/Payables						
1.6	1.8	2.1	Sales/Working Capital				1.3	1.8	4.7
3.9	4.5	4.3					2.8	2.5	10.1
8.6	9.8	11.2					4.3	10.3	16.8
11.7	34.4	46.5	EBIT/Interest					28.6	70.6
(25) 3.5	(27) 4.0	(43) 8.8					(10) 1.8	(22) 22.5
-.9	-2.1	.9						-1.9	4.3
			Net Profit + Depr., Dep., Amort./Cur. Mat. L/T/D						
.3	.3	.3	Fixed/Worth				.3	.5	.4
.4	.5	.5					.5	.6	.5
.8	.8	.8					1.0	.8	.7
.1	.1	.0	Debt/Worth				.1	.1	.0
.2	.1	.2					.2	.3	.2
.5	.5	.4					.5	.5	.4
8.6	13.3	11.2	% Profit Before Taxes/Tangible Net Worth				8.5	13.2	12.4
(43) 1.6	2.5	3.7					1.2	3.9	7.2
-1.2	-1.5	-.5					.5	-3.8	.2
7.7	10.5	8.6	% Profit Before Taxes/Total Assets				6.9	11.1	9.4
1.4	2.3	2.6					.7	2.3	4.7
-1.1	-1.3	-.4					.3	-2.4	.2
9.1	12.8	7.5	Sales/Net Fixed Assets				2.1	2.7	13.4
2.4	3.0	2.7					1.7	2.2	6.1
1.6	1.7	1.6					.9	1.0	4.2
2.4	3.5	2.7	Sales/Total Assets				1.4	1.3	4.3
1.0	1.3	1.4					.7	.6	2.9
.5	.6	.6					.4	.5	1.7
.8	.7	1.0	% Depr., Dep., Amort./Sales					2.0	.6
(40) 2.4	(42) 2.5	(60) 2.0						3.6	1.1
4.4	4.6	4.4						5.4	1.6
			% Officers', Directors' Owners' Comp/Sales						
1311142M	1371581M	2323371M	Net Sales ($)	1512M	8186M	31594M	75970M	251085M	1955024M
1024404M	860227M	1421356M	Total Assets ($)	1875M	13384M	33604M	133673M	369501M	869319M

© RMA 2019
M = $ thousand   MM = $ million
See Pages viii through xx for Explanation of Ratios and Data

Current Data Sorted by Assets

Comparative Historical Data

0-500M	500M-2MM	2-10MM	10-50MM	50-100MM	100-250MM		4/1/14-3/31/15 ALL	4/1/15-3/31/16 ALL
	2	15	17	2		**Type of Statement** Unqualified	27	39
	1					Reviewed	2	2
						Compiled	1	
1	1	1	1			Tax Returns	2	
	6	7	3			Other	12	15
	43 (4/1-9/30/18)		14 (10/1/18-3/31/19)					
1	10	23	21	2		**NUMBER OF STATEMENTS**	44	56
%	%	%	%	%	%	**ASSETS**	%	%
	28.9	18.0	11.7			Cash & Equivalents	21.0	19.3
	12.9	5.9	7.8			Trade Receivables (net)	12.2	9.6
	.6	.2	.9			Inventory	.3	.4
	2.2	4.3	2.6			All Other Current	3.4	2.2
	44.6	28.4	23.0			Total Current	36.9	31.5
	48.5	59.1	59.7			Fixed Assets (net)	48.4	58.4
	2.9	.1	1.7			Intangibles (net)	.1	.0
	4.0	12.5	15.6			All Other Non-Current	14.5	10.1
	100.0	100.0	100.0			Total	100.0	100.0
						LIABILITIES		
	.1	.7	1.6			Notes Payable-Short Term	2.9	1.8
	.6	.7	1.5			Cur. Mat.-L.T.D.	.3	1.0
	3.2	2.2	2.5			Trade Payables	6.1	4.8
	.0	.0	.0			Income Taxes Payable	.0	.0
	3.8	2.4	4.4			All Other Current	5.2	3.9
	7.7	6.1	10.0			Total Current	14.6	11.6
	7.5	20.0	21.8			Long-Term Debt	23.0	15.6
	.0	.0	.0			Deferred Taxes	.0	.0
	5.5	3.7	2.4			All Other Non-Current	2.1	2.0
	79.3	70.2	65.8			Net Worth	60.3	70.8
	100.0	100.0	100.0			Total Liabilties & Net Worth	100.0	100.0
						INCOME DATA		
	100.0	100.0	100.0			Net Sales	100.0	100.0
						Gross Profit		
	89.5	92.0	100.5			Operating Expenses	98.2	97.3
	10.5	8.0	-.5			Operating Profit	1.8	2.7
	-.2	.5	-.9			All Other Expenses (net)	-.8	.8
	10.7	7.5	.4			Profit Before Taxes	2.7	1.9
						RATIOS		
	18.7	6.4	5.8			Current	9.5	7.8
	4.7	5.0	2.8				4.4	3.5
	3.1	2.1	1.2				1.8	1.9
	15.6	5.5	5.0			Quick	8.3	7.4
	4.7	3.6	2.3				3.1	3.0
	3.0	1.1	.6				1.5	1.6
	3 112.0	10 35.3	4 81.8			Sales/Receivables	2 158.2	4 87.4
	19 19.3	18 20.7	34 10.7				28 12.9	25 14.6
	56 6.5	48 7.6	62 5.9				44 8.3	43 8.4
						Cost of Sales/Inventory		
						Cost of Sales/Payables		
	3.0	2.2	2.1			Sales/Working Capital	2.3	2.8
	6.5	3.0	4.9				5.0	5.5
	12.7	10.4	168.9				10.7	14.0
		18.3	8.4			EBIT/Interest	16.5	18.0
		(17) 1.0	(16) 3.0				(28) 2.4	(35) 2.4
		-.6	-4.6				-3.5	-2.9
						Net Profit + Depr., Dep., Amort./Cur. Mat. L/T/D		
	.4	.5	.6			Fixed/Worth	.4	.6
	.7	.8	.8				.7	.8
	1.0	1.5	1.9				1.1	1.1
	.1	.1	.1			Debt/Worth	.1	.1
	.2	.3	.3				.4	.3
	.5	.7	1.3				1.0	.7
	27.4	6.4	7.9			% Profit Before Taxes/Tangible Net Worth	6.5	7.3
	7.2	(20) 1.6	2.2				(42) 1.9	(55) 1.0
	-3.5	-3.9	-5.5				-3.0	-4.9
	25.5	5.6	4.9			% Profit Before Taxes/Total Assets	4.4	5.5
	5.7	1.0	1.0				1.3	.3
	-2.7	-2.4	-3.8				-1.8	-3.2
	18.9	2.2	1.9			Sales/Net Fixed Assets	5.0	2.7
	4.2	1.0	.8				2.0	1.2
	1.1	.6	.4				.8	.8
	3.4	1.0	1.0			Sales/Total Assets	1.7	1.4
	1.4	.6	.6				.9	.7
	.7	.4	.3				.4	.5
		1.9	2.6			% Depr., Dep., Amort./Sales	1.6	2.1
		(22) 3.7	5.1				(37) 3.4	(47) 3.8
		5.9	8.7				5.8	4.8
						% Officers', Directors' Owners' Comp/Sales		
304M	18384M	81820M	253560M	56927M		Net Sales ($)	254241M	490257M
89M	11095M	118109M	461199M	167879M		Total Assets ($)	481712M	708693M

(Columns 50-100MM and 100-250MM marked: DATA NOT AVAILABLE)

Comparative Historical Data / Current Data Sorted by Sales

Type of Statement	4/1/16-3/31/17 ALL	4/1/17-3/31/18 ALL	4/1/18-3/31/19 ALL	0-1MM	1-3MM	3-5MM	5-10MM	10-25MM	25MM & OVER
Unqualified	25	39	36	1	12	3	7	10	3
Reviewed	2	3	1	1					
Compiled	2	1							
Tax Returns	1	1	4	2	1			1	
Other	16	20	16	1	7	5	1	2	
					43 (4/1-9/30/18)			14 (10/1/18-3/31/19)	
NUMBER OF STATEMENTS	46	64	57	5	20	8	8	13	3
	%	%	%	%	%	%	%	%	%
ASSETS									
Cash & Equivalents	14.7	19.7	17.9		16.3			14.1	
Trade Receivables (net)	8.8	9.1	8.2		6.1			10.7	
Inventory	.1	.7	.5		1.2			.3	
All Other Current	1.9	1.8	3.1		2.3			1.7	
Total Current	25.5	31.4	29.8		25.9			26.9	
Fixed Assets (net)	64.4	56.2	57.1		60.1			52.7	
Intangibles (net)	1.1	1.0	1.2		.1			.6	
All Other Non-Current	9.1	11.4	12.0		13.9			19.8	
Total	100.0	100.0	100.0		100.0			100.0	
LIABILITIES									
Notes Payable-Short Term	1.8	1.5	.9		.4			1.0	
Cur. Mat.-L.T.D.	1.4	1.4	1.0		.5			1.1	
Trade Payables	2.4	2.8	2.6		1.7			3.4	
Income Taxes Payable	.0	.0	.0		.0			.0	
All Other Current	5.0	4.9	3.5		3.1			4.5	
Total Current	10.7	10.6	8.0		5.7			10.1	
Long-Term Debt	14.3	17.6	18.1		21.4			14.3	
Deferred Taxes	.0	.0	.0		.0			.0	
All Other Non-Current	1.7	2.4	3.3		3.3			3.8	
Net Worth	73.4	69.3	70.6		69.6			71.8	
Total Liabilities & Net Worth	100.0	100.0	100.0		100.0			100.0	
INCOME DATA									
Net Sales	100.0	100.0	100.0		100.0			100.0	
Gross Profit									
Operating Expenses	98.2	91.9	95.3		97.8			96.6	
Operating Profit	1.8	8.1	4.7		2.2			3.4	
All Other Expenses (net)	-.6	.1	-.1		-.5			-.8	
Profit Before Taxes	2.4	8.0	4.8		2.8			4.2	
RATIOS									
Current	5.8	6.3	6.3		6.2			5.9	
Current	2.9	3.8	4.3		4.7			2.8	
Current	1.4	1.7	1.7		2.4			1.0	
Quick	5.8	6.0	5.5		5.0			5.6	
Quick	2.8	3.3	3.4		3.9			2.4	
Quick	1.4	1.3	1.1		2.0			.9	
Sales/Receivables	3 104.5	1 306.3	9 41.9		9 38.6			6 58.1	
Sales/Receivables	25 14.4	24 15.3	24 15.5		19 19.5			35 10.3	
Sales/Receivables	42 8.6	48 7.6	52 7.0		46 7.9			65 5.6	
Cost of Sales/Inventory									
Cost of Sales/Payables									
Sales/Working Capital	3.1	2.7	2.4		2.2			2.9	
Sales/Working Capital	7.3	5.6	4.7		4.0			6.7	
Sales/Working Capital	18.9	15.1	14.6		9.9			211.6	
EBIT/Interest	20.9	18.5	8.0		18.3				
EBIT/Interest	(32) 1.3	(43) 6.0	(38) 1.3	(13) 1.0				
EBIT/Interest	-.8	1.3	-2.1		-.6				
Net Profit + Depr., Dep., Amort./Cur. Mat. L/T/D									
Fixed/Worth	.7	.6	.5		.6			.4	
Fixed/Worth	.9	.9	.8		.9			.7	
Fixed/Worth	1.2	1.1	1.5		1.5			1.0	
Debt/Worth	.1	.1	.1		.1			.1	
Debt/Worth	.4	.3	.3		.4			.2	
Debt/Worth	.7	.9	.8		.8			1.0	
% Profit Before Taxes/Tangible Net Worth	8.6	14.8	8.5		6.4			10.6	
% Profit Before Taxes/Tangible Net Worth	(45) 1.0	(62) 6.7	(56) 1.8		2.6			3.5	
% Profit Before Taxes/Tangible Net Worth	-2.7	.0	-4.1		-2.5			-6.6	
% Profit Before Taxes/Total Assets	5.6	10.1	6.8		5.3			9.0	
% Profit Before Taxes/Total Assets	.8	4.2	1.0		1.4			2.7	
% Profit Before Taxes/Total Assets	-1.8	-.1	-3.1		-1.5			-4.4	
Sales/Net Fixed Assets	1.7	2.5	2.5		2.5			2.5	
Sales/Net Fixed Assets	1.1	1.2	1.1		1.0			1.5	
Sales/Net Fixed Assets	.5	.7	.6		.5			.8	
Sales/Total Assets	1.1	1.2	1.1		1.1			1.0	
Sales/Total Assets	.7	.7	.6		.6			.9	
Sales/Total Assets	.4	.5	.4		.4			.5	
% Depr., Dep., Amort./Sales	2.7	2.3	2.5		3.3			2.5	
% Depr., Dep., Amort./Sales	(40) 4.1	(56) 3.9	(53) 4.0	(18) 4.0				4.0	
% Depr., Dep., Amort./Sales	5.5	5.8	7.2		7.0			5.2	
% Officers', Directors' Owners' Comp/Sales									
Net Sales ($)	311409M	442637M	410995M	3518M	42898M	32021M	60154M	189039M	83365M
Total Assets ($)	496189M	805147M	758371M	4823M	85455M	88594M	137472M	255766M	186261M

© RMA 2019

M = $ thousand   MM = $ million
See Pages viii through xx for Explanation of Ratios and Data

Current Data Sorted by Assets

Comparative Historical Data

0-500M	500M-2MM	2-10MM	10-50MM	50-100MM	100-250MM	Type of Statement	4/1/14-3/31/15 ALL	4/1/15-3/31/16 ALL
1	5	22	33	6	5	Unqualified	93	96
		1				Reviewed	1	2
		1				Compiled		1
2		2				Tax Returns	7	6
	10	16	18	1		Other	31	46
	82 (4/1-9/30/18)		41 (10/1/18-3/31/19)				31 4/1/14-3/31/15	46 4/1/15-3/31/16
3	15	42	51	7	5	NUMBER OF STATEMENTS	132	151
%	%	%	%	%	%	**ASSETS**	%	%
	21.0	13.4	15.5			Cash & Equivalents	13.2	14.9
	19.8	11.6	8.3			Trade Receivables (net)	9.0	9.2
	1.9	2.6	1.3			Inventory	2.1	2.2
	4.5	3.5	3.6			All Other Current	4.5	4.0
	47.1	31.1	28.7			Total Current	28.8	30.3
	40.3	43.5	42.3			Fixed Assets (net)	50.5	45.7
	2.6	.3	1.4			Intangibles (net)	.5	.8
	10.0	25.1	27.5			All Other Non-Current	20.3	23.2
	100.0	100.0	100.0			Total	100.0	100.0
						LIABILITIES		
	9.9	3.9	2.1			Notes Payable-Short Term	2.8	2.3
	.2	2.2	1.9			Cur. Mat.-L.T.D.	2.2	1.9
	6.0	2.8	3.5			Trade Payables	3.7	2.9
	.0	.0	.0			Income Taxes Payable	.0	.1
	5.4	6.0	7.7			All Other Current	6.2	6.2
	21.5	14.8	15.3			Total Current	14.9	13.4
	11.6	22.3	29.5			Long-Term Debt	33.5	29.3
	.0	.0	.0			Deferred Taxes	.0	.0
	2.9	2.9	2.4			All Other Non-Current	4.2	3.2
	64.0	59.9	52.8			Net Worth	47.4	54.0
	100.0	100.0	100.0			Total Liabilities & Net Worth	100.0	100.0
						INCOME DATA		
	100.0	100.0	100.0			Net Sales	100.0	100.0
						Gross Profit		
	98.1	90.3	87.0			Operating Expenses	94.2	91.7
	1.9	9.7	13.0			Operating Profit	5.8	8.3
	1.7	3.3	.9			All Other Expenses (net)	3.4	4.0
	.2	6.4	12.1			Profit Before Taxes	2.4	4.3
						RATIOS		
	8.4	4.6	4.7				4.9	6.0
	4.5	2.2	1.9			Current	1.9	2.4
	1.2	1.0	1.0				.9	1.1
	4.8	3.3	3.5				3.9	5.0
	2.9	2.1	1.4			Quick	1.3	1.9
	1.2	.8	.8				.6	.7
	0 UND	0 UND	14 26.4				3 121.7	2 184.0
	9 38.6	14 26.9	24 15.2			Sales/Receivables	16 23.4	16 22.7
	54 6.8	41 9.0	54 6.8				45 8.2	47 7.8
						Cost of Sales/Inventory		
						Cost of Sales/Payables		
	2.3	2.1	1.9				2.1	2.0
	4.3	5.9	5.1			Sales/Working Capital	6.6	4.5
	33.1	NM	144.4				-166.4	46.8
		7.3	17.1				8.0	11.7
		(31) 2.2	(39) 4.5			EBIT/Interest	(98) 2.4	(103) 3.1
		-1.0	1.4				.4	.0
						Net Profit + Depr., Dep., Amort./Cur. Mat. L/T/D		
	.0	.3	.2				.4	.3
	.9	.6	.7			Fixed/Worth	1.0	.7
	1.0	1.4	1.4				2.2	1.6
	.3	.2	.5				.3	.3
	.5	.6	.8			Debt/Worth	1.2	.7
	.8	1.5	2.4				3.2	2.4
	20.9	10.5	13.7				13.4	9.3
	6.0	2.7	(50) 7.0			% Profit Before Taxes/Tangible Net Worth	(122) 3.6	(149) 4.1
	-3.3	-4.4	1.3				-.9	-2.4
	15.2	6.1	7.1				4.7	5.3
	4.2	1.3	3.2			% Profit Before Taxes/Total Assets	1.3	1.6
	-3.0	-2.0	.8				-.7	-1.2
	232.0	4.9	10.2				5.2	5.9
	2.3	1.5	1.1			Sales/Net Fixed Assets	1.2	1.3
	.8	.7	.5				.4	.5
	2.8	1.0	.8				1.1	1.1
	1.3	.5	.5			Sales/Total Assets	.5	.4
	.5	.3	.2				.2	.2
		1.5	1.5				2.0	1.4
		(34) 3.2	(44) 3.6			% Depr., Dep., Amort./Sales	(108) 4.2	(124) 3.8
		7.2	7.8				11.9	11.9
							4.7	3.2
						% Officers', Directors' Owners' Comp/Sales	(12) 11.7	(10) 5.5
							26.4	12.0
271M	31868M	182393M	821952M	108954M	84167M	Net Sales ($)	1135819M	1392193M
1045M	19816M	216478M	1324653M	438150M	731090M	Total Assets ($)	2406965M	3099963M

M = $ thousand   MM = $ million
See Pages viii through xx for Explanation of Ratios and Data

Comparative Historical Data | Current Data Sorted by Sales

			Type of Statement						
102	87	72	Unqualified	4	14	11	13	20	10
5	1	1	Reviewed		1				
2	3	1	Compiled			1			
5	8	4	Tax Returns	2	1	1			
37	45	45	Other	9	13	3	12	5	3
4/1/16-3/31/17 ALL	4/1/17-3/31/18 ALL	4/1/18-3/31/19 ALL		82 (4/1-9/30/18)			41 (10/1/18-3/31/19)		
				0-1MM	1-3MM	3-5MM	5-10MM	10-25MM	25MM & OVER
151	144	123	NUMBER OF STATEMENTS	15	29	16	25	25	13
%	%	%	ASSETS	%	%	%	%	%	%
16.7	16.5	14.6	Cash & Equivalents	10.9	13.2	17.1	15.1	15.3	17.0
7.9	8.3	10.3	Trade Receivables (net)	5.6	5.5	11.5	12.5	7.9	25.7
2.0	2.5	2.1	Inventory	4.5	2.6	3.4	1.5	.4	.9
3.7	4.0	3.7	All Other Current	1.2	3.7	2.8	5.0	4.9	2.5
30.3	31.3	30.7	Total Current	22.2	25.0	34.8	34.0	28.5	46.1
45.2	43.7	42.1	Fixed Assets (net)	51.7	40.2	37.2	41.9	44.0	38.5
1.4	1.9	1.1	Intangibles (net)	.0	1.4	.0	1.6	1.4	1.2
23.1	23.1	26.1	All Other Non-Current	26.1	33.5	28.0	22.6	26.1	14.3
100.0	100.0	100.0	Total	100.0	100.0	100.0	100.0	100.0	100.0
			LIABILITIES						
3.0	2.0	3.7	Notes Payable-Short Term	2.9	5.1	1.2	4.3	2.1	6.8
1.8	2.6	1.8	Cur. Mat.-L.T.D.	1.2	2.2	1.9	1.4	1.2	3.1
2.9	3.4	3.3	Trade Payables	.6	1.8	2.2	4.4	2.9	10.2
.0	.0	.0	Income Taxes Payable	.0	.0	.0	.0	.0	.0
6.4	4.8	6.5	All Other Current	3.6	3.8	8.3	4.3	7.9	14.9
14.1	12.7	15.3	Total Current	8.3	12.8	13.6	14.4	14.1	35.0
27.1	27.9	25.9	Long-Term Debt	30.8	20.8	23.4	34.4	24.7	20.4
.0	.0	.0	Deferred Taxes	.0	.0	.0	.0	.0	.0
3.9	2.9	2.5	All Other Non-Current	2.2	.4	3.0	4.9	2.9	1.4
54.9	56.5	56.3	Net Worth	58.7	66.0	60.0	46.3	58.3	43.1
100.0	100.0	100.0	Total Liabilties & Net Worth	100.0	100.0	100.0	100.0	100.0	100.0
			INCOME DATA						
100.0	100.0	100.0	Net Sales	100.0	100.0	100.0	100.0	100.0	100.0
			Gross Profit						
92.2	92.7	89.0	Operating Expenses	85.9	85.5	96.1	80.2	95.0	96.7
7.8	7.3	11.0	Operating Profit	14.1	14.5	3.9	19.8	5.0	3.3
2.5	1.8	3.2	All Other Expenses (net)	8.3	3.4	-.9	4.2	2.3	1.9
5.3	5.5	7.8	Profit Before Taxes	5.8	11.0	4.8	15.6	2.8	1.4
			RATIOS						
6.1	6.0	4.9	Current	10.2	5.8	4.1	5.0	4.3	3.3
2.3	2.5	2.3		3.1	3.0	2.6	2.8	2.0	1.1
1.1	1.2	1.0		.6	.9	1.2	1.3	1.1	.9
4.2	4.4	3.6	Quick	4.8	3.7	2.7	4.0	3.2	3.2
1.7	2.1	1.8		2.7	2.8	2.1	1.5	1.9	1.0
.6	.8	.8		.5	.4	1.0	1.0	.8	.8
4 87.4	1 255.6	3 104.6	Sales/Receivables	0 UND	0 UND	20 18.7	12 29.8	13 27.4	18 19.8
21 17.6	18 20.6	23 16.0		3 104.6	5 66.6	36 10.2	27 13.7	31 11.9	47 7.7
42 8.6	44 8.3	51 7.1		46 8.0	24 15.3	57 6.4	68 5.4	54 6.7	63 5.8
			Cost of Sales/Inventory						
			Cost of Sales/Payables						
1.8	2.2	1.9	Sales/Working Capital	1.1	1.5	2.0	1.7	2.1	7.1
4.2	4.5	5.1		2.1	2.8	4.8	4.9	7.4	52.3
45.5	19.3	144.4		-11.0	-21.3	588.9	14.8	118.7	-28.7
9.9	9.9	10.5	EBIT/Interest		16.0	5.5	10.9	10.5	18.9
(114) 3.3	(103) 3.3	(86) 3.3		(21) 2.2	(11) 2.2	(18) 5.6	(18) 2.1		(12) 3.1
1.0	-.3	.1			-1.2	-.9	3.3	.3	-6.5
			Net Profit + Depr., Dep., Amort./Cur. Mat. L/T/D						
.2	.3	.2	Fixed/Worth	.2	.1	.1	.1	.3	.3
.7	.7	.7		.9	.5	.6	.7	.7	.9
1.4	1.5	1.4		1.2	1.0	1.3	1.6	1.6	1.6
.3	.3	.3	Debt/Worth	.1	.2	.3	.5	.3	.7
.8	.7	.7		.6	.4	.5	.9	.7	1.0
1.7	1.5	2.1		2.3	.9	1.9	3.8	1.4	3.8
11.9	12.9	12.6	% Profit Before Taxes/Tangible Net Worth	8.3	13.5	8.8	31.9	9.0	15.2
(147) 3.2	(140) 4.6	(122) 5.0		3.3	2.6	1.6	(24) 9.2	3.7	2.0
-1.9	-2.9	-2.0		-3.3	-4.1	-1.2	5.5	-3.1	-7.5
5.1	6.8	7.0	% Profit Before Taxes/Total Assets	4.5	8.7	5.1	10.0	6.3	7.2
1.6	2.3	1.9		.3	1.3	1.3	4.5	1.8	.8
.9	-1.3	-1.0		-1.9	-2.7	-.8	.9	-1.1	-2.7
6.5	7.8	8.8	Sales/Net Fixed Assets	2.0	4.6	7.1	14.4	10.0	30.0
1.3	1.6	1.5		.6	1.3	1.5	1.5	1.2	6.4
.5	.6	.5		.2	.7	.5	.4	.6	1.7
1.1	1.2	1.0	Sales/Total Assets	.3	.6	.7	1.4	1.0	2.8
.5	.5	.5		.2	.4	.4	.5	.5	1.3
.2	.2	.2		.1	.2	.2	.2	.2	.9
1.4	1.5	1.4	% Depr., Dep., Amort./Sales		2.0	1.3	1.1	1.4	.6
(133) 3.6	(121) 3.4	(100) 3.3			(22) 3.5	(15) 1.8	(21) 2.5	(24) 3.8	(12) 1.5
9.3	8.5	7.8			7.2	10.4	8.2	7.8	3.1
	3.0		% Officers', Directors' Owners' Comp/Sales						
	(11) 4.7								
	10.6								
1784083M	1183880M	1229605M	Net Sales ($)	6602M	53233M	62049M	171854M	357439M	578428M
3860376M	2939447M	2731232M	Total Assets ($)	33510M	204555M	210552M	718961M	1087197M	476457M

© RMA 2019   **M = $ thousand   MM = $ million**
See Pages viii through xx for Explanation of Ratios and Data

Current Data Sorted by Assets | | | | | Comparative Historical Data

0-500M	500M-2MM	2-10MM	10-50MM	50-100MM	100-250MM	Type of Statement	ALL	ALL
	5	32	46	10	2	Unqualified	131	128
		1	1			Reviewed	2	4
		1				Compiled	2	7
4	2	1				Tax Returns	13	10
4	10	23	22	6	1	Other	72	61
	101 (4/1-9/30/18)		70 (10/1/18-3/31/19)				4/1/14-3/31/15	4/1/15-3/31/16
8	17	58	69	16	3	NUMBER OF STATEMENTS	220	210
%	%	%	%	%	%	ASSETS	%	%
	23.3	25.9	22.6	23.0		Cash & Equivalents	23.0	21.8
	25.5	18.2	15.7	8.6		Trade Receivables (net)	19.4	19.2
	.3	2.5	2.8	7.7		Inventory	2.3	2.9
	5.8	3.0	3.6	2.1		All Other Current	2.6	2.7
	54.8	49.6	44.7	41.3		Total Current	47.3	46.6
	28.4	41.5	40.3	43.0		Fixed Assets (net)	40.9	41.3
	5.6	2.7	1.7	5.6		Intangibles (net)	2.1	1.6
	11.2	6.1	13.3	10.1		All Other Non-Current	9.7	10.5
	100.0	100.0	100.0	100.0		Total	100.0	100.0
						LIABILITIES		
	6.3	1.4	2.7	1.0		Notes Payable-Short Term	3.0	2.0
	8.7	1.7	1.7	2.0		Cur. Mat.-L.T.D.	2.0	2.0
	10.6	5.2	5.3	4.9		Trade Payables	7.8	6.5
	.0	.0	.0	.0		Income Taxes Payable	.0	.0
	21.1	9.3	9.1	15.9		All Other Current	10.7	10.6
	46.7	17.6	18.8	23.8		Total Current	23.5	21.1
	8.7	15.6	15.0	12.5		Long-Term Debt	17.3	15.4
	.0	.0	.0	.0		Deferred Taxes	.0	.0
	2.5	3.7	1.6	6.4		All Other Non-Current	5.3	3.6
	42.1	63.2	64.6	57.3		Net Worth	53.8	59.8
	100.0	100.0	100.0	100.0		Total Liabilties & Net Worth	100.0	100.0
						INCOME DATA		
	100.0	100.0	100.0	100.0		Net Sales	100.0	100.0
						Gross Profit		
	98.7	97.5	98.1	97.4		Operating Expenses	97.3	96.9
	1.3	2.5	1.9	2.6		Operating Profit	2.7	3.1
	1.3	.0	.0	.4		All Other Expenses (net)	.3	.4
	.0	2.5	1.9	2.1		Profit Before Taxes	2.3	2.8
						RATIOS		
	3.4	5.4	4.6	5.4		Current	4.3	3.9
	1.7	3.5	2.8	1.5			2.4	2.4
	.9	1.7	1.7	1.2			1.4	1.5
	3.2	5.1	3.9	4.9		Quick	3.9	3.6
	1.5	3.1	2.2	1.2			2.1	2.0
	.3	1.5	1.4	.8			1.2	1.2
	10　37.3	17　22.0	12　29.3	8　46.1		Sales/Receivables	15　24.4	15　24.6
	32　11.3	33　11.1	31　11.8	20　18.6			33　11.0	35　10.5
	46　8.0	45　8.1	46　8.0	27　13.7			45　8.1	50　7.3
						Cost of Sales/Inventory		
						Cost of Sales/Payables		
	7.5	3.9	3.6	3.0		Sales/Working Capital	4.2	4.2
	17.1	7.3	6.3	13.3			8.1	8.1
	NM	13.0	14.3	37.1			26.2	18.0
	17.6	32.7	18.4	9.8		EBIT/Interest	12.3	15.1
	(10)　5.5	(42)　3.2	(64)　5.2	5.0			(168)　3.3	(158)　2.8
	-2.9	1.3	1.3	1.9			.2	.3
						Net Profit + Depr., Dep., Amort./Cur. Mat. L/T/D		
	.1	.3	.4	.7		Fixed/Worth	.3	.3
	.5	.6	.7	1.0			.8	.7
	1.8	1.2	1.0	1.3			1.2	1.2
	.5	.2	.2	.3		Debt/Worth	.3	.3
	1.0	.5	.5	1.0			.7	.6
	3.6	1.0	.9	1.7			1.5	1.1
	50.0	13.3	10.7	6.9		% Profit Before Taxes/Tangible Net Worth	13.3	12.4
	(15)　16.2	(56)　4.3	(68)　4.9	(14)　2.5			(207)　3.9	(205)　4.2
	-6.0	-.2	.6	-.9			-2.2	-1.6
	12.2	6.8	7.4	4.0		% Profit Before Taxes/Total Assets	7.3	6.8
	6.5	2.5	3.1	2.8			2.2	2.3
	-5.9	-.4	.3	.5			-1.4	-.9
	551.4	17.8	7.3	5.0		Sales/Net Fixed Assets	19.4	13.0
	27.3	4.1	3.5	3.3			4.1	4.0
	3.1	1.6	1.8	1.9			2.0	1.9
	5.8	2.9	2.1	2.6		Sales/Total Assets	2.9	2.5
	2.2	1.8	1.3	1.5			1.7	1.5
	1.6	.8	.8	.8			1.1	1.0
	.7	1.2	1.6	1.8		% Depr., Dep., Amort./Sales	1.3	1.2
	(13)　1.1	(52)　2.1	(68)　2.5	(15)　3.0			(192)　2.6	(190)　2.4
	1.9	4.1	4.2	4.6			3.9	3.8
						% Officers', Directors' Owners' Comp/Sales	2.5	3.5
							(24)　6.1	(25)　7.5
							17.2	14.2
20561M	77203M	656453M	2562733M	1765878M	819264M	Net Sales ($)	6341712M	6488866M
2612M	19587M	305859M	1477684M	1097020M	503066M	Total Assets ($)	3806409M	4061031M

M = $ thousand　　MM = $ million
See Pages viii through xx for Explanation of Ratios and Data

Comparative Historical Data | | | | Current Data Sorted by Sales

Hist 1	Hist 2	Hist 3	Type of Statement	0-1MM	1-3MM	3-5MM	5-10MM	10-25MM	25MM & OVER
125	111	95	Unqualified		8	6	18	29	34
2	3	2	Reviewed					1	1
3	2	1	Compiled						1
9	9	7	Tax Returns	2	2	2		1	
51	60	66	Other	2	11	4	12	15	22
4/1/16-3/31/17 ALL	4/1/17-3/31/18 ALL	4/1/18-3/31/19 ALL			101 (4/1-9/30/18)		70 (10/1/18-3/31/19)		
190	185	171	**NUMBER OF STATEMENTS**	4	21	12	30	46	58
%	%	%	**ASSETS**	%	%	%	%	%	%
23.0	22.6	25.0	Cash & Equivalents		21.4	28.1	25.8	27.8	21.8
19.7	19.4	17.1	Trade Receivables (net)		13.1	15.0	17.8	16.1	19.7
2.5	2.2	2.8	Inventory		.1	1.3	1.7	3.1	4.6
3.0	2.7	3.8	All Other Current		4.4	2.7	4.4	3.2	2.7
48.3	46.9	48.6	Total Current		39.0	47.1	49.7	50.3	48.7
39.4	40.3	38.4	Fixed Assets (net)		50.7	38.8	38.8	35.7	36.8
2.7	2.3	2.7	Intangibles (net)		5.7	.3	1.5	3.0	2.8
9.7	10.5	10.2	All Other Non-Current		4.6	13.8	10.0	11.0	11.7
100.0	100.0	100.0	Total		100.0	100.0	100.0	100.0	100.0
			LIABILITIES						
2.7	3.3	2.8	Notes Payable-Short Term		1.5	.5	1.0	3.1	4.3
1.7	1.6	2.4	Cur. Mat.-L.T.D.		1.5	4.3	2.8	1.4	1.7
6.4	6.8	5.8	Trade Payables		2.4	7.2	5.0	5.6	7.3
.0	.0	.0	Income Taxes Payable		.0	.0	.0	.0	.0
14.1	9.8	11.1	All Other Current		8.9	5.2	9.3	10.2	13.8
25.0	21.5	22.1	Total Current		14.3	17.3	18.1	20.3	27.1
17.0	20.0	15.3	Long-Term Debt		17.5	13.0	17.0	12.9	13.3
.0	.0	.0	Deferred Taxes		.0	.0	.0	.0	.0
3.9	2.9	4.4	All Other Non-Current		11.6	2.7	.6	4.9	3.9
54.2	55.7	58.3	Net Worth		56.6	67.1	64.3	61.8	55.7
100.0	100.0	100.0	Total Liabilities & Net Worth		100.0	100.0	100.0	100.0	100.0
			INCOME DATA						
100.0	100.0	100.0	Net Sales		100.0	100.0	100.0	100.0	100.0
			Gross Profit						
97.0	97.1	97.4	Operating Expenses		98.8	96.9	96.7	97.2	98.0
3.0	2.9	2.6	Operating Profit		1.2	3.1	3.3	2.8	2.0
.4	-.4	.2	All Other Expenses (net)		2.5	-.8	.6	-.6	-.1
2.6	3.2	2.4	Profit Before Taxes		-1.3	3.9	2.7	3.3	2.1
			RATIOS						
4.3	4.4	5.0	Current		10.1	6.4	5.0	5.3	3.5
2.5	2.5	2.8			5.0	3.3	3.3	3.1	1.9
1.4	1.6	1.5			2.1	1.6	1.6	1.9	1.2
3.9	3.9	4.5	Quick		9.3	6.1	4.4	4.8	3.5
2.1	2.2	2.2			4.3	2.5	3.1	2.8	1.6
1.2	1.3	1.3			1.7	1.4	1.4	1.5	1.0
10 36.4	13 27.9	10 35.7	Sales/Receivables	0 UND	15 24.6	15 24.2	9 39.0	14 25.9	
32 11.4	32 11.3	29 12.5		31 11.8	28 13.2	34 10.6	28 13.2	24 15.0	
49 7.4	48 7.6	43 8.4		55 6.6	40 9.2	47 7.8	43 8.4	41 8.8	
			Cost of Sales/Inventory						
			Cost of Sales/Payables						
3.9	4.4	4.0	Sales/Working Capital		3.0	2.6	4.2	3.6	5.8
7.8	8.5	8.2			8.3	6.7	8.2	5.6	9.5
17.8	18.8	18.2			15.4	20.2	17.3	14.3	26.3
11.0	14.0	18.4	EBIT/Interest		9.0		26.2	30.8	11.6
(149) 3.5	(142) 3.9	(140) 4.4			(16) .9		(22) 2.6	(37) 7.7	(55) 5.3
-.9	.5	1.3			-4.0		1.2	2.0	1.9
			Net Profit + Depr., Dep., Amort./Cur. Mat. L/T/D						
.3	.3	.3	Fixed/Worth		.4	.2	.2	.2	.4
.7	.8	.7			1.1	.5	.6	.5	.7
1.2	1.2	1.1			1.3	1.1	1.0	1.0	1.1
.3	.3	.2	Debt/Worth		.1	.1	.3	.2	.4
.6	.6	.5			.4	.5	.5	.4	.8
1.1	1.2	1.2			.8	1.0	1.0	.9	1.9
10.0	16.4	13.3	% Profit Before Taxes/Tangible Net Worth		7.1	14.4	19.4	13.8	13.3
(178) 4.6	(174) 5.1	(162) 4.7			(19) .6	5.7	3.9	(43) 5.3	(55) 5.4
-1.5	-.1	.4			-14.5	1.6	.4	.1	1.1
5.9	9.7	7.6	% Profit Before Taxes/Total Assets		7.4	6.7	10.7	6.8	7.8
2.4	3.2	3.1			.3	2.7	2.4	4.3	3.3
-1.1	-.1	.3			-8.8	1.0	.3	-.1	.9
17.7	16.6	14.4	Sales/Net Fixed Assets		25.9	26.3	14.8	17.2	13.2
4.1	4.2	4.0			1.4	3.2	3.3	4.1	5.0
2.0	2.0	2.1			.8	1.7	1.6	2.4	2.5
2.8	2.7	2.7	Sales/Total Assets		2.2	4.5	3.1	2.7	2.8
1.7	1.7	1.8			.8	1.3	1.7	1.8	2.0
1.0	1.0	.9			.5	.9	.8	1.0	1.3
1.1	1.3	1.4	% Depr., Dep., Amort./Sales		1.7		1.7	1.5	1.0
(174) 2.4	(162) 2.4	(152) 2.3			(18) 3.8		(27) 2.5	(41) 2.4	(55) 2.0
3.7	3.9	4.0			6.7		4.2	3.9	3.0
2.5	1.8	3.8	% Officers', Directors' Owners' Comp/Sales						
(17) 7.4	(19) 7.0	(15) 5.4							
16.8	13.3	14.5							
6298007M	6263608M	5902092M	Net Sales ($)	2720M	42362M	46764M	225679M	819241M	4765326M
3650583M	3657007M	3405828M	Total Assets ($)	1549M	75423M	38260M	197950M	564736M	2527910M

M = $ thousand   MM = $ million
See Pages viii through xx for Explanation of Ratios and Data

Current Data Sorted by Assets | Comparative Historical Data

Type of Statement	0-500M	500M-2MM	2-10MM	10-50MM	50-100MM	100-250MM	4/1/14-3/31/15 ALL	4/1/15-3/31/16 ALL
Unqualified	3	12	21	17	2	3	84	81
Reviewed	11	2	6	4			13	16
Compiled	130	12	6	4			70	60
Tax Returns	87	58	34		1	2	319	282
Other		63	40	10		1	239	269
	92 (4/1-9/30/18)			437 (10/1/18-3/31/19)				
NUMBER OF STATEMENTS	231	147	107	35	3	6	725	708

	%	%	%	%	%	%	%	%
ASSETS								
Cash & Equivalents	42.3	24.8	13.4	22.4			26.5	25.0
Trade Receivables (net)	2.0	5.4	7.6	8.9			4.4	4.7
Inventory	.6	.1	.1	.9			.1	.2
All Other Current	3.3	2.7	1.8	2.3			2.8	2.4
Total Current	48.1	33.0	22.9	34.5			33.7	32.4
Fixed Assets (net)	32.8	46.2	67.2	55.5			48.6	48.1
Intangibles (net)	8.9	9.8	5.2	2.6			7.7	9.7
All Other Non-Current	10.2	11.1	4.8	7.4			10.0	9.9
Total	100.0	100.0	100.0	100.0			100.0	100.0
LIABILITIES								
Notes Payable-Short Term	7.5	4.3	1.6	2.9			6.8	6.0
Cur. Mat.-L.T.D.	4.3	2.4	2.2	2.6			3.1	3.3
Trade Payables	2.7	2.5	4.2	7.4			3.6	4.1
Income Taxes Payable	.0	.0	.0	.0			.1	.0
All Other Current	23.6	11.7	7.7	8.2			16.9	16.0
Total Current	38.0	20.9	15.7	21.0			30.5	29.5
Long-Term Debt	29.1	37.2	51.3	29.3			36.5	37.7
Deferred Taxes	.0	.0	.0	.3			.1	.1
All Other Non-Current	14.8	4.4	2.8	4.6			9.4	10.5
Net Worth	18.1	37.5	30.2	44.9			23.5	22.3
Total Liabilties & Net Worth	100.0	100.0	100.0	100.0			100.0	100.0
INCOME DATA								
Net Sales	100.0	100.0	100.0	100.0			100.0	100.0
Gross Profit								
Operating Expenses	92.0	84.5	79.6	89.9			86.4	86.2
Operating Profit	8.0	15.5	20.4	10.1			13.6	13.8
All Other Expenses (net)	.4	4.6	9.1	.8			4.3	4.3
Profit Before Taxes	7.6	10.9	11.3	9.4			9.3	9.5

RATIOS

	0-500M	500M-2MM	2-10MM	10-50MM	50-100MM	100-250MM	4/1/14-3/31/15 ALL	4/1/15-3/31/16 ALL
Current	7.0	4.5	3.5	3.4			4.2	3.8
	2.1	1.6	1.3	1.9			1.4	1.3
	.7	.4	.3	1.0			.4	.4
Quick	6.4	4.0	3.0	3.3			3.7	3.5
	1.8	1.4	1.3	1.8			1.3	1.1
	.5	.3	.3	1.0			.3	.3
Sales/Receivables	0 UND	0 UND	0 UND	4 83.0			0 UND	0 UND
	0 UND	0 UND	0 UND	14 26.2			0 UND	0 UND
	0 UND	3 124.8	20 17.9	32 11.5			3 113.2	2 167.3
Cost of Sales/Inventory								
Cost of Sales/Payables								
Sales/Working Capital	11.7	6.2	6.1	2.9			12.5	13.7
	39.9	53.5	50.5	12.2			71.0	87.9
	-72.0	-25.7	-16.2	211.7			-20.6	-19.5
EBIT/Interest	56.5	25.9	6.5	15.4			16.9	14.3
	(124) 13.3	(85) 7.1	(73) 2.5	(28) 5.3			(449) 4.4	(418) 3.9
	3.1	1.6	1.1	2.1			1.7	1.3
Net Profit + Depr., Dep., Amort./Cur. Mat. L/T/D							3.8	3.5
							(19) 2.5	(15) 2.3
							1.1	1.1
Fixed/Worth	.2	.3	1.2	.6			.4	.4
	.8	1.2	4.0	1.1			1.7	2.2
	-2.0	14.7	13.6	3.4			UND	-33.6
Debt/Worth	.2	.3	.9	.5			.6	.5
	1.1	2.2	4.5	1.2			2.4	3.3
	-4.8	19.5	15.7	4.0			-46.3	-17.5
% Profit Before Taxes/Tangible Net Worth	191.1	91.8	57.4	53.1			141.0	118.2
	(158) 80.0	(117) 37.3	(89) 20.4	(32) 6.9			(534) 47.8	(500) 40.3
	28.6	13.5	2.2	4.6			10.5	8.2
% Profit Before Taxes/Total Assets	91.1	29.5	9.0	10.9			46.7	37.8
	37.1	10.0	4.3	4.4			12.2	9.3
	8.1	2.7	.2	2.0			2.3	1.7
Sales/Net Fixed Assets	103.7	28.0	3.3	6.1			48.6	45.1
	29.5	6.9	.9	2.1			11.2	11.1
	12.1	1.1	.5	1.2			1.3	1.2
Sales/Total Assets	9.9	3.7	1.5	1.8			7.6	6.3
	6.1	1.6	.7	1.2			3.1	2.9
	4.2	.9	.4	.8			.9	.9
% Depr., Dep., Amort./Sales	.6	1.1	2.4	1.3			.9	.9
	(129) 1.1	(95) 2.8	(85) 4.8	(34) 2.9			(495) 2.4	(504) 2.4
	2.8	6.3	10.1	4.8			4.5	5.2
% Officers', Directors' Owners' Comp/Sales	3.0	3.6	2.1				3.1	3.0
	(117) 5.7	(52) 5.4	(30) 3.5				(255) 5.2	(260) 5.3
	8.2	9.6	6.0				8.7	9.8
Net Sales ($)	312517M	381824M	796651M	1451306M	1898291M	4365042M	10650520M	5950804M
Total Assets ($)	50869M	158570M	444951M	849668M	192586M	944751M	3178088M	2512408M

Comparative Historical Data | Current Data Sorted by Sales

4/1/16-3/31/17 ALL	4/1/17-3/31/18 ALL	4/1/18-3/31/19 ALL		0-1MM	1-3MM	3-5MM	5-10MM	10-25MM	25MM & OVER
			Type of Statement		92 (4/1-9/30/18)		437 (10/1/18-3/31/19)		
70	59	58	Unqualified	3	12	8	10	11	14
17	11	12	Reviewed		1	2	1	5	3
41	39	33	Compiled	7	15	6	1	3	1
237	226	225	Tax Returns	83	119	12	6	2	3
228	229	201	Other	65	98	11	6	8	13
593	564	529	**NUMBER OF STATEMENTS**	158	245	39	24	29	34
%	%	%	**ASSETS**	%	%	%	%	%	%
28.2	27.9	30.0	Cash & Equivalents	25.6	33.9	34.6	29.0	22.3	24.2
3.9	4.8	4.5	Trade Receivables (net)	1.7	1.9	11.5	11.3	13.3	16.3
.1	.4	.4	Inventory	.1	.5	.1	.0	.3	1.0
4.4	2.9	2.7	All Other Current	1.6	3.7	1.2	4.7	1.8	2.1
36.6	36.1	37.6	Total Current	29.0	40.0	47.3	45.2	37.7	43.6
44.5	46.4	45.1	Fixed Assets (net)	53.6	39.7	41.0	45.6	53.6	41.1
9.3	9.3	8.1	Intangibles (net)	9.0	10.0	2.9	.2	2.3	7.5
9.5	8.3	9.2	All Other Non-Current	8.4	10.2	8.8	9.0	6.4	7.8
100.0	100.0	100.0	Total	100.0	100.0	100.0	100.0	100.0	100.0
			LIABILITIES						
7.7	7.7	5.1	Notes Payable-Short Term	6.6	4.2	6.9	1.4	5.8	4.1
3.7	3.4	3.2	Cur. Mat. L.T.D.	4.0	3.0	1.9	1.0	5.1	2.7
4.2	4.7	3.2	Trade Payables	1.8	1.9	2.8	5.7	9.3	12.8
.2	.0	.0	Income Taxes Payable	.0	.0	.0	.0	.1	.0
19.0	16.7	15.8	All Other Current	13.4	19.2	14.8	11.2	10.9	11.1
34.8	32.4	27.3	Total Current	25.8	28.3	26.4	19.3	31.2	30.7
34.4	37.6	35.7	Long-Term Debt	42.5	36.1	20.3	19.4	50.4	18.7
.1	.1	.0	Deferred Taxes	.0	.0	.0	.0	.0	.4
9.1	8.7	8.6	All Other Non-Current	12.0	9.2	1.8	3.6	2.4	5.2
21.6	21.2	28.3	Net Worth	19.7	26.4	51.6	57.7	16.0	45.0
100.0	100.0	100.0	Total Liabilties & Net Worth	100.0	100.0	100.0	100.0	100.0	100.0
			INCOME DATA						
100.0	100.0	100.0	Net Sales	100.0	100.0	100.0	100.0	100.0	100.0
			Gross Profit						
86.9	87.4	87.3	Operating Expenses	80.1	89.7	87.0	93.5	93.4	94.7
13.1	12.6	12.7	Operating Profit	19.9	10.3	13.0	6.5	6.6	5.3
3.8	3.8	3.4	All Other Expenses (net)	8.4	1.5	1.2	.2	.7	.2
9.3	8.7	9.3	Profit Before Taxes	11.5	8.8	11.9	6.3	5.9	5.1
			RATIOS						
3.7	3.7	5.0		4.2	6.7	6.0	6.3	2.8	2.5
1.2	1.4	1.7	Current	1.1	2.0	2.1	2.4	1.1	1.4
.5	.5	.5		.2	.7	.9	1.1	.7	1.0
3.1	3.3	4.7		3.7	6.0	5.9	6.3	2.5	2.4
1.0	1.3	1.6	Quick	1.0	1.7	1.7	2.3	1.1	1.4
.4	.4	.5		.2	.5	.8	1.1	.6	1.0
0 UND	0 UND	0 UND		0 UND	0 UND	0 UND	0 UND	0 UND	4 90.8
0 UND	0 UND	0 UND	Sales/Receivables	0 UND	0 UND	1 351.2	13 27.7	8 44.6	8 45.1
2 193.2	4 99.2	3 120.6		0 UND	0 UND	26 13.9	36 10.2	31 11.8	29 12.4
			Cost of Sales/Inventory						
			Cost of Sales/Payables						
11.6	12.1	8.6		9.1	8.8	8.6	3.6	9.1	11.1
98.7	62.0	41.7	Sales/Working Capital	154.9	33.4	18.9	9.8	78.0	49.4
-21.1	-26.7	-36.9		-6.9	-70.8	-182.5	116.1	-37.6	NM
19.1	16.9	24.4		6.4	37.2	35.0	13.0	8.6	23.5
(366) 4.7	(351) 4.3	(318) 5.8	EBIT/Interest	(65) 3.0	(166) 10.1	(27) 13.9	(14) 2.9	(20) 4.4	(26) 8.5
1.2	1.7	1.6		.4	1.9	5.6	-1.3	2.3	2.5
9.6	15.5	17.6	Net Profit + Depr., Dep.,						
(21) 3.0	(16) 5.4	(20) 6.4	Amort./Cur. Mat. L/T/D						
1.0	1.8	1.1							
.4	.4	.3		.5	.2	.1	.2	.5	.5
1.6	2.1	1.3	Fixed/Worth	4.4	1.2	.8	.8	2.2	1.1
-17.7	-14.8	31.2		-8.6	-18.9	1.6	1.2	8.9	3.9
.6	.6	.4		.6	.3	.4	.2	.5	.5
3.0	2.8	2.1	Debt/Worth	5.1	1.9	1.0	.6	3.1	.9
-12.9	-13.5	608.5		-9.8	-16.1	2.0	2.3	9.9	10.4
139.8	137.3	115.0	% Profit Before Taxes/Tangible	111.0	126.3	194.4	41.8	103.4	66.1
(419) 46.1	(396) 48.9	(402) 42.9	Net Worth	(111) 39.0	(176) 63.9	(38) 41.4	(24) 2.6	10.3	(29) 13.9
9.0	11.6	10.3		8.7	25.2	15.5	-3.7	1.8	5.7
41.8	45.6	45.7	% Profit Before Taxes/Total	27.9	64.3	76.5	17.9	16.7	24.9
10.7	12.0	11.3	Assets	6.2	23.5	18.3	1.8	5.9	6.6
1.0	2.2	2.3		.1	5.1	8.1	-2.5	1.6	1.9
46.5	48.0	42.9		29.0	65.4	60.7	23.3	16.7	28.0
11.4	11.1	11.9	Sales/Net Fixed Assets	5.4	19.2	12.1	8.6	3.4	7.9
1.6	1.5	1.5		.5	3.4	2.0	1.0	2.0	2.7
6.2	7.1	6.4		4.6	7.5	7.2	4.2	6.2	6.7
3.2	3.1	3.0	Sales/Total Assets	1.8	4.3	3.2	2.0	2.2	3.1
1.0	1.0	1.0		.4	1.3	1.4	.9	1.1	1.3
.8	.8	1.0		1.6	.8	1.1	.5	1.4	.6
(403) 2.3	(379) 2.2	(348) 2.6	% Depr., Dep., Amort./Sales	(93) 4.4	(159) 1.8	(24) 2.2	(20) 1.7	(24) 2.7	(28) 2.6
4.2	4.2	5.1		15.2	4.3	5.5	3.2	4.1	4.0
3.1	3.0	2.9	% Officers', Directors'	5.0	2.6	2.4			
(203) 5.4	(204) 5.3	(208) 5.2	Owners' Comp/Sales	(57) 8.0	(116) 4.4	(14) 4.6			
8.3	9.1	8.3		11.4	6.9	5.6			
4721961M	7100620M	9205631M	Net Sales ($)	87439M	452066M	147547M	175467M	443745M	7899367M
2859249M	2797997M	2641395M	Total Assets ($)	137403M	256166M	104513M	167534M	262508M	1713271M

M = $ thousand   MM = $ million
See Pages viii through xx for Explanation of Ratios and Data

ARTS, ENTERTAINMENT, AND RECREATION

Current Data Sorted by Assets							Comparative Historical Data	
						Type of Statement		
2	6	10	19	6	4	Unqualified	56	55
1				1		Reviewed	3	7
		1				Compiled	5	3
5	3	1				Tax Returns	16	12
5	3	12	8	4	2	Other	42	52
	59 (4/1-9/30/18)		34 (10/1/18-3/31/19)				4/1/14-3/31/15	4/1/15-3/31/16
0-500M	500M-2MM	2-10MM	10-50MM	50-100MM	100-250MM		ALL	ALL
13	13	23	27	11	6	**NUMBER OF STATEMENTS**	122	129
%	%	%	%	%	%	**ASSETS**	%	%
39.2	29.4	15.1	18.5	30.3		Cash & Equivalents	21.9	22.0
15.5	9.7	6.6	4.7	3.5		Trade Receivables (net)	5.6	5.2
1.6	.5	.2	.3	.2		Inventory	.9	1.6
5.2	3.7	4.5	5.4	4.0		All Other Current	3.7	3.2
61.6	43.3	26.4	28.9	38.1		Total Current	32.2	32.0
13.9	40.7	56.1	48.4	40.2		Fixed Assets (net)	47.1	41.3
10.8	4.0	3.5	4.7	.6		Intangibles (net)	2.7	2.8
13.9	12.0	14.0	18.0	21.2		All Other Non-Current	18.1	23.8
100.0	100.0	100.0	100.0	100.0		Total	100.0	100.0
						LIABILITIES		
8.8	1.9	5.7	1.1	.0		Notes Payable-Short Term	3.4	3.9
6.6	14.9	1.3	1.2	2.8		Cur. Mat.-L.T.D.	2.5	1.8
13.7	14.0	3.6	2.5	2.6		Trade Payables	4.7	4.6
.0	.8	.8	.0	.0		Income Taxes Payable	.3	1.1
31.4	19.3	18.7	10.2	7.6		All Other Current	9.7	12.1
60.5	50.8	30.2	14.9	13.0		Total Current	20.6	23.5
18.7	19.2	18.0	16.3	14.2		Long-Term Debt	15.2	13.4
.0	.0	.0	.0	.0		Deferred Taxes	.1	.1
11.8	10.4	5.2	2.6	2.8		All Other Non-Current	7.0	9.1
9.0	19.6	46.6	66.2	70.0		Net Worth	57.1	53.9
100.0	100.0	100.0	100.0	100.0		Total Liabilities & Net Worth	100.0	100.0
						INCOME DATA		
100.0	100.0	100.0	100.0	100.0		Net Sales	100.0	100.0
						Gross Profit		
103.9	100.9	93.7	97.7	90.0		Operating Expenses	95.2	93.7
-3.9	-.9	6.3	2.3	10.0		Operating Profit	4.8	6.3
-1.1	1.1	2.8	1.2	-1.5		All Other Expenses (net)	.3	1.4
-2.8	-2.0	3.5	1.1	11.5		Profit Before Taxes	4.5	4.9
						RATIOS		
7.6	5.1	8.4	6.2	8.8			3.7	3.9
1.9	1.2	.9	1.5	3.6		Current	1.6	1.3
.5	.5	.5	.7	1.3			.7	.7
5.7	5.0	4.1	5.9	6.1			2.9	3.5
1.9	1.2	.7	1.4	3.5		Quick	1.1	1.0
.5	.4	.6	.6	1.2			.5	.5
0 UND	0 UND	0 UND	4 92.5	2 175.0			0 UND	0 UND
3 126.9	4 94.8	7 52.6	18 20.6	9 40.0		Sales/Receivables	8 45.8	5 67.5
17 21.9	15 23.8	32 11.4	46 7.9	60 6.1			22 16.8	28 13.0
						Cost of Sales/Inventory		
						Cost of Sales/Payables		
7.8	3.9	3.9	1.5	.6			4.3	4.4
42.2	19.0	-49.3	8.9	.7		Sales/Working Capital	20.1	21.5
-14.4	-13.3	-5.7	-12.9	8.8			-26.7	-14.4
		2.7	6.9				9.0	7.5
	(18) -.3		(17) 1.8			EBIT/Interest	(74) 1.7	(74) 1.7
		-3.7	-6.0				-3.2	-3.1
						Net Profit + Depr., Dep., Amort./Cur. Mat. L/T/D		
.0	.6	.6	.3	.4			.2	.1
.3	2.1	1.3	1.0	.5		Fixed/Worth	.8	.7
-.4	NM	3.1	1.5	.8			1.4	1.3
.5	.3	.5	.2	.3			.2	.2
-43.0	3.1	.9	.5	.4		Debt/Worth	.4	.5
-3.0	NM	2.3	.9	.5			2.0	1.7
	53.9	11.8	6.6	13.8			22.3	22.9
(10) 2.2	(22) -.2	1.2	6.0			% Profit Before Taxes/Tangible Net Worth	(113) 3.0	(118) 3.5
-11.0	-20.4	-4.4	-1.6				-4.2	-2.4
71.9	26.1	9.3	3.1	10.0			11.6	10.0
24.5	.6	.0	.8	4.0		% Profit Before Taxes/Total Assets	2.4	2.0
-30.8	-27.4	-4.4	-2.7	-1.3			-2.5	-2.2
UND	55.0	5.5	2.7	1.6			10.7	15.6
85.5	6.3	1.8	1.5	.9		Sales/Net Fixed Assets	2.2	2.9
22.7	2.2	.7	.6	.5			.7	.8
10.9	3.3	1.9	.8	.5			2.3	2.0
6.2	2.0	1.0	.5	.3		Sales/Total Assets	.7	.7
3.8	1.3	.3	.3	.2			.5	.4
		1.6	2.5	1.0			2.0	1.2
	(20) 3.2	(25) 5.2	5.8			% Depr., Dep., Amort./Sales	(97) 4.2	(101) 3.4
		9.0	8.2	9.3			8.5	7.0
							3.6	2.0
						% Officers', Directors' Owners' Comp/Sales	(22) 7.7	(19) 7.9
							10.8	11.0
17277M	32319M	107157M	398461M	345325M	507529M	Net Sales ($)	3664785M	2172589M
2304M	13481M	102076M	700155M	862855M	909175M	Total Assets ($)	2750140M	3259557M

Comparative Historical Data | Current Data Sorted by Sales

4/1/16-3/31/17 ALL	4/1/17-3/31/18 ALL	4/1/18-3/31/19 ALL	Type of Statement	0-1MM	1-3MM	3-5MM	5-10MM	10-25MM	25MM & OVER
60	50	47	Unqualified	1	9	8	8	12	9
1	1	2	Reviewed	1					1
6	4	1	Compiled		1				
9	11	9	Tax Returns	3	2	2	2		
34	48	34	Other	7	6	4	4	8	5
					59 (4/1-9/30/18)			34 (10/1/18-3/31/19)	
110	114	93	NUMBER OF STATEMENTS	12	18	14	14	20	15
%	%	%	**ASSETS**	%	%	%	%	%	%
19.3	20.0	22.9	Cash & Equivalents	20.4	30.7	19.4	22.4	22.4	19.8
5.4	6.9	7.1	Trade Receivables (net)	12.3	7.8	7.5	6.3	5.8	4.3
.6	.5	.5	Inventory	1.3	.3	.4	.4	.3	.8
3.7	4.5	4.5	All Other Current	1.1	9.3	3.0	4.0	5.0	2.8
28.9	31.9	35.0	Total Current	35.1	48.1	30.3	33.1	33.4	27.7
43.5	46.6	43.6	Fixed Assets (net)	51.6	38.1	51.9	45.4	36.4	43.9
4.4	2.8	4.5	Intangibles (net)	11.5	.1	3.7	2.3	8.1	2.2
23.2	18.8	16.9	All Other Non-Current	2.0	13.7	14.1	19.1	22.1	26.1
100.0	100.0	100.0	Total	100.0	100.0	100.0	100.0	100.0	100.0
			LIABILITIES						
2.4	2.0	3.2	Notes Payable-Short Term	5.1	5.4	5.9	.6	2.4	.3
2.6	2.0	4.0	Cur. Mat.-L.T.D.	8.0	.9	14.4	2.2	.6	1.3
3.3	3.7	6.0	Trade Payables	8.1	6.3	12.6	2.9	3.6	4.0
.1	.2	.3	Income Taxes Payable	.0	.0	.0	2.0	.0	.0
14.2	15.7	16.0	All Other Current	29.9	7.8	12.4	13.6	23.2	10.9
22.5	23.5	29.6	Total Current	51.0	20.3	45.4	21.3	29.7	16.6
14.1	12.5	18.4	Long-Term Debt	37.9	12.9	13.1	24.6	12.2	16.6
.0	.0	.0	Deferred Taxes	.0	.0	.0	.0	.0	.0
7.9	4.8	6.2	All Other Non-Current	1.2	11.2	11.0	2.5	3.7	6.6
55.5	59.2	45.8	Net Worth	9.8	55.5	30.6	51.5	54.3	60.2
100.0	100.0	100.0	Total Liabilities & Net Worth	100.0	100.0	100.0	100.0	100.0	100.0
			INCOME DATA						
100.0	100.0	100.0	Net Sales	100.0	100.0	100.0	100.0	100.0	100.0
			Gross Profit						
94.2	93.7	97.3	Operating Expenses	101.0	96.7	97.3	98.0	96.5	95.3
5.8	6.3	2.7	Operating Profit	-1.0	3.3	2.7	2.0	3.5	4.7
1.2	.4	1.0	All Other Expenses (net)	5.9	-1.6	1.6	4.2	-1.1	-.8
4.7	5.9	1.8	Profit Before Taxes	-6.9	4.9	1.1	-2.2	4.6	5.4
			RATIOS						
4.5	4.7	6.3		10.3	8.8	5.0	3.0	6.3	4.1
1.7	1.6	1.5	Current	2.1	3.1	.7	1.9	1.4	1.5
.8	.8	.6		.3	1.0	.4	.9	.7	.5
3.8	3.3	5.6		9.1	7.0	4.9	2.4	6.1	3.6
1.3	1.3	1.4	Quick	2.1	2.1	.7	1.6	1.3	1.4
.6	.5	.5		.3	.2	.3	.7	.5	.5
1 297.2	1 382.1	0 UND		0 UND	0 UND	0 UND	4 88.9	1 385.5	5 74.9
7 51.0	4 90.3	9 40.8	Sales/Receivables	0 UND	5 79.9	5 76.4	19 19.4	12 30.7	11 32.0
35 10.3	33 11.1	33 10.9		30 12.0	13 28.6	26 13.9	34 10.7	49 7.5	46 7.9
			Cost of Sales/Inventory						
			Cost of Sales/Payables						
4.4	4.0	2.1		4.6	1.9	53.3	1.9	.8	1.6
14.0	17.8	14.4	Sales/Working Capital	NM	8.8	-12.9	6.2	8.4	9.7
-21.4	-21.8	-11.6		-3.5	NM	-5.6	-39.6	-14.9	-9.3
14.2	13.5	7.4				7.8		14.9	14.3
(67) 3.8	(66) 2.3	(62) 1.3	EBIT/Interest			(10) 1.0		(14) 6.2	(11) -2.3
.1	-4.5	-3.2				-3.7		1.7	-8.3
			Net Profit + Depr., Dep., Amort./Cur. Mat. L/T/D						
.3	.3	.3		1.2	.1	.7	.3	.2	.4
.7	.8	.9	Fixed/Worth	8.0	.5	1.5	1.0	.9	.5
1.6	1.4	2.3		-6.0	1.3	NM	2.1	2.0	1.0
.2	.2	.3		1.5	.3	.4	.3	.2	.3
.5	.5	.6	Debt/Worth	NM	.5	1.1	1.0	.6	.4
2.1	1.6	3.0		-4.7	1.1	NM	2.5	1.6	.6
23.2	18.1	11.5			8.3	82.0	18.4	11.4	13.9
(101) 3.4	(102) 3.5	(80) 1.6	% Profit Before Taxes/Tangible Net Worth		(17) -.4	(11) 2.3	-1.4	(19) 3.5	(13) 3.3
-1.3	-2.0	-5.5			-22.4	-3.2	-7.8	-1.9	-1.3
9.6	11.2	9.6		19.0	13.3	23.3	6.7	5.9	10.0
2.2	2.6	.8	% Profit Before Taxes/Total Assets	-.8	.0	1.1	.7	1.9	2.1
-.5	-1.9	-4.0		-37.3	-13.5	-3.6	-3.6	-.8	-4.8
8.4	10.8	12.5		71.0	58.4	12.8	21.2	7.9	2.4
1.9	1.7	1.8	Sales/Net Fixed Assets	9.8	2.6	3.9	.8	2.1	1.2
.7	.7	.7		.2	1.3	1.4	.5	.6	1.0
1.7	1.6	2.0		6.4	3.0	3.3	2.0	.9	1.0
.7	.8	.8	Sales/Total Assets	1.3	1.3	1.7	.5	.6	.5
.4	.4	.3		.2	.7	.7	.2	.3	.3
2.0	1.3	1.6			1.1		2.2	1.2	2.4
(92) 4.4	(93) 3.4	(75) 3.6	% Depr., Dep., Amort./Sales		(13) 2.9	(12) 6.4	(19) 2.5		(14) 5.9
8.3	7.5	8.0			5.9	11.7	5.2		8.3
	1.4	2.9							
	(11) 8.9	(10) 8.4	% Officers', Directors' Owners' Comp/Sales						
	14.1	19.2							
1886923M	1543875M	1408068M	Net Sales ($)	6144M	31745M	55645M	91502M	309128M	913904M
3123076M	2346468M	2590046M	Total Assets ($)	21691M	47560M	61850M	285243M	670614M	1503088M

M = $ thousand   MM = $ million
See Pages viii through xx for Explanation of Ratios and Data

Current Data Sorted by Assets   Comparative Historical Data

0-500M	500M-2MM	2-10MM	10-50MM	50-100MM	100-250MM	Type of Statement	4/1/14-3/31/15 ALL	4/1/15-3/31/16 ALL
2	1	6	1	2		Unqualified	18	17
	1					Reviewed	1	2
						Compiled		1
3						Tax Returns	3	2
3	6	6	2		1	Other	18	20
	21 (4/1-9/30/18)		13 (10/1/18-3/31/19)					
8	8	12	3	2	1	NUMBER OF STATEMENTS	40	42
%	%	%	%	%	%	**ASSETS**	%	%
		24.4				Cash & Equivalents	27.7	25.0
		5.3				Trade Receivables (net)	9.1	10.3
		.2				Inventory	.3	2.7
		8.7				All Other Current	5.9	5.7
		38.6				Total Current	43.0	43.7
		13.1				Fixed Assets (net)	18.7	14.9
		7.5				Intangibles (net)	5.5	5.5
		40.7				All Other Non-Current	33.0	36.0
		100.0				Total	100.0	100.0
						LIABILITIES		
		3.8				Notes Payable-Short Term	11.4	10.7
		1.0				Cur. Mat.-L.T.D.	1.5	.1
		4.3				Trade Payables	7.0	6.0
		.0				Income Taxes Payable	1.6	.0
		12.7				All Other Current	12.6	13.0
		21.9				Total Current	34.2	29.7
		16.2				Long-Term Debt	8.2	1.5
		.0				Deferred Taxes	.0	.0
		18.0				All Other Non-Current	4.9	10.4
		43.9				Net Worth	52.7	58.5
		100.0				Total Liabilties & Net Worth	100.0	100.0
						INCOME DATA		
		100.0				Net Sales	100.0	100.0
						Gross Profit		
		84.0				Operating Expenses	92.1	95.1
		16.0				Operating Profit	7.9	4.9
		3.3				All Other Expenses (net)	-.2	.5
		12.7				Profit Before Taxes	8.1	4.4
						RATIOS		
		33.9				Current	4.7	3.8
		1.8					1.2	1.5
		.4					.7	.8
		22.7				Quick	3.8	3.5
		1.5					1.1	1.3
		.3					.5	.6
		0 UND				Sales/Receivables	0 UND	0 UND
		5 75.3					12 30.7	15 23.7
		18 19.8					30 12.1	53 6.9
						Cost of Sales/Inventory		
						Cost of Sales/Payables		
		2.0				Sales/Working Capital	5.4	3.0
		41.4					36.0	15.0
		-7.9					-14.1	-58.0
						EBIT/Interest	23.9	52.3
							(23) .8	(19) -1.0
							-1.0	-21.5
						Net Profit + Depr., Dep., Amort./Cur. Mat. L/T/D		
		.0				Fixed/Worth	.0	.0
		.0					.2	.1
		NM					1.6	.6
		.1				Debt/Worth	.1	.1
		.2					.4	.3
		-53.1					1.8	3.5
						% Profit Before Taxes/Tangible Net Worth	38.4	24.4
							(31) 5.0	(38) .8
							-.5	-3.6
		16.3				% Profit Before Taxes/Total Assets	28.0	8.7
		1.3					3.5	.2
		-7.7					-1.2	-3.0
		457.3				Sales/Net Fixed Assets	155.1	140.3
		84.0					20.1	35.9
		13.6					2.7	8.1
		2.8				Sales/Total Assets	4.1	3.6
		.7					1.1	1.0
		.3					.6	.4
						% Depr., Dep., Amort./Sales	.6	.3
							(28) 1.9	(27) 1.1
							4.3	2.2
						% Officers', Directors' Owners' Comp/Sales		
8938M	125671M	80019M	100108M	116946M	34411M	Net Sales ($)	304798M	448019M
1821M	6624M	54797M	101556M	149802M	197802M	Total Assets ($)	809524M	772124M

© RMA 2019

M = $ thousand   MM = $ million
See Pages viii through xx for Explanation of Ratios and Data

Comparative Historical Data | Current Data Sorted by Sales

			Type of Statement						
17	11	12	Unqualified	1	7			2	2
1			Reviewed						
		1	Compiled						1
6	2	3	Tax Returns	1	2				
14	17	18	Other	1	5	1	2	5	4
4/1/16- 3/31/17	4/1/17- 3/31/18	4/1/18- 3/31/19		21 (4/1-9/30/18)			13 (10/1/18-3/31/19)		
ALL	ALL	ALL		0-1MM	1-3MM	3-5MM	5-10MM	10-25MM	25MM & OVER
38	30	34	NUMBER OF STATEMENTS	3	14	1	2	7	7
%	%	%	ASSETS	%	%	%	%	%	%
33.0	35.5	36.0	Cash & Equivalents		33.1				
9.5	6.9	11.3	Trade Receivables (net)		9.8				
.7	.4	2.6	Inventory		.9				
5.2	4.0	6.9	All Other Current		5.2				
48.4	46.7	56.7	Total Current		49.0				
14.5	21.5	11.1	Fixed Assets (net)		11.5				
3.4	6.8	4.5	Intangibles (net)		2.5				
33.7	25.0	27.7	All Other Non-Current		37.0				
100.0	100.0	100.0	Total		100.0				
			LIABILITIES						
11.9	23.0	12.5	Notes Payable-Short Term		14.0				
5.4	1.1	5.7	Cur. Mat.-L.T.D.		9.1				
3.0	5.8	11.1	Trade Payables		11.8				
.0	.0	.0	Income Taxes Payable		.0				
9.5	8.7	26.4	All Other Current		24.1				
29.8	38.6	55.7	Total Current		59.0				
5.0	15.9	11.1	Long-Term Debt		15.4				
.0	.0	.0	Deferred Taxes		.0				
14.3	4.4	8.3	All Other Non-Current		.2				
50.9	41.1	24.9	Net Worth		25.4				
100.0	100.0	100.0	Total Liabilities & Net Worth		100.0				
			INCOME DATA						
100.0	100.0	100.0	Net Sales		100.0				
			Gross Profit						
97.9	91.7	93.3	Operating Expenses		89.8				
2.1	8.3	6.7	Operating Profit		10.2				
1.2	-1.0	-.8	All Other Expenses (net)		2.8				
.9	9.2	5.9	Profit Before Taxes		7.5				
			RATIOS						
10.0	10.2	6.3			9.1				
1.7	1.5	1.3	Current		1.1				
.8	.4	.6			.4				
9.2	8.3	5.8			7.4				
1.6	1.4	1.1	Quick		1.0				
.7	.3	.5			.3				
1 370.1	0 UND	0 UND		0 UND					
10 37.8	2 231.0	7 50.2	Sales/Receivables	4 95.8					
30 12.1	35 10.4	20 18.1		20 18.3					
			Cost of Sales/Inventory						
			Cost of Sales/Payables						
3.2	2.5	4.2			2.1				
11.9	11.7	25.6	Sales/Working Capital		112.7				
-34.3	-16.6	-22.0			-8.2				
14.2	24.4	41.2							
(20) 1.3	(17) 4.5	(16) 3.7	EBIT/Interest						
-21.5	-8.6	-7.1							
			Net Profit + Depr., Dep., Amort./Cur. Mat. L/T/D						
.0	.1	.0			.0				
.1	.3	.1	Fixed/Worth		.0				
.6	1.2	1.1			.2				
.1	.1	.1			.1				
.2	.3	.7	Debt/Worth		.4				
1.9	3.7	-37.1			-3.7				
15.7	78.2	44.0			17.5				
(32) -.4	(24) 6.6	(24) 4.0	% Profit Before Taxes/Tangible Net Worth	(10) 2.6					
-5.1	.1	-6.2			-11.1				
9.5	21.7	21.7			21.7				
.0	6.2	2.0	% Profit Before Taxes/Total Assets		9.7				
-4.8	-.9	-7.4			-8.7				
176.6	123.5	438.3			999.8				
30.1	11.2	73.3	Sales/Net Fixed Assets		84.0				
8.3	2.8	18.1			21.1				
3.4	3.0	8.0			4.9				
1.2	1.2	2.5	Sales/Total Assets		.8				
.4	.4	.6			.4				
.3	.3	.2			.2				
(23) 1.0	(21) .9	(17) .6	% Depr., Dep., Amort./Sales						
1.9	4.1	1.5							
			% Officers', Directors' Owners' Comp/Sales						
275747M	286351M	466093M	Net Sales ($)	1299M	24231M	4444M	12453M	98954M	324712M
782763M	751230M	512402M	Total Assets ($)	691M	42552M	1202M	3179M	84087M	380691M

M = $ thousand   MM = $ million
See Pages viii through xx for Explanation of Ratios and Data

Current Data Sorted by Assets   Comparative Historical Data

						Type of Statement		
1		2	7	4	23	Unqualified	40	37
				1		Reviewed	4	3
	1	2				Compiled	5	8
7	6	3	2	5	18	Tax Returns	19	17
7	8	8				Other	73	52
	48 (4/1-9/30/18)		65 (10/1/18-3/31/19)				4/1/14-3/31/15	4/1/15-3/31/16
0-500M	**500M-2MM**	**2-10MM**	**10-50MM**	**50-100MM**	**100-250MM**		**ALL**	**ALL**
15	15	15	17	10	41	NUMBER OF STATEMENTS	141	117
%	%	%	%	%	%	**ASSETS**	%	%
27.8	37.3	11.0	14.0	15.2	12.9	Cash & Equivalents	20.6	18.3
14.6	6.7	4.3	4.8	20.4	12.5	Trade Receivables (net)	10.2	9.8
5.2	1.6	1.8	1.1	2.5	.1	Inventory	1.3	1.3
1.4	1.1	1.3	2.6	7.8	6.9	All Other Current	5.1	4.3
49.1	46.7	18.5	22.5	45.8	32.4	Total Current	37.2	33.7
33.7	43.8	23.2	28.6	20.2	15.1	Fixed Assets (net)	23.7	23.9
9.5	4.6	21.3	27.7	14.9	28.5	Intangibles (net)	18.0	21.7
7.3	4.9	37.0	21.2	19.1	24.0	All Other Non-Current	21.1	20.7
100.0	100.0	100.0	100.0	100.0	100.0	Total	100.0	100.0
						LIABILITIES		
5.1	5.0	4.0	2.0	.0	5.3	Notes Payable-Short Term	5.1	12.7
4.3	15.7	2.6	2.4	3.7	2.1	Cur. Mat.-L.T.D.	2.1	2.3
27.9	4.1	3.6	4.8	8.3	16.0	Trade Payables	9.3	6.6
.1	.0	.3	.0	.0	.0	Income Taxes Payable	.4	.0
9.3	12.0	15.7	16.8	36.2	31.2	All Other Current	29.2	25.3
46.7	36.8	26.2	26.0	48.3	54.6	Total Current	46.1	46.9
34.8	20.2	9.0	16.1	58.8	105.3	Long-Term Debt	48.8	47.3
.0	.0	.0	.4	1.2	.1	Deferred Taxes	.1	.1
3.1	8.7	9.4	3.6	39.1	44.6	All Other Non-Current	22.4	20.4
15.3	34.3	55.4	53.9	-47.3	-104.6	Net Worth	-17.4	-14.7
100.0	100.0	100.0	100.0	100.0	100.0	Total Liabilities & Net Worth	100.0	100.0
						INCOME DATA		
100.0	100.0	100.0	100.0	100.0	100.0	Net Sales	100.0	100.0
						Gross Profit		
92.0	85.7	99.0	91.9	98.7	91.7	Operating Expenses	94.4	96.8
8.0	14.3	1.0	8.1	1.3	8.3	Operating Profit	5.6	3.2
1.4	1.4	4.9	2.7	2.6	5.7	All Other Expenses (net)	3.4	2.0
6.5	12.9	-3.9	5.4	-1.3	2.6	Profit Before Taxes	2.2	1.2
						RATIOS		
5.2	6.8	1.2	3.2	4.1	1.0		2.4	1.9
1.3	2.9	.7	.9	1.0	.6	Current	.9	.9
.5	.7	.3	.4	.5	.4		.4	.4
5.2	6.6	1.0	2.9	3.4	.8		2.0	1.7
1.1	2.9	.6	.7	.8	.4	Quick	.7	.7
.5	.7	.2	.3	.3	.2		.3	.3
0 UND	0 UND	2 180.9	5 77.3	16 22.6	11 32.0		1 440.6	1 256.4
0 UND	0 UND	19 18.9	15 25.0	24 14.9	21 17.3	Sales/Receivables	16 23.4	15 24.2
38 9.5	3 107.5	28 13.0	38 9.6	61 6.0	63 5.8		47 7.8	45 8.2
						Cost of Sales/Inventory		
						Cost of Sales/Payables		
4.6	3.7	15.2	5.3	4.0	NM		9.3	10.6
33.4	13.3	-15.5	-32.8	NM	-6.1	Sales/Working Capital	-34.0	-47.5
-12.0	-21.1	-4.4	-4.0	-5.8	-3.3		-4.6	-4.5
19.5	21.0	40.6	57.0		3.1		6.3	5.9
(10) 11.5	(10) 5.0	(12) -1.1	(12) 3.6		(34) 1.1	EBIT/Interest	(101) 1.8	(84) 1.3
5.1	.4	-11.1	1.3		-.6		-1.7	-1.2
						Net Profit + Depr., Dep., Amort./Cur. Mat. L/T/D		
.1	.2	.2	.4	.0	-1.3		.3	.5
.9	1.9	.6	.7	.6	-.1	Fixed/Worth	7.0	3.3
-1.8	-9.3	12.9	-4.2	-.1	.0		-.2	-.1
.3	.1	.7	.3	.3	-4.7		1.3	1.4
3.4	1.2	1.8	.9	NM	-1.7	Debt/Worth	-17.3	-104.9
-3.1	-11.6	20.9	-7.2	-1.4	-1.3		-1.9	-1.8
70.5	64.7	59.3	36.4			% Profit Before Taxes/Tangible Net Worth	73.2	66.8
(10) 24.2	(11) 30.0	(13) 3.5	(12) 8.5				(68) 11.0	(58) 12.3
.7	-.4	-66.8	-1.3				1.0	-2.5
45.1	44.7	12.3	11.7	7.1	10.6	% Profit Before Taxes/Total Assets	11.8	10.1
38.7	10.6	-.3	2.1	1.0	.6		2.3	2.3
1.3	-1.3	-10.7	-2.6	-5.3	-5.8		-10.0	-4.7
26.5	18.5	9.2	7.7	112.8	51.0		81.1	66.0
12.6	9.8	5.4	4.3	25.7	17.7	Sales/Net Fixed Assets	15.3	14.6
5.2	1.8	3.1	1.6	4.3	5.9		4.0	3.6
5.3	3.0	1.4	.9	2.6	1.7		2.3	2.1
2.8	1.8	.7	.7	1.8	1.1	Sales/Total Assets	1.3	1.3
.9	.9	.4	.5	.6	.8		.7	.7
		2.0	3.3		1.2		.9	1.0
		2.8	(11) 5.1		(26) 1.6	% Depr., Dep., Amort./Sales	(89) 2.1	(76) 2.5
		6.7	10.9		2.5		5.1	5.0
						% Officers', Directors' Owners' Comp/Sales	2.8	2.9
							(22) 5.8	(19) 5.1
							13.0	17.0
10273M	36308M	67826M	272781M	1366889M	8568164M	Net Sales ($)	9978980M	9269023M
3041M	17956M	84219M	366101M	780475M	6834578M	Total Assets ($)	8185541M	8112489M

M = $ thousand   MM = $ million
See Pages viii through xx for Explanation of Ratios and Data

Comparative Historical Data / Current Data Sorted by Sales

38	31	37	Type of Statement						
			Unqualified	1	1	1	2	5	27
4	2	1	Reviewed						1
4	10	3	Compiled			3			
14	16	18	Tax Returns	8	4	2	3	1	
46	44	54	Other	5	12	6	3	7	21
4/1/16-3/31/17 ALL	4/1/17-3/31/18 ALL	4/1/18-3/31/19 ALL		48 (4/1-9/30/18)			65 (10/1/18-3/31/19)		
				0-1MM	1-3MM	3-5MM	5-10MM	10-25MM	25MM & OVER
106	103	113	NUMBER OF STATEMENTS	14	17	12	8	13	49
%	%	%	**ASSETS**	%	%	%	%	%	%
16.3	21.0	18.2	Cash & Equivalents	25.4	28.8	19.6		15.6	15.0
10.5	11.5	10.5	Trade Receivables (net)	11.8	6.6	7.2		4.5	14.8
1.7	3.3	1.6	Inventory	5.9	1.1	1.3		1.1	.6
5.5	4.6	4.1	All Other Current	1.5	1.1	1.2		.7	8.0
33.9	40.4	34.4	Total Current	44.7	37.5	29.3		21.9	38.3
22.8	24.7	24.9	Fixed Assets (net)	43.9	24.7	35.6		33.7	14.4
23.8	17.4	20.5	Intangibles (net)	6.9	16.3	13.9		23.7	24.8
19.4	17.4	20.1	All Other Non-Current	4.1	21.6	21.2		20.7	22.5
100.0	100.0	100.0	Total	100.0	100.0	100.0		100.0	100.0
			LIABILITIES						
8.6	6.3	4.1	Notes Payable-Short Term	2.6	5.9	6.2		2.7	3.9
1.6	1.9	4.5	Cur. Mat. L.T.D.	2.5	17.1	1.1		1.4	2.5
6.6	7.8	12.0	Trade Payables	30.3	3.0	4.3		4.0	15.4
.0	.0	.1	Income Taxes Payable	.0	.1	.4		.0	.0
33.3	28.2	22.0	All Other Current	4.4	16.0	11.3		13.8	35.3
50.2	44.2	42.6	Total Current	39.9	42.0	23.3		21.8	57.1
51.1	49.5	54.3	Long-Term Debt	35.2	18.3	13.0		22.6	96.5
.1	.2	.2	Deferred Taxes	.0	.0	.0		.5	.3
22.7	26.1	23.0	All Other Non-Current	.5	8.1	10.7		7.6	45.2
-24.1	-20.0	-20.1	Net Worth	24.3	31.6	53.1		47.6	-99.2
100.0	100.0	100.0	Total Liabilties & Net Worth	100.0	100.0	100.0		100.0	100.0
			INCOME DATA						
100.0	100.0	100.0	Net Sales	100.0	100.0	100.0		100.0	100.0
			Gross Profit						
92.6	89.9	92.6	Operating Expenses	86.4	93.3	105.8		77.2	97.6
7.4	10.1	7.4	Operating Profit	13.6	6.7	-5.8		22.8	2.4
3.8	3.9	3.7	All Other Expenses (net)	3.5	4.1	.6		5.7	2.4
3.6	6.2	3.7	Profit Before Taxes	10.1	2.6	-6.4		17.2	.1
			RATIOS						
1.6	2.6	2.0		5.1	5.8	4.8		6.7	1.0
.8	.9	.8	Current	1.7	.7	1.3		1.4	.7
.5	.5	.4		.8	.3	.4		.4	.4
1.5	2.3	1.8		5.1	5.8	4.4		6.5	.9
.7	.7	.7	Quick	1.7	.7	1.2		1.3	.5
.3	.3	.3		.6	.2	.4		.3	.3
0 UND	4 100.8	2 225.5		0 UND	0 UND	0 UND		0 UND	14 25.9
15 24.3	21 17.8	17 21.6	Sales/Receivables	0 UND	2 163.4	21 17.1		16 22.5	27 13.7
43 8.4	43 8.4	41 8.9		43 8.4	27 13.3	33 11.0		33 11.2	63 5.8
			Cost of Sales/Inventory						
			Cost of Sales/Payables						
9.4	6.2	7.6		4.4	6.5	4.0		3.3	104.4
-24.4	-98.6	-15.5	Sales/Working Capital	18.8	-32.9	33.0		9.0	-6.6
-4.3	-5.9	-5.1		-13.1	-6.7	-9.3		-4.8	-3.9
(81) 6.2	(76) 10.4	(87) 9.1			18.2			67.2	4.4
2.3	3.8	2.4	EBIT/Interest	(12) 3.4			(10) 3.0	(41) 1.2	
-.8	.5	-.2			-2.8			.6	-.5
			Net Profit + Depr., Dep., Amort./Cur. Mat. L/T/D						
.5	.3	.4		.3	.2	.1		.6	2.0
325.5	4.2	3.8	Fixed/Worth	1.4	2.2	1.5		.7	-.1
-.1	-.3	-.1		UND	-1.6	3.6		-3.0	.0
1.2	.8	.8		.3	.1	.5		.5	-9.5
-5.2	-7.8	29.0	Debt/Worth	2.1	5.2	1.3		1.1	-1.7
-1.6	-1.6	-1.7		UND	-4.4	3.9		-6.2	-1.3
(45) 31.3	(48) 43.3	(58) 39.8	% Profit Before Taxes/Tangible Net Worth	39.6	6.8	59.9			30.7
10.8	19.8	6.9		(11) 19.5	(11) 1.4	(10) 30.1		(11) 2.2	
.0	.8	-.7		-.4	-66.3	-2.0			-17.1
12.9	21.8	18.4	% Profit Before Taxes/Total Assets	41.7	42.1	25.5		18.7	11.3
3.1	5.6	2.8		7.7	3.2	5.6		5.4	.6
-4.3	-1.7	-4.5		-.1	-5.3	-13.9		-.2	-6.0
52.1	78.7	36.4		73.6	18.8	12.8		8.0	51.0
14.7	10.7	9.2	Sales/Net Fixed Assets	4.7	11.3	6.0		4.3	17.7
3.5	3.5	3.6		.9	5.1	3.5		1.1	6.6
2.0	2.1	2.1		2.5	4.5	2.9		1.0	2.0
1.0	1.3	1.1	Sales/Total Assets	.9	1.8	1.3		.9	1.5
.6	.6	.6		.8	.6	.4		.3	.9
(70) .9	(74) .9	(77) 1.4	% Depr., Dep., Amort./Sales		1.9	1.3			1.2
2.3	2.4	2.6			(10) 3.8	(10) 3.8			(34) 1.6
4.1	5.0	5.6			7.0	5.8			2.5
(12) 1.8	(14) 2.7	(18) 4.7	% Officers', Directors' Owners' Comp/Sales						
6.2	10.7	6.5							
10.1	10.7	11.1							
9815570M	7878697M	10322241M	Net Sales ($)	5822M	34713M	46989M	61019M	214622M	9959076M
8346296M	6547713M	8086370M	Total Assets ($)	6036M	39625M	80893M	270795M	705038M	6983983M

M = $ thousand   MM = $ million
See Pages viii through xx for Explanation of Ratios and Data

Current Data Sorted by Assets

Comparative Historical Data

						Type of Statement		
			2	1	4	Unqualified	7	5
	3			1		Reviewed	1	4
						Compiled		
1	1					Tax Returns	3	5
1	2	1	5	3		Other	14	14
	3 (4/1-9/30/18)		22 (10/1/18-3/31/19)				4/1/14-3/31/15	4/1/15-3/31/16
0-500M	500M-2MM	2-10MM	10-50MM	50-100MM	100-250MM		ALL	ALL
2	3	4	7	5	4	NUMBER OF STATEMENTS	25	28
%	%	%	%	%	%	ASSETS	%	%
						Cash & Equivalents	12.9	15.0
						Trade Receivables (net)	3.7	4.9
						Inventory	2.3	5.0
						All Other Current	1.8	3.0
						Total Current	20.7	27.9
						Fixed Assets (net)	61.1	57.1
						Intangibles (net)	2.6	2.7
						All Other Non-Current	15.6	12.3
						Total	100.0	100.0
						LIABILITIES		
						Notes Payable-Short Term	6.0	2.2
						Cur. Mat.-L.T.D.	2.4	2.2
						Trade Payables	3.4	2.9
						Income Taxes Payable	.0	.0
						All Other Current	16.5	19.2
						Total Current	28.2	26.5
						Long-Term Debt	17.8	20.0
						Deferred Taxes	1.5	1.2
						All Other Non-Current	4.1	4.1
						Net Worth	48.3	48.2
						Total Liabilties & Net Worth	100.0	100.0
						INCOME DATA		
						Net Sales	100.0	100.0
						Gross Profit		
						Operating Expenses	92.9	90.4
						Operating Profit	7.1	9.6
						All Other Expenses (net)	.0	.5
						Profit Before Taxes	7.1	9.1
						RATIOS		
							2.6	3.2
						Current	.9	1.1
							.3	.5
							1.4	1.9
						Quick	.6	.8
							.2	.2
							1 316.8	1 435.5
						Sales/Receivables	6 60.7	5 78.5
							15 23.7	29 12.7
						Cost of Sales/Inventory		
						Cost of Sales/Payables		
							13.0	12.0
						Sales/Working Capital	-71.8	327.0
							-5.9	-9.1
							35.7	17.6
						EBIT/Interest	(18) 9.5	(25) 6.0
							-.8	.6
						Net Profit + Depr., Dep., Amort./Cur. Mat. L/T/D		
							.7	.7
						Fixed/Worth	1.2	1.1
							2.0	2.5
							.2	.5
						Debt/Worth	.8	.8
							2.0	2.1
							23.2	21.6
						% Profit Before Taxes/Tangible Net Worth	(22) 10.7	(24) 9.7
							1.9	2.1
							12.2	11.2
						% Profit Before Taxes/Total Assets	4.1	5.4
							-1.2	.7
							4.1	5.2
						Sales/Net Fixed Assets	1.8	2.0
							.8	1.1
							1.7	2.7
						Sales/Total Assets	1.1	1.1
							.5	.7
							2.7	4.1
						% Depr., Dep., Amort./Sales	(21) 5.1	(22) 7.4
							10.8	11.2
						% Officers', Directors' Owners' Comp/Sales		
2069M	3858M	43464M	252538M	329858M	657823M	Net Sales ($)	908136M	1016918M
200M	3265M	24254M	172242M	369031M	566159M	Total Assets ($)	1133837M	1233620M

© RMA 2019

M = $ thousand   MM = $ million
See Pages viii through xx for Explanation of Ratios and Data

Comparative Historical Data				Current Data Sorted by Sales					
			Type of Statement						
6	8	7	Unqualified				1		6
1	2	4	Reviewed				1	2	1
			Compiled						
2	2	2	Tax Returns		2				
11	9	12	Other	3			2	1	6
					3 (4/1-9/30/18)		22 (10/1/18-3/31/19)		
4/1/16-3/31/17 ALL	4/1/17-3/31/18 ALL	4/1/18-3/31/19 ALL		0-1MM	1-3MM	3-5MM	5-10MM	10-25MM	25MM & OVER
20	21	25	**NUMBER OF STATEMENTS**	3	2		4	3	13
%	%	%	**ASSETS**	%	%	%	%	%	%
17.1	16.5	19.1	Cash & Equivalents			D			16.9
8.9	7.3	8.2	Trade Receivables (net)			A			8.9
4.3	1.1	2.1	Inventory			T			.8
3.8	2.5	6.1	All Other Current			A			7.3
34.1	27.3	35.5	Total Current						33.9
51.5	62.0	51.3	Fixed Assets (net)			N			50.0
4.7	4.0	6.8	Intangibles (net)			O			5.9
9.6	6.6	6.5	All Other Non-Current			T			10.2
100.0	100.0	100.0	Total						100.0
			LIABILITIES			A			
5.7	1.2	.6	Notes Payable-Short Term			V			.3
3.6	2.0	1.5	Cur. Mat.-L.T.D.			A			1.7
7.4	5.8	10.9	Trade Payables			I			13.7
.0	.3	.2	Income Taxes Payable			L			.3
15.2	14.8	12.3	All Other Current			A			16.0
31.9	24.1	25.4	Total Current			B			32.1
22.3	21.9	23.3	Long-Term Debt			L			13.1
3.3	.8	.9	Deferred Taxes			E			1.5
2.9	6.3	12.2	All Other Non-Current						6.3
39.6	46.9	38.1	Net Worth						47.1
100.0	100.0	100.0	Total Liabilties & Net Worth						100.0
			INCOME DATA						
100.0	100.0	100.0	Net Sales						100.0
			Gross Profit						
92.6	90.3	94.9	Operating Expenses						91.9
7.4	9.7	5.1	Operating Profit						8.1
.6	1.9	1.1	All Other Expenses (net)						.9
6.8	7.8	4.0	Profit Before Taxes						7.2
			RATIOS						
3.8	2.2	3.1							2.6
1.4	1.0	1.3	Current						1.1
.7	.7	.9							.8
2.4	2.0	2.6							1.5
1.0	.9	1.1	Quick						1.0
.3	.3	.4							.4
4 101.3	**4** 102.7	**3** 130.0							**4** 101.4
14 26.7	**8** 44.6	**8** 48.4	Sales/Receivables						**15** 23.8
37 9.8	**31** 11.8	**36** 10.2							**38** 9.7
			Cost of Sales/Inventory						
			Cost of Sales/Payables						
6.5	11.2	8.5							6.6
19.9	999.8	35.5	Sales/Working Capital						73.2
-18.5	-19.5	-38.2							-38.2
19.9	14.7	10.3							
(16) 6.5	(17) 7.7	(20) 6.4	EBIT/Interest						
1.6	2.9	2.0							
			Net Profit + Depr., Dep., Amort./Cur. Mat. L/T/D						
.6	.9	.7							.7
.8	1.2	1.0	Fixed/Worth						1.0
2.1	4.2	8.3							2.5
.3	.4	.3							.4
.9	.9	1.2	Debt/Worth						1.2
4.9	6.6	21.3							2.8
23.1	20.4	22.0							27.1
(17) 12.8	(19) 13.6	(20) 10.9	% Profit Before Taxes/Tangible Net Worth						(12) 11.7
7.2	5.8	4.0							5.4
10.4	9.6	11.2							12.0
7.0	7.5	5.2	% Profit Before Taxes/Total Assets						5.9
3.2	3.0	.9							2.2
8.1	3.8	6.3							4.2
3.4	1.6	2.5	Sales/Net Fixed Assets						1.9
1.3	1.0	1.3							1.4
2.2	2.0	2.2							1.7
1.4	1.1	1.3	Sales/Total Assets						1.1
.8	.6	.7							1.0
2.7	2.0	2.6							1.8
(17) 5.3	(16) 3.4	(20) 4.8	% Depr., Dep., Amort./Sales						(11) 3.6
9.8	7.7	8.1							5.2
			% Officers', Directors' Owners' Comp/Sales						
661151M	1093900M	1289610M	Net Sales ($)	1607M	4320M		29503M	53461M	1200719M
652940M	1008085M	1135151M	Total Assets ($)	2637M	828M		47462M	27179M	1057045M

M = $ thousand MM = $ million

See Pages viii through xx for Explanation of Ratios and Data

Current Data Sorted by Assets   **Comparative Historical Data**

Type of Statement	0-500M	500M-2MM	2-10MM	10-50MM	50-100MM	100-250MM		4/1/14-3/31/15 ALL	4/1/15-3/31/16 ALL
Unqualified	2	3	8	14	7	6		41	53
Reviewed			2	3				7	8
Compiled		4	3	1				14	10
Tax Returns	7	5	4					39	36
Other	7	7	17	10	4	2		68	63
	50 (4/1-9/30/18)			66 (10/1/18-3/31/19)					
NUMBER OF STATEMENTS	16	19	34	28	11	8		169	170
ASSETS	%	%	%	%	%	%		%	%
Cash & Equivalents	32.1	26.1	22.1	26.2	10.7			20.8	22.0
Trade Receivables (net)	9.5	17.5	8.9	5.7	4.7			9.5	10.1
Inventory	2.6	.1	2.2	2.9	1.1			1.8	1.5
All Other Current	11.2	4.7	1.8	6.9	8.3			3.1	3.6
Total Current	55.4	48.4	34.9	41.7	24.9			35.1	37.2
Fixed Assets (net)	28.0	47.2	47.4	37.7	49.3			44.6	40.8
Intangibles (net)	7.8	1.8	5.9	4.3	.7			6.6	6.2
All Other Non-Current	8.7	2.7	11.8	16.3	25.1			13.7	15.9
Total	100.0	100.0	100.0	100.0	100.0			100.0	100.0
LIABILITIES									
Notes Payable-Short Term	5.8	10.9	3.2	1.6	.3			8.2	12.2
Cur. Mat.-L.T.D.	9.1	8.5	2.7	.5	.6			3.8	2.8
Trade Payables	13.8	15.0	5.3	6.3	4.4			5.4	6.6
Income Taxes Payable	.0	.0	.0	.3	.5			.1	.1
All Other Current	24.7	21.4	12.2	15.3	14.9			16.4	18.2
Total Current	53.3	55.8	23.5	24.1	20.7			34.0	39.8
Long-Term Debt	35.9	24.8	20.1	11.9	4.5			23.4	19.7
Deferred Taxes	.0	.0	.0	.0	.0			.5	.1
All Other Non-Current	3.7	16.8	6.2	3.4	14.2			8.7	6.6
Net Worth	7.1	2.6	50.2	60.6	60.7			33.5	33.8
Total Liabilities & Net Worth	100.0	100.0	100.0	100.0	100.0			100.0	100.0
INCOME DATA									
Net Sales	100.0	100.0	100.0	100.0	100.0			100.0	100.0
Gross Profit									
Operating Expenses	100.2	91.8	89.6	89.1	90.2			88.3	90.6
Operating Profit	-.2	8.2	10.4	10.9	9.8			11.7	9.4
All Other Expenses (net)	.6	2.6	2.1	3.4	.1			2.8	4.1
Profit Before Taxes	-.8	5.7	8.2	7.5	9.7			8.9	5.4
RATIOS									
Current	21.5	2.6	2.8	4.5	2.3			2.3	2.9
	1.7	.9	1.4	2.0	1.3			1.0	1.1
	.6	.3	.9	1.1	.8			.4	.5
Quick	8.4	2.6	2.7	3.4	1.9			2.2	2.3
	1.3	.9	1.4	1.5	.7			.9	1.0
	.4	.2	.7	1.1	.3			.3	.4
Sales/Receivables	0 UND	0 UND	1 263.2	2 151.4	4 95.6			0 UND	0 UND
	1 376.7	3 122.2	10 35.6	7 53.1	16 22.2			5 75.1	6 62.2
	5 75.2	31 11.9	27 13.7	24 15.2	29 12.5			26 14.2	24 15.4
Cost of Sales/Inventory									
Cost of Sales/Payables									
Sales/Working Capital	5.3	9.5	4.6	2.3	6.3			8.3	6.6
	50.8	-29.5	15.2	8.6	9.2			123.1	78.1
	-33.1	-9.0	-140.4	126.0	-13.8			-10.7	-9.8
EBIT/Interest	32.9	46.0	23.2	24.1				23.8	15.6
	(10) .3	(13) 4.2	(24) 5.4	(13) 6.4				(106) 6.3	(108) 3.2
	-29.2	.0	.7	3.7				1.0	-1.2
Net Profit + Depr., Dep., Amort./Cur. Mat. L/T/D									
Fixed/Worth	.0	.2	.4	.0	.3			.2	.2
	.5	1.7	1.0	.5	.9			1.1	.9
	13.4	-.5	2.0	1.1	1.1			9.3	4.4
Debt/Worth	.1	.8	.4	.2	.2			.3	.2
	3.0	5.1	1.0	.4	.3			1.5	1.1
	UND	-42.9	3.3	1.7	1.3			16.9	125.3
% Profit Before Taxes/Tangible Net Worth	98.6	58.7	62.3	26.4	13.3			55.6	50.4
	(13) 33.9	(14) 11.0	(31) 10.4	(26) 6.5	(10) .3			(132) 15.2	(130) 7.4
	-61.8	-.7	-.6	1.0	-5.7			3.6	-1.7
% Profit Before Taxes/Total Assets	34.6	27.7	22.6	10.9	8.0			20.6	20.1
	-3.6	6.6	6.3	4.7	.3			6.5	3.7
	-42.8	-.2	-.8	1.3	-2.5			.1	-1.5
Sales/Net Fixed Assets	UND	248.3	17.9	137.2	2.7			37.2	82.7
	36.3	7.2	3.3	1.5	.9			4.9	5.4
	11.6	1.0	1.0	.8	.2			.7	.9
Sales/Total Assets	11.5	5.2	2.8	1.5	.9			3.1	3.1
	6.8	2.3	1.3	.7	.4			1.3	1.3
	3.6	.8	.5	.4	.2			.4	.5
% Depr., Dep., Amort./Sales		1.0	2.4	3.2				1.2	.7
		(13) 3.1	(26) 4.4	(22) 5.1				(118) 4.5	(114) 4.1
		6.9	13.8	7.2				9.0	7.8
% Officers', Directors' Owners' Comp/Sales								2.0	2.9
								(44) 4.8	(37) 5.9
								9.9	10.6
Net Sales ($)	24425M	78707M	233720M	620643M	443321M	1332745M		3158096M	4168083M
Total Assets ($)	4207M	23364M	160083M	637845M	800624M	1290074M		2986386M	3180138M

M = $ thousand   MM = $ million
See Pages viii through xx for Explanation of Ratios and Data

Comparative Historical Data | Current Data Sorted by Sales

4/1/16-3/31/17 ALL	4/1/17-3/31/18 ALL	4/1/18-3/31/19 ALL	Type of Statement	0-1MM	1-3MM	3-5MM	5-10MM	10-25MM	25MM & OVER
39	39	40	Unqualified	3	3	5	8	7	14
7	3	5	Reviewed				2	1	2
5	9	7	Compiled		1		6		
26	19	17	Tax Returns					2	1
50	56	47	Other	5	8	1		2	1
				8	6	7	9	9	8
				50 (4/1-9/30/18)			**66 (10/1/18-3/31/19)**		
127	**126**	**116**	**NUMBER OF STATEMENTS**	**16**	**18**	**13**	**25**	**19**	**25**
%	%	%	**ASSETS**	%	%	%	%	%	%
21.9	26.3	23.5	Cash & Equivalents	18.5	20.8	34.6	22.2	23.1	24.6
6.9	6.7	8.8	Trade Receivables (net)	5.3	10.9	8.9	9.7	9.9	7.6
2.0	2.4	2.1	Inventory	.6	1.8	.3	2.6	.9	4.8
3.4	4.8	5.6	All Other Current	2.4	8.7	.8	9.9	2.3	6.2
34.3	40.2	40.0	Total Current	26.7	42.2	44.6	44.5	36.1	43.2
48.4	40.6	42.7	Fixed Assets (net)	62.5	42.1	40.0	44.0	42.4	30.9
6.7	4.6	4.3	Intangibles (net)	7.3	2.4	3.4	1.6	11.2	1.7
10.6	14.6	13.0	All Other Non-Current	3.5	13.4	12.1	9.9	10.3	24.3
100.0	100.0	100.0	Total	100.0	100.0	100.0	100.0	100.0	100.0
			LIABILITIES						
7.3	4.6	4.0	Notes Payable-Short Term	3.1	5.3	3.4	5.1	5.3	1.7
4.8	1.8	3.7	Cur. Mat.-L.T.D.	7.8	3.6	.5	4.3	5.6	.7
8.0	6.0	8.3	Trade Payables	12.8	6.4	5.9	6.9	8.7	9.2
.2	.2	.1	Income Taxes Payable	.0	.0	.0	.0	.5	.2
18.1	16.4	16.1	All Other Current	11.5	16.4	7.6	15.9	18.6	21.6
38.4	29.0	32.2	Total Current	35.2	31.6	17.4	32.2	38.8	33.4
31.9	17.4	19.3	Long-Term Debt	58.0	31.7	8.4	10.9	10.2	6.5
.1	.0	.0	Deferred Taxes	.0	.0	.0	.0	.0	.0
9.5	8.7	8.4	All Other Non-Current	15.3	7.6	3.2	6.5	2.9	13.2
20.1	44.9	40.2	Net Worth	-8.5	29.1	71.0	50.4	48.1	46.9
100.0	100.0	100.0	Total Liabilties & Net Worth	100.0	100.0	100.0	100.0	100.0	100.0
			INCOME DATA						
100.0	100.0	100.0	Net Sales	100.0	100.0	100.0	100.0	100.0	100.0
			Gross Profit						
86.1	94.8	91.0	Operating Expenses	87.8	97.3	89.7	97.2	91.4	82.7
13.9	5.2	9.0	Operating Profit	12.2	2.7	10.3	2.8	8.6	17.3
3.4	1.3	2.8	All Other Expenses (net)	9.6	1.8	.5	-.2	.4	5.0
10.5	3.9	6.2	Profit Before Taxes	2.6	1.0	9.8	3.0	8.1	12.3
			RATIOS						
2.9	4.5	3.5	Current	9.2	2.4	11.3	4.6	2.9	2.3
1.1	1.6	1.5		1.5	1.0	2.8	1.6	1.5	1.5
.4	.8	.8		.2	.5	1.2	1.0	.6	1.0
2.5	3.6	2.6	Quick	9.1	2.4	11.1	2.9	2.8	1.8
.8	1.2	1.2		1.2	.9	2.6	1.2	1.0	1.2
.2	.5	.5		.2	.4	1.2	.4	.6	.5
0 UND	0 UND	1 276.3	Sales/Receivables	0 UND	0 UND	3 141.0	1 251.1	0 844.7	2 146.3
3 125.9	6 59.2	7 53.5		0 UND	3 114.8	8 43.6	12 31.1	3 110.4	12 30.9
27 13.7	25 14.6	25 14.6		8 46.1	43 8.4	29 12.6	35 10.3	18 19.9	29 12.4
			Cost of Sales/Inventory						
			Cost of Sales/Payables						
5.6	3.4	4.6	Sales/Working Capital	5.3	9.9	4.5	2.4	2.4	4.9
97.4	11.0	14.3		17.0	NM	9.3	11.1	22.0	11.3
-7.8	-27.6	33.1		-15.1	-12.3	21.8	-188.6	-11.6	NM
18.4	12.7	30.3	EBIT/Interest		30.3		7.6	42.3	59.3
(82) 3.6	(72) 3.1	(75) 4.8		(15)	3.6	(15)	(15) 5.3	(15) 7.5	(15) 3.0
.8	.2	.5			-10.0		.7	3.9	.3
			Net Profit + Depr., Dep., Amort./Cur. Mat. L/T/D						
.5	.2	.2	Fixed/Worth	.4	.1	.1	.3	.5	.1
1.2	.0	.0		1.8	2.6	.8	1.0	.9	.3
-27.5	1.8	2.2		7.8	UND	1.1	1.5	1.9	1.1
.2	.2	.2	Debt/Worth	.1	.9	.1	.2	.2	.3
1.9	.9	1.0		1.1	6.1	.3	.8	.6	1.2
-13.2	4.8	4.9		16.4	UND	1.9	3.7	3.4	3.4
45.6	73.0	50.0	% Profit Before Taxes/Tangible Net Worth	20.6	90.2	53.2	49.7	25.4	57.6
(89) 8.8	(107) 8.7	(101) 6.9		(13) 1.1	(15) 14.0	14.7	(22) 7.3	(16) 8.1	(22) 6.5
.8	.2	-1.3		-5.9	-33.4	2.0	-1.4	-1.3	-.1
17.2	25.0	15.8	% Profit Before Taxes/Total Assets	6.7	16.1	37.2	11.9	33.8	20.1
5.2	4.1	4.1		.2	3.9	9.1	3.7	4.3	6.8
-.1	-.4	-1.4		-7.2	-15.9	1.3	-3.0	2.6	.1
22.9	35.8	36.3	Sales/Net Fixed Assets	10.7	109.0	31.9	116.3	25.2	131.7
2.5	3.4	4.3		2.3	11.2	2.1	4.2	7.4	4.5
.8	1.1	.8		.2	1.5	.7	1.2	.9	.8
3.2	3.2	3.6	Sales/Total Assets	4.5	4.5	3.0	2.9	4.0	2.6
1.0	1.1	1.2		.8	2.2	1.0	1.3	1.1	1.1
.4	.6	.4		.2	.7	.5	.4	.5	.4
1.8	1.6	1.7	% Depr., Dep., Amort./Sales	4.2	.8		1.6	1.8	.4
(91) 4.1	(90) 4.5	(84) 4.5		(10) 9.8	(12) 4.5		(18) 3.8	(17) 4.4	(19) 5.7
9.7	8.4	11.7		28.8	24.9		7.9	6.2	13.7
4.0	1.4	1.9	% Officers', Directors' Owners' Comp/Sales						
(26) 7.2	(23) 5.0	(24) 4.0							
13.5	9.6	8.3							
4257561M	3798963M	2733561M	Net Sales ($)	9593M	34628M	50219M	178630M	288049M	2172442M
3743422M	3000224M	2916197M	Total Assets ($)	36155M	59353M	108089M	368541M	431216M	1912843M

M = $ thousand   MM = $ million
See Pages viii through xx for Explanation of Ratios and Data

Current Data Sorted by Assets							Comparative Historical Data	
						Type of Statement		
	1	2	3			Unqualified	5	5
		1	1			Reviewed	2	
	1	3				Compiled	5	1
5	4	2				Tax Returns	7	12
5	3	5	3	3		Other	20	26
	10 (4/1-9/30/18)		32 (10/1/18-3/31/19)				**4/1/14-3/31/15 ALL**	**4/1/15-3/31/16 ALL**
0-500M	**500M-2MM**	**2-10MM**	**10-50MM**	**50-100MM**	**100-250MM**			
10	9	13	7	3		**NUMBER OF STATEMENTS**	39	44
%	%	%	%	%	%	**ASSETS**	%	%
35.3		26.6			D	Cash & Equivalents	28.4	25.1
11.1		17.4			A	Trade Receivables (net)	17.8	12.9
3.6		6.2			T	Inventory	6.0	3.9
1.7		3.7			A	All Other Current	5.6	6.5
51.7		53.9				Total Current	57.9	48.3
29.2		19.4			N	Fixed Assets (net)	16.4	23.6
12.4		12.1			O	Intangibles (net)	11.8	12.7
7.4		14.6			T	All Other Non-Current	13.9	15.4
100.0		100.0				Total	100.0	100.0
					A	**LIABILITIES**		
34.8		4.8			V	Notes Payable-Short Term	7.6	11.7
.2		1.8			A	Cur. Mat.-L.T.D.	1.4	4.3
18.9		11.6			I	Trade Payables	13.3	8.1
.0		.0			L	Income Taxes Payable	.0	.0
12.7		35.2			A	All Other Current	27.4	26.8
66.6		53.4			B	Total Current	49.7	50.9
39.1		5.0			L	Long-Term Debt	19.8	17.1
.0		.0			E	Deferred Taxes	.3	.1
8.2		3.8				All Other Non-Current	6.2	8.4
-13.2		37.8				Net Worth	24.0	23.5
100.0		100.0				Total Liabilties & Net Worth	100.0	100.0
						INCOME DATA		
100.0		100.0				Net Sales	100.0	100.0
						Gross Profit		
98.5		96.3				Operating Expenses	91.4	90.1
1.5		3.7				Operating Profit	8.6	9.9
.4		.4				All Other Expenses (net)	.9	1.6
1.1		3.3				Profit Before Taxes	7.7	8.3
						RATIOS		
2.9		5.9					2.9	3.0
.7		3.5				Current	1.3	1.1
.4		.3					.9	.4
2.7		5.1					2.5	1.9
.5		2.0				Quick	1.0	.8
.2		.2					.5	.3
0 UND		**1** 317.4					**0** UND	**0** UND
1 636.6		**19** 19.1				Sales/Receivables	**8** 48.3	**8** 43.6
20 18.7		**26** 14.2					**34** 10.6	**35** 10.4
						Cost of Sales/Inventory		
						Cost of Sales/Payables		
48.2		3.5					7.3	5.8
-22.3		7.1				Sales/Working Capital	27.2	63.4
-11.8		-5.3					-79.7	-9.4
		265.8					102.9	49.5
		(11) 46.0				EBIT/Interest	(25) 12.1	(33) 8.7
		9.0					3.0	1.6
						Net Profit + Depr., Dep., Amort./Cur. Mat. L/T/D		
.0		.1					.0	.0
NM		.3				Fixed/Worth	.4	.7
-.6		-6.3					4.1	-.7
10.4		.3					.6	.6
-3.0		.8				Debt/Worth	1.8	2.3
-2.3		-9.8					-11.2	-3.1
							112.9	82.3
						% Profit Before Taxes/Tangible Net Worth	(29) 44.4	(29) 35.7
							9.2	3.6
34.8		50.6					30.8	28.5
8.7		11.7				% Profit Before Taxes/Total Assets	16.7	11.7
-7.4		-5.9					2.4	1.1
UND		288.5					417.1	217.4
37.9		33.1				Sales/Net Fixed Assets	66.8	50.7
10.6		8.0					13.5	5.5
10.0		4.3					5.5	3.6
7.4		2.5				Sales/Total Assets	3.1	2.7
3.5		2.0					1.8	1.2
							.3	.2
						% Depr., Dep., Amort./Sales	(24) .7	(29) .7
							1.5	3.7
								1.8
						% Officers', Directors' Owners' Comp/Sales		(12) 4.9
								13.1
17761M	**25221M**	**223870M**	**378474M**	**797710M**		Net Sales ($)	**1435546M**	**1025290M**
2117M	**10678M**	**76848M**	**180203M**	**204278M**		Total Assets ($)	**721861M**	**689181M**

M = $ thousand MM = $ million

See Pages viii through xx for Explanation of Ratios and Data

Comparative Historical Data			Type of Statement	Current Data Sorted by Sales					
10	5	6	Unqualified			1	1	3	1
2	1	2	Reviewed				1	1	1
2	2	4	Compiled		1		2	1	
9	9	11	Tax Returns	2	3	2	3	1	
26	30	19	Other	6	2			4	7
4/1/16-3/31/17 ALL	4/1/17-3/31/18 ALL	4/1/18-3/31/19 ALL		0-1MM	10 (4/1-9/30/18) 1-3MM	3-5MM	5-10MM	32 (10/1/18-3/31/19) 10-25MM	25MM & OVER
49	47	42	**NUMBER OF STATEMENTS**	8	6	3	6	10	9
%	%	%	**ASSETS**	%	%	%	%	%	%
34.5	30.4	24.3	Cash & Equivalents					25.8	
10.6	10.1	13.4	Trade Receivables (net)					15.2	
3.6	3.1	8.2	Inventory					8.0	
4.3	9.1	8.4	All Other Current					2.7	
52.9	52.8	54.3	Total Current					51.7	
18.8	19.1	20.4	Fixed Assets (net)					15.8	
12.3	11.7	13.4	Intangibles (net)					31.4	
15.9	16.5	12.0	All Other Non-Current					1.1	
100.0	100.0	100.0	Total					100.0	
			LIABILITIES						
6.5	9.3	14.8	Notes Payable-Short Term					11.0	
3.1	3.5	1.0	Cur. Mat.-L.T.D.					2.4	
7.3	10.4	13.7	Trade Payables					9.4	
.0	.0	.0	Income Taxes Payable					.0	
21.4	27.5	25.2	All Other Current					35.1	
38.2	50.8	54.7	Total Current					57.8	
12.3	15.0	16.6	Long-Term Debt					9.8	
.0	.1	.0	Deferred Taxes					.0	
7.4	9.5	5.1	All Other Non-Current					1.4	
42.1	24.6	23.7	Net Worth					31.0	
100.0	100.0	100.0	Total Liabilities & Net Worth					100.0	
			INCOME DATA						
100.0	100.0	100.0	Net Sales					100.0	
			Gross Profit						
91.0	90.8	96.2	Operating Expenses					98.2	
9.0	9.2	3.8	Operating Profit					1.8	
.3	1.4	1.4	All Other Expenses (net)					.9	
8.7	7.7	2.4	Profit Before Taxes					.9	
			RATIOS						
3.8 1.5 .7	4.8 1.3 .6	3.8 .9 .4	Current					5.0 1.4 .3	
3.3 1.3 .4	3.2 .9 .3	3.0 .5 .2	Quick					4.2 .9 .2	
1 695.3 9 42.5 27 13.3	0 UND 6 58.5 26 14.2	1 509.2 8 45.7 28 13.2	Sales/Receivables					2 229.2 19 18.8 29 12.5	
			Cost of Sales/Inventory						
			Cost of Sales/Payables						
5.4 23.2 -19.4	6.4 64.2 -16.1	5.5 UND -11.8	Sales/Working Capital					5.2 NM -4.5	
63.9 (35) 11.8 2.2	41.8 (32) 8.0 .8	63.1 (33) 6.6 -1.3	EBIT/Interest						
			Net Profit + Depr., Dep., Amort./Cur. Mat. L/T/D						
.0 .5 -8.6	.1 .6 -.8	.0 .5 -.6	Fixed/Worth					.1 NM .0	
.3 1.6 -12.8	.2 5.2 -5.4	.3 3.4 -2.5	Debt/Worth					.3 NM -1.3	
99.4 (35) 37.3 6.3	100.0 (31) 27.6 6.9	57.6 (25) 19.1 -1.8	% Profit Before Taxes/Tangible Net Worth						
38.5 9.3 2.2	22.4 10.6 .1	28.0 3.6 -4.6	% Profit Before Taxes/Total Assets					46.5 11.0 -8.9	
232.1 62.3 10.0	199.8 29.7 9.4	284.6 34.1 10.9	Sales/Net Fixed Assets					177.1 30.4 11.2	
3.9 2.2 1.2	5.3 2.3 1.4	4.8 2.8 1.8	Sales/Total Assets					4.0 2.5 1.4	
.3 (35) .7 2.9	.4 (27) .7 3.2	.3 (25) .8 2.9	% Depr., Dep., Amort./Sales						
1.6 (11) 5.6 15.6		2.4 (11) 5.4 13.5	% Officers', Directors' Owners' Comp/Sales						
1112225M 650222M	1260114M 628477M	1443036M 474124M	Net Sales ($) Total Assets ($)	3411M 4457M	9536M 7094M	10517M 3117M	45890M 29849M	171168M 110201M	1202514M 319406M

© RMA 2019

M = $ thousand   MM = $ million
See Pages viii through xx for Explanation of Ratios and Data

Current Data Sorted by Assets   **Comparative Historical Data**

0-500M	500M-2MM	2-10MM	10-50MM	50-100MM	100-250MM	Type of Statement	4/1/14-3/31/15 ALL	4/1/15-3/31/16 ALL
			1	3	2	Unqualified	9	6
	1	2	1		2	Reviewed	2	1
1	1	3	1	1	4	Compiled	1	3
9	4	3				Tax Returns	13	18
	1 (4/1-9/30/18)		38 (10/1/18-3/31/19)			Other	11	28
10	6	9	5	1	8	**NUMBER OF STATEMENTS**	36	56
%	%	%	%	%	%	**ASSETS**	%	%
36.7						Cash & Equivalents	39.4	31.5
10.3						Trade Receivables (net)	16.8	14.8
.0						Inventory	.9	2.5
10.2						All Other Current	5.2	4.2
57.2						Total Current	62.2	52.9
9.9						Fixed Assets (net)	14.5	14.5
11.8						Intangibles (net)	11.6	12.0
21.1						All Other Non-Current	11.7	20.6
100.0						Total	100.0	100.0
						LIABILITIES		
35.3						Notes Payable-Short Term	9.1	13.1
.0						Cur. Mat.-L.T.D.	11.6	1.1
7.5						Trade Payables	10.5	7.4
.1						Income Taxes Payable	.1	.0
34.5						All Other Current	15.5	21.2
77.3						Total Current	46.7	42.9
3.8						Long-Term Debt	25.3	23.9
.0						Deferred Taxes	.1	.1
.0						All Other Non-Current	11.8	11.5
18.9						Net Worth	16.0	21.6
100.0						Total Liabilities & Net Worth	100.0	100.0
						INCOME DATA		
100.0						Net Sales	100.0	100.0
						Gross Profit		
88.3						Operating Expenses	84.2	88.3
11.7						Operating Profit	15.8	11.7
-.5						All Other Expenses (net)	2.2	2.2
12.2						Profit Before Taxes	13.6	9.5
						RATIOS		
3.0							5.0	3.9
.8						Current	1.4	1.5
.4							.8	.7
2.7							4.6	3.8
.7						Quick	1.3	1.3
.1							.8	.4
0 UND							0 UND	0 UND
0 UND						Sales/Receivables	8 47.3	0 999.8
18 19.8							53 6.9	36 10.1
						Cost of Sales/Inventory		
						Cost of Sales/Payables		
60.9							5.5	4.9
NM						Sales/Working Capital	28.3	23.5
-8.3							-43.8	-52.5
							34.5	78.6
						EBIT/Interest	(22) 3.9	(36) 11.3
							.8	1.7
						Net Profit + Depr., Dep., Amort./Cur. Mat. L/T/D		
.0							.0	.0
.1						Fixed/Worth	.3	.5
NM							-1.8	-.8
.3							1.2	.4
1.5						Debt/Worth	4.6	5.5
-2.7							-4.6	-3.6
							348.4	238.3
						% Profit Before Taxes/Tangible Net Worth	(22) 56.4	(35) 78.5
							11.6	.9
111.5							74.1	71.6
44.1						% Profit Before Taxes/Total Assets	11.8	16.6
10.4							-.3	-1.5
UND							494.6	223.6
91.5						Sales/Net Fixed Assets	93.2	63.6
25.7							31.7	20.1
15.7							8.1	7.4
5.2						Sales/Total Assets	3.7	2.9
3.2							.8	1.6
							.3	.4
						% Depr., Dep., Amort./Sales	(21) .6	(30) .9
							1.4	2.6
							4.3	1.9
						% Officers', Directors' Owners' Comp/Sales	(10) 8.4	(22) 5.6
							15.7	25.1
27534M	38256M	67913M	295888M	44631M	2078428M	Net Sales ($)	685819M	1678300M
2509M	6222M	39833M	155447M	52083M	1397946M	Total Assets ($)	674871M	991687M

© RMA 2019

M = $ thousand   MM = $ million
See Pages viii through xx for Explanation of Ratios and Data

Comparative Historical Data | Current Data Sorted by Sales

	4/1/16-3/31/17 ALL	4/1/17-3/31/18 ALL	4/1/18-3/31/19 ALL	0-1MM	1-3MM	3-5MM	5-10MM	10-25MM	25MM & OVER
Type of Statement									
Unqualified	5	9	6		1			1	4
Reviewed	2	1	1					1	1
Compiled		1	5	1			2	1	2
Tax Returns	8	4	5		3		1		
Other	18	17	22	4	4		4	3	6

1 (4/1-9/30/18) spans 1-3MM / 3-5MM; 38 (10/1/18-3/31/19) spans 5-10MM / 10-25MM / 25MM & OVER

	4/1/16-3/31/17 ALL	4/1/17-3/31/18 ALL	4/1/18-3/31/19 ALL	0-1MM	1-3MM	3-5MM	5-10MM	10-25MM	25MM & OVER
NUMBER OF STATEMENTS	33	32	39	5	8		7	6	13
	%	%	%	%	%	%	%	%	%
ASSETS									
Cash & Equivalents	25.5	29.5	23.6						16.1
Trade Receivables (net)	20.6	14.0	15.4						16.2
Inventory	2.6	2.4	.1	DATA	NOT	AVAILABLE			.1
All Other Current	5.9	8.8	9.6						7.6
Total Current	54.6	54.7	48.6						40.0
Fixed Assets (net)	14.9	13.4	19.3						16.0
Intangibles (net)	18.6	14.0	14.0						25.7
All Other Non-Current	11.8	17.9	18.0						18.3
Total	100.0	100.0	100.0						100.0
LIABILITIES									
Notes Payable-Short Term	10.5	5.6	13.2						6.1
Cur. Mat.-L.T.D.	1.6	.8	.9						1.4
Trade Payables	10.3	7.4	11.5						11.0
Income Taxes Payable	.0	.0	.0						.0
All Other Current	12.8	21.4	19.8						18.0
Total Current	35.2	35.3	45.5						36.6
Long-Term Debt	18.9	28.8	23.3						42.8
Deferred Taxes	.2	.1	.1						.3
All Other Non-Current	6.1	6.6	7.0						18.8
Net Worth	39.5	29.3	24.2						1.5
Total Liabilities & Net Worth	100.0	100.0	100.0						100.0
INCOME DATA									
Net Sales	100.0	100.0	100.0						100.0
Gross Profit									
Operating Expenses	90.7	91.0	90.1						93.3
Operating Profit	9.3	9.0	9.9						6.7
All Other Expenses (net)	.9	2.3	2.1						1.4
Profit Before Taxes	8.5	6.7	7.9						5.3
RATIOS									
Current	5.5	3.2	2.5						2.3
	1.3	1.3	1.2						1.1
	.9	.8	.4						.8
Quick	5.3	2.8	2.0						2.3
	1.2	.9	.9						.9
	.6	.5	.3						.4
Sales/Receivables	2 148.1	0 UND	0 UND						0 UND
	24 15.3	2 206.6	6 56.5						10 35.7
	61 6.0	33 11.2	44 8.3						66 5.5
Cost of Sales/Inventory									
Cost of Sales/Payables									
Sales/Working Capital	2.6	6.9	14.5						14.5
	17.5	56.2	76.4						37.8
	-26.6	-32.9	-10.1						-19.4
EBIT/Interest	27.0	11.5	18.2						14.0
	(23) 6.3	(20) 8.5	(29) 6.2						2.4
	1.2	.2	1.0						-1.0
Net Profit + Depr., Dep., Amort./Cur. Mat. L/T/D									
Fixed/Worth	.1	.1	.0						2.5
	.9	1.6	.6						-.6
	-.2	-.3	-.6						-.2
Debt/Worth	.4	.6	.4						3.9
	6.9	16.5	3.9						-3.6
	-3.8	-4.7	-2.9						-2.2
% Profit Before Taxes/Tangible Net Worth	72.1	204.5	90.5						
	(18) 34.1	(19) 69.3	(25) 53.4						
	11.7	8.2	10.7						
% Profit Before Taxes/Total Assets	46.0	29.6	44.3						19.5
	7.3	10.2	13.7						2.7
	.9	1.4	1.0						-4.3
Sales/Net Fixed Assets	311.1	305.2	999.8						29.2
	52.0	65.8	30.3						14.0
	11.0	13.6	9.2						9.0
Sales/Total Assets	3.0	4.1	5.0						2.1
	1.8	2.4	2.1						1.6
	.7	1.0	1.2						1.2
% Depr., Dep., Amort./Sales	.4	.3	.3						
	(18) 1.7	(18) .9	(13) 1.3						
	4.6	2.9	9.2						
% Officers', Directors' Owners' Comp/Sales	3.6		2.2						
	(11) 7.6	(14)	8.6						
	15.6		20.0						
Net Sales ($)	1391120M	1850353M	2552650M	2824M	11562M		45931M	95939M	2396394M
Total Assets ($)	1127126M	877759M	1654040M	5242M	10715M		10927M	45845M	1581311M

© RMA 2019

M = $ thousand   MM = $ million
See Pages viii through xx for Explanation of Ratios and Data

Current Data Sorted by Assets

Comparative Historical Data

0-500M	500M-2MM	2-10MM	10-50MM	50-100MM	100-250MM	Type of Statement		4/1/14-3/31/15 ALL	4/1/15-3/31/16 ALL
			1		1	Unqualified		1	1
		1				Reviewed		1	3
2		1	2			Compiled		1	6
3	2	1				Tax Returns		6	13
8	6	2	1	3		Other		13	18
	1 (4/1-9/30/18)			33 (10/1/18-3/31/19)					
13	8	5	4	3	1	NUMBER OF STATEMENTS		22	41
%	%	%	%	%	%	ASSETS		%	%
33.8						Cash & Equivalents		34.9	27.2
.2						Trade Receivables (net)		7.3	11.7
3.3						Inventory		.4	5.6
10.0						All Other Current		3.4	1.2
47.4						Total Current		46.0	45.7
23.4						Fixed Assets (net)		32.7	34.0
7.9						Intangibles (net)		1.0	5.7
21.4						All Other Non-Current		20.2	14.5
100.0						Total		100.0	100.0
						LIABILITIES			
24.7						Notes Payable-Short Term		26.8	36.9
1.5						Cur. Mat.-L.T.D.		4.2	1.8
.8						Trade Payables		6.1	9.2
.0						Income Taxes Payable		.0	.1
58.5						All Other Current		21.4	28.1
85.5						Total Current		58.6	76.0
.0						Long-Term Debt		23.7	22.5
.0						Deferred Taxes		.0	.2
29.3						All Other Non-Current		6.2	7.1
-14.9						Net Worth		11.5	-5.8
100.0						Total Liabilties & Net Worth		100.0	100.0
						INCOME DATA			
100.0						Net Sales		100.0	100.0
						Gross Profit			
92.3						Operating Expenses		72.9	92.1
7.7						Operating Profit		27.1	7.9
.4						All Other Expenses (net)		4.1	1.5
7.3						Profit Before Taxes		23.0	6.4
						RATIOS			
2.7								2.4	2.1
.8						Current		1.0	.8
.2								.4	.3
2.1								2.3	1.6
.5						Quick		.6	.6
.1								.4	.2
0 UND							0 UND	0 UND	
0 UND						Sales/Receivables	0 UND	1 391.4	
0 UND							11 31.9	24 15.4	
						Cost of Sales/Inventory			
						Cost of Sales/Payables			
20.5								12.9	13.2
-27.7						Sales/Working Capital		NM	-320.3
-7.0								-10.4	-9.5
								99.0	20.7
						EBIT/Interest	(11)	21.3	(27) 2.5
								-1.6	-1.1
						Net'Profit + Depr., Dep., Amort./Cur. Mat. L/T/D			
.0								.0	.1
.6						Fixed/Worth		.3	1.1
-.5								-11.0	-5.6
.2								.3	.7
2.1						Debt/Worth		1.5	5.2
-2.1								-4.6	-4.2
						% Profit Before Taxes/Tangible Net Worth		124.1	144.8
							(14)	73.6	(26) 33.6
								18.1	6.6
63.2								119.5	36.7
28.8						% Profit Before Taxes/Total Assets		22.5	4.9
-8.1								3.5	-7.6
UND								211.2	723.8
28.4						Sales/Net Fixed Assets		22.2	15.1
9.3								8.9	3.4
9.2								11.6	12.6
4.7						Sales/Total Assets		3.0	2.7
1.7								.8	1.3
									1.8
						% Depr., Dep., Amort./Sales		(19)	3.4
									4.9
									4.4
						% Officers', Directors' Owners' Comp/Sales		(15)	14.6
									21.6
33389M	45244M	58162M	70570M	475400M	30754M	Net Sales ($)		206190M	886282M
3261M	9408M	22869M	55719M	250383M	249453M	Total Assets ($)		271261M	450103M

© RMA 2019

M = $ thousand   MM = $ million
See Pages viii through xx for Explanation of Ratios and Data

Comparative Historical Data | | Type of Statement | Current Data Sorted by Sales

Hist 1	Hist 2	Hist 3	Type of Statement	0-1MM	1-3MM	3-5MM	5-10MM	10-25MM	25MM & OVER
3	1	2	Unqualified					1	1
		1	Reviewed					1	1
2	2	5	Compiled	2		1	1	1	1
12	11	6	Tax Returns	4	1	2	1		1
24	23	20	Other	6	3		3	2	4
4/1/16- 3/31/17	4/1/17- 3/31/18	4/1/18- 3/31/19			1 (4/1-9/30/18)			33 (10/1/18-3/31/19)	
ALL	ALL	ALL							
41	37	34	**NUMBER OF STATEMENTS**	12	4	3	5	4	6
%	%	%	**ASSETS**	%	%	%	%	%	%
30.2	33.3	22.2	Cash & Equivalents	29.8					
7.2	13.2	6.0	Trade Receivables (net)	.3					
5.7	4.6	4.5	Inventory	2.8					
5.8	1.5	11.5	All Other Current	6.5					
48.9	52.6	44.1	Total Current	39.3					
33.5	25.3	32.0	Fixed Assets (net)	39.9					
4.8	5.7	7.9	Intangibles (net)	4.4					
12.8	16.4	16.0	All Other Non-Current	16.4					
100.0	100.0	100.0	Total	100.0					
			LIABILITIES						
8.4	7.8	14.3	Notes Payable-Short Term	26.8					
1.2	1.1	2.1	Cur. Mat.-L.T.D.	3.8					
6.1	6.2	4.6	Trade Payables	.3					
.9	.0	.0	Income Taxes Payable	.0					
29.2	28.2	26.5	All Other Current	34.9					
45.8	43.3	47.6	Total Current	65.8					
9.5	10.8	18.5	Long-Term Debt	12.7					
.3	.3	.0	Deferred Taxes	.0					
10.0	.4	16.9	All Other Non-Current	32.1					
34.5	45.2	16.9	Net Worth	-10.7					
100.0	100.0	100.0	Total Liabilities & Net Worth	100.0					
			INCOME DATA						
100.0	100.0	100.0	Net Sales	100.0					
			Gross Profit						
88.2	79.5	85.6	Operating Expenses	83.3					
11.8	20.5	14.4	Operating Profit	16.7					
2.4	1.0	3.2	All Other Expenses (net)	5.8					
9.5	19.5	11.2	Profit Before Taxes	10.9					
			RATIOS						
3.3	4.6	5.4		5.7					
1.1	.9	1.5	Current	1.0					
.6	.5	.6		.3					
2.2	4.3	4.5		5.6					
.9	.9	1.0	Quick	1.0					
.4	.4	.1		.0					
0 UND	0 UND	0 UND		0 UND					
0 UND	0 999.8	0 UND	Sales/Receivables	0 UND					
19 18.9	36 10.2	15 24.4		0 UND					
			Cost of Sales/Inventory						
			Cost of Sales/Payables						
12.2	7.1	5.5		3.5					
97.5	-118.5	42.7	Sales/Working Capital	NM					
-12.1	-16.2	-11.8		-3.4					
25.3	87.8	39.3							
(21) 7.2	(17) 9.1	(18) 4.1	EBIT/Interest						
.2	.5	1.0							
			Net Profit + Depr., Dep., Amort./Cur. Mat. L/T/D						
.1	.0	.1		.1					
.7	.3	.9	Fixed/Worth	1.2					
13.1	2.6	-9.9		-.8					
.3	.2	.3		.2					
1.7	1.5	1.2	Debt/Worth	1.3					
45.2	-17.8	-8.8		-4.2					
109.4	156.7	114.6							
(32) 38.9	(27) 94.9	(24) 46.3	% Profit Before Taxes/Tangible Net Worth						
2.4	35.3	6.7							
46.8	86.6	44.2		39.2					
8.3	30.8	7.4	% Profit Before Taxes/Total Assets	9.8					
.1	.4	.0		.1					
362.5	UND	325.8		33.9					
14.3	72.9	24.8	Sales/Net Fixed Assets	8.5					
2.6	3.5	2.9		.7					
8.9	6.6	5.9		3.6					
2.8	3.0	2.2	Sales/Total Assets	1.3					
1.1	1.5	1.1		.5					
1.0	.8	.5							
(15) 3.8	(10) 3.2	(16) 3.2	% Depr., Dep., Amort./Sales						
9.5	18.8	15.4							
2.1	4.0	3.6							
(14) 14.8	(12) 9.8	(13) 8.2	% Officers', Directors' Owners' Comp/Sales						
24.1	26.8	15.9							
656426M	587256M	713519M	Net Sales ($)	6558M	6467M	9547M	38663M	79800M	572484M
470612M	269155M	591093M	Total Assets ($)	21731M	5756M	2285M	20271M	19191M	521859M

© RMA 2019

M = $ thousand   MM = $ million
See Pages viii through xx for Explanation of Ratios and Data

Current Data Sorted by Assets   Comparative Historical Data

0-500M	500M-2MM	2-10MM	10-50MM	50-100MM	100-250MM	Type of Statement	4/1/14-3/31/15 ALL	4/1/15-3/31/16 ALL
1		11	24	13	4	Unqualified	86	86
		1				Reviewed	3	3
		1	1			Compiled	4	3
3	1	1	1			Tax Returns	3	6
3	6	4	12	8	6	Other	49	37
		55 (4/1-9/30/18)		46 (10/1/18-3/31/19)				
7	7	18	38	21	10	**NUMBER OF STATEMENTS**	145	135
%	%	%	%	%	%	**ASSETS**	%	%
		16.2	10.9	10.1	12.2	Cash & Equivalents	12.1	13.9
		2.2	2.8	1.8	3.9	Trade Receivables (net)	4.2	3.5
		1.0	.7	.2	.9	Inventory	2.4	1.1
		4.8	1.8	4.5	.6	All Other Current	1.2	1.6
		24.2	16.2	16.6	17.7	Total Current	19.9	20.1
		44.0	53.5	47.9	51.4	Fixed Assets (net)	55.7	50.7
		2.7	.5	1.9	.3	Intangibles (net)	.7	.4
		29.2	29.8	33.6	30.6	All Other Non-Current	23.7	28.7
		100.0	100.0	100.0	100.0	Total	100.0	100.0
						LIABILITIES		
		2.0	.8	.7	.8	Notes Payable-Short Term	3.1	1.8
		2.1	.6	1.2	.5	Cur. Mat.-L.T.D.	.6	.6
		3.7	1.3	1.3	1.6	Trade Payables	2.4	2.5
		.0	.0	.0	.0	Income Taxes Payable	.1	.1
		2.5	2.3	1.9	2.4	All Other Current	2.2	2.3
		10.3	5.0	5.2	5.3	Total Current	8.4	7.2
		9.6	8.0	12.7	7.4	Long-Term Debt	11.7	10.0
		.0	.0	.0	.0	Deferred Taxes	.0	.0
		1.9	3.6	1.1	1.9	All Other Non-Current	6.6	3.0
		78.2	83.5	81.0	85.4	Net Worth	73.3	79.7
		100.0	100.0	100.0	100.0	Total Liabilties & Net Worth	100.0	100.0
						INCOME DATA		
		100.0	100.0	100.0	100.0	Net Sales	100.0	100.0
						Gross Profit		
		96.3	98.4	97.1	86.9	Operating Expenses	93.0	98.8
		3.7	1.6	2.9	13.1	Operating Profit	7.0	1.2
		1.5	2.3	6.2	-1.8	All Other Expenses (net)	1.0	3.5
		2.2	-.7	-3.3	14.8	Profit Before Taxes	6.1	-2.3
						RATIOS		
		5.9	6.2	7.6	6.3		7.7	6.9
		2.2	2.6	3.5	2.8	Current	2.7	3.0
		.7	1.4	1.2	2.0		1.2	1.1
		3.8	5.5	6.3	4.8		6.8	5.6
		1.1	2.1	1.7	2.0	Quick	2.3	2.6
		.3	.9	.9	1.6		.9	.8
		(1) 409.4	(2) 211.0	(3) 143.4	(21) 17.8		(2) 175.6	(1) 258.5
		(7) 53.2	(9) 41.1	(17) 21.8	(45) 8.2	Sales/Receivables	(13) 28.5	(14) 26.2
		(25) 14.7	(27) 13.6	(46) 7.9	(69) 5.3		(48) 7.6	(45) 8.1
						Cost of Sales/Inventory		
						Cost of Sales/Payables		
		2.6	1.8	1.2	2.9		2.1	1.6
		8.8	4.7	2.5	4.2	Sales/Working Capital	4.7	4.5
		-10.6	20.9	33.2	7.9		49.6	29.9
		10.0	3.4	10.8			12.6	8.1
		(12) -7.7	(24) -2.7	(17) -.1		EBIT/Interest	(92) 1.4	(92) -2.3
		-61.2	-23.2	-4.4			-4.5	-18.6
						Net Profit + Depr., Dep., Amort./Cur. Mat. L/T/D		
		.3	.4	.4	.4		.4	.3
		.5	.6	.7	.6	Fixed/Worth	.8	.7
		.9	.9	.9	.8		1.0	1.0
		.1	.0	.1	.0		.0	.1
		.2	.1	.2	.1	Debt/Worth	.2	.1
		.4	.4	.4	.4		.5	.4
		8.6	4.6	2.6	7.4		9.4	6.0
		-1.4	-1.3	-1.3	3.2	% Profit Before Taxes/Tangible Net Worth	(138) 1.3	(133) -1.2
		-5.3	-6.1	-3.7	-.4		-3.2	-3.8
		6.9	3.6	2.5	7.3		6.1	4.8
		-1.3	-1.0	-1.1	2.7	% Profit Before Taxes/Total Assets	.6	-1.0
		-4.0	-4.9	-2.9	-.3		-2.7	-3.5
		3.1	1.0	1.0	1.0		1.2	1.3
		1.2	.5	.4	.5	Sales/Net Fixed Assets	.6	.5
		.7	.3	.2	.3		.3	.3
		.6	.4	.4	.4		.5	.5
		.5	.2	.2	.2	Sales/Total Assets	.3	.3
		.3	.2	.1	.1		.2	.1
		3.5	6.5	8.0			6.3	6.3
		(15) 7.0	(35) 12.5	(20) 12.5		% Depr., Dep., Amort./Sales	(128) 10.6	(118) 10.6
		15.6	19.9	19.4			17.0	18.8
						% Officers', Directors' Owners' Comp/Sales		
5576M	8298M	63629M	298615M	383399M	409119M	Net Sales ($)	1582494M	1639916M
1706M	7261M	116557M	981015M	1475635M	1366508M	Total Assets ($)	4717176M	6469564M

© RMA 2019

M = $ thousand   MM = $ million
See Pages viii through xx for Explanation of Ratios and Data

Comparative Historical Data			Type of Statement	Current Data Sorted by Sales					
64	51	53	Unqualified	1	12	8	15	13	4
5	2	1	Reviewed			1			
1	3	2	Compiled		1	1			
6	2	6	Tax Returns			3			
39	51	39	Other	3	7	2	8	8	8
4/1/16-3/31/17	4/1/17-3/31/18	4/1/18-3/31/19		6		55 (4/1-9/30/18)		46 (10/1/18-3/31/19)	
ALL	ALL	ALL		0-1MM	1-3MM	3-5MM	5-10MM	10-25MM	25MM & OVER
115	109	101	NUMBER OF STATEMENTS	10	20	15	23	21	12
%	%	%	ASSETS	%	%	%	%	%	%
13.8	20.5	15.7	Cash & Equivalents	31.1	20.8	10.5	14.7	11.0	10.9
3.7	3.3	3.4	Trade Receivables (net)	7.4	3.5	1.0	1.8	3.9	5.0
1.9	1.6	1.8	Inventory	10.6	.4	1.8	.4	.5	1.7
1.7	1.9	2.9	All Other Current	.2	4.3	4.1	1.2	2.0	6.4
21.1	27.3	23.8	Total Current	49.4	29.1	17.4	18.1	17.4	24.0
51.4	47.1	46.1	Fixed Assets (net)	25.2	46.0	53.2	49.7	47.6	45.4
.4	2.8	1.7	Intangibles (net)	6.0	.1	2.7	1.1	.2	3.1
27.0	22.8	28.4	All Other Non-Current	19.4	24.8	26.7	31.1	34.9	27.5
100.0	100.0	100.0	Total	100.0	100.0	100.0	100.0	100.0	100.0
			LIABILITIES						
1.3	1.9	2.3	Notes Payable-Short Term	13.7	1.4	.9	.9	1.0	.8
.8	1.1	1.0	Cur. Mat.-L.T.D.	.5	.5	3.0	.7	.8	.9
1.5	3.7	2.0	Trade Payables	1.5	1.8	1.7	2.6	1.7	2.2
.0	.0	.0	Income Taxes Payable	.0	.0	.0	.0	.0	.0
1.9	7.4	2.5	All Other Current	5.1	1.8	1.4	3.0	1.8	3.1
5.4	14.1	7.8	Total Current	20.8	5.6	7.1	7.1	5.4	6.9
8.4	11.6	8.5	Long-Term Debt	.0	5.1	18.5	10.0	5.8	10.4
.0	.0	.0	Deferred Taxes	.0	.0	.0	.0	.0	.0
4.0	4.1	6.0	All Other Non-Current	9.0	15.9	2.3	2.6	1.5	5.8
82.2	70.2	77.8	Net Worth	70.1	73.5	72.1	80.3	87.4	77.0
100.0	100.0	100.0	Total Liabilties & Net Worth	100.0	100.0	100.0	100.0	100.0	100.0
			INCOME DATA						
100.0	100.0	100.0	Net Sales	100.0	100.0	100.0	100.0	100.0	100.0
			Gross Profit						
96.2	87.4	95.3	Operating Expenses	93.5	102.0	90.4	104.5	90.0	83.1
3.8	12.6	4.7	Operating Profit	6.5	-2.0	9.6	-4.5	10.0	16.9
4.0	.6	2.2	All Other Expenses (net)	-.5	.9	3.3	2.9	2.0	4.4
-.2	12.0	2.5	Profit Before Taxes	7.1	-2.9	6.3	-7.3	8.0	12.5
			RATIOS						
8.8	8.7	7.1	Current	20.3	18.7	3.4	6.1	4.5	8.2
3.3	2.6	3.0		9.3	5.8	1.4	2.7	3.1	2.2
1.5	1.1	1.3		.6	1.4	.4	1.1	1.4	1.6
7.1	7.5	6.1	Quick	20.2	13.2	1.4	5.7	4.1	3.9
2.3	2.1	2.1		4.2	4.6	1.1	2.3	2.1	1.7
1.0	.9	.9		.6	1.2	.2	1.0	1.0	1.5
1 343.1	0 UND	2 225.2	Sales/Receivables	0 UND	0 UND	0 UND	5 69.5	8 46.4	13 28.8
10 35.1	6 60.5	11 32.5		0 UND	9 41.3	2 196.7	9 39.1	19 19.3	30 12.1
45 8.2	32 11.3	44 8.3		51 7.2	27 13.3	12 31.4	48 7.6	52 7.0	61 6.0
			Cost of Sales/Inventory						
			Cost of Sales/Payables						
1.6	1.4	1.8	Sales/Working Capital	3.1	1.2	12.5	1.4	1.7	2.2
4.5	4.9	4.4		6.7	2.6	18.0	3.3	4.1	4.2
17.5	67.4	23.6		9.1	12.6	-6.1	24.9	20.0	10.7
13.7	26.3	9.4	EBIT/Interest		.0	12.4	-.2	12.2	
(72) .0	(67) 4.8	(66) -.4		(12) -7.7	(11) 3.5	(14) -2.7	(15) .1		
-7.4	-.2	-11.3		-15.6	-4.2	-22.2	-5.2		
			Net Profit + Depr., Dep., Amort./Cur. Mat. L/T/D						
.3	.2	.4	Fixed/Worth	.0	.4	.3	.4	.3	.3
.7	.7	.6		.4	.0	.6	.6	.6	.6
.9	1.2	.9		.8	.8	1.5	.9	.8	1.0
.0	.0	.0	Debt/Worth	.0	.0	.1	.1	.0	.0
.1	.2	.2		.2	.1	.2	.1	.1	.3
.4	.7	.4		1.9	.2	.8	.5	.3	.8
5.8	11.0	6.4	% Profit Before Taxes/Tangible Net Worth	23.4	3.6	64.6	1.2	6.4	18.3
(114) .0	(101) 3.7	(100) -.1		5.5	(19) -2.0	3.3	-1.5	.9	4.8
-3.2	-1.0	-3.8		-.7	-3.8	-6.0	-5.8	-3.0	-1.4
4.6	10.2	5.2	% Profit Before Taxes/Total Assets	9.0	3.6	16.2	1.1	5.6	10.8
.0	3.6	-.1		4.8	-1.9	2.2	-1.4	.7	3.6
2.5	-.9	-3.3		-.6	-3.6	-4.2	-4.7	-2.7	-1.1
1.2	2.0	2.4	Sales/Net Fixed Assets	302.8	1.3	2.4	.8	1.7	2.8
.5	.7	.7		24.9	.4	1.1	.5	.5	1.0
.3	.4	.3		2.8	.3	.3	.2	.3	.5
.4	.6	.6	Sales/Total Assets	3.4	.5	.6	.4	.4	.8
.2	.3	.3		1.1	.3	.4	.2	.3	.5
.1	.2	.2		.6	.2	.2	.1	.2	.3
5.7	3.1	6.0	% Depr., Dep., Amort./Sales		14.2	3.4	6.7	5.9	3.5
(91) 11.2	(82) 8.0	(86) 9.7		(15) 18.0	(14) 6.9	(20) 14.0	(19) 8.6	7.7	
18.7	13.3	18.4		26.5	14.7	19.7	16.3	12.0	
			% Officers', Directors' Owners' Comp/Sales						
1324622M	1334809M	1168636M	Net Sales ($)	5069M	44061M	59815M	175996M	306173M	577522M
5288719M	4441287M	3948682M	Total Assets ($)	5672M	232290M	202087M	917823M	1323838M	1266972M

Current Data Sorted by Assets   Comparative Historical Data

Type of Statement					
	2-10MM	10-50MM	50-100MM	100-250MM	
Unqualified	2	8	3	4	
Reviewed			1		
Compiled	1	1			
Tax Returns	1				
Other	1	4	1	4	

Comparative Historical: Unqualified 15 / 18; Reviewed — / 1; Compiled — / 2; Tax Returns 1 / 1; Other 7 / 7
Dates: 4/1/14-3/31/15 ALL; 4/1/15-3/31/16 ALL

	0-500M	500M-2MM	2-10MM	9 (4/1-9/30/18) / 22 (10/1/18-3/31/19) 10-50MM	50-100MM	100-250MM		4/1/14-3/31/15 ALL	4/1/15-3/31/16 ALL
NUMBER OF STATEMENTS			5	13	5	8		22	29
	%	%	%	%	%	%		%	%
ASSETS									
Cash & Equivalents	D	D		24.1				23.2	16.9
Trade Receivables (net)	A	A		1.1				6.6	2.8
Inventory	T	T		.5				.3	.6
All Other Current	A	A		6.6				2.1	3.8
Total Current				32.4				32.3	24.1
Fixed Assets (net)	N	N		47.7				56.1	60.0
Intangibles (net)	O	O		.0				.1	.3
All Other Non-Current	T	T		20.0				11.4	15.5
Total				100.0				100.0	100.0
LIABILITIES	A	A							
Notes Payable-Short Term	V	V		1.3				.5	.5
Cur. Mat.-L.T.D.	A	A		.5				1.5	1.0
Trade Payables	I	I		2.2				4.1	3.5
Income Taxes Payable	L	L		.0				.0	.0
All Other Current	A	A		3.9				5.1	2.7
Total Current	B	B		7.9				11.3	7.7
Long-Term Debt	L	L		12.3				13.7	24.1
Deferred Taxes	E	E		.0				.0	.1
All Other Non-Current				3.4				2.6	4.1
Net Worth				76.5				72.3	64.0
Total Liabilities & Net Worth				100.0				100.0	100.0
INCOME DATA									
Net Sales				100.0				100.0	100.0
Gross Profit									
Operating Expenses				88.2				89.6	86.4
Operating Profit				11.8				10.4	13.6
All Other Expenses (net)				2.4				4.3	7.3
Profit Before Taxes				9.4				6.1	6.3
RATIOS									
Current				12.0				7.3	6.7
				6.0				2.3	2.9
				2.8				1.4	1.6
Quick				9.9				6.2	6.5
				4.6				2.1	2.3
				1.5				1.3	1.2
Sales/Receivables				0 UND				4 99.2	0 UND
				2 164.1				15 23.9	6 60.7
				11 31.8				42 8.7	17 21.9
Cost of Sales/Inventory									
Cost of Sales/Payables									
Sales/Working Capital				.7				2.3	2.0
				1.7				5.0	5.1
				4.0				15.8	13.3
EBIT/Interest								37.9	10.0
								(14) 11.1	(20) 5.7
								-.7	.6
Net Profit + Depr., Dep., Amort./Cur. Mat. L/T/D									
Fixed/Worth				.2				.3	.6
				.8				.8	.9
				1.1				1.2	1.6
Debt/Worth				.1				.1	.1
				.2				.3	.3
				.4				.8	1.2
% Profit Before Taxes/Tangible Net Worth				14.1				12.3	8.1
				6.0				3.5	(26) 2.0
				-.8				.7	-.3
% Profit Before Taxes/Total Assets				7.0				7.3	7.8
				4.8				3.4	2.0
				-.5				.4	-.1
Sales/Net Fixed Assets				6.4				6.4	2.5
				.7				.5	.7
				.5				.3	.4
Sales/Total Assets				.8				.9	1.0
				.4				.4	.5
				.2				.2	.3
% Depr., Dep., Amort./Sales				2.1				1.5	2.9
			(12)	7.6				(20) 9.3	(25) 9.6
				10.9				12.1	15.0
% Officers', Directors' Owners' Comp/Sales									
Net Sales ($)			33004M	192183M	98234M	348615M		470808M	672537M
Total Assets ($)			29930M	401334M	321578M	1413531M		1424330M	1960657M

M = $ thousand   MM = $ million
See Pages viii through xx for Explanation of Ratios and Data

Comparative Historical Data | **Current Data Sorted by Sales**

4/1/16-3/31/17 ALL	4/1/17-3/31/18 ALL	4/1/18-3/31/19 ALL		0-1MM	1-3MM	3-5MM	5-10MM	10-25MM	25MM & OVER
			Type of Statement						
19	20	17	Unqualified		1	2	3	3	8
		1	Reviewed					1	
	1	2	Compiled		1			1	
1	2	1	Tax Returns					1	
10	7	10	Other		1	1	2	4	2
				9 (4/1-9/30/18)		22 (10/1/18-3/31/19)			
30	30	31	**NUMBER OF STATEMENTS**		3	3	5	10	10
%	%	%	**ASSETS**	%	%	%	%	%	%
24.6	27.4	21.4	Cash & Equivalents	D				28.1	18.5
2.1	2.2	2.0	Trade Receivables (net)	A				1.3	4.4
.6	1.8	.9	Inventory	T				1.5	.3
2.8	2.6	4.9	All Other Current	A				5.1	3.0
30.0	34.0	29.2	Total Current					36.1	26.3
56.7	49.1	56.4	Fixed Assets (net)	N				48.8	55.8
.6	.7	.2	Intangibles (net)	O				.1	.0
12.6	16.3	14.1	All Other Non-Current	T				15.0	17.9
100.0	100.0	100.0	Total					100.0	100.0
			LIABILITIES	A					
2.4	.9	1.0	Notes Payable-Short Term	V				1.1	1.6
1.2	1.1	.7	Cur. Mat.-L.T.D.	A				.8	.3
3.8	4.0	2.2	Trade Payables	I				2.3	2.5
.0	.0	.0	Income Taxes Payable	L				.0	.0
4.8	5.7	3.4	All Other Current	A				4.1	2.9
12.2	11.7	7.3	Total Current	B				8.3	7.4
7.9	10.6	12.8	Long-Term Debt	L				17.0	7.2
.0	.0	.0	Deferred Taxes	E				.0	.0
2.3	3.2	2.4	All Other Non-Current					2.3	1.1
77.6	74.5	77.5	Net Worth					72.4	84.4
100.0	100.0	100.0	Total Liabilties & Net Worth					100.0	100.0
			INCOME DATA						
100.0	100.0	100.0	Net Sales					100.0	100.0
			Gross Profit						
92.5	88.6	90.5	Operating Expenses					84.7	91.9
7.5	11.4	9.5	Operating Profit					15.3	8.1
1.5	-3.2	1.7	All Other Expenses (net)					5.5	2.0
6.0	14.6	7.8	Profit Before Taxes					9.9	6.1
			RATIOS						
9.3	7.6	10.3						11.2	5.4
2.9	2.5	4.2	Current					2.8	4.0
1.2	1.3	1.9						1.2	1.8
8.7	7.1	9.0						10.3	5.0
2.7	2.4	4.2	Quick					2.3	3.3
.9	1.1	1.7						.4	1.6
1 468.3	**1** 330.2	**0** UND						**0** UND	**7** 51.7
6 56.3	**7** 55.4	**5** 76.5	Sales/Receivables					**3** 136.4	**12** 29.6
18 20.3	**21** 17.7	**14** 26.6						**11** 32.0	**27** 13.5
			Cost of Sales/Inventory						
			Cost of Sales/Payables						
1.8	1.6	.8						.5	1.5
5.3	5.2	3.2	Sales/Working Capital					4.0	3.3
23.6	11.9	7.8						NM	10.6
34.8	91.6	42.4							
(22) 6.2	(19) 16.8	(23) 9.5	EBIT/Interest						
-2.5	3.3	3.2							
			Net Profit + Depr., Dep., Amort./Cur. Mat. L/T/D						
.5	.3	.5						.4	.3
.8	.8	.8	Fixed/Worth					.7	.8
1.1	1.0	1.1						1.1	1.1
.1	.1	.1						.1	.1
.2	.2	.3	Debt/Worth					.3	.2
.5	.5	.4						.6	.4
11.0	23.4	9.3						24.5	8.6
3.7	(29) 6.7	3.5	% Profit Before Taxes/Tangible Net Worth					6.0	2.7
-2.4	3.0	-.5						-1.1	-2.1
8.6	18.4	7.6						11.2	7.6
2.8	5.8	2.9	% Profit Before Taxes/Total Assets					5.1	2.0
-2.0	1.8	.4						-.7	-1.6
2.7	5.7	1.4						7.0	3.5
.6	1.2	.6	Sales/Net Fixed Assets					.7	.5
.5	.5	.4						.5	.4
.8	1.3	.6						.8	.6
.4	.5	.3	Sales/Total Assets					.4	.4
.3	.3	.2						.2	.2
4.1	2.3	4.4							1.4
(25) 11.2	(28) 5.7	(28) 10.0	% Depr., Dep., Amort./Sales						12.7
12.5	10.0	15.9							17.0
			% Officers', Directors' Owners' Comp/Sales						
663501M	680607M	672036M	Net Sales ($)		6289M	12883M	38954M	185905M	428005M
1831886M	1572153M	2166373M	Total Assets ($)		32413M	32174M	188931M	651839M	1261016M

M = $ thousand MM = $ million

See Pages viii through xx for Explanation of Ratios and Data

ENTERTAINMENT—Amusement and Theme Parks NAICS 713110

Current Data Sorted by Assets | **Comparative Historical Data**

Type of Statement

0-500M	500M-2MM	2-10MM	10-50MM	50-100MM	100-250MM	Type of Statement	ALL 4/1/14-3/31/15	ALL 4/1/15-3/31/16
		3	5	4	2	Unqualified	11	16
		2	4	2		Reviewed	8	8
3		1	2			Compiled	10	8
3	4	1	1			Tax Returns	25	12
3	4	5	16	3	1	Other	32	24
	10 (4/1-9/30/18)		58 (10/1/18-3/31/19)					
9	8	11	28	9	3	**NUMBER OF STATEMENTS**	86	68

0-500M	500M-2MM	2-10MM	10-50MM	50-100MM	100-250MM		ALL 4/1/14-3/31/15	ALL 4/1/15-3/31/16
%	%	%	%	%	%	**ASSETS**	%	%
		10.4	16.1			Cash & Equivalents	15.6	18.4
		3.3	2.6			Trade Receivables (net)	4.1	1.8
		7.4	4.9			Inventory	6.3	4.5
		1.4	1.6			All Other Current	3.4	1.5
		22.6	25.1			Total Current	29.4	26.1
		63.8	64.1			Fixed Assets (net)	57.7	64.7
		7.6	4.2			Intangibles (net)	5.1	2.6
		5.9	6.6			All Other Non-Current	7.8	6.5
		100.0	100.0			Total	100.0	100.0
						LIABILITIES		
		.5	2.6			Notes Payable-Short Term	5.1	4.1
		6.6	5.0			Cur. Mat.-L.T.D.	4.3	4.8
		3.1	2.7			Trade Payables	5.7	3.6
		.0	.2			Income Taxes Payable	.1	.1
		15.2	6.7			All Other Current	15.7	17.1
		25.4	17.2			Total Current	30.9	29.8
		45.4	34.5			Long-Term Debt	32.3	33.9
		1.9	.4			Deferred Taxes	1.0	.9
		1.9	6.9			All Other Non-Current	20.2	8.2
		25.4	41.0			Net Worth	15.6	27.2
		100.0	100.0			Total Liabilities & Net Worth	100.0	100.0
						INCOME DATA		
		100.0	100.0			Net Sales	100.0	100.0
						Gross Profit		
		76.4	89.4			Operating Expenses	85.3	85.8
		23.6	10.6			Operating Profit	14.7	14.2
		9.1	3.4			All Other Expenses (net)	1.9	3.3
		14.5	7.2			Profit Before Taxes	12.8	10.9
						RATIOS		
		1.8	2.7			Current	2.5	2.7
		.4	1.7				1.3	.9
		.3	.5				.4	.4
		1.7	2.2			Quick	1.9	2.1
		.3	1.0				.7	.6
		.1	.2				.2	.3
		0 999.8	0 999.8			Sales/Receivables	0 UND	0 UND
		2 218.7	3 134.8				1 455.4	0 987.0
		4 100.1	5 69.8				6 58.3	3 119.0
						Cost of Sales/Inventory		
						Cost of Sales/Payables		
		6.5	6.2			Sales/Working Capital	11.1	7.4
		-12.4	22.7				60.0	-30.1
		-7.4	-8.4				-8.5	-7.9
			6.6			EBIT/Interest	16.5	12.6
			(26) 3.5				(68) 5.2	(50) 6.3
			-.1				1.9	1.7
						Net Profit + Depr., Dep., Amort./Cur. Mat. L/T/D		6.0
							(10)	2.7
								2.2
		1.3	1.3			Fixed/Worth	.8	.9
		2.4	1.8				2.5	1.8
		-15.9	4.4				-8.3	4.4
		.9	.7			Debt/Worth	.7	.7
		2.1	1.5				3.1	1.6
		-17.1	5.1				-7.9	7.2
			28.6			% Profit Before Taxes/Tangible Net Worth	58.2	52.1
			(26) 16.2				(60) 27.8	(56) 30.5
			-6.5				9.4	10.1
		20.6	11.3			% Profit Before Taxes/Total Assets	25.9	23.7
		8.7	5.9				8.9	11.2
		2.2	-1.7				3.5	1.8
		4.1	2.9			Sales/Net Fixed Assets	7.4	4.5
		2.4	1.3				2.6	1.8
		.3	.6				.8	.9
		2.1	1.5			Sales/Total Assets	2.9	2.3
		1.6	.9				1.3	1.3
		.3	.5				.7	.7
		5.0	4.4			% Depr., Dep., Amort./Sales	4.1	5.3
		(10) 7.5	(27) 12.2				(67) 7.3	(53) 7.8
		20.5	16.3				12.0	11.7
						% Officers', Directors' Owners' Comp/Sales	3.9	3.5
							(30) 6.0	(13) 8.4
							10.3	22.3
13129M	23504M	73261M	811523M	362686M	284417M	Net Sales ($)	1520750M	1455059M
2803M	9055M	56250M	750139M	605488M	504855M	Total Assets ($)	1979686M	1735164M

© RMA 2019

M = $ thousand   MM = $ million
See Pages viii through xx for Explanation of Ratios and Data

Comparative Historical Data | Current Data Sorted by Sales

Type of Statement	4/1/16-3/31/17 ALL	4/1/17-3/31/18 ALL	4/1/18-3/31/19 ALL	0-1MM	1-3MM	3-5MM	5-10MM	10-25MM	25MM & OVER
					10 (4/1-9/30/18)		58 (10/1/18-3/31/19)		
Unqualified	7	12	11				3	3	8
Reviewed	5	11	9					4	2
Compiled	5	7	7	3	1	1	2		2
Tax Returns	23	13	9	4	2	1			
Other	29	26	32	2	4	3	5	8	10
NUMBER OF STATEMENTS	69	69	68	9	7	5	10	15	22
ASSETS	%	%	%	%	%	%	%	%	%
Cash & Equivalents	13.3	16.6	13.0				13.2	13.5	13.7
Trade Receivables (net)	2.3	2.1	2.9				7.6	.8	3.1
Inventory	2.3	4.5	3.7				7.6	1.6	5.8
All Other Current	2.2	1.3	1.4				3.5	1.3	1.3
Total Current	20.2	24.5	20.9				31.8	17.2	23.9
Fixed Assets (net)	64.4	61.9	67.1				52.2	69.8	67.9
Intangibles (net)	2.6	6.8	4.2				6.8	5.4	2.0
All Other Non-Current	12.8	6.8	7.7				9.2	7.6	6.1
Total	100.0	100.0	100.0				100.0	100.0	100.0
LIABILITIES									
Notes Payable-Short Term	5.8	6.2	2.8				.0	.2	4.0
Cur. Mat.-L.T.D.	4.2	3.3	4.9				3.9	4.4	6.7
Trade Payables	2.1	2.8	3.2				4.4	2.8	3.4
Income Taxes Payable	.0	.3	.1				.0	.4	.1
All Other Current	16.1	19.7	9.6				11.9	5.8	8.3
Total Current	28.3	32.3	20.6				20.2	13.7	22.5
Long-Term Debt	31.1	41.7	33.2				28.1	48.0	19.1
Deferred Taxes	.6	.9	.6				1.0	1.0	.7
All Other Non-Current	5.8	3.2	6.2				7.9	6.5	2.7
Net Worth	34.2	21.9	39.4				42.8	30.9	55.0
Total Liabilties & Net Worth	100.0	100.0	100.0				100.0	100.0	100.0
INCOME DATA									
Net Sales	100.0	100.0	100.0				100.0	100.0	100.0
Gross Profit									
Operating Expenses	84.5	82.9	86.4				89.1	91.9	86.3
Operating Profit	15.5	17.1	13.6				10.9	8.1	13.7
All Other Expenses (net)	2.5	5.0	3.4				1.3	5.4	.7
Profit Before Taxes	13.0	12.1	10.2				9.6	2.8	13.0
RATIOS									
Current	2.1 .9 .3	2.5 .7 .3	2.1 .8 .4				4.7 1.3 .3	2.2 1.0 .5	2.0 .8 .3
Quick	1.7 .7 .2	2.3 .6 .2	1.8 .6 .2				2.7 .5 .2	2.0 .7 .2	1.8 .5 .2
Sales/Receivables	0 UND 0 905.8 4 92.2	0 UND 1 485.6 5 71.2	0 UND 1 276.5 4 85.9				0 UND 3 121.7 6 63.9	0 999.8 1 260.1 3 126.4	0 UND 3 116.3 6 58.6
Cost of Sales/Inventory									
Cost of Sales/Payables									
Sales/Working Capital	13.7 -75.8 -8.1	8.0 -81.2 -7.1	9.0 -71.0 -8.0				3.4 NM -7.0	6.5 999.8 -14.7	8.8 -77.9 -5.5
EBIT/Interest	14.5 (54) 4.9 2.5	11.0 (54) 4.1 1.2	10.7 (53) 4.1 .8					6.4 (19) 3.8 .1	47.4 10.2 2.9
Net Profit + Depr., Dep., Amort./Cur. Mat. L/T/D		9.4 (12) 3.1 1.5	7.4 (10) 2.8 .6						
Fixed/Worth	.9 1.6 4.3	1.2 2.1 17.8	1.2 1.8 4.8				.1 1.5 2.8	1.7 2.0 7.8	.7 1.6 2.2
Debt/Worth	.5 1.4 9.5	.7 1.7 113.4	.7 1.3 5.1				.6 1.2 4.4	.8 4.9 8.4	.4 1.2 1.6
% Profit Before Taxes/Tangible Net Worth	46.2 (55) 25.1 10.9	39.6 (53) 25.6 6.5	55.3 (61) 25.8 .9					52.9 (13) 27.5 -8.7	28.2 22.1 5.7
% Profit Before Taxes/Total Assets	21.4 11.5 3.9	20.7 8.2 1.6	16.9 8.7 1.3				17.2 8.3 -1.0	11.6 7.3 -3.1	15.6 8.8 3.0
Sales/Net Fixed Assets	5.8 1.6 .8	5.4 1.7 .7	4.9 1.7 .6				105.1 2.4 .7	2.3 1.0 .3	3.4 1.3 .7
Sales/Total Assets	2.2 1.0 .6	2.1 1.2 .6	2.1 1.1 .5				1.9 1.2 .5	1.4 .6 .3	1.8 1.1 .6
% Depr., Dep., Amort./Sales	2.8 (59) 7.5 11.5	5.5 (59) 8.3 12.4	6.0 (57) 10.9 14.9					4.4 12.2 29.9	5.5 8.6 13.1
% Officers', Directors' Owners' Comp/Sales	3.8 (17) 5.7 7.8	1.4 (15) 5.1 8.4	1.6 (10) 6.6 9.8						
Net Sales ($)	1435053M	1329146M	1568520M	6355M	12381M	21344M	78855M	223258M	1226327M
Total Assets ($)	1746486M	1468063M	1928590M	16786M	8778M	17445M	90054M	433179M	1362348M

M = $ thousand   MM = $ million
See Pages viii through xx for Explanation of Ratios and Data

Current Data Sorted by Assets | Comparative Historical Data

	0-500M	500M-2MM	2-10MM	10-50MM	50-100MM	100-250MM	Type of Statement	4/1/14-3/31/15 ALL	4/1/15-3/31/16 ALL
		1	7	5	10	8	Unqualified	30	27
			3	1			Reviewed	2	2
			1	1			Compiled	3	1
	1		3	1			Tax Returns	21	18
	6	10	1	9	3	13	Other	34	32
		18 (4/1-9/30/18)		66 (10/1/18-3/31/19)					
	0-500M	500M-2MM	2-10MM	10-50MM	50-100MM	100-250MM	NUMBER OF STATEMENTS	90	80
	7	11	15	17	13	21			

	0-500M	500M-2MM	2-10MM	10-50MM	50-100MM	100-250MM		ALL	ALL
	%	%	%	%	%	%	**ASSETS**	%	%
		39.1	38.9	32.0	17.0	13.6	Cash & Equivalents	21.3	25.6
		.7	1.3	1.2	1.9	1.0	Trade Receivables (net)	1.2	1.4
		1.1	2.0	.8	.7	.5	Inventory	1.8	1.6
		7.5	.9	3.1	2.0	1.3	All Other Current	1.6	1.7
		48.3	43.1	37.1	21.6	16.4	Total Current	25.9	30.4
		32.0	48.6	50.7	73.8	71.3	Fixed Assets (net)	53.7	56.2
		14.3	4.5	8.9	2.1	11.0	Intangibles (net)	11.8	6.6
		5.4	3.8	3.2	2.6	1.3	All Other Non-Current	8.6	6.9
		100.0	100.0	100.0	100.0	100.0	Total	100.0	100.0
							LIABILITIES		
		.5	1.2	.3	.6	.8	Notes Payable-Short Term	3.4	2.8
		2.6	1.2	3.0	3.0	4.1	Cur. Mat.-L.T.D.	10.0	7.6
		4.3	6.1	4.9	3.4	2.6	Trade Payables	7.3	5.9
		.0	.0	.0	.0	.1	Income Taxes Payable	.1	.0
		18.8	18.2	9.7	7.9	7.2	All Other Current	13.5	18.3
		26.2	26.7	18.0	14.8	14.8	Total Current	34.4	34.6
		15.4	3.7	20.2	22.9	33.0	Long-Term Debt	34.5	36.2
		.0	.0	.1	.0	.0	Deferred Taxes	.2	.0
		6.3	4.2	1.7	.5	3.2	All Other Non-Current	3.4	3.3
		52.1	65.4	60.1	61.8	49.1	Net Worth	27.6	25.8
		100.0	100.0	100.0	100.0	100.0	Total Liabilties & Net Worth	100.0	100.0
							INCOME DATA		
		100.0	100.0	100.0	100.0	100.0	Net Sales	100.0	100.0
							Gross Profit		
		87.7	76.5	78.8	72.1	77.1	Operating Expenses	86.0	80.0
		12.3	23.5	21.2	27.9	22.9	Operating Profit	14.0	20.0
		2.3	12.7	4.1	4.2	2.9	All Other Expenses (net)	3.1	2.6
		10.0	10.8	17.1	23.7	20.0	Profit Before Taxes	10.9	17.4
							RATIOS		
		6.6	4.8	4.2	2.1	1.5		2.6	2.2
		1.6	1.7	2.4	1.4	1.3	Current	1.1	1.2
		1.0	.9	1.3	1.0	.9		.6	.6
		6.5	4.2	3.7	1.9	1.3		2.3	2.2
		1.4	1.3	2.3	1.4	1.0	Quick	1.0	1.1
		.8	.9	1.3	1.0	.8		.5	.5
	0 UND	0 UND	1 639.8	2 185.3	1 301.7			0 UND	0 UND
	0 UND	1 304.3	2 222.4	5 71.3	3 109.0		Sales/Receivables	1 356.4	1 352.4
	0 UND	2 211.4	4 81.2	8 43.0	5 76.1			3 118.0	4 88.3
							Cost of Sales/Inventory		
							Cost of Sales/Payables		
		14.9	5.7	3.7	8.1	20.0		11.9	13.4
		88.0	19.6	7.0	23.4	29.2	Sales/Working Capital	127.4	78.3
		-621.8	-107.4	NM	NM	-57.2		-18.8	-15.6
				63.0	142.5	27.3		13.9	27.6
			(13) 7.3	(10) 43.0	(20) 14.3		EBIT/Interest	(71) 5.7	(65) 10.8
				2.7	7.7	3.4		1.7	3.3
							Net Profit + Depr., Dep., Amort./Cur. Mat. L/T/D		
		.1	.4	.5	.9	1.0		.8	.8
		.6	.9	.9	1.1	2.0	Fixed/Worth	1.9	1.7
		2.0	1.4	1.8	2.4	5.4		-6.1	-14.6
		.1	.2	.1	.2	.3		.4	.3
		.6	.4	.8	.3	1.5	Debt/Worth	1.9	1.4
		1.1	1.3	1.4	2.0	5.7		-7.3	-21.4
		114.4	101.3	56.4	76.5	54.4	% Profit Before Taxes/Tangible Net Worth	72.6	82.8
		(10) 41.4	11.2	(15) 24.3	51.1	(18) 31.3		(63) 31.3	(57) 42.9
		19.1	-5.6	9.5	27.4	11.1		9.9	21.2
		51.9	42.9	32.4	43.1	24.8	% Profit Before Taxes/Total Assets	31.3	43.7
		17.7	9.3	19.9	25.2	18.8		11.7	18.2
		.6	-3.7	3.0	16.8	6.0		2.8	6.5
		64.2	8.0	5.4	2.3	1.5	Sales/Net Fixed Assets	13.9	12.4
		21.7	5.3	3.4	1.5	1.2		2.8	2.2
		11.1	2.6	1.3	1.1	1.0		1.4	1.2
		9.0	3.9	2.1	1.5	1.1	Sales/Total Assets	3.2	3.4
		6.7	2.3	1.3	1.2	.9		1.5	1.2
		4.4	1.4	.9	.9	.7		.9	.8
		.5	1.3	2.3	4.7	6.4	% Depr., Dep., Amort./Sales	2.0	1.7
		(10) .9	(14) 1.9	(16) 4.4	7.0	(11) 7.3		(68) 5.3	(61) 5.3
		2.0	3.3	7.5	8.0	9.5		7.8	8.4
							% Officers', Directors' Owners' Comp/Sales		
	32524M	79229M	210310M	719209M	1296930M	3182857M	Net Sales ($)	5789045M	5344487M
	1920M	11997M	83408M	469054M	1006298M	3500414M	Total Assets ($)	4927874M	4928359M

© RMA 2019

M = $ thousand   MM = $ million
See Pages viii through xx for Explanation of Ratios and Data

Comparative Historical Data | Current Data Sorted by Sales

Type of Statement groupings — Historical columns: ALL. Current columns grouped as **18 (4/1-9/30/18)** spanning 0-1MM / 1-3MM / 3-5MM, and **66 (10/1/18-3/31/19)** spanning 5-10MM / 10-25MM / 25MM & OVER.

4/1/16-3/31/17 ALL	4/1/17-3/31/18 ALL	4/1/18-3/31/19 ALL	Type of Statement	0-1MM	1-3MM	3-5MM	5-10MM	10-25MM	25MM & OVER
26	26	31	Unqualified				2	6	23
	1	3	Reviewed		1	1		1	
4	2	3	Compiled		1	1	1	1	
14	10	10	Tax Returns	2	1	2	4		
32	49	37	Other	1			5	5	26
76	88	84	**NUMBER OF STATEMENTS**	3	3	4	12	13	49
%	%	%	**ASSETS**	%	%	%	%	%	%
23.4	21.6	27.7	Cash & Equivalents				43.6	43.4	19.8
1.6	1.5	1.7	Trade Receivables (net)				2.0	.8	1.3
1.9	1.3	1.3	Inventory				3.7	1.2	.6
1.7	2.3	2.6	All Other Current				1.8	5.9	2.0
28.5	26.7	33.3	Total Current				51.1	51.4	23.8
53.6	58.5	54.6	Fixed Assets (net)				35.7	41.4	65.3
10.1	10.2	9.2	Intangibles (net)				8.4	1.8	8.6
7.8	4.6	2.9	All Other Non-Current				4.8	5.4	2.3
100.0	100.0	100.0	Total				100.0	100.0	100.0
			LIABILITIES						
8.2	1.3	.7	Notes Payable-Short Term				.1	.3	.8
6.0	6.0	3.3	Cur. Mat.-L.T.D.				3.5	2.3	3.5
9.2	4.7	7.5	Trade Payables				24.9	5.0	4.2
.0	.0	.0	Income Taxes Payable				.0	.0	.0
14.7	14.8	12.9	All Other Current				21.4	19.1	9.4
38.0	26.8	24.4	Total Current				49.9	26.6	17.9
40.2	27.8	22.8	Long-Term Debt				21.1	15.9	25.7
.2	.0	.0	Deferred Taxes				.0	.0	.0
5.5	2.7	2.8	All Other Non-Current				.0	5.3	2.1
16.1	42.7	50.0	Net Worth				29.1	52.2	54.3
100.0	100.0	100.0	Total Liabilities & Net Worth				100.0	100.0	100.0
			INCOME DATA						
100.0	100.0	100.0	Net Sales				100.0	100.0	100.0
			Gross Profit						
80.3	79.4	79.7	Operating Expenses				93.8	79.6	75.6
19.7	20.6	20.3	Operating Profit				6.2	20.4	24.4
2.3	2.9	4.8	All Other Expenses (net)				2.2	10.6	4.9
17.4	17.8	15.5	Profit Before Taxes				4.0	9.8	19.5
			RATIOS						
1.8	2.1	2.3					5.5	4.7	2.0
1.2	1.4	1.5	Current				2.9	1.9	1.3
.8	.8	.9					1.7	1.0	.9
1.7	1.9	2.3					5.4	4.2	1.7
1.0	1.0	1.3	Quick				2.9	1.8	1.2
.5	.7	.8					1.4	.8	.8
0 UND	0 942.3	0 999.8					0 UND	0 UND	1 301.7
1 318.0	3 118.3	2 243.2	Sales/Receivables				0 925.6	0 999.8	3 109.0
4 98.8	5 70.4	4 86.3					2 219.2	2 225.8	5 68.4
			Cost of Sales/Inventory						
			Cost of Sales/Payables						
12.0	8.3	8.8					4.0	5.6	9.0
65.6	81.9	22.5	Sales/Working Capital				20.7	14.9	23.4
-38.1	-31.8	-113.7					83.6	-810.8	-57.2
39.0	60.9	62.6							62.1
(64) 7.8	(72) 13.9	(59) 11.4	EBIT/Interest					(40) 15.3	
3.2	5.2	3.3							4.4
			Net Profit + Depr., Dep., Amort./Cur. Mat. L/T/D						
1.0	.9	.6					.4	.2	.9
2.0	1.4	1.0	Fixed/Worth				.6	.7	1.6
-46.9	3.8	2.3					.9	1.2	2.6
.6	.4	.2					.1	.2	.3
2.0	.9	.7	Debt/Worth				.4	.7	.9
-42.2	4.5	2.2					.6	1.0	2.6
137.4	78.7	72.3					116.0	95.1	60.7
(55) 48.5	(72) 37.3	(76) 36.1	% Profit Before Taxes/Tangible Net Worth			(11) 11.2		(12) 36.3	(44) 40.4
24.6	18.3	9.7					2.0	.9	15.6
47.3	34.7	33.7					25.9	48.1	27.5
18.6	18.1	18.8	% Profit Before Taxes/Total Assets				6.9	16.3	19.2
6.0	5.3	2.6					.9	-4.1	7.9
13.4	5.3	8.4					63.3	148.5	3.1
2.5	1.7	2.4	Sales/Net Fixed Assets				34.8	6.8	1.5
1.3	1.1	1.2					3.0	2.2	1.1
3.8	2.4	3.3					24.7	7.9	1.4
1.2	1.1	1.3	Sales/Total Assets				4.8	3.3	1.1
.9	.8	.9					1.4	1.3	.9
1.9	3.1	1.4					.2	.8	3.5
(55) 4.2	(70) 5.9	(69) 4.1	% Depr., Dep., Amort./Sales		(10) 1.0		(11) 1.8		(39) 6.5
7.0	8.1	7.1					2.1	4.4	8.0
			% Officers', Directors' Owners' Comp/Sales						
5589145M	7706304M	5521059M	Net Sales ($)	2324M	7485M	15689M	87937M	182250M	5225374M
5015534M	7329265M	5073091M	Total Assets ($)	1471M	5995M	6092M	39529M	90690M	4929314M

See Pages viii through xx for Explanation of Ratios and Data

Current Data Sorted by Assets   Comparative Historical Data

0-500M	500M-2MM	2-10MM	10-50MM	50-100MM	100-250MM	Type of Statement	4/1/14-3/31/15 ALL	4/1/15-3/31/16 ALL
		4	7	2	5	Unqualified	27	33
		1				Reviewed	4	1
		1				Compiled	2	1
2	1	1				Tax Returns	4	4
2	6	3	14	5	5	Other	56	42
		20 (4/1-9/30/18)	39 (10/1/18-3/31/19)					
0-500M	**500M-2MM**	**2-10MM**	**10-50MM**	**50-100MM**	**100-250MM**			
4	7	10	21	7	10	NUMBER OF STATEMENTS	93	81
%	%	%	%	%	%	ASSETS	%	%
		25.5	22.7		16.3	Cash & Equivalents	19.7	20.4
		12.8	5.4		1.8	Trade Receivables (net)	5.1	4.1
		7.9	3.5		1.4	Inventory	3.4	3.4
		2.1	3.1		.9	All Other Current	2.3	2.5
		48.3	34.8		20.4	Total Current	30.5	30.5
		35.5	48.0		56.6	Fixed Assets (net)	57.5	59.3
		10.7	7.6		21.1	Intangibles (net)	6.9	6.6
		5.4	9.6		1.9	All Other Non-Current	5.1	3.6
		100.0	100.0		100.0	Total	100.0	100.0
						LIABILITIES		
		2.3	2.8		7.3	Notes Payable-Short Term	2.3	1.7
		11.0	8.8		6.6	Cur. Mat.-L.T.D.	6.4	6.0
		13.0	4.4		7.5	Trade Payables	5.5	4.7
		.0	.0		.0	Income Taxes Payable	.0	.4
		12.8	24.4		2.2	All Other Current	11.4	12.0
		39.1	40.4		23.6	Total Current	25.6	24.8
		12.5	35.1		38.9	Long-Term Debt	36.5	31.4
		.0	.3		.0	Deferred Taxes	.1	.3
		1.8	1.6		.1	All Other Non-Current	4.2	5.5
		46.7	22.6		37.4	Net Worth	33.6	38.0
		100.0	100.0		100.0	Total Liabilities & Net Worth	100.0	100.0
						INCOME DATA		
		100.0	100.0		100.0	Net Sales	100.0	100.0
						Gross Profit		
		80.5	75.3		87.0	Operating Expenses	78.9	78.9
		19.5	24.7		13.0	Operating Profit	21.1	21.1
		3.0	2.3		2.8	All Other Expenses (net)	2.9	2.7
		16.6	22.4		10.2	Profit Before Taxes	18.2	18.4
						RATIOS		
		1.8	2.1		1.4		1.8	2.1
		1.1	1.4		.7	Current	1.2	1.3
		.7	.4		.6		.7	.8
		1.6	1.9		1.3		1.7	1.8
		.8	.8		.7	Quick	1.0	1.1
		.7	.4		.4		.6	.6
		0 UND	0 999.8		0 999.8		1 488.9	1 618.7
		3 105.7	5 79.1		1 441.5	Sales/Receivables	3 142.3	2 148.4
		41 8.8	27 13.3		11 33.7		16 22.4	7 55.3
						Cost of Sales/Inventory		
						Cost of Sales/Payables		
		12.0	8.4		NM		10.6	9.1
		113.3	21.9		-12.5	Sales/Working Capital	38.5	22.4
		-9.1	-5.1		-8.4		-15.0	-25.4
			23.9		19.7		21.6	47.9
			(19) 9.4		4.4	EBIT/Interest	(76) 9.6	(70) 12.7
			5.8		2.9		1.9	3.3
						Net Profit + Depr., Dep., Amort./Cur. Mat. L/T/D		
		.3	.8		1.9		.8	.8
		1.0	1.3		6.4	Fixed/Worth	1.5	1.5
		1.7	-2.8		-1.8		5.4	11.2
		.7	.5		1.2		.4	.4
		1.1	1.7		6.5	Debt/Worth	1.2	1.3
		3.7	-7.3		-4.4		6.9	17.1
			86.1				80.8	99.9
			(13) 65.7			% Profit Before Taxes/Tangible Net Worth	(74) 40.0	(65) 36.4
			24.9				16.8	16.4
		62.8	43.7		19.2		31.9	34.7
		13.3	24.8		10.0	% Profit Before Taxes/Total Assets	15.3	16.9
		6.3	11.8		2.1		5.0	4.6
		21.3	16.4		3.4		4.4	4.3
		8.0	2.7		1.7	Sales/Net Fixed Assets	2.2	1.7
		2.1	1.6		.9		1.1	1.2
		3.4	2.8		1.2		1.9	2.0
		2.0	1.4		1.0	Sales/Total Assets	1.1	1.1
		1.2	1.0		.6		.9	.9
		1.2	1.8				4.2	3.9
		3.0	(17) 4.6			% Depr., Dep., Amort./Sales	(67) 7.0	(60) 6.7
		23.4	15.4				10.2	9.3
						% Officers', Directors' Owners' Comp/Sales		
14642M	29188M	96703M	917434M	641587M	1424938M	Net Sales ($)	7511002M	7225971M
1010M	6688M	46658M	529815M	514692M	1565508M	Total Assets ($)	5961257M	6237778M

© RMA 2019

M = $ thousand   MM = $ million
See Pages viii through xx for Explanation of Ratios and Data

Comparative Historical Data | Current Data Sorted by Sales

Type of Statement										
	37	28	18	Unqualified		1		2	4	11
	—	1	1	Reviewed				1		
	3	3	1	Compiled				1		
	4	5	4	Tax Returns	1	2		1		
	48	35	35	Other	2	1	2	1	5	21
	4/1/16- 3/31/17	4/1/17- 3/31/18	4/1/18- 3/31/19			20 (4/1-9/30/18)		39 (10/1/18-3/31/19)		
	ALL	ALL	ALL		0-1MM	1-3MM	3-5MM	5-10MM	10-25MM	25MM & OVER
NUMBER OF STATEMENTS	92	72	59		3	4	2	9	9	32
	%	%	%	**ASSETS**	%	%	%	%	%	%
Cash & Equivalents	21.6	27.5	25.0							21.3
Trade Receivables (net)	3.6	5.3	6.4							5.0
Inventory	2.2	3.2	5.4							3.7
All Other Current	2.8	3.2	2.8							2.8
Total Current	30.1	39.1	39.7							32.8
Fixed Assets (net)	61.3	46.3	42.5							46.6
Intangibles (net)	4.2	8.6	12.0							12.9
All Other Non-Current	4.3	5.9	5.8							7.7
Total	100.0	100.0	100.0							100.0
				LIABILITIES						
Notes Payable-Short Term	2.6	2.6	5.3							4.2
Cur. Mat.-L.T.D.	6.2	6.5	6.6							7.9
Trade Payables	4.8	6.1	8.9							5.3
Income Taxes Payable	.0	.5	.2							.3
All Other Current	12.1	12.5	14.7							17.9
Total Current	25.8	28.1	35.6							35.6
Long-Term Debt	29.3	32.2	35.5							41.6
Deferred Taxes	.3	.4	.3							.2
All Other Non-Current	5.3	6.7	2.7							3.0
Net Worth	39.3	32.6	26.0							19.6
Total Liabilities & Net Worth	100.0	100.0	100.0							100.0
				INCOME DATA						
Net Sales	100.0	100.0	100.0							100.0
Gross Profit										
Operating Expenses	74.2	81.3	82.6							81.2
Operating Profit	25.8	18.7	17.4							18.8
All Other Expenses (net)	2.6	3.1	2.3							2.4
Profit Before Taxes	23.3	15.6	15.1							16.4
				RATIOS						
Current	2.0	2.5	2.6							2.4
	1.2	1.6	1.3							.8
	.9	.9	.6							.5
Quick	1.8	2.3	1.9							1.9
	1.1	1.4	.8							.7
	.6	.7	.4							.4
Sales/Receivables	2 242.5	0 UND	0 UND							0 999.8
	3 123.5	4 101.8	3 132.7							4 99.0
	8 44.0	20 18.2	27 13.4							28 13.2
Cost of Sales/Inventory										
Cost of Sales/Payables										
Sales/Working Capital	8.1	7.0	9.4							9.8
	37.5	17.8	31.1							-36.0
	-42.5	-38.4	-9.3							-8.3
EBIT/Interest	38.1	31.8	19.8							19.7
	(78) 13.1	(62) 9.0	(49) 8.3						(30)	8.7
	5.8	3.7	3.9							4.0
Net Profit + Depr., Dep., Amort./Cur. Mat. L/T/D										
Fixed/Worth	.9	.7	.5							.7
	1.4	1.4	1.4							6.4
	3.2	-4.6	3.9							-1.9
Debt/Worth	.5	.5	.5							.8
	1.1	1.7	1.3							6.9
	4.1	-6.6	-7.7							-4.6
% Profit Before Taxes/Tangible Net Worth	99.9	86.2	84.2							89.1
	(78) 52.4	(53) 50.5	(39) 59.2						(18)	51.2
	20.6	15.0	7.9							7.2
% Profit Before Taxes/Total Assets	38.3	38.7	39.1							35.8
	23.0	21.8	16.5							17.5
	8.6	5.2	3.8							5.4
Sales/Net Fixed Assets	4.0	12.8	19.4							6.0
	1.5	3.4	3.4							3.2
	1.0	1.4	1.9							1.4
Sales/Total Assets	1.7	2.7	2.9							2.4
	1.0	1.3	1.3							1.2
	.8	.9	.8							.8
% Depr., Dep., Amort./Sales	4.4	2.2	1.8							2.9
	(63) 6.7	(50) 4.7	(43) 3.8						(23)	5.9
	9.5	7.5	8.4							8.4
% Officers', Directors' Owners' Comp/Sales			1.0							
		(11)	3.3							
			4.3							
Net Sales ($)	9439214M	3893906M	3124492M		1790M	8564M	7532M	68188M	148556M	2889862M
Total Assets ($)	8160653M	3640510M	2664371M		1524M	5224M	1436M	82023M	124140M	2450024M

Current Data Sorted by Assets

Comparative Historical Data

						Type of Statement		
1		45	101	16	4	Unqualified	219	191
1	8	23	18			Reviewed	85	81
1	7	13	6			Compiled	80	69
21	25	30	4			Tax Returns	103	113
13	29	89	67	7	5	Other	291	279
	124 (4/1-9/30/18)		410 (10/1/18-3/31/19)				4/1/14-3/31/15 ALL	4/1/15-3/31/16 ALL
0-500M	500M-2MM	2-10MM	10-50MM	50-100MM	100-250MM			
37	69	200	196	23	9	NUMBER OF STATEMENTS	778	733
%	%	%	%	%	%	ASSETS	%	%
27.0	10.0	8.7	8.7	9.0		Cash & Equivalents	8.8	9.3
2.9	4.9	5.6	4.3	4.2		Trade Receivables (net)	5.3	4.9
9.8	2.8	2.3	1.4	1.1		Inventory	2.6	2.6
.9	.5	1.6	1.7	.6		All Other Current	1.3	1.5
40.6	18.1	18.2	16.1	14.9		Total Current	18.0	18.4
44.6	69.0	75.8	78.2	76.0		Fixed Assets (net)	74.3	73.5
4.2	7.3	2.7	1.1	.5		Intangibles (net)	2.5	2.6
10.5	5.6	3.2	4.5	8.6		All Other Non-Current	5.2	5.6
100.0	100.0	100.0	100.0	100.0		Total	100.0	100.0
						LIABILITIES		
9.0	6.7	2.7	.9	.0		Notes Payable-Short Term	4.1	4.5
21.6	4.7	3.7	2.1	1.3		Cur. Mat.-L.T.D.	3.5	3.6
10.7	6.5	3.1	2.2	2.3		Trade Payables	3.5	3.6
.0	.0	.1	.0	.0		Income Taxes Payable	.1	.1
29.7	13.7	9.3	8.1	9.5		All Other Current	11.2	13.0
71.0	31.7	19.0	13.5	13.2		Total Current	22.4	24.7
38.4	61.5	38.6	22.9	20.6		Long-Term Debt	37.6	38.4
.0	.0	.1	.1	.0		Deferred Taxes	.1	.1
40.8	12.9	6.3	9.5	6.0		All Other Non-Current	10.4	10.2
-50.3	-6.1	36.0	54.0	60.2		Net Worth	29.5	26.6
100.0	100.0	100.0	100.0	100.0		Total Liabilities & Net Worth	100.0	100.0
						INCOME DATA		
100.0	100.0	100.0	100.0	100.0		Net Sales	100.0	100.0
						Gross Profit		
96.8	96.8	97.3	99.1	100.5		Operating Expenses	99.4	98.1
3.2	3.2	2.7	.9	-.5		Operating Profit	.6	1.9
1.1	2.7	1.1	-.7	-.4		All Other Expenses (net)	1.2	1.7
2.1	.5	1.7	1.6	.0		Profit Before Taxes	-.6	.3
						RATIOS		
1.6	.9	1.9	2.3	2.1			1.8	1.8
1.0	.5	1.2	1.4	1.3		Current	1.1	1.0
.4	.3	.6	.9	.8			.6	.5
1.3	.8	1.4	1.9	1.8			1.5	1.4
.8	.4	.9	1.1	1.2		Quick	.8	.8
.1	.2	.4	.7	.7			.3	.3
0 UND	0 UND	4 97.7	14 25.8	13 28.2			2 240.6	1 314.8
0 UND	1 459.0	22 16.7	27 13.6	24 15.3		Sales/Receivables	20 18.6	17 20.9
1 272.6	17 21.8	36 10.2	40 9.1	40 9.1			36 10.1	35 10.4
						Cost of Sales/Inventory		
						Cost of Sales/Payables		
18.2	-70.8	10.0	5.4	4.6			9.3	9.5
UND	-16.8	37.2	14.3	12.7		Sales/Working Capital	77.4	220.6
-8.6	-5.6	-11.6	-26.9	-25.9			-10.4	-8.7
2.4	3.2	3.8	4.7	4.6			2.8	3.1
(25) .5	(62) 1.2	(175) 1.5	(168) 1.6	(21) 2.8		EBIT/Interest	(666) 1.1	(620) 1.1
-7.3	-.6	.2	-.9	-1.1			-1.0	-.9
		4.4	5.9				4.6	4.1
	(13) 1.8	(12) 2.9				Net Profit + Depr., Dep., Amort./Cur. Mat. L/T/D	(31) 2.0	(41) 1.8
		.6	1.0				.7	.8
.3	1.3	1.2	1.0	1.0			1.1	1.1
1.9	3.8	2.0	1.3	1.3		Fixed/Worth	1.8	1.8
-1.1	-1.3	6.7	1.7	1.5			9.7	9.4
.9	1.3	.6	.2	.3			.4	.5
7.1	4.0	1.5	.6	.6		Debt/Worth	1.4	1.4
-2.5	-2.6	7.6	1.3	1.0			15.8	14.2
80.0	22.1	10.7	5.6	5.9			5.8	8.5
(19) 18.8	(44) 2.3	(156) 2.3	(178) 1.6	(22) .5		% Profit Before Taxes/Tangible Net Worth	(610) .6	(575) 1.2
-25.7	-12.9	-4.1	-2.0	-7.1			-5.1	-5.0
23.3	6.8	5.0	3.2	2.5			3.2	3.6
.0	1.5	1.2	.7	.3		% Profit Before Taxes/Total Assets	.1	.3
-11.4	-4.9	-2.1	-1.0	-4.7			-3.6	-3.0
49.8	3.0	1.4	.9	.9			1.4	1.5
9.3	1.6	.9	.6	.6		Sales/Net Fixed Assets	.8	.8
2.6	.8	.6	.5	.4			.5	.5
6.2	1.8	1.0	.7	.6			1.0	1.0
3.0	1.2	.7	.5	.4		Sales/Total Assets	.6	.6
1.7	.7	.5	.4	.3			.4	.4
2.1	3.0	6.3	8.4	8.3			6.6	6.4
(20) 3.8	(59) 5.5	(172) 8.2	(188) 10.9	10.9		% Depr., Dep., Amort./Sales	(698) 9.3	(648) 9.2
8.8	8.3	11.3	13.5	14.2			12.7	12.6
4.2	2.9	2.6	3.1				3.4	3.0
(11) 6.3	(17) 4.9	(25) 4.6	(12) 8.4			% Officers', Directors' Owners' Comp/Sales	(105) 7.8	(104) 5.4
8.2	8.2	11.3	24.4				13.0	13.9
32090M	119437M	847798M	2276117M	741742M	725164M	Net Sales ($)	6600089M	4951355M
8237M	84386M	1038220M	3892889M	1584631M	1534982M	Total Assets ($)	9066574M	8732429M

M = $ thousand   MM = $ million
See Pages viii through xx for Explanation of Ratios and Data

Comparative Historical Data | | | | ## Current Data Sorted by Sales

			Type of Statement						
182	181	167	Unqualified	1	7	29	58	55	17
68	57	50	Reviewed	2	16	13	14	4	1
60	47	27	Compiled	3	11	7	5	1	
107	99	80	Tax Returns	33	30	7	6	3	1
234	233	210	Other	21	53	39	32	32	10
4/1/16- 3/31/17	4/1/17- 3/31/18	4/1/18- 3/31/19		124 (4/1-9/30/18)			410 (10/1/18-3/31/19)		
ALL	ALL	ALL		0-1MM	1-3MM	3-5MM	5-10MM	10-25MM	25MM & OVER
651	617	534	**NUMBER OF STATEMENTS**	60	117	95	138	95	29
%	%	%	**ASSETS**	%	%	%	%	%	%
9.3	9.6	10.1	Cash & Equivalents	14.6	10.0	8.7	9.6	9.5	10.4
4.9	5.0	4.7	Trade Receivables (net)	2.7	3.9	5.2	5.8	5.2	4.4
2.4	2.5	2.5	Inventory	5.7	2.5	2.1	1.9	1.9	1.8
1.4	1.4	1.4	All Other Current	.6	1.3	1.0	1.1	2.8	1.4
18.0	18.5	18.7	Total Current	23.7	17.6	17.0	18.3	19.5	18.0
73.8	74.0	73.7	Fixed Assets (net)	64.5	73.6	75.7	76.5	73.5	74.7
2.5	2.7	2.8	Intangibles (net)	7.2	4.8	1.2	1.2	1.7	1.7
5.7	4.7	4.8	All Other Non-Current	4.6	4.0	6.1	4.0	5.4	5.7
100.0	100.0	100.0	Total	100.0	100.0	100.0	100.0	100.0	100.0
			LIABILITIES						
3.9	3.4	2.9	Notes Payable-Short Term	8.0	5.5	1.7	1.2	.7	1.0
3.5	3.3	4.4	Cur. Mat.-L.T.D.	14.6	5.0	3.1	2.8	1.6	1.5
3.3	3.7	3.7	Trade Payables	8.1	4.1	3.2	2.3	3.3	3.3
.1	.0	.0	Income Taxes Payable	.0	.1	.0	.0	.1	.0
14.1	12.6	10.9	All Other Current	15.8	12.2	9.1	8.8	11.3	9.7
24.8	23.1	21.9	Total Current	46.5	26.9	17.1	15.1	16.9	15.5
36.8	36.8	34.7	Long-Term Debt	50.8	52.8	33.5	24.4	22.4	21.7
.1	.1	.1	Deferred Taxes	.0	.2	.0	.0	.1	.0
9.7	12.8	10.8	All Other Non-Current	25.9	11.4	4.6	9.5	8.1	12.1
28.6	27.3	32.6	Net Worth	-23.3	8.7	44.8	51.1	52.5	50.7
100.0	100.0	100.0	Total Liabilties & Net Worth	100.0	100.0	100.0	100.0	100.0	100.0
			INCOME DATA						
100.0	100.0	100.0	Net Sales	100.0	100.0	100.0	100.0	100.0	100.0
			Gross Profit						
99.4	99.0	98.0	Operating Expenses	96.5	97.0	97.4	99.8	97.8	99.7
.6	1.0	2.0	Operating Profit	3.5	3.0	2.6	.2	2.2	.3
.9	1.4	.5	All Other Expenses (net)	3.1	3.1	-.3	-1.3	-.5	-.1
-.3	-.4	1.4	Profit Before Taxes	.4	-.1	3.0	1.5	2.7	.4
			RATIOS						
1.8	1.7	1.9		1.5	1.5	2.0	2.2	1.9	1.7
1.0	1.0	1.2	Current	.7	.7	1.2	1.4	1.4	1.2
.5	.5	.6		.2	.4	.7	.9	.9	.8
1.4	1.5	1.5		1.2	1.0	1.9	1.8	1.6	1.5
(650) .7	.8	.9	Quick	.4	.5	1.0	1.1	1.0	1.0
.3	.4	.4		.1	.2	.5	.6	.7	.6
2 182.6	2 239.9	3 130.0		0 UND	0 UND	9 42.7	16 22.5	13 27.9	13 27.8
18 19.8	19 19.4	20 18.5	Sales/Receivables	0 UND	4 81.3	24 15.0	29 12.8	22 16.6	19 18.8
35 10.4	35 10.3	34 10.6		2 150.6	32 11.4	36 10.2	41 8.8	35 10.3	34 10.8
			Cost of Sales/Inventory						
			Cost of Sales/Payables						
8.9	9.5	8.5		24.0	16.5	6.7	6.6	6.2	9.5
-214.9	162.3	37.4	Sales/Working Capital	-27.7	-20.7	25.4	17.5	18.4	29.5
-8.0	-9.5	-12.4		-4.3	-6.2	-16.0	-19.0	-39.0	-25.6
2.9	3.4	4.0		2.4	2.7	3.4	5.2	9.5	4.5
(546) .9	(534) 1.2	(459) 1.5	EBIT/Interest	(49) .9	(101) .9	(83) 1.3	(114) 1.9	(85) 2.7	(27) 2.3
-1.3	-1.5	-.4		-.5	-.8	-.3	.3	.1	.5
3.3	4.7	4.6						5.9	
(35) 1.8	(39) 2.2	(36) 2.8	Net Profit + Depr., Dep., Amort./Cur. Mat. L/T/D				(12) 3.5		
1.1	1.2	1.2						1.0	
1.1	1.1	1.0		1.0	1.6	1.0	1.1	1.0	1.0
1.7	1.7	1.5	Fixed/Worth	3.9	3.4	1.5	1.3	1.2	1.5
0.0	11.1	4.0		-1.5	-4.3	3.3	2.0	1.7	1.7
.5	.5	.4		.6	1.2	.4	.4	.3	.4
1.3	1.2	1.2	Debt/Worth	4.8	3.4	1.0	.7	.5	.7
10.4	15.1	5.5		-2.7	-6.3	3.5	2.0	1.2	1.4
7.7	7.9	9.2		23.2	12.4	6.6	7.2	6.8	7.1
(511) .6	(486) 1.2	(427) 2.0	% Profit Before Taxes/Tangible Net Worth	(35) 3.0	(74) .4	(80) 1.0	(128) 2.4	(83) 2.2	(27) 2.8
-5.8	-5.3	-3.1		-7.8	-8.1	-3.9	-1.7	-1.4	-2.2
3.7	4.2	4.6		7.0	4.6	4.5	3.9	5.3	4.4
.1	.3	.9	% Profit Before Taxes/Total Assets	.3	.1	.6	1.5	1.9	2.0
-3.5	-3.4	-2.1		-5.2	-4.8	-1.3	-.7	-1.0	-.7
1.4	1.4	1.4		8.4	1.9	1.3	1.1	1.0	1.0
.8	.8	.8	Sales/Net Fixed Assets	1.7	1.0	.7	.7	.8	.8
.5	.6	.6		.6	.6	.6	.5	.6	.5
1.0	1.0	1.0		2.7	1.2	.9	.8	.8	.8
.7	.7	.6	Sales/Total Assets	1.1	.8	.6	.6	.6	.5
.4	.5	.5		.5	.5	.4	.4	.5	.4
6.2	6.0	6.5		2.9	4.0	6.7	7.5	7.7	6.6
(579) 9.3	(556) 9.0	(470) 9.4	% Depr., Dep., Amort./Sales	(41) 7.9	(101) 6.6	(87) 9.8	(123) 10.2	(91) 10.1	(27) 10.9
12.4	12.6	12.5		12.0	10.0	12.7	13.3	12.8	13.1
3.7	3.0	2.9		5.2	3.2	3.6		1.5	
(84) 6.1	(95) 5.9	(67) 5.2	% Officers', Directors' Owners' Comp/Sales	(15) 7.0	(20) 4.4	(10) 9.5		(10) 2.7	
12.5	12.5	10.6		8.9	6.4	25.5		5.5	
4408480M	4406159M	4742348M	Net Sales ($)	35377M	223748M	375664M	985375M	1383716M	1738468M
8492048M	8750095M	8143345M	Total Assets ($)	52039M	331314M	729570M	1807622M	2533335M	2689465M

M = $ thousand   MM = $ million
See Pages viii through xx for Explanation of Ratios and Data

Current Data Sorted by Assets   Comparative Historical Data

0-500M	500M-2MM	2-10MM	10-50MM	50-100MM	100-250MM	Type of Statement	4/1/14-3/31/15 ALL	4/1/15-3/31/16 ALL
		1	4		1	Unqualified	11	13
	1		4			Reviewed	7	3
		1	2			Compiled	4	8
		1	1			Tax Returns	9	3
1	1	4	10	1		Other	27	20
	18 (4/1-9/30/18)		15 (10/1/18-3/31/19)					
1	3	7	20	1	1	NUMBER OF STATEMENTS	58	47
%	%	%	%	%	%		%	%
						ASSETS		
			17.7			Cash & Equivalents	14.3	12.0
			1.3			Trade Receivables (net)	1.7	1.5
			2.6			Inventory	3.0	4.6
			1.4			All Other Current	4.0	1.6
			23.0			Total Current	22.9	19.7
			66.7			Fixed Assets (net)	62.4	68.4
			3.9			Intangibles (net)	8.2	5.7
			6.4			All Other Non-Current	6.5	6.2
			100.0			Total	100.0	100.0
						LIABILITIES		
			.2			Notes Payable-Short Term	4.2	3.1
			2.2			Cur. Mat.-L.T.D.	2.3	5.2
			3.6			Trade Payables	5.9	5.4
			.0			Income Taxes Payable	.1	.1
			12.3			All Other Current	11.2	10.4
			18.3			Total Current	23.7	24.2
			25.4			Long-Term Debt	34.9	27.2
			.7			Deferred Taxes	1.5	1.5
			3.4			All Other Non-Current	9.0	7.5
			52.3			Net Worth	30.9	39.6
			100.0			Total Liabilities & Net Worth	100.0	100.0
						INCOME DATA		
			100.0			Net Sales	100.0	100.0
						Gross Profit		
			85.3			Operating Expenses	89.6	92.6
			14.7			Operating Profit	10.4	7.4
			.7			All Other Expenses (net)	3.5	2.8
			14.0			Profit Before Taxes	6.9	4.6
						RATIOS		
			1.8				2.2	1.6
			1.2			Current	.7	.6
			1.0				.3	.3
			1.6				1.8	1.3
			1.0			Quick	.4	.4
			.7				.2	.2
		1	381.5				0 UND	0 876.0
		5	76.3			Sales/Receivables	3 122.9	5 74.1
		10	35.3				9 42.6	10 36.9
						Cost of Sales/Inventory		
						Cost of Sales/Payables		
			9.5				7.2	9.9
			34.8			Sales/Working Capital	-16.0	-14.0
			NM				-4.8	-4.4
			62.3				18.4	18.8
			14.4			EBIT/Interest	(51) 5.1	(42) 4.5
			5.7				1.1	-.5
						Net Profit + Depr., Dep., Amort./Cur. Mat. L/T/D		
			1.0				1.0	1.1
			1.2			Fixed/Worth	2.3	2.3
			2.1				49.4	12.2
			.4				.6	.4
			.8			Debt/Worth	2.1	2.0
			1.7				57.2	13.0
			39.8				39.0	27.6
		(19)	21.6			% Profit Before Taxes/Tangible Net Worth	(45) 18.8	(39) 11.9
			14.5				1.2	-4.8
			16.1				16.5	12.7
			12.0			% Profit Before Taxes/Total Assets	5.7	4.8
			6.3				.3	-3.3
			2.2				2.8	2.3
			1.2			Sales/Net Fixed Assets	1.6	1.5
			.8				1.0	.7
			1.2				1.5	1.3
			.9			Sales/Total Assets	.9	.9
			.6				.6	.5
			6.7				5.6	6.0
			8.6			% Depr., Dep., Amort./Sales	(53) 7.1	(41) 9.0
			10.1				12.8	12.5
						% Officers', Directors' Owners' Comp/Sales		
1163M	5852M	53342M	418916M	26168M	100337M	Net Sales ($)	2004204M	1661747M
217M	3904M	38591M	512728M	50886M	125348M	Total Assets ($)	2077005M	2060419M

© RMA 2019

M = $ thousand   MM = $ million
See Pages viii through xx for Explanation of Ratios and Data

Comparative Historical Data | Current Data Sorted by Sales

Type of Statement

			Type of Statement	0-1MM	1-3MM	3-5MM	5-10MM	10-25MM	25MM & OVER
11	8	6	Unqualified				1	3	2
7	8	5	Reviewed		1		2	1	1
4	8	3	Compiled		1			1	1
5	4	2	Tax Returns						
22	26	17	Other	1	1	1	1	8	5
4/1/16-3/31/17	4/1/17-3/31/18	4/1/18-3/31/19				18 (4/1-9/30/18)		15 (10/1/18-3/31/19)	
ALL	ALL	ALL							
49	54	33	NUMBER OF STATEMENTS	1	3	3	5	13	9

Hist %	Hist %	Hist %		0-1MM %	1-3MM %	3-5MM %	5-10MM %	10-25MM %	25MM & OVER %
			ASSETS						
13.6	12.2	17.0	Cash & Equivalents					19.1	
1.5	1.5	1.2	Trade Receivables (net)					1.3	
3.7	2.9	4.3	Inventory					2.6	
2.7	1.8	2.0	All Other Current					1.7	
21.6	18.5	24.5	Total Current					24.6	
63.7	67.7	64.8	Fixed Assets (net)					64.4	
9.0	7.0	4.9	Intangibles (net)					2.6	
5.7	6.8	5.8	All Other Non-Current					8.4	
100.0	100.0	100.0	Total					100.0	
			LIABILITIES						
4.7	3.1	1.5	Notes Payable-Short Term					.4	
2.6	3.3	2.2	Cur. Mat.-L.T.D.					2.4	
4.7	4.7	3.5	Trade Payables					4.2	
.0	.3	.0	Income Taxes Payable					.1	
14.4	14.2	16.3	All Other Current					18.7	
26.3	25.6	23.5	Total Current					25.8	
25.0	34.8	22.5	Long-Term Debt					17.2	
1.0	1.2	.5	Deferred Taxes					.8	
13.6	12.2	3.5	All Other Non-Current					4.6	
34.1	26.2	50.1	Net Worth					51.6	
100.0	100.0	100.0	Total Liabilities & Net Worth					100.0	
			INCOME DATA						
100.0	100.0	100.0	Net Sales					100.0	
			Gross Profit						
92.4	90.6	89.2	Operating Expenses					84.1	
7.6	9.4	10.8	Operating Profit					15.9	
2.6	2.0	.9	All Other Expenses (net)					.3	
5.1	7.3	9.9	Profit Before Taxes					15.7	
			RATIOS						
1.6	1.2	1.8	Current					1.9	
.7	.7	1.0						1.0	
.4	.4	.6						1.0	
1.4	.9	1.3	Quick					1.5	
.4	.4	.9						1.0	
.2	.2	.3						.7	
0 UND	0 999.8	0 UND	Sales/Receivables					1 699.5	
3 118.5	3 110.8	2 193.4						6 62.8	
8 45.4	8 43.8	8 45.5						10 37.6	
			Cost of Sales/Inventory						
			Cost of Sales/Payables						
12.6	25.8	9.7	Sales/Working Capital					7.6	
-26.8	-15.1	76.9						76.9	
-5.1	-5.8	-11.8						-231.8	
18.1	10.9	37.7	EBIT/Interest					47.2	
(43) 2.9	(52) 3.7	(31) 7.3						7.3	
-1.0	1.3	1.3						5.1	
			Net Profit + Depr., Dep., Amort./Cur. Mat. L/T/D						
1.2	1.2	1.0	Fixed/Worth					1.0	
3.1	2.8	1.2						1.2	
-44.7	-6.4	4.0						1.9	
.5	.7	.4	Debt/Worth					.5	
3.2	3.1	.8						.9	
-27.4	-8.9	3.5						1.6	
33.1	40.2	43.8	% Profit Before Taxes/Tangible Net Worth					51.9	
(35) 10.8	(37) 18.8	(30) 21.0						(12) 28.1	
-6.8	2.6	5.7						4.6	
14.7	13.7	15.9	% Profit Before Taxes/Total Assets					19.6	
4.1	6.8	11.7						14.7	
-2.4	1.0	.8						4.5	
2.1	2.1	2.6	Sales/Net Fixed Assets					2.1	
1.4	1.5	1.6						1.6	
.9	.9	.9						.7	
1.3	1.5	1.4	Sales/Total Assets					1.2	
1.0	.9	1.0						1.0	
.6	.6	.6						.5	
5.7	5.6	5.3	% Depr., Dep., Amort./Sales					5.7	
(43) 7.5	(51) 8.5	(29) 8.1						(12) 8.6	
11.5	11.7	9.5						10.4	
			% Officers', Directors' Owners' Comp/Sales						
1198273M	1829321M	605778M	Net Sales ($)	133M	2531M	13121M	36564M	202205M	351224M
1276982M	1748678M	731674M	Total Assets ($)	574M	1755M	7591M	38570M	296080M	387104M

M = $ thousand   MM = $ million
See Pages viii through xx for Explanation of Ratios and Data

Current Data Sorted by Assets

Comparative Historical Data

0-500M	500M-2MM	2-10MM	10-50MM	50-100MM	100-250MM	Type of Statement	4/1/14-3/31/15 ALL	4/1/15-3/31/16 ALL
	1		4	1		Unqualified	8	11
	1	5	4			Reviewed	17	19
1	6	5	1			Compiled	17	24
3	19	14	1			Tax Returns	38	41
4	14	29	11	3	2	Other	91	85
13 (4/1-9/30/18)			116 (10/1/18-3/31/19)					
8	41	53	21	4	2	**NUMBER OF STATEMENTS**	171	180
%	%	%	%	%	%	**ASSETS**	%	%
	13.8	7.7	9.7			Cash & Equivalents	12.5	12.5
	7.0	3.4	2.1			Trade Receivables (net)	4.9	4.6
	13.0	9.7	5.5			Inventory	10.4	7.2
	2.0	1.3	.3			All Other Current	1.4	1.6
	35.8	22.1	17.5			Total Current	29.2	25.9
	48.8	60.7	72.5			Fixed Assets (net)	58.8	60.1
	5.3	5.4	1.8			Intangibles (net)	4.2	7.6
	10.1	11.7	8.2			All Other Non-Current	7.8	6.5
	100.0	100.0	100.0			Total	100.0	100.0
						LIABILITIES		
	6.8	4.6	2.6			Notes Payable-Short Term	8.2	6.8
	7.8	2.9	8.7			Cur. Mat.-L.T.D.	3.1	2.8
	8.8	2.0	3.4			Trade Payables	3.4	3.1
	.0	.0	.1			Income Taxes Payable	.0	.1
	9.6	6.8	6.5			All Other Current	13.0	16.9
	33.1	16.3	21.4			Total Current	27.7	29.6
	58.5	55.1	47.2			Long-Term Debt	59.9	49.2
	.0	.0	1.4			Deferred Taxes	.1	.1
	2.2	6.6	5.6			All Other Non-Current	7.7	4.5
	6.2	22.0	24.3			Net Worth	4.7	16.5
	100.0	100.0	100.0			Total Liabilities & Net Worth	100.0	100.0
						INCOME DATA		
	100.0	100.0	100.0			Net Sales	100.0	100.0
						Gross Profit		
	87.6	79.1	77.7			Operating Expenses	84.6	85.4
	12.4	20.9	22.3			Operating Profit	15.4	14.6
	5.4	8.3	10.8			All Other Expenses (net)	6.0	5.1
	7.0	12.6	11.4			Profit Before Taxes	9.4	9.5
						RATIOS		
	3.2	3.0	1.7				3.3	2.5
	1.5	1.4	1.3			Current	1.6	1.4
	.6	.6	.4				.8	.6
	2.3	2.1	1.5				2.4	2.0
	.6	1.0	1.1			Quick	.9	.9
	.3	.3	.2				.3	.3
	0 UND	0 UND	4 84.1				3 114.9	3 140.9
	14 25.3	5 72.0	12 29.3			Sales/Receivables	12 29.7	11 34.1
	25 14.6	27 13.5	21 17.1				30 12.2	28 13.2
						Cost of Sales/Inventory		
						Cost of Sales/Payables		
	4.6	4.6	7.8				4.1	4.8
	13.0	15.0	15.7			Sales/Working Capital	12.7	17.7
	-18.7	-12.8	-1.9				-23.5	-12.3
	9.0	6.2	4.8				6.6	7.5
	(32) 4.5	(41) 3.5	(15) 3.7			EBIT/Interest	(147) 2.8	(142) 3.0
	1.3	1.4	1.7				1.4	1.4
						Net Profit + Depr., Dep., Amort./Cur. Mat. L/T/D		
	.9	1.1	1.0				1.0	1.0
	2.5	3.0	6.0			Fixed/Worth	3.8	2.1
	-1.4	-9.9	-16.7				-2.6	-6.3
	1.0	1.1	.7				1.0	.8
	5.4	3.2	6.1			Debt/Worth	5.7	2.8
	-3.5	-16.5	-23.2				-7.6	-7.1
	57.5	44.0	22.8				35.9	31.7
	(25) 19.6	(38) 18.4	(14) 14.5			% Profit Before Taxes/Tangible Net Worth	(110) 12.5	(123) 14.8
	8.1	7.1	3.2				3.5	2.4
	19.1	9.7	8.9				10.2	12.2
	7.0	4.7	3.1			% Profit Before Taxes/Total Assets	4.6	5.1
	1.4	1.5	.8				.5	.5
	8.6	4.1	1.0				4.0	2.9
	2.0	.7	.5			Sales/Net Fixed Assets	1.2	1.1
	1.1	.4	.3				.5	.4
	1.6	.9	.7				1.3	1.2
	1.2	.4	.4			Sales/Total Assets	.6	.6
	.6	.3	.2				.4	.3
	2.4	4.3	6.3				2.6	4.2
	(31) 7.7	(39) 7.8	(20) 11.3			% Depr., Dep., Amort./Sales	(140) 7.9	(141) 8.3
	13.8	12.3	15.2				13.5	13.3
	1.4						2.6	3.4
	(14) 4.0					% Officers', Directors' Owners' Comp/Sales	(42) 4.3	(41) 5.5
	9.1						9.6	8.8
7454M	59443M	207660M	186629M	135270M	84764M	Net Sales ($)	739892M	848263M
2167M	46855M	253240M	393589M	277441M	327092M	Total Assets ($)	1442615M	1893686M

M = $ thousand MM = $ million

See Pages viii through xx for Explanation of Ratios and Data

Comparative Historical Data | Current Data Sorted by Sales

			Type of Statement						
7	9	6	Unqualified	1	1		1	2	1
7	11	10	Reviewed	2	2	1	4	1	
14	17	13	Compiled	4	8			1	
32	37	37	Tax Returns	15	15	5	2		
74	78	63	Other	16	17	7	10	10	3
4/1/16-3/31/17 ALL	4/1/17-3/31/18 ALL	4/1/18-3/31/19 ALL		13 (4/1-9/30/18)			116 (10/1/18-3/31/19)		
				0-1MM	1-3MM	3-5MM	5-10MM	10-25MM	25MM & OVER
134	152	129	NUMBER OF STATEMENTS	38	43	13	17	14	4
%	%	%	ASSETS	%	%	%	%	%	%
11.4	11.0	10.4	Cash & Equivalents	8.8	12.0	13.8	8.7	10.0	
5.2	4.4	4.4	Trade Receivables (net)	1.9	6.5	5.6	5.2	2.6	
10.1	8.6	9.6	Inventory	1.9	9.3	14.7	11.4	22.6	
1.1	1.4	1.4	All Other Current	2.0	.5	4.0	.1	2.1	
27.8	25.3	25.8	Total Current	14.6	28.3	38.0	25.4	37.3	
57.7	57.4	57.3	Fixed Assets (net)	70.6	55.4	42.3	55.2	44.9	
7.3	6.9	6.7	Intangibles (net)	4.0	9.0	8.1	1.7	9.7	
7.2	10.4	10.2	All Other Non-Current	10.8	7.4	11.6	17.7	8.1	
100.0	100.0	100.0	Total	100.0	100.0	100.0	100.0	100.0	
			LIABILITIES						
6.6	4.5	5.6	Notes Payable-Short Term	2.6	5.3	9.5	2.2	13.4	
3.4	3.3	6.4	Cur. Mat.-L.T.D.	5.2	6.9	3.2	9.7	2.0	
3.6	4.9	4.8	Trade Payables	4.6	4.7	6.2	6.1	2.3	
.1	.0	.0	Income Taxes Payable	.0	.0	.0	.1	.0	
17.2	8.6	8.3	All Other Current	6.2	10.7	7.7	9.2	4.9	
30.9	21.3	25.1	Total Current	18.6	27.6	26.6	27.4	22.6	
52.7	60.8	52.7	Long-Term Debt	64.7	48.4	62.0	44.6	41.1	
.0	.0	.3	Deferred Taxes	.0	.0	.0	1.7	.0	
5.0	4.1	4.9	All Other Non-Current	3.1	3.8	2.4	4.8	15.0	
11.4	13.8	17.1	Net Worth	13.6	20.3	9.0	21.6	21.3	
100.0	100.0	100.0	Total Liabilties & Net Worth	100.0	100.0	100.0	100.0	100.0	
			INCOME DATA						
100.0	100.0	100.0	Net Sales	100.0	100.0	100.0	100.0	100.0	
			Gross Profit						
86.4	82.4	82.4	Operating Expenses	75.1	85.0	82.8	83.9	90.6	
13.6	17.6	17.6	Operating Profit	24.9	15.0	17.2	16.1	9.4	
6.5	6.6	7.5	All Other Expenses (net)	11.7	6.7	5.3	5.7	4.1	
7.1	11.0	10.1	Profit Before Taxes	13.2	8.3	11.9	10.4	5.2	
			RATIOS						
2.3	3.1	2.3		4.4	2.8	2.4	1.5	2.1	
1.3	1.2	1.3	Current	1.3	1.3	1.7	1.3	1.4	
.5	.6	.5		.2	.6	1.0	.5	1.2	
1.7	2.3	1.8		2.5	2.2	1.7	1.3	1.6	
.7	.8	.7	Quick	.6	1.0	.7	.6	1.1	
.2	.3	.3		.1	.3	.3	.4	.1	
1 331.9	1 577.9	1 474.4		0 UND	2 171.5	2 218.1	9 40.4	2 164.4	
8 43.6	8 43.9	11 32.1	Sales/Receivables	0 UND	16 22.3	6 62.1	20 18.6	12 30.5	
24 14.9	24 15.2	24 15.3		15 24.5	38 9.5	18 20.1	24 15.0	18 19.8	
			Cost of Sales/Inventory						
			Cost of Sales/Payables						
5.5	6.3	5.0		4.5	4.3	6.8	10.5	3.9	
18.8	29.8	16.6	Sales/Working Capital	35.0	19.2	13.0	18.3	13.1	
-9.4	-15.0	-11.3		-2.7	-11.4	NM	-8.7	19.7	
6.5	5.3	6.1		6.8	6.1	6.2	9.7	5.9	
(108) 2.7	(121) 3.3	(99) 3.5	EBIT/Interest	(22) 1.9	(36) 2.9	(10) 3.6	(15) 3.8	(12) 4.5	
1.2	1.5	1.4		.7	1.3	1.7	3.5	1.8	
			Net Profit + Depr., Dep., Amort./Cur. Mat. L/T/D						
1.1	1.1	1.0		1.2	1.0	.7	.9	.9	
3.9	2.9	3.4	Fixed/Worth	6.1	2.7	28.3	2.1	1.6	
-3.9	-6.2	-4.8		-4.8	-1.4	-5.4	-16.7	NM	
.9	1.2	1.1		1.4	1.0	2.8	.8	1.4	
5.8	4.6	5.4	Debt/Worth	6.3	3.2	50.8	2.1	5.7	
-4.6	-9.2	-7.0		-7.5	-3.2	-9.0	-23.2	NM	
36.7	44.9	38.1	% Profit Before Taxes/Tangible Net Worth	22.4	36.9		45.1	43.6	
(84) 12.1	(101) 18.5	(82) 17.3		(23) 10.6	(27) 15.2	(11)	17.4	(11) 19.7	
.3	4.1	5.7		2.7	6.5		11.5	4.0	
10.9	10.7	11.6	% Profit Before Taxes/Total Assets	9.3	12.1	31.7	10.9	11.8	
3.4	5.3	5.5		2.7	6.0	9.1	7.8	4.6	
.0	1.2	1.3		-.7	1.3	3.5	2.5	-.4	
4.7	3.3	4.4		2.1	6.4	39.6	4.2	4.7	
1.2	1.1	1.3	Sales/Net Fixed Assets	.6	1.4	2.3	1.6	1.3	
.4	.5	.4		.2	.5	.6	.4	.9	
1.5	1.3	1.3		.9	1.3	3.9	1.1	1.8	
.7	.6	.7	Sales/Total Assets	.3	.8	.8	.7	.7	
.4	.3	.3		.1	.4	.5	.4	.5	
4.4	3.8	3.9		4.5	3.3		3.4	1.4	
(108) 8.4	(114) 8.4	(100) 8.3	% Depr., Dep., Amort./Sales	(28) 9.3	(35) 8.3	(14)	6.3	(11) 7.7	
16.6	14.2	14.0		26.7	12.5		13.3	14.9	
2.2	3.3	1.6							
(37) 4.1	(29) 5.5	(29) 3.3	% Officers', Directors' Owners' Comp/Sales						
8.1	9.0	8.7							
661237M	1046680M	681220M	Net Sales ($)	21183M	75186M	45386M	121557M	222046M	195862M
1265092M	1334247M	1300384M	Total Assets ($)	71823M	168746M	58427M	215696M	481107M	304585M

© RMA 2019

M = $ thousand   MM = $ million

See Pages viii through xx for Explanation of Ratios and Data

Current Data Sorted by Assets   Comparative Historical Data

		2	10	29	13	12	Type of Statement			
1		5	16	12			Unqualified		53	69
3		6	8	5	1	1	Reviewed		37	43
55		39	36				Compiled		66	78
46		52	62	40	11	19	Tax Returns		168	183
	57 (4/1-9/30/18)			427 (10/1/18-3/31/19)			Other		302	333
									4/1/14-	4/1/15-
									3/31/15	3/31/16
0-500M	500M-2MM	2-10MM	10-50MM	50-100MM	100-250MM			ALL	ALL
105	104	132	86	25	32	**NUMBER OF STATEMENTS**		626	706
%	%	%	%	%	%	**ASSETS**		%	%
26.4	19.1	9.1	11.1	6.0	6.6	Cash & Equivalents		14.5	15.8
2.2	2.1	3.1	2.5	2.7	1.6	Trade Receivables (net)		2.7	2.7
3.0	1.7	.6	.4	.9	.2	Inventory		1.8	1.4
4.4	3.5	3.1	1.2	2.4	1.2	All Other Current		2.6	3.3
36.1	26.4	15.9	15.2	12.0	9.6	Total Current		21.6	23.3
48.9	54.2	73.4	70.7	59.6	62.7	Fixed Assets (net)		62.0	60.7
7.1	7.4	5.1	6.7	23.9	22.8	Intangibles (net)		7.5	7.8
7.9	12.0	5.5	7.4	4.4	4.9	All Other Non-Current		8.8	8.2
100.0	100.0	100.0	100.0	100.0	100.0	Total		100.0	100.0
						LIABILITIES			
10.7	4.8	1.2	1.2	1.5	1.3	Notes Payable-Short Term		4.6	5.3
7.2	4.3	4.3	4.3	4.6	3.5	Cur. Mat.-L.T.D.		4.9	4.4
2.8	2.2	2.3	2.5	3.0	3.2	Trade Payables		2.9	3.4
.0	.1	.0	.1	.0	.0	Income Taxes Payable		.3	.2
18.4	14.8	7.1	7.2	9.1	8.0	All Other Current		13.1	12.9
39.1	26.3	14.8	15.4	18.3	16.0	Total Current		25.7	26.1
35.9	34.2	48.1	40.4	70.1	51.7	Long-Term Debt		40.9	38.5
.0	.4	.0	.1	.0	.4	Deferred Taxes		.1	.1
19.8	10.1	6.1	4.2	18.5	9.4	All Other Non-Current		15.4	10.7
5.3	29.0	31.0	39.8	-6.9	22.6	Net Worth		17.8	24.6
100.0	100.0	100.0	100.0	100.0	100.0	Total Liabilities & Net Worth		100.0	100.0
						INCOME DATA			
100.0	100.0	100.0	100.0	100.0	100.0	Net Sales		100.0	100.0
						Gross Profit			
86.2	87.7	85.4	87.4	87.6	94.8	Operating Expenses		86.5	87.1
13.8	12.3	14.6	12.6	12.4	5.2	Operating Profit		13.5	12.9
1.6	3.7	6.3	3.6	6.5	5.2	All Other Expenses (net)		4.2	3.1
12.2	8.6	8.3	9.1	5.9	.0	Profit Before Taxes		9.3	9.7
						RATIOS			
3.6	5.0	2.1	2.3	1.5	1.1			2.6	2.7
1.0	1.4	.9	1.2	1.0	.4	Current		.9	1.0
.3	.4	.4	.5	.3	.3			.3	.4
3.0	4.4	1.5	2.1	1.2	.8			2.1	2.3
.8	.9	.7	1.0	.9	.4	Quick	(625) .7	(703) .8
.2	.2	.2	.4	.2	.2			.2	.3
0 UND	0 UND	0 UND	0 UND	0 999.8	1 529.6			0 UND	0 UND
0 UND	0 UND	2 163.3	5 78.4	3 114.4	3 128.7	Sales/Receivables		0 UND	0 UND
0 UND	2 216.5	13 28.7	14 25.3	11 32.4	9 38.5			8 45.0	6 59.7
						Cost of Sales/Inventory			
						Cost of Sales/Payables			
12.8	5.5	7.5	7.9	18.7	76.2			11.6	12.1
UND	67.9	-68.7	67.4	213.4	-11.9	Sales/Working Capital		-92.4	-390.7
-14.9	-15.7	-12.2	-9.9	-5.3	-4.4			-8.0	-9.6
22.0	13.7	6.6	8.8	3.8	2.4			11.2	11.9
(74) 7.5	(73) 2.5	(113) 2.9	(80) 3.2	(23) 2.1	(30) 1.6	EBIT/Interest	(481) 3.7	(530) 4.4
2.7	.4	1.2	1.3	.4	-.6			1.0	1.1
		10.6				Net Profit + Depr., Dep.,		6.7	7.6
	(12) 2.5					Amort./Cur. Mat. L/T/D	(33) 3.3	(43) 3.7
		1.3						1.3	2.2
.5	.5	1.3	1.2	2.7	1.8			1.1	1.0
2.0	2.2	2.8	2.3	-1.8	-4.8	Fixed/Worth		2.8	2.4
-3.7	-36.6	9.3	6.6	-.7	-1.7			-7.9	-14.6
.7	.4	.8	.6	2.0	1.3			.8	.6
2.7	2.1	2.6	1.8	-3.2	-6.3	Debt/Worth		3.2	2.7
-6.2	-25.0	14.7	5.8	-1.8	-3.0			-9.2	-18.8
184.1	76.2	47.1	33.5	50.7	11.0			83.8	89.0
(71) 84.0	(76) 26.1	(109) 15.9	(72) 5.7	(11) 6.6	(13) 2.5	% Profit Before Taxes/Tangible Net Worth	(435) 24.4	(510) 24.2
7.1	1.8	2.3	.7	3.7	-8.6			3.4	3.5
74.9	26.4	12.2	13.3	12.2	5.1			24.0	29.9
23.4	5.0	3.7	4.3	3.5	1.3	% Profit Before Taxes/Total Assets		6.8	8.6
.0	-.9	.5	.6	-.7	-3.5			.2	.4
19.9	9.8	2.3	1.9	2.1	1.4			6.2	7.1
7.6	4.4	.9	1.1	1.3	1.1	Sales/Net Fixed Assets		1.7	2.1
4.1	.9	.4	.6	.7	.7			.7	.8
6.2	3.0	1.1	1.1	1.0	.9			2.4	2.7
3.2	1.5	.7	.7	.6	.6	Sales/Total Assets		1.0	1.3
2.1	.7	.4	.4	.5	.5			.6	.6
1.7	1.7	5.9	6.0	4.3	5.6			4.1	3.6
(62) 3.7	(69) 4.1	(116) 8.8	(79) 7.9	(16) 8.9	(12) 7.7	% Depr., Dep., Amort./Sales	(486) 7.6	(497) 6.7
7.6	9.0	14.0	11.5	12.4	12.3			11.6	10.4
4.0	2.2	2.9						2.9	2.6
(43) 5.5	(36) 4.7	(25) 5.4				% Officers', Directors' Owners' Comp/Sales	(146) 5.5	(176) 5.3
10.0	8.7	8.0						10.3	9.5
97699M	208553M	523803M	1691326M	1504864M	3251418M	Net Sales ($)		5645089M	8518135M
25995M	110473M	623241M	1880879M	1830617M	5038992M	Total Assets ($)		7226387M	9636648M

Comparative Historical Data / Current Data Sorted by Sales

			Type of Statement						
74	73	66	Unqualified		8	2	12	12	32
49	37	34	Reviewed	6	5	6	5	7	5
62	32	24	Compiled	2	7	4	4	4	3
144	129	130	Tax Returns	58	50	15	5	2	
269	258	230	Other	70	52	21	28	20	39
4/1/16-3/31/17 ALL	4/1/17-3/31/18 ALL	4/1/18-3/31/19 ALL		57 (4/1-9/30/18)		427 (10/1/18-3/31/19)			
				0-1MM	1-3MM	3-5MM	5-10MM	10-25MM	25MM & OVER
598	529	484	NUMBER OF STATEMENTS	136	122	48	54	45	79
%	%	%	ASSETS	%	%	%	%	%	%
13.3	15.0	15.0	Cash & Equivalents	18.1	17.0	17.6	11.5	14.6	7.8
2.9	2.3	2.5	Trade Receivables (net)	1.0	3.0	2.1	4.3	2.3	3.4
1.1	1.5	1.3	Inventory	1.9	1.5	1.1	1.2	.5	.5
2.7	3.1	3.0	All Other Current	2.4	3.5	4.2	5.4	1.2	1.8
20.0	21.9	21.8	Total Current	23.4	25.0	25.0	22.4	18.6	13.5
64.3	60.7	62.1	Fixed Assets (net)	62.3	59.9	57.0	67.9	64.9	62.5
8.4	9.2	8.5	Intangibles (net)	7.6	4.5	8.3	4.0	9.7	18.6
7.3	8.2	7.7	All Other Non-Current	6.7	10.6	9.7	5.7	6.7	5.4
100.0	100.0	100.0	Total	100.0	100.0	100.0	100.0	100.0	100.0
			LIABILITIES						
3.6	4.7	4.1	Notes Payable-Short Term	8.8	2.9	1.9	2.8	1.4	1.3
4.6	4.9	4.9	Cur. Mat.-L.T.D.	5.5	4.4	7.3	3.2	4.8	4.4
3.5	2.9	2.5	Trade Payables	1.3	2.2	2.9	3.5	3.1	3.7
.1	.1	.1	Income Taxes Payable	.0	.1	.0	.1	.1	.1
17.2	13.5	11.4	All Other Current	10.5	14.7	8.4	10.8	10.8	10.4
28.9	26.0	22.9	Total Current	26.2	24.2	20.6	20.4	20.2	20.0
41.3	40.8	42.5	Long-Term Debt	44.9	42.2	37.0	30.4	30.7	56.9
.2	.2	.1	Deferred Taxes	.0	.0	.0	.0	1.2	.2
11.4	11.6	10.4	All Other Non-Current	7.0	19.6	7.1	6.2	7.3	9.0
18.2	21.5	24.0	Net Worth	22.0	14.0	35.2	43.0	40.5	13.9
100.0	100.0	100.0	Total Liabilties & Net Worth	100.0	100.0	100.0	100.0	100.0	100.0
			INCOME DATA						
100.0	100.0	100.0	Net Sales	100.0	100.0	100.0	100.0	100.0	100.0
			Gross Profit						
88.3	86.8	87.2	Operating Expenses	81.4	88.5	91.1	89.3	88.6	90.4
11.7	13.2	12.8	Operating Profit	18.6	11.5	8.9	10.7	11.4	9.6
4.0	4.0	4.2	All Other Expenses (net)	6.9	2.9	2.3	2.3	2.9	4.3
7.6	9.2	8.7	Profit Before Taxes	11.7	8.6	6.6	8.4	8.5	5.2
			RATIOS						
1.9	2.3	2.5		5.0	2.7	2.1	2.5	2.3	1.3
.8	.9	1.0	Current	1.2	1.0	.8	1.2	1.3	.6
.3	.3	.4		.3	.4	.5	.6	.5	.3
1.5	1.9	2.1		4.5	2.3	1.4	2.2	2.0	1.1
(597) .6	(528) .7	.8	Quick	.9	.9	.7	1.0	1.2	.5
.2	.2	.2		.2	.2	.3	.4	.5	.2
0 UND	0 UND	0 UND		0 UND	0 UND	0 UND	0 UND	0 UND	0 999.8
0 973.3	0 UND	0 UND	Sales/Receivables	0 UND	0 UND	2 216.5	5 68.8	3 109.8	3 114.4
8 44.8	6 57.3	7 55.3		0 UND	7 49.5	6 60.1	20 18.2	10 36.1	14 25.8
			Cost of Sales/Inventory						
			Cost of Sales/Payables						
17.2	10.8	9.7		6.1	10.7	19.9	6.3	7.6	23.4
-59.4	-109.3	999.9	Sales/Working Capital	67.9	-147.6	-37.5	31.5	63.7	-17.8
-8.1	-9.9	-11.3		-10.1	-13.7	-15.0	-16.8	-10.7	-5.6
11.2	12.3	9.9		10.2	12.2	9.1	16.6	14.7	4.3
(484) 3.1	(419) 3.8	(393) 2.9	EBIT/Interest	(88) 3.6	(97) 2.9	(44) 3.2	(48) 3.3	(42) 6.1	(74) 2.3
.7	1.2	1.0		.6	1.1	1.0	1.2	1.7	.9
5.7	8.1	8.5	Net Profit + Depr., Dep.,						12.1
(37) 3.7	(35) 5.3	(23) 4.5	Amort./Cur. Mat. L/T/D					(10) 6.4	
1.0	2.0	2.1							2.9
1.2	1.0	1.1		1.0	.9	.9	1.1	1.0	1.7
3.3	2.6	2.7	Fixed/Worth	2.8	2.5	1.7	1.8	1.7	15.7
-9.7	-9.7	-33.1		UND	-6.2	12.0	4.3	NM	-1.1
.8	.7	.7		.8	.6	.6	.6	.6	1.4
3.4	2.8	2.6	Debt/Worth	2.8	2.6	2.1	1.9	1.1	15.9
-12.7	-11.0	-38.5		-62.1	-12.7	15.6	4.8	NM	-2.3
74.9	62.6	61.7	% Profit Before Taxes/Tangible	98.9	79.6	71.3	57.6	44.6	44.9
(406) 22.0	(373) 15.5	(352) 18.3	Net Worth	(101) 24.4	(88) 24.3	(38) 14.5	(50) 18.1	(34) 10.4	(41) 6.5
2.1	2.7	1.8		1.1	1.4	1.7	1.1	1.3	2.4
23.3	21.4	19.9	% Profit Before Taxes/Total	30.7	22.9	13.0	20.5	19.1	11.9
5.6	5.7	4.9	Assets	4.5	6.1	4.7	5.5	8.6	3.5
-.6	.5	.0		-.9	.0	.3	.6	1.3	.0
5.7	6.7	6.0		7.7	9.8	13.1	4.0	3.1	2.5
1.7	1.8	1.7	Sales/Net Fixed Assets	2.6	2.6	1.8	1.2	1.3	1.3
.8	.7	.8		.4	.7	.8	.8	.9	.9
2.4	2.7	2.3		2.7	3.2	2.7	2.2	1.6	1.3
1.1	1.0	1.0	Sales/Total Assets	1.3	1.4	1.0	1.0	1.0	.9
.6	.5	.5		.4	.5	.6	.6	.7	.5
4.0	3.7	4.0		3.2	2.8	4.5	5.1	5.9	4.2
(469) 7.2	(395) 7.1	(354) 7.1	% Depr., Dep., Amort./Sales	(85) 8.3	(94) 5.9	(40) 6.9	(44) 7.8	(42) 6.9	(49) 6.9
11.0	11.6	11.4		19.2	10.2	10.2	10.4	10.7	9.6
3.1	3.0	3.3		3.8	3.0	1.3			
(151) 5.1	(110) 5.9	(112) 5.0	% Officers', Directors' Owners' Comp/Sales	(38) 6.0	(36) 4.6	(17) 5.1	(13) 4.4		
10.5	11.6	8.4		15.0	10.3	9.6	6.7		
8008132M	8804421M	7277663M	Net Sales ($)	71991M	225717M	196060M	380594M	713728M	5689573M
9108202M	9127115M	9510197M	Total Assets ($)	148800M	293074M	218928M	582129M	894548M	7372718M

M = $ thousand   MM = $ million
See Pages viii through xx for Explanation of Ratios and Data

Current Data Sorted by Assets							Comparative Historical Data	
	3	3				Type of Statement		
						Unqualified		
6	8	1				Reviewed	6	1
14	11	4				Compiled	42	22
8	7	12	2	2		Tax Returns	53	47
						Other	38	44
	13 (4/1-9/30/18)		68 (10/1/18-3/31/19)				4/1/14-3/31/15	4/1/15-3/31/16
0-500M	500M-2MM	2-10MM	10-50MM	50-100MM	100-250MM		ALL	ALL
28	29	20	2	2		NUMBER OF STATEMENTS	139	120
%	%	%	%	%	%	**ASSETS**	%	%
31.7	19.3	11.1				Cash & Equivalents	14.4	13.3
.9	.2	.1			D	Trade Receivables (net)	.5	.9
5.3	2.3	1.1			A	Inventory	3.3	2.7
1.3	6.3	.7			T	All Other Current	1.2	1.6
39.2	28.0	13.0			A	Total Current	19.3	18.5
41.6	58.8	77.4				Fixed Assets (net)	64.6	67.6
8.3	3.7	2.7			N	Intangibles (net)	5.8	6.3
10.8	9.6	6.9			O	All Other Non-Current	10.2	7.7
100.0	100.0	100.0			T	Total	100.0	100.0
						LIABILITIES		
7.0	1.1	1.7			A	Notes Payable-Short Term	5.9	7.2
7.2	6.0	2.8			V	Cur. Mat.-L.T.D.	5.1	4.7
16.0	2.9	1.2			A	Trade Payables	7.1	7.1
.9	.3	.0			I	Income Taxes Payable	.1	.0
28.0	11.0	2.9			L	All Other Current	19.1	14.5
59.2	21.3	8.6			A	Total Current	37.2	33.5
37.5	54.0	68.9			B	Long-Term Debt	59.2	58.9
.1	.0	.3			L	Deferred Taxes	.2	.1
44.6	19.5	5.8			E	All Other Non-Current	22.0	19.5
-41.5	5.3	16.4				Net Worth	-18.6	-12.0
100.0	100.0	100.0				Total Liabilities & Net Worth	100.0	100.0
						INCOME DATA		
100.0	100.0	100.0				Net Sales	100.0	100.0
						Gross Profit		
95.7	90.5	85.1				Operating Expenses	91.8	89.2
4.3	9.5	14.9				Operating Profit	8.2	10.8
1.2	3.5	5.4				All Other Expenses (net)	4.7	3.9
3.1	6.0	9.5				Profit Before Taxes	3.5	6.9
						RATIOS		
2.8	2.3	2.9					1.2	1.7
.7	1.0	1.6				Current	.7	.7
.4	.4	.3					.3	.3
2.5	1.9	2.6					1.0	1.3
.6	.6	1.1				Quick	.5	.5
.3	.3	.2					.2	.2
0 UND	0 UND	0 UND					0 UND	0 UND
0 UND	0 UND	0 UND				Sales/Receivables	0 UND	0 UND
0 UND	0 885.4	1 405.3					1 322.8	1 327.0
						Cost of Sales/Inventory		
						Cost of Sales/Payables		
16.8	11.3	8.9					46.0	24.7
-34.5	-715.8	15.7				Sales/Working Capital	-32.5	-44.3
-8.8	-7.7	-15.7					-6.9	-7.2
16.4	13.6	4.4					4.3	5.0
(16) 2.5	(24) 2.4	(18) 2.4				EBIT/Interest	(115) 1.6	(103) 2.2
.6	.8	1.3					.7	1.0
						Net Profit + Depr., Dep., Amort./Cur. Mat. L/T/D		
1.1	1.1	1.7					2.4	2.2
-3.8	17.0	11.0				Fixed/Worth	-22.9	-87.3
-.3	-2.1	-4.8					-1.5	-1.9
1.8	2.1	1.1					2.9	2.1
-9.4	31.8	12.1				Debt/Worth	-38.7	-51.1
-1.7	-3.7	-7.2					-2.7	-3.6
92.9	117.6	25.5				% Profit Before Taxes/Tangible	76.4	64.3
(12) 26.5	(16) 47.9	(11) 12.8				Net Worth	(64) 21.4	(57) 27.1
5.8	23.9	5.5					1.1	9.4
26.5	21.7	11.7				% Profit Before Taxes/Total	15.2	11.6
8.2	6.5	4.6				Assets	3.3	5.9
-4.6	.0	1.4					-1.8	-.2
16.3	6.1	1.2					5.0	4.6
9.2	3.1	.9				Sales/Net Fixed Assets	1.8	1.8
6.8	1.2	.6					.8	.9
5.8	2.3	1.0					2.5	2.8
3.6	1.6	.6				Sales/Total Assets	1.3	1.2
2.7	.9	.5					.7	.7
1.8	3.4	4.3					3.2	3.2
(22) 2.9	(22) 7.2	(18) 7.6				% Depr., Dep., Amort./Sales	(121) 5.8	(106) 6.0
4.7	12.3	12.9					10.5	9.5
2.9	3.2						3.4	2.3
(13) 4.3	(14) 5.4					% Officers', Directors' Owners' Comp/Sales	(47) 5.1	(42) 5.7
10.8	7.3						8.6	8.6
26652M	52678M	65605M	59904M	90558M		Net Sales ($)	462393M	660538M
6952M	32357M	92665M	60284M	148652M		Total Assets ($)	449203M	583049M

M = $ thousand   MM = $ million
See Pages viii through xx for Explanation of Ratios and Data

Comparative Historical Data   Current Data Sorted by Sales

Type of Statement									
	4	2	6		1	5			
	10	18	15		7	7	1		
	39	28	29		11	16	2		
	34	31	31		10	8	6	3	1	3
	4/1/16-3/31/17 ALL	4/1/17-3/31/18 ALL	4/1/18-3/31/19 ALL		13 (4/1-9/30/18)			68 (10/1/18-3/31/19)		
					0-1MM	1-3MM	3-5MM	5-10MM	10-25MM	25MM & OVER

	ALL	ALL	ALL	0-1MM	1-3MM	3-5MM	5-10MM	10-25MM	25MM & OVER
NUMBER OF STATEMENTS	95	80	81	29	36	9	3	1	3
	%	%	%	%	%	%	%	%	%
ASSETS									
Cash & Equivalents	14.7	17.3	20.9	20.0	25.4				
Trade Receivables (net)	.8	.8	.4	.8	.2				
Inventory	5.0	3.5	3.0	4.9	2.2				
All Other Current	2.4	1.2	2.9	2.6	4.1				
Total Current	23.0	22.8	27.2	28.3	32.0				
Fixed Assets (net)	63.5	63.5	58.8	53.2	56.5				
Intangibles (net)	3.7	4.3	5.1	5.8	5.6				
All Other Non-Current	9.8	9.4	8.9	12.6	5.9				
Total	100.0	100.0	100.0	100.0	100.0				
LIABILITIES									
Notes Payable-Short Term	6.6	5.0	3.5	6.6	2.0				
Cur. Mat.-L.T.D.	5.8	4.3	5.5	7.7	4.5				
Trade Payables	4.7	4.0	6.9	12.7	4.5				
Income Taxes Payable	.1	.3	.4	.1	.9				
All Other Current	20.0	12.6	14.5	19.7	14.6				
Total Current	37.2	26.1	30.9	46.8	26.6				
Long-Term Debt	63.7	56.6	52.8	44.7	51.1				
Deferred Taxes	.0	.1	.1	.1	.1				
All Other Non-Current	15.5	23.6	23.9	42.1	18.4				
Net Worth	-16.4	-6.4	-7.7	-33.9	3.8				
Total Liabilties & Net Worth	100.0	100.0	100.0	100.0	100.0				
INCOME DATA									
Net Sales	100.0	100.0	100.0	100.0	100.0				
Gross Profit									
Operating Expenses	90.7	89.5	90.8	91.2	92.6				
Operating Profit	9.3	10.5	9.2	8.8	7.4				
All Other Expenses (net)	4.7	4.3	3.3	3.6	2.2				
Profit Before Taxes	4.6	6.2	5.9	5.2	5.2				
RATIOS									
Current	1.8	2.0	2.4	2.6	2.4				
	.9	.8	.9	.7	1.2				
	.3	.4	.3	.3	.4				
Quick	1.1	1.4	2.1	2.5	1.9				
	.5	(79) .7	.6	.5	.9				
	.2	.3	.3	.2	.3				
Sales/Receivables	0 UND	0 UND	0 UND	0 UND	0 UND				
	0 UND	0 999.8	0 UND	0 UND	0 UND				
	1 509.2	2 237.3	0 806.1	1 674.0	0 UND				
Cost of Sales/Inventory									
Cost of Sales/Payables									
Sales/Working Capital	17.8	15.0	12.1	14.4	10.7				
	-56.5	-81.8	-139.0	-36.3	78.6				
	-7.3	-8.9	-8.5	-6.2	-13.4				
EBIT/Interest	4.2	4.6	8.9	10.3	16.8				
	(81) 2.2	(68) 2.2	(62) 2.4	(19) 2.2	(27) 2.3				
	.5	.2	1.2	.5	1.2				
Net Profit + Depr., Dep., Amort./Cur. Mat. L/T/D									
Fixed/Worth	1.8	2.2	1.7	2.4	.7				
	-544.5	UND	92.0	-3.6	54.5				
	-1.1	-2.4	-2.1	-1.2	-1.5				
Debt/Worth	1.7	1.5	1.7	2.6	.8				
	-16.4	UND	132.5	-7.6	77.3				
	-2.8	-4.4	-3.7	-2.5	-2.8				
% Profit Before Taxes/Tangible Net Worth	48.1	111.6	80.0	60.1	90.9				
	(45) 17.3	(41) 17.0	(41) 27.8	(12) 20.2	(19) 39.1				
	4.2	.0	9.8	4.3	19.9				
% Profit Before Taxes/Total Assets	11.4	13.3	20.0	17.4	26.0				
	4.8	5.4	5.9	4.9	6.0				
	-1.2	-2.3	.2	3.2	.6				
Sales/Net Fixed Assets	7.4	6.1	8.5	12.8	12.3				
	1.7	1.9	3.4	5.9	3.6				
	.8	.8	1.0	1.1	1.3				
Sales/Total Assets	2.7	2.8	3.2	3.8	2.9				
	1.2	1.2	1.6	2.3	2.1				
	.7	.6	.8	.9	.9				
% Depr., Dep., Amort./Sales	2.9	3.9	2.6	1.8	3.1				
	(84) 5.4	(63) 6.2	(66) 5.6	(24) 3.7	(28) 6.4				
	9.2	11.2	9.9	8.0	9.6				
% Officers', Directors' Owners' Comp/Sales	2.2	1.9	2.5	2.8	2.7				
	(36) 4.8	(24) 3.9	(36) 4.4	(12) 7.1	(18) 4.4				
	8.4	6.0	8.1	10.3	7.5				
Net Sales ($)	359134M	544928M	295397M	18529M	70556M	32982M	22868M	17001M	133461M
Total Assets ($)	351477M	584498M	340910M	15103M	52132M	37342M	27397M	30020M	178916M

© RMA 2019   M = $ thousand   MM = $ million
See Pages viii through xx for Explanation of Ratios and Data

Current Data Sorted by Assets   **Comparative Historical Data**

Type of Statement	0-500M	500M-2MM	2-10MM	10-50MM	50-100MM	100-250MM		4/1/14-3/31/15 ALL	4/1/15-3/31/16 ALL
Unqualified	2	1	9	9	2	8		44	34
Reviewed	2	6	8	4				20	28
Compiled	27	31	5	3				34	32
Tax Returns	28	55	18	11	6	1		129	111
Other			43					168	137
		36 (4/1-9/30/18)		243 (10/1/18-3/31/19)					
NUMBER OF STATEMENTS	59	93	83	27	8	9		395	342
	%	%	%	%	%	%	**ASSETS**	%	%
Cash & Equivalents	31.4	21.2	15.6	12.9				21.5	18.0
Trade Receivables (net)	3.3	3.3	3.6	3.4				4.4	5.0
Inventory	6.3	6.8	4.0	4.6				4.7	5.5
All Other Current	.7	1.8	3.1	2.0				3.0	2.5
Total Current	41.7	33.2	26.3	22.9				33.6	31.0
Fixed Assets (net)	40.9	50.8	62.8	63.2				49.5	52.6
Intangibles (net)	8.2	7.5	4.7	4.4				7.1	7.7
All Other Non-Current	9.2	8.5	6.1	9.5				9.8	8.7
Total	100.0	100.0	100.0	100.0				100.0	100.0
							LIABILITIES		
Notes Payable-Short Term	19.2	8.7	3.5	4.7				7.0	7.1
Cur. Mat.-L.T.D.	6.5	4.6	3.2	5.7				3.4	3.2
Trade Payables	4.8	6.0	3.3	4.1				4.7	5.5
Income Taxes Payable	.1	.1	.1	.1				.1	.1
All Other Current	12.2	17.2	13.1	7.0				11.1	11.8
Total Current	42.8	36.6	23.1	21.6				26.4	27.7
Long-Term Debt	31.2	33.8	33.0	31.9				30.5	34.3
Deferred Taxes	.0	.0	.1	.4				.2	.2
All Other Non-Current	23.2	17.1	5.2	6.9				9.5	11.7
Net Worth	2.7	12.5	38.5	39.3				33.4	26.2
Total Liabilities & Net Worth	100.0	100.0	100.0	100.0				100.0	100.0
							INCOME DATA		
Net Sales	100.0	100.0	100.0	100.0				100.0	100.0
Gross Profit									
Operating Expenses	93.6	85.8	88.6	88.0				86.9	87.1
Operating Profit	6.4	14.2	11.4	12.0				13.1	12.9
All Other Expenses (net)	1.7	3.0	4.5	2.9				3.0	3.3
Profit Before Taxes	4.7	11.2	6.9	9.1				10.1	9.5
							RATIOS		
	12.1	2.6	3.9	2.3				4.7	3.2
Current	2.0	.9	1.1	.9				1.3	1.2
	.5	.3	.4	.3				.4	.6
	6.6	1.8	2.8	2.2				3.8	2.4
Quick	1.8	.6	.8	.7				.9 (341)	.8
	.2	.2	.2	.1				.2	.3
	0 UND	0 UND	0 UND	1 547.7				0 UND	0 UND
Sales/Receivables	0 UND	0 UND	1 264.2	6 64.4				999.8	1 558.8
	0 UND	2 242.4	11 32.7	21 17.4				9 42.0	10 36.3
							Cost of Sales/Inventory		
							Cost of Sales/Payables		
	8.9	11.5	6.8	8.1				6.6	9.1
Sales/Working Capital	30.4	-98.9	41.5	-150.4				31.3	50.6
	-9.6	-7.7	-7.3	-5.3				-12.1	-15.9
	12.3	19.6	13.1	7.6				14.4	11.7
EBIT/Interest	(36) 4.9	(71) 4.9	(67) 3.9	(21) 2.8				(281) 4.2	(248) 4.2
	-.1	-.2	1.0	1.4				1.4	1.0
							Net Profit + Depr., Dep.,	5.6	3.4
							Amort./Cur. Mat. L/T/D	(21) 3.5 (20) 2.3	
								2.2	1.3
	.2	.7	.8	1.0				.5	.6
Fixed/Worth	1.8	2.5	2.1	2.2				1.5	2.0
	-1.4	-3.0	5.7	6.1				19.6	185.6
	.3	.6	.5	.5				.4	.5
Debt/Worth	2.4	3.5	1.9	2.1				1.7	2.2
	-2.5	-5.3	6.6	11.8				-175.0	-61.2
	145.3	129.9	47.9	38.8				75.5	74.4
% Profit Before Taxes/Tangible Net Worth	(38) 38.3	(62) 56.4	(72) 10.8	(24) 13.7				(296) 22.6	(253) 23.5
	2.3	10.5	.0	.4				5.0	3.7
	30.5	34.7	17.3	10.9				25.8	24.7
% Profit Before Taxes/Total Assets	15.7	9.7	3.1	5.4				8.5	7.3
	-2.6	-2.2	-.4	.0				1.4	.3
	37.9	18.0	3.6	2.9				18.4	14.8
Sales/Net Fixed Assets	10.1	4.1	1.2	1.2				3.4	2.9
	3.9	1.6	.7	.6				1.0	1.0
	5.8	3.5	2.2	1.5				3.3	3.0
Sales/Total Assets	3.4	1.9	.9	.8				1.4	1.4
	1.9	1.0	.5	.5				.7	.6
	.9	1.8	4.3	3.8				2.4	2.8
% Depr., Dep., Amort./Sales	(30) 4.9	(59) 4.9	(69) 7.3	(26) 7.4				(282) 4.9	(251) 5.8
	9.6	9.9	12.3	12.8				9.4	10.5
	2.6	2.8	2.4					3.9	2.2
% Officers', Directors' Owners' Comp/Sales	(29) 5.7	(34) 4.6	(23) 3.8					(119) 6.6	(92) 4.3
	10.8	7.3	6.4					10.3	9.3
Net Sales ($)	51343M	264797M	471228M	597017M	561017M	1813378M		4973487M	4896963M
Total Assets ($)	13976M	105858M	403018M	624973M	531065M	1509842M		5284458M	4449555M

M = $ thousand   MM = $ million
See Pages viii through xx for Explanation of Ratios and Data

Comparative Historical Data | Current Data Sorted by Sales

	4/1/16-3/31/17 ALL	4/1/17-3/31/18 ALL	4/1/18-3/31/19 ALL	0-1MM	1-3MM	3-5MM	5-10MM	10-25MM	25MM & OVER
Type of Statement				36 (4/1-9/30/18)			243 (10/1/18-3/31/19)		
Unqualified	26	30	28		2	3	6	3	14
Reviewed	15	14	15	1	4	2	5	3	
Compiled	30	23	16	3	7	3	1	2	
Tax Returns	93	92	76	29	25	9	10	3	
Other	123	125	144	38	47	16	15	19	9
NUMBER OF STATEMENTS	287	284	279	71	85	33	37	30	23
	%	%	%	%	%	%	%	%	%
ASSETS									
Cash & Equivalents	18.5	16.2	20.4	20.8	22.8	18.0	21.2	16.9	16.5
Trade Receivables (net)	4.7	4.0	3.6	2.4	2.3	3.2	4.9	7.2	5.2
Inventory	4.2	6.1	5.6	3.6	5.2	5.6	9.0	6.7	6.4
All Other Current	3.0	4.1	2.1	.6	2.3	1.1	2.4	4.3	4.4
Total Current	30.4	30.5	31.6	27.4	32.7	27.9	37.5	35.1	32.4
Fixed Assets (net)	53.2	52.7	54.0	57.4	53.0	59.8	48.0	49.9	54.0
Intangibles (net)	8.4	7.9	6.4	8.5	5.6	5.1	7.0	4.6	6.5
All Other Non-Current	7.9	8.9	7.9	6.7	8.7	7.1	7.6	10.4	7.0
Total	100.0	100.0	100.0	100.0	100.0	100.0	100.0	100.0	100.0
LIABILITIES									
Notes Payable-Short Term	6.4	6.1	8.6	16.9	8.6	4.1	4.5	2.7	4.0
Cur. Mat.-L.T.D.	4.9	4.4	4.5	4.5	4.7	4.8	4.7	3.4	5.0
Trade Payables	5.0	5.0	4.7	2.1	4.1	6.5	8.7	5.3	5.6
Income Taxes Payable	.1	.2	.1	.0	.1	.1	.0	.2	.0
All Other Current	11.7	12.9	13.3	9.1	11.6	8.4	24.2	24.6	7.6
Total Current	28.1	28.5	31.3	32.6	29.0	23.8	42.2	36.2	22.2
Long-Term Debt	36.1	34.5	33.3	37.5	33.6	42.7	19.0	28.5	35.4
Deferred Taxes	.2	.3	.1	.0	.1	.0	.2	.3	.3
All Other Non-Current	8.9	8.4	13.7	13.1	22.0	4.8	9.3	5.8	15.0
Net Worth	26.7	28.3	21.5	16.8	15.2	28.6	29.2	29.2	27.2
Total Liabilities & Net Worth	100.0	100.0	100.0	100.0	100.0	100.0	100.0	100.0	100.0
INCOME DATA									
Net Sales	100.0	100.0	100.0	100.0	100.0	100.0	100.0	100.0	100.0
Gross Profit									
Operating Expenses	87.1	87.9	88.4	86.3	88.9	89.7	92.4	89.7	82.8
Operating Profit	12.9	12.1	11.6	13.7	11.1	10.3	7.6	10.3	17.2
All Other Expenses (net)	3.3	2.8	3.1	5.4	3.8	1.9	.4	1.1	2.5
Profit Before Taxes	9.6	9.3	8.5	8.3	7.3	8.4	7.3	9.2	14.6
RATIOS									
Current	2.9	2.9	3.6	6.5	5.4	3.5	2.5	2.0	3.8
	1.1	1.2	1.1	1.1	1.3	1.2	.9	1.0	1.3
	.5	.5	.4	.2	.5	.6	.4	.7	.7
Quick	2.3	1.7	3.1	6.0	5.1	3.0	1.5	1.3	3.6
	.8	.7	.8	1.0	1.0	.9	.6	.7	1.2
	.3	.2	.2	.1	.3	.3	.2	.3	.2
Sales/Receivables	0 UND	0 UND	0 UND	0 UND	0 UND	0 UND	0 UND	0 999.8	3 106.4
	0 999.8	0 999.8	0 UND	0 UND	0 UND	1 552.8	1 264.2	6 64.7	7 48.9
	10 35.2	7 54.4	6 60.2	0 UND	3 120.4	9 38.8	11 33.5	12 30.4	31 11.7
Cost of Sales/Inventory									
Cost of Sales/Payables									
Sales/Working Capital	7.4	7.4	8.2	10.6	5.0	8.4	7.3	11.9	3.2
	57.2	42.2	88.7	373.5	30.4	35.0	-150.4	732.8	30.9
	-10.5	-12.4	-8.0	-3.0	-10.7	-14.1	-6.3	-22.4	-26.2
EBIT/Interest	14.4	16.2	13.1	11.3	11.1	19.6	26.1	23.8	30.1
	(211) 3.4	(206) 3.4	(211) 3.9	(43) 4.6	(67) 1.6	(27) 4.2	(29) 5.2	(25) 6.0	(20) 3.0
	.9	.8	.6	-.3	-.7	1.1	1.0	2.1	1.9
Net Profit + Depr., Dep., Amort./Cur. Mat. L/T/D		18.2	6.8						
		(10) 5.0	(13) 4.1						
		2.0	1.9						
Fixed/Worth	.7	.5	.8	.7	.7	.9	.6	.8	.8
	1.8	1.7	2.0	2.5	2.1	2.0	1.5	2.1	1.4
	-10.9	NM	24.2	-8.2	-5.0	11.0	4.3	11.5	2.5
Debt/Worth	.5	.6	.5	.6	.3	.6	.5	.9	.2
	2.3	2.6	2.1	3.5	2.2	2.0	1.6	2.7	1.6
	-14.8	-21.1	371.5	-8.5	-7.3	12.7	8.6	12.2	4.6
% Profit Before Taxes/Tangible Net Worth	72.8	56.8	77.6	88.8	85.2	75.0	85.8	130.4	34.9
	(204) 24.6	(206) 22.4	(212) 23.4	(49) 19.5	(61) 23.5	(26) 27.8	(30) 16.0	(25) 41.0	(21) 15.9
	3.0	1.0	1.3	-3.1	-.2	1.4	.0	12.3	5.9
% Profit Before Taxes/Total Assets	23.8	21.8	23.9	19.1	25.6	34.7	25.0	35.0	28.2
	6.9	6.7	6.2	4.0	3.7	6.2	9.9	8.8	10.4
	.3	-.4	-1.1	-3.0	-3.0	-1.0	.0	3.3	3.1
Sales/Net Fixed Assets	11.3	15.0	12.3	13.7	12.9	9.6	12.9	58.6	5.0
	2.7	2.4	3.0	2.2	3.7	2.5	3.2	4.0	1.7
	.9	.8	1.0	.4	1.2	.9	1.1	1.3	1.0
Sales/Total Assets	2.7	2.6	2.9	2.6	3.2	3.3	3.0	3.1	2.1
	1.2	1.3	1.5	1.1	1.6	1.5	1.5	2.2	1.0
	.6	.6	.7	.4	.8	.8	.7	1.1	.7
% Depr., Dep., Amort./Sales	2.8	2.1	2.8	5.5	2.8	1.6	1.7	1.6	1.4
	(206) 7.8	(204) 5.8	(195) 6.1	(36) 9.4	(62) 6.1	(24) 4.3	(33) 6.9	(22) 4.3	(18) 6.0
	12.5	10.3	11.3	15.5	11.1	6.4	11.3	11.8	12.4
% Officers', Directors' Owners' Comp/Sales	2.8	3.2	2.6	3.3	2.6	2.5	2.7		
	(84) 4.8	(77) 5.1	(88) 4.8	(21) 6.4	(34) 4.5	(12) 4.6	(12) 4.4		
	9.9	7.6	7.0	10.8	6.8	7.2	5.7		
Net Sales ($)	3593561M	3506465M	3758780M	34640M	161130M	121246M	254032M	462661M	2725071M
Total Assets ($)	3264854M	3720372M	3188732M	68073M	171070M	111083M	272260M	455349M	2110897M

© RMA 2019

M = $ thousand   MM = $ million
See Pages viii through xx for Explanation of Ratios and Data

ACCOMMODATION AND FOOD SERVICES

Current Data Sorted by Assets							Comparative Historical Data	
						Type of Statement		
2	1	14	25	7	11	Unqualified	99	67
	1	17	18	5	2	Reviewed	60	67
8	21	82	12	5	2	Compiled	185	147
57	135	270	32	2		Tax Returns	758	717
33	84	281	180	27	21	Other	613	562
	63 (4/1-9/30/18)		1,292 (10/1/18-3/31/19)				4/1/14-3/31/15	4/1/15-3/31/16
0-500M	500M-2MM	2-10MM	10-50MM	50-100MM	100-250MM		ALL	ALL
100	242	664	267	46	36	**NUMBER OF STATEMENTS**	1715	1560
%	%	%	%	%	%	**ASSETS**	%	%
37.4	13.2	9.3	7.1	9.4	10.6	Cash & Equivalents	11.4	11.7
3.3	1.5	1.4	2.0	2.1	3.8	Trade Receivables (net)	2.1	2.1
1.8	.8	.5	.5	.5	.5	Inventory	.5	.6
2.9	1.6	1.6	2.8	2.5	3.7	All Other Current	1.9	2.0
45.4	17.0	12.9	12.4	14.4	18.6	Total Current	15.8	16.4
42.4	72.3	76.6	76.9	67.0	63.5	Fixed Assets (net)	74.1	72.5
2.8	3.2	4.7	5.7	4.9	7.8	Intangibles (net)	3.5	3.8
9.4	7.4	5.8	5.0	13.6	10.1	All Other Non-Current	6.5	7.4
100.0	100.0	100.0	100.0	100.0	100.0	Total	100.0	100.0
						LIABILITIES		
16.1	3.2	1.9	1.1	2.2	2.9	Notes Payable-Short Term	2.3	3.4
2.6	2.8	3.0	2.4	2.2	1.7	Cur. Mat.-L.T.D.	3.1	3.3
8.9	2.5	1.6	2.3	2.3	2.4	Trade Payables	2.7	2.3
.2	.1	.0	.1	.2	.1	Income Taxes Payable	.2	.1
21.4	7.9	4.5	6.0	12.3	13.1	All Other Current	9.7	9.0
49.2	16.5	11.0	11.9	19.3	20.3	Total Current	18.0	18.1
27.4	55.1	69.9	61.8	45.4	43.8	Long-Term Debt	61.4	59.9
.0	.0	.1	.1	.1	.0	Deferred Taxes	.0	.1
23.0	10.0	4.7	4.1	5.2	2.0	All Other Non-Current	6.6	7.2
.2	18.3	14.4	22.0	30.0	34.0	Net Worth	13.9	14.7
100.0	100.0	100.0	100.0	100.0	100.0	Total Liabilties & Net Worth	100.0	100.0
						INCOME DATA		
100.0	100.0	100.0	100.0	100.0	100.0	Net Sales	100.0	100.0
						Gross Profit		
89.4	83.5	80.4	81.8	85.8	88.9	Operating Expenses	81.2	81.5
10.6	16.5	19.6	18.2	14.2	11.1	Operating Profit	18.8	18.5
2.4	6.5	8.5	9.1	7.0	6.7	All Other Expenses (net)	7.6	7.4
8.2	10.0	11.1	9.0	7.2	4.4	Profit Before Taxes	11.2	11.2
						RATIOS		
5.0	3.3	3.1	2.5	1.8	1.9		2.6	2.6
1.4	1.2	1.4	1.0	1.0	1.0	Current	1.1	1.1
.6	.4	.5	.5	.4	.4		.4	.5
4.8	3.0	2.8	2.0	1.6	1.5		2.2	2.3
1.1 (241)	1.1 (663)	1.1	.8	.7	.7	Quick (1711)	.9 (1559)	.9
.4	.4	.4	.3	.4	.2		.3	.3
0 UND	0 UND	0 UND	2 164.8	3 118.9	6 57.3		0 UND	0 UND
0 UND	0 UND	2 222.9	5 69.2	6 61.2	8 43.0	Sales/Receivables	2 182.6	2 155.1
1 303.8	2 160.7	7 54.7	11 33.9	15 23.9	28 13.2		8 44.8	8 46.8
						Cost of Sales/Inventory		
						Cost of Sales/Payables		
11.7	9.2	6.7	6.6	8.1	4.2		9.0	8.3
63.8	72.7	33.6	277.5	999.8	547.9	Sales/Working Capital	146.9	100.1
-20.1	-14.2	-13.6	-10.4	-6.5	-5.2		-9.6	-11.2
12.9	5.5	4.4	4.2	4.5	2.7		4.8	5.2
(46) 3.9	(195) 2.6	(588) 2.5	(219) 2.1	(38) 2.5	(30) 1.5	EBIT/Interest (1411)	2.6 (1290)	2.7
2.0	1.3	1.3	.9	.7	.8		1.3	1.4
			8.6	4.2			5.2	8.3
		(22) 4.0	(20) 2.7			Net Profit + Depr., Dep., Amort./Cur. Mat. L/T/D (60)	3.1 (58)	5.4
		1.9	1.3				1.2	2.1
.3	1.7	2.6	2.3	1.1	1.0		2.0	1.8
1.3	3.7	6.0	5.0	2.7	2.3	Fixed/Worth	5.3	5.0
-2.8	50.1	-20.7	-86.3	14.2	NM		-21.8	-17.9
.4	1.5	2.3	1.7	1.2	.7		1.8	1.6
2.3	3.6	6.3	5.0	2.6	2.1	Debt/Worth	5.7	5.2
-4.7	96.9	-23.2	-53.6	17.5	NM		-21.7	-18.0
147.7	63.5	55.4	34.5	24.9	12.9	% Profit Before Taxes/Tangible	60.8	66.1
(66) 48.6	(190) 26.2	(465) 23.2	(195) 10.4	(37) 12.5	(27) 2.8	Net Worth (1190)	25.8 (1083)	25.6
13.3	5.7	6.2	-1.5	-.4	-1.3		6.4	7.4
52.0	16.5	11.0	7.6	8.6	5.0		12.5	12.7
16.7	6.1	5.1	3.4	4.0	1.6	% Profit Before Taxes/Total Assets	5.4	5.7
-.9	.7	1.0	-.5	-.5	-.4		.9	1.2
120.4	1.9	1.0	.8	1.2	1.9		1.3	1.3
14.7	.8	.6	.4	.6	.6	Sales/Net Fixed Assets	.6	.6
4.1	.5	.4	.3	.4	.3		.4	.4
10.0	1.3	.7	.6	.7	.8		.9	.9
5.2	.6	.5	.4	.4	.3	Sales/Total Assets	.5	.5
1.7	.4	.3	.3	.3	.2		.4	.3
1.0	4.5	5.8	7.7	6.4	5.1		5.6	5.3
(60) 3.4	(197) 7.7	(565) 8.9	(206) 11.3	(39) 10.7	(29) 7.8	% Depr., Dep., Amort./Sales (1438)	8.5 (1310)	8.3
6.8	12.0	13.4	17.4	13.6	12.8		12.8	12.6
3.1	2.7	1.8	2.3				2.0	2.1
(37) 5.3	(91) 4.5	(147) 3.8	(17) 4.2			% Officers', Directors' Owners' Comp/Sales (410)	3.7 (373)	3.9
11.1	6.8	6.9	15.9				6.4	7.8
124142M	364032M	2032821M	3924343M	3031259M	3272028M	Net Sales ($)	13080200M	12995042M
23900M	307446M	3272115M	5710105M	3271233M	6072957M	Total Assets ($)	17654329M	17528009M

© RMA 2019

M = $ thousand   MM = $ million
See Pages viii through xx for Explanation of Ratios and Data

Comparative Historical Data | | | | Current Data Sorted by Sales

			Type of Statement						
77	51	60	Unqualified	3	7	7	6	15	22
53	60	43	Reviewed	3	4	10	8	7	11
110	105	130	Compiled	20	65	21	11	4	9
529	521	496	Tax Returns	148	239	69	20	17	3
519	567	626	Other	93	224	114	84	65	46
4/1/16-3/31/17	4/1/17-3/31/18	4/1/18-3/31/19			63 (4/1-9/30/18)		1,292 (10/1/18-3/31/19)		
ALL	ALL	ALL		0-1MM	1-3MM	3-5MM	5-10MM	10-25MM	25MM & OVER
1288	1304	1355	**NUMBER OF STATEMENTS**	267	539	221	129	108	91
%	%	%	**ASSETS**	%	%	%	%	%	%
12.6	11.5	11.7	Cash & Equivalents	11.3	11.3	13.0	8.6	13.8	13.9
2.8	1.9	1.8	Trade Receivables (net)	.9	1.1	2.3	1.9	3.3	5.5
.6	.5	.6	Inventory	.2	.4	.4	1.3	1.5	1.5
1.9	1.8	2.0	All Other Current	.9	1.8	2.4	2.1	3.1	4.1
17.9	15.8	16.1	Total Current	13.4	14.7	18.1	13.9	21.6	25.0
71.4	72.9	72.7	Fixed Assets (net)	76.6	74.9	73.2	72.3	64.7	57.2
3.7	4.1	4.6	Intangibles (net)	3.8	4.3	3.4	6.5	4.8	8.2
7.1	7.3	6.6	All Other Non-Current	6.2	6.2	5.3	7.2	8.8	9.5
100.0	100.0	100.0	Total	100.0	100.0	100.0	100.0	100.0	100.0
			LIABILITIES						
2.2	2.6	3.1	Notes Payable-Short Term	3.8	3.9	1.7	2.9	.6	2.9
3.3	3.3	2.8	Cur. Mat.-L.T.D.	2.9	3.0	2.7	2.1	2.6	2.7
2.7	2.4	2.5	Trade Payables	1.6	1.8	2.8	3.3	4.6	4.8
.1	.1	.1	Income Taxes Payable	.0	.1	.0	.0	.2	.2
8.4	8.1	7.1	All Other Current	5.2	6.3	5.9	6.5	10.4	17.5
16.6	16.4	15.5	Total Current	13.6	15.0	13.1	14.8	18.3	28.1
59.4	59.7	61.0	Long-Term Debt	56.6	65.2	65.9	69.3	46.5	42.2
.1	.1	.1	Deferred Taxes	.0	.1	.1	.1	.1	.1
7.8	6.3	6.8	All Other Non-Current	12.0	6.0	3.4	6.8	7.7	3.5
16.1	17.5	16.6	Net Worth	17.8	13.7	17.4	9.0	27.5	26.1
100.0	100.0	100.0	Total Liabilities & Net Worth	100.0	100.0	100.0	100.0	100.0	100.0
			INCOME DATA						
100.0	100.0	100.0	Net Sales	100.0	100.0	100.0	100.0	100.0	100.0
			Gross Profit						
81.6	82.8	82.3	Operating Expenses	79.6	82.2	80.6	84.0	86.3	87.6
18.4	17.2	17.7	Operating Profit	20.4	17.8	19.4	16.0	13.7	12.4
7.1	7.4	7.7	All Other Expenses (net)	10.4	7.8	7.1	7.3	5.2	4.2
11.2	9.9	10.0	Profit Before Taxes	9.9	10.0	12.3	8.6	8.5	8.2
			RATIOS						
2.8	2.9	2.9		3.9	3.2	3.1	2.5	2.3	1.8
1.2	1.1	1.2	Current	1.2	1.4	1.4	.9	1.2	.9
.5	.4	.5		.4	.5	.5	.5	.6	.4
2.4	2.5	2.5		3.3	2.9	2.8	1.8	2.0	1.5
(1287) 1.0	(1301) .9	(1353) 1.0	Quick	1.2 (538)	1.1 (220)	1.1	.7	.9	.7
.3	.3	.4		.3	.4	.4	.2	.4	.3
0 UND	0 UND	0 UND		0 UND	0 UND	0 999.8	1 297.4	2 206.2	4 85.2
3 142.2	3 135.5	2 171.9	Sales/Receivables	0 UND	1 527.3	4 103.4	4 95.9	5 67.6	8 48.6
8 46.2	8 47.4	7 50.7		1 444.0	6 65.3	8 43.9	10 37.3	12 31.6	16 22.2
			Cost of Sales/Inventory						
			Cost of Sales/Payables						
7.6	8.3	7.5		7.5	7.3	5.7	9.0	9.2	10.1
66.2	85.5	51.3	Sales/Working Capital	48.7	34.9	32.8	-136.3	46.1	-102.3
-12.5	-9.7	-12.7		-8.2	-14.3	-14.6	-10.5	-18.3	-8.4
5.5	5.1	4.6		3.5	4.2	5.2	4.5	9.5	6.8
(1065) 2.7	(1067) 2.6	(1116) 2.4	EBIT/Interest	(185) 2.0	(462) 2.5	(191) 2.9	(114) 2.1	(90) 3.2	(74) 2.3
1.4	1.2	1.2		1.1	1.2	1.4	.8	1.5	1.0
5.5	5.0	5.1	Net Profit + Depr., Dep.,		8.9	6.6		4.3	6.4
(65) 2.9	(55) 2.6	(54) 2.9	Amort./Cur. Mat. L/T/D	(10) 2.0	(11) 3.7		(13) 2.7	(10) 3.4	
1.7	1.6	1.5		.7	2.0		1.7	1.0	
1.7	1.8	2.0		2.1	2.3	2.1	3.2	.9	.9
4.4	4.6	5.0	Fixed/Worth	4.4	5.4	4.7	13.2	2.5	2.3
-120.4	-39.9	-41.8		130.9	-97.8	-40.8	-4.7	NM	103.5
1.6	1.5	1.7		1.8	2.1	1.6	2.9	.8	1.2
4.7	4.7	5.0	Debt/Worth	4.4	5.7	5.0	18.9	2.4	3.6
-64.1	-44.5	-37.1		UND	-43.5	-50.4	-7.0	-319.5	-19.5
68.1	54.0	55.0	% Profit Before Taxes/Tangible	47.0	56.5	60.8	41.4	67.2	45.0
(942) 25.4	(937) 20.6	(980) 20.4	Net Worth	(202) 16.9	(394) 23.2	(161) 26.1	(76) 11.8	(80) 16.9	(67) 15.0
5.8	3.1	4.0		3.5	5.6	5.3	-3.4	4.9	2.8
14.1	11.8	11.6		8.7	11.4	13.0	11.0	15.6	11.7
5.9	5.4	4.8	% Profit Before Taxes/Total Assets	3.1	5.2	6.2	3.9	5.6	4.3
1.2	.2	.4		.0	.5	1.7	-1.0	1.9	.2
1.4	1.3	1.2		.8	1.1	1.2	1.3	3.3	4.8
.7	.6	.6	Sales/Net Fixed Assets	.5	.6	.7	.6	.9	1.2
.4	.4	.4		.3	.4	.4	.4	.5	.6
.9	.9	.8		.6	.7	.8	.9	1.3	1.2
.5	.5	.5	Sales/Total Assets	.4	.5	.5	.5	.7	.8
.3	.3	.3		.3	.3	.3	.3	.4	.4
5.0	5.3	5.5		6.7	5.4	5.6	5.6	4.6	4.6
(1085) 8.1	(1049) 8.6	(1096) 8.9	% Depr., Dep., Amort./Sales	(215) 10.2	(433) 8.4	(182) 8.4	(108) 9.0	(86) 9.0	(72) 6.6
13.0	13.3	13.6		16.1	13.0	14.5	14.3	12.8	11.5
2.2	2.1	2.1		3.8	2.0	1.9	1.7	1.4	
(283) 3.9	(281) 4.0	(298) 4.3	% Officers', Directors' Owners' Comp/Sales	(77) 5.9	(146) 3.9	(35) 3.1	(14) 3.7	(18) 1.7	
7.4	7.5	7.0		11.0	6.9	6.9	5.5	6.3	
10880361M	11546159M	12748625M	Net Sales ($)	151884M	1010633M	839201M	870313M	1689078M	8187516M
15717480M	17471763M	18657756M	Total Assets ($)	512541M	2405960M	1876796M	2118677M	3337306M	8406476M

© RMA 2019

M = $ thousand   MM = $ million
See Pages viii through xx for Explanation of Ratios and Data

Current Data Sorted by Assets   **Comparative Historical Data**

Type of Statement — time period groupings: **20 (4/1-9/30/18)** covers 0-500M / 500M-2MM / 2-10MM; **61 (10/1/18-3/31/19)** covers 10-50MM / 50-100MM / 100-250MM.

Type of Statement	0-500M	500M-2MM	2-10MM	10-50MM	50-100MM	100-250MM	4/1/14-3/31/15 ALL	4/1/15-3/31/16 ALL
Unqualified			2	9	9	10	24	22
Reviewed	1		2	1			4	1
Compiled	1		1	1			3	2
Tax Returns			1	1			2	1
Other	2	1	3	11	11	14	59	54
NUMBER OF STATEMENTS	4	1	9	23	20	24	92	80

0-500M	500M-2MM	2-10MM	10-50MM	50-100MM	100-250MM		4/1/14-3/31/15 ALL	4/1/15-3/31/16 ALL
%	%	%	%	%	%	**ASSETS**	%	%
			19.2	15.6	15.0	Cash & Equivalents	15.9	16.4
			1.1	1.1	1.4	Trade Receivables (net)	1.4	1.4
			.8	.7	.6	Inventory	1.0	.9
			4.1	1.4	.9	All Other Current	3.9	1.8
			25.2	18.6	17.9	Total Current	22.2	20.6
			64.0	71.6	73.7	Fixed Assets (net)	68.2	70.2
			6.0	6.3	5.9	Intangibles (net)	5.4	5.4
			4.8	3.4	2.5	All Other Non-Current	4.3	3.7
			100.0	100.0	100.0	Total	100.0	100.0
						LIABILITIES		
			.6	.0	1.2	Notes Payable-Short Term	.6	.6
			9.6	5.5	4.0	Cur. Mat.-L.T.D.	5.4	5.3
			3.1	2.1	3.0	Trade Payables	2.6	2.9
			.1	.0	.0	Income Taxes Payable	.0	.1
			9.3	8.8	8.5	All Other Current	8.4	12.8
			22.5	16.4	16.7	Total Current	17.1	21.7
			39.9	41.2	30.1	Long-Term Debt	34.5	37.8
			.2	.0	.0	Deferred Taxes	.2	.2
			13.9	12.0	3.6	All Other Non-Current	6.4	6.3
			23.5	30.4	49.6	Net Worth	41.8	34.0
			100.0	100.0	100.0	Total Liabilities & Net Worth	100.0	100.0
						INCOME DATA		
			100.0	100.0	100.0	Net Sales	100.0	100.0
						Gross Profit		
			88.0	81.0	79.8	Operating Expenses	81.8	81.4
			12.0	19.0	20.2	Operating Profit	18.2	18.6
			3.2	3.7	3.4	All Other Expenses (net)	3.8	5.1
			8.8	15.3	16.8	Profit Before Taxes	14.5	13.5
						RATIOS		
			2.7	2.0	1.5		2.0	1.9
			1.2	1.2	1.1	Current	1.1	1.1
			.8	.7	.8		.8	.5
			2.3	1.8	1.4		1.4	1.6
			.9	1.1	1.0	Quick	.9	.9
			.7	.7	.7		.5	.4
			1 572.8	1 273.8	3 138.6		1 297.3	1 268.0
			3 143.2	3 113.7	5 80.8	Sales/Receivables	3 144.2	3 134.6
			5 80.8	4 83.4	7 49.9		6 59.2	6 59.0
						Cost of Sales/Inventory		
						Cost of Sales/Payables		
			7.0	12.6	12.3		12.3	10.4
			67.1	41.9	128.7	Sales/Working Capital	49.6	534.4
			-37.0	NM	-24.2		-21.4	-13.2
			6.3	13.0	27.6		17.5	13.3
			(20) 2.8	(17) 4.9	(21) 4.7	EBIT/Interest	(78) 6.2	(61) 4.4
			.9	1.9	1.2		1.7	1.8
						Net Profit + Depr., Dep., Amort./Cur. Mat. L/T/D		
			1.0	1.0	1.0		1.0	1.0
			2.6	1.8	1.7	Fixed/Worth	2.0	2.5
			16.2	NM	3.4		3.9	7.8
			.8	.2	.5		.6	.5
			1.9	1.7	1.0	Debt/Worth	1.8	1.9
			20.3	NM	2.8		4.0	8.9
			44.5	72.5	58.4		71.4	64.0
			(19) 13.9	(15) 32.9	(22) 25.7	% Profit Before Taxes/Tangible Net Worth	(77) 29.9	(64) 21.9
			2.1	15.1	8.2		4.5	6.8
			14.8	24.3	24.5		23.8	29.8
			3.1	14.0	9.5	% Profit Before Taxes/Total Assets	11.3	7.5
			-.1	4.0	2.9		.4	2.0
			4.1	1.7	1.7		2.0	2.0
			1.4	1.3	1.1	Sales/Net Fixed Assets	1.3	1.3
			1.1	1.1	.8		1.0	.9
			1.5	1.4	1.1		1.3	1.3
			1.0	1.0	.9	Sales/Total Assets	1.0	1.0
			.8	.8	.6		.8	.7
			4.5	4.8	5.0		4.2	4.6
			(22) 6.7	(17) 6.1	(12) 5.9	% Depr., Dep., Amort./Sales	(72) 6.4	(53) 6.8
			8.2	8.3	7.7		8.5	8.6
						% Officers', Directors' Owners' Comp/Sales		
3086M	174M	55851M	938821M	1537247M	3700890M	Net Sales ($)	9459067M	8185263M
1268M	1695M	40281M	718794M	1408087M	3939138M	Total Assets ($)	8108965M	7982125M

M = $ thousand   MM = $ million
See Pages viii through xx for Explanation of Ratios and Data

Comparative Historical Data / Current Data Sorted by Sales

Type of Statement — Current Data date groupings: **20 (4/1-9/30/18)** covers the 1-3MM band; **61 (10/1/18-3/31/19)** covers the 5-10MM band.

	4/1/16-3/31/17 ALL	4/1/17-3/31/18 ALL	4/1/18-3/31/19 ALL	0-1MM	1-3MM	3-5MM	5-10MM	10-25MM	25MM & OVER
Type of Statement									
Unqualified	42	41	30				1	3	26
Reviewed	2	2	3					1	2
Compiled	1	3	4		3				1
Tax Returns	1	1	2		2				
Other	48	50	42	4		1	1	4	32
NUMBER OF STATEMENTS	94	97	81	4	5	1	3	10	58
ASSETS (%)	%	%	%	%	%	%	%	%	%
Cash & Equivalents	16.2	16.9	18.6					22.3	17.3
Trade Receivables (net)	1.4	1.4	1.3					.7	1.3
Inventory	.9	1.0	.7					.8	.7
All Other Current	2.8	2.2	2.1					5.3	1.9
Total Current	21.3	21.4	22.7					29.0	21.1
Fixed Assets (net)	69.3	68.6	66.1					58.6	70.0
Intangibles (net)	7.1	7.1	5.5					5.9	6.0
All Other Non-Current	2.3	2.8	5.7					6.5	2.9
Total	100.0	100.0	100.0					100.0	100.0
LIABILITIES									
Notes Payable-Short Term	1.3	.6	.6					2.2	.5
Cur. Mat.-L.T.D.	4.7	5.9	5.5					3.3	6.7
Trade Payables	3.1	3.9	2.7					3.1	2.7
Income Taxes Payable	.1	.1	.0					.1	.0
All Other Current	9.6	9.6	9.1					10.5	9.5
Total Current	18.8	20.1	17.9					19.2	19.5
Long-Term Debt	41.5	38.9	36.2					35.9	35.9
Deferred Taxes	.3	.1	.1					.0	.1
All Other Non-Current	19.2	7.3	9.0					2.1	10.7
Net Worth	20.2	33.6	36.9					42.8	33.8
Total Liabilities & Net Worth	100.0	100.0	100.0					100.0	100.0
INCOME DATA									
Net Sales	100.0	100.0	100.0					100.0	100.0
Gross Profit									
Operating Expenses	82.7	83.1	85.5					91.7	81.5
Operating Profit	17.3	16.9	14.5					8.3	18.5
All Other Expenses (net)	3.7	3.6	2.9					2.9	3.6
Profit Before Taxes	13.6	13.4	11.6					5.4	14.9
RATIOS									
Current	1.9	2.0	2.5					2.7	2.1
	1.1	1.1	1.2					1.4	1.1
	.7	.8	.9					.7	.8
Quick	1.7	1.7	2.1					1.9	1.7
	1.0	.9	1.1					1.1	1.0
	.5	.6	.8					.7	.7
Sales/Receivables	2 221.0	2 232.5	1 281.8					1 614.9	2 179.2
	3 131.1	3 107.6	3 119.5					2 158.7	4 103.2
	5 78.0	5 67.5	5 74.2					5 67.1	5 74.9
Cost of Sales/Inventory									
Cost of Sales/Payables									
Sales/Working Capital	9.2	9.2	7.9					8.3	10.5
	97.1	47.6	31.8					NM	63.8
	-17.3	-18.4	-48.5					-28.9	-34.2
EBIT/Interest	21.7	15.1	11.1						15.9
	(79) 6.0	(85) 5.6	(65) 3.5						(49) 4.7
	2.1	1.8	1.4						1.3
Net Profit + Depr., Dep., Amort./Cur. Mat. L/T/D									
Fixed/Worth	1.1	1.0	1.0					.5	1.0
	2.1	2.2	1.8					1.7	2.2
	21.2	5.1	4.5					3.9	6.0
Debt/Worth	.5	.4	.4					1.0	.4
	1.9	1.8	1.6					1.2	1.8
	26.0	6.4	4.8					3.8	6.3
% Profit Before Taxes/Tangible Net Worth	81.1	58.8	53.2					44.5	61.1
	(76) 28.1	(77) 30.0	(67) 22.5					5.1	(47) 31.3
	12.6	11.0	5.2					2.2	10.3
% Profit Before Taxes/Total Assets	21.6	21.0	19.9					14.1	25.5
	9.7	9.2	7.7					2.2	11.9
	3.3	2.7	1.3					.8	2.8
Sales/Net Fixed Assets	2.2	2.1	2.4					5.3	2.0
	1.3	1.3	1.3					1.2	1.3
	.9	1.0	1.0					1.1	1.0
Sales/Total Assets	1.3	1.3	1.3					1.5	1.3
	.9	1.0	1.0					1.0	1.0
	.7	.7	.8					.7	.8
% Depr., Dep., Amort./Sales	4.8	4.6	4.5						4.6
	(60) 7.0	(79) 6.7	(62) 6.0						(42) 6.0
	9.0	8.2	8.2						8.2
% Officers', Directors', Owners' Comp/Sales									
Net Sales ($)	9904686M	8667336M	6236069M	1334M	6853M	4642M	20150M	166526M	6036564M
Total Assets ($)	8958103M	8246073M	6109263M	4155M	17561M	5104M	19474M	211206M	5851763M

© RMA 2019

M = $ thousand   MM = $ million
See Pages viii through xx for Explanation of Ratios and Data

Current Data Sorted by Assets

Comparative Historical Data

Type of Statement	0-500M	500M-2MM	2-10MM	10-50MM	50-100MM	100-250MM		4/1/14-3/31/15 ALL	4/1/15-3/31/16 ALL
Unqualified									
Reviewed								1	
Compiled	1	2	1	2				1	2
Tax Returns	11	5	3	1				9	17
Other	6	6	1					5	1
		0 (4/1-9/30/18)		39 (10/1/18-3/31/19)					
NUMBER OF STATEMENTS	18	13	5	3				16	20
	%	%	%	%	%	%		%	%
ASSETS									
Cash & Equivalents	34.1	15.0						13.4	16.0
Trade Receivables (net)	1.1	5.8		D	D			.2	3.1
Inventory	2.0	1.1		A	A			3.1	2.0
All Other Current	.7	6.1		T	T			4.1	1.7
Total Current	37.9	28.0		A	A			20.8	22.8
Fixed Assets (net)	41.8	64.6						66.5	62.8
Intangibles (net)	6.2	4.4		N	N			5.8	7.9
All Other Non-Current	14.0	2.9		O	O			6.8	6.5
Total	100.0	100.0		T	T			100.0	100.0
LIABILITIES				A	A				
Notes Payable-Short Term	1.6	.5		V	V			2.4	5.2
Cur. Mat.-L.T.D.	.6	2.7		A	A			.8	2.4
Trade Payables	7.7	6.7		I	I			.2	3.7
Income Taxes Payable	.0	.4		L	L			.0	.8
All Other Current	51.9	16.7		A	A			8.5	16.9
Total Current	61.8	27.0		B	B			11.9	29.1
Long-Term Debt	10.7	37.5		L	L			56.7	35.1
Deferred Taxes	.0	.0		E	E			.0	.0
All Other Non-Current	27.8	5.2						15.1	19.1
Net Worth	-.3	30.3						16.4	16.8
Total Liabilties & Net Worth	100.0	100.0						100.0	100.0
INCOME DATA									
Net Sales	100.0	100.0						100.0	100.0
Gross Profit									
Operating Expenses	100.2	78.8						84.5	97.4
Operating Profit	-.2	21.2						15.5	2.6
All Other Expenses (net)	1.8	15.2						10.5	4.6
Profit Before Taxes	-2.0	6.0						5.1	-2.0

RATIOS

Ratio	0-500M	500M-2MM					4/1/14-3/31/15 ALL	4/1/15-3/31/16 ALL
Current	2.5	8.2					11.2	3.0
	1.1	1.7					1.7	.6
	.2	.6					.4	.3
Quick	2.1	8.2					5.1	2.6
	.4	1.3					1.2	.4
	.1	.2					.3	.2
Sales/Receivables	0 UND	0 UND					0 UND	0 UND
	0 UND	0 UND					0 UND	0 UND
	1 283.3	2 187.2					1 303.9	1 586.6
Cost of Sales/Inventory								
Cost of Sales/Payables								
Sales/Working Capital	16.6	6.1					4.2	13.5
	UND	29.7					58.4	-21.6
	-10.5	-44.2					-9.7	-11.0
EBIT/Interest							4.8	15.5
							(10) 1.2	(11) .2
							.9	-.7
Net Profit + Depr., Dep., Amort./Cur. Mat. L/T/D								
Fixed/Worth	.1	.8					2.3	1.1
	UND	2.4					7.0	4.1
	-2.4	14.4					UND	NM
Debt/Worth	.7	1.3					1.4	.4
	UND	2.8					6.2	3.5
	-4.6	14.5					UND	NM
% Profit Before Taxes/Tangible Net Worth	35.7	125.4					56.4	41.4
	(11) 16.2	(11) 15.5					(13) 7.1	(15) 14.0
	-37.5	4.8					-2.5	-18.1
% Profit Before Taxes/Total Assets	20.7	23.3					22.4	9.5
	-1.9	2.1					1.0	.7
	-24.6	-1.7					-.6	-6.1
Sales/Net Fixed Assets	65.4	5.2					5.2	12.8
	9.6	.7					.4	2.9
	4.2	.3					.3	.3
Sales/Total Assets	5.8	2.6					2.1	3.0
	3.5	.5					.3	1.6
	1.7	.3					.2	.3
% Depr., Dep., Amort./Sales							6.6	3.0
							(12) 9.0	(14) 10.3
							15.5	16.9
% Officers', Directors' Owners' Comp/Sales								

	0-500M	500M-2MM	2-10MM	10-50MM			4/1/14-3/31/15	4/1/15-3/31/16
Net Sales ($)	8450M	18167M	18901M	28298M			12912M	21525M
Total Assets ($)	2660M	14137M	13434M	62719M			30940M	21190M

Comparative Historical Data　　　　　　　Current Data Sorted by Sales

			Type of Statement						
	1		Unqualified						
			Reviewed						
			Compiled						
2	1	4	Tax Returns	2	1	1		1	2
20	21	21	Other	16	2	2		1	1
7	11	14		9	2	2			
4/1/16-	4/1/17-	4/1/18-		0 (4/1-9/30/18)			39 (10/1/18-3/31/19)		
3/31/17	3/31/18	3/31/19							
ALL	ALL	ALL		0-1MM	1-3MM	3-5MM	5-10MM	10-25MM	25MM & OVER
29	34	39	NUMBER OF STATEMENTS	27	5	3	2	2	
%	%	%	ASSETS	%	%	%	%	%	%
23.9	16.1	22.5	Cash & Equivalents	21.4					D
.5	2.2	3.8	Trade Receivables (net)	.8					A
.8	1.3	1.4	Inventory	.8					T
1.8	1.9	4.9	All Other Current	3.0					A
27.0	21.5	32.5	Total Current	26.0					
62.9	60.8	52.1	Fixed Assets (net)	59.2					N
4.4	4.2	4.9	Intangibles (net)	5.3					O
5.6	13.5	10.4	All Other Non-Current	9.5					T
100.0	100.0	100.0	Total	100.0					
			LIABILITIES						A
3.0	5.7	1.0	Notes Payable-Short Term	1.2					V
8.6	1.0	1.7	Cur. Mat.-L.T.D.	1.8					A
.7	4.6	6.4	Trade Payables	6.9					I
.1	.2	.1	Income Taxes Payable	.0					L
16.3	22.8	31.6	All Other Current	32.4					A
28.6	34.3	40.9	Total Current	42.3					B
38.8	40.8	29.6	Long-Term Debt	30.0					L
.0	.0	.0	Deferred Taxes	.0					E
22.2	12.3	16.7	All Other Non-Current	16.3					
10.3	12.7	12.9	Net Worth	11.4					
100.0	100.0	100.0	Total Liabilities & Net Worth	100.0					
			INCOME DATA						
100.0	100.0	100.0	Net Sales	100.0					
			Gross Profit						
87.6	88.0	89.5	Operating Expenses	89.1					
12.4	12.0	10.5	Operating Profit	10.9					
6.7	4.8	7.7	All Other Expenses (net)	10.6					
5.7	7.3	2.9	Profit Before Taxes	.3					
			RATIOS						
4.4	1.4	3.4		8.2					
1.1	.7	1.2	Current	1.2					
.4	.3	.2		.1					
3.7	1.4	2.1		5.0					
.9	.5	(38) .9	Quick	.9					
.3	.2	.1		.1					
0 UND	0 UND	0 UND		0 UND					
0 UND	0 UND	0 UND	Sales/Receivables	0 UND					
0 UND	1 305.9	2 165.7		0 UND					
			Cost of Sales/Inventory						
			Cost of Sales/Payables						
10.5	29.7	9.1		7.6					
74.0	-25.6	36.8	Sales/Working Capital	47.3					
-9.0	-8.6	-11.8		-11.8					
14.5	5.9	4.8		5.1					
(22) 2.4	(20) 3.3	(16) 1.7	EBIT/Interest	(10) 1.3					
.7	.7	.8		-2.2					
			Net Profit + Depr., Dep., Amort./Cur. Mat. L/T/D						
.7	.9	.2		.9					
4.8	4.4	3.0	Fixed/Worth	3.0					
-15.3	-7.6	-4.9		-4.9					
.7	1.1	1.2		1.2					
4.1	4.6	3.9	Debt/Worth	2.8					
-18.7	-9.3	-9.4		-9.4					
102.3	51.5	65.7	% Profit Before Taxes/Tangible Net Worth	34.7					
(21) 49.3	(24) 30.8	(28) 19.3		(20) 8.9					
-12.6	5.0	-6.5		-12.0					
44.8	18.6	16.5	% Profit Before Taxes/Total Assets	13.1					
6.5	4.9	3.2		.7					
-2.6	-2.9	-5.6		-12.7					
12.0	11.6	28.0	Sales/Net Fixed Assets	10.5					
1.5	4.1	3.8		1.9					
.3	.6	.4		.3					
2.3	3.9	4.6	Sales/Total Assets	3.4					
1.1	1.9	1.5		.8					
.3	.5	.4		.3					
2.0	1.4	3.0	% Depr., Dep., Amort./Sales	3.8					
(19) 9.8	(24) 3.9	(22) 4.2		(16) 5.7					
16.1	8.4	10.0		10.1					
	2.5		% Officers', Directors' Owners' Comp/Sales						
	(13) 5.4								
	13.0								
38792M	77322M	73816M	Net Sales ($)	10119M	7906M	11716M	13890M	30185M	
38106M	81512M	92950M	Total Assets ($)	17949M	5005M	15322M	28664M	26010M	

© RMA 2019

M = $ thousand　　MM = $ million
See Pages viii through xx for Explanation of Ratios and Data

Current Data Sorted by Assets | Comparative Historical Data

	0-500M	500M-2MM	2-10MM	10-50MM	50-100MM	100-250MM	Type of Statement	4/1/14-3/31/15 ALL	4/1/15-3/31/16 ALL
							Unqualified		
				1		1	Reviewed	2	4
			2		1	1	Compiled	2	1
	2	2	3			1	Tax Returns	7	7
	2	5	8				Other	10	8
								4/1/14-3/31/15	4/1/15-3/31/16
			4 (4/1-9/30/18)	25 (10/1/18-3/31/19)				ALL	ALL
NUMBER OF STATEMENTS	4	7	13	1	1	3		21	20
	%	%	%	%	%	%	ASSETS	%	%
			6.7				Cash & Equivalents	16.0	15.4
			10.3				Trade Receivables (net)	20.4	17.6
			1.1				Inventory	1.0	1.6
			1.4				All Other Current	5.4	2.1
			19.5				Total Current	42.8	36.6
			69.6				Fixed Assets (net)	36.1	40.8
			2.3				Intangibles (net)	8.6	7.4
			8.6				All Other Non-Current	12.6	15.1
			100.0				Total	100.0	100.0
							LIABILITIES		
			8.0				Notes Payable-Short Term	6.4	3.4
			.6				Cur. Mat.-L.T.D.	1.6	3.1
			4.9				Trade Payables	3.2	4.0
			.0				Income Taxes Payable	.1	.0
			9.0				All Other Current	20.9	24.5
			22.5				Total Current	32.2	35.0
			37.3				Long-Term Debt	26.6	36.4
			.0				Deferred Taxes	2.2	1.7
			15.4				All Other Non-Current	6.9	4.9
			24.8				Net Worth	32.1	22.0
			100.0				Total Liabilties & Net Worth	100.0	100.0
							INCOME DATA		
			100.0				Net Sales	100.0	100.0
							Gross Profit		
			74.1				Operating Expenses	90.9	86.3
			25.9				Operating Profit	9.1	13.7
			13.7				All Other Expenses (net)	5.6	5.5
			12.2				Profit Before Taxes	3.5	8.2
							RATIOS		
			10.4				Current	2.6	1.3
			1.3					1.1	.9
			.9					.4	.4
			5.5				Quick	2.4	1.2
			1.1					.8	.9
			.8					.3	.3
			0 UND				Sales/Receivables	0 UND	0 UND
			3 104.9					10 35.3	3 136.8
			21 17.1					53 6.9	48 7.6
							Cost of Sales/Inventory		
							Cost of Sales/Payables		
			6.8				Sales/Working Capital	7.5	22.9
			28.5					16.9	-73.2
			NM					-5.9	-3.6
							EBIT/Interest	23.2	16.0
								(15) 1.3	(15) 7.3
								-1.3	1.7
							Net Profit + Depr., Dep., Amort./Cur. Mat. L/T/D		
			1.4				Fixed/Worth	.2	.9
			3.1					1.5	2.5
			-23.3					3.9	-253.6
			1.8				Debt/Worth	1.2	1.3
			3.7					2.7	7.8
			-24.8					16.1	-7.9
							% Profit Before Taxes/Tangible Net Worth	89.7	52.5
								(17) 20.8	(13) 25.2
								-7.8	6.3
			14.8				% Profit Before Taxes/Total Assets	23.6	19.1
			2.9					5.9	8.4
			-.2					-2.9	1.7
			16.6				Sales/Net Fixed Assets	137.9	123.3
			.5					3.6	3.8
			.3					.5	.4
			1.5				Sales/Total Assets	3.1	4.3
			.5					1.0	.9
			.2					.3	.3
							% Depr., Dep., Amort./Sales	2.1	2.5
								(14) 6.1	(14) 4.5
								16.1	13.7
							% Officers', Directors' Owners' Comp/Sales		
	6982M	12762M	127219M	1762M	38253M	317829M	Net Sales ($)	345351M	289828M
	1344M	8027M	62462M	15111M	58752M	402261M	Total Assets ($)	324369M	587727M

M = $ thousand   MM = $ million
See Pages viii through xx for Explanation of Ratios and Data

Comparative Historical Data | Current Data Sorted by Sales

			Type of Statement	0-1MM	1-3MM	3-5MM	5-10MM	10-25MM	25MM & OVER
4	3	2	Unqualified						2
1	3	1	Reviewed					1	1
1	1	2	Compiled			1			
5	4	7	Tax Returns		1	2	1		
8	9	17	Other	3	1	3	1		2
4/1/16-3/31/17 ALL	4/1/17-3/31/18 ALL	4/1/18-3/31/19 ALL		6	5				
				4 (4/1-9/30/18)			25 (10/1/18-3/31/19)		
19	20	29	NUMBER OF STATEMENTS	9	6	6	2	1	5
%	%	%		%	%	%	%	%	%
			ASSETS						
16.5	11.8	16.7	Cash & Equivalents						
13.1	13.3	10.0	Trade Receivables (net)						
2.2	2.1	1.1	Inventory						
2.5	3.8	.9	All Other Current						
34.4	31.1	28.7	Total Current						
52.2	48.6	56.5	Fixed Assets (net)						
5.4	9.0	7.4	Intangibles (net)						
8.0	11.4	7.4	All Other Non-Current						
100.0	100.0	100.0	Total						
			LIABILITIES						
5.7	7.4	5.2	Notes Payable-Short Term						
1.8	4.5	2.2	Cur. Mat.-L.T.D.						
5.9	4.5	5.3	Trade Payables						
.1	.0	.0	Income Taxes Payable						
21.2	17.8	11.8	All Other Current						
34.6	34.2	24.6	Total Current						
38.4	26.9	37.6	Long-Term Debt						
1.9	1.3	.5	Deferred Taxes						
8.0	22.2	15.0	All Other Non-Current						
17.1	15.5	22.3	Net Worth						
100.0	100.0	100.0	Total Liabilties & Net Worth						
			INCOME DATA						
100.0	100.0	100.0	Net Sales						
			Gross Profit						
88.8	87.5	81.3	Operating Expenses						
11.2	12.5	18.7	Operating Profit						
2.7	4.5	9.1	All Other Expenses (net)						
8.5	7.9	9.7	Profit Before Taxes						
			RATIOS						
1.9	1.8	7.7							
1.1	1.3	1.7	Current						
.7	.4	.6							
1.9	1.6	7.2							
1.1	1.1	1.6	Quick						
.6	.2	.5							
0 UND	0 UND	0 UND							
2 186.4	5 73.9	1 356.0	Sales/Receivables						
50 7.3	26 14.3	20 18.7							
			Cost of Sales/Inventory						
			Cost of Sales/Payables						
5.5	5.0	3.4							
68.7	35.9	28.5	Sales/Working Capital						
-41.5	-36.9	-15.3							
22.7	37.2	7.5							
(12) 3.7	(17) 2.1	(20) 2.1	EBIT/Interest						
.8	1.3	.2							
			Net Profit + Depr., Dep., Amort./Cur. Mat. L/T/D						
.7	.2	.8							
2.4	2.2	2.9	Fixed/Worth						
5.8	4.0	-23.3							
1.1	.7	.5							
4.2	2.8	2.4	Debt/Worth						
100.9	37.0	-8.7							
96.6	79.0	40.0							
(16) 21.0	(16) 16.4	(20) 20.2	% Profit Before Taxes/Tangible Net Worth						
5.6	1.7	13.8							
21.2	14.7	20.1							
4.9	4.4	4.4	% Profit Before Taxes/Total Assets						
.3	-1.4	-.2							
30.3	215.4	52.3							
3.2	3.0	1.3	Sales/Net Fixed Assets						
.3	.6	.4							
4.3	3.0	2.2							
1.0	1.0	.8	Sales/Total Assets						
.3	.4	.4							
1.4	.4	.9							
(13) 4.8	(14) 6.6	(20) 4.5	% Depr., Dep., Amort./Sales						
15.2	9.3	12.9							
		2.6							
	(11)	3.7	% Officers', Directors' Owners' Comp/Sales						
		6.5							
281929M	743016M	504807M	Net Sales ($)	4558M	8831M	24994M	12897M	13288M	440239M
432907M	871196M	547957M	Total Assets ($)	20088M	24563M	19602M	8116M	7397M	468191M

© RMA 2019

M = $ thousand   MM = $ million
See Pages viii through xx for Explanation of Ratios and Data

Current Data Sorted by Assets   **Comparative Historical Data**

0-500M	500M-2MM	2-10MM	10-50MM	50-100MM	100-250MM	Type of Statement	4/1/14-3/31/15 ALL	4/1/15-3/31/16 ALL
		1	1		1	Unqualified	6	4
	1	3	2			Reviewed	9	6
	4	11			1	Compiled	17	9
10	10	10				Tax Returns	52	62
7	10	15	3	1		Other	37	35
	4 (4/1-9/30/18)		86 (10/1/18-3/31/19)					
17	25	40	6		2	**NUMBER OF STATEMENTS**	121	116
%	%	%	%	%	%	**ASSETS**	%	%
24.1	6.9	6.9				Cash & Equivalents	12.3	11.3
5.2	.3	.4				Trade Receivables (net)	1.4	1.1
4.1	2.8	3.9				Inventory	1.7	3.2
.2	3.1	1.1				All Other Current	2.0	1.8
33.6	13.1	12.3				Total Current	17.5	17.3
61.0	81.2	71.4				Fixed Assets (net)	68.5	68.9
2.6	4.5	8.4				Intangibles (net)	8.7	7.3
2.7	1.3	7.9				All Other Non-Current	5.3	6.5
100.0	100.0	100.0				Total	100.0	100.0
						LIABILITIES		
30.0	3.9	3.4				Notes Payable-Short Term	4.7	5.0
6.8	4.0	2.0				Cur. Mat.-L.T.D.	8.6	2.9
6.9	.3	.6				Trade Payables	2.5	.8
.0	.1	.0				Income Taxes Payable	.1	.0
11.4	1.8	8.1				All Other Current	7.9	6.2
55.1	10.1	14.1				Total Current	23.8	15.0
84.1	57.4	53.6				Long-Term Debt	59.1	51.9
.0	.0	.0				Deferred Taxes	.0	.0
39.5	4.3	10.6				All Other Non-Current	9.9	6.9
-78.7	28.2	21.7				Net Worth	7.2	26.1
100.0	100.0	100.0				Total Liabilties & Net Worth	100.0	100.0
						INCOME DATA		
100.0	100.0	100.0				Net Sales	100.0	100.0
						Gross Profit		
89.3	72.0	76.9				Operating Expenses	79.3	77.3
10.7	28.0	23.1				Operating Profit	20.7	22.7
.7	13.3	10.8				All Other Expenses (net)	7.5	7.6
10.0	14.7	12.2				Profit Before Taxes	13.2	15.1
						RATIOS		
1.6	3.4	2.3					3.3	3.4
.7	.6	.9				Current	1.0	1.3
.3	.3	.4					.3	.4
1.5	3.4	1.8					2.1	2.5
.5	.4	.8				Quick	.7	.9
.2	.2	.2					.2	.3
0 UND	0 UND	0 UND					0 UND	0 UND
0 UND	0 UND	0 UND				Sales/Receivables	0 UND	0 UND
0 UND	0 UND	0 UND					1 248.5	1 686.2
						Cost of Sales/Inventory		
						Cost of Sales/Payables		
30.8	5.9	10.1					11.4	9.3
-46.7	-26.2	-102.9				Sales/Working Capital	-292.0	44.7
-9.8	-8.5	-7.3					-7.8	-9.8
13.9	3.9	4.8					6.3	4.8
(10) 6.6	(20) 2.7	(36) 2.9				EBIT/Interest	(93) 2.7	(87) 2.6
-4.4	1.1	1.2					1.4	1.3
						Net Profit + Depr., Dep., Amort./Cur. Mat. L/T/D		
3.3	2.1	2.1					1.6	1.3
-2.1	3.2	6.3				Fixed/Worth	5.3	3.2
-.4	NM	-9.9					-2.7	-63.8
2.4	1.3	1.4					1.4	.9
-7.0	2.3	9.0				Debt/Worth	5.2	3.1
-1.7	NM	-17.8					-4.3	-46.2
	23.7	56.4					60.0	54.1
	(19) 10.1	(27) 25.2				% Profit Before Taxes/Tangible Net Worth	(78) 27.9	(84) 23.7
	5.2	-1.5					8.5	6.7
90.3	11.9	9.8					12.8	13.5
25.8	4.3	5.5				% Profit Before Taxes/Total Assets	6.1	6.2
-1.1	1.2	-.2					1.1	.9
23.1	.8	.9					2.2	2.2
4.4	.5	.5				Sales/Net Fixed Assets	.8	.7
1.0	.3	.3					.4	.4
8.0	.6	.6					1.3	1.3
3.3	.4	.4				Sales/Total Assets	.5	.5
.8	.3	.2					.3	.3
.5	8.6	7.8					4.5	4.0
(14) 4.8	(18) 15.5	(30) 13.9				% Depr., Dep., Amort./Sales	(104) 9.9	(102) 9.5
10.5	21.0	24.5					15.0	15.8
							2.9	4.0
						% Officers', Directors' Owners' Comp/Sales	(41) 6.9	(38) 7.1
							9.6	10.5
10028M	16441M	92402M	68923M		141401M	Net Sales ($)	322136M	387255M
3810M	32881M	168059M	113080M		276347M	Total Assets ($)	615685M	604326M

Note: columns 10-50MM, 50-100MM, and 100-250MM are marked "DATA NOT AVAILABLE" for the Assets, Liabilities, Income Data, and Ratios sections.

M = $ thousand   MM = $ million
See Pages viii through xx for Explanation of Ratios and Data

Comparative Historical Data

Current Data Sorted by Sales

© RMA 2019

			Type of Statement						
4	3	3	Unqualified					2	1
6	7	6	Reviewed	2	2		1	1	1
15	8	15	Compiled	5	0		1	1	
40	41	30	Tax Returns	17	10	2	1		1
39	44	36	Other	22	9	1	3		1
4/1/16- 3/31/17	4/1/17- 3/31/18	4/1/18- 3/31/19		4 (4/1-9/30/18)		86 (10/1/18-3/31/19)			
ALL	ALL	ALL		0-1MM	1-3MM	3-5MM	5-10MM	10-25MM	25MM & OVER
104	103	90	NUMBER OF STATEMENTS	46	30	3	5	4	2
%	%	%	ASSETS	%	%	%	%	%	%
10.8	10.1	10.8	Cash & Equivalents	11.4	6.4				
1.4	1.9	1.9	Trade Receivables (net)	2.1	.2				
2.2	3.1	3.3	Inventory	1.4	6.1				
2.9	.8	1.5	All Other Current	1.7	1.0				
17.3	15.8	17.5	Total Current	16.6	13.7				
69.9	71.5	70.1	Fixed Assets (net)	77.2	71.7				
5.4	6.5	6.1	Intangibles (net)	3.9	9.9				
7.4	6.2	6.2	All Other Non-Current	2.3	4.7				
100.0	100.0	100.0	Total	100.0	100.0				
			LIABILITIES						
4.5	2.7	8.4	Notes Payable-Short Term	11.4	6.9				
4.9	6.0	3.4	Cur. Mat.-L.T.D.	4.8	2.1				
.9	.7	1.8	Trade Payables	.2	4.2				
.2	.1	.0	Income Taxes Payable	.0	.0				
9.5	8.4	6.9	All Other Current	3.7	10.7				
20.0	17.8	20.6	Total Current	20.2	24.0				
54.2	56.0	57.6	Long-Term Debt	68.3	60.4				
.0	.0	.0	Deferred Taxes	.0	.0				
12.1	14.9	13.8	All Other Non-Current	12.9	14.8				
13.7	11.3	8.0	Net Worth	-1.3	.8				
100.0	100.0	100.0	Total Liabilties & Net Worth	100.0	100.0				
			INCOME DATA						
100.0	100.0	100.0	Net Sales	100.0	100.0				
			Gross Profit						
79.3	79.8	77.9	Operating Expenses	74.9	81.4				
20.7	20.2	22.1	Operating Profit	25.1	18.6				
7.8	8.6	8.7	All Other Expenses (net)	11.7	8.3				
12.9	11.6	13.4	Profit Before Taxes	13.5	10.4				
			RATIOS						
2.5	2.4	2.5		2.2	1.9				
.9	.9	.9	Current	1.0	.9				
.3	.4	.3		.3	.3				
2.0	2.2	2.0		2.2	1.0				
.6	.6	.6	Quick	.8	.5				
.2	.2	.2		.2	.1				
0 UND	0 UND	0 UND		0 UND	0 UND				
0 UND	0 UND	0 UND	Sales/Receivables	0 UND	0 UND				
0 874.0	1 356.0	0 UND		0 UND	0 UND				
			Cost of Sales/Inventory						
			Cost of Sales/Payables						
9.9	11.2	10.2		10.5	23.7				
-81.7	-60.9	-62.4	Sales/Working Capital	NM	-54.0				
-10.3	-7.1	-9.0		-7.8	-6.5				
6.6	8.3	5.7		6.2	4.6				
(84) 2.9	(87) 3.5	(71) 2.8	EBIT/Interest	(30) 2.6	2.6				
1.4	1.5	1.1		1.1	.9				
			Net Profit + Depr., Dep., Amort./Cur. Mat. L/T/D						
1.4	1.5	1.6		2.1	4.0				
4.0	4.1	4.1	Fixed/Worth	4.1	-28.7				
-32.4	-11.4	-8.2		-14.2	-2.1				
.9	1.5	1.3		1.4	3.8				
3.9	4.7	4.0	Debt/Worth	3.5	-39.9				
-36.3	-12.9	-13.8		-17.0	-4.3				
65.8	51.8	40.8	% Profit Before Taxes/Tangible Net Worth	29.8	62.5				
(74) 20.6	(69) 17.6	(62) 18.2		(34) 11.0	(14) 31.5				
3.1	6.4	4.9		.5	9.6				
18.1	16.5	12.9	% Profit Before Taxes/Total Assets	12.6	10.8				
7.1	5.9	5.5		5.0	5.2				
.6	1.3	.6		.4	-.5				
2.9	2.2	1.9	Sales/Net Fixed Assets	1.0	1.3				
.9	.8	.6		.4	.7				
.4	.4	.3		.3	.4				
1.4	1.1	.8	Sales/Total Assets	.7	.8				
.6	.6	.5		.3	.5				
.3	.3	.3		.2	.3				
4.3	5.3	4.0	% Depr., Dep., Amort./Sales	7.6	6.7				
(83) 10.3	(84) 10.9	(69) 11.3		(32) 13.8	(25) 12.4				
17.9	17.8	18.9		20.6	22.7				
4.7	4.4	3.7	% Officers', Directors' Owners' Comp/Sales		3.7				
(39) 6.5	(33) 8.1	(25) 8.3			(10) 6.6				
10.6	13.7	9.7			9.8				
440456M	387728M	329195M	Net Sales ($)	22331M	49113M	10429M	41834M	64087M	141401M
653536M	685417M	594177M	Total Assets ($)	66945M	102393M	14501M	74699M	59292M	276347M

M = $ thousand   MM = $ million
See Pages viii through xx for Explanation of Ratios and Data

Current Data Sorted by Assets   **Comparative Historical Data**

Type of Statement

Type of Statement	0-500M	500M-2MM	2-10MM	10-50MM	50-100MM	100-250MM		4/1/14-3/31/15 ALL	4/1/15-3/31/16 ALL
Unqualified		1	4	5				7	7
Reviewed			2					5	7
Compiled		1	3					2	6
Tax Returns	1	2	4					15	12
Other	1	9	10	4				28	14
	15 (4/1-9/30/18)		32 (10/1/18-3/31/19)						

Data

Columns: 0-500M, 500M-2MM, 2-10MM, 10-50MM, 50-100MM, 100-250MM | Comparative 4/1/14-3/31/15 ALL, 4/1/15-3/31/16 ALL

(50-100MM and 100-250MM columns: DATA NOT AVAILABLE)

	0-500M	500M-2MM	2-10MM	10-50MM	4/1/14-3/31/15 ALL	4/1/15-3/31/16 ALL
NUMBER OF STATEMENTS	2	13	23	9	57	46
ASSETS	%	%	%	%	%	%
Cash & Equivalents		21.3	17.8		18.7	17.8
Trade Receivables (net)		1.7	2.6		2.1	1.7
Inventory		1.4	.3		1.5	.8
All Other Current		5.2	3.1		1.5	4.0
Total Current		29.6	23.9		23.8	24.3
Fixed Assets (net)		59.2	55.8		62.5	61.6
Intangibles (net)		4.0	8.1		6.5	6.0
All Other Non-Current		7.3	12.2		7.2	8.2
Total		100.0	100.0		100.0	100.0
LIABILITIES						
Notes Payable-Short Term		2.5	5.3		6.3	1.9
Cur. Mat.-L.T.D.		2.5	4.0		2.1	3.4
Trade Payables		4.2	1.1		1.9	2.9
Income Taxes Payable		.2	.0		.2	.0
All Other Current		18.1	17.8		14.9	22.5
Total Current		27.5	28.1		25.4	30.7
Long-Term Debt		24.8	25.4		36.1	34.1
Deferred Taxes		.0	.0		.2	.0
All Other Non-Current		40.9	10.8		9.1	11.3
Net Worth		6.8	35.7		29.2	23.8
Total Liabilties & Net Worth		100.0	100.0		100.0	100.0
INCOME DATA						
Net Sales		100.0	100.0		100.0	100.0
Gross Profit						
Operating Expenses		91.9	87.5		88.4	90.9
Operating Profit		8.1	12.5		11.6	9.1
All Other Expenses (net)		1.0	4.3		3.0	1.8
Profit Before Taxes		7.2	8.3		8.6	7.4
RATIOS						
Current		3.9	2.0		3.8	2.4
		1.3	1.0		1.0	1.2
		.7	.5		.4	.5
Quick		3.7	1.8		3.0	2.2
		.6	.8		.8	1.0
		.4	.4		.4	.3
Sales/Receivables	0 UND	0 UND		0 UND	0 UND	
	0 999.8	0 UND		0 999.8	1 327.5	
	7 49.5	3 120.8		5 69.4	7 55.9	
Cost of Sales/Inventory						
Cost of Sales/Payables						
Sales/Working Capital		8.3	8.2		7.1	7.5
		54.9	-285.9		-420.9	43.4
		-42.9	-5.1		-10.1	-9.1
EBIT/Interest			25.4		6.4	5.2
			(20) 3.9		(42) 3.6	(33) 3.3
			-.9		1.2	1.3
Net Profit + Depr., Dep., Amort./Cur. Mat. L/T/D						
Fixed/Worth		.4	.8		.9	.7
		2.0	2.0		2.3	2.1
		NM	-44.3		-24.6	-4.5
Debt/Worth		.5	.2		.3	.3
		5.0	3.2		3.0	3.2
		NM	-14.8		-14.0	-17.1
% Profit Before Taxes/Tangible Net Worth		117.7	34.3		36.7	28.1
		(10) 12.8	(16) 6.6		(41) 11.1	(32) 9.6
		-.2	-.1		3.8	.2
% Profit Before Taxes/Total Assets		25.1	12.4		19.5	9.4
		3.3	3.2		5.3	4.4
		-.4	-.8		1.4	.2
Sales/Net Fixed Assets		8.2	6.2		3.6	3.5
		2.9	1.1		1.1	1.2
		.8	.7		.5	.6
Sales/Total Assets		3.0	1.3		1.8	1.8
		1.6	.8		.9	.8
		.5	.4		.4	.5
% Depr., Dep., Amort./Sales			3.6		3.2	3.3
		(18)	5.2		(43) 5.4	(39) 6.1
			8.8		9.3	8.7
% Officers', Directors' Owners' Comp/Sales					3.2	2.9
					(19) 6.2	(19) 3.7
					11.7	6.1
Net Sales ($)	2635M	27932M	118486M	141066M	236445M	234975M
Total Assets ($)	509M	14487M	128629M	181059M	292814M	344311M

Comparative Historical Data | Current Data Sorted by Sales

			Type of Statement					
9	9	10	Unqualified	1	4	3	1	1
4	4	2	Reviewed			2		
4	3	4	Compiled	2		2		
11	13	7	Tax Returns	2	1	2		
17	25	24	Other	5	8	3	2	1
4/1/16-3/31/17 ALL	4/1/17-3/31/18 ALL	4/1/18-3/31/19 ALL		0-1MM	15 (4/1-9/30/18) 1-3MM	3-5MM	32 (10/1/18-3/31/19) 5-10MM	10-25MM	25MM & OVER

45	54	47	**NUMBER OF STATEMENTS**	7	13	10	12	3	2
%	%	%	**ASSETS**	%	%	%	%	%	%
20.5	18.5	20.7	Cash & Equivalents	16.7	12.9	26.5			
1.3	2.1	2.3	Trade Receivables (net)		1.2	1.5	6.0		
1.1	1.5	.6	Inventory		.8	.3	.9		
2.5	2.4	4.4	All Other Current		4.2	4.0	4.0		
25.5	24.5	28.0	Total Current		22.9	18.6	37.4		
59.4	61.7	54.3	Fixed Assets (net)		59.1	67.0	41.3		
2.9	4.8	5.9	Intangibles (net)		3.9	3.7	5.8		
12.3	9.0	11.8	All Other Non-Current		14.1	10.6	15.6		
100.0	100.0	100.0	Total		100.0	100.0	100.0		
			LIABILITIES						
3.0	1.6	3.9	Notes Payable-Short Term		2.5	8.8	.4		
3.5	2.1	2.9	Cur. Mat.-L.T.D.		2.4	2.5	1.4		
3.3	2.0	2.0	Trade Payables		1.9	2.1	1.8		
.0	.0	.0	Income Taxes Payable		.0	.2	.0		
12.6	12.2	15.2	All Other Current		11.0	12.5	29.0		
22.4	17.9	24.1	Total Current		17.8	26.1	32.5		
27.8	33.1	24.0	Long-Term Debt		26.1	22.7	19.6		
.1	.1	.1	Deferred Taxes		.0	.0	.0		
16.2	12.1	17.1	All Other Non-Current		43.3	4.3	2.0		
33.5	36.8	34.7	Net Worth		12.8	47.0	45.9		
100.0	100.0	100.0	Total Liabilties & Net Worth		100.0	100.0	100.0		
			INCOME DATA						
100.0	100.0	100.0	Net Sales		100.0	100.0	100.0		
			Gross Profit						
88.4	91.6	90.6	Operating Expenses		89.0	97.7	91.3		
11.6	8.4	9.4	Operating Profit		11.0	2.3	8.7		
2.5	2.0	3.0	All Other Expenses (net)		.6	1.6	.8		
9.1	6.4	6.4	Profit Before Taxes		10.5	.7	7.9		
			RATIOS						
2.6	2.8	2.6			5.0	3.5	2.4		
1.3	1.3	1.2	Current		1.7	.9	1.2		
.7	.7	.6			.7	.4	.8		
2.6	2.5	1.9			4.8	3.4	1.7		
1.2	1.0	.9	Quick		.9	.5	1.0		
.5	.4	.5			.4	.2	.6		
0 UND	0 UND	0 UND		0 UND	0 UND	0 UND			
1 346.4	1 435.3	0 968.0	Sales/Receivables	0 UND	3 122.5	0 890.5			
5 68.9	4 88.6	3 112.6		3 140.9	5 70.3	8 47.0			
			Cost of Sales/Inventory						
			Cost of Sales/Payables						
4.4	6.9	4.9			6.7	9.1	5.2		
24.9	31.6	44.0	Sales/Working Capital		28.9	-348.3	49.4		
-12.7	-11.8	-8.3			-42.9	-4.9	-87.0		
19.9	14.8	17.7							
(33) 4.5	(41) 3.5	(33) 2.7	EBIT/Interest						
1.4	.0	-.7							
			Net Profit + Depr., Dep., Amort./Cur. Mat. L/T/D						
.6	.8	.6			.6	.8	.1		
1.1	1.2	1.5	Fixed/Worth		2.8	1.3	.7		
52.3	152.2	8.6			-2.4	2.0	2.6		
.2	.2	.2			.2	.6	.2		
1.2	.7	1.5	Debt/Worth		3.4	.9	2.1		
241.7	154.7	29.8			4.0	3.5	12.1		
45.3	25.6	52.9					116.2		
(37) 8.0	(42) 9.2	(36) 7.6	% Profit Before Taxes/Tangible Net Worth			(10) 10.1		
.4	.1	-.3					-10.5		
12.3	12.9	12.4			12.1	24.2	19.2		
3.9	5.9	3.3	% Profit Before Taxes/Total Assets		10.1	2.3	7.9		
.2	.0	-.7			-.4	-1.3	-3.3		
4.9	4.8	6.9			6.0	3.0	179.3		
1.5	1.1	1.4	Sales/Net Fixed Assets		1.8	.8	1.4		
.6	.6	.7			.9	.5	1.1		
1.9	1.4	2.0			2.3	2.2	1.4		
1.0	.8	.8	Sales/Total Assets		1.0	.5	.9		
.4	.5	.4			.5	.3	.6		
3.7	4.1	2.5					2.8		
(36) 5.6	(44) 6.7	(35) 4.9	% Depr., Dep., Amort./Sales				5.0		
11.8	12.3	8.6					10.9		
3.4	2.3	2.6							
(14) 5.5	(16) 4.0	(17) 5.5	% Officers', Directors' Owners' Comp/Sales						
8.3	6.4	7.7							
183387M	386179M	290119M	Net Sales ($)	3762M	24769M	41928M	79360M	46543M	93757M
271317M	446915M	324684M	Total Assets ($)	14607M	30266M	88849M	86196M	72618M	32148M

M = $ thousand   MM = $ million
See Pages viii through xx for Explanation of Ratios and Data

Current Data Sorted by Assets   **Comparative Historical Data**

0-500M	500M-2MM	2-10MM	10-50MM	50-100MM	100-250MM	Type of Statement	4/1/14-3/31/15 ALL	4/1/15-3/31/16 ALL
		2				Unqualified	4	6
		1	5			Reviewed	1	1
		2	2			Compiled	3	4
1	7					Tax Returns	11	3
3	3	5		2		Other	9	7
	18 (4/1-9/30/18)		15 (10/1/18-3/31/19)					
4	10	10	7	2		**NUMBER OF STATEMENTS**	28	21
%	%	%	%	%	%	**ASSETS**	%	%
	11.7	10.8				Cash & Equivalents	17.3	15.3
	6.6	.6				Trade Receivables (net)	1.4	1.4
	.0	.0				Inventory	1.3	1.9
	.3	4.3				All Other Current	.7	3.2
	18.7	15.7				Total Current	20.7	21.8
	76.7	82.4				Fixed Assets (net)	75.3	71.3
	.4	.1				Intangibles (net)	.8	.9
	4.3	1.7				All Other Non-Current	3.2	6.0
	100.0	100.0				Total	100.0	100.0
						LIABILITIES		
	4.2	.7				Notes Payable-Short Term	.5	4.5
	.9	2.0				Cur. Mat.-L.T.D.	1.0	4.4
	2.4	.3				Trade Payables	.9	2.8
	.0	.0				Income Taxes Payable	.0	.0
	14.1	1.4				All Other Current	6.5	3.0
	21.6	4.3				Total Current	9.0	14.8
	45.6	45.4				Long-Term Debt	45.0	47.2
	.0	.0				Deferred Taxes	.4	.0
	5.9	.2				All Other Non-Current	3.7	8.5
	26.9	50.2				Net Worth	42.0	29.5
	100.0	100.0				Total Liabilties & Net Worth	100.0	100.0
						INCOME DATA		
	100.0	100.0				Net Sales	100.0	100.0
						Gross Profit		
	89.7	78.1				Operating Expenses	79.7	75.5
	10.3	21.9				Operating Profit	20.3	24.5
	12.9	15.1				All Other Expenses (net)	8.5	13.7
	-2.6	6.8				Profit Before Taxes	11.8	10.8
						RATIOS		
	26.6	10.2					15.8	5.2
	1.4	4.6				Current	3.8	1.8
	.4	1.3					2.1	.6
	26.5	9.5					15.8	5.2
	1.2	2.7				Quick	3.8	.9
	.4	1.1					1.5	.3
	0 UND	0 UND					0 UND	0 UND
	0 UND	1 397.3				Sales/Receivables	0 UND	2 196.3
	24 15.2	3 119.0					17 22.1	18 20.3
						Cost of Sales/Inventory		
						Cost of Sales/Payables		
	3.3	.9					1.2	3.0
	NM	3.0				Sales/Working Capital	3.5	10.5
	-8.4	17.3					8.4	-4.7
							4.0	
						EBIT/Interest	(12) 1.7	
							1.0	
						Net Profit + Depr., Dep., Amort./Cur. Mat. L/T/D		
	1.4	1.0					.9	1.0
	2.8	1.7				Fixed/Worth	1.7	2.5
	-11.2	3.3					24.3	-7.1
	.9	.3					.3	.4
	3.1	1.0				Debt/Worth	1.2	3.0
	-12.8	2.5					26.5	-12.7
		9.2					16.5	20.2
		4.7				% Profit Before Taxes/Tangible Net Worth	(23) 6.2	(14) 10.3
		.2					-.2	-6.1
	5.1	3.6					7.4	12.6
	-.1	1.9				% Profit Before Taxes/Total Assets	2.1	5.9
	-3.1	.2					-.6	-.7
	.6	.4					1.0	.8
	.3	.2				Sales/Net Fixed Assets	.5	.5
	.2	.1					.2	.2
	.5	.3					.6	.5
	.3	.1				Sales/Total Assets	.3	.4
	.2	.1					.2	.2
		13.0					6.9	7.7
		20.0				% Depr., Dep., Amort./Sales	(22) 11.5	(16) 14.4
		24.1					19.6	26.0
						% Officers', Directors' Owners' Comp/Sales		
7006M	12198M	10134M	29863M	739627M		Net Sales ($)	55571M	58449M
1009M	10453M	51518M	160534M	135993M		Total Assets ($)	249951M	135473M

(100-250MM column: DATA NOT AVAILABLE)

Comparative Historical Data   Current Data Sorted by Sales

5	8	7	Type of Statement						
					4	3			
			Unqualified						
			Reviewed						
4	4	1	Compiled	1					
11	11	10	Tax Returns	10					
8	9	15	Other	7					
4/1/16-3/31/17 ALL	4/1/17-3/31/18 ALL	4/1/18-3/31/19 ALL		0-1MM	18 (4/1-9/30/18) 1-3MM	3-5MM	15 (10/1/18-3/31/19) 5-10MM	10-25MM	25MM & OVER
28	32	33	NUMBER OF STATEMENTS	18	7	4	2		1
%	%	%	ASSETS	%	%	%	%	%	%
16.5	16.9	16.9	Cash & Equivalents	17.0					
5.0	4.0	4.8	Trade Receivables (net)	.9					
.2	.0	.0	Inventory	.0					
1.5	1.3	1.8	All Other Current	2.3					
23.2	22.2	23.6	Total Current	20.2					
68.3	70.1	66.3	Fixed Assets (net)	78.4					
1.3	.2	1.2	Intangibles (net)	1.1					
7.1	7.5	8.9	All Other Non-Current	.3					
100.0	100.0	100.0	Total	100.0					
			LIABILITIES						
5.3	3.4	3.7	Notes Payable-Short Term	2.6					
2.2	4.7	1.9	Cur. Mat.-L.T.D.	.9					
9.6	3.1	3.5	Trade Payables	1.8					
.0	.0	.0	Income Taxes Payable	.0					
3.6	12.5	9.7	All Other Current	11.1					
20.7	23.6	18.8	Total Current	16.4					
57.9	51.5	45.1	Long-Term Debt	46.3					
.0	.1	.0	Deferred Taxes	.0					
2.0	.8	4.3	All Other Non-Current	3.4					
19.3	24.0	31.7	Net Worth	34.0					
100.0	100.0	100.0	Total Liabilities & Net Worth	100.0					
			INCOME DATA						
100.0	100.0	100.0	Net Sales	100.0					
			Gross Profit						
77.4	79.1	82.8	Operating Expenses	82.9					
22.6	20.9	17.2	Operating Profit	17.1					
11.9	9.0	11.7	All Other Expenses (net)	14.8					
10.7	12.0	5.5	Profit Before Taxes	2.3					
			RATIOS						
3.2	4.2	6.5	Current	7.3					
1.6	1.4	1.8		3.2					
.7	.6	.8		.9					
3.0	3.7	5.9	Quick	6.9					
1.4	1.4	1.6		2.0					
.5	.4	.7		.7					
0 UND	0 UND	0 UND	Sales/Receivables	0 UND					
0 UND	0 UND	3 109.7		0 UND					
9 42.4	8 44.0	18 20.6		4 97.3					
			Cost of Sales/Inventory						
			Cost of Sales/Payables						
2.6	3.7	2.9	Sales/Working Capital	3.0					
8.0	13.3	10.2		3.6					
-20.1	-26.5	-209.8		-298.7					
6.2	5.7	7.4	EBIT/Interest	2.8					
(21) 2.0	(19) 3.2	(20) 2.7		(11) 2.5					
.6	1.4	1.3		.1					
			Net Profit + Depr., Dep., Amort./Cur. Mat. L/T/D						
1.1	1.0	1.0	Fixed/Worth	1.3					
1.8	2.8	2.1		2.3					
9.9	NM	6.7		8.3					
.6	.7	.7	Debt/Worth	.7					
1.9	2.6	2.8		2.2					
12.4	-20.3	14.8		7.6					
15.7	45.1	14.6	% Profit Before Taxes/Tangible Net Worth	26.1					
(23) 9.4	(23) 11.2	(26) 6.1		(15) 3.1					
-3.1	4.5	.2		-4.7					
6.8	11.5	6.8	% Profit Before Taxes/Total Assets	3.9					
2.7	4.3	2.3		1.7					
-1.3	.4	.1		-2.6					
.5	1.0	.7	Sales/Net Fixed Assets	.6					
.3	.4	.3		.3					
.2	.2	.2		.1					
.4	.8	.5	Sales/Total Assets	.5					
.2	.3	.2		.2					
.2	.2	.1		.1					
9.8	3.9	10.6	% Depr., Dep., Amort./Sales	10.6					
(24) 17.6	(29) 12.9	(29) 16.5		(17) 19.2					
22.1	22.5	24.2		24.7					
			% Officers', Directors' Owners' Comp/Sales						
106044M	57154M	798828M	Net Sales ($)	8859M	15589M	17285M	17468M	12632M	726995M
231862M	175916M	359507M	Total Assets ($)	46720M	71788M	81680M	23326M	51629M	84364M

M = $ thousand   MM = $ million
See Pages viii through xx for Explanation of Ratios and Data

Current Data Sorted by Assets

Comparative Historical Data

						Type of Statement		
1		1	5	1	2	Unqualified	17	14
1	1	6	6			Reviewed	10	14
2	2	4				Compiled	16	10
15	12	3	2			Tax Returns	62	68
15	12	15	13	8	4	Other	70	74
	15 (4/1-9/30/18)		116 (10/1/18-3/31/19)				4/1/14-3/31/15	4/1/15-3/31/16
0-500M	500M-2MM	2-10MM	10-50MM	50-100MM	100-250MM		ALL	ALL
34	27	29	26	9	6	NUMBER OF STATEMENTS	175	180
%	%	%	%	%	%	ASSETS	%	%
30.0	17.9	9.2	13.7			Cash & Equivalents	17.2	18.9
4.2	11.9	22.5	31.1			Trade Receivables (net)	17.7	16.4
12.1	3.6	9.9	9.8			Inventory	9.3	7.0
8.1	7.9	4.6	3.3			All Other Current	2.5	2.4
54.4	41.3	46.2	57.8			Total Current	46.9	44.7
26.3	31.4	29.0	21.5			Fixed Assets (net)	32.5	35.5
7.0	11.5	12.4	4.2			Intangibles (net)	9.6	10.3
12.5	15.8	12.4	16.5			All Other Non-Current	11.0	9.6
100.0	100.0	100.0	100.0			Total	100.0	100.0
						LIABILITIES		
13.0	8.4	10.0	5.3			Notes Payable-Short Term	9.3	8.3
2.4	1.9	5.0	2.7			Cur. Mat.-L.T.D.	2.5	3.7
6.0	9.5	17.1	14.3			Trade Payables	12.9	12.5
.8	.0	.0	.2			Income Taxes Payable	.1	.1
27.1	23.1	12.2	22.0			All Other Current	20.6	16.4
49.4	43.0	44.3	44.5			Total Current	45.4	41.1
17.3	22.2	26.1	18.0			Long-Term Debt	22.5	24.2
.0	.1	.0	.3			Deferred Taxes	.3	.1
.8	5.1	6.3	6.3			All Other Non-Current	9.9	9.9
32.7	29.7	23.2	30.9			Net Worth	21.9	24.8
100.0	100.0	100.0	100.0			Total Liabilties & Net Worth	100.0	100.0
						INCOME DATA		
100.0	100.0	100.0	100.0			Net Sales	100.0	100.0
						Gross Profit		
93.4	90.6	96.3	92.5			Operating Expenses	93.5	92.6
6.6	9.4	3.7	7.5			Operating Profit	6.5	7.4
.7	2.9	.8	.6			All Other Expenses (net)	1.3	1.6
5.8	6.6	2.9	6.9			Profit Before Taxes	5.2	5.8
						RATIOS		
8.7	1.9	1.5	1.8				2.3	2.5
1.9	1.0	1.0	1.5			Current	1.2	1.2
.5	.4	.5	.8				.7	.5
4.5	1.5	1.0	1.6				1.6	1.7
1.0	.7	.5	1.0			Quick	.9	.9
.1	.3	.3	.5				.4	.3

0	UND	0	UND	3	129.1	12	29.7	Sales/Receivables	0	UND	0	UND	
0	UND	2	154.2	22	16.4	32	11.4		5	81.1	2	170.2	
1	677.1	18	20.3	37	9.8	45	8.2		33	11.2	29	12.6	

Cost of Sales/Inventory

Cost of Sales/Payables

	8.5	19.2	25.2	9.7		Sales/Working Capital	15.6	13.7
	31.1	416.9	360.1	25.1			50.4	87.8
	-11.9	-17.5	-9.8	-21.0			-30.4	-24.0
	21.9	13.5	19.7	30.4		EBIT/Interest	25.2	27.4
(15)	14.2	(20) 6.5	(28) 5.9	(22) 16.8			(130) 6.8	(132) 4.7
	.7	2.5	2.2	4.1			1.6	1.1
						Net Profit + Depr., Dep., Amort./Cur. Mat. L/T/D	12.9	10.4
							(21) 4.1	(20) 3.4
							1.3	1.7
	.1	.2	.4	.1		Fixed/Worth	.2	.4
	.6	2.5	2.3	.4			1.2	1.2
	3.8	-18.8	-2.2	1.9			-4.7	-37.7
	.2	1.1	1.3	1.3		Debt/Worth	.7	.7
	1.3	4.9	5.2	2.6			2.4	2.4
	NM	-29.1	-7.5	5.7			-8.3	-25.1
	285.3	70.9	81.3	97.3		% Profit Before Taxes/Tangible Net Worth	89.9	103.7
(26)	47.0	(20) 33.6	(19) 46.4	(23) 41.6			(119) 30.8	(130) 37.2
	18.9	9.0	6.6	14.0			8.1	10.5
	63.5	25.1	24.4	17.5		% Profit Before Taxes/Total Assets	27.2	27.5
	29.4	14.5	9.8	13.9			11.8	9.0
	9.6	1.4	1.4	3.5			1.1	1.9
	378.6	30.6	72.0	73.4		Sales/Net Fixed Assets	59.1	81.3
	26.1	23.2	15.9	35.6			16.7	14.6
	9.2	8.4	4.7	7.7			4.7	4.9
	8.5	5.5	5.3	5.6		Sales/Total Assets	5.7	5.8
	4.2	3.7	3.0	3.3			3.3	3.5
	2.6	1.3	1.5	1.9			2.1	2.1
	.5	1.0	.7	.6		% Depr., Dep., Amort./Sales	.8	.7
(19)	1.2	(18) 2.4	(22) 1.5	(25) 1.0			(124) 2.1	(131) 1.8
	2.8	7.5	2.9	2.4			3.7	3.9
	3.7	2.1				% Officers', Directors' Owners' Comp/Sales	1.6	2.4
(10)	5.5	(12) 3.7					(69) 3.8	(54) 4.1
	13.3	4.9					5.4	7.1

40359M	99113M	620801M	1939956M	1309802M	2756162M	Net Sales ($)	6697222M	7366974M
7694M	25161M	146212M	542251M	589152M	1046200M	Total Assets ($)	2405132M	2544152M

M = $ thousand   MM = $ million
See Pages viii through xx for Explanation of Ratios and Data

Comparative Historical Data | Current Data Sorted by Sales

	4/1/16-3/31/17 ALL	4/1/17-3/31/18 ALL	4/1/18-3/31/19 ALL		15 (4/1-9/30/18)			116 (10/1/18-3/31/19)		
				0-1MM	1-3MM	3-5MM	5-10MM	10-25MM	25MM & OVER
Type of Statement									
Unqualified	10	8	10		1				9
Reviewed	12	13	14	1		1	1	3	8
Compiled	9	13	8		2	3	1	2	
Tax Returns	36	34	32	10	12	6	1	2	1
Other	65	57	67	11	9	6	8	4	29
NUMBER OF STATEMENTS	132	125	131	22	24	16	11	11	47
	%	%	%	%	%	%	%	%	%
ASSETS									
Cash & Equivalents	19.2	16.2	16.7	22.3	26.4	17.1	15.7	9.1	11.1
Trade Receivables (net)	18.6	18.0	16.5	3.7	5.5	10.1	24.4	14.7	28.8
Inventory	9.8	8.9	8.8	9.9	7.8	6.6	9.8	6.1	10.0
All Other Current	3.2	4.0	5.9	8.2	9.3	7.0	3.3	2.7	4.1
Total Current	50.8	47.1	48.0	44.1	49.0	40.8	53.2	32.7	54.0
Fixed Assets (net)	30.4	33.2	27.3	33.9	24.7	24.9	26.2	48.2	21.8
Intangibles (net)	9.5	12.0	10.5	7.7	13.0	13.8	8.9	9.1	10.2
All Other Non-Current	9.4	7.6	14.2	14.3	13.2	20.5	11.7	10.1	14.0
Total	100.0	100.0	100.0	100.0	100.0	100.0	100.0	100.0	100.0
LIABILITIES									
Notes Payable-Short Term	9.6	9.1	8.7	13.7	9.7	9.7	9.8	.3	7.2
Cur. Mat.-L.T.D.	3.8	3.8	3.1	.4	3.4	4.5	2.8	6.4	2.9
Trade Payables	14.1	15.3	11.3	1.6	8.7	13.8	17.1	11.6	14.8
Income Taxes Payable	.0	.2	.2	.0	1.1	.0	.3	.0	.0
All Other Current	20.2	19.8	20.8	33.3	23.3	11.7	18.9	12.2	19.4
Total Current	47.7	48.1	44.1	49.0	46.2	39.7	48.9	30.6	44.3
Long-Term Debt	27.8	28.3	22.9	22.0	19.4	26.2	19.1	34.5	22.0
Deferred Taxes	.1	.1	.1	.0	.0	.0	.3	.0	.2
All Other Non-Current	9.5	7.5	5.1	.9	.5	4.4	5.3	10.1	8.4
Net Worth	14.9	15.9	27.9	28.2	33.9	29.7	26.4	24.8	25.1
Total Liabilities & Net Worth	100.0	100.0	100.0	100.0	100.0	100.0	100.0	100.0	100.0
INCOME DATA									
Net Sales	100.0	100.0	100.0	100.0	100.0	100.0	100.0	100.0	100.0
Gross Profit									
Operating Expenses	93.2	94.5	93.1	88.3	91.9	96.4	98.7	93.4	93.4
Operating Profit	6.8	5.5	6.9	11.7	8.1	3.6	1.3	6.6	6.6
All Other Expenses (net)	1.8	1.4	1.3	3.4	1.2	.5	.5	1.5	.8
Profit Before Taxes	5.0	4.1	5.6	8.4	6.9	3.1	.8	5.1	5.8
RATIOS									
Current	2.6	2.3	1.9	11.3	5.7	1.3	1.9	1.5	1.7
	1.3	1.2	1.1	1.4	1.1	.9	1.2	1.0	1.1
	.7	.6	.6	.4	.4	.5	.6	.5	.9
Quick	2.0	1.7	1.5	3.4	3.2	1.0	1.5	1.4	1.3
	.9	.8	.7	.6	1.1	.5	.6	.5	.8
	.4	.3	.3	.0	.2	.3	.3	.4	.4
Sales/Receivables	0 UND	0 UND	0 UND	0 UND	0 UND	0 UND	7 54.2	0 999.8	11 33.5
	10 38.2	7 52.7	8 47.3	0 UND	0 UND	0 UND	13 28.9	9 39.9	26 14.2
	33 11.1	32 11.3	36 10.2	0 UND	2 226.2	25 14.6	48 7.6	25 14.7	42 8.6
Cost of Sales/Inventory									
Cost of Sales/Payables									
Sales/Working Capital	10.8	13.2	19.0	6.3	13.1	50.2	19.2	20.2	19.0
	38.7	57.3	167.9	UND	126.2	NM	47.8	360.1	100.5
	-30.6	-16.6	-18.0	-4.1	-12.9	-10.9	-15.0	-20.6	-54.6
EBIT/Interest	24.0	21.5	18.6		18.5	25.3	11.0	17.7	19.6
	(102) 6.3	(101) 7.9	(99) 7.3	(18) 11.5	(13) 6.5	(10) 2.2	(10) 9.4	(43) 7.3	
	1.3	1.7	2.2		5.5	2.1	.1	1.7	2.5
Net Profit + Depr., Dep., Amort./Cur. Mat. L/T/D	7.2	9.1	6.3						8.4
	(18) 3.7	(22) 3.9	(20) 2.0					(12)	2.0
	1.1	1.9	.7						1.1
Fixed/Worth	.3	.3	.2	.1	.2	.3	.1	1.3	.2
	1.5	1.5	1.1	.4	1.0	.7	2.3	2.9	1.1
	-1.9	-2.4	-18.8	7.2	NM	-20.6	-3.3	-1.3	-14.8
Debt/Worth	.9	1.3	1.0	.2	.4	1.1	1.6	1.3	1.5
	3.7	4.6	3.8	1.1	5.0	2.6	5.2	2.6	4.8
	-5.3	7.2	-16.4	-4.6	NM	-38.7	-5.8	-5.0	-22.4
% Profit Before Taxes/Tangible Net Worth	71.1	110.8	92.3	49.1	497.0	71.5			112.3
	(89) 34.6	(82) 53.1	(94) 39.3	(16) 27.1	(18) 94.3	(11) 23.3		(34)	59.9
	11.7	12.4	13.6	11.4	18.7	6.6			17.2
% Profit Before Taxes/Total Assets	26.4	26.6	28.9	31.3	60.8	23.5	8.4	32.3	17.8
	9.1	10.3	13.5	12.7	25.5	12.2	1.5	13.9	11.4
	1.4	2.4	2.1	-3.2	11.9	2.4	-5.8	1.0	4.6
Sales/Net Fixed Assets	79.0	60.8	68.7	281.2	202.6	55.4	66.3	35.2	68.7
	19.6	13.2	19.6	13.2	24.7	23.8	23.2	15.1	19.6
	6.0	5.3	6.7	1.6	10.5	8.6	4.1	3.2	7.3
Sales/Total Assets	5.6	6.0	5.6	3.9	8.1	5.8	7.4	5.5	5.6
	3.6	3.6	3.5	2.0	4.5	3.1	2.5	3.0	3.6
	2.2	2.1	1.7	.8	2.9	1.8	1.2	1.1	2.1
% Depr., Dep., Amort./Sales	.6	.8	.7	1.2	.4				.7
	(92) 1.3	(78) 1.8	(96) 1.5	(12) 3.7	(17) 1.1			(41)	1.4
	3.4	4.8	3.5	17.1	1.9				2.0
% Officers', Directors' Owners' Comp/Sales	1.6	1.3	1.5		1.4	1.3			
	(37) 3.6	(33) 2.9	(34) 3.7		(12) 4.9	(10) 3.5			
	6.5	6.0	5.6		5.6	4.5			
Net Sales ($)	5934489M	7986263M	6766193M	10103M	43770M	62165M	77836M	147174M	6425145M
Total Assets ($)	2088261M	2785763M	2356670M	8976M	12781M	23217M	43357M	64006M	2204333M

M = $ thousand   MM = $ million
See Pages viii through xx for Explanation of Ratios and Data

Current Data Sorted by Assets   Comparative Historical Data

						Type of Statement		
	2					Unqualified	4	3
	5	3	6			Reviewed	14	10
18	16	6	2			Compiled	17	19
25	23	7				Tax Returns	43	61
	17 (4/1-9/30/18)	17	5			Other	50	56
			119 (10/1/18-3/31/19)				4/1/14-3/31/15	4/1/15-3/31/16
0-500M	500M-2MM	2-10MM	10-50MM	50-100MM	100-250MM		ALL	ALL
43	46	33	13		1	**NUMBER OF STATEMENTS**	128	149
%	%	%	%	%	%	**ASSETS**	%	%
32.5	20.2	17.8	21.0			Cash & Equivalents	22.7	24.8
11.1	13.7	13.2	11.0			Trade Receivables (net)	14.4	12.3
3.3	3.1	3.2	3.4			Inventory	4.6	3.2
2.0	2.1	4.9	3.4			All Other Current	3.2	3.6
49.0	39.0	39.2	38.8			Total Current	45.0	43.8
37.7	40.4	42.3	36.7			Fixed Assets (net)	37.9	39.5
2.8	10.1	4.5	12.4			Intangibles (net)	5.2	6.0
10.5	10.5	13.9	12.1			All Other Non-Current	12.1	10.7
100.0	100.0	100.0	100.0			Total	100.0	100.0
						LIABILITIES		
48.8	6.1	7.0	1.1			Notes Payable-Short Term	8.2	12.7
3.1	3.1	1.8	4.4			Cur. Mat.-L.T.D.	2.5	2.6
8.7	9.4	13.6	15.0			Trade Payables	10.9	11.3
.3	.2	.0	.6			Income Taxes Payable	.5	.3
24.0	17.9	22.3	18.1			All Other Current	22.4	24.6
85.0	36.5	44.7	39.2			Total Current	44.6	51.6
34.9	26.2	25.8	24.5			Long-Term Debt	21.5	23.9
.0	.1	.1	.3			Deferred Taxes	.1	.1
7.1	2.2	4.2	1.0			All Other Non-Current	11.9	6.8
-27.0	35.0	25.2	35.0			Net Worth	21.9	17.5
100.0	100.0	100.0	100.0			Total Liabilties & Net Worth	100.0	100.0
						INCOME DATA		
100.0	100.0	100.0	100.0			Net Sales	100.0	100.0
						Gross Profit		
95.4	93.0	89.7	93.7			Operating Expenses	92.9	93.0
4.6	7.0	10.3	6.3			Operating Profit	7.1	7.0
1.1	.8	2.8	1.1			All Other Expenses (net)	.9	.4
3.5	6.2	7.5	5.2			Profit Before Taxes	6.2	6.6
						RATIOS		
2.4	2.7	1.5	1.3				2.4	2.1
.7	1.2	1.0	1.0			Current	1.0	1.0
.4	.5	.2	.6				.5	.5
2.3	2.6	1.1	1.3				2.1	2.0
.7	.9	.8	.7			Quick	.8 (148)	.8
.3	.4	.2	.4				.3	.4
0 UND	0 UND	1 271.5	2 189.9				0 UND	0 UND
0 UND	6 59.7	10 36.0	15 23.9			Sales/Receivables	4 87.1	4 83.5
12 30.4	19 19.0	21 17.1	18 20.8				19 19.5	16 23.2
						Cost of Sales/Inventory		
						Cost of Sales/Payables		
18.1	12.0	15.7	29.4				13.6	18.0
-59.2	83.3	179.5	-999.8			Sales/Working Capital	-472.1	-277.3
-9.1	-10.5	-5.3	-19.0				-17.7	-15.0
20.1	22.6	59.3	38.3				31.7	33.0
(29) 3.9	(35) 7.0	(25) 11.0	14.2			EBIT/Interest	(90) 7.8	(103) 11.6
.0	1.8	5.4	4.5				1.3	3.2
						Net Profit + Depr., Dep., Amort./Cur. Mat. L/T/D	5.2	
							(11) 1.9	
							1.5	
.7	.4	.6	.6				.3	.4
-24.9	2.1	1.7	1.8			Fixed/Worth	1.7	1.6
-.5	-18.5	130.3	4.9				-10.1	-45.8
1.3	.8	1.3	1.8				.9	.9
-19.6	3.0	4.4	2.3			Debt/Worth	3.1	3.3
-2.6	-25.4	299.8	7.5				-17.9	-67.8
158.2	103.9	112.4	97.2			% Profit Before Taxes/Tangible Net Worth	123.9	129.7
(19) 103.8	(33) 50.1	(26) 42.7	(12) 43.3				(89) 55.5	(108) 65.0
10.3	14.9	18.6	25.1				21.5	21.6
49.3	36.6	22.3	16.2			% Profit Before Taxes/Total Assets	34.9	42.6
9.0	13.4	12.8	12.6				14.8	15.6
-11.3	3.1	5.8	7.4				1.8	4.5
71.9	48.3	21.0	22.6			Sales/Net Fixed Assets	44.8	37.0
22.8	8.4	7.9	10.9				19.2	12.7
7.5	2.6	2.1	2.5				4.2	4.4
11.4	4.7	3.5	4.1			Sales/Total Assets	7.2	5.8
5.5	2.7	2.9	2.7				3.8	3.9
3.1	1.7	1.5	1.1				1.9	2.2
.8	.9	.7	.8			% Depr., Dep., Amort./Sales	1.0	.9
(22) 1.3	(32) 2.4	(25) 2.0	2.3				(88) 1.7	(103) 2.0
2.2	5.3	4.3	4.8				3.9	3.7
2.7	3.1	2.1				% Officers', Directors' Owners' Comp/Sales	2.8	2.7
(20) 3.7	(24) 4.9	(12) 2.5					(55) 4.5	(65) 5.3
8.1	7.1	4.7					8.0	9.4
69660M	157855M	373463M	870537M	642618M		Net Sales ($)	1277563M	1078142M
10431M	48717M	136673M	278079M	198343M		Total Assets ($)	422899M	403643M

Note: Columns "50-100MM" and "100-250MM" marked "DATA NOT AVAILABLE" for the percentage/ratio sections.

Comparative Historical Data   Current Data Sorted by Sales

			Type of Statement						
4	3	3	Unqualified		1		1		1
11	13	9	Reviewed					5	4
23	22	13	Compiled		1	3	4	3	1
44	48	41	Tax Returns	1	1	9	4	1	
65	64	70	Other	12	15	9	14	7	5
4/1/16-3/31/17	4/1/17-3/31/18	4/1/18-3/31/19		14	20	10			
ALL	ALL	ALL		17 (4/1-9/30/18)			119 (10/1/18-3/31/19)		
				0-1MM	1-3MM	3-5MM	5-10MM	10-25MM	25MM & OVER
147	150	136	NUMBER OF STATEMENTS	27	37	23	22	16	11
%	%	%	ASSETS	%	%	%	%	%	%
25.5	22.4	23.5	Cash & Equivalents	30.5	17.7	22.4	25.9	21.8	25.3
11.4	11.8	12.7	Trade Receivables (net)	3.3	11.7	14.1	19.9	13.7	20.2
5.0	3.9	3.2	Inventory	1.7	3.6	3.1	4.3	2.9	4.7
3.0	3.4	2.9	All Other Current	.8	3.5	1.0	5.1	3.4	5.3
45.0	41.6	42.3	Total Current	36.2	36.4	40.7	55.2	41.8	55.5
39.6	42.2	39.7	Fixed Assets (net)	50.0	47.5	35.0	26.7	38.3	26.0
6.3	6.2	6.6	Intangibles (net)	3.0	5.7	12.2	5.6	9.1	5.2
9.1	10.0	11.4	All Other Non-Current	10.8	10.4	12.1	12.6	10.8	13.2
100.0	100.0	100.0	Total	100.0	100.0	100.0	100.0	100.0	100.0
			LIABILITIES						
8.1	9.0	19.3	Notes Payable-Short Term	23.2	40.2	10.6	8.7	3.1	2.0
3.3	3.2	2.9	Cur. Mat.-L.T.D.	2.0	3.9	3.0	1.9	3.5	2.4
11.4	9.6	10.8	Trade Payables	2.2	9.3	11.8	12.5	15.5	24.6
.2	.2	.2	Income Taxes Payable	.1	.4	.2	.0	.3	.3
26.3	29.0	21.0	All Other Current	10.2	28.1	19.3	21.1	24.9	21.1
49.3	50.9	54.2	Total Current	37.7	81.9	45.0	44.2	47.4	50.4
24.2	26.4	28.7	Long-Term Debt	54.4	29.9	24.4	13.2	18.7	16.6
.1	.0	.1	Deferred Taxes	.0	.1	.0	.0	.2	.3
11.0	11.7	4.1	All Other Non-Current	5.2	6.7	2.7	1.5	2.7	3.3
15.4	10.9	12.9	Net Worth	2.7	-18.5	27.8	41.0	31.1	29.4
100.0	100.0	100.0	Total Liabilties & Net Worth	100.0	100.0	100.0	100.0	100.0	100.0
			INCOME DATA						
100.0	100.0	100.0	Net Sales	100.0	100.0	100.0	100.0	100.0	100.0
			Gross Profit						
93.2	92.1	93.1	Operating Expenses	85.2	96.0	94.3	95.3	92.9	96.1
6.8	7.9	6.9	Operating Profit	14.8	4.0	5.7	4.7	7.1	3.9
1.0	2.5	1.4	All Other Expenses (net)	6.3	.2	.4	-.5	.8	.0
5.8	5.5	5.5	Profit Before Taxes	8.5	3.8	5.3	5.1	6.3	3.9
			RATIOS						
1.9	2.2	2.2		3.2	2.1	2.4	2.3	1.5	1.2
.9	1.0	1.0	Current	1.5	.5	.9	1.5	1.0	1.0
.5	.4	.4		.3	.2	.5	.4	.6	1.0
1.5	1.6	1.9		3.1	1.7	2.0	2.1	1.4	1.2
.8	.7	.8	Quick	1.2	.4	.8	.9	.9	.8
.4	.2	.3		.1	.1	.4	.4	.5	.7
0 UND	0 UND	0 UND		0 UND	0 UND	0 UND	4 86.5	2 229.9	10 36.7
4 83.0	5 79.2	6 62.0	Sales/Receivables	0 UND	4 89.5	4 83.7	16 23.5	10 36.1	17 21.2
18 20.4	18 20.2	19 19.2		6 61.2	15 23.9	19 19.1	20 17.9	25 14.6	23 15.9
			Cost of Sales/Inventory						
			Cost of Sales/Payables						
18.7	19.2	15.9		8.1	24.2	21.7	10.4	20.0	29.5
-174.2	-134.9	806.4	Sales/Working Capital	19.0	-34.2	-206.8	24.8	-101.0	179.5
-11.3	-10.5	-9.3		-8.8	-1.6	-13.8	-15.1	-13.7	-999.8
24.3	29.9	32.4		14.3	12.2	28.7	35.0	78.4	48.7
(108) 8.4	(104) 5.1	(103) 7.9	EBIT/Interest	(16) 3.5	(26) 3.2	(17) 7.8	(18) 11.1	17.9	(10) 26.6
1.0	1.9	1.8		.9	-.5	3.6	2.5	6.7	5.8
17.1		6.7							
(10) 3.7		(14) 4.4	Net Profit + Depr., Dep., Amort./Cur. Mat. L/T/D						
2.8		1.0							
.5	.5	.6		1.0	.9	.6	.2	.8	.5
2.7	2.6	2.8	Fixed/Worth	8.5	17.0	4.6	.0	1.9	.7
-2.5	-3.0	-6.6		-3.3	-.7	-10.8	5.8	6.0	3.4
1.0	.9	1.0		1.2	1.1	.8	.7	1.7	1.9
4.0	4.4	5.5	Debt/Worth	32.0	-60.1	15.2	1.8	2.2	4.4
-6.7	-11.8	-8.7		-7.6	-3.8	-24.9	12.5	10.7	8.0
104.8	101.3	107.8		106.8	105.3	269.6	152.3	82.1	141.5
(95) 41.9	(101) 49.3	(91) 50.1	% Profit Before Taxes/Tangible Net Worth	(15) 35.6	(17) 31.0	(16) 65.7	(19) 58.5	(13) 37.5	53.6
15.1	15.1	17.1		8.8	8.3	24.3	14.6	22.0	30.5
34.3	23.0	29.3		32.4	28.3	42.6	36.8	23.7	17.6
11.3	9.9	12.7	% Profit Before Taxes/Total Assets	3.3	8.0	17.5	15.3	12.2	16.0
.0	.7	1.7		-6.9	-10.3	6.7	7.3	8.6	11.7
57.2	36.4	42.1		34.4	53.4	60.0	67.3	23.6	22.6
10.6	9.7	10.9	Sales/Net Fixed Assets	4.8	12.2	17.8	17.3	8.5	21.8
3.9	3.0	4.4		1.2	3.6	5.4	7.3	3.6	8.3
6.0	5.1	5.7		3.4	7.5	6.9	5.2	4.0	7.5
3.6	3.3	3.3	Sales/Total Assets	1.6	3.7	3.7	3.8	2.9	3.9
1.9	1.5	1.9		.8	1.9	2.6	2.4	1.4	3.2
.8	.7	.8		1.2	1.1	.7	.4	1.1	
(99) 1.8	(106) 2.0	(92) 1.8	% Depr., Dep., Amort./Sales	(18) 3.1	(22) 2.1	(15) 1.5	(12) .8	1.8	
4.5	3.5	4.4		10.3	5.4	4.7	2.4	4.5	
2.7	2.7	2.5			2.7	1.8	2.5		
(55) 5.0	(59) 4.9	(56) 4.0	% Officers', Directors' Owners' Comp/Sales		(18) 5.1	(13) 3.5	(12) 3.8		
8.8	8.2	6.2			7.9	5.5	5.6		
2280896M	2485004M	2114133M	Net Sales ($)	16326M	65962M	86823M	157517M	279235M	1508270M
840411M	877452M	672243M	Total Assets ($)	21282M	35270M	25874M	47836M	148207M	393774M

M = $ thousand   MM = $ million
See Pages viii through xx for Explanation of Ratios and Data

Current Data Sorted by Assets   Comparative Historical Data

	0-500M	500M-2MM	2-10MM	10-50MM	50-100MM	100-250MM	Type of Statement		4/1/14- 3/31/15 ALL	4/1/15- 3/31/16 ALL
				1	1		Unqualified		2	3
	1		3	3			Reviewed		2	3
	6	4	2	1			Compiled		30	34
	58	21	8	1		2	Tax Returns		130	136
	33	35	15	4		2	Other		89	97
		4 (4/1-9/30/18)		198 (10/1/18-3/31/19)						
NUMBER OF STATEMENTS	98	60	29	10	1	4			253	273
	%	%	%	%	%	%	**ASSETS**		%	%
	25.4	13.0	9.8	11.3			Cash & Equivalents		19.0	21.2
	.7	1.4	1.6	2.1			Trade Receivables (net)		1.8	.8
	10.8	7.9	5.8	6.2			Inventory		10.1	11.4
	3.7	2.9	3.6	2.0			All Other Current		2.4	2.1
	40.5	25.1	20.8	21.6			Total Current		33.3	35.5
	37.4	52.7	53.0	60.0			Fixed Assets (net)		45.8	44.1
	12.5	8.8	10.9	7.0			Intangibles (net)		10.5	10.0
	9.5	13.4	15.3	11.5			All Other Non-Current		10.4	10.4
	100.0	100.0	100.0	100.0			Total		100.0	100.0
							LIABILITIES			
	11.0	3.9	3.3	3.3			Notes Payable-Short Term		5.1	7.3
	.6	1.1	2.8	4.0			Cur. Mat.-L.T.D.		2.2	3.3
	4.6	4.1	6.2	4.8			Trade Payables		7.4	7.6
	.3	.3	.0	.0			Income Taxes Payable		.4	.1
	23.6	16.9	12.0	6.5			All Other Current		21.9	18.4
	40.1	26.4	24.4	18.6			Total Current		37.0	36.7
	16.4	33.6	36.6	41.5			Long-Term Debt		25.4	20.7
	.1	.0	.0	.0			Deferred Taxes		.0	.0
	14.4	8.8	11.1	14.7			All Other Non-Current		18.8	15.1
	28.9	31.2	28.0	25.2			Net Worth		18.8	27.5
	100.0	100.0	100.0	100.0			Total Liabilities & Net Worth		100.0	100.0
							INCOME DATA			
	100.0	100.0	100.0	100.0			Net Sales		100.0	100.0
	62.8	65.4	65.8	59.0			Gross Profit		61.6	62.4
	55.9	58.5	59.1	51.0			Operating Expenses		55.4	56.0
	6.9	6.9	6.6	8.0			Operating Profit		6.2	6.4
	.6	1.0	2.5	1.3			All Other Expenses (net)		.9	.1
	6.3	6.0	4.1	6.7			Profit Before Taxes		5.3	6.3
							RATIOS			
	4.5	3.0	1.7	1.7					3.4	3.6
	1.7	1.1	1.2	1.0			Current		1.5	1.5
	.5	.5	.4	.7					.5	.5
	3.0	1.8	1.0	1.0					2.3	2.3
	1.0	.7	.5	.6			Quick	(251)	.8	.8
	.2	.2	.2	.5					.2	.2
	0 UND	0 UND	0 UND	0 UND					0 UND	0 UND
	0 UND	0 UND	0 UND	1 516.1			Sales/Receivables		0 UND	0 UND
	0 UND	1 452.6	5 80.7	6 65.3					0 999.8	0 UND
	8 46.5	10 36.3	12 31.1	7 49.3					6 56.9	10 38.3
	14 26.5	18 20.0	27 13.4	27 13.3			Cost of Sales/Inventory		16 22.7	20 18.6
	24 14.9	31 11.6	68 5.4	44 8.3					34 10.6	32 11.5
	0 UND	0 UND	16 23.4	9 40.6					0 UND	0 UND
	0 UND	11 34.7	30 12.0	18 19.9			Cost of Sales/Payables		5 80.5	4 82.5
	11 33.6	29 12.5	68 5.4	41 8.8					25 14.5	22 16.9
	18.9	19.5	21.0	14.3					17.0	15.8
	46.1	175.8	66.4	NM			Sales/Working Capital		61.7	53.1
	-35.4	-27.5	-11.3	-43.2					-29.4	-33.0
	33.3	37.9	17.0	14.0					21.3	31.9
(45)	8.9	(44) 6.0	(25) 1.8	4.4			EBIT/Interest	(166)	5.6	(141) 6.3
	2.7	1.0	-1.6	.7					1.3	1.4
							Net Profit + Depr., Dep., Amort./Cur. Mat. L/T/D			
	.3	.6	.9	1.1					.6	.4
	1.0	1.7	2.3	1.6			Fixed/Worth		1.6	1.1
	-4.7	-4.1	NM	-1.0					-4.2	-13.4
	.2	.3	1.2	.7					.5	.3
	1.8	1.8	4.3	1.1			Debt/Worth		2.1	1.7
	-8.7	-5.3	NM	-2.7					-6.0	-15.8
	181.2	145.0	68.6						134.9	104.8
(66)	78.9	(42) 34.7	(22) 43.1				% Profit Before Taxes/Tangible Net Worth	(180)	44.7	(193) 44.0
	41.1	6.9	-3.1						15.1	10.7
	58.2	35.8	26.5	22.1					39.3	44.3
	31.6	8.8	8.7	7.4			% Profit Before Taxes/Total Assets		13.2	15.1
	4.6	1.0	-5.3	-1.6					.7	.6
	80.4	18.9	6.7	7.7					28.4	35.3
	18.3	5.8	3.7	3.3			Sales/Net Fixed Assets		9.2	10.6
	8.0	2.8	2.2	1.8					3.2	3.7
	8.7	4.5	2.5	3.0					6.3	6.0
	6.0	2.5	1.7	2.0			Sales/Total Assets		3.2	3.6
	3.2	1.7	.9	1.0					1.7	2.0
	.6	.9	1.1						1.1	.9
(61)	1.2	(46) 2.4	(20) 3.1				% Depr., Dep., Amort./Sales	(188)	2.0	(172) 1.9
	2.3	6.1	6.8						3.7	3.6
	2.6	1.8							2.4	2.4
(48)	4.8	(15) 3.8					% Officers', Directors' Owners' Comp/Sales	(102)	4.4	(110) 4.4
	8.2	6.7							7.7	7.9
	124701M	195301M	203480M	487495M	51935M	2352046M	Net Sales ($)		1737451M	5147093M
	22068M	65115M	108785M	177346M	67321M	565200M	Total Assets ($)		876761M	995225M

M = $ thousand   MM = $ million
See Pages viii through xx for Explanation of Ratios and Data

Comparative Historical Data

				Type of Statement						

Current Data Sorted by Sales

1		3		2	Type of Statement						1	1
2		7		6	Unqualified						1	1
14		19		15	Reviewed	1	1	1	1	1	1	2
115		106		90	Compiled	2	5	4	1	1	1	3
84		82		89	Tax Returns	31	35	12	8	1	1	4
					Other	24	32	16	3	10		
4/1/16- 3/31/17 ALL		4/1/17- 3/31/18 ALL		4/1/18- 3/31/19 ALL		4 (4/1-9/30/18)			198 (10/1/18-3/31/19)			
						0-1MM	1-3MM	3-5MM	5-10MM	10-25MM	25MM & OVER	
216		217		202	**NUMBER OF STATEMENTS**	58	73	33	13	14	11	
%		%		%	**ASSETS**	%	%	%	%	%	%	
18.6		18.4		18.4	Cash & Equivalents	16.1	23.0	18.2	10.3	16.2	13.2	
1.0		1.2		1.2	Trade Receivables (net)	.2	1.2	.6	4.9	1.2	4.9	
9.0		9.2		9.0	Inventory	9.9	9.8	8.3	5.7	6.6	7.9	
3.8		2.2		3.6	All Other Current	.9	5.1	3.8	2.8	3.9	9.0	
32.4		31.0		32.3	Total Current	27.0	39.0	30.9	23.6	27.9	34.9	
49.0		46.4		45.0	Fixed Assets (net)	47.1	36.4	53.2	56.3	54.1	41.7	
10.8		13.2		11.3	Intangibles (net)	15.4	9.1	8.7	12.8	4.3	19.7	
7.8		9.4		11.4	All Other Non-Current	10.5	15.4	7.2	7.3	13.7	3.7	
100.0		100.0		100.0	Total	100.0	100.0	100.0	100.0	100.0	100.0	
					LIABILITIES							
5.9		5.4		7.2	Notes Payable-Short Term	11.6	7.9	3.2	4.2	.3	2.8	
2.9		2.5		1.3	Cur. Mat.-L.T.D.	.9	.8	1.5	2.0	2.5	3.0	
7.3		4.7		4.7	Trade Payables	2.5	5.4	4.9	5.6	8.2	6.4	
.1		.2		.2	Income Taxes Payable	.3	.0	.5	.5	.0	.1	
17.5		17.0		18.8	All Other Current	17.9	22.2	18.9	18.3	12.3	10.2	
33.6		29.9		32.2	Total Current	33.1	36.4	28.9	30.6	23.4	22.6	
25.9		25.0		25.8	Long-Term Debt	32.4	16.5	26.8	35.1	30.8	32.2	
.0		.0		.1	Deferred Taxes	.2	.0	.0	.0	.0	.0	
12.7		20.2		12.0	All Other Non-Current	11.0	10.9	19.2	7.2	7.9	13.9	
27.8		24.9		30.0	Net Worth	23.3	36.2	25.0	27.1	37.9	31.3	
100.0		100.0		100.0	Total Liabilities & Net Worth	100.0	100.0	100.0	100.0	100.0	100.0	
					INCOME DATA							
100.0		100.0		100.0	Net Sales	100.0	100.0	100.0	100.0	100.0	100.0	
61.9		62.4		63.5	Gross Profit	61.0	64.5	65.4	66.9	65.0	58.1	
55.8		57.0		56.6	Operating Expenses	55.2	58.1	55.8	60.2	57.2	52.5	
6.1		5.4		6.8	Operating Profit	5.9	6.4	9.6	6.8	7.8	5.6	
.8		.4		1.0	All Other Expenses (net)	1.6	.6	.5	1.2	2.3	1.2	
5.3		5.0		5.8	Profit Before Taxes	4.3	5.8	9.1	5.6	5.5	4.3	
					RATIOS							
3.4		3.3		3.6		4.3	3.8	4.3	1.7	1.3	3.9	
1.3		1.5		1.3	Current	1.5	1.4	1.5	.8	1.2	1.3	
.5		.5		.5		.3	.5	.5	.6	1.0	.7	
2.3		2.0		2.2		2.5	2.8	2.6	.9	1.0	2.6	
(214) .7		(216) .9		.7	Quick	.9	.9	.5	.6	.8	.7	
.2		.2		.2		.1	.2	.3	.3	.6	.4	
0 UND		0 UND		0 UND		0 UND	0 UND	0 UND	0 UND	0 UND	0 UND	
0 UND		0 UND		0 UND	Sales/Receivables	0 UND	0 UND	0 UND	2 197.4	0 856.7	0 UND	
0 999.8		0 UND		0 969.2		0 UND	0 UND	0 864.5	10 37.1	5 72.5	8 44.9	
7 51.6		7 48.8		9 42.5		8 45.3	8 48.6	13 29.1	11 33.2	8 45.7	3 115.0	
16 22.6		18 20.3		17 22.0	Cost of Sales/Inventory	15 24.1	13 27.1	18 20.2	17 20.9	19 19.5	22 16.7	
34 10.8		32 11.3		31 11.7		33 11.2	29 12.7	35 10.4	29 12.4	27 13.5	33 10.9	
0 UND		0 UND		0 UND		0 UND	0 UND	0 UND	2 214.2	12 31.0	0 UND	
5 71.8		4 89.0		7 50.1	Cost of Sales/Payables	0 UND	6 59.2	9 40.8	19 18.8	24 15.3	34 10.8	
26 13.9		21 17.7		29 12.7		13 28.3	24 14.9	30 12.2	35 10.5	50 7.3	49 7.5	
18.0		15.7		18.5		19.7	13.8	19.9	41.9	45.5	12.9	
107.0		52.8		58.1	Sales/Working Capital	48.4	52.1	53.1	-98.9	87.8	15.9	
-26.8		-29.5		-27.8		-18.3	-24.1	-33.1	-26.9	999.8	-43.0	
22.9		15.9		22.7		7.0	39.8	45.0	15.3	127.8		
(152) 6.2		(132) 4.9		(126) 6.6	EBIT/Interest	(28) 4.0	(43) 11.4	(23) 9.6	(11) 1.8	(13) 9.0		
.8		.5		1.0		1.0	1.3	2.9	1.1	-.5		
					Net Profit + Depr., Dep., Amort./Cur. Mat. L/T/D							
.6		.6		.4		.3	.3	.6	1.2	.9	.3	
1.6		1.7		1.4	Fixed/Worth	2.8	.9	1.1	3.8	1.3	1.3	
-19.1		-4.2		-5.4		-3.6	NM	NM	-41.8	2.4	-.8	
.3		.4		.4		.4	.3	.2	.9	.8	.3	
1.7		2.3		2.0	Debt/Worth	10.0	1.4	1.2	4.9	1.9	2.7	
-27.8		-5.4		-8.7		-5.4	NM	NM	-5.1	2.6	-2.3	
114.0		100.6		139.8		182.1	107.9	173.4		426.5		
(159) 43.9		(144) 45.9		(141) 50.6	% Profit Before Taxes/Tangible Net Worth	(33) 50.0	(55) 50.6	(25) 64.9		(13) 47.2		
16.4		11.6		10.6		11.7	11.1	13.2		9.1		
40.4		36.8		43.0		37.4	49.4	47.1	39.3	69.5	44.8	
16.5		12.2		14.0	% Profit Before Taxes/Total Assets	13.3	18.6	31.7	3.2	13.7	6.2	
.7		-1.5		1.2		.0	3.0	7.1	-1.8	-1.1	-6.4	
25.0		27.0		26.1		41.5	64.9	22.0	11.0	9.3	16.4	
7.4		8.9		8.7	Sales/Net Fixed Assets	8.4	16.1	5.7	6.1	5.7	6.1	
3.5		3.7		3.6		2.9	6.5	2.9	2.4	3.2	3.6	
6.2		6.0		6.6		7.0	7.2	5.9	5.0	5.0	3.2	
3.0		3.0		3.3	Sales/Total Assets	3.0	4.4	2.7	3.5	3.0	2.5	
1.8		1.9		1.8		1.6	2.4	1.8	1.4	1.7	1.7	
1.2		1.2		.8		1.0	.5	1.0	2.0	.7		
(157) 2.3		(154) 2.2		(139) 1.8	% Depr., Dep., Amort./Sales	(34) 2.1	(48) 1.0	(27) 1.5	(11) 2.6	(10) 2.7		
4.2		3.9		3.8		3.7	2.9	3.9	7.4	7.0		
2.4		2.8		2.2		3.6	2.6	1.1				
(81) 4.4		(94) 4.6		(72) 4.6	% Officers', Directors' Owners' Comp/Sales	(21) 4.7	(34) 5.5	(11) 1.9				
7.4		8.3		8.2		7.0	10.9	3.9				
831851M		2392791M		3414958M	Net Sales ($)	37121M	130263M	126941M	84197M	193389M	2843047M	
399377M		671715M		1005835M	Total Assets ($)	20321M	53038M	48124M	41661M	81056M	761635M	

© RMA 2019

M = $ thousand   MM = $ million
See Pages viii through xx for Explanation of Ratios and Data

Current Data Sorted by Assets   Comparative Historical Data

Type of Statement	0-500M	500M-2MM	2-10MM	10-50MM	50-100MM	100-250MM		4/1/14-3/31/15 ALL	4/1/15-3/31/16 ALL
Unqualified	5	6	5	39	19	18		98	113
Reviewed	18	7	26	29	4			117	140
Compiled	108	68	53	10	1	1		381	326
Tax Returns	512	332	95	8	6	2		1263	1172
Other	345	388	205	135	34	32		1212	1264
		169 (4/1-9/30/18)		2,342 (10/1/18-3/31/19)					
NUMBER OF STATEMENTS	988	801	384	221	64	53		3071	3015
	%	%	%	%	%	%		%	%
ASSETS									
Cash & Equivalents	29.0	18.8	13.7	12.2	10.8	7.2		19.4	20.1
Trade Receivables (net)	1.2	1.9	2.2	2.3	1.8	4.0		1.9	1.9
Inventory	8.6	4.4	3.6	3.5	4.3	2.8		6.5	6.2
All Other Current	4.5	3.2	3.0	3.3	2.2	2.8		2.5	2.3
Total Current	43.3	28.3	22.6	21.2	19.1	16.9		30.3	30.6
Fixed Assets (net)	38.7	48.3	53.5	56.5	54.0	46.1		47.4	47.1
Intangibles (net)	9.1	10.5	10.8	12.8	20.4	28.7		11.1	11.2
All Other Non-Current	8.9	13.0	13.1	9.4	6.5	8.3		11.2	11.2
Total	100.0	100.0	100.0	100.0	100.0	100.0		100.0	100.0
LIABILITIES									
Notes Payable-Short Term	9.9	4.9	2.8	1.9	3.3	.9		5.2	6.6
Cur. Mat.-L.T.D.	2.9	3.1	3.1	4.7	5.6	5.9		3.4	3.2
Trade Payables	11.9	8.1	6.9	8.1	6.7	4.4		11.0	9.2
Income Taxes Payable	.5	.2	.1	.1	.1	.0		.2	.3
All Other Current	31.8	19.0	15.2	14.4	12.8	12.5		21.6	20.0
Total Current	57.0	35.3	28.1	29.2	28.6	23.7		41.4	39.4
Long-Term Debt	22.2	31.7	37.4	37.7	43.3	47.1		28.9	28.6
Deferred Taxes	.0	.0	.1	.1	.4	.9		.2	.1
All Other Non-Current	15.2	7.8	6.4	11.7	13.0	10.1		14.6	12.9
Net Worth	5.6	25.1	28.0	21.4	14.7	18.2		14.9	18.9
Total Liabilities & Net Worth	100.0	100.0	100.0	100.0	100.0	100.0		100.0	100.0
INCOME DATA									
Net Sales	100.0	100.0	100.0	100.0	100.0	100.0		100.0	100.0
Gross Profit	61.1	62.6	62.9	64.7	64.4	65.8		59.9	60.7
Operating Expenses	55.8	56.9	57.2	59.3	61.9	62.5		55.0	54.8
Operating Profit	5.2	5.7	5.7	5.4	2.5	3.3		4.9	5.9
All Other Expenses (net)	.6	.8	1.1	2.3	1.6	2.3		.7	.7
Profit Before Taxes	4.6	4.9	4.6	3.2	.9	1.0		4.2	5.2
RATIOS									
	2.8	2.0	1.7	1.2	1.0	.8		2.0	2.0
Current	1.1	.9	.8	.7	.6	.6		.8	.9
	.4	.3	.4	.3	.3	.4		.4	.4
	2.1	1.5	1.3	.9	.8	.7		1.5	1.5
Quick	(986) .7	(798) .6	(383) .6	(220) .4	(63) .5	.4		(3053) .6	(2999) .6
	.2	.2	.2	.2	.2	.2		.2	.2
	0 UND	0 UND	0 UND	0 999.8	0 UND	0 883.2		0 UND	0 UND
Sales/Receivables	0 UND	0 UND	0 999.8	1 272.4	2 231.2	2 176.7		0 UND	0 UND
	0 UND	1 451.4	2 163.5	6 65.4	4 81.9	8 46.0		1 396.8	1 406.7
	3 112.9	5 69.0	7 53.7	8 47.3	7 50.6	7 49.0		5 71.9	5 74.9
Cost of Sales/Inventory	8 46.5	9 38.7	11 32.9	12 29.6	13 28.6	11 33.1		9 38.9	10 38.4
	14 26.7	15 24.0	18 20.2	21 17.6	21 17.5	16 23.0		16 22.6	17 21.2
	0 UND	1 631.0	8 47.5	17 22.0	15 23.6	16 23.1		0 999.8	0 UND
Cost of Sales/Payables	3 112.3	15 23.6	21 17.6	34 10.8	30 12.1	24 15.4		15 24.8	13 27.3
	18 20.3	30 12.0	38 9.6	61 6.0	51 7.2	37 9.9		33 11.1	31 11.7
	27.4	21.9	24.2	50.0	350.0	-74.6		28.9	28.5
Sales/Working Capital	346.8	-157.9	-82.2	-33.1	-19.9	-22.8		-127.1	-174.9
	-26.6	-16.4	-13.6	-10.8	-10.6	-13.8		-16.1	-17.6
	33.0	23.9	13.1	12.1	4.7	4.8		16.5	21.4
EBIT/Interest	(475) 6.9	(601) 6.3	(332) 4.3	(196) 3.0	(60) 1.6	1.6		(2095) 4.8	(2061) 5.9
	.1	.9	1.2	.3	-1.7	-.2		1.1	1.7
Net Profit + Depr., Dep.,		11.9	7.0	5.4	4.5			5.4	6.1
Amort./Cur. Mat. L/T/D		(11) 1.9	(14) 2.9	(45) 3.1	(15) 1.9			(147) 2.9	(159) 3.1
		1.5	1.4	1.3	1.1			1.8	1.8
	.4	.6	1.0	1.2	2.2	3.0		.7	.7
Fixed/Worth	1.3	1.9	2.7	3.4	-116.1	-3.2		2.5	2.2
	-1.5	-3.9	-19.3	-3.4	-1.1	-.7		-3.0	-3.8
	.4	.6	1.0	1.0	1.7	3.2		.7	.6
Debt/Worth	2.7	2.3	3.6	3.8	-144.9	-6.3		3.8	2.9
	-3.4	-6.1	-18.9	-5.8	-2.8	-2.3		-5.3	-6.0
% Profit Before Taxes/Tangible	216.4	112.5	69.0	49.3	45.8	78.5		111.5	127.5
Net Worth	(618) 85.7	(535) 52.4	(271) 33.9	(146) 19.8	(31) 16.9	(25) 13.1		(1989) 46.1	(1998) 55.3
	28.0	18.1	8.5	4.4	-18.0	2.9		13.0	20.3
% Profit Before Taxes/Total	76.7	35.5	17.5	11.5	9.9	7.3		33.2	40.3
Assets	28.3	15.4	8.4	5.4	2.4	1.6		12.2	15.7
	2.4	.9	1.3	-2.1	-5.7	-4.0		1.2	3.5
	83.7	18.5	10.5	6.7	7.8	7.1		25.3	25.9
Sales/Net Fixed Assets	22.8	8.0	5.1	4.0	3.4	3.9		9.0	9.1
	10.1	3.9	2.0	2.2	2.2	2.4		3.9	4.0
	12.0	4.8	3.3	2.9	2.9	2.2		6.6	6.6
Sales/Total Assets	7.4	3.2	2.1	1.9	1.7	1.5		3.7	3.7
	4.5	2.1	1.2	1.3	1.2	1.0		2.1	2.1
	.6	1.1	1.6	2.5	2.9	2.5		1.0	1.0
% Depr., Dep., Amort./Sales	(627) 1.2	(600) 2.1	(305) 2.8	(198) 3.8	(54) 4.3	(18) 2.9		(2346) 2.1	(2198) 2.1
	2.3	3.7	4.6	5.3	5.7	4.8		3.7	3.7
	2.3	1.6	1.2	.5	.5			2.0	2.0
% Officers', Directors'	(444) 4.1	(304) 3.0	(121) 2.5	(21) 2.5	(11) .7			(1151) 3.6	(1095) 3.8
Owners' Comp/Sales	6.8	5.0	4.5	5.4	4.2			6.3	6.2
Net Sales ($)	1697626M	2888398M	4280589M	13577781M	14795687M	17617126M		65424628M	67934375M
Total Assets ($)	234732M	810727M	1752837M	5626702M	4600500M	8569450M		24350184M	27861960M

Comparative Historical Data | | | | ## Current Data Sorted by Sales

			Type of Statement						
101	99	92	Unqualified	2	5	3	3	6	73
103	104	84	Reviewed	1	16	6	12	16	33
273	272	241	Compiled	21	108	46	33	24	9
946	1046	955	Tax Returns	175	455	176	92	39	18
1129	1163	1139	Other	100	441	194	105	119	180
4/1/16-3/31/17 ALL	4/1/17-3/31/18 ALL	4/1/18-3/31/19 ALL		169 (4/1-9/30/18)			2,342 (10/1/18-3/31/19)		
				0-1MM	1-3MM	3-5MM	5-10MM	10-25MM	25MM & OVER
2552	2684	2511	**NUMBER OF STATEMENTS**	299	1025	425	245	204	313
%	%	%	**ASSETS**	%	%	%	%	%	%
19.8	20.0	21.0	Cash & Equivalents	22.4	23.2	23.5	19.8	16.6	12.8
1.8	2.0	1.7	Trade Receivables (net)	1.5	1.0	2.0	2.9	2.2	2.7
5.9	5.8	5.8	Inventory	7.6	6.3	5.6	5.7	4.6	3.8
2.8	3.4	3.7	All Other Current	2.7	4.5	3.3	3.3	3.0	3.0
30.3	31.2	32.2	Total Current	34.2	35.0	34.5	31.7	26.4	22.4
47.2	46.6	46.1	Fixed Assets (net)	47.3	44.5	43.0	44.6	50.1	53.4
11.3	11.7	10.8	Intangibles (net)	10.8	9.6	9.9	10.5	11.8	15.9
11.2	10.6	10.8	All Other Non-Current	7.7	11.0	12.6	13.2	11.7	8.3
100.0	100.0	100.0	Total	100.0	100.0	100.0	100.0	100.0	100.0
			LIABILITIES						
6.0	6.0	6.2	Notes Payable-Short Term	13.5	6.4	5.2	3.8	4.6	2.4
3.8	3.5	3.3	Cur. Mat.-L.T.D.	2.9	3.0	2.6	3.2	3.4	5.6
9.4	9.4	9.3	Trade Payables	8.8	8.5	11.2	12.0	9.0	7.9
.2	.2	.3	Income Taxes Payable	.1	.4	.3	.3	.1	.1
22.6	22.6	22.8	All Other Current	32.7	25.0	19.3	23.6	15.6	14.9
42.0	41.7	41.8	Total Current	57.9	43.2	38.6	42.9	32.7	30.9
30.9	30.3	30.0	Long-Term Debt	29.4	28.6	26.9	28.4	31.4	39.8
.1	.1	.1	Deferred Taxes	.0	.0	.0	.0	.1	.3
11.3	11.8	11.0	All Other Non-Current	18.8	11.3	9.2	6.2	6.0	12.3
15.7	16.1	17.1	Net Worth	-6.1	16.9	25.2	22.5	29.9	16.6
100.0	100.0	100.0	Total Liabilties & Net Worth	100.0	100.0	100.0	100.0	100.0	100.0
			INCOME DATA						
100.0	100.0	100.0	Net Sales	100.0	100.0	100.0	100.0	100.0	100.0
62.3	62.1	62.3	Gross Profit	61.3	61.8	62.6	62.5	63.6	63.6
56.8	57.1	57.0	Operating Expenses	58.2	56.6	54.7	57.0	57.3	60.0
5.5	5.0	5.3	Operating Profit	3.1	5.2	7.9	5.4	6.4	3.6
.9	.8	1.0	All Other Expenses (net)	1.4	.9	.7	.3	1.3	1.6
4.6	4.1	4.4	Profit Before Taxes	1.6	4.4	7.3	5.1	5.0	2.0
			RATIOS						
1.8	1.9	2.0		3.0	2.5	2.3	1.7	1.6	1.1
.8	.9	.9	Current	1.0	1.0	1.0	.9	.8	.6
.4	.4	.4		.3	.4	.5	.3	.4	.4
1.3	1.4	1.5		2.2	1.7	1.8	1.3	1.2	.8
(2541) .5	(2679) .5	(2503) .6	Quick	(298) .5	(1021) .6	(424) .7	.6	.6	(311) .5
.2	.2	.2		.1	.2	.3	.2	.3	.2
0 UND	0 UND	0 UND		0 UND	0 UND	0 UND	0 UND	0 UND	0 999.8
0 UND	0 UND	0 UND	Sales/Receivables	0 UND	0 UND	0 UND	0 999.8	0 999.8	1 258.0
1 352.7	1 356.9	1 352.7		0 UND	0 UND	1 366.2	1 271.4	3 128.0	5 72.4
5 69.5	5 80.0	5 76.6		3 122.0	4 97.2	5 71.5	6 59.2	7 52.6	7 50.5
10 37.3	9 39.3	9 39.0	Cost of Sales/Inventory	9 42.6	8 43.5	9 39.0	10 35.5	11 32.9	12 31.5
17 21.4	16 22.5	16 23.5		20 18.5	14 26.6	15 24.1	15 23.6	18 20.5	18 20.8
1 701.0	0 UND	0 UND		0 UND	0 UND	5 72.2	7 50.3	13 28.5	15 23.8
15 24.0	14 26.4	14 26.0	Cost of Sales/Payables	0 UND	6 59.7	17 21.9	19 19.1	26 13.9	29 12.7
32 11.3	31 11.7	31 11.9		15 25.1	22 16.5	33 11.1	36 10.0	43 8.5	51 7.1
32.3	28.6	26.6		26.0	25.0	20.1	27.5	32.9	92.9
-92.5	-130.0	-171.3	Sales/Working Capital	UND	999.9	701.5	-127.5	-75.9	-30.1
-14.7	-15.4	-16.7		-12.5	-20.2	-22.5	-14.0	-13.9	-11.6
20.9	17.9	19.7		7.5	21.2	34.6	21.8	17.1	10.0
(1805) 5.8	(1824) 4.2	(1717) 4.5	EBIT/Interest	(163) 1.5	(610) 5.2	(291) 9.8	(190) 5.3	(176) 5.0	(287) 2.5
1.1	.5	.6		-2.5	.5	2.8	1.2	1.7	-.1
6.1	5.6	5.2	Net Profit + Depr., Dep.,					9.1	4.9
(138) 2.7	(139) 3.1	(97) 3.1	Amort./Cur. Mat. L/T/D				(10) 5.5		(66) 2.6
1.3	1.5	1.5						-.3	1.3
.8	.7	.6		.6	.5	.5	.8	.9	1.4
2.6	2.4	2.1	Fixed/Worth	3.2	1.7	1.5	2.0	2.3	6.1
-2.5	-2.4	-2.7		-1.4	-2.7	-5.1	-5.1	-34.6	-1.6
.7	.7	.6		.6	.4	.5	.8	.9	1.3
3.8	3.8	3.1	Debt/Worth	8.7	2.7	1.8	3.0	2.8	7.0
-4.6	-4.8	-4.6		3.0	-4.6	-8.9	-7.8	-61.8	-3.4
129.4	131.8	121.1	% Profit Before Taxes/Tangible	114.2	144.3	144.7	136.4	97.4	57.1
(1621) 52.7	(1703) 51.6	(1626) 49.8	Net Worth	(168) 53.0	(666) 52.8	(293) 72.7	(166) 49.4	(152) 42.1	(181) 19.9
16.5	13.8	15.5		9.3	17.6	32.3	12.9	10.1	2.9
39.0	38.9	40.3	% Profit Before Taxes/Total	35.4	49.1	56.5	41.1	24.9	13.1
14.1	12.4	13.3	Assets	8.4	17.3	22.7	15.1	10.9	4.4
1.5	.2	.4		-10.0	.7	7.1	1.8	2.1	-3.9
24.2	27.3	27.5		38.1	46.9	30.1	25.5	12.8	7.9
8.6	9.1	9.6	Sales/Net Fixed Assets	10.9	12.6	12.0	10.3	6.4	4.6
3.7	3.9	4.2		3.8	5.3	5.8	5.0	3.1	2.6
6.4	6.8	6.9		8.1	8.5	6.9	6.7	4.7	3.4
3.5	3.8	3.8	Sales/Total Assets	4.0	4.7	4.1	3.9	2.7	2.2
2.0	2.0	2.1		2.0	2.5	2.5	2.2	1.6	1.5
1.1	1.1	1.0		1.1	.8	.8	.9	1.6	2.2
(1852) 2.2	(1892) 2.2	(1802) 2.1	% Depr., Dep., Amort./Sales	(189) 2.3	(684) 1.7	(313) 1.6	(192) 1.9	(174) 2.6	(250) 3.6
4.0	3.9	3.8		4.5	3.4	2.9	3.6	3.7	5.1
2.1	1.8	1.8		3.0	2.1	1.5	1.0	.9	.6
(929) 3.7	(993) 3.4	(905) 3.4	% Officers', Directors' Owners' Comp/Sales	(130) 5.8	(425) 3.8	(161) 2.9	(94) 2.0	(60) 2.0	(35) 1.8
6.3	6.0	5.9		8.2	5.9	4.2	4.0	3.5	5.8
61030740M	61047366M	54857207M	Net Sales ($)	194718M	1931186M	1625597M	1732915M	3214606M	46158185M
24449388M	25810096M	21594948M	Total Assets ($)	76842M	644071M	578498M	662405M	1585306M	18047826M

M = $ thousand   MM = $ million
See Pages viii through xx for Explanation of Ratios and Data

Current Data Sorted by Assets								Comparative Historical Data	
Type of Statement									
Unqualified	2	8	15	38	25	31		97	103
Reviewed	2	7	34	40	4			95	94
Compiled	90	200	283	90	4	4		783	894
Tax Returns	263	154	71	7	2	2		669	658
Other	259	223	322	236	60	68		1110	1321
	201 (4/1-9/30/18)			2,343 (10/1/18-3/31/19)				4/1/14- 3/31/15	4/1/15- 3/31/16
	0-500M	500M-2MM	2-10MM	10-50MM	50-100MM	100-250MM		ALL	ALL
NUMBER OF STATEMENTS	616	592	725	411	95	105		2754	3070
	%	%	%	%	%	%		%	%
ASSETS									
Cash & Equivalents	25.2	19.2	16.9	13.1	9.9	7.9		18.6	18.5
Trade Receivables (net)	1.2	1.0	1.2	1.3	2.2	2.6		.9	1.1
Inventory	7.0	3.0	2.3	2.0	1.7	2.1		3.8	3.4
All Other Current	3.0	3.2	1.7	2.2	1.9	1.6		1.7	1.7
Total Current	36.3	26.5	22.1	18.7	15.8	14.2		24.9	24.8
Fixed Assets (net)	39.7	47.0	44.3	46.4	44.2	40.3		45.9	45.0
Intangibles (net)	14.9	18.0	25.7	27.9	31.6	38.8		20.2	21.6
All Other Non-Current	9.1	8.6	7.9	7.0	8.5	6.7		9.0	8.7
Total	100.0	100.0	100.0	100.0	100.0	100.0		100.0	100.0
LIABILITIES									
Notes Payable-Short Term	8.3	2.4	2.0	1.2	.8	.2		3.1	2.8
Cur. Mat.-L.T.D.	5.9	6.7	7.8	7.0	6.7	5.0		6.6	6.8
Trade Payables	8.2	5.9	6.2	5.9	5.1	4.6		7.3	6.7
Income Taxes Payable	.5	.0	.1	.0	.1	.1		.1	.1
All Other Current	31.2	17.6	10.6	10.4	9.4	9.1		18.1	17.3
Total Current	54.1	32.5	26.6	24.5	22.1	19.0		35.2	33.8
Long-Term Debt	35.0	40.6	45.4	47.2	55.9	58.4		39.5	39.7
Deferred Taxes	.0	.0	.0	.1	.3	.8		.2	.1
All Other Non-Current	16.2	8.8	6.5	4.6	3.7	6.9		9.3	8.7
Net Worth	-5.2	18.1	21.5	23.6	18.1	14.9		15.9	17.7
Total Liabilities & Net Worth	100.0	100.0	100.0	100.0	100.0	100.0		100.0	100.0
INCOME DATA									
Net Sales	100.0	100.0	100.0	100.0	100.0	100.0		100.0	100.0
Gross Profit	62.5	64.4	65.7	64.0	64.8	63.7		61.9	62.5
Operating Expenses	56.9	59.5	61.3	59.4	58.2	57.2		56.5	56.8
Operating Profit	5.6	4.9	4.4	4.6	6.6	6.5		5.4	5.8
All Other Expenses (net)	.7	1.0	.9	1.3	1.7	2.6		.8	.7
Profit Before Taxes	4.9	4.0	3.5	3.3	4.9	3.9		4.6	5.1
RATIOS									
Current	2.8	2.2	1.5	1.1	1.0	.9		1.6	1.7
	1.1	.9	.8	.7	.6	.6		.8	.8
	.4	.4	.4	.4	.3	.3		.3	.4
Quick	2.0	1.6	1.2	.9	.8	.7		1.3	1.3
	(613) .8	(589) .6	(723) .7	.5	.5	.4		(2748) .6	(3067) .6
	.2	.2	.3	.3	.3	.2		.2	.2
Sales/Receivables	0 UND	0 UND	0 UND	0 UND	0 UND	0 999.8		0 UND	0 UND
	0 UND	0 UND	0 999.8	0 999.8	1 704.7	2 190.9		0 UND	0 UND
	0 UND	0 UND	1 355.8	2 198.6	3 105.2	5 77.6		1 570.5	1 555.5
Cost of Sales/Inventory	3 125.9	5 69.1	6 57.5	6 58.8	5 69.2	5 76.7		5 68.6	5 70.8
	7 53.5	8 46.5	8 43.4	9 42.8	8 43.7	7 53.0		8 46.3	8 45.7
	11 32.3	11 34.5	10 36.1	11 34.3	12 31.4	11 33.8		10 35.1	10 34.9
Cost of Sales/Payables	0 UND	1 294.4	6 59.5	13 28.7	15 24.8	13 28.7		2 180.7	2 207.5
	3 133.3	11 33.9	17 21.5	24 15.2	29 12.5	29 12.4		12 29.6	12 30.2
	13 27.7	24 15.5	33 11.0	39 9.4	47 7.7	45 8.1		26 14.1	26 14.1
Sales/Working Capital	26.8	22.2	35.5	95.0	228.3	-139.8		39.5	37.4
	443.8	-208.2	-64.8	-33.9	-26.0	-25.3		-68.5	-75.4
	-28.7	-16.9	-18.1	-14.4	-14.0	-13.8		-16.3	-17.0
EBIT/Interest	23.7	12.9	8.8	7.0	4.7	4.0		14.3	15.3
	(346) 6.1	(496) 4.7	(688) 3.6	(402) 3.1	(93) 3.1	(102) 2.2		(2214) 5.2	(2521) 6.1
	1.3	1.0	1.0	1.4	1.8	1.0		1.8	2.4
Net Profit + Depr., Dep., Amort./Cur. Mat. L/T/D		14.5	4.4	5.0	3.9	3.8		4.6	4.7
		(10) 4.2	(36) 2.6	(53) 2.5	(19) 2.9	(32) 2.1		(156) 2.4	(187) 2.8
		1.3	2.1	1.4	1.4	.9		1.7	1.6
Fixed/Worth	.4	1.2	1.7	2.1	3.1	-36.5		1.1	1.1
	2.0	12.0	-19.3	-10.8	-2.8	-1.7		13.9	13.2
	-1.1	-1.5	-.9	-.9	-.9	-.8		-1.2	-1.2
Debt/Worth	.5	1.4	1.8	2.5	4.5	-50.9		1.3	1.3
	5.9	31.6	-32.5	-14.2	-5.7	-3.3		32.5	30.2
	-2.3	-3.6	-2.5	-2.5	-2.2	-2.0		-2.8	-2.9
% Profit Before Taxes/Tangible Net Worth	188.9	105.8	79.2	76.9	51.0	87.4		139.1	141.9
	(341) 80.0	(311) 53.1	(346) 32.6	(183) 30.1	(32) 26.5	(25) 28.8		(1435) 51.9	(1616) 60.3
	29.0	16.2	11.4	12.9	11.0	13.6		19.5	22.6
% Profit Before Taxes/Total Assets	64.1	26.7	16.1	10.9	11.1	8.7		28.5	28.7
	26.3	11.3	7.3	5.5	6.4	4.8		11.5	13.1
	3.6	.2	.2	.8	2.3	.4		2.7	4.2
Sales/Net Fixed Assets	70.1	17.9	11.9	9.1	6.5	7.2		19.3	18.0
	18.2	7.9	7.4	5.1	4.4	4.1		7.9	7.9
	7.1	4.1	4.2	3.0	2.7	2.6		3.9	4.0
Sales/Total Assets	10.8	4.9	3.8	2.7	2.2	1.9		5.5	5.0
	5.9	3.1	2.7	2.0	1.6	1.4		3.2	3.1
	3.5	2.0	1.8	1.5	1.1	1.0		1.9	1.9
% Depr., Dep., Amort./Sales	1.0	1.9	2.2	2.9	3.0	2.5		1.6	1.7
	(399) 1.9	(469) 3.0	(607) 3.6	(372) 4.3	(84) 3.9	(55) 3.0		(2185) 2.9	(2461) 3.0
	3.8	4.9	5.3	5.8	6.1	3.7		4.5	4.7
% Officers', Directors' Owners' Comp/Sales	2.4	1.3	.9	.6				1.3	1.2
	(263) 3.9	(186) 2.5	(253) 1.3	(99) 1.4				(887) 2.3	(941) 2.5
	6.1	4.5	3.1	3.7				4.8	5.0
Net Sales ($)	898348M	2405322M	10280755M	20804065M	12320285M	26495645M		62704616M	73146340M
Total Assets ($)	143860M	634638M	3576904M	9236027M	6545536M	16388967M		29967440M	33902458M

Comparative Historical Data | Current Data Sorted by Sales

			Type of Statement						
114	131	119	Unqualified		4	3	4	15	93
97	111	87	Reviewed	2	3	6	9	25	42
804	803	671	Compiled	27	143	87	121	181	112
630	549	499	Tax Returns	147	199	59	40	33	21
1223	1196	1168	Other	125	255	96	125	213	354
4/1/16-3/31/17	4/1/17-3/31/18	4/1/18-3/31/19		201 (4/1-9/30/18)			2,343 (10/1/18-3/31/19)		
ALL	ALL	ALL		0-1MM	1-3MM	3-5MM	5-10MM	10-25MM	25MM & OVER
2868	2790	2544	**NUMBER OF STATEMENTS**	301	604	251	299	467	622
%	%	%	**ASSETS**	%	%	%	%	%	%
19.4	18.4	18.2	Cash & Equivalents	20.5	20.1	23.6	17.3	18.6	13.2
1.1	1.3	1.3	Trade Receivables (net)	1.0	.9	1.2	1.3	1.3	1.7
3.2	3.2	3.5	Inventory	6.6	4.0	3.5	3.2	2.8	2.3
1.9	2.3	2.4	All Other Current	2.2	3.0	3.7	2.3	1.7	2.2
25.5	25.1	25.4	Total Current	30.4	28.0	32.0	24.1	24.3	19.5
44.8	43.8	44.0	Fixed Assets (net)	46.2	44.1	41.0	40.8	44.0	45.4
22.2	24.0	22.4	Intangibles (net)	15.7	16.8	18.2	26.9	25.1	28.6
7.5	7.1	8.2	All Other Non-Current	7.6	11.0	8.9	8.2	6.6	6.5
100.0	100.0	100.0	Total	100.0	100.0	100.0	100.0	100.0	100.0
			LIABILITIES						
2.8	3.2	3.4	Notes Payable-Short Term	10.4	4.9	1.3	1.8	2.0	1.1
6.8	7.0	6.8	Cur. Mat.-L.T.D.	4.8	5.8	6.2	8.2	8.4	7.0
6.2	6.0	6.4	Trade Payables	3.7	5.9	7.4	7.3	7.4	6.8
.1	.2	.2	Income Taxes Payable	.2	.4	.1	.1	.1	.0
17.3	15.9	17.1	All Other Current	20.5	25.4	16.7	17.0	12.4	11.0
33.1	32.3	33.8	Total Current	39.6	42.4	31.6	34.2	30.3	26.0
42.2	43.5	43.0	Long-Term Debt	42.0	36.1	39.6	45.0	43.5	50.0
.1	.1	.1	Deferred Taxes	.0	.0	.0	.0	.0	.3
7.2	8.7	9.0	All Other Non-Current	14.3	12.6	11.0	7.6	5.5	5.3
17.5	15.5	14.2	Net Worth	4.1	8.9	17.7	13.2	20.7	18.4
100.0	100.0	100.0	Total Liabilties & Net Worth	100.0	100.0	100.0	100.0	100.0	100.0
			INCOME DATA						
100.0	100.0	100.0	Net Sales	100.0	100.0	100.0	100.0	100.0	100.0
63.0	63.4	64.2	Gross Profit	61.8	64.3	63.9	65.7	65.1	64.2
56.9	58.2	59.2	Operating Expenses	56.6	58.4	57.8	61.3	61.3	59.3
6.1	5.2	5.0	Operating Profit	5.2	5.8	6.1	4.4	3.8	4.9
.8	1.0	1.0	All Other Expenses (net)	1.6	.8	.7	.7	.8	1.4
5.3	4.2	4.0	Profit Before Taxes	3.6	5.0	5.4	3.7	3.0	3.5
			RATIOS						
1.6	1.7	1.8	Current	3.8	2.4	2.6	1.4	1.5	1.1
.8	.8	.8		1.4	.9	1.0	.8	.8	.7
.4	.4	.4		.4	.4	.5	.4	.4	.4
1.3	1.3	1.3	Quick	2.7	1.7	1.8	1.1	1.2	.9
(2863) .6	(2773) .6	(2536) .6		(298) .9	(602) .7	.7	(298) .6	(465) .6	.5
.2	.2	.3		.2	.2	.3	.2	.3	.3
0 UND	0 UND	0 UND	Sales/Receivables	0 UND	0 UND	0 UND	0 UND	0 UND	0 UND
0 UND	0 UND	0 UND		0 UND	0 UND	0 UND	0 999.8	0 999.8	0 820.4
1 409.6	1 399.7	1 383.2		0 UND	0 999.8	1 598.5	1 552.3	2 213.0	2 158.7
5 73.4	5 72.5	5 69.8	Cost of Sales/Inventory	2 179.0	4 90.8	4 81.8	6 58.1	7 55.2	6 65.9
8 47.0	8 44.5	8 45.5		7 48.8	7 51.1	8 46.6	8 43.5	8 43.4	8 43.9
10 35.7	10 35.0	11 34.6		15 25.1	10 35.6	11 33.7	10 35.1	10 36.5	10 34.8
3 124.7	2 235.5	2 152.6	Cost of Sales/Payables	0 UND	0 UND	2 180.4	4 88.3	8 44.6	13 29.1
13 28.7	12 29.9	13 27.3		0 UND	7 53.9	13 28.8	15 24.0	17 20.9	24 15.0
26 13.9	26 13.8	30 12.3		9 38.9	19 19.0	26 13.8	30 12.1	33 10.9	41 8.9
33.4	34.0	33.1	Sales/Working Capital	17.3	27.7	19.0	51.3	36.0	154.2
-77.4	-68.8	-82.2		101.6	-308.6	-563.0	-63.9	-73.6	-33.2
-15.8	-16.8	-17.2		-26.7	-17.4	-21.8	-15.4	-18.4	-15.0
17.3	12.9	10.7	EBIT/Interest	7.7	15.5	19.7	10.1	10.0	6.3
(2387) 6.5	(2333) 4.5	(2127) 3.7		(171) 2.5	(431) 5.3	(196) 6.5	(275) 3.8	(449) 4.0	(605) 3.0
2.4	1.5	1.1		-1.0	1.2	1.5	1.0	1.1	1.3
4.5	4.4	4.6	Net Profit + Depr., Dep., Amort./Cur. Mat. L/T/D					3.9	4.4
(163) 2.8	(169) 2.6	(150) 2.5						(31) 2.7	(102) 2.5
1.9	1.6	1.4						1.7	1.3
1.2	1.3	1.3	Fixed/Worth	.6	.7	.7	1.7	1.6	2.7
18.1	-222.0	UND		3.3	4.2	4.2	-8.7	-12.9	-3.9
-1.1	-.9	-1.0		-1.8	-1.3	-1.5	-.6	-1.0	-.9
1.5	1.6	1.4	Debt/Worth	.8	.6	.7	2.0	2.0	3.1
61.5	-35.4	-48.3		10.4	9.2	5.5	-22.1	-26.1	-7.1
-2.8	-2.5	-2.6		-3.2	-2.8	-3.4	-2.2	-2.7	-2.5
151.3	129.1	111.9	% Profit Before Taxes/Tangible Net Worth	136.3	134.2	106.5	129.2	91.1	84.5
(1468) 62.4	(1349) 54.3	(1238) 43.8		(168) 48.6	(330) 66.4	(142) 44.2	(138) 52.3	(220) 32.9	(240) 32.1
25.3	18.2	16.0		14.2	22.9	17.2	17.0	11.4	13.2
30.8	24.2	23.4	% Profit Before Taxes/Total Assets	33.1	43.6	31.8	20.9	16.6	11.8
13.9	10.0	8.8		11.9	16.9	14.4	8.1	8.1	6.0
4.1	1.8	.9		5.7	2.8	2.8	.3	.6	1.1
16.8	16.8	16.7	Sales/Net Fixed Assets	34.4	32.4	28.2	19.0	12.7	9.6
7.5	7.7	7.7		8.3	9.2	9.5	8.6	7.9	5.6
3.7	3.8	4.0		3.6	4.3	4.7	4.9	4.4	3.3
4.9	4.7	4.8	Sales/Total Assets	6.2	7.0	6.2	5.0	4.3	3.3
2.8	2.8	2.9		3.2	3.6	3.4	2.9	2.8	2.2
1.8	1.7	1.8		1.9	2.1	2.0	1.9	1.9	1.5
1.8	1.9	1.9	% Depr., Dep., Amort./Sales	1.3	1.5	1.6	2.1	2.2	2.6
(2269) 3.2	(2150) 3.4	(1986) 3.3		(201) 3.2	(437) 2.6	(184) 2.7	(228) 3.5	(406) 3.7	(530) 3.8
5.1	5.3	5.0		5.1	4.5	4.2	5.3	5.3	5.1
1.1	1.1	1.1	% Officers', Directors' Owners' Comp/Sales	3.0	2.2	1.3	.9	.8	.5
(924) 2.3	(949) 2.3	(815) 2.5		(109) 4.8	(222) 3.4	(84) 2.6	(113) 1.6	(164) 1.2	(123) 1.3
4.8	5.1	4.7		7.6	5.3	4.4	3.2	2.3	3.8
65826704M	72785686M	73204420M	Net Sales ($)	187878M	1151823M	970892M	2212588M	7562019M	61119220M
32656933M	35551122M	36525932M	Total Assets ($)	83995M	428170M	387005M	901642M	3150698M	31574422M

M = $ thousand   MM = $ million
See Pages viii through xx for Explanation of Ratios and Data

Current Data Sorted by Assets **Comparative Historical Data**

						Type of Statement		
		3			2	Unqualified	1	4
4		1	2			Reviewed	1	13
2	1	5	2			Compiled	18	19
27	10	4				Tax Returns	36	58
22	13	22	5	1	2	Other	57	64
	8 (4/1-9/30/18)		120 (10/1/18-3/31/19)				4/1/14-3/31/15	4/1/15-3/31/16
0-500M	500M-2MM	2-10MM	10-50MM	50-100MM	100-250MM		ALL	ALL
55	24	35	9	1	4	NUMBER OF STATEMENTS	113	158
%	%	%	%	%	%	ASSETS	%	%
25.3	13.2	16.9				Cash & Equivalents	16.7	15.4
.6	3.4	4.0				Trade Receivables (net)	3.7	4.5
5.3	5.1	5.2				Inventory	6.0	3.9
3.6	1.4	1.0				All Other Current	5.1	4.3
34.8	23.1	27.1				Total Current	31.5	28.0
38.8	54.3	51.6				Fixed Assets (net)	45.9	47.5
19.3	13.0	15.7				Intangibles (net)	11.8	16.8
7.2	9.5	5.6				All Other Non-Current	10.7	7.6
100.0	100.0	100.0				Total	100.0	100.0
						LIABILITIES		
11.4	16.0	2.4				Notes Payable-Short Term	12.2	6.3
8.0	8.3	5.6				Cur. Mat.-L.T.D.	4.3	4.9
5.8	8.3	6.6				Trade Payables	10.4	9.1
.0	.0	.1				Income Taxes Payable	.0	.1
11.5	9.4	8.1				All Other Current	14.6	11.4
36.7	42.0	22.7				Total Current	41.5	31.8
33.2	55.5	39.2				Long-Term Debt	46.1	36.6
.0	.0	.2				Deferred Taxes	.1	.2
7.3	10.9	9.6				All Other Non-Current	10.2	13.5
22.5	-8.4	28.3				Net Worth	2.1	17.9
100.0	100.0	100.0				Total Liabilities & Net Worth	100.0	100.0
						INCOME DATA		
100.0	100.0	100.0				Net Sales	100.0	100.0
						Gross Profit		
95.4	98.9	92.3				Operating Expenses	94.8	93.3
4.6	1.1	7.7				Operating Profit	5.2	6.7
1.0	2.2	2.3				All Other Expenses (net)	1.1	1.4
3.6	-1.0	5.4				Profit Before Taxes	4.1	5.3
						RATIOS		
2.7	.7	2.0					1.9	1.9
1.1	.6	1.3				Current	.8	.9
.4	.3	.6					.3	.4
2.3	.6	1.6					1.2	1.3
.9	.4	(34) 1.0				Quick	.6	.6
.2	.2	.4					.1	.2
0 UND	0 UND	0 999.8					0 UND	0 UND
0 UND	0 UND	2 214.2				Sales/Receivables	0 UND	0 UND
0 UND	0 UND	6 56.7					2 228.0	2 176.4
						Cost of Sales/Inventory		
						Cost of Sales/Payables		
24.6	-64.4	14.2					19.2	18.9
101.2	-24.2	67.2				Sales/Working Capital	-82.8	-78.9
-17.4	-11.4	-28.2					-11.4	-13.0
9.3	12.3	16.2					14.7	13.8
(35) 2.2	(22) 2.6	(32) 6.8				EBIT/Interest	(90) 3.5	(128) 5.1
-.3	-1.0	1.7					-.7	1.4
						Net Profit + Depr., Dep.,		3.8
						Amort./Cur. Mat. L/T/D	(11) 1.8	
								.8
.8	2.4	1.2					.9	1.0
8.2	-12.3	3.1				Fixed/Worth	11.4	4.7
-.8	-.8	-76.4					-1.9	-2.0
.5	2.7	1.4					1.3	1.3
16.0	-14.7	4.5				Debt/Worth	14.2	9.8
-3.4	-2.5	-82.8					-3.8	-3.7
147.7	116.0	91.3				% Profit Before Taxes/Tangible	137.1	155.7
(31) 65.6	(11) 33.6	(26) 51.1				Net Worth	(61) 34.9	(94) 48.5
9.8	-40.2	18.6					3.5	21.8
42.1	20.7	22.7				% Profit Before Taxes/Total	25.9	26.6
10.7	10.0	10.8				Assets	9.0	9.7
-4.5	-10.0	1.5					-3.7	1.6
54.1	9.1	8.8					17.3	14.1
9.5	4.8	5.0				Sales/Net Fixed Assets	6.6	5.3
3.4	2.6	3.3					2.5	2.8
7.0	3.4	3.6					4.5	4.1
3.4	2.5	2.3				Sales/Total Assets	2.4	2.4
1.6	1.2	1.7					1.3	1.4
1.7	2.6	2.5					2.0	1.9
(32) 4.3	(14) 4.6	(27) 4.0				% Depr., Dep., Amort./Sales	(84) 3.6	(111) 3.3
6.1	5.5	5.6					6.0	5.7
2.3	3.2					% Officers', Directors'	3.0	2.4
(16) 4.0	(10) 5.4					Owners' Comp/Sales	(36) 5.2	(51) 5.2
5.9	7.4						8.4	9.8
38285M	62323M	426710M	287952M	61360M	973403M	Net Sales ($)	2297316M	3865173M
10578M	24070M	172760M	175751M	62236M	735005M	Total Assets ($)	1056123M	1299308M

© RMA 2019

M = $ thousand   MM = $ million
See Pages viii through xx for Explanation of Ratios and Data

Comparative Historical Data / Current Data Sorted by Sales

	4/1/16-3/31/17 ALL	4/1/17-3/31/18 ALL	4/1/18-3/31/19 ALL		0-1MM	1-3MM	3-5MM	5-10MM	10-25MM	25MM & OVER
Type of Statement										
Unqualified	1	7	5		4				3	2
Reviewed	3	2	7						1	2
Compiled	15	12	10		1	2	1	1	5	
Tax Returns	46	48	41		19	19	1		2	
Other	69	69	65		24	8	5	4	19	5
					8 (4/1-9/30/18)			120 (10/1/18-3/31/19)		
NUMBER OF STATEMENTS	134	138	128		48	29	7	5	30	9
	%	%	%		%	%	%	%	%	%
ASSETS										
Cash & Equivalents	20.2	18.1	19.4		23.4	19.0			18.5	
Trade Receivables (net)	1.5	1.4	2.6		.7	1.7			4.4	
Inventory	5.6	4.5	5.3		4.5	5.0			6.2	
All Other Current	3.6	3.2	2.3		4.0	.7			1.7	
Total Current	30.9	27.2	29.6		32.6	26.5			30.8	
Fixed Assets (net)	45.9	42.9	45.6		44.9	45.6			47.0	
Intangibles (net)	14.2	19.0	17.6		19.1	15.7			15.5	
All Other Non-Current	9.0	10.9	7.2		3.5	12.3			6.7	
Total	100.0	100.0	100.0		100.0	100.0			100.0	
LIABILITIES										
Notes Payable-Short Term	8.5	6.9	8.7		11.4	6.6			3.1	
Cur. Mat.-L.T.D.	4.5	5.4	7.3		5.6	12.1			6.0	
Trade Payables	4.8	4.7	6.5		4.0	7.7			8.0	
Income Taxes Payable	.0	.2	.0		.0	.0			.1	
All Other Current	12.9	11.6	9.8		9.0	12.5			9.1	
Total Current	30.8	28.9	32.3		30.0	38.9			26.3	
Long-Term Debt	37.5	39.7	41.1		31.6	63.5			34.3	
Deferred Taxes	.1	.1	.1		.0	.0			.2	
All Other Non-Current	12.1	8.9	8.1		7.8	7.0			8.7	
Net Worth	19.5	22.4	18.3		30.2	-9.4			30.5	
Total Liabilties & Net Worth	100.0	100.0	100.0		100.0	100.0			100.0	
INCOME DATA										
Net Sales	100.0	100.0	100.0		100.0	100.0			100.0	
Gross Profit										
Operating Expenses	92.6	92.3	95.4		96.5	94.2			93.4	
Operating Profit	7.4	7.7	4.6		3.5	5.8			6.6	
All Other Expenses (net)	1.4	1.9	1.5		1.8	1.7			1.3	
Profit Before Taxes	6.0	5.8	3.1		1.7	4.1			5.3	
RATIOS										
Current	3.8	2.7	2.0		3.2	1.1			1.9	
	1.4	1.0	.9		1.3	.6			1.4	
	.6	.4	.4		.4	.2			.7	
Quick	3.0	1.8	1.5		2.3	.9			1.5	
	(131) 1.1	(137) .6	(127) .7		.8	.4			(29) 1.0	
	.3	.2	.3		.3	.1			.4	
Sales/Receivables	0 UND	0 UND	0 UND		0 UND	0 UND			0 UND	
	0 UND	0 UND	0 UND		0 UND	0 UND			2 197.7	
	1 480.6	1 257.4	3 144.5		0 UND	0 UND			7 55.3	
Cost of Sales/Inventory										
Cost of Sales/Payables										
Sales/Working Capital	14.6	16.1	21.8		20.9	142.4			14.8	
	65.2	UND	-134.7		69.3	-19.7			40.2	
	-27.3	-14.5	-17.4		-14.3	-12.8			-31.5	
EBIT/Interest	13.9	12.0	10.6		10.5	7.0			21.9	
	(97) 6.5	(95) 4.7	(103) 2.7		(30) 2.2	(24) 2.5			(28) 7.5	
	2.0	.1	.7		-.8	.5			2.3	
Net Profit + Depr., Dep., Amort./Cur. Mat. L/T/D		5.9								
		(11) 2.4								
		.7								
Fixed/Worth	.7	.8	1.2		.8	2.8			1.2	
	2.7	2.9	6.7		5.1	-5.3			3.0	
	-5.4	-2.8	-1.3		-1.4	-.7			13.8	
Debt/Worth	.6	.9	1.3		.3	4.4			1.4	
	3.7	4.3	7.9		6.9	-11.3			4.4	
	-8.9	-4.8	-5.0		-4.7	-2.3			19.2	
% Profit Before Taxes/Tangible Net Worth	152.4	114.9	113.8		120.8	194.1			114.0	
	(92) 60.5	(88) 52.9	(79) 50.5		(29) 60.0	(11) 24.6			(24) 53.2	
	26.0	19.5	1.7		-1.0	-3.5			15.2	
% Profit Before Taxes/Total Assets	34.3	31.7	23.7		38.7	27.8			23.0	
	15.1	10.6	8.4		6.2	13.1			12.3	
	3.9	.4	1.3		-8.2	-1.4			4.3	
Sales/Net Fixed Assets	18.1	17.1	14.7		21.2	63.8			12.8	
	6.4	6.6	5.5		5.5	5.6			6.5	
	3.6	3.1	3.0		2.8	2.7			3.6	
Sales/Total Assets	4.5	4.2	4.2		5.7	5.9			3.7	
	2.7	2.4	2.4		2.3	2.8			2.6	
	1.6	1.5	1.5		1.2	1.7			1.8	
% Depr., Dep., Amort./Sales	1.6	1.6	2.4		2.0	1.8			2.2	
	(92) 2.8	(88) 3.8	(82) 4.3		(28) 4.6	(19) 4.4			(22) 3.0	
	4.9	6.1	6.0		7.2	5.6			5.1	
% Officers', Directors' Owners' Comp/Sales	2.3	2.9	2.7		2.7	2.4				
	(56) 5.1	(39) 5.5	(35) 5.1		(11) 4.6	(15) 5.4				
	9.0	11.3	8.5		8.5	7.0				
Net Sales ($)	1595578M	2376716M	1850033M		24486M	51552M	28941M	33480M	482087M	1229487M
Total Assets ($)	858397M	932947M	1180400M		12403M	29654M	15102M	15973M	206405M	900863M

© RMA 2019

M = $ thousand   MM = $ million
See Pages viii through xx for Explanation of Ratios and Data

OTHER SERVICES (EXCEPT PUBLIC ADMINISTRATION)

Current Data Sorted by Assets   Comparative Historical Data

	0-500M	500M-2MM	2-10MM	10-50MM	50-100MM	100-250MM	Type of Statement	4/1/14-3/31/15 ALL	4/1/15-3/31/16 ALL
	4	2				2	Unqualified	7	11
	1	4	5	1			Reviewed	10	8
	14	13	7	1			Compiled	59	42
	166	64	12	1		2	Tax Returns	291	320
	84	53	27	6	1	1	Other	209	177
		46 (4/1-9/30/18)		425 (10/1/18-3/31/19)					
NUMBER OF STATEMENTS	269	136	51	9	1	5		576	558
	%	%	%	%	%	%	**ASSETS**	%	%
	31.4	16.0	15.2				Cash & Equivalents	23.7	23.0
	8.0	13.0	11.7				Trade Receivables (net)	9.3	10.2
	15.0	15.7	25.4				Inventory	13.9	15.2
	2.1	2.9	1.9				All Other Current	2.7	1.9
	56.5	47.6	54.2				Total Current	49.6	50.4
	28.0	34.9	35.0				Fixed Assets (net)	33.3	32.5
	7.4	11.2	7.1				Intangibles (net)	7.8	7.8
	8.0	6.3	3.7				All Other Non-Current	9.3	9.3
	100.0	100.0	100.0				Total	100.0	100.0
							LIABILITIES		
	16.2	8.0	10.0				Notes Payable-Short Term	12.4	15.0
	5.1	3.0	1.9				Cur. Mat.-L.T.D.	3.4	4.3
	12.0	11.2	11.6				Trade Payables	14.6	12.7
	1.0	.1	.1				Income Taxes Payable	.2	.3
	22.0	8.5	6.0				All Other Current	14.7	14.4
	56.3	30.7	29.6				Total Current	45.3	46.6
	31.5	28.0	26.1				Long-Term Debt	28.3	26.2
	.0	.0	.3				Deferred Taxes	.0	.0
	11.0	3.7	3.0				All Other Non-Current	11.9	8.2
	1.1	37.5	41.0				Net Worth	14.5	18.9
	100.0	100.0	100.0				Total Liabilities & Net Worth	100.0	100.0
							INCOME DATA		
	100.0	100.0	100.0				Net Sales	100.0	100.0
							Gross Profit		
	94.1	89.4	88.1				Operating Expenses	92.8	92.9
	5.9	10.6	11.9				Operating Profit	7.2	7.1
	.4	2.6	3.4				All Other Expenses (net)	1.8	1.5
	5.5	8.0	8.5				Profit Before Taxes	5.5	5.6
							RATIOS		
	3.5	3.7	3.8				Current	3.2	3.3
	1.3	1.8	1.8					1.3	1.4
	.6	.7	1.1					.7	.6
	2.6	2.2	1.4				Quick	2.3	2.1
	.8	.9	1.0					.8 (557)	.8
	.3	.4	.5					.3	.3
	0 UND	0 UND	4 93.9				Sales/Receivables	0 UND	0 UND
	0 UND	7 52.1	11 33.7					2 204.0	2 155.2
	7 50.8	24 15.3	33 10.9					11 31.8	15 25.0
							Cost of Sales/Inventory		
							Cost of Sales/Payables		
	15.1	7.0	4.7				Sales/Working Capital	12.5	11.2
	84.1	18.4	12.3					49.8	41.3
	-27.3	-35.6	50.4					-31.9	-30.8
	19.7	20.3	50.3				EBIT/Interest	15.7	17.4
	(172) 5.1	(100) 5.1	(44) 7.9					(394) 4.4	(379) 4.9
	1.0	1.6	1.8					1.3	1.3
							Net Profit + Depr., Dep., Amort./Cur. Mat. L/T/D	4.6	6.4
								(24) 3.1	(22) 2.9
								1.5	1.2
	.2	.2	.2				Fixed/Worth	.3	.2
	1.0	.9	.9					1.5	1.1
	-1.3	50.3	5.5					-6.0	UND
	.6	.6	.4				Debt/Worth	.7	.6
	3.8	1.9	1.2					3.4	2.7
	-3.3	NM	18.1					-10.3	-13.2
	159.4	67.7	66.0				% Profit Before Taxes/Tangible Net Worth	101.5	108.0
	(172) 68.3	(102) 32.5	(44) 34.6					(402) 41.8	(403) 39.5
	24.2	8.3	7.7					14.6	11.9
	55.6	28.1	22.3				% Profit Before Taxes/Total Assets	35.0	34.1
	23.5	10.8	11.6					13.3	10.9
	3.9	2.3	2.2					1.4	1.7
	134.3	46.3	23.5				Sales/Net Fixed Assets	70.0	97.9
	36.7	15.1	11.6					22.8	18.7
	14.2	3.6	2.4					7.4	7.1
	10.5	3.9	4.0				Sales/Total Assets	7.9	7.5
	6.1	2.8	2.4					4.5	4.2
	3.6	1.5	1.2					2.4	2.2
	.6	1.0	.9				% Depr., Dep., Amort./Sales	.7	.6
	(141) 1.3	(79) 1.7	(38) 2.1					(368) 1.5	(353) 1.5
	2.9	4.1	3.8					2.8	3.3
	4.7	3.2	1.1				% Officers', Directors' Owners' Comp/Sales	3.0	3.1
	(172) 6.5	(71) 5.3	(19) 1.6					(340) 5.5	(334) 5.4
	10.0	8.3	3.2					8.8	8.8
	332866M	394529M	544184M	569913M	87268M	3102413M	Net Sales ($)	11124484M	10060428M
	55105M	137856M	207356M	185990M	52912M	867578M	Total Assets ($)	2374527M	2532170M

M = $ thousand   MM = $ million
See Pages viii through xx for Explanation of Ratios and Data

Comparative Historical Data | Current Data Sorted by Sales

Hist 1	Hist 2	Hist 3	Type of Statement	0-1MM	1-3MM	3-5MM	5-10MM	10-25MM	25MM & OVER
9	6	8	Unqualified	2	2	2	1	3	2
7	8	11	Reviewed		2	3	9	1	2
34	34	35	Compiled	8	13	3	9	1	1
278	252	245	Tax Returns	101	103	18	13	6	4
184	193	172	Other	54	65	19	10	15	9
4/1/16-3/31/17	4/1/17-3/31/18	4/1/18-3/31/19		46 (4/1-9/30/18)			425 (10/1/18-3/31/19)		
ALL	ALL	ALL		0-1MM	1-3MM	3-5MM	5-10MM	10-25MM	25MM & OVER
512	493	471	**NUMBER OF STATEMENTS**	165	185	45	33	25	18
%	%	%	**ASSETS**	%	%	%	%	%	%
24.3	23.1	24.6	Cash & Equivalents	27.8	24.6	24.1	18.8	20.6	11.9
10.2	9.5	9.8	Trade Receivables (net)	5.3	10.8	13.2	22.6	10.8	7.7
15.1	14.5	16.3	Inventory	13.3	14.7	24.7	17.8	28.8	20.0
2.6	2.6	2.4	All Other Current	1.7	2.4	2.3	5.4	2.1	4.0
52.2	49.7	53.1	Total Current	48.1	52.5	64.4	64.6	62.3	43.5
32.4	33.5	31.3	Fixed Assets (net)	36.9	28.9	25.1	25.2	23.5	41.0
7.0	7.9	8.4	Intangibles (net)	7.9	10.3	6.7	3.2	9.5	7.0
8.5	8.9	7.2	All Other Non-Current	7.2	8.3	3.9	6.9	4.8	8.5
100.0	100.0	100.0	Total	100.0	100.0	100.0	100.0	100.0	100.0
			LIABILITIES						
12.2	12.6	12.8	Notes Payable-Short Term	13.1	12.2	15.0	16.3	8.2	11.3
4.0	3.5	4.0	Cur. Mat.-L.T.D.	5.6	3.2	4.8	3.3	1.7	1.6
13.6	12.3	11.5	Trade Payables	6.6	13.4	14.7	18.7	18.3	6.9
.2	.1	.6	Income Taxes Payable	.2	1.3	.2	.2	.2	.0
12.9	15.4	16.0	All Other Current	15.9	20.9	8.7	8.1	8.2	9.8
42.9	43.9	45.0	Total Current	41.4	50.9	43.3	46.5	36.6	29.6
27.2	28.2	29.9	Long-Term Debt	38.9	26.9	27.6	15.6	20.2	24.5
.1	.2	.1	Deferred Taxes	.0	.0	.4	.0	.2	.1
8.2	4.8	8.0	All Other Non-Current	10.6	7.1	10.6	.7	2.7	8.9
21.6	22.9	17.0	Net Worth	9.0	15.1	18.0	37.2	40.4	36.9
100.0	100.0	100.0	Total Liabilities & Net Worth	100.0	100.0	100.0	100.0	100.0	100.0
			INCOME DATA						
100.0	100.0	100.0	Net Sales	100.0	100.0	100.0	100.0	100.0	100.0
			Gross Profit						
92.4	93.9	92.1	Operating Expenses	87.1	94.8	95.7	93.8	94.4	95.3
7.6	6.1	7.9	Operating Profit	12.9	5.2	4.3	6.2	5.6	4.7
1.2	1.3	1.3	All Other Expenses (net)	3.2	.5	.1	.1	-.6	-.2
6.4	4.8	6.6	Profit Before Taxes	9.7	4.6	4.2	6.1	6.2	4.9
			RATIOS						
3.2	3.1	3.5		4.5	3.4	3.5	2.8	2.3	2.4
1.5	1.4	1.4	Current	1.4	1.4	2.0	1.4	1.8	1.4
.8	.7	.7		.6	.6	.9	.9	1.2	.9
2.3	2.2	2.3		3.0	2.5	2.3	1.7	1.3	1.2
(510) .9	.9	.9	Quick	.9	.8	.9	1.0	1.1	.7
.4	.3	.3		.3	.3	.4	.3	.7	.4
0 UND	0 UND	0 UND		0 UND	0 UND	0 UND	4 90.9	2 241.3	2 147.3
3 138.4	3 141.6	2 153.1	Sales/Receivables	0 UND	2 161.0	11 32.7	13 28.8	6 56.5	12 29.2
14 25.2	15 23.6	14 25.3		6 61.4	15 24.3	24 15.0	36 10.0	16 23.2	16 23.0
			Cost of Sales/Inventory						
			Cost of Sales/Payables						
9.9	11.1	9.1		7.6	11.5	7.8	8.4	8.1	10.9
31.1	34.6	32.4	Sales/Working Capital	69.5	49.3	14.5	29.0	14.6	29.2
-55.8	35.8	-31.7		-29.4	-23.2	-105.1	NM	79.6	-83.7
20.8	16.0	22.8		13.2	17.4	53.6	58.3	41.5	21.6
(364) 5.7	(351) 5.0	(330) 5.5	EBIT/Interest	(93) 3.3	(136) 7.3	(36) 2.8	(26) 15.6	(22) 15.5	(17) 6.7
1.8	1.4	1.4		.8	1.5	.3	1.9	3.6	3.0
7.9	8.9	5.1	Net Profit + Depr., Dep.,						
(28) 2.2	(19) 4.0	(16) 2.0	Amort./Cur. Mat. L/T/D						
1.4	1.5	1.0							
.2	.2	.2		.2	.2	.2	.2	.2	.7
1.0	1.0	1.0	Fixed/Worth	1.6	1.1	.6	.4	.5	1.4
-13.3	-53.9	-13.4		-6.3	-3.4	-3.9	3.1	4.1	9.1
.6	.6	.6		.6	.6	.5	.5	.8	1.0
2.2	2.4	2.8	Debt/Worth	2.7	4.5	1.5	1.2	1.2	1.7
-17.2	-12.2	-10.5		-6.1	-4.9	-6.3	13.0	6.4	20.5
95.6	90.2	105.2	% Profit Before Taxes/Tangible	144.4	106.5	61.6	73.6	82.1	109.5
(364) 40.1	(355) 37.6	(331) 47.0	Net Worth	(112) 52.3	(123) 50.6	(32) 39.4	(27) 39.4	(21) 39.8	(16) 39.2
10.8	10.7	15.9		16.2	19.1	4.0	6.9	21.9	20.4
36.6	32.8	40.0	% Profit Before Taxes/Total	51.0	34.9	35.7	41.0	33.3	19.0
12.3	10.6	15.2	Assets	15.1	15.9	13.6	18.1	16.8	11.5
3.1	1.9	3.0		2.5	3.2	-.4	4.6	7.6	4.7
73.3	80.7	76.0		71.4	88.3	65.0	79.3	51.6	13.2
19.4	19.4	21.9	Sales/Net Fixed Assets	18.2	23.0	29.8	26.3	22.0	8.4
6.6	7.2	8.3		4.5	11.3	9.5	15.3	10.4	3.0
7.2	6.8	7.5		8.2	8.2	6.9	6.6	5.3	4.3
4.0	4.2	4.0	Sales/Total Assets	3.8	4.6	3.9	4.5	4.0	3.2
2.1	2.1	2.2		1.5	2.7	2.3	3.1	2.4	1.3
.7	.7	.7		.9	.7	.6	.6	.5	.7
(344) 1.5	(305) 1.5	(268) 1.6	% Depr., Dep., Amort./Sales	(92) 2.3	(105) 1.3	(23) 1.4	(19) 1.2	(15) 1.2	(14) 1.7
3.2	3.0	3.4		6.2	3.2	3.5	2.4	2.8	2.5
3.2	3.4	3.8	% Officers', Directors'	6.3	4.1	2.4	1.5	1.2	
(301) 5.5	(287) 6.0	(268) 5.8	Owners' Comp/Sales	(85) 9.2	(124) 5.3	(21) 4.3	(19) 2.1	(13) 1.4	
9.4	10.4	9.2		12.4	8.7	5.4	4.9	2.9	
10931004M	6211809M	5031173M	Net Sales ($)	94654M	324200M	166636M	205032M	357539M	3883112M
3009945M	1781716M	1506797M	Total Assets ($)	55136M	98632M	60089M	56917M	112299M	1123724M

M = $ thousand   MM = $ million
See Pages viii through xx for Explanation of Ratios and Data

Current Data Sorted by Assets   Comparative Historical Data

Asset-size column date-range labels: **8 (4/1-9/30/18)** covers 0-500M / 500M-2MM / 2-10MM group; **40 (10/1/18-3/31/19)** covers 10-50MM / 50-100MM / 100-250MM group.

Columns for the middle asset groups (10-50MM, 50-100MM, 100-250MM) are marked **DATA NOT AVAILABLE**.

0-500M	500M-2MM	2-10MM	10-50MM	50-100MM	100-250MM	Type of Statement	4/1/14-3/31/15 ALL	4/1/15-3/31/16 ALL
		1		1		Unqualified	2	3
						Reviewed		3
	3	3				Compiled	9	9
12	8	2	1			Tax Returns	26	27
5	7	4		1		Other	24	25
17	18	10	1	2		**NUMBER OF STATEMENTS**	61	67
%	%	%	%	%	%	**ASSETS**	%	%
27.7	15.2	23.1				Cash & Equivalents	17.8	17.6
14.4	18.5	12.6				Trade Receivables (net)	12.3	14.7
15.9	18.1	25.7				Inventory	18.4	21.7
1.6	1.8	7.6				All Other Current	2.0	1.5
59.6	53.5	69.1				Total Current	50.6	55.5
23.5	38.2	22.7				Fixed Assets (net)	27.6	27.6
11.4	3.1	1.8				Intangibles (net)	6.6	4.8
5.7	5.1	6.4				All Other Non-Current	15.2	12.1
100.0	100.0	100.0				Total	100.0	100.0
						LIABILITIES		
4.4	9.2	10.2				Notes Payable-Short Term	9.4	8.0
11.0	2.1	1.4				Cur. Mat.-L.T.D.	3.4	2.8
14.2	8.6	20.5				Trade Payables	12.5	16.6
.2	.1	.0				Income Taxes Payable	.7	.3
15.7	9.4	18.3				All Other Current	12.0	9.5
45.6	29.3	50.3				Total Current	38.1	37.1
3.5	16.5	8.3				Long-Term Debt	20.3	19.7
.0	.0	.0				Deferred Taxes	.7	.6
9.6	2.0	.6				All Other Non-Current	14.1	13.8
41.4	52.3	40.8				Net Worth	26.9	28.8
100.0	100.0	100.0				Total Liabilities & Net Worth	100.0	100.0
						INCOME DATA		
100.0	100.0	100.0				Net Sales	100.0	100.0
						Gross Profit		
93.6	92.2	89.0				Operating Expenses	92.6	91.0
6.4	7.8	11.0				Operating Profit	7.4	9.0
.2	1.1	.7				All Other Expenses (net)	1.3	1.8
6.2	6.8	10.3				Profit Before Taxes	6.2	7.2
						RATIOS		
3.0 / 1.3 / .8	3.4 / 2.3 / 1.4	4.4 / 1.2 / .8				Current	3.6 / 1.5 / .9	3.5 / 1.5 / 1.0
2.8 / 1.1 / .4	2.7 / 1.4 / .6	3.3 / .7 / .3				Quick	1.9 / .8 / .6	2.6 / .9 / .5
0 UND / 0 UND / 21 17.1	0 UND / 13 28.5 / 38 9.5	0 UND / 22 16.9 / 40 9.1				Sales/Receivables	0 UND / 11 34.1 / 24 15.1	0 UND / 14 25.3 / 36 10.2
						Cost of Sales/Inventory		
						Cost of Sales/Payables		
10.8 / 37.8 / -59.2	5.2 / 8.6 / NM	5.4 / 16.3 / -21.3				Sales/Working Capital	7.3 / 23.9 / -238.2	5.8 / 15.2 / -969.0
	11.0 / (16) 7.0 / 2.2					EBIT/Interest	19.1 / (44) 5.7 / 1.4	13.2 / (52) 6.1 / 1.5
						Net Profit + Depr., Dep., Amort./Cur. Mat. L/T/D		
.2 / .6 / 4.4	.3 / .6 / 1.2	.1 / .3 / NM				Fixed/Worth	.1 / .8 / 11.5	.1 / .8 / 2.9
.4 / 1.3 / 27.6	.4 / .8 / 2.0	.3 / 1.1 / NM				Debt/Worth	.6 / 1.4 / 30.5	.5 / 1.7 / 9.9
430.1 / (14) 77.2 / 23.3	59.3 / (17) 42.4 / 12.4					% Profit Before Taxes/Tangible Net Worth	71.7 / (48) 24.2 / 3.9	68.5 / (54) 22.3 / 3.4
101.2 / 19.5 / 3.4	31.3 / 18.3 / 4.2	26.4 / 19.8 / 6.9				% Profit Before Taxes/Total Assets	33.4 / 8.8 / 1.6	23.5 / 7.0 / .9
114.8 / 25.6 / 14.3	39.2 / 11.8 / 4.0	59.8 / 12.7 / 9.7				Sales/Net Fixed Assets	107.2 / 25.9 / 8.6	116.6 / 29.3 / 5.7
8.8 / 7.5 / 2.6	4.4 / 2.5 / 2.2	3.0 / 1.9 / 1.3				Sales/Total Assets	5.4 / 3.1 / 1.7	5.0 / 2.9 / 1.8
.5 / (11) 1.5 / 2.3	.4 / (11) 1.2 / 3.7					% Depr., Dep., Amort./Sales	.7 / (37) 1.8 / 4.5	1.0 / (40) 2.0 / 3.8
						% Officers', Directors' Owners' Comp/Sales	2.4 / (29) 6.4 / 8.6	2.2 / (33) 4.0 / 7.8
20753M	67492M	65524M	45055M	120291M		Net Sales ($)	405161M	529245M
3561M	20234M	32241M	13910M	142319M		Total Assets ($)	250483M	283581M

© RMA 2019

M = $ thousand   MM = $ million
See Pages viii through xx for Explanation of Ratios and Data

Comparative Historical Data   Current Data Sorted by Sales

1		2				Type of Statement							
		1		1		Unqualified							
7		3		7		Reviewed				3	1	2	1
20		30		22		Compiled	7	10	2	3			
22		24		18		Tax Returns	3	6	2	3	2		2
4/1/16-		4/1/17-		4/1/18-		Other		8 (4/1-9/30/18)			40 (10/1/18-3/31/19)		
3/31/17		3/31/18		3/31/19									
ALL		ALL		ALL			0-1MM	1-3MM	3-5MM	5-10MM	10-25MM	25MM & OVER
50		60		48		**NUMBER OF STATEMENTS**	10	17	7	7	4	3
%		%		%		**ASSETS**	%	%	%	%	%	%
23.2		16.8		20.6		Cash & Equivalents	32.1	13.4				
19.6		14.1		16.0		Trade Receivables (net)	11.9	11.3				
17.7		20.0		18.2		Inventory	19.3	20.8				
3.0		.9		2.9		All Other Current	1.7	2.9				
63.5		51.8		57.7		Total Current	65.0	48.4				
27.1		33.4		31.2		Fixed Assets (net)	20.8	39.8				
3.5		6.5		5.6		Intangibles (net)	6.5	10.0				
5.9		8.3		5.5		All Other Non-Current	7.8	1.9				
100.0		100.0		100.0		Total	100.0	100.0				
						LIABILITIES						
9.2		10.6		8.0		Notes Payable-Short Term	3.2	5.4				
3.2		4.2		5.2		Cur. Mat.-L.T.D.	.0	12.2				
16.5		10.8		13.5		Trade Payables	12.5	12.4				
.2		.2		.1		Income Taxes Payable	.2	.0				
12.2		8.1		13.1		All Other Current	17.0	18.8				
41.2		34.0		39.9		Total Current	32.9	48.8				
15.4		26.3		10.1		Long-Term Debt	4.9	15.5				
.7		.6		.0		Deferred Taxes	.0	.0				
3.4		9.4		4.3		All Other Non-Current	14.8	.5				
39.3		29.7		45.7		Net Worth	47.6	35.2				
100.0		100.0		100.0		Total Liabilities & Net Worth	100.0	100.0				
						INCOME DATA						
100.0		100.0		100.0		Net Sales	100.0	100.0				
						Gross Profit						
93.7		93.6		91.8		Operating Expenses	94.2	88.3				
6.3		6.4		8.2		Operating Profit	5.8	11.7				
1.0		1.0		.7		All Other Expenses (net)	.3	1.0				
5.4		5.4		7.4		Profit Before Taxes	5.5	10.7				
						RATIOS						
3.6		3.4		3.2			12.0	2.9				
1.5		1.6		1.7		Current	2.7	1.2				
1.0		1.0		.9			1.3	.6				
2.3		2.1		2.5			10.4	1.7				
.9		1.0		1.0		Quick	2.4	.6				
.5		.4		.4			.7	.3				
4	99.1	0	UND	0	UND		0	UND	0	UND		
15	24.9	13	28.8	11	33.9	Sales/Receivables	4	90.5	0	UND		
35	10.5	33	11.1	26	14.2		23	15.8	22	16.4		
						Cost of Sales/Inventory						
						Cost of Sales/Payables						
6.1		6.0		6.9			4.6	5.8				
18.1		26.3		22.9		Sales/Working Capital	10.8	76.5				
767.7		406.1		-253.6			39.7	-16.4				
22.6		15.1		17.4				29.5				
(36)	6.8	(46) 6.7		(32) 9.4		EBIT/Interest	(14)	10.1				
1.2		1.2		3.1				1.1				
4.6												
(11)	1.8					Net Profit + Depr., Dep.,						
1.3						Amort./Cur. Mat. L/T/D						
.1		.2		.2			.0	.6				
.7		1.0		.6		Fixed/Worth	.3	1.4				
4.4		10.2		1.7			2.5	NM				
.5		.5		.4			.2	.6				
1.1		1.7		1.0		Debt/Worth	.6	1.8				
14.2		21.6		3.1			15.4	NM				
52.4		131.0		75.0				220.5				
(41)	21.0	(49) 46.3		(42) 43.2		% Profit Before Taxes/Tangible	(13)	59.8				
5.0		10.9		16.1		Net Worth		35.6				
28.7		28.9		35.2			68.4	53.3				
9.4		9.5		18.6		% Profit Before Taxes/Total	15.5	27.5				
1.3		1.6		5.1		Assets	-10.5	4.2				
49.0		63.3		56.7			UND	25.7				
25.7		14.5		14.6		Sales/Net Fixed Assets	98.4	14.3				
8.1		4.6		6.7			6.8	4.6				
5.5		5.2		7.1			8.5	7.1				
3.5		2.8		2.7		Sales/Total Assets	2.6	2.4				
1.9		1.8		2.1			2.4	1.6				
.8		.7		.4				.5				
(37)	1.7	(40) 1.8		(33) 1.5		% Depr., Dep., Amort./Sales	(14)	2.2				
3.2		4.2		3.2				3.7				
1.9		2.5		3.0								
(26)	4.5	(31) 5.1		(21) 5.0		% Officers', Directors'						
6.3		7.8		7.7		Owners' Comp/Sales						
489023M		535349M		319115M		Net Sales ($)	5560M	29216M	27998M	44213M	46782M	165346M
256478M		312067M		212265M		Total Assets ($)	3087M	13572M	9837M	13071M	16469M	156229M

© RMA 2019   M = $ thousand   MM = $ million
See Pages viii through xx for Explanation of Ratios and Data

Current Data Sorted by Assets   Comparative Historical Data

	0-500M	500M-2MM	2-10MM	10-50MM	50-100MM	100-250MM	Type of Statement	4/1/14-3/31/15 ALL	4/1/15-3/31/16 ALL
	7	1	8	2			Unqualified	3	3
	10	10	7	4			Reviewed	8	16
	56	45	6	6			Compiled	34	33
	50	41	36	8	2	2	Tax Returns	178	154
					2	2	Other	125	141
	33 (4/1-9/30/18)		254 (10/1/18-3/31/19)						
NUMBER OF STATEMENTS	113	97	57	14	2	4		348	347
	%	%	%	%	%	%		%	%
							ASSETS		
Cash & Equivalents	29.0	21.7	14.0	19.4				21.4	25.4
Trade Receivables (net)	15.3	10.6	15.4	12.1				13.5	12.3
Inventory	7.1	8.7	10.4	22.1				10.9	7.8
All Other Current	3.1	3.6	4.1	3.7				4.5	3.1
Total Current	54.6	44.5	43.9	57.2				50.2	48.6
Fixed Assets (net)	31.4	35.7	34.4	32.7				32.1	33.1
Intangibles (net)	6.0	7.7	14.5	4.0				7.0	6.9
All Other Non-Current	8.1	12.1	7.3	6.2				10.7	11.4
Total	100.0	100.0	100.0	100.0				100.0	100.0
							LIABILITIES		
Notes Payable-Short Term	15.6	9.5	8.1	11.8				10.0	11.1
Cur. Mat.-L.T.D.	4.7	2.5	3.2	1.3				2.8	2.9
Trade Payables	16.7	12.0	13.6	9.9				15.3	13.3
Income Taxes Payable	.3	.1	.1	.4				.4	.5
All Other Current	26.2	12.8	14.2	14.7				17.0	18.2
Total Current	63.3	36.9	39.2	38.0				45.5	45.9
Long-Term Debt	24.5	23.0	32.0	16.9				24.0	22.3
Deferred Taxes	.0	.0	.0	.4				.1	.1
All Other Non-Current	3.0	8.0	7.2	4.1				9.5	10.5
Net Worth	9.1	32.1	21.5	40.6				20.9	21.1
Total Liabilities & Net Worth	100.0	100.0	100.0	100.0				100.0	100.0
							INCOME DATA		
Net Sales	100.0	100.0	100.0	100.0				100.0	100.0
Gross Profit									
Operating Expenses	94.3	93.8	90.6	93.4				94.2	92.9
Operating Profit	5.7	6.2	9.4	6.6				5.8	7.1
All Other Expenses (net)	.0	.6	2.4	.6				.9	.9
Profit Before Taxes	5.7	5.6	7.0	5.9				4.9	6.2

RATIOS

Ratio	0-500M	500M-2MM	2-10MM	10-50MM			4/1/14-3/31/15	4/1/15-3/31/16
Current	2.3	2.8	1.6	3.2			2.6	3.0
	1.0	1.4	1.1	1.6			1.3	1.3
	.5	.7	.7	.8			.7	.6
Quick	2.1	1.9	1.2	1.6			1.9	2.2
	.9	1.0	.7	.9			(347) .8	1.0
	.4	.3	.5	.4			.4	.4
Sales/Receivables	0 UND	0 UND	5 67.4	5 68.9			0 UND	0 UND
	4 102.5	7 53.7	13 27.6	8 45.8			7 53.5	7 51.0
	13 28.5	16 22.3	28 12.9	36 10.1			16 22.3	16 23.3
Cost of Sales/Inventory								
Cost of Sales/Payables								
Sales/Working Capital	15.2	11.9	13.8	3.8			13.3	13.6
	455.1	37.4	104.7	9.6			43.4	53.0
	-32.5	-73.7	-29.4	-42.2			-38.3	-29.7
EBIT/Interest	23.8	36.2	28.5	14.1			23.9	32.0
	(76) 8.0	(67) 9.6	(50) 8.4	(13) 10.4			(246) 6.3	(232) 12.1
	3.3	2.3	2.0	5.9			1.0	3.7
Net Profit + Depr., Dep., Amort./Cur. Mat. L/T/D							14.6	17.2
							(19) 3.0	(18) 4.5
							1.1	2.7
Fixed/Worth	.3	.4	.7	.2			.3	.2
	1.3	1.0	2.1	1.0			1.1	1.1
	-2.1	-34.7	-13.9	3.6			-6.4	-27.0
Debt/Worth	.8	.5	2.1	.5			.8	.6
	3.8	1.9	8.0	1.8			2.8	2.1
	-4.3	-332.0	-11.2	4.1			-11.0	-27.7
% Profit Before Taxes/Tangible Net Worth	198.2	79.0	105.2	65.6			114.5	112.2
	(74) 100.5	(72) 46.3	(37) 60.5	(12) 43.8			(246) 47.5	(254) 54.3
	36.8	17.1	21.4	15.5			11.9	21.9
% Profit Before Taxes/Total Assets	61.4	31.7	22.6	20.0			30.7	38.1
	24.1	14.9	14.5	13.2			14.2	18.0
	9.9	2.2	1.9	5.5			1.5	6.2
Sales/Net Fixed Assets	88.3	35.2	32.9	54.6			58.8	55.8
	36.3	12.5	12.7	14.5			21.7	21.8
	13.8	6.1	5.2	3.5			8.3	8.2
Sales/Total Assets	10.4	5.2	4.3	2.8			7.7	7.3
	6.4	3.6	2.9	2.4			4.8	4.5
	3.9	2.5	1.8	2.0			2.4	2.5
% Depr., Dep., Amort./Sales	.5	.9	.6	.7			.5	.7
	(60) 1.0	(67) 1.8	(44) 1.6	(10) 1.6			(233) 1.3	(219) 1.4
	2.0	3.4	2.3	2.9			2.5	2.5
% Officers', Directors', Owners' Comp/Sales	2.9	2.5	1.6				2.9	2.7
	(72) 5.2	(61) 4.0	(26) 2.5				(208) 4.9	(196) 4.6
	7.9	6.5	5.3				7.3	7.6
Net Sales ($)	204954M	369351M	754335M	719684M	577779M	6486005M	1572821M	6216008M
Total Assets ($)	29271M	103379M	243340M	279790M	109414M	632089M	536329M	890657M

© RMA 2019   M = $ thousand   MM = $ million

See Pages viii through xx for Explanation of Ratios and Data

Comparative Historical Data / Current Data Sorted by Sales

			Type of Statement	0-1MM	1-3MM	3-5MM	5-10MM	10-25MM	25MM & OVER
5	2		Unqualified	1			2	6	2
10	12	11	Reviewed						
21	25	28	Compiled	3	7	6	3	6	3
141	144	111	Tax Returns	18	44	28	12	5	4
116	139	137	Other	19	45	21	21	19	12
4/1/16-3/31/17	4/1/17-3/31/18	4/1/18-3/31/19		33 (4/1-9/30/18)			254 (10/1/18-3/31/19)		
ALL	ALL	ALL							
293	322	287	**NUMBER OF STATEMENTS**	41	96	55	38	36	21
%	%	%	**ASSETS**	%	%	%	%	%	%
25.0	24.6	22.8	Cash & Equivalents	20.6	26.3	25.4	18.1	20.3	17.1
11.6	13.3	13.9	Trade Receivables (net)	10.2	12.6	13.4	13.6	18.2	21.4
7.8	8.0	8.9	Inventory	5.8	5.8	11.6	10.8	10.7	15.4
2.6	3.9	3.5	All Other Current	2.3	2.5	3.8	6.4	3.9	3.7
47.0	49.8	49.1	Total Current	38.9	47.1	54.2	49.0	53.1	57.6
35.1	32.2	33.1	Fixed Assets (net)	49.0	33.1	31.7	26.4	30.7	21.9
7.8	9.1	8.6	Intangibles (net)	4.9	8.8	4.3	16.7	8.4	11.8
10.1	8.9	9.3	All Other Non-Current	7.2	11.0	9.8	7.9	7.8	8.7
100.0	100.0	100.0	Total	100.0	100.0	100.0	100.0	100.0	100.0
			LIABILITIES						
10.2	10.0	11.6	Notes Payable-Short Term	11.0	12.8	7.6	19.1	9.6	7.9
3.3	3.4	3.4	Cur. Mat.-L.T.D.	5.8	3.5	2.9	2.3	3.4	1.2
12.4	12.3	14.3	Trade Payables	4.1	14.5	15.7	20.0	15.7	17.7
.4	.2	.2	Income Taxes Payable	.0	.1	.5	.1	.1	.2
17.8	16.0	18.6	All Other Current	23.7	19.4	15.2	17.0	18.7	16.8
44.2	42.0	48.2	Total Current	44.6	50.3	42.0	58.5	47.6	43.9
25.7	24.6	25.3	Long-Term Debt	38.8	27.3	18.1	22.7	20.6	21.3
.2	.1	.0	Deferred Taxes	.0	.0	.0	.0	.1	.2
6.9	5.3	5.9	All Other Non-Current	2.5	5.5	6.2	7.6	7.6	7.4
23.1	28.1	20.6	Net Worth	14.2	16.9	33.7	11.2	24.1	27.1
100.0	100.0	100.0	Total Liabilities & Net Worth	100.0	100.0	100.0	100.0	100.0	100.0
			INCOME DATA						
100.0	100.0	100.0	Net Sales	100.0	100.0	100.0	100.0	100.0	100.0
			Gross Profit						
90.8	93.0	93.3	Operating Expenses	83.7	94.2	95.9	94.5	94.7	97.0
9.2	7.0	6.7	Operating Profit	16.3	5.8	4.1	5.5	5.3	3.0
2.4	1.1	.7	All Other Expenses (net)	5.9	.0	-.5	.3	-.7	-.1
6.8	5.9	6.0	Profit Before Taxes	10.3	5.8	4.6	5.2	5.9	3.1
			RATIOS						
2.4	2.6	2.3		3.8	2.2	2.7	1.8	1.6	2.4
1.2	1.3	1.2	Current	1.0	1.1	1.6	1.2	1.1	1.2
.6	.7	.6		.2	.5	1.0	.5	.8	.8
1.9	1.9	1.7		2.9	2.1	1.7	1.2	1.3	1.6
.9	1.0	.9	Quick	.8	.9	1.1	.8	.7	.9
.4	.4	.4		.2	.3	.6	.2	.5	.5
0 UND	0 UND	0 UND		0 UND	0 UND	3 104.7	3 144.0	6 57.1	6 57.6
6 58.6	6 56.7	7 53.7	Sales/Receivables	0 UND	4 100.5	7 48.9	7 51.6	17 21.6	9 39.5
15 24.3	16 23.0	19 19.1		13 27.9	18 19.9	14 25.5	15 23.7	33 11.0	29 12.7
			Cost of Sales/Inventory						
			Cost of Sales/Payables						
13.7	13.9	12.9		8.9	14.1	10.7	18.7	13.3	7.2
76.7	54.8	72.8	Sales/Working Capital	182.3	486.3	26.5	91.1	92.8	25.5
-25.8	-32.5	-34.5		-4.6	-29.2	-192.8	-16.2	-34.9	-78.5
31.0	27.3	27.0		19.0	27.0	40.2	17.6	46.6	17.0
(199) 8.7	(223) 7.0	(210) 8.8	EBIT/Interest	(23) 5.1	(65) 6.7	(40) 11.7	(30) 8.0	(35) 12.9	(17) 10.4
1.8	1.4	2.7		2.3	2.7	2.2	4.2	2.0	5.6
9.4	13.1	18.5	Net Profit + Depr., Dep.,						
(21) 1.6	(19) 2.5	(17) 10.7	Amort./Cur. Mat. L/T/D						
.4	.4	2.7							
.4	.3	.4		.3	.4	.3	.3	.7	.2
1.5	1.3	1.3	Fixed/Worth	2.2	1.5	.0	1.0	1.8	.6
UND	-87.6	-12.4		UND	-1.9	3.2	-.9	-19.1	3.3
.8	.6	.9		.5	.6	.7	1.1	1.3	1.2
3.1	2.6	3.4	Debt/Worth	3.1	5.6	2.0	6.8	2.9	2.9
-39.9	-110.6	8.6		UND	-3.9	8.3	-2.8	-35.1	-19.1
102.2	122.7	112.1	% Profit Before Taxes/Tangible	182.4	144.9	93.9	138.6	81.4	75.2
(217) 51.6	(240) 50.5	(197) 59.3	Net Worth	(31) 55.6	(58) 64.7	(45) 57.6	(22) 67.9	(26) 51.9	(15) 51.7
17.9	17.3	21.0		22.9	23.2	17.0	11.6	22.0	23.4
38.4	36.1	35.2	% Profit Before Taxes/Total	38.7	44.1	33.8	26.1	34.8	24.7
14.9	14.9	16.9	Assets	15.7	23.1	17.3	16.0	15.1	15.2
2.8	2.7	5.3		3.9	7.5	1.5	4.2	3.7	7.4
50.1	61.0	58.9		30.9	64.1	73.8	66.8	23.7	130.2
21.1	22.0	19.9	Sales/Net Fixed Assets	8.8	24.1	23.8	29.7	13.6	21.0
6.7	8.4	7.2		.7	7.0	7.5	13.3	8.4	6.8
7.7	7.5	6.6		5.3	8.0	8.2	7.7	5.1	6.7
4.4	4.5	4.0	Sales/Total Assets	2.7	4.4	4.5	5.5	3.5	2.9
2.2	2.3	2.6		.5	3.2	2.5	2.5	2.8	2.3
.7	.7	.6		1.7	.6	.4	.9	.7	.6
(184) 1.5	(209) 1.5	(182) 1.4	% Depr., Dep., Amort./Sales	(25) 2.9	(54) 1.3	(35) .8	(23) 1.5	(33) 1.3	(12) 1.4
2.8	2.6	2.4		15.7	2.7	2.1	2.1	1.9	2.7
2.7	2.6	2.3		1.9	3.4	2.5	1.6	1.5	
(165) 4.3	(183) 5.0	(166) 4.1	% Officers', Directors' Owners' Comp/Sales	(19) 4.5	(61) 4.6	(39) 4.3	(21) 4.5	(20) 1.9	
7.7	8.4	6.7		14.1	7.1	6.3	6.9	3.4	
7577440M	2395532M	9112108M	Net Sales ($)	21466M	182366M	208098M	247988M	564171M	7888019M
1007633M	997018M	1397283M	Total Assets ($)	27212M	48378M	57000M	114252M	176063M	974378M

© RMA 2019   M = $ thousand   MM = $ million
See Pages viii through xx for Explanation of Ratios and Data

Current Data Sorted by Assets

Comparative Historical Data

						Type of Statement		
						Unqualified		
	1		2		1	Reviewed		
10	1	1	4			Compiled	3	3
16	14	2	6	1	1	Tax Returns	5	5
20	7	13		1		Other	11	8
	3 (4/1-9/30/18)		104 (10/1/18-3/31/19)				51	50
							44	55
							4/1/14-3/31/15	4/1/15-3/31/16
0-500M	500M-2MM	2-10MM	10-50MM	50-100MM	100-250MM		ALL	ALL
46	23	22	12	2	2	NUMBER OF STATEMENTS	114	121
%	%	%	%	%	%	ASSETS	%	%
33.9	16.3	12.9	12.2			Cash & Equivalents	14.0	18.3
3.8	2.4	1.7	.6			Trade Receivables (net)	5.5	4.6
13.0	12.4	5.8	4.6			Inventory	10.5	11.7
2.8	1.7	4.1	4.9			All Other Current	1.3	1.4
53.4	32.8	24.6	22.2			Total Current	31.3	35.9
30.5	50.4	49.7	45.2			Fixed Assets (net)	42.1	41.3
11.5	14.9	15.8	21.2			Intangibles (net)	16.3	11.3
4.7	1.9	10.0	11.4			All Other Non-Current	10.4	11.5
100.0	100.0	100.0	100.0			Total	100.0	100.0
						LIABILITIES		
14.8	5.7	3.7	.9			Notes Payable-Short Term	5.4	3.8
2.2	2.7	4.1	6.0			Cur. Mat.-L.T.D.	2.9	2.9
17.3	7.5	7.5	4.5			Trade Payables	7.8	11.5
.2	.1	.0	.0			Income Taxes Payable	.1	.0
21.2	11.8	5.7	5.0			All Other Current	15.5	14.0
55.7	27.8	21.0	16.3			Total Current	31.6	32.2
10.8	40.9	59.2	35.0			Long-Term Debt	42.8	39.1
.0	.0	.0	.2			Deferred Taxes	.2	.2
6.0	9.8	2.8	17.3			All Other Non-Current	6.0	9.0
27.6	21.5	17.0	31.1			Net Worth	19.3	19.5
100.0	100.0	100.0	100.0			Total Liabilties & Net Worth	100.0	100.0
						INCOME DATA		
100.0	100.0	100.0	100.0			Net Sales	100.0	100.0
						Gross Profit		
90.4	79.3	78.3	89.2			Operating Expenses	86.9	87.1
9.6	20.7	21.7	10.8			Operating Profit	13.1	12.9
4.9	5.8	8.9	-.1			All Other Expenses (net)	2.9	2.9
4.7	14.9	12.8	10.9			Profit Before Taxes	10.2	10.0
						RATIOS		
4.2	5.2	2.3	3.3				2.4	3.2
1.2	1.1	1.2	1.3			Current	1.0	1.2
.5	.3	.3	.9				.5	.6
2.4	3.8	2.0	1.2				1.5	1.8
.7	.8	.7	.8			Quick	(112) .5	.7
.3	.1	.2	.5				.1	.3
0 UND	0 UND	0 UND	0 UND				0 UND	0 UND
0 UND	1 323.3	1 266.6	2 228.3			Sales/Receivables	1 340.6	1 248.8
1 273.4	3 141.1	2 166.3	3 140.9				6 66.1	7 55.1
						Cost of Sales/Inventory		
						Cost of Sales/Payables		
20.4	9.9	9.6	8.4				15.0	12.5
67.4	593.8	47.9	26.1			Sales/Working Capital	UND	61.9
-19.9	-7.5	-11.9	NM				-18.1	-15.2
17.4	18.0	16.3					17.5	22.4
(20) 5.0	(17) 5.4	(17) 6.2				EBIT/Interest	(92) 5.1	(89) 5.4
-4.7	2.9	4.1					2.1	1.8
						Net Profit + Depr., Dep., Amort./Cur. Mat. L/T/D	18.9	
							(10) 5.0	
							3.5	
.1	2.1	1.7	.9				.8	.6
.8	5.2	10.3	4.7			Fixed/Worth	4.0	3.2
UND	-2.3	-2.6	NM				-1.6	-3.1
.2	1.7	4.0	2.0				1.4	.9
1.5	10.8	17.8	4.6			Debt/Worth	7.9	4.0
-4.2	-3.9	-7.4	NM				-3.4	-4.8
194.9	148.1	99.4					158.2	106.5
(34) 41.7	(13) 49.3	(15) 64.0				% Profit Before Taxes/Tangible Net Worth	(70) 50.3	(80) 39.2
14.8	14.0	41.7					24.3	17.5
83.6	59.2	25.2	27.1				30.8	22.2
17.6	11.2	11.4	13.3			% Profit Before Taxes/Total Assets	12.7	10.4
1.4	4.7	2.4	6.7				3.5	2.3
109.3	34.4	13.8	6.2				38.9	48.2
29.2	6.8	3.2	3.8			Sales/Net Fixed Assets	8.6	9.9
9.9	.6	.6	1.8				1.5	1.5
8.9	4.2	3.2	1.7				5.2	5.0
5.5	1.6	1.3	1.5			Sales/Total Assets	2.3	2.3
4.1	.6	.5	1.3				.9	.9
.5	.7	1.9	1.0				1.5	1.3
(28) 1.3	(17) 2.5	(16) 4.6	(10) 1.8			% Depr., Dep., Amort./Sales	(82) 2.9	(91) 2.8
2.5	5.7	15.5	4.2				6.0	5.5
2.5	2.8						1.4	1.8
(16) 4.2	(11) 4.2					% Officers', Directors' Owners' Comp/Sales	(43) 4.7	(41) 4.4
10.8	6.5						8.0	7.6
48484M	70196M	130162M	416985M	105121M	329418M	Net Sales ($)	1210777M	1038619M
9394M	27571M	95502M	274037M	121816M	338535M	Total Assets ($)	902204M	767538M

M = $ thousand   MM = $ million
See Pages viii through xx for Explanation of Ratios and Data

Comparative Historical Data | | Current Data Sorted by Sales

4/1/16-3/31/17 ALL	4/1/17-3/31/18 ALL	4/1/18-3/31/19 ALL	Type of Statement	0-1MM	1-3MM	3-5MM	5-10MM	10-25MM	25MM & OVER
3	2	3	Unqualified					2	3
6	5	6	Reviewed		1				3
6	11	15	Compiled	5	7				2
51	42	36	Tax Returns	14	12	4	4	3	2
50	62	47	Other	15	14	5	3	6	4
				3 (4/1-9/30/18)			104 (10/1/18-3/31/19)		
116	122	107	NUMBER OF STATEMENTS	34	34	9	7	11	12
%	%	%	**ASSETS**	%	%	%	%	%	%
17.0	21.0	22.3	Cash & Equivalents	16.5	31.3			13.3	11.4
6.1	3.7	2.7	Trade Receivables (net)	1.9	4.5			3.5	1.4
12.2	9.4	10.1	Inventory	10.2	11.6			9.1	4.8
1.6	2.5	3.0	All Other Current	3.4	.7			9.1	1.8
36.9	36.6	38.1	Total Current	32.0	48.1			35.0	19.5
38.7	43.9	41.7	Fixed Assets (net)	50.7	33.8			35.2	51.6
16.2	10.1	14.3	Intangibles (net)	13.5	12.4			23.3	15.9
8.2	9.5	6.0	All Other Non-Current	3.9	5.8			6.5	13.0
100.0	100.0	100.0	Total	100.0	100.0			100.0	100.0
			LIABILITIES						
4.8	4.6	8.8	Notes Payable-Short Term	14.0	9.6			1.2	4.1
3.9	3.0	3.2	Cur. Mat.-L.T.D.	1.6	3.2			6.0	6.1
13.5	10.9	11.2	Trade Payables	12.7	13.4			10.8	5.2
.0	.1	.1	Income Taxes Payable	.0	.4			.0	.0
20.4	15.7	13.5	All Other Current	22.8	8.5			11.7	4.6
42.6	34.3	36.8	Total Current	51.1	35.1			29.8	20.0
43.9	42.6	30.9	Long-Term Debt	26.2	25.3			37.7	37.4
.0	.1	.1	Deferred Taxes	.0	.0			.0	.9
7.4	5.2	7.3	All Other Non-Current	8.9	5.9			6.6	12.2
6.0	17.8	24.9	Net Worth	13.7	33.6			25.9	29.5
100.0	100.0	100.0	Total Liabilities & Net Worth	100.0	100.0			100.0	100.0
			INCOME DATA						
100.0	100.0	100.0	Net Sales	100.0	100.0			100.0	100.0
			Gross Profit						
89.2	86.2	85.4	Operating Expenses	82.5	84.9			91.8	89.1
10.8	13.8	14.6	Operating Profit	17.5	15.1			8.2	10.9
2.1	3.1	5.2	All Other Expenses (net)	7.5	8.2			.1	.8
8.7	10.7	9.4	Profit Before Taxes	10.0	6.9			8.1	10.0
			RATIOS						
2.4	2.6	3.4	Current	4.2	3.3			2.9	1.7
1.1	1.1	1.2		.7	1.3			1.1	1.1
.5	.6	.5		.3	.5			.8	.7
1.4	1.9	2.0	Quick	1.2	2.9			1.3	1.0
.6	.7	.7		.4	1.0			.5	.6
.2	.3	.3		.1	.4			.1	.4
0 UND	0 UND	0 UND	Sales/Receivables	0 UND	0 UND			1 278.0	1 410.0
1 247.9	1 329.1	1 602.0		0 UND	0 999.8			2 176.0	2 234.7
4 89.2	4 93.2	2 180.6		1 273.4	2 186.0			3 121.6	2 156.9
			Cost of Sales/Inventory						
			Cost of Sales/Payables						
15.5	12.9	12.6	Sales/Working Capital	23.2	15.2			12.0	18.3
159.4	104.9	67.9		-38.3	61.8			68.5	148.3
-17.3	-20.4	-15.4		-6.3	-17.5			-36.5	-21.9
14.9	12.5	15.3	EBIT/Interest	10.8	9.0			39.3	
(89) 5.2	(87) 5.0	(66) 6.0		(18) 2.7	(17) 3.9			(10) 12.3	
1.9	2.0	2.7		-2.9	2.7			5.1	
			Net Profit + Depr., Dep., Amort./Cur. Mat. L/T/D						
.8	.7	.6	Fixed/Worth	.6	.3			.9	1.5
5.3	3.9	3.2		3.3	.9			3.6	5.4
-.9	-3.2	-3.9		-91.5	-1.9			-1.2	NM
1.2	.7	1.0	Debt/Worth	1.2	.6			2.8	2.0
10.7	5.6	4.6		4.8	1.7			5.9	5.2
-2.8	-7.0	-8.1		-38.7	-4.7			-5.3	NM
101.5	137.5	146.7	% Profit Before Taxes/Tangible Net Worth	187.4	126.2				
(66) 50.9	(78) 41.5	(74) 49.6		(24) 49.6	(23) 32.2				
26.1	13.0	16.2		13.6	6.0				
27.2	26.3	33.5	% Profit Before Taxes/Total Assets	21.7	53.0			29.0	23.9
12.8	12.8	12.6		3.7	12.2			12.8	13.3
4.5	3.2	3.1		-2.7	4.1			9.7	3.9
51.2	62.2	37.5	Sales/Net Fixed Assets	47.1	91.8			36.8	4.0
13.8	7.1	10.0		8.8	20.7			14.7	2.9
2.6	1.2	1.9		.6	3.5			2.5	1.3
6.1	4.8	5.2	Sales/Total Assets	5.2	8.9			3.8	1.7
3.0	1.9	2.6		2.2	4.7			2.4	1.4
1.3	.8	1.0		.5	1.3			1.6	.9
.8	1.0	.8	% Depr., Dep., Amort./Sales	1.6	.6				1.6
(85) 1.8	(88) 2.5	(75) 2.0		(21) 2.7	(25) 1.7			(10)	2.7
4.0	6.9	4.3		15.6	4.4				3.9
2.2	2.3	1.8	% Officers', Directors' Owners' Comp/Sales	2.6	3.2				
(48) 4.1	(49) 4.2	(38) 3.6		(10) 4.5	(14) 4.5				
7.1	6.0	5.9		14.9	9.2				
3571957M	1159135M	1100366M	Net Sales ($)	18948M	53980M	35006M	54806M	158044M	779582M
1070397M	728017M	866855M	Total Assets ($)	34325M	34480M	24072M	13883M	91583M	668512M

M = $ thousand   MM = $ million
See Pages viii through xx for Explanation of Ratios and Data

Current Data Sorted by Assets   Comparative Historical Data

	0-500M	500M-2MM	2-10MM	10-50MM	50-100MM	100-250MM	Type of Statement	4/1/14-3/31/15 ALL	4/1/15-3/31/16 ALL
							Unqualified	3	3
	1				1		Reviewed	9	20
			2	12	1		Compiled	66	38
	11	7	13	1	1		Tax Returns	171	152
	38	40	20		1		Other	125	137
	28	39	56	10	11				
	12 (4/1-9/30/18)		281 (10/1/18-3/31/19)						
NUMBER OF STATEMENTS	78	86	91	23	15			374	350

	%	%	%	%	%	%		%	%
							ASSETS		
Cash & Equivalents	38.0	16.3	9.0	11.2	4.9			14.2	14.8
Trade Receivables (net)	3.6	1.5	1.0	.6	.4			1.8	2.4
Inventory	4.5	1.6	.8	1.2	.6			2.3	3.0
All Other Current	3.4	1.4	1.0	.8	.4			1.9	2.1
Total Current	49.5	20.7	11.8	13.8	6.2			20.3	22.3
Fixed Assets (net)	35.9	62.4	77.4	73.6	83.8			65.6	63.9
Intangibles (net)	4.6	10.6	3.5	5.6	7.5			6.1	5.5
All Other Non-Current	10.0	6.2	7.3	7.0	2.5			8.0	8.3
Total	100.0	100.0	100.0	100.0	100.0			100.0	100.0
							LIABILITIES		
Notes Payable-Short Term	7.5	4.9	2.0	.2	5.9			7.6	6.7
Cur. Mat.-L.T.D.	3.2	2.8	3.3	4.3	3.2			5.1	4.0
Trade Payables	7.6	2.5	1.0	2.7	1.7			3.1	2.6
Income Taxes Payable	.4	.1	.0	.0	.1			.2	.1
All Other Current	18.6	6.8	2.9	4.7	3.3			11.3	12.1
Total Current	37.3	17.1	9.2	11.9	14.1			27.3	25.5
Long-Term Debt	37.9	56.0	65.0	46.9	46.6			65.2	62.7
Deferred Taxes	.0	.0	.0	.3	.0			.0	.0
All Other Non-Current	18.1	5.1	1.8	3.7	36.5			13.7	8.3
Net Worth	6.7	21.8	24.0	37.3	2.8			-6.2	3.6
Total Liabilities & Net Worth	100.0	100.0	100.0	100.0	100.0			100.0	100.0
							INCOME DATA		
Net Sales	100.0	100.0	100.0	100.0	100.0			100.0	100.0
Gross Profit									
Operating Expenses	89.6	78.8	73.5	83.9	71.0			84.2	83.4
Operating Profit	10.4	21.2	26.5	16.1	29.0			15.8	16.6
All Other Expenses (net)	3.1	4.7	11.0	2.6	4.9			6.2	6.2
Profit Before Taxes	7.4	16.5	15.5	13.5	24.1			9.6	10.5
							RATIOS		
Current	8.4	5.0	4.2	2.5	.9			2.2	3.0
	1.8	1.2	1.2	1.1	.7			.8	.9
	.5	.4	.2	.5	.1			.3	.3
Quick	5.5	4.3	3.7	2.4	.8			1.6	2.0
	1.3	1.0	(90) .9	.8	.6			(373) .6	(349) .7
	.5	.2	.1	.5	.1			.2	.2
Sales/Receivables	0 UND	0 UND	0 UND	0 UND	0 999.8			0 UND	0 UND
	0 UND	0 UND	0 UND	1 447.2	0 820.3			0 UND	0 UND
	1 355.2	1 606.7	1 622.3	3 110.2	3 113.8			1 299.1	1 352.1
Cost of Sales/Inventory									
Cost of Sales/Payables									
Sales/Working Capital	8.0	6.5	6.2	13.1	-307.0			15.9	13.2
	34.2	71.5	63.5	109.1	-12.0			-44.0	-233.0
	-16.6	-8.7	-6.2	-10.5	-2.8			-7.2	-7.9
EBIT/Interest	21.2	9.8	7.3	9.8	9.2			7.0	8.9
	(45) 8.1	(65) 3.4	(68) 3.4	(22) 5.6	(14) 4.9			(287) 2.7	(263) 3.5
	1.3	1.4	1.7	2.6	3.6			1.1	1.5
Net Profit + Depr., Dep., Amort./Cur. Mat. L/T/D									5.0
									(12) 1.8
									.4
Fixed/Worth	.1	.8	1.8	1.1	1.8			1.7	1.2
	.9	5.2	6.2	2.9	4.5			9.1	8.4
	-2.2	-4.2	-35.4	4.8	25.8			-2.7	-3.6
Debt/Worth	.3	.5	1.2	.7	1.0			1.6	1.4
	1.8	6.5	5.4	2.8	3.9			10.7	10.4
	-3.0	-5.0	-64.9	4.9	25.3			-4.2	-5.1
% Profit Before Taxes/Tangible Net Worth	147.0	97.0	91.2	44.6	205.7			79.5	100.0
	(51) 41.9	(48) 40.2	(65) 34.6	(21) 30.0	(12) 35.8			(215) 33.7	(203) 44.8
	5.9	10.3	13.3	11.9	6.8			10.4	11.4
% Profit Before Taxes/Total Assets	60.1	32.2	14.6	20.0	15.5			18.5	23.2
	14.5	11.3	5.1	9.3	8.7			6.8	7.5
	1.4	2.6	1.9	6.5	2.0			.3	.6
Sales/Net Fixed Assets	184.5	4.4	1.1	1.8	1.9			7.2	9.1
	14.2	1.5	.5	1.0	.5			1.1	1.2
	3.7	.6	.3	.7	.4			.5	.5
Sales/Total Assets	6.6	1.8	.8	1.3	1.5			2.8	2.7
	3.9	1.0	.5	.9	.4			.8	.8
	1.5	.5	.2	.6	.3			.4	.4
% Depr., Dep., Amort./Sales	1.0	3.0	6.9	3.9	4.6			3.2	3.1
	(45) 3.5	(60) 7.3	(61) 12.0	(21) 7.0	(11) 9.2			(293) 8.3	(271) 8.6
	11.0	11.8	23.0	14.2	15.3			17.1	17.0
% Officers', Directors' Owners' Comp/Sales	5.5	2.8	1.5					2.0	3.0
	(26) 10.1	(26) 6.2	(25) 2.4					(124) 5.4	(110) 5.9
	13.6	10.5	6.0					8.7	8.9
Net Sales ($)	60753M	128053M	254030M	533607M	826951M			2196612M	4690098M
Total Assets ($)	17580M	92816M	362510M	505296M	1117394M			1389725M	1539557M

(Column 100-250MM: DATA NOT AVAILABLE)

M = $ thousand   MM = $ million
See Pages viii through xx for Explanation of Ratios and Data

Comparative Historical Data | Current Data Sorted by Sales

Type of Statement	4/1/16-3/31/17 ALL	4/1/17-3/31/18 ALL	4/1/18-3/31/19 ALL	0-1MM	1-3MM	3-5MM	5-10MM	10-25MM	25MM & OVER
Unqualified	6	3	2	1					1
Reviewed	24	24	15				5	6	4
Compiled	59	35	33	12	14	4	2		1
Tax Returns	128	132	99	58	33	3	1	3	1
Other	155	135	144	51	54	8	12	8	11
				12 (4/1-9/30/18)			281 (10/1/18-3/31/19)		
NUMBER OF STATEMENTS	372	329	293	122	101	15	20	17	18
	%	%	%	%	%	%	%	%	%
ASSETS									
Cash & Equivalents	14.9	15.3	18.8	19.0	20.6	24.8	16.9	14.6	8.8
Trade Receivables (net)	2.7	2.5	1.8	.8	2.5	1.3	4.8	.9	2.7
Inventory	2.0	2.4	2.0	1.6	2.8	1.1	1.9	2.7	.8
All Other Current	1.4	1.6	1.7	2.0	1.7	2.0	1.4	1.2	.3
Total Current	21.0	21.9	24.3	23.3	27.5	29.2	25.1	19.4	12.7
Fixed Assets (net)	64.9	62.6	62.0	62.7	59.4	54.1	61.0	66.1	75.8
Intangibles (net)	7.4	6.4	6.3	6.8	5.2	14.0	1.5	5.8	7.6
All Other Non-Current	6.7	9.1	7.4	7.1	7.9	2.7	12.5	8.7	3.9
Total	100.0	100.0	100.0	100.0	100.0	100.0	100.0	100.0	100.0
LIABILITIES									
Notes Payable-Short Term	4.0	4.8	4.4	5.8	3.0	6.9	3.2	1.2	4.9
Cur. Mat.-L.T.D.	3.8	4.5	3.2	3.3	3.2	1.1	3.3	3.7	3.2
Trade Payables	2.9	2.5	3.3	3.8	3.3	1.3	3.6	3.0	2.2
Income Taxes Payable	.1	.1	.1	.2	.0	.0	.1	.0	.1
All Other Current	10.5	9.9	8.4	7.9	11.3	1.9	7.1	3.9	6.4
Total Current	21.3	21.8	19.4	21.0	20.9	11.3	17.4	11.9	16.6
Long-Term Debt	60.6	57.1	52.8	58.6	53.4	45.5	37.3	46.4	39.7
Deferred Taxes	.0	.1	.0	.0	.0	.0	.0	.3	.0
All Other Non-Current	9.1	12.2	9.0	8.8	7.7	.9	8.3	1.0	33.2
Net Worth	8.9	8.9	18.7	11.6	18.0	42.4	37.0	40.4	10.5
Total Liabilties & Net Worth	100.0	100.0	100.0	100.0	100.0	100.0	100.0	100.0	100.0
INCOME DATA									
Net Sales	100.0	100.0	100.0	100.0	100.0	100.0	100.0	100.0	100.0
Gross Profit									
Operating Expenses	82.5	81.3	80.0	80.3	78.9	79.7	80.2	79.1	85.7
Operating Profit	17.5	18.7	20.0	19.7	21.1	20.3	19.8	20.9	14.3
All Other Expenses (net)	6.5	6.4	6.1	9.5	4.0	2.9	3.2	3.2	2.4
Profit Before Taxes	11.0	12.3	13.9	10.1	17.1	17.4	16.6	17.7	11.9
RATIOS									
Current	3.1	3.0	4.3	3.6	5.2	7.7	4.4	3.6	1.3
	1.2	1.2	1.3	1.0	1.6	4.4	1.3	1.3	.8
	.4	.4	.3	.3	.4	1.5	.5	.5	.2
Quick	2.6	2.5	3.7	2.6	4.4	7.1	3.9	2.5	1.0
	1.0	.9 (292)	1.0	.8 (100)	1.3	4.2	.9	1.3	.7
	.3	.3	.2	.2	.2	1.3	.4	.5	.1
Sales/Receivables	0 UND	0 UND	0 UND	0 UND	0 UND	0 UND	0 UND	0 999.8	0 999.8
	0 UND	0 UND	0 UND	0 UND	0 UND	0 UND	1 723.5	1 358.0	0 782.9
	2 194.8	2 198.2	1 397.3	0 UND	2 219.2	1 503.8	8 43.0	4 85.5	3 112.9
Cost of Sales/Inventory									
Cost of Sales/Payables									
Sales/Working Capital	9.3	10.4	7.9	9.5	6.2	3.6	8.1	8.8	85.6
	109.1	70.1	58.9	UND	32.8	12.3	18.6	28.0	-55.5
	-9.5	-11.0	-8.1	4.9	-18.0	85.2	-7.9	-11.3	-2.8
EBIT/Interest	7.7	7.6	9.9	8.0	10.0		16.4	16.1	26.1
	(295) 3.2	(260) 3.8	(214) 4.2	(80) 2.2	(76) 4.8		(18) 6.2	(15) 5.7	(16) 4.4
	1.5	1.4	1.6	1.2	1.8		1.6	2.7	2.7
Net Profit + Depr., Dep., Amort./Cur. Mat. L/T/D	6.2	89.4	4.8						
	(22) 4.2	(11) 4.5	(14) 3.0						
	1.7	1.6	1.9						
Fixed/Worth	1.3	1.3	.9	1.0	.7	.1	.9	.9	1.1
	6.3	6.3	4.1	6.3	3.9	1.4	1.6	2.4	3.5
	-5.1	-4.9	-11.8	-4.3	-18.4	10.9	7.5	8.3	21.8
Debt/Worth	1.2	1.5	.7	.9	.6	.1	.7	.5	1.1
	8.6	7.9	4.0	10.4	3.9	1.0	1.3	1.9	3.5
	-6.1	-7.4	-7.9	-5.3	-18.0	-4.6	8.0	8.3	31.1
% Profit Before Taxes/Tangible Net Worth	94.0	110.5	100.0	101.8	104.7	80.3	48.2	72.8	232.1
	(232) 35.3	(203) 37.0	(197) 34.9	(72) 22.0	(67) 50.5	(11) 34.6	(18) 28.9	(14) 44.5	(15) 27.0
	9.5	10.2	10.5	2.2	15.1	13.7	13.0	33.5	4.5
% Profit Before Taxes/Total Assets	20.9	18.9	23.9	16.9	34.7	49.5	23.2	22.3	18.4
	8.3	8.7		5.3	14.6	12.6	7.3	12.2	11.9
	.9	.6	2.1	.2	3.9	3.7	4.5	7.5	1.6
Sales/Net Fixed Assets	6.5	5.4	7.2	7.7	8.7	64.6	7.0	3.0	2.4
	1.0	1.1	1.2	.8	1.5	1.9	1.4	1.4	1.7
	.5	.5	.5	.3	.6	.9	.9	.6	.5
Sales/Total Assets	2.1	1.9	2.2	2.2	2.5	4.2	2.8	1.6	1.6
	.7	.8	.9	.6	1.0	1.4	1.0	.9	1.3
	.4	.4	.4	.3	.5	.7	.6	.6	.4
% Depr., Dep., Amort./Sales	3.8	3.7	3.4	4.3	2.8	3.1	3.1	3.3	2.3
	(300) 8.2	(252) 9.1	(198) 7.5	(77) 10.9	(68) 7.0	(11) 7.0	(14) 9.6	(14) 8.1	(14) 5.4
	16.5	17.7	15.4	20.4	12.0	11.3	14.2	13.9	9.5
% Officers', Directors' Owners' Comp/Sales	3.9	3.0	1.6	4.7	2.2				
	(103) 7.0	(98) 5.6	(89) 5.5	(29) 9.9	(35) 5.4				
	10.9	10.5	10.5	12.0	10.5				
Net Sales ($)	2661045M	1910084M	1803394M	64378M	159781M	57759M	137909M	275271M	1108296M
Total Assets ($)	1880202M	2488637M	2095596M	157608M	194413M	59258M	259088M	380261M	1044968M

© RMA 2019

M = $ thousand   MM = $ million
See Pages viii through xx for Explanation of Ratios and Data

Current Data Sorted by Assets   Comparative Historical Data

0-500M	500M-2MM	2-10MM	10-50MM	50-100MM	100-250MM	Type of Statement	ALL 4/1/14-3/31/15	ALL 4/1/15-3/31/16
		1	1		1	Unqualified	3	2
1		3	1			Reviewed	4	7
1	2	1				Compiled	19	8
22	10	9	1			Tax Returns	49	41
15	12	3	3			Other	40	34
	9 (4/1-9/30/18)		78 (10/1/18-3/31/19)					
39	24	17	6		1	NUMBER OF STATEMENTS	115	92
%	%	%	%	%	%	**ASSETS**	%	%
36.4	18.6	16.3				Cash & Equivalents	19.9	22.2
13.6	8.5	15.2				Trade Receivables (net)	13.6	11.6
16.2	15.2	27.9				Inventory	17.8	18.4
1.0	2.4	2.8				All Other Current	2.5	2.3
67.2	44.6	62.2				Total Current	53.8	54.4
21.1	33.4	23.6				Fixed Assets (net)	33.0	32.3
5.7	13.9	5.9				Intangibles (net)	5.9	5.4
6.1	8.0	8.4				All Other Non-Current	7.5	7.9
100.0	100.0	100.0				Total	100.0	100.0
						LIABILITIES		
9.7	6.0	8.6				Notes Payable-Short Term	8.9	15.0
.9	2.9	2.1				Cur. Mat.-L.T.D.	4.8	4.9
8.3	8.9	9.5				Trade Payables	13.5	9.8
.1	.1	.4				Income Taxes Payable	.1	.1
14.3	13.4	15.2				All Other Current	12.8	13.8
33.3	31.3	36.0				Total Current	40.1	43.5
20.7	29.7	18.9				Long-Term Debt	26.1	24.2
.0	.0	.8				Deferred Taxes	.1	.2
15.0	8.0	5.6				All Other Non-Current	11.3	12.0
31.0	31.0	38.7				Net Worth	22.4	20.0
100.0	100.0	100.0				Total Liabilties & Net Worth	100.0	100.0
						INCOME DATA		
100.0	100.0	100.0				Net Sales	100.0	100.0
						Gross Profit		
92.1	94.1	91.6				Operating Expenses	92.2	93.9
7.9	5.9	8.4				Operating Profit	7.8	6.1
.9	.4	3.0				All Other Expenses (net)	1.8	.6
7.0	5.5	5.3				Profit Before Taxes	6.0	5.5
						RATIOS		
7.3	4.2	3.8					3.2	3.3
2.3	1.7	1.6				Current	1.5	1.6
1.0	.7	1.0					.9	.7
6.7	2.0	2.5					1.8	2.1
2.0	1.2	.9				Quick	.9	.8
.6	.4	.3					.4	.4
0 UND	0 UND	1 437.6					0 UND	0 UND
0 999.8	10 36.5	13 28.6				Sales/Receivables	6 65.5	6 56.2
19 19.1	23 16.0	34 10.6					22 16.3	21 17.0
						Cost of Sales/Inventory		
						Cost of Sales/Payables		
6.1	5.9	3.8					9.5	7.9
12.2	16.6	9.5				Sales/Working Capital	34.9	18.5
740.0	-26.1	NM					-69.1	-36.2
32.5	8.9	46.6					11.9	18.3
(19) 4.5	(15) 4.2	(15) 4.0				EBIT/Interest	(80) 4.2	(67) 7.1
.8	1.1	2.6					.9	2.2
						Net Profit + Depr., Dep., Amort./Cur. Mat. L/T/D		
.1	.2	.0					.2	.3
.4	2.2	.2				Fixed/Worth	.9	1.5
3.8	-6.8	9.3					-13.4	-10.2
.3	.5	.6					.5	.6
1.2	3.8	1.2				Debt/Worth	2.3	3.6
254.0	-8.5	49.9					-23.3	-13.2
125.0	61.2	52.0				% Profit Before Taxes/Tangible	69.9	75.4
(30) 62.6	(15) 25.1	(14) 14.6				Net Worth	(84) 30.7	(65) 48.3
32.1	2.4	-1.4					4.5	6.1
66.7	23.1	27.6				% Profit Before Taxes/Total	24.5	31.5
27.8	13.9	8.1				Assets	8.6	11.5
2.7	1.6	.5					.2	1.0
346.0	60.0	92.6					74.1	65.8
56.8	12.8	27.1				Sales/Net Fixed Assets	24.2	17.7
11.7	3.2	9.4					5.4	7.2
9.6	3.7	3.4					6.0	6.6
5.2	2.5	2.7				Sales/Total Assets	3.8	3.8
3.6	1.4	1.4					1.9	1.9
.2	1.3	.6					.5	.7
(15) 1.8	(10) 3.2	(15) 1.5				% Depr., Dep., Amort./Sales	(71) 1.6	(57) 1.4
5.1	7.4	3.2					4.6	3.4
3.7		1.1					2.2	2.0
(17) 7.6		(10) 2.0				% Officers', Directors' Owners' Comp/Sales	(52) 3.6	(45) 4.7
10.3		5.5					8.3	10.0
56231M	72865M	188664M	404124M		234425M	Net Sales ($)	1854744M	1304427M
9175M	22169M	77411M	156156M		237909M	Total Assets ($)	718577M	808005M

(DATA NOT AVAILABLE for the 10-50MM, 50-100MM, and 100-250MM asset-size columns.)

Comparative Historical Data | Current Data Sorted by Sales

			Type of Statement	0-1MM	1-3MM	3-5MM	5-10MM	10-25MM	25MM & OVER
3	3	3	Unqualified					1	2
5	4	5	Reviewed		1			3	1
7	10	4	Compiled	3	1				
36	54	42	Tax Returns	18	12	4	3	3	2
26	41	33	Other	8	11	5	3	2	4
4/1/16-3/31/17 ALL	4/1/17-3/31/18 ALL	4/1/18-3/31/19 ALL			9 (4/1-9/30/18)		78 (10/1/18-3/31/19)		

4/1/16-3/31/17 ALL	4/1/17-3/31/18 ALL	4/1/18-3/31/19 ALL		0-1MM	1-3MM	3-5MM	5-10MM	10-25MM	25MM & OVER
77	112	87	**NUMBER OF STATEMENTS**	29	25	9	6	9	9
%	%	%	**ASSETS**	%	%	%	%	%	%
21.2	18.2	25.3	Cash & Equivalents	29.7	29.2				
11.6	14.2	13.1	Trade Receivables (net)	6.4	15.5				
17.3	12.4	18.5	Inventory	11.7	21.0				
5.6	2.6	1.7	All Other Current	.7	1.7				
55.8	47.4	58.7	Total Current	48.6	67.4				
30.7	34.8	25.6	Fixed Assets (net)	38.2	18.2				
8.2	7.9	8.5	Intangibles (net)	5.1	11.3				
5.3	9.8	7.2	All Other Non-Current	8.1	3.1				
100.0	100.0	100.0	Total	100.0	100.0				
			LIABILITIES						
5.9	10.6	8.4	Notes Payable-Short Term	5.6	7.1				
5.0	2.9	1.9	Cur. Mat.-L.T.D.	2.0	1.2				
10.6	12.7	9.1	Trade Payables	4.7	11.9				
.1	.0	.1	Income Taxes Payable	.1	.1				
17.2	19.0	14.1	All Other Current	8.9	14.7				
38.8	45.3	33.7	Total Current	21.4	35.0				
23.8	23.2	22.9	Long-Term Debt	36.9	16.0				
.1	.2	.2	Deferred Taxes	.0	.0				
14.0	2.1	10.4	All Other Non-Current	7.5	7.1				
23.2	29.2	32.7	Net Worth	34.2	42.0				
100.0	100.0	100.0	Total Liabilties & Net Worth	100.0	100.0				
			INCOME DATA						
100.0	100.0	100.0	Net Sales	100.0	100.0				
			Gross Profit						
92.0	90.1	93.1	Operating Expenses	91.8	91.2				
8.0	9.9	6.9	Operating Profit	8.2	8.8				
.9	1.3	1.2	All Other Expenses (net)	2.9	.9				
7.2	8.6	5.7	Profit Before Taxes	5.3	7.9				
			RATIOS						
4.0	2.3	5.9	Current	6.4	9.2				
1.5	1.3	1.9		2.1	3.4				
.9	.6	.8		.8	1.1				
2.5	1.8	4.3	Quick	5.1	8.9				
.8	.8	1.2		1.6	2.2				
.3	.4	.4		.6	.5				
0 UND	0 UND	0 UND	Sales/Receivables	0 UND	0 784.5				
8 44.4	7 51.6	6 64.7		0 UND	10 38.4				
21 17.7	24 15.0	25 14.8		16 22.8	20 18.7				
			Cost of Sales/Inventory						
			Cost of Sales/Payables						
6.5	9.7	5.7	Sales/Working Capital	5.2	6.3				
26.9	33.6	13.8		7.6	11.1				
-76.1	-30.8	-893.5		207.8	408.0				
16.9	16.8	14.9	EBIT/Interest	12.1	23.2				
(52) 6.3	(79) 5.5	(55) 4.5		(21) 3.0	(10) 5.4				
1.9	2.5	1.3		1.0	-5.9				
			Net Profit + Depr., Dep., Amort./Cur. Mat. L/T/D						
.2	.2	.1	Fixed/Worth	.1	.0				
.9	1.2	.7		1.3	.2				
28.8	8.5	14.7		10.2	1.6				
.8	.6	.5	Debt/Worth	.5	.1				
2.8	2.1	1.8		1.9	.8				
329.6	UND	-41.3		16.7	-8.6				
91.7	96.1	81.9	% Profit Before Taxes/Tangible Net Worth	78.5	89.4				
(59) 42.1	(84) 44.9	(64) 42.7		(24) 36.3	(18) 61.0				
10.0	14.4	14.5		4.2	27.3				
29.3	34.4	34.9	% Profit Before Taxes/Total Assets	33.2	71.4				
14.0	12.2	15.4		9.2	23.9				
2.1	4.9	2.7		.6	2.7				
55.3	57.5	136.7	Sales/Net Fixed Assets	41.5	454.5				
20.4	16.2	27.1		10.9	58.0				
6.0	3.0	9.1		1.7	19.4				
5.4	5.5	5.7	Sales/Total Assets	4.9	9.0				
3.3	2.9	3.4		2.3	5.0				
1.7	1.6	1.8		1.1	2.8				
.6	.6	.9	% Depr., Dep., Amort./Sales	1.0					
(48) 1.9	(70) 2.1	(45) 1.8		(18) 3.8					
4.0	5.2	6.2		7.0					
3.2	1.8	2.1	% Officers', Directors' Owners' Comp/Sales	4.7					
(36) 5.4	(54) 4.6	(36) 5.0		(15) 8.1					
9.1	8.6	9.5		11.1					
753759M	1278609M	956309M	Net Sales ($)	17657M	48455M	34597M	35763M	121561M	698276M
445969M	805010M	502820M	Total Assets ($)	18453M	14394M	12351M	10045M	35572M	412005M

M = $ thousand   MM = $ million
See Pages viii through xx for Explanation of Ratios and Data

Current Data Sorted by Assets   **Comparative Historical Data**

0-500M	500M-2MM	2-10MM	10-50MM	50-100MM	100-250MM	Type of Statement	4/1/14-3/31/15 ALL	4/1/15-3/31/16 ALL
			2	1	1	Unqualified	3	5
	1		1			Reviewed	8	5
1		2			1	Compiled	4	4
1		10	5		2	Tax Returns	17	13
1	2					Other	21	22
	2 (4/1-9/30/18)		31 (10/1/18-3/31/19)					
3	3	14	8	1	4	**NUMBER OF STATEMENTS**	53	49
%	%	%	%	%	%		%	%

ASSETS

2-10MM	Item	ALL 4/1/14-3/31/15	ALL 4/1/15-3/31/16
16.5	Cash & Equivalents	17.8	17.3
39.5	Trade Receivables (net)	33.2	34.5
18.6	Inventory	19.4	14.0
5.3	All Other Current	2.6	4.8
79.9	Total Current	72.9	70.5
14.0	Fixed Assets (net)	16.7	13.4
3.2	Intangibles (net)	5.0	10.1
2.9	All Other Non-Current	5.3	6.0
100.0	Total	100.0	100.0

LIABILITIES

2-10MM	Item	ALL 4/1/14-3/31/15	ALL 4/1/15-3/31/16
10.2	Notes Payable-Short Term	9.4	12.7
1.8	Cur. Mat.-L.T.D.	1.3	.6
13.8	Trade Payables	18.9	22.1
.0	Income Taxes Payable	1.0	1.0
18.1	All Other Current	13.9	12.5
43.9	Total Current	44.5	48.9
8.3	Long-Term Debt	13.1	10.4
.0	Deferred Taxes	.0	.0
3.4	All Other Non-Current	6.2	12.7
44.5	Net Worth	36.1	28.0
100.0	Total Liabilities & Net Worth	100.0	100.0

INCOME DATA

2-10MM	Item	ALL 4/1/14-3/31/15	ALL 4/1/15-3/31/16
100.0	Net Sales	100.0	100.0
	Gross Profit		
84.6	Operating Expenses	93.7	93.7
15.4	Operating Profit	6.3	6.3
2.2	All Other Expenses (net)	.2	2.3
13.3	Profit Before Taxes	6.1	4.0

RATIOS

2-10MM	Ratio	ALL 4/1/14-3/31/15	ALL 4/1/15-3/31/16
3.1	Current	3.8	2.5
1.9		1.7	1.5
1.3		1.0	.9
2.1	Quick	2.4	2.1
1.4		1.2	1.1
.8		.6	.5
28 12.9	Sales/Receivables	12 30.7	20 18.1
41 9.0		41 9.0	41 8.9
63 5.8		61 6.0	60 6.1
	Cost of Sales/Inventory		
	Cost of Sales/Payables		
6.0	Sales/Working Capital	6.0	6.8
10.2		12.1	12.9
NM		116.7	-64.9
	EBIT/Interest	65.3	38.5
		(35) 16.7	(33) 7.2
		4.4	2.1
	Net Profit + Depr., Dep., Amort./Cur. Mat. L/T/D		
.1	Fixed/Worth	.1	.0
.3		.3	.2
2.0		.9	2.1
.5	Debt/Worth	.6	.6
1.0		1.4	3.6
12.9		6.0	-17.5
96.9	% Profit Before Taxes/Tangible Net Worth	(44) 87.6	(36) 91.6
(13) 72.0		41.5	43.1
7.3		12.5	13.3
46.4	% Profit Before Taxes/Total Assets	37.9	28.2
18.1		12.9	9.7
1.5		4.8	2.6
83.0	Sales/Net Fixed Assets	102.1	279.3
54.9		37.4	44.9
24.8		11.9	18.1
4.5	Sales/Total Assets	4.3	4.0
3.3		3.3	3.0
2.5		2.3	2.2
.1	% Depr., Dep., Amort./Sales	(34) .3	(26) .2
(10) .5		.9	.4
2.5		1.8	1.7
	% Officers', Directors' Owners' Comp/Sales	(24) 2.9	(15) 1.7
		3.9	3.5
		11.6	16.3

0-500M	500M-2MM	2-10MM	10-50MM	50-100MM	100-250MM		ALL 4/1/14-3/31/15	ALL 4/1/15-3/31/16
2178M	18643M	180769M	450493M	99200M	753608M	Net Sales ($)	890734M	1195441M
714M	4391M	55982M	166689M	63497M	694224M	Total Assets ($)	288348M	564419M

M = $ thousand   MM = $ million
See Pages viii through xx for Explanation of Ratios and Data

Comparative Historical Data | Current Data Sorted by Sales

			Type of Statement						
4	3	4	Unqualified						4
5	3	2	Reviewed					1	1
2	1	4	Compiled	1			1	1	1
11	9	3	Tax Returns	1			2		
22	23	20	Other	1	1	1	2	7	8
4/1/16-3/31/17	4/1/17-3/31/18	4/1/18-3/31/19		0-1MM	1-3MM	3-5MM	5-10MM	10-25MM	25MM & OVER
ALL	ALL	ALL			2 (4/1-9/30/18)			31 (10/1/18-3/31/19)	
44	39	33	NUMBER OF STATEMENTS	3	1	1	5	9	14
%	%	%	ASSETS	%	%	%	%	%	%
16.5	22.8	18.5	Cash & Equivalents						19.3
27.3	29.8	31.9	Trade Receivables (net)						31.4
14.0	11.9	14.3	Inventory						7.1
4.4	4.7	4.4	All Other Current						4.9
62.2	69.2	69.1	Total Current						62.6
19.1	12.1	11.3	Fixed Assets (net)						7.9
7.8	8.5	13.0	Intangibles (net)						23.2
10.9	10.2	6.6	All Other Non-Current						6.2
100.0	100.0	100.0	Total						100.0
			LIABILITIES						
9.6	7.0	7.1	Notes Payable-Short Term						4.5
4.2	2.9	4.6	Cur. Mat.-L.T.D.						5.3
16.3	13.4	11.8	Trade Payables						12.1
.6	.7	.0	Income Taxes Payable						.0
14.9	10.9	15.5	All Other Current						15.7
45.6	34.9	39.1	Total Current						37.6
13.7	6.8	15.2	Long-Term Debt						16.8
.8	.3	.5	Deferred Taxes						1.0
11.0	10.6	11.9	All Other Non-Current						21.2
28.9	47.4	33.4	Net Worth						23.4
100.0	100.0	100.0	Total Liabilties & Net Worth						100.0
			INCOME DATA						
100.0	100.0	100.0	Net Sales						100.0
			Gross Profit						
90.3	94.1	89.8	Operating Expenses						96.6
9.7	5.9	10.2	Operating Profit						3.4
1.3	.4	1.4	All Other Expenses (net)						.7
8.3	5.5	8.8	Profit Before Taxes						2.7
			RATIOS						
2.1	3.8	2.9							2.4
1.5	2.1	1.7	Current						1.7
.9	1.2	1.2							1.1
1.9	3.6	2.4							2.4
1.1	1.6	1.4	Quick						1.3
.5	.9	.8							.8
20 18.6	19 19.1	28 13.0							36 10.0
39 9.4	46 8.0	41 8.8	Sales/Receivables						46 8.0
52 7.0	59 6.2	59 6.2							60 6.1
			Cost of Sales/Inventory						
			Cost of Sales/Payables						
7.7	4.9	5.5							4.9
22.3	9.5	10.4	Sales/Working Capital						8.6
-44.8	32.2	111.7							NM
41.4	37.0	23.1							14.6
(33) 7.2	(21) 8.9	(22) 4.5	EBIT/Interest					(11) 2.6	2.6
1.5	2.8	.1							-1.3
			Net Profit + Depr., Dep., Amort./Cur. Mat. L/T/D						
.1	.0	.1							.2
.7	.3	.4	Fixed/Worth						-1.1
19.9	.5	-.3							-.2
.9	.3	.9							1.7
3.1	1.2	2.2	Debt/Worth						-9.0
NM	4.0	-4.8							-2.7
91.2	62.0	122.2							
(33) 33.5	(32) 27.1	(22) 66.3	% Profit Before Taxes/Tangible Net Worth						
5.7	-1.9	18.5							
35.4	31.8	30.4							16.8
13.3	14.2	13.2	% Profit Before Taxes/Total Assets						9.6
2.2	.0	2.9							-1.1
89.0	117.1	115.8							129.9
33.9	44.8	55.6	Sales/Net Fixed Assets						36.9
12.2	20.0	25.7							24.4
3.7	3.7	3.9							3.6
2.6	2.6	2.9	Sales/Total Assets						2.4
2.0	1.8	1.9							1.3
.4	.2	.3							
(24) .8	(19) .9	(18) .5	% Depr., Dep., Amort./Sales						
2.0	1.5	2.0							
1.9	2.4								
(12) 7.5	(12) 9.4		% Officers', Directors' Owners' Comp/Sales						
18.5	13.4								
850895M	823807M	1504891M	Net Sales ($)	1186M	1448M	3260M	35117M	133390M	1330490M
418176M	410939M	985497M	Total Assets ($)	3639M	433M	1393M	11875M	37641M	930516M

M = $ thousand   MM = $ million
See Pages viii through xx for Explanation of Ratios and Data

	Current Data Sorted by Assets						Comparative Historical Data	
Type of Statement								
Unqualified			1	4			5	5
Reviewed		1	10	5			9	14
Compiled		2	4				12	11
Tax Returns	7	8	4	1			33	36
Other	5	13	12	3	2		35	40
		8 (4/1-9/30/18)		74 (10/1/18-3/31/19)			4/1/14-3/31/15 ALL	4/1/15-3/31/16 ALL
	0-500M	500M-2MM	2-10MM	10-50MM	50-100MM	100-250MM		
NUMBER OF STATEMENTS	12	24	31	13	2		94	106
ASSETS	%	%	%	%	%	%	%	%
Cash & Equivalents	35.5	21.1	15.4	10.0		DATA NOT AVAILABLE	13.8	12.1
Trade Receivables (net)	29.2	30.3	36.3	31.6			32.3	33.0
Inventory	11.7	23.5	20.9	24.8			15.2	17.4
All Other Current	1.0	1.7	1.7	2.9			1.2	1.4
Total Current	77.4	76.6	74.3	69.4			62.4	64.0
Fixed Assets (net)	14.6	12.3	16.9	9.7			23.3	22.3
Intangibles (net)	5.1	3.4	5.2	18.3			8.4	7.5
All Other Non-Current	3.0	7.8	3.6	2.6			5.9	6.2
Total	100.0	100.0	100.0	100.0			100.0	100.0
LIABILITIES								
Notes Payable-Short Term	71.7	10.6	8.4	11.3			9.9	14.8
Cur. Mat.-L.T.D.	3.3	2.4	3.4	1.3			2.9	3.3
Trade Payables	17.8	15.5	15.5	13.4			16.5	16.4
Income Taxes Payable	.0	.0	.1	.0			.1	.1
All Other Current	16.3	12.3	14.1	11.5			10.8	15.4
Total Current	109.0	40.8	41.6	37.5			40.2	50.0
Long-Term Debt	17.2	6.8	9.6	8.2			16.3	16.0
Deferred Taxes	.0	.0	.3	.4			.5	.4
All Other Non-Current	.0	10.5	2.3	3.9			8.9	5.9
Net Worth	-26.2	41.9	46.2	50.1			34.1	27.7
Total Liabilties & Net Worth	100.0	100.0	100.0	100.0			100.0	100.0
INCOME DATA								
Net Sales	100.0	100.0	100.0	100.0			100.0	100.0
Gross Profit								
Operating Expenses	94.9	88.5	93.4	92.5			93.0	93.6
Operating Profit	5.1	11.5	6.6	7.5			7.0	6.4
All Other Expenses (net)	.4	.1	.7	.6			1.7	.7
Profit Before Taxes	4.7	11.3	5.9	7.0			5.3	5.7
RATIOS								
Current	2.5	4.7	3.2	4.5			3.3	2.7
	1.2	2.0	2.1	1.8			1.6	1.4
	.7	1.1	1.2	1.2			1.0	1.0
Quick	2.1	3.3	2.7	2.8			2.1	2.3
	.8	1.2	1.2	1.1			1.2	(105) 1.0
	.4	.4	.9	.5			.7	.5
Sales/Receivables	0 UND	10 37.9	29 12.6	51 7.2			23 16.2	20 17.9
	6 58.1	38 9.7	51 7.2	61 6.0			38 9.5	38 9.5
	41 8.8	54 6.8	59 6.2	68 5.4			59 6.2	58 6.3
Cost of Sales/Inventory								
Cost of Sales/Payables								
Sales/Working Capital	27.3	4.4	4.9	3.7			6.1	6.5
	59.2	12.9	9.7	7.1			13.4	19.4
	-38.2	36.4	26.8	19.7			204.5	-309.2
EBIT/Interest		52.2	21.5	44.1			32.0	35.5
		(20) 15.3	(26) 8.5	(11) 12.1			(72) 9.1	(92) 10.7
		4.7	4.7	2.5			2.0	2.0
Net Profit + Depr., Dep., Amort./Cur. Mat. L/T/D								4.8
								(13) 2.7
								1.3
Fixed/Worth	.0	.1	.1	.1			.2	.2
	.3	.3	.3	.2			.7	.7
	NM	.6	1.2	NM			3.5	2.5
Debt/Worth	1.3	.3	.5	.4			.7	.7
	14.1	1.2	.9	1.3			1.6	2.2
	-3.5	3.5	4.1	NM			158.8	13.3
% Profit Before Taxes/Tangible Net Worth		73.4	53.1	50.0			60.9	75.5
		(22) 51.4	(27) 36.9	(10) 34.1			(72) 30.3	(88) 42.1
		12.0	8.8	16.6			8.3	17.9
% Profit Before Taxes/Total Assets	75.4	44.9	22.5	21.4			24.5	26.8
	28.3	20.0	13.4	14.3			9.0	12.5
	7.5	3.0	3.0	2.3			2.3	3.2
Sales/Net Fixed Assets	538.0	186.3	134.3	92.6			47.8	46.0
	278.8	51.1	19.8	30.7			17.0	21.9
	41.5	19.1	13.1	16.3			9.4	9.4
Sales/Total Assets	19.0	4.4	3.7	2.5			4.2	4.6
	8.4	2.9	2.8	2.0			3.3	3.2
	4.8	1.9	2.0	1.2			1.7	1.8
% Depr., Dep., Amort./Sales		.1	.4	.5			1.0	.5
		(11) 1.1	(20) 1.7	(10) 1.2			(68) 1.6	(72) 1.3
		2.7	2.8	1.6			3.1	2.5
% Officers', Directors' Owners' Comp/Sales		3.2	1.3				2.5	2.2
		(14) 5.6	(13) 3.1				(45) 4.4	(51) 3.7
		15.4	4.5				8.2	9.1
Net Sales ($)	27673M	92091M	423850M	653075M	329037M		1002501M	2540096M
Total Assets ($)	2504M	25763M	149424M	339882M	121205M		543378M	1188688M

M = $ thousand MM = $ million

See Pages viii through xx for Explanation of Ratios and Data

Comparative Historical Data | Current Data Sorted by Sales

				Type of Statement	0-1MM	1-3MM	3-5MM	5-10MM	10-25MM	25MM & OVER
	1	3	5	Unqualified		1		1	1	3
	16	14	16	Reviewed		1	1	4	6	6
	11	11	6	Compiled		1	1	2	2	2
	17	30	20	Tax Returns	3	7	3	4	2	1
	34	44	35	Other	2	5	5	7	9	2
	4/1/16-3/31/17 ALL	4/1/17-3/31/18 ALL	4/1/18-3/31/19 ALL			8 (4/1-9/30/18)		74 (10/1/18-3/31/19)		
	79	102	82	**NUMBER OF STATEMENTS**	5	15	10	18	20	14
	%	%	%	**ASSETS**	%	%	%	%	%	%
Cash & Equivalents	11.9	16.8	19.3			17.8	32.0	16.3	17.5	11.5
Trade Receivables (net)	35.1	30.7	32.6			28.7	38.0	28.4	33.6	41.2
Inventory	18.0	20.3	20.5			20.9	12.7	20.6	26.1	17.9
All Other Current	3.2	1.7	1.9			.2	2.5	1.6	2.9	2.3
Total Current	68.2	69.5	74.3			67.6	85.2	66.9	80.1	72.8
Fixed Assets (net)	16.9	21.1	13.8			19.6	9.5	18.5	10.5	10.8
Intangibles (net)	7.4	2.9	6.8			6.0	.7	6.6	6.6	11.8
All Other Non-Current	7.5	6.5	5.0			6.8	4.6	8.0	2.8	4.6
Total	100.0	100.0	100.0			100.0	100.0	100.0	100.0	100.0
				LIABILITIES						
Notes Payable-Short Term	10.3	12.9	18.6			19.4	13.7	8.2	8.5	8.0
Cur. Mat.-L.T.D.	4.5	3.9	2.7			1.7	4.7	4.1	1.7	1.9
Trade Payables	16.3	12.2	15.2			19.0	10.5	11.2	14.7	18.1
Income Taxes Payable	.1	.1	.1			.0	.0	.0	.0	.3
All Other Current	14.2	13.2	13.4			10.2	17.9	14.2	14.0	12.2
Total Current	45.4	42.3	50.0			50.3	46.9	37.7	38.9	40.6
Long-Term Debt	17.1	17.9	10.2			5.8	12.2	19.2	4.7	10.8
Deferred Taxes	.7	.1	.2			.6	.0	.0	.1	.3
All Other Non-Current	2.9	5.6	4.5			.7	2.7	13.0	2.9	2.9
Net Worth	33.9	34.1	35.0			42.5	38.3	30.0	53.3	45.4
Total Liabilities & Net Worth	100.0	100.0	100.0			100.0	100.0	100.0	100.0	100.0
				INCOME DATA						
Net Sales	100.0	100.0	100.0			100.0	100.0	100.0	100.0	100.0
Gross Profit										
Operating Expenses	95.6	91.6	91.9			92.0	91.9	92.0	93.0	94.9
Operating Profit	4.4	8.4	8.1			8.0	8.1	8.0	7.0	5.1
All Other Expenses (net)	1.3	1.3	.5			.0	.3	.6	.5	.3
Profit Before Taxes	3.1	7.1	7.6			8.0	7.8	7.3	6.4	4.8
				RATIOS						
Current	2.7	3.1	3.8			2.5	3.7	3.2	4.8	3.9
	1.5	1.7	1.8			1.2	2.4	2.0	2.6	1.7
	1.1	1.2	1.1			1.0	1.3	1.1	1.5	1.2
Quick	1.8	2.3	2.7			2.5	3.6	2.4	3.0	2.9
	1.1	1.2	1.2			.9	1.8	1.1	1.5	1.3
	.7	.8	.7			.4	.8	.7	.8	1.0
Sales/Receivables	33 11.0	20 18.2	23 15.9			12 29.2	0 UND	24 15.4	25 14.8	47 7.8
	45 8.1	39 9.3	45 8.2			40 9.2	46 7.9	49 7.4	38 9.6	54 6.7
	57 6.4	57 6.4	59 6.2			45 8.2	63 5.8	58 6.3	61 6.0	65 5.6
Cost of Sales/Inventory										
Cost of Sales/Payables										
Sales/Working Capital	6.1	4.7	4.8			9.4	4.6	4.7	4.8	4.6
	11.2	11.2	10.4			28.4	9.0	14.9	8.0	8.6
	34.6	41.3	38.7			64.0	42.4	43.2	24.9	27.6
EBIT/Interest	41.4	25.6	38.7			43.6		17.8	50.8	55.7
	(72) 4.7	(81) 6.8	(66) 9.7			(12) 9.7		(15) 7.5	(16) 15.2	(13) 12.1
	.7	1.6	4.3			4.4		4.8	4.5	1.1
Net Profit + Depr., Dep., Amort./Cur. Mat. L/T/D	11.5	6.2	13.0							
	(14) 6.6	(13) 1.5	(13) 5.4							
	2.0	-.4	2.2							
Fixed/Worth	.1	.2	.1			.1	.0	.2	.0	.1
	.5	.4	.3			.4	.1	.8	.2	.2
	2.3	2.2	1.0			1.0	.5	-8.6	.4	3.6
Debt/Worth	.6	.5	.5			1.1	.4	.5	.3	.5
	2.4	1.7	1.3			1.8	.9	1.0	.7	2.1
	16.7	7.8	4.6			4.2	NM	-198.4	3.3	11.2
% Profit Before Taxes/Tangible Net Worth	46.2	59.2	63.2			81.1		51.8	68.2	55.2
	(63) 23.0	(87) 30.6	(68) 37.7			52.6		(13) 36.9	(18) 35.1	(12) 34.1
	2.5	10.9	16.7			8.8		15.1	20.5	11.2
% Profit Before Taxes/Total Assets	22.3	24.8	25.7			31.1	46.9	21.3	25.6	16.5
	4.7	10.5	16.0			14.5	41.3	12.8	21.6	13.5
	-.8	2.5	3.2			.9	13.6	4.0	5.8	1.0
Sales/Net Fixed Assets	66.2	65.3	146.3			320.2	288.9	56.0	129.9	104.9
	21.4	21.8	35.9			27.0	80.6	18.9	48.4	32.0
	10.6	10.5	16.4			9.3	31.4	12.0	21.6	15.6
Sales/Total Assets	4.0	4.1	4.8			4.6	8.1	3.1	4.9	4.5
	2.7	2.8	2.9			2.8	3.2	2.6	2.9	2.5
	1.8	1.7	1.9			1.6	2.9	1.7	2.4	1.7
% Depr., Dep., Amort./Sales	.7	.6	.3					1.2	.1	.2
	(56) 1.4	(68) 1.5	(46) 1.2					(11) 2.5	(11) .6	(11) 1.3
	2.9	2.9	2.6					3.1	1.2	1.9
% Officers', Directors' Owners' Comp/Sales	2.3	3.2	2.2						.6	
	(31) 4.9	(37) 6.7	(35) 4.0						(10) 2.0	
	8.0	12.0	6.6						3.4	
Net Sales ($)	1521079M	1566972M	1525726M		2706M	27627M	38156M	137798M	311134M	1008305M
Total Assets ($)	903608M	618241M	638778M		1072M	14086M	9540M	67551M	116608M	429921M

© RMA 2019   M = $ thousand   MM = $ million
See Pages viii through xx for Explanation of Ratios and Data

Current Data Sorted by Assets   **Comparative Historical Data**

							Type of Statement		
	2	3	4	7	3	4	Unqualified	36	30
	4	12	20	7			Reviewed	53	39
	33	54	23	1	1	1	Compiled	52	65
	31	65	20	2	6	5	Tax Returns	175	158
			74	30			Other	197	225
	42 (4/1-9/30/18)			370 (10/1/18-3/31/19)				4/1/14-3/31/15	4/1/15-3/31/16
	0-500M	500M-2MM	2-10MM	10-50MM	50-100MM	100-250MM		ALL	ALL
NUMBER OF STATEMENTS	70	134	141	47	10	10		513	517
	%	%	%	%	%	%	**ASSETS**	%	%
	29.8	15.5	10.1	10.8	6.8	6.3	Cash & Equivalents	12.7	14.4
	18.8	29.5	34.5	28.1	25.1	24.3	Trade Receivables (net)	28.5	29.1
	13.6	21.1	22.9	15.7	15.4	21.4	Inventory	18.9	18.5
	3.8	2.4	2.9	5.0	3.8	7.7	All Other Current	2.8	2.9
	66.0	68.5	70.4	59.6	51.0	59.8	Total Current	62.9	64.9
	25.5	24.5	18.9	25.9	20.6	11.0	Fixed Assets (net)	24.9	24.1
	1.0	2.8	5.2	6.9	18.7	17.0	Intangibles (net)	5.4	4.6
	7.5	4.3	5.5	7.6	9.7	12.2	All Other Non-Current	6.9	6.5
	100.0	100.0	100.0	100.0	100.0	100.0	Total	100.0	100.0
							LIABILITIES		
	16.4	12.8	10.3	9.0	15.9	14.4	Notes Payable-Short Term	12.2	12.8
	7.1	5.3	3.8	3.5	2.3	6.2	Cur. Mat.-L.T.D.	3.9	3.4
	9.4	15.4	14.3	12.7	5.9	12.5	Trade Payables	13.7	11.7
	.1	.2	.3	.7	.0	.1	Income Taxes Payable	.3	.2
	16.4	8.6	9.8	13.7	8.4	7.5	All Other Current	10.2	12.0
	49.4	42.2	38.4	38.9	32.6	40.7	Total Current	40.3	40.1
	23.3	24.2	13.3	14.5	31.1	46.0	Long-Term Debt	20.5	17.6
	.0	.0	.2	.7	.6	1.0	Deferred Taxes	.5	.4
	6.1	3.9	5.0	6.4	2.1	4.4	All Other Non-Current	6.5	6.4
	21.2	29.7	43.1	39.5	33.6	7.9	Net Worth	32.2	35.5
	100.0	100.0	100.0	100.0	100.0	100.0	Total Liabilities & Net Worth	100.0	100.0
							INCOME DATA		
	100.0	100.0	100.0	100.0	100.0	100.0	Net Sales	100.0	100.0
							Gross Profit		
	91.4	92.9	94.0	91.9	95.3	95.7	Operating Expenses	92.5	92.4
	8.6	7.1	6.0	8.1	4.7	4.3	Operating Profit	7.5	7.6
	1.9	.9	.5	1.2	2.0	1.1	All Other Expenses (net)	1.1	1.0
	6.7	6.2	5.5	6.9	2.7	3.1	Profit Before Taxes	6.4	6.6
							RATIOS		
	3.8	3.4	3.2	2.8	2.6	2.3		2.9	3.6
	1.8	1.7	1.8	1.5	1.8	1.7	Current	1.8	1.8
	1.0	1.1	1.2	1.1	1.4	1.2		1.1	1.1
	3.0	2.4	2.1	2.1	1.9	1.6		2.1	2.4
	1.1	1.1	1.2	1.1	1.1	.8	Quick	1.1 (516)	1.1
	.5	.5	.6	.6	.3	.4		.6	.6
	0 UND	12 31.3	35 10.5	38 9.6	27 13.6	0 UND		20 18.3	21 17.2
	8 46.5	33 11.0	51 7.2	59 6.2	66 5.5	57 6.4	Sales/Receivables	40 9.2	40 9.2
	32 11.3	49 7.4	69 5.3	78 4.7	85 4.3	70 5.2		56 6.5	57 6.4
							Cost of Sales/Inventory		
							Cost of Sales/Payables		
	8.0	6.0	4.6	4.5	3.4	7.4		5.7	5.1
	17.4	13.2	7.9	7.5	4.8	11.5	Sales/Working Capital	10.5	10.2
	-547.7	68.2	22.8	40.5	NM	NM		43.8	47.4
	32.1	21.7	27.0	17.5	8.6	9.9		20.9	25.1
	(48) 9.8	(118) 6.2	(125) 7.3	(42) 6.1	4.0	3.3	EBIT/Interest	(445) 6.9	(439) 7.5
	.1	1.0	2.4	2.5	.9	2.7		2.1	2.0
			9.2					8.2	7.2
		(15) 3.3					Net Profit + Depr., Dep., Amort./Cur. Mat. L/T/D	(72) 2.9	(53) 3.8
			1.1					1.3	1.8
	.1	.1	.1	.4	.4	.4		.2	.2
	.6	.6	.4	.7	.7	2.7	Fixed/Worth	.6	.5
	3.5	5.1	1.0	2.5	NM	-.2		3.1	2.2
	.6	.7	.7	.7	1.4	3.7		.7	.5
	2.6	2.5	1.5	2.2	5.0	21.2	Debt/Worth	1.8	1.8
	-104.3	19.4	3.5	5.5	NM	-2.2		10.5	7.5
	138.2	90.6	65.6	49.5				67.8	70.9
	(52) 72.9	(108) 39.4	(129) 28.0	(39) 26.6			% Profit Before Taxes/Tangible Net Worth	(421) 30.3	(434) 27.3
	22.0	7.2	14.4	6.9				10.3	8.8
	52.6	27.2	23.7	16.7	10.7	15.3		23.9	24.7
	19.0	11.7	9.9	7.2	5.2	8.3	% Profit Before Taxes/Total Assets	10.4	9.8
	-2.7	.3	3.2	2.5	-.1	5.0		2.5	2.2
	150.1	62.6	61.9	15.5	25.9	57.6		47.2	55.6
	35.9	22.2	20.0	8.4	13.6	21.7	Sales/Net Fixed Assets	17.2	16.8
	8.3	6.1	8.2	3.6	7.1	14.1		6.8	6.8
	6.3	4.1	3.3	2.2	2.7	3.6		3.7	3.9
	4.5	3.1	2.4	1.6	1.4	2.1	Sales/Total Assets	2.6	2.6
	2.8	2.0	1.5	.9	1.0	1.8		1.7	1.6
	.4	1.0	.8	1.3				.7	.7
	(33) 1.4	(67) 1.7	(94) 1.7	(39) 2.3			% Depr., Dep., Amort./Sales	(374) 1.7	(355) 1.9
	3.4	3.2	2.8	4.5				3.5	3.4
	4.5	2.1	1.4					2.2	2.1
	(38) 8.9	(82) 4.1	(58) 1.9				% Officers', Directors' Owners' Comp/Sales	(248) 4.6	(238) 4.8
	14.7	7.0	4.1					7.6	8.4
	98696M	501407M	1616889M	1668843M	1411242M	7418108M	Net Sales ($)	10865912M	12168142M
	20050M	154769M	655686M	1038233M	628841M	1939151M	Total Assets ($)	4978464M	5037809M

© RMA 2019   M = $ thousand   MM = $ million

See Pages viii through xx for Explanation of Ratios and Data

Comparative Historical Data | Current Data Sorted by Sales

			Type of Statement						
25	17	18	Unqualified			1	2		15
40	33	32	Reviewed	1	2	2	5	15	7
41	43	40	Compiled	3	9	6	10	12	
127	145	111	Tax Returns	16	40	16	25	9	5
205	217	211	Other	22	37	38	38	46	30
4/1/16-3/31/17 ALL	4/1/17-3/31/18 ALL	4/1/18-3/31/19 ALL		42 (4/1-9/30/18)			370 (10/1/18-3/31/19)		
				0-1MM	1-3MM	3-5MM	5-10MM	10-25MM	25MM & OVER
438	455	412	NUMBER OF STATEMENTS	42	88	63	80	82	57
%	%	%	ASSETS	%	%	%	%	%	%
12.1	14.2	15.1	Cash & Equivalents	27.7	17.8	17.5	13.1	9.1	10.6
28.4	28.5	29.0	Trade Receivables (net)	16.9	22.4	27.0	36.2	34.8	32.1
19.4	18.9	19.7	Inventory	13.6	18.0	20.0	21.0	25.4	16.5
2.2	2.2	3.2	All Other Current	4.0	2.4	3.8	2.0	3.3	5.1
62.2	63.8	67.1	Total Current	62.1	60.5	68.2	72.2	72.7	64.3
26.5	25.3	22.5	Fixed Assets (net)	29.6	29.7	19.4	20.6	18.5	18.1
4.9	4.8	4.5	Intangibles (net)	.7	3.9	6.6	3.0	3.2	9.8
6.4	6.2	5.9	All Other Non-Current	7.5	6.0	5.7	4.2	5.6	7.9
100.0	100.0	100.0	Total	100.0	100.0	100.0	100.0	100.0	100.0
			LIABILITIES						
13.3	12.7	12.2	Notes Payable-Short Term	9.8	15.6	11.4	11.8	12.7	9.9
4.2	3.9	4.8	Cur. Mat.-L.T.D.	9.2	4.6	4.1	5.6	3.4	3.6
13.0	11.8	13.4	Trade Payables	7.1	10.3	14.5	17.0	15.7	13.0
.5	.2	.2	Income Taxes Payable	.0	.1	.0	.7	.1	.1
12.1	10.5	10.9	All Other Current	13.9	9.7	10.3	9.1	11.7	12.4
43.1	39.2	41.5	Total Current	40.0	40.3	40.3	44.1	43.6	39.0
20.1	19.8	19.9	Long-Term Debt	28.0	25.4	21.5	16.2	11.4	21.2
.3	.2	.2	Deferred Taxes	.0	.0	.0	.2	.4	.6
6.4	7.2	4.9	All Other Non-Current	10.8	4.4	5.5	2.9	5.3	2.8
30.0	33.5	33.5	Net Worth	21.2	29.9	32.7	36.5	39.4	36.4
100.0	100.0	100.0	Total Liabilities & Net Worth	100.0	100.0	100.0	100.0	100.0	100.0
			INCOME DATA						
100.0	100.0	100.0	Net Sales	100.0	100.0	100.0	100.0	100.0	100.0
			Gross Profit						
93.6	92.5	93.0	Operating Expenses	84.1	93.6	92.7	96.0	94.2	93.1
6.4	7.5	7.0	Operating Profit	15.9	6.4	7.3	4.0	5.8	6.9
1.1	1.3	1.0	All Other Expenses (net)	5.1	.3	.4	.2	.9	.8
5.4	6.2	6.0	Profit Before Taxes	10.7	6.1	6.8	3.8	4.9	6.1
			RATIOS						
3.1	3.0	3.3	Current	3.8	4.7	3.4	2.9	2.5	2.8
1.6	1.8	1.7		1.9	2.2	1.7	1.7	1.7	1.7
1.0	1.1	1.1		1.0	.9	1.2	1.1	1.2	1.3
2.1	2.3	2.3	Quick	2.4	3.3	2.8	2.0	1.8	2.2
1.0	1.1	1.1		1.2	1.1	1.1	1.3	1.1	1.1
.6	.6	.6		.6	.4	.5	.7	.6	.5
22 16.7	18 20.4	19 18.8	Sales/Receivables	0 UND	4 98.9	10 34.8	27 13.7	36 10.0	32 11.5
40 9.2	37 9.9	40 9.1		7 49.6	29 12.4	38 9.6	42 8.7	51 7.2	54 6.7
59 6.2	55 6.6	62 5.9		50 7.3	46 8.0	58 6.3	62 5.9	72 5.1	72 5.1
			Cost of Sales/Inventory						
			Cost of Sales/Payables						
5.5	5.6	5.1	Sales/Working Capital	3.7	5.1	4.8	5.4	5.4	4.8
11.7	10.3	10.5		10.1	13.5	9.2	13.1	9.4	8.5
UND	41.6	44.2		UND	-77.3	47.9	52.1	23.2	22.7
19.1	23.4	20.5	EBIT/Interest	19.4	22.2	20.2	30.5	21.1	16.0
(387) 5.4	(377) 7.5	(353) 6.6		(27) 6.6	(71) 7.1	(53) 5.5	(75) 6.2	(75) 6.7	(52) 7.2
1.3	2.5	1.9		.4	1.1	2.1	1.7	2.4	3.2
5.7	9.1	10.4	Net Profit + Depr., Dep., Amort./Cur. Mat. L/T/D					10.2	14.8
(52) 2.4	(50) 2.5	(37) 4.6						(10) 4.7	(15) 4.6
.7	1.1	1.9						2.6	2.1
.3	.2	.1	Fixed/Worth	.0	.2	.1	.1	.2	.3
.7	.6	.6		.6	.9	.5	.5	.5	.6
3.0	2.1	2.3		3.7	5.5	5.7	1.5	1.1	1.3
.7	.6	.7	Debt/Worth	.6	.5	.8	.6	.7	.7
2.1	1.7	2.1		2.5	2.1	2.4	1.8	1.9	2.5
11.2	8.8	7.2		17.9	60.3	9.9	6.1	4.1	9.4
70.6	70.8	74.5	% Profit Before Taxes/Tangible Net Worth	130.5	85.8	101.2	81.2	64.8	68.9
(350) 24.7	(378) 29.4	(342) 32.6		(33) 30.8	(67) 41.5	(49) 49.0	(70) 26.8	(75) 27.0	(48) 31.9
6.6	11.4	12.6		14.7	11.5	14.6	4.1	8.7	20.4
22.5	24.3	26.0	% Profit Before Taxes/Total Assets	44.2	28.1	30.7	24.9	22.4	22.7
7.1	9.5	10.5		11.9	15.0	11.9	9.3	9.1	9.6
1.1	2.8	2.5		-.1	.8	2.5	2.2	2.3	5.4
42.7	53.8	61.9	Sales/Net Fixed Assets	174.1	49.9	100.4	62.7	60.2	43.5
15.3	18.2	19.7		14.4	14.1	33.0	25.7	19.6	15.4
5.1	6.2	6.9		1.6	5.5	8.0	9.3	7.2	8.4
3.8	4.1	3.9	Sales/Total Assets	3.9	4.7	5.1	4.0	3.3	3.4
2.6	2.7	2.7		2.1	2.9	2.5	3.2	2.5	2.2
1.6	1.7	1.6		.7	1.9	1.6	2.1	1.6	1.6
.9	.9	.9	% Depr., Dep., Amort./Sales	.8	1.0	.7	1.0	.8	.8
(300) 2.0	(292) 2.0	(247) 1.7		(17) 3.1	(49) 1.8	(31) 1.4	(48) 1.9	(59) 1.6	(43) 1.4
4.3	3.8	3.1		15.3	3.5	2.4	3.3	3.0	2.8
2.2	2.3	1.8	% Officers', Directors' Owners' Comp/Sales	6.2	4.4	1.8	1.5	1.4	.8
(201) 4.4	(205) 4.6	(188) 3.9		(15) 14.3	(51) 7.0	(37) 3.7	(41) 3.0	(33) 1.9	(11) 1.7
8.6	8.1	7.0		19.5	9.3	4.8	4.3	3.9	4.5
8175899M	8953986M	12715185M	Net Sales ($)	23840M	172303M	233524M	573343M	1205030M	10507145M
4452576M	4608879M	4436730M	Total Assets ($)	19197M	76464M	130745M	245200M	657786M	3307338M

© RMA 2019

M = $ thousand   MM = $ million
See Pages viii through xx for Explanation of Ratios and Data

Current Data Sorted by Assets   Comparative Historical Data

							Type of Statement		
			1				Unqualified	4	
			2				Reviewed	3	3
		2	2				Compiled	6	6
21	16	2	2	2		1	Tax Returns	63	59
11	15		7	3		1	Other	39	38
	5 (4/1-9/30/18)			81 (10/1/18-3/31/19)				4/1/14-3/31/15	4/1/15-3/31/16
0-500M	500M-2MM	2-10MM	10-50MM	50-100MM	100-250MM			ALL	ALL
32	33	14	5		2		NUMBER OF STATEMENTS	115	106
%	%	%	%	%	%		ASSETS	%	%
34.0	16.8	17.6					Cash & Equivalents	21.5	25.4
17.4	25.7	29.8					Trade Receivables (net)	16.9	16.9
12.0	6.0	3.6					Inventory	16.1	12.5
.5	2.4	5.3					All Other Current	2.8	5.8
63.9	50.8	56.3					Total Current	57.2	60.5
17.3	28.6	29.4					Fixed Assets (net)	27.5	23.4
10.6	11.0	4.6					Intangibles (net)	5.4	6.7
8.2	9.5	9.7					All Other Non-Current	9.8	9.4
100.0	100.0	100.0					Total	100.0	100.0
							LIABILITIES		
20.8	5.4	16.8					Notes Payable-Short Term	13.1	13.5
2.7	4.9	2.0					Cur. Mat.-L.T.D.	3.5	4.3
5.3	9.8	5.7					Trade Payables	12.5	10.9
.0	1.3	.3					Income Taxes Payable	.0	.1
23.3	9.8	14.4					All Other Current	15.4	16.3
52.2	31.2	39.2					Total Current	44.6	45.1
17.3	25.2	10.8					Long-Term Debt	25.1	21.7
.0	.0	.0					Deferred Taxes	.2	.0
4.6	7.2	10.8					All Other Non-Current	13.4	8.0
26.1	36.3	39.2					Net Worth	16.8	25.2
100.0	100.0	100.0					Total Liabilities & Net Worth	100.0	100.0
							INCOME DATA		
100.0	100.0	100.0					Net Sales	100.0	100.0
							Gross Profit		
92.9	86.6	89.3					Operating Expenses	90.2	90.6
7.1	13.4	10.7					Operating Profit	9.8	9.4
1.1	2.2	2.2					All Other Expenses (net)	2.1	1.1
5.9	11.1	8.4					Profit Before Taxes	7.7	8.3
							RATIOS		
4.2	6.4	8.6						3.7	8.7
1.9	2.1	2.7					Current	1.4	2.3
.8	.7	.7						.7	.8
3.0	5.7	8.4						3.1	6.3
1.5	1.4	2.4					Quick	1.0	1.5
.6	.4	.6						.2	.4
0 UND	5 68.7	0 UND						0 UND	0 UND
4 91.6	17 21.0	26 13.9					Sales/Receivables	5 67.5	4 82.3
24 15.5	38 9.7	73 5.0						26 13.9	26 14.3
							Cost of Sales/Inventory		
							Cost of Sales/Payables		
10.1	5.8	4.2						7.4	4.6
30.3	17.0	10.7					Sales/Working Capital	23.1	17.0
-72.9	-17.5	-42.5						-28.5	-95.4
30.4	57.8	84.5						26.6	42.3
(15) .9	(25) 3.6	(11) 21.5					EBIT/Interest	(89) 6.2	(73) 10.2
-13.2	2.3	6.7						2.2	2.5
							Net Profit + Depr., Dep., Amort./Cur. Mat. L/T/D		
.0	.1	.2						.1	.1
.4	1.3	.8					Fixed/Worth	.6	.5
NM	-2.3	3.2						110.9	5.8
.5	.4	.4						.8	.4
1.8	1.0	1.1					Debt/Worth	2.2	1.5
-6.2	-4.9	4.6						-8.3	341.5
162.0	75.4	85.9						102.2	105.3
(22) 75.3	(21) 46.7	(12) 50.4					% Profit Before Taxes/Tangible Net Worth	(84) 41.3	(82) 52.6
30.4	11.1	10.7						11.5	9.8
81.1	48.7	39.3						45.3	51.8
29.4	14.2	15.9					% Profit Before Taxes/Total Assets	13.7	18.6
-1.4	3.0	3.0						3.5	2.4
UND	39.9	56.8						112.0	87.8
41.6	16.7	15.0					Sales/Net Fixed Assets	29.8	29.0
14.7	5.7	6.0						8.7	13.0
13.8	4.3	6.7						6.3	6.3
5.1	2.6	2.6					Sales/Total Assets	4.1	3.9
3.6	1.6	1.1						2.1	2.4
.6	1.9	.8						.5	.6
(13) 1.4	(14) 2.9	(11) 1.7					% Depr., Dep., Amort./Sales	(62) 1.1	(58) 1.2
2.5	5.8	3.6						4.2	2.8
5.7	2.8							2.7	2.5
(16) 10.0	(16) 3.4						% Officers', Directors' Owners' Comp/Sales	(66) 5.1	(65) 5.7
19.2	4.8							9.7	12.7
24826M	115869M	286104M	1380477M		1461787M		Net Sales ($)	771449M	2372840M
5198M	37181M	58513M	108120M		397309M		Total Assets ($)	295155M	129419M

M = $ thousand   MM = $ million
See Pages viii through xx for Explanation of Ratios and Data

Comparative Historical Data | Current Data Sorted by Sales

Hist 1	Hist 2	Hist 3	Type of Statement	0-1MM	1-3MM	3-5MM	5-10MM	10-25MM	25MM & OVER
			Unqualified					1	
			Reviewed		2				2
1	1	1	Compiled						
4	4	2	Tax Returns	19	13	3	3	2	4
42	41	4	Other	8	10	6	6	5	2
36	56	42							
		37							
4/1/16-3/31/17 ALL	4/1/17-3/31/18 ALL	4/1/18-3/31/19 ALL			5 (4/1-9/30/18)		81 (10/1/18-3/31/19)		
83	102	86	NUMBER OF STATEMENTS	27	25	10	9	7	8
%	%	%	ASSETS	%	%	%	%	%	%
27.4	19.9	24.1	Cash & Equivalents	34.4	16.4	17.5			
18.9	18.7	22.8	Trade Receivables (net)	13.9	26.8	26.5			
7.1	9.9	7.6	Inventory	13.3	2.0	9.1			
4.8	2.4	2.0	All Other Current	.1	3.1	1.0			
58.1	50.9	56.6	Total Current	61.8	48.3	54.1			
30.5	30.6	25.0	Fixed Assets (net)	24.6	24.7	21.8			
5.2	8.8	9.1	Intangibles (net)	9.3	14.1	8.4			
6.2	9.6	9.4	All Other Non-Current	4.4	12.9	15.7			
100.0	100.0	100.0	Total	100.0	100.0	100.0			
			LIABILITIES						
8.5	14.8	18.6	Notes Payable-Short Term	22.4	7.6	4.3			
4.9	3.9	3.8	Cur. Mat.-L.T.D.	2.1	4.8	4.1			
6.7	8.1	8.0	Trade Payables	3.3	5.1	10.2			
.0	.1	.6	Income Taxes Payable	.0	1.8	.0			
18.3	14.9	16.0	All Other Current	21.6	11.3	14.0			
38.3	41.8	47.0	Total Current	49.4	30.6	32.6			
30.6	29.8	19.2	Long-Term Debt	24.0	18.5	16.8			
.0	.2	.0	Deferred Taxes	.0	.0	.0			
3.9	3.2	6.7	All Other Non-Current	2.5	9.5	4.7			
27.1	24.9	27.1	Net Worth	24.2	41.4	46.0			
100.0	100.0	100.0	Total Liabilities & Net Worth	100.0	100.0	100.0			
			INCOME DATA						
100.0	100.0	100.0	Net Sales	100.0	100.0	100.0			
			Gross Profit						
89.6	90.4	89.8	Operating Expenses	87.2	88.3	91.8			
10.4	9.6	10.2	Operating Profit	12.8	11.7	8.2			
1.1	1.2	1.7	All Other Expenses (net)	3.3	1.9	.0			
9.2	8.4	8.5	Profit Before Taxes	9.4	9.8	8.2			
			RATIOS						
7.6	3.7	6.2	Current	4.5	10.6	9.0			
2.1	1.3	1.9		2.0	1.9	4.8			
.9	.7	.7		.4	.7	1.0			
6.3	2.9	5.4	Quick	3.1	9.3	8.6			
1.5	1.0	1.5		1.5	1.9	4.7			
.6	.4	.5		.3	.5	.8			
0 UND	0 UND	0 UND	Sales/Receivables	0 UND	1 270.1	16 22.9			
10 38.3	10 35.2	15 25.0		0 UND	18 20.4	18 19.9			
31 11.6	31 11.7	34 10.7		16 23.5	62 5.9	33 10.9			
			Cost of Sales/Inventory						
			Cost of Sales/Payables						
6.1	8.8	6.5	Sales/Working Capital	9.8	4.3	6.4			
13.9	57.3	18.7		35.0	19.7	7.9			
-88.2	-28.8	-39.2		-12.9	-32.7	NM			
46.2	17.3	46.8	EBIT/Interest	20.8	84.3				
(58) 8.5	(75) 7.5	(57) 8.0		(13) 2.4	(17) 7.0				
2.7	2.5	1.4		-6.5	2.3				
			Net Profit + Depr., Dep., Amort./Cur. Mat. L/T/D						
.2	.3	.1	Fixed/Worth	.0	.1	.1			
.7	1.4	.6		.6	1.0	.6			
-43.4	2.2	2.5		14.0	-2.1	-25.5			
.3	.5	.5	Debt/Worth	.6	.4	.3			
1.8	2.1	1.5		1.8	1.5	.6			
-15.4	-9.5	-6.2		-6.2	-4.0	-89.8			
131.5	133.1	95.3	% Profit Before Taxes/Tangible Net Worth	129.8	79.5				
(60) 59.5	(71) 70.0	(60) 53.6		(19) 72.7	(17) 52.9				
25.3	26.4	14.1		15.1	13.5				
52.7	58.4	54.4	% Profit Before Taxes/Total Assets	80.4	52.8	76.6			
27.6	24.2	21.2		29.6	13.4	17.4			
6.5	5.5	2.6		1.2	3.4	-4.4			
52.9	64.1	78.3	Sales/Net Fixed Assets	UND	278.4	106.6			
20.1	18.3	20.5		24.6	16.6	22.9			
6.2	7.6	10.0		7.3	8.3	8.6			
5.8	6.4	6.4	Sales/Total Assets	9.4	4.2	4.7			
3.4	3.9	3.7		4.4	2.6	4.1			
2.1	2.5	1.9		1.6	1.7	2.2			
.6	1.1	1.1	% Depr., Dep., Amort./Sales	.9	1.1				
(47) 1.4	(51) 2.0	(41) 2.3		(12) 2.0	(10) 2.7				
5.0	4.1	3.8		20.1	4.1				
2.6	2.6	3.2	% Officers', Directors' Owners' Comp/Sales	8.0	3.0				
(50) 5.2	(52) 4.6	(39) 5.0		(10) 13.2	(16) 4.6				
8.0	8.3	11.5		21.2	6.0				
4137714M	2020809M	3269063M	Net Sales ($)	11166M	46275M	40115M	66486M	107439M	2997582M
321840M	276771M	606321M	Total Assets ($)	9278M	22979M	14711M	18194M	45551M	495608M

© RMA 2019

M = $ thousand   MM = $ million
See Pages viii through xx for Explanation of Ratios and Data

Current Data Sorted by Assets   Comparative Historical Data

Type of Statement

	0-500M	500M-2MM	2-10MM	10-50MM	50-100MM	100-250MM		4/1/14-3/31/15 ALL	4/1/15-3/31/16 ALL
Unqualified					2			4	3
Reviewed			1	2				5	4
Compiled	1	3	4					13	12
Tax Returns	44	8	5	1				77	91
Other	24	28	17	5	4			69	77
	14 (4/1-9/30/18)			135 (10/1/18-3/31/19)					
NUMBER OF STATEMENTS	69	39	27	8	6			168	187

	0-500M %	500M-2MM %	2-10MM %	10-50MM %	50-100MM %	100-250MM %		ALL %	ALL %
ASSETS									
Cash & Equivalents	28.9	14.8	17.8			D		23.1	23.7
Trade Receivables (net)	.1	2.0	1.1			A		1.5	2.4
Inventory	13.5	6.6	6.7			T		12.0	11.2
All Other Current	1.2	5.6	2.4			A		1.6	2.5
Total Current	43.8	29.1	27.9					38.2	39.8
Fixed Assets (net)	39.0	45.2	37.4			N		39.5	40.1
Intangibles (net)	4.8	12.1	14.8			O		10.0	10.3
All Other Non-Current	12.6	13.6	19.8			T		12.2	9.8
Total	100.0	100.0	100.0					100.0	100.0
LIABILITIES						A			
Notes Payable-Short Term	14.7	6.4	3.2			V		12.3	12.8
Cur. Mat.-L.T.D.	2.7	2.0	1.7			A		3.9	3.9
Trade Payables	5.8	3.6	7.1			I		5.0	4.0
Income Taxes Payable	.0	.0	.1			L		.1	.2
All Other Current	31.5	13.3	22.7			A		22.5	22.7
Total Current	54.7	25.3	34.7			B		43.8	43.6
Long-Term Debt	34.1	34.6	25.9			L		27.2	27.4
Deferred Taxes	.0	.0	.0			E		.0	.0
All Other Non-Current	11.9	3.1	3.3					16.6	9.3
Net Worth	-.7	37.0	36.1					12.3	19.7
Total Liabilties & Net Worth	100.0	100.0	100.0					100.0	100.0
INCOME DATA									
Net Sales	100.0	100.0	100.0					100.0	100.0
Gross Profit									
Operating Expenses	92.9	86.2	93.5					93.1	92.3
Operating Profit	7.1	13.8	6.5					6.9	7.7
All Other Expenses (net)	.9	4.0	.6					1.4	1.4
Profit Before Taxes	6.2	9.8	5.8					5.5	6.3

RATIOS

	0-500M	500M-2MM	2-10MM	10-50MM	50-100MM	100-250MM		ALL	ALL
	2.7	2.0	2.1					2.3	2.6
Current	1.2	.9	.8					1.0	1.1
	.4	.3	.6					.4	.5
	1.8	1.7	1.3					1.6	1.7
Quick	(68) .7	(38) .6	.6					.6 (185)	.5
	.2	.2	.4					.2	.3
	0 UND	0 UND	0 UND					0 UND	0 UND
Sales/Receivables	0 UND	0 UND	0 UND					0 UND	0 UND
	0 UND	0 999.8	2 205.8					0 UND	0 UND
Cost of Sales/Inventory									
Cost of Sales/Payables									
	18.1	22.3	22.9					19.3	17.1
Sales/Working Capital	86.0	-103.3	-47.6					UND	781.4
	-15.9	-8.4	-19.9					-14.4	-17.7
	16.0	12.5	58.1					17.4	23.5
EBIT/Interest	(43) 3.4	(29) 3.9	(24) 23.1					(112) 5.6	(120) 6.6
	1.1	1.1	2.4					1.3	1.9
Net Profit + Depr., Dep., Amort./Cur. Mat. L/T/D									
	.2	.5	.7					.4	.3
Fixed/Worth	1.1	2.0	1.2					1.7	1.5
	104.3	-7.9	-1.7					-3.4	-7.1
	.4	.5	.4					.5	.5
Debt/Worth	2.3	1.9	3.4					3.1	2.6
	-3.2	-9.9	-6.4					-4.8	-5.0
	116.1	48.1	88.2					174.7	117.8
% Profit Before Taxes/Tangible Net Worth	(47) 47.5	(29) 27.8	(19) 27.1					(110) 58.7	(123) 39.8
	2.3	2.8	13.6					14.2	11.3
	45.0	27.9	20.5					41.8	41.3
% Profit Before Taxes/Total Assets	13.2	9.9	10.4					17.2	14.6
	-.7	.7	3.5					1.6	2.6
	91.9	14.8	20.3					36.5	49.4
Sales/Net Fixed Assets	15.9	9.3	10.5					12.6	13.0
	5.2	1.6	4.3					6.0	4.1
	10.1	4.5	3.6					7.7	7.2
Sales/Total Assets	5.1	2.0	2.2					4.1	3.8
	2.7	.8	1.1					2.3	1.8
	.7	.8	1.0					1.1	.9
% Depr., Dep., Amort./Sales	(44) 1.3	(24) 2.3	(20) 1.8					(113) 1.8	(132) 1.7
	3.2	10.3	4.6					4.0	3.8
	4.0	1.6						2.8	3.6
% Officers', Directors' Owners' Comp/Sales	(42) 6.4	(14) 2.7						(69) 6.2	(78) 6.3
	11.2	3.9						14.0	10.8
Net Sales ($)	72810M	123536M	279651M	291616M	945934M			1280622M	3514928M
Total Assets ($)	14196M	42535M	120013M	150928M	438230M			543192M	905731M

© RMA 2019

M = $ thousand   MM = $ million
See Pages viii through xx for Explanation of Ratios and Data

Comparative Historical Data | Current Data Sorted by Sales

Type of Statement									
Unqualified	3	4	2						2
Reviewed	1	1	3						3
Compiled	7	5	8	1	1	2	1	3	
Tax Returns	87	66	58	33	15	3	4	3	
Other	80	77	78	26	17	8	13	7	7
	4/1/16-3/31/17 ALL	4/1/17-3/31/18 ALL	4/1/18-3/31/19 ALL	14 (4/1-9/30/18) 0-1MM	1-3MM	3-5MM	135 (10/1/18-3/31/19) 5-10MM	10-25MM	25MM & OVER
NUMBER OF STATEMENTS	178	153	149	60	33	13	18	13	12
ASSETS	%	%	%	%	%	%	%	%	%
Cash & Equivalents	22.5	21.2	21.6	21.9	24.0	31.8	15.5	18.9	14.4
Trade Receivables (net)	1.2	1.8	1.7	.2	2.2	1.0	.8	3.0	8.4
Inventory	10.5	10.3	11.1	10.2	10.0	9.6	12.4	12.4	16.8
All Other Current	3.4	1.2	2.7	1.1	5.4	.2	5.4	3.1	2.3
Total Current	37.6	34.5	37.1	33.3	41.6	42.6	34.1	37.4	41.8
Fixed Assets (net)	43.5	46.9	40.7	46.8	36.8	33.8	30.0	37.6	47.9
Intangibles (net)	10.3	9.7	8.7	9.3	4.8	6.0	18.6	6.7	6.6
All Other Non-Current	8.6	8.8	13.5	10.7	16.9	17.6	17.3	18.3	3.6
Total	100.0	100.0	100.0	100.0	100.0	100.0	100.0	100.0	100.0
LIABILITIES									
Notes Payable-Short Term	8.5	9.9	9.6	12.0	10.4	7.5	8.4	3.0	6.2
Cur. Mat.-L.T.D.	2.9	2.8	2.2	2.1	3.1	1.2	2.8	2.5	.4
Trade Payables	4.5	5.2	6.1	5.3	2.9	13.7	6.6	3.9	11.7
Income Taxes Payable	.3	.2	.1	.0	.0	.2	.0	.0	.5
All Other Current	22.0	23.4	24.1	26.7	24.1	18.3	18.5	22.9	26.6
Total Current	38.2	41.5	42.0	46.1	40.5	40.9	36.3	32.4	45.4
Long-Term Debt	33.6	30.8	30.8	41.8	23.1	36.6	29.0	11.8	14.5
Deferred Taxes	.0	.0	.0	.0	.0	.0	.0	.0	.0
All Other Non-Current	5.9	8.6	8.3	3.1	18.0	10.2	4.4	4.7	15.5
Net Worth	22.2	19.2	18.9	9.0	18.5	12.2	30.3	51.1	24.6
Total Liabilties & Net Worth	100.0	100.0	100.0	100.0	100.0	100.0	100.0	100.0	100.0
INCOME DATA									
Net Sales	100.0	100.0	100.0	100.0	100.0	100.0	100.0	100.0	100.0
Gross Profit									
Operating Expenses	89.0	91.1	91.4	86.8	94.6	88.8	96.9	94.1	96.6
Operating Profit	11.0	8.9	8.6	13.2	5.4	11.2	3.1	5.9	3.4
All Other Expenses (net)	2.1	1.5	1.8	3.4	.9	.6	.2	-.9	2.7
Profit Before Taxes	8.9	7.4	6.9	9.8	4.5	10.6	2.9	6.8	.7
RATIOS									
Current	2.4	3.1	2.2	3.4	2.1	5.5	1.9	1.7	1.2
	1.1	1.1	1.0	.8	1.1	2.0	.9	.9	.8
	.5	.4	.4	.2	.5	.5	.7	.7	.4
Quick	1.4	1.8	1.5	2.0	1.8	5.1	.9	.8	.7
	.7	.6 (147)	.6	(58) .4	.9	1.3	.5	.7	.4
	.2	.2	.2	.2	.3	.3	.2	.5	.3
Sales/Receivables	0 UND	0 UND	0 UND	0 UND	0 UND	0 UND	0 UND	0 UND	0 UND
	0 UND	0 UND	0 UND	0 UND	0 UND	0 UND	0 UND	0 999.8	1 364.1
	0 UND	0 UND	0 UND	0 UND	0 UND	0 UND	1 455.9	2 165.9	20 18.7
Cost of Sales/Inventory									
Cost of Sales/Payables									
Sales/Working Capital	20.7	21.2	20.5	16.1	27.5	12.3	21.4	23.6	46.2
	198.3	256.0	-330.8	-49.5	96.0	34.0	-93.3	-90.4	-65.4
	-14.9	-18.6	-15.0	-7.3	-22.3	-17.4	-19.3	-32.7	-12.7
EBIT/Interest	15.3	20.7	20.7	11.0	21.6		12.1	58.1	49.9
	(115) 4.7	(110) 4.7	(109) 4.2	(31) 3.4	(28) 4.6		(17) 2.1	(12) 16.5	9.4
	1.4	1.2	1.3	1.3	.2		1.1	3.5	-1.0
Net Profit + Depr., Dep., Amort./Cur. Mat. L/T/D									
Fixed/Worth	.5	.8	.4	.3	.4	.3	.5	.6	1.3
	2.0	2.3	1.4	1.5	1.1	.6	2.5	.9	4.3
	-8.8	-5.7	104.3	12.0	-37.0	-1.4	-.4	1.3	9.4
Debt/Worth	.6	.7	.5	.4	.5	.5	.6	.3	1.8
	3.0	4.0	2.8	3.2	2.1	7.2	3.1	.8	6.6
	-8.8	-7.3	-9.2	-3.0	-93.1	-3.0	-2.7	3.4	158.9
% Profit Before Taxes/Tangible Net Worth	177.9	97.9	75.9	70.2	97.4		24.6	68.9	111.3
	(125) 61.3	(100) 48.6	(107) 32.5	(42) 30.5	(24) 50.7		(11) 10.4	(12) 21.5	(10) 32.7
	21.2	12.8	10.1	9.2	17.4		-1.1	10.4	-61.8
% Profit Before Taxes/Total Assets	47.7	41.9	28.3	37.5	32.4	27.9	15.0	26.2	16.5
	20.0	13.9	10.6	10.7	11.9	20.1	6.4	10.4	5.2
	3.8	1.1	.6	.1	-1.0	13.8	.5	3.1	-8.0
Sales/Net Fixed Assets	25.7	21.6	35.1	32.5	50.1	353.8	41.2	17.5	16.8
	10.7	8.2	11.6	6.4	12.5	15.8	12.4	12.3	5.3
	4.6	3.6	3.6	2.0	5.3	7.1	7.9	6.7	3.6
Sales/Total Assets	6.6	6.5	5.8	5.3	7.0	8.7	4.9	5.1	4.2
	3.8	3.5	3.0	2.7	3.4	2.7	3.8	3.4	2.0
	1.9	1.9	1.5	.8	1.9	1.5	1.7	2.2	1.8
% Depr., Dep., Amort./Sales	.9	.9	.8	.5	.5		.7	1.0	.9
	(114) 2.1	(102) 1.7	(98) 1.8	(36) 2.8	(24) 1.3		(13) 1.6	(10) 1.7	(10) 2.4
	4.2	4.6	4.7	6.4	3.3		4.7	2.5	10.3
% Officers', Directors' Owners' Comp/Sales	2.4	3.0	2.0	4.3	2.5		1.1		
	(78) 5.3	(58) 6.2	(67) 5.1	(27) 7.7	(19) 5.1		(10) 2.1		
	9.5	11.8	9.2	19.8	7.5		3.8		
Net Sales ($)	1477259M	1786901M	1713547M	27055M	63325M	52442M	135917M	216677M	1218131M
Total Assets ($)	492389M	573232M	765902M	23880M	27627M	22368M	62170M	81422M	548435M

M = $ thousand   MM = $ million
See Pages viii through xx for Explanation of Ratios and Data

Current Data Sorted by Assets   Comparative Historical Data

0-500M	500M-2MM	2-10MM	10-50MM	50-100MM	100-250MM		4/1/14-3/31/15 ALL	4/1/15-3/31/16 ALL
						Type of Statement		
		3		1	1	Unqualified	4	2
1	1					Reviewed		
10	2			1		Compiled		
8	5	2	1	1	1	Tax Returns	14	15
	3 (4/1-9/30/18)		35 (10/1/18-3/31/19)			Other	10	19
0-500M	500M-2MM	2-10MM	10-50MM	50-100MM	100-250MM			
19	8	5	1	3	2	**NUMBER OF STATEMENTS**	28	36
%	%	%	%	%	%	**ASSETS**	%	%
31.0						Cash & Equivalents	23.4	24.7
5.5						Trade Receivables (net)	3.7	4.5
1.7						Inventory	5.1	4.7
9.7						All Other Current	4.4	3.3
47.9						Total Current	36.6	37.1
39.2						Fixed Assets (net)	45.6	37.4
11.1						Intangibles (net)	10.8	12.5
1.8						All Other Non-Current	7.0	13.0
100.0						Total	100.0	100.0
						LIABILITIES		
26.3						Notes Payable-Short Term	13.4	14.2
1.4						Cur. Mat.-L.T.D.	2.9	4.7
4.0						Trade Payables	5.9	7.0
.0						Income Taxes Payable	.0	.0
19.7						All Other Current	7.1	25.9
51.4						Total Current	29.3	51.8
6.1						Long-Term Debt	37.2	32.3
.0						Deferred Taxes	.1	.3
27.2						All Other Non-Current	13.2	9.0
15.5						Net Worth	20.2	6.6
100.0						Total Liabilties & Net Worth	100.0	100.0
						INCOME DATA		
100.0						Net Sales	100.0	100.0
						Gross Profit		
85.0						Operating Expenses	90.6	90.4
15.0						Operating Profit	9.4	9.6
.2						All Other Expenses (net)	1.8	1.1
14.7						Profit Before Taxes	7.6	8.5
						RATIOS		
3.7							5.3	2.1
1.0						Current	1.7	.9
.4							.4	.3
2.8							3.2	1.5
.5						Quick	.9	.6
.3							.1	.2
0 UND							0 UND	0 UND
0 UND						Sales/Receivables	0 UND	0 UND
0 UND							4 81.7	4 94.5
						Cost of Sales/Inventory		
						Cost of Sales/Payables		
10.1							14.1	16.7
UND						Sales/Working Capital	51.2	-280.2
-18.6							-57.7	-10.3
							8.8	29.6
						EBIT/Interest	(20) 5.0	(28) 10.9
							1.6	1.6
						Net Profit + Depr., Dep., Amort./Cur. Mat. L/T/D		
.6							.4	.4
1.6						Fixed/Worth	2.8	2.2
-1.3							-1.1	-.5
.2							.3	.6
1.2						Debt/Worth	4.6	2.7
-3.6							-3.6	-2.0
434.1							265.9	121.5
(14) 100.1						% Profit Before Taxes/Tangible Net Worth	(17) 97.8	(20) 58.3
18.2							36.3	14.6
106.6							45.5	74.0
52.3						% Profit Before Taxes/Total Assets	25.8	30.4
-9.1							6.4	3.5
269.0							29.6	30.6
9.7						Sales/Net Fixed Assets	10.8	17.5
6.7							3.4	6.3
9.5							6.9	7.5
5.3						Sales/Total Assets	3.6	4.2
3.2							1.7	1.7
							.6	.8
						% Depr., Dep., Amort./Sales	(18) 1.8	(25) 2.3
							5.9	3.1
							1.1	3.3
						% Officers', Directors' Owners' Comp/Sales	(10) 1.9	(13) 6.6
							9.0	13.4
13371M	18334M	41205M	4867M	482315M	1383772M	Net Sales ($)	867410M	1442691M
2951M	8570M	26341M	17825M	201427M	399622M	Total Assets ($)	400775M	503718M

© RMA 2019

M = $ thousand   MM = $ million
See Pages viii through xx for Explanation of Ratios and Data

Comparative Historical Data | Current Data Sorted by Sales

4/1/16-3/31/17 ALL	4/1/17-3/31/18 ALL	4/1/18-3/31/19 ALL	Type of Statement	0-1MM	1-3MM	3-5MM	5-10MM	10-25MM	25MM & OVER
1	1	2	Unqualified					1	1
		3	Reviewed				2	1	
	2	2	Compiled						
11	14	13	Tax Returns	9	2	1			1
12	8	18	Other	3	9	2	2		2
				3 (4/1-9/30/18)			35 (10/1/18-3/31/19)		
24	25	38	**NUMBER OF STATEMENTS**	14	11	3	4	2	4
%	%	%	**ASSETS**	%	%	%	%	%	%
16.8	24.6	24.8	Cash & Equivalents	39.0	5.9				
4.2	3.1	4.5	Trade Receivables (net)	2.1	6.7				
9.6	4.4	5.8	Inventory	1.3	10.2				
2.5	4.3	8.6	All Other Current	5.2	18.6				
33.2	36.4	43.6	Total Current	47.7	41.5				
38.4	36.5	38.2	Fixed Assets (net)	45.4	34.5				
15.7	23.2	15.0	Intangibles (net)	5.2	21.5				
12.8	3.9	3.3	All Other Non-Current	1.8	2.4				
100.0	100.0	100.0	Total	100.0	100.0				
			LIABILITIES						
30.9	4.2	15.4	Notes Payable-Short Term	34.9	4.2				
3.2	8.0	2.3	Cur. Mat.-L.T.D.	1.5	2.9				
8.9	6.2	5.4	Trade Payables	3.8	4.3				
.0	.1	.0	Income Taxes Payable	.0	.0				
35.9	25.6	21.3	All Other Current	16.1	30.7				
78.9	44.2	44.4	Total Current	56.4	42.2				
24.6	26.9	18.9	Long-Term Debt	10.4	22.7				
.0	.5	.0	Deferred Taxes	.0	.0				
17.8	22.2	30.8	All Other Non-Current	37.0	.6				
-21.2	6.2	6.1	Net Worth	-3.5	34.6				
100.0	100.0	100.0	Total Liabilities & Net Worth	100.0	100.0				
			INCOME DATA						
100.0	100.0	100.0	Net Sales	100.0	100.0				
			Gross Profit						
95.6	91.7	90.6	Operating Expenses	83.9	88.1				
4.4	8.3	9.4	Operating Profit	16.1	11.9				
2.1	2.4	1.9	All Other Expenses (net)	.7	2.2				
2.4	5.9	7.5	Profit Before Taxes	15.3	9.6				
			RATIOS						
1.1	2.5	2.8		2.6	6.8				
.6	.8	.9	Current	1.0	.9				
.4	.3	.4		.4	.4				
.7	1.5	2.2		2.6	2.6				
.4	.7	.5	Quick	.5	.3				
.2	.2	.2		.3	.0				
0 UND	0 UND	0 UND		0 UND	0 UND				
0 UND	0 UND	0 UND	Sales/Receivables	0 UND	0 UND				
4 103.4	2 213.7	1 501.0		0 UND	0 UND				
			Cost of Sales/Inventory						
			Cost of Sales/Payables						
NM	13.2	9.0		16.1	9.8				
-33.9	-55.4	-171.4	Sales/Working Capital	UND	-92.9				
-7.0	-6.0	-14.1		-14.1	-3.6				
20.1	4.0	26.9							
(15) 2.9	(12) 1.6	(18) 1.2	EBIT/Interest						
-1.5	-.2	-.3							
			Net Profit + Depr., Dep., Amort./Cur. Mat. L/T/D						
.8	.4	.6		.7	.4				
5.1	2.0	6.1	Fixed/Worth	1.9	5.9				
-.7	-.5	-1.1		-41.6	-1.1				
.7	.9	.3		.3	.1				
NM	4.5	17.9	Debt/Worth	1.4	8.8				
-2.0	-1.4	-3.4		-43.9	-2.4				
118.6	167.8	151.4	% Profit Before Taxes/Tangible Net Worth	UND					
(12) 58.6	(14) 49.1	(22) 56.4		(10) 100.1					
7.0	10.2	27.9		-32.1					
40.9	47.9	67.4	% Profit Before Taxes/Total Assets	124.9	80.5				
9.1	8.6	27.5		35.6	38.2				
.3	-2.0	-4.4		-18.3	-.2				
23.3	23.9	33.5	Sales/Net Fixed Assets	UND	32.7				
14.2	10.2	9.2		9.0	8.4				
3.9	4.1	3.6		3.6	5.1				
6.4	5.3	5.7	Sales/Total Assets	11.2	5.3				
3.5	3.5	3.4		5.4	2.8				
1.5	1.6	1.2		2.8	1.3				
.6	.9	.9	% Depr., Dep., Amort./Sales						
(14) 1.8	(17) 3.4	(15) 4.4							
5.4	6.7	6.6							
	6.2	1.2	% Officers', Directors' Owners' Comp/Sales						
(10)	7.9	(11) 5.1							
	10.7	10.4							
1581674M	1302690M	1943864M	Net Sales ($)	4219M	16536M	11138M	28488M	37561M	1845922M
473141M	477291M	656736M	Total Assets ($)	2426M	7647M	19987M	21742M	72173M	532761M

© RMA 2019   M = $ thousand   MM = $ million
See Pages viii through xx for Explanation of Ratios and Data

Current Data Sorted by Assets   Comparative Historical Data

						Type of Statement		
		1		4	1	Unqualified	10	8
			2	1		Reviewed		2
		3				Compiled	4	7
1		4	4		1	Tax Returns	48	33
24		17	12		1	Other	48	40
22				1	1		4/1/14-	4/1/15-
	5 (4/1-9/30/18)			94 (10/1/18-3/31/19)			3/31/15	3/31/16
0-500M	500M-2MM	2-10MM	10-50MM	50-100MM	100-250MM		ALL	ALL
47	25	18	6	3		NUMBER OF STATEMENTS	110	90
%	%	%	%	%	%	ASSETS	%	%
38.1	23.5	25.4				Cash & Equivalents	23.7	23.0
1.0	.7	8.5			D	Trade Receivables (net)	4.4	3.9
6.9	2.0	4.1			A	Inventory	4.3	7.4
1.8	5.2	2.9			T	All Other Current	1.4	2.0
47.9	31.4	40.9			A	Total Current	33.8	36.4
30.0	37.2	38.9				Fixed Assets (net)	40.5	42.9
13.2	24.2	10.7			N	Intangibles (net)	13.0	10.3
9.1	7.1	9.5			O	All Other Non-Current	12.7	10.4
100.0	100.0	100.0			T	Total	100.0	100.0
					A	LIABILITIES		
8.8	3.8	2.1			V	Notes Payable-Short Term	10.4	14.4
5.5	3.2	2.8			A	Cur. Mat.-L.T.D.	3.6	3.1
3.5	3.3	5.2			I	Trade Payables	6.5	5.6
1.4	.2	.0			L	Income Taxes Payable	.1	.1
31.2	11.6	18.7			A	All Other Current	20.7	16.5
50.4	22.2	28.8			B	Total Current	41.3	39.7
51.8	42.3	23.4				Long-Term Debt	28.3	31.7
.0	.0	.0			E	Deferred Taxes	.3	.0
13.3	8.7	5.7				All Other Non-Current	15.8	12.4
-15.4	26.9	42.1				Net Worth	14.3	16.1
100.0	100.0	100.0				Total Liabilties & Net Worth	100.0	100.0
						INCOME DATA		
100.0	100.0	100.0				Net Sales	100.0	100.0
						Gross Profit		
86.6	90.4	87.8				Operating Expenses	89.5	90.7
13.4	9.6	12.2				Operating Profit	10.5	9.3
.9	3.6	3.3				All Other Expenses (net)	1.4	1.1
12.5	6.1	8.8				Profit Before Taxes	9.1	8.2
						RATIOS		
7.3	4.2	5.2					5.6	4.3
1.8	1.4	1.4				Current	1.2	1.1
.3	.8	.6					.4	.5
5.7	4.0	3.8					4.3	4.2
1.2	1.2	1.1				Quick	1.0	.6
.2	.5	.3					.3	.3
0 UND	0 UND	0 UND					0 UND	0 UND
0 UND	0 UND	0 UND				Sales/Receivables	0 UND	0 UND
0 UND	0 UND	9 42.6					4 101.3	1 386.5
						Cost of Sales/Inventory		
						Cost of Sales/Payables		
13.4	9.6	8.7					9.9	10.2
214.4	25.9	17.0				Sales/Working Capital	74.8	197.2
-16.7	-88.0	-12.9					-11.1	-12.4
23.6	17.3	38.2					15.0	19.4
(28) 8.9	(20) 3.6	(14) 6.8				EBIT/Interest	(80) 6.5	(66) 5.4
4.0	-1.7	.7					1.0	1.7
						Net Profit + Depr., Dep., Amort./Cur. Mat. L/T/D		
.3	.5	.1					.5	.6
3.4	2.5	.9				Fixed/Worth	3.5	3.4
-.4	-1.1	3.8					-2.5	-1.7
.5	.6	.5					1.0	.8
5.0	3.9	1.6				Debt/Worth	5.4	6.4
-2.2	-1.7	6.3					-5.4	-3.2
386.5	122.9	152.3					100.0	157.3
(27) 175.8	(15) 57.2	(15) 25.3				% Profit Before Taxes/Tangible Net Worth	(69) 39.8	(55) 73.9
88.9	31.8	7.8					21.8	26.2
105.4	32.6	36.2					35.4	39.6
48.6	14.8	9.6				% Profit Before Taxes/Total Assets	17.3	12.3
22.2	2.8	-1.1					1.2	1.5
72.3	25.7	37.7					18.7	18.2
23.7	6.0	7.5				Sales/Net Fixed Assets	7.2	8.6
8.5	2.2	3.5					2.9	4.1
8.3	2.3	2.9					3.6	4.7
5.5	1.5	2.0				Sales/Total Assets	2.3	2.8
3.2	1.1	.7					1.2	1.8
.5	2.1	.6					1.3	.8
(21) 1.4	(10) 3.7	(13) 2.1				% Depr., Dep., Amort./Sales	(72) 3.6	(59) 2.2
2.2	6.5	6.1					8.0	5.9
3.5							3.6	2.1
(20) 5.4						% Officers', Directors' Owners' Comp/Sales	(34) 5.0	(43) 4.5
11.4							9.6	10.6
42228M	61967M	145948M	132404M	525204M		Net Sales ($)	1204037M	1143395M
9470M	26867M	69540M	119807M	188117M		Total Assets ($)	851069M	622926M

© RMA 2019   M = $ thousand   MM = $ million
See Pages viii through xx for Explanation of Ratios and Data

Comparative Historical Data | Current Data Sorted by Sales

			Type of Statement	0-1MM	1-3MM	3-5MM	5-10MM	10-25MM	25MM & OVER
5	3	6	Unqualified				1	3	2
1	3	3	Reviewed				1	2	
10	3	4	Compiled	1	2	1			
40	42	33	Tax Returns	17	10	2	3	1	2
34	38	53	Other	24	15	1	6	5	2
4/1/16-3/31/17 ALL	4/1/17-3/31/18 ALL	4/1/18-3/31/19 ALL		5 (4/1-9/30/18)			94 (10/1/18-3/31/19)		
90	89	99	**NUMBER OF STATEMENTS**	42	27	6	9	10	5
%	%	%	**ASSETS**	%	%	%	%	%	%
24.6	21.4	30.0	Cash & Equivalents	37.6	24.2			22.8	
3.1	4.7	2.9	Trade Receivables (net)	1.1	.2			14.9	
6.7	4.4	5.0	Inventory	4.2	6.9			5.5	
3.3	3.5	2.9	All Other Current	2.5	2.4			3.2	
37.8	34.1	40.9	Total Current	45.4	33.7			46.5	
38.5	36.9	33.9	Fixed Assets (net)	31.5	38.5			37.2	
14.4	16.7	16.7	Intangibles (net)	17.6	16.7			9.3	
9.4	12.3	8.4	All Other Non-Current	5.6	11.1			7.0	
100.0	100.0	100.0	Total	100.0	100.0			100.0	
			LIABILITIES						
6.3	14.0	5.6	Notes Payable-Short Term	8.7	4.4			.3	
4.4	2.4	4.4	Cur. Mat.-L.T.D.	3.6	6.5			5.9	
4.7	3.2	4.0	Trade Payables	1.0	5.6			7.3	
.2	.8	.7	Income Taxes Payable	1.6	.0			.0	
26.3	19.5	23.3	All Other Current	24.4	23.1			26.4	
41.8	39.9	37.9	Total Current	39.3	39.6			39.9	
32.1	34.7	45.4	Long-Term Debt	64.0	29.9			29.5	
.2	.0	.0	Deferred Taxes	.0	.0				
14.1	10.8	10.2	All Other Non-Current	14.3	9.6			2.1	
11.7	14.6	6.5	Net Worth	-17.5	20.9			28.6	
100.0	100.0	100.0	Total Liabilities & Net Worth	100.0	100.0			100.0	
			INCOME DATA						
100.0	100.0	100.0	Net Sales	100.0	100.0			100.0	
			Gross Profit						
92.1	90.2	88.8	Operating Expenses	82.0	94.7			97.3	
7.9	9.8	11.2	Operating Profit	18.0	5.3			2.7	
1.2	1.6	2.3	All Other Expenses (net)	3.2	.8			2.4	
6.7	8.2	8.9	Profit Before Taxes	14.8	4.5			.3	
			RATIOS						
2.6	3.4	5.5		7.6	3.0			3.5	
1.0	1.0	1.4	Current	3.6	1.2			2.0	
.6	.3	.5		.6	.3			.5	
2.0	2.9	5.0		6.1	3.0			3.1	
.7	.6	1.1	Quick	3.0	1.1			1.8	
.3	.2	.3		.3	.1			.2	
0 UND	0 UND	0 UND		0 UND	0 UND			0 UND	
0 UND	0 UND	0 UND	Sales/Receivables	0 UND	0 UND			0 UND	
1 247.9	1 298.5	0 UND		0 UND	0 UND			68 5.4	
			Cost of Sales/Inventory						
			Cost of Sales/Payables						
12.3	9.9	10.5		9.0	17.4			4.9	
-916.9	167.9	32.3	Sales/Working Capital	24.6	56.6			34.8	
-17.2	-14.6	-16.7		-18.6	-16.7			-9.5	
24.1	10.5	21.4		10.4	24.6			57.3	
(63) 8.7	(61) 4.9	(71) 6.8	EBIT/Interest	(24) 6.7	(20) 8.3			6.8	
.8	.9	1.6		1.7	-.4			-.9	
			Net Profit + Depr., Dep., Amort./Cur. Mat. L/T/D						
.7	.4	.4		.2	.9			.4	
2.1	2.0	2.4	Fixed/Worth	4.7	2.5			1.1	
-2.2	-1.4	-.7		-.3	-.6			NM	
1.0	.8	.5		.5	.8			.5	
6.7	8.1	4.1	Debt/Worth	4.6	4.6			1.4	
-4.2	-3.0	-2.6		-1.6	-3.0			NM	
122.8	122.1	210.0		241.1	267.4				
(52) 63.4	(50) 53.4	(60) 87.7	% Profit Before Taxes/Tangible Net Worth	(23) 122.7	(16) 66.6				
18.7	14.5	26.8		42.8	17.3				
33.9	34.8	54.4		83.6	50.0			36.3	
11.6	19.6	28.9	% Profit Before Taxes/Total Assets	30.5	30.4			13.1	
2.4	2.5	2.5		5.8	.4			-8.3	
23.0	39.5	49.5		127.3	28.7			14.3	
8.5	8.2	12.5	Sales/Net Fixed Assets	24.4	12.5			5.6	
4.5	4.2	4.3		3.8	4.3			3.2	
4.6	4.5	5.9		7.2	5.9			3.5	
2.8	2.6	2.6	Sales/Total Assets	3.7	2.7			2.4	
1.9	1.5	1.4		1.5	1.3			1.4	
1.3	1.1	1.0		.5	1.2			1.7	
(66) 2.6	(55) 2.5	(52) 2.1	% Depr., Dep., Amort./Sales	(15) 1.8	(14) 2.3			3.4	
5.0	4.9	5.2		2.9	5.9			7.6	
2.8	3.9	3.0		2.3					
(42) 5.3	(40) 6.6	(34) 5.3	% Officers', Directors' Owners' Comp/Sales	(16) 5.4					
8.9	9.5	10.0		11.5					
1812197M	690021M	907751M	Net Sales ($)	24907M	41288M	22465M	69075M	164126M	585890M
812539M	481520M	413801M	Total Assets ($)	15861M	22339M	14825M	23816M	86394M	250566M

M = $ thousand   MM = $ million
See Pages viii through xx for Explanation of Ratios and Data

Current Data Sorted by Assets   Comparative Historical Data

Type of Statement	0-500M	500M-2MM	2-10MM	10-50MM	50-100MM	100-250MM		4/1/14-3/31/15 ALL	4/1/15-3/31/16 ALL
Unqualified			3					4	7
Reviewed			3	2				18	12
Compiled	5	13	9	6				61	50
Tax Returns	29	45	19	1	2			113	148
Other	13	39	18	8	1	1		102	89
	39 (4/1-9/30/18)			178 (10/1/18-3/31/19)					
NUMBER OF STATEMENTS	47	97	52	17	3	1		298	306
	%	%	%	%	%	%	**ASSETS**	%	%
Cash & Equivalents	25.0	12.4	13.6	13.8				13.9	16.4
Trade Receivables (net)	15.4	9.7	7.4	9.4				14.1	13.0
Inventory	4.7	3.0	2.3	6.3				3.6	4.3
All Other Current	2.8	2.5	.8	2.5				2.2	1.7
Total Current	47.9	27.7	24.1	32.0				33.8	35.4
Fixed Assets (net)	30.3	46.4	49.0	32.6				42.5	39.5
Intangibles (net)	14.5	10.6	11.1	12.4				9.8	9.5
All Other Non-Current	7.4	15.3	15.8	23.1				13.9	15.6
Total	100.0	100.0	100.0	100.0				100.0	100.0
							LIABILITIES		
Notes Payable-Short Term	7.7	3.1	3.6	5.5				4.7	6.1
Cur. Mat.-L.T.D.	5.7	3.7	2.7	1.3				3.1	3.5
Trade Payables	5.2	3.7	3.0	1.8				5.0	4.7
Income Taxes Payable	.1	.2	.1	.3				.1	.2
All Other Current	12.7	7.6	6.0	6.5				10.3	8.9
Total Current	31.4	18.3	15.4	15.5				23.2	23.4
Long-Term Debt	30.6	35.5	34.1	21.8				40.6	35.5
Deferred Taxes	.0	.0	.9	.2				.1	.2
All Other Non-Current	21.5	9.5	11.7	19.4				10.5	11.6
Net Worth	16.5	36.7	38.0	43.2				25.6	29.3
Total Liabilities & Net Worth	100.0	100.0	100.0	100.0				100.0	100.0
							INCOME DATA		
Net Sales	100.0	100.0	100.0	100.0				100.0	100.0
Gross Profit									
Operating Expenses	92.9	86.9	81.9	83.4				89.6	89.0
Operating Profit	7.1	13.1	18.1	16.6				10.4	11.0
All Other Expenses (net)	-.1	3.2	2.8	3.8				2.5	2.4
Profit Before Taxes	7.2	10.0	15.3	12.9				7.9	8.7
							RATIOS		
Current	6.6	5.5	4.4	4.5				4.7	4.6
	2.2	2.0	1.9	2.4				2.1	1.7
	.6	.6	.7	1.3				.8	.6
Quick	6.6	4.2	4.0	3.6				4.2	3.8
	1.8	1.6	1.5	1.4				1.6	1.3
	.5	.5	.6	.4				.6	.5
Sales/Receivables	0 UND	0 UND	9 38.5	10 37.2				8 48.1	0 UND
	9 40.8	19 19.0	21 17.2	18 20.3				26 14.2	21 17.5
	27 13.7	38 9.7	36 10.1	54 6.7				42 8.6	40 9.2
Cost of Sales/Inventory									
Cost of Sales/Payables									
Sales/Working Capital	8.9	5.0	3.9	1.7				5.3	5.9
	23.4	10.4	8.8	3.8				13.5	19.7
	-31.6	-10.7	-16.6	15.1				-37.1	-16.8
EBIT/Interest	18.9	11.0	10.3	10.5				9.7	11.3
	(30) 8.7	(78) 3.6	(36) 3.4	(16) 4.5				(238) 3.4	(228) 3.9
	2.1	1.0	1.7	2.6				1.4	1.5
Net Profit + Depr., Dep., Amort./Cur. Mat. L/T/D								3.7	4.1
								(26) 2.0	(30) 1.7
								.7	.7
Fixed/Worth	.4	.5	.7	.5				.6	.5
	1.4	2.0	2.0	.7				1.9	1.7
	-.8	-10.2	10.8	2.1				-11.3	-6.7
Debt/Worth	.4	.4	.8	.9				.8	.6
	3.0	2.5	1.8	1.7				3.2	2.3
	-3.6	-24.2	21.9	8.7				-19.4	-13.8
% Profit Before Taxes/Tangible Net Worth	178.6	35.5	43.2	25.4				55.9	63.1
	(31) 70.1	(69) 13.8	(42) 22.4	(15) -12.4				(214) 23.5	(220) 23.0
	32.6	3.3	6.2	10.3				6.1	8.5
% Profit Before Taxes/Total Assets	36.8	12.7	11.4	8.6				18.0	20.9
	19.7	4.4	7.1	5.7				6.4	8.6
	2.6	.5	2.9	3.0				1.1	1.7
Sales/Net Fixed Assets	38.7	8.4	3.3	3.8				12.2	15.4
	13.7	3.8	1.8	1.6				4.2	4.4
	8.9	1.0	.9	1.1				1.4	1.5
Sales/Total Assets	6.1	2.0	1.3	.7				2.6	2.7
	3.9	1.1	.6	.5				1.3	1.4
	2.3	.6	.4	.3				.6	.7
% Depr., Dep., Amort./Sales	1.1	1.5	2.4	2.7				1.6	1.5
	(27) 1.6	(81) 3.8	(48) 4.8	4.1				(259) 3.0	(244) 3.2
	3.7	8.4	8.2	5.4				5.8	6.0
% Officers', Directors' Owners' Comp/Sales	6.7	6.2	3.9					6.0	5.6
	(32) 10.7	(62) 8.6	(29) 8.2					(173) 10.1	(179) 9.3
	15.0	17.4	13.1					14.4	15.6
Net Sales ($)	45570M	140074M	189566M	162614M	124284M	26350M		910023M	983586M
Total Assets ($)	12056M	105359M	231278M	345903M	242410M	110526M		1572146M	1717879M

M = $ thousand   MM = $ million
See Pages viii through xx for Explanation of Ratios and Data

Comparative Historical Data				Type of Statement	Current Data Sorted by Sales					
4		3	5	Unqualified			1	1	1	2
0		8	5	Reviewed			2	2	1	
40		45	33	Compiled	7	9	5	10	2	
107		134	94	Tax Returns	44	39	8	3		
83		84	80	Other	32	31	6	5	5	1
4/1/16-3/31/17 ALL		4/1/17-3/31/18 ALL	4/1/18-3/31/19 ALL		39 (4/1-9/30/18)			178 (10/1/18-3/31/19)		
					0-1MM	1-3MM	3-5MM	5-10MM	10-25MM	25MM & OVER
243		274	217	NUMBER OF STATEMENTS	83	79	22	21	9	3
%		%	%	ASSETS	%	%	%	%	%	%
14.3		14.4	15.4	Cash & Equivalents	15.6	15.4	17.4	15.8		
12.1		11.2	10.5	Trade Receivables (net)	7.5	12.6	11.7	13.3		
3.0		3.7	3.5	Inventory	3.3	3.0	3.6	5.7		
2.3		1.1	2.2	All Other Current	.8	4.0	1.4	1.7		
31.7		30.4	31.6	Total Current	27.1	35.0	34.1	36.5		
42.8		47.3	42.3	Fixed Assets (net)	46.9	38.5	44.3	35.6		
8.8		9.8	11.5	Intangibles (net)	13.6	11.6	7.8	7.5		
16.7		12.4	14.5	All Other Non-Current	12.4	14.9	13.8	20.4		
100.0		100.0	100.0	Total	100.0	100.0	100.0	100.0		
				LIABILITIES						
4.4		4.1	4.4	Notes Payable-Short Term	3.5	3.9	8.0	7.4		
4.6		3.6	3.7	Cur. Mat.-L.T.D.	4.1	3.7	2.7	3.8		
3.7		3.9	3.7	Trade Payables	2.9	3.9	4.7	5.3		
.3		.2	.1	Income Taxes Payable	.0	.1	.1	.8		
10.7		8.4	8.3	All Other Current	11.3	5.1	9.2	7.8		
23.6		20.2	20.2	Total Current	21.8	16.7	24.7	25.2		
37.4		39.0	32.7	Long-Term Debt	36.7	34.9	29.6	18.6		
.2		.2	.2	Deferred Taxes	.2	.1	1.0	.2		
8.1		9.8	13.6	All Other Non-Current	16.1	11.7	11.4	12.0		
30.7		30.8	33.3	Net Worth	25.2	36.6	33.3	44.0		
100.0		100.0	100.0	Total Liabilities & Net Worth	100.0	100.0	100.0	100.0		
				INCOME DATA						
100.0		100.0	100.0	Net Sales	100.0	100.0	100.0	100.0		
				Gross Profit						
88.9		87.0	86.6	Operating Expenses	79.3	92.1	93.8	87.1		
11.1		13.0	13.4	Operating Profit	20.7	7.9	6.2	12.9		
1.5		2.2	2.4	All Other Expenses (net)	5.6	-.1	.3	1.0		
9.5		10.8	11.0	Profit Before Taxes	15.1	8.0	5.9	11.9		
				RATIOS						
4.0		4.2	5.2	Current	4.9	6.3	3.8	3.1		
1.6		1.7	2.0		1.5	2.4	2.0	1.6		
.6		.6	.6		.3	.8	.9	1.0		
3.1		3.5	4.1	Quick	4.5	5.6	3.1	2.8		
1.3		1.4	1.6		1.3	2.0	1.7	1.3		
.5		.4	.5		.3	.6	.6	.6		

								Sales/Receivables						
6	59.9	5	75.3	3	122.4	0	UND	9	42.5	14	26.3	10	38.4	
21	17.1	18	19.8	17	21.0	9	40.8	19	19.1	34	10.8	18	20.3	
36	10.0	34	10.6	36	10.2	26	13.8	37	9.8	49	7.5	33	11.1	

Cost of Sales/Inventory

Cost of Sales/Payables

Comparative Historical Data					Current Data Sorted by Sales				
5.2	5.7	4.3	Sales/Working Capital		4.9	5.0	4.0	3.1	
15.8	16.9	13.1			26.7	10.4	8.4	6.2	
20.0	18.0	-19.6			-4.6	-43.7	-93.7	NM	

							EBIT/Interest						
	11.0		16.5		12.0		10.3		19.6		50.8		9.4
(199)	4.2	(219)	5.0	(163)	4.2	(54)	3.1	(65)	4.1	(16)	3.8	(19)	5.4
	1.8		1.5		1.6		1.0		1.9		1.8		3.1

							Net Profit + Depr., Dep., Amort./Cur. Mat. L/T/D						
	4.8		5.2		4.3								
(26)	2.1	(27)	2.0	(18)	1.8								
	1.1		1.1		.8								

					Fixed/Worth				
.7	.7	.5			1.0	.5	.7	.4	
1.7	1.8	1.0			2.9	1.3	1.0	.7	
-16.0	56.7	-84.2			-1.1	6.8	-5.3	2.1	

					Debt/Worth				
.7	.6	.6			.9	.4	.4	.7	
2.2	2.2	2.1			4.5	1.6	2.6	1.1	
-27.4	57.3	-103.0			-5.3	17.5	-7.4	3.0	

							% Profit Before Taxes/Tangible Net Worth						
	54.7		63.6		49.6		45.8		72.1		63.1		34.7
(175)	21.4	(209)	25.8	(161)	22.3	(53)	23.8	(62)	28.6	(14)	15.1	(20)	15.4
	6.0		7.8		7.3		9.7		6.2		-1.2		8.8

					% Profit Before Taxes/Total Assets				
16.9	18.3	15.8			18.2	19.7	15.5	12.1	
6.3	7.7	7.0			5.6	7.6	6.4	6.2	
1.3	1.5	1.9			.8	2.6	-.2	3.6	

					Sales/Net Fixed Assets				
12.9	10.4	10.6			10.5	12.9	5.3	9.5	
3.9	3.5	3.7			3.1	5.8	3.4	3.5	
1.5	1.5	1.2			.6	1.8	1.7	1.5	

					Sales/Total Assets				
2.5	2.5	2.3			2.2	3.1	2.2	2.6	
1.3	1.3	1.1			.7	1.6	1.4	.6	
.7	.7	.5			.3	.8	.6	.5	

							% Depr., Dep., Amort./Sales						
	1.8		1.6		1.6		2.9		1.4		2.0		1.3
(194)	3.6	(235)	3.2	(177)	3.7	(61)	6.7	(63)	2.7	(21)	3.2		2.4
	5.8		5.8		6.7		14.1		4.4		6.7		4.1

							% Officers', Directors' Owners' Comp/Sales						
	5.9		5.4		5.6		6.6		5.5		6.7		4.9
(139)	9.5	(170)	9.4	(130)	9.0	(38)	10.9	(61)	8.3	(14)	9.2	(14)	5.8
	14.4		14.2		15.3		19.0		15.4		14.5		10.8

Comparative Historical Data				Current Data Sorted by Sales					
865028M	860876M	688458M	Net Sales ($)	45693M	141717M	82379M	143540M	143547M	131582M
1500900M	1355548M	1047532M	Total Assets ($)	74658M	133154M	98260M	247239M	215386M	278835M

M = $ thousand   MM = $ million
See Pages viii through xx for Explanation of Ratios and Data

Current Data Sorted by Assets   Comparative Historical Data

						Type of Statement	1	3
				2		Unqualified	1	3
	1	2		2		Reviewed	3	2
5	5	2	1	1		Compiled	6	3
2	6	1	3	2		Tax Returns	15	15
		3				Other	26	33
	3 (4/1-9/30/18)		29 (10/1/18-3/31/19)				4/1/14-3/31/15	4/1/15-3/31/16
0-500M	500M-2MM	2-10MM	10-50MM	50-100MM	100-250MM		ALL	ALL
7	12	8	3	2		NUMBER OF STATEMENTS	51	56
%	%	%	%	%	%	ASSETS	%	%
	16.1					Cash & Equivalents	15.9	10.8
	15.1					Trade Receivables (net)	11.4	8.5
	10.9					Inventory	8.7	7.7
	2.4				D	All Other Current	3.1	1.0
	44.4				A	Total Current	39.2	28.1
	36.2				T	Fixed Assets (net)	30.6	32.9
	8.5				A	Intangibles (net)	6.4	3.3
	10.9					All Other Non-Current	23.8	35.7
	100.0				N	Total	100.0	100.0
					O	LIABILITIES		
	8.6				T	Notes Payable-Short Term	4.3	3.8
	1.4					Cur. Mat.-L.T.D.	2.8	1.2
	2.4				A	Trade Payables	3.2	4.5
	2.2				V	Income Taxes Payable	.0	.0
	7.3				A	All Other Current	13.5	11.5
	21.9				I	Total Current	23.9	21.0
	14.6				L	Long-Term Debt	32.7	22.1
	.0				A	Deferred Taxes	.0	.0
	12.9				B	All Other Non-Current	22.2	33.4
	50.7				L	Net Worth	21.2	23.5
	100.0				E	Total Liabilities & Net Worth	100.0	100.0
						INCOME DATA		
	100.0					Net Sales	100.0	100.0
						Gross Profit		
	88.7					Operating Expenses	88.6	92.4
	11.3					Operating Profit	11.4	7.6
	-.2					All Other Expenses (net)	1.4	1.4
	11.5					Profit Before Taxes	10.0	6.2
						RATIOS		
	3.5						6.1	6.6
	2.1					Current	3.3	3.0
	1.1						1.0	1.0
	3.0						4.0	4.6
	1.8					Quick	1.7	1.5
	.5						.9	.6
22	16.8						12 31.1	11 34.4
42	8.6					Sales/Receivables	40 9.2	36 10.0
56	6.5						96 3.8	87 4.2
						Cost of Sales/Inventory		
						Cost of Sales/Payables		
	1.8						2.1	2.5
	5.3					Sales/Working Capital	5.5	6.1
	31.5						UND	UND
				18.0			18.0	11.4
						EBIT/Interest	(35) 6.7	(45) 2.9
							2.3	.8
						Net Profit + Depr., Dep., Amort./Cur. Mat. L/T/D		
	.1						.4	.3
	1.0					Fixed/Worth	.9	1.3
	5.7						8.5	53.1
	.5						.8	.7
	1.2					Debt/Worth	3.0	3.5
	5.3						UND	466.3
	70.3					% Profit Before Taxes/Tangible	49.6	40.9
(10)	27.4					Net Worth	(40) 15.6	(44) 8.5
	2.3						1.6	-1.1
	36.3					% Profit Before Taxes/Total	25.0	11.2
	8.3					Assets	4.2	2.0
	-.2						.2	-.5
	9.5						8.9	7.4
	6.3					Sales/Net Fixed Assets	4.6	3.0
	1.6						1.6	1.2
	2.6						3.0	2.0
	1.3					Sales/Total Assets	.9	.4
	.5						.2	.2
						% Depr., Dep., Amort./Sales	1.2	2.1
							(40) 3.0	(45) 3.7
							4.0	8.7
						% Officers', Directors'	4.3	4.9
						Owners' Comp/Sales	(18) 7.0	(11) 8.4
							9.3	10.7
6750M	18652M	30700M	29420M	25500M		Net Sales ($)	157963M	199704M
2159M	13562M	42993M	66780M	127412M		Total Assets ($)	432733M	844719M

Comparative Historical Data | Current Data Sorted by Sales

4/1/16-3/31/17 ALL	4/1/17-3/31/18 ALL	4/1/18-3/31/19 ALL	Type of Statement	0-1MM	1-3MM	3-5MM	5-10MM	10-25MM	25MM & OVER
4	4	2	Unqualified					1	1
3	2	2	Reviewed				1	1	
2	3	3	Compiled		2			1	
13	13	11	Tax Returns	8	2	1			
15	8	14	Other	3	6	1	3	1	
					3 (4/1-9/30/18)		29 (10/1/18-3/31/19)		
37	30	32	NUMBER OF STATEMENTS	11	10	3	6	2	
%	%	%	**ASSETS**	%	%	%	%	%	%
16.2	15.1	15.2	Cash & Equivalents	12.0	18.3				
12.2	13.5	12.8	Trade Receivables (net)	11.0	15.7				
9.8	11.7	11.1	Inventory	11.4	3.7				
1.8	6.3	8.6	All Other Current	16.8	2.7				
39.9	46.5	47.7	Total Current	51.2	40.4				
36.6	32.6	30.5	Fixed Assets (net)	29.0	38.2				
7.0	6.0	7.1	Intangibles (net)	6.4	12.5				
16.4	14.8	14.7	All Other Non-Current	13.3	8.9				
100.0	100.0	100.0	Total	100.0	100.0				
			LIABILITIES						
2.7	8.7	4.9	Notes Payable-Short Term	6.4	4.4				
5.5	2.7	2.3	Cur. Mat.-L.T.D.	2.7	.3				
2.8	3.2	2.5	Trade Payables	1.6	3.2				
.0	.7	.8	Income Taxes Payable	2.4	.0				
11.1	15.4	13.7	All Other Current	18.1	16.3				
22.1	30.6	24.3	Total Current	31.2	24.2				
21.9	33.3	12.9	Long-Term Debt	12.0	17.7				
.1	.0	.0	Deferred Taxes	.0	.0				
17.1	9.3	15.6	All Other Non-Current	13.0	12.8				
38.8	26.8	47.3	Net Worth	43.8	45.3				
100.0	100.0	100.0	Total Liabilties & Net Worth	100.0	100.0				
			INCOME DATA						
100.0	100.0	100.0	Net Sales	100.0	100.0				
			Gross Profit						
87.5	89.1	90.8	Operating Expenses	93.4	88.6				
12.5	10.9	9.2	Operating Profit	6.6	11.4				
1.8	-.1	1.2	All Other Expenses (net)	.8	1.1				
10.6	10.9	8.0	Profit Before Taxes	5.7	10.3				
			RATIOS						
11.7	8.7	12.9	Current	15.8	29.5				
3.0	3.1	2.7		2.3	2.6				
.9	.7	1.2		1.1	.7				
7.0	6.0	2.7	Quick	2.3	25.2				
1.6	1.7	1.7		1.1	2.1				
.6	.2	.5		.1	.7				
11 32.6	1 369.2	14 26.0	Sales/Receivables	1 662.0	17 21.2				
43 8.5	33 11.0	41 9.0		47 7.8	24 15.0				
91 4.0	64 5.7	72 5.1		74 4.9	68 5.4				
			Cost of Sales/Inventory						
			Cost of Sales/Payables						
1.8	2.0	1.3	Sales/Working Capital	1.1	5.7				
3.4	4.8	4.1		3.2	13.2				
-119.3	-11.8	31.8		34.7	-42.5				
23.1	31.1	26.7	EBIT/Interest						
(26) 2.8	(24) 4.8	(23) 3.7							
.5	1.6	.6							
			Net Profit + Depr., Dep., Amort./Cur. Mat. L/T/D						
.3	.3	.2	Fixed/Worth	.1	.5				
.8	.7	.6		.0	1.0				
5.6	NM	3.3		2.0	-4.5				
.2	.2	.5	Debt/Worth	.5	.4				
1.0	1.0	.7		.8	2.3				
6.9	NM	5.4		2.8	-8.2				
42.9	49.1	60.7	% Profit Before Taxes/Tangible Net Worth	28.4					
(29) 14.8	(23) 17.3	(27) 10.7		(10) 7.4					
-.3	6.0	1.1		-8.3					
24.8	18.2	14.9	% Profit Before Taxes/Total Assets	8.0	38.0				
7.7	9.5	6.1		2.4	20.9				
-.1	1.5	-.8		-4.1	2.6				
7.5	8.5	10.0	Sales/Net Fixed Assets	11.6	10.8				
2.5	3.1	5.8		7.5	5.8				
1.1	1.7	1.2		.6	3.6				
1.3	2.4	2.5	Sales/Total Assets	1.5	2.9				
.8	.9	.9		.5	2.5				
.3	.5	.4		.3	.7				
2.5	1.7	1.7	% Depr., Dep., Amort./Sales						
(29) 3.8	(28) 2.6	(26) 3.3							
7.3	3.6	5.6							
6.8	3.4		% Officers', Directors' Owners' Comp/Sales						
(10) 10.8	(10) 6.0								
12.6	17.4								
197657M	92530M	111022M	Net Sales ($)	6164M	18447M	11138M	40800M	34473M	
565381M	245857M	252906M	Total Assets ($)	13773M	16171M	6775M	117405M	98782M	

(Right-side columns 3-5MM through 25MM & OVER: DATA NOT AVAILABLE)

© RMA 2019

M = $ thousand   MM = $ million
See Pages viii through xx for Explanation of Ratios and Data

Current Data Sorted by Assets   Comparative Historical Data

						Type of Statement		
				1	1	Unqualified	1	1
				1		Reviewed	3	3
		2				Compiled	6	4
1		3	1			Tax Returns	31	33
20	10	1		1		Other	28	23
6	9	4	1		1		4/1/14-	4/1/15-
	6 (4/1-9/30/18)		56 (10/1/18-3/31/19)				3/31/15	3/31/16
0-500M	500M-2MM	2-10MM	10-50MM	50-100MM	100-250MM		ALL	ALL
27	19	10	2	2	2	NUMBER OF STATEMENTS	69	64
%	%	%	%	%	%	ASSETS	%	%
20.9	10.9	11.1				Cash & Equivalents	12.9	14.3
.2	3.1	.9				Trade Receivables (net)	2.2	2.8
.8	1.4	7.4				Inventory	2.7	2.7
.9	4.2	3.6				All Other Current	3.2	3.0
22.9	19.6	23.1				Total Current	21.0	22.7
52.3	65.2	56.4				Fixed Assets (net)	62.1	56.9
8.9	12.2	11.3				Intangibles (net)	9.6	12.8
15.9	3.0	9.1				All Other Non-Current	7.2	7.6
100.0	100.0	100.0				Total	100.0	100.0
						LIABILITIES		
9.4	3.1	3.9				Notes Payable-Short Term	8.1	17.7
4.9	3.8	8.7				Cur. Mat.-L.T.D.	4.3	3.6
.5	2.4	5.2				Trade Payables	1.3	3.7
1.0	.0	.0				Income Taxes Payable	.2	.3
23.1	5.3	11.3				All Other Current	8.8	14.9
38.9	14.6	29.0				Total Current	22.7	40.2
44.8	51.5	40.9				Long-Term Debt	44.2	41.5
.0	.0	.0				Deferred Taxes	.0	.0
13.2	2.5	.5				All Other Non-Current	8.2	15.0
3.0	31.5	29.6				Net Worth	24.8	3.3
100.0	100.0	100.0				Total Liabilities & Net Worth	100.0	100.0
						INCOME DATA		
100.0	100.0	100.0				Net Sales	100.0	100.0
						Gross Profit		
85.8	81.7	74.8				Operating Expenses	83.6	83.9
14.2	18.3	25.2				Operating Profit	16.4	16.1
3.2	2.6	5.3				All Other Expenses (net)	4.7	4.0
11.1	15.7	19.8				Profit Before Taxes	11.6	12.1
						RATIOS		
5.5	16.7	1.2					4.4	2.1
1.4	1.5	.5				Current	1.1	1.0
.2	.7	.3					.3	.4
5.5	13.3	.5					2.5	1.9
1.4	.7	.2				Quick	.8	.7
.2	.4	.4					.2	.3
0 UND	0 UND	0 UND					0 UND	0 UND
0 UND	0 UND	0 UND				Sales/Receivables	0 UND	0 UND
0 UND	6 62.8	6 64.1					0 UND	2 175.9
						Cost of Sales/Inventory		
						Cost of Sales/Payables		
9.2	5.0	19.0					8.8	15.2
32.7	30.6	-20.8				Sales/Working Capital	230.8	UND
-9.0	-23.8	-8.1					-13.0	-7.6
19.7	20.8	54.0					13.3	10.1
(16) 6.6	(17) 5.8	3.6				EBIT/Interest	(56) 4.1	(49) 5.4
1.8	2.4	.8					2.3	1.8
						Net Profit + Depr., Dep., Amort./Cur. Mat. L/T/D		
.4	1.3	1.6					.9	1.1
2.3	4.6	2.3				Fixed/Worth	2.4	3.0
-3.3	-10.7	NM					-22.0	-12.9
.4	1.5	1.4					.7	.9
2.1	4.0	1.9				Debt/Worth	2.6	4.1
-5.1	-14.1	NM					-14.2	-8.8
60.4	148.4						64.9	102.7
(17) 30.8	(13) 35.6					% Profit Before Taxes/Tangible Net Worth	(50) 25.6	(45) 32.7
14.4	18.6						11.1	13.8
35.3	15.2	27.8					19.5	22.6
20.6	12.9	8.9				% Profit Before Taxes/Total Assets	8.8	10.6
2.0	4.4	-.8					2.5	1.4
21.4	4.1	5.9					6.0	7.2
4.7	2.1	3.1				Sales/Net Fixed Assets	2.0	2.0
1.2	.6	1.0					.7	1.0
3.8	2.0	2.3					1.9	1.9
1.6	1.3	2.1				Sales/Total Assets	.9	1.3
.8	.5	.5					.5	.6
3.6	2.8						5.9	4.9
(17) 12.5	(13) 8.4					% Depr., Dep., Amort./Sales	(52) 8.9	(42) 8.9
18.1	11.8						16.8	12.9
							4.1	2.7
						% Officers', Directors' Owners' Comp/Sales	(27) 5.7	(23) 4.9
							8.9	11.5
12338M	31315M	98437M	69198M	177801M	70365M	Net Sales ($)	318497M	353822M
6522M	20949M	54833M	63113M	139842M	347012M	Total Assets ($)	276568M	235858M

© RMA 2019   M = $ thousand   MM = $ million
See Pages viii through xx for Explanation of Ratios and Data

Comparative Historical Data & Current Data Sorted by Sales

				Type of Statement	6 (4/1-9/30/18)			56 (10/1/18-3/31/19)		
					0-1MM	1-3MM	3-5MM	5-10MM	10-25MM	25MM & OVER
2	1	2		Unqualified					1	2
5	1	3		Reviewed						2
5	8	5		Compiled	2			1	1	
24	25	31		Tax Returns	20	9	2	3	1	2
15	25	21		Other	13	2				
4/1/16-3/31/17 ALL	4/1/17-3/31/18 ALL	4/1/18-3/31/19 ALL								
51	60	62		**NUMBER OF STATEMENTS**	35	12	2	4	3	6
%	%	%		**ASSETS**	%	%	%	%	%	%
11.7	16.5	14.7		Cash & Equivalents	15.6	14.4				
3.7	1.1	1.9		Trade Receivables (net)	1.1	1.6				
4.6	1.6	2.4		Inventory	.6	1.5				
2.8	4.0	2.6		All Other Current	.7	7.4				
22.7	23.2	21.6		Total Current	17.9	25.0				
53.1	57.7	56.8		Fixed Assets (net)	58.7	59.8				
11.5	6.5	12.1		Intangibles (net)	10.3	13.0				
12.7	12.6	9.4		All Other Non-Current	13.2	2.2				
100.0	100.0	100.0		Total	100.0	100.0				
				LIABILITIES						
3.5	7.0	5.9		Notes Payable-Short Term	8.2	1.3				
5.0	9.7	5.1		Cur. Mat.-L.T.D.	2.4	9.9				
3.3	2.0	2.2		Trade Payables	.7	2.7				
.1	.1	.5		Income Taxes Payable	.8	.0				
12.6	16.8	13.9		All Other Current	20.0	1.9				
24.6	35.5	27.6		Total Current	32.0	15.8				
48.1	38.7	45.7		Long-Term Debt	50.4	46.8				
.0	.1	.2		Deferred Taxes	.0	.0				
12.2	6.1	7.1		All Other Non-Current	9.6	5.7				
15.2	19.6	19.5		Net Worth	8.0	31.7				
100.0	100.0	100.0		Total Liabilities & Net Worth	100.0	100.0				
				INCOME DATA						
100.0	100.0	100.0		Net Sales	100.0	100.0				
				Gross Profit						
85.1	79.6	83.2		Operating Expenses	82.7	80.4				
14.9	20.4	16.8		Operating Profit	17.3	19.6				
4.2	3.7	4.3		All Other Expenses (net)	3.9	3.3				
10.7	16.7	12.5		Profit Before Taxes	13.4	16.3				
				RATIOS						
3.2	2.9	2.9		Current	5.5	3.9				
1.0	.9	1.2			1.2	1.6				
.3	.2	.4			.2	.7				
2.1	2.7	2.3		Quick	5.5	2.2				
.7	.7	.8			1.1	.8				
.2	.2	.2			.1	.4				
0 UND	0 UND	0 UND		Sales/Receivables	0 UND	0 UND				
0 UND	0 UND	0 UND			0 UND	0 UND				
6 58.8	0 UND	2 162.7			0 UND	3 112.7				
				Cost of Sales/Inventory						
				Cost of Sales/Payables						
10.8	9.8	9.0		Sales/Working Capital	9.1	7.5				
-260.8	-156.1	37.4			42.2	128.9				
-8.2	-6.7	-13.5			-9.0	-29.5				
6.3	9.0	15.4		EBIT/Interest	9.7	44.0				
(40) 3.2	(49) 4.5	(47) 5.0			(23) 4.4	(11) 9.7				
2.1	2.1	2.0			1.5	3.5				
				Net Profit + Depr., Dep., Amort./Cur. Mat. L/T/D						
.8	1.2	1.1		Fixed/Worth	.9	1.1				
3.5	2.0	2.7			3.8	3.2				
-9.0	-6.2	-6.9			-3.7	-8.8				
.8	.7	1.2		Debt/Worth	.8	.9				
3.6	1.7	2.3			4.8	2.8				
-5.8	-8.9	-9.1			-6.6	-11.2				
50.6	147.4	78.6		% Profit Before Taxes/Tangible Net Worth	49.6					
(33) 21.2	(42) 40.0	(42) 32.6			(23) 19.6					
11.8	12.8	14.2			14.2					
20.5	34.5	32.9		% Profit Before Taxes/Total Assets	29.5	88.5				
6.8	12.8	11.7			8.7	14.4				
2.6	4.2	2.5			2.0	7.3				
10.8	6.3	6.3		Sales/Net Fixed Assets	7.0	5.8				
2.7	2.5	2.5			1.7	2.9				
.8	1.5	1.1			.6	2.1				
2.5	2.5	2.5		Sales/Total Assets	1.8	2.7				
1.6	1.6	1.4			1.0	1.9				
.6	.6	.5			.5	1.3				
2.1	4.0	3.5		% Depr., Dep., Amort./Sales	4.2	2.6				
(34) 8.3	(39) 9.6	(39) 8.7			(21) 12.5	(10) 8.7				
16.3	17.5	13.7			17.6	13.4				
3.0	2.9	2.5		% Officers', Directors' Owners' Comp/Sales						
(22) 7.8	(23) 4.1	(15) 4.1								
13.8		8.2								
291659M	318471M	459454M		Net Sales ($)	13415M	21971M	7130M	24940M	51301M	340697M
221996M	220984M	632271M		Total Assets ($)	19231M	29587M	2830M	14259M	23997M	542367M

M = $ thousand   MM = $ million
See Pages viii through xx for Explanation of Ratios and Data

Current Data Sorted by Assets / Comparative Historical Data

	0-500M	500M-2MM	2-10MM	10-50MM	50-100MM	100-250MM	4/1/14-3/31/15 ALL	4/1/15-3/31/16 ALL
Type of Statement								
Unqualified				4		1	6	4
Reviewed		1	7	2		1	11	8
Compiled	4	3	7			1	22	17
Tax Returns	17	16	6				59	64
Other	21	12	14	11			48	53
	20 (4/1-9/30/18)			108 (10/1/18-3/31/19)				
NUMBER OF STATEMENTS	42	32	34	17		3	146	146
ASSETS	%	%	%	%	%	%	%	%
Cash & Equivalents	34.9	7.8	7.9	14.7	DATA NOT AVAILABLE		14.2	12.9
Trade Receivables (net)	3.2	4.3	14.8	13.1			9.2	9.0
Inventory	1.0	.9	3.4	7.0			2.3	3.3
All Other Current	2.2	3.2	1.6	1.1			.7	1.8
Total Current	41.3	16.2	27.7	35.9			26.4	27.0
Fixed Assets (net)	29.5	54.0	51.4	51.1			51.8	52.8
Intangibles (net)	17.6	20.3	14.4	5.9			14.3	11.8
All Other Non-Current	11.5	9.5	6.5	7.1			7.4	8.5
Total	100.0	100.0	100.0	100.0			100.0	100.0
LIABILITIES								
Notes Payable-Short Term	29.8	7.1	3.1	3.8			6.3	9.3
Cur. Mat.-L.T.D.	6.4	6.2	7.0	4.5			6.2	5.9
Trade Payables	2.4	1.9	5.5	6.0			5.1	4.9
Income Taxes Payable	.0	.0	.0	.0			.0	.0
All Other Current	51.9	10.2	5.9	9.2			9.2	7.8
Total Current	90.5	25.5	21.5	23.6			26.9	27.9
Long-Term Debt	38.1	60.0	42.9	26.0			50.6	40.4
Deferred Taxes	.0	.0	.0	.4			.3	.2
All Other Non-Current	5.0	8.5	12.0	1.0			9.8	5.3
Net Worth	-33.6	6.0	23.7	49.0			12.4	26.2
Total Liabilties & Net Worth	100.0	100.0	100.0	100.0			100.0	100.0
INCOME DATA								
Net Sales	100.0	100.0	100.0	100.0			100.0	100.0
Gross Profit								
Operating Expenses	93.7	86.5	91.9	91.7			91.7	91.2
Operating Profit	6.3	13.5	8.1	8.3			8.3	8.8
All Other Expenses (net)	1.6	3.8	1.8	.3			2.5	2.2
Profit Before Taxes	4.7	9.7	6.3	8.0			5.8	6.6
RATIOS								
Current	4.9	3.9	1.8	3.3			2.7	2.4
	1.5	.6	1.3	1.7			1.0	1.2
	.4	.3	.6	.9			.4	.4
Quick	4.6	2.8	1.7	2.3			2.3	2.1
	1.5	.5	1.0	1.2			.8	.9
	.3	.2	.4	.5			.3	.3
Sales/Receivables	0 UND	0 UND	5 72.7	27 13.3			0 UND	0 UND
	0 UND	0 UND	29 12.7	31 11.6			4 96.1	2 183.9
	0 UND	3 106.1	38 9.6	49 7.5			28 13.0	26 13.8
Cost of Sales/Inventory								
Cost of Sales/Payables								
Sales/Working Capital	14.9	9.8	11.5	6.7			13.7	13.0
	55.1	-245.1	31.5	12.6			983.7	76.3
	-16.6	-9.4	-27.5	-85.8			-12.6	-13.6
EBIT/Interest	14.7	7.1	5.6	16.8			9.9	9.8
	(24) 4.2	(22) 3.5	(33) 3.3	(15) 4.7			(124) 2.7	(115) 4.3
	1.1	.2	.9	2.4			1.4	1.6
Net Profit + Depr., Dep., Amort./Cur. Mat. L/T/D							3.5	
							(13) 2.3	
							1.3	
Fixed/Worth	.2	2.0	1.9	.7			.9	.9
	1.0	NM	2.7	1.1			3.0	2.5
	-1.5	-1.2	-7.4	2.0			-2.9	-5.5
Debt/Worth	.4	2.0	1.8	.6			1.0	.9
	8.6	NM	3.9	1.3			3.9	2.8
	-1.7	-3.2	-13.8	3.3			-5.1	-8.7
% Profit Before Taxes/Tangible Net Worth	224.0	108.9	63.8	65.0			86.5	72.2
	(24) 34.6	(16) 38.0	(23) 18.0	10.2			(97) 27.2	(105) 30.0
	10.6	15.7	-3.1	5.9			9.8	10.5
% Profit Before Taxes/Total Assets	35.8	16.3	11.8	13.8			18.0	22.5
	15.5	9.3	6.9	7.1			6.0	9.1
	-3.9	.1	.0	3.2			1.5	2.0
Sales/Net Fixed Assets	127.8	7.8	9.3	7.1			14.9	10.5
	18.6	2.6	4.7	2.4			4.8	5.4
	7.2	1.6	1.6	1.4			2.0	1.9
Sales/Total Assets	10.8	2.2	3.0	1.9			3.6	3.4
	4.3	1.6	1.8	1.4			2.1	1.9
	2.9	.9	1.2	.8			1.2	1.1
% Depr., Dep., Amort./Sales	1.6	3.5	2.6	3.5			2.2	2.3
	(19) 2.9	(22) 6.9	(28) 5.3	(16) 5.5			(121) 5.0	(112) 4.3
	5.0	9.9	8.0	8.5			8.4	8.1
% Officers', Directors' Owners' Comp/Sales	2.9	3.4	2.4				2.9	3.0
	(29) 5.8	(12) 5.7	(20) 3.4				(82) 4.2	(76) 4.9
	8.9	8.0	5.0				7.0	9.4
Net Sales ($)	38814M	60258M	287639M	473568M		308105M	757940M	688150M
Total Assets ($)	9120M	37111M	156875M	375491M		350421M	469614M	414262M

M = $ thousand MM = $ million

See Pages viii through xx for Explanation of Ratios and Data

Comparative Historical Data **Current Data Sorted by Sales**

Type of Statement	4/1/16-3/31/17 ALL	4/1/17-3/31/18 ALL	4/1/18-3/31/19 ALL		0-1MM	1-3MM	3-5MM	5-10MM	10-25MM	25MM & OVER
					20 (4/1-9/30/18)			108 (10/1/18-3/31/19)		
Unqualified	2	1	5					4	3	2
Reviewed	11	14	11			1		4	4	2
Compiled	15	10	15		4	3	2	4	1	1
Tax Returns	36	41	39		14	15	4	5	1	
Other	40	46	58		21	12	2	8	8	7
NUMBER OF STATEMENTS	104	112	128		39	31	8	21	17	12
	%	%	%		%	%	%	%	%	%
ASSETS										
Cash & Equivalents	14.9	15.0	17.5		27.5	18.1		9.1	11.8	9.2
Trade Receivables (net)	9.7	9.0	8.0		1.4	5.1		16.3	13.1	17.1
Inventory	3.5	4.4	3.7		1.0	1.0		3.1	4.5	21.0
All Other Current	1.3	.9	2.1		2.2	3.5		1.7	1.0	.9
Total Current	29.5	29.4	31.4		32.1	27.7		30.2	30.3	48.2
Fixed Assets (net)	53.8	47.6	43.9		37.1	44.6		52.0	48.5	38.5
Intangibles (net)	8.4	13.6	16.0		20.7	15.9		11.2	14.0	6.2
All Other Non-Current	8.3	9.4	8.8		10.1	11.8		6.5	7.1	7.1
Total	100.0	100.0	100.0		100.0	100.0		100.0	100.0	100.0
LIABILITIES										
Notes Payable-Short Term	9.9	7.4	13.6		27.6	12.3		3.8	4.9	8.5
Cur. Mat.-L.T.D.	6.0	7.1	6.1		4.5	8.4		8.0	5.8	3.9
Trade Payables	6.9	4.2	3.7		1.2	3.3		4.7	6.0	9.4
Income Taxes Payable	.0	.1	.0		.0	.0		.1	.0	.1
All Other Current	14.2	10.7	22.7		58.0	8.7		4.1	8.5	10.8
Total Current	36.9	29.4	46.2		91.3	32.7		20.7	25.2	32.7
Long-Term Debt	42.8	42.1	42.8		45.7	50.0		47.9	31.2	22.9
Deferred Taxes	.5	.5	.1		.0	.0		.0	.1	.6
All Other Non-Current	7.9	10.1	7.1		3.3	12.2		13.2	6.0	.5
Net Worth	11.8	17.8	3.9		-40.4	5.1		18.3	37.5	43.3
Total Liabilities & Net Worth	100.0	100.0	100.0		100.0	100.0		100.0	100.0	100.0
INCOME DATA										
Net Sales	100.0	100.0	100.0		100.0	100.0		100.0	100.0	100.0
Gross Profit										
Operating Expenses	94.6	91.3	91.2		85.0	94.3		92.9	93.9	95.1
Operating Profit	5.4	8.7	8.8		15.0	5.7		7.1	6.1	4.9
All Other Expenses (net)	2.1	1.3	2.1		5.0	.5		1.9	-.9	1.9
Profit Before Taxes	3.2	7.5	6.7		10.0	5.2		5.2	7.0	3.0
RATIOS										
Current	1.5	2.4	3.1		4.2	3.3		2.7	1.8	2.4
	.9	1.3	1.4		1.3	1.1		1.3	1.2	1.7
	.4	.5	.5		.2	.4		.5	.7	1.3
Quick	1.4	2.1	2.7		3.1	2.7		2.7	1.5	2.1
	.6	1.0	1.0		1.3	.5		.9	.9	1.1
	.3	.4	.4		.2	.2		.4	.5	.5
Sales/Receivables	0 UND	0 UND	0 UND		0 UND	0 UND		16 22.7	6 65.1	30 12.3
	8 47.1	7 49.7	0 980.2		0 UND	0 UND		33 11.2	21 17.5	31 11.7
	30 12.3	29 12.7	30 12.1		0 UND	9 41.7		41 9.0	37 9.8	49 7.5
Cost of Sales/Inventory										
Cost of Sales/Payables										
Sales/Working Capital	18.4	12.9	10.9		8.2	11.3		10.4	13.9	3.9
	-135.3	78.6	42.7		210.5	112.4		31.3	31.8	12.0
	-15.9	-15.7	-17.6		-11.5	-10.7		-16.5	-25.7	32.7
EBIT/Interest	8.6	10.3	7.9		4.7	11.7		5.0	15.5	10.6
	(93) 2.2	(92) 4.5	(97) 3.6		(18) 1.7	(23) 4.8		3.3	(15) 5.3	4.3
	.4	2.0	1.0		.0	.9		1.1	1.6	.2
Net Profit + Depr., Dep., Amort./Cur. Mat. L/T/D	3.8	3.1	2.8							
	(15) 2.2	(13) 2.4	(13) 2.0							
	1.7	1.4	.9							
Fixed/Worth	.9	.8	.8		.2	.8		2.1	.7	.6
	2.7	2.1	2.5		3.2	7.8		2.8	1.5	1.2
	-6.6	-6.5	-3.1		-.9	-1.2		NM	-10.9	1.9
Debt/Worth	1.2	.7	1.2		1.4	1.2		2.0	.6	.6
	3.9	2.5	4.4		-5.7	9.8		4.2	1.4	1.4
	-7.0	-11.7	-4.1		-1.7	-3.3		NM	-19.0	4.1
% Profit Before Taxes/Tangible Net Worth	62.8	84.3	79.0		141.0	185.0		74.0	65.6	23.1
	(71) 19.3	(76) 23.4	(82) 28.5		(19) 27.0	(17) 31.0	(16) 52.2		(12) 10.9	(11) 9.5
	-2.3	8.1	7.6		-10.2	14.8		2.0	3.8	-5.6
% Profit Before Taxes/Total Assets	19.2	23.7	19.4		20.4	27.9		12.8	20.8	7.4
	4.7	8.4	8.5		8.4	12.9		8.1	9.1	4.2
	-1.2	3.1	.1		-8.0	2.7		.5	2.6	-1.8
Sales/Net Fixed Assets	18.2	14.3	18.1		143.3	23.1		12.7	7.2	11.9
	4.7	6.1	6.1		7.7	11.1		2.8	4.8	5.3
	2.0	2.8	2.3		1.5	2.4		1.4	2.2	2.0
Sales/Total Assets	4.6	4.0	3.6		10.0	4.5		2.8	2.9	1.8
	2.1	2.2	2.0		2.7	2.3		1.6	1.9	1.3
	1.3	1.2	1.2		.9	1.6		1.2	1.3	.8
% Depr., Dep., Amort./Sales	2.3	2.4	2.7		2.7	2.2		2.2	2.7	2.1
	(84) 5.3	(84) 4.1	(86) 4.8		(20) 4.8	(17) 3.9	(17) 6.8		(16) 3.8	(10) 5.0
	7.6	7.2	8.1		9.4	7.1		12.0	7.0	6.3
% Officers', Directors' Owners' Comp/Sales	2.7	2.6	2.9		2.8	4.7		2.7		
	(44) 5.2	(47) 5.2	(63) 4.6		(20) 5.8	(17) 6.7	(16) 3.4			
	7.6	11.0	7.0		9.0	8.7		5.2		
Net Sales ($)	2194195M	2299661M	1168384M		19072M	56316M	29172M	155713M	245892M	662219M
Total Assets ($)	656804M	779235M	929018M		18909M	27426M	13716M	112959M	151901M	604107M

© RMA 2019   M = $ thousand   MM = $ million
See Pages viii through xx for Explanation of Ratios and Data

		Current Data Sorted by Assets						Comparative Historical Data	
		1	4	1		Type of Statement			
		3	7			Unqualified		8	12
		6				Reviewed		16	16
1	7	4	7			Compiled		9	10
8		7	6	4	1	Tax Returns		11	18
	12 (4/1-9/30/18)		48 (10/1/18-3/31/19)			Other		28	41
								4/1/14- 3/31/15	4/1/15- 3/31/16
0-500M	500M-2MM	2-10MM	10-50MM	50-100MM	100-250MM			ALL	ALL
1	15	21	17	5	1	NUMBER OF STATEMENTS		72	97
%	%	%	%	%	%	ASSETS		%	%
	15.9	11.2	12.4			Cash & Equivalents		10.0	12.0
	16.0	22.7	18.6			Trade Receivables (net)		19.3	19.5
	16.9	6.4	7.5			Inventory		9.2	11.5
	2.6	2.8	1.6			All Other Current		1.9	1.6
	51.4	43.1	40.0			Total Current		40.4	44.7
	32.7	41.3	38.0			Fixed Assets (net)		44.3	39.3
	2.7	6.9	4.2			Intangibles (net)		7.3	8.7
	13.2	8.8	17.9			All Other Non-Current		8.0	7.3
	100.0	100.0	100.0			Total		100.0	100.0
						LIABILITIES			
	7.8	5.5	4.3			Notes Payable-Short Term		7.7	11.4
	5.9	4.9	3.3			Cur. Mat.-L.T.D.		6.6	5.7
	7.2	8.6	10.4			Trade Payables		9.2	9.1
	.0	.1	.0			Income Taxes Payable		.4	.3
	4.7	6.2	6.9			All Other Current		7.7	7.9
	25.5	25.4	25.0			Total Current		31.6	34.4
	35.7	30.2	14.7			Long-Term Debt		29.6	24.4
	.0	.0	1.2			Deferred Taxes		.3	.2
	5.2	1.2	5.1			All Other Non-Current		7.1	7.0
	33.6	43.2	54.0			Net Worth		31.3	34.0
	100.0	100.0	100.0			Total Liabilities & Net Worth		100.0	100.0
						INCOME DATA			
	100.0	100.0	100.0			Net Sales		100.0	100.0
						Gross Profit			
	94.9	94.1	94.6			Operating Expenses		92.0	90.6
	5.1	5.9	5.4			Operating Profit		8.0	9.4
	-.4	.7	-.1			All Other Expenses (net)		2.3	1.8
	5.5	5.1	5.5			Profit Before Taxes		5.7	7.6
						RATIOS			
	8.7	4.0	2.5					2.5	2.6
	1.9	1.7	1.8			Current		1.4	1.5
	.9	1.0	1.4					.7	.8
	1.8	3.6	2.0					1.8	2.0
	1.5	1.6	1.6			Quick		1.0	1.0
	.5	.6	.9					.5	.5
0 UND		27 13.4	28 13.2					26 14.1	24 15.4
17 21.4		33 10.9	35 10.4			Sales/Receivables		32 11.5	31 11.6
26 14.1		45 8.1	42 8.6					36 10.0	40 9.1
						Cost of Sales/Inventory			
						Cost of Sales/Payables			
	3.8	5.8	8.7					6.8	6.9
	17.6	9.7	12.0			Sales/Working Capital		18.7	15.1
	-191.5	-530.4	16.7					-16.0	-30.8
	22.8	25.4	11.0					15.3	22.6
	(13) 3.1	(19) 7.5	(13) 7.7			EBIT/Interest		(63) 5.1	(86) 6.2
	1.7	1.2	4.6					1.1	2.4
						Net Profit + Depr., Dep.,		9.2	7.3
						Amort./Cur. Mat. L/T/D		(16) 1.8	(17) 2.7
								1.0	1.2
	.1	.5	.2					.5	.5
	.6	1.0	.7			Fixed/Worth		1.2	1.0
	-2.3	3.3	1.4					27.7	6.3
	.1	.6	.5					.6	.6
	.9	1.0	.6			Debt/Worth		1.6	1.4
	-6.4	12.6	2.2					37.8	NM
	90.9	65.4	22.4			% Profit Before Taxes/Tangible		35.2	42.6
	(11) 10.3	(18) 16.6	(16) 11.1			Net Worth		(55) 17.9	(73) 18.0
	5.3	4.1	2.8					5.8	7.6
	25.4	20.6	13.9			% Profit Before Taxes/Total		13.0	16.7
	4.9	10.4	7.0			Assets		6.3	8.7
	2.3	.5	2.0					1.1	3.2
	62.2	11.8	9.2					11.0	13.4
	15.5	4.4	5.0			Sales/Net Fixed Assets		4.4	5.9
	4.1	2.5	2.6					2.3	3.0
	3.7	3.0	2.3					2.7	3.1
	2.9	2.1	1.6			Sales/Total Assets		1.8	2.1
	1.9	1.6	1.2					1.2	1.5
	.8	3.1	2.2					2.5	2.1
	(12) 3.3	(16) 4.0	(16) 3.9			% Depr., Dep., Amort./Sales		(63) 4.5	(81) 4.3
	8.6	5.3	9.2					8.5	8.7
		1.7						1.9	1.9
	(12)	3.2				% Officers', Directors'		(25) 4.4	(32) 3.3
		6.6				Owners' Comp/Sales		6.0	6.5
1164M	62791M	239387M	760780M	496138M	290132M	Net Sales ($)		1927628M	2510496M
124M	20181M	109393M	417079M	351613M	195988M	Total Assets ($)		1098413M	1391023M

M = $ thousand   MM = $ million
See Pages viii through xx for Explanation of Ratios and Data

Comparative Historical Data / Current Data Sorted by Sales

4/1/16-3/31/17 ALL	4/1/17-3/31/18 ALL	4/1/18-3/31/19 ALL	Type of Statement	0-1MM	1-3MM	3-5MM	5-10MM	10-25MM	25MM & OVER
				12 (4/1-9/30/18)			48 (10/1/18-3/31/19)		
3	4	6	Unqualified					2	4
17	12	10	Reviewed					4	6
5	6	6	Compiled			1	2	3	
17	9	12	Tax Returns		3	3	4	2	
28	34	26	Other		4	4	4	3	11
70	65	60	NUMBER OF STATEMENTS		7	8	10	14	21
%	%	%	**ASSETS**	%	%	%	%	%	%
7.7	11.1	13.3	Cash & Equivalents	DATA NOT AVAILABLE			12.1	9.3	12.7
20.1	18.4	18.8	Trade Receivables (net)				19.0	22.1	19.0
15.7	9.6	10.0	Inventory				6.1	8.9	7.6
1.4	1.8	2.3	All Other Current				.2	3.2	2.3
45.0	40.9	44.3	Total Current				37.3	43.4	41.6
37.1	41.8	37.8	Fixed Assets (net)				44.4	37.8	37.3
10.9	8.5	5.4	Intangibles (net)				5.8	8.1	5.9
6.9	8.8	12.5	All Other Non-Current				12.5	10.7	15.2
100.0	100.0	100.0	Total				100.0	100.0	100.0
			LIABILITIES						
11.6	8.3	5.8	Notes Payable-Short Term				4.5	9.8	2.1
6.1	4.6	4.3	Cur. Mat.-L.T.D.				5.7	3.6	2.8
9.3	9.3	8.8	Trade Payables				8.2	9.5	10.9
.1	.1	.1	Income Taxes Payable				.0	.1	.1
6.7	9.1	7.5	All Other Current				4.1	5.1	7.3
33.7	31.4	26.5	Total Current				22.5	28.2	23.2
25.6	21.6	29.1	Long-Term Debt				50.1	23.7	19.3
.4	.2	.3	Deferred Taxes				.0	.9	.3
8.7	2.8	3.9	All Other Non-Current				6.9	4.3	2.9
31.7	44.0	40.2	Net Worth				20.4	43.0	54.4
100.0	100.0	100.0	Total Liabilties & Net Worth				100.0	100.0	100.0
			INCOME DATA						
100.0	100.0	100.0	Net Sales				100.0	100.0	100.0
			Gross Profit						
93.5	91.6	94.9	Operating Expenses				94.8	95.9	95.7
6.5	8.4	5.1	Operating Profit				5.2	4.1	4.3
1.3	1.2	.3	All Other Expenses (net)				-.1	1.0	.3
5.2	7.1	4.9	Profit Before Taxes				5.3	3.1	4.0
			RATIOS						
2.4	2.4	3.7					4.2	3.3	2.4
1.5	1.5	1.7	Current				2.5	1.7	1.6
.8	.7	1.2					.8	1.1	1.3
1.8	1.7	2.2					3.4	2.8	2.0
.9	.8	1.5	Quick				1.6	1.3	1.4
.5	.5	.7					.6	.6	.9
26 14.0	**23** 15.7	**24** 15.2					**11** 32.0	**29** 12.7	**28** 13.1
35 10.4	**31** 11.8	**31** 11.9	Sales/Receivables				**26** 13.9	**34** 10.6	**34** 10.6
45 8.2	**40** 9.1	**41** 8.8					**39** 9.3	**43** 8.5	**41** 9.0
			Cost of Sales/Inventory						
			Cost of Sales/Payables						
7.2	6.5	6.3					7.4	7.3	8.5
15.6	16.4	12.7	Sales/Working Capital				21.3	9.3	13.0
-28.5	-33.6	41.1					-40.1	NM	27.0
15.3	23.0	17.7					34.7	10.0	11.9
(64) 5.4	(56) 7.5	(52) 6.8	EBIT/Interest				11.0	(13) 4.1	(16) 7.6
1.2	2.7	1.2					1.7	.9	.6
8.5	9.0	4.8							
(11) 3.0	(14) 3.3	(11) 2.9	Net Profit + Depr., Dep., Amort./Cur. Mat. L/T/D						
2.0	1.3	.9							
.5	.5	.3					.5	.4	.4
1.2	1.1	.7	Fixed/Worth				5.8	1.0	.7
NM	2.8	2.6					-2.9	NM	1.4
.6	.5	.5					.9	.6	.5
1.6	1.3	1.0	Debt/Worth				11.2	1.0	.6
-10.0	4.2	5.4					-6.2	NM	3.1
46.3	36.1	31.8						27.0	24.2
(52) 19.3	(57) 16.6	(51) 10.3	% Profit Before Taxes/Tangible Net Worth					(11) 11.0	9.0
5.9	5.2	2.8						1.1	.3
15.4	17.4	15.2					39.2	14.4	13.1
7.9	7.1	4.9	% Profit Before Taxes/Total Assets				11.2	8.7	4.9
.5	2.5	.6					2.5	.2	.1
19.0	11.4	15.5					25.7	29.9	10.0
6.2	4.6	5.0	Sales/Net Fixed Assets				8.0	5.0	5.0
2.5	2.7	2.9					2.3	2.9	2.8
2.9	3.1	2.9					3.8	2.6	2.6
1.9	2.1	2.1	Sales/Total Assets				2.9	2.1	1.6
1.4	1.4	1.5					1.7	1.2	1.4
2.2	2.6	2.4						2.5	2.4
(58) 3.9	(49) 3.6	(50) 4.0	% Depr., Dep., Amort./Sales					(12) 4.0	(18) 4.6
7.4	7.5	6.3						6.6	8.2
1.5	1.8	1.7							
(32) 3.2	(26) 2.4	(25) 3.6	% Officers', Directors' Owners' Comp/Sales						
6.2	5.7	6.6							
1629543M	1711367M	1850392M	Net Sales ($)		12584M	31703M	70913M	197523M	1537669M
961463M	974337M	1094378M	Total Assets ($)		7091M	17107M	29106M	108432M	932642M

M = $ thousand MM = $ million

See Pages viii through xx for Explanation of Ratios and Data

Current Data Sorted by Assets

Comparative Historical Data

0-500M	500M-2MM	2-10MM	10-50MM	50-100MM	100-250MM	Type of Statement	4/1/14-3/31/15 ALL	4/1/15-3/31/16 ALL
	1	1	6	1		Unqualified	5	7
1	3	3		2		Reviewed	2	4
22	10	2				Compiled	14	2
19	14	19				Tax Returns	48	56
						Other	66	51
	16 (4/1-9/30/18)		88 (10/1/18-3/31/19)					
42	28	25	6	3		NUMBER OF STATEMENTS	135	120
%	%	%	%	%	%	ASSETS	%	%
38.4	19.2	23.6				Cash & Equivalents	23.3	27.6
1.5	3.7	.8				Trade Receivables (net)	1.9	2.2
3.4	.9	2.2				Inventory	5.0	3.3
1.8	1.5	1.3				All Other Current	3.4	2.2
45.3	25.3	27.8				Total Current	33.5	35.3
35.7	60.6	55.8				Fixed Assets (net)	49.8	47.8
10.4	9.2	3.6				Intangibles (net)	6.5	7.0
8.6	4.8	12.8				All Other Non-Current	10.1	9.9
100.0	100.0	100.0				Total	100.0	100.0
						LIABILITIES		
13.9	13.8	.9				Notes Payable-Short Term	8.2	6.5
2.3	1.9	1.4				Cur. Mat.-L.T.D.	3.8	3.2
1.4	2.2	.8				Trade Payables	4.2	3.7
.1	.0	.0				Income Taxes Payable	.1	.0
35.4	6.2	3.1				All Other Current	15.8	11.2
53.2	24.1	6.2				Total Current	32.1	24.7
20.0	37.4	32.3				Long-Term Debt	30.4	25.0
.0	.0	.0				Deferred Taxes	.0	.0
13.1	.3	2.5				All Other Non-Current	15.5	9.7
13.8	38.2	59.0				Net Worth	22.1	40.6
100.0	100.0	100.0				Total Liabilities & Net Worth	100.0	100.0
						INCOME DATA		
100.0	100.0	100.0				Net Sales	100.0	100.0
						Gross Profit		
87.0	85.1	84.3				Operating Expenses	87.0	88.6
13.0	14.9	15.7				Operating Profit	13.0	11.4
2.3	4.4	7.1				All Other Expenses (net)	2.3	1.4
10.7	10.5	8.7				Profit Before Taxes	10.7	10.0
						RATIOS		
4.0	8.3	26.6					6.3	6.2
1.3	2.0	6.1				Current	1.8	1.9
.7	.6	1.5					.3	.8
3.6	8.3	26.6					4.4	6.2
1.2	1.7	3.7				Quick	1.0	1.6
.4	.5	1.1					.2	.5
0 UND	0 UND	0 UND					0 UND	0 UND
0 UND	0 UND	0 999.8				Sales/Receivables	0 UND	0 UND
0 UND	0 UND	5 68.8					2 199.4	2 184.1
						Cost of Sales/Inventory		
						Cost of Sales/Payables		
14.5	5.2	1.7					10.8	8.1
57.6	23.0	3.9				Sales/Working Capital	55.3	26.7
-121.3	-30.4	51.3					-12.6	-52.0
41.7	12.5	18.0					22.6	31.3
(23) 14.8	(20) 4.0	(14) 6.7				EBIT/Interest	(88) 5.9	(75) 6.4
3.5	.8	1.9					1.5	2.0
						Net Profit + Depr., Dep., Amort./Cur. Mat. L/T/D		
.2	.7	.4					.5	.3
1.2	2.0	1.0				Fixed/Worth	1.6	1.1
UND	19.7	3.2					-3.0	3.4
.5	.5	.0					.3	.2
1.9	1.4	.5				Debt/Worth	2.1	1.1
-18.1	20.8	2.9					-6.1	5.5
481.6	41.2	28.4				% Profit Before Taxes/Tangible	136.3	103.3
(31) 125.6	(22) 25.3	(23) 11.6				Net Worth	(94) 59.4	(100) 38.7
44.1	8.7	-.7					14.0	14.7
94.2	20.9	17.6				% Profit Before Taxes/Total	72.3	40.8
31.8	11.2	5.6				Assets	25.1	15.2
5.3	-.3	-.7					5.2	2.7
82.2	6.4	3.6					32.3	25.3
22.6	2.1	.9				Sales/Net Fixed Assets	6.5	5.9
6.7	.8	.4					1.7	1.4
9.6	2.3	.8					6.0	4.8
4.7	1.2	.5				Sales/Total Assets	3.1	2.4
2.5	.7	.2					1.1	.9
.5	3.5	2.8					1.3	1.4
(23) 1.1	(19) 5.5	(22) 5.7				% Depr., Dep., Amort./Sales	(73) 2.7	(80) 2.8
3.6	11.5	10.2					5.1	5.4
4.7	7.0						5.0	4.9
(25) 7.9	(14) 9.2					% Officers', Directors' Owners' Comp/Sales	(52) 7.3	(48) 8.3
11.8	11.8						14.4	12.5
40223M	40336M	95674M	89589M	115276M		Net Sales ($)	402475M	460953M
8795M	28772M	139468M	180177M	261191M		Total Assets ($)	497778M	467932M

(Columns 10-50MM, 50-100MM, and 100-250MM for the ASSETS through RATIOS sections are marked "DATA NOT AVAILABLE.")

M = $ thousand   MM = $ million
See Pages viii through xx for Explanation of Ratios and Data

Comparative Historical Data / Current Data Sorted by Sales

		Comparative Historical Data		Type of Statement	Current Data Sorted by Sales					
				Unqualified	1			3	3	1
				Reviewed						
				Compiled	3	2	1		1	
				Tax Returns	19	15				
				Other	18	24	5	4	1	2
	9	8	9							
	2	2								
	6	5	7							
	34	44	34							
	60	59	54		16 (4/1-9/30/18)		88 (10/1/18-3/31/19)			
	4/1/16-3/31/17	4/1/17-3/31/18	4/1/18-3/31/19		0-1MM	1-3MM	3-5MM	5-10MM	10-25MM	25MM & OVER
	ALL	ALL	ALL							
	111	118	104	NUMBER OF STATEMENTS	41	41	7	7	5	3
	%	%	%	ASSETS	%	%	%	%	%	%
	26.3	24.3	27.5	Cash & Equivalents	33.1	25.8				
	2.7	1.5	1.9	Trade Receivables (net)	1.6	1.0				
	3.9	1.8	2.2	Inventory	2.5	1.6				
	1.9	2.6	1.5	All Other Current	2.1	1.5				
	34.8	30.2	33.1	Total Current	39.2	29.9				
	47.0	51.5	48.4	Fixed Assets (net)	44.5	51.0				
	10.8	10.7	9.8	Intangibles (net)	9.0	9.7				
	7.4	7.6	8.7	All Other Non-Current	7.3	9.4				
	100.0	100.0	100.0	Total	100.0	100.0				
				LIABILITIES						
	4.6	7.9	9.8	Notes Payable-Short Term	17.7	5.8				
	2.6	3.5	1.8	Cur. Mat.-L.T.D.	1.9	1.7				
	4.1	4.3	1.5	Trade Payables	.8	2.3				
	.2	.1	.1	Income Taxes Payable	.1	.0				
	12.7	17.1	17.0	All Other Current	31.7	9.3				
	24.2	32.9	30.1	Total Current	52.3	19.1				
	25.5	31.1	27.6	Long-Term Debt	30.4	28.2				
	.0	.0	.0	Deferred Taxes	.0	.0				
	7.6	7.5	6.5	All Other Non-Current	10.1	5.1				
	42.7	28.5	35.8	Net Worth	7.2	47.6				
	100.0	100.0	100.0	Total Liabilties & Net Worth	100.0	100.0				
				INCOME DATA						
	100.0	100.0	100.0	Net Sales	100.0	100.0				
				Gross Profit						
	87.7	85.8	86.1	Operating Expenses	83.8	86.1				
	12.3	14.2	13.9	Operating Profit	16.2	13.9				
	3.0	3.1	3.9	All Other Expenses (net)	7.4	2.1				
	9.3	11.1	10.0	Profit Before Taxes	8.8	11.8				
				RATIOS						
	5.1	4.0	7.4	Current	5.6	7.9				
	1.9	1.2	1.9		1.5	2.1				
	.5	.5	.8		.6	1.0				
	4.1	3.4	6.2	Quick	5.2	7.3				
	1.6	1.1	1.7		1.3	1.8				
	.4	.4	.6		.2	.8				
0	UND	0 UND	0 UND	Sales/Receivables	0 UND	0 UND				
0	UND	0 UND	0 UND		0 UND	0 UND				
1	472.0	0 873.4	1 547.8		0 UND	0 UND				
				Cost of Sales/Inventory						
				Cost of Sales/Payables						
	8.1	12.0	4.9	Sales/Working Capital	5.2	8.2				
	30.3	84.2	26.3		51.2	26.6				
	-17.2	-18.1	-85.0		-17.3	NM				
	34.9	18.6	26.8	EBIT/Interest	29.9	30.5				
(70)	8.4	(83) 7.3	(62) 5.5		(18) 6.6	(29) 5.9				
	1.9	1.8	2.0		3.2	1.8				
				Net Profit + Depr., Dep., Amort./Cur. Mat. L/T/D						
	.4	.6	.5	Fixed/Worth	.2	.4				
	1.1	1.7	1.2		2.5	1.2				
	5.8	75.0	12.3		UND	12.0				
	.3	.4	.3	Debt/Worth	.6	.2				
	1.2	2.0	1.1		4.4	1.1				
	16.3	-398.3	24.1		-13.8	16.5				
	133.9	123.6	71.1	% Profit Before Taxes/Tangible Net Worth	127.4	144.1				
(88)	43.5	(88) 39.5	(82) 29.3		(30) 42.7	(34) 34.6				
	10.8	7.4	5.6		2.8	8.7				
	38.1	40.6	33.6	% Profit Before Taxes/Total Assets	41.9	42.4				
	18.0	13.1	12.3		9.7	17.0				
	1.9	.7	-.1		-.4	-.6				
	21.9	21.4	15.5	Sales/Net Fixed Assets	43.3	12.4				
	7.9	5.3	4.6		6.4	4.8				
	1.3	1.2	1.0		.8	1.3				
	5.2	5.0	4.0	Sales/Total Assets	4.8	3.5				
	2.2	2.3	1.5		2.0	2.2				
	.7	.7	.6		.4	.7				
	1.1	1.3	1.4	% Depr., Dep., Amort./Sales	1.0	1.6				
(77)	3.1	(78) 2.8	(72) 4.2		(27) 3.9	(26) 4.1				
	8.1	7.9	7.8		8.7	7.1				
	4.5	4.0	4.4	% Officers', Directors' Owners' Comp/Sales	4.8	4.9				
(47)	8.7	(45) 7.3	(45) 7.9		(19) 7.9	(20) 7.4				
	13.1	10.7	11.1		13.0	10.2				
	1012435M	290419M	381098M	Net Sales ($)	21038M	69717M	28779M	48525M	97763M	115276M
	530901M	385880M	618403M	Total Assets ($)	35279M	74578M	37679M	95305M	114371M	261191M

M = $ thousand   MM = $ million
See Pages viii through xx for Explanation of Ratios and Data

Current Data Sorted by Assets   Comparative Historical Data

0-500M	500M-2MM	2-10MM	10-50MM	50-100MM	100-250MM	Type of Statement	4/1/14-3/31/15 ALL	4/1/15-3/31/16 ALL
		2	5	2	3	Unqualified	8	7
1		3	1			Reviewed	3	5
1	1	1	2			Compiled	2	8
1	1	4				Tax Returns	16	11
3	2	12	15	1	6	Other	48	50
		6 (4/1-9/30/18)	60 (10/1/18-3/31/19)					
4	5	22	23	3	9	NUMBER OF STATEMENTS	77	81
%	%	%	%	%	%	ASSETS	%	%
		14.8	17.4			Cash & Equivalents	14.7	19.8
		11.3	12.2			Trade Receivables (net)	14.1	12.6
		4.9	1.9			Inventory	.3	1.1
		5.7	5.6			All Other Current	3.0	4.1
		36.6	37.0			Total Current	32.1	37.6
		42.6	36.1			Fixed Assets (net)	49.7	40.9
		12.2	15.5			Intangibles (net)	8.1	6.5
		8.5	11.3			All Other Non-Current	10.2	15.0
		100.0	100.0			Total	100.0	100.0
						LIABILITIES		
		.9	4.6			Notes Payable-Short Term	6.6	4.4
		2.1	3.1			Cur. Mat.-L.T.D.	2.5	2.4
		10.3	7.4			Trade Payables	7.9	9.5
		.3	.4			Income Taxes Payable	.1	.2
		21.4	19.4			All Other Current	15.0	20.3
		35.0	35.0			Total Current	32.1	36.9
		35.3	44.6			Long-Term Debt	49.9	30.9
		.0	.0			Deferred Taxes	.5	.4
		5.2	9.1			All Other Non-Current	2.5	5.0
		24.5	11.3			Net Worth	15.1	26.9
		100.0	100.0			Total Liabilties & Net Worth	100.0	100.0
						INCOME DATA		
		100.0	100.0			Net Sales	100.0	100.0
						Gross Profit		
		66.4	74.6			Operating Expenses	77.8	82.0
		33.6	25.4			Operating Profit	22.2	18.0
		8.2	8.6			All Other Expenses (net)	10.9	4.4
		25.4	16.8			Profit Before Taxes	11.4	13.6
						RATIOS		
		2.7	2.4				2.3	2.8
		1.2	1.0			Current	1.1	1.3
		.7	.7				.5	.6
		1.9	1.7				1.9	2.4
		.9	.9			Quick	.9	.9
		.4	.5				.5	.4
		0 UND	4 87.9				0 UND	0 UND
		1 299.3	17 21.9			Sales/Receivables	10 35.6	6 62.2
		27 13.6	34 10.8				26 13.8	23 16.0
						Cost of Sales/Inventory		
						Cost of Sales/Payables		
		4.9	7.4				7.9	9.0
		289.1	207.0			Sales/Working Capital	131.1	42.8
		-14.6	-14.8				-14.5	-15.5
		22.2	12.0				12.7	26.3
		(16) 3.8	(18) 2.9			EBIT/Interest	(54) 6.2	(61) 7.1
		1.1	1.4				2.7	2.5
						Net Profit + Depr., Dep., Amort./Cur. Mat. L/T/D		
		.8	.9				1.0	.3
		5.6	49.6			Fixed/Worth	3.5	1.8
		-1.0	-1.4				-15.3	-6.1
		.8	2.2				1.8	.7
		5.1	511.6			Debt/Worth	9.6	2.7
		-6.3	-2.9				-7.8	-13.1
		57.7	344.2				90.1	91.8
		(13) 20.3	(12) 19.3			% Profit Before Taxes/Tangible Net Worth	(53) 33.3	(59) 34.3
		4.8	9.3				8.4	9.8
		23.1	12.8				18.8	25.7
		7.6	5.5			% Profit Before Taxes/Total Assets	6.2	9.3
		1.3	3.3				2.6	2.3
		49.2	51.3				37.2	109.2
		4.9	8.8			Sales/Net Fixed Assets	3.1	10.8
		.2	.4				.4	.6
		3.5	3.8				4.3	5.0
		.5	.6			Sales/Total Assets	1.1	1.6
		.2	.2				.3	.4
		.6	.8				1.2	.4
		(15) 3.4	(17) 2.8			% Depr., Dep., Amort./Sales	(58) 4.3	(57) 1.7
		14.2	13.1				12.0	9.4
							.5	.7
						% Officers', Directors' Owners' Comp/Sales	(14) 2.5	(15) 1.6
							8.7	5.0
4763M	24818M	229806M	735993M	316924M	1553009M	Net Sales ($)	3155100M	2284118M
776M	5330M	103828M	395269M	176590M	1386264M	Total Assets ($)	2176667M	1477493M

M = $ thousand   MM = $ million
See Pages viii through xx for Explanation of Ratios and Data

Comparative Historical Data   Current Data Sorted by Sales

			Type of Statement						
12	14	12	Unqualified				1	3	7
3	3	5	Reviewed	1				2	2
6	11	4	Compiled			1	1	1	1
8	5	6	Tax Returns	3	1	1	1		
46	31	39	Other	10	5	4	4	6	10
4/1/16-3/31/17 ALL	4/1/17-3/31/18 ALL	4/1/18-3/31/19 ALL		0-1MM	6 (4/1-9/30/18) 1-3MM	3-5MM	5-10MM	60 (10/1/18-3/31/19) 10-25MM	25MM & OVER
75	64	66	NUMBER OF STATEMENTS	14	6	7	7	12	20
%	%	%	ASSETS	%	%	%	%	%	%
16.1	17.4	16.9	Cash & Equivalents	15.3				26.9	18.8
14.8	15.2	12.2	Trade Receivables (net)	5.4				19.5	19.1
.0	.0	2.3	Inventory	.0				.8	1.7
6.6	4.9	5.4	All Other Current	10.5				3.1	8.4
37.5	37.5	36.9	Total Current	31.2				50.3	47.9
44.7	39.4	39.2	Fixed Assets (net)	53.3				34.1	16.3
5.7	9.6	15.1	Intangibles (net)	13.8				1.8	25.9
12.1	13.5	8.9	All Other Non-Current	1.7				13.9	10.0
100.0	100.0	100.0	Total	100.0				100.0	100.0
			LIABILITIES						
8.1	6.8	7.2	Notes Payable-Short Term	3.3				4.6	5.0
2.8	3.3	3.6	Cur. Mat.-L.T.D.	2.6				1.3	4.2
7.6	7.6	8.3	Trade Payables	2.6				9.9	15.5
.2	.3	.2	Income Taxes Payable	.0				.7	.1
20.7	13.4	18.7	All Other Current	9.7				22.4	27.3
39.4	31.4	38.0	Total Current	18.2				38.9	52.1
34.5	42.9	42.3	Long-Term Debt	45.6				27.6	21.5
.3	.1	.0	Deferred Taxes	.0				.0	.1
4.5	6.9	6.7	All Other Non-Current	6.3				4.2	13.1
21.3	18.7	12.9	Net Worth	29.9				29.4	13.3
100.0	100.0	100.0	Total Liabilites & Net Worth	100.0				100.0	100.0
			INCOME DATA						
100.0	100.0	100.0	Net Sales	100.0				100.0	100.0
			Gross Profit						
80.5	78.8	75.7	Operating Expenses	56.5				83.2	95.6
19.5	21.2	24.3	Operating Profit	43.5				16.8	4.4
6.2	6.6	8.4	All Other Expenses (net)	10.7				8.5	3.1
13.3	14.6	15.9	Profit Before Taxes	32.8				8.3	1.3
			RATIOS						
2.5	1.9	2.4		2.9				2.7	1.2
1.1	1.1	1.1	Current	1.4				1.9	.9
.7	.8	.7		.9				1.0	.7
1.7	1.8	1.9		1.4				2.5	1.0
.9	1.0	.8	Quick	1.0				1.7	.7
.5	.6	.5		.4				.8	.5
0 UND	2 150.6	0 UND		0 UND				16 22.9	6 62.1
9 41.0	19 19.6	10 36.3	Sales/Receivables	0 UND				31 11.9	11 32.3
26 13.8	34 10.6	29 12.4		33 11.2				60 6.1	28 13.0
			Cost of Sales/Inventory						
			Cost of Sales/Payables						
9.2	9.3	5.7		.5				2.5	38.9
80.0	85.0	131.1	Sales/Working Capital	12.9				16.0	-83.7
-16.8	-20.0	-14.7		-28.6				NM	-15.3
17.0	21.8	17.6							6.6
(56) 7.9	(51) 5.7	(49) 3.0	EBIT/Interest					(16)	2.2
3.0	1.3	1.5							.4
6.8	6.7		Net Profit + Depr., Dep.,						
(13) 2.8	(12) 1.8		Amort./Cur. Mat. L/T/D						
1.6	.4								
.7	.6	1.0		.5				.1	1.7
2.0	2.6	12.5	Fixed/Worth	2.1				.5	-4.4
-26.2	-2.7	-1.1		-29.3				33.2	.2
.9	1.4	1.5		1.0				.9	7.4
3.2	11.7	18.7	Debt/Worth	1.6				2.1	-35.1
-61.2	-8.4	-3.0		-42.8				35.2	-2.3
83.3	65.4	101.9	% Profit Before Taxes/Tangible	24.7				66.2	
(53) 28.1	(40) 19.4	(38) 20.3	Net Worth	(10) 8.9				(11) 20.3	
8.1	6.2	6.2		5.4				-.2	
19.1	18.3	19.1	% Profit Before Taxes/Total	6.7				22.6	18.5
6.9	6.3	5.5	Assets	4.4				4.9	5.4
2.1	.7	1.8		2.6				-.1	.4
67.6	48.1	46.8		7.7				93.0	65.4
7.9	11.2	6.8	Sales/Net Fixed Assets	.2				11.2	38.1
.4	.5	.4		.1				.8	24.7
5.0	4.3	3.6		.3				4.9	5.4
1.7	1.6	.7	Sales/Total Assets	.2				1.6	3.5
.2	.4	.2		.1				.4	1.3
.4	1.2	.7		1.7				.6	.5
(59) 3.0	(45) 2.8	(48) 3.3	% Depr., Dep., Amort./Sales	(10) 14.2				(10) 3.3	(15) .7
10.8	11.8	14.0		20.5				19.2	1.8
1.3	1.0		% Officers', Directors'						
(13) 4.0	(10) 5.8		Owners' Comp/Sales						
6.7	18.1								
2604637M	3075798M	2865313M	Net Sales ($)	6166M	12023M	27148M	52228M	181054M	2586694M
1345716M	1713825M	2068057M	Total Assets ($)	49870M	38942M	165514M	72596M	495720M	1245415M

© RMA 2019

M = $ thousand   MM = $ million

See Pages viii through xx for Explanation of Ratios and Data

Current Data Sorted by Assets   Comparative Historical Data

0-500M	500M-2MM	2-10MM	10-50MM	50-100MM	100-250MM	Type of Statement	ALL	ALL
	1	7	5	1	4	Unqualified	18	23
	2	5	1			Reviewed	5	5
3	5	7	2		2	Compiled	32	25
81	51	23	2	1		Tax Returns	186	198
69	43	37	13	1	2	Other	158	177
	29 (4/1-9/30/18)		340 (10/1/18-3/31/19)				4/1/14-3/31/15	4/1/15-3/31/16
0-500M	500M-2MM	2-10MM	10-50MM	50-100MM	100-250MM		ALL	ALL
153	102	79	23	6	6	NUMBER OF STATEMENTS	399	428
%	%	%	%	%	%	**ASSETS**	%	%
36.5	21.0	20.1	10.5			Cash & Equivalents	26.8	27.3
7.6	12.5	21.8	15.4			Trade Receivables (net)	15.5	13.5
4.6	5.6	8.4	9.8			Inventory	4.3	5.1
2.3	2.8	4.2	5.4			All Other Current	3.0	2.9
51.0	41.9	54.5	41.1			Total Current	49.6	48.8
28.6	37.3	28.4	35.3			Fixed Assets (net)	30.4	31.3
8.3	8.1	4.9	7.3			Intangibles (net)	8.2	8.0
12.2	12.7	12.2	16.3			All Other Non-Current	11.8	11.9
100.0	100.0	100.0	100.0			Total	100.0	100.0
						LIABILITIES		
19.5	7.1	9.1	18.8			Notes Payable-Short Term	10.0	15.8
4.8	3.6	3.7	4.4			Cur. Mat.-L.T.D.	4.1	2.7
12.7	4.8	7.3	8.8			Trade Payables	9.2	8.0
.4	.1	.0	.1			Income Taxes Payable	.3	.0
25.4	13.7	20.0	30.1			All Other Current	18.1	16.0
62.8	29.3	40.0	62.2			Total Current	41.7	42.5
28.5	25.4	19.3	12.3			Long-Term Debt	23.6	28.0
.0	.0	.0	.0			Deferred Taxes	.1	.0
7.8	4.3	2.8	3.3			All Other Non-Current	10.8	14.3
.9	41.0	37.9	22.0			Net Worth	23.9	15.1
100.0	100.0	100.0	100.0			Total Liabilities & Net Worth	100.0	100.0
						INCOME DATA		
100.0	100.0	100.0	100.0			Net Sales	100.0	100.0
						Gross Profit		
88.0	86.9	87.8	86.1			Operating Expenses	88.4	89.1
12.0	13.1	12.2	13.9			Operating Profit	11.6	10.9
1.1	2.2	1.6	.7			All Other Expenses (net)	1.6	1.6
10.9	10.9	10.6	13.2			Profit Before Taxes	10.0	9.3
						RATIOS		
4.8	5.2	3.8	1.6			Current	3.4	4.4
1.6	1.4	1.5	1.2				1.3	1.4
.5	.4	.9	.8				.6	.6
4.8	3.8	2.9	1.3			Quick	2.8	3.4
1.3	1.2	1.4	.9				(398) 1.2	1.1
.3	.3	.6	.2				.4	.4
0 UND	0 UND	1 553.7	8 46.4			Sales/Receivables	0 UND	0 UND
0 UND	0 UND	24 15.0	27 13.4				0 819.0	0 UND
1 251.0	23 16.2	57 6.4	62 5.9				27 13.3	29 12.6
						Cost of Sales/Inventory		
						Cost of Sales/Payables		
14.3	7.3	5.2	8.2			Sales/Working Capital	10.5	8.7
48.1	29.5	15.4	27.8				48.1	42.5
-12.3	-18.2	-46.2	-19.6				-25.0	-36.2
26.2	23.3	40.5	23.8			EBIT/Interest	35.6	32.9
(93) 10.0	(74) 6.8	(60) 5.5	(15) 9.9				(269) 7.4	(294) 6.7
1.9	2.9	1.9	2.8				2.0	1.2
						Net Profit + Depr., Dep., Amort./Cur. Mat. L/T/D	20.4	6.8
							(15) 6.2	(12) 2.6
							1.9	.7
.1	.1	.1	.3			Fixed/Worth	.1	.1
.7	.9	.6	.7				.9	1.1
-4.7	21.1	3.3	5.1				UND	-17.9
.5	.2	.4	.7			Debt/Worth	.5	.5
3.2	2.2	1.4	2.1				2.8	2.8
-4.8	UND	8.6	22.0				-18.5	-13.2
256.5	79.8	65.3	49.7			% Profit Before Taxes/Tangible Net Worth	151.3	115.8
(99) 104.3	(78) 45.4	(69) 33.8	(19) 30.3				(289) 69.1	(298) 47.2
42.9	12.4	6.4	7.2				22.3	14.7
88.4	34.0	25.9	18.8			% Profit Before Taxes/Total Assets	55.9	41.1
40.9	15.9	10.6	11.2				17.2	14.1
6.7	5.3	1.3	3.9				3.9	1.6
365.4	66.2	143.2	26.4			Sales/Net Fixed Assets	213.6	146.7
32.3	14.1	20.4	5.5				24.5	20.8
7.9	3.0	3.8	1.7				6.3	4.7
8.7	4.2	4.1	2.7			Sales/Total Assets	6.3	6.0
4.8	2.7	2.5	1.6				3.6	3.2
2.6	1.3	1.1	.5				1.9	1.5
.8	.6	.4	.7			% Depr., Dep., Amort./Sales	.6	.6
(60) 2.1	(64) 1.7	(55) 1.3	(19) 2.4				(219) 1.9	(241) 2.1
4.9	7.8	5.1	6.1				4.3	5.3
4.2	3.6	1.2				% Officers', Directors' Owners' Comp/Sales	2.4	2.8
(70) 7.1	(45) 5.2	(34) 3.9					(182) 5.3	(201) 5.5
11.9	8.6	7.4					11.5	11.9
181583M	348291M	890539M	1012490M	1392467M	1245174M	Net Sales ($)	3760368M	6021358M
32893M	112485M	338477M	567258M	405570M	945453M	Total Assets ($)	1939890M	2240259M

M = $ thousand   MM = $ million
See Pages viii through xx for Explanation of Ratios and Data

Comparative Historical Data   Current Data Sorted by Sales

4/1/16-3/31/17 ALL	4/1/17-3/31/18 ALL	4/1/18-3/31/19 ALL	Type of Statement	0-1MM	1-3MM	3-5MM	5-10MM	10-25MM	25MM & OVER
							29 (4/1-9/30/18)	340 (10/1/18-3/31/19)	
8	18	18	Unqualified		2		4	3	9
3	8	8	Reviewed				2	3	2
17	16	17	Compiled	2	4	4	1	5	1
128	176	158	Tax Returns	61	54	17	12	10	4
122	199	168	Other	47	49	16	21	18	17
278	417	369	**NUMBER OF STATEMENTS**	110	109	38	40	39	33
%	%	%	**ASSETS**	%	%	%	%	%	%
23.0	25.2	26.1	Cash & Equivalents	28.4	28.9	32.6	20.6	23.7	11.3
13.3	14.4	12.8	Trade Receivables (net)	3.5	10.1	15.6	24.0	23.7	22.5
4.1	6.4	6.1	Inventory	3.1	4.8	5.8	10.1	9.2	12.6
4.7	3.4	3.1	All Other Current	1.0	4.7	3.3	2.0	3.8	4.6
45.0	49.4	48.1	Total Current	36.0	48.5	57.3	56.7	60.5	51.0
34.7	32.0	31.6	Fixed Assets (net)	42.3	31.4	23.1	22.6	21.5	28.7
7.9	7.2	7.7	Intangibles (net)	8.0	7.9	8.6	6.9	4.1	10.5
12.4	11.4	12.7	All Other Non-Current	13.7	12.2	10.9	13.8	13.9	9.8
100.0	100.0	100.0	Total	100.0	100.0	100.0	100.0	100.0	100.0
			LIABILITIES						
12.7	10.9	14.0	Notes Payable-Short Term	20.7	8.3	7.2	9.2	13.1	25.3
3.8	3.6	4.2	Cur. Mat.-L.T.D.	4.5	4.4	4.1	3.4	4.0	3.7
6.5	5.8	8.9	Trade Payables	6.1	8.8	5.2	18.4	11.8	8.1
.4	.1	.2	Income Taxes Payable	.1	.1	.0	1.1	.0	.0
20.1	17.0	20.9	All Other Current	21.0	22.0	20.0	15.0	24.2	21.0
43.4	37.5	48.2	Total Current	52.4	43.6	36.5	47.1	53.1	58.3
25.4	23.8	24.8	Long-Term Debt	32.3	29.7	21.4	13.6	10.7	17.3
.0	.0	.0	Deferred Taxes	.0	.0	.0	.0	.1	.1
8.2	8.6	5.4	All Other Non-Current	7.8	4.5	7.1	3.0	2.7	4.9
23.0	30.2	21.6	Net Worth	7.6	22.1	35.0	36.3	33.5	19.5
100.0	100.0	100.0	Total Liabilities & Net Worth	100.0	100.0	100.0	100.0	100.0	100.0
			INCOME DATA						
100.0	100.0	100.0	Net Sales	100.0	100.0	100.0	100.0	100.0	100.0
			Gross Profit						
87.9	88.9	87.8	Operating Expenses	82.1	87.2	91.9	93.0	91.0	94.3
12.1	11.1	12.2	Operating Profit	17.9	12.8	8.1	7.0	9.0	5.7
1.8	1.8	1.5	All Other Expenses (net)	4.0	.9	.1	-.4	.2	.5
10.3	9.4	10.7	Profit Before Taxes	13.9	12.0	7.9	7.4	8.9	5.3
			RATIOS						
2.8	4.1	4.1	Current	4.8	4.2	7.9	4.2	3.3	1.7
1.3	1.6	1.4		1.0	1.6	2.1	1.7	1.5	1.3
.5	.7	.6		.3	.6	1.0	.5	.8	.9
2.4	3.2	3.4	Quick	4.8	3.3	7.5	3.5	2.2	1.4
(277) 1.0	1.2	1.1		.9	1.3	1.9	1.3	1.1	.8
.4	.5	.4		.2	.6	.8	.4	.5	.4
0 UND	0 UND	0 UND	Sales/Receivables	0 UND	0 UND	0 UND	0 843.8	2 211.1	14 26.3
0 UND	1 613.5	0 UND		0 UND	0 UND	1 334.6	29 12.8	15 23.9	32 11.5
25 14.7	29 12.7	28 13.1		0 UND	10 37.4	29 12.5	54 6.7	43 8.5	57 6.4
			Cost of Sales/Inventory						
			Cost of Sales/Payables						
10.3	7.6	8.3	Sales/Working Capital	9.9	9.2	8.7	3.8	9.4	9.4
49.3	29.4	30.1		UND	29.9	28.6	11.9	35.6	22.5
-12.9	-34.0	-19.3		-5.4	-21.4	NM	-42.9	-26.4	-44.5
28.8	32.5	24.6	EBIT/Interest	14.8	25.8	53.8	35.4	47.7	22.6
(185) 8.4	(287) 9.0	(253) 7.2		(63) 4.5	(80) 9.7	(26) 7.1	(26) 7.9	(30) 12.6	(28) 7.9
2.3	2.1	2.4		1.6	3.0	2.8	1.0	2.4	3.3
13.6	17.7	48.4	Net Profit + Depr., Dep., Amort./Cur. Mat. L/T/D						
(12) 4.0	(20) 3.9	(11) 4.7							
1.8	2.0	1.9							
.2	.2	.1	Fixed/Worth	.1	.1	.1	.0	.1	.3
1.1	.9	.7		1.4	.9	.3	.3	.5	1.0
162.1	42.6	28.6		-8.1	-13.8	4.5	1.1	2.4	8.5
.6	.5	.4	Debt/Worth	.5	.4	.2	.2	.5	.7
2.9	2.1	2.2		2.9	2.3	2.1	.8	1.9	3.3
-14.4	UND	-53.1		-5.6	-17.6	NM	4.8	11.3	25.4
118.8	114.8	116.0	% Profit Before Taxes/Tangible Net Worth	213.8	161.1	123.0	68.7	84.5	91.9
(201) 60.4	(314) 46.8	(275) 49.7		(73) 66.4	(76) 65.0	(29) 52.9	(35) 33.8	(35) 45.7	(27) 26.9
17.0	12.5	16.6		28.7	17.4	14.3	2.2	12.2	8.9
41.3	41.4	48.7	% Profit Before Taxes/Total Assets	58.2	68.5	44.5	26.5	41.0	17.1
16.1	16.3	16.4		18.3	24.6	17.4	13.5	16.4	9.5
4.0	3.0	3.7		3.1	7.8	3.4	.3	3.1	4.4
84.2	103.5	146.5	Sales/Net Fixed Assets	158.9	112.0	174.2	307.3	191.6	42.3
14.4	19.5	20.3		8.5	20.3	39.0	36.2	39.0	16.4
4.2	4.5	4.6		2.0	5.7	11.4	5.4	12.9	5.0
5.0	5.5	5.2	Sales/Total Assets	4.7	6.8	6.2	4.4	5.1	3.6
2.9	3.2	3.0		2.3	3.8	3.5	3.0	3.9	2.7
1.4	1.5	1.6		.8	2.1	2.1	1.5	2.5	1.6
.9	.7	.6	% Depr., Dep., Amort./Sales	1.5	.7	.4	.3	.2	.7
(156) 2.3	(231) 2.0	(205) 1.7		(52) 4.6	(56) 1.9	(20) 1.0	(23) 1.4	(29) .7	(25) 1.4
5.9	5.2	5.4		11.6	5.7	2.1	7.0	3.1	2.8
3.3	2.8	3.4	% Officers', Directors' Owners' Comp/Sales	4.7	4.7	2.9	2.2	.9	
(117) 5.8	(177) 5.0	(156) 6.1		(41) 9.3	(54) 6.8	(21) 4.3	(17) 3.7	(16) 1.4	
11.6	9.5	10.3		12.3	10.2	6.4	7.1	5.7	
2320997M	4111414M	5070544M	Net Sales ($)	55253M	197243M	146087M	271854M	631473M	3768634M
933803M	1934741M	2402136M	Total Assets ($)	55600M	112961M	51184M	132044M	294913M	1755434M

© RMA 2019

M = $ thousand   MM = $ million
See Pages viii through xx for Explanation of Ratios and Data

Current Data Sorted by Assets   Comparative Historical Data

						Type of Statement		
	7	66	209	33	28	Unqualified	475	506
1	7	116	50	3	1	Reviewed	261	245
8	22	116	24		1	Compiled	290	263
1	2	1				Tax Returns	15	18
94	170	496	215	22	8	Other	1271	1315
	571 (4/1-9/30/18)		1,130 (10/1/18-3/31/19)				4/1/14- 3/31/15	4/1/15- 3/31/16
0-500M	500M-2MM	2-10MM	10-50MM	50-100MM	100-250MM		ALL	ALL
104	208	795	498	58	38	NUMBER OF STATEMENTS	2312	2347
%	%	%	%	%	%	ASSETS	%	%
55.3	22.3	12.6	12.3	20.9	28.1	Cash & Equivalents	14.9	15.2
1.8	1.0	.6	1.2	2.8	5.4	Trade Receivables (net)	1.0	1.4
.1	.3	.1	.2	.3	.6	Inventory	.2	.2
.7	.9	.7	1.0	3.1	1.8	All Other Current	1.0	1.1
57.9	24.4	14.0	14.6	27.0	36.0	Total Current	17.1	17.8
35.6	71.2	82.8	78.0	52.5	30.1	Fixed Assets (net)	76.8	75.5
.2	.2	.3	.3	1.6	.5	Intangibles (net)	.3	.4
6.3	4.2	2.9	7.1	18.8	33.4	All Other Non-Current	5.8	6.3
100.0	100.0	100.0	100.0	100.0	100.0	Total	100.0	100.0
						LIABILITIES		
3.2	2.0	1.3	.7	1.2	2.8	Notes Payable-Short Term	1.4	1.3
2.0	1.4	1.6	1.7	.7	.7	Cur. Mat.-L.T.D.	2.1	1.7
3.7	1.1	.5	1.0	1.8	1.8	Trade Payables	1.0	1.0
.2	.0	.0	.0	.0	.0	Income Taxes Payable	.0	.0
13.7	4.8	1.5	2.7	7.2	9.5	All Other Current	3.2	3.3
22.8	9.3	5.0	6.1	10.8	14.7	Total Current	7.6	7.5
28.3	32.3	29.1	22.1	16.7	12.4	Long-Term Debt	29.8	30.1
.0	.0	.0	.0	.0	.0	Deferred Taxes	.0	.0
.9	1.2	.8	1.9	7.4	19.2	All Other Non-Current	1.8	2.2
48.0	57.2	65.1	69.9	65.1	53.7	Net Worth	60.7	60.2
100.0	100.0	100.0	100.0	100.0	100.0	Total Liabilties & Net Worth	100.0	100.0
						INCOME DATA		
100.0	100.0	100.0	100.0	100.0	100.0	Net Sales	100.0	100.0
						Gross Profit		
86.9	86.6	86.6	89.0	90.6	86.8	Operating Expenses	87.9	87.8
13.1	13.4	13.4	11.0	9.4	13.2	Operating Profit	12.1	12.2
1.7	5.4	4.8	3.1	4.1	2.1	All Other Expenses (net)	5.0	5.0
11.4	8.0	8.6	7.9	5.3	11.1	Profit Before Taxes	7.1	7.2
						RATIOS		
13.8	11.3	10.8	7.4	12.0	15.7		8.7	8.7
3.7	3.1	3.7	3.0	3.4	2.5	Current	2.8	3.0
1.2	.9	1.4	1.5	1.5	.9		1.1	1.2
13.8	10.4	10.4	7.1	11.3	12.1		8.3	8.3
3.6	2.9	3.4	2.8	3.0	2.4	Quick	2.6	2.8
1.1	.9	1.3	1.3	1.1	.8		1.0	1.1
0 UND	0 UND	0 UND	0 UND	0 UND	2 199.9		0 UND	0 UND
0 UND	0 UND	0 UND	0 UND	1 285.0	18 20.4	Sales/Receivables	0 UND	0 UND
0 UND	0 UND	0 UND	2 166.9	26 13.9	101 3.6		0 999.8	0 865.4
						Cost of Sales/Inventory		
						Cost of Sales/Payables		
2.4	3.0	2.5	2.6	1.0	.5		2.9	2.8
7.2	7.5	5.1	5.3	3.4	2.2	Sales/Working Capital	7.0	6.2
55.9	-207.5	26.7	20.7	22.1	-112.4		134.8	47.7
6.0	5.2	5.0	6.8	5.6	20.5		4.1	4.3
(23) 2.7	(117) 2.2	(590) 2.2	(385) 2.4	(41) 2.3	(24) 5.8	EBIT/Interest	(1627) 1.9	(1635) 2.0
1.7	1.0	.9	.8	-.1	2.6		.8	.8
						Net Profit + Depr., Dep., Amort./Cur. Mat. L/T/D		
.0	.8	1.0	.9	.3	.1		1.0	.9
.3	1.3	1.3	1.1	.8	.3	Fixed/Worth	1.3	1.3
1.4	2.2	1.8	1.5	1.2	.8		1.9	1.8
.1	.1	.2	.1	.2	.3		.2	.2
.3	.6	.5	.4	.4	1.0	Debt/Worth	.6	.5
1.6	1.5	1.0	.8	1.1	2.0		1.2	1.2
49.8	13.2	7.7	7.5	5.7	9.2		7.6	7.7
(96) 19.8	(199) 4.6	(786) 2.7	(493) 2.3	(56) 2.5	3.9	% Profit Before Taxes/Tangible Net Worth	(2260) 2.4	(2276) 2.4
2.6	.0	-.1	-.4	-.9	1.0		-.3	-.4
34.4	8.3	4.4	4.9	3.4	4.9		4.4	4.3
8.8	2.4	1.7	1.5	1.2	1.8	% Profit Before Taxes/Total Assets	1.3	1.4
.2	-.1	-.1	-.3	-.6	.6		-.3	-.3
UND	1.7	.6	.6	2.3	3.3		.7	.7
23.0	.5	.3	.4	.5	1.9	Sales/Net Fixed Assets	.4	.4
.9	.3	.2	.2	.3	.5		.2	.2
3.5	.8	.5	.5	.4	.4		.5	.5
1.5	.4	.3	.3	.3	.2	Sales/Total Assets	.3	.3
.6	.2	.2	.2	.2	.1		.2	.2
1.1	2.2	5.4	5.6	2.2	1.9		4.9	4.7
(19) 5.3	(69) 6.2	(403) 8.6	(336) 8.9	(44) 7.6	(34) 4.1	% Depr., Dep., Amort./Sales	(1229) 8.6	(1246) 8.5
7.1	10.6	12.5	12.6	10.6	7.8		12.9	12.6
7.0	5.7	5.3	5.0				6.0	6.2
(13) 22.5	(25) 18.7	(65) 12.6	(44) 7.7			% Officers', Directors' Owners' Comp/Sales	(245) 13.1	(236) 12.7
34.8	34.0	19.6	25.9				23.0	22.8
43126M	192060M	1654635M	4200119M	1515309M	1526947M	Net Sales ($)	12476779M	12101461M
25559M	259426M	4172247M	10402101M	3962802M	5779348M	Total Assets ($)	31232591M	34247576M

© RMA 2019

M = $ thousand MM = $ million
See Pages viii through xx for Explanation of Ratios and Data

Comparative Historical Data				Current Data Sorted by Sales					
Type of Statement									
401	362	343	Unqualified	3	38	56	79	119	48
217	199	178	Reviewed	18	82	51	17	9	1
201	216	171	Compiled	63	83	17	5	2	1
14	11	4	Tax Returns	2	2				
1093	1035	1005	Other	441	345	83	79	45	12
4/1/16-3/31/17 ALL	4/1/17-3/31/18 ALL	4/1/18-3/31/19 ALL		571 (4/1-9/30/18)			1,130 (10/1/18-3/31/19)		
				0-1MM	1-3MM	3-5MM	5-10MM	10-25MM	25MM & OVER
1926	1823	1701	**NUMBER OF STATEMENTS**	527	550	207	180	175	62
%	%	%	**ASSETS**	%	%	%	%	%	%
15.8	15.9	16.9	Cash & Equivalents	18.3	14.3	14.4	19.5	18.0	26.3
1.1	1.0	1.1	Trade Receivables (net)	.6	.8	1.2	1.4	2.1	4.3
.2	.2	.1	Inventory	.1	.0	.1	.1	.2	.9
1.1	1.2	.9	All Other Current	.3	.9	.6	1.4	2.0	2.3
18.3	18.3	19.1	Total Current	19.4	16.0	16.3	22.5	22.3	33.8
75.7	76.3	74.9	Fixed Assets (net)	77.6	79.8	79.4	68.5	65.0	39.1
.4	.3	.3	Intangibles (net)	.2	.2	.2	.4	1.1	.5
5.7	5.1	5.7	All Other Non-Current	2.9	3.9	4.1	8.6	11.6	26.6
100.0	100.0	100.0	Total	100.0	100.0	100.0	100.0	100.0	100.0
			LIABILITIES						
1.7	1.1	1.4	Notes Payable-Short Term	1.8	1.2	1.5	1.0	.8	1.1
1.8	1.8	1.6	Cur. Mat.-L.T.D.	1.3	1.8	1.7	1.3	2.2	.8
.8	.8	1.0	Trade Payables	.9	.5	.8	1.1	1.6	3.9
.0	.0	.0	Income Taxes Payable	.0	.0	.0	.0	.0	.1
3.4	3.0	3.4	All Other Current	4.1	2.0	2.2	3.9	5.4	6.4
7.6	6.7	7.3	Total Current	8.1	5.5	6.3	7.3	10.1	12.3
29.9	28.6	26.6	Long-Term Debt	31.0	26.8	28.3	23.0	21.1	8.4
.0	.0	.0	Deferred Taxes	.0	.0	.0	.0	.0	.0
1.9	1.4	1.8	All Other Non-Current	.7	1.0	1.4	3.2	3.8	10.2
60.6	63.3	64.3	Net Worth	60.2	66.8	64.0	66.5	65.1	69.0
100.0	100.0	100.0	Total Liabilities & Net Worth	100.0	100.0	100.0	100.0	100.0	100.0
			INCOME DATA						
100.0	100.0	100.0	Net Sales	100.0	100.0	100.0	100.0	100.0	100.0
			Gross Profit						
88.2	86.5	87.5	Operating Expenses	82.9	88.2	88.5	90.1	92.8	93.2
11.8	13.5	12.5	Operating Profit	17.1	11.8	11.5	9.9	7.2	6.8
4.9	4.3	4.1	All Other Expenses (net)	6.1	3.9	4.5	2.9	1.3	-.7
6.9	9.3	8.4	Profit Before Taxes	11.0	7.9	7.0	7.0	5.9	7.5
			RATIOS						
8.4	9.5	10.1	Current	11.8	11.3	7.5	10.3	7.8	8.1
3.1	3.3	3.4		3.4	4.0	3.1	3.2	3.0	2.6
1.2	1.4	1.3		1.0	1.6	1.7	1.5	1.3	1.2
8.0	9.0	9.6	Quick	11.2	10.7	7.0	9.2	7.4	8.1
2.9	3.1	3.1		3.2	3.5	2.9	3.0	2.7	2.5
1.1	1.2	1.2		.9	1.4	1.6	1.4	1.1	1.1
0 UND	0 UND	0 UND	Sales/Receivables	0 UND	0 UND	0 UND	0 UND	0 UND	0 UND
0 UND	0 UND	0 UND		0 UND	0 UND	0 UND	0 999.8	1 680.7	6 62.3
0 999.8	0 999.8	0 827.2		0 UND	0 UND	0 755.3	4 91.7	5 68.0	32 11.5
			Cost of Sales/Inventory						
			Cost of Sales/Payables						
2.6	2.5	2.5	Sales/Working Capital	2.3	2.5	3.0	2.3	2.9	2.3
5.7	5.4	5.4		6.7	4.8	6.0	5.3	4.9	5.0
36.9	24.5	29.2		-294.7	22.5	15.5	15.5	26.2	28.1
4.4	5.6	5.8	EBIT/Interest	4.2	5.0	5.5	6.8	9.5	24.9
(1370) 2.0	(1313) 2.5	(1180) 2.3		(297) 2.3	(395) 2.0	(173) 1.8	(131) 2.6	(138) 2.8	(46) 8.8
.7	1.1	.9		1.2	.7	.7	.6	.8	2.9
			Net Profit + Depr., Dep., Amort./Cur. Mat. L/T/D						
.9	.9	.9	Fixed/Worth	1.0	1.0	1.0	.8	.6	.2
1.2	1.2	1.2		1.3	1.2	1.2	1.1	1.1	.4
1.0	1.7	1.7		1.8	1.7	1.8	1.5	1.5	.9
.2	.2	.2	Debt/Worth	.2	.2	.2	.1	.2	.1
.5	.5	.5		.5	.4	.5	.4	.5	.5
1.1	1.0	1.0		1.2	.9	1.0	.9	.9	1.0
7.9	8.9	9.0	% Profit Before Taxes/Tangible Net Worth	9.8	8.2	8.0	10.6	9.0	12.9
(1871) 2.3	(1784) 3.1	(1668) 2.9		(514) 3.1	(540) 2.0	(205) 1.7	(176) 3.4	(171) 3.6	4.2
-.6	.2	-.2		.1	-.2	-1.1	-.6	-.6	.5
4.4	5.3	5.4	% Profit Before Taxes/Total Assets	5.4	5.2	5.1	5.6	5.6	7.6
1.4	2.0	1.8		2.0	1.4	1.2	2.4	2.6	3.2
-.4	.1	-.1		.1	-.2	-.7	-.3	-.4	.5
.7	.7	.8	Sales/Net Fixed Assets	.6	.6	.7	1.0	1.3	6.0
.4	.4	.4		.3	.4	.4	.5	.6	2.6
.2	.2	.2		.2	.2	.3	.4	.4	.9
.5	.5	.5	Sales/Total Assets	.4	.5	.5	.6	.6	1.1
.3	.3	.3		.2	.3	.4	.4	.4	.6
.2	.2	.2		.1	.2	.2	.3	.3	.4
4.9	5.0	4.7	% Depr., Dep., Amort./Sales	4.9	6.2	6.3	4.8	3.8	1.1
(1051) 8.6	(958) 8.6	(905) 8.4		(144) 8.7	(272) 9.2	(142) 9.3	(133) 8.0	(152) 7.5	2.4
12.6	12.3	12.2		15.3	13.3	12.1	12.3	10.6	6.2
6.5	5.7	5.1	% Officers', Directors' Owners' Comp/Sales	6.0	4.1	4.3	7.1	5.2	
(203) 12.7	(192) 13.6	(150) 12.6		(59) 16.0	(52) 10.2	(15) 9.9	(11) 7.7	(10) 10.1	
25.5	24.8	25.2		27.6	19.6	15.8	38.4	35.4	
9853625M	10078992M	9132196M	Net Sales ($)	277640M	1001262M	799788M	1250219M	2673919M	3129368M
27434485M	25880483M	24601483M	Total Assets ($)	1407902M	3936792M	2826387M	4005318M	6944902M	5480182M

© RMA 2019

M = $ thousand   MM = $ million
See Pages viii through xx for Explanation of Ratios and Data

Current Data Sorted by Assets   Comparative Historical Data

						Type of Statement		
1	2	13	25	6	12	Unqualified	44	53
	1	2				Reviewed	1	2
		1	1			Compiled		
1			1			Tax Returns	5	1
2	2	8	9	6	4	Other	28	30
	66 (4/1-9/30/18)		31 (10/1/18-3/31/19)				4/1/14-3/31/15	4/1/15-3/31/16
0-500M	500M-2MM	2-10MM	10-50MM	50-100MM	100-250MM		ALL	ALL
4	5	24	36	12	16	NUMBER OF STATEMENTS	78	86
%	%	%	%	%	%	ASSETS	%	%
		39.6	25.9	24.5	26.7	Cash & Equivalents	36.2	31.7
		2.0	9.5	8.7	3.3	Trade Receivables (net)	5.0	6.6
		1.3	.1	1.2	.0	Inventory	.4	.7
		8.4	7.4	1.7	1.9	All Other Current	4.5	3.9
		51.3	42.9	36.2	32.0	Total Current	46.2	43.0
		26.7	28.8	30.7	23.7	Fixed Assets (net)	22.0	25.9
		.8	.2	.0	.2	Intangibles (net)	.1	.2
		21.1	28.1	33.1	44.2	All Other Non-Current	31.7	31.0
		100.0	100.0	100.0	100.0	Total	100.0	100.0
						LIABILITIES		
		1.8	1.4	.0	3.7	Notes Payable-Short Term	1.1	2.2
		.8	1.1	2.4	2.2	Cur. Mat.-L.T.D.	.6	1.1
		1.7	2.0	3.0	.7	Trade Payables	2.4	3.4
		.0	.0	.0	.0	Income Taxes Payable	.0	.1
		7.6	5.0	5.0	3.6	All Other Current	4.3	6.0
		11.8	9.5	10.3	10.2	Total Current	8.4	12.7
		4.7	19.1	23.8	23.4	Long-Term Debt	11.1	12.6
		.0	.0	.0	.0	Deferred Taxes	.0	.0
		6.5	4.5	1.5	1.3	All Other Non-Current	2.7	2.6
		76.9	66.8	64.4	65.1	Net Worth	77.8	72.1
		100.0	100.0	100.0	100.0	Total Liabilities & Net Worth	100.0	100.0
						INCOME DATA		
		100.0	100.0	100.0	100.0	Net Sales	100.0	100.0
						Gross Profit		
		82.7	78.7	85.7	74.8	Operating Expenses	75.7	87.6
		17.3	21.3	14.3	25.2	Operating Profit	24.3	12.4
		6.5	7.2	6.7	9.6	All Other Expenses (net)	1.9	5.1
		10.8	14.0	7.6	15.6	Profit Before Taxes	22.5	7.3
						RATIOS		
		32.9	29.6	7.2	6.8		32.5	13.8
		11.2	4.7	3.6	3.0	Current	7.7	4.7
		3.2	1.4	1.5	1.6		2.7	1.9
		29.8	18.7	7.1	4.2		24.5	10.5
		8.0	3.7	3.5	2.9	Quick	5.5	4.3
		3.0	1.2	1.0	1.4		2.6	1.8
0 UND	0 UND	0 UND	0 UND				0 UND	0 UND
0 UND	20 18.4	6 61.7	15 25.1			Sales/Receivables	12 29.9	11 33.9
15 23.9	47 7.7	34 10.7	94 3.9				53 6.9	37 9.9
						Cost of Sales/Inventory		
						Cost of Sales/Payables		
		.5	.9	.8	.6		.5	.7
		2.5	2.5	2.3	1.4	Sales/Working Capital	1.5	2.3
		11.8	12.8	24.8	8.4		4.7	7.2
			18.8				25.8	23.2
		(20)	3.7			EBIT/Interest	(35) 4.3	(44) 1.6
			.4				.8	-10.4
						Net Profit + Depr., Dep., Amort./Cur. Mat. L/T/D		
		.0	.0	.1	.0		.0	.0
		.2	.3	.5	.0	Fixed/Worth	.1	.2
		.9	1.0	.8	1.1		.6	.8
		.0	.1	.1	.1		.1	.1
		.1	.3	.4	.5	Debt/Worth	.1	.2
		.5	.8	1.3	1.5		.4	.6
		16.2	13.2	9.9	7.5		13.6	8.3
		5.0	(33) 3.9	.1	1.8	% Profit Before Taxes/Tangible Net Worth	(77) 5.6	(83) 1.1
		-4.2	.3	-9.0	.6		.1	-1.8
		8.8	8.9	7.7	4.6		11.7	4.1
		3.3	2.8	-.1	1.1	% Profit Before Taxes/Total Assets	4.3	.4
		-4.0	.3	-4.2	.5		.1	-1.3
		UND	739.9	4.9	UND		468.8	165.7
		25.6	5.3	2.8	5.3	Sales/Net Fixed Assets	7.1	4.5
		2.2	.8	.6	.4		.9	.7
		1.9	.7	1.0	.2		.8	.9
		.6	.3	.3	.1	Sales/Total Assets	.3	.3
		.2	.2	.1	.1		.1	.1
		.9	.9	1.0			.4	.9
	(15)	2.1	(25) 2.8	(11) 3.2		% Depr., Dep., Amort./Sales	(49) 2.3	(54) 2.5
		5.7	11.9	6.0			6.5	5.5
						% Officers', Directors' Owners' Comp/Sales		
3786M	6014M	162645M	443561M	482117M	321509M	Net Sales ($)	792826M	878085M
1436M	5200M	121265M	839281M	796565M	2136625M	Total Assets ($)	3082230M	3335339M

M = $ thousand   MM = $ million
See Pages viii through xx for Explanation of Ratios and Data

Comparative Historical Data | Current Data Sorted by Sales

Comparative Historical Data			Type of Statement	Current Data Sorted by Sales					
40	48	59	Unqualified	5	10	6	9	20	9
1	2	3	Reviewed	2	1				
1			Compiled		1		1		1
			Tax Returns	1					
2	5	2	Other	4	7	4	7	4	5
21	34	31							
4/1/16-3/31/17 ALL	4/1/17-3/31/18 ALL	4/1/18-3/31/19 ALL		66 (4/1-9/30/18)			31 (10/1/18-3/31/19)		
				0-1MM	1-3MM	3-5MM	5-10MM	10-25MM	25MM & OVER
65	89	97	**NUMBER OF STATEMENTS**	12	19	10	17	24	15
%	%	%	**ASSETS**	%	%	%	%	%	%
31.9	32.4	32.7	Cash & Equivalents	57.9	42.1	37.1	22.6	20.6	28.3
7.2	6.2	6.4	Trade Receivables (net)	1.3	3.4	2.3	13.6	7.2	7.4
.6	.4	.5	Inventory	.0	.2	.2	.2	.3	2.4
3.3	7.0	5.6	All Other Current	.3	7.8	4.9	7.5	3.4	9.2
43.1	46.0	45.2	Total Current	59.5	53.4	44.5	43.9	31.5	47.2
20.1	25.5	26.9	Fixed Assets (net)	22.6	23.8	33.1	26.1	26.0	32.7
1.8	.6	.4	Intangibles (net)	1.6	.0	.0	.2	.4	.2
35.1	27.8	27.5	All Other Non-Current	16.4	22.8	22.4	29.7	42.1	19.9
100.0	100.0	100.0	Total	100.0	100.0	100.0	100.0	100.0	100.0
			LIABILITIES						
1.4	7.5	2.0	Notes Payable-Short Term	3.2	2.6	.0	1.0	.8	4.9
.9	1.4	1.5	Cur. Mat.-L.T.D.	2.9	.5	1.2	.8	2.5	1.1
2.1	2.0	2.2	Trade Payables	3.3	1.3	1.0	1.5	1.0	5.6
.0	.0	.0	Income Taxes Payable	.0	.0	.0	.0	.0	.0
9.8	11.9	6.5	All Other Current	1.8	9.6	1.8	7.1	6.5	8.9
14.2	22.8	12.2	Total Current	11.2	14.0	3.9	10.4	10.8	20.6
8.9	12.8	16.0	Long-Term Debt	14.9	3.2	26.8	19.6	20.1	15.0
.0	.0	.0	Deferred Taxes	.0	.0	.0	.0	.0	.0
3.0	4.0	4.0	All Other Non-Current	7.1	2.4	5.7	2.0	2.0	7.7
73.9	60.4	67.9	Net Worth	66.7	80.3	63.5	68.0	67.1	56.8
100.0	100.0	100.0	Total Liabilities & Net Worth	100.0	100.0	100.0	100.0	100.0	100.0
			INCOME DATA						
100.0	100.0	100.0	Net Sales	100.0	100.0	100.0	100.0	100.0	100.0
			Gross Profit						
90.3	81.3	81.8	Operating Expenses	76.2	87.3	82.3	74.8	77.2	94.1
9.7	18.7	18.2	Operating Profit	23.8	12.7	17.7	25.2	22.8	5.9
3.7	4.1	6.7	All Other Expenses (net)	8.9	6.1	4.1	15.1	3.0	3.6
6.0	14.6	11.6	Profit Before Taxes	14.8	6.7	13.6	10.1	19.8	2.2
			RATIOS						
12.6	11.3	20.0		88.5	51.2	68.0	26.1	6.0	4.4
5.1	4.2	5.1	Current	7.8	19.5	11.6	12.1	3.0	2.4
2.1	1.7	1.5		3.8	.9	4.2	1.6	1.4	1.5
12.5	10.8	14.1		87.9	49.0	68.0	16.1	4.1	4.3
4.5	3.1	4.3	Quick	7.7	7.8	9.1	11.6	2.6	1.6
1.4	.9	1.4		3.7	.7	2.2	1.6	1.2	.8
0 UND	0 UND	0 UND		0 UND	0 UND	0 UND	0 UND	8 47.4	0 999.8
17 20.9	6 57.6	6 57.1	Sales/Receivables	0 UND	0 UND	1 512.8	7 51.1	21 17.3	6 58.4
45 8.1	30 12.0	37 9.8		0 UND	13 27.8	34 10.8	261 1.4	94 3.9	39 9.3
			Cost of Sales/Inventory						
			Cost of Sales/Payables						
.6	.5	.7		.5	.4	.3	.9	.9	1.8
2.0	3.7	1.9	Sales/Working Capital	.8	1.1	1.7	1.3	3.2	6.0
5.9	14.7	12.9		1.8	-141.9	6.8	32.8	13.3	20.5
15.2	17.7	11.6						35.2	13.7
(31) 6.1	(42) 5.4	(47) 3.4	EBIT/Interest					(10) 5.7	(10) 3.9
.1	1.5	-.4						2.0	-3.8
			Net Profit + Depr., Dep., Amort./Cur. Mat. L/T/D						
.0	.0	.0		.0	.0	.0	.0	.0	.1
.1	.2	.2	Fixed/Worth	.0	.0	.1	.3	.2	.7
.5	.7	.9		2.5	.7	1.2	.6	.7	1.2
.1	.1	.1		.0	.0	.0	.1	.1	.3
.2	.3	.3	Debt/Worth	.2	.1	.1	.4	.4	.8
.5	1.0	1.0		2.0	.3	2.2	1.2	1.3	1.2
5.8	11.6	11.2		18.2	8.1		13.6	11.2	22.0
(62) 1.0	(84) 4.3	(92) 3.8	% Profit Before Taxes/Tangible Net Worth	(11) 5.1	(18) 1.4	(16) 2.8	4.3	(14) 2.4	
-4.5	.8	-.7		-4.0	-4.6	-1.3	.7	-10.6	
4.2	7.5	8.8		12.3	5.4	7.5	10.2	9.3	12.2
.7	2.5	2.4	% Profit Before Taxes/Total Assets	3.3	.3	4.8	1.3	2.3	1.9
-2.5	.6	-.6		-2.6	-4.2	.5	-.6	.5	-4.5
999.8	353.1	656.7		UND	UND	299.8	UND	13.9	32.7
10.0	7.4	6.4	Sales/Net Fixed Assets	43.0	361.7	2.3	9.7	5.0	6.2
.8	.9	1.0		2.7	.4	.9	.6	.8	1.9
.7	.9	1.0		1.2	.7	.8	.6	.7	2.6
.3	.4	.3	Sales/Total Assets	.3	.3	.3	.3	.2	1.3
.1	.2	.2		.1	.2	.1	.2	.1	.4
.5	.8	1.0			.2		1.5	1.3	.8
(44) 1.5	(59) 3.0	(63) 2.8	% Depr., Dep., Amort./Sales		(10) 6.5		(10) 5.3	(18) 3.4	(13) 1.7
8.3	6.4	8.2			22.6		13.6	7.9	3.7
			% Officers', Directors' Owners' Comp/Sales						
708863M	1121600M	1419632M	Net Sales ($)	7635M	38559M	38761M	117645M	387527M	829505M
3048929M	3803872M	3900372M	Total Assets ($)	36323M	278781M	298990M	470153M	1868840M	947285M

© RMA 2019

M = $ thousand   MM = $ million
See Pages viii through xx for Explanation of Ratios and Data

Current Data Sorted by Assets

Comparative Historical Data

0-500M	500M-2MM	2-10MM	10-50MM	50-100MM	100-250MM	Type of Statement	4/1/14-3/31/15 ALL	4/1/15-3/31/16 ALL
	2	14	8	2	3	Unqualified	35	39
						Reviewed		
						Compiled		
						Tax Returns		
2	5 (35 4/1-9/30/18)	6	1 (11 10/1/18-3/31/19)	1	2	Other	2 (15 4/1/14-3/31/15)	3 (16 4/1/15-3/31/16)
2	7	20	9	3	5	**NUMBER OF STATEMENTS**	52	58
%	%	%	%	%	%		%	%
		20.6				Cash & Equivalents	31.0	29.9
		17.0				Trade Receivables (net)	21.1	17.3
		.3				Inventory	.4	.4
		5.3				All Other Current	4.4	2.0
		43.1				Total Current	56.9	49.6
		42.1				Fixed Assets (net)	31.5	31.2
		.2				Intangibles (net)	1.2	2.8
		14.6				All Other Non-Current	10.4	16.4
		100.0				Total	100.0	100.0
						LIABILITIES		
		2.8				Notes Payable-Short Term	1.4	1.4
		1.9				Cur. Mat.-L.T.D.	1.2	1.0
		7.9				Trade Payables	7.0	7.3
		.0				Income Taxes Payable	.0	.0
		6.7				All Other Current	19.7	13.5
		19.4				Total Current	29.2	23.3
		10.2				Long-Term Debt	11.5	13.7
		.0				Deferred Taxes	.0	.0
		1.4				All Other Non-Current	3.5	2.8
		69.0				Net Worth	55.8	60.3
		100.0				Total Liabilities & Net Worth	100.0	100.0
						INCOME DATA		
		100.0				Net Sales	100.0	100.0
						Gross Profit		
		97.6				Operating Expenses	96.7	94.7
		2.4				Operating Profit	3.3	5.3
		-.3				All Other Expenses (net)	-.5	1.0
		2.7				Profit Before Taxes	3.8	4.2
						RATIOS		
		4.5				Current	4.1	3.6
		2.3					2.3	2.4
		1.0					1.5	1.4
		4.4				Quick	3.6	3.6
		2.0					2.2	2.1
		.6					1.2	1.3
		9　42.2				Sales/Receivables	21　17.4	12　30.8
		35　10.4					36　10.2	29　12.4
		51　7.2					56　6.5	45　8.1
						Cost of Sales/Inventory		
						Cost of Sales/Payables		
		4.2				Sales/Working Capital	3.1	3.7
		9.5					5.3	7.2
		465.1					15.3	19.8
		7.6				EBIT/Interest	(33) 16.4	(36) 14.3
		(15) 4.7					6.2	4.4
		2.5					1.0	-.6
						Net Profit + Depr., Dep., Amort./Cur. Mat. L/T/D		
		.2				Fixed/Worth	.1	.2
		.6					.6	.5
		1.2					1.0	1.1
		.1				Debt/Worth	.3	.3
		.4					.7	.6
		1.0					1.3	1.2
		7.4				% Profit Before Taxes/Tangible Net Worth	(50) 12.3	(55) 17.5
		4.2					7.0	4.9
		-.3					.0	-4.4
		4.6				% Profit Before Taxes/Total Assets	8.8	8.4
		2.9					3.8	3.2
		-.2					-.4	-2.9
		10.7				Sales/Net Fixed Assets	32.9	37.5
		3.0					6.3	7.9
		2.2					2.4	2.4
		2.1				Sales/Total Assets	2.7	2.5
		1.5					1.6	1.5
		.7					1.0	.9
		.8				% Depr., Dep., Amort./Sales	(51) .9	(52) .7
		(18) 1.8					1.6	1.8
		3.7					3.0	2.9
						% Officers', Directors' Owners' Comp/Sales		
2208M	24880M	129984M	235809M	2374010M	850282M	Net Sales ($)	3420213M	3806426M
843M	7306M	89598M	187182M	203593M	854142M	Total Assets ($)	1064583M	1575642M

© RMA 2019

M = $ thousand　　MM = $ million
See Pages viii through xx for Explanation of Ratios and Data

OTHER SERVICES—Voluntary Health Organizations NAICS 813212   1607

	Comparative Historical Data				Current Data Sorted by Sales					
Type of Statement										
Unqualified					1	3	3	9	4	9
Reviewed	39	30	29							
Compiled		1								
Tax Returns	2									
Other	2 11	2 18	17		4	1	3	4	4	1
	4/1/16- 3/31/17 ALL	4/1/17- 3/31/18 ALL	4/1/18- 3/31/19 ALL		0-1MM	35 (4/1-9/30/18) 1-3MM	3-5MM	11 (10/1/18-3/31/19) 5-10MM	10-25MM	25MM & OVER
NUMBER OF STATEMENTS	54	51	46		5	4	6	13	8	10
	%	%	%	ASSETS	%	%	%	%	%	%
Cash & Equivalents	30.5	29.9	24.1					14.3		34.2
Trade Receivables (net)	21.3	19.1	19.3					21.9		18.5
Inventory	.7	.3	1.4					2.3		1.1
All Other Current	3.7	4.9	3.6					7.3		3.0
Total Current	56.1	54.2	48.4					45.9		56.9
Fixed Assets (net)	27.3	30.5	34.1					34.1		21.0
Intangibles (net)	2.0	1.5	1.0					.8		2.4
All Other Non-Current	14.6	13.8	16.6					19.2		19.7
Total	100.0	100.0	100.0					100.0		100.0
				LIABILITIES						
Notes Payable-Short Term	2.5	4.4	2.5					6.7		.0
Cur. Mat.-L.T.D.	1.0	.4	1.1					.9		.2
Trade Payables	6.7	6.6	7.6					9.2		7.8
Income Taxes Payable	.0	.1	.0					.0		.0
All Other Current	15.5	13.0	10.1					13.4		17.0
Total Current	25.7	24.5	21.3					30.2		25.1
Long-Term Debt	6.2	7.0	9.9					13.9		1.6
Deferred Taxes	.0	.0	.0					.0		.0
All Other Non-Current	4.0	4.3	4.0					1.4		.9
Net Worth	64.1	64.1	64.8					54.5		72.3
Total Liabilties & Net Worth	100.0	100.0	100.0					100.0		100.0
				INCOME DATA						
Net Sales	100.0	100.0	100.0					100.0		100.0
Gross Profit										
Operating Expenses	98.4	95.8	97.2					96.7		98.4
Operating Profit	1.6	4.2	2.8					3.3		1.6
All Other Expenses (net)	.0	-1.0	-.8					-2.0		-1.3
Profit Before Taxes	1.6	5.2	3.6					5.3		2.9
				RATIOS						
	4.0	4.8	4.9					2.5		4.2
Current	2.7	2.7	2.6					1.9		2.9
	1.5	1.5	1.3					.9		1.6
	3.6	4.8	3.9					2.3		4.2
Quick	2.5	2.6	2.3					.7		2.5
	1.4	1.2	.9					.5		1.2
	6 57.4	12 30.0	13 27.1					0 UND		19 19.3
Sales/Receivables	36 10.1	27 13.5	33 11.2					27 13.7		33 11.1
	55 6.6	46 7.9	51 7.2					52 7.0		41 8.8
				Cost of Sales/Inventory						
				Cost of Sales/Payables						
	3.1	3.0	4.0					6.1		4.3
Sales/Working Capital	5.7	7.0	6.4					11.2		6.2
	13.2	16.8	95.5					NM		NM
	21.7	56.0	9.3					27.0		
EBIT/Interest	(32) 2.3	(34) 19.6	(29) 4.6				(10)	5.2		
	-5.0	1.5	.2					2.3		
				Net Profit + Depr., Dep., Amort./Cur. Mat. L/T/D						
	.1	.1	.1					.2		.1
Fixed/Worth	.3	.4	.4					.5		.3
	.7	.7	.8					.9		.6
	.2	.2	.2					.2		.2
Debt/Worth	.5	.4	.4					.7		.3
	.9	1.1	.9					1.0		.9
% Profit Before Taxes/Tangible	19.0	23.0	8.2					18.2		9.4
Net Worth	(52) 5.7	(49) 7.9	(44) 3.6				(12)	8.3		3.9
	-3.2	1.8	-1.6					4.1		-1.8
% Profit Before Taxes/Total	10.5	11.7	4.9					9.4		7.5
Assets	2.9	5.0	2.8					5.2		3.0
	-2.7	1.4	-.9					3.1		-.5
	63.7	53.6	49.0					52.7		83.9
Sales/Net Fixed Assets	9.7	9.4	6.2					3.4		11.7
	2.4	2.1	1.6					2.1		6.6
	2.5	3.2	2.4					3.7		2.9
Sales/Total Assets	1.5	1.6	1.4					1.5		1.7
	.7	.8	.7					.7		1.0
	.5	.4	.4					.9		.3
% Depr., Dep., Amort./Sales	(48) 1.2	(42) 1.2	(38) 1.4				(11)	1.8		1.1
	3.4	3.3	2.9					2.9		1.9
				% Officers', Directors' Owners' Comp/Sales						
Net Sales ($)	4827849M	4043912M	3617173M		3204M	5923M	23632M	98139M	121472M	3364803M
Total Assets ($)	1442100M	968901M	1342664M		5468M	7644M	24048M	83525M	356293M	865686M

© RMA 2019   M = $ thousand   MM = $ million
See Pages viii through xx for Explanation of Ratios and Data

Current Data Sorted by Assets

Comparative Historical Data

Type of Statement

Type of Statement	ALL (4/1/14-3/31/15)	ALL (4/1/15-3/31/16)
Unqualified	41	43
Reviewed	2	1
Compiled		1
Tax Returns	5	
Other	10	8

Current data statement types (by asset size): Unqualified 3 (500M-2MM), 14 (2-10MM), 12 (10-50MM), 4 (50-100MM), 4 (100-250MM); Reviewed 1 (10-50MM); Compiled 3 (500M-2MM); Other 2 (0-500M), 5 (500M-2MM), 7 (2-10MM), 9 (10-50MM), 2 (50-100MM), 1 (100-250MM). Current period counts: 41 (4/1-9/30/18) and 26 (10/1/18-3/31/19).

0-500M	500M-2MM	2-10MM	10-50MM	50-100MM	100-250MM		ALL 4/1/14-3/31/15	ALL 4/1/15-3/31/16
2	11	21	22	6	5	**NUMBER OF STATEMENTS**	58	53
%	%	%	%	%	%	**ASSETS**	%	%
	16.9	28.6	34.9			Cash & Equivalents	31.9	31.8
	15.7	14.1	12.6			Trade Receivables (net)	14.5	13.8
	.6	.5	1.5			Inventory	3.1	2.9
	1.4	5.3	3.9			All Other Current	2.2	3.5
	34.6	48.5	52.8			Total Current	51.7	52.0
	62.5	36.5	28.7			Fixed Assets (net)	23.4	20.1
	.1	.2	.1			Intangibles (net)	.5	1.6
	2.7	14.8	18.4			All Other Non-Current	24.4	26.4
	100.0	100.0	100.0			Total	100.0	100.0
						LIABILITIES		
	.3	2.8	2.0			Notes Payable-Short Term	2.1	1.7
	.8	.9	.6			Cur. Mat.-L.T.D.	.9	1.0
	5.6	5.8	4.7			Trade Payables	4.9	5.0
	.0	.0	.0			Income Taxes Payable	.0	.0
	6.9	10.8	11.5			All Other Current	11.3	11.1
	13.6	20.4	18.9			Total Current	19.3	18.8
	20.8	14.5	13.6			Long-Term Debt	10.0	7.9
	.0	.0	.0			Deferred Taxes	.0	.0
	6.6	1.5	9.6			All Other Non-Current	3.9	2.4
	59.0	63.6	57.9			Net Worth	66.8	70.9
	100.0	100.0	100.0			Total Liabilities & Net Worth	100.0	100.0
						INCOME DATA		
	100.0	100.0	100.0			Net Sales	100.0	100.0
						Gross Profit		
	94.9	87.0	89.1			Operating Expenses	94.1	95.2
	5.1	13.0	10.9			Operating Profit	5.9	4.8
	1.0	5.1	3.3			All Other Expenses (net)	-1.6	.3
	4.2	7.8	7.7			Profit Before Taxes	7.5	4.5
						RATIOS		
	4.0	6.4	7.4				9.4	9.5
	2.4	2.9	3.5			Current	4.3	3.9
	1.2	1.3	1.4				2.1	1.3
	4.0	6.1	5.8				7.1	8.4
	2.4	2.7	3.0			Quick	3.8	3.0
	1.0	1.0	1.3				1.6	1.1
	0 UND	1 561.0	2 195.9				5 72.9	5 70.1
	17 22.0	19 19.0	28 13.2			Sales/Receivables	33 11.0	23 16.1
	48 7.6	50 7.3	101 3.6				69 5.3	68 5.4
						Cost of Sales/Inventory		
						Cost of Sales/Payables		
	4.5	3.0	2.1				1.6	1.6
	15.9	6.3	4.6			Sales/Working Capital	4.5	3.4
	167.3	27.3	12.3				13.8	13.2
	9.7	10.2	42.6				41.1	14.3
	(10) 3.4	(13) 9.0	(11) 6.1			EBIT/Interest	(34) 4.5	(25) 4.3
	.2	1.0	-3.7				.8	.1
						Net Profit + Depr., Dep., Amort./Cur. Mat. L/T/D		
	.7	.0	.1				.0	.0
	1.1	.7	.5			Fixed/Worth	.2	.1
	2.0	1.1	1.0				.7	.7
	.2	.2	.1				.1	.1
	.7	.5	.4			Debt/Worth	.4	.3
	1.1	1.5	1.1				.7	.6
	47.1	19.1	18.4				16.4	8.5
	1.0	(20) 9.9	(19) 6.4			% Profit Before Taxes/Tangible Net Worth	(57) 5.2	(51) 3.7
	-1.0	-2.1	-3.0				-.2	-.8
	18.7	12.9	9.5				8.1	5.5
	.7	6.2	3.9			% Profit Before Taxes/Total Assets	4.2	2.2
	-.8	-1.4	-2.0				-.2	-1.6
	4.9	142.0	22.3				70.3	49.2
	3.4	5.7	5.5			Sales/Net Fixed Assets	12.3	10.9
	.8	1.4	2.5				3.0	1.4
	2.8	2.6	1.8				2.3	1.7
	2.1	1.3	1.2			Sales/Total Assets	1.0	.7
	.8	.5	.6				.5	.3
		.3	.6				.5	.6
	(18)	1.1	(21) 1.2			% Depr., Dep., Amort./Sales	(49) 1.0	(44) 1.1
		3.5	3.5				2.6	3.0
						% Officers', Directors' Owners' Comp/Sales		
1570M	28592M	164582M	787541M	1162058M	208770M	Net Sales ($)	2105927M	1270834M
310M	13501M	109819M	424412M	399621M	858453M	Total Assets ($)	1691538M	2357262M

© RMA 2019

M = $ thousand   MM = $ million
See Pages viii through xx for Explanation of Ratios and Data

Comparative Historical Data			Type of Statement	Current Data Sorted by Sales					
31	24	37	Unqualified	7	1	8	7	14	
		1	Reviewed		1				
			Compiled						
4	1	3	Tax Returns	2	1	1			
11	15	26	Other	4	5		4	7	5
4/1/16-3/31/17	4/1/17-3/31/18	4/1/18-3/31/19		41 (4/1-9/30/18)		26 (10/1/18-3/31/19)			
ALL	ALL	ALL		0-1MM	1-3MM	3-5MM	5-10MM	10-25MM	25MM & OVER
46	40	67	NUMBER OF STATEMENTS	6	13	2	13	14	19
%	%	%	ASSETS	%	%	%	%	%	%
31.0	31.4	31.9	Cash & Equivalents		21.9		39.7	31.2	36.1
13.4	11.9	12.9	Trade Receivables (net)		7.8		15.4	13.4	18.6
2.4	2.0	.9	Inventory		.9		.2	.9	1.5
4.4	6.6	4.5	All Other Current		9.1		1.2	.9	7.5
51.2	51.9	50.1	Total Current		39.7		56.6	46.5	63.7
23.9	27.8	33.2	Fixed Assets (net)		51.6		30.7	28.4	17.3
.2	1.9	.7	Intangibles (net)		.2		.0	1.7	1.0
24.7	18.5	16.0	All Other Non-Current		8.5		12.7	23.4	18.0
100.0	100.0	100.0	Total		100.0		100.0	100.0	100.0
			LIABILITIES						
1.4	.8	2.9	Notes Payable-Short Term		6.4		2.1	3.8	1.5
2.2	2.1	.7	Cur. Mat.-L.T.D.		.7		.4	1.2	.6
4.3	5.1	5.2	Trade Payables		2.6		9.3	4.8	5.8
.0	.0	.0	Income Taxes Payable		.0		.0	.0	.0
10.4	10.0	14.5	All Other Current		3.6		12.2	14.8	25.5
18.2	18.0	23.2	Total Current		13.4		24.1	24.6	33.4
11.8	17.3	13.3	Long-Term Debt		21.4		10.1	6.9	11.8
.0	.0	.0	Deferred Taxes		.0		.0	.0	.0
1.6	4.5	6.0	All Other Non-Current		10.2		2.1	2.1	11.3
68.4	60.2	57.4	Net Worth		55.0		63.7	66.4	43.5
100.0	100.0	100.0	Total Liabilities & Net Worth		100.0		100.0	100.0	100.0
			INCOME DATA						
100.0	100.0	100.0	Net Sales		100.0		100.0	100.0	100.0
			Gross Profit						
95.0	91.8	89.8	Operating Expenses		85.0		84.3	94.5	94.8
5.0	8.2	10.2	Operating Profit		15.0		15.7	5.5	5.2
.5	-.4	3.8	All Other Expenses (net)		4.0		2.5	3.7	.1
4.5	8.6	6.4	Profit Before Taxes		11.0		13.2	1.7	5.1
			RATIOS						
8.2	9.2	6.3	Current	8.0		6.6	3.3	6.1	
3.5	4.3	2.8		3.4		2.7	2.5	4.7	
1.1	1.5	1.4		1.1		1.4	1.2	1.6	
6.5	8.7	5.8	Quick	6.6		6.4	3.3	5.5	
2.1	3.6	2.6		2.0		2.7	2.5	3.0	
1.0	1.2	1.2		.9		1.3	1.1	1.2	
1 508.8	1 538.6	1 482.9	Sales/Receivables	1 445.0	2 205.8	2 183.4	5 77.0		
26 14.0	27 13.6	19 19.0		17 22.0	17 22.0	23 15.7	33 10.9		
85 4.3	104 3.5	59 6.2		65 5.6	55 6.6	49 7.4	89 4.1		
			Cost of Sales/Inventory						
			Cost of Sales/Payables						
1.6	1.0	2.2	Sales/Working Capital	1.9		1.7	2.9	1.6	
4.2	2.8	5.3		8.5		6.3	6.0	4.5	
15.6	10.1	13.2		39.1		10.8	20.2	12.8	
5.1	10.6	12.3	EBIT/Interest	9.6					
(21) -.7	(21) 3.1	(38) 8.4		(12) 8.4					
-9.9	.4	-.5		1.3					
			Net Profit + Depr., Dep., Amort./Cur. Mat. L/T/D						
.0	.0	.1	Fixed/Worth	.5		.0	.1	.0	
.1	.4	.5		1.0		.5	.3	.3	
.7	1.0	1.1		2.5		.9	.8	.8	
.1	.1	.2	Debt/Worth	.2		.2	.2	.1	
.3	.6	.5		.5		.6	.5	.7	
.8	1.6	1.4		2.3		1.1	.9	-23.9	
8.1	11.6	18.5	% Profit Before Taxes/Tangible Net Worth	43.4		20.1	11.4	11.0	
(45) 1.2	(38) 6.0	(60) 7.1		(12) 11.5		9.6	3.4	(14) 6.7	
-5.7	.2	-2.5		.0		-18.0	-3.9	2.3	
6.0	6.3	9.7	% Profit Before Taxes/Total Assets	19.6		16.3	7.4	8.1	
.2	3.0	3.8		7.4		5.1	2.9	3.8	
4.6	-2.0	-1.7		.3		-8.1	-2.5	-4.5	
55.9	62.9	32.1	Sales/Net Fixed Assets	6.4		70.4	8.8	140.9	
9.7	7.4	5.2		3.4		5.1	5.3	19.4	
1.6	1.4	1.6		.6		1.5	3.3	4.7	
1.3	1.5	2.5	Sales/Total Assets	2.7		2.9	2.4	3.6	
.9	.6	1.3		1.0		1.0	1.6	1.6	
.4	.3	.5		.3		.4	.7	.5	
.6	.8	.6	% Depr., Dep., Amort./Sales	.5		.4	.5	.7	
(39) 1.2	(30) 1.5	(52) 1.3		(10) 2.8	(11) 1.2	(13) 1.2	(14) 1.2		
4.1	4.8	4.2		10.5		4.3	4.2	1.6	
			% Officers', Directors' Owners' Comp/Sales						
997463M	673856M	2353113M	Net Sales ($)	2412M	26059M	8312M	92261M	225847M	1998222M
1366086M	1093866M	1806116M	Total Assets ($)	12683M	53906M	6207M	137401M	400553M	1195366M

© RMA 2019

M = $ thousand   MM = $ million
See Pages viii through xx for Explanation of Ratios and Data

Current Data Sorted by Assets | Comparative Historical Data

0-500M	500M-2MM	2-10MM	10-50MM	50-100MM	100-250MM	Type of Statement	4/1/14-3/31/15 ALL	4/1/15-3/31/16 ALL
	2	5	11	3	2	Unqualified	18	28
1			1			Reviewed		1
	1		1			Compiled		
		1	1			Tax Returns	1	3
	4	7	7	2		Other	17	24
		28 (4/1-9/30/18)	21 (10/1/18-3/31/19)					
1	7	13	21	5	2	**NUMBER OF STATEMENTS**	36	56
%	%	%	%	%	%	**ASSETS**	%	%
		39.1	19.7			Cash & Equivalents	30.7	30.4
		11.0	14.3			Trade Receivables (net)	12.1	12.0
		2.6	3.7			Inventory	2.0	2.1
		3.9	5.0			All Other Current	1.4	1.5
		56.7	42.7			Total Current	46.2	45.9
		36.5	35.5			Fixed Assets (net)	33.7	29.4
		.2	2.2			Intangibles (net)	.8	.1
		6.5	19.6			All Other Non-Current	19.3	24.6
		100.0	100.0			Total	100.0	100.0
						LIABILITIES		
		.2	.4			Notes Payable-Short Term	.8	3.0
		.8	1.2			Cur. Mat.-L.T.D.	2.4	.6
		6.2	6.3			Trade Payables	5.9	4.5
		.0	.0			Income Taxes Payable	.0	.0
		7.6	3.5			All Other Current	4.5	4.7
		14.8	11.5			Total Current	13.7	12.8
		8.6	7.7			Long-Term Debt	7.5	4.1
		.0	.0			Deferred Taxes	.0	.1
		6.0	3.4			All Other Non-Current	5.9	4.3
		70.6	77.4			Net Worth	72.9	78.7
		100.0	100.0			Total Liabilities & Net Worth	100.0	100.0
						INCOME DATA		
		100.0	100.0			Net Sales	100.0	100.0
						Gross Profit		
		95.6	89.3			Operating Expenses	91.2	91.9
		4.4	10.7			Operating Profit	8.8	8.1
		-1.1	4.0			All Other Expenses (net)	-.7	-.1
		5.6	6.6			Profit Before Taxes	9.5	8.2
						RATIOS		
		17.1	9.7				7.4	11.5
		4.7	4.1			Current	4.1	3.9
		1.9	1.6				2.5	2.8
		16.8	7.8				6.7	10.2
		4.7	3.3			Quick	3.6	3.7
		1.5	.9				1.6	2.4
		1 534.3	11 34.3				2 206.1	5 79.9
		18 20.0	28 13.2			Sales/Receivables	17 22.1	23 16.2
		53 6.9	91 4.0				47 7.7	68 5.4
						Cost of Sales/Inventory		
						Cost of Sales/Payables		
		1.1	1.3				1.9	1.3
		2.8	4.0			Sales/Working Capital	4.2	2.6
		21.2	10.1				9.3	5.5
							33.3	22.4
						EBIT/Interest	(21) 9.1	(25) 1.6
							.8	-1.9
						Net Profit + Depr., Dep., Amort./Cur. Mat. L/T/D		
		.1	.1				.1	.1
		.4	.5			Fixed/Worth	.4	.3
		1.2	.7				.8	.7
		.1	.1				.1	.1
		.3	.3			Debt/Worth	.2	.2
		.6	.5				.5	.4
		12.8	10.0				18.9	16.3
		(12) 4.8	4.6			% Profit Before Taxes/Tangible Net Worth	5.5	(55) 5.5
		-8.4	-2.1				-.1	.0
		14.5	9.3				12.4	12.0
		3.9	4.3			% Profit Before Taxes/Total Assets	3.1	3.8
		-5.2	-.7				-.1	-.2
		32.9	17.4				16.2	17.6
		4.6	1.7			Sales/Net Fixed Assets	2.8	3.5
		1.4	.7				.9	1.1
		2.1	1.8				1.7	1.5
		.9	.5			Sales/Total Assets	.9	.7
		.7	.3				.5	.4
		.2	1.3				1.2	.8
		(11) 1.5	(16) 2.7			% Depr., Dep., Amort./Sales	(31) 2.0	(45) 2.4
		3.0	3.9				4.9	5.1
						% Officers', Directors' Owners' Comp/Sales		
755M	8716M	94021M	453473M	156182M	222018M	Net Sales ($)	960684M	1394472M
93M	5570M	70551M	517250M	371849M	339936M	Total Assets ($)	945031M	1796722M

© RMA 2019

M = $ thousand   MM = $ million
See Pages viii through xx for Explanation of Ratios and Data

Comparative Historical Data | Current Data Sorted by Sales

Type of Statement

25	21	23		1	2	3	4		6	7	
		1	Unqualified				1				
	1	2	Reviewed	2							
	2	2	Compiled		1	1					
			Tax Returns								
16	13	21	Other	2	4	3	3		6	3	

4/1/16-3/31/17 ALL	4/1/17-3/31/18 ALL	4/1/18-3/31/19 ALL		0-1MM	1-3MM	3-5MM	5-10MM	10-25MM	25MM & OVER
					28 (4/1-9/30/18)		21 (10/1/18-3/31/19)		
41	37	49	**NUMBER OF STATEMENTS**	5	7	7	8	12	10
%	%	%	**ASSETS**	%	%	%	%	%	%
21.1	23.9	28.7	Cash & Equivalents					25.6	21.6
13.4	11.4	14.3	Trade Receivables (net)					7.5	29.5
1.1	1.3	3.8	Inventory					1.3	7.9
5.4	3.8	3.8	All Other Current					2.2	3.2
41.0	40.4	50.5	Total Current					36.5	62.2
30.2	36.9	33.2	Fixed Assets (net)					38.8	15.8
1.3	.4	1.2	Intangibles (net)					.4	.0
27.5	22.4	15.1	All Other Non-Current					24.3	21.9
100.0	100.0	100.0	Total					100.0	100.0
			LIABILITIES						
1.8	1.6	2.3	Notes Payable-Short Term					.8	.2
.8	1.3	1.1	Cur. Mat.-L.T.D.					1.7	.2
6.3	3.9	6.6	Trade Payables					3.2	12.3
.0	.0	.0	Income Taxes Payable					.0	.0
8.4	5.3	5.8	All Other Current					7.6	6.3
17.2	12.0	15.9	Total Current					13.3	19.0
4.5	12.5	7.6	Long-Term Debt					10.5	2.2
.2	.0	.0	Deferred Taxes					.0	.0
2.8	2.7	3.3	All Other Non-Current					.5	7.5
75.3	72.8	73.2	Net Worth					75.6	71.3
100.0	100.0	100.0	Total Liabilities & Net Worth					100.0	100.0
			INCOME DATA						
100.0	100.0	100.0	Net Sales					100.0	100.0
			Gross Profit						
98.9	98.6	90.0	Operating Expenses					92.5	93.4
1.1	1.4	10.0	Operating Profit					7.5	6.6
-.8	-.3	2.0	All Other Expenses (net)					4.8	-1.3
2.0	1.7	8.0	Profit Before Taxes					2.7	7.9
			RATIOS						
6.3	7.7	11.8						6.7	5.2
3.5	4.4	4.4	Current					4.2	3.8
1.4	1.5	1.6						1.2	2.7
6.1	6.4	8.9						6.6	4.4
2.8	3.6	3.5	Quick					3.8	3.4
1.1	1.1	1.2						.9	2.2
5 70.2	3 145.0	7 49.7						1 290.9	18 20.4
20 18.5	17 21.5	22 16.8	Sales/Receivables					10 36.0	44 8.3
65 5.6	81 4.5	66 5.5						41 9.0	118 3.1
			Cost of Sales/Inventory						
			Cost of Sales/Payables						
1.5	1.3	1.3						2.0	2.4
4.6	3.5	3.2	Sales/Working Capital					4.5	4.4
11.2	18.2	10.1						28.5	6.4
67.7	32.6	53.9							
(20) 8.7	(21) 2.7	(20) 14.1	EBIT/Interest						
-1.9	-3.1	.7							
			Net Profit + Depr., Dep., Amort./Cur. Mat. L/T/D						
.1	.1	.0						.2	.0
.3	.4	.4	Fixed/Worth					.5	.1
.7	.9	.7						.7	.4
.1	.1	.1						.1	.1
.2	.3	.2	Debt/Worth					.3	.3
.4	.6	.6						.6	.6
7.6	10.9	10.2	% Profit Before Taxes/Tangible Net Worth					9.1	13.4
(40) 1.2	(36) 4.6	(47) 4.6						2.6	6.0
-5.2	-1.5	-1.1						-3.5	-2.9
6.9	9.6	9.2	% Profit Before Taxes/Total Assets					8.5	11.0
1.0	3.1	3.9						2.2	4.9
-2.6	-1.8	-.7						-3.1	-.6
23.5	27.2	37.1						19.7	78.5
2.8	2.3	3.4	Sales/Net Fixed Assets					1.5	19.0
.9	.7	.8						.8	6.4
1.6	1.6	1.9						2.0	2.2
.7	.7	.7	Sales/Total Assets					.5	1.8
.3	.3	.4						.4	.9
1.1	.9	.8						.9	
(33) 2.7	(30) 1.8	(36) 2.1	% Depr., Dep., Amort./Sales					(10) 2.1	
6.6	6.8	3.9						6.0	
			% Officers', Directors' Owners' Comp/Sales						
1319610M	834411M	935165M	Net Sales ($)	2958M	12337M	26534M	58513M	184571M	650252M
1637978M	1047066M	1305249M	Total Assets ($)	42141M	9731M	82471M	219998M	423079M	527829M

© RMA 2019

M = $ thousand   MM = $ million
See Pages viii through xx for Explanation of Ratios and Data

Current Data Sorted by Assets | Comparative Historical Data

	0-500M	500M-2MM	2-10MM	10-50MM	50-100MM	100-250MM		Type of Statement	4/1/14-3/31/15 ALL	4/1/15-3/31/16 ALL
	2	17	62	48	14	9		Unqualified	214	216
	1							Reviewed	6	5
	1	1	5					Compiled	8	8
	2	3						Tax Returns	17	11
	12	23	29	23	4	2		Other	119	109
		183 (4/1-9/30/18)		75 (10/1/18-3/31/19)						
NUMBER OF STATEMENTS	18	44	96	71	18	11			364	349
	%	%	%	%	%	%		**ASSETS**	%	%
Cash & Equivalents	41.1	29.8	28.3	24.2	30.3	38.9			24.4	25.7
Trade Receivables (net)	10.5	20.1	13.7	12.0	15.2	6.6			13.1	13.5
Inventory	.3	1.3	1.9	3.1	1.2	1.5			1.7	2.1
All Other Current	9.8	5.2	4.6	3.3	1.8	2.2			4.7	4.5
Total Current	61.7	56.3	48.5	42.6	48.6	49.2			43.9	45.8
Fixed Assets (net)	31.5	24.2	36.6	39.0	22.4	29.0			37.3	34.4
Intangibles (net)	.0	.4	1.0	1.3	1.4	.1			.8	.8
All Other Non-Current	7.3	19.1	13.9	17.2	27.6	21.7			18.0	19.0
Total	100.0	100.0	100.0	100.0	100.0	100.0			100.0	100.0
								LIABILITIES		
Notes Payable-Short Term	5.3	1.8	3.0	1.6	.0	.2			2.9	1.9
Cur. Mat.-L.T.D.	.8	1.1	2.8	1.7	2.1	1.6			1.6	1.3
Trade Payables	7.6	5.8	6.9	4.4	3.4	4.2			5.6	6.2
Income Taxes Payable	.0	.0	.0	.0	.0	.0			.0	.0
All Other Current	12.2	13.6	10.6	6.2	5.4	13.8			8.4	8.6
Total Current	26.0	22.2	23.3	14.0	10.9	19.9			18.6	18.0
Long-Term Debt	6.6	9.5	14.0	19.9	14.3	19.8			15.8	13.8
Deferred Taxes	.0	.0	.0	.0	.0	.0			.0	.0
All Other Non-Current	.0	2.1	1.4	3.4	5.6	5.4			4.7	3.4
Net Worth	67.4	66.2	61.3	62.7	69.2	54.9			60.9	64.7
Total Liabilities & Net Worth	100.0	100.0	100.0	100.0	100.0	100.0			100.0	100.0
								INCOME DATA		
Net Sales	100.0	100.0	100.0	100.0	100.0	100.0			100.0	100.0
Gross Profit										
Operating Expenses	98.4	94.0	98.0	94.2	89.7	96.6			95.1	95.6
Operating Profit	1.6	6.0	2.0	5.8	10.3	3.4			4.9	4.4
All Other Expenses (net)	.6	-.3	.7	1.7	1.0	-1.1			.7	1.3
Profit Before Taxes	.9	6.3	1.4	4.1	9.3	4.6			4.2	3.1
								RATIOS		
Current	13.9	7.4	6.1	7.3	8.4	4.5			6.5	6.2
	2.3	3.5	2.6	3.2	4.7	2.2			2.7	3.0
	1.0	1.4	1.2	1.9	2.9	1.6			1.4	1.4
Quick	13.9	7.2	5.6	6.3	8.3	4.5			5.4	5.4
	2.1	3.5	2.3	2.7	3.9	1.8			2.3	2.5
	.6	1.2	1.0	1.4	2.8	1.3			1.1	1.2
Sales/Receivables	0 UND	0 UND	7 50.9	9 42.1	6 65.3	9 40.7			3 109.3	3 118.3
	0 UND	17 21.3	25 14.5	31 11.7	35 10.5	21 17.4			26 14.3	26 13.8
	17 21.2	51 7.1	53 6.9	57 6.4	166 2.2	69 5.3			51 7.2	53 6.9
Cost of Sales/Inventory										
Cost of Sales/Payables										
Sales/Working Capital	3.7	3.4	2.3	1.7	.7	1.9			2.2	2.3
	9.1	6.9	5.7	2.7	2.5	4.2			6.0	5.6
	NM	20.8	17.7	7.4	5.2	8.3			20.3	20.4
EBIT/Interest		33.7	6.7	7.9	27.9				15.7	13.2
		(22) 8.0	(60) 1.6	(48) 3.0	(11) 5.0				(230) 2.4	(200) 2.9
		.6	-3.5	-.9	-1.3				-.9	-1.9
Net Profit + Depr., Dep., Amort./Cur. Mat. L/T/D										
Fixed/Worth	.1	.0	.2	.2	.0	.0			.1	.1
	.2	.2	.5	.6	.2	.4			.5	.5
	.9	.5	1.1	1.1	.5	1.4			1.1	1.0
Debt/Worth	.1	.2	.2	.1	.1	.5			.2	.2
	.2	.4	.4	.5	.3	.5			.5	.4
	.9	1.2	1.4	1.7	1.4	2.0			1.3	1.1
% Profit Before Taxes/Tangible Net Worth	11.5	31.8	9.6	9.9	11.9	13.8			11.8	11.3
	(17) .0	4.5	(91) 2.2	4.0	3.2	4.3			(349) 3.6	(337) 2.4
	-9.8	-3.3	-6.0	-2.0	.3	-.9			-1.6	-3.6
% Profit Before Taxes/Total Assets	6.7	15.7	5.5	4.2	7.2	5.7			6.9	6.9
	.0	2.2	.8	2.0	1.8	2.7			1.9	1.5
	-8.0	-2.1	-3.8	-1.0	.0	-.6			-1.1	-2.3
Sales/Net Fixed Assets	91.5	226.2	47.8	8.4	91.9	43.9			28.2	33.4
	29.2	31.9	2.8	2.2	7.2	2.9			3.5	3.9
	1.9	3.4	1.2	.9	2.1	1.2			1.1	1.3
Sales/Total Assets	5.1	4.3	2.1	1.5	1.1	1.9			1.9	1.9
	3.0	1.8	1.1	.7	.7	.7			.9	1.0
	1.1	.9	.5	.3	.2	.6			.4	.5
% Depr., Dep., Amort./Sales		.5	.7	1.2	.7				1.0	.8
	(29) 1.4	(80) 2.1	(62) 2.6	(16) 1.3					(303) 2.3	(288) 2.3
		3.5	3.5	4.3	4.0				4.6	4.4
% Officers', Directors' Owners' Comp/Sales									2.8	1.2
									(17) 7.5	(19) 5.2
									16.3	10.5
Net Sales ($)	17443M	164231M	759098M	2365086M	1108348M	2273567M			5669057M	7976385M
Total Assets ($)	5065M	54583M	472677M	1631600M	1213458M	1744226M			6336394M	6987063M

© RMA 2019

M = $ thousand   MM = $ million
See Pages viii through xx for Explanation of Ratios and Data

Comparative Historical Data				Type of Statement	Current Data Sorted by Sales					
183	167	152		Unqualified	5	30	17	31	33	36
7	4	1		Reviewed		1				
1	6	7		Compiled	2	4			1	
10	9	5		Tax Returns	3	2				
76	93	93		Other	15	24	16	14	12	12
4/1/16-3/31/17 ALL	4/1/17-3/31/18 ALL	4/1/18-3/31/19 ALL			183 (4/1-9/30/18)			75 (10/1/18-3/31/19)		
					0-1MM	1-3MM	3-5MM	5-10MM	10-25MM	25MM & OVER
277	279	258		NUMBER OF STATEMENTS	25	61	33	45	46	48
%	%	%		ASSETS	%	%	%	%	%	%
24.2	28.1	28.9		Cash & Equivalents	24.2	28.0	27.5	30.9	27.2	33.3
13.8	15.6	13.9		Trade Receivables (net)	5.7	11.6	13.0	15.7	17.9	16.1
2.4	2.5	1.9		Inventory	1.7	2.4	.7	1.7	1.0	3.4
5.4	3.4	4.4		All Other Current	.8	5.5	3.3	5.3	4.8	4.2
45.8	49.6	49.2		Total Current	32.4	47.6	44.6	53.7	51.0	57.1
34.1	33.9	33.5		Fixed Assets (net)	42.6	33.3	41.1	32.5	28.0	29.7
1.5	1.1	.9		Intangibles (net)	.0	1.2	.2	1.5	.7	1.2
18.7	15.4	16.5		All Other Non-Current	25.4	17.9	14.1	12.3	20.3	12.0
100.0	100.0	100.0		Total	100.0	100.0	100.0	100.0	100.0	100.0
				LIABILITIES						
2.6	3.5	2.3		Notes Payable-Short Term	2.6	1.6	3.7	3.3	2.4	.8
1.8	1.9	1.9		Cur. Mat.-L.T.D.	1.5	2.4	2.8	2.3	1.7	.9
6.0	5.7	5.7		Trade Payables	1.8	4.2	3.6	6.2	7.7	8.7
.0	.0	.0		Income Taxes Payable	.0	.0	.0	.0	.0	.0
7.9	9.6	9.8		All Other Current	3.9	8.2	12.3	10.7	8.3	13.9
18.4	20.7	19.7		Total Current	9.7	16.5	22.4	22.4	20.1	24.3
13.1	14.4	14.6		Long-Term Debt	17.7	14.8	18.0	11.9	17.0	10.4
.0	.0	.0		Deferred Taxes	.0	.0	.0	.0	.0	.0
3.1	3.4	2.5		All Other Non-Current	.8	1.5	2.2	2.8	3.9	3.1
65.4	61.5	63.3		Net Worth	71.8	67.2	57.4	62.9	59.0	62.2
100.0	100.0	100.0		Total Liabilities & Net Worth	100.0	100.0	100.0	100.0	100.0	100.0
				INCOME DATA						
100.0	100.0	100.0		Net Sales	100.0	100.0	100.0	100.0	100.0	100.0
				Gross Profit						
96.2	96.1	95.6		Operating Expenses	92.5	93.8	96.7	95.8	96.7	97.8
3.8	3.9	4.4		Operating Profit	7.5	6.2	3.3	4.2	3.3	2.2
.7	.2	.7		All Other Expenses (net)	2.0	1.3	2.0	-.1	.7	-.7
3.1	3.6	3.6		Profit Before Taxes	5.5	4.9	1.3	4.3	2.7	2.9
				RATIOS						
6.0	7.2	7.0			8.0	9.7	5.9	6.6	6.7	6.0
2.8	3.3	3.2		Current	2.8	3.8	2.4	3.2	3.1	2.6
1.5	1.6	1.6			.8	1.7	1.2	1.6	1.4	1.7
5.2	6.0	6.4			7.8	9.3	5.7	5.9	6.4	4.5
2.3	2.6	2.7		Quick	2.7	3.2	2.4	2.7	2.4	2.4
1.2	1.3	1.2			.8	1.3	1.0	1.2	1.2	1.5
3 124.2	4 94.2	3 111.7			0 UND	0 UND	12 29.9	14 25.2	4 92.2	9 39.6
23 16.2	26 14.0	24 15.1		Sales/Receivables	0 UND	13 27.1	24 15.2	30 12.3	28 13.1	28 13.2
54 6.7	55 6.6	53 6.9			20 18.4	60 6.1	57 6.4	61 6.0	54 6.8	51 7.2
				Cost of Sales/Inventory						
				Cost of Sales/Payables						
2.3	2.0	2.1			1.9	1.8	2.3	1.8	1.9	2.7
5.7	5.0	4.9		Sales/Working Capital	4.5	4.3	4.2	3.8	6.1	5.8
15.9	16.7	12.5			-25.6	11.5	14.2	9.8	18.6	12.4
14.3	13.0	10.7			11.9	21.0	4.0	11.7	8.1	15.1
(167) 3.1	(165) 3.1	(154) 2.6		EBIT/Interest	(14) .6	(33) 3.5	(18) .2	(30) 1.4	(28) 2.4	(31) 4.2
.2	.1	-2.2			-3.7	-3.3	-6.2	-2.6	-1.3	1.4
				Net Profit + Depr., Dep., Amort./Cur. Mat. L/T/D						
.1	.1	.1			.0	.1	.2	.1	.1	.2
.4	.5	.4		Fixed/Worth	.4	.4	.6	.4	.3	.4
.9	1.0	.9			1.3	.9	1.5	.9	.9	.8
.2	.2	.1			.1	.1	.2	.1	.3	.2
.4	.5	.4		Debt/Worth	.3	.3	.4	.4	.6	.5
1.1	1.2	1.4			.8	1.0	2.3	1.5	1.9	1.4
10.4	13.1	11.3		% Profit Before Taxes/Tangible Net Worth	16.1	14.7	6.1	12.7	10.4	9.9
(272) 2.7	(267) 4.2	(252) 3.0			3.6 (58)	2.8 (31)	2.0	3.2	4.9 (47)	3.1
-3.5	-1.4	-3.9			-4.9	-4.1	-5.0	-4.4	-5.0	-.6
6.0	7.8	6.0		% Profit Before Taxes/Total Assets	7.3	8.7	2.6	6.9	5.8	5.9
1.7	2.8	1.7			2.0	1.7	.7	2.2	2.4	2.2
-2.1	-1.1	-2.5			-3.2	-3.7	-3.8	-2.6	-2.5	-.5
34.8	40.8	47.5		Sales/Net Fixed Assets	71.1	73.1	15.3	72.4	98.7	38.9
3.9	4.5	4.2			2.0	4.2	2.2	2.8	10.9	6.0
1.3	1.4	1.4			.8	.9	1.2	1.2	2.0	2.9
2.0	2.2	2.2		Sales/Total Assets	1.2	1.8	1.3	2.3	3.0	3.0
1.0	1.1	1.0			.6	.8	.7	1.1	1.3	1.7
.5	.6	.5			.3	.4	.3	.5	.6	.8
.8	.8	.8		% Depr., Dep., Amort./Sales	.6	1.0	1.0	.8	.8	.5
(226) 2.1	(225) 1.9	(204) 2.1			(13) 3.7	(47) 3.2	(28) 2.2	(38) 2.2	(38) 1.5	(40) 1.4
4.0	3.5	3.9			6.5	4.4	4.6	3.4	3.1	2.7
1.2	1.9	.8		% Officers', Directors' Owners' Comp/Sales						
(11) 3.6	(17) 4.7	(17) 4.1								
9.8	15.9	10.4								
5719178M	6468043M	6687773M		Net Sales ($)	13136M	118341M	131427M	343803M	734045M	5347021M
5393618M	5392987M	5121609M		Total Assets ($)	35055M	212522M	329182M	548578M	989267M	3007005M

M = $ thousand   MM = $ million
See Pages viii through xx for Explanation of Ratios and Data

Current Data Sorted by Assets | | | | | | | | **Comparative Historical Data**

Type of Statement	0-500M	500M-2MM	2-10MM	10-50MM	50-100MM	100-250MM	4/1/14-3/31/15 ALL	4/1/15-3/31/16 ALL
Unqualified		19	54	101	23	14	295	299
Reviewed	1	2	4				21	15
Compiled	1	3	5	1			22	16
Tax Returns	5	16	7	1		1	46	51
Other	14	33	62	39	9		147	181
		246 (4/1-9/30/18)		169 (10/1/18-3/31/19)				
NUMBER OF STATEMENTS	21	73	132	142	32	15	531	562
	%	%	%	%	%	%	%	%
ASSETS								
Cash & Equivalents	46.6	35.8	25.0	21.6	18.2	14.1	25.3	25.4
Trade Receivables (net)	2.0	12.8	8.5	4.4	3.2	5.4	7.8	8.1
Inventory	1.2	2.2	1.0	.8	1.6	.8	1.1	1.0
All Other Current	1.6	1.0	2.6	2.5	1.7	3.6	2.3	2.9
Total Current	51.4	51.8	37.2	29.3	24.6	23.9	36.5	37.3
Fixed Assets (net)	40.4	43.3	47.6	45.0	57.7	39.3	48.3	46.4
Intangibles (net)	3.1	.8	1.5	1.2	.7	.2	.9	1.1
All Other Non-Current	5.1	4.0	13.8	24.6	17.1	36.6	14.2	15.2
Total	100.0	100.0	100.0	100.0	100.0	100.0	100.0	100.0
LIABILITIES								
Notes Payable-Short Term	15.7	2.3	2.6	1.2	.4	.2	1.7	2.3
Cur. Mat.-L.T.D.	.6	1.7	1.4	1.1	2.0	1.7	1.8	1.3
Trade Payables	1.7	6.7	4.3	2.7	2.4	3.2	4.2	5.1
Income Taxes Payable	.0	.0	.0	.0	.0	.0	.0	.0
All Other Current	2.5	7.6	5.8	6.6	3.1	1.8	7.7	7.0
Total Current	20.5	18.3	14.1	11.6	7.9	7.0	15.5	15.6
Long-Term Debt	14.4	17.1	17.8	11.6	19.3	23.5	16.7	18.4
Deferred Taxes	.0	.0	.1	.0	.0	.0	.0	.1
All Other Non-Current	4.1	4.6	1.9	3.1	4.2	4.3	4.5	3.5
Net Worth	61.0	59.9	66.2	73.7	68.5	65.3	63.4	62.3
Total Liabilities & Net Worth	100.0	100.0	100.0	100.0	100.0	100.0	100.0	100.0
INCOME DATA								
Net Sales	100.0	100.0	100.0	100.0	100.0	100.0	100.0	100.0
Gross Profit								
Operating Expenses	94.8	95.2	91.6	97.5	94.6	90.0	94.1	93.3
Operating Profit	5.2	4.8	8.4	2.5	5.4	10.0	5.9	6.7
All Other Expenses (net)	.4	1.3	2.3	-.3	3.2	2.3	1.0	2.4
Profit Before Taxes	4.8	3.5	6.1	2.8	2.2	7.7	5.0	4.3
RATIOS								
Current	36.3	10.5	8.0	4.7	5.2	8.8	8.2	8.0
	10.0	3.8	2.9	2.7	2.9	2.8	3.0	3.0
	2.8	1.2	1.4	1.4	1.4	2.0	1.3	1.4
Quick	35.8	10.4	7.5	4.3	4.5	5.8	7.4	7.1
	10.0	3.8	2.5	2.5	2.5	2.8	2.6	2.6
	2.6	1.1	1.0	1.0	1.3	1.7	1.1	1.1
Sales/Receivables	0 UND	0 UND	1 341.1	3 112.2	4 102.9	8 43.9	1 284.0	1 253.9
	0 UND	7 52.8	11 31.9	12 31.1	16 22.9	27 13.7	12 31.3	13 29.1
	4 95.4	37 9.9	38 9.5	33 11.0	30 12.3	49 7.5	36 10.0	35 10.3
Cost of Sales/Inventory								
Cost of Sales/Payables								
Sales/Working Capital	1.9	2.5	2.1	2.3	2.0	1.0	2.1	2.0
	3.1	5.3	4.8	5.2	4.4	2.5	5.0	4.5
	12.0	32.4	13.8	14.4	30.0	8.7	19.9	17.4
EBIT/Interest		6.0	11.8	8.3	6.7	10.2	9.4	7.9
		(24) 1.5	(80) 2.8	(90) 1.4	(27) 1.2	(12) 5.9	(314) 2.1	(342) 2.6
		-5.0	-1.2	-4.1	-1.6	.9	-.4	-.4
Net Profit + Depr., Dep., Amort./Cur. Mat. L/T/D								
Fixed/Worth	.0	.1	.2	.3	.5	.3	.3	.2
	.7	.6	.7	.5	.9	.7	.7	.7
	1.5	1.9	1.3	.9	1.3	1.0	1.2	1.3
Debt/Worth	.0	.1	.1	.1	.2	.2	.2	.1
	.2	.4	.4	.3	.4	.5	.4	.4
	1.6	1.9	1.1	.7	.9	1.1	.9	1.0
% Profit Before Taxes/Tangible Net Worth	17.2	11.2	12.8	5.4	4.9	10.4	9.6	10.6
	(19) .0	(70) 2.3	(129) 2.8	(140) .7	(31) 1.5	3.7	(511) 3.1	(541) 3.0
	-9.5	-3.8	-1.6	-2.5	-1.8	-.3	-.9	-1.7
% Profit Before Taxes/Total Assets	9.4	7.8	8.4	4.2	3.0	7.2	6.3	6.0
	.0	1.8	1.9	.5	.4	2.3	1.8	1.5
	-5.3	-2.7	-1.1	-2.1	-1.4	-.3	-.6	-1.2
Sales/Net Fixed Assets	UND	52.9	8.0	2.8	1.7	4.0	7.1	7.2
	3.9	4.5	1.6	1.4	1.0	.7	1.4	1.4
	1.3	.7	.7	.7	.6	.3	.6	.6
Sales/Total Assets	2.8	2.4	1.1	.7	.8	.5	1.2	1.2
	1.0	1.2	.6	.5	.5	.2	.7	.7
	.6	.4	.4	.4	.3	.1	.4	.4
% Depr., Dep., Amort./Sales		.6	1.3	2.7	3.7	4.5	1.7	1.8
	(49) 1.9	(103) 4.1	(132) 4.8	(31) 7.3	(14) 7.9		(439) 4.2	(451) 4.3
		8.6	7.1	7.9	10.0	12.2	8.4	8.2
% Officers', Directors' Owners' Comp/Sales							3.5	3.0
							(39) 6.6	(48) 9.1
							17.5	21.0
Net Sales ($)	9494M	143918M	598511M	2063562M	1283190M	1210409M	5000302M	5855873M
Total Assets ($)	6211M	87609M	670699M	3319551M	2260171M	2404637M	8029595M	9985259M

M = $ thousand   MM = $ million
See Pages viii through xx for Explanation of Ratios and Data

Comparative Historical Data | | Current Data Sorted by Sales

					Type of Statement						
227		236		211	Unqualified	10	23	26	45	67	40
10		12		7	Reviewed	2	4			1	
16		13		10	Compiled	3	3	2	2		
49		38		30	Tax Returns	20	5	2	2	1	
157		166		157	Other	34	47	21	25	20	10
4/1/16-3/31/17 ALL		4/1/17-3/31/18 ALL		4/1/18-3/31/19 ALL		246 (4/1-9/30/18)			169 (10/1/18-3/31/19)		
						0-1MM	1-3MM	3-5MM	5-10MM	10-25MM	25MM & OVER
459		465		415	**NUMBER OF STATEMENTS**	69	82	51	74	89	60
%		%		%	**ASSETS**	%	%	%	%	%	%
23.7		23.1		25.9	Cash & Equivalents	25.1	30.3	30.2	26.2	20.6	24.4
7.7		7.7		7.0	Trade Receivables (net)	2.4	8.1	9.0	9.9	5.6	7.8
1.2		1.0		1.2	Inventory	.7	1.7	.6	1.5	1.2	1.4
3.0		2.7		2.2	All Other Current	2.7	.8	1.3	1.7	3.6	3.0
35.5		34.5		36.3	Total Current	30.9	40.9	41.0	39.3	31.0	36.6
46.3		46.0		46.1	Fixed Assets (net)	61.0	45.4	42.5	40.6	40.3	48.5
1.4		1.3		1.2	Intangibles (net)	1.1	1.6	1.6	1.7	.4	1.2
16.7		18.2		16.4	All Other Non-Current	7.0	12.2	14.9	18.5	28.3	13.6
100.0		100.0		100.0	Total	100.0	100.0	100.0	100.0	100.0	100.0
					LIABILITIES						
1.9		1.7		2.5	Notes Payable-Short Term	4.5	3.2	2.3	2.5	1.3	.7
1.5		1.6		1.4	Cur. Mat.-L.T.D.	1.6	1.3	2.3	1.0	1.2	1.1
4.0		4.0		3.9	Trade Payables	1.1	3.9	2.8	6.3	3.8	5.1
.0		.0		.0	Income Taxes Payable	.0	.0	.0	.0	.0	.0
8.0		7.1		5.8	All Other Current	2.0	7.8	3.9	5.5	7.0	8.3
15.4		14.4		13.6	Total Current	9.2	16.2	11.3	15.4	13.4	15.1
17.3		17.6		15.7	Long-Term Debt	30.0	12.2	15.0	12.0	12.9	13.3
.0		.2		.0	Deferred Taxes	.0	.1	.0	.0	.0	.0
4.1		3.3		3.2	All Other Non-Current	2.4	2.1	1.4	4.7	2.9	6.0
63.3		64.6		67.5	Net Worth	58.4	69.5	72.2	68.0	70.8	65.6
100.0		100.0		100.0	Total Liabilties & Net Worth	100.0	100.0	100.0	100.0	100.0	100.0
					INCOME DATA						
100.0		100.0		100.0	Net Sales	100.0	100.0	100.0	100.0	100.0	100.0
					Gross Profit						
94.1		95.1		94.6	Operating Expenses	88.6	93.4	97.4	95.3	97.0	96.4
5.9		4.9		5.4	Operating Profit	11.4	6.6	2.6	4.7	3.0	3.6
1.4		.2		1.2	All Other Expenses (net)	5.9	.3	.7	.3	-.4	.9
4.5		4.7		4.2	Profit Before Taxes	5.5	6.3	1.9	4.4	3.4	2.7
					RATIOS						
8.3		6.7		7.0		14.1	9.7	10.0	6.3	4.8	5.0
2.9		2.8		3.0	Current	4.5	3.5	3.6	2.9	2.7	2.5
1.4		1.3		1.4		1.0	1.1	2.4	1.6	1.2	1.5
7.4		6.2		6.5		12.4	9.3	10.0	6.1	4.3	4.6
2.5		2.3		2.7	Quick	3.8	3.1	3.2	2.6	2.4	2.3
1.0		1.0		1.2		1.0	1.0	1.9	1.3	1.0	1.3
1 586.2	1	422.6	1	361.8		0 UND	0 UND	4 98.2	4 84.3	4 93.7	8 43.8
11 33.6	11	32.2	12	31.3	Sales/Receivables	0 UND	6 63.8	17 21.7	13 27.3	12 30.1	18 19.9
36 10.2	35	10.5	32	11.3		13 28.3	40 9.2	53 6.9	35 10.3	35 10.5	29 12.5
					Cost of Sales/Inventory						
					Cost of Sales/Payables						
2.0		2.3		2.2		1.4	2.4	2.1	2.4	2.5	2.6
5.1		5.4		5.0	Sales/Working Capital	3.6	4.8	3.2	5.5	5.2	5.4
23.3		31.2		16.2		NM	42.9	8.4	10.1	19.2	17.7
10.3		8.6		8.8		6.7	12.3	3.6	8.2	9.4	10.6
(279) 2.9	(280)	2.0	(242)	1.9	EBIT/Interest	(30) 2.3	(41) 2.0	(35) .5	(41) 1.9	(57) 2.6	(38) 1.7
-.3		-.4		-1.7		-.3	-2.4	-5.7	-2.4	-2.4	.5
					Net Profit + Depr., Dep., Amort./Cur. Mat. L/T/D						
.3		.2		.3		.3	.1	.2	.2	.3	.3
.7		.7		.6	Fixed/Worth	1.1	.6	.6	.5	.5	.7
1.3		1.2		1.2		1.9	1.2	1.0	1.0	.8	1.2
.1		.1		.1		.1	.1	.1	.1	.1	.2
.4		.4		.3	Debt/Worth	.4	.3	.2	.3	.3	.5
1.1		1.0		.9		2.0	1.0	.6	.8	.8	.9
10.3		9.4		9.3	% Profit Before Taxes/Tangible Net Worth	9.6	12.8	8.2	11.8	5.7	9.5
(443) 2.6	(446)	2.4	(404)	1.8		(65) .9	(81) 3.0	(48) 1.3	(73) 1.3	(88) 1.3	(49) 2.7
-2.5		-2.0		-2.3		-3.2	-1.1	-2.4	-3.5	-2.5	-1.1
5.7		5.9		6.7	% Profit Before Taxes/Total Assets	6.7	8.5	6.7	7.8	3.9	6.5
1.8		1.8		1.1		.6	1.8	1.0	.9	1.1	1.4
-1.7		-1.4		-1.5		-2.3	-1.1	-2.2	-2.7	-1.8	-.6
6.1		7.1		6.8		2.6	28.8	6.1	19.2	4.0	5.5
1.6		1.5		1.5	Sales/Net Fixed Assets	.6	1.6	1.6	2.0	1.7	1.4
.7		.6		.7		.3	.7	.7	.8	.9	.7
1.2		1.2		1.1		.8	1.3	1.1	1.5	.9	1.4
.6		.6		.6	Sales/Total Assets	.4	.7	.6	.6	.6	.7
.3		.4		.4		.2	.3	.3	.4	.4	.5
1.9		1.8		1.7		4.5	.9	1.5	1.4	2.0	2.3
(380) 4.2	(380)	4.6	(335)	4.7	% Depr., Dep., Amort./Sales	(41) 9.7	(52) 3.3	(42) 4.0	(67) 4.2	(85) 4.5	(48) 5.5
8.1		8.8		8.3		17.5	6.9	8.5	6.4	6.9	8.0
2.7		3.4		1.9	% Officers', Directors' Owners' Comp/Sales						
(33) 5.9	(33)	6.3	(26)	5.7							
15.5		10.8		19.4							
5555412M		5602766M		5309084M	Net Sales ($)	36160M	162862M	194925M	544803M	1453270M	2917064M
9125330M		8923874M		8748878M	Total Assets ($)	133157M	430941M	403319M	1084355M	3009597M	3687509M

Current Data Sorted by Assets   **Comparative Historical Data**

	0-500M	500M-2MM	2-10MM	10-50MM	50-100MM	100-250MM		4/1/14-3/31/15 ALL	4/1/15-3/31/16 ALL
		76 (4/1-9/30/18)		127 (10/1/18-3/31/19)			**Type of Statement**		
Unqualified	1	8	22	41	9	8		134	138
Reviewed	1	2	2					10	9
Compiled	3	3	1					13	7
Tax Returns	7	3	2	1				6	9
Other	12	19	19	27	6	6		71	84
NUMBER OF STATEMENTS	24	35	46	69	15	14		234	247
	%	%	%	%	%	%	**ASSETS**	%	%
	50.1	40.9	43.0	41.4	36.5	54.7	Cash & Equivalents	41.3	43.6
	4.5	12.7	8.7	7.3	20.4	6.7	Trade Receivables (net)	10.4	10.6
	1.7	5.4	.5	1.2	4.4	.1	Inventory	2.0	2.0
	1.2	8.6	4.9	5.8	2.1	5.4	All Other Current	3.6	4.5
	57.5	67.6	57.0	55.7	63.3	66.9	Total Current	57.2	60.7
	23.8	17.1	29.3	21.0	16.0	13.9	Fixed Assets (net)	26.5	20.9
	7.1	3.1	.6	1.1	2.2	2.2	Intangibles (net)	.9	.9
	11.5	12.2	13.1	22.2	18.5	17.0	All Other Non-Current	15.3	17.6
	100.0	100.0	100.0	100.0	100.0	100.0	Total	100.0	100.0
							LIABILITIES		
	16.8	3.4	1.7	.8	.1	.0	Notes Payable-Short Term	2.0	2.6
	3.9	.9	1.3	.4	.3	.1	Cur. Mat.-L.T.D.	1.1	1.1
	2.2	7.9	6.4	8.6	9.8	2.8	Trade Payables	7.9	8.7
	.0	.5	.0	.0	.0	.0	Income Taxes Payable	.1	.1
	17.5	26.8	14.3	11.0	21.5	5.0	All Other Current	14.0	14.1
	40.3	39.5	23.7	20.8	31.7	7.9	Total Current	25.1	26.6
	21.3	7.6	8.0	10.0	2.6	4.3	Long-Term Debt	9.1	8.4
	.0	.0	.0	.0	.5	.0	Deferred Taxes	.1	.1
	7.2	7.1	9.2	12.0	14.8	16.4	All Other Non-Current	13.3	15.5
	31.2	45.7	59.1	57.2	50.5	71.3	Net Worth	52.3	49.4
	100.0	100.0	100.0	100.0	100.0	100.0	Total Liabilities & Net Worth	100.0	100.0
							INCOME DATA		
	100.0	100.0	100.0	100.0	100.0	100.0	Net Sales	100.0	100.0
							Gross Profit		
	89.8	91.8	99.0	94.8	97.0	94.8	Operating Expenses	96.3	97.5
	10.2	8.2	1.0	5.2	3.0	5.2	Operating Profit	3.7	2.5
	4.9	2.3	.5	1.4	1.3	6.8	All Other Expenses (net)	.3	1.8
	5.3	5.9	.6	3.8	1.7	-1.6	Profit Before Taxes	3.4	.8
							RATIOS		
	7.1	6.2	12.4	6.7	6.6	26.9		5.4	5.3
	2.5	1.9	2.9	2.9	2.3	8.7	Current	2.6	2.6
	1.0	1.0	1.3	1.5	1.3	3.1		1.3	1.4
	7.0	5.0	11.1	6.6	6.4	26.7		5.1	4.9
	2.0	1.4	2.6	2.5	1.9	8.7	Quick	2.3	2.3
	.8	1.0	1.1	1.2	.9	3.1		1.0	1.3
	0 UND	0 UND	4 94.6	2 151.2	26 14.1	6 60.2		5 70.6	4 82.2
	0 UND	5 77.6	16 23.3	14 26.8	37 9.9	23 15.8	Sales/Receivables	18 20.0	19 19.0
	11 33.8	22 16.8	34 10.7	38 9.6	107 3.4	64 5.7		38 9.6	43 8.5
							Cost of Sales/Inventory		
							Cost of Sales/Payables		
	3.3	1.7	1.1	1.2	1.1	.4		1.7	1.7
	21.1	4.7	2.9	3.0	3.7	.8	Sales/Working Capital	3.7	3.5
	-343.1	48.1	10.4	9.7	13.5	2.8		18.5	13.0
		106.0	12.7	20.1				20.3	8.9
	(16) 8.8		(17) 4.9	(25) 2.3			EBIT/Interest	(95) 4.2	(97) 2.9
		2.2	1.1	-1.9				.1	-.3
							Net Profit + Depr., Dep., Amort./Cur. Mat. L/T/D		
	.0	.0	.1	.1	.1	.0		.1	.0
	.2	.1	.4	.2	.1	.1	Fixed/Worth	.3	.2
	2.1	1.1	.9	.6	1.0	.1		.9	.9
	.2	.1	.2	.3	.3	.1		.3	.3
	.8	.8	.4	.6	1.1	.3	Debt/Worth	.7	.8
	NM	21.6	1.2	1.5	2.6	.7		1.5	1.8
	39.4	47.7	10.0	10.9	12.5	6.0		14.8	9.3
	(18) 14.6	(28) 6.5	(43) 1.8	(67) 2.7	(14) 4.2	-.7	% Profit Before Taxes/Tangible Net Worth	(225) 5.8	(228) 1.9
	-1.6	1.8	-6.0	-2.4	-3.0	-5.4		-1.0	-4.9
	24.0	16.3	6.9	5.4	5.4	3.4		8.4	5.2
	8.9	2.7	1.3	1.2	3.1	-.5	% Profit Before Taxes/Total Assets	3.3	1.1
	-.5	.3	-2.3	-1.5	-6.3	-2.7		-1.0	-2.8
	UND	UND	27.8	35.3	25.4	52.8		30.7	61.2
	115.6	132.6	3.6	10.3	15.0	8.2	Sales/Net Fixed Assets	7.6	12.5
	2.4	17.8	1.5	2.3	2.7	4.0		1.7	2.7
	8.6	2.9	1.4	1.3	1.0	.5		1.7	1.9
	2.2	1.0	.8	.8	.9	.4	Sales/Total Assets	.9	1.0
	.9	.4	.5	.4	.5	.2		.6	.6
	.2	.5	.7	.7	1.1	.7		.9	.8
	(10) 3.3	(15) 1.1	(35) 2.8	(55) 1.6	(11) 1.8	(12) 1.8	% Depr., Dep., Amort./Sales	(181) 2.2	(194) 1.9
	17.0	4.9	4.6	4.1	4.6	4.5		3.6	3.7
								1.4	4.3
							% Officers', Directors' Owners' Comp/Sales	(11) 9.1	(13) 15.5
								15.2	33.8
	32403M	99083M	259265M	1785551M	1083620M	1237071M	Net Sales ($)	5164314M	6372448M
	6022M	44422M	258816M	1402269M	1047177M	2374947M	Total Assets ($)	4869525M	5405523M

M = $ thousand   MM = $ million
See Pages viii through xx for Explanation of Ratios and Data

Comparative Historical Data | Current Data Sorted by Sales

			Type of Statement						
102	104	89	Unqualified	4	10	11	15	22	27
8	5	5	Reviewed	2	2		1		
6	1	7	Compiled	5		1	1		
9	8	13	Tax Returns	7	1	2	2	1	
75	98	89	Other	20	15	15	6	15	18
4/1/16-3/31/17	4/1/17-3/31/18	4/1/18-3/31/19		76 (4/1-9/30/18)			127 (10/1/18-3/31/19)		
ALL	ALL	ALL		0-1MM	1-3MM	3-5MM	5-10MM	10-25MM	25MM & OVER
200	216	203	NUMBER OF STATEMENTS	38	28	29	25	38	45
%	%	%	ASSETS	%	%	%	%	%	%
38.1	41.7	43.3	Cash & Equivalents	43.2	38.6	43.3	43.2	46.9	43.2
11.8	9.9	9.1	Trade Receivables (net)	2.6	8.0	9.3	8.4	9.9	15.0
1.6	2.0	2.0	Inventory	2.6	.2	.8	2.4	1.6	3.4
4.1	3.8	5.2	All Other Current	7.8	3.9	5.3	4.7	3.7	5.4
55.6	57.4	59.6	Total Current	56.2	50.6	58.7	58.6	62.1	67.1
21.7	22.5	21.7	Fixed Assets (net)	26.0	26.5	26.4	24.2	18.9	12.9
2.5	.6	2.2	Intangibles (net)	4.3	3.2	.6	1.4	1.1	2.2
20.1	19.4	16.5	All Other Non-Current	13.5	19.6	14.3	15.8	17.9	17.7
100.0	100.0	100.0	Total	100.0	100.0	100.0	100.0	100.0	100.0
			LIABILITIES						
3.0	4.5	3.2	Notes Payable-Short Term	5.7	10.0	.6	1.4	.9	1.6
.9	1.0	1.1	Cur. Mat.-L.T.D.	1.2	2.9	1.9	.6	.4	.2
8.9	5.5	6.9	Trade Payables	5.3	3.2	3.8	6.5	8.2	11.8
.1	.0	.1	Income Taxes Payable	.4	.0	.0	.2	.0	.0
15.7	16.7	15.6	All Other Current	16.0	22.8	13.1	16.0	14.3	13.2
28.6	27.8	26.9	Total Current	28.6	38.9	19.4	24.7	23.8	26.8
9.0	8.5	9.5	Long-Term Debt	17.2	13.5	11.7	5.7	7.1	3.3
.1	.1	.1	Deferred Taxes	.0	.0	.1	.0	.0	.2
12.1	9.4	10.5	All Other Non-Current	5.0	5.2	8.7	15.3	13.9	13.9
50.2	54.2	53.0	Net Worth	49.2	42.4	60.2	54.2	55.2	55.8
100.0	100.0	100.0	Total Liabilties & Net Worth	100.0	100.0	100.0	100.0	100.0	100.0
			INCOME DATA						
100.0	100.0	100.0	Net Sales	100.0	100.0	100.0	100.0	100.0	100.0
			Gross Profit						
95.0	95.1	94.8	Operating Expenses	89.8	90.1	95.3	101.0	98.3	95.3
5.0	4.9	5.2	Operating Profit	10.2	9.9	4.7	-1.0	1.7	4.7
1.6	-.1	2.1	All Other Expenses (net)	5.3	3.7	.6	-.6	.7	2.2
3.4	5.1	3.1	Profit Before Taxes	4.9	6.2	4.1	-.3	1.0	2.5
			RATIOS						
4.5	6.0	8.7		11.2	6.1	13.8	8.0	6.3	6.8
2.3	2.6	2.7	Current	2.6	2.3	5.2	2.6	2.8	2.7
1.2	1.2	1.4		1.0	.7	1.5	1.6	1.3	1.5
4.2	5.8	7.4		8.0	5.4	12.4	6.7	6.2	6.6
1.9	2.3	2.4	Quick	2.0	2.0	4.3	1.8	2.6	2.4
1.1	1.0	.7		1.0	.7	1.4	1.3	1.3	1.3
4 90.9	3 121.8	1 271.0		0 UND	0 UND	4 95.6	1 632.3	5 75.0	12 31.3
18 20.5	14 26.3	13 27.6	Sales/Receivables	1 562.5	12 30.7	11 34.6	8 47.6	17 22.0	30 12.1
42 8.6	39 9.3	34 10.6		11 32.5	40 9.1	32 11.4	30 12.2	43 8.5	58 6.3
			Cost of Sales/Inventory						
			Cost of Sales/Payables						
1.9	1.7	1.1		.8	1.6	1.0	1.4	1.2	1.2
4.5	4.2	3.3	Sales/Working Capital	2.9	4.4	3.3	2.8	3.4	3.1
25.3	23.3	20.8		UND	-14.2	10.4	16.1	35.3	11.7
12.8	19.6	22.0		6.5		64.0		18.6	35.2
(81) 2.7	(84) 4.6	(77) 4.0	EBIT/Interest	(12) 3.3		(13) 12.0		(16) 2.7	(19) 2.6
-.5	.8	-.1		-4.0		3.3		-10.1	-12.1
			Net Profit + Depr., Dep., Amort./Cur. Mat. L/T/D						
.0	.0	.0		.0	.0	.0	.1	.0	.1
.2	.2	.2	Fixed/Worth	.1	.3	.3	.3	.2	.1
.9	.8	.8		2.0	1.1	.9	.8	.0	.3
.3	.2	.3		.1	.1	.2	.3	.3	.3
.7	.6	.6	Debt/Worth	.7	.6	.4	.5	.6	.7
2.4	1.7	1.8		4.2	134.7	1.5	1.2	1.5	1.5
13.8	17.1	12.8		17.5	14.7	17.0	5.0	12.0	12.6
(184) 3.5	(200) 6.4	(184) 3.2	% Profit Before Taxes/Tangible Net Worth	(32) 1.7	(22) 2.8	(28) 4.7	(24) 1.7	(36) 1.3	(42) 5.0
-3.5	-.3	-2.4		-2.8	-.8	1.6	-6.0	-5.8	-2.2
7.0	8.7	6.9		8.3	9.2	9.9	4.8	6.8	6.8
1.5	3.2	1.7	% Profit Before Taxes/Total Assets	1.3	1.5	2.9	.9	.8	2.5
-1.8	-.5	-1.6		-2.4	-.4	.7	-3.3	-3.2	-1.8
80.4	71.6	89.5		UND	871.6	90.0	56.8	35.6	44.3
11.9	12.4	13.0	Sales/Net Fixed Assets	46.9	5.2	13.1	7.0	11.2	16.2
2.6	2.3	2.2		1.2	1.4	1.4	1.4	3.5	6.0
1.9	1.8	1.5		1.2	1.6	1.4	1.4	1.3	1.7
.9	1.0	.9	Sales/Total Assets	.6	.8	.7	.7	.9	.9
.5	.5	.4		.3	.3	.4	.5	.7	.5
.9	1.0	.7		1.5	1.1	1.1	.3	.7	.6
(147) 2.1	(152) 2.1	(138) 1.9	% Depr., Dep., Amort./Sales	(18) 4.0	(17) 3.5	(19) 1.8	(18) 2.1	(32) 1.5	(34) 1.5
3.6	3.7	4.7		8.2	6.9	4.2	4.4	3.3	2.6
1.3	2.2	1.7	% Officers', Directors' Owners' Comp/Sales						
(11) 9.3	(11) 11.1	(18) 8.5							
30.5	36.6	19.2							
6020362M	4987810M	4496993M	Net Sales ($)	18546M	59536M	110408M	164585M	582066M	3561852M
4130676M	5797476M	5133653M	Total Assets ($)	47420M	175159M	226471M	239723M	757662M	3687218M

© RMA 2019

M = $ thousand   MM = $ million
See Pages viii through xx for Explanation of Ratios and Data

Current Data Sorted by Assets   Comparative Historical Data

0-500M	500M-2MM	2-10MM	10-50MM	50-100MM	100-250MM	Type of Statement	4/1/14-3/31/15 ALL	4/1/15-3/31/16 ALL
	5	19	37	7	14	Unqualified	122	128
	2					Reviewed	6	3
		1				Compiled	6	4
2		1	1			Tax Returns	6	5
8	10	15	9		2	Other	48	66
	68 (4/1-9/30/18)		65 (10/1/18-3/31/19)					
10	17	36	47	7	16	**NUMBER OF STATEMENTS**	188	206
%	%	%	%	%	%	**ASSETS**	%	%
45.1	46.6	42.0	52.3		43.4	Cash & Equivalents	39.9	42.2
18.8	8.7	11.4	5.1		4.4	Trade Receivables (net)	8.4	10.0
.0	.8	.2	.5		1.6	Inventory	1.1	.8
.4	3.7	4.4	2.8		.9	All Other Current	3.2	3.3
64.3	59.8	58.0	60.7		50.3	Total Current	52.6	56.2
11.2	19.5	20.5	19.7		12.9	Fixed Assets (net)	24.0	22.3
8.5	9.3	4.8	1.5		.5	Intangibles (net)	2.5	1.8
16.0	11.3	16.7	18.0		36.3	All Other Non-Current	20.9	19.7
100.0	100.0	100.0	100.0		100.0	Total	100.0	100.0
						LIABILITIES		
25.8	10.3	.2	1.7		.5	Notes Payable-Short Term	1.7	2.2
.4	.9	2.4	2.3		.5	Cur. Mat.-L.T.D.	.7	.6
.5	7.5	8.5	4.7		4.7	Trade Payables	6.6	7.1
.0	.0	.0	.0		.0	Income Taxes Payable	.3	.2
17.5	17.4	12.1	11.6		5.7	All Other Current	16.5	13.9
44.2	36.0	23.2	20.3		11.5	Total Current	25.8	24.1
8.4	8.7	7.1	6.2		11.6	Long-Term Debt	11.5	9.5
.0	.0	.0	.0		.2	Deferred Taxes	.1	.1
12.3	7.5	8.8	12.5		13.9	All Other Non-Current	12.4	11.3
35.0	47.8	60.8	61.0		62.8	Net Worth	50.2	55.0
100.0	100.0	100.0	100.0		100.0	Total Liabilties & Net Worth	100.0	100.0
						INCOME DATA		
100.0	100.0	100.0	100.0		100.0	Net Sales	100.0	100.0
						Gross Profit		
89.8	97.0	95.9	97.3		92.0	Operating Expenses	94.6	96.4
10.2	3.0	4.1	2.7		8.0	Operating Profit	5.4	3.6
.4	1.4	-.8	-.7		7.9	All Other Expenses (net)	-.6	.7
9.8	1.6	4.9	3.4		.1	Profit Before Taxes	6.0	2.9
						RATIOS		
11.3	25.8	5.3	13.0		9.3		5.0	6.1
3.8	2.1	3.1	2.4		4.3	Current	2.2	2.6
1.0	1.0	1.4	1.3		1.7		1.1	1.2
11.3	25.7	5.0	13.0		8.6		4.7	5.5
3.8	1.7	2.5	2.2		3.8	Quick	2.1	2.3
1.0	.6	1.1	1.3		1.6		1.0	1.0
0 UND	0 UND	3 123.6	3 119.3		18 20.8		3 125.2	4 84.6
0 UND	11 33.4	16 22.7	9 40.8		26 13.8	Sales/Receivables	15 24.4	15 24.8
19 19.6	34 10.7	47 7.8	29 12.8		47 7.8		29 12.5	36 10.2
						Cost of Sales/Inventory		
						Cost of Sales/Payables		
9.2	1.1	1.1	.9		.7		1.8	1.3
27.5	9.0	3.9	2.4		1.5	Sales/Working Capital	5.5	3.3
UND	NM	9.1	7.6		8.9		25.4	21.6
		5.6	10.5				20.9	19.7
		(13) 2.3	(20) .0			EBIT/Interest	(74) 5.4	(92) 5.7
		.4	-16.3				1.9	.4
							9.6	
						Net Profit + Depr., Dep., Amort./Cur. Mat. L/T/D	(13) 5.3	
							2.6	
.0	.0	.0	.1		.0		.1	.1
.2	.0	.3	.3		.1	Fixed/Worth	.3	.3
3.5	4.5	.6	.6		.3		1.0	.8
.1	.2	.3	.3		.2		.3	.3
2.3	.9	.6	.6		.5	Debt/Worth	.7	.7
NM	NM	1.1	1.2		1.2		1.7	1.6
	78.9	10.1	8.7		4.2	% Profit Before Taxes/Tangible Net Worth	15.0	10.6
	(13) 5.0	3.6	(46) 2.5		.9		(176) 5.6	(197) 3.2
	-4.1	-1.8	-6.5		-10.1		.8	-3.9
134.8	22.3	5.2	5.5		3.5	% Profit Before Taxes/Total Assets	8.7	6.5
69.1	2.5	2.1	1.6		.6		3.3	2.0
-25.8	-7.1	-1.3	-3.4		-3.6		.3	-2.5
UND	UND	71.4	14.9		58.5		31.6	34.0
82.7	118.2	11.2	7.4		5.2	Sales/Net Fixed Assets	6.9	7.0
47.1	6.4	2.0	2.1		3.4		2.1	2.4
24.2	4.4	1.5	.9		.6		1.6	1.4
6.3	1.5	.7	.7		.5	Sales/Total Assets	.8	.7
3.4	.5	.5	.5		.3		.5	.5
	.2	.7	1.3		.9		1.2	1.3
	(12) .8	(30) 1.8	(44) 2.2		(13) 1.7	% Depr., Dep., Amort./Sales	(162) 2.3	(175) 2.5
	1.3	3.7	4.0		3.7		4.1	3.8
							8.0	6.3
						% Officers', Directors' Owners' Comp/Sales	(14) 17.0	(21) 10.3
							32.8	16.6
10317M	53945M	235097M	858373M	222769M	1363602M	Net Sales ($)	4875051M	6629713M
2018M	23811M	188879M	1056903M	517543M	2624545M	Total Assets ($)	5647142M	7023447M

© RMA 2019

M = $ thousand   MM = $ million

See Pages viii through xx for Explanation of Ratios and Data

	Comparative Historical Data			Current Data Sorted by Sales					
Type of Statement									
Unqualified	84	79	82	3	10	6	11	28	24
Reviewed	4	1	2	1	1				
Compiled		2	1	1					
Tax Returns	2	2	4				1		
Other	37	38	44	8	12	4		8	5
	4/1/16-3/31/17 ALL	4/1/17-3/31/18 ALL	4/1/18-3/31/19 ALL	68 (4/1-9/30/18)			65 (10/1/18-3/31/19)		
				0-1MM	1-3MM	3-5MM	5-10MM	10-25MM	25MM & OVER
NUMBER OF STATEMENTS	127	122	133	16	23	10	19	36	29
ASSETS	%	%	%	%	%	%	%	%	%
Cash & Equivalents	45.1	44.8	46.6	38.4	39.8	54.4	37.2	60.1	43.2
Trade Receivables (net)	8.8	7.5	8.1	6.9	8.6	11.3	6.7	5.6	11.2
Inventory	.7	.4	.5	.0	.2	.0	.5	.7	1.0
All Other Current	2.9	3.0	2.8	.5	5.3	3.7	2.0	2.7	2.6
Total Current	57.6	55.7	58.0	45.9	53.9	69.5	46.4	69.1	57.9
Fixed Assets (net)	21.7	21.8	18.2	24.6	17.7	4.7	25.6	18.9	14.2
Intangibles (net)	2.9	3.7	3.8	9.2	9.4	.4	3.3	.9	1.4
All Other Non-Current	17.9	18.9	19.9	20.2	18.9	25.4	24.7	11.2	26.4
Total	100.0	100.0	100.0	100.0	100.0	100.0	100.0	100.0	100.0
LIABILITIES									
Notes Payable-Short Term	1.1	2.4	4.0	20.6	1.5	1.1	3.3	1.6	1.1
Cur. Mat.-L.T.D.	1.2	.8	1.7	.5	.6	.1	7.9	1.1	.6
Trade Payables	6.7	6.8	5.8	1.0	5.5	6.4	7.0	5.4	7.9
Income Taxes Payable	.0	.2	.0	.0	.0	.0	.0	.0	.0
All Other Current	14.7	17.2	12.0	12.1	10.5	5.7	16.1	14.0	10.0
Total Current	23.7	27.3	23.4	34.2	18.2	13.2	34.3	22.0	19.6
Long-Term Debt	10.2	10.1	8.3	18.3	6.4	10.2	4.2	6.5	8.5
Deferred Taxes	.0	.0	.0	.0	.0	.0	.0	.0	.1
All Other Non-Current	12.3	10.2	11.1	.4	16.6	6.2	9.0	12.0	14.3
Net Worth	53.7	52.3	57.2	47.0	58.7	70.3	52.5	59.5	57.4
Total Liabilities & Net Worth	100.0	100.0	100.0	100.0	100.0	100.0	100.0	100.0	100.0
INCOME DATA									
Net Sales	100.0	100.0	100.0	100.0	100.0	100.0	100.0	100.0	100.0
Gross Profit									
Operating Expenses	98.1	97.5	95.2	89.0	95.5	86.8	99.7	95.9	97.5
Operating Profit	1.9	2.5	4.8	11.0	4.5	13.2	.3	4.1	2.5
All Other Expenses (net)	.4	-2.1	.9	2.2	-.7	7.4	-1.2	-.1	2.0
Profit Before Taxes	1.5	4.6	3.8	8.8	5.3	5.8	1.4	4.1	.5
RATIOS									
Current	5.7	5.6	9.9	22.4	14.1	12.9	4.4	13.0	7.6
	2.6	2.3	3.4	3.2	4.1	5.3	1.3	2.5	3.4
	1.3	1.3	1.3	1.1	1.3	4.1	.7	1.9	1.3
Quick	5.4	5.5	9.8	22.4	14.1	12.5	4.4	12.8	7.5
	2.4	2.1	2.8	3.2	3.7	4.9	1.1	2.3	2.4
	1.2	1.1	1.2	1.1	.9	4.1	.7	1.7	1.3
Sales/Receivables	5 76.7	4 99.6	3 129.7	0 UND	0 UND	5 70.8	3 124.0	3 133.1	14 26.3
	14 26.8	15 23.7	15 24.5	0 UND	12 30.4	33 10.9	6 58.6	10 38.4	26 14.2
	34 10.8	31 11.6	36 10.1	36 10.0	33 11.0	45 8.2	26 14.0	31 11.6	46 7.9
Cost of Sales/Inventory									
Cost of Sales/Payables									
Sales/Working Capital	1.2	1.3	1.0	.7	1.1	.8	3.2	1.0	.8
	3.3	3.1	3.3	7.3	4.3	2.1	12.8	2.4	2.2
	15.9	20.1	13.2	52.4	33.3	4.3	-7.8	5.2	11.3
EBIT/Interest	9.4	16.0	10.6		31.2			12.6	7.1
	(62) 1.2	(55) 5.5	(55) 3.3		(10) 5.6			(15) -.3	(13) 2.9
	-2.1	.3	-3.1		-3.1			-20.7	-7.9
Net Profit + Depr., Dep., Amort./Cur. Mat. L/T/D									
Fixed/Worth	.1	.1	.0	.0	.0	.0	.0	.1	.1
	.3	.3	.2	.1	.2	.0	.2	.3	.2
	.7	.7	.5	.0	.7	.1	1.4	.6	.3
Debt/Worth	.4	.3	.2	.1	.4	.2	.3	.3	.4
	.7	.8	.6	.3	.7	.2	.7	.7	.6
	1.5	1.4	1.4	6.4	1.5	1.0	2.0	1.2	1.4
% Profit Before Taxes/Tangible Net Worth	8.0	14.2	10.5	76.2	49.5	34.8	10.4	12.0	8.0
	(121) 1.7	(113) 5.0	(126) 3.6	(14) 4.6	(21) 5.0	4.4	(17) .4	(35) 6.7	1.5
	-4.8	.9	-3.2	-1.8	1.8	-.2	-6.5	-5.4	-7.4
% Profit Before Taxes/Total Assets	5.2	7.9	6.0	8.1	7.0	12.3	6.5	6.1	4.3
	1.4	2.6	1.8	1.2	2.5	1.6	.3	3.8	1.2
	-2.9	-.8	-2.3	-2.8	-.1	-.1	-4.4	-2.9	-2.7
Sales/Net Fixed Assets	30.9	26.8	65.2	UND	118.2	UND	21.7	16.8	19.4
	5.8	6.6	11.4	62.9	14.9	241.4	10.7	7.8	5.2
	1.8	2.1	3.2	.7	2.9	35.0	2.0	2.5	3.7
Sales/Total Assets	1.2	1.2	1.3	4.3	1.7	3.0	1.4	1.2	1.0
	.7	.7	.7	.4	.7	.7	.7	.8	.6
	.5	.5	.5	.2	.6	.3	.5	.6	.5
% Depr., Dep., Amort./Sales	1.0	1.2	.9		.7		1.3	1.3	1.1
	(109) 2.5	(99) 2.1	(105) 1.9	(14) 1.2		(17) 2.3	(35) 2.0	(25) 2.1
	4.4	3.2	3.7		4.7		3.8	3.7	3.6
% Officers', Directors' Owners' Comp/Sales	7.5		3.2						
	(11) 17.4		(10) 12.4						
	32.1		29.1						
Net Sales ($)	3143404M	2861658M	2744103M	9661M	43974M	37699M	147887M	577426M	1927456M
Total Assets ($)	3826603M	3905722M	4413699M	36620M	61616M	281171M	201292M	750986M	3082014M

Current Data Sorted by Assets

Comparative Historical Data

						Type of Statement		
	1	12	6	5	4	Unqualified	47	50
			1			Reviewed	1	2
						Compiled	1	2
	1					Tax Returns	5	3
	2	6	11			Other	29	29
		32 (4/1-9/30/18)		18 (10/1/18-3/31/19)			4/1/14-3/31/15	4/1/15-3/31/16
0-500M	500M-2MM	2-10MM	10-50MM	50-100MM	100-250MM		ALL	ALL
	4	18	18	5	5	NUMBER OF STATEMENTS	83	86
%	%	%	%	%	%	ASSETS	%	%

2-10MM	10-50MM		Hist 4/1/14-3/31/15	Hist 4/1/15-3/31/16
36.1	48.7	Cash & Equivalents	42.5	49.9
1.6	4.4	Trade Receivables (net)	3.8	4.9
.0	.3	Inventory	.1	.1
1.0	5.2	All Other Current	2.7	3.0
38.6	58.6	Total Current	49.0	57.8
50.5	34.0	Fixed Assets (net)	36.1	29.2
.1	1.1	Intangibles (net)	1.1	1.1
10.8	6.3	All Other Non-Current	13.8	12.1
100.0	100.0	Total	100.0	100.0
		LIABILITIES		
.0	.0	Notes Payable-Short Term	1.3	.6
4.1	.5	Cur. Mat.-L.T.D.	.9	.8
1.2	2.7	Trade Payables	3.9	3.7
.0	.0	Income Taxes Payable	.0	.0
2.4	6.2	All Other Current	4.8	8.4
7.8	9.5	Total Current	11.0	13.6
20.0	9.6	Long-Term Debt	13.7	14.2
.0	.0	Deferred Taxes	.2	.1
1.4	16.9	All Other Non-Current	6.0	7.1
70.9	64.1	Net Worth	69.2	65.1
100.0	100.0	Total Liabilties & Net Worth	100.0	100.0
		INCOME DATA		
100.0	100.0	Net Sales	100.0	100.0
		Gross Profit		
90.3	88.0	Operating Expenses	92.1	90.2
9.7	12.0	Operating Profit	7.9	9.8
.8	2.4	All Other Expenses (net)	-.1	1.1
8.9	9.6	Profit Before Taxes	8.0	8.7
		RATIOS		
46.5	22.6	Current	21.4	45.4
9.8	8.5		7.3	6.9
3.1	3.6		2.4	2.6
45.9	22.6	Quick	21.2	45.0
9.1	7.9		7.1	6.5
3.1	2.8		2.2	2.5
0 UND	0 UND	Sales/Receivables	0 UND	0 UND
0 UND	4 96.3		0 792.6	4 81.2
25 14.4	19 19.1		28 12.9	30 12.0
		Cost of Sales/Inventory		
		Cost of Sales/Payables		
1.0	1.0	Sales/Working Capital	1.2	1.0
1.8	2.6		2.4	1.9
7.2	5.0		6.7	5.1
5.6	81.0	EBIT/Interest	22.3	10.7
(11) 3.5	(11) 2.9		(45) 2.6	(39) 1.6
1.6	-.9		-1.8	-3.8
		Net Profit + Depr., Dep., Amort./Cur. Mat. L/T/D		
.2	.0	Fixed/Worth	.1	.0
.9	.4		.4	.2
1.4	1.1		1.1	1.1
.0	.1	Debt/Worth	.0	.0
.4	.3		.3	.3
.9	.8		.9	1.2
14.2	13.8	% Profit Before Taxes/Tangible Net Worth	13.9	13.3
6.2	(16) 5.7		(79) 5.3	(79) 3.9
1.4	.6		-2.5	-3.2
7.2	14.7	% Profit Before Taxes/Total Assets	11.1	6.7
4.3	5.0		3.0	3.3
1.3	.4		-2.3	-1.6
3.4	999.8	Sales/Net Fixed Assets	27.5	97.5
1.1	3.3		3.7	5.1
.6	1.6		.9	1.5
1.0	1.4	Sales/Total Assets	1.3	1.4
.5	.7		.8	.8
.3	.5		.4	.4
1.6	1.1	% Depr., Dep., Amort./Sales	1.3	.5
(16) 2.7	(11) 3.7		(56) 2.3	(60) 2.3
5.5	6.9		5.3	3.7
		% Officers', Directors' Owners' Comp/Sales	1.9	.8
			(13) 6.8	(12) 7.5
			19.6	19.8

500M-2MM	2-10MM	10-50MM	50-100MM	100-250MM		Hist	Hist
4889M	51415M	516990M	293377M	692013M	Net Sales ($)	1807514M	2363900M
5008M	81850M	439999M	321454M	809092M	Total Assets ($)	2236759M	3001996M

(Left-hand columns 0-500M, 500M-2MM, 50-100MM and 100-250MM marked: DATA NOT AVAILABLE)

M = $ thousand   MM = $ million
See Pages viii through xx for Explanation of Ratios and Data

Comparative Historical Data				Current Data Sorted by Sales					

Type of Statement

42	33	28	Unqualified	2	5	6	3	4	8
1	1	1	Reviewed		1				
1			Compiled						
	2	1	Tax Returns	1					
32	32	20	Other	1	5	1	1	5	7

4/1/16-3/31/17 ALL	4/1/17-3/31/18 ALL	4/1/18-3/31/19 ALL		32 (4/1-9/30/18)			18 (10/1/18-3/31/19)		
				0-1MM	1-3MM	3-5MM	5-10MM	10-25MM	25MM & OVER
76	68	50	**NUMBER OF STATEMENTS**	4	11	7	4	9	15
%	%	%	**ASSETS**	%	%	%	%	%	%
43.7	53.1	50.0	Cash & Equivalents		41.5				64.4
5.9	5.5	3.4	Trade Receivables (net)		1.9				7.0
.2	.0	.2	Inventory		.0				.5
2.5	3.2	2.5	All Other Current		.8				4.9
52.3	61.8	56.1	Total Current		44.2				76.7
32.3	29.8	35.3	Fixed Assets (net)		48.4				14.2
1.1	.1	.4	Intangibles (net)		.0				.2
14.3	8.3	8.2	All Other Non-Current		7.4				8.9
100.0	100.0	100.0	Total		100.0				100.0
			LIABILITIES						
.6	.2	.0	Notes Payable-Short Term		.0				.0
4.1	.9	1.7	Cur. Mat.-L.T.D.		5.6				.2
4.1	3.2	2.1	Trade Payables		1.0				3.6
.0	.0	.0	Income Taxes Payable		.0				.0
7.9	11.9	4.7	All Other Current		1.6				9.8
16.7	16.2	8.5	Total Current		8.3				13.6
14.4	13.9	12.2	Long-Term Debt		12.7				4.5
.0	.0	.0	Deferred Taxes		.0				.0
6.3	5.6	8.0	All Other Non-Current		1.6				25.1
62.6	64.4	71.3	Net Worth		77.4				56.8
100.0	100.0	100.0	Total Liabilities & Net Worth		100.0				100.0
			INCOME DATA						
100.0	100.0	100.0	Net Sales		100.0				100.0
			Gross Profit						
94.8	90.0	86.9	Operating Expenses		91.2				85.5
5.2	10.0	13.1	Operating Profit		8.8				14.5
1.0	.9	.7	All Other Expenses (net)		1.5				-1.7
4.2	9.2	12.4	Profit Before Taxes		7.3				16.2
			RATIOS						
15.5	23.2	54.5			55.5				59.1
7.9	8.0	10.8	Current		16.4				10.9
2.5	2.1	3.6			3.4				3.0
14.5	21.9	46.5			54.7				58.6
7.0	7.8	10.8	Quick		16.3				10.8
2.5	2.1	3.4			3.4				2.1
0 UND	0 UND	0 UND			0 UND				0 UND
0 UND	9 38.6	1 584.7	Sales/Receivables		0 UND				17 21.8
29 12.5	27 13.5	25 14.4			27 13.6				29 12.6
			Cost of Sales/Inventory						
			Cost of Sales/Payables						
1.2	1.2	1.0			.9				1.0
2.6	2.1	1.7	Sales/Working Capital		1.8				1.8
8.1	5.2	4.3			3.4				4.3
13.8	61.4	75.8							
(36) 2.7	(33) 8.3	(28) 3.8	EBIT/Interest						
.6	1.8	.9							
			Net Profit + Depr., Dep., Amort./Cur. Mat. L/T/D						
.0	.0	.1			.2				.0
.4	.2	.4	Fixed/Worth		.6				.1
1.3	1.2	1.1			1.1				.4
.1	.0	.0			.0				.0
.3	.3	.3	Debt/Worth		.3				.3
1.1	1.2	.8			.5				2.1
13.4	18.9	15.4			9.5				45.8
(69) 4.4	(63) 6.0	(48) 7.6	% Profit Before Taxes/Tangible Net Worth		3.1			(13)	20.2
-.7	2.5	1.6			1.2				7.4
8.4	11.4	14.5			7.1				29.4
3.5	4.7	5.9	% Profit Before Taxes/Total Assets		2.0				20.1
-.6	1.5	1.3			.9				7.2
242.5	176.0	20.6			3.2				999.8
4.2	5.3	2.8	Sales/Net Fixed Assets		1.1				17.1
1.5	1.4	.9			.7				3.7
1.6	1.4	1.3			.9				1.9
.8	.8	.7	Sales/Total Assets		.5				1.4
.4	.5	.4			.3				.6
1.2	.9	1.1							.5
(43) 2.2	(43) 2.1	(37) 2.3	% Depr., Dep., Amort./Sales					(10)	1.2
4.9	4.3	5.3							1.7
1.4									
(11) 6.5			% Officers', Directors' Owners' Comp/Sales						
19.5									
1759630M	1981377M	1558684M	Net Sales ($)	2303M	21733M	25753M	28791M	141293M	1338811M
1965210M	1840978M	1657403M	Total Assets ($)	9262M	45393M	48913M	73495M	224887M	1255453M

M = $ thousand   MM = $ million
See Pages viii through xx for Explanation of Ratios and Data

Current Data Sorted by Assets   **Comparative Historical Data**

0-500M	500M-2MM	2-10MM	10-50MM	50-100MM	100-250MM	Type of Statement	4/1/14-3/31/15 ALL	4/1/15-3/31/16 ALL
7	18	24	13	5	2	Unqualified	116	103
4	7	5	1			Reviewed	18	21
5	5	1				Compiled	14	17
5	4	3	1		1	Tax Returns	18	17
52	49	30	10	2		Other	129	153
	75 (4/1-9/30/18)		179 (10/1/18-3/31/19)					
73	83	63	25	7	3	**NUMBER OF STATEMENTS**	295	311
%	%	%	%	%	%	**ASSETS**	%	%
76.5	63.2	37.7	31.7			Cash & Equivalents	47.2	46.0
4.5	6.7	6.7	6.2			Trade Receivables (net)	6.5	6.8
.3	.2	.8	1.2			Inventory	.9	.9
4.0	6.4	6.2	3.6			All Other Current	5.2	5.1
85.3	76.5	51.4	42.7			Total Current	59.8	58.9
6.3	12.4	32.6	44.4			Fixed Assets (net)	25.5	25.0
.1	.8	.5	.5			Intangibles (net)	1.1	1.6
8.2	10.3	15.5	12.4			All Other Non-Current	13.6	14.5
100.0	100.0	100.0	100.0			Total	100.0	100.0
						LIABILITIES		
21.9	4.0	3.9	1.6			Notes Payable-Short Term	3.3	2.8
2.9	4.7	2.4	1.1			Cur. Mat.-L.T.D.	3.3	3.2
6.4	3.4	9.7	6.9			Trade Payables	6.2	5.3
.1	.1	.0	.0			Income Taxes Payable	.0	.1
9.0	9.4	15.5	11.4			All Other Current	10.6	13.0
40.2	21.6	31.5	21.0			Total Current	23.5	24.5
24.8	26.3	13.2	12.4			Long-Term Debt	31.7	24.4
.0	.0	.1	.0			Deferred Taxes	.2	.0
7.4	6.2	7.5	1.5			All Other Non-Current	4.2	4.7
27.5	45.9	47.6	65.1			Net Worth	40.5	46.4
100.0	100.0	100.0	100.0			Total Liabilties & Net Worth	100.0	100.0
						INCOME DATA		
100.0	100.0	100.0	100.0			Net Sales	100.0	100.0
						Gross Profit		
92.5	90.6	94.8	95.2			Operating Expenses	89.8	89.9
7.5	9.4	5.2	4.8			Operating Profit	10.2	10.1
1.5	2.9	.8	-1.3			All Other Expenses (net)	3.1	2.6
6.1	6.5	4.4	6.1			Profit Before Taxes	7.1	7.5
						RATIOS		
23.8	17.9	6.5	4.8				6.5	8.4
4.6	5.0	2.7	3.5			Current	3.0	3.2
1.7	2.0	1.2	1.4				1.5	1.2
23.8	17.9	6.1	4.5				6.0	8.1
4.6	4.7	2.3	2.2			Quick	2.6	2.6
1.6	1.6	1.1	1.0				1.1	1.0
0 UND	0 UND	1 371.3	2 175.5				0 824.6	0 999.8
1 353.0	3 122.0	8 45.6	14 27.0			Sales/Receivables	6 64.1	5 75.9
8 43.4	8 43.6	33 11.2	42 8.7				20 18.7	18 20.1
						Cost of Sales/Inventory		
						Cost of Sales/Payables		
1.6	1.2	1.8	1.1				1.6	1.6
2.9	2.0	3.6	2.9			Sales/Working Capital	3.4	4.0
10.8	6.1	19.2	12.6				15.3	21.5
21.7	13.0	15.7	25.9				10.2	13.5
(28) 6.4	(33) 6.6	(28) 3.3	(15) 16.8			EBIT/Interest	(143) 3.1	(145) 3.0
1.5	.5	-.8	1.9				.9	.8
						Net Profit + Depr., Dep.,		2.3
						Amort./Cur. Mat. L/T/D	(12) .6	.6
								-1.3
.0	.0	.0	.2				.0	.0
.0	.0	.4	.8			Fixed/Worth	.1	.1
.0	.2	1.3	.9				.9	1.1
.1	.2	.2	.1				.2	.2
.6	.7	.6	.3			Debt/Worth	.7	.7
5.5	3.3	1.8	2.3				3.7	3.6
41.4	16.6	12.0	5.4			% Profit Before Taxes/Tangible	20.0	21.8
(60) 14.8	(72) 3.4	(59) 4.1	(23) 2.8			Net Worth	(251) 5.5	(268) 6.7
-5.3	-11.1	-2.2	1.1				-2.3	-.3
29.6	13.8	7.3	7.9			% Profit Before Taxes/Total	13.8	13.4
8.7	4.1	2.7	2.3			Assets	3.9	4.2
-3.3	-4.4	-1.2	1.2				-1.4	-.5
UND	UND	229.9	11.2				UND	UND
UND	UND	7.1	2.5			Sales/Net Fixed Assets	33.3	84.2
UND	25.1	.9	.7				1.3	1.4
2.9	1.6	1.4	1.3				1.8	1.8
2.1	1.1	.8	.6			Sales/Total Assets	1.1	1.0
1.2	.8	.4	.3				.5	.5
	.3	.6	1.6				1.0	1.0
	(20) 2.3	(37) 2.0	(23) 3.4			% Depr., Dep., Amort./Sales	(154) 3.1	(142) 4.2
	5.7	5.4	7.5				8.8	9.0
						% Officers', Directors'		3.8
						Owners' Comp/Sales	(24) 8.9	(39) 8.2
							17.0	24.6
35757M	141845M	347155M	603063M	355422M	96245M	Net Sales ($)	1617982M	2818770M
14324M	95201M	301037M	558099M	490281M	464403M	Total Assets ($)	2088548M	3132487M

© RMA 2019   M = $ thousand   MM = $ million
See Pages viii through xx for Explanation of Ratios and Data

Comparative Historical Data   Current Data Sorted by Sales

			Type of Statement						
90	103	69	Unqualified	11	17	11	8	14	8
8	24	17	Reviewed	12	2		2		1
8	13	11	Compiled	7	3			1	
14	18	14	Tax Returns	8	3			1	2
91	137	143	Other	66	43	14	11	6	3
4/1/16-3/31/17	4/1/17-3/31/18	4/1/18-3/31/19		75 (4/1-9/30/18)			179 (10/1/18-3/31/19)		
ALL	ALL	ALL		0-1MM	1-3MM	3-5MM	5-10MM	10-25MM	25MM & OVER
211	295	254	NUMBER OF STATEMENTS	104	68	25	21	22	14
%	%	%	**ASSETS**	%	%	%	%	%	%
46.6	49.1	55.8	Cash & Equivalents	69.8	54.6	46.6	49.3	29.3	25.7
8.0	6.7	6.0	Trade Receivables (net)	4.9	3.1	7.6	11.8	8.8	12.0
.7	.5	.5	Inventory	.2	.3	.1	.3	2.8	.7
4.9	5.4	5.1	All Other Current	5.4	2.9	6.8	13.4	2.9	2.6
60.2	61.7	67.4	Total Current	80.3	60.9	61.1	74.8	43.7	41.1
24.9	23.3	20.8	Fixed Assets (net)	12.3	21.4	19.7	18.4	46.3	46.9
1.6	1.0	.5	Intangibles (net)	.1	1.3	.1	.5	.5	.7
13.4	13.9	11.3	All Other Non-Current	7.3	16.5	19.1	6.3	9.5	11.3
100.0	100.0	100.0	Total	100.0	100.0	100.0	100.0	100.0	100.0
			LIABILITIES						
2.4	7.3	8.9	Notes Payable-Short Term	15.9	2.5	.0	6.4	.2	22.0
4.2	3.9	3.1	Cur. Mat.-L.T.D.	3.3	3.8	3.2	2.8	.6	2.1
7.3	6.7	6.1	Trade Payables	4.1	4.1	4.5	5.7	8.5	31.2
.2	.0	.0	Income Taxes Payable	.0	.0	.0	.0	.2	.0
12.2	9.8	10.9	All Other Current	9.9	9.4	9.5	17.2	13.0	15.0
26.3	27.7	29.1	Total Current	33.3	19.8	17.3	32.1	22.5	70.2
34.7	25.3	20.7	Long-Term Debt	26.2	18.0	15.5	26.7	7.1	13.8
.0	.0	.0	Deferred Taxes	.0	.0	.3	.0		.1
6.4	6.2	6.2	All Other Non-Current	5.8	8.4	8.1	7.5	1.5	1.2
32.6	40.6	44.0	Net Worth	34.7	53.8	59.2	33.4	68.9	14.8
100.0	100.0	100.0	Total Liabilities & Net Worth	100.0	100.0	100.0	100.0	100.0	100.0
			INCOME DATA						
100.0	100.0	100.0	Net Sales	100.0	100.0	100.0	100.0	100.0	100.0
			Gross Profit						
91.0	89.5	93.0	Operating Expenses	89.4	93.9	96.1	98.8	95.9	97.6
9.0	10.5	7.0	Operating Profit	10.6	6.1	3.9	1.2	4.1	2.4
2.7	3.1	1.5	All Other Expenses (net)	3.0	1.5	-.1	-.7	-1.4	.9
6.2	7.5	5.5	Profit Before Taxes	7.7	4.6	4.0	1.8	5.4	1.5
			RATIOS						
7.4	9.4	11.2		27.9	16.6	6.8	6.1	4.9	2.3
3.3	3.6	3.9	Current	5.3	3.8	5.0	2.8	3.3	1.1
1.3	1.4	1.6		1.7	1.7	1.6	1.5	1.6	.7
6.9	8.7	10.9		27.9	16.2	6.6	5.1	4.6	2.0
2.8	3.2	3.5	Quick	4.7	3.7	4.7	2.2	2.7	1.1
1.2	1.2	1.3		1.5	1.6	1.4	1.3	.7	.7
1 429.3	0 999.8	0 UND		0 UND	0 UND	2 184.4	0 UND	5 70.8	11 33.7
6 57.4	5 75.8	4 88.9	Sales/Receivables	1 299.7	3 117.6	10 37.1	8 48.6	16 23.2	18 20.3
26 14.1	24 15.5	17 21.2		8 43.0	11 31.9	44 8.3	49 7.5	38 9.7	48 7.6
			Cost of Sales/Inventory						
			Cost of Sales/Payables						
1.5	1.5	1.4		1.1	1.4	2.1	1.7	1.7	6.6
3.5	3.3	3.0	Sales/Working Capital	2.2	3.1	4.3	3.1	3.0	360.7
12.1	13.6	11.5		5.8	12.6	9.6	11.1	11.8	-5.9
14.6	11.0	16.0		14.7	14.9		35.0	21.4	22.1
(104) 3.9	(138) 4.5	(113) 5.7	EBIT/Interest	(43) 5.6	(29) 8.0		(11) 4.6	(10) 13.1	(13) 6.1
.3	1.1	.3		1.0	.0		-.8	-1.0	-2.9
			Net Profit + Depr., Dep., Amort./Cur. Mat. L/T/D						
.0	.0	.0		.0	.0	.0	.0	.2	.8
.2	.1	.0	Fixed/Worth	.0	.0	.1	.2	.8	1.0
1.0	1.0	.8		.0	.8	1.0	.7	1.0	NM
.2	.2	.2		.1	.1	.2	.4	.1	.2
.7	.7	.6	Debt/Worth	.6	.6	.6	1.1	.3	.8
6.8	3.5	2.6		4.2	2.1	1.7	2.7	.7	NM
15.8	23.4	19.6		29.7	13.4	15.7	23.0	17.3	16.4
(168) 4.6	(251) 8.0	(224) 4.2	% Profit Before Taxes/Tangible Net Worth	(88) 8.3	(60) 2.5	(19) 4.1	(21) 3.8	(11) 2.8	3.9
-2.4	-.3	-2.4		-1.4	-5.5	-5.0	-6.7	.7	-.9
11.1	16.6	13.1		24.3	7.5	6.9	10.3	11.1	14.3
3.1	4.7	2.9	% Profit Before Taxes/Total Assets	4.9	2.1	2.7	3.6	2.2	2.9
-1.7	-.2	-1.5		-1.4	-3.1	-1.6	-2.4	.7	-1.2
UND	UND	UND		UND	UND	148.3	UND	41.1	54.4
27.3	107.3	252.4	Sales/Net Fixed Assets	UND	133.9	21.7	10.4	1.2	2.0
1.4	1.6	3.0		497.1	3.1	3.5	4.8	.7	.7
1.6	2.1	2.0		2.2	1.6	2.0	2.2	1.5	5.2
1.0	1.0	1.1	Sales/Total Assets	1.2	1.0	1.1	1.2	.7	1.3
.5	.5	.6		.7	.6	.7	.8	.3	.5
1.0	1.0	.8		.3	1.1	.5	1.1	1.4	.3
(109) 3.8	(129) 3.4	(96) 3.3	% Depr., Dep., Amort./Sales	(16) 4.3	(19) 3.2	(14) 1.6	(13) 1.7	(20) 5.8	4.4
8.2	8.4	6.7		6.7	6.3	3.7	4.5	14.3	8.7
3.2	2.7	4.4							
(15) 8.2	(29) 7.0	(20) 6.2	% Officers', Directors' Owners' Comp/Sales						
17.5	14.5	11.9							
1747123M	2117726M	1579487M	Net Sales ($)	43956M	114633M	98597M	144878M	292810M	884613M
2056557M	2631522M	1923345M	Total Assets ($)	63129M	164608M	114956M	135294M	735613M	709745M

Current Data Sorted by Assets / Comparative Historical Data

Current Data Sorted by Assets							Comparative Historical Data	
						Type of Statement		
	1		1			Unqualified	2	2
						Reviewed	6	3
1		2				Compiled	7	5
6	7	5				Tax Returns	19	25
7	6	15	3			Other	32	23
	1 (4/1-9/30/18)		53 (10/1/18-3/31/19)				**4/1/14-3/31/15 ALL**	**4/1/15-3/31/16 ALL**
0-500M	**500M-2MM**	**2-10MM**	**10-50MM**	**50-100MM**	**100-250MM**			
14	14	22	4			**NUMBER OF STATEMENTS**	66	58
%	%	%	%	%	%	**ASSETS**	%	%
31.4	14.8	16.4		DATA NOT AVAILABLE	DATA NOT AVAILABLE	Cash & Equivalents	12.6	13.8
6.7	9.0	1.0				Trade Receivables (net)	14.6	12.7
3.2	5.4	2.6				Inventory	10.5	6.5
3.3	6.8	12.8				All Other Current	6.7	6.2
44.6	36.0	32.9				Total Current	44.5	39.3
34.3	47.2	34.0				Fixed Assets (net)	35.8	41.4
5.3	3.5	1.7				Intangibles (net)	6.7	2.5
15.8	13.4	31.5				All Other Non-Current	13.0	16.7
100.0	100.0	100.0				Total	100.0	100.0
						LIABILITIES		
26.7	3.7	3.1				Notes Payable-Short Term	13.5	4.9
3.6	1.8	.8				Cur. Mat.-L.T.D.	3.0	2.2
14.7	8.2	.1				Trade Payables	9.0	5.7
.0	.0	.0				Income Taxes Payable	.1	.1
34.8	10.6	.3				All Other Current	12.0	9.0
79.8	24.3	4.3				Total Current	37.7	21.8
33.4	37.7	19.0				Long-Term Debt	21.8	26.1
.0	.0	.0				Deferred Taxes	.5	.9
9.5	1.0	.0				All Other Non-Current	12.6	10.6
-22.7	37.0	76.6				Net Worth	27.4	40.6
100.0	100.0	100.0				Total Liabilties & Net Worth	100.0	100.0
						INCOME DATA		
100.0	100.0	100.0				Net Sales	100.0	100.0
						Gross Profit		
70.3	44.2	27.3				Operating Expenses	72.6	62.4
29.7	55.8	72.7				Operating Profit	27.4	37.6
3.2	9.6	3.2				All Other Expenses (net)	4.1	5.9
26.5	46.2	69.5				Profit Before Taxes	23.4	31.7
						RATIOS		
1.8	5.7	218.7					6.0	11.9
.7	1.5	111.2				Current	1.5	2.5
.4	1.0	1.3					1.1	1.0
1.2	4.2	94.7					2.9	5.4
.7	1.2	17.1				Quick	1.0	1.7
.4	.3	1.1					.4	.5
0 UND	0 UND	0 UND					0 UND	0 UND
0 UND	0 UND	0 UND				Sales/Receivables	1 591.0	0 UND
0 UND	13 28.1	0 UND					35 10.4	30 12.0
						Cost of Sales/Inventory		
						Cost of Sales/Payables		
32.6	.7	.2					4.1	1.5
-75.6	5.8	.6				Sales/Working Capital	12.8	9.7
-14.6	NM	5.1					58.0	NM
							26.2	79.2
						EBIT/Interest	(41) 7.3	(33) 10.2
							2.8	2.1
						Net Profit + Depr., Dep., Amort./Cur. Mat. L/T/D		
.0	.5	.2					.3	.1
.5	.8	.3				Fixed/Worth	.7	.6
-.9	2.6	.6					3.0	2.4
.5	.4	.1					.5	.3
2.5	1.3	.2				Debt/Worth	1.2	.8
-2.7	2.2	.4					6.9	3.3
	60.3	15.8					43.7	34.2
	(13) 28.6	9.6				% Profit Before Taxes/Tangible Net Worth	(54) 21.9	(50) 10.1
	16.3	2.9					3.2	3.3
82.9	23.2	12.8					16.8	15.5
29.2	11.0	7.4				% Profit Before Taxes/Total Assets	9.5	7.4
1.5	7.4	2.6					2.1	1.9
UND	14.6	.7					47.8	22.6
19.7	.4	.5				Sales/Net Fixed Assets	7.0	1.0
5.6	.2	.2					.8	.3
11.9	1.8	.2					3.4	3.6
5.7	.2	.1				Sales/Total Assets	1.9	.6
1.0	.1	.1					.2	.1
							.6	.7
						% Depr., Dep., Amort./Sales	(39) 1.5	(27) 1.8
							4.6	14.0
							2.0	1.9
						% Officers', Directors' Owners' Comp/Sales	(14) 8.1	(13) 5.6
							11.5	10.4
22146M	25015M	22589M	37541M			Net Sales ($)	513057M	298316M
3772M	17235M	112980M	134715M			Total Assets ($)	436771M	347530M

M = $ thousand MM = $ million

See Pages viii through xx for Explanation of Ratios and Data

Comparative Historical Data							Type of Statement	Current Data Sorted by Sales					
	2		3		2		Unqualified		1				1
	2		2				Reviewed						
	4		2		3		Compiled		1	1			1
	18		29		18		Tax Returns	12	3	1	2		
	28		31		31		Other	21	5	2	2	1	
	4/1/16-3/31/17		4/1/17-3/31/18		4/1/18-3/31/19				1 (4/1-9/30/18)		53 (10/1/18-3/31/19)		
	ALL		ALL		ALL			0-1MM	1-3MM	3-5MM	5-10MM	10-25MM	25MM & OVER
	54		67		54		NUMBER OF STATEMENTS	33	10	4	4	3	
	%		%		%		ASSETS	%	%	%	%	%	%
	21.5		23.0		19.1		Cash & Equivalents	17.9	19.5				D
	10.2		6.8		5.5		Trade Receivables (net)	.0	4.4				A
	8.5		8.7		3.7		Inventory	.8	3.1				T
	4.9		5.8		8.0		All Other Current	12.0	.3				A
	45.2		44.4		36.4		Total Current	30.7	27.3				
	37.2		35.6		39.9		Fixed Assets (net)	38.1	53.2				N
	4.0		4.3		3.0		Intangibles (net)	1.9	9.4				O
	13.6		15.5		20.8		All Other Non-Current	29.3	10.1				T
	100.0		100.0		100.0		Total	100.0	100.0				
							LIABILITIES						A
	17.3		10.5		9.3		Notes Payable-Short Term	3.2	10.9				V
	2.0		2.6		2.0		Cur. Mat.-L.T.D.	.1	8.3				A
	5.5		3.8		6.0		Trade Payables	4.8	5.5				I
	.0		.0		.0		Income Taxes Payable	.0	.0				L
	16.9		18.6		12.3		All Other Current	.6	13.0				A
	41.7		35.5		29.7		Total Current	8.7	37.7				B
	18.5		30.3		28.3		Long-Term Debt	26.3	42.1				L
	.0		.1		.0		Deferred Taxes	.0	.0				E
	.6		3.6		2.7		All Other Non-Current	.6	13.0				
	39.2		30.4		39.3		Net Worth	64.4	7.3				
	100.0		100.0		100.0		Total Liabilties & Net Worth	100.0	100.0				
							INCOME DATA						
	100.0		100.0		100.0		Net Sales	100.0	100.0				
							Gross Profit						
	65.2		65.6		46.4		Operating Expenses	23.0	75.5				
	34.8		34.4		53.6		Operating Profit	77.0	24.5				
	3.9		4.4		5.6		All Other Expenses (net)	5.8	5.9				
	31.0		30.0		48.1		Profit Before Taxes	71.2	18.7				
							RATIOS						
	12.8		5.5		51.0			190.6	3.1				
	2.2		1.7		2.5		Current	9.0	.9				
	1.0		.8		.9			1.1	.3				
	11.6		4.8		14.8			30.8	1.9				
	1.4		1.1		1.4		Quick	5.9	.7				
	.5		.3		.6			.7	.2				
0	UND	0	UND	0	UND			0 UND	0 UND				
0	UND	0	UND	0	UND		Sales/Receivables	0 UND	0 UND				
15	24.3	3	104.3	1	386.9			0 UND	17 21.2				
							Cost of Sales/Inventory						
							Cost of Sales/Payables						
	1.1		5.0		.6			.2	3.4				
	7.7		24.1		4.2		Sales/Working Capital	1.3	NM				
	-352.7		-101.0		-771.5			50.3	-16.1				
	25.7		20.0		29.8								
(30)	4.4	(31)	6.8	(26)	4.9		EBIT/Interest						
	1.9		3.6		1.7								
							Net Profit + Depr., Dep., Amort./Cur. Mat. L/T/D						
	.2		.2		.2			.2	.5				
	.5		.7		.5		Fixed/Worth	.5	3.2				
	1.5		2.2		1.6			.8	-.9				
	.2		.4		.2			.2	.3				
	.7		1.2		.6		Debt/Worth	.3	2.8				
	3.2		5.3		2.2			1.7	-2.9				
	79.6		73.2		43.8			27.5					
(48)	24.2	(58)	36.4	(47)	15.8		% Profit Before Taxes/Tangible Net Worth	(32) 15.6					
	2.8		12.2		5.7			5.9					
	20.0		38.7		21.6			13.9	44.7				
	10.9		13.4		8.8		% Profit Before Taxes/Total Assets	8.8	22.5				
	1.6		5.2		2.6			4.5	.6				
	62.4		64.9		9.1			.7	18.2				
	2.8		5.9		.6		Sales/Net Fixed Assets	.4	7.5				
	.3		.5		.3			.2	.9				
	3.9		4.6		1.9			.2	7.5				
	1.1		2.7		.2		Sales/Total Assets	.1	1.9				
	.2		.2		.1			.1	.4				
	.5		.5		.7								
(28)	1.6	(30)	1.7	(19)	6.0		% Depr., Dep., Amort./Sales						
	5.1		7.0		15.3								
	2.0		2.9		3.3								
(10)	5.4	(16)	6.5	(11)	5.3		% Officers', Directors' Owners' Comp/Sales						
	26.0		18.7		11.6								
	232666M		539598M		107291M		Net Sales ($)	10847M	16440M	14528M	26505M	38971M	
	201131M		463630M		268702M		Total Assets ($)	101912M	22060M	52149M	27438M	65143M	

PUBLIC ADMINISTRATION

PUBLIC
ADMINISTRATION

Current Data Sorted by Assets | Comparative Historical Data

0-500M	500M-2MM	2-10MM	10-50MM	50-100MM	100-250MM	Type of Statement	4/1/14-3/31/15 ALL	4/1/15-3/31/16 ALL
1	6	19	40	26	41	Unqualified	227	238
		1				Reviewed	1	3
						Compiled	1	2
						Tax Returns	1	1
2	4	4	4	3	2	Other	20	35
	127 (4/1-9/30/18)			26 (10/1/18-3/31/19)				
3	10	24	44	29	43	**NUMBER OF STATEMENTS**	250	279
%	%	%	%	%	%	**ASSETS**	%	%
	59.5	46.7	44.8	41.7	22.5	Cash & Equivalents	33.0	36.9
	11.7	11.8	6.9	6.0	3.6	Trade Receivables (net)	7.4	7.6
	3.3	.3	.3	.1	.1	Inventory	.3	.3
	7.7	2.8	9.1	5.8	3.7	All Other Current	5.4	7.7
	82.3	61.5	61.1	53.6	30.0	Total Current	46.1	52.4
	5.9	31.8	35.0	37.4	60.4	Fixed Assets (net)	45.7	38.4
	.8	.0	.0	.6	.4	Intangibles (net)	.1	.4
	11.0	6.6	3.9	8.4	9.2	All Other Non-Current	8.1	8.8
	100.0	100.0	100.0	100.0	100.0	Total	100.0	100.0
						LIABILITIES		
	.4	.0	.2	.2	.1	Notes Payable-Short Term	.9	1.2
	.0	1.5	1.9	1.4	2.3	Cur. Mat.-L.T.D.	1.5	1.4
	11.0	5.1	3.6	2.8	1.8	Trade Payables	3.2	3.8
	.0	.0	.1	.0	.0	Income Taxes Payable	.2	.0
	5.3	4.8	4.9	3.6	1.8	All Other Current	5.1	5.7
	16.7	11.5	10.7	8.0	5.9	Total Current	10.9	12.1
	.0	14.8	14.8	17.6	25.4	Long-Term Debt	19.1	19.8
	.0	.0	.4	.0	.0	Deferred Taxes	.0	.0
	6.3	10.0	9.7	12.9	31.8	All Other Non-Current	3.7	8.5
	77.0	63.7	64.4	61.5	36.9	Net Worth	66.3	59.6
	100.0	100.0	100.0	100.0	100.0	Total Liabilities & Net Worth	100.0	100.0
						INCOME DATA		
	100.0	100.0	100.0	100.0	100.0	Net Sales	100.0	100.0
						Gross Profit		
	80.4	92.9	90.5	87.7	88.5	Operating Expenses	89.8	88.6
	19.6	7.1	9.5	12.3	11.5	Operating Profit	10.2	11.4
	2.4	3.7	4.6	4.0	2.6	All Other Expenses (net)	4.7	5.0
	17.2	3.3	4.9	8.3	8.9	Profit Before Taxes	5.6	6.5
						RATIOS		
	27.2	12.4	12.2	11.4	6.8	Current	7.8	9.9
	16.7	5.8	5.8	6.5	5.0		4.4	5.2
	3.4	3.1	2.7	4.5	2.8		2.9	2.4
	21.4	12.1	10.4	10.8	6.4	Quick	7.2	8.4
	8.9	5.7	4.8	6.0	4.3		4.2	4.5
	1.5	3.1	2.6	4.3	2.5		2.4	2.1
	0 UND	0 UND	4 103.7	7 51.4	13 27.8	Sales/Receivables	10 35.2	6 63.1
	9 41.1	23 15.6	17 22.1	25 14.4	28 13.1		29 12.6	24 15.1
	21 17.0	51 7.1	36 10.1	55 6.6	57 6.4		52 7.0	47 7.8
						Cost of Sales/Inventory		
						Cost of Sales/Payables		
	1.2	1.1	1.3	.8	1.0	Sales/Working Capital	1.3	1.3
	1.7	2.2	2.1	1.3	1.5		2.3	2.3
	8.8	4.1	4.1	2.5	3.0		3.8	4.8
		20.8	7.5	9.4	16.7	EBIT/Interest	9.1	10.2
	(14) 1.9	(30) 2.9	(24) 2.9	(40) 3.7			(192) 2.5	(207) 3.2
	-1.5	1.0	1.3	.8			.8	1.0
						Net Profit + Depr., Dep., Amort./Cur. Mat. L/T/D		
	.0	.0	.0	.0	1.0	Fixed/Worth	.0	.0
	.0	.4	.0	.7	1.2		.9	.8
	.0	1.0	1.5	1.3	3.6		1.2	1.4
	.0	.2	.2	.2	.3	Debt/Worth	.2	.2
	.1	.5	.4	.4	1.2		.4	.5
	.4	.8	1.0	1.0	4.3		.9	1.2
		18.4	10.1	7.5	6.2	% Profit Before Taxes/Tangible Net Worth	8.9	12.4
	(23) 4.6	(41) 3.3	(27) 4.6	(37) 4.6			(243) 2.5	(266) 4.5
	-1.5	-1.1	.6	.4			-.9	-.3
	38.0	13.1	7.2	4.7	3.8	% Profit Before Taxes/Total Assets	5.8	7.0
	13.3	1.7	2.2	2.9	2.3		1.7	2.9
	4.1	-1.4	-.6	.5	.0		-.6	-.2
	UND	UND	UND	UND	.9	Sales/Net Fixed Assets	UND	UND
	UND	UND	UND	.9	.5		.7	1.1
	UND	.6	.4	.4	.3		.4	.4
	4.5	1.8	1.9	1.2	.5	Sales/Total Assets	1.2	1.6
	1.5	.7	.7	.4	.3		.4	.5
	.6	.4	.3	.2	.2		.3	.3
		5.9	8.1	8.7	4.9	% Depr., Dep., Amort./Sales	7.1	5.8
	(11) 10.2	(20) 11.9	(14) 15.2	(32) 8.8			(137) 11.1	(136) 10.6
	24.6	17.1	20.3	14.0			16.9	15.0
						% Officers', Directors' Owners' Comp/Sales	1.0	2.1
							(12) 8.0	(19) 8.5
							13.0	16.7
261M	37953M	167764M	1302646M	1572270M	3804120M	Net Sales ($)	10399613M	11175513M
878M	13581M	132991M	1145054M	2070754M	6898477M	Total Assets ($)	15884529M	14672181M

© RMA 2019

M = $ thousand   MM = $ million
See Pages viii through xx for Explanation of Ratios and Data

Comparative Historical Data | Current Data Sorted by Sales

					Type of Statement						
	179		153	133	Unqualified	4	11	6	16	32	64
	3				Reviewed						
	1				Compiled						
	2			1	Tax Returns				1		
	21		27	19	Other	4		3		4	4
	4/1/16-		4/1/17-	4/1/18-			127 (4/1-9/30/18)		26 (10/1/18-3/31/19)		
	3/31/17		3/31/18	3/31/19							
	ALL		ALL	ALL		0-1MM	1-3MM	3-5MM	5-10MM	10-25MM	25MM & OVER
	206		181	153	**NUMBER OF STATEMENTS**	8	14	9	18	36	68
	%		%	%	**ASSETS**	%	%	%	%	%	%
	34.1		36.8	39.5	Cash & Equivalents		38.7		35.9	38.9	41.1
	6.1		6.9	6.8	Trade Receivables (net)		5.9		8.1	8.8	6.7
	.3		.2	.4	Inventory		.1		.3	.9	.2
	4.6		5.3	5.8	All Other Current		6.9		1.4	3.6	8.7
	45.0		49.2	52.5	Total Current		51.6		45.8	52.2	56.6
	46.0		42.4	40.2	Fixed Assets (net)		44.7		48.8	39.0	36.4
	.7		.9	.3	Intangibles (net)		.0		.0	.7	.3
	8.3		7.6	7.1	All Other Non-Current		3.7		5.4	8.2	6.7
	100.0		100.0	100.0	Total		100.0		100.0	100.0	100.0
					LIABILITIES						
	.8		.8	.1	Notes Payable-Short Term		.0		.0	.4	.1
	1.5		1.4	1.7	Cur. Mat.-L.T.D.		2.0		1.4	1.8	1.5
	3.1		2.8	3.6	Trade Payables		2.5		7.7	3.2	3.6
	.1		.0	.0	Income Taxes Payable		.0		.0	.0	.0
	5.2		3.9	4.0	All Other Current		2.5		5.2	1.6	4.8
	10.6		9.0	9.5	Total Current		7.0		14.3	7.1	10.0
	20.8		17.4	17.4	Long-Term Debt		19.5		24.2	19.2	14.9
	.1		.2	.1	Deferred Taxes		.0		.0	.0	.3
	12.5		12.5	16.2	All Other Non-Current		6.1		5.0	17.0	23.0
	56.0		61.0	56.9	Net Worth		67.3		56.6	56.7	51.8
	100.0		100.0	100.0	Total Liabilities & Net Worth		100.0		100.0	100.0	100.0
					INCOME DATA						
	100.0		100.0	100.0	Net Sales		100.0		100.0	100.0	100.0
					Gross Profit						
	90.4		89.2	88.6	Operating Expenses		82.7		85.8	89.6	92.5
	9.6		10.8	11.4	Operating Profit		17.3		14.2	10.4	7.5
	4.8		5.1	3.6	All Other Expenses (net)		6.0		4.7	2.0	3.3
	4.8		5.7	7.8	Profit Before Taxes		11.3		9.5	8.4	4.1
					RATIOS						
	9.3		10.6	11.2			22.9		5.9	12.7	9.9
	5.0		6.1	5.7	Current		8.9		3.3	7.3	5.3
	2.6		3.3	3.3			2.9		2.3	4.9	3.6
	8.2		9.2	9.8			20.3		5.7	11.6	8.4
	4.5		5.3	4.8	Quick		5.5		3.3	6.5	4.7
	2.2		2.8	2.7			1.9		2.2	4.2	2.9
6	62.9	8	46.5	5	78.6		0	UND	5	67.2	10	38.1	6	57.1
25	14.7	27	13.5	22	16.4	Sales/Receivables	16	22.9	33	11.2	27	13.7	23	16.1
46	8.0	47	7.7	45	8.2		36	10.0	51	7.1	65	5.6	39	9.3
					Cost of Sales/Inventory						
					Cost of Sales/Payables						
	1.3		1.2	1.0			.8		1.0	.8	1.3
	2.1		1.7	1.8	Sales/Working Capital		1.3		2.0	1.4	2.1
	4.0		3.6	3.2			2.9		4.3	2.5	3.4
	7.0		8.6	10.5					36.4	16.2	9.3
(143)	3.0	(130)	3.2	(112)	3.0	EBIT/Interest	(12)	4.4	(31)	4.9	(52)	2.8
	1.2		.5	1.0					2.9	1.6	1.0
					Net Profit + Depr., Dep., Amort./Cur. Mat. L/T/D						
	.0		.0	.0			.0		.0	.0	.0
	1.0		.9	.9	Fixed/Worth		.8		1.0	.8	.9
	1.7		1.3	1.5			1.4		1.5	1.7	1.5
	.2		.2	.2			.1		.4	.2	.2
	.5		.5	.5	Debt/Worth		.5		.7	.4	.5
	1.7		1.4	1.4			.8		1.2	1.5	1.8
	10.2		9.3	10.7	% Profit Before Taxes/Tangible Net Worth		29.1		21.4	12.5	9.8
(194)	3.9	(169)	2.8	(140)	4.5		(13)	3.9	(17)	5.3	(32)	4.0	(62)	4.3
	.1		-.7	.2			-1.8		.7	.6	-1.2
	5.4		4.9	5.7	% Profit Before Taxes/Total Assets		22.5		7.8	6.5	4.8
	2.0		1.9	2.5			2.4		3.0	2.5	2.4
	.1		-.5	-.1			-1.8		-.4	.3	-.6
	UND		UND	UND	Sales/Net Fixed Assets		UND		UND	UND	UND
	.7		.7	.9			.8		.5	.9	1.2
	.3		.3	.4			.3		.3	.4	.5
	1.3		1.3	1.3	Sales/Total Assets		.8		1.3	1.3	1.8
	.4		.4	.4			.5		.3	.4	.7
	.2		.2	.2			.3		.2	.2	.3
	6.3		7.1	6.0					11.5	8.2	4.5
(111)	11.2	(95)	11.7	(77)	10.2	% Depr., Dep., Amort./Sales	(11)	16.4	(19)	12.0	(30)	6.8
	16.1		16.4	16.7					36.6	16.7	11.7
	1.6		2.6	2.5	% Officers', Directors' Owners' Comp/Sales						
(26)	6.3	(17)	6.0	(10)	6.4						
	8.9		10.0	8.5							
	7390199M		6000030M	6885014M	Net Sales ($)	3311M	25200M	35687M	135298M	585180M	6100338M
	13204009M		10646873M	10261735M	Total Assets ($)	7772M	73833M	217094M	493129M	1979427M	7490480M

Current Data Sorted by Assets

Comparative Historical Data

	0-500M	500M-2MM	2-10MM	10-50MM	50-100MM	100-250MM	Type of Statement	4/1/14-3/31/15 ALL	4/1/15-3/31/16 ALL
		2	6	16	25	38	Unqualified	140	155
				1			Reviewed		1
		1			1		Compiled		1
							Tax Returns		
		1	3	5	2	2	Other	19	28
		88 (4/1-9/30/18)		15 (10/1/18-3/31/19)					
		4	9	22	28	40	**NUMBER OF STATEMENTS**	159	185
	%	%	%	%	%	%	**ASSETS**	%	%
				28.7	16.0	18.7	Cash & Equivalents	19.1	23.7
				4.8	4.5	5.8	Trade Receivables (net)	6.1	5.7
D				.4	.4	.4	Inventory	.2	.2
A				6.9	6.5	3.2	All Other Current	4.2	3.6
T				40.7	27.3	28.1	Total Current	29.6	33.3
A				47.2	65.3	62.1	Fixed Assets (net)	63.0	60.0
				.2	.5	.6	Intangibles (net)	.5	.3
N				11.9	6.9	9.1	All Other Non-Current	7.0	6.4
O				100.0	100.0	100.0	Total	100.0	100.0
T							**LIABILITIES**		
				.0	.0	.1	Notes Payable-Short Term	.4	.0
A				1.8	2.2	2.4	Cur. Mat.-L.T.D.	2.5	2.6
V				2.0	1.9	1.5	Trade Payables	2.4	2.3
A				.0	.0	.0	Income Taxes Payable	.0	.0
I				3.0	2.4	4.5	All Other Current	4.2	4.0
L				6.8	6.5	8.5	Total Current	9.6	8.9
A				17.3	23.0	31.6	Long-Term Debt	27.6	23.1
B				.0	.0	.0	Deferred Taxes	.0	.2
L				10.6	17.2	17.3	All Other Non-Current	4.4	12.9
E				65.2	53.3	42.6	Net Worth	58.5	55.0
				100.0	100.0	100.0	Total Liabilities & Net Worth	100.0	100.0
							INCOME DATA		
				100.0	100.0	100.0	Net Sales	100.0	100.0
							Gross Profit		
				98.9	90.4	90.4	Operating Expenses	89.5	91.0
				1.1	9.6	9.6	Operating Profit	10.5	9.0
				4.0	2.7	3.6	All Other Expenses (net)	4.2	2.6
				-3.0	6.8	6.0	Profit Before Taxes	6.3	6.5
							RATIOS		
				7.4	6.5	5.8		5.4	7.3
				5.8	4.8	4.0	Current	3.8	4.6
				3.1	2.5	2.4		2.1	2.3
				6.3	4.4	5.1		5.0	6.6
				4.0	3.9	3.8	Quick	3.3	4.3
				3.0	2.3	2.2		1.8	1.9
				7　52.7	22　16.5	29　12.4		15　24.1	20　18.4
				34　10.6	42　8.6	47　7.7	Sales/Receivables	36　10.1	34　10.6
				57　6.4	87　4.2	126　2.9		68　5.4	60　6.1
							Cost of Sales/Inventory		
							Cost of Sales/Payables		
				.9	.8	.9		1.2	1.1
				1.4	1.4	1.3	Sales/Working Capital	1.8	1.6
				2.5	3.1	2.2		4.4	3.4
				4.7	8.4	7.8		6.2	9.0
				(17)　1.0	(26)　2.4	(38)　2.8	EBIT/Interest	(142)　2.5	(123)　3.4
				-.4	.6	1.5		.4	1.3
							Net Profit + Depr., Dep., Amort./Cur. Mat. L/T/D		
				.0	.9	1.0		.9	.9
				.9	1.2	1.2	Fixed/Worth	1.1	1.2
				1.3	1.8	2.0		1.5	1.5
				.2	.3	.4		.3	.3
				.5	.7	.9	Debt/Worth	.5	.6
				1.1	2.2	2.3		1.1	1.5
				2.5	7.5	5.9		7.5	8.0
				-1.2	(27)　3.5	(36)　3.0	% Profit Before Taxes/Tangible Net Worth	(152)　3.0	(177)　2.9
				-5.3	-.4	1.0		-.9	-.5
				1.5	4.9	2.8		4.4	4.1
				-.5	1.9	1.9	% Profit Before Taxes/Total Assets	1.8	1.9
				-2.1	-.1	.5		-.7	-.2
				UND	.7	.6		.8	.8
				.7	.3	.4	Sales/Net Fixed Assets	.4	.4
				.2	.2	.3		.2	.3
				.7	.4	.4		.5	.5
				.4	.2	.3	Sales/Total Assets	.3	.3
				.1	.1	.2		.2	.2
				5.1	9.3	9.2		8.2	6.4
				(15)　10.0	(26)　14.3	(37)　12.2	% Depr., Dep., Amort./Sales	(129)　13.6	(147)　10.2
				25.2	23.1	23.0		20.2	15.9
							% Officers', Directors' Owners' Comp/Sales	.7	
								(10)　4.0	
								20.5	
		6878M	70923M	382606M	621796M	1811587M	Net Sales ($)	4433141M	5347995M
		4761M	55524M	658687M	2129460M	6126742M	Total Assets ($)	12355999M	14201129M

The vertical notation **DATA NOT AVAILABLE** spans the 0-500M, 500M-2MM and 2-10MM columns across the ASSETS, LIABILITIES, INCOME DATA and RATIOS sections.

Comparative Historical Data | Current Data Sorted by Sales

				Type of Statement						
144		109	87	Unqualified	2	3	4	8	31	39
1			1	Reviewed		1				
1		3	2	Compiled			1		1	
				Tax Returns						
33		32	13	Other	3	1		2	5	2
4/1/16-		4/1/17-	4/1/18-			88 (4/1-9/30/18)			15 (10/1/18-3/31/19)	
3/31/17		3/31/18	3/31/19							
ALL		ALL	ALL		0-1MM	1-3MM	3-5MM	5-10MM	10-25MM	25MM & OVER
179		144	103	**NUMBER OF STATEMENTS**	5	5	5	10	37	41
%		%	%	**ASSETS**	%	%	%	%	%	%
23.4		20.6	24.2	Cash & Equivalents				13.7	28.1	22.4
4.6		6.4	4.9	Trade Receivables (net)				5.2	4.4	6.5
.2		.3	.3	Inventory				.4	.3	.4
3.5		4.1	5.1	All Other Current				7.8	2.4	7.2
31.7		31.4	34.5	Total Current				27.1	35.2	36.6
58.6		59.5	56.0	Fixed Assets (net)				66.4	55.5	55.3
1.0		.6	.4	Intangibles (net)				.3	.4	.6
8.7		8.5	9.1	All Other Non-Current				6.1	8.9	7.4
100.0		100.0	100.0	Total				100.0	100.0	100.0
				LIABILITIES						
.3		.4	.1	Notes Payable-Short Term				.0	.0	.1
2.0		2.0	2.1	Cur. Mat.-L.T.D.				1.3	1.9	2.4
1.8		1.7	2.1	Trade Payables				1.5	2.5	2.1
.1		.0	.0	Income Taxes Payable				.0	.0	.0
2.8		3.0	3.5	All Other Current				4.4	1.8	4.9
7.0		7.1	7.8	Total Current				7.2	6.2	9.6
22.0		24.0	23.0	Long-Term Debt				17.0	19.8	30.4
.2		.2	.0	Deferred Taxes				.0	.0	.0
17.0		17.8	14.9	All Other Non-Current				9.8	10.0	22.1
53.8		50.8	54.3	Net Worth				65.9	64.0	37.9
100.0		100.0	100.0	Total Liabilities & Net Worth				100.0	100.0	100.0
				INCOME DATA						
100.0		100.0	100.0	Net Sales				100.0	100.0	100.0
				Gross Profit						
93.2		93.9	92.1	Operating Expenses				89.1	90.2	92.1
6.8		6.1	7.9	Operating Profit				10.9	9.8	7.9
2.5		2.5	3.9	All Other Expenses (net)				3.4	3.2	3.7
4.3		3.7	4.0	Profit Before Taxes				7.6	6.7	4.2
				RATIOS						
7.4		8.3	6.7					9.0	6.6	6.1
4.4		4.4	4.7	Current				4.9	4.9	4.4
2.6		2.8	2.7					1.8	3.1	2.8
7.1		7.3	5.9					8.3	6.1	5.5
4.3		3.9	4.0	Quick				3.4	4.3	3.8
2.2		2.4	2.3					1.3	3.0	2.3
13 28.4	21 17.0	17 21.9		Sales/Receivables	36 10.1	22 16.5	20 18.5			
34 10.6	46 8.0	37 9.9			40 9.1	41 8.9	37 9.9			
57 6.4	96 3.8	99 3.7			60 6.1	89 4.1	114 3.2			
				Cost of Sales/Inventory						
				Cost of Sales/Payables						
1.0		1.0	.9					.7	.9	1.0
1.7		1.6	1.4	Sales/Working Capital				.9	1.4	1.4
3.1		3.0	2.6					2.8	2.3	3.3
7.2		7.1	7.2						10.4	9.5
(116) 2.0	(121) 2.0	(91) 2.6		EBIT/Interest		(31) 2.8	(38) 2.6			
.2		-.4	.8						1.0	1.2
				Net Profit + Depr., Dep., Amort./Cur. Mat. L/T/D						
.8		.9	.8					.9	.8	.9
1.1		1.2	1.1	Fixed/Worth				1.2	1.0	1.3
1.5		1.7	1.5					1.3	1.3	2.3
.3		.4	.3					.2	.2	.5
.6		.8	.6	Debt/Worth				.6	.5	1.5
1.4		1.8	1.9					.8	1.0	2.7
6.4		7.8	6.8	% Profit Before Taxes/Tangible Net Worth				3.6	5.8	8.8
(167) 1.9	(136) 2.9	(98) 2.7				(36) 2.6	(37) 3.7	1.9		
-1.4		-1.4	-.8					.0	-1.2	.9
3.8		3.2	3.4	% Profit Before Taxes/Total Assets				2.1	4.2	3.7
1.2		1.3	1.5					1.2	1.6	2.1
-.8		-.8	-.4					.0	-.5	.1
.9		.8	.9					.5	.8	1.1
.4		.5	.5	Sales/Net Fixed Assets				.2	.4	.6
.3		.3	.2					.1	.1	.4
.4		.4	.5					.3	.4	.5
.3		.3	.3	Sales/Total Assets				.1	.3	.4
.2		.2	.2					.1	.1	.3
7.7		8.3	8.2					11.7	10.7	5.0
(141) 13.5	(123) 12.1	(83) 12.9		% Depr., Dep., Amort./Sales		(29) 19.5	(35) 9.6	14.7		
24.2		19.0	22.0					23.1	32.3	12.4
3.4		3.5								
(35) 5.9	(14) 7.0			% Officers', Directors' Owners' Comp/Sales						
7.1		21.1								
4541697M		4372161M	2893790M	Net Sales ($)	3281M	8553M	20055M	78165M	618226M	2165510M
14209168M		13031694M	8975174M	Total Assets ($)	15289M	47047M	100635M	509006M	2870097M	5433100M

M = $ thousand   MM = $ million
See Pages viii through xx for Explanation of Ratios and Data

Current Data Sorted by Assets							Comparative Historical Data	

		5	11	11	7		Type of Statement		
							Unqualified	47	40
							Reviewed	3	5
						1	Compiled		
							Tax Returns		1
	2	4	3	1			Other	1	4
	38 (4/1-9/30/18)		7 (10/1/18-3/31/19)					4/1/14-3/31/15	4/1/15-3/31/16
0-500M	500M-2MM	2-10MM	10-50MM	50-100MM	100-250MM			ALL	ALL
	2	9	14	12	8		NUMBER OF STATEMENTS	51	50
%	%	%	%	%	%		ASSETS	%	%
			23.0	32.2			Cash & Equivalents	34.6	43.7
			2.6	4.2			Trade Receivables (net)	7.2	5.8
			.1	.1			Inventory	2.2	1.3
			3.0	14.0			All Other Current	7.1	5.2
			28.7	50.6			Total Current	51.2	55.9
			61.8	41.0			Fixed Assets (net)	39.2	36.3
			5.5	4.4			Intangibles (net)	.2	.5
			4.0	4.0			All Other Non-Current	9.5	7.3
			100.0	100.0			Total	100.0	100.0
							LIABILITIES		
			.0	.3			Notes Payable-Short Term	1.0	1.2
			1.8	1.3			Cur. Mat.-L.T.D.	2.3	1.3
			1.4	1.7			Trade Payables	4.7	4.5
			.0	.0			Income Taxes Payable	.0	.0
			6.1	3.7			All Other Current	8.0	7.0
			9.3	6.9			Total Current	16.0	14.1
			36.0	29.2			Long-Term Debt	21.0	18.6
			.0	.0			Deferred Taxes	.0	.0
			3.3	23.4			All Other Non-Current	5.1	11.2
			51.4	40.5			Net Worth	57.9	56.1
			100.0	100.0			Total Liabilties & Net Worth	100.0	100.0
							INCOME DATA		
			100.0	100.0			Net Sales	100.0	100.0
							Gross Profit		
			78.9	83.2			Operating Expenses	89.8	85.8
			21.1	16.8			Operating Profit	10.2	14.2
			9.4	4.7			All Other Expenses (net)	4.1	6.2
			11.7	12.2			Profit Before Taxes	6.1	8.1
							RATIOS		
			8.0	18.1				8.7	11.3
			6.1	7.0			Current	3.8	4.5
			2.2	3.5				2.1	2.5
			7.6	12.5				7.3	10.9
			6.1	6.1			Quick	3.4	3.8
			2.2	3.5				1.8	2.3

		0	UND	4	90.7			6	57.0	2	146.0
		16	23.1	16	23.1		Sales/Receivables	21	17.8	13	27.4
		37	9.9	49	7.4			42	8.7	41	9.0

							Cost of Sales/Inventory		

							Cost of Sales/Payables		

			1.0	1.1				1.4	.9
			1.3	1.5		Sales/Working Capital	3.2	2.4
			3.5	2.2			5.7	3.8
			12.7	37.3			14.1	14.4
		(11)	5.7	(10)	2.2	EBIT/Interest	(36)	3.0	(29)	2.2
			1.4	-.6			-.1	1.0

							Net Profit + Depr., Dep., Amort./Cur. Mat. L/T/D		

			1.1	.0				.0	.0
			1.3	.8		Fixed/Worth	.7	.8
			2.7	3.4			1.2	1.4
			.6	.2			.3	.2
			.9	1.2		Debt/Worth	.5	.6
			3.0	19.2			.8	1.7
			16.3	35.1			15.0	11.3
			8.9	(10)	6.9	% Profit Before Taxes/Tangible Net Worth	(49)	3.8	(47)	4.6
			2.6	2.8			-1.7	1.7
			6.4	9.8			7.9	7.3
			2.7	1.9		% Profit Before Taxes/Total Assets	3.3	2.9
			.5	-.6			-1.1	1.0
			.9	UND			UND	UND
			.3	.8		Sales/Net Fixed Assets	1.5	3.0
			.1	.3			.4	.4
			.4	1.1			2.0	1.6
			.2	.4		Sales/Total Assets	.6	.5
			.1	.2			.3	.2
			9.1				4.5	5.5
		(11)	13.0			% Depr., Dep., Amort./Sales	(27)	7.1	(23)	9.8
			62.9				17.6	17.1

							% Officers', Directors' Owners' Comp/Sales		

	7228M	57092M	260855M	637791M	523755M	Net Sales ($)	1433400M	1290007M
	3058M	40173M	328571M	860420M	1455075M	Total Assets ($)	2460674M	2057953M

M = $ thousand   MM = $ million
See Pages viii through xx for Explanation of Ratios and Data

(Left-side columns 0-500M through 2-10MM marked: DATA NOT AVAILABLE)

Comparative Historical Data				Current Data Sorted by Sales					

			Type of Statement						
41	28	34	Unqualified	3	6	1	3	5	16
2			Reviewed						
		1	Compiled					1	
			Tax Returns						
16	32	10	Other	1	2	2	3	1	1
4/1/16-	4/1/17-	4/1/18-			38 (4/1-9/30/18)		7 (10/1/18-3/31/19)		
3/31/17	3/31/18	3/31/19		0-1MM	1-3MM	3-5MM	5-10MM	10-25MM	25MM & OVER
ALL	ALL	ALL							
59	60	45	**NUMBER OF STATEMENTS**	4	8	3	6	7	17
%	%	%	**ASSETS**	%	%	%	%	%	%
29.2	32.4	28.2	Cash & Equivalents						29.8
6.2	6.7	4.9	Trade Receivables (net)						4.4
.1	.3	.1	Inventory						.3
7.0	6.6	8.1	All Other Current						13.2
42.5	46.0	41.3	Total Current						47.7
49.8	45.3	48.0	Fixed Assets (net)						41.7
1.6	2.2	2.9	Intangibles (net)						3.0
6.1	6.6	7.8	All Other Non-Current						7.6
100.0	100.0	100.0	Total						100.0
			LIABILITIES						
1.7	1.7	1.0	Notes Payable-Short Term						.2
1.8	1.1	1.5	Cur. Mat.-L.T.D.						1.6
2.8	2.6	2.2	Trade Payables						3.0
.0	.4	.0	Income Taxes Payable						.0
6.0	5.0	5.0	All Other Current						7.0
12.3	10.8	9.7	Total Current						11.8
32.6	17.7	27.0	Long-Term Debt						26.5
.0	.0	.0	Deferred Taxes						.0
16.7	16.4	11.4	All Other Non-Current						22.2
38.4	55.1	51.9	Net Worth						39.4
100.0	100.0	100.0	Total Liabilities & Net Worth						100.0
			INCOME DATA						
100.0	100.0	100.0	Net Sales						100.0
			Gross Profit						
86.5	89.1	84.9	Operating Expenses						89.8
13.5	10.9	15.1	Operating Profit						10.2
7.1	3.5	5.8	All Other Expenses (net)						4.5
6.4	7.4	9.2	Profit Before Taxes						5.7
			RATIOS						
9.5	17.6	10.1							9.2
4.2	8.0	5.7	Current						6.1
2.6	3.3	2.5							2.5
8.1	17.0	8.4							6.9
3.7	7.7	4.6	Quick						4.6
2.1	2.9	2.0							1.7
6 62.7	5 75.9	3 110.9						4	100.1
30 12.1	34 10.6	28 12.9	Sales/Receivables					15	24.4
60 6.1	55 6.6	51 7.2						41	8.8
			Cost of Sales/Inventory						
			Cost of Sales/Payables						
1.3	1.0	1.1							1.4
2.3	1.4	1.7	Sales/Working Capital						2.3
3.8	3.8	2.8							2.9
4.9	13.3	15.6							14.1
(46) 2.0	(37) 2.5	(31) 3.8	EBIT/Interest					(13)	2.2
.4	.6	.5							-4.0
			Net Profit + Depr., Dep., Amort./Cur. Mat. L/T/D						
.4	.2	.0							.0
1.2	.8	1.1	Fixed/Worth						1.1
2.0	1.5	1.8							4.2
.2	.2	.4							.4
.7	.6	.8	Debt/Worth						.9
2.7	1.9	2.5							9.5
7.2	11.2	14.7	% Profit Before Taxes/Tangible Net Worth						15.1
(51) 3.3	(54) 5.4	(43) 5.4						(15)	7.9
.1	.1	-.8							3.2
3.9	5.0	6.9	% Profit Before Taxes/Total Assets						7.4
1.8	2.8	2.0							3.3
-.4	.1	-1.1							-2.4
244.6	17.1	UND	% Sales/Net Fixed Assets						UND
.5	.8	.6							.9
.3	.3	.2							.5
1.1	.9	.9	Sales/Total Assets						1.1
.3	.3	.3							.5
.2	.2	.2							.3
6.9	4.0	5.7	% Depr., Dep., Amort./Sales						5.0
(37) 9.9	(41) 8.4	(29) 9.6						(10)	6.1
16.4	17.6	24.6							13.4
			% Officers', Directors' Owners' Comp/Sales						
1700748M	1101592M	1486721M	Net Sales ($)	1967M	13549M	10698M	42152M	127363M	1290992M
3764080M	2286745M	2687297M	Total Assets ($)	26746M	76936M	32239M	198563M	465917M	1886896M

M = $ thousand   MM = $ million
See Pages viii through xx for Explanation of Ratios and Data

Current Data Sorted by Assets · **Comparative Historical Data**

0-500M	500M-2MM	2-10MM	10-50MM	50-100MM	100-250MM	Type of Statement	ALL 4/1/14-3/31/15	ALL 4/1/15-3/31/16
1		1	14	15	14	Unqualified	133	138
						Reviewed		
						Compiled	2	1
						Tax Returns		
1		2	1	2	2	Other	14	9
	45 (4/1-9/30/18)		8 (10/1/18-3/31/19)					
2		3	15	17	16	**NUMBER OF STATEMENTS**	149	148
%	%	%	%	%	%	**ASSETS**	%	%
			36.1	31.4	22.3	Cash & Equivalents	30.6	35.8
			6.1	4.9	5.2	Trade Receivables (net)	6.5	8.5
			.7	.2	.2	Inventory	.4	.3
			10.2	4.0	3.0	All Other Current	5.5	8.8
			53.1	40.6	30.7	Total Current	43.0	53.3
			43.2	48.9	58.6	Fixed Assets (net)	49.8	37.7
			.0	.0	.5	Intangibles (net)	.4	.8
			3.7	10.5	10.2	All Other Non-Current	6.8	8.2
			100.0	100.0	100.0	Total	100.0	100.0
						LIABILITIES		
			.4	.1	.2	Notes Payable-Short Term	.2	.8
			2.2	1.1	2.5	Cur. Mat.-L.T.D.	1.7	2.1
			3.6	2.3	2.5	Trade Payables	3.5	5.0
			.0	.0	.0	Income Taxes Payable	.0	.0
			5.7	7.4	2.0	All Other Current	7.0	6.6
			12.0	10.9	7.1	Total Current	12.4	14.4
			22.7	15.8	20.9	Long-Term Debt	18.6	20.1
			.0	.1	.0	Deferred Taxes	.0	.0
			4.7	8.2	24.7	All Other Non-Current	3.2	11.2
			60.7	65.0	47.3	Net Worth	65.7	54.3
			100.0	100.0	100.0	Total Liabilities & Net Worth	100.0	100.0
						INCOME DATA		
			100.0	100.0	100.0	Net Sales	100.0	100.0
						Gross Profit		
			88.9	87.6	87.2	Operating Expenses	92.1	88.3
			11.1	12.4	12.8	Operating Profit	7.9	11.7
			5.9	5.2	2.8	All Other Expenses (net)	2.9	5.0
			5.3	7.2	10.0	Profit Before Taxes	5.0	6.7
						RATIOS		
			15.3	8.1	9.8		7.2	10.4
			6.6	5.1	4.8	Current	3.5	4.0
			1.9	2.7	1.8		2.1	2.0
			13.5	7.7	9.5		6.6	8.9
			5.9	4.6	4.0	Quick	3.2	3.4
			1.5	2.3	1.7		1.8	1.5
			0 UND	15 24.7	20 18.1		12 31.7	9 41.7
			30 12.2	29 12.5	54 6.7	Sales/Receivables	27 13.5	23 15.6
			54 6.7	45 8.1	83 4.4		51 7.2	46 7.9
						Cost of Sales/Inventory		
						Cost of Sales/Payables		
			1.4	.9	.8		1.5	1.2
			1.8	1.4	1.7	Sales/Working Capital	2.3	2.4
			5.5	2.8	5.1		4.1	6.9
			12.6	10.5	8.1		7.7	9.3
			(14) 3.9	(15) 2.6	4.1	EBIT/Interest	(116) 2.1	(107) 3.4
			-1.0	-1.6	2.6		.0	.9
						Net Profit + Depr., Dep., Amort./Cur. Mat. L/T/D		
			.0	.0	.9		.0	.0
			1.0	.9	1.1	Fixed/Worth	.9	.7
			1.5	1.1	2.1		1.2	1.2
			.3	.3	.3		.2	.2
			.6	.5	.6	Debt/Worth	.5	.6
			1.3	1.0	2.4		.8	1.2
			11.9	6.8	7.3	% Profit Before Taxes/Tangible Net Worth	6.0	11.3
			7.4	3.3	(14) 4.7		(147) 1.6	(143) 4.8
			-4.1	-2.8	2.3		-1.9	-1.5
			7.5	4.6	4.2	% Profit Before Taxes/Total Assets	3.7	6.3
			3.4	1.6	2.6		1.1	2.8
			-3.1	-1.6	.8		-1.0	-.5
			UND	UND	1.0		UND	UND
			.5	.4	.4	Sales/Net Fixed Assets	.5	1.0
			.3	.3	.3		.3	.4
			1.5	.7	.4		1.3	1.3
			.4	.3	.3	Sales/Total Assets	.4	.5
			.2	.2	.2		.2	.3
				12.1	5.5		7.7	7.4
			(11)	13.1	(11) 13.7	% Depr., Dep., Amort./Sales	(94) 11.1	(72) 10.6
				19.2	17.4		15.9	14.4
						% Officers', Directors', Owners' Comp/Sales		
3927M		10557M	409588M	653921M	1382556M	Net Sales ($)	5678566M	6532647M
689M		17187M	405052M	1191736M	2832753M	Total Assets ($)	10145391M	8685709M

(The 0-500M, 500M-2MM and 2-10MM spreads are marked "DATA NOT AVAILABLE" for all ratio/percentage rows.)

M = $ thousand   MM = $ million
See Pages viii through xx for Explanation of Ratios and Data

Comparative Historical Data   Current Data Sorted by Sales

Comparative Historical Data			Type of Statement						
52	49	45	Unqualified		3	3	3	12	24
			Reviewed						
1	1		Compiled						
			Tax Returns						
10	12	8	Other		1	1	1	2	3
4/1/16-3/31/17	4/1/17-3/31/18	4/1/18-3/31/19			45 (4/1-9/30/18)			8 (10/1/18-3/31/19)	
ALL	ALL	ALL		0-1MM	1-3MM	3-5MM	5-10MM	10-25MM	25MM & OVER
63	62	53	**NUMBER OF STATEMENTS**	4	4	4	14	27	
%	%	%	**ASSETS**	%	%	%	%	%	%
30.3	32.3	30.0	Cash & Equivalents	D				23.0	36.7
8.9	5.7	6.2	Trade Receivables (net)	A				3.7	6.8
.4	.2	1.4	Inventory	T				.4	.4
9.4	6.9	5.4	All Other Current	A				2.0	8.5
48.9	45.1	43.0	Total Current					29.1	52.5
44.3	46.0	48.1	Fixed Assets (net)	N				66.2	36.4
.8	1.2	.2	Intangibles (net)	O				.1	.3
6.0	7.7	8.7	All Other Non-Current	T				4.7	10.9
100.0	100.0	100.0	Total					100.0	100.0
			LIABILITIES	A					
.4	.1	.2	Notes Payable-Short Term	V				.2	.1
1.7	1.6	1.8	Cur. Mat. L.T.D.	A				1.5	2.1
2.9	1.9	4.7	Trade Payables	I				1.5	3.9
.0	.0	.0	Income Taxes Payable	L				.0	.0
5.4	4.0	5.5	All Other Current	A				1.4	7.9
10.4	7.7	12.2	Total Current	B				4.6	14.1
15.2	17.8	19.1	Long-Term Debt	L				23.6	14.2
.1	.0	.0	Deferred Taxes	E				.1	.0
11.8	12.7	14.1	All Other Non-Current					5.3	18.2
62.6	61.9	54.6	Net Worth					66.5	53.6
100.0	100.0	100.0	Total Liabilties & Net Worth					100.0	100.0
			INCOME DATA						
100.0	100.0	100.0	Net Sales					100.0	100.0
			Gross Profit						
87.1	87.8	86.9	Operating Expenses					84.2	91.4
12.9	12.2	13.1	Operating Profit					15.8	8.6
6.2	4.5	5.1	All Other Expenses (net)					1.6	5.6
6.7	7.7	8.0	Profit Before Taxes					14.1	3.0
			RATIOS						
11.1	10.3	8.7						10.4	8.1
5.0	6.1	4.8	Current					6.3	4.8
2.1	2.7	2.3						3.0	1.9
8.6	9.1	7.9						10.3	7.4
4.3	5.2	4.5	Quick					5.0	4.5
1.9	2.2	2.1						2.8	1.5

	10	35.1	2	149.3	12	30.7				19	18.8	14	26.9
	24	14.9	31	11.9	35	10.3	Sales/Receivables			31	11.6	40	9.1
	72	5.1	62	5.9	62	5.9				45	8.2	69	5.3

Cost of Sales/Inventory

Cost of Sales/Payables

Comparative Historical Data				10-25MM	25MM & OVER
1.1	1.0	1.0	Sales/Working Capital	.9	1.1
1.6	1.4	1.8		1.3	1.8
4.8	3.7	4.1		2.2	5.4
10.1	10.2	9.5	EBIT/Interest	18.8	6.9
(53) 4.6	(51) 3.0	(48) 3.9		8.1	(24) 3.0
1.4	.8	.8		1.6	-.6
			Net Profit + Depr., Dep., Amort./Cur. Mat. L/T/D		
.0	.0	.0	Fixed/Worth	.9	.0
.9	1.0	1.0		1.0	.9
1.3	1.4	1.4		1.4	1.2
.2	.3	.3	Debt/Worth	.3	.3
.5	.6	.6		.4	.6
1.0	1.3	1.5		.9	1.7
8.5	7.6	8.2	% Profit Before Taxes/Tangible Net Worth	8.7	7.7
(62) 4.3	(61) 3.3	(49) 4.3		6.8	(25) 3.3
.8	-.7	-.9		2.5	-3.7
5.1	4.5	4.9	% Profit Before Taxes/Total Assets	5.3	4.1
2.8	1.8	2.4		4.6	1.2
.3	-.3	-.6		2.0	-2.8
UND	UND	UND	Sales/Net Fixed Assets	.4	UND
.7	.5	.5		.3	1.0
.4	.3	.3		.2	.4
1.2	.8	1.0	Sales/Total Assets	.3	1.4
.4	.3	.3		.3	.6
.3	.2	.2		.2	.3
7.5	8.2	8.9	% Depr., Dep., Amort./Sales	10.4	4.6
(36) 11.2	(34) 11.8	(31) 13.7		(12) 14.3	(12) 10.1
18.9	14.9	18.0		21.3	14.5
			% Officers', Directors' Owners' Comp/Sales		

4251626M	2741364M	2460549M	Net Sales ($)	7115M	17736M	28470M	231786M	2175442M	
5280369M	4639038M	4447417M	Total Assets ($)	17116M	85184M	159250M	1033892M	3151975M	

© RMA 2019   M = $ thousand   MM = $ million
See Pages viii through xx for Explanation of Ratios and Data

Current Data Sorted by Assets							Comparative Historical Data	
						Type of Statement		
		2	2	4	4	Unqualified	18	12
						Reviewed		
						Compiled	1	
						Tax Returns	2	
	2	1	5	5	8	Other	22	21
	8 (4/1-9/30/18)		25 (10/1/18-3/31/19)				**4/1/14-3/31/15**	**4/1/15-3/31/16**
0-500M	**500M-2MM**	**2-10MM**	**10-50MM**	**50-100MM**	**100-250MM**		**ALL**	**ALL**
	2	3	7	9	12	**NUMBER OF STATEMENTS**	43	33
%	%	%	%	%	%	**ASSETS**	%	%
DATA NOT AVAILABLE					23.4	Cash & Equivalents	17.1	26.4
					7.5	Trade Receivables (net)	5.7	6.5
					.3	Inventory	1.2	1.1
					3.0	All Other Current	2.5	3.9
					34.3	Total Current	26.5	38.0
					60.6	Fixed Assets (net)	65.7	58.2
					.1	Intangibles (net)	3.4	.9
					5.0	All Other Non-Current	4.4	3.0
					100.0	Total	100.0	100.0
						LIABILITIES		
					1.2	Notes Payable-Short Term	1.5	.9
					1.6	Cur. Mat.-L.T.D.	2.5	2.2
					3.5	Trade Payables	3.2	4.8
					.0	Income Taxes Payable	.0	.1
					12.4	All Other Current	9.8	11.4
					18.7	Total Current	17.2	19.4
					15.5	Long-Term Debt	23.7	19.1
					.0	Deferred Taxes	.1	.2
					1.8	All Other Non-Current	.9	1.6
					64.0	Net Worth	58.1	59.7
					100.0	Total Liabilties & Net Worth	100.0	100.0
						INCOME DATA		
					100.0	Net Sales	100.0	100.0
						Gross Profit		
					78.6	Operating Expenses	78.4	77.4
					21.4	Operating Profit	21.6	22.6
					2.1	All Other Expenses (net)	1.8	1.7
					19.3	Profit Before Taxes	19.8	20.9
						RATIOS		
					3.6		2.3	3.1
					2.1	Current	1.7	2.0
					1.3		1.1	1.4
					3.4		1.9	2.9
					1.6	Quick	1.4	1.8
					1.1		.8	1.1
					3 115.3		**1** 472.9	**2** 236.8
					5 72.4	Sales/Receivables	**3** 138.3	**2** 165.2
					21 17.0		**7** 52.7	**12** 31.5
						Cost of Sales/Inventory		
						Cost of Sales/Payables		
					3.2		6.0	5.2
					9.2	Sales/Working Capital	13.3	10.3
					20.1		82.6	18.2
					28.7		76.4	55.4
					(10) 23.7	EBIT/Interest	(30) 18.3	(26) 33.4
					5.2		4.5	6.6
						Net Profit + Depr., Dep., Amort./Cur. Mat. L/T/D		
					.6		.8	.6
					.9	Fixed/Worth	1.1	.9
					1.1		1.9	1.7
					.2		.2	.2
					.4	Debt/Worth	.6	.6
					1.0		1.8	1.6
					62.9		89.3	110.1
					26.6	% Profit Before Taxes/Tangible Net Worth	(42) 29.5	37.0
					10.4		3.2	5.5
					48.1		41.7	50.9
					15.5	% Profit Before Taxes/Total Assets	17.7	16.5
					7.3		1.9	4.6
					3.1		3.2	4.7
					1.9	Sales/Net Fixed Assets	1.4	1.8
					1.2		.8	1.1
					2.0		1.7	1.8
					1.0	Sales/Total Assets	1.1	1.1
					.8		.6	.9
							1.8	2.3
						% Depr., Dep., Amort./Sales	(28) 5.9	(23) 5.9
							8.2	7.3
						% Officers', Directors' Owners' Comp/Sales		
	3326M	**20909M**	**486333M**	**821345M**	**2975786M**	Net Sales ($)	**4694925M**	**4278381M**
	1962M	**23920M**	**224804M**	**650862M**	**2278468M**	Total Assets ($)	**3981717M**	**3409761M**

M = $ thousand MM = $ million

See Pages viii through xx for Explanation of Ratios and Data

Comparative Historical Data				Current Data Sorted by Sales					
17	15	12	**Type of Statement**			1	1		10
			Unqualified						
			Reviewed						
			Compiled						
			Tax Returns						
			Other	1		1	1	2	16
22 4/1/16- 3/31/17 ALL	21 4/1/17- 3/31/18 ALL	21 4/1/18- 3/31/19 ALL		0-1MM	8 (4/1-9/30/18) 1-3MM	3-5MM	25 (10/1/18-3/31/19) 5-10MM	10-25MM	25MM & OVER
39	36	33	**NUMBER OF STATEMENTS**	1	2	2	2	2	26
%	%	%	**ASSETS**	%	%	%	%	%	%
23.6	21.9	27.6	Cash & Equivalents						24.8
4.0	6.0	5.2	Trade Receivables (net)						5.3
.7	1.0	.6	Inventory						.7
4.8	4.0	4.0	All Other Current						4.2
33.2	32.9	37.4	Total Current						34.9
60.8	61.9	58.1	Fixed Assets (net)						60.4
1.4	2.1	1.1	Intangibles (net)						.9
4.6	3.2	3.5	All Other Non-Current						3.7
100.0	100.0	100.0	Total						100.0
			LIABILITIES						
.5	.9	1.2	Notes Payable-Short Term						.7
3.1	3.3	3.7	Cur. Mat.-L.T.D.						3.4
2.3	3.3	2.5	Trade Payables						2.8
.0	.0	.0	Income Taxes Payable						.0
11.0	10.1	12.8	All Other Current						12.3
17.1	17.6	20.2	Total Current						19.3
18.7	15.4	17.0	Long-Term Debt						18.1
.4	.1	.0	Deferred Taxes						.0
3.3	1.9	1.2	All Other Non-Current						1.1
60.5	65.0	61.6	Net Worth						61.5
100.0	100.0	100.0	Total Liabilties & Net Worth						100.0
			INCOME DATA						
100.0	100.0	100.0	Net Sales						100.0
			Gross Profit						
73.3	76.9	77.4	Operating Expenses						73.7
26.7	23.1	22.6	Operating Profit						26.3
1.9	1.8	2.7	All Other Expenses (net)						2.5
24.8	21.3	19.8	Profit Before Taxes						23.8
			RATIOS						
4.1	3.9	3.4							2.9
2.5	1.8	2.0	Current						2.1
1.1	1.2	1.3							1.2
3.5	3.8	3.2							2.6
2.4	1.5	1.5	Quick						1.3
1.0	1.0	1.1							1.0
2 232.8	3 118.1	3 116.8							3 114.4
3 127.0	5 68.4	5 66.8	Sales/Receivables						5 69.6
8 44.8	12 30.4	14 26.3							9 38.5
			Cost of Sales/Inventory						
			Cost of Sales/Payables						
3.6	4.1	4.0							4.9
8.1	13.8	8.4	Sales/Working Capital						11.2
59.8	70.3	29.2							25.0
59.3	69.8	43.1							67.6
(26) 34.4	(28) 30.9	(26) 19.1	EBIT/Interest						(22) 25.8
7.1	8.2	4.3							8.3
			Net Profit + Depr., Dep., Amort./Cur. Mat. L/T/D						
.7	.7	.5							.5
.9	.9	.9	Fixed/Worth						.9
1.6	1.4	1.4							1.4
.3	.2	.2							.2
.5	.5	.5	Debt/Worth						.4
1.6	1.1	1.0							1.0
132.4	100.5	72.1	% Profit Before Taxes/Tangible Net Worth						84.8
30.6	27.3	(32) 31.6							(25) 34.5
6.9	4.8	9.4							13.7
61.3	58.6	50.0	% Profit Before Taxes/Total Assets						58.2
14.1	13.7	13.4							21.3
4.6	3.0	6.6							8.9
4.0	3.0	4.8							4.6
1.7	1.8	1.9	Sales/Net Fixed Assets						1.9
1.1	1.2	1.3							1.3
2.1	1.7	1.8							2.0
1.1	1.2	1.2	Sales/Total Assets						1.3
.7	.8	.8							.9
2.4	2.3	1.8							2.1
(23) 4.6	(26) 5.6	(22) 4.8	% Depr., Dep., Amort./Sales						(17) 4.4
6.7	7.2	7.0							6.8
			% Officers', Directors' Owners' Comp/Sales						
5389492M	4314500M	4307699M	Net Sales ($)	107M		6322M	14720M	29727M	4256823M
4120891M	3364110M	3180016M	Total Assets ($)	895M		10370M	19029M	24090M	3125632M

Note: Columns 1-3MM show "DATA NOT AVAILABLE" (displayed vertically through the 0-1MM/1-3MM region).

© RMA 2019

M = $ thousand   MM = $ million
See Pages viii through xx for Explanation of Ratios and Data

Current Data Sorted by Assets — Comparative Historical Data

Type of Statement	0-500M	500M-2MM	2-10MM	10-50MM	50-100MM	100-250MM		4/1/14-3/31/15 ALL	4/1/15-3/31/16 ALL
Unqualified	1	3	13	34	24	32		199	186
Reviewed								6	4
Compiled								2	3
Tax Returns								1	1
Other		4	6	6	5	5		46	32
			118 (4/1-9/30/18)		15 (10/1/18-3/31/19)				
NUMBER OF STATEMENTS	1	7	19	40	29	37		254	226
	%	%	%	%	%	%	**ASSETS**	%	%
			34.9	28.0	21.7	26.7	Cash & Equivalents	29.8	37.0
			9.4	4.9	7.2	5.9	Trade Receivables (net)	7.5	9.4
			.1	.2	.2	.2	Inventory	1.2	.7
			3.7	7.1	4.5	3.2	All Other Current	4.1	6.1
			48.0	40.2	33.7	36.0	Total Current	42.5	53.2
			40.0	50.2	56.7	51.1	Fixed Assets (net)	48.7	37.3
			.0	.0	.9	.1	Intangibles (net)	.5	1.2
			12.0	9.5	8.7	12.8	All Other Non-Current	8.3	8.3
			100.0	100.0	100.0	100.0	Total	100.0	100.0
							LIABILITIES		
			.2	.1	.4	.1	Notes Payable-Short Term	1.9	1.0
			1.9	1.7	2.9	1.8	Cur. Mat.-L.T.D.	2.1	1.7
			3.6	2.8	2.3	3.1	Trade Payables	4.7	4.7
			.0	.0	.0	.1	Income Taxes Payable	.1	.2
			7.0	6.2	3.7	3.8	All Other Current	6.6	8.0
			12.7	10.8	9.4	8.8	Total Current	15.3	15.6
			20.7	16.1	33.7	25.8	Long-Term Debt	19.3	15.9
			.4	.0	.6	.0	Deferred Taxes	.2	.0
			18.8	20.4	17.5	29.7	All Other Non-Current	5.1	15.0
			47.4	52.8	38.8	35.7	Net Worth	60.1	53.5
			100.0	100.0	100.0	100.0	Total Liabilties & Net Worth	100.0	100.0
							INCOME DATA		
			100.0	100.0	100.0	100.0	Net Sales	100.0	100.0
							Gross Profit		
			94.7	92.5	88.1	93.5	Operating Expenses	89.4	88.7
			5.3	7.5	11.9	6.5	Operating Profit	10.6	11.3
			3.1	2.1	4.4	3.4	All Other Expenses (net)	3.6	3.8
			2.2	5.4	7.6	3.1	Profit Before Taxes	6.9	7.4
							RATIOS		
			9.4	9.0	7.2	7.1	Current	6.1	7.7
			4.1	4.0	4.3	4.4		3.3	4.2
			1.4	2.7	2.3	2.0		1.7	2.1
			8.3	8.8	7.0	6.1	Quick	5.2	7.0
			3.4	3.2	3.4	4.2		3.0	3.7
			1.3	2.1	1.7	2.0		1.5	1.8
	0 UND	0 UND	4 86.4	14 26.9			Sales/Receivables	4 86.0	7 53.6
	13 27.2	21 17.0	29 12.6	35 10.3				26 14.0	23 15.9
	63 5.8	40 9.1	83 4.4	54 6.7				44 8.3	47 7.8
							Cost of Sales/Inventory		
							Cost of Sales/Payables		
			.9	1.4	1.3	1.3	Sales/Working Capital	1.5	1.6
			3.2	2.4	2.4	1.9		2.8	2.6
			11.0	4.2	4.9	3.8		7.4	5.4
			4.2	11.6	7.0	8.7	EBIT/Interest	8.8	13.2
			(10) 3.2	(30) 3.2	(26) 4.2	(30) 2.0		(178) 3.7	(148) 4.6
			-.9	.1	1.9	-.2		1.0	1.3
							Net Profit + Depr., Dep., Amort./Cur. Mat. L/T/D		
			.0	.7	.8	.8	Fixed/Worth	.1	.0
			1.1	.9	1.5	1.3		.9	.8
			1.6	1.4	2.5	NM		1.2	1.2
			.4	.2	.4	.4	Debt/Worth	.2	.2
			.7	.6	1.1	1.2		.5	.6
			2.7	1.5	3.5	NM		1.0	1.4
			6.2	6.6	13.8	6.1	% Profit Before Taxes/Tangible Net Worth	9.5	13.1
			(18) 2.5	(37) 2.5	(26) 5.4	(28) 3.6		(242) 4.1	(208) 5.1
			-1.8	-.5	3.3	-3.8		.0	.7
			3.0	4.2	4.6	3.4	% Profit Before Taxes/Total Assets	6.6	7.4
			1.3	1.7	3.1	1.6		2.8	3.5
			-1.0	-.6	1.6	-1.8		.0	.3
			UND	4.1	1.7	1.4	Sales/Net Fixed Assets	44.0	UND
			1.6	.7	.7	.7		.8	2.2
			.6	.4	.4	.4		.3	.4
			2.3	.9	.8	.6	Sales/Total Assets	1.5	1.8
			.6	.4	.4	.4		.4	.6
			.3	.2	.2	.3		.2	.3
			3.0	4.1	4.1	4.5	% Depr., Dep., Amort./Sales	4.3	3.6
			(10) 7.9	(32) 12.4	(22) 10.2	(27) 7.3		(180) 9.1	(123) 7.8
			15.4	17.7	16.3	16.6		15.8	13.9
							% Officers', Directors' Owners' Comp/Sales	5.0	3.2
								(18) 9.2	(31) 5.3
								28.8	16.0
	1180M	10028M	149040M	847843M	1357158M	3137176M	Net Sales ($)	7806894M	10425969M
	138M	8933M	107158M	978566M	2090038M	5675789M	Total Assets ($)	14994326M	13120394M

M = $ thousand   MM = $ million
See Pages viii through xx for Explanation of Ratios and Data

Comparative Historical Data | | Current Data Sorted by Sales

			Type of Statement						
144	127	106	Unqualified	3	8	7	11	29	48
2			Reviewed						
3			Compiled						
1	2	1	Tax Returns		1				
40	44	26	Other	4	5	1	3	4	9
4/1/16-	4/1/17-	4/1/18-			118 (4/1-9/30/18)		15 (10/1/18-3/31/19)		
3/31/17	3/31/18	3/31/19							
ALL	ALL	ALL		0-1MM	1-3MM	3-5MM	5-10MM	10-25MM	25MM & OVER
190	173	133	**NUMBER OF STATEMENTS**	7	14	8	14	33	57
%	%	%	**ASSETS**	%	%	%	%	%	%
32.3	28.0	27.9	Cash & Equivalents		34.0		22.7	18.4	33.5
9.8	8.9	6.6	Trade Receivables (net)		2.7		6.3	5.4	8.0
.5	.7	.2	Inventory		.0		.3	.3	.2
4.6	3.8	4.7	All Other Current		2.6		3.9	5.1	6.2
47.2	41.3	39.4	Total Current		39.4		33.2	29.2	47.8
42.3	46.2	49.3	Fixed Assets (net)		50.2		55.3	61.0	39.5
1.7	1.0	.3	Intangibles (net)		.0		1.8	.1	.1
8.9	11.4	11.1	All Other Non-Current		10.4		9.7	9.7	12.6
100.0	100.0	100.0	Total		100.0		100.0	100.0	100.0
			LIABILITIES						
1.8	1.3	.5	Notes Payable-Short Term		3.3		.2	.1	.2
2.0	1.5	1.9	Cur. Mat.-L.T.D.		2.5		1.8	1.6	2.3
4.6	3.8	3.1	Trade Payables		4.5		1.4	2.5	4.1
.0	.0	.0	Income Taxes Payable		.0		.0	.0	.0
6.6	6.3	4.9	All Other Current		2.9		3.5	5.1	5.2
15.1	12.9	10.5	Total Current		13.2		7.0	9.3	11.8
20.5	16.5	23.0	Long-Term Debt		17.1		17.8	22.0	25.3
.2	.2	.2	Deferred Taxes		.6		.0	.5	.0
16.9	14.7	25.4	All Other Non-Current		39.2		21.4	18.2	30.2
47.1	55.7	41.0	Net Worth		29.9		53.9	50.0	32.7
100.0	100.0	100.0	Total Liabilities & Net Worth		100.0		100.0	100.0	100.0
			INCOME DATA						
100.0	100.0	100.0	Net Sales		100.0		100.0	100.0	100.0
			Gross Profit						
91.6	92.2	91.4	Operating Expenses		96.4		88.4	90.2	94.3
8.4	7.8	8.6	Operating Profit		3.6		11.6	9.8	5.7
4.3	2.8	3.4	All Other Expenses (net)		1.3		1.3	3.1	3.5
4.1	5.1	5.2	Profit Before Taxes		2.3		10.3	6.7	2.2
			RATIOS						
7.9	8.8	7.6			8.2		8.9	7.7	7.0
4.4	4.0	4.3	Current		2.4		5.6	4.3	3.9
2.3	2.0	2.1			1.0		2.5	2.7	2.1
7.4	8.2	7.1			8.1		7.3	7.0	6.1
4.0	3.8	3.4	Quick		2.3		5.6	4.1	3.2
1.9	1.8	1.8			1.0		2.0	2.5	1.8
5 69.7	5 73.5	2 175.9		0 UND		1 298.0	5 68.4	2 175.9	
26 13.9	24 14.9	26 13.8	Sales/Receivables	2 227.4		39 9.3	32 11.3	27 13.7	
51 7.1	57 6.4	52 7.0		35 10.4		68 5.4	59 6.2	49 7.4	
			Cost of Sales/Inventory						
			Cost of Sales/Payables						
1.2	1.2	1.3			1.0		1.2	1.3	1.8
2.5	2.3	2.3	Sales/Working Capital		2.5		1.4	2.2	2.9
6.7	6.2	5.3			NM		3.6	3.3	7.1
8.6	12.1	7.1					22.2	9.8	4.9
(130) 2.4	(133) 2.9	(96) 3.2	EBIT/Interest	(13) 7.3		(27) 3.2	(40) 2.6		
-1.0	.4	.6					4.4	-1.4	.6
			Net Profit + Depr., Dep., Amort./Cur. Mat. L/T/D						
.0	.4	.7			.7		.7	.8	.0
.0	.0	1.1	Fixed/Worth		1.2		.8	1.1	1.0
1.5	1.4	2.0			1.5		1.5	1.7	13.8
.3	.2	.4			.4		.2	.4	.4
.6	.6	.8	Debt/Worth		.8		.7	.6	1.2
2.3	1.4	3.0			1.3		1.1	1.5	28.2
10.0	8.6	9.2			9.9		8.0	6.5	10.1
(168) 3.2	(161) 4.3	(116) 3.8	% Profit Before Taxes/Tangible Net Worth	(13) 3.2		(13) 5.5	(31) 3.6	(44) 4.0	
-1.6	-1.0	-.3			-1.8		2.4	-1.2	-.4
6.5	4.9	4.3			4.9		4.7	3.4	4.7
1.8	1.5	2.1	% Profit Before Taxes/Total Assets		1.8		3.8	2.1	1.8
-1.3	-.7	-.8			-2.1		1.9	-1.2	-1.1
UND	56.9	6.2			24.0		1.0	.9	UND
.8	.7	.8	Sales/Net Fixed Assets		.9		.6	.4	1.2
.4	.4	.4			.4		.4	.2	.7
1.7	1.1	.9			1.4		.6	.5	1.5
.5	.4	.4	Sales/Total Assets		.6		.3	.3	.6
.2	.2	.3			.3		.2	.2	.4
3.9	4.0	4.1					7.2	7.0	2.4
(114) 10.1	(120) 9.1	(93) 8.5	% Depr., Dep., Amort./Sales	(12) 13.5		(29) 15.3	(35) 5.2		
14.4	15.0	17.2					17.0	19.2	7.0
5.8	3.2								
(12) 9.8	(19) 7.3		% Officers', Directors' Owners' Comp/Sales						
13.7		18.8							
6942565M	6005178M	5502425M	Net Sales ($)	3729M	26868M	30202M	107255M	540714M	4793657M
10594079M	10748169M	8860622M	Total Assets ($)	26650M	70477M	115140M	336128M	2196017M	6116210M

© RMA 2019   M = $ thousand   MM = $ million
See Pages viii through xx for Explanation of Ratios and Data

Current Data Sorted by Assets | Comparative Historical Data

						Type of Statement		
1	8	16	5	2		Unqualified	53	52
1		4				Reviewed	10	9
		2	1			Compiled	6	5
2	1	2				Tax Returns	10	9
2	8	7	3			Other	22	17
	39 (4/1-9/30/18)		26 (10/1/18-3/31/19)				4/1/14-3/31/15 ALL	4/1/15-3/31/16 ALL
0-500M	500M-2MM	2-10MM	10-50MM	50-100MM	100-250MM	NUMBER OF STATEMENTS	101	92
6	17	31	9	2				
%	%	%	%	%	%	ASSETS	%	%
	29.5	25.5			D	Cash & Equivalents	29.8	28.2
	11.5	11.7			A	Trade Receivables (net)	7.7	7.5
	2.4	.9			T	Inventory	.7	.7
	.5	1.8			A	All Other Current	1.8	1.5
	43.8	39.8				Total Current	40.0	37.9
	53.6	54.4			N	Fixed Assets (net)	54.8	55.6
	.0	.0			O	Intangibles (net)	1.3	.8
	2.6	5.8			T	All Other Non-Current	4.0	5.7
	100.0	100.0				Total	100.0	100.0
					A	LIABILITIES		
	4.3	1.3			V	Notes Payable-Short Term	1.7	1.4
	2.9	3.0			A	Cur. Mat.-L.T.D.	2.8	3.1
	6.7	3.4			I	Trade Payables	7.4	2.4
	.0	.2			L	Income Taxes Payable	.1	.0
	2.0	4.8			A	All Other Current	3.4	4.9
	15.8	12.6			B	Total Current	15.4	11.7
	24.3	29.8			L	Long-Term Debt	26.2	23.9
	.0	.4			E	Deferred Taxes	.1	.0
	.0	6.2				All Other Non-Current	3.0	14.2
	59.9	51.1				Net Worth	55.4	50.2
	100.0	100.0				Total Liabilities & Net Worth	100.0	100.0
						INCOME DATA		
	100.0	100.0				Net Sales	100.0	100.0
						Gross Profit		
	89.3	83.6				Operating Expenses	91.6	91.1
	10.7	16.4				Operating Profit	8.4	8.9
	1.3	1.4				All Other Expenses (net)	3.0	3.2
	9.4	15.0				Profit Before Taxes	5.5	5.7
						RATIOS		
	10.2	14.3					9.3	10.7
	3.5	4.1				Current	4.3	4.8
	1.9	1.9					2.1	1.9
	10.2	14.3					8.9	10.2
	3.5	4.0				Quick	4.2	4.3
	1.9	1.8					1.8	1.9
0	UND	0 UND					0 UND	0 UND
9	38.6	0 UND				Sales/Receivables	4 83.8	3 117.7
32	11.3	38 9.5					25 14.5	22 16.5
						Cost of Sales/Inventory		
						Cost of Sales/Payables		
	.9	1.0					1.5	1.4
	4.5	2.9				Sales/Working Capital	3.0	2.8
	7.8	5.8					11.0	6.7
	8.5	32.7					4.6	7.8
	(12) 3.4	(27) 6.5				EBIT/Interest	(74) 1.7	(82) 3.3
	-1.4	3.4					-.2	.4
						Net Profit + Depr., Dep., Amort./Cur. Mat. L/T/D		
	.4	.5					.6	.6
	.8	1.0				Fixed/Worth	1.0	1.0
	1.6	1.6					1.5	1.8
	.2	.3					.2	.2
	.6	1.0				Debt/Worth	.7	.7
	2.1	1.8					1.3	1.9
	12.2	25.4				% Profit Before Taxes/Tangible Net Worth	8.9	16.6
	3.5	(28) 11.5					(95) 2.3	(83) 5.0
	-6.2	7.3					-2.7	-1.5
	6.0	9.4				% Profit Before Taxes/Total Assets	5.8	9.0
	3.2	5.8					1.6	3.0
	-1.7	3.6					-2.0	-.9
	6.4	1.9					3.7	1.9
	.7	.9				Sales/Net Fixed Assets	.9	.9
	.5	.5					.4	.4
	2.2	1.0					1.2	1.1
	.6	.5				Sales/Total Assets	.5	.5
	.3	.3					.3	.3
	5.0	3.2					5.3	6.1
	(10) 18.4	(26) 8.6				% Depr., Dep., Amort./Sales	(74) 9.5	(69) 10.1
	23.4	14.2					23.6	19.6
						% Officers', Directors' Owners' Comp/Sales	2.0	
							(10) 5.7	
							9.5	
880M	26042M	146057M	233399M	87140M		Net Sales ($)	711642M	412469M
923M	23291M	163570M	227378M	119229M		Total Assets ($)	719994M	560960M

M = $ thousand   MM = $ million
See Pages viii through xx for Explanation of Ratios and Data

Comparative Historical Data / Current Data Sorted by Sales

			Type of Statement						
35	27	32	Unqualified	9	10	3	4	4	2
5	8	5	Reviewed	1	3			1	
9	3	3	Compiled		1	1		1	
9	11	5	Tax Returns	4			1		
22	14	20	Other	7	4		4	2	3
4/1/16-3/31/17	4/1/17-3/31/18	4/1/18-3/31/19			39 (4/1-9/30/18)		26 (10/1/18-3/31/19)		
ALL	ALL	ALL		0-1MM	1-3MM	3-5MM	5-10MM	10-25MM	25MM & OVER
80	63	65	**NUMBER OF STATEMENTS**	21	18	4	9	8	5
%	%	%	**ASSETS**	%	%	%	%	%	%
24.1	22.1	28.6	Cash & Equivalents	37.4	32.0				
10.1	14.1	12.6	Trade Receivables (net)	.4	5.7				
2.5	.9	1.6	Inventory	.0	.0				
4.0	2.8	1.8	All Other Current	.4	.7				
40.6	39.9	44.7	Total Current	38.2	38.5				
53.8	49.7	48.0	Fixed Assets (net)	57.2	57.0				
1.1	1.5	.1	Intangibles (net)	.2	.0				
4.5	8.8	7.3	All Other Non-Current	4.7	4.5				
100.0	100.0	100.0	Total	100.0	100.0				
			LIABILITIES						
3.4	1.2	2.2	Notes Payable-Short Term	.1	.2				
3.4	3.8	2.7	Cur. Mat.-L.T.D.	2.3	3.4				
4.0	4.0	4.8	Trade Payables	1.6	2.3				
.0	.0	.1	Income Taxes Payable	.0	.0				
6.0	5.0	5.5	All Other Current	3.7	3.5				
16.8	14.0	15.3	Total Current	7.6	9.5				
26.1	27.4	25.3	Long-Term Debt	27.7	28.7				
.1	.3	.2	Deferred Taxes	.0	.0				
14.3	11.6	9.5	All Other Non-Current	1.0	3.2				
42.7	46.7	49.8	Net Worth	63.9	58.6				
100.0	100.0	100.0	Total Liabilities & Net Worth	100.0	100.0				
			INCOME DATA						
100.0	100.0	100.0	Net Sales	100.0	100.0				
			Gross Profit						
87.5	90.9	87.2	Operating Expenses	80.2	86.9				
12.5	9.1	12.8	Operating Profit	19.8	13.1				
2.4	3.3	1.0	All Other Expenses (net)	2.9	.5				
10.1	5.8	11.8	Profit Before Taxes	16.9	12.6				
			RATIOS						
7.6	9.4	15.7		34.1	12.1				
3.7	3.1	3.6	Current	6.5	4.9				
1.5	1.9	2.0		2.1	2.6				
7.4	7.2	15.7		34.1	12.1				
2.9	2.8	3.6	Quick	6.5	4.4				
1.3	1.7	1.8		2.1	2.5				
0 UND	0 UND	0 UND		0 UND	0 UND				
3 119.1	2 168.7	8 44.3	Sales/Receivables	0 UND	0 UND				
35 10.3	59 6.2	51 7.2		7 50.3	27 13.3				
			Cost of Sales/Inventory						
			Cost of Sales/Payables						
1.5	1.8	.9		.8	.9				
3.1	4.1	3.5	Sales/Working Capital	2.8	2.4				
10.2	10.6	7.1		4.7	5.9				
17.9	13.3	28.9		7.1	11.1				
(63) 3.4	(50) 4.0	(49) 6.2	EBIT/Interest	(13) 3.4	(15) 5.3				
.9	1.5	2.8		-.4	3.3				
			Net Profit + Depr., Dep., Amort./Cur. Mat. L/T/D						
.6	.3	.4		.4	.5				
1.1	1.3	.9	Fixed/Worth	.8	1.1				
2.1	2.0	1.6		1.5	1.9				
.3	.4	.3		.1	.1				
.9	1.0	1.0	Debt/Worth	.6	.5				
2.7	1.9	2.2		1.1	1.8				
17.6	24.3	20.9	% Profit Before Taxes/Tangible Net Worth	16.1	12.4				
(66) 7.3	(55) 7.3	(60) 9.9		6.6 (17) 8.0					
-.5	.9	4.6		3.4	4.4				
9.1	9.1	11.2	% Profit Before Taxes/Total Assets	9.4	7.9				
3.9	3.8	5.1		3.6	4.9				
-.1	.4	2.0		2.7	2.7				
2.9	13.8	6.7	Sales/Net Fixed Assets	1.4	2.1				
1.0	1.2	1.1		.7	.9				
.4	.4	.6		.4	.5				
1.0	1.6	1.6	Sales/Total Assets	.7	.8				
.6	.7	.6		.4	.5				
.3	.3	.3		.2	.3				
4.0	2.6	3.3	% Depr., Dep., Amort./Sales	16.1	7.0				
(55) 9.3	(48) 7.2	(47) 7.8		(11) 21.9	(13) 10.9				
15.9	17.8	16.1		31.6	18.0				
			% Officers', Directors' Owners' Comp/Sales						
1221153M	505316M	493518M	Net Sales ($)	8931M	31402M	14421M	64485M	134686M	239593M
1045080M	564267M	534391M	Total Assets ($)	35295M	65986M	27097M	57516M	188216M	160281M

M = $ thousand   MM = $ million
See Pages viii through xx for Explanation of Ratios and Data

Current Data Sorted by Assets   Comparative Historical Data

	0-500M	500M-2MM	2-10MM	10-50MM	50-100MM	100-250MM		4/1/14-3/31/15 ALL	4/1/15-3/31/16 ALL
Type of Statement									
Unqualified	2		10	12	8	9		118	81
Reviewed			1					1	2
Compiled	1	1							
Tax Returns									1
Other	2	3	3		1	2		12	15
		47 (4/1-9/30/18)		8 (10/1/18-3/31/19)					
NUMBER OF STATEMENTS	5	4	14	12	9	11		131	99
	%	%	%	%	%	%		%	%
ASSETS									
Cash & Equivalents			37.2	46.6		25.3		23.2	31.0
Trade Receivables (net)			10.1	14.0		5.8		9.7	10.2
Inventory			.0	.3		.0		.3	.4
All Other Current			.7	7.5		9.4		2.6	3.2
Total Current			48.0	68.4		40.5		35.9	44.7
Fixed Assets (net)			33.4	24.2		38.3		52.8	40.9
Intangibles (net)			1.8	.7		13.0		.4	3.2
All Other Non-Current			16.7	6.6		8.3		10.9	11.2
Total			100.0	100.0		100.0		100.0	100.0
LIABILITIES									
Notes Payable-Short Term			1.0	1.5		.0		.5	.5
Cur. Mat.-L.T.D.			1.5	.9		2.0		2.4	1.8
Trade Payables			2.3	6.3		3.2		3.4	4.5
Income Taxes Payable			.0	.0		.0		.0	.0
All Other Current			22.7	12.4		14.7		9.1	11.6
Total Current			27.5	21.2		19.9		15.4	18.4
Long-Term Debt			19.9	3.9		20.9		24.2	22.9
Deferred Taxes			.0	.0		1.7		.1	.1
All Other Non-Current			3.0	16.3		25.7		5.2	25.7
Net Worth			49.5	58.7		31.8		55.1	33.0
Total Liabilties & Net Worth			100.0	100.0		100.0		100.0	100.0
INCOME DATA									
Net Sales			100.0	100.0		100.0		100.0	100.0
Gross Profit									
Operating Expenses			90.3	92.7		88.6		96.3	94.5
Operating Profit			9.7	7.3		11.4		3.7	5.5
All Other Expenses (net)			.1	.3		4.4		.3	.2
Profit Before Taxes			9.6	6.9		7.0		3.4	5.3
RATIOS									
Current			14.7	7.0		7.3		5.1	4.5
			4.1	4.2		3.4		2.3	2.5
			.6	2.2		.4		1.3	1.4
Quick			14.7	6.4		7.3		5.0	4.4
			4.1	4.0		3.0		2.2	2.4
			.5	1.9		.3		1.2	1.2
Sales/Receivables			3 134.8	4 102.1		2 155.9		5 78.3	3 121.2
			12 31.5	36 10.0		10 35.2		16 22.7	14 25.2
			17 21.3	61 6.0		41 9.0		50 7.3	59 6.2
Cost of Sales/Inventory									
Cost of Sales/Payables									
Sales/Working Capital			1.7	1.7		1.4		3.0	2.8
			4.6	2.8		4.0		5.5	4.5
			-19.6	4.2		-3.5		17.1	12.8
EBIT/Interest						15.7		6.3	6.7
				(10) 2.1				(102) 1.9	(70) 2.7
						.6		.2	.8
Net Profit + Depr., Dep., Amort./Cur. Mat. L/T/D									
Fixed/Worth			.0	.0		.7		.6	.0
			.4	.2		2.2		1.0	1.1
			1.8	.9		-5.0		1.6	4.0
Debt/Worth			.0	.2		1.0		.3	.5
			.5	.5		2.4		.7	1.4
			8.1	1.5		-7.5		1.5	5.9
% Profit Before Taxes/Tangible Net Worth			28.1	26.9				8.3	15.0
			(12) 3.5	(11) 5.3				(125) 2.7	(82) 4.6
			-6.4	-.3				-2.7	-1.8
% Profit Before Taxes/Total Assets			19.4	22.6		5.5		4.5	5.6
			2.1	6.4		.3		1.4	2.0
			-4.0	.2		-2.0		-1.8	-.7
Sales/Net Fixed Assets			640.2	UND		9.5		4.5	43.4
			18.7	17.2		1.4		1.1	1.6
			.8	2.0		.6		.6	.8
Sales/Total Assets			2.6	1.9		1.1		1.2	1.9
			.7	1.5		.5		.7	.8
			.5	.7		.3		.4	.5
% Depr., Dep., Amort./Sales			.2					2.5	2.0
			(10) 1.9					(114) 4.1	(71) 3.6
			6.3					7.0	5.9
% Officers', Directors' Owners' Comp/Sales									
Net Sales ($)	3485M	5627M	170006M	347580M	370503M	1311206M		5142439M	4980128M
Total Assets ($)	1463M	3459M	72892M	304673M	624235M	1484370M		7416075M	5456810M

M = $ thousand   MM = $ million
See Pages viii through xx for Explanation of Ratios and Data

Comparative Historical Data   **Current Data Sorted by Sales**

			Type of Statement						
47	43	41	Unqualified	3	3	2	4	12	17
2	2	1	Reviewed		1				
1		2	Compiled	2					
			Tax Returns			2			
13	9	11	Other	3	2	2		1	3
4/1/16-3/31/17 ALL	4/1/17-3/31/18 ALL	4/1/18-3/31/19 ALL		47 (4/1-9/30/18)			8 (10/1/18-3/31/19)		
				0-1MM	1-3MM	3-5MM	5-10MM	10-25MM	25MM & OVER
63	54	55	**NUMBER OF STATEMENTS**	8	5	5	4	13	20
%	%	%	**ASSETS**	%	%	%	%	%	%
29.6	31.2	35.8	Cash & Equivalents					39.8	32.7
8.3	8.9	9.0	Trade Receivables (net)					12.9	11.2
.4	.1	.1	Inventory					.3	.1
5.1	5.9	6.7	All Other Current					6.1	8.9
43.4	46.1	51.6	Total Current					59.1	52.9
42.1	39.6	30.7	Fixed Assets (net)					22.7	33.9
5.0	2.7	4.7	Intangibles (net)					4.4	4.7
9.4	11.5	12.9	All Other Non-Current					13.7	8.5
100.0	100.0	100.0	Total					100.0	100.0
			LIABILITIES						
.4	.4	1.9	Notes Payable-Short Term					.0	1.3
1.5	2.3	1.2	Cur. Mat.-L.T.D.					1.5	1.7
4.5	4.3	4.1	Trade Payables					3.0	5.1
.0	.0	.0	Income Taxes Payable					.0	.0
10.5	8.0	12.9	All Other Current					7.7	15.7
16.9	15.0	20.2	Total Current					12.2	23.8
23.7	19.8	16.3	Long-Term Debt					8.6	16.0
.2	.4	.3	Deferred Taxes					.0	.9
22.5	23.0	15.0	All Other Non-Current					8.9	33.8
36.7	41.8	48.2	Net Worth					70.3	25.5
100.0	100.0	100.0	Total Liabilties & Net Worth					100.0	100.0
			INCOME DATA						
100.0	100.0	100.0	Net Sales					100.0	100.0
			Gross Profit						
95.0	96.6	89.6	Operating Expenses					91.4	91.7
5.0	3.4	10.4	Operating Profit					8.6	8.3
1.3	2.7	1.1	All Other Expenses (net)					2.3	1.6
3.6	.7	9.2	Profit Before Taxes					6.3	6.7
			RATIOS						
4.7	7.6	9.6	Current					6.9	6.5
2.8	3.1	5.0						3.3	3.4
1.5	1.9	1.3						2.4	1.6
4.3	5.8	7.3	Quick					6.3	5.6
2.6	2.6	3.3						3.3	2.9
1.4	1.5	1.0						2.0	.7
3 145.1	0 999.8	1 380.9	Sales/Receivables					4 101.9	2 154.5
19 19.2	12 30.0	13 27.6						19 19.7	18 20.4
47 7.7	41 9.0	35 10.5						46 8.0	49 7.5
			Cost of Sales/Inventory						
			Cost of Sales/Payables						
3.0	1.8	1.6	Sales/Working Capital					2.4	2.2
4.3	3.6	4.0						4.1	4.2
9.0	6.4	10.4						5.1	9.7
6.2	7.5	30.9	EBIT/Interest						37.3
(46) 2.2	(39) 3.6	(34) 7.0						(16)	5.6
.8	-.4	1.1							1.2
			Net Profit + Depr., Dep., Amort./Cur. Mat. L/T/D						
.6	.0	.0	Fixed/Worth					.0	.1
1.3	1.0	.7						.2	1.3
3.8	2.8	1.9						.8	NM
.6	.3	.2	Debt/Worth					.2	.9
1.2	1.0	.8						.4	2.4
7.6	3.6	3.6						1.1	NM
15.7	11.3	26.5	% Profit Before Taxes/Tangible Net Worth					26.4	18.9
(51) 3.8	(47) 1.4	(46) 5.1						5.3	(15) 4.9
.3	-3.8	.0						.8	.6
5.7	4.8	15.4	% Profit Before Taxes/Total Assets					16.8	6.8
1.7	.9	2.1						3.4	1.7
-.3	-1.8	-.1						.6	-.6
11.0	66.2	322.0	Sales/Net Fixed Assets					UND	66.7
1.5	1.9	5.3						35.8	3.7
.7	.7	.8						.8	.9
1.6	1.4	1.7	Sales/Total Assets					2.3	1.7
.7	.7	.9						1.2	.9
.4	.4	.4						.4	.5
2.2	1.6	1.0	% Depr., Dep., Amort./Sales						1.0
(51) 3.6	(42) 4.1	(33) 3.6						(13)	2.9
6.7	8.5	7.0							5.7
			% Officers', Directors' Owners' Comp/Sales						
2573676M	2373122M	2208407M	Net Sales ($)	3586M	10049M	17803M	30766M	243404M	1902799M
3335013M	3014500M	2491092M	Total Assets ($)	9920M	14467M	21058M	177470M	519658M	1748519M

© RMA 2019

M = $ thousand   MM = $ million
See Pages viii through xx for Explanation of Ratios and Data

Current Data Sorted by Assets | | | | | Comparative Historical Data

0-500M	500M-2MM	2-10MM	10-50MM	50-100MM	100-250MM	Type of Statement	4/1/14-3/31/15 ALL	4/1/15-3/31/16 ALL
	2	4	10	7	5	Unqualified	39	42
						Reviewed		
		1				Compiled	3	
						Tax Returns		1
3	2	6	2	2		Other	6	12
	36 (4/1-9/30/18)		8 (10/1/18-3/31/19)					
3	4	11	12	9	5	NUMBER OF STATEMENTS	48	55
%	%	%	%	%	%		%	%
		21.6	30.7			Cash & Equivalents	32.5	37.1
		13.1	13.3			Trade Receivables (net)	22.0	19.0
		.2	1.0			Inventory	1.6	.8
		14.1	1.7			All Other Current	3.4	3.2
		49.0	46.6			Total Current	59.5	59.9
		36.4	36.6			Fixed Assets (net)	28.9	25.6
		.1	3.8			Intangibles (net)	.7	1.1
		14.5	12.9			All Other Non-Current	10.8	13.4
		100.0	100.0			Total	100.0	100.0
						LIABILITIES		
		2.4	1.8			Notes Payable-Short Term	1.2	.9
		1.3	.9			Cur. Mat.-L.T.D.	1.4	1.2
		8.6	9.7			Trade Payables	11.1	7.9
		.1	.0			Income Taxes Payable	.5	.0
		17.7	9.8			All Other Current	15.1	17.8
		30.1	22.1			Total Current	29.3	27.9
		21.1	12.0			Long-Term Debt	8.9	11.0
		.0	.0			Deferred Taxes	.0	.0
		6.1	13.1			All Other Non-Current	3.4	7.2
		42.7	52.7			Net Worth	58.3	53.9
		100.0	100.0			Total Liabilities & Net Worth	100.0	100.0
						INCOME DATA		
		100.0	100.0			Net Sales	100.0	100.0
						Gross Profit		
		86.6	96.4			Operating Expenses	97.3	93.7
		13.4	3.6			Operating Profit	2.7	6.3
		4.6	-.6			All Other Expenses (net)	-1.5	1.3
		8.8	4.2			Profit Before Taxes	4.3	5.0
						RATIOS		
		5.1	5.1				5.2	5.3
		2.9	2.1			Current	2.7	2.7
		1.0	1.1				1.4	1.4
		5.1	5.1				4.9	4.9
		1.7	2.0			Quick	2.4	2.4
		.4	1.0				1.3	1.2
		1 272.3	16 23.0				10 37.1	14 26.6
		15 23.7	30 12.0			Sales/Receivables	43 8.4	33 10.9
		43 8.4	43 8.4				56 6.5	44 8.3
						Cost of Sales/Inventory		
						Cost of Sales/Payables		
		3.1	3.3				2.9	2.8
		6.6	10.9			Sales/Working Capital	5.4	5.9
		-999.8	98.2				18.8	25.6
							16.7	30.5
						EBIT/Interest	(24) 4.9	(31) 9.3
							-1.5	2.3
						Net Profit + Depr., Dep., Amort./Cur. Mat. L/T/D		
		.2	.2				.1	.1
		1.0	.7			Fixed/Worth	.4	.4
		1.5	2.1				.8	.9
		.3	.3				.2	.3
		1.0	.9			Debt/Worth	.5	.6
		6.3	2.3				1.9	3.0
			25.2				16.5	21.5
		(11) 16.6				% Profit Before Taxes/Tangible Net Worth	(54) 4.7	8.8
			1.5				-3.3	1.4
		9.3	12.8				9.5	11.9
		2.1	3.9			% Profit Before Taxes/Total Assets	3.0	2.3
		-.2	.3				-1.8	.0
		24.4	21.1				59.0	116.5
		3.5	3.8			Sales/Net Fixed Assets	7.1	5.8
		.8	2.4				2.1	2.8
		3.2	2.3				2.9	2.7
		1.3	1.6			Sales/Total Assets	1.7	1.6
		.5	.7				.8	.8
			1.1				.7	.5
		(10) 1.7				% Depr., Dep., Amort./Sales	(40) 2.2	(44) 1.6
			4.6				4.3	4.4
						% Officers', Directors' Owners' Comp/Sales		
2657M	14773M	140505M	500043M	799750M	1462204M	Net Sales ($)	2699987M	3548925M
357M	4526M	57106M	324878M	595407M	783968M	Total Assets ($)	1410293M	2552554M

© RMA 2019   M = $ thousand   MM = $ million
See Pages viii through xx for Explanation of Ratios and Data

Comparative Historical Data | | | | Current Data Sorted by Sales

40	37	28	Type of Statement	1	1	1	2	7	16
			Unqualified						
	1	1	Reviewed						
			Compiled		1				
			Tax Returns						
13	21	15	Other	3	2	2	1	2	5
4/1/16-3/31/17 ALL	4/1/17-3/31/18 ALL	4/1/18-3/31/19 ALL		0-1MM	36 (4/1-9/30/18) 1-3MM	3-5MM	8 (10/1/18-3/31/19) 5-10MM	10-25MM	25MM & OVER
53	60	44	**NUMBER OF STATEMENTS**	4	4	3	3	9	21
%	%	%	**ASSETS**	%	%	%	%	%	%
31.9	29.8	30.9	Cash & Equivalents						26.1
18.9	15.0	14.0	Trade Receivables (net)						17.1
.6	.5	.6	Inventory						.7
4.6	7.3	5.6	All Other Current						9.7
56.0	52.5	51.1	Total Current						53.7
27.3	30.2	32.6	Fixed Assets (net)						27.4
1.2	2.7	2.8	Intangibles (net)						4.6
15.5	14.6	13.5	All Other Non-Current						14.4
100.0	100.0	100.0	Total						100.0
			LIABILITIES						
.4	2.0	7.4	Notes Payable-Short Term						.9
.9	.8	.8	Cur. Mat.-L.T.D.						.7
8.2	8.0	10.3	Trade Payables						14.1
.0	.0	.0	Income Taxes Payable						.0
14.3	15.3	15.9	All Other Current						19.8
23.9	26.0	34.5	Total Current						35.5
12.1	9.7	13.9	Long-Term Debt						12.5
.0	.0	.1	Deferred Taxes						.0
12.3	9.8	7.3	All Other Non-Current						3.6
51.6	54.4	44.2	Net Worth						48.3
100.0	100.0	100.0	Total Liabilties & Net Worth						100.0
			INCOME DATA						
100.0	100.0	100.0	Net Sales						100.0
			Gross Profit						
96.7	95.6	96.3	Operating Expenses						97.7
3.3	4.4	3.7	Operating Profit						2.3
.5	.6	.8	All Other Expenses (net)						.3
2.7	3.8	2.9	Profit Before Taxes						2.1
			RATIOS						
5.4	6.4	5.1							3.1
3.1	2.3	2.4	Current						2.2
1.4	1.4	1.0							1.0
5.0	5.4	4.9							2.8
2.6	2.2	1.8	Quick						1.4
1.4	1.0	1.0							.9
12 · 31.7	6 · 58.6	6 · 61.9							9 · 42.5
33 · 10.9	29 · 12.5	29 · 12.7	Sales/Receivables						28 · 13.0
56 · 6.5	49 · 7.5	45 · 8.2							46 · 8.0
			Cost of Sales/Inventory						
			Cost of Sales/Payables						
2.9	3.0	3.1							4.7
5.3	5.3	8.8	Sales/Working Capital						10.1
13.6	20.4	171.5							594.8
27.1	21.9	9.6							9.6
(33) 5.2	(34) 6.4	(28) 2.2	EBIT/Interest						(16) 2.3
-.7	-1.1	-6.2							-2.3
			Net Profit + Depr., Dep., Amort./Cur. Mat. L/T/D						
.1	.1	.1							.1
.5	.5	.6	Fixed/Worth						.7
.8	.9	1.4							1.3
.2	.2	.3							.4
.5	.5	.8	Debt/Worth						.8
2.9	1.9	5.6							6.1
17.7	19.4	17.6							17.6
(49) 5.6	(54) 4.9	(38) 4.1	% Profit Before Taxes/Tangible Net Worth						(18) 1.7
-1.3	-1.2	-4.2							7.9
10.3	9.0	8.9							8.6
2.1	2.5	1.1	% Profit Before Taxes/Total Assets						.2
-.9	-1.2	-1.9							-3.3
88.6	139.5	44.1							84.6
5.9	4.6	4.5	Sales/Net Fixed Assets						11.0
2.7	1.7	1.7							2.8
2.8	3.0	3.4							3.4
1.7	1.5	1.6	Sales/Total Assets						1.8
.8	.7	.6							1.3
.7	.6	.7							.4
(45) 1.6	(49) 2.5	(34) 1.7	% Depr., Dep., Amort./Sales						(17) 1.6
4.0	4.8	5.2							5.1
			% Officers', Directors' Owners' Comp/Sales						
3307977M	3170420M	2919932M	Net Sales ($)	2734M	6671M	11515M	18819M	152412M	2727781M
2438295M	2113431M	1766242M	Total Assets ($)	5252M	7140M	11072M	23129M	420556M	1299093M

M = $ thousand   MM = $ million
See Pages viii through xx for Explanation of Ratios and Data

Current Data Sorted by Assets   Comparative Historical Data

						Type of Statement		
3	3	4	12	4	9	Unqualified	79	85
		1				Reviewed	3	
						Compiled	3	5
						Tax Returns	1	1
1	2	5	1	1	1	Other	1	
	33 (4/1-9/30/18)		14 (10/1/18-3/31/19)				20	22
							4/1/14-	4/1/15-
							3/31/15	3/31/16
0-500M	500M-2MM	2-10MM	10-50MM	50-100MM	100-250MM		ALL	ALL
4	5	10	13	5	10	NUMBER OF STATEMENTS	106	113
%	%	%	%	%	%	ASSETS	%	%
		33.3	28.2		16.5	Cash & Equivalents	18.8	21.2
		15.3	3.5		1.8	Trade Receivables (net)	6.9	4.6
		.2	.5		.3	Inventory	.3	.3
		7.1	4.1		2.9	All Other Current	2.2	1.6
		55.9	36.3		21.4	Total Current	28.2	27.6
		33.5	55.4		67.7	Fixed Assets (net)	63.5	61.7
		2.5	.2		.4	Intangibles (net)	.9	1.4
		8.0	8.0		10.6	All Other Non-Current	7.4	9.3
		100.0	100.0		100.0	Total	100.0	100.0
						LIABILITIES		
		2.5	.0		.0	Notes Payable-Short Term	1.3	.5
		.8	2.5		1.5	Cur. Mat.-L.T.D.	2.3	3.3
		3.7	2.3		.9	Trade Payables	2.9	3.0
		.0	.0		.0	Income Taxes Payable	.0	.0
		16.2	3.1		1.2	All Other Current	4.0	4.5
		23.1	7.9		3.6	Total Current	10.6	11.3
		27.0	21.0		31.5	Long-Term Debt	27.2	36.2
		.0	.0		.0	Deferred Taxes	.0	.0
		5.4	3.1		7.8	All Other Non-Current	2.2	5.2
		44.5	68.0		57.1	Net Worth	60.0	47.2
		100.0	100.0		100.0	Total Liabilities & Net Worth	100.0	100.0
						INCOME DATA		
		100.0	100.0		100.0	Net Sales	100.0	100.0
						Gross Profit		
		87.0	83.3		74.0	Operating Expenses	83.1	79.9
		13.0	16.7		26.0	Operating Profit	16.9	20.1
		2.4	3.0		8.1	All Other Expenses (net)	6.9	10.1
		10.6	13.7		17.9	Profit Before Taxes	10.0	10.0
						RATIOS		
		11.8	8.0		5.1		6.7	6.1
		4.9	4.1		3.9	Current	3.6	3.4
		1.2	3.4		2.9		1.7	1.4
		11.6	7.9		5.0		6.6	5.8
		4.8	3.7		3.3	Quick	3.3	2.9
		1.0	2.8		2.5		1.3	1.2
26	14.2	1 417.7		1 259.9			22 16.8	18 19.8
48	7.6	43 8.4		35 10.4		Sales/Receivables	38 9.6	33 10.9
83	4.4	50 7.3		57 6.4			51 7.1	49 7.4
						Cost of Sales/Inventory		
						Cost of Sales/Payables		
		1.1	.9		1.4		1.1	.9
		2.8	1.5		1.7	Sales/Working Capital	2.1	1.8
		12.2	2.0		2.4		7.3	13.3
			23.2				5.9	5.0
			(11) 13.6			EBIT/Interest	(82) 3.4	(87) 2.6
			2.5				1.0	1.1
						Net Profit + Depr., Dep., Amort./Cur. Mat. L/T/D		
		.0	.7		1.0		.8	.9
		.8	.9		1.2	Fixed/Worth	1.1	1.3
		UND	1.2		1.5		1.5	2.2
		.1	.2		.3		.3	.4
		1.2	.3		.7	Debt/Worth	.5	.9
		UND	.8		1.2		1.3	2.1
			6.7				9.9	8.6
			(12) 5.1			% Profit Before Taxes/Tangible Net Worth	(101) 4.2	(103) 2.7
			4.2				.2	-.2
		19.1	5.3		4.6		4.7	4.5
		3.3	3.4		2.8	% Profit Before Taxes/Total Assets	2.4	1.6
		-2.3	1.9		.1		.1	.0
		UND	.9		.3		.9	.8
		3.0	.6		.2	Sales/Net Fixed Assets	.3	.3
		.3	.2		.2		.2	.2
		1.3	.6		.2		.5	.4
		.5	.4		.1	Sales/Total Assets	.2	.2
		.2	.1		.1		.2	.1
			8.4				7.6	8.9
			(11) 15.0			% Depr., Dep., Amort./Sales	(90) 16.2	(97) 17.4
			24.4				22.2	24.3
						% Officers', Directors' Owners' Comp/Sales		
543M	3387M	33114M	139331M	88061M	253147M	Net Sales ($)	1769847M	1370472M
386M	5424M	41082M	353305M	357555M	1600890M	Total Assets ($)	5102744M	5730331M

© RMA 2019   M = $ thousand   MM = $ million
See Pages viii through xx for Explanation of Ratios and Data

Comparative Historical Data | Current Data Sorted by Sales

			Type of Statement						
37	40	35	Unqualified	8	3	1	10	8	5
1	1		Reviewed						
1	1	1	Compiled	1					
			Tax Returns						
11	12	11	Other	3	2	1	3		2
4/1/16-	4/1/17-	4/1/18-			33 (4/1-9/30/18)		14 (10/1/18-3/31/19)		
3/31/17	3/31/18	3/31/19							
ALL	ALL	ALL		0-1MM	1-3MM	3-5MM	5-10MM	10-25MM	25MM & OVER
50	54	47	NUMBER OF STATEMENTS	12	5	2	13	8	7
%	%	%	ASSETS	%	%	%	%	%	%
19.7	23.8	30.2	Cash & Equivalents	49.4			31.3		
6.2	5.2	7.0	Trade Receivables (net)	9.9			8.6		
.5	.3	.3	Inventory	.1			.4		
1.6	2.1	3.6	All Other Current	.9			3.5		
28.0	31.4	41.1	Total Current	60.3			43.8		
60.3	60.9	49.3	Fixed Assets (net)	25.4			49.9		
.8	2.5	.7	Intangibles (net)	.0			.4		
10.9	5.3	8.9	All Other Non-Current	14.3			5.9		
100.0	100.0	100.0	Total	100.0			100.0		
			LIABILITIES						
1.2	.4	12.9	Notes Payable-Short Term	49.2			.0		
1.9	2.3	1.5	Cur. Mat.-L.T.D.	.5			2.7		
3.0	3.8	12.0	Trade Payables	41.0			3.6		
.0	.0	.0	Income Taxes Payable	.0			.0		
2.2	2.7	5.2	All Other Current	5.5			2.2		
8.4	9.1	31.6	Total Current	96.2			8.5		
35.3	29.4	24.4	Long-Term Debt	18.6			29.9		
.0	.1	.0	Deferred Taxes	.0			.0		
5.3	4.9	4.8	All Other Non-Current	.0			7.0		
51.0	56.6	39.1	Net Worth	-14.8			54.6		
100.0	100.0	100.0	Total Liabilties & Net Worth	100.0			100.0		
			INCOME DATA						
100.0	100.0	100.0	Net Sales	100.0			100.0		
			Gross Profit						
83.2	82.5	83.0	Operating Expenses	87.1			85.5		
16.8	17.5	17.0	Operating Profit	12.9			14.5		
5.9	4.2	3.5	All Other Expenses (net)	-.6			7.1		
10.9	13.3	13.5	Profit Before Taxes	13.5			7.4		
			RATIOS						
7.7	6.5	7.0		20.5			8.0		
4.1	3.8	4.2	Current	5.2			5.4		
2.0	2.4	3.1		1.3			3.5		
6.8	6.4	7.0		20.1			7.9		
3.5	3.6	3.9	Quick	4.5			5.0		
1.7	2.2	2.5		1.2			2.9		

							Sales/Receivables							
23	15.6	23	15.8	7	50.0		0	UND			10	36.2		
36	10.1	36	10.0	34	10.6		23	15.8			34	10.6		
47	7.7	51	7.1	57	6.4		87	4.2			58	6.3		

			Cost of Sales/Inventory						

			Cost of Sales/Payables						

			Sales/Working Capital						
.9	1.0	.8		.5			.8		
1.9	1.6	1.6		1.3			1.3		
4.3	3.0	2.8		NM			2.8		

							EBIT/Interest							
	5.9		11.0		15.7							15.4		
(36)	2.7	(42)	5.2	(36)	6.6					(11)		2.5		
	1.5		1.6		1.7							-1.5		

			Net Profit + Depr., Dep., Amort./Cur. Mat. L/T/D						

			Fixed/Worth						
.8	.7	.2		.0			.4		
1.1	1.2	1.0		.2			1.1		
1.9	1.9	1.4		1.9			1.6		

			Debt/Worth						
.3	.3	.2		.1			.2		
.7	.6	.5		.4			.8		
2.4	1.7	1.3		UND			1.3		

							% Profit Before Taxes/Tangible Net Worth							
	7.7		11.7		13.2			50.9				12.2		
(46)	5.1	(49)	4.9	(41)	5.5		(10)	8.9		(11)		5.3		
	1.2		2.3		2.1			-4.8				1.0		

			% Profit Before Taxes/Total Assets						
4.9	5.8	7.4		17.8			6.6		
2.1	3.1	3.8		5.7			2.7		
.7	.9	.6		-1.1			-.4		

			Sales/Net Fixed Assets						
.8	1.7	198.0		UND			486.5		
.3	.3	.5		106.5			.6		
.2	.2	.2		.5			.2		

			Sales/Total Assets						
.4	.6	.6		1.0			1.0		
.2	.2	.2		.4			.4		
.1	.1	.2		.2			.1		

							% Depr., Dep., Amort./Sales							
	6.2		9.6		7.0									
(42)	16.8	(45)	16.6	(32)	15.7									
	27.2		26.6		22.0									

			% Officers', Directors' Owners' Comp/Sales						

							Net Sales ($) / Total Assets ($)							
564011M	767938M	517583M	Net Sales ($)	5166M	10516M	6371M	92181M	142055M	261294M
2521270M	2915497M	2358642M	Total Assets ($)	19784M	40920M	30341M	359453M	1094833M	813311M

M = $ thousand   MM = $ million
See Pages viii through xx for Explanation of Ratios and Data

Current Data Sorted by Assets

Comparative Historical Data

						Type of Statement		
	1	16	21	7	4	Unqualified	81	79
		1				Reviewed	1	2
		1				Compiled	1	3
						Tax Returns		2
4	6	7	13	1	2	Other	29	36
	64 (4/1-9/30/18)		20 (10/1/18-3/31/19)				4/1/14-3/31/15	4/1/15-3/31/16
0-500M	500M-2MM	2-10MM	10-50MM	50-100MM	100-250MM		ALL	ALL
4	8	24	34	8	6	NUMBER OF STATEMENTS	112	122
%	%	%	%	%	%	ASSETS	%	%
		20.3	17.6			Cash & Equivalents	16.1	17.8
		4.3	1.6			Trade Receivables (net)	3.8	5.1
		1.9	1.5			Inventory	1.0	2.6
		3.9	2.2			All Other Current	2.7	2.6
		30.4	22.9			Total Current	23.5	28.1
		50.8	55.4			Fixed Assets (net)	55.2	47.8
		2.6	.5			Intangibles (net)	.7	.7
		16.1	21.2			All Other Non-Current	20.6	23.5
		100.0	100.0			Total	100.0	100.0
						LIABILITIES		
		1.2	1.0			Notes Payable-Short Term	1.6	1.9
		1.5	2.6			Cur. Mat.-L.T.D.	2.3	2.4
		3.4	1.2			Trade Payables	1.9	1.9
		.0	.1			Income Taxes Payable	.0	.0
		4.7	5.2			All Other Current	4.8	5.7
		10.7	10.1			Total Current	10.7	11.9
		20.2	23.5			Long-Term Debt	24.4	23.8
		.0	.0			Deferred Taxes	.0	.0
		7.7	7.0			All Other Non-Current	4.4	5.4
		61.4	59.4			Net Worth	60.5	58.9
		100.0	100.0			Total Liabilties & Net Worth	100.0	100.0
						INCOME DATA		
		100.0	100.0			Net Sales	100.0	100.0
						Gross Profit		
		91.8	93.8			Operating Expenses	93.7	89.4
		8.2	6.2			Operating Profit	6.3	10.6
		6.1	1.2			All Other Expenses (net)	3.1	5.0
		2.1	4.9			Profit Before Taxes	3.2	5.7
						RATIOS		
		7.3	7.3				7.6	8.4
		3.1	3.3			Current	3.4	3.6
		1.6	1.4				1.4	1.4
		7.2	6.3				7.1	7.1
		1.9	3.2			Quick	2.6	2.9
		1.0	.8				1.1	1.1
	3	107.2	2 174.5				2 236.9	1 261.0
	9	39.8	13 27.7			Sales/Receivables	7 52.7	8 43.4
	29	12.7	26 14.3				27 13.4	27 13.5
						Cost of Sales/Inventory		
						Cost of Sales/Payables		
		1.4	1.0				1.5	1.2
		4.3	2.5			Sales/Working Capital	4.4	3.4
		11.4	21.9				13.9	14.1
		9.5	4.3				5.4	5.9
	(15)	2.3	(25) 1.5			EBIT/Interest	(81) 1.3	(82) 2.1
		.0	-1.4				-1.6	-1.2
						Net Profit + Depr., Dep., Amort./Cur. Mat. L/T/D		
		.3	.6				.4	.2
		.8	.9			Fixed/Worth	.9	.8
		4.2	1.5				1.4	1.3
		.1	.2				.2	.2
		.4	.8			Debt/Worth	.5	.5
		5.3	1.5				1.3	1.6
		13.5	4.0				7.1	7.1
	(23)	3.5	.7			% Profit Before Taxes/Tangible Net Worth	(108) .8	(119) .9
		-1.7	-4.5				-3.1	-2.9
		7.0	2.6				3.5	3.9
		1.3	.4			% Profit Before Taxes/Total Assets	.5	.6
		-1.3	-2.3				-2.2	-1.5
		9.3	1.6				2.0	2.9
		.9	.6			Sales/Net Fixed Assets	.7	.9
		.3	.3				.4	.4
		.8	.6				.7	.7
		.5	.3			Sales/Total Assets	.3	.4
		.2	.2				.2	.2
		.5	3.9				3.1	2.9
	(22)	6.4	(28) 9.2			% Depr., Dep., Amort./Sales	(98) 8.7	(101) 6.7
		27.4	14.4				17.0	13.4
						% Officers', Directors' Owners' Comp/Sales		
5465M	3525M	92340M	379465M	218676M	285841M	Net Sales ($)	1816022M	1908267M
671M	10338M	138795M	858322M	601141M	1032338M	Total Assets ($)	4543874M	4846705M

M = $ thousand   MM = $ million
See Pages viii through xx for Explanation of Ratios and Data

Comparative Historical Data / Current Data Sorted by Sales

Hist 1	Hist 2	Hist 3	Type of Statement	0-1MM	1-3MM	3-5MM	5-10MM	10-25MM	25MM & OVER
72	66	49		4	5	8	13	9	10
			Unqualified						
			Reviewed						
2	1	1	Compiled	1					
1	2	1	Tax Returns	1					
24	31	33	Other	11	8	2	4	3	5
4/1/16-3/31/17 ALL	4/1/17-3/31/18 ALL	4/1/18-3/31/19 ALL			64 (4/1-9/30/18)			20 (10/1/18-3/31/19)	
99	100	84	**NUMBER OF STATEMENTS**	17	13	10	17	12	15
%	%	%	**ASSETS**	%	%	%	%	%	%
18.7	17.9	21.0	Cash & Equivalents	30.0	14.2	19.4	22.0	19.7	17.6
4.4	3.1	2.3	Trade Receivables (net)	1.2	.8	4.0	3.7	2.5	1.9
1.7	1.0	1.9	Inventory	3.4	2.6	3.6	.6	.3	1.1
3.4	4.5	2.9	All Other Current	4.1	2.9	4.3	2.9	1.7	1.7
28.2	26.5	28.1	Total Current	38.7	20.5	31.2	29.2	24.2	22.3
51.0	49.8	51.2	Fixed Assets (net)	56.6	59.1	52.1	40.3	43.4	56.4
1.4	1.0	1.1	Intangibles (net)	.2	.4	3.0	2.1	1.4	.2
19.4	22.7	19.6	All Other Non-Current	4.5	20.0	13.7	28.4	31.0	21.1
100.0	100.0	100.0	Total	100.0	100.0	100.0	100.0	100.0	100.0
			LIABILITIES						
2.2	1.7	1.3	Notes Payable-Short Term	3.7	.9	.3	1.9	.1	.1
2.5	2.0	3.1	Cur. Mat.-L.T.D.	4.6	2.6	3.4	3.0	.6	3.4
1.7	1.5	2.1	Trade Payables	3.6	.8	1.0	2.6	1.6	2.0
.0	.0	.0	Income Taxes Payable	.0	.0	.0	.0	.1	.1
5.7	4.8	5.0	All Other Current	6.6	3.4	5.4	4.4	7.1	3.5
12.1	10.0	11.6	Total Current	18.6	7.7	10.1	11.9	9.5	9.2
32.7	25.2	23.1	Long-Term Debt	30.1	38.7	25.0	15.9	13.5	16.0
.0	.0	.0	Deferred Taxes	.0	.0	.0	.0	.0	.0
10.1	8.1	9.4	All Other Non-Current	13.1	6.2	4.3	5.8	11.4	13.8
45.1	56.7	56.0	Net Worth	38.2	47.4	60.6	66.4	65.6	61.0
100.0	100.0	100.0	Total Liabilities & Net Worth	100.0	100.0	100.0	100.0	100.0	100.0
			INCOME DATA						
100.0	100.0	100.0	Net Sales	100.0	100.0	100.0	100.0	100.0	100.0
			Gross Profit						
89.9	91.7	91.5	Operating Expenses	85.4	78.9	89.6	98.0	94.9	100.2
10.1	8.3	8.5	Operating Profit	14.6	21.1	10.4	2.0	5.1	-.2
6.3	4.8	3.8	All Other Expenses (net)	11.5	4.3	1.6	1.5	.6	1.2
3.8	3.5	4.8	Profit Before Taxes	3.1	16.8	8.8	.5	4.4	-1.4
			RATIOS						
5.6	7.3	7.3	Current	14.9	10.7	4.1	10.0	7.6	5.8
3.0	3.1	3.4		4.1	3.5	2.9	6.8	3.7	3.5
1.4	1.3	1.3		1.1	1.6	1.0	1.2	1.5	1.0
5.3	5.8	6.7	Quick	14.9	9.1	3.7	8.7	7.4	5.3
2.5	2.6	3.1		3.4	3.5	1.7	4.6	3.7	3.2
1.1	1.0	.9		.6	.6	.9	1.0	1.0	.8
1 421.5	2 232.4	2 165.2	Sales/Receivables	0 UND	1 439.4	1 285.2	2 157.3	4 95.3	3 125.3
9 42.5	7 51.1	10 36.3		2 150.5	18 20.5	8 45.8	14 26.9	14 26.7	9 42.7
24 15.3	23 16.2	27 13.6		32 11.3	37 9.9	33 11.1	49 7.5	18 20.4	18 19.9
			Cost of Sales/Inventory						
			Cost of Sales/Payables						
1.6	1.5	1.4	Sales/Working Capital	1.0	.8	1.6	1.8	2.3	5.2
3.8	3.8	3.5		3.4	1.3	2.9	3.3	6.1	9.3
11.8	24.2	23.7		NM	3.4	NM	18.1	18.6	163.5
6.4	10.2	4.0	EBIT/Interest		3.3		3.6		2.5
(71) 1.8	(74) 1.6	(58) 1.6		(10) 2.5		(13) 1.8		(13) -.7	
-1.1	-.7	-.6			.9		.8		-12.9
			Net Profit + Depr., Dep., Amort./Cur. Mat. L/T/D						
.5	.3	.4	Fixed/Worth	.5	.9	.2	.2	.2	.6
1.0	.8	.9		1.2	1.1	1.2	.6	.7	1.0
2.3	1.9	2.0		NM	2.7	2.0	.9	1.1	2.3
.3	.3	.2	Debt/Worth	.2	.3	.2	.1	.2	.2
.8	.6	.6		1.4	1.6	.7	.4	.4	.6
3.1	2.2	2.6		-31.2	6.8	2.1	1.1	1.0	2.8
8.9	10.2	6.8	% Profit Before Taxes/Tangible Net Worth	6.6	9.3	22.5	4.7	11.7	3.5
(85) 2.5	(96) 1.1	(79) .6		(12) -2.3	2.4	6.6	.5	1.7	-2.8
-2.6	-2.2	-2.8		-6.4	-.2	-2.5	-.9	-1.4	-8.9
4.4	4.4	3.4	% Profit Before Taxes/Total Assets	3.6	4.9	8.8	2.0	3.7	1.1
1.3	.7	.4		-1.0	2.4	1.4	.3	1.4	-2.3
-1.5	-1.1	-2.2		-2.7	.0	-1.8	-.2	-1.3	-3.5
6.5	3.7	2.2	Sales/Net Fixed Assets	7.7	.6	17.6	2.0	9.3	2.1
.7	.9	.8		.4	.2	.8	.9	1.9	1.3
.4	.4	.3		.2	.2	.3	.4	.4	.5
.7	.7	.6	Sales/Total Assets	.7	.3	.6	.8	1.0	1.2
.4	.4	.4		.3	.2	.4	.3	.4	.6
.2	.2	.2		.1	.1	.3	.2	.3	.3
2.0	2.2	3.4	% Depr., Dep., Amort./Sales	11.7			1.3	1.4	3.4
(88) 7.4	(89) 7.0	(71) 7.8		(12) 24.3			(16) 5.9	(10) 6.6	6.1
18.3	14.1	16.5		31.9			10.2	10.2	11.1
	1.6		% Officers', Directors' Owners' Comp/Sales						
	(10) 6.3								
	20.5								
1451460M	1651795M	985312M	Net Sales ($)	7592M	25414M	40966M	117556M	156325M	637459M
3325197M	3801076M	2641605M	Total Assets ($)	33198M	183338M	113397M	505180M	338848M	1467644M

© RMA 2019

M = $ thousand   MM = $ million
See Pages viii through xx for Explanation of Ratios and Data

Current Data Sorted by Assets							Comparative Historical Data	
						Type of Statement		
	3	4	15	2	5	Unqualified	50	44
		1				Reviewed	1	2
		1	1			Compiled		
						Tax Returns	1	1
	1	1	7	2	2	Other	14	13
	27 (4/1-9/30/18)		18 (10/1/18-3/31/19)				**4/1/14-3/31/15 ALL**	**4/1/15-3/31/16 ALL**
0-500M	**500M-2MM**	**2-10MM**	**10-50MM**	**50-100MM**	**100-250MM**			
	4	7	23	4	7	**NUMBER OF STATEMENTS**	66	60
%	%	%	%	%	%	**ASSETS**	%	%
DATA NOT AVAILABLE			26.5			Cash & Equivalents	24.0	23.2
			3.3			Trade Receivables (net)	9.9	11.7
			.3			Inventory	1.6	2.4
			6.6			All Other Current	3.6	4.1
			36.6			Total Current	39.2	41.3
			32.9			Fixed Assets (net)	40.1	37.6
			1.2			Intangibles (net)	2.0	1.4
			29.3			All Other Non-Current	18.6	19.6
			100.0			Total	100.0	100.0
						LIABILITIES		
			.1			Notes Payable-Short Term	4.1	2.6
			1.5			Cur. Mat.-L.T.D.	2.5	2.9
			2.2			Trade Payables	3.8	5.0
			.0			Income Taxes Payable	.0	.0
			4.1			All Other Current	7.6	8.8
			7.9			Total Current	18.0	19.3
			25.7			Long-Term Debt	34.0	44.8
			.0			Deferred Taxes	.0	.0
			9.7			All Other Non-Current	6.3	7.4
			56.7			Net Worth	41.6	28.5
			100.0			Total Liabilties & Net Worth	100.0	100.0
						INCOME DATA		
			100.0			Net Sales	100.0	100.0
						Gross Profit		
			78.3			Operating Expenses	71.5	72.2
			21.7			Operating Profit	28.5	27.8
			9.0			All Other Expenses (net)	13.2	13.2
			12.7			Profit Before Taxes	15.3	14.6
						RATIOS		
			7.3				5.4	6.0
			2.8			Current	2.4	2.0
			1.4				1.2	1.0
			6.4				4.8	4.5
			2.7			Quick	2.0	1.8
			.9				.9	.8
			0 UND				**0** UND	**0** UND
			1 501.8			Sales/Receivables	**16** 23.0	**20** 18.4
			31 11.8				**60** 6.1	**81** 4.5
						Cost of Sales/Inventory		
						Cost of Sales/Payables		
			.8				1.1	.9
			2.4			Sales/Working Capital	3.2	2.5
			14.7				12.3	-40.9
			35.2				11.1	7.8
			(12) 3.2			EBIT/Interest	(37) 5.9	(34) 3.5
			-1.4				1.6	.8
						Net Profit + Depr., Dep., Amort./Cur. Mat. L/T/D		
			.0				.1	.1
			.3			Fixed/Worth	.8	.9
			1.4				1.4	2.2
			.2				.4	.3
			.6			Debt/Worth	.9	1.6
			1.7				3.5	6.8
			16.1				18.5	13.9
			(22) 3.9			% Profit Before Taxes/Tangible Net Worth	(59) 4.6	(53) 4.6
			.3				-.7	-4.0
			8.0				10.1	7.2
			2.1			% Profit Before Taxes/Total Assets	2.1	1.6
			.0				-.5	-1.2
			67.1				55.5	62.8
			2.2			Sales/Net Fixed Assets	1.3	.9
			.4				.3	.3
			.7				.5	.7
			.3			Sales/Total Assets	.3	.3
			.1				.1	.1
			.6				.9	.9
			(17) 2.8			% Depr., Dep., Amort./Sales	(48) 3.9	(46) 4.3
			14.7				15.2	15.6
						% Officers', Directors' Owners' Comp/Sales		
	6396M	**19269M**	**214347M**	**41498M**	**137681M**	Net Sales ($)	**601056M**	**635469M**
	4529M	**37076M**	**496769M**	**236241M**	**1124460M**	Total Assets ($)	**2533778M**	**2614733M**

M = $ thousand MM = $ million

See Pages viii through xx for Explanation of Ratios and Data

Comparative Historical Data

Current Data Sorted by Sales

			Type of Statement						
44	44	29	Unqualified	2	8		8	8	3
1	1	1	Reviewed			1			
4	1	2	Compiled		1				1
2			Tax Returns						
17	16	13	Other		4	3	3	3	
4/1/16-	4/1/17-	4/1/18-			27 (4/1-9/30/18)		18 (10/1/18-3/31/19)		
3/31/17	3/31/18	3/31/19							
ALL	ALL	ALL		0-1MM	1-3MM	3-5MM	5-10MM	10-25MM	25MM & OVER
68	62	45	**NUMBER OF STATEMENTS**	2	13	4	11	11	4
%	%	%	**ASSETS**	%	%	%	%	%	%
23.3	19.8	25.5	Cash & Equivalents		24.3		19.0	33.6	
5.5	10.0	5.4	Trade Receivables (net)		8.1		4.1	5.7	
2.9	.4	.2	Inventory		.0		.0	.0	
4.7	4.0	6.1	All Other Current		7.7		3.2	9.4	
36.5	34.2	37.3	Total Current		40.1		26.4	48.8	
45.8	42.4	33.6	Fixed Assets (net)		34.4		42.5	21.0	
1.8	4.1	.8	Intangibles (net)		.7		1.3	.3	
15.9	19.3	28.4	All Other Non-Current		24.8		29.9	30.0	
100.0	100.0	100.0	Total		100.0		100.0	100.0	
			LIABILITIES						
3.3	2.3	4.8	Notes Payable-Short Term		9.5		.5	7.2	
2.9	2.6	2.1	Cur. Mat.-L.T.D.		3.5		1.5	.7	
3.3	4.9	3.1	Trade Payables		5.2		1.5	2.2	
.0	.0	.0	Income Taxes Payable		.0		.0	.0	
6.6	9.3	5.8	All Other Current		8.8		3.0	4.0	
16.1	19.1	15.8	Total Current		27.0		6.5	14.1	
58.7	43.9	29.4	Long-Term Debt		39.5		31.4	21.7	
.0	.0	.0	Deferred Taxes		.0		.0	.0	
4.4	11.9	14.6	All Other Non-Current		9.8		29.2	10.2	
20.8	25.0	40.2	Net Worth		23.7		32.9	54.0	
100.0	100.0	100.0	Total Liabilities & Net Worth		100.0		100.0	100.0	
			INCOME DATA						
100.0	100.0	100.0	Net Sales		100.0		100.0	100.0	
			Gross Profit						
78.5	81.2	82.0	Operating Expenses		82.2		88.5	69.8	
21.5	18.8	18.0	Operating Profit		17.8		11.5	30.2	
9.0	7.1	7.0	All Other Expenses (net)		11.2		.4	10.8	
12.5	11.7	11.0	Profit Before Taxes		6.6		11.1	19.4	
			RATIOS						
5.4	5.4	5.7			3.0		6.5	7.3	
2.3	2.1	2.1	Current		1.6		2.5	5.5	
.7	1.1	1.3			.9		1.7	1.3	
5.2	4.8	5.3			2.8		6.4	7.0	
1.8	1.7	2.0	Quick		1.4		2.5	5.2	
.6	.8	.9			.8		1.6	.9	
0 UND	0 UND	0 UND		0 UND		0 UND	0 UND		
3 111.1	17 21.2	16 22.4	Sales/Receivables	7 54.4		31 11.7	24 14.9		
42 8.6	51 7.1	51 7.2		83 4.4		44 8.3	55 6.6		
			Cost of Sales/Inventory						
			Cost of Sales/Payables						
.9	1.4	.9			1.0		.8	.5	
2.5	2.7	2.8	Sales/Working Capital		3.8		2.8	1.4	
-16.9	101.0	17.6			NM		14.7	2.6	
7.5	18.1	7.3							
(29) 2.1	(26) 5.2	(24) 3.2	EBIT/Interest						
.3	-1.1	1.0							
			Net Profit + Depr., Dep., Amort./Cur. Mat. L/T/D						
.0	.0	.0			.0		.1	.0	
1.1	1.0	.7	Fixed/Worth		.8		.9	.7	
11.6	6.1	1.7			-1.6		3.4	1.1	
.4	.4	.4			.6		.2	.2	
1.7	1.8	1.1	Debt/Worth		1.4		1.1	1.0	
108.4	-183.3	3.8			-6.1		21.2	2.3	
16.4	12.4	15.1					11.8	16.1	
(52) 3.3	(46) 4.4	(40) 5.3	% Profit Before Taxes/Tangible Net Worth			(10)	5.3	9.0	
-.5	-3.0	.5					1.4	-.1	
7.1	4.6	7.8			7.8		4.3	12.5	
1.3	1.3	2.3	% Profit Before Taxes/Total Assets		.9		2.1	2.9	
-.3	-1.7	-.1			-.2		-.7	.0	
31.5	65.7	39.4			40.9		6.3	85.8	
.6	1.3	1.7	Sales/Net Fixed Assets		1.0		.8	1.9	
.2	.2	.4			.4		.3	.6	
.5	.8	.7			.7		.4	.8	
.2	.3	.2	Sales/Total Assets		.2		.2	.2	
.1	.1	.1			.1		.1	.1	
1.6	.6	.9			.3				
(52) 8.7	(51) 3.8	(35) 4.0	% Depr., Dep., Amort./Sales		(11) 1.3				
37.0	31.5	13.2			13.2				
			% Officers', Directors' Owners' Comp/Sales						
456291M	559441M	419191M	Net Sales ($)	1455M	25717M	15916M	75000M	174337M	126766M
2027105M	2229036M	1899075M	Total Assets ($)	7884M	158629M	54218M	411324M	898422M	368598M

M = $ thousand   MM = $ million
See Pages viii through xx for Explanation of Ratios and Data

Current Data Sorted by Assets | Comparative Historical Data

	0-500M	500M-2MM	2-10MM	10-50MM	50-100MM	100-250MM		4/1/14-3/31/15 ALL	4/1/15-3/31/16 ALL
Type of Statement									
Unqualified		3	7	22	2	6		71	69
Reviewed			1	1				2	1
Compiled								3	2
Tax Returns								1	1
Other	2	3	4	3	3	4		24	22
		48 (4/1-9/30/18)		13 (10/1/18-3/31/19)					
NUMBER OF STATEMENTS	2	6	12	26	5	10		101	95
	%	%	%	%	%	%		%	%
ASSETS									
Cash & Equivalents			17.1	36.7		10.7		23.1	26.1
Trade Receivables (net)			4.7	4.9		2.6		7.3	8.5
Inventory			.1	.7		.0		1.1	1.0
All Other Current			10.3	3.3		4.3		5.7	4.5
Total Current			32.1	45.8		17.6		37.1	40.0
Fixed Assets (net)			48.4	29.2		53.2		45.5	36.7
Intangibles (net)			.0	.5		.0		.5	1.6
All Other Non-Current			19.5	24.5		29.1		16.9	21.7
Total			100.0	100.0		100.0		100.0	100.0
LIABILITIES									
Notes Payable-Short Term			.2	1.2		.0		1.5	1.5
Cur. Mat.-L.T.D.			2.6	2.3		2.9		2.3	3.0
Trade Payables			1.7	4.6		2.5		3.5	4.8
Income Taxes Payable			.0	.0		.0		.0	.0
All Other Current			3.4	4.6		9.6		5.4	8.8
Total Current			7.9	12.7		14.9		12.8	18.0
Long-Term Debt			21.3	21.9		32.9		36.1	33.9
Deferred Taxes			.0	.0		.0		.0	.0
All Other Non-Current			4.9	8.2		8.4		6.3	7.1
Net Worth			65.8	57.2		43.8		44.8	41.0
Total Liabilties & Net Worth			100.0	100.0		100.0		100.0	100.0
INCOME DATA									
Net Sales			100.0	100.0		100.0		100.0	100.0
Gross Profit									
Operating Expenses			101.4	83.6		69.1		81.7	81.5
Operating Profit			-1.4	16.4		30.9		18.3	18.5
All Other Expenses (net)			1.4	6.3		11.5		6.9	7.9
Profit Before Taxes			-2.7	10.0		19.5		11.5	10.6
RATIOS									
Current			12.7	5.3		2.5		7.0	5.0
			6.4	3.2		1.1		2.7	2.1
			2.5	2.0		.3		1.6	1.3
Quick			10.0	4.3		2.1		5.1	3.9
			4.6	2.8		.7		2.1	2.0
			1.8	1.8		.2		1.1	.9
Sales/Receivables			0 UND	0 UND		4 96.5		1 278.4	2 240.8
			9 38.7	23 16.0		14 26.7		16 22.8	22 16.3
			76 4.8	46 8.0		47 7.8		44 8.3	42 8.6
Cost of Sales/Inventory									
Cost of Sales/Payables									
Sales/Working Capital			.7	.7		1.2		1.0	1.3
			1.1	1.2		NM		2.7	3.0
			3.7	2.7		-4.2		10.8	14.5
EBIT/Interest				10.4				6.6	9.6
				(17) 2.1				(61) 2.3	(61) 2.8
				1.1				.2	1.0
Net Profit + Depr., Dep., Amort./Cur. Mat. L/T/D									
Fixed/Worth			.3	.0		.1		.2	.1
			.9	.3		1.2		.9	1.0
			1.1	1.3		1.5		1.9	1.6
Debt/Worth			.2	.4		.7		.4	.5
			.6	.6		1.1		1.0	1.2
			1.2	1.3		4.5		2.2	3.1
% Profit Before Taxes/Tangible Net Worth			4.4	7.9		36.8		11.6	23.6
			2.3	2.5		4.4		(96) 3.7	(86) 5.0
			-3.6	.3		-.2		.4	-1.6
% Profit Before Taxes/Total Assets			2.9	3.7		20.4		5.7	7.4
			1.3	1.4		.9		1.9	1.2
			-2.1	.1		-.2		-.2	-.6
Sales/Net Fixed Assets			4.5	302.5		1.5		15.2	44.0
			.9	8.8		.4		.8	1.4
			.1	.3		.1		.3	.3
Sales/Total Assets			.9	.5		.5		.9	.9
			.2	.3		.1		.3	.3
			.1	.2		.1		.1	.1
% Depr., Dep., Amort./Sales			2.4	.6				1.2	.6
			(11) 11.6	(20) 5.5				(82) 6.6	(79) 3.4
			26.2	11.6				16.9	12.9
% Officers', Directors' Owners' Comp/Sales									
Net Sales ($)	2111M	12265M	27331M	254618M	1325898M	882670M		1179864M	1487755M
Total Assets ($)	179M	5855M	68097M	575229M	345088M	1588741M		2971785M	3587985M

M = $ thousand   MM = $ million
See Pages viii through xx for Explanation of Ratios and Data

Comparative Historical Data — Current Data Sorted by Sales

59	50	40	Type of Statement	4	7	7	8	8	6
			Unqualified						
			Reviewed						
1		2	Compiled	1		1			
			Tax Returns						
27	21	19	Other	6	4		3	1	5
4/1/16-3/31/17 ALL	4/1/17-3/31/18 ALL	4/1/18-3/31/19 ALL		0-1MM	1-3MM (48 4/1-9/30/18)	3-5MM	5-10MM (13 10/1/18-3/31/19)	10-25MM	25MM & OVER
87	71	61	NUMBER OF STATEMENTS	11	11	8	11	9	11
%	%	%	ASSETS	%	%	%	%	%	%
23.5	25.4	31.3	Cash & Equivalents	22.0	29.1		28.3		37.9
7.1	7.1	3.6	Trade Receivables (net)	1.0	3.1		4.1		6.3
1.2	.1	.3	Inventory	.0	.0		.1		1.7
5.2	5.5	8.2	All Other Current	6.0	9.3		6.6		19.2
37.0	38.0	43.5	Total Current	29.0	41.4		39.0		65.1
40.3	37.0	35.4	Fixed Assets (net)	47.8	25.2		40.0		27.5
.7	.9	.2	Intangibles (net)	.0	.0		.3		.1
22.0	24.0	20.9	All Other Non-Current	23.2	33.4		20.7		7.4
100.0	100.0	100.0	Total	100.0	100.0		100.0		100.0
			LIABILITIES						
1.7	5.7	1.0	Notes Payable-Short Term	.3	2.5		.3		.0
2.4	2.8	2.4	Cur. Mat.-L.T.D.	2.3	3.3		3.0		2.0
3.3	3.4	3.8	Trade Payables	.5	5.0		5.5		6.5
.0	.0	.0	Income Taxes Payable	.0	.0		.0		.2
7.4	4.6	6.7	All Other Current	1.1	2.5		4.8		21.0
14.8	16.4	13.9	Total Current	4.2	13.3		13.6		29.8
25.6	27.2	24.2	Long-Term Debt	25.9	20.1		23.2		26.2
.0	.1	.0	Deferred Taxes	.0	.0		.0		.0
9.4	7.2	6.3	All Other Non-Current	1.8	3.6		3.2		6.8
50.2	49.2	55.6	Net Worth	68.1	63.1		59.9		37.2
100.0	100.0	100.0	Total Liabilties & Net Worth	100.0	100.0		100.0		100.0
			INCOME DATA						
100.0	100.0	100.0	Net Sales	100.0	100.0		100.0		100.0
			Gross Profit						
87.9	88.5	84.4	Operating Expenses	93.0	98.3		85.8		69.6
12.1	11.5	15.6	Operating Profit	7.0	1.7		14.2		30.4
5.7	2.5	5.3	All Other Expenses (net)	3.1	3.3		1.7		2.3
6.5	9.0	10.3	Profit Before Taxes	3.9	-1.6		12.5		28.2
			RATIOS						
5.0	7.2	8.0		13.3	5.4		4.0		5.3
2.7	2.4	3.2	Current	8.2	2.2		2.6		1.8
1.4	1.3	1.7		3.4	1.4		1.3		1.0
4.9	5.4	6.2		11.1	5.4		3.4		3.6
2.4	2.1	2.5	Quick	5.8	1.6		1.9		.8
1.1	.9	1.4		2.0	1.3		1.2		.1
1 318.3	2 149.0	0 UND		0 UND	1 500.0		0 UND		0 UND
16 22.7	19 19.5	9 39.5	Sales/Receivables	0 UND	26 13.9		6 57.2		5 68.4
52 7.0	40 9.1	43 8.4		53 6.9	42 8.6		62 5.9		25 14.8
			Cost of Sales/Inventory						
			Cost of Sales/Payables						
1.3	.9	.8		.4	1.1		1.0		2.1
2.6	2.6	1.8	Sales/Working Capital	.8	2.2		2.2		12.8
12.4	14.7	4.7		1.7	22.2		44.6		-115.5
4.6	7.9	11.4							
(52) 1.7	(43) 2.1	(37) 2.2	EBIT/Interest						
.0	.6	1.0							
			Net Profit + Depr., Dep., Amort./Cur. Mat. L/T/D						
.1	.0	.0		.1	.1		.0		.0
.9	.6	.5	Fixed/Worth	.9	.2		.3		.5
1.4	1.4	1.2		1.2	.9		1.3		1.5
.3	.3	.2		.1	.2		.5		.4
.9	.7	.7	Debt/Worth	.5	.3		.7		1.2
2.0	1.7	1.6		1.0	1.5		.9		2.6
8.0	10.4	9.0		3.2	4.4		6.8		107.7
(82) 1.4	(66) 2.0	(60) 3.2	% Profit Before Taxes/Tangible Net Worth	1.4	.5		4.4	(10) 38.2	
-2.9	-1.7	-.9		-1.2	-5.9		2.2		3.7
4.0	4.7	4.1		2.4	3.7		4.1		67.6
.6	1.3	1.4	% Profit Before Taxes/Total Assets	1.4	.1		1.4		18.5
-1.3	-1.0	-.4		-1.0	-3.3		1.1		-2.4
36.1	55.1	50.5		2.4	49.0		540.5		999.8
1.0	2.5	2.4	Sales/Net Fixed Assets	.3	5.0		3.1		21.8
.2	.3	.3		.1	.4		.2		1.1
.8	1.0	.9		.3	1.4		.7		4.5
.3	.3	.3	Sales/Total Assets	.1	.2		.2		.9
.1	.1	.1		.1	.1		.1		.7
1.1	.9	1.0							
(69) 6.5	(54) 4.7	(47) 5.0	% Depr., Dep., Amort./Sales						
16.1	14.5	15.1							
			% Officers', Directors' Owners' Comp/Sales						
800417M	746537M	2504893M	Net Sales ($)	4204M	19713M	30976M	83427M	143787M	2222786M
2605149M	2319176M	2583189M	Total Assets ($)	55084M	189122M	119851M	370081M	852721M	996330M

M = $ thousand   MM = $ million
See Pages viii through xx for Explanation of Ratios and Data

CONSTRUCTION— PERCENTAGE OF COMPLETION BASIS OF ACCOUNTING*

CONSTRUCTION—
PERCENTAGE OF
COMPLETION BASIS OF
ACCOUNTING*

Current Data Sorted by Revenue   **Comparative Historical Data**

0-1MM	1-10MM	10-50MM	50 & OVER	ALL	Type of Statement	4/1/14-3/31/15 ALL	4/1/15-3/31/16 ALL	4/1/16-3/31/17 ALL	4/1/17-3/31/18 ALL	4/1/18-3/31/19 ALL
	1	1	2	4	Unqualified	5	9	3	3	4
	6	8		14	Reviewed	17	12	13	13	14
	3	2	1	6	Compiled	16	12	5	6	6
	13	5	1	19	Tax Returns	31	31	27	28	19
1	26	12	3	42	Other	37	50	28	30	42
	4 (4/1-9/30/18)	81 (10/1/18-3/31/19)								
1	49	28	7	85	**NUMBER OF STATEMENTS**	106	114	76	80	85
%	%	%	%	%	**ASSETS**	%	%	%	%	%
	9.4	12.1		10.2	Cash & Equivalents	12.9	11.0	13.5	9.7	10.2
	17.9	21.1		17.4	A/R - Progress Billings	8.7	9.6	11.5	12.1	17.4
	1.3	.6		1.0	A/R - Current Retention	1.0	.4	.6	.8	1.0
	36.1	33.3		37.5	Inventory	50.2	43.4	44.2	45.3	37.5
	2.8	5.8		4.5	Cost & Est. Earnings In Excess Billings	2.2	4.2	3.6	3.7	4.5
	8.3	4.6		6.5	All Other Current	4.3	8.2	7.5	4.5	6.5
	75.8	77.5		77.0	Total Current	79.2	76.9	81.0	76.1	77.0
	12.6	12.1		11.4	Fixed Assets (net)	8.4	11.0	11.5	13.6	11.4
	4.0	1.3		2.8	Joint Ventures & Investments	3.0	.8	1.5	1.2	2.8
	.0	.2		.1	Intangibles (net)	2.2	.4	.4	.4	.1
	7.6	9.0		8.7	All Other Non-Current	7.2	10.9	5.9	8.7	8.7
	100.0	100.0		100.0	Total	100.0	100.0	100.0	100.0	100.0
					LIABILITIES					
	23.5	23.7		25.1	Notes Payable-Short Term	24.6	25.3	22.2	29.3	25.1
	9.5	17.6		11.6	A/P - Trade	8.4	10.9	12.7	9.6	11.6
	.4	.8		.5	A/P - Retention	.6	.9	.2	.3	.5
	4.9	6.6		5.0	Billings in Excess of Costs & Est. Earnings	2.2	2.9	5.2	3.3	5.0
	.1	.0		.1	Income Taxes Payable	.3	.0	.0	.5	.1
	.9	3.3		1.9	Cur. Mat.-L/T/D	6.8	3.3	2.9	3.1	1.9
	10.7	7.8		9.4	All Other Current	8.1	10.7	10.0	9.9	9.4
	50.0	59.9		53.7	Total Current	51.0	54.0	53.3	55.9	53.7
	16.3	9.2		13.2	Long-Term Debt	11.2	12.4	16.8	13.5	13.2
	.2	.4		.3	Deferred Taxes	.8	1.0	.4	.5	.3
	6.2	5.4		6.2	All Other Non-Current	13.0	6.4	4.4	7.4	6.2
	27.2	25.1		26.6	Net Worth	23.9	26.3	25.1	22.8	26.6
	100.0	100.0		100.0	Total Liabilities & Net Worth	100.0	100.0	100.0	100.0	100.0
					INCOME DATA					
	100.0	100.0		100.0	Contract Revenues	100.0	100.0	100.0	100.0	100.0
		15.2		17.5	Gross Profit	18.3	18.2	15.4	16.9	17.5
	13.3	11.1		12.5	Operating Expenses	12.5	11.4	11.0	11.3	12.5
	5.2	4.1		5.0	Operating Profit	5.9	6.8	4.3	5.6	5.0
	-.1	.0		.0	All Other Expenses (net)	.9	.6	.3	.3	.0
	5.3	4.1		5.0	Profit Before Taxes	5.0	6.2	4.0	5.3	5.0
					RATIOS					
	3.7	1.7		2.5		3.6	2.4	2.4	2.2	2.5
	1.4	1.3		1.3	Current	1.6	1.4	1.6	1.4	1.3
	1.0	1.0		1.0		1.1	1.1	1.1	1.0	1.0
	4.6	1.5		2.0		1.7	1.3	1.7	2.1	2.0
	(37) .5	(26) .8	(71) .7		Receivables/Payables	(75) .1	(90) .1	(58) .4	(59) .5	(71) .7
	.0	.1		.0		.0	.0	.0	.0	.0
0 UND	1 722.6	0 UND				0 UND	0 UND	0 UND	0 UND	0 UND
1 565.0	15 24.9	2 172.4			Revenues/Receivables	0 UND	0 UND	0 999.8	0 UND	2 172.4
24 15.5	36 10.0	22 16.8				8 48.0	21 17.8	27 13.3	22 16.9	22 16.8
0 UND	6 57.0	0 840.4				0 UND	0 UND	0 UND	0 UND	0 840.4
6 56.8	24 15.4	12 30.3			Cost of Revenues/Payables	9 42.1	14 26.5	18 20.2	12 29.4	12 30.3
24 15.4	38 9.7	30 12.2				29 12.6	34 10.7	29 12.5	24 15.0	30 12.2
	4.2	5.3		4.3		2.7	3.7	4.0	5.1	4.3
	8.5	12.2		9.7	Revenues/Working Capital	6.6	8.8	9.1	10.6	9.7
	-244.2	NM		NM		27.8	26.7	51.2	86.7	NM
	18.6	27.2		21.5		32.3	25.7	33.6	28.2	21.5
	(34) 3.3	(26) 10.6	(67) 6.0		EBIT/Interest	(84) 8.1	(91) 5.0	(64) 7.6	(67) 6.0	(67) 6.0
	.7	2.0		1.2		3.2	1.6	2.9	2.1	1.2
					Net Profit + Depr., Dep., Amort./Cur. Mat. L/T/D					
	.0	.0		.0		.0	.0	.0	.0	.0
	.2	.2		.2	Fixed/Worth	.1	.1	.1	.2	.2
	1.0	1.3		1.0		.6	1.0	1.0	3.4	1.0
	1.4	1.4		1.4		1.1	1.2	1.1	1.5	1.4
	4.0	3.5		3.5	Debt/Worth	2.7	2.9	2.5	3.6	3.5
	30.0	11.5		13.3		9.6	12.2	12.2	31.3	13.3
	99.7	82.2		80.4		69.2	78.8	64.4	70.6	80.4
	(42) 25.0	(26) 48.2	(75) 32.0		% Profit Before Taxes/ Tangible Net Worth	(93) 24.8	(102) 26.1	(62) 30.1	(66) 33.1	(75) 32.0
	3.7	4.4		4.4		14.1	12.4	11.6	7.3	4.4
	18.1	17.0		16.6		15.7	15.8	16.6	14.5	16.6
	8.6	8.3		8.1	% Profit Before Taxes/ Total Assets	7.9	6.5	7.6	7.6	8.1
	.3	3.2		1.4		2.7	1.9	2.6	1.5	1.4
	.2	.1		.1		.2	.2	.2	.2	.1
	(27) .6	(21) .5	(52) .5		% Depr., Dep., Amort./ Revenues	(56) .4	(63) .4	(38) .3	(46) .4	(52) .5
	1.8	1.2		1.3		.7	.8	.6	1.1	1.3
	1.8			1.0		1.3	1.0	1.5	.8	1.0
	(24) 3.4		(36) 2.7		% Officers', Directors' Owners' Comp/Revenues	(45) 2.6	(49) 2.1	(28) 2.7	(37) 2.0	(36) 2.7
	4.3					4.8	4.0	5.1	2.8	4.0
843M	211457M	667071M	7403090M	8282461M	Contract Revenues ($)	60010895M	9538203M	2891894M	2693554M	8282461M
1982M	131146M	390461M	6907593M	7431182M	Total Assets ($)	42293155M	11728185M	2878707M	2597932M	7431182M

© RMA 2019

M = $ thousand   MM = $ million

See Pages viii through xx for Explanation of Ratios and Data

Current Data Sorted by Revenue | **Comparative Historical Data**

Current period splits: 2 (4/1-9/30/18); 21 (10/1/18-3/31/19)

0-1MM	1-10MM	10-50MM	50 & OVER	ALL		4/1/14-3/31/15 ALL	4/1/15-3/31/16 ALL	4/1/16-3/31/17 ALL	4/1/17-3/31/18 ALL	4/1/18-3/31/19 ALL
					Type of Statement					
			1	1	Unqualified	1		5	6	1
	1	2	2	5	Reviewed	5	6	8	5	5
					Compiled		1		2	
	2	2	2	4	Tax Returns	1	3	3	5	4
2	2	2	8	13	Other	1	11	4	11	13
2	4	6	11	23	**NUMBER OF STATEMENTS**	8	21	20	29	23
%	%	%	%	%		%	%	%	%	%
					ASSETS					
			16.3	13.1	Cash & Equivalents		17.9	15.9	15.2	13.1
			45.6	37.4	A/R - Progress Billings		34.4	40.0	25.0	37.4
			17.4	9.5	A/R - Current Retention		5.6	5.4	4.1	9.5
			.7	14.7	Inventory		12.3	5.9	22.1	14.7
			2.9	3.0	Cost & Est. Earnings In Excess Billings		4.0	5.7	3.6	3.0
			.8	2.8	All Other Current		3.1	5.5	3.4	2.8
			83.7	80.5	Total Current		77.3	78.4	73.4	80.5
			6.8	10.9	Fixed Assets (net)		11.0	13.3	11.9	10.9
			.0	.2	Joint Ventures & Investments		.0	1.9	1.4	.2
			4.2	2.2	Intangibles (net)		1.1	.4	.4	2.2
			5.3	6.3	All Other Non-Current		10.6	5.9	12.8	6.3
			100.0	100.0	Total		100.0	100.0	100.0	100.0
					LIABILITIES					
			1.1	7.8	Notes Payable-Short Term		15.2	10.3	18.6	7.8
			37.1	28.1	A/P - Trade		26.8	32.2	24.6	28.1
			9.8	5.9	A/P - Retention		1.1	4.2	2.9	5.9
			8.8	7.8	Billings in Excess of Costs & Est. Earnings		4.2	4.6	5.3	7.8
			.0	.0	Income Taxes Payable		.1	.2	.0	.0
			1.2	2.0	Cur. Mat.-L/T/D		3.1	2.6	1.4	2.0
			8.4	12.8	All Other Current		4.8	6.6	27.0	12.8
			66.4	64.3	Total Current		55.3	60.7	79.8	64.3
			8.4	8.9	Long-Term Debt		8.7	3.8	7.4	8.9
			.1	.0	Deferred Taxes		.0	.2	.0	.0
			1.4	1.6	All Other Non-Current		5.0	2.7	1.9	1.6
			23.7	25.2	Net Worth		31.0	32.7	10.9	25.2
			100.0	100.0	Total Liabilities & Net Worth		100.0	100.0	100.0	100.0
					INCOME DATA					
			100.0	100.0	Contract Revenues		100.0	100.0	100.0	100.0
			9.7	14.2	Gross Profit		18.2	13.8	14.7	14.2
			5.7	10.5	Operating Expenses		13.1	12.5	10.5	10.5
			4.0	3.7	Operating Profit		5.1	1.3	4.2	3.7
			.0	.0	All Other Expenses (net)		.4	-.5	.0	.0
			3.9	3.7	Profit Before Taxes		4.8	1.8	4.2	3.7
					RATIOS					
			1.4	2.1	Current		2.5	1.4	1.5	2.1
			1.2	1.2			1.3	1.3	1.2	1.2
			1.1	1.1			1.1	1.2	1.0	1.1
			2.2	2.2	Receivables/Payables		2.4	1.6	1.4	2.2
			1.4	(19) 1.4			(18) 1.6	(17) 1.4	(22) 1.0	(19) 1.4
			1.1	1.1			.9	.9	.6	1.1
			51 7.2	24 15.2	Revenues/Receivables		21 17.3	25 14.8	0 UND	24 15.2
			58 6.3	53 6.9			57 6.4	57 6.4	18 20.1	53 6.9
			73 5.0	83 4.4			79 4.6	69 5.3	65 5.6	83 4.4
			36 10.0	18 20.5	Cost of Revenues/Payables		11 32.8	18 20.8	0 UND	18 20.5
			48 7.6	43 8.5			27 13.6	41 8.9	32 11.5	43 8.5
			64 5.7	61 6.0			54 6.8	65 5.3	69 5.3	61 6.0
			8.0	8.0	Revenues/Working Capital		8.3	10.4	9.3	8.0
			24.2	28.6			15.6	19.4	31.7	28.6
			61.4	62.6			38.4	26.1	NM	62.6
				108.3	EBIT/Interest		38.0	62.6	66.5	108.3
				(16) 17.5			(17) 12.0	(13) 8.1	(16) 8.4	(16) 17.5
				4.6			4.0	-3.0	3.3	4.6
					Net Profit + Depr., Dep., Amort./Cur. Mat. L/T/D					
			.0	.0	Fixed/Worth		.0	.0	.0	.0
			.1	.2			.1	.2	.2	.2
			.3	1.4			.6	.8	.7	1.4
			1.8	1.8	Debt/Worth		.9	1.0	1.4	1.8
			6.6	6.5			3.1	2.6	4.6	6.5
			7.7	8.4			8.7	4.4	9.3	8.4
			115.8	104.7	% Profit Before Taxes/Tangible Net Worth		96.4	45.8	66.0	104.7
			(10) 62.7	(20) 44.9			(20) 49.9	(19) 11.8	(28) 35.7	(20) 44.9
			39.3	20.8			10.7	.5	7.7	20.8
			15.8	18.5	% Profit Before Taxes/Total Assets		18.3	14.7	14.4	18.5
			11.7	10.2			10.0	3.8	7.5	10.2
			8.6	5.4			4.4	.6	1.7	5.4
				.1	% Depr., Dep., Amort./Revenues		.1	.1	.1	.1
				(18) .4			(17) .4	(18) .4	(20) .5	(18) .4
				1.0			1.9	1.6	1.4	1.0
					% Officers', Directors', Owners' Comp/Revenues					
821M	10977M	121597M	2988996M	3122391M	Contract Revenues ($)	2120709M	756835M	1776918M	2470406M	3122391M
326M	4021M	57107M	1299923M	1361377M	Total Assets ($)	1721518M	361279M	799092M	1430802M	1361377M

M = $ thousand   MM = $ million
See Pages viii through xx for Explanation of Ratios and Data

Current Data Sorted by Revenue   Comparative Historical Data

0-1MM	1-10MM	10-50MM	50 & OVER	ALL		4/1/14-3/31/15 ALL	4/1/15-3/31/16 ALL	4/1/16-3/31/17 ALL	4/1/17-3/31/18 ALL	4/1/18-3/31/19 ALL
					Type of Statement					
1	1		1	3	Unqualified	2	1	2	2	3
	1			2	Reviewed	4	2	3	6	3
1	5	1		7	Compiled	2	6	3	2	2
1	5	3	4	13	Tax Returns	4	8	3	5	7
					Other	3	13	2	10	13
1 (4/1-9/30/18)		24 (10/1/18-3/31/19)								
3	12	5	5	25	**NUMBER OF STATEMENTS**	15	30	13	25	25
%	%	%	%	%		%	%	%	%	%
					ASSETS					
	4.3			6.7	Cash & Equivalents	9.9	7.8	9.2	9.2	6.7
	7.7			4.8	A/R - Progress Billings	6.7	3.3	8.2	10.0	4.8
	.0			.0	A/R - Current Retention	.0	.0	1.6	1.3	.0
	49.1			53.8	Inventory	55.9	55.2	46.8	55.0	53.8
	12.5			6.5	Cost & Est. Earnings In Excess Billings	2.2	2.0	6.7	3.5	6.5
	8.2			11.5	All Other Current	1.3	2.1	1.3	5.0	11.5
	81.7			83.3	Total Current	75.9	70.3	73.8	84.0	83.3
	11.4			9.9	Fixed Assets (net)	16.0	13.2	8.9	5.5	9.9
	2.3			1.1	Joint Ventures & Investments	2.8	1.5	9.7	2.2	1.1
	.0			.1	Intangibles (net)	1.0	2.0	.0	.1	.1
	4.6			5.5	All Other Non-Current	4.3	12.9	7.6	8.2	5.5
	100.0			100.0	Total	100.0	100.0	100.0	100.0	100.0
					LIABILITIES					
	37.3			36.4	Notes Payable-Short Term	18.5	33.7	28.4	31.1	36.4
	8.0			7.3	A/P - Trade	11.2	8.1	14.1	12.1	7.3
	.0			.0	A/P - Retention	.0	.0	1.2	1.1	.0
	6.2			3.2	Billings in Excess of Costs & Est. Earnings	.8	6.0	3.3	9.2	3.2
	.7			.4	Income Taxes Payable	.1	.0	.0	.0	.4
	.0			.0	Cur. Mat.-L/T/D	8.7	1.4	3.4	.1	.0
	19.8			23.2	All Other Current	4.6	8.6	7.6	7.3	23.2
	72.1			70.3	Total Current	43.9	57.8	58.0	60.9	70.3
	20.2			11.8	Long-Term Debt	12.8	10.5	7.7	7.6	11.8
	.0			.0	Deferred Taxes	.0	1.5	.0	.0	.0
	2.1			7.0	All Other Non-Current	5.1	13.1	13.8	5.9	7.0
	5.6			10.9	Net Worth	38.2	17.1	20.4	25.6	10.9
	100.0			100.0	Total Liabilities & Net Worth	100.0	100.0	100.0	100.0	100.0
					INCOME DATA					
	100.0			100.0	Contract Revenues	100.0	100.0	100.0	100.0	100.0
	22.4			19.0	Gross Profit	25.3	14.3	14.7	16.3	19.0
	18.2			13.8	Operating Expenses	14.5	10.6	9.0	12.5	13.8
	4.2			5.3	Operating Profit	10.7	3.7	5.8	3.8	5.3
	.8			.6	All Other Expenses (net)	.0	.8	.0	.1	.6
	3.3			4.6	Profit Before Taxes	10.7	2.8	5.7	3.7	4.6
					RATIOS					
	1.4			1.6	Current	2.0	1.8	1.7	1.7	1.6
	1.1			1.2		1.6	1.4	1.5	1.2	1.2
	.9			1.0		1.4	1.1	1.0	1.0	1.0
				.6	Receivables/Payables	.5	.3	.3	1.2	.6
			(18)	.0		(12) .1	(23) .0	(12) .1	(20) .2	(18) .0
				.0		.0	.0	.0	.0	.0
0 UND	0 UND			0 UND	Revenues/Receivables	0 UND	0 UND	0 UND	0 UND	0 UND
0 UND	0 UND			0 UND		1 548.5	0 UND	1 294.2	0 UND	0 UND
1 260.2			1	312.4		4 101.3	4 95.1	5 68.8	11 33.8	1 312.4
0 UND	0 UND			0 UND	Cost of Revenues/Payables	10 36.4	0 UND	12 30.0	0 UND	0 UND
9 40.1			11	34.6		25 14.5	12 30.7	26 14.1	23 15.9	11 34.6
24 15.3			28	13.2		44 8.3	33 11.2	39 9.4	49 7.4	28 13.2
	8.4			5.4	Revenues/Working Capital	2.9	3.2	2.4	2.8	5.4
	11.6			10.7		7.1	8.1	11.1	11.2	10.7
	NM			55.8		13.4	NM	NM	NM	55.8
	45.3			18.9	EBIT/Interest		8.7		7.6	18.9
	(11) 8.2		(22)	6.3			(23) 3.9		(17) 2.9	(22) 6.3
	.9			1.5			1.9		1.2	1.5
					Net Profit + Depr., Dep., Amort./Cur. Mat. L/T/D					
	.0			.0	Fixed/Worth	.0	.0	.0	.0	.0
	.0			.0		.1	.2	.1	.2	.0
	2.6			1.8		.8	1.4	.5	.5	1.8
	3.6			2.6	Debt/Worth	1.0	1.7	1.4	1.1	2.6
	49.7			6.1		2.0	3.4	2.4	3.2	6.1
	NM			135.1		3.7	30.7	28.1	8.3	135.1
				82.5	% Profit Before Taxes/Tangible Net Worth	62.5	70.7	107.0	32.6	82.5
			(20)	40.9		35.2	(25) 30.3	(11) 51.9	(21) 19.6	(20) 40.9
				20.6		11.5	10.4	15.8	7.5	20.6
	13.0			14.1	% Profit Before Taxes/Total Assets	19.8	10.5	22.5	9.5	14.1
	5.9			8.7		11.6	5.7	10.9	5.8	8.7
	.0			.7		3.5	2.0	2.0	.5	.7
				.1	% Depr., Dep., Amort./Revenues		.1		.1	.1
			(13)	.2			(14) .3		(12) .4	(13) .2
				1.1			.7		1.4	1.1
				.8	% Officers', Directors' Owners' Comp/Revenues					.8
			(10)	1.7					(10)	1.7
				3.6						3.6
1362M	51415M	141356M	7389661M	7583794M	Contract Revenues ($)	513056M	1343512M	665647M	6566310M	7583794M
382M	39247M	78516M	10366040M	10484185M	Total Assets ($)	573614M	1135387M	395936M	9957878M	10484185M

M = $ thousand   MM = $ million
See Pages viii through xx for Explanation of Ratios and Data

Current Data Sorted by Revenue | **Comparative Historical Data**

0-1MM	1-10MM	10-50MM	50 & OVER	ALL	Type of Statement	4/1/14-3/31/15 ALL	4/1/15-3/31/16 ALL	4/1/16-3/31/17 ALL	4/1/17-3/31/18 ALL	4/1/18-3/31/19 ALL
	1		5	6	Unqualified	2	6	8	7	6
2	2	14	4	22	Reviewed	14	21	17	17	22
					Compiled		2	1	1	
			1	1	Tax Returns		1	1	1	
	4	9	12	25	Other	4	1	3	5	1
						10	20	22	22	25
5 (4/1-9/30/18)		49 (10/1/18-3/31/19)								
2	7	23	22	54	**NUMBER OF STATEMENTS**	30	50	51	52	54
%	%	%	%	%	**ASSETS**	%	%	%	%	%
		18.7	20.2	20.7	Cash & Equivalents	20.1	19.6	20.7	20.6	20.7
		43.3	46.0	41.9	A/R - Progress Billings	46.0	40.4	37.8	41.7	41.9
		5.0	5.6	4.9	A/R - Current Retention	3.5	4.0	3.1	2.3	4.9
		1.3	1.1	1.0	Inventory	1.6	3.1	2.4	1.9	1.0
		7.3	3.2	5.9	Cost & Est. Earnings In Excess Billings	5.1	7.3	7.0	7.0	5.9
		6.6	2.8	4.2	All Other Current	2.6	5.9	4.3	4.3	4.2
		82.2	78.9	78.6	Total Current	79.0	80.4	75.3	77.7	78.6
		13.6	14.4	14.7	Fixed Assets (net)	13.6	12.7	18.1	16.4	14.7
		.1	.8	.4	Joint Ventures & Investments	.4	.0	.5	.3	.4
		.8	1.7	1.1	Intangibles (net)	1.1	.8	1.0	.9	1.1
		3.3	4.3	5.2	All Other Non-Current	5.9	6.1	5.0	4.7	5.2
		100.0	100.0	100.0	Total	100.0	100.0	100.0	100.0	100.0
					LIABILITIES					
		2.1	2.9	2.7	Notes Payable-Short Term	3.8	4.1	3.7	3.2	2.7
		34.5	34.6	31.3	A/P - Trade	33.0	31.7	25.5	30.4	31.3
		2.4	2.3	2.1	A/P - Retention	2.6	2.3	1.4	3.8	2.1
		8.4	15.4	11.7	Billings in Excess of Costs & Est. Earnings	6.3	8.3	10.2	6.7	11.7
		.0	.2	.1	Income Taxes Payable	.9	.5	.7	.1	.1
		1.4	2.1	1.9	Cur. Mat.-L/T/D	1.8	1.3	2.2	1.6	1.9
		6.3	8.5	6.7	All Other Current	10.8	6.8	9.0	8.8	6.7
		55.1	65.9	56.4	Total Current	59.2	55.0	52.8	54.5	56.4
		4.3	5.5	5.1	Long-Term Debt	6.1	5.9	7.1	6.0	5.1
		.0	.3	.3	Deferred Taxes	.5	.3	.4	.2	.3
		1.0	2.8	2.0	All Other Non-Current	2.1	2.7	2.3	3.9	2.0
		39.6	25.5	35.9	Net Worth	32.1	36.0	37.5	35.3	35.9
		100.0	100.0	100.0	Total Liabilties & Net Worth	100.0	100.0	100.0	100.0	100.0
					INCOME DATA					
		100.0	100.0	100.0	Contract Revenues	100.0	100.0	100.0	100.0	100.0
		15.9	9.2	14.8	Gross Profit	14.4	15.9	16.9	15.8	14.8
		10.1	6.9	10.2	Operating Expenses	12.8	11.9	12.2	12.5	10.2
		5.8	2.4	4.6	Operating Profit	1.6	4.0	4.7	3.3	4.6
		-.6	.3	-.3	All Other Expenses (net)	.0	.1	.0	-.1	-.3
		6.3	2.1	4.9	Profit Before Taxes	1.5	3.9	4.7	3.4	4.9
					RATIOS					
		2.1	1.4	2.0	Current	1.5	1.9	1.9	2.1	2.0
		1.6	1.2	1.3		1.3	1.4	1.3	1.5	1.3
		1.1	1.1	1.1		1.1	1.2	1.1	1.2	1.1
		2.8	2.2	2.7	Receivables/Payables	2.2	1.9	2.7	2.2	2.7
		1.4	1.3	1.3		1.2	1.4	(51) 1.8	1.4	1.3
		.9	1.1	1.1		1.0	1.0	1.1	1.0	1.1
		48 7.6	51 7.1	49 7.5	Revenues/Receivables	48 7.6	34 10.6	36 10.0	33 11.0	49 7.5
		68 5.4	63 5.8	68 5.4		63 5.8	54 6.7	58 6.3	54 6.7	68 5.4
		79 4.6	83 4.4	79 4.6		73 5.0	74 4.9	72 5.1	65 5.6	79 4.6
		25 14.5	30 12.1	23 16.1	Cost of Revenues/Payables	33 11.2	23 15.7	22 16.8	25 14.5	23 16.1
		48 7.6	49 7.4	46 8.0		47 7.7	42 8.7	35 10.5	39 9.3	46 8.0
		83 4.4	63 5.8	68 5.4		65 5.6	65 6.5	56 6.5	66 5.5	68 5.4
		7.3	13.9	7.3	Revenues/Working Capital	11.1	6.7	7.1	8.1	7.3
		11.0	24.0	17.4		17.4	12.3	15.8	13.9	17.4
		39.2	57.6	55.5		29.4	23.7	31.4	27.5	55.5
		270.3	51.6	117.7	EBIT/Interest	27.7	152.4	99.1	31.6	117.7
		(18) 59.2	(15) 8.7	(38) 16.7		(22) 13.8	(41) 22.7	(39) 17.6	(45) 12.2	(38) 16.7
		9.0	3.3	5.2		3.6	7.2	5.2	2.9	5.2
					Net Profit + Depr., Dep., Amort./Cur. Mat. L/T/D					
		.1	.1	.1	Fixed/Worth	.1	.1	.1	.2	.1
		.3	.5	.3		.4	.2	.4	.4	.3
		.6	1.1	.7		.7	.6	.9	.9	.7
		.8	1.9	.9	Debt/Worth	1.5	1.0	.7	.9	.9
		1.5	3.2	2.0		2.1	2.0	2.0	2.1	2.0
		5.5	9.7	6.1		4.7	3.7	4.7	5.1	6.1
		55.2	84.9	61.2	% Profit Before Taxes/Tangible Net Worth	41.6	48.0	51.2	58.5	61.2
		(22) 42.8	(21) 24.2	(52) 38.1		(29) 16.2	(47) 24.1	(49) 25.6	(47) 19.6	(52) 38.1
		25.5	6.6	10.3		7.5	9.6	5.9	10.6	10.3
		21.4	10.3	18.4	% Profit Before Taxes/Total Assets	10.1	18.0	20.3	14.7	18.4
		16.2	5.7	9.5		5.4	9.4	7.2	6.1	9.5
		7.8	2.4	3.8		1.5	3.6	2.8	2.6	3.8
		.2	.1	.2	% Depr., Dep., Amort./Revenues	.2	.2	.2	.2	.2
		(18) .4	.4	(49) .5		(27) .4	(41) .5	(44) .7	(42) .5	(49) .5
		1.3	.8	1.7		1.7	1.3	1.4	.9	1.7
					% Officers', Directors' Owners' Comp/Revenues	.4	.9	.9	1.2	
						(12) 1.0	(12) 2.1	(16) 2.3	(11) 1.4	
						4.5	5.0	5.3	4.6	
54M	44139M	507804M	7264011M	7816008M	Contract Revenues ($)	8239732M	14422594M	4183996M	7781008M	7816008M
27M	40785M	197802M	3567517M	3806131M	Total Assets ($)	5190510M	7917088M	1837917M	5271663M	3806131M

M = $ thousand   MM = $ million
See Pages viii through xx for Explanation of Ratios and Data

Current Data Sorted by Revenue   Comparative Historical Data

					Type of Statement					
	3	11	21	35	Unqualified	28	28	38	35	35
7	37	79	23	146	Reviewed	77	121	134	130	146
	6	6		12	Compiled	12	10	12	16	12
	7	2	1	10	Tax Returns	17	14	19	16	10
7	23	35	48	113	Other	52	98	84	108	113
						4/1/14-	4/1/15-	4/1/16-	4/1/17-	4/1/18-
39 (4/1-9/30/18)		277 (10/1/18-3/31/19)				3/31/15	3/31/16	3/31/17	3/31/18	3/31/19
0-1MM	1-10MM	10-50MM	50 & OVER	ALL		ALL	ALL	ALL	ALL	ALL
14	76	133	93	316	NUMBER OF STATEMENTS	186	271	287	305	316
%	%	%	%	%	ASSETS	%	%	%	%	%
35.1	24.9	22.0	23.1	23.6	Cash & Equivalents	24.3	23.6	25.4	21.8	23.6
36.5	40.7	44.1	48.4	44.2	A/R - Progress Billings	41.8	43.7	43.7	44.6	44.2
13.7	3.9	6.0	9.0	6.7	A/R - Current Retention	3.9	4.7	4.6	4.8	6.7
.0	.9	1.1	.9	.9	Inventory	.4	1.7	1.0	1.1	.9
2.6	7.6	6.2	5.6	6.2	Cost & Est. Earnings In Excess Billings	5.3	5.8	5.7	6.4	6.2
.2	6.3	3.5	2.1	3.6	All Other Current	4.5	4.4	4.3	3.9	3.6
88.0	84.3	82.9	89.1	85.3	Total Current	80.3	83.9	84.6	82.7	85.3
8.3	11.2	11.0	7.4	9.8	Fixed Assets (net)	10.7	9.8	9.3	10.4	9.8
.0	.1	.5	.4	.4	Joint Ventures & Investments	1.0	.3	.6	.6	.4
.6	.1	.1	.4	.2	Intangibles (net)	1.7	.8	.4	1.1	.2
3.0	4.2	5.6	2.7	4.3	All Other Non-Current	6.3	5.1	5.0	5.2	4.3
100.0	100.0	100.0	100.0	100.0	Total	100.0	100.0	100.0	100.0	100.0
					LIABILITIES					
7.6	4.6	3.0	1.1	3.0	Notes Payable-Short Term	4.1	3.6	3.4	4.3	3.0
35.3	28.4	36.3	42.1	36.0	A/P - Trade	34.4	37.0	35.8	36.9	36.0
4.3	1.1	3.5	6.7	3.9	A/P - Retention	2.9	3.3	3.4	3.2	3.9
11.9	7.8	11.0	10.9	10.3	Billings in Excess of Costs & Est. Earnings	8.6	9.8	10.0	9.8	10.3
.4	.3	.2	.0	.2	Income Taxes Payable	.1	.3	.3	.2	.2
.1	2.6	1.3	.6	1.3	Cur. Mat.-L/T/D	2.2	1.2	1.1	1.1	1.3
14.3	5.7	5.6	7.6	6.6	All Other Current	7.6	7.5	6.8	7.0	6.6
73.9	50.6	60.9	69.0	61.4	Total Current	59.8	62.8	60.9	62.4	61.4
.7	5.1	4.6	3.7	4.3	Long-Term Debt	6.6	4.5	4.2	5.0	4.3
.0	.4	.2	.1	.2	Deferred Taxes	.2	.3	.2	.2	.2
.4	1.9	1.8	2.7	2.0	All Other Non-Current	2.4	1.4	3.2	1.5	2.0
24.1	42.1	32.5	24.5	32.1	Net Worth	31.0	31.0	31.5	30.9	32.1
100.0	100.0	100.0	100.0	100.0	Total Liabilties & Net Worth	100.0	100.0	100.0	100.0	100.0
					INCOME DATA					
100.0	100.0	100.0	100.0	100.0	Contract Revenues	100.0	100.0	100.0	100.0	100.0
15.9	18.8	12.6	8.8	13.1	Gross Profit	14.2	12.7	12.1	12.3	13.1
12.6	14.6	9.3	5.7	9.7	Operating Expenses	11.6	9.6	9.0	9.8	9.7
3.2	4.1	3.4	3.0	3.4	Operating Profit	2.5	3.1	3.1	2.5	3.4
-.2	-.4	-.1	.1	-.1	All Other Expenses (net)	.1	.1	.0	-.1	-.1
3.5	4.5	3.5	3.0	3.6	Profit Before Taxes	2.5	3.1	3.1	2.5	3.6
					RATIOS					
2.2	2.8	1.7	1.4	1.8		1.8	1.7	1.8	1.7	1.8
1.2	1.7	1.3	1.2	1.3	Current	1.3	1.3	1.4	1.3	1.3
1.1	1.3	1.2	1.1	1.1		1.1	1.1	1.2	1.1	1.1

	2.1		2.8		1.6		1.6		2.0	Receivables/Payables		1.8		1.7		1.8		1.8		2.0
	1.2		1.4	(132)	1.3		1.1	(315)	1.2		(179)	1.2	(265)	1.2	(284)	1.2	(302)	1.2	(315)	1.2
	1.1		1.1		.9		.9		1.0			.9		.9		1.0		1.0		1.0
29	12.8	32	11.5	37	9.8	45	8.1	39	9.4	Revenues/Receivables	38	9.6	34	10.6	38	9.7	41	9.0	39	9.4
61	6.0	56	6.5	54	6.7	62	5.9	57	6.4		56	6.5	53	6.9	57	6.4	58	6.3	57	6.4
76	4.8	78	4.7	79	4.6	83	4.4	81	4.5		74	4.9	74	4.9	78	4.7	76	4.8	81	4.5
28	13.2	18	20.6	31	11.6	40	8.8	29	12.4	Cost of Revenues/Payables	26	14.1	28	12.9	31	11.8	28	12.9	29	12.4
47	7.8	36	10.1	48	7.6	54	6.7	49	7.5		56	6.5	49	7.5	52	7.0	49	7.4	49	7.5
73	5.0	62	5.9	69	5.3	74	4.9	72	5.1		73	5.0	73	5.0	72	5.1	72	5.1	72	5.1
	4.9		6.1		9.7		11.2		8.3	Revenues/Working Capital		7.6		8.8		8.0		9.2		8.3
	17.0		9.2		16.7		20.6		16.0			15.7		18.6		14.5		17.6		16.0
	52.5		22.0		33.2		38.1		33.4			41.5		36.0		31.8		45.1		33.4
			80.5		68.5		266.4		95.7	EBIT/Interest		58.7		72.6		116.0		100.9		95.7
		(62)	31.2	(101)	18.6	(68)	58.2	(232)	30.8		(131)	14.4	(188)	20.1	(203)	26.0	(227)	22.0	(232)	30.8
			4.3		4.2		17.6		5.4			3.8		3.6		6.0		5.3		5.4
			22.1		9.8		114.5		25.3	Net Profit + Depr., Dep., Amort./Cur. Mat. L/T/D		17.2		9.3		11.6		13.7		25.3
		(10)	10.5	(14)	5.0	(15)	21.2	(39)	9.4		(21)	4.0	(34)	3.7	(30)	4.9	(27)	7.6	(39)	9.4
			1.7		2.4		3.1		2.8			1.6		1.5		1.6		1.8		2.8
	.1		.1		.1		.1		.1	Fixed/Worth		.1		.1		.1		.1		.1
	.2		.2		.2		.2		.2			.2		.2		.2		.2		.2
	.5		.5		.5		.5		.5			.5		.5		.4		.6		.5
	.8		.6		1.2		2.0		1.1	Debt/Worth		1.2		1.2		1.1		1.3		1.1
	3.2		1.3		2.2		3.9		2.4			2.5		2.6		2.4		2.6		2.4
	7.3		3.5		3.6		5.7		4.5			5.1		5.1		4.3		4.8		4.5
	79.2		61.0		60.5		69.2		63.6	% Profit Before Taxes/ Tangible Net Worth		43.5		56.4		50.6		56.0		63.6
(13)	34.7	(72)	30.1	(127)	29.9	(90)	43.7	(302)	34.0		(174)	17.6	(258)	23.1	(273)	24.2	(290)	28.0	(302)	34.0
	23.6		8.7		8.2		16.8		10.4			4.2		7.8		9.8		7.9		10.4
	16.0		25.4		18.3		14.1		18.1	% Profit Before Taxes/ Total Assets		12.2		14.8		14.2		15.6		18.1
	11.5		12.8		7.7		8.7		8.7			5.6		6.2		7.3		7.2		8.7
	3.8		3.3		1.8		4.0		2.9			.9		1.7		2.4		1.9		2.9
			.3		.2		.1		.2	% Depr., Dep., Amort./ Revenues		.2		.2		.2		.1		.2
		(54)	.6	(118)	.4	(82)	.2	(256)	.4		(162)	.4	(226)	.3	(246)	.3	(260)	.4	(256)	.4
			1.3		.9		.5		.9			.7		.7		.8		.8		.9
			1.1		.8		.4		.8	% Officers', Directors' Owners' Comp/Revenues		1.3		.8		.9		.9		.8
		(27)	3.3	(43)	1.4	(16)	.8	(89)	1.5		(52)	2.5	(76)	1.7	(79)	1.8	(89)	1.6	(89)	1.5
			6.6		2.4		2.1		2.9			4.5		3.2		3.3		3.2		2.9

3426M	469601M	3379039M	25697510M	29549576M	Contract Revenues ($)	19127331M	33440803M	30528046M	53721644M	29549576M
1793M	173150M	1177955M	11276652M	12629550M	Total Assets ($)	9312033M	14873327M	13842618M	30148484M	12629550M

Current Data Sorted by Revenue | Comparative Historical Data

Current data period split: 7 (4/1-9/30/18), 48 (10/1/18-3/31/19)

0-1MM	1-10MM	10-50MM	50 & OVER	ALL	Type of Statement	4/1/14-3/31/15 ALL	4/1/15-3/31/16 ALL	4/1/16-3/31/17 ALL	4/1/17-3/31/18 ALL	4/1/18-3/31/19 ALL
		5		5	Unqualified	2	3	3	5	5
	11	13	1	25	Reviewed	13	26	26	23	25
	1			1	Compiled	4	3	1	3	1
			1	1	Tax Returns	2			2	1
	1	11	11	23	Other	19	21	22	35	23
	13	29	13	55	**NUMBER OF STATEMENTS**	40	53	54	67	55
%	%	%	%	%	**ASSETS**	%	%	%	%	%
	15.3	9.4	15.5	12.2	Cash & Equivalents	12.5	15.0	17.2	14.4	12.2
D	26.6	33.9	28.1	30.8	A/R - Progress Billings	35.9	30.0	29.9	33.5	30.8
A	3.0	3.0	6.2	3.8	A/R - Current Retention	3.0	3.8	3.5	3.4	3.8
T	2.0	1.0	1.8	1.4	Inventory	3.0	2.8	.8	1.3	1.4
A	4.1	6.5	9.2	6.6	Cost & Est. Earnings In Excess of Billings	5.9	8.0	6.0	5.2	6.6
N	4.1	2.4	3.7	3.1	All Other Current	3.4	2.5	3.3	2.5	3.1
O	55.1	56.2	64.4	57.9	Total Current	63.7	62.1	60.6	60.5	57.9
T	40.8	38.2	25.8	35.9	Fixed Assets (net)	29.2	32.2	33.1	32.7	35.9
	.0	.0	.0	.0	Joint Ventures & Investments	.0	.0	.0	.1	.0
A	.0	.8	7.5	2.2	Intangibles (net)	.7	1.3	1.6	2.6	2.2
V	4.1	4.8	2.3	4.1	All Other Non-Current	6.3	4.5	4.7	4.2	4.1
A	100.0	100.0	100.0	100.0	Total	100.0	100.0	100.0	100.0	100.0
I					**LIABILITIES**					
L	7.4	4.6	1.5	4.5	Notes Payable-Short Term	9.6	6.0	3.9	3.9	4.5
A	11.3	16.8	15.7	15.3	A/P - Trade	22.0	18.5	15.1	16.6	15.3
B	.1	.1	1.6	.5	A/P - Retention	.9	.6	.2	.5	.5
L	4.2	3.4	8.7	4.9	Billings in Excess of Costs & Est. Earnings	4.3	6.7	6.4	6.6	4.9
E	.9	.1	.0	.3	Income Taxes Payable	.1	.1	.3	.2	.3
	5.7	6.4	7.6	6.5	Cur. Mat.-L/T/D	4.4	5.3	5.5	6.5	6.5
	2.6	5.4	5.9	4.9	All Other Current	6.0	3.4	3.9	5.6	4.9
	32.2	36.8	41.1	36.7	Total Current	47.3	40.7	35.3	39.9	36.7
	11.0	15.4	13.5	13.9	Long-Term Debt	11.6	15.4	14.5	17.8	13.9
	1.1	.2	.1	.4	Deferred Taxes	.7	.5	.5	.2	.4
	.3	1.0	10.3	3.0	All Other Non-Current	6.2	2.7	1.8	1.8	3.0
	55.4	46.6	35.0	45.9	Net Worth	34.2	40.6	47.8	40.3	45.9
	100.0	100.0	100.0	100.0	Total Liabilities & Net Worth	100.0	100.0	100.0	100.0	100.0
					INCOME DATA					
	100.0	100.0	100.0	100.0	Contract Revenues	100.0	100.0	100.0	100.0	100.0
	21.7	21.0	12.9	19.2	Gross Profit	19.2	19.5	17.9	20.7	19.2
	12.1	13.6	9.5	12.3	Operating Expenses	15.6	15.0	11.8	15.2	12.3
	9.6	7.3	3.4	6.9	Operating Profit	3.6	4.5	6.1	5.5	6.9
	.2	.8	.9	.7	All Other Expenses (net)	-.4	.7	-.2	.7	.7
	9.4	6.5	2.5	6.3	Profit Before Taxes	4.0	3.8	6.2	4.9	6.3
					RATIOS					
	4.5	2.0	2.0	2.3	Current	1.8	2.2	2.4	2.1	2.3
	1.8	1.4	1.6	1.5		1.5	1.6	1.7	1.6	1.5
	1.2	1.1	1.4	1.1		1.1	1.1	1.3	1.1	1.1
	6.0	3.1	2.7	3.2	Receivables/Payables	3.0	3.2	3.5	3.3	3.2
	2.6	2.1	2.3	2.3		1.7	1.8	2.4 (66)	2.5	2.3
	2.2	1.6	1.4	1.6		1.3	1.4	1.6	1.7	1.6
	33 10.9	58 6.3	51 7.2	53 6.9	Revenues/Receivables	48 7.6	51 7.2	45 8.2	49 7.4	53 6.9
	56 6.5	66 5.5	60 6.1	65 5.6		66 5.5	64 5.7	64 5.7	68 5.4	65 5.6
	96 3.8	79 4.6	73 5.0	81 4.5		85 4.3	87 4.2	76 4.8	94 3.9	81 4.5
	10 38.0	24 14.9	22 16.5	22 16.5	Cost of Revenues/Payables	26 14.2	27 13.4	20 18.7	24 15.2	22 16.5
	29 12.7	39 9.3	29 12.7	31 11.6		46 7.9	40 9.2	31 11.7	38 9.5	31 11.6
	52 7.0	47 7.8	48 7.6	47 7.8		66 5.5	54 6.7	42 8.7	57 6.4	47 7.8
	5.0	7.1	5.6	5.8	Revenues/Working Capital	7.7	4.8	4.9	5.0	5.8
	8.7	12.5	9.2	9.9		10.5	8.1	8.0	9.4	9.9
	43.9	48.4	12.2	45.5		30.1	25.1	20.5	40.4	45.5
	137.6	28.8	143.3	85.8	EBIT/Interest	27.5	26.7	45.0	32.9	85.8
	28.9	9.9	21.9	17.1		(36) 8.0	(50) 6.7	(49) 10.7	(64) 8.6	17.1
	3.2	4.5	.3	2.6		1.2	2.7	4.5	2.7	2.6
					Net Profit + Depr., Dep., Amort./Cur. Mat. L/T/D					
	.4	.5	.3	.4	Fixed/Worth	.4	.5	.4	.4	.4
	.7	.9	.7	.8		.9	.8	.7	.6	.8
	1.1	1.3	2.7	1.2		1.4	1.3	1.3	1.3	1.2
	.3	.6	.7	.5	Debt/Worth	.9	.8	.7	.8	.5
	.7	1.2	1.5	1.2		1.7	1.5	1.1	1.3	1.2
	2.1	1.9	6.0	2.4		2.6	2.8	2.3	2.5	2.4
	32.1	38.5	38.5	37.4	% Profit Before Taxes/ Tangible Net Worth	25.2	30.9	42.7	32.8	37.4
	23.7	28.1	(11) 28.1	(53) 27.2		(39) 11.9	(52) 15.7	26.3	(63) 18.6	(53) 27.2
	9.8	8.1	3.3	8.1		6.2	5.8	10.2	4.8	8.1
	19.2	19.9	18.6	18.5	% Profit Before Taxes/ Total Assets	11.4	13.9	20.7	15.6	18.5
	14.3	9.3	9.6	11.0		5.5	6.7	10.1	8.2	11.0
	4.2	3.1	-2.0	2.4		1.9	2.1	4.0	1.8	2.4
	4.3	2.3		2.3	% Depr., Dep., Amort./ Revenues	1.3	2.0	2.2	1.9	2.3
(11)	5.4	(28) 3.3		(47) 3.5		(33) 2.8	(46) 3.6	(45) 3.1	(56) 3.7	(47) 3.5
	6.7	5.0		5.4		3.7	4.9	4.7	4.8	5.4
				1.0	% Officers', Directors' Owners' Comp/Revenues	1.0	1.4	1.5	1.2	1.0
				(12) 2.2		(14) 1.9	(14) 2.8	(17) 2.6	(22) 2.5	(12) 2.2
				4.8		2.3	4.2	4.6	4.4	4.8
	82383M	640809M	7744705M	8467897M	Contract Revenues ($)	8772107M	9600858M	5864044M	7965229M	8467897M
	51518M	357593M	4443126M	4852237M	Total Assets ($)	4298240M	5037781M	3899553M	4834355M	4852237M

© RMA 2019

M = $ thousand   MM = $ million
See Pages viii through xx for Explanation of Ratios and Data

Current Data Sorted by Revenue | **Comparative Historical Data**

Type of Statement

Type of Statement	0-1MM	1-10MM	10-50MM	50 & OVER	ALL		4/1/14-3/31/15 ALL	4/1/15-3/31/16 ALL	4/1/16-3/31/17 ALL	4/1/17-3/31/18 ALL	4/1/18-3/31/19 ALL
Unqualified				1	1					1	2
Reviewed	1	3		2	6			6	8	6	6
Compiled				1	1					1	
Tax Returns								3			
Other	3	2		16	21			13	12	20	21
	4 (4/1-9/30/18)		27 (10/1/18-3/31/19)								
NUMBER OF STATEMENTS	6	5		20	31			22	22	29	31

Columns 0-1MM, 1-10MM, 10-50MM (Current Data) and 4/1/14-3/31/15 (Historical) are marked DATA NOT AVAILABLE for the percentage and ratio rows below.

ASSETS (%)

	50 & OVER	ALL	4/1/15-3/31/16 ALL	4/1/16-3/31/17 ALL	4/1/17-3/31/18 ALL	4/1/18-3/31/19 ALL
Cash & Equivalents	7.7	10.4	17.5	5.8	11.0	10.4
A/R - Progress Billings	30.1	28.3	28.7	39.4	31.1	28.3
A/R - Current Retention	1.5	1.7	.9	1.2	1.4	1.7
Inventory	2.3	1.7	1.2	1.6	2.3	1.7
Cost & Est. Earnings In Excess Billings	10.0	7.7	9.1	10.7	8.7	7.7
All Other Current	3.1	4.6	4.9	2.4	2.3	4.6
Total Current	54.7	54.4	62.3	61.1	56.9	54.4
Fixed Assets (net)	28.5	30.5	22.8	27.0	30.2	30.5
Joint Ventures & Investments	.1	.2	.1	.1	.1	.2
Intangibles (net)	14.1	10.7	11.5	9.4	7.2	10.7
All Other Non-Current	2.5	4.2	3.3	2.3	5.5	4.2
Total	100.0	100.0	100.0	100.0	100.0	100.0

LIABILITIES (%)

	50 & OVER	ALL	4/1/15-3/31/16 ALL	4/1/16-3/31/17 ALL	4/1/17-3/31/18 ALL	4/1/18-3/31/19 ALL
Notes Payable-Short Term	3.1	3.2	8.0	6.6	7.4	3.2
A/P - Trade	10.8	9.5	12.3	16.5	9.5	9.5
A/P - Retention	.1	.1	.0	.1	.1	.1
Billings in Excess of Costs & Est. Earnings	1.6	1.7	2.4	3.6	4.3	1.7
Income Taxes Payable	.1	.1	.8	.2	.3	.1
Cur. Mat.-L/T/D	3.7	4.0	3.0	3.7	3.7	4.0
All Other Current	9.0	8.7	10.2	8.6	12.3	8.7
Total Current	28.4	27.2	36.7	39.3	37.6	27.2
Long-Term Debt	25.9	21.9	16.9	17.2	18.5	21.9
Deferred Taxes	1.4	.9	1.6	1.5	1.1	.9
All Other Non-Current	6.1	5.9	9.7	3.9	4.3	5.9
Net Worth	38.1	44.1	35.0	38.1	38.5	44.1
Total Liabilties & Net Worth	100.0	100.0	100.0	100.0	100.0	100.0

INCOME DATA (%)

	50 & OVER	ALL	4/1/15-3/31/16 ALL	4/1/16-3/31/17 ALL	4/1/17-3/31/18 ALL	4/1/18-3/31/19 ALL
Contract Revenues	100.0	100.0	100.0	100.0	100.0	100.0
Gross Profit	16.9	23.3	23.3	19.0	24.4	23.3
Operating Expenses	11.7	16.2	17.1	14.4	17.1	16.2
Operating Profit	5.2	7.2	6.3	4.6	7.3	7.2
All Other Expenses (net)	1.7	1.1	1.3	.9	1.0	1.1
Profit Before Taxes	3.6	6.1	4.9	3.7	6.3	6.1

RATIOS

	50 & OVER	ALL	4/1/15-3/31/16 ALL	4/1/16-3/31/17 ALL	4/1/17-3/31/18 ALL	4/1/18-3/31/19 ALL
Current	2.5	2.5	2.6	2.3	2.5	2.5
	2.1	2.0	1.7	1.7	1.7	2.0
	1.6	1.6	1.2	1.1	1.1	1.6
Receivables/Payables	4.5	6.9	4.4	4.7	4.6	6.9
	3.6	(29) 3.8	(19) 3.2	2.9	(27) 2.9	(29) 3.8
	2.3	2.5	1.9	2.2	2.4	2.5
Revenues/Receivables	49 7.5	46 7.9	36 10.0	52 7.0	52 7.0	46 7.9
	57 6.4	57 6.4	51 7.1	74 4.9	64 5.7	57 6.4
	73 5.0	78 4.7	74 4.9	91 4.0	78 4.7	78 4.7
Cost of Revenues/Payables	17 21.3	12 30.6	9 41.0	19 19.6	19 19.7	12 30.6
	20 18.2	18 20.1	25 14.5	24 15.2	23 15.8	18 20.1
	31 11.7	32 11.5	32 11.5	45 8.2	35 10.3	32 11.5
Revenues/Working Capital	5.3	4.8	6.4	6.6	5.2	4.8
	8.2	8.0	8.7	9.1	8.4	8.0
	9.9	9.8	25.7	29.2	85.9	9.8
EBIT/Interest	13.3	18.4	51.0	23.1	18.8	18.4
	5.2	(30) 9.5	(21) 13.6	8.0	(30) 7.9	(30) 9.5
	1.0	2.3	1.0	1.9	1.7	2.3
Net Profit + Depr., Dep., Amort./Cur. Mat. L/T/D						
Fixed/Worth	.7	.7	.4	.7	.6	.7
	1.0	.9	.8	.9	1.1	.9
	5.0	1.8	5.2	2.3	2.1	1.8
Debt/Worth	1.0	.6	.8	1.1	.8	.6
	2.1	1.9	2.5	2.2	2.0	1.9
	19.7	3.6	14.5	5.6	4.1	3.6
% Profit Before Taxes/Tangible Net Worth	36.5	41.8	95.1	57.3	52.1	41.8
	(16) 26.6	(26) 29.7	(18) 35.2	(19) 20.7	(25) 22.2	(26) 29.7
	17.2	15.1	19.6	7.3	8.7	15.1
% Profit Before Taxes/Total Assets	15.1	18.0	34.8	12.6	17.0	18.0
	6.8	10.9	10.4	6.8	9.1	10.9
	-.6	3.2	-.2	2.7	1.7	3.2
% Depr., Dep., Amort./Revenues		2.6	1.3	.9	1.4	2.6
	(17) 4.1	4.1	(12) 2.9	(14) 2.6	(17) 3.4	(17) 4.1
		6.2	4.5	4.5	4.2	6.2
% Officers', Directors' Owners' Comp/Revenues						

Dollar Figures

	0-1MM	1-10MM	10-50MM	50 & OVER	ALL	4/1/15-3/31/16 ALL	4/1/16-3/31/17 ALL	4/1/17-3/31/18 ALL	4/1/18-3/31/19 ALL
Contract Revenues ($)	36983M	135684M		28584538M	28757205M	17963308M	20083660M	25282194M	28757205M
Total Assets ($)	17375M	85009M		18731998M	18834382M	11810312M	12913073M	17557095M	18834382M

Current Data Sorted by Revenue						Comparative Historical Data				
		1	1	2	**Type of Statement**					
		2	2	2	Unqualified	1				2
				3	Reviewed	3	5	2	2	2
2	1			22	Compiled	3		1	1	
7	9	5	1		Tax Returns	6	2	5	3	3
2 (4/1-9/30/18)		27 (10/1/18-3/31/19)			Other	9	13	11	4	22
0-1MM	1-10MM	10-50MM	50 & OVER	ALL		4/1/14-3/31/15	4/1/15-3/31/16	4/1/16-3/31/17	4/1/17-3/31/18	4/1/18-3/31/19
						ALL	ALL	ALL	ALL	ALL
9	10	6	4	29	**NUMBER OF STATEMENTS**	22	20	20	10	29
%	%	%	%	%	**ASSETS**	%	%	%	%	%
	8.6			7.6	Cash & Equivalents	8.2	5.9	4.3	3.5	7.6
	.3			2.6	A/R - Progress Billings	3.3	10.1	9.0	10.0	2.6
	.0			.5	A/R - Current Retention	.1	.1	.0	.3	.5
	20.9			33.0	Inventory	27.5	34.9	26.0	38.5	33.0
	.0			.5	Cost & Est. Earnings In Excess Billings	4.7	1.8	1.2	.7	.5
	7.9			4.4	All Other Current	7.6	4.3	16.7	5.8	4.4
	37.7			48.5	Total Current	51.3	57.1	57.2	58.9	48.5
	40.2			26.5	Fixed Assets (net)	34.3	16.8	17.5	16.8	26.5
	4.0			3.9	Joint Ventures & Investments	4.4	1.2	4.4	1.1	3.9
	.5			3.5	Intangibles (net)	.8	1.8	1.6	.0	3.5
	17.7			17.6	All Other Non-Current	9.2	23.2	19.4	23.2	17.6
	100.0			100.0	Total	100.0	100.0	100.0	100.0	100.0
					LIABILITIES					
	6.6			10.5	Notes Payable-Short Term	11.1	11.3	16.1	19.0	10.5
	1.6			4.2	A/P - Trade	3.7	6.9	7.0	6.3	4.2
	.0			.1	A/P - Retention	.0	.7	.0	.0	.1
	.0			1.8	Billings in Excess of Costs & Est. Earnings	1.0	5.2	2.3	2.5	1.8
	.0			.0	Income Taxes Payable	.0	.0	.0	.1	.0
	.0			.9	Cur. Mat.-L/T/D	5.5	2.0	7.0	9.0	.9
	10.7			12.4	All Other Current	4.9	13.4	10.4	18.9	12.4
	18.8			29.9	Total Current	26.1	39.5	42.8	55.8	29.9
	32.2			26.6	Long-Term Debt	27.7	19.8	25.4	19.3	26.6
	.0			.1	Deferred Taxes	.2	.7	.5	1.4	.1
	.1			9.2	All Other Non-Current	9.0	4.4	17.6	19.5	9.2
	48.9			34.2	Net Worth	37.1	35.6	13.8	4.1	34.2
	100.0			100.0	Total Liabilties & Net Worth	100.0	100.0	100.0	100.0	100.0
					INCOME DATA					
	100.0			100.0	Contract Revenues	100.0	100.0	100.0	100.0	100.0
					Gross Profit					
	59.8			70.0	Operating Expenses	83.0	85.1	90.7	91.7	70.0
	40.2			30.0	Operating Profit	17.0	14.9	9.3	8.3	30.0
	2.2			4.0	All Other Expenses (net)	7.5	-.4	8.7	1.7	4.0
	38.0			26.0	Profit Before Taxes	9.5	15.4	.6	6.6	26.0
					RATIOS					
	5.7			3.1		5.7	4.6	2.3	1.7	3.1
	2.1			1.3	Current	1.9	1.2	1.4	1.4	1.3
	.6			.4		1.0	.7	1.0	.8	.4
				.6		3.0	2.6	1.8		.6
			(19)	.0	Receivables/Payables	(20) .1	.5	(19) .2	(19)	.0
				.0		.0	.1	.0		.0
0 UND			0 UND		0 UND	0 767.2	0 UND	0 UND	0 UND	
0 UND			0 UND	Revenues/Receivables	0 UND	10 38.0	4 100.7	5 76.4	0 UND	
0 UND			0 UND		6 58.9	36 10.0	46 8.0	54 6.8	0 UND	
					Cost of Revenues/Payables					
	1.0			1.0		1.1	2.0	2.8	1.7	1.0
	2.1			10.0	Revenues/Working Capital	9.0	8.6	12.9	21.4	10.0
	-41.7			-4.1		NM	-19.2	NM	-6.4	-4.1
				23.1		9.9	58.0	11.5		23.1
			(22)	7.0	EBIT/Interest	(15) 3.0	(17) 7.2	(18) 3.7	(22)	7.0
				3.2		1.0	2.2	.7		3.2
					Net Profit + Depr., Dep., Amort./Cur. Mat. L/T/D					
	.0			.0		.0	.0	.0	.0	.0
	.8			.3	Fixed/Worth	.5	.1	.3	.4	.3
	3.3			1.3		3.1	2.7	3.3	3.6	1.3
	.3			.9		.4	.6	2.1	1.7	.9
	.9			2.1	Debt/Worth	2.6	2.9	4.2	5.3	2.1
	7.9			6.9		11.9	7.3	26.0	NM	6.9
	93.1			50.9		20.1	34.5	55.2		50.9
	17.2		(27)	22.3	% Profit Before Taxes/ Tangible Net Worth	(19) 5.6	(17) 14.6	(16) 38.3	(27)	22.3
	.2			6.1		-11.0	8.2	2.0		6.1
	42.8			15.6		10.9	14.0	8.2	5.2	15.6
	10.8			5.3	% Profit Before Taxes/ Total Assets	1.2	4.7	2.4	3.1	5.3
	1.1			1.4		-.5	2.1	-1.2	.2	1.4
					% Depr., Dep., Amort./ Revenues	.5	.2	.3		
						(15) 4.2	(11) .3	(10) 1.7		
						10.5	1.5	4.8		
					% Officers', Directors' Owners' Comp/Revenues					
4110M	43222M	134039M	2026885M	2208256M	Contract Revenues ($)	1362515M	7506277M	4071781M	1890891M	2208256M
23249M	120200M	154795M	1914596M	2212840M	Total Assets ($)	1039196M	13305020M	9492346M	1049686M	2212840M

M = $ thousand   MM = $ million
See Pages viii through xx for Explanation of Ratios and Data

Current Data Sorted by Revenue					Type of Statement	Comparative Historical Data				
	1	10	4	15	Unqualified	15	22	22	13	15
1	12	21	5	39	Reviewed	25	34	48	37	39
		1	1	1	Compiled	1	3	3	3	1
	2	1	3	6	Tax Returns	4	2	5	3	6
3	12	21	48	84	Other	48	87	76	84	84
	18 (4/1-9/30/18)		127 (10/1/18-3/31/19)			4/1/14-3/31/15	4/1/15-3/31/16	4/1/16-3/31/17	4/1/17-3/31/18	4/1/18-3/31/19
0-1MM	1-10MM	10-50MM	50 & OVER	ALL		ALL	ALL	ALL	ALL	ALL
4	27	53	61	145	NUMBER OF STATEMENTS	93	148	154	140	145
%	%	%	%	%	ASSETS	%	%	%	%	%
	15.5	21.3	17.1	18.2	Cash & Equivalents	20.0	17.6	19.3	15.7	18.2
	30.8	29.4	22.5	26.8	A/R - Progress Billings	28.2	29.0	28.2	29.5	26.8
	3.6	2.9	3.0	3.1	A/R - Current Retention	1.9	2.1	2.0	2.3	3.1
	1.3	2.3	4.3	3.2	Inventory	3.5	3.6	2.8	2.9	3.2
	5.4	5.0	5.9	5.3	Cost & Est. Earnings In Excess Billings	4.3	4.1	3.8	4.6	5.3
	2.7	2.0	3.7	2.8	All Other Current	3.8	3.9	3.1	2.7	2.8
	59.3	63.0	56.4	59.4	Total Current	61.7	60.3	59.2	57.7	59.4
	33.4	31.3	32.8	32.5	Fixed Assets (net)	28.3	31.5	31.9	34.1	32.5
	.0	1.1	.2	.5	Joint Ventures & Investments	1.1	.7	.2	.1	.5
	.2	.6	3.0	1.5	Intangibles (net)	1.6	1.3	1.7	2.1	1.5
	7.1	4.0	7.6	6.1	All Other Non-Current	7.3	6.2	7.0	6.1	6.1
	100.0	100.0	100.0	100.0	Total	100.0	100.0	100.0	100.0	100.0
					LIABILITIES					
	6.4	2.5	1.8	3.1	Notes Payable-Short Term	4.9	3.2	2.5	2.7	3.1
	9.4	14.2	14.7	13.7	A/P - Trade	16.1	15.9	15.3	15.0	13.7
	.0	.6	.8	.6	A/P - Retention	.4	.4	.4	.4	.6
	3.9	7.1	7.5	6.5	Billings in Excess of Costs & Est. Earnings	4.3	6.4	6.7	6.7	6.5
	.2	.0	.1	.1	Income Taxes Payable	.3	.1	.2	.1	.1
	4.6	4.2	3.9	4.2	Cur. Mat.-L/T/D	4.0	4.5	4.7	4.8	4.2
	5.8	5.7	6.2	5.9	All Other Current	5.4	6.7	5.9	5.6	5.9
	30.3	34.3	34.9	34.0	Total Current	35.6	37.1	35.7	35.4	34.0
	13.4	12.8	13.9	13.5	Long-Term Debt	13.4	14.6	12.5	14.0	13.5
	1.3	.6	1.2	1.0	Deferred Taxes	.7	.9	1.2	.9	1.0
	.9	2.0	2.7	2.1	All Other Non-Current	4.0	2.9	3.9	2.7	2.1
	54.1	50.3	47.3	49.4	Net Worth	46.3	44.5	46.6	47.0	49.4
	100.0	100.0	100.0	100.0	Total Liabilties & Net Worth	100.0	100.0	100.0	100.0	100.0
					INCOME DATA					
	100.0	100.0	100.0	100.0	Contract Revenues	100.0	100.0	100.0	100.0	100.0
	26.8	17.0	13.3	17.4	Gross Profit	16.2	17.0	17.3	18.3	17.4
	22.5	11.3	9.0	12.5	Operating Expenses	12.6	12.0	12.3	12.9	12.5
	4.4	5.7	4.3	5.0	Operating Profit	3.6	5.0	5.0	5.3	5.0
	-.1	.2	.3	.1	All Other Expenses (net)	-.4	.1	.3	-.1	.1
	4.4	5.5	4.0	4.8	Profit Before Taxes	4.0	4.9	4.7	5.5	4.8
					RATIOS					
	4.3	2.8	2.3	2.8	Current	2.8	2.1	2.1	2.2	2.8
	2.6	1.7	1.6	1.7		1.8	1.6	1.6	1.6	1.7
	1.2	1.4	1.2	1.3		1.3	1.3	1.3	1.3	1.3
	13.9	4.3	2.3	3.4	Receivables/Payables	3.2	3.0	3.1	3.5	3.4
	(26) 4.2	2.7	1.8	(144) 2.2		(92) 2.0	(145) 1.9	2.0	(144) 2.1	2.2
	2.2	1.5	1.1	1.4		1.4	1.4	1.5	1.4	1.4
34 10.6	35 10.4	37 9.8	36 10.2		Revenues/Receivables	32 11.5	34 10.7	33 11.0	39 9.3	36 10.2
66 5.5	54 6.7	52 7.0	56 6.5			49 7.4	54 6.8	56 6.5	57 6.4	56 6.5
101 3.6	85 4.3	66 5.5	78 4.7			69 5.3	78 4.7	73 5.0	78 4.7	78 4.7
6 58.9	14 25.7	23 15.6	16 22.9		Cost of Revenues/Payables	15 24.2	19 19.3	18 20.2	20 18.0	16 22.9
16 23.1	25 14.6	31 11.6	26 13.9			28 12.9	29 12.5	30 12.3	30 12.1	26 13.9
33 11.0	43 8.4	42 8.7	41 8.8			44 8.3	49 7.4	45 8.2	46 8.0	41 8.8
	3.6	3.7	4.8	4.0	Revenues/Working Capital	4.9	5.7	5.2	5.3	4.0
	6.1	7.5	8.9	8.0		8.8	10.2	8.6	9.1	8.0
	10.8	13.9	17.9	14.4		17.1	16.7	17.2	18.4	14.4
	73.5	56.5	27.1	39.8	EBIT/Interest	29.0	24.7	28.0	36.8	39.8
	(25) 14.4	(51) 14.3	(56) 10.2	(134) 12.3		(85) 8.9	(135) 10.5	(140) 10.5	(130) 11.4	(134) 12.3
	1.2	4.7	3.2	3.1		3.2	3.6	4.4	4.9	3.1
				8.2	Net Profit + Depr., Dep., Amort./Cur. Mat. L/T/D	3.8	4.0	5.3	6.5	8.2
			(20)	2.4		(15) 2.6	(26) 2.3	(34) 2.4	(22) 2.3	(20) 2.4
				1.7		1.5	1.4	1.5	1.7	1.7
	.2	.3	.4	.4	Fixed/Worth	.3	.4	.4	.5	.4
	.5	.6	.7	.6		.7	.7	.7	.8	.6
	1.2	.9	1.2	1.1		1.1	1.2	1.1	1.1	1.1
	.2	.6	.8	.5	Debt/Worth	.5	.8	.7	.7	.5
	.9	1.0	1.2	1.0		1.4	1.2	1.2	1.2	1.0
	1.5	1.7	2.0	1.8		2.7	1.9	2.0	1.9	1.8
	28.3	26.1	21.6	23.3	% Profit Before Taxes/Tangible Net Worth	27.1	33.6	32.1	35.9	23.3
	(26) 11.1	(52) 13.7	(60) 14.0	(141) 13.1		(89) 16.6	(145) 21.4	(151) 18.8	(137) 16.4	(141) 13.1
	.4	6.2	5.3	5.1		7.3	7.7	8.3	10.0	5.1
	13.7	15.0	10.6	12.0	% Profit Before Taxes/Total Assets	14.6	14.1	14.3	15.5	12.0
	4.3	7.0	5.9	6.1		6.1	7.7	8.4	7.6	6.1
	-2.4	3.3	1.8	2.0		2.0	2.7	2.9	4.5	2.0
	1.9	1.8	2.2	2.0	% Depr., Dep., Amort./Revenues	1.7	1.8	1.8	2.2	2.0
	(22) 4.5	(50) 3.2	(41) 3.6	(116) 3.6		(86) 2.9	(124) 2.9	(136) 3.4	(115) 3.3	(116) 3.6
	6.9	5.1	4.7	5.1		3.9	3.8	4.7	5.2	5.1
	1.8	.7	.5	.8	% Officers', Directors' Owners' Comp/Revenues	.9	.7	.8	.7	.8
	(11) 3.3	(21) 1.5	(13) 1.2	(46) 1.5		(34) 1.8	(43) 1.6	(47) 1.6	(46) 2.0	(46) 1.5
	8.3	3.1	1.4	3.1		3.3	3.5	3.5	3.8	3.1
1731M	144041M	1290031M	35740165M	37175968M	Contract Revenues ($)	56098378M	81015156M	23196241M	32171024M	37175968M
1105M	89143M	758388M	21239185M	22087821M	Total Assets ($)	27121628M	39686187M	15199500M	20252181M	22087821M

© RMA 2019

M = $ thousand   MM = $ million
See Pages viii through xx for Explanation of Ratios and Data

Current Data Sorted by Revenue · **Comparative Historical Data**

Type of Statement										
		5	2	7	Unqualified	5	5	10	8	7
3	2	12	1	18	Reviewed	12	17	25	26	18
	1	1	1	3	Compiled	2	4	4	2	3
2	1	1	1	3	Tax Returns	1	7	2	2	3
4		13	15	32	Other	11	23	27	36	32

8 (4/1-9/30/18) · 55 (10/1/18-3/31/19)

0-1MM	1-10MM	10-50MM	50 & OVER	ALL		4/1/14-3/31/15 ALL	4/1/15-3/31/16 ALL	4/1/16-3/31/17 ALL	4/1/17-3/31/18 ALL	4/1/18-3/31/19 ALL
3	9	32	19	63	**NUMBER OF STATEMENTS**	31	56	68	74	63
%	%	%	%	%	**ASSETS**	%	%	%	%	%
		10.3	14.7	14.6	Cash & Equivalents	22.3	10.8	16.8	13.9	14.6
		33.5	27.0	30.9	A/R - Progress Billings	29.4	30.4	31.9	31.5	30.9
		2.3	4.6	3.3	A/R - Current Retention	2.4	2.9	3.1	3.0	3.3
		2.5	1.2	1.9	Inventory	1.0	1.4	1.6	1.8	1.9
		7.3	7.8	6.7	Cost & Est. Earnings In Excess Billings	6.5	7.0	5.3	5.8	6.7
		3.2	5.2	4.6	All Other Current	6.3	9.0	4.7	5.4	4.6
		59.0	60.6	61.9	Total Current	67.9	61.3	63.5	61.3	61.9
		34.5	26.5	29.2	Fixed Assets (net)	26.1	30.6	29.0	28.7	29.2
		1.1	1.0	.8	Joint Ventures & Investments	.3	.0	.3	.8	.8
		1.2	3.8	1.9	Intangibles (net)	1.8	2.4	2.6	2.8	1.9
		4.2	8.1	6.2	All Other Non-Current	3.8	5.6	4.4	6.3	6.2
		100.0	100.0	100.0	Total	100.0	100.0	100.0	100.0	100.0
					LIABILITIES					
		5.0	1.5	4.2	Notes Payable-Short Term	3.1	5.3	4.0	4.7	4.2
		19.4	15.4	18.2	A/P - Trade	18.3	18.3	19.1	17.9	18.2
		.3	1.0	.9	A/P - Retention	.8	.7	1.0	.7	.9
		3.6	10.7	6.1	Billings in Excess of Costs & Est. Earnings	8.3	4.3	6.9	5.1	6.1
		.2	.1	.1	Income Taxes Payable	.1	.8	.3	.4	.1
		4.7	2.2	3.7	Cur. Mat.-L/T/D	3.8	4.3	3.9	4.7	3.7
		4.9	11.3	7.4	All Other Current	11.3	7.1	5.9	4.9	7.4
		38.1	42.3	40.6	Total Current	45.8	40.9	41.1	38.4	40.6
		13.4	13.0	11.9	Long-Term Debt	9.3	16.3	13.1	12.2	11.9
		.5	.8	.7	Deferred Taxes	.8	1.6	1.2	1.3	.7
		3.3	4.0	2.9	All Other Non-Current	1.5	2.7	.6	1.5	2.9
		44.8	39.9	43.9	Net Worth	42.6	38.6	43.9	46.7	43.9
		100.0	100.0	100.0	Total Liabilities & Net Worth	100.0	100.0	100.0	100.0	100.0
					INCOME DATA					
		100.0	100.0	100.0	Contract Revenues	100.0	100.0	100.0	100.0	100.0
		20.4	11.6	17.7	Gross Profit	18.9	17.7	17.3	19.8	17.7
		15.9	9.5	13.6	Operating Expenses	13.1	12.2	12.0	15.1	13.6
		4.5	2.1	4.1	Operating Profit	5.7	5.5	5.3	4.8	4.1
		.6	.9	.6	All Other Expenses (net)	.0	1.1	.3	.6	.6
		3.9	1.1	3.5	Profit Before Taxes	5.7	4.4	5.0	4.2	3.5
					RATIOS					
		2.1	2.0	2.1	Current	2.2	1.8	2.3	2.0	2.1
		1.4	1.4	1.4		1.4	1.4	1.5	1.6	1.4
		1.2	1.1	1.2		1.2	1.2	1.1	1.2	1.2
		3.6	3.3	3.1	Receivables/Payables	2.6	3.3	3.5	3.3	3.1
		1.9	2.4	(62) 2.0		2.1	1.8	2.0	2.0	(62) 2.0
		1.3	.9	1.2		1.1	1.2	1.3	1.3	1.2
		49 7.4	33 11.2	41 8.9	Revenues/Receivables	31 11.8	40 9.1	40 9.2	41 8.8	41 8.9
		60 6.1	60 6.1	59 6.2		72 5.1	57 6.4	55 6.6	64 5.7	59 6.2
		76 4.8	91 4.0	79 4.6		94 3.9	83 4.4	85 4.3	85 4.3	79 4.6
		26 14.2	25 14.4	25 14.4	Cost of Revenues/Payables	23 15.7	23 15.6	21 17.5	22 16.8	25 14.4
		42 8.6	43 8.5	42 8.6		34 10.6	34 10.7	34 10.6	38 9.7	42 8.6
		55 6.6	50 7.3	54 6.8		64 5.7	53 6.9	49 7.5	54 6.8	54 6.8
		5.3	6.0	5.4	Revenues/Working Capital	4.8	6.4	5.4	5.2	5.4
		16.2	11.4	13.9		8.9	11.0	11.1	7.9	13.9
		23.4	24.8	23.5		20.8	25.6	51.4	23.0	23.5
		36.0	26.4	26.4	EBIT/Interest	71.9	12.6	35.1	17.9	26.4
		(28) 5.8	5.7	(55) 6.0		(27) 11.2	(53) 4.9	(61) 9.2	(66) 8.3	(55) 6.0
		1.6	1.5	1.5		3.7	1.0	1.9	1.9	1.5
					Net Profit + Depr., Dep., Amort./Cur. Mat. L/T/D		27.5	10.1	3.9	
						(12)	3.5	(11) 3.7	(12) 2.5	
							1.4	.6	1.0	
		.2	.3	.2	Fixed/Worth	.3	.4	.3	.2	.2
		.8	.8	.8		.6	.9	.7	.7	.8
		1.3	1.4	1.2		1.1	1.6	1.2	1.1	1.2
		.9	1.2	.9	Debt/Worth	.7	.8	.8	.7	.9
		1.5	1.9	1.5		1.2	1.7	1.5	1.2	1.5
		2.3	3.7	2.7		3.3	3.6	3.0	2.3	2.7
		33.9	24.1	34.5	% Profit Before Taxes/Tangible Net Worth	43.1	37.8	42.6	37.0	34.5
		(31) 15.7	13.2	(62) 17.2		(29) 13.9	(52) 13.7	(66) 23.9	(72) 19.6	(62) 17.2
		8.3	4.3	4.2		8.3		7.0	4.1	4.2
		15.3	5.6	12.7	% Profit Before Taxes/Total Assets	14.0	14.2	16.8	15.5	12.7
		6.0	4.0	5.6		6.1	5.3	7.5	7.6	5.6
		4.3	2.3	2.3		2.0	.1	2.1	1.9	2.3
		1.6	.5	.9	% Depr., Dep., Amort./Revenues	.9	.8	.7	1.2	.9
		(29) 3.7	(11) 1.3	(49) 2.1		(24) 1.9	(44) 2.8	(58) 1.8	(58) 3.0	(49) 2.1
		7.7	2.8	5.4		3.1	4.5	4.6	6.0	5.4
				.7	% Officers', Directors' Owners' Comp/Revenues	1.7	.7	1.4	1.0	.7
				(15) 2.1		(10) 2.6	(15) 2.1	(20) 2.9	(21) 2.5	(15) 2.1
				6.8		4.7	4.4	4.2	5.0	6.8
111M	47328M	810828M	17471826M	18330093M	Contract Revenues ($)	3454815M	8372884M	8012980M	10661423M	18330093M
41M	24801M	466620M	12690174M	13181636M	Total Assets ($)	2564511M	5176419M	4675307M	6848109M	13181636M

© RMA 2019

M = $ thousand   MM = $ million
See Pages viii through xx for Explanation of Ratios and Data

Current Data Sorted by Revenue

Comparative Historical Data

Type of Statement

1-10MM	10-50MM	50 & OVER	ALL	Type of Statement					
1	1		2	Unqualified	1	1	1		2
5	7	1	13	Reviewed	10	16	15	16	13
2	3		5	Compiled	4	4	6	1	5
2	3	1	5	Tax Returns	3	4	5	8	5
3	8	2	13	Other	12	12	9	14	13

2 (4/1-9/30/18)   36 (10/1/18-3/31/19)

0-1MM	1-10MM	10-50MM	50 & OVER	ALL		4/1/14-3/31/15 ALL	4/1/15-3/31/16 ALL	4/1/16-3/31/17 ALL	4/1/17-3/31/18 ALL	4/1/18-3/31/19 ALL
	13	21	4	38	**NUMBER OF STATEMENTS**	30	37	36	39	38
%	%	%	%	%	**ASSETS**	%	%	%	%	%
	10.0	10.8		9.6	Cash & Equivalents	10.7	14.3	15.2	14.0	9.6
	44.9	42.0		44.9	A/R - Progress Billings	40.4	48.7	44.8	40.5	44.9
	3.2	8.6		6.3	A/R - Current Retention	4.6	2.0	3.2	5.7	6.3
	1.1	.6		.8	Inventory	.7	1.5	.8	1.2	.8
D	6.4	6.7		6.4	Cost & Est. Earnings In Excess Billings	3.4	4.8	3.8	2.6	6.4
A	8.8	.3		3.2	All Other Current	7.8	4.0	3.1	4.3	3.2
T	74.3	69.0		71.3	Total Current	67.5	75.4	70.9	68.3	71.3
A	17.2	25.5		22.2	Fixed Assets (net)	22.9	18.8	23.1	21.0	22.2
N	.0	.0		.0	Joint Ventures & Investments	.8	.0	.0	5.6	.0
O	1.9	.7		1.1	Intangibles (net)	1.6	.7	.9	1.2	1.1
T	6.6	4.8		5.4	All Other Non-Current	7.3	5.2	5.0	3.8	5.4
	100.0	100.0		100.0	Total	100.0	100.0	100.0	100.0	100.0
A					**LIABILITIES**					
V	12.0	6.5		9.0	Notes Payable-Short Term	20.4	12.6	9.3	5.9	9.0
A	11.4	19.5		17.7	A/P - Trade	16.1	21.8	17.8	18.0	17.7
I	.5	.5		.5	A/P - Retention	.0	.1	.3	.6	.5
L	2.5	4.1		3.3	Billings in Excess of Costs & Est. Earnings	3.6	6.5	5.7	7.0	3.3
A	.2	.0		.1	Income Taxes Payable	.1	.0	.0	.0	.1
B	3.0	3.3		3.0	Cur. Mat.-L/T/D	3.3	3.0	3.9	2.6	3.0
L	9.5	9.9		10.4	All Other Current	12.0	8.0	7.0	8.7	10.4
E	39.0	43.9		43.9	Total Current	55.5	52.1	44.1	42.8	43.9
	8.5	11.3		9.3	Long-Term Debt	7.4	7.3	13.8	7.9	9.3
	.0	.4		.2	Deferred Taxes	1.1	.7	.4	.3	.2
	2.5	1.9		1.9	All Other Non-Current	10.7	6.8	3.4	2.1	1.9
	50.0	42.6		44.6	Net Worth	25.5	33.1	38.3	46.8	44.6
	100.0	100.0		100.0	Total Liabilities & Net Worth	100.0	100.0	100.0	100.0	100.0
					INCOME DATA					
	100.0	100.0		100.0	Contract Revenues	100.0	100.0	100.0	100.0	100.0
	22.9	16.6		18.7	Gross Profit	20.4	20.1	18.5	22.8	18.7
	18.8	11.8		14.4	Operating Expenses	15.6	14.5	12.8	15.9	14.4
	4.1	4.8		4.3	Operating Profit	4.8	5.6	5.7	6.9	4.3
	.3	.2		.2	All Other Expenses (net)	.0	.2	.1	.8	.2
	3.9	4.6		4.1	Profit Before Taxes	4.7	5.4	5.6	6.1	4.1
					RATIOS					
	4.1	2.3		2.8	Current	2.7	2.1	2.3	2.5	2.8
	2.5	1.4		1.6		1.7	1.7	1.6	1.5	1.6
	1.5	1.2		1.2		1.1	1.2	1.4	1.2	1.2
	14.7	4.5		4.7	Receivables/Payables	7.6	3.4	3.4	8.8	4.7
	(12) 4.8	3.0		(37) 3.0		(29) 2.9	(36) 2.2	(34) 2.6	(38) 2.5	(37) 3.0
	2.6	1.8		2.1		2.2	2.0	2.2	1.9	2.1
	31 11.7	51 7.1	50 7.3		Revenues/Receivables	37 9.9	43 8.5	43 8.4	39 9.4	50 7.3
	72 5.1	74 4.9	76 4.8			62 5.9	74 4.9	66 5.5	81 4.5	76 4.8
	104 3.5	87 4.2	91 4.0			91 4.0	99 3.7	89 4.1	99 3.7	91 4.0
	3 122.0	16 23.4	11 33.3		Cost of Revenues/Payables	6 56.3	20 18.4	17 21.0	11 33.8	11 33.3
	22 16.5	27 13.5	28 13.2			22 16.8	38 9.6	28 13.1	34 10.6	28 13.2
	62 5.9	50 7.3	54 6.8			38 9.5	52 7.0	45 8.2	53 6.9	54 6.8
	3.8	6.4		5.3	Revenues/Working Capital	5.1	6.2	6.0	5.4	5.3
	6.8	13.2		13.3		10.0	9.3	9.1	11.1	13.3
	20.7	23.8		25.8		113.5	32.8	18.8	23.9	25.8
	39.5	13.9		18.0	EBIT/Interest	45.1	39.6	29.3	43.0	18.0
	8.7	(19) 7.6		(36) 8.1		(28) 14.3	(33) 14.4	(31) 14.6	(31) 13.9	(36) 8.1
	-6.8	1.7		1.6		3.4	5.0	2.3	2.0	1.6
					Net Profit + Depr., Dep., Amort./Cur. Mat. L/T/D					
	.1	.2		.2	Fixed/Worth	.2	.1	.2	.2	.2
	.3	.6		.6		.6	.4	.5	.4	.6
	.7	1.0		.8		1.1	.8	.9	.8	.8
	.5	.9		.6	Debt/Worth	.7	.9	.7	.5	.6
	.8	1.4		1.2		1.3	1.3	1.4	1.4	1.2
	1.7	2.2		2.3		4.6	3.3	2.6	3.1	2.3
	37.2	44.1		39.6	% Profit Before Taxes/Tangible Net Worth	42.1	58.2	51.5	62.4	39.6
	(12) 24.0	21.2		(37) 21.5		(26) 21.4	(36) 30.5	(32) 34.8	(38) 28.9	(37) 21.5
	2.1	6.6		6.6		8.8	9.9	20.7	17.7	6.6
	19.4	18.6		18.1	% Profit Before Taxes/Total Assets	17.8	21.2	23.2	22.6	18.1
	13.1	10.0		9.4		11.1	12.8	11.6	13.6	9.4
	-7.7	1.4		1.0		3.3	5.3	4.0	4.7	1.0
	1.2	.8		.8	% Depr., Dep., Amort./Revenues	.5	.6	.5	.5	.8
	1.7	1.2		(37) 1.3		(26) 1.7	(33) 1.1	(31) 1.5	(33) 1.4	(37) 1.3
	2.7	1.8		2.2		2.6	2.6	2.4	3.3	2.2
		.4		.6	% Officers', Directors' Owners' Comp/Revenues	2.3	1.7	.9	1.1	.6
	(10)	1.1		(15) 1.4		(13) 3.2	(17) 2.7	(15) 3.3	(14) 2.5	(15) 1.4
		2.4		3.2		5.0	5.3	5.2	4.9	3.2
	59965M	601259M	8356562M	9017786M	Contract Revenues ($)	807173M	7130822M	909099M	924640M	9017786M
	24478M	267958M	1743540M	2035976M	Total Assets ($)	269439M	1470048M	334659M	373608M	2035976M

(0-1MM column: DATA NOT AVAILABLE)

M = $ thousand   MM = $ million
See Pages viii through xx for Explanation of Ratios and Data

	Current Data Sorted by Revenue						**Comparative Historical Data**				
Type of Statement	0-1MM	1-10MM	10-50MM	50 & OVER	ALL		4/1/14-3/31/15	4/1/15-3/31/16	4/1/16-3/31/17	4/1/17-3/31/18	4/1/18-3/31/19
Unqualified							1				
Reviewed		6	4		10		11	6	8	8	10
Compiled		1	1		1		3	3	2	5	1
Tax Returns		1	1		1		1		2	1	
Other		4	7	2	13		5	11	11	14	13
		3 (4/1-9/30/18)	22 (10/1/18-3/31/19)				ALL	ALL	ALL	ALL	ALL
NUMBER OF STATEMENTS		10	13	2	25		21	20	22	29	25
	%	%	%	%	%		%	%	%	%	%
ASSETS											
Cash & Equivalents		10.9	5.1		7.1		16.9	13.5	11.5	9.3	7.1
A/R - Progress Billings		36.2	46.6		42.5		45.9	44.9	45.7	43.5	42.5
A/R - Current Retention		1.2	4.2		3.1		2.0	5.7	2.4	4.3	3.1
Inventory		.8	4.6		3.0		2.1	3.1	2.2	2.6	3.0
Cost & Est. Earnings In Excess Billings		4.2	6.1		5.7		5.8	7.6	5.4	5.7	5.7
All Other Current		4.4	1.2		2.9		1.1	1.2	7.2	7.3	2.9
Total Current		57.6	67.8		64.3		73.8	76.0	74.5	72.7	64.3
Fixed Assets (net)		34.2	23.9		26.8		15.6	19.0	16.8	16.9	26.8
Joint Ventures & Investments		.0	.0		.0		.1	.0	.0	.0	.0
Intangibles (net)		2.8	.2		1.3		3.7	.2	.1	2.9	1.3
All Other Non-Current		5.3	8.1		7.6		6.9	4.9	8.4	7.4	7.6
Total		100.0	100.0		100.0		100.0	100.0	100.0	100.0	100.0
LIABILITIES											
Notes Payable-Short Term		4.8	11.4		8.1		21.4	4.5	6.4	5.3	8.1
A/P - Trade		11.2	19.9		16.2		14.8	14.9	13.3	18.5	16.2
A/P - Retention		.0	.0		.1		.0	.4	.3	.5	.1
Billings in Excess of Costs & Est. Earnings		4.9	4.8		5.5		5.5	7.4	10.6	9.1	5.5
Income Taxes Payable		.1	.0		.1		.0	.0	.1	.2	.1
Cur. Mat.-L/T/D		2.8	4.6		4.0		2.1	1.6	1.5	2.9	4.0
All Other Current		5.6	8.2		7.2		5.5	11.1	8.3	8.8	7.2
Total Current		29.4	49.0		41.1		49.3	40.0	40.4	45.2	41.1
Long-Term Debt		17.7	7.6		11.5		8.8	6.0	7.9	7.8	11.5
Deferred Taxes		.0	.1		.1		.0	.0	.0	.3	.1
All Other Non-Current		.9	4.2		2.6		.6	.0	4.0	3.1	2.6
Net Worth		51.9	39.1		44.8		41.4	54.0	47.5	43.6	44.8
Total Liabilities & Net Worth		100.0	100.0		100.0		100.0	100.0	100.0	100.0	100.0
INCOME DATA											
Contract Revenues		100.0	100.0		100.0		100.0	100.0	100.0	100.0	100.0
Gross Profit		24.2	14.2		18.7		22.5	21.1	19.2	20.2	18.7
Operating Expenses		27.2	11.2		17.9		17.8	13.3	13.8	13.8	17.9
Operating Profit		-3.0	3.0		.8		4.8	7.8	5.4	6.3	.8
All Other Expenses (net)		.9	-.3		.2		.2	1.0	.4	.7	.2
Profit Before Taxes		-4.0	3.3		.6		4.6	6.8	5.0	5.7	.6
RATIOS											
Current		2.5	1.9		2.0		3.8	2.8	3.0	2.2	2.0
		1.7	1.5		1.5		1.8	1.9	1.9	1.6	1.5
		1.3	.9		1.2		1.1	1.4	1.4	1.2	1.2
Receivables/Payables		11.3	6.8		7.3		9.2	5.6	7.9	8.1	7.3
		4.1	3.1		3.2		(20) 4.1	4.2	3.2	3.8	3.2
		2.0	1.6		2.0		2.0	2.2	2.1	1.5	2.0
Revenues/Receivables	35 10.4	69 5.3		69 5.3			51 7.2	47 7.7	64 5.7	56 6.5	69 5.3
	94 3.9	78 4.7		83 4.4			64 5.7	72 5.1	89 4.1	78 4.7	83 4.4
	152 2.4	96 3.8		122 3.0			104 3.5	104 3.5	122 3.0	99 3.7	122 3.0
Cost of Revenues/Payables	8 47.3	16 22.6		16 22.6			8 45.1	18 20.8	14 26.3	12 30.1	16 22.6
	33 11.2	26 14.1		32 11.5			19 19.1	24 15.3	27 13.5	26 13.8	32 11.5
	54 6.8	46 8.0		48 7.6			45 8.1	36 10.0	36 10.0	57 6.4	48 7.6
Revenues/Working Capital		3.7	5.9		4.9		3.8	4.0	3.5	5.2	4.9
		7.0	10.8		8.3		8.2	6.8	6.2	10.4	8.3
		13.8	NM		28.2		22.9	15.2	13.1	29.6	28.2
EBIT/Interest			21.3		22.1		29.8	109.9	62.0	133.1	22.1
		(12)	4.3	(23)	3.1		(15) 10.0	(17) 40.0	(10) 10.9	(24) 7.4	(23) 3.1
			1.1		-3.7		1.3	10.7	2.9	1.5	-3.7
Net Profit + Depr., Dep., Amort./Cur. Mat. L/T/D											
Fixed/Worth		.4	.2		.2		.1	.2	.1	.1	.2
		.6	.6		.5		.3	.4	.4	.4	.5
		1.2	2.0		1.2		.6	.4	.7	.9	1.2
Debt/Worth		.5	.7		.7		.3	.4	.4	.6	.7
		.8	1.3		1.3		1.0	.8	1.1	1.3	1.3
		1.7	4.3		3.3		1.7	2.6	3.4	4.0	3.3
% Profit Before Taxes/Tangible Net Worth			40.8		23.0		37.3	75.4	46.9	75.2	23.0
		(12)	12.4	(23)	8.1		(20) 28.2	30.9	(20) 33.2	(26) 25.9	(23) 8.1
			6.2		-4.5		.9	7.4	6.7	8.9	-4.5
% Profit Before Taxes/Total Assets		4.6	16.1		10.6		22.0	28.2	23.7	20.9	10.6
		-1.4	4.1		3.2		12.8	16.5	12.0	8.1	3.2
		-7.4	.3		-2.5		.6	3.6	4.0	3.3	-2.5
% Depr., Dep., Amort./Revenues			1.1		1.1		.8	.5	.8	1.0	1.1
		(11)	1.6	(22)	1.8		(16) 1.2	(15) .9	(16) 1.6	(21) 1.8	(22) 1.8
			3.5		4.1		2.0	1.9	2.4	3.0	4.1
% Officers', Directors' Owners' Comp/Revenues							1.0				
							(12) 2.1				
							6.3				
Contract Revenues ($)		58808M	288800M	591490M	939098M		409427M	719249M	693200M	818300M	939098M
Total Assets ($)		47474M	143476M	308946M	499896M		185042M	295537M	315141M	396722M	499896M

Note: 0-1MM column — DATA NOT AVAILABLE

© RMA 2019

M = $ thousand   MM = $ million
See Pages viii through xx for Explanation of Ratios and Data

Current Data Sorted by Revenue						Comparative Historical Data				
					Type of Statement					
					Unqualified			1		
1	7	8		16	Reviewed	7	8	14	13	16
	1			1	Compiled		1	1	3	1
					Tax Returns	2	4	1	2	
	1	4		5	Other	4	7	4	7	5
3 (4/1-9/30/18)		19 (10/1/18-3/31/19)				4/1/14-3/31/15	4/1/15-3/31/16	4/1/16-3/31/17	4/1/17-3/31/18	4/1/18-3/31/19
0-1MM	1-10MM	10-50MM	50 & OVER	ALL		ALL	ALL	ALL	ALL	ALL
1	9	12		22	NUMBER OF STATEMENTS	13	20	21	25	22
%	%	%	%	%	**ASSETS**	%	%	%	%	%
		24.0	DATA NOT AVAILABLE	18.4	Cash & Equivalents	22.7	20.8	14.9	10.6	18.4
		35.0		39.6	A/R - Progress Billings	36.0	42.5	48.3	46.3	39.6
		7.1		9.4	A/R - Current Retention	8.1	2.6	4.3	7.1	9.4
		.5		1.2	Inventory	.0	1.0	1.0	1.2	1.2
		3.9		3.7	Cost & Est. Earnings In Excess Billings	3.5	4.1	6.6	4.9	3.7
		2.5		3.6	All Other Current	3.5	2.5	4.7	4.3	3.6
		73.0		75.9	Total Current	73.8	73.5	79.9	74.3	75.9
		14.7		16.4	Fixed Assets (net)	18.4	15.7	16.9	17.5	16.4
		.0		.0	Joint Ventures & Investments	.0	.0	.1	.0	.0
		4.8		2.9	Intangibles (net)	.0	.1	.7	1.8	2.9
		7.5		4.9	All Other Non-Current	7.7	10.6	2.5	6.3	4.9
		100.0		100.0	Total	100.0	100.0	100.0	100.0	100.0
					LIABILITIES					
		2.9		3.2	Notes Payable-Short Term	10.2	8.4	15.9	11.2	3.2
		9.4		8.4	A/P - Trade	8.5	14.1	17.4	10.8	8.4
		1.2		.7	A/P - Retention	.0	.4	.6	.3	.7
		6.9		7.7	Billings in Excess of Costs & Est. Earnings	6.2	5.8	5.2	5.5	7.7
		.6		.3	Income Taxes Payable	.5	1.5	.1	1.0	.3
		4.8		3.2	Cur. Mat.-L/T/D	.9	3.4	1.9	1.1	3.2
		8.4		7.5	All Other Current	18.8	5.9	7.3	11.1	7.5
		34.2		31.2	Total Current	45.0	39.5	48.4	41.0	31.2
		5.5		4.0	Long-Term Debt	4.4	8.1	6.1	5.8	4.0
		.2		.5	Deferred Taxes	.9	.5	.3	.6	.5
		2.9		2.2	All Other Non-Current	3.0	.4	2.4	2.6	2.2
		57.1		62.1	Net Worth	46.7	51.6	42.9	50.0	62.1
		100.0		100.0	Total Liabilties & Net Worth	100.0	100.0	100.0	100.0	100.0
					INCOME DATA					
		100.0		100.0	Contract Revenues	100.0	100.0	100.0	100.0	100.0
		25.2		22.7	Gross Profit	22.8	27.9	20.6	21.0	22.7
		16.9		16.2	Operating Expenses	20.5	22.9	15.4	17.0	16.2
		8.2		6.5	Operating Profit	2.3	5.0	5.2	4.0	6.5
		.7		.5	All Other Expenses (net)	-.8	.1	.1	-.4	.5
		7.6		6.0	Profit Before Taxes	3.2	4.8	5.1	4.4	6.0
					RATIOS					
		3.6		4.1		3.1	3.5	2.5	3.1	4.1
		2.2		2.4	Current	1.8	2.5	1.9	2.0	2.4
		1.3		1.8		1.2	1.3	1.3	1.3	1.8
		6.1		8.5		UND	10.1	6.0	17.3	8.5
		3.4		5.0	Receivables/Payables	7.0	3.3	3.1	(24) 6.0	5.0
		2.6		3.1		1.8	1.9	2.0	2.8	3.1
		52 7.0		**52** 7.0		**28** 13.0	**45** 8.1	**49** 7.5	**55** 6.6	**52** 7.0
		60 6.1		**63** 5.8	Revenues/Receivables	**60** 6.1	**64** 5.7	**69** 5.3	**85** 4.3	**63** 5.8
		83 4.4		**96** 3.8		**104** 3.5	**81** 4.5	**85** 4.3	**118** 3.1	**96** 3.8
		14 26.5		**11** 33.8		**0** UND	**9** 39.0	**16** 22.6	**2** 222.2	**11** 33.8
		22 16.9		**18** 20.1	Cost of Revenues/Payables	**16** 23.5	**27** 13.7	**20** 18.3	**16** 23.1	**18** 20.1
		31 11.6		**26** 14.2		**38** 9.7	**41** 8.9	**46** 8.0	**28** 13.1	**26** 14.2
		4.5		4.4		3.5	4.9	6.1	4.7	4.4
		5.1		5.6	Revenues/Working Capital	8.5	6.5	9.0	7.7	5.6
		20.4		7.6		19.7	13.8	16.8	14.9	7.6
		110.3		63.9		25.9	31.9	51.7	13.0	63.9
		(11) 38.1		(19) 24.6	EBIT/Interest	(10) 16.3	(16) 11.2	(20) 20.7	(21) 8.3	(19) 24.6
		2.7		2.7		2.9	7.8	5.7	2.0	2.7
					Net Profit + Depr., Dep., Amort./Cur. Mat. L/T/D					
		.1		.1		.2	.1	.2	.1	.1
		.2		.2	Fixed/Worth	.3	.1	.4	.4	.2
		.4		.4		.6	.9	.6	.6	.4
		.4		.4		.5	.4	.6	.5	.4
		.8		.6	Debt/Worth	1.1	.9	.9	.8	.6
		2.9		.9		3.0	1.6	5.0	2.2	.9
		50.4		49.8		31.9	33.3	61.9	45.8	49.8
		46.7		34.5	% Profit Before Taxes/ Tangible Net Worth	16.0	(19) 16.4	(20) 32.8	(24) 22.3	34.5
		23.0		9.0		7.2	7.4	13.7	3.0	9.0
		27.8		28.1		10.4	23.6	23.7	23.5	28.1
		18.6		17.9	% Profit Before Taxes/ Total Assets	6.0	10.3	15.3	8.2	17.9
		5.3		3.6		1.9	4.7	4.1	.5	3.6
		.6		.6		.5	.4	.8	.8	.6
		1.3		(20) 1.3	% Depr., Dep., Amort./ Revenues	1.1	(14) 1.0	(17) 1.2	(19) 1.1	(20) 1.3
		2.7		2.5		1.7	2.0	2.2	1.6	2.5
				1.0			1.7		1.4	1.0
				(11) 3.0	% Officers', Directors' Owners' Comp/Revenues		(10) 4.4		(12) 3.1	(11) 3.0
				6.5			11.4		5.7	6.5
7M	59569M	241500M		301076M	Contract Revenues ($)	132405M	212457M	415596M	276990M	301076M
3M	22148M	111950M		134101M	Total Assets ($)	61342M	84326M	149797M	109536M	134101M

M = $ thousand MM = $ million

See Pages viii through xx for Explanation of Ratios and Data

Current Data Sorted by Revenue						Comparative Historical Data				
					Type of Statement					
1	3	10		14	Unqualified	8	16	15	11	14
	1			1	Reviewed		1	1	1	1
					Compiled		1	2	1	
					Tax Returns	1	3	2	3	
	2	3	1	6	Other	2	2	5	4	6
3 (4/1-9/30/18)		18 (10/1/18-3/31/19)				2 4/1/14-3/31/15	2 4/1/15-3/31/16	5 4/1/16-3/31/17	4 4/1/17-3/31/18	6 4/1/18-3/31/19
0-1MM	1-10MM	10-50MM	50 & OVER	ALL		ALL	ALL	ALL	ALL	ALL
1	6	13	1	21	**NUMBER OF STATEMENTS**	11	23	25	20	21
%	%	%	%	%	**ASSETS**	%	%	%	%	%
		7.8		15.5	Cash & Equivalents	16.7	13.6	13.2	11.4	15.5
		51.8		47.7	A/R - Progress Billings	52.1	54.2	55.2	48.3	47.7
		12.4		11.4	A/R - Current Retention	8.8	7.5	6.3	7.5	11.4
		.6		.7	Inventory	2.6	3.6	1.3	2.1	.7
		6.7		5.8	Cost & Est. Earnings In Excess Billings	3.2	4.9	7.4	4.3	5.8
		.9		.7	All Other Current	.8	2.1	2.7	3.1	.7
		80.2		81.7	Total Current	84.2	85.9	86.1	76.6	81.7
		16.3		12.9	Fixed Assets (net)	9.2	8.8	11.4	18.8	12.9
		.0		.0	Joint Ventures & Investments	.0	.6	.0	.0	.0
		1.7		3.4	Intangibles (net)	.0	.2	1.0	.2	3.4
		1.8		2.0	All Other Non-Current	6.5	4.5	1.5	4.4	2.0
		100.0		100.0	Total	100.0	100.0	100.0	100.0	100.0
					LIABILITIES					
		10.7		9.0	Notes Payable-Short Term	8.8	8.4	11.8	10.1	9.0
		18.9		21.2	A/P - Trade	19.9	17.8	20.8	17.0	21.2
		.2		.3	A/P - Retention	.1	.0	.1	.1	.3
		9.8		9.4	Billings in Excess of Costs & Est. Earnings	6.5	9.0	9.6	8.1	9.4
		.1		.5	Income Taxes Payable	.3	.3	.6	.1	.5
		1.6		1.6	Cur. Mat.-L/T/D	.8	.9	1.7	1.3	1.6
		5.6		6.0	All Other Current	7.5	8.4	7.0	5.8	6.0
		46.9		48.0	Total Current	43.9	44.9	51.4	42.5	48.0
		5.0		4.1	Long-Term Debt	2.0	2.7	8.0	8.1	4.1
		.2		.3	Deferred Taxes	.0	.3	.3	.6	.3
		1.3		3.1	All Other Non-Current	4.2	2.6	1.8	1.7	3.1
		46.7		44.4	Net Worth	49.9	49.6	38.4	47.1	44.4
		100.0		100.0	Total Liabilities & Net Worth	100.0	100.0	100.0	100.0	100.0
					INCOME DATA					
		100.0		100.0	Contract Revenues	100.0	100.0	100.0	100.0	100.0
		26.5		27.8	Gross Profit	29.0	26.2	25.5	28.0	27.8
		17.7		20.6	Operating Expenses	25.4	21.2	18.3	21.8	20.6
		8.8		7.1	Operating Profit	3.6	5.0	7.2	6.2	7.1
		.2		.2	All Other Expenses (net)	-.3	.4	.3	.4	.2
		8.6		7.0	Profit Before Taxes	3.9	4.6	6.9	5.8	7.0
					RATIOS					
		2.6		2.6	Current	3.9	3.4	2.7	2.2	2.6
		1.6		1.6		2.2	1.9	1.9	1.9	1.6
		1.3		1.2		1.4	1.4	1.2	1.4	1.2
		5.7		5.7	Receivables/Payables	7.3	7.2	5.0	6.7	5.7
		3.8		3.7		4.3	3.8	4.0	(18) 4.0	3.7
		2.4		2.3		1.7	2.4	2.1	2.2	2.3
	76	4.8	76	4.8	Revenues/Receivables	51 7.2	59 6.2	73 5.0	55 6.6	76 4.8
	87	4.2	94	3.9		76 4.8	83 4.4	96 3.8	76 4.8	94 3.9
	107	3.4	118	3.1		111 3.3	107 3.4	111 3.4	111 3.3	118 3.1
	24	15.0	22	16.4	Cost of Revenues/Payables	12 31.3	11 33.0	22 16.5	15 25.1	22 16.4
	34	10.8	34	10.8		30 12.0	25 14.8	31 11.9	24 15.0	34 10.8
	43	8.5	49	7.5		79 4.6	40 9.2	58 6.3	40 9.1	49 7.5
		5.0		4.6	Revenues/Working Capital	4.4	4.1	4.6	5.6	4.6
		7.2		9.6		5.0	7.4	7.2	9.5	9.6
		16.9		16.9		23.8	11.7	20.8	14.0	16.9
		90.4		60.1	EBIT/Interest		99.6	104.5	114.8	60.1
	(12)	37.0	(16)	16.0		(19) 20.0	(23) 15.3	(19) 23.4	(16) 16.0	16.0
		9.6		4.2		3.6	4.5	6.1		4.2
					Net Profit + Depr., Dep., Amort./Cur. Mat. L/T/D					
		.1		.1	Fixed/Worth	.1	.1	.1	.1	.1
		.4		.4		.1	.2	.2	.2	.4
		.7		.8		.7	.4	1.1	.8	.8
		.7		.7	Debt/Worth	.5	.3	.5	.6	.7
		1.4		1.5		.6	1.1	1.5	1.0	1.5
		1.9		3.9		1.8	2.1	6.1	2.5	3.9
		71.0		45.8	% Profit Before Taxes/Tangible Net Worth	43.2	45.2	60.4	58.1	45.8
	(12)	36.7	(19)	33.7		19.8	(22) 24.3	(23) 35.1	40.1	(19) 33.7
		28.8		22.8		3.9	10.3	17.1	25.8	22.8
		31.1		21.6	% Profit Before Taxes/Total Assets	26.0	18.3	23.0	24.3	21.6
		17.1		11.2		12.9	9.4	14.5	16.5	11.2
		10.0		6.7		2.5	5.3	4.8	9.3	6.7
		.7		.7	% Depr., Dep., Amort./Revenues	.2	.3	.4		.7
	(12)	.8	(18)	.8		(18) .4	.6	.8	(18) .8	.8
		1.2		1.2		.9	1.2	1.0		1.2
					% Officers', Directors' Owners' Comp/Revenues		2.7	1.6		
						(11)	3.5	(11) 1.8		
							5.9	6.1		
50M	47703M	240989M	151363M	440105M	Contract Revenues ($)	579496M	859188M	537296M	244279M	440105M
28M	33035M	100341M	93550M	226954M	Total Assets ($)	228680M	294759M	224035M	95645M	226954M

© RMA 2019

M = $ thousand   MM = $ million
See Pages viii through xx for Explanation of Ratios and Data

Current Data Sorted by Revenue   Comparative Historical Data

Current Data period spans: **5 (4/1-9/30/18)** covers 0-1MM and 1-10MM; **35 (10/1/18-3/31/19)** covers 10-50MM and 50 & OVER.

0-1MM	1-10MM	10-50MM	50 & OVER	ALL		4/1/14-3/31/15 ALL	4/1/15-3/31/16 ALL	4/1/16-3/31/17 ALL	4/1/17-3/31/18 ALL	4/1/18-3/31/19 ALL
					Type of Statement					
			1	1	Unqualified					
	7	11		18	Reviewed	18	24	31	23	18
	1	1		2	Compiled	3	1	1	4	2
	4	2		6	Tax Returns	6	5	2	4	6
1	2	8	2	13	Other	7	11	15	23	13
1	14	22	3	40	**NUMBER OF STATEMENTS**	34	41	49	55	40
%	%	%	%	%		%	%	%	%	%
					ASSETS					
	15.5	13.7		14.6	Cash & Equivalents	16.1	15.2	11.5	10.9	14.6
	35.9	48.3		43.7	A/R - Progress Billings	44.8	44.7	45.6	47.0	43.7
	.7	6.6		3.9	A/R - Current Retention	2.7	3.7	1.7	3.2	3.9
	4.7	6.1		5.6	Inventory	7.0	5.7	4.9	6.7	5.6
	4.6	5.9		6.1	Cost & Est. Earnings In Excess Billings	3.5	6.2	5.8	6.1	6.1
	.8	2.2		1.6	All Other Current	5.2	3.5	5.5	2.1	1.6
	62.1	82.7		75.4	Total Current	79.2	78.9	74.9	76.0	75.4
	27.4	12.3		17.7	Fixed Assets (net)	14.9	16.0	20.4	17.9	17.7
	.1	.6		.4	Joint Ventures & Investments	.2	.0	.2	.5	.4
	.5	.7		.6	Intangibles (net)	.2	.9	1.9	1.5	.6
	9.9	3.7		5.7	All Other Non-Current	5.5	4.2	2.6	4.2	5.7
	100.0	100.0		100.0	Total	100.0	100.0	100.0	100.0	100.0
					LIABILITIES					
	16.0	11.5		12.1	Notes Payable-Short Term	8.7	7.1	9.2	9.6	12.1
	13.3	19.4		16.7	A/P - Trade	19.3	18.1	17.7	16.5	16.7
	.0	.1		.1	A/P - Retention	.0	.1	.0	.2	.1
	4.4	7.3		6.4	Billings in Excess of Costs & Est. Earnings	5.6	8.3	6.0	7.2	6.4
	.0	.0		.0	Income Taxes Payable	.0	.2	.2	.2	.0
	3.2	1.8		2.2	Cur. Mat.-L/T/D	2.0	2.5	3.5	2.6	2.2
	12.8	9.2		11.4	All Other Current	12.3	9.9	10.8	9.6	11.4
	49.6	49.3		48.9	Total Current	47.9	46.1	47.5	45.9	48.9
	8.9	4.0		5.9	Long-Term Debt	6.0	6.8	10.2	7.8	5.9
	.4	.3		.3	Deferred Taxes	.1	.2	.3	.3	.3
	1.8	2.8		2.5	All Other Non-Current	3.5	3.8	2.6	2.8	2.5
	39.2	43.7		42.5	Net Worth	42.5	43.0	39.4	43.2	42.5
	100.0	100.0		100.0	Total Liabilties & Net Worth	100.0	100.0	100.0	100.0	100.0
					INCOME DATA					
	100.0	100.0		100.0	Contract Revenues	100.0	100.0	100.0	100.0	100.0
	32.7	22.2		26.9	Gross Profit	21.3	22.9	25.5	27.3	26.9
	26.3	17.6		21.7	Operating Expenses	18.3	17.2	20.3	22.1	21.7
	6.4	4.6		5.2	Operating Profit	3.0	5.6	5.2	5.2	5.2
	.3	.0		.1	All Other Expenses (net)	-.2	.1	.2	.1	.1
	6.0	4.6		5.1	Profit Before Taxes	3.2	5.6	5.0	5.2	5.1
					RATIOS					
	2.9	2.1		2.6		3.3	3.0	2.0	2.2	2.6
	2.2	1.6		1.6	Current	1.8	1.6	1.6	1.6	1.6
	.6	1.4		1.3		1.3	1.3	1.2	1.3	1.3
	5.4	4.1		4.5		5.2	5.1	4.2	4.4	4.5
	(12) 2.7	2.9	(38) 2.9		Receivables/Payables	(33) 2.7	(39) 3.2	(48) 2.9	(54) 3.7	(38) 2.9
	1.5	2.4		2.3		1.7	2.2	1.7	2.1	2.3
14 26.1	52 7.0	40 9.2				41 8.8	36 10.1	37 9.9	43 8.5	40 9.2
46 8.0	70 5.2	58 6.3			Revenues/Receivables	63 5.8	62 5.9	55 6.6	62 5.9	58 6.3
60 6.1	83 4.4	79 4.6				76 4.8	83 4.4	79 4.6	78 4.7	79 4.6
7 56.1	21 17.7	15 23.6				16 23.5	14 25.9	16 23.3	18 20.3	15 23.6
21 17.2	24 15.5	23 16.0			Cost of Revenues/Payables	27 13.3	24 15.5	22 16.7	22 16.7	23 16.0
28 13.1	47 7.8	31 11.6				40 9.1	40 9.1	41 8.9	38 9.5	31 11.6
	5.5	6.4		6.3		5.5	5.9	7.0	6.6	6.3
	8.0	9.9		9.9	Revenues/Working Capital	9.4	10.2	12.5	11.1	9.9
	-22.1	12.7		17.5		18.0	20.8	25.5	20.6	17.5
	22.0	54.1		46.3		47.5	36.2	60.4	33.4	46.3
	(11) 3.7	(20) 7.2	(34) 6.8		EBIT/Interest	(25) 5.6	(35) 19.3	(46) 14.3	(50) 10.3	(34) 6.8
	.8	1.6		1.6		.0	4.0	1.7	4.8	1.6
					Net Profit + Depr., Dep., Amort./Cur. Mat. L/T/D					
	.1	.2		.1		.2	.2	.2	.2	.1
	.3	.3		.3	Fixed/Worth	.3	.3	.5	.4	.3
	2.1	.4		.6		.6	.6	1.0	.7	.6
	.4	.7		.6		.5	.8	.9	.9	.6
	.9	1.5		1.2	Debt/Worth	1.0	1.4	1.4	1.3	1.2
	2.2	2.3		2.1		2.1	3.3	3.4	2.5	2.1
	59.6	52.1		57.6		49.2	72.1	51.6	49.3	57.6
	(13) 26.9	29.2	(39) 26.7		% Profit Before Taxes/ Tangible Net Worth	(30) 21.2	(40) 35.5	(47) 29.5	(54) 28.8	(39) 26.7
	3.3	2.2		2.8		3.6	8.2	7.7	12.1	2.8
	32.0	22.3		21.1		20.0	28.2	24.0	22.6	21.1
	8.3	8.7		8.4	% Profit Before Taxes/ Total Assets	7.1	11.2	12.2	9.5	8.4
	.9	1.0		1.4		.6	2.8	1.1	4.2	1.4
	.5	.8		.7		.6	.7	.7	.8	.7
	(13) .8	(20) 1.3	(36) 1.0		% Depr., Dep., Amort./ Revenues	(32) 1.1	(37) .9	(41) 1.2	(50) 1.1	(36) 1.0
	1.6	1.7		1.5		1.6	1.5	2.0	1.6	1.5
		1.2		2.0		1.2	1.8	1.8	1.7	2.0
	(10)	3.1	(19)	3.8	% Officers', Directors' Owners' Comp/Revenues	(17) 2.3	(19) 2.2	(18) 3.5	(23) 2.3	(19) 3.8
		4.3				3.4	3.4	5.0	4.7	4.5
53M	80808M	471453M	967348M	1519662M	Contract Revenues ($)	917604M	1360831M	6267642M	2002182M	1519662M
12M	28247M	163307M	534328M	725894M	Total Assets ($)	460124M	620308M	2904902M	861094M	725894M

© RMA 2019

M = $ thousand   MM = $ million
See Pages viii through xx for Explanation of Ratios and Data

Current Data Sorted by Revenue						**Comparative Historical Data**				

Type of Statement

0-1MM	1-10MM	10-50MM	50 & OVER	ALL	Type of Statement	4/1/14-3/31/15	4/1/15-3/31/16	4/1/16-3/31/17	4/1/17-3/31/18	4/1/18-3/31/19
	1	7	5	13	Unqualified	4	11	11	11	13
2	29	59	10	100	Reviewed	64	75	86	81	100
	8	3		11	Compiled	7	10	10	8	11
1	6	2		9	Tax Returns	13	11	8	14	9
4	12	30	27	73	Other	27	52	49	73	73
33 (4/1-9/30/18)		173 (10/1/18-3/31/19)								
0-1MM	1-10MM	10-50MM	50 & OVER	**ALL**		**ALL**	**ALL**	**ALL**	**ALL**	**ALL**
7	56	101	42	206	**NUMBER OF STATEMENTS**	115	159	164	187	206
%	%	%	%	%		%	%	%	%	%

ASSETS

0-1MM	1-10MM	10-50MM	50 & OVER	ALL	ASSETS	4/1/14-3/31/15	4/1/15-3/31/16	4/1/16-3/31/17	4/1/17-3/31/18	4/1/18-3/31/19
	15.6	13.3	11.0	14.3	Cash & Equivalents	14.9	13.5	13.5	13.9	14.3
	48.6	52.6	53.7	51.2	A/R - Progress Billings	46.6	49.6	48.5	51.0	51.2
	3.5	3.7	4.9	4.1	A/R - Current Retention	3.4	3.7	4.5	3.4	4.1
	3.1	1.9	1.4	2.1	Inventory	3.0	2.4	2.6	2.1	2.1
	7.9	9.5	7.8	8.6	Cost & Est. Earnings In Excess Billings	7.7	6.8	9.2	7.6	8.6
	1.8	2.0	2.4	2.0	All Other Current	3.9	4.9	2.5	2.6	2.0
	80.5	83.0	81.3	82.3	Total Current	79.5	80.9	80.8	80.6	82.3
	12.3	11.4	11.5	11.4	Fixed Assets (net)	13.3	13.6	13.1	12.7	11.4
	.3	.3	.0	.3	Joint Ventures & Investments	.2	.3	.1	.1	.3
	2.3	1.9	3.4	2.3	Intangibles (net)	2.7	1.6	2.0	2.1	2.3
	4.6	3.4	3.8	3.7	All Other Non-Current	4.3	3.6	4.0	4.3	3.7
	100.0	100.0	100.0	100.0	Total	100.0	100.0	100.0	100.0	100.0

LIABILITIES

0-1MM	1-10MM	10-50MM	50 & OVER	ALL	LIABILITIES	4/1/14-3/31/15	4/1/15-3/31/16	4/1/16-3/31/17	4/1/17-3/31/18	4/1/18-3/31/19
	7.2	9.5	5.0	7.8	Notes Payable-Short Term	9.2	8.5	7.4	6.9	7.8
	17.3	18.3	17.7	18.5	A/P - Trade	21.5	19.8	17.5	18.3	18.5
	.1	.2	.4	.2	A/P - Retention	.2	.1	.3	.2	.2
	6.6	10.8	13.8	10.7	Billings in Excess of Costs & Est. Earnings	8.3	10.1	10.8	11.7	10.7
	.2	.3	.2	.2	Income Taxes Payable	.3	.5	.2	.4	.2
	2.7	1.7	2.4	2.1	Cur. Mat.-L/T/D	2.0	2.1	2.3	1.8	2.1
	8.2	9.3	13.7	9.7	All Other Current	8.7	7.4	7.7	10.6	9.7
	42.3	50.0	53.0	49.3	Total Current	50.2	48.3	46.1	49.9	49.3
	8.7	4.4	4.5	5.7	Long-Term Debt	8.3	7.8	5.5	7.9	5.7
	.2	.5	.6	.4	Deferred Taxes	.8	.6	.6	.3	.4
	3.4	2.0	3.6	4.5	All Other Non-Current	3.4	3.4	2.7	3.1	4.5
	45.5	43.1	38.3	40.2	Net Worth	37.3	39.9	45.1	38.7	40.2
	100.0	100.0	100.0	100.0	Total Liabilities & Net Worth	100.0	100.0	100.0	100.0	100.0

INCOME DATA

0-1MM	1-10MM	10-50MM	50 & OVER	ALL	INCOME DATA	4/1/14-3/31/15	4/1/15-3/31/16	4/1/16-3/31/17	4/1/17-3/31/18	4/1/18-3/31/19
	100.0	100.0	100.0	100.0	Contract Revenues	100.0	100.0	100.0	100.0	100.0
	22.5	21.8	14.8	20.9	Gross Profit	22.8	20.7	20.6	22.9	20.9
	18.6	16.1	10.7	15.9	Operating Expenses	18.3	16.2	15.6	17.8	15.9
	3.9	5.7	4.2	5.1	Operating Profit	4.5	4.5	5.1	5.1	5.1
	.1	-.1	.2	.0	All Other Expenses (net)	.3	.5	.2	.2	.0
	3.8	5.8	4.0	5.0	Profit Before Taxes	4.3	4.0	4.9	4.9	5.0

RATIOS

0-1MM	1-10MM	10-50MM	50 & OVER	ALL	RATIOS	4/1/14-3/31/15	4/1/15-3/31/16	4/1/16-3/31/17	4/1/17-3/31/18	4/1/18-3/31/19
	2.7	2.3	1.7	2.3	Current	2.4	2.5	2.4	2.4	2.3
	1.9	1.6	1.5	1.7		1.7	1.8	1.7	1.6	1.7
	1.5	1.3	1.3	1.4		1.3	1.4	1.4	1.3	1.4
	5.6	4.7	4.7	5.1	Receivables/Payables	4.1	4.8	5.1	4.7	5.1
(55)	3.2	3.1	(41) 3.4	(204) 3.2		(113) 2.5	(155) 3.0	(163) 3.0	(185) 3.1	(204) 3.2
	2.1	2.2	2.3	2.3		1.6	2.1	2.2	2.2	2.3
53 6.9	54 6.8	74 4.9	59 6.2		Revenues/Receivables	42 8.7	53 6.9	54 6.8	55 6.6	59 6.2
69 5.3	70 5.2	83 4.4	74 4.9			68 5.4	70 5.2	73 5.0	76 4.8	74 4.9
96 3.8	89 4.1	99 3.7	94 3.9			85 4.0	91 4.0	87 4.2	91 4.0	94 3.9
15 23.7	18 20.2	20 18.3	18 20.6	Cost of Revenues/Payables	18 20.3	16 22.3	16 22.7	20 18.6	18 20.6
22 16.4	29 12.7	25 14.4	27 13.6		28 13.2	27 13.7	28 13.2	31 11.8	27 13.6
51 7.1	37 9.8	44 8.3	41 8.9		51 7.2	43 8.5	39 9.3	41 8.8	41 8.9
	4.5	5.9	7.0	5.7	Revenues/Working Capital	5.7	5.2	5.6	5.8	5.7
	6.9	9.1	9.6	8.6		8.9	8.0	8.6	9.0	8.6
	12.6	15.8	14.7	14.8		16.2	16.1	13.8	16.1	14.8
	33.6	81.3	30.5	42.4	EBIT/Interest	30.6	35.4	45.7	78.2	42.4
(51) 10.3	(91) 16.0	(37) 17.0	(180) 15.7		(97) 10.6	(139) 12.6	(150) 16.0	(159) 17.9	(180) 15.7
	2.0	4.1	7.4	4.1		2.2	3.4	5.1	4.0	4.1
	23.5	14.6		11.3	Net Profit + Depr., Dep., Amort./Cur. Mat. L/T/D	11.0	12.4	10.0	8.9	11.3
(13) 3.7	(14) 3.3		(34) 4.0		(25) 3.3	(33) 5.2	(23) 4.6	(22) 5.7	(34) 4.0
	1.4	1.9		1.8		1.5	1.6	2.0	2.8	1.8
	.1	.1	.1	.1	Fixed/Worth	.1	.1	.1	.1	.1
	.2	.2	.3	.2		.3	.2	.2	.3	.2
	.5	.5	.5	.5		.8	.6	.5	.6	.5
	.6	.7	1.2	.8	Debt/Worth	.8	.8	.7	.7	.8
	1.2	1.5	1.8	1.5		1.6	1.3	1.2	1.7	1.5
	2.9	2.4	3.6	2.8		3.0	2.7	2.2	2.7	2.8
	57.4	50.3	46.1	51.8	% Profit Before Taxes/ Tangible Net Worth	49.8	47.2	52.6	52.2	51.8
(53) 21.5	(96) 31.3	28.6	(197) 30.6		(103) 21.9	(149) 20.8	(159) 27.2	(174) 29.9	(197) 30.6
	1.8	14.3	14.9	9.6		5.7	6.7	8.9	11.1	9.6
	27.8	26.1	14.5	23.1	% Profit Before Taxes/ Total Assets	18.3	21.0	18.5	21.1	23.1
	10.6	13.6	9.4	11.4		8.9	7.9	10.0	11.3	11.4
	1.0	3.2	4.7	3.4		3.2	1.7	4.1	4.0	3.4
	.5	.5	.4	.5	% Depr., Dep., Amort./ Revenues	.4	.4	.5	.5	.5
(51) 1.0	(90) .9	(32) .6	(173) .9		(98) .8	(142) .7	(139) 1.1	(154) .9	(173) .9
	1.6	1.5	1.1	1.5		1.7	1.3	1.8	1.5	1.5
	1.7	1.4		1.4	% Officers', Directors' Owners' Comp/Revenues	1.5	1.7	1.5	1.7	1.4
(27) 2.9	(43) 2.1		(78) 2.7		(54) 2.7	(74) 2.8	(79) 2.6	(72) 3.0	(78) 2.7
	4.4	3.7		4.0		5.4	6.0	4.8	5.8	4.0
913M	364759M	2111590M	70614286M	73091548M	Contract Revenues ($)	9317505M	12280364M	13843400M	16501013M	73091548M
228M	147023M	753843M	37958450M	38859544M	Total Assets ($)	4674046M	5840437M	6826431M	7691788M	38859544M

M = $ thousand   MM = $ million
See Pages viii through xx for Explanation of Ratios and Data

Current Data Sorted by Revenue

Comparative Historical Data

					Type of Statement					
1		3	4	8	Unqualified	4	6	5	6	8
2	24	78	8	112	Reviewed	59	81	105	103	112
4	5	5	9		Compiled	5	8	9	15	9
10	3	2	15		Tax Returns	16	20	10	9	15
2	9	29	17	57	Other	27	51	46	57	57
	42 (4/1-9/30/18)	159 (10/1/18-3/31/19)				4/1/14- 3/31/15	4/1/15- 3/31/16	4/1/16- 3/31/17	4/1/17- 3/31/18	4/1/18- 3/31/19
0-1MM	1-10MM	10-50MM	50 & OVER	ALL		ALL	ALL	ALL	ALL	ALL
5	47	118	31	201	NUMBER OF STATEMENTS	111	166	175	190	201
%	%	%	%	%	ASSETS	%	%	%	%	%
	15.4	15.8	8.9	14.3	Cash & Equivalents	14.8	14.0	15.2	14.9	14.3
	47.7	50.9	50.0	50.3	A/R - Progress Billings	44.1	51.5	48.4	49.2	50.3
	3.5	5.5	7.0	5.5	A/R - Current Retention	3.3	4.1	5.2	4.2	5.5
	5.9	3.2	2.8	3.8	Inventory	5.1	4.4	3.8	3.8	3.8
	5.0	6.3	5.8	6.0	Cost & Est. Earnings In Excess of Billings	4.6	5.9	6.3	6.2	6.0
	1.1	1.7	3.0	1.7	All Other Current	4.4	2.1	2.1	2.1	1.7
	78.6	83.4	77.6	81.5	Total Current	76.3	82.0	81.1	80.4	81.5
	13.4	11.8	10.5	11.8	Fixed Assets (net)	14.9	12.5	13.6	12.9	11.8
	.0	.0	.1	.0	Joint Ventures & Investments	.0	.1	.0	.2	.0
	.8	1.2	8.0	2.1	Intangibles (net)	3.0	2.0	1.4	2.5	2.1
	7.2	3.5	3.8	4.4	All Other Non-Current	5.8	3.3	3.9	3.9	4.4
	100.0	100.0	100.0	100.0	Total	100.0	100.0	100.0	100.0	100.0
					LIABILITIES					
	6.9	5.8	6.8	6.2	Notes Payable-Short Term	8.6	7.5	7.1	6.6	6.2
	19.5	23.6	19.8	22.4	A/P - Trade	21.0	24.2	20.2	21.1	22.4
	.2	.9	1.0	.7	A/P - Retention	.4	.7	.7	.6	.7
	10.7	12.8	13.2	12.4	Billings in Excess of Costs & Est. Earnings	9.1	9.6	11.1	11.7	12.4
	.2	.1	.0	.1	Income Taxes Payable	.2	.2	.2	.2	.1
	2.2	1.8	1.3	1.8	Cur. Mat.-L/T/D	3.6	2.0	2.2	2.1	1.8
	8.8	9.2	13.6	9.9	All Other Current	11.0	9.5	10.7	10.5	9.9
	48.4	54.1	55.8	53.5	Total Current	53.8	53.7	52.2	52.8	53.5
	9.3	4.9	8.9	6.5	Long-Term Debt	10.2	6.2	6.2	6.5	6.5
	.4	.2	.1	.2	Deferred Taxes	.2	.4	.3	.3	.2
	4.5	3.4	1.8	3.4	All Other Non-Current	4.6	3.8	3.4	2.0	3.4
	37.5	37.3	33.5	36.5	Net Worth	31.3	35.9	37.9	38.4	36.5
	100.0	100.0	100.0	100.0	Total Liabilties & Net Worth	100.0	100.0	100.0	100.0	100.0
					INCOME DATA					
	100.0	100.0	100.0	100.0	Contract Revenues	100.0	100.0	100.0	100.0	100.0
	28.6	21.6	17.4	22.3	Gross Profit	26.1	22.1	20.0	21.8	22.3
	25.5	16.4	12.9	17.8	Operating Expenses	23.3	18.1	16.4	17.3	17.8
	3.1	5.2	4.5	4.5	Operating Profit	2.8	4.0	3.7	4.5	4.5
	-.2	.1	.6	.1	All Other Expenses (net)	.2	.7	.2	.1	.1
	3.3	5.2	3.9	4.4	Profit Before Taxes	2.6	3.3	3.4	4.4	4.4
					RATIOS					
	2.7	2.0	1.8	2.1		2.1	2.2	2.2	2.2	2.1
	1.8	1.6	1.3	1.5	Current	1.5	1.6	1.6	1.5	1.5
	1.2	1.3	1.2	1.2		1.3	1.2	1.3	1.2	1.2
	5.5	4.0	3.8	4.4		3.4	4.2	4.4	4.2	4.4
(45)	3.5	2.7	2.6 (199)	2.7	Receivables/Payables	(101) 2.3	2.5 (174)	2.8 (186)	2.8 (199)	2.7
	2.0	1.8	2.3	2.0		1.6	1.7	1.9	2.0	2.0
48 7.6	59 6.2	63 5.8	58 6.3			45 8.2	54 6.8	51 7.1	51 7.2	58 6.3
60 6.1	74 4.9	76 4.8	74 4.9		Revenues/Receivables	66 5.5	69 5.3	65 5.6	70 5.2	74 4.9
89 4.1	89 4.1	89 4.1	89 4.1			85 4.3	87 4.2	83 4.4	89 4.1	89 4.1
13 28.1	24 15.1	23 16.0	20 18.6			18 20.7	21 17.1	17 21.4	19 18.8	20 18.6
24 15.2	36 10.0	31 11.6	33 11.2		Cost of Revenues/Payables	31 11.7	33 10.9	27 13.4	29 12.5	33 11.2
47 7.7	50 7.3	41 8.9	49 7.5			49 7.5	47 7.8	42 8.6	47 7.8	49 7.5
	5.8	6.0	8.1	6.2		6.1	6.2	6.6	6.5	6.2
	8.7	9.2	14.1	10.1	Revenues/Working Capital	11.5	10.1	10.4	9.7	10.1
	28.9	17.3	25.6	21.8		23.7	18.4	22.0	20.3	21.8
	31.8	91.9	31.5	61.5		35.6	54.0	50.6	60.2	61.5
(44)	13.1 (108)	27.2 (25)	7.4 (177)	17.8	EBIT/Interest	(94) 12.1 (143)	13.4 (152)	13.2 (167)	15.3 (177)	17.8
	4.8	6.4	3.1	5.1		2.8	2.5	4.3	4.8	5.1
		14.3		11.3		9.2	12.5	5.1	16.6	11.3
	(20)	6.3	(28)	5.8	Net Profit + Depr., Dep., Amort./Cur. Mat. L/T/D	(15) 3.0 (19)	3.4 (22)	2.2 (28)	3.1 (28)	5.8
		2.7		2.5		.3	1.7	.8	1.9	2.5
	.1	.1	.1	.1		.1	.1	.1	.2	.1
	.3	.3	.4	.3	Fixed/Worth	.3	.3	.3	.3	.3
	.8	.5	.8	.6		.7	.6	.6	.7	.6
	.6	.9	1.7	.9		.9	.8	.9	.8	.9
	1.2	1.5	2.7	1.7	Debt/Worth	1.6	1.6	1.6	1.7	1.7
	3.2	3.4	4.5	3.7		3.6	3.4	3.1	3.3	3.7
	62.3	52.8	51.4	52.5		36.9	40.6	42.0	52.7	52.5
(42)	21.1 (113)	31.9 (28)	25.0 (188)	29.1	% Profit Before Taxes/ Tangible Net Worth	(98) 18.7 (152)	21.0 (167)	23.0 (177)	23.9 (188)	29.1
	8.6	14.1	9.5	12.5		4.8	6.9	7.1	8.0	12.5
	20.1	20.4	14.3	19.3		13.7	15.8	15.4	19.4	19.3
	9.7	12.3	6.9	10.3	% Profit Before Taxes/ Total Assets	5.6	6.8	8.6	8.7	10.3
	3.7	4.7	2.5	3.7		1.6	2.1	2.3	3.2	3.7
	.5	.5	.4	.5		.4	.5	.5	.5	.5
(37)	1.0 (106)	.8 (26)	.6 (171)	.9	% Depr., Dep., Amort./ Revenues	(96) .7 (147)	.8 (151)	.9 (174)	.9 (171)	.9
	1.8	1.4	1.6	1.5		1.1	1.3	1.3	1.5	1.5
	2.6	.8		1.0		1.9	1.6	1.1	1.2	1.0
(29)	4.9 (50)	1.4	(83)	2.1	% Officers', Directors' Owners' Comp/Revenues	(46) 3.8 (68)	2.9 (66)	2.0 (71)	2.2 (83)	2.1
	10.2	2.4		3.9		7.9	4.7	3.6	3.9	3.9
336M	257621M	2731886M	14531720M	17521563M	Contract Revenues ($)	7079000M	11722886M	8116401M	8883444M	17521563M
103M	95369M	1073536M	5168784M	6337792M	Total Assets ($)	2194368M	4099448M	4489301M	3578060M	6337792M

M = $ thousand   MM = $ million
See Pages viii through xx for Explanation of Ratios and Data

Current Data Sorted by Revenue | **Comparative Historical Data**

Current Data size ranges: 5 (4/1-9/30/18), 34 (10/1/18-3/31/19)

	0-1MM	1-10MM	10-50MM	50 & OVER	ALL	Type of Statement	4/1/14-3/31/15 ALL	4/1/15-3/31/16 ALL	4/1/16-3/31/17 ALL	4/1/17-3/31/18 ALL	4/1/18-3/31/19 ALL
			2		2	Unqualified	2	3	3	3	2
	1	3	12	4	20	Reviewed	13	17	19	25	20
		3			3	Compiled		2	8	1	3
	1	1			2	Tax Returns	4	1	1	2	2
		4	4	4	12	Other	6	16	12	10	12
NUMBER OF STATEMENTS	2	11	18	8	39		25	39	43	41	39
	%	%	%	%	%	**ASSETS**	%	%	%	%	%
Cash & Equivalents		10.5	12.5		11.4		14.8	9.0	12.3	11.6	11.4
A/R - Progress Billings		53.0	59.7		55.8		50.4	57.3	51.0	55.9	55.8
A/R - Current Retention		5.1	6.1		7.1		6.3	7.0	6.6	6.5	7.1
Inventory		1.7	1.2		1.3		2.2	2.1	2.9	1.5	1.3
Cost & Est. Earnings In Excess Billings		4.9	4.8		5.9		5.6	4.5	7.2	7.3	5.9
All Other Current		3.5	4.1		2.9		6.2	3.1	6.4	4.0	2.9
Total Current		78.8	88.4		84.4		85.6	83.1	86.4	86.8	84.4
Fixed Assets (net)		9.7	4.6		7.8		9.3	7.7	7.5	6.6	7.8
Joint Ventures & Investments		.0	.0		.1		.0	.1	.0	.0	.1
Intangibles (net)		.2	1.2		.6		.2	.1	.2	.4	.6
All Other Non-Current		11.4	5.8		6.9		4.9	8.7	5.7	6.2	6.9
Total		100.0	100.0		100.0		100.0	100.0	100.0	100.0	100.0
						LIABILITIES					
Notes Payable-Short Term		15.0	11.6		12.0		9.3	13.5	10.9	6.6	12.0
A/P - Trade		15.4	12.2		14.4		14.7	17.2	18.1	14.5	14.4
A/P - Retention		.0	1.5		1.3		.8	.5	.4	.8	1.3
Billings in Excess of Costs & Est. Earnings		6.1	16.1		12.8		5.6	7.4	10.3	12.8	12.8
Income Taxes Payable		.2	.1		.1		.0	.1	.0	.0	.1
Cur. Mat.-L/T/D		.6	.2		.4		4.5	1.0	1.2	.7	.4
All Other Current		12.0	9.9		11.1		11.5	10.4	11.8	12.2	11.1
Total Current		49.3	51.6		52.1		46.5	50.0	52.7	47.6	52.1
Long-Term Debt		3.1	2.3		3.4		3.6	4.5	4.7	2.5	3.4
Deferred Taxes		1.2	.0		.3		.3	.0	.2	.2	.3
All Other Non-Current		3.1	.2		1.5		4.6	14.7	7.7	2.2	1.5
Net Worth		43.3	45.9		42.9		45.0	30.6	34.7	47.5	42.9
Total Liabilities & Net Worth		100.0	100.0		100.0		100.0	100.0	100.0	100.0	100.0
						INCOME DATA					
Contract Revenues		100.0	100.0		100.0		100.0	100.0	100.0	100.0	100.0
Gross Profit		21.2	19.4		19.5		19.4	22.4	19.8	20.7	19.5
Operating Expenses		16.9	13.2		14.3		14.8	17.4	15.7	14.9	14.3
Operating Profit		4.2	6.3		5.2		4.6	5.0	4.1	5.7	5.2
All Other Expenses (net)		.3	.3		.1		.2	.9	.4	-.2	.1
Profit Before Taxes		3.9	6.0		5.1		4.4	4.1	3.8	5.9	5.1
						RATIOS					
Current		3.1	2.6		2.2		3.9	3.7	2.6	2.6	2.2
		1.6	1.7		1.7		1.8	2.1	1.8	1.8	1.7
		1.3	1.3		1.3		1.3	1.3	1.3	1.4	1.3
Receivables/Payables		5.1	11.6		8.1		11.3	10.0	8.0	8.8	8.1
		4.6	6.8	(38)	4.7		(24) 5.1	(38) 5.1	3.8	5.2	(38) 4.7
		2.3	3.8		2.9		2.3	3.3	2.5	3.2	2.9
Revenues/Receivables		54 6.7	79 4.6		78 4.7		47 7.8	58 6.3	50 7.3	63 5.8	78 4.7
		87 4.2	94 3.9		87 4.2		96 3.8	83 4.4	76 4.8	79 4.6	87 4.2
		111 3.3	101 3.6		104 3.5		114 3.2	101 3.6	87 4.2	89 4.1	104 3.5
Cost of Revenues/Payables		10 37.4	7 49.0		11 34.6		8 44.4	8 48.2	11 34.0	11 34.0	11 34.6
		33 11.2	17 21.9		24 15.3		20 18.0	25 14.8	22 16.6	19 18.9	24 15.3
		43 8.4	35 10.5		42 8.7		42 8.7	35 10.3	33 11.0	39 9.4	42 8.7
Revenues/Working Capital		5.4	4.6		5.4		4.5	5.3	4.7	5.6	5.4
		9.1	8.3		9.1		8.7	8.6	8.3	6.8	9.1
		12.4	14.4		12.8		19.9	19.7	15.9	14.2	12.8
EBIT/Interest			35.8		36.9		46.3	65.1	66.8	145.0	36.9
		(12)	13.0	(28)	13.0		(18) 8.7	(30) 10.6	(37) 21.0	(33) 56.9	(28) 13.0
			3.5		3.7		4.3	2.3	3.2	12.6	3.7
Net Profit + Depr., Dep., Amort./Cur. Mat. L/T/D											
Fixed/Worth		.0	.0		.0		.0	.0	.0	.0	.0
		.1	.1		.1		.2	.1	.1	.1	.1
		.6	.2		.3		.5	.3	.4	.2	.3
Debt/Worth		.5	.6		.7		.4	.6	.5	.7	.7
		.9	1.1		1.2		1.4	1.4	1.4	1.2	1.2
		2.7	3.0		2.7		3.8	2.5	2.8	2.5	2.7
% Profit Before Taxes/Tangible Net Worth		28.4	53.2		44.7		84.6	55.5	72.5	60.0	44.7
	(10)	12.7	20.9	(38)	25.1		23.3	(34) 28.6	(38) 28.6	34.1	(38) 25.1
		1.3	14.6		5.8		7.0	4.8	6.0	13.4	5.8
% Profit Before Taxes/Total Assets		14.9	18.5		16.4		22.7	21.1	22.5	22.9	16.4
		6.5	12.4		10.5		10.1	10.3	8.8	14.5	10.5
		2.3	4.2		2.6		3.1	1.0	2.7	7.1	2.6
% Depr., Dep., Amort./Revenues			.2		.2		.3	.2	.2	.3	.2
		(17)	.4	(32)	.4		(22) .5	(29) .4	(34) .3	(37) .5	(32) .4
			.5		.6		.8	.5	.6	.6	.6
% Officers', Directors' Owners' Comp/Revenues				(14)	2.0		1.3	1.0	1.0	.9	2.0
					3.5		(12) 3.8	(15) 1.3	(18) 1.6	(16) 2.4	(14) 3.5
					7.7		4.6	4.3	4.7	4.4	7.7
Contract Revenues ($)	353M	67921M	409867M	736019M	1214160M		491045M	1676824M	1153186M	1328511M	1214160M
Total Assets ($)	158M	34095M	155075M	276464M	465792M		192245M	534504M	398448M	481843M	465792M

M = $ thousand   MM = $ million
See Pages viii through xx for Explanation of Ratios and Data

Current Data Sorted by Revenue						**Comparative Historical Data**				
		2		2	**Type of Statement**				1	2
		5		5	Unqualified	6	4	2	8	5
		4		4	Reviewed	1	2	2	1	4
		2		2	Compiled	2	1	3		2
5		1	1	7	Tax Returns	5	6	10	7	7
2 (4/1-9/30/18)		**18 (10/1/18-3/31/19)**			Other					
0-1MM	**1-10MM**	**10-50MM**	**50 & OVER**	**ALL**		**4/1/14-3/31/15**	**4/1/15-3/31/16**	**4/1/16-3/31/17**	**4/1/17-3/31/18**	**4/1/18-3/31/19**
5		14	1	20	**NUMBER OF STATEMENTS**	**ALL** 14	**ALL** 13	**ALL** 17	**ALL** 17	**ALL** 20
%	%	%	%	%	**ASSETS**	%	%	%	%	%
		18.6		17.3	Cash & Equivalents	16.4	16.0	18.9	23.7	17.3
		46.7		44.4	A/R - Progress Billings	37.0	36.4	39.7	42.5	44.4
		1.0		1.1	A/R - Current Retention	.6	.6	1.4	1.8	1.1
		1.0		1.4	Inventory	2.1	2.1	.5	.5	1.4
D		7.9		7.3	Cost & Est. Earnings In Excess Billings	7.4	6.3	9.2	7.0	7.3
A		4.1		3.1	All Other Current	9.0	2.4	1.1	.8	3.1
T		79.4		74.5	Total Current	72.6	63.8	70.8	76.3	74.5
A		16.2		20.0	Fixed Assets (net)	21.1	29.9	17.7	15.9	20.0
		.0		.5	Joint Ventures & Investments	.0	.0	3.2	.8	.5
N		1.1		.8	Intangibles (net)	.0	.9	.3	1.1	.8
O		3.3		4.2	All Other Non-Current	6.2	5.4	8.0	5.9	4.2
T		100.0		100.0	Total	100.0	100.0	100.0	100.0	100.0
					LIABILITIES					
A		16.5		14.9	Notes Payable-Short Term	10.1	8.9	7.9	9.2	14.9
V		10.0		9.3	A/P - Trade	7.8	9.0	8.4	10.0	9.3
A		.0		.0	A/P - Retention	.0	.1	.0	.0	.0
I		6.1		5.1	Billings in Excess of Costs & Est. Earnings	5.3	4.0	8.9	6.0	5.1
L				.0	Income Taxes Payable	.1	.2	.1	.8	.0
A		2.7		2.5	Cur. Mat.-L/T/D	3.5	4.5	1.5	1.7	2.5
B		4.0		4.7	All Other Current	8.9	7.7	7.7	5.7	4.7
L		39.3		36.5	Total Current	35.6	34.3	34.5	33.5	36.5
E		6.7		8.4	Long-Term Debt	6.3	16.8	6.4	9.7	8.4
		.0		.0	Deferred Taxes	1.4	.3	.0	.5	.0
		1.1		2.2	All Other Non-Current	.8	2.6	1.4	2.1	2.2
		52.8		52.8	Net Worth	55.9	46.0	57.7	54.2	52.8
		100.0		100.0	Total Liabilities & Net Worth	100.0	100.0	100.0	100.0	100.0
					INCOME DATA					
		100.0		100.0	Contract Revenues	100.0	100.0	100.0	100.0	100.0
		23.5		23.2	Gross Profit	17.5	23.0	28.2	23.6	23.2
		19.4		19.4	Operating Expenses	16.7	22.2	20.1	17.0	19.4
		4.1		3.7	Operating Profit	.7	.8	8.1	6.6	3.7
		.5		.3	All Other Expenses (net)	-.3	.1	-.7	.1	.3
		3.6		3.5	Profit Before Taxes	1.0	.7	8.8	6.4	3.5
					RATIOS					
		5.0		4.3		4.8	3.2	3.3	4.4	4.3
		2.0		2.0	Current	2.0	1.8	2.0	2.4	2.0
		1.3		1.4		1.4	1.1	1.6	1.6	1.4
		10.4		12.4		29.2	9.3	10.2	11.3	12.4
		5.6		5.5	Receivables/Payables	5.9 (12)	4.5 (16)	4.8	5.0	5.5
		2.7		2.8		2.9	2.1	3.1	3.3	2.8
	34	10.6	36	10.1		32 11.5	20 18.2	36 10.0	52 7.0	36 10.1
	53	6.9	55	6.6	Revenues/Receivables	51 7.1	54 6.8	61 6.0	79 4.6	55 6.6
	122	3.0	107	3.4		99 3.7	70 5.2	68 5.4	91 4.0	107 3.4
	9	39.7	8	43.8		2 232.4	4 93.1	5 71.0	9 40.9	8 43.8
	13	28.6	14	26.4	Cost of Revenues/Payables	9 41.0	12 29.5	11 32.7	13 27.5	14 26.4
	25	14.7	23	15.6		29 12.7	25 14.6	21 17.1	30 12.3	23 15.6
		3.9		3.8		3.8	4.4	4.1	3.7	3.8
		8.8		8.0	Revenues/Working Capital	7.3	14.9	5.7	5.9	8.0
		12.5		12.8		16.4	NM	15.2	8.3	12.8
		22.6		18.8		30.1	10.5	123.1	142.0	18.8
		10.6	(19)	10.3	EBIT/Interest	(13) 9.9	4.5 (13)	20.1 (16)	38.0 (19)	10.3
		3.6		3.6		1.4	1.4	6.3	3.2	3.6
					Net Profit + Depr., Dep., Amort./Cur. Mat. L/T/D					
		.2		.2		.2	.2	.2	.2	.2
		.3		.3	Fixed/Worth	.3	.5	.3	.3	.3
		.4		.6		.5	1.3	.5	.5	.6
		.2		.3		.4	.5	.4	.3	.3
		1.2		1.0	Debt/Worth	.7	1.0	.8	.9	1.0
		2.9		2.7		1.5	3.0	1.4	2.2	2.7
		40.2		36.2		60.1	35.3	51.5	41.7	36.2
		19.8		14.9	% Profit Before Taxes/ Tangible Net Worth	12.2 (12)	3.7	42.0	21.4 (16)	14.9
		2.5		1.6		1.2	1.2	25.8	10.1	1.6
		13.1		10.5		25.9	11.3	30.9	27.9	10.5
		7.7		7.5	% Profit Before Taxes/ Total Assets	10.5	2.7	23.2	9.3	7.5
		1.1		1.1		.5	.4	12.1	4.2	1.1
		.9		.9		.4	1.1	.6	.7	.9
	(12)	2.1	(17)	2.2	% Depr., Dep., Amort./ Revenues	(13) .9	1.9 (15)	1.2 (16)	1.8 (17)	2.2
		3.9		4.2		5.8	3.4	2.7	3.7	4.2
					% Officers', Directors' Owners' Comp/Revenues					
	27618M	247517M	57329M	332464M	Contract Revenues ($)	144379M	167736M	382153M	363994M	332464M
	16954M	103882M	15344M	136180M	Total Assets ($)	59395M	60271M	159793M	177568M	136180M

© RMA 2019

M = $ thousand   MM = $ million

See Pages viii through xx for Explanation of Ratios and Data

Current Data Sorted by Revenue | **Comparative Historical Data**

0-1MM	1-10MM	10-50MM	50 & OVER	ALL	Type of Statement	4/1/14-3/31/15 ALL	4/1/15-3/31/16 ALL	4/1/16-3/31/17 ALL	4/1/17-3/31/18 ALL	4/1/18-3/31/19 ALL
					Unqualified					
	3	10		13	Reviewed	2	10	11	12	13
	2	1		3	Compiled		1		1	3
					Tax Returns	1				
	3	4		7	Other		3	6	7	7
1 (4/1-9/30/18)		22 (10/1/18-3/31/19)								
	8	15		23	**NUMBER OF STATEMENTS**	3	14	17	20	23
%	%	%	%	%	**ASSETS**	%	%	%	%	%
DATA NOT AVAILABLE		8.4	DATA NOT AVAILABLE	8.8	Cash & Equivalents		8.1	9.2	13.7	8.8
		49.7		51.5	A/R - Progress Billings		56.0	50.3	44.5	51.5
		5.9		4.4	A/R - Current Retention		3.2	4.4	5.5	4.4
		4.5		5.6	Inventory		3.2	6.9	7.0	5.6
		8.8		9.5	Cost & Est. Earnings In Excess Billings		14.1	10.3	11.5	9.5
		4.3		3.0	All Other Current		2.4	2.5	1.5	3.0
		81.6		82.9	Total Current		87.0	83.7	83.8	82.9
		10.2		8.7	Fixed Assets (net)		8.2	6.4	11.1	8.7
		.4		.3	Joint Ventures & Investments		.0	.0	.1	.3
		.7		.6	Intangibles (net)		2.4	4.0	.7	.6
		7.2		7.5	All Other Non-Current		2.5	5.7	4.4	7.5
		100.0		100.0	Total		100.0	100.0	100.0	100.0
					LIABILITIES					
		14.2		13.5	Notes Payable-Short Term		21.8	6.0	10.0	13.5
		17.6		17.0	A/P - Trade		17.3	15.7	13.7	17.0
		.5		.4	A/P - Retention		.2	.3	.5	.4
		9.9		7.3	Billings in Excess of Costs & Est. Earnings		7.3	10.8	11.0	7.3
		.1		.2	Income Taxes Payable		.6	.4	.3	.2
		1.4		1.2	Cur. Mat.-L/T/D		1.3	1.3	1.6	1.2
		9.4		9.1	All Other Current		8.2	6.4	9.4	9.1
		53.0		48.7	Total Current		56.7	40.8	46.5	48.7
		7.1		5.7	Long-Term Debt		3.6	4.3	6.3	5.7
		.1		.1	Deferred Taxes		.0	.2	.2	.1
		2.8		8.9	All Other Non-Current		2.4	4.8	1.4	8.9
		37.0		36.6	Net Worth		37.3	50.0	45.6	36.6
		100.0		100.0	Total Liabilties & Net Worth		100.0	100.0	100.0	100.0
					INCOME DATA					
		100.0		100.0	Contract Revenues		100.0	100.0	100.0	100.0
		27.8		27.3	Gross Profit		21.5	24.4	22.7	27.3
		21.9		21.8	Operating Expenses		17.8	18.8	18.2	21.8
		5.9		5.6	Operating Profit		3.7	5.6	4.5	5.6
		.4		.4	All Other Expenses (net)		.2	-.3	.1	.4
		5.5		5.2	Profit Before Taxes		3.5	5.8	4.4	5.2
					RATIOS					
		1.8		2.5			2.1	3.2	3.0	2.5
		1.5		1.6	Current		1.6	1.9	1.6	1.6
		1.3		1.4			1.1	1.5	1.4	1.4
		7.9		7.4			5.1	6.9	5.9	7.4
		5.0		3.6	Receivables/Payables		3.2	3.6	4.3	3.6
		2.3		2.4			2.7	2.2	3.0	2.4
		55 6.6		**55** 6.6			**58** 6.3	**58** 6.3	**46** 8.0	**55** 6.6
		73 5.0		**73** 5.0	Revenues/Receivables		**81** 4.5	**74** 4.9	**74** 4.9	**73** 5.0
		94 3.9		**94** 3.9			**91** 4.0	**94** 3.9	**83** 4.4	**94** 3.9
		13 28.5		**15** 24.7			**18** 20.6	**15** 25.1	**14** 26.0	**15** 24.7
		29 12.7		**26** 13.8	Cost of Revenues/Payables		**26** 13.8	**23** 15.7	**25** 14.8	**26** 13.8
		50 7.3		**39** 9.4			**40** 9.2	**37** 9.8	**35** 10.5	**39** 9.4
		6.0		5.5			5.6	4.4	4.5	5.5
		9.7		8.1	Revenues/Working Capital		10.0	6.4	7.2	8.1
		20.0		16.9			26.7	9.9	10.9	16.9
		30.7		31.5			22.8	36.9	37.0	31.5
		(12) 8.2		(20) 11.9	EBIT/Interest		(12) 8.3	(13) 12.3	(19) 15.9	(20) 11.9
		6.2		3.0			1.8	5.4	5.7	3.0
					Net Profit + Depr., Dep., Amort./Cur. Mat. L/T/D					
		.1		.1			.1	.1	.1	.1
		.2		.1	Fixed/Worth		.2	.1	.1	.1
		.4		.4			.3	.2	.3	.4
		1.0		.8			.9	.5	.7	.8
		1.8		1.6	Debt/Worth		1.6	1.3	1.3	1.6
		3.5		3.2			11.9	2.2	2.6	3.2
		48.6		49.4			25.7	42.8	44.0	49.4
		38.0		(22) 41.2	% Profit Before Taxes/ Tangible Net Worth		(13) 19.7	(16) 29.6	26.8	(22) 41.2
		24.9		24.6			8.5	15.7	9.3	24.6
		21.9		24.9			16.1	25.2	19.1	24.9
		16.4		17.1	% Profit Before Taxes/ Total Assets		8.0	12.2	11.9	17.1
		6.6		5.1			1.3	6.1	3.0	5.1
		.3		.3			.1	.3	.4	.3
		(14) .4		(21) .4	% Depr., Dep., Amort./ Revenues		(13) .5	(13) .4	(18) .5	(21) .4
		.8		.9			1.1	1.0	1.1	.9
					% Officers', Directors' Owners' Comp/Revenues					
	49700M	353830M		403530M	Contract Revenues ($)	35744M	276559M	367104M	420830M	403530M
	18828M	131394M		150222M	Total Assets ($)	17348M	101360M	137211M	168324M	150222M

M = $ thousand MM = $ million

See Pages viii through xx for Explanation of Ratios and Data

Current Data Sorted by Revenue   **Comparative Historical Data**

0-1MM	1-10MM	10-50MM	50 & OVER	ALL	Type of Statement	4/1/14-3/31/15 ALL	4/1/15-3/31/16 ALL	4/1/16-3/31/17 ALL	4/1/17-3/31/18 ALL	4/1/18-3/31/19 ALL
	1	2		3	Unqualified	10	7	6	8	3
2	17	26	1	46	Reviewed	29	42	45	45	46
	2			2	Compiled	6	7	3	3	2
1	2	2		5	Tax Returns	14	9	6	4	5
1	15	16	14	46	Other	16	30	33	42	46
14 (4/1-9/30/18)		88 (10/1/18-3/31/19)								
4	37	46	15	102	**NUMBER OF STATEMENTS**	75	95	93	102	102
%	%	%	%	%	**ASSETS**	%	%	%	%	%
	7.0	10.8	13.0	9.8	Cash & Equivalents	11.6	10.5	13.2	9.5	9.8
	31.2	37.2	34.4	34.7	A/R - Progress Billings	31.4	34.0	33.5	33.9	34.7
	2.8	5.4	7.5	4.6	A/R - Current Retention	3.6	2.4	2.6	4.2	4.6
	1.6	.8	.4	1.1	Inventory	2.4	2.7	2.2	1.2	1.1
	2.3	4.7	4.9	3.9	Cost & Est. Earnings In Excess Billings	3.4	4.1	5.3	4.7	3.9
	4.6	.9	.3	2.1	All Other Current	3.0	3.5	4.4	3.2	2.1
	49.7	59.7	60.4	56.3	Total Current	55.4	57.3	61.2	56.7	56.3
	41.7	36.4	34.6	37.9	Fixed Assets (net)	36.1	37.5	34.8	38.5	37.9
	.5	.0	.0	.3	Joint Ventures & Investments	1.5	.4	.4	.4	.3
	1.6	.4	.2	.8	Intangibles (net)	2.6	.2	.2	.2	.8
	6.5	3.5	4.7	4.8	All Other Non-Current	4.4	4.6	3.4	4.2	4.8
	100.0	100.0	100.0	100.0	Total	100.0	100.0	100.0	100.0	100.0
					LIABILITIES					
	7.8	3.9	1.4	4.8	Notes Payable-Short Term	7.9	5.4	5.4	5.9	4.8
	12.2	20.3	18.7	16.9	A/P - Trade	15.6	14.2	15.7	15.9	16.9
	.0	.4	.9	.3	A/P - Retention	.1	.1	.2	.3	.3
	2.5	5.7	12.6	5.4	Billings in Excess of Costs & Est. Earnings	4.1	5.1	5.7	5.5	5.4
	.0	.1	.2	.1	Income Taxes Payable	.3	.2	.4	.3	.1
	4.9	5.7	5.3	5.3	Cur. Mat.-L/T/D	5.8	6.1	6.7	6.2	5.3
	6.3	4.9	5.4	5.7	All Other Current	4.6	4.8	6.7	6.1	5.7
	33.7	40.9	44.5	38.4	Total Current	38.4	35.8	40.7	40.1	38.4
	15.8	14.5	12.8	14.7	Long-Term Debt	18.8	18.5	17.1	16.2	14.7
	.8	.8	.4	.6	Deferred Taxes	1.9	1.3	1.2	.8	.6
	3.7	.8	.9	1.9	All Other Non-Current	2.9	3.9	2.3	1.8	1.9
	45.9	43.3	41.4	44.2	Net Worth	38.0	40.5	38.7	41.1	44.2
	100.0	100.0	100.0	100.0	Total Liabilities & Net Worth	100.0	100.0	100.0	100.0	100.0
					INCOME DATA					
	100.0	100.0	100.0	100.0	Contract Revenues	100.0	100.0	100.0	100.0	100.0
	24.3	18.4	15.2	20.6	Gross Profit	23.9	23.8	21.8	24.2	20.6
	19.6	12.8	8.3	15.1	Operating Expenses	17.6	17.5	16.3	18.1	15.1
	4.7	5.5	6.9	5.5	Operating Profit	6.3	6.3	5.5	6.2	5.5
	.2	-.1	-.2	.0	All Other Expenses (net)	.2	.1	.1	.2	.0
	4.4	5.6	7.1	5.4	Profit Before Taxes	6.1	6.2	5.4	6.0	5.4
					RATIOS					
	2.7	1.8	1.5	2.0	Current	2.3	2.2	2.4	2.0	2.0
	1.5	1.4	1.4	1.4		1.6	1.5	1.4	1.4	1.4
	1.1	1.1	1.1	1.1		1.1	1.2	1.2	1.1	1.1
	5.0	2.8	2.8	3.3	Receivables/Payables	4.7	4.6	4.0	4.0	3.3
	2.8	2.1	2.4	2.3		(70) 2.3	(90) 2.4	(87) 2.5	(97) 2.3	2.3
	1.7	1.6	1.7	1.7		1.6	1.8	1.8	1.7	1.7
49 7.5	60 6.1	70 5.2	55 6.6		Revenues/Receivables	33 10.9	50 7.3	44 8.3	54 6.8	55 6.6
70 5.2	79 4.6	89 4.1	74 4.9			63 5.8	65 5.6	62 5.9	74 4.9	74 4.9
91 4.0	96 3.8	94 3.9	91 4.0			89 4.1	83 4.4	94 3.9	96 3.8	91 4.0
15 24.3	27 13.3	37 9.9	24 15.1		Cost of Revenues/Payables	11 32.0	15 23.9	19 18.8	22 16.8	24 15.1
28 13.0	40 9.1	42 8.7	37 9.8			31 11.9	31 11.9	30 12.0	36 10.2	37 9.8
49 7.5	58 6.3	48 7.6	54 6.7			46 8.0	47 7.8	49 7.4	52 7.0	54 6.7
	5.5	6.8	7.6	6.5	Revenues/Working Capital	5.5	6.1	5.9	6.3	6.5
	9.8	12.4	10.5	10.5		11.0	10.5	12.5	11.3	10.5
	28.7	59.5	41.4	30.5		173.6	34.6	27.2	42.4	30.5
	19.3	36.6	45.1	28.8	EBIT/Interest	31.5	23.5	41.1	36.6	28.8
	(45) 3.7	11.7	(99) 24.5	8.7		(67) 10.6	(88) 11.4	(83) 12.7	(97) 9.2	(99) 8.7
	-1.3	4.4	12.6	2.4		2.8	4.7	3.8	2.3	2.4
				3.1	Net Profit + Depr., Dep., Amort./Cur. Mat. L/T/D	3.8	5.0	3.9	4.1	3.1
			(11)	2.2		(16) 2.3	(18) 3.6	(16) 1.8	(14) 2.7	(11) 2.2
				.9		1.8	2.0	.7	1.8	.9
	.7	.5	.5	.5	Fixed/Worth	.5	.5	.4	.6	.5
	1.1	.9	.8	.9		.8	.9	.8	.9	.9
	1.4	1.5	1.1	1.4		1.7	1.5	1.4	1.4	1.4
	.6	.9	1.2	.9	Debt/Worth	.7	.7	.8	.7	.9
	1.4	1.5	1.6	1.4		1.3	1.4	1.4	1.5	1.4
	2.0	2.0	1.9	2.0		2.9	2.5	3.0	2.9	2.0
	32.9	36.9	48.1	37.5	% Profit Before Taxes/Tangible Net Worth	49.6	55.1	42.7	44.3	37.5
(35)	8.5	(44) 22.2	26.8	(98) 19.5		(67) 25.2	(89) 24.2	(90) 24.0	(97) 28.6	(98) 19.5
	-18.8	8.2	14.4	6.0		12.6	12.6	9.6	10.6	6.0
	16.1	17.9	16.8	16.7	% Profit Before Taxes/Total Assets	20.0	20.2	21.3	20.2	16.7
	4.0	8.5	16.1	7.4		10.9	9.5	12.1	10.2	7.4
	-3.5	4.0	5.6	2.2		2.6	4.4	2.9	2.0	2.2
	3.1	2.2	2.0	2.7	% Depr., Dep., Amort./Revenues	2.1	2.2	1.9	2.7	2.7
(35)	5.8	(44) 4.0	(14) 3.5	(95) 4.2		(62) 3.6	(81) 3.7	(83) 4.1	(93) 4.7	(95) 4.2
	8.0	6.4	5.2	6.5		5.2	4.7	5.2	6.8	6.5
	2.5	.7		1.0	% Officers', Directors' Owners' Comp/Revenues	1.2	1.3	1.5	1.0	1.0
(16)	4.1	(14) 1.2		(38) 1.9		(34) 2.0	(41) 2.5	(46) 2.6	(41) 2.1	(38) 1.9
	8.5	1.9		5.1		5.8	5.9	4.6	3.6	5.1
1705M	184350M	993251M	1409820M	2589126M	Contract Revenues ($)	8302901M	10332243M	1781747M	2790964M	2589126M
1427M	113069M	520702M	781444M	1416642M	Total Assets ($)	1606466M	1609953M	937055M	1459420M	1416642M

M = $ thousand   MM = $ million
See Pages viii through xx for Explanation of Ratios and Data

Current Data Sorted by Revenue   **Comparative Historical Data**

Type of Statement

0-1MM	1-10MM	10-50MM	50 & OVER	ALL	Type of Statement	4/1/14-3/31/15 ALL	4/1/15-3/31/16 ALL	4/1/16-3/31/17 ALL	4/1/17-3/31/18 ALL	4/1/18-3/31/19 ALL
	3	4	3	10	Unqualified		5	5	7	10
	5	11	2	18	Reviewed	19	33	22	21	18
	6	3		9	Compiled	5	8	6	4	9
1	7	1	1	10	Tax Returns	13	11	5	9	10
1	14	7	7	29	Other	24	37	36	30	29
	5 (4/1-9/30/18)	71 (10/1/18-3/31/19)								
2	35	26	13	76	NUMBER OF STATEMENTS	61	94	74	71	76

Main Data

0-1MM %	1-10MM %	10-50MM %	50 & OVER %	ALL %		4/1/14-3/31/15 ALL %	4/1/15-3/31/16 ALL %	4/1/16-3/31/17 ALL %	4/1/17-3/31/18 ALL %	4/1/18-3/31/19 ALL %
					ASSETS					
	11.9	14.3	7.7	11.8	Cash & Equivalents	15.8	12.7	12.2	12.7	11.8
	32.7	38.6	37.2	35.5	A/R - Progress Billings	35.0	42.8	41.3	40.9	35.5
	1.5	3.0	.4	2.1	A/R - Current Retention	.5	1.0	1.5	1.9	2.1
	4.5	4.0	5.0	4.4	Inventory	4.5	3.2	3.9	2.2	4.4
	5.2	7.9	4.6	5.9	Cost & Est. Earnings In Excess Billings	3.7	5.0	4.6	5.5	5.9
	3.8	3.9	2.5	3.5	All Other Current	5.0	2.7	2.7	4.5	3.5
	59.6	71.7	57.3	63.1	Total Current	64.6	67.4	66.2	67.7	63.1
	30.3	20.5	25.7	26.6	Fixed Assets (net)	24.2	24.0	21.8	22.7	26.6
	.8	.6	.6	.7	Joint Ventures & Investments	.3	.4	.6	.3	.7
	1.5	1.8	11.1	3.2	Intangibles (net)	3.5	2.3	3.5	2.8	3.2
	7.8	5.3	5.2	6.3	All Other Non-Current	7.4	5.9	7.9	6.4	6.3
	100.0	100.0	100.0	100.0	Total	100.0	100.0	100.0	100.0	100.0
					LIABILITIES					
	16.9	5.2	8.1	11.0	Notes Payable-Short Term	7.2	8.9	8.1	10.5	11.0
	17.7	14.9	19.6	17.0	A/P - Trade	14.3	15.2	16.9	15.5	17.0
	.0	.7	.0	.3	A/P - Retention	.4	.2	.2	.5	.3
	6.2	5.4	9.0	6.5	Billings in Excess of Costs & Est. Earnings	4.4	7.1	5.9	5.1	6.5
	.7	.2	.1	.4	Income Taxes Payable	.0	.4	.4	.3	.4
	3.7	3.4	3.6	3.5	Cur. Mat.-L/T/D	4.0	3.5	3.7	3.3	3.5
	5.2	9.4	3.8	6.3	All Other Current	8.8	8.3	7.8	10.2	6.3
	50.4	39.3	44.2	45.0	Total Current	39.1	43.6	43.0	45.5	45.0
	19.2	10.3	14.8	15.2	Long-Term Debt	30.8	18.5	17.2	14.3	15.2
	4.6	.3	.8	2.4	Deferred Taxes	1.5	.9	1.2	.4	2.4
	4.4	7.9	10.5	7.8	All Other Non-Current	4.9	6.3	4.1	1.5	7.8
	21.3	42.3	29.6	29.6	Net Worth	23.7	30.6	34.5	38.3	29.6
	100.0	100.0	100.0	100.0	Total Liabilities & Net Worth	100.0	100.0	100.0	100.0	100.0
					INCOME DATA					
	100.0	100.0	100.0	100.0	Contract Revenues	100.0	100.0	100.0	100.0	100.0
	32.6	24.6	20.9	27.5	Gross Profit	28.9	26.6	27.0	23.8	27.5
	27.7	18.9	16.0	22.5	Operating Expenses	25.9	19.9	21.3	19.0	22.5
	4.8	5.8	4.8	5.0	Operating Profit	3.1	6.6	5.6	4.9	5.0
	.5	.5	1.4	.7	All Other Expenses (net)	.8	.8	.5	.0	.7
	4.3	5.3	3.4	4.4	Profit Before Taxes	2.3	5.8	5.1	4.9	4.4
					RATIOS					
	2.0	2.8	1.9	2.3	Current	3.9	2.7	2.2	2.4	2.3
	1.4	1.8	1.3	1.5		2.0	1.5	1.7	1.7	1.5
	.8	1.4	1.1	1.1		1.2	1.2	1.2	1.2	1.1
	6.7	4.2	3.0	4.2	Receivables/Payables	7.0	6.9	6.0	6.2	4.2
	(31) 3.2	2.9	(72) 2.1	2.7		(53) 3.6	(92) 3.8	3.0	(68) 3.1	(72) 2.7
	1.3	2.0	1.6	1.6		2.1	1.9	1.9	1.8	1.6
	27 13.3	29 12.6	54 6.8	38 9.6	Revenues/Receivables	22 16.8	42 8.6	50 7.3	43 8.5	38 9.6
	51 7.2	70 5.2	85 4.3	61 6.0		60 6.1	62 5.9	62 5.9	62 5.9	61 6.0
	72 5.1	91 4.0	101 3.6	85 4.3		83 4.4	89 4.1	83 4.4	85 4.3	85 4.3
	10 36.0	16 22.5	30 12.0	16 23.0	Cost of Revenues/Payables	6 57.1	9 38.6	13 27.3	13 28.6	16 23.0
	20 18.7	28 13.0	49 7.4	27 13.5		19 19.3	22 16.7	28 13.2	25 14.5	27 13.5
	54 6.8	41 8.8	69 5.3	53 6.9		36 10.1	40 9.1	47 7.8	40 9.1	53 6.9
	6.1	4.0	8.0	5.6	Revenues/Working Capital	4.7	5.7	6.3	5.6	5.6
	14.8	8.2	13.9	10.5		8.7	9.9	10.1	10.6	10.5
	-20.8	13.4	54.2	113.4		36.5	22.3	25.1	31.9	113.4
	32.7	53.0	9.0	26.3	EBIT/Interest	18.8	20.5	32.7	37.4	26.3
	(30) 5.9	(24) 16.7	3.4	(68) 5.9		(53) 6.0	(83) 12.0	(70) 10.6	(65) 8.6	(68) 5.9
	-1.7	3.5	1.1	1.7		1.6	2.9	2.9	3.4	1.7
				5.8	Net Profit + Depr., Dep., Amort./Cur. Mat. L/T/D		11.8	5.6		5.8
			(14) 3.1			(17) 5.6	(10) 3.4		(14) 3.1	
			1.3			1.5	3.1		1.3	
	.3	.2	.6	.3	Fixed/Worth	.2	.3	.2	.2	.3
	.9	.4	1.2	.7		.6	.8	.5	.4	.7
	3.1	.9	-1.7	2.4		2.5	2.0	1.5	1.3	2.4
	.7	.5	1.0	.6	Debt/Worth	.6	.8	.8	.7	.6
	1.8	1.2	3.5	1.8		2.0	1.7	1.3	1.6	1.8
	9.5	2.7	-6.0	8.2		9.2	8.9	4.5	4.9	8.2
	78.4	64.0		65.1	% Profit Before Taxes/Tangible Net Worth	47.1	62.6	51.6	62.7	65.1
	(30) 45.6	(25) 21.0		(65) 25.4		(48) 21.9	(79) 32.6	(64) 29.1	(63) 27.2	(65) 25.4
	-1.7	7.3		6.4		5.0	16.4	10.1	13.4	6.4
	29.1	30.7	9.4	26.2	% Profit Before Taxes/Total Assets	13.4	23.3	20.5	25.9	26.2
	15.1	11.5	3.0	9.8		7.0	12.5	13.0	10.1	9.8
	-1.8	2.4	-.1	1.8		1.8	4.9	3.6	3.2	1.8
	.3	.8		1.0	% Depr., Dep., Amort./Revenues	.4	.6	.5	.5	1.0
	(29) 2.5	(20) 1.2		(59) 1.9		(44) 1.6	(66) 1.2	(47) 1.3	(51) 1.4	(59) 1.9
	4.5	2.6		3.9		3.6	3.1	2.7	2.6	3.9
	2.2			1.5	% Officers', Directors' Owners' Comp/Revenues	2.1	1.6	1.0	1.1	1.5
	(20) 3.4			(29) 3.0		(29) 4.2	(29) 2.7	(22) 3.3	(19) 2.2	(29) 3.0
	7.4			6.1		9.6	5.7	6.8	4.3	6.1
751M	157621M	529709M	2860179M	3548260M	Contract Revenues ($)	4974014M	4914162M	6021729M	69123459M	3548260M
287M	95301M	248569M	1921740M	2265897M	Total Assets ($)	2594912M	2953927M	4180307M	30165778M	2265897M

© RMA 2019

M = $ thousand   MM = $ million
See Pages viii through xx for Explanation of Ratios and Data

TEXT—KEY WORD INDEX
OF INDUSTRIES APPEARING
IN THE STATEMENT
STUDIES

STATEMENT STUDIES KEY WORD INDEX

A complete description of each industry category listed below begins on page 33.

A

Abrasive Product Manufacturing, 482-483, mfg

Adhesive Manufacturing, 426-427, mfg

Administration of Air and Water Resource and Solid Waste Management Programs, 1646-1647, pub admin

Administration of Education Programs, 1642-1643, pub admin

Administration of General Economic Programs, 1652-1653, pub admin

Administration of Housing Programs, 1648-1649, pub admin

Administration of Public Health Programs, 1644-1645, pub admin

Administration of Urban Planning and Community and Rural Development, 1650-1651, pub admin

Administrative Management and General Management Consulting Services, 1274-1275, prof serv

Advertising Agencies, 1294-1295, prof serv

Agents and Managers for Artists, Athletes, Entertainers, and Other Public Figures, 1504-1505, ent

Air and Gas Compressor Manufacturing, 614-615, mfg

Air-Conditioning and Warm Air Heating Equipment and Commercial and Industrial Refrigeration Equipment Manufacturing, 598-599, mfg

Aircraft Engine and Engine Parts Manufacturing, 710-711, mfg

Aircraft Manufacturing, 708-709, mfg

All Other Amusement and Recreation Industries, 1528-1529, ent

All Other Automotive Repair and Maintenance, 1570-1571, other

All Other Basic Organic Chemical Manufacturing, 410-411, mfg

All Other Business Support Services, 1344-1345, Admin

All Other Consumer Goods Rental, 1218-1219, R/E

All Other Converted Paper Product Manufacturing, 392-393, mfg

All Other General Merchandise Stores, 990-991, rtl

All Other Grain Farming, 106-107, ag

All Other Health and Personal Care Stores, 964-965, rtl

All Other Home Furnishings Stores, 922-923, rtl

All Other Information Services, 1128-1129, info

All Other Insurance Related Activities, 1180-1181, fin

All Other Leather Good and Allied Product Manufacturing, 356-357, mfg

All Other Legal Services, 1238-1239, prof serv

All Other Miscellaneous Ambulatory Health Care Services, 1452-1453, HC

All Other Miscellaneous Chemical Product and Preparation Manufacturing, 438-439, mfg

All Other Miscellaneous Crop Farming, 132-133, ag

All Other Miscellaneous Electrical Equipment and Component Manufacturing, 684-685, mfg

All Other Miscellaneous Fabricated Metal Product Manufacturing, 570-571, mfg

All Other Miscellaneous Food Manufacturing, 316-317, mfg

All Other Miscellaneous General Purpose Machinery Manufacturing, 630-631, mfg

All Other Miscellaneous Manufacturing, 760-761, mfg

All Other Miscellaneous Nonmetallic Mineral Product Manufacturing, 486-487, mfg

All Other Miscellaneous Schools and Instruction, 1408-1409, edu

All Other Miscellaneous Store Retailers (except Tobacco Stores), 1008-1009, rtl

All Other Miscellaneous Textile Product Mills, 342-343, mfg

All Other Miscellaneous Waste Management Services, 1388-1389, Admin

All Other Miscellaneous Wood Product Manufacturing, 376-377, mfg

All Other Nondepository Credit Intermediation, 1138-1139, fin

All Other Outpatient Care Centers, 1440-1441, HC

All Other Personal Services, 1600-1601, other

All Other Plastics Product Manufacturing, 460-461, mfg

All Other Professional, Scientific, and Technical Services, 1314-1315, prof serv

All Other Publishers, 1102-1103, info

All Other Rubber Product Manufacturing, 466-467, mfg

All Other Specialty Food Stores, 952-953, rtl

All Other Specialty Trade Contractors, 260-261, cons-g

All Other Specialty Trade Contractors, 1677, cons-%

All Other Support Activities for Transportation, 1080-1081, trans

All Other Support Services, 1370-1371, Admin

All Other Telecommunications, 1122-1123, info

All Other Transit and Ground Passenger Transportation, 1054-1055, trans

All Other Transportation Equipment Manufacturing, 720-721, mfg

All Other Travel Arrangement and Reservation Services, 1350-1351, Admin

All Other Traveler Accommodation, 1538-1539, rest/lodg

Aluminum Foundries (except Die-Casting), 510-511, mfg

Ambulance Services, 1448-1449, HC

American Indian and Alaska Native Tribal Governments, 1636-1637, pub admin

Amusement and Theme Parks, 1512-1513, ent

Analytical Laboratory Instrument Manufacturing, 664-665, mfg

Animal (except Poultry) Slaughtering, 288-289, mfg

Apparel Accessories and Other Apparel Manufacturing, 352-353, mfg

Apple Orchards, 112-113, ag

Architectural Services, 1248-1249, prof serv

Art Dealers, 1002-1003, rtl

Asphalt Paving Mixture and Block Manufacturing, 402-403, mfg

Assisted Living Facilities for the Elderly, 1470-1471, HC

Audio and Video Equipment Manufacturing, 640-641, mfg

Automatic Environmental Control Manufacturing for Residential, Commercial, and Appliance Use, 658-659, mfg

Automobile and Other Motor Vehicle Merchant Wholesalers, 764-765, wsle

Automobile Manufacturing, 686-687, mfg

Automotive Body, Paint, and Interior Repair and Maintenance, 1564-1565, other

Automotive Oil Change and Lubrication Shops, 1566-1567, other

Automotive Parts and Accessories Stores, 914-915, rtl

B

Baked Goods Stores, 948-949, rtl

Ball and Roller Bearing Manufacturing, 564-565, mfg

Bare Printed Circuit Board Manufacturing, 642-643, mfg

Beauty Salons, 1580-1581, other

Bed-and-Breakfast Inns, 1536-1537, rest/lodg

Beef Cattle Ranching and Farming, 134-135, ag

Beer and Ale Merchant Wholesalers, 882-883, wsle

Beer, Wine, and Liquor Stores, 954-955, rtl

Blood and Organ Banks, 1450-1451, HC

Boat Building, 716-717, mfg

Boat Dealers, 910-911, rtl

Bolt, Nut, Screw, Rivet, and Washer Manufacturing, 548-549, mfg

Book Publishers, 1100-1101, info

Book, Periodical, and Newspaper Merchant Wholesalers, 888-889, wsle

Bottled Water Manufacturing, 320-321, mfg

Bowling Centers, 1526-1527, ent

Breweries, 322-323, mfg

Brick, Stone, and Related Construction Material Merchant Wholesalers, 778-779, wsle

Broadwoven Fabric Mills, 330-331, mfg

Business Associations, 1616-1617, other

Business to Business Electronic Markets, 898-899, wsle

C

Cable and Other Subscription Programming, 1114-1115, info

Capacitor, Resistor, Coil, Transformer, and Other Inductor Manufacturing, 646-647, mfg

Car Washes, 1568-1569, other

Carpet and Rug Mills, 336-337, mfg

Carpet and Upholstery Cleaning Services, 1362-1363, Admin

Casino Hotels, 1534-1535, rest/lodg

Casinos (except Casino Hotels), 1514-1515, ent

Caterers, 1548-1549, rest/lodg

Cattle Feedlots, 136-137, ag

Cement Manufacturing, 474-475, mfg

Cemeteries and Crematories, 1588-1589, other

Charter Bus Industry, 1052-1053, trans

Cheese Manufacturing, 284-285, mfg

Chicken Egg Production, 142-143, ag

Child and Youth Services, 1474-1475, HC

Child Day Care Services, 1488-1489, HC

Civic and Social Organizations, 1614-1615, other

Claims Adjusting, 1176-1177, fin

Clay Building Material and Refractories Manufacturing, 468-469, mfg

Clothing Accessories Stores, 976-977, rtl

Coal and Other Mineral and Ore Merchant Wholesalers, 798-799, wsle

Coastal and Great Lakes Freight Transportation, 1030-1031, trans

Coffee and Tea Manufacturing, 306-307, mfg

Coin-Operated Laundries and Drycleaners, 1590-1591, other

Collection Agencies, 1342-1343, Admin

Colleges, Universities, and Professional Schools, 1396-1397, edu

Commercial Air, Rail, and Water Transportation Equipment Rental and Leasing, 1222-1223, R/E

Commercial and Industrial Machinery and Equipment (except Automotive and Electronic) Repair and Maintenance, 1576-1577, other

Commercial and Institutional Building Construction, 212-213, cons-g

Commercial and Institutional Building Construction, 1660, cons-%

Commercial Bakeries, 298-299, mfg

Commercial Photography, 1308-1309, prof serv

Commercial Printing (except Screen and Books), 394-395, mfg

Commercial Screen Printing, 396-397, mfg

Commercial, Industrial, and Institutional Electric Lighting Fixture Manufacturing, 670-671, mfg

Commodity Contracts Dealing, 1150-1151, fin

STATEMENT STUDIES KEY WORD INDEX

A complete description of each industry category listed below begins on page 33.

Community Food Services, 1480-1481, HC

Computer and Computer Peripheral Equipment and Software Merchant Wholesalers, 788-789, wsle

Computer and Office Machine Repair and Maintenance, 1572-1573, other

Computer Facilities Management Services, 1270-1271, prof serv

Computer Systems Design Services, 1268-1269, prof serv

Computer Terminal and Other Computer Peripheral Equipment Manufacturing, 634-635, mfg

Concrete Block and Brick Manufacturing, 478-479, mfg

Confectionery and Nut Stores, 950-951, rtl

Confectionery Manufacturing from Purchased Chocolate, 272-273, mfg

Confectionery Merchant Wholesalers, 860-861, wsle

Construction and Mining (except Oil Well) Machinery and Equipment Merchant Wholesalers, 814-815, wsle

Construction Machinery Manufacturing, 576-577, mfg

Construction Sand and Gravel Mining, 176-177, mng

Construction, Mining, and Forestry Machinery and Equipment Rental and Leasing, 1224-1225, R/E

Consumer Electronics and Appliances Rental, 1214-1215, R/E

Consumer Lending, 1134-1135, fin

Continuing Care Retirement Communities, 1468-1469, HC

Convenience Stores, 942-943, rtl

Convention and Trade Show Organizers, 1368-1369, Admin

Conveyor and Conveying Equipment Manufacturing, 618-619, mfg

Cookie and Cracker Manufacturing, 300-301, mfg

Copper Rolling, Drawing, Extruding, and Alloying, 498-499, mfg

Corn Farming, 102-103, ag

Corporate, Subsidiary, and Regional Managing Offices, 1320-1321, mgmt

Corrugated and Solid Fiber Box Manufacturing, 380-381, mfg

Cosmetics, Beauty Supplies, and Perfume Stores, 958-959, rtl

Cosmetology and Barber Schools, 1400-1401, edu

Cotton Farming, 130-131, ag

Cotton Ginning, 152-153, ag

Couriers and Express Delivery Services, 1082-1083, trans

Crop Harvesting, Primarily by Machine, 156-157, ag

Crude Petroleum Extraction, 168-169, mng

Crushed and Broken Limestone Mining and Quarrying, 172-173, mng

Current-Carrying Wiring Device Manufacturing, 682-683, mfg

Curtain and Linen Mills, 338-339, mfg

Custom Architectural Woodwork and Millwork Manufacturing, 732-733, mfg

Custom Compounding of Purchased Resins, 436-437, mfg

Custom Computer Programming Services, 1266-1267, prof serv

Cut and Sew Apparel Contractors, 344-345, mfg

Cut Stock, Resawing Lumber, and Planing, 368-369, mfg

Cut Stone and Stone Product Manufacturing, 484-485, mfg

Cutting Tool and Machine Tool Accessory Manufacturing, 604-605, mfg

D

Dairy Cattle and Milk Production, 138-139, ag

Dairy Product (except Dried or Canned) Merchant Wholesalers, 856-857, wsle

Data Processing, Hosting, and Related Services, 1124-1125, Info

Deep Sea Freight Transportation, 1028-1029, trans

Dental Equipment and Supplies Manufacturing, 744-745, mfg

Dental Laboratories, 746-747, mfg

Diagnostic Imaging Centers, 1444-1445, HC

Diet and Weight Reducing Centers, 1582-1583, other

Dimension Stone Mining and Quarrying, 170-171, mng

Direct Health and Medical Insurance Carriers, 1164-1165, fin

Direct Life Insurance Carriers, 1162-1163, fin

Direct Mail Advertising, 1300-1301, prof serv

Direct Property and Casualty Insurance Carriers, 1166-1167, fin

Direct Title Insurance Carriers, 1168-1169, fin

Distilleries, 326-327, mfg

Dog and Cat Food Manufacturing, 264-265, mfg

Doll, Toy, and Game Manufacturing, 752-753, mfg

Dried and Dehydrated Food Manufacturing, 280-281, mfg

Drilling Oil and Gas Wells, 178-179, mng

Drinking Places (Alcoholic Beverages), 1550-1551, rest/lodg

Drugs and Druggists' Sundries Merchant Wholesalers, 842-843, wsle

Drycleaning and Laundry Services (except Coin-Operated), 1592-1593, other

Drywall and Insulation Contractors, 246-247, cons-g

Drywall and Insulation Contractors, 1673, cons-%

E

Educational Support Services, 1410-1411, edu

Electric Power Distribution, 192-193, util

Electrical Apparatus and Equipment, Wiring Supplies, and Related Equipment Merchant Wholesalers, 800-801, wsle

Electrical Contractors and Other Wiring Installation Contractors, 240-241, cons-g

Electrical Contractors and Other Wiring Installation Contractors, 1671, cons-%

Electromedical and Electrotherapeutic Apparatus Manufacturing, 654-655, mfg

Electronic Computer Manufacturing, 632-633, mfg

Electronic Connector Manufacturing, 648-649, mfg

Electronic Shopping and Mail-Order Houses, 1010-1011, rtl

Electronics Stores, 926-927, rtl

Electroplating, Plating, Polishing, Anodizing, and Coloring, 554-555, mfg

Elementary and Secondary Schools, 1392-1393, edu

Employment Placement Agencies, 1328-1329, Admin

Engineering Services, 1252-1253, prof serv

Environment, Conservation and Wildlife Organizations, 1610-1611, other

Environmental Consulting Services, 1284-1285, prof serv

Ethyl Alcohol Manufacturing, 408-409, mfg

Executive and Legislative Offices, Combined, 1634-1635, pub admin

Executive Offices, 1628-1629, pub admin

Executive Search Services, 1330-1331, Admin

Exterminating and Pest Control Services, 1356-1357, Admin

F

Fabricated Pipe and Pipe Fitting Manufacturing, 568-569, mfg

Fabricated Structural Metal Manufacturing, 524-525, mfg

Facilities Support Services, 1326-1327, Admin

Family Clothing Stores, 974-975, rtl

Family Planning Centers, 1432-1433, HC

Farm and Garden Machinery and Equipment Merchant Wholesalers, 816-817, wsle

Farm Machinery and Equipment Manufacturing, 572-573, mfg

Farm Management Services, 160-161, ag

Farm Product Warehousing and Storage, 1090-1091, trans

Farm Supplies Merchant Wholesalers, 886-887, wsle

Fertilizer (Mixing Only) Manufacturing, 416-417, mfg

Fiber, Yarn, and Thread Mills, 328-329, mfg

Financial Transactions Processing, Reserve, and Clearinghouse Activities, 1142-1143, fin

Fine Arts Schools, 1404-1405, edu

Finfish Fishing, 148-149, ag

Finish Carpentry Contractors, 254-255, cons-g

Fire Protection, 1640-1641, pub admin

Fish and Seafood Merchant Wholesalers, 862-863, wsle

Fitness and Recreational Sports Centers, 1524-1525, ent

Flat Glass Manufacturing, 470-471, mfg

Flavoring Syrup and Concentrate Manufacturing, 308-309, mfg

Floor Covering Stores, 920-921, rtl

Flooring Contractors, 250-251, cons-g

Flooring Contractors, 1675, cons-%

Floriculture Production, 126-127, ag

Florists, 992-993, rtl

Flour Milling, 268-269, mfg

Flower, Nursery Stock, and Florists' Supplies Merchant Wholesalers, 890-891, wsle

Fluid Milk Manufacturing, 282-283, mfg

Fluid Power Valve and Hose Fitting Manufacturing, 558-559, mfg

Folding Paperboard Box Manufacturing, 382-383, mfg

Food (Health) Supplement Stores, 962-963, rtl

Food Product Machinery Manufacturing, 582-583, mfg

Food Service Contractors, 1546-1547, rest/lodg

Footwear Manufacturing, 354-355, mfg

Footwear Merchant Wholesalers, 850-851, wsle

Fossil Fuel Electric Power Generation, 184-185, util

Framing Contractors, 230-231, cons-g

Freestanding Ambulatory Surgical and Emergency Centers, 1438-1439, HC

Freight Transportation Arrangement, 1076-1077, trans

Fresh Fruit and Vegetable Merchant Wholesalers, 866-867, wsle

Frozen Fruit, Juice, and Vegetable Manufacturing, 274-275, mfg

Frozen Specialty Food Manufacturing, 276-277, mfg

Fruit and Tree Nut Combination Farming, 118-119, ag

Fruit and Vegetable Canning, 278-279, mfg

Fruit and Vegetable Markets, 946-947, rtl

Fuel Dealers, 1014-1015, rtl

Full-Service Restaurants, 1552-1553, rest/lodg

Funeral Homes and Funeral Services, 1586-1587, other

Furniture Merchant Wholesalers, 772-773, wsle

Furniture Stores, 918-919, rtl

G

Gasket, Packing, and Sealing Device Manufacturing, 756-757, mfg

Gasoline Stations with Convenience Stores, 966-967, rtl

General Automotive Repair, 1560-1561, other

STATEMENT STUDIES KEY WORD INDEX

A complete description of each industry category listed below begins on page 33.

General Freight Trucking, Local, 1034-1035, trans

General Freight Trucking, Long-Distance, Less Than Truckload, 1038-1039, trans

General Freight Trucking, Long-Distance, Truckload, 1036-1037, trans

General Line Grocery Merchant Wholesalers, 852-853, wsle

General Medical and Surgical Hospitals, 1454-1455, HC

General Medical and Surgical Hospitals (Non-Profit), 1456-1457, HC

General Rental Centers, 1220-1221, R/E

General Warehousing and Storage, 1086-1087, trans

Gift, Novelty, and Souvenir Stores, 996-997, rtl

Glass and Glazing Contractors, 234-235, cons-g

Glass and Glazing Contractors, 1669, cons-%

Glass Product Manufacturing Made of Purchased Glass, 472-473, mfg

Golf Courses and Country Clubs, 1518-1519, ent

Grain and Field Bean Merchant Wholesalers, 870-871, wsle

Grantmaking Foundations, 1604-1605, other

Grape Vineyards, 114-115, ag

Graphic Design Services, 1262-1263, prof serv

H

Hardware Manufacturing, 538-539, mfg

Hardware Merchant Wholesalers, 806-807, wsle

Hardware Stores, 932-933, rtl

Hardwood Veneer and Plywood Manufacturing, 362-363, mfg

Hazardous Waste Treatment and Disposal, 1376-1377, Admin

Heating Equipment (except Warm Air Furnaces) Manufacturing, 596-597, mfg

Heavy Duty Truck Manufacturing, 688-689, mfg

Highway, Street, and Bridge Construction, 222-223, cons-g

Highway, Street, and Bridge Construction, 1664, cons-%

Hobby, Toy, and Game Stores, 986-987, rtl

Hog and Pig Farming, 140-141, ag

Home Centers, 928-929, rtl

Home Furnishing Merchant Wholesalers, 774-775, wsle

Home Health Care Services, 1446-1447, HC

Home Health Equipment Rental, 1216-1217, R/E

Hotels (except Casino Hotels) and Motels, 1532-1533, rest/lodg

Household Appliance Stores, 924-925, rtl

Household Appliances, Electric Housewares, and Consumer Electronics Merchant Wholesalers, 802-803, wsle

Human Resources Consulting Services, 1276-1277, prof serv

I

Ice Cream and Frozen Dessert Manufacturing, 286-287, mfg

Independent Artists, Writers, and Performers, 1506-1507, ent

Industrial and Commercial Fan and Blower and Air Purification Equipment Manufacturing, 594-595, mfg

Industrial and Personal Service Paper Merchant Wholesalers, 840-841, wsle

Industrial Building Construction, 210-211, cons-g

Industrial Building Construction, 1659, cons-%

Industrial Design Services, 1260-1261, prof serv

Industrial Machinery and Equipment Merchant Wholesalers, 818-819, wsle

Industrial Mold Manufacturing, 600-601, mfg

Industrial Process Furnace and Oven Manufacturing, 628-629, mfg

Industrial Supplies Merchant Wholesalers, 820-821, wsle

Industrial Truck, Tractor, Trailer, and Stacker Machinery Manufacturing, 622-623, mfg

Industrial Valve Manufacturing, 556-557, mfg

Inland Water Freight Transportation, 1032-1033, trans

Institutional Furniture Manufacturing, 728-729, mfg

Instrument Manufacturing for Measuring and Testing Electricity and Electrical Signals, 662-663, mfg

Instruments and Related Products Manufacturing for Measuring, Displaying, and Controlling Industrial Process Variables, 660-661, mfg

Insurance Agencies and Brokerages, 1174-1175, fin

Interior Design Services, 1258-1259, prof serv

Internet Publishing and Broadcasting and Web Search Portals, 1126-1127, info

Investment Advice, 1156-1157, fin

Investment Banking and Securities Dealing, 1146-1147, fin

Iron and Steel Forging, 512-513, mfg

Iron and Steel Mills and Ferroalloy Manufacturing, 488-489, mfg

Iron and Steel Pipe and Tube Manufacturing from Purchased Steel, 490-491, mfg

Iron Foundries, 504-505, mfg

J

Janitorial Services, 1358-1359, Admin

Jewelry and Silverware Manufacturing, 748-749, mfg

Jewelry Stores, 982-983, rtl

Jewelry, Watch, Precious Stone, and Precious Metal Merchant Wholesalers, 832-833, wsle

Junior Colleges, 1394-1395, edu

K

Kidney Dialysis Centers, 1436-1437, HC

L

Labor Unions and Similar Labor Organizations, 1620-1621, other

Laminated Plastics Plate, Sheet (except Packaging), and Shape Manufacturing, 450-451, mfg

Land Subdivision, 220-221, cons-g

Land Subdivision, 1663, cons-%

Landscape Architectural Services, 1250-1251, prof serv

Landscaping Services, 1360-1361, Admin

Lawn and Garden Tractor and Home Lawn and Garden Equipment Manufacturing, 574-575, mfg

Legislative Bodies, 1630-1631, pub admin

Lessors of Miniwarehouses and Self-Storage Units, 1194-1195, R/E

Lessors of Nonfinancial Intangible Assets (except Copyrighted Works), 1230-1231, R/E

Lessors of Nonresidential Buildings (except Miniwarehouses), 1192-1193, R/E

Lessors of Other Real Estate Property, 1196-1197, R/E

Lessors of Residential Buildings and Dwellings, 1190-1191, R/E

Limited-Service Restaurants, 1554-1555, rest/lodg

Limousine Service, 1048-1049, trans

Line-Haul Railroads, 1026-1027, trans

Linen Supply, 1594-1595, other

Local Messengers and Local Delivery, 1084-1085, trans

Logging, 146-147, ag

Lumber, Plywood, Millwork, and Wood Panel Merchant Wholesalers, 776-777, wsle

M

Machine Shops, 544-545, mfg

Machine Tool Manufacturing, 606-607, mfg

Manufactured (Mobile) Home Dealers, 1004-1005, rtl

Marinas, 1522-1523, ent

Marine Cargo Handling, 1066-1067, trans

Marketing Consulting Services, 1278-1279, prof serv

Marketing Research and Public Opinion Polling, 1304-1305, prof serv

Masonry Contractors, 232-233, cons-g

Masonry Contractors, 1668, cons-%

Materials Recovery Facilities, 1384-1385, Admin

Mattress Manufacturing, 738-739, mfg

Mayonnaise, Dressing, and Other Prepared Sauce Manufacturing, 310-311, mfg

Measuring, Dispensing, and Other Pumping Equipment Manufacturing, 616-617, mfg

Meat and Meat Product Merchant Wholesalers, 864-865, wsle

Meat Markets, 944-945, rtl

Meat Processed from Carcasses, 290-291, mfg

Mechanical Power Transmission Equipment Manufacturing, 610-611, mfg

Medical Laboratories, 1442-1443, HC

Medical, Dental, and Hospital Equipment and Supplies Merchant Wholesalers, 792-793, wsle

Medicinal and Botanical Manufacturing, 420-421, mfg

Men's and Boys' Cut and Sew Apparel Manufacturing, 346-347, mfg

Men's and Boys' Clothing and Furnishings Merchant Wholesalers, 846-847, wsle

Men's Clothing Stores, 970-971, rtl

Metal Coating, Engraving (except Jewelry and Silverware), and Allied Services to Manufacturers, 552-553, mfg

Metal Crown, Closure, and Other Metal Stamping (except Automotive), 516-517, mfg

Metal Heat Treating, 550-551, mfg

Metal Kitchen Cookware, Utensil, Cutlery, and Flatware (except Precious) Manufacturing, 518-519, mfg

Metal Service Centers and Other Metal Merchant Wholesalers, 796-797, wsle

Metal Tank (Heavy Gauge) Manufacturing, 534-535, mfg

Metal Window and Door Manufacturing, 528-529, mfg

Mining Machinery and Equipment Manufacturing, 578-579, mfg

Miscellaneous Financial Investment Activities, 1160-1161, fin

Miscellaneous Intermediation, 1152-1153, fin

Mortgage and Nonmortgage Loan Brokers, 1140-1141, fin

Motion Picture and Video Production, 1106-1107, info

Motion Picture Theaters (except Drive-Ins), 1108-1109, info

Motor and Generator Manufacturing, 676-677, mfg

Motor Vehicle Body Manufacturing, 690-691, mfg

Motor Vehicle Electrical and Electronic Equipment Manufacturing, 698-699, mfg

Motor Vehicle Gasoline Engine and Engine Parts Manufacturing, 696-697, mfg

Motor Vehicle Metal Stamping, 704-705, mfg

Motor Vehicle Parts (Used) Merchant Wholesalers, 770-771, wsle

Motor Vehicle Seating and Interior Trim Manufacturing, 702-703, mfg

Motor Vehicle Supplies and New Parts Merchant Wholesalers, 766-767, wsle

Motor Vehicle Towing, 1072-1073, trans

Motor Vehicle Transmission and Power Train Parts Manufacturing, 700-701, mfg

STATEMENT STUDIES KEY WORD INDEX

A complete description of each industry category listed below begins on page 33.

Motorcycle, ATV, and All Other Motor Vehicle Dealers, 912-913, rtl
Motorcycle, Bicycle, and Parts Manufacturing, 718-719, mfg
Museums, 1508-1509, ent
Mushroom Production, 122-123, ag
Musical Groups and Artists, 1494-1495, ent
Musical Instrument and Supplies Stores, 988-989, rtl
Musical Instrument Manufacturing, 758-759, mfg

N

Natural Gas Distribution, 194-195, util
Navigational Services to Shipping, 1068-1069, trans
New Car Dealers, 904-905, rtl
New Housing For-Sale Builders, 206-207, cons-g
New Housing For-Sale Builders, 1658, cons-%
New Multifamily Housing Construction (except For-Sale Builders), 204-205, cons-g
New Multifamily Housing Construction (except For-Sale Builders), 1657, cons-%
New Single-Family Housing Construction (except For-Sale Builders), 202-203, cons-g
New Single-Family Housing Construction (except For-Sale Builders), 1656, cons-%
Newspaper Publishers, 1096-1097, info
Nitrogenous Fertilizer Manufacturing, 414-415, mfg
Nonchocolate Confectionery Manufacturing, 270-271, mfg
Nonferrous Metal (except Copper and Aluminum) Rolling, Drawing, and Extruding, 500-501, mfg
Nonferrous Metal Die-Casting Foundries, 508-509, mfg
Nonresidential Property Managers, 1202-1203, R/E
Nonscheduled Chartered Passenger Air Transportation, 1022-1023, trans
Nonupholstered Wood Household Furniture Manufacturing, 726-727, mfg
Nonwoven Fabric Mills, 332-333, mfg
Nursery and Tree Production, 124-125, ag
Nursery, Garden Center, and Farm Supply Stores, 938-939, rtl
Nursing Care Facilities (Skilled Nursing Facilities), 1462-1463, HC

O

Office Administrative Services, 1324-1325, Admin
Office Equipment Merchant Wholesalers, 786-787, wsle
Office Furniture (except Wood) Manufacturing, 734-735, mfg
Office Machinery and Equipment Rental and Leasing, 1226-1227, R/E
Office Supplies and Stationery Stores, 994-995, rtl
Offices of All Other Miscellaneous Health Practitioners, 1430-1431, HC
Offices of Certified Public Accountants, 1240-1241, prof serv
Offices of Chiropractors, 1420-1421, HC
Offices of Dentists, 1418-1419, HC
Offices of Lawyers, 1234-1235, prof serv
Offices of Mental Health Practitioners (except Physicians), 1424-1425, HC
Offices of Optometrists, 1422-1423, HC
Offices of Other Holding Companies, 1318-1319, mgmt
Offices of Physical, Occupational and Speech Therapists, and Audiologists, 1426-1427, HC
Offices of Physicians (except Mental Health Specialists), 1414-1415, HC
Offices of Physicians, Mental Health Specialists, 1416-1417, HC
Offices of Podiatrists, 1428-1429, HC

Offices of Real Estate Agents and Brokers, 1198-1199, R/E
Offices of Real Estate Appraisers, 1204-1205, R/E
Oil and Gas Field Machinery and Equipment Manufacturing, 580-581, mfg
Oil and Gas Pipeline and Related Structures Construction, 216-217, cons-g
Oilseed and Grain Combination Farming, 104-105, ag
Open-End Investment Funds, 1182-1183, fin
Optical Goods Stores, 960-961, rtl
Optical Instrument and Lens Manufacturing, 590-591, mfg
Ornamental and Architectural Metal Work Manufacturing, 532-533, mfg
Other Accounting Services, 1246-1247, prof serv
Other Activities Related to Credit Intermediation, 1144-1145, fin
Other Activities Related to Real Estate, 1206-1207, R/E
Other Aircraft Parts and Auxiliary Equipment Manufacturing, 712-713, mfg
Other Airport Operations, 1058-1059, trans
Other Aluminum Rolling, Drawing, and Extruding, 496-497, mfg
Other Animal Food Manufacturing, 266-267, mfg
Other Automotive Mechanical and Electrical Repair and Maintenance, 1562-1563, other
Other Basic Inorganic Chemical Manufacturing, 406-407, mfg
Other Building Equipment Contractors, 244-245, cons-g
Other Building Finishing Contractors, 256-257, cons-g
Other Building Material Dealers, 934-935, rtl
Other Business Service Centers (including Copy Shops), 1340-1341, Admin
Other Chemical and Allied Products Merchant Wholesalers, 876-877, wsle
Other Clothing Stores, 978-979, rtl
Other Commercial and Industrial Machinery and Equipment Rental and Leasing, 1228-1229, R/E
Other Commercial and Service Industry Machinery Manufacturing, 592-593, mfg
Other Commercial Equipment Merchant Wholesalers, 790-791, wsle
Other Communications Equipment Manufacturing, 638-639, mfg
Other Community Housing Services, 1484-1485, HC
Other Computer Related Services, 1272-1273, prof serv
Other Concrete Product Manufacturing, 480-481, mfg
Other Construction Material Merchant Wholesalers, 782-783, wsle
Other Crushed and Broken Stone Mining and Quarrying, 174-175, mng
Other Cut and Sew Apparel Manufacturing, 350-351, mfg
Other Direct Insurance (except Life, Health, and Medical) Carriers, 1170-1171, fin
Other Direct Selling Establishments, 1016-1017, rtl
Other Electric Power Generation, 190-191, util
Other Electronic and Precision Equipment Repair and Maintenance, 1574-1575, other
Other Electronic Component Manufacturing, 652-653, mfg
Other Electronic Parts and Equipment Merchant Wholesalers, 804-805, wsle
Other Engine Equipment Manufacturing, 612-613, mfg
Other Fabricated Wire Product Manufacturing, 542-543, mfg
Other Farm Product Raw Material Merchant Wholesalers, 872-873, wsle
Other Financial Vehicles, 1186-1187, fin

Other Foundation, Structure, and Building Exterior Contractors, 238-239, cons-g
Other Gambling Industries, 1516-1517, ent
Other Gasoline Stations, 968-969, rtl
Other General Government Support, 1638-1639, pub admin
Other Grantmaking and Giving Services, 1608-1609, other
Other Grocery and Related Products Merchant Wholesalers, 868-869, wsle
Other Heavy and Civil Engineering Construction, 224-225, cons-g
Other Heavy and Civil Engineering Construction, 1665, cons-%
Other Individual and Family Services, 1478-1479, HC
Other Industrial Machinery Manufacturing, 588-589, mfg
Other Lighting Equipment Manufacturing, 672-673, mfg
Other Management Consulting Services, 1282-1283, prof serv
Other Measuring and Controlling Device Manufacturing, 666-667, mfg
Other Metal Container Manufacturing, 536-537, mfg
Other Metal Valve and Pipe Fitting Manufacturing, 562-563, mfg
Other Millwork (including Flooring), 370-371, mfg
Other Miscellaneous Durable Goods Merchant Wholesalers, 834-835, wsle
Other Miscellaneous Nondurable Goods Merchant Wholesalers, 896-897, wsle
Other Motor Vehicle Parts Manufacturing, 706-707, mfg
Other Noncitrus Fruit Farming, 120-121, ag
Other Nonhazardous Waste Treatment and Disposal, 1380-1381, Admin
Other Nonscheduled Air Transportation, 1024-1025, trans
Other Paperboard Container Manufacturing, 384-385, mfg
Other Personal and Household Goods Repair and Maintenance, 1578-1579, other
Other Personal Care Services, 1584-1585, other
Other Professional Equipment and Supplies Merchant Wholesalers, 794-795, wsle
Other Residential Care Facilities, 1472-1473, HC
Other Scientific and Technical Consulting Services, 1286-1287, prof serv
Other Services Related to Advertising, 1302-1303, prof serv
Other Services to Buildings and Dwellings, 1364-1365, Admin
Other Similar Organizations (except Business, Professional, Labor, and Political Organizations), 1622-1623, other
Other Snack Food Manufacturing, 304-305, mfg
Other Social Advocacy Organizations, 1612-1613, other
Other Specialized Design Services, 1264-1265, prof serv
Other Support Activities for Air Transportation, 1060-1061, trans
Other Support Activities for Road Transportation, 1074-1075, trans
Other Support Activities for Water Transportation, 1070-1071, trans
Other Technical and Trade Schools, 1402-1403, edu
Other Vegetable (except Potato) and Melon Farming, 110-111, ag
Other Warehousing and Storage, 1092-1093, trans
Other Waste Collection, 1374-1375, Admin
Outdoor Advertising, 1298-1299, prof serv
Outdoor Power Equipment Stores, 936-937, rtl
Outpatient Mental Health and Substance Abuse Centers, 1434-1435, HC

STATEMENT STUDIES KEY WORD INDEX

A complete description of each industry category listed below begins on page 33.

Overhead Traveling Crane, Hoist, and Monorail System Manufacturing, 620-621, mfg

P

Packaged Frozen Food Merchant Wholesalers, 854-855, wsle
Packaging and Labeling Services, 1366-1367, Admin
Packaging Machinery Manufacturing, 626-627, mfg
Packing and Crating, 1078-1079, trans
Paint and Coating Manufacturing, 424-425, mfg
Paint and Wallpaper Stores, 930-931, rtl
Paint, Varnish, and Supplies Merchant Wholesalers, 894-895, wsle
Painting and Wall Covering Contractors, 248-249, cons-g
Painting and Wall Covering Contractors, 1674, cons-%
Paper (except Newsprint) Mills, 378-379, mfg
Paper Bag and Coated and Treated Paper Manufacturing, 386-387, mfg
Parking Lots and Garages, 1598-1599, other
Passenger Car Leasing, 1210-1211, R/E
Passenger Car Rental, 1208-1209, R/E
Payroll Services, 1244-1245, prof serv
Periodical Publishers, 1098-1099, info
Perishable Prepared Food Manufacturing, 314-315, mfg
Pesticide and Other Agricultural Chemical Manufacturing, 418-419, mfg
Pet and Pet Supplies Stores, 1000-1001, rtl
Pet Care (except Veterinary) Services, 1596-1597, other
Petroleum and Petroleum Products Merchant Wholesalers (except Bulk Stations and Terminals), 880-881, wsle
Petroleum Bulk Stations and Terminals, 878-879, wsle
Petroleum Lubricating Oil and Grease Manufacturing, 404-405, mfg
Petroleum Refineries, 400-401, mfg
Pharmaceutical Preparation Manufacturing, 422-423, mfg
Pharmacies and Drug Stores, 956-957, rtl
Photographic Equipment and Supplies Merchant Wholesalers, 784-785, wsle
Photography Studios, Portrait, 1306-1307, prof serv
Piece Goods, Notions, and Other Dry Goods Merchant Wholesalers, 844-845, wsle
Plastics Bag and Pouch Manufacturing, 440-441, mfg
Plastics Bottle Manufacturing, 456-457, mfg
Plastics Material and Resin Manufacturing, 412-413, mfg
Plastics Materials and Basic Forms and Shapes Merchant Wholesalers, 874-875, wsle
Plastics Packaging Film and Sheet (including Laminated) Manufacturing, 442-443, mfg
Plastics Pipe and Pipe Fitting Manufacturing, 448-449, mfg
Plastics Plumbing Fixture Manufacturing, 458-459, mfg
Plate Work Manufacturing, 526-527, mfg
Plumbing and Heating Equipment and Supplies (Hydronics) Merchant Wholesalers, 808-809, wsle
Plumbing Fixture Fitting and Trim Manufacturing, 560-561, mfg
Plumbing, Heating, and Air-Conditioning Contractors, 242-243, cons-g
Plumbing, Heating, and Air-Conditioning Contractors, 1672, cons-%
Polish and Other Sanitation Good Manufacturing, 430-431, mfg
Polystyrene Foam Product Manufacturing, 452-453, mfg
Port and Harbor Operations, 1064-1065, trans
Portfolio Management, 1154-1155, fin

Postharvest Crop Activities (except Cotton Ginning), 158-159, ag
Potato Farming, 108-109, ag
Poultry and Poultry Product Merchant Wholesalers, 858-859, wsle
Poultry Processing, 292-293, mfg
Poured Concrete Foundation and Structure Contractors, 226-227, cons-g
Poured Concrete Foundation and Structure Contractors, 1666, cons-%
Powder Metallurgy Part Manufacturing, 514-515, mfg
Power and Communication Line and Related Structures Construction, 218-219, cons-g
Power and Communication Line and Related Structures Construction, 1662, cons-%
Power, Distribution, and Specialty Transformer Manufacturing, 674-675, mfg
Precision Turned Product Manufacturing, 546-547, mfg
Prefabricated Metal Building and Component Manufacturing, 522-523, mfg
Prefabricated Wood Building Manufacturing, 374-375, mfg
Printed Circuit Assembly (Electronic Assembly) Manufacturing, 650-651, mfg
Printing and Writing Paper Merchant Wholesalers, 836-837, wsle
Printing Ink Manufacturing, 434-435, mfg
Printing Machinery and Equipment Manufacturing, 586-587, mfg
Private Households, 1624-1625, other
Process, Physical Distribution, and Logistics Consulting Services, 1280-1281, prof serv
Professional and Management Development Training, 1398-1399, edu
Professional Employer Organizations, 1334-1335, Admin
Professional Organizations, 1618-1619, other
Promoters of Performing Arts, Sports, and Similar Events with Facilities, 1500-1501, ent
Promoters of Performing Arts, Sports, and Similar Events without Facilities, 1502-1503, ent
Psychiatric and Substance Abuse Hospitals, 1458-1459, HC
Public Finance Activities, 1632-1633, pub admin
Public Relations Agencies, 1296-1297, prof serv

R

Racetracks, 1498-1499, ent
Radio and Television Broadcasting and Wireless Communications Equipment Manufacturing, 636-637, mfg
Radio Stations, 1110-1111, info
Ready-Mix Concrete Manufacturing, 476-477, mfg
Real Estate Credit, 1136-1137, fin
Recreational and Vacation Camps (except Campgrounds), 1542-1543, rest/lodg
Recreational Vehicle Dealers, 908-909, rtl
Recyclable Material Merchant Wholesalers, 830-831, wsle
Refrigerated Warehousing and Storage, 1088-1089, trans
Refrigeration Equipment and Supplies Merchant Wholesalers, 812-813, wsle
Reinsurance Carriers, 1172-1173, fin
Relay and Industrial Control Manufacturing, 680-681, mfg
Religious Organizations, 1602-1603, other
Remediation Services, 1382-1383, Admin
Research and Development in Biotechnology (except Nanobiotechnology), 1288-1289, prof serv
Research and Development in the Physical, Engineering, and Life Sciences (except Nanotechnology and Biotechnology), 1290-1291, prof serv

Research and Development in the Social Sciences and Humanities, 1292-1293, prof serv
Residential Electric Lighting Fixture Manufacturing, 668-669, mfg
Residential Intellectual and Developmental Disability Facilities, 1464-1465, HC
Residential Mental Health and Substance Abuse Facilities, 1466-1467, HC
Residential Property Managers, 1200-1201, R/E
Residential Remodelers, 208-209, cons-g
Retail Bakeries, 296-297, mfg
Roasted Nuts and Peanut Butter Manufacturing, 302-303, mfg
Rolled Steel Shape Manufacturing, 492-493, mfg
Rolling Mill and Other Metalworking Machinery Manufacturing, 608-609, mfg
Roofing Contractors, 236-237, cons-g
Roofing Contractors, 1670, cons-%
Roofing, Siding, and Insulation Material Merchant Wholesalers, 780-781, wsle
Rooming and Boarding Houses, 1544-1545, rest/lodg
Rubber and Plastics Hoses and Belting Manufacturing, 462-463, mfg
Rubber Product Manufacturing for Mechanical Use, 464-465, mfg
RV (Recreational Vehicle) Parks and Campgrounds, 1540-1541, rest/lodg

S

Sales Financing, 1132-1133, fin
Sanitary Paper Product Manufacturing, 390-391, mfg
Saw Blade and Handtool Manufacturing, 520-521, mfg
Sawmill, Woodworking, and Paper Machinery Manufacturing, 584-585, mfg
Sawmills, 358-359, mfg
Scenic and Sightseeing Transportation, Water, 1056-1057, trans
Scheduled Passenger Air Transportation, 1020-1021, trans
School and Employee Bus Transportation, 1050-1051, trans
Seafood Product Preparation and Packaging, 294-295, mfg
Search, Detection, Navigation, Guidance, Aeronautical, and Nautical System and Instrument Manufacturing, 656-657, mfg
Secondary Smelting, Refining, and Alloying of Nonferrous Metal (except Copper and Aluminum), 502-503, mfg
Securities Brokerage, 1148-1149, fin
Security Guards and Patrol Services, 1352-1353, Admin
Security Systems Services (except Locksmiths), 1354-1355, Admin
Semiconductor and Related Device Manufacturing, 644-645, mfg
Septic Tank and Related Services, 1386-1387, Admin
Service Establishment Equipment and Supplies Merchant Wholesalers, 822-823, wsle
Services for the Elderly and Persons with Disabilities, 1476-1477, HC
Sewage Treatment Facilities, 198-199, util
Sheet Metal Work Manufacturing, 530-531, mfg
Shellfish Fishing, 150-151, ag
Ship Building and Repairing, 714-715, mfg
Shoe Stores, 980-981, rtl
Showcase, Partition, Shelving, and Locker Manufacturing, 736-737, mfg
Sign Manufacturing, 754-755, mfg
Site Preparation Contractors, 258-259, cons-g
Site Preparation Contractors, 1676, cons-%
Skiing Facilities, 1520-1521, ent
Small Arms, Ordnance, and Ordnance Accessories Manufacturing, 566-567, mfg

STATEMENT STUDIES KEY WORD INDEX

A complete description of each industry category listed below begins on page 33.

Snack and Nonalcoholic Beverage Bars, 1556-1557, rest/lodg
Soap and Other Detergent Manufacturing, 428-429, mfg
Soft Drink Manufacturing, 318-319, mfg
Software Publishers, 1104-1105, info
Soil Preparation, Planting, and Cultivating, 154-155, ag
Solar Electric Power Generation, 186-187, util
Solid Waste Collection, 1372-1373, Admin
Solid Waste Landfill, 1378-1379, Admin
Soybean Farming, 98-99, ag
Special Die and Tool, Die Set, Jig, and Fixture Manufacturing, 602-603, mfg
Specialized Freight (except Used Goods) Trucking, Local, 1042-1043, trans
Specialized Freight (except Used Goods) Trucking, Long-Distance, 1044-1045, trans
Specialty (except Psychiatric and Substance Abuse) Hospitals, 1460-1461, HC
Spice and Extract Manufacturing, 312-313, mfg
Sporting and Athletic Goods Manufacturing, 750-751, mfg
Sporting and Recreational Goods and Supplies Merchant Wholesalers, 826-827, wsle
Sporting Goods Stores, 984-985, rtl
Sports and Recreation Instruction, 1406-1407, edu
Sports Teams and Clubs, 1496-1497, ent
Spring Manufacturing, 540-541, mfg
Stationery and Office Supplies Merchant Wholesalers, 838-839, wsle
Stationery Product Manufacturing, 388-389, mfg
Steel Foundries (except Investment), 506-507, mfg
Steel Wire Drawing, 494-495, mfg
Structural Steel and Precast Concrete Contractors, 228-229, cons-g
Structural Steel and Precast Concrete Contractors, 1667, cons-%
Supermarkets and Other Grocery (except Convenience) Stores, 940-941, rtl
Support Activities for Animal Production, 162-163, ag
Support Activities for Forestry, 164-165, ag
Support Activities for Oil and Gas Operations, 180-181, mng
Support Activities for Printing, 398-399, mfg
Support Activities for Rail Transportation, 1062-1063, trans
Surgical and Medical Instrument Manufacturing, 740-741, mfg
Surgical Appliance and Supplies Manufacturing, 742-743, mfg
Surveying and Mapping (except Geophysical) Services, 1254-1255, prof serv
Switchgear and Switchboard Apparatus Manufacturing, 678 679, mfg

T

Tax Preparation Services, 1242-1243, prof serv
Taxi Service, 1046-1047, trans
Telecommunications Resellers, 1120-1121, info
Telemarketing Bureaus and Other Contact Centers, 1338-1339, Admin
Telephone Answering Services, 1336-1337, Admin
Television Broadcasting, 1112-1113, info
Temporary Help Services, 1332-1333, Admin
Temporary Shelters, 1482-1483, HC
Testing Laboratories, 1256-1257, prof serv
Textile and Fabric Finishing Mills, 334-335, mfg
Textile Bag and Canvas Mills, 340-341, mfg
Theater Companies and Dinner Theaters, 1492-1493, ent
Third Party Administration of Insurance and Pension Funds, 1178-1179, fin
Tile and Terrazzo Contractors, 252-253, cons-g
Timber Tract Operations, 144-145, ag
Tire and Tube Merchant Wholesalers, 768-769, wsle
Tire Dealers, 916-917, rtl
Title Abstract and Settlement Offices, 1236-1237, prof serv
Tobacco and Tobacco Product Merchant Wholesalers, 892-893, wsle
Tobacco Farming, 128-129, ag
Tobacco Stores, 1006-1007, rtl
Toilet Preparation Manufacturing, 432-433, mfg
Tour Operators, 1348-1349, Admin
Toy and Hobby Goods and Supplies Merchant Wholesalers, 828-829, wsle
Translation and Interpretation Services, 1310-1311, prof serv
Transportation Equipment and Supplies (except Motor Vehicle) Merchant Wholesalers, 824-825, wsle
Travel Agencies, 1346-1347, Admin
Travel Trailer and Camper Manufacturing, 694-695, mfg
Tree Nut Farming, 116-117, ag
Truck Trailer Manufacturing, 692-693, mfg
Truck, Utility Trailer, and RV (Recreational Vehicle) Rental and Leasing, 1212-1213, R/E
Truss Manufacturing, 364-365, mfg
Trust, Fiduciary, and Custody Activities, 1158-1159, fin
Trusts, Estates, and Agency Accounts, 1184-1185, fin

U

Unlaminated Plastics Film and Sheet (except Packaging) Manufacturing, 444-445, mfg
Unlaminated Plastics Profile Shape Manufacturing, 446-447, mfg

Upholstered Household Furniture Manufacturing, 724-725, mfg
Urethane and Other Foam Product (except Polystyrene) Manufacturing, 454-455, mfg
Used Car Dealers, 906-907, rtl
Used Household and Office Goods Moving, 1040-1041, trans
Used Merchandise Stores, 998-999, rtl

V

Vending Machine Operators, 1012-1013, rtl
Veterinary Services, 1312-1313, prof serv
Vocational Rehabilitation Services, 1486-1487, HC
Voluntary Health Organizations, 1606-1607, other

W

Warm Air Heating and Air-Conditioning Equipment and Supplies Merchant Wholesalers, 810-811, wsle
Water and Sewer Line and Related Structures Construction, 214-215, cons-g
Water and Sewer Line and Related Structures Construction, 1661, cons-%
Water Supply and Irrigation Systems, 196-197, util
Welding and Soldering Equipment Manufacturing, 624-625, mfg
Wheat Farming, 100-101, ag
Wholesale Trade Agents and Brokers, 900-901, wsle
Wind Electric Power Generation, 188-189, util
Wine and Distilled Alcoholic Beverage Merchant Wholesalers, 884-885, wsle
Wineries, 324-325, mfg
Wired Telecommunications Carriers, 1116-1117, info
Wireless Telecommunications Carriers (except Satellite), 1118-1119, info
Women's, Girls', and Infants' Cut and Sew Apparel Manufacturing, 348-349, mfg
Women's Clothing Stores, 972-973, rtl
Women's, Children's, and Infants' Clothing and Accessories Merchant Wholesalers, 848-849, wsle
Wood Container and Pallet Manufacturing, 372-373, mfg
Wood Kitchen Cabinet and Countertop Manufacturing, 722-723, mfg
Wood Office Furniture Manufacturing, 730-731, mfg
Wood Preservation, 360-361, mfg
Wood Window and Door Manufacturing, 366-367, mfg

Z

Zoos and Botanical Gardens, 1510-1511, ent

CONSTRUCTION
FINANCIAL MANAGEMENT
ASSOCIATION DATA

About the Construction Financial Management Association (CFMA)
Web site: www.cfma.org

Once again, we are delighted to include excerpts from *CFMA's 2019 Construction Industry Financial Benchmarker*. CFMA is **The Source and Resource for Construction Financial Professionals** and has more than 8,000 members in 98 chapters throughout the U.S. and Canada. CFMA's 2019 Benchmarker Website includes aggregate financial data broken down by industry classification, region, revenue and can accessed at www.financialbenchmarker.com.

The 2019 Annual Survey Questionnaire was distributed to approximately 8,000 firms including CFMA member construction firms, non-member construction firms as well as member CPA and CICPAC firms who represent both member and non-member construction companies (mostly companies that are based in or have significant employment in the U.S. and Canada. Responses were received in early 2019. In all, 1,475 companies submitted data for the study. Companies that submitted data for other sections of the Online Questionnaire and general information that enabled us to classify the respondents were included in those appropriate sections' results. The data submitted were compiled and analyzed by a third party vendor, in cooperation with CFMA, and was not engaged to and did not audit or review this information and, accordingly, does not express an opinion or any other form of assurance on it.

Fiscal year-end closing dates reflected in the CFMA survey range from 3/31/18 through 3/31/19. The CFMA data are most comparable to the RMA contractor data from 4/1/18 through 3/31/19 appearing in this edition.

The survey respondents were classified into four categories of construction based on the type of work performed. Classification was based on the level of contract volume reported for various NAICS codes. A contractor was included in a classification if at least one half of its annual contract revenue was attributable to that classification. CFMA categorized certain NAICS codes together. The classifications and NAICS codes included in each are as follows:

NAICS Codes

RESIDENTIAL CONTRACTORS:

236115 New Single-Family Housing Construction (Except Operative Builders)
236116 New Multifamily Housing Construction (Except Operative Builders)
236117 New Housing Operative Builders
236118 Residential Remodelers

INDUSTRIAL AND NONRESIDENTIAL CONTRACTORS:

236210 Industrial Building Construction
236220 Commercial and Institutional Building Construction

HEAVY AND HIGHWAY CONTRACTORS:

237110 Water and Sewer Line and Related Structures Construction
237120 Oil and Gas Pipeline and Related Structures Construction
237130 Power and Communication Line and Related Structures Construction
237310 Highway, Street, and Bridge Construction
237990 Other Heavy and Civil Engineering Construction

SPECIALTY TRADES CONTRACTORS:

238110 Poured Concrete Foundation and Structure Contractors
238120 Structural Steel and Precast Concrete Contractors
238130 Framing Contractors
238140 Masonry Contractors
238150 Glass and Glazing Contractors
238160 Roofing Contractors
238170 Siding Contractors
238190 Other Foundation, Structure, and Building Exterior Contractors
238210 Electrical Contractors
238220 Plumbing, Heating, and Air-Conditioning Contractors
238290 Other Building Equipment Contractors
238310 Drywall and Insulation Contractors
238320 Painting and Wall Covering Contractors
238330 Flooring Contractors
238340 Tile and Terrazzo Contractors

238350 Finish Carpentry Contractors
238390 Other Building Finishing Contractors
238910 Site Preparation Contractors
238990 All Other Specialty Trade Contractors
561621 Security Systems Services (except Locksmiths)
562910 Environmental Remediation Services

The CFMA financial data includes balance sheets, statements of earnings, and financial ratios. The balance sheets and statements of earnings represent a weighted average of all companies included in each classification. Percentages are presented for each dollar amount in the financial statements. Due to rounding, the totals may not agree to the sum of various accounts. Such variations are few and insignificant.

The financial ratios are calculated from the composite balance sheets and statements of earnings data. They are not averages of ratios for all companies included in the classification.

If you wish to purchase 2019 Financial Benchmarking reports (www.financialbenchmarker.com) or have questions regarding the data, contact Mike Elek; Construction Financial Management Association, 100 Village Blvd, Suite 200, Princeton, NJ 08540; Phone 609-452-8000; E-mail melek@cfma.org.

Interpretation of the Construction Financial Management Association (CFMA) Data

CFMA's data should only be regarded as general information. It cannot be used to establish industry norms for a number of reasons, including the following:

(1) The financial statements used in the composite are not selected by any random or statistically reliable method. CFMA members voluntarily submitted their financial data. Note that contractors' statements have no upper asset/sales limit.

(2) Many companies provide varied services; CFMA includes a contractor in a classification if at least one-half (1/2) of its annual contract revenue was completed within that classification.

(3) Some of the NAICS group samples may be rather small in relation to the total number of firms in a given industry category. A relatively small sample can increase the chances that some of our composites do not fully represent an industry group.

(4) There is the chance that an extreme statement can be present in a sample, causing a disproportionate influence on the industry composite. This is particularly true in a relatively small sample.

(5) Companies within the same industry may differ in their method of operations, which in turn can directly influence their financial statements. Since such differences affect financial data included in our sample, our composite calculations could be significantly affected.

(6) Other considerations that can result in variation among different companies engaged in the same general line of business are: different labor markets; geographical location; different accounting methods; quality of service rendered; sources and methods of financing; and terms of sale.

The use of CFMA data may be helpful when considered with other methods of financial analysis. Nevertheless, RMA and CFMA do not recommend the use of CFMA's data to establish norms or parameters for a given industry or grouping, or the industry as a whole. Although CFMA believes that its data is accurate and representative within the confines of the aforementioned reasons, RMA and CFMA specifically make no representations regarding the accuracy of representativeness of the figures printed in this supplement of the RMA Annual Statement Studies.

CFMA's ANNUAL FINANCIAL SURVEY - 2019

	All Companies	Industrial & Non-Residential All Companies	Heavy & Highway All Companies	Specialty Trade All Companies
FINANCIAL INFORMATION				
KEY RATIOS - ALL SHOWN AS MEDIANS EXCEPT INVENTORY DAYS				
Number of Participants	*1,475*	*372*	*242*	*530*
LIQUIDITY RATIOS				
Current Ratio	1.5	1.3	1.7	1.8
Quick Ratio	1.3	1.2	1.4	1.5
Days of Cash	20.0	24.1	25.3	15.0
Working Capital Turnover	**8.9**	**15.5**	**7.3**	**7.2**
PROFITABILITY RATIOS				
Return on Assets	9.5%	7.3%	9.1%	11.8%
Return on Equity	27.1%	29.7%	19.1%	29.0%
Times Interest Earned	20.8	34.4	11.6	18.2
LEVERAGE RATIOS				
Debt to Equity	1.5	2.8	1.0	1.1
Revenue to Equity	6.4	12.6	4.0	5.8
Asset Turnover	2.6	3.3	1.9	2.6
Fixed Asset Ratio	27.4%	16.6%	58.2%	28.4%
Equity to SG&A Expenses	1.6	1.4	2.8	1.4
Underbillings to Equity	8.6%	9.9%	5.6%	9.2%
Average Backlog to Equity	5.1	10.6	3.0	3.5
EFFICIENCY RATIOS				
Average Backlog to Working Capital	6.8	12.4	6.2	4.3
Average Months in Backlog	7.4	8.5	8.7	6.6
Days in Accounts Receivable	55.9	46.6	45.6	63.8
Days in Inventory	3.6	0.3	4.1	4.2
Days in Accounts Payable	33.6	43.7	29.2	26.2
Operating Cycle	46.5	30.2	50.6	55.5
PRODUCTIVITY RATIOS				
Revenue per FTE Employee	$377,423	$937,348	$354,502	$238,578
Gross Profit per FTE Employee	$55,757	$71,606	$53,478	$43,783

CFMA's ANNUAL FINANCIAL SURVEY - 2019 (*continued*)

	All Companies	Industrial & Non-Residential All Companies	Heavy & Highway All Companies	Specialty Trade All Companies
Revenue per Production FTE Employee	$495,911	$1,321,967	$472,870	$300,796
Gross Profit per Production FTE Employee	$72,482	$102,054	$64,470	$53,617
SALES MEASURES				
2017 Total Revenue ($000's)	$83,929	$134,022	$81,107	$51,245
2017 Sales Growth	7.4%	3.9%	8.1%	7.6%
DETAILED FINANCIAL VALUES - ALL SHOWN AS AVERAGES				
Average total Backlog Contract Revenue as of year-end.	$124,948,402	$191,724,871	$140,202,077	$66,286,800
BALANCE SHEET				
Current Assets:				
Cash and cash equivalents	18.7%	24.2%	17.7%	15.2%
Marketable securities and short-term investments	2.2%	3.7%	2.5%	1.7%
Accounts receivable:				
Contract Receivables currently due	40.5%	43.2%	27.6%	43.5%
Retainages on contracts	7.7%	10.5%	6.0%	7.7%
Unbilled work	0.5%	0.2%	0.6%	0.5%
Other receivables	0.8%	0.9%	0.5%	0.8%
(Less) Allowance for doubtful accounts	0.2%	0.1%	0.1%	0.3%
Total Accounts Receivable, Net	49.3%	54.8%	34.6%	52.2%
Notes receivable, current	0.4%	0.3%	0.4%	0.5%
Inventories	1.5%	0.2%	1.6%	1.9%
Costs and recognized earnings in excess of billings on uncompleted contracts	5.2%	4.4%	5.2%	5.7%
Investments in and advances to construction joint ventures	0.3%	0.3%	0.2%	0.1%
Income taxes	0.1%	0.1%	0.2%	0.2%
Other current assets	2.2%	1.7%	2.2%	1.7%
Total Current Assets	80.0%	89.7%	64.7%	79.2%
Total Property Plant & Equipment	43.9%	19.2%	82.7%	48.6%
(Less) accumulated depreciation	28.0%	11.7%	52.2%	31.5%
Property, Plant and Equipment, Net	15.9%	7.5%	30.5%	17.0%

CFMA's ANNUAL FINANCIAL SURVEY - 2019 *(continued)*

	All Companies	Industrial & Non-Residential All Companies	Heavy & Highway All Companies	Specialty Trade All Companies
Noncurrent Assets:				
Long-term investments	0.6%	0.5%	1.2%	0.3%
Notes receivable	0.7%	0.7%	1.0%	0.8%
Investments in and advances to construction joint ventures	0.1%	0.1%	0.1%	0.0%
Investments in unconsolidated affiliates	0.2%	0.1%	0.2%	0.2%
Deferred income taxes	0.1%	0.1%	0.2%	0.1%
Goodwill	0.6%	0.1%	0.6%	0.9%
Other Intangible assets	0.2%	0.1%	0.1%	0.3%
Other Noncurrent Assets	1.6%	1.1%	1.5%	1.2%
Total Other Noncurrent Assets	2.4%	1.3%	2.1%	2.4%
Total Noncurrent Assets	4.1%	2.8%	4.8%	3.8%
Total Assets	100.0%	100.0%	100.0%	100.0%
Current Liabilities:				
Trade, including currently due subcontractors	22.7%	36.2%	15.2%	16.0%
Subcontractors retainages	3.6%	9.7%	1.5%	0.7%
Other payables	1.1%	1.2%	0.9%	1.3%
Total Accounts Payable	27.5%	47.0%	17.6%	18.0%
Accrued expenses	4.9%	4.9%	4.0%	6.1%
Billings in excess of costs and recognized earnings on uncompleted contracts	10.8%	11.2%	7.8%	11.5%
Income taxes Payable	0.2%	0.1%	0.2%	0.2%
Total Other Current Liabilities	2.1%	0.7%	0.9%	1.9%
Notes payable and lines of credit	3.4%	1.7%	2.5%	5.2%
Current maturities of long-term debt, including capitalized leases	2.0%	0.8%	3.7%	2.1%
Total Current Liabilities	50.8%	66.4%	36.6%	45.0%
Noncurrent Liabilities:				
Long-term debt, excluding current maturities	7.0%	3.7%	10.7%	8.3%
Deferred income taxes	0.4%	0.2%	0.7%	0.5%
Other	1.7%	1.1%	1.7%	1.7%
Total Noncurrent Liabilities	9.1%	5.0%	13.1%	10.5%
Total Liabilities	59.9%	71.3%	49.7%	55.4%
Minority Interests	0.1%	0.0%	0.2%	0.2%

CFMA's ANNUAL FINANCIAL SURVEY - 2019 (*continued*)

	All Companies	Industrial & Non-Residential All Companies	Heavy & Highway All Companies	Specialty Trade All Companies
Net Worth:				
Corporation:				
Common stock, par value	1.4%	1.1%	1.3%	1.8%
Preferred stock, stated value	0.2%	0.1%	0.4%	0.2%
(Less) treasury stock	2.0%	1.9%	1.8%	2.4%
Additional paid-in capital	4.2%	3.2%	4.4%	4.7%
Retained earnings	31.5%	21.7%	37.9%	36.0%
Net Corporate Stock	35.3%	24.2%	42.1%	40.4%
Partnership/LLC Capital	4.3%	3.9%	6.9%	4.2%
Other equity	0.5%	0.5%	1.1%	-0.2%
Total Net Worth	40.0%	28.6%	50.1%	44.4%
Total Liabilities and Net Worth	**100.0%**	**100.0%**	**100.0%**	**100.0%**
Total Revenue	100.0%	100.0%	100.0%	100.0%
Direct Costs				
Direct Labor	17.2%	8.5%	18.1%	23.3%
Materials	18.9%	9.4%	21.3%	25.2%
Subcontracts	29.0%	59.7%	18.1%	11.9%
Equipment	3.4%	0.9%	8.1%	3.4%
Other Direct Costs	12.2%	10.1%	14.6%	11.7%
Total Direct Costs	80.7%	88.7%	80.3%	75.5%
Indirect Costs	2.7%	1.1%	4.1%	3.8%
Total Costs	83.4%	89.7%	84.4%	79.3%
Gross Profit	16.6%	10.3%	15.7%	20.7%
SG&A Expenses				
Base Payroll / Payroll Related (Exclusive of Owner Bonuses)	5.9%	3.7%	4.7%	7.6%
Professional Fees	0.5%	0.3%	0.5%	0.6%
Sales & Marketing Costs	0.3%	0.2%	0.1%	0.4%
Technology Costs	0.2%	0.2%	0.2%	0.3%
Administrative Bonuses	0.6%	0.4%	0.5%	0.8%
Other Expenses	4.5%	2.6%	4.0%	5.9%
Total SG&A Expenses	12.0%	7.4%	10.0%	15.6%
Income (Loss) from Operations	4.6%	2.9%	5.6%	5.2%
Interest income	0.1%	0.1%	0.1%	0.1%
Other investment income (loss)	0.1%	0.0%	0.1%	0.2%
Other income (expense)	0.1%	0.1%	0.1%	0.1%
Interest expense	0.3%	0.1%	0.4%	0.4%
Total Other Income (Expense), net	-0.1%	0.1%	-0.1%	-0.1%

CFMA's ANNUAL FINANCIAL SURVEY - 2019 (*continued*)

	All Companies	Industrial & Non-Residential All Companies	Heavy & Highway All Companies	Specialty Trade All Companies
Net Income (Loss) Before Income Taxes	4.5%	3.0%	5.6%	5.1%
Income taxes (benefit)	0.1%	0.1%	0.1%	0.2%
Net Income (LOSS)	4.4%	2.9%	5.5%	4.9%
DETAILED FINANCIAL VALUES - ALL SHOWN AS AVERAGES				
Typical total Backlog Contract Revenue as of year-end.	$124,948,402	$191,724,871	$140,202,077	$66,286,800
BALANCE SHEET				
Current Assets:				
Cash and cash equivalents	$5,398	$8,218	$7,064	$2,293
Marketable securities and short-term investments	$1,693	$4,481	$1,577	$405
Accounts receivable:				
Contract Receivables currently due	$12,996	$18,172	$10,699	$9,412
Retainages on contracts	$3,249	$6,089	$2,845	$1,991
Unbilled work	$152	$69	$422	$155
Other receivables	$395	$302	$296	$225
(Less) Allowance for doubtful accounts	$43	$24	$61	$48
Total Accounts Receivable, Net	$16,750	$24,608	$14,200	$11,735
Notes receivable, current	$119	$70	$275	$49
Inventories	$389	$49	$989	$298
Costs and recognized earnings in excess of billings on uncompleted contracts	$1,717	$1,498	$2,312	$1,643
Investments in and advances to construction joint ventures	$79	$141	$66	$36
Income taxes	$23	$10	$33	$30
Other current assets	$692	$550	$1,115	$367
Total Current Assets	$26,839	$39,624	$27,634	$16,798
Total Property Plant & Equipment	$11,109	$4,413	$34,256	$7,676
(Less) accumulated depreciation	$6,319	$2,484	$20,250	$4,061
Property, Plant and Equipment, Net	$4,791	$1,928	$14,005	$3,615
Noncurrent Assets:				
Long-term investments	$204	$294	$382	$73
Notes receivable	$148	$232	$213	$78
Investments in and advances to construction joint ventures	$57	$34	$210	$10

CFMA's ANNUAL FINANCIAL SURVEY - 2019 (continued)

	All Companies	Industrial & Non-Residential All Companies	Heavy & Highway All Companies	Specialty Trade All Companies
Investments in unconsolidated affiliates	$84	$60	$263	$34
Deferred income taxes	$34	$44	$47	$35
Goodwill	$567	$599	$1,134	$497
Other Intangible assets	$96	$24	$263	$97
Other Noncurrent Assets	$875	$392	$744	$322
Total Other Noncurrent Assets	$1,539	$1,016	$2,140	$915
Total Noncurrent Assets	$2,065	$1,681	$3,255	$1,145
Total Assets	$33,695	$43,233	$44,895	$21,558
Current Liabilities:				
Trade, including currently due subcontractors	$8,522	$15,924	$6,117	$3,609
Subcontractors retainages	$2,080	$6,068	$851	$206
Other payables	$367	$811	$260	$204
Total Accounts Payable	$10,969	$22,804	$7,228	$4,020
Accrued expenses	$1,944	$2,653	$2,622	$1,592
Billings in excess of costs and recognized earnings on uncompleted contracts	$4,100	$5,168	$4,685	$3,385
Income taxes Payable	$37	$25	$71	$37
Total Other Current Liabilities	$1,081	$518	$513	$560
Notes payable and lines of credit	$519	$238	$689	$738
Current maturities of long-term debt, including capitalized leases	$475	$205	$1,365	$369
Total Current Liabilities	$19,125	$31,609	$17,174	$10,701
Noncurrent Liabilities:				
Long-term debt, excluding current maturities	$2,352	$1,622	$4,478	$2,712
Deferred income taxes	$131	$32	$434	$95
Other	$945	$743	$980	$442
Total Noncurrent Liabilities	$3,427	$2,397	$5,892	$3,249
Total Liabilities	$22,552	$34,006	$23,066	$13,949
Minority Interests	$58	$38	$76	$56
Net Worth:				
Corporation:				
Common stock, par value	$350	$483	$420	$262
Preferred stock, stated value	$69	$12	$299	$22
(Less) treasury stock	$652	$965	$472	$596
Additional paid-in capital	$1,292	$1,648	$1,376	$978

CFMA's ANNUAL FINANCIAL SURVEY - 2019 (*continued*)

	All Companies	Industrial & Non-Residential All Companies	Heavy & Highway All Companies	Specialty Trade All Companies
Retained earnings	$8,675	$6,511	$17,055	$6,505
Net Corporate Stock	$9,734	$7,689	$18,678	$7,170
Partnership/LLC Capital	$1,202	$1,735	$2,125	$474
Other equity	$148	-$235	$949	-$92
Total Net Worth	$11,084	$9,189	$21,752	$7,552
Total Liabilities and Net Worth	$33,695	$43,233	$44,895	$21,558
Total Revenue	$83,929	$134,022	$81,107	$51,245
Direct Costs				
Direct Labor	$13,232	$8,606	$16,611	$14,653
Materials	$10,885	$7,300	$15,059	$12,471
Subcontracts	$33,415	$84,758	$16,710	$6,202
Equipment	$2,570	$773	$7,486	$2,114
Other Direct Costs	$13,270	$23,079	$12,529	$5,878
Total Direct Costs	$73,373	$124,516	$68,394	$41,318
Indirect Costs	$1,136	$559	$1,875	$1,399
Total Costs	$74,509	$125,075	$70,269	$42,717
Gross Profit	$9,420	$8,947	$10,838	$8,528
SG&A Expenses				
Base Payroll / Payroll Related (Exclusive of Owner Bonuses)	$3,128	$3,045	$2,909	$2,930
Professional Fees	$227	$178	$285	$216
Sales & Marketing Costs	$180	$165	$77	$191
Technology Costs	$178	$184	$175	$170
Administrative Bonuses	$496	$565	$509	$405
Other Expenses	$1,998	$1,438	$2,352	$1,898
Total SG&A Expenses	$6,207	$5,575	$6,308	$5,811
Income (Loss) from Operations	$3,212	$3,372	$4,530	$2,718
Interest income	$76	$165	$66	$25
Other investment income (loss)	$23	$16	$64	$22
Other income (expense)	-$62	-$46	-$67	-$52
Interest expense	$146	$106	$225	$190
Total Other Income (Expense), net	-$110	$28	-$161	-$195
Net Income (Loss) Before Income Taxes	$3,103	$3,401	$4,368	$2,523
Income taxes (benefit)	$163	$59	$279	$153
Net Income (LOSS)	$2,940	$3,342	$4,089	$2,370

RMA'S CREDIT &
LENDING DICTIONARY

A

Absentee Owner: landlord who does not reside in his or her rental property.

Abstract of Title: condensed history of title to land and real property, consisting of ownership transfers and any conveyances or liens that may affect future ownership.

Acceleration Clause: provision in note or contract that allows holder to declare remaining balance due and payable immediately upon default in an obligation. Usual causes of default are failure to pay interest or principal installments in a timely manner, an adverse change in financing conditions, or failure to meet loan covenants.

Acceptance: drawee's signed agreement to honor draft as presented, which consists of signature alone, but will frequently be evidenced by drawee writing word "accepted," date it is payable, and signature. Sometimes called Trade Acceptance or Banker's Acceptance, depending upon function of acceptor.

Accommodation: 1. lending or extending credit to borrower. 2. loan or commitment to lend money.

Accord and Satisfaction: agreement between two or more persons or entities that satisfies or discharges obligation or settles claim or lawsuit. Generally involves disputed matter in which one party agrees to give and other party agrees to accept something in satisfaction different from, and usually less than, that originally asked for.

Account: 1. statement showing balance along with detailed explanation covering debits and credits. 2. right of payment for goods sold or leased or for services rendered on open account basis. 3. summarized record of financial transaction. 4. customer.

Accountant: person in charge of and skilled in the recording of financial transactions and maintenance of financial records.

Accounting: 1. theory and system of classifying, recording, summarizing, and auditing books of firm. 2. art of analyzing, interpreting, and reporting financial position and operating results of business.

Account Manager: 1. sometimes called Relationship Manager or Account Officer. 2. person responsible for overseeing all matters relating to a specific client or group of customers.

Account Number: unique identification number used to designate specific customer.

Accounts Payable: short-term liability representing amounts due trade creditors.

Accounts Payable Department: section of business office responsible for processing open account balances and paying amounts owed for goods and services purchased.

Accounts Receivable: money due to a business by its customers for goods sold or services performed on open account (or credit). Usually refers to short-term receivables.

Accounts Receivable Aging Report: report by customer that lists age of accounts receivable generally by 30-day intervals from invoice or due date. See also Aging of Accounts Receivable.

Accounts Receivable Financing: form of secured lending in which borrowings are typically limited to percentage of receivables pledged as collateral.

Accrual Accounting: basis of accounting in which expenses are recorded when incurred and revenues are recognized when earned, regardless of when cash is actually paid or received.

Accrue: 1. something gained, added, or accumulated, such as profit from a business transaction. 2. right to sue has become exercisable.

Accrued Expenses: short-term liabilities that represent expenses for goods used but not yet paid.

Accrued Income: income earned but not yet collected.

Accrued Interest: interest accumulated since last interest payment due date.

Accrued Liabilities: expenses or obligations for goods or services incurred but not yet paid.

ACH: see Automated Clearinghouse.

Acid Test: ratio between company's most liquid assets (generally, cash and accounts receivable) and current liabilities that represents the degree to which current liabilities can be paid with those assets.

Acknowledgment: 1. declaration making known receipt of something done or to be done; confirmation of receipt of order or of terms of contract. 2. statement of notary or other competent officer certifying that signature on document was personally signed by individual whose signature is affixed to instrument.

Acquisition: merger or taking over of controlling interest of one business by another.

Acquisition and Development Loan: loan made for the purpose of purchasing a property and completing all on-site improvements such as street layout, utility installation, and community area grading necessary to bring the site to a buildable state.

Acquittal: 1. release from obligation or contract. 2. to have accusation of crime dismissed by some formal legal procedure.

Active Account: 1. customer who makes frequent purchases. 2. bank account in which regular deposits or withdrawals are made.

Activity Charge: service charge imposed for check or deposit activity or any other maintenance charge.

Act of God: event that could not be prevented by reasonable foresight, is ca exclusively by forces and violence of nature, and is uninfluenced by hu power (storm, flood, earthquake, or lightning).

Additional Dating: means of extending credit beyond normal sales terms, gra to induce buyers to place orders in advance of season or for other specia sons. See also Advance Dating and Dating.

Adjudication: judgment rendered by court, primarily used in bankruptcy proc ings.

Adjustable Interest Rate: interest rate on loan that may be adjusted up or c at specific intervals. Index used in determining adjusted interest rate potential frequency of adjustments must be stated in loan documents.

Adjustable Rate Mortgage: loan is pursuant to an agreement executed a inception of the loan that permits creditor to adjust interest rate from tir time based on a specific interest rate index.

Adjuster: person who deals with insured party to settle amount of loss, clair debt.

Adjustment: 1. settlement of disputed account. 2. change or concession in or terms. 3. determining amount one is to receive in settlement of claim. accounting, entry made to correct or compensate for error or differenc account.

Adjustment Bureau: organization that supervises debt extensions and com mise arrangements or oversees orderly liquidation of troubled businesses benefit of creditors.

Advance: 1. payment made before it is due. 2. disbursement of loan proceeds

Advance Dating: additional time granted customers to pay for goods rece and to earn available discounts. See also Additional Dating and Dating.

Advancement of Costs: prepayment of necessary legal expenses. Such char set by law, may be for commencement of suit and vary in different courts states. Some items for which prepaid costs may be requested are filing f process serving, premiums on court bonds, trial fees, posting security costs, entering judgment, recording abstract of judgment, issue execut and discovery actions after judgment.

Advertising Allowance: promotional discount in price or payment given tomers who share expense of advertising supplier's product.

Affidavit: voluntary written statement of facts pertaining to a transaction or ev signed under oath and witnessed by an authorized person.

Affiliate: business entity connected with another through common ownershi management, usually responsible for payment of its own obligations.

After-Acquired Property: security interest by which secured creditor autom cally obtains interest in assets that debtor acquires after lien had been filed

Agency: legal relationship between two parties in which one is authorized to for another.

Agent: person legally authorized to act for another.

Agent Bank: formal designation that applies to a bank responsible for negotiat structuring, and overseeing a loan or commitment to a borrower in wl more than one bank is involved. See also Lead Bank.

Aggregate Balances: combined total of two or more demand deposit accou money markets, or time certificates of deposit. Term can also be appliee credit facility totals.

Aging of Accounts Receivable: accounting record of customer's receivab showing how long receivables have remained unpaid beyond regular term sale. Used as basis for advancing credit.

Agreement: a contract involving an offer and an acceptance between two or m parties, governing the terms of the contract and binding on the parties to agreement (e.g., a loan agreement, security agreement, or guaranty).

AKA: see Also Known As.

Alert Action: a series of information services provided by credit reporting ag cies; provides subscribers with listing of specific accounts on which unfav able payment condition has recently been reported.

Allegation: statement of party to action, setting out what he or she intends prove or contend.

ALLL: see Allowance for Loan and Lease Losses.

Allocation: sub-limit within a total credit facility that is to be used for a spec purpose.

Allonge: paper attached to a negotiable instrument for additional endorseme or other terms and conditions.

Allowance: accounting provision used to set aside amounts for depreciati returns, or bad debts.

Allowance for Bad Debts: contra account against which uncollectible receivab are charged. See also Bad Debt Reserve.

Allowance for Loan and Lease Losses (ALLL): contra account, generally fou on asset side of balance sheet as deduction from total loans outstandir amount is intended to cover future losses of loans currently in the financ institution's portfolio. The ALLL should be adjusted monthly, concurren with the generation of current financial statements.

Also Known As (AKA): sometimes used to designate a fictitious trade style name.

Policy: an extended coverage title insurance policy that protects the lender against losses resulting from any defects in the title or claims against the property. The policy's coverage includes encroachments, mechanic's liens, and other matters that a physical inspection or inquiry of the parties would disclose.

...ed Check: check on which original entries have been changed (date, payee, or amount); financial institutions generally refuse to honor or pay checks that have been altered.

...nd: to correct, add to, or alter legal document.

...cus Curiae: friend of court; uninvolved third party who intervenes in lawsuit, with court's permission, to introduce information or arguments in respect to the issue or principle of law to be decided.

...rtization: 1. reduction of loan by periodic principal payments. 2. decline in the book value of an intangible asset over the period owned.

...rtization Tables: calculation charts showing amounts required periodically to discharge debts over various periods of time and at different interest rates.

...rtize: 1. to write off the value of an intangible asset over the period owned. 2. to reduce or pay off debt or obligation by making periodic payments of principal.

...ual Percentage Rate (APR): annual cost of credit expressed as percentage; creditors are required under Federal Truth in Lending Act to disclose true annual interest on consumer loans, as well as the total dollar cost and other terms of loan.

...ual Report: yearly report detailing a company's comparative financial and organizational conditions.

...uity: series of fixed periodic payments made at regular intervals.

...ecedent Credit Information: historical record of significant business information concerning individuals who are involved in ownership or management of business enterprise.

...cipation: bridge loan made to a municipal or government borrower to cover expenses until revenue or tax proceeds are collected.

...eal: complaint made to higher court by either plaintiff or defendant for court's review, correction, or reversal of lower court's decision.

...earance: coming into court formally as plaintiff or defendant in lawsuit.

...raisal: opinion of current value of real or personal property based upon cost of replacement, market, income, or fair value analysis.

...reciation: increase in value of asset over its cost due to economic and other conditions. Property that increases in value as result of improvements or additions is not considered to have appreciated.

...ropriation: sum of money designated for a special purpose only.

...R: See *Annual Percentage Rate*.

...itration: submission for settlement of disputed matter, by nonjudicial means, to one or more impartial or disinterested third persons selected by disputants.

...'s Length: business transaction between two or more parties that is open, sincere, and without personal influence, favoritism, or close relations.

...angement: plan for corporate reorganization for rescheduling or extension of time for payment of unsecured debts, such as an arrangement under Chapter 11 or 13 of the U. S. Bankruptcy Code.

...ears: total or partial debt amounts that remain unpaid and past due.

...icles of Agreement: any written statement or contract, terms to which all parties consent.

...icles of Incorporation: formal papers that set forth pertinent data for formation of corporation and are filed with appropriate state agency.

...sess: 1. to fix rate or amount. 2. to set value of real and personal property, as for tax purposes.

...sessed Value: in the case of real property, value set by government agency for purpose of levying taxes.

...set: 1. anything owned having monetary value. 2. item listed on left-hand side of balance sheet representing cash, or property, real or personal, belonging to an individual or company and convertible to cash.

...signed Account: 1. account receivable pledged by borrower to factor or lender as security. 2. past-due customer whose account has been placed with collection agency.

...signed Risk: insurance plan that provides coverage for risks rejected by regular markets and in which all licensed insurers are made to participate by various state laws.

...signee: person to whom some rights, authority, or property is assigned.

...signment: 1. written contract for transfer of one's title, legal rights, or property from one person to another. 2. in some states, form used to transfer claim to agency that undertakes collection of account for benefit of assigning creditor.

...signment for the Benefit of Creditors: A liquidation technique in which an insolvent debtor goes out of business and an assignee facilitates the transfer of the insolvent debtor's estate for administration and payment of debts. Property transferred to assignee places such assets beyond control of debtor or reach of creditors.

...signment of Claim: claim assigned to third party for collection.

...signor: 1. one who transfers claim, right, or property. 2. individual, partnership, or corporation making assignment.

Assumed Liability: acknowledgment of responsibility for payment of obligation by third party.

At Sight: words used in negotiable instrument directing that payment be made upon presentation or demand.

Attached Account: legally frozen account on which payments have been suspended; release or disbursement of funds can be made only after court order.

Attachment: 1. legal writ or process by which debtor's property (or any interest therein) is seized and placed in custody of law. 2. Supplemental data provided as clarifying information to a document.

Attorney-in-Fact: private attorney who has written authorization to act for another. This authority is given by an instrument called power of attorney.

Attorney of Record: lawyer whose name must appear in permanent court records as person acting on behalf of party in legal matter.

Auction: public sale of property that is sold to highest bidder.

Audit: to examine a firm's records, accounts, or procedures for purpose of substantiating or verifying individual transactions or to confirm if assets and liabilities are properly accounted for, including income and expense items.

Audited Financial Statements: financial statements that have been examined by an independent certified public accountant to determine if the financial statements present fairly the financial position, results of operations, and cash flows in conformity with generally accepted accounting principles.

Auditor: person who deals with examination and verification of financial accounts and with making financial reports.

Auditor's Report: part of complete set of financial statements that explains degree of responsibility that independent accountant assumed for expressing an opinion on management's financial statements and assurance that is provided by said opinion.

Automated Cash Application: computerized procedures enabling payments to be quickly and automatically applied to accounts receivable.

Automated Clearinghouse (ACH): computer-based clearing and settlement facility for interchange of electronic debits and credits among financial institutions. ACH entries can be substituted for checks in recurring payments such as mortgages or in direct deposit distribution of federal and corporate benefits payments. Federal Reserve Banks furnish data processing services for most ACHs, although some are privately operated. Final settlement, or net settlement, of ACH transfers is made against reserve accounts at Federal Reserve Banks.

Available Balance: checking account balance that the customer actually may use; that is, current balance less deposits not yet cleared through the account.

Average Collected Balances: average dollar amount on deposit in checking accounts defined as the difference between ledger balance and deposit float, or those deposits posted to the account but having not yet cleared the financial institution upon which they are drawn. See also Uncollected Funds.

Average Collection Period: average number of days required to convert accounts receivable to cash.

Average Daily Balance: average amount of money that depositor keeps on deposit when calculated on a daily basis.

B

Backdating: predating document prior to date on which it was drawn.

Backlog: amount of revenue expected to be realized from work to be performed on uncompleted contracts, including new contractual agreements on which work has not begun.

Bad Check Laws: laws enacted in various states to encourage and facilitate lawful use of checks; statutes differ in various jurisdictions and are generally enforced according to state laws as well as local custom and usage.

Bad Debt: account receivable that proves uncollectible in normal course of business; full payment is doubtful.

Bad Debt Ratio: ratio of bad debt expense to sales, used as measure of quality of accounts receivable.

Bad Debt Reserve: reserve or provision for accounts receivables to be charged off company's books based on historical levels of bad debts or industry averages.

Balance: amount owed or unpaid on loan or credit transaction. Also called outstanding or unpaid balance.

Balance Due: total amount owed after applying debits and credits of account.

Balance Sheet: A financial statement listing the assets, liabilities, and owner's equity of a business entity or individual as of a specific date.

Balloon Payment: lump-sum payment of principal and sometimes accrued interest, usually due at end of term of installment loan in which periodic installments of principal and interest did not fully amortize loan.

Bank: financial institution chartered by state or federal government to transact financial business that includes receiving deposits, lending money, exchanging currencies, providing safekeeping, and investing money.

Bank Draft: sight or demand draft (order to pay) drawn by a bank (drawer) on its account at another bank (drawee).

Banker's Acceptance: draft or order to pay specified amount at specified time not to exceed 270 days, drawn on individuals, business firms, or financial institutions; draft becomes accepted when a financial institution formally acknowledges its obligation to honor such draft, usually by writing or stamping "Accepted" on face of instrument. When accepted in this manner, draft becomes liability of bank. See also *Draft* and *Time Draft*.

Bank Overdraft: check presented for collection for which there are not sufficient funds on deposit to make normal payment. Financial institution may honor such check, considering payment as loan to depositor for which the institution will usually collect interest or service charge.

Bankrupt: debtor who is unable to meet debt obligations as they become due or is insolvent and whose assets are administered for benefit of creditors.

Bankruptcy: Legal action taken under the U.S. Bankruptcy Code by or against an insolvent debtor who is unable to meet obligations as they become due. The bankrupt, if given discharge, is released from further liability of most debts listed as of the date of the bankruptcy filing.

- *Voluntary Bankruptcy:* any individual, partnership, corporation, estate, trust, or governmental unit may be afforded protection of debtor under U.S. Bankruptcy Code by filing petition. Exceptions: railroads, insurance or banking corporations, building and loan associations.
- *Involuntary Bankruptcy:* involuntary petition can be filed in bankruptcy court by three or more creditors or, if there are fewer than 12 creditors, by any one creditor. Petitioning creditors' claims must aggregate at least $5,000 in excess of value of any collateral of debtor. Involuntary cases may be filed against individuals, partnerships, or corporations other than farmers and nonprofit corporations and may be instituted under either Chapter 7 or Chapter 11 of the U.S. Bankruptcy Code. Involuntary petition must allege one of two grounds for relief: either that the debtor is generally not paying debts as they become due, or that the non-bankruptcy custodian, other than one appointed to enforce lien on less than substantially all of debtor's property, was appointed for, or took possession of, substantially all of debtor's property within 120 days of filing.
- *Chapter 7 Cases:* liquidation proceedings, formerly referred to as "straight bankruptcy," wherein nonexempt assets of debtor are converted to cash and proceeds distributed pro rata among creditors.
- *Chapter 9 Cases:* reorganization proceedings wherein municipality that is insolvent or unable to meet debts as they mature effects plan to adjust such debts.
- *Chapter 11 Cases:* reorganization proceedings available to all business enterprises; may be instituted either by debtor or creditor(s). For plan to be confirmed by court under Chapter 11, each class of creditors, as set forth in such plan, must accept plan or each class must receive at least that which it would receive on liquidation. Class of creditors has accepted plan when majority in number and two-thirds in dollar amount of those creditors actually voting approve it.
- *Chapter 12 Cases:* reorganization proceedings for agricultural concerns and small family-owned farms having debts under $1.5 million.
- *Chapter 13 Cases:* reorganization cases that may be instituted only by individuals with regular income who owe unsecured debts of less than $100,000 and secured debts of less than $350,000, other than stockbroker or commodity broker. For plan to be confirmed, it must provide for submission to trustee of all or any portion of debtor's future earnings as necessary for execution of plan, payment in full of all priority claims, and equal treatment of each member of class of creditors. While consent of unsecured creditors is not required, value of what they receive under plan may not be less than if debtor were liquidated.

Bankruptcy Judge: presiding judge of court in which bankruptcy cases are heard. (Formerly called Referee in Bankruptcy.) Duties of judge include supervising administrative details of bankrupt estates and ruling on all matters involving debtor-creditor problems.

Basis: 1. number of days used in calculating interest earned in investment or interest payable on bank loan. Also called accrual base. 2. original cost of asset plus capital improvements from which any taxable gains (or losses) are determined after deducting depreciation expenses.

Basis Point: 1/100th of a percent; 100 basis points equal 1%.

Bearer: negotiable item (check, note, bill, or draft) in which no payee is indicated or payee is shown as "cash" or "bearer." Item is payable to person in possession of it or to person who presents it for payment.

Bearer Paper: instrument that is made "payable to bearer." When negotiable instrument is endorsed in blank, it becomes bearer paper and can be transferred by delivery since it does not require endorsement.

Beneficiary: 1. person or organization named in will to inherit or receive property. 2. person or organization to whom insurance policy is payable. 3. person or organization for whose benefit trust is created.

Bid Bond: bond issued by surety on behalf of contractor that provides assurance to recipient of contractor's bid that if bid is accepted, contractor will execute contract and provide performance bond. Under bond, surety is obligated to pay recipient difference between contractor's bid and bid of next lowest responsible bidder if bid is accepted and contractor fails to execute cor... or to provide performance bond.

Billing Cycle: number of days between payment due dates.

Bill of Costs: certified itemization of costs associated with lawsuit.

Bill of Lading: written instrument signed by common carrier or agent identi... freight and representing both receipt and contract for shipment. It must s... name of consignee, description of goods, terms of carrier's contract, ... directions for assigning to specific person at specific place. In form of n... tiable instrument, it is evidence of holding title to goods being shipped.

Bill of Sale: written instrument evidencing transfer of title of specific pers... property to buyer.

Binder: 1. written agreement that provides temporary legal protection per... issuance of final contract or policy. 2. temporary insurance contract; ma... oral or written; also called cover note.

Blank Endorsement: endorser's writing on check, promissory note, or b... exchange without indicating party to whom it is payable. Endorser m... signs his or her name, making the instrument "payable to bearer." Also ca... endorsement in blank.

Blanket Coverage: property coverage applicable to group of exposures (b... ings, inventory, equipment, etc., combined or individually, at one or r... locations), in single total amount of insurance; contrasts with Specific Cc... age.

Blanket Mortgage: mortgage secured by two or more parcels of real prop... frequently used by developers who acquire large tract of land for subdivi... and resale to individual homeowners. Also called blanket trust deed.

Bond: contract issued by insurance or bonding company in support of princi... obligation to obligee. See also *Fidelity Bond* and *Surety Bond*.

Bonded Warehouse: federally approved warehouse under bond for strict ob... vance of revenue laws; used for storing goods until duties are paid or p... erty is otherwise released. Bonded warehouse assures owner of property ... operators of warehouse are insured against loss by fraud and will keep pr... inventory and accounting of goods in transit.

Bonding Company: company authorized to issue bid bonds, performance bo... labor and materials bonds, or other types of surety bonds.

Book Value: 1. company's net worth calculated by adding total assets minus t... liabilities. 2. value of asset (cost plus additions, less depreciation) shown ... books or financial report of an entity.

Borrower's Certificate: A document required under a loan or other agreemen... be submitted by the borrower or another designated party to certify the va... of collateral and compliance with the terms of the agreement.

Bottom Line: (colloq.) final price, net profit, or end results.

Branch Banking: multioffice banking. Branch is any banking facility away fr... bank's main office that accepts deposits or makes loans. State laws stri... control opening of new banking offices by state-chartered banks, nati... banks, and thrift institutions.

Breach of Contract: failure to fulfill terms of contract, in part or whole.

Breach of Warranty: 1. failure to fully disclose information about conditio... property or insured party. 2. failure to perform as promised.

Break-Even Analysis: A method of determining the number of units that mus... sold at a given price to recover all fixed and variable costs.

Break-even Point: 1. point at which total sales are equal to total expenses. N... be expressed in units or dollars. 2. amount received from sale that exa... equals amount of expense or cost.

Bridge Loan: loan that provides liquidity until defined event occurs that will g... erate cash, such as sale of noncurrent asset, replacement financing, or eq... infusion.

Bulk Sales Acts: statutes designed to prevent defrauding of creditors throu... secret sale in bulk of merchant's goods. Most states require notice of p... posed sale to all creditors.

Burden of Proof: 1. duty of producing sufficient evidence to prove position tal... in lawsuit. 2. necessity of proving fact or facts as to truth of claim.

Business: 1. commercial, industrial, or mercantile activity engaged in by indiv... ual, partnership, corporation, or other form of organization for purpose ... making, buying, or selling goods or services at profit. 2. occupation, prof... sion, or trade.

Business Failure: 1. suspension of business resulting from insolvency or ba... ruptcy. 2. inability to fulfill normal business obligations.

Business Interruption Insurance: property insurance written to cover loss ... profits and continuing expenses as result of shutdown by insured peril; exp... sure is classified as consequential loss. Also called earnings insurance.

Buyer's Market: market condition in which supply exceeds demand, whi... causes prices to decline.

Buy Out: to purchase at least a controlling percentage of a company's stock ... take over its assets.

Bylaws: set of rules or regulations adopted to control internal affairs of organi... tion.

C

...f Credit: the "Five C's" of credit. A longstanding means of evaluating a customer by investigating Character, Collateral, Capacity, Conditions, and Capital.

...ndar Year: 12-month accounting period ending December 31.

...ble Loan: loan payable on demand.

...celed Check: check that has been paid by a financial institution and on which the financial institution has imprinted evidence of payment so that it cannot be presented again.

...cellation Clause: provision in contract or agreement allowing parties to rescind agreement under certain conditions.

...acity: one of the "Five C's" of credit; a customer's ability to successfully absorb merchandise and to pay for the merchandise. Refers to customer's ability to produce sufficient cash so as to meet obligations when due.

...ital: 1. one of the "Five Cs" of credit; refers to financial resources the customer has at the time order is placed and those that he or she is likely to have when payment is due. 2. amount invested in business by owners or stockholders. 3. owner's equity in the business.

...h: 1. money readily available for current expenditures; usually consists of cash on hand or money in a financial institution. 2. money equivalent, such as a check, paid at time of purchase. 3. any medium of exchange that the financial institution will accept at face value upon deposit.

...h Basis Accounting: basis of accounting in which revenues and expenses are reported in the income statement when cash is received or paid out for the time period in which the revenues and expenses occur.

...sh Basis Loan: loan on which interest payments are recorded when collected from borrower. This is a loan in which the borrower has fallen behind on interest payments and is classified as a nonaccrual asset.

...sh Concentration and Disbursement (CCD): corporate electronic payment used in business-to-business and intracompany transfers of funds. Funds are cleared on overnight basis through nationwide automated clearinghouse network.

...sh Equivalents: accounting term for actual cash on hand and total of bank deposits.

...sh Flow: is based on an activity format, which classifies cash inflows and outflows in terms of operating, investing, and financing activities.

...shier's Check: check drawn on financial institution's account, becoming direct obligation of the financial institution.

...sh Management Account: special type of deposit service that permits corporate customers to invest cash in demand deposit account until needed for operations.

...sh Surrender Value: in life insurance, amount payable under whole life policy when terminated by insured.

...sualty Insurance: coverage for automobile, liability, crime, boiler and machinery, health, bonds, aviation, workers' compensation, and other miscellaneous lines; contrasts with Property Insurance.

...rtificate of Insurance: written statement issued by insurer indicating that insurance policy has been issued and showing details of coverage at time certificate was written; used as evidence of insurance.

...rtified Check: depositor's check confirmed on its face as good by a financial institution and stamped "certified." It is then dated and signed by an authorized officer of the institution. Such check becomes an obligation of the financial institution, which guarantees that it is holding sufficient funds to cover payment of check on demand.

...rtified Copy of Policy: document that provides evidence of insurance as of certain date; coverage may be terminated or changed after certification.

...rtified Public Accountant (CPA): one who has been trained to do accounting and who has passed state test and received title of CPA; title certifies holder's qualification to practice accounting, audit, prepare reports, and analyze accounting information.

...GL: see *Comprehensive General Liability*.

...haracter: one of the "Five Cs" of credit; refers to evaluating qualities that would impel debtor to meet his or her obligations. Generally identified as customer's reputation, responsibility, integrity, and honesty.

...harge-Off: portion of principal balance of a loan or account receivable that an entity considers uncollectible; this amount may be partially or fully recovered in future. Also called a *Write-Off*.

...hart of Accounts: listing of all financial accounts or categories (usually numbered) into which business transactions are classified and recorded.

...hattel: item of tangible personal property, animate or inanimate, as distinguished from real property.

...hattel Mortgage: instrument of sale in which debtor transfers title in property to creditor as security for debt. Failure by debtor to comply with terms of contract may cause creditor's title in property to become absolute.

...heck: order on a financial institution for payment of funds from depositor's account and payable on demand.

...laim: 1. action to recover payment, reimbursement, or compensation from entity legally liable for damage or injury.

...laimant: one who makes claim or asserts right.

Cleanup: period during which particular loan or entire borrowing has been paid off; out-of-debt period required under line of credit.

Clearinghouse: association of financial institutions or security dealers created to permit daily settlement and exchange of checks or delivery of stocks and other items between members in local geographic area.

Closed-End Credit: consumer installment loan made for predetermined amount, calling for periodic payments of principal and interest over specified period or term. Finance charge may be fixed or variable rate. Borrower does not have option of obtaining extra funds under original loan agreement. Contrasts with Open-End Credit.

Cloud on Title: outstanding claim or encumbrance on property that may impair owner's title.

Cognovit Note: form of promissory note or statement that allows creditor, in case of default by debtor, to enter judgment without trial. (Not recognized in all jurisdictions.)

Collateral: 1. one of the "Five C's" of credit; refers to real or personal property that may be available as security. 2. asset pledged by borrower in support of loan. See also *Secured Loan*.

Collateral Note: form of promissory note given for loan, pledging real or personal property as security for payment of debt.

Collectible: account capable of being collected.

Collection Agency: professional business service employed as agent to collect creditors' unpaid (past-due) accounts. Collection agency is usually compensated by receiving agreed upon contingent percentage of amount collected.

Collection Agency Report: report from collection agency that informs client of results of collection efforts, investigations, or recommendations.

Collection Charges: 1. fees charged by bank for collecting drafts, notes, coupons, or other instruments. 2. compensation paid to collection agency or attorney for collecting delinquent accounts.

Collection Item: 1. term for item received for collection that is to be credited to depositor's account after payment. Most financial institutions charge special (collection) fees for handling such items. 2. past due account assigned for collection.

Collection Period: number of days required for company's receivables to be collected and converted to cash.

Comaker: person who signs (and guarantees) note of another and by so doing promises to pay in full. See also *Cosigner*.

Commensurate: describes deposit balances that are in acceptable proportion to size of loan or commitment.

Commercial Debt: loan or obligation incurred for business purposes.

Commercial Law League of America (C.L.L.A.): national membership organization of commercial attorneys, commercial credit and collection agencies, credit insurance companies, and law list publishers. Objectives include setting standards for honorable dealings among members, improving the practice of commercial law, and promoting uniformity of legislation affecting commercial law.

Commercial Paper: short-term securities such as notes, drafts, bills of exchange, and other negotiable paper that arise out of commercial activity and become due on a definite maturity date.

Commercial Property: real estate used for business purposes or managed so as to produce income from rents and leases.

Commitment: agreement between a financial institution and borrower to make funds available under certain conditions for a specified period of time.

Commitment Fee: lender's charge for holding credit available, usually replaced with interest when funds are advanced, as in revolving credit. In business credit, a commitment fee is often charged for unused portion of line of credit.

Commitment Letter: letter from lender stating willingness to advance funds to named borrower, repayable at specified rate and time period, subject to escape clause(s) allowing lender to rescind agreement in event of materially adverse changes in borrower's financial condition.

Committee Approval: credit is approved by several people acting as group.

Common Law: body of law that was originated, developed, and administered in England.

Community Property: property shared by husband and wife, each having one-half interest in earnings of other; form of joint property ownership in some states.

Community Reinvestment Act of 1977 (CRA): federal law that requires mortgage lenders to demonstrate their commitment to home mortgage financing in economically disadvantaged areas. Prohibits redlining or credit allocation based on geographic region and requires lenders to file annual compliance statements.

Compensating Balance: demand deposit balance that must be maintained by borrower to compensate financial institution for loan accommodations and other services.

Compound Interest: interest calculated by adding accumulated interest to date to original principal. New balance becomes principal for additional interest calculations.

Comprehensive General Liability (CGL): policy form providing automatic coverage for all insured's business operations; may include auto exposures; newer form of CGL is called commercial general liability.

Concession: 1. granting of special privilege to digress from regular terms or previous conditions. 2. allowance or rebate from established price. 3. business enterprise operated under special permission.

Conditional Sales Contract: contract for sale of goods under which possession is delivered to buyer but title retained by seller until goods are paid for in full or until other conditions are met. In most states, conditional sales contracts have been replaced by security agreements having substantially the same definition under Uniform Commercial Code.

Conditions: one of the "Five C's" of credit; refers to general business environment and status of borrower's industry.

Confession of Judgment Note: note in which (after maturity) debtor permits attorney to appear in court and have judgment entered if payment is not made as agreed. Acceptance of note varies by state. See also *Cognovit Note.*

Confirmation: 1. supplier's written acknowledgment that he or she has accepted buyer's order. 2. customer's written verification of order previously placed. 3. proof verifying agreement or existence of assets and liabilities or claims against assets and liabilities.

Consent Judgment: judgment that debtor allows to be entered against him or her by motion filed with court.

Consideration: 1. element in contract without which contract is not binding. Contract is generally not valid without consideration. 2. reason for contracting parties to enter into contract. Act, promise, price, or motive for which agreement is entered into. 3. value given in exchange for benefit that is to be derived from contract. 4. compensation. Exchange of consideration is usually mutual, each party giving something up to other.

Consign: to send or forward goods to merchant, factor, or agent for sale with title retained by seller and with payment delayed, generally until sale is made.

Consignee: person or entity to which goods or property is consigned or shipped; ultimate recipient of shipment.

Consignment: arrangement under which consignor (seller) remains owner of property until such time as consignee (buyer) pays for goods; usually consignee pays consignor when goods are sold or holds proceeds of sale in trust for benefit of consignor.

Consignor: 1. one who delivers shipment or turns it over to carrier for transportation and delivery. 2. one who consigns goods to be sold without giving up title.

Consolidated Financial Statement: combined statement showing financial condition of parent corporation and its subsidiaries.

Consolidating Financial Statement: combined statement of subsidiary and parent companies that shows complete statement for each entity without netting intercompany transactions.

Construction Loan: interim financing for development and construction of real property, generally converted to long-term financing upon completion of construction.

Consumer Credit: debt incurred for personal, family, or household use.

Consumer Credit Protection Act (Truth in Lending Act of 1968): law that requires most lenders and those who extend consumer credit to disclose true credit costs. Act provides for limits on garnishment of wages, prohibits excessive interest, and makes available contents of consumer credit reports.

Consumer Sale Disclosure Statement: form required to be provided by creditor to customer, disclosing finance charge details as required under Consumer Credit Protection Act.

Contingent Fee: fee to be paid only in event of specific occurrence, usually successful results. Arrangement, for example, in which collection agency will receive stated percentage of any amounts recovered or in which lawyer will receive payment only if successful in prosecuting lawsuit.

Contingent Liability: liability in which a person(s) or business(es) is indirectly responsible for obligations of a third party. Such indirect liability is usually established by guaranty or endorsement, and the liability holder may turn to guarantors or endorsers for satisfaction of debt. See also Endorsement and Guaranty.

Contra Account: account that partially or wholly offsets another account or balance.

Contract: agreement between two or more entities or legally competent persons that creates, modifies, or destroys legal arrangement.

Controlled Disbursement: funds management technique in corporate cash management designed to maximize funds available for temporary investment in money market or for payment to trade creditors. Controls flow of checks through banking system to meet corporate investment and funds management requirements. Contrasts with delayed disbursement. See also *Federal Reserve Float* and *Treasury Workstation.*

Controller: person in business organization responsible for finances, internal auditing, and accounting systems in use in company's operations.

Conversion: process of consolidating or transferring data from one system to another.

Conveyance: 1. transfer of right, generally instrument transferring interest in estate in form of deed. 2. transfer of property ownership (sometimes incl leases and mortgages) from one person or organization to another.

Copyright: intangible right granted to author or originator by federal governm to solely and exclusively reproduce or publish specific literary, musica artistic work for certain number of years.

Corporate Reorganization: see *Bankruptcy.*

Corporate Veil: convention that corporate organization insulates organizat owners from liability for corporate activities.

Corporation: artificial person or legal entity organized under and treated by s laws, legally distinct from its shareholders and vested with capacity of con uous succession irrespective of changes in its ownership either in perpe or for limited term. It may be set up to contract, own, and discharge busi within boundaries of powers granted it by its corporate charter.

Correspondent: organization or individual that carries on business relations acts as agent with others in different cities or countries.

Cosigner: one of joint signers of loan documents. One who signs note of ano as support for credit of the principal maker.

Cost of Funds: dollar cost of interest paid or accrued on funds acquired from ious sources within bank and borrowed funds acquired from other finan institutions, including time deposits, advances at Federal Reserve disco window, federal funds purchased, and Eurodollar deposits. Financial inst tion may use internal cost of funds in pricing loans it makes.

Covenant: written agreement, convention, or promise between parties w pledge to do or not to do certain things or that stipulates truth of certain fa

CPA: see *Certified Public Accountant.*

CRA: see *Community Reinvestment Act of 1977.*

Crash: sudden sharp decrease in business activity that can negatively affect st market volumes and prices.

Credit: 1. privilege of buying goods and services, or for borrowing money return for promise of future payment. 2. in bookkeeping, entry on ledger s nifying cash payment, merchandise returned, or allowance to reduce debt accounting entry on right side of ledger sheet.

Credit Advisory Board (CAB): agency established by Financial Institutio Reform, Recovery, and Enforcement Act of 1989 "to monitor the credit sta dards and lending practices of insured depository institutions and the sup vision of such standards and practices by the federal financial regulators" well as to "ensure that insured depository institutions can meet the deman of a modern and globally competitive world." This board was granted perm nent authorization by the Federal Deposit Insurance Corporation Improvem Act of 1991. Formerly known as Credit Standards Advisory Committ (CSAC).

Credit Analyst: person who evaluates the financial history and financial sta ments of credit applicants to assess creditworthiness. Analysts are trained evaluate applicant's financial strength and to opine on the probability of repayment, collateral adequacy, or whether a credit enhancement through cosigner or guarantor is needed.

Credit Application: form completed by potential borrower and used by creditor determine applicant's creditworthiness.

Credit Approval: decision to extend credit.

Credit Approval System: internal methods by which credit decisions are made.

Credit Bureau: agency that gathers information and provides its subscribers wi credit reports on consumers.

Credit Checking: examining and analyzing creditworthiness of customer by co tacting references, reviewing credit reports, etc.

Credit Department: department within a financial institution that performs oper tions and credit support functions for underwriting activities. May inclu maintenance of credit files, credit investigations, financial statement analys and spreading, customers' accounts receivable audits, lender training, portf lio reporting, facilitation of credit meetings, etc.

Credit Enhancement: enhancement to creditworthiness of loans underlyin asset-backed security or municipal bond, generally to get investment-grad rating from bond rating agency and to improve marketability of debt securitie to investors. There are two general classifications of credit enhancements:

- third-party enhancement, in which third party pledges its own creditworth ness and guarantees repayment in form of standby letter of credit or com mercial letter of credit issued by a financial institution, surety bond fro insurance company, or special reserve fund managed by financial guarant firm in exchange for fee.

- self-enhancement, which is generally done by issuer through over-collatera ization—that is, pledging loans with book value greater than face value o bonds offered for sale.

Credit File: creditor's file that compiles information about customer, includin correspondence, credit memorandums and analyses, credit ratings, a credi history, payment patterns, and credit inquiries.

Credit Granting: approval and extension of credit to a customer.

Credit Inquiry: request made by a financial institution or trade creditor concern ing the responding bank's own customer.

...it Insurance: life and health insurance issued in conjunction with borrowing by individuals; covers payments or unpaid balance when borrower is disabled or dies; in business, covers loss of receivables when debtor becomes insolvent. '

...it Interchange: exchange of credit information between individuals or groups.

...it Interchange Bureau (CIB): 1. local bureaus offering members or subscribers credit reports usually based on recent ledger experiences. Generally refers to organized system of cooperating bureaus operated by regional credit associations. 2. credit agency that may limit its reporting to a particular trade.

...it Investigation: inquiry made by a financial institution or trade creditor concerning subject that is not the responding financial institution's customer.

...it Limit: maximum amount of credit made available to customer by specific creditor.

...it Line: commitment by a financial institution to lend funds to a borrower up to a given amount over a specified future period under certain pre-established conditions. Normally reviewed annually.

...it Management: function of planning, organizing, implementing, and supervising credit policies of a company.

...ditor: 1. one to whom debt is owed by another as a result of a financial transaction. 2. one who extends credit and to whom money is due.

...ditors' Committee: voluntary representative group of creditors that may examine affairs of insolvent debtor. Group will usually advise as to continuation of business, study accountant's and appraiser's reports, act as watchdog over operating business, make recommendations to appropriate groups or legal body so that creditors will realize largest settlement possible, and advise as to acceptability of settlement.

...ditors' Remedies: legal rights enabling creditors to collect delinquent debts owed them.

...edit Policy: company's written procedures for making credit decisions. Used to aid company in meeting its overall risk management objectives.

...edit Process Review: assessment of entire credit-granting process concerning specific financial institution loan portfolio(s).

...edit Rating: appraisal made by a financial institution or credit agency as to creditworthiness of a person or company. Such a report will include background on owners, estimate of financial strength and ability to pay when due, and company's payment record.

...edit Record: written history of how well a customer has handled debt repayment.

...edit Report: 1. report to aid management in reaching credit, sales, and financial decisions. 2. confidential report containing information obtained by mercantile agency that has investigated a company's background, credit history, financial strength, and payment record.

...edit Reporting Agency: company or trade interchange group that confidentially supplies subscribers or members with credit information and other relevant data as to a company's ability or likelihood to pay for goods and services purchased on credit.

...edit Research Foundation (CRF): education and research affiliate of National Association of Credit Management.

...edit Review: follow-up monitoring of loan or extension of credit by credit review officer or department, senior loan committee, auditor, or regulatory agency intended to determine whether loan was made in accordance with lender's written credit standards and policies and in compliance with banking regulations. Errors, omissions, concentrations, etc., if detected by credit review process, can then be corrected by lending officers, thus preventing deterioration in credit quality and possible loan losses. Also called loan review.

...edit Risk: 1. evaluation of a customer's ability or willingness to pay debts on time. 2. risk that a financial institution assumes when it makes an irrevocable payment on behalf of its customer against insufficient funds.

...edit Scoring: statistical model used to predict the creditworthiness of credit applicants. Credit scoring estimates repayment probability based on information in credit application and credit bureau report. The two main types of credit scoring are application scoring for new accounts and behavior scoring for accounts that have been activated and are carrying balances.

...redit Terms: stated and agreed on terms for debt repayment.

...redit Union: nonprofit cooperative financial organization chartered by state or federal government to provide financial services such as deposit and loan activities to a specific and limited group of people.

...reditworthy: term used to describe individual or entity deemed worthy of extension of credit.

...SAC: see Credit Advisory Board.

...urrent Assets: short-term assets of company, including cash, accounts receivable, temporary investments, and goods and materials in inventory.

...urrent Liabilities: short-term obligations due within one year, including current maturities of long-term debts.

Current Open Account: sale of goods or services for which customer does not pay for each purchase but rather is required to settle in full periodically or within specified time period after each transaction.

Current Ratio: total of current assets divided by total current liabilities; used as indication of a company's liquidity and ability to service current obligations.

D

D&B: see Dun & Bradstreet, Inc.

Dating (Terms): extension of credit terms beyond normal terms because of industry's seasonality or unusual circumstance.

Days Sales Outstanding (DSO): a calculation that expresses the average time in days that receivables are outstanding.

DBA: see Doing Business As.

DDA: see Demand Deposit Account.

Dealer Loan: see Floor Plan.

Debenture: unsecured, long-term indebtedness or corporate obligation.

Debit: entry on left side of accounting ledger.

Debit Card: magnetized plastic card that permits customers to withdraw cash from automatic teller machines and make purchases with charges deducted from funds on deposit at a predesignated account.

Debt: 1. specified amount of money, goods, or services that is owed from one to another, including not only obligation of debtor to pay but also right of creditor to receive and enforce payment. 2. financial obligation of debtor.

Debtor: person or entity indebted to or owing money to another.

Debtor in Possession (DIP): In a Chapter 11 bankruptcy, a debtor may continue to maintain possession of its assets and use them in normal business operations.

Debtor-in-Possession Financing: credit facilities extended to borrower who is reorganizing under Chapter 11 bankruptcy.

Debt Ratio: measure of firm's leverage position derived by dividing total debts by equity.

Debt Service: total interest and scheduled principal payments on debt due within given time frame.

Decision: judgment, decree, or verdict pronounced by court in determination of case.

Declarations Page: policy form containing data regarding insured, policy term, premium, type and amount of coverage, designation of forms and endorsements incorporated at time policy is issued, name of insurer, and countersignature of agent.

Deductible: portion of loss that is not insured; may be stated amount deducted from loss or percentage of loss or of value of property at time of loss.

Deduction: partial amount of payment that is withheld.

Deed: legal, written document used to transfer ownership of real property from one party to another.

Deed of Trust: legal document used in some states in lieu of mortgage. Title to real property passes from seller to trustee, who holds mortgaged property until mortgage has been fully paid and then releases title to borrower. Trustee is authorized to sell property if borrower defaults, paying amount of mortgage loan to lender and any remaining balance to former owner.

Defalcation: misappropriation of funds held in trust for another.

Defamation: injury to person's or entity's character, reputation, or good name by false and malicious statements (includes both libel and slander).

Default: to fail to meet obligation or terms of loan agreement such as payment of principal or interest.

Default Charge: legally agreed upon charge or penalty added to account when payment of debt is late or another event of default occurs under a loan agreement.

Defendant: person or entity defending or denying claim; party against which suit or charge has been filed in court of law. See also Plaintiff.

Defer: to postpone or delay action.

Deferred Payment Sale: selling on installment plan with payments delayed or postponed until future date.

Deficiency Judgment: decree requiring debtor to pay amount remaining due under defaulted contract after secured property has been liquidated.

Deficit: difference between receipts and expenses when expenses are greater.

Defraud: to deprive person of property by fraud, deceit, or artifice.

Defunct: business that has ceased to exist and is without assets; concern that has failed.

Delayed Disbursement: practice in cash management whereby a firm pays vendors and other corporations by disbursing payments from a financial institution in a remote city. Also called remote disbursement. Contrasts with controlled disbursement. See also Federal Reserve Float.

Delinquent: 1. past-due obligation; overdue and unpaid account. 2. to be in arrears in payment of debts, loans, taxes. 3. to have failed in duty or responsibility.

Demand Deposit Account (DDA): funds on deposit in checking account that are payable by a financial institution upon demand of depositor. See also *Time Deposit.*

Demand Draft: written order directing that payment be made, on sight, to a third party.

Demand Letter: correspondence sent by creditor, collection agency, or lawyer to debtor requesting payment of obligation by specific date.

Demand Loan: loan with no fixed due date and payable on demand by maker of loan; loan that can be "called" by lender at any time.

Demurrage: charge that is fixed by contract and payable by recipient of goods for detaining freight car or ship longer than agreed in order to load or unload. Purpose is remuneration to owner of vessel for earnings he or she was improperly caused to lose.

Deposit: 1. amount of money given as down payment for goods or as consideration for contract. 2. funds retained in customer's bank account.

Depreciation: decline in value of fixed assets, allocating purchase cost of an asset plus additions to value over its useful economic life as outlined by the Federal Tax Code.

Derivatives: broad family of financial instruments with characteristics of forward or option contracts.

Derogatory Account Information: adverse information on customers who have not paid accounts with other creditors according to payment terms, as reported to a credit bureau.

Directors and Officers Liability Insurance: legal liability coverage for wrongful acts including breach of duty but not fraud or dishonesty. Often known as E & O, or Errors and Omissions Insurance.

Disbursement: full or partial advancement of funds.

Discharge: 1. to cancel or release obligation. 2. to release debtor from all or most debts in bankruptcy.

Disclaimer Statement: notice disclaiming responsibility for accuracy, completeness, or timeliness of credit information. Most disclaimer statements urge recipients of the information not to rely unduly on it and stress the confidential nature of information being disclosed.

Discontinued Operations: operations of a segment of a company, usually a subsidiary whose activities represent a separate line of business that, although still operating, is the subject of a formal plan of disposal approved by management.

Discount: 1. interest deducted from face amount of note at time loan is made. 2. trade term used for reduction of invoice amount when payment has been made within specified terms.

Discounted Note: 1. borrowing arrangement in which interest is deducted from face amount of note before proceeds are advanced (see also *Note*). 2. term used when customer endorses note received from another party and presents it to a financial institution to obtain funds.

Dishonor: to fail to make payment of negotiable instrument on its due date.

Disintermediation: withdrawal of funds from interest-bearing deposit accounts when rates on competing financial instruments, such as money market mutual funds, stocks, and bonds, offer better returns.

Dismissal: court order or judgment disposing action, suit, or motion without trial.

Dispossess: legal action taken by landlord to put individual or business tenant out of his or her property.

Dissolution of Corporation: termination of entity's existence by law, expiration of charter, loss of all members, or failure to meet statutory level of members.

Distribution: one or more payments made to creditors who have approved claims filed in a bankruptcy proceeding, assignment for the benefit of creditors, or receivership.

Distributor: business engaged in the distribution or marketing of manufacturer's goods to customers or dealers. See also *Wholesaler.*

Dividend: 1. periodic distribution of cash or property to shareholders of corporation as return on their investment.

Document: any written instrument that records letters with figures or marks that may be used as evidence.

Documentary Evidence: any written record or inanimate object, as distinguished from oral evidence.

Documents of Title: Include bill of lading, dock warrant, dock receipt, warehouse receipt, order for the delivery of goods, and any other document that in the regular course of business or financing is treated as adequately evidencing that the person in possession of it is entitled to receive, hold, and dispose of the document and the goods it covers. To be a document of title, a document must purport to be issued by, or addressed to, a bailee and purport to cover goods in the bailee's possession that are either identified or are fungible portions of an identified mass.

Doing Business As (DBA): reference term placed before trade name under which business operates. Sometimes used as fictitious trade style acknowledging that name is not part of corporation title or registered trademark.

Domestic Corporation: company doing business in state in which it is incorporated.

Dormant Account: inactive deposit account in which there have been no deposits or withdrawals for a long period of time.

Doubtful Assets: assets that have all weaknesses inherent in substandard assets with added characteristic that weaknesses make collection or liquidation in full, on basis of currently existing facts, conditions, and values, highly questionable and improbable. Possibility of loss is extremely high. Because of certain important and reasonably specific pending factors that may strengthen assets, classification as estimated loss is deferred until more exact status may be determined. Pending factors include proposed merger, acquisition, liquidation procedures, capital injection, perfecting liens on additional collateral, and refinancing plans.

Downgrading: 1. lowering of assessment of customer's creditworthiness. 2. worsening the internally assigned credit quality rating of a loan or relationship in order to appropriately report risk.

Down Payment: up-front partial payment made to secure right to purchase goods.

Downstream Funding: funds borrowed by holding company for a subsidiary's use, generally to obtain more favorable rate; contrasts with Upstream Funding.

Draft: written order by one party (drawer) directing second party (drawee) to pay sum of money to third party (payee). See also *Banker's Acceptance, Letter of Credit, Sight Draft,* and *Time Draft.*

Drawee: person or entity that is expected to pay check or draft when instrument is presented for payment.

Drawer: party instructing drawee to pay someone else by writing or drawing check or draft. Also called maker or writer.

Drop Shipment: shipment of goods delivered directly from manufacturer to customer.

DSO: see *Days Sales Outstanding.*

Dual Banking: banking system in U.S., consisting of state banks, chartered and supervised by state banking departments, and national banks, chartered and regulated by Office of the Comptroller of the Currency.

Due Date: stated maturity date for debt obligation.

Due Diligence: 1. responsibility of an entity's directors and officers to act in prudent manner in evaluating credit applications; in essence, using same degree of care that an ordinary person would use in making same analysis or review that is made of a loan portfolio of a potential merger candidate by an acquiring institution.

Due Process of Law: law in its regular course of administration through courts, guaranteed by U.S. Constitution.

Dun: to repeatedly demand payment of debt; to be insistent in following debtor for payment.

Dun & Bradstreet, Inc. (D&B): international mercantile agency supplying information and credit ratings on all types of businesses.

Dun Letter: letter or notice sent by creditor requesting payment of past-due debt.

D-U-N-S Number: (Data Universal Numbering System) code developed by Dun & Bradstreet that identifies specific business name and location.

Durable Goods: goods that provide long-lasting qualities and continuing service.

Duress: unlawful constraint that forces person to do what he or she would not have done by choice.

Duty: 1. legal, moral, or ethical obligation. 2. tax collected on import or export goods.

E

Earnest Money: money that one contracting party gives to another at the time of entering into the contract in order to bind the contract in good faith, and which will be forfeited if the purchaser fails to carry out the contract.

Earnings Report: 1. income statement showing a business's or individual's revenues and expenses for stated period of time.

Easement: right of owner of one parcel of land to use land of another for special purpose. Usually easement rights pass with land when it is sold.

Edge Act: banking legislation, passed in 1919, that allows national banks to conduct foreign lending operations through federal or state-chartered subsidiaries called Edge Act corporations. Such corporations can be chartered by other states and are allowed to own banks in foreign countries and to invest in foreign commercial and industrial firms.

EFT: see *Electronic Funds Transfer.*

Electronic Funds Transfer (EFT): computerized system enabling funds to be debited, credited, or transferred between financial institution accounts and vendors.

Embezzlement: fraudulent appropriation of one's property by person to whom it was entrusted.

Encumbrance: any right or interest in real or other property that diminishes the property's value and alters control of disposition.

Endorsement: 1. act of writing one's name on back of note, bill, check, or similar written instrument for payment of money; required on negotiable instrument to pass title properly to another. By signing such instrument, endorser

becomes party to it and thereby liable, under certain conditions, for its payment. 2. change or addition to insurance policy, informally called rider.

ntrepreneur: person who plans, organizes, and runs operation of new business.

OM Terms: Shipments during a month are invoiced in a single statement dated as of the last day of that month or the first day of the following month.

qual Credit Opportunity Act of 1974: Federal Reserve Regulation B that prohibits creditors from discriminating against credit applicants on basis of age, race, color, religion, national origin, sex, marital status, age, or receipt of public assistance.

quitable Subordination: principles in section 510 (c) of U.S. Bankruptcy Code that permit bankruptcy court to subordinate, for purposes of distribution, all or part of creditor's claim against debtor's estate to claims of another creditor of that debtor after court has determined that first creditor has engaged in some form of wrongful conduct that has improved position relative to other creditors.

quity: value of ownership, calculated by subtracting total liabilities from total assets.

scheat: right of state to claim property or money if there is no legal claim made to it.

scrow Account: deposit account to which access is restricted or limited by terms of written agreement entered into by three parties, including a financial institution.

state: any right, title, or interest that a person may have in lands or other personal property.

stimate: amount of labor, materials, and other costs that a contractor anticipates for a project, as summarized in contractor's bid proposal for project.

vent of Default: a breach of an agreement between parties to a contract; a violation of one or more of the loan covenants as set forth in either the loan agreement, commitment letter, or promissory note.

vergreen Revolving Credit: commitment to lend money that remains in effect unless lender takes specific action to terminate agreement; agreement may provide that, in event of termination, any outstanding amount will convert to term loan.

xchange Rate: value of one country's currency to that of another country at a particular point in time.

xclusive Sales Agreement: contractual arrangement, generally between a retailer and a manufacturer or wholesaler, giving retailer exclusive rights for sale of articles or services within a defined geographic area or through a defined distribution channel.

xecute: to complete and give validity to a legal document by signing, sealing, and delivering it.

xempt: 1. to release, discharge, or waive from a liability to which others in the same general class are subject. 2. property not available for seizure.

xemption: 1. immunity from general burden, tax, or charge. 2. legal right of debtor to hold portion of property free from claims or judgments.

xpense: cost or outlay of money used in business operating cycle.

xport-Import Bank: also called Ex-Im Bank. Provides guarantees of working capital loans for U.S. exporters; guarantees the repayment of loans or makes loans to foreign purchasers of U.S. goods and services. Ex-Im Bank also provides credit insurance that protects U.S. exporters against the risks of nonpayment by foreign buyers for political or commercial reasons. Ex-Im Bank does not compete with commercial lenders, but assumes the risks they cannot accept.

F

Face Amount: indicated value of a financial instrument, as shown on its front.

Facility Fee: lender's charge for making a line of credit or other credit facility available to borrower (for example, a commitment fee).

Facsimile: exact copy of an original.

Factor: entity that purchases borrower's accounts receivable and may extend funds to borrower prior to collection of receivables.

Factoring: short-term financing from nonrecourse sale of accounts receivable to third party or factor. Factor assumes full risk of collection, including credit losses. Factoring is most common in the garment industry, but has been used in other industries as well. There are two basic types of factoring:
- discount factoring, in which factor pays discounted price for receivables before maturity date.
- maturity factoring, in which factor pays the client purchase price of factored accounts at maturity.

Fair Credit Billing Act of 1974 (FCBA): Federal Reserve Regulation Z details the provisions of this act by prescribing uniform methods of computing the cost of consumer credit, disclosure of credit terms, and procedures for resolving billing errors on certain kinds of credit accounts.

Fair Credit Reporting Act: federal legislation that regulates consumer credit reporting activities and gives consumer right to learn contents of his or her credit bureau file.

Fair Market Value: price that property would sell for between willing buyer and willing seller, neither of whom is obligated to effect transaction.

Fannie Mae: see *Federal National Mortgage Association.*

FASB: see *Financial Accounting Standards Board.*

FFB: see *Federal Financing Bank.*

FCBA: see *Fair Credit Billing Act of 1974.*

FDIC: see *Federal Deposit Insurance Corporation.*

FDICIA: see *Federal Deposit Insurance Corporation Improvement Act of 1991.*

Federal Deposit Insurance Corporation (FDIC): 1. federal agency that insures bank accounts for up to $100,000 at both commercial banks and thrifts through Bank Insurance Fund and Savings Association Fund. 2. federal regulator for state-chartered banks that are not members of Federal Reserve System.

Federal Deposit Insurance Corporation Improvement Act of 1991 (FDICIA): legislation that provides for recapitalization of Bank Insurance Fund and restructuring of financial services industry through:
- emphasis on more capital.
- government standards for lending, operations, and asset growth.
- quicker government seizure of struggling institutions.
- reduced liquidity options for all but the strongest banks.
- incentives for uninsured depositors to use only the largest and strongest banks.
- sharply increased regulatory costs and fees.
- easier rules for acquiring banks and thrifts.

Federal Financial Institutions Examination Council (FFIEC): interagency group of federal banking regulators formed in 1979 to maintain uniform standards for federal examination and supervision of federally insured depository institutions, bank holding companies, and savings and loan holding companies. Also runs schools for examiners employed by banks, thrifts, and credit union agencies. Council produces Uniform Bank Performance Report.

Federal Financing Bank (FFB): agency in U.S. Treasury established by Congress in 1973 to centralize borrowing by federal agencies. Instead of selling securities directly to financial markets, all but largest federal agencies raise capital by borrowing from U.S. Treasury through FFB. FFB makes loans at favorable rates to agencies that do not have ready access to credit markets; its debt is direct obligation of U.S. Treasury.

Federal Funds: unsecured advances of immediately available funds from excess balances in reserve accounts held at Federal Reserve Banks. Technically, these funds are not borrowings but purchases of immediately available funds. Banks advancing federal funds sell excess reserves; banks receiving federal funds buy excess reserves from selling banks. Federal funds sold are credit transactions on account of selling banks. See also *Federal Funds Rate.*

Federal Funds Rate: rate charged in interbank market for purchases of excess reserve balances. Rate of interest is key money market interest rate and correlates with rates on other short-term credit arrangements. Because the federal funds rate re-prices with each transaction, it is the most sensitive of money market rates and is watched carefully by the Federal Reserve Board.

Federal Home Loan Bank Board (FHLBB): federal agency established by Federal Home Loan Bank Act of 1932 to supervise reserve credit system, Federal Home Loan Bank System, for savings institutions. Board also acted as chartering agency and primary regulator of federal savings and loan associations under Home Owners Loan Act of 1933. Financial Institutions Reform, Recovery, and Enforcement Act of 1989 abolished board, transferring its powers in examination and supervision of federally chartered savings institutions to new agency, Office of Thrift Supervision, bureau of U.S. Treasury Department. Regulatory oversight of district Home Loan Banks was transferred to the five-member Federal Housing Finance Board.

Federal Home Loan Bank System: system of 11 regional banks established by Federal Home Loan Bank Act of 1932, acting as central credit system for savings and loan institutions. District Home Loan Banks make short-term credit advances to savings institutions, much like Federal Reserve System acts as lender of last resort to commercial banks. Each Home Loan Bank operates independently and has its own board of directors.

Federal Home Loan Mortgage Corporation (FHLMC): corporation authorized by Congress in 1970 as secondary market conduit for residential mortgages. Corporation purchases loans from mortgage originators and sells its own obligations and mortgage-backed bonds issued by Government National Mortgage Association to private investors, namely financial institution trust funds, insurance companies, pension funds, and thrift institutions. Also called Freddie Mac.

Federal Housing Administration (FHA): federal agency that insures residential mortgages. Created by National Housing Act of 1934, FHA is now part of Department of Housing and Urban Development. Both FHA and Department of Veterans Affairs have single-family mortgage programs to assist homebuyers who are unable to obtain financing from conventional mortgage lenders (banks, savings and loans, and other financial institutions).

Federal Housing Finance Board (FHFB): independent federal agency regulating credit advance activities of 11 Federal Home Loan Banks. This board, estab-

lished by Financial Institutions Reform, Recovery, and Enforcement Act of 1989, has five members, including secretary of Housing and Urban Development, and four directors appointed by the President with Senate confirmation to serve seven-year terms. At least one director must represent the interests of community groups.

Federal National Mortgage Association (FNMA): federally chartered, stockholder-owned corporation that purchases residential mortgages insured or guaranteed by federal agencies, as well as conventional mortgages, in secondary mortgage market. Corporation raises capital to support its operations through collection of insurance and commitment fees, issuance of stock, and sale of debentures and notes. Also called Fannie Mae.

Federal Open Market Committee (FOMC): policy committee in Federal Reserve System that sets short-term monetary policy objectives for Fed. Committee is made up of seven governors of Federal Reserve Board, plus the presidents of six Federal Reserve Banks. President of Federal Reserve Bank of New York is permanent FOMC member. The other five slots are filled on rotating basis by presidents of other 11 Federal Reserve Banks. Committee carries out monetary objectives by instructing Open Market Desk at Federal Reserve Bank of New York to buy or sell government securities from special account, called open market account, at New York Fed.

Federal Reserve Board (FRB): U.S.'s central bank responsible for conduct of monetary policy; also oversees state-chartered banks that are members of Federal Reserve System, bank holding companies, and Edge Act corporations.

Federal Reserve Float: total amount of funds that Federal Reserve Banks, in their role as clearing agents, have credited to depositing institutions but have not charged to paying institutions.

Federal Reserve System: central bank of U.S. created by Federal Reserve Act of 1913. System consists of Board of Governors, made up of seven members, and a network of 12 Federal Reserve Banks and 25 branches throughout U.S. Board of Governors is responsible for setting monetary policy and reserve requirements. Board and banks share responsibility for setting the discount rate, the interest rate that depository institutions are charged for borrowing from Federal Reserve Banks.

Federal Trade Commission (FTC): federal regulatory agency that administers and enforces rules to prevent unfair business practices.

Fee Simple: estate in which owner is entitled to entire property and has unconditional power over its disposition.

FFIEC: see *Federal Financial Institutions Examination Council.*

FHA: see *Federal Housing Administration.*

FHLBB: see *Federal Home Loan Bank Board.*

FHLMC: see *Federal Home Loan Mortgage Corporation.*

Fictitious Name: pretend name used by firm in business transactions. Company is usually required to register this name with local authorities, along with true names and addresses of company's owners.

Fidelity Bond: contract issued by insurer to employer to cover loss caused by dishonest acts of employees; form of suretyship. Also called dishonesty insurance.

Fiduciary: person or entity acting in capacity of trustee for another.

Field Warehousing: method of using company's inventory to secure business loan. In leased and separate storage area of borrower's facility, goods act as security for loan and are released by custodian only upon lender's order.

FIFO: see *First-In First-Out.*

File: 1. organized folder containing accumulation of information and items retained for preservation or reference. 2. to deposit legal document with proper authority.

File Revision: routine gathering of credit information by credit grantor to update files on borrowers.

Filing Claims: 1. depositing of formal papers with proper public office and in manner and time frame prescribed by law in order to preserve creditor's rights. 2. method used to perfect security interest accomplished by recording in proper public office.

Finance Charges: total costs to an individual or business of obtaining credit, including interest and any fees.

Financial Analysis: evaluation by credit analyst of customer's financial situation to determine whether customer has ability to meet his or her obligations as they become due. Factors such as general condition of customer's industry, organizational structure, available collateral or guarantors, and past financial performance are considered.

Financial Accounting Standards Board (FASB): independent board responsible for establishing and interpreting generally accepted accounting principles, formed in 1973 to succeed and continue activities of Accounting Principles Board.

Financial Institutions Reform, Recovery, and Enforcement Act of 1989 (FIRREA): act signed into law on August 9, 1989, to provide funding and regulatory structure necessary to close several hundred insolvent savings associations and liquidate their assets, to consolidate federal insurance of banks and savings associations under direction of the Federal Deposit Insurance Corporation, to provide regulatory agencies with sweeping new enforcement pow-

ers, and to increase substantially civil and criminal penalties for violation federal banking statutes and regulations. Act substantially alters relation between savings institutions and regulators and imposes new requireme that must be observed in day-to-day operations of institutions.

Financial Position: standing of company, combining assets and liabilities entered on balance sheet.

Financial Statements: reports consisting of individual's or company's bala sheet, income statement, and statement of cash flows, footnotes, and supplemental schedules.

Financing Statement: form required to be completed by creditor and filed v appropriate county and state authorities in order to perfect creditor's secu interest in collateral and to give public notice of such interest.

FIRREA: see *Financial Institutions Reform, Recovery, and Enforcement Ac 1989.*

First Deed of Trust: first recorded deed of trust that acts as first lien on prope it describes.

First-In First-Out (FIFO): method of valuing inventory in which the first goo received are the first goods used or sold. Using this method, costs of inve tory used to determine cost of goods sold are related to costs that w incurred first.

First Mortgage: mortgage on property that is superior to any others by fact having been filed first.

Fiscal: anything involving financial matters or issues.

Fiscal Agent: person or organization serving as another's financial agent or r resentative.

Fiscal Year: fixed accounting year used as basis for annual financial reporting business or government.

Five C's of Credit: method of evaluating potential borrower's creditworthine based on five criteria: Capacity, Capital, Character, Collateral, and Conditions

Fixed Assets: property used in normal course of business that is of a long-te nature, such as land, machinery, fixtures, and equipment.

Fixed-Rate Loan: loan with interest rate that does not vary over term of loan.

Fixture: that which is permanently attached or affixed to real property.

Flagging an Account: temporarily identifying an account for specific purpose reason; may involve suspending activity.

Float: uncollected funds represented by checks deposited in one bank but not y cleared through bank on which they are drawn.

Floating Interest Rate: loan interest rate that changes whenever the stated ind rate, or base rate, changes.

Floating Lien: loan or credit facility secured by inventory or receivables. This ty of security agreement gives lender interest in assets acquired by borrow after agreement, as well as those owned when agreement was made. Whe agreement covers proceeds from sales, lender also has recourse against cas collected from the payment of receivables.

Floor Plan: loan made to dealer for purchase of inventory acquired for resale ar secured by that inventory, such as automobiles or appliances.

FNMA: see *Federal National Mortgage Association.*

FOB: see *Free on Board.*

FOB Point: point at which responsibility for freight charges begins and tit passes. See also *Free on Board.*

FOMC: see *Federal Open Market Committee.*

Forbearance: Temporarily giving up the right to enforce a valid claim, in retur for a promise. It is sufficient consideration to make a promise binding (fo example, protracted payment arrangements or interest rate reduction i exchange for additional collateral or guarantors).

Forced Sale: 1. court-ordered sale of property, usually without owner's approva 2. voluntary sale of goods or property to raise cash or to reduce inventory.

Foreclosure: legal termination of all of debtor's rights in property secured b mortgage after debtor has defaulted on obligation supported by such mort gage.

Foreign Corporation: corporation established under laws of a state other tha that in which it is doing business.

Foreign Exchange: conversion of money of one country into its equivalent in cur rency of another country.

Foreign Item: check drawn on any financial institution other than the financia institution where it is presented for payment. Also called transit item.

Foreign Judgment: judgment obtained in state or country other than the one where the debtor now lives, is doing business, or has assets.

Forfeiture: penalty resulting in automatic loss of cash, property, or rights for no complying with legal terms of agreement.

Forgery: false making or material altering of any writing with intent to defraud.

Form 8K: report disclosing significant events potentially affecting corporation's financial condition or market value of its shares, required by Securities and Exchange Commission. Report is filed within 30 days after event (pending merger, amendment to corporate charter, charge to earnings for credit losses took place and summarizes information that any reasonable investor would want to know before buying or selling securities.

Form 10K: annual financial report filed with Securities and Exchange Commission. Issuers of registered securities are required to file 10K, as are corporations with 500 or more shareholders or assets of $2 million and exchange-listed corporations. Report, which becomes public information once filed, summarizes key financial information, including sources and uses of funds by type of business, net pretax operating income, provision for income taxes and credit losses, plus comparative financial statements for past two fiscal years. Summary of 10K report is included in annual report to stockholders.

Form 10Q: quarterly financial report filed by companies with listed securities and those corporations required to file annual 10K report with Securities and Exchange Commission. 10Q report, which does not have to be audited, summarizes key financial data on earnings and expenses and compares current financial information with data reported in same quarter of previous year.

Forwarding: referral or placement of out-of-town claims with attorney who then acts on behalf of creditor. In collection process, when authorized, agency may forward account to attorney for collection or suit.

Franchise: business agreement whereby one company allows another the right to conduct business under its name and/or distribute its products in exchange for royalties or another agreed upon method of payment.

Fraud: any act of deceit, omission, or commission used to deprive someone of right or property. Elements of fraud consist of intentional misrepresentation of fact, relied on by another to his or her detriment, that results in damages.

Fraudulent Conveyance: a transfer of property by a debtor, for the intent and purpose of defrauding creditors. Such property may be reached by the creditors through appropriate legal proceedings.

FRB: see *Federal Reserve Board.*

Freddie Mac: see *Federal Home Loan Mortgage Corporation.*

Free and Clear: 1. property with an unencumbered title. 2. title that is free of defects.

Free and Clear Delivery Receipt: delivery receipt signed by consignee completely absolving carrier from any claim for loss or damages.

Free Astray: freight shipment that has been lost. If it is carrier's fault and shipment is located, it is carrier's obligation to make delivery to original destination at no additional cost to shipper or consignee.

Free Demand Letter Service: pre-collection letter sent by collection agency to debtor, requesting that payment be made directly to creditor by given date. No charge is made for payments received within free demand period, but balances remaining unpaid are followed for collection by agency at its regular rates.

Free on Board (FOB): term identifying shipping point from which buyer assumes all responsibilities and costs for transportation.

Free Port: place where goods are imported or exported free of any duty.

Freight Forwarder: business that receives goods for transportation; services include consolidation of small freight shipments of less than carload, truckload, or container lots assembled for lower shipping rates.

Frozen Account: 1. account to which customer no longer has access. 2. account suspended by court order, violation of loan covenants, or checking account agreement, etc.

Frozen Assets: any assets that cannot be used by owner because of pending legal action.

FTC: see *Federal Trade Commission.*

Fund: cash or equivalents set aside for specific purpose.

Fund Accounting: fiscal and accounting entity with self-balancing set of accounts recording cash and other financial resources, together with all related liabilities and residual equities or balances, and changes therein, which are segregated for purpose of carrying on specific activities or obtaining certain objectives in accordance with special regulations, restrictions, or limitations.

Funded Debt: mortgages, bonds, debentures, notes, or other obligations with maturity of more than one year from statement date.

G

GAAP: see *Generally Accepted Accounting Principles.*

Garnishee: 1. person or entity that has possession of money or property belonging to defendant and is served with writ of garnishment to hold money or property for payment of defendant's debt to plaintiff. 2. one against whom garnishment has been served.

Garnishment: legal warning or procedure to one in possession of another's property not to allow owner access to such property as it will be used to satisfy judgment against owner.

General Contractor: contractor who enters into a contract with an owner for construction of a project and who takes full responsibility for its completion. Contractor may enter into subcontracts with various subcontractors for performance of specific parts or phases of project.

General Ledger: bookkeeping record comprising all assets, liabilities, proprietorship, revenue, and expense accounts. Entries for each account are posted, and balances are included for each entry.

Generally Accepted Accounting Principles (GAAP): conventions, rules, and procedures that define accepted accounting practices, including broad guidelines as well as detailed procedures. Financial Accounting Standards Board, an independent self-regulatory organization, is responsible for promulgating these principles.

General Obligation Debt: long-term debt or bond repaid from all otherwise unrestricted revenues, sales taxes, property taxes, license fees, property sales, rents, and so forth of municipality.

General Partner: participant in a business relationship who is personally liable, without limitation, for all partnership debts.

Ginnie Mae: see *Government National Mortgage Association.*

GNMA: see *Government National Mortgage Association.*

Going Concern: assumes that a business entity has a reasonable expectation of continuing in business and generating a profit for an indefinite period of time.

Goods on Approval: goods offered by seller to buyer with option of examining goods for specific period of time before deciding to purchase them.

Goodwill: 1. intangible assets of business consisting of its good reputation, valuable clientele, or desirable location that results in above normal earning power. 2. value or amount for which business could be sold above book value of its physical property and receivables.

Government National Mortgage Association (GNMA): corporation created by Congress that administers mortgage-backed securities program that channels new sources of funds into residential mortgages through sale of securities. Also called Ginnie Mae.

Grace Period: specified length of time beyond payment due date during which late fee will not be assessed.

Grantee: person to whom title in property is made.

Grantor: person who transfers title to property.

Gross Margin: gross profit as a percentage of sales.

Gross Profit: net sales less cost of sales.

Gross Sales: sales before returns and allowances; discounts are deducted to arrive at net sales.

Guarantor: person who agrees by execution of a contract to repay the debt of another if that person defaults.

Guaranty: separate agreement by which a party (or parties) other than debtor assumes responsibility for payment of obligation if principal debtor defaults or is subsequently unable to perform under the terms of the obligation.

Guardian: person who is legally responsible for the care and management of a minor or individual who is not mentally or legally competent (or of such person's property).

H

Hard Goods: durable consumer goods, usually including such items as major appliances and furniture, with relatively long, useful lives.

Heavy Industry: industry involved in manufacturing basic products such as metals, machinery, or other equipment.

Hidden Assets: assets not easily identified and either intentionally not disclosed or publicly reported at lower value than their true worth.

High Credit: largest amount of credit used by borrower during specified period of time.

Holder in Due Course: person who has taken negotiable instrument (check or note) for value, in good faith, and on assurance that it is complete and regular, not overdue or dishonored, and has no defect in ownership on part of previous holder or endorser.

Holding Company: company organized to hold and control stock in other companies.

Homestead Exemption: state's law allowing householder or head of family to exempt residence from attachment by creditors.

Housing and Urban Development, Department of: cabinet-level federal agency, founded in 1965, that promotes housing development in U.S. through direct loans, mortgage insurance, and guaranties. It houses Federal Housing Administration and Government National Mortgage Association.

HUD: see *Housing and Urban Development, Department of.*

Hypothecate: to pledge or assign property owned by one entity as security or collateral for loan to second entity.

Hypothecation: 1. offer of stocks, bonds, or other assets owned by party other than borrower as collateral for loan, without transferring title. Borrower retains possession but gives lender right to sell property in event of default by borrower. 2. pledging of negotiable securities to collateralize broker's margin loan. If broker pledges same securities to bank as collateral for broker's loan, process is referred to as re-hypothecation.

I

Immunity: condition of being exempt from duty that others are generally required to perform.

Import Letter of Credit: commercial letter of credit issued to finance import of goods.

Import Duty: government tax on imported items.

Impound: to seize or take into legal custody, usually at order of court. Cash, documents, or records may be impounded.

Inactive Account: account that has shown little or no activity over a substantial period of time.

Inactive Files: 1. accounts on which collection activity has been completed or suspended (claims either collected or found to be uncollectible) and on which no further work is being done. Also called closed or dead files. 2. stored records available for reference.

In Arrears: amounts due but not yet paid.

Income Property: real property acquired as investment and managed for profit.

Income Statement: summary of revenue and expenses covering a specified period.

Income Tax: tax levied by federal, state, or local governments on personal or business earnings.

Incorporation: formation of legal entity, with qualities of perpetual existence and succession.

Incumbrance: see *Encumbrance.*

Indebtedness: total amount of money or liabilities owed.

In Default: failing to abide by terms and conditions of note or loan agreement. This can include payments on interest or principal (or both) being past due.

Indemnity: 1. contract or assurance to reimburse another against anticipated loss, damage, or failure to fulfill obligation. 2. type of insurance that provides coverage for losses of this nature.

Indirect Liability: contingent liability such as a continuing guarantee.

Individual Signature: credit approved by one person on his or her own authority.

Indorsement: see *Endorsement.*

Industrial Consumer: purchaser who buys goods or services for business purposes.

Inquiry: request for credit information on a bank's customer.

Insider Loans: loans to directors and officers of bank, which must be reported to bank regulators under Financial Institutions Reform Act of 1978. Banking laws require that loans to insiders be made at substantially the same rate and credit terms as loans to other borrowers.

Insolvency: 1. inability to meet debts as they become due in ordinary course of business. 2. financial condition in which assets are not sufficient to satisfy liabilities.

Installment Sale: contract sale in which merchandise is purchased with down payment and balance is made in partial payments over agreed period of time.

Instrument: written formal or legal document.

In-Substance Foreclosure Assets: loans for which borrower is perceived to have little or no equity in the asset or project and the financial institution can reasonably anticipate proceeds for repayment only from the operation or sale of collateral.

Insufficient Funds: see *Non-sufficient Funds.*

Insurable Interest: interest such that loss or damage inflicts economic loss.

Insurable Value: maximum possible loss to which property is exposed; actual amount depends on basis of calculation per insurance policy.

Intangible Assets: nonmaterial assets of business that have no value in themselves but that represent value. Examples include trademarks, goodwill, patents, and copyrights.

Interchange: confidential exchange of credit information between individuals and trade groups.

Interchange Bureau: association organized to record and exchange or furnish confidential credit information about a member's payment experience and manner in which customers meet obligations.

Interchange Group: trade membership group within specific industry that meets regularly to exchange credit experiences and other confidential information.

Interchange Report: report usually obtained through credit interchange bureau showing recent credit experience as supplied by participating members.

Inter-creditor Agreement: document used when there is more than one lender involved in credit transaction to spell out each lender's rights and obligations.

Interest: 1. legally allowed or agreed upon compensation to lender for use of borrowed money. 2. any right in property but less than title to it.

Interest Bearing: term describing note or contract calling for payment of agreed interest.

Interest Only: loan term during which no principal repayments are made.

Interest Rate: cost of borrowing money expressed as an annualized percentage of the loan.

Internal Guidance Line of Credit: credit facility similar to a line of credit, but customer may or may not be advised of it; established for internal financial institution purposes, it provides financing for recurrent requests without referring each one to credit committee or other approval source.

International Consumer Credit Association: professional trade association of retail credit professionals. Association keeps members informed of latest developments in consumer credit and provides educational courses, seminars, textbooks, and other published material.

Intestate: dying without leaving valid will or any other specific instructions as disposition of property.

Inventory: current assets of business that represent goods for sale, including materials, work in process, and finished goods.

Investigation: 1. gathering of credit information on a person or entity. 2. systematic research for information necessary for a business decision.

Investment: use of money for purpose of earning profit or return.

Investor: person or entity that puts money to use for capital appreciation or pr or to receive regular dividends.

Invoice: seller's descriptive, itemized billing for goods or services sold, show date, terms, cost, purchase order number, method of shipment, and oth identifying information.

Involuntary Bankruptcy: see *Bankruptcy.*

Itemized Statement: detailed listing of activity on account for particular period time.

J

Jobber: see *Wholesaler.*

Joint Account: financial institution account shared or owned in name of two more persons with full privileges available to each person.

Joint and Several: relative to liability, a term used when creditor has option pursuing one or more signers of an agreement individually or all signe together.

Joint Tenancy with Rights of Survivorship: interest in property held by two more persons that includes right of survivorship in which deceased person interest passes to survivors. See also *Tenancy by Entirety.*

Joint Venture: business or undertaking entered into on one-time basis by two more parties in which profits, losses, and control are shared.

Journal: account book of original entry in which all money receipts and expens are chronologically recorded.

Judgment: court's determination of rights of parties to claim.

Judgment Creditor: one who has obtained judgment against debtor and ca enforce it.

Judgment Debtor: one against whom judgment has been recovered but not satis fied.

Judgment Note: see *Cognovit Note.*

Judgment Lien: claim or encumbrance on property, allowed by law, usual against real estate of judgment debtor.

Judgment-Proof: term to describe judgment debtor from whom collection cann be obtained or person who has no money or assets or has concealed removed property subject to execution.

Judicial Sale: see *Forced Sale.*

Junior Mortgage: any mortgage filed after and subject to satisfaction of firs mortgage.

Jurisdiction: 1. legal authority, power, capacity, and right of court to act. 2. geo graphic area within which court or government agency exercises power.

K

Keyperson Life Insurance: insurance policy written on owner or principa employee in which death benefits are payable to company.

Key Ratios: performance measures used to determine probable ability of busi ness to operate profitably. Results are expressed in percentages that are the weighed against average percentages in each industry.

L

Landlord's Waiver: the relinquishment of a right(s) contained in a lease agree ment by a lessor.

Last-In First-Out (LIFO): method of valuating inventory in which last goods received are the first ones sold. Using this method, inventory costs used to determine cost of goods sold are related to costs of inventory that were incurred last.

Late Charge: special legally agreed upon fee, charged by creditor, on any pay ment that is not made when due.

Lawful Money: legal tender for payment of all debts.

Law List: compiled publication of names and addresses of those in legal profes sion, often including court calendars, private investigators, and other informa tion of interest to legal profession.

Lawsuit: suit, action, or cause instituted by one person against another in a court of law.

Lead Bank: financial institution that has the primary deposit or lending relation ship in a multi-bank situation; usually in the context of shared credit and sometimes defined within an inter-creditor agreement. See also *Agent Bank.*

Leaseback: agreement by which one party sells property to another and, after completing sale, the first party rents it from second party.

Lease Contract: written agreement for which equipment or facilities can be obtained on rental payment basis for specified period of time.

...ed Department: section of department store not operated by store but by ...ndependent outside organization on contract or percentage-of-sales arrange-...ent.

...ehold: rights tenant holds in property as conferred by terms of lease.

...ehold Improvement: permanent improvements made to rented property. ...easehold improvements are considered fixtures and depreciate over lease ...eriod.

...ehold Interest: lessee's equity or ownership in leasehold improvements.

...e-Purchase Agreement: contract providing for set amount of lease pay-...ments to be applied to purchase of property.

...er: in accounting, book of permanent records containing series of accounts ...o which debits and credits of transactions are posted from books of original ...ntry.

...ger Experience: trade experience reported by credit manager or interchange ...group. Such reports provide picture of account's paying habits, high credit, ...nd terms of repayment.

...al and Sovereign Risk: risk that government may intervene to affect bank's ...system or any participant of such system detrimentally.

...al Composition: identification and description of lawful ownership or title to ...business entity.

...al Entity: business organization that has capacity to make contract or agree-...ment or assume obligation. Such organization may consist of individual pro-...prietorship, partnership, corporation, or association.

...al Right: natural right, right created by contract, and right created or recog-...nized by law.

...al Tender: any money that is recognized by law for payment of debt unless ...contract exists specifically calling for payment in another type of money.

...al Title: document establishing right of ownership to property that is recog-...nized and upheld by law.

...der: one who extends funds to another with expectation of repayment with ...interest.

...der's Loss Payable Endorsement: form attached to property insurance poli-...cies to cover lender's interest in what is insured; extends coverage to give ...lender protection beyond that in basic policy; language may be prescribed by ...banking industry, standard form prepared by insurance industry, or specified ...by lender. See also *Loss Payee Clause.*

...ssee: one to whom lease is given and therefore has right to use property in ...exchange for rental payments.

...sor: owner who grants lease for use of property in return for rent.

...ter of Agreement: letter stating terms of agreement between addressor and ...addressee, usually prepared for signature by addressee as indication of ...acceptance of those terms as legally binding.

...ter of Credit: letter or document issued by bank on behalf of customer that is ...evidence of financial background of bank and ensures that payment will be ...made when proper documents confirm completion of related transaction. ...Such letters authorize drawing of sight or time drafts when certain terms and ...conditions are fulfilled. See also *Banker's Acceptance, Draft, Sight Draft, Standby Letter of Credit,* and *Time Draft.*

...ter of Intent: letter signifying intention to enter into formal agreement and ...usually setting forth general terms of such agreement.

...able: duty or obligation enforceable by law.

...abilities: indebtedness of an individual or entity.

...bel: written or published false and malicious statements about another that ...tend to defame or harm another's reputation.

...BOR: see *London Interbank Offered Rate.*

...en: legal right or encumbrance to secure payment performance on property ...pledged as collateral until the debt it secures is satisfied.

...FO: see *Last-In First-Out.*

...imited Liability Company: legal entity that offers shareholders the same limita-...tions on personal liability available to corporate shareholders. The owners of a ...limited liability company (LLC) have limited liability. They are not liable for the ...debts, liabilities, acts, or omissions of the company. Only their investment is ...at risk.

...imited Liability: legal exemption corporate stockholders or limited liability com-...panies have from full financial responsibilities for debts of company.

...imited Partnership: partnership of one or more general partners who are per-...sonally, jointly, and separately responsible, with one or more special partners ...whose liabilities are limited to amount of investment.

...ne of Credit: see *Credit Line.*

...iquid Assets: assets that can be readily converted into cash.

...quidate: 1. to pay off or settle current obligation. 2. to sell off or convert assets ...into cash. 3. to dissolve business in order to raise cash for payment of debts.

...iquidation: process of dissolving a business, settling accounts, and paying off ...any claims or obligations; remaining cash is distributed to the owners of the ...business.

...iquidation Value: cash that can be realized from sale of assets in dissolving ...business, as distinct from its value as ongoing entity.

Liquidity: measure of quality and adequacy of current assets to meet current obligations as they come due.

Liquidity Ratio: company's most liquid assets (generally cash and accounts receivable) divided by current liabilities. Also called quick ratio.

List Price: generally advertised or posted price. Sometimes subject to trade or cash discounts.

Litigation: lawsuit brought to court for purpose of enforcing a right.

LLC: see *Limited Liability Company.*

Loan: money advanced to a borrower with agreement of repayment usually with interest within a specified period of time.

Loan Agreement: legal contract between a financial institution and a borrower that governs the terms and conditions for the life of a loan. Elements usually include description of loan, representations, and warranties reaffirming known facts about the borrower such as legal structure, affirmative and nega-tive covenants, conditions that must be met before the loan is granted, delin-quent payment penalties, and statement of remedies that the financial institu-tion may take in event of default.

Loan Participation: sharing of loan(s) by a group of financial institutions that join together to make said loan(s), affording an opportunity to share the risk of a very large transaction. Arranged through correspondent banking networks in which smaller financial institutions buy a portion of an overall financing pack-age. Participations are a convenient way for smaller financial institutions to book loans that would otherwise exceed their legal lending limits. Also called participation financing.

Loan Policy: principles that reflect a financial institution's credit culture, under-writing procedures, and overall approach to lending.

Loans Past Due: loans with interest or principal payments that are contractually past due a certain number of days.

Loan-to-Value Ratio (LTV): relationship, expressed as percent, between principal amount of loan and appraised value of the asset securing financing.

Loan Value: amount of money that can be borrowed against real or personal property.

Lockbox: regional financial institution depository used by corporations to obtain earlier receipt and collection of customer payments. Arrangement provides creditor with better control of accounts receivable and earlier availability of cash balances. Many large financial institutions offer lockbox processing as a cash management service to corporate customers. Lockboxes can be:
- retail, designed for remittance processing for consumer accounts.
- wholesale, in which payments from other entities are collected and submit-ted through depository transfer check or electronic debit into a concentra-tion account for investment and disbursement as needed.

London Interbank Offered Rate (LIBOR): key rate index used in international lending. LIBOR is the rate at which major financial institutions in London are willing to lend Eurodollars to each other. This index is often used to determine interest rate charged to creditworthy borrowers.

Long-Arm Statutes: state statutes that allow state courts to exercise jurisdiction over nonresident persons or property outside their state's borders.

Long-Term Capital Gain (Loss): gain or loss realized from sale or exchange of capital asset held for longer than 12 months.

Long-Term Liabilities: all senior debt, including bonds, debentures, bank debt, mortgages, deferred portions of long term-debt, and capital lease obligations owed for longer than 12 months.

Loss: 1. circumstance in which expenses exceed revenues. 2. result if an asset is sold for less than its depreciated book value.

Loss Assets: assets considered uncollectible and of such little value that their continuance as realizable assets is not warranted.

Loss Leader: deliberate sale of product or service at or below cost in order to attract new customers.

Loss Payee Clause: provision in insurance policy or added by endorsement to cover lender/mortgagee's interest in property loss settlement. Provision is not as broad as lender's loss payable endorsement. Also called mortgagee clause and loss payable clause.

LTV: see *Loan-to-Value Ratio.*

Lump-sum Settlement: payment made in full with single, one-time payment.

M

Magnetic Ink Character Recognition (MICR): description of numbers and sym-bols that are printed in magnetic ink on documents for automated processing. Fully inscribed MICR line of information may include item's serial number, routing and transit number, check digit, account number, process control number, and amount.

Mail-Fraud Statute: federal law against using mails to defraud creditors by mail-ing false financial statements. Prosecution under mail-fraud statute must prove beyond reasonable doubt that:
- statement is false.
- statement was made with intention it should be relied on.
- it was made for the purpose of securing money or property.

• statement was delivered by mail.

• money or property was obtained by means of false statement.

Mailgram: telegraphic message transmitted electronically by Western Union and delivered by U.S. Postal Service.

Mail Teller: employee of a financial institution who receives mail deposits, checks them for accuracy, and returns stamped receipts for deposits to customers.

Majority Stockholder: person or entity that owns more than 50% of voting stock of a corporation, thereby having controlling interest.

Maker: one who signs or executes negotiable instrument.

Malpractice: professional misconduct with negligence.

Management: persons responsible for administrating and carrying out policy of business or other organization.

Management Information System (MIS): established flow of information developed to keep managers informed of what is happening within their organization and to do it within a time frame that permits effective reaction when required. Efficient MIS helps managers make better decisions.

Management Report: statement in unaudited financial statements that says financials are representations of firm's management.

Manifest: shipping document that lists freight's origin, contents, value, destination, carrier, and other pertinent information for use at terminals or custom house.

Manufacturers Representative (Agent): independent, commissioned sales agent who represents several noncompeting manufacturers for sale of their products to related businesses within agreed, exclusive sales territory.

Marginal Account: borderline credit risk that does not have sufficient operating capital and from which payment may be delayed.

Markdown: price reduction of goods below normal selling price.

Market: 1. customer base for a company's goods or services. 2. securities exchange and its associated institutions.

Marketability: ease and rapidity with which product, service, or other asset can be sold or converted to cash.

Marketing: 1. activities necessary to facilitate the sale of goods or services through planned research, manufacturing, promotion, advertising, and distribution. 2. business promotion devoted to getting the maximum purchases of products or services by consumers.

Market Value: price that goods or property would bring in current market of willing buyers and sellers.

Markup: amount or percentage added to cost of goods to arrive at selling price.

Maturity Date: date when financial obligation, note, draft, bond, or instrument becomes due for payment.

Mechanic's Lien: enforceable claim, permitted by law in most states, securing payment to contractors, subcontractors, and suppliers of materials for work performed in constructing or repairing buildings. Lien attaches to real property, plus buildings and improvements situated on land, and remains in effect until workers have been paid in full or, in event of liquidation, gives contractor priority of lien ahead of other creditors.

Medium of Exchange: money or commodity accepted in payment or settlement of debt.

Memorandum (Consignment) Sale: sale of goods for which seller is not paid until retailer has sold merchandise. Seller retains title to such goods until retailer has sold merchandise and payment is made to retailer.

Mercantile Agency: organization that compiles credit and financial information and supplies subscribers or members with reports on applicants for credit; can also perform other functions such as collection of accounts or compiling of statistical trade information.

Merchandise Shortage: goods purchased but not included in shipment.

Merger: combining of two or more businesses to form a single organization.

Mezzanine Financing: 1. in corporate finance, leveraged buyout or restructuring financed through subordinated debt, such as preferred stock or convertible debentures. Transaction is financed by expanding equity, as opposed to debt. 2. second- or third-level financing of companies financed by venture capital. Senior to venture capital but junior to financial institution financing, it adds creditworthiness to firm. Generally used as intermediate-stage financing, preceding a company's initial public offering, it is considered less risky than start-up financing.

MICR: see *Magnetic Ink Character Recognition.*

Middle-of-Month (M.O.M.) Billing Term: billing system in which all shipments are charged on one invoice issued twice a month. For first half of month, credit period runs to the 25th and, for the second half, to the tenth of the following month.

MIS: see *Management Information System.*

Modified Accrual Accounting: basis of accounting in which expenditures are recognized when liability is incurred. Revenues are recognized when measurable and available. Exception is in debt service funds in which expenditures are recorded only when due.

M.O.M.: see *Middle-of-Month Billing Term.*

Money Judgment: court decision that adjudges payment of money rather requiring act to be performed or property transferred.

Monitoring: service available through many credit reporting or interch bureaus enabling subscribers to request that certain listed accounts be matically monitored and reviewed and that updated reports be issued pe cally.

Moratorium: 1. temporary extension or delay of normal period for payme account. 2. Formal postponement during which debtor is permitted to payment of obligations.

Mortgage: debt instrument giving conditional ownership of asset to borr secured by the asset being financed. The instrument by which real esta hypothecated as security for the repayment of a loan. Borrower gives len mortgage in exchange for the right to use property while mortgage is in and agrees to make regular payments of principal and interest. Mortgage is lender's security interest and is recorded in title documents in public records. Lien is removed when debt is paid in full. Mortgage norr involves real estate and is considered long-term debt.

Mortgagee: lender who arranges mortgage financing, collects loan payme and takes security interest in property financed.

Mortgagee Clause: provision in property policy, or added by endorsement, extends protection, in limited manner, to mortgagee; not as broad as len loss payable endorsement.

Mortgagee Waiver: the relinquishment of right(s) contained in a mortgage mortgagee.

Mortgage Verification: request made by mortgagee to applicant's financial i tution for information on applicant's accounts, as part of mortgagee's c approval process.

Mortgagor: borrower in a mortgage contract who mortgages property exchange for a loan.

Multinational Corporation: corporation whose operations are conducted o international basis.

Multiple Signature Credit Approval: describes credit approval process in w credit is approved by two or more persons acting together.

Mutual Account Revision: routine exchange of credit information between tw more credit grantors that have extended credit to subject of inquiry.

N

NACM: see *National Association of Credit Management.*

National Association of Credit Management (NACM): national business org zation of credit and financial professionals that promotes laws for so credit, protects businesses against fraudulent debtors, improves the in change of commercial credit information, develops credit practices, and p vides education and certification programs for its members.

Negligence: failure to use reasonable care that an ordinarily prudent pers would in like circumstances.

Negotiable: anything capable of being transferred by endorsement or delivery.

Negotiable Instrument: any written evidence of indebtedness, transferable endorsement and delivery or by delivery only, that contains uncondition promise to pay specified sum on demand or at some fixed date.

Negotiate: to discuss, bargain, or work out plan of settlement, terms, or comp mise in business transaction.

Net: amount left after necessary deductions have been made from gross amoun

Net Assets: sum of individual's or entity's total assets less total liabilities.

Net Earnings: total sales, less total operating, administrative, and overhe expenses, but before other expenses and income such as interest and d dends.

Net Income: amount of income remaining after deducting all expenses from to revenues.

Net Lease: agreement in which tenant assumes payment of other prope expenses, such as taxes, maintenance, and insurance, in addition to ren payments.

Net Price: actual price paid after all discounts, allowances, and other authoriz deductions have been taken.

Net Profit: income earned by business over specific period of time. Profit fro transaction or sale, after deducting all costs, expenses, and miscellaneo reserves and adjustments from gross receipts.

Net Sales: total sales less returns, allowances, and discounts.

Net Working Capital: current assets less current liabilities; used as measure o company's liquidity and indicates its ability to finance current operations.

Net Worth: total assets less total liabilities; reflects owners' net interest in co pany.

No Account: notation on rejected check when check writer does not have accou at the financial institution on which check is drawn.

No Asset Case: insolvent or bankrupt estate with no assets available for payme of creditors' claims.

No Funds: notation on rejected check when check writer has account but n funds to cover check.

...inal Balance: an account balance of less than $100.

...inal Owner: person whose name appears on title to asset, but who has no interest in it.

...accrual: loan on which a financial institution does not accrue interest; also known as a nonperforming loan.

...orrowing Account: banking relationship in which no extension of credit is involved.

...inancial Information: facts used to evaluate a customer's creditworthiness; focuses on background and history rather than financial measures.

...payment: failure or neglect to pay or discharge debt in accordance with terms of agreement.

...performing Assets: total of earning assets listed as nonaccrual; formerly, earning assets acquired in foreclosure and through in-substance foreclosures.

...performing Loans: amount of loans not meeting original terms of agreement, including renegotiated, restructured, and nonaccrual loans. Loans included in this total vary according to bank policy and regulation.

...profit Corporation: organization specifically classified by the IRS as generally tax exempt and whose primary purpose for existence is to provide services of a charitable, fraternal, religious, social, or civic nature.

...recourse: inability of holder in due course to demand payment from endorser of debt instrument if party(ies) primarily liable fail to make payment.

...-sufficient Funds (NSF): term used when collected demand deposit balances are less than the amount of the check being presented for payment and check is returned to payee's financial institution. See also Overdraft.

Protest (N.P.): instructions given by one financial institution to another not to protest check or note when presented for payment. N.P. is usually stamped on instrument to avoid protest fee.

...th American Industrial Classification System (NAICS): the Standard Industrial Classification (SIC) code is being replaced by the NAICS code. NAICS classifies establishments by their primary type of activity within a six-digit code. NAICS provides structural enhancements over SIC and identifies over 350 new industries. See also *SIC* and *Standard Industrial Classification*.

...tary Public: public officer authorized to administer oaths, attest and certify certain types of documents, and to take acknowledgements of conveyances.

...te: unconditional written promise by borrower to pay certain amount of money to lender on demand or at specified or determinable date. This instrument should meet all requirements of laws pertaining to negotiable instruments.

...tes Payable: liabilities represented by promissory notes, excluding trade debts, that are payable in future.

...tes Receivable: assets represented by promissory notes, excluding amounts due from customers for credit sales, to be collected in future.

...tice of Protest: formal statement that a certain bill of exchange, check, or promissory note was presented for payment or acceptance and that such payment or acceptance was not made. Such notice will also state that because instrument has been dishonored, maker, endorsers, or other parties to document will be held responsible for payment.

...ovation: substitution of old contract for new one between same or different parties; substitution of new debtor or creditor for previous one, by mutual agreement.

...SF: see *Non-sufficient Funds*.

...lla Bona: report made by sheriff when no assets are found within his or her jurisdiction on which to satisfy judgment against debtor.

O

...ligation: 1. law or duty binding parties to an agreement. 2. written promise to pay money or to do a specific thing.

...ligee: person or entity to which payment is due.

...ligor: person or entity required by contract to perform specific act.

...bsolescence: decline in perceived value of asset, frequently because of technological innovations, changes in an industry's processes, or changes required by law.

...CC: see *Office of the Comptroller of the Currency*.

...ffer: proposal to make contract, usually presented by one party to another for acceptance.

...ffering Basis: customer's loan requests considered individually on merits of each proposal.

...ffice of the Comptroller of the Currency (OCC): branch of the Treasury Department that regulates federally chartered banks.

...ffice of Thrift Supervision (OTS): branch of the Treasury Department that regulates state and federally chartered thrifts as well as those institutions in conservatorship.

...ffset: amount allowed to be netted against another.

...n Account: generally describes partial payment made toward settlement of unpaid balance.

...n Account Payment: partial payment not intended as payment in full.

...n Demand: debt instrument that is due and payable on presentation.

Open (Book) Account: credit extended without a formal written contract and represented on books and records of the seller as an unsecured account receivable for which payment is expected within a specified period after purchase.

Open-End Credit: consumer line of credit that may be added to, up to preset credit limit, or paid down at any time. Customer has option of paying off outstanding balance, without penalty, or making several installment payments. Contrasts with Closed-End Credit. Also called revolving credit or charge account credit.

Open Terms: selling on credit terms as opposed to having customer pay cash.

Operating Performance Ratios: financial measures designed to assist in evaluation of management performance.

Operating Statement: report of an individual's or entity's income and expenses for a specified period of time. See also Income Statement.

Operational Risk: risk concerning computer network failure due to system overload or other disruptions; also includes potential losses from fraud, malicious damage to data, and error.

Oral Contract: agreement that may or may not be written in whole or in part or signed but is legally enforceable.

Order: informal bill of exchange or letter or request identifying person to be paid.

Order for Relief: order issued by bankruptcy court judge upon filing of petition by debtor or filing of petition by creditors.

Order to Order: agreement for payment to be made for prior shipment before next delivery will be made.

OREO: see *Other Real Estate Owned*.

Other Real Estate Owned: real property usually taken as collateral and subsequently acquired through foreclosure, or by obtaining a deed in lieu of foreclosure, in satisfaction of the debts previously contracted. Real property formerly used as banking premises, or real property sold in a "covered transaction" as defined by banking regulations.

OTS: see *Office of Thrift Supervision*.

Outlet Store: retail operation where manufacturers' production overruns, discontinued merchandise, or irregular goods are sold at discount.

Out-of-Court Settlement: 1. settlement made by distressed debtor through direct negotiations with creditors or through creditors' committee; acceptance of such settlement is not obligatory to nonconsenting creditors. 2. agreement reached between opposing parties to settle pending lawsuit before matter has been decided by court.

Out-of-Pocket Expense: business expenses for which individual pays.

Out-of-Trust: an event occurring in floor plan financing where a borrower sells inventory securing the financial institution's loan and fails to promptly remit the proceeds to the financial institution in accordance with the loan agreement.

Outstanding: 1. amount of credit facility that is being used versus total amount made available. 2. unpaid or uncollected account.

Overdraft: negative account balance created when a check is paid when collected demand deposit balances are less than amount of check being presented for payment. See also Non-sufficient Funds.

Overdue: debt obligation on which payments are past due.

Overhead: selling and administrative business costs as contrasted with costs of goods sold.

Oversold: condition in which manufacturer or wholesaler finds itself after taking more orders than it can deliver within an agreed period of time.

Owed: debt that is due and payable.

Own: to have legal title to property.

Owner: person or entity that owns or has title to property.

Owner's Equity: mathematical difference between total assets and total liabilities that represents shareholders' equity or an individual's net worth.

Ownership: exclusive rights that one has to property, to exclusion of all others; having complete title to property.

Owner's Risk: term used in transportation contracts to exempt carrier from responsibility for loss or damage to goods.

P

Packing List: detailed listing of information on shipment's contents (enclosed for inspection with package).

Paid Direct: payment made by debtor directly to original creditor instead of to collection agency or attorney handling account for collection.

Paper Profit: unrealized income or gain on asset.

Paralegal: trained aide to attorney who handles various legal tasks.

Parent Company: an entity that holds controlling majority interest in subsidiaries.

Partial Payment: payment not in full for amount owed.

Participation: purchase or sale of a loan or credit facility among two or more financial institutions in which the acquiring institution(s) has no formal or direct role in establishing the terms and conditions binding the borrower. Participants do not participate in the document negotiation between the originating financial institution and the borrower.

Partnership: business arrangement in which two or more persons agree to engage, upon terms of mutual participation, in profits and losses.

Party: person concerned or taking part in a transaction or proceeding.

Past Due: payment or account that remains outstanding and unpaid after its agreed-upon payment or maturity date.

Pay: to satisfy, or make partial payments on, a debt obligation.

Payable: obligation that is due now or in future.

Payables: liabilities owed to trade creditors for purchase of supplies. Also called accounts payable.

Payee: person or entity named on a negotiable instrument as the one to whom the obligation is due.

Payer: party responsible for making payment as shown on check, note, or other type of negotiable instrument; also called maker or writer.

Payment: discharge, in whole or in part, of debt or performance of agreement.

Payment for Honor: payment of past-due obligation by someone else to save credit or reputation of person responsible for payment.

Payoff: receipt of payment in full on an obligation.

Penalty: 1. legal fine, forfeiture, or payment imposed for defaulting or violating terms of contract. 2. interest charge imposed for late payments that is permissible by law and imposed with customer's prior agreement or knowledge of seller's terms of sale.

Percentage Lease: lease of real property in which rental payments are based on percentage of retailer's sales.

Percentage of Completion: method of accounting commonly used by contractors and developers in which costs are related to percentage of job completion.

Perfection: with respect to security interests in personal property under Article 9 of the UCC, the action required to give the secured party rights in the collateral as against third parties with competing claims. In general, a security interest is not perfected until a properly executed financing statement has been recorded or the secured party is in the possession of the collateral, whichever applies as to that specific collateral type.

Performance: fulfillment of promise or agreement according to terms of contract or obligation.

Performance Bond: guaranty to project owner that the contractor will perform the work called for by the contract in accordance with the plans and specifications. Customarily issued by bonding and insurance companies, although financial institution letters of credit may be used.

Perjury: willfully and knowingly giving false testimony under oath.

Person: individual (natural person) or incorporated enterprise (artificial person) having certain legal rights and responsibilities.

Personal Check: check drawn by individual on his or her own bank account.

Personality: legal term for personal property or possessions that are not real estate.

Personally Liable: individual's responsibility for payment of obligation, generally used to refer to owner's or guarantor's responsibility.

Personal Property: movable or chattel property of any kind.

Petition: written application, made in contradiction to motion. Also used in some states in place of complaint.

Petition in Bankruptcy: document filed in court to declare bankruptcy. Petition can be either voluntary (filed by debtor) or involuntary (filed by creditors), depending on bankruptcy chapter rules.

Petty Cash: cash on hand or in designated bank account that is available for small, miscellaneous purchases.

Physical Inventory: inventory verification obtained by visual observation of items and itemization of quantities of goods on hand.

Piercing the Corporate Veil: legal action taken by creditor, when fraud or unjust enrichment may be involved, to hold principals of corporation (or other entities) liable for debts of corporation.

Plaintiff: person or entity that initiates legal action against another.

Plan of Arrangement: procedure in bankruptcy under Chapter 11 for debtor to restructure debts or rehabilitate by arriving at arrangement with creditors. See also Bankruptcy, Chapter 11 Cases.

Pledge: promise of personal property as security for performance of act, payment of debt, or satisfaction of obligation.

Points: 1. percentage fee charged to obtain a mortgage loan. 2. in shares of stock, one point equals $1.00.

Policy: 1. written statement by management that explains an organization's philosophy and approach to doing business. 2. written contract of insurance between insured and the insurance company.

Pooling Accounts: arrangement by a debtor listing all his or her debts with a debt management or pro-rating service with the understanding that the service will receive, as its fee, a portion of debtor's payments to his or her creditors and proportionately distribute the balance of payments to each creditor on a scheduled basis. Activities of such services may be covered by individual state statutes.

Postdated Check: check written for payment, effective at future date.

Power of Attorney: written document that authorizes one person to act as another's agent.

Preference: 1. right of a creditor to be paid before other creditors by virtue of having lien or collateral. 2. improperly paying or securing of one or [more] creditors, in whole or part, by an insolvent debtor to the exclusion of [other] creditors.

Preference Period: in bankruptcy, the 90-day period immediately prece[ding] debtor entering into bankruptcy. If a creditor files new or additional [claims] against a debtor during this time, such claims may be disallowed by b[ank]ruptcy court.

Preferred Creditor: creditor whose account takes legal preference for pay[ment] over claims of others.

Prepaid Expenses: payment for goods or services not yet received.

Prepayment: payment of loan or debt before it actually becomes due.

Prime Contractor: contractor who enters into contract with the owner of the [pro]ject for completion of all or portion of the project and takes full responsi[bility] for its completion. See also General Contractor.

Prime Rate: an index or base rate published or publicly announced by a fina[ncial] institution from time to time as the rate it is generally willing to give its m[ost] creditworthy customers.

Principal: 1. amount of money loaned or borrowed. 2. key decision make[r in] management of entity.

Priority: legal preferences that secured creditors have over general credito[rs in] bankruptcy.

Priority Lien: lien recorded before other secured claims and payable ahea[d of] other liens if liquidation of pledged collateral occurs. First mortgage has pr[ior]ity over second and third mortgages, known as junior liens. Secured cred[itor] holding perfected security interest has priority over liens filed afterward.

Private Enterprise: business established to take economic risks for purpose [of] making profit.

Privilege: right that nature of debt gives to one debt holder over others.

Proceeds: actual amount of money given to or received from creditor after [all] deductions are made.

Profit: 1. amount of net income made by an entity in course of doing business[. 2.] increase in value of an asset over its depreciated book value at the time [of] sale.

Profit and Loss Statement (P & L): financial report of an individual's or enti[ty's] revenue and expenses for a given period of time. See also Income Statem[ent] and Operating Statement.

Pro Forma: projected financial statements.

Progress Payments: partial payments made on a long-term contract as it p[ro]gresses. Required when a manufacturer or contractor cannot afford, or d[oes] not wish, to finance a project.

Projection: borrower's estimate of future performance over designated ti[me] period.

Promissory Note: written promise to make unconditional payment of specif[ic] amount on designated date, signed by maker.

Proof of Claim: creditor's formal document filed with court against estate [of] debtor if creditor is owed funds.

Proof of Loss: sworn statement filed by insured when making claim.

Property: something of value that is legally owned and in which person has exc[lu]sive and unrestricted right or interest.

Property Insurance: coverage that applies to loss caused by physical damage [to] property (buildings, contents, earnings, etc.) owned by insured.

Proposal: oral or written offer that, if accepted, constitutes a contract.

Proprietorship: single and exclusive ownership of a business by one person.

Pro Rata: share calculated in proportion to total amount.

Pro Rata Distribution: payment proportionate to uniform percentage of oblig[a]tions to all creditors.

Protest: formal, written, notarized notice stating credit instrument has not be[en] honored and that makers or endorsers will be held responsible for payment.

Prox.: see Proximo.

Proximo (Prox.): sales term used in invoices to mean next month after month [of] invoice. This term is sometimes used instead of EOM terms.

Proxy: written statement or power of attorney, authorizing an individual to act [or] speak for another.

Public Credit: debt incurred by government, federal and local, for a use that me[ets] the needs of its citizens.

Purchase Money Lien: manufacturer's legal right to goods and products until th[e] buyer makes payment. Under the Uniform Commercial Code, manufacturer['s] rights can take priority over lender's lien rights if both claim interest in sam[e] inventory. Lender may receive such priority if funds were provided to pu[r]chase asset, provided liens are filed within 20 days of borrower taking pos[s]ession of collateral and noticing requirements have been met.

Purchase Money Mortgage: mortgage given by buyer to seller in lieu of cash, a[s] partial payment on property.

Purchasing Power: value of money and its ability to buy goods and services in [a] given period.

Q

Qualified Acceptance: agreement to terms of contract only if certain conditions are meet. This constitutes counteroffer and rejection of original offer.

Qualified Endorsement: transfer of debt instrument to endorsee without recourse or liability to endorser.

Qualified Financial Statement: audit report issued by independent accountants that indicates restrictions on scope of audit performed, uncertainties, or disagreements with management.

Qualified Prospect: potential customer whose background and credit have been checked and approved.

Quantity Discount: price reduction extended to purchaser of a large volume of goods.

Quarterly Accounts Receivable Survey: index, compiled by Credit Research Foundation in affiliation with the National Association of Credit Management and published quarterly, that shows average days' sales outstanding for manufacturers and wholesalers.

Quick Assets: current assets that can be readily converted into cash (generally, accounts receivable).

Quick Assets Ratio: cash and cash equivalents plus trade receivables (net) divided by total current liabilities; used as measure of liquidity.

Quid Pro Quo: 1. giving of one valuable thing for another. 2. mutual consideration between parties to contract.

Quitclaim: to release or relinquish claim or title.

R

Rack Jobber: wholesale distributor who sells housewares and other convenience-type merchandise through retail stores and assumes responsibility for stocking and maintaining store's inventory.

Rate of Exchange: amount of one country's currency that can be bought with another country's currency at a particular point in time.

Rate of Interest: cost of borrowing money, usually expressed as annual percentage charge.

Rating: 1. assessment of borrower's financial strength and creditworthiness. 2. symbol used to denote borrower's creditworthiness.

Ratios: mathematical relationship between two or more things, used as indication of a company's financial strength relative to other companies of comparable size or in same industry.

Real Property: land and anything erected or growing on it or affixed to it.

Receivables: money due or collectible for goods sold, services performed, or money loaned. Also called accounts receivable.

Receivables Turnover: measurement of how effective a company is in collecting on its trade receivables.

Receiver: person appointed by the court to receive, take charge, and hold in trust a property in litigation or bankruptcy until a legal decision is made as to its disposition.

Receivership: 1. court action whereby money or property is placed under control, and administration of receiver is to be preserved for benefit of persons or creditors ultimately entitled to it. 2. procedure used to help a distressed debtor or to resolve a dispute.

Reclamation: 1. legal action by titleholder to recover property from another's possession. 2. process used to restore land to usable state.

Record: written account of act, transaction, or instrument drawn by proper legal authority that remains as permanent evidence.

Recourse: right of holder in due course to demand payment from anyone who endorsed instrument if original signer fails to pay.

Recovery: amount finally collected; amount of judgment.

Reference Check: contacting and interviewing business or professional associates of credit applicant to gain information about his or her creditworthiness.

References: names of trade suppliers or creditors provided by a customer to be used as a source of information about that customer.

Refer to Maker: term stamped by financial institution on a check to indicate its rejection.

Refinance: to reorganize existing debts by obtaining new debt that incorporates or pays off existing debts.

Register: book of factual public information, kept by a public official.

Regulation 9: regulation issued by the Comptroller of Currency allowing national banks to operate trust departments and act as fiduciaries. Under Regulation 9, a national bank is permitted to act as trustee, administrator, and registrar of stocks and bonds and engage in related activities, such as management of a collective investment fund, as long as these activities do not violate state legislation.

Regulation A: Federal Reserve Board regulation governing advances by Federal Reserve Banks to depository institutions at a Federal Reserve discount window. Credit advances are available to any bank or savings institution maintaining transaction accounts or non-personal time deposits. The Fed has two different programs for handling discount window borrowings:

- adjustment credit to meet temporary needs for funds when other sources are not available.
- extended credit, designed to assist financial institutions with longer-term needs for funds. This includes seasonal credit privileges extended to smaller financial institutions that do not have ready access to money market funds. Federal Reserve Banks may also extend emergency credit to financial institutions other than depository institutions in which failure to obtain credit would affect the economy adversely.

Regulation B: Federal Reserve regulation prohibiting discrimination against consumer credit applicants and establishing guidelines for collecting and evaluating credit information. Regulation B prohibits creditors from discriminating on the basis of age, sex, race, color, religion, national origin, marital status, or receipt of public assistance. Regulation B also requires creditors to give written notification of rejection, statement of applicant's rights under Equal Credit Opportunity Act of 1974, and statement listing reasons for rejection, or applicant has right to request reasons. If applicant is denied credit because of adverse information in credit bureau report, applicant is entitled to receive copy of bureau report at no cost. Creditors who furnish credit information when reporting information on married borrowers must report information in name of each spouse.

Regulation C: Federal Reserve regulation implementing Home Mortgage Disclosure Act of 1975, requiring depository institutions to make annual disclosure of location of certain residential loans to determine whether depository institutions are meeting credit needs of their local communities. Specifically exempted are institutions with assets of $10 million or less. Regulation C requires lenders of mortgages that are insured or guaranteed by a federal agency to disclose number and total dollar amount of mortgage loans originated or purchased in recent calendar year, itemized by census tract where property is located.

Regulation D: Federal Reserve regulation that sets uniform reserve requirements for depository financial institutions holding transaction accounts or non-personal time deposits. Reserves are maintained in form of vault cash or non-interest-bearing balance at a Federal Reserve Bank or at a correspondent bank.

Regulation E: Federal Reserve regulation that sets rules, liabilities, and procedures for electronic funds transfers (EFT) and establishes consumer protections using EFT systems. This regulation prescribes rules for solicitation and issuance of EFT debit cards, governs consumer liability for unauthorized transfers, and requires financial institutions to disclose annually terms and conditions of EFT services.

Regulation F: Federal Reserve regulation requiring state-chartered banks with 500 or more stockholders and at least $1 million in assets to file financial statements with the Board of Governors of the Federal Reserve System. In general, these state-chartered member banks must file registration statements, periodic financial statements, proxy statements, and various other disclosures of interest to investors. These regulations are substantially similar to those issued by Securities and Exchange Commission.

Regulation G: Federal Reserve regulation governing credit secured by margin securities extended or arranged by parties other than banks or broker/dealers. It requires lenders to register credit extensions of $200,000, secured by margin stock, or $500,000 in total credit, within 30 days after end of quarter.

Regulation H: Federal Reserve regulation defining membership requirements for state-chartered banks that become members of the Federal Reserve System. The regulation sets forth procedures as well as privileges and requirements for membership. The regulation also requires state-chartered banks acting as securities transfer agents to register with board.

Regulation I: Federal Reserve regulation requiring each member bank joining the Federal Reserve System to purchase stock in its Federal Reserve Bank equal to 6% of its capital and surplus. Federal Reserve Bank stock, which pays interest semiannually, is nontransferable and cannot be used as collateral. When bank increases or decreases its capital base, it must adjust its ownership of Federal Reserve stock accordingly.

Regulation J: Federal Reserve regulation providing legal framework for collection of checks and other cash items and net settlement of balances through Federal Reserve System. It specifies terms and conditions under which Federal Reserve Banks will receive checks for collection from depository institutions, presentment to paying banks, and return of unpaid items. It is supplemented by operating circulars issued by Federal Reserve Banks.

Regulation K: Federal Reserve regulation governing international banking operations by bank holding companies and foreign banks in the U.S. The regulation permits Edge Act corporations to engage in range of international banking and financial activities. It also permits U.S. banks to own up to 100% of non-financial companies located outside the U.S. Regulation K also imposes reserve requirements on Edge Act corporations, as specified in Regulation D, and limits interstate activities of foreign banks in the U.S.

Regulation L: Federal Reserve regulation prohibiting interlocking director arrangements in member banks or bank holding companies. Management official of state member bank or bank holding company may not act simulta-

neously as management official of another depository institution if both are not affiliated, are very large banks, or are located in same local area. Regulation L provides 10-year grandfather period for certain interlocks and allows some on exception basis, such as organizations owned by women or minority groups, newly chartered organizations, and in situations in which implementing regulation would endanger safety and soundness.

Regulation M: Federal Reserve regulation implementing consumer leasing provisions of Truth in Lending Act of 1968. It covers leases on personal property for more than four months for family, personal, or household use. It requires leasing companies to disclose in writing the cost of lease, including security deposit and monthly payments, taxes, and other payments, and in case of an open-end lease, whether a balloon payment may be applied. It also requires written disclosure of terms of lease, including insurance, guaranties, responsibility for servicing property, and whether lessor has an option to buy property at lease termination.

Regulation N: Federal Reserve regulation governing transactions among Federal Reserve Banks and transactions involving Federal Reserve Banks and foreign banks and governments. This regulation gives the board responsibility for approving in advance negotiations or agreements by Federal Reserve Banks and foreign banks, bankers, and governments. The Federal Reserve Bank may, under direction of the Federal Open Market Committee, undertake negotiations, agreements, or facilitate open market transactions. Reserve Banks must report quarterly to the Board of Governors on accounts they maintain with foreign banks.

Regulation O: Federal Reserve regulation limiting amount of credit member banks may extend to their own executive officers. Regulation O also implements reporting requirements of Financial Institutions Regulatory and Interest Rate Control Act of 1978 and Garn-St. Germain Depository Institutions Act of 1982.

Regulation P: Federal Reserve regulation that sets minimum standards for security devices, such as bank vaults and currency handling equipment, including automated teller machines. Member bank must appoint security officer to develop and administer program to deter thefts and file the annual compliance statement with its Federal Reserve Bank.

Regulation Q: Federal Reserve regulation requiring depository institutions to state clearly terms for depositing and renewing time deposits and certificates of deposit and also any penalties for early withdrawal of savings accounts.

Regulation R: Federal Reserve regulation prohibiting individuals who are engaged in securities underwriting, sale, and distribution from serving as directors, officers, or employees of member banks. Regulation R specifically exempts those involved in government securities trading and general obligations of states and municipalities.

Regulation S: Federal Reserve regulation implementing section of Right to Financial Privacy Act of 1978 requiring government authorities to pay reasonable fees to financial institutions for financial records of individuals and small partnerships available to federal agencies in connection with government loan programs or Internal Revenue Service summons.

Regulation T: Federal Reserve regulation governing credit extensions by securities brokers and dealers, including all members of national securities exchanges. Brokers/dealers may not extend credit to their customers unless such loans are secured by margin securities—securities listed and traded on national securities exchange, mutual funds, and over-the-counter stock designated by Securities and Exchange Commission as eligible for trading in national market system. Generally, brokers/dealers may not extend credit on margin securities in excess of percentage of current market value permitted by board.

Regulation U: Federal Reserve regulation governing extensions of credit by banks for purchasing and carrying margin securities. Whenever lender makes loan secured by margin securities, bank must have customer execute purpose statement regardless of use of loan.

Regulation V: Federal Reserve regulation dealing with financing of contractors, subcontractors, and others involved in national defense work. The regulation spells out the authority granted to Federal Reserve Banks under the Defense Production Act of 1950 to assist federal departments and agencies in making and administering loan guaranties to defense-related contractors and sets maximum interest rates, guaranty fees, and commitment fees.

Regulation X: Federal Reserve regulation extending provisions of other securities-related regulations—Regulations G, T, and U—to foreign persons or organizations who obtain credit outside U.S. for purchase of U.S. Treasury securities.

Regulation Y: Federal Reserve regulation governing banking and nonbanking activities of bank holding companies and divestiture of impermissible nonbank activities. Regulation Y spells out procedures for forming bank holding company and procedures to be followed by bank holding companies acquiring voting shares in bank or nonbank companies. Regulation Y also lists those nonbank activities that are deemed closely related to banking and therefore permissible for bank holding companies.

Regulation Z: Federal Reserve regulation implementing consumer credit provisions in the Truth in Lending Act of 1968. Major areas of regulation require lenders to:
- give borrowers written disclosure on essential credit terms, including cost of credit expressed as finance charge and annual percentage rate.
- respond to consumer complaints of billing errors on certain credit accounts within specified period.
- identify credit transactions on periodic statements of open-end credit accounts.
- provide certain rights regarding credit cards.
- inform customers of right of rescission in certain mortgage-related loans within specified period.
- comply with special requirements when advertising credit.

Regulation AA: Federal Reserve regulation establishing procedures for handling consumer complaints about alleged unfair or deceptive practices by a state member bank.

Regulation BB: Federal Reserve regulation implementing Community Reinvestment Act of 1977 (CRA). Banks are required to make available to public statement indicating communities served, type of credit the lender is prepared to extend, and public comments to its CRA statement.

Regulation CC: Federal Reserve regulation implementing Expedited Funds Availability Act of 1987, setting endorsement standards on checks collected by depository financial institutions. Endorsement standard is designed to facilitate identification of endorsing bank and prompt return of unpaid checks. The regulation specifies funds availability schedules that banks must comply with and procedures for returning dishonored checks.

Release: to discharge debt or give up claim against party from whom it is due to party to whom it is due.

Remedy: legal means by which right is enforced or violation of right is prevented or compensated.

Rent: periodic payments made by tenant to owner in return for leasing land, building space, or equipment.

Reorganization: 1. voluntary or court-ordered change in capital structure of corporation in which all assets of an old corporation are transferred to a new formed corporation. 2. restructuring of business entity, whether in or out of bankruptcy.

Replevin: legal action taken to recover possession of property unlawfully taken.

Repossess: action taken by creditor in which he or she takes possession of goods purchased under credit agreement or pledged as collateral if debtor defaults on terms of contract.

Rescind: to void contract from its inception. Result is that parties are restored to relative positions before contract was made.

Rescission: agreement by parties to contract that effects cancellation of contract.

Reserve: in accounting, funds set aside for specific purpose.

Reserve for Bad Debts: valuation account established for accounts receivable that may prove uncollectible.

Residence: place where person legally lives part or full time.

Residual Value: the estimated recoverable amount of a depreciable asset as of the time of its removal from service.

Resolution Trust Corporation (RTC): federal agency established in 1989 to oversee the savings and loan bailout.

Restraint of Trade: any action, by agreement or by combination, that tends to eliminate competition, artificially sets up prices, or results in monopoly.

Restrictive Endorsement: endorsement on negotiable instrument that limits any further negotiability, for example, "for deposit only" written on back of check.

Restructured Loan: loan on which a bank, for economic or legal reasons related to debtor's financial difficulties, grants concession to debtor that would not be considered otherwise.

Retailer: company that sells its product directly to end-user.

Retained Earnings: cumulative earnings and losses of company that remain undistributed to shareholders.

Retentions: amounts withheld by customer from total billings until contractor has satisfactorily completed project.

Retroactive: 1. effective as of past date. 2. having reference to prior time.

Return: rate of profit or earnings on sales or investment.

Return Items/Returned Checks: checks, drafts, or notes returned unpaid to originating bank by drawee bank so that originator can correct any errors or irregularities and may present items for collection again.

Revenue: 1. income from sales, interest, or dividends. 2. income from investment or wages.

Reviewed Financial Statements: business financial statements that are reviewed by independent accountants through inquiries of management and performance of analytical procedures on financials to provide limited assurance that no material modifications are necessary for statements to conform to generally accepted accounting principles. Independent accountants do not express opinion on review statements.

olving Charge: credit type that allows borrower to become indebted up to an approved credit limit, with no fixed maturity date. Finance costs are assessed monthly on unpaid balance, and periodic payments are required.

olving Credit: commitment under which funds can be borrowed, repaid, and re-borrowed during life of credit. Such credits have stated maturity date at which time borrower may have option of converting outstanding balance into term loan. See also *Evergreen Revolving Credit*.

er: any schedule or amendment attached to a contract or document that becomes part of it.

ht of Rescission: consumer's right as prescribed by Truth in Lending Act of 1968 to rescind certain credit and mortgage contracts within three days without penalty.

ht of Setoff: right of financial institution to apply borrower's funds on deposit to debt owed to the financial institution in event that payment on the debt is not made as agreed.

k-Based Capital: level of capital that bank is required to maintain; level is determined by relating capital to risk by type of asset.

IA: see *Risk Management Association*.

IA General Figure Ranges: dollar amount ranges established by RMA to ensure accuracy and consistency when exchanging credit information. There are four ranges: low, 1-1.9; moderate, 2-3.9; medium, 4-6.9; and high, 7-9.9. Ranges can be applied to any figure category. Sample figure categories are: nominal = under $100; 3 figures = from $100 to $999; 4 figures = from $1,000 to $9,999; 5 figures = from $10,000 to $99,999; and 6 figures = from $100,000 to $999,999. Information is reported, using both range description and figure category; for example, "average balances are in medium 4-figure range."

k Management Association (RMA): association of lending, credit, and risk management professionals. Originally, RMA was founded to facilitate the exchange of credit information. Today, RMA works continuously to improve practices of the financial services industry and to provide members with networking opportunities, training, research publications, and seminars.

binson-Patman Act: federal legislation prohibiting firms engaged in interstate commerce from charging different buyers different prices for the same goods unless there is difference in costs or the price does not restrict competition.

O.G. Dating: payment term that uses date customer is in receipt of goods as effective sale date.

yalty: compensation made to another for use of his or her work.

TC: see *Resolution Trust Corporation*.

le of 72: method commonly used to approximate time required for sum of money to double at given rate of interest. Rule of 72 is computed by dividing interest rate by 72.

le of 78s: mathematical formula used in computing interest rebated when borrower pays off loan before maturity. Rule of 78s is applied mostly to consumer loans in which finance charges were computed using add-on interest or discounted interest method of interest calculation. Also called sum of digits method.

S

ale: agreement or contract that transfers title of goods or property from one person or entity to another for consideration.

ale and Lease Back: arrangement whereby company sells goods with intent to lease those same goods from buyer.

ale on Approval: purchase of goods conditioned on buyer approval of goods or retention of them beyond reasonable time.

alvage Value: estimated worth of a depreciated asset at the end of its useful life.

atisfaction: paying debt in full.

atisfaction of Judgment: legal evidence that recorded judgment has been paid or settled and entered in court records.

atisfaction Piece: legal evidence that debt has been paid in full or settled and that liens on collateral have been released.

BA: see *Small Business Administration*.

chedule: listing by account name or number of total sales, current sales, monies owing or paid, chargebacks, or credits. Also called aging schedule or trial balance.

cheduled Liability: 1. in property insurance, listing of property—items or locations—covered. 2. in dishonesty insurance (fidelity bonding), listing of persons or positions covered.

cheduled Payment: partial payments made at dates specified in credit agreement.

chedules: in bankruptcy, lists showing debtor's property—location, quantity, and money value; names and addresses of creditors and their class; or names and addresses of stockholders of each class.

crap Value: worth of asset that is going to be destroyed or used for its components.

easonal Loans: loans used to finance cyclical buildup of current (working capital) assets until those assets can be converted to cash.

Second Lien: lien that can be honored only after first lien is satisfied.

Second Mortgage: mortgage secured by equity in property but one that cannot enforce payment until claims of first mortgage are satisfied.

Secret Partner: partner in business whose interest in partnership is not publicly known.

Secured Creditor: lender or other person whose claim is supported by taking collateral.

Secured Loan: loan supported by borrower's pledge of an asset such as marketable securities, accounts receivable, inventories, real estate, equipment, etc.

Secured Note: note that provides, upon default, certain pledged or mortgaged property that may be applied or sold in payment of debt.

Secured Party: 1. lender or other person to whom or in whose favor security interest has been given. Includes person to whom accounts or chattel paper have been sold. 2. trustee or agent representing holders of obligations issued under indenture of trust, equipment trust agreement, or the like.

Securities: 1. documents that evidence debt or property pledged in fulfillment of obligation. 2. evidence of indebtedness or right to participate in earnings and distribution of corporate, trust, and other property.

Security: guaranty or assets pledged that can be applied to loan or obligation.

Security Agreement: formally executed document that gives lender rights to property pledged by borrower in support of debt.

Security Interest: right that lender or lienholder obtains to debtor's goods as evidenced by security agreement.

Seller's Market: economic condition in which demand is greater than supply, and that typically causes prices to increase.

Sequestered Account: account that has been attached by court order with disbursements subject to court approval.

Service Business: firm that performs functions for its customers rather than sells goods.

Setoff: 1. defendant's counterdemand against plaintiff. 2. right of parties to contract to reduce debt owed to one party by netting it against amount owed by other. See also *Right of Setoff*.

Settle: 1. to mutually reach agreement for adjustment or liquidation of debt. 2. to negotiate payment of obligation or lawsuit for less than amount claimed.

Settlement: 1. adjustment or liquidation of accounts. 2. full and final payment of debt. See also *Out-of-Court Settlement*.

Shared National Credit (SNC): any loan originally $20 million or more that is shared at its inception by two or more financial institutions under a formal intercreditor or participation agreement or sold in part to one or more financial institutions with purchasing financial institution assuming its pro rata share of credit risk.

Shareholder: person or entity that legally owns stock in a corporation.

Sheriff's Sale: court-ordered sale of property to satisfy judgment, mortgage, lien, or other outstanding debt against debtor.

Sherman Antitrust Act: federal legislation aimed at prevention of business monopoly; act declares illegal every contract, combination, or conspiracy in restraint of normal trade.

Short-Term Liabilities: current debts that are due within one year.

Short-Term Loan: current debt obligation that matures within one year, evidenced by promissory note that spells out terms of agreement.

SIC: see *Standard Industrial Classification*.

Sight Draft: draft payable on demand when presented to drawee. See also *Draft, Letter of Credit*, and *Time Draft*.

Signal Action: notices that provide subscriber with list of accounts in which subscriber has interest and on which delinquent payments have been reported.

Signature Loan: unsecured loan backed only by borrower's signature on promissory note. No collateral is taken by lender. This loan is generally offered to individuals with good credit standing. Also called good faith loan or character loan.

Signature Verification: examination of signature on negotiable instrument to determine whether handwriting is genuine and whether person signing check is authorized to use account.

Simple Interest: interest calculated on outstanding principal amount of debt or investment only.

Single Proprietorship: ownership of company by one person.

Skip Tracing: process used to obtain information to locate debtor's whereabouts in order to collect payment on debts. Sources used include other creditors, friends, relatives, neighbors, directories, credit bureaus, court records, and other informants or references.

Slander: oral defamation of another's reputation.

Small Business Administration (SBA): federal agency whose function is to advise and assist small businesses; provides loan guaranties for small businesses, minorities, and veterans plus financial assistance to small businesses that have suffered catastrophes.

SNC: see *Shared National Credit*.

Soft Goods: nondurable consumer goods such as clothing and linen, having a short-term useful life.

Soldier's and Sailor's Relief Act: federal act, also passed by various states, under which right to legally enforce an obligation against a person is suspended during the period that person is in military service or for period thereafter.

Sole Owner: one with title to proprietorship.

Solvency: ability to pay one's debts in usual and ordinary course of business as they mature.

Special Material: made-to-order material or work done to customer's specifications that has no value to seller if order is canceled.

Special Mention Assets: as it relates to risk assessment of bank assets, assets that deserve management's close attention. If left uncorrected, these potential weaknesses may result in deterioration of repayment prospects for asset or in institution's credit position at some future date. Special mention assets are not adversely classified and do not expose institution to sufficient risk to warrant adverse classification.

Specific Coverage: property coverage on designated property or item. Contrasts with Blanket Coverage.

Specific Performance: court order directing party guilty of breach of contract to undertake complete performance of contractual obligation in instances in which damages would inadequately compensate injured party.

Speculation: investment made with hope of achieving large financial gain.

Speculator: one who makes risky investments for quick financial gain rather than long-term investment.

Stale Check: negotiable draft that has been held too long to be honored for payment; time varies from state to state.

Standard Industrial Classification (SIC): statistical classification standard underlying all establishment-based federal economic statistics classified by industry. SIC is used to promote comparability of establishment data describing various facets of the U.S. economy. Classification covers entire field of economic activities and defines industries in accordance with composition and structure of economy. It is revised periodically to reflect economy's changing industrial organization. See also *North American Industrial Classification System* and *NAICS.*

Standby Letter of Credit: type of letter of credit issued by bank that may be drawn on by payee only if party that makes letter of credit (drawer) defaults or does not perform according to terms of specific contract or agreement. See also Letter of Credit.

Statement: 1. itemized summary and accounting of charges, payments, and balance outstanding at close of billing period. 2. financial report.

Statement of Cash Flows: financial statement that shows cash receipts and disbursements for given period.

Statement of Changes in Owner's Equity: financial statement that reconciles changes in capital accounts (capital stock, paid in surplus, and retained earnings).

Statute: written law.

Statute of Frauds: law prohibiting filing of actions or suits against certain types of contracts unless the contracts are in writing.

Statute of Limitations: law that sets time frame for bringing action against another. Time frame varies according to nature of claim and jurisdiction.

Stay: act of arresting judicial proceeding by court order.

Stipulation: agreement between opposing attorneys in lawsuit, usually required to be in writing.

Stock: 1. merchandise or inventory on hand and available for sale. 2. certificate that indicates number of shares of ownership in corporation.

Stock Power: document executed in form of power of attorney by which owner of stock authorizes another party to sell or transfer stock.

Stop Payment Order: instructions given by depositor to a financial institution to dishonor, or not make payment on, a certain check.

Subchapter S: business concern chartered as corporation that is taxed as partnership. An S corporation has 35 or fewer shareholders and can use cash basis of accounting. Corporate gains (or losses) from operations are taxed to shareholders as individuals.

Subcontract: contract between prime contractor and another contractor or supplier to perform specified work or to supply specified materials in accordance with plans and specifications for project.

Subject: party on which credit information is requested.

Sublimit: specified, partial amount of credit facility that is designated for special use.

Subordination: 1. signed agreement acknowledging that one's claim or interest is inferior to another's. 2. act of agreeing to take secondary position.

Subpoena: process to demand person to appear in court and give testimony.

Subrogation: substitution of one creditor for another so that substituted creditor succeeds to rights, remedies, or proceeds of claim.

Subsidiary: business entity owned or controlled by another organization.

Substandard Assets: as it relates to risk assessment of bank assets, assets that are inadequately protected by current sound worth and paying capacity of obligor or of collateral pledged, if any. Assets so classified must have well-defined weakness or weaknesses that jeopardize liquidation of debt. They are characterized by distinct possibility that bank will sustain some loss if deficiencies are not corrected.

Summons: formal notice served on defendant stating that action has been instituted against him or her and requiring defendant to appear in court to answer it.

Supplementary Proceedings: statutory action requiring judgment debtor to appear in court to discover property against which action can be taken by creditor to enforce collection of judgment.

Supplier: business that sells goods, materials, or services to customers. Also called vendor.

Surety: one who agrees to be primarily liable with another and to fulfill another's obligations under terms of agreement.

Surety Bond: guaranty that payment or performance of some specific act will be completed under penalty or forfeiture of bond usually issued by a bonding company.

Suretyship: undertaking by person or entity to pay obligation of obligee in favor of principal when obligee defaults; such undertaking by individual is known as personal suretyship and by insurance company as corporate suretyship.

Suspense File: group of accounts, records, or other items held temporarily until final disposition is determined.

Swap: A financial derivative contract between two parties to exchange fixed-rate interest payments for floating-rate interest payments, or floating-rate interest payments on different bases (e.g., prime rate versus LIBOR), calculated on specific floating indices by reference to a notional principal amount for a specified term.

Sweep Account: type of cash management tool in which, when prearranged amount of cash accumulates in account, amount is automatically invested.

Swindle: 1. to obtain money or property by deceitful misrepresentation. 2. to cheat or fraudulently induce individual to give up his or her property willingly.

Swing Loan: see *Bridge Loan.*

Syndicate: temporary association of persons or firms formed to carry out business venture or project of mutual interest.

Syndication: project financing whereby commercial or investment bankers agree to advance portion of funding. Syndicator acts as investment manager, collecting loan origination fee or commitment fee from borrower and arranging for sale to other banks in group. Typically, syndicator keeps only a small portion of total financing. A syndicated loan differs from loan participation because syndicate members are known at outset to borrower. Syndication also separates lead bank from group of financial institutions that ultimately fund obligation.

T

Takeover: acquisition, seizure, control, or management of one business by another.

Tangible Assets: assets that can be weighed, measured, or counted, including cash, property, machinery, and buildings.

Tax: payments imposed by legislative authority for support of government and its functions.

Taxable Income: portion of individual's or entity's income that is subject to taxation.

Tax Avoidance: act of using legal deductions, exemptions, and tax code provisions to reduce taxes payable.

Tax Evasion: failure to report taxable income to avoid proper payment of taxes.

Tax Foreclosure: legal seizure and sale of property by authorized public official to satisfy unpaid taxes.

Tax Levy: legislative action by which tax is imposed.

Tax Lien: statutory claim by state or municipality against property of person owing taxes. Property may be sold to satisfy obligation or judgment filed against it.

Tax Sale: sale of property seized by governmental taxing body for nonpayment of taxes.

Tenancy by Entirety: ownership in property by husband and wife in which each becomes whole owner of the entire estate upon the other's death. See also Joint Tenancy with Rights of Survivorship.

Tenancy in Common: two or more persons who hold title to land or other property in undivided ownership.

Tender: 1. unconditional offer of money or performance to satisfy claim. 2. offer to buy stock to take control of company.

Term Loan: fixed-term business loan with a maturity of more than one year and with defined periodic payments, providing borrower with working capital to acquire assets or inventory or to finance plant and equipment.

Terms: conditions and requirements as set forth in sales proposal, contract, or promissory note.

Terms of Sale: mutually agreed upon conditions for transfer of title or ownership of goods or property.

Testimony: written or oral evidence given in court under oath.

d Party: one who is not directly related to action between two parties but who may be affected by its outcome.

d-Party Claim: demand made by person who is not party to action for delivery or possession of personal property, title to which is claimed by third party.

e Deposit: 1. interest-bearing funds deposited in a financial institution for a specified period of time, such as certificates of deposit and savings accounts. 2. under Regulation D, deposit in which depositor is not permitted to make withdrawals within six days after date of deposit unless deposit is subject to early withdrawal penalty.

e Draft: draft payable on fixed date or certain number of days after sight or date of draft. See also *Banker's Acceptance, Draft, Letter of Credit,* and *Sight Draft.*

e: document that evidences legal ownership and possession of property.

e Company: business that as contracted researches specific property's history through real estate records and issues policy to purchaser or lienholder guaranteeing that there are no known defects in title.

e Insurance: a guarantee by a title insurance company that it will indemnify the insured, in a specific amount, against losses resulting from defects in the title to a property. The insured may be the owner of the property, that person's heirs and devises, or the lender and future assignees.

e Search: to review history of property's ownership and any judgments or liens filed against it.

ing the Statute: act of debtor to freeze statute of limitations that extends period for creditor to legally enforce payment of account. Individual state laws and statutes apply.

t: violation of legal duty that results in injury or damage to another.

de Acceptance: draft, accepted by buyer, sent with shipment of goods, requiring customer to pay amount involved at specific date and place.

de Credit: accounts payable; credit extended from one company to another.

de Debts: liabilities due from one business to another for purchase of supplies, inventory, etc.

de-in: property accepted by seller as partial down payment on purchase of new item.

de Information: confidential exchange of payment history and credit information among suppliers.

demark: distinctive identifying mark, word, or logo of product or service; protected when registered with U.S. Patent Office.

de Name: name used by a company to identify itself in the course of business. Also known as Trade Style or Fictitious Name.

de Payment Record: summary of performance of company in meeting terms of its credit obligations.

de References: names of suppliers or business creditors with whom credit information on customer can be exchanged.

easury Workstation: microcomputer-based information management system that allows corporate treasurer to automate daily balance reporting of collected balances, to invest idle funds in short-term money market, and to disburse funds to trade creditors. Overall aim is improvement in productivity and eventual integration of funds management and corporate accounting systems, such as order entry and invoicing.

ial Balance: listing of all account balances from general ledger used in preparing financial statements.

uck Jobber: wholesale merchant who sells and delivers products from truck inventory at time of sale. Also called *Wagon Distributor.*

ust: right to real or personal property that is held by one for benefit of another.

ust Company: business that acts as fiduciary and agent, handling trusts, estates, and guardianships for individuals and businesses.

ustee: one who holds or is entrusted with management of property or funds for benefit of another.

ustee in Bankruptcy: person appointed by court or elected by creditors to manage bankrupt property and carry out responsibilities of trust in proceedings.

ust Receipt: trust agreement (in receipt form) between a financial institution and borrower. It is temporarily substituted for possessory collateral securing creditor's loan so that creditor may release instruments, documents, or other property without releasing title to property. Borrower agrees to keep property (collateral), as well as any funds received from its sale, separate and distinct from borrower's own property and subject to repossession by the financial institution in event that he or she fails to comply with conditions specified in trust agreement.

ruth in Lending Act of 1968: See *Regulation Z.*

urnkey: something that is constructed, supplied, or installed and fully ready as intended.

U

CC: see *Uniform Commercial Code.*

ltra Vires: unauthorized acts taken by corporation beyond powers conferred on it by corporate charter.

Umbrella Policy: in liability insurance, policy that applies excess coverage to primary or underlying contract; provides large limits and broad coverage or may cover only primary basis risks not otherwise insured.

Unaudited Financial Statement: financial statement or report based on figures that have not been verified by a qualified accountant.

Uncollected Funds: deposits not yet collected by a financial institution, such as checks that have not yet cleared.

Uncollectible Accounts: receivables or debts not capable of being settled or recovered.

Underwriter: 1. person who reviews application for insurance and decides whether or not to accept risk. 2. one who agrees to purchase entire issue of bonds or securities at end of certain period.

Undue Influence: improper or illegal pressure used to wrongfully take advantage of person or to influence his or her actions or decisions.

Unearned Discount: A term used to reflect a reduced price (from the face value of an invoice) taken by a buyer without the consent of the seller.

Unearned Income: income received in advance of being earned.

Unencumbered Property: property that has no legal defects in its title; a property free and clear of any liens or debts.

Unenforceable Claim: debt on which all collection efforts have failed.

Unfair Competition: any fraudulent or dishonest practice intended to harm or unfairly attract competitor's customers.

Uniform Commercial Code (UCC): comprehensive set of statutes created to provide uniformity in business laws in all states, as approved by National Conference of Commissioners on Uniform State Laws. Statutes can vary from state to state.

Unit Banking: banking system in several states that prohibits branching or operation of more than one full-service banking office by state-chartered or national banks. Limited branching laws encourage chartering of large numbers of small, independently owned state banks and large multi-bank holding companies that own numerous unit banks.

Unjust Enrichment: doctrine whereby one is not allowed to profit inequitably at another's expense.

Unsatisfied Judgment: recorded judgment that has not been released or discharged.

Unsecured Creditor: one who grants credit without taking collateral in support of it.

Unsecured Loan: loan made on strength of borrower's general financial condition. Contrasts with Secured Loan.

Upstream Funding: funds borrowed by a subsidiary of a holding company for holding company's use. Contrasts with Downstream Funding.

Usury: The rate of interest that exceeds the legal limit allowed to be charged for the use of another's money. Legal limit of interest for different types of loan transactions is established by state law.

V

Valuable Consideration: see *Consideration.*

Valuation: 1. the estimated or determined worth of something. 2. process of appraising or affixing value of something.

Value Received: phrase used in bill of exchange or promissory note to denote that lawful consideration has been given.

Variable Interest Rate: interest rate that fluctuates with changes in an identified base rate or index.

Vendor: trade supplier or service provider.

Venture Capital: capital invested or available for investment in the ownership element of a new enterprise.

Verdict: formal decision of judge or jury on matter submitted in trial.

Verification: 1. affidavit or statement under oath swearing to truth or accuracy of written document. 2. in accounting, confirmation of entries in books of account.

Verification of Deposit (VOD): formal request by creditor to debtor's bank for account balance information.

Vest: 1. to give immediate transfer of title to property. 2. to obtain absolute ownership.

VOD: see *Verification of Deposit.*

Void: having no legal force.

Voidable Contract: contract that is nullified as to party who committed invalid act but not with respect to other party, unless he or she agrees to treat it as such.

Voluntary Bankruptcy: bankruptcy initiated by debtor petitioning court to be declared bankrupt.

Voucher: 1. statement itemizing payment or receipt of money. 2. detachable portion of check that describes purpose for which check was issued.

W

Wage Assignment: agreement by borrower that permits creditor to collect certain portion of borrower's wages from employer in the event of a default.

Wage Garnishment: court order requiring that percentage of debtor's earnings be withheld by employer and paid directly to creditor.

Waiver: intentional or voluntary relinquishing of known legal right.

Warehouse Loans: loans made against warehouse receipts that are evidence of collateral for material stored in public warehouse.

Warehouse Receipt: receipt issued by person engaged in business of storing goods for hire. It is document of title that gives evidence that person in possession of warehouse receipt is entitled to receive, hold, and dispose of document and goods it covers. Warehouse receipt in turn obligates warehouser to keep goods safely and to redeliver them upon surrender of receipt, properly endorsed, and payment of storage charges.

Wholesaler: company whose primary function is as intermediary between manufacturer of goods and retailer or other wholesalers.

Will: legal declaration by person making disposition of property, effective only after death.

Windfall Profit: large, unexpected return or income.

Wire Fate: instructions to financial institution requesting confirmation by wire that out-of-town check, sent for collection, has been paid.

Without Exception: see *Free and Clear*.

Without Prejudice: legal term used in offer, motion, or suit to indicate that parties' rights or privileges involved remain intact and to allow new suit to be brought on same cause of action.

Without Recourse: term used in endorsing negotiable instrument excluding endorser from responsibility should obligation not be paid.

With Prejudice: legal term used for dismissal of lawsuit that bars any future action and that, if prosecuted to final adjudication, would have been adverse to plaintiff.

With Recourse: endorsement of negotiable instrument on which endorser remains responsible should obligation not be paid.

Working Capital: 1. current assets less current liabilities, used as measure of firm's liquidity. 2. funds available to finance company's current operations.

Working Papers: information or schedules used by accountant in preparing financial reports.

Work in Process (WIP): goods in act of being manufactured, but not yet finished and ready for sale, representing a portion of inventory.

Workout: problem loan on which the financial institution is working closely with borrower for repayment, restructuring, or modification because of noncompliance with loan covenants.

Wrap-Around Mortgage: A second or junior mortgage with a face value of both the amount it secures and the balance due under the first mortgage. Covenant contained within second mortgage used to induce sellers of commercial properties to sell to buyer who has small down payment, normally when interest rates are high.

Writ of Execution: 1. writ issued by court ordering sheriff to attach debtor's property to enforce payment of judgment.

Write-down: partial reduction in book value of asset as result of obsolescence or depreciation.

Write-off: see *Charge-off*.

Writ of Attachment: court order directing sheriff to seize property of debtor held as security for satisfaction of judgment.

Y

Yield: rate of return on investment.

Z

Zero Balance Account: a checking account (subordinate account) used for disbursing or collecting funds in which no balances are maintained. At the end of the processing day, funds are transferred from a master account or concentration account to cover activity in the subordinate account.

Zoning Ordinance: municipal regulation dividing land into districts and prescribing structural, architectural, and nature of use of buildings within these districts.

NOTES

NOTES

NOTES

NOTES

NOTES

NOTES

NOTES

NOTES